YEARBOOK OF THE
UNITED NATIONS
2000

Volume 54

Yearbook of the United Nations, 2000

Volume 54   Sales No. E.02.I.1

Prepared by the Yearbook Section of the Department of Public Information, United Nations, New York. Although the *Yearbook* is based on official sources, it is not an official record.

Chief Editor: Kathryn Gordon

Senior Editors: Elizabeth Baldwin-Penn, Melody C. Pfeiffer

Editors/Writers: Barbara Christiani, Federigo Magherini

Contributing Editors/Writers: Peter Jackson, Nancy Seufert-Barr, Juanita B. Phelan, Luisa Balacco, Alexandre Slavashevich, Sharon McPherson, Anvita Sharma

Senior Copy Editor: Alison M. Koppelman

Copy Editor: Peter Homans

Production Coordinator: Leonard M. Simon

Editorial Assistants: Lawri M. Moore, Margaret O'Donnell, Rodney Pascual

Senior Typesetter: Sunita Chabra

Indexer: David Golante

Jacket design adapted by Nancy Settecasi

Photographs in Special Section on Millennium Summit: UN/DPI

YEARBOOK
OF THE
UNITED
NATIONS
2000

Volume 54

Department of Public Information
United Nations, New York

UNITED NATIONS PUBLICATIONS
SALES NO. E.02.I.1

Printed in the United States of America

Foreword

In September 2000, an unprecedented number of heads of State and Government gathered at United Nations Headquarters in New York for the Millennium Summit. In adopting the Millennium Declaration, they reaffirmed the purposes and principles of the United Nations, pledged their collective responsibility to uphold the principles of human dignity and equality, and established a range of ambitious goals and targets for human progress in the twenty-first century.

Governments were not the only ones to seize the occasion of the millennium to set forth their views; civil society groups, parliamentarians and religious organizations each held landmark meetings during the year, seeking new levels of cooperation with each other and with the United Nations.

Throughout the year, however, we were reminded of the gap between the Declaration's aspirations and the deprivation and despair that characterize the lives of so much of humankind. Violence escalated in the Middle East, continued in Afghanistan and raged on in a number of countries in sub-Saharan Africa. Poverty and natural disasters blighted lives on all continents. The AIDS epidemic continued to spread rapidly, and with it the devastation it wreaks on families, communities and, indeed, entire countries.

This volume of the *Yearbook of the United Nations* provides a comprehensive review of the Organization's efforts throughout the year 2000 to address these and other challenges on the international agenda. It is intended as a tool for scholars, journalists, diplomats and others interested in the United Nations and international affairs. I hope it will serve as a contribution to the effort to create the wide-ranging partnerships and policies needed to address the global challenges of our times.

KOFI A. ANNAN

Secretary-General of the United Nations
New York, September 2002

Contents

Part One: *Political and security questions*

Part Two: *Human Rights*

Part Three: *Economic and social questions*

Part Four: *Legal questions*

Part Five: *Institutional, administrative and budgetary questions*

Part Six: *Intergovernmental organizations related to the United Nations*

Appendices

Indexes

About the 2000 edition of the *Yearbook*

This volume of the *YEARBOOK OF THE UNITED NATIONS* continues the tradition of providing the most comprehensive coverage of the activities of the United Nations. It is an indispensable reference tool for the research community, diplomats, government officials and the general public seeking readily available information on the UN system and its related organizations.

Efforts by the Department of Public Information to achieve a more timely publication have resulted in having to rely on provisional documentation and other materials to prepare the relevant articles. Largely, Security Council resolutions and presidential statements, Economic and Social Council resolutions and some other texts in the present volume are provisional.

Structure and scope of articles

The *Yearbook* is subject-oriented and divided into six parts covering political and security questions; human rights issues; economic and social questions; legal questions; institutional, administrative and budgetary questions; and intergovernmental organizations related to the United Nations. Chapters and topical headings present summaries of pertinent UN activities, including those of intergovernmental and expert bodies, major reports, Secretariat activities and, in selected cases, the views of States in written communications.

Activities of United Nations bodies. All resolutions, decisions and other major activities of the principal organs and, on a selective basis, those of subsidiary bodies are either reproduced or summarized in the appropriate chapter. The texts of all resolutions and decisions of substantive nature adopted in 2000 by the General Assembly, the Security Council and the Economic and Social Council are reproduced or summarized under the relevant topic. These texts are preceded by procedural details giving date of adoption, meeting number and vote totals (in favour–against–abstaining) if any; and an indication of their approval by a sessional or subsidiary body prior to final adoption. The texts are followed by details of any recorded or roll-call vote on the resolution/decision as a whole.

Major reports. Most reports of the Secretary-General, in 2000, along with selected reports from other UN sources, such as seminars and working groups, are summarized briefly.

Secretariat activities. The operational activities of the United Nations for development and humanitarian as-sistance are described under the relevant topics. For major activities financed outside the UN regular budget, selected information is given on contributions and expenditures.

Views of States. Written communications sent to the United Nations by Member States and circulated as documents of the principal organs have been summarized in selected cases, under the relevant topics. Substantive actions by the Security Council have been analysed and brief reviews of the Council's deliberations given, particularly in cases where an issue was taken up but no resolution was adopted.

Related organizations. The *Yearbook* also briefly describes the 2000 activities of the specialized agencies and other related organizations of the UN system.

Multilateral treaties. Information on signatories and parties to multilateral treaties and conventions is taken from *Multilateral Treaties Deposited with the Secretary-General: Status as at 31 December 2000* (ST/LEG/SER.E/19 (vols. I & II)), Sales No. E.01.V.5.

Terminology

Formal titles of bodies, organizational units, conventions, declarations and officials are given in full on first mention in an article or sequence of articles. They are also used in resolution/decision texts, and in the SUBJECT INDEX under the key word of the title. Short titles may be used in subsequent references.

How to find information in the *Yearbook*

The user may locate information on the United Nations activities contained in this volume by the use of the Table of Contents, the Subject Index, the Index of Resolutions and Decisions and the Index of Security Council Presidential Statements. The volume also has five appendices: Appendix I comprises a roster of Member States; Appendix II reproduces the Charter of the United Nations, including the Statute of the International Court of Justice; Appendix III gives the structure of the principal organs of the United Nations; Appendix IV provides the agenda for each session of the principal organs in 2000; and Appendix V gives the addresses of the United Nations information centres and services worldwide.

For more information on the United Nations and its activities, visit our Internet site at:

http://www.un.org

ABBREVIATIONS COMMONLY USED IN THE *YEARBOOK*

ACABQ	Advisory Committee on Administrative and Budgetary Questions
ACC	Administrative Committee on Coordination
CEDAW	Committee on the Elimination of Discrimination against Women
CIS	Commonwealth of Independent States
DPKO	Department of Peacekeeping Operations
DPRK	Democratic People's Republic of Korea
DRC	Democratic Republic of the Congo
ECA	Economic Commission for Africa
ECE	Economic Commission for Europe
ECLAC	Economic Commission for Latin America and the Caribbean
ECOWAS	Economic Community of West African States
ESC	Economic and Social Council
ESCAP	Economic and Social Commission for Asia and the Pacific
ESCWA	Economic and Social Commission for Western Asia
EU	European Union
FAO	Food and Agriculture Organization of the United Nations
FRY	Federal Republic of Yugoslavia
FYROM	The former Yugoslav Republic of Macedonia
GA	General Assembly
GDP	gross domestic product
GNP	gross national product
HIPC	Heavily Indebted Poor Countries
IAEA	International Atomic Energy Agency
ICAO	International Civil Aviation Organization
ICJ	International Court of Justice
ICRC	International Committee of the Red Cross
ICTR	International Criminal Tribunal for Rwanda
ICTY	International Tribunal for the Former Yugoslavia
IDA	International Development Association
IFAD	International Fund for Agricultural Development
ILO	International Labour Organization
IMF	International Monetary Fund
IMO	International Maritime Organization
INCB	International Narcotics Control Board
ITC	International Trade Centre (UNCTAD/WTO)
ITU	International Telecommunication Union
JIU	Joint Inspection Unit
LDC	least developed country
MINURCA	United Nations Mission in the Central African Republic
MINURSO	United Nations Mission for the Referendum in Western Sahara
MIPONUH	United Nations Civilian Police Mission in Haiti
MONUA	United Nations Observer Mission in Angola
MONUC	United Nations Mission in the Democratic Republic of the Congo
NATO	North Atlantic Treaty Organization
NGO	non-governmental organization
NSGT	Non-Self-Governing Territory
OAS	Organization of American States
OAU	Organization of African Unity
ODA	official development assistance
OECD	Organisation for Economic Cooperation and Development
OHCHR	Office of the United Nations High Commissioner for Human Rights
OIOS	Office of Internal Oversight Services
OPEC	Organization of Petroleum Exporting Countries
OSCE	Organization for Security and Cooperation in Europe
PLO	Palestine Liberation Organization
SC	Security Council
UN	United Nations
UNAMSIL	United Nations Mission in Sierra Leone
UNCTAD	United Nations Conference on Trade and Development
UNDCP	United Nations International Drug Control Programme
UNDOF	United Nations Disengagement Observer Force (Golan Heights)
UNDP	United Nations Development Programme
UNEP	United Nations Environment Programme
UNESCO	United Nations Educational, Scientific and Cultural Organization
UNFICYP	United Nations Peacekeeping Force in Cyprus
UNFPA	United Nations Population Fund
UNHCR	Office of the United Nations High Commissioner for Refugees
UNIC	United Nations Information Centre
UNICEF	United Nations Children's Fund
UNIDO	United Nations Industrial Development Organization
UNIFIL	United Nations Interim Force in Lebanon
UNIKOM	United Nations Iraq-Kuwait Observation Mission
UNMEE	United Nations Mission in Ethiopia and Eritrea
UNMIBH	United Nations Mission in Bosnia and Herzegovina
UNMIK	United Nations Interim Administration Mission in Kosovo
UNMOGIP	United Nations Military Observer Group in India and Pakistan
UNMOP	United Nations Mission of Observers in Prevlaka
UNMOT	United Nations Mission of Observers in Tajikistan
UNMOVIC	United Nations Monitoring, Verification and Inspection Commission
UNOMIG	United Nations Observer Mission in Georgia
UNOPS	United Nations Office for Project Services
UNRWA	United Nations Relief and Works Agency for Palestine Refugees in the Near East
UNTAET	United Nations Transitional Administration in East Timor
UNTSO	United Nations Truce Supervision Organization
UPU	Universal Postal Union
WFP	World Food Programme
WHO	World Health Organization
WIPO	World Intellectual Property Organization
WMO	World Meteorological Organization
WTO	World Trade Organization
YUN	*Yearbook of the United Nations*

EXPLANATORY NOTE ON DOCUMENTS

References in square brackets in each chapter of Parts One to Five of this volume give the symbols of the main documents issued in 2000 on the topic. The following is a guide to the principal document symbols:

A/- refers to documents of the General Assembly, numbered in separate series by session. Thus, A/55/- refers to documents issued for consideration at the fifty-fifth session, beginning with A/55/1. Documents of special and emergency special sessions are identified as A/S- and A/ES-, followed by the session number.

A/C.- refers to documents of the Assembly's Main Committees, e.g. A/C.1/- is a document of the First Committee, A/C.6/-, a document of the Sixth Committee. A/BUR/- refers to documents of the General Committee. A/AC.- documents are those of the Assembly's ad hoc bodies and A/CN.-, of its commissions; e.g. A/AC.105/- identifies documents of the Assembly's Committee on the Peaceful Uses of Outer Space, A/CN.4/-, of its International Law Commission. Assembly resolutions and decisions since the thirty-first (1976) session have been identified by two arabic numerals; the first indicates the session of adoption; the second, the sequential number in the series. Resolutions are numbered consecutively from 1 at each session. Decisions of regular sessions are numbered consecutively, from 301 for those concerned with elections and appointments, and from 401 for all other decisions. Decisions of special and emergency special sessions are numbered consecutively, from 11 for those concerned with elections and appointments, and from 21 for all other decisions.

E/- refers to documents of the Economic and Social Council, numbered in separate series by year. Thus, E/2000/- refers to documents issued for consideration by the Council at its 2000 sessions, beginning with E/2000/1. E/AC.-, E/C.- and E/CN.-, followed by identifying numbers, refer to documents of the Council's subsidiary ad hoc bodies, committees and commissions. For example, E/CN.5/- refers to documents of the Council's Commission for Social Development, E/C.2/-, to documents of its Committee on Non-Governmental Organizations. E/ICEF/- documents are those of the United Nations Children's Fund (UNICEF). Symbols for the Council's resolutions and decisions, since 1978, consist of two arabic numerals: the first indicates the year of adoption and the second, the sequential number in the series. There are two series: one for resolutions, beginning with 1 (resolution 2000/1); and one for decisions, beginning with 201 (decision 2000/201).

S/- refers to documents of the Security Council. Its resolutions are identified by consecutive numbers followed by the year of adoption in parentheses, beginning with resolution 1(1946).

ST/-, followed by symbols representing the issuing department or office, refers to documents of the United Nations Secretariat.

Documents of certain bodies bear special symbols, including the following:

ACC/-	Administrative Committee on Coordination
CD/-	Conference on Disarmament
CERD/-	Committee on the Elimination of Racial Discrimination
DC/-	Disarmament Commission
DP/-	United Nations Development Programme
HS/-	Commission on Human Settlements
ITC/-	International Trade Centre
TD/-	United Nations Conference on Trade and Development
UNEP/-	United Nations Environment Programme

Many documents of the regional commissions bear special symbols. These are sometimes preceded by the following:

E/ECA/-	Economic Commission for Africa
E/ECE/-	Economic Commission for Europe
E/ECLAC/-	Economic Commission for Latin America and the Caribbean
E/ESCAP/-	Economic and Social Commission for Asia and the Pacific
E/ESCWA/-	Economic and Social Commission for Western Asia

"L" in a symbol refers to documents of limited distribution, such as draft resolutions; "CONF." to documents of a conference; "INF." to those of general information. Summary records are designated by "SR.", verbatim records by "PV.", each followed by the meeting number.

United Nations sales publications each carry a sales number with the following components separated by periods: a capital letter indicating the language(s) of the publication; two arabic numerals indicating the year; a Roman numeral indicating the subject category; a capital letter indicating a subdivision of the category, if any; and an arabic numeral indicating the number of the publication within the category. Examples: E.00.II.A.2; E/F/R.00.II.E.7; E.00.X.1.

Report of the Secretary-General

Report of the Secretary-General on the work of the Organization

*Following is the Secretary-General's report on the work of the Organization, submitted to the fifty-fifth session of the General Assembly and dated 30 August 2000. The Assembly took note of it on 28 September (**decision 55/404**). On 23 December, the Assembly decided that the agenda item would remain for consideration during the resumed fifty-fifth (2001) session (**decision 55/458**).*

Introduction

1. The turn of the millennium provides a unique vantage point from which to view humanity's progress and challenges. In my report to the Millennium Summit, *We the Peoples: The Role of the United Nations in the Twenty-first Century,* I offered my own assessment, and suggested ways in which the entire international community can work together to better the lives of people still left behind.

2. The past year has reminded us that the international community is not yet close enough to meeting that goal. Since last September, new wars have erupted in several parts of the world, and many long-running conflicts have continued to defy the best efforts of mediators to end them. The devastation caused by natural disasters continued to increase, with drought, floods and earthquakes blighting the lives of millions. Demands on United Nations humanitarian agencies vastly exceeded worst-case predictions.

3. While living standards in much of the developing world continued to improve, in many of the least developed countries they remained in decline. This is particularly so in sub-Saharan Africa, where AIDS, violent conflict, and in some instances predatory behaviour by Governments and political factions have taken a heavy toll, while per capita economic assistance from the richer world has declined dramatically.

4. In Africa, AIDS is now killing at least four times as many people each year as the continent's numerous armed conflicts. In other parts of the world, the pandemic continues to spread with frightening rapidity. The gravity of the threat HIV/AIDS poses is at last being widely recognized, but this provides small comfort. What is needed is a stronger commitment to action.

5. During the year, the creation of three new peace missions resulted in a tripling of the numbers of authorized United Nations peacekeepers to 45,000, straining United Nations Headquarters resources to the very limits. United Nations operations in East Timor and in Kosovo, Federal Republic of Yugoslavia, are the most complex, and in some ways the most demanding, in the Organization's history. We are charged with nothing less than helping to rebuild shattered societies almost from scratch.

6. In 1999, in the wake of the war in Kosovo, the question how the international community should respond to gross violations of human rights was fiercely debated. For the Organization this had already been a critical issue for some time, not least because the inability of the international community to help prevent the genocide in Rwanda in 1994 or the massacre of thousands of unarmed men and boys from the United Nations "safe area" of Srebrenica in 1995 continued to weigh on our conscience.

7. Two United Nations reviews were conducted in 1999 to determine what had caused those failures—a Secretariat study on Srebrenica and an Independent Inquiry study of Rwanda. Both reviews revealed how lack of political will, inappropriate Security Council mandates and inadequate resources contributed to failure, together with doctrinal and institutional misjudgements and shortcomings on the part of the United Nations itself.

8. While both studies offered valuable recommendations, it was evident that a more comprehensive diagnosis was required of the deep-rooted problems that have plagued so many of our missions, and above all a prescription for avoiding such failures in the future. Therefore,

in March 2000, I established a high-level panel, chaired by Lakhdar Brahimi, to undertake a major review and recommend ways of ensuring that future peace operations will be more effective.

9. The Panel's report has just been issued. It contains a frank and clear-sighted analysis of the problems we continue to face in mounting effective peace operations. The Panel's recommendations for change are realistic and cogently argued. They go to the very heart of the dilemmas that we confront in seeking to meet our commitment, under the Charter, "to save succeeding generations from the scourge of war". I trust that Member States will give them the most serious consideration, and join me in putting them into effect swiftly.

10. No objective observer could doubt that the current level of Secretariat support for peace operations is inadequate. The 12,000 troops currently serving in the United Nations Mission in Sierra Leone, for example, are supported by just five people at Headquarters. No national Government would dream of deploying a comparably sized military mission overseas with such a minimal headquarters support unit.

11. Not surprisingly, therefore, some of the Panel's recommendations will require additional resources to implement. The international community must accept that these are indeed essential if we are to meet our international peace and security commitments. The estimated cost of all United Nations peacekeeping operations in 2000 amounts to less than one half of 1 per cent of the approximately $800 billion that Member States spend on national defence. The additional resources needed to implement the Panel's recommendations are very modest by comparison.

12. Security has not been the only contentious issue during the past year. The protests at the World Trade Organization meeting in Seattle indicated a growing potential backlash against globalization. Concern is by no means restricted to street demonstrators in the developed countries; albeit largely for different reasons, it is also evident in the capitals of many developing countries.

13. To some, globalization is imbued with great promise; to others it appears deeply threatening. Few deny that the economic and technological forces that drive it have the potential to lift the dreadful burdens of poverty and disease that still weigh on half the world's population. But in the face of persistent poverty, rising inequality and the volatility of global markets and financial flows many doubt that this potential will be realized. Others are concerned that open markets will threaten both the integrity of cultures and the sovereignty of States.

14. That there should be such disagreements is not surprising. Like other great changes in history, globalization creates losers as well as winners.

15. It is clear that no country has developed successfully by rejecting the opportunities offered by international trade and foreign direct investment. The developing countries that have become most effectively integrated into the global economy, notably those of East Asia, have not only grown faster than the rest, they have also been far more successful in reducing poverty levels. At the same time, engagement with the global economy alone is no panacea for rapid development, and additional measures, domestic as well as international, are necessary to make globalization work for all.

16. I firmly believe that thriving markets and human security go hand in hand. But if support for open markets and financial liberalization is to be sustained, globalization must be made more inclusive and its benefits must be spread more equitably. These goals cannot be achieved without more effective global institutions.

17. Here the international community confronts a major problem. The international economic institutions that were created in the aftermath of the Second World War were designed to manage a much less complex and fast-moving set of issues. Even more importantly, they were designed to manage the flow of *international* economic transactions. We have however moved into the era of *global* economic transactions.

18. Economic liberalization has unleashed extraordinary growth but, as the East Asia crisis of 1997-1998 reminded us, it has also reduced the ability of Governments to resist the influence of the global economic environment. There is a need for more effective global governance, by which I mean the cooperative management of global affairs.

19. In some instances, far-reaching institutional changes are called for, but governance does not have to involve formal institutions, regulations or mechanisms of enforcement. It can also be achieved through informal dialogue and cooperation. It can involve agreements with non-State actors as well as between and among Governments.

20. Indeed, during the past decade many informal coalitions have emerged to pursue cooperative solutions to common problems—not only among Governments but also encompassing international institutions, civil society organizations and sometimes the private sector. Such engagement does not threaten Governments. On the contrary, it increases their power by bringing them willing and able allies. All partners can gain

in such coalitions, because each achieves through cooperation what none could achieve alone.

21. Sometimes called "coalitions for change", global policy networks transcend both geographical and political boundaries. They focus attention on specific issues, disseminate knowledge, set global agendas and mobilize people for change. Recent examples can be seen in the campaigns to reduce global warming, roll back malaria, ban landmines, create an international criminal court and provide debt relief for developing countries.

22. The United Nations, with its universality, legitimacy and broad mandates, has unique convening and consensus-building roles to play in such coalitions for change.

23. Much is already being done. In the past year the United Nations has forged global partnerships that would hardly have been conceivable even a decade ago. Last year, at the World Economic Forum in Davos, I proposed a Global Compact by which private corporations would commit themselves to observing, in their own corporate domains, good practices, as defined by the broader international community, in the areas of human rights, labour and the environment. In July 2000, in New York, I convened the inaugural meeting of the Compact partners, which was attended by representatives of the international trade union movement and major civil society organizations, as well as the leaders of some 50 multinational companies.

24. The Global Compact is not intended as a substitute for international agreements or effective action by Governments, but as a complement to them. The corporations that have joined it did so because the values that the Compact promotes will help to create the stable and secure environment that business needs if it is to flourish in the long term. Labour and civil society organizations have joined because the values that the Global Compact upholds are also their values, and because they recognize the importance of having corporations support them.

25. We are also working with business, philanthropic foundations and civil society organizations on an ever-increasing range of partnership projects at the country level. One will bring Internet-delivered medical information to developing countries, another will provide communications equipment and expertise for use in disasters and humanitarian emergencies, while a third seeks to significantly increase vaccine coverage among the world's children.

26. Other cooperative activities that the United Nations is pursuing with international organizations, the private sector and civil society organizations, and with individual Member States, are described in the body of this report.

27. In my report, *We the Peoples*, I review some of the major challenges confronting the international community in the twenty-first century, suggest a series of targets and actions for the Millennium Summit and Assembly to consider and call on Member States to renew their commitment to the United Nations.

28. I am gratified that my proposals have met with such a positive reception. I sincerely hope that Member States will use the opportunities presented by the Millennium Summit and Assembly to go beyond supportive sentiment, and commit themselves firmly to action.

Chapter I

Achieving peace and security

Introduction

29. Sustainable peace and security for all countries and peoples remains a central objective of the United Nations at the dawn of the twenty-first century, as it was when the Organization was founded over half a century ago. No issue commands more of our attention and resources, as the intense pace of work in the Security Council over the past year has again shown. The international community has sought to respond to complex crises in situations as diverse as those in Afghanistan, Burundi, the Democratic Republic of the Congo, East Timor, Eritrea-Ethiopia, Kosovo and Sierra Leone.

30. The demands made on the United Nations reflect a shift in the nature of the threats to peace and security since the end of the cold war: from inter-State conflict to intra-State conflict; from the violation of borders to a much greater emphasis on the violation of people. Where conflicts were once driven by the ideological divisions of a bipolar world, they are now fuelled by ethnic and religious intolerance, political ambition and greed, and are often exacerbated by the illicit traffic in arms, gems and drugs.

31. The demands we face also reflect a growing consensus that collective security can no longer be narrowly defined as the absence of armed conflict, be it between or within States. Gross abuses of human rights, the large-scale displacement of civilian populations, international terrorism, the AIDS pandemic, drug and arms trafficking and environmental disasters present a direct threat to human security, forcing us to adopt a much more coordinated approach to a range of issues. Such an approach, as I made clear in my report to the Millennium Assembly, is

one that compels us to think creatively. It requires us, above all, to understand that the various elements that contribute to human security must be addressed in a comprehensive way if we are to sustain durable peace in the future.

32. That we are already embarked on this path is evidenced by changes in the way we manage our numerous and far-flung peace operations, where there is increasing readiness to work across administrative and institutional boundaries in pursuit of lasting solutions to complex problems.

33. United Nations peacemakers, peacekeepers and peace-builders around the world have begun to cooperate more closely than ever with Governments and other actors within the United Nations system, with regional bodies, with nongovernmental organizations and with the private sector to help create the basis for good governance and the peaceable resolution of differences between parties. The activities now pursued are far more extensive and complex than those of traditional peacekeeping. They include providing emergency relief; demobilizing and reintegrating former combatants; assistance in clearing and destroying mines; constitutional and legal reform; providing advice on the enhancement of human rights; and the creation and reform of state institutions and electoral assistance. Traditional activities, such as monitoring ceasefires, continue to play a critical role in peacekeeping operations.

34. We have confronted major challenges during the past year and it is clear that there is no room for complacency. Both the United Nations and the Member States that determine its mandates and authorize the resources to accomplish them still have much to learn.

35. Three major studies issued in the past year have sought to promote a better understanding of the needs and the potential of United Nations peace operations. By commissioning reports on the tragedies that happened in Srebrenica and Rwanda, I hoped to clarify what went wrong—including within the United Nations—in order to suggest what we might do differently in the future. Certain clear lessons emerged from those two reports, which have since been reinforced by experience, particularly that of the United Nations Mission in Sierra Leone. Those lessons include the importance of joint action by Member States and the Secretariat to strengthen the instrument of peacekeeping; the need to understand clearly whether peacekeeping or enforcement is needed in a specific situation; the importance of providing adequate resources to meet mission needs and having, even within peacekeeping operations, a credible deterrent capacity; the importance of preparedness for "worst-case" scenarios; the requirement to improve information flows, both between Member States and the Secretariat and within the Secretariat; and the need for more effective and timely analysis of information from the field. Mutual respect by Member States and the Secretariat for each other's roles and responsibilities, including arrangements of command and control in the field, is critical, as is the need for political commitment to initiate and sustain operations.

36. Those two reports also helped us to reflect on the difficult questions surrounding what, in my millennium report, I termed "the dilemma of intervention". It is, of course, relatively easy for the international community to assert that the tragedies of Rwanda and Srebrenica should never be allowed to happen again. But if the reaction to my address last year to the General Assembly is any guide, I fear we may still prove unable to give a credible answer to the question of what happens next time we are faced with a comparable crime against humanity.

37. Recognition that many States have serious and legitimate concerns about intervention does not answer the question I posed in my report, namely, if humanitarian intervention is, indeed, an unacceptable assault on sovereignty, how should we respond to a Rwanda, to a Srebrenica—to gross and systematic violations of human rights that offend every precept of our common humanity? In essence the problem is one of responsibility: in circumstances in which universally accepted human rights are being violated on a massive scale we have a responsibility to act.

38. In recognition of the increasingly complex task faced by the United Nations as it seeks to prevent and resolve conflict, and to keep and build the peace, I requested a panel of experts led by the former Minister for Foreign Affairs of Algeria, Lakhdar Brahimi, to produce a report that would provide an overview of peace operations and suggest how they might be strengthened for the future. The report of the Panel on United Nations Peace Operations has just been issued. I am gratified that the Panel's recommendations, some of which I discuss in the introduction to the present report, parallel many of my own proposals, outlined below.

39. If we do not commit ourselves to these vital reforms, there is a real risk that we will continue to fail to meet the challenge of saving the innocent from the scourge of war. I urge Member States to join with me in acting upon the Panel's key recommendations.

Conflict prevention and peacemaking

40. In recent years the international community has agreed that preventing armed conflict is critical to achieving lasting human security. Conflict prevention, as I put it in my millennium report, is where it all begins. Shifting from a culture of reaction to one of prevention is highly cost-effective both in human and in financial terms. In the early stages of a dispute, parties tend to be less polarized and more flexible and thus more inclined to settle their disputes peacefully than after violent conflict has become entrenched. Prevention also offers the best possible chance to address the root causes of a conflict, and not just its consequences, thus providing a real opportunity to sow the seeds of a durable peace.

41. Confronting new outbreaks of violent conflict around the world and recognizing the importance of acting proactively, I have continued to strengthen our early warning and conflict prevention capacities. My primary objective has been to make early warning and conflict prevention a day-to-day concern for United Nations staff, both at Headquarters and in the field.

42. In this context the Department of Political Affairs, serving as the focal point for conflict prevention within the United Nations system, has established a Prevention Team, which meets regularly to identify conflict situations that may offer potential for preventive action. Other departments and agencies have also strengthened their capacity in this area; once a developing crisis has been identified by a United Nations department or agency, consultations are held within the new interdepartmental Framework for Coordination. Meanwhile, the United Nations Staff College at Turin, Italy, in close cooperation with the Secretariat, has launched a conflict prevention training course, so far attended by more than 400 staff members from 22 departments, agencies, offices and programmes.

43. Experience shows that the success of the United Nations in helping to prevent conflicts will hinge upon close collaboration with Member States and a large number of other actors, including regional arrangements, non-governmental organizations and others. Following a high-level meeting held in New York in July 1998, we established a programme for coordination in conflict prevention with regional organizations, and have sought to improve our contacts with a variety of non-governmental actors. Such efforts should not obscure the fact that the primary responsibility for the prevention of conflict lies with Member States. Successful conflict prevention, under United Nations auspices, ultimately requires the political will to provide the necessary leadership and resources for action.

44. I therefore welcome the growing attention Member States have paid to conflict prevention. This was most vividly demonstrated in the general debate during the fifty-fourth session of the General Assembly, as well as in the groundbreaking open debates on conflict prevention held by the Security Council in November 1999 and July 2000 and the comprehensive action plan adopted by the Group of Eight in July. The far-reaching presidential statements adopted by the Security Council indicated the broad commitment of Member States to improving the capacity of the United Nations for effective preventive action. It is important that this momentum is maintained and I look forward to engaging with Member States directly on this issue in the coming months.

45. No region in the world illustrates the need to prevent conflict, and the costs of the failure to do so, more dramatically than Africa. The dreadful human cost inflicted by conflicts in Angola, the Democratic Republic of the Congo, Eritrea-Ethiopia, Sierra Leone, the Sudan and elsewhere is self-evident. Tragically, despite the collective efforts of the international community to avert a resumption of hostilities between Eritrea and Ethiopia, including a visit to both countries by a delegation of the Security Council, fierce fighting resumed in May 2000, inflicting high levels of casualties and widespread destruction.

46. Assisting Eritrea and Ethiopia to resolve their conflict through support for the mediation efforts of the Organization of African Unity (OAU) has been a major preoccupation during the past year. I urged the leaders of the parties to pursue a peaceful settlement and asked my Special Envoy on Africa to assist OAU in this regard. On 18 June, an agreement on the cessation of hostilities was signed—a necessary first step towards the restoration of peace through a comprehensive peace settlement. The United Nations Mission in Ethiopia and Eritrea will soon be deployed on the border between the two countries, and we will assist in implementing the agreement and providing support for the mediation efforts of OAU.

47. In Burundi, the designation of former President Nelson Mandela as the new facilitator of the peace process, after the death of former President Julius Nyerere in October 1999, brought new momentum to the Arusha process. United Nations assistance to the peace process increased with the provision of technical and conference service support, in addition to the assignment of a senior political adviser to the facilitator. I have also raised the profile of our in-

volvement by designating a Special Representative for the Great Lakes region, with special emphasis on Burundi.

48. In the quest for peace in Somalia there have been many false dawns. The Government of Djibouti's peace initiative for Somalia is therefore something I have warmly welcomed. The Somali National Peace Conference, which opened at Arta, Djibouti, in May, has seen considerable success and secured the participation of a wide spectrum of Somalis. The extent of participation by a number of Somali groups and individuals remains mixed, however, "Somaliland", in particular, remaining firmly outside the peace process. Success will continue to depend on the extent of unity that Somalis can achieve in reaching agreement on future political arrangements for their country.

49. Meanwhile, the war in Angola, which resumed in October 1998, continues to cause terrible suffering. Almost 3.7 million people are internally displaced and hundreds of thousands more have been forced to flee their country. While the Government of Angola has weakened the military capabilities of UNITA, it is aware that military force alone will not bring peace to the country and has reiterated its commitment to the Lusaka Protocol. The United Nations is committed to working closely with the Government of Angola and all others concerned to help bring the war to an end and restore peace in the country. To this end, I have asked my Adviser for Special Assignments in Africa to pay particular attention to Angola.

50. It is encouraging to note that African States themselves are increasingly determined to work together to avert the outbreak of new conflicts and to promote peace in the region. This was demonstrated when a sudden and unconstitutional change of government occurred in Côte d'Ivoire in December 1999 and States of the region took the lead, with support from the United Nations, in seeking to help Côte d'Ivoire to restore constitutional order.

51. An area of renewed engagement of United Nations efforts in the last year—and one that has seen significant progress—is the Middle East. For 22 years, United Nations peacekeepers have served in southern Lebanon in one of our longest standing peacekeeping commitments anywhere in the world. Following several missions to the region by my Special Envoy, I reported to the Security Council on 16 June that Israeli forces had withdrawn from Lebanon in compliance with Council resolution 425(1978). Soon afterwards, I visited the countries of the region to encourage the parties and other regional leaders to support the efforts to consolidate the restoration of peace and stability in Lebanon. Notwithstanding the reservations of the Governments of Lebanon and Israel about the withdrawal line, they both confirmed that they would respect the line as identified by the United Nations. After Israel withdrew its forces, the Government of Lebanon began to reassert law and order functions throughout the area.

52. The United Nations Interim Force in Lebanon is being reinforced so that it may carry out its responsibilities under the resolution. I trust that the international community will be quick to assist Lebanon with the task of reconstructing the economy in the south and rebuilding its links with the rest of the country. In August 2000, I appointed a Personal Representative for Southern Lebanon to coordinate United Nations efforts and assist in bringing peace and stability to the region.

53. I have also been encouraged by the renewed bilateral and multilateral efforts in search of a just and comprehensive peace in the Middle East. At the Camp David summit hosted by President Clinton, the quest for a lasting peace between Israel and the Palestinians reached a crucial stage. I hope that the parties will persist in their efforts to bring the Israeli-Palestinian negotiations on the permanent status agreement to a successful conclusion.

54. Iraq's lack of compliance with various Security Council resolutions continues to be of grave concern. After lengthy negotiations, the Security Council adopted resolution 1284(1999) on 17 December 1999, replacing the United Nations Special Commission with a new inspection agency for Iraq, the United Nations Monitoring, Verification and Inspection Commission (UNMOVIC). I appointed an Executive Chairman of UNMOVIC and a College of Commissioners to act as an advisory body. Iraq, however, has not accepted the resolution.

55. There has been no United Nations presence in Iraq since December 1998 to ensure Iraq's compliance with Security Council resolutions concerning its programmes of weapons of mass destruction. In its resolution 1284(1999) the Security Council also reiterated Iraq's obligations to repatriate all Kuwaiti and third-country missing nationals and return all Kuwaiti property. Iraq has not agreed to cooperate with the high-level coordinator I appointed to deal with these issues, and the matter remains unresolved.

56. The challenge of bringing peace to Afghanistan, another of the world's intractable conflicts, remains daunting. The past year has seen scant progress, as the warring factions have evidenced little enthusiasm for a negotiated settlement. Meanwhile, there has been a continuing in-

flux of war materiel from outside powers, in clear violation of General Assembly and Security Council resolutions and the Tashkent Declaration signed by the "six plus two" group of countries in July 1999. Since his appointment in February 2000 my Personal Representative and Head of the United Nations Special Mission to Afghanistan has established an ongoing dialogue with Afghan leaders, including the Taliban and the United Front, as well as with other countries whose assistance will be essential if an overall settlement is to be achieved.

57. The fragility of the region remains evident in the continuing tensions between India and Pakistan. It is regrettable that the two countries, both of which tested nuclear devices two years ago, have not been able to resume their bilateral dialogue. In Kashmir the situation along the line of control remains precarious and the level of violence and insecurity has increased. This is unacceptable. In this context, proposals currently under discussion aimed at resolving the conflict should be encouraged. Meanwhile, the worsening of the internal conflict in Sri Lanka has increased the concern of the international community, which has offered its backing to Norway's facilitation efforts.

58. I have paid close attention to positive developments on the Korean peninsula, where the follow-up to the recent historic inter-Korean summit offers an opportunity to establish trust between the two parties and resolve a bitter conflict that has persisted for half a century. I attach particular importance to enhancing the United Nations humanitarian and development effort in the Democratic People's Republic of Korea.

59. On a very different scale are developments in Bougainville, Papua New Guinea, where the work of the United Nations Political Office illustrates how effectively a small presence can help to maintain the integrity of a peace process. The Office was instrumental in assisting the Government of Papua New Guinea and the Bougainville parties to arrive at the Loloata Understanding in March 2000 and the Gateway communiqué in June 2000, which laid the basis for further talks on a political settlement of the crisis in Bougainville.

60. In April 2000, I appointed a new Special Envoy for Myanmar. While I am not able to report substantive progress in our efforts, I am heartened to note that, with the agreement of the Government of Myanmar, the International Committee of the Red Cross began its humanitarian work in the country in 1999.

61. In Fiji, in response to the crisis precipitated by the detention of Prime Minister Mahendra Chaudhry and others, I immediately dispatched my Personal Envoy, who conveyed to the leaders of the political parties my deep concern about the use of violence against a democratically elected government. While I welcome the release of the hostages, much more needs to be done to return the country to normalcy. Sustainable peace, stability and the prosperity of Fiji can be assured only if the aspirations of all communities within Fijian society are taken into account and when all its citizens can play a meaningful role in the political and economic life of the country. I stand ready to work with the Commonwealth and the international community to this end. Recent setbacks in the democratic process in another Pacific country, Solomon Islands, have also caused deep concern.

62. In Europe, I have been encouraged by the continuing improvement in relations between Greece and Turkey. This evolution, bolstered by the Helsinki decision of the European Union regarding Turkey, should help to support efforts directed towards a comprehensive settlement of the Cyprus problem. A continuous process of proximity talks involving Glafcos Clerides and Rauf Denktash is under way under my auspices. With the assistance of my Special Adviser, attempts are being made to develop a conceptual framework for future progress.

63. My Special Representative for Georgia has made a great effort to reinvigorate the Georgian/Abkhaz peace process, in particular by convening the Coordinating Council and by meeting regularly with the Russian Federation, in its capacity as facilitator, the Group of Friends of the Secretary-General and the Organization for Security and Cooperation in Europe (OSCE). He has shifted attention back to the core issue of the conflict, the political status of Abkhazia, Georgia, while continuing to negotiate, with both sides, issues such as the return of refugees and internally displaced persons and economic rehabilitation. While some progress has been achieved, the parties still lack the necessary political will to move towards a comprehensive political settlement.

64. In Latin America, taking note of the growing international concern about the security and human rights situation in Colombia, I appointed a Special Adviser on International Assistance to Colombia in December 1999. He has established contact with a range of actors both within and outside the country and helped to heighten international awareness of the need for a settlement of the country's conflict.

Peacekeeping and peace-building

65. The efforts to gain a better understanding of the needs of United Nations peace operations, outlined in the introduction to this chapter, have

been made in the context of extraordinarily rapid developments on the ground. Over the past year, there has been a dramatic increase in peacekeeping activities, and recognition of the critically important links between peacekeeping and peace-building is increasingly reflected in practice in the field. As the Panel on United Nations Peace Operations noted in its recently released report, peacekeepers and peace-builders are "inseparable partners", and the only ready exit for peacekeeping forces is sustainable peace.

66. The operation in Kosovo, Federal Republic of Yugoslavia, is now fully established; new operations were launched in East Timor and the Democratic Republic of the Congo during the year, and another is contemplated for Eritrea and Ethiopia; major changes have taken place or are envisaged for operations in Sierra Leone and southern Lebanon; and peacekeeping operations in the Central African Republic and Tajikistan have been successfully concluded and succeeded by smaller peace-building offices.

67. United Nations authorized deployment stands at approximately 45,000 uniformed personnel (troops, observers and civilian police) and a further 13,000 international and local civilian staff for peacekeeping operations mandated by the Security Council; the corresponding figures for this time last year were less than 17,000 uniformed personnel and less than 10,000 civilians. Operations broadly described as peace-building, and under the authority of the General Assembly, have 341 international personnel in the field, supported by 455 local staff, up from 203 and 244 respectively this time last year. However, these numbers in themselves do not indicate the extent of the challenges that increasingly confront peacekeeping operations. I have identified eight of these challenges below; many of them are echoed in the report of the Panel on United Nations Peace Operations.

New types of tasks

68. Peacekeeping has become more complicated because peacekeepers must now undertake a greatly expanded range of tasks. Beyond interposition forces and multidisciplinary operations to assist the parties to implement agreements, peacekeepers over the past year have assumed responsibility for interim administrations in Kosovo and East Timor, balancing the competing and sometimes contradictory tasks of governing those territories, supporting the emergence of local institutions and maintaining law and order.

New types of personnel

69. The assumption of these new responsibilities has required that the United Nations expand and adapt the profile of peacekeepers in the field. Over a little more than a year, reflecting in particular the deployment of the United Nations Interim Administration Mission in Kosovo and the United Nations Transitional Authority in East Timor, the authorized deployment of police has jumped from approximately 2,500 to over 8,600, a more than threefold increase. In addition, these new missions have obliged the United Nations to recruit lawyers and judges; city administrators; and experts in customs, fiscal management, public utilities, health, education, sanitation and agriculture.

Deterrent capacity

70. This past year offered further evidence, in particular in Sierra Leone, of the precarious environments in which today's operations are deployed, environments that can threaten the effectiveness of operations and the security of peacekeepers. As the Panel on United Nations Peace Operations notes, these operational experiences have underlined the importance of the United Nations deploying credible deterrent capacity with "robust rules of engagement". There is also a clear need for further efforts in three areas: we need more and better equipped and trained troops; ongoing capacity-building efforts in developing countries, drawing upon bilateral and multilateral partnerships, to expand the pool of potential peacekeepers; and more effective use of United Nations standby capacities to provide equipment to peacekeeping troops in the field.

Readiness/rapid deployment

71. Events over the past year have demonstrated once again how important it is to be able to deploy forces rapidly, and have revealed the constraints in the critical areas of logistics, finance and human resources. Supplies of mission equipment at the United Nations Logistics Base at Brindisi, Italy, are now largely depleted. Yet, as a result of additional and more complex mandates, we face increased demands on the same or fewer resources. In this context I am gratified that the Panel on Peace Operations recommends that the Secretary-General be allowed funds to start planning a mission before the Security Council approves it.

Timely and predictable financial support within peace processes

72. The effective disarmament, demobilization and reintegration of former combatants can

be crucial to the success of a peace process, without some degree of predictability of funding for such operations, the entire enterprise risks failure. To avoid such an outcome I have urged Member States to consider a more flexible approach to the use of assessed funding in this area.

The role of economic incentives in perpetuating conflict

73. The United Nations experiences in Angola, the Democratic Republic of the Congo, Sierra Leone and elsewhere have revealed what damage struggles for control over diamonds, timber, drugs, guns and other resources can do to a peace process. The importance of this issue was highlighted during the year by debates in the Security Council and by the report of the panel of experts on sanctions against UNITA in Angola. The report revealed the extent to which violations of sanctions, in the form of exports of illicitly mined diamonds, were sustaining the war in Angola.

Cooperation with regional organizations

74. Over the past year, cooperation with regional organizations and others in peace-building has proved fruitful on several occasions, but practical, political and organizational problems continue to make it a complicated undertaking. Those who will be responsible for implementing a peace agreement must be present during the negotiation phase to ensure that the operation is based on realistic assumptions. Furthermore, the lines of reporting and division of labour should be as unambiguous as possible; the Organization's relationships with OSCE and the European Union in Kosovo represent an important step in the right direction. Efforts to improve working arrangements with respect to peace-keeping, will continue, and the forthcoming high-level meeting between the United Nations and regional organizations will be dedicated to cooperation in peace-building.

Staffing at Headquarters

75. The past year's events have underlined the importance of adequate staffing at Headquarters, an issue which is dealt with in some depth by the Panel on United Nations Peace Operations. I am in complete agreement with the Panel's view that Headquarters support for peacekeeping should be funded primarily through the regular United Nations budget rather than via the current Support Account, which has to be justified on a post-by-post basis every year.

76. I welcomed the decision of the General Assembly in November 1999 to approve a number of posts within the Department of Peacekeeping Operations. However, the significant loss of personnel and expertise previously incurred through the departure of gratis personnel severely constrained the Secretariat's efforts to support new deployments, expansions and changes of mandate, as well as the liquidation of completed missions. The fact that so much was achieved with so few resources should be acknowledged as a major achievement of the Organization. Recognizing the extraordinary constraints under which the Secretariat has been required to operate and the impact those constraints have had on the planning and execution of missions, the Panel on Peace Operations has recommended an urgent increase in funding. In particular it urges the creation of a new information and analysis unit that will service all departments with peace and security responsibilities.

* * *

77. No two operations have demonstrated the extent of the challenges outlined above more comprehensively than those in the Democratic Republic of the Congo and Sierra Leone. The conflict in the Democratic Republic of the Congo, Africa's third largest country, involves a number of regional States and continues to threaten the stability of the region as a whole. In accordance with my recommendations of 17 January 2000 for the United Nations Organization Mission in the Democratic Republic of the Congo (MONUC), the Security Council authorized the deployment of a total of 5,537 officers and men. The task of that force was to provide secure logistics bases for the operations of up to 500 military observers charged with monitoring the implementation of the Lusaka Ceasefire Agreement.

78. MONUC has experienced serious problems from the outset, including persistent restrictions on its freedom of movement by the Government and other parties; repeated outbreaks of fighting, including major military offensives, in violation of the ceasefire; and logistical challenges arising from the degraded state of the infrastructure in the Democratic Republic of the Congo and the huge size of the country. MONUC operations are continually constrained by the deep suspicion that exists between the parties and, from time to time, by hostility towards the United Nations itself.

79. The overall situation in Sierra Leone remains tense and critical. The successive and unprovoked attacks on, and detentions of, United Nations personnel by the Revolutionary United

Front fighters, initiated in May 2000, have seriously undermined the prospects for peace in that country and continue to pose serious challenges to the operations of the United Nations Mission in Sierra Leone.

80. Despite the difficulties in implementation, I share the view reaffirmed by both the Economic Community of West African States (ECOWAS) and the Security Council that the broad terms of the Lomé Peace Agreement reached in July 1999 remain important as a basis for moving towards durable peace. However, the determined and cohesive support of the neighbouring States and subregional organizations, particularly ECOWAS, and of troop contributors as well as the international community, remain vital if the Mission is to secure the credible military strength necessary to fulfil the broad objectives of the Peace Agreement.

81. Meanwhile, in Western Sahara, nine years have passed since the plan for the settlement of the conflict between Morocco and the Frente POLISARIO was agreed to, yet the settlement plan has still to be implemented and the situation remains delicate. In my recent report to the Security Council on the United Nations Mission for the Referendum in Western Sahara (MINURSO), I have included suggestions that may assist in resolving the multiple problems relating to the implementation of the settlement plan. The presence of MINURSO remains critical to prevent any worsening of the conflict.

82. Challenges of a different kind confront the United Nations in Kosovo and East Timor. In Kosovo, the United Nations Interim Administration Mission in Kosovo (UNMIK) has continued to work closely with the international security presence (KFOR) to create a safe and secure environment for all the residents of the province.

83. A particular challenge has been the development and implementation of the rule of law in Kosovo. In cooperation with OSCE, the Mission is pursuing a comprehensive strategy to rebuild and reform the judicial, police and penal systems. UNMIK has also made progress in ensuring the direct involvement of the local population in the administration of the province. This involvement will be further enhanced following municipal elections later this year. With the assistance of the European Union, good progress has been made in establishing a macroeconomic framework in Kosovo. On the humanitarian front, the United Nations High Commissioner for Refugees and her staff in Kosovo, together with key partners in the United Nations system, the International Federation of Red Cross and Red Crescent Societies and non-governmental organiza-

tions, successfully met the challenges of the emergency relief needs of Kosovo throughout the winter. As a result, the humanitarian "pillar" of UNMIK was terminated at the end of June, and the Mission is now focusing on reconstruction and development.

84. The presence of the United Nations in Kosovo complements its long-standing engagement in the region, particularly through the United Nations Mission in Bosnia and Herzegovina (UNMIBH), which continues to assist in the establishment of the rule of law as part of the implementation of the Dayton/Paris Peace Agreement. After lengthy efforts to overcome political obstruction, in June 2000, UNMIBH finally inaugurated the first unit of the new multi-ethnic State Border Service. This is the first and only executive law enforcement organ that is under the joint institutions of the State, rather than its ethnically based entities. Efforts to redress the ethnic imbalance in the police forces are, however, proceeding exceedingly slowly.

85. The past year has seen extraordinary developments in East Timor. The popular consultation in the territory on 30 August 1999 resulted in 78.5 per cent of voters rejecting the autonomy option offered by Indonesia, thereby expressing their preference for a transition towards independence under United Nations auspices. Unfortunately, that success was marred by the subsequent violence, destruction and forcible displacement of hundreds of thousands of East Timorese, a direct result of the failure of the Indonesian authorities to fulfil their security responsibilities under the agreements of 5 May 1999.

86. The speedy and resolute action of the Security Council in authorizing the deployment of the International Force, East Timor (INTERFET), led by Australia, and the subsequent establishment of UNTAET helped to bring to an end a long and sad chapter in East Timor's history. The complex and difficult task of rebuilding East Timor and preparing it for full independence is proceeding but faces formidable challenges. Political skill, patience and a high level of international and local-level cooperation and coordination are the necessary conditions for success, and cooperation between UNTAET and the East Timorese has proceeded with vigour and goodwill. UNTAET intends gradually to expand the participation of the East Timorese in the administration so as to ensure a seamless transition to independence. The positive disposition of the President of Indonesia, Abdurrahman Wahid, and the East Timorese leadership, particularly Xanana Gusmão, bodes well for good relations in the future.

87. While we have confronted major difficulties and resource constraints in mounting these operations, I am gratified to report that the past year has also seen a considerable reduction in the level of United Nations engagement in the Central African Republic and Tajikistan.

88. The United Nations Mission in the Central African Republic, which completed its work in February 2000, played a crucial role in restoring peace and security to the country. It also helped to create conditions conducive to holding national elections, restructuring the security forces, training the national police and gendarmerie and launching major economic and social reforms. I have since established, with the concurrence of the Security Council, the United Nations Peace-building Support Office. The new office will assist the Government and people of the Central African Republic in the peace process, and help to nurture democratic institutions and build socio-economic recovery and respect for human rights and the rule of law, demonstrating how much can be done to promote peace and national reconciliation when missions are conducted with a clear mandate, appropriate resources, the commitment of the parties and the sustained support of the international community.

89. As in the Central African Republic, our objective in Guinea-Bissau and Liberia, where United Nations peace-building offices are also in place, is not simply to deal with the immediate challenges of post-conflict stabilization, but also to promote sustainable peace in the longer term. Here and elsewhere the United Nations is working with local actors to address the root causes of conflict and thus minimize the chance that violence will reoccur.

90. The United Nations Peace-building Support Office in Tajikistan, which was established in May 2000, will provide the political framework and leadership for the peace-building activities of the United Nations system in that country. It builds on the success of more than seven years of United Nations peacemaking and peacekeeping efforts in Tajikistan. The United Nations Mission of Observers in Tajikistan, working closely with regional guarantor States and international organizations, assisted the Tajik parties in overcoming many obstacles to peace, national reconciliation and development. However, the conflict in neighbouring Afghanistan and the complexities of domestic politics mean that renewed instability cannot be ruled out. Consequently, the continuing support of the international community in the post-conflict phase will be important for Tajikistan's ability to sustain and build on the achievements of the peace process.

91. Haiti presents another example of a country in which the United Nations presence has recently changed. In this case the shift came about after a series of peacekeeping missions deployed since 1995 came to an end, including the joint United Nations/Organization of American States International Civilian Mission in Haiti. Those multidimensional missions were not mandated to re-establish or maintain peace in the wake of an armed conflict, but rather to solve a serious internal crisis by re-establishing democracy, improving respect for human rights and reforming state institutions, particularly the police.

92. In order to consolidate the Mission's achievements I recommended to the General Assembly that it establish the International Civilian Support Mission in Haiti (MICAH), which has taken over the task of assisting the ongoing transition to democratic constitutional rule. MICAH has three substantive pillars of activity: human rights, police and justice.

93. The United Nations Verification Mission in Guatemala remains the largest of the United Nations peace-building missions. It continues to provide good offices and advisory and public information functions to support the implementation of the peace agreements. Many substantive reforms remain incomplete, however. Although 2000 is the final year in the official implementation calendar, the parties to the agreements have proposed that the implementation timetable be extended. Consequently, I am conducting consultations on means of consolidating the peace-building process in order to allow me to make an appropriate recommendation to the General Assembly.

94. Peace-building in practice involves initiatives to help promote national reconciliation and justice, respect for human rights and the rule of law, and the organization of free and fair elections. It also includes measures to create propitious conditions for sustainable economic growth, a necessary condition for reconstruction. In pursuing these goals, our offices maintain regular contacts with relevant donor countries and with representatives of the international financial institutions.

95. United Nations peace-building activities have been strengthened by a closer working relationship between peace operations and the field offices of the Office of the United Nations High Commissioner for Human Rights. Such field offices are currently in place in Bosnia, Burundi, Cambodia, Colombia, Croatia, the Democratic Republic of the Congo and the Federal Republic of Yugoslavia.

96. Another far-reaching aspect of our peace-building work is that related to mine clear-

ing. The Mine Action Service of the Department of Peacekeeping Operations works with its partners in missions all over the world to help locate and clear mines—a task that is growing as the number of mine-affected countries continues to rise and new mines are laid in countries previously cleared. These developments have further strained the limited resources that are available. Access to resources is only part of the problem, however, and once again I would like to stress the need to stigmatize the production, distribution and use of these indiscriminate weapons.

Electoral assistance

97.   The United Nations provides assistance to electoral institutions for two reasons, namely, to enhance administrative capacity to hold credible, transparent and fair elections and to assist in the institutional consolidation required during the post-election period. Over the medium and long term such assistance aims to prevent the democratic breakdown and erosion that may sometimes occur after the first elections are held in societies in transition and to stabilize the electoral institutions themselves.

98.   The provision of electoral assistance is a vital component of the United Nations system's overall peace-building and democratization strategies. Over the past eight years, the United Nations has experienced a significant increase in the number and complexity of requests for electoral assistance. Since its establishment in 1992, the Electoral Assistance Division has provided assistance in 150 electoral processes, ranging from the organization of elections to the provision of technical support. Particularly notable during the past year has been the United Nations participation in the electoral processes in Mexico and Nigeria.

Sanctions

99.   Sanctions have had an uneven track record in encouraging compliance with Security Council resolutions and in recent years their efficacy has been increasingly questioned. In the case of comprehensive economic sanctions, concerns have been expressed about their negative effects on civilians and on neighbouring States, whose trading relations are harmed by sanctions but which receive no compensation for the harm suffered. The costs of sanctions have too often been borne by ordinary people, not by the authoritarian Governments against which they were directed. Paradoxically, the political élites that compose the regimes themselves have often benefited economically from the black markets

that have sprung up to circumvent the sanctions intended to exert pressure upon them.

100.   I therefore share the view, emerging as a consensus among Member States, that the design and implementation of Security Council sanctions need to be improved, and their administration enhanced, to allow a more prompt and effective response to present and future threats to international peace and security. Future sanctions regimes should be designed so as to maximize the chance of inducing the target to comply with Security Council resolutions while minimizing the negative effects of the sanctions on the civilian population and neighbouring and other affected States.

101.   The debate on sanctions held in the Security Council in April and the subsequent establishment of an informal working group of the Council, with a mandate to draw up general recommendations on how to improve the effectiveness of sanctions, demonstrated the Council's readiness to consider practical steps to improve sanctions regimes. This is a welcome development that should help the Council to oversee the evolution of sanctions into a more potent instrument of deterrence and conflict prevention.

Disarmament

102.   Disarmament is a critical element of the United Nations strategy for peace and security. Steps to reduce the level of arms and curb proliferation not only make the world a safer place by reducing the propensity for conflict but also lessen the temptation for States to embark on costly arms races. The latest figures indicate that global military expenditures increased in 1999 for the first time in the post-cold-war period, bringing total spending to approximately $780 billion, or 2.6 per cent of the world's gross national product.

103.   Despite some progress in the reduction of nuclear weapons—in particular the Russian Federation's ratification of the second Treaty on the Reduction of Strategic Arms (START II)—there is deep concern within the international community at the continuing risk posed by such weapons. The results of the 2000 Review Conference of the Parties to the Treaty on the Non-Proliferation of Nuclear Weapons are therefore of considerable importance. The unequivocal undertaking by the nuclear-weapon States to accomplish the total elimination of their nuclear arsenals, a reinvigorated effort to halt the global spread of nuclear weapons and a strengthening of the standards governing the peaceful uses of nuclear energy—all issues crucial to the security of the peoples of the United Nations—provide grounds for encouragement. Much, however, re-

mains to be done. The universalization of the Chemical Weapons Convention and the speedy negotiation of a protocol to strengthen the Biological Weapons Convention are achievable goals; I strongly urge their pursuit.

104. While the number of ratifications of the Comprehensive Nuclear-Test-Ban Treaty has increased during the past year, the challenges that confront its entry into force persist, especially after the United States Senate's rejection of ratification in October 1999. It is essential that the Final Declaration of the Conference on facilitating the entry into force of the Treaty, held in October 1999, be implemented. I therefore reiterate my call to all States to ratify the Treaty, particularly those whose ratification is necessary for it to enter into force.

105. Last year, I drew attention to the dangers posed by the development and testing of long-range missiles. While that danger remains, there is also danger from another quarter, namely, the growing pressure to deploy national missile defences. Within the scientific community there is widespread scepticism that such systems could ever work effectively, and real concern that their deployment could lead to a new arms race, set back nuclear disarmament and non-proliferation policies, and create new incentives for missile proliferation. I trust that States will weigh these factors very carefully before embarking on a path that could jeopardize the Anti-Ballistic Missile Treaty and that may reduce, rather than enhance, global security.

106. With respect to conventional arms, preparations are being made for the United Nations Conference on the Illicit Trade in Small Arms and Light Weapons in All Its Aspects, scheduled for 2001. Since these are the weapons that kill most people in most wars, the outcome of the Conference is of crucial importance. We must reduce the risks to the people most threatened by those weapons, including the children who are often recruited as soldiers to use them. Some progress is already being made as States tighten their arms export legislation and collect and destroy surplus weapons. Innovative approaches such as "weapons for development" and "weapons for food" programmes are yielding concrete results as practical disarmament measures at the community level. This progress is due to close cooperation between States, the business sector, groups in civil society and the international community.

107. Although the United Nations is a global Organization, it recognizes that regional approaches to arms control and disarmament may also play a crucial role in enhancing security. The three United Nations regional centres for peace and disarmament have been revitalized but a chronic lack of resources unfortunately continues to limit their effectiveness.

108. During the 2000 Review Conference of the parties to the Non-Proliferation Treaty, non-governmental organizations working in the field of disarmament had an unprecedented opportunity to express their views to States parties at a meeting organized for that purpose. They also continued to play an unofficial but vital monitoring role under the Ottawa Convention, on anti-personnel mines. I trust that Member States will bear in mind the constructive contribution that civil society makes to disarmament when they decide how non-governmental organizations are to participate in the conference on small arms in 2001.

Chapter II

Meeting humanitarian commitments

109. The past year has been marked by humanitarian emergencies that far surpassed predicted worst-case scenarios. Protracted conflicts in Afghanistan, Angola, Colombia, the Democratic Republic of the Congo, Somalia, Sri Lanka and the Sudan continued unabated. Crises escalated or erupted in the Republic of the Congo, Kosovo, East Timor and Chechnya, and between Ethiopia and Eritrea. The situation in Burundi deteriorated because of Government-led mass forced relocation programmes, and the outbreak of violence in Sierra Leone in May 2000 has had serious humanitarian consequences. Civilians continue to bear the brunt of these violent conflicts, as victims of direct attacks, indiscriminate bombings, rape and sexual torture, forced relocation, the denial or restriction of access to humanitarian assistance and numerous other human rights violations.

110. Apart from these complex emergencies, natural disasters have once again wrought devastation in many developing countries. Mongolia, Turkey, India, Venezuela and southern Africa, among others, were severely affected by the consequences of snowstorms, earthquakes, cyclones, mudslides and floods, while drought spread in the Horn of Africa and gained momentum in Central Asia. The number and scale of natural disasters are growing rapidly, demanding greater international cooperation for the provision of assistance to affected populations.

Coordinating humanitarian action

111. This past year, improved coordination of international humanitarian action has been characterized by the implementation of innova-

tive approaches in major emergencies in Kosovo and East Timor, and by the challenges of providing protection to internally displaced persons and civilians in armed conflict. In response to the humanitarian crisis in the Balkans, the Office for the Coordination of Humanitarian Affairs seconded personnel to perform coordination functions in support of the lead role of the Office of the United Nations High Commissioner for Refugees (UNHCR) in the region. They helped to create the Emergency Management Group in Albania, and later established an Inter-Agency Coordination Unit and a Humanitarian Community Information Centre in Kosovo.

112. In response to the East Timor crisis, a senior humanitarian coordinator was immediately deployed by the Office for the Coordination of Humanitarian Affairs to lead an inter-agency team of specialists. This deployment provided vital coordination services until the humanitarian component of the United Nations Transitional Administration in East Timor (UNTAET) could be established. The Office also supported my Special Representative for East Timor in designing, staffing and providing initial funding for the humanitarian component of UNTAET.

113. An inter-agency response was developed to address the rapid growth of internally displaced persons in a number of countries, including Afghanistan, Angola, Burundi, Colombia and the Democratic Republic of the Congo. The Emergency Relief Coordinator and the members of the Inter-Agency Standing Committee also intensified their efforts to improve the coordination and delivery of programmes for internally displaced persons.

114. Since internally displaced persons remain by definition citizens of their own country, international responses to specific situations are designed in collaboration with Governments and local authorities in each affected country. It had been clear for some time that the international response mechanisms needed to be reviewed, and that clearer lines of responsibility and accountability had to be agreed upon. A series of reviews were undertaken and a policy paper on the protection of internally displaced persons has been produced. The central premise of the policy is that the responsibility for internally displaced persons lies first and foremost with their national Government, but it is recognized that the capacity and willingness of authorities to fulfil their responsibilities may be insufficient or lacking altogether in some conflict situations. The policy therefore urges humanitarian agencies to cooperate with national and local authorities and other relevant actors to support and supplement their efforts on behalf of the displaced. In adopting these guidelines, the Inter-Agency Standing Committee has sought to resolve some of the ambiguities that impede effective humanitarian action in crises.

115. The Committee also advocates strengthening the legal and physical protection of civilians caught in armed conflict. In September 1999, I presented to the Security Council my report on the protection of civilians in armed conflict, which contained 40 recommendations aimed at reducing the threats to civilians in armed conflict. The report was transmitted to the General Assembly in November. The Security Council has adopted several resolutions supporting my recommendations, and has undertaken to give special emphasis to the protection and rights of children in armed conflict. Those resolutions constitute a significant milestone in the humanitarian community's long-standing efforts to ensure that the causes of humanitarian crises are addressed politically at the highest international level.

116. The response so far to the consolidated inter-agency appeals for the year 2000 has been disappointing. As at 30 June 2000, midway through the appeal cycle, just 34 per cent of the total requirements were available. This amount is lower, in percentage terms, than pledges made to the 1999 consolidated appeals by the same time last year, despite acknowledged improvements in the quality of the appeals. Further efforts are being made to strengthen the consolidated appeal process in the coming year and more innovative approaches are being considered to help mobilize resources for these "forgotten emergencies".

117. In the consolidated appeals for 2000, requests for funding to meet security needs were introduced for the first time, US$ 8.5 million being sought for security-related activities in 10 countries or regions. All future consolidated appeals will include a comprehensive review of security requirements.

118. Efforts to improve the United Nations response to the growing number of natural and environmental disasters include the appointment by the Office for the Coordination of Humanitarian Affairs of regional natural disaster response advisers in Asia, Latin America and the Pacific. The advisers counsel and assist Governments and regional networks in natural disaster preparations. They also assist in the deployment of United Nations Disaster Assessment and Coordination teams from within the disaster region and elsewhere around the world.

119. In 1999, those teams were deployed on 12 occasions. The Office for the Coordination of Humanitarian Affairs also assisted the members of the International Search and Rescue Advisory

Group in coordinating the international search and rescue teams that were deployed in response to earthquakes in three continents.

120. Member States recognized the achievements of the International Decade for Natural Disaster Reduction, and the need to continue disaster reduction activities under the leadership of the United Nations system, in Economic and Social Council resolution 1999/63 and General Assembly resolution 54/219, concerning future arrangements for natural disaster reduction. The new strategy helps communities to resist the effects of natural, technological and environmental hazards and reduce their social and economic costs. The initiative also seeks to integrate risk-prevention strategies into sustainable development activities. During the past year increasing emphasis has been placed on multidisciplinary approaches to disaster reduction. Priority is being given to using scientific and technological innovations relevant to disaster reduction and to engaging local decision makers and citizens' groups in developing sustainable long-term disaster reduction strategies at the regional and national levels. An inter-agency task force has been established to facilitate the new multidisciplinary approach. The United Nations Development Programme (UNDP) chairs a working group to develop measures to quantify risk, vulnerability and impact indicators; the United Nations Environment Programme chairs a working group on early warning systems; and the World Meteorological Organization chairs a working group on forecasting the socio-economic impacts of future occurrences of El Niño, climate change and variability.

Delivering humanitarian services

121. During the past year, areas receiving United Nations humanitarian assistance included Afghanistan, Angola, Burundi, Colombia, the Republic of the Congo, the Democratic Republic of the Congo, East Timor, Kosovo, Mozambique, Mongolia, the Russian Federation, Rwanda, Sierra Leone, Somalia, the Sudan, Tajikistan, Turkey, Uganda, Venezuela, and the Great Lakes region in Africa.

122. In 1999, the World Food Programme (WFP) provided food aid to nearly 89 million people worldwide, much of it in the form of emergency and recovery operations. The number of people assisted represented a 17 per cent increase over the 1998 total. Some 41 million of those assisted were victims of natural disasters. Approximately 18 million more vulnerable civilians caught in conflict situations, including internally displaced persons and refugees, were also assisted.

123. Seventy-five per cent of the people reached by WFP humanitarian activities in 1999 were women and children. In nearly all ongoing humanitarian operations, in compliance with the policies of the Inter-Agency Standing Committee and its own "commitments to women" policy, WFP and its partners have concentrated efforts to tackle the gender-related aspects and social dimensions of food insecurity, embedding gender concerns within humanitarian assistance programmes.

124. The response of WFP to rapid onset crises, like those in the Balkans and East Timor, demonstrated the Programme's ability to facilitate effective food aid coordination and provide logistic and telecommunication support to humanitarian partners from the very outset of such crises. WFP and its partners are now able to rapidly develop coordinated intervention strategies that target the needs of the most vulnerable.

125. As a consequence of its improved analytic and forecasting capabilities, WFP was one of the first agencies to detect signals of an impending, drought-related regional food crisis in the Horn of Africa late in 1999, and alert the international community to the severity of the situation. In response to that crisis, in March 2000 I appointed the Executive Director of WFP as my Special Representative for the Drought in the Horn of Africa.

126. Staff security continues to be of great concern to the World Food Programme. Seven staff members lost their lives in the field in 1999. WFP persists in its efforts to strengthen the Organization's capacity to protect its staff in the field and nearly all staff have now undergone security training.

127. The Food and Agriculture Organization of the United Nations (FAO) provides early warning of impending food emergencies, produces information on crop and food supplies, assesses emergency needs in the agricultural sector, provides agricultural inputs so that people can grow their own food and reduce their dependence on food aid, assists Governments in coping with crises and gives technical advice to non-governmental organizations active in agriculture.

128. Thanks to donor funding, and United Nations system partners such as WFP, UNHCR and UNDP, FAO together with its non-governmental organization partners has been able to conduct major campaigns to provide agricultural inputs to internally displaced persons, returnees and refugees and to implement early rehabilitation programmes. FAO has also continued to work closely with WFP and UNHCR in assisting refugees, internally displaced persons, returnees and host populations to improve their food security

situation. FAO has provided technical assistance for disaster mapping and for establishing integrated information management systems for disaster management.

129. Immunizations, nutrition, pharmaceuticals, controlling epidemics and mental health remain World Health Organization (WHO) priorities. This past year, WHO has called attention to such critical global health threats as malaria, poliomyelitis, HIV/AIDS and maternal mortality. Efforts to overcome these challenges have been complicated by the increased number of natural disasters and complex humanitarian emergencies. With the support of the Organization's central management bodies, intensified efforts have been made to enhance the readiness of WHO country offices and to assess and address the health needs of those affected by natural and human-induced disasters in a timely manner.

130. In the field, and with enhanced support from regional offices and headquarters, WHO has focused on health and nutritional surveillance, providing the data that is critical for coordinated planning and implementation of assistance, both in emergencies and post-crisis reconstruction.

131. In 1999-2000, special efforts have been made to eradicate polio, to control malaria, and to define new strategies for HIV/AIDS control and safe motherhood in complex emergencies. WHO has also continued to monitor the equitable distribution of commodities imported into Iraq under Security Council resolution 986(1995). Work continued in the Palestinian self-rule areas to reform health-care systems. Strengthening the dialogue and coordination between national and international health actors, and bridging the gap between recovery, rehabilitation and health development, have continued to be high priority issues for the Organization.

132. The United Nations Children's Fund (UNICEF), together with its United Nations and non-governmental organization partners, provided humanitarian aid and protection to more than 48 million children and women affected by man-made and natural disasters in the past year. In response to the resolution adopted in August 1999 by the Security Council, stressing the need for greater and more effective efforts to protect children caught in armed conflict, UNICEF developed a comprehensive package of programmes and interventions for children and mothers in emergency situations, including baby care, pre-school and primary education, recreational activities, and education about health and nutrition. UNICEF also increased its support for demobilization and reintegration programmes for children in Sierra Leone and the Democratic Re-public of the Congo, and strengthened and expanded programmes in Angola, the Democratic Republic of the Congo, Kosovo and East Timor supporting the reunification of families separated by conflict. Psycho-social support for children affected by conflict and displacement was provided in Albania, the former Yugoslav Republic of Macedonia and Turkey. In Kosovo, East Timor and many other emergency situations, UNICEF support to basic education and schooling has helped to restore some normalcy to children's lives.

133. National Immunization Days were conducted throughout the year in an effort to eradicate polio in Afghanistan, Angola, Burundi, the Democratic People's Republic of Korea, the Democratic Republic of the Congo, the Sudan and the United Republic of Tanzania. In pursuing these campaigns in countries embroiled in violent conflict, UNICEF worked with WHO to negotiate "days of tranquillity" to enable children to be immunized safely.

134. In 1999, UNICEF launched a Global Peace and Security Agenda to help guide international efforts on behalf of children and women in armed conflict. The set of goals, presented to the Security Council by the Executive Director, calls for an end to the use of children as soldiers; the protection of children from the effects of sanctions; the inclusion of specific provisions for children in peace-building; an end to impunity from war crimes—especially those committed against children; early warning and preventive action for children; and improvements in the safety of humanitarian workers.

135. During the past year my Special Representative for Children and Armed Conflict has focused on engaging regional, intergovernmental and civil society organizations with the plight of children in armed conflict and advocating the application of relevant norms and standards; raising the age-limit for the recruitment and participation of young persons in armed conflict; addressing cross-border issues affecting children, with special attention to the West Africa region; seeking to bring those who have violated international human rights and humanitarian law to justice; working to ensure that children's rights are protected within the rules of evidence and procedure of the International Criminal Court; and encouraging the involvement of children and young people in peacemaking and peace-building efforts.

136. I am gratified that this year the Security Council, building on the more general resolution 1261(1999), has adopted another resolution (1314(2000)) on children affected by armed conflict, by which it puts in place a number of con-

crete provisions for the protection of war-affected children. I am also pleased to announce that these initiatives have led to commitments from the Governments of Burundi, Colombia, Rwanda, Sierra Leone and the Sudan to protect children.

137. The United Nations Relief and Works Agency for Palestine Refugees in the Near East (UNRWA) combines humanitarian and developmental strategies in providing education, health and relief and social services to approximately 3.7 million refugees in its five fields of operation: Jordan, Lebanon, the West Bank, the Gaza Strip and the Syrian Arab Republic. In May 2000, the Agency commemorated 50 years of service in the field. The work of UNRWA, carried out principally by more than 20,000 dedicated local staff, has continued to produce impressive achievements, often under challenging circumstances including emergencies and conflict situations. However, serious shortfalls in funding the Agency's budget have inevitably had a negative impact on the level and standard of services. The voluntary donor contributions on which UNRWA depends must be secured and enhanced if the Agency is to meet the challenges it is sure to face in the years ahead.

138. In recognition of its unique role in promoting reproductive health and preventing sexual violence in emergency situations, the United Nations Population Fund (UNFPA) became a full member of the Inter-Agency Standing Committee in April 2000. Following an assessment of the extent of sexual violence towards Kosovar women, UNFPA set up an office in Kosovo to re-establish reproductive health care and to provide counselling and services to women and their families. The guidelines in the Inter-Agency Field Manual for Reproductive Health in Refugee Situations were updated and training was provided to staff from UNFPA, other United Nations bodies, non-governmental organizations and national agencies in the use of the guidelines and to sensitize them to the reproductive health needs of refugees. UNFPA also participated in discussions with the Department of Peacekeeping Operations on HIV prevention within peacekeeping missions. At its annual session in June 2000, the Executive Board of UNDP/UNFPA endorsed the use of up to $1 million from special UNFPA interregional programme funds as a leveraging base from which to build appeals for extrabudgetary resources to tackle this problem.

139. An integral component of the overall planning framework of UNDP is to reduce the incidence and impact of complex emergencies and disasters—natural, environmental and technological—and to accelerate the recovery process towards sustainable human development. The main objectives in disaster reduction and recovery are to achieve a sustainable reduction in disaster risks and the protection of development gains; reduce the loss of life and livelihood due to disasters, and ensure that disaster recovery serves to consolidate sustainable human development. To achieve these goals, UNDP works through its system of country-based resident representatives, regional bureaux and specialized programmes, such as the Division for Sustainable Energy and Environment, co-sponsorship of the Global Environment Fund and the Office to Combat Desertification and Drought. The UNDP Disaster Reduction Programme, a component of its Emergency Response Division, is the focal point for ensuring that disaster reduction concerns are integrated into development strategies. A central objective of the Division is to strengthen, at all levels, the capacity of institutions to manage disasters more effectively and to promote and develop disaster reduction strategies.

140. UNICEF continued to promote the Convention on the Prohibition of the Use, Stockpiling, Production and Transfer of Anti-personnel Mines and on Their Destruction, and to advocate its universal ratification. As at 21 August 2000, the Convention has been signed by 133 countries, and ratified by 101. UNDP, in close collaboration with the Mine Action Service of the Department of Peacekeeping Operations, is responsible for supporting national and local capacity-building, and addressing the socio-economic consequences of landmines. With 12 active UNDP programmes, and 5 new initiatives, the UNDP Mine Action Team, which is an advisory element of the Emergency Response Division, is responsible for policy development, policy guidance, and operational support for UNDP mine action programmes.

141. Since the phases of relief, rehabilitation, reconstruction and development often overlap in post-conflict situations, UNDP has adopted a comprehensive and integrated approach to countries in and emerging from crisis. Humanitarian and development strategies that focus on preventing crises, mitigating their consequences and promoting sustainable recovery must be carried out in concert if they are to be effective. In order to achieve this goal, capacity-building, infrastructure rehabilitation, promotion of the rule of law, and reintegration programmes which assist displaced as well as local communities have become an integral part of UNDP activities in post-conflict situations.

142. In all countries, UNDP works through the resident coordinator system, emphasizing joint

planning, demand-driven rather than agency-driven assessments of needs and local capacities, the importance of a clearly agreed division of labour through inter-agency collaboration, and the need for more flexible financing systems for transitional programming. Every effort is made to support the central role of national authorities in the management of these processes and to engage all international actors in a common, inclusive and participatory approach.

143. Since the end of 1996 the "oil-for-food" programme, established by the Security Council and administered by the Office of the Iraq Programme, has provided a means for Iraq to sell its oil and use two thirds of the revenue to purchase, with sanctions Committee approval, humanitarian supplies and, more recently, spare parts and equipment for damaged infrastructure including the oil industry. Thirty per cent is used by the United Nations Compensation Commission in Geneva for war reparations. Tight limits on the value of oil sold in each 180-day phase were eased in 1998 and then lifted completely in 1999. As at the end of July 2000, Iraq had sold $32 billion worth of oil and received $8 billion worth of supplies, with another $5 billion approved and en route. Nevertheless, the people of Iraq continue to suffer from the effects of sanctions.

Protecting and assisting refugees

144. Although in global terms there was relatively little change in the number of refugees and persons of concern to the Office of the United Nations High Commissioner for Refugees between the beginning and the end of 1999 (21.5 million as against 22.3 million), it was, nevertheless, a year of major challenges. Conflicts in Kosovo, East Timor and Chechnya, Russian Federation, dominated the media and absorbed a large share of UNHCR resources, but there were many other humanitarian crises around the world, especially in Africa, that received less media attention. These disparate situations posed dilemmas and difficult decisions, not only for the United Nations refugee agency but also for the wider humanitarian community.

145. In Kosovo, the massive emergency that erupted late in March 1999, leading to the exodus of over 800,000 people, was followed 10 weeks later by one of the most spectacular reverse population movements in contemporary history, obliging humanitarian agencies to shift gears from a large-scale emergency operation to one supporting return and reintegration. The continuation of ethnic violence in Kosovo, primarily by ethnic Albanians against the Serb and Roma minorities, has frustrated one of the declared purposes of international action, namely, to pre-

serve a multi-ethnic society in Kosovo. Against this troubled background, UNHCR is attempting to ensure a smooth transition to longer-term reconstruction, and has handed over its responsibility as head of the humanitarian "pillar" of the United Nations Interim Administration Mission in Kosovo to the civil administration and economic reconstruction pillars. Elsewhere in the region, the first half of 2000 has witnessed encouraging signs of minority communities returning to their homes in Bosnia and Herzegovina and Croatia.

146. The bitter conflict in East Timor led to the displacement of more than 75 per cent of the population, many of whom crossed into West Timor. Following the deployment of the Australian-led multinational force in October, thousands of refugees began to return home. UNHCR and its partners provided protection and assistance to some 160,000 refugees, including extensive reconstruction of housing in East Timor. Continuing intimidation of refugees in the camps in West Timor has required ongoing humanitarian assistance in the region.

147. The situation around Chechnya deteriorated sharply in the second half of 1999, and led to over 200,000 people fleeing into neighbouring republics, several thousand more into Georgia and others further afield to Kazakhstan. Working closely with its partners in the United Nations system, the International Federation of Red Cross and Red Crescent Societies and non-governmental organizations, UNHCR has continued to assist these internally displaced persons and refugees, despite severe operating constraints. Limited aid is also being provided to those returning to Chechnya on a voluntary basis.

148. The intensification of the war between Eritrea and Ethiopia that marked the early months of 2000 forced close to 100,000 refugees to flee from Eritrea into the Sudan, while hundreds of thousands more have been internally displaced. Since the beginning of this conflict more than two years ago, over 1 million people have abandoned their homes in both countries. With the ceasefire brokered by the Organization of African Unity in June 2000, there were hopes for lasting peace and solutions for the victims. An appeal to meet the needs of those returning was launched by UNHCR in July 2000. Meanwhile, plans are under way to resume the repatriation of other Eritrean refugees who had been residing in the Sudan for many years. The programme had been suspended owing to the renewed conflict.

149. Many other refugee movements have occurred away from the glare of the media, and the international response, particularly in support of peace, has been slow, timid and piecemeal. In the

Great Lakes region, continued fighting between Government and rebel forces in the Democratic Republic of the Congo, despite the Lusaka Ceasefire Agreement of July 1999, caused over 136,000 people to flee into neighbouring countries, with thousands of new arrivals in Zambia and the United Republic of Tanzania. Heightened rebel activity in Burundi caused new movements into the United Republic of Tanzania, bringing the number of refugees from Burundi there to nearly half a million. Although the situation in the Republic of the Congo improved slightly, a further 49,000 Congolese fled to the neighbouring Democratic Republic of the Congo. Gabon was also confronted with the sudden arrival of more than 12,000 refugees from the Republic of the Congo. The list of these and other ongoing refugee situations, many of them protracted, is depressingly long. In West Africa more than 15,000 Sierra Leoneans and 8,000 Liberians fled to Guinea during 1999, bringing the total number of refugees in the country to well over 460,000. This has led to large-scale demand for humanitarian assistance with little prospect of voluntary repatriation despite the Lomé Peace Agreement of May 1999.

150. The escalation of the armed conflict in Sri Lanka since March 2000 has meant that the number of internally displaced persons in the Jaffna Peninsula climbed to 170,000, giving rise to concern for the fate of civilians trapped in the conflict areas. Together with the International Committee of the Red Cross, UNHCR and its partners continue to provide emergency relief aid to those in need.

151. The most severe drought in 30 years has struck south-western Afghanistan and adjacent areas in Pakistan and the Islamic Republic of Iran, further complicating the provision of assistance to refugee populations, many of whom have been awaiting an opportunity to return home for many years. On a more positive note, a joint programme with the Government of the Islamic Republic of Iran for the voluntary repatriation of Afghan refugees has been launched, allowing the return of some 29,000 persons since April 2000. The programme has now been suspended largely because of circumstances linked to the drought.

152. The challenges for the coming year remain daunting. Among the most serious of these remains the plight of internally displaced persons. The growing tendency to deny humanitarian agencies access to war-affected areas for long periods, thus exacerbating the suffering of civilian victims, is an issue of particular concern. Security poses further major challenges including the protection of refugees and refugee operations; the security of refugee-populated areas; the safety of States jeopardized by mass population movements; and the well-being of humanitarian staff. UNHCR has made a series of proposals to address these issues comprehensively, including a strategy aimed at improving security in refugee-populated areas, camps or settlements. The emphasis is increasingly on prevention. To this end, UNHCR is in the process of establishing standby arrangements with a number of Governments for the provision of public security experts to be deployed as an integral component of UNHCR emergency response teams at the beginning of a refugee crisis. In addition, the Department of Peacekeeping Operations has indicated its willingness, within the limits of available resources, to evaluate situations of insecurity that pose a threat to regional peace and security, and recommend an appropriate response.

153. Another major undertaking in respect of the international protection of refugees is the reaffirmation of the 1951 Convention Relating to the Status of Refugees as the universal foundation of refugee protection. The fiftieth anniversary of the Convention falls next year, following that of UNHCR in December 2000. To strengthen refugee protection policies, UNHCR will soon initiate a process of global consultations with senior government representatives and refugee protection experts. A central aim will be to clarify the provisions for refugee protection in situations not fully covered by the Convention.

Chapter III

Cooperating for development

Development in a globalizing world

154. As we confront the complex and profound changes being wrought by globalization, the most important development goal of the United Nations must continue to be the elimination of poverty worldwide. The most important means to this end is the promotion of sustainable and equitable growth, which in turn requires open markets and the stable legal and regulatory institutions that markets need in order to flourish. Adequate levels of development finance are also critical; for the poorest countries that find it difficult to attract private capital, this means continued reliance on official development assistance. Effective social development policies in the areas of health, education and welfare, which are important United Nations goals in their own right, also support the growth process.

155. As we enter the new millennium, arguments over the costs and benefits of globalization have intensified. The controversies surrounding

this issue were manifested by the violent protests at the World Trade Organization (WTO) meeting in Seattle at the end of 1999 and by subsequent demonstrations against the World Bank and the International Monetary Fund (IMF) in Washington. The disquiet is evident not only in the streets, however. Concerns about the consequences of globalization pervade much of the developing world. The tenth session of the United Nations Conference on Trade and Development (UNCTAD) in February reflected many of these concerns. The Conference examined a range of issues central to the globalization debate and urged that the benefits of globalization be more widely shared both within and among countries.

156. During the past year I have been engaged in an intensive process of reflection on the institutional and policy implications of globalization. At a meeting held with the executive heads of key United Nations agencies last April, two challenges clearly emerged. First, how can we ensure the effective participation of all countries in the global trading system? Second, how do we integrate the advancement of our social and environmental objectives with our economic and financial strategies?

157. These critical challenges have resonated throughout the United Nations system during the past year. The Economic and Social Council, for example, has devoted priority attention to the relationship between globalization and the eradication of poverty. The special high-level meeting of the Council with the Bretton Woods institutions, held in April 2000, focused on strengthening financial arrangements as well as eradicating poverty. The easing of the economic and financial crises of the late 1990s has provided a window of opportunity to consider reforms, including the reform of elements of the international financial architecture. System-wide discussion of these issues is continuing.

158. In the course of the July session of the Economic and Social Council, the need to integrate development, finance, trade and social policies more effectively was stressed, as was the need for better coordination among the United Nations system, the Bretton Woods institutions and WTO. Achieving greater policy coherence and consistency in the decisions taken by different intergovernmental forums remains a daunting task, however.

159. The discussions in the Economic and Social Council were held in the context of a global recovery from the economic crises of the previous two years. The *World Economic and Social Survey 2000*, produced by the Department of Economic and Social Affairs, highlights the prospect of solid global economic growth continuing for some years to come. The global financial system remains vulnerable to disruption, however, and many of the problems that caused or exacerbated the Asian crisis of 1997 remain unresolved. There is no room for complacency and a continuing need for reform.

Development finance

160. The high-level event on financing for development planned for 2001 will provide an opportunity to advance a range of policies to promote financial stability and crisis prevention. I attach great importance to the work of the Preparatory Committee for that meeting, which will be the first ever to involve the world's finance, trade and development organizations in a global consultation on issues of common concern. It is encouraging that the Preparatory Committee has already agreed on a broad agenda that includes the mobilization of domestic and international resources for development, trade, development assistance and debt relief.

The need for reliable statistics

161. Effective development policies require reliable statistical data, but the diverse and often inadequate statistical capacities of different countries make the task of developing standardized statistical indicators daunting. Responding to this need, the Economic and Social Council has called on international organizations to improve coordination of the production and dissemination of statistical indicators. It has also urged the need for increased statistical capacity-building at the national level. Enhancing the quality of information available to policy makers also emerged from the fifteenth meeting of the Group of Experts on the United Nations Programme in Public Administration and Finance, held in May 2000, as a fundamental prerequisite for addressing the challenges of globalization.

162. In response to these requests, the United Nations is supporting capacity-building in national statistical offices, in particular in census-taking. We are also helping to strengthen statistical capacity in several subregions, including those of the Caribbean Community (CARICOM) and the Association of South-East Asian Nations (ASEAN).

Engaging with other actors

163. During recent years the United Nations has engaged in a regular dialogue with a diverse range of actors involved in the development process, particularly civil society organizations and, increasingly, the private sector. In the past year,

we have pursued a number of major initiatives with the private sector. The Global Alliance for Vaccines and Immunization, supported by the Bill and Melinda Gates Foundation, and the agreement with major drug companies to provide HIV/AIDS drug treatments at reduced cost to developing countries are two prominent examples. The Global Compact, whose partners met for the first time late in July, is but the latest demonstration of the increasing cooperation between the United Nations, the private sector and civil society.

Improving operational performance

164. Building on my reform programme launched in 1997, the United Nations system is making steady progress in improving the coherence and effectiveness of its operations, particularly at the country level. Since May 1999, 17 countries have participated in the United Nations Development Assistance Framework and 38 more will take part before the end of the year. To date 37 common country assessments of national development needs have been finalized and 55 more are being prepared. Another 19 assessments are in the planning phase.

Eradication of poverty

165. While there has been considerable progress in addressing the challenges of poverty during the last decade, particular success being achieved in Asia, half of the world's population still must try to survive on less than $2 a day. Some 1.2 billion subsist on less than $1 a day. The five-year review of the outcome of the World Summit for Social Development committed the international community to halving the proportion of people living on $1 a day by 2015. This commitment must now be translated into effective action. The 2015 target must be central to our collective development efforts and I call on the Millennium Assembly to endorse it and to commit the resources necessary to achieve it.

166. In July 2000, a report entitled *A Better World for All: Progress towards the International Development Goals* was submitted to the Group of Eight industrialized countries at their summit meeting in Okinawa. Produced at the request of the G-8, the report was the result of an unprecedented collaboration between the United Nations, the Organisation for Economic Co-operation and Development (OECD), the World Bank and IMF. It charts the progress made towards achieving seven interrelated international development goals set by United Nations conferences in the 1990s.

167. The report shows that, while some countries and regions have made progress, others continue to fall behind. In my letter to the G-8 forwarding the report, I called for a commitment to ensure financial stability; for policies that promote sustainable economic growth that favours the poor; for greater investment in health, education and welfare services; for greater openness to trade; for better access to markets, and for more effective dissemination of technology, together with the knowledge and the capacity to use it.

168. Greater access to resources coupled with appropriate policies ensuring that those resources are deployed to maximum effect are critical to promoting development. Above all we need a new commitment on the part of developing and industrialized countries to transform paper targets into concrete achievements.

169. External aid will continue to play an important part in supporting development, particularly in those countries that have not succeeded in attracting private capital. I have urged the G-8 countries to recommit themselves to reversing the decline in aid and to meeting the globally agreed targets of 0.7 per cent of GNP, with 0.15 per cent going to the least developed countries. I have also urged that greater efforts be made on all sides to enact the debt relief commitments already made.

170. Poverty eradication is a complex and difficult task. To help clarify what our priorities should be, a working group of the United Nations Development Group, chaired by UNDP, has prepared a proposal for a system-wide poverty reduction strategy. Practical options for country teams to implement the strategy are currently being developed.

Education

171. Girls' education is a critical factor in the eradication of poverty, as I stressed in my millennium report. At my request, the United Nations Development Group has established an informal task force, chaired by UNICEF, to design a 10-year initiative on girls' education. I launched this initiative at the World Education Forum at Dakar in April.

172. The initiative puts into place a set of five strategic objectives, and will bring greater coherence to the efforts undertaken within the United Nations system to promote girls' education. It is intended primarily to support those Governments that are committed to ending the gender gap in the school system.

Health

173. Protecting and improving health standards, particularly of the poor and vulnerable, is crucial to social and economic development. Societies cannot prosper unless their people are healthy. Children cannot learn and adults cannot earn if they succumb to illness. Households are devastated when breadwinners fall ill or die prematurely. Protecting and improving health is a development issue, and is recognized as such by the World Health Organization's strategic framework on health and poverty reduction, centred on collaborative efforts with partner agencies.

174. A number of significant health initiatives are now under way, involving partnerships between United Nations agencies, the private sector and civil society. These include the Roll Back Malaria and Stop Tuberculosis campaigns, a programme to reduce maternal mortality through increased availability and use of emergency obstetric care in developing countries, and the Global Alliance for Vaccines and Immunization.

Urbanization

175. Over the course of the next two decades, the global urban population will double, from 2.5 billion to 5 billion people. Almost all of the increase will be in developing countries. Understanding and managing the dynamics of urbanization and addressing issues of secure land tenure are also critical elements in any comprehensive poverty reduction policy. Two initiatives, the Global Campaign for Good Urban Governance and the Global Campaign for Secure Tenure, have been launched by the United Nations Centre for Human Settlements (Habitat) to address these issues. The World Bank and Habitat are building a global alliance of cities and their development programme includes the Cities without Slums action plan, whose patron is President Nelson Mandela. The aim of the programme is to improve the living conditions of 100 million slum-dwellers in the developing countries by 2020.

Working together more effectively

176. With the introduction of the poverty reduction strategy papers by the World Bank and IMF, the United Nations system as a whole is increasing its assistance to Governments that are committed to strengthening their own poverty reduction strategies. By drawing on United Nations presence and experience, and by using such tools as the common country assessment and United Nations Development Assistance Framework, we can assist national Governments to improve the effectiveness of development assist-

ance. The United Nations, the World Bank and IMF have agreed to jointly monitor the progress made in this area in 14 countries, a number expected to increase to more than 20 in the near future.

Sustainable development

177. The overriding aim of sustainable development is twofold: to meet the economic needs of the present generation without compromising the ability of future generations to meet their needs also, and to protect the environment in the process. We are, unfortunately, far from meeting these goals.

178. The challenges of achieving sustainability are complex and multifaceted. As countries have struggled to work themselves out of financial crises, to restore growth and raise incomes, environmental concerns have become less salient. Our efforts are frustrated by growing environmental degradation, pollution, delays in reducing the increase in greenhouse gas emissions, the depletion of resources and the threats to biodiversity that are exacerbated by unsustainable levels of consumption in the developed world, and by poverty-induced environmental stresses in the developing world.

179. These challenges are compounded by the burden that continuing population growth is placing on the planet's physical resources. The medium scenario, long-range world population projection issued in December 1999 by the Population Division of the Department of Economic and Social Affairs indicates that population is likely to increase from 6 billion in 1999 to 9.7 billion in 2150, before stabilizing at just above 10 billion. Virtually all world population growth between now and 2030 will be absorbed by the urban areas of the less developed regions.

180. Within the United Nations, the Commission on Sustainable Development has been the main high-level intergovernmental forum for promoting integrated and cross-cutting proposals to achieve sustainable development. Since its establishment, and through its recent policy debates with stakeholders, the Commission has been a key forum for enhancing policy dialogue and for monitoring progress in sustainable development.

181. Of the various programme activities undertaken under the auspices of the Commission, the work of the Intergovernmental Forum on Forests is particularly noteworthy. The Forum, which successfully concluded its fourth session in February 2000, focuses on forest issues from the perspective of sustainable forest management, looking not only at the underlying causes of deforestation but also at the trade in forest products

and the use of economic instruments for forest conservation. Looking ahead, the Forum has proposed that new international arrangements, including a United Nations Forum on Forests, be established with a view to promoting the implementation of internationally agreed actions on forests and to providing a coherent, transparent and participatory global framework for sustainable forest management.

182. The Commission on Sustainable Development at its eighth session in April and May 2000 considered a range of agricultural issues and the question of integrated planning and management of land resources. At high-level meetings, ministers of agriculture, environment, trade, economics, and development cooperation conducted a candid and in-depth dialogue on land resource problems, sustainable agriculture, trade, economic growth and globalization. These multi-stakeholder dialogues also enable representative civil society organizations and private companies to make known to government officials their perspectives on both problems and possible solutions.

183. The Commission also discussed the upcoming 10-year review of the outcome of the United Nations Conference on Environment and Development (Rio de Janeiro, 1992), stressing the need for early and effective preparations. It recommended that the General Assembly consider convening a summit-level review conference in 2002, preferably in a developing country. The 10-year review provides an important opportunity to reassess what progress has or has not been made towards meeting the ambitious targets established by the Conference. It is imperative that the international community take advantage of this event to reinvigorate the global partnerships needed to achieve sustainable development goals.

184. The inaugural Global Ministerial Environment Forum—the sixth special session of the Governing Council of the United Nations Environment Programme (UNEP)—was held in Sweden in May 2000. The resulting Malmö Ministerial Declaration spelled out the major environmental challenges of the twenty-first century, and the role and responsibility of the private sector and of civil society in meeting those challenges in an increasingly globalized world.

185. With regard to multilateral environmental agreements, a major milestone was the successful negotiation of the Cartagena Protocol on Biosafety to the Convention on Biological Diversity. The Protocol was adopted by more than 130 countries at Montreal in January 2000. This is the first global treaty that reaffirms, incorporates and operationalizes the precautionary principle enunciated in the Rio Declaration on Environment and Development. It outlines procedures to deal with issues arising from the transboundary movement, transit, handling and use of genetically modified organisms that may adversely affect the conservation and sustainable use of biological diversity, or pose risks to human health and the environment. The Protocol was opened for signature at the fifth meeting of the Conference of the Parties to the Convention, held at Nairobi in May 2000, and was signed by 68 Governments.

186. Progress has also been made towards creating a global treaty to reduce and eliminate the use of certain persistent organic pollutants. The Protocol on Liability and Compensation to the Basel Convention on the Control of Transboundary Movements of Hazardous Wastes and Their Disposal was adopted in December 1999. Further steps have been taken with regard to the implementation of the Global Programme of Action for the Protection of the Marine Environment from Land-based Activities and the Global International Waters Assessment. With respect to the former, a clearing house was launched at the special session of the General Assembly on small island developing States, held in September 1999, which will facilitate access to information on the issue. A strategic action plan on municipal wastewater has been developed in close collaboration with WHO, Habitat and the Water Supply and Sanitation Collaborative Council.

187. Efforts continue to be made to improve Member States' understanding of the interlinkages and complementarities between environment, trade and development issues. UNEP and UNCTAD, for example, have established a task force to increase national capacity to develop mutually supportive environment and trade policies.

188. The United Nations Environment Programme has taken a leadership role in developing the environment components of the Global Compact, building on its long-standing relationship with the private sector. With the help of a grant from the United Nations Foundation, UNEP, in partnership with the Coalition for Environmentally Responsible Economics, the World Business Council for Sustainable Development, the Association of Chartered Accountants, the Stockholm Environment Institute and Imperial College, London, is working to promote sustainability reporting guidelines, prepared under the Global Reporting Initiative.

189. At the regional level, a number of initiatives have been successfully implemented. For example, the Economic Commission for Europe (ECE) has four major areas of activity, namely, the

negotiation and adoption of international legal instruments at the regional level; the Ministerial Conference "Environment for Europe"; the promotion of sustainable quality of life in human settlements; and environmental performance reviews.

190.   Instruments adopted include the Protocol to Abate Acidification, Eutrophication and Ground-level Ozone to the Convention on Long-range Transboundary Air Pollution (November 1999); the Convention on the Transboundary Effects of Industrial Accidents, which entered into force in April 2000; and a protocol on water and health to the Convention on the Protection and Use of Transboundary Watercourses and International Lakes.

191.   The environmental performance reviews help to foster effective environmental management policies in countries with economies in transition. During the year, initial reviews of Armenia, Kazakhstan and Kyrgyzstan were undertaken, as were a second review of Bulgaria and follow-up reviews of Latvia, Lithuania, the Republic of Moldova and Slovenia. Reviews are also being scheduled for Romania and Uzbekistan.

192.   In Latin America, the Economic Commission for Latin America and the Caribbean, together with UNEP, UNDP, the World Bank and the Inter-American Development Bank, is supporting the work of the Forum of Ministers of the Environment, established to help implement regional environmental priorities.

193.   A new, joint initiative of UNDP and the European Commission on Poverty and Environment outlines a set of concrete policy options for reducing poverty while at the same time protecting the natural resource base on which the poor depend for their livelihoods.

194.   Achieving sustainable development will continue to require commitment, enhanced policy dialogue, more effective cooperation within the United Nations system, and innovative and practical solutions in the field.

Social development and the advancement of women

195.   In June 2000 the General Assembly held special sessions, at Geneva and New York, to conduct five-year reviews of the outcome of the World Summit for Social Development (Copenhagen, March 1995) and the Fourth World Conference on Women (Beijing, September 1995), during which it reiterated the commitment to put people at the centre of development efforts.

Five-year review of the Copenhagen Summit

196.   The outcome of the special session of the General Assembly held at Geneva to review the World Summit for Social Development, demonstrated that agreements can be reached on sensitive social development issues. The General Assembly supported a wide array of initiatives to reduce poverty, spur the growth of employment and promote greater inclusiveness in the decision-making process, and issued an agreement spelling out specific targets and strategies.

197.   Prominent among the special session's achievements were commitments to launch a global campaign against poverty; implement debt relief arrangements; empower the poor via access to microcredit schemes; ensure access to social services even during times of financial crisis; seek new and innovative sources of development finance; encourage corporate social responsibility and combat corruption, bribery, money-laundering and the illegal transfer of funds; attack the use of tax shelters that undermine national tax systems; promote dialogue between government, labour and employer groups to achieve broad-based social progress, and promote an international strategy to increase access to employment.

198.   To address problems of social exclusion and deprivation more effectively, it is vital that the resolutions adopted by United Nations conferences be followed up at the country level. National policy must benefit from the evolving international consensus on better ways of promoting human development. I recognize the importance of supporting Member States in the follow-up process, and I look forward to seeing, for example, how the Administrative Committee on Coordination Inter-Agency Task Force on basic social services for all, chaired by UNFPA, will take up this challenge in its new guidelines for country teams.

Five-year review of the Beijing Conference

199.   At the special session held in New York, entitled "Women 2000: Gender Equality, Development and Peace for the Twenty-first Century", the outcome document on the review of the Fourth World Conference on Women was adopted by consensus by the General Assembly. We are gratified that the Beijing Platform for Action has been strengthened by sharpening its focus in some areas, and by encompassing new issues that have emerged or become more salient during the last five years. Notable progress was made with regard to promoting the human rights of women, the issue of violence against women, and that of trafficking in women and girls. All these issues are now being addressed in a more

holistic manner. The outcome document requests changes in legislation to remove any discriminatory provisions by 2005, and to eliminate legislative gaps that leave women and girls without effective legal protection or recourse against gender-based discrimination. It also urges Member States to sign and ratify the 1999 Optional Protocol to the Convention on the Elimination of All Forms of Discrimination against Women, one of the greatest legislative achievements in the area of women's rights.

200. Throughout the United Nations system consistent efforts are being made to incorporate a gender perspective into the substantive work of the Organization, particularly through the Inter-Agency Committee on Women and Gender Equality. At the country level, United Nations teams under the leadership of the resident coordinators continue to work with national partners to address gender issues, with support from the United Nations Development Fund for Women (UNIFEM). Initiatives in over 100 countries work to support women's economic empowerment, leadership and participation in peacemaking, as well as to promote women's human rights and eliminate gender-based violence. More than half of the United Nations country teams around the world are working on joint programmes and projects on gender. Some 30 countries reported on gender advocacy initiatives. Furthermore, 17 country teams reported developing gender initiatives within the United Nations system itself.

Coping with ageing and disability

201. One of the most complex social development problems that increasing numbers of States confront is the problem of ageing populations. The International Year of Older Persons (1999) helped to advance our understanding of ageing, and its theme, "A society for all ages", was illustrated by a range of activities that focused on the situation of older persons, multigenerational relationships, and the interplay between ageing and development. During the special plenary meetings on the follow-up to the Year, held during the fifty-fourth session of the General Assembly, many Member States noted that the commemoration of the Year provided a unique opportunity both to evaluate the impact of the demographic revolution in different societies and to develop appropriate strategies to meet the challenges presented by that revolution.

202. Promoting equal opportunities for disabled persons continues to be a high priority. During the past year, our primary concerns in this area were accessibility; employment and sustainable livelihoods; and social services and social safety nets. A number of activities were organized

to explore the role of technological progress in facilitating access, especially to information, as a resource for persons with disabilities.

Drug control and crime prevention

203. The Office for Drug Control and Crime Prevention, which consists of the United Nations International Drug Control Programme and the Centre for International Crime Prevention, has been leading the Organization's efforts to fight the spread of illicit drug cultivation and production, trafficking and abuse, transnational organized crime, trafficking in human beings, and corruption and money-laundering.

204. The Office for Drug Control and Crime Prevention has assisted in the design and realization of innovative strategies for reducing illicit drug cultivation and abuse, including the elaboration of the first ever convention against transnational organized crime and the launching of initiatives to counter money-laundering, corruption and trafficking in human beings.

205. The United Nations International Drug Control Programme is assisting several Andean countries to implement a set of national plans for reducing drug production and trafficking, including direct assistance to provide poor farmers with economically viable alternatives to illicit crop cultivation. The Programme is working increasingly in partnership with the World Bank and bilateral donors in these projects. In Asia, the Programme has helped to develop a regional plan of action for reducing drug production, as well as country-specific initiatives in Afghanistan, the Lao People's Democratic Republic and Myanmar.

206. During the past year, the activities of the Centre for International Crime Prevention included supporting the negotiation process on the draft United Nations Convention against Transnational Organized Crime and its three protocols, on trafficking in persons, migrants and firearms. It is expected that the text will be submitted to the General Assembly for adoption during its millennium session, and heads of State are invited to join the United Nations in celebrating the first ever convention against transnational organized crime at a special signing in December, hosted at Palermo by the Government of Italy. The Centre also worked closely with the United Nations Interregional Crime and Research Institute and other international organizations to generate improved data and knowledge on transnational organized crime, trafficking in human beings and corruption, and to promote appropriate responses by the international community to those problems. In March 2000, the United Nations Offshore Forum was launched. The Forum

seeks to obtain global commitments to internationally accepted anti-money-laundering standards, and to provide technical assistance where necessary to assist jurisdictions in meeting them.

HIV/AIDS

207. The HIV/AIDS epidemic has become a serious development crisis. The pandemic is destroying the economic and social fabric in the countries most affected, reversing years of declining death rates and causing dramatic rises in mortality among young adults. At the end of 1999, it is estimated that 34.3 million adults and children around the world were living with HIV/AIDS, and that 18.8 million people have died since the beginning of the epidemic. According to the latest *Report on the Global HIV/AIDS Epidemic*, released by UNAIDS in June 2000, there were 5.4 million new infections in 1999, while the number of children orphaned by AIDS reached 13.2 million.

208. Africa south of the Sahara is the most affected region, with a total of 24.5 million people living with HIV/AIDS. In that region, AIDS is now the leading cause of mortality. HIV prevalence rates among those aged 15 to 49 have already reached or exceeded 10 per cent in 16 countries, all in sub-Saharan Africa. In Eastern Europe and in South and East Asia a rapid increase in the number of HIV infections is cause for serious concern. In the Caribbean, several island States have worse epidemics than any other countries outside sub-Saharan Africa.

209. In the last year, the United Nations has made significant efforts to help countries address these daunting challenges. In an unprecedented move, the Security Council addressed the impact of the epidemic on Africa in January 2000. Following the debate in the Council, a reference group was established by the Inter-Agency Standing Committee Working Group to examine the relationship between war and civil strife and the spread of HIV/AIDS.

210. In June 1999, the international community responded to the epidemic by setting a new development target. The General Assembly, in its five-year review of the International Conference on Population and Development, called for reductions in new infections by 25 per cent among 15 to 24-year-olds in the most affected countries by 2005. Twenty-four of these countries are in Africa. I call on the Millennium Summit to adopt this as a goal, and also to support the goal of ensuring that at least 90 per cent of young people have access to the necessary information, education and services to protect themselves against HIV infection by 2005, and at least 95 per cent by 2010.

211. System-wide efforts have been made to deal with the gender and drug aspects of HIV/AIDS. In an attempt to integrate gender awareness into HIV/AIDS policy and direct gender-focused research, advocacy and responses at the national and local levels, pilot programmes in nine developing countries were implemented by an inter-agency partnership between UNIFEM, UNAIDS and UNFPA. HIV/AIDS prevention activities have been increased by the United Nations International Drug Control Programme as part of its worldwide drug abuse prevention programmes.

212. In collaboration with the UNAIDS secretariat and other co-sponsors, WHO is developing a global health sector strategy for improving the response of health systems to HIV/AIDS. A United Nations inter-agency task force chaired by WHO has developed a strategy for improving the access of AIDS victims to anti-AIDS drugs.

213. UNAIDS and its co-sponsors have established a close dialogue with pharmaceutical companies. As a result five companies have agreed to discuss reductions in the prices of AIDS drugs for Africa and other poor regions. This is a most welcome step, but not sufficient. As well as increasing overall drug supplies to affected regions, there is an urgent need to strengthen the capacity of weak and overburdened health-care systems in developing countries. To help realize this goal, WHO is developing a strategy for comprehensive care and support for people living with HIV/AIDS.

214. Major challenges in the fight against AIDS remain. There is a critical need for additional financial resources and development assistance. UNAIDS estimates that, to fight AIDS effectively in Africa alone, a minimum of $3 billion per year is needed. Money is by no means the only problem. In many countries official reluctance to speak out against the risks that HIV/AIDS poses is still causing unnecessary death and suffering.

Bridging the digital divide

215. Information and communication technologies provide unique opportunities to help advance economic and social development goals and to reduce poverty. As only 5 per cent of the world's population has access to the Internet, however, the vast majority of the world's peoples are denied the economic and social benefits that the information and communication technology revolution can offer. Bridging the "digital divide" between rich and poor has become an increasingly important development goal.

216. The Ministerial Declaration adopted by the Economic and Social Council at its July ses-

sion makes a forceful call for concerted action at national, regional and international levels to bridge the digital divide and put information and communication technologies at the service of development for all. It stresses the need to involve all relevant stakeholders in mobilizing those technologies for development. The Council's session brought together ministers, representatives of civil society and an unprecedented number of major private sector companies from the information and communication technology sector to discuss how the digital divide might be bridged.

217. National programmes for promoting information and communication technologies should be an integral part of development strategies. Connecting poor communities to the Internet will give people access to telemedicine, distance learning and many other valuable social development resources; but achieving connectivity will require major investments in infrastructure, education and capacity-building.

218. The provision of hardware is of little use, however, unless the necessary human resources are available to install, service and repair the equipment. Such expertise is often lacking in developing countries and it was for this reason that I announced the creation of the United Nations Information Technology Service (UNITeS) in my millennium report. UNITeS, a high-tech volunteer corps, will help train communities in the developing world in the use of information technologies. Content is also a critical issue, as 80 per cent of the Internet is in English, a language which less than 30 per cent of the world speaks.

219. The commitment to bridging the digital divide is evident right across the United Nations system. In 1999, UNDP adopted a comprehensive strategy to guide its support to national partners. The key elements of the strategy are the promotion of awareness about the knowledge revolution; advocacy and policy formulation; helping to build connectivity to secure universal and affordable access to telecommunications infrastructure; developing national and human capacities; strengthening national language content; and fostering creative solutions to problems.

220. At the regional level, the Internet Initiative for Africa focuses on assisting 15 sub-Saharan countries to develop Internet connectivity and build the capacities required for their operation. In Asia and the Pacific, the Asia-Pacific Development Information Programme helped to establish connectivity for several countries, including Bhutan, East Timor, the Lao People's Democratic Republic and Tuvalu. UNDP, through its Sustainable Development Networking Programme and partnerships with the private sector, has pro-

moted the use of open-source and public software and made available information on sustainable development in numerous languages.

221. The Sustainable Cities Programme, managed by Habitat, builds resources for computer hardware and software into the budget of every city demonstration project it undertakes. Habitat has also developed an Internet-based networking system that electronically connects over 1,000 municipalities and 1,500 community-based organizations in Latin America.

222. In its policy and advocacy work, through training and seminars, UNCTAD has vigorously promoted e-commerce as a development tool. The UNCTAD Reference Service, for example, has created an "e-bookshelf" on trade and development issues with material obtained from a large number of sources worldwide, and it is currently creating a virtual library of its own documents and publications.

223. UNCTAD also continued to implement its Automated System for Customs Data, which uses information technologies to modernize and simplify customs procedures, to increase government revenue and to improve the transparency of customs administrations. Used by over 80 countries, this system has become the de facto international standard for customs modernization, and is available to developing countries and countries with economies in transition at a fraction of the cost of alternative systems.

224. The regional commissions actively promoted information and communication technologies in their regions in 1999. The Economic Commission for Europe, in collaboration with the European Electronic Messaging Association, held a two-day Forum on E-Commerce for Transition Economies in the Digital Age at Geneva in June 2000. The ECE Committee for Trade, Industry and Enterprise Development will establish a team of specialists on Internet enterprise development to promote the free flow of information and exploit the business potential of new technologies. ECE and UNCTAD are collaborating on a programme to promote electronic commerce for the transition economies.

225. The Economic and Social Commission for Asia and the Pacific has undertaken analyses of recent trends in the development and application of information technologies and their impact on the social and economic development of countries in the region.

226. The theme of the first African Development Forum, organized by the Economic Commission for Africa and held at Addis Ababa in October 1999, was "The challenge to Africa of globalization and the information age". Programmes initiated by the participants at that con-

ference include NGOnet Africa (an action group to engage civil society in the promotion of information and communication technology for African development), a telecentre network, a programme to harness the digital African diaspora for African information technology development, and the formation of the Alliance for African Business, which aims to promote the development of information and communication infrastructure in Africa.

227. Information technologies can also assist the United Nations in its advocacy activities for development. The launch of NetAid in 1999 was the largest syndicated Internet broadcast ever. The NetAid web site has received more than 40 million hits and helped raise support for a number of poverty reduction projects. Initial grants for Africa and Kosovo have reached $1.7 million.

Africa

228. Africa continues to face a range of complex and extraordinarily difficult economic, health and security challenges. These are now being addressed as a matter of priority by the Security Council and the General Assembly, as well as by United Nations programmes and agencies.

229. The political, economic and social challenges faced by Africa were spelled out in detail in my 1998 report on the causes of conflict and the promotion of durable peace and sustainable development in Africa. Adoption of the recommendations in that report was widely recognized as being essential if sub-Saharan Africa were to overcome the challenges it confronted and realize its extraordinary potential. In December 1998, the General Assembly established an open-ended ad hoc Working Group to monitor the implementation of those recommendations. In February 2000, the mandate of the Working Group was altered and it will now focus its work on a number of priority areas. These include poverty eradication, development finance, debt relief, HIV/AIDS, refugees and internally displaced persons and support to countries in post-conflict situations.

230. A review conducted by the Working Group reveals that major obstacles to progress remain—lack of political will, weak governance in a number of countries, armed conflict, difficulty in mobilizing financial resources, lack of adequate human resource capacity, public health issues—notably HIV/AIDS and malaria—the inappropriate structure of some economies, and limited access to technology.

231. The breadth and depth of United Nations involvement in Africa is extraordinary. It includes preventive diplomacy, peacekeeping, electoral assistance, humanitarian and emergency relief, post-conflict reconstruction, environmental advice, support for Internet connectivity and economic and social development assistance.

232. The World Food Programme assisted 22 million people in Africa over the past year. Of these, 15.7 million were refugees, internally displaced persons and other persons affected by natural disasters in some 26 countries. Some 6.3 million people benefited from WFP development assistance. A total of 44 per cent of WFP operational expenditures were for sub-Saharan Africa. WFP also provided some $37.1 million in support of human resource development through basic education (early childhood development, primary education and literacy), nutrition, health and training. Together with the World Bank and the United Nations Educational, Scientific and Cultural Organization (UNESCO), WFP is assisting 15 countries in Africa that have signed country-specific action plans to increase primary school enrolment.

233. One of Africa's greatest challenges is to protect and nurture its children. Yet the gap between what is being done and what needs be done is widening; the variety of interventions required is increasing. In war-torn countries like Burundi, the Democratic Republic of the Congo, Sierra Leone and the Sudan, for instance, UNICEF advocacy has focused attention on the special needs of children in the delivery of humanitarian assistance. In natural disasters, in Madagascar and Mozambique, UNICEF was able to combine immediate relief with the longer term reopening of schools, to create the normalcy children need most in putting such sudden disruptions behind them.

234. High priority has been given to the survival of children and improvements in child and maternal health, centred on the revitalization of health systems. Efforts to improve children's access to good quality basic education, especially for girls, continue to be pursued.

235. The WHO Roll Back Malaria initiative, which was launched in Africa, is committed to halving the malaria burden by 2010. A summit of over 50 African heads of State, G-8 heads of State, development agencies and OECD health ministers, held at Abuja in April 2000, focused on the means of combating Africa's malaria problem. The initiative is a joint venture of WHO with UNICEF, UNDP, the World Bank and development groups, private agencies and Governments. The WHO Kick Polio out of Africa campaign, with African political support, aims to eradicate polio from Africa in this year.

236. The earlier discussion of the HIV/AIDS pandemic indicated what an extraordinary

threat it poses not just to individuals in Africa but to the continent's overall development prospects. Sub-Saharan Africa accounts for only one tenth of the global population, but it carries the burden of more than 80 per cent of AIDS-related deaths worldwide. It is in this tragic context that the Economic Commission for Africa has decided that the theme of the African Development Forum 2000 will be "AIDS: the greatest leadership challenge for Africa". The Forum, which will be held at Addis Ababa in October 2000, is being organized in collaboration with UNAIDS, the World Bank, UNICEF and UNDP.

237. The International Partnership against AIDS in Africa, a major, multi-agency endeavour, is charged with intensifying efforts and mobilizing additional resources for the battle against AIDS. Six countries—Burkina Faso, Ethiopia, Ghana, Malawi, Mozambique and the United Republic of Tanzania—have been selected for intensified action.

238. Prevention is critical to the containment of AIDS; in Africa, UNFPA is providing adolescents with greater access to youth-friendly reproductive health information, counselling and services. UNICEF has also geared many of its country programmes, particularly in eastern and southern Africa, to giving high priority to the control of HIV/AIDS.

239. The United Nations Environment Programme is working with African Governments to provide policy support and capacity-building for international negotiations. A major goal is the revitalization of the African Ministerial Conference on the Environment as the main African policy forum in the field of the environment. UNEP also hosted expert and ministerial-level consultations to facilitate the development of a common African position on the issues of desertification, climate change, biosafety, and forest protection.

240. The United Nations Environment Programme continues to support the strengthening of Africa's human, managerial and institutional capacity to address the immense environmental challenges facing the continent as well as undertaking a number of programme initiatives to protect its land, water and biological resources. UNEP is working with Habitat, for example, to implement the new Managing Water for African Cities programme, which will assist major cities to improve water supply and management.

241. Trade is critical to Africa's future. In 1999, UNCTAD continued its cooperation with WTO and the International Trade Centre, acting as lead agency in promoting trade access for African countries. UNCTAD has also strengthened its programme of technical assistance and advisory services for debt management and negotiations for African countries during the past year, extending assistance to 18 African countries. The total long-term foreign debt of those 18 African countries stood at $95 billion at the end of 1998.

Chapter IV

The international legal order and human rights

Human rights development

242. In the field of human rights, the past year has been one of consolidation, progress and challenge, both within the United Nations system and at the State level. Our capacity to uphold a code of human rights continues to develop internationally and nationally. Strategies developed by the Office of the United Nations High Commissioner for Human Rights to promote cooperation with regional and subregional organizations and the international financial institutions have been key to this progress. The Office of the High Commissioner has strengthened its relations with the Department of Peacekeeping Operations, improving the effectiveness of United Nations field operations by integrating the promotion and protection of human rights with peacemaking, peacekeeping and peacebuilding initiatives. Other organizations also promoted programmes centred on human rights in 1999 and 2000. The United Nations Population Fund has followed a rights-based approach in advocating for the protection of the sexual and reproductive rights of women and girls, and the United Nations Development Programme devoted its *Human Development Report 2000* to human rights and human development.

New developments

243. The Economic and Social Council, at its substantive session of 2000, on the recommendation of the Commission on Human Rights, decided to establish a Permanent Forum on Indigenous Issues as a subsidiary organ of the Council. The Permanent Forum will serve as an advisory body to the Council on a range of issues of concern to indigenous peoples.

244. In April 2000, the Commission on Human Rights adopted two ground-breaking resolutions, on good governance and women's rights to land. In the first, the Commission identifies the key components of good governance as transparency, responsibility, accountability, participation and responsiveness to the needs and as-

ance to an environment conducive to the enjoyment of human rights and the promotion of growth and sustainable human development. In the second resolution the Commission affirms that discrimination in law against women with respect to acquiring and securing land, property and housing, as well as the related financing, constitutes a violation of women's human rights.

245. The Commission on Human Rights also decided to appoint two new special rapporteurs and an independent expert, and requested the Secretary-General to appoint a special representative. The special rapporteurs will serve for a three-year period. One will focus on adequate housing as a component of the right to an adequate standard of living, while the other will address the right to food. Combining two old mandates, the Commission appointed an independent expert to examine the effects of structural adjustment policies and foreign debt on the full enjoyment of all human rights, particularly economic, social and cultural rights. The Commission, further, recommended the appointment of a special representative of the Secretary-General to report on the situation of human rights defenders. The Economic and Social Council approved the new mandates on 16 June 2000.

246. In April 2000, the Commission on Human Rights held a special debate on poverty and the enjoyment of human rights. The United Nations High Commissioner for Human Rights, representatives of United Nations organizations and experts led the special debate with statements on poverty and human rights issues. The Commission endorsed a human-rights-based approach to poverty alleviation and development.

247. On the occasion of the third Ministerial Conference of the World Trade Organization, the Committee on Economic, Social and Cultural Rights urged the World Trade Organization to review international trade and investment policies and rules to ensure that they were consistent with the promotion and protection of human rights. The Committee recognized the wealth-generating potential of trade liberalization, but noted that liberalization in trade, investment and finance do not necessarily create a favourable environment for the realization of economic, social and cultural rights. The Committee stated that trade liberalization is not an end in itself, but should promote human well-being within the context of existing international human rights instruments.

248. In October 1999, the General Assembly adopted the Optional Protocol to the Convention on the Elimination of All Forms of Discrimination against Women. The Optional Protocol, once ratified by 10 Member States, establishes a mechanism whereby individuals or groups of individuals may submit communications, claiming to be victims of violations of rights protected under the Convention, to the Committee on the Elimination of Discrimination against Women. As at 21 August 2000, there were 43 signatories and 5 ratifications. In May 2000, the General Assembly also adopted two Optional Protocols to the Convention on the Rights of the Child. The first concerns the involvement of children in armed conflict and prohibits the compulsory recruitment or use in hostilities of persons under 18 by Governments or non-governmental armed groups. The second Optional Protocol relates to the sale of children, child prostitution and child pornography and reflects the General Assembly's concern about the widespread and increasing traffic in children and the continuing practice of sex tourism.

Challenges ahead

249. In spite of the positive developments in the promotion and protection of human rights over the past year, gross violations of human rights are still too common. The trafficking of women and children is a matter of grave concern. Similarly, the rights of migrants, minorities and indigenous peoples are often vulnerable to abuse, while racism and xenophobia continue to threaten the dignity, peace and security of many. In September 2001, the issues of discrimination on the grounds of race, colour or ethnic origin will be addressed at the World Conference against Racism, Racial Discrimination, Xenophobia and Related Intolerance, to be held in South Africa.

250. The year 2000 marks the halfway point in the United Nations Decade for Human Rights Education, a process critical to ensuring the promotion and protection of human rights throughout the world. It is vital that the momentum and progress towards the respect for human rights and the promotion of human well-being generated over the last five years be augmented and secured in the remainder of the decade.

The International Criminal Court

251. The Preparatory Commission for the International Criminal Court held its fourth session in March 2000 and its fifth session in June 2000. A sixth session will be held in November-December 2000.

252. In June 2000, the Preparatory Commission adopted the final draft texts of two instruments that are essential for the functioning of the Court: the Rules of Procedure and Evidence and the Elements of Crimes. These draft instruments

are the result of extensive negotiations held during the first five sessions of the Preparatory Commission in 1999 and 2000. They still have to be adopted by the Assembly of States Parties to the Rome Statute of the International Criminal Court.

253.   The Rules of Procedure and Evidence regulate the composition and administration of the Court, jurisdiction and admissibility, disclosure, trial procedure, evidence and other important aspects of the Rome Statute. Special attention has been paid to rules relating to the protection of victims and witnesses.

254.   The Elements of Crimes assist the Court in the interpretation and application of the definitions of the crime of genocide, crimes against humanity and war crimes that are contained in articles 6, 7 and 8 of the Rome Statute. They contain a detailed description of the acts that constitute the most heinous crimes and represent a major contribution to the field of international criminal law.

255.   At its next session, the Preparatory Commission will continue to consider the definition of the crime of aggression and how the Court shall exercise jurisdiction with respect to that crime. The Preparatory Commission will also begin considering three of the remaining items within its mandate: the draft relationship agreement between the United Nations and the Court; draft financial regulations and rules; and a draft agreement on the privileges and immunities of the Court.

256.   As at 24 August 2000, 98 States had signed the Rome Statute, while 15 had ratified it. These figures are encouraging. They are, however, far short of the 60 ratifications that are needed to bring the Statute into force and enable the Court to operate.

257.   By adopting the Rome Statute, States took a decisive step, showing their determination to take concrete measures to enforce the rules of international humanitarian law that have been developed over the course of the last 100 years. They displayed their resolve that those whose deeds offend the conscience of humankind should no longer go unpunished. They made known their conviction that, in the affairs of men and women of all nations, the rule of law should finally prevail. I encourage States, in that same spirit, to establish their consent to be bound by the Rome Statute of the International Criminal Court as soon as possible.

The International Tribunals

258.   In November 1999, the group of independent experts I had appointed, at the request of the General Assembly, to review all aspects of the operation and functioning of the Tribunals for Rwanda and the former Yugoslavia submitted its report. The Expert Group concluded that the operations and functioning of the Tribunals were reasonably effective, but made some 46 recommendations with a view to improving them. The experts cautioned however that, in view of the fundamental constraints encountered by the two Tribunals, proceedings would continue to be lengthy. In March and April 2000, the Tribunals reported that they had implemented, or were implementing, the great majority of the recommendations of the Expert Group.

International Tribunal for the former Yugoslavia

259.   Several landmark events occurred in the past year, including the arrest in April 2000 of Momcilo Krajisnik, former President of the Bosnian Serb Assembly and the highest ranking political figure apprehended to date. Another was the trial of General Radoslav Krstic, which began in March 2000. General Krstic is alleged to be responsible for the worst massacre of civilians in Europe since the Second World War, following the fall of Srebrenica.

260.   The Tribunal experienced a significant increase in the rate of arrests of indicted suspects; 10 people have been apprehended and transferred to the Tribunal's detention unit in the past year. As at August 2000, there were 37 detainees in the detention unit. Three other accused were provisionally released, pending the commencement of their trial.

261.   Proceedings commenced or continued in the pre-trial, trial and appeal stages of 20 cases, involving a total of 39 accused. The Tribunal handed down decisions in four cases, involving eight accused. It convicted seven of these and handed down sentences of imprisonment ranging from 6 to 45 years—the latter being the longest sentence that the Tribunal has pronounced to date. It also found one accused not guilty of the charge against him and ordered his release.

262.   The Appeals Chamber handed down decisions in two cases, rejecting the appeals of the accused in both cases and, in one case, finding the accused guilty on nine additional counts. It varied sentences pronounced by the Trial Chambers in both cases. Negotiations are under way for the transfer of the convicted persons to States which will undertake the enforcement of their sentences. The total number of States that have concluded agreements to enforce the Tribunal's sentences increased to seven: France and Spain signed agreements in February and March 2000, respectively.

263.   Following the cessation of the NATO air campaign, the Prosecutor undertook intensive

investigations in Kosovo, the scale and pace of which were unprecedented. With the assistance of specialist forensic teams seconded by 14 Member States, the Prosecutor reported to the Security Council that work had been completed at 159 of 529 identified grave sites and that 2,108 bodies had been exhumed by November 1999. A second forensic programme began in April 2000 and will continue throughout the year. The Prosecutor's Office is also pursuing approximately 24 further investigations, involving crimes in Bosnia and Herzegovina, Croatia and Kosovo, Federal Republic of Yugoslavia.

264. The Tribunal established regional outreach offices at Zagreb and Banja Luka, which provide accurate and timely information in local languages on the Tribunal's work so as to counter misinformation and promote understanding of the Tribunal in the region.

International Tribunal for Rwanda

265. The Tribunal continued to consolidate and expand on its achievements. The Trial Chambers handed down judgements in three cases, the Appeals Chamber in one. To date, the Tribunal has, in seven judgements, convicted a total of eight individuals. These verdicts remain the first for the crime of genocide by an international court, and set important precedents for other jurisdictions.

266. In December 1999, Trial Chamber I handed down its verdict in *The Prosecutor v. Georges Rutaganda*. It found the accused, a businessman and national vice-president of the Interahamwe militia, guilty of genocide and crimes against humanity and sentenced him to life imprisonment. In January and June 2000, the Tribunal convicted two more individuals of genocide and crimes against humanity and of incitement to genocide, respectively. The June trial involved the first non-Rwandan convicted by the Tribunal.

267. In another trial—that of a former mayor, who was also charged with genocide and crimes against humanity—the judges visited and inspected the sites of certain of the massacres in which the accused allegedly participated. This was the first visit to Rwanda to be made by the judges acting in their judicial capacity. Several further trials are scheduled to begin in the second half of 2000.

268. In its first judgement on appeal in a case completed by a Trial Chamber, the Appeals Chamber in February 2000 dismissed the appeal of a local leader of the Interahamwe militia, who had pleaded guilty to the charges against him, and confirmed the sentence of 15 years' imprisonment handed down by Trial Chamber I.

269. As of August 2000, the Tribunal's detention facility in Arusha held a total of 43 detainees. Over the course of the past year, there were a number of arrests of individuals subject to warrants issued by the Tribunal. Belgium, France, the United Republic of Tanzania and the United States of America transferred a total of five accused to Arusha.

270. The Tribunal implements a vigorous outreach programme in Rwanda, designed to bring its work closer to the Rwandan people and so facilitate long-term reconciliation. Its relations with the Government and people of Rwanda have greatly improved as its effectiveness in bringing to justice high-level planners and perpetrators of the 1994 genocide has become increasingly recognized.

Other tribunals

271. The Office of Legal Affairs played a central role in the discussions between the United Nations and the Government of Cambodia on the establishment and operation of a special court to prosecute leaders of the Khmer Rouge. In particular, it advised the Government on drafting the necessary national legislation, and led negotiations on the conclusion of an agreement setting out the mutual obligations of the parties.

272. The Office of Legal Affairs has been entrusted with the responsibility of implementing Security Council resolution 1315(2000) of 14 August 2000 on the establishment of an independent special court for Sierra Leone. Its jurisdiction will include, notably, crimes against humanity, war crimes and other serious violations of international humanitarian law, as well as crimes under relevant Sierra Leonean law committed in the territory of Sierra Leone. The special court will have personal jurisdiction over those most responsible for such crimes. The Office of Legal Affairs is preparing the legal instruments to implement the resolution, and discussions are under way with representatives of the Government of Sierra Leone in this regard and with Member States on the financing of the court.

Enhancing the rule of law

273. The new millennium is an appropriate occasion to reaffirm the primary objectives of our Organization and focus on them anew. Establishing the rule of law in international affairs is a central priority.

274. Treaties are one of the two main sources of international law, and I have decided to launch a campaign during the Millennium Summit to

promote the signature and ratification of, and accession to, treaties of which I am the depositary. In May 2000, I wrote to all heads of State and Government inviting them to use the opportunity of the Millennium Summit to sign and ratify, or accede to, those treaties. I encouraged them to pay special attention to a core group of 25 multilateral treaties that are representative of the objectives of the Charter of the United Nations and reflect the Organization's key values. A booklet, entitled *Millennium Summit—Multilateral Treaty Framework: An Invitation to Universal Participation*, containing that letter and a list of the core treaties that are the focus of this campaign is available. I am pleased to report that, as at 25 August 2000, 69 States have responded to my request to ratify those treaties.

275. As of August 2000, I am the depositary of 517 treaties. Many of them have a profound impact on the lives and livelihood of individuals, as they relate to questions such as human rights, refugees and stateless persons, international criminal law, commodities, trade, transportation, the sea, disarmament and the environment. Some of those treaties have been open for signature, ratification or accession for a number of years but have not yet succeeded in attracting universal participation.

276. I would remind Member States that the third objective proclaimed in the preamble to the Charter of the United Nations is to establish conditions under which justice and respect for the obligations arising from treaties and other sources of international law can be maintained. One of our most important tasks is to entrench the application of the rules set out in those treaties and help to sustain and enhance the values that underpin them.

277. It is not enough for States simply to give their consent to be bound by treaties. If the peoples of all nations are to participate in the emerging global legal order and enjoy its benefits, States must also respect and implement the obligations that the treaties in question embody. Realizing the promise of the framework of global norms developed by the international community is of critical importance. Without such a commitment the rule of law in international affairs will remain little more than a remote abstraction.

278. Much remains to be done; all too often, individuals and corporations find that they are denied the rights and benefits that international law and treaties provide for. Sometimes, national authorities refuse to recognize and respect their obligations under international law, even where the State has voluntarily subscribed to the relevant treaties. More often, though, such authorities simply lack the necessary expertise or resources to ensure that their obligations are properly implemented and applied—to draft and adopt the needed legislation, to put in place the necessary procedure and administrative arrangements, to train those involved in the application of such legislation, procedure and arrangements and to familiarize them with the international rules they are designed to implement. To support efforts to implement international treaty commitments we already provide Governments, on request, with assistance in drafting national laws and running training programmes in particular aspects of international law for those involved in its application, such as law enforcement officers, prison officers, social workers and immigration officers.

279. In order to build national capacities to implement treaties more effectively, I have requested every office, department, programme, fund and agency of the United Nations to review its current activities and to consider what else it might do, within its existing mandate and given existing resources, to promote the application of international law, and to provide technical assistance to help Governments implement their commitments under the treaties to which they are or might wish to become parties.

280. More generally, I have also requested all United Nations entities, not simply those immediately involved with legal issues, to indicate how they might help to increase awareness of international law, both among the public and among those involved in the application of the law, particularly legal practitioners and judges. I would also encourage the wider teaching of international law at universities and other institutions of higher education. To this end, the Legal Counsel has written to the deans of law schools throughout the world and enlisted the assistance of a team of prominent academic lawyers to provide universities with assistance in developing suitable curricula and identifying relevant teaching materials.

281. As international law develops and affects ever greater areas of daily life and business, it will also increasingly affect the laws of each country. This reality imposes a special responsibility on lawyers and on those who educate and train them. International law can no longer—if it ever could—be considered an optional extra, in which lawyers may or may not be trained. To satisfy the demands of the rule of law, lawyers need to be familiar with international law, to be schooled in its methods and know how to research it when the occasion demands.

Chapter V

Managing change

Enhancing communication

282. Broad-based, global support for the United Nations depends on timely and effective communication. In 2000, the Department of Public Information implemented a range of innovations that will increase the breadth and depth of communication about who we are, what we do and why we do it. One such initiative has been the system-wide "UN works" campaign, which explains how the Organization is addressing the main challenges of the twenty-first century, in particular those relating to economic and social development. Driving these efforts is a commitment to embrace new communications technology as a means of enhancing the impact of our activities and the productivity of our staff.

283. Use of the United Nations web site continues to increase at an extraordinary rate, the number of hits on the site now exceeding 400 million a year. Significant improvements in the web site's content and design were made in the past year and several new features in all six official languages were introduced, including live webcasts of major events. The redesign currently under way will present the same look and feel to all users in all official languages. Meeting the General Assembly's requirement to maintain the web site in all six official languages has proved a real challenge, despite the modest increase in resources allocated for web site development.

284. The Millennium Summit and Assembly provide a major opportunity for the Department to mobilize public interest in the Organization and its global role through a worldwide promotional campaign. Unprecedented media coverage has already been generated for the Summit with the publication of my millennium report and the series of teleconferenced briefings to journalists around the world that promoted it. The Department also widely promoted the Secretary-General's multilateral treaty signing initiative in connection with the Summit. In May, the Millennium Forum of civil society organizations featured simultaneous coverage by United Nations television, videoconferencing and webcasting.

285. As the number and scope of United Nations peace operations continue to rise, the need for public information and outreach in the field has risen with them. In Kosovo and East Timor, the role of public information has been critical and in new missions such as those in the Democratic Republic of the Congo, Ethiopia/Eritrea and Sierra Leone, the Department has been fully involved from the outset. The introduction of rapid-deployment information teams on new peace missions will further strengthen the capacity of the Department to achieve its goals in the field.

286. Initiatives to build partnerships with other entities of the United Nations system, non-governmental organizations, educational institutions and the business community continue to develop through the co-sponsorship of conferences, briefings, exhibits, and events such as the World Television Forum and World AIDS Day. Contact with the 1,600 non-governmental organizations associated with the Department has been dramatically enhanced through the use of videoconferencing and live webcasting.

287. The programme for broadcasters and journalists from developing countries, now in its twentieth year, and the programme for Palestinian journalists continue to provide training while raising awareness of the work of the United Nations in the developing world. Other media outreach programmes took 12 senior editors and broadcasters from developing countries to Geneva for intensive briefings on human rights in December 1999, and brought 15 senior African editors and broadcasters to Headquarters in June for a week to familiarize them with the United Nations role and activities in Africa. Direct e-mail links to journalists around the world are part of another innovative project that will provide electronic alerts of breaking news from the United Nations system almost as it happens.

288. The advent of a 24-hour global news cycle has generated a number of new initiatives to increase the reporting of United Nations activities. Information and other materials are now available in real time to regional media through the web-based United Nations News Centre. Established nearly a year ago, the Centre provides United Nations news updates throughout the day. The Department's ultimate goal is the development of a fully integrated, multimedia United Nations news service, delivering news directly to media worldwide.

289. A pilot project is under way that will enable United Nations Radio to produce and deliver daily 15-minute news bulletins, in all six official languages, to radio stations around the globe. By the end of the year, the Department expects to have all United Nations Radio outputs on the United Nations web site, enabling broadcasters from around the world with Internet access to use the material at any time. The radio initiative will be replicated by the television service: news packages highlighting United Nations

system-wide developments will be disseminated daily for use by television broadcasters in 2001.

290. These are major developments, but their success will be entirely dependent on the Secretariat being able to meet the challenge of adapting to the digital revolution. The goal is to create an information technology infrastructure capable of instantaneously transmitting text, image and voice messages from the Organization to almost anywhere in the world. Major investment, including by other departments, will be needed if the United Nations is to avoid becoming marginalized in the new information environment. Investment is also needed to replace the crumbling communication infrastructure at Headquarters, much of which is 50 years old. Total failure of this communication system, which carries television and radio materials from Headquarters to the world's media, is a real threat.

291. The United Nations information centres are instrumental in bringing the United Nations messages and concerns to communities all over the world. They are the Organization's direct link with media representatives, nongovernmental organizations and the public at large, and draw the attention of local communities to the work of the United Nations. Staff of the centres lead the development of national information strategies for United Nations country teams, helping to ensure that the Organization speaks with a consistent voice. Thirty-four centres already have separate web sites; others are in the planning stage.

292. The Dag Hammarskjöld Library continues to focus on delivering electronic information; outreach to depository libraries; training mission, Secretariat and non-governmental organization staff in documentation and Internet use; and supporting multilingualism. The Library's web pages had 1.5 million hits in 1999, while its major databases are now installed on a web platform as UNBISNET. The programme to digitize and add to the optical disk data storage system documents of all major United Nations bodies from the Library's microfiche collection continues apace.

293. Technological change has enhanced the range and reach of one of the most traditional areas of activity, publications, and related client-specific services. The first half-century of the *Yearbook of the United Nations* will shortly be placed in electronic format as a readily retrievable resource of the Organization's history. *Development Business*, which focuses on business procurement opportunities in developing countries, has been revitalized by a process of constructive collaboration between the Organization and the World Bank, leading to the launch of an active,

revenue-generating electronic edition of the journal. Both print and web site editions of the *UN Chronicle* have been revitalized—while continuing to draw eminent contributors. *Africa Recovery*, a journal that seeks to enhance the prospects for development and the achievement of peace and security on the continent, appeals to a broad readership, and has received increasing recognition in African media and government circles during the past year. Sales of United Nations publications have increased, with the United Nations publications web site providing a solid platform for expanding global sales.

294. The Cartographic Section plays a critical role in supporting the substantive activities of the Organization. The technical services of our cartographers are used almost daily by the Security Council, and provide crucial information for peacemaking and peacekeeping activities. In March 2000, a Geographic Information Working Group was formally established, bringing together on a regular basis all cartographic and geographic specialists across the United Nations system.

Reaching out

295. One of the most fundamental challenges facing the United Nations is coping with increased workloads without a compensatory increase in resources. Our ongoing reform programme seeks to address the resource challenge through increases in efficiency, not least through greater reliance on information technologies.

296. We have made considerable progress over the past three years in this regard, but our commitments still remain greater than the resources available to meet them and our financial difficulties are compounded by the non-payment of dues. We can do more with less, but only up to a point. It is in this context that the generosity of individual Member States, the private sector and philanthropic foundations assumes particular importance.

297. Over the years generous assistance from individual Member States has enabled United Nations bodies to embark on innovative programmes in conflict prevention, peace-building and development that would otherwise never have been funded.

298. More recent is the burgeoning co-operation between the United Nations and the private sector that I discuss earlier in the present report. The United Nations increasingly benefits from the ideas, expertise and resources that the private sector can provide. The private sector, in turn, benefits from a stronger United Nations that promotes international norms and stand-

ards, the "soft infrastructure" on which global commerce increasingly depends.

299. To ensure that public-private co-operation conforms to the priorities and rules of the United Nations, I have issued guidelines on United Nations partnerships with the business community, which may be reviewed as our experience in this area accumulates.

300. While philanthropic foundations have always given generous support to our activities, it is only in the last three years that the United Nations has benefited from a major partnership through a generous gift from Ted Turner. This has supported work on United Nations projects as diverse as the prevention of mother-to-child transmission of HIV/AIDS, the creation of electricity from biomass in India and biodiversity conservation in the Galapagos. The precedent created by that donation has already encouraged others to assist the United Nations as it addresses the world's pressing problems.

301. The United Nations Fund for International Partnerships, created to serve as the distribution channel for Mr. Turner's gift and to promote other new partnerships, is entering its third year of operations. To date the Fund has programmed funds totalling $310 million in 112 countries, in four specific areas: children's health, women and population, environment and peace, and security and human rights. Its work in coming years will continue to focus on these areas and on priorities spelled out in my millennium report.

302. The United Nations system's own in-house research network, much of which is part of the United Nations University (UNU), produces policy-relevant research across a broad range of disciplines and subjects. At the UNU institute in Helsinki, for example, United Nations researchers are examining the relationship between information technology, poverty and economic growth; in Hamilton, Ontario, Canada, the focus is on water security for the developing world; in Geneva, on restricting the proliferation of small arms; in Legon, Ghana, on natural resource management in Africa; in Reykjavik, on geothermal energy; and in Tokyo, on sustainable development and on humanitarian intervention.

303. In my reform plan of 1997, I stressed the need for the Organization to develop research and utilize its results more effectively. Since then significant efforts have been made to increase communication between those who do research in UNU and other research institutions, on the one hand, and those who use the research in the United Nations Secretariat, programmes and agencies, on the other. Making research more relevant and useful to those who create and im-

plement policy, and making policy makers more aware of what the United Nations research community has to offer, is critically important. Furthering such a dialogue is a fundamental rationale for the annual Geneva research and policy dialogue that was inaugurated in 2000.

304. Over the past decade, civil society organizations have played an increasingly important role in helping to formulate, implement and deliver United Nations programmes, and as advocates of change. Thanks to the global reach of the Internet, which has become a powerful tool for advocacy as well as an extraordinary source of information and analysis, civil society organizations are now better placed than ever to form coalitions, organize and mobilize on a global scale.

305. During the past year civil society organizations played a vital role in the regional hearings preparatory to the Millennium Assembly. The Millennium Forum held at United Nations Headquarters in May brought together representatives from more than 1,000 civil society organizations from more than 100 countries to discuss how the United Nations should be strengthened to meet the challenges of the twenty-first century. Even greater numbers attended the special sessions of the General Assembly held in June in New York, to review progress since the Fourth World Conference on Women, and at Geneva, to review progress since the World Summit for Social Development.

306. The term civil society is a broad one and encompasses more than activist and advocacy groups. Some extraordinary civil society meetings are being held in the run-up to the Millennium Summit. They include a round table to launch the United Nations Year of Dialogue among Civilizations, convened by the United Nations Educational, Scientific and Cultural Organization with the support of the President of the Islamic Republic of Iran, S. M. Khatami; the annual Department of Public Information/ Non-Governmental Organization Conference; a three-day conference organized by the Inter-Parliamentary Union which will bring presiding officers of parliaments from all over the world to the United Nations; and a summit of religious and spiritual leaders representing some 75 different faiths.

Administration and management

307. I am pleased to note that considerable progress has been made during the past year towards achieving my goal of creating an "organizational culture that is responsive and results-oriented". Important developments were the drafting of a human resources reform package, an information technology policy and a capital

master plan. I commend these proposals to the Member States for their approval. Their implementation will greatly enhance the effectiveness of the Organization.

Human resources reform

308. As the United Nations evolves from a Headquarters-based organization into one with a stronger field presence, the Secretariat needs to be increasingly flexible in using its human resources. The goal of the reform proposals is to modernize human resource management, to have empowered, responsible and accountable managers, and skilled, competent and well-motivated staff.

309. The reform package consists of nine building blocks, which rest on the principles of transparency, simplicity and timeliness. It proposes fundamental changes in four main areas, namely, accountability; mobility; recruitment, placement and promotion; and contractual mechanisms. Other reforms will include improvements in the use of human resource planning and performance management, the streamlining of rules and procedure, the enhancement of skills and competency development, better conditions of service, and strengthening the administration of justice.

Information technology policy

310. To ensure that the Organization keeps up with the rapid developments in information and communication technology, a United Nations information technology policy has been developed. Using in-house expertise, the policy will address both the introduction and management of new information technologies and their use as vehicles for the distribution and management of information.

311. Once the policy is implemented, senior managers will benefit from timely access to comprehensive information on policy, administrative and operational matters and from the greater overall productivity this access will generate. Member States will also benefit from enhanced support and services.

312. The information technology policy will also allow for more effective dissemination of greater amounts of information within the United Nations. Our external partners will also benefit from these changes. The United Nations broader goal of "bridging the digital divide" between the developed and the developing world will be facilitated by a Secretariat that can take greater advantage of the information and communication technology revolution.

313. In this context, the Integrated Management Information System is playing an increasingly important role in the Organization's central administrative operations, and is proving to be a powerful management tool. It will be deployed at all other major duty stations from September 2000.

314. The Integrated Management Information System has allowed significant re-engineering and standardization of administrative processes throughout the Organization. Owing to the system's internal controls and monitoring capabilities, responsibility for managing programmes has been firmly placed back in the hands of programme managers. Currently, seven organizations make use of the system, which has been implemented at 11 different sites around the world.

Capital master plan

315. The United Nations Headquarters complex in New York, despite its superb design and construction, is ageing and requires major repairs and refurbishment. The present ad hoc and reactive approach to maintenance cannot sustain our buildings in the long term and may also pose serious financial problems if costs for repair and maintenance accelerate. In the long-term capital master plan, I put forward a number of possible solutions, and propose various financing options. The plan demonstrates quite clearly that, while the costs of a major upgrade of the complex are high, they are considerably less than the resources that will have to be expended—particularly on energy—if we continue to pursue the current reactive maintenance policy.

Other challenges

316. I remain committed to improving the productivity of the Organization—that is to continuous improvement in the quality, impact and cost-effectiveness of United Nations programmes. Making staff productivity the responsibility of each manager is central to this goal.

317. Efficiency and transparency in the procurement process has increased, thanks to Internet technology that now allows a variety of procurement information to be placed in the public domain on the Procurement Division's home page.

318. The process of simplifying and streamlining the rules and procedure of the Organization has continued throughout the past year. The first phase will be completed by the end of the year and will improve management performance and accountability throughout the United Nations. We expect that rules and procedure will be

applied more consistently as information about them is transmitted more efficiently through electronic means.

319. Preparations to shift to results-based budgeting, with widespread use of performance indicators, are continuing. My programme budget for the biennium 2000-2001 was the beginning of that process and included statements of expected accomplishments for all substantive areas. This new budgetary concept will be the last element to link the various components that comprise my plan to create a more results-oriented management system.

320. The greatest challenge to improving management and productivity over the last three biennia continues to be financial constraint. While the funding available to the Organization has become more stable, the level of unpaid assessments, particularly for peacekeeping activities, remains unacceptably high.

Legal affairs

321. The past year has been one of quiet accomplishment in the field of legal affairs. The United Nations Commission on International Trade Law (UNCITRAL) made good progress towards finalizing a draft convention on assignment in receivables financing. This will facilitate financing based on receivables and allow access by commercial entities to credit at lower rates. UNCITRAL also made progress on unifying rules on electronic signatures. In July 2000, the Commission adopted a Legislative Guide on Privately Financed Infrastructure Projects, designed to assist Governments to establish appropriate legislation to attract investment where private parties construct and operate public infrastructure facilities under a public licensing system.

322. The International Law Commission continued its work on a set of draft articles on State responsibility, with a view to their final adoption in 2001. It also reviewed the question of the jurisdictional immunities of States and their property, revisiting issues arising out of its previous work on the topic. Member States have given a very positive reception to the draft articles on nationality of natural persons in relation to the succession of States, which the Commission adopted in July 1999. The draft articles are currently before the Sixth Committee, which is considering adopting them as a declaration of the General Assembly.

323. In December 1999, the General Assembly adopted the International Convention for the Suppression of the Financing of Terrorism—the latest in a series of related conventions in this field. As at 25 August 2000, 22 States had signed the Convention, which will enter into force once ratified by 22 States. I call upon Member States to sign and ratify this very important legal instrument. Since adopting the Convention, the Ad Hoc Committee and the Sixth Committee have focused on another important instrument in this field—a convention intended to suppress acts of nuclear terrorism.

324. The General Assembly in December 1999 established a consultative process to facilitate its annual review of developments relating to the oceans and the law of the sea. The first meeting, held early in June 2000, offered an opportunity to examine this issue in some depth and to seek pragmatic solutions to the remaining problems. The General Assembly will consider the recommendations of this consultation at its fifty-fifth session.

325. The Office of Legal Affairs was also responsible for developing the legislative mechanisms for the United Nations Interim Administration Mission in Kosovo and the United Nations Transitional Administration in East Timor, the first of the Organization's peacekeeping missions to exercise legislative and executive authority. The Office also drafted the basic legal framework under which those missions were to operate and administer the territories placed under their charge. The Office has provided legal support and advice to the missions from the time of their establishment, as well as to other United Nations peacekeeping missions. The Office provided particularly valuable assistance to the Secretary-General's Special Coordinator for the Middle East Peace Process on the implementation of Security Council resolution 425(1978) and the withdrawal by Israel of its forces from Lebanon.

326. The Office of Legal Affairs successfully defended the Organization in complex arbitration proceedings involving a $50 million claim; assisted in developing comprehensive guidelines for the Organization's cooperation with the business community; aided in negotiating and drafting agreements with the private sector; supported the successful prosecution of former staff members in cases of fraud against the Organization and helped recover its assets; prevented, before United States courts, an attempt by a private entity to attach the assets in a United Nations escrow account of the "oil-for-food" programme; advised on the implementation of the oil-for-food programme; and helped to draft a new set of financial regulations for the United Nations Development Programme. The Office also continued to seek Malaysia's implementation of the advisory opinion of the International Court of Justice, of 29 April 1999, confirming the immu-

nity from legal process of a Special Rapporteur of the Commission on Human Rights.

Project services

327. The only completely self-financing entity in the Organization, the United Nations Office for Project Services works on a fee-for-service basis for United Nations bodies and other organizations around the world. Since its services may be requested on a voluntary basis, the Office must compete for business in the open services market. In 1999, it acquired new business valued at more than $1.2 billion and delivered a record $560 million in project services. These included purchasing equipment and goods, hiring consultants, contracting for services and works, and administering training. In addition, the disbursement of $196 million in loans was authorized for projects that the Office is supervising on behalf of the International Fund for Agricultural Development.

328. As the proportion of new projects funded from UNDP regular resources continued to decline, the volume of services requested by non-development-oriented entities within the United Nations system increased substantially. The Department of Political Affairs, the Department of Peacekeeping Operations and the Office of the United Nations High Commissioner for Human Rights, all of which used the services of the Office for Project Services for the first time in 1998, increased their use by 22 per cent in 1999. Demand for service from more traditional sources of business, such as the United Nations International Drug Control Programme and associated United Nations organizations based in Vienna, almost tripled during the year.

329. Responding to these new demands, the Office for Project Services has expanded its management expertise into fields beyond the development arena. In Kosovo, for example, its mine action services provided rapid support for mine clearance and related services, at the request of the Department of Peacekeeping Operations, and the Office will work with UNDP to provide housing and electrification in the province. Responding to an initiative of member organizations of the United Nations Development Group, the Office also formulated an UNMIK programme to build up local management capacities, both public and private.

330. An agreement with the United Nations Institute for Training and Research has enabled the Office for Project Services to assist local authorities in both developing and donor countries to strengthen their capacities; and it will provide specialized procurement services to UNTAET

under an operational agreement currently under discussion.

331. The Office for Project Services is also developing specialized management services in support of democratization, and now has experience in over a dozen countries in this area. Acting on behalf of the Department of Political Affairs, and with funding from the European Commission, it assembled an electoral observation team in Nigeria in less than four weeks in 1999. The team monitored voting in locations right across the country.

332. To backstop project personnel in areas of concentrated demand, substantive management support units are being established. One such unit operates through the Geneva office and is focusing on the design, monitoring and evaluation of programmes fostering social and economic development at the local level, with particular emphasis on rehabilitation in post-conflict societies. A similar substantive unit focusing on public sector reform is being developed.

333. The pursuit of operational partnerships with the private sector is another new initiative of the Office for Project Services. In the spring of 2000, 12 such partnerships between the United Nations and the business sector were launched. These joint projects range from developing local economic development in Guatemala and Mozambique to stemming the spread of HIV/AIDS in Asia and making high-tech satellite imagery more affordable and accessible to United Nations agencies and others working in post-conflict rehabilitation and natural disaster prevention.

334. In a further attempt to combine private sector practices with United Nations goals, the Office for Project Services has created new contracting mechanisms for the procurement of goods and services, generating innovative partnership agreements with non-governmental organizations and developing new tools and instruments for public-private partnerships that will expand the impact of the work of the United Nations.

Accountability and oversight

335. The Office of Internal Oversight Services provides United Nations entities with reviews of their performance and guidance on their methods of work. It has become an important agent for change within the Organization, particularly with regard to strengthening internal controls and improving management performance. More and more managers within the system are seeking its advice. The independence of the Office is assured by the fact that the Under-Secretary-General for Internal Oversight

Services serves for a single, non-renewable, five-year term.

336. The work of the Office has had a positive impact on the whole Organization. Internal oversight bodies in the specialized agencies and separately administered funds and programmes, as well as the Secretariat, are increasingly working together, sharing experiences, and benefiting from lessons learned.

Audit and management consulting

337. Last year, the Audit and Management Consulting Division placed special emphasis on peacekeeping operations, humanitarian and related activities, human resources management, procurement, problems associated with establishing new bodies, and information technology management. In addition to monetary savings, the audits resulted in improvements in the overall administration and management of the Secretariat as well as strengthening the internal control environment.

338. Audits were also conducted in the Department of Peacekeeping Operations in New York and in most peacekeeping missions in the field. They focused on the staffing of peacekeeping missions, managing air operations and other logistical support functions, and planning and executing the liquidation of missions.

339. In response to a request from the Office of the United Nations High Commissioner for Human Rights, the Office of Internal Oversight Services conducted comprehensive audits of human rights field operations in Burundi and Rwanda and followed up with audits at the headquarters of the Office of the High Commissioner. Recommendations were made aimed at improving the Office of the High Commissioner's management of field operations and strengthening its internal control systems.

340. The Audit Section of the Office of the United Nations High Commissioner for Refugees at Geneva, with resident auditors at Nairobi and Abidjan, audited UNHCR field operations in 22 countries, with a focus on operations in Africa. At UNHCR headquarters, the Office of Internal Oversight Services audited support services. UNHCR implementing partners were also assessed.

Investigations

341. Work continued to ensure that the Organization's resources and staff are being used properly. For example, an important case involving the misdirection of Member States' contributions to the United Nations Environment Programme was resolved. The misappropriated funds, totalling over $700,000, were restored, and the individual responsible is facing criminal proceedings.

342. The Office of Internal Oversight Services also worked with law enforcement authorities in the criminal prosecution of a former staff member accused of defrauding the Organization of $800,000. The individual concerned was tried, convicted and sentenced to 41 months in prison, but only $110,000 of the funds stolen has been repaid to the Organization to date. Further repayments are expected, as ordered by the court.

Central Monitoring and Inspection Unit

343. The Central Monitoring and Inspection Unit prepared my report on the programme performance of the United Nations for the biennium 1998-1999, which was discussed by the Committee for Programme and Coordination in the spring of 2000. A qualitative assessment of programme performance found a programme implementation rate of 88 per cent, the highest this decade, which was attributed to the Organization's determination to promote managerial efficiency and accountability. In particular, the use of electronic monitoring and reporting systems was found to reduce reliance on paper-based reports, to strengthen intra-departmental discipline in performance monitoring, and to facilitate the flow of management information.

344. An inspection of the Office for the Coordination of Humanitarian Affairs concluded that streamlining and reorganization had enhanced its capabilities to respond to emerging humanitarian crises and strengthened its coordination role. Follow-up inspections of the Economic Commission for Africa (ECA), UNEP and the United Nations Centre for Human Settlements (Habitat) were undertaken. The Office reported that ECA had undergone profound change, with a marked improvement in the quality of its products, and a revitalized relevance to its constituents, partners (especially the Organization of African Unity) and host country. The Office of Internal Oversight Services concluded that UNEP had addressed the recommendations of my 1998 task force on UNEP and that Habitat had recaptured the confidence of its stakeholders and was moving in the right direction. In Habitat, the Office of Internal Oversight Services found a new culture emerging, one that prioritized initiative, creativity and flexibility. A backlog of unresolved problems in financial and personnel management has, however, delayed the implementation of administrative reforms.

Central Evaluation Unit

345. Two in-depth evaluations were conducted by the Central Evaluation Unit. The first examined the Department for Disarmament Affairs and found that Member States were, in general, satisfied with the support that the Department provided to multilateral disarmament bodies. An evaluation of the electoral assistance programme revealed that valuable electoral assistance was provided to a total of 68 Member States during the period 1992-1998. The Unit also conducted triennial reviews of the implementation of the recommendations made in 1996 by the Committee for Programme and Coordination on the Department of Public Information and the termination phase of peacekeeping operations.

Millennium Summit

United Nations Headquarters, New York

The world did celebrate as the clock struck midnight on New Year's Eve, in one time zone after another, from Kiribati and Fiji westward around the globe to Samoa. People of all cultures joined in—not only those for whom the millennium might be thought to have a special significance. The Great Wall of China and the Pyramids of Giza were lit as brightly as Manger Square in Bethlehem and St. Peter's Square in Rome. Tokyo, Jakarta and New Delhi joined Sydney, Moscow, Paris, New York, Rio de Janeiro and hundreds of other cities in hosting millennial festivities. Children's faces reflected the candlelight from Spitsbergen in Norway to Robben Island in South Africa. For 24 hours the human family celebrated its unity through an unprecedented display of its rich diversity.

—Secretary-General Kofi Annan

The General Assembly Hall

The Millennium Summit of the United Nations General Assembly

Largest gathering of world leaders. For three days (6-8 September), the largest-ever gathering of world leaders, representing the 189 United Nations Member States, met at Headquarters in New York to mark the advent of the new millennium and to set the course for the United Nations in the new era. Convened in response to General Assembly resolution 53/202 [YUN 1998, p. 598], by which the Assembly decided to designate its fifty-fifth (2000) session as the Millennium Assembly and to convene as part of the Assembly a Millennium Summit, the Summit was organized around six plenary meetings and four interactive round-table sessions. During those three days, speeches were heard from 99 heads of State, 3 Crown Princes and 47 heads of Government on the theme "The United Nations in the twenty-first century" and its

sub-topics (peace and security, including disarmament; development, including poverty eradication; human rights; and strengthening the United Nations), as well as the world drug problem, as requested by the Economic and Social Council (**resolution 2000/16**). World leaders also met on 7 September [S/2000/772] in a special session of the Security Council to consider the topic "Ensuring an effective role of the Security Council in the maintenance of international peace and security, particularly in Africa" as a contribution towards achieving the major purpose of the Millennium Summit.

Also before the Summit for consideration was the Ministerial Declaration "Development and international cooperation in the twenty-first century: the role of information technology in the context of a knowledge-based global economy" (see p. 799), which the

Flanked by Secretary-General Annan and President Nujoma, Co-Chairperson Tarja Halonen, President of Finland, presides over the Assembly

high-level segment of the 2000 substantive session of the Economic and Social Council had recommended for endorsement by the Summit.

To assist the Summit in its deliberations, the Secretary-General submitted a report entitled "We the peoples: the role of the United Nations in the twenty-first century" [A/54/2000], in which he set out his recommendations to the Summit (see p. 55).

Charting a new course for the future. The Millennium Summit was opened on the morning of 6 September by Tarja Halonen, President of Finland and Co-Chairperson of the Summit, who told the gathering that "we meet today at the United Nations to celebrate the new millennium and declare our vision for the future .... Our task is threefold: we need to meet the demands of the outside world, we need to clarify the role of the United Nations in world affairs and we need to change the United Nations to be a modern, effective organization .... The Millennium Summit is the moment to reflect on the future of the United Nations. The United Nations is often the only one in the field to assist, to advise and to build institutions .... We cannot expect the United Nations to accomplish everything alone. To be successful and credible, it must act in partnership with other organizations and with the civil society. We must make the Organization reflect the world as it is today."

The President of Namibia and Co-Chairperson of the Summit, Sam Nujoma, in his opening address, said that "peoples of the world have high expectations for social change; determination to put things right; to put men and women on the same footing before the law; to conquer fear, poverty and alienation in society; and to use the benefits of science and technology for peace, human security, empowerment of the poor, poverty eradication and sustainable development .... We are here because we believe in the United Nations, in its Charter and in the common objectives and principles for which our indispensable Organization stands."

United States President William Jefferson Clinton, in his address to the Summit as the host country President, said "We come together not just at a remarkable moment on our calendar, but at the dawn of a new era in human affairs, when globalization and the revolution in information technology have brought us closer together than ever before .... Fifty-five years ago the United Nations was formed to 'save succeeding generations from the scourge of war' .... We find today fewer wars between nations, but more wars within them .... We must work as well to prevent conflict; to get more children in school; to relieve more debt in developing countries; to do more to fight malaria, tuberculosis and AIDS ...; to do more to promote prevention and to stimulate the development of and affordable access to drugs and vaccines; and to do more to curb the trade in items that generate money that make conflict more profitable than peace, whether

President Sam Nujoma of Namibia, Summit Co-Chairperson, addressing the Assembly

diamonds in Africa or drugs in Colombia. All these things come with a price tag, and all nations, including the United States, must pay it. The price must be fairly apportioned, and the United Nations structure of finances must be fairly reformed so that the Organization can do its job .... The leaders here assembled can rewrite human history in the new millennium. If we have learned the lessons of the past, we can leave a very different legacy for our children."

At the end of the three days of statements, debate, frank and free exchange of views in the round-table sessions (see p. 57), consultations and negotiations, the General Assembly, on 8 September, adopted the draft United Nations Millennium Declaration, contained in the annex to **resolution 54/282** of 5 September, which was referred to it by the Assembly's fifty-fourth session. By that Declaration, world leaders renewed their commitment to the principles and purposes of the United Nations and set out their vision for the future course of the Organization.

United Nations Millennium Declaration

An eight-part United Nations Millennium Declaration, set out in **resolution 55/2** [draft: A/55/L.2], was adopted by the General Assembly on 8 September [meeting 8] without vote [agenda item 60 *(b)*].

I. Values and principles

1. We, heads of State and Government, have gathered at United Nations Headquarters in New York from 6 to 8 September 2000, at the dawn of a new millennium, to reaffirm our faith in the Organization and its Charter as indispensable foundations of a more peaceful, prosperous and just world.

2. We recognize that, in addition to our separate responsibilities to our individual societies, we have a collective responsibility to uphold the principles of human dignity, equality and equity at the global level. As leaders we have a duty therefore to all the world's people, especially the most vulnerable and, in particular, the children of the world, to whom the future belongs.

3. We reaffirm our commitment to the purposes and principles of the Charter of the United Nations, which have proved timeless and universal. Indeed, their relevance and capacity to inspire have increased, as nations and peoples have become increasingly interconnected and interdependent.

4. We are determined to establish a just and lasting peace all over the world in accordance with the purposes and principles of the Charter. We rededicate ourselves to support all efforts to uphold the sovereign equality of all States, respect for their territorial integrity and political independence, resolution of disputes by peaceful means and in conformity with the principles of justice and international law, the right to self-determination of peoples which remain under colonial domination and foreign occupation, non-interference in the internal affairs of States, respect for human rights and fundamental freedoms, respect for the equal rights of all without distinction as to race, sex, language or religion and international cooperation in solving international problems of an economic, social, cultural or humanitarian character.

5. We believe that the central challenge we face today is to ensure that globalization becomes a positive force for all the world's people. For while globalization offers great opportunities, at present its benefits are very unevenly shared, while its costs are unevenly distributed. We recognize that developing countries and countries with economies in transition face special difficulties in responding to this central challenge. Thus, only through broad and sustained efforts to create a shared future, based upon our common humanity in all its diversity, can globalization be made fully inclusive and equitable. These efforts must include policies and measures, at the global level, which correspond to the needs of developing countries and economies in transition and are formulated and implemented with their effective participation.

6. We consider certain fundamental values to be essential to international relations in the twenty-first century. These include:

- **Freedom.** Men and women have the right to live their lives and raise their children in dignity, free from hunger and from the fear of violence, oppression or injustice. Democratic and participatory governance based on the will of the people best assures these rights.

- **Equality.** No individual and no nation must be denied the opportunity to benefit from development. The equal rights and opportunities of women and men must be assured.

- **Solidarity.** Global challenges must be managed in a way that distributes the costs and burdens fairly in accordance with basic principles of equity and social justice. Those who suffer or who benefit least deserve help from those who benefit most.

- **Tolerance.** Human beings must respect one other, in all their diversity of belief, culture and language. Differences within and between societies should be neither feared nor repressed, but cherished as a precious asset of humanity. A culture of peace and dialogue among all civilizations should be actively promoted.

- **Respect for nature.** Prudence must be shown in the management of all living species and natural resources, in accordance with the precepts of sustainable development. Only in this way can the immeasurable riches provided to us by nature be preserved and passed on to our descendants. The current unsustainable patterns of production and consumption must be changed in the interest of our future welfare and that of our descendants.

- **Shared responsibility.** Responsibility for managing worldwide economic and social development, as well as threats to international peace and security, must be shared among the nations of the world and should be exercised multilaterally. As the most universal and most representative organization in the world, the United Nations must play the central role.

7. In order to translate these shared values into actions, we have identified key objectives to which we assign special significance.

II. Peace, security and disarmament

8. We will spare no effort to free our peoples from the scourge of war, whether within or between States, which has claimed more than 5 million lives in the past decade. We will also seek to eliminate the dangers posed by weapons of mass destruction.

9. We resolve therefore:

- To strengthen respect for the rule of law in international as in national affairs and, in particular, to ensure compliance by Member States with the decisions of the International Court of Justice, in compliance with the Charter of the United Nations, in cases to which they are parties.

- To make the United Nations more effective in maintaining peace and security by giving it the resources and tools it needs for conflict prevention, peaceful resolution of disputes, peacekeeping, post-conflict peace-building and reconstruction. In this context, we take note of the report of the Panel on United Nations Peace Operations, and request the General Assembly to consider its recommendations expeditiously.

- To strengthen cooperation between the United Nations and regional organizations, in accordance with the provisions of Chapter VIII of the Charter.

- To ensure the implementation, by States Parties, of treaties in areas such as arms control and disarmament and of international humanitarian law and human rights law, and call upon all States to consider signing and ratifying the Rome Statute of the International Criminal Court.

- To take concerted action against international terrorism, and to accede as soon as possible to all the relevant international conventions.

- To redouble our efforts to implement our commitment to counter the world drug problem.

- To intensify our efforts to fight transnational crime in all its dimensions, including trafficking as well as smuggling in human beings and money laundering.

- To minimize the adverse effects of United Nations economic sanctions on innocent populations, to subject such sanctions regimes to regular reviews and to eliminate the adverse effects of sanctions on third parties.

- To strive for the elimination of weapons of mass destruction, particularly nuclear weapons, and to keep all options open for achieving this aim, including the possibility of convening an international conference to identify ways of eliminating nuclear dangers.

- To take concerted action to end illicit traffic in small arms and light weapons, especially by making arms transfers more transparent and supporting regional disarmament measures, taking account of all the recommendations of the forthcoming United Nations Conference on Illicit Trade in Small Arms and Light Weapons.

- To call on all States to consider acceding to the Convention on the Prohibition of the Use, Stockpiling, Production and Transfer of Anti-personnel Mines and on Their Destruction, as well as the amended mines protocol to the Convention on conventional weapons.

10. We urge Member States to observe the Olympic Truce, individually and collectively, now and in the future, and to support the International Olympic Committee in its efforts to promote peace and human understanding through sport and the Olympic Ideal.

III. Development and poverty eradication

11. We will spare no effort to free our fellow men, women and children from the abject and dehumanizing conditions of extreme poverty, to which more than a billion of them are currently subjected. We are committed to making the right to development a reality for everyone and to freeing the entire human race from want.

12. We resolve therefore to create an environment—at the national and global levels alike—which is conducive to development and to the elimination of poverty.

13. Success in meeting these objectives depends, inter alia, on good governance within each country. It also depends on good governance at the international level and on transparency in the financial, monetary and trading systems. We are committed to an open, equitable, rule-based, predictable and non-discriminatory multilateral trading and financial system.

14. We are concerned about the obstacles developing countries face in mobilizing the resources needed to finance their sustained development. We will therefore make every effort to ensure the success of the high-level international intergovernmental event on financing for development, to be held in 2001.

15. We also undertake to address the special needs of the least developed countries. In this context, we welcome the Third United Nations Conference on the Least Developed Countries to be held in May 2001 and will endeavour to ensure its success. We call on the industrialized countries:

- To adopt, preferably by the time of that Conference, a policy of duty- and quota-free access for essentially all exports from the least developed countries;

- To implement the enhanced programme of debt relief for the heavily indebted poor countries without further delay and to agree to cancel all official bilateral debts of those countries in return for their making demonstrable commitments to poverty reduction; and

- To grant more generous development assistance, especially to countries that are genuinely making an effort to apply their resources to poverty reduction.

16. We are also determined to deal comprehensively and effectively with the debt problems of low- and middle-income developing countries, through various national and international measures designed to make their debt sustainable in the long term.

17. We also resolve to address the special needs of small island developing States, by implementing the Barbados Programme of Action and the outcome of the twenty-second special session of the General

Assembly rapidly and in full. We urge the international community to ensure that, in the development of a vulnerability index, the special needs of small island developing States are taken into account.

18. We recognize the special needs and problems of the landlocked developing countries, and urge both bilateral and multilateral donors to increase financial and technical assistance to this group of countries to meet their special development needs and to help them overcome the impediments of geography by improving their transit transport systems.

19. We resolve further:

- To halve, by the year 2015, the proportion of the world's people whose income is less than one dollar a day and the proportion of people who suffer from hunger and, by the same date, to halve the proportion of people who are unable to reach or to afford safe drinking water.

- To ensure that, by the same date, children everywhere, boys and girls alike, will be able to complete a full course of primary schooling and that girls and boys will have equal access to all levels of education.

- By the same date, to have reduced maternal mortality by three quarters, and under-five child mortality by two thirds, of their current rates.

- To have, by then, halted, and begun to reverse, the spread of HIV/AIDS, the scourge of malaria and other major diseases that afflict humanity.

- To provide special assistance to children orphaned by HIV/AIDS.

- By 2020, to have achieved a significant improvement in the lives of at least 100 million slum dwellers as proposed in the "Cities Without Slums" initiative.

20. We also resolve:

- To promote gender equality and the empowerment of women as effective ways to combat poverty, hunger and disease and to stimulate development that is truly sustainable.

- To develop and implement strategies that give young people everywhere a real chance to find decent and productive work.

- To encourage the pharmaceutical industry to make essential drugs more widely available and affordable by all who need them in developing countries.

- To develop strong partnerships with the private sector and with civil society organizations in pursuit of development and poverty eradication.

- To ensure that the benefits of new technologies, especially information and communication technologies, in conformity with recommendations contained in the Economic and Social Council 2000 Ministerial Declaration, are available to all.

IV. Protecting our common environment

21. We must spare no effort to free all of humanity, and above all our children and grandchildren, from the threat of living on a planet irredeemably spoilt by human activities, and whose resources would no longer be sufficient for their needs.

22. We reaffirm our support for the principles of sustainable development, including those set out in Agenda 21, agreed upon at the United Nations Conference on Environment and Development.

23. We resolve therefore to adopt in all our environmental actions a new ethic of conservation and stewardship and, as first steps, we resolve:

- To make every effort to ensure the entry into force of the Kyoto Protocol, preferably by the tenth anniversary of the United Nations Conference on Environment and Development in 2002, and to embark on the required reduction in emissions of greenhouse gases.

- To intensify our collective efforts for the management, conservation and sustainable development of all types of forests.

- To press for the full implementation of the Convention on Biological Diversity and the Convention to

Combat Desertification in those Countries Experiencing Serious Drought and/or Desertification, particularly in Africa.

- To stop the unsustainable exploitation of water resources by developing water management strategies at the regional, national and local levels, which promote both equitable access and adequate supplies.

- To intensify cooperation to reduce the number and effects of natural and man-made disasters.

- To ensure free access to information on the human genome sequence.

V. Human rights, democracy and good governance

24. We will spare no effort to promote democracy and strengthen the rule of law, as well as respect for all internationally recognized human rights and fundamental freedoms, including the right to development.

25. We resolve therefore:

- To respect fully and uphold the Universal Declaration of Human Rights.

- To strive for the full protection and promotion in all our countries of civil, political, economic, social and cultural rights for all.

- To strengthen the capacity of all our countries to implement the principles and practices of democracy and respect for human rights, including minority rights.

- To combat all forms of violence against women and to implement the Convention on the Elimination of All Forms of Discrimination against Women.

- To take measures to ensure respect for and protection of the human rights of migrants, migrant workers and their families, to eliminate the increasing acts of racism and xenophobia in many societies and to promote greater harmony and tolerance in all societies.

- To work collectively for more inclusive political processes, allowing genuine participation by all citizens in all our countries.

- To ensure the freedom of the media to perform their essential role and the right of the public to have access to information.

VI. Protecting the vulnerable

26. We will spare no effort to ensure that children and all civilian populations that suffer disproportionately the consequences of natural disasters, genocide, armed conflicts and other humanitarian emergencies are given every assistance and protection so that they can resume normal life as soon as possible.

We resolve therefore:

- To expand and strengthen the protection of civilians in complex emergencies, in conformity with international humanitarian law.

- To strengthen international cooperation, including burden sharing in, and the coordination of humanitarian assistance to, countries hosting refugees and to help all refugees and displaced persons to return voluntarily to their homes, in safety and dignity and to be smoothly reintegrated into their societies.

- To encourage the ratification and full implementation of the Convention on the Rights of the Child and its optional protocols on the involvement of children in armed conflict and on the sale of children, child prostitution and child pornography.

VII. Meeting the special needs of Africa

27. We will support the consolidation of democracy in Africa and assist Africans in their struggle for lasting peace, poverty eradication and sustainable development, thereby bringing Africa into the mainstream of the world economy.

28. We resolve therefore:

- To give full support to the political and institutional structures of emerging democracies in Africa.

- To encourage and sustain regional and subregional mechanisms for preventing conflict and promoting political stability, and to ensure a reliable flow of resources for peacekeeping operations on the continent.

- To take special measures to address the challenges of poverty eradication and sustainable development in Africa, including debt cancellation, improved market access, enhanced Official Development Assistance and increased flows of Foreign Direct Investment, as well as transfers of technology.

- To help Africa build up its capacity to tackle the spread of the HIV/AIDS pandemic and other infectious diseases.

VIII. *Strengthening the United Nations*

29. We will spare no effort to make the United Nations a more effective instrument for pursuing all of these priorities: the fight for development for all the peoples of the world, the fight against poverty, ignorance and disease; the fight against injustice; the fight against violence, terror and crime; and the fight against the degradation and destruction of our common home.

30. We resolve therefore:

- To reaffirm the central position of the General Assembly as the chief deliberative, policy-making and representative organ of the United Nations, and to enable it to play that role effectively.

- To intensify our efforts to achieve a comprehensive reform of the Security Council in all its aspects.

- To strengthen further the Economic and Social Council, building on its recent achievements, to help it fulfil the role ascribed to it in the Charter.

- To strengthen the International Court of Justice, in order to ensure justice and the rule of law in international affairs.

- To encourage regular consultations and coordination among the principal organs of the United Nations in pursuit of their functions.

- To ensure that the Organization is provided on a timely and predictable basis with the resources it needs to carry out its mandates.

- To urge the Secretariat to make the best use of those resources, in accordance with clear rules and procedures agreed by the General Assembly, in the interests of all Member States, by adopting the best management practices and technologies available and by concentrating on those tasks that reflect the agreed priorities of Member States.

- To promote adherence to the Convention on the Safety of United Nations and Associated Personnel.

- To ensure greater policy coherence and better cooperation between the United Nations, its agencies, the Bretton Woods Institutions and the World Trade Organization, as well as other multilateral bodies, with a view to achieving a fully coordinated approach to the problems of peace and development.

- To strengthen further cooperation between the United Nations and national parliaments through their world organization, the Inter-Parliamentary Union, in various fields, including peace and security, economic and social development, international law and human rights and democracy and gender issues.

- To give greater opportunities to the private sector, non-governmental organizations and civil society, in general, to contribute to the realization of the Organization's goals and programmes.

31. We request the General Assembly to review on a regular basis the progress made in implementing the provisions of this Declaration, and ask the Secretary-General to issue periodic reports for consideration by the General Assembly and as a basis for further action.

32. We solemnly reaffirm, on this historic occasion, that the United Nations is the indispensable common house of the entire human family, through which we will seek to realize our universal aspirations for peace, cooperation and development. We therefore pledge our unstinting support for these common objectives and our determination to achieve them.

"We the peoples: the role of the United Nations in the twenty-first century"

To chart the new course for the Organization, the Secretary-General, in his report to the General Assembly entitled "We the peoples: the role of the United Nations in the twenty-first century" [A/54/2000], proposed action the Organization could take to make its work more relevant to the changing times.

He said that the Assembly had convened the gathering of heads of State and Government to address the role of the United Nations in the twenty-first century. Both the occasion and the subject required a broader, longer-term view of the state of the world and the challenges it posed for the Organization.

According to the Secretary-General, there was much to be grateful for. Most people could expect to live longer than their parents. They were better nourished, enjoyed better health, were better educated, and on the whole faced more favourable economic prospects. However, there were also many things to deplore, and to correct. The century just ended was disfigured, time and again, by ruthless conflict. Grinding poverty and striking inequality persisted within and among countries even amidst unprecedented wealth. Diseases, old and new, threatened to undo painstaking progress and nature's life-sustaining services were being seriously disrupted and degraded.

The United Nations could succeed in helping to meet those challenges only if all felt a renewed sense of mission. Clear answers were necessary to energize and focus the Organization's work in the decades ahead, and it was those answers that the Millennium Summit had to provide. The Summit offered an unparalleled opportunity to reshape the United Nations well into the twenty-first century, enabling it to make a real and measurable difference to people's lives.

The Secretary-General said that his report identified some of the pressing challenges faced by the world's people that fell within the UN ambit. It proposed a number of priorities for Member States to consider, and recommended several immediate steps that the Summit itself could take. All those proposals were set in the context of globalization, which was transforming the world as it entered the twenty-first century. Globalization offered great opportunities, but its benefits were unevenly distributed while its costs were borne by all. The central challenge, therefore, was to ensure that globalization became a positive force for all the world's people. Inclusive globalization should be built on market forces, as well as on a broader effort to create a shared future, based upon our common humanity and diversity.

Secretary-General's charge to the Summit

The Secretary-General declared that the values of freedom, equity and solidarity, tolerance, non-violence, respect for nature and shared responsibility, which reflected the spirit of the UN Charter and were shared by all nations, were of particular importance for the age we were entering. In applying those values to the new century, our priorities had to be clear.

First, no effort should be spared to free our fellow men and women from the abject and dehumanizing poverty in which more than 1 billion of them were currently confined. He urged the Summit to resolve: to halve, by the time the century was 15 years old, the proportion of the world's people (currently 22 per cent) whose income was less than one dollar a day, and the proportion of people (currently 20 per cent) unable to reach, or to afford, safe drinking water; that by the same date all children everywhere would be able to complete a full course of primary schooling, and girls and boys would have equal access to all levels of education; and that by then the spread of HIV/AIDS would have been halted, and begun to reverse. By 2020, the lives of at least 100 million slum-dwellers around the world would be significantly improved; strategies developed to give young people everywhere the chance of finding decent work; the benefits of new technology, especially information technology, made available to all; and every Government committed to national policies and programmes to reduce poverty.

At the international level, the more fortunate countries owed a duty of solidarity to the less fortunate. In that regard, the Secretary-General urged leaders to: grant free access to their markets for goods produced in poor countries, and, as a first step, be prepared, at the Third United Nations Conference on the Least Developed Countries in May 2001, to adopt a policy of duty-free and quota-free access for essentially all exports from the least developed countries; remove the shackles of debt that currently kept many of the poorest countries imprisoned in their poverty, and, as first steps, implement the expansion of the debt relief programme for heavily indebted poor countries [YUN 1999, p. 895] without further delay and be prepared to cancel all official debts of those countries, in return for them making demonstrable commitments to poverty reduction; grant more generous development assistance, particularly to those countries that were genuinely applying their resources to poverty reduction; and work with the pharmaceutical industry and other partners to develop an effective and affordable vaccine against HIV, and make HIV-related drugs more widely accessible in developing countries.

At both the national and international levels, private investment had an indispensable role to play. Countries should develop strong partnerships with the private sector to combat poverty in all its aspects. Extreme poverty in sub-Saharan Africa affected a higher proportion of the population than in any other region. It was compounded by a higher incidence of conflict, HIV/AIDS and many other ills. Special provision should be made for the needs of Africa, and full support given to Africans in their struggle to overcome the continent's problems.

The Secretary-General drew attention to the four new initiatives he had proposed in the report: a Health InterNetwork, to provide hospitals and clinics in developing countries with access to up-to-date medical information; a United Nations Information Technology Service, to train groups in developing countries in the uses and opportunities of information technology; a disaster response initiative, "First on the Ground", which would provide uninterrupted communications access to areas affected by natural disasters and emergencies; and a global policy network to explore viable new approaches to the problem of youth employment.

Second, no effort should be spared to free our fellow men and women from the scourge of war, as required by the Charter, and especially from the violence of civil conflict and the fear of weapons of mass destruction, two great sources of terror in the current age. The Secretary-General urged States therefore to strengthen respect for law, in international as in national affairs, in particular the agreed provisions of treaties on the control of armaments, and international humanitarian and human rights law. All Governments that had not done so should sign and ratify the various conventions, covenants and treaties that formed the central corpus of international law. He also urged States to make the United Nations more effective in its work of maintaining peace and security, notably by strengthening its capacity to conduct peace operations, and adopt measures to make economic sanctions adopted by the Security Council less harsh on innocent populations and more effective in penalizing delinquent rulers.

States should take action to curb the illegal traffic in small arms by: creating greater transparency in arms transfers; supporting regional disarmament measures, such as the moratorium on the importing, exporting or manufacturing of light weapons in West Africa; and extending to other areas, especially post-conflict situations, the "weapons for goods" programmes that had worked well in Albania, El Salvador, Mozambique and Panama. They should also examine the possibility of convening a major international conference to identify ways of eliminating nuclear dangers.

Third, no effort should be spared to free our fellow men and women, and above all our children and grandchildren, from the danger of living on a planet irredeemably spoilt by human activities, and whose resources could no longer provide for their needs. The Secretary-General urged leaders to adopt a new ethic of conservation and stewardship, and, as first steps: to adopt and ratify the Kyoto Protocol to the United Nations Framework Convention on Climate Change [YUN 1997, p. 1048], so that it could enter into force by 2002, and to ensure that its goals were met, as a step towards reducing emissions of greenhouse gases; to consider seriously incorporating the UN system of "green accounting" into national accounts; and to provide financial support for, and become actively engaged in, the Millennium Ecosystem Assessment (see p. 977).

Finally, no effort should be spared to make the United Nations a more effective instrument in the

hands of the world's peoples for pursuing those three priorities: the fight against poverty, ignorance and disease; the fight against violence and terror; and the fight against the degradation and destruction of our common home. Leaders should therefore: reform the Security Council so that it could carry out its responsibilities more effectively and give it greater legitimacy; ensure that the Organization was given the necessary resources to carry out its mandates and that the Secretariat made best use of those resources in the interests of all Member States, by allowing it to adopt the best management practices and technologies available, and to concentrate on those tasks that reflected the current priorities of Member States; and give full opportunities to non-governmental organizations (NGOs) and other non-state actors to make their contributions to the Organization's work.

Further documentation

Other documents before the Summit included the report of the Panel on United Nations Peace Operations (the Brahimi report) [A/55/305-S/2000/809] (see p. 80); a Secretariat note [A/54/959] transmitting the final document of the Millennium Forum of NGOs and civil society actors (see p. 65); the Declaration of the Council of Presidents of the General Assembly on the occasion of the Millennium Summit [A/55/372]; the Declaration of the Heads of State of the Commonwealth of Independent States [A/55/330]; messages from Turkmenistan [A/55/309] and the Federal Republic of Yugoslavia [A/55/362-S/2000/855] to the Millennium Summit; and a position paper by China [A/54/882].

Round-table sessions

More open and informal discussions of the Summit's theme and the Secretary-General's report took place, for the first time in UN history, in four interactive round-table sessions, each of which was chaired by a head of State or Government. Each regional grouping (Africa, Asia, Eastern Europe, Latin America and the Caribbean, and Western European and other States) was represented in the round tables, in accordance with General Assembly **resolution 54/261** of 10 May (see p. 1366).

During the concluding plenary of the Millennium Summit, the Chairpersons of the four round tables, in accordance with Assembly **resolution 54/281** of

11 August (see p. 1367), made oral presentations on the deliberations of their respective groups.

Round Table 1. The Chairperson of the first round table, Prime Minister Goh Chok Tong of Singapore, said that all the leaders felt that globalization was a reality that had to be faced, but while there were enormous benefits for those who could take advantage of it, those who lacked the capacity to do so would find themselves falling further and further behind in the economic race. The negative effects of globalization had therefore to be moderated. One key point was that, while individual countries had national institutions to regulate the domestic market and moderate its social impact, there were no international institutions to regulate the global market and check the adverse effects of globalization on countries.

On the "digital divide", many leaders felt that bridging it would help close the widening income gulf, but others felt that they needed first to deal with more fundamental problems, such as the lack of basic education and reliable electricity and water supplies. Several leaders argued that the rules of the international financial institutions were written to favour strong, rich countries. Undemocratic decision-making at the International Monetary Fund (IMF) and the World Trade Organization (WTO) was cited. The decision-making procedures of WTO, IMF and the World Bank should be made more democratic, consultative, inclusive and transparent, and take into account the different social and economic needs of various countries.

Many said that a basic problem impeding their country's development was their debt burden, and urged debt relief.

The leaders offered several solutions to the problems they had identified, such as the importance of development assistance in capacity-building so that countries could benefit from globalization, and training in international trade negotiations. They said that the United Nations had to be given the resources to run such programmes and Member States should show their political will and sincerity in wanting to help the poorer countries by paying their UN dues.

To raise resources, an international tax or some other fiscal measure was suggested to help in finding a solution to the problems created by globalization. Other proposals included: the creation of an economic security council within the United Nations, with the same binding authority as the political Security Council, to monitor the global market and make recommendations to deal with economic developments that threatened the security of countries; and an international anti-trust law to combat price-fixing and the abuse of power by monopolies, cartels and large companies.

There was discussion on whether new institutions should be created to deal with the new challenges of the era, or old ones reformed. Some participants cautioned that it would be hard to find resources for new institutions, as the cost of participating in existing ones was already a great burden for small countries. Moreover, it was pointless to establish new institutions unless the decision-making process was made more democratic.

As to follow-up action on the round-table discussion, participants proposed that the Millennium Declaration be used as a plan of action to be implemented and monitored at both the national and United Nations levels.

The Chairperson said that he had suggested that a round table for leaders every few years should be built into the UN process to allow interactive discussion among leaders in an informal setting. Such a format could give rise to fresh, useful and innovative ideas and foster closer friendship and understanding between leaders and hence warmer relations among nations.

Round Table 2. President Aleksander Kwasniewski of Poland, Chairperson of the second round table, said that participants shared the same view concerning the nature of the challenges facing the world in the twenty-first century: security risks and local conflicts, poverty, development gaps, endemic illnesses and environmental hazards, among others. The discussion offered some new ideas and new approaches to solving those problems. There was common agreement that the United Nations should play a crucial role in defining the right answers to those problems and in implementing them.

They considered that the main challenge ahead was the development and equal distribution of the benefits resulting from globalization. It was broadly agreed that its benefits should be more evenly and universally spread. Technology offered a great chance, but the fundamental needs of peoples, including food, health and education, had to be satisfied first. Globalization should become human and better managed. At the institutional level, it meant reform of the international

financial and trading systems to make them more equitable. It should also address the risks posed by the new "digital divide". Negative aspects, such as drug trafficking, money-laundering, the illicit arms trade and transnational crime, needed to be addressed as well. The process of globalization had to be based on moral principles and values, the most important being solidarity, especially with Africa. A strong plea was made to recognize the special circumstances of that continent and for the international community to undertake a concerted effort to address the plight the continent faced: poverty, conflicts and HIV/AIDS. A new partnership for Africa was called for. That "new deal" would require a fundamental change of attitude, based on independent thinking and active participation by Africans themselves, a non-parochial, forthcoming and comprehensive approach by their partners, a rejection of a welfare approach and an emphasis on the root causes of the problems.

The most pressing challenge was the fight against poverty, which was often the root cause of instability, conflicts, social tensions and environmental threats. Several participants stressed the need to elaborate workable mechanisms at all levels to alleviate poverty and close the gap between rich and poor, and to intensify international cooperation towards that goal. Leaders reaffirmed their commitment to achieving the goal of halving the proportion of people living in extreme poverty by 2015 and suggested that a coordinated UN global action plan for poverty eradication should be elaborated.

Among the priorities for action, participants mentioned debt relief and increasing official development assistance. It was suggested that some means to mediate between creditors and debtors might be helpful to better meet the needs and interests of both sides. Debt reduction for the poorest nations would enable them to address the most acute problems of social development.

Grave concern was expressed over HIV/AIDS, malaria and other pandemic diseases as a major threat to the achievement of development goals. To control those diseases, access to treatment and medical drugs at affordable prices should be assured, particularly for developing countries. There was a call to launch global programmes with the participation of all stakeholders, including the United Nations, Governments, NGOs and the pharmaceutical industry. In that regard, there was widespread support for the proposals contained in the Secretary-General's report to the Summit [A/54/2000].

The importance of investing in education and the promotion of the rights of children and youth were also stressed. Many participants underlined that stable development was not possible without effective protection of human rights and strong democracy. The conditions for democracy needed to be addressed in both developed and developing countries.

The leaders stressed the link between poverty alleviation and environmental protection, emphasizing that environment be placed high on the global agenda. Ratification of legally binding international instruments, such as the Kyoto Protocol to the United Nations Framework Convention on Climate Change [YUN 1997, p. 1048], was also called for.

Ensuring security, preventing deadly conflicts and maintaining peace were still among the priority tasks of the United Nations. There was an urgent need to adapt peacekeeping operations to the new circumstances, and to pay increased attention to conflict prevention, peace-making and peace-building. If the capacity of the United Nations quickly to deploy robust operations was not strengthened, if Member States failed to provide on time the necessary resources and personnel and if the Organization failed to improve the planning and management of those operations, the United Nations might lose its credibility. There was widespread support for the report of the Panel on United Nations Peace Operations and for its recommendations [A/55/305-S/2000/809] (see p. 80).

The call for reform of the Security Council was reiterated. Support was expressed for the early establishment of the International Criminal Court and some participants pointed out the need to assess critically the instrument of sanctions.

There was a commonly shared view that the United Nations should be strengthened and it should adapt to the changing international environment. The Organization was seen as an important vehicle to manage globalization. Several participants drew attention to the need to ensure democracy in international relations, and hence coherence and coordination among international organizations, both at the global and the regional levels.

Round Table 3. President Hugo Rafael Chávez Frías of Venezuela, Chairperson of the third round table, reported that the group's first recommendation

was for continuity, frequency and institutionalization of the round tables as a way of reclaiming the ethical nature of participation and of restoring the ethical character of the dialogue and creativity. As to meeting the goals of reducing poverty by half by 2015 and ensuring that by 2015 all boys and girls received a complete education of good quality, leaders agreed with Round Table 1 on the establishment of an independent development council to confront the enormous challenge of reducing poverty levels and raising living standards, particularly of the poorest and most backward countries. They also proposed the establishment of a development council in the United Nations with great authority and strong decision-making powers, representative and democratic.

Secondly, the leaders proposed institutionalizing and reinforcing regional groups that would meet frequently, table recommendations and offer avenues to resolve the many tragedies before existing UN bodies. Thirdly, they agreed with almost all the round tables, as an urgent matter, to reactivate the South-South dialogue and re-establish a North-South dialogue.

Round Table 4. The Chairperson of the fourth round table, President Abdelaziz Bouteflika of Algeria, said that the fourth round table was an excellent opportunity to exchange views on the crucial issues of globalization, peace and security and the role of the United Nations.

In today's new world, national interests needed to be defined in broader terms. Globalization, while offering enormous opportunities, ran the risk of exclusion and marginalization. Rules needed to be established to steer globalization. The United Nations had a crucial role to play in that regard in order to transform it into a positive force.

At the national level, leaders said that they needed to give priority to education, to take advantage of fresh opportunities and to reduce the gap between poor and rich. At the regional level, they should develop strategies for common action to open up more our economic spaces, to reduce conflicts and to make real progress together in education. At the global level, they needed to open up markets more to the commodities of the developing countries; to create a world compact with the private sector to increase investments in African and other low-income countries; and to provide debt relief and increase official development assistance to stimulate growth in the poor countries. They hoped that the process launched in the United Nations on financing for development would offer an opportunity to make great progress.

In order to combat poverty, national efforts were necessary, but the consistent support of the international community was also crucial to mainstream the human and environmental dimensions into the globalization process. A consistent, global approach in the economic, social and environmental protection areas should be developed, and the question of the relationship between trade, the environment and social standards should be dealt with. Health, nutrition, employment, respect for cultural identity and, in particular, education were all essential areas. Education had to be central to international concerns.

The development of strategies for debt relief in Africa had been proposed but the continent was still awaiting the results. African countries definitely needed investment in manufactured goods and intermediate goods. To that end, it was essential that national infrastructures be built to attract private investment. A proposal was made to analyse the debts of the indebted countries to understand how the debt was accumulated. That might be done in a South-South framework, in which the United Nations could be involved as a partner.

Africa had to create wider economic spaces, which were essential for the success of its industrial development. Participants said that they were in favour of a conference of the countries of the South, the theme of which would be "Revisiting globalization". They also deplored the fact that the new international economic order, which was debated in the United Nations in the 1960s and 1970s, was no longer relevant.

IMF, in the view of the round table, should be reformed. Attention was drawn to the current discussion in the countries of the North about the new role of that institution. However, the South was not a participant and that situation had to be redressed.

Concerning peace and security, troop-contributing countries should be more involved in the negotiations and in the follow-up work in the Security Council. Harmonizing regional mechanisms with the work of the Security Council should be guaranteed. As was the case in the other round tables, participants stressed the fact that the composition of the current Council no longer reflected today's realities. While much of the work of the Council concerned the situation in Africa, the continent had no permanent seat on that body.

On the subject of terrorism, no one in the interactive dialogue challenged the idea that there was interaction between democracy and the concept of terrorism. There could be no democracy as long as there was terrorism. The eradication of terrorism was a condition for the establishment and the strengthening of the democratic process. Terrorism was a worldwide scourge and it should be discussed by the entire world community. It was disquieting that terrorism was acquiring increasingly internationalized forms and that it had particular links with organized crime, including drug trafficking. The General Assembly needed to remain actively involved in that question and to consider ways to combat that scourge. The leaders particularly recommended to the Secretary-General that a fund be established, or a way be found, for the United Nations to finance a study or studies on terrorism and on its sources of financing, particularly countries that were bridgeheads for terrorist activities in the world.

The need to strengthen the United Nations in the area of peacekeeping was reaffirmed, and the recommendations contained in the Brahimi report (see p. 80) were welcomed. Everyone agreed to recommend the reform of the Security Council, IMF, the Bretton Woods agreements and all post–Second World War institutions.

Closing session

During its closing session on 8 September, the Millennium Summit also heard statements by the Secretary-General of the League of Arab States, the President of the European Commission, the Secretary-General of the Organization of the Islamic Conference, the Secretary-General of the Commonwealth Secretariat, the Secretary-General of the Economic Cooperation Organization, the President of the International Committee of the Red Cross, the Grand Chancellor of the Sovereign Military Order of Malta, the President of the Conference of Presiding Officers of National Parliaments (see p. 67) and the Co-Chairperson of the NGO Millennium Forum (see p. 65).

Secretary-General's closing statement

The Secretary-General of the United Nations, in his closing remarks, said that he was struck by the note-worthy convergence of views expressed concerning the challenge before the international community and by the urgency of the appeal for action. He declared:

"You have said that your first priority is the eradication of extreme poverty. You have set specific targets to that goal, and you have prescribed measures for achieving them. If the measures are really taken, we all know the targets can be reached. Many of you have said that you understand the potential benefits of globalization but that your peoples have yet to feel them. You have acknowledged that part of the solution lies in the hands of sovereign States, which must give priority to needs of their people, especially the poorest. We all know that States alone cannot solve the problems of globalization. They need to work in partnership with the private sector and with civil society in the broadest sense.

"You have also called for a more equitable world economy in which all countries have a fair chance to compete and in which those who have more will do more for those who have less. Speaker after speaker has stressed the urgent need to release poor countries from their burden of debt. You expressed interest in finding new approaches to this problem, including a system of arbitration or mediation, which would balance the interests of creditors with those of sovereign debtors. I will give further thought to this idea and suggest ways in which it could be done.

"You have said that it is intolerable, as we enter a new century, that millions of innocent people, especially women and children, should still fall victim to brutal conflict. We all know that in this area the United Nations has fallen short of the world's expectations. We must strengthen our capacity and improve our performance so that vulnerable communities feel able to count on us in their hour of need. That is why so many of you have welcomed the report of the Panel on United Nations Peace Operations and promised to act quickly on its recommendations.

"You have reaffirmed the vital importance of international law, which is the common language of our global community. Over 80 of you have taken action during this Summit to adhere to international legal instruments that are central to the spirit of our Charter [see p. 68]. Most of these actions concerned protocols that seek to protect children from abuses that bring shame to all humankind. Your action is a welcome sign that humankind is coming together at last to put an end to them.

"You have called for higher priority to be given to the special needs of Africa, where poverty and all its attendant ills seem most intractable.

"You have said that we need more effective international institutions, starting with the United Nations. In your minds, clearly, the reform we began together three years ago is not complete. I agree and look forward to working with you to take it further. Almost every one of you has called for a comprehensive reform of the Security Council. That surely must give new impetus to the search for consensus on this thorny but unavoidable issue. You are rightly concerned with the effectiveness of this Organization. You want action and, above all, you want results. You are right, and I look forward to working with you over the coming year to ensure that the United Nations of the twenty-first century can deliver real improvements in the life of the world's peoples.

"Excellencies, you have sketched out clear directions for adapting this Organization to its role in the new century. But ultimately, you are yourselves the United Nations. It lies in your power, and therefore it is your responsibility, to reach the goals that you have defined. Only you can determine whether the United Nations rises to the challenge. For my part, I hereby rededicate myself as from today to carrying out your mandate. I know that the whole staff of the United Nations does the same."

Millennium Summit follow-up

In order to effect an integrated, coordinated, comprehensive and balanced approach in the implementation of the Millennium Declaration, Algeria, Finland, Namibia, Poland, Singapore and Venezuela requested, on 6 October [A/55/235], that the fifty-fifth regular session of the General Assembly consider the follow-up to the outcome of the Millennium Summit. They said that there was no shortage of challenges to the United Nations. Thus, what was important were the implementation and follow-up of the Millennium Declaration and the maintainence of the momentum created by the Summit.

The General Assembly, on 14 December [meeting 85], adopted without vote **resolution 55/162** [draft: A/55/L.56/ Rev.1], which called on relevant organs, organizations and bodies of the United Nations system to be involved in the follow-up to the Summit [agenda item 182].

Follow-up to the outcome of the Millennium Summit

The General Assembly,

Recalling its resolution 55/2 of 8 September 2000,

Having considered the United Nations Millennium Declaration,

Expressing satisfaction that, for the first time in history, so many heads of State and Government gathered at a summit in New York, which reached a successful conclusion with the adoption of the Millennium Declaration,

Stressing the need for maintaining the political will and momentum of the Millennium Summit at the national, regional and international levels in order to translate commitments into concrete action,

Recognizing the necessity for creating a framework for the implementation of the Millennium Declaration,

Guided by the purposes and principles of the Charter of the United Nations,

Stressing the importance of a comprehensive and balanced approach in implementation and follow-up,

1. *Calls* for an integrated, coordinated, comprehensive and balanced approach in the implementation of the United Nations Millennium Declaration at the national, regional and international levels;

2. *Recognizes* that Governments bear the main responsibility, individually and collectively, for action and implementation of the Millennium Declaration;

3. *Calls upon* the entire United Nations system to assist Member States in every way possible in the implementation of the Millennium Declaration;

4. *Decides* to use existing structures and mechanisms and upcoming events and special sessions of the General Assembly, as well as related conferences and events, to the maximum extent possible in the implementation of the Millennium Declaration, and requests the President of the General Assembly to follow up these processes;

5. *Requests* the Main Committees of the General Assembly to ensure that the outcome of the Millennium Summit is taken into account in their work;

6. *Calls upon* all relevant organs, organizations and bodies of the United Nations system to become involved in the follow-up to the Summit, and invites specialized agencies and related organizations of the United Nations system to strengthen and adjust their activities, programmes and medium-term strategies, as appropriate, to take into account the follow-up to the Summit;

7. *Invites* the regional commissions, in cooperation with regional intergovernmental organizations and regional development banks, to review progress made towards implementing the Millennium Declaration;

8. *Requests* the United Nations system to take action to meet the special needs of Africa and to strengthen the broad range of its engagement in Africa, with a view to intensifying support for poverty eradication and sustainable development, for combating diseases and pandemics and for the process of conflict prevention and the consolidation of democracy;

9. *Recognizes* that the implementation of the Millennium Declaration will require resources and adequate financing at the national, regional and international levels and that additional financial resources are needed, in particular in Africa and the least developed countries, landlocked developing countries and small island developing States;

10. *Requests* the appropriate bodies to consider urgently how the implementation of the Millennium Declaration should relate to the biennial budget process and the medium-term plan;

11. *Requests* the Secretary-General to ensure system-wide coordination to assist with the implementation of the Millennium Declaration, and invites him to identify, within the framework of the Administrative Committee on Coordination, innovative ways of enhancing cooperation and coherence throughout the United Nations system;

12. *Invites* the Bretton Woods institutions to become involved actively in the implementation of and follow-up to the Summit and to enhance their cooperation with other parts of the United Nations system for coherent implementation of the Millennium Declaration;

13. *Invites* the World Trade Organization to contribute to the implementation of the Millennium Declaration;

14. *Calls* for enhanced partnership and cooperation with national parliaments as well as civil society, including nongovernmental organizations and the private sector, as set out in the Millennium Declaration, to ensure their contribution to the implementation of the Declaration;

15. *Requests* the specialized agencies, the Bretton Woods institutions and the World Trade Organization to keep the General Assembly informed about how they contribute to the implementation of the Millennium Declaration;

16. *Requests* that the events and conferences referred to in paragraph 4 above keep the General Assembly informed about how they contribute to the implementation of the Millennium Declaration;

17. *Reiterates* the call to assess, on a regular basis, progress towards implementing the Millennium Declaration;

18. *Requests* the Secretary-General urgently to prepare a long-term "road map" towards the implementation of the Millennium Declaration within the United Nations system and to submit it to the General Assembly at its fifty-sixth session;

19. *Also requests* the Secretary-General to prepare a comprehensive report every five years, supplemented by an annual report on progress achieved towards implementing the Millennium Declaration, taking into account the following:

(a) The annual reports should reflect the broad array of specific goals and commitments enunciated in the Millennium Declaration, though each could explore in greater depth one or two areas covered in the Declaration;

(b) All reports should focus, in this respect, on the results and benchmarks achieved, identify gaps in implementation and strategies for reducing them, and highlight in particular cross-sectoral issues and cross-cutting themes on development and peace and security;

(c) Reports should draw on the work of the entire United Nations system, including the Bretton Woods institutions and the World Trade Organization;

(d) The reporting system should be appraised with a view to strengthening its coherence and integration;

20. *Decides* to include in the provisional agenda of its fifty-sixth session the item entitled "Follow-up to the outcome of the Millennium Summit".

The Assembly, by **decision 55/458** of 23 December, decided that the item "Follow-up to the outcome of the Millennium Summit" would remain for consideration during its resumed fifty-fifth (2001) session.

High-level Security Council meeting

The Security Council

As part of the Millennium Summit, the Security Council met on 7 September for the second time in its history, the first being in 1992 [YUN 1992, p. 33], at the level of heads of State and Government to discuss ways of ensuring an effective role of the Security Council in the maintenance of international peace. The meeting was attended by 9 Presidents (Argentina, China, France, Mali, Namibia, the Russian Federation, Tunisia, Ukraine and the United States), 5 Prime Ministers (Bangladesh, Canada, Jamaica, the Netherlands and the United Kingdom) and the Minister of Foreign Affairs of Malaysia of the Council's 15 members.

The Council President (Mali) told the meeting that the United Nations Development Programme (UNDP) indicators had shown how far we were from eliminating poverty and creating the conditions for a better life for all. Conflicts had not ceased but had become internal, particularly in the form of civil wars. The Organization had made progress but there had been some failures over the last 10 years, which in some ways had affected its credibility, as Africa had unfortunately illustrated. The tragic events that took place in Sierra Leone, the need to better protect communities and individuals, including UN and humanitarian personnel, and the need to better meet the new security challenges were not in conflict with the shared determination to fine-tune the actions of the Council to enhance its ability to prevent crises and to respond to them in an appropriate fashion. At a time when the world was scrutinizing the UN's role in the twenty-first century, we needed more than ever to send strong clear signals to peoples and States of the determination and ability of the United Nations to carry out effective peacekeeping operations.

The Secretary-General said that the Council and the Organization were facing a crisis of credibility in discharging their responsibility for the maintenance of international peace and security. Too many vulnerable communities in too many regions now hesitated to look to the United Nations to assist them in their hour of need. Only determined action could restore the reputation of the United Nations as a credible force for peace and justice. However, the United Nations and its peacekeepers could not be the answer to every crisis, conflict or threat to human life, nor could it be a substitute for the political will of the parties to achieve a peaceful settlement, but where it was the answer, it should be given the means to make the difference between life and death. The Secretary-General said that he was already committed to implementing those changes recommended by the Panel on United Nations Peace Operations (see p. 80), which he had appointed in March to provide frank and realistic recommendations to assist the Council and the larger membership in fulfilling its mission of peace.

Security Council declaration

Following statements by all the Council members, the Council's action came in the form of a declaration on ensuring an effective role for the Security Council in the maintenance of international peace and security, particularly in Africa, adopted unanimously on 7 September [meeting 4194] and annexed to **resolution 1318(2000)**. The draft [S/2000/845] was prepared in consultations among Council members.

The Security Council

Decides to adopt the attached declaration on ensuring an effective role for the Security Council in the maintenance of international peace and security, particularly in Africa.

ANNEX

The Security Council,

Meeting at the level of heads of State and Government in the course of the Millennium Summit to discuss the need to ensure an effective role for the Security Council in the maintenance of international peace and security, particularly in Africa,

I   *Pledges* to uphold the purposes and principles of the Charter of the United Nations, reaffirms its commitment to the principles of sovereign equality, national sovereignty, territorial integrity and political independence of all States, and underlines the need for respect for human rights and the rule of law;

Reaffirms the importance of adhering to the principles of the non-threat or non-use of force in international relations in any manner inconsistent with the purposes of the United Nations, and the peaceful settlement of international disputes;

Recalls its primary responsibility for the maintenance of international peace and security, and resolves to strengthen the central role of the United Nations in peace-keeping and to ensure the effective functioning of the collective security system established by the Charter;

II   *Pledges* to enhance the effectiveness of the United Nations in addressing conflict at all stages from prevention to settlement to post-conflict peace-building;

Reaffirms its determination to give equal priority to the maintenance of international peace and security in every region of the world and, in view of the particular needs of Africa, to give special attention to the promotion of durable peace and sustainable development in Africa, and to the specific characteristics of African conflicts;

III *Strongly encourages* the development within the United Nations system and more widely of comprehensive and integrated strategies to address the root causes of conflicts, including their economic and social dimensions;

Affirms its determination to strengthen United Nations peacekeeping operations by:

- Adopting clearly defined, credible, achievable and appropriate mandates;
- Including in those mandates effective measures for the security and safety of United Nations personnel and, wherever feasible, for the protection of the civilian population;
- Taking steps to assist the United Nations to obtain trained and properly equipped personnel for peacekeeping operations;
- Strengthening consultations with troop-contributing countries when deciding on such operations;

Agrees to support:

- The upgrading of United Nations capacity for planning,

establishing, deploying and conducting peacekeeping operations;

- The provision of a more up-to-date and sounder foundation for financing peacekeeping operations;

Underlines the importance of enhancing the United Nations capacity for rapid deployment of peacekeeping operations, and urges Member States to provide sufficient and timely resources;

IV *Welcomes* the report of the Panel on United Nations Peace Operations of 17 August 2000, and decides to consider expeditiously the recommendations that fall within its area of responsibility;

V *Stresses* the critical importance of the disarmament, demobilization and reintegration of ex-combatants, and emphasizes that such programmes should normally be integrated into the mandates of peacekeeping operations;

VI *Calls* for effective international action to prevent the illegal flow of small arms into areas of conflict;

Decides to continue to take resolute action in areas where the illegal exploitation and trafficking of high-value commodities contributes to the escalation or continuation of conflicts;

Stresses that the perpetrators of crimes against humanity, crimes of genocide, war crimes, and other serious violations of international humanitarian law should be brought to justice;

Emphasizes its determination to continue to sensitize peacekeeping personnel in the prevention and control of HIV/AIDS in all operations;

VII *Calls* for the strengthening of cooperation and communication between the United Nations and regional or subregional organizations or arrangements, in accordance with Chapter VIII of the Charter, and in particular in respect of peacekeeping operations;

Emphasizes the importance of continued cooperation and effective coordination between the United Nations, the Organization of African Unity and African subregional organizations in addressing conflicts in Africa, and of enhanced support for the Mechanism for Conflict Prevention, Management and Resolution of the Organization of African Unity;

VIII *Underlines* the fact that the ultimate responsibility for resolving disputes and conflicts lies with the parties themselves and that peacekeeping operations aimed at helping to implement a peace accord can succeed only to the extent that there is a genuine and lasting commitment to peace by all parties concerned;

Calls upon all States to intensify efforts to secure a world free of the scourge of war.

Other millennium gatherings

The occasion of the Millennium Summit was also the opportunity for several other bodies to gather so that their views and proposals could be taken into account by the heads of State and Government during their deliberations and in the finalization of the Summit's final document. Those gatherings included the Women Leaders Summit, bringing together women heads of State and Government, past and present, and women heads of UN agencies, funds and programmes; the Millennium World Peace Summit of Religious and Spiritual Leaders; the Interreligious and International Federation for World Peace Assembly 2000; and the Conference of Presiding Officers of National Parliaments. Earlier in the year, the Millennium Forum of non-governmental and civil society organizations took place in New York.

Also, regional hearings in preparation for the Millennium Assembly had been organized in 1999 by the Economic Commission for Africa [YUN 1999, p. 914], the Economic and Social Commission for Asia and the Pacific [ibid., p. 934], the Economic Commission for Europe [ibid., p. 941], the Economic Commission for Latin America and the Caribbean [ibid., p. 948] and the Economic and Social Commission for Western Asia [ibid., p. 957].

NGO Millennium Forum

As a contribution to the Millennium Summit activities, the Millennium Forum, which was held at UN Headquarters from 22 to 26 May, brought together NGOs and other civil society actors. The Forum was attended by representatives of over 1,000 NGOs and other civil society organizations from more than 100 countries. Their objective was to build upon the common vision and the work begun at civil society conferences and the UN world conferences during the 1990s, to draw the attention of Governments to the urgency of implementing the commitments they had made and to channel their collective energies by reclaiming globalization for and by the people.

The final document of the Forum [A/54/959], entitled "We the Peoples Millennium Forum Declaration and Agenda for Action: strengthening the United Nations in the twenty-first century", outlined a vision of a world that was human-centred and genuinely democratic, just, sustainable and peaceful, guided by the universal principles of democracy, equality, inclusion, voluntarism and non-discrimination; and a world where peace and human security replaced armaments, violent conflicts and wars, and where everyone lived in a clean environment with a fair distribution of the Earth's resources. The vision also included a special role for the dynamism of young people and the experience of the elderly and reaffirmed the universality of all human rights. The Forum identified the challenges facing the new millennium, including rising violence and armed conflicts, widespread violations of human rights and unacceptably large numbers of people who were denied the means for a minimal human existence. At the same time, new and emerging diseases, such as HIV/AIDS, threatened to devastate entire societies. Globalization and advances in technology created significant opportunities for people to connect, share and learn from each other. At the same time, corporate-driven globalization increased inequalities between and within countries, undermined local traditions and cultures and escalated disparities between rich and poor, marginalizing large numbers of people in urban and rural areas. The Forum proposed action to strengthen cooperation among all actors at the international, regional, national and local levels to make its vision a reality. The Agenda for Action included steps that should be taken by civil society, Governments and the United Nations in the eradication of poverty; peace, security and disarmament; facing the challenge of globalization: equity, justice and diversity; human rights; sustainable development and the environment; and strengthening and democratizing the United Nations and international organizations.

Speaking before the General Assembly's Millennium Summit on 8 September, the Co-Chairperson of the Millennium Forum, Techeste Ahderom, declared that, after listening to the speeches over the preceding three days, the Forum's vision and plan of action were consonant with much of what had been said. Civil society stood ready to work with the leaders and their Governments in a strong new partnership to create a new world. At the same time, it stood ready to hold leaders to their commitments if they did not deliver on their words. The Forum asked that leaders review carefully the Millennium Forum Declaration, which was simply calling on Governments to live up to the commitments and the principles that they had agreed to in the global conferences of the 1990s. It was also seeking increased access for NGOs to the General Assembly and its Main Committees.

World Peace Assembly 2000

Two weeks before the Millennium Summit (17-19 August), the Interreligious and International Federation for World Peace (IIFWP) Assembly 2000: Renewing the United Nations and Building a Culture of Peace was held in New York at UN Headquarters and the Waldorf-Astoria Hotel. Sponsored by IIFWP and the Permanent Missions to the United Nations of Indonesia, Mongolia and Uganda, the conference was attended by dignitaries from over 100 nations, including former heads of State and Government, and religious and parliamentary leaders, as well as academic, business and media leaders. The conference was chaired by Makarim Wibisono, Indonesia's Permanent Representative to the United Nations. The conference discussed religion and politics as partners for peace, the quest for economic justice, UN reform and renewal, conflict resolution and religion's role, the global importance of the family, and globalization and sustainable development. Assembly 2000 hoped to convey to the world's religious and political leaders substantial recommendations and conclusions as to how best to create a culture of peace. Among the recommendations endorsed in the statement of affirmation adopted at the end of the conference was that an assembly of religious representatives be formed within the UN structure, a UN council consisting of respected spiritual leaders appointed by Member States. That council would especially advocate a universal, transnational ideal of peace. Those persons would be considered global ambassadors of the United Nations.

Millennium World Peace Summit

For the first time in history, religious and spiritual leaders of the world's diverse faith traditions came together in a Millennium World Peace Summit of Religious and Spiritual Leaders, which was held at Headquarters on

28 and 29 August and continued in working sessions at the Waldorf-Astoria Hotel on 30 and 31 August. Attended by over 1,000 religious leaders, activists, scholars and observers, the Summit sought to identify ways that the worldwide religious and spiritual communities could work together as interfaith allies with the United Nations on specific peace, poverty and environmental initiatives. Religious leaders could work together to support the United Nations.

In his address to the Summit, the Secretary-General called on the spiritual leaders to set an example of interfaith dialogue and communication and help bridge the chasms of ignorance, fear and misunderstanding. He suggested that the Summit presented an opportunity for religious, spiritual and political leaders to consider what they could do to promote justice, equality, reconciliation and peace, and to inspire people to new levels of commitment and public service. Their presence at the United Nations signified their commitment to its global mission of tolerance, development and peace.

The main document emerging from the Summit was the statement Commitment to Global Peace, in which the religious and spiritual leaders condemned all violence in the name of religion and appealed to all religious, ethnic and national groups to respect the right to freedom of religion. The Commitment pledged collaboration with the United Nations in the pursuit of peace, in promoting the eradication of poverty and assuming a shared responsibility for expanding education, health care and an opportunity to achieve a secure and sustainable livelihood. Signatories to the Commitment also pledged to educate their communities to make environment a priority. Religious leaders agreed to form a Steering Committee to explore ways to bring about future collaboration with the United Nations, identify specific mechanisms to further that process and present a plan as soon as possible. Another initiative was an agreement of the women delegates to form their own international religious council.

Conference of Presiding Officers of National Parliaments

The Inter-Parliamentary Union (IPU) held its first Conference of Presiding Officers of National Parliaments at Headquarters from 30 August to 1 September. Reporting to the Millennium Summit during its closing plenary on 8 September, the President of the Conference, Najma Heptulla, said that the Conference, attended by 148 Presidents of chambers from 140 countries, represented the commitment of the parliaments to work closely with the United Nations to ensure that the twenty-first century was a century without fear, without deprivation and want, a century that allowed for the fullest development of the inherent potential of each and every human being that would represent the real globalization. The Conference unanimously adopted a declaration encapsulating the participants' parliamentary vision for international cooperation at the dawn of the third millennium and setting out the main challenges facing societies and expressing their political resolve to successfully overcome them through international cooperation. It also contained recommendations on the role of parliaments in a reformed multilateral cooperation system.

The President declared that parliaments stood firmly behind the United Nations and that support was both political and practical. They were committed to offering the necessary political backing to the United Nations as the cornerstone of the international cooperation system, and to allocating the resources that the United Nations and the other intergovernmental institutions needed to accomplish their noble mission.

Participants were unanimous in identifying a democratic deficit in the United Nations and the intergovernmental regime at large. They declared that, if UN decisions were to interpret the concerns and aspirations of the peoples and if international agreements were to effectively find their way to national reality, parliament, as the institution that legitimately represented society in its diversity and was accountable to it, should have a better say in the international cooperation process.

They noted that the Millennium Declaration (see p. 49) called for a strengthening of cooperation between the United Nations and national parliaments through IPU. They were determined to see that the necessary work was done at the national level, and especially within national parliaments, so that the parliamentary dimension of international cooperation could be developed. To create that new partnership, parliaments intended to act in close consultation with Governments and with intergovernmental organizations.

Because it was a unique instrument for relaying the views of parliaments, IPU looked forward to identifying with the General Assembly a status for the organization that was commensurate with the constitutional status of parliaments and with IPU's mission, instead of the current classification as an NGO.

Women Leaders Summit

On 5 September, the day before the Millennium Summit of the General Assembly, women heads of State and Government gathered at Headquarters to focus on issues arising from the Millennium Summit's theme, "The role of the United Nations in the twenty-first century", that affected women.

Organized by the Council of Women Leaders, located at the John F. Kennedy School of Government at Harvard University (Cambridge, Massachusetts, United States), the Women Leaders Summit made recommendations in areas the leaders considered critical to the advancement of women: peace, security and disarmament, development and poverty eradication, protecting the environment, good governance, democracy and human rights, protecting vulnerable groups and strengthening the United Nations.

They called on the United Nations, among other things, to: ensure greater participation of women in peacekeeping operations and peace-negotiating tables and acknowledge and promote their participation in the identification of solutions to prevent conflicts; focus on developing enabling conditions for women to combat poverty, including by guaranteeing their equal access to education, credit and information and by providing affordable health care; reaffirm its commitment to gender-sensitive development and support women's role in sustainable, ecologically sound consumption and production patterns; support their advancement in government; ensure the prevention and punishment of discrimination and violence against women, including in conflict situations; adopt policies to protect and promote the human rights of indigenous women; and improve women's representation at all levels within the UN system.

The meeting was also attended by eight women heads of UN agencies, funds and programmes, the wife of the United Nations Secretary-General, the Secretary-General of the Council of Women Leaders and the United States Secretary of State. It was chaired by Mary Robinson, United Nations High Commissioner for Human Rights and former President of Ireland.

Treaty-signing ceremony

During the Summit, an exceptional response was generated to the Secretary-General's invitation of 15 May to all heads of State and Government to use the unique opportunity afforded by the convening of the Millennium Summit to rededicate themselves to the international legal framework by becoming parties to the core group of multilateral treaties that reflected the key policy goals of the United Nations and the spirit of its Charter. In an unprecedented treaty-signing ceremony held throughout the three-day Summit, some 40 instruments of international law were signed, ratified or acceded to by 84 countries (59 at the level of heads of State or Government). A total of 273 treaty actions took place during that time (187 signatures and 86 ratifications), ranging from human rights treaties to conventions on refugees and stateless persons, international criminal matters, disarmament and the environment. The treaties that attracted the most attention were the Optional Protocols to the Convention on the Rights of the Child on the involvement of children in armed conflict (59 signatures and 2 ratifications) and on the sale of children, child prostitution and child pornography (57 signatures and 1 ratification), adopted by General Assembly **resolution 54/263** (see p. 615); the Optional Protocol to the Convention on the Elimination of All Forms of Discrimination against Women (18 signatures and 4 ratifications), adopted by Assembly resolution 54/4 [YUN 1999, p. 1100]; the Rome Statute of the International Criminal Court (12 signatures and 4 ratifications) [YUN 1998, p. 1209]; the International Convention for the Suppression of the Financing of Terrorism (10 signatures and 2 ratifications), adopted by Assembly resolution 54/109 [YUN 1999, p. 1232]; and the Convention on the Safety of United Nations and Associated Personnel (7 ratifications and accessions), adopted by Assembly resolution 49/59 [YUN 1994, p. 1289].

As a result of the success of the event, it was proposed to make similar appeals prior to each annual session of the General Assembly, inviting heads of State and Government to sign and ratify those treaties deposited with the Secretary-General to which their States were not yet party.

PART ONE

Political and security questions

Chapter I

International peace and security

In 2000, the United Nations took action to reform its peacekeeping activities by laying secure and adequate foundations for an effective peacekeeping structure, while providing daily direction and support to the operations in the field. In March, the Secretary-General established a high-level panel to undertake a major review of UN peace and security activities and recommend ways to ensure that future peacekeeping operations were more effective. The panel's recommendations, contained in what was known as the "Brahimi report", after the panel's chairman, Lakhdar Brahimi, were endorsed by the General Assembly in December. In October, the Secretary-General presented a number of practical measures, including resource requirements, to support the broad objectives identified by the panel.

Equally important for the Organization were the growing concerns for the prevention of conflicts and the effectiveness of UN efforts towards post-conflict peace-building. In July, the Security Council held an open debate on conflict prevention during which Member States indicated their broad commitment to improving UN capacity for effective preventive action. In that regard, it took action to prevent the trade in illicit diamonds that were fuelling conflict in Africa. The Council also reviewed the role of disarmament, demobilization and reintegration of ex-combatants in enhancing the effectiveness of UN peacekeeping and peace-building activities. Moreover, the Council, recognizing that wars and conflicts contributed to the spread of HIV/AIDS, discussed ways to incorporate HIV/AIDS prevention awareness skills and advice in UN peacekeeping operations.

During the year, the United Nations deployed 18 peacekeeping operations worldwide, with some 37,719 military personnel and civilian police serving under UN command as at 31 December 2000. The year began with 17 operations in place. Three missions ended during the year, one each in Africa, the Americas and Europe, and one new one was established in Africa. The total number of missions in place at the end of the year stood at 15.

The Special Committee on Peacekeeping Operations, the body responsible for reviewing UN peacekeeping operations in all their aspects, and its open-ended working group made proposals and recommendations to guide the principles, definitions and implementation of mandates and to enhance the capacity of the United Nations for peacekeeping and cooperation with regional groups, particularly in Africa.

The cost of UN peacekeeping operations amounted to $1,756.8 million for the period 1 July 1999 to 30 June 2000, compared to $837.8 million during the previous 12-month period, while unpaid assessed contributions for peacekeeping operations amounted to $2,128.9 million as at 30 June 2000, compared to $1,687.6 million in 1999.

The Assembly considered various aspects of peacekeeping financing, financial performance and proposed budgets, the peacekeeping support account and the Peacekeeping Reserve Fund. It changed the procedure for apportioning the expenses of peacekeeping operations among States and reviewed the new procedure for the reimbursement of contingent-owned equipment and the management of peacekeeping assets, including the operation of the United Nations Logistics Base in Brindisi, Italy.

In addition to its peacekeeping operations, the United Nations addressed peace-building and other conflict situations through a number of political and human rights missions and the deployment of the Secretary-General's Special Representatives in Afghanistan, Angola, Burundi, the Central African Republic, the Democratic People's Republic of Korea, Guatemala, Guinea-Bissau, Liberia, Papua New Guinea, Somalia and Tajikistan.

Maintenance of international peace and security

Heads of State and Government Security Council Summit

In a 4 August statement to the media [S/2000/772], the Security Council President indicated the Council's intention, as a contribution to the General Assembly's Millennium Summit (see p. 47), to meet on 7 September at the level of heads of State and Government to consider the topic "Ensuring an effective role of the Security

Council in the maintenance of international peace and security, particularly in Africa".

At that meeting, which was attended by the Presidents of Argentina, China, France, Mali, Namibia, the Russian Federation, Tunisia, Ukraine and the United States, the Prime Ministers of Bangladesh, Canada, Jamaica, the Netherlands and the United Kingdom, and the Minister for Foreign Affairs of Malaysia, the Council, by **resolution 1318(2000)** (see p. 64), adopted the Millennium Summit declaration in which it resolved to strengthen the United Nations role in peacekeeping and pledged to enhance its effectiveness in addressing conflict at all stages from prevention to settlement to post-conflict peace-building.

Conflict prevention and peace-building

Preventive diplomacy and peacemaking

In a March report "We the peoples: the role of the United Nations in the twenty-first century" [A/54/2000], the Secretary-General said that there was near-universal agreement that prevention was preferable to cure, and that prevention strategies had to address the root causes of conflicts, not simply their violent symptoms. Consensus was not always matched by practical actions, however. Political leaders found it hard to sell prevention policies abroad to their public at home, because the costs were palpable and immediate, while the benefits were more difficult for the leaders to convey and the public to grasp. Thus, prevention was, first, a challenge of political leadership. To be successful at preventing deadly conflicts, there had to be a clear understanding of their causes, but no single strategy would be universally effective.

Noting that the majority of current wars were among the poor, the Secretary-General stated that every step taken towards reducing poverty and achieving broad-based economic growth was a step towards conflict prevention. All those engaged in conflict prevention and development, therefore—the United Nations, the Bretton Woods institutions (the World Bank Group and the International Monetary Fund), Governments and civil society organizations—should address those challenges in a more integrated fashion.

The Secretary-General further observed that in many poor countries at war, poverty was coupled with sharp ethnic or religious cleavages; the rights of subordinate groups were insufficiently respected, the institutions of government were insufficiently inclusive and the allocation of resources favoured the dominant faction over others. The solution was clear, even if difficult to achieve: promote human rights, protect minority rights and institute political arrangements in which all groups were represented.

Some armed conflicts, however, were driven by greed, not grievance. Often, the control over natural resources was at stake, drugs were often involved, the conflicts were abetted by opportunistic neighbours, and private sector actors were complicit—buying ill-gotten gains, helping to launder funds and feeding a steady flow of weapons into the conflict zone. The best preventive strategy in that context was transparency: "naming and shaming". Civil society actors had an enormous role to play in that regard, but Governments and the Security Council should exercise their responsibility. Greater social responsibility on the part of global companies, including banks, was also essential.

Successful strategies for prevention required that old conflicts did not start up again, and that support was provided for post-conflict peace-building. However, it had to be recognized that even the best preventive and deterrence strategies could fail. Other measures, therefore, might be called for, including strengthening the commitment to protecting vulnerable people.

Security Council consideration. Speaking before the Security Council on 20 July [S/PV.4174], during its consideration of the agenda item on the role of the Security Council in conflict prevention, the Secretary-General stated that it was high time that prevention was given primacy in all the Organization's work. However, he observed that no two wars were alike and no single prevention strategy would be effective everywhere. There was no panacea. Prevention was multidimensional and effective prevention had to address the structural faults that predisposed a society to conflict. The best form of long-term conflict prevention was healthy and balanced economic development and the United Nations had a special role to play in that regard. The Department of Political Affairs, the designated focal point for conflict prevention within the UN system, had set up a Prevention Team to identify situations where UN preventive action could help, and other UN departments and agencies had taken similar measures to strengthen their preventive capacity. The Secretary-General had established a Framework for Coordination to improve interdepartmental and inter-agency links, and the Organization was working more closely with regional organizations. In addition, more than 400 staff system-wide had been trained in prevention and early warning at the United Nations Staff College in Turin, Italy.

The Secretary-General intended to continue to strengthen the Secretariat's information-gathering and analysis capacity and looked forward to a systematic exchange with Council members on ways to do that. He recalled his earlier suggestions on steps the Council could take with regard to prevention, including making greater use of fact-finding missions, encouraging States to bring potential conflicts to the Council's attention and setting up an informal working group or a subsidiary organ to study early warning and prevention. He further suggested that some of the UN Charter's provisions relating to prevention had been underutilized and proposed that the Council hold periodic meetings at the Foreign Minister level, as provided for in Article 28, to discuss thematic or actual prevention issues; work more closely with the other principal UN organs; and place prevention issues on the agenda of the monthly meeting between the Presidents of the General Assembly and the Council. The Council could also obtain useful information and other assistance from the Economic and Social Council, as envisaged in Article 65; request under Article 96 an advisory opinion on any legal question from the International Court of Justice; and examine ways to interact more closely with non-State actors with expertise in prevention or that could make a difference to it. Civil society, including the corporate sector, also had a vital role to play in defusing or avoiding conflicts.

The Secretary-General believed that the time had come to review all those proposals and those put forward by Council members, and to agree on the most practical ideas for action. He thanked those Governments that had contributed a total of $7.4 million to the Trust Fund for Preventive Action. He believed that, although prevention cost money, intervention, relief and rebuilding broken societies and lives cost far more. Leaders would have to acknowledge that the international community could play a constructive role in internal situations and that that could strengthen sovereignty rather than weaken it. States would also have to give prevention institutions the backing they so urgently needed. Conflict prevention should become the cornerstone of collective security in the twenty-first century.

SECURITY COUNCIL ACTION

On 20 July [meeting 4174], following the Security Council's discussion of its role in the prevention of armed conflicts and consultations among Council members, the President made statement **S/PRST/2000/25** on behalf of the Council:

The Security Council recalls the statements by its President of 16 and 24 September and 30 November 1998, 30 November 1999 and 23 March 2000, and recalls also resolutions 1196(1998) of 16 September 1998, 1197(1998) of 18 September 1998, and 1208

(1998) and 1209(1998) of 19 November 1998. Bearing in mind its primary responsibility under the Charter of the United Nations for the maintenance of international peace and security, it reaffirms its role in taking appropriate steps aimed at the prevention of armed conflicts. It affirms its commitment to the principles of the political independence, sovereign equality and territorial integrity of all States. The Council also affirms the need for respect for human rights and the rule of law.

The Council stresses the need for the maintenance of regional and international peace and stability and friendly relations among all States, and underlines the overriding humanitarian and moral imperative as well as the economic advantages of preventing the outbreak and escalation of conflicts. It highlights, in this regard, the need to create a culture of prevention. The Council reaffirms its belief that early warning, preventive diplomacy, preventive deployment, preventive disarmament and post-conflict peace-building are interdependent and complementary components of a comprehensive conflict-prevention strategy. The Council emphasizes its continuing commitment to addressing the prevention of armed conflicts in all regions of the world.

The Council recognizes that peace is not only the absence of conflict, but that it requires a positive, dynamic, participatory process where dialogue is encouraged and conflicts are resolved in a spirit of mutual understanding and cooperation. Bearing in mind that causes of conflict are often nurtured in the minds of human beings, the Council calls upon Member States, relevant bodies of the United Nations system and other relevant organizations to promote a culture of peace. It recognizes the importance of appropriate implementation of the Declaration and Programme of Action on a Culture of Peace, adopted by the General Assembly on 13 September 1999, for preventing violence and conflicts as well as strengthening efforts aimed at the creation of conditions of peace, and consolidation thereof through post-conflict peace-building.

The Council recalls its important role in the peaceful settlement of disputes under Chapter VI of the Charter. It reaffirms the importance of its consideration of all situations that might deteriorate into armed conflicts, and of considering follow-up action, as appropriate. In this regard, it expresses continued willingness to consider the use of Council missions, with the consent of host countries, in order to determine whether any dispute, or any situation that might lead to international friction or give rise to a dispute, is likely to endanger the maintenance of international peace and security, and to make recommendations for action by the Council, as appropriate.

The Council highlights the importance of the full support of all States for the efforts of the Council and other relevant United Nations organs and agencies in developing and implementing appropriate strategies for the prevention of armed conflicts in accordance with the provisions of the Charter. The Council underlines the importance of the peaceful settlement of disputes and recalls the obligation of parties to disputes to seek actively a peaceful solution in accordance with the provisions of Chapter VI of the Charter. The Council also recalls the obligation of all Member States to accept and carry out its decisions, including those for the prevention of armed conflicts.

The Council also stresses the importance of a co-ordinated international response to economic, social, cultural and humanitarian problems, which are often the root causes of armed conflicts.

The Council recalls the essential role of the Secretary-General in the prevention of armed conflicts, in accordance with Article 99 of the Charter, and expresses its willingness to take appropriate preventive action in response to matters brought to its attention by States or the Secretary-General, which it deems likely to endanger the maintenance of international peace and security. The Council encourages the ongoing efforts within the United Nations system to enhance its early warning capacity, and notes in this regard the importance of drawing on information from a variety of sources, given the multiple factors that contribute to conflict. It invites the Secretary-General to make recommendations to the Council, taking into account the views of Member States and, in the light of past experience, on the most effective and appropriate early warning strategies, bearing in mind the need to link early warning with early response. The Council invites the Secretary-General to submit to the Council reports on such disputes, including, as appropriate, early warning and proposals for preventive measures.

The Council recognizes the important role regional organizations and arrangements play in the prevention of armed conflicts, including through the development of confidence- and security-building measures, and re-emphasizes the need for effective and sustained cooperation and coordination between the United Nations and such regional organizations and arrangements in the prevention of armed conflict, in accordance with the provisions of Chapter VIII of the Charter. It expresses its willingness, within its responsibilities, to support the efforts of the Secretary-General in collaborating with the leadership of regional organizations and arrangements in order to develop strategies and programmes to be employed at the regional level. In this regard, it encourages the strengthening of the modalities of cooperation between the United Nations and regional organizations and arrangements, including in early warning and the mutual exchange of information. It recognizes the need to enhance the capacity of the Organization of African Unity, in particular, its Mechanism for Conflict Prevention, Management and Resolution.

The Council recognizes the importance of effective post-conflict peace-building strategies in preventing the re-emergence of conflicts. In this context, it recognizes also the need for close cooperation among bodies of the United Nations system and with other organizations and arrangements in the area of post-conflict peace-building, and expresses its willingness to consider ways to improve such cooperation. It also stresses that the design of peacekeeping mandates that fully take into account operational military requirements and other relevant situations on the ground could help to prevent the re-emergence of conflicts. The Council highlights the importance of strengthening its cooperation with the Economic and Social Council, in accordance with Article 65 of the Charter, in the area of the prevention of armed conflicts, including in addressing the economic, social, cultural and humanitarian problems that are often the root causes of conflicts. It underlines the fact that economic rehabilitation and reconstruction constitute important elements in the long-term development of post-conflict societies and the maintenance of lasting peace, and stresses the importance of international assistance in this regard.

The Council highlights the importance of preventive deployment in armed conflicts, and reiterates its willingness to consider the deployment, with the consent of the host country, of preventive missions in appropriate circumstances.

The Council recalls the emphasis it placed in its statement of 23 March 2000 on the process of disarmament, demobilization and reintegration, which can be vital in stabilizing post-conflict situations, reducing the likelihood of renewed violence and facilitating the transition from conflict to normalcy and development. The Council will take appropriate measures, with the consent of the State concerned, aimed at preventing the recurrence of armed conflicts, by, inter alia, developing adequate programmes for the disarmament, demobilization and reintegration of ex-combatants, including child soldiers.

The Council recognizes the important role of women in the prevention and resolution of conflicts and in peace-building. It stresses the importance of their increased participation in all aspects of the conflict prevention and resolution process.

The Council recognizes the fact that the illegal exploitation of and trade in natural resources, particularly diamonds, can contribute to the escalation of conflicts. The Council is particularly concerned that the proceeds from the illegal exploitation of and trade in high value commodities such as diamonds are providing funds for arms purchases, thus aggravating conflicts and humanitarian crises, in particular in Africa. It therefore expresses its willingness to seek the cooperation of Member States and the business community in curbing the illegal exploitation of and trade in these resources, particularly diamonds, and in effectively implementing the measures imposed by its relevant resolutions aimed at curbing illicit diamond flows.

The Council, while fully conscious of the responsibilities of other United Nations organs, emphasizes the crucial importance of disarmament and the non-proliferation of weapons of mass destruction and the means of their delivery for the maintenance of international peace and security.

The Council highlights, in particular, the importance of preventive disarmament in averting armed conflicts, and expresses concern that the proliferation and excessive and destabilizing accumulation and circulation of small arms and light weapons in many parts of the world have contributed to the intensity and duration of armed conflicts and pose a threat to peace and security. It calls upon States, international organizations and the business community to increase their efforts aimed at the prevention of illicit trafficking in small arms and light weapons.

The Council also emphasizes the importance of continued coordinated regional and international action with regard to small arms and welcomes initiatives such as the Inter-American Convention against the Illicit Manufacturing of and Trafficking in Firearms, Ammunition, Explosives and other Related Materials, adopted by the General Assembly of the Organization of American States at its twenty-fourth special session, held in Washington D.C. on 13 and 14 November 1997, the Regional Action Programme for Tackling Arms Trafficking in Southern Africa, ratified in November 1998 by the European Union/Southern African Development Community ministerial meeting, and the Moratorium on the Importation, Exportation and Manufacture of Small Arms and Light Weapons in West Africa, adopted in Abuja on 31 October 1998 by the heads of State and Government of the Economic Community of West African States. It welcomes and encourages efforts to prevent and combat the excessive and destabilizing accumulation of and the illicit trafficking in small arms.

The Council underlines the vital importance of effective national regulations and controls on small arms transfers. The Council encourages Governments to exercise the highest degree of responsibility in these transactions. It calls for complementary supply- and demand-side measures, including those against illegal diversion and re-export. It underlines the obligation of all States to enforce existing arms interdiction measures. The Council emphasizes that the prevention of illicit trafficking is of immediate concern in the global search for ways and means to curb the excessive and destabilizing accumulation of small arms, especially in regions of conflict.

The Council recognizes the importance of adequate, stable and predictable resources for preventive action. The Council also recognizes the importance of consistent funding for long-term preventive activities. The Council encourages consideration of conflict prevention in development assistance strategies and recognition of the need to ensure a smooth transition from emergency humanitarian assistance to development in the post-conflict stage.

The Council acknowledges the important activities supported by the Trust Fund for Preventive Action, and encourages Member States to contribute to the Fund.

The Council recognizes the increasing demand for civilian police as a critical element in peacekeeping operations, as part of the general approach to conflict prevention. It calls upon Member States to explore ways to meet this demand in a timely and effective way. The Council invites the Secretary-General to include his recommendations in this respect in the report on conflict prevention requested below.

The Council underlines the need for continued in-depth consideration of this issue and, in this regard, invites the Secretary-General to submit to the Council, by May 2001, a report containing an analysis, and recommendations on initiatives within the United Nations, taking into account previous experience and the views and considerations expressed by Member States on the prevention of armed conflict.

The Council affirms that a reformed, strengthened and effective United Nations remains central to the maintenance of peace and security, of which prevention is a key component, and underlines the importance of enhancing the capacity of the Organization in preventive action, peacekeeping and peace-building.

The Council recalls the statement by its President of 30 November 1999, and reaffirms its willingness to consider the possibility of a meeting at the level of Ministers for Foreign Affairs on the issue of the prevention of armed conflicts during the Millennium Assembly.

The Council will remain seized of the matter.

Miyazaki Initiatives for Conflict Prevention. By an 18 July letter [A/55/161-S/2000/714], Japan transmitted to the Secretary-General the G-8 Miyazaki Initiatives for Conflict Prevention, adopted by the Foreign Ministers of the Group of Eight major industrialized countries at their meeting in Miyazaki, Japan, on 13 July. The Ministers outlined a basic conceptual framework for conflict prevention efforts and identified initiatives in the areas of small arms and light weapons, conflict and development, illicit trade in diamonds, children in armed conflict and international civilian police.

Report of Secretary-General. The Secretary-General, in his report on the work of the Organization [A/55/1] (see p. 3), said that shifting from a culture of reaction to one of prevention was highly cost-effective in human and financial terms, offering the best possible chance to address the root causes of a conflict and providing a real opportunity to sow the seeds of a durable peace. However, the primary responsibility for conflict prevention lay with Member States, and successful conflict prevention, under UN auspices, required the political will to provide the necessary leadership and resources for action. The Secretary-General welcomed the growing attention Member States were paying to conflict prevention. The far-reaching presidential statements adopted by the Security Council and the G-8 action plan (see above) indicated their broad commitment to improving UN capacity for effective preventive action and it was important that the momentum be maintained. He noted that no region in the world illustrated the need to prevent conflict, and the cost of the failure to do so, more dramatically than Africa.

Conflict diamonds

The United Nations, since 1998, had recognized the link between the illegal exploitation of and trade in diamonds and the escalation of conflicts in Africa. In that year, the Security Council, by resolution 1173(1998) [YUN 1998, p. 108], prohibited the import from Angola of all diamonds that were not controlled through the certificate-of-origin regime of the Government of Angola, as part of its sanctions regime imposed on the National Union for the Total Independence of Angola (UNITA). Following the failure of that regime to work effectively, the Council, by resolution 1237(1999) [YUN 1999, p. 112], established an independent Panel of Experts to investigate violations of its sanctions, including the diamond trade.

The Panel of Experts, in its final report submitted in March 2000 [S/2000/203], concluded that UNITA's ability to sell diamonds was based on its access to diamond-rich territories, its easy and protected access to external locations where diamond deals could be transacted and the ease with which illegal diamonds could be sold and traded on major diamond markets, particularly in Antwerp, Belgium, the largest diamond market. The lax controls and regulations governing the Antwerp diamond market facilitated and perhaps encouraged illegal trading activity, while lax controls in Angola facilitated diamond smuggling in that country.

The Panel made recommendations to discourage diamond smuggling and sanctions busting, including the convening of a conference of experts to determine a system of controls that would allow for increased transparency and accountability from the source or origin to the bourses; and the development of a mechanism for identifying diamonds entering diamond centres without a customs declaration, including the establishment of a comprehensive database on diamond characteristics and trends (see also p. 154).

The World Diamond Congress adopted a July resolution in support of the objectives of the measures contained in resolution 1173(1998), which led to the creation of the World Diamond Council.

In a 16 October note verbale [S/2000/998], Angola transmitted to the Security Council President its strategy against conflict diamonds and trade in illicit diamonds.

With regard to Sierra Leone, the Security Council, following the breakdown of the Lomé Peace Agreement [YUN 1999, p. 159], in July placed a mandatory prohibition on the purchase of diamonds from Sierra Leone that were not certified by the Government (**resolution 1306(2000)**) (see p. 201). It also encouraged the International Diamond Manufacturers Association, the World Federation of Diamond Bourses, the Diamond High Council and other representatives of the diamond industry to help develop methods and working practices to facilitate the effective implementation of that prohibition. In statement **S/PRST/2000/25** of 20 July (see p. 73), the Council expressed its willingness to seek the cooperation of Member States and the business community in curbing the illegal exploitation of and trade in diamonds, and in effectively implementing the measures imposed by its relevant resolutions aimed at curbing illicit diamond flows.

In July [S/2000/662], India transmitted to the Security Council President a resolution on conflict diamonds adopted by the Gems and Jewellery Export Promotion Council of India on 2 May. India also expressed its support for the rules of the diamond industry with respect to stopping all trade in conflict diamonds and for the relevant UN resolutions on the issue.

The Kimberley Process. The Kimberley Process, initiated in May 2000 in Kimberley, South Africa, with subsequent meetings in Luanda (Angola), London and Windhoek (Namibia), evolved out of an inclusive approach by Governments, industry and civil society in the diamond exporting, processing and importing States to find solutions to the problem of conflict diamonds.

Within that framework, a ministerial meeting was held (Pretoria, South Africa, 21 September) [A/55/638], at the invitation of African diamond-producing countries, of Ministers and representatives of the world's leading diamond exporting, processing and importing States. In a statement adopted at that meeting, the Ministers expressed concern that the trade in conflict diamonds was prolonging wars in parts of Africa, frustrating development efforts and causing immense suffering. Conflict diamonds were understood to be rough diamonds that were illicitly traded by rebel movements to finance their attempts to overthrow legitimate Governments. The Ministers resolved to work together to deny those conflict diamonds access to world markets, while recognizing the difficulty of devising and enforcing measures to prevent their smuggling.

The Ministers welcomed important progress made, including the role of the Security Council in addressing the problem; the initiative of the G-8 summit meeting (Okinawa, Japan, 21-23 July) [A/55/257-S/2000/766] to support practical approaches, including consideration of an international agreement on certification of rough diamonds; national initiatives, especially by Angola (see above) and Sierra Leone, to put in place effective certification schemes, as well as the efforts by trading and marketing centres in Belgium, India and Israel to strengthen regulation of and transparency in the trade; and the proposed steps by the industry, including the resolution agreed at the World Diamond Congress to address the problem (see above).

The Ministers agreed that a comprehensive approach should be explored to deal with the causes and drivers of conflict. The establishment of an intergovernmental body to monitor compliance with the certification system should be investigated, including the relationship between such a body and the World Diamond Council. They expressed their resolve to maintain the momentum of the Kimberley Process by moving ahead into an intergovernmental process to design a workable international certification scheme for rough diamonds, favouring a simple and effective scheme that did not place undue burden on Governments and industry, particularly smaller producers. The Ministers welcomed the convening of an intergovernmental conference in London to bring together other interested States and to take the multilateral process forward.

London intergovernmental meeting. Representatives of 36 Governments, representing the world's leading rough diamond exporting, processing and importing States, the European Commission and the World Diamond Council met in London on 25 and 26 October to build on the momentum of the Kimberley Process [A/55/628]. They welcomed the Kimberley joint ministerial statement (see p. 76) and the action taken by the Security Council to address the problem of conflict diamonds. Participants emphasized the urgency of curbing the trade in conflict diamonds and underlined the need to devise effective and pragmatic measures to address the problem that complied with international law and that would not impede the legitimate diamond industry or impose undue burden on Governments or industry. Participants welcomed the start of a broader process to address the problem, consideration of the key elements of which would include: the creation and implementation of a simple and workable international certification scheme for rough diamonds, based primarily on national certification schemes; the need for national practices to meet internationally agreed minimum standards; securing the widest possible participation; the need for diamond exporting, processing and importing States to act in concert; appropriate arrangements to help secure compliance; and transparency. Participants agreed that the General Assembly debate was an important opportunity to further negotiations on an international rough diamonds certification scheme and agreed to work to ensure that the momentum of the Kimberley Process was maintained and strengthened.

GENERAL ASSEMBLY ACTION

On 1 December [meeting 79], the General Assembly adopted **resolution 55/56** [draft: A/55/L.52 & Add.1] without vote [agenda item 175].

The role of diamonds in fuelling conflict: breaking the link between the illicit transaction of rough diamonds and armed conflict as a contribution to prevention and settlement of conflicts

The General Assembly,

Expressing its concern over the problem of conflict diamonds fuelling conflicts in a number of countries and the devastating impact of these conflicts on peace, safety and security for people in affected countries,

Understanding conflict diamonds to be rough diamonds which are used by rebel movements to finance their military activities, including attempts to undermine or overthrow legitimate Governments,

Recognizing that the vast majority of rough diamonds produced in the world are from legitimate sources,

Recognizing also that the legitimate trade in diamonds makes a critical contribution to economic development in many countries worldwide,

Acknowledging that the problem of conflict diamonds is of serious international concern, and that measures to address the problem should involve all concerned parties, including producing, processing, exporting and importing countries, as well as the diamond industry,

Recognizing the need to address the problem of rough diamonds originating from territories of diamond-producing countries under military occupation by another country,

Emphasizing that these measures should be effective and pragmatic, consistent with international law, including relevant trade provisions and commitments, and should not impede the current legitimate trade in diamonds or impose an undue burden on Governments or industry, particularly smaller producers, and not hinder the development of the diamond industry,

Recalling all the relevant resolutions of the Security Council, including its resolutions 1173(1998) of 12 June 1998, 1295(2000) of 18 April 2000 and 1306(2000) of 5 July 2000, as well as resolution 1304(2000) of 16 June 2000,

Highlighting the additional important initiatives already taken to address this problem, in particular by the Governments of Angola and Sierra Leone and by other key producing, processing, exporting and importing countries, as well as by the diamond industry and civil society, including the creation by the industry of the World Diamond Council,

Welcoming with appreciation the initiative by the African diamond-producing countries to launch an inclusive consultation process of Governments, industry and civil society, referred to as the Kimberley Process, to deal with the issue,

Taking note of the ministerial statement issued at the conclusion of the meeting on diamonds held in Pretoria on 21 September 2000,

Also taking note of the communiqué issued by the London Intergovernmental Meeting on Conflict Diamonds, held on 25 and 26 October 2000,

1. *Calls upon* all States to implement fully Security Council measures targeting the link between the trade in conflict diamonds and the supply to rebel movements of weapons, fuel or other prohibited materiel;

2. *Urges* all States to support efforts of the diamond producing, processing, exporting and importing countries and the diamond industry to find ways to break the link between conflict diamonds and armed conflict, and encourages other appropriate initiatives to this end, including improved international cooperation on law enforcement;

3. *Expresses* the need to give urgent and careful consideration to devising effective and pragmatic measures to address the problem of conflict diamonds, the elements of which would include:

(a) The creation and implementation of a simple and workable international certification scheme for rough diamonds;

(b) Basing the scheme primarily on national certification schemes;

(c) The need for national practices to meet internationally agreed minimum standards;

(d) The aim of securing the widest possible participation;

(e) The need for diamond processing, exporting and importing States to act in concert;

(f) The need for appropriate arrangements to help to ensure compliance, acting with respect for the sovereignty of States;

(g) The need for transparency;

4. *Welcomes* the offer by the Government of Namibia to convene a workshop of the world's leading diamond processing, exporting and importing countries, continuing the momentum of the Kimberley Process to consider technical aspects pertaining to the envisaged international certification scheme for rough diamonds;

5. *Encourages* the countries participating in the Kimberley Process to consider expanding the membership of the Process in order to allow all key States with a significant interest in the world diamond industry to participate in further meetings, and to move ahead with the intergovernmental negotiating process to develop detailed proposals for the envisaged international certification scheme for rough diamonds, in close collaboration with the diamond industry and taking into account the views of relevant elements of civil society;

6. *Requests* the countries participating in the Kimberley Process to submit to the General Assembly, no later than at its fifty-sixth session, a report on progress made;

7. *Decides* to include in the provisional agenda of its fifty-sixth session the item entitled "The role of diamonds in fuelling conflict".

On 23 December, the Assembly decided that the agenda item "The role of diamonds in fuelling conflict" would remain for consideration during its resumed fifty-fifth (2001) session (**decision 55/458**).

Post-conflict peace-building

The Secretary-General, in his report on the role of the United Nations in the twenty-first century [A/54/2000] (see p. 55), said that while traditional peacekeeping had focused mainly on monitoring ceasefires, the objective of the current complex peace operations of the United Nations was to assist the parties engaged in conflict to pursue their interests through political channels instead. To that end, the Organization helped to create and strengthen political institutions and to broaden their base. It worked alongside Governments, non-governmental organizations (NGOs) and local citizens' groups to provide emergency relief, demobilize former fighters and reintegrate them into society, clear mines, or-

ganize and conduct elections, and promote sustainable development practices.

International assistance to rebuild the economy was an essential complement to that work, as people would quickly become disillusioned with fledgling institutions, and even the peace process itself, if they saw no prospect for any material improvement in their condition. Post-conflict peace-building had helped to prevent the breakdown of numerous peace agreements and to build the foundations for sustainable peace.

Review of disarmament, demobilization and reintegration

As requested in Security Council statement S/PRST/1999/21 [YUN 1999, p. 50], the Secretary-General submitted a February report on the role of United Nations peacekeeping in disarmament, demobilization and reintegration [S/2000/101]. The report reviewed the evolution of UN involvement in the area, identified key elements that favoured the success of the disarmament, demobilization and reintegration process, highlighted ways in which peacekeeping operations had assisted in the past and suggested ways in which the Organization could better support future efforts.

The report noted that, in civil conflicts of the post-cold-war era, a process of disarmament, demobilization and reintegration had repeatedly proved to be vital in stabilizing a post-conflict situation, reducing the likelihood of renewed violence and facilitating a society's transition from conflict to normalcy and development, as well as contributing to strengthening confidence between former factions and enhancing the momentum towards stability. The success of the process depended on the political will of the parties to commit themselves to peace, political leaders building working relationships through commitment to reconciliation and undertaking necessary institutional reforms, and the widespread support and engagement of civil society. However, the complexity and fragility of that process often required the assistance of the international community. An impartial UN peacekeeping operation could play an essential role by helping to create an environment where the disarmament, demobilization and reintegration process could ultimately be successful, including paying special attention to the needs of child soldiers.

Although the engagement of UN operations in the process was relatively recent, it had rapidly become a well-established feature of post-cold-war peacekeeping. The first operation to be involved in the process was the United Nations Observer Group in Central America in 1989, which was followed by other UN operations with key responsibilities for disarmament, demobilization and reintegration: in Angola, Cambodia, Croatia, El Salvador, Guatemala, Liberia, Sierra Leone and Tajikistan. In others, such as the Central African Republic and Somalia, the Organization had assumed responsibility for only some elements.

The report observed that a UN operation might bring key advantages of impartiality, legitimacy, security, political momentum and resources to a disarmament, demobilization and reintegration process and had the unique ability to coordinate simultaneous efforts in many different areas. It went on to suggest a number of measures for a peacekeeping operation to advance the process: the basis for it should be provided for in a peace agreement, and the international community's advocacy might be essential in ensuring its inclusion; and expertise and resources should be provided to a peacekeeping operation that allowed it to offer incentives to combatants, to undertake the destruction of weapons and to monitor and help control regional arms traffic. It might also be necessary for the international community to focus on the economic dimension of arms flows. With regard to demobilization, a review of past experience showed the importance of a strong political role and ample resources for peacekeeping operations, including at times a deterrent capacity. A peacekeeping operation might make direct contributions to reintegration and assist in fostering an appropriate political and socio-economic framework. However, further efforts were necessary to enhance UN access to the skills and resources required. The ability of peacekeeping operations to advance reintegration could also be strengthened through enhancement of institutional coordination within the international community. The international community could respond to the needs of children in the conflict area by promoting the inclusion of child protection in peace agreements and integrating it into the staffing and mandates of UN peacekeeping operations. However, donors should adopt a holistic and long-term view of the demobilization and reintegration of child soldiers, which also embraced social healing and economic development. Given the significant staffing and resource implications of those measures, real progress would require sustained political, moral and financial support by the Secretariat and Member States.

The ultimate success of a disarmament, demobilization and reintegration process might require efforts long after the withdrawal of a peacekeeping operation, including the deployment of a follow-on mission. Such missions might take the form of police or political missions, but it remained crucial that such operations should have a sufficiently broad mandate to make a difference, together with the resources and personnel to achieve that goal. The international community's key role in post-conflict disarmament, demobilization and reintegration was to provide clear, consistent and determined support to an overall peace process and to offer long-term assistance with development.

SECURITY COUNCIL ACTION

On 23 March [meetings 4118 & 4119], following the Security Council's consideration of the Secretary-General's report on the role of the United Nations in disarmament, demobilization and reintegration and consultations among its members, the President made statement **S/PRST/2000/10** on behalf of the Council:

The Security Council recalls the statement of its President of 8 July 1999 and welcomes the report of the Secretary-General on the role of United Nations peacekeeping in disarmament, demobilization and reintegration of 11 February 2000. The Council recalls its primary responsibility for the maintenance of international peace and security and reaffirms its commitment to the principles of the political independence, sovereignty and territorial integrity of all States in conducting all peacekeeping and peace-building activities and the need for States to comply with their obligations under international law.

The Council has considered the matter of disarmament, demobilization and reintegration of ex-combatants in a peacekeeping environment as part of its overall and continuing effort to contribute to enhancing the effectiveness of United Nations peacekeeping and peace-building activities in conflict situations around the world.

The Council underlines that disarmament, demobilization and reintegration of ex-combatants are mutually supportive and that the success of the process is dependent on the success of each of its steps. The Council stresses that the political commitment of the parties involved in a peace process is a precondition for the success of disarmament, demobilization and reintegration programmes. The Council reaffirms that disarmament and demobilization must take place in a secure and safe environment, which will give ex-combatants the confidence to lay down their arms, and underlines the importance of international assistance for long-term economic and social development to facilitate successful reintegration. In this regard, the Council notes that disarmament, demobilization and reintegration must be addressed comprehensively so as to facilitate a smooth transition from peacekeeping to peace-building.

The Council recognizes that the mandates of peacekeeping missions increasingly include oversight of disarmament, demobilization and reintegration as one of their functions. The Council further recognizes the importance of incorporating, as appropriate, within specific peace agreements, with the consent of the parties, and on a case-by-case basis within United Nations peacekeeping mandates, clear terms for the disarmament, demobilization and reintegration of ex-combatants, including the safe and timely collection and disposal of arms and ammunition. The Council emphasizes that the advocacy of the international community is essential in this regard. The Council also underlines the necessity of a clear definition of tasks and division of responsibilities among all actors involved in the disarmament, demobilization and reintegration process, including United Nations agencies and programmes, and that this should be reflected, where relevant, in the mandates of peacekeeping operations.

The Council recognizes that effective action to curb the illegal flow of small arms and light weapons into areas of conflict can contribute to the success of disarmament, demobilization and reintegration programmes, and encourages further efforts and cooperation at the national, subregional, regional and global levels to this end.

The Council underlines in particular the importance of disarming, demobilizing and reintegrating child soldiers, as well as taking into account the problems faced by war-affected children in mission areas. It is therefore imperative that child soldiers be fully included in disarmament, demobilization and reintegration programmes, and that programmes also be designed to address the special needs of all war-affected children, taking into account differences in sex and age, and their differing experiences in the course of armed conflict, with particular attention to girls. In this regard, the Council requests the Secretary-General to consult relevant United Nations agencies, including the United Nations Children's Fund, the Office of the Special Representative of the Secretary-General for Children and Armed Conflict, and other relevant organizations with expertise in the field with a view to the development of appropriate programmes, and underlines the importance of coordination in this regard.

The Council welcomes the initiative of the Secretary-General to include within all peacekeeping operations personnel with appropriate training in international, humanitarian, human rights and refugee law, including child- and gender-related provisions. In this regard, the Council welcomes the inclusion of a child protection adviser in some of the recent peacekeeping operations, and encourages the Secretary-General to include such personnel in future operations as appropriate. The Council stresses the importance of addressing, in particular, the needs of women ex-combatants, notes the role of women in conflict resolution and peace-building and requests the Secretary-General to take that into account.

The Council recognizes that adequate and timely funding for disarmament, demobilization and reintegration is critical to the successful implementation of a peace process, and calls for coordination of voluntary and assessed funding to that end, including among all elements of the United Nations system. The Council welcomes the increasing involvement of the World Bank in disarmament, demobilization and reintegration processes and stresses the impor-

tance of support of Member States for its activities in this area. The Council further encourages other international financial institutions to become involved.

The Council stresses that training of peacekeepers in the disarmament, demobilization and reintegration of ex-combatants continues to be an important asset in the implementation of these activities in mission areas. In that regard, the Council notes that the review by the Secretary-General of lessons learned from disarmament, demobilization and reintegration experiences may assist Member States and others in their training efforts. The Council encourages the Secretary-General to explore avenues of cooperation with existing and new peacekeeping training centres in the implementation of such training programmes.

The Council takes note that the ultimate success of the disarmament, demobilization and reintegration process may require efforts long after the withdrawal of multidisciplinary peacekeeping operations. In this regard, the post-conflict United Nations presence, including the deployment, as appropriate, of a follow-on mission, may help support the advances made and further make progress on the matter.

The Council encourages the Secretary-General to continue to address this issue on a regular basis and to draw to its attention any new developments in this area.

The Council will remain seized of the matter.

Recommendations of the Panel on UN Peace Operations

The Panel on United Nations Peace Operations (see p. 83), in its August report [A/55/305-S/2000/809], said that peace-building support offices or United Nations political offices might be established as follow-ons to other peace operations, as in Haiti or Tajikistan, or as independent initiatives, as in Guatemala or Guinea-Bissau. They helped to support the consolidation of peace in post-conflict countries, working with Governments and non-governmental parties and complementing ongoing UN development activities. Effective peace-building required active, multidimensional engagements with local parties. Free and fair elections should be part of broader efforts to strengthen governance institutions, and UN civilian police should be tasked to reform, train and restructure local police forces according to international standards. Where required, international judicial experts, penal experts and human rights specialists, as well as civilian police, should be available in sufficient numbers to strengthen rule of law institutions, and be authorized to further the work of apprehension and prosecution of persons indicted for war crimes in support of UN tribunals. The human rights component of a peacekeeping operation was critical to effective peace-building, especially in helping to implement a comprehensive programme for national reconciliation, and the disarmament, demobilization and reintegration of former combatants was an area in which peace-building made a direct contribution to public security and law and order.

The Panel's recommendations included that the Executive Committee on Peace and Security should propose a plan to strengthen UN capacity to develop peace-building strategies and to implement accompanying support programmes.

In October [A/55/502], the Secretary-General reported that he had instructed the Executive Committee to formulate such a plan by the end of March 2001 to help identify ways in which different parts of the UN system might properly work together to devise country-specific peace-building strategies and to implement them together in the context of the country team.

Other action

The Security Council, in statement **S/PRST/ 2000/7** of 9 March (see p. 855), recognized the importance of the humanitarian dimension to the maintenance of international peace and security and that full and timely support for humanitarian components could be critical in ensuring and enhancing the sustainability of any peace agreement and post-conflict peace-building.

In July [A/55/138-S/2000/693], Namibia transmitted to the General Assembly and the Council the Windhoek Declaration and the Namibia Plan of Action on Mainstreaming a Gender Perspective in Multidimensional Peace Support Operations, adopted at a seminar (Windhoek, 29-31 May) organized by the Lessons Learned Unit of the Department of Peacekeeping Operations (DPKO) and the Office of the Special Adviser on Gender Issues and Advancement of Women.

In **resolution 1325(2000)** of 31 October (see p. 1113), the Council recognized that an understanding of the impact of armed conflict on women and girls, effective institutional arrangements to guarantee their protection and full participation in the peace process could significantly contribute to the maintenance and promotion of peace and security. It urged the increased representation of women at all decision-making levels in national, regional and international institutions and mechanisms for the prevention, management and resolution of conflict.

Impact of AIDS on peace and security

On 10 January [S/PV.4087], the Security Council considered the agenda item entitled "The situation in Africa", focusing on the impact of AIDS on peace and security. The Executive Director of the Joint United Nations Programme on HIV/AIDS (UNAIDS) told the meeting that war was one of the instruments of AIDS, as rape was one of the instruments of war. Conflict and the resulting movements of people fuelled the epidemic. Refugee men, and particularly women, became vulnerable to HIV infection. Humanitarian aid workers and military and police forces that were well trained in HIV prevention and behaviour change could be a tremendous force for prevention if that was made one of their priorities.

In a 31 January letter [S/2000/75], the Council President informed the General Assembly President that, as a result of those discussions and following further consultations, members of the Council recognized the negative impact of AIDS on peace and security in Africa and worldwide and considered that the United Nations should elaborate a comprehensive and effective agenda for action against the HIV/AIDS epidemic. The Council suggested that the Assembly review the problem in all its aspects and consider proposing new strategies, methods, practical activities and specific measures to strengthen international cooperation (see p. 1166).

On 17 July, the Council continued consideration of HIV/AIDS and international peacekeeping operations in the context of its responsibility for the maintenance of international peace and security. It had before it a 5 July letter from the Secretary-General [S/2000/657], transmitting a note from UNAIDS, which summarized actions taken as a follow-up to the Council's 10 January meeting on HIV/AIDS in Africa. They included the endorsement by the Inter-Agency Standing Committee of a plan to integrate HIV/AIDS into humanitarian action, focusing on the role of the military and peacekeeping forces in the prevention and spread of HIV, the epidemic's potential to contribute to social instability and emergency situations, and the need for a set of basic measures to ensure minimum standards of prevention and care before, during and immediately after conflicts or disasters occurred. The UNAIDS secretariat would implement the plan.

Discussions had been held with DPKO and the Civil Military Alliance, a UNAIDS collaborating centre, focusing on ways in which conflict and humanitarian situations sometimes brought about an elevated risk of HIV transmission for refugees and host communities, as well as for UN and NGO personnel. The goal was to promote responsible and safe behaviour among staff providing humanitarian aid and peacekeeping troops and to ensure they were aware of preventive measures to protect themselves. Specific follow-up actions included the development of a UN medical policy on HIV/AIDS for personnel associated with UN missions. The UNAIDS secretariat would work closely with the World Health Organization, the United Nations Population Fund and DPKO on the issue. In addition, the Framework for Action of the International Partnership against AIDS in Africa, comprising a set of agreed principles, goals and targets, was completed and endorsed by the Conference of African Ministers of Health (Ouagadougou, Burkina Faso, May) and the UNAIDS Programme Coordinating Board. It brought together, under the leadership of African Governments, the UN system, donor Governments, the private sector and the community sector. The note also summarized progress made at the country level.

(For further details on HIV/AIDS, see PART THREE, Chapter XIII.)

Special Committee on Peacekeeping Operations. The Special Committee on Peacekeeping Operations (11 February–10 March) [A/54/839] recognized the concerns of Member States regarding medical aspects of peacekeeping operations, including the high risk of transmission and contraction of HIV/AIDS and other communicable diseases facing UN peacekeeping and other personnel in the field. It requested DPKO to incorporate language into the "Guidelines for Military and CIVPOL Participation in Peacekeeping Operations" manuals, to raise peacekeepers' awareness of those diseases, and the Training Unit to promote that awareness through the train-the-trainers programme.

SECURITY COUNCIL ACTION

On 17 July [meeting 4172], the Security Council unanimously adopted **resolution 1308(2000).** The draft text [S/2000/696] was prepared in consultations among Council members.

The Security Council,

Deeply concerned by the extent of the HIV/AIDS pandemic worldwide, and by the severity of the crisis in Africa in particular,

Recalling its meeting of 10 January 2000 on "The situation in Africa: the impact of AIDS on peace and security in Africa", taking note of the note of 5 July 2000 from the Joint United Nations Programme on HIV/AIDS, which summarizes follow-up actions taken to date, and recalling also the letter dated 31 January 2000 from the President of the Security Council addressed to the President of the General Assembly,

Emphasizing the important roles of the General Assembly and the Economic and Social Council in addressing HIV/AIDS,

Stressing the need for coordinated efforts of all relevant United Nations organizations to address the HIV/AIDS pandemic in line with their respective mandates and to assist, wherever possible, in global efforts against the pandemic,

Commending the efforts of the Joint United Nations Programme on HIV/AIDS to coordinate and intensify efforts to address HIV/AIDS in all appropriate forums,

Recalling the special meeting of the Economic and Social Council of 28 February 2000, held in partnership with the President of the Security Council, on the development aspects of the HIV/AIDS pandemic,

Welcoming the decision by the General Assembly to include in the agenda of its fifty-fourth session an additional item of an urgent and important character entitled "Review of the problem of human immunodeficiency virus/acquired immunodeficiency syndrome (HIV/AIDS) in all its aspects", and encouraging further action to address the problem of HIV/AIDS,

Recognizing that the spread of HIV/AIDS can have a uniquely devastating impact on all sectors and levels of society,

Reaffirming the importance of a coordinated international response to the HIV/AIDS pandemic, given its possible growing impact on social instability and emergency situations,

Recognizing that the HIV/AIDS pandemic is also exacerbated by conditions of violence and instability, which increase the risk of exposure to the disease through large movements of people, widespread uncertainty over conditions and reduced access to medical care,

Stressing that the HIV/AIDS pandemic, if unchecked, may pose a risk to stability and security,

Recognizing the need to incorporate HIV/AIDS prevention awareness skills and advice in aspects of the training provided to peacekeeping personnel by the Department of Peacekeeping Operations of the Secretariat, and welcoming the report of the United Nations Special Committee on Peacekeeping Operations of 20 March 2000, which affirmed this need and the efforts already made by the Secretariat in this regard,

Taking note of the call by the Secretary-General, in his report to the Millennium Assembly, for coordinated and intensified international action to reduce HIV infection rates in persons between 15 and 24 years of age by 25 per cent by the year 2010,

Noting with satisfaction the thirteenth International AIDS Conference, held from 9 to 14 July 2000 in Durban, South Africa, which was the first conference of this type to be held in a developing country and drew significant attention to the magnitude of the HIV/AIDS pandemic in sub-Saharan Africa, and noting that the conference was an important opportunity for leaders and scientists to discuss the epidemiology of HIV/AIDS and estimates of resources needed to address HIV/AIDS, as well as issues related to access to care, mother-to-child transmission, prevention, and development of vaccines,

Bearing in mind the primary responsibility of the Security Council for the maintenance of international peace and security,

1. *Expresses concern* at the potentially damaging impact of HIV/AIDS on the health of international peacekeeping personnel, including support personnel;

2. *Recognizes* the efforts of those Member States that have acknowledged the problem of HIV/AIDS and, where applicable, have developed national programmes, and encourages all interested Member States that have not already done so to consider developing, in cooperation with the international community and the Joint United Nations Programme on

HIV/AIDS, where appropriate, effective long-term strategies for HIV/AIDS education, prevention, voluntary and confidential testing and counselling, and treatment of their personnel, as an important part of their preparation for participation in peacekeeping operations;

3. *Requests* the Secretary-General to take further steps towards the provision of training for peacekeeping personnel on issues related to preventing the spread of HIV/AIDS and to continue the further development of pre-deployment orientation and ongoing training for all peacekeeping personnel on these issues;

4. *Encourages* interested Member States to increase international cooperation among their relevant national bodies to assist with the creation and execution of policies for HIV/AIDS prevention, voluntary and confidential testing and counselling, and treatment for personnel to be deployed in international peacekeeping operations;

5. *Encourages*, in this context, the Joint United Nations Programme on HIV/AIDS to continue to strengthen its cooperation with interested Member States to further develop its country profiles in order to reflect best practices in and country policies on HIV/AIDS prevention education, testing, counselling and treatment;

6. *Expresses keen interest* in additional discussion among relevant United Nations bodies, Member States, industry and relevant organizations to make progress, inter alia, on the question of access to treatment and care, and on prevention.

Peacekeeping operations

In recognition of the increasingly complex task faced by the United Nations as it sought to prevent and resolve conflict, and to keep and build the peace, the Secretary-General established a panel of experts led by the former Minister for Foreign Affairs of Algeria, Lakhdar Brahimi, to produce a report that would provide an overview of peace operations and suggest how they might be strengthened. That report—the Brahimi report—was considered by the Security Council and the General Assembly.

The Special Committee on Peacekeeping Operations, whose mandate was to review the whole question of peacekeeping operations in all their aspects, held a general debate on 11, 14 and 15 February [A/54/839] and, at an extraordinary session in November [A/C.4/55/6], created an open-ended working group to examine the Brahimi report's recommendations.

Report of Panel on UN Peace Operations

On 21 August [A/55/305-S/2000/809], the Secretary-General transmitted to the Presidents of the General Assembly and the Security Coun-

cil the report of the Chairman of the Panel on United Nations Peace Operations (the Brahimi report). The Panel, which the Secretary-General appointed in March to assess the shortcomings of the existing system and to make specific and realistic recommendations for change, comprised individuals experienced in various aspects of conflict prevention, peacekeeping and peace-building and was headed by Lakhdar Brahimi (Algeria). It examined the need for change, the doctrine, strategy and decision-making for peace operations, UN capacities to deploy operations rapidly and effectively, Headquarters resources and structure for planning and supporting peacekeeping, adapting peace operations to the information age and challenges to implementation.

The Panel endorsed the Secretary-General's recommendations with respect to conflict prevention contained in the Millennium Report [A/54/2000] (see p. 55) and in his remarks before the Security Council's July meeting on conflict prevention (see p. 72), in particular his appeal that all those engaged in conflict prevention and development should address those challenges in a more integrated fashion. It also supported the Secretary-General's more frequent use of fact-finding missions and stressed Member States' obligations under the Charter to give "every assistance" to such UN activities.

In terms of a peace-building strategy, the Panel recommended: that a small percentage of a mission's first-year budget should be used to fund quick-impact projects; a doctrinal shift in the use of civilian police, other rule of law elements and human rights experts in complex peace operations to reflect an increased focus on strengthening rule of law institutions and improving respect for human rights in post-conflict environments; that demobilization and reintegration programmes should be consolidated into the assessed budgets of complex peace operations in their first phase to facilitate the rapid disassembly of fighting factions and reduce the likelihood of resumed conflict; and that the Executive Committee on Peace and Security (ECPS) should recommend to the Secretary-General a plan to strengthen the permanent UN capacity to develop peace-building strategies and implement supporting programmes.

With regard to doctrine and strategy, the Panel stated that UN peacekeepers should be able to carry out their mandates professionally and successfully. In order to be able to defend themselves and the mission's mandate against those who would renege on their commitments to a peace accord, they should be provided with robust rules of engagement. As to mandates, the Security

Council should assure that ceasefire or peace agreements with a UN-led peacekeeping operation met threshold conditions, such as consistency with international human rights standards and practicability of specified tasks and timeliness, and should leave authorizing resolutions in draft form until the Secretary-General had firm commitments of troops and other critical mission support elements from Member States. "Rapid and effective deployment capacities" should be defined as the ability to fully deploy traditional peacekeeping operations within 30 days of the adoption of a Council resolution and within 90 days in the case of complex peacekeeping operations. The Council's resolutions should meet the requirements of peacekeeping operations deployed into potentially dangerous situations, especially the need for a clear chain of command and unity of effort. Troop contributors should have access to Secretariat briefings to the Council on matters affecting the safety and security of their personnel, especially those meetings with implications for a mission's use of force.

Concerning information and analysis, the Secretary-General should establish the ECPS Information and Strategic Analysis Secretariat (EISAS) to support the information and analysis needs of all members of ECPS, administered by and reporting jointly to the Department of Political Affairs (DPA) and the Department of Peacekeeping Operations (DPKO).

In connection with transitional civil administration, the Panel recommended that the Secretary-General invite a panel of international legal experts to evaluate the feasibility of developing an interim criminal code for use pending the re-establishment of local rule of law and local law enforcement capacity.

Regarding mission leadership, the Secretary-General should systematize the method of selecting mission leaders, and the entire leadership of a mission should be selected and assembled at Headquarters as early as possible to enable their participation in key aspects of the mission planning process. The Secretariat should routinely provide the mission leadership with strategic guidance and plans for anticipating and overcoming challenges to mandate implementation.

As for military personnel, Member States should enter into partnerships with one another, within the context of the United Nations standby arrangements system (UNSAS), to form several brigade-size forces for rapid and effective deployment. The Secretary-General should be given the authority to canvass Member States to contribute troops to a potential operation once it appeared likely that a ceasefire accord or agreement envisaging an implementing role for the Organization

might be reached. The Secretariat should confirm the preparedness of each potential troop contributor to meet the provisions of the memorandums of understanding on the requisite training and equipment requirements prior to deployment. A revolving "on-call list" of about 100 military officers should be created in UNSAS to be available on seven days' notice to augment the nuclei of DPKO planners with teams trained to create a mission headquarters for a new peacekeeping operation.

Concerning civilian police personnel, the Panel encouraged Member States to establish a national pool of civilian police officers for deployment to UN peace operations on short notice, within the context of UNSAS; to enter into regional training partnerships for civilian police in the respective national pools to promote a common level of preparedness; and to designate a single point of contact within their governmental structures for the provision of civilian police to UN peace operations. It recommended that a revolving on-call list of about 100 police officers and related experts be created in UNSAS to be available on seven days' notice to train incoming personnel and give the component greater coherence at an early date. Parallel arrangements should be established for judicial, penal, human rights and other relevant specialists.

As to civilian specialists, the Secretariat should establish a central Internet/Intranet-based roster of pre-selected civilian candidates available to deploy to peace operations on short notice, and field missions should be delegated the authority to recruit candidates from it. The Field Service category of personnel should be reformed, especially at the mid- to senior levels in the administrative and logistics areas, and conditions of service for externally recruited civilian staff should be revised to attract the most highly qualified candidates and to offer greater career prospects. DPKO should formulate a comprehensive staffing strategy for peace operations.

The Panel suggested that additional resources should be devoted in mission budgets to public information and associated personnel and for information technology. The Secretariat should prepare a global logistics support strategy to enable rapid and effective mission deployment within proposed timeliness and planning assumptions. The General Assembly should approve the maintenance of at least five mission start-up kits at the UN Logistics Base in Brindisi, Italy, to be routinely replenished from the assessed contributions to operations drawing on them. The Secretary-General should be given authority to draw up to $50 million from the Peacekeeping Reserve Fund, once an operation was likely to be established, with the approval of the Advisory Committee on Administrative and Budgetary Questions (ACABQ) but prior to the adoption of a Security Council resolution. The Secretariat should review procurement policies and procedures and those governing the management of financial resources in the field missions to provide such missions with greater flexibility in the management of their budgets. The level of procurement authority delegated to the field missions should be increased from $200,000 to as much as $1 million for local goods and services not covered under systems contracts or standing commercial services contracts.

The Panel recommended a substantial increase in resources for Headquarters support of peacekeeping operations, and urged the Secretary-General to submit to the Assembly his requirements in full. Headquarters support for peacekeeping should be treated as a core activity of the United Nations and funded through the regular biennial programme budget. Pending the preparation of the next regular budget, the Secretary-General should request from the Assembly an emergency supplemental increase to the peacekeeping support account to allow immediate recruitment of additional personnel, particularly in DPKO.

Integrated mission task forces should be the standard vehicle for mission-specific planning and support, serving as the first point of contact for all such support. Other structural adjustments in DPKO should include the restructuring of the Military and Civilian Police Division, moving the Civilian Police Unit out of the military reporting chain; the upgrading of the rank and level of the Civilian Police Adviser; the restructuring of the Military Adviser's Office to correspond more closely to that of the military field headquarters; the establishment of a new unit to provide advice on criminal law issues that were critical to the effective use of civilian police in UN peace operations; the delegation by the Under-Secretary-General for Management of authority and responsibility for peacekeeping-related budgeting and procurement functions to the Under-Secretary-General for Peacekeeping Operations for a two-year trial period; the enhancement of the Lessons Learned Unit, which should be moved into a revamped DPKO Office of Operations; consideration given to increasing the number of Assistant Secretaries-General in DPKO from two to three, with one of the three designated as the "Principal Assistant Secretary-General" and functioning as the deputy to the Under-Secretary-General; and the establishment of a unit for operational planning and support of public information in peace operations.

With regard to peace-building, the Panel supported the Secretariat's effort to create a pilot Peace-building Unit within DPA and suggested that regular budgetary support for that unit be revisited if the programme worked well. That programme should be evaluated and, if considered the best available option, it should be presented to the Secretary-General as part of the plan to strengthen the Organization's permanent peace-building capacity. The Panel also recommended that regular budget resources for Electoral Assistance Division programmatic expenses be increased to meet the growing demand for its services, in lieu of voluntary contributions, and that procurement, logistics, staff recruitment and other support services for smaller, non-military field missions be provided by the UN Office for Project Services (UNOPS).

The Panel recommended that the field mission planning and preparation capacity of the Office of the United Nations High Commissioner for Human Rights be enhanced, with funding partly from the regular budget and partly from peace operations mission budgets.

In the context of the information age, the Panel said that Headquarters peace and security departments needed a responsibility centre to devise and oversee the implementation of common information technology strategy and training for peace operations. EISAS, in cooperation with the Information Technology Services Division, should implement an enhanced peace operations element on the current UN Intranet and link it to the missions through a Peace Operations Extranet.

The Security Council, in **resolution 1318(2000)** of 7 September (see p. 64), welcomed the Panel's report and decided to consider the recommendations that fell within its responsibility expeditiously. The heads of State and Government attending the Millennium Summit, in **resolution 55/2** of 8 September (see p. 49), took note of the Panel's report and requested the General Assembly to consider its recommendations expeditiously.

Implementation of the Panel's report

Report of Secretary-General. In October, the Secretary-General submitted to the General Assembly [A/55/502] and the Security Council [S/2000/1081] his report on the implementation of the report of the Panel on United Nations Peace Operations. He stated that he had already implemented the Panel's recommendation to designate a senior official to oversee the report's implementation, by assigning the Deputy Secretary-General that responsibility. The Secretary-General's initial proposals for implementing the recommendations were in the areas of enhancing the effectiveness of key peace and security instruments;

new mechanisms for improving system-wide integration; enhancing rapid and effective deployment capacities; funding of Headquarters support to peacekeeping operations; the proposed restructuring of DPKO; strengthening other parts of the UN system; and information technology and knowledge management.

With regard to conflict prevention, the Secretary-General said that he would submit, in response to Security Council presidential statement S/PRST/2000/25 (see p. 73), a report on conflict prevention in May 2001. He had also asked the Executive Committees on Peace and Security and on Humanitarian Affairs to explore, together with the Bretton Woods institutions, additional initiatives on conflict prevention, in addition to those he had described in his 2000 annual report on the work of the Organization (see p. 7). He also proposed that the United Nations serve as the focal point for various inter-agency coordinating mechanisms for the formulation of conflict prevention strategies.

In the area of peace-building, the Secretary-General had instructed ECPS to formulate a plan to address stronger measures to reduce poverty and promote economic growth as important dimensions of peace-building, and intended to seek legislative approval for a percentage of a mission's first-year budget to fund quick-impact projects. He also intended to include comprehensive disarmament, demobilization and reintegration programmes in plans for future peacekeeping operations so that they could be included in the operations' mandates. Future concepts of operations and missions budgets would spell out more clearly what the UN system could collectively do to help strengthen the rule of law and human rights institutions.

As to transitional administration, work on developing an interim criminal code for use by UN operations with transitional administrative mandates had begun and the first draft of interim rules of criminal law and procedure was expected by July 2001.

With regard to peacekeeping operations themselves, the Secretary-General outlined measures that the Secretariat could take to help peacekeepers carry out their mandates and requested an increase in resources for the Military Division (including for the Training Unit) and the Lessons Learned Unit of DPKO.

In order to improve system-wide integration, the Secretary-General proposed creating the ECPS Information and Strategic Analysis Secretariat by January 2001 by consolidating resources of various departments and offices. In addition to providing secretariat services for the Executive Committee and serving as the focal point for cross-cutting strategies and information technology, EISAS would be assigned the role of coordinating the formulation of system-wide peace-building strategies. In that connection, the Secretary-General intended to establish a Peace-building Unit, within EISAS, to be financed from extrabudgetary resources. Further details on the structure and required resources of EISAS would be presented in the report on resource requirements (see p. 91). Concerning the institution of integrated mission task forces, the Secretary-General indicated his intention to do so for the planning and initial deployment phases of all new multidisciplinary operations, as well as in support of peacemaking efforts. The Bretton Woods institutions would also participate in the integrated task force structure during peacemaking and mission planning stages.

Additional resources would be requested to allow DPKO and DPA to perform their coordinating roles effectively.

With regard to enhancing rapid deployment capacities, the Secretary-General said he had asked relevant parts of the Secretariat to use the timelines proposed by the Panel as a basis for evaluating the capacity of existing systems to provide field missions with the human, material, financial and information assets that they required, in quantitative and qualitative terms. As for the selection process for mission leaders, the Secretary-General had decided to form a senior appointments group to oversee the formulation of recommendations. That group, as from February 2001, would, among other functions, expand and centralize the existing senior appointment roster system by consolidating one roster for all senior appointments to peace operations. It would also be asked to recommend training/briefing procedures, to be made standard practice. The United Nations Development Programme (UNDP) and the United Nations Development Group would be asked to make recommendations by March 2001 on improving the selection, training and support of resident coordinators sent to posts with strong prevention and peace-building demands, as well as on procedures for reviewing those currently serving in such posts. Training teams from Headquarters would also deploy in field missions to conduct training in situ, and training cells would be established in each mission to train mission personnel at all levels. Provision would be made in the budgets of peace operations for such training. In addition, the Office of Human Resources Management (OHRM) Learning Service, together with the United Nations Institute for Training and Research, would develop a systematic approach for briefing and debriefing Special Representatives. Annual seminars, the first of which would be held in 2001, would be organized as a forum for sharing experiences and discussion with Headquarters personnel.

In connection with military personnel, the Secretary-General invited participants in UNSAS to inform DPKO by 1 December 2000 if the assets they had listed in the system were in fact available for immediate deployment. He noted that it would be preferable to have a much smaller number of assets listed than having a large figure that was unrealistic. He also invited participants to indicate at the end of each month any changes to the status of availability of assets. He added that he had asked DPKO to institute procedures to contact UNSAS participants regarding the availability of assets in a mission-specific context and maintain statistics on response rates. To better manage the system, he would be requesting additional resources. Regarding civilian police and related personnel, work had already begun to assist Member States to identify civilian police for peace operations. DPKO had developed "Principles and guidelines for United Nations civilian police operations", which would be published in February 2001, and additional resources were being sought to strengthen the Civilian Police Unit.

In terms of logistics support and expenditure management, the Secretary-General had asked the DPKO Field Administration and Logistics Division, supported by the Department of Management, to address all the issues raised by the Panel that related to that area and to prepare a set of detailed proposals, along with financial implications, for presentation to the General Assembly. To allow the Division to complete the work, he was requesting additional resources, in particular for the Logistics and Communications Service. Concerning the funding of Headquarters support to peacekeeping operations, he was requesting, on an emergency basis, additional resources through the Support Account for 2000-2001. Proposals were also being developed to properly define a predictable baseline level and funding mechanism for Headquarters support to peacekeeping and for temporary increases in activity. He would also be initiating the review called for by the Special Committee on Peacekeeping Operations (see p. 90).

The Secretary-General also proposed strengthening and extensively restructuring the Military Division and agreed to establish a distinct unit in the DPKO Office of Operations responsible for operational planning and support of public information components in peace operations.

Report of Security Council Working Group. Pursuant to Security Council resolution 1318 (2000) (see p. 64), the Council established the Working Group on the Report of the Panel on United Nations Peace Operations on 3 October to undertake a comprehensive review of the recommendations of the Panel that fell within the purview of the Council, in particular peacekeeping operations.

The Working Group discussed ways to ensure clear, credible and achievable mandates and procedures for handling Council resolutions; mechanisms and procedures for strengthening consultations with troop contributors; benchmarks for ensuring consistency of peacekeeping operations with international human rights conventions; means of ensuring the rapid deployment of adequately equipped missions and ensuring a clear, unified chain of command; and ways to ensure that the rules of engagement were clearly understood. Also discussed were systems to enhance the provision of accurate, timely and comprehensive information, possibilities for involving the Council during peace negotiations and modalities for its involvement in conflict prevention and post-conflict peace-building. The results of those discussions were contained in a draft resolution attached to the Group's report [S/2000/1084].

SECURITY COUNCIL ACTION

On 13 November [meeting 4220], the Security Council unanimously adopted **resolution 1327 (2000)**. The draft text [S/2000/1085] was prepared in consultations among Council members.

The Security Council,

Recalling its resolution 1318(2000) of 7 September 2000, adopted at its meeting at the level of heads of State and Government in the course of the Millennium Summit,

Reaffirming its determination to strengthen United Nations peacekeeping operations,

Stressing that peacekeeping operations should strictly observe the purposes and principles of the Charter of the United Nations,

Having welcomed the report of the Panel on United Nations Peace Operations, and welcoming the report of the Secretary-General on its implementation,

Having considered the recommendations in the report of the Panel on United Nations Peace Operations which fall within its area of responsibility,

1. *Agrees* to adopt the decisions and recommendations contained in the annex to the present resolution;

2. *Decides* to review periodically the implementation of the provisions contained in the annex;

3. *Decides* to remain actively seized of the matter.

ANNEX

The Security Council,

I

Resolves to give peacekeeping operations clear, credible and achievable mandates;

Recognizes the critical importance of peacekeeping operations having, where appropriate and within their mandates, a credible deterrent capability;

Urges the parties to prospective peace agreements, including regional and subregional organizations and arrangements, to coordinate and cooperate fully with the United Nations from an early stage in negotiations, bearing in mind the need for any provisions for a peacekeeping operation to meet minimum conditions, including the need for a clear political objective, the practicability of the designated tasks and timeliness, and compliance with the rules and principles of international law, in particular international humanitarian, human rights and refugee law;

Requests the Secretary-General, in this regard, to make necessary arrangements for the appropriate involvement of the United Nations in peace negotiations that are likely to provide for the deployment of United Nations peacekeepers;

Also requests the Secretary-General to keep the Council regularly and fully informed of the progress in such negotiations with his analysis, assessment and recommendations, and to report to the Council, upon the conclusion of any such peace agreement, as to whether it meets the minimum conditions for United Nations peacekeeping operations;

Requests the Secretariat to continue to provide comprehensive political briefings on relevant issues before the Council;

Requests regular military briefings from the Secretariat, including by the Military Adviser, the Force Commander or the Force Commander–designate, both prior to the establishment of a peacekeeping operation and in the implementation phase, and requests that those briefings report on key military factors such as, where appropriate, the chain of command, force structure, unity and cohesion of the force, training and equipment, risk assessment and rules of engagement;

Also requests regular civilian police briefings from the Secretariat in a similar vein, both prior to the establishment and in the implementation phase of peacekeeping operations with significant civilian police components;

Requests the Secretariat to provide the Council with regular, comprehensive humanitarian briefings for countries where there are United Nations peacekeeping operations;

Encourages the Secretary-General, during the planning and preparation of a peacekeeping operation, to take all possible measures at his disposal to facilitate rapid deployment, and agrees to assist the Secretary-General, wherever appropriate, with specific planning mandates, requesting him to take the necessary administrative steps to prepare the rapid deployment of a mission;

Undertakes, when establishing or enlarging a peacekeeping operation, to request formally that the Secretary-General proceed to the implementation phase of the mandate upon receipt of firm commitments to provide sufficient numbers of adequately trained and equipped troops and other critical mission support elements;

Encourages the Secretary-General to begin his consultations with potential troop contributors well in advance of the establishment of peacekeeping operations, and requests him to report on his consultations during the consideration of new mandates;

Recognizes that the problem of the commitment gap with regard to personnel and equipment for peacekeeping operations requires the assumption by all Member States of the shared responsibility to support United Nations peacekeeping;

Emphasizes the importance of Member States taking the necessary and appropriate steps to ensure the capability of their peacekeepers to fulfil the mandates assigned to them, underlines the importance of international cooperation in this regard, including the training of peacekeepers, and invites Member States to incorporate HIV/AIDS awareness training into their national programmes in preparation for deployment;

Underlines the importance of an improved system of consultations among the troop-contributing countries, the Secretary-General and the Security Council, in order to foster a common understanding of the situation on the ground, of the mandate of the mission and of its implementation;

Agrees, in this regard, to strengthen significantly the existing system of consultations through the holding of private meetings with troop-contributing countries, including at their request and without prejudice to the provisional rules of procedure of the Security Council, in particular when the Secretary-General has identified potential troop-contributing countries for a new or ongoing peacekeeping operation, during the implementation phase of an operation, when considering a change in, or renewal or completion of a peacekeeping mandate, or when a rapid deterioration in the situation on the ground threatens the safety and security of United Nations peacekeepers;

II

Undertakes to ensure that the mandated tasks of peacekeeping operations are appropriate to the situation on the ground, including such factors as the prospects for success, the potential need to protect civilians and the possibility that some parties may seek to undermine peace through violence;

Emphasizes that the rules of engagement for United Nations peacekeeping forces should be fully consistent with the legal basis of the operation and any relevant Security Council resolutions and clearly set out the circumstances in which force may be used to protect all mission components and personnel, military or civilian, and that the rules of engagement should support the accomplishment of the mandate of the mission;

Requests the Secretary-General, following full consultations with the United Nations membership, in particular troop-contributing countries, to prepare a comprehensive operational doctrine for the military component of United Nations peacekeeping operations and submit it to the Security Council and the General Assembly;

III

Stresses the need to improve the information gathering and analysis capacity of the Secretariat, with a view to improving the quality of advice to both the Secretary-General and the Security Council, and welcomes, in this regard, the clarification provided by the Secretary-General in his implementation report on plans for the establishment of the Executive Committee on Peace and Security Information and Strategic Analysis Secretariat;

IV

Stresses the importance of the United Nations being able to respond and deploy a peacekeeping operation rapidly upon the adoption by the Security Council of a resolution establishing its mandate, and notes that rapid deployment is a comprehensive concept that will require improvements in a number of areas;

Calls upon all relevant parties to work towards the objective of meeting the timeliness for United Nations peacekeeping operations, that is, deploying a traditional peacekeeping operation within thirty days and a complex operation within ninety days of the adoption of a Security Council resolution establishing its mandate;

Welcomes the intention of the Secretary-General to use these timelines as the basis for evaluating the capacity of existing systems to provide field missions with the human, material, financial and information assets that they require;

Welcomes also the proposal of the Panel on United Nations Peace Operations to create integrated mission task forces, and urges the Secretary-General to pursue this or any other related capabilities that would improve United Nations planning and support capacities;

Emphasizes the need for the Secretariat to provide the leadership of a peacekeeping operation with strategic guidance and plans for anticipating and overcoming any challenges to the implementation of a mandate, and stresses that such guidance should be formulated in cooperation with the leadership of the mission;

Welcomes the proposals of the Panel on United Nations Peace Operations for improving the capacity of the United Nations to deploy military, civilian police and other personnel rapidly, including through the United Nations standby arrangements system, and urges the Secretary-General to consult current and potential troop-contributing countries on how best to achieve this important objective;

Undertakes to consider the possibility of using the Military Staff Committee as one of the means of enhancing the United Nations peacekeeping capacity;

V

Emphasizes that the greatest deterrent to violent conflict is addressing the root causes of conflict, including through the promotion of sustainable development and a democratic society based on a strong rule of law and civic institutions, as well as adherence to all human rights—civil, political, economic, social and cultural;

Concurs with the Secretary-General that every step taken towards reducing poverty and achieving broad-based economic growth is a step towards conflict prevention;

Stresses the important role of the Secretary-General in the prevention of armed conflicts, and looks forward to his report on that issue, which is to be submitted to Member States by May 2001;

Expresses its continued willingness to consider the use of Security Council missions, with the consent of host countries, in order to determine whether any dispute, or situation that might lead to international tension or give rise to a dispute, is likely to endanger the maintenance of international peace and security, and to make recommendations for action by the Council where appropriate;

Recalls the statements by its President of 30 November 1999 and 20 July 2000 on the prevention of armed conflict, and welcomes, in this context, the intention of the Secretary-General to send fact-finding missions to areas of tension more frequently;

Recalls also resolution 1296(2000) of 19 April 2000 on the protection of civilians in armed conflict, and looks forward to receiving the follow-up report of the Secretary-General in this context;

Reaffirms the important role of women in the prevention and resolution of conflicts and in post-conflict peace-building, and fully endorses the urgent need to mainstream a gender perspective into peacekeeping operations;

Calls for the full implementation of its resolution 1325(2000) of 31 October 2000;

VI

Welcomes the decision by the Secretary-General to instruct the Executive Committee on Peace and Security to formulate a plan on the strengthening of the United Nations capacity to develop peace-building strategies and to implement programmes in support thereof, and requests the Secretary-General to submit recommendations to the Security Council and the General Assembly on the basis of that plan;

Recognizes that stronger measures to reduce poverty and promote economic growth are important for the success of peace-building;

Emphasizes, in this regard, the need for more effective coordination of disarmament, demobilization and reintegration programmes, and reaffirms that adequate and timely funding for these programmes is critical to the success of peace processes;

Welcomes the intention of the Secretary-General to spell out more clearly, when submitting future concepts of operations, what the United Nations system can do to help to strengthen local rule of law and human rights institutions, drawing on existing civilian police, human rights, gender and judicial expertise;

VII

Welcomes the intention of the Secretary-General to conduct a needs assessment of the areas in which it would be feasible and useful to draft a simple, common set of interim rules of criminal procedure.

Special Committee on Peacekeeping Operations. The Special Committee on Peacekeeping Operations convened in November in an extraordinary session [A/C.4/55/6] and created an open-ended working group to examine the recommendations of the Panel on United Nations Peace Operations, in the light of the Secretary-General's implementation plan (see p. 85).

The Special Committee supported, endorsed or noted most of the Secretary-General's proposals for implementing the Panel's recommendations. It specifically stated that, if the proposal for funding quick-impact projects were implemented, it should be done following consultations with local authorities in an impartial and transparent manner. Details of such projects should be reflected in the relevant reports of the Secretary-General. The Special Committee recommended that, when mandated by the Security Council as part of a peacekeeping operation, programmes for disarmament, demobilization and integration should be provided with adequate and timely resources. It urged that those programmes be brought into assessed budgets of relevant peacekeeping operations and that their funding be reviewed during examination of the mission's budget.

The Special Committee emphasized the need for clear, credible and achievable mandates and the necessity for strengthening and formalizing the consultation process between the Security Council and troop contributors, especially during the implementation phase of an operation. Concerning the safety and security of personnel, the Special Committee urged that Secretariat briefings to troop-contributing countries should be timely, comprehensive and professional and be accompanied by written briefs.

The Secretariat was urged to work towards deploying peacekeeping operations within 30 days of the adoption of a mandate and within 90 days for a complex operation. Those time frames would require political will and more effective operational capabilities, including an efficient standby arrangements system. The Special Committee recommended that, in the selection of mission leadership, due regard be given to contributions by countries providing troops and civilian police; the expenses of candidates called for interview should be borne by the United Nations, and all concerned permanent missions should be informed of the outcome of the selection process.

The Committee reiterated its request for an expeditious and comprehensive review of the management, structure, recruitment processes and interrelationships of relevant elements within the Secretariat that played a role in peacekeeping operations. That review would be essential for the thorough consideration of DPKO's resource requirements and those of other departments backstopping peacekeeping operations. Pending that review, additional resources should be made available on an emergency basis for staffing DPKO. The Special Committee stressed that approved increases in DPKO's staff should be carried out in an open and transparent manner and requested the Secretary-General to submit a report on the subject for consideration by the relevant bodies of the General Assembly. The Special Committee recognized the need to restructure DPKO's Military and Civilian Planning Division, including separating the Civilian Police Unit from the Division. It requested the Secretariat to clarify, at its next regular session, its intention to develop a "military doctrine", a term that was

open to several interpretations, thus causing concern to the Special Committee.

The Special Committee expressed deep concern at the delay in reimbursing troop contributors. It encouraged the Secretariat to continue to expedite the processing of all claims and asked the Secretary-General to present a progress report in that regard to the Committee's next regular session. It underlined the need to explore the possibilities for improving the safety and security of UN and associated personnel working in peacekeeping operations.

The Special Committee said it would resume consideration of the Panel's report and the implementation plan at its next session, after completion of the comprehensive review, and requested the Secretary-General to report on the implementation of the recommendations of the Special Committee's special session at that time.

GENERAL ASSEMBLY ACTION

On 8 December [meeting 83], the General Assembly, on the recommendation of the Fourth (Special Political and Decolonization) Committee [A/55/572], adopted **resolution 55/135** without vote [agenda item 86].

Comprehensive review of the whole question of peacekeeping operations in all their aspects

The General Assembly,

Recalling its resolution 2006(XIX) of 18 February 1965 and all other relevant resolutions,

Recalling in particular its resolution 54/81 B of 25 May 2000,

Taking note of the report of the Secretary-General on the work of the Organization, the report of the Panel on United Nations Peace Operations and the report of the Secretary-General on the implementation of the report of the Panel,

1. *Welcomes* the report of the Special Committee on Peacekeeping Operations;

2. *Endorses* the proposals, recommendations and conclusions of the Special Committee, contained in its report;

3. *Urges* Member States, the Secretariat and relevant organs of the United Nations to take all necessary steps to implement the proposals, recommendations and conclusions of the Special Committee;

4. *Decides* that the Special Committee, in accordance with its mandate, shall continue its efforts for a comprehensive review of the whole question of peacekeeping operations in all their aspects and shall review the implementation of its previous proposals and consider any new proposals so as to enhance the capacity of the United Nations to fulfil its responsibilities in this field;

5. *Requests* the Special Committee to submit a report on its work to the General Assembly at its fifty-fifth session;

6. *Decides* to keep open during its fifty-fifth session the item entitled "Comprehensive review of the whole question of peacekeeping operations in all their aspects".

Resource requirements

Report of Secretary-General. In October [A/55/507 & Add.1], the Secretary-General outlined the resource requirements of his proposals to implement the recommendations of the Panel on United Nations Peace Operations. He requested $14,675,600, including an increase of 214 posts, on an emergency basis through the support account for the 2000-2001 biennium, and $7,527,300, including an increase of 35 posts, under the regular budget for the same biennium.

Requirements for the 2002-2003 biennium would total $71.4 million, of which $12 million would relate to the regular budget and $59.4 million to the support account.

Report of ACABQ. In December [A/55/676], ACABQ said that although the Secretary-General described his resource estimates as emergency requests, not all of his proposals could be so classified. It also noted that some of the Panel's recommendations required further study and their financial implications would be submitted to the General Assembly in 2001. In addition, the Special Committee on Peacekeeping Operations had requested a comprehensive review of DPKO's management structure, recruitment processes and interrelationships. ACABQ had also considered the report of the Special Committee and Security Council resolution 1327(2000) (see p. 87).

ACABQ recommended that the Assembly appropriate an additional amount of $363,000 under section 3, Political affairs, $37,200 under section 27, Management and central support services, and $19,200 under section 32, Staff assessment, of the 2000-2001 programme budget. It also recommended that the Assembly finance an additional amount of $9,190,200 under the support account for peacekeeping operations for the period 1 July 2000 to 30 June 2001.

ACABQ recommended acceptance of 93 of the 214 posts requested under the support account and the deferral of consideration of 117. Of the 35 posts requested under the regular budget in the 2000-2001 biennium, ACABQ recommended acceptance of 2 and deferred consideration of 33.

The Assembly, on 23 December, in **resolution 55/238** (see p. 1300), approved ACABQ's recommendations.

General aspects

Standby arrangements and rapid deployment

The Secretary-General, in a January report [A/54/670] on the implementation of the 1999 recommendations of the Special Committee on Peacekeeping Operations [YUN 1999, p. 51], said that further expansion of the standby arrange-

ments system might be of assistance in enhancing access to expertise in such areas as law, public information and engineering. It was essential that the Secretariat and Member States continue to explore ways to improve the ability to tap such expertise. The two mission start-up kits, held at the UN Logistics Base in Brindisi, Italy, had amply proved their value by facilitating the rapid deployment in support of recent major missions, and the Secretariat was working on their urgent replenishment. The Secretariat was also working to identify staff serving in existing field missions who could be deployed at short notice to provide start-up support. In addition, personnel from the Military and Civilian Police Division had been used in the start-up phase of a mission. However, that at times imposed an unmanageable burden on staff at Headquarters, particularly where the Secretariat had to explore start-up of more than one mission concurrently. The Secretariat had been unable to obtain full staffing for the rapidly deployable mission headquarters. Filling the six additional posts through redeployment proved to be impossible in view of other immediate demands on staff time. The Secretariat intended to explore other options through which that could be achieved. It also considered that the concept of linking the standby arrangements system with procedures for contingent-owned equipment merited further consideration.

At its 2000 session [A/54/839], the Special Committee on Peacekeeping Operations, noting that contingent-owned equipment was an indispensable element in an effective rapid deployment capability, urged the Secretariat to expedite its work to link such equipment to the standby arrangements system in order to realize its full potential for rapid deployment capability. Where critical start-up materiel and services were subject to extended procurement lead time, the Secretariat should maintain a minimum stock of such items on hand. Appropriate General Assembly bodies should explore additional contracting authority mechanisms to permit accelerated procurement of such items, and formulate a mechanism to facilitate third-party loans of operational equipment to Member States participating in peacekeeping operations within the context of the contingent-owned equipment concept.

Expressing dissatisfaction over the lack of progress in implementing further the concept of the rapidly deployable mission headquarters, the Special Committee regretted that the remaining six mission headquarters military positions had not been established. It recommended that they be established and filled as quickly as possible, and that the rapidly deployable mission headquarters requirement be incorporated into the structural review of the management of peace-keeping operations requested by the Special Committee. The Special Committee called on the Secretariat to recommend measures, particularly with regard to the ability of missions to accept and deploy civilian police personnel, to overcome the problem of delays caused by the lack of suitable accommodation, in consultation with troop-contributing States, as part of the mission start-up kit concept.

The Special Committee reiterated its support for funding to permit immediate replenishment of the mission start-up kits at the Logistics Base so as to restore that element of rapid deployment capacity to its full effectiveness. It encouraged the Secretariat to review the role and function of the Base to promote its potential as a forward logistics and materiel staging area for peacekeeping operations.

Consultations with troop contributors

In its March report [A/54/839], the Special Committee on Peacekeeping Operations emphasized that the planning process within DPKO should be more transparent and effective and troop-contributing countries should be consulted at the earliest stages of mission planning. Consultations between the Security Council and troop-contributing countries should be used to their fullest extent in the elaboration, change and extension of UN peacekeeping mandates and, when authorizing force, the Council should, in all cases, adhere to the relevant provisions of the Charter.

The Special Committee reiterated its request that copies of the Secretary-General's reports to the Council be provided to troop-contributing countries in a timely manner prior to the convening of troop and police contributor meetings. It regretted that progress reports did not reflect the Secretary-General's undertaking to ensure that the Special Committee was consulted in the development of policy and issues affecting peacekeeping personnel and reiterated the request that it be consulted prior to the finalization of all such policies and issues.

The Special Committee recommended that Member States concerned be fully consulted and provided on a timely basis with a copy of all UN internal investigations or inquiries into incidents, including the final outcome reached, which involved the death or injury of personnel from Member States or loss/theft of property of Member States. Consultation with Member States was also necessary when mission authorities took any action, including repatriation or investigation in the event of misconduct by

peacekeeping personnel. In that context, the Special Committee emphasized that the national contingent commanders had the sole authority for any disciplinary action in respect of misconduct by a member of their contingent. The Special Committee noted the difficulties experienced by Member States in prosecuting personnel repatriated from mission areas who were accused of having committed serious crimes. It recommended that, in cases of gross misconduct, Member States concerned be invited to take part in the investigation, including through representation in the force-level international military police unit, bearing in mind the need to maintain discipline in the mission area and the desirability of justice being done in all such cases.

Civilian police

The Special Committee on Peacekeeping Operations [A/54/839] recognized that the increased role of civilian police components in UN peacekeeping operations should be adequately reflected in DPKO structures and stressed the need further to strengthen the Civilian Police Unit and enhance the Civilian Police Adviser's role. Care should be taken that police and military tasks were clearly defined and differentiated. The Secretariat should urgently develop, in consultation with Member States, a comprehensive set of policies on civilian police activities to be articulated through the guidelines for civilian police that the Special Committee had asked the Secretariat to prepare. The development of those guidelines should be finalized as soon as possible and should include procedures and standards for the selection, training and deployment of civilian police, as well as for the effective coordination of civilian police matters at Headquarters and the conduct of operations in the field. Where UN peacekeeping operations were mandated to develop a domestic police service, activities such as recruitment, selection and training of local police officers should be undertaken at an early stage in the operation. In that regard, mission budgets should contain sufficient resources for the establishment of local police academies.

The Special Committee viewed with concern the inability of the international community to meet the requirements for UN civilian police and requested the Secretariat to explore alternatives for meeting the increasing demand, including the use of qualified non-active service personnel. Noting that the use of English as the only accepted language of work in most UN civilian police operations denied the participation of many non-English-speaking countries, it recommended that the Secretariat expand ways to ensure wider participation by Member States, keeping in mind the need to maintain safe, secure, efficient and effective field missions. The Special Committee also recommended that the modalities of the Selection Assistance Team concept be clarified and incorporated into the civilian police guidelines and that operationally effective Selection Assistance Team testing standards be developed. Rules of engagement for UN civilian police personnel mandated to carry arms should be formulated and the development, finalization and implementation of rules of engagement should be undertaken in all cases in consultation with Member States.

Safety and security

The Special Committee on Peacekeeping Operations [A/54/839] emphasized that appropriate protection and security measures should be included in the design and planning of peacekeeping operations, that initial mission cost estimates should provide for personnel safety, that missions should be provided with the necessary logistics support, that personnel safety and security should be stressed in pre-deployment training standards and that status-of-forces agreements/status-of-mission agreements should include measures to enhance personnel safety, based on the 1994 Convention on the Safety of United Nations and Associated Personnel [YUN 1994, p. 1289]. The Special Committee urged DPKO to complete as soon as possible a general and comprehensive review of security arrangements and encouraged the Secretariat to convene a seminar on the safety and security of UN personnel in peacekeeping operations to facilitate the review. DPKO's Air Safety Unit should also be considered a part of the Secretary-General's comprehensive review. All peacekeeping personnel should receive security briefings upon arrival in the mission area, be briefed on major potential threats associated with the environment and given specific guidance to avoid hazardous situations. The Special Committee requested that a reference to the need to strictly observe mandatory air safety requirements of Member States be incorporated in the Operations Manual and specific provisions to that effect included in Secretariat contracts with commercial carriers for night flying operations.

The Special Committee reiterated the role that UN public information, especially radio, could play in enhancing personnel safety and security in peacekeeping operations. It expressed support for the Secretariat's efforts to address public information requirements in the planning and start-up of peacekeeping operations and for close cooperation between DPKO and the Department of Public Information.

The Security Council, in statement **S/PRST/2000/4** of 9 February, encouraged the Secretary-General to complete a general and comprehensive review of security in peacekeeping operations with a view to elaborating and undertaking further specific and practical measures to increase the safety of UN and associated personnel (see p. 1345).

Protection of civilians in armed conflict

On 14 February [S/2000/119], the Security Council President informed the General Assembly President of the request of the Council's informal working group on the protection of civilians in armed conflict that the Assembly's Special Committee on Peacekeeping Operations consider four of the recommendations contained in the Secretary-General's 1999 report on the subject [YUN 1999, p. 648]. The recommendations related to taking steps to strengthen the Organization's capacity to plan and deploy rapidly, including enhancing participation in the UN standby arrangements system; support for a public ombudsman to be attached to all peacekeeping operations to deal with complaints from the public about the behaviour of UN peacekeepers and the establishment of an ad hoc fact-finding commission to examine reports on alleged breaches of international humanitarian and human rights law committed by members of UN forces; requesting deploying Member States to report to the United Nations on measures taken to prosecute members of their armed forces who violated those laws while in the service of the United Nations; and mobilizing international support for national security forces, from logistical and operational assistance to technical advice, training and supervision.

On 7 April [S/2000/298], the Assembly President transmitted to the Council President a letter of 1 April from the Chairman of the Special Committee that drew attention to the paragraphs of the Special Committee's report addressing the issues of rapid deployment and planning capacity and troop-contributing countries reporting to the United Nations on measures taken to prosecute those of its members violating international humanitarian and human rights law. The letter stated that the Special Committee's schedule did not allow for substantive consideration of the establishment of a public ombudsman or mobilizing international support for national security forces. Those issues would be taken up in 2001.

The Council, in **resolution 1296(2000)** of 19 April (see p. 667), welcomed the Special Committee's work and encouraged the General Assembly to continue consideration of protection of civilians in armed conflict.

Integrating the protection of children in UN peacekeeping operations

The Secretary-General, in his July report on children and armed conflict [A/55/163-S/2000/712], said that, in recognition of the critical roles peacekeeping missions played in protecting children, the Security Council, in resolutions 1260(1999) [YUN 1999, p. 161] and 1279(1999) [ibid., p. 92] had incorporated the protection of children into the mandates of the missions in Sierra Leone and in the Democratic Republic of the Congo and had adopted the proposal that senior child protection officers be deployed with peacekeeping operations. DPKO, the Office of the Special Representative of the Secretary-General for Children and Armed Conflict, and the United Nations Children's Fund (UNICEF), in collaboration with other UN agencies, had finalized the terms of reference for child protection advisers. Two peacekeeping operations currently had senior child protection advisers on the ground; two were seconded from UNICEF and a third was previously with a UN peacekeeping operation. The United Nations, in keeping with the affirmation in Council resolution 1296(2000) that peacekeeping operations should include a mass media component to disseminate information about child protection, was working with radio stations in Bosnia and Herzegovina, Cambodia, the Kosovo province of the Federal Republic of Yugoslavia and Liberia to ensure responsible broadcasting practices and programmes. Entities such as UNICEF, the Office of the United Nations High Commissioner for Refugees and UNDP often worked with local and international broadcasters to produce radio material that addressed key themes, such as the rights of children and their protection.

The Secretary-General recommended that the Council ensure that the mandates of all relevant UN peacekeeping operations included monitoring and reporting on the protection of children, and that Member States ensure the appropriate training and education of all civilian, military, police and humanitarian personnel involved in UN peacekeeping operations on international humanitarian, human rights and refugee law, especially on the rights and protection of children and women. Such training should be provided in advance of deploying troops to UN operations.

The Council, in **resolution 1314(2000)** of 11 August (see p. 723), reaffirmed its readiness to continue to include child protection advisers in future peacekeeping operations.

Status-of-forces and status-of-mission agreements

The Special Committee on Peacekeeping Operations [A/54/839] expressed disappointment that the compendium of instances in which the Organization was due restitution, as a result of non-compliance with status-of-forces agreements or other agreements, was still not completed, and reiterated the need for the Secretary-General to fulfil ACABQ's 1996 request [YUN 1996, p. 36] that the compendium be provided and that claims submitted by Member States be withheld until the matter of expenditures was resolved. It concurred with the requirement for flexible application of the model status-of-forces agreement to accommodate changing developments in peacekeeping practice and welcomed the inclusion in future agreements of provisions regarding the responsibility of host Governments in respect of the safety and security of UN and associated personnel.

The Special Committee attached the same importance to status-of-mission agreements as it did to status-of-forces agreements and requested the Secretariat to report to it on the possibility of developing a model status-of-mission agreement, in consultation with Member States.

Training

The Special Committee on Peacekeeping Operations [A/54/839] stressed the importance of participants in peacekeeping operations being given, prior to deployment, specific training that addressed local cultural sensitivities, including gender-sensitivity training, and encouraged the Secretariat, as well as Member States, to include and develop that aspect in their efforts to promote training norms for UN peacekeeping personnel. It expressed concern that the shortfall in staff in DPKO's Training Unit would have a negative effect on its work and recommended that it be corrected.

The Special Committee noted the Secretariat's efforts to provide training materials in all UN official languages and asked the Secretary-General for an update on the issue, including measures taken to secure funding. It recommended that the United Nations Training and Assistance Team concept be broadened to include additional functional areas of peacekeeping, such as communications, finances, personnel administration, engineering and other more specific areas of general logistics.

The Special Committee encouraged the Secretariat to continue to provide assistance for the conduct of regional training programmes, and to continue to pay attention to gender-sensitivity training. It requested that consideration be given to including a member of the Training Unit in the pre-mission technical survey team to assess the unique training requirements for each mission. The Special Committee emphasized that activities of the Training Unit should take into account the increased requirements of civilian police in peacekeeping operations and called for enhanced cooperation between Member States in training civilian police personnel for UN peacekeeping operations, pursuant to UN training standards.

Comprehensive review of peacekeeping

Special Committee on Peacekeeping Operations

As requested by the General Assembly in resolution 54/81 A [YUN 1999, p. 56], the Special Committee on Peacekeeping Operations continued its comprehensive review of the whole question of peacekeeping operations in all their aspects [A/54/839]. In response to the Committee's request, the Secretary-General submitted in January a report on the implementation of its recommendations [A/54/670].

The Special Committee held an organizational meeting on 11 February and a general debate on 11, 14 and 15 February; the informal open-ended working group met from 16 February to 10 March. The Special Committee held a special session in November to consider the report of the Panel on United Nations Peace Operations (see p. 83).

The Special Committee, noting that during the preceding year there had been a sudden surge in UN peacekeeping efforts in different parts of the world, considered it essential for the Organization to be in an effective position to maintain international peace and security, including by improving the capacity to assess conflict situations, by effective planning and management of peacekeeping operations and by responding quickly and effectively to any Security Council mandate. The Special Committee, taking note that the Council had recently mandated peacekeeping operations that, in addition to the traditional tasks of monitoring and reporting, included a number of other mandated activities, stressed the importance of an effective DPKO that was structured efficiently and staffed adequately. It stressed the importance of consistently applying the principles and standards it had set forth for the establishment and conduct of peacekeeping operations and emphasized the need to continue to consider those principles, as well as peacekeeping definitions, in a systematic fashion. New proposals or conditions concerning peacekeeping operations should be discussed in the Special Committee.

The Special Committee stressed the importance of a correctly staffed and flexible DPKO, capable of responding swiftly and effectively to the increased demands placed on it by the planning and deployment of missions, and the need for a comprehensive and coordinated management of peacekeeping operations, at Headquarters and in the field. It reinforced the need to ensure that DPKO's structure and staffing contained an effective and efficient medical planning and support capacity.

The Special Committee encouraged the Secretariat to continue using coordination mechanisms within the Secretariat to avoid duplication and overlap and to maintain contact with UN agencies and regional organizations. It noted that the increasing complexity of peacekeeping operations placed additional demands on the Special Representatives of the Secretary-General in discharging that critical coordination function in the field and stressed that they be granted the authority and resources to fulfil their responsibilities efficiently and effectively.

The Special Committee reiterated the importance of transparency in selecting troop contributors, particularly in the use of the UN standby arrangements system, welcomed increased contributions of Member States to the system, and encouraged Member States that had not already done so to join it. The Secretariat was encouraged to consult first with contributors to the system and also with other Member States regarding capabilities to overcome the deficiencies referred to by the Secretary-General in his 1999 report [YUN 1999, p. 52].

The Special Committee stressed the importance of timely, efficient, transparent and cost-effective procurement of goods and services in support of peacekeeping operations, and invited the Secretariat to explore ways to enhance the logistics readiness of the Organization, in particular through a broader use of the United Nations Logistics Base in Brindisi, reserve stocks and a reassessment of the start-up kits, including their scope and number. The Secretariat was asked for a status report on procurement from developing countries and countries with economies in transition. The Special Committee requested the Secretary-General to undertake a comprehensive review of the procurement and requisitioning process, to include in his annual report on procurement reform a detailed section addressing field procurement, with particular emphasis on a more flexible and timely contracting mechanism for new missions, including local procurement, and to address, in detail, peacekeeping procurement in his next report to the Special Committee.

The Committee, while noting progress made in developing the Operational Support Manual, recommended that it be harmonized with other related mission support manuals. It emphasized the urgent need to develop an overarching logistics concept to guide the efficient coordination between planning and management, establish a cost-effective use of resources, integrate support to civilian, military and civilian police staff in the field and produce an up-to-date set of contractual and procurement regulations. The Special Committee expressed the hope that its recommendations would be further considered by the contingent-owned equipment post–Phase V Working Group (see p. 108) in 2001. In that regard, Member States were asked to submit the data required. The Special Committee welcomed the circulation of the revised Manual on Policies and Procedures concerning Reimbursement and Control of Contingent-owned Equipment of Troop-contributing Countries Participating in Peacekeeping Missions (the COE Manual-2000) for comments by Member States and requested the Secretariat to update the Manual and to make it available at the earliest opportunity in all UN official languages.

The Special Committee recommended that the Lessons Learned Unit convene a meeting of interested Member States to develop mechanisms for validating lessons learned at the field level, that the Secretary-General include an update on that issue in his next report, and that experience derived from past peacekeeping operations be incorporated into peacekeeping policy and planning to improve the efficiency and effectiveness of future missions. The Secretary-General was asked to address the need for full commitment and additional resources to be given to the conduct of peacekeeping operations in Africa in his next progress report to the Special Committee.

The Special Committee encouraged the Secretariat to formalize a mechanism for retaining lessons learned from disarmament, demobilization and reintegration programmes and recommended that those programmes be provided with adequate resources. To promote compliance with the objectives of those programmes within a peacekeeping operation, mission planners should ensure that the security of disarmed soldiers was an integral part of any programme. Mission planning for disarmament, demobilization and reintegration aspects of peacekeeping operations should accommodate the special needs of women and children in such programmes.

The Special Committee emphasized the need to differentiate between peacekeeping operations and humanitarian assistance. However, if protection of humanitarian assistance was a mandated task of a UN peacekeeping operation, both should be coordinated to ensure that they were not working at cross purposes and that humanitarian assistance was impartial.

GENERAL ASSEMBLY ACTION

On 25 May [meeting 97], the General Assembly, on the recommendation of the Fourth Committee [A/54/577/Add.1], adopted **resolution 54/81 B** without vote [agenda item 90].

Comprehensive review of the whole question of peacekeeping operations in all their aspects

The General Assembly,

Recalling its resolution 2006(XIX) of 18 February 1965 and all other relevant resolutions,

Recalling in particular its resolution 54/81 A of 6 December 1999,

Affirming that the efforts of the United Nations in the peaceful settlement of disputes, including through its peacekeeping operations, are indispensable,

Convinced of the need for the United Nations to continue to improve its capabilities in the field of peacekeeping and to enhance the effective and efficient deployment of its peacekeeping operations,

Considering the contribution that all States Members of the Organization make to peacekeeping,

Noting the widespread interest in contributing to the work of the Special Committee on Peacekeeping Operations expressed by many Member States, in particular troop-contributing countries,

Bearing in mind the continuous necessity of preserving the efficiency and strengthening the effectiveness of the work of the Special Committee,

1. *Welcomes* the report of the Special Committee on Peacekeeping Operations;

2. *Endorses* the proposals, recommendations and conclusions of the Special Committee, contained in paragraphs 46 to 171 of its report;

3. *Urges* Member States, the Secretariat and relevant organs of the United Nations to take all necessary steps to implement the proposals, recommendations and conclusions of the Special Committee;

4. *Reiterates* that those Member States that become personnel contributors to United Nations peacekeeping operations in years to come or participate in the future in the Special Committee for three consecutive years as observers shall, upon request in writing to the Chairman of the Special Committee, become members at the following session of the Special Committee;

5. *Decides* that the Special Committee, in accordance with its mandate, shall continue its efforts for a comprehensive review of the whole question of peacekeeping operations in all their aspects and shall review the implementation of its previous proposals and consider any new proposals so as to enhance the capacity of the United Nations to fulfil its responsibilities in this field;

6. *Requests* the Special Committee to submit a report on its work to the General Assembly at its fifty-fifth session;

7. *Decides* to include in the provisional agenda of its fifty-fifth session the item entitled "Comprehensive re-

view of the whole question of peacekeeping operations in all their aspects".

On 23 December, the Assembly decided that the agenda item "Comprehensive review of the whole question of peacekeeping operations in all their aspects" would remain for consideration during the resumed fifty-fifth (2001) session (**decision 55/458**).

Exit strategy in peacekeeping operations

In a 6 November letter [S/2000/1072], the Netherlands informed the Secretary-General of its intention to organize an open debate in the Security Council on the Council's decision-making in respect of mission closure and mission transition. The Netherlands said that the Council often had to decide whether to extend, modify or terminate the mandate of a particular operation, and there had been cases in which the Council decided to end a mission or to reduce significantly its military component, only to have those situations remain unstable or, worse, descend again into violence and chaos soon thereafter. That seemed to contradict the Council's mandate, as contained in the Charter, to facilitate the establishment of a self-sustaining peace, or at least a durable absence of violence.

In a paper annexed to its letter, the Netherlands further explained that the use of the term "exit strategy" to refer to the withdrawal or termination phase of a peacekeeping operation was misleading because it did not link the end of a mission to the mission's objectives. What was required, rather, was an overall strategy: a long-term plan designed to lead to a self-sustaining peace in the conflict area. "Exit" should be based on the successful fulfilment of a mission mandate as signified by the achievement of a lasting peace, which in turn rendered a continued mission presence unnecessary. That could be the result of a transition from one type of peace operation to another, reflecting the changing nature and intensity of a conflict. Such an approach would entail more careful consideration of the objectives to be pursued by the proposed mission and the resources required to achieve them. When such a strategy was not viable, an alternative might be to provide a stabilizing presence in the conflict area. In such cases, however, the Council would have to acknowledge the long-term commitment involved. The Council should also ponder whether a prolonged presence would be beneficial to peace efforts. It should therefore engage in more realistic and frank debates and negotiations regarding the true nature of the situation under consideration and the desired outcome.

The Netherlands used the examples of UN experiences in Haiti, Liberia and Mozambique as case studies to support its argument.

On 15 November [meeting 4223], the Security Council discussed the letter from the Netherlands.

By a 30 November letter [S/2000/1141], the Council President informed the Secretary-General that the Council considered its debate a useful input on an issue that merited further study and requested him to submit by April 2001 a report on the issue, including an analysis and recommendations, taking into account the responsibilities of different organs of the UN system and the views expressed during the debate. In that regard, the Council invited Member States to facilitate the preparation of the report, which should be made available also as a document of the General Assembly.

Operations in 2000

On 1 January, 17 UN peacekeeping operations were in place—3 in Africa, 1 in the Americas, 5 in Asia, 5 in Europe and 3 in the Middle East. During the year, 3 operations ended and 1 was launched. The total number of operations deployed in 2000 was 18; the number in place at the end of the year was 15.

Africa

In Africa, the United Nations Mission in the Central African Republic (MINURCA) ended in February. On 31 July, the Security Council established the United Nations Mission in Ethiopia and Eritrea to put into operation the mechanism for verifying the cessation of hostilities between the two countries and to prepare for the establishment of the Military Coordination Commission provided for in the Agreement on Cessation of Hostilities. In February, the Council expanded the mandate of the United Nations Mission in Sierra Leone (UNAMSIL) and the strength of its military component to ensure that the provisions of the 1999 Lomé Peace Agreement [YUN 1999, p. 159] were implemented in full. The Council extended UNAMSIL several times during the year; in December it extended the Mission to 31 March 2001. The United Nations Organization Mission in the Democratic Republic of the Congo (MONUC) continued to help implement the 1999 Lusaka Ceasefire Agreement [ibid., p. 87]. Its mandate, which the Council expanded in February to monitor implementation of the Ceasefire Agreement and investigate violations of its implementation, was extended until 15 June 2001. The United Nations Mission for the Referendum in Western Sahara (MINURSO) continued to monitor the ceasefire and otherwise conduct peace-keeping tasks. In October, the Council extended its mandate until 28 February 2001. (See next chapter.)

The Americas

In the Americas, the United Nations Civilian Police Mission in Haiti (MIPONUH) ended in March (see p. 250).

Asia

In Asia, the United Nations Iraq-Kuwait Observation Mission (UNIKOM) continued to monitor the demilitarized zone along the border between the two countries. In May, the United Nations Mission of Observers in Tajikistan (UN-MOT) ended.

Elsewhere in Asia, the United Nations Military Observer Group in India and Pakistan (UNMOGIP) remained in place to monitor the ceasefire in Jammu and Kashmir (see p. 319). The United Nations Transitional Administration in East Timor (UNTAET), responsible for the Territory's overall administration, remained in place (see p. 278).

Europe

The Security Council extended the mandate of the United Nations Mission in Bosnia and Herzegovina (UNMIBH), which included the International Police Task Force (IPTF), until 21 June 2001. It also extended the mandate of the United Nations Observer Mission in Georgia (UNOMIG) until 31 January 2001; and the mandate of the United Nations Mission of Observers in Prevlaka (UNMOP) until 15 January 2001. The United Nations Interim Administration Mission in Kosovo (UNMIK), Federal Republic of Yugoslavia, remained in place. In the Mediterranean, the mandate of the United Nations Peacekeeping Force in Cyprus (UNFICYP) was extended until 15 June 2001. (See PART ONE, Chapter V.)

Middle East

In the Middle East, the mandates of the United Nations Interim Force in Lebanon (UNIFIL) and the United Nations Disengagement Observer Force (UNDOF) were extended until 31 January 2001 and 31 May 2001, respectively. The United Nations Truce Supervision Organization (UNTSO) continued to assist both peacekeeping operations in their tasks.

Other missions

In addition to peacekeeping, the United Nations supported a number of political and human rights missions worldwide. In Africa, the United Nations Peace-building Support Office in Guinea-Bissau continued to assist in the transition from conflict management to post-conflict peace-building and reconstruction. The Security Council extended the mandate of the United Nations Office in Angola until October to assist in capacity-building, humanitarian assistance and the promotion of human rights. The Organization continued to support the United Nations Political Office for Somalia, located in Nairobi, Kenya, the United Nations Office in Burundi and the United Nations Peace-building Support Office in Liberia. In February, the Council welcomed the Secretary-General's decision to establish, until 15 February 2001, the United Nations Peace-building Support Office in the Central African Republic to support efforts to consolidate peace and national reconciliation, as well as national reconstruction and economic recovery.

In the Americas, the General Assembly extended the mandate of the United Nations Verification Mission in Guatemala until 31 December 2001, while the International Civilian Support Mission in Haiti continued to assist in that country's economic rehabilitation and reconstruction.

In Asia and the Pacific, the United Nations Monitoring, Verification and Inspection Commission, established by Security Council resolution 1284(1999) [YUN 1999, p. 230] to monitor Iraq's compliance with Council resolutions on its disarmament, had not been deployed. The United Nations Special Mission to Afghanistan continued its efforts to facilitate a political process aimed at achieving a lasting political settlement of the internal conflict there. In June, the Secretary-General established the United Nations Peace-building Support Office in Tajikistan to provide a political framework and leadership for post-conflict peace-building. In Papua New Guinea, the United Nations Political Office in Bougainville continued to assist in the promotion of political dialogue among parties to the 1998 Lincoln Agreement [YUN 1998, p. 319]. In the Democratic People's Republic of Korea, the United Nations Command continued in 2000 to implement the maintenance of the 1953 Armistice Agreement [YUN 1953, p. 136]. In November, the Council supported the Townsville Peace Agreement for the cessation of hostilities in Solomon Islands and welcomed the establishment of the International Peace Monitoring Team composed of unarmed military personnel and civilian police from Australia and New Zealand.

(For the financing of UN political missions, see PART FIVE, Chapter II.)

Roster of 2000 operations

UNTSO

United Nations Truce Supervision Organization
Established: June 1948.
Mandate: To assist in supervising the observance of the truce in Palestine.
Strength as at December 2000: 150 military observers.

UNMOGIP

United Nations Military Observer Group in India and Pakistan
Established: January 1949.
Mandate: To supervise the ceasefire between India and Pakistan in Jammu and Kashmir.
Strength as at December 2000: 46 military observers.

UNFICYP

United Nations Peacekeeping Force in Cyprus
Established: March 1964.
Mandate: To prevent the recurrence of fighting between the two Cypriot communities.
Strength as at December 2000: 1,213 troops, 33 civilian police.

UNDOF

United Nations Disengagement Observer Force
Established: June 1974.
Mandate: To supervise the ceasefire between Israel and the Syrian Arab Republic and the disengagement of Israeli and Syrian forces in the Golan Heights.
Strength as at December 2000: 1,034 troops.

UNIFIL

United Nations Interim Force in Lebanon
Established: March 1978.
Mandate: To confirm the withdrawal of Israeli forces from southern Lebanon, restore peace and security, and assist the Lebanese Government in ensuring the return of its effective authority in the area.
Strength as at December 2000: 5,802 troops.

UNIKOM

United Nations Iraq-Kuwait Observation Mission
Established: April 1991.
Mandate: To monitor the demilitarized zone along the border between Iraq and Kuwait.
Strength as at December 2000: 903 troops, 193 military observers.

MINURSO

United Nations Mission for the Referendum in Western Sahara
Established: April 1991.
Mandate: To monitor and verify the implementation of a settlement plan for Western Sahara and assist in the holding of a referendum in the Territory.
Strength as at December 2000: 27 troops, 203 military observers, 31 civilian police.

UNOMIG

United Nations Observer Mission in Georgia
Established: August 1993.
Mandate: To verify compliance with a ceasefire agreement between the parties to the conflict in Georgia and investigate ceasefire violations; expanded in 1994 to include monitoring the implementation of an agreement on a ceasefire and separation of forces and observing the operation of a multinational peacekeeping force.
Strength as at December 2000: 103 military observers.

UNMOT

United Nations Mission of Observers in Tajikistan
Established: December 1994.
Terminated: May 2000.
Mandate: To assist in monitoring a temporary ceasefire agreement between the parties to the conflict in Tajikistan.
Strength as at May 2000: 1 military observer, 2 civilian police.

UNMIBH

United Nations Mission in Bosnia and Herzegovina (including the International Police Task Force (IPTF))
Established: December 1995.
Mandate: To monitor and facilitate law enforcement activities in Bosnia and Herzegovina, train and assist law enforcement personnel in carrying out their responsibilities, advise government authorities on the organization of civilian law enforcement agencies, and assess threats to public order and the agencies' capability to deal with such threats.
Strength as at December 2000: 1,808 civilian police, 5 military observers.

UNMOP

United Nations Mission of Observers in Prevlaka
Established: January 1996.
Mandate: To monitor the demilitarization of the Prevlaka peninsula.

Strength as at December 2000: 27 military observers.

MIPONUH

United Nations Civilian Police Mission in Haiti

Established: November 1997.

Terminated: March 2000.

Mandate: To continue to assist the Government of Haiti by supporting and contributing to the professionalization of the Haitian National Police, including monitoring Haitian National Police field performance.

Strength as at February 2000: 201 civilian police.

MINURCA

United Nations Mission in the Central African Republic

Established: March 1998.

Terminated: February 2000.

Mandate: To assist in maintaining and enhancing security and stability in Bangui and the immediate vicinity of the city; to supervise, control storage and monitor the final disposition of all weapons retrieved in the course of the disarmament exercise; and to assist in a short-term police trainers programme and in other capacity-building efforts of the national police and provide advice on the restructuring of the national police and special police forces.

Strength as at February 2000: 429 troops, 9 civilian police.

UNMIK

United Nations Interim Administration Mission in Kosovo

Established: June 1999.

Mandate: To promote, among other things, the establishment of substantial autonomy and self-government in Kosovo, perform basic civilian administrative functions, organize and oversee the development of provisional institutions, facilitate a political process to determine Kosovo's future status, support reconstruction of key infrastructure, maintain civil law and order, protect human rights and assure the return of refugees and displaced persons.

Strength as at December 2000: 4,411 civilian police, 39 military observers.

UNTAET

United Nations Transitional Administration in East Timor

Established: October 1999.

Mandate: To provide security and maintain law and order, establish an effective administration,

assist in the development of civil and social services, ensure the coordination and delivery of humanitarian assistance, rehabilitation and development assistance, support capacity-building for self-government and assist in the establishment of conditions for sustainable development.

Strength as at December 2000: 7,765 troops, 1,398 civilian police, 124 military observers.

UNAMSIL

United Nations Mission in Sierra Leone

Established: October 1999.

Mandate: To cooperate with the Government of Sierra Leone and other parties in the implementation of the Peace Agreement signed at Lomé, Togo, on 7 July 1999, including, among other things, to assist in the implementation of the disarmament, demobilization and reintegration plan, monitor adherence to the ceasefire agreement of 18 May 1999, facilitate the delivery of humanitarian assistance and provide support to the elections.

Strength as at December 2000: 10,137 troops, 249 military observers, 34 civilian police.

MONUC

United Nations Organization Mission in the Democratic Republic of the Congo

Established: November 1999.

Mandate: To establish contacts with the signatories to the Ceasefire Agreement, provide technical assistance in implementation of the Agreement, provide information on security conditions, plan for the observation of the ceasefire, facilitate the delivery of humanitarian assistance and assist in the protection of human rights.

Strength as at December 2000: 24 troops, 183 military observers.

UNMEE

United Nations Mission in Ethiopia and Eritrea

Established: July 2000.

Mandate: To establish and put into operation the mechanism for verifying the cessation of hostilities and prepare for the establishment of the Military Coordination Commission.

Strength as at December 2000: 1,633 troops, 144 military observers.

Financial and administrative aspects of peacekeeping operations

General aspects

Expenditures for peacekeeping activities amounted to $1,756.8 million for the period

1 July 1999 to 30 June 2000, compared to $837.8 million during the previous 12-month period.

The financial situation of UN peacekeeping operations continued to be affected by serious cash shortages, necessitating borrowing from and among peacekeeping funds, while substantial amounts of obligations for reimbursement to Member States for troop costs and contingent-owned equipment remained unpaid.

As at 30 June 2000, the total unpaid assessed contributions for peacekeeping operations amounted to $2,128.9 million, compared to $1,687.6 million in 1999. Available cash for all operations totalled $787 million, while total liabilities were more than twice as much, at $1,942.5 million.

Notes of Secretary-General. In accordance with General Assembly resolution 49/233 A [YUN 1994, p. 1338], the Secretary-General submitted to the Assembly's Fifth (Administrative and Budgetary) Committee a January note [A/C.5/54/48] updating the budgetary information on requirements for all peacekeeping operations from 1 July 1999 to 30 June 2000 and reflecting the appropriations provided to date by the Assembly for those operations for that period, inclusive of support account requirements. The updated level of requirements totalled $1.4 billion gross, compared to the initial estimate of $644,199,100.

In May [A/C.5/54/61], the Secretary-General submitted proposed budgetary requirements for the period 1 July 2000 to 30 June 2001 of $2,072,562,000, including $782,316,600 for military personnel costs and $767,109,300 for civilian personnel costs.

On 23 December, the Assembly decided that the item "Administrative and budgetary aspects of the financing of the United Nations peacekeeping operations" would remain for consideration during its resumed fifty-fifth (2001) session (**decision 55/458**) and that the Fifth Committee should continue to consider it at that session (**decision 55/455**).

Review exercise

In its March report [A/54/839], the Special Committee on Peacekeeping Operations stressed that all Member States should pay their assessed contributions in full, on time and without conditions. The Committee remained concerned at the delay in reimbursements to troop contributors. It encouraged the Secretariat to continue to expedite the processing of all claims and to sensitize all departments involved to resolve current delays as soon as funds were available.

The Special Committee noted the conditions governing the operation of UN trust funds and requested the Secretariat to provide a regular update during the Assembly's next regular session on their impact on applicable peacekeeping operations, advise on steps taken or contemplated to ensure timely and efficient disbursement of funds from those trust funds, and undertake to keep the Committee informed of the terms of any future peacekeeping trust fund established. The Special Committee urged the Secretariat to accelerate the verification and claims payment process for injured peacekeepers, as well as for the families of those who had died in the service of the United Nations. In that regard, it urged the Secretary-General to ensure the completion of the process of disbursement of death compensation to the families of the victims of the UN flights that crashed in Angola in 1998 [YUN 1998, p. 120] and 1999 [YUN 1999, p. 103]. The Secretary-General should provide an update on the issue in his next report.

Apportionment of costs

In 2000, the General Assembly again considered the question of the placement of Member States into groups for the apportionment of peacekeeping expenses. First specified in resolution 3101(XXVIII) [YUN 1973, p. 222], the groups were subsequently adjusted several times, most recently by resolution 52/230 [YUN 1998, p. 49]. The original four groups were: (A) permanent members of the Security Council; (B) specifically named economically developed Member States not permanent members of the Council; (C) economically less developed Member States; and (D) economically less developed Member States that were specifically named.

The Assembly, by **decision 54/486** of 15 June, deferred until its fifty-fifth session a decision on the question of reallocating South Africa to the group of Member States (economically less developed) set out in paragraph 3 *(c)* of Assembly resolution 43/232 [YUN 1989, p. 793].

In December, by **resolution 55/235**, the Assembly changed the procedure for apportioning the expenses of peacekeeping operations among States, establishing 10 categories of countries (A to J). The new levels of contribution would go into effect as from 1 July 2001.

Communications. In a 13 April letter [A/C.5/54/55] addressed to the Chairman of the Fifth Committee, the United States said that the current ad hoc system for apportioning peacekeeping expenses, which concentrated the responsibility for peacekeeping finance in a small group of Member States and did not take into account changes in Members' financial circumstances or the addition of new Member States, was outmoded and in need of review and revision. It proposed that the General Assembly conduct such a review to create a more up-to-date scale of assessment, which would provide a stronger foundation for financing peacekeeping operations. That request was supported by 38 other Member States, which requested on 30 June [A/55/141 & A/55/224] that the Assembly include the item in the provisional agenda of its fifty-fifth session.

By a 20 October note verbale [A/C.5/55/16], Cambodia requested reallocation from group C to group D. It stated that it had been placed in group C since 1973. However, after three decades of conflicts, unrest and economic crisis, Cambodia had been categorized as one of the least developed countries, with an average per capita gross national product of $260 per annum, lower than that of a number of countries in group D.

GENERAL ASSEMBLY ACTION

On 23 December [meeting 89], the General Assembly, on the recommendation of the Fifth Committee [A/55/712], adopted **resolution 55/235** without vote [agenda item 169].

Scale of assessments for the apportionment of the expenses of United Nations peacekeeping operations

The General Assembly,

I

Reaffirming the principles set out in its resolutions 1874(S-IV) of 27 June 1963 and 3101(XXVIII) of 11 December 1973,

1. *Reaffirms* the following general principles underlying the financing of United Nations peacekeeping operations:

(*a*) The financing of such operations is the collective responsibility of all States Members of the United Nations and, accordingly, the costs of peacekeeping operations are expenses of the Organization to be borne by Member States in accordance with Article 17, paragraph 2, of the Charter of the United Nations;

(*b*) In order to meet the expenditures caused by such operations, a different procedure is required from that applied to meet expenditures under the regular budget of the United Nations;

(*c*) Whereas the economically more developed countries are in a position to make relatively larger contributions to peacekeeping operations, the economically less developed countries have a relatively limited capacity to contribute towards peacekeeping operations involving heavy expenditures;

(*d*) The special responsibilities of the permanent members of the Security Council for the maintenance of peace and security should be borne in mind in connection with their contributions to the financing of peace and security operations;

(*e*) Where circumstances warrant, the General Assembly should give special consideration to the situation of any Member States which are victims of, and those which are otherwise involved in, the events or actions leading to a peacekeeping operation;

2. *Recognizes* the need to reform the current methodology for apportioning the expenses of peacekeeping operations;

3. *Notes with appreciation* voluntary contributions made to peacekeeping operations and, without prejudice to the principle of collective responsibility, invites Member States to consider making such contributions;

II

4. *Decides* that assessment rates for the financing of peacekeeping operations should be based on the scale of assessments for the regular budget of the United Nations, with an appropriate and transparent system of adjustments based on levels of Member States, consistent with the principles outlined above;

5. *Decides also* that the permanent members of the Security Council should form a separate level and that, consistent with their special responsibilities for the maintenance of peace and security, they should be assessed at a higher rate than for the regular budget;

6. *Decides further* that all discounts resulting from adjustments to the regular budget assessment rates of Member States in levels C through J shall be borne on a pro rata basis by the permanent members of the Security Council;

7. *Decides* that the least developed countries should be placed in a separate level and receive the highest rate of discount available under the scale;

8. *Decides also* that the statistical data used for setting the rates of assessment for peacekeeping should be the same as the data used in preparing the regular budget scale of assessments, subject to the provisions of the present resolution;

9. *Decides further* to create levels of discount to facilitate automatic, predictable movement between categories on the basis of the per capita gross national product of Member States;

10. *Decides* that, as from 1 July 2001, the rates of assessment for peacekeeping should be based on the ten levels of contribution and parameters set forth in the table below:

Peacekeeping scale levels based on average per capita gross national product (PCGNP) of all Member States

Level	Threshold	Thresholds in United States dollars (2001-2003)	Target discount (Percentage)	Transition period for new contributors (2001-2003 scale)
A	Permanent members of the Security Council		Premium	
B	All Member States (except level A contributors)	N/A	0	3 years
C	N/A	N/A	7.5	3 years
D	Below 2X average PCGNP of all Member States (except level A contributors)	Under 9,594	20	3 years
E	Below 1.8X average PCGNP of all Member States (except level A contributors)	Under 8,634	40	2 years

Level	Threshold	Thresholds in United States dollars (2001-2003)	Target discount (Percentage)	Transition period for new contributors (2001-2003 scale)
F	Below 1.6X average PCGNP of all Member States (except level A contributors)	Under 7,675	60	N/A
G	Below 1.4X average PCGNP of all Member States (except level A contributors)	Under 6,715	70	N/A
H	Below 1.2X average PCGNP of all Member States (except level A contributors)	Under 5,756	80 (or 70 on a voluntary basis)	N/A
I	Below average PCGNP of all Member States	Under 4,797	80	N/A
J	Least developed countries (except level A contributors)		90	N/A

11. *Decides also* that Member States will be assigned to the lowest level of contribution with the highest discount for which they are eligible, unless they indicate a decision to move to a higher level;

12. *Decides further* that for purposes of determining the eligibility of Member States for contribution in particular levels during the 2001-2003 scale period, the average per capita gross national product of all Member States will be 4,797 United States dollars and the per capita gross national product of Member States will be the average of 1993 to 1998 figures;

13. *Decides* that transitions as specified above will occur in equal increments over the transition period as designated above;

14. *Decides also* that after 2001-2003, transition periods of two years will apply to countries moving up by two levels, and that transition periods of three years will apply to countries moving up by three levels or more without prejudice to paragraph 11 above;

15. *Requests* the Secretary-General to update the composition of the levels described above on a triennial basis, in conjunction with the regular budget scale of assessment reviews, in accordance with the criteria established above, and to report thereon to the General Assembly;

16. *Decides* that the structure of levels to be implemented from 1 July 2001 shall be reviewed after nine years;

17. *Decides also* that Member States may agree upon adjustments to their assessment rates under the ad hoc scale in the light of the special transitional circumstances applying during the period 1 January to 30 June 2001;

III

18. *Decides* that, as an ad hoc arrangement until 30 June 2001, in respect of the composition of groups set out in paragraphs 3 and 4 of its resolution 43/232 of 1 March 1989, as adjusted by subsequent relevant resolutions and decisions, for the apportionment of peacekeeping appropriations, Tuvalu should be included in the group of Member States set out in para-

graph 3 (*d*) of resolution 43/232 and that its contributions to peacekeeping operations should be calculated in accordance with the provisions of the relevant resolutions adopted and to be adopted by the General Assembly regarding the scale of assessments;

19. *Decides also* that, as an ad hoc arrangement until 30 June 2001, in respect of the composition of groups set out in paragraphs 3 and 4 of its resolution 43/232, as adjusted by subsequent relevant resolutions and decisions, for the apportionment of peacekeeping appropriations, the Federal Republic of Yugoslavia should be included in the group of Member States set out in paragraph 3 (*c*) of resolution 43/232 and that its contributions to peacekeeping operations should be calculated in accordance with the provisions of the relevant resolutions adopted and to be adopted by the General Assembly regarding the scale of assessments;

20. *Decides further* that, as an ad hoc arrangement until 30 June 2001, in respect of the composition of groups set out in paragraphs 3 and 4 of its resolution 43/232, as adjusted by subsequent relevant resolutions and decisions, for the apportionment of peacekeeping appropriations, as from 1 January 2001, South Africa should be included in the group of Member States set out in paragraph 3 (*c*) of resolution 43/232 and that its contributions to peacekeeping operations should be calculated in accordance with the provisions of the relevant resolutions adopted and to be adopted by the General Assembly regarding the scale of assessments;

21. *Decides* that, as an ad hoc arrangement until 30 June 2001, in respect of the composition of groups set out in paragraphs 3 and 4 of its resolution 43/232, as adjusted by subsequent relevant resolutions and decisions, for the apportionment of peacekeeping appropriations, as from 1 January 2001, Cambodia should be included in the group of Member States set out in paragraph 3 (*d*) of resolution 43/232 and that its contributions to peacekeeping operations should be calculated in accordance with the provisions of the relevant resolutions adopted and to be adopted by the General Assembly regarding the scale of assessments;

22. *Decides also*, as an ad hoc arrangement, to assess the share of the Republic of Korea, which currently belongs to Group C, in the costs of peacekeeping operations in the following manner: 36 per cent of the regular budget assessment beginning on 1 July 2001, 52 per cent in 2002, 68 per cent in 2003, 84 per cent in 2004 and 100 per cent in 2005.

ANNEX
Assignment of contribution levels for 2001-2003

Level A

Permanent members of the Security Council: China, France, Russian Federation, United Kingdom of Great Britain and Northern Ireland, United States of America

Level B

Andorra, Australia, Austria, Belgium, Canada, Cyprus, Denmark, Finland, Germany, Greece, Iceland, Ireland, Israel, Italy, Japan, Liechtenstein, Luxembourg, Monaco, Netherlands, New Zealand, Norway, Portugal, San Marino, Spain, Sweden

Level C

Brunei Darussalam, Kuwait, Qatar, Singapore, United Arab Emirates

Level D
Bahamas, Republic of Korea
Level E
Antigua and Barbuda, Bahrain, Malta, Slovenia
Level F
Argentina, Barbados, Seychelles
Level G
Oman, Palau, Saudi Arabia
Level H
Saint Kitts and Nevis, Uruguay
Level I
Albania, Algeria, Armenia, Azerbaijan, Belarus, Belize, Bolivia, Bosnia and Herzegovina, Botswana, Brazil, Bulgaria, Cameroon, Chile, Colombia, Congo, Costa Rica, Côte d'Ivoire, Croatia, Cuba, Czech Republic, Democratic People's Republic of Korea, Dominica, Dominican Republic, Ecuador, Egypt, El Salvador, Estonia, Fiji, Gabon, Georgia, Ghana, Grenada, Guatemala, Guyana, Honduras, Hungary, India, Indonesia, Iran, Iraq, Jamaica, Jordan, Kazakhstan, Kenya, Kyrgyzstan, Latvia, Lebanon, Libyan Arab Jamahiriya, Lithuania, Malaysia, Marshall Islands, Mauritius, Mexico, Micronesia, Mongolia, Morocco, Namibia, Nauru, Nicaragua, Nigeria, Pakistan, Panama, Papua New Guinea, Paraguay, Peru, Philippines, Poland, Republic of Moldova, Romania, Saint Lucia, Saint Vincent and the Grenadines, Senegal, Slovakia, South Africa, Sri Lanka, Suriname, Swaziland, Syrian Arab Republic, Tajikistan, Thailand, the former Yugoslav Republic of Macedonia, Tonga, Trinidad and Tobago, Tunisia, Turkey, Turkmenistan, Ukraine, Uzbekistan, Venezuela, Viet Nam, Yugoslavia, Zimbabwe
Level J
The least developed countries: Afghanistan, Angola, Bangladesh, Benin, Bhutan, Burkina Faso, Burundi, Cambodia, Cape Verde, Central African Republic, Chad, Comoros, Democratic Republic of the Congo, Djibouti, Equatorial Guinea, Eritrea, Ethiopia, Gambia, Guinea, Guinea-Bissau, Haiti, Kiribati, Lao People's Democratic Republic, Lesotho, Liberia, Madagascar, Malawi, Maldives, Mali, Mauritania, Mozambique, Myanmar, Nepal, Niger, Rwanda, Samoa, Sao Tome and Principe, Sierra Leone, Solomon Islands, Somalia, Sudan, Togo, Tuvalu, Uganda, United Republic of Tanzania, Vanuatu, Yemen, Zambia

Also on 23 December [meeting 89], the Assembly, on the recommendation of the Fifth Committee [A/55/712], adopted **resolution 55/236** without vote [agenda item 169].

Voluntary movements in connection with the apportionment of the expenses of United Nations peacekeeping operations

The General Assembly,

Recalling its resolution 55/235 of 23 December 2000,

1. *Welcomes with appreciation* the commitment of certain Member States to undertake voluntarily to contribute to peacekeeping operations at a rate higher than required by their per capita income;

2. *Welcomes* the voluntary decision made by Estonia and Israel to be reclassified for the purpose of the apportionment of the expenses of United Nations peacekeeping operations;

3. *Decides* that, as an ad hoc arrangement until 30 June 2001, in respect of the composition of groups set out in paragraphs 3 and 4 of its resolution 43/232 of 1 March 1989, as adjusted by subsequent relevant resolutions and decisions, for the apportionment of peacekeeping appropriations, from 1 January 2001 Estonia should be included in the group of Member States set out in paragraph 3 *(b)* of resolution 43/232, and that its contributions to peacekeeping operations should be calculated in accordance with the provisions of the relevant resolutions adopted and to be adopted by the General Assembly regarding the scale of assessments;

4. *Decides also* that, as an ad hoc arrangement until 30 June 2001, in respect of the composition of groups set out in paragraphs 3 and 4 of its resolution 43/232, as adjusted by subsequent relevant resolutions and decisions, for the apportionment of peacekeeping appropriations, from 1 January 2001 Israel should be included in the group of Member States set out in paragraph 3 *(b)* of resolution 43/232, and that its contributions to peacekeeping operations should be calculated in accordance with the provisions of the relevant resolutions adopted and to be adopted by the General Assembly regarding the scale of assessments;

5. *Welcomes* the following voluntary commitments:
Bulgaria: from Level I to Level H;
Czech Republic: from Level I to Level H;
Estonia: to move to Level B immediately upon the effective date of the new scale, forgoing its transition time;
Hungary: from Level I to Level B, with a transition time of five years, starting from 1 July 2001 as follows: from Level I to Level H from 1 July 2001; from Level H to Level F from 1 July 2002; from Level F to Level E from 1 July 2003; from Level E to Level D from 1 July 2004; and from Level D to Level B from 1 July 2005;
Israel: to move to Level B immediately upon the effective date of the new scale, forgoing its transition time;
Latvia: from Level I to Level H;
Lithuania: from Level I to Level H;
Malta: from Level E to Level B;
Philippines: from Level I to Level H;
Poland: from Level I to Level H;
Romania: from Level I to Level H;
Slovakia: from Level I to Level H;
Slovenia: from Level E to Level B immediately upon the effective date of the new scale, forgoing its transition time;
Turkey: from Level I to Level H from the effective date of the new scale until 2002, and from Level H to Level F for the remainder of the scale period;

6. *Decides* that, at any time during the scale period, a Member State may make a voluntary commitment to contribute at a rate higher than its current rate by informing the General Assembly through the Secretary-General, and the Assembly may take note of that decision.

On 23 December, the Assembly decided that the item "Scale of assessments for the apportionment of the expenses of United Nations peacekeeping operations" would remain for consideration during its resumed fifty-fifth (2001) session (**decision 55/458**) and that the Fifth Committee should continue to consider it at that session (**decision 55/455**).

Financial performance and proposed budgets

In April [A/54/841], ACABQ considered the financial performance reports for the period 1 July 1998 to 30 June 1999 and the proposed budgets for the period 1 July 2000 to 30 June 2001 of UNDOF, UNIFIL, UNIKOM, UNFICYP, UNOMIG, UNMIBH, MINURSO and the United Nations Logistics Base in Brindisi. It also considered the financial performance reports for the period 1 July 1998 to 30 June 1999 for MIPONUH, UNMOT, the United Nations Preventive Deployment Force (UNPREDEP) and the United Nations Observer Mission in Sierra Leone (UNOMSIL). In addition, ACABQ considered the financial performance report for the period 1 July 1998 to 30 June 1999 and the revised budget for the period 1 July 1999 to 30 June 2000 for the United Nations Observer Mission in Angola (MONUA); the revised budget for the period 1 July 1999 to 30 June 2000 and the proposed budget for the period 1 July 2000 to 30 June 2001 for UNOMSIL and UNAMSIL; the financial report for the United Nations Mission in East Timor (UNAMET) from 5 May to 30 November 1999 and the request for additional appropriation; and the estimates for UNTAET from 1 July 1999 to 30 June 2000. ACABQ further considered, on a preliminary basis, the proposed budget for the period 1 July 2000 to 30 June 2001 for UNMIK and the Secretary-General's request for authority to enter into commitments in an amount not exceeding $200 million to meet the most immediate anticipated requirements of MONUC. It also considered the report on losses of UN property in peacekeeping operations (see p. 111).

ACABQ welcomed the enhancements in the information contained in the performance reports and refinements in the additional complementary information on budget implementation. However, in some cases, the information given needed to be more accurate. Information on steps taken to manage authorized funds more effectively and on economy measures taken should be included in the performance reports. ACABQ intended to monitor the variations in expenditures to ascertain whether the frequency of unbudgeted expenditures resulted from unforeseen circumstances or reflected weaknesses in the methods used to identify requirements. It was concerned at the number of voluntary contributions for which no value was given and which failed to comply with the requirement for full-cost budgeting. Recalling the draft technical guidelines for voluntary contributions [YUN 1998, p. 53], ACABQ trusted that that deficiency would be remedied in future budget submissions. It requested that, in future budget presentations, organization charts indicating personnel proposed for each mission's organizational unit be provided to facilitate a comprehensive analysis of the budget proposals for various missions.

ACABQ continued to be concerned about the screening, selection and deployment of police personnel and was of the view that a more effective selection process and better management of those personnel could result in savings. The organizational set-up and the role and capacity of the DPKO Civilian Police Unit needed to be examined, and the structure of the Military and Civilian Police Division monitored to ensure organizational efficiency.

ACABQ recommended that an analysis be undertaken to determine the effect of continuing high vacancy rates on mission operations, as well as the impact that inter-mission loans of personnel and equipment might have on mission implementation. That analysis should also address measures to increase mobility between missions and from headquarters duty stations to the field and to improve recruitment. It encouraged the practice of converting international General Service posts to local posts and believed that in new missions the number of National Professional Officers should be increased. ACABQ called for greater involvement of the Office of Human Resources Management in developing job descriptions and classifying posts to ensure the overall uniformity of peacekeeping post levels with respect to the rest of the Secretariat. The Secretary-General should analyse the problems of attracting and retaining qualified personnel for peacekeeping operations. Efforts should be made to increase the number of United Nations Volunteers and local staff and a study should be made of the potential for wider use of Volunteers to meet the requirements of peacekeeping operations.

ACABQ requested that the criteria for setting training priorities be stated in a more transparent manner, and training areas and costs be more clearly stated in budget reports. The number of personnel to be trained and institutions and facilities to be used for training should also be given.

ACABQ considered that there was a need for a comprehensive system-wide approach, under the aegis of the United Nations, of the costs and related policy issues of civilian security in the field to avoid the potential for conflict in policy, activities and guidelines that endangered the security and safety of UN personnel and family members. The report on the issue should be expedited.

ACABQ requested that information be given indicating the mechanisms for coordination and the various roles and functions of partners. In relation to coordination with funding partners, it was of the view that the establishment, financing and expenditure of trust funds and other extrabudgetary funds to implement mission mandates needed to be more transparent. The costs for environmental activities in peacekeeping operations should also be studied, as well as experience in field missions to identify lessons learned for wide application and for establishing the best method for dealing with the environmental consequences of the activities and operations of UN forces in the field. The Secretariat should collect and evaluate data on incidents giving rise to high insurance premiums to determine the best way for management to deal with them.

Accounts and auditing

At its resumed fifty-fourth session, the General Assembly considered the financial report and audited financial statements for UN peacekeeping operations for the 12-month period from 1 July 1998 to 30 June 1999 [A/54/5, vol. II & Corr.1], the Secretary-General's February report on the implementation of the recommendations of the Board of Auditors [A/54/748] and the related report of ACABQ [A/54/801].

On 15 June [meeting 98], the General Assembly, on the recommendation of the Fifth Committee [A/54/506/Add.2], adopted **resolution 54/13 C** without vote [agenda item 117].

Financial reports and audited financial statements, and reports of the Board of Auditors
The General Assembly,

Having considered the financial report and audited financial statements for the twelve-month period from 1 July 1998 to 30 June 1999 and the report of the Board of Auditors on United Nations peacekeeping operations, the related report of the Advisory Committee on Administrative and Budgetary Questions and the report of the Secretary-General on the implementation of the recommendations of the Board of Auditors concerning United Nations peacekeeping operations for the period ending 30 June 1999,

1. *Accepts* the audited financial statements and the report of the Board of Auditors on United Nations peacekeeping operations;

2. *Approves* all the recommendations and conclusions contained in the report of the Board of Auditors, and endorses the observations and recommendations contained in the report of the Advisory Committee on Administrative and Budgetary Questions;

3. *Takes note* of the report of the Secretary-General on the implementation of the recommendations of the Board of Auditors concerning United Nations peacekeeping operations for the period ending 30 June 1999.

Peacekeeping support account

The Secretary-General, in March [A/54/797], submitted the financial performance report of the support account for peacekeeping operations for the period 1 July 1998 to 30 June 1999. Of the $34,400,000 for post and non-post requirements authorized by the General Assembly in resolution 52/248 [YUN 1998, p. 51], expenditures amounted to $32,821,600, resulting in an unutilized balance of $1,578,400.

In response to General Assembly resolutions 53/12 B [YUN 1999, p. 64] and 54/243 A [ibid., p. 66], the Secretary-General submitted, also in March [A/54/800], resource requirements for the support account for peacekeeping operations for the period 1 July 2000 to 30 June 2001, estimated at $51,736,600, which provided for a staffing establishment of 471 posts, including 4 new ones.

In April [A/54/832], ACABQ recommended that the Assembly approve total staffing and non-staffing requirements of $50,699,900 gross ($43,237,900 net) for the period 1 July 2000 to 30 June 2001, and that the unencumbered balance of $2,179,400 from the period 1 July 1998 to 30 June 1999 be applied to the resources required for the period 1 July 2000 to 30 June 2001.

On 15 June [meeting 98], the General Assembly, on the recommendation of the Fifth Committee [A/54/684/Add.2], adopted **resolution 54/243 B** without vote [agenda item 151 *(a)*].

Support account for peacekeeping operations
The General Assembly,

Recalling its resolutions 45/258 of 3 May 1991, 47/218 A of 23 December 1992, 48/226 A of 23 December 1993, 48/226 B of 5 April 1994, 48/226 C of 29 July 1994, 49/250 of 20 July 1995, 50/11 of 2 November 1995, 50/221 A of 11 April 1996, 50/221 B of 7 June 1996, 51/226 of 3 April 1997, 51/239 A of 17 June 1997, 51/239 B and 51/243 of 15 September 1997, 52/220 of 22 December 1997, 52/234 and 52/248 of 26 June 1998, 53/12 A of 26 October 1998, 53/208 B of 18 December 1998, 53/12 B of 8 June 1999 and 54/243 A of 23 December 1999 and its decisions 48/489 of 8 July 1994, 49/469 of 23 December 1994 and 50/473 of 23 December 1995,

Having considered the report of the Secretary-General on the support account for peacekeeping operations, the performance report on the use of support account resources for the period from 1 July 1998 to 30 June 1999 and the related report of the Advisory Committee on Administrative and Budgetary Questions,

Reaffirming the need to continue to improve the administrative and financial management of peacekeeping operations,

Recognizing the need for adequate support during all phases of peacekeeping operations, including the liquidation and termination phases,

1. *Takes note* of the report of the Secretary-General on the support account for peacekeeping operations and the separate performance report on the use of support account resources in respect of the period from 1 July 1998 to 30 June 1999;

2. *Recognizes* the importance of the United Nations being able to respond and deploy rapidly a peacekeeping operation upon the adoption of a Security Council mandate;

3. *Endorses* the conclusions and recommendations contained in the report of the Advisory Committee on Administrative and Budgetary Questions, and requests the Secretary-General to ensure their full implementation;

4. *Affirms* the need for adequate funding for the backstopping of peacekeeping operations;

5. *Reaffirms* that the expenses of the Organization, including the backstopping of peacekeeping operations, shall be borne by Member States and, to that effect, that the Secretary-General should request adequate funding to maintain the capacity of the Department of Peacekeeping Operations of the Secretariat;

6. *Decides* to maintain for the period from 1 July 2000 to 30 June 2001 the funding mechanism for the support account used in the current period, from 1 July 1999 to 30 June 2000, as approved in paragraph 3 of its resolution 50/221 B;

7. *Approves* the establishment of four hundred and sixty-nine support account–funded temporary posts, including one P-3 and one General Service post for the Training Unit of the Department of Peacekeeping Operations;

8. *Notes* the importance of the continuing efforts of the Secretary-General to develop a comprehensive concept of the United Nations rapid deployment capability, invites, in this regard, the Special Committee on Peacekeeping Operations to review the concept of the Rapid Deployment Management Unit, including its compatibility with the rapidly deployable mission headquarters, in accordance with paragraph 24 of the report of the Advisory Committee, and requests the Secretary-General to report thereon to the General Assembly at its fifty-fifth session;

9. *Requests* the Secretary-General to take into account the mandate of relevant committees before requesting any human or financial resources;

10. *Also requests* the Secretary-General timeously to inform Member States of all job vacancies in the Department of Peacekeeping Operations and in field missions;

11. *Reiterates its requests* to the Secretary-General to continue his efforts to avoid duplication and overlapping among departments of the Secretariat related to backstopping peacekeeping activities, and requests him, in this regard, to keep the General Assembly informed about concrete measures taken;

12. *Reaffirms* the need for the Secretary-General to ensure that delegation of authority to the Department of Peacekeeping Operations and field missions is in strict compliance with relevant resolutions and decisions, as well as relevant rules and procedures of the General Assembly on this matter;

13. *Approves* the support account post and non-post requirements in the amount of 50,699,900 United States dollars gross (43,237,900 dollars net) for the period from 1 July 2000 to 30 June 2001;

14. *Decides* to apply the unencumbered balance of 2,179,000 dollars from the period from 1 July 1998 to 30 June 1999, inclusive of 601,000 dollars in miscellaneous and interest income, and to prorate the balance of 48,520,900 dollars gross (41,058,900 dollars net) among the individual active peacekeeping operation budgets, to meet the resources required for the support account for the period from 1 July 2000 to 30 June 2001;

15. *Stresses* the importance of providing detailed and comprehensive information on activities related to training, including information on how it serves the interests of the United Nations.

The Secretary-General, in an October report on the resource requirements for the implementation of the recommendations of the Panel on United Nations Peace Operations [A/55/507 & Add.1] (see p. 91), requested support account funding for 214 posts in an amount of $14,675,600 for the period 1 July 2000 to 30 June 2001.

ACABQ, in December [A/55/676], recommended that the Assembly finance 93 posts in an additional amount of $9,190,200 under the support account for the period 1 July 2000 to 31 June 2001.

By **resolution 55/238** of 23 December, the Assembly approved ACABQ's recommendation.

Reimbursement issues

Troops

Responding to the General Assembly's request in resolution 51/218 E, section V [YUN 1997, p. 54], that he carry out a new survey of troop-contributing States, the Secretary-General submitted a February review of the rates of reimbursement to the Governments of troop-contributing States [A/54/763]. For the purpose of the survey, cost information based on military salary scales in effect as at December 1996 was requested from 64 Member States providing troops and military observers to UN peacekeeping operations at that time. Cost information was made available by 26 Member States providing troops and 11 providing military observers.

The Secretary-General observed that, regarding the consideration that the rates of reimbursement should compensate all troop-contributing States for at least the actual overseas allowance paid to their troops, the data showed that 15 of the 26 States were not being fully reimbursed for overseas allowance. The overall average allowance (excluding salary) amounted to $1,416, compared with the current average UN reimbursement for troop costs (including basic pay and supplementary allowance for some specialists) of $1,028. As to the consideration that no Government should receive a higher reimbursement than its actual cost, the Secretary-General noted that only 11 of the 26 Governments recovered their expenses in full or more. Based on the cost information provided, the overall average absorption factor for 1996 was 53.9 per cent, reflecting an increase of 21.1 per cent above the average absorption factor of 32.8 per cent reported in 1991. The Secretary-General suggested that the Assembly might wish to decide whether an upward adjustment to the current rates was warranted.

ACABQ, commenting on the Secretary-General's report in May [A/54/859], said that some of the Organization's expenses, such as direct per diem payments and leave allowance to military personnel, had not been reflected. The results of the analysis would also have been significantly affected if an approximation of the average cost of services provided by UN peacekeeping missions per member of a contingent had been included. ACABQ was of the opinion that it was appropriate to adjust the current methodology of calculating the standard rates of reimbursement to include those payments and there was a strong argument in favour of deducting those amounts from the reimbursements to troop-contributing States. There also appeared to be a number of inconsistencies in the data provided by troop-contributing States, making a comparative analysis difficult. ACABQ invited the General Assembly to provide further guidelines with a view to refining the methodology to ensure that more timely and comprehensive data were provided to establish whether a change in the standard rates of reimbursement to troop-contributing States was warranted.

GENERAL ASSEMBLY ACTION

On 15 June, the General Assembly, by **decision 54/485**, took note of the Secretary-General's review of the rates of reimbursement and decided to postpone consideration of the question to the main part of its fifty-fifth session.

On 23 December [meeting 89], the Assembly, on the recommendation of the Fifth Committee [A/55/534], adopted **resolution 55/229** without vote [agenda item 153 (a)].

Review of the rates of reimbursement to the Governments of troop-contributing States

The General Assembly,

Having considered the report of the Secretary-General on the review of the rates of reimbursement to the Governments of troop-contributing States and the related

report of the Advisory Committee on Administrative and Budgetary Questions,

1. *Takes note* of the report of the Secretary-General on the review of the rates of reimbursement to the Governments of troop-contributing States and of the related report of the Advisory Committee on Administrative and Budgetary Questions;

2. *Decides* to request the post–Phase V Working Group on reform procedures for determining reimbursement of contingent-owned equipment to consider the current methodology underlying the calculations of standard rates of reimbursement to troop-contributing States, including ways to produce timely and more representative data;

3. *Requests* the post–Phase V Working Group to report on the results of the review to the General Assembly at its resumed fifty-fifth session through the Advisory Committee.

Equipment

The Secretary-General, in a March note on reform of the procedure for determining reimbursement to Member States for contingent-owned equipment [A/54/795], summarized the proposals and recommendations contained in the report of the Phase V Working Group on reform procedures [A/C.5/54/49], established by General Assembly decision 53/480 [YUN 1999, p. 67]. The Working Group, which met from 24 to 28 January, reviewed and updated the Phase II and Phase III standards and rates of major equipment and self-sustainment categories, in accordance with Assembly resolution 49/233 A [YUN 1994, p. 1338]. It also reviewed levels of medical support and established rates of reimbursement.

The Secretary-General said the Group had proposed a methodology for the periodic revision of the rates in major equipment, self-sustainment and special cases, recommended improvements with regard to some performance standards and reimbursement procedures and adopted, with amendments, the Secretariat's proposal on medical support services. Owing to time constraints and the unavailability of sufficient data from troop contributors, the Working Group was unable to develop new rates for major equipment and self-sustainment categories. It recommended that the Assembly convene a post–Phase V Working Group to validate a methodology by which revised rates would be recommended to the Assembly for approval. That Group would meet for 10 working days in early 2001 and would be open to all Member States.

The Secretary-General said that the enhanced procedures developed for major equipment, self-sustainment and medical support services and the progress made on developing a methodology for the systematic review of standards and rates would greatly facilitate the Secretariat's work in reimbursing troop-contributing countries for their contingent-owned equipment in peacekeeping operations. He recommended that the Assembly adopt the triennial review of rates using indices for generic categories to be applied to all major equipment and self-sustainment categories listed in the contingent-owned equipment manual; approve the subcategories and changes with respect to major equipment; amend the performance standards for catering, furniture and welfare; include in the soldier's kit a basic flak jacket; approve the medical support services proposal; convene an expert group to review and specify the rates for medical support services; convene a meeting of experts to review pre-deployment immunization and post-repatriation medical examination costs for peacekeeping personnel; and convene a post–Phase V Working Group to complete the mandate of the Phase V Working Group in January 2001.

ACABQ, in April [A/54/826], said that the convening of a post–Phase V Working Group should be contingent upon the receipt of sufficient data from Member States and recommended that the Secretariat collect data from Member States and report to the Assembly on its success in that regard. The Assembly could then convene the Working Group. ACABQ also recommended that the 1995 rates continue to be used until sufficient replies and data were received for a review to be conducted. The Manual on Policies and Procedures concerning Reimbursement and Control of Contingent-owned Equipment of Troop-contributing Countries Participating in Peacekeeping Missions (the COE Manual) should be revised immediately after the Assembly had taken action on the Phase V Working Group's recommendations and be translated into the UN working languages.

OIOS report

In February [A/54/765 & Corr.1], the Secretary-General transmitted to the General Assembly the report of the Office of Internal Oversight Services (OIOS) on the audit of contingent-owned equipment (COE) procedures and payments to troop-contributing countries. OIOS, recalling the adoption by the Assembly in resolution 50/222 [YUN 1996, p. 35] of revised procedures for reimbursing troop-contributing countries for equipment used in peacekeeping missions, found that those procedures had resulted in greater economy and efficiency. However, improvements were needed in several areas to fully realize the cost savings and efficiency gains anticipated when the revised procedures were introduced.

OIOS made nine recommendations, including measures for enhancing the process of negotiat-

ing memorandums of understanding, improving DPKO's administrative arrangements for reimbursing troop contributors, strengthening procedures to reimburse Member States for equipment preparation and inland transport costs, and simplifying COE reporting procedures.

GENERAL ASSEMBLY ACTION

On 15 June [meeting 98], the General Assembly, on the recommendation of the Fifth Committee [A/54/684/Add.2], adopted **resolution 54/19 B** without vote [agenda item 151 (a)].

Reformed procedures for determining reimbursement to Member States for contingent-owned equipment

The General Assembly,

Recalling its resolutions 49/233 A of 23 December 1994, 50/222 of 11 April 1996, 51/218 E of 17 June 1997 and 54/19 A of 29 October 1999,

Recalling also its decision 53/480 of 8 June 1999, by which the Secretary-General was requested to convene the Phase V Working Group,

Recalling further the report of the Secretary-General and the related report of the Advisory Committee on Administrative and Budgetary Questions on the reform of the procedure for determining reimbursement to Member States for contingent-owned equipment,

Having considered the report of the Phase V Working Group on reform procedures for determining reimbursement of contingent-owned equipment, as transmitted by the Chairman of the Working Group to the Chairman of the Fifth Committee and the note by the Secretary-General and the related report of the Advisory Committee on the reform of the procedure for determining reimbursement to Member States for contingent-owned equipment,

Having considered also the report of the Office of Internal Oversight Services on the audit of contingent-owned equipment procedures and payments to troop-contributing countries,

1. *Endorses* the recommendations of the Phase V Working Group on reform procedures for determining reimbursement of contingent-owned equipment;

2. *Requests* the Secretary-General to collect the data from Member States referred to in the recommendations made by the Phase V Working Group in paragraphs 44 and 45 of its report concerning the cost of painting and repainting major equipment;

3. *Takes note* of the views of the Secretariat regarding replacement of the term "force-wide" with the term "force level", the inclusion of climatic and environmental changes under inland transportation costs, and the medical equipment threshold of 1,500 United States dollars, and invites the post–Phase V Working Group to reconsider these issues;

4. *Endorses* the recommendations of the Advisory Committee on Administrative and Budgetary Questions, subject to the provisions of the present resolution;

5. *Decides* to convene, for not less than ten working days, in accordance with annex IX to the report of the Phase V Working Group, a post–Phase V Working Group in January/February 2001, to review rates for major equipment, self-sustainment and medical support services, and to include, within the post–Phase V Working Group, appropriate expertise to conduct the

vaccination cost review recommended by the Phase V Working Group in paragraph 87 *(a)* (iii) of its report;

6. *Requests* the Secretary-General to ensure that adequate and sufficient conference facilities are provided for the post–Phase V Working Group, taking duly into consideration the structure and needs of the Working Group;

7. *Also requests* the Secretary-General to collect data from Member States and to report to the General Assembly on the extent of his success;

8. *Urges* Member States, in this regard, to provide the data pertaining to major equipment and self-sustainment to the Secretariat by 31 October 2000 at the latest, in order for the Secretariat to report to the General Assembly in November 2000 on the adequacy of the data, with a view to ascertaining whether the data are available for holding the meeting of the post–Phase V Working Group in January/February 2001;

9. *Emphasizes* that the Secretary-General should strictly ensure that in future, when the reports of the Office of Internal Oversight Services are transmitted, a reference to General Assembly resolution 54/244 of 23 December 1999 is included in addition to a reference to Assembly resolution 48/218 B of 29 July 1994, and issue a corrigendum to the current report;

10. *Decides* to keep this matter under review at its fifty-fifth session.

Responding to the Assembly's request to collect data pertaining to major equipment and self-sustainment from Member States, the Secretary-General, in a November note [A/55/650], reported that the Secretariat had received data from 30 troop contributors, which it considered sufficient for the post–Phase V Working Group to be able to conduct a further analysis. The Secretary-General recommended that the Assembly convene a post–Phase V Working Group meeting from 15 to 26 January 2001.

On 23 December, the Assembly, by **decision 55/452**, took note of the Secretary-General's note and decided to convene the post–Phase V meeting on the dates recommended.

Management of peacekeeping assets

Liquidation

The Secretary-General, in his report on the implementation of the recommendations of the Special Committee on Peacekeeping Operations [A/54/670], said that concerted efforts had been made to complete liquidation of missions closed prior to December 1997, and that that exercise was expected to be finalized in the current fiscal year (2000/01). As for missions closed after January 1998, procedures had been instituted to allow for the preparation of their liquidation well before termination of the mandates. As a result, it had been possible to conduct the liquidation of the United Nations Transitional Administration for Eastern Slavonia, Baranja and Western Sir-

mium (UNTAES) and the United Nations Preventive Deployment Force (UNPREDEP) within the initial liquidation time frame. The Secretariat would continue to pursue that approach in dealing with missions that were scheduled for liquidation so as to ensure that that was carried out in a timely manner.

The General Assembly, by **decision 54/462 B** of 15 June, deferred consideration of the OIOS report on the audit of the liquidation of peacekeeping missions [YUN 1999, p. 69].

Procurement and inventory

The General Assembly, by **resolution 54/257** of 7 April, took note of the 1998 OIOS report on the inquiry into allegations of insufficient use of expertise in procurement planning of aviation services in peacekeeping missions [YUN 1998, p. 59].

By **decision 54/462 B** of 15 June, the Assembly deferred to its fifty-fifth (2000) session consideration of the 1999 OIOS reports on the investigation into the award of a fresh-rations contract in a UN peacekeeping mission and on the audit of the management of service and ration contracts on peacekeeping missions [YUN 1999, p. 70].

ACABQ, in an April report [A/54/841], stressed the need for further information on the impact of the decentralization of procurement and of the increase in the threshold of procurement handled by field missions under delegated authority on the staffing and other resources at Headquarters. Resources released as a result of such decentralization could be used to increase further the capacity for procurement planning at Headquarters to reduce the lead time for mission needs. That and the issue of procurement levels and executing units at Headquarters, in the field and in regional areas, in terms of value and the number of procurement actions, should be examined. Reserve stock for peacekeeping missions, including alternative methods of maintaining standby arrangements, should be reviewed and the results reported to ACABQ in the next review of the 2001/02 budgets. An enhanced role for the Logistics Base in Brindisi to increase the capacity for procurement for peacekeeping operations and start-up of new or expanded peacekeeping missions needed to be examined. The efficiency of the procedure for recouping the costs for the work done at the Base should be reviewed and the full cost of those activities disclosed in the next budget presentations. ACABQ endorsed the view of the UN Board of Auditors that the cost-effectiveness of any proposed transfer of assets should be properly evaluated in all missions under liquidation.

With respect to the use of new technology in peacekeeping missions, ACABQ acknowledged the need to provide missions with additional capacity, such as data processing and communications. However, it cautioned against the tendency to automatically requisition state-of-the-art equipment in all cases. The current replacement cycles for various inventory items should be made more transparent and the reasons for replacement provided. Given the new surge in peacekeeping operations and the high inventory values involved, ACABQ reiterated that all stages of the field assets control system should be implemented within the shortest possible time, a progress report on the implementation of its initial stage should be submitted to the Assembly's fifty-fifth session and summary reports of inventory should be readily available.

Improving procurement in the field

In response to General Assembly resolution 54/17 A [YUN 1999, p. 117], the Secretary-General submitted a May report on measures taken to improve procurement activities in the field [A/54/866]. The report provided observations on the outcome of procurement audits in Angola [YUN 1998, p. 123 & YUN 1999, p. 117] and summarized ongoing efforts by the Administration to strengthen procurement activities in the field.

The Secretary-General said that the sharp increase in the number and complexity of peacekeeping operations in the early 1990s had caught the UN procurement system unprepared to meet the new challenges in terms of its organizational structure and human resources capacity. Also, the expansion of peacekeeping operations was accompanied by an increase in the complexity of mandates. Those factors, coupled with an outdated procurement system, contributed to the problems experienced in Angola. While the audits and investigations did not reveal any severe misconduct in the United Nations Angola Verification Mission (UNAVEM), the Secretariat recognized the importance of addressing procedural and systemic weaknesses to prevent any opportunity for misuse of UN resources. Therefore, much had been done to make the procurement system more responsive to the requirements of peacekeeping operations and to ensure transparency and accountability at all stages of the process. Among the measures implemented were the introduction of procurement planning on the basis of the annual budget cycle, the initiation of preparatory processes in advance of commitment authority, which enhanced procurement authority, and new arrangements governing contingent-owned equipment and self-sustainment, reducing the amount of direct support provided by the United Nations. A particularly effective measure was the introduction

of start-up kits for new missions as a first-line procurement support mechanism at the United Nations Logistics Base in Brindisi (see below). The Secretariat had also tried to consolidate most of its generic requirements under system contracts at Headquarters and in the field, resulting in reductions in procurement price and lead times, as well as the number of ex post facto cases submitted to the Committee on Contracts. In that context, the Secretariat was increasing the practice of sharing systems contracts with other UN agencies and programmes as part of the Secretary-General's common services initiative. The Secretariat was also designing a comprehensive procurement training programme targeting field procurement and contract administration personnel. Staff from the DPKO Field Administration and Logistics Division were more frequently deployed to missions at short notice during the start-up phase.

The General Assembly, by **decision 54/462 B** of 15 June, deferred consideration of the Secretary-General's report until its fifty-fifth session.

Property losses

ACABQ, in its April report [A/54/841], considered the Secretary-General's 1999 report on losses of UN property in peacekeeping operations [YUN 1999, p. 71]. It requested that the issue of the definition of loss due to negligence, in particular what constituted gross carelessness in the definition of negligence and the relationship between that definition and the threshold of gross negligence, be clarified in the next report. It said that further progress needed to be made in the methods of collecting, classifying and analysing the data presented in the report, including statistics on recovery and loss over the same time period. The causes of loss should also be analysed, with particular emphasis on the distinction between negligence and gross negligence.

The General Assembly, on 15 June, took note of the Secretary-General's report and concurred with ACABQ's observations and recommendations thereon (**decision 54/484**).

UN Logistics Base

In a January report [A/54/711], the Secretary-General submitted the financial performance report of the United Nations Logistics Base in Brindisi for the period 1 July 1998 to 30 June 1999. Expenditures for the period totalled $6,690,000, against approved cost estimates of $7,141,800, resulting in an unencumbered balance of $451,800. The Secretary-General recommended that that amount, as well as interest income of $114,000 and miscellaneous income of

$1,166,000 (a total of $1,731,800), be applied to the resources required for the period 1 July 2000 to 30 June 2001.

In February [A/54/733], the Secretary-General presented the proposed budget for the maintenance of the Base for the period 1 July 2000 to 30 June 2001 in the amount of $9,317,400 gross ($8,481,300 net), representing a 25 per cent increase in resources over the period 1 July 1999 to 30 June 2000. The increase reflected a 6 per cent increase in civilian personnel costs, a 24.1 per cent increase in operational costs and a 7.5 per cent increase under other programmes. The budget provided for a staffing establishment of 23 international and 83 local staff.

In relation to the financial performance report, ACABQ, in April [A/54/841/Add.8], recommended acceptance of the Secretary-General's proposal regarding the unencumbered balance. It welcomed the trend of procurement by the Base on behalf of other entities and recommended that the potential capacity for its wider use be explored. It requested that the related workload be monitored and appropriate reimbursement sought for those services. ACABQ recommended that the potential of the Base for use as a regional procurement centre be explored with the missions in the area. It was of the opinion that, regardless of the funding source, there was a need for more transparency regarding the total cost of the operation of the Base. It recommended that the efficiency of the procedure for accounting and settlement of the cost for work done at the Base be reviewed and that the full cost of those activities be disclosed in the next budget presentation.

ACABQ recommended approval of the proposed 2000/01 budget, including the staffing arrangements. It welcomed the proposed review of the Base's operations by DPKO in 2000-2001, the results of which and the changes proposed would be reflected in the next budget proposal.

In June [A/C.5/54/63], the Secretary-General submitted to the Fifth Committee a note on the amounts to be apportioned in respect of each peacekeeping mission, including the prorated share of the support account and of the Logistics Base.

GENERAL ASSEMBLY ACTION

On 15 June [meeting 98], the General Assembly, on the recommendation of the Fifth Committee [A/54/684/Add.2], adopted **resolution 54/278** without vote [agenda item 151 (a)].

Financing of the United Nations Logistics Base at Brindisi, Italy

The General Assembly,

Recalling section XIV of its resolution 49/233 A of 23 December 1994,

Recalling also its decision 50/500 of 17 September 1996 on the financing of the United Nations Logistics Base at Brindisi, Italy, and its subsequent resolutions thereon, the latest of which was resolution 53/236 of 8 June 1999,

Having considered the reports of the Secretary-General on the financing of the Logistics Base and the related reports of the Advisory Committee on Administrative and Budgetary Questions,

Reiterating the importance of establishing an accurate inventory of assets,

1. *Takes note* of the reports of the Secretary-General on the financing of the United Nations Logistics Base at Brindisi, Italy;

2. *Endorses* the observations and recommendations contained in the report of the Advisory Committee on Administrative and Budgetary Questions;

3. *Welcomes,* in this regard, the recent positive developments in the utilization of the Logistics Base, especially the contribution of crucial logistical support to the launching of large new missions;

4. *Reiterates* the need to implement, as a matter of priority, an effective inventory management standard, especially in respect of peacekeeping operations involving high inventory value;

5. *Welcomes* the intention of the Secretary-General to review the concept of the operations of the Logistics Base, and requests him, as part of that review, to consider fully the observations and recommendations of the Advisory Committee and report thereon to the General Assembly as soon as possible during its fifty-fifth session;

6. *Approves* the cost estimates for the Logistics Base amounting to 9,317,400 United States dollars gross (8,481,300 dollars net) for the period from 1 July 2000 to 30 June 2001;

7. *Decides* to apply the unencumbered balance of 451,800 dollars in respect of the period from 1 July 1998 to 30 June 1999, the interest income of 114,000 dollars and miscellaneous income of 1,166,000 dollars (1,731,800 dollars in total) to the resources required for the period from 1 July 2000 to 30 June 2001;

8. *Decides also* to prorate the balance of 7,585,600 dollars gross (6,479,500 dollars net) among the individual active peacekeeping operation budgets to meet the financing requirements of the Logistics Base for the period from 1 July 2000 to 30 June 2001;

9. *Authorizes* the Secretary-General to provide for a civilian establishment consisting of ten Professional, thirteen Field Service and eighty-three locally recruited staff;

10. *Decides* to consider during its fifty-fifth session the question of the financing of the United Nations Logistics Base at Brindisi.

In December [A/55/714], the Secretary-General presented the financial performance report for the Base for the period 1 July 1999 to 30 June 2000, which showed expenditures totalling $7,026,000, resulting in an unencumbered balance of $430,500. The Secretary-General requested that that amount, as well as interest income of $289,000 and miscellaneous income of $340,000 ($1,059,500 in total), be applied to resources for 1 July 2001 to 30 June 2002.

Personnel matters

Death and disability benefits

In January [A/C.5/54/47], the Secretary-General submitted his tenth quarterly report showing that, of the original backlog of 564 death and disability claims awaiting processing as at 19 May 1997, only 19 remained (9 for Austria, 9 for Bangladesh and 1 for the Russian Federation), most of which had already been certified for settlement. In the circumstances, the Secretary-General recommended that the tenth quarterly report be the last such report to be submitted.

ACABQ, in March [A/54/782], said that, while there was no need to continue reporting on the backlog of cases, annual reports should be submitted. ACABQ was of the opinion that the information provided should be more complete and recommended that information on incidents should distinguish between accidents, injuries and deaths, and include the total number of claims, those being processed and the number settled, as well as the dollar amounts involved. Some assessment could be given regarding which incidents were likely to lead to claims.

The General Assembly, by **decision 54/459 B** of 7 April, took note of the Secretary-General's report and the related report of ACABQ. It concurred with ACABQ's observations and recommendations and decided that annual reports should be submitted on the status of all death and disability claims, commencing with the period ending 31 December 2000.

Other peacekeeping matters

Cooperation with regional arrangements

The Special Committee on Peacekeeping Operations [A/54/839] urged the strengthening of cooperation between the United Nations and relevant regional arrangements and agencies to enhance the capabilities of the international community in the maintenance of international peace and security. It encouraged the Secretary-General to take steps towards that end, but recognized that such cooperation posed considerable challenges. The Special Committee recommended that the Secretary-General elaborate in his next progress report on how those challenges could best be tackled. It was of the view that efforts to enhance the capacity of African countries in various aspects of peacekeeping were complementary to the obligations of Member States under the Charter and were not intended to replace or reduce engagement of non-African countries in peacekeeping operations in the continent. International efforts to strengthen the collective capacity of African countries to participate in peacekeeping operations should focus on enhancing the institutional capacity of the Organization of African Unity (OAU) and, in particular, its Mechanism for Conflict Prevention, Management and Resolution, through the provision of financial and technical assistance. In that connection, the Special Committee urged Member States to contribute to the OAU Peace Fund. It also encouraged partnerships between States and with OAU and subregional organizations in training, logistics, equipment and financial support. The United Nations should play an active role, especially in coordinating those efforts. Member States were urged to contribute to the Trust Fund established by the Secretary-General for that purpose and to provide financial and other support to the current study of peacekeeping operations conducted by African subregional organizations. The Special Committee looked forward to the establishment of a group on the enhancement of African peacekeeping capacity and urged the Secretariat to continue its consultations on the terms of reference of the group with a view to establishing it in a timely manner. It urged, in accordance with General Assembly resolution 54/94 [YUN 1999, p. 191], that discussion on the exchange of staff between the United Nations and OAU secretariats be concluded at the earliest opportunity. The Special Committee welcomed Secretariat efforts in subregional peacekeeping training and seminars conducted with the Southern African Development Community and the Economic Community of West African States, and encouraged the Secretariat to extend those efforts to all other African subregional organizations.

Chapter II

Africa

Armed conflict and political discord continued to trouble a number of African countries in 2000, most seriously in the Democratic Republic of the Congo (DRC), Eritrea, Ethiopia and Sierra Leone. Africa's political and security challenges were complicated by the pervasive problems of economic stagnation and the rapid spread of HIV/AIDS, both of which had consequences for peace in the continent.

In 2000, the Security Council and the General Assembly considered ways to implement the Secretary-General's 1998 recommendations on the causes of conflict and the promotion of durable peace and sustainable development in Africa. A working group established by the Assembly reported in July on those recommendations, covering areas such as conflict prevention and maintenance of peace, and strengthening peacekeeping capabilities. The Council, under the presidency of the United States, devoted the month of January to discussing the problems of Africa.

The war in the DRC continued to dominate events in the Great Lakes region where the situation remained unstable and the conflict continued between the DRC Government, supported by Angola, Namibia and Zimbabwe, and various rebel groups, loosely allied with the neighbouring countries of Burundi, Rwanda and Uganda. Among other diplomatic efforts to seek a solution, a Security Council mission visited the country in mid-May when a ceasefire was briefly in effect. However, the situation deteriorated rapidly in June with heavy fighting in and around the city of Kisangani, and the DRC forces encountered opposition there from the armies of Burundi, Rwanda and Uganda as well as from armed groups. By the end of the year, the situation had improved; Rwandan and Ugandan troops withdrew from Kisangani and the fighting diminished and shifted to other parts of the country.

In Burundi, efforts to end the ethnic conflict were spearheaded by the Facilitator of that process, former President Nelson Mandela of South Africa. The Arusha Agreement on Peace and Reconciliation, a framework for political reform, was signed by 19 political parties, but some of the main combatant rebel forces were not parties to it. By the end of the year, armed groups continued to carry out attacks against government forces and civilians. Burundi accused certain neighbouring countries of supporting the rebel groups.

In contrast to other Great Lakes countries, the security situation in Rwanda improved and the Government began laying the foundation for the transition to democracy. Steps were made to draw up a new constitution, overhaul the justice system and promote the observance of human rights. In April, the Security Council considered the 1999 report of the Independent Inquiry it had commissioned to evaluate the UN role during the 1994 genocide in Rwanda.

The situation in Sierra Leone reached a new crisis point in May and June when rebel groups detained hundreds of peacekeepers of the United Nations Mission in Sierra Leone (UNAMSIL) and seized their weapons. By the end of July, most of the UN troops had either been rescued during UN operations or released by their captors, but nine UN peacekeepers were reported killed and others were missing. Despite those developments, UNAMSIL continued its efforts to bring peace to the country under the terms of the 1999 Lomé Peace Agreement, signed by the Government and the main opposition force. Following the attacks on UN personnel, the Security Council increased the size of the Mission from 6,000 to 13,000 peacekeepers and expanded its mandate. The Council also took action to restrict the capacity of rebel groups to wage war by prohibiting the importation of rough diamonds from Sierra Leone without official certification of their origin and by strengthening the arms embargo against those groups. The Council was also considering a proposal to establish a special court in order to bring to justice those responsible for serious crimes and atrocities against the people of Sierra Leone and UNAMSIL peacekeepers. UNAMSIL and the Economic Community of West African States (ECOWAS) continued their efforts to mediate with the parties. On 10 November, the Government and the main rebel group reached a ceasefire agreement, agreeing that UNAMSIL would supervise and monitor the ceasefire. Opposition forces displayed reluctance to fulfil their commitments under the new agreement; however, the situation was relatively calm, but tense, at the end of the year.

The instability in Sierra Leone and the activities of rebel groups there affected other countries in West Africa. In December, the Council condemned recent incursions into Guinea by rebel groups from Liberia and Sierra Leone along the length of Guinea's border. ECOWAS was also active in efforts to consolidate peace in the subregion, participating in the summit meeting of Guinea, Liberia and Sierra Leone that dealt with shared political, security and socio-economic concerns. In December, the three countries agreed that an ECOWAS interposition force be sent to the border areas.

In Liberia, where the internal situation remained fragile, the United Nations Peacebuilding Support Office in Liberia (UNOL) continued to work towards the consolidation of peace and democracy in cooperation with the Government and ECOWAS. The Secretary-General reported that, despite the transition from civil conflict to an elected Government in 1997, Liberia was beset with governance problems and inadequate external support for its reconstruction programme.

Guinea-Bissau was also in the early stages of a new, democratically elected Government. In January, it held the second and final round of presidential elections in accordance with the 1998 Abuja Peace Accord that ended the civil conflict there. The military establishment continued to interfere in the establishment of democratic institutions and, in November, led an attempted coup d'état. By the end of the year, the situation was relatively calm, but tense.

Angola continued to be one of the most unstable countries in Africa in 2000. Implementation of the 1994 Lusaka Protocol, by which the Government and the opposition guerrilla group agreed to the extension of the State administration, remained at a standstill. In April, the Security Council reiterated that the primary cause of the crisis was the refusal of the National Union for the Total Independence of Angola (UNITA) to comply with the Lusaka Protocol. The Government continued its offensive against the UNITA guerrilla forces and was able to re-establish its authority in several UNITA strongholds. Military operations in southern and south-eastern border areas spilled into neighbouring Namibia and Zambia, where bombing and shelling incidents were reported and refugee flows occurred. The Expert Panel established by the Security Council in 1999 to investigate sanctions against UNITA determined that the sanctions were ineffective. Angola approved the status of the United Nations Office in Angola (UNOA), which had replaced the United Nations Observer Mission in Angola (MONUA) in 1999, and agreed that the Office should aim to build the country's capacity in humanitarian assistance and human rights.

The border war between Eritrea and Ethiopia intensified in May despite the fact that both parties had agreed to abide by the terms of the Framework Agreement drawn up by the Organization of African Unity (OAU) in 1998. Under OAU auspices, the two Governments resumed proximity talks and signed a ceasefire agreement on 18 June. By its terms, they agreed to seek a UN peacekeeping mission under OAU auspices, to redeploy troops to their positions before the war, and to establish a temporary security zone between the two sides. To monitor that plan, the Security Council decided on 31 July to establish the United Nations Mission in Ethiopia and Eritrea (UNMEE) with a deployment of up to 4,200 personnel. The ceasefire agreement was followed by the signing of a Peace Agreement in December.

In Somalia, new steps were made in the peace process under the proposals suggested by the President of Djibouti. Preparatory meetings organized by Djibouti in early 2000 brought together representatives of most of Somalia's numerous clans, and during the year agreement was reached on a Transitional National Charter, the election of a Transitional National Assembly and the election of a president to head the transitional Government. Following his inauguration, the President made efforts to bring Somaliland and Puntland, two factions that had boycotted the peace conference, into the peace process. In June, the Security Council urged representatives of all forces in Somalia to participate in the peace process. By the end of the year, the new transitional Government had only limited control of the country and banditry and lawlessness prevailed.

Following the establishment of a new democratically elected Government in the Central African Republic in 1999, the United Nations withdrew its mission from that country in February 2000 and replaced it with the United Nations Peace-building Support Office (BONUCA). The situation in 2000 was dominated by the confrontational approach between the ruling party and the numerous opposition parties.

The United Nations pursued its goal of holding a referendum in Western Sahara for the self-determination of its people, as agreed in 1990 by Morocco and the Frente Popular para la Liberación de Saguia el-Hamra y de Río de Oro (POLISARIO), but progress remained elusive. Direct meetings between Morocco and POLISARIO in May, July and September, organized by the Secretary-General's Personal Envoy, failed to make progress on the main issues. The Secretary-General concluded that further meetings of the parties to seek a political solution could not succeed unless Morocco, as administrative Power, was prepared to support some genuine devolution of governmental authority for all inhabitants and former inhabitants of the Territory.

A number of regional organizations sought to lift the Security Council sanctions against the Libyan Arab Jamahiriya, which were suspended in 1999 but not completely removed. It was argued that removal was called for since the two Libyan suspects charged with the 1988 bombing of Pan Am flight 103 over Lockerbie, Scotland, were currently being tried by a Scottish court sitting in the Netherlands.

Promotion of peace in Africa

During 2000, the General Assembly and the Security Council continued to consider ways to implement the recommendations made by the Secretary-General in his 1998 report on the causes of conflict and the promotion of durable peace and sustainable development in Africa [YUN 1998, p. 66]. In that report, the Secretary-General had highlighted three areas to which Africa should devote particular attention: it should demonstrate the political will to rely on political rather than military responses to problems; it should take good governance seriously; and it should meet and adhere to reforms needed to promote economic growth. In addition, the international community should summon the political will to intervene where it could have an impact and invest where resources were needed, the Secretary-General had stated.

In order to follow up on the Secretary-General's recommendations, the General Assembly had established an open-ended working group, which issued its report in July 2000. Covering such areas as conflict prevention and maintenance of peace, refugees, strengthening peacekeeping capacities and arms sanctions, the report outlined where progress had been made and areas where obstacles remained. It also made proposals for further action and called for continued monitoring. In December, the Assembly endorsed those proposals, and extended the mandate of the working group for a year so that it could continue to monitor progress in implementing the Secretary-General's recommendations.

The United States, as President of the Security Council, declared January 2000 the "month of Africa". The Council discussed African issues at six open Council meetings and in four informal consultations. Particular attention was paid to

AIDS (see p. 81) and the situation of refugees and internally displaced persons (see p. 1154).

Report of Working Group. The Open-ended Ad Hoc Working Group on the Causes of Conflict and the Promotion of Durable Peace and Sustainable Development in Africa, established by the General Assembly in resolution 53/92 [YUN 1998, p. 77] to monitor the Secretary-General's recommendations, issued a report in July [A/55/45] covering progress made in implementing the recommendations, obstacles encountered and modalities for further action. The Working Group held three sessions during the year (7 and 13-15 March, 15-19 May and 17-21 July), as well as a number of informal meetings.

In the area of peacemaking and peacekeeping, the Working Group noted that progress made was described in a report submitted by the Secretary-General to the Security Council in September 1999 [YUN 1999, p. 78]. Peacemaking activities included such measures as the Secretary-General's appointment of special envoys and representatives to help resolve conflicts in a number of countries and coordinating mediation efforts with other organizations involved in the process. Progress had also been made in post-conflict peace-building to promote the transition from relief to development, financing recovery, coordinating political, human rights, humanitarian and development activities, promotion of human rights, elimination of discrimination against women, social development, food security, debt relief and opening international markets.

However, the Working Group identified a number of obstacles that remained, including insufficient political will on the part of some African countries and the international community, inadequate financial resources and human resource capacity, deficiencies in governance in some African countries, the persistence of armed conflict, limited access to technology, poor public health and the major threat of HIV/AIDS, a weak private sector and economic structure and coordination difficulties. The Working Group presented a list of modalities for further action, at both the national and international levels, towards further implementation, and stated that there was a need for regular monitoring in order to ensure effective implementation. It made specific proposals in the areas of poverty eradication, debt relief, financing for development, HIV/AIDS and malaria, conflict prevention and post-conflict peace-building, refugees and internally displaced persons, coordination and follow-up.

With regard to finding solutions to the ongoing armed conflicts in Africa, the Working

Group welcomed the efforts of the Organization of African Unity (OAU) to strengthen its mechanism for conflict prevention and resolution and to promote peace and stability, while emphasizing that further efforts were needed to prevent violent conflicts at their earliest stages. It recognized the need to strengthen the early warning capacity of the United Nations, OAU and African subregional organizations to respond to conflict situations. The Group also supported the Conference on Security, Stability, Development and Cooperation in Africa process initiated by Africa and called on the Secretary-General to explore ways to provide support to that initiative. It proposed that the Economic and Social Council create an ad hoc advisory group on countries emerging from conflict, with a view to assessing their economic needs and elaborating a long-term programme of support beginning with the integration of relief into development. It further proposed that greater financial support be given for demobilization, demilitarization and reintegration programmes, with funding provided through peacekeeping operations' budgets as a solution to the shortfall in resources. Postconflict peace-building should include assisting the reintegration of demobilized soldiers and other war-affected groups, including child soldiers.

The Working Group recommended that the Secretary-General, in consultation with the President of the World Bank, strengthen coordination mechanisms, including the United Nations Development Assistance Framework, the United Nations System-wide Special Initiative on Africa and the Comprehensive Development Framework of the World Bank, with a view to streamlining them and creating complementarity and synergy.

The Working Group emphasized that the General Assembly had primary responsibility for monitoring progress in implementing the Secretary-General's recommendations, with due regard being given to the competences of the other main UN organs. The review had revealed a need for continued monitoring in all areas included in the Secretary-General's report. It therefore proposed: that its mandate be extended; that applicable benchmarks be developed to assess impact and measure performance; and that thematic working groups be established to make specific proposals on issues that had not yet been covered in the Working Group's sessions.

In a September note [A/55/431], the Secretary-General informed the Assembly that the Secretariat had provided assistance and information to

the Working Group for the preparation of its report. In view of that, he did not see the need to submit another report to the Assembly on the same subject.

Security Council consideration. The United States, as President of the Security Council, declared January the "month of Africa". The Council discussed African issues at six open meetings, some of which were attended by heads of State, and four informal consultations. Two presidential statements were issued, one on the situation of refugees in Africa (**S/PRST/2000/1**), in which the Council underlined the importance of taking measures aimed at conflict prevention and resolution in Africa in order to avoid circumstances that led to internal displacement and the outflow of refugees (see p. 1154), and the other on support for the peace agreement in the Democratic Republic of the Congo (**S/PRST/2000/2**) (see p. 121). A resolution on support for the Burundi peace process was also adopted (**resolution 1286(2000)**) (see p. 144). Also in January, the Council held an open debate to discuss the devastating impact of AIDS in Africa and its consequences for regional peace and security (see p. 81), Angola (see p. 149) and Sierra Leone (see p. 189).

On 4 August [S/2000/772], the Council decided to meet on 7 September, during the Millennium Summit, at the level of heads of State and Government, to consider the topic "Ensuring an effective role of the Security Council in the maintenance of international peace and security, particularly in Africa". At the 7 September meeting [S/PV.4194], the Council adopted **resolution 1318(2000)** on the topic (see p. 64).

Adviser for Special Assignments. On 7 November [S/2000/1082], the Secretary-General informed the Security Council of his decision to extend the appointment of Ibrahim Gambari as his Adviser for Special Assignments in Africa until 28 February 2002. Mr. Gambari had pursued the peaceful resolution of conflicts in Africa with particular attention to Angola (see p. 149). The Council took note of the decision on 10 November [S/2000/1083].

GENERAL ASSEMBLY ACTION

On 21 December [meeting 88], the General Assembly adopted **resolution 55/217** [draft: A/55/L.37/Rev.1 & Corr.1 & Add.1] without vote [agenda item 50].

Causes of conflict and the promotion of durable peace and sustainable development in Africa

The General Assembly,

Recalling its resolutions 53/92 of 7 December 1998 and 54/234 of 22 December 1999 on the causes of conflict and the promotion of durable peace and sustainable development in Africa,

Having considered the report of the Open-ended Ad Hoc Working Group on the Causes of Conflict and the Promotion of Durable Peace and Sustainable Development in Africa, as well as the note by the Secretary-General on the implementation of resolution 54/234,

Recalling its resolution 46/151 of 18 December 1991, the annex to which contains the United Nations New Agenda for the Development of Africa in the 1990s, its resolutions 48/214 of 23 December 1993, 49/142 of 23 December 1994 and 51/32 of 6 December 1996, on the mid-term review of the New Agenda, as well as its resolution 53/90 of 7 December 1998 on the implementation of the New Agenda, as well as chapter VII of the United Nations Millennium Declaration,

Reaffirming the close linkage between peace, security and sustainable development and the need for a comprehensive implementation of the recommendations contained in the report of the Secretary-General,

Expressing deep concern about the obstacles to the effective implementation of the recommendations of the Secretary-General, including the lack of financial and technical resources for development in Africa,

Emphasizing the need to strengthen further the political will that is indispensable for the successful implementation of the recommendations of the Secretary-General and the proposals of the Working Group,

1. *Takes note with appreciation* of the report of the Open-ended Ad Hoc Working Group on the Causes of Conflict and the Promotion of Durable Peace and Sustainable Development in Africa;

2. *Endorses* the proposals of the Working Group contained in paragraphs 25 to 57 of chapter IV of its report, entitled "Modalities for further action", and the follow-up action proposed in paragraph 60 of the report;

3. *Encourages* Member States, the organizations of the United Nations system and other relevant international and regional institutions, within their respective mandates, to take necessary measures to implement fully the proposals made by the Working Group in its report;

4. *Decides* to extend the mandate of the Working Group until the fifty-sixth session of the General Assembly, to enable it to continue to monitor the implementation of all of the recommendations made by the Secretary-General in his report;

5. *Requests* the Working Group, in devising the modalities for its work, to consider the need for a comprehensive follow-up to the recommendations of the Secretary-General and the necessity of ensuring efficiency by focusing on selected thematic areas;

6. *Invites* the Security Council to pursue its consideration of the follow-up to the recommendations in the areas of peace and security, with a view to ensuring coordinated and integrated implementation of the recommendations contained in the report of the Secretary-General;

7. *Requests* the Economic and Social Council, at its substantive session of 2001, to consider the proposals of the Working Group contained in chapter IV of its report, including the creation of an ad hoc advisory group on countries emerging from conflict, with a view to assessing their humanitarian and economic needs and elaborating a long-term programme of support for

implementation that begins with the integration of relief into development;

8. *Requests* that, where applicable, benchmarks be developed by the Secretary-General to assess the impact of and measure performance in the implementation of the recommendations contained in his report and that he submit them to the Working Group for its consideration;

9. *Requests* the Working Group to submit a report to the General Assembly at its fifty-sixth session;

10. *Requests* the Secretary-General to submit to the General Assembly at its fifty-sixth session a progress report on the implementation of the recommendations contained in his report.

In other action related to the maintenance of peace in Africa, the Assembly, in **resolution 55/56**, called on States to implement Security Council measures aimed at breaking the link between the illicit trade in rough diamonds and the supply to rebel movements of weapons, fuel or other prohibited materiel (see p. 77). In **resolution 55/77**, the Assembly expressed its particular concern about the impact of large-scale refugee populations on the security, socio-economic situation and environment of African countries of asylum (see p. 1158).

By **decision 55/458** of 23 December, the Assembly decided that the agenda item on causes of conflict and the promotion of durable peace and sustainable development in Africa would remain for consideration during its resumed fifty-fifth (2001) session.

Great Lakes region

In the Great Lakes region of Africa, the situation remained tense and unpredictable in 2000, particularly in the Democratic Republic of the Congo (DRC), where the conflict showed no sign of ending, despite the efforts of both the United Nations and OAU. Fighting in the DRC, which had been engulfed in war since the beginning of the armed rebellion in August 1998, had resulted in the death of hundreds of civilians and caused massive harm to an already fragile economy. Insecurity and the lack of serious commitment to the peace process by the various warring parties and their supporters from several neighbouring countries continued to hamper the full deployment of UN peacekeepers and military observers.

Optimism was generated by efforts to implement the 1999 Lusaka Ceasefire Agreement on the DRC [YUN 1999, p. 87] and to pursue the Arusha peace process on Burundi, but that gave way later to caution and some scepticism. The breakdown of mediation efforts in the DRC further reduced the likelihood of a constructive dialogue between the Government and the warring factions. In Burundi, despite some progress to achieve a settlement, concrete results remained elusive. The situation in Rwanda was marked by increasing tension, particularly in the north-west of the country.

Communications. The Secretary-General, on 21 September [S/2000/907], informed the Security Council of his intention to extend until the end of December 2001 the mandate of his Special Representative for the Great Lakes Region, Berhanu Dinka, whom he had appointed in December 1999 [YUN 1999, p. 81]. In that capacity, Mr. Dinka had been sounding out the views of countries in the region regarding the proposed organization of an international conference on the Great Lakes; representing the Secretary-General at meetings under the Arusha peace process on Burundi; and addressing the regional dimensions of the conflict in the DRC through, among other steps, close interaction with his Special Representative in that country. With respect to Burundi (see p. 143), the signing of the Arusha peace agreement on 28 August 2000 had created a momentum towards a comprehensive agreement to which all parties subscribed. It was therefore desirable for Mr. Dinka to stay engaged in the efforts to address the political and humanitarian situation in Burundi and its regional dimensions. On 26 September [S/2000/908], the Council took note of the Secretary-General's intention.

Uganda, on 26 January, transmitted to the Council a document by President Yoweri Kaguta Museveni, which described the historical background to the conflicts in the Great Lakes region [S/2000/73].

On 13 December [S/2000/1186], Rwanda requested the Council to support Zambia in disarming and repatriating the ex-Rwandese Armed Forces and Interahamwe forces currently on Zambian territory who had fled the DRC after having provoked fighting there. Rwanda's main concern was that, if allowed to return to the DRC, they would fuel more war in the region.

Democratic Republic of the Congo

In 2000, the United Nations continued its efforts to support the implementation of the 1999 Lusaka Ceasefire Agreement, which was signed by the Government of the DRC, one of the two main rebel movements and five regional States. The Agreement provided for a ceasefire to be monitored by the United Nations Organization Mission in the Democratic Republic of the Congo (MONUC), OAU and Zambia; withdrawal of foreign forces from the country; and re-establishment of State administration throughout the country. Although some progress was made in implementation, such as the positioning of UN military liaison officers in the DRC and agreement on a disengagement plan, obstacles encountered included lack of cooperation on the part of the DRC Government and other parties to facilitate deployment of MONUC, continued fighting between the parties, especially in eastern DRC, and the DRC's refusal to meet with the neutral Facilitator appointed by the Secretary-General

Throughout the year, the DRC remained in the throes of a crisis that continued to elude attempts to solve it. Since 1998 the country had been the scene of a conflict involving seven neighbouring countries and numerous rebel groups that threatened to destabilize the Central African region and exacerbated the already dire socio-economic and political situation of the country. The protagonists in the war were the country's neighbours to the east—Burundi, Rwanda and Uganda—in a loose alliance with various rebel factions, and the DRC Government, supported, at its request, by Angola, Namibia and Zimbabwe, member countries of the Southern African Development Community. A number of diplomatic missions were undertaken to the DRC during the year to try to maintain momentum for peace, but they made little headway. They included a Security Council mission in mid-May, which reported that the ceasefire was holding at that time. However, the agreements were subsequently subjected to many major breaches caused by fighting between government forces and rebels, as well as forces from neighbouring countries.

Some of the heaviest fighting occurred in and around the city of Kisangani in June, when clashes took place between Ugandan and Rwandan troops and their affiliated rebel groups. The conflict between the Government and the Rassemblement congolais pour la démocratie (RCD) flared up in August, when the DRC encountered opposition from the armies of Burundi, Rwanda, Uganda and RCD-Goma and other armed groups. For its part, the Government relied on counter-rebel militias for its defence. The DRC complained that the Burundian and Rwandan armies, as well as RCD, had carried out attacks on the civilian population. By the end of the year, Rwandan and Ugandan troops had withdrawn from Kisangani to a distance of 100 kilometres from the city, although rebel groups remained there. The scene of the fighting shifted at that time to other areas of the country in the north, south and east.

The Security Council responded to the crisis in February by authorizing the expansion of MONUC from a force of 90 to over 5,500 military personnel, with a mandate to facilitate the implementation of the Agreement and liaise with the parties' forces. However, largely due to the lack of cooperation on the part of the parties, particularly the Government, further deployment of troops remained blocked and by the end of the year the strength of the Mission remained at just over 200.

The Secretary-General's Special Representative for the DRC, Kamel Morjane (Tunisia), was based in Kinshasa throughout the year.

Implementation of Lusaka Peace Agreement

Report of Secretary-General (January). The Secretary-General reported on 17 January [S/2000/30] on MONUC, as requested by the Security Council in resolution 1279(1999) [YUN 1999, p. 92]. MONUC, which comprised UN military liaison personnel, together with civilian, political, humanitarian and administrative staff, was established by the Council under resolution 1258(1999) [ibid., p. 89] to assist in developing modalities for implementing the Lusaka Ceasefire Agreement [ibid., p. 87]. By the Agreement, a Joint Military Commission (JMC) was established which, together with the United Nations and OAU, would be responsible for executing peacekeeping operations until the deployment of the UN peacekeeping force. In late 1999, JMC began work on a number of issues [ibid., p. 93], including the question of the stationing of UN liaison officers in the DRC.

The military and security situation in the DRC deteriorated in late 1999 [ibid., p. 94] and early 2000, with fighting reported between government troops and rebel forces in several areas and alleged atrocities against women and children.

The Secretary-General stated that MONUC, in its preliminary deployment in the DRC, was able to position officers at eight locations (Gbadolite, Goma, Kananga, Kindu, Gemena, Isiro, Lisala and Boende), although it continued to encounter difficulties in positioning military liaison officers at the rear military headquarters of the belligerents and other key locations. At the time of the report, 79 UN military liaison officers were deployed in the DRC and in the capitals of the belligerent parties and elsewhere in the subregion. MONUC was prepared to deploy additional military officers to assist JMC to assume its tasks under the Lusaka Agreement.

Implementation of the Lusaka Agreement required close cooperation between the United Nations, the parties to the conflict, JMC and OAU, said the Secretary-General. The United Nations,

at Headquarters and through MONUC, continued to develop that cooperation through such efforts as deploying two military liaison officers at Addis Ababa, Ethiopia, to improve links with OAU, providing training to OAU observers deployed by JMC and providing assistance for JMC deployment. While progress had been made in implementing the Agreement, some setbacks had been registered, particularly the fighting in some parts of the country and obstacles and delays encountered in receiving the necessary clearances to position personnel, thus prohibiting MONUC from performing all its tasks.

The Secretary-General was of the view that the deployment of additional UN military personnel would contribute to restoring momentum for the implementation of the Agreement. The signatories bore a crucial responsibility for ensuring implementation. In that context, no military offensives should be launched, the security and freedom of movement of UN personnel should be guaranteed, and the spreading of hostile propaganda, especially incitements to attack unarmed civilians, should cease.

In view of its essential role, JMC needed to be established on a permanent basis and be able to react swiftly to events. The inter-Congolese dialogue to be conducted under the auspices of the neutral Facilitator, Sir Ketumile Masire, former President of Botswana, with OAU assistance, was an indispensable step towards national reconciliation.

Subject to the parties' agreement to taking those steps, the Secretary-General recommended the expansion of MONUC to 3,400 troops, as follows: deployment of four reinforced protected infantry battalion groups, accompanied by up to 500 military observers; two marine companies (for river patrol) with supporting military personnel and equipment; and the additional civilian personnel required. Its main tasks would be: to liaise with all the parties' military forces and with JMC; to assist the parties in developing modalities for implementing the Agreement; to monitor the ceasefire; in cooperation with JMC, to investigate violations of the ceasefire; and to verify the disengagement of forces. Other tasks would include facilitating the release of prisoners of war and humanitarian operations, supervising the redeployment of the parties' forces to defensive positions or administrative assembly areas and preparing for the next phase of UN deployment. Until the full deployment of a UN force, the role of JMC remained crucial and the Secretary-General appealed to donors to provide it with the resources to support its operations.

SADC summit (January)

The Southern African Development Community (SADC) held an extraordinary summit meeting in Maputo, Mozambique, on 16 January, at the invitation of President Joaquim Alberto Chissano in his capacity as Chairman of SADC. The objective of the summit, as stated in the final communiqué transmitted to the Security Council on 18 January [S/2000/36], was to evaluate the degree of implementation of the Lusaka Ceasefire Agreement and to review the work of the commissions set up by the Agreement on the modalities and mechanisms of implementation, with a view to the adoption of appropriate measures for the rapid normalization of the DRC situation.

While applauding the appointment of Sir Ketumile Masire by the Congolese parties as the Facilitator of the national dialogue between the political forces in the DRC, the summit noted with concern the lack of progress in implementing the Agreement. The summit urged the signatories to cooperate more actively in the implementation and called on the Security Council to send urgently a full peacekeeping force to the DRC and to provide the logistical means for its operation. It also appealed to the international community to provide humanitarian assistance to refugees and displaced populations and to provide resources for national reconstruction.

SECURITY COUNCIL ACTION (January)

On 24 and 26 January [meeting 4092], the Security Council discussed the situation in the DRC. The meeting, at which the United States Secretary of State presided, was attended by the heads of State of Angola, the DRC, Mozambique, Rwanda, Uganda, Zambia and Zimbabwe and at the ministerial level by Belgium, Burundi, Canada, France, Mali, Namibia, South Africa and the United Kingdom. The OAU Secretary-General and the Facilitator of the inter-Congolese dialogue also addressed the Council.

On 26 January, the Council President made statement **S/PRST/2000/2** on behalf of the members:

> The Security Council expresses its appreciation to the heads of State of Angola, the Democratic Republic of the Congo, Mozambique, Rwanda, Uganda, Zambia and Zimbabwe, and to the Ministers for Foreign Affairs of Burundi, Canada, Namibia, South Africa and the United States of America, the Vice-Prime Minister and Minister for Foreign Affairs of Belgium, the Minister Delegate for Cooperation and Francophonie of France, the Minister of State for Foreign and Commonwealth Affairs of the United Kingdom of Great Britain and Northern Ireland and the Minister of the Armed Forces of Mali, who participated in its meeting of 24 January 2000 on the situation in the Democratic Republic of the Congo. The Council also expresses its appreciation to the Secretary-General of the Organization of African Unity, the representative of the current Chairman of the Assembly of Heads of State and Government of the Organization of African Unity, and the Facilitator of the Inter-Congolese Dialogue nominated by the Organization of African Unity. Their presence and their statements attest to their renewed commitment to the Ceasefire Agreement signed at Lusaka on 10 July 1999 and to the search for a durable peace in the Democratic Republic of the Congo and the region. Their presence in New York also reinforces the progress made at the summit of the Southern African Development Community, held in Maputo on 16 January 2000, and the meeting of the Political Committee for the implementation of the Lusaka Ceasefire Agreement, held in Harare on 18 January 2000. The Council expects that this progress will continue at the next Political Committee meeting and summit of the signatories to the Agreement.

> The Council urges all the parties to the Ceasefire Agreement to build on the momentum of those meetings in order to create and sustain the climate necessary for the full implementation of the Agreement. It underlines the importance of a revised implementation calendar for the full and effective implementation of the tasks set forth in the Agreement.

> The Council reaffirms the territorial integrity and national sovereignty of the Democratic Republic of the Congo, including over its natural resources, in accordance with the principles of the Charter of the United Nations and the Charter of the Organization of African Unity. In this regard, it reiterates its call for the immediate cessation of hostilities and the orderly withdrawal of all foreign forces from the territory of the Democratic Republic of the Congo, in accordance with the Ceasefire Agreement. The Council reaffirms its support for the Agreement, and also reaffirms its resolutions 1234(1999) of 9 April 1999, 1258(1999) of 6 August 1999, 1273 (1999) of 5 November 1999 and 1279(1999) of 30 November 1999.

> The Council welcomes the report of the Secretary-General of 17 January 2000. The Council expresses its determination to support the implementation of the Ceasefire Agreement. Accordingly, it has now begun consideration of a draft resolution authorizing the expansion of the present mandate of the United Nations Organization Mission in the Democratic Republic of the Congo along the lines recommended by the Secretary-General in that report. It expresses its intention to act promptly on this basis. It expresses its intention also to consider at the appropriate time preparations for an additional phase of United Nations deployment and further action. It welcomes the statements by the heads of State and delegation in support of the proposals of the Secretary-General. The Council welcomes the arrival of the Special Representative of the Secretary-General in the Democratic Republic of the Congo, expresses its support for his efforts, and urges all parties to provide him with the assistance and cooperation he will require to carry out his functions.

The Council supports the establishment of a co-ordinated Mission and Joint Military Commission structure with co-located headquarters and joint support arrangements. The Council believes this is a vital step in enhancing the ability of the United Nations to support the Ceasefire Agreement. In this regard, the Council urges Member States and donor organizations to continue to provide assistance to the Commission.

The Council underlines the absolute necessity of security and access for United Nations personnel deployed in support of the Lusaka process, and stresses that such a climate of cooperation is an essential prerequisite for the successful implementation of the mandate of the Mission in the Democratic Republic of the Congo. The Council calls upon all signatories to the Ceasefire Agreement to provide assurances of safety, security and freedom of movement of United Nations and associated personnel, and, in this regard, attaches importance to the statement by the President of the Democratic Republic of the Congo on the security of the Mission and the Special Representative of the Secretary-General.

The Council stresses the importance of the national dialogue as called for in the Ceasefire Agreement, and affirms that it must be an open, inclusive and democratic process conducted independently by the Congolese people under the established facilitation. It affirms that the national dialogue is the best means for all Congolese parties to address the political future of the Democratic Republic of the Congo.

The Council strongly supports the designation of the former President of Botswana, Sir Ketumile Masire, as the Facilitator of the Inter-Congolese Dialogue as provided for by the Ceasefire Agreement, and calls upon Member States to provide full financial and other support for his efforts and the process as a whole. The Council welcomes the declared readiness of the President of the Democratic Republic of the Congo to begin the national dialogue, and to guarantee the security of all participants.

The Council stresses the need for the continued operation by the United Nations and other agencies of humanitarian relief operations and the promotion and monitoring of human rights, under acceptable conditions of security, freedom of movement and access to affected areas. The Council expresses its serious concern at the humanitarian situation in the Democratic Republic of the Congo as well as the shortfall in responses to the United Nations consolidated humanitarian appeal. It therefore urges Member States and donor organizations to make available the necessary funds to carry out urgent humanitarian operations in the Democratic Republic of the Congo.

The Council expresses its concern that the presence in the Democratic Republic of the Congo of non-signatory armed groups that have yet to be demobilized constitutes a threat to the Lusaka process. The Council recognizes that disarmament, demobilization, resettlement and reintegration are among the fundamental objectives of the Ceasefire Agreement. The Council underlines the fact that a credible plan for disarmament, demobilization, resettlement and reintegration must be based on an agreed and comprehensive set of principles.

The Council expresses deep concern at the illicit flow of arms into the region, and calls upon all concerned to halt such flows.

The Council values the continuing leadership of the peace process by the President of Zambia and the vital contribution of the Southern African Development Community through its Chairman, the President of Mozambique. It expresses its appreciation to the current Chairman of the Assembly of Heads of State and Government of the Organization of African Unity, President of Algeria, and to the Secretary-General of the Organization of African Unity for the vital role of that organization in the Lusaka process. It urges them to continue their essential efforts in close cooperation with the Council and the Secretary-General.

Communications (January/February). On 31 January [S/2000/81], South Africa requested the Security Council to adopt a resolution authorizing the expansion of MONUC and providing for disarmament, demobilization, reintegration and resettlement of all armed groups. It believed that no conditionalities should be attached to the deployment of MONUC, such as linkage to the need for progress in the national dialogue.

The DRC, in letters to the Council, reported new outbreaks of violence in north-eastern parts of the country, stating that Ugandan forces were involved in the fighting. Uganda responded to allegations against it. On 28 January [S/2000/67], the DRC said that massacres were taking place in the Blukwa district, which was occupied by Ugandan forces. The DRC urged the Council to adopt binding measures for the immediate withdrawal of the occupying forces. Uganda, on 3 February [S/2000/89], rejected allegations of genocide and urged the Council to condemn the DRC's attempts to disrupt the Lusaka peace process by inflammatory language against the other signatories of the Agreement.

On 11 February [S/2000/122], the DRC claimed that as a result of massacres and atrocities committed by Ugandan armed forces, backed by RCD, there was a humanitarian catastrophe in Blukwa district, near the Ugandan border. The DRC called on the international community to condemn the aggression, order all uninvited foreign forces to withdraw from DRC territory and dispatch an international commission of inquiry to investigate. MONUC was requested to ensure the opening of a humanitarian corridor to the affected population. On 24 February [S/2000/147], Uganda denied that it had ever been involved in any human rights abuse on DRC territory and stated that it welcomed impartial investigations into the causes of those massacres. The clashes between ethnic groups in Blukwa district had nothing to do with the presence of Ugandan defence forces, which were in the area to counter

Ugandan rebels there. Uganda was ready to co-operate with JMC and the United Nations to provide security and humanitarian relief to the affected communities.

Expansion of MONUC

The January report of the Secretary-General on MONUC (see p. 120) was considered by the Security Council on 24 February. The Council expanded the size of MONUC to up to 5,537 military personnel and authorized it to establish a joint structure with JMC.

SECURITY COUNCIL ACTION (February)

On 24 February [meeting 4104], the Security Council unanimously adopted **resolution 1291 (2000)**. The draft [S/2000/143] was prepared in consultations among Council members.

The Security Council,

Recalling its resolutions 1234(1999) of 9 April 1999, 1258(1999) of 6 August 1999, 1273(1999) of 5 November 1999, 1279(1999) of 30 November 1999, and other relevant resolutions, and the statements by its President of 13 July, 31 August and 11 December 1998, 24 June 1999 and 26 January 2000,

Reaffirming the purposes and principles of the Charter of the United Nations and the primary responsibility of the Security Council for the maintenance of international peace and security, and the obligation of all States to refrain from the threat or use of force against the territorial integrity or political independence of any State or in any other manner inconsistent with the purposes of the United Nations,

Reaffirming also the sovereignty, territorial integrity and political independence of the Democratic Republic of the Congo and all States in the region,

Reaffirming further the sovereignty of the Democratic Republic of the Congo over its natural resources, and noting with concern reports of the illegal exploitation of the assets of that country and the potential consequences of these actions on security conditions and the continuation of hostilities,

Expressing its strong support for the Ceasefire Agreement signed at Lusaka on 10 July 1999, which represents the most viable basis for the peaceful resolution of the conflict in the Democratic Republic of the Congo,

Reiterating its call for the orderly withdrawal of all foreign forces from the territory of the Democratic Republic of the Congo, in accordance with the Ceasefire Agreement,

Noting the commitment of all parties to the Ceasefire Agreement to locate, identify, disarm and assemble all members of all armed groups in the Democratic Republic of the Congo referred to in chapter 9.1 of annex A to the Ceasefire Agreement and the commitment of all countries of origin of those armed groups to take the steps necessary for their repatriation, and noting also that these tasks must be conducted by the parties in accordance with the Agreement,

Endorsing the selection by the Congolese parties, with the assistance of the Organization of African Unity, of the Facilitator of the Inter-Congolese Dialogue provided for in the Ceasefire Agreement, and calling upon all Member States to provide political, financial and material support to the facilitation,

Recalling the report of the Secretary-General of 17 January 2000,

Stressing its commitment to work with the parties to implement fully the Ceasefire Agreement, while underlining the fact that its successful implementation rests first and foremost on the will of all parties to the Agreement,

Stressing also the importance of the re-establishment of state administration throughout the national territory of the Democratic Republic of the Congo, as called for in the Ceasefire Agreement,

Stressing further the importance of the Joint Military Commission, and urging all States to continue to provide it with assistance,

Emphasizing that phase II of the deployment of the United Nations Organization Mission in the Democratic Republic of the Congo should be based on the following considerations:

(a) That the parties respect and uphold the Ceasefire Agreement and the relevant Council resolutions,

(b) That a valid plan is developed for the disengagement of the forces of the parties and their redeployment to positions approved by the Joint Military Commission,

(c) That the parties provide firm and credible assurances, prior to the deployment of the forces of the Mission, for the security and freedom of movement of United Nations and related personnel,

Recalling the relevant principles contained in the Convention on the Safety of United Nations and Associated Personnel of 9 December 1994 and the statement by the President of the Security Council of 10 February 2000,

Welcoming and encouraging efforts by the United Nations to sensitize peacekeeping personnel in the prevention and control of HIV/AIDS and other communicable diseases in all its peacekeeping operations,

Expressing its serious concern at the humanitarian situation in the Democratic Republic of the Congo, and encouraging donors to respond to the United Nations consolidated humanitarian appeal,

Stressing the importance to the effectiveness of such humanitarian assistance and other international operations in the Democratic Republic of the Congo of favourable conditions for local procurement and recruitment by international organizations and agencies,

Expressing its deep concern at all violations and abuses of human rights and international humanitarian law, in particular those alleged violations referred to in the report of the Secretary-General,

Expressing its deep concern also at the limited access of humanitarian workers to refugees and internally displaced persons in some areas of the Democratic Republic of the Congo, and stressing the need for the continued operation by the United Nations and other agencies of relief operations as well as the promotion and monitoring of human rights, under acceptable conditions of security, freedom of movement and access to affected areas,

Determining that the situation in the Democratic Republic of the Congo constitutes a threat to international peace and security in the region,

1. *Calls upon* all parties to fulfil their obligations under the Ceasefire Agreement signed at Lusaka;

2. *Reiterates its strong support* for the Special Representative of the Secretary-General in the Democratic Republic of the Congo and his overall authority over United Nations activities in that country, and calls upon all parties to cooperate fully with him;

3. *Decides* to extend the mandate of the United Nations Organization Mission in the Democratic Republic of the Congo until 31 August 2000;

4. *Authorizes* the expansion of the Mission to consist of up to 5,537 military personnel, including up to 500 observers, or more, provided that the Secretary-General determines that there is a need and that it can be accommodated within the overall size and structure of the force, and appropriate civilian support staff in the areas of, inter alia, human rights, humanitarian affairs, public information, child protection, political affairs, medical support and administrative support, and requests the Secretary-General to recommend immediately any additional force requirements that might become necessary to enhance force protection;

5. *Decides* that the phased deployment of personnel referred to in paragraph 4 above will be carried out as and if the Secretary-General determines that Mission personnel will be able to deploy to their assigned locations and carry out their functions as described in paragraph 7 below, in conditions of adequate security and with the cooperation of the parties, and that he has received firm and credible assurances from the parties to the Ceasefire Agreement to that effect, and requests the Secretary-General to keep the Council informed in this regard;

6. *Decides also* that the Mission will establish, under the overall authority of the Special Representative of the Secretary-General, a joint structure with the Joint Military Commission that will ensure close coordination during the period of deployment of the Mission, with co-located headquarters and joint support and administrative structures;

7. *Decides further* that the Mission, in cooperation with the Joint Military Commission, shall have the following mandate:

(a) To monitor the implementation of the Ceasefire Agreement and investigate violations of the ceasefire;

(b) To establish and maintain continuous liaison with the field headquarters of the military forces of all the parties;

(c) To develop, within forty-five days of adoption of the present resolution, an action plan for the overall implementation of the Ceasefire Agreement by all concerned, with particular emphasis on the following key objectives: the collection and verification of military information on the forces of the parties, the maintenance of the cessation of hostilities and the disengagement and redeployment of the parties' forces, the comprehensive disarmament, demobilization, resettlement and reintegration of all members of all armed groups referred to in chapter 9.1 of annex A to the Agreement and the orderly withdrawal of all foreign forces;

(d) To work with the parties to obtain the release of all prisoners of war, military captives and remains, in cooperation with international humanitarian agencies;

(e) To supervise and verify the disengagement and redeployment of the forces of the parties;

(f) Within its capabilities and areas of deployment, to monitor compliance with the provisions of the Ceasefire Agreement on the supply of ammunition, weaponry and other war-related materiel to the field, including to all armed groups referred to in chapter 9.1 of annex A;

(g) To facilitate humanitarian assistance and human rights monitoring, with particular attention to vulnerable groups including women, children and demobilized child soldiers, as the Mission deems within its capabilities and under acceptable security conditions, in close cooperation with other United Nations agencies, related organizations and non-governmental organizations;

(h) To cooperate closely with the Facilitator of the Inter-Congolese Dialogue, provide support and technical assistance to him, and coordinate the activities of other United Nations agencies to this effect;

(i) To deploy mine action experts to assess the scope of the mine and unexploded ordnance problems, coordinate the initiation of mine action activities, develop a mine action plan, and carry out emergency mine action activities as required in support of its mandate;

8. *Decides*, acting under Chapter VII of the Charter of the United Nations, that the Mission may take the necessary action, in the areas of deployment of its infantry battalions and as it deems within its capabilities, to protect United Nations and co-located Joint Military Commission personnel, facilities, installations and equipment, ensure the security and freedom of movement of its personnel, and protect civilians under imminent threat of physical violence;

9. *Calls upon* the parties to the Ceasefire Agreement to support actively the deployment of the Mission to the areas of operations deemed necessary by the Special Representative of the Secretary-General, including through the provision of assurances of security and freedom of movement as well as the active participation of liaison personnel;

10. *Requests* the Governments of the States in the region to conclude, as necessary, status-of-forces agreements with the Secretary-General within thirty days of adoption of the present resolution, and recalls that pending the conclusion of such agreements the model status-of-forces agreement dated 9 October 1990 should apply provisionally;

11. *Requests* the Secretary-General, on the basis of concrete and observed military and political progress in the implementation of the Ceasefire Agreement and relevant Council resolutions, to continue to plan for any additional United Nations deployments in the Democratic Republic of the Congo and to make recommendations for further action by the Council;

12. *Calls upon* all parties to ensure the safe and unhindered access of relief personnel to all those in need, and recalls that the parties must also provide guarantees for the safety, security and freedom of movement for United Nations and associated humanitarian relief personnel;

13. *Also calls upon* all parties to cooperate with the International Committee of the Red Cross to enable it to carry out its mandates as well as the tasks entrusted to it under the Ceasefire Agreement;

14. *Condemns* all massacres carried out in and around the territory of the Democratic Republic of the Congo, and urges that an international investigation into all such events be carried out with a view to bringing to justice those responsible;

15. *Calls upon* all parties to the conflict in the Democratic Republic of the Congo to protect human rights and respect international humanitarian law and the Convention on the Prevention and Punishment of the Crime of Genocide of 9 December 1948, and calls upon all parties to refrain from or cease any support to, or association with, those suspected of involvement in the crime of genocide, crimes against humanity or war crimes, and to bring to justice those responsible and facilitate measures in accordance with international law to ensure accountability for violations of international humanitarian law;

16. *Expresses its deep concern* at the illicit flow of arms into the region, calls upon all concerned to halt such flows, and expresses its intention to consider this issue further;

17. *Expresses its serious concern* at reports of illegal exploitation of the natural resources and other forms of wealth of the Democratic Republic of the Congo, including in violation of the sovereignty of that country, calls for an end to such activities, expresses its intention to consider the matter further, and requests the Secretary-General to report to the Council within ninety days on ways to achieve this goal;

18. *Reaffirms* the importance of holding, at the appropriate time, an international conference on peace, security, democracy and development in the Great Lakes region under the auspices of the United Nations and the Organization of African Unity, with the participation of all the Governments of the region and all others concerned;

19. *Requests* the Secretary-General to provide a report every sixty days to the Council on progress in the implementation of the Ceasefire Agreement and the present resolution;

20. *Decides* to remain actively seized of the matter.

By a 28 February letter [S/2000/172], the Secretary-General informed the Security Council of his intention to appoint Major-General Mountaga Diallo (Senegal) as Force Commander of MONUC. The Council took note of the decision on 2 March [S/2000/173].

Political and military developments

Communications. On 17 March [S/2000/229], the DRC stated that Rwandan Patriotic Army troops had entered two Congolese towns on 14 March, thereby demonstrating that Rwanda was trying to prevent further MONUC deployment. The DRC called on the Security Council to condemn the attack by the armed coalition of Uganda, Rwanda and Burundi on the DRC, which began on 2 August 1998; demand that Rwanda comply with the Lusaka Ceasefire Agreement; and demand the disengagement of the regular Rwandan troops and their redeployment to the positions they occupied prior to 1 March 2000.

Responding on 22 March [S/2000/239], Uganda rejected allegations and insinuations of Ugandan involvement and affirmed its commitment to the Lusaka Agreement. Rwanda, on 21 March [S/2000/234], complained of violations of the Agreement by the "Kabila forces" over the previous three days in the northern Katanga region. It identified those forces as DRC troops, ex-Rwandese Armed Forces (ex-FAR), the Interahamwe and Burundi rebels. On 31 March [S/2000/273], the DRC charged that Rwandan and Ugandan regular armies were currently reinforcing their positions around the town of Kisangani. Such deployments could provoke a new clash between their armies in the DRC, and the DRC urged the Council to call for their withdrawal from DRC territory.

The OAU Chairman, in a communiqué of 24 March [A/54/814-S/2000/254], expressed deep concern at the resumption of armed conflict in the DRC, in violation of the Lusaka Ceasefire Agreement, which jeopardized the security and stability of the region. He called on the parties to respect the ceasefire and cooperate with the United Nations and JMC in order to establish the conditions required for implementation of the Agreement.

On 3 March [S/2000/187], Portugal transmitted to the Secretary-General a European Union (EU) statement of 29 February expressing concern that Archbishop Emmanuel Kataliko had been prevented from returning to his archdiocese in Bukavu to resume his work. It appealed to RCD leaders, in accordance with their verbal undertaking, and the Rwandan Government to ensure that the Archbishop could return. The EU Presidency issued a 12 April statement [S/2000/317] expressing concern at the continuing tension in the DRC and reiterating support for the Lusaka Agreement. It stressed that responsibility for implementation rested with the parties themselves, including the assurance that conditions were in place to enable early MONUC deployment.

In a 17 April letter [S/2000/333], the DRC provided the Security Council with a list of violations of the Lusaka Agreement by the rebels and their allies that had occurred between 10 July 1999 and 7 March 2000. It requested Sir Ketumile Masire to continue his work and to organize the inter-Congolese dialogue as soon as possible, in Kinshasa, and urged the speedy deployment of MONUC with a view to securing the withdrawal of aggressor forces.

Report of Secretary-General (April). On 18 April, the Secretary-General, as requested in Security Council resolution 1291(2000), submitted his second report on MONUC [S/2000/330 & Corr.1]. He reported that the Under-Secretary-General for Peacekeeping Operations had visited the DRC and the other belligerent States and rebel movements in March. He had stressed to DRC officials the need for MONUC to enjoy freedom of movement within the country. Authorities in several cases had refused or delayed clearances for MONUC aircraft to leave Kinshasa airport. Despite affirmations of cooperation with MONUC and adherence to the Lusaka Peace Agreement, the authorities continued to limit MONUC flights and access to certain parts of the country. Flights were further hampered by explosions on 14 April that devastated Kinshasa airport.

JMC met in Kampala, Uganda, on 4 April to discuss a draft plan for the disengagement from confrontation lines of belligerent forces and their redeployment to designated assembly points under MONUC monitoring. The plan, drawn up by MONUC and adopted by the Political Committee on 8 April, set a date for cessation of hostilities (14 April) and a schedule for disengagement. It provided for the withdrawal of all forces to a distance of 15 kilometres from the confrontation line and the creation of a 30-kilometre zone of disengagement. All parties undertook to provide a secure environment in the areas under their control and to facilitate the access of UN personnel and guarantee their freedom of movement. The plan also called for the deployment of MONUC phase II between mid-May and mid-September.

The Secretary-General reported that, during February, fighting continued around Mbandaka, where government troops and troops of the Movement for the Liberation of the Congo were reportedly engaged in clashes; around Ikela, where Zimbabwean, Namibian and Congolese troops relieved the encirclement of an allied force; and in the east, where clashes between armed groups and Rwandan and rebel forces were reported. The Secretariat had also received reports of fighting between the Lendu and Hema communities in the north-east. Unrest was also reported from Goma and Bukavu, where the local population conducted strikes against the RCD authorities. The disturbances were accompanied by the re-emergence of Radio patriotique, which had broadcast anti-Tutsi messages in August 1998 inciting massacres of Tutsis. In March, RCD-Goma reportedly launched an offensive in central DRC. Such military activities raised questions about the commitment of the parties to the ceasefire.

The inter-Congolese dialogue had not advanced, according to the report, despite the discussions with some of the parties held by the neutral Facilitator, Sir Ketumile Masire. There was increasing awareness that a peaceful solution of the conflict might not be possible in the absence of progress in the national dialogue. Furthermore, the human rights situation remained grave (see p. 736) and humanitarian needs had attained massive proportions, with some 1.3 million internally displaced persons and 300,000 refugees, and a further estimated 14 million in need of humanitarian assistance.

Overall, the Secretary-General observed that there had been a number of recent indications of progress in the Lusaka process, including, in particular, the undertakings of cooperation made by the leaders of the DRC and the other signatory States during the visit of the Under-Secretary-General for Peacekeeping Operations; the decision of the Political Committee on 8 April to adopt the disengagement and redeployment plan; the communiqué issued by the allied Presidents the following day calling for the speedy deployment of MONUC military observers; and the outcome of the special cabinet meeting of the DRC on 10 April. However, the Secretary-General was disturbed at the resumed fighting, ethnic violence and evidence that some of the parties could be preparing for new military activities. Delays continued to arise in the granting of flight clearances for MONUC but it was hoped that the deployment of military liaison officers to Bukavu, Kabalo, Kabinda, Kalemie, Mbandaka and Mbuji Mayi would be completed in a short period of time.

The Security Council held a private meeting on 25 April [meeting 4132] to consider the situation in the DRC, at which it was briefed by Sir Ketumile Masire.

Communications. On 1 May [A/54/853-S/2000/369], Algeria forwarded a communiqué issued by the OAU summit on the DRC situation (Algiers, 30 April), in which the heads of State called on the parties concerned to respect the Lusaka Ceasefire Agreement and expressed support for the disengagement plan adopted by the Political Committee. They appealed to the parties to organize and convene the inter-Congolese dialogue.

On 5 May [S/2000/386], the DRC said that fighting had resumed that day between troops of the regular armies of Rwanda and Uganda in the Congolese city of Kisangani, which had been under the control of those armies since 1998. The clashes were taking place under the same circumstances as those in which the same protagonists clashed in August 1999 [YUN 1999, p. 90] in the same city. According to the DRC, the fighting, which was taking place during a ceasefire and shortly before a Security Council mission was to visit the area (see p. 127), was the result of Uganda's determination to regain control over the diamond trade in the region. The DRC called on the Council to condemn the aggression by Burundi, Rwanda and Uganda and to put an end to the illegal exploitation of DRC riches (see p. 128), which had motivated the war of aggression.

SECURITY COUNCIL ACTION (May)

On 5 May [meeting 4135], following consultations among Council members, the President made statement **S/PRST/2000/15** on behalf of the Council:

> The Security Council expresses its grave concern at renewed fighting between Ugandan and Rwandan forces in Kisangani, Democratic Republic of the Congo, which began on 5 May 2000. The Council endorses the statement made by its mission to the Democratic Republic of the Congo, on 5 May 2000, in Kinshasa, calling for an immediate halt to the fighting.
>
> The Council condemns unreservedly the outbreak of military hostilities in Kisangani. This renewed fighting is, once more, threatening the implementation of the Ceasefire Agreement signed at Lusaka on 10 July 1999. The Council is also concerned at reports of the killing of innocent Congolese civilians.
>
> The Council demands that these latest hostilities cease immediately and that those involved in the fighting at Kisangani reaffirm their commitment to the Lusaka process and comply with all relevant Council resolutions. The Council reaffirms its commitment to the national sovereignty, territorial integrity and political independence of the Democratic Republic of the Congo.
>
> The Council considers that this violent action directly violates the Ceasefire Agreement, the Kampala Disengagement Plan of 8 April 2000, the ceasefire of 14 April 2000, the subsequent written instructions to field commanders to abide by this ceasefire, and relevant Council resolutions.
>
> The Council will remain actively seized of the matter.

Security Council mission to DRC

The Security Council informed the Secretary-General on 24 April [S/2000/344] that it had decided to send a mission to the DRC, from 2 to 8 May. The terms of reference of the mission were annexed to the letter. Concerned by developments since the signing of the Lusaka Ceasefire Agreement, the mission would attempt to facilitate the parties' agreement on concrete ways to ensure its implementation. It would focus on the conditions necessary for the full deployment of MONUC, including adherence to the ceasefire, an adequate status-of-forces agreement, guarantees of security and freedom of movement for UN personnel, the relocation of JMC to Kinshasa and its establishment as a permanent body, and the need for progress on the disengagement of forces.

The mission, which comprised seven Council members and was headed by United States Ambassador Richard Holbrooke, visited the DRC, Zambia, Zimbabwe, Rwanda and Uganda. It met with the heads of State of those countries, the leaders of the two factions of RCD (RCD-Goma and RCD-Kisangani), representatives of Congolese civil society and political parties, the Political Committee and JMC. DRC President Laurent-Désiré Kabila, expressing concern over the fragility of the ceasefire, called for the speedy deployment of the second phase of MONUC. He said that his Government would interpose no obstacle to that deployment and would continue to facilitate humanitarian access as long as prior notification was received. During the visit, the status-of-forces agreement was signed by the Special Representative of the Secretary-General and the DRC Foreign Minister, reflecting an improvement in relations between MONUC and the DRC.

In its report to the Council [S/2000/416], the mission stated that the ceasefire agreed by the parties as part of the disengagement plan of 8 April largely continued to hold during the visit; however, there were serious outbreaks of fighting at Kisangani between Rwandan and Ugandan troops. Approximately 100 Congolese civilians had reportedly been killed or injured in that fighting. The acceptance by President Paul Kagame of Rwanda and President Yoweri Kaguta Museveni of Uganda of a proposal to withdraw their forces from Kisangani in a balanced manner under UN supervision, and for the rapid deployment of MONUC units in the city, had helped to ease a source of tension that had hampered the Lusaka peace process and caused many deaths of civilians and property damage. The mission accepted that the disarmament, demobilization, reintegration and resettlement of the armed groups, including ex-FAR and Interahamwe militia, was an essential element in restoring confidence in eastern DRC. Unless it was resolved, it would be very difficult to restore the rule of law or ensure the security of borders. Much more needed to be done to address that question.

In regard to the inter-Congolese dialogue, the mission noted the reservations expressed by President Kabila that the facilitation programme had been drawn up without adequate consultation and reference to the timetable contained in the Ceasefire Agreement. The mission believed that progress in the dialogue, in conjunction with the deployment of MONUC and implementation of the other military aspects of the Agreement, represented the path to lasting security in the country.

The mission reported that the ceasefire of 8 April, though fragile, was a basis for future peacemaking. While the Kisangani incident and other violations were deplorable, they did not represent breakdowns between the parties. Interim measures were needed since deployment of an enlarged MONUC would take more time. The requirement for ceasefire monitoring and verification as mandated by resolution 1291(2000) was evident; however, the mission cautioned that MONUC would face risks, noting that lessons could be learned from the Sierra Leone tragedy (see p. 189) about the deployment of peacekeepers before a conflict had run its course. At the same time, the Sierra Leone situation should not be allowed to cloud the international community's responsibility in the DRC.

The mission recommended that the Secretary-General, before making his final decision on deployment, should seek the commitment of each party to the Agreement to assist in deploying phase II of MONUC. In the event of a positive decision, it was essential for the Lusaka and UN processes to interact effectively. As stated in resolution 1291(2000), MONUC and JMC had to work jointly from a co-located headquarters, whose location should be decided by those concerned on the ground.

Noting the agreement of 8 May signed in Kampala by Rwanda and Uganda on the demilitarization of Kisangani, the mission said that implementation was the only true test, and reports of fresh shelling and troop movements had already been received. The mission urged the Special Representative to explore whether a demilitarized Kisangani, under the temporary authority of MONUC in the early stages of its deployment, could provide the parties with secure, neutral facilities for future political and military exchanges.

The mission remained convinced of the importance of establishing a national dialogue on the future of the DRC. Sir Ketumile Masire's facilitation needed immediate access to funds and the support of all the Lusaka signatories. It was hoped that he would address the question of the venue for the first stages of dialogue with renewed vigour. While Kinshasa was the natural eventual home of the political process, the mission recommended that an interim solution, with the venue possibly at Kisangani, could be explored and Kinshasa re-examined at a later date when confidence between the parties had grown. The issue of a disarmament, demobilization, reintegration and resettlement programme had been broached by the mission with the parties, and the issue should be taken forward in New York in June, with prior preparation by the parties and by MONUC. At the mission's instigation,

particular parties offered to take steps to exchange prisoners of war. In the mission's view, the Council should urge the International Committee of the Red Cross to renew its approaches to turn the expressed willingness into practical results.

The Security Council discussed the results of its mission on 17 May [S/PV.4143].

Exploitation of natural resources

The Secretary-General, referring to Security Council resolution 1291(2000) (see p. 123), which expressed concern at reports of illegal exploitation of natural resources in the DRC, suggested, in an 18 April letter [S/2000/334], that the Council consider creating a panel of experts to undertake a preliminary investigation into the situation and to revert to the Council with recommendations. The panel, which would be financed from the regular UN budget, would be organizationally separate from MONUC, although it could request logistical support. Members would be selected for their expertise and the panel would be based at the UN Office in Nairobi. The DRC made a similar proposal on 26 April [S/2000/350].

The Council, in a 28 April reply [S/2000/362], stated that it would make a decision on an expert panel expeditiously, taking into account the conclusions of the Council's mission to the DRC. During that mission (see above), President Kabila accused Rwanda, Uganda and Burundi of paying for weapons with diamonds taken from his country and said that it was up to the Council to put a stop to that activity through peaceful means. The mission recommended the early establishment of an expert panel to take the matter forward.

On 1 June [S/2000/515], the DRC welcomed the mission's recommendation.

SECURITY COUNCIL ACTION (June)

On 2 June [meeting 4151], following consultations among Security Council members, the President made statement **S/PRST/2000/20** on behalf of the Council:

The Security Council recalls the letter dated 18 April 2000 from the Secretary-General and the letter dated 28 April 2000 from the President of the Council. The Council also recalls the letters dated 26 April 2000 and 1 June 2000 from the Permanent Representative of the Democratic Republic of the Congo to the United Nations addressed to the President of the Council.

The Council welcomes the recommendation made by its mission to the Democratic Republic of the Congo, contained in paragraph 77 of its report of 11 May 2000, to proceed with the early establishment of an expert panel on the illegal exploitation of the natural resources and other forms of wealth of the Democratic Republic of the Congo.

The Council requests the Secretary-General to establish this panel, for a period of six months, with the following mandate:

—To follow up on reports and collect information on all activities of illegal exploitation of the natural resources and other forms of wealth of the Democratic Republic of the Congo, including those in violation of the sovereignty of that country;

—To research and analyse the links between the exploitation of the natural resources and other forms of wealth of the Democratic Republic of the Congo and the continuation of the conflict;

—To revert to the Council with recommendations.

The Council stresses that in order to implement its mandate, the expert panel, which will be based at the United Nations Office at Nairobi, may receive logistical support from the United Nations Organization Mission in the Democratic Republic of the Congo and make visits to various countries of the region, making contact during its visits with diplomatic missions in the capitals concerned, and, if necessary, to other relevant countries.

The Council requests the Secretary-General to appoint the members of the panel, in consultation with the Council, on the basis of the professional expertise and impartiality of the candidates, and their knowledge of the subregion. The Council stresses that the Chairman of the panel should be an eminent personality with the necessary experience, and decides that the panel will consist of five members, including its Chairman. The Council underlines the fact that the panel might call upon the technical expertise of the Secretariat and of the United Nations funds and programmes and the specialized agencies, as required. Voluntary contributions to support the panel would be welcomed.

The Council requests the Secretary-General to report to it on the steps taken to establish the expert panel. The Council requests also that the expert panel, once established, submit to the Council, through the Secretary-General, a preliminary report with initial findings after three months and a final report, with recommendations, at the end of its mandate.

The Secretary-General informed the Council on 31 July [S/2000/796] of his intention to appoint as Chairperson of the five-member expert panel Safiatou Ba-N'Daw (Côte d'Ivoire), former Minister of Energy and former senior World Bank official. The other proposed members were François Ekoko (Cameroon), Moustapha Tall (Senegal), Henri Maire (Switzerland) and Mel Holt (United States). The Council took note of the Secretary-General's intention and proposal on 14 August [S/2000/797]. The panel, established in Nairobi on 18 September following briefings at UN Headquarters [S/2001/49], undertook consultations with the parties and visits within the region.

The DRC, by a 17 August letter [S/2000/810], forwarded to the Council a report of the non-governmental organization (NGO) Observatoire Gouvernance-Transparence on the alleged systematic trafficking by Rwanda and Uganda of the mineral, agricultural and forestry resources of the DRC provinces under their control.

Further developments

Communications. In May and June, the DRC, in letters to the Security Council, protested military activity by foreign troops in the eastern part of the country, called for an international investigation and requested the rapid deployment of MONUC. On 18 May [S/2000/453], it alleged that troops of the Rwandan Patriotic Army had murdered some 30 inhabitants of a village in South Kivu province. It called on the Council to condemn Rwanda, which it said was responsible for the massacre [S/2000/468]. On the same date [S/2000/452], the DRC asked the Council to demand that Burundi, Rwanda and Uganda withdraw their troops from DRC territory, and that those forces not be redeployed to other fronts and conflict zones within the country. A similar appeal was made to the international community on 19 May [S/2000/466]. On 7 June [S/2000/548], the DRC reported fighting in Kisangani between Rwandan and Ugandan forces, which had claimed the lives of some 100 civilians and caused material damage, and it called on the Council to impose sanctions on those two countries.

Referring to the hostilities in Kisangani on 5 May, Uganda and Rwanda put forward their assessments of the situation in letters to the Council. Uganda, on 8 May [S/2000/397], said that Rwandan troops had fired on Ugandan troops. On 17 and 26 May [S/2000/442, S/2000/503], Uganda stated that the Presidents of the two countries, at a meeting in Mwanza, United Republic of Tanzania, on 14 May, had reaffirmed their commitment to the 8 May declaration on the demilitarization of Kisangani. Rwanda, on 17 May [S/2000/445], forwarded a joint statement signed by both countries on 15 May, in which they agreed to withdraw their forces 100 kilometres from Kisangani, among other things. However, on 5 June [S/2000/537 & Corr.1], Rwanda complained that Ugandan troops had attacked its troops in Kisangani, and Uganda, on 9 June [S/2000/558], claimed that Rwanda had repeatedly violated the ceasefire in that city. Uganda added that it remained committed to the Lusaka Ceasefire Agreement and the demilitarization of Kisangani.

On 10 June [S/2000/559], Rwanda said that heavy fighting had been going on between Ugandan and Rwandan forces for six days. The conflict was sparked off when Ugandan troops attacked Rwandan forces who were withdrawing from Kisangani. A series of ceasefire agreements, largely negotiated through MONUC, had failed to hold owing to the intransigence of Ugandan commanders on the ground. Large numbers of Congolese civilians had been killed and property destroyed. Rwanda announced it would effect a unilateral withdrawal from Kisangani. Uganda, on 12 June [S/2000/562], claimed that Rwandan forces were not interested in a ceasefire, but Uganda would withdraw from positions it held on 5 June in order to minimize the loss of lives and destruction of property in Kisangani.

The EU, on 9 June [S/2000/584], expressed its concern at the renewed fighting between Rwandan and Ugandan forces in Kisangani, which had resulted in the deaths of civilians and damage to property and had put the safety of UN personnel at risk. It urged Rwanda and Uganda to cease hostilities, to implement the ceasefire and the demilitarization plan previously agreed by them, and to withdraw from Kisangani.

Presidents Kagame of Rwanda and Museveni of Uganda held a meeting in Entebbe, Uganda, on 2 July at which they agreed to work towards the implementation of the Lusaka Ceasefire Agreement and reaffirmed their commitment to the demilitarization of Kisangani [S/2000/648].

Uganda, by a letter of 16 June to the Council [S/2000/605], transmitted a press statement by the Chairman of the Political Committee on the Implementation of the Lusaka Ceasefire Agreement issued at the conclusion of a joint session with the Security Council (New York, 15-16 June). The Committee informed the Council that although the Agreement had suffered violations, it had generally held. Uganda and Rwanda had confirmed that the fighting had stopped and that the withdrawal of their forces from Kisangani had commenced that day. The Council was urged to expedite MONUC's deployment in order to enhance the security situation. On the issue of national dialogue, the Political Committee informed the Council of the Facilitator's efforts to start them, including a recent preparatory meeting in Cotonou, Benin.

Report of Secretary-General (June). In his third report on MONUC, issued on 12 June [S/2000/566 & Corr.1], the Secretary-General stated that persistent outbreaks of heavy fighting between the belligerents—the Rwandan Patriotic Army (RPA) and the Ugandan People's Defence Force (UPDF)—in Kisangani had caused an estimated 150 civilian deaths and more than 1,000 casualties, as well as severe property damage. Following the visit of the Security Council mission in May, the fighting eased briefly with the signing of a MONUC-brokered agreement, but resumed on 5 June with heavy fighting resulting in serious damage to the power station, the hydroelectric dam and a hospital, and the disruption of electricity and water supplies. On 12 June, Ugandan forces had reportedly withdrawn northwards and a ceasefire was in place. Fighting was also reported in Equateur province between the Movement for the Liberation of the Congo (MLC) and DRC troops, and along the central eastern border in North and South Kivu provinces, where clashes between armed groups and Rwandan troops, as well as attacks on civilians and interethnic clashes, had taken place. RCD and its allies, who were nominally responsible for security there, seemed unable to prevent killings by the ex-FAR and Rwandan and Burundi rebel groups, including the Interahamwe.

In May, the Facilitator of the inter-Congolese dialogue, Sir Ketumile Masire, met with representatives of the parties to discuss the planning and preparations for the dialogue. A planning meeting was held in Cotonou on 6 June. However, the DRC Government did not attend and prevented representatives of civil society and the unarmed opposition from leaving Kinshasa. The dialogue itself was scheduled to commence no later than 3 July and to last 45 days. On 9 June, the DRC released a statement criticizing the Facilitator for remaining silent in the face of renewed fighting in Kisangani and announced it was withdrawing its confidence in him. It called on OAU to propose a new neutral Facilitator.

As at 12 June, MONUC had a total of 228 military observers and military liaison officers deployed in and around the DRC, 200 of whom were stationed at 12 sites in the country and 28 in the capitals of surrounding countries.

The Secretary-General concluded that the fighting in certain locations had cast into doubt the implementation of the 8 April ceasefire agreement despite widespread adherence to that agreement elsewhere in the country. The Government's decision not to participate in the preparatory meeting for the inter-Congolese dialogue, its blocking of the participation of the unarmed opposition in Kinshasa and the chronic shortages and delays in the provision of resources for the Facilitator's operations raised serious doubts about the future course of the dialogue. Furthermore, the fighting and the difficulties encountered in the inter-Congolese dialogue augured ill for the deployment of the second phase of MONUC. Despite the signing of the status-of-forces agreement, MONUC operations were denied full freedom of movement. Once the signatories of the Lusaka Ceasefire Agreement had demonstrated commitment to its terms, the United Nations could proceed with the deployment of the second phase of MONUC, provided the necessary facilities were made available and the military units were fully equipped.

Communication (15 June). On 15 June [S/2000/596], Uganda transmitted to the Security Council a chronology of events and ceasefire violations in Kisangani by RPA, rejected allegations levelled at UPDF and affirmed its commitment to the Lusaka peace process.

SECURITY COUNCIL ACTION (June)

On 16 June [meeting 4159], the Security Council, having met in private with the members of the Political Committee for the Implementation of the Lusaka Ceasefire Agreement [S/PV.4157, S/PV.4158], unanimously adopted **resolution 1304(2000)**. The draft [S/2000/587] was prepared in consultations among Council members.

The Security Council,

Recalling its resolutions 1234(1999) of 9 April 1999, 1258(1999) of 6 August 1999, 1265(1999) of 17 September 1999, 1273(1999) of 5 November 1999, 1279(1999) of 30 November 1999, 1291(2000) of 24 February 2000 and 1296(2000) of 19 April 2000, and the statements by its President of 13 July, 31 August and 11 December 1998, 24 June 1999, 26 January, 5 May and 2 June 2000,

Reaffirming the purposes and principles of the Charter of the United Nations and the primary responsibility of the Security Council for the maintenance of international peace and security,

Reaffirming also the obligation of all States to refrain from the use of force against the territorial integrity or political independence of any State or in any other manner inconsistent with the purposes of the United Nations,

Reaffirming further the sovereignty, territorial integrity and political independence of the Democratic Republic of the Congo and all States in the region,

Reaffirming the sovereignty of the Democratic Republic of the Congo over its natural resources, and noting with concern reports of the illegal exploitation of the assets of that country and the potential consequences of these actions on security conditions and the continuation of hostilities,

Calling, in this regard, upon all the parties to the conflict in the Democratic Republic of the Congo and others concerned to cooperate fully with the expert panel on the illegal exploitation of the natural resources and other forms of wealth of the Democratic Republic of the Congo in its investigation and visits in the region,

Expressing its deep concern at the continuation of the hostilities in the country,

Expressing in particular its outrage at renewed fighting between Ugandan and Rwandan forces in Kisangani, Democratic Republic of the Congo, which began on 5 June 2000, and at the failure of Uganda and Rwanda to comply with their commitment to cease hostilities and withdraw from Kisangani, made in their joint statements of 8 May and 15 May 2000, and deploring the loss of civilian lives, the threat to the civilian population and the damage to property inflicted by the forces of Uganda and Rwanda on the Congolese population,

Recalling its strong support for the Ceasefire Agreement signed at Lusaka on 10 July 1999, and insisting that all parties honour their obligations under that Agreement,

Deploring the delays in the implementation of the Ceasefire Agreement and the Kampala Disengagement Plan of 8 April 2000, and stressing the need for new momentum to ensure progress in the peace process,

Expressing its deep concern at the lack of cooperation of the Government of the Democratic Republic of the Congo with the Facilitator of the Inter-Congolese Dialogue designated with the assistance of the Organization of African Unity, including the fact that the delegates were prevented from attending the preparatory meeting held in Cotonou on 6 June 2000,

Welcoming the report of the Secretary-General of 12 June 2000,

Recalling the responsibility of all parties to the conflict in the Democratic Republic of the Congo for ensuring the safety and security of United Nations and associated personnel throughout the country,

Welcoming the participation in its meetings, held on 15 and 16 June 2000, of the members of the Political Committee for the implementation of the Lusaka Ceasefire Agreement,

Expressing its serious concern at the humanitarian situation in the Democratic Republic of the Congo resulting mainly from the conflict, and stressing the need for substantial humanitarian assistance to the Congolese population,

Expressing its alarm at the dire consequences of the prolonged conflict for the security of the civilian population throughout the territory of the Democratic Republic of the Congo, and its deep concern at all violations and abuses of human rights and international humanitarian law, in particular in the eastern part of the country, especially in North Kivu and South Kivu, and Kisangani,

Determining that the situation in the Democratic Republic of the Congo continues to constitute a threat to international peace and security in the region,

Acting under Chapter VII of the Charter,

1. *Calls upon* all parties to cease hostilities throughout the territory of the Democratic Republic of the Congo and to fulfil their obligations under the Ceasefire Agreement signed at Lusaka and the relevant provisions of the Kampala Disengagement Plan;

2. *Reiterates its unreserved condemnation* of the fighting between Ugandan and Rwandan forces in Kisangani in violation of the sovereignty and territorial integrity of the Democratic Republic of the Congo, and demands that these forces and those allied to them desist from further fighting;

3. *Demands* that Ugandan and Rwandan forces as well as forces of the Congolese armed opposition and other armed groups immediately and completely withdraw from Kisangani, and calls upon all parties to the Ceasefire Agreement to respect the demilitarization of the city and its environs;

4. *Demands also:*

(a) That Uganda and Rwanda, which have violated the sovereignty and territorial integrity of the Democratic Republic of the Congo, withdraw all their forces from the territory of the Democratic Republic of the Congo without further delay, in conformity with the timetable of the Ceasefire Agreement and the Kampala Disengagement Plan;

(b) That each phase of withdrawal completed by Ugandan and Rwandan forces be reciprocated by the other parties, in conformity with the same timetable;

(c) That all other foreign military presence and activity, direct and indirect, in the territory of the Democratic Republic of the Congo be brought to an end, in conformity with the provisions of the Ceasefire Agreement;

5. *Demands*, in this context, that all parties abstain from any offensive action during the process of disengagement and of withdrawal of foreign forces;

6. *Requests* the Secretary-General to keep under review the arrangements for the deployment of the personnel of the United Nations Organization Mission in the Democratic Republic of the Congo, as authorized and in conditions defined by resolution 1291(2000), to monitor the cessation of hostilities, disengagement of forces and withdrawal of foreign forces as described in paragraphs 1 to 5 above and to assist in the planning of these tasks, and also requests the Secretary-General to recommend any adjustment that may become necessary in this regard;

7. *Calls upon* all parties, in complying with paragraphs 1 to 5 above, to cooperate with the efforts of the Mission to monitor the cessation of hostilities, disengagement of forces and withdrawal of foreign forces;

8. *Demands* that the parties to the Ceasefire Agreement cooperate with the deployment of the Mission to the areas of operation deemed necessary by the Special Representative of the Secretary-General for the Democratic Republic of the Congo, including by lifting restrictions on the freedom of movement of Mission personnel and by ensuring their security;

9. *Calls upon* all the Congolese parties to engage fully in the national dialogue process as provided for in the Ceasefire Agreement, and calls in particular on the Government of the Democratic Republic of the Congo to reaffirm its full commitment to the dialogue, to honour its obligations in this respect and to cooperate with the Facilitator of the Inter-Congolese Dialogue designated with the assistance of the Organization of African Unity and to allow for the full participation of political opposition and civil society groups in the dialogue;

10. *Demands* that all parties cease all forms of assistance and cooperation with the armed groups referred to in chapter 9.1 of annex A to the Ceasefire Agreement;

11. *Welcomes* efforts made by the parties to engage in a dialogue on the question of disarmament, demobilization, resettlement and reintegration of members of all armed groups referred to in chapter 9.1 of annex A to the Ceasefire Agreement, and urges the parties, in particular the Government of the Democratic Republic of the Congo and the Government of Rwanda, to continue these efforts in full cooperation;

12. *Demands* that all parties comply in particular with the provisions of chapter 12 of annex A to the Ceasefire Agreement relating to the normalization of the security situation along the borders between the Democratic Republic of the Congo and its neighbours;

13. *Condemns* all massacres and other atrocities carried out in the territory of the Democratic Republic of the Congo, and urges that an international investigation into all such events be carried out with a view to bringing to justice those responsible;

14. *Expresses the view* that the Governments of Uganda and Rwanda should make reparations for the loss of life and the property damage they have inflicted on the civilian population in Kisangani, and requests the Secretary-General to submit an assessment of the damage as a basis for such reparations;

15. *Calls upon* all parties to the conflict in the Democratic Republic of the Congo to protect human rights and respect international humanitarian law;

16. *Also calls upon* all parties to ensure the safe and unhindered access of relief personnel to all those in need, and recalls that the parties must also provide guarantees for the safety, security and freedom of movement of United Nations and associated humanitarian relief personnel;

17. *Further calls upon* all parties to cooperate with the International Committee of the Red Cross to enable it to carry out its mandate as well as the tasks entrusted to it under the Ceasefire Agreement;

18. *Reaffirms* the importance of holding, at the appropriate time, an international conference on peace, security, democracy and development in the Great Lakes region under the auspices of the United Nations and the Organization of African Unity, with the participation of all the Governments of the region and all others concerned;

19. *Expresses its readiness* to consider possible measures that could be imposed in accordance with its responsibility under the Charter of the United Nations in case of failure by the parties to comply fully with the present resolution;

20. *Decides* to remain actively seized of the matter.

ICJ case. The International Court of Justice (ICJ), by a 1 July letter [S/2000/654], informed the Secretary-General that it had rendered its order on the request for the indication of provisional measures submitted on 19 June 2000 by the DRC in the case concerning *Armed activities on the territory of the Congo (Democratic Republic of the Congo v. Uganda)* (see p. 1217). Pending a decision, the Court ordered both parties to refrain from action that might prejudice the rights of the other party in respect of any ICJ judgment, or which might aggravate the dispute. The parties were also ordered to comply with their obligations under international law and to respect fundamental human rights in the zone of conflict.

On 4 July [S/2000/649], the DRC welcomed the ICJ provisional orders and pointed out that the Council was responsible for seeing that ICJ decisions were respected.

Communications (June-August). On 22 June [S/2000/616], Uganda affirmed that its forces had been withdrawn from Kisangani under the supervision of MONUC, while some forces remained in other parts of the DRC in accordance with the Lusaka Agreement.

Botswana, in a press release of 17 June [S/2000/606], expressed concern about reports that the DRC had demanded the withdrawal of former President Sir Ketumile Masire from his assignment as Facilitator for the inter-Congolese dialogue, which it described as a serious setback to the peace process.

The DRC continued to complain of serious violations of human rights and of international humanitarian law perpetrated by Ugandan, Burundian and Rwandan forces against civilians in the eastern part of the DRC. On 6 July [S/2000/658], the DRC said that attacks continued even though Ugandan and Rwandan troops had moved away from the centre of Kisangani and that more than 104,000 people had been forced to flee their homes. The DRC called on the Security Council to take action that would cause those three countries to abide strictly by the Lusaka Agreement. A similar request was made on 21 July [S/2000/725], when the DRC complained of fresh large-scale massacres against the civilian population that had left several hundred dead. On 1 August [S/2000/767], the DRC forwarded eyewitness accounts of massacres allegedly perpetrated by the armies of Burundi, Rwanda and Uganda. On 21 August [S/2000/817], the DRC said that regular Ugandan troops were preparing a large-scale offensive in Equateur province. The DRC outlined its position on the Lusaka Agreement and its support for MONUC deployment in a 29 August letter [S/2000/837], noting that it had made its position known at the SADC summit in Lusaka on 14 and 15 August. It affirmed that repeated violations of the Lusaka Agreement by the other parties were to blame for the failure of the Agreement, which it said should be revised. The DRC believed that the war of aggression waged by Burundi, Rwanda and Uganda must be separated out from the political conflict between the Government and a number of armed Congolese factions.

Rwanda, on 21 July [S/2000/740], denied reports of recent RPA movements, adding that its army had fully respected the Lusaka Agreement. On 8 August [S/2000/782], Rwanda forwarded a proposal for a disengagement plan as a move towards implementation of the Lusaka Agreement, which, in its view, the DRC had thwarted, and full deployment of MONUC. Rwanda said it would begin to disengage from certain positions on the front line in order to provide a 200-kilometre-wide zone that could be secured by MONUC.

Extension of MONUC mandate

The Secretary-General, in a letter of 14 August [S/2000/799], alerted the Council to the adverse climate that had so far prevented full MONUC de-

ployment. He described the situation as characterized by persistent large-scale fighting in many parts of the country, severe restrictions imposed by the Government and other parties on the Mission's freedom of movement, the refusal of the Government to permit the deployment of UN armed troops, and a sustained campaign of vilification conducted against MONUC and individual members of its staff, which had created risks to their security. The Lusaka peace process was currently undergoing an extremely challenging phase that required substantial re-evaluation. In particular, he warned, the role MONUC could play under current circumstances remained unclear. At the same time, other developments needed to be studied before recommendations could be made; therefore, the Secretary-General requested that the Council consider an interim extension of MONUC's mandate until 30 September.

SECURITY COUNCIL ACTION (August)

On 23 August [meeting 4189], the Security Council unanimously adopted **resolution 1316(2000)**. The draft text [S/2000/823] was prepared in consultations among Council members.

The Security Council,

Recalling its resolutions 1273(1999) of 5 November 1999, 1291(2000) of 24 February 2000 and 1304(2000) of 16 June 2000, and all other resolutions and statements by its President on the situation in the Democratic Republic of the Congo,

Taking note of the letter dated 14 August 2000 from the Secretary-General to the President of the Security Council,

Reaffirming the sovereignty, territorial integrity and political independence of the Democratic Republic of the Congo and all States in the region,

Reaffirming its commitment to assisting in the implementation of the Ceasefire Agreement signed at Lusaka on 10 July 1999, and noting the results of the summit of the Southern African Development Community, held on 6 and 7 August 2000, and the second summit of parties to the Ceasefire Agreement in the Democratic Republic of the Congo, held on 14 August 2000,

Noting with concern that the lack of adequate conditions of access, security and cooperation has restricted the ability of the United Nations Organization Mission in the Democratic Republic of the Congo to deploy up to its authorized strength,

Reaffirming its will to work with the parties to the Ceasefire Agreement and other interested parties, including potential troop contributors, in order to create the conditions necessary for deployment as authorized under resolution 1291(2000),

Expressing its appreciation to all States that have declared their willingness to provide the military units required for the deployment of phase II of the Mission,

Calling upon the Government of the Democratic Republic of the Congo and other parties to lift all obstacles to the full deployment and operation of the Mission,

Recalling the responsibility of all parties to the conflict in the Democratic Republic of the Congo for ensuring the safety and security of United Nations and associated personnel throughout the country,

Commending the outstanding work of Mission personnel in challenging conditions, and noting the strong leadership of the Special Representative of the Secretary-General for the Democratic Republic of the Congo,

1. *Decides* to extend the mandate of the United Nations Organization Mission in the Democratic Republic of the Congo until 15 October 2000;

2. *Emphasizes* that this technical extension of the mandate of the Mission is designed to allow time for further diplomatic activities in support of the Ceasefire Agreement signed at Lusaka and for reflection by the Council on the future mandate of the Mission and possible adjustments thereto;

3. *Requests* the Secretary-General to report to the Council, by 21 September 2000, on progress in the implementation of the Ceasefire Agreement and relevant Council resolutions and to make recommendations for further action by the Council;

4. *Decides* to remain actively seized of the matter.

General Assembly consideration. The DRC, on 21 August [A/54/969], requested the Secretary-General to include in the agenda of the fifty-fifth session of the General Assembly the item entitled "Armed aggression against the Democratic Republic of the Congo". The DRC wished the item to be considered in plenary meeting, without reference to a Main Committee.

On 5 September, the Assembly decided to include that item in the fifty-fifth session's agenda (**decision 54/502**). By **decision 55/458** of 23 December, the Assembly decided that the agenda item would remain for consideration during its resumed fifty-fifth (2001) session.

Assessment mission to Kisangani

The Secretary-General, in response to Security Council resolution 1304(2000) (see p. 131), sent an inter-agency mission to the DRC from 13 to 24 August to assess the loss of life and property damage inflicted on Kisangani as a result of the fighting between Uganda and Rwanda in June. The report of the mission [S/2000/1153] described the team's findings concerning the events in Kisangani and its effects on the population and infrastructure. It also described the immediate reaction of the international community. According to the report, over 760 civilians were killed and an estimated 1,700 wounded in six days of indiscriminate shelling. More than 4,000 houses were partially damaged, destroyed or made uninhabitable, 69 schools were shelled and other public buildings were badly damaged. Medical facilities and the cathedral were also damaged during

the shelling, and 65,000 residents were forced to flee and seek refuge in nearby forests.

The team noted that the recent war in the DRC, which was preceded by decades of political and economic mismanagement that had resulted in widespread poverty, poor infrastructure and ineffective governmental institutions, involved seven neighbouring countries and was intensifying the country's already critical socio-economic and political situation. The major humanitarian crisis currently affected over 20 million people, including 1.8 million internally displaced people and over 400,000 refugees. The city of Kisangani was one of the worst casualties. The latest conflict there erupted on 5 June between the occupying forces of Uganda and Rwanda. Those forces and their affiliated rebel groups were vying for control of the lucrative diamond industry centred in the city.

The international humanitarian community responded by sending over 240 tons of relief supplies. At the time of the report, there were some signs that normal life was resuming in the city, although large-scale reconstruction of homes and public buildings was needed. However, it was the uncertain security environment that remained the main obstacle to people resettling into their communities. The mission recommended that urgent efforts be made to strengthen field security in order to provide a safer working environment for all UN and international humanitarian workers on the ground. The United Nations needed to pursue the international dialogue with the current and potential donors on peacebuilding initiatives within the country. It should draw up a country strategy in collaboration with civil society and NGOs, aimed at rehabilitation and promoting peace and reconciliation. The mission also recommended that MONUC continue to facilitate the delivery of humanitarian assistance and help to create an environment conducive to the provision of rehabilitation support to war-affected communities. It suggested that the United Nations field a follow-up technical mission to Kisangani to obtain costs of the actual damage to buildings and infrastructure and called for increased funding for humanitarian assistance by the international donor community.

SECURITY COUNCIL ACTION (September)

On 7 September [meeting 4194], following a discussion on ensuring an effective role of the Security Council in the maintenance of international peace and security, particularly in Africa, and the adoption of **resolution 1318(2000)** (see p. 64), the President of the Council made statement **S/PRST/2000/28** on behalf of the Council:

The Security Council is deeply concerned at the continuation of hostilities in the Democratic Republic of the Congo, at the dire consequences of the conflict for the humanitarian situation and at reports of abuses of human rights and of illegal exploitation of the natural resources of that country.

The Council reaffirms the sovereignty, territorial integrity and political independence of the Democratic Republic of the Congo and all States in the region.

The Council calls upon all parties to the conflict to cease hostilities and to fulfil their obligations under the Ceasefire Agreement signed at Lusaka on 10 July 1999 and the relevant resolutions of the Council.

The Council takes note in this context of the statements issued by Uganda and Rwanda relating to measures towards disengagement and withdrawal of their forces which are present in the Democratic Republic of the Congo. It calls for the accelerated withdrawal of Ugandan and Rwandan forces and of all other foreign forces from the territory of the Democratic Republic of the Congo in full compliance with resolution 1304(2000) of 16 June 2000.

The Council calls upon all parties to respect human rights and international humanitarian law, and provide access for humanitarian relief personnel.

The Council calls upon all the Congolese parties, in particular on the Government of the Democratic Republic of the Congo, to engage fully in the national dialogue process as provided for in the Ceasefire Agreement and to support, in this regard, the efforts of the facilitation.

The Council calls on the parties to the Ceasefire Agreement to engage in a sincere dialogue to implement that Agreement and to agree upon ways to give a new momentum to the peace process. It expresses its support for the efforts of Mr. Frederick J. T. Chiluba, President of Zambia, and other leaders of the region to this end.

The Council is ready to assist in the peace process, in particular through the United Nations Organization Mission in the Democratic Republic of the Congo, in accordance with resolution 1291(2000) of 24 February 2000. It deplores the fact that the continuation of the hostilities and the lack of cooperation by the parties have prevented the full deployment of the Mission. The Council takes note of the commitments made by the Government of the Democratic Republic of the Congo to support the deployment of the Mission and urges it to honour its particular responsibilities as the host Government of the Mission. It calls upon the parties to demonstrate their will to move the peace process forward and to cooperate effectively with the Mission in order to allow its deployment.

Report of Secretary-General (September). In response to Security Council resolution 1316 (2000) (see p. 133), the Secretary-General submitted on 21 September his fourth report on MONUC [S/2000/888]. He noted that, despite the efforts of all concerned, the peace process remained at an impasse. Following a 28 July meeting of the Political Committee, an SADC summit on the issue was convened in Windhoek, Namibia, on 7 August. Subsequently, President Chiluba of Zambia convened a summit of the parties to the Lusaka Agreement and SADC countries in Lusaka on 14 August, which also failed to make progress, principally because of the DRC's reluctance to allow the deployment of MONUC troops to government-controlled territory and to accept Sir Ketumile Masire as the neutral Facilitator.

The Secretary-General maintained contacts with regional leaders and appointed General Abdulsalami Abubakar, former head of State of Nigeria, as his Special Envoy. General Abubakar travelled to the region from 20 to 24 August. He requested the Government to cease all hostilities, extend full freedom of movement to MONUC, comply with the status-of-forces agreement and proceed with the inter-Congolese dialogue. President Kabila maintained that the obstacles to implementation were not caused by the Government but by the "aggressors".

The DRC, which had withdrawn its support for Sir Ketumile as Facilitator and requested OAU to propose a new one, closed his Kinshasa office on 20 June. The absence of President Kabila at the thirty-sixth ordinary session of the OAU summit (Lomé, Togo, 10-12 July) frustrated efforts to address the issue at the highest level. The Government announced on 25 July that the newly established Constituent Assembly was the appropriate forum for a national dialogue. The Assembly, whose 300 members were appointed by presidential decree, was inaugurated on 21 August with the mandate to examine the draft constitution, elaborate laws on political institutions and oversee government activities. A special parliamentary commission was established for the inter-Congolese dialogue on 13 September.

Since the Secretary-General's June report, the parties had continued to conduct significant military operations, particularly in Equateur province, and there were indications of intensive military preparations. The military and security situation in the eastern part of the country remained highly volatile. RCD had complained that pro-government armed groups continued to launch attacks in North and South Kivu. With regard to Kisangani, Rwanda and Uganda withdrew their forces to a distance of 100 kilometres from the centre of the city, although military and political elements of RCD maintained control over it. Uganda began withdrawing its troops from the DRC on 22 June, and Rwanda announced the return of 1,000 of its troops from the DRC and a proposal for its troops to disengage from certain positions on the front line on

8 August [S/2000/782], redeploying them 200 kilometres away.

At a meeting of the Political Committee in July, the DRC representative contended that Council **resolution 1304(2000)** recognized that his country was being occupied by foreign armed forces and that his Government would therefore seek revisions to the Lusaka Ceasefire Agreement and the mandate of MONUC. In response, the RCD and MLC movements stated their support for the Agreement.

As at 15 September, MONUC had a total of 258 liaison officers and military observers. Within the DRC, teams of military liaison officers were deployed at the headquarters of the rebel movements and the four regional joint military commissions, in addition to Kinshasa. Military observer teams were also stationed in six other locations, and 24 liaison officers were stationed in the capitals of neighbouring countries. MONUC's plans for new sites for military observer teams met with limited success because of the severe restrictions imposed on the Mission's movement.

The Secretary-General concluded that the lack of progress in implementing the Lusaka Agreement and the intensified fighting between government and rebel and UPDF forces not only had imperilled the peace process, but also had spilled over into the Republic of the Congo and the Central African Republic. At the same time, the volatile environment in the Kivus, marked by clashes between the RCD/RPA troops and the armed groups, was of serious concern. During the reporting period, recruitment of troops and the purchase of weapons continued, as did attempts by rebel movements to achieve a united front against the DRC Government. Further uncertainty remained over the Government's refusal to deal with the Facilitator and its request to revise the Lusaka Agreement. The deteriorating humanitarian and human rights situation was another cause for grave concern, particularly since the fighting had hindered access by humanitarian agencies to many areas.

In view of the situation, the Secretary-General recommended that the Council extend MONUC's mandate for two months, giving the United Nations time to make plans for further deployment and signalling UN determination to remain committed to the peace process. A lack of progress would make it difficult to justify not only further deployment but also the continued presence of MONUC in the DRC.

Communication. On 25 September [S/2000/917], France forwarded an EU statement of 22 September that expressed alarm at proposals to suspend application of the Lusaka Agreement. The

EU appealed to the DRC Government and other signatories to respect the ceasefire, implement the withdrawal of forces and guarantee security and freedom of movement for MONUC.

SECURITY COUNCIL ACTION (October)

On 13 October [meeting 4207], the Security Council unanimously adopted **resolution 1323(2000)**. The draft [S/2000/979] was prepared in consultations among Council members.

The Security Council,

Recalling its resolutions 1291(2000) of 24 February 2000, 1304(2000) of 16 June 2000 and 1316(2000) of 23 August 2000, the statement adopted at its meeting of 7 September 2000, held at the level of heads of State and Government, and all previous resolutions and statements by its President relating to the situation in the Democratic Republic of the Congo,

Reaffirming the sovereignty, territorial integrity and political independence of the Democratic Republic of the Congo and all States of the region,

Deploring the continuation of hostilities in the Democratic Republic of the Congo, the lack of cooperation with the United Nations, and the lack of progress on the national dialogue,

Taking note of the report of the Secretary-General of 21 September 2000 and the recommendations therein, as well as the observations contained in paragraphs 82 and 85,

Reaffirming its readiness to assist in the peace process, in particular through the United Nations Organization Mission in the Democratic Republic of the Congo, in accordance with resolution 1291(2000),

Expressing its deep concern at the dire consequences of the conflict for the humanitarian and human rights situations, as well as at reports of the illegal exploitation of the natural resources of the Democratic Republic of the Congo,

1. *Decides* to extend the mandate of the United Nations Organization Mission in the Democratic Republic of the Congo until 15 December 2000;

2. *Decides* to remain actively seized of the matter.

Communications (October). The DRC described the effects of the war on women, children and civilians in two letters of 20 October [S/2000/1008, S/2000/1009]. By the first, it transmitted a document by prominent Congolese women denouncing the violence committed in their country, including the burial of 15 women alive by RCD and other barbarous acts. The second letter contained a statement by women parliamentarians aimed at drawing the international community's attention to the pernicious effects of war on women.

On 25 October [S/2000/1045], Rwanda denounced violations of the Lusaka Ceasefire Agreement by DRC forces and their allies in attacks against RCD and RPA positions.

Regional mediation efforts

In late 2000, a number of diplomatic efforts were made by regional leaders to encourage the disengagement of forces in the DRC.

A mini-summit on the situation in the DRC (Maputo, Mozambique, 16 October) addressed disengagement issues and the security concerns of the participants in the conflict [S/2000/1017]. The Presidents of the DRC, Mozambique, Namibia, Rwanda, South Africa, Uganda and Zimbabwe participated in the meeting, at which it was agreed that all the armed forces in the DRC would immediately start disengaging to positions set out in the Kampala disengagement plan adopted by the Political Committee on 8 April (see p. 126). Rwanda and Uganda undertook voluntarily to move even further than the agreed lines. The other parties agreed that once MONUC had verified that process of further disengagement, they would reciprocate. It was also agreed that President Chiluba should continue to address all other issues arising from the Lusaka Agreement, especially the urgent matter of the internal political process in the DRC. Any proposal on possible adjustments to the Lusaka Agreement would also be addressed through that process.

The Summit Meeting of the Heads of State of Central Africa (Kinshasa, DRC, 27 October) [S/2000/1050] welcomed the new dynamic that had emerged from the Maputo summit meeting and appealed for a stronger commitment by the United Nations and OAU to resolving the Congolese crisis. The meeting, attended by the Presidents of Angola, the Congo, the DRC and Gabon, and the Prime Ministers of the Central African Republic and Equatorial Guinea, demanded the unconditional withdrawal of the aggressors from the DRC and suggested the deployment of neutral intervention troops on the common frontier of protagonist States as a solution to the security concerns expressed by Burundi, Rwanda and Uganda. To follow up on their decisions, the heads of State established an ad hoc ministerial committee.

A mini-summit of parties to the conflict in the DRC (7-8 November, Tripoli, Libyan Arab Jamahiriya) was convened at the invitation of Colonel Muammar Qaddafi and attended by the Presidents of Mali, Rwanda, Uganda and Zimbabwe, and by representatives of Angola, the DRC, Namibia and South Africa [S/2000/1079]. The participants agreed on the deployment of a neutral African force in the DRC to guarantee the security of the borders of Rwanda and Uganda and to assess the size and strength of the armed groups in the DRC with the objective of disarming, disbanding and resettling them. They also agreed that Ugandan and Rwandan forces should withdraw from the DRC in accordance with the Lusaka Agreement, followed by the withdrawal of all other foreign forces.

On 9 November, Colonel Qaddafi suggested to the Secretary-General that Egypt, Libya, Nigeria and South Africa should participate in the neutral force and proposed that the United Nations should undertake the leadership, funding and supervision of those forces.

The heads of State of the DRC, Mozambique, Rwanda, South Africa and Zimbabwe and representatives of Angola and Namibia met to discuss the situation in the DRC (Maputo, 27 November). They agreed to reaffirm the Kampala disengagement plan of 8 April, confirmed the role of MONUC in monitoring the disengagement of forces, and confirmed that the DRC Government was responsible for the timely resolution of the remaining difficulties hindering the deployment of MONUC. The DRC confirmed that MONUC flights need not be routed through Kinshasa and agreed in principle to the deployment of armed UN troops at Kinshasa airport. No agreement was reached on the disarmament and demobilization of armed groups and the withdrawal of foreign forces from DRC territory.

At its 29 November meeting in Lusaka, the Political Committee established by the Lusaka Agreement adopted disengagement sub-plans, which were signed by the military chiefs of staff of all the parties except one (MLC) at Harare, Zimbabwe, on 6 December. They drew up detailed sub-plans for disengagement and redeployment. Subsequently, MONUC received notification from Angola, the DRC, Namibia, Rwanda, Uganda and Zimbabwe that executive orders had been issued to their military forces to begin the disengagement process. No notification was received from the rebel movements. The Harare disengagement plan stipulated that the military forces would undertake a 15-kilometre disengagement over a two-week period starting 21 January 2001.

Communications (November). On 8 November [S/2000/1076], Zimbabwe dismissed Rwandan allegations of violations of the Lusaka Ceasefire Agreement by SADC allied forces, adding that its forces were not deployed anywhere near the theatre of operations as claimed by Rwanda. The SADC forces were fulfilling their obligations under the Lusaka Agreement and subsequent agreements.

On 1 November [S/2000/1062], Rwanda said that DRC forces and their allies, including Namibian and Zimbabwean forces, continued to attack RCD and RPA positions and had intensified their military offensive in Katanga province. Rwanda requested the Security Council and MONUC to verify those violations. Namibia, on 7 November [S/2000/1074], denied those allegations.

Security Council consideration. On 28 November [S/PV.4237], the Security Council was briefed by the Emergency Relief Coordinator of the UN Office for the Coordination of Humanitarian Affairs on the humanitarian situation in the DRC.

Report of Secretary-General (December). On 6 December [S/2000/1156], the Secretary-General reported to the Security Council for the fifth time on MONUC. He described diplomatic efforts to pursue implementation of the Lusaka Ceasefire Agreement, in particular the subregional summits (see p. 137), noting that the rebel movements had not been invited to any of them. Efforts were also made by his Special Representative, who met with the OAU Chairman to discuss the difficulties encountered by JMC and the process of the inter-Congolese dialogue. The Chairman acknowledged the need for better coordination of diplomatic initiatives and said he was attempting to establish contacts between President Kabila and the rebel movements. On 7 November, the Secretary-General met with SADC ambassadors who expressed disappointment at the lack of progress in the peace process and their concern that it might lead to MONUC's termination.

Despite the DRC Government's continued rejection of the neutral Facilitator of the inter-Congolese dialogue, the Facilitator renewed his efforts to revive the dialogue process and maintained that he would remain in that position since only one party to the Lusaka Agreement opposed him. The DRC, in discussions with the Special Representative, said it recognized the need for political negotiations among the Congolese parties. In the Government's view, the purpose of those negotiations was not to achieve transitional power-sharing arrangements but to agree on a new constitution and an electoral commission. In contrast, the rebel movements supported the inter-Congolese dialogue, as provided by the Lusaka Agreement, and Sir Ketumile Masire as the neutral Facilitator.

Recent fighting had complicated and imperilled ongoing peace efforts and threatened to spill over into the Republic of the Congo and the Central African Republic to the north and into Zambia to the south. The main military activity during the reporting period, which included aerial bombing raids against rebel-held locations causing civilian casualties, took place in Equateur province (north), in Katanga province (south) and in the east of the country. The situation in Kisangani remained generally calm. Rwanda and Uganda continued to limit their forces to a dis-

tance of 100 kilometres from the city, but RCD troops and other rebel groups remained there. Fighting appeared to abate in late November but there were reports of bombing attacks at Kalemie in early December. Heavy fighting was also reported near Pweto, which drove some 60,000 people across the border into Zambia.

As at 1 December, MONUC had a total of 224 liaison officers and military observers deployed at various locations in the country, including 23 liaison officers stationed in the capitals of surrounding countries. MONUC continued to plan sites for the sector headquarters required for implementing the Kampala disengagement plan of 8 April. The most serious threat facing MONUC personnel was the volatile confrontations between the belligerent parties. An inflammatory propaganda campaign conducted in some pro-Government media against MONUC had abated following protests from the United Nations. Although the Government continued to restrict MONUC flights through advance notification requirements, there had been a more positive attitude and a relaxation in regard to other restrictions. MONUC and government officials had been meeting since 30 September in order to assess the Government's compliance with the status-of-forces agreement and had achieved some positive results, in particular with regard to customs clearances, exemption of taxes, authorization for telecommunications, facilities at Kinshasa airport and joint reconnaissance missions. In field locations, MONUC military observers had encountered some limitations on their freedom of movement imposed by local commanders.

The Secretary-General welcomed the agreements reached at Maputo on 27 November, which, he said, represented forward movement, and the recent improvements in the Government's attitude towards MONUC deployment. With some exceptions, the security guarantees provided by the parties at the time of the deployment of UN liaison officers had been honoured, and it had been possible to keep the liaison officers and military observers in the field supplied, despite the serious restrictions placed on the Mission's freedom of movement. For that reason, the Secretariat had developed plans to monitor actions taken by the parties in compliance with the Kampala disengagement plan, including local ceasefire arrangements and disengagement movements and eventual withdrawal from DRC territory, through the use of unarmed military observers in static and mobile teams. They would also monitor the continuing demilitarization of Kisangani, investigate ceasefire violations and maintain contact with the parties.

While welcoming the restoration of calm around Kisangani after the June fighting, the Secretary-General said that the terms of the Lusaka Agreement and other demands made on the parties under **resolution 1304(2000)**, such as cooperation with the deployment of MONUC and full engagement in the national dialogue process, had yet to be implemented. Therefore, he recommended that the Council extend the mandate of MONUC for another six months, until 15 June 2001. During that period, MONUC should deploy additional military observers, accompanied by the necessary medical, air, riverine and logistical support units. Broader agreement needed to be reached on key unresolved questions, and that could be approached through building on the recent diplomatic initiatives. Those questions included the withdrawal of foreign forces, the disarmament and demobilization of armed groups, the security of the borders of Burundi, Rwanda and Uganda with the DRC, the return of refugees in safety, the inter-Congolese dialogue and regional economic reconstruction and cooperation.

SECURITY COUNCIL ACTION (December)

On 14 December [meeting 4247], the Security Council unanimously adopted **resolution 1332 (2000)**. The draft [S/2000/1182], which was orally amended, was prepared in consultations with Council members.

The Security Council,

Recalling its resolutions 1234(1999) of 9 April 1999, 1258(1999) of 6 August 1999, 1265(1999) of 17 September 1999, 1273(1999) of 5 November 1999, 1279(1999) of 30 November 1999, 1291(2000) of 24 February 2000, 1296(2000) of 19 April 2000, 1304(2000) of 16 June 2000 and 1323(2000) of 13 October 2000, and the statements by its President of 13 July, 31 August and 11 December 1998, 24 June 1999, 26 January, 5 May, 2 June and 7 September 2000,

Reaffirming the sovereignty, territorial integrity and political independence of the Democratic Republic of the Congo and all States in the region,

Reaffirming also the obligation of all States to refrain from the use of force against the territorial integrity and political independence of any State or in any other manner inconsistent with the purposes of the United Nations,

Reaffirming further the sovereignty of the Democratic Republic of the Congo over its natural resources, and noting with concern reports of the illegal exploitation of the assets of that country and the potential consequences of these actions on security conditions and the continuation of hostilities,

Deploring the continuation of hostilities in the Democratic Republic of the Congo, the numerous ceasefire violations and the lack of progress on the inter-Congolese dialogue,

Reaffirming its support for the Ceasefire Agreement signed at Lusaka on 10 July 1999,

Welcoming the agreements reached at Maputo, on 27 November 2000, concerning the disengagement of forces, as well as the signing, on 6 December 2000, of the Harare Agreement, pursuant to the Kampala Disengagement Plan of 8 April 2000,

Taking note of recent statements, assurances and actions of the Government of the Democratic Republic of the Congo supporting the deployment of the United Nations Organization Mission in the Democratic Republic of the Congo, and expressing the hope that the practical measures necessary to facilitate the full deployment of the Mission will be taken accordingly,

Recalling the responsibilities of all parties to cooperate in the full deployment of the Mission,

Taking note with appreciation of the report of the Secretary-General of 6 December 2000 and the recommendations therein,

Recalling the responsibility of all parties to the conflict in the Democratic Republic of the Congo for ensuring the safety and security of United Nations military and civilian staff and associated personnel throughout the country,

Expressing its serious concern at the humanitarian situation in the Democratic Republic of the Congo resulting mainly from the conflict, and stressing the need for increased humanitarian assistance to the Congolese population,

Expressing its serious concern also at the severe political, economic and humanitarian consequences of the conflict on the neighbouring countries,

Expressing its alarm at the dire consequences of the prolonged conflict for the civilian population throughout the territory of the Democratic Republic of the Congo, and its deep concern at all violations and abuses of human rights and international humanitarian law, including atrocities against civilian populations, especially in the eastern provinces,

Deeply concerned at the increased rate of HIV/AIDS infection, in particular amongst women and girls, as a result of the conflict,

Gravely concerned by the continued recruitment and use of child soldiers by armed forces and groups, including cross-border recruitment and abduction of children,

Expressing serious concern at the difficulties, including those created by continued hostilities, faced by humanitarian agencies in delivering assistance to a large number of refugees and internally displaced persons,

Commending the outstanding work of Mission personnel in challenging conditions, and noting the strong leadership of the Special Representative of the Secretary-General for the Democratic Republic of the Congo,

Welcoming the diplomatic initiatives by African leaders, and stressing the need for a coordinated approach involving the United Nations and the Organization of African Unity to create new momentum for further progress in the peace process,

1. *Decides* to extend the mandate of the United Nations Organization Mission in the Democratic Republic of the Congo until 15 June 2001;

2. *Calls upon* all parties to the Ceasefire Agreement signed at Lusaka to cease hostilities and to continue to intensify their dialogue to implement the Agreement, as well as the Kampala, Maputo and Harare agreements,

and to take additional steps, within the framework of these agreements, to accelerate the peace process;

3. *Also calls upon* all parties, and in particular the Government of the Democratic Republic of the Congo, to continue to cooperate in the deployment and operations of the Mission, including through the full implementation of the provisions of the status-of-forces agreement;

4. *Endorses* the proposal made by the Secretary-General to deploy, as soon as he considers that conditions will allow it and in accordance with the relevant provisions of resolution 1291(2000), additional military observers, in order to monitor and verify the implementation by the parties of the ceasefire and disengagement plans adopted in Lusaka and Maputo;

5. *Invites* the Secretary-General to consult the Organization of African Unity and all parties concerned with regard to the possibility of organizing, in February 2001, a follow-up meeting between the signatories of the Ceasefire Agreement and the members of the Security Council;

6. *Requests* the Secretary-General, in that connection, to submit to the Council, prior to the convening of the meeting suggested in paragraph 5 above, a review of the implementation of the current mandate of the Mission, including an assessment of the implementation by the parties of the ceasefire and disengagement plans and elements for an updated concept of operation;

7. *Also requests* the Secretary-General to submit in that report proposals to the Council on ways to address the situation in the eastern provinces of the Democratic Republic of the Congo, including in the areas bordering Rwanda, Uganda and Burundi;

8. *Expresses its readiness* to support the Secretary-General, as soon as he considers that conditions allow it, in the deployment of infantry units in support of the military observers in Kisangani and Mbandaka in due course and, subject to the proposals submitted by him under paragraph 7 above, to other areas he may deem necessary, including possibly to Goma or Bukavu;

9. *Requests* the Secretary-General to submit to the Council, in consultation with all parties concerned, detailed proposals concerning the establishment of a permanent follow-up mechanism that could address, in consultation with existing mechanisms in an integrated and coordinated manner, the issues of the full withdrawal of foreign forces, the disarmament and demobilization of armed groups, the security of the borders of the Democratic Republic of the Congo with Rwanda, Uganda and Burundi, the return of refugees and internally displaced persons in safety, the inter-Congolese dialogue and regional economic reconstruction and cooperation;

10. *Calls* for the withdrawal of Ugandan and Rwandan forces, and all other foreign forces, from the territory of the Democratic Republic of the Congo in compliance with resolution 1304(2000) and the Ceasefire Agreement, and urges the forces to take urgent steps to accelerate this withdrawal;

11. *Calls upon* all parties to the conflict to cooperate in moving forward the disarmament, demobilization, repatriation/resettlement and reintegration of all armed groups referred to in chapter 9.1 of annex A to the Ceasefire Agreement, in particular the Forces for the Defence of Democracy of Burundi, the ex-Rwandese Armed Forces, Interahamwe, and the Allied Democratic Forces;

12. *Calls upon* all Congolese parties concerned to cooperate fully in the inter-Congolese dialogue as called for in the Ceasefire Agreement;

13. *Reiterates its call* on all parties to the conflict, including all armed groups referred to in chapter 9.1 of annex A to the Ceasefire Agreement, to take immediate steps to prevent human rights abuses and violations of international humanitarian law and to ensure safe and unhindered access for humanitarian personnel providing assistance to all those in need, including the refugees and internally displaced persons;

14. *Calls upon* all armed forces and groups immediately to cease all campaigns for the recruitment, abduction, cross-border deportation and use of children, and demands immediate steps for the demobilization, disarmament, return and rehabilitation of all such children, with the assistance of relevant United Nations and other agencies and organizations;

15. *Stresses* the need to strengthen the human rights component of the Mission, and requests the Secretary-General to take appropriate measures to that end, including through active cooperation and coordination with the Commission on Human Rights in a country-wide effort;

16. *Calls once again upon* all parties to the conflict in the Democratic Republic of the Congo and others concerned to cooperate fully with the expert panel on the illegal exploitation of the natural resources and other forms of wealth of the Democratic Republic of the Congo in its investigation and visits in the region;

17. *Calls upon* all parties fully to implement their commitments under the Ceasefire Agreement;

18. *Expresses again its readiness* to consider possible measures that could be imposed in accordance with its responsibility and obligations under the Charter of the United Nations, in case of failure by the parties to comply fully with the present resolution;

19. *Decides* to remain actively seized of the matter.

Communications (December). On 13 December [S/2000/1186], Rwanda called on the Council to support Zambia in disarming and repatriating ex-FAR and Interahamwe forces currently on Zambian territory. Those forces were not bona fide refugees and should be disarmed, demobilized and repatriated to Rwanda. If allowed to return to the DRC, they could fuel the war there, Rwanda said.

The DRC, on 26 December [S/2000/1237], complained to the Council of the resurgence of military activities in the DRC, which were the result, it said, of offensives led by RPA forces in Katanga province, leading to a major influx of Congolese refugees into Zambia, and by Ugandan forces in Equateur province. The DRC called on the Council to impose an international embargo on the delivery, sale or transfer of arms to Rwanda and Uganda; an economic, trade and financial blockade against them; and the freezing of diplomatic relations between UN Member States and those two Governments. On 28 December [S/2000/1245], the DRC stated that a brigade of RPA, supported by National Union for the Total Independence of Angola (UNITA) forces, had launched attacks on Katanga province from Zambian territory. That claim was later denied by Rwanda [S/2001/4], and Zambia denied the claim that it had granted use of its territory to launch attacks against the DRC [S/2001/77].

Rwanda, on 28 December [S/2000/1244], accused President Kabila and his allies of conducting a campaign of misinformation against it. Rwanda reiterated its commitment to withdraw its forces 200 kilometres, a distance much further than the Kampala disengagement plan of 15 kilometres. It had already pulled back in Kasai province, but had been attacked by the Congolese Armed Forces (FAC). In similar circumstances, RPA and RCD forces were preparing to disengage in Katanga when they were attacked by Kabila forces and Interahamwe militias, forcing RPA to withdraw to Pweto. Rwanda said it would withdraw from Pweto if MONUC deployed there. Rwanda urged the Council fully to deploy MONUC without delay. The next day [S/2000/1256], Rwanda warned of continued fighting, and urged the United Nations to play its part in the situation, in particular the deployment of MONUC forces to oversee the withdrawal of troops.

Uganda, on 29 December [S/2000/1257], denied that its troops were involved in an offensive in Equateur province. It said that it remained ready to withdraw its troops in accordance with the Kampala disengagement plan and subsequent agreements.

Situation at year's end. In December [S/2001/128], over 5,000 combatants and refugees fled into Zambia to escape fighting in Katanga; some 3,000 FAC and 200 Zimbabwean soldiers were disarmed and escorted back to the DRC. Fighting was also reported in Equateur province and the security situation in parts of the eastern areas remained volatile. Rwanda and Uganda continued to keep their forces some 100 kilometres from Kisangani; however, RCD elements remained in the city.

MONUC financing

Following the Security Council's 24 February decision in **resolution 1291(2000)** to expand the size of MONUC to up to 5,537 military personnel, the Secretary-General, on 23 March [A/54/808], provided an estimate of the required resources in the amount of $200 million, inclusive of the $41 million commitment authority granted previously by the Advisory Committee on Administrative and Budgetary Questions (ACABQ) for MONUC's preliminary deployment. ACABQ, in its

28 March report [A/54/813], noted the amount and recommended that efforts be made to use locally available expertise as much as possible.

GENERAL ASSEMBLY ACTION (April)

On 7 April [meeting 95], the General Assembly, on the recommendation of the Fifth (Administrative and Budgetary) Committee [A/54/830], adopted **resolution 54/260 A** without vote [agenda item 175].

Financing of the United Nations Organization Mission in the Democratic Republic of the Congo

The General Assembly,

Having considered the report of the Secretary-General on the financing of the United Nations Organization Mission in the Democratic Republic of the Congo and the related report of the Advisory Committee on Administrative and Budgetary Questions,

Bearing in mind Security Council resolutions 1258(1999) of 6 August 1999 and 1279(1999) of 30 November 1999 regarding, respectively, the deployment to the Congo region of military liaison personnel and the establishment of the United Nations Organization Mission in the Democratic Republic of the Congo, and Security Council resolution 1291(2000) of 24 February 2000, by which the Council extended the mandate of the Mission until 31 August 2000,

Recognizing that the costs of the Mission are expenses of the Organization to be borne by Member States in accordance with Article 17, paragraph 2, of the Charter of the United Nations,

Recognizing also that, in order to meet the expenditures caused by the Mission, a different procedure is required from that applied to meet expenditures of the regular budget of the United Nations,

Taking into account the fact that the economically more developed countries are in a position to make relatively larger contributions and that the economically less developed countries have a relatively limited capacity to contribute towards such an operation,

Bearing in mind the special responsibilities of the States permanent members of the Security Council, as indicated in General Assembly resolution 1874(S-IV) of 27 June 1963, in the financing of such operations,

Noting with appreciation that voluntary contributions have been made to the Trust Fund to Support the Peace Process in the Democratic Republic of the Congo,

Mindful of the fact that it is essential to provide the Mission with the necessary financial resources to enable it to fulfil its responsibilities under the relevant resolutions of the Security Council,

1. *Expresses concern* about the financial situation with regard to peacekeeping activities, in particular as regards the reimbursements to troop contributors that bear additional burdens owing to overdue payments by Member States of their assessments;

2. *Urges* all Member States to make every possible effort to ensure payment of their assessed contributions to the United Nations Organization Mission in the Democratic Republic of the Congo in full and on time;

3. *Expresses concern* at the delay experienced by the Secretary-General in deploying and providing adequate resources to some recent peacekeeping missions, in particular those in Africa;

4. *Emphasizes* that all existing and future peace-keeping missions shall be given equal and non-discriminatory treatment in respect of financial and administrative arrangements;

5. *Also emphasizes* that all peacekeeping missions shall be provided with adequate resources for the effective and efficient discharge of their respective mandates;

6. *Requests* the Secretary-General to make the fullest possible use of facilities and equipment at the United Nations Logistics Base at Brindisi, Italy, in order to minimize the costs of procurement for the Mission, and for this purpose requests the Secretary-General to speed up the implementation of the asset management system at all peacekeeping missions in accordance with General Assembly resolution 52/1 of 15 October 1997;

7. *Endorses* the conclusions and recommendations contained in the report of the Advisory Committee on Administrative and Budgetary Questions, and requests the Secretary-General to ensure their full implementation;

8. *Requests* the Secretary-General to take all necessary action to ensure that the Mission is administered with a maximum of efficiency and economy;

9. *Also requests* the Secretary-General, in order to reduce the cost of employing General Service staff, to employ locally recruited staff for the Mission against General Service posts, commensurate with the requirements of the Mission;

10. *Authorizes* the Secretary-General to enter into commitments for the Mission for the period from 6 August 1999 to 30 June 2000 in an amount not exceeding 200 million United States dollars gross (199,760,000 dollars net), inclusive of the amount of 41,011,200 dollars gross (40,771,200 dollars net) previously authorized by the Advisory Committee, and requests the Secretary-General to establish a special account for the Mission;

11. *Decides*, as an ad hoc arrangement, to apportion the amount of 200 million dollars gross (199,760,000 dollars net) among Member States in accordance with the composition of groups set out in paragraphs 3 and 4 of General Assembly resolution 43/232 of 1 March 1989, as adjusted by the Assembly in its resolutions 44/192 B of 21 December 1989, 45/269 of 27 August 1991, 46/198 A of 20 December 1991, 47/218 A of 23 December 1992, 49/249 A of 20 July 1995, 49/249 B of 14 September 1995, 50/224 of 11 April 1996, 51/218 A to C of 18 December 1996 and 52/230 of 31 March 1998 and its decisions 48/472 A of 23 December 1993, 50/451 B of 23 December 1995 and 54/456 to 54/458 of 23 December 1999, and taking into account the scale of assessments for the years 1999 and 2000, as set out in its resolutions 52/215 A of 22 December 1997 and 54/237 A of 23 December 1999;

12. *Decides also* that, in accordance with the provisions of its resolution 973(X) of 15 December 1955, there shall be set off against the apportionment among Member States, as provided for in paragraph 11 above, their respective share in the Tax Equalization Fund of the estimated staff assessment income of 240,000 dollars approved for the Mission for the period from 6 August 1999 to 30 June 2000;

13. *Emphasizes* that no peacekeeping mission shall be financed by borrowing funds from other active peacekeeping missions;

14. *Encourages* the Secretary-General to continue to take additional measures to ensure the safety and security of all personnel under the auspices of the United Nations participating in the Mission;

15. *Invites* voluntary contributions to the Mission in cash and in the form of services and supplies acceptable to the Secretary-General, to be administered, as appropriate, in accordance with the procedure and practices established by the General Assembly;

16. *Requests* the Secretary-General to submit to the General Assembly, in September 2000, a comprehensive report on the financing of the Mission, including full budget estimates and information on the utilization of resources until the time of the submission of the report, to enable the Assembly to take action on it at the main part of its fifty-fifth session;

17. *Notes* the intention of the Secretary-General to submit to the General Assembly, during the second part of its resumed fifty-fourth session, a preliminary expenditure report for the Mission for the period from 6 August 1999 to 30 June 2000;

18. *Decides* to keep under review during its fifty-fourth session the item entitled "Financing of the United Nations Organization Mission in the Democratic Republic of the Congo".

In response to that resolution, the Secretary-General, on 19 May [A/54/872], prepared a preliminary expenditure report for MONUC covering 6 August 1999 to 30 June 2000. He revised the requirements for the Mission for that period from $200 million to $58,681,000 gross ($58,441,000 net), to cover the costs of preliminary deployment of military and civilian personnel to the Congo region, the immediate initial requirements for the establishment of MONUC, as well as resources for vehicles, communications and data-processing equipment required for up to 500 UN military observers and 100 civilian support staff. The amount of $141,319,000 gross, representing the balance of the commitment authority of $200 million gross granted by the Assembly for 1999-2000 would be carried over and used for 1 July 2000 to 30 June 2001.

GENERAL ASSEMBLY ACTION (June)

On 15 June [meeting 98], the General Assembly, on the recommendation of the Fifth Committee [A/54/830/Add.1], adopted **resolution 54/260 B** without vote [agenda item 175].

Financing of the United Nations Organization Mission in the Democratic Republic of the Congo

The General Assembly,

Having considered the report of the Secretary-General on the financing of the United Nations Organization Mission in the Democratic Republic of the Congo and the related oral report of the Advisory Committee on Administrative and Budgetary Questions,

Bearing in mind Security Council resolution 1291(2000) of 24 February 2000 concerning the extension of the mandate of the Mission,

1. *Notes* that, by 30 June 2000, only 500 United Nations military observers and 100 civilian support staff out of up to 5,537 military personnel, including up to 500 military observers, as indicated by the Secretary-General in his report, will have been deployed to the United Nations Organization Mission in the Democratic Republic of the Congo;

2. *Requests* the Secretary-General to take the necessary measures with a view to ensuring the deployment of military personnel and the provision of adequate resources to the Mission without any unnecessary delay;

3. *Decides* to reduce the commitment authority provided for in its resolution 54/260 A of 7 April 2000, totalling 200 million United States dollars gross (199,760,000 dollars net) for the operation of the Mission for the period from 6 August 1999 to 30 June 2000, to the amount of 58,681,000 dollars gross (58,441,000 dollars net);

4. *Authorizes* the Secretary-General to enter into commitments for the operation of the Mission for the period from 1 July 2000 to 30 June 2001 in an amount not exceeding 141,319,000 dollars gross (140,827,100 dollars net), which represents the difference between the commitment authority provided for in its resolution 54/260 A for the period from 6 August 1999 to 30 June 2000 and the reduced commitment authority provided for in paragraph 3 above;

5. *Reiterates its request* to the Secretary-General to submit to the General Assembly, in September 2000, a comprehensive report on the financing of the Mission, including full budget estimates and information on the utilization of resources up to the time of the submission of the report, to enable the Assembly to take action on it at the main part of its fifty-fifth session.

The Assembly, on 23 December, decided that the agenda item on MONUC financing would remain for consideration during its resumed fifty-fifth (2001) session (**decision 55/458**). By **decision 55/455** of the same date, the Assembly decided that the Fifth Committee would continue to consider the item.

In other action, the Assembly, in **resolution 55/166** on special assistance for the economic recovery and reconstruction of the DRC, invited Governments to continue to provide support (see p. 878). In **resolution 55/117**, the Assembly addressed the human rights situation in the DRC (see p. 738).

Burundi

Former President Nelson Mandela of South Africa, appointed in late 1999 as Facilitator of the Burundi peace process, undertook mediation efforts to move that process forward in 2000. At the beginning of the year, Burundi faced ongoing violence, in particular by rebel groups who refused to participate in the peace process, and mounting tension as the two main ethnic groups

remained hostile to each other. Coordinated mediation efforts were carried out not only by the Facilitator, but also at the regional level through a series of summits and by representatives of the Secretary-General.

Those efforts resulted in significant progress on 28 August with the signing of the Arusha Agreement on Peace and Reconciliation, a framework for political reform, which was eventually signed by 19 political parties. Some of the main combatant rebel forces, however, were not parties to the Agreement although they had joined the negotiations. The Security Council and the Facilitator called on the parties that remained outside the peace process to cease hostilities and to participate in the process. At the end of the year, armed groups continued to carry out attacks against government forces and on civilians. Burundi claimed that certain neighbouring countries were fuelling the war by supporting the rebel groups. As a result of the uncertain situation and the monitoring role foreseen for the United Nations under the Arusha Agreement, the Secretary-General recommended that the mandate of the United Nations Office in Burundi be extended until the end of the year, to which the Security Council agreed.

Political situation

The Secretary-General, at a 19 January meeting of the Security Council [S/PV.4091], warned that the situation in Burundi remained tense, with two ethnic groups remaining hostile to one another, a steadily escalating spiral of violence and killing and a faltering peace process in which the different parties paid lip service at best. Some progress had been achieved in the peace process but disagreements remained on key issues, such as the future composition of the army, the electoral system and the transition period, while others, such as guarantees for the minority community and the question of reconciliation versus impunity, had yet to be seriously addressed. There was also the larger volatile regional context of wars in neighbouring countries and the fluid refugee situation. The Burundian refugee population was estimated at 500,000 and more than 800,000 were internally displaced, many of them as a result of a government policy of forcibly relocating civilians.

The Facilitator of the Burundi peace process, Nelson Mandela, said that progress had been made in the past 18 months in the Arusha (United Republic of Tanzania) peace process, named for the series of regional summits on Burundi that began in 1996 [YUN 1996, p. 81]. The four committees had achieved progress. Two—those dealing with the nature of the conflict and the issue of genocide and with reconstruction and development—had nearly completed their work. The major outstanding issues were, respectively, the appropriate mechanism for dealing with the past and the recovery of property by returning refugees. The other two committees were dealing with democracy and good governance and with peace and security. Most of the parties were agreed on the principle of universal franchise, but differences remained on whether the parliament should be balanced in ethnic, gender or other terms. With regard to peace and security, the parties had agreed on principles for the organization of the defence and security forces, but they failed to agree on reform of the existing security forces or on the integration of armed groups into the security forces. Mr. Mandela, who had met with Burundian political parties and role players in Arusha on 16 January, noted the importance of making the process inclusive by inviting all groups to join.

Also addressing the Council, Burundi said that the security situation had significantly improved compared to 1995 and 1996 and the overall situation was under control. Only 4 provinces out of 17 still suffered from a lack of security. With respect to rural Bujumbura province, the Government had been obliged to establish regroupment camps for the protection of the people and to prevent destabilization of the capital through terrorist acts. Rejecting claims that the camps were an ethnic cleansing system, Burundi said it intended to close about 10 of the 50 camps within two weeks and the remainder once security was restored. It elaborated on those plans in a 17 January statement [S/2000/33]. Burundi appealed to the international community to provide Burundi with support in view of its dire socio-economic situation.

SECURITY COUNCIL ACTION (January)

On 19 January [meeting 4091], the Security Council unanimously adopted **resolution 1286(2000)**. The draft [S/2000/29] was prepared in consultations among Council members.

The Security Council,

Reaffirming its previous resolutions and the statements by its President on the situation in Burundi,

Expressing concern at the dire economic, humanitarian and social conditions in Burundi,

Expressing deep concern at the ongoing violence and insecurity in Burundi marked by increased attacks by armed groups on the civilian population in and around the capital,

Noting with concern the implications of the situation in Burundi for the region as well as the consequences for Burundi of continued regional instability,

Recognizing the important role of the States of the region, in particular the United Republic of Tanzania,

which is host to hundreds of thousands of Burundian refugees and home to the Julius Nyerere Foundation, which has provided outstanding support to the talks,

Noting that the United Nations agencies and regional and non-governmental organizations, in cooperation with host Governments, are making use of the Guiding Principles on Internal Displacement, inter alia, in Africa,

Welcoming the human rights programme undertaken by the United Nations and the cooperation afforded to it by·the Government of Burundi and political parties in Burundi,

Reaffirming that the renewed Arusha peace process represents the most viable basis for a resolution of the conflict, together with the continued efforts to build an internal political partnership in Burundi,

1. *Warmly endorses and strongly supports* the designation by the Eighth Arusha Regional Summit, on 1 December 1999, of Nelson Mandela, former President of the Republic of South Africa, as the new Facilitator of the Arusha peace process, successor to the late Mwalimu Julius Nyerere, expresses its strongest support for his efforts to achieve a peaceful solution to the conflict in Burundi, and welcomes the successful meeting in Arusha, on 16 January 2000, launching his initiative;

2. *Reiterates its strong support* for the renewed Arusha peace process, endorses the call at the Eighth Arusha Regional Summit for all parties to the conflict in Burundi to extend maximum cooperation to the new Facilitator of the peace process, and calls for increased efforts to build an internal political partnership in Burundi;

3. *Endorses* efforts by the Secretary-General to enhance the role of the United Nations in Burundi, in particular the continued work of his Special Representative for the Great Lakes region;

4. *Commends* those Burundian parties, including the Government, that have demonstrated their commitment to continue negotiations, and calls upon all parties that remain outside the Arusha peace process to cease hostilities and to participate fully in that process;

5. *Expresses appreciation* for international donor support, and appeals for increased assistance for the Arusha peace process;

6. *Condemns* continuing violence perpetrated by all parties, in particular by those non-State actors that refuse to participate in the Arusha peace process, and strongly urges all parties to end the ongoing armed conflict and to resolve their differences peacefully;

7. *Condemns also* attacks against civilians in Burundi, and calls for an immediate end to these criminal acts;

8. *Strongly condemns* the murder of United Nations Children's Fund and World Food Programme personnel and Burundian civilians in Rutana province, in October 1999, and urges that the perpetrators be effectively brought to justice;

9. *Calls* for all parties to ensure the safe and unhindered access of humanitarian assistance to those in need in Burundi, and to guarantee fully the safety, security and freedom of movement of United Nations and associated personnel;

10. *Calls also* for the immediate, full, safe and unhindered access of humanitarian workers and human rights observers to all regroupment camps, and calls

further for internees to have access to their livelihoods outside these camps;

11. *Encourages* further progress between the United Nations and the Government of Burundi and political parties in Burundi in establishing appropriate security guarantees for United Nations humanitarian agencies to resume field operations;

12. *Calls upon* neighbouring States, where appropriate, to take measures to halt cross-border insurgent activity and the illicit flow of arms and ammunition, and to ensure the neutrality, security and civilian character of refugee camps;

13. *Calls* for donors to provide humanitarian and human rights assistance to Burundi and to resume substantial economic and development assistance with due regard to security conditions;

14. *Urges* the international community to examine the economic development needs of Burundi, with a view to establishing stable long-term conditions for the well-being of the Burundian people and the return of refugees;

15. *Decides* to remain actively seized of the matter.

Arusha Summit (February). On 21 February, the Presidents of Burundi, Mozambique, Rwanda, South Africa, Uganda and the United Republic of Tanzania and the Vice-President of Kenya met in Arusha to discuss the political and security situation in Burundi and the peace negotiations [S/2000/165].

The Arusha Summit noted with regret that the security situation was deteriorating as fighting continued, claiming innocent lives and destroying property. It further noted the Government's announcement that it had disbanded 11 regroupment camps. It recalled, however, that the decision of the Eighth Arusha Regional Summit (December 1999) was to immediately disband all of them and called on the Government of Burundi to take appropriate measures accordingly.

Communications (February/March). In a 4 February statement [S/2000/97], the EU Presidency said that the resumption of the Arusha process and the subsequent Council discussion on Burundi marked a new phase that it hoped would give a fresh impetus to the peace process. The EU, however, remained concerned at the ongoing violence and insecurity in Burundi, as well as the increasing flow of refugees and internally displaced people. It called on the Government to proceed with the dismantling of the regroupment camps. Concerned over cross-border insurgent activity, the EU welcomed the agreement between Burundi and the United Republic of Tanzania to hold consultations on border issues.

In a 24 March statement [S/2000/275], the EU expressed concern about the assassination in November 1999 of Gabriel Gisabwamana, a Burundian member of parliament who was engaged in inter-Burundian talks.

Political reforms. Burundi, in a 5 May letter to the Security Council President [S/2000/406], responded to concerns expressed with regard to the functioning of political parties, certain detainees regarded as political prisoners, assembly sites and freedom of the press. It said that there were 14 registered political parties that participated in the political life of the country. They were governed by the Transitional Constitution and the law on political parties. With regard to the so-called political prisoners, Burundi made the point that all prisoners whose cases had been raised by certain politicians had in fact been detained for ordinary crimes, including assassination attempts, massacres, participation in armed gangs or terrorist attacks, and arming themselves against the State authority. It acknowledged that the prison population had increased from 4,500 in 1993 to 10,200 at the start of 1999, as a result of the recent crisis, and the Burundian judicial system was not prepared to handle such a workload. Since 1999, the Government had taken specific measures to reduce overcrowding in the prisons, including the release of prisoners not held on serious charges, more expeditious trials and conditional release, thereby reducing the prison population to 8,700. The situation of protected sites in rural Bujumbura province was not a result of a policy of concentrating the population but rather of a situation of insecurity. It was adopted to protect the population from acts of violence on the part of the armed bands and to prevent people from being caught in the crossfire between government troops and rebels. Since the security situation had improved, the Government had begun dismantling the sites in February 2000, releasing nearly 100,000 persons, with the remainder to be released within the next two months. Public and private media were operating in Burundi and Burundians could express their views through the national and some foreign media. The public press was regulated by national law. The supposed restraints on the media were false, Burundi said.

Appointments. The Secretary-General informed the Security Council on 11 May [S/2000/423] of his intention to appoint Jean Arnault (France) as his Representative and Head of the United Nations Office in Burundi as of 1 June. The Council took note of that decision on the same day [S/2000/424].

On 30 June [S/2000/650], the Secretary-General said that the Arusha peace process relating to the Burundi peace negotiations had just entered a crucial phase, and the possibility could not be ruled out that a peace agreement would be reached by the end of the year. Therefore, he had decided to extend until 31 October 2000 the appointment of Ayité Jean-Claude Kpakpo (Benin), Senior United Nations Adviser to the Facilitator, which expired on 30 June. By a letter of 5 July [S/2000/651], the Council took note of the decision.

Regional summit (July). The Eleventh Arusha Regional Consultative Summit on Burundi (19 July) issued a press communiqué [S/2000/836] in which it noted with satisfaction that the negotiations under the Facilitator had reached a very advanced and encouraging stage. In that regard, the Summit commended the Facilitator, members of the facilitation team and the Burundian negotiating parties whose efforts had made the progress possible. The Summit met separately with leaders of the Burundian negotiating parties and called on them to redouble their efforts and commitment to the negotiations in a spirit of give and take so as to resolve all outstanding differences. The Summit was attended by the Presidents of Burundi, Kenya, Uganda, the United Republic of Tanzania and Zambia, the Prime Minister of Ethiopia and a minister representing the President of Rwanda.

Arusha Agreement

The peace process moved forward significantly on 28 August with the signing of the Arusha Agreement on Peace and Reconciliation in Burundi. The Secretary-General, addressing the Security Council on 29 September [S/PV.4201], described it as a comprehensive blueprint for the reform of Burundian society, which addressed the root causes of the conflict, such as exclusion and genocide, as well as the tragic consequences of the war, such as the plight of hundreds of thousands of refugees and internally displaced people. He noted, however, that before that ambitious programme could be fully implemented, a number of obstacles needed to be overcome.

The draft compromise proposal had been based on the inputs received by the facilitation team led by Mr. Mandela. A majority of participating parties signed the document drafted by the team, and a number of parties that did not sign on 28 August subsequently did so. The Facilitator informed the Council that the significance of the Agreement was that the 19 political parties represented a united forum that could deal with the remaining issues and with the combatant forces that were not yet part of the process.

One of the most crucial issues—the integration of a Burundi national defence force—was settled. Both Hutu and Tutsi leaders had agreed that 50 per cent of the defence force would be from the Hutu community and 50 per cent from the Tutsi community, with accommodation being made for the Twa community as well. It was further agreed that a body of respected persons, inde-

pendent from the defence force, would oversee that process.

The political agreement was not yet the final and comprehensive agreement, Mr. Mandela said, as some of the main combatant rebel forces were not parties to the signed agreement. However, they had been invited to join the Arusha process. He called on the rebel groups to announce a ceasefire to halt the slaughter of innocent civilians. As to the regroupment camps, President Buyoya had given his assurances that they had been closed but that some inmates refused to leave because of the security situation inside the country, which Mr. Mandela had no reason to doubt.

In a letter to the Security Council [S/2000/1096], the Secretary-General said that the Arusha Agreement called for the establishment of the Implementation Monitoring Committee, to be chaired by the United Nations, which would supervise the implementation of the Agreement; ensure respect for the implementation timetable and accurate interpretation of the Agreement; arbitrate on disputes that might arise among the signatories; give guidance to and coordinate the commissions and subcommissions set up to implement the Agreement; and assist the transitional Government in mobilizing the resources required for implementation.

In a 19 September statement [S/2000/890], the EU welcomed the mediator's decision to hold a further session of negotiations in Nairobi on 20 September with the participation of the Burundian Government, representatives of the rebel movements and those parties that had not yet signed the Agreement but had undertaken to do so at the Nairobi meeting. Pointing to the urgency of finalizing a peace accord that had the agreement of all parties, the EU called for an immediate general ceasefire.

SECURITY COUNCIL ACTION (September)

On 29 September [meeting 4201], following consultations among Security Council members, the President made statement **S/PRST/2000/29** on behalf of the Council:

> The Security Council expresses its warm appreciation to former President Nelson Mandela, in his capacity as Facilitator of the Burundi peace process in Arusha, for his briefing to the Council on 29 September 2000. It commends him for his tireless efforts in the cause of peace in Burundi, and encourages him to continue his efforts.
>
> The Council welcomes the signature, on 28 August 2000, of the Arusha Peace Accord, as well as the signatures added to that Accord at a regional summit, held on 20 September 2000, in Nairobi. It commends those Burundian parties, including the Gov-

ernment of Burundi, that have demonstrated their commitment to continued negotiations.

The Council stresses that the key to achieving a lasting peace agreement in Burundi lies with the Burundian parties. It is convinced that compromise is the only means to reach such an agreement, and to this end urges all parties to work towards resolving any remaining differences over the Peace Accord, and to proceed to its implementation.

The Council reiterates its call, in resolution 1286(2000) of 19 January 2000, on all parties that remain outside the peace process to cease hostilities and to participate fully in that process. In this regard, it supports the call of the Facilitator to the rebel groups to clarify their positions by 20 October 2000.

The Council is encouraged by the engagement of regional States. It urges them to continue their efforts and, especially, to use their influence to draw the armed groups firmly into the peace process.

The Council condemns all attacks on civilians populations. It remains deeply concerned at the continuing level of violence in Burundi, in particular at acts perpetrated by rebel groups, despite the call made to them to hold direct negotiations with the Burundian Government to secure a lasting ceasefire agreement.

The Council remains deeply concerned at the dire economic, humanitarian and social conditions in Burundi, and calls upon all parties to cooperate fully with non-governmental organizations and international organizations involved in the implementation of the Peace Accord. It urges all concerned to ensure that former camp inhabitants are protected, respected and enabled to return voluntarily and in safety and dignity to their homes.

The Council notes the holding of a meeting of donor countries in Brussels on 15 September 2000. It welcomes the call made at that meeting for progressive resumption of assistance to Burundi, including development aid, to alleviate its urgent humanitarian and economic problems as it makes progress in its internal peace negotiations. In this regard, it also welcomes the plan to hold a donor conference in Paris in due course.

The Council stands ready to consider practical ways in which it can best support the peace process. To this end, the Council requests the Secretary-General urgently to report to it on specific actions the United Nations can undertake in the consolidation of peace and economic recovery in Burundi.

The Council will remain actively seized of the matter.

Following the issuance of the statement, the Council held a private meeting, at which it held an exchange of views with Mr. Mandela [S/PV.4202]. On 20 October [S/2000/1014], Burundi requested the Council to alter misleading wording in the French translation of the 29 September presidential statement and urged it to commend the total dismantling of the regroupment camps in Burundi.

Situation at year's end. In the months following the signing of the Arusha Agreement, the situation remained unclear. In a 20 October statement [S/2000/1059], the EU Presidency expressed concern at the scale and intensity of attacks by armed groups in Burundi and at the effects of clashes between those groups and government forces on the population. Disquieted by the risks that such violence entailed for the peace process, the EU reaffirmed its support for Mr. Mandela's efforts and those of the signatories to consolidate the Arusha Agreement. It condemned the use of force to settle disputes and urged the armed groups to respond to the calls made at the Thirteenth Regional Summit on Burundi (Nairobi, Kenya, 20 September) for an unconditional suspension of hostilities and for the urgent resumption of negotiations to flesh out and implement the Arusha Agreement. It called on countries able to influence the armed groups, in particular the DRC, the United Republic of Tanzania and Zimbabwe, to urge those groups to choose the path of peace and negotiation without delay.

Burundi, on 20 December [S/2000/1220], urged the Council to publicly condemn the rebels who continued to commit acts of violence against the population, and to use its full authority to persuade those groups to end the violence and come to the negotiating table so that a ceasefire could be reached. Burundi charged that certain neighbouring countries were fuelling the war in Burundi. It said that the Council should help to disarm, arrest and repatriate to Burundi the rebels of two groups that had taken refuge in Zambia. Burundi thanked the Council for mobilizing the donor community to resume cooperation and assistance to Burundi with a view to supporting the Arusha Agreement and alleviating the suffering of the population caused by a war that had lasted seven years. A donors' conference was held in Paris on 11 and 12 December. President Buyoya's statement to that conference was annexed to Burundi's 20 December letter.

Extension of UNOB mandate

The Secretary-General, in a 10 November letter [S/2000/1096], noted that under the Arusha Agreement, the United Nations was requested to chair the Implementation Monitoring Committee (see p. 146). For the range of activities required, it would be necessary to adjust the current political mandate and strengthen UN capacity in Burundi. Further study was required to determine what was expected of the United Nations in that role but, in the meantime, he recommended that the Security Council extend the mandate of the United Nations Office in Burundi (UNOB) until 31 December 2001. On 15 November [S/2000/1097], the Council took note of the information and agreed with the recommendation.

Appointment extended. On 9 November [S/2000/1098], the Secretary-General, noting that several issues remained to be negotiated after the signing of the Arusha Agreement, informed the Security Council of his decision to extend the appointment of Mr. Kpakpo, Senior Adviser to the Facilitator, until 31 January 2001. The Council took note of the decision on 15 November [S/2000/1099].

Rwanda

Rwanda carried out fundamental changes in several areas in 2000: decentralization of government and the transition to democracy, moves to draw up a new constitution, overhauling of the justice system and the introduction of *gacaca*, a traditional system of justice, and the promotion of a culture of human rights, unity and reconciliation. With those steps, Rwanda began moving out of the shadow of the 1994 genocide and laying the foundation for the transition to democracy. The regional crisis remained relevant as the ongoing conflicts (see under the DRC, above) created a feeling of insecurity and fear among the population and blocked efforts towards reconciliation. In general, however, the security situation continued to improve in 2000, resulting in a corresponding decline in alleged abuses by the Rwandan armed forces, despite some incidents of infiltration and related violence in March. The drought and food shortages in the eastern part of the country led to population movements. Meanwhile, some 45,000 Rwandan refugees returned from the DRC between January and May and some 60,000 more were expected later in the year.

Inquiry into UN response to 1994 genocide

The Security Council, on 14 April [S/PV.4127], considered the 1999 report of the Independent Inquiry into the actions of the United Nations during the 1994 genocide in Rwanda [S/1999/1257]. Addressing the Council, the Chairman of the Inquiry, Ingvar Carlsson, said that the purpose of the report was to establish the facts related to the UN role during the genocide and to make recommendations for the future. Summarizing the Inquiry's findings [YUN 1999, p. 95], Mr. Carlsson stated that the overriding failure of the United Nations was lack of resources and the lack of political will to act. He further summarized a number of recommendations made by the Inquiry for future peacekeeping efforts [ibid., p. 96],

key among them the need to improve UN peacekeeping capacity.

The representative of Rwanda said the report clearly showed that the world had failed his country. The victims of the genocide were still suffering from physical, psychological and post-trauma hardships. What the country currently needed was a mini–Marshall plan as Rwanda struggled to rebuild itself.

Having heard speakers from 16 countries, the Council concluded the current stage of its consideration of the agenda item on the situation concerning Rwanda.

In a 17 August letter [S/2000/818], Bangladesh, referring to the Inquiry's report, said that some of the remarks made about the Bangladesh contingent lacked clarity, objectivity and factual accuracy or were seriously misleading.

Throughout the year, the International Tribunal for Rwanda continued to try a number of persons accused of the crime of genocide and/or crimes against humanity committed during the 1994 conflict (see PART FOUR, Chapter II).

Arms embargo

On 20 December [S/2000/1227], the Chairman of the Security Council Committee established pursuant to resolution 918(1994) concerning the arms embargo against Rwanda [YUN 1994, p. 285] submitted to the Council a report on its 2000 activities. The Committee was mandated to seek information regarding the implementation of the arms embargo. It recalled that it had no specific monitoring mechanism to ensure implementation of the embargo and relied solely on the cooperation of States and organizations in a position to provide pertinent information. During the year, no violations were brought to the Committee's attention.

Financing of UNAMIR

The General Assembly, by **decision 54/500** of 5 September, included in the draft agenda of its fifty-fifth session the item on financing of the United Nations Assistance Mission for Rwanda (UNAMIR). The military component of UNAMIR had been withdrawn from Rwanda in 1996 [YUN 1996, p. 62] and the liquidation process was begun at that time. On 23 December, the Assembly decided that the agenda item would remain for consideration at its resumed fifty-fifth (2001) session (**decision 55/458**); it decided that the Fifth Committee should continue to consider the item (**decision 55/455**).

Angola

In 2000, the overall situation in Angola remained unstable and guerrilla activities by the National Union for the Total Independence of Angola (UNITA) exacerbated an already alarming humanitarian situation. The Government continued its successful offensive, re-establishing its authority in the central, northern and eastern regions in a number of UNITA strongholds and capturing areas in the south and south-eastern parts of the country. Military operations on the southern and eastern Angolan borders spilled into neighbouring Namibia and Zambia, where, in addition to the refugee influx, bombing and shelling incidents were reported. By year's end, the number of persons internally displaced due to the conflict had increased to more than 2.7 million. The Secretary-General, concerned that the situation appeared to be entering a new phase of political and military impasse, said that if the current trend continued, security and humanitarian problems, especially in the border regions of neighbouring Namibia and Zambia, could worsen and further threaten the peace and security of the entire subregion.

Implementation of the 1994 Lusaka Protocol [YUN 1994, p. 348], by which the two sides agreed that the State administration would be extended, remained at a standstill. In July, the Government stated that UNITA should return to the peace process to complete its outstanding tasks under the Protocol as the Government had already concluded its part of the agreement. On the other hand, UNITA's leader, Jonas Savimbi, had said it was the Government's prerogative to initiate talks with UNITA, which had earlier in the year reiterated its readiness to hold talks with the Angolan Government, noting that it did not object to an all-inclusive national dialogue to end the conflict. President José Eduardo dos Santos stressed that the Lusaka Protocol was still a valid basis for the peace process and outlined a programme of action expected to culminate in legislative and presidential elections. However, the Government maintained it did not consider Mr. Savimbi a credible partner for dialogue, but it permitted his supporters who surrendered to government forces to carry out political activities.

During the year, the Panel of Experts established by Security Council resolution 1237(1999) [YUN 1999, p. 112] to investigate violations of Council sanctions against UNITA stated in its final report that it was clear that the sanctions were ineffective. UNITA could still procure its needs for war and sell its diamonds, its officials travelled with little restriction and UNITA continued to be active in international capitals through "unofficial" offices and representatives.

In April, the Council reiterated that the primary cause of the crisis in Angola was UNITA's refusal to comply with its obligations under the Lusaka Protocol and relevant Council resolutions. It demanded that UNITA comply immediately and without condition and stressed the obligation of all Member States to comply fully with the measures imposed against UNITA, emphasizing that non-compliance constituted a violation of the provisions of the UN Charter.

Also during the year, the Government of Angola approved the status-of-mission agreement for the United Nations Office in Angola (UNOA), noting that the new Office, which replaced the United Nations Observer Mission in Angola (MONUA) in 1999, should aim to strengthen and build the country's capacity in the areas of humanitarian assistance and human rights and serve as a liaison between the Government and the Secretary-General.

Political and military developments

The Government of Angola continued to gain ground in 2000, reinforcing its military action and campaign for the political isolation of UNITA. In Luanda and some provincial capitals, the UNITA Restoration Committee continued to call for an end to the conflict by Jonas Savimbi's group, in accordance with the provisions of the 1994 Lusaka Protocol [YUN 1994, p. 348]. That agreement covered, among other matters, the withdrawal, quartering and demilitarization of all UNITA forces; the disarming of civilians; integration of forces into a national military; police functions; the electoral process; and national reconciliation. A number of political parties and church groups also appealed for resumed national dialogue and cessation of hostilities, and some civic organizations emphasized the need for a general amnesty law and for holding an all-inclusive national conference to discuss the country's problems. President dos Santos announced that general elections would be held in 2001 and it was promised that all political parties would be consulted prior to fixing an election date. While opposition parties welcomed the announcement of elections, they questioned the timeliness of the initiative because of the continuing civil war.

In February, Angola approved the status-of-mission agreement for UNOA, which the Government expected would assist in capacity-building in the areas of human rights and humanitarian assistance.

Report of Secretary-General (January). The Secretary-General, in a January report [S/2000/23] submitted in response to Security Council resolution 1268(1999) [YUN 1999, p. 109], described developments in Angola since October 1999 [ibid., p. 110]. He stated that, following the Government's successful military campaign, State authority had been re-established in the vast territory previously occupied by UNITA. However, hostilities continued and the escalation of fighting into Namibia caused concern.

Meanwhile, the Government continued to reinforce its military action and campaign for political isolation of UNITA. In Luanda and some provincial capitals, the UNITA Restoration Committee continued calling for an end to the conflict by Mr. Savimbi's group. A number of political parties and church groups also appealed for resumed national dialogue and cessation of hostilities.

The report noted that the expert panel of the Security Council Committee established pursuant to resolution 864(1993) [YUN 1993, p. 256] visited Angola and other countries in Southern Africa in October 1999 to discuss ways to improve implementation of measures imposed against UNITA. In January, the Committee's Chairman consulted with Angolan authorities on the impact of those sanctions and to discuss additional measures to strengthen their implementation.

The intensified military operations and precarious security conditions throughout Angola had reportedly been accompanied by human rights abuses. The United Nations had been unable to verify such information because it lacked access to most of Angola, but it appeared that various military elements, including UNITA, were responsible for looting of crops and destruction of property. The intensification of the conflict and re-establishment of the Government in areas previously held by UNITA also sparked debate on the country's democratization process. Since relocation of its personnel to Luanda in early 1999 [YUN 1999, p. 106], MONUA's Human Rights Division discontinued its activities outside the Angolan capital, except in Benguela province, where it set up human rights centres. It also carried out assessment missions and identified new projects for expanded operations in several other provinces. The Government had identified six provinces for priority human rights activities in 2000.

The humanitarian situation in the country remained precarious, with the war-affected population estimated at 3.7 million persons, of whom nearly 2 million were internally displaced. Forty-two per cent of children under 5 years were underweight, and agricultural production for 2000 was projected to be unsatisfactory for the popula-

tion. Moreover, the humanitarian status of one third of the population living in inaccessible areas remained unknown. Landmine incidents had also increased, with 409 civilians, mainly women, falling victim to landmines between January and November 1999. The Secretary-General hoped the donor community would respond to the funding requirement of the 2000 UN consolidated inter-agency appeal for Angola amounting to $258 million [YUN 1999, p. 832].

The Secretary-General observed that UNITA, through its refusal to comply with obligations under the Lusaka Protocol, bore the primary responsibility for the current state of affairs in Angola. Welcoming the indication by the Angolan authorities that the Lusaka Protocol remained a valid basis for the peace process, the Secretary-General urged UNITA to demonstrate its preparedness to fulfil its commitments under the Protocol for genuine national reconciliation.

Communication (January). In a 17 January declaration on the situation in Angola [S/2000/32], the EU Presidency urged UNITA to cease immediately its military activities and appealed for its compliance with the Lusaka Protocol. The EU encouraged the Angolan Government to create the appropriate political, social and economic environment for democracy and rule of law to flourish, and called for an end to mine-laying activities by the Government and UNITA. It also stated its readiness to consider assistance for the Government of Angola in rebuilding and reconstruction in a democratic environment.

Report of Secretary-General (April). In an 11 April report on UNOA [S/2000/304 & Corr.1], submitted pursuant to resolution 1268(1999), the Secretary-General covered political developments, the military situation, human rights aspects, humanitarian aspects and the socio-economic situation of Angola since January. He stated that the Government continued to call on the followers of UNITA to abandon Mr. Savimbi, and President dos Santos expressed his readiness to forgive all those who renounced the use of force to attain political power. A number of civic organizations had underlined the need for a general amnesty law and for holding an all-inclusive national conference to discuss the country's problems. The President had announced that general elections would be held in 2001, and the Secretary-General of the ruling Popular Movement for the Liberation of Angola (MPLA) had promised that all political parties would be consulted prior to fixing a date for the elections. Consultations had begun on a draft constitution proposed by the MPLA members of Parliament. In the meantime, while opposition parties welcomed the announcement of elections, they questioned the prematurity of the initiative because of the continuing civil war.

The Secretary-General reported that the Government reiterated its rejection of any negotiation with Mr. Savimbi, and a recent offer of mediation by the Government of South Africa for a negotiated end of the conflict had been rejected by the Angolan Government, which had justified the rejection on the grounds that, among other factors, South Africa was a member of the Southern African Development Community, which had declared Mr. Savimbi a war criminal and an invalid interlocutor in the Angolan peace process. In March, the UNITA Secretary-General stated that it was the Government's prerogative to initiate discussions with UNITA to end the fighting. He said UNITA had written to the Secretary-General seeking a change in the composition of the three observer States of the Lusaka peace process (Portugal, the Russian Federation and the United States), as the neutrality of the three countries was compromised by their national interests. He reiterated UNITA's readiness to hold talks with the Angolan Government, noting that it did not object to an all-inclusive national dialogue to end the conflict.

The security situation along the border with Zambia had reportedly improved, and Zambia had agreed to increase efforts to tighten UN sanctions against UNITA. The Office of the United Nations High Commissioner for Refugees was also able, with the cooperation of Zambian authorities, to complete the transfer of the last group of Angolan refugees further inland. The Angolan Government had been undertaking diplomatic initiatives to explain its position on the war and the new political dispensation it planned leading to elections, as well as to continue efforts to further isolate Mr. Savimbi.

In March, the report of the Panel of Experts on violations of Security Council sanctions against UNITA was issued and considered by the Council (see p. 154). A number of Governments and corporations announced that they would be taking measures to comply with the sanctions. UNITA dismissed allegations in the sanctions report on the grounds that they were based on statements made by defectors.

Regarding the general military situation, reports indicated that in spite of military clashes in several regions in the country, government forces continued to be effective in further reducing the conventional war capability of UNITA, forcing it to resort to guerrilla attacks. Military developments continued to exacerbate the deplorable humanitarian situation affecting the civilian population and to cause instability in much of the country and along the border with Namibia and Zambia. Government forces effectively controlled the major cities, but the continuous influx of internally displaced persons fleeing the countryside, where fighting, road ambushes and mine incidents were common, concerned relief organizations.

The Secretary-General referred to allegations of grave human rights violations that had surfaced against both government and UNITA forces, noting that UNOA addressed mainly capacity-building initiatives designed to overcome structural problems in areas not affected directly by the conflict. UNOA continued to promote gradual acceptance by the Government of the existence of serious human rights problems and had been supporting the Office of the Prosecutor-General with training and material to develop a computerized case-tracking system, expected to be fully operational in Luanda, Benguela and Huíla provinces by the end of March. A workshop was organized to address recognized deficiencies in Angola's fulfilment of its international obligations when producing required reports for 6 of the 20 international human rights treaties to which it was signatory. UNOA identified three basic human rights issues that required attention in Angola: the need to ensure respect for the human rights of internally displaced persons; the lack of the necessary government structures to ensure respect for human rights in areas recently captured from UNITA forces; and the continuing decline of basic socio-economic benefits for a substantial majority of the population.

Of a total population estimated at 12.6 million, 3.7 million were affected by the war, of which 1.6 million were internally displaced. Owing to increased guerrilla warfare activities at the beginning of 2000, internally displaced population numbers began increasing. The lack of security for humanitarian relief operations continued to constrain the work of the international community, confining the scope of humanitarian activities to areas inside and around the provincial capitals. Mine clearance, which had been curtailed since the conflict reignited, was important for any safe resumption of agricultural and commercial activities and for the eventual return of internally displaced persons to their homes in rural areas. In March, at the request of the Secretary-General, a delegation travelled to the provinces of Bié, Huambo and Uíge to determine challenges posed by internally displaced persons and the capacity of relief agencies to respond, and to assess gaps in the humanitarian response. Other needs assessment missions were also planned to review short-term requirements of vulnerable populations, the capacity of agencies to respond and additional resources needed in accessible locations. The Secretary-General noted that 25 per cent of the required $258 million for the 2000 inter-agency consolidated appeal for Angola was covered, but the majority of aid received was for food, while complementary sectors of intervention remained underfunded. Despite the constraints of the war situation, which obliged UN operational agencies to review their programmes and intervention strategies, the United Nations Development Programme (UNDP) continued to assist the Government to address the humanitarian and development crisis. Among other activities, UNDP, in March, organized a conference to define a national policy for social assistance.

The Secretary-General reiterated that UNITA clearly bore the primary responsibility for Angola's state of affairs. He observed that the Government had announced plans to re-establish political and military stability, confine the war to controlled areas and complete the extension of State administration throughout Angolan territory. It also planned to institute monetary stability, further economic development and establish humanitarian and social service assistance programmes for the civilian population. The United Nations would continue humanitarian relief and assistance in human rights capacity-building activities in Angola. The Secretary-General announced his intention to designate the head of UNOA and recommended that the Security Council continue the Office's activities for a further six-month period.

SECURITY COUNCIL ACTION (April)

On 13 April [meeting 4126], the Security Council unanimously adopted **resolution 1294(2000)**. The draft [S/2000/307] was prepared during consultations among Council members.

The Security Council,

Reaffirming its resolution 696(1991) of 30 May 1991 and all subsequent relevant resolutions, in particular resolution 1268(1999) of 15 October 1999,

Reaffirming also its view that a continued presence of the United Nations in Angola can contribute greatly to the promotion of peace, national reconciliation, human rights and regional security,

Having considered the report of the Secretary-General of 11 April 2000,

1. *Endorses* the decision contained in paragraph 51 of the report of the Secretary-General to extend the mandate of the United Nations Office in Angola for a period of six months until 15 October 2000;

2. *Requests* the Secretary-General to continue his efforts to implement the tasks of the United Nations Office in Angola as outlined in resolution 1268(1999);

3. *Also requests* the Secretary-General to provide every three months a report on developments in Angola, including his recommendations about additional measures the Council might consider to promote the peace process in Angola;

4. *Decides* to remain actively seized of the matter.

Report of Secretary-General (July). In a 12 July report [S/2000/678], submitted pursuant to resolution 1294(2000), the Secretary-General stated that despite the Government's efforts to consolidate its authority throughout Angola, the absence of dialogue continued to create an unstable political and military situation. UNITA continued its guerrilla activities, impeding people's movement in certain areas and causing an increase in the total numbers of internally displaced persons and refugees. In addition to an influx of refugees into neighbouring countries, particularly Namibia and Zambia, and the accompanying adverse socio-economic consequences, the conflict also caused an increase in tensions between Angola and Zambia. However, on 1 July, it was announced that the two countries had agreed to investigate charges of border violations and to create a permanent communication link between their regional military commanders and security chiefs in Moxico and Cuando Cubango provinces in Angola and in the north-western and western provinces in Zambia.

Internal efforts to promote dialogue for peace continued and, in April, a coalition of Angolan opposition political parties presented a list of proposals, "Agenda for Peace", to the Government. In May, the Secretary-General's Adviser for Special Assignments in Africa, Ibrahim Gambari (Nigeria), visited Angola to discuss the prospects for peace and the terms of reference of UNOA. With regard to the military situation, the report noted that government forces continued to be effective in reducing the conventional war capability of UNITA, which pursued guerrilla activities, particularly along the border with Zambia.

While the human rights situation remained grave, the Government had indicated it was prepared to recognize the existence of abuses and to develop regular procedures to redress them with the support of the international community and members of Angolan society. Meanwhile, the plight of children was particularly acute after the long years of conflict, and the Secretary-General suggested that, to increase the level of child protection, greater efforts should be made to refrain from targeting civilians, to secure access to vulnerable populations comprising women and children and to ensure the disarmament, demobilization and reintegration of former child combatants. The special needs of children who were victims of mine injuries and of internally displaced women and children should also be stressed. In addition, UNOA should continue its efforts to include child protection advisers as an integral part of its operations.

The humanitarian situation remained precarious, with more than 1 million persons relying on food distributions to survive and about 2.5 million receiving humanitarian assistance. The World Food Programme (WFP) was facing a possible breakdown in the food pipeline from the end of August and it was forced to cut the number of its beneficiaries. In other developments, a detailed plan of action for implementing the rapid assessment of critical needs was drafted and was expected to form the framework for humanitarian interventions during the second half of the year. It was also reported that humanitarian access to populations at risk increased as new locations came under government administration.

The Secretary-General again stated that UNITA was primarily responsible for the return to war in Angola because it refused to comply with key provisions of the Lusaka Protocol, in particular its failure to demilitarize its forces and to allow State administration to be extended throughout the country. Expressing deep concern regarding the protracted conflicts and absence of any meaningful attempt to reach a political settlement, the Secretary-General said his Adviser for Special Assignments in Africa would hold further talks with Angolan authorities. He announced that the UNOA head had been selected and he would inform the Council shortly of the appointment.

Communications (July/August). On 31 July [S/2000/760], the Secretary-General informed the Council that he had appointed Mussagy Jeichande (Mozambique) to be his Representative and Head of UNOA. On 2 August [S/2000/761], the Council President informed the Secretary-General that Council members took note of his decision.

Report of Secretary-General (October). In an October report [S/2000/977], submitted pursuant to Council resolution 1294(2000), the Secretary-General provided an update of developments in Angola, stating that the overall situation remained unstable. UNITA's continued guerrilla activities were exacerbating the already alarming humanitarian situation. In August, President dos Santos announced that he had been informed that some 10,000 UNITA soldiers had so far surrendered to the Government. Also in August, the Secretary-General's Adviser for Special Assignments in Africa visited Namibia and Zambia to consult with senior officials and UN offices there to ascertain the extent of the security, socio-economic and humanitarian problems arising from the Angolan war on the two neighbouring countries and make recommendations for re-

sponding to those problems. Debate continued on whether dialogue between the Government and UNITA should be resumed. It was felt that the Government was not heeding appeals from civil society, particularly the Church, for a dialogue that would include UNITA. In July, the Government indicated that UNITA should return to the peace process to complete its outstanding tasks under the Lusaka Protocol as the Government had already concluded its part of the agreement.

In July, the Angolan National Assembly approved the ratification of the 1997 Ottawa Convention [YUN 1997, p. 503] banning the production and use of landmines. In addition, the Government invited the United Nations to contribute to its efforts to meet its legal obligations to respect the human rights of all its citizens. In a related development, UNOA helped extend the work of Angola's first public interest litigation group to four provinces, in addition to Luanda.

The Secretary-General reported that the humanitarian situation in Angola remained serious and, as in previous months, conflict-related displacement continued with new movements occurring in 13 provinces. The total number of internally displaced persons had increased to more than 2.7 million persons by the end of August. Inflationary pressures in the economy and fluctuations in local labour and agricultural markets led to increasing destitution. However, in a positive development, the Government was relocating populations living in unsustainable camps and transit centres to new resettlement sites. Also, a large number of internally displaced persons living in sub-standard shelters were relocated to more suitable areas. Although the pace of resettlement initiatives increased during the reporting period, the majority of displaced populations did not yet have access to adequate agricultural land. In July and August, a campaign to distribute agricultural inputs for internally displaced persons with land was organized in keeping with the new WFP strategy, which aimed to improve targeting of the most vulnerable and to support transition activities through food-for-work and other programmes. In spite of other coordinated activities by the Ministry of Agriculture and the Food and Agriculture Organization of the United Nations, food security of war-affected populations continued to be at risk because of persistent insecurity and displacement. To improve humanitarian coverage, other initiatives included the identification by the United Nations of newly administered areas in 13 provinces where security assessments were expected to be conducted during the upcoming months. The Government also finalized a national Plan of Emergency Action with UN agencies and NGOs, which included a new nationwide water and sanitation emergency programme and a multifaceted programme for protection of vulnerable groups.

The Secretary-General, concerned that the situation appeared to be entering a new phase of political and military impasse, said if the current trend continued the situation in Angola could worsen the security and humanitarian problems, especially in the border regions of Namibia and Zambia, and further threaten the peace and security of the entire subregion. He suggested that the quest for national reconciliation should be broad-based and seek to overcome the enmity and mistrust reinforced by hostility and violence. A genuine process of national reconciliation could be initiated and enhanced by building and developing, in partnership with civil society, the Government's institutional capacities for promoting and protecting human rights, providing justice and security, and improving the living conditions of the Angolan people.

The Secretary-General recommended that the Security Council extend the mandate of UNOA for a further six-month period, until 15 April 2001.

Communications (October/November). On 13 October [S/2000/987], the Security Council President informed the Secretary-General that the Council had considered his report and concurred with the recommendation to extend UNOA's mandate until 15 April 2001.

By a 16 October note verbale [S/2000/998], Angola transmitted to the Council President a document entitled "The strategy of the Angolan Government against conflict diamonds and trade in illicit diamonds", in which it was stated that the Government believed that, as a result of measures already taken, "conflict diamonds" were no longer to be found in Angola.

On 7 November [S/2000/1082], the Secretary-General informed the Council President that he had decided to extend the appointment of Ibrahim Gambari as his Adviser for Special Assignments in Africa until 28 February 2002. Mr. Gambari's efforts with regard to Angola had led to improvements in the relationship between the Angolan Government and the United Nations.

Later developments. In late 2000 [S/2001/351], the Government of Angola was reported to be consolidating its military advantage over UNITA, while continuing to reaffirm the validity of the Lusaka Protocol. On 10 November, President dos Santos announced a general amnesty and declared that the war no longer constituted an obstacle to Angola's development. He subsequently announced the establishment of the Fund for Peace and National Reconciliation, intended to facilitate the social reintegration of those who abandoned war. On 31 December, he indicated that general elections would be held during the second half of 2002, provided that there was security, a new constitution and a new electoral law and the displaced population was resettled to permit an electoral census. UNITA reacted negatively to the amnesty proclamation and vowed to prevent the elections from taking place. On 13 November, its secretary-general stated that the Government had no legitimacy to grant the amnesty. Some opposition political parties and individual UNITA parliamentarians also agreed that there was a need to address the root causes of the conflict.

Sanctions

In February, the Security Council Committee established pursuant to resolution 864(1993) [YUN 1993, p. 256] to monitor sanctions against UNITA submitted its annual report covering January to December 1999 [S/2000/83]. It noted that public awareness of the sanctions increased in 1999, and they seemed to have been more effective. The work of the Panel of Experts, established pursuant to resolution 1237(1999) [YUN 1999, p. 112], should render the sanctions more effective and further hamper UNITA from conducting military activities.

Report of Panel of Experts. In its final report [S/2000/203], the Panel of Experts on violations of Security Council sanctions against UNITA stated that it was clear to all concerned that the sanctions were ineffective. UNITA could still procure its war needs and sell its diamonds, its officials still travelled with little restriction and it continued to be active in international capitals through "unofficial" offices and representatives. Panel members had visited almost 30 countries and met with government officials, members of the diplomatic community, NGOs, police and intelligence sources, industry associations and commercial companies, journalists and others. They also conducted interviews with UNITA defectors during a visit to Luanda in January, when they received a large amount of detailed and valuable information. The Panel made recommendations with regard to preventing sanctions busting on arms and military equipment, petroleum and petroleum products, diamonds, UNITA finances and assets, and UNITA representation and travel abroad.

On 8 March [S/2000/200], Uganda transmitted to the Council President the record of a meeting held between Panel members and Ugandan government representatives regarding allegations that Uganda was collaborating with UNITA in contravention of the UN sanctions. In a 15 March letter [S/2000/225], Gabon requested further information on allegations that 150,000 litres of fuel were delivered to UNITA from Libreville. Also on 15 March [S/2000/228], Belgium discussed the omission from the Panel's report of action taken by Belgium in response to allegations of its involvement in illegal diamond trading. On 17 March [S/2000/230], Portugal objected to the reference in the report that it was regarded as a key country for UNITA in mobilizing political support, and a source of commercial and logistical support. A 22 March note verbale from Bulgaria [S/2000/240] informed the Council that it had established a special interdepartmental commission to investigate allegations against it. The commission's findings were conveyed to the Council in July [S/2000/680] and a decree was adopted on implementation of the sanctions [S/2000/721]. Burkina Faso informed the Council on 24 March [S/2000/249] that it had established an inter-ministerial committee to investigate allegations contained in the report. In addition, its security services had been instructed to take steps to strengthen existing measures for implementing the sanctions. In June, it presented a report on its review of measures taken to address the situation [S/2000/607]. The Government of Togo also established a commission of inquiry to consider allegations made against it and requested all information used by the Panel in its review [S/2000/256]; the report on its findings was presented to the Council in April [S/2000/326]. On 24 March [S/2000/252], Uganda denied allegations in the report, noting that it had only one international airport that was open to and used by many aircraft, making it impossible to conduct secret flights and refuelling exercises without being noticed. Rwanda, on 29 March [S/2000/283], transmitted its comments on the Panel's report.

SECURITY COUNCIL ACTION (April)

On 18 April [meeting 4129], the Security Council unanimously adopted **resolution 1295(2000)**. The draft [S/2000/323] was prepared in consultations among Council members.

The Security Council,

Reaffirming its resolution 864(1993) of 15 September 1993 and all subsequent relevant resolutions, in particular resolutions 1127(1997) of 28 August 1997, 1173(1998) of 12 June 1998 and 1237(1999) of 7 May 1999,

Reaffirming also its commitment to preserve the sovereignty and territorial integrity of Angola,

Expressing its alarm at the impact of the continuing civil war on the civilian population of Angola,

Reiterating that the primary cause of the present crisis in Angola is the refusal of the União Nacional Para a Independência Total de Angola, under the leadership of Mr. Jonas Savimbi, to comply with its obligations under the "Accordos de Paz", the Lusaka Protocol and relevant Security Council resolutions, and reiterating its demand that the União Nacional Para a Independência Total de Angola comply immediately and without condition with those obligations, in particular the complete demilitarization of its forces and full cooperation in the immediate and unconditional extension of State administration throughout the territory of Angola,

Noting that the measures against the União Nacional Para a Independência Total de Angola are intended to promote a political settlement to the conflict in Angola by requiring the União Nacional Para a Independência Total de Angola to comply with the obligations that it undertook under the "Accordos de Paz" and the Lusaka Protocol, and by curtailing the ability of the União Nacional Para a Independência Total de Angola to pursue its objectives by military means,

Emphasizing its concern at violations of the measures concerning arms and related materiel, petroleum and petroleum products, diamonds, funds and financial assets and travel and representation, imposed against the União Nacional Para a Independência Total de Angola, contained in resolutions 864(1993), 1127(1997) and 1173(1998),

Recalling the provisions of resolution 864(1993), and expressing its concern at the reports of supply to the União Nacional Para a Independência Total de Angola of military assistance, including weapons-related training and advice, and at the presence of foreign mercenaries,

Expressing its appreciation and strong support for the efforts of the Chairman of the Security Council Committee established pursuant to resolution 864(1993) aimed at improving the effectiveness of the measures imposed against the União Nacional Para a Independência Total de Angola,

Noting with appreciation the decisions taken by the Organization of African Unity and the Southern African Development Community in support of the implementation of the measures imposed against the União Nacional Para a Independência Total de Angola,

Recalling the Final Communiqué of the meeting of Ministers for Foreign Affairs and Heads of Delegation of the Movement of Non-Aligned Countries, held in New York on 23 September 1999, and noting the Final Document adopted by the Thirteenth Ministerial Conference of the Movement of Non-Aligned Countries, held at Cartagena, Colombia, on 8 and 9 April 2000, in support of the implementation of the measures imposed against the União Nacional Para a Independência Total de Angola,

A

Determining that the situation in Angola constitutes a threat to international peace and security in the region,

Acting under Chapter VII of the Charter of the United Nations,

1. *Stresses* the obligation of all Member States to comply fully with the measures imposed against the União Nacional Para a Independência Total de Angola contained in resolutions 864(1993), 1127(1997) and 1173(1998), and emphasizes that non-compliance with those measures constitutes a violation of the provisions of the Charter of the United Nations;

2. *Welcomes* the report of the Panel of Experts established pursuant to resolution 1237(1999), and takes

note of the conclusions and recommendations contained therein;

3. *Requests* the Secretary-General to establish a monitoring mechanism composed of up to five experts, for a period of six months from its effective entry into operation, to collect additional relevant information and investigate relevant leads relating to any allegations of violations of the measures contained in resolutions 864(1993), 1127(1997) and 1173(1998), including any relevant leads initiated by the Panel of Experts, including through visits to relevant countries, and to report periodically to the Security Council Committee established pursuant to resolution 864(1993), including by providing a written report by 18 October 2000, with a view to improving the implementation of the measures imposed against the União Nacional Para a Independência Total de Angola, and further requests the Secretary-General, within thirty days of adoption of the present resolution and acting in consultation with the Committee, to appoint experts to serve on the monitoring mechanism;

4. *Calls upon* all States to cooperate with the monitoring mechanism in the discharge of its mandate;

5. *Expresses its intention* to review the situation regarding the implementation of the measures contained in resolutions 864(1993), 1127(1997) and 1173 (1998) on the basis of information provided, inter alia, by the Panel of Experts, by States, including in particular any that are mentioned in the report of the Panel of Experts, and by the monitoring mechanism established by the present resolution, expresses its readiness, on the basis of the results of this review, to consider appropriate action in accordance with the Charter in relation to States it determines to have violated the measures contained in those resolutions, and establishes 18 November 2000 as the deadline for an initial decision in this regard;

6. *Undertakes* to consider, by 18 November 2000, the application of additional measures against the União Nacional Para a Independência Total de Angola under Article 41 of the Charter and the development of additional tools to render more effective the existing measures imposed against the União Nacional Para a Independência Total de Angola;

7. *Welcomes* the decision of several of the States referred to in the report of the Panel of Experts to establish interdepartmental commissions and other mechanisms to investigate the allegations contained in the report, invites those States to keep the Committee informed of the results of such investigations, invites other States referred to in the report to consider the allegations contained therein, takes note of the information provided to the Security Council by States in response to the conclusions and recommendations of the Panel of Experts, and requests the Committee to consider fully all such information, including, where appropriate, through discussion with representatives of the States concerned, and to invite the submission of additional information where appropriate;

B

With regard to the trade in arms,

8. *Encourages* all States to exercise all due diligence, in order to prevent the diversion or trans-shipment of weapons to unauthorized end-users or unauthorized destinations where such diversion or trans-shipment

risks resulting in the violation of the measures contained in resolution 864(1993), including by requiring end-use documentation or equivalent measures before exports from their territories are allowed, and further encourages all States to ensure effective monitoring and regulation in the export of weapons, including by private arms brokers, where they do not already do so;

9. *Invites* States to consider the proposal to convene one or more conferences of representatives of countries that are manufacturers and, in particular, exporters of weapons for the purpose of developing proposals to stem the illicit flow of arms into Angola, calls for the provision of necessary financial support for such conferences by States, and urges that representatives of the States members of the Southern African Development Community be invited to participate in any such conference or conferences;

C

With regard to the trade in petroleum and petroleum products,

10. *Encourages* the convening of a conference of experts to devise a regime for curbing the illegal supply of petroleum and petroleum products into areas controlled by the União Nacional Para a Independência Total de Angola, including physical inspection as well as the broader monitoring of petroleum supply in the area, and further encourages any such conference to focus on the role and capacity of the Southern African Development Community in the implementation of such a regime;

11. *Invites* the Southern African Development Community to consider the establishment of monitoring activities in the border areas adjacent to Angola for the purpose of reducing the opportunities for the smuggling of petroleum and petroleum products into areas under the control of the União Nacional Para a Independência Total de Angola, including through the monitoring of fuel supplies and transfers thereof;

12. *Also invites* the Southern African Development Community to take the lead in establishing an information-exchange mechanism involving petroleum companies and governments to facilitate the flow of information regarding possible illegal diversions of fuel to the União Nacional Para a Independência Total de Angola;

13. *Further invites* the Southern African Development Community to take the lead in carrying out chemical analysis of fuel samples obtained from petroleum suppliers in the region of the Community and, using the results, to create a database for the purpose of determining the sources of fuel obtained or captured from the União Nacional Para a Independência Total de Angola;

14. *Calls upon* the Government of Angola to implement additional internal controls and inspection procedures with respect to the distribution of petroleum and petroleum products, for the purpose of enhancing the effectiveness of the measures contained in resolution 864(1993), and invites the Government of Angola to inform the Committee of the steps taken in this regard;

15. *Calls upon* all States to enforce strictly safety and control regulations relating to the transportation by air of fuel and other hazardous commodities, in particular in the area around Angola, urges States to develop such

regulations where they do not exist already, and, in this regard, requests all States to provide relevant information to the International Air Transport Association, the International Civil Aviation Organization and the Committee;

D

With regard to the trade in diamonds,

16. *Expresses its concern* that illicit trade in diamonds constitutes a principal source of funding for the União Nacional Para a Independência Total de Angola, encourages States hosting diamond markets to impose significant penalties for the possessing of rough diamonds imported in contravention of the measures contained in resolution 1173(1998), emphasizes, in this connection, that the implementation of the measures contained in that resolution requires an effective certificate-of-origin regime, welcomes the introduction by the Government of Angola of new control arrangements involving redesigned and reconcilable certificates of origin, and invites the Government of Angola to provide Member States with full details of the certificate-of-origin scheme and to brief the Committee on this scheme;

17. *Welcomes* the steps announced by the Government of Belgium, on 3 March 2000, in support of the more effective implementation of the measures contained in resolution 1173(1998), welcomes also the establishment by the Government of Belgium of an inter-ministerial task force to curb sanctions violations, further welcomes the measures taken by the Diamond High Council, in conjunction with the Government of Angola, to render sanctions more effective, invites the Government of Belgium and the Diamond High Council to continue to cooperate with the Committee to devise practical measures to limit access by the União Nacional Para a Independência Total de Angola to the legitimate diamond market and welcomes their public affirmations in this regard, and further invites other States hosting diamond markets, as well as other States closely involved with the diamond industry, also to cooperate with the Committee to devise practical measures to the same end and to inform the Committee of measures taken in this regard;

18. *Welcomes also* the proposal that a meeting of experts be convened for the purpose of devising a system of controls to facilitate the implementation of the measures contained in resolution 1173(1998), including arrangements that would allow for increased transparency and accountability in the control of diamonds from their point of origin to the bourses, emphasizes that it is important that, in devising such controls, every effort be made to avoid inflicting collateral damage on the legitimate diamond trade, and welcomes the intention of the Republic of South Africa to host a relevant conference this year;

19. *Calls upon* relevant States to cooperate with the diamond industry to develop and implement more effective arrangements to ensure that members of the diamond industry worldwide abide by the measures contained in resolution 1173(1998), and to inform the Committee regarding progress in this regard;

E

With regard to funds and financial measures,

20. *Encourages* States to convene a conference of experts to explore possibilities to strengthen the implementation of the financial measures imposed against the União Nacional Para a Independência Total de Angola contained in resolution 1173(1998);

21. *Calls upon* all States to work with financial institutions on their territory to develop procedures to facilitate the identification of funds and financial assets that may be subject to the measures contained in resolution 1173(1998) and the freezing of such assets;

F

With regard to measures relating to travel and representation,

22. *Emphasizes* the importance of States acting to prevent the circumvention on or from their territory of the measures contained in resolutions 864(1993), 1127(1997) and 1173(1998), and invites States to review the status of officials and representatives of the União Nacional Para a Independência Total de Angola, as well as all adult members of their families, designated by the Committee pursuant to resolution 1127(1997) and believed to be residing on their territory, with a view to suspending or cancelling their travel documents, visas and residence permits in conformity with that resolution;

23. *Calls upon* States that have issued passports to officials of the União Nacional Para a Independência Total de Angola and adult members of their families designated by the Committee pursuant to resolution 1127(1997) to cancel those passports in conformity with paragraph 4 *(b)* of that resolution and to report to the Committee on the status of their efforts in this regard;

24. *Requests* the Committee, in consultation with the Government of Angola, to update the list of officials of the União Nacional Para a Independência Total de Angola and adult members of their immediate families who are subject to travel restrictions and to expand the information contained in that list, including date and place of birth and any known addresses, and further requests the Committee to consult relevant States, including the Government of Angola, regarding the possible expansion of that list, drawing on the information set out in paragraphs 140 to 154 of the report of the Panel of Experts;

G

With regard to additional steps,

25. *Invites* the Southern African Development Community to consider the introduction of measures to strengthen air traffic control systems in the subregion for the purpose of detecting illegal flight activities across national borders, and further invites the Community to liaise with the International Civil Aviation Organization to consider the establishment of an air traffic regime for the control of regional air space;

26. *Urges* all States to make available to the Committee any information on the violation of the measures contained in resolutions 864(1993), 1127(1997) and 1173(1998);

27. *Also urges* all States, including those geographically close to Angola, to take immediate steps to enforce, strengthen or enact legislation making it a criminal offence under domestic law for their nationals or other individuals operating on their territory to violate the measures imposed by the Council against the União Nacional Para a Independência Total de Angola, where they have not already done so, and to inform the Committee of the adoption of such measures,

and invites States to report the results of all related investigations or prosecutions to the Committee;

28. *Encourages* States to inform the relevant professional associations and certification bodies of the measures contained in resolutions 864(1993), 1127(1997) and 1173(1998), to seek action by those bodies where those measures are violated, and to consult with such bodies with a view to improving the implementation of those measures;

29. *Invites* the Secretary-General to strengthen collaboration between the United Nations and regional and international organizations, including Interpol, that may be involved in monitoring or enforcing the implementation of the measures contained in resolutions 864(1993), 1127(1997) and 1173(1998);

30. *Also invites* the Secretary-General to develop an information package and media campaign designed to educate the public at large on the measures contained in resolutions 864(1993), 1127(1997) and 1173(1998);

31. *Welcomes* the appeal by the Council of Ministers of the Organization of African Unity at its seventieth ordinary session, held in Algiers from 8 to 10 July 1999, to all States members of the Organization of African Unity to work strenuously for the implementation of all Security Council resolutions, especially those relating to measures imposed against the União Nacional Para a Independência Total de Angola, undertakes to convey the report of the Panel of Experts to the Chairman of the Organization of African Unity, and requests the Secretary-General of the United Nations to transmit the report to the Secretary-General of the Organization of African Unity;

32. *Underlines* the important role played by the Southern African Development Community in the implementation of the measures contained in resolutions 864(1993), 1127(1997) and 1173(1998) and its determination to strengthen the implementation of the measures against the União Nacional Para a Independência Total de Angola, invites the Community to make known to the Committee what assistance the Community requires in implementing the present and previous relevant resolutions, expresses its intention to initiate a dialogue with the Community with regard to the implementation of activities contained in the present resolution, strongly urges States and international organizations to consider the provision of financial and technical assistance to the Community in this regard, recalls the Final Communiqué of the Summit of the Heads of State or Government of the Southern African Development Community adopted at Grand Baie, Mauritius, on 14 September 1998, relating to the application of measures imposed against the União Nacional Para a Independência Total de Angola, undertakes to convey the report of the Panel of Experts to the Chairman of the Southern African Development Community, and requests the Secretary-General of the United Nations to transmit the report to the Executive Secretary of the Southern African Development Community;

33. *Decides* to remain actively seized of the matter.

Communications (May-July). Côte d'Ivoire, in a 3 May letter to the Security Council President [S/2000/379], said that it had long served as an intermediary to facilitate contacts between UNITA

and the Angolan Government. However, following the signing of the Lusaka Protocol and the failure of UNITA to respect its provisions, Côte d'Ivoire had decided to freeze its relations with UNITA. The letter also contested allegations against Côte d'Ivoire contained in the Panel of Experts' report.

On 24 May [S/2000/480], Togo informed the Council that, as of 18 May, 56 Angolan nationals connected with UNITA had left Togo's territory, on instructions from its President. A subsequent note verbale from Angola [S/2000/484] stressed that the action taken by the Togolese Government clearly confirmed accounts in the report of Togolese involvement with UNITA. The action was therefore insufficient for Togo's redemption considering the degree of its involvement in the Angolan conflict.

Namibia, by a 27 July letter to the Council [S/2000/752], discussed allegations that significant quantities of UNITA diamonds were marketed through the country. On investigation, it had become obvious that Namibia had been used by certain individuals who had violated the sanctions without the Government's knowledge. Investigations into the matter would continue.

Monitoring mechanism. On 11 July [S/2000/677], the Secretary-General, referring to resolution 1295(2000), informed the Security Council of the appointment of five experts to serve on a monitoring mechanism for six months to collect additional relevant information and investigate leads relating to allegations of violations of the sanctions against UNITA.

A 25 October interim report of the Monitoring Mechanism on Angola Sanctions [S/2000/1026] stated that members had visited a number of African and European countries and had attended the World Diamond Congress in Belgium and the Southern African Regional Police Chiefs Cooperation Organization meeting in Malawi. The information it had received on the military situation suggested a weakening of UNITA's operational capabilities and it was generally accepted that the sanctions, combined with military factors, were hampering UNITA's capacity. During the second stage of its work, the Mechanism intended to concentrate on whether the cooperation it initially received could be translated into effective action to diminish UNITA's military capability. It would also develop proposals to enable strengthening of the sanctions and encourage a more targeted and focused approach for strategic monitoring.

In its final report [S/2000/1225 & Corr.1,2], the Mechanism described its approach and presented findings on several issues, including sanctions-busting on arms and military equipment in Bulgaria, Burkina Faso, Romania, Togo, Ukraine and Zaire; UNITA representation and travel and residence of senior UNITA officials and their adult family members; the role of transport in the violation of the sanctions; and sanctions on diamond trading and financial assets. It also made recommendations on those issues and for maintaining the effectiveness of sanctions. Annexed to the report were lists of confiscated military materiel and equipment and of senior UNITA officials and immediate family members.

Report of Sanctions Committee. In its annual report covering the period from January to 28 December 2000 [S/2000/1255], the Sanctions Committee summarized its activities and noted that the Chairman had briefed the Council on 18 January on his visit to Angola earlier in the month. The purpose of that visit was to consult with the Government on worldwide application of the UNITA sanctions, to visit the areas and see the military equipment recently captured from UNITA and to meet with UNITA defectors or supporters who had been captured in the fighting. The report also provided Member States' responses to the Expert Panel's report and a summary of activities of the Monitoring Mechanism, and discussed implementation of resolution 1295(2000). The Committee stated that in 2000 it was clear that the measures against UNITA were successful in preventing it from pursuing its objectives through military means.

Financing of UN missions

In March [A/54/809], the Secretary-General presented the financial performance report of MONUA for the period 1 July 1998 to 30 June 1999. Expenditures for the period totalled $132,949,580 gross ($129,664,280 net), as compared with an appropriation of $133,099,080 gross ($128,876,680 net), resulting in an unencumbered balance of $149,000 gross ($787,600 net). The unencumbered balance resulted from reduced requirements under all categories of expenditure, due to the expiration of the mandate of MONUA on 26 February 1999, repatriation of military and civilian personnel and commencement of its technical liquidation. Unutilized resources were used to absorb unbudgeted additional requirements arising from implementation of the new contingent-owned equipment reimbursement procedures of eight troop contributors in the United Nations Angola Verification Mission (UNAVEM).

Also in March [A/54/812], the Secretary-General presented the revised liquidation budget of MONUA for the period from 1 July 1999 to 30 June 2000 and the cost estimates for continuing liquidation activities at United Nations Headquarters afterwards. The revised budget for the period amounted to $15,049,440 gross ($14,306,540 net), representing an increase of $7,607,900 gross, compared with the initial budget of MONUA for the same period. The increase was mainly attributable to the retention of military and civilian personnel in the mission area because liquidation activities were extended beyond the originally envisaged deadline. For the 2000/01 period, $143,500 gross ($130,500 net) was requested for eight work-months of staff activities at Headquarters.

In an April report [A/54/831], ACABQ recommended that the General Assembly take note of the unencumbered balance of $149,500 gross and additional requirements of $787,600 net for MONUA for 1 July 1998 to 30 June 1999, but defer action until the review of the final performance information of UNAVEM and MONUA was completed.

Procurement procedures

In regard to General Assembly resolution 54/17 A [YUN 1999, p. 117], the Secretary-General submitted a May report [A/54/866] containing additional information on measures being taken to improve procurement activities in the field and commenting on the outcome of the procurement audits in Angola [YUN 1998, p. 123]. The Secretary-General stated that the sharp increase in the number and complexity of peacekeeping operations in the early 1990s, which caught the UN procurement system unprepared to meet the new challenges, coupled with a procurement system designed in the early days of the Organization, had contributed to the problems experienced in Angola. While the audits and investigations did not reveal severe misconduct as was originally feared, the Secretariat recognized the importance of addressing procedural and systemic weaknesses to prevent misuse of UN resources.

GENERAL ASSEMBLY ACTION

On 15 June [meeting 98], the General Assembly, on the recommendation of the Fifth Committee [A/54/504/Add.1], adopted **resolution 54/17 B** without vote [agenda item 129].

Financing of the United Nations Angola Verification Mission and the United Nations Observer Mission in Angola

The General Assembly,
Having considered the reports of the Secretary-General on the financing of the United Nations Observer Mission in Angola and the related reports of the Advisory Committee on Administrative and Budgetary Questions,

Having considered also the report of the Office of Internal Oversight Services on the investigation into the 6.9 million United States dollars procurement of quartering area goods in the United Nations Angola Verification Mission,

Bearing in mind Security Council resolutions 626 (1988) of 20 December 1988, by which the Council established the United Nations Angola Verification Mission, 696(1991) of 30 May 1991, by which the Council decided to entrust a new mandate to the United Nations Angola Verification Mission (thenceforth called the United Nations Angola Verification Mission II), 976(1995) of 8 February 1995, by which the Council authorized the establishment of a peacekeeping operation (thenceforth called the United Nations Angola Verification Mission III), 1118(1997) of 30 June 1997, by which the Council decided to establish, as from 1 July 1997, the United Nations Observer Mission in Angola, and its subsequent resolutions, the latest of which was resolution 1229(1999) of 26 February 1999,

Recalling its resolution 43/231 of 16 February 1989 on the financing of the Verification Mission and its subsequent resolutions and decisions thereon, and resolution 53/228 of 8 June 1999 on the financing of the Observer Mission,

Reaffirming that the costs of the Observer Mission are expenses of the Organization to be borne by Member States in accordance with Article 17, paragraph 2, of the Charter of the United Nations,

Recalling its previous decisions regarding the fact that, in order to meet the expenditures caused by the Observer Mission, a different procedure is required from that applied to meet expenditures of the regular budget of the United Nations,

Taking into account the fact that the economically more developed countries are in a position to make relatively larger contributions and that the economically less developed countries have a relatively limited capacity to contribute towards such an operation,

Bearing in mind the special responsibilities of the States permanent members of the Security Council, as indicated in General Assembly resolution 1874(S-IV) of 27 June 1963, in the financing of such operations,

Noting with appreciation that voluntary contributions have been made to the Observer Mission,

Mindful of the fact that it is essential to provide the Observer Mission with the necessary financial resources to enable it to meet its outstanding liabilities,

1. *Takes note* of the status of contributions to the United Nations Angola Verification Mission and the United Nations Observer Mission in Angola as at 30 April 2000, including the contributions outstanding in the amount of 90.6 million United States dollars, representing 7 per cent of the total assessed contributions, notes that some 40 per cent of the Member States have paid their assessed contributions in full, and urges all other Member States concerned, in particular those in arrears, to ensure payment of their outstanding assessed contributions;

2. *Expresses its appreciation* to those Member States which have paid their assessed contributions in full;

3. *Expresses concern* about the financial situation with regard to peacekeeping activities, in particular as regards the reimbursements to troop contributors that bear additional burdens owing to overdue payments by Member States of their assessments;

4. *Urges* all other Member States to make every possible effort to ensure payment of their assessed contributions to the Verification Mission and the Observer Mission in full and on time;

5. *Expresses concern* at the delay experienced by the Secretary-General in deploying and providing adequate resources to some recent peacekeeping missions, in particular those in Africa;

6. *Emphasizes* that all future and existing peacekeeping missions shall be given equal and non-discriminatory treatment in respect of financial and administrative arrangements;

7. *Also emphasizes* that all peacekeeping missions shall be provided with adequate resources for the effective and efficient discharge of their respective mandates;

8. *Endorses* the conclusions and recommendations contained in the report of the Advisory Committee on Administrative and Budgetary Questions, and requests the Secretary-General to ensure their full implementation;

9. *Takes note* of the report of the Office of Internal Oversight Services on the investigation into the 6.9 million dollars procurement of quartering area goods in the United Nations Angola Verification Mission;

10. *Requests* the Secretary-General to take all necessary action to ensure that the liquidation of the Observer Mission is administered with a maximum of efficiency and economy;

11. *Decides* to appropriate to the Special Account for the United Nations Observer Mission in Angola the amount of 7,607,900 dollars gross (7,222,700 dollars net) for the liquidation of the Observer Mission for the period from 1 July 1999 to 30 June 2000, in addition to the amount of 7,441,540 dollars gross (7,083,840 dollars net) already appropriated under the terms of General Assembly resolution 53/228 and inclusive of the amount of 5,274,800 dollars gross (4,875,100 dollars net) authorized by the Advisory Committee under the terms of section IV of Assembly resolution 49/233 A of 23 December 1994;

12. *Decides also,* as an ad hoc arrangement, taking into account the amount of 7,441,540 dollars gross (7,083,840 dollars net) already apportioned under the terms of its resolution 53/228, to apportion among Member States the additional amount of 7,607,900 dollars gross (7,222,700 dollars net) for the period from 1 July 1999 to 30 June 2000, in accordance with the composition of groups set out in paragraphs 3 and 4 of General Assembly resolution 43/232 of 1 March 1989, as adjusted by the Assembly in its resolutions 44/192 B of 21 December 1989, 45/269 of 27 August 1991, 46/198 A of 20 December 1991, 47/218 A of 23 December 1992, 49/249 A of 20 July 1995, 49/249 B of 14 September 1995, 50/224 of 11 April 1996, 51/218 A to C of 18 December 1996 and 52/230 of 31 March 1998 and its decisions 48/472 A of 23 December 1993, 50/451 B of 23 December 1995 and 54/456 to 54/458 of 23 December 1999, and taking into account the scale of assessments for the year 2000, as set out in its resolutions 52/215 A of 22 December 1997 and 54/237 A of 23 December 1999;

13. *Decides further* that, in accordance with the provisions of its resolution 973(X) of 15 December 1955, there shall be set off against the apportionment among Member States, as provided for in paragraph 12 above,

their respective share in the Tax Equalization Fund of the estimated additional staff assessment income of 385,200 dollars approved for the Observer Mission for the period from 1 July 1999 to 30 June 2000;

14. *Decides* to appropriate the amount of 151,916 dollars gross (137,671 dollars net) for the liquidation of the Observer Mission for the period from 1 July 2000 to 30 June 2001, inclusive of the amount of 7,278 dollars gross (6,159 dollars net) for the support account for peacekeeping operations and the amount of 1,138 dollars gross (1,012 dollars net) for the United Nations Logistics Base at Brindisi, Italy, and decides also that no action shall be taken on the apportionment of the said amounts at this stage;

15. *Takes note* of the unencumbered balance of 149,500 dollars gross and of the additional requirements of 787,600 dollars net in respect of the period from 1 July 1998 to 30 June 1999, and decides to defer action thereon until its review of the final performance information on the Verification Mission and the Observer Mission;

16. *Requests* the Secretary-General to present a more detailed explanation of the amounts required for reimbursement of contingent-owned equipment, including the impact of the retroactive application of the new procedures for contingent-owned equipment for the Verification Mission and the Observer Mission, to be provided no later than at its resumed fifty-fifth session;

17. *Decides* to keep under review the amounts budgeted for provision for reimbursement of contingent-owned equipment;

18. *Emphasizes* that no peacekeeping mission shall be financed by borrowing funds from other active peacekeeping missions;

19. *Decides* to include in the provisional agenda of its fifty-fifth session the item entitled "Financing of the United Nations Angola Verification Mission and the United Nations Observer Mission in Angola".

On 23 December, the Assembly decided that the agenda item on the financing of UNAVEM and MONUA remained for consideration at its resumed fifty-fifth (2001) session (**decision 55/458**) and that the Fifth Committee should continue to consider the item at that session (**decision 55/455**).

Central African Republic

The United Nations Mission in the Central African Republic (MINURCA) concluded successfully in February 2000. Established in 1998 [YUN 1998, p. 134], the Mission had contributed much towards the restoration of peace and security in the Central African Republic and the creation of conditions conducive to holding national legislative and presidential elections, restructuring the security forces, training the national police and

launching major economic and social reforms. In order to remain involved in addressing the challenges facing the new Government, the United Nations established the Peace-Building Support Office (BONUCA) to take over from MINURCA. With UN support, the Government of the Central African Republic continued its efforts to implement the 1997 Bangui Agreements [YUN 1997, p. 91], an arrangement to end a crisis stemming from a 1996 army rebellion that had resulted in ex-rebels and militia retaining a large supply of weapons. The Bangui Agreements were followed by and supplemented with the 1998 National Reconciliation Pact [YUN 1998, p. 133].

The Secretary-General described the situation in the Central African Republic as dominated by the confrontational approach between the ruling party and the numerous opposition parties. In addition to the lack of dialogue, the Government was faced with dire economic circumstances already strained by the oil crisis and inflation.

Political situation and MINURCA withdrawal

Political developments in late 1999 and early 2000 were dominated by the investiture of President Ange-Félix Patassé to a second term as the head of State [YUN 1999, p. 125] and by the formation of the new Government under the reappointed Prime Minister, Anicet Georges Dologuélé.

Report of Secretary-General. As requested in Security Council resolution 1271(1999) [YUN 1999, p. 127], the Secretary-General on 14 January reported on MINURCA [S/2000/24], his ninth report on the Mission. Following the presidential election of 19 September 1999 [YUN 1999, p. 125], the Government took steps towards reintegrating some ex-mutineers into the Armed Forces, as called for in the Bangui Agreements. Other elements of the Agreements, such as the modification of some procedures under the Penal Code, the regulation of access to the University of Bangui, the revision of certain articles in the Constitution and the negotiation of a social pact with the trade unions, had not yet been implemented. A number of provisions of the National Reconciliation Pact had been implemented, including the independence of the judiciary and the privatization of some public services (energy and water supply and banking).

The military and security situation in Bangui and the environs remained relatively calm at the beginning of 2000. MINURCA, which as at 6 January comprised 815 troops and civilian police observers, was in the process of a phased withdrawal and was making the transition from peacekeeping to the post-conflict peace-building phase to be taken over by BONUCA. The Mission coordinated its withdrawal action with the Central African authorities in order to ensure a progressive transfer of its security functions to government security and police forces, and the Central African gendarmerie, police and armed forces began to take over those duties. Four long-awaited bills on the restructuring of the Armed Forces were promulgated and the Government began to take measures for their implementation. With regard to the statutory functions of the Special Force for the Defence of the Republican Institutions (FORSDIR), a decree was issued indicating that the Force would be constituted by drawing from various sections of the Armed Forces and would be restricted to the defence of republican institutions; its command would remain within the purview of the Chief of Staff of the Central African Armed Forces. Additional steps were needed in order that FORSDIR be truly restricted to the duties ascribed to the security forces under the Constitution.

The Secretary-General observed that, by successfully conducting two national elections and the ongoing reforms, the people and Government of the Central African Republic had demonstrated their commitment to democracy and peaceful development. What remained to be done was the restructuring of the security and armed forces. The sizeable number of Central African police and gendarmes who had been trained by MINURCA still lacked the resources to ensure security in the country. At the same time, the Central African Republic remained vulnerable to the volatile situation in the subregion, in particular the neighbouring DRC (see p. 119). Security concerns in Bangui had decreased somewhat following the voluntary repatriation of military elements from the DRC and the relocation of refugees to rural sites. Some 50,000 refugees from neighbouring States remained in the Central African Republic and required international support. As the Government had emphasized, the crisis in the Central African Republic was rooted, to a considerable extent, in the poverty and economic deterioration of the country.

Communication. The President of Chad, on 22 February [S/2000/145], informed the Security Council of his concern at the withdrawal of MINURCA. While welcoming the return of peace to the Central African Republic, he warned that certain institutions important to ensuring peace, security and stability had not been put in place, particularly the army, which had not been restructured. For that reason, African regional and subregional organizations felt the withdrawal

was premature, particularly as instability existed in the subregion, characterized by the continuing war in the DRC and in southern Sudan, and the fragility of the political situation in the Republic of the Congo, all neighbouring countries of the Central African Republic. In his threefold capacity as President of the UN Standing Advisory Committee on Security Questions in Central Africa, President of the Central African Economic and Monetary Community and President of the Community of Sahelo-Saharan States, he requested the Council to review the political and security situation in the Central African Republic with a view to extending the MINURCA mandate.

Establishment of BONUCA

MINURCA gradually withdrew from the Central African Republic during the last month of 1999 and the first months of 2000. The United Nations Peace-Building Support Office in the Central African Republic (BONUCA) took over from MINURCA on 15 February to provide assistance in the peace-building effort. The establishment of the Office had been proposed by the Secretary-General in December 1999 [YUN 1999, p. 128].

SECURITY COUNCIL ACTION

On 10 February [meeting 4101], following consultations among Security Council members, the President made statement **S/PRST/2000/5** on behalf of the Council:

> The Security Council has considered the report of the Secretary-General of 14 January 2000 submitted in accordance with resolution 1271(1999) of 22 October 1999.
>
> The Council commends the United Nations Mission in the Central African Republic and the Special Representative of the Secretary-General for the contribution they have made to the restoration of peace and security in the Central African Republic, and for their important and tangible support for the holding of free and fair legislative and presidential elections, the restructuring of the security forces, the training of the police force and the launching of vital reforms in the political, social and economic fields in the Central African Republic. The Council expresses its thanks to all the countries that took part in and contributed to the success of the Mission, particularly the troop-contributing countries.
>
> The Council recognizes the significant progress made by the Government of the Central African Republic in implementing the Bangui Agreements and the National Reconciliation Pact, which are the foundations of peace and stability in the country.
>
> The Council strongly encourages the Government of the Central African Republic to do all it can to build on the progress made while the Inter-African Mission to Monitor the Implementation of the Bangui Agreements and the United Nations Mission in

the Central African Republic were present in the country, and to work with determination to strengthen democratic institutions, broaden the scope of reconciliation and national unity and promote economic reform and recovery. The Council urges the Government of the Central African Republic to continue to conform to the requirements of the programmes for economic reform and financial consolidation agreed upon with the international financial institutions. The Council calls upon the members of the international community and upon bilateral and multilateral donors in particular to give their active support to the efforts being made to this end by the Government of the Central African Republic. The Council wishes to stress the importance of providing international assistance to the refugees and displaced persons in the Central African Republic and the other countries of the region in order to contribute to regional stability.

The Council welcomes the promulgation by the Central African authorities of three laws on the restructuring of the armed forces and the decrees issued by the Government so that these laws can be implemented. The Council encourages the Central African authorities actively to prepare and to submit, with the help of the United Nations, specific plans for the holding of a meeting in New York to mobilize the financial and other resources necessary for the effective implementation of the programme for the restructuring of the Central African Armed Forces, and the demobilization and reintegration programme. The Council calls upon the members of the international community to support these programmes.

The Council welcomes in particular the decision by the Government of the Central African Republic to disband the Special Force for the Defence of the Republican Institutions, and notes with satisfaction that the Force will be replaced by a unit fully integrated in the national security forces, under the command of the Chief of Staff of the Central African Armed Forces, and that its mission will be strictly limited to protecting State authorities at the highest level.

The Council also welcomes the decision by the Secretary-General, which has been accepted by the Government of the Central African Republic, to establish, for an initial period of one year, beginning on 15 February 2000, the United Nations Peace-Building Support Office in the Central African Republic, headed by a representative of the Secretary-General, and encourages the Central African authorities and the Office to work closely together. The Council notes with satisfaction that the principal mission of the Office will be to support the efforts of the Government to consolidate peace and national reconciliation, strengthen democratic institutions and facilitate the mobilization at the international level of political support and resources for national reconstruction and economic recovery in the Central African Republic, and that the Office is also tasked with monitoring developments in, and promoting public awareness of, human rights issues.

The Council requests the Secretary-General to continue to keep it regularly informed of the activities of the Office, the situation in the Central African Republic and, in particular, the progress achieved in political, social and economic reforms, and to submit a report to the Council by 30 June 2000 and every six months thereafter.

The Secretary-General informed the Security Council on 26 April [S/2000/366] that BONUCA was established on 15 February with an initial mandate of one year and operational under an officer-in-charge. Following consultations with the Government of the Central African Republic, he intended to appoint Cheikh Tidiane Sy (Senegal), currently his Representative in Burundi, as his Representative in the Central African Republic and head of BONUCA. The Council took note of the Secretary-General's intention on 1 May [S/2000/367].

Report of Secretary-General. In response to the Council's request (see above), the Secretary-General reported on 29 June on the situation in the Central African Republic and on BONUCA activities [S/2000/639]. The primary purpose of the Office was to support the Government's efforts to consolidate peace and national reconciliation, strengthen democratic institutions and facilitate the mobilization of international political support and resources for national reconstruction and economic recovery. The Office was also expected to promote public awareness of human rights issues and monitor developments in that field.

The political situation had been dominated by the challenge to the Government of Prime Minister Dologuélé. The ruling Movement for the Liberation of the Central African People (MLPC) expressed its dissatisfaction to President Patassé at the distribution of cabinet posts and particularly objected to the selection of Mr. Dologuélé as Prime Minister. The Government was also involved in major financial scandals. The political situation appeared to improve with the nomination of additional MLPC members to the Cabinet and the launching of a government investigation into the financial scandals. However, the suspended jail sentences and financial penalties imposed on two journalists revived tensions between the Government and the opposition.

During his visit to the Central African Republic on 30 April and 1 May, the Secretary-General met with President Patassé, Prime Minister Dologuélé and members of the Government, as well as with members of the Bureau of the National Assembly.

Implementation of the Bangui Agreements and the National Reconciliation Pact was facilitated during the reporting period: two ex-mutineers were rehabilitated and appointed to key government positions; the revision of the Electoral Code was completed; the Electoral Independent and Mixed Commission was strengthened with a control organ to further assure its transparency and credibility; and the Government institutionalized the payment of pension allowances to former heads of State, as provided under the Bangui Agreements. It was agreed that a general amnesty would be granted to people who had been identified by a parliamentary audit as having embezzled public funds and who were recommended for appropriate sanctions.

A disquieting development was the increase in reports of extrajudicial killings and summary executions. In May, a special anti-crime police squad reportedly executed eight alleged armed robbery suspects without due process. The Secretary-General suggested that an accelerated rehabilitation of local prisons and rejuvenation of a credible judicial system to permit secure detention of criminals awaiting arraignment could help eliminate the recourse to summary executions and arbitrary detentions. A short training session, co-sponsored by BONUCA and the Ministry of Defence, was held for 50 police officers, 50 gendarmes and 50 armed forces officers, to acquaint them with ways to uphold international human rights law (Bangui, 3-19 May).

The military and security situation in the Central African Republic had remained relatively calm since the transfer of security functions from MINURCA to the Government. As part of the military reforms, FORSDIR was dissolved and replaced by a Special Unit in charge of Presidential Security (UPS), under the authority of the Chief of Staff of the Armed Forces. Due to lack of resources, UPS had been called on to undertake law-and-order tasks that would normally fall outside the scope of its mandate. An increasingly dangerous situation was being caused by armed bandits' attacks, which disrupted the movement of people and goods both within the country and on roads to neighbouring countries. Scores of people had been killed by such bandits.

With regard to the economic situation, improvements had taken place in the area of revenue generation, which showed an increase of almost 20 per cent over the previous year, largely attributable to the Government's fiscal reforms. A joint IMF/World Bank mission visited the Central African Republic in February/March to assess the country's economic performance since an earlier visit in November 1999. Salaries had been paid to civil servants without interruption since March 1999. However, there was a need for the Government to control expenditures. Following recent scandals in State corporations, the Government had stressed its commitment to fight corruption and mismanagement. At the same time, the Government was facing new diffi-

culties with an unforeseen fuel supply problem. The United Nations organized a donors' conference (New York, 15-16 May) to mobilize funds to assist the Government in security and development projects; pledges totalling $38 million were made.

Extension of BONUCA mandate. Following consultations with the Government of the Central African Republic, the Secretary-General proposed to the Security Council on 28 September [S/2000/943] that the mandate of BONUCA be extended until 31 December 2001. The initial mandate was due to expire on 14 February 2001. In the light of the difficult situation in the country and the climate of instability in the subregion, the extension would allow the Office to continue to support the efforts of the Government to consolidate peace and national reconciliation and to strengthen democratic institutions and the rule of law. The Council, on 3 October [S/2000/944], took note of the Secretary-General's proposal.

Later developments. The political situation in the Central African Republic in late 2000 was dominated by tension between the ruling party and the opposition [S/2001/35]. The Government had not engaged in a dialogue with the opposition, and the opposition tended to adopt a confrontational approach in its activities and was attempting to seize the power it was unable to win through the ballot box. Dissension within the ruling MLPC also had a negative impact on the political landscape. The situation was aggravated by a strike of civil service workers that the opposition was trying to exploit for political ends. In June, President Patassé agreed in principle to hold a meeting with political stakeholders and other key national players; however, he did not do so during the year, stating that no constructive dialogue was possible with political opponents who were calling for his resignation. Meanwhile, the opposition, with the exception of former President David Dacko, rejected the notion of a national conference or a new forum, claiming that the conclusions of any such event would not be implemented. On 19 December, the 15 opposition parties attempted to hold a public rally in an outdoor stadium in Bangui, in defiance of a government ban announced the previous evening because of the tense social climate. When the organizers went ahead with the rally, security forces dispersed the crowd and detained 73 persons. Following that incident, the opposition deputies boycotted parliament meetings until its closure on 29 December.

The social situation, already strained by the oil crisis, was aggravated by unpaid arrears of wages (up to 30 months). Civil servants had frequently been on strike since October. As a result, the

2000/01 school year had not begun by the end of 2000. The human rights situation showed some improvement with a reduction in summary and extrajudicial executions. BONUCA and the Government collaborated in training 300 law enforcement officers in human rights and humanitarian law, and a training workshop was organized in December for NGOs for the promotion of human rights. However, another form of human rights violation had appeared in the Central African Republic—"neighbourhood justice". That type of popular justice had become commonplace, particularly in Bangui, where victims were often beaten to death. Concerns were also raised about the conditions of prisoners.

The security situation was relatively calm. Since the murder on 20 August of the Ambassador of the Libyan Arab Jamahiriya by a group of armed individuals, no further acts of a serious nature had been reported. Incidents of hold-ups, armed robbery and illegal roadblocks were reported, especially in the countryside. In order to strengthen law enforcement capacities, BONUCA organized civilian police training courses. Disarmament efforts continued and, by the end of the year, 95 per cent of the heavy weapons that had been in circulation since the mutinies of 1996 and 1997 had been recovered, as well as 65 per cent of light weapons. Illicit circulation of new weapons remained a concern. The process of restructuring the defence and security forces was continuing, but due to lack of financial resources only limited progress had been made in the demobilization and reintegration programme.

The overall economic situation worsened as a result of the continuing fuel crisis, and inflation surged while internal and exernal debt accumulated. A joint World Bank/IMF mission visited the country in October to undertake another assessment of the economy. Later, the World Bank approved a partial waiver of the conditions attached to the release of the $5 million second tranche of the fiscal consolidation credit.

Within the region, fighting in the DRC had caused a large number of refugees to flee to border towns in the Central African Republic. The number of refugees, most of them in makeshift camps, reached a peak of 10,000 in July and August, but declined to approximately 8,000 by December.

In the light of the situation, the Secretary-General sent Amara Essy, the former Foreign Minister of Côte d'Ivoire, as his Special Envoy to assess the multidimensional impact of the conflict in the DRC on the Central African Republic and the Republic of the Congo, in particular its humanitarian, economic, social and security implications. It was clear, however, that a solution to instability in the subregion depended on the restoration of peace in the DRC.

Financing of MINURCA and BONUCA

In April, the Secretary-General presented the financial performance report of MINURCA for the period from 1 July 1998 to 30 June 1999 [A/54/851]. The General Assembly, by resolution 53/238 [YUN 1999, p. 129], had appropriated $63,415,650 gross ($62,230,050 net) for that period, excluding voluntary contributions in kind. Expenditure for the period totalled $60,221,750 gross ($58,991,550 net), resulting in an unencumbered balance of $3,193,900 gross ($3,238,500 net). The unencumbered balance resulted mainly from the lower deployment levels of military and civilian personnel and reduced operational requirements under premises/accommodation, air operations and other equipment.

In a May report on MINURCA financing [A/54/857], the Secretary-General presented the revised budget for 1 July 1999 to 30 June 2000, including requirements for the Mission's liquidation and the cost estimates for the continuation of the liquidation activities in New York thereafter. The revised 1999-2000 budget amounted to $41,098,075 gross ($40,069,275 net), exclusive of budgeted voluntary contributions in kind of $736,300, and represented an increase of $7,730,200 in gross terms compared with the initial budget. The increase was attributable to additional requirements for the extension of the Mission's mandate until 15 February 2000 and the consequential retention of military and civilian personnel and logistical support beyond the original deadlines. Of the total revised budget, personnel costs accounted for 75 per cent of the budget. With regard to the 1 July 2000 to 30 June 2001 period, provision of $115,800 gross ($102,800 net) was requested for six work-months of staff activities at UN Headquarters and for the liquidation audit. The report proposed that the Assembly appropriate and assess the additional amount of $7,730,200 gross for the 1999/2000 period, inclusive of the commitment authority of $6,701,900 granted by ACABQ. It also suggested that the Assembly appropriate and assess the amount of $115,800 gross for the 2000/01 period.

Having considered the Secretary-General's two reports on MINURCA financing, ACABQ, in a May report [A/54/865], recommended that the unencumbered balance for the 1998/99 period ($3,193,900 gross ($3,238,500 net)) be credited to Member States in a manner to be decided by the Assembly. Regarding the revised budget for the 1999/2000 period, it recommended that the Assembly appropriate and assess the additional amount of $7,730,200 gross ($7,496,600 net), inclusive of the commitment authority already granted. ACABQ also recommended that the Assembly appropriate $115,800 gross ($102,800 net) for the 2000/01 period. Due to the cash position of the Mission account, the Committee did not believe that an assessment in that case was necessary at that time.

The Secretary-General, in a March report to the Fifth Committee [A/C.5/54/52], responded to an Assembly request made in resolution 54/250 A [YUN 1999, p. 1303] dealing with a budget for special political missions. The report contained proposed resource requirements of two political missions whose mandates were recently approved, one of which was BONUCA. The estimated requirements for BONUCA from 15 February 2000 to 14 February 2001 totalled $3,431,300.

GENERAL ASSEMBLY ACTION

On 15 June [meeting 98], the General Assembly, on the recommendation of the Fifth Committee [A/54/908], adopted **resolution 54/277** without vote [agenda item 149].

Financing of the United Nations Mission in the Central African Republic

The General Assembly,

Having considered the reports of the Secretary-General on the financing of the United Nations Mission in the Central African Republic and the related report of the Advisory Committee on Administrative and Budgetary Questions,

Bearing in mind Security Council resolution 1159(1998) of 27 March 1998, by which the Council decided to establish the United Nations Mission in the Central African Republic, and the subsequent resolutions by which the Council extended the mandate of the Mission, the latest of which was resolution 1271(1999) of 22 October 1999,

Recalling its resolution 52/249 of 26 June 1998 on the financing of the Mission and its subsequent resolutions thereon, the latest of which was resolution 53/238 of 8 June 1999,

Reaffirming that the costs of the Mission are expenses of the Organization to be borne by Member States in accordance with Article 17, paragraph 2, of the Charter of the United Nations,

Recalling its previous decisions regarding the fact that, in order to meet the expenditures caused by the Mission, a different procedure is required from that applied to meet expenditures of the regular budget of the United Nations,

Taking into account the fact that the economically more developed countries are in a position to make relatively larger contributions and that the economically less developed countries have a relatively limited capacity to contribute towards such an operation,

Bearing in mind the special responsibilities of the States permanent members of the Security Council, as indicated in General Assembly resolution 1874(S-IV) of 27 June 1963, in the financing of such operations,

Noting with appreciation that voluntary contributions have been made to the Mission,

Mindful of the fact that it is essential to provide the account of the Mission with the necessary financial resources to enable it to meet its outstanding liabilities,

1. *Takes note* of the status of contributions to the United Nations Mission in the Central African Republic as at 30 April 2000, including the contributions outstanding in the amount of 36.6 million United States dollars, representing 32 per cent of the total assessed contributions, notes that some 41 per cent of the Member States have paid their assessed contributions in full, and urges all other Member States concerned, in particular those in arrears, to ensure payment of their outstanding assessed contributions;

2. *Expresses its appreciation* to those Member States which have paid their assessed contributions in full;

3. *Expresses concern* about the financial situation with regard to peacekeeping activities, in particular as regards the reimbursements to troop contributors that bear additional burdens owing to overdue payments by Member States of their assessments;

4. *Urges* all other Member States to make every possible effort to ensure payment of their assessed contributions to the Mission in full and on time;

5. *Expresses concern* at the delay experienced by the Secretary-General in deploying and providing adequate resources to some recent peacekeeping missions, in particular those in Africa;

6. *Emphasizes* that all future and existing peacekeeping missions shall be given equal and nondiscriminatory treatment in respect of financial and administrative arrangements;

7. *Also emphasizes* that all peacekeeping missions shall be provided with adequate resources for the effective and efficient discharge of their respective mandates;

8. *Endorses* the conclusions and recommendations contained in the report of the Advisory Committee on Administrative and Budgetary Questions, and requests the Secretary-General to ensure their full implementation;

9. *Requests* the Secretary-General to take all necessary action to ensure that the liquidation of the Mission is administered with a maximum of efficiency and economy;

10. *Decides* to appropriate to the Special Account for the United Nations Mission in the Central African Republic the amount of 7,730,200 dollars gross (7,496,600 dollars net) for the maintenance and liquidation of the Mission for the period ending 30 June 2000, in addition to the amount of 33,367,875 dollars gross (32,572,675 dollars net) already appropriated under the terms of General Assembly resolution 53/238 and inclusive of an amount of 6,701,900 dollars gross and net authorized by the Advisory Committee under the terms of section IV of Assembly resolution 49/233 A of 23 December 1994;

11. *Decides also*, as an ad hoc arrangement, taking into account the amount of 33,367,875 dollars gross (32,572,675 dollars net) already apportioned under the terms of its resolution 53/238, to apportion among Member States the additional amount of 7,730,200 dollars gross (7,496,600 dollars net) for the period ending 30 June 2000, in accordance with the composition of groups set out in paragraphs 3 and 4 of General Assembly resolution 43/232 of 1 March 1989, as adjusted by the Assembly in its resolutions 44/192 B of 21 Decem-

ber 1989, 45/269 of 27 August 1991, 46/198 A of 20 December 1991, 47/218 A of 23 December 1992, 49/249 A of 20 July 1995, 49/249 B of 14 September 1995, 50/224 of 11 April 1996, 51/218 A to C of 18 December 1996 and 52/230 of 31 March 1998 and its decisions 48/472 A of 23 December 1993, 50/451 B of 23 December 1995 and 54/456 to 54/458 of 23 December 1999, and taking into account the scale of assessments for the year 2000, as set out in its resolutions 52/215 A of 22 December 1997 and 54/237 A of 23 December 1999;

12. *Decides further* that, in accordance with the provisions of its resolution 973(X) of 15 December 1955, there shall be set off against the apportionment among Member States, as provided for in paragraph 11 above, their respective share in the Tax Equalization Fund of the estimated additional staff assessment income of 233,600 dollars approved for the Mission for the period ending 30 June 2000;

13. *Decides* to appropriate the amount of 119,726 dollars gross (106,147 dollars net) for the period from 1 July 2000 to 30 June 2001, for the continuation of activities relating to the liquidation of the Mission, inclusive of the amount of 3,396 dollars gross (2,874 dollars net) for the support account for peacekeeping operations and the amount of 530 dollars gross (473 dollars net) for the United Nations Logistics Base at Brindisi, Italy, and decides also that no action be taken on the apportionment of the said amount at this stage;

14. *Decides also* that, for Member States that have fulfilled their financial obligations to the Mission, there shall be set off against their apportionment, as provided for in paragraph 11 above, their respective share of the unencumbered balance of 3,193,900 dollars gross (3,238,500 dollars net) in respect of the period ending 30 June 1999;

15. *Decides further* that, for Member States that have not fulfilled their financial obligations to the Mission, their share of the unencumbered balance of 3,193,900 dollars gross (3,238,500 dollars net) in respect of the period ending 30 June 1999 shall be set off against their outstanding obligations;

16. *Emphasizes* that no peacekeeping mission shall be financed by borrowing funds from other active peacekeeping missions;

17. *Decides* to include in the provisional agenda of its fifty-fifth session the item entitled "Financing of the United Nations Mission in the Central African Republic".

On 23 December, the Assembly decided that the item on MINURCA financing would remain for consideration during its resumed fifty-fifth (2001) session (**decision 55/458**) and that the Fifth Committee would continue to consider the item at that session (**decision 55/455**).

Eritrea-Ethiopia

The border dispute between Eritrea and Ethiopia increased in intensity in May with the resumption of large-scale hostilities. However, the year ended on a more hopeful note when the two countries signed a Peace Agreement that allowed the expansion of the United Nations Mission in Ethiopia and Eritrea (UNMEE), which was established in July.

In 1999, Eritrea and Ethiopia had agreed to settle their conflict through restoration of the status quo ante as of 6 May 1998, when hostilities broke out, and delimitation and demarcation of their entire border with the help of the United Nations; they had also agreed on the sequence of mutual withdrawal from occupied territories in order to return to the status quo ante. Ethiopia had accepted those proposals, which were contained in the Framework Agreement put forward by OAU in November 1998 [YUN 1998, p. 149], and Eritrea indicated its acceptance of the terms in February 1999 [YUN 1999, p. 134]. However, the text remained unsigned and OAU continued its mediation efforts in 2000.

By the end of May 2000, Ethiopian forces had made major advances and the Security Council called for an arms embargo against both countries. The two Governments resumed proximity talks under OAU auspices. A ceasefire agreement was signed on 18 June, by which the two countries committed themselves to seeking a UN peacekeeping mission to monitor the ceasefire, the redeployment of Ethiopian forces to their earlier positions and the establishment of a temporary security zone between the two sides. Having received requests from Ethiopia and Eritrea, the Council, on 31 July, established UNMEE in anticipation of a future peacekeeping operation. The Secretary-General, in August, put forward proposals for a peacekeeping operation with up to 4,200 personnel, and the Council authorized the expansion of the Mission to that size on 15 September.

On 12 December, Eritrea and Ethiopia signed a Peace Agreement in Algiers that provided for the two parties to terminate hostilities, respect the provisions of the earlier agreement and release prisoners of war. They also agreed to an investigation to determine the origins of the conflict and to establish a neutral boundary commission to demarcate the border. By the end of the year, the agreement appeared to be holding and the United Nations began accelerating the expansion of the peacekeeping mission.

Border dispute

The border dispute between Eritrea and Ethiopia, which began in 1998 [YUN 1998, p. 145] and flared into a full-scale war in 1999, continued in early 2000. By May, large-scale hostilities were taking place along the border. Peace initiatives were carried out by the Secretary-General and his representatives, the current OAU Chairman, President Abdelaziz Bouteflika of Algeria, and others. OAU held proximity talks with the two parties based on the Framework Agreement and the Modalities for Implementation, and work continued on a third document, the Technical Arrangements.

Communications. In early 2000, Eritrea and Ethiopia, in letters to the Security Council, exchanged charges of aggression and of insincerity and intransigence in mediation efforts. Ethiopia, in letters of 6 and 22 March, 7 and 27 April and 11 and 12 May [S/2000/185, S/2000/241, S/2000/296, S/2000/356, S/2000/422, S/2000/421], claimed that Eritrea was committing aggression against it, while Ethiopia was committed to the peace process. Ethiopia had accepted the Framework Agreement and the modalities for its implementation, but had found some problems with the implementation plan's Technical Arrangements; meanwhile, Eritrea was engaged in posturing and in a game of brinkmanship. In Ethiopia's view, the peace process was in trouble due to the intransigence of the Eritrean regime and its reluctance to return to the status quo ante. The issue, according to Ethiopia, was not a border dispute but a question of aggression by Eritrea against another country. Ethiopia reviewed the events of the dispute and said that its bottom line for peace was the restoration of the status quo ante; it called on the Council to assist in stopping the war. Eritrea denied the allegations of aggression and put forward its position on 23 March and 5 May [S/2000/247, S/2000/389]. Regarding the status of the OAU negotiations, Eritrea claimed that the Ethiopian ruling party was blocking progress by refusing to agree to the Technical Arrangements. Annexed to the 5 May letter were Eritrea's proposals submitted to OAU for the April/May proximity talks (see below).

Eritrea, on 23 February [A/54/770-S/2000/161], transmitted to the Secretary-General copies of the case and supplemental application it had made to the International Court of Justice concerning the dispute with Ethiopia.

Germany, on 13 April [S/2000/312], warned of a pending tragedy in the Horn of Africa due to the looming natural disaster compounded by longstanding armed conflicts. It suggested that the Security Council appeal to Ethiopia and Eritrea to avoid any military conflict and request all countries to end the sale of arms in the region.

Mediation efforts

OAU proximity talks

The OAU proximity talks held in Algiers from 29 April to 5 May concluded unsuccessfully, owing to disagreements between the parties over whether the Framework Agreement, the Modalities for Implementation and a ceasefire agreement should be signed prior to the finalization of consolidated technical arrangements. In a 5 May communiqué on the talks [A/54/863, S/2000/394], the OAU Chairman, Abdelaziz Bouteflika, stated that the aim of the indirect talks was to enable the two parties to reach an agreement on consolidated technical arrangements that would lead to the implementation of the plan for a settlement as contained in the Framework Agreement and the Modalities accepted by the two parties and endorsed by the OAU summit in July 1999 [YUN 1999, p. 136]. Recapitulating the events prior to the talks, the communiqué outlined the points of convergence and said that substantive talks could not take place because Eritrea called for the prior signing of the Framework Agreement, the Modalities and a ceasefire agreement, while Ethiopia maintained its July 1999 position, namely, that those documents could not be signed until the technical arrangements had been finalized. All efforts by the Special Envoy of the OAU Chairman, with the support of the representatives of the United States and the EU, failed to change those positions. As a result, the talks ended in an impasse.

The EU Presidency, in a 10 May statement [S/2000/437], expressed support for the OAU efforts and called on the Governments of Ethiopia and Eritrea to enter immediately and without preconditions into further negotiations and to refrain from military action.

Security Council mission

Concerned by the ongoing conflict between Eritrea and Ethiopia, the Security Council, on 7 May [S/2000/392], authorized its special mission to the DRC (see p. 127) to visit those two countries on 9 and 10 May.

The special mission to Eritrea and Ethiopia, in a report to the Council [S/2000/413], warned that the two sides were on the verge of resuming a senseless war, despite progress achieved over time by the OAU negotiations. Those negotiations had produced agreements and drafts on a ceasefire, withdrawal, interim arrangements and arbitration and final demarcation of the disputed territory. The final elements of the technical arrangements to be agreed upon represented a small proportion of the whole and could be resolved by negotiations. However, Ethiopia continued to accuse Eritrea of stringing out negotiations to avoid redressing its offensive of May 1998, while Eritrea accused Ethiopia of actively holding to the option of resuming the conflict while negotiations continued.

The special mission tried to find a mechanism to get past that blockage without going into the details of the OAU negotiations. That mechanism took the form of a draft Security Council resolution calling for proximity talks to resume and insisting that the parties refrain from the use of force.

Renewed hostilities

Eritrea, in a 12 May letter to the Council [S/2000/420], stated that Ethiopia had resumed its war of aggression against Eritrea by launching a large-scale offensive. Eritrea claimed that Ethiopia had frustrated the peace process by reneging on its commitments and rejecting the technical arrangements after seven months of stalling. Ethiopia's resort to force was in violation of the OAU Framework Agreement and Modalities. Therefore, Eritrea called on the Council to condemn Ethiopia's resumption of the war and support Eritrea's right to self-defence.

Also on 12 May [A/54/867-S/2000/427], the OAU Chairman forwarded to the Secretary-General and the Security Council a communiqué expressing concern at the resumption of fighting between Ethiopia and Eritrea. At that time, the two parties' acceptance of the Framework Agreement and the Modalities had aroused hope that there would be a settlement of the dispute, he said. Although those documents had not been implemented, there were points of convergence between the two parties as to the process for implementing the peace plan. Despite an appeal to both sides to show restraint and to continue the talks, the use of force had replaced dialogue and negotiation. In view of those developments, the Chairman appealed to the two Governments to end the hostilities immediately and unconditionally and to the international community to urge an immediate cessation of the fighting so that OAU could pursue its peace effort.

SECURITY COUNCIL ACTION (May)

On 12 May [meeting 4142], the Security Council unanimously adopted **resolution 1297(2000)**. The draft [S/2000/419] was prepared in consultations among Council members.

The Security Council,

Recalling its resolutions 1177(1998) of 26 June 1998, 1226(1999) of 29 January 1999 and 1227(1999) of 10 February 1999,

Deeply disturbed by the outbreak of renewed fighting between Eritrea and Ethiopia,

Stressing the need for both parties to achieve a peaceful resolution of the conflict,

Reaffirming the commitment of all Member States to the sovereignty, independence and territorial integrity of Eritrea and Ethiopia,

Expressing its strong support for the efforts of the Organization of African Unity to achieve a peaceful resolution of the conflict,

Welcoming the efforts of its Mission to the region and its report of 11 May 2000,

Convinced of the need for further and immediate diplomatic efforts,

Noting with concern that the renewed fighting has serious humanitarian implications for the civilian population of the two countries,

Stressing that the situation between Eritrea and Ethiopia constitutes a threat to peace and security,

Stressing also that renewed hostilities constitute an even greater threat to the stability, security and economic development of the subregion,

1. *Strongly condemns* the renewed fighting between Eritrea and Ethiopia;

2. *Demands* that both parties cease immediately all military action and refrain from the further use of force;

3. *Also demands* the earliest possible reconvening, without preconditions, of substantive peace talks, under the auspices of the Organization of African Unity, on the basis of the Framework Agreement approved on 17 December 1998 and the Modalities for Implementation and of the work conducted by the Organization of African Unity as recorded in the communiqué issued by its current Chairman on 5 May 2000;

4. *Resolves* to meet again within seventy-two hours of the adoption of the present resolution to take immediate steps to ensure compliance with the present resolution in the event that hostilities continue;

5. *Reaffirms its full support* for the continuing efforts of the Organization of African Unity, of Algeria, its current Chairman, and of other interested parties to achieve a peaceful resolution of the conflict;

6. *Endorses* the Framework Agreement and the Modalities for Implementation as the basis for the peaceful resolution of the dispute between the two parties;

7. *Also endorses* the communiqué of 5 May 2000 issued by the current Chairman of the Organization of African Unity, which records the achievements of the Organization of African Unity–led negotiations up to that point, including the areas of convergence already established between the two parties;

8. *Calls upon* both parties to ensure the safety of civilian populations and fully to respect human rights and international humanitarian law;

9. *Requests* the Secretary-General to keep the Council fully and regularly informed on the situation;

10. *Decides* to remain seized of the matter.

Communications. Referring to resolution 1297(2000), Ethiopia, on 15 May [S/2000/430], said that the call for reconvening peace talks without preconditions under OAU auspices could not be directed to Ethiopia because Ethiopia was not responsible for the collapse of the latest talks, but was prepared to proceed to the proximity talks and commence from where it had left off in Algiers on 5 May.

The Central Organ of the OAU Mechanism for Conflict Prevention, Management and Resolution, at an ambassadorial-level meeting in Addis Ababa on 14 May, issued a communiqué [S/2000/435] in which it expressed concern at the resumption of hostilities between Ethiopia and Eritrea and the consequences for both countries and for security in the region. Appealing for the resumption of the proximity talks under OAU auspices, it took note of the Ethiopian statement on its readiness to resume talks and the Eritrean statement that both parties were expected to respond to the OAU appeal.

On 17 May [S/2000/444], Eritrea complained of Ethiopia's latest aggression, which had resulted in its occupation of western Eritrea; consequently, over 500,000 Eritreans were fleeing from the invading army. Eritrea called on the United Nations to fulfil its duties by preventing the annihilation of Eritrean independence or the dismemberment of its territory through collective security measures. On the same day [S/2000/454], the EU Presidency issued a statement condemning the resumption of hostilities between the two countries and welcoming Council resolution 1297(2000). On 18 May, the Intergovernmental Authority on Development (IGAD) appealed to the two parties to show restraint and promote the proximity talks [S/2000/479].

Arms embargo

On 17 May [meeting 4144], the Security Council unanimously adopted **resolution 1298(2000)**. The draft text [S/2000/440] was submitted by Bangladesh, Canada, the Netherlands, the United Kingdom and the United States.

The Security Council,

Recalling its resolutions 1177(1998) of 26 June 1998, 1226(1999) of 29 January 1999, 1227(1999) of 10 February 1999 and 1297(2000) of 12 May 2000,

Recalling in particular its urging of all States in its resolution 1227(1999) to end all sales of arms and munitions to Eritrea and Ethiopia,

Deeply disturbed by the continuation of fighting between Eritrea and Ethiopia,

Deploring the loss of human life resulting from the fighting, and strongly regretting the negative impact the diversion of resources to the conflict continues to have on efforts to address the ongoing humanitarian food crisis in the region,

Stressing the need for both parties to achieve a peaceful resolution of the conflict,

Reaffirming the commitment of all Member States to the sovereignty, independence and territorial integrity of Eritrea and Ethiopia,

Expressing its strong support for the efforts of the Organization of African Unity to achieve a peaceful resolution of the conflict,

Noting that the proximity talks held in Algiers from 29 April to 5 May 2000 and reported in the Organization of African Unity communiqué of 5 May 2000 were intended to assist the two parties to arrive at a final detailed peace implementation plan acceptable to each of them, which would lead to the peaceful resolution of the conflict,

Recalling the efforts of the Security Council, including through its Mission to the region, to achieve a peaceful resolution of the situation,

Convinced of the need for further and immediate diplomatic efforts,

Noting with concern that the fighting has serious humanitarian implications for the civilian population of the two States,

Stressing that the hostilities constitute an increasing threat to the stability, security and economic development of the subregion,

Determining that the situation between Eritrea and Ethiopia constitutes a threat to regional peace and security,

Acting under Chapter VII of the Charter of the United Nations,

1. *Strongly condemns* the continued fighting between Eritrea and Ethiopia;

2. *Demands* that both parties cease immediately all military action and refrain from the further use of force;

3. *Demands also* that both parties withdraw their forces from military engagement and take no action that would aggravate tensions;

4. *Demands further* the earliest possible reconvening, without preconditions, of substantive peace talks, under the auspices of the Organization of African Unity, on the basis of the Framework Agreement approved on 17 December 1998 and the Modalities for Implementation and of the work conducted by the Organization of African Unity as recorded in the communiqué issued by its current Chairman on 5 May 2000, which would conclude a peaceful, definitive settlement of the conflict;

5. *Requests* that the current Chairman of the Organization of African Unity consider dispatching urgently his Personal Envoy to the region to seek immediate cessation of hostilities and resumption of the peace talks;

6. *Decides* that all States shall prevent:

(a) The sale or supply to Eritrea and Ethiopia, by their nationals or from their territories, or using their flag vessels or aircraft, of arms and related materiel of all types, including weapons and ammunition, military vehicles and equipment, paramilitary equipment and spare parts for the aforementioned, whether or not originating in their territory;

(b) Any provision to Eritrea and Ethiopia, by their nationals or from their territories, of technical assistance or training related to the provision, manufacture, maintenance or use of the items in (a) above;

7. *Decides also* that the measures imposed by paragraph 6 above shall not apply to supplies of non-lethal military equipment intended solely for humanitarian use, as approved in advance by the committee established by paragraph 8 below;

8. *Decides further* to establish, in accordance with rule 28 of its provisional rules of procedure, a committee of the Security Council consisting of all the members of the Council, to undertake the following tasks and to report on its work to the Council with its observations and recommendations:

(*a*) To seek from all States further information regarding the action taken by them with a view to implementing effectively the measures imposed by paragraph 6 above, and thereafter to request from them whatever further information it may consider necessary;

(*b*) To consider information brought to its attention by States concerning violations of the measures imposed by paragraph 6 above and to recommend appropriate measures in response thereto;

(*c*) To make periodic reports to the Council on information submitted to it regarding alleged violations of the measures imposed by paragraph 6 above, identifying where possible persons or entities, including vessels and aircraft, reported to be engaged in such violations;

(*d*) To promulgate such guidelines as may be necessary to facilitate the implementation of the measures imposed by paragraph 6 above;

(*e*) To give consideration to, and decide upon, requests for the exceptions set out in paragraph 7 above;

(*f*) To examine the reports submitted pursuant to paragraphs 11 and 12 below;

9. *Calls upon* all States and all international and regional organizations to act strictly in conformity with this resolution, notwithstanding the existence of any rights granted or obligations conferred or imposed by any international agreement or of any contract entered into or any licence or permit granted prior to the entry into force of the measures imposed by paragraph 6 above;

10. *Requests* the Secretary-General to provide all necessary assistance to the Committee established by paragraph 8 above and to make the necessary arrangements in the Secretariat for this purpose;

11. *Requests* States to report in detail to the Secretary-General within thirty days of the date of adoption of the present resolution on the specific steps they have taken to give effect to the measures imposed by paragraph 6 above;

12. *Requests* all States, relevant United Nations bodies and, as appropriate, other organizations and interested parties to report information on possible violations of the measures imposed by paragraph 6 above to the Committee established by paragraph 8 above;

13. *Requests* the Committee established by paragraph 8 above to make information it considers relevant publicly available through appropriate media, including through the improved use of information technology;

14. *Requests* the Governments of Eritrea and Ethiopia and other concerned parties to establish appropriate arrangements for the provision of humanitarian assistance and to endeavour to ensure that such assistance responds to local needs and is safely delivered to, and used by, its intended recipients;

15. *Requests* the Secretary-General to submit an initial report to the Council within fifteen days of the date of adoption of the present resolution on compliance with paragraphs 2, 3 and 4 above, and thereafter every

sixty days after the date of adoption of the present resolution on its implementation and on the humanitarian situation in Eritrea and Ethiopia;

16. *Decides* that the measures imposed by paragraph 6 above are established for twelve months and that, at the end of this period, the Council will decide whether the Governments of Eritrea and Ethiopia have complied with paragraphs 2, 3 and 4 above and, accordingly, whether to extend these measures for a further period with the same conditions;

17. *Decides also* that the measures imposed by paragraph 6 above shall be terminated immediately if the Secretary-General reports that a peaceful, definitive settlement of the conflict has been concluded;

18. *Decides* to remain seized of the matter.

Communications. Both Ethiopia and Eritrea responded to the Security Council's imposition of an arms embargo in letters to the President. Ethiopia, on 18 May [S/2000/448], said that, although the arms embargo was ostensibly aimed at both countries, the intent and objective of the initiators of the text were obviously focused on Ethiopia. The United Kingdom and the United States, which had wanted a harsher punishment of Ethiopia, did not succeed. On 19 May [S/2000/464], Eritrea said that it had complied with the demand to halt military action while Ethiopia had not. Eritrea objected to the arms embargo on the grounds that it punished equally Eritrea and Ethiopia, thus depriving Eritrea of its legitimate right to defend itself against Ethiopia's invasion and occupation of Eritrean territory.

Further military and mediation developments

Communications. On 19 May [A/54/876-S/2000/456], the OAU Chairman, President Bouteflika, appealed to the two parties for an immediate ceasefire and invited them to participate in a new round of proximity talks. Declaring his readiness to organize such indirect talks immediately, the Chairman stated that he would await positive reactions from the parties. He later informed the Secretary-General that he had dispatched his Special Envoy, Ahmed Ouyahia, to the region from 21 to 24 May [A/54/885].

On 24 May, the OAU Chairman issued a communiqué [S/2000/477] regarding Mr. Ouyahia's diplomatic efforts to encourage Eritrea and Ethiopia to take steps to de-escalate the conflict. On the same day [S/2000/481], Eritrea announced that, in response to that communiqué, it had decided to redeploy its forces to positions held before 6 May 1998 and would begin redeployment on 25 May in the Zalanbessa area. Eritrea also expressed readiness to finalize consolidated technical arrangements and to attend the Algiers proximity talks.

On 25 May, Ethiopia announced that its forces had recaptured the town of Zalanbessa [S/2000/483]. Ethiopia stated that the Eritrean announcement of withdrawal had come as its forces were being evicted from the Mereb-Zalanbessa-Alitena front and that fighting was continuing in areas on that front. It also claimed that large areas of territory in the eastern and north-eastern part of Ethiopia were still occupied by Eritrea. Ethiopia said it had no desire to remain in Eritrean territory that it held temporarily for the purpose of military expediency. It also re-affirmed its commitment to the peace process under OAU auspices.

In a communiqué of 26 May [A/54/886-S/2000/495], the OAU Chairman identified the following points on which the two parties were committed: to redeploy their respective forces to positions held prior to 6 May 1998; to resolve their border dispute in conformity with the Framework Agreement and the Modalities; and to pursue negotiations under OAU auspices with a view to finalizing the consolidated technical arrangements. The communiqué also noted that the OAU Chairman had invited the two parties to resume the proximity talks on 29 May. The Chairman considered that the Eritrean initiative to withdraw would lead to the rapid cessation of fighting.

In letters to the Secretary-General of 27 May [S/2000/498] and 29 May [S/2000/499], Eritrea accused Ethiopia of continuing military action against Eritrea even after Eritrea's full compliance with the OAU proposal for redeployment of troops to positions prior to 6 May 1998. It called on the Council to lift the sanctions against Eritrea. However, in a statement of 30 May [S/2000/505], Ethiopia claimed that, while Eritrean troops had fled Bure, it had not been verified that they had vacated Badda on the northeast frontier; Ethiopia was taking measures to verify if indeed Eritrean troops had withdrawn from all occupied territories in the area.

In a 2 June letter to the Security Council [S/2000/523], the Foreign Minister of Ethiopia announced that the Government had verified that all its territories had been cleared of Eritrean troops and that the war was over as far as Ethiopia was concerned. He acknowledged that the Ethiopian army was in Eritrean territories on the Zalanbessa front and declared that whether Ethiopia would redeploy to the 6 May 1998 positions would depend on what the international community would provide by way of security guarantees.

Report of Secretary-General (June). In accordance with resolution 1298(2000), the Secretary-General submitted a 2 June report on Eritrea and Ethiopia [S/2000/530]. He stated that Eritrea and Ethiopia had resumed proximity talks on 30 May. He described the military and diplomatic developments since the adoption of resolution 1298(2000) and noted that progress had been made towards meeting the requirements of paragraphs 2, 3 and 4 of the resolution, mainly through OAU diplomatic efforts. The Secretary-General observed that the Secretariat's capacity to monitor and report on the military situation between Eritrea and Ethiopia was extremely limited as there were no UN observers on the ground. Nevertheless, the broad outline of developments seemed sufficiently clear from official statements by both Eritrea and Ethiopia.

Since Ethiopia's declaration of the end of the war on 31 May, no major combat had been reported. However, reports of some fighting had been received and the parties continued to accuse each other of attacks. Noting that proximity talks under OAU auspices were under way, the Secretary-General urged both parties to cooperate fully with OAU and other members of the international community to continue to support OAU efforts to achieve a definitive, peaceful resolution of the conflict without further delay.

Resumed OAU proximity talks

The diplomatic efforts to find a solution to the border dispute, in particular the resumed proximity talks in Algiers (30 May–10 June), were described by OAU in communiqués of 1, 9 and 12 June [S/2000/535, S/2000/557, A/54/913-S/2000/560]. OAU announced that Eritrea had accepted its proposal for an immediate cessation of hostilities. The OAU proposal also provided for the withdrawal of Ethiopian troops from Eritrean territory, after the deployment of "a peacekeeping mission deployed by the United Nations under the auspices of OAU". The mandate of the mission would extend until the demarcation of the border between the two countries. Eritrea, which had earlier redeployed its troops to the positions they held before the outbreak of the conflict and from additional areas on the basis of an OAU appeal, asked that Ethiopia follow suit. Ethiopia, however, presented preconditions for redeployment, namely, the provision by the international community of "security guarantees". Although Eritrea initially rejected the Ethiopian position as unjustified, it decided to respond positively to OAU's appeal. Eritrea called on the international community to take strong action against Ethiopia in the event that it rejected the OAU proposal or pretended to accept while continuing its war against Eritrea. The border dispute would be settled in conformity with the Framework Agreement and the Modalities, on the basis of the relevant colonial treaties and of applicable international law, through delimitation and demarcation with UN assistance and, if necessary, through arbitration. A security zone in Eritrea would be designed to separate the forces of the two countries following the withdrawal of Ethiopian troops to the 6 May 1998 line. Despite agreement on those points, there was still disagreement on two points, namely, the exact definition of the security zone between the two forces, and certain aspects of the composition and functioning of the international peacekeeping force.

During the period when proximity talks were taking place in Algiers, both Eritrea [S/2000/532, S/2000/554] and Ethiopia [S/2000/534] complained of attacks by the other party.

Human rights violations

Eritrea and Ethiopia accused each other of committing human rights violations against their nationals. Eritrea complained that Ethiopia was committing acts of violence against civilians in the occupied Eritrean territories [A/54/912-S/2000/561, A/54/922-S/2000/592, A/54/923-S/2000/593, S/2000/610, A/55/438-S/2000/931] and against ethnic Eritreans in Ethiopia [A/54/965-S/2000/816, A/54/962-S/2000/812]. Ethiopia protested about the human rights violations suffered by Ethiopian nationals residing in Eritrea, including acts of extrajudicial killings, abductions, detentions and torture [S/2000/542, A/54/898, S/2000/568, S/2000/619, S/2000/793, S/2000/811]. Eritrea denied those claims [A/54/970-S/2000/838, A/55/630-S/2000/1101].

Ceasefire agreement

By letters of 14 and 15 June, respectively, Ethiopia [S/2000/576] and Eritrea [S/2000/579] indicated to the Security Council their acceptance of the OAU proposal for a cessation of hostilities. The EU, on 14 June [S/2000/585], welcomed the outcome of the proximity talks and confirmed its commitment to support the implementation of the peace settlement, in particular the deployment of a peacekeeping mission, the demarcation of the common border, mine clearance and efforts to support refugees and displaced persons. On 20 June [S/2000/612], Eritrea requested the United Nations to take the measures necessary to assist the parties in implementing the cessation of hostilities. On 26 June [S/2000/627], Ethiopia addressed a similar request to the Organization.

Report of Secretary-General (June). The OAU proximity talks, which culminated in the signing on 18 June of the Agreement on Cessation of Hostilities between Ethiopia and Eritrea by the Foreign Ministers of both countries, were high-

lighted by the Secretary-General in his 30 June report on Ethiopia and Eritrea [S/2000/643]. Although under OAU auspices, the talks also had the assistance of representatives of the EU and the United States. Under the Agreement, which was circulated on 19 June as a document of the Security Council [S/2000/601] and the General Assembly [A/54/925], the parties agreed to a cessation of hostilities and reaffirmed their acceptance of the OAU Framework Agreement and the modalities for its implementation. They called on the United Nations, in cooperation with OAU, to deploy a peacekeeping mission to assist in implementing the Agreement and guaranteed to ensure free movement and access for the mission and its supplies and to respect its members, installations and equipment.

As stipulated in the Agreement, Ethiopia would submit to the peacekeeping mission redeployment plans for its troops from positions taken after 6 February 1999 that were not under Ethiopian administration before 6 May 1998. For its part, Eritrea would maintain its forces 25 kilometres (artillery range) from positions to which the Ethiopian forces would redeploy. That zone of separation would be called the "temporary security zone". The United Nations and OAU would establish a Military Coordination Commission to coordinate and resolve issues relating to implementation of the mission's mandate. In particular, the peacekeeping mission was mandated to: monitor the cessation of hostilities; monitor and ensure the redeployment of Ethiopian forces; ensure the observance of the security commitments agreed to by the two parties; and monitor the temporary security zone. The Agreement also called on the Security Council to adopt "appropriate measures" should one or both parties violate the commitments. Other provisions concerned demining activities with UN technical assistance and the return of civilian administration and of the population. The mandate of the peacekeeping operation would terminate when the delimitation/demarcation process was completed.

The Secretary-General described the Agreement as the first but an extremely vital step towards restoring peace between Ethiopia and Eritrea. The protracted conflict had compounded the effects of the drought in the two countries. It was estimated that 1.2 million people, 70 per cent of them women, children and the elderly, had been displaced by the war. Many of them lived without shelter, proper sanitation or regular access to food and water. Many thousands had fled across the border into the Sudan. In order to facilitate the implementation of the Agreement, the Secretary-General intended to send a reconnaissance mission to the region to make recommendations on a UN mission. He also would send liaison officers to each capital to liaise with the parties and OAU, to be followed by the deployment of a military observer group of up to 100 members, pending the establishment of a mission.

On 7 July [S/2000/676], the Security Council endorsed the Secretary-General's decision to dispatch reconnaissance and liaison teams to the region to expedite planning and coordination activities to start up a possible peacekeeping mission.

Communications. By a 21 July letter [S/2000/726], Eritrea requested the Council to investigate the violation of the Agreement on 17 July by three Ethiopian aircraft that flew deep into Eritrean airspace. Two of the fighter planes were hit as they attacked Eritrean defence installations. Ethiopia was also demolishing homes and villages in southern Eritrea. Ethiopia rejected the charges as totally false [S/2000/704].

Establishment of UNMEE

Having considered the Secretary-General's report on Ethiopia and Eritrea following the Agreement on Cessation of Hostilities, the Security Council, in July, established the United Nations Mission in Ethiopia and Eritrea (UNMEE) as requested by the two countries and recommended by the Secretary-General. The Mission would consist initially of up to 100 military observers. In September, the Council authorized the deployment of up to 4,200 troops until 15 March 2001.

SECURITY COUNCIL ACTION (July)

On 31 July [meeting 4181], the Security Council unanimously adopted **resolution 1312(2000)**. The draft [S/2000/729] was prepared in consultations among Council members.

The Security Council,

Recalling its resolutions 1298(2000) of 17 May 2000 and 1308(2000) of 17 July 2000 and all its resolutions and statements by its President pertaining to the Ethiopia-Eritrea conflict,

Commending the Organization of African Unity for successfully facilitating the Agreement on Cessation of Hostilities between the Government of the Federal Democratic Republic of Ethiopia and the Government of the State of Eritrea, signed in Algiers on 18 June 2000,

Recalling the official communications by the Governments of Eritrea and Ethiopia dated 20 and 26 June 2000 respectively to the Secretary-General requesting United Nations assistance in implementing the Agreement on Cessation of Hostilities,

Recalling also the relevant principles contained in the Convention on the Safety of United Nations and Associated Personnel of 9 December 1994,

Welcoming the report of the Secretary-General of 30 June 2000, and recalling the letter of its President dated 7 July 2000 endorsing the decision of the Secretary-General to dispatch reconnaissance and liaison teams to the region,

1. *Decides* to establish the United Nations Mission in Ethiopia and Eritrea consisting of up to one hundred military observers and the necessary civilian support staff until 31 January 2001, in anticipation of a peacekeeping operation subject to future Security Council authorization, and to undertake the following mandate:

(a) To establish and maintain liaison with the parties;

(b) To visit the military headquarters and other units of the parties in all areas of operation of the mission deemed necessary by the Secretary-General;

(c) To establish and put into operation the mechanism for verifying the cessation of hostilities;

(d) To prepare for the establishment of the Military Coordination Commission provided for in the Agreement on Cessation of Hostilities;

(e) To assist in planning for a future peacekeeping operation as necessary;

2. *Welcomes* the discussions between the secretariats of the United Nations and the Organization of African Unity on cooperation in the implementation of the Agreement on Cessation of Hostilities;

3. *Calls upon* the parties to provide the Mission with the access, assistance, support and protection required for the performance of its duties;

4. *Requests* the parties to facilitate the deployment of mine action experts and assets under the United Nations Mine Action Service to assess further the mine and unexploded ordnance problem and to provide technical assistance to the parties to carry out emergency mine action required;

5. *Decides* that the measures imposed by paragraph 6 of its resolution 1298(2000) shall not apply to the sale or supply of equipment and related materiel for the use of the United Nations Mine Action Service, or to the provision of related technical assistance and training by that Service;

6. *Stresses* the importance of the rapid delimitation and demarcation of the common border between the parties in accordance with the Organization of African Unity Framework Agreement approved on 17 December 1998 and the Agreement on Cessation of Hostilities;

7. *Requests* the Secretary-General to continue planning for a peacekeeping operation and to begin to take the administrative measures for assembling such a mission, which would be subject to future Council authorization;

8. *Also requests* the Secretary-General to provide periodic reports, as necessary, on the establishment and work of the Mission;

9. *Decides* to remain actively seized of the matter.

Report of Secretary-General (August). As requested by the Council in resolution 1312(2000), the Secretary-General submitted a 9 August report on Ethiopia and Eritrea [S/2000/785], which paid particular attention to plans for UNMEE. He noted that OAU was continuing to encourage the two parties to resolve their outstanding differences. During the latest round of proximity talks (Washington, D.C., 3, 5 and 6 July), the parties discussed modalities for the delimitation and demarcation of the border and the issue of compensation. The Secretary-General also described the humanitarian situation in the two countries. In Eritrea, the number of internally displaced persons and other war-affected persons was more than 1.1 million in June, and another 94,000 Eritreans had sought refuge in the Sudan. Since the conclusion of the Agreement on Cessation of Hostilities, refugees had begun repatriating voluntarily. A revised country appeal called for $87.3 million to address humanitarian needs for 1.1 million Eritreans. In Ethiopia, the severe drought had caused significant migrations, increased malnutrition, livestock losses and a higher incidence of diseases. As of early July, Ethiopia estimated that over 10 million people were in need of emergency food assistance.

With regard to UNMEE, liaison officers had been deployed to each capital and were consulting the parties' military headquarters and OAU to prepare for the Mission's deployment. A reconnaissance mission visited the region from 4 to 18 July to assess needs for the political, military, public information, mine action and administrative components. UNMEE's area of operations would be the temporary security zone and areas adjacent to it. The Mission would be headed by the Secretary-General's special representative, who, with the force commander, would maintain offices at Asmara and Addis Ababa. The main support base would be located in Asmara, given its proximity to the area of operations and its transport facilities.

The political component of the Mission would assist the special representative in liaison with the parties, address any political issues in implementing the Mission's mandate, keep abreast of political developments, and assist in coordinating UN activities. The military component, headed by a force commander, would monitor observance of the Agreement on Cessation of Hostilities, confirm the redeployment of Ethiopian troops and supervise the temporary security zone. UNMEE would chair and provide the secretariat for the Military Coordination Commission, which would be one of the main instruments for addressing the military concerns of the parties. The Secretary-General estimated that UNMEE would require a total military strength of up to 4,200 personnel, including 220 military observers, three infantry battalions and the necessary support units. The military observers would liaise with the parties' military headquarters, investigate incidents and patrol, and the battalions would maintain static checkpoints and provide security for the Military Coordination Commission. The Mission would also require an engineering company, military police, an administration company, a medical unit and a transport unit. The Mission would also require significant air assets, including rotary and fixed-wing aircraft.

Given the presence of landmines and unexploded ordnance in the conflict area, the United Nations Mine Action Service (UNMAS) was preparing a programme with two objectives—to support operational needs of the peacekeeping force, mainly inside the temporary security zone, including technical advice and monitoring of the Ethiopian and Eritrean mine-clearance activities, and to facilitate international mine action assistance in support of humanitarian relief efforts, including the repatriation of refugees and internally displaced persons. If requested by the parties, the mine action component would prepare national mine action assistance programmes. An initial activity would be to carry out a mine survey of the temporary security zone.

The public information component would disseminate information on the activities and mandate of the Mission and on progress in implementing the Agreement on Cessation of Hostilities. An office of communications and public information would be established, headed by a chief of information/spokesperson, who would conduct press briefings and advise the Mission on media policy. Adequate airtime on television and radio stations in both countries should be provided to UNMEE free of charge.

Coordination with OAU was necessary to carry out the tasks under the Agreement on Cessation of Hostilities and discussions were held by the reconnaissance mission and OAU in that regard. Three OAU liaison officers would be stationed in each capital during the initial stage of UNMEE, pending full deployment. UNMEE would provide logistic assistance and securitiy for OAU participation in joint activities.

The Secretary-General noted that the parties were expected to cooperate with UNMEE in the establishment of the temporary security zone and in providing information and personnel necessary for mine action activities. So far, the parties had shown commitment to ensure the implementation of the Agreement.

Security Council consideration (August). On 14 August [meeting 4187], the Security Council considered the Secretary-General's report and the representatives of Eritrea and Ethiopia gave their views on the situation. Eritrea, while welcoming the report's recommendations, considered significant the omission of mention of the 71,000 Eritreans and Ethiopians of Eritrean origin who had been expelled from Ethiopia, of civilian casualties and of the destruction of economic and social infrastructure by the Ethiopian army. Also welcoming the recommendations, Ethiopia said that while it was upholding the Agreement, Eritrea continued to deport Ethiopians under inhumane conditions.

Troop contributors. On 29 August [S/2000/841], the Secretary-General proposed that 19 countries be included in the initial list of Member States contributing military personnel to UNMEE. The Security Council took note of that proposal on 31 August [S/2000/842]. On 20 October [S/2000/1018], the Secretary-General proposed that another 23 countries be added to the list of troop contributors. The Council took note of that proposal on 24 October [S/2000/1019].

SECURITY COUNCIL ACTION (September)

On 15 September [meeting 4197], the Security Council unanimously adopted **resolution 1320 (2000)**. The draft [S/2000/867] was prepared in consultations among Council members.

The Security Council,

Recalling its resolutions 1298(2000) of 17 May 2000 and 1308(2000) of 17 July 2000, and all resolutions and statements by its President pertaining to the Ethiopia-Eritrea conflict,

Reaffirming the commitment of all Member States to the sovereignty, independence and territorial integrity of Ethiopia and Eritrea,

Reaffirming also the need for both parties to fulfil all their obligations under international humanitarian, human rights and refugee law,

Recalling the relevant principles contained in the Convention on the Safety of United Nations and Associated Personnel adopted by the General Assembly in its resolution 49/59 of 9 December 1994,

Expressing its strong support for the Agreement on Cessation of Hostilities between the Government of the Federal Democratic Republic of Ethiopia and the Government of the State of Eritrea, signed on 18 June 2000 in Algiers, and the official communications by each Government requesting United Nations assistance in the implementation of this Agreement,

Stressing its commitment to work in coordination with the Organization of African Unity and the parties to implement fully the Agreement on Cessation of Hostilities, while underlining that its successful implementation rests first and foremost on the will of the parties to the Agreement,

Welcoming the report of the Secretary-General of 9 August 2000,

Recalling its resolution 1312(2000) of 31 July 2000, which established the United Nations Mission in Ethiopia and Eritrea,

1. *Calls upon* the parties to fulfil all their obligations under international law, including the Agreement on Cessation of Hostilities;

2. *Authorizes* the deployment within the United Nations Mission in Ethiopia and Eritrea of up to 4,200 troops, including up to 220 military observers, until 15 March 2001, with a mandate to:

(a) Monitor the cessation of hostilities;

(b) Assist, as appropriate, in ensuring the observance of the security commitments agreed upon by the parties;

(c) Monitor and verify the redeployment of Ethiopian troops from positions taken after 6 February 1999 that were not under Ethiopian administration before 6 May 1998;

(d) Monitor the positions of Ethiopian forces once redeployed;

(e) Simultaneously, monitor the positions of Eritrean forces that are to redeploy in order to remain at a distance of 25 kilometres from positions to which Ethiopian forces shall redeploy;

(f) Monitor the temporary security zone to assist in ensuring compliance with the Agreement on Cessation of Hostilities;

(g) Chair the Military Coordination Commission to be established by the United Nations and the Organization of African Unity in accordance with the Agreement on Cessation of Hostilities;

(h) Coordinate and provide technical assistance for humanitarian mine action activities in the temporary security zone and areas adjacent to it;

(i) Coordinate the activities of the Mission in the temporary security zone and areas adjacent to it with humanitarian and human rights activities of the United Nations and other organizations in those areas;

3. *Welcomes* the intention of the Secretary-General to appoint a special representative who will be responsible for all aspects of the United Nations work in fulfilment of the mandate of the Mission;

4. *Requests* the Secretary-General to coordinate with the Organization of African Unity in the implementation of the Agreement on Cessation of Hostilities;

5. *Calls upon* the parties to take whatever action may be necessary to ensure the access, safety and freedom of movement of the Mission, and to provide the assistance, support and protection required for the performance of its mandate in all areas of its operation deemed necessary by the Secretary-General;

6. *Requests* the Governments of Ethiopia and Eritrea to conclude, as necessary, status-of-forces agreements with the Secretary-General within thirty days of adoption of the present resolution, and recalls that pending the conclusion of such agreements, the model status-of-forces agreement of 9 October 1990 should apply provisionally;

7. *Urges* the parties to proceed immediately with demining, in order to ensure safe access of United Nations and associated personnel to the areas being monitored, drawing on United Nations technical assistance as needed;

8. *Calls upon* the parties to ensure the safe and unhindered access of humanitarian personnel to all those in need;

9. *Calls upon* all parties to cooperate with the International Committee of the Red Cross;

10. *Acting* under Chapter VII of the Charter of the United Nations and further to the provisions of paragraph 5 of its resolution 1312(2000), decides that the

measures imposed by paragraph 6 of its resolution 1298(2000) shall not apply to the sale and supply of:

(a) Arms and related materiel for the sole use in Ethiopia or Eritrea of the United Nations, and

(b) Equipment and related materiel, including technical assistance and training, for use solely for demining within Ethiopia or Eritrea under the auspices of the United Nations Mine Action Service;

11. *Encourages* all States and international organizations to assist and participate in the longer-term tasks of reconstruction and development, as well as in the economic and social recovery of Ethiopia and Eritrea;

12. *Requests* the Secretary-General to keep the Council closely and regularly informed of progress towards the implementation of the present resolution;

13. *Emphasizes* that the Agreement on Cessation of Hostilities links the termination of the United Nations peacekeeping mission with the completion of the process of delimitation and demarcation of the Ethiopian-Eritrean border, and requests the Secretary-General to provide regular updates on the status of this issue;

14. *Calls upon* the parties to continue negotiations and conclude without delay a comprehensive and final peace settlement;

15. *Decides* that the Council, in considering the renewal of the mandate of the Mission, will take into account whether the parties have made adequate progress as called for in paragraphs 13 and 14 above;

16. *Decides* to remain actively seized of the matter.

Report of Secretary-General (September). On 18 September, the Secretary-General reported on Ethiopia and Eritrea [S/2000/879], as requested by the Council in resolution 1298(2000). He stated that under the 18 June Agreement, implementation of the plan would begin with the withdrawal of Ethiopian forces from positions taken by them since 6 February 1999 and end with the settlement of the border dispute through delimitation and demarcation and, if necessary, through arbitration. However, at Ethiopia's request and with Eritrea's consent, it had been agreed to first finalize a cessation of hostilities agreement and then negotiate and finalize a second agreement on the other outstanding issues.

On the humanitarian front, Ethiopia and the UN country team estimated that nearly 350,000 people had been displaced as a result of the conflict in the northern regions of Tigray and Afar. While most of those were accommodated in host communities, local basic infrastructure was insufficient to support their presence. Since the signing of the Agreement, 30 per cent had started rebuilding their lives in their home towns and needed assistance. The continuing drought had left over 10 million people in Ethiopia in need of emergency food assistance. In Eritrea, some 400,000 internally displaced persons had returned to their areas of origin bordering Ethiopia. Of 94,000 Eritrean refugees in the Sudan, 23,881 had returned under the UNHCR repatriation plan and an estimated 25,000 had returned

spontaneously. There were still over 200,000 internally displaced persons in camps and other settlements who required a wide array of humanitarian services, including food assistance, health services and shelter.

Since the establishment of UNMEE, preparations had continued for the deployment of both the first group of 100 military observers and the civilian support staff to Ethiopia and Eritrea. The first group of military liaison officers had undertaken field visits to military positions of Ethiopia and Eritrea and had completed a survey of potential deployment areas in both countries. A deployment timetable for military observers had been prepared. Logistical build-up continued, with the arrival of supplies and equipment from the UN Logistics Base in Brindisi, Italy. The mine action component of the Mission was established and a landmine/unexploded ordnance survey, conducted by a British NGO, the Halo Trust, was under way and was expected to be completed by mid-December.

The Secretary-General reported that Ethiopia and Eritrea had shown commitment to implementing the Agreement signed in June. He counted on them to continue to cooperate with the Mission, in particular in the establishment of the temporary security zone and the early start of mine clearance. He urged Member States to provide the Mission with the necessary military personnel, equipment and other resources. He was concerned by the continuing mutual accusations of human rights abuses by the two countries, even after the signing of the Agreement, and he intended to establish a component within the Mission to follow human rights issues.

Appointments. On 21 September [S/2000/909], the Secretary-General informed the Security Council of his intention to extend the appointment of his Special Adviser, Mohamed Sahnoun, until 31 December 2001. Mr. Sahnoun had been engaged in efforts to resolve the Eritrea-Ethiopia conflict and had also been following developments in other countries in the Horn of Africa subregion, especially Somalia and the Sudan.

On 29 September [S/2000/947], the Secretary-General announced his intention to appoint, with immediate effect, Legwaila Joseph Legwaila (Botswana) as his Special Representative for Ethiopia and Eritrea. The Council took note of that decision on 3 October [S/2000/948].

Similarly, on 25 October [S/2000/1037], the Secretary-General, following the usual consultations, announced his intention to appoint Brigadier General Patrick C. Cammaert (Netherlands) as Force Commander of UNMEE, with effect from 1 November. He was expected to arrive in the Mission area during the first half of November.

The Council took note of that intention on 27 October [S/2000/1038].

Situation update (November). The Security Council, on 17 November [meeting 4227], considered the situation between Eritrea and Ethiopia. Addressing the Council, the Secretary-General said that UNMEE deployment was proceeding on schedule and was expected to be completed by early 2001. The situation on the ground appeared to have stabilized in recent weeks and the cease-fire was holding. However, humanitarian conditions remained a source of serious concern. More than 300,000 persons were internally displaced in Eritrea and some 350,000 in Ethiopia. The most critical obstacle to their return was the presence of landmines and unexploded ordnance along the border. UNMEE had begun to conduct demining surveys and both Governments had established national commissions for demining. Both sides had agreed to open the first land access route for UNMEE convoys and other uses on 28 November. One step that could contribute to maintaining peace was the establishment of the Military Coordination Commission, as called for in the Agreement on Cessation of Hostilities.

The Council President (Netherlands), having visited the area, proposed five confidence-building measures to reduce the level of mistrust between the two Governments. Those measures were incorporated in his statement of 21 November.

SECURITY COUNCIL ACTION (November)

On 21 November [meeting 4230], following consultations among Security Council members, the President made statement **S/PRST/2000/34** on behalf of the Council:

The Security Council reaffirms its resolutions regarding the situation in Ethiopia and Eritrea, in particular resolutions 1298(2000) of 17 May 2000, 1312(2000) of 31 July 2000 and 1320(2000) of 15 September 2000, which established the United Nations Mission in Ethiopia and Eritrea.

The Council reaffirms the commitment of all Member States to the sovereignty, independence and territorial integrity of Ethiopia and Eritrea.

The Council notes with appreciation the commitment of both parties towards a final and comprehensive peace settlement. The Council also notes with appreciation the rounds of proximity talks that have taken place and, pursuant to paragraph 14 of resolution 1320(2000), calls upon the parties to continue negotiations and to conclude without delay a final and comprehensive peace settlement. The Council emphasizes that the deployment of the Mission should contribute to a positive climate for negotiations and that it does not replace the need for such a peace settlement.

The Council reiterates its strong support for the Agreement on Cessation of Hostilities between the Government of the Federal Democratic Republic of Ethiopia and the Government of the State of Eritrea signed in Algiers on 18 June 2000.

The Council underlines the important role that confidence-building measures could play in dispelling the remaining distrust between Ethiopia and Eritrea, and encourages both States to agree on a package of such measures. In particular, the Council encourages the parties to agree on the immediate release and voluntary and orderly return of interned civilians, under the auspices of the International Committee of the Red Cross, the opening of land and air corridors for the Mission, an exchange of maps showing mined areas, the prompt release of prisoners of war and their return under the auspices of the International Committee of the Red Cross and a moratorium on expulsions.

The Council reaffirms the need for both parties to fulfil all their obligations under international humanitarian, human rights and refugee law. The Council calls upon the parties to cooperate with the Mission in this regard.

The Council expresses its continuing support for the efforts of the Secretary-General and his Special Envoy, the Organization of African Unity, the President of Algeria and his Special Envoy, and concerned Member States to find a peaceful and lasting solution to the conflict.

The Council underlines the importance of the full compliance of Member States with the arms embargo imposed by resolution 1298(2000).

The Council remains actively seized of the matter.

Communications (November). In a 21 November statement [S/2000/1146], the EU welcomed the establishment of UNMEE and urged both parties to intensify the peace process under the aegis of OAU, supported by the EU and the United States, in order to reach a comprehensive and sustainable peace settlement.

Ethiopia, on 29 November [A/55/669-S/2000/1157], welcomed the confidence-building measures proposed by the Council and said that it had assisted in the opening of a land corridor for UNMEE to use. It had also begun demobilizing its army and called on Eritrea to do the same.

Financing of UNMEE

Following the Security Council's establishment of UNMEE in July and its expansion in September, the Secretary-General, on 4 December, presented the proposed budget for the establishment and operation of the Mission for the period from 31 July 2000 to 30 June 2001 [A/55/666]. The suggested budget amounted to $199,075,800 gross ($196,313,700 net), inclusive of the commitment authority of $50 million gross ($49,715,100 net) granted by ACABQ to meet initial requirements and the costs related to dispatching reconnaissance and liaison teams in July. The estimates provided for the deployment of up to 4,200 military personnel, including 220 military observers, supported by 619 civilian staff (282 international, 322 local and 15 United Nations Volunteers). Of the total budget, operational costs accounted for 50.2 per cent, military personnel costs reflected 36.1 per cent, civilian personnel costs amounted to 11.1 per cent, staff assessment comprised 1.4 per cent and 1.2 per cent of total resources were related to other programmes.

ACABQ issued its comments on the Secretary-General's proposed budget on 13 December [A/55/688]. It had several areas of concern, especially with respect to how the concept of operations affected and could justify the proposed structure of the Mission. Under the circumstances and given the timing of the report's submission, ACABQ intended to resume consideration of the report in 2001. Pending its review, it recommended that the General Assembly authorize commitment authority of $150 million gross.

GENERAL ASSEMBLY ACTION

On 23 December [meeting 89], the General Assembly, on the recommendation of the Fifth Committee [A/55/711], adopted **resolution 55/237** without vote [agenda item 176].

Financing of the United Nations Mission in Ethiopia and Eritrea

The General Assembly,

Having considered the report of the Secretary-General on the financing of the United Nations Mission in Ethiopia and Eritrea and the related report of the Advisory Committee on Administrative and Budgetary Questions,

Bearing in mind Security Council resolution 1312(2000) of 31 July 2000 regarding the establishment of the United Nations Mission in Ethiopia and Eritrea,

Recognizing that the costs of the Mission are expenses of the Organization to be borne by Member States in accordance with Article 17, paragraph 2, of the Charter of the United Nations,

Recognizing also that, in order to meet the expenditures caused by the Mission, a different procedure is required from that applied to meet expenditures of the regular budget of the United Nations,

Taking into account the fact that the economically more developed countries are in a position to make relatively larger contributions and that the economically less developed countries have a relatively limited capacity to contribute towards such operations,

Bearing in mind the special responsibilities of the States permanent members of the Security Council, as indicated in General Assembly resolution 1874(S-IV) of 27 June 1963, in the financing of such operations,

Mindful of the fact that it is essential to provide the Mission with the necessary financial resources to enable it to fulfil its responsibilities under the relevant resolutions of the Security Council,

1. *Expresses concern* about the financial situation with regard to peacekeeping activities, in particular as regards the reimbursements to troop contributors that bear additional burdens owing to overdue payments by Member States of their assessments;

2. *Urges* all Member States to make every possible effort to ensure payment of their assessed contributions to the United Nations Mission in Ethiopia and Eritrea in full and on time;

3. *Expresses concern* at the delay experienced by the Secretary-General in deploying and providing adequate resources to some recent peacekeeping missions, in particular those in Africa;

4. *Emphasizes* that all future and existing peacekeeping missions shall be given equal and non-discriminatory treatment in respect of financial and administrative arrangements;

5. *Also emphasizes* that all peacekeeping missions shall be provided with adequate resources for the effective and efficient discharge of their respective mandates;

6. *Requests* the Secretary-General to make the fullest possible use of facilities and equipment at the United Nations Logistics Base at Brindisi, Italy, in order to minimize the costs of procurement for the Mission, and for this purpose requests the Secretary-General to speed up the implementation of the asset management system at all peacekeeping missions in accordance with its resolution 52/1 A of 15 October 1997;

7. *Endorses* the conclusions and recommendations contained in the report of the Advisory Committee on Administrative and Budgetary Questions;

8. *Requests* the Secretary-General to take all necessary action to ensure that the Mission is administered with a maximum of efficiency and economy;

9. *Also requests* the Secretary-General, in order to reduce the cost of employing General Service staff, to recruit local staff for the Mission against General Service posts, commensurate with the requirements of the Mission;

10. *Authorizes* the Secretary-General to enter into commitments for the establishment and operation of the Mission for the period from 31 July 2000 to 30 June 2001 in an amount not exceeding 150 million United States dollars gross (148,220,200 dollars net), inclusive of the amount of 50 million dollars gross (49,715,100 dollars net) authorized by the Advisory Committee under the terms of section IV of General Assembly resolution 49/233 A of 23 December 1994, and of the costs related to the dispatch of reconnaissance and liaison teams to the Mission area, and requests the Secretary-General to establish a special account for the Mission;

11. *Decides,* as an ad hoc arrangement, to apportion among Member States the amount of 102,192,982 dollars gross (100,980,428 dollars net) for the period from 31 July 2000 to 15 March 2001, in accordance with the composition of groups set out in paragraphs 3 and 4 of its resolution 43/232 of 1 March 1989, as adjusted by the Assembly in its resolutions 44/192 B of 21 December 1989, 45/269 of 27 August 1991, 46/198 A of 20 December 1991, 47/218 A of 23 December 1992, 49/249 A of 20 July 1995, 49/249 B of 14 September 1995, 50/224 of 11 April 1996, 51/218 A to C of 18 December 1996, 52/230 of 31 March 1998 and 55/236 of 23 December 2000 and its decisions 48/472 A of 23 December 1993, 50/451 B of 23 December 1995 and 54/456 to 54/458 of 23 December 1999, the scale of assessments for 2000 to be applied against a portion thereof, that is,

68,421,052 dollars gross (67,609,214 dollars net), which is the amount pertaining to the period ending 31 December 2000, and the scale of assessments for 2001 to be applied against the balance, that is, 33,771,930 dollars gross (33,371,214 dollars net) for the period from 1 January to 15 March 2001;

12. *Decides also* that, in accordance with the provisions of its resolution 973(X) of 15 December 1955, there shall be set off against the apportionment among Member States, as provided for in paragraph 11 above, their respective share in the Tax Equalization Fund of the estimated staff assessment income of 1,212,554 dollars approved for the Mission for the period from 31 July 2000 to 15 March 2001, 811,838 dollars being the amount pertaining to the period ending 31 December 2000 and the balance, that is, 400,716 dollars, pertaining to the period from 1 January to 15 March 2001;

13. *Decides further,* as an ad hoc arrangement, to apportion among Member States the amount of 47,807,018 dollars gross (47,239,772 dollars net) for the period from 16 March to 30 June 2001 at a monthly rate of 13,596,491 dollars gross (13,435,164 dollars net), in accordance with the scheme set out in the present resolution and taking into account the scale of assessments for the year 2001, subject to any decision by the Security Council to extend the mandate of the Mission beyond 15 March 2001;

14. *Decides* that, in accordance with the provisions of its resolution 973(X), there shall be set off against the apportionment among Member States, as provided for in paragraph 13 above, their respective share in the Tax Equalization Fund of the estimated staff assessment income of 567,246 dollars approved for the Mission for the period from 16 March to 30 June 2001;

15. *Decides also* to appropriate to the Special Account for the United Nations Mission in Ethiopia and Eritrea the additional amount of 9,190,200 dollars gross (8,741,600 dollars net) for the support account for peacekeeping operations for the period from 1 July 2000 to 30 June 2001, to be apportioned, as an ad hoc arrangement, among Member States in accordance with the scheme set out in the present resolution, the scale of assessments for the year 2000 to be applied against a portion thereof, that is 4,595,100 dollars gross (4,370,800 dollars net), which is the amount pertaining to the period ending 31 December 2000, and the scale of assessments for the year 2001 to be applied against the balance, that is, 4,595,100 dollars gross (4,370,800 dollars net) for the period from 1 January to 30 June 2001;

16. *Decides further* that, in accordance with the provisions of its resolution 973(X), there shall be set off against the apportionment among Member States, as provided for in paragraph 15 above, their respective share in the Tax Equalization Fund of the estimated staff assessment income of 448,600 dollars approved for the support account for peacekeeping operations for the period from 1 July 2000 to 30 June 2001, 224,300 dollars being the amount pertaining to the period ending 31 December 2000 and the balance, that is, 224,300 dollars, pertaining to the period from 1 January to 30 June 2001;

17. *Emphasizes* that no peacekeeping mission shall be financed by borrowing funds from other active peacekeeping missions;

18. *Encourages* the Secretary-General to continue to take additional measures to ensure the safety and security of all personnel under the auspices of the United Nations participating in the Mission;

19. *Invites* voluntary contributions to the Mission in cash and in the form of services and supplies acceptable to the Secretary-General, to be administered, as appropriate, in accordance with the procedure and practices established by the General Assembly;

20. *Decides* to keep under review during its fifty-fifth session the item entitled "Financing of the United Nations Mission in Ethiopia and Eritrea".

Also on 23 December, the Assembly decided that the agenda item on the financing of UNMEE would remain for consideration during its resumed fifty-fifth (2001) session (**decision 55/458**). On the same day, it decided that the Fifth Committee should continue to consider the item at that session (**decision 55/455**).

Peace Agreement

Following negotiations led by President Bouteflika, President Isaias Afwerki of Eritrea and Prime Minister Meles Zenawi of Ethiopia signed the Peace Agreement between the two countries on 12 December in Algiers.

On 6 December [A/55/673-S/2000/1162], the Presidency of Algeria issued a communiqué announcing the forthcoming event, which was the result of efforts led by Mr. Bouteflika under the OAU mandate, with the support of the United States and in consultation with the EU, OAU and the United Nations.

The text of the Agreement was transmitted to the United Nations by Algeria on 12 December [A/55/686-S/2000/1183]. By that document, the Governments agreed to permanently terminate military hostilities between them, refrain from the threat or use of force and repatriate all prisoners of war. They agreed that an independent body under OAU auspices would carry out an investigation to determine the origins of the conflict. The Agreement also envisaged a neutral Boundary Commission that would delimit and demarcate the border based on pertinent colonial treaties (1900, 1902 and 1908) and international law, with the UN Cartographer serving as Secretary to the Commission. A neutral Claims Commission would be established to arbitrate claims for loss, damage or injury by one Government against the other, and by nationals of one party against the Government of the other.

On 14 December [S/2000/1194], the Secretary-General, in a letter to the Security Council, said that the 12 December Agreement marked an important victory for peace between the two countries and a major achievement for the African continent as a whole. In welcoming the historic document, he said the United Nations was prepared to work closely with the Eritrean and Ethiopian authorities, OAU and all other parties concerned to ensure the early implementation of the Agreements of 18 June and 12 December.

Also welcoming the Peace Agreement, the EU Presidency, in a 12 December statement [S/2000/1207], said the event might represent a turning point towards peace and development in the region and affirmed its commitment to supporting action to implement the peace settlement.

By letters of 19 and 21 December, Ethiopia [S/2000/1213] and Eritrea [S/2000/1230], respectively, informed the Council of their intention to release prisoners of war. Ethiopia said it had begun releasing 390 wounded Eritreans under arrangements made with the International Committee of the Red Cross (ICRC). Eritrea said it would begin repatriating Ethiopians in a few days' time under ICRC auspices and noted that it had unilaterally released 71 Ethiopian prisoners of war during the early phase of the conflict.

Later developments. The first meeting of the Military Coordination Commission (MCC), established in accordance with the ceasefire Agreement of 18 June, was held in Nairobi on 2 December under the chairmanship of the UNMEE Force Commander, with the participation of representatives of the two parties and of OAU [S/2001/45]. At the meeting, the Eritrean and Ethiopian authorities confirmed their agreement to open two additional land access routes on 7 December, following the opening of the first such route on 28 November, to enable UNMEE convoys to cross the front lines in all of its three deployment sectors. The parties also agreed to submit to the Force Commander their redeployment plans by 12 December, and to provide UNMEE by 14 December with information on known and suspected minefields. The Mission received some information from Ethiopia and was awaiting a response from Eritrea. There was also an agreement on the removal of bodies of those killed in action on the Manda-Assab road. As planned, 20 bodies were recovered and returned in solemn ceremonies on 6 and 14 December.

MCC reconvened in Nairobi on 28 December. At that meeting, the parties agreed to develop protocols to improve the freedom of movement of UNMEE aircraft in the Mission area. However, the parties could not reach an agreement on the redeployment of Ethiopian forces and repositioning of Eritrean forces, and maintained differing views over which areas were or were not under Ethiopian administration before 6 May 1998. MCC decided therefore that the matter be referred to the Secretary-General's Special Representative. Ethiopia submitted its redeployment plans to UNMEE on 12 December. Four cross-border land access routes were opened by the end of the month, and the Mine Action Coordination Centre of the Mission organized the clearance of mines and unexploded ordnance from those routes.

Although several incidents involving small exchanges of fire between Eritrean and Ethiopian forces on or near the front lines were reported, UNMEE concluded that they did not constitute deliberate breaches of the ceasefire by either side.

The release of prisoners of war, detainees and internees was begun in late 2000. On 28 November, 836 persons of Ethiopian origin were repatriated from Eritrea with the assistance of ICRC, and another 3,500 Ethiopians were repatriated in December. On 23 and 24 December, ICRC undertook the first repatriation of 360 Ethiopian and 359 Eritrean soldiers.

Other developments

Arms embargo

The Security Council Committee established pursuant to resolution 1298(2000) concerning the situation between Eritrea and Ethiopia was established in May (see p. 170). By that resolution, the Council decided that all States would prevent the sale or supply to Eritrea and Ethiopia of arms and related materiel of all types and the provision to Eritrea and Ethiopia of technical assistance or training related to the prohibited items. In a report forwarded to the Council on 29 December [S/2000/1259], the Chairman said that the Secretary-General had sent to all States a note verbale asking about specific steps they had taken to give effect to the measures imposed by that resolution. The Committee did not have any specific monitoring mechanism to ensure the implementation of the arms embargo and relied on the cooperation of States and organizations to provide pertinent information. As of 8 December, replies had been received from 40 States [S/2001/39].

Guinea

In December, the Security Council condemned recent incursions into Guinea by rebel groups from Liberia and Sierra Leone that had affected villages and towns along the entire length of Guinea's border. The Government had affirmed that 350 people were killed.

Border incursions

The Secretary-General discussed the border situation of Guinea in his seventh report on the United Nations Mission in Sierra Leone (UNAMSIL) of 7 November [S/2000/1055]. That report, which covered regional aspects of the situation in several West African countries, stated that in September and October there had been at least 15 attacks against Guinean border villages by armed insurgents, reportedly operating from Liberia and Sierra Leone. Guinea reported that 350 people were killed and it accused Liberia and Burkina Faso of complicity in the attacks. Both Governments denied any involvement. The violence in the border areas caused the internal displacement of an estimated 40,000 Guineans. In October, the Mediation and Security Council of the Economic Community of West African States (ECOWAS) called for the deployment of ECOWAS military observers along the common borders of Guinea, Liberia and Sierra Leone.

In his eighth UNAMSIL report of 15 December [S/2000/1199], the Secretary-General again noted that several cross-border incursions had occurred in southern Guinea and fighting had resulted in heavy civilian casualties and large-scale displacement of people. Guinea accused Liberia and rebel groups in Sierra Leone of being responsible for those attacks, while Liberia accused Guinea of supporting Liberian dissidents. Both Governments denied the other's accusations.

The heads of State and Government of ECOWAS countries, at a meeting held in Bamako, Mali, on 15 and 16 December [S/2000/1201], issued a final communiqué stating, among other things, that they had held in-depth discussions on the deterioration in the climate of peace and security among Guinea, Liberia and Sierra Leone. The meeting took due note of the undertaking by each of those three countries: to ensure that its national territory was not used by national or foreign armed individuals to attack neighbouring countries; to disarm any irregular armed groups present in its territory; and to refrain from acts or statements that might appear hostile to the other parties. The heads of State and Government agreed to the immediate deployment of interposition forces along the borders between the three countries and called for an urgent meeting of heads of State of the three countries under the auspices of ECOWAS and OAU. The proposed mandate of an interposition force of 1,796 troops would include monitoring the border areas; neutralizing irregular armed groups; facilitating the movement of persons, goods and services; ensuring the security of refugees and displaced persons; and creating a conducive environment for humanitarian assistance.

A Security Council mission to Sierra Leone visited the region in October and also addressed the question of the Guinean border (see p. 207).

(see p. 207).

SECURITY COUNCIL ACTION

On 21 December [meeting 4252], following consultations among Security Council members, the President made statement **S/PRST/2000/41** on behalf of the Council:

The Security Council expresses its deep concern at developments on the border that Guinea shares with Liberia and Sierra Leone.

The Council condemns in the strongest terms the recent incursions into Guinea by rebel groups coming from Liberia and Sierra Leone that have affected villages and towns along the entire length of Guinea's border, including in Guékédou on 6 December 2000 and in Kissidougou on 10 December 2000. The Council deplores the fact that these attacks claimed many lives, in particular the lives of civilians, and caused an exodus of local inhabitants and refugees, further exacerbating an already grave humanitarian situation. The Council also condemns the recent looting of the facilities of the Office of the United Nations High Commissioner for Refugees and other humanitarian organizations. The Council demands an immediate halt to all acts of violence, especially those directed against civilians, as well as the infiltration of displaced persons camps by armed elements, and demands that those responsible for the violations of international humanitarian law be brought to justice.

The Council reaffirms its commitment to the sovereignty, political independence and territorial integrity of Guinea. It expresses its serious concern, in this regard, over reports that external military support is being provided to those rebel groups. It calls upon all States, particularly Liberia, to refrain from providing any such military support and from any act that might contribute to further destabilization of the situation on the borders between Guinea, Liberia and Sierra Leone. The Council further calls upon all States in the region to prevent armed individuals from using their national territory to prepare and commit attacks in neighbouring countries.

The Council notes with interest the common undertakings assumed by Guinea, Liberia and Sierra Leone at the twenty-fourth ordinary session of the Authority of Heads of State and Government of the Economic Community of West African States held in Bamako on 15 and 16 December 2000 and calls upon them to implement those undertakings fully and without delay. It again pays tribute to the current Chairman of the Economic Community of West African States and to that organization for the important role they play towards restoring peace and security to the three countries of the Mano River Union. The Council requests the Secretary-General to consider what support the international community, and in particular the United Nations, might provide to the Economic Community of West African States in order to ensure security on the border that Guinea shares with Liberia and Sierra Leone, and to report in that connection to the Council as soon as possible. The Council supports the appeal made by the heads of State and Government of the Economic Community of West African States for an urgent meeting of the heads of State of Guinea, Liberia and Sierra Leone under the auspices of the Community and the Organization of African Unity.

The Council expresses its deep appreciation to the Government of Guinea for hosting a large number of refugees. The Council is concerned by the growing hostile attitude among the local population towards refugees, and urges the Government of Guinea to take urgent measures to discourage the propagation of such anti-refugee feelings.

The Council expresses its deep concern over the fate of all those who continue to live in a state of insecurity, especially the local populations and the tens of thousands of refugees and displaced persons. It urges all the competent organizations to ensure that humanitarian relief continues, and it underlines the importance of integrated action by the United Nations agencies, acting in coordination with the Government of Guinea and with the support of the Economic Community of West African States. The Council believes that humanitarian assistance in secure locations must be made available not only to displaced refugees and Guineans, but also to those refugees returning to Sierra Leone. The Council calls on the Secretary-General and the Office of the United Nations High Commissioner for Refugees to ensure that suitable programmes of reintegration and assistance exist and are enhanced where security permits in Sierra Leone. It also recognizes the important role of the international community and the competent non-governmental organizations in providing the humanitarian relief that the local populations, the refugees and the displaced persons so sorely need. The Council is concerned over the security of humanitarian personnel working in Sierra Leone and Guinea. It calls upon all the parties concerned to facilitate the work of the humanitarian organizations. It urges the parties to guarantee the security of refugees and displaced persons, and the security of the staff of the United Nations and humanitarian organizations. The Council also reaffirms the need to respect the civilian character of refugee camps.

The Council welcomes the proposed inter-agency multidisciplinary mission to West Africa, supports its earliest possible departure to the region and looks forward to its report and recommendations.

Guinea-Bissau

On 16 January, the second round of presidential elections in Guinea-Bissau was held, thus completing the formation of a new Government and bringing to a close the transitional Government established in accordance with the Abuja Peace Accord of 1 November 1998 [YUN 1998, p. 153]. That agreement had ended an armed conflict between forces supporting President João Bernardo Vieira and his former Army Chief of Staff, General Ansoumane Mane. The elections led to the swearing in of President Kumba Yala, under whom the new Government focused on establishing democratic institutions in the face of continued interference from the military establishment, culminating in an attempted coup d'état by General Mane on 20 November. General Mane was killed in a shoot-out with the army following that attempt.

Internal friction was not the only cause for concern as tensions along the Guinea-Bissau/Senegal border were reported and the threat of military intervention remained ever present. In view of those dangers, the mandate of the United Nations Peace-building Support Office in Guinea-Bissau (UNOGBIS), established in 1999 [YUN 1999, p. 140], was extended. Despite the troubling climate of tension, Guinea-Bissau continued its efforts to consolidate its fragile democratization process.

Formation of new Government

Report of Secretary-General (March). The Secretary-General, in response to Security Council resolution 1233(1999) [YUN 1999, p. 140], submitted a 24 March report on developments in Guinea-Bissau [S/2000/250], updating the Council on events since his previous report in December 1999 [YUN 1999, p. 144].

The second round of presidential elections, held on 16 January as the result of inconclusive results in the first round on 28 November 1999, brought an end to the post-conflict transitional period in Guinea-Bissau. President Kumba Yala, who obtained 72 per cent of the vote, was invested on 17 February, following which a new Government was formed and the new pluralist National Assembly was inaugurated. In view of the new political situation, the revised mandate of UNOGBIS was approved by the Council on 10 March (see p. 187). Among the priorities identified by the new Government were the consolidation of the country's nascent democracy, the depoliticization of the military, the demobilization and reintegration of retired military personnel, the revitalization of State institutions and the relaunching of the economy. In a move to promote national reconciliation, the Chief of Staff and a member of the former military junta was appointed as Defence Minister; however, under pressure from the military establishment the Minister resigned. Negotiations were under way with the former military junta to identify a replacement and to redefine the role of the military in a new, democratic Guinea-Bissau. Those negotiations were led by a group of mediators from civil society, including the Bishop of Bissau. The Secretary-General's Representative, Samuel Nana-Sinkam, was also providing his good offices as needed.

Despite the restoration of constitutional rule, the military continued to maintain a high public posture and to perform police functions, even as the presence of police units increased. The maintenance of public law and order was severely constrained by a lack of appropriate training and poor logistic support for the police. In the Secretary-General's view, that situation underscored the need for the international community to assist in that regard. The continuing circulation of large quantities of small arms in civilian communities compounded the security situation. In that connection, efforts continued, under the coordination of UNOGBIS and with the support of the World Food Programme and the Food and Agriculture Organization of the United Nations, to develop a package of incentives to encourage civilians to surrender their weapons. Relations with neighbouring countries continued to improve. Bilateral cooperation to resolve concerns over border security issues, especially along the border with Guinea (see p. 181), was evolving in the right direction.

The trials of those detained following the events of May 1999 began in late February 2000. From the original 385 detained, 50 remained in detention, some having been released for lack of evidence or pending further investigation. UNOGBIS provided assistance to the new justice system by training 37 new judges in order to increase the capacity of the judiciary to speed up trial proceedings.

The humanitarian situation in the country improved significantly, as more and more Bissau Guinean refugees and internally displaced persons returned to their homes in different parts of the country. The return of refugees and displaced persons had put additional pressure on the demand for social services, in particular water and electricity. To meet that demand, the United Nations Children's Fund (UNICEF) and NGOs had begun digging wells and rehabilitating small water refilling systems in Bissau and in the countryside. UNICEF was also active in repairing damaged hospitals, restarting inoculation projects and distributing medicines.

Addressing the Council on 29 March [meeting 4121] when it considered the Secretary-General's report, Under-Secretary-General for Political Affairs, Kieran Prendergast, said that the overall situation was peaceful and the humanitarian situation had improved, but the economic situation remained worrying. He warned of the difficulties encountered in redefining the relationship between the new Government and the military establishment in the post-electoral period. However, it was encouraging, he said, that negotiations between the Government and the former military junta were continuing, led by the Bishop of Bissau and a group of mediators from civil society. In view of the situation, the Secretary-General had urged the international community to provide urgent assistance for the Government's 100-day transitional programme, which was critical for the credibility of the new Government as it faced pressures from ordinary citizens who were demanding basic services such as water and electricity.

SECURITY COUNCIL ACTION (March)

On 29 March [meeting 4122], following consultations among Security Council members, the President made statement **S/PRST/2000/11** on behalf of the Council:

> The Security Council has considered the report of the Secretary-General of 24 March 2000 on developments in Guinea-Bissau.
>
> The Council pays tribute to the people of Guinea-Bissau for the success of the transitional process that has led to the organization of free, fair and transparent elections. It congratulates the Representative of the Secretary-General, the staff of the United Nations Peace-building Support Office in Guinea-Bissau and the States Members of the United Nations for all they have done to assist the people of Guinea-Bissau in this task. The Council also thanks the Economic Community of West African States, the Community of Portuguese-speaking Countries, Member States that contributed to the Trust Fund established to support the activities of the Support Office and the Friends of the Secretary-General for Guinea-Bissau for their contributions to consolidating peace and stability in Guinea-Bissau.
>
> The Council welcomes the swearing in of President Kumba Yala on 17 February 2000 and the return to constitutional and democratic order in Guinea-Bissau following the holding of free and fair presidential and legislative elections. The Council affirms that all concerned, particularly the former military junta, are obligated to recognize and uphold the results of these elections, as part of the Abuja Accord.
>
> The Council encourages all concerned in Guinea-Bissau to work together closely in a spirit of tolerance to strengthen democratic values, protect the rule of law, depoliticize the army and safeguard human rights. The Council supports the efforts made by the Government of Guinea-Bissau to redefine the role of the military in Guinea-Bissau in accordance with the rule of law and democracy.
>
> The Council expresses its support for the newly elected Government of Guinea-Bissau and encourages the new authorities to develop and to implement programmes devised to consolidate peace and national reconciliation. The Council calls upon the international community to support the three-month transitional programme of the Government

of Guinea-Bissau pending the organization of a new round-table conference. The Council agrees with the comment made by the Secretary-General, in paragraph 24 of his report, to the effect that sustained support of the international community is crucial for the consolidation of the progress achieved so far, and for helping Guinea-Bissau lay a durable foundation for a better life for its people.

Communication. In a 19 May statement [S/2000/487], the EU expressed concern at the ongoing climate of tension and insecurity in Guinea-Bissau and at reports of indiscipline in some sectors of the armed forces. It urged all in Guinea-Bissau, in particular the military, to continue to take forward the positive developments of the previous year and stressed the need for a full return to civil rule, effective functioning of democratic institutions and a peaceful environment as prerequisites for the continuation of foreign investments and financial and economic aid.

Report of Secretary-General (June). The Secretary-General, in a 28 June report on developments in Guinea-Bissau and on UNOGBIS activities [S/2000/632], said that while important progress had been made on the ground since his last report, many challenges remained as Guinea-Bissau sought to restore lasting peace, stability and sustainable development and to improve the living standards of its people. During the period under review, the Government of President Yala had focused on consolidating the authority of the newly established democratic institutions in the face of continued interference from the military establishment, following protracted consultations with a wide spectrum of actors. The continued high profile of the former military junta on the political scene and the lack of a constitution anchored in democratic principles presented difficult challenges. Some progress was reported in discussions mediated by civil society leaders under the leadership of the Bishop of Bissau and facilitated by the Secretary-General's Representative, aimed at redefining the role of the military. The National Assembly had established a Commission of Good Offices to bridge differences between the Government and the military establishment.

The appointment on 7 April of a new Attorney-General and a civilian as Minister of Defence and the decision of the military establishment not to challenge the President's decree replacing the Chief of Naval Staff further strengthened the authority of the constitutional order. In June, the military reaffirmed its intention to resume its traditional role and to subjugate itself to the civilian authorities.

On 15 May, ECOWAS sent a Special Envoy to Guinea-Bissau to discuss with the authorities and other parties the latest developments. At a summit meeting on 28 and 29 May, the ECOWAS members expressed concern over continuing tensions between the President and the former military junta.

A worrying development concerned religious and ethnic tensions in some northern parts of the country between the Fula and Felupe communities and in the east between the Fula and Mandingo communities.

In an effort to restore the economy, the National Assembly approved the Government's four-year programme of work and the 2000 budget. In order to strengthen the democratic process, the Supreme Court of Justice set up a commission to review the current constitution. The authorities announced plans to hold municipal elections in 2000.

The security situation along the Guinea-Bissau/Senegal border, which had deteriorated in April, was significantly improved by the visit to Bissau on 29 April of newly elected President Wade of Senegal. The leaders of the two countries agreed to de-escalate tensions and discussed cooperative strategies for securing their common border. The Secretary-General's Representative, during meetings with President Wade and Senegalese officials in Dakar in early May, discussed ways to sustain the initiatives on border security generated during the President's visit to Bissau.

Internally, there was a rise in armed criminality and banditry attributable, in part, to the prevailing difficult economic situation, the weak police force and uncontrolled circulation of weapons. Another security issue was the presence of landmines throughout the country. With support from UNDP, a demining project was scheduled to begin in July. The Government also prepared a demobilization and reintegration programme. Endemic poverty remained the single most debilitating social and economic problem. The unemployment level remained high and the Government experienced persistent difficulties in paying the civil servants who constituted the bulk of all formally employed Bissau Guinean citizens.

The Secretary-General said that the restructuring of the armed forces was crucial for the democratization process and remained one of the Government's priorities. However, in the absence of adequate resources, that remained a daunting and potentially problematic challenge. He therefore appealed to the international community to provide the necessary financial and material support to enable the Government to address that issue effectively, to strengthen its institutional capacity and to implement its rehabilitation, reconstruction and development priorities.

Report of Secretary-General (September). On 29 September, the Secretary-General submitted a further report on developments in Guinea-Bissau and UNOGBIS activities [S/2000/920], in which he said that the country had continued to make progress towards consolidating its democratization process; however, the overall situation remained worrying. The threat of military intervention, the precarious border situation and chronic poverty continued to confront the Government, which had neither the means nor the capacity to address them on its own.

In early September, President Yala dismissed five ministers belonging to the rival Guinea-Bissau Resistance Party from the coalition Government, but later reinstated them following peaceful negotiations. The Secretary-General's Representative played a facilitation role in that matter. Another positive development was the normal functioning of the National Assembly. The Assembly, in collaboration with UNOGBIS, conducted in June a five-day seminar on democratic ethics and parliamentary protocols and procedures for parliamentarians.

Internal friction and tensions in the border area with Senegal continued to cause concern. The temporary closure of border crossings on the Senegalese side led to steep price increases in Guinea-Bissau for imported fuel and goods, while segments of the military were trying to capitalize on the instability to increase their visibility in the political process. The leaders of Guinea-Bissau and Senegal continued to work to defuse the tensions, and a bilateral commission met in Senegal to discuss border issues. On 7 September, the Prime Ministers of the two countries met in Dakar and signed a document that called on the international community, through the United Nations, to institute mechanisms to complement their joint military patrolling of the border. Following that meeting, the borders were reopened.

In a related development, President Yala, in a letter to the Secretary-General of 5 September, formally requested that an international military observer force be established to serve along with contingents from the two countries.

The institutional and logistical weakness of the national police continued to hamper its ability to deal with the rising incidence of banditry. A mine-clearance programme was begun in the capital, with support from UNOGBIS, NGOs and other donors. Out of the 378 political and military prisoners detained since the events of 7 May 1999, only four were still being held by the time of the report. A number of released detainees had already been tried, while others were awaiting trial.

With assistance from UN agencies, the Government finalized an interim poverty reduction strategic paper to be submitted to the World Bank. Meanwhile, the World Bank had made available some $25 million to allow the Government to meet its budgetary obligations. An increase in the harvest of cashew nuts, the country's most important cash crop and its principal source of revenue, and proceeds from offshore oil drilling were expected to boost the country's revenue base.

Addressing the Security Council on 29 November [meeting 4238], the Secretary-General reported an armed showdown during the previous week between the head of the former military junta, General Ansoumane Mane, who was killed following the attempted coup d'état, and the elected President, which nearly plunged the country back into turmoil, underscoring the precariousness of the stability of the country. Post-conflict peace-building would require measures to prevent a relapse into a cycle of conflict and instability and needed to address the root causes of conflict, which included weak State institutions, a disgruntled and highly politicized army, endemic poverty, a crippling debt and an insecure internal and external environment. Addressing such a range of causes required, on the part of the Government and the international community, a long-term commitment and was a multidimensional process.

SECURITY COUNCIL ACTION (November)

On 29 November [meeting 4239], following consultations among Security Council members, the President made statement **S/PRST/2000/37** on behalf of the Council:

> The Security Council reiterates its support for the democratically elected Government of Guinea-Bissau, and underlines the fact that all parties concerned, especially the members of the former military junta, must continue to uphold the results of the elections and the principles of democracy, the rule of law and respect for human rights and civilian rule in the country.
>
> The Council welcomes the return to peace, democracy and constitutional order in Guinea-Bissau, and urges all parties to work towards the consolidation of peace in a spirit of cooperation and reconciliation.
>
> The Council notes with satisfaction the political progress made so far in Guinea-Bissau, and stresses the importance of continued cooperation by all parties towards the consolidation of sustainable peace in Guinea-Bissau. The Council calls upon the members of the former military junta to subordinate themselves fully to the civilian institutions and to with-

draw from the political process. The Council underlines the fact that the primary responsibility for the consolidation of peace lies with all the parties and the people of Guinea-Bissau, and is concerned that renewed political unrest may be harmful to the consolidation of peace and the commitment of donors to support the reconstruction of Guinea-Bissau.

In this connection, the Council underlines the importance of an energetic continuation of the disarmament, demobilization and reintegration process and the need for an urgent and accurate census of all military forces. It recalls the statement by its President of 23 March 2000, and underlines the fact that timely funding for disarmament, demobilization and reintegration is a critical factor in the successful implementation of the peace process in Guinea-Bissau. The Council commends the support provided by the Bretton Woods institutions to the disarmament, demobilization and reintegration process in Guinea-Bissau, and stresses the importance of the coordinated support of Member States for these activities.

The Council recalls the statement by its President of 29 December 1998, and recognizes that the challenges of the post-conflict situation in Guinea-Bissau require an integrated and consolidated approach by all actors to support the Government of Guinea-Bissau, inter alia, the United Nations system, the World Bank and the International Monetary Fund, as well as bilateral donors. In this regard, the Council once again underlines the importance of ensuring a smooth transition from conflict management to post-conflict peace-building and reconstruction, which can be greatly enhanced through adequate coordination of the efforts of all. The Council stresses the special position of the United Nations Peace-building Support Office in Guinea-Bissau in this regard.

The Council recognizes and commends the important role played by the Support Office towards helping to consolidate peace, democracy and the rule of law, including the strengthening of democratic institutions, and expresses its appreciation for the activities of the Office. In order to optimize the efforts of the Office, some degree of flexibility on the part of donors and financial institutions is required concerning issues such as debt relief, trade policies and internal budget constraints.

The Council reiterates that economic rehabilitation and reconstruction constitutes one of the major tasks facing Guinea-Bissau as it emerges from conflict, and that significant international assistance is indispensable for promoting sustainable development there. The Council underlines the fact that an integrated and coordinated approach is required for Guinea-Bissau, combining sustainable post-conflict peace-building and economic and development issues.

The Council calls upon Member States to provide generous support at the next round table scheduled for February 2001 in Geneva.

The Council acknowledges the relevance of the regional dimension. It welcomes the initiatives that the President of Guinea-Bissau and the President of Senegal have taken towards stabilization of their common border region. The Council encourages both Governments to explore further possibilities to achieve peace and stability along the regional borders. It commends the Economic Community of West African States and the Community of Portuguese-speaking Countries for their continuing contributions towards the return of peace and democracy to Guinea-Bissau.

The Council expresses its intention to keep the situation in Guinea-Bissau under regular review and to coordinate with all actors in the post-conflict peace-building process.

Communication. In a 29 November statement [S/2000/1148], the EU Presidency expressed its pleasure that Guinea-Bissau's constitution had been upheld, despite the recent attempt at destabilization and the clashes that had cast a shadow over the country. It also expressed support for the legitimate authorities in their efforts to bring about national reconciliation and consolidate democracy, as well as concern that the programme of demobilization and restructuring of the armed forces should be brought to a successful conclusion. The EU reaffirmed its readiness to assist in the national reconstruction effort and called on the international community to join in that task.

Extension of UNOGBIS mandate

The Secretary-General, at the request of President Yala, extended the mandate of the United Nations Peace-building Support Office in Guinea-Bissau (UNOGBIS) twice in 2000.

On 3 March [S/2000/201], the Secretary-General informed the Security Council that Mr. Yala, while President-elect, had requested that the UNOGBIS mandate be extended for at least two years to help his Government cope with the post-electoral challenges. After a review of the request, the Secretary-General proposed that the mandate be extended for one year after the current one expired on 31 March 2000. The revised mandate would be: to support national efforts to maintain peace, democracy and the rule of law and towards reconciliation and tolerance; to encourage initiatives aimed at building confidence and maintaining friendly relations with its neighbours; to seek a programme of voluntary arms collection; to provide the political framework and leadership for harmonizing UN activities in the country; and to facilitate the mobilization of international political support and resources for rehabilitation, reconstruction and development. The Council, on 10 March [S/2000/202], took note of the Secretary-General's proposal.

In a report of 20 March to the Fifth Committee [A/C.5/54/52], the Secretary-General provided estimates for two political missions in the context of actions taken by the Security Council regarding good offices, preventive diplomacy and post-conflict missions. One of those missions was UNOGBIS, for which the proposed resource requirement was $2,723,300, to be charged against the programme budget for the 2000-2001 biennium.

The Secretary-General, in a 28 September letter to the Security Council [S/2000/941], proposed that the UNOGBIS mandate be extended again until the end of 2001 in the light of events in Guinea-Bissau and the situation in the entire subregion that continued to require the United Nations to play a constructive role in the consolidation of peace. The Council, on 3 October [S/2000/942], took note of the proposal.

Liberia

The United Nations Peace-building Support Office in Liberia (UNOL) continued in 2000 to work towards the consolidation of peace and democracy in cooperation with the Government and ECOWAS. In a June report on assistance for the rehabilitation and reconstruction of Liberia [A/55/90-E/2000/81] (see p. 862), the Secretary-General said that the inauguration of an elected Government headed by President Charles G. Taylor in August 1997 had constituted a significant landmark in Liberia's transition from civil conflict to peace and resumption of normal development activities; however, two and a half years later, the path to sustainable peace and recovery remained uncertain, owing mainly to residual governance problems and inadequate external support to the country's reconstruction programme. The restoration of peace had not brought sustainable social and economic recovery, despite programmes initiated by the Government aimed at reconstruction, and supported by ECOWAS, the UN system and other donors.

The political and security situation was susceptible to subregional events, especially in neighbouring Sierra Leone, where significant progress in the peace process had been difficult to achieve and relations between members of the Revolutionary United Front, the defunct Armed Forces Revolutionary Council and some officials in the Liberian Government had been a source of regional tensions. ECOWAS intensified its efforts to help consolidate peace in the subregion, including support for the meeting of the heads of State of Guinea, Liberia and Sierra Leone (Bamako, Mali, 2 March), and that of their Foreign Ministers (Monrovia, Liberia, 18 March). The decision to revitalize the Mano River Union (MRU) institutions to deal with political, security and socio-economic concerns between the three States was among the outcomes.

Extension of UNOL

The Secretary-General, in a 28 September letter to the Security Council [S/2000/945], proposed that UNOL's mandate be extended for one year, until 31 December 2001. The proposal was made following his consultations with the Liberian Government, which was faced with a difficult political situation and instability in the subregion. An extension, he said, would enable UNOL to support the Government's efforts to consolidate democracy and promote national reconciliation and the rule of law, including the protection of human rights, and would allow UNOL to contribute to subregional efforts to normalize relations between Liberia and its neighbours. On 3 October [S/2000/946], the Council took note of his proposal.

Sanctions committee

The Security Council Committee established pursuant to resolution 985(1995) [YUN 1995, p. 355] to monitor sanctions against Liberia issued a report on 22 December covering its activities in 2000 [S/2000/1233]. The arms embargo was imposed by the Council by resolution 788(1992) [YUN 1992, p. 192].

The Committee said that Ugandan customs officials had informed it that they had seized a consignment of arms that were believed to have been destined for Monrovia in violation of the sanctions. The Committee noted that it did not have any specific monitoring mechanism to ensure the implementation of the arms embargo; therefore, it urged Member States and organizations to provide information pertinent to the arms embargo to the Committee.

Border incursions

In a 28 August letter to the Secretary-General [S/2000/844], the Liberian President complained of repeated violations of its territorial integrity by armed insurgents from the area of the Guinea–Sierra Leone borders (see also under "Sierra Leone"), including a recent attack emanating from Guinea, which was ongoing. Liberia called for a UN presence at those borders to monitor all crossing points.

At its fourth ministerial meeting (Abuja, Nigeria, 4 October), the ECOWAS Mediation and Security Council decided to deploy an ECOWAS observer mission on the border between Guinea and Liberia. Mali, informing the Security Council of that decision on 11 December [S/2000/1191], requested, on behalf of ECOWAS, UN assistance in the deployment of the mission, which could make a useful contribution towards ensuring security and stability in the West African subregion.

Financing of UNOMIL

By **decision 54/499** of 5 September, the General Assembly decided to include in the draft agenda of its fifty-fifth (2000) session the item on financing of the United Nations Observer Mission in Liberia, whose mandate ended in 1997 [YUN 1997, p. 123]. On 23 December, the Assembly decided that the item would remain for consideration during its resumed fifty-fifth (2001) session (**decision 55/458**) and that the Fifth Committee should continue to consider the item at that session (**decision 55/455**).

Libyan Arab Jamahiriya

Following the Security Council's 1999 suspension of the sanctions imposed on the Libyan Arab Jamahiriya under resolution 748(1992) [YUN 1992, p. 55] and strengthened under resolution 883(1993) [YUN 1993, p. 101], a number of regional organizations sought in 2000 to have those sanctions completely lifted. The organizations proposed that action in view of the fact that the two Libyan suspects charged with the 1988 bombing of Pan Am flight 103 over Lockerbie, Scotland, were being tried under a Scottish court sitting in the Netherlands. The sanctions covered air links with, provision of military supplies to, restrictions on diplomatic and consular personnel of, and restrictions on suspected terrorist nationals of Libya.

Trial of Pan Am 103 bombing suspects

In 2000, the trial of two Libyan nationals suspected of the 1988 bombing of Pan Am flight 103 began in the Scottish court sitting in the Netherlands. Arrangements for the trial had been approved by the Security Council in resolution 1192(1998) [YUN 1998, p. 161]. The Secretary-General, in a letter of 25 April to the Council [S/2000/349], listed five international observers he had nominated to attend the trial, all of whom represented entities that had demonstrated an interest in the matter.

Suspension of sanctions

Libya, by an 8 March letter [S/2000/243], transmitted to the Security Council a report concerning the damage, in both material and human terms, that was caused by the sanctions imposed by the Council in resolutions 748(1992) and 883(1993) and maintained from 15 April 1992 until suspended on 5 April 1999. The report covered alleged damage sustained by the Libyan people in the areas of health, agriculture, livestock, communications, transport, industry, finance, trade and energy. Total financial losses were estimated at $33.6 billion.

In further letters to the Council, Libya transmitted a decision adopted by the OAU heads of State and Government (Lomé, Togo, 10-12 July) [S/2000/770] and a resolution adopted by the Islamic Conference of Foreign Ministers (Kuala Lumpur, Malaysia, 27-30 June) [S/2000/773], both calling for the total and final lifting of the sanctions against Libya. On 11 September [S/2000/864], Algeria, Egypt, Libya, Mauritania, Morocco, the Syrian Arab Republic and Tunisia transmitted a resolution adopted by the Council of the League of Arab States also calling for the lifting of the sanctions and urging the United States to engage in direct dialogue with Libya to resolve issues that might be preventing normalization of relations between them. In a 13 September letter [S/2000/881], Cameroon, Ghana, Tunisia, Uganda and Zimbabwe, as the five-member committee entrusted by OAU to follow up the question of Lockerbie, called on the Council to lift the sanctions immediately and irrevocably. Burkina Faso, Cuba, the Lao People's Democratic Republic, Malaysia, South Africa and Zimbabwe, as the Committee of Six of the Non-Aligned Movement, on 15 September [S/2000/906] expressed disappointment at the Council's failure to lift the sanctions and urged it to do so.

1986 attack against Libya

The General Assembly, by **decision 55/430** of 14 December, deferred consideration of the item "Declaration of the Assembly of Heads of State and Government of the Organization of African Unity on the aerial and naval military attack against the Socialist People's Libyan Arab Jamahiriya by the present United States Administration in April 1986" and included it in the provisional agenda of its fifty-sixth (2001) session.

Sierra Leone

Throughout most of 2000, the situation in Sierra Leone was tense and critical until a ceasefire agreement was signed by the Government and the rebel group, the Revolutionary United Front (RUF), in November. Throughout the year, the United Nations attempted to assist in implementing the Lomé Peace Agreement, signed by the Government and RUF on 7 July 1999 [YUN 1999, p. 159].

At the beginning of the year, the United Nations Mission in Sierra Leone (UNAMSIL) had an authorized force of 6,000 military personnel, with a mandate to work together with the forces of the ECOWAS Monitoring Group (ECOMOG) in implementing the Lomé Peace Agreement, to assist the Government in implementing its disarmament plan, to ensure freedom of movement of UN personnel, to monitor the ceasefire and to facilitate the delivery of humanitarian aid. As ECOMOG began to withdraw, the Security Council in February authorized an expansion of UNAMSIL to a maximum of 11,100 military personnel, subject to periodic review in the light of conditions on the ground and progress made in the peace process. UNAMSIL was later expanded again to 13,000 troops.

The situation deteriorated rapidly in May when RUF forces stepped up attacks against government forces and UNAMSIL and held hundreds of UNAMSIL personnel hostage. For months, RUF continued to attack UN peacekeepers and pro-Government forces and to detain UN personnel. By the end of July, nine peacekeepers had been killed and others were missing. During that month, the Council took action to limit the capacity of rebel groups to wage war by prohibiting the importation of rough diamonds from Sierra Leone, except those with a certificate of origin issued by the Government, and by strengthening the arms embargo to non-government forces. In August, the Council strengthened the UNAMSIL mandate to include new tasks of countering the threat of RUF attacks by responding robustly to hostile actions or threats of force, deploying at key strategic locations and main population centres, assisting the Government to extend State authority, and providing protection to civilians in areas of deployment.

Also in August, the Council proposed that a special court on Sierra Leone be established in order to bring to justice those responsible for serious crimes and atrocities against the people of Sierra Leone and UNAMSIL peacekeepers. The Secretary-General drew up proposals for such a court, which the Council was reviewing at the end of the year.

By the ceasefire agreement signed by the Government and RUF on 10 November, the two parties agreed that UNAMSIL would supervise and monitor the ceasefire and report any violations.

Initially, RUF displayed reluctance to follow through with its commitments, and the security situation remained precarious, but relatively calm, at the end of the year.

The Special Representative of the Secretary-General for Sierra Leone was Oluyemi Adeniji (Nigeria).

UNAMSIL

In response to resolution 1270(1999) [YUN 1999, p. 165], the Secretary-General reported to the Security Council every 45 days on UNAMSIL and on developments in Sierra Leone, including the status of the peace process. The UNAMSIL Force Commander until October was Major-General Vijay Kumar Jetley (India). He was succeeded by Lieutenant-General Daniel Ishmael Opande (Kenya).

Expansion of mission

Report of Secretary-General (January). In an 11 January report [S/2000/13], the second on UNAMSIL, the Secretary-General said that the situation in Sierra Leone had gone through a difficult period over the preceding two weeks as ECOMOG continued its withdrawal from several key locations in the provinces and the RUF Party (RUFP) challenged the implementation of some of the aspects of the peace process. The resulting tensions subsided somewhat with the deployment of UNAMSIL troops to areas under RUFP control. A rising level of lawlessness and banditry was reported, especially in and around Freetown and in Lungi and Port Loko, and security deteriorated in several disarmament centres. Ceasefire violations and incidents were apparently committed by former Sierra Leonean army elements based in the Occra Hills region.

Progress in the disarmament, demobilization and reintegration programme had been very slow and was compounded by unrest among the 6,000 ex-combatants in the disarmament centres. Discharge from the camps had been delayed due to logistical problems. With ECOMOG's decision to repatriate its forces [YUN 1999, p. 167], the only alternative was to expand UNAMSIL in order to keep the peace process on track. In addition to its current mandate, the Secretary-General said, UNAMSIL would need to assume tasks that had been assigned to ECOMOG, such as guarding weapons and ammunition retrieved during the disarmament process and assisting in their destruction. The expanded force would also contribute to the free circulation of people and goods and delivery of humanitarian assistance along selected roads. In accordance with its current mandate as stipulated in resolution 1270(1999), the Mission would continue, within its capabilities, to afford protection to civilians under imminent threat of physical violence. In addition to its current mandate, the Secretary-General proposed that UNAMSIL operations should include: establishing a presence at key locations, in particular in Freetown, important intersections and major airports; providing additional security at disarmament, demobilization and reintegration sites and guarding weapons collected from ex-combatants; conducting mobile patrols and, if necessary, providing armed escorts to ensure the free flow of people, goods and humanitarian assistance along main thoroughfares; affirming, when necessary, through rapid deployment, UN commitment to the peace process; maintaining adequate reserves to ensure flexibility and reaction capabilities and reinforcing its positions or patrols when necessary; and maintaining close coordination with the Sierra Leonean law enforcement authorities.

The expanded force would require up to 11,100 military personnel, including 260 military observers, 12 infantry battalions, force and sector headquarters personnel, two military engineer companies, medical personnel, communications and transport units and an aviation element. The engineering companies would engage in demining and repair of roads and bridges. The new tasks falling to UNAMSIL would require robust rules of engagement for the entire force. Up to 60 UN civilian police advisers would assist the Government and local police in the restructuring and training of the Sierra Leonean police forces. They would assist in maintaining law and order at disarmament, demobilization and reintegration sites to make up for the role ECOMOG had played in that regard.

Overall, the situation remained difficult and progress in the implementation of the Lomé Agreement had been very slow. In addition, members of some armed groups continued to attack, rob and rape civilians in parts of the country, while humanitarian workers were denied access to large sections of the population. After more than eight years of brutal conflict, the Secretary-General stated, building trust and confidence would take time. It was crucial that the Government take the lead in developing a comprehensive plan for the restructuring of the police and armed forces so that they could safeguard the stability and security of the country once UNAMSIL began its withdrawal following the elections in 2001.

In a 21 January addendum [S/2000/13/Add.1] to his report, the Secretary-General outlined the financial implications of the recommended UNAMSIL expansion. For the period 15 February to 30 June 2000, additional requirements would be $110.8 million, based on the assumption of a phased induction of an additional 5,100 troops, 54 civilian police and 170 civilian international and local staff. On that basis, the total estimated cost of the UN peacekeeping operations in Sierra Leone from 1 July 1999 to 30 June 2000 was projected at $310.8 million, inclusive of $200 million already appropriated by General Assembly resolution 54/241 A [YUN 1999, p. 168].

Sierra Leone, on 17 January [S/2000/31], endorsed the Secretary-General's recommendations, in particular the expansion of UNAMSIL.

SECURITY COUNCIL ACTION (February)

On 7 February [meeting 4099], the Security Council unanimously adopted **resolution 1289(2000)**. The draft [S/2000/34] was prepared in consultations among Council members.

The Security Council,

Recalling its resolutions 1171(1998) of 5 June 1998, 1181(1998) of 13 July 1998, 1231(1999) of 11 March 1999, 1260(1999) of 20 August 1999, 1265(1999) of 17 September 1999 and 1270(1999) of 22 October 1999 and other relevant resolutions and the statement by its President of 15 May 1999,

Affirming the commitment of all States to respect the sovereignty, political independence and territorial integrity of Sierra Leone,

Recalling the relevant principles contained in the Convention on the Safety of United Nations and Associated Personnel of 9 December 1994,

Welcoming and encouraging efforts by the United Nations to sensitize peacekeeping personnel in the prevention and control of HIV/AIDS and other communicable diseases in all its peacekeeping operations,

Taking note of the letter dated 17 January 2000 from the Minister for Foreign Affairs and International Cooperation of Sierra Leone to the President of the Security Council,

Having considered the reports of the Secretary-General of 23 September and 6 December 1999 and 11 January 2000 and the letter dated 23 December 1999 from the Secretary-General to the President of the Security Council,

Determining that the situation in Sierra Leone continues to constitute a threat to international peace and security in the region,

1. *Notes* that the deployment of the United Nations Mission in Sierra Leone as established by resolution 1270(1999) is in the process of completion;

2. *Welcomes* the efforts made by the Government of Sierra Leone, the leadership of the Revolutionary United Front Party of Sierra Leone, the Monitoring Group of the Economic Community of West African States and the Mission towards the implementation of the Peace Agreement signed in Lomé on 7 July 1999;

3. *Reiterates its call* upon the parties to fulfil all their commitments under the Peace Agreement to facilitate the restoration of peace, stability, national reconciliation and development in Sierra Leone, and stresses that the responsibility for the success of the peace pro-

cess ultimately lies with the people and leaders of Sierra Leone;

4. *Notes with concern* that, despite the progress that has been made, the peace process thus far has been marred by the limited and sporadic participation in the disarmament, demobilization and reintegration programme, by the lack of progress on the release of abductees and child soldiers and by continued hostage-taking and attacks on humanitarian personnel, and expresses its conviction that the expansion of the Mission as provided for in paragraphs 9 to 12 below will create conditions under which all parties can work to ensure that the provisions of the Peace Agreement are implemented in full;

5. *Also notes with concern* the continuing human rights violations against the civilian population of Sierra Leone, and emphasizes that the amnesty extended under the Peace Agreement does not extend to such violations committed after the date of its signing;

6. *Calls upon* the parties and all others involved to take steps to ensure that the disarmament, demobilization and reintegration programme is fully implemented throughout the country, and in particular urges the Revolutionary United Front, the Civil Defence Force, the former Sierra Leone Armed Forces/Armed Forces Revolutionary Council and all other armed groups to participate fully in the programme and cooperate with all those responsible for its implementation;

7. *Takes note* of the decision of the Governments of Nigeria, Guinea and Ghana to withdraw their remaining Monitoring Group contingents from Sierra Leone, as reported in the letter from the Secretary-General dated 23 December 1999;

8. *Expresses its appreciation* to the Monitoring Group for its indispensable contribution towards the restoration of democracy and the maintenance of peace, security and stability in Sierra Leone, commends highly the forces and the Governments of its contributing States for their courage and sacrifice, and encourages all States to assist the contributing States further in meeting the costs they have incurred in making possible the deployment of the Monitoring Group forces in Sierra Leone;

9. *Decides* that the military component of the Mission shall be expanded to a maximum of 11,100 military personnel, including the 260 military observers already deployed, subject to periodic review in the light of conditions on the ground and progress made in the peace process, in particular in the disarmament, demobilization and reintegration programme, and takes note of paragraph 33 of the report of the Secretary-General of 11 January 2000;

10. *Also decides*, acting under Chapter VII of the Charter of the United Nations, that the mandate of the Mission shall be revised to include the following additional tasks, to be performed by the Mission within its capabilities and areas of deployment, and in the light of conditions on the ground:

(a) To provide security at key locations and Government buildings, in particular in Freetown, and at important intersections and major airports, including the Lungi airport;

(b) To facilitate the free flow of people, goods and humanitarian assistance along specified thoroughfares;

(c) To provide security in and at all sites of the disarmament, demobilization and reintegration programme;

(d) To coordinate with and assist, in common areas of deployment, the Sierra Leone law enforcement authorities in the discharge of their responsibilities;

(e) To guard weapons, ammunition and other military equipment collected from ex-combatants and to assist in their subsequent disposal or destruction;

authorizes the Mission to take the necessary action to fulfil the additional tasks set out above, and affirms that, in the discharge of its mandate, the Mission may take the necessary action to ensure the security and freedom of movement of its personnel and, within its capabilities and areas of deployment, afford protection to civilians under imminent threat of physical violence, taking into account the responsibilities of the Government of Sierra Leone;

11. *Decides further* that the mandate of the Mission, as revised, shall be extended for a period of six months from the date of adoption of the present resolution;

12. *Authorizes* the increases in the civil affairs, civilian police, administrative and technical personnel of the Mission proposed by the Secretary-General in his report of 11 January 2000;

13. *Welcomes* the intention of the Secretary-General, as indicated in his report of 11 January 2000, to establish within the Mission a landmine action office responsible for awareness training of Mission personnel and for the coordination of mine action activities of non-governmental organizations and humanitarian agencies operating in Sierra Leone;

14. *Stresses* the importance of a smooth transition between the Monitoring Group and the Mission for the successful implementation of the Peace Agreement and the stability of Sierra Leone, and in that regard urges all those concerned to consult over the timing of troop movements and withdrawals;

15. *Reiterates* the importance of the safety, security and freedom of movement of United Nations and associated personnel, notes that the Government of Sierra Leone and the Revolutionary United Front have agreed in the Peace Agreement to provide guarantees in this regard, and calls upon all parties in Sierra Leone to respect fully the status of United Nations and associated personnel;

16. *Reiterates its request* to the Government of Sierra Leone to conclude a status-of-forces agreement with the Secretary-General within thirty days of the adoption of the present resolution, and recalls that pending the conclusion of such an agreement the model status-of-forces agreement dated 9 October 1990 should apply provisionally;

17. *Reiterates* the continued need to promote peace and national reconciliation and to foster accountability and respect for human rights in Sierra Leone, and urges the Government of Sierra Leone, specialized agencies, other multilateral organizations, civil society and Member States to accelerate their efforts to establish the Truth and Reconciliation Commission, the Human Rights Commission and the Commission for the Consolidation of Peace as fully-functioning and effective institutions, as provided for under the Peace Agreement;

18. *Emphasizes* the importance of the exercise by the Government of Sierra Leone of full control over the exploitation of gold, diamonds and other resources for

the benefit of the people of the country and in accordance with article VII, paragraph 6, of the Peace Agreement, and, to that end, calls for the early and effective operation of the Commission of the Management of Strategic Resources, National Reconstruction and Development;

19. *Welcomes* the contributions that have been made to the multi-donor trust fund established by the International Bank for Reconstruction and Development to finance the disarmament, demobilization and reintegration process, and urges all States and international and other organizations that have not yet done so to contribute generously to the fund so that the process is adequately financed and the provisions of the Peace Agreement can be fully implemented;

20. *Underlines* the ultimate responsibility of the Government of Sierra Leone for the provision of adequate security forces in the country, calls upon it, in that regard, to take urgent steps towards the establishment of professional and accountable national police and armed forces, and stresses the importance to this objective of generous support and assistance from the international community;

21. *Reiterates* the continued need for urgent and substantial assistance for the people of Sierra Leone, as well as for sustained and generous assistance for the longer-term tasks of peace-building, reconstruction, economic and social recovery and development in Sierra Leone, and urges all States and international and other organizations to provide such assistance as a priority;

22. *Requests* the Secretary-General to continue to report to the Council every forty-five days to provide, inter alia, assessments of security conditions on the ground so that troop levels and the tasks to be performed by the Mission can be kept under review, as indicated in the report of the Secretary-General of 11 January 2000;

23. *Decides* to remain actively seized of the matter.

Report of Secretary-General (March). In his third report on UNAMSIL, issued on 7 March [S/2000/186], the Secretary-General said that progress had been made in the establishment and functioning of the various bodies envisaged in the Lomé Peace Agreement. The Commission for the Consolidation of Peace, an implementation organ, under the chairmanship of Lieutenant Colonel Johnny Paul Koroma, had set up its offices. The 16-member Constitutional Review Committee had also begun its work and was expected to report to President Ahmad Tejan Kabbah in the near future. Parliament had begun confirmation hearings for nominees to serve on other commissions. Mr. Koroma, leader of the Armed Forces Revolutionary Council (AFRC), had resigned from the Sierra Leone Army, but remained leader of his party. However, his faction would be dissolved on the reinstatement of ex–Sierra Leone Army elements into the current armed forces. The Ministry of Defence was preparing a military reintegration plan that would screen ex-combatants to decide whether they would be accepted into the new army or would enter the demobilization programme.

On 24 January, the ECOWAS Chairman convened the second meeting of the Joint Implementation Committee. The Government of Sierra Leone was represented by the Attorney-General while RUFP was represented by its Secretary-General, Momoh Rogers. Mr. Koroma attended in his capacity as Chairman of the Commission for the Consolidation of Peace. The Committee adopted recommendations aimed at accelerating the implementation of the Lomé Agreement, especially regarding the disarmament process, the ceasefire agreement and unhindered humanitarian access. It demanded that UN troops be allowed to carry out their mandate without restrictions and that the weapons confiscated from some of the contingents by the armed groups be returned. Progress in disarmament had been slow, particularly in the northern and eastern parts of the country, and rebel groups continued to interfere with humanitarian activities and UNAMSIL patrols and to harass the civilian population in those areas. During the reporting period, RUF, including its leader, Foday Sankoh, made hostile public statements about UNAMSIL.

The security situation remained tense and volatile, although there were some improvements, particularly in the Lungi area where UNAMSIL was patrolling extensively. In other areas, such as the Occra Hills and the Northern and Eastern Provinces, ceasefire violations included ambushes against civilians, illegal roadblocks, RUF troop movements and obstruction of peacekeeping operations. There were serious incidents involving UNAMSIL and former rebel elements or combatants, including RUF elements seizing weapons and vehicles from a convoy of Guinean troops, ex-army combatants seizing weapons, and RUF fighters stopping a convoy and blocking a UN landing strip.

The strength of UNAMSIL reached 7,391 military personnel as at 1 March. With the deployment of UNAMSIL military units, access for humanitarian aid had improved, but delays in disarmament and continuing RUF resistance to the deployment of UN troops continued to slow humanitarian access to 2.6 million war-affected Sierra Leoneans in the Northern and Eastern Provinces. The human rights situation remained a cause for serious concern, in particular in the Port Loko area where looting, house burnings, harassment and abduction of civilians, rape and sexual abuse continued, mostly perpetrated by ex-army elements from the surrounding Occra Hills.

The Secretary-General stated that one of the Mission's main priorities remained the speedy establishment of a credible peacekeeping presence throughout the country to create the necessary climate of confidence and security conditions for the implementation of the peace process. The Sierra Leonean parties, in particular RUF, needed to cooperate with UNAMSIL and provide unrestricted access to all parts of the country. The main steps ahead in the peace process were in four areas—the early disarmament, demobilization and reintegration of all ex-combatants; the extension of State authority, including law enforcement, throughout the country; national reconciliation and democratization; and the improvement of Sierra Leone's capacity to ensure its own security. Progress would require commitment by the Government, RUFP and other Sierra Leonean parties, and on the part of the international community.

The Secretary-General noted that serious doubts remained about the commitment of RUFP to the peace process and expressed concern about the often negative and confusing approach taken by Mr. Sankoh to key elements of the peace process and the role entrusted to the United Nations. Also, the continuing ceasefire violations perpetrated against civilians and peacekeepers could not be tolerated by the international community, and the obstruction of UNAMSIL patrols and deployments was unacceptable.

Attacks against UNAMSIL

The situation in Sierra Leone erupted in a new crisis on 1 May and the peace process suffered a very serious setback as the result of unprovoked armed attacks on UN peacekeepers by RUF fighters, the detention of several hundred UN personnel (the great majority of them Zambians), and the destruction of disarmament and demobilization camps by RUF fighters. UNAMSIL increased in strength to 9,495 (over a third contributed by Nigeria), replacing ECOMOG completely by mid-May.

SECURITY COUNCIL ACTION (4 May)

On 4 May [meeting 4134], following consultations among Security Council members, the President made statement **S/PRST/2000/14** on behalf of the Council:

The Security Council expresses its grave concern at the outbreak of violence in Sierra Leone in recent days. It condemns in the strongest terms the armed attacks perpetrated by the Revolutionary United Front against the forces of the United Nations Mission in Sierra Leone, and its continued detention of a large number of United Nations and other international personnel. The Council expresses its outrage at the killing of a number of United Nations peacekeepers from the Kenyan battalion and its deep concern for the troops of the United Nations Mission in Sierra Leone who have been wounded or remain unaccounted for.

The Council demands that the Revolutionary United Front end its hostile actions, release immediately and unharmed all detained United Nations and other international personnel, cooperate in establishing the whereabouts of those unaccounted for and comply fully with the terms of the Peace Agreement signed in Lomé on 7 July 1999.

The Council considers Mr. Foday Sankoh, as leader of the Revolutionary United Front, to be responsible for those actions, which are unacceptable and in clear violation of their obligations under the Peace Agreement. The Council condemns the fact that Mr. Sankoh has deliberately failed to fulfil his responsibility to cooperate with the Mission in bringing these incidents to an end. The Council believes that he must be held accountable, together with the perpetrators, for their actions.

The Council commends the forces of the Mission and the Force Commander for the courage, resolve and sacrifice they have shown in attempting to bring this situation under control. It expresses its full support for their continued efforts to this end, and for the overall fulfilment of their mandate. It calls upon all States in a position to do so to assist the Mission in this regard. The Council also expresses its support for the regional and other international efforts under way to resolve the crisis, including by the Economic Community of West African States.

The Council will continue to monitor the situation closely, and consider further action, as necessary.

On 10 May [S/2000/408], the Group of African States requested an open emergency meeting of the Council to address the situation in Sierra Leone. That request, forwarded by Eritrea, was supported by separate requests on the next day by Mali [S/2000/409] and Namibia [S/2000/410].

The Council held an open meeting on 11 May [meeting 4139] at which members and other States expressed their views on expanding UNAMSIL and revising its mandate. Kenya [S/2000/418] and South Africa [S/2000/417] forwarded statements that they had intended to make at that meeting but were unable to do so.

The Secretary-General informed the Council on 17 May [S/2000/446] that the UNAMSIL authorized strength of 11,100 would be exceeded in the following several days as reinforcements arrived. He suggested that the Council consider authorizing the interim expansion of the Mission pending his report and recommendations regarding the situation in Sierra Leone.

Report of Secretary-General (May). The Secretary-General stated in his fourth (19 May) report on UNAMSIL [S/2000/455] that the attacks on UN peacekeepers overshadowed the limited progress achieved in the implementation of the Lomé Peace Agreement through a series of meetings of the parties and international stakeholders. Among those meetings was one convened by President Kabbah on 9 March, at which all faction leaders agreed to grant UNAMSIL access to all parts of the country; to relinquish territory they occupied and allow the Government to have full control; and to allow disarmament to take place. Despite some movement towards those goals, RUF fighters continued to obstruct UNAMSIL deployment in the Kono District, the number of RUF ex-combatants reporting for disarmament remained very low and some checkpoints operated by rebel forces remained in place. A donors' conference was convened in London on 27 March to affirm political support for the peace process and mobilize resources. New pledges totalling $70 million were made. The conference called on the rebels to end human rights abuses, to disarm their combatants, to release women and children still detained, and to allow access for humanitarian assistance to all areas of the country. Speaking before the Sierra Leone Parliament on 15 March, Mr. Sankoh said that he was committed to the peace process and claimed he was ready to work with Parliament.

During the reporting period, there were unconfirmed reports of the formation of a new faction by a former RUF commander, Sam Bockarie, who was said to be engaged in recruiting and training of rebels in Liberia. Liberia denied those reports. On 22 March, Sierra Leone arrested 16 persons suspected of organizing a group of dissidents to invade Liberia.

Prior to the serious attacks on UN peacekeepers which erupted on 1 May, the overall security situation had improved gradually; however, in the areas controlled by rebel groups, particularly RUF and AFRC/ex-army strongholds, the security situation remained precarious and there were several serious incidents, some involving UN peacekeepers. Those attacks included firing by RUF and ex-army forces on the Kenyan and Ghanaian battalions of UNAMSIL. A soldier of the Nigerian contingent was shot and seriously wounded when he refused to surrender his weapon to a large group of men (presumably ex-army personnel).

The Secretary-General noted some progress towards the objectives he had outlined in his previous report. The disarmament and demobilization process, which had been making slow but steady progress, came to a standstill after hostilities erupted early in May. As at 15 May, some 24,042 ex-combatants had been disarmed: 4,949 from RUF, 10,055 from AFRC/ex-army and 9,038 from the Civil Defence Forces. The number

(10,840) and quality of weapons surrendered remained an issue of concern. On 17 April, the four disarmament, demobilization and reintegration camps became operational. An effort towards democratization was made on 20 March when the National Electoral Commission was sworn into office and subsequently began work. Although there was some improvement in the functioning of the police force, the restructuring process was proceeding slowly.

The situation reached a crisis point on 1 May when RUF ex-combatants approached the disarmament centre in Makeni, made threatening demands and detained seven UNAMSIL members. At Magburaka, armed RUF ex-combatants surrounded the UNAMSIL team site. The next day, when RUF tried to disarm UNAMSIL troops at Magburaka, the troops resisted. The exchange of fire, which lasted all day, resulted in three soldiers of the Kenyan battalion being injured. RUF also destroyed and looted the disarmament, demobilization and reintegration facilities at Magburaka and Makeni. Also on 2 May, a UN helicopter and its crew were detained by RUF, as was a 23-man unit of the Indian battalion. Some 400 UN troops were believed to have fallen into the hands of RUF within the next few days. From 2 May, several clashes took place between RUF and UNAMSIL troops, as well as elements of the Sierra Leone Army and the Civil Defence Forces at several locations. On 9 May, the Indian quick reaction company and a Kenyan company, which had been surrounded at Magburaka, broke through RUF lines and managed to reach UN positions at Mile 91. On the same day, the remaining troops of the Kenyan battalion broke out of Makeni and managed to reach areas controlled by the ex-army at Kabala and Bumbuna. Through negotiations, other detainees were released and, as at 15 May, RUF held 352 UN staff, comprising 297 Zambian soldiers, 29 Kenyans, 23 Indians and 3 military observers. Fifteen UN soldiers remained missing.

A pivotal factor in restoring stability was the arrival of United Kingdom troops on 7 May and of a substantial British naval presence offshore a week later. The deployment of British troops at Lungi airport and in Freetown had as its objective the evacuation of United Kingdom nationals but it also enabled UNAMSIL to redeploy troops east of Freetown; an additional stabilizing factor was the arrival on 12 May of 300 Jordanian troops.

Following the outbreak of hostilities, the Secretary-General contacted leaders in the region to seek their assistance. Representatives of several Governments were in touch with Mr. Sankoh to secure the release of the detainees. The Special Representative also met with Mr. Sankoh and demanded the release of all detained UNAM-SIL troops. On 8 May, a crowd gathered outside Mr. Sankoh's house to protest the RUF attacks. After violence broke out and several people were killed, Mr. Sankoh disappeared with some of his body guards but was apprehended on 17 May.

On 9 May, a summit meeting of the ECOWAS Committee on Sierra Leone, consisting of Burkina Faso, Côte d'Ivoire, Ghana, Guinea, Liberia, Mali, Nigeria and Togo, met in Abuja, Nigeria. The summit condemned RUF, called for the release of the detainees, and warned RUF leaders that they could be tried for war crimes if they continued to flout the Lomé Peace Agreement. A meeting of the Joint Implementation Committee was held in Freetown on 13 May [S/2000/494], chaired by the Foreign Minister of Mali and attended by representatives of several countries, OAU and UNAMSIL. Mr. Koroma attended but RUF was not represented. It was agreed that a dual approach would be pursued, namely, by exerting diplomatic pressure on RUF and displaying military strength by enhancing UNAMSIL capabilities. The meeting condemned the taking of UNAMSIL hostages by RUF and the murder of some UNAM-SIL personnel and of innocent civilians by RUF.

As at 15 May, there had been few indications that RUF leaders were willing to change their course of action, although some individual members had conveyed their willingness to disarm. At the same time, RUF continued to detain hundreds of UNAMSIL personnel and also to attack UNAM-SIL and Sierra Leonean troops at various locations in the country.

The Secretary-General made a number of recommendations for immediate measures. Stressing the need to maintain political pressure on RUF, as well as a strong military posture, including on the part of the United Nations, to deter RUF from pursuing the military option, he called for the immediate reinforcement of UNAMSIL. In particular, the Mission should enhance its capability to defend its positions at Lungi airport, on the Freetown peninsula and other locations in the western and southern parts of the country. The immediate reinforcement would bring the military strength of UNAMSIL from its current strength of 9,250 to 13,000, including 260 military observers. The Mission should be further expanded in order to stabilize the situation in the country. The first priority would be the consolidation of UNAMSIL units at strong positions and strategic locations to ensure the protection of the civilian population in Freetown and the security of government institutions, as well as maintaining a sufficient strength in the areas under government control to deter and, if necessary, repel further attacks by RUF. UNAMSIL would then seek

to stabilize the situation and assist the Government to restore law and order in the areas outside RUF control. Once strengthened, UNAMSIL would begin to gradually deploy forward to secure strategic locations in the western and southern parts of the country. To achieve that goal, UNAMSIL would need additional battalions and logistics, with a total military strength of up to 16,500 military personnel and an increase in the civilian administrative staff. To ensure proper control and unity of command, the Secretary-General believed that all international forces in Sierra Leone, with the exception of those sent for a brief period for strictly national purposes, should be integrated into UNAMSIL. He also suggested that UNAMSIL should establish a countrywide public information campaign and set up its own radio station.

Of immediate concern were the safe return of all UN personnel being detained by RUF, an end to the hostile acts of the RUF fighters, and their cooperation in retrieving the dead, wounded and missing. In addition, the Secretary-General suggested that the Security Council consider strengthening the sanctions regime, including measures to prevent RUF commanders from reaping the benefits of their illegal exploitation of mineral resources, in particular diamonds. The international community should hold Mr. Sankoh accountable for his actions and those of RUF, and for the safety and well-being of those detained. Political efforts and humanitarian aid to assist the people should be supplemented by credible military force. Ultimately, a lasting resolution of the crisis could be found only through political means; it could not be imposed by military force alone, nor could a solution be the result of international involvement alone.

The United Nations needed to draw lessons from its experiences in Sierra Leone, the Secretary-General stated. Deployed as a peacekeeping force, it was forced into actual combat with one of the parties that had pledged to cooperate with it. In the course of the ensuing events, problems emerged within the Mission, including with regard to command and control, cohesiveness of the force, the flow of information, equipment and preparedness of troops, and coordination between and within UNAMSIL components.

SECURITY COUNCIL ACTION (19 May)

On 19 May [meeting 4145], the Security Council unanimously adopted **resolution 1299(2000)**. The draft [S/2000/449] was prepared in consultations among Council members.

The Security Council,
Recalling its previous resolutions and the statements by its President on the situation in Sierra Leone,

Having considered the letter dated 17 May 2000 from the Secretary-General to the President of the Security Council, and awaiting his next report,

Convinced that the deterioration in security conditions on the ground necessitates the rapid reinforcement of the military component of the United Nations Mission in Sierra Leone to provide the mission with additional resources to fulfil its mandate,

1. *Decides* that the military component of the United Nations Mission in Sierra Leone shall be expanded to a maximum of 13,000 military personnel, including the 260 military observers already deployed;

2. *Expresses its appreciation* to all States which, in order to expedite the rapid reinforcement of the Mission, have accelerated the deployment of their troops to the Mission, made available additional personnel and offered logistical, technical and other forms of military assistance, and calls upon all those in a position to do so to provide further support;

3. *Decides*, acting under Chapter VII of the Charter of the United Nations, that the restrictions set out in paragraph 2 of its resolution 1171(1998) of 5 June 1998 do not apply to the sale or supply of arms and related materiel for the sole use in Sierra Leone of those Member States cooperating with the Mission and the Government of Sierra Leone;

4. *Decides* to remain actively seized of the matter.

Communications (May). In May, Sierra Leone expressed its views on the situation in a series of letters to the Security Council [S/2000/373, S/2000/380, S/2000/391, S/2000/401, S/2000/433, S/2000/434, S/2000/469, S/2000/470]. Warning on 2 May that violence perpetrated by ex-combatants against peacekeepers was causing concern, Sierra Leone reminded the Council of UNAMSIL's mandate to protect the people of Sierra Leone if and when they were under threat of physical violence. The national Parliament, on 4 May, issued a resolution in which it, among other things, called on UNAMSIL to disarm all combatants unwilling to hand in their weapons. On 8 May, President Kabbah issued an appeal to the people of his country to desist from violence; on 14 May he appealed to RUF fighters to lay down their arms. Sierra Leone issued its comments on the meeting of the Joint Implementation Committee on the Lomé Peace Agreement (Freetown, 13 May), in which it criticized the assault on UN peacekeepers and put forward proposals for returning to the peace process. On 19 May, the Government confirmed that it had custody of Mr. Sankoh and it issued a list of conditions that needed to be met by RUF in order for the Lomé Agreement to continue to be implemented. A government statement of 23 May denied claims by Liberia that Sierra Leone forces were attacking RUF positions inside Liberia.

Some regional organizations transmitted letters criticizing the attacks against UNAMSIL. On 5 May [S/2000/404], the EU Presidency, condemning actions by RUF and expressing its concern at reports of the killing of UNAMSIL personnel, called on RUF, in particular its leader, Mr. Sankoh, to cease all such attacks, to release all detainees and to implement their commitments under the Lomé Peace Agreement. On 9 May [S/2000/441], Mali transmitted the communiqué of the summit of the ECOWAS heads of State members of the Committee on Sierra Leone of the Lomé Peace Agreement (Abuja, 9 May). The Committee condemned the action of the RUF fighters who had taken UNAMSIL soldiers hostage. They approved the mandate given by the ECOWAS Chairman and by the heads of State of the Mano River Union to the President of Liberia, Charles Taylor, to seek the release of the hostages and the resumption of the peace process. Algeria, on 26 May [S/2000/492], forwarded a communiqué issued by the OAU Mechanism for Conflict Prevention, Management and Resolution, in which it condemned the RUF action, called for the transformation of UNAMSIL's mandate from peacekeeping to peace enforcement, and expressed support for the Secretary-General's proposal to broaden the sanctions against RUF, including measures to counter the illegal trade in diamonds from Sierra Leone.

On 5 May [S/2000/400], Burkina Faso expressed its indignation and concern at the developments in Sierra Leone, particularly the attacks on UN peacekeeping forces that had resulted in the death of several UNAMSIL peacekeepers and the abduction of many more.

SECURITY COUNCIL ACTION (June)

On 21 June [meeting 4163], the Security Council held a private meeting with a delegation of the ECOWAS Mediation and Security Council Committee of Six on Sierra Leone. In an official communiqué issued after the meeting, Council members and the ECOWAS Committee condemned the continued detention by RUF of UN peacekeepers of the Indian contingent of UNAMSIL and the denial of freedom of movement to UN personnel in the east of the country. They demanded the immediate and unconditional release of all UN personnel detained or surrounded, and recalled the ECOWAS mandate given to the President of Liberia to obtain the release of the remaining hostages. They expressed concern about the humanitarian situation in Sierra Leone and called on all parties to ensure unhindered access of humanitarian assistance to those in need. Council members informed ECOWAS of ongoing discussions within the Council on draft resolutions concerning the strengthening of UNAMSIL, the control of diamond exports and arms imports and on the provision of justice.

Communications. In June and July, Sierra Leone submitted four letters to the Security Council. In a government statement of 1 June [S/2000/524], it expressed pleasure at the release of all the abducted UN peacekeepers by RUF and acknowledged the role played by Liberian President Taylor in achieving that objective. The Government continued to demand that RUF return all the weapons and equipment seized from the peacekeepers and release all abducted Sierra Leoneans. In July, however, the Secretary-General reported that hundreds of UNAMSIL peacekeepers were still held hostage by RUF (see above). On 17 July [S/2000/698], Sierra Leone welcomed the rescue of UN peacekeepers who had been held by RUF in Kailahun.

President Kabbah, in a statement of 22 June [S/2000/620 & Corr.1], criticized RUF for not abiding by the Lomé Agreement and mounting attacks against the Government. Although the Government in principle remained committed to the Agreement, it reserved the right not to be bound by all its provisions in view of the RUF action; it would set its own priorities regarding implementation, with security and humanitarian provisions of primary concern.

Another statement by the President [S/2000/727] was made on 22 July at the ceremony marking the completion of a training session for Sierra Leone armed forces under the United Kingdom short-term training programme.

SECURITY COUNCIL ACTION (July)

On 17 July [meeting 4173], following consultations among Security Council members, the President made statement **S/PRST/2000/24** on behalf of the Council:

> The Security Council expresses its full support for the decision taken by the Secretary-General to mount a military operation by the United Nations Mission in Sierra Leone to relieve its surrounded peacekeepers and military observers at Kailahun. It expresses its satisfaction at the successful outcome of the operation, with the minimum of casualties among United Nations personnel. The Council expresses its admiration for the professionalism, determination and robustness displayed by all the Mission forces involved in this difficult and dangerous operation, and for the leadership and skill of the Force Commander, General Jetley, under whose personal command it was carried out.
>
> The Council believes that the hostile stance taken by the Revolutionary United Front towards Mission personnel at Kailahun had become intolerable. It fully concurs with the assessment of the Secretary-General in this regard. It is firmly of the view that, after the denial of freedom of movement by the Front for over two months, the exhaustion of intensive diplomatic and political efforts and the recent decision by the Front to impede the resupply to Kai-

lahun, the Force Commander, under those circumstances, had no choice but to take resolute action to restore the security and freedom of movement of Mission personnel, as authorized under the mandate of the Mission.

> The Council pays tribute to the forces of the Indian contingent of the Mission, which took the lead in the execution of the operation. The Council expresses its profound condolences to the family of the Indian sergeant, Krishna Kumar, who gave his life in the cause of peace. It also expresses its sympathies to those who were wounded. The Council commends equally the critical role played by the Nigerian and Ghanaian contingents that provided essential flank and rear support, without which the operation would not have been possible, as well as the contribution of the force as a whole. The Council also expresses its appreciation to the United Kingdom of Great Britain and Northern Ireland for the valuable logistical support provided. The cooperation, coherence and sense of common purpose displayed by all concerned should be considered an example of the very best in United Nations multilateral peacekeeping.

> The Council believes that there is now a firm foundation on which the Mission can build as it continues to implement its mandate and work towards a lasting peaceful settlement to the conflict in Sierra Leone. While noting these positive developments, the Council recognizes that there is still much to be done, and expresses its full support to the Mission in its efforts to implement its mandate.

Report of Secretary-General (July). In response to Security Council resolution 1289 (2000), the Secretary-General on 31 July issued his fifth report on UNAMSIL [S/2000/751]. Since his previous report of 19 May, the situation in Sierra Leone had remained tense and volatile under conditions that resembled civil war. RUF continued to attack UN peacekeepers and pro-Government forces and, until recently, to detain and surround UN personnel. During the reporting period, nine peacekeepers, seven from Nigeria, one from India and one from Jordan, were killed, and another eight soldiers were still missing. The programme for disarmament, demobilization and reintegration came to a standstill as various pro-Government groups rearmed and formed an alliance to fight RUF. President Kabbah announced in June that his Government intended to pursue a two-track approach, based on both military and political action, to end the hostilities, and would apply the terms of the Lomé Agreement selectively. The civil society of Sierra Leone and the Commission for the Consolidation of Peace, headed by Johnny Paul Koroma, were also engaged in exploring ways to restart the peace process. The various groups within RUF reportedly lacked unanimity of views on its strategy and leadership. Owing to the resumption of hostilities, no further progress was made in efforts to restore civil authority throughout the country.

On 12 June, President Kabbah requested UN assistance to establish a special court to try Foday Sankoh and other senior RUF members for crimes against the people of Sierra Leone and for taking UN peacekeepers as hostages. The UN Office of Legal Affairs was researching the request to assess the needs and requirements of the local justice system.

ECOWAS remained engaged in seeking a solution to the crisis. At a summit (Abuja, 28-29 May), it established a six-member committee to facilitate a cessation of hostilities and to insist on a return by the parties to positions they held at the signing of the Lomé Agreement. Additional troops from ECOWAS States would be made available to participate in UNAMSIL, whose mandate, as recommended by ECOWAS, should be revised to include peace-enforcement elements. On 21 June, a Committee delegation met with the Security Council and submitted an eight-point plan to resolve the crisis [S/2000/631] (see above). A meeting of the ECOWAS Defence and Security Commission (Accra, Ghana, 19-20 July) discussed modalities for deploying additional troops for UNAMSIL and commended UNAMSIL for extracting its troops surrounded by RUF at Kailahun and called on those countries that had promised to do so to equip troops from ECOWAS countries serving in UNAMSIL. The ongoing hostilities aggravated tensions between Sierra Leone and Liberia, which alleged that Sierra Leone was supporting Liberian dissidents and accused Guinea of supporting the recent incursion by dissidents into northern Liberia. Guinea denied those accusations. For its part, Sierra Leone alleged that Liberia was supporting and arming RUF.

The volatile security situation was marked by continuing RUF attacks on UNAMSIL and on an alliance of pro-Government forces, which consisted of the Sierra Leone Army (SLA), the Civil Defence Force and some of the forces loyal to AFRC/ex-SLA. In the Freetown and Lungi peninsulas, the situation was relatively stable owing to the deployment of UNAMSIL, pro-Government forces and the troops deployed by the United Kingdom at Lungi. There were, however, a few serious incidents in Freetown and other locations during which UN peacekeepers were killed and injured. On 22 July, UNAMSIL launched a successful military operation to remove illegal checkpoints and to clear the Occra Hills area of armed groups. Efforts were made at all levels to seek the release of UN personnel, resulting in the release of 461 UN peacekeepers who were held by RUF in Kono district. Liberian President Taylor played an important role in the release of those peacekeepers. A UNAMSIL military operation on 15 and 16 July, conducted by troops from the Indian contingent with support provided by units from Ghana and Nigeria and logistical support by the United Kingdom, successfully removed the UN personnel from Kailahun. One Indian soldier was killed during the operation. The troop strength of UNAMSIL was 12,428 as at 22 July.

The disarmament and demobilization process remained at a standstill. Two demobilization centres were destroyed by RUF rebels and operations were suspended at four of the remaining seven centres.

Following the resumption of hostilities in Sierra Leone, more than 150,000 new internally displaced persons were registered by aid agencies, bringing the total number to 310,000. More than 1.5 million war-affected individuals were also in need of assistance, 1 million of whom were in inaccessible areas.

As the Secretary-General had recommended, the UNAMSIL public information unit was strengthened, with Radio UNAMSIL continuing as the focal point of the Mission's public information strategy.

. The Secretary-General sent an assessment team to Sierra Leone to review UNAMSIL operations (2-8 June). The team found a lack of cohesion within the Mission and other shortcomings; in particular, it found that there was no commonly shared understanding of the mandate and rules of engagement, as well as other problems in command and control. There were also serious problems related to internal communication and coordination between the civilian and military components, as well as within each component. The team noted a lack of integrated planning and logistic support as well as insufficient coordination and sharing of information with UN agencies and others. Some military units showed a lack of training and others had shortfalls in equipment. Public information efforts and relations with the public could be improved. Many of those problems had since been addressed.

The Secretary-General reported that the threat posed by RUF remained a matter of grave concern as it had shown no credible sign that it was ready to resume the peace process and had continued to attack UNAMSIL and pro-Government forces. To achieve the goals of a durable peace, the restoration of government authority throughout the country, the establishment of national institutions, and democratic elections and respect for human rights, efforts should be focused on a political solution based on a robust and credible international military presence. The Secretary-General recommended, therefore, that the UNAMSIL mandate, due to expire on 7 August, be extended for another six months.

On 4 August [meeting 4184], the Security Council unanimously adopted **resolution 1313(2000)**. The draft [S/2000/764] was prepared in consultations among Council members.

The Security Council,

Recalling all its previous resolutions and the statements by its President concerning the situation in Sierra Leone,

Condemning in the strongest terms the armed attacks against and the detention of the personnel of the United Nations Mission in Sierra Leone, and commending the Mission and the Force Commander for the recent resolute action taken in response to the continuing threat to the mission from the Revolutionary United Front and other armed elements in Sierra Leone,

Having considered the reports of the Secretary-General of 19 May 2000 and 31 July 2000,

1. *Decides* to extend the mandate of the United Nations Mission in Sierra Leone until 8 September 2000;

2. *Considers* that the widespread and serious violations of the Peace Agreement signed in Lomé on 7 July 1999 by the Revolutionary United Front since early May 2000 constitute a breakdown of the prior, generally permissive environment based on the Peace Agreement and predicated on the cooperation of the parties, that until security conditions have been established allowing progress towards the peaceful resolution of the conflict in Sierra Leone there will continue to be a threat to the Mission and the security of the State of Sierra Leone, and that in order to counter that threat, the structure, capability, resources and mandate of the Mission require appropriate strengthening;

3. *Expresses its intention,* in this context, taking into account the views of the Government of Sierra Leone, the Economic Community of West African States and the troop-contributing countries, to strengthen the mandate of the Mission as established in resolutions 1270(1999) of 22 October 1999 and 1289(2000) of 7 February 2000 with the following priority tasks:

(*a*) To maintain the security of the Lungi and Freetown peninsulas, and their major approach routes;

(*b*) To deter and, where necessary, decisively counter the threat of attack by the Revolutionary United Front by responding robustly to any hostile actions or threat of imminent and direct use of force;

(*c*) To deploy progressively in a coherent operational structure and in sufficient numbers and density at key strategic locations and main population centres and, in coordination with the Government of Sierra Leone, to assist, through its presence and within the framework of its mandate, the efforts of the Government of Sierra Leone to extend state authority, restore law and order and further stabilize the situation progressively throughout the entire country, and, within its capabilities and areas of deployment, to afford protection to civilians under threat of imminent physical violence;

(*d*) To patrol actively on strategic lines of communication, specifically main access routes to the capital in order to dominate ground, ensure freedom of movement and facilitate the provision of humanitarian assistance;

(*e*) To assist in the promotion of the political process leading, inter alia, to a renewed disarmament, demobilization and reintegration programme, where possible;

4. *Considers* that, in order to allow the restructuring of the force and provide the additional capability required for the achievement of the priority tasks set out in paragraph 3 above, the military component of the Mission should be reinforced through accelerated troop rotations, as appropriate, and with, inter alia, further aviation and maritime assets, a strengthened force reserve, upgraded communications and specialist combat and logistic support assets;

5. *Recognizes* that the offensive by the Revolutionary United Front against the Mission since May 2000 revealed serious inherent weaknesses in the structure, command and control and resources of the Mission, as referred to in paragraph 54 of the report of the Secretary-General of 31 July 2000, reflecting the findings of the United Nations assessment mission that visited Sierra Leone from 2 to 8 June 2000, welcomes the recommendations made and action already taken to address those deficiencies, and requests the Secretary-General to take further urgent steps to implement those recommendations, to improve the performance and capacity of the mission;

6. *Stresses* that the successful achievement of the objectives of the mission, including the priority tasks set out in paragraph 3 above, will depend on the provision to the Mission of fully equipped, complete units, with the required capabilities, effective command and control structure and capacity, a single chain of command, adequate resources and the commitment to implement the mandate of the mission in full as authorized by the Council;

7. *Requests* the Secretary-General, after further consultations with troop-contributing countries, to provide a further report to the Council as soon as possible on the proposals in paragraphs 2 to 6 above, with recommendations for the restructuring and strengthening of the Mission, and expresses its intention to take a decision on those recommendations expeditiously;

8. *Decides* to remain actively seized of the matter.

Sanctions and justice system

As the internal conflict in Sierra Leone continued in mid-2000, the Security Council took action to control the illicit trade in diamonds from the country, which was considered to be linked to trade in arms and related materiel in violation of Council sanctions. The Council's arms sanctions against non-governmental forces in Sierra Leone, imposed by resolution 1132(1997) [YUN 1997, p. 135] and revised by resolution 1171(1998) [YUN 1998, p. 169], remained in force. The EU Presidency, however, in a 7 June statement [S/2000/583], questioned the effectiveness of the arms embargo, stating that fighting between the Government and RUF continued as a result of the continuing supplies of arms from outside.

In August, the Council requested the Secretary-General to negotiate an agreement with Sierra Leone to create an independent court to bring to justice those responsible for committing serious crimes against the people of Sierra Leone.

Role of diamonds in conflict

Sierra Leone forwarded to the Security Council a 28 June memorandum [S/2000/641] on the role of diamonds in the conflict in Sierra Leone and the establishment of a certificate-of-origin regime for the export of rough diamonds from Sierra Leone. The Government, being of the view that the illicit export of Sierra Leone diamonds, especially through Liberia, was a major cause of the conflict in Sierra Leone and constituted the most formidable impediment to a peaceful resolution of the conflict, concurred with the idea that the export of diamonds should be temporarily prohibited until such time that a certificate-of-origin scheme was in full operation. That concurrence was based on the understanding that the temporary prohibition and the process of assessment by the Council's Sanctions Committee and endorsement by the Council would not be prolonged.

SECURITY COUNCIL ACTION

On 5 July [meeting 4168], the Security Council adopted **resolution 1306(2000)** by vote (14-0-1). The draft [S/2000/635] was submitted by the United Kingdom.

The Security Council,

Recalling its previous resolutions and the statements by its President concerning the situation in Sierra Leone, in particular resolutions 1132(1997) of 8 October 1997, 1171(1998) of 5 June 1998 and 1299(2000) of 19 May 2000,

Affirming the commitment of all States to respect the sovereignty, political independence and territorial integrity of Sierra Leone,

Having considered the report of the Secretary-General of 19 May 2000, in particular paragraph 94 thereof,

Determining that the situation in Sierra Leone continues to constitute a threat to international peace and security in the region,

Acting under Chapter VII of the Charter of the United Nations,

A

Expressing its concern at the role played by the illicit trade in diamonds in fuelling the conflict in Sierra Leone, and at reports that such diamonds transit neighbouring countries, including the territory of Liberia,

Welcoming ongoing efforts by interested States, the International Diamond Manufacturers Association, the World Federation of Diamond Bourses, the Diamond High Council, other representatives of the diamond industry and non-governmental experts to im-

prove the transparency of the international diamond trade, and encouraging further action in this regard,

Emphasizing that the legitimate diamond trade is of great economic importance for many States and can make a positive contribution to prosperity and stability and to the reconstruction of countries emerging from conflict, and emphasizing also that nothing in the present resolution is intended to undermine the legitimate diamond trade or to diminish confidence in the integrity of the legitimate diamond industry,

Welcoming the decision taken by States members of the Economic Community of West African States at their Abuja summit on 28 and 29 May 2000 to undertake a regional inquiry into the illegal trade in diamonds,

Taking note of the letter dated 29 June 2000 from the Permanent Representative of Sierra Leone to the United Nations addressed to the President of the Security Council and its enclosure,

1. *Decides* that all States shall take the necessary measures to prohibit the direct or indirect import of all rough diamonds from Sierra Leone to their territory;

2. *Requests* the Government of Sierra Leone to ensure, as a matter of urgency, that an effective certificate-of-origin regime for trade in diamonds is in operation in Sierra Leone;

3. *Requests* States, relevant international organizations and other bodies in a position to do so to offer assistance to the Government of Sierra Leone to facilitate the full operation of an effective certificate-of-origin regime for Sierra Leone rough diamonds;

4. *Requests* the Government of Sierra Leone to notify the Security Council Committee established pursuant to resolution 1132(1997) of the details of such a certificate-of-origin regime when it is fully in operation;

5. *Decides* that rough diamonds controlled by the Government of Sierra Leone through the certificate-of-origin regime shall be exempt from the measures imposed in paragraph 1 above when the Security Council Committee has reported to the Council, taking into account expert advice obtained at the request of the Committee through the Secretary-General, that an effective regime is fully in operation;

6. *Decides also* that the measures referred to in paragraph 1 above are established for an initial period of eighteen months, and affirms that, at the end of that period, it will review the situation in Sierra Leone, including the extent of the Government's authority over the diamond-producing areas, in order to decide whether to extend those measures for a further period and, if necessary, to modify them or adopt further measures;

7. *Decides further* that the Security Council Committee shall also undertake the following tasks:

(a) To seek from all States further information regarding the action taken by them with a view to implementing effectively the measures imposed by paragraph 1 above;

(b) To consider information brought to its attention concerning violations of the measures imposed by paragraph 1 above, identifying where possible persons or entities, including vessels, reported to be engaged in such violations;

(c) To make periodic reports to the Council on information submitted to it regarding alleged violations

of the measures imposed by paragraph 1 above, identifying where possible persons or entities, including vessels, reported to be engaged in such violations;

(d) To promulgate such guidelines as may be necessary to facilitate the implementation of the measures imposed by paragraph 1 above;

(e) To continue its cooperation with other relevant sanctions committees, in particular that established pursuant to resolution 985(1995) of 13 April 1995 concerning the situation in Liberia and that established pursuant to resolution 864(1993) of 15 September 1993 concerning the situation in Angola;

8. *Requests* all States to report to the Security Council Committee established pursuant to resolution 1132(1997), within thirty days of the adoption of the present resolution, on the actions they have taken to implement the measures imposed by paragraph 1 above;

9. *Calls upon* all States, in particular those through which rough diamonds from Sierra Leone are known to transit, and all relevant international and regional organizations to act strictly in accordance with the provisions of the present resolution, notwithstanding the existence of any rights or obligations conferred or imposed by any international agreement or any contract entered into or any licence or permit granted prior to the date of adoption of the present resolution;

10. *Encourages* the International Diamond Manufacturers Association, the World Federation of Diamond Bourses, the Diamond High Council and all other representatives of the diamond industry to work with the Government of Sierra Leone and the Security Council Committee to develop methods and working practices to facilitate the effective implementation of the present resolution;

11. *Invites* States, international organizations, members of the diamond industry and other relevant entities in a position to do so to offer assistance to the Government of Sierra Leone to contribute to the further development of a well-structured and well-regulated diamond industry that provides for the identification of the provenance of rough diamonds;

12. *Requests* the Security Council Committee to hold an exploratory hearing in New York, no later than 31 July 2000, to assess the role of diamonds in the Sierra Leone conflict and the link between trade in Sierra Leone diamonds and trade in arms and related materiel in violation of resolution 1171(1998), involving representatives of interested States and regional organizations, the diamond industry and other relevant experts, requests the Secretary-General to provide the necessary resources, and further requests the Committee to report on the hearing to the Council;

13. *Welcomes* the commitments made by certain members of the diamond industry not to trade in diamonds originating from conflict zones, including in Sierra Leone, urges all other companies and individuals involved in trading in rough diamonds to make similar declarations in respect of Sierra Leone diamonds, and underlines the importance of relevant financial institutions encouraging such companies to do so;

14. *Stresses* the need for the extension of government authority to the diamond-producing areas for a durable solution to the problem of illegal exploitation of diamonds in Sierra Leone;

15. *Decides* to conduct a first review on the measures imposed by paragraph 1 above, no later than 15 September 2000, and further reviews every six months following the date of adoption of the present resolution, and to consider at those times what further measures may be necessary;

16. *Urges* all States, relevant United Nations bodies and, as appropriate, other organizations and interested parties to report to the Security Council Committee information on possible violations of the measures imposed by paragraph 1 above;

B

Stressing the need to ensure effective implementation of the measures concerning arms and related materiel imposed by paragraph 2 of resolution 1171(1998),

Stressing also the obligation of all Member States, including those neighbouring Sierra Leone, to comply fully with the measures imposed by the Council,

Recalling the Moratorium on the Importation, Exportation and Manufacture of Light Weapons in West Africa adopted in Abuja on 31 October 1998 by the heads of State and Government of the Economic Community of West African States,

17. *Reminds* States of their obligation to implement fully the measures imposed by resolution 1171(1998), and calls upon them, where they have not already done so, to enforce, strengthen or enact, as appropriate, legislation making it a criminal offence under domestic law for their nationals or other persons operating on their territory to act in violation of the measures imposed by paragraph 2 of that resolution, and to report to the Security Council Committee no later than 31 July 2000 on the implementation of those measures;

18. *Urges* all States, relevant United Nations bodies and, as appropriate, other organizations and interested parties to report to the Security Council Committee information on possible violations of the measures imposed by the Council;

19. *Requests* the Secretary-General, in consultation with the Security Council Committee, to establish a panel of experts, for an initial period of four months, consisting of no more than five members:

(a) To collect information on possible violations of the measures imposed by paragraph 2 of resolution 1171(1998) and the link between trade in diamonds and trade in arms and related materiel, including through visits to Sierra Leone and other States, as appropriate, and making contact with those they consider appropriate, including diplomatic missions;

(b) To consider the adequacy, for the purpose of detecting flights by aircraft suspected of carrying arms and related materiel across national borders in violation of the measures imposed by paragraph 2 of resolution 1171(1998), of air traffic control systems in the region;

(c) To participate, if possible, in the hearing referred to in paragraph 12 above;

(d) To report to the Council through the Security Council Committee with observations and recommendations on strengthening the implementation of the measures imposed by paragraph 2 of resolution 1171(1998), and those imposed by paragraph 1 above, no later than 31 October 2000;

and also requests the Secretary-General to provide the necessary resources;

20. *Expresses its readiness*, on the basis, inter alia, of the report produced pursuant to paragraph 19 *(d)* above, to consider appropriate action in relation to States that it determines to have violated the measures imposed by paragraph 2 of resolution 1171(1998) and paragraph 1 above;

21. *Urges* all States to cooperate with the panel in the discharge of its mandate, and underlines, in this regard, the importance of the cooperation and technical expertise of the Secretariat and other parts of the United Nations system;

22. *Requests* the Security Council Committee to strengthen existing contacts with regional organizations, in particular the Economic Community of West African States and the Organization of African Unity, and relevant international organizations, including Interpol, with a view to identifying ways to improve effective implementation of the measures imposed by paragraph 2 of resolution 1171(1998);

23. *Also requests* the Security Council Committee to make information it considers relevant publicly available through appropriate media, including through the improved use of information technology;

24. *Requests* the Secretary-General to publicize the provisions of the present resolution and the obligations imposed thereby;

25. *Decides* to remain actively seized of the matter.

VOTE ON RESOLUTION 1306(2000):

In favour: Argentina, Bangladesh, Canada, China, France, Jamaica, Malaysia, Namibia, Netherlands, Russian Federation, Tunisia, Ukraine, United Kingdom, United States.
Against: None.
Abstaining: Mali.

Before the vote, Mali, as Chairman of ECOWAS, explained that the draft's open accusation of an ECOWAS member State, whose President had played a constructive role in the Sierra Leone peace process, was unacceptable.

Sanctions Committee

The Chairman of the Security Council Committee established pursuant to resolution 1132(1997) concerning Sierra Leone reported to the Council several times in 2000 on the arms embargo and the ban on the export of rough diamonds. In four July letters [S/2000/659, S/2000/660, S/2000/730, S/2000/739], the Chairman notified the Council that the United Kingdom had informed it of exports of military goods to the Government of Sierra Leone for use by its army and for use by the Ghanaian contingent of UNAMSIL. In November [S/2000/1127], the United Kingdom reported that it had again sent military equipment for use by UNAMSIL forces.

The Committee held public hearings on 31 July and 1 August to assess the role of diamonds in the Sierra Leone conflict and the link between trade in Sierra Leone diamonds and trade in arms. The discussions, involving representatives of interested States and regional organizations, the diamond industry and other relevant experts, were summarized in a December report [S/2000/1150]. Recommendations included ways and means to develop a sustainable and well regulated diamond industry in Sierra Leone. The Libyan Arab Jamahiriya, on 4 August [S/2000/771], rejected allegations made by the United States at those hearings that Libya was involved in the smuggling of arms to RUF. Libya gave examples of its efforts to promote national reconciliation in Sierra Leone.

The Chairman of the Sanctions Committee reported that, as at 4 December [S/2000/861 & Add.1], 21 countries had replied to the Council's request for information on any legislation on the arms embargo. The Chairman also reported that, as at 4 December [S/2000/862 & Add.1], 36 countries had replied to the Council's request for information on legislation pertaining to the ban on import of rough diamonds from Sierra Leone.

On 6 October [S/2000/966], the Chairman stated that the Government of Sierra Leone had submitted to the Committee a new mining, export and monitoring regime for rough and uncut diamonds from Sierra Leone, together with a draft new forgery-proof certificate-of-origin document and a copy of the Mines and Minerals (Amendments) Act of 1999. The Committee had no objection to the new procedures; therefore, rough diamonds controlled by the Government through the new certification regime would be exempt from the import ban on rough diamonds from Sierra Leone. Details of the new regime were transmitted to the Council on 4 December [S/2000/1151].

The Chairman, on 26 December [S/2000/1238], transmitted to the Council a report on the Committee's activities since the beginning of 2000. During the year, it held seven meetings. The Committee granted exemptions to the travel ban on officials of Sierra Leone opposition groups and on the export to Sierra Leone of arms. In addition to the hearings on conflict diamonds, the Committee reviewed Sierra Leone's proposed certification process and information regarding alleged violations of sanctions. Since the Committee had no specific monitoring mechanism to ensure implementation of the sanctions, it urged all Member States and organizations to provide it with pertinent information. In particular, reports from UNAMSIL and ECOWAS could assist the Committee.

In December, the General Assembly took action on the role of diamonds in fuelling conflict: breaking the link between the illicit transaction of rough diamonds and armed conflict as a contribution to prevention and settlement of conflicts (**resolution 55/56**) (see p. 77).

Panel of experts on diamonds and arms

In response to resolution 1306(2000), the Secretary-General, on 2 August [S/2000/756], informed the Security Council that he had established a panel of five experts to collect information on possible violations of the arms embargo and the ban on rough diamond exports, and to consider the adequacy of air traffic control systems in the region. Liberia, in a 13 December letter to the Secretary-General [S/2000/1192], welcomed the concept and the mandate of the panel, but noted that some Council members had mounted pressure on panel members in order to undermine the objectivity of the panel's report; therefore, Liberia was concerned that the report might lack objectivity and fairness.

The report of the Panel of Experts on Sierra Leone Diamonds and Arms was submitted to the Council on 20 December [S/2000/1195]. Estimates of the volume of RUF diamonds varied from $25 million to $125 million per annum. It represented a major primary source of income for RUF and was more than enough to sustain its military activities. The bulk of the RUF diamonds left Sierra Leone through Liberia. Such trade could not be conducted without the permission and the involvement of Liberian government officials at the highest level. Regarding Sierra Leone's new certification system, the report said it was largely irrelevant where RUF's conflict diamonds were concerned. As long as there were no controls in neighbouring countries, RUF would continue to move its diamonds out with impunity. For that reason, a standardized global certification scheme was necessary. A large volume of diamonds entering Europe was disguised as Liberian, Guinean and Gambian in order to evade taxation and launder money, and there was much fraudulent commercial reporting, flagrant examples of which in Belgium were provided.

In the absence of a global system, it was recommended that certification systems similar to that adopted by Sierra Leone be required of all diamond-exporting countries in West Africa, with special and immediate reference to Côte d'Ivoire and Guinea, to protect their indigenous industries and prevent their exposure to conflict diamonds. The Panel further recommended a complete embargo on all diamonds from Liberia until it stopped the trafficking of arms to, or diamonds from, Sierra Leone. Special attention was required to imports from a number of other African States, in particular by the importing countries, including India, Israel, South Africa, Switzerland, the United Kingdom and the United States. Those major trading centres plus Belgium needed to reach agreement on the recording and documentation of rough diamond imports that was consistent and that designated the country of origin in addition to country of provenance (last exporting country). An annual statistical production report should be compiled by each exporting country and gathered into a central annual report.

In addition to the numerous specific recommendations dealing with diamonds, the Panel made recommendations on weapons and the use of aircraft for sanctions-busting and the movement of illicit weapons. Many of those recommendations and the problems they addressed were related to the primary support of RUF, namely Liberia—its President, its Government and the individuals and companies it did business with. Liberia was actively breaking the Council embargoes regarding weapons imports into its own territory and into Sierra Leone. It was being assisted actively by Burkina Faso and tacitly by countries allowing weapons to pass through or over their territory without question, and by those countries that provided a base for the aircraft used in such operations. The report gave technical details on the adequacy of air traffic control and surveillance systems within the region.

The Panel noted with concern that Council resolutions on diamonds and weapons were being broken with impunity. It recommended that a travel ban similar to that already imposed on senior Liberian officials and diplomats by the United States be considered by all UN Member States until Liberia ended its support to RUF. The principals in Liberia's timber industry were also involved in a variety of illicit activities, and large amounts of the proceeds were used to pay for weapons, among other things. Consideration should be given to a temporary embargo on Liberian timber exports until Liberia demonstrated that it was no longer involved in the trafficking of arms to, or diamonds from, Sierra Leone. It was further suggested that consideration should be given to creating capacity within the Secretariat to carry out ongoing monitoring of Council sanctions and embargoes.

Switzerland, on 21 December [S/2000/1232], said that it had been singled out with regard to customs warehouses. Switzerland would study the report's recommendations. However, it had already taken measures to strengthen controls on the transit of diamonds that had not been reflected in the report. The Gambia, on 28 December [S/2001/8], said that while it was likely that diamonds might be transiting through the Gambia, the Government had neither condoned nor involved itself in such transactions and did not derive any revenue from that trade.

Proposal for special court

President Kabbah, in a 12 June letter to the Security Council, forwarded on 9 August [S/2000/786], called on the United Nations to set up a special court for Sierra Leone in order to try and bring to justice those RUF members and others responsible for committing crimes against the people of Sierra Leone and for taking UN peacekeepers as hostages. Mr. Kabbah also requested the Council's assistance in establishing a court to meet the objectives of bringing justice and ensuring lasting peace. Under the Lomé Agreement, amnesty had been granted to the RUF leadership, but it had since reneged on that Agreement and had resumed atrocities, including murder, amputation and the use of women and girls as sex slaves. Its members had abducted over 500 UN peacekeepers and seized their arms, and killed some of the peacekeepers. In order to expedite the establishment of a special court, Mr. Kabbah invited the Council to send a team of inquiry to assess the needs and concerns regarding Sierra Leone's ability to provide justice. With regard to the magnitude and extent of the crimes committed, Sierra Leone did not have the resources or expertise to conduct trials for such crimes. Annexed to the letter was a suggested framework for the proposed special court.

SECURITY COUNCIL ACTION (August)

On 14 August [meeting 4186], the Security Council unanimously adopted **resolution 1315(2000)**. The draft [S/2000/789] was prepared in consultations among Council members.

The Security Council,

Deeply concerned at the very serious crimes committed within the territory of Sierra Leone against the people of Sierra Leone and United Nations and associated personnel and at the prevailing situation of impunity,

Commending the efforts of the Government of Sierra Leone and the Economic Community of West African States to bring lasting peace to Sierra Leone,

Noting that the heads of State and Government of the Economic Community of West African States agreed at the twenty-third summit of that organization, held in Abuja on 28 and 29 May 2000, to dispatch a regional investigation of the resumption of hostilities,

Noting also the steps taken by the Government of Sierra Leone in creating a national truth and reconciliation process, as required by article XXVI of the Peace Agreement signed in Lomé on 7 July 1999 to contribute to the promotion of the rule of law,

Recalling that the Special Representative of the Secretary-General appended to his signature of the Peace Agreement a statement that the United Nations holds the understanding that the amnesty provisions of the Agreement shall not apply to international crimes of genocide, crimes against humanity, war crimes and other serious violations of international humanitarian law,

Reaffirming the importance of compliance with international humanitarian law, and reaffirming also that persons who commit or authorize serious violations of international humanitarian law are individually responsible and accountable for those violations and that the international community will exert every effort to bring those responsible to justice in accordance with international standards of justice, fairness and due process of law,

Recognizing that, in the particular circumstances of Sierra Leone, a credible system of justice and accountability for the very serious crimes committed there would end impunity and would contribute to the process of national reconciliation and to the restoration and maintenance of peace,

Taking note in this regard of the letter dated 12 June 2000 from the President of Sierra Leone to the Secretary-General and the suggested framework transmitted therewith,

Recognizing the desire of the Government of Sierra Leone for assistance from the United Nations in establishing a strong and credible court that will meet the objectives of bringing justice and ensuring lasting peace,

Taking note of the report of the Secretary-General of 31 July 2000, and, in particular, taking note with appreciation of the steps already taken by the Secretary-General in response to the request by the Government of Sierra Leone to assist it in establishing a special court,

Noting the negative impact of the security situation on the administration of justice in Sierra Leone and the pressing need for international cooperation to assist in strengthening the judicial system of Sierra Leone,

Acknowledging the important contribution that can be made to that effort by qualified persons from West African States, the Commonwealth, other States Members of the United Nations and international organizations, to expedite the process of bringing justice and reconciliation to Sierra Leone and the region,

Reiterating that the situation in Sierra Leone continues to constitute a threat to international peace and security in the region,

1. *Requests* the Secretary-General to negotiate an agreement with the Government of Sierra Leone to create an independent special court consistent with the present resolution, and expresses its readiness to take further steps expeditiously upon receiving and reviewing the report of the Secretary-General referred to in paragraph 6 below;

2. *Recommends* that the subject matter jurisdiction of the special court should include notably crimes against humanity, war crimes and other serious violations of international humanitarian law, as well as crimes under relevant Sierra Leonean law committed within the territory of Sierra Leone;

3. *Recommends also* that the special court should have personal jurisdiction over persons who bear the greatest responsibility for the commission of the crimes referred to in paragraph 2 above, including those leaders who, in committing such crimes, have threatened the establishment and implementation of the peace process in Sierra Leone;

4. *Emphasizes* the importance of ensuring the impartiality, independence and credibility of the process,

in particular with regard to the status of the judges and the prosecutors;

5. *Requests*, in this connection, that the Secretary-General, if necessary, send a team of experts to Sierra Leone as may be required to prepare the report referred to in paragraph 6 below;

6. *Requests* the Secretary-General to submit a report to the Security Council on the implementation of the present resolution, in particular on his consultations and negotiations with the Government of Sierra Leone concerning the establishment of the special court, including recommendations, no later than thirty days from the date of the present resolution;

7. *Also requests* the Secretary-General to address in his report the questions of the temporal jurisdiction of the special court, an appeals process, including the advisability, feasibility, and appropriateness of an appeals chamber in the special court or of sharing the Appeals Chamber of the International Tribunals for the Former Yugoslavia and Rwanda or other effective options, and a possible alternative host State, should it be necessary to convene the special court outside the seat of the court in Sierra Leone, if circumstances so require;

8. *Further requests* the Secretary-General to include recommendations on the following:

(*a*) Any additional agreements that may be required for the provision of the international assistance that will be necessary for the establishment and functioning of the special court;

(*b*) The level of participation, support and technical assistance of qualified persons from States Members of the United Nations, including, in particular, States members of the Economic Community of West African States and the Commonwealth, and from the United Nations Mission in Sierra Leone that will be necessary for the efficient, independent and impartial functioning of the special court;

(*c*) The amount of voluntary contributions, as appropriate, of funds, equipment and services to the special court, including through the offer of expert personnel that may be needed from States, intergovernmental organizations and non-governmental organizations;

(*d*) Whether the special court could receive, as necessary and feasible, expertise and advice from the International Tribunals for the Former Yugoslavia and Rwanda;

9. *Decides* to remain actively seized of the matter.

Sierra Leone, on 14 August [S/2000/803], welcomed the Council's firm commitment to establish an independent special court, which, it said, went beyond the mere expression of abhorrence at the atrocities committed against the people of Sierra Leone and sent a message to the perpetrators that collective action was currently being taken to end impunity in the country.

Report of Secretary-General. In response to resolution 1315(2000), the Secretary-General, on 4 October, reported on the establishment of a special court for Sierra Leone [S/2000/915]. He examined and analysed the nature and specificity of the Special Court, its jurisdiction (subject matter, temporal and personal), the organizational

structure (the Chambers and the nature of the appeals process, the Prosecutor's Office and the Registry), enforcement of sentences in third States and the choice of the alternative seat. It also dealt with the practical arrangements for the Court's operation and the financial mechanism envisaged. Annexed to the report were the draft Agreement between the United Nations and the Government of Sierra Leone on the Establishment of a Special Court for Sierra Leone and a draft Statute of the Court. The Secretary-General also recommended that a broad public information and education campaign be undertaken as part of the Court's activities.

Noting that a credible system of justice for the serious crimes committed in Sierra Leone would end impunity and contribute to the process of national reconciliation and to the restoration and maintenance of peace, the Secretary-General stated that the Council should bear in mind the expectations that had been created and the state of urgency that permeated all discussions of the problem of impunity in Sierra Leone.

The Council reviewed the Secretary-General's report and issued its comments in a 22 December letter [S/2000/1234]. Reaffirming its support for resolution 1315(2000), the Council suggested that the draft Agreement and the proposed Statute be amended to incorporate the Council's suggestions in regard to personal jurisdiction, funding and court size.

Later developments

Report of Secretary-General (August). The Secretary-General issued his sixth report on UNAMSIL on 24 August [S/2000/832], as requested by the Council in resolution 1313(2000). Reviewing the strengthened mandate of the force under that resolution, the Secretary-General said that the main objectives would be to assist the Government's efforts to extend State authority, restore law and order and stabilize the situation progressively throughout the country, and to assist in the promotion of the political process, leading to a renewed disarmament, demobilization and reintegration programme where possible. The key elements of a political process included the restoration of civil authority throughout the country, the establishment and/or strengthening of national institutions, including democratically accountable armed forces and a national police force, free and fair elections, national reconciliation and respect for human rights and provision of emergency relief assistance. Achieving those objectives would require a robust military presence by the international community for the foreseeable future in order to maintain a level of security. In due course, the Government would have to assume full responsibility for its own security; therefore, the military training assistance provided to the armed forces of Sierra Leone by the United Kingdom and other Member States and the assistance provided by the Commonwealth for the training of the police force were welcomed. Offers of further assistance to improve Sierra Leone's operational capacity would be of significant value.

In reviewing UNAMSIL's strength, account had to be taken of the precarious security situation, the RUF threat and the regional dimension of the conflict. In addition, the country's infrastructure had suffered tremendous damage. In many cases, resupply of troops could be provided only by air. The dense vegetation was favourable to guerrilla tactics such as ambushes and concealed movement. On 21 August, RUF announced it had designated Issa Sesay as its interim leader to replace Foday Sankoh, following diplomatic efforts by ECOWAS leaders. Nevertheless, it continued its forcible recruitment of new fighters and the RUF threat against the general population, government forces and UNAMSIL remained real. The forces fighting for the Government, mainly SLA and the Civil Defence Force, were still in the process of training, and they continued to experience problems with command and control and logistical support. The United Kingdom was providing training to the new SLA. The most urgent tasks for UNAMSIL were restructuring the force, strengthening its headquarters, equipping its battalions and strengthening deployment in areas close to RUF positions, to the extent that its authorized strength of 13,000 military personnel allowed.

To achieve its objectives, UNAMSIL would be required to deploy progressively to strategic positions throughout the country in an operational structure and in sufficient numbers and density. The Secretary-General outlined a plan for phased deployment, to be accompanied by coordinated political steps, involving the Government of Sierra Leone, ECOWAS and the United Nations, as well as a public information campaign. Such efforts would be aimed at seeking the compliance of rebel groups with the peace process and encouraging them to join the disarmament, demobilization and reintegration programme. In order to deploy fully as outlined by the Secretary-General, the total strength of the force would need to be 20,500, and subsequent deployment to key areas not currently under government control would require additional resources. In addition to expanding UNAMSIL's strength, the Secretary-General recommended that the Council authorize an extension of its mandate,

due to expire on 8 September, for another six months.

The report's addendum [S/2000/832/Add.1] indicated that the expansion of the Mission would entail an additional expense of $305.5 million for the 2000-2001 financial period.

SECURITY COUNCIL ACTION (September)

On 5 September [meeting 4193], the Security Council unanimously adopted **resolution 1317 (2000)**. The draft [S/2000/846] was prepared in consultations among Council members.

The Security Council,
Recalling its resolutions 1270(1999) of 22 October 1999, 1289(2000) of 7 February 2000 and 1313(2000) of 4 August 2000 and all other relevant resolutions and the statements by its President concerning the situation in Sierra Leone,
1. *Decides* to extend the present mandate of the United Nations Mission in Sierra Leone until 20 September 2000;
2. *Decides* to remain actively seized of the matter.

On 20 September [meeting 4199], the Council unanimously adopted **resolution 1321(2000)**. The draft [S/2000/882] was prepared in consultations among Council members.

The Security Council,
Recalling its resolutions 1270(1999) of 22 October 1999, 1289(2000) of 7 February 2000, 1313(2000) of 4 August 2000, 1317(2000) of 5 September 2000 and all other relevant resolutions and the statements by its President concerning the situation in Sierra Leone,
1. *Decides* to extend the present mandate of the United Nations Mission in Sierra Leone until 31 December 2000;
2. *Decides also* to review the situation no later than 31 October 2000;
3. *Decides* to remain actively seized of the matter.

The Security Council, on 20 September [S/2000/886], informed the Secretary-General of its decision to send a mission to Sierra Leone from 7 to 14 October. The mission's terms of reference were: to consider ways to ensure the full application of the Council's resolutions on Sierra Leone and the implementation of measures taken by the Secretary-General to enhance - UNAMSIL's effectiveness; to support the Government's efforts and review with it progress made in implementing the Lomé Peace Agreement; to consider the regional dimensions of the crisis, including its humanitarian aspects, and, in particular, to work with the leaders of neighbouring States and ECOWAS to promote a solution to the conflict; and to follow up the report of the Secretary-General on the establishment of a special court for Sierra Leone as envisaged in Council resolution 1315(2000) (see p. 205).

On 26 September [S/2000/903], the Council informed the Secretary-General of the composition of the 10-member mission (later expanded to 11 members) and requested that arrangements be made for its support.

Report of Security Council mission. The Security Council's mission to Sierra Leone issued its report on 16 October [S/2000/992] after an eight-day visit to the region (Guinea, Sierra Leone, Mali, Nigeria and Liberia). It found that UNAMSIL had begun to make progress after the setbacks and pressures caused by RUF attacks against peacekeepers and renewed fighting in May. It noted, however, that different contingents had different perceptions of UNAMSIL's mandate and tasks. Since the visit of an assessment team from 31 May to 8 June, progress had been made with regard to communication and coordination within UNAMSIL, as well as with UN agencies and NGOs; however, key areas that still needed to be addressed were full integration with headquarters, better coordination of logistics and arrangements for contingent-owned equipment. The planned withdrawal of the Indian contingent in November constituted a serious loss for UNAMSIL and the civilian component of the Mission was understaffed. It was generally agreed that the strength of the force needed to be increased in order to deploy in strength throughout Sierra Leone, including the border with Liberia and the diamond-producing areas. Nigeria had indicated its readiness to contribute either to UNAMSIL or to a mission authorized by ECOWAS, but needed equipment to bring its units to the required levels.

The mission concluded that the highest priority should be given to the coordination of a comprehensive strategy with clear objectives. Its first recommendation, therefore, was for the establishment of a UN-based mechanism for overall coordination. It also suggested military measures to enhance security in the country and on its borders. The current tentative indications of RUF interest in dialogue should be thoroughly explored, and the Secretary-General's Special Representative might give priority to the coordination of contacts, liaising in particular, beyond UNAMSIL itself, with the Presidents of Sierra Leone, Guinea, Mali, Nigeria and Liberia.

Regarding the peace process, the fundamental principles of the Lomé Peace Agreement remained valid. The conclusion of a ceasefire and the withdrawal of RUF forces from key areas of the country, in particular the diamond fields, should remain prime objectives. Renewed dialogue with both RUF leadership and with commanders at the local level should be pursued and the process should also include the return of all

seized UNAMSIL weapons and equipment and the opening up of humanitarian and other access in the north and east of the country. The peace process should also focus on disarmament, demobilization and reintegration. In that context, the Security Council and the Sierra Leonean authorities would need to reflect before taking any final decisions on the scope of the Special Court. A balance had to be struck between the requirements of justice and the need to minimize any potential disincentive to entering the disarmament, demobilization and reintegration process that the threat of prosecution might represent, especially to child combatants.

The military track remained an indispensable element of the peace process to maintain pressure on RUF and create incentives for dialogue and disarmament. To meet those demands, UNAMSIL needed to be strengthened in terms of numbers, effectiveness and capability, as recommended by the Secretary-General, taking advantage of the offers of further troops from, among others, ECOWAS countries.

Instability in the West African region, in particular in the Mano River Union (MRU) countries, also needed to be addressed. Regional leaders believed that the relationship of President Taylor of Liberia with RUF was a key to the situation in Sierra Leone. Illicit trafficking in diamonds and arms, the proliferation and encouragement of militias and armed groups, and the massive flows of refugees and internally displaced persons resulting from their activities had to be addressed directly. The region, through ECOWAS, was showing willingness to take the lead, under its current Chairman, in undertaking specific action in those areas. The Council and individual Governments should consider support for the ECOWAS decision to deploy an observer force on the borders of the three MRU countries, in coordination with UNAMSIL. Guinea, in particular, needed support to provide access and protection for humanitarian personnel and aid.

The disarmament, demobilization and reintegration programme needed to be reoriented, and the Council should decide on a proper balance of responsibilities in the programme among the Government, the World Bank, UNAMSIL and bilateral agencies. The primary responsibility for the resolution of the conflict rested with the Government, Parliament and people of Sierra Leone, and the Government needed to communicate its vision for taking the peace process forward as well as for development. Advice and financial help on a communications and public awareness strategy would be useful. The mission recommended that UNAMSIL and ECOWAS explore with RUF the possibility of access under conditions of security for a needs assessment to be conducted in areas under its control, and for safe access for the delivery of humanitarian assistance. The vacant UNAMSIL human rights posts should be filled as soon as possible and the proposed Human Rights Commission should be established at an early date.

As to coordination, the mission stated that, at a minimum, the Security Council and the Secretariat, ECOWAS, UNAMSIL troop-contributing countries and the Government of Sierra Leone needed to consult through some form of continuous structure. As a first step, the mission recommended international assistance to help the ECOWAS secretariat to develop its capacity, including the placing of UNAMSIL liaison staff at ECOWAS headquarters.

Report of Secretary-General (October). The Secretary-General, in his seventh report on UNAMSIL dated 31 October and reissued on 7 November [S/2000/1055], said that the situation in Sierra Leone had been at a political and military standstill since the events of May/June. Since 24 August, the efforts of UNAMSIL and ECOWAS had been focused on creating a political and security environment conducive to resuming the peace process. In spite of the designation of a new interim RUF leader, Issa Sesay, which was facilitated by the Presidents of Mali and Nigeria, there had been no progress towards establishing a political dialogue and possible ceasefire. There were reports that some RUF field commanders were reluctant to recognize Mr. Sesay's authority. The designation of Mr. Sesay as interim leader had enabled UNAMSIL to establish limited informal contacts with RUF, focusing on the return of weapons and equipment seized from UNAMSIL and on humanitarian access to areas under RUF control. UNAMSIL received reports that RUF was preparing for military operations in Guinea and some RUF commanders refused to disarm or give up diamond-mining areas under their control. At the same time, the Government continued military operations against RUF.

During the reporting period, relative calm had prevailed although the security situation remained unpredictable and precarious, and was marked by the increase in cross-border attacks along the border area of Guinea, Liberia and Sierra Leone (see above, under "Guinea"). Within Sierra Leone, there was no change in the areas controlled by either RUF or pro-Government forces. RUF largely maintained a defensive posture, but also continued to mobilize its forces in its strongholds and to dig craters on major roads. There were several attacks on UNAMSIL by RUF and by ex-SLA/AFRC, known as the West Side group, the leadership of which had been taken over by Foday Kallay. On 25 August, 11 British military personnel, involved in training the Sierra Leone Army, and one Sierra Leone Army officer were taken hostage by the West Side group. A successful rescue mission dislodged the group from its Occra Hills base. The group lost most of its fighting capability and Kallay and other key combatants were captured. The training programme, led by United Kingdom soldiers, continued, but the Sierra Leone Army suffered from lack of leadership and logistics.

UNAMSIL military strength stood at 12,510 as at 30 October; peacekeepers conducted patrols and cordon and search operations and provided humanitarian assistance to the local population in their areas of operation. The disarmament, demobilization and reintegration activities were limited due to ongoing hostilities. A total of 706 ex-combatants joined the programme during the period from 8 May to 13 October. Civilian police advisers focused on the promotion of community policy in Freetown and in the south, where the effectiveness of the Sierra Leone Police Force was gradually being restored. Civil affairs activities included further contacts with local leaders and surveys to identify areas needing immediate assistance. The public information section produced regular radio broadcasts, press briefings and printed materials.

With regard to human rights, the Secretary-General expressed the view that the establishment of the Special Court for Sierra Leone and the Truth and Reconciliation Commission could contribute to ending impunity and developing respect for the rule of law, and bring closure to victims of human rights abuses. The Government had approved the establishment of a commission for war-affected children. The humanitarian situation continued to deteriorate with lack of access severely restricting humanitarian operations inside the country. Since the resumption of hostilities in May, approximately 300,000 Sierra Leoneans had been displaced, bringing the total number of internally displaced persons in the country to 500,000.

In an effort to expand UNAMSIL to its full strength, the United Nations had held discussions with possible troop-contributing countries. India and Jordan announced their decisions to withdraw from the Mission. That and other troop movements would put a heavy strain on the Mission's logistic capabilities.

The Secretary-General supported the comprehensive approach suggested by the Security Council's mission to Sierra Leone (see p. 208), based on the continued provision of security by UNAMSIL in key areas. That would require an increase in the force's strength to 20,500, as he had recommended earlier. He appealed to Member States, in particular those with large and well-equipped armed forces, to participate in UNAMSIL so that the credibility of the international community's military presence in Sierra Leone was not undermined. In the meantime, the implementation of the Mission's mandate, in particular its deployment on the ground, would have to be adjusted in the light of the available resources. In the final analysis, the Secretary-General said, no lasting progress could be made in Sierra Leone without comprehensive action being taken to tackle the instability in the West African region, particularly the MRU countries.

Appointment. On 30 October [S/2000/1060], the Secretary-General informed the Security Council of his intention to appoint Lieutenant-General Daniel Ishmael Opande (Kenya) as Force Commander of UNAMSIL. The Council took note of the decision on 2 November [S/2000/1061].

SECURITY COUNCIL ACTION (November)

On 3 November [meeting 4216], following consultations among Security Council members, the President made statement **S/PRST/2000/31** on behalf of the Council:

The Security Council expresses its concern at the continued fragile situation in Sierra Leone and the related instability in the wider subregion. It condemns the continued cross-border attacks along the border area of Guinea, Liberia and Sierra Leone. The Council stresses that only through a comprehensive regional approach can security and stability be restored. In this regard, it expresses its support for the efforts undertaken by the Economic Community of West African States to address the situation, and calls upon Member States to provide support.

In this context, and following the return of its mission to Sierra Leone, the Council welcomes the recommendations made in the report of the mission. It expresses its support in particular for the establishment of a continuous, United Nations–based process for overall strategic coordination on Sierra Leone, bringing together members of the Council, the Secretariat, the Economic Community of West African States, countries contributing troops to the United Nations Mission in Sierra Leone and the Government of Sierra Leone. The Council notes the support of the Secretary-General for this proposal in his report of 31 October 2000 and encourages him to take early steps to put such a process into effect.

The Council underlines that such a coordinated strategy for lasting peace in Sierra Leone must combine both political and military elements. The Council fully supports efforts to strengthen the State institutions of Sierra Leone and to maintain the principles of democratic accountability and the rule of law. It also places emphasis on the humanitarian and human rights aspects. It welcomes the current efforts of the Economic Community of West African States to explore the possibilities for dialogue towards peace, but stresses that this should be pursued only under terms acceptable to the Government of Sierra Leone. In this context, the Council underlines the importance of the Revolutionary United Front relinquishing control of the diamond-producing areas, full freedom of movement for the Mission leading to its deployment throughout the country, proper provision for the disarmament and demobilization of all non-governmental forces, full and secure humanitarian access and the extension of the authority of the Government throughout its territory. The Council also calls upon those armed groups responsible for continuing human rights abuses to put an immediate end to such activities.

The Council is convinced that the continuation of a credible military presence of the international community in Sierra Leone remains an indispensable element of the peace process. The Council concurs with the view of the Secretary-General that a key aspect of the overall approach on Sierra Leone is continued provision of security by the Mission in key areas of the country. The Council reiterates its view that to achieve this, the Mission requires strengthening. The Council also underlines the importance of continued action to improve the effectiveness of the Mission through the full implementation of the recommendations of the May assessment mission. The Council notes the decisions by the Governments of India and Jordan to end participation by their troops in the Mission and expresses its appreciation for the important contribution made by these two contingents. It also warmly welcomes the new commitments made by Bangladesh and Ghana of additional battalions, by Ukraine of equipment and support personnel and by Slovakia of equipment to enhance force capability. The Council urges both departing and incoming contingents to display all possible flexibility to ensure that force capability is maintained as the Mission moves into this period of transition.

The Council supports the appeal by the Secretary-General to Member States, as set out in paragraph 55 of his report, urgently to consider participating in the Mission or otherwise contributing to its reinforcement, and encourages him to intensify his consultations to this end. The Council reiterates its firm intention to take action to strengthen the Mission at the appropriate time, taking into account the readiness of troop-contributing countries to provide sufficient forces to this end.

Abuja ceasefire agreement

On 10 November, the Government of Sierra Leone and RUF, at a meeting in Abuja, signed the Agreement on the Ceasefire and Cessation of Hostilities. By that text, forwarded to the Security Council by Mali on 13 November [S/2000/1091], the two parties agreed to a ceasefire to be supervised and monitored by UNAMSIL. UNAMSIL would report any violations to a committee comprising the ECOWAS Committee of Six on Sierra Leone, the ECOWAS secretariat, the United Nations, the Government of Sierra Leone and RUF.

The parties agreed that UNAMSIL would have full liberty to deploy its troops and other personnel throughout Sierra Leone, including the diamond-producing areas. They undertook to ensure free movement of persons and goods, and unimpeded movement of humanitarian agencies and of refugees and displaced persons. They agreed to recommence immediately the disarmament, demobilization and reintegration programme. RUF committed itself to return all weapons and other equipment it had seized. Implementation of the agreement would be reviewed after 30 days.

Report of Secretary-General (December). On 15 December, the Secretary-General issued his eighth report on UNAMSIL [S/2000/1199]. During the period under review, UNAMSIL attempted to follow up on its monitoring role in the light of the ceasefire agreement reached on 10 November. However, after an initial approach, efforts to contact the RUF leader were ignored until 8 December, and there were conflicting signals emanating from RUF about its intentions. The media quoted RUF officials as saying that the group was divided over the ceasefire and that the majority of combatants were no longer taking orders from Issa Sesay, a report that was later denied. On 8 December, the Force Commander met with RUF leader Sesay who pledged to cooperate with UNAMSIL and to uphold the ceasefire agreement; subsequently, UNAMSIL worked on modalities for monitoring the agreement. On 13 December, RUF returned 11 armoured vehicles, but they were stripped of all mounted weapons and equipment. No personal weapons were surrendered. The following day, as announced in a statement attributed to RUF, UNAMSIL was barred from entering RUF-controlled territory until certain "non-negotiable" conditions, including the release of Foday Sankoh, were met.

A meeting of the United Nations, ECOWAS and the Government of Sierra Leone Coordination Mechanism (Abuja, 8-9 November) discussed the ceasefire negotiations with RUF and ways to reactivate the peace process. The Coordination Mechanism agreed that RUF should be prevailed upon to accelerate the process of returning all remaining UN equipment and called on Member States and organizations concerned to facilitate the establishment of the ECOWAS commissions of investigation into the resumption of hostilities and into the illegal trade in Sierra Leonean diamonds. While endorsing the recommendations of the Security Council mission relating to ECOWAS, the meeting also agreed to seek further clarifications on some of the issues. Regarding the recommendation to establish a mechanism for the overall coordination of a comprehensive strategy for Sierra Leone, the Secretary-General's Special Representative had established

a contact group in Freetown, which consisted of the representatives of ECOWAS countries, members of the Security Council represented in Sierra Leone and major troop contributors.

The Secretary-General visited Sierra Leone on 2 and 3 December to assess UN operations and met with President Kabbah and other personalities to consider the way forward. He noted that, on the one hand, UNAMSIL had made progress in recovering from the May crisis and that significant efforts had been made to implement the recommendations of the assessment mission as well as those of the Security Council mission; on the other hand, the challenges confronting Sierra Leone were still daunting. UNAMSIL needed to strike a balance between its limited presence and the need to be proactive. Large areas of the country remained outside government control and were not accessible to humanitarian agencies. Furthermore, the regional dimension of the conflict needed to be addressed. If UNAMSIL was to assume new responsibilities in the disarmament, demobilization and reintegration programme as proposed, such as the provision of managerial, logistical and coordination support to demobilization camps and disarmament/reception sites, there would be significant implications for the Mission's mandate as well as its additional financial, human and other resources. The military strength, for example, would need to be expanded well beyond its current size of 12,455.

The security situation had remained relatively stable, with the exception of the border area with Guinea. Elsewhere, the ceasefire appeared to be holding. The Government continued to face considerable constraints in its efforts to restore its authority, even in those areas already under its control, due to lack of financial and logistical resources and, in some cases, security concerns. The human rights situation was exacerbated by the cross-border attacks against Guinea, allegedly by RUF, and reported human rights abuses committed by RUF in its harassment of civilians persisted, as did forcible recruitment of adults and children for fighting as well as forced labour. The humanitarian situation continued to deteriorate as Sierra Leonean refugees fleeing violence in neighbouring Guinea began returning home. Since early September, the Government of Sierra Leone had assisted in repatriating more than 20,000 Sierra Leonean refugees from Guinea by boat and an additional 11,500 refugees moved over land to the Lungi areas where they were receiving community-based assistance.

In general, despite some positive developments, the situation remained precarious. The fighting along the borders with Guinea and Liberia further complicated the situation. The reported involvement of RUF in those incursions raised serious questions about the sincerity of their commitment to disarmament and the peace process. The signing of the ceasefire agreement constituted a first step towards creating an environment conducive to the reactivation of the peace process. However, RUF needed to demonstrate its good faith by opening roads in areas it controlled so that the United Nations had access, and by returning to UNAMSIL all weapons seized from peacekeepers and proceeding with the disarmament, demobilization and reintegration of its combatants. Should RUF comply with the 10 November ceasefire agreement, UNAMSIL would be able to deploy forward gradually in the discharge of its mandate. However, that might require the Mission to expand beyond its authorized strength. The Secretary-General therefore urged all militarily capable countries to consider contributing equipped contingents to the Mission, and reiterated his recommendation to increase the strength to 20,500 personnel. In the meantime, he recommended the extension of UNAMSIL's mandate for another three months, to allow the Mission to respond to the requirements of the Abuja ceasefire agreement. The challenges confronting the country remained daunting and required the active support of the international community, he concluded.

SECURITY COUNCIL ACTION (December)

On 22 December [meeting 4253], the Security Council unanimously adopted **resolution 1334 (2000)**. The draft [S/2000/1224] was prepared in consultations among Council members.

The Security Council,

Recalling its resolutions 1270(1999) of 22 October 1999, 1289(2000) of 7 February 2000, 1313(2000) of 4 August 2000, 1317(2000) of 5 September 2000, 1321(2000) of 20 September 2000, the statement by its President of 3 November 2000, and all other relevant resolutions and the statements by its President concerning the situation in Sierra Leone,

Having considered the report of the Secretary-General of 15 December 2000,

1. *Expresses its continued concern* at the continuing fragile situation in Sierra Leone and neighbouring States;

2. *Takes note* of the Agreement on the Ceasefire and Cessation of Hostilities between the Government of the Republic of Sierra Leone and the Revolutionary United Front, signed in Abuja on 10 November 2000, expresses its concern at the failure of the Front fully to meet its obligations under the agreement, and calls upon it to give a more convincing demonstration of commitment to the ceasefire and the peace process;

3. *Recalls* that the main objectives of the United Nations Mission in Sierra Leone, as set out in resolution 1313(2000) and confirmed in the concept of operations proposed by the Secretary-General in his report of 24

August 2000, remain to assist the efforts of the Government of Sierra Leone to extend State authority, restore law and order and further stabilize the situation progressively throughout the entire country and to assist in the promotion of the political process, leading to a renewed disarmament, demobilization and reintegration programme where possible, and reiterates that, to that end, the structure, capability, resources and mandate of the Mission require appropriate strengthening;

4. *Commends* the continued efforts of the Secretary-General in that regard to seek further firm commitments of troops for the Mission, strongly urges all States in a position to do so seriously to consider contributing peacekeeping forces for Sierra Leone, and expresses its appreciation to those States which have already made such offers;

5. *Expresses its intention*, in that context, following consultations with troop-contributing countries, to respond promptly to any additional specific recommendations made by the Secretary-General in the next period on the force strength and tasks of the Mission;

6. *Decides* to extend the present mandate of the Mission until 31 March 2001;

7. *Decides* to remain actively seized of the matter.

UNOMSIL/UNAMSIL financing

The Secretary-General, in March [A/54/778], presented to the General Assembly the financial performance report of the United Nations Observer Mission in Sierra Leone (UNOMSIL), the mission that preceded UNAMSIL, for the period from its inception on 13 July 1998 to 30 June 1999. The Assembly had appropriated $22 million gross ($21,279,800 net) for that period, from which $16,167,100 gross ($15,706,550 net) had been assessed on Member States. Expenditures for the period totalled $12,883,800 gross ($12,397,000 net), resulting in an unutilized balance of $9,116,200 gross ($8,882,800 net). The unutilized balance of assessments amounted to $3,283,300 gross ($3,309,550 net). The unutilized balance of appropriations was attributable to the scaling back of UNOMSIL following the outbreak of hostilities in Freetown in mid-December 1998 and early January 1999. The Secretary-General recommended that the Assembly reduce the appropriation for UNOMSIL from $22 million gross to $16,167,100 gross, corresponding to the amount actually assessed on Member States, and make a decision on the treatment of the unutilized balance of $3,283,300.

In April [A/54/820], the Secretary-General reported on the revised budget for the operation of UNAMSIL for the period from 1 July 1999 to 30 June 2000, as well as the proposed budget for the period from 1 July 2000 to 30 June 2001. The 1999/2000 budget was revised after the Security Council, by **resolution 1289(2000)**, expanded UNAMSIL's military strength to 11,100 personnel. The revised 1999/2000 budget amounted to

$265,789,000 gross ($264,371,600 net) and represented an increase of some 33 per cent in gross terms over resources already appropriated for UNAMSIL by the Assembly in resolution 54/241 A [YUN 1999, p. 168]. The proposed budget for 1 July 2000 to 30 June 2001 amounted to $476,726,400 gross ($472,965,600 net).

The Secretary-General recommended that the Assembly appropriate and assess the additional amount of $65,789,000 gross ($66,606,500 net) for the maintenance of UNAMSIL from 1 July 1999 to 30 June 2000. He also recommended that it appropriate $476,726,400 gross ($472,965,600 net) to cover the following 12 months. Assessments in the amount of $47,672,640 gross ($47,296,560 net) were suggested for UNAMSIL maintenance from 1 July to 6 August 2000, as were assessments of $429,053,760 gross ($425,669,040 net) for the period from 7 August 2000 to 30 June 2001, at the monthly rate of $39,727,200 gross ($39,413,800 net), subject to the Council's extension of the UNAMSIL mandate.

ACABQ considered the Secretary-General's reports on UNOMSIL's financial performance and UNAMSIL's revised budget and, in May [A/54/858], recommended that the Assembly approve the proposal to reduce the appropriation for the establishment and operation of UNOMSIL as suggested, and that the unutilized balance be credited to Member States. It also recommended the approval of the request for the appropriation and assessment of the additional amount of $65,789,000 gross ($66,606,500 net) for the maintenance of UNAMSIL for the 1999/2000 period, and the appropriation and assessment of $476,726,400 gross ($472,965,600 net) for the maintenance of the Mission for the 2000/01 period.

GENERAL ASSEMBLY ACTION

On 15 June [meeting 98], the General Assembly, on the recommendation of the Fifth Committee [A/54/686/Add.1], adopted **resolution 54/241 B** without vote [agenda items 150 and 172].

Financing of the United Nations Observer Mission in Sierra Leone and financing of the United Nations Mission in Sierra Leone

The General Assembly,

Having considered the reports of the Secretary-General on the financing of the United Nations Observer Mission in Sierra Leone and the United Nations Mission in Sierra Leone and the related report of the Advisory Committee on Administrative and Budgetary Questions,

Bearing in mind Security Council resolutions 1181(1998) of 13 July 1998, by which the Council established the United Nations Observer Mission in Sierra Leone, 1270(1999) of 22 October 1999, by which the Council established the United Nations Mission in Si-

erra Leone, and 1289(2000) of 7 February 2000, by which the Council revised and extended the mandate of the Mission,

Recalling its resolutions 53/29 of 20 November 1998 and 54/241 A of 23 December 1999 on the financing of the Observer Mission and the United Nations Mission in Sierra Leone,

Reaffirming that the costs of the Mission are expenses of the Organization to be borne by Member States in accordance with Article 17, paragraph 2, of the Charter of the United Nations,

Recalling its previous decisions regarding the fact that, in order to meet the expenditures caused by the Mission, a different procedure is required from that applied to meet expenditures of the regular budget of the United Nations,

Taking into account the fact that the economically more developed countries are in a position to make relatively larger contributions and that the economically less developed countries have a relatively limited capacity to contribute towards such an operation,

Bearing in mind the special responsibilities of the States permanent members of the Security Council, as indicated in General Assembly resolution 1874(S-IV) of 27 June 1963, in the financing of such operations,

Noting with appreciation that voluntary contributions have been made to the Mission,

Mindful of the fact that it is essential to provide the Mission with the necessary financial resources to enable it to fulfil its responsibilities under the relevant resolutions of the Security Council,

1. *Takes note* of the status of contributions to the United Nations Mission in Sierra Leone as at 30 April 2000, including the contributions outstanding in the amount of 83.7 million United States dollars, representing 39 per cent of the total assessed contributions, notes that some 18 per cent of the Member States have paid their assessed contributions in full, and urges all other Member States concerned, in particular those in arrears, to ensure payment of their outstanding assessed contributions;

2. *Expresses its appreciation* to those Member States which have paid their assessed contributions in full;

3. *Expresses concern* about the financial situation with regard to peacekeeping activities, in particular as regards the reimbursements to troop contributors that bear additional burdens owing to overdue payments by Member States of their assessments;

4. *Urges* all other Member States to make every possible effort to ensure payment of their assessed contributions to the Mission in full and on time;

5. *Expresses concern* at the delay experienced by the Secretary-General in deploying and providing adequate resources to some recent peacekeeping missions, in particular those in Africa;

6. *Emphasizes* that all future and existing peacekeeping missions shall be given equal and non-discriminatory treatment in respect of financial and administrative arrangements;

7. *Also emphasizes* that all peacekeeping missions shall be provided with adequate resources for the effective and efficient discharge of their respective mandates;

8. *Reiterates its request* to the Secretary-General to make the fullest possible use of facilities and equipment at the United Nations Logistics Base at Brindisi,

Italy, in order to minimize the costs of procurement for the Mission, and for this purpose requests the Secretary-General to speed up the implementation of the asset management system at all peacekeeping missions in accordance with General Assembly resolution 52/1 A of 15 October 1997;

9. *Endorses* the conclusions and recommendations contained in the report of the Advisory Committee on Administrative and Budgetary Questions, and requests the Secretary-General to ensure their full implementation;

10. *Requests* the Secretary-General to take all necessary action to ensure that the Mission is administered with a maximum of efficiency and economy;

11. *Also requests* the Secretary-General, in order to reduce the cost of employing General Service staff, to continue efforts to recruit local staff for the Mission against General Service posts, commensurate with the requirements of the Mission;

12. *Decides* to reduce the appropriation authorized for the United Nations Observer Mission in Sierra Leone in respect of the period from 13 July 1998 to 30 June 1999 under the terms of General Assembly resolution 53/29 from the amount of 22 million dollars gross (21,279,800 dollars net) to the amount of 16,167,100 dollars gross (15,706,550 dollars net), equal to the amount apportioned among Member States in respect of the period from 13 July 1998 to 13 March 1999, and to extend the period covered by the apportionment until 30 June 1999;

13. *Decides also* to appropriate to the Special Account for the United Nations Mission in Sierra Leone the amount of 65,789,000 dollars gross (66,606,500 dollars net) for the maintenance of the Mission for the period from 1 July 1999 to 30 June 2000, in addition to the amount of 200 million dollars gross (197,765,100 dollars net) already appropriated under the terms of General Assembly resolution 54/241 A;

14. *Decides further,* as an ad hoc arrangement, taking into account the amount of 200 million dollars gross (197,765,100 dollars net) already apportioned under the terms of General Assembly resolution 54/241 A, to apportion among Member States the additional amount of 65,789,000 dollars gross (66,606,500 dollars net) for the period from 1 July 1999 to 30 June 2000, in accordance with the composition of groups set out in paragraphs 3 and 4 of General Assembly resolution 43/232 of 1 March 1989, as adjusted by the Assembly in its resolutions 44/192 B of 21 December 1989, 45/269 of 27 August 1991, 46/198 A of 20 December 1991, 47/218 A of 23 December 1992, 49/249 A of 20 July 1995, 49/249 B of 14 September 1995, 50/224 of 11 April 1996, 51/218 A to C of 18 December 1996 and 52/230 of 31 March 1998 and its decisions 48/472 A of 23 December 1993, 50/451 B of 23 December 1995 and 54/456 to 54/458 of 23 December 1999, and taking into account the scale of assessments for the year 2000, as set out in its resolutions 52/215 A of 22 December 1997 and 54/237 A of 23 December 1999;

15. *Decides* that, in accordance with the provisions of its resolution 973(X) of 15 December 1955, the apportionment among Member States, as provided for in paragraph 14 above, shall take into consideration the decrease in their respective share in the Tax Equalization Fund of the estimated staff assessment income of

817,500 dollars approved for the Mission for the period from 1 July 1999 to 30 June 2000;

16. *Decides also* to appropriate the amount of 504,399,051 dollars gross (496,545,461 dollars net) for the maintenance of the Mission for the period from 1 July 2000 to 30 June 2001, inclusive of the amount of 23,931,281 dollars gross (20,250,873 dollars net) for the support account for peacekeeping operations and the amount of 3,741,370 dollars gross (3,328,988 dollars net) for the United Nations Logistics Base;

17. *Decides further,* as an ad hoc arrangement, to apportion among Member States the amount of 50,168,723 dollars gross (49,387,586 dollars net) for the period from 1 July to 6 August 2000, in accordance with the scheme set out in the present resolution and the scale of assessments for the year 2000, as set out in its resolutions 52/215 A and 54/237 A;

18. *Decides* that, in accordance with the provisions of its resolution 973(X), there shall be set off against the apportionment among Member States, as provided for in paragraph 17 above, their respective share in the Tax Equalization Fund of the estimated staff assessment income of 781,137 dollars approved for the Mission for the period from 1 July to 6 August 2000;

19. *Decides also,* as an ad hoc arrangement, to apportion among Member States the amount of 454,230,328 dollars gross (447,157,875 dollars net) for the period from 7 August 2000 to 30 June 2001 at a monthly rate of 42,033,254 dollars gross (41,378,788 dollars net), in accordance with the scheme set out in the present resolution and the scale of assessments for the year 2000, as set out in its resolutions 52/215 A and 54/237 A, and for the year 2001, subject to the decision of the Security Council to extend the mandate of the Mission beyond 6 August 2000;

20. *Decides further* that, in accordance with the provisions of its resolution 973(X), there shall be set off against the apportionment among Member States, as provided for in paragraph 19 above, their respective share in the Tax Equalization Fund of the estimated staff assessment income of 7,072,453 dollars approved for the Mission for the period from 7 August 2000 to 30 June 2001;

21. *Decides* that, for Member States that have fulfilled their financial obligations to the Mission, there shall be set off against the apportionment, as provided for in paragraph 14 above, their respective share of the unencumbered balance of 3,283,300 dollars gross (3,309,550 dollars net) in respect of the period from 13 July 1998 to 30 June 1999;

22. *Decides also* that, for Member States that have not fulfilled their financial obligations to the Mission, their share of the unencumbered balance of 3,283,300 dollars gross (3,309,550 dollars net) in respect of the period from 13 July 1998 to 30 June 1999 shall be set off against their outstanding obligations;

23. *Emphasizes* that no peacekeeping mission shall be financed by borrowing funds from other active peacekeeping missions;

24. *Encourages* the Secretary-General to continue to take additional measures to ensure the safety and security of all personnel under the auspices of the United Nations participating in the Mission;

25. *Invites* voluntary contributions to the Mission in cash and in the form of services and supplies acceptable to the Secretary-General, to be administered, as

appropriate, in accordance with the procedure and practices established by the General Assembly;

26. *Decides* to include in the provisional agenda of its fifty-fifth session the item entitled "Financing of the United Nations Mission in Sierra Leone".

On 23 December, the Assembly decided that the item on UNAMSIL financing would remain for consideration during its resumed fifty-fifth (2001) session (**decision 55/458**) and that the Fifth Committee should continue to consider the item at that session (**decision 55/455**).

Somalia

The quest for peace in Somalia took a step forward in 2000 as the international community and Somali leaders worked together to implement the Djibouti initiative for peace in Somalia, which the President of Djibouti, Ismail Omar Guelleh, had presented to the General Assembly in 1999.

Preparatory meetings organized by Djibouti in the early part of the year were followed by the Somali National Peace Conference in May and June in Arta, Djibouti. The Conference was attended by 810 delegates representing most of Somalia's clans and from all parts of the county. The initiative progressed further following the Conference with the approval of a Transitional National Charter, the election of a Transitional National Assembly, and the election in August of a President (Abdikassim Salad Hassan) to head Somalia's Transitional National Government. Following his inauguration, President Hassan made determined efforts to bring Somaliland and Puntland, two factions that boycotted the Conference, into the peace process. The Secretary-General's Special Representative also assisted in the effort towards reconciliation.

The United Nations Political Office in Somalia (UNPOS) continued to monitor the political situation and to encourage Somali leaders and the international community to work together to restore peace; UN agencies continued to provide support and technical assistance.

However, even with the Transitional National Government in place, banditry and other criminal acts remained rampant, as the Government had only limited control. Several local and international aid workers and non-governmental staff lost their lives in 2000.

In June, the Security Council urged representatives of all social and political forces in Somalia to participate actively and constructively in the peace process and urged the warlords and faction leaders to desist from obstructing and undermining peace efforts.

In December, the General Assembly, in **resolution 55/168**, called on the Secretary-General to continue to mobilize international humanitarian, rehabilitation and reconstruction assistance for Somalia.

Peace process

Communication. On 5 April [S/2000/287], Djibouti transmitted to the Security Council President the final communiqué of the Technical Consultative Symposium on the Somali Peace Process (Djibouti, 21-30 March). The Symposium, the first inclusive civil society–based peace initiative of its kind, was opened by the President of Djibouti, and attended by over 60 intellectuals and peace activists from Somalia and the diaspora. The participants recommended that the upcoming National Peace Conference be open to all Somalis who wanted to bring peace, progress and speedy reconstruction to the country and stated that there was a need to consider an extension of the Conference's time frame to allow Somalis to fully prepare for it.

National Peace Conference. The first phase of the Somali National Peace Conference, a meeting of 810 traditional and clan leaders, took place in Arta, Djibouti, from 2 May to 13 June. The Conference focused on the issue of reconciliation among the clans and prepared for the second phase (15 June–15 July) by drawing up an agenda.

Somaliland and Puntland had withdrawn their support, in February and March respectively, for the Djibouti initiative, and rejected the outcome of the Somali peace process.

The Conference approved the Transitional National Charter, which provided for governance in a transition phase of three years, culminating in elections; regional autonomy; structures for executive, legislative and judicial powers; and the rights of individuals. For the first time in Somali history, there was a specific requirement that 25 seats in parliament be set aside for women. In addition 24 seats were allotted for minority clans. The Charter, which would be the supreme law until a definitive federal constitution for Somalia was adopted, also provided for the election of a 225-person Transitional National Assembly. The Assembly was selected in August. However, due to serious differences about the number of seats allotted to each clan, the Somali National Peace Conference later gave President Guelleh the right to use his own discretion to select a further 20 parliamentarians. The Assembly met for the first time on 13 August.

Transitional Government. The presidential elections for the Transitional National Government were won by Abdikassim Salad Hassan. President Hassan, who was inaugurated in Arta on 27 August, was the first Somali leader since 1991 to be readmitted to Somalia's seat in the Intergovernmental Authority on Development (IGAD). Acceptance of the Transitional National Government by Somalia's immediate neighbours represented an important development in the country's return to the community of nations.

By October, appointments were made to the Transitional National Government and priorities, such as security, demobilization and disarmament, were established. In a move towards reconciliation, President Hassan, with the aid of the Government of Italy, met twice with some faction leaders from Mogadishu.

SECURITY COUNCIL ACTION

On 29 June [S/PV.4166], the Security Council was briefed on the situation in Somalia by the Under-Secretary-General for Political Affairs. He observed that the most serious obstacle to the peace process was the absence of the leaders of the self-styled Somaliland and "Puntland". He noted that Djibouti was continuing its efforts to persuade certain faction leaders, particularly the Hawiye clan in the Mogadishu area, to revise their hostile attitude towards the Somali National Peace Conference. The Under-Secretary-General described the serious humanitarian situation in Somalia, noting that 750,000 people across the country were highly vulnerable following three consecutive years of below-normal rainfall (see also p. 859). Personal safety and security remained part of the risk of humanitarian assistance delivery in Somalia and the lives of humanitarian staff continued to be lost or put at risk.

The Permanent Representative of Djibouti also addressed the Council, providing details of the Peace Conference.

Also on 29 June [meeting 4167], following consultations among Council members, the President made statement **S/PRST/2000/22** on behalf of the Council:

> The Security Council reaffirms its commitment to a comprehensive and lasting settlement of the situation in Somalia, consistent with the principles of the Charter of the United Nations, bearing in mind respect for the sovereignty, territorial integrity, political independence and unity of Somalia. It reiterates that full responsibility for achieving national reconciliation and peace rests with the Somali people themselves.
> The Council expresses its full support for the efforts exerted by the Intergovernmental Authority on Development to find a political solution to the crisis in Somalia. It welcomes and fully supports the

initiative of the President of Djibouti aimed at restoring peace and stability in Somalia, and urges States and international organizations, in a position to do so, to give these efforts political support and to provide financial and technical assistance to the Government of Djibouti to this end.

> The Council expresses its deep concern at the ongoing abuse of human rights and grave deterioration of the humanitarian situation in Somalia, which has led to death, displacement and the outbreak of diseases among the civilian population, particularly among children and other vulnerable groups. It expresses appreciation for the efforts of all United Nations agencies, other organizations and individuals carrying out humanitarian activities in Somalia. The Council strongly condemns attacks by armed groups on innocent civilians and all humanitarian personnel. It strongly urges the Somali factions to respect international humanitarian and human rights law, ensure the safety and freedom of movement of all humanitarian personnel and facilitate the delivery of humanitarian relief to all those in need.
> The Council underlines the importance of the widest participation by representatives of all parts of Somali society in an effort to rehabilitate Somalia. The Council strongly urges representatives of all social and political forces of Somali society to participate actively and in a constructive spirit in the work of the Somali National Peace and Reconciliation Conference in Arta, Djibouti. In this regard, it urges the warlords and faction leaders to desist from obstructing and undermining efforts to achieve peace. The Council expresses its readiness to consider taking appropriate steps regarding the warlords and faction leaders who engage in such activities. It also urges all States to stop providing those individuals with the means to carry on their destructive activities.
> The Council reminds all States of their obligation to comply with the measures imposed by resolution 733(1992) of 23 January 1992, and urges them to take all necessary steps to ensure full implementation and enforcement of the arms embargo. The Council further urges all States, the United Nations and other international organizations and entities to report to the Committee established pursuant to resolution 751(1992) of 24 April 1992 any information on possible violations of the arms embargo.
> The Council will remain seized of the matter.

Communication. On 13 July [S/2000/691], Djibouti transmitted to the Security Council a decision on Somalia adopted by the seventy-second ordinary session of the OAU Council of Ministers, and subsequently endorsed by the Summit of the Heads of State and Government of OAU. The Council welcomed and fully supported the Djibouti initiative on Somalia and the resulting National Peace Conference; urged all warlords and other leaders not involved in the Conference to join and participate; called on the international community to exert pressure on those who engaged in hostile activities towards undermining and obstructing the peace process; and appealed to the international community to provide assistance to the potential national transitional administration in Somalia, particularly reconstruction and development assistance and rebuilding of institutions.

Security Council consideration. On 14 September, the Security Council held a private meeting to consider the situation in Somalia [S/PV.4196], at which it was briefed by President Ismail Omar Guelleh of Djibouti. Among other things, President Guelleh requested the Council to give serious consideration to a UN post-conflict peace-building mission in Somalia. Members of the Council posed questions, to which President Guelleh responded.

Further communications. On 8 September [S/2000/916], the EU indicated its willingness to enter into dialogue with the new Somali authorities and to support their efforts to rebuild the country. It called on the authorities in Somaliland and Puntland to establish constructive relations with the institutions that emerged from the Arta process, and urged the future Transitional Government to establish a constructive dialogue with the aforementioned authorities for the purpose of re-establishing national unity in peace.

By a 22 September communiqué [S/2000/923], the Libyan Arab Jamahiriya stated that President Hassan of Somalia visited Libya (20-22 September) and had met with Colonel Muammar Qadhafi with whom he discussed the national reconciliation process in Somalia and the need for support in order to achieve security, stability and development. Mr. Hassan also met with the leaders of the Somali National Alliance, present in Libya at that time. The two parties expressed an understanding of the need for dispatch in taking the necessary measures to build the executive institutions established by the Peace Conference.

By a communiqué [S/2000/1126], Ethiopia informed the Security Council that President Hassan had paid a three-day visit to Ethiopia starting on 15 November when he met with Prime Minister Meles Zenawi and Foreign Minister Seyoum Mesfin. The Ethiopian Government was encouraged by President Hassan's assurance that the Somali Transitional Government would do everything possible to remove all elements using Somali territory as a springboard to threaten regional peace and stability; and by his conviction of the need to bring into the peace process the other Somali parties that had not participated in the Arta Conference. Ethiopia affirmed that that Conference constituted a major achievement in the Somali peace process.

Report of Secretary-General. In a 19 December report [S/2000/1211], submitted in response to a request contained in Security Council state-

ment S/PRST/1999/16 [YUN 1999, p. 171], the Secretary-General described events in Somalia since his August 1999 report [ibid., p. 172], particularly the Djibouti President's peace initiative and the Arta Peace Conference and its follow-up (see above). He also described activities of the Transnational National Assembly and the Transitional National Government, including President Hassan's efforts to reconcile the Somali factions that had stayed away from the peace process.

With regard to the UN role, the Secretary-General stated that UNPOS continued to monitor the political situation in Somalia and to encourage Somali leaders and the international community to work together to restore peace. The Secretary-General's Special Representative for Somalia, David Stephen, had travelled to Djibouti in February to assist and support Djibouti's efforts and remained there until the conclusion of the process. Mr. Stephen made several attempts to engage the "Somaliland administration" and succeeded in establishing direct talks between President Guelleh and Mohamed Ibrahim Egal, a Somaliland leader. Nevertheless, the Egal administration did not participate in the Arta Conference. In September, he tried to encourage dialogue between Mr. Egal and President Hassan but Mr. Egal stated that he would not talk to Mr. Hassan as long as the latter claimed to be President of all of Somalia.

The security situation in north-western and north-eastern Somalia remained relatively calm, with occasional incidents of banditry and other criminal acts. In the central and southern parts of the country, the situation was uncertain and sometimes extremely tense. Extended parts of coastal areas were not under the control of any effective regional authority and continued to be dominated by pirates. The risk for the personal safety of international staff was very high. Banditry was rampant in Mogadishu where there was no single authority for the maintenance of law and order. Significant parts of the city continued to be under the control of different militias, including the seaport and the airport, which remained closed, the former government blocks and the main city market. The Transitional National Government had only limited control of the Greater Mogadishu area. Several Somali aid workers had lost their lives during the period under review and there had been killings and kidnappings of foreign nationals.

With regard to humanitarian conditions, the Secretary-General stated that there had been favourable environmental conditions since June. Thus, humanitarian needs had decreased significantly across most of Somalia. In response, UN agencies were developing assistance strategies to promote the mid-term recovery of the livelihood of poor and displaced populations. While humanitarian concerns had lessened on the national level, pockets of vulnerability remained. As of October, field reports indicated that the bumper harvest might provide only temporary respite for many communities in southern Somalia and, without further improvements in their livelihood, many communities would face more food and water insecurity.

The Secretary-General observed that the Transitional National Government, currently located in Mogadishu, had begun the process of establishing itself on Somali soil and expanding the areas under its influence. It had three years in which to prepare for the installation of permanent governance arrangements, during which basic political, economic and development challenges would have to be addressed.

Arms embargo

On 20 December, the Chairman of the Security Council Committee established pursuant to resolution 751(1992) [YUN 1992, p. 202] concerning Somalia submitted to the Council a report covering the Committee's activities in 2000 [S/2000/1226]. The Committee had been established to monitor the military and weapons embargo against Somalia imposed by resolution 733(1992) [YUN 1992, p. 199].

On 8 March, the Committee reviewed measures for enhancing the effective implementation of the arms embargo, with a view to curbing the continued flow of arms to Somalia. Towards that end, the Committee decided to seek the assistance of OAU and IGAD and, in letters of 20 March, appealed to both organizations to provide the Committee with any information they might have relating to violations or suspected violations of the embargo.

On 22 March, the Committee addressed a note verbale to all Permanent Representatives/Permanent Observers to the United Nations, reminding them of their obligations under resolutions 733(1992) and 954(1994) [YUN 1994, p. 325], and requesting their assistance towards the effective implementation of the arms embargo.

The Committee reiterated that it did not have any specific monitoring mechanism to ensure the effective implementation of the arms embargo, and that it relied solely on the cooperation of States and organizations in a position to provide information on violations.

UNOSOM II financing

The United Nations Operation in Somalia (UNOSOM), established by Security Council resolution 751(1992) [YUN 1992, p. 202], was withdrawn from Somalia in March 1995 [YUN 1995, p. 400].

On 5 September, the General Assembly decided to include in the draft agenda of its fifty-fifth session the item entitled "Financing of the United Nations Operation in Somalia II" (**decision 54/496**).

On 23 December, the Assembly decided that the item would remain for consideration at its resumed fifty-fifth (2001) session (**decision 55/458**). On the same date, it decided that the Fifth Committee should continue its consideration of the item at that session (**decision 55/455**).

Sudan

In 2000, the Sudan made serious efforts to cooperate with the international community. In order to improve relations and mend any rifts, the Sudan brokered many agreements with its neighbours through joint ministerial meetings. It also acceded to international conventions against terrorism.

Given its concerted efforts to discharge its obligations under various Security Council resolutions, the Sudan requested that the Council lift the sanctions imposed against it in 1996.

Despite improved international relations, the Sudan remained entangled in internal conflict. It informed the Council and the General Assembly that the Sudanese People's Liberation Movement/Army (SPLM/A) was in frequent violation of the ceasefire agreement between it and the Government. Although the Sudan remained committed to the ceasefire, it affirmed its right to respond to aggression.

In December, the Sudan held presidential elections, which were considered by an observer team of the Intergovernmental Authority on Development (IGAD) to have been conducted in a satisfactory manner and in a conducive atmosphere.

Sanctions

On 1 June [S/2000/513], the Sudan informed the Security Council that it had taken practical and concrete measures to fully discharge its obligations under Council resolutions 1044(1996) [YUN 1996, p. 129], 1054(1996) [ibid., p. 130] and 1070(1996) [ibid., p. 131], and on that basis requested that the sanctions imposed in 1996 be lifted. Those sanctions called for States to reduce the level of diplomatic staff in the Sudan and restrict travel of Sudanese government officials and armed forces into or through their territories, and to deny Sudanese aircraft the right to use other countries' airspace.

Describing the actions taken, the Sudan stated that on the issue of the surrender of the three persons suspected in the attempt to assassinate President Hosni Mubarak of Egypt in 1995, in Addis Ababa [YUN 1995, p. 412], its inquiries showed no trace of the suspects in the Sudan. The findings were shared with Egypt and Ethiopia, the two parties concerned, which expressed satisfaction with the honest efforts made by the Sudan and signed security agreements or memorandums of understanding with the Sudan with a view to promoting future cooperation in that area.

With regard to desisting from engaging in any terrorist activities, the Sudan expressed its desire to cooperate with the international community in combating terrorism. Putting words into deeds, the Sudan, in March, enacted legislation for the suppression of terrorist offences, and, in May, it acceded to or signed all of the international conventions for the elimination of international terrorism. It was also a party to regional agreements, had participated in regional programmes for the suppression and elimination of terrorism in the African continent, and had taken measures regarding the regulation of entry into the country.

The Sudan also took steps to improve relations with its neighbours, as exemplified by the conclusion of different agreements by joint ministerial committees convened to discuss political, economic and social interests; it also made sustained efforts to mend any rifts in the country's foreign relations at the inter-African and inter-Arab levels, demonstrating its political will to cooperate.

The Sudan's request that the sanctions be lifted drew letters of endorsement from the League of Arab States [S/2000/517, S/2000/863], from the Coordinating Bureau of the Movement of Non-Aligned Countries [S/2000/521] and from the African Group at the United Nations [S/2000/533].

Internal conflict

Communications. In a 28 March letter [S/2000/288], the President of IGAD communicated to the Security Council the Authority's concern that if the Council took up the question of peace in the Sudan, it could have a negative impact on the peace process being guided by IGAD. Although IGAD fully recognized that the Council had primary responsibility for the maintenance of international peace and security, IGAD hoped that the Council would give it the opportunity to resolve the conflict in the Sudan.

In 5 May [S/2000/402] and 30 June [S/2000/656] statements, the EU welcomed the Sudan's announcement that it had ordered the cessation of aerial bombings of targets in southern Sudan; reiterated its commitment to the renewed political dialogue; expressed concern regarding the offensive launched by SPLM/A in the region of Bahr al-Ghazal; and appealed to the Government of the Sudan and SPLM/A to decide on a comprehensive cessation of hostilities and to advance the ongoing IGAD peace process. It also called for the humanitarian ceasefire commitments given to be respected and expressed the hope that a global and unlimited ceasefire might be proclaimed as soon as possible.

On 27 June [A/54/933], the Sudan informed the Secretary-General that SPLM/A had resumed its attacks in various areas on 20 and 21 June, in a breach of the ceasefire it had declared on 8 May. The Sudan called on the world community, IGAD member countries, the IGAD partners forum and all the forces supporting the rebel movement to condemn the irresponsible behaviour of SPLM/A, and reiterated that it reserved the right to repulse attacks launched by the rebel movement, without affecting its commitment to the ceasefire and its pledge to strive for peace.

In follow-up letters of 30 June [A/54/934], 19 July [A/54/943] and 2 August [A/54/956], the Sudan informed the Secretary-General that the continuous attacks by SPLM/A had resulted in the seizure of the town of Gogrial in the Bahr al-Ghazal region and in the injury of a staff member of the United Nations Children's Fund aboard a UN boat. The Sudan confirmed its commitment to the ceasefire, renewed its call for agreement on a comprehensive ceasefire and reaffirmed its right to respond to aggression.

Elections

The Sudan held presidential elections from 5 to 23 December. On 29 December [A/55/722], OAU informed the Secretary-General that, at the invitation of the General Elections Authority of the Sudan, it had dispatched a nine-member team to observe the elections.

The team witnessed various aspects of the electoral process, including administrative arrangements, campaigns and polling activities, and held discussions with all five presidential candidates and other parties, including those who boycotted the elections, and noted their concerns. Although some major political parties boycotted the elections, the leaders from all sides expressed their readiness and commitment to embark on a dialogue after the elections.

The OAU team commended the General Elections Authority for making arrangements to allow the Sudanese people, including those outside the country, to freely exercise their democratic rights and noted that the exercise, an important step towards democratization, was conducted in a satisfactory manner and in a conducive atmosphere.

Sudan-Uganda

On 8 November [S/2000/1086], Uganda informed the Security Council of a meeting it had hosted (Kampala, 26-27 September) to discuss relations between it and the Sudan. The participants were the Foreign Ministers of Egypt, the Sudan and Uganda and the Minister of African Unity of the Libyan Arab Jamahiriya.

Uganda and the Sudan reiterated their commitment to refrain from interfering in each other's internal affairs and from doing anything that would undermine the security and stability of the other.

Sudan–United States

On 28 November [A/55/651-S/2000/1135], the Sudan informed the Secretary-General of a breach of its sovereignty on 19 and 20 November by a United States official and accompanying delegation, who entered the country without visas and without the permission of the Sudanese Government, thereby violating the domestic laws and international norms governing the movement of persons between States.

The Sudan asked the Secretary-General to draw the attention of the United States to the fact that it had taken steps incompatible with the UN Charter and to alert the Security Council to the incident.

Western Sahara

In 2000, the United Nations continued efforts to hold a referendum to enable the people of Western Sahara to make a choice between independence or integration with Morocco, in accordance with a settlement plan approved by the Security Council in resolution 658(1990) [YUN 1990, p. 920]. The plan, agreed to by both Morocco and the Frente Popular para la Liberación de Saguia el-Hamra y de Río de Oro (POLISARIO), established the conditions for the referendum.

The United Nations Mission for the Referendum in Western Sahara (MINURSO) was established by Council resolution 690(1991) [YUN 1991, p. 794] to implement the plan.

In January, the second round of the appeals process was launched by the Identification Commission. The second part of the provisional list of applicants eligible to vote contained the names of 2,135 applicants out of 51,220 interviewed from tribal groupings H41, H61 and J51/52. Together with the 84,251 eligible applicants in the first part of the provisional list, issued in July 1999, the number of those eligible to vote totalled 86,386. In accordance with the MINURSO appeals procedures, all those excluded from the provisional voter list had the right to appeal, while those found eligible could also challenge the inclusion of others.

At the suggestion of the Secretary-General's Personal Envoy, James A. Baker III, and following preliminary discussions with the two parties and two neighbouring countries, Algeria and Mauritania, a meeting was held between the parties in London in May to consider the problems in implementing the settlement plan and the 1997 Houston agreements [YUN 1997, p. 149], as well as other possible approaches. However, despite that meeting and subsequent meetings in London, Geneva and Berlin, a resolution of the parties' dispute had still not been achieved. While POLISARIO reiterated its commitment to the settlement plan and to the holding of the referendum as the only solution to the conflict, Morocco said that it was willing, within the framework of respect for the sovereignty and territorial integrity of Morocco, to respond positively to the Security Council's request pursuant to resolution 1309(2000) to search for a political solution to the situation in Western Sahara.

At the end of the year, the Secretary-General observed that further meetings to seek a political solution could not succeed unless the Government of Morocco was prepared to offer or support some devolution of governmental authority for all inhabitants and former inhabitants of the Territory that was genuine, substantial and in keeping with international norms. If Morocco could not agree on that issue, MINURSO should begin expeditiously hearing the pending appeals from the identification process.

MINURSO's mandate was extended several times during the year; in October, the Council extended the mandate until 28 February 2001.

Report of Secretary-General (February). In response to Security Council resolution 1282(1999) [YUN 1999, p. 186], the Secretary-General submitted a 17 February progress report [S/2000/131] on the implementation of the 1990 settlement plan. He stated that his Special Representative, William Eagleton, had consulted with Moroccan and POLISARIO representatives on moving the process forward, particularly with respect to the new round of appeals following the issuance of the second part of the provisional voter list on 17 January and the preparatory work for repatriation of Saharan refugees. POLISARIO continued to express concern over delays resulting from the large number of appeals expected from the second part of the provisional voter list. Meanwhile, the Moroccan authorities reiterated the right of every applicant to appeal by presenting witnesses who could provide new information to support his or her inclusion in the list. Following the release of the second part of the provisional list, the Moroccan authorities, surprised at the small number of applicants found to be eligible, emphasized the importance of an appeals process in which all Saharans rejected by the MINURSO Identification Commission were given the opportunity to restate their case. Moroccan officials again questioned the impartiality and objectivity of the Identification Commission and warned that the referendum would not be held if any person originating from the Sahara were denied the right to participate. At the same time, POLISARIO warned against any attempt to delay the referendum and called for the speedy implementation of the settlement plan. POLISARIO officials expressed the view that if the process were delayed much longer, the presence of MINURSO would become irrelevant and there could be a return to armed hostilities.

MINURSO had opened appeal centres in the Territory, in the Tindouf area of Algeria, in Morocco and in Mauritania to receive appeals from tribal groupings H41, H61 and J51/52. As at 11 February, 29,690 appeals had been received. The Identification Commission had almost completed the processing of the 79,000 appeals received from the first part of the provisional voter list.

On 26 January, the Government of Morocco informed the International Committee of the Red Cross (ICRC) that it was prepared to receive all Moroccan prisoners of war whose names had been submitted to the Secretary-General's Special Representative in 1999 [YUN 1999, p. 186]. ICRC subsequently informed the Special Representative that it was proceeding with the necessary arrangements in consultation with the parties.

As at 17 February, the strength of MINURSO's military component, which continued to monitor the ceasefire between the Royal Moroccan Army and the POLISARIO forces, was 230. The strength of the civilian police component, which had been assisting at appeal centres since 17 January, stood at 81.

During the reporting period, UNHCR continued preparations for the repatriation of Saharan refugees, consolidating its presence in the mission area by assigning additional personnel to Laayoune and Tindouf. It completed its pre-registration exercise to ascertain the refugees' willingness to repatriate and to determine their final destinations in the Territory. The total number of pre-registered refugees reached 107,149. The Special Representative and UNHCR initiated cross-border confidence-building measures, including family visits. However, no progress was made because POLISARIO continued to be concerned about the absence of security guarantees in the area of the Territory west of the berm and, although initially welcoming the proposed measures, the refugees in the Tindouf camps also remained concerned for their safety and security.

The Secretary-General noted that the developments during the nine years since MINURSO's establishment, and particularly those in recent months, raised doubts about the possibility of achieving a smooth and consensual implementation of the settlement plan and agreements adopted by the parties, despite the support given by the international community. Furthermore, even assuming that a referendum were held pursuant to the settlement plan and agreements of the parties, should the results not be recognized and accepted by one party, no enforcement mechanism was envisioned by the settlement plan nor was one likely to be proposed, calling for the use of military means to effect enforcement. The Secretary-General felt that it would be wise to review the situation and he intended to ask his Personal Envoy to consult with the parties and to explore ways to achieve an early, durable and agreed resolution of their dispute. The Secretary-General therefore recommended that the Council extend MINURSO's mandate for a three-month period, until 31 May.

Communication. In a 24 February letter to the Council [S/2000/148], Morocco conveyed its views on the implementation of the settlement plan, the progress of the identification process and prospects for implementing the appeals procedure.

SECURITY COUNCIL ACTION (February)

On 29 February [meeting 4106], the Security Council unanimously adopted **resolution 1292 (2000)**. The draft [S/2000/149] was prepared in consultations among Council members.

The Security Council,

Recalling all its resolutions on the question of Western Sahara, in particular resolution 1108(1997) of 22 May 1997,

Recalling also the relevant principles contained in the Convention on the Safety of United Nations and Associated Personnel of 9 December 1994,

Welcoming and encouraging efforts by the United Nations to sensitize peacekeeping personnel in the prevention and control of HIV/AIDS and other communicable diseases in all its peacekeeping operations,

Welcoming the report of the Secretary-General of 17 February 2000 and the observations and recommendations contained therein,

Reiterating its full support for the continued efforts exerted by the Secretary-General, his Personal Envoy, his Special Representative and the United Nations Mission for the Referendum in Western Sahara to implement the settlement plan and agreements adopted by the parties, to hold a free, fair and impartial referendum for the self-determination of the people of Western Sahara,

Noting the concern expressed in the report about the possibility of achieving a smooth and consensual implementation of the settlement plan and agreements adopted by the parties, despite the support given by the international community, and urging the parties to cooperate so as to achieve a lasting solution,

1. *Decides* to extend the mandate of the United Nations Mission for the Referendum in Western Sahara until 31 May 2000;

2. *Supports* the intention of the Secretary-General, as stated, inter alia, in his report, to ask his Personal Envoy to consult the parties and, taking into account existing and potential obstacles, to explore ways and means to achieve an early, durable and agreed resolution of their dispute;

3. *Requests* the Secretary-General to provide an assessment of the situation before the end of the present mandate of the Mission;

4. *Decides* to remain seized of the matter.

Communication. On 7 March [A/55/58-S/2000/197], Namibia transmitted a memorandum from POLISARIO to the General Assembly and the Security Council that stated that a new problem was hindering the implementation of the settlement plan, namely the large number of appeals in the identification process lodged by Morocco. POLISARIO was of the view that the new problem could be resolved through implementation of the May 1999 protocols, concluded in conformity with Council resolutions 1238(1999) [YUN 1999, p. 181] and 1263(1999) [ibid., p. 185]. Those instruments warned that the appeals process should not turn into a new identification operation.

Report of Secretary General (May). In accordance with Security Council resolution 1292 (2000), the Secretary-General submitted a 22 May report [S/2000/461], in which he provided an assessment of the situation concerning Western Sahara. He said his Personal Envoy visited the region from 8 to 11 April for preliminary discussions with the two parties and the two neighbouring countries, Algeria and Mauritania. Following those contacts, the Personal Envoy thought it necessary to convene a meeting between the parties to consider the problems in implementing the settlement plan and the 1997 Houston agreements, as well as other possible approaches. The high-level face-to-face discussions between the parties (London, 14 May), at which observer delegations from the two neighbouring countries were also present, were inconclusive. At the close of those discussions, the Personal Envoy proposed another meeting, possibly in June, to discuss other ways to achieve resolution of the dispute.

As at 16 May, the strength of MINURSO's military component stood at 230 and the civilian police component numbered 80. Progress continued to be made in implementing the military agreements between MINURSO and the two parties on the marking and disposal of mines and unexploded ordnance and the related exchange of detailed information. The Royal Moroccan Army and POLISARIO forces conducted 21 operations for disposing of explosives and ammunition.

UNHCR continued the refugee pre-registration exercise for repatriation in Tindouf of those refugees who were away from the camps during the earlier registration phase. By May, 119,698 refugees and their immediate family members had been pre-registered from the MINURSO provisional lists of voters since the exercise started in August 1997. Efforts by the Special Representative and UNHCR to initiate cross-border confidence-building measures could not overcome the parties' reservations to implementing such measures. POLISARIO, in particular, continued to express security concerns about the Territory west of the berm.

The Secretary-General hoped that, as requested by his Personal Envoy, the parties would come forward with concrete proposals at the proposed June meeting. As they had been unable to bridge their recurrent differences over the years and taking into account that no enforcement mechanism was envisaged in the settlement plan, it was essential for the parties to offer specific solutions to the problems related to implementing the plan or, alternatively, be prepared to consider other ways to achieve an early, durable and agreed resolution of their dispute over Western Sahara. The Secretary-General therefore recommended that the Council extend MINURSO's mandate for a further two months, until 31 July.

SECURITY COUNCIL ACTION (May)

On 31 May [meeting 4149], the Security Council adopted by vote (12-1-2) **resolution 1301(2000).**

The draft [S/2000/500] was submitted by France, the Russian Federation, the United Kingdom and the United States.

The Security Council,

Recalling all its resolutions on the question of Western Sahara, in particular resolution 1108(1997) of 22 May 1997 and resolution 1292(2000) of 29 February 2000,

Recalling also the relevant principles contained in the Convention on the Safety of United Nations and Associated Personnel of 9 December 1994,

Welcoming and encouraging efforts by the United Nations to sensitize peacekeeping personnel in the prevention and control of HIV/AIDS and other communicable diseases in all its peacekeeping operations,

Welcoming the report of the Secretary-General of 22 May 2000 and the efforts of his Personal Envoy in his mission as outlined therein, and endorsing the observations and recommendations contained therein,

Reiterating its full support for the continued efforts exerted by the United Nations Mission for the Referendum in Western Sahara to implement the settlement plan and agreements adopted by the parties to hold a free, fair and impartial referendum for the self-determination of the people of Western Sahara, noting that fundamental differences between the parties over the interpretation of the main provisions remain to be resolved,

1. *Decides* to extend the mandate of the United Nations Mission for the Referendum in Western Sahara until 31 July 2000, with the expectation that the parties will offer the Personal Envoy of the Secretary-General specific and concrete proposals that can be agreed to, in order to resolve the multiple problems relating to the implementation of the settlement plan and explore all ways and means to achieve an early, durable and agreed resolution to their dispute over Western Sahara;

2. *Requests* the Secretary-General to provide an assessment of the situation before the end of the present mandate of the Mission;

3. *Decides* to remain seized of the matter.

VOTE ON RESOLUTION 1301(2000):

In favour: Argentina, Bangladesh, Canada, China, France, Malaysia, Netherlands, Russian Federation, Tunisia, Ukraine, United Kingdom, United States.
Against: Namibia.
Abstaining: Jamaica, Mali.

Speaking before the vote, Namibia said that, although it fully supported the extension of MINURSO's mandate, it could not endorse observations in the Secretary-General's report that sought to diverge from the implementation of the settlement plan. Jamaica and Mali could not support the final phrase of operative paragraph 1.

Communication. Namibia transmitted to the Council a 31 May letter [S/2000/545] from POLISARIO referring to the fourth preambular and first operative paragraphs of resolution 1301(2000). POLISARIO considered that the only valid framework for a just and final settlement of the question of Western Sahara was the settlement plan, agreed to by the two parties and approved by the Council. Any approach other than implementa-

tion of the settlement plan could not achieve that objective and would undermine the international community's efforts to enable the Saharan people to express itself freely concerning its future. POLISARIO therefore could not support such an approach.

Report of Secretary-General (July). In response to resolution 1301(2000), the Secretary-General submitted a 12 July report [S/2000/683] on the situation concerning Western Sahara. The second meeting of the parties, under the auspices of the Secretary-General's Personal Envoy, took place in London on 28 June. There had been a frank and full exchange of views during which POLISARIO identified two areas of difficulty: the conduct of the appeals process and the repatriation of refugees. POLISARIO reiterated its willingness to cooperate with the United Nations to resolve all problems encountered in implementing the settlement plan and examine any proposals aimed at launching the appeals process, and reconfirmed its commitment to continue cooperating with UNHCR in carrying out its mission according to normal practices and principles concerning repatriation. It reiterated its promise to respect the results of the referendum of self-determination, hoping that Morocco would do the same. POLISARIO, however, did not offer specific proposals to resolve the multiple problems of the settlement plan to which the parties could agree.

Morocco identified four areas that it felt were impeding implementation of the settlement plan: the conduct of the appeals process; the reversal of the identification results for 7,000 applicants, which, in Morocco's view, should be reinstated; the repatriation of Saharan refugees; and the issue of Saharans who had reached voting age after December 1993, but had been excluded from the identification process. Those individuals should be identified or at least permitted to lodge appeals so all Saharans could participate in the referendum. Morocco would not participate in a referendum where Saharans who were entitled to vote were not allowed to do so. While promising to remain a partner with the United Nations in search of a solution to the question of Western Sahara, Morocco did not present any proposals to resolve the issue.

The Secretary-General's Personal Envoy indicated that other issues also remained unresolved: enforcement of the referendum's results; release of prisoners of war and Saharan political detainees; and possible problems related to the implementation of the code of conduct for the referendum campaign. He was also concerned about the high level of animosity between the parties. Indeed, he felt that the meeting, instead of resolving problems, had moved things backwards as it had deepened differences between the parties. The Personal Envoy appealed to the parties not to return to violence as an acceptable alternative, and suggested that they should meet again to arrive at a political solution. Options relevant to that solution could be a negotiated agreement for full integration of Western Sahara with Morocco, or for full independence, although, in his view, neither prospect appeared likely. Alternatively, a negotiated agreement could produce a solution somewhere between the two results. Another political solution could be agreement that would permit successful implementation of the settlement plan. He reiterated to the two parties that if they should agree to discuss a political solution other than the settlement plan, they would not prejudice their final positions, as according to the rules of the consultations, nothing would be agreed to until agreement could be reached on every issue. The Personal Envoy requested the parties to participate in expert-level meetings in Geneva to discuss the appeals process, prisoners of war and refugees. A meeting was scheduled for the end of July with participation of the Secretary-General's Special Representative, the Deputy to the Personal Envoy and representatives of ICRC, UNHCR and the parties.

During the reporting period, the Special Representative and the Chairman of the Identification Commission maintained contact with the parties in Rabat and Tindouf to ensure follow-up on the implementation of Security Council resolution 1301(2000). The Secretary-General himself visited Morocco on 17 June where he met with King Mohammed VI and Prince Moulay Rachid.

Concerning the appeals process, the Secretary-General stated that the Identification Commission had almost completed its work on data processing and analysis of the files received during the first round of appeals. It also completed a family research programme with a view to ascertaining the claims of the appellants regarding the existence of immediate family members included in the provisional voter lists. Other achievements included the finalization of a training manual and a training programme for all Commission staff.

As at 3 July, the military component of MINURSO stood at the authorized strength of 230 personnel; the civilian police component totalled 46 officers, down from 80 in May. During the reporting period, 278 mines and unexploded ordnance were marked and 124 destroyed on the Moroccan side, while 488 were marked and 177 destroyed on the POLISARIO side.

Regarding preparatory work for repatriating Saharan refugees, consultations continued between UNHCR and the parties. However, it was noted that certain activities, such as the cross-border confidence-building measures, could start only after the parties and refugees had agreed to the modalities for implementation.

The Secretary-General observed that, following the June meeting between the parties, it was obvious that arriving at a political solution was preferable to a breakdown of the process that could lead to a return to hostilities, which had to be avoided. He therefore suggested that the Council reflect on the problem of ensuring that the results of the referendum, should one be held, were respected by both parties. In that regard, he recalled that there was no enforcement mechanism provided in the settlement plan, nor was one likely to be proposed, calling for the use of military means to effect enforcement. He hoped that progress could be achieved during the forthcoming expert-level meetings in Geneva and expected his Personal Envoy, following those consultations, to meet with the parties, in the presence of the two observer countries, to try once again to resolve the problems relating to the settlement plan. Meanwhile, he was recommending that the Council extend MINURSO's mandate for a further three months, until 31 October.

Communication. In a 17 July letter [S/2000/699], Morocco pointed out to the Secretary-General that his 12 July report did not accurately reflect Morocco's position on the question of the review of the identification results. It explained that it was not calling for the reversal of the identification results. Rather, it had requested that candidates whose names had been included by the identification centres in official lists, but subsequently withdrawn by the review commission, be reinstated and included once again on the list of eligible persons. The report should be amended to reflect accurately Morocco's position on the issue.

SECURITY COUNCIL ACTION (July)

On 25 July [meeting 4175], the Security Council unanimously adopted **resolution 1309(2000)**. The draft [S/2000/728] was prepared in consultations among Council members.

The Security Council,
Reaffirming all its resolutions on the question of Western Sahara, in particular resolutions 1108(1997) of 22 May 1997, 1292(2000) of 29 February 2000 and 1301(2000) of 31 May 2000, as well as its resolution 1308(2000) of 17 July 2000,
Recalling the relevant principles contained in the Convention on the Safety of United Nations and Associated Personnel of 9 December 1994,
Welcoming the report of the Secretary-General of 12 July 2000 and the observations and recommendations

contained therein, and expressing full support for the role and work of his Personal Envoy,

Reiterating its full support for the continued efforts exerted by the United Nations Mission for the Referendum in Western Sahara to implement the settlement plan and agreements adopted by the parties to hold a free, fair and impartial referendum for the self-determination of the people of Western Sahara,

Noting that fundamental differences between the parties over the interpretation of the main provisions of the settlement plan remain to be resolved,

Regretting that there was no progress made during the meeting held in London on 28 June 2000 between the parties,

1. *Decides* to extend the mandate of the United Nations Mission for the Referendum in Western Sahara until 31 October 2000, with the expectation that the parties will meet in direct talks under the auspices of the Personal Envoy of the Secretary-General to try to resolve the multiple problems relating to the implementation of the settlement plan and to try to agree upon a mutually acceptable political solution to their dispute over Western Sahara;

2. *Requests* the Secretary-General to provide an assessment of the situation before the end of the present mandate of the Mission;

3. *Decides* to remain seized of the matter.

Communications. By a 12 September letter [A/55/384-S/2000/870], Namibia transmitted to the Security Council and General Assembly a POLISARIO memorandum alluding to what POLISARIO perceived as Morocco's obstructionist attitude to the identification process and accusing Morocco of presenting obstacles to the repatriation of Saharawi refugees. POLISARIO stated that the undeclared objective of the Moroccan side was to sabotage the referendum process or at least to delay the time frame. As a result, MINURSO's civil activity had been reduced to a minimum since the completion in December 1999 of the process of identification of the tribes whose inclusion in the list had been challenged. Faced with that situation, neither the Secretary-General nor the Council continued to show the same determination to compel Morocco to honour its commitments and to cooperate loyally with MINURSO. POLISARIO observed that, since December 1999, the Secretary-General's reports had negatively evaluated implementation of the settlement plan; the considerable progress achieved in the settlement process was either being ignored or minimized. Indeed the Secretary-General's July report suggested searching for a new path towards settling the conflict outside the settlement plan and the referendum. Within the Council, efforts to abandon the settlement plan had also been gaining ground since December 1999. Attempts were being made to abandon the referendum process in favour of a political solution to be negotiated between Morocco and

POLISARIO that would ignore the right to self-determination of the people of Western Sahara. Those efforts had led to division among Council members.

The memorandum stated that throughout the direct consultations in May and July, POLISARIO reiterated its commitment to the settlement plan and to the holding of the referendum as the only solution to the conflict in Western Sahara and cautioned that it could not support any other approach that ignored the inalienable right of the people of Western Sahara.

In letters of 9 October to the Council and the Secretary-General [A/55/468-S/2000/975], Algeria stated that it was convinced that the settlement plan remained the only framework for settling the conflict between Morocco and POLISARIO and supported the efforts of the Secretary-General, his Personal Envoy and his Special Representative to organize, in cooperation with OAU, a referendum for self-determination of the people of Western Sahara.

By a 17 October letter to the Secretary-General [A/55/500-S/2000/1000], Namibia transmitted a letter from POLISARIO outlining its position on the latest developments and reaffirming its commitment to the settlement plan.

In 19 October letters to the Secretary-General and the Council President [S/2000/1003], Morocco recalled that the Sahara was an integral part of its territory and that, as a gesture of goodwill, it had initiated the referendum process to end the artificial dispute that had been created over its territorial integrity. The letter listed a number of proposals that Morocco had made in response to resolution 1309(2000). Morocco was convinced that the other parties involved wanted a specially contrived referendum, excluding the majority of Saharans from the referendum consultation and taking no account of the consequences of such a position. It shared the assessment of the Secretary-General regarding the near impossibility of finding compromise solutions concerning implementation of the settlement plan. That explained Morocco's readiness to respond positively to the Council's request for the search for a political solution in the framework of respect for the sovereignty and territorial integrity of Morocco.

Report of Secretary-General (October). The Secretary-General's 25 October report on the situation concerning Western Sahara [S/2000/1029] included an account of the expert-level technical meetings of the parties (Geneva, 20-21 July). Separate meetings were held between the United Nations and the two parties on the first day concerning the 1,686 Moroccan prisoners of war still held by POLISARIO and the list of 207 presumed political detainees compiled and submitted by the independent jurist to the Government of Morocco in 1998. POLISARIO indicated that it was not in a position to discuss the release of prisoners of war while refugees in the Tindouf camps were living under unacceptable conditions. The fate of the prisoners of war was raised by the Moroccan delegation, which also provided a general account of the current status of Saharans whose names had been provided by the independent jurist, and reported that only one among those listed was still detained in Morocco. Separate meetings were also held on practical steps for implementing confidence-building measures and both parties agreed in principle to allow exchanges of family visits between the Laayoune and the Tindouf refugee camps under the auspices of UNHCR and MINURSO. On 21 July, the Moroccan delegation said it was not authorized to discuss the appeals process because problems regarding that issue were political and not technical. At the end of the meeting, POLISARIO accepted the draft proposal by the United Nations, while the Moroccan delegation undertook to obtain its Government's endorsement or suggested amendments. However, later discussions failed to produce a set of operational points acceptable to the Moroccan party.

The report also covered the third meeting of the parties under the auspices of the Personal Envoy (Berlin, 28 September). The two neighbouring countries, Algeria and Mauritania, were again invited to attend as observers. A member of the Personal Envoy's delegation reviewed outstanding issues impeding implementation of the settlement plan and the Special Representative reviewed the results of the July expert-level technical meetings. It was noted that the failure of the parties to agree on implementation of the pilot project on confidence-building family visits proposed at the July meeting was yet another example of the difficulties still lying ahead. Both parties also reiterated their positions on implementation of the settlement plan. POLISARIO felt remaining obstacles could be overcome with the cooperation of the parties and expressed its willingness to discuss implementation of the appeals procedures immediately. Regarding other issues, such as the prisoners of war, POLISARIO stated they should be dealt with in the framework of the settlement plan. The Moroccan delegation believed that the difficulties connected with the settlement plan were not merely technical, but were errors and distortions in implementing the plan which could not satisfy the thousands of rejected applicants. Morocco was of the opinion that, despite all good will, the difficulties faced in the implementation of the plan could not be overcome.

Concerning the proposed confidence-building measures on family visits, the Personal Envoy asked both parties to accept a compromise and suggested various formulations for selecting candidates for such visits. POLISARIO eventually accepted the proposed formulations. However, the Moroccan delegation stated that the issue had become almost irrelevant given the current atmosphere, which was not conducive to considering the issue. Morocco suggested that the matter be put on hold until better conditions prevailed. The Personal Envoy felt that there was no political will on either side; under such circumstances, he was unsure as to the next steps and whether there would be another meeting. Reiterating that there were many ways of achieving self-determination, he asked the parties whether they would be willing to try to reach agreement, as had been done by parties to other disputes, without abandoning the settlement plan. POLISARIO restated its commitment to the plan and its readiness to discuss the appeals process, and Morocco, while also committed to the plan, observed that the way in which it was being implemented meant that two thirds of the Saharan population would be excluded from the referendum. The Personal Envoy then suggested that since POLISARIO had expressed interest in discussing the appeals process and the Security Council had also requested that the parties try to agree on a mutually acceptable political solution, the two parties should explore ways to move the appeals process forward and simultaneously search for a political solution. Morocco pointed out that the appeals question was exhausted and the issue deadlocked. Meanwhile, the Moroccan delegation wished to explore other ways to settle the conflict with the assistance of the Personal Envoy and reaffirmed its willingness to engage in such dialogue within the next few weeks, as long as the country's national sovereignty and territorial integrity were respected. Rejecting the Moroccan proposal, POLISARIO reiterated that it would cooperate and adhere to any dialogue within the framework of the settlement plan. The Personal Envoy indicated that the plan was not being abandoned. Also, Morocco had expressed readiness for the first time to engage in direct dialogue. The Secretary-General noted that both Morocco and POLISARIO had indicated to him in writing that they accepted his Personal Envoy's Berlin proposals on implementation of the confidence-building measures.

As at 24 October, the military component of MINURSO stood at the authorized strength of 230. The civilian police component was 47.

During the period under review, UNHCR completed the pre-registration and needs assessment of the refugees in the Tindouf camps, using MINURSO's provisional voter lists. UNHCR was also finalizing the electronic data processing of information gathered on all pre-registered refugees.

The Secretary-General regretted that he could not report any progress in implementing the settlement plan. He shared the view of his Personal Envoy that further meetings of the parties to seek a political solution could not succeed, and that if the Government of Morocco was not prepared to offer or support some devolution of governmental authority that could be discussed at a meeting of the parties during the next extension of MINURSO's mandate, then the Mission should begin hearing the pending appeals from the identification process expeditiously without regard as to how long it might be expected to take to complete them. The Secretary-General recommended that the Security Council extend the mandate of MINURSO for four more months, until 28 February 2001.

SECURITY COUNCIL ACTION (October)

On 30 October [meeting 4211], the Security Council unanimously adopted **resolution 1324 (2000)**. The draft [S/2000/1040] was prepared during consultations among Council members.

The Security Council,

Reaffirming all its resolutions on the question of Western Sahara, in particular resolutions 1108(1997) of 22 May 1997, 1292(2000) of 29 February 2000, 1301(2000) of 31 May 2000 and 1309(2000) of 25 July 2000, as well as its resolution 1308(2000) of 17 July 2000,

Recalling the relevant principles contained in the Convention on the Safety of United Nations and Associated Personnel of 9 December 1994,

Welcoming the report of the Secretary-General of 26 October 2000, and the observations and recommendations contained therein, and expressing its full support for the role and work of the Personal Envoy,

Reiterating its full support for the continued efforts exerted by the United Nations Mission for the Referendum in Western Sahara to implement the settlement plan and agreements adopted by the parties to hold a free, fair and impartial referendum for the self-determination of the people of Western Sahara,

Noting that fundamental differences between the parties over the interpretation of the main provisions of the settlement plan remain to be resolved,

1. *Decides* to extend the mandate of the United Nations Mission for the Referendum in Western Sahara until 28 February 2001, with the expectation that the parties, under the auspices of the Personal Envoy of the Secretary-General, will continue to try to resolve the multiple problems relating to the implementation of the settlement plan and try to agree upon a mutually acceptable political solution to their dispute over Western Sahara;

2. *Requests* the Secretary-General to provide an assessment of the situation before the end of the present mandate of the Mission;

3. *Decides* to remain seized of the matter.

On 8 December [meeting 83], the General Assembly, having considered the Secretary-General's report [A/55/303] summarizing developments from 1 September 1999 to 31 August 2000, on the recommendation of the Fourth (Special Political and Decolonization) Committee [A/55/578], adopted **resolution 55/141** without vote [agenda item 18].

Question of Western Sahara

The General Assembly,

Having considered in depth the question of Western Sahara,

Reaffirming the inalienable right of all peoples to self-determination and independence, in accordance with the principles set forth in the Charter of the United Nations and in General Assembly resolution 1514(XV) of 14 December 1960, containing the Declaration on the Granting of Independence to Colonial Countries and Peoples,

Recalling its resolution 54/87 of 6 December 1999,

Recalling also the agreement in principle given on 30 August 1988 by the Kingdom of Morocco and the Frente Popular para la Liberación de Saguia el-Hamra y de Río de Oro to the proposals of the Secretary-General of the United Nations and the Chairman of the Assembly of Heads of State and Government of the Organization of African Unity in the context of their joint mission of good offices,

Recalling further Security Council resolutions 658(1990) of 27 June 1990 and 690(1991) of 29 April 1991, by which the Council approved the settlement plan for Western Sahara,

Recalling all the Security Council and General Assembly resolutions relating to the question of Western Sahara,

Reaffirming the responsibility of the United Nations towards the people of Western Sahara, as provided for in the settlement plan,

Noting with satisfaction the entry into force of the ceasefire in accordance with the proposal of the Secretary-General, and stressing the importance it attaches to the maintenance of the ceasefire as an integral part of the settlement plan,

Noting also with satisfaction the agreements reached by the two parties during their private direct talks aimed at the implementation of the settlement plan, and stressing the importance it attaches to a full, fair and faithful implementation of the settlement plan and the agreements aimed at its implementation,

Noting that, despite the progress achieved, difficulties remain in the implementation of the settlement plan which must be overcome,

Taking note of the Security Council resolutions relating to the question, including resolutions 1301(2000) of 31 May 2000 and 1309(2000) of 25 July 2000,

Welcoming the acceptance by the two parties of the detailed modalities for the implementation of the Secretary-General's package of measures relating to the identification of voters and the appeals process,

Having examined the relevant chapter of the report of the Special Committee on the Situation with regard to the Implementation of the Declaration on the Granting of Independence to Colonial Countries and Peoples,

Having also examined the report of the Secretary-General,

1. *Takes note* of the report of the Secretary-General;

2. *Commends* the Secretary-General and his Personal Envoy for their outstanding efforts and the two parties for the spirit of cooperation they have shown in the support they provided for those efforts;

3. *Takes note* of the agreements reached between the Kingdom of Morocco and the Frente Popular para la Liberación de Saguia el-Hamra y de Rio de Oro for the implementation of the settlement plan during their private direct talks under the auspices of James Baker III, the Personal Envoy of the Secretary-General, and urges the parties to implement those agreements fully and in good faith;

4. *Urges* the two parties to continue their cooperation with the Secretary-General and his Personal Envoy, as well as with his Special Representative, and to refrain from undertaking anything that would undermine the implementation of the settlement plan and the agreements reached for its implementation as well as the continued efforts of the Secretary-General and his Personal Envoy;

5. *Calls upon* the two parties to cooperate fully with the Secretary-General, his Personal Envoy and his Special Representative in implementing the various phases of the settlement plan and in overcoming the difficulties that remain despite the progress so far achieved;

6. *Urges* the two parties to implement faithfully and loyally the Secretary-General's package of measures relating to the identification of voters and the appeals process;

7. *Reaffirms* the responsibility of the United Nations towards the people of Western Sahara, as provided for in the settlement plan;

8. *Reiterates its support* for further efforts of the Secretary-General for the organization and the supervision by the United Nations, in cooperation with the Organization of African Unity, of a referendum for self-determination of the people of Western Sahara that is impartial and free of all constraints, in conformity with Security Council resolutions 658(1990) and 690(1991), by which the Council approved the settlement plan for Western Sahara;

9. *Takes note* of the relevant Security Council resolutions, including resolutions 1301(2000) and 1309(2000);

10. *Requests* the Special Committee on the Situation with regard to the Implementation of the Declaration on the Granting of Independence to Colonial Countries and Peoples to continue to consider the situation in Western Sahara, bearing in mind the positive ongoing implementation of the settlement plan, and to report thereon to the General Assembly at its fifty-sixth session;

11. *Invites* the Secretary-General to submit to the General Assembly at its fifty-sixth session a report on the implementation of the present resolution.

Further developments. On 14 December, 201 of the Moroccan prisoners held by POLISARIO, more than half of whom had been held for more than 20 years, were repatriated to Morocco under ICRC auspices.

UN Mission for the Referendum in Western Sahara

The United Nations Mission for the Referendum in Western Sahara (MINURSO) reported that the situation remained calm during 2000 and there had been no indications that either side intended to resume hostilities in the near future. Under the command of General Claude Buze (Belgium), the MINURSO military component continued to monitor the ceasefire between the Royal Moroccan Army and the POLISARIO military forces which came into effect on 6 September 1991 [YUN 1991, p. 796]. The Mission's military component remained at the authorized strength of 230 throughout the year. The civilian police, under the command of Inspector-General Om Prakash Rathor (India), fell from 81 officers in January to 47 officers at the end of the year. The civilian police continued to protect files and sensitive material at the Identification Commission centres at Laayoune and Tindouf, and to undertake training and planning for possible future activities.

Financing of MINURSO

In March [A/54/780], the Secretary-General reported on MINURSO's financial performance for the period 1 July 1998 to 30 June 1999. Expenditures totalled $44,607,700 gross ($42,398,200 net), resulting in an unutilized balance of appropriation of $15,392,300 gross ($13,520,600 net). The unutilized balance of assessments amounted to $1,423,377 gross ($603,627 net). The unutilized balance resulted primarily from the early repatriation of the military engineering support unit, a higher than projected vacancy rate for international civilian staff and reduced operational requirements due to the suspension of identification activities.

Also in March [A/54/785], the Secretary-General presented the proposed budget to maintain MINURSO from 1 July 2000 to 30 June 2001, which amounted to $46,611,600 gross ($42,772,800 net). In an April report [A/54/841/Add.7], ACABQ recommended that the General Assembly assess the requested amount at a monthly rate of $3,884,300 gross ($3,564,400 net) should the Security Council decide to extend MINURSO's mandate beyond 31 May 2000.

GENERAL ASSEMBLY ACTION

On 15 June [meeting 98], the General Assembly, on the recommendation of the Fifth Committee [A/54/899], adopted **resolution 54/268** without vote [agenda item 131].

Financing of the United Nations Mission for the Referendum in Western Sahara

The General Assembly,

Having considered the reports of the Secretary-General on the financing of the United Nations Mission for the Referendum in Western Sahara and the related reports of the Advisory Committee on Administrative and Budgetary Questions,

Bearing in mind Security Council resolution 690(1991) of 29 April 1991, by which the Council established the United Nations Mission for the Referendum in Western Sahara, and the subsequent resolutions by which the Council extended the mandate of the Mission, the latest of which was resolution 1301(2000) of 31 May 2000,

Recalling its resolution 45/266 of 17 May 1991 on the financing of the Mission and its subsequent resolutions and decisions thereon, the latest of which was resolution 53/18 B of 8 June 1999,

Reaffirming that the costs of the Mission are expenses of the Organization to be borne by Member States in accordance with Article 17, paragraph 2, of the Charter of the United Nations,

Recalling its previous decisions regarding the fact that, in order to meet the expenditures caused by the Mission, a different procedure is required from that applied to meet expenditures of the regular budget of the United Nations,

Taking into account the fact that the economically more developed countries are in a position to make relatively larger contributions and that the economically less developed countries have a relatively limited capacity to contribute towards such an operation,

Bearing in mind the special responsibilities of the States permanent members of the Security Council, as indicated in General Assembly resolution 1874(S-IV) of 27 June 1963, in the financing of such operations,

Noting with appreciation that voluntary contributions have been made to the Mission,

Mindful of the fact that it is essential to provide the Mission with the necessary financial resources to enable it to fulfil its responsibilities under the relevant resolutions of the Security Council,

1. *Takes note* of the status of contributions to the United Nations Mission for the Referendum in Western Sahara as at 30 April 2000, including the contributions outstanding in the amount of 77.2 million United States dollars, representing 19 per cent of the total assessed contributions, notes that some 3 per cent of the Member States have paid their assessed contributions in full, and urges all other Member States concerned, in particular those in arrears, to ensure payment of their outstanding assessed contributions;

2. *Expresses its appreciation* to those Member States which have paid their assessed contributions in full;

3. *Expresses concern* about the financial situation with regard to peacekeeping activities, in particular as regards the reimbursements to troop contributors that bear additional burdens owing to overdue payments by Member States of their assessments;

4. *Urges* all other Member States to make every possible effort to ensure payment of their assessed contributions to the Mission in full and on time;

5. *Expresses concern* at the delay experienced by the Secretary-General in deploying and providing adequate resources to some recent peacekeeping missions, in particular those in Africa;

6. *Emphasizes* that all future and existing peacekeeping missions shall be given equal and non-discriminatory treatment in respect of financial and administrative arrangements;

7. *Also emphasizes* that all peacekeeping missions shall be provided with adequate resources for the effective and efficient discharge of their respective mandates;

8. *Reiterates its request* to the Secretary-General to make the fullest possible use of facilities and equipment at the United Nations Logistics Base at Brindisi, Italy, in order to minimize the costs of procurement for the Mission, and for this purpose requests the Secretary-General to speed up the implementation of the asset management system at all peacekeeping missions in accordance with General Assembly resolution 52/1 A of 15 October 1997;

9. *Endorses* the conclusions and recommendations contained in the report of the Advisory Committee on Administrative and Budgetary Questions, and requests the Secretary-General to ensure their full implementation;

10. *Requests* the Secretary-General to take all necessary action to ensure that the Mission is administered with a maximum of efficiency and economy;

11. *Also requests* the Secretary-General, in order to reduce the cost of employing General Service staff, to continue efforts to recruit local staff for the Mission against General Service posts, commensurate with the requirements of the Mission;

12. *Decides* to reduce the appropriation authorized for the Mission in respect of the period from 1 July 1998 to 30 June 1999 under the terms of General Assembly resolutions 52/228 B of 26 June 1998 and 53/18 A of 2 November 1998 from the amount of 60 million dollars gross (55,918,800 dollars net) to the amount of 46,031,077 dollars gross (43,001,827 dollars net), equal to the amount apportioned among Member States in respect of the period from 1 July 1998 to 31 March 1999, and to extend the period covered by the apportionment until 30 June 1999;

13. *Decides also* to appropriate to the Special Account for the United Nations Mission for the Referendum in Western Sahara the amount of 49,317,037 dollars gross (45,078,102 dollars net) for the maintenance of the Mission for the period from 1 July 2000 to 30 June 2001, inclusive of the amount of 2,339,659 dollars gross (1,979,841 dollars net) for the support account for peacekeeping operations and the amount of 365,778 dollars gross (325,461 dollars net) for the United Nations Logistics Base, to be apportioned, as an ad hoc arrangement, among Member States at a monthly rate of 4,109,753 dollars gross (3,756,509 dollars net), in accordance with the composition of groups set out in paragraphs 3 and 4 of General Assembly resolution 43/232 of 1 March 1989, as adjusted by the Assembly in its resolutions 44/192 B of 21 December 1989, 45/269 of 27 August 1991, 46/198 A of 20 December 1991, 47/218 A of 23 December 1992, 49/249 A of 20 July 1995, 49/249 B of 14 September 1995, 50/224 of 11 April 1996, 51/218 A to C of 18 December 1996 and 52/230 of 31 March 1998 and its decisions 48/472 A of 23 December 1993, 50/451 B of 23 December 1995 and 54/456 to 54/458 of 23 December 1999, and taking into account the scale of assessments for the year 2000,

as set out in its resolutions 52/215 A of 22 December 1997 and 54/237 A of 23 December 1999, and for the year 2001, subject to the decision of the Security Council to extend the mandate of the Mission beyond 31 July 2000;

14. *Decides further* that, in accordance with the provisions of its resolution 973(X) of 15 December 1955, there shall be set off against the apportionment among Member States, as provided for in paragraph 13 above, their respective share in the Tax Equalization Fund of the estimated staff assessment income of 4,238,935 dollars approved for the Mission for the period from 1 July 2000 to 30 June 2001;

15. *Decides* that, for Member States that have fulfilled their financial obligations to the Mission, there shall be set off against their apportionment, as provided for in paragraph 13 above, their respective share of the unencumbered balance of 1,423,377 dollars gross (603,627 dollars net) in respect of the period from 1 July 1998 to 30 June 1999;

16. *Decides also* that, for Member States that have not fulfilled their financial obligations to the Mission, their share of the unencumbered balance of 1,423,377 dollars gross (603,627 dollars net) in respect of the period from 1 July 1998 to 30 June 1999 shall be set off against their outstanding obligations;

17. *Emphasizes* that no peacekeeping mission shall be financed by borrowing funds from other active peacekeeping missions;

18. *Encourages* the Secretary-General to continue to take additional measures to ensure the safety and security of all personnel under the auspices of the United Nations participating in the Mission;

19. *Invites* voluntary contributions to the Mission in cash and in the form of services and supplies acceptable to the Secretary-General, to be administered, as appropriate, in accordance with the procedure and practices established by the General Assembly;

20. *Decides* to include in the provisional agenda of its fifty-fifth session the item entitled "Financing of the United Nations Mission for the Referendum in Western Sahara".

On 23 December, the Assembly decided that the item on MINURSO financing would remain for consideration at its resumed fifty-fifth (2001) session (**decision 55/458**) and that the Fifth Committee should continue consideration of the item at that session (**decision 55/455**).

Other questions

Côte d'Ivoire

In a letter to the Secretary-General [A/55/825], Côte d'Ivoire explained the situation in that country following the coup d'état in December 1999 [YUN 1999, p. 190]. A difficult transition period culminated in the swearing in of a new President on 26 October 2000. Since then, a Government had been in place and had been func-

tioning normally. The letter gave a historical background of the country in an effort to show its political and social inclusiveness and cited some legislative actions taken by the new President. It also stated that Côte d'Ivoire was a democratic State that respected human and citizens' rights. It hoped to reconcile itself with the international community and wished to be able to count on the understanding and contribution of its friends and donors.

Djibouti

By a letter dated 22 February [S/2000/153], Portugal, on behalf of the EU, informed the Secretary-General of the framework agreement signed on 7 February between the armed Front for the Restoration of Unity and Democracy and the Government of Djibouti. The agreement envisaged the suspension of hostilities between the two sides and the liberation of prisoners.

Mozambique

In accordance with decision 54/465 [YUN 1999, p. 190], the General Assembly retained for consideration at its resumed fifty-fourth (2000) session the item "Financing of the United Nations Operation in Mozambique" (ONUMOZ). ONUMOZ began operations in 1992 [YUN 1992, p. 196] and was liquidated in 1995 [YUN 1995, p. 368].

On 5 September 2000, the Assembly included the item in the draft agenda of its fifty-fifth session (**decision 54/497**).

On 23 December, the Assembly decided that the item should remain for consideration at the resumed fifty-fifth (2001) session (**decision 55/458**) and that the Fifth Committee should continue its consideration of the item at that session (**decision 55/455**).

Cooperation between OAU and the UN system

In response to General Assembly resolution 54/94 [YUN 1999, p. 191], the Secretary-General submitted an October report [A/55/498] on cooperation between the United Nations and the Organization of African Unity (OAU).

At a meeting in Addis Ababa, Ethiopia, on 10 and 11 April, the two organizations reviewed and assessed the activities undertaken as a result of the two-year programme of cooperation they adopted in 1998. They also discussed ways and means to enhance their work and adopted an action-oriented programme for the period 2000-2002.

The Secretary-General outlined the collaborative work undertaken in the areas of peace and security involving the Departments of Political Affairs and of Peacekeeping Operations of the UN Secretariat and African subregional organizations, such as the Economic Community of West African States (ECOWAS) and the Southern African Development Community (SADC), and in the area of human rights, involving the Office of the High Commissioner for Human Rights. The report also described cooperative activities in economic and social development involving the UN Department of Economic and Social Affairs and the United Nations Conference on Trade and Development. Other UN agencies and programmes involved in the programme of cooperation were the Office for the Coordination of Humanitarian Affairs, the Office of the United Nations High Commissioner for Refugees, the World Health Organization, the United Nations Children's Fund, the United Nations Development Programme, the United Nations Population Fund and the Economic Commission for Africa.

On 3 August [A/55/286], Ghana transmitted to the Secretary-General the decisions adopted by the OAU Council of Ministers at its seventy-second ordinary session (Lomé, Togo, 6-8 July), and the declarations and decisions adopted by the OAU Assembly of Heads of State and Government at its thirty-sixth ordinary session (Lomé, 10-12 July).

GENERAL ASSEMBLY ACTION

On 21 December [meeting 88], the General Assembly adopted **resolution 55/218** [draft: A/55/L.67, orally revised] without vote [agenda item 27].

Cooperation between the United Nations and the Organization of African Unity

The General Assembly,

Having considered the report of the Secretary-General,

Recalling the provisions of Chapter VIII of the Charter of the United Nations and the agreement on cooperation between the United Nations and the Organization of African Unity, as well as all its resolutions on cooperation between the United Nations and the Organization of African Unity, including resolution 54/94 of 8 December 1999,

Taking note of the declarations and decisions adopted by the Assembly of Heads of State and Government of the Organization of African Unity at its thirty-sixth ordinary session, held in Lomé from 10 to 12 July 2000, in particular the decision relating to the adoption of the Constitutive Act of the African Union and the declaration on the Conference on Security, Stability, Development and Cooperation in Africa,

Mindful of the need for continued and closer cooperation between the United Nations and its specialized agencies and the Organization of African Unity in

the peace and security, political, economic, social, technical, cultural and administrative fields,

Acknowledging the contribution of the United Nations Liaison Office in strengthening coordination and cooperation between the Organization of African Unity and the United Nations since its establishment in Addis Ababa in April 1998,

Emphasizing the importance of the effective implementation of the United Nations Millennium Declaration, and welcoming in this regard the commitments of Member States to respond to the special needs of Africa,

Noting the efforts being made by the Organization of African Unity and its member States in the area of economic integration and the need to accelerate the process of implementation of the Treaty establishing the African Economic Community,

Noting also the progress made by the Organization of African Unity in developing the capacity of its Mechanism for Conflict Prevention, Management and Resolution, including with the assistance of the United Nations and the international community,

Stressing the urgent need to address the plight of refugees and internally displaced persons in Africa, and noting in this context the efforts made to implement the recommendations of the Organization of African Unity Ministerial Meeting on Refugees, Returnees and Displaced Persons in Africa, held in Khartoum on 13 and 14 December 1998, as well as the endorsement by the Council of Ministers of the Organization of African Unity, at its seventy-second session, of the Comprehensive Implementation Plan adopted at the special meeting of governmental and non-governmental technical experts organized by the Organization of African Unity and the Office of the United Nations High Commissioner for Refugees at Conakry from 27 to 29 March 2000,

Recognizing the importance of developing and maintaining a culture of peace, tolerance and harmonious relationships based on the promotion of economic development, democratic principles, good governance, the rule of law, human rights, social justice and international cooperation,

1. *Takes note with satisfaction* of the report of the Secretary-General;

2. *Encourages* the Secretary-General to strengthen the capacity of the United Nations Liaison Office with the Organization of African Unity;

3. *Welcomes* the continuing participation in and constructive contribution of the Organization of African Unity to the work of the United Nations, its organs and specialized agencies, and calls upon the two organizations to enhance the involvement of the Organization of African Unity in all United Nations activities concerning Africa;

4. *Calls upon* the Secretary-General closely to involve the Organization of African Unity in the implementation of the commitments contained in the United Nations Millennium Declaration, especially those that relate to meeting the special needs of Africa;

5. *Requests* the Secretary-General to take the necessary measures to implement the recommendations of the annual meeting of the two organizations held in Addis Ababa on 10 and 11 April 2000, in particular those relating to priority programmes of the Organization of African Unity as specified in section III of the report of the Secretary-General;

6. *Requests* the United Nations to intensify its assistance to the Organization of African Unity in strengthening the institutional and operational capacity of its Mechanism for Conflict Prevention, Management and Resolution, in particular in the following areas:

(a) Development of its early warning system;

(b) Technical assistance and training of civilian and military personnel, including a staff exchange programme;

(c) Exchange and coordination of information, including between the early warning systems of the two organizations;

(d) Logistical support, including in the area of mine clearance;

(e) Mobilization of financial support, including through the trust funds of the United Nations and the Organization of African Unity;

7. *Urges* the United Nations to encourage donor countries, in consultation with the Organization of African Unity, to contribute to adequate funding, training and logistical support for African countries in their efforts to enhance their peacekeeping capabilities, with a view to enabling those countries to participate actively in peacekeeping operations within the framework of the United Nations;

8. *Requests* the agencies of the United Nations system working in Africa to include in their programmes at the national, subregional and regional levels activities to support African countries in their efforts to enhance regional economic cooperation and integration;

9. *Calls upon* the United Nations agencies to intensify the coordination of their regional programmes in Africa to ensure the effective harmonization of their programmes with those of the African regional and subregional economic organizations and contribute to creating a positive environment for economic development and investment;

10. *Calls upon* the international community to support and enhance the capacity of African countries to take advantage of the opportunities offered by globalization and to overcome the challenges it poses, as a means of ensuring sustained economic growth and sustainable development;

11. *Calls upon* the United Nations to support actively the efforts of the Organization of African Unity in urging the donor community and, where appropriate, multilateral institutions to strive to meet the agreed target of 0.7 per cent of gross national product for official development assistance, to implement fully, speedily and effectively the enhanced programme of debt relief for the heavily indebted poor countries, and to achieve the goal of securing debt relief in a comprehensive and effective manner in favour of African countries through various national and international measures designed to make their debt sustainable in the long term;

12. *Calls upon* all Member States and regional and international organizations, in particular those of the United Nations system, as well as non-governmental organizations, to provide additional assistance to the Organization of African Unity and those Governments in Africa concerned with the problems of refugees, returnees and displaced persons;

13. *Calls upon* the relevant organizations of the United Nations system to ensure the effective and equitable representation of African men and women at senior and policy levels at their respective headquarters and in their regional field of operations;

14. *Requests* the Secretary-General to report to the General Assembly at its fifty-sixth session on the implementation of the present resolution.

Cooperation between the UN and ECCAS

On 6 September [A/55/233], Equatorial Guinea transmitted to the Secretary-General an explanatory memorandum from its President, in his capacity as Chairman of the Economic Community of Central African States (ECCAS), with the request that an item on cooperation between the United Nations and ECCAS be included in the agenda of the fifty-fifth session of the General Assembly. The memorandum stated that, since the Community's establishment in 1983, the heads of State of the ECCAS member countries had sought to show their resolve to join forces to achieve subregional integration as a means of better ensuring the well-being of their peoples. The President was convinced of the need to establish an institutional framework to enable the States of the Central African subregion to continue to benefit from the rich experience of the United Nations in such areas as preventive diplomacy, peacekeeping and peace-building, democratic institution-building, human rights and support for economic development.

GENERAL ASSEMBLY ACTION

On 10 November [meeting 58], the General Assembly adopted **resolution 55/22** [draft: A/55/L.6/Rev.1 & Add.1] without vote [agenda item 180].

Cooperation between the United Nations and the Economic Community of Central African States

The General Assembly,

Bearing in mind the charter establishing the Economic Community of Central African States, by which the Central African countries have agreed to work for the economic development of their subregion, to promote economic cooperation and to establish a Common Market of Central Africa,

Welcoming the establishment by the Secretary-General, at the initiative of the States members of the Economic Community of Central African States, of the United Nations Standing Advisory Committee on Security Questions in Central Africa on 28 May 1992, pursuant to resolution 46/37 B of 6 December 1991, and recalling its subsequent resolutions on the programme of work of the Committee,

Bearing in mind the report of the Secretary-General on the causes of conflict and the promotion of durable peace and sustainable development in Africa and resolutions 1196(1998) and 1197(1998) pertaining thereto, adopted by the Security Council on 16 and 18 September 1998 respectively,

Noting that, at the ninth regular session of the Economic Community of Central African States, held in

Malabo on 24 June 1999, the heads of State and Government of the member States decided to resume the activities of the Community, inter alia, by providing it with sufficient financial and human resources to enable it to become a real tool for the integration of their economies and to foster the development of cooperation between their peoples, with the ultimate aim of making it one of the five pillars of the African Economic Community and of helping Central Africa to meet the challenges of globalization,

Welcoming the fact that, in their desire to instil a climate of peace and security and to strengthen democratic institutions and practice, together with respect for the rule of law and human rights in their subregion, the States of the Economic Community of Central African States have established the Council for Peace and Security in Central Africa and have decided to set up an early warning mechanism in Central Africa as a tool for preventing armed conflicts, a subregional parliament and a subregional centre for human rights and democracy in Central Africa to promote democratic values and experience and human rights,

Bearing in mind the United Nations Millennium Declaration, adopted on 8 September 2000 by the heads of State and Government at the Millennium Summit of the United Nations, and especially chapter VII thereof,

Aware of the importance of the support of the United Nations system and the international community, which is essential to ensuring that the members of the Economic Community of Central African States are successful in promoting economic development and integration and in consolidating peace, democracy and human rights in their subregion,

1. *Recognizes* that the purposes and objectives of the Economic Community of Central African States are in conformity with the principles and ideals embodied in the Charter of the United Nations;

2. *Requests* the Secretary-General to take the appropriate steps to establish cooperation between the United Nations and the Economic Community of Central African States;

3. *Welcomes* the support provided by the Secretary-General to the States members of the Economic Community of Central African States in strengthening confidence-building measures at the subregional level and promoting human rights, the rule of law and democratic institutions, in implementation of the programme of work of the United Nations Standing Advisory Committee on Security Questions in Central Africa;

4. *Requests* the Secretary-General to continue this support and, within the existing United Nations budget, extend it to all the fields to be covered in the framework of cooperation between the United Nations system and the Economic Community of Central African States, especially the reinforcement of the structures of the Community and the attainment of its objectives in favour of peace and security, democracy and human rights, so as to facilitate the operation of the early warning mechanism in Central Africa as a tool for preventing armed conflicts and to establish a subregional parliament and a subregional centre for human rights and democracy in Central Africa to promote democratic values and experience and human rights;

5. *Emphasizes* the importance of appropriate coordination between the United Nations system, including the Bretton Woods institutions, and the Economic Community of Central African States;

6. *Urges* all Member States and the international community to contribute to the efforts of the Economic Community of Central African States to achieve economic integration and development, promote democracy and human rights and consolidate peace and security in Central Africa;

7. *Welcomes and calls* for the continuation of the efforts made by a number of States, notably in the form of multinational exercises, to enhance the peacekeeping capacities of the States members of the Economic Community of Central African States, so as to enable them to play a larger part in United Nations operations;

8. *Requests* the Secretary-General to submit to the General Assembly at its fifty-sixth session a report on the implementation of the present resolution;

9. *Decides* to include in the provisional agenda of its fifty-sixth session the item entitled "Cooperation between the United Nations and the Economic Community of Central African States".

Regional cooperation

By an 18 February letter [A/54/760], Gabon transmitted to the Secretary-General the Declaration on the Economic and Social Agenda for Africa at the Dawn of the Third Millennium, adopted at the Summit of African Heads of State and Government (Libreville, 18-19 January).

On 25 April [A/55/70-S/2000/364], Japan transmitted the summary report on the International Symposium on the Roles of Subregional and Non-Governmental Organizations in Conflict Prevention and Peace Initiatives in Sub-Saharan Africa (Tokyo, 28-29 March). The symposium discussed the recognition of conflicts in Africa as matters of serious international concern; the need for cooperation and collaboration among a variety of actors; efforts made by subregional organizations to enhance their capacities and concrete measures for improvements; and the roles and functions of NGOs and the need for further participation.

On 1 June [S/2000/522], Mali transmitted to the Security Council the final communiqué of the twenty-third summit meeting of heads of State and Government of ECOWAS (Abuja, Nigeria, 28-29 May).

By an 8 August letter [A/55/287], Namibia transmitted the final communiqué of the Summit of Heads of State or Government of SADC (Windhoek, Namibia, 6-7 August).

On 19 December [A/55/726-S/2001/3], the Sudan transmitted to the Secretary-General the Khartoum Declaration issued by the Eighth Summit of Heads of State and Government of IGAD (Khartoum, 23 November).

Chapter III

Americas

During 2000, the United Nations continued to assist countries in the Americas region in the attainment of political stability, security, economic and social development, judicial reform and respect for human rights. Although there was an increase in the level of crime in some countries of Central America, progress was made in consolidating democracy in the subregion.

The United Nations Verification Mission in Guatemala (MINUGUA), established in 1994, continued to fulfil its mandate of verifying compliance with the peace accords signed in 1996 between the Government of Guatemala and the Unidad Revolucionaria Nacional Guatemalteca. In December, the General Assembly extended MINUGUA's mandate until 31 December 2001. After four years, a number of commitments on the peace agenda still had not been implemented or were in the process of implementation. The Commission to Follow Up the Implementation of the Peace Agreements rescheduled the pending commitments in an implementation timetable for 2000-2004. The new Government of President Alfonso Portillo took office in January.

In Haiti, the political and institutional crisis continued to worsen throughout the year, stalling the implementation of much-needed structural reforms and further polarizing political and civil society. Parliamentary and local elections were held on 21 May amid a climate of violence. A flawed method of electoral calculation allotted all but one of the contested Senate seats to the ruling Fanmi Lavalas party, headed by former President Jean-Bertrand Aristide. Based on those elections, a new Parliament was installed on 28 August, despite calls for rectification of the results by the international community. Haiti's main bilateral donors suspended all forms of international assistance, deciding to channel their technical support through non-governmental organizations (NGOs). Elections for President and a third of the remaining Senate seats were held on 26 November but were boycotted by the opposition parties. Mr. Aristide was elected President and Fanmi Lavalas won all the contested Senate seats. The International Civilian Support Mission in Haiti (MICAH) was launched on 16 March in order to consolidate the results already achieved by the United Nations Civilian Police

Mission in Haiti and the International Civilian Mission to Haiti. The Security Council had extended the mandates of those two Missions in November 1999 to ensure a phased transition to MICAH by 15 March. By mid-October, the three pillars of MICAH—justice, police and human rights—had deployed a total of 68 advisers in Haiti. In November, due to the political turmoil and instability in the country, the Secretary-General recommended that the Mission be terminated at the end of its mandate on 6 February 2001 and called for a new programme of assistance for the Haitian people that was commensurate with the country's political realities.

In November, the General Assembly again called on States to refrain from promulgating laws and measures such as the ongoing United States economic embargo against Cuba. It also adopted resolutions on strengthening cooperation with the Organization of American States and the Caribbean Community.

Central America

In response to General Assembly resolution 54/118 [YUN 1999, p. 197], the Secretary-General submitted an October report on the situation in Central America [A/55/465], describing progress achieved by Central American countries in the areas of peace, freedom, democracy and development since September 1999. The report focused on the five signatories to the Esquipulas II process [YUN 1987, p. 188] (Costa Rica, El Salvador, Guatemala, Honduras, Nicaragua).

The Secretary-General said that a new Government took office in Guatemala on 14 January, following the first general election (November/ December 1999) [YUN 1999, p. 194] held since the signing of the 1996 Agreement on a Firm and Lasting Peace [YUN 1996, p. 168]. Ongoing verification of political rights by MINUGUA had exposed the need to deepen electoral reforms to increase voter participation and improve conditions for the free exercise of political rights. To that end, the approval by Congress of the Political Parties and Electoral Law was crucial.

Congressional and municipal elections took place in El Salvador on 12 March and voting proceeded without incident. Both the peaceful fashion in which the polling unfolded and the voting patterns exhibited were signs that the rancour of the past had been replaced by a new political maturity. However, 62 per cent of the nation's 3 million voters chose not to vote. Implementation of the 1995 electoral reforms would encourage greater participation.

In Nicaragua, municipal elections were scheduled to take place on 5 November under new electoral rules. The strengthening of citizen participation throughout Central America in electoral and other political processes, in particular by women and indigenous people, was assuming greater urgency. It was hoped that reformed electoral regulations would foster increasingly democratic and pluralistic processes. In that regard, democratic governance was fundamental to ongoing efforts to achieve regional stability.

The region's deteriorating public security situation was a major threat to the enjoyment of fundamental rights. The rise in common crime and social violence was linked to the inability to investigate and punish crimes and human rights violations. Regional and international criminal networks posed an additional challenge to fragile public security structures. The trafficking in firearms was a constant threat to security. Irregularities and long delays in processing accused persons undermined public confidence in the judicial process. Prison reform was urgently needed, in particular the approval of new legislation, the training of personnel and upgrading of the infrastructure. Acts of so-called social cleansing, as well as lynching, continued. In addition, domestic violence and violence against women remained a problem.

The establishment in El Salvador and Guatemala of the National Civil Police, bringing public security forces under civilian control, represented one of the most important achievements of the peace agreements and a key element of the democratization process in the region. In Guatemala, Congress approved legislation allowing for joint patrols by the police and the army. Similar joint patrols were conducted in rural parts of El Salvador. The Secretary-General said that the need to address the population's feeling of insecurity should not be made at the cost of remilitarizing public security. The participation of police officers in criminal acts and human rights violations seriously undermined the credibility of the security forces. Salvadoran authorities had established a special commission to strengthen discipline and internal control mechanisms. Similar functions were fulfilled in Guatemala by

the Office of Professional Responsibility within the National Civil Police. Criminal investigative capacity was still deficient throughout the region, giving rise to numerous due process violations and lack of confidence in the administration of justice. The adoption in Guatemala of the Career Judicial Service Act, together with the setting up of the ad hoc commission on the strengthening of the justice system, should strengthen the rule of law, while inadequacy of the national penitentiary system was being addressed by means of new legislation and increasing budgetary allocations. However, serious deficiencies in infrastructure, trained personnel and prison security persisted, leading to overcrowding and deplorable living conditions for the inmates. Lengthy periods of pre-trial detention remained a problem throughout the region.

Meeting for the twelfth time in March, Central American ombudsmen made a collective call to Central American Governments to ensure that globalization would not negatively impact the enjoyment of social, economic, cultural and political rights. They recommended a cautious approach towards privatizing basic services such as health, education, housing and communications, in order to avoid increasing extreme poverty. At the national level, the ombudsmen played a central role in the defence of democracy and the rule of law by ensuring public accountability of government actions. For that reason, it was important that the independence of those institutions be strengthened and that problems related to the lack of leadership and proper funding be adequately addressed. The establishment in Nicaragua of the Ombudsman's Office represented an important development.

Hurricane Mitch, which devastated parts of Central America in October 1998 [YUN 1998, p. 876], revealed the region's extreme social and ecological vulnerability. After the May 1999 meeting of the Consultative Group for the Reconstruction and Transformation of Central America and the adoption of the Stockholm Declaration [YUN 1999, p. 195], national follow-up meetings were held for Costa Rica, Honduras and El Salvador in February 2000. The national meetings recognized significant progress in the process of reconstruction in all the countries examined. It was also recognized that the agenda of transformation, including the strengthening of democratic governance, transparency, environmental protection and poverty reduction, should become the focus of national efforts with the support of the international community.

According to the Economic Commission for Latin America and the Caribbean (ECLAC), the gross national product for the Central American region grew by 3.4 per cent in 1999 compared to 4.4 per cent in 1998. That drop mirrored similar stagnation throughout Latin America and the Caribbean. The gross domestic product (GDP) growth rates ranged from a high of 7.5 per cent in Costa Rica to a low of 2 per cent in Honduras. The major factor in that contraction was the devastation caused by hurricane Mitch. Overall, however, the 1990s brought significant economic growth to Central America. Advances had been made in the area of structural economic reform, though the capacity of Governments to transform and create sustainable economic growth depended largely on reducing the burden of external debt. In July, the International Monetary Fund and the World Bank agreed to support a comprehensive debt reduction package for Honduras under the Heavily Indebted Poor Countries Initiative. As a sign of increasing trade and cooperation within and outside the region, El Salvador, Guatemala and Honduras, in May, signed a free trade agreement with Mexico, which committed those countries to pursuing regional trade liberalization to further economic integration in the western hemisphere. In the same month, the United States extended the benefits of the Caribbean Basin Initiative to a number of Central American countries, ensuring their increased duty-free access to the United States market. In addition, cooperation continued or was projected with the European Union (EU), the Andean Community (Bolivia, Colombia, Ecuador, Peru, Venezuela) and Canada.

On 15 and 16 May, Colombia hosted the fourteenth Summit Meeting of Heads of State and Government of the Rio Group, which served as a mechanism for political coordination. For the first time, Central American countries participated in the Summit, with heads of State from Latin America and the Caribbean. The role of the United Nations, personal and environmental safety and the reform of the international financial system dominated the agenda. Ministers of Trade from six Central American countries met in Panama in March to continue discussions on a regional free trade agreement. At that meeting, ministers from Costa Rica, El Salvador, Guatemala, Honduras and Nicaragua began talks with Panama on a comprehensive trade pact.

Closer regional integration remained the key to consolidating peace and fostering development throughout the isthmus. The secretariat of the Central American Integration System (SICA) continued to work towards the execution and coordination of the mandates established at the summits of the Central American Presidents, as well as the decisions of the Council of Ministers of External Relations. On 2 May, the Presidents

of El Salvador, Guatemala and Nicaragua signed an integration pact, the Declaración Trinacional para el siglo XXI, containing economic and political proposals to accelerate the integration process (see p. 237). Furthermore, at a meeting of Ministers for Foreign Affairs from Central American States in Panama that same month, ways to advance the goal of regional integration established by SICA were explored.

The Ministers of External Relations of the Central American countries attended the thirtieth regular session of the General Assembly of the Organization of American States (OAS) (Windsor, Canada, 4-6 June). The session focused on democracy and human security, adopting various resolutions on Central America, and, in particular, reaffirming the need to continue joint efforts between the OAS and SICA secretariats. It also adopted a resolution for the continued support of the mine-clearing programme in Central America, as well as the Special Programme of Support for Guatemala. Finally, the Assembly resolved to establish a permanent fund for the peaceful resolution of territorial disputes among member States.

OAS played a leading role in reducing tensions and seeking a political solution to border disputes, such as in the case of the dispute between Honduras and Nicaragua that flared up in late 1999 [YUN 1999, p. 208]. Under the auspices of the OAS Secretary-General, Costa Rica and Nicaragua reached an understanding on the San Juan River [ibid.].

The United Nations continued to support the process of peace-building and development in Central America. In El Salvador, the United Nations Development Programme (UNDP) followed up on the implementation of outstanding commitments of the 1992 Peace Agreement [YUN 1992, p. 222] and was assisting the Government to that end. The Secretary-General said that much remained to be done to implement the recommendations of the Commission on the Truth [YUN 1993, p. 314]. Also outstanding was the enactment of an agrarian code. Other concerns included the non-fulfilment by the authorities of their obligation to provide benefits to handicapped combatants and the dependants of combatants killed during the conflict; the deteriorating public security situation; and the failure to strengthen the role of the ombudsman.

In Guatemala, the United Nations continued to verify compliance with the 1996 Agreement on a Firm and Lasting Peace [YUN 1996, p. 168]. The Secretary-General was encouraged by the fact that, upon taking office in January, President Alfonso Portillo embraced the accords as an obligation of the State and pledged to reinvigorate the peace process by promoting social policies based on the accords. Equally important was the commitment shown by the Unidad Revolucionaria Nacional Guatemalteca (URNG) to fully implement the peace agenda. However, the Secretary-General expressed concern about signs of a qualitative deterioration in the human rights situation.

UNDP was elaborating a regional strategy, within the framework of the 1999 Stockholm Declaration [YUN 1999, p. 195], on the effects of hurricane Mitch. The strategy would focus on democratic governance, poverty and equality, protection of the environment and reduction of the region's vulnerability to natural disasters. A regional strategy for reducing disasters, which included the five Central American countries plus Belize and Panama, had been drawn up. With regard to other operational activities, Guatemalan civil society and, in particular, women's and indigenous organizations, had contributed policy proposals related to the peace accords with the support of UNDP and bilateral donors. UNDP had supported the Nicaraguan Government in creating national forums for the discussion of public policy and in drafting an environmental curriculum. It had also assisted Nicaragua and Honduras in preparing national reconstruction plans and monitoring their implementation and in preparing the poverty reduction strategy papers required by the World Bank in order to enter into relief programmes for highly indebted countries. In El Salvador and Guatemala, UNDP supported the modernization of the justice sector by focusing on institutional strengthening, law reforms and personnel training. In Guatemala and Nicaragua, UNDP was supporting initiatives to increase the access of excluded populations to the justice system.

The Secretary-General observed that nearly two decades after the United Nations first became involved in the region, it seemed clear that the success of the peacekeeping operations was due to the comprehensive peace-building strategy put in place by Central American countries and civil societies. Furthermore, the international community had consistently supported, through political and economic means, the exemplary engagement of local actors. As a result of that multifaceted effort, Central America was a region transformed. However, the effective completion of the peace-building stage, such as greater regional integration, continued to be a challenge for the consolidation of democracy.

Communication. On 4 May [A/54/862], El Salvador, Guatemala and Nicaragua transmitted to the Secretary-General three documents they had signed on 2 May on ways to facilitate political and economic integration and cooperation in Central America.

GENERAL ASSEMBLY ACTION

On 19 December [meeting 86], the General Assembly adopted **resolution 55/178** [draft: A/55/L.42/Rev.1 & Add.1] without vote [agenda item 43].

The situation in Central America: procedures for the establishment of a firm and lasting peace and progress in fashioning a region of peace, freedom, democracy and development

The General Assembly,

Considering the relevant resolutions of the Security Council, particularly resolution 637(1989) of 27 July 1989, and its own resolutions, particularly resolution 43/24 of 15 November 1988, in which it requests the Secretary-General to continue his good offices and to afford the fullest possible support to the Central American Governments in their efforts to achieve the objectives of peace, reconciliation, democracy, development and justice established in the agreement on "Procedures for the establishment of a firm and lasting peace in Central America" of 7 August 1987,

Reaffirming its resolutions in which it recognizes and stresses the importance of international economic, financial and technical cooperation and assistance, both bilateral and multilateral, aimed at promoting economic and social development in the region with a view to furthering and supplementing the efforts of the Central American peoples and Governments to achieve peace and democratization, particularly resolution 52/169 G of 16 December 1997, concerning international assistance to and cooperation with the Alliance for the Sustainable Development of Central America, as well as its resolution 53/1 C of 2 November 1998, concerning emergency assistance to Central America, owing to the destruction caused by hurricane Mitch,

Emphasizing the importance of the development of the Central American Integration System, which has as its main objective the promotion of the integration process, the Alliance for the Sustainable Development of Central America as the integrated programme for national and regional development, which contains the commitments and priorities of the countries of the area for the promotion of sustainable development, the establishment of the subsystem and of the regional social policy, the model of democratic Central American security, and the implementation of other agreements adopted at the presidential summit meetings, which taken together constitute the global frame of reference for consolidating peace, freedom, democracy and development and the basis for the promotion of mutually advantageous relations between Central America and the international community,

Recognizing the considerable success achieved in the fulfilment of the commitments contained in the Guatemala Peace Agreements, implementation of which is being verified by the United Nations Verification Mission in Guatemala,

Noting at the same time the delays in the fulfilment of some of the commitments contained in the Guatemala Peace Agreements, which has led the Commission to Follow up the Implementation of the Peace Agreements to reschedule its fulfilment for the period 2001-2004, and having considered the report of the Secretary-General on the work of the United Nations Verification Mission in Guatemala and the recommendations contained therein aimed at ensuring that the Mission is able to respond adequately to the demands of the peace process until December 2001,

Taking note with satisfaction of the successful implementation of the Peace Agreements and the continuous consolidation of the process of democratization in El Salvador, as a result of the efforts of its people and Government,

Recognizing with satisfaction the role played by the peacekeeping operations and observer and monitoring missions of the United Nations, which carried out successfully their mandate in Central America pursuant to the relevant resolutions of the Security Council and the General Assembly, respectively,

Recognizing with satisfaction also the organization and holding of general elections in Guatemala at the end of 1999, of municipal and parliamentary elections in El Salvador in March 2000 and of municipal elections in Nicaragua in November 2000,

Emphasizing the importance of the end of a critical period in Central American history and the start of a new phase free from armed conflict, with freely elected Governments in each country and with political, economic, social and other changes which are creating a climate conducive to the promotion of economic growth and further progress towards the consolidation and further development of democratic, just and equitable societies,

Noting with gratification that the Third Meeting of the States Parties to the Convention on the Prohibition of the Use, Stockpiling, Production and Transfer of Antipersonnel Mines and on Their Destruction will be held in Nicaragua in September 2001,

Reaffirming that the consolidation and establishment of firm and lasting peace and democracy in Central America is a dynamic and ongoing process that faces serious structural challenges,

Stressing the importance of progress in human development, especially the alleviation of extreme poverty, the promotion of economic and social justice, judicial reform, the safeguarding of human rights and fundamental freedoms, respect for minorities and the satisfaction of the basic needs of the most vulnerable groups among the peoples in the region, issues which have been a primary source of tension and conflict and which deserve to be discussed with the same urgency and dedication as was the case in the settlement of armed conflicts,

Considering with concern that it has not yet been possible to overcome the devastating effects of hurricanes Mitch and Keith on sectors of Central American countries and which are causing setbacks in the efforts of the peoples and the Governments of Central America,

Emphasizing the solidarity of the international community with the victims of hurricane Mitch, as demonstrated by the Stockholm Declaration, the subsequent meetings of the Consultative Group for the Reconstruction and Transformation of Central America and the next meeting of the Group in Madrid in January 2001,

· *Bearing in mind* the efforts made by the Central American Governments to reduce the risks and miti-

gate the consequences of natural disasters in the region, as demonstrated by the adoption, by the Presidents of the isthmus, of the Declaration of Guatemala II of 19 October 1999, the subsequent adoption of the Strategic Framework for the Reduction of Vulnerability and Disasters in Central America, as well as the adoption of the Central American Five-Year Plan for the Reduction of Vulnerability to and the Impact of Disasters, 2000 to 2004,

1. *Takes note with appreciation* of the report of the Secretary-General;

2. *Commends* the efforts of the peoples and the Governments of the Central American countries to re-establish peace and democracy throughout the region and promote sustainable development by implementing the commitments adopted at the summit meetings in the region, and supports the decision of the Presidents that Central America should become a region of peace, freedom, democracy and development;

3. *Reaffirms* the need to continue to improve the electoral processes that have been taking place in Central America, which are conducive to the consolidation of democracy in the region, and encourages greater participation of citizens in elections;

4. *Recognizes* the need to continue to follow closely the situation in Central America according to the objectives and principles established in the Stockholm Declaration in order to support national and regional efforts to overcome the underlying causes that have led to armed conflicts, avoid setbacks and consolidate peace and democratization in the area and promote the objectives of the Alliance for the Sustainable Development of Central America;

5. *Stresses* the importance of lending support to the meeting of the Consultative Group for the Reconstruction and Transformation of Central America, which will be held in Madrid in January 2001, in order to continue to help to consolidate the modernization and improvement of the principal structures of the region in accordance with the model established by the Alliance for Sustainable Development;

6. *Welcomes* the Declaration of Guatemala II which provides for the necessary measures to prevent vulnerability to and mitigate the effects of natural disasters;

7. *Also welcomes* the progress achieved in implementing the Guatemala Peace Agreements, calls upon all parties to take further measures to implement the commitments in the Peace Agreements, and urges all sectors of society to combine efforts and work with courage and determination to consolidate peace;

8. *Requests* the Secretary-General, the bodies and programmes of the United Nations system and the international community to continue to support and verify in Guatemala the implementation of all the peace agreements signed under United Nations auspices, compliance with which is an essential condition for a firm and lasting peace in that country, and to consider the implementation of the Peace Agreements as the framework for their technical and financial assistance programmes and projects, stressing the importance of constant and close cooperation among them in the context of the United Nations Development Assistance Framework for Guatemala;

9. *Expresses its appreciation with satisfaction* to the people and the Government of El Salvador for their efforts to fulfil the commitments set forth in the Peace Agree-

ments, which has made a substantial contribution to the strengthening of the process of democratization in that country;

10. *Recognizes* the importance of the Central American Integration System as the body set up to coordinate and harmonize efforts to achieve integration, and calls upon the international community, the United Nations system and other international organizations, both governmental and non-governmental, to extend generous and effective cooperation with a view to improving the competence and efficiency of the Integration System in the fulfilment of its mandate;

11. *Underlines* the efforts carried out in the Central American region towards integration, such as the Trinational Declaration between Guatemala, El Salvador and Nicaragua, as well as the Customs Union between those countries, as means for promoting integration while respecting different stages of development, through a pragmatic mechanism open to the participation of the other countries of the region;

12. *Encourages* the Central American Governments to continue to carry out their historic responsibilities by fully implementing the commitments they have assumed under national, regional or international agreements, especially the commitments to implement the social programme to overcome poverty and unemployment, establish a more just and equitable society, improve public safety, strengthen the judiciary, consolidate a modern and transparent public administration and eliminate corruption, impunity, acts of terrorism and drug and arms trafficking, all of which are necessary and urgent measures for establishing a firm and lasting peace in the region;

13. *Reiterates its deep appreciation* to the Secretary-General, his special representatives, the groups of countries for the peace processes in El Salvador (Colombia, Mexico, Spain, United States of America and Venezuela), and Guatemala (Colombia, Mexico, Norway, Spain, United States of America and Venezuela), to the Support Group for Nicaragua (Canada, Mexico, Netherlands, Spain and Sweden), to the European Union and to other countries that have contributed significantly and to the international community in general for its support and solidarity in the building of peace, democracy and development in Central America;

14. *Reaffirms* the importance of international cooperation, in particular cooperation with the bodies, funds and programmes of the United Nations system and the donor community in the new stage of consolidating firm and lasting peace and democracy in Central America, and urges them to continue to support Central American efforts to achieve those goals;

15. *Notes with satisfaction* the determination of the Central American Governments to settle their disputes through peaceful means, thereby avoiding any setback in the efforts to consolidate firm and lasting peace in the region;

16. *Requests* the Secretary-General to continue to lend his full support to the initiatives and activities of the Central American Governments, particularly their efforts to consolidate peace and democracy through the promotion of integration and the implementation of the comprehensive sustainable development programme, emphasizing, inter alia, the potential repercussions of natural disasters, in particular the persist-

ing effects of hurricane Mitch, for the peace processes and the vulnerable economies of the region, and to report to the General Assembly at its fifty-sixth session on the implementation of the present resolution;

17. *Decides* to include in the provisional agenda of its fifty-sixth session the item entitled "The situation in Central America: procedures for the establishment of a firm and lasting peace and progress in fashioning a region of peace, freedom, democracy and development".

On 23 December, the Assembly decided that the agenda item on the situation in Central America would remain for consideration during its resumed fifty-fifth (2001) session (**decision 55/458**).

Guatemala

In 2000, the peace process in Guatemala continued to be implemented, although its impact on the lives of the people was marginal, a situation that was affecting governance and the process itself. There was a marked deterioration in public security, reflected in, among other things, an increase in crime and actions by armed criminal groups.

The United Nations Verification Mission in Guatemala (MINUGUA) continued to verify the implementation of the 1996 Agreement on a Firm and Lasting Peace [YUN 1996, p. 168] and the Agreement on the Implementation, Compliance and Verification Timetable for the Peace Agreements (the Timetable Agreement) [YUN 1997, p. 176], signed by the Government of Guatemala and URNG. After four years, a number of commitments were still in the process of implementation or had not been implemented. The Commission to Follow Up the Implementation of the Peace Agreements therefore completely rescheduled pending commitments in an implementation timetable for 2000-2004. The Secretary-General transmitted to the General Assembly reports by the MINUGUA Director covering the Mission's activities throughout 2000. The Assembly renewed the Mission's mandate until 31 December 2001.

MINUGUA

The mandate of MINUGUA, which was extended to 31 December 2000 by General Assembly resolution 54/99 [YUN 1999, p. 205], included verification of all agreements signed by the Government of Guatemala and URNG covering human rights, the parties' compliance with the ceasefire, separation and concentration of the respective forces, and disarmament and demobilization of former URNG combatants. The Mission's functions also comprised good offices, advisory and support services and public information. The parties to the agreements had requested that the duration of MINUGUA's mandate be the same as that of the implementation timetable, namely four years, up to 31 December 2000.

By a 28 July letter [A/54/950], the Secretary-General informed the General Assembly of his decision to appoint Gerd D. Merrem (Germany) as his Special Representative in Guatemala and Head of MINUGUA, succeeding Jean Arnault (France). The appointment would take effect on 1 August 2000.

Report of Secretary-General. In response to General Assembly resolution 54/99, the Secretary-General submitted a September report [A/55/389] covering the state of implementation of the peace agreements (see below) and the structure and staffing of MINUGUA. He noted that March 2000 marked the tenth anniversary of direct UN involvement in the Guatemalan peace process. Citing the relevance and extent of the outstanding agenda, the parties to the peace agreements had requested the United Nations to continue to support the consolidation of the process until 2003, although the duration of MINUGUA's mandate had been the same as that of the implementation timetable, namely four years, up to 31 December 2000. A considerable number of commitments remained to be fully accomplished in the third and last phase (1998-2000), which would necessitate monitoring the further implementation of the agreements, with a special focus on socio-economic issues, rural development, strengthening of civilian power and various forms of increased citizen participation. The implementation of the agreements was to be based on a revised calendar that was being considered by the Commission to Follow Up the Implementation of the Peace Agreements (Follow-up Commission), which was expected to reschedule pending commitments and establish timelines for items that were not initially included in the agreements.

For the 2001-2003 period, the Secretary-General planned to scale down the Mission's operation, starting with an important reduction in staffing, which would ensure substantive savings in 2001. The achievements already registered in the implementation of the peace process formed the basis for an important restructuring of personnel. Regional offices and sub-offices would be redeployed without sacrificing geographical coverage. In order to ensure a steady transition through the three-year period towards a nationally driven process, the Mission's functions were being refocused with the aim of strengthening national actors, both governmental and non-governmental. MINUGUA would continue to assist the parties in providing good offices, verification, assistance in specific fields and public infor-

mation. In 2001, the Mission was expected to have a total of six regional offices (reduced from eight), four sub-offices (reduced from five) and five mobile offices (increased from three). The number of political affairs officers would be reduced by approximately 45 per cent. An 80 per cent reduction of military and police observers was also envisaged, as well as corresponding reductions of 40 per cent in international and national administrative support staff. That would result in an overall 45 per cent decrease in Mission staff. The structure of the Mission's headquarters would continue to consist of four substantive areas, namely: human rights; juridical affairs; socio-economic affairs, resettlement and incorporation; and public security and military affairs. The Public Information Office would remain unchanged. The offices of the Military and Police Advisers would merge under public security and military affairs. With a view to enhancing cooperation within the UN system, MINUGUA would begin a gradual transfer of projects, funded by an existing trust fund for peace in Guatemala, to relevant UN agencies. The Mission would, however, continue to guide core projects to ensure their timely implementation and coherence with the overall MINUGUA strategy and the priorities established by the Follow-up Commission. The Mission would provide, with the parties' consent, specific technical support to other entities, such as NGOs and State structures involved in the implementation of the peace process. The Secretary-General recommended that the Assembly authorize the renewal of MINUGUA's mandate for a further period of one year, until 31 December 2001.

Verification of compliance

In response to General Assembly resolution 54/99, the Secretary-General, in July, submitted his fifth report [A/55/175] on the verification of compliance with the agreements signed by the Government of Guatemala and URNG [YUN 1996, p. 168].

The implementation of the commitments entered into by the two parties was governed by the Timetable Agreement [YUN 1997, p. 176], which divided the period from 1997 to 2000 into three phases. The report covered part of the third phase (1998-2000), from 1 November 1999 to 30 June 2000, and focused on the priority areas identified in 1999 by the Follow-up Commission [YUN 1999, p. 201].

The Secretary-General said that there was a need to implement the outstanding agenda, which included commitments such as the implementation of fiscal reforms, the expansion of judicial reforms, the reform of the electoral system and the armed forces, and critical aspects related to public security. At the same time, the labour and housing situations, the sustainable reintegration of the uprooted and demobilized population and the problems of compensation and national reconciliation remained outstanding and the failure to solve them was affecting both the peace process and governance. The challenge was to ensure the sustainability of the progress achieved, to make adequate provision for the multicultural and multi-ethnic characteristics of Guatemala society in all areas of national life, and to extend the benefits of peace to the areas of the country where the social debt remained greatest.

Noting that Alfonso Portillo had taken office as President on 15 January, the Secretary-General recalled that he had expressed his satisfaction at President Portillo's strong reaffirmation, in his inaugural speech, of the validity of the peace process and his recognition that its full implementation was a State commitment. In late January, President Portillo presented his proposal for a democratic governance pact, intended as a mechanism for reaching consensus among State representatives and political and social leaders on a national agenda, based on the peace agreements, that would be submitted to local authorities for discussion in order to secure broad consensus throughout the country. The President specifically requested the help of the UN system and MINUGUA.

In March, the Chairman of the Presidential Commission for Coordinating Executive Policy in the Field of Human Rights set out the policy adopted by the Government in the area of human rights. The proposed measures included ratification of international human rights instruments and acknowledgement of the State's responsibility in cases submitted to the Inter-American Court of Human Rights. In May, the Peace Secretariat (SEPAZ) presented its Strategic Guidelines for the Implementation of the Peace Agreements, 2000-2004, which envisaged a renewed effort to implement the agreements and the strengthening of institutions set out under the peace process.

MINUGUA reported that, in the early months of the new Government, a number of bodies had been created and mechanisms set in motion that, in some cases, paralleled or duplicated the institutions derived from or provided for in the agreements. Lack of coordination among government agencies responsible for the broad strategic outlines of the peace agenda could hamper their ability to carry out their mandates properly, and that could weaken both the institutions created by the peace process and the State's organiza-

tional capacity to implement the agreements. SEPAZ announced that priority would be given to allocating resources and building State institutions in areas of the country hardest hit by the internal armed conflict, where a significant percentage of the uprooted and demobilized population were living. MINUGUA believed that SEPAZ's approach would promote reconciliation in those areas, though it should not take the place of fulfilling the commitments undertaken towards the resettlement of population groups uprooted by the civil war and the integration of former combatants. The delay in fulfilling those commitments was undermining legal certainty as to land tenure and the economic self-sufficiency of the intended beneficiaries.

While the Mission noted the urgent need to overcome the population's feelings of insecurity, it was deeply concerned that measures were being adopted that were not conducive to the demilitarization of public security or to the strengthening of civilian authority. Despite the perception that the National Civil Police (PNC) was given to excesses, no serious effort had been made to improve its operational, technical and training capacities. The Secretary-General had recommended that the Government should fulfil its commitments under the peace agreements with regard to public security, namely: to set up the Advisory Council on Security; to implement the judicial reform in order to combat impunity; to increase the capacity of the new PNC in all its aspects; and to adopt a comprehensive public security policy as soon as possible.

The Secretary-General reiterated his deep satisfaction at the signing of the Fiscal Pact for a Future with Peace and Development, the outcome of an extensive process of national consultation to define a long-term fiscal policy [YUN 1999, p. 202]. That process, which was supported by MINUGUA as part of its good offices and technical assistance mandate, was without precedent in Guatemala's history and involved the participation of broad sectors of society.

As to the 1994 Comprehensive Agreement on Human Rights [YUN 1994, p. 407], MINUGUA had observed substantial delays in implementing the 1999 National Programme of Compensation for and/or Assistance to the Victims of Human Rights Violations during the Armed Conflict [YUN 1999, p. 201]. SEPAZ had identified the readjustment of that programme as a priority in its strategic guidelines. MINUGUA monitored the execution of two pilot programmes of assistance to victims of human rights violations, which covered the areas of health, education, housing, infrastructure, exhumation and restoration of dignity to the victims. The purpose of the pilot projects was to provide information to help finalize the design of the national compensation and assistance programme. The Mission had found that communities in which some of those projects had been carried out were pleased with them. The beneficiaries saw the projects as a reparation for the losses suffered during the armed conflict, but did not associate them with forgiveness and reconciliation. The Secretary-General noted that in reformulating the national compensation programme, it would be important to incorporate those missing dimensions. A national programme of reconciliation had to be launched as a matter of urgency and its technical and financial sustainability ensured as part of a long-term effort to fulfil the State's legal and moral obligation to the victims.

The Follow-up Commission submitted to the Guatemalan Congress the preliminary draft of a bill setting up a commission for peace and harmony, the text of which was based on a draft prepared by the Multi-institutional Forum for Peace and Harmony, a group of civil society organizations formed in 1999 to advance the implementation of the Commission for Historical Clarification recommendations [YUN 1999, p. 199]. In April 2000, the Congressional Committee for Peace and Mine Clearance issued a new, unfavourable ruling on the draft bill, which had still to be submitted to the full Congress. MINUGUA considered it important for the national reconciliation process that the bill be debated and approved in the Congress as soon as possible. The establishment of a commission for peace and harmony, as provided for in SEPAZ strategic guidelines, would make it easier to address such critical issues as comprehensive policies on the search for the disappeared and on exhumations.

Regarding compliance with the 1994 Agreement on Resettlement of the Population Groups Uprooted by the Armed Conflict [YUN 1994, p. 407], the Secretary-General said that the implementation of a comprehensive, long-term rural development policy was essential for consolidating the bases for sustainable productive integration, and thereby ensuring the definitive reintegration of the uprooted population in conditions of dignity. It was important to move ahead in fulfilling a number of commitments made with regard to rural development, land management plans, the promotion of public investment in rural areas and the allocation of specific resources to the competent institutions. At the same time, the formulation of long-term social development policies should include: the allocation of resources and the identification of institutional mechanisms that would facilitate the integration of the uprooted population and allow for the incorpo-

ration of elements of the special education plan into the official educational system; reaffirmation in the new public health policy of the priority accorded to 13 specific projects, to help ensure that the goal of bringing comprehensive health care to 100 per cent of the uprooted population was attained by the end of 2001; and disbursement of the fund of 200 million quetzales (approximately $25 million) announced by the Government in order to provide housing for uprooted and demobilized populations. Access to land and legal security of tenure continued to be priority issues for the uprooted population. The purchase of agricultural estates for Communities in Resistance had been completed, but resources had yet to be earmarked for ensuring that the process of socio-economic reintegration was sustainable. For the internally displaced population, only two more estates were acquired in addition to the two previously purchased. The Land Trust Fund (FONTIERRAS) did not have sufficient funds to purchase the remaining 19 estates needed to reach the target of 23 estates pledged in 1999. Moreover, for the estates already purchased, no specific funds had been allocated for moving in the new owners or providing basic services. FONTIERRAS had also assumed responsibility for completing the process of regularizing title to public lands awarded to the uprooted population. Little had been accomplished in terms of sustainable productive integration. The Trust Fund of the Consultative Assembly of Uprooted Population Groups/Ministry of Agriculture, Livestock and Food was still at the negotiation stage. Congress adopted a decree that fulfilled the commitment to provide the uprooted population with personal documentation, although there had been constraints on its implementation.

Under the 1995 Agreement on Identity and Rights of Indigenous Peoples [YUN 1995, p. 432], a number of ministries were carrying out decentralization projects based on new social participation structures, chiefly in the areas of health and education. In some cases, that process overlooked existing forms of participation, notably those of indigenous communities and their traditional authorities. MINUGUA recommended that the recognition of the legal personality of indigenous communities should be made effective and reiterated the importance of the commitment to create consultation mechanisms allowing indigenous people to participate in decision-making on public matters that concerned them. The Permanent National Commission for the Official Recognition of Indigenous Languages and the Academy of Mayan Languages of Guatemala had prepared a preliminary draft of a bill on languages, but lack of funds had prevented it from being submitted to the linguistic communities for endorsement. The Joint Commission on Reform and Participation proposed amendments to the Municipal Code and the Development Councils Act, but discussions on both proposals were at a standstill pending the formulation of a decentralization strategy. The Government and SEPAZ were refocusing the Commission's work towards broader proposals covering issues of decentralization, participation and governance. MINUGUA trusted that the intention of broadening the opportunities for debate with other social actors would respect the nature of that Commission, which had been judged an important mechanism for participation and consensus-building between the Government and indigenous peoples. The Mission welcomed the appointment of members of the Maya people to high-level political posts, though the number of such appointments was still very small. The Joint Commission on Rights relating to Indigenous Peoples' Land continued its work, although it faced difficulties owing to the turnover of its membership and the absence of technical, logistical and economic support. The Mission noted that the commitments concerning land and natural resources were a key issue that transcended the economic use of land, was highly sensitive and offered considerable potential for social conflict. It was therefore urgent that the commitments relating to land contained in the peace agreements should be addressed comprehensively, especially those relating to the recognition and regulation of indigenous communities' land tenure. The proposal submitted by the Joint Commission on Educational Reform, which envisaged an intercultural, bilingual education system in keeping with Guatemala's cultural and linguistic diversity, was welcomed by the Advisory Commission of the Ministry of Education. MINUGUA noted with satisfaction the increase in the number of studies on indigenous customary law carried out by educational institutions and research centres, but expressed concern that the Guatemalan Government had committed limited resources to the funding of the Office for the Defence of Indigenous Women's Rights.

Under the 1996 Agreement on Social and Economic Aspects and the Agrarian Situation [YUN 1996, p. 165], the Fiscal Pact for a Future with Peace and Development was signed on 25 May by over 130 organizations representing a broad spectrum of society. The Pact set forth the principles and commitments that should guide fiscal policy in the coming decade. On 20 June, representatives of civil society and business signed the Political Agreement for Funding Peace, Development and

Democracy in Guatemala, which set forth measures for beginning the tax and administrative changes needed to build a new fiscal system. On 28 June, the signatories to that Agreement and representatives of the executive branch and the Congress completed negotiations on a set of fiscal measures to be implemented beginning in July and, progressively, throughout the rest of the year.

Crucial commitments concerning the agrarian situation remained to be implemented, including the establishment of an agrarian and environmental jurisdiction and the promulgation of a land registry act. The agricultural policy for 2000-2004 presented by the Ministry of Agriculture, Livestock and Food included guidelines for assisting small farmers but lacked specific investment plans for promoting their development.

MINUGUA noted that there was a glaring disproportion between the magnitude and complexity of the country's labour problems and the human and material resources allocated by the State to overcome them. It also noted that labour issues played a secondary role in political decision-making. On the other hand, the Mission welcomed the increase in the minimum wage and in the bonuses decreed in early 2000, as well as the bill sent by the President to Congress containing amendments to the Labour Code that would bring national legislation into line with the standards set by International Labour Organization (ILO) conventions.

Progress in fulfilling the commitments on social development encountered serious obstacles. Public investment in the social sphere was delayed and an almost 20-per-cent cut in the approved budget, except for health, education and security, affected the State's physical and financial investment capacity. The budget cuts affected not only public investment in the country's poorest areas, but also the funding of many commitments scheduled for implementation in 2000. As a result, in the first six months of the year, very little progress was made in meeting targets for social investment and for coverage and quality of social services. The social sector budget for 2000 was approximately $500.6 million, but only 31 per cent of that amount had been disbursed as at 31 May. The Ministry of Education announced the implementation of a national literacy programme that it hoped would reduce the illiteracy rate to around 15 per cent within four years and would benefit 2.8 million people.

The 2000 budget for the health sector amounted to $263.6 million, of which only 29.2 per cent had been disbursed by May. The basic objectives of the National Health Plan 2000-2004 included plans for promoting women's health, such as adequate access to prenatal care and childbirth services. The 2000 budget for the housing sector amounted to $38.4 million, none of which was distributed due to, among other things, the suspension of the activities of the Guatemalan Housing Fund.

With regard to social participation and consultation, the development councils had made progress as forums for allocating the budget of the Solidarity Fund for Community Development and for approving municipal projects. However, civil society organizations were still not participating in the councils as fully as they should. MINUGUA welcomed the establishment of the Presidential Secretariat for Women as an advisory and public policy coordinating body for promoting the advancement of Guatemalan women and the development of a culture of democracy.

Under the 1996 Agreement on the Strengthening of Civilian Power and on the Role of the Armed Forces in a Democratic Society [YUN 1996, p. 167], an important landmark in the administration of justice was achieved with the entry into force of the Career Judicial Service Act. In January, the National Commission for Monitoring and Supporting the Strengthening of the Justice System, responsible for advising on and supporting the modernization and reform of the judicial system, took up its functions. It had since prepared a five-year strategic plan. In May, judges' and magistrates' representatives were elected to the Career Judicial Service Council. MINUGUA noted with concern, however, that the commitment to amend the Penal Code was still unfulfilled and scant progress was made in strengthening the Public Prosecutor's Office. Guatemalan prisons continued to experience serious deficiencies in infrastructure and trained personnel.

During the period under review, the public perception of heightened insecurity and criminal violence continued to grow. Frequent changes in the PNC command structure created the feeling that the institution was unstable. A number of reforms in police rules and regulations were introduced, including the creation of an anti-kidnapping squad as a specialized unit for preventing, investigating and prosecuting the crimes of abduction or kidnapping and extortion. In that connection, MINUGUA expressed its concern at the withholding of the identity of investigators and operatives for a 10-year period, a provision that could undermine the principles of accusatory criminal proceedings in force in Guatemala. PNC was deployed in all 22 of the country's departments and covered 307 of its 331 municipalities, with a force of 16,205 members, of whom 1,692 were women. The number of indigenous people who applied and were selected, trained

and deployed remained low. The Mission noted that, in general, the PNC regime of confinement to barracks was affecting police morale and preventing better public service and the development of a relationship with the community. The Police Academy had continued to train new police recruits and had completed the retraining process of former police members. The Mission stressed the need to recruit throughout the country, particularly in indigenous areas, and to strengthen police training at all levels. It reiterated its concern at the lack of development of the PNC information and criminal investigation services. Three years after its creation, the Criminal Investigation Service was deployed in only 14 departments and its staff had not increased significantly. Notwithstanding efforts to modernize the disciplinary section and the PNC Office of Professional Accountability, MINUGUA considered it essential to create higher oversight mechanisms to monitor the overall functioning of the police. With the change of government, progress had been made in ensuring that the Strategic Analysis Secretariat was made up of civilian personnel. In June, the Secretariat submitted a plan of work, which included the restructuring and functional rethinking of State intelligence mechanisms. The plan indicated that the Secretariat's mission was to advise the President on the creation of democratic institutions by providing information and forward-looking analysis for decision-making purposes.

With regard to the reduction of the armed forces budget as provided for in the peace agreements, the sum allocated—approximately $118.6 million—failed to meet the agreed reduction target. Some progress in the redeployment of governmental troops from areas they had occupied during the armed conflict took place following the inauguration of the new Government. The proposed doctrinal manual of the armed forces, submitted in late 1999, did not meet expectations of fulfilling the commitment on the formulation of a new doctrine. The new Government expressed its willingness to include more sectors in its discussions of the manual. It also made some progress towards disbanding the Presidential General Staff by including that commitment in its draft amendments to the Act establishing the armed forces. The Mission was extremely concerned at the potential impact of the recently adopted Support for the Civil Security Forces Act. The Act provided for the participation of the armed forces in public security tasks, and thus was a major setback for the process of demilitarizing public security pursuant to the peace agreements. Moreover, in MINUGUA's view, the Act contained legal ambiguities and reflected a public security policy that did not include the strengthening of PNC.

As to the 1996 Agreement on Constitutional Reforms and the Electoral Regime [YUN 1997, p. 178], the draft amendments to the Elections and Political Parties Act were discussed in the Electoral Affairs Committee of the Congress. The Committee had launched a broad debate on the amendments and was receiving proposals on that issue from women's organizations and civic committees.

During the period under review, the Mission observed that the unease that demobilized population groups were feeling at implementation delays had evolved into a perception that compliance with the 1996 Agreement on the Basis for the Legal Integration of URNG [YUN 1996, p. 169] was at a standstill. However, implementation of the programme of production projects began after a delay of over a year. It was hoped that the programme would benefit nearly 1,500 demobilized combatants—approximately half of the total demobilized population. The integration of demobilized women faced additional difficulties since no specific measures had been envisaged to facilitate their access to production projects. A comprehensive programme for disabled former combatants and civilians had been completed. Also, 891 housing units were being built for uprooted and demobilized population groups. The Secretary-General reiterated his recommendation that the Guillermo Toriello Foundation be strengthened and called on Governments to provide it with the support it needed to perform its tasks in the integration process.

The Secretary-General observed that the increased mobilization of national resources that would result from the tax measures agreed within the framework of the Fiscal Pact would give the State the capacity to finance adequately a large number of commitments whose fulfilment had been affected by lack of resources and budget cuts. The depth and extent of poverty and social exclusion in rural areas required a comprehensive rural development strategy. The commitments relating to redeployment and to the elaboration of a new doctrine of the armed forces had to be complied with fully, while military intelligence had to be transformed and the Presidential Military Staff disbanded. At the same time, there was a need to continue the professionalization of PNC. The new educational policy should aim to establish new models for democratic pluralism and promote technical and scientific progress. In order to overcome the historical exclusion of large population groups from Guatemala's political life, priority should be given to reforming the electoral system. There was also a need to put in place a public policy of fostering collective bargaining that would promote the development of consensus methods of dealing with labour disputes. The Secretary-General said that in order to attain the goals of decentralization specified in the agreements, it was essential for the Government to define its strategy with regard to functional and territorial decentralization. Defining that strategy would allow the proposed reforms to the Development Council Acts and the Municipal Code to be taken into account by the Congress. The process of building national unity required the full integration of indigenous people and women in the political, economic and cultural life of the country.

In a later report [A/55/973], the Secretary-General said that, in December, the Follow-up Commission rescheduled pending commitments in an implementation timetable for 2000-2004, to which the Government pledged its support. The execution of public spending for 2000 on items related to the peace process was generally satisfactory. However, actual spending by key ministries, such as the Ministry of Agriculture, Livestock and Food, the Ministry of Communications, Infrastructure and Housing and the Ministry of Labour and Social Security, was unsatisfactory. With regard to revenues, the estimated tax burden at the end of 2000 was 9.44 per cent of GDP; if that situation continued, it would be impossible to reach the 12-per-cent target rescheduled for 2002 in the Fiscal Pact. The draft General Budget of State Revenues and Expenditures, which the executive branch transmitted to the Congress in September, gave priority to spending for peace. However, it underwent significant cuts in the course of its approval by Parliament. The Government requested the suspension of the Consultative Group on Reconstruction and Transformation meeting that had been scheduled to take place before the end of 2000, due to delays in fulfilling pending commitments, the difficulties in increasing tax collection and the rescheduling carried out by the Follow-up Commission. In November, a further one-year extension of the Special Temporary Act on Personal Documentation was approved because some internally displaced persons and women still did not have documentation and were therefore unable to obtain credit, land, housing and other social benefits.

Human rights

In July [A/55/174], the Secretary-General transmitted to the General Assembly the MINUGUA Head's eleventh report on human rights, which described the Mission's activities between 1 December 1999 and 30 June 2000.

In March, the new Government announced that it intended to ratify certain international human rights treaties and that it was prepared to recognize the State's responsibility in 52 cases of human rights violations that were before the Inter-American Commission on Human Rights. The State also acknowledged its responsibility in the cases of Myrna Mack (an anthropologist who was killed in Guatemala City in 1990), the 1982 Dos Erres massacre and the 1994 death of street child Marcos Fidel Quisquinay. The new Government also condemned the fact that the files on the investigation of high-profile cases, such as the assassination of Monsignor Juan José Gerardi Conedera [YUN 1998, p. 219] and Myrna Mack, were missing and that some confidential files in the possession of the Strategic Affairs Secretariat in the Office of the President had been partially destroyed. The general perception of an increase in criminal activity and lack of public security was heightened by the discovery of a large number of corpses of alleged criminals bearing signs of torture, possibly as part of so-called social cleansing between individuals or criminal gangs. Also filed were complaints of death threats and selective searches and robberies at the headquarters of social organizations. Those acts of intimidation were aimed mainly at social, human rights and victims' organizations, and judges, prosecutors and journalists involved in the criminal trials of State agents or investigations into the activities of the intelligence services. Notwithstanding the Government's new human rights policy and its clear willingness to move forward with the implementation of its commitments under the 1994 Comprehensive Agreement on Human Rights [YUN 1994, p. 407], the human rights situation in Guatemala was deteriorating.

During the period under review, the Mission admitted 285 complaints, compared with 316 during the previous reporting period [YUN 1999, p. 204]. There was a slight increase in the number of alleged violations of the rights accorded priority under the Comprehensive Agreement, as well as in the number of confirmed violations. The comprehensive analysis by category of right showed an increase in confirmed violations of the right to freedom of association and assembly and of political rights. In the case of political rights, nearly all the violations were connected with the general election. There was also an increase in violations of the right to individual liberty and security of person. The number of violations of the right to life decreased, though there was an increase in the involvement of PNC members in such violations. As for the right to integrity of person, 91 confirmed violations were reported—63 from the period under review and 28 from previous periods. Confirmed violations of due process of law totalled 2,991, of which 1,639 corresponded to complaints submitted during the period under review.

The persistent and widespread failure of the State to fulfil its obligation to prevent, investigate and punish crimes and human rights violations and to enforce the guarantees that constituted due process of law was one of the main factors contributing to the situation of impunity prevailing in Guatemala. Major progress had been made in February with the ratification of the Inter-American Convention on Forced Disappearances of Persons, even though that was marred by the attachment of a reservation to the effect that the extradition to or from the country of Guatemalans alleged to be responsible for enforced disappearances would not be facilitated. Illegal security forces and clandestine groups continued to be active and the Government had not devised a policy to combat them. The operational capacity of those groups, their links with public officials at the local and national level and the impunity that prevailed for most of their actions were all factors that contributed to the people's perception of insecurity.

In order to strengthen the mechanisms to ensure effective exercise of human rights, it was particularly important to deal with legal provisions, such as the reform of the Elections and Political Parties Act, the characterization of discrimination and sexual harassment as offences, the law which regulated the civil service and the law on arms and munitions. The State also had to bring domestic legislation into line with the precepts of the 1989 Convention on the Rights of the Child, annexed to General Assembly resolution 44/25 [YUN 1989, p. 561].

MINUGUA noted that, despite legal and infrastructural constraints, there had been considerable improvement in the management of the Supreme Electoral Tribunal during the electoral process in 1999. In order to surmount the exclusion of broad sectors of society from political life and to approve the reforms of the Elections and Political Parties Act, the Mission recommended that the Tribunal should consider sectoral voter registration campaigns, particularly for women and indigenous people, and ensure that officials working to register voters in the interior were familiar with Mayan languages.

PNC, which bore primary responsibility for human rights violations during the period under review, had to adopt without delay a democratic policy that was respectful of the rule of law and consistent with human rights and the concept of public service. Some of the violations committed by police officers could be prevented by redoubling efforts to enhance police training, particularly as regards arrest procedures, treatment of those detained and proportional use of force. In addition, in order for the State to fulfil its duty to investigate and punish human rights violations, priority had to be given to dealing with the inadequacies and interferences that prevented the Public Prosecutor's Office from playing its role in criminal investigations and the fight against impunity. Prosecutors, like judges, had to be free from pressure and threats, and the judiciary had to be reformed and modernized. The Government had to separate military intelligence agencies from civil matters and particularly from judicial investigations. It also had to put a stop to lynchings and so-called social cleansing and establish the Advisory Council on Security, which was provided for in the peace agreements.

In a later report [A/56/273], MINUGUA stated that, in September, Guatemala signed the Optional Protocol to the Convention on the Elimination of All Forms of Discrimination against Women, adopted by General Assembly resolution 54/4 [YUN 1999, p. 1100], and the Optional Protocol to the Convention on the Rights of the Child on involvement of children in armed conflict, adopted by Assembly resolution 54/263 (see p. 615). In October, it ratified the Additional Protocol to the American Convention on Human Rights in the Area of Economic, Social and Cultural Rights, and in November it ratified the Optional Protocol to the International Covenant on Civil and Political Rights, adopted by Assembly resolution 2200 A (XXI) [YUN 1966, p. 423]. Lynchings and acts of mob violence, both spontaneous and premeditated, continued, undermining governance in various municipalities.

GENERAL ASSEMBLY ACTION

On 19 December [meeting 86], the General Assembly adopted **resolution 55/177** [draft: A/55/L.33/Rev.1 & Add.1] without vote [agenda item 43].

United Nations Verification Mission in Guatemala

The General Assembly,

Recalling its resolution 54/99 of 8 December 1999, in which it decided to authorize the renewal of the mandate of the United Nations Verification Mission in Guatemala from 1 January to 31 December 2000,

Taking into account that, for the first time since the signing of the peace agreements, Guatemala held general elections during the period from November to December 1999 and that the peaceful transfer of power signals significant progress towards the consolidation of an inclusive and democratic political system,

Underlining the fact that substantive aspects of the agenda of the peace agreements are yet to be implemented and that their implementation requires a revised calendar prepared by the Commission to Follow Up the Implementation of the Peace Agreements,

Taking into account that the parties have requested the United Nations to support the consolidation of the peace-building process until 2003,

Taking into account also the tenth and eleventh reports of the Mission on human rights,

Taking into account further the fourth and fifth reports of the Secretary-General on the verification of compliance with the peace agreements,

Taking into account the report of the Commission for Historical Clarification,

Stressing the positive role played by the Mission in support of the Guatemala peace process, and emphasizing the need for the Mission to continue to enjoy the full support of all parties concerned,

Having considered the report of the Secretary-General on the work of the Mission,

1. *Welcomes* the tenth and eleventh reports of the United Nations Verification Mission in Guatemala on human rights;

2. *Also welcomes* the fourth and fifth reports of the Secretary-General on the verification of compliance with the peace agreements;

3. *Recalls* the report of the Commission for Historical Clarification and the recommendations contained therein;

4. *Welcomes* the commitment made by the new Government of Guatemala in January 2000 to the implementation of the peace agreements and to reinvigorating the peace process through the adoption of social policies anchored to the agreements;

5. *Takes note* of the agreement reached by the parties regarding the importance of the continuing presence of the Mission in Guatemala until 2003;

6. *Also takes note* of the recommendations contained in the report of the Secretary-General which are aimed at ensuring that the Mission can respond adequately to the demands of the peace process until 31 December 2001, as well as of his proposals relating to the changes in the structure and staffing of the Mission for the period 2001-2003;

7. *Notes with satisfaction* the progress made in the implementation of the peace agreements, in particular the process towards the finalization of the Fiscal Pact for a Future with Peace and Development which establishes the basis for increased public spending on the peace agenda and paves the way for the modernization of the economic system, the reinforcement of the operational capacities and training of the National Civil Police and the establishment by decree of the Women's Secretariat;

8. *Welcomes* the rescheduling of pending commitments by the Commission to Follow Up the Implementation of the Peace Agreements and the inclusion of commitments not initially scheduled in a revised calendar for implementation, and urges the rapid approval of the new timetable;

9. *Notes* that the consolidation of the peace-building process remains a significant challenge that requires the strengthening of achievements to date and the completion of the outstanding agenda;

10. *Underlines with concern* that key reforms envisaged in the peace agreements remain outstanding, including the fiscal, judicial, military, electoral and land reforms, as well as decentralization and rural development, and therefore urges the finalization of the Fiscal Pact, notes the need to strengthen the institutions es-

tablished under the agreements, and stresses the importance of continued compliance with the peace agreements;

11. *Notes* that the present Government has assigned priority to national and international human rights obligations;

12. *Encourages* the Government to implement the recommendations contained in the reports of the Mission on human rights, in particular in view of the persistent shortcomings in the overall human rights situation and the troubling increase in incidents directed at people working on such issues;

13. *Underlines* the importance of implementing fully the Agreement on identity and rights of indigenous peoples as a key to achieving peace in Guatemala, and highlights the need to implement fully the Agreement on Social and Economic Aspects and the Agrarian Situation as a means of addressing the root causes of the armed conflict;

14. *Calls upon* the Government to follow up the recommendations of the Commission for Historical Clarification, with a view to promoting national reconciliation, upholding the right to truth and providing redress, in accordance with Guatemalan law, for the victims of human rights abuses and violence committed during the thirty-six-year conflict, and calls upon Congress to establish the Commission for Peace and Harmony;

15. *Encourages* the parties and all sectors of Guatemalan society to intensify their efforts to achieve the goals of the peace agreements, in particular the observance of human rights, including the rights of indigenous peoples, equitable development, participation and national reconciliation;

16. *Invites* the international community and, in particular, the agencies, programmes and funds of the United Nations, to continue to support the consolidation of the peace-building process and to consider the implementation of the peace agreements as the framework for their technical and financial assistance programmes and projects, and stresses the continued importance of close cooperation among them in the context of the United Nations Development Assistance Framework for Guatemala;

17. *Urges* the international community to support financially the strengthening of the capacities of the United Nations agencies and programmes as they assume a more active role in working in a closely coordinated relationship with the Mission in order to ensure the consolidation of the peace process in Guatemala;

18. *Stresses* that the Mission has a key role to play in promoting the consolidation of peace and the observance of human rights and in verifying compliance with the newly approved timetable for the implementation of pending commitments under the peace agreements;

19. *Decides* to authorize the renewal of the mandate of the Mission from 1 January to 31 December 2001;

20. *Requests* the Secretary-General to submit, as early as possible, an updated report to the General Assembly at its fifty-sixth session, together with his recommendations regarding the continuation of the peace-building phase after 31 December 2001;

21. *Also requests* the Secretary-General to keep the General Assembly fully informed of the implementation of the present resolution.

Financing of Military Observer Group

The MINUGUA Military Observer Group was deployed for three months—from 3 March to 27 May 1997 [YUN 1997, p. 172]—to verify the Agreement on the Definitive Ceasefire of 4 December 1996 [YUN 1996, p. 168] between the Government of Guatemala and URNG.

On 23 December, the General Assembly decided that the item on the financing of the Military Observer Group would remain for consideration at its resumed fifty-fifth (2001) session (**decision 55/458**) and that the Fifth (Administrative and Budgetary) Committee should continue to consider the item at that session (**decision 55/455**).

Nicaragua

In a report on international assistance for the rehabilitation and reconstruction of Nicaragua [YUN 1999, p. 207], the Secretary-General noted that, at the Consultative Group meeting for Nicaragua (Washington, D.C., 23-24 May 2000), the country's sound economic performance during the 1998-1999 biennium, with economic growth and decreasing inflation, was emphasized. There was general agreement that combating poverty was the most important development goal for Nicaragua. The Government was commended for the progress achieved in the preparation of a comprehensive poverty reduction strategy. President Arnoldo Alemán underlined the importance of governance as an indispensable precondition for confronting poverty and creating the structures for stable development. The international community stressed the importance of transparency in public spending and urged the Nicaraguan authorities to apply the new instruments at their disposition in order to resolve cases of corruption.

The most important political event was the agreement achieved by the two political parties, the Partido Liberal Constitucionalista and Frente Sandinista de Liberación Nacional, around issues of constitutional reform, which were approved in January. Among the reforms were the automatic membership in parliament of former Presidents, the increased number of judges for the Supreme Court and the replacement of judges in the Supreme Electoral Council. An additional element of the agreement became the new Electoral Law, criticized by international experts on the grounds that it made political participation unduly difficult, with numerous requirements that appeared to serve no purpose other than imposing a bipartisan model for Nicaragua. At the beginning of May, the National Assembly approved the Law for the Creation of the Public Ministry as the entity for opening criminal proceedings, a major step in the consolidation of the rule of law.

Haiti

During 2000, Haiti's three-year-old political and institutional crisis deepened, further eroding the moral, economic and social fabric of the country. After repeated delays, the first round of parliamentary and local elections was held on 21 May. Although election day went unexpectedly well, with a higher than usual turnout and little violence, the electoral process unfolded in a climate of violence and intimidation and fell short of the desired goal. A flawed method of calculating percentages in the Senate race wrongly gave front-runners, all of whom belonged to the ruling Fanmi Lavalas party headed by former President Jean-Bertrand Aristide, an absolute majority in the first round. Despite calls by the international community for rectification of the methods of calculation of the Senate results, a new Parliament was seated on 28 August. That decision compelled all main bilateral donors to cut direct international assistance to the Haitian Government and to channel aid through NGOs. Despite the failure to correct the error, Haitian authorities held elections for President and a third of the Senate on 26 November. Since the opposition parties boycotted the elections in protest over the 21 May results, Mr. Aristide won the presidential race and Fanmi Lavalas took all the Senate seats up for contest. In response to the electoral and political crisis, and after intensive examination of Haiti's Provisional Electoral Council (CEP) and its practices, the United Nations withdrew a technical team of electoral experts in mid-October.

The International Civilian Support Mission in Haiti (MICAH), which was launched on 16 March, was expected to consolidate and develop the results already achieved by the United Nations Civilian Police Mission in Haiti (MIPONUH) and the OAS/UN International Civilian Mission to Haiti (MICIVIH) with regard to respect for human rights and reinforcement of the institutional effectiveness of the Haitian police and judiciary. The MIPONUH and MICIVIH mandates had been extended in November 1999 by Security Council resolution 1277(1999) [YUN 1999, p. 215] in order to ensure a phased transition to MICAH by 15 March. Despite initial budgetary shortfalls, the first MICAH advisers arrived in Haiti in mid-June. By mid-October, a total of 68 advisers were in place. However, due to the political turmoil

and instability in Haiti, the Secretary-General recommended in November that MICAH be terminated on 6 February 2001 and that new forms of technical assistance be devised in order to allow the UN system to continue supporting the Haitian people.

Civilian Police Mission

Report of Secretary-General. On 25 February [S/2000/150], the Secretary-General updated the activities of MIPONUH and developments in its mission area since his November 1999 report [YUN 1999, p. 213]. The Mission had been established by Security Council resolution 1141(1997) [YUN 1997, p. 193] to assist the Government of Haiti by supporting and contributing to the professionalization of the Haitian National Police (HNP) in close cooperation with MICIVIH.

The Secretary-General said that during the reporting period, the security situation in Haiti was characterized by frequent demonstrations and by incidents of violence and robbery. The political climate had been dominated by pre-electoral activities. Despite some election-related disturbances and organizational delays, CEP had proceeded with the implementation of its electoral timetable. It was hoped that the process would culminate in the holding of legislative and local elections as scheduled on 19 March. On 4 January, CEP held a conference with the political parties to obtain their commitment to an electoral code of ethics binding them to pursue their electoral objectives by non-violent means. Numerous parties, including Fanmi Lavalas, signed the code. The voter registration campaign was launched on 24 January. Despite reported irregularities, delays and protests, more than 3 million voters had registered by the middle of February.

As at 21 February, MIPONUH was composed of 219 civilian police officers from 10 countries, including a 110-strong special police unit. The police continued to be deployed in all of Haiti's nine departments, while the special police unit remained in the capital. The curriculum of training courses designed by MIPONUH in cooperation with HNP had been taught comprehensively and had met all the objectives established by HNP. Civilian police officers continued to discharge their mentoring (accompagnement) responsibilities at the Offices of the Director-General and Inspector-General of HNP, as well as alongside the departmental directors of the police force. The emphasis remained on community policing, the maintenance of law and order, the fight against capital crimes and drug trafficking, and the reinforcement of police administration and logistics. A disengagement plan had been established to ensure the progressive withdrawal of MIPONUH civilian police personnel. The special police unit was scheduled to be withdrawn on 16 March.

While the security situation in Haiti remained of concern, HNP had been able to work with increased efficiency during the period under review. In fact, HNP had undertaken several successful operations in the fight against delinquency and drug trafficking and, in most cases, had provided adequate security during election-related events.

In the context of the transition to MICAH, both MIPONUH and MICIVIH held a series of coordination meetings with a view to harmonizing their activities and preparing the transition. In February, meetings were conducted by the Prime Minister and the Minister of Justice with the Secretary-General's Representative, the UNDP representative and bilateral donors to prepare the assistance to judicial reform in the context of MICAH. The joint working groups composed of Haitian officials and international experts established in 1999 by the Minister of Justice [YUN 1999, p. 214] continued to work on the drafting of legal texts in order to promote the judicial reform process.

The UN system continued to implement and support development activities (see also p. 815), such as the launching of a United Nations Capital Development Fund programme to strengthen governance for the environment, and the organization by the United Nations Children's Fund (UNICEF), the Office of the United Nations High Commissioner for Human Rights and MICIVIH of a national workshop for the preparation of the first report on the implementation of the Convention on the Rights of the Child, annexed to General Assembly resolution 44/25 [YUN 1989, p. 561].

By early February, the withdrawal plans for MIPONUH's civilian police personnel were finalized and their repatriation was expected to be concluded by 15 March. The Mission had earmarked some assets to be retained by MICAH. The liquidation phase was expected to be completed by 30 June. The recruitment of police advisers for MICAH was under way. The advisers were expected to provide continued training and mentoring support to HNP decision makers, who still did not have all the necessary experience to command and administer their young police force. Concerning the new Mission, the UN Secretariat had identified and recommended candidates for the majority of the positions to be financed under the regular budget. Those positions would need to be complemented by personnel that would be financed by extrabudgetary means.

The Secretary-General observed that, by deciding to establish MICAH, the international community had confirmed that it was committed to continuing to assist the Haitian Government in reinforcing the country's democratic institutions. MICAH was expected to consolidate and develop the results already achieved by MIPONUH and MICIVIH as regards respect for human rights and reinforcement of the institutional effectiveness of the police and the judiciary, and to coordinate and facilitate the international community's dialogue with political and social actors in Haiti. Subject to the availability of resources, MICAH's relatively short-term objectives would be situated in the longer-term perspective of facilitating the passage from security to development priorities. The Secretary-General called on Member States to assist in the transition from peacekeeping to peace-building and to contribute to the Trust Fund established for MICAH. The Fund would allow for the recruitment of over 100 advisers in the areas of police, justice and human rights.

SECURITY COUNCIL ACTION

On 15 March [meeting 4112], following consultations among Security Council members, the President made statement **S/PRST/2000/8** on behalf of the Council:

The Security Council has considered the report of the Secretary-General dated 25 February 2000 submitted in accordance with resolution 1277(1999) of 30 November 1999.

The Council commends the Representative of the Secretary-General, the United Nations Civilian Police Mission in Haiti, the International Civilian Mission in Haiti and all previous missions deployed in Haiti for assisting the Haitian Government in supporting the professionalization of the Haitian National Police force, consolidating the system of justice and other national institutions of Haiti, and promoting human rights. The Council expresses its thanks to all the countries that took part in, and contributed to the success of, the United Nations Civilian Police Mission in Haiti, the International Civilian Mission in Haiti and all previous missions deployed in Haiti, particularly the troop-contributing countries.

The Council recognizes that the people and the Government of Haiti bear the ultimate responsibility for national reconciliation, the maintenance of a secure and stable environment, the administration of justice and the reconstruction of their country, and that the Government of Haiti bears particular responsibility for the further strengthening and effective functioning of the Haitian National Police and the justice system. The Council considers that timely, free and fair elections are crucial to democracy and all aspects of Haiti's development, and strongly urges the Haitian authorities to work cooperatively together in order to finalize arrangements for holding credible elections as rapidly as possible so as to restore, promptly and fully, the lapsed parliament and independent local governments.

The Council commends the Secretary-General for ensuring a phased transition to the International Civilian Support Mission in Haiti and recognizes that economic rehabilitation and reconstruction constitute a major task facing the Government and people of Haiti and that significant international assistance is indispensable for the sustainable development of Haiti.

The Council recognizes the success of cooperative efforts in bringing about the mandate for this new mission in Haiti, and notes with satisfaction the contributions made by the General Assembly and the Economic and Social Council in this regard. The Council welcomes the initiative of the Economic and Social Council to develop a strategic framework and a comprehensive approach for a long-term United Nations programme of support for Haiti, and underlines the vital link between national stability and economic and social development.

The Council expects the Secretary-General to keep it informed, as appropriate, of the situation in Haiti and, in particular, the progress achieved in the electoral process.

Communications. On 15 March [A/54/806-S/2000/232], the EU Presidency noted the postponement of legislative and local elections in Haiti and the new dates (9 April–21 May 2000) proposed by CEP. The EU expressed regret that, 14 months after Parliament was officially prorogued and one year after CEP was appointed, the Haitian authorities were, despite large-scale international aid, unable to fulfil all the conditions necessary for the holding of fair and transparent elections.

On 31 March [A/54/819], the Secretary-General informed the General Assembly President that no contributions had been received for the MICAH Trust Fund. As a result, MICAH began its mandate on 16 March with only core staff. In the light of the lack of financial resources, the Assembly might wish to consider whether the Mission should be closed and its substantive activities transferred to UNDP.

International Civilian Support Mission

On 17 July [A/55/154], the Secretary-General submitted the first report on the activities of the International Civilian Support Mission in Haiti (MICAH), covering the period since the Mission's inception on 16 March. MICAH had been established by General Assembly resolution 54/193 [YUN 1999, p. 218] to consolidate the results achieved by MICIVIH, MIPONUH and previous UN missions.

The Secretary-General said that although parliamentary and local elections were held in Haiti, the electoral process, which unfolded in a climate of violence, intimidation and unpredictability, fell short of the desired goal. A dispute over the method used to calculate the Senate results remained unresolved. While the first round of elections was originally set for 28 November 1999, the polling was rescheduled three additional times and finally held on 21 May 2000. The delay was due in part to the unexpectedly high number of citizens seeking voter identity cards. Concern about the repeated postponements was raised by the Group of Friends of the Secretary-General for Haiti (Argentina, Canada, Chile, France, the United States and Venezuela) and other envoys in several meetings with President René Préval and Prime Minister Jacques-Édouard Alexis. In a 15 March letter to President Préval, the Secretary-General stated that the prompt holding of free and transparent elections was an essential step towards the consolidation of democracy. Three days of violent protests against early elections by members of pro–Fanmi Lavalas groups (popular organizations) in Port-au-Prince from 27 to 29 March caused additional disquiet. According to the OAS Electoral Observation Mission (EOM), more than 70 acts of violence were committed in the three-month run-up to the May elections. In the department of Grand'Anse, elections were postponed to a later date due to an internal political dispute.

The election itself went unexpectedly well, with a turnout of over 50 per cent, little violence and a visible, disciplined police presence throughout the country. However, signs of electoral mismanagement abounded, including inadequate planning for the receipt of voting urns, which meant that ballots were mixed up, mislaid or even scattered in the street, rendering any recount impossible. The major opposition parties asserted that there had been massive fraud and refused to participate in any second round. More than 30 opposition candidates and activists were arrested on 23 May on the grounds that they had staged violent protests. EOM's initial evaluation did not support the opposition's claim of systematic fraud, although it acknowledged many minor irregularities and a few serious ones, but those irregularities were isolated and did not affect the overall credibility of the elections. A similar assessment was issued by the Conseil National d'Observation Electorale, the umbrella organization of several thousand Haitian electoral observers. On close examination, it was discovered that CEP's Senate results had not been calculated according to the electoral law. All 17 of the Senate contests held on 21 May were won in the first round (16 of them by Fanmi Lavalas and one by an independent). If properly calculated, however, a run-off would have been required for eight of those seats, for which no candidate obtained an absolute majority of all votes cast, as required by the electoral law. In the view of EOM, the credibility of the entire electoral process would be jeopardized if that serious error were not corrected. Haitian officials strongly rejected suggestions that the results be recalculated, justifying the decision in part because it obviated the need for costly run-offs. Fanmi Lavalas called on its supporters to defend its election victory, resulting in two days of aggressive demonstrations by hundreds of protesters outside embassies and offices of the international community in Port-au-Prince. On 14 June, the Secretary-General expressed his expectation that the electoral authorities would calculate the final results in accordance with the electoral law. Statements were also issued by OAS and other international organizations. Meanwhile, the nine-member CEP came under conflicting pressure, forcing two members to resign. The CEP President fled the country and subsequently announced that he had been under pressure, from the Government in particular, to confirm the provisional Senate results. After continued violence and demonstration on the part of Fanmi Lavalas supporters, the six remaining CEP members issued final results for the Senate elections, using the same disputed system of calculation and confirming the first-round victory of the 16 Fanmi Lavalas candidates and one independent. According to CEP's final results for the first round of the Chamber of Deputies elections, in which the percentages appeared to have been calculated correctly, Fanmi Lavalas won about a third of the seats outright and was front-runner in run-offs for most of the other seats. Fanmi Lavalas also won most municipal councils overwhelmingly.

On 28 June, a delegation of the Caribbean Community (CARICOM) arrived in Haiti and submitted a proposal for resolving the Senate results issue to former President Aristide, head of Fanmi Lavalas. In order to pre-empt that effort, President Préval issued a decree fixing the second round for 9 July. The second round was held on that day, with run-offs being held only for the lower Chamber of Deputies. EOM did not observe the second round on the grounds that the unrevised Senate results could not be the basis for a credible electoral process. It also reported that, since 21 May, the electoral process had become increasingly flawed by such irregularities as the inaccurate transmission of results, the arbitrary treatment of challenges filed by candidates and political parties, and other irregularities. On 6 July, the Security Council President issued a statement to the press expressing the Council's concern about the violence and desire that Haitian authorities address electoral irregularities. On 10 July, the Secretary-General also expressed

his regret that Haitian authorities had chosen to proceed to hold run-off elections without having resolved outstanding issues related to the first round. The delayed elections in Grand'Anse on 11 June were marred by the theft of counted ballots and tally sheets, as a result of which polling had to be reheld in two places. The theft of voting urns from several polling stations also disrupted the polling when it was reheld on 6 July. According to CEP provisional results for Grand'Anse, the department's two Senate seats were also won in the first round by Fanmi Lavalas, giving it a total of 18 out of 19 Senate seats.

Sufficient voluntary contributions had been received to allow for recruitment of MICAH's justice, human rights and police advisers. The first advisers arrived in Haiti in mid-June 2000. Discussions had been held with government authorities, UN agencies and representatives of NGOs and civil society in order to define the advisers' specific activities and responsibilities and to clarify the kind of support they could bring to development and institutional strengthening.

The resignation in April of the Inspector-General, Luc Eucher Joseph, raised new concerns about the politicization of HNP; Mr. Joseph's departure had been among the demands of Fanmi Lavalas supporters. Evidence of politicization was also seen in the passivity of the police in the face of the often violent protests by Fanmi Lavalas supporters at various stages of the electoral process between late March and mid-June, compared with resolute police interventions against opposition protests in late May. It was also alleged that certain elements of the police participated in the theft of ballots and the falsification of vote tallies after the 21 May election. As the technical assistance to be provided by the MICAH police pillar was different from the work of preceding missions, a new framework for its activities had to be created. By mid-June, 26 of the projected 34 advisers had been selected and several had arrived in the Mission area, where they were assigned to posts throughout the nine departments.

At the outset of MICAH, senior staff of the human rights pillar crafted a programme of human rights capacity-building and monitoring to be implemented by its 31 advisers, the first of whom arrived in June. Activities likely to have a long-term impact, such as work with human rights trainers, were identified as priorities. Teams deployed in the capital and the interior would develop a programme of monitoring activities to focus on the human rights aspects of the electoral process.

During the reporting period, the Ministry of Justice drafted a series of laws to be submitted to Parliament that reinforced the independence of the judiciary. MICAH's justice pillar had been providing technical assistance to the Ministry of Justice and had held discussions with bilateral donors and within the UN system in order to ensure that justice sector work would be coordinated, complementary and sustainable. Other activities envisaged by the justice pillar included support for legal aid programmes and training of court clerks and prison staff.

Among development programmes, UNDP, the World Health Organization, the World Food Programme (WFP) and UNICEF helped prepare the first national plan for risk and disaster prevention and management, while the Joint United Nations Programme on HIV/AIDS (UNAIDS) launched a public information campaign on HIV/AIDS in 10 major cities. UNICEF supported the Ministry of Health in a measles immunization campaign.

The Secretary-General observed that the 21 May elections had led to a deepening of the political crisis, increased tension and violence and the possible installation of a Senate that—if the crucial calculation question was not addressed—would cast a shadow over the Parliament's democratic legitimacy, thereby threatening the resumption of international financial assistance. Although EOM's initial assessment of the elections did not support the claim of widespread systematic fraud, the decision of the electoral authorities, supported by the Government and the ruling Fanmi Lavalas party, to stand by the erroneous Senate results was cause for serious concern.

The rule of law had suffered as a result of the passivity or even complicity of some police and judicial authorities in the face of violent demonstrations by members of so-called popular organizations, which targeted opposition parties, journalists and the general population. The Secretary-General said it was regrettable that political leaders had not consistently and publicly urged their supporters to refrain from such activity. The reliance on street violence to impose objectives at every crucial juncture in the political process had set dangerous precedents that bode ill for the future. Developments related to HNP were also cause for increasing concern; events in the aftermath of the 21 May election suggested that some Haitian political leaders sought to use the police for their own ends.

MICAH's capacity to support Haiti's fledgling democratic institutions risked being jeopardized by a climate of political turmoil and intolerance, which could place significant constraints on the ability of its advisers to do their work. Strong, independent justice sector institutions were the best guarantors of the rule of law. MICAH's support hinged on the existence of credible interlocutors in Haiti who enjoyed the support of their people as well as of the international community. Canada, Norway and the United States had contributed to MICAH's Trust Fund, while the Friends of the Secretary-General for Haiti had played a supportive role during the transition from MIPONUH/MICIVIH to MICAH.

On 9 November [A/55/618], the Secretary-General described MICAH's activities and developments in the Mission area since July. He said that Haiti's political and electoral crisis had again deepened, polarizing its political class and civil society, jeopardizing its international relations and sapping an already declining economy. Disregarding all calls for rectification of the calculation method of the Senate results and other irregularities in the 21 May elections, and with the opposition maintaining its boycott, the authorities completed the drawn-out electoral process, promulgated the final results and seated a new Parliament. Former President Aristide's Fanmi Lavalas party took 18 of the 19 contested Senate seats and 72 of the 83 seats in the Chamber of Deputies. Without consulting the opposition, President Préval named three new CEP members to replace its President, who fled the country in June, and two opposition representatives who had resigned. He then empowered CEP to organize elections for President and the remaining one third of the Senate seats on 26 November. Most of the opposition, grouped in a tactical alliance known as the Democratic Convergence, adhered, throughout the period under review, to the position that the 21 May elections were so fraudulent that they should be annulled and held again under a new CEP, but only after President Préval had stood down and been replaced by a provisional government. In the meantime, the opposition ruled out any participation in the November elections. While not backing the opposition call for the complete annulment of the elections, civil society organizations urged the authorities to address the electoral irregularities in order to avoid exacerbating the political crisis and jeopardizing international assistance.

The international community always held that the errors of the 21 May elections could be rectified, although its appeals to that end at every stage in the process had no effect. After an OAS mission in mid-August and several visits by envoys of CARICOM and the United States had failed to stop the seating of the new Parliament on 28 August, Haiti's main bilateral donors announced that they would not finance the November elections or any electoral observer mission, would not recognize the new Parliament, and would henceforth provide little or no assistance to the Government of Haiti, channelling it all through NGOs. The United States Administration also stated that it would consider opposing Haitian loan requests from international financial institutions. All that was to stay in effect until an independent and credible CEP was established; accommodations were made with regard to the 21 May elections, especially the contested Senate seats; and a dialogue was started with the opposition on ways to strengthen Haitian democracy. At a ministerial-level meeting (New York, 13 September), the Group of Friends of the Secretary-General for Haiti voiced disappointment and concern at the failure of the Haitian authorities to rectify the flaws of the 21 May elections. The United Nations decided that it was not in a position to continue its technical assistance to CEP in its preparations for the November elections, given the fact that it did not meet required standards. The UN technical assistance team—deployed under the auspices of UNDP—left the country on 15 October.

The deepening political crisis and the continued suspension of much financial assistance by international financial institutions precipitated a fall in the Haitian currency (gourde). Since July, there had also been an increase in violent crime, with allegations of police involvement in robbery, extortion and abduction, as well as drug trafficking. Political pressures on HNP had contributed to the demoralization of the police force and had eroded its operational capacity and credibility.

By mid-October, MICAH's three pillars—justice, police and human rights—had a total of 68 advisers assigned to the Ministry of Justice, HNP, the Prison Authority, the Judges School and the Office of the Ombudsman, as well as to MICAH regional offices, a human rights verification unit and units working with civil society partners. MICAH worked with UNDP and bilateral donors to identify short-term projects that would best be undertaken by the Mission and took part in discussions with all United Nations agencies on the common country assessment conducted throughout June.

MICAH's justice pillar, which had 17 advisers by mid-October, provided logistical and organizational support for a process of discussion and revision of five newly prepared draft laws concerning the organization and independence of the judiciary, drug trafficking and money-laundering. Two landmark trials were held in the fight against impunity: one of a group of police officers accused of carrying out executions in 1999; and the other of a group of former army officers, soldiers and civilians accused of a 1994 massacre. Building on the work of UNDP, the jus-

tice pillar helped to organize the Prison Authority and attempted to address problems in prison conditions.

The police section of MICAH had 24 advisers by mid-October. The equipment and materiel necessary for the police to operate were found to be in extremely short supply in most units. After the installation of the new Parliament, several Fanmi Lavalas senators embarked on a campaign of almost daily criticism of the police, accusing the service of incompetence and inactivity in the face of soaring crime and of having corrupted elements within its ranks.

MICAH's human rights section had 27 advisers by the start of October. A training programme was developed for human rights instructors at the Police Academy and for prison guard recruits, in order to reinforce their knowledge of human rights. MICAH organized a number of activities to raise public awareness of human rights, such as International Peace Day (19 September), which was used as a vehicle to promote the values of a culture of peace through the media, meetings and other activities organized jointly with the United Nations Educational, Scientific and Cultural Organization (UNESCO). The human rights section also began carrying out verification activities, following up incidents of violence that could be of a political nature. Respect of the rights to individual liberty and a fair trial within a reasonable time limit continued to be the most frequent human rights violations (see also p. 628).

The UN system was engaged in formulating a United Nations Development Assistance Framework for Haiti, which was expected to be finalized in January 2001. Other UN activities included the launching of a justice programme by UNDP, aimed at, among other things, promoting the participation of civil society in the debate on judicial reform, and a special assistance drive by WFP to stabilize the food security situation in drought-stricken northern and north-eastern regions.

The Secretary-General observed that the political polarization of Haiti was highlighted by the Inter-American Commission of Human Rights, which visited Port-au-Prince from 21 to 25 August. The Commission stated that the most critical and worrying aspect of the human rights situation in Haiti was the deterioration of the political climate to such a point that no consensus seemed to exist about the ways in which to consolidate the country's fledgling democracy. A disturbing element of that polarization was the widely held perception among opponents of Fanmi Lavalas that the party might establish a dictatorial and repressive regime if, as was widely expected, Mr. Aristide regained the presidency. On the other hand, it was evident that Mr. Aristide enjoyed the loyalty of broad sectors of the urban and rural poor. The disinclination of the parties to work towards a compromise was a fundamental cause of the polarization. Many in the opposition seemed to hope that, under the pressure of international isolation and internal unrest, Fanmi Lavalas would somehow disintegrate and that compromise was therefore unnecessary. The consequences of that attitude could be seen in Haiti's political stalemate, soon to enter its fourth year.

In the absence of any solution to the crisis, popular discontent seemed likely to mount in response to the rising prices and increasing poverty. A combination of rampant crime, violent street protests and incidents of violence targeted at the international community could severely limit MICAH's ability to fulfil its mandate. In that climate of political turmoil and instability, and with national counterparts often lacking or distracted by political concerns, it would be necessary to devise new forms of technical assistance that might better allow the UN system to continue supporting the Haitian people. The Secretary-General expressed the view that, in the light of the conditions in Haiti, a renewal of MICAH's mandate was not advisable, and recommended, with regret, that the Mission be terminated at the end of its mandate on 6 February 2001. In preparation, discussions had already commenced among UNDP, MICAH and the Friends of the Secretary-General for Haiti, in consultation with other members of the UN system, with the aim of designing a programme of assistance to the Haitian people that was commensurate with the country's political realities and absorption capacity.

In a later report [A/55/905], the Secretary-General detailed, among other things, developments in the Mission area during the last two months of 2000. Elections for President and a third of the Senate were held on 26 November, despite the absence of an accord between Fanmi Lavalas and opposition parties to resolve the irregularities of the 21 May elections. The opposition boycotted the electoral process and former President Aristide faced no serious opposition candidates. As a result, Mr. Aristide won the presidential race with 92 per cent of the vote, while Fanmi Lavalas took all nine Senate seats up for election, giving it a total of 26 of the Senate's 27 seats.

EOM's final report on the 21 May elections, published in December, noted that there should have been run-offs for eight Senate seats where a flawed method of calculating percentages wrongly gave front-runners an absolute majority in the first round. In addition, vote tally discrepancies indicated that run-offs should also have been held for at least one other Senate seat and perhaps as many as three Deputy seats. The report cited many other irregularities, including the mishandling of challenges and irregular complementary elections in several districts.

Mr. Aristide's offer, after the 26 November election, to include persons from outside Fanmi Lavalas in his Government was rejected by the opposition parties. The only negotiations that took place were between Mr. Aristide and two United States envoys. They resulted in an eight-point accord contained in a 27 December letter to the President of the United States, William J. Clinton, in which Mr. Aristide pledged to: hold run-offs for the disputed Senate seats (or rectify the 21 May election problems by other credible means); create a credible new electoral council in consultation with the opposition; endeavour to form a broad-based government; and request a semi-permanent OAS commission to facilitate dialogue and reinforce democratic institutions. The accord also contained commitments on drug trafficking, money-laundering, illegal migration, reinforcement of the police and economic reforms. Though rejected by the opposition as insufficient and insincere, action was taken by the authorities to implement some of the points. In mid-December, the opposition parties announced their intention to form a provisional government to fill what they considered a constitutional void that would be left at the end of President Préval's term. Although the leaders of the Democratic Convergence gave private assurances that they had no intention of trying to install their alternative government by force, their public statements sometimes created a different impression. Haitian authorities responded with a series of critical and implicitly threatening statements and urged the popular organizations to mobilize against what they viewed as a coup d'état.

A second national forum on judicial reform was organized jointly by the Ministry of Justice and MICAH from 4 to 8 December. Four draft laws were debated, including a code of ethics for the judiciary and legislation regulating the Judicial Inspectorate, the Judicial Police and legal aid. MICAH supported the drafting of a series of judicial reform bills, which included legislation to combat drug trafficking and money-laundering.

UNAIDS supported several activities for World AIDS Day on 1 December, in particular a mobilization and sensitization campaign throughout the country. Following heavy floods in northern

Haiti in early November, the United Nations Disaster Management Team reacted swiftly, coordinated immediate assistance and formulated a joint integrated proposal for local risk and disaster management.

On 23 December, the General Assembly decided that the item on the situation of democracy and human rights in Haiti would remain for consideration at its resumed fifty-fifth (2001) session **(decision 55/458)**.

Financing of missions

In February [A/54/757], the Secretary-General submitted to the General Assembly MIPONUH's financial performance report for the period from 1 July 1998 to 30 June 1999. Expenditures for the period totalled $26,261,000 gross ($25,101,100 net), excluding budgeted voluntary contributions in kind of $1,788,000, resulting in an unencumbered balance of $3,707,700 gross ($3,435,600 net).

In April [A/54/825], ACABQ suggested that the Assembly might consider crediting the unencumbered balance to Member States or to MICAH's Trust Fund.

GENERAL ASSEMBLY ACTION

On 15 June [meeting 98], the General Assembly, on the recommendation of the Fifth Committee [A/54/907], adopted **resolution 54/276** without vote [agenda item 147].

Financing of the United Nations Civilian Police Mission in Haiti

The General Assembly,

Having considered the report of the Secretary-General on the financing of the United Nations Support Mission in Haiti, the United Nations Transition Mission in Haiti and the United Nations Civilian Police Mission in Haiti and the related reports of the Advisory Committee on Administrative and Budgetary Questions,

Bearing in mind Security Council resolutions 1063(1996) of 28 June 1996, by which the Council established the United Nations Support Mission in Haiti, and 1086(1996) of 5 December 1996, by which the Council extended the mandate of the Mission until 31 July 1997,

Bearing in mind also Security Council resolution 1123(1997) of 30 July 1997, by which the Council established the United Nations Transition Mission in Haiti for a single four-month period,

Bearing in mind further Security Council resolutions 1141(1997) of 28 November 1997, by which the Council established the United Nations Civilian Police Mission in Haiti, and 1277(1999) of 30 November 1999, by which the Council continued the Mission until 15 March 2000,

Recalling its resolution 51/15 A of 4 November 1996 on the financing of the Support Mission and its subsequent decisions and resolutions thereon, the latest of which was resolution 53/222 B of 8 June 1999,

Reaffirming that the costs of the Missions are expenses of the Organization to be borne by Member States in accordance with Article 17, paragraph 2, of the Charter of the United Nations,

Recalling its previous decisions regarding the fact that, in order to meet the expenditures caused by the Missions, a different procedure is required from that applied to meet expenditures of the regular budget of the United Nations,

Taking into account the fact that the economically more developed countries are in a position to make relatively larger contributions and that the economically less developed countries have a relatively limited capacity to contribute towards such an operation,

Bearing in mind the special responsibilities of the States permanent members of the Security Council, as indicated in General Assembly resolution 1874(S-IV) of 27 June 1963, in the financing of such operations,

Noting with appreciation that voluntary contributions have been made to the United Nations Civilian Police Mission in Haiti by certain Governments,

Mindful of the fact that it is essential to continue to provide the account of the Missions with the necessary financial resources to enable them to meet their outstanding liabilities,

1. *Takes note* of the status of contributions to the United Nations Support Mission in Haiti, the United Nations Transition Mission in Haiti and the United Nations Civilian Police Mission in Haiti as at 30 April 2000, including the contributions outstanding in the amount of 23 million United States dollars, representing 24 per cent of the total assessed contributions from the inception of the Support Mission to the period ending 30 June 2000, notes that some 29 per cent of the Member States have paid their assessed contributions in full, and urges all other Member States concerned, in particular those in arrears, to ensure payment of their outstanding contributions;

2. *Expresses its appreciation* to those Member States which have paid their assessed contributions in full;

3. *Expresses concern* about the financial situation with regard to peacekeeping activities, in particular as regards the reimbursements to troop contributors that bear additional burdens owing to overdue payments by Member States of their assessments;

4. *Urges* all other Member States to make every possible effort to ensure payment of their assessed contributions to the United Nations Civilian Police Mission in Haiti in full;

5. *Expresses concern* at the delay experienced by the Secretary-General in deploying and providing adequate resources to some recent peacekeeping missions, in particular those in Africa;

6. *Emphasizes* that all future and existing peacekeeping missions shall be given equal and non-discriminatory treatment in respect of financial and administrative arrangements;

7. *Also emphasizes* that all peacekeeping missions shall be provided with adequate resources for the effective and efficient discharge of their respective mandates;

8. *Takes note* of the observations contained in the report of the Advisory Committee on Administrative and Budgetary Questions;

9. *Decides* that Member States that have fulfilled their financial obligations to the Civilian Police Mis-

sion shall be credited their respective share of the un-encumbered balance of 3,707,700 dollars gross (3,435,600 dollars net) in respect of the period ending 30 June 1999;

10. *Decides also* that, for Member States that have not fulfilled their obligations to the Civilian Police Mission, their share of the unencumbered balance of 3,707,700 dollars gross (3,435,600 dollars net) in respect of the period ending 30 June 1999 shall be set off against their outstanding obligations;

11. *Emphasizes* that no peacekeeping mission shall be financed by borrowing funds from other active peacekeeping missions;

12. *Decides* to include in the provisional agenda of its fifty-fifth session the item entitled "Financing of the United Nations Support Mission in Haiti, the United Nations Transition Mission in Haiti and the United Nations Civilian Police Mission in Haiti".

On 5 September, the Assembly decided to include in the draft agenda of its fifty-fifth session the item entitled "Financing of the United Nations Mission in Haiti" (**decision 54/498**).

In December [A/55/667], the Secretary-General submitted a report on the final disposition of the assets of the United Nations Support Mission in Haiti (UNSMIH), which ended in July 1997, the United Nations Transition Mission in Haiti (UNTMIH), which terminated in November 1997, and MIPONUH, which terminated on 15 March 2000. The inventory value of the Missions' assets as at 15 March amounted to some $27.2 million, 46 per cent of which had been transferred to other peacekeeping operations or to the United Nations Logistics Base in Brindisi, Italy, for temporary storage. The disposal of the assets had been guided by the principles endorsed by the Assembly in section VII of resolution 49/233 A [YUN 1994, p. 1340].

On 23 December, the Assembly decided that the items on the financing of the United Nations Mission in Haiti and of UNSMIH, UNTMIH and MIPONUH would remain for consideration at its resumed fifty-fifth (2001) session (**decision 55/458**), and that the Fifth Committee should continue its consideration of those items at that session (**decision 55/455**).

Other questions

Cuba–United States

In July [A/55/172], the Secretary-General, in response to General Assembly resolution 54/21 [YUN 1999, p. 222], submitted information received from 54 States, the EU and 10 UN bodies on the implementation of the resolution, by which the Assembly had called on States to refrain from

unilateral application of economic and trade measures against States, and urged them to repeal or invalidate such measures. The preamble to resolution 54/21 had made particular reference to the Helms-Burton Act, promulgated by the United States in 1996, which had strengthened sanctions against Cuba. In a September report [A/55/172/Add.1], the Secretary-General submitted information received from six States and one UN body.

GENERAL ASSEMBLY ACTION

On 9 November [meeting 56], the General Assembly adopted **resolution 55/20** [draft: A/55/L.7] by recorded vote (167-3-4) [agenda item 35].

Necessity of ending the economic, commercial and financial embargo imposed by the United States of America against Cuba

The General Assembly,

Determined to encourage strict compliance with the purposes and principles enshrined in the Charter of the United Nations,

Reaffirming, among other principles, the sovereign equality of States, non-intervention and non-interference in their internal affairs and freedom of international trade and navigation, which are also enshrined in many international legal instruments,

Recalling the statements of the heads of State or Government at the Ibero-American Summits concerning the need to eliminate the unilateral application of economic and trade measures by one State against another that affect the free flow of international trade,

Concerned about the continued promulgation and application by Member States of laws and regulations, such as that promulgated on 12 March 1996 known as the "Helms-Burton Act", the extraterritorial effects of which affect the sovereignty of other States, the legitimate interests of entities or persons under their jurisdiction and the freedom of trade and navigation,

Taking note of declarations and resolutions of different intergovernmental forums, bodies and Governments that express the rejection by the international community and public opinion of the promulgation and application of regulations of the kind referred to above,

Recalling its resolutions 47/19 of 24 November 1992, 48/16 of 3 November 1993, 49/9 of 26 October 1994, 50/10 of 2 November 1995, 51/17 of 12 November 1996, 52/10 of 5 November 1997, 53/4 of 14 October 1998 and 54/21 of 9 November 1999,

Concerned that, since the adoption of its resolutions 47/19, 48/16, 49/9, 50/10, 51/17, 52/10, 53/4 and 54/21, further measures of that nature aimed at strengthening and extending the economic, commercial and financial embargo against Cuba continue to be promulgated and applied, and concerned also about the adverse effects of such measures on the Cuban people and on Cuban nationals living in other countries,

1. *Takes note* of the report of the Secretary-General on the implementation of resolution 54/21;

2. *Reiterates its call* on all States to refrain from promulgating and applying laws and measures of the kind referred to in the preamble to the present resolu-

tion in conformity with their obligations under the Charter of the United Nations and international law, which, inter alia, reaffirm the freedom of trade and navigation;

3. *Once again urges* States that have and continue to apply such laws and measures to take the necessary steps to repeal or invalidate them as soon as possible in accordance with their legal regime;

4. *Requests* the Secretary-General, in consultation with the appropriate organs and agencies of the United Nations system, to prepare a report on the implementation of the present resolution in the light of the purposes and principles of the Charter and international law and to submit it to the General Assembly at its fifty-sixth session;

5. *Decides* to include in the provisional agenda of its fifty-sixth session the item entitled "Necessity of ending the economic, commercial and financial embargo imposed by the United States of America against Cuba".

RECORDED VOTE ON RESOLUTION 55/20:

In favour: Afghanistan, Albania, Algeria, Andorra, Angola, Antigua and Barbuda, Argentina, Armenia, Australia, Austria, Azerbaijan, Bahamas, Bahrain, Bangladesh, Barbados, Belarus, Belgium, Belize, Benin, Bhutan, Bolivia, Botswana, Brazil, Brunei Darussalam, Bulgaria, Burkina Faso, Burundi, Cambodia, Cameroon, Canada, Cape Verde, Chad, Chile, China, Colombia, Comoros, Congo, Costa Rica, Côte d'Ivoire, Croatia, Cuba, Cyprus, Czech Republic, Democratic People's Republic of Korea, Democratic Republic of the Congo, Denmark, Djibouti, Dominica, Dominican Republic, Ecuador, Egypt, Equatorial Guinea, Eritrea, Ethiopia, Fiji, Finland, France, Gabon, Gambia, Georgia, Germany, Ghana, Greece, Grenada, Guatemala, Guinea, Guyana, Haiti, Honduras, Hungary, Iceland, India, Indonesia, Iran, Ireland, Italy, Jamaica, Japan, Jordan, Kazakhstan, Kenya, Kuwait, Kyrgyzstan, Lao People's Democratic Republic, Lebanon, Lesotho, Libyan Arab Jamahiriya, Liechtenstein, Lithuania, Luxembourg, Madagascar, Malawi, Malaysia, Maldives, Mali, Malta, Mauritius, Mexico, Monaco, Mongolia, Mozambique, Myanmar, Namibia, Nauru, Nepal, Netherlands, New Zealand, Nigeria, Norway, Oman, Pakistan, Panama, Papua New Guinea, Paraguay, Peru, Philippines, Poland, Portugal, Qatar, Republic of Korea, Republic of Moldova, Romania, Russian Federation, Rwanda, Saint Kitts and Nevis, Saint Lucia, Saint Vincent and the Grenadines, Samoa, San Marino, Sao Tome and Principe, Saudi Arabia, Senegal, Sierra Leone, Singapore, Slovakia, Slovenia, Solomon Islands, South Africa, Spain, Sri Lanka, Sudan, Suriname, Swaziland, Sweden, Syrian Arab Republic, Tajikistan, Thailand, The former Yugoslav Republic of Macedonia, Togo, Tonga, Trinidad and Tobago, Tunisia, Turkey, Turkmenistan, Uganda, Ukraine, United Arab Emirates, United Kingdom, United Republic of Tanzania, Uruguay, Vanuatu, Venezuela, Viet Nam, Yemen, Yugoslavia, Zambia, Zimbabwe.

Against: Israel, Marshall Islands, United States.

Abstaining: El Salvador, Latvia, Morocco, Nicaragua.

Communications. On 14 January [A/54/715-S/2000/44], Cuba informed the Secretary-General that on 1 January an aircraft from the United States violated Cuban airspace by flying at a low altitude over the capital city of Havana.

On 20 June [A/55/316], Cuba transmitted to the Secretary-General a submission from the Cuban people to the Government of the United States for economic damage to Cuba.

Panama–United States

On 15 September [A/55/392-S/2000/874], Panama transmitted to the Secretary-General a note concerning the contamination of several thousand hectares of Panamanian territory with materials, explosives and toxic waste left behind by the armed forces of the United States after the clo-

sure of United States military bases in Panama and the transfer of the Panama Canal to exclusive Panamanian control on 31 December 1999. Panama said that when the 1977 Panama Canal Treaties were signed [YUN 1978, p. 160], it was agreed that the United States had a broad responsibility without any time limit for the decontamination of the areas used by it for target and bombing practice. According to Panama, the United States was reluctant to meet its obligations, claiming that it could not improve on the clean-up operations already performed. Panama requested the United Nations to investigate that alleged United States breach of its obligations.

Cooperation with OAS

In response to General Assembly resolution 53/9 [YUN 1998, p. 237], the Secretary-General submitted a July report on cooperation between the United Nations and the Organization of American States (OAS) [A/55/184]. The report reviewed their joint participation in the International Civilian Mission to Haiti (see p. 249), described consultations and information exchange on matters of mutual interest, and provided information on collaborative activities undertaken with OAS by the UN Secretariat, ECLAC, the United Nations Conference on Trade and Development (UNCTAD), the Office of the United Nations High Commissioner for Refugees (UNHCR), the United Nations International Drug Control Programme (UNDCP), ILO, UNESCO, the International Civil Aviation Organization (ICAO), the World Bank, the International Maritime Organization (IMO) and the United Nations Industrial Development Organization (UNIDO).

In June, the United Nations was represented at the thirtieth session of the General Assembly of OAS, at which a resolution was adopted requesting the OAS Secretary-General to continue to strengthen cooperation between the two organizations.

GENERAL ASSEMBLY ACTION

On 3 November [meeting 51], the General Assembly adopted **resolution 55/15** [draft: A/55/L.21 & Add.1] without vote [agenda item 21].

Cooperation between the United Nations and the Organization of American States

The General Assembly,

Recalling its resolution 53/9 of 22 October 1998 relating to the promotion of cooperation between the United Nations and the Organization of American States,

Having examined the report of the Secretary-General on cooperation between the United Nations and the Organization of American States,

Recalling that the purposes of the United Nations are, inter alia, to achieve international cooperation in solving international problems of an economic, social, cultural or humanitarian character and in promoting and encouraging respect for human rights and fundamental freedoms and to be a centre for harmonizing the actions of nations in the attainment of these common ends,

Recalling also that the Charter of the Organization of American States reaffirms these purposes and principles and provides that that organization is a regional agency under the terms of the Charter of the United Nations,

Recalling further its resolutions 47/20 A of 24 November 1992, 47/20 B of 20 April 1993, 48/27 B of 8 July 1994, 49/5 of 21 October 1994, 49/27 B of 12 July 1995, 50/86 B of 3 April 1996, 51/4 of 24 October 1996 and 53/9 of 22 October 1998,

Welcoming the upcoming Summit of the Americas to be held in Quebec City, Canada, from 20 to 22 April 2001,

Welcoming also resolution AG/RES.1733(XXX-O/00), adopted by the General Assembly of the Organization of American States at its thirtieth regular session, by which it declared 2001 as the Inter-American Year of the Child and the Adolescent, and related efforts in the Americas to address emerging issues for children in the twenty-first century, during lead-up to the special session of the General Assembly of the United Nations in 2001 for follow-up to the World Summit for Children,

1. *Takes note with satisfaction* of the report of the Secretary-General on cooperation between the United Nations and the Organization of American States and his efforts to strengthen that cooperation;

2. *Also takes note with satisfaction* of the exchanges of information between the United Nations and the Organization of American States in the context of the work of the International Civilian Support Mission in Haiti and of the United Nations Verification Mission in Guatemala;

3. *Recognizes* the work of the Organization of American States towards the promotion of democracy in the Americas, in the field of regional cooperation and in connection with its task of coordination with the United Nations;

4. *Welcomes* the efforts of the Economic Commission for Latin America and the Caribbean to strengthen cooperation with inter-American institutions in various fields, including hemispheric integration, statistics and women and development;

5. *Recommends* that a general meeting of representatives of the United Nations system and of the Organization of American States be held in 2001 for the continued review and appraisal of cooperation programmes and of other matters to be mutually decided upon;

6. *Expresses its satisfaction* at the exchange with the Organization of American States of information and substantive reports on the advancement in the status of women, on matters relating to youth and on the eradication of poverty;

7. *Emphasizes* that the cooperation between the United Nations and the Organization of American States should be undertaken in accordance with their respective mandates, scope and composition and be suited to each specific situation, in accordance with the Charter of the United Nations;

8. *Requests* the Secretary-General to submit to the General Assembly at its fifty-seventh session a report on the implementation of the present resolution;

9. *Decides* to include in the provisional agenda of its fifty-seventh session the item entitled "Cooperation between the United Nations and the Organization of American States".

Cooperation with CARICOM

In response to General Assembly resolution 53/17 [YUN 1998, p. 238], the Secretary-General submitted an August report on cooperation between the United Nations and the Caribbean Community (CARICOM) [A/55/215]. He described consultations and information exchange between the two organizations and provided information on collaborative activities undertaken with CARICOM by the UN Secretariat, ECLAC, UNCTAD, UNDP, the United Nations Environment Programme, the United Nations Population Fund, UNHCR, UNDCP, ILO, the Food and Agriculture Organization of the United Nations, UNESCO, ICAO, the World Bank, the Universal Postal Union, IMO and UNIDO.

The second general meeting between representatives of CARICOM and its associated institutions and the UN system (Nassau, Bahamas, 27-28 March) recognized existing collaboration between the United Nations and CARICOM and welcomed new areas of possible cooperation, which, it was agreed, should be further explored and developed, subject to financial and human resources. At the invitation of CARICOM, the United Nations was represented by the UNDP Resident Representative in Trinidad and Tobago and Barbados at the twentieth and twenty-first Conferences of Heads of State and Government of CARICOM, held in Trinidad and Tobago in July 1999 and in Saint Vincent and the Grenadines in July 2000.

GENERAL ASSEMBLY ACTION

On 7 November [meeting 54], the General Assembly adopted **resolution 55/17** [draft: A/55/L.24/Rev.1 & Add.1] without vote [agenda item 23].

Cooperation between the United Nations and the Caribbean Community

The General Assembly,

Recalling its resolutions 46/8 of 16 October 1991, 49/141 of 20 December 1994, 51/16 of 11 November 1996 and 53/17 of 29 October 1998,

Noting with satisfaction the report of the Secretary-General on cooperation between the United Nations and the Caribbean Community,

Bearing in mind the provisions of Chapter VIII of the Charter of the United Nations on the existence of regional arrangements or agencies for dealing with such matters relating to the maintenance of international peace and security as are appropriate for regional action and other activities consistent with the purposes and principles of the United Nations,

Bearing in mind also the assistance given by the United Nations towards the maintenance of peace and security in the Caribbean region,

Noting with satisfaction that the first general meeting between representatives of the Caribbean Community and its associated institutions and of the United Nations system was held in New York on 27 and 28 May 1997, and that the second general meeting was held in Nassau on 27 and 28 March 2000,

Bearing in mind that, in its resolution 54/225 of 22 December 1999, it recognized the importance of adopting an integrated management approach to the Caribbean Sea area in the context of sustainable development,

Bearing in mind also that in the United Nations Millennium Declaration, adopted by resolution 55/2 of 8 September 2000, heads of State and Government resolved to address the special needs of small island developing States by implementing the Barbados Programme of Action and the outcome of the twenty-second special session of the General Assembly rapidly and in full,

Affirming the need to strengthen the cooperation that already exists between entities of the United Nations system and the Caribbean Community in the areas of economic and social development, as well as of political and humanitarian affairs,

Convinced of the need for the coordinated utilization of available resources to promote the common objectives of the two organizations,

1. *Takes note* of the report of the Secretary-General on cooperation between the United Nations and the Caribbean Community, as well as efforts to strengthen that cooperation;

2. *Welcomes* the signing on 27 May 1997 by the Secretary-General of the United Nations and the Secretary-General of the Caribbean Community of a cooperation agreement between the secretariats of the two organizations;

3. *Calls upon* the Secretary-General of the United Nations, in consultation with the Secretary-General of the Caribbean Community, to continue to assist in furthering the development and maintenance of peace and security within the Caribbean region;

4. *Invites* the Secretary-General to continue to promote and expand cooperation and coordination between the United Nations and the Caribbean Community in order to increase the capacity of the two organizations to attain their objectives;

5. *Urges* the specialized agencies and other organizations and programmes of the United Nations system to cooperate with the Secretary-General of the United Nations and the Secretary-General of the Caribbean Community in order to initiate, maintain and increase consultations and programmes with the Caribbean Community and its associated institutions in the attainment of their objectives, with special attention to the areas and issues identified at the second general meeting, as set out in the report of the Secretary-General, as well as resolutions 54/225 and 55/2;

6. *Welcomes* the initiatives of Member States in assisting in the cooperation between the United Nations and the Caribbean Community;

7. *Recommends* that the third general meeting between representatives of the Caribbean Community and its associated institutions and of the United Nations system be held in 2002 in New York in order to review and appraise progress in the implementation of the agreed areas and issues and to hold consultations on such additional measures and procedures as may be required to facilitate and strengthen cooperation between the two organizations;

8. *Requests* the Secretary-General to submit to the General Assembly at its fifty-seventh session a report on the implementation of the present resolution;

9. *Decides* to include in the provisional agenda of its fifty-seventh session the item entitled "Cooperation between the United Nations and the Caribbean Community".

Chapter IV

Asia and the Pacific

In 2000, the United Nations continued to face challenges to regional security and peace in Asia and the Pacific, mainly in Afghanistan, East Timor, Iraq and Tajikistan.

In Afghanistan, the military confrontation between the Taliban and the United Front continued. In October, however, the two warring factions agreed to enter into a dialogue under UN auspices. The prolonged civil conflict, combined with the worst drought in 30 years and gross human rights violations, especially against women and girls, exacerbated the already tenuous living conditions of the Afghan population. On 19 December, the Security Council imposed new sanctions against the Taliban regime for its failure, among other things, to turn over Osama bin Laden—a Saudi Arabian national indicted by the United States for terrorist activities—to appropriate authorities to face trial. The Council also called on the Taliban authorities to close all terrorist camps operating in their territory and decided that all States should close immediately all Taliban offices in their territories and freeze funds and other financial assets. The United Nations Special Mission to Afghanistan continued to promote political dialogue and deployed a Civil Affairs Unit inside Afghanistan.

In East Timor, progress was made in the transition towards independence and the attainment of peace and security, despite continued militia-led violence and the displacement of thousands of people. The United Nations was confronted with the task of rebuilding, managing and governing a territory for the first time in its history when, in February, the United Nations Transitional Administration in East Timor replaced the International Force in East Timor as the sole legitimate governing and military body. Following the killing of three UN humanitarian staff by a militia-led mob, the Council, which closely monitored the situation in East Timor throughout the year, called on Indonesia to disband the militia groups and to ensure the safety of refugees and humanitarian workers. A Council mission visited East Timor and Indonesia in November.

In Iraq, UN activities to verify Baghdad's compliance with its weapons-related obligations under Council resolution 687(1991), which brought a formal ceasefire to the 1991 Gulf war, continued to be stalled following the withdrawal in December 1998 of the United Nations Special Commission (UNSCOM) and the International Atomic Energy Agency (IAEA) from Iraq. UNSCOM's monitoring and verification activities were assumed by the United Nations Monitoring, Verification and Inspection Commission, which began operations in March 2000. The United Nations Iraq-Kuwait Observation Mission continued to carry out its surveillance functions in the demilitarized zone between the two countries. The Council extended the humanitarian programme, based on an oil-for-food formula, twice during the year, each time for another 180 days.

In Tajikistan, the United Nations Mission of Observers in Tajikistan completed its mandate and withdrew from the country on 15 May. In view of the fact that armed elements continued to operate outside the Government's control, and in order to sustain and build upon the achievements of the peace process, the United Nations Tajikistan Office of Peace-building was established on 1 June, with the aim of providing the political framework and leadership for UN post-conflict peace-building activities. In spite of serious problems and shortcomings, the first multiparty and pluralistic parliamentary elections were held on 27 February, for the lower house, and on 23 March, for the upper house.

Other matters brought to the attention of the United Nations were the long-standing dispute between India and Pakistan over Jammu and Kashmir, violations reported by Iran and Iraq of their 1988 ceasefire agreement and of the area of separation between them, as well as the continued occupation by Iran of Greater Tunb, Lesser Tunb and Abu Musa, three islands claimed by the United Arab Emirates. The Democratic People's Republic of Korea (DPRK) and the Republic of Korea held their first summit meeting since the division of the peninsula in 1945 and produced a joint declaration based on the principles of independence, peaceful reunification and national unity. IAEA continued to maintain an inspector presence in the DPRK to monitor the freeze of its graphite moderated reactors and related facilities. The United Nations continued to discuss with Cambodia the establishment of a court to try top Khmer Rouge leaders for crimes committed during the period of Democratic Kampuchea. The United Nations Political Office in

Bougainville (UNPOB) in Papua New Guinea continued to monitor and report on the implementation of the 1998 Lincoln Agreement on Peace, Security and Development on Bougainville by the parties to that Agreement, as well as by the Peace Monitoring Group composed of Australia, Fiji, New Zealand and Vanuatu. At the request of the Government, the Secretary-General, with the concurrence of the Security Council, extended UNPOB's mandate for a further 12-month period to 31 December 2001. In Solomon Islands, the Council supported a peace agreement, concluded in October 2000, for the cessation of hostilities between two rival militia groups following an attempt to overthrow the legitimate Government in June.

Afghanistan

Developments in Afghanistan throughout 2000 gave little ground for optimism. It was an exceptionally difficult year for most Afghans as the country faced a combination of war, with its consequent displacement and suffering of civilians, widespread poverty exacerbated by the worst drought in 30 years, continued gross violations of human rights, particularly against women and girls, and the destruction and criminalization of the economy. However, the November agreement by the two warring factions—the Taliban and the United Front (UF)—to enter into a dialogue under UN auspices provided a glimmer of hope.

The conditions under which humanitarian assistance was provided became progressively more complicated as the year progressed. The Taliban instituted a firman (edict), banning the employment of women by the United Nations and non-governmental organizations (NGOs), with the exception of the health sector, and issued a statute containing regulations governing the activities of UN agencies and programmes. Taliban forces also made forced entries into UN premises and intimidated UN staff. In addition, funding for the consolidated appeal for Afghanistan for 2000 reached only 50 per cent of the amount needed.

During the year, the Office of the United Nations High Commissioner for Refugees (UNHCR) assisted in the voluntary repatriation of 210,170 Afghans; however, reports showed that the returnees faced enormous difficulties. The onset of the harsh winter, extremely precarious food security and the massive displacement inside Afghanistan temporarily halted the repatriation programme.

The role and presence of the United Nations Special Mission to Afghanistan (UNSMA) were strengthened on the ground. Francesc Vendrell (Spain) was appointed Personal Representative of the Secretary-General and Head of Mission, and UNSMA's Civil Affairs Unit was in place and functioning. Topics raised by the Personal Representative during his talks with senior Taliban and UF officials included the Security Council's repeated demands for an immediate ceasefire; the non-targeting of civilians; other humanitarian and human rights matters; issues of terrorism and poppy cultivation; and the possibility of establishing a broadly based, multi-ethnic and representative government. Discussions also touched on relations with third countries, in which connection each side complained of persistent outside interference in support of the other.

In April, the Security Council again demanded that the Taliban turn over indicted terrorist Osama bin Laden to appropriate authorities. It also stressed the need for the Taliban to comply without delay with the Council's repeated demands to conclude a ceasefire and resume negotiations. In December, the Council imposed further sanctions on Afghanistan, including a decision that all States should close immediately all Taliban offices and Ariana Afghan Airlines offices in their territories and freeze funds and other financial assests of Osama bin Laden and individuals and entities associated with him. In the light of that action, the Taliban said that they no longer accepted the United Nations as an impartial broker in the dialogue that they had agreed to pursue with the UF.

Situation in Afghanistan

The situation in Afghanistan during 2000 was described by the Secretary-General in four progress reports, submitted in response to General Assembly resolution 54/189 A [YUN 1999, p. 258]. The first three were quarterly, issued on 10 March [A/54/791-S/2000/205], 16 June [A/54/918-S/2000/581] and 18 September [A/55/393-S/2000/875]; the fourth was an annual report issued in the last quarter of the year (see p. 269). The reports gave accounts of the political and military developments in the country; the peacemaking activities of the Secretary-General's Personal Representative, of UNSMA and at UN Headquarters in New York; UN assistance and programmes to alleviate the progressively deteriorating humanitarian and human rights situations of the war victims; and UN efforts to curb terrorism within and from Afghanistan, as well as to reduce the illicit cultivation, production and trafficking of drugs.

Report of Secretary-General (March). In his 10 March report [A/54/791-S/2000/205], the

Secretary-General noted that he had appointed Francesc Vendrell as his Personal Representative and Head of UNSMA; Mr. Vendrell had taken up his appointment on 1 February. From 3 to 23 February, he visited senior officials of both sides in Afghanistan and neighbouring countries in the region and beyond, including some members of the "six plus two" group—the countries bordering Afghanistan (China, Iran, Pakistan, Tajikistan, Turkmenistan and Uzbekistan) plus the Russian Federation and the United States. He had earlier visited Washington, D.C.

The two Afghan parties stated their readiness to cooperate with Mr. Vendrell in the search for a political solution to the Afghan conflict and both expressed their opposition to terrorism and their commitment to progressively eradicate drug cultivation. Regarding the Security Council demand that the Taliban turn over Osama bin Laden, Mullah Mohammad Rabbani, Chairman of the Taliban Council of Ministers, reminded the Personal Representative that Mr. bin Laden had taken up residence when Afghanistan was under the control of the previous regime and maintained that there was not sufficient evidence to link him to the 1998 terrorist bombings of United States embassies in Nairobi, Kenya, and Dar es Salaam, United Republic of Tanzania [YUN 1998, 1218]. He further stated that Mr. bin Laden was no longer able to carry out activities from Afghan territory.

In discussions with the Personal Representative, Governments of the "six plus two" group expressed concern at the absence of a political solution to the Afghan conflict; shared the view that international terrorism, illicit drug production and trafficking, and extremism emanating from the country posed a serious threat to the stability of the region; reaffirmed their commitment to work with the United Nations; and conveyed their interest in strengthening the role of the group as a means of bringing the parties to the negotiating table and assisting in the search for a lasting political settlement. In that connection, the group held a meeting (New York, 28 February) at which it focused on the issue of illicit drugs.

Under the auspices of the Organization of the Islamic Conference (OIC), talks involving the Taliban and the UF took place in Jeddah, Saudi Arabia, from 7 to 9 March. The sides agreed to hold another round of indirect talks after the hajj season.

As to the military situation, the Secretary-General noted that the fighting, although at a low ebb during the winter months and the holy month of Ramadan, had never completely halted. Most recently, Taliban forces on 1 March initiated fresh fighting in the province of Kunduz and the Sho-mali Plains and continued their attacks in the province of Samangan in the Dara-e-Souf area where the UF renewed efforts to resist. Although the Taliban initially achieved significant progress, the UF succeeded in recapturing ground lost in Kunduz and claimed to have recaptured towns taken by the Taliban in other conflict areas.

In view of the impact of the continued fighting on the Afghan population and reports indicating that a major offensive was being prepared for the spring, the Secretary-General asked his Personal Representative to concentrate his efforts to persuade the parties to enter into a process of dialogue that might lead to a stable and verifiable ceasefire and, eventually, to an agreement on the establishment of a broadly based, multi-ethnic and fully representative government.

Communication. In identical letters of 15 March [A/54/798-S/2000/218] to the Secretary-General and the Security Council President, Afghanistan's representative to the United Nations reported on alleged Pakistani-Taliban military operations in Government-held territories.

Security Council consideration. On 7 April [meeting 4124], the Security Council was briefed by a Department of Political Affairs (DPA) official on the situation in Afghanistan. Having reviewed the events covered in the Secretary-General's 10 March report, the official described later developments. With regard to the humanitarian situation, he noted that the Organization was worried by the situation in Kandahar, where searches of UN premises and intimidation of staff in recent days had caused the withdrawal of all international staff from the area. As to the situation of women and girls, he recalled that the abhorrent measures imposed on them by the Taliban had been repeatedly deplored by the Secretary-General and had been condemned by the Council, the General Assembly, the Commission on Human Rights and the Commission on the Status of Women (see also pp. 750 and 1120). While there had been limited progress with regard to the Taliban's position on the access of women to health services, education and employment opportunities, the overall situation remained unacceptable and required the continuous and sustained attention of the international community.

SECURITY COUNCIL ACTION

On 7 April [meeting 4125], following consultations among Security Council members, the President made statement **S/PRST/2000/12** on behalf of the Council:

The Security Council has considered the report of the Secretary-General of 10 March 2000 concerning the situation in Afghanistan and its implications for international peace and security.

The Council reiterates its grave concern at the continued Afghan conflict, which is a serious and growing threat to regional and international peace and security. It strongly condemns the Taliban for the launching of new offensives, most notably that of 1 March 2000. The Council expresses its deep concern at the reports that both parties to the conflict are preparing for renewed large-scale fighting and recalls its repeated demands that the Afghan parties cease fighting. These events add to the enormous suffering of the civilian population of Afghanistan.

The Council reiterates that there is no military solution to the conflict in Afghanistan and that only a negotiated political settlement aimed at the establishment of a broad-based, multi-ethnic and fully representative government acceptable to all Afghans can lead to peace and national reconciliation. It notes that the United Front of Afghanistan is willing to talk with the Taliban and recalls its demand that the parties, in particular the Taliban, resume negotiations under the auspices of the United Nations without delay or preconditions in full compliance with the relevant resolutions of the General Assembly and the Council.

The Council calls upon all Afghan parties to comply with their obligations under international humanitarian law and to ensure the full and unhindered access of international humanitarian assistance and personnel to all those in need. It expresses its grave concern at the further deterioration of the humanitarian situation in Afghanistan as a result of ongoing hostilities. The Taliban has the primary responsibility for this.

The Council strongly condemns the Taliban for the repeated forced entries on 26, 27 and 29 March 2000 by its armed groups into, and their searches of, the United Nations premises in Kandahar and for the intimidation of the United Nations personnel. It stresses that responsibility for the subsequent withdrawal of all international staff from Kandahar and suspension of humanitarian assistance activities in southern Afghanistan rests solely with the Taliban. The Council demands that the Taliban stop these unacceptable practices and ensure the safety and security of all United Nations and associated personnel and humanitarian personnel working in Afghanistan in accordance with international law.

The Council stresses its grave concern at the human rights situation in Afghanistan, which is unacceptable. It expresses particular alarm at the continuing disregard by the Taliban of the concerns expressed by the international community. The Council strongly condemns the forced displacement of the civilian population, notably that conducted by the Taliban in 1999, the deliberate targeting of civilians and the destruction of their assets and means of survival, summary executions, arbitrary detention of civilians and forced labour of those in detention, the separation of men from their families, indiscriminate bombing and other violations of human rights and international humanitarian law. It calls upon all Afghan parties, especially the Taliban, to put an end to such practices and to ensure the protection of civilians.

The Council reaffirms the principle of non-refoulement of refugees, as provided for in relevant instruments of international law, welcomes recent efforts of countries neighbouring Afghanistan to support the voluntary repatriation of Afghan refugees in safety and dignity, and urges those host States to continue to provide international protection to Afghan refugees in need of it. It encourages the international community to provide the necessary assistance in this regard.

The Council condemns the continuing grave violations of the human rights of women and girls, including all forms of discrimination against them, in all areas of Afghanistan, particularly in areas under the control of the Taliban. It remains deeply concerned about continued restrictions on their access to health care, to education and to employment outside the home, and about restrictions on their freedom of movement and freedom from intimidation, harassment and violence. The Council notes the recent reports of modest progress regarding the access of women and girls to certain services, but considers that such incremental improvements, while welcome, still fall far short of the minimum expectations of the international community, and calls upon all parties, particularly the Taliban, to take measures to end all violations of human rights of women and girls.

The Council reiterates that outside interference in the internal affairs of Afghanistan, including the involvement of foreign combatants and military personnel and the supply of weapons and other materials used in the conflict, should cease immediately. It calls upon all States to take resolute measures to prohibit their military personnel from planning and participating in combat operations in Afghanistan, and immediately to withdraw their personnel and to assure that the supply of ammunition and other war-making materials is halted. The Council expresses its deep concern at the continuing involvement in the fighting in Afghanistan, on the side of the Taliban forces, of thousands of non-Afghan nationals.

The Council reiterates its position that the United Nations must continue to play its central and impartial role in international efforts towards a peaceful resolution of the Afghan conflict. It welcomes the appointment of a new Personal Representative of the Secretary-General and the activities of the United Nations Special Mission to Afghanistan to facilitate a political process aimed at achieving a lasting political settlement to the conflict. The Council supports the phased deployment of the Civil Affairs Unit of the Mission inside Afghanistan, as the security conditions permit.

The Council welcomes the renewed commitment of members of the "six plus two" group to contribute to a peaceful resolution of the Afghan conflict in support of the efforts of the United Nations, and urges the members of the group and the Afghan parties to implement the Tashkent Declaration on Fundamental Principles for a Peaceful Settlement of the Conflict in Afghanistan, particularly the agreement of members of the group not to provide military support to any Afghan party and to prevent the use of their territories for such purposes.

The Council expresses its appreciation for the efforts undertaken by the Organization of the Islamic Conference, in support of and in coordination with the United Nations, to facilitate the convening of negotiations between the two Afghan parties. It encourages the process launched in Rome to convene a loya jirga in Afghanistan and acknowledges other recent efforts to promote peace in Afghanistan, such as those of the groups meeting in Cyprus and in Tokyo.

The Council strongly condemns the continuing use of Afghan territory, especially areas controlled by the Taliban, for the sheltering and training of terrorists and planning of terrorist acts, and reaffirms its conviction that the suppression of international terrorism is essential for the maintenance of international peace and security. It insists that the Taliban cease the provision of sanctuary and training for international terrorists and their organizations, take effective measures to ensure that the territory under its control is not used for terrorist installations and camps or for the preparation or organization of terrorist acts against other States or their citizens, and cooperate with efforts to bring indicted terrorists to justice.

The Council demands once again that the Taliban turn over indicted terrorist Osama bin Laden to appropriate authorities as set out in resolution 1267(1999) of 15 October 1999. It stresses that the continued failure of the Taliban to comply with this demand is unacceptable. The Council will ensure effective implementation of the measures imposed by that resolution. It condemns the recent attacks and planned attacks by terrorists affiliated with Osama bin Laden, which constitute a continuing threat to the international community.

The Council reiterates that the capture by the Taliban of the Consulate-General of the Islamic Republic of Iran and the murder of Iranian diplomats and a journalist in Mazar-e-Sharif as well as the murders of United Nations personnel constitute flagrant violations of international law. It expresses its concern at the failure of the Taliban effectively to bring to justice those responsible for these crimes. The Council reiterates its demand that the Taliban cooperate fully with the United Nations in this regard.

The Council is deeply disturbed by an alarming increase in the cultivation, production and trafficking of drugs in Afghanistan, especially in areas controlled by the Taliban, and by its consequences for the continuation of the conflict. It demands that the Taliban, as well as others, halt all illegal drug activities. The Council encourages the initiative of the "six plus two" group to address the drug-related issues in a coordinated manner with the support of the Office for Drug Control and Crime Prevention. It also encourages Member States and others concerned to increase their support for the efforts aimed at strengthening the drug control capacities of countries bordering Afghanistan.

The Council stresses the need for prompt and effective implementation by all Member States of the measures imposed by resolution 1267(1999), and reminds Member States of their obligations under that resolution, including assisting in the identification of Taliban assets and aircraft. It underlines the fact that sanctions are not aimed at the Afghan people, but are imposed against the Taliban because of its non-compliance with that resolution. The Council reaffirms its decision to assess the impact, including the humanitarian implications, of the measures imposed by that resolution. It encourages the Security Council Committee established pursuant to resolution 1267(1999) to report in this respect as soon as practicable.

The Council holds the leadership of the Taliban responsible for not taking measures to comply with the demands made in its resolutions, especially to conclude a ceasefire and to resume negotiations, and stresses the need for the Taliban to comply with these demands without delay.

In this context, the Council reaffirms its readiness to consider the imposition of further targeted measures, in accordance with its responsibility under the Charter of the United Nations, with the aim of achieving the full implementation of all its relevant resolutions.

Reports of Secretary-General (June and September). In his 16 June report [A/54/918-S/2000/581], the Secretary-General observed that the situation of the Afghan people remained deplorable. The country remained in a state of acute crisis with its resources depleted, its intelligentsia in exile, its people disfranchised, its traditional political structures shattered and its human development indices among the lowest in the world.

In his 18 September report [A/55/393-S/2000/875], the Secretary-General again updated the Afghan situation, stating that it was hard not to be repetitive when commenting on the continuing tragedy. Fighting between the two warring parties had taken place throughout the summer, with the regular seasonal offensive, and the drought, the worst for over 30 years, was having a devastating effect on the population.

Communications. By a 19 June letter [A/55/86-S/2000/604], Kazakhstan, Kyrgyzstan, Tajikistan and Uzbekistan transmitted an appeal to the Secretary-General in which they expressed concern about the escalation of military and political confrontation in Afghanistan, which continued to cause enormous suffering, destruction and senseless sacrifices. They appealed to the United Nations, the Organization for Security and Cooperation in Europe (OSCE), OIC and the States permanent members of the Security Council to use their influence and authority and all the resources available to them to bring about a speedy and just settlement of the Afghan conflict with a view to putting a stop to the sufferings of the people of Afghanistan and maintaining regional and international security.

On 20 July [A/54/945-S/2000/723], Afghanistan submitted information on the renewed summer offensive allegedly launched by the Taliban-Pakistan–bin Laden axis; incriminating remarks by the Pakistani Chief Executive; and heightened

Pakistani-Taliban terrorist activities, their perilous impact on the safety and security of the Afghan people and implications for regional peace and stability. The letter also discussed the option of convening a loya jirga (grand assembly) as a political solution to the conflict in Afghanistan.

The European Union (EU), in a 14 July statement [A/55/223-S/2000/762], condemned the resumption of wide-scale hostilities in Afghanistan and expressed concern that the military operations were impeding humanitarian assistance. It urged the various factions to stop fighting and work, with UN help, on a political process to restore peace. It reiterated its call to Afghanistan's neighbours to desist from interfering in the conflict.

By a 25 August letter [A/55/326-S/2000/834], the heads of State of Kazakhstan, Kyrgyzstan, Tajikistan and Uzbekistan and the Special Representative of the President of the Russian Federation submitted to the Secretary-General a statement adopted at their meeting (Bishkek, Kyrgyzstan, 20 August). They expressed concern about Central Asia in relation to the terrorist activities of international gangs and appealed to the Security Council, OSCE, OIC and all States not only to condemn international terrorism and extremism but also to move beyond declarations to devise practical coordinated measures designed to eradicate that global threat.

In an 11 October statement [A/55/533-S/2000/1054], the heads of State of Armenia, Belarus, Kazakhstan, Kyrgyzstan, the Russian Federation and Tajikistan expressed concern about the increasing manifestations of international terrorism and extremism in Central Asia. The basic source of instability in the region, they stated, was the ongoing conflict in Afghanistan, and they urged the international community to expedite a settlement of the situation. They also proposed that a special Security Council meeting be convened to elaborate specific measures for the settlement of the Afghan problem, with the participation of all sides involved in the conflict.

By identical letters of 8 November [A/55/548-S/2000/1077], the Secretary-General transmitted to the Presidents of the General Assembly and the Security Council letters dated 30 October from the two Afghan warring parties expressing their agreement to a process of dialogue under the good offices of the Secretary-General, aimed at bringing about an end to the armed conflict in Afghanistan through political means.

Further report of Secretary-General (November). The Secretary-General's fourth progress report, dated 20 November [A/55/633-S/2000/1106] (see p. 269), summarized developments since the issuance of his 16 November 1999 annual report [YUN 1999, p. 261].

On 19 December [meeting 86], the General Assembly adopted **resolution 55/174 A** [draft: A/55/L.62/Rev.1 & Add.1] without vote [agenda items 20 (d) & 46].

The situation in Afghanistan and its implications for international peace and security

The General Assembly,

Recalling its resolutions 51/195 B of 17 December 1996, 52/211 B of 19 December 1997, 53/203 A of 18 December 1998 and 54/189 A of 17 December 1999,

Recalling also Security Council resolutions 1193 (1998) of 28 August 1998, 1214(1998) of 8 December 1998 and 1267(1999) of 15 October 1999 and all statements by the President of the Council on the situation in Afghanistan,

Noting all recent declarations by participants of regional international meetings and by international organizations on the situation in Afghanistan,

Reaffirming its continued strong commitment to the sovereignty, independence, territorial integrity and national unity of Afghanistan, and respecting its multicultural, multi-ethnic and historical heritage,

Reiterating that the United Nations, as a universally recognized and impartial intermediary, must continue to play its central role in international efforts towards a peaceful resolution of the Afghan conflict, and expressing its appreciation and strong support for the ongoing efforts made in this regard by the Secretary-General, by his Personal Representative and by the United Nations Special Mission to Afghanistan,

Convinced that there is no military solution to the Afghan conflict and that only a political settlement aimed at the establishment of a broad-based, multi-ethnic and fully representative government acceptable to the Afghan people can lead to peace and reconciliation,

Stressing the importance of non-intervention and non-interference in the internal affairs of Afghanistan, and deeply concerned at all forms of continued external support, which is causing the prolongation and intensification of the conflict,

Expressing its grave concern at the failure of all Afghan parties, in particular the Taliban, to put an end to the conflict, which seriously threatens stability and peace in the region, despite the repeated demands by the Security Council to the warring sides to desist from fighting,

Strongly condemning the resumption of major offensives by the Taliban in summer 2000, especially in the Taloqan area, and the resulting negative humanitarian consequences, including the loss of human life, the deliberate abuse, indiscriminate bombing and arbitrary detention of civilians, refugee flows, the recruitment of children for use in armed conflict, harassment, the forcible displacement of innocent civilians, in particular of women and children, in the Shomali Plains and north-eastern Afghanistan, and the indiscriminate destruction of their homes and agricultural land, thereby eliminating their source of income,

Expressing its grave concern at persistent violations of human rights and at breaches of international humanitarian law in Afghanistan as well as at the continuing and substantiated reports of systematic human rights violations against women and girls, including all forms of discrimination against them, notably in areas under the control of the Taliban,

Expressing concern at the growing spread of the Afghan conflict beyond its borders and at actions undermining the security of States' frontiers,

Deeply disturbed by the continuing use of Afghan territory in areas controlled by the Taliban for the recruitment, sheltering and training of terrorists, including international terrorists, and the planning of terrorist acts within and outside Afghanistan,

Deeply disturbed also by the continuing use of Afghan territory, especially areas controlled by the Taliban, for the continuing cultivation, production and trafficking of narcotic drugs, which contribute to the war-making capabilities of the Afghans and have dangerous repercussions reaching Afghanistan's neighbours and far beyond,

Welcoming the written agreement communicated by the Taliban and the United Front in separate letters dated 30 October 2000 to enter into a process of dialogue, without preconditions and under the good offices of the Secretary-General or his Personal Representative, aimed at achieving a political solution to the conflict in Afghanistan,

Stressing that a lasting cessation of hostilities is essential for meaningful dialogue, and welcoming in particular the stated commitment of the two sides to negotiate with serious intent and in good faith and not to abandon the process unilaterally until the negotiating agenda is exhausted,

Welcoming the high-level meetings of the "six plus two" group, held at United Nations Headquarters in September and November 2000, and the active role played by the group, leading, inter alia, to the adoption of a regional action plan aimed at eliminating illicit drug production and trafficking in Afghanistan,

Welcoming also the contacts between the Special Mission and various non-warring Afghan parties and personalities, and supporting calls by these independent Afghans for an end to the fighting and any proposals that might advance the cause of peace, including the efforts of independent Afghan personalities, many of whom support the proposal of the former King of Afghanistan, Zahir Shah, for the convening of a loya jirga to promote a political settlement,

Expressing its appreciation for the efforts undertaken by the Organization of the Islamic Conference, in support of and in coordination with the United Nations, to facilitate the convening of talks between the two Afghan parties, held in Jeddah in March and May 2000,

1. *Takes note* of the report of the Secretary-General;

2. *Stresses* that the main responsibility for finding a political solution to the conflict lies with the Afghan parties, and urges all of them to respond to the repeated calls for peace by the United Nations;

3. *Reiterates its position* that the United Nations must continue to play its central and impartial role in international efforts towards a peaceful resolution of the Afghan conflict, and reaffirms its full support for the efforts of the United Nations in facilitating the political process towards the goal of national reconciliation and a lasting political settlement with the participation of all parties to the conflict and all segments of Afghan society;

4. *Urges* the Taliban and the United Front to honour the written agreement communicated to the Personal Representative of the Secretary-General in separate letters dated 30 October 2000 to enter into a process of dialogue, without preconditions and under the good offices of the Secretary-General or his Personal Representative, aimed at achieving a political solution to the conflict in Afghanistan;

5. *Calls upon* the Afghan parties, in particular the Taliban, to cease immediately all armed hostilities, to renounce the use of force and to pursue without delay the political dialogue under United Nations auspices aimed at achieving a lasting political settlement of the conflict, leading to the establishment of a broad-based, multi-ethnic and fully representative government which would protect the rights of all Afghans and observe the international obligations of Afghanistan;

6. *Strongly urges* the Taliban and other Afghan parties to refrain from all acts of violence against civilians, in particular women and children;

7. *Strongly condemns* the resumption of major hostilities by the Taliban starting in July 2000, and strongly calls upon all Afghan parties to end all armed hostilities and not to pursue a military solution to the conflict in Afghanistan;

8. *Notes with alarm* reports indicating that a significant number of non-Afghan personnel, mainly on the side of the Taliban forces and largely from religious schools, are actively involved in various military activities;

9. *Strongly condemns* the fact that foreign military support to the Afghan parties continued unabated through 2000, and calls upon all States to refrain strictly from any outside interference and to end immediately the supply of arms, ammunition, military equipment, training or any other military support to all parties to the conflict in Afghanistan;

10. *Calls upon* all States to take resolute measures to prohibit their military personnel from planning and participating in combat operations in Afghanistan and immediately to withdraw their personnel, and to assure that the supply of ammunition and other war-making materials is halted;

11. *Supports* the United Nations Special Mission to Afghanistan with a view to assuring its primary role in United Nations peacemaking activities in Afghanistan, especially by the resumption of a dialogue between the Afghan parties through a negotiating process based on a comprehensive agenda to be agreed by the two sides that addresses the core problems of the Afghan situation and leads to a durable ceasefire and the formation of a broad-based, multi-ethnic and fully representative government;

12. *Also supports* the continuing cooperation of the Special Mission with all countries that are willing to help find a peaceful solution to the Afghan conflict, in particular with the members of the "six plus two" group, while continuing to monitor closely and to encourage the various peace initiatives of non-warring Afghan parties and personalities;

13. *Welcomes* the deployment of the Civil Affairs Unit of the Special Mission to Faizabad, Herat, Jalalabad, Kabul, Kandahar and Mazar-e-Sharif and its ongoing dialogue on political and human rights issues

with high-ranking representatives of the local and regional authorities of both Afghan sides, and supports
the intention of the Secretary-General to strengthen
the political capacity of the Special Mission and increase the number of military advisers from two to
four;

14. *Supports* the activities of groups of interested
States to coordinate their efforts as well as the activities
of international organizations, in particular the Organization of the Islamic Conference, and encourages
these organizations and States, in particular the "six
plus two" group, to use their influence in a constructive
manner in support of and in close coordination with
the United Nations to promote peace in Afghanistan;

15. *Encourages* the international community to support the Afghan people in their right to express themselves on their main needs and their future through
democratic or traditional means by developing a
framework for institution- and capacity-building that
could lead to the eventual structure for a broad-based
government;

16. *Calls upon* all signatories to the Tashkent Declaration on Fundamental Principles for a Peaceful Settlement of the Conflict in Afghanistan and the Afghan
parties to implement the principles contained in that
Declaration in support of the efforts of the United Nations towards a peaceful resolution of the Afghan conflict, in particular the agreement not to provide military support to any Afghan party and to prevent the use
of their territories for such purposes, and recalls their
appeal to the international community to take identical
measures to prevent the delivery of weapons to Afghanistan;

17. *Strongly condemns* the armed attacks on and the
killing of United Nations and other humanitarian personnel, strongly calls upon the Taliban to fulfil their
stated commitment to cooperate in urgent investigations of these heinous crimes with a view to bringing
those responsible to justice, and urges all Afghan parties to demonstrate their full commitment to the safety
and security of all United Nations and other humanitarian personnel so as to facilitate their continued work
in support of the affected population;

18. *Reiterates its strong condemnation* of the killing of
the diplomatic and consular staff of the Consulate-
General of the Islamic Republic of Iran in Mazar-e-
Sharif and the correspondent of the Islamic Republic
News Agency in August 1998, stresses that these unacceptable acts which constitute flagrant violations of
established international law must not go unpunished,
expresses deep concern at the lack of progress in the
Taliban investigation of the murders, and once again
urges the Taliban to carry out, without further delay, a
credible investigation with a view to prosecuting the
guilty parties and to inform the Government of the Islamic Republic of Iran and the United Nations about
the results thereof;

19. *Strongly condemns* the widespread violations and
abuses of human rights, including summary executions and an alleged mass killing of detainees in
Samangan in May 2000, and strongly urges all Afghan
parties to recognize, protect and promote all human
rights and freedoms, including the right to life, liberty
and security of persons, regardless of gender, ethnicity
or religion;

20. *Calls upon* all Afghan parties, in particular the
Taliban, to bring an end without delay to all violations
of human rights and discriminatory policies against
women and girls and to recognize, protect and promote
the equal rights and dignity of men and women, especially in the fields of education, work and equal health
care;

21. *Condemns* the continuing widespread violations
of international humanitarian law in Afghanistan, and
urgently calls upon all Afghan parties to respect strictly
all its provisions that provide essential protection for
the civilian population in armed conflicts;

22. *Reiterates its concern* that the continuing conflict
in Afghanistan poses a growing risk to peace and stability in the region;

23. *Condemns* the acts of terrorists based in Afghanistan, including those in support of extremist
groups operating against the interests of Member
States and against their citizens, and strongly demands
that in particular the Taliban refrain from providing
safe haven to international terrorists and their organizations, cease the recruitment of terrorists, close down
terrorist training camps inside Afghanistan, take
effective measures to ensure that the territory under its
control is not used to sponsor international terrorist
operations and take the necessary steps to cooperate
with efforts to bring indicted terrorists to justice without delay;

24. *Strongly urges* the Taliban to comply without preconditions and without further delay with its obligations under Security Council resolution 1267(1999)
and other relevant resolutions;

25. *Reiterates its call* to all Afghan parties, in particular the Taliban, to halt all illegal drug activities and to
support international efforts to ban illicit drug production and trafficking, and calls upon all Member States
and all parties concerned to undertake concerted
measures to stop the trafficking of illegal drugs from
Afghanistan;

26. *Notes with interest* in this regard the decree issued
by the Taliban in July 2000 imposing a total ban on
opium poppy cultivation, and calls upon the Taliban to
implement fully this decree;

27. *Notes* the severe impact of illicit drug production
and trafficking on Afghanistan's immediate neighbours, and calls for further international cooperation
in support of the efforts of the neighbouring States to
stop the trafficking of illegal drugs from Afghanistan
and to cope with its adverse social and economic consequences;

28. *Requests* the United Nations International Drug
Control Programme to continue its crop monitoring
work inside Afghanistan, within the context of the
United Nations common programme and, with particular regard to assessing the impact of the July 2000
decree, to consider enlarging its alternative development work there should the assessment show significant implementation of the decree, and further to develop international measures against drug trafficking;

29. *Calls upon* the international community to continue providing financial resources to the United Nations International Drug Control Programme for the
implementation of the above activities;

30. *Reiterates* that the cultural and historic relics
and monuments of Afghanistan belong to the common
heritage of humankind, calls upon all Afghan parties

to protect the cultural and historic relics and monuments of Afghanistan from acts of vandalism, damage and theft, and requests all Member States to take appropriate measures to prevent the looting of cultural artefacts and to ensure their return to Afghanistan;

31. *Requests* the Secretary-General to report to the General Assembly every four months during its fifty-fifth session on the progress of the Special Mission and to report to the Assembly at its fifty-sixth session on the progress made in the implementation of the present resolution;

32. *Decides* to include in the provisional agenda of its fifty-sixth session the item entitled "The situation in Afghanistan and its implications for international peace and security".

Also on 19 December, the Assembly adopted **resolution 55/174 B** on emergency international assistance for peace, normalcy and reconstruction of war-stricken Afghanistan (see p. 864).

By **decision 55/458** of 23 December, the Assembly decided that the agenda item on the situation in Afghanistan and its implications for international peace and security would remain for consideration at its resumed fifty-fifth (2001) session.

Military and political developments

In his 20 November report [A/55/633-S/2000/1106], the Secretary-General stated that the fighting season in 2000 had started earlier than usual. The Taliban, with superiority in numbers and logistics, took the initiative from the outset. The intensity of the fighting indicated that the flow of arms and other war-making materiel into the country continued unabated, and even rose to new levels during the last few months of the year.

The season's full-scale fighting started in the north of Kabul with major offensives by the Taliban on 1 and 9 July. In September and October, they secured wider areas around Taloqan and, to the north, captured the districts of Khwajaghar, Dashti Archi and Emam Saheb in Takhar province. At that point, Badakhshan was the sole province left entirely under UF control. The UF recaptured the districts in a counter-attack launched on 14 October. However, after 10 days of progress, the UF counter-offensive ebbed and the Taliban pushed the attacking forces back. As at 5 November, the confrontation lines were more or less the same as at 13 October and a stalemate had developed.

The year's military setback put the UF under intense pressure. Meetings were hurriedly convened in an effort to save the alliance from disintegrating and to invite non-UF commanders to join the fight against the Taliban. It was agreed that the UF leaders would establish a new military council, to include themselves and other key alliance commanders.

The political situation was marked by the increasing impact that the conflict in Afghanistan was having in Central and South Asia. Afghanistan's neighbours and countries farther afield were worried about spillover effects from the ongoing fighting. The Central Asian States held two meetings (April and August) at the presidential level to discuss the Afghan conflict (see p. 266).

After holding separate talks under OIC auspices in March and May, the two warring parties agreed on a comprehensive exchange of prisoners of war, to be conducted through the International Committee of the Red Cross (ICRC). They further agreed to respect their existing commitments not to target the civilian population and to allow the unimpeded passage of humanitarian convoys to the civilian population on both sides of the front lines. The Personal Representative attended both rounds of talks as an observer. Although the prisoner exchange process was interrupted by the fighting in July, the two sides continued with an informal exchange of smaller groups of prisoners.

In mid-May, Taliban Interior Minister Mullah Abdur Razzaq paid an official visit to Islamabad to hold discussions with Pakistani authorities on the extradition of criminals, terrorism and drug trafficking and on the Afghanistan Transit Trade Agreement.

The United States and the Russian Federation held two rounds of high-level talks (Washington D.C., August, and Moscow, October) on the situation in Afghanistan, and it was reported that the two countries agreed to put international pressure on the Taliban. In March, United States President William J. Clinton, on a visit to Islamabad, had discussed the question of terrorism and the continued presence in Afghanistan of Osama bin Laden.

In September, the President of the Russian Federation, Vladimir Putin, dispatched a Special Envoy to Islamabad for discussions on Afghanistan with senior Pakistani officials. During a visit to India in October, President Putin agreed with Prime Minister Atal Behari Vajpayee to coordinate efforts to counter terrorism in the region, in particular that emanating from Afghanistan. An Indian and Russian working group was formed in that regard.

In other developments, the Under-Secretary of State for Foreign Affairs of Italy, Ugo Intini, visited the two warring factions in September in an attempt to create a "humanitarian corridor" between the war-divided territories of Afghanistan. Supporters of the loya jirga initiative [YUN 1999, p. 262], led by former King Zahir Shah, the so-called Rome process, dispatched delegations to UN Headquarters, Washington, D.C., Paris, Berlin, London, Islamabad and Kandahar to explain their activities and to seek support. A representative of a parallel initiative, known as the Cyprus process, visited New York to explain its activities and, at its fourth meeting (Cyprus, 15 September), discussed the mechanism to convene a grand national assembly inside Afghanistan. Although the United Nations and a number of Member States attended as observers, both the UF and the Taliban declined their invitations. The Council for Peace and National Unity of Afghanistan, a group with links to the Rome process, held a meeting (Bonn, Germany, 4-6 October) to discuss practical ways to accelerate the convening of an emergency loya jirga. OIC launched a diplomatic initiative in February and invited the UF and the Taliban to Jeddah for two rounds of talks (7-9 March and 8-10 May).

UN activities

"Six plus two" group

The "six plus two" group met several times during 2000, starting with a February meeting at which it focused on the issue of illicit drugs (see p. 272). The Secretary-General's Personal Representative convened a "six plus two" meeting in Islamabad on 22 May, which was followed on 30 May, also in Islamabad, by a meeting of the "group of 21"—a larger group of Governments with influence in Afghanistan. That group had not met since 1998 [YUN 1998, p. 300].

Taking advantage of the presence of Ministers for Foreign Affairs in New York for the General Assembly session, the Secretary-General convened a meeting of the "six plus two" group on 15 September at the ministerial level of Foreign Ministers at which his Personal Representative gave a briefing on the latest developments in Afghanistan and on his peacemaking efforts. In the concluding statement of the meeting, which was annexed to the Secretary-General's September report [A/55/393-S/2000/875], the group expressed concern about the intensification of fighting in Afghanistan and its negative humanitarian consequences. Emphasizing that there could be no military solution to the conflict, the Ministers requested the Personal Representative to enter into contact with all relevant Afghan parties and report back on the outcome.

On 3 November, another meeting of the "six plus two" group took place in New York, as agreed by the Foreign Ministers in September, to consider the Personal Representative's report on his contacts. The group welcomed the written agreement by the two sides to enter into a dialogue without preconditions (see p. 266) and requested the Personal Representative to report to the group by 1 February 2001 on progress achieved in the dialogue process. The statement of the group's meeting was annexed to the Secretary-General's November report [A/55/633-S/2000/1106].

Personal Representative of the Secretary-General

By identical letters of 12 January to the General Assembly and Security Council Presidents [A/54/706-S/2000/20], the Secretary-General, referring to his 1999 decision to freeze the activities of his Special Envoy for Afghanistan, Lakhdar Brahimi [YUN 1999, p. 262], stated that he remained convinced of the need to strengthen UNSMA, which was playing the primary role in conducting UN peacemaking activities in Afghanistan. He had therefore decided to appoint Mr. Vendrell as his Personal Representative and Head of UNSMA. On 14 January [S/2000/21], the Council members took note of his decision.

In his 20 November report [A/55/633-S/2000/1106], the Secretary-General described the work of his Personal Representative during the year. He noted that, soon after taking up his appointment on 1 February, Mr. Vendrell met with the UF, the Taliban supreme leader, and the Governments of the "six plus two" group, which were also the signatories of the Tashkent Declaration on Fundamental Principles for a Peaceful Settlement of the Conflict in Afghanistan [YUN 1999, p. 256].

In November, the Personal Representative was successful in securing letters of agreement from the two warring factions to initiate a process of dialogue, in an effort to end the armed conflict in Afghanistan through political means, utilizing the Secretary-General's good offices. However, by December, the Taliban stated that, in view of the imminent adoption of new sanctions by the Security Council (see p. 274), the United Nations would no longer be accepted as an impartial broker and that, while they were willing to pursue a dialogue with the UF, they were not willing to do so under UN auspices.

Mr. Vendrell met with the former King of Afghanistan, Zahir Shah, in June and October for discussions on the situation in Afghanistan and the king's ideas on how a loya jirga could be convened inside Afghanistan.

UN Special Mission to Afghanistan

In his November report [A/55/633-S/2000/1106], the Secretary-General stated that the role and political presence of UNSMA in Afghanistan and the region had been strengthened. With its full complement of political officers on board, it had opened a liaison office in Tehran and re-established its political presence in Kabul.

In the first quarter of the year, the Civil Affairs Unit, which comprised a Coordinator and seven Civil Affairs Officers, became operational. By year's end, it had offices in the six major urban centres of Faizabad, Herat, Jalalabad, Kabul, Kandahar and Mazar-e-Sharif. The Unit also wished to open an office in Bamyan in the central highlands and had deployed missions to the Hazarajat and Ghor regions in that area.

With its mandate defined by Security Council resolution 1214(1998) [YUN 1998, p. 297], the Civil Affairs Unit spent its first full year laying the foundations for deeper involvement with the Afghan people. It was attempting to build and strengthen an ongoing persuasive dialogue with Afghan authorities at both the regional and local levels, in areas such as administration, law enforcement, the judiciary and the media, with a view to fostering human rights awareness among those key groups. The Unit monitored and reported on political, social, economic and cultural trends, including highlights on the human rights situation in the country, and studied such areas as administration, judiciary, legislature, constitution, media and economic activities, in order to better map the current and future situation of Afghanistan and to respond to the needs of the people.

UNSMA's military component succeeded in establishing solid contacts with the military authorities of both warring factions and had provided reliable and informative support to the Head of Mission. The Secretary-General stated that, in view of the fruitful interaction between the political and military components, he would increase the number of military advisers from two to four.

As Head of Mission, Mr. Vendrell maintained close contact with Afghanistan's neighbours (Iran, Pakistan, Tajikistan, Turkmenistan and Uzbekistan) and held several meetings with their leaders. The focus of discussions on the Afghan situation remained, among other things, the implications for regional and international security, the prospects for peace, the means of achieving a lasting settlement and the question of human rights.

Humanitarian assistance

The Secretary-General observed that the conditions under which assistance was provided in Afghanistan became more complicated as the year progressed [A/55/633-S/2000/1106]. The UN country team and its NGO partners continued their efforts to alleviate the problems faced by the Afghan people and to provide assistance to improve the dire humanitarian situation. However, funding for the consolidated appeal for 2000, and specifically for the drought appeal, had reached less than 50 per cent of the amount needed (see p. 864). Implementation of assistance programmes in some parts of the country had been hampered by restrictions on access to those in need of humanitarian assistance and constrained by high levels of insecurity. However, security conditions away from the front lines and zones of conflict had been adequate for the implementation of humanitarian programmes, although volatility remained. Early in the year, UNHCR successfully negotiated an agreement with Iran for the repatriation of Afghan refugees. Since the implementation of the joint programme in April, forcible return of Afghan refugees from Iran had decreased drastically to several thousands (from 70,000 in 1999) and contributed significantly to increased protection of the refugees who were unable or unwilling to return. On the other hand, the number of Afghan refugees who returned voluntarily from Pakistan and Iran, with the assistance of UNHCR, the World Food Programme (WFP) and the International Organization for Migration, had doubled compared to 1999, with 170,000 returnees by September. Initial reintegration assistance in the form of transport, individual household support, potable water and emergency shelter construction, in addition to programmes of education, health and income generation, was provided on a continual basis throughout the year.

The UN specialized agencies, along with NGO partners, conducted priority health activities, including human resource development, integrated disease control activities and safe motherhood and water and sanitation programmes. The United Nations Children's Fund (UNICEF), the World Health Organization (WHO) and a wide range of NGOs supported the national immunization days during May, June, October and November. During the spring round, about 5.3 million children under 5 were vaccinated against polio, the highest coverage since 1994. WHO also carried out malaria and tuberculosis control programmes. The Poverty Eradication and Community Empowerment Programme of the United Nations Development Programme (UNDP) successfully established and strengthened over 2,000 multi-ethnic, community-based organizations and interest groups that formed sustainable linkages in terms of reconciliation, peace-building, good governance and refugee reintegration. Implementing projects through the United Nations Office for Project Services (UN-OPS), the Food and Agriculture Organization of the United Nations (FAO) and the United Nations Centre for Human Settlements (Habitat), the programme contributed substantially to the international aid community's collective efforts in food security, access to basic social services and livelihood opportunities.

Afghanistan continued to rank as one of the most severely landmine-contaminated countries in the world, with 720 square kilometres of land containing mines. Since its inception in 1989 and as at October, the Mine Action Programme for Afghanistan had cleared 518 square kilometres of mined and battlefield areas, with 79 square kilometres being cleared in 2000 alone. Significant inroads in the survey of mine and battlefield areas had been made with over 619 square kilometres covered. Mine-awareness training and materials had been provided to over 6.8 million Afghans. Funding for the programme decreased substantially in 2000, with a shortfall of $3.5 million for activities for the period from September through December. The Programme cleared only 64 per cent of the sites targeted for the year.

Human rights violations

During the year, Afghans continued to suffer a wide range of deprivations, violations, policies and practices that severely restricted or denied their human rights (see also p. 750). The situation of women and girls in particular remained dismal due to the unconscionable policies of the Taliban and the general socio-economic decline. In July, the firman (decree) imposed by the Taliban banned the employment of women in UN and NGO programmes, except in the health sector. A clear violation of the right to work, the firman constituted an unacceptable precedent and undermined the ability of aid agencies to reach those who were most vulnerable and marginalized in Afghan society.

The Secretary-General expressed regret that Taliban authorities continued to deny access to the Special Rapporteur of the Commission on Human Rights on the situation of human rights in Afghanistan.

Drug control

The Secretary-General stated in November [A/55/633-S/2000/1106] that the United Nations International Drug Control Programme (UNDCP), in its annual opium poppy survey in Afghanistan, showed a slight decline in the area under cultivation of 10 per cent, from 91,000 hectares in 1999 to around 82,000 hectares in 2000. That figure, however, did not live up to the Taliban decree of September 1999 to reduce opium poppy cultivation by one third in the 1999/2000 planting season. The year's opium harvest had fallen by 28 per cent from a record of 4,581 tons in 1999 to 3,275 tons in 2000, mainly due to the severe drought.

The Secretary-General noted the success of UNDCP's alternative development pilot programme, which had reduced the opium harvest by 50 per cent in Ghorak, Khakrez and Maiwand districts. He stated that it demonstrated that alternative development was the right strategy for illicit crop reduction in the Afghan context, but that lack of funds might lead to a lack of credibility in the future and jeopardize the sustainability of the poppy reduction achieved in the target districts in 2000. He added that, with the increase in drug trafficking from Afghanistan posing a serious threat, UNDCP had initiated a drug law enforcement programme in the countries around Afghanistan, a "security belt", aimed at containing at the regional level a problem having its source in Afghanistan.

The "six plus two" group held a high-level meeting (New York, 28 February) to address the problem of illicit drugs in the country. The Security Council President subsequently encouraged the group to address drug-related issues in a coordinated manner with UNDCP, and urged Member States to help strengthen the drug control capacities of countries bordering Afghanistan (**S/PRST/2000/12**). In May, UNDCP, the "six plus two" group and donor countries met in Vienna to endorse the formulation of a regional action plan to promote an exchange of information, the interdiction of cross-border drug shipments and control of chemicals used to produce drugs, as well as the elimination of illicit crops in Afghanistan and subsequent alternative development activities. The regional action plan was approved by the "six plus two" group on 13 September.

Meanwhile, in July, the Taliban supreme leader, Mullah Omar, issued a decree imposing for the first time a total ban on opium poppy cultivation in Afghanistan.

Sanctions

Security Council consideration. At informal consultations on 13 December, Security Council members were briefed by the Chairman of the Committee established pursuant to resolution 1267(1999) [YUN 1999, p. 265] (see p. 276) on the humanitarian aspects of the sanctions against Afghanistan, which had been imposed under that resolution.

Communications. By a 19 December letter [A/55/704-S/2000/1214], Pakistan forwarded to the Secretary-General the text of a statement by its

Foreign Minister regarding the disastrous humanitarian consequences that would result from the adoption of the draft resolution being considered by the Security Council (see below). Pakistan said that millions of innocent Afghans, already stricken by famine, would be exposed to starvation as UN aid agencies and NGOs withdrew their personnel, warning that the sanctions would make their task difficult, if not impossible. Aid agencies and relief organizations operating inside Afghanistan were unanimously of the view that the additional sanctions would further aggravate the humanitarian crisis and as many as 1 million people would face starvation during Afghanistan's bitter winter and unprecedented drought conditions.

Also on 19 December [S/2000/1212], Kazakhstan forwarded to the Council a position paper on the situation in Afghanistan, in which it noted that Afghanistan had been turned into a major world centre for drug production and exportation and that its territory, where an enormous amount of weapons had accumulated and where terrorist training centres had been established, had become a springboard for spreading extremism and international terrorism in Central Asia. Although Kazakhstan gave a generally positive assessment of the work of the Sanctions Committee, it also called for a balanced approach to the adoption of further measures. It was important to ensure that, before taking additional measures, the Council should weigh the effects of the sanctions on all aspects of the settlement of the situation in Afghanistan and their possible unintended implications for the civilian population.

SECURITY COUNCIL ACTION

On 19 December [meeting 4251], the Security Council adopted **resolution 1333(2000)** by vote (13-0-2). The draft [S/2000/1202] was submitted by India, Kyrgyzstan, the Russian Federation, Tajikistan and the United States.

The Security Council,

Reaffirming its previous resolutions, in particular resolution 1267(1999) of 15 October 1999 and the statements by its President on the situation in Afghanistan,

Reaffirming its strong commitment to the sovereignty, independence, territorial integrity and national unity of Afghanistan, and its respect for the cultural and historical heritage of Afghanistan,

Recognizing the critical humanitarian needs of the Afghan people,

Supporting the efforts of the Personal Representative of the Secretary-General for Afghanistan to advance a peace process through political negotiations between the Afghan parties aimed at the establishment of a broad-based, multi-ethnic, and fully representative government, and calling for the warring factions to cooperate fully with those efforts to conclude a ceasefire and begin discussions leading to a political settlement,

by moving forward promptly in the process of dialogue to which they have committed themselves,

Taking note of the seventh meeting of the Afghan Support Group, held in Montreux, Switzerland, on 7 and 8 December 2000, which emphasized that the situation in Afghanistan is a complex one that requires a comprehensive, integrated approach to a peace process and issues of narcotics trafficking, terrorism, human rights and international humanitarian and development aid,

Recalling the relevant international counter-terrorism conventions and in particular the obligations of parties to those conventions to extradite or prosecute terrorists,

Strongly condemning the continuing use of the areas of Afghanistan under the control of the Afghan faction known as Taliban, which also calls itself the Islamic Emirate of Afghanistan (hereinafter known as the Taliban), for the sheltering and training of terrorists and planning of terrorist acts, and reaffirming its conviction that the suppression of international terrorism is essential for the maintenance of international peace and security,

Noting the importance of the Taliban acting in accordance with the 1961 Single Convention, the 1971 Convention on Psychotropic Substances, and the 1988 United Nations Convention against Illicit Traffic in Narcotic Drugs and Psychotropic Substances, and the commitments made at the twentieth special session of the General Assembly on narcotic drugs held in 1998, including the commitment to work closely with the United Nations Drug Control Programme,

Noting also that the Taliban benefits directly from the cultivation of illicit opium by imposing a tax on its production and indirectly benefits from the processing and trafficking of such opium, and recognizing that these substantial resources strengthen the capacity of the Taliban to harbour terrorists,

Deploring the fact that the Taliban continues to provide safe haven to Osama bin Laden and to allow him and others associated with him to operate a network of terrorist training camps from Taliban-controlled territory and to use Afghanistan as a base from which to sponsor international terrorist operations,

Noting the indictment of Osama bin Laden and his associates by the United States of America for, inter alia, the bombings on 7 August 1998 of the United States embassies in Nairobi and Dar es Salaam, and for conspiring to kill American nationals outside the United States, and noting also the request of the United States to the Taliban to surrender them for trial,

Reiterating its deep concern over the continuing violations of international humanitarian law and of human rights, particularly discrimination against women and girls, and over the significant rise in the illicit production of opium,

Stressing that the capture by the Taliban of the Consulate-General of the Islamic Republic of Iran and the murder of Iranian diplomats and a journalist in Mazar-e-Sharif constituted flagrant violations of established international law,

Determining that the failure of the Taliban authorities to respond to the demands in paragraph 13 of resolution 1214(1998) of 8 December 1998 and paragraph 2 of resolution 1267(1999) constitutes a threat to international peace and security,

Stressing its determination to ensure respect for its resolutions,

Reaffirming the necessity for sanctions to contain adequate and effective exemptions to avoid adverse humanitarian consequences for the people of Afghanistan, and that they should be structured in a way that would not impede, thwart or delay the work of international humanitarian assistance organizations or governmental relief agencies providing humanitarian assistance to the civilian population in the country,

Underlining the responsibility of the Taliban for the well-being of the population in the areas of Afghanistan under its control, and in this context calling upon the Taliban to ensure the safe and unhindered access of relief personnel and aid to all those in need in the territory under its control,

Recalling the relevant principles contained in the Convention on the Safety of United Nations and Associated Personnel adopted by the General Assembly in its resolution 49/59 of 9 December 1994,

Acting under Chapter VII of the Charter of the United Nations,

1. *Demands* that the Taliban comply with resolution 1267(1999) and, in particular, cease the provision of sanctuary and training for international terrorists and their organizations, take appropriate effective measures to ensure that the territory under its control is not used for terrorist installations and camps or for the preparation or organization of terrorist acts against other States or their citizens, and cooperate with international efforts to bring indicted terrorists to justice;

2. *Demands also* that the Taliban comply without further delay with the demand of the Security Council in paragraph 2 of resolution 1267(1999) that requires the Taliban to turn over Osama bin Laden to appropriate authorities in a country where he has been indicted, or to appropriate authorities in a country where he will be returned to such a country, or to appropriate authorities in a country where he will be arrested and effectively brought to justice;

3. *Demands further* that the Taliban act swiftly to close all camps where terrorists are trained within the territory under its control, and calls for the confirmation of such closures by the United Nations, inter alia, through information made available to the United Nations by Member States in accordance with paragraph 19 below and through such other means as are necessary to assure compliance with the present resolution;

4. *Reminds* all States of their obligation to implement strictly the measures imposed by paragraph 4 of resolution 1267(1999);

5. *Decides* that all States shall:

(a) Prevent the direct or indirect supply, sale and transfer to the territory of Afghanistan under Taliban control as designated by the Security Council Committee established pursuant to resolution 1267(1999), hereinafter known as the Committee, by their nationals or from their territories, or using their flag vessels or aircraft, of arms and related materiel of all types including weapons and ammunition, military vehicles and equipment, paramilitary equipment, and spare parts for the aforementioned;

(b) Prevent the direct or indirect sale, supply and transfer to the territory of Afghanistan under Taliban control, as designated by the Committee, by their nationals or from their territories, of technical advice, assistance, or training related to the military activities of the armed personnel under the control of the Taliban;

(c) Withdraw any of their officials, agents, advisers, and military personnel employed by contract or other arrangement present in Afghanistan to advise the Taliban on military or related security matters, and in this context urge other nationals to leave the country;

6. *Decides* that the measures imposed by paragraph 5 above shall not apply to supplies of non-lethal military equipment intended solely for humanitarian or protective use and related technical assistance or training, as approved in advance by the Committee, and affirms that the measures imposed by paragraph 5 above do not apply to protective clothing, including flak jackets and military helmets, exported to Afghanistan by United Nations personnel, representatives of the media, and humanitarian workers for their personal use only;

7. *Urges* all States that maintain diplomatic relations with the Taliban to reduce significantly the number and level of the staff at Taliban missions and posts and restrict or control the movement within their territory of all such staff who remain; in the case of Taliban missions to international organizations, the host State may, as it deems necessary, consult the organization concerned on the measures required to implement this paragraph;

8. *Decides* that all States shall take further measures:

(a) To close immediately and completely all Taliban offices in their territories;

(b) To close immediately all offices of Ariana Afghan Airlines in their territories;

(c) To freeze without delay funds and other financial assets of Osama bin Laden and individuals and entities associated with him as designated by the Committee, including those in al-Qa'idah, and including funds derived or generated by property owned or controlled directly or indirectly by Osama bin Laden and individuals and entities associated with him, and to ensure that neither they nor any other funds or financial resources are made available, by their nationals or by any persons within their territory, directly or indirectly for the benefit of Osama bin Laden, his associates or any entities owned or controlled, directly or indirectly, by Osama bin Laden or individuals and entities associated with him, including al-Qa'idah, and requests the Committee to maintain an updated list, based on information provided by States and regional organizations, of the individuals and entities designated as being associated with Osama bin Laden, including those in al-Qa'idah;

9. *Demands* that the Taliban, as well as others, halt all illegal drug activities and work to virtually eliminate the illicit cultivation of opium poppy, the proceeds of which finance Taliban terrorist activities;

10. *Decides* that all States shall prevent the sale, supply or transfer, by their nationals or from their territories, of the chemical acetic anhydride to any person in the territory of Afghanistan under Taliban control as designated by the Committee, or to any person for the purpose of any activity carried on in, or operated from, the territory under Taliban control as designated by the Committee;

11. *Decides also* that all States are required to deny any aircraft permission to take off from, land in or over-fly their territories if that aircraft has taken off from, or is destined to land at, a place in the territory of Afghanistan designated by the Committee as being un-

der Taliban control, unless the particular flight has been approved in advance by the Committee on the grounds of humanitarian need, including religious obligations such as the performance of the Hajj, or on the grounds that the flight promotes discussion of a peaceful resolution of the conflict in Afghanistan, or is likely to promote Taliban compliance with the present resolution or with resolution 1267(1999);

12. *Decides further* that the Committee shall maintain a list of approved organizations and governmental relief agencies that are providing humanitarian assistance to Afghanistan, including the United Nations and its agencies, governmental relief agencies providing humanitarian assistance, the International Committee of the Red Cross and non-governmental organizations as appropriate, that the prohibition imposed by paragraph 11 above shall not apply to humanitarian flights operated by, or on behalf of, organizations and governmental relief agencies on the list approved by the Committee, that the Committee shall keep the list under regular review, adding new organizations and governmental relief agencies as appropriate, and that the Committee shall remove organizations and governmental agencies from the list if it decides that they are operating, or are likely to operate, flights for other than humanitarian purposes, and shall notify such organizations and governmental agencies immediately that any flights operated by them, or on their behalf, are thereby subject to the provisions of paragraph 11 above;

13. *Calls upon* the Taliban to ensure the safe and unhindered access of relief personnel and aid to all those in need in the territory under its control, and underlines the fact that the Taliban must provide guarantees for the safety, security and freedom of movement of United Nations and associated humanitarian relief personnel;

14. *Urges* States to take steps to restrict the entry into or transit through their territory of all senior officials of the rank of Deputy Minister or higher in the Taliban, the equivalent rank of armed personnel under the control of the Taliban, and other senior advisers and dignitaries of the Taliban, unless those officials are travelling for humanitarian purposes, including religious obligation such as the performance of the Hajj, or where the travel promotes discussion of a peaceful resolution of the conflict in Afghanistan or involves compliance with the present resolution or resolution 1267(1999);

15. *Requests* the Secretary-General, in consultation with the Committee:

(a) To appoint a committee of experts to make recommendations to the Council within sixty days of the adoption of the present resolution regarding ways in which the arms embargo and the closure of terrorist training camps demanded in paragraphs 3 and 5 above can be monitored, including, inter alia, the use of information obtained by Member States through their national means and provided by them to the Secretary-General;

(b) To consult with relevant Member States to put into effect the measures imposed by the present resolution and resolution 1267(1999) and report the results of such consultations to the Council;

(c) To report on the implementation of the existing measures, assess problems involved in enforcing these measures, make recommendations for strengthening

enforcement, and evaluate actions of the Taliban to come into compliance;

(d) To review the humanitarian implications of the measures imposed by the present resolution and resolution 1267(1999), and report back to the Council within ninety days of the adoption of the present resolution with an assessment and recommendations, to report at regular intervals thereafter on any humanitarian implications, and to present a comprehensive report on this issue and any recommendations no later than thirty days prior to the expiration of those measures;

16. *Requests* the Committee to fulfil its mandate by undertaking the following tasks in addition to those set out in resolution 1267(1999):

(a) To establish and maintain updated lists, based on information provided by States, and international and regional organizations, of all points of entry and landing-areas for aircraft within the territory of Afghanistan under Taliban control, and to notify Member States of the contents of such lists;

(b) To establish and maintain updated lists, based on information provided by States and regional organizations, of individuals and entities designated as being associated with Osama bin Laden, in accordance with paragraph 8 (c) above;

(c) To give consideration to, and decide upon, requests for the exceptions set out in paragraphs 6 and 11 above;

(d) To establish no later than one month after the adoption of the present resolution, and maintain an updated list of approved organizations and governmental relief agencies that are providing humanitarian assistance to Afghanistan, in accordance with paragraph 12 above;

(e) To make relevant information regarding implementation of these measures publicly available through appropriate media, including through improved use of information technology;

(f) To consider, where and when appropriate, a visit to countries in the region by the Chairman of the Committee and such other members as may be required to enhance the full and effective implementation of the measures imposed by the present resolution and resolution 1267(1999) with a view to urging States to comply with relevant Council resolutions;

(g) To make periodic reports to the Council on information submitted to it regarding the present resolution and resolution 1267(1999), including possible violations of the measures reported to the Committee and recommendations for strengthening the effectiveness of those measures;

17. *Calls upon* all States and all international and regional organizations, including the United Nations and the specialized agencies, to act strictly in accordance with the provisions of the present resolution, notwithstanding the existence of any rights or obligations conferred or imposed by any international agreement or any contract entered into or any licence or permit granted prior to the date of coming into force of the measures imposed by paragraphs 5, 8, 10 and 11 above;

18. *Calls upon* States to bring proceedings against persons and entities within their jurisdiction that violate the measures imposed by paragraphs 5, 8, 10 and 11 above and to impose appropriate penalties;

19. *Calls upon* all States to cooperate fully with the Committee in the fulfilment of its tasks, including sup-

plying such information as may be required by the Committee in pursuance of the present resolution;

20. *Requests* all States to report to the Committee within thirty days of the coming into force of the measures imposed by paragraphs 5, 8, 10 and 11 above on the steps they have taken with a view to effectively implementing the present resolution;

21. *Requests* the Secretariat to submit for consideration by the Committee information received from Governments and public sources on possible violations of the measures imposed by paragraphs 5, 8, 10 and 11 above;

22. *Decides* that the measures imposed by paragraphs 5, 8, 10 and 11 above shall come into force at 0001 hours, eastern standard time, one month after the adoption of the present resolution;

23. *Also decides* that the measures imposed by paragraphs 5, 8, 10 and 11 above are established for twelve months and that, at the end of this period, the Council shall decide whether the Taliban has complied with paragraphs 1, 2 and 3 above, and, accordingly, whether to extend these measures for a further period with the same conditions;

24. *Further decides* that, if the Taliban complies with the conditions of paragraphs 1, 2 and 3 above, before the twelve-month period has elapsed, the Council shall terminate the measures imposed by paragraphs 5, 8, 10 and 11 above;

25. *Expresses its readiness* to consider the imposition of further measures, in accordance with its responsibility under the Charter of the United Nations, with the aim of achieving full implementation of the present resolution and resolution 1267(1999), inter alia, taking into account the impact assessment referred to in paragraph 15 *(d)* with a view to enhancing the effectiveness of sanctions and avoiding humanitarian consequences;

26. *Decides* to remain actively seized of the matter.

VOTE ON RESOLUTION 1333(3000):

In favour: Argentina, Bangladesh, Canada, France, Jamaica, Mali, Namibia, Netherlands, Russian Federation, Tunisia, Ukraine, United Kingdom, United States.
Against: None.
Abstaining: China, Malaysia.

Afghanistan's representative to the United Nations stated before the vote that the Pakistan/Taliban/bin Laden alliance had categorically refused to cooperate with the international community or to put an end to the training and haven it provided to international terrorists. Afghanistan was grateful to Council members for having included in the draft resolution clear and explicit provision for the implementation of sanctions in such a way that they would not hamper the provision of humanitarian assistance to the Afghan population.

Malaysia, while condemning terrorism in all its forms and manifestations, intended to abstain on the draft resolution as the imposition of additional sanctions might lead to the deterioration of the humanitarian operational environment in the Taliban-controlled areas, especially if the Taliban were to withhold its cooperation with the

international humanitarian agencies there. In addition, every care should have been taken to ensure that the sanctions regime against the Taliban was not politicized.

Speaking after the vote, China stated that it had abstained as the Afghan people could not cope with the effects of any measures that could lead to the further deterioration of the humanitarian situation in the country. China also felt that a new round of sanctions would have a negative impact on the peace process.

Sanctions Committee activities

The Security Council Committee established pursuant to resolution 1267(1999) [YUN 1999, p. 265] (the Afghanistan Sanctions Committee) submitted a report [S/2000/1254] covering its activities from 15 October 1999 to 28 December 2000. During that period, the Committee held two meetings and 13 informal consultations at the expert level.

On 14 November 1999, the Security Council had imposed a flight ban on any aircraft owned, leased or operated by or on behalf of the Taliban, as well as the freezing of funds directly or indirectly owned or controlled by the Taliban. The sanctions went into effect when the Taliban failed to meet the Council's demand, made in the same resolution, that the Taliban turn over Osama bin Laden to appropriate authorities.

On 22 December 1999, the Committee issued a list of aircraft owned, leased or operated by or on behalf of the Taliban and, on 10 February 2000, it added an additional aircraft to the list. The Committee stated that the list would be revised as necessary and encouraged Member States to bring to its attention any information they might have concerning aircraft that did not appear on the list.

On 4 April [S/2000/282], the Chairman transmitted to the Council a list of 51 Member States that had responded to his request to provide information regarding the measures imposed against the Taliban. On 31 August [S/2000/282/Add.1], the Chairman transmitted a list of a further 18 Member States.

On 12 April, the Committee, by a note verbale to all States, designated the funds and other financial resources to be frozen, in accordance with resolution 1267(1999). On 24 October and 20 November, the Committee issued press releases identifying additional financial entities.

On 14 April, the Chairman circulated a Secretariat note containing recommendations for improving the monitoring of the implementation of the measures imposed for the Committee's consideration and action. In that connection, the International Civil Aviation Organization (ICAO) and the International Air Transport Association

(IATA) expressed their willingness to undertake technical missions with a view to assisting the Committee.

On 12 December, the Afghanistan Sanctions Committee held informal consultations with representatives of the UN Department of Political Affairs (on behalf of UNSMA) and the Office for the Coordination of Humanitarian Affairs, to assess the humanitarian impact of the sanctions. On 13 December, the Chairman of the Committee briefed the Security Council on the subject.

During the reporting period, the Committee approved all 11 humanitarian flights requested. It also approved requests by the Taliban for 90 return trips for Ariana Afghan Airlines to transport 12,000 Afghan pilgrims to perform the hajj; 10 return trips for Air Gulf Falcon of Sharjah, United Arab Emirates (operating on behalf of Ariana Afghan Airlines), to transport additional Afghan pilgrims to perform the hajj; and a return flight of a hijacked Ariana Afghan Airlines aeroplane from London to Kabul.

On 5 December, the Committee granted an exemption to the measures in respect of payment by IATA to the aeronautical authority of Afghanistan, on behalf of international airlines for air traffic control services. The authorization was subject to representatives of IATA and ICAO conducting a survey of the facilities of the Ministry of Civil Aviation and Tourism every two months and reporting back to the Committee, including copies of financial transactions between escrow accounts, and the Ministry providing the Committee, through IATA, with a report on the uses to which the funds had been put.

On 15 December, the Committee authorized ICAO's request for an exemption to unfreeze a specific amount of funds from the Civil Aviation Purchasing Service account for Afghanistan with ICAO, and additional funds to be transferred from the overflight charges collected by IATA on behalf of the Ministry of Civil Aviation and Tourism, for aeronautical communications equipment, back-up communications equipment, certain air traffic control tower equipment and aviation security equipment. ICAO would report to the Committee on the delivery and the installation of the equipment.

On 28 December, the Sanctions Committee issued a note verbale requesting all States to submit lists of organizations and governmental relief agencies providing humanitarian assistance to Afghanistan pursuant to resolution 1333 (2000). It also issued a press release stating that it was compiling a list of organizations and governmental relief agencies providing humanitarian assistance to Afghanistan that would be exempt from the prohibition imposed by paragraph 11 of that resolution.

East Timor

Despite setbacks during 2000, including continued militia-led violence, the security situation in East Timor was stable, and the territory was well advanced in the transition to independence.

In February, the United Nations Transitional Administration in East Timor (UNTAET) assumed full responsibility for military security and overall administration of the territory from the Australian-led International Force, East Timor. UNTAET, which was entrusted with a governance operation, compelled the United Nations to confront pressures that it had never before faced in the field, starting with the complete administrative, political, judicial, military and socio-economic reconstruction of the territory. Great progress was made in the transition towards self-government with the establishment of an East Timor National Council, as an interim step towards a democratic legislative institution, as well as the appointment of a joint United Nations–Timorese cabinet to increase local participation in the administration of the territory.

The Security Council held nine open meetings during the year to discuss the situation in East Timor [meetings, 4097, 4133, 4147, 4165, 4180, 4182, 4191, 4203, 4236]; at those meetings it was briefed on developments in the territory by the Special Representative of the Secretary-General and Transitional Administrator in East Timor, Sergio Vieira de Mello, and the Assistant Secretary-General for Peacekeeping Operations, Hédi Annabi. The Council issued two presidential statements, which called for, among other things, a timetable and mechanisms for a constitution and elections in the territory. Following the killing on 6 September of three UN humanitarian staff by a militia-led mob in West Timor, the Council unanimously adopted a resolution calling on Indonesia to disarm and disband the militia, restore law and order in West Timor and ensure the safety and security of refugees and humanitarian workers. A Council mission visited East Timor and Indonesia from 9 to 17 November. The Secretary-General also visited East Timor and Indonesia in February.

In December, the General Assembly, by **resolution 55/172** (see p. 867), called on the international community to continue to address the remaining humanitarian relief needs of East Timor and to support the transition from relief and rehabilitation to development in preparation for independence.

Withdrawal of INTERFET

In accordance with Security Council resolution 1264(1999) [YUN 1999, p. 290], Australia submitted to the Council, through the Secretary-General, the last two periodic reports of the International Force, East Timor (INTERFET). The sixth report [S/2000/92], which covered the period from 10 December 1999 to 31 January 2000, stated that INTERFET had fulfilled its mandate under resolution 1264(1999) to restore peace and security to all parts of East Timor, except some areas of the border region of the Oecussi enclave. It had succeeded in establishing a credible deterrent security presence in all parts of the territory; preventing armed violence by any group in East Timor, including militia groups; developing, in cooperation with Indonesia, agreed procedures for border management along the East Timor–West Timor border; and creating conditions and providing escort support for large numbers of displaced persons to return to their homes in East Timor. INTERFET's mandate to support wider UN operations and humanitarian assistance programmes had also been met through the continued facilitation of the transition from the United Nations Mission in East Timor (UNAMET) to UNTAET; and the facilitation of the conduct of humanitarian operations across East Timor. In addition, INTERFET undertook national reconstruction tasks, governance and administration, policing and law and order functions, as well as investigations into possible crimes against humanity.

Militia groups operating from West Timor continued to pose an unacceptable threat to peace and security in some parts of the border regions of the Oecussi enclave. Also, the future of the Armed Forces for the National Liberation of East Timor (FALINTIL), the former pro-independence guerrilla force, remained an unresolved issue. Although the objective of disarming FALINTIL proved unachievable, arrangements to secure FALINTIL within its cantonment in Aileu had been effective.

Border management protocols established under the memorandum signed between the Indonesian armed forces (TNI) and INTERFET in November 1999 (the so-called Holbrooke agreement) [YUN 1999, p. 295] had worked well and had been important in rapidly and effectively resolving low-level incidents on the border. The border management framework was formalized on 13 January 2000 with the signing of a memorandum of understanding between INTERFET, UNTAET and TNI, which outlined an agreed border for East Timor operations, in the hope of further reducing border incidents, and established a number of junction points on the Oecussi and West Timor–East Timor borders, some of which would be staffed by UN military observers to facilitate refugee return. An agreement had also been reached that gave refugees unhindered personal passage across the border, and provided that TNI and INTERFET would disarm individuals not authorized to carry firearms and non-traditional weapons.

The transition from INTERFET to a UN peacekeeping operation, which commenced on 1 February, was to be completed by the end of the month. Several countries participating in INTERFET had begun to withdraw their troops and assets from East Timor.

The seventh report [S/2000/236], which covered activities from 1 to 23 February, noted that on 23 February INTERFET formally transferred full responsibility for military security in all parts of East Timor to UNTAET. INTERFET's experience demonstrated the advantages of selecting a coalition leader from the immediate region, which included proximity to the crisis zone and the ability to respond quickly to a crisis, commensurate with a knowledge of the conditions surrounding the intervention. INTERFET also benefited from having a clear UN mandate and operational end state; resolution 1264(1999) provided INTERFET with an unambiguous mission statement, while resolution 1272(1999) [YUN 1999, p. 293] gave it a clear end state and identified the preconditions necessary to transfer military responsibility to UNTAET, vital factors in the implementation of military plans for the operation and transition. In addition, INTERFET's ability under Chapter VIII of the UN Charter to deliver appropriate force decisively and quickly was critical to success and the prevention of widespread loss of life. The transition arrangements also proved very effective, with INTERFET and UNTAET executing a progressive transition, rather than the traditional comprehensive, single-step transition. That approach enabled the embryonic UNTAET peacekeeping operation headquarters to accept responsibility in a phased manner commensurate with its developing capability.

UN Transitional Administration for East Timor

In February, UNTAET, established under Security Council resolution 1272(1999) [YUN 1999, p. 293], assumed overall responsibility from INTERFET for the administration of East Timor. Its responsibilities included the maintenance of law and order, assistance in the development of civil and social services, coordination and delivery of humanitarian assistance and capacity-building support for self-government.

On 25 January [S/2000/62], the Secretary-General proposed that the military component of UNTAET be composed of 32 countries, which he listed. On 28 January [S/2000/63], the Security Council took note of the Secretary-General's proposal.

On 7 July [S/2000/671], the Secretary-General informed the Council of his intention to appoint Lieutenant General Boonsrang Niumpradit (Thailand) as the new Force Commander of UNTAET with effect from 19 July. Lieutenant General Jaime de los Santos (Philippines), who had served as Force Commander since January 2000, would relinquish his post on 21 July. On 10 July [S/2000/672], the Council took note of the Secretary-General's intention.

Reports of Secretary-General (January and July). In response to resolution 1272(1999), the Secretary-General submitted to the Security Council a report [S/2000/53 & Add.1] covering UNTAET activities and developments in East Timor between 25 October and 31 December 1999 [YUN 1999, p. 294] and the first three weeks of 2000. The report noted that humanitarian assistance had brought some relief to the East Timorese, but conditions were very difficult owing to the extent of destruction, lack of opportunity to earn a living and high prices. Crime was on the rise, especially in Dili and other urban sectors, mainly due to the large number of unemployed. From the beginning of January, there were a number of violent clashes in Baucau and Dili between groups of East Timorese, many of whom were armed with machetes, stones and sticks and some reportedly with firearms.There were also a number of border incidents between West and East Timor, including exchanges of fire between TNI and INTERFET. As at 24 January, 185 military observers were deployed in the mission area.

With regard to governance and public administration, an independent Public Service Commission was established on 21 January to oversee the selection and recruitment of a new, leaner East Timorese civil service and the setting up of administrative support arrangements, such as a payroll and payment system. The Transitional Judicial Service Commission, established on 5 January, proceeded to select an initial corps of 10 judges and prosecutors and suggested a list of 6 defence lawyers from among 20 East Timorese who participated in a 1999 judicial training programme. Training of judges, prosecutors and lawyers nevertheless remained an urgent requirement. In mid-January, INTERFET handed over its functions related to arrest and detention to the UN civilian police and the East Timorese judiciary. The Police Commissioner assumed his position on 7 January. Some 400 civilian police personnel had been dispatched to the mission area from 29 countries.

On 3 January, the Indonesian commercial airline Merpati conducted a test flight to Dili; regular flights were expected to begin in February. Those on board included the Governor of West Timor, a senior official from the Ministry of Foreign Affairs, a member of the Indonesian parliament and other officials. That was the first official Indonesian delegation to visit East Timor since the departure of Indonesian troops.

As at 24 January, 991 civilian staff were in the mission area, while 391 additional international staff were in the process of recruitment. However, there was a shortage of experts in the fields of electricity; water; public health; education; telecommunications; road maintenance; post; airport, port and harbour management; procurement; treasury; budgeting; and prison management.

In accordance with resolution 1272(1999), the Secretary-General submitted a report [S/2000/738] on the activities of UNTAET and developments in East Timor covering the period from 27 January to 26 July.

The 15-member National Consultative Council [YUN 1999, p. 294], which served as the primary mechanism through which the East Timorese participated in UNTAET's decision-making, was replaced on 14 July by the National Council (NC). The new Council would be composed of 33 members, all Timorese, appointed by the Transitional Administrator. Consultations were under way regarding their selection. At the same time, UNTAET reorganized itself to resemble more closely the future government and to increase the direct participation of the Timorese, who thus assumed a greater share of political responsibility. Eight portfolios were created: internal administration, infrastructure, economic affairs, social affairs, finance, justice, police and emergency services, and political affairs. The first four had been entrusted to East Timorese, and the other four to senior UNTAET staff members. The eight officials formed a Cabinet chaired by the Special Representative of the Secretary-General, Sergio Vieira de Mello, and were responsible for formulating policies and recommending regulations and directives for consideration by the NC. The Special Representative retained full responsibility as Transitional Administrator in accordance with Council resolution 1272(1999).

The report noted that when UNTAET was established, there was no history of open and democratic political activity in East Timor. Since then, the National Council of Timorese Resistance

(CNRT) and its component parties had been active, and new political organizations had emerged. However, there had been cases of intimidation against groups and parties not under the CNRT umbrella. Ethnic and religious minorities had also been the targets of harassment. In order to counter those tendencies and to prepare the population for democratic elections, UNTAET had launched a programme to promote civic education, constitutional development, the rule of law and political education. It had also disseminated information on human rights and was working with local community leaders to develop a culture of tolerance. In addition, UNTAET had promoted the free flow of information by supporting local media and through its own radio, limited television broadcasts and fortnightly newsletters.

The normalization of relations between Indonesia and East Timor had progressed well. On the occasion of Indonesian President Wahid's visit to Dili on 29 February, various trade and communications agreements were signed. On 6 April, Indonesia and UNTAET concluded a memorandum of understanding on cooperation in legal, judicial and human rights matters. In accordance with the memorandum, UNTAET assisted Indonesian authorities in their efforts to identify and prosecute those responsible for human rights violations in East Timor in 1999. To that end, UNTAET had located and interviewed witnesses and provided the results to Indonesian investigators. On 5 July, agreement was reached on the establishment of a Joint Border Committee, which was responsible for managing all cross-border matters. UNTAET established offices in Jakarta, Indonesia, and Kupang, West Timor, while Indonesia had a mission in East Timor. The office in Kupang helped coordinate UNTAET's assistance to flood victims on both sides of the border between East and West Timor in May. It had also been closely involved with UNHCR in initiatives designed to encourage reconciliation and the return of refugees who remained in West Timor and Java.

More than 167,000 refugees had returned from Indonesia, primarily from West Timor. The repatriation effort was coordinated by UNHCR; the International Organization for Migration arranged their movement to their destinations. That activity had proceeded with few incidents and the reintegration of the refugees into their original communities was conducted without any major problem. UNTAET supported UNHCR's work at the political level by promoting reconciliation and preparing the communities in East Timor for the return of those refugees who had opposed independence. Despite those efforts, an estimated 85,000 to 120,000 refugees remained in camps in West Timor, where militias opposed to independence continued to exercise great influence and impeded UNHCR's work by intimidation and violence. As a result, an important UNHCR effort to register refugees and determine whether they wished to return or to be resettled was repeatedly delayed and had to be postponed indefinitely in July, when militia members attacked UNHCR workers. UNHCR had increased its efforts to persuade the Indonesian authorities to assume their obligations and act on commitments made, which included free and unhindered access to the refugees and ensuring the safety of humanitarian workers.

UNTAET continued to build the foundations of governance, including a legal framework, a central financial capacity and a civil service structure, in order to transfer administrative functions to a sustainable East Timorese administration. The Civil Service Academy was inaugurated in May and UNDP, in cooperation with UNTAET, was preparing a comprehensive project for capacity-building in governance and public administration. During the reporting period, UNTAET established the Central Fiscal Authority and the Central Payments Office. The Treasury had been formed within the Central Fiscal Authority, responsible for the execution of the budget. Disbursements on public spending from the UNTAET Trust Fund totalled over $3 million, and a further $7.9 million had been committed. The collapse of both the public and private sectors following the wave of violence in 1999, in conjunction with large-scale destruction, had a devastating effect on the economy. The gross domestic product (GDP) was estimated to have shrunk in 1999 by as much as 38 per cent. Unemployment soared, while the price of fuel and other basic goods rose steeply. To provide relief and launch the repair of the infrastructure, quick-impact projects had been carried out throughout the country. Business activity had expanded on a moderate scale , and the agricultural sector saw a fairly strong recovery in the first half of 2000, owing to a good coffee crop and strong domestic demand.

Although the vast majority of schoolchildren and teachers were back in school by the end of April, the conditions they faced remained very difficult. Supplies were insufficient and many schools were structurally unsound. A $13.9 million project had been agreed between UNTAET and the World Bank for a rehabilitation programme. Owing to the collapse of the public health-care system, NGOs had become the main health service providers.

The Secretary-General noted that there had been a notable increase in low-level personal and property crime. Since January, UNTAET's civilian police grew from 400 to 1,270 officers. UNTAET's Border Control Unit maintained operations at Dili's port and airport and at two crossings points on the border with West Timor. The Unit's main functions were the control and monitoring of customs, immigration and quarantine, and the establishment and training of the Border Service of East Timor. As at 21 July, UNTAET had 2,684 civilian staff, of whom 1,886 were recruited locally and 798 internationally.

A phased transfer of responsibility from IN-TERFET, which began deployment in September 1999 [YUN 1999, p. 291], to UNTAET's military component took place in February. Since then, UN-TAET's force had conducted security operations throughout the country and had supported the activities of other components, notably the police, helped with the delivery of relief goods in remote areas, and provided medical care to civilians. The security situation was generally stable, though there was a period from late February to mid-March during which UNTAET's military positions near the border came under fire and four significant cross-border incursions were carried out by militia groups operating from West Timor. Following those attacks, UNTAET and Indonesian officials met and, on 11 April, UNTAET's Force Commander and the commander of the Indonesian forces in West Timor signed a memorandum of understanding regarding tactical cooperation in the border area. Thereafter, the situation along the border was quieter. However, a grenade attack against an UNTAET post on 28 May injured an Australian soldier, while on 24 July a New Zealand soldier was killed during an attack against an UNTAET patrol. Since October 1999, FALINTIL's troops had been cantoned in the Aileu district. Difficult living conditions, lack of supplies and lack of clarity about their future role had led to concerns over discipline and morale. UNTAET had allocated $100,000 from the consolidated budget of East Timor to provide food for two months to FALINTIL personnel and their dependants.

In planning for UNTAET's military component in 1999, the aim was to create a sufficiently robust force so as not to invite challenges after it took over from INTERFET. It was envisaged that the strength of the force could be reduced if the situation remained stable. Since that had turned out to be the case, especially in the eastern sector, and given also the improved capacity of the police, the Secretary-General intended to effect a reduction in that sector from 1,850 to a battalion-size force of 500 by the end of January 2001. The military observers would be reduced to 150 and a

further reduction was being considered. CNRT, in a reversal of its initial position, advocated the establishment of a national security force as a necessary element in the transition to independence. With financial support from the United Kingdom, a team organized by King's College, London, was undertaking a study of East Timor's future defence and security needs and their practical and financial implications.

The Secretary-General observed that the first six months of 2000 had made it clear how daunting the UN task was in East Timor. The United Nations had never before attempted to build and manage a State. Nor did it have an opportunity to prepare for that assignment; the team in East Timor had to be assembled ad hoc and still lacked important expertise in a number of fields. The relationship between UNTAET and the East Timorese was crucial for the attainment of the mandate. While Council resolution 1272(1999) had given the United Nations exclusive authority, the Special Representative had chosen to proceed only in the closest possible consultation with the East Timorese and with their full consent. During his visit to East Timor in February, the Secretary-General asked the Special Representative to establish benchmarks to guide the activities of the mission towards achieving minimum goals that would provide the population with a sound platform for governing their country when independence was achieved. The key areas were: to ensure security during the transitional period and arrangements for East Timor's security once it was independent; to establish a credible system of justice in which fundamental human rights were respected; to achieve a reasonable level of reconstruction of public services and infrastructure; to establish an administration that was financially sustainable; and to manage a political transition to independence, culminating in the adoption of a constitution and democratic elections. The last objective was the most important, since it entailed the establishment of a political system that was responsive to the citizens and a political leadership that was responsible in its decisions.

SECURITY COUNCIL ACTION

On 3 August [meeting 4182], following consultations among Security Council members, the President made statement **S/PRST/2000/26** on behalf of the Council:

> The Security Council recalls its previous resolutions and the statements by its President on the situation in East Timor. It welcomes the report of the Secretary-General of 26 July 2000 on the United Nations Transitional Administration in East Timor. It takes note with warm appreciation of the progress

made by the Transitional Administration and pays tribute to the leadership of the Special Representative of the Secretary-General. The Council also welcomes the significant progress made in building healthy relations between East Timor and Indonesia. The Council acknowledges in this regard the cooperation shown by the Government of Indonesia, the Transitional Administration and the people of East Timor.

The Council strongly supports the steps taken by the Transitional Administration to strengthen the involvement and direct participation of the East Timorese people in the administration of their territory, in particular the establishment, on 14 July 2000, of the National Council and the reorganization of the Transitional Administration, with a view to building capacity in the territory in the run up to independence. The Council invites the Secretary-General to report at an early date, on the basis of close consultations with the East Timorese, on the process for adopting a constitution and holding democratic elections.

The Council notes that the National Council of Timorese Resistance is advocating the creation of a national security force. In this regard, it welcomes work being done on the future defence and security needs of East Timor and their practical and financial implications. It urges the East Timorese people to conduct a broad discussion of these issues. The Council welcomes the humanitarian relief given by the Transitional Administration to the cantoned troops of the Armed Forces for the National Liberation of East Timor and encourages further assistance in this regard.

The Council condemns the murder on 24 July 2000 of a New Zealand soldier serving with the Transitional Administration and expresses its sympathy to the Government and people of New Zealand and to the family of the murdered peacekeeper. The Council is determined to ensure the safety and security of United Nations personnel in East Timor. In this regard, it requests the Secretary-General to inform the Council as soon as possible on the outcome of his investigation into the incident. It welcomes the establishment, on 31 July 2000, of a joint investigation by the Transitional Administration and the Government of Indonesia and welcomes also the cooperation of the Government of Indonesia to bring the perpetrators to justice.

The Council expresses its profound concern at the continuing presence of large numbers of refugees from East Timor in camps in West Timor, at the continuing presence of militia in the camps and at their intimidation of staff of the Office of the United Nations High Commissioner for Refugees. It expresses particular concern that this intimidation reached such a level that the Office of the High Commissioner was forced to postpone indefinitely its important effort to register refugees and determine whether they wished to return to East Timor or to be resettled, a task that should be completed as soon as possible given the impending rainy season. The Council calls for a more determined involvement in this problem by the Government of Indonesia, including implementation of the memorandum of understanding with the Office of the High Commis-

sioner of 14 October 1999 and of a recent security agreement concluded between local authorities and the Office of the High Commissioner. The Council calls upon the Government of Indonesia to take effective steps to restore law and order, to establish conditions of security for refugees and international humanitarian personnel, to allow free access by such personnel to the camps, to separate the former military personnel, police and civil servants from the refugees and to arrest those militia extremists who are attempting to sabotage the resettlement process.

The Council acknowledges that the Government of Indonesia has approached these challenges with an attitude of cooperation, manifested, inter alia, by the signing of such important agreements with the Transitional Administration as the memorandum of understanding of 6 April 2000 on legal, judicial and human rights matters, and the memorandum of understanding of 11 April 2000 on Tactical Coordination, and the establishment, on 5 July 2000, of a joint border commission. The Council regrets, however, that serious problems persist and looks forward to these agreements being translated into concrete progress on the ground. It also calls upon the Government of Indonesia to cooperate more closely with the Transitional Administration in the field to end cross-border incursions from West Timor, to disarm and disband the militias and to bring to justice those militia members guilty of crimes.

The Council takes note of the intention of the Secretary-General to reduce the size of the military component of the Transitional Administration in the eastern sector of East Timor to a battalion-size force of 500 by the end of January 2001, in the light of the situation on the ground.

The Council requests the Secretary-General to keep it closely informed of the situation in East Timor, including through provision of a military assessment of the security situation and its implications for the structure of the military component of the Transitional Administration. It also requests the Secretary-General to continue to report to it in line with the requirements set out in resolution 1272 (1999) of 25 October 1999. It further requests the Secretary-General to submit to it, in his next regular report, detailed plans on the transition to independence for East Timor, which should be drawn up in close consultation with the East Timorese people.

The Council will remain actively seized of the matter.

Attack on UNHCR office

On 8 September, the Security Council received briefings by the Under-Secretary-General for Peacekeeping Operations and the United Nations High Commissioner for Refugees on an attack against the UNHCR office in the vicinity of Atambua, West Timor, in which three international staff members were killed and three others wounded.

SECURITY COUNCIL ACTION (September)

On 8 September [meeting 4195], the Security Council unanimously adopted **resolution 1319**

(2000). The draft [S/2000/853] was prepared in consultations among Council members.

The Security Council,

Recalling its previous resolutions and the statements by its President on the situation in East Timor, in particular the statement of 3 August 2000, in which it expressed profound concern at the continuing presence of large numbers of refugees from East Timor in camps in West Timor, at the continuing presence of militia in the camps and at their intimidation of refugees and staff of the Office of the United Nations High Commissioner for Refugees,

Appalled by the brutal murder of three United Nations personnel killed, on 6 September 2000, by a militia-led mob, and supporting the statement on this subject made by the Secretary-General at the outset of the Millennium Summit and the expressions of concern by several heads of State and Government during the Summit proceedings,

Condemning this outrageous and contemptible act against unarmed international staff who were in West Timor to help the refugees, and reiterating its condemnation of the murder of two peacekeepers of the United Nations Transitional Administration in East Timor and attacks on the United Nations presence in East Timor,

Recalling that the declaration of the Millennium Summit included specific reference to the need for effective measures for the safety and security of United Nations personnel,

Expressing its outrage at the reported attacks in Betun, West Timor, on 7 September 2000, in which a number of refugees reportedly were killed,

Welcoming the letter of the President of Indonesia to the Secretary-General on 7 September 2000, in which he expressed outrage at the killing of the staff of the Office of the United Nations High Commissioner for Refugees and stated his intention to conduct a full-scale investigation and to take firm measures against those found guilty,

1. *Insists* that the Government of Indonesia take immediate additional steps, in fulfilment of its responsibilities, to disarm and disband the militia immediately, restore law and order in the affected areas in West Timor, ensure safety and security in the refugee camps and for humanitarian workers, and prevent cross-border incursions into East Timor;

2. *Stresses* that those responsible for the attacks on international personnel in West and East Timor must be brought to justice;

3. *Recalls,* in this regard, the letter of 18 February 2000 from the President of the Security Council to the Secretary-General, in which it was noted that grave violations of international humanitarian and human rights law had been committed and that those responsible for these violations should be brought to justice, and reiterates its belief that the United Nations has a role to play in the process in order to safeguard the rights of the people of East Timor;

4. *Calls upon* the Indonesian authorities to take immediate and effective measures to ensure the safe return of refugees who choose to go back to East Timor, and stresses the need for parallel programmes to resettle individuals who choose not to return;

5. *Notes* that the Government of Indonesia has decided to deploy additional troops to West Timor to improve the serious security situation, but stresses that workers of the Office of the United Nations High Commissioner for Refugees cannot return to West Timor until there is a credible security guarantee, including real progress towards disarming and disbanding the militias;

6. *Underlines* that the United Nations Transitional Administration in East Timor should respond robustly to the militia threat in East Timor, consistent with its resolution 1272(1999) of 22 October 1999;

7. *Requests* the Secretary-General to report to the Council within one week of the adoption of the present resolution on the situation on the ground;

8. *Decides* to remain seized of the matter.

The Council, on 19 September [meeting 4198], held a private meeting with the Special Envoy of Indonesia. A frank and constructive discussion took place on the need for early and full implementation of resolution 1319(2000).

Communications from Indonesia (25 September–4 October). In two letters to the Security Council President, dated 25 September [S/2000/899] and 26 September [S/2000/901], Indonesia provided information regarding the follow-up to the briefing given by its Special Envoy to the Council on 19 September. It recalled that the Special Envoy had conveyed the urgent need for achieving a comprehensive resolution of the problems concerning the situation in West Timor through the attainment of four objectives: investigation of the 6 September incident and bringing the perpetrators to justice; disarming the militias; reaching a lasting solution to the refugee question; and promoting reconciliation among the East Timorese of all political persuasions. The disarming process had commenced, and Indonesia had extended the period for the voluntary surrender of weapons from 25 to 27 September, in order to ensure an orderly and complete transfer of those arms by the militias. Beyond that date, strict enforcement measures would be taken against those found in possession of weapons. In the humanitarian field, Indonesia would continue to meet its responsibilities to render aid to the refugees.

In identical letters to the Security Council and the Secretary-General, dated 29 September [S/2000/922] and 3 October [A/55/446], respectively, Indonesia provided information on its response to resolution 1319(2000) on the question of East Timorese refugees in West Timor. Among other things, Indonesia noted that it had questioned individuals suspected of involvement in the attack against the UNHCR Atambua office and that investigations were ongoing. It also welcomed the establishment of a Joint Border Committee with UNTAET on 14 September, which would provide a mechanism and institutionalized processes to address border-related issues. Indonesia said that it was necessary to approach the Atambua incident within the wider context of the important progress that had been achieved over the past year in dealing with residual issues arising from the transfer of authority over East Timor. The best guarantee against a repeat of that incident was by addressing the root causes of all the outstanding issues, in particular the question of refugees.

On 3 October [S/2000/949], Indonesia informed the Council of the latest developments concerning the process of disarming the militias in Atambua.

By a 4 October letter [S/2000/955], Indonesia provided information on developments regarding the situation in West Timor.

Security Council mission

On 25 October [S/2000/1030], the Security Council President informed the Secretary-General that the Council members had agreed to dispatch a mission to East Timor and Indonesia in November. The composition and terms of reference of the mission were included.

On 21 November [S/2000/1105], the mission (9-17 November) reported on its findings and recommendations to the Council. The report also included the texts of statements made by Indonesia's Foreign Minister on the mission's visit to Indonesia and by Ambassador Martin Andjaba (Namibia), leader of the mission.

With regard to the implementation of resolution 1272(1999), the mission said that the overall security situation in East Timor was relatively stable, with remarkably little general crime. Civilian police had been deployed to all districts and to all but 10 subdistricts. Training of the local police force continued, but budgetary constraints meant that the requisite force of 3,000 would not be realized until 2006. Consequently, it was likely that there would be a need for the international civilian police to remain beyond the date of independence.

The establishment of a fully functioning judicial system had proved challenging in the light of the total absence of local capacity in that area and other priorities placed on UNTAET at the beginning of its operations. The judicial sector remained seriously under-resourced and thus could not process those suspects already in detention. It was therefore particularly important for UNTAET to consider all available ways of attracting the necessary resources and that decisions on handling serious crimes investigations should reflect East Timorese expectations. The Special Representative intended to conduct a review of the justice sector. The mission welcomed the initiative and urged the Council to give it priority considera-

tion. UNTAET had made substantial progress in addressing the security threat posed by militia infiltration from West Timor. As with the police, however, it seemed likely that East Timor would require an international military presence in some form for some time after independence.

The humanitarian situation had passed its most pressing phase. However, East Timor would need continued resources as people reestablished their livelihoods and as long as the prospect of large additional refugee returns remained. UNTAET had put in place the necessary contingency plans to cope with a significant refugee influx. The mission noted that it was important that that readiness should be maintained as a component of UNTAET's refugee return strategy.

A particularly positive and important development in fulfilment of UNTAET's mandate of capacity-building for self-governance had been the acceleration of the Timorization of the administration. A number of Timorese District or Deputy District Administrators had been appointed, while legislative responsibility was exercised through the all-Timorese NC and executive powers by a Transitional Cabinet comprising five Timorese and four internationals, under the chairmanship of the Transitional Administrator. The mission endorsed UNTAET's efforts and emphasized the need for capacity-building among the East Timorese.

There had been major rehabilitation of public buildings and utilities in Dili. The mission was told that the education system was functioning throughout East Timor, together with a basic level of health care in many areas. Nevertheless, implementation of projects had been slow due to lack of resources. The mission recommended that consideration be given to increased flexibility in the use of assessed resources allocated to complex peacekeeping operations such as UNTAET.

The mission recognized that in all likelihood there would be a need for a strong international commitment to East Timor after independence through the provision of financial, technical and security assistance, if the aspirations of the East Timorese were to be fully realized.

With regard to the implementation of resolution 1319(2000), Ambassador Andjaba welcomed Indonesia's efforts to address the situation in West Timor, although much remained to be done. In East Timor, over 170,000 refugees had returned, and the process of reconciliation was beginning. However, information from refugees returning to East Timor indicated that intimidation was still present in the camps in West Timor. The mission took note of the request of the Indonesian Attorney-General for international assistance to ensure adequate expertise in bringing to justice those responsible for human rights violations. It also welcomed the passage of human rights law and awaited the establishment of ad hoc courts.

There was agreement on the high priority of resuming international assistance to the refugees to supplement Indonesia's efforts. For that to happen, the security of international humanitarian workers would need to be assured. Indonesia would be discussing with UN offices in Jakarta arrangements to facilitate an assessment by UN security experts of the situation in West Timor, in cooperation with the police, TNI and other responsible authorities.

The mission underscored the importance of internationally observed registration of refugees, a view shared by Indonesia. Fair treatment and support had to be provided to those refugees who wanted to stay in Indonesia and those who wanted to return to East Timor. The mission encouraged Indonesia to promulgate a detailed plan for registration, return and resettlement. It also believed that ad hoc returns could be an important factor in helping to create the conditions necessary for resolving the issue. In that context, it welcomed plans for the return of the ex-TNI reservists from East Timor.

The mission welcomed the statements by East Timorese leaders that they were anxious to welcome the refugees back and to pursue reconciliation. It also stressed the need for continued talks between Indonesia and UNTAET on residual issues that would arise during the transition period.

Communications from Indonesia (13-27 November). On 13 November, in identical letters to the Secretary-General and the Council President [A/55/626-S/2000/1090], Indonesia reported on developments in East Nusa Tenggara, a region on the border with East Timor. Indonesia planned to dispatch an additional company of marines to patrol the waters in the border area. In addition, Indonesia reported that the refugee situation had improved and approximately 500 East Timorese had decided to return to East Timor.

On 27 November [S/2000/1125], Indonesia transmitted to the Council a document entitled "The visit of the mission of the Security Council to Indonesia: Indonesia's constructive response to Security Council resolution 1319(2000)". Indonesia welcomed the visit as an expression of the existing positive line of communication with the United Nations. It also reaffirmed that, through concrete actions and deeds, it had endeavoured to create a conducive atmosphere for East Timor during the transition phase. A prosperous, peaceful, stable and democratic East Timor was in Indonesia's national interest.

SECURITY COUNCIL ACTION (December)

On 6 December [meeting 4244], following consultations among Security Council members, the President made statement **S/PRST/2000/39** on behalf of the Council:

The Security Council welcomes the report of the Security Council mission to East Timor and Indonesia of 21 November 2000, and endorses the recommendations that it contains. It notes in particular the view of the mission that a strong international presence will be required in East Timor after independence, inter alia for the provision of financial, technical and security assistance, and agrees that planning for such a presence should begin as soon as possible. It requests the Secretary-General to report on this matter in his next regular report to the Council.

The Council pays tribute to the work of the United Nations Transitional Administration in East Timor. It welcomes in particular the creation of the National Council in East Timor, and stresses the importance of further work on the transition to independence, including a timetable and mechanisms for a constitution and elections. It stresses that urgent consideration should be given to expediting the training of the Timor Lorosae Police Service and to attracting sufficient resources to develop the judicial system. It notes the views of the Special Representative of the Secretary-General on the need to use assessed funding more flexibly.

The Council emphasizes that urgent action is necessary to resolve the problem of the East Timorese refugees in West Timor. While acknowledging the efforts of the Government of Indonesia so far, the Council expresses its belief that a number of further steps must be taken, including:

(i) Decisive action to disarm and disband the militia and put an end to their activities, including by the separation of militia leaders from the refugees in West Timor and the expeditious prosecution of those responsible for criminal acts. The Council welcomes the steps already taken by the Government of Indonesia and urges it to make further progress on eradicating intimidation in the camps;

(ii) Action to allow the international relief agencies to return to West Timor, which will in turn require that the security of their staff be guaranteed. The Council looks forward, in this context, to discussions between the Government of Indonesia and the United Nations on arrangements to facilitate an expert assessment of the security situation in West Timor. This should be in accordance with the usual modalities employed by the Office of the United Nations Security Coordinator;

(iii) Action to improve the flow of information to the refugees. The Council urges the Government of Indonesia, the Transitional Administration and the Office of the United Nations High Commissioner for Refugees to work together to develop an information strategy that will allow the refugees to make an informed decision about their future;

(iv) Credible, apolitical and internationally observed registration of the refugees, carried out in close cooperation with United Nations agencies and other relevant actors.

The Council emphasizes the need for measures to address shortcomings in the implementation of justice in East Timor. The Council welcomes the adoption of Indonesian legislation for the establishment of ad hoc human rights tribunals. Also, it underlines the need to bring to justice those responsible for violent attacks in East and West Timor, including attacks on United Nations personnel and in particular the murder of three humanitarian workers and two United Nations peacekeepers. The Council regrets that those responsible for the murder of the peacekeepers have not been arrested, and calls for action in this regard and for an early start to the trials of those accused of killing the humanitarian workers.

The Council highlights the importance of the bilateral relationship between the Transitional Administration and the Government of Indonesia. The Council underlines the need to resolve the outstanding issues of payment of pensions to former civil servants and the proposed transit arrangements between the Oecussi enclave and the remainder of East Timor. It encourages in this regard further progress in the dialogue between the Government of Indonesia and the Transitional Administration.

The Council will remain actively seized of the matter.

Further report of Secretary-General. In a later report [S/2001/42], the Secretary-General reported on UNTAET's activities and developments in East Timor during the latter part of 2000. One of the main political developments was the emergence of a growing consensus among the Timorese people to seek independence by the end of 2001. On 12 December, the NC endorsed the outlines of a political calendar proposed by Xanana Gusmão in his capacity as CNRT president. Broad public consultations on the proposed calendar resulted in agreement on the following sequence of steps. Phase one included nationwide consultation and decisions regarding the electoral modalities and the composition of the Constituent Assembly. In phase two, the Assembly would draft a constitution. The modalities for its adoption, whether by the Assembly itself of by referendum, were still under discussion. That would be followed by the establishment of a government. If a presidential form of government was adopted, elections might be held. It was anticipated that under the shortest possible time frame, elections could be held in the summer of 2001 and independence declared late in the year. UNTAET would be fully responsible for the conduct of the elections. The UN Secretariat carried out an initial need-assessment mission in August and an electoral pre-planning session in Canberra, Australia, in September. It also dispatched an electoral system education team in October and an advance planning and design team had

been in East Timor since mid-November. The establishment of the NC on 23 October significantly enhanced the participation of the Timorese in the political decision-making process. At its first session, Mr. Gusmão was elected Speaker. On 19 October, José Ramos-Horta was sworn in as cabinet member for foreign affairs, so that East Timorese held five of the nine cabinet portfolios; the others were held by international staff, who would be gradually replaced by East Timorese.

During the summer, the situation in the western districts gave cause for concern, as a result of a relatively high level of activity by militia groups that had infiltrated from West Timor. The activities of the militias, which caused the temporary displacement of more than 3,000 persons, decreased towards the end of September, following the launching of operations by UNTAET that put pressure on the militias. In the light of that situation, UNTAET suspended a planned reduction of the military component, brought in an additional rifle company and strengthened its surveillance and information capacity as well as its civil-military affairs elements.

No tangible progress was made in the disbanding of the militias entrenched inside refugee camps in West Timor and, thus, the refugees were not yet free to decide whether to return to their homes or to resettle in Indonesia. Following the killing of three UNHCR staff members on 6 September in Atambua, all UN international staff were withdrawn from West Timor. The Security Council's mission to East Timor and Indonesia in November found that despite the collection of some arms, resolution 1319(2000), which called on Indonesia to disarm and disband the militia and ensure safety in the refugee camps, remained largely unfulfilled. On 22 December, Indonesia convened a meeting with the UN resident coordinator in Jakarta to discuss the question of a mission to assess security conditions in West Timor, as called for by the Council in statement S/PRST/2000/39. There had been no further developments on that matter so far.

The East Timor Transitional Administration was established on 7 August to integrate East Timorese into all major decision-making areas and the Department of Foreign Affairs was created in October. Relations with Indonesia continued to be affected by the problem of the militias and refugees in West Timor.

Based on a study coordinated by King's College, London (see p. 281), the Cabinet decided in September to establish the East Timor Defence Force (ETDF) as a light infantry force of 1,500 regular soldiers and 1,500 reservists, drawn initially from FALINTIL. In November, UNTAET met with representatives of a number of interested

Governments to discuss how the new force might best be set up. Training, infrastructure and equipment for ETDF depended on voluntary contributions, while personnel, operating and maintenance costs would be borne by the Government of East Timor.

The justice system was investigating more than 180 cases. The Serious Crimes Investigation Unit focused on cases to be tried under the Indonesian penal code and prosecuting suspects accused of crimes against humanity. Public safety had improved. During the second half of 2000, civilian police deployment had risen to 1,439 officers. The police had set up a special unit to prepare for security during the electoral process.

More than 820 schools were operating with about 200,000 students enrolled at the primary and secondary levels. The National University of East Timor opened in November, with an enrolment of over 4,000 students. Three hospitals were functioning, as well as 71 community health centres at the district and subdistrict levels.

Efforts to promote economic activity, including foreign investment, continued. However, unemployment was very high, and the needs far exceeded the available resources and capacity. Agriculture was the single largest contributor to GDP. Efforts to increase crop productivity with the aim of ensuring food self-sufficiency and food security had been increased. The humanitarian situation improved during the second half of 2000. However, some communities remained vulnerable, and recovery from the widespread destruction of September 1999 had moved forward slowly.

As at 31 December, the strength of the UNTAET military component was 7,886 all ranks, including 120 military observers, from 31 countries. The international civilian police comprised 1,402 officers from 38 countries and included two rapid response units of 120 each from Jordan and Portugal. UNTAET comprised 2,668 civilian staff, 877 of whom were internationally recruited and 1,791 locally recruited. In addition, the mission was supported by 513 UN Volunteers.

The Secretary-General observed that during the period under review there had been a concerted effort to accelerate the transfer of authority to the Timorese. While the United Nations retained overall responsibility, he envisaged the further progressive delegation of authority, until authority was finally transferred to the Government of the independent State. That was an innovative approach, which required understanding and flexibility from all involved. Another innovation was the involvement of UNTAET in the creation of ETDF as a consequence of its responsibility to prepare East Timor for independence. The estab-

lishment of that force was coordinated by the East Timor Transitional Administration, but depended entirely on the support of the Governments that had expressed their readiness to assist. The question of security remained a matter of concern; although infiltration by militia groups from West Timor had decreased, the threat was bound to remain as long as the Government of Indonesia did not disband those groups. That was also an essential step towards the overdue solution of the problem of the refugees in West Timor.

By **decision 55/435** of 19 December, the General Assembly deferred consideration of the item "The situation in East Timor during its transition to independence" and included it in the provisional agenda of its fifty-sixth (2001) session.

Financing of UN operations

During 2000, the General Assembly considered the financing of two UN missions in East Timor—UNAMET and UNTAET. UNAMET was established by Security Council resolution 1246 (1999) [YUN 1999, p. 283] to conduct the 1999 popular consultation on East Timor's autonomy [ibid., p. 288]; its mandate was extended until 30 November 1999 by resolution 1262(1999) [ibid., p. 287]. UNTAET was established by Council resolution 1272(1999) [ibid., p. 293] to administer East Timor during its transition to independence.

UNAMET

The General Assembly had before it the Secretary-General's March report on UNAMET's financing [A/54/775], which requested an additional appropriation of $26,913,800 gross ($26,499,800 net), representing the difference between expenditures and the initial appropriation, and assessment in the amount of $23,241,600 gross ($22,827,600 net). The Assembly also considered a related report of the Advisory Committee on Administrative and Budgetary Questions (ACABQ) [A/54/802], which concurred with the Secretary-General's request.

GENERAL ASSEMBLY ACTION

On 7 April [meeting 95], on the recommendation of the Fifth (Administrative and Budgetary) Committee [A/54/505/Add.1], the General Assembly adopted **resolution 54/20 B** without vote [agenda item 169].

Financing of the United Nations Mission in East Timor

The General Assembly,

Having considered the report of the Secretary-General on the financing of the United Nations Mission in East Timor and the related report of the Advisory Committee on Administrative and Budgetary Questions,

1. *Endorses* the observations and recommendations contained in the report of the Advisory Committee on Administrative and Budgetary Questions;

2. *Decides* to appropriate to the Special Account for the United Nations Mission in East Timor an additional amount of 26,913,800 United States dollars gross (26,499,800 dollars net);

3. *Also decides*, as an ad hoc arrangement, to apportion the amount of 23,241,600 dollars gross (22,827,600 dollars net) among Member States in accordance with the composition of groups set out in paragraphs 3 and 4 of General Assembly resolution 43/232 of 1 March 1989, as adjusted by the Assembly in its resolutions 44/192 B of 21 December 1989, 45/269 of 27 August 1991, 46/198 A of 20 December 1991, 47/218 A of 23 December 1992, 49/249 A of 20 July 1995, 49/249 B of 14 September 1995, 50/224 of 11 April 1996, 51/218 A to C of 18 December 1996 and 52/230 of 31 March 1998 and its decisions 48/472 A of 23 December 1993, 50/451 B of 23 December 1995 and 54/456 to 54/458 of 23 December 1999, and taking into account the scale of assessments for the year 1999, as set out in its resolutions 52/215 A of 22 December 1997 and 54/237 A of 23 December 1999.

On 23 December, the Assembly decided that the agenda item on the financing of UNAMET would remain for consideration during its resumed fifty-fifth (2001) session (**decision 55/458**) and that the Fifth Committee should continue its consideration of the item at that session (**decision 55/455**).

UNTAET

On 7 March [A/54/769], the Secretary-General submitted to the General Assembly a report on the financing of UNTAET, which contained the proposed budget for the period from 1 December 1999 to 30 June 2000 for the maintenance of the mission, which amounted to $386,341,400 gross ($377,425,700 net).

On 17 March [A/54/804], ACABQ recommended that the Assembly appropriate for the establishment and maintenance of UNTAET an amount of $350 million for the period from 1 December 1999 to 30 June 2000, inclusive of the amount of $200 million authorized by the Assembly in resolution 54/246 A [YUN 1999, p. 297]. In addition, ACABQ recommended that the Assembly authorize the assessment of $150 million for the period from 1 December 1999 to 30 June 2000, taking into account the $200 million already assessed on Member States in accordance with resolution 54/246 A. ACABQ recommended that the UN Secretariat submit the budget for the mission for the period from 1 July 2000 to 30 June 2001 in September 2000, taking fully into account the results of the review referred to in the Secretary-General's January 2000 report on UNTAET (see p. 279). ACABQ trusted that the Secretariat would be able to gain performance experience and estimate

more accurately UNTAET's requirements for the next financial period. Should the Secretary-General require additional resources for the maintenance of UNTAET from 1 July to the time the Assembly authorized the budget for 1 July 2000 to 30 June 2001, ACABQ recommended that the Secretariat submit a progress report in May 2000 indicating such additional requirements.

GENERAL ASSEMBLY ACTION

On 7 April [meeting 95], the General Assembly, on the recommendation of the Fifth Committee [A/54/687/Add.1], adopted **resolution 54/246 B** without vote [agenda item 173].

Financing of the United Nations Transitional Administration in East Timor

The General Assembly,

Having considered the report of the Secretary-General on the financing of the United Nations Transitional Administration in East Timor and the related report of the Advisory Committee on Administrative and Budgetary Questions,

Bearing in mind Security Council resolution 1272(1999) of 25 October 1999 regarding the establishment of the United Nations Transitional Administration in East Timor,

Recalling its resolution 54/246 A of 23 December 1999,

Reaffirming that the costs of the Transitional Administration are expenses of the Organization to be borne by Member States in accordance with Article 17, paragraph 2, of the Charter of the United Nations,

Recalling its previous decisions regarding the fact that, in order to meet the expenditures caused by the Transitional Administration, a different procedure is required from that applied to meet expenditures of the regular budget of the United Nations,

Taking into account the fact that the economically more developed countries are in a position to make relatively larger contributions and that the economically less developed countries have a relatively limited capacity to contribute towards such an operation,

Bearing in mind the special responsibilities of the States permanent members of the Security Council, as indicated in General Assembly resolution 1874(S-IV) of 27 June 1963, in the financing of such operations,

Noting with appreciation that voluntary contributions have been made to the trust fund for the multinational force,

Noting also with appreciation that voluntary contributions have been made to the Trust Fund for the United Nations Transitional Administration in East Timor, and inviting further such contributions to the Fund,

Mindful of the fact that it is essential to provide the Transitional Administration with the necessary financial resources to enable it to fulfil its responsibilities under the relevant resolutions of the Security Council,

1. *Takes note* of the status of contributions to the United Nations Transitional Administration in East Timor as at 24 March 2000, including the contributions outstanding in the amount of 130.8 million United States dollars, representing 65 per cent of the total assessed contributions, notes that some 18 per cent of the Member States have paid their assessed contribu-

tions in full, and urges all other Member States concerned, in particular those in arrears, to ensure the payment of their outstanding assessed contributions;

2. *Expresses its appreciation* to those Member States which have paid their assessed contributions in full;

3. *Expresses concern* about the financial situation with regard to peacekeeping activities, in particular as regards the reimbursements to troop contributors that bear additional burdens owing to overdue payments by Member States of their assessments;

4. *Urges* all other Member States to make every possible effort to ensure payment of their assessed contributions to the Transitional Administration in full and on time;

5. *Expresses concern* at the delay experienced by the Secretary-General in deploying and providing adequate resources to some recent peacekeeping missions, in particular those in Africa;

6. *Emphasizes* that all future and existing peacekeeping missions shall be given equal and non-discriminatory treatment in respect of financial and administrative arrangements;

7. *Also emphasizes* that all peacekeeping missions shall be provided with adequate resources for the effective and efficient discharge of their respective mandates;

8. *Reiterates its request* to the Secretary-General to make the fullest possible use of facilities and equipment at the United Nations Logistics Base at Brindisi, Italy, in order to minimize the costs of procurement for the Transitional Administration, and for this purpose requests the Secretary-General to speed up the implementation of the asset management system at all peacekeeping missions in accordance with General Assembly resolution 52/1 A of 15 October 1997;

9. *Endorses* the conclusions and recommendations contained in the report of the Advisory Committee on Administrative and Budgetary Questions, and requests the Secretary-General to ensure their full implementation;

10. *Requests* the Secretary-General to take all necessary action to ensure that the Transitional Administration is administered with a maximum of efficiency and economy;

11. *Also requests* the Secretary-General, in order to reduce the cost of employing General Service staff, to continue efforts to employ locally recruited staff for the Transitional Administration against General Service posts, commensurate with the requirements of the Transitional Administration;

12. *Decides* to appropriate to the Special Account for the United Nations Transitional Administration in East Timor the amount of 350 million dollars gross (341,084,300 dollars net) for the establishment and maintenance of the Transitional Administration for the period from 1 December 1999 to 30 June 2000, inclusive of the amount of 200 million dollars authorized by the General Assembly in its resolution 54/246 A;

13. *Decides also*, as an ad hoc arrangement, to apportion the amount of 150 million dollars gross (141,084,300 dollars net) for the period from 1 December 1999 to 30 June 2000, taking into account the amount of 200 million dollars already apportioned among Member States in accordance with General Assembly resolution 54/246 A and in accordance with the composition of groups set out in paragraphs 3 and 4 of Assembly resolution 43/232 of 1 March 1989, as adjusted by the Assembly in its resolutions 44/192 B of 21

December 1989, 45/269 of 27 August 1991, 46/198 A of 20 December 1991, 47/218 A of 23 December 1992, 49/249 A of 20 July 1995, 49/249 B of 14 September 1995, 50/224 of 11 April 1996, 51/218 A to C of 18 December 1996 and 52/230 of 31 March 1998 and its decisions 48/472 A of 23 December 1993, 50/451 B of 23 December 1995 and 54/456 to 54/458 of 23 December 1999, and taking into account the scale of assessments for the years 1999 and 2000, as set out in its resolutions 52/215 A of 22 December 1997 and 54/237 A of 23 December 1999;

14. *Decides further* that, in accordance with the provisions of its resolution 973(X) of 15 December 1955, there shall be set off against the apportionment among Member States, as provided for in paragraph 13 above, their respective share in the Tax Equalization Fund of the estimated staff assessment income of 8,915,700 dollars approved for the Transitional Administration for the period from 1 December 1999 to 30 June 2000;

15. *Emphasizes* that no peacekeeping mission shall be financed by borrowing funds from other active peacekeeping missions;

16. *Encourages* the Secretary-General to continue to take additional measures to ensure the safety and security of all personnel under the auspices of the United Nations participating in the Transitional Administration;

17. *Invites* voluntary contributions to the Transitional Administration in cash and in the form of services and supplies acceptable to the Secretary-General, to be administered, as appropriate, in accordance with the procedure and practices established by the General Assembly;

18. *Decides* to keep under review during its fifty-fourth session the item entitled "Financing of the United Nations Transitional Administration in East Timor".

On 10 March [A/54/769/Add.1], the Secretary-General submitted a report containing the first full 12-month proposed budget for UNTAET's maintenance from 1 July 2000 to 30 June 2001, which amounted to $584,138,100 gross ($567,377,100 net).

On 19 May [A/54/875], ACABQ drew attention to a 5 May letter on the financing of UNTAET from the UN Controller to ACABQ's Chairman. The Controller said that the comprehensive review of UNTAET's requirements commenced during the third week of April and that it was expected to be finalized in late June. ACABQ recommended that the Assembly authorize commitment authority of $292,069,000 gross ($283,688,500 net) and that it also authorize assessment of $200 million. In addition, it recommended that the funding be granted without prejudice to recommendations that might be made to the Assembly in the autumn of 2000.

GENERAL ASSEMBLY ACTION

On 15 June [meeting 98], the General Assembly, on the recommendation of the Fifth Committee [A/54/687/Add.2], adopted **resolution 54/246 C** without vote [agenda item 173].

Financing of the United Nations Transitional Administration in East Timor

The General Assembly,

Having considered the report of the Secretary-General on the financing of the United Nations Transitional Administration in East Timor and the related report of the Advisory Committee on Administrative and Budgetary Questions,

Bearing in mind Security Council resolution 1272(1999) of 25 October 1999 regarding the establishment of the United Nations Transitional Administration in East Timor,

Recalling its resolutions 54/246 A of 23 December 1999 and 54/246 B of 7 April 2000 on the financing of the Transitional Administration,

Reaffirming that the costs of the Transitional Administration are expenses of the Organization to be borne by Member States in accordance with Article 17, paragraph 2, of the Charter of the United Nations,

Recalling its previous decisions regarding the fact that, in order to meet the expenditures caused by the Transitional Administration, a different procedure is required from that applied to meet expenditures of the regular budget of the United Nations,

Taking into account the fact that the economically more developed countries are in a position to make relatively larger contributions and that the economically less developed countries have a relatively limited capacity to contribute towards such an operation,

Bearing in mind the special responsibilities of the States permanent members of the Security Council, as indicated in General Assembly resolution 1874(S-IV) of 27 June 1963, in the financing of such operations,

Noting with appreciation that voluntary contributions have been made to the trust fund for the multinational force,

Noting with appreciation also that voluntary contributions have been made to the Trust Fund for the United Nations Transitional Administration in East Timor, and inviting further such contributions to the Fund,

Mindful of the fact that it is essential to provide the Transitional Administration with the necessary financial resources to enable it to fulfil its responsibilities under the relevant resolutions of the Security Council,

1. *Takes note* of the status of contributions to the United Nations Transitional Administration in East Timor as at 30 April 2000, including the contributions outstanding in the amount of 217.2 million United States dollars, representing some 63 per cent of the total assessed contributions from the inception of the Transitional Administration to the period ending 30 June 2000, notes that some 2 per cent of the Member States have paid their assessed contributions in full, and urges all other Member States concerned, in particular those in arrears, to ensure payment of their outstanding assessed contributions;

2. *Expresses its appreciation* to those Member States which have paid their assessed contributions in full;

3. *Expresses concern* about the financial situation with regard to peacekeeping activities, in particular as regards the reimbursements to troop contributors that bear additional burdens owing to overdue payments by Member States of their assessments;

4. *Urges* all other Member States to make every possible effort to ensure payment of their assessed contributions to the Transitional Administration in full and on time;

5. *Expresses concern* at the delay experienced by the Secretary-General in deploying and providing adequate resources to some recent peacekeeping missions, in particular those in Africa;

6. *Emphasizes* that all future and existing peacekeeping missions shall be given equal and non-discriminatory treatment in respect of financial and administrative arrangements;

7. *Also emphasizes* that all peacekeeping missions shall be provided with adequate resources for the effective and efficient discharge of their respective mandates;

8. *Reiterates its request* to the Secretary-General to make the fullest possible use of facilities and equipment at the United Nations Logistics Base at Brindisi, Italy, in order to minimize the costs of procurement for the Transitional Administration, and for this purpose requests the Secretary-General to speed up the implementation of the asset management system at all peacekeeping missions in accordance with General Assembly resolution 52/1 A of 15 October 1997;

9. *Endorses* the conclusions and recommendations contained in the report of the Advisory Committee on Administrative and Budgetary Questions;

10. *Requests* the Secretary-General to take all necessary action to ensure that the Transitional Administration is administered with a maximum of efficiency and economy;

11. *Also requests* the Secretary-General, in order to reduce the cost of employing General Service staff, to continue efforts to recruit local staff for the Transitional Administration against General Service posts, commensurate with the requirements of the Transitional Administration;

12. *Authorizes* the Secretary-General to enter into commitments in an amount not exceeding 292,069,000 dollars gross (283,688,500 dollars net) for the operation of the Transitional Administration for the period from 1 July to 31 December 2000;

13. *Decides,* as an ad hoc arrangement, to apportion the amount of 200 million dollars gross (194,261,300 dollars net) for the period from 1 July to 31 December 2000 among Member States in accordance with the composition of groups set out in paragraphs 3 and 4 of General Assembly resolution 43/232 of 1 March 1989, as adjusted by the Assembly in its resolutions 44/192 B of 21 December 1989, 45/269 of 27 August 1991, 46/198 A of 20 December 1991, 47/218 A of 23 December 1992, 49/249 A of 20 July 1995, 49/249 B of 14 September 1995, 50/224 of 11 April 1996, 51/218 A to C of 18 December 1996 and 52/230 of 31 March 1998 and its decisions 48/472 A of 23 December 1993, 50/451 B of 23 December 1995 and 54/456 to 54/458 of 23 December 1999, and taking into account the scale of assessments for the year 2000, as set out in its resolutions 52/215 A of 22 December 1997 and 54/237 A of 23 December 1999;

14. *Decides also* that, in accordance with the provisions of its resolution 973(X) of 15 December 1955, there shall be set off against the apportionment among Member States, as provided for in paragraph 13 above, their respective share in the Tax Equalization Fund of the estimated staff assessment income of 5,738,700 dollars approved for the Transitional Administration for the period from 1 July to 31 December 2000;

15. *Emphasizes* that no peacekeeping mission shall be financed by borrowing funds from other active peacekeeping missions;

16. *Encourages* the Secretary-General to continue to take additional measures to ensure the safety and security of all personnel under the auspices of the United Nations participating in the Transitional Administration;

17. *Invites* voluntary contributions to the Transitional Administration in cash and in the form of services and supplies acceptable to the Secretary-General, to be administered, as appropriate, in accordance with the procedure and practices established by the General Assembly;

18. *Decides* to include in the provisional agenda of its fifty-fifth session the item entitled "Financing of the United Nations Transitional Administration in East Timor".

On 3 October [A/55/443 & Corr.1-3], the Secretary-General submitted to the Assembly a report on the financing of UNTAET that contained the proposed budget for the 12-month period from 1 July 2000 to 30 June 2001 and which superseded the budget submission contained in his 10 March report (see above). The new proposed budget amounted to $592,306,800 gross ($574,466,400 net).

On 30 October [A/55/531], ACABQ recommended that the Assembly appropriate for the maintenance of UNTAET an amount of $563 million for the period from 1 July 2000 to 30 June 2001, reflecting a reduction of approximately 5 per cent from the amount proposed by the Secretary-General. It further recommended that the Assembly approve the assessment of $363 million and that the unencumbered balance of $48,973,500 as at 30 June 2000 be credited among Member States.

GENERAL ASSEMBLY ACTION

On 23 December [meeting 89], the General Assembly, on the recommendation of the Fifth Committee [A/55/664], adopted **resolution 55/228 A** without vote [agenda item 134].

Financing of the United Nations Transitional Administration in East Timor

The General Assembly,

Having considered the report of the Secretary-General on the financing of the United Nations Transitional Administration in East Timor and the related report of the Advisory Committee on Administrative and Budgetary Questions,

Bearing in mind Security Council resolution 1272 (1999) of 25 October 1999 regarding the establishment of the United Nations Transitional Administration in East Timor,

Recalling its resolution 54/246 A of 23 December 1999 on the financing of the Transitional Administration and its subsequent resolutions thereon, the latest of which was resolution 54/246 C of 15 June 2000,

Reaffirming that the costs of the Transitional Administration are expenses of the Organization to be borne by Member States in accordance with Article 17, paragraph 2, of the Charter of the United Nations,

Recalling its previous decisions regarding the fact that, in order to meet the expenditures caused by the Transitional Administration, a different procedure is required from that applied to meet expenditures of the regular budget of the United Nations,

Taking into account the fact that the economically more developed countries are in a position to make relatively larger contributions and that the economically less developed countries have a relatively limited capacity to contribute towards such operations,

Bearing in mind the special responsibilities of the States permanent members of the Security Council, as indicated in General Assembly resolution 1874(S-IV) of 27 June 1963, in the financing of such operations,

Noting with appreciation that voluntary contributions have been made to the trust fund for the multinational force,

Also noting with appreciation that voluntary contributions have been made to the Trust Fund for the United Nations Transitional Administration in East Timor, and inviting further such contributions to the Fund,

Mindful of the fact that it is essential to provide the Transitional Administration with the necessary financial resources to enable it to fulfil its responsibilities under the relevant resolutions of the Security Council,

1. *Takes note* of the status of contributions to the United Nations Transitional Administration in East Timor as at 31 October 2000, including the contributions outstanding in the amount of 149 million United States dollars, representing some 28 per cent of the total assessed contributions from the inception of the Transitional Administration to the period ending 31 December 2000, notes that some 21 per cent of the Member States have paid their assessed contributions in full, and urges all other Member States concerned, in particular those in arrears, to ensure payment of their outstanding assessed contributions;

2. *Expresses its appreciation* to those Member States which have paid their assessed contributions in full;

3. *Expresses concern* about the financial situation with regard to peacekeeping activities, in particular as regards the reimbursements to troop contributors that bear additional burdens owing to overdue payments by Member States of their assessments;

4. *Urges* all other Member States to make every possible effort to ensure payment of their assessed contributions to the Transitional Administration in full and on time;

5. *Expresses concern* at the delay experienced by the Secretary-General in deploying and providing adequate resources to some recent peacekeeping missions, in particular those in Africa;

6. *Emphasizes* that all future and existing peacekeeping missions shall be given equal and non-discriminatory treatment in respect of financial and administrative arrangements;

7. *Also emphasizes* that all peacekeeping missions shall be provided with adequate resources for the effective and efficient discharge of their respective mandates;

8. *Reiterates its request* to the Secretary-General to make the fullest possible use of facilities and equipment at the United Nations Logistics Base at Brindisi,

Italy, in order to minimize the costs of procurement for the Transitional Administration, and for this purpose requests the Secretary-General to speed up the implementation of the asset management system at all peacekeeping missions in accordance with its resolution 52/1 of 15 October 1997;

9. *Endorses* the conclusions and recommendations contained in the report of the Advisory Committee on Administrative and Budgetary Questions, subject to the provisions of the present resolution;

10. *Decides* to retain the post of the Chief of Staff to the Special Representative of the Secretary-General at the level of Assistant Secretary-General;

11. *Requests* the Secretary-General, in future budget proposals and pending further guidance by the Advisory Committee, to consider using United Nations Volunteers for the fourteen posts mentioned in paragraph 60 of his report, taking into account the opinion of the Advisory Committee in paragraph 38 of its report, and bearing in mind the need of the Transitional Administration for human rights officers in the light of the evolution of the situation in the territory;

12. *Also requests* the Secretary-General to take all necessary action to ensure that the Transitional Administration is administered with a maximum of efficiency and economy;

13. *Further requests* the Secretary-General, in order to reduce the cost of employing General Service staff, to continue efforts to recruit local staff for the Transitional Administration against General Service posts, commensurate with the requirements of the Transitional Administration;

14. *Decides* to appropriate to the Special Account for the United Nations Transitional Administration in East Timor the amount of 563 million dollars gross (546,051,600 dollars net) for the operation of the Transitional Administration for the period from 1 July 2000 to 30 June 2001, inclusive of the amount of 292,069,000 dollars gross (283,688,500 dollars net) authorized by the General Assembly in its resolution 54/246 C;

15. *Decides also*, as an ad hoc arrangement and taking into account the amount of 200 million dollars gross (194,261,300 dollars net) already apportioned in accordance with General Assembly resolution 54/246 C for the period from 1 July to 31 December 2000, to apportion the additional amount of 128,416,670 dollars gross (124,268,800 dollars net) for the period from 1 July 2000 to 31 January 2001 among Member States in accordance with the composition of groups set out in paragraphs 3 and 4 of its resolution 43/232 of 1 March 1989, as adjusted by the Assembly in its resolutions 44/192 B of 21 December 1989, 45/269 of 27 August 1991, 46/198 A of 20 December 1991, 47/218 A of 23 December 1992, 49/249 A of 20 July 1995, 49/249 B of 14 September 1995, 50/224 of 11 April 1996, 51/218 A to C of 18 December 1996, 52/230 of 31 March 1998 and 55/236 of 23 December 2000 and its decisions 48/472 A of 23 December 1993, 50/451 B of 23 December 1995 and 54/456 to 54/458 of 23 December 1999, the scale of assessments for the year 2000 to be applied against a portion thereof, that is, 81.5 million dollars gross (78,764,500 dollars net), which is the amount pertaining to the period ending 31 December 2000, and the scale of assessments for the year 2001 to be applied against the balance, that is, 46,916,670 dollars gross (45,504,300 dollars net) for the period from 1 to 31 January 2001;

16. *Decides further* that, in accordance with the provisions of its resolution 973(X) of 15 December 1955, there shall be set off against the apportionment among Member States, as provided for in paragraph 15 above, their respective share in the Tax Equalization Fund of the estimated additional staff assessment income of 4,147,870 dollars approved for the Transitional Administration for the period from 1 July 2000 to 31 January 2001, 2,735,500 dollars being the amount pertaining to the period ending 31 December 2000, and the balance, that is, 1,412,370 dollars, for the period from 1 to 31 January 2001;

17. *Decides*, as an ad hoc arrangement, to apportion among Member States the amount of 234,583,330 dollars gross (227,521,500 dollars net) for the period from 1 February to 30 June 2001, at a monthly rate of 46,916,666 dollars gross (45,504,300 dollars net), in accordance with the scheme set out in the present resolution and taking into account the scale of assessments for the year 2001, subject to the decision of the Security Council to extend the mandate of the Transitional Administration beyond 31 January 2001;

18. *Decides also* that, in accordance with the provisions of its resolution 973(X), there shall be set off against the apportionment among Member States, as provided for in paragraph 17 above, their respective share in the Tax Equalization Fund of the estimated staff assessment income of 7,061,830 dollars approved for the Transitional Administration for the period from 1 February to 30 June 2001;

19. *Emphasizes* that no peacekeeping mission shall be financed by borrowing funds from other active peacekeeping missions;

20. *Encourages* the Secretary-General to continue to take additional measures to ensure the safety and security of all personnel under the auspices of the United Nations participating in the Transitional Administration;

21. *Invites* voluntary contributions to the Transitional Administration in cash and in the form of services and supplies acceptable to the Secretary-General, to be administered, as appropriate, in accordance with the procedure and practices established by the General Assembly;

22. *Decides* to keep under review during its fifty-fifth session the item entitled "Financing of the United Nations Transitional Administration in East Timor".

On 23 December, the Assembly decided that the agenda item on the financing of UNTAET would remain for consideration during its resumed fifty-fifth (2001) session (**decision 55/458**) and that the Fifth Committee should continue consideration of the item at that session (**decision 55/455**).

Iraq

During 2000, relations between the Security Council and Iraq continued to be overshadowed by the stalemate precipitated by the withdrawal in

December 1998 [YUN 1998, p. 262] of the United Nations Special Commission (UNSCOM) and the International Atomic Energy Agency (IAEA)— both mandated by the Council's ceasefire resolution 687(1991) [YUN 1991, p. 172] to disarm Iraq of its weapons of mass destruction and to ensure that it did not reconstitute or reacquire them. UNSCOM's monitoring and verification responsibilities were assumed by the United Nations Monitoring, Verification and Inspection Commission (UNMOVIC), which was established by Council resolution 1284(1999) [YUN 1999, p. 230] and began operations on 1 March 2000. However, since Iraq refused to accept resolution 1284(1999), UNMOVIC was not able to carry out its work inside Iraqi territory. In February 2000, the Secretary-General appointed Hans Blix as Executive Chairman of UNMOVIC and in March he nominated 16 UNMOVIC Commissioners. UNMOVIC submitted to the Council three quarterly reports, while IAEA submitted biannual reports on its activities. In January, IAEA inspectors were able to verify the presence of known nuclear material under safeguards during an inspection carried out in Iraq.

The Secretary-General transmitted three reports on the repatriation or return of all Kuwaiti and third-country nationals from Iraq, and on the return of all Kuwaiti property seized by Iraq during its 1990 invasion and occupation of Kuwait [YUN 1990, p. 189]. Yuli M. Vorontsov was appointed as the high-level Coordinator for compliance by Iraq with its obligations regarding the repatriation of Kuwaiti nationals and return of Kuwaiti property.

The United Nations Iraq-Kuwait Observation Mission (UNIKOM) continued to carry out its functions of surveillance, control and investigation in the demilitarized zone between Kuwait and Iraq, and maintained liaison with authorities from both countries. The Council, on the Secretary-General's recommendation, decided to maintain UNIKOM and to review its functions in 2001.

In the context of the continuing sanctions against Iraq, the temporary arrangements for the humanitarian programme for the Iraqi people, based on an oil-for-food formula, was extended twice during the year, each time for another 180 days. The Council, based on the recommendations of a group of experts that visited Iraq in January, decided to increase Iraqi spending on oil equipment and spare parts, in order to sustain production levels and to offset permanent damage to oil-bearing structures.

By **decisions 55/431** and **55/432** of 14 December, the General Assembly deferred consideration of, respectively, Israel's armed aggression against Iraqi nuclear installations and its grave consequences for the established international system on the peaceful uses of nuclear energy, the non-proliferation of nuclear weapons and international peace and security; and the consequences of Iraq's occupation of and aggression against Kuwait. It included both items in the provisional agenda of its fifty-sixth (2001) session.

UN Monitoring, Verification and Inspection Commission and IAEA activities

UNMOVIC

In 2000, UNMOVIC assumed UNSCOM's responsibilities connected with verifying Iraq's compliance with its weapons-related obligations under resolution 687(1991) [YUN 1991, p. 172] and other relevant resolutions, established and operated a reinforced ongoing monitoring and verification (OMV) system and addressed unresolved disarmament issues within that framework. UNMOVIC was established on 17 December 1999 by Security Council resolution 1284(1999) [YUN 1999, p. 230] as a successor body to UNSCOM.

On 26 January [S/2000/60], the Secretary-General recommended that Hans Blix (Sweden) be appointed Executive Chairman of UNMOVIC. On 27 January [S/2000/61], the Council approved the appointment. The Council had earlier considered Rolf Ekéus but did not reach a consensus on his nomination.

On 7 February [S/2000/90], the Secretary-General said that he had appointed Mr. Blix as the Executive Chairman effective 1 March. On 10 March [S/2000/207], the Secretary-General appointed 16 UNMOVIC Commissioners, who would review the implementation of resolution 1284(1999) and other relevant resolutions and provide advice and guidance to the Executive Chairman. Mr. Blix would chair meetings of the College of Commissioners.

Organizational plan

On 6 April [S/2000/292 & Corr.1], the Secretary-General transmitted to the Security Council the organizational plan for UNMOVIC, as called for in paragraph 6 of resolution 1284(1999). The plan, which was prepared by the Executive Chairman, described the Commission's management and organizational structure, staffing and responsibilities as well as Iraq's obligations. On 13 April [S/2000/311], the Council approved the plan and looked forward to consultations on its implementation.

By a 14 April letter to the Secretary-General [S/2000/321], the Russian Federation said that UNMOVIC's organizational plan did not clearly prescribe procedures for conducting inspections, taking samples or aerial monitoring and failed to mention anything about the need to reach agreement on those procedures with Baghdad. It was in connection with those questions, Russia asserted, that many serious problems arose during the period in which UNSCOM was operating in Iraq. The practical aspects of the new Commission's activities required substantial revision.

Reports of UNMOVIC (June, August, December). As called for by Security Council resolution 1284(1999), UNMOVIC submitted to the Council, through the Secretary-General, three quarterly reports, on 1 June [S/2000/516], 28 August [S/2000/835] and 1 December [S/2000/1134]. The June report, covering the period from 1 March to 31 May, noted that the first meeting of the UNMOVIC College of Commissioners took place on 23 and 24 May. Representatives of IAEA and the Organization for the Prohibition of Chemical Weapons (OPCW) also attended. The Commissioners discussed, among other matters, possible operational procedures for UNMOVIC, the recruitment and training of personnel and the Joint Unit for Export/Import Monitoring. The Joint Unit continued to receive notifications from States and international organizations of exports to Iraq of dual-use goods subject to the provisions of Council resolution 1051(1996) [YUN 1996, p. 218]. Despite its obligations under that resolution, Iraq had not provided UNMOVIC with any notifications during the review period. A technical and cultural training programme had been created to establish a sufficient pool of experts for work related to inspection and monitoring in Iraq on behalf of the United Nations.

The August report, which covered the period from 1 June to 31 August, stated that the second meeting of the College of Commissioners took place on 23 and 24 August. Observers from IAEA and OPCW attended. The Executive Chairman reported on the results of the first UNMOVIC training course and on recruitment, and introduced discussion papers on operating procedures under a reinforced OMV system and on a draft action plan for the resumption of activities in Iraq. The Commissioners had before them an informal paper on the experience of UNSCOM in respect to modalities for the inspection of sensitive sites. They also discussed procedures applied, and to be applied, for the operations in the field, in particular for sensitive sites. The recruitment and training of staff continued, with the first UNMOVIC training programme being held from 11 July to 10 August. UNMOVIC's staff began a systematic review of the Commission's databases with a view to creating a single, secure, central system, which would also be capable of being accessed from the Commission's premises in Baghdad. The staff had also started examining inspec-

tion procedures in order to define appropriate operational procedures to be applied under the reinforced OMV system. Iraq failed to provide the Export/Import Joint Unit with any notifications or other mandated declarations during the period under review.

The December report covered the period from 1 September to 30 November. The principal issue discussed at the third meeting of the College of Commissioners (27-29 November) was preparations for the commencement of work by UNMOVIC in Iraq. The Commissioners were consulted on and supported principles for sampling and analysis, which would form the basis of detailed guidelines for such activities in Iraq. The College was also briefed on the oil-for-food programme by the Office of the Iraq Programme (OIP). The Executive Chairman continued his practice of providing monthly briefings to the President of the Security Council. The Commission was preparing a web site and had distributed a first newsletter to all experts who had undergone UNMOVIC training. The second month-long training course commenced on 7 November and would conclude on 8 December. The Commission continued to revise and update the lists of dual-use items and materials to which the export/import monitoring mechanism applied. Work on the elaboration of inspection guidelines and procedures for use in the field continued.

IAEA

IAEA reports (April and October). In accordance with Security Council resolution 1051 (1996), IAEA submitted to the Security Council, through the Secretary-General, two consolidated six-monthly reports, on 11 April [S/2000/300] and on 11 October [S/2000/983], on the Agency's verification activities in Iraq. The Agency had not been in a position, since its withdrawal from Iraq on 16 December 1998 [YUN 1998, p. 267], to implement its mandate in Iraq. It was thus unable to provide any measure of assurance with regard to Iraq's compliance with its obligations under relevant Council resolutions. In that context, IAEA had not received from Iraq the semi-annual declarations required by the Agency's OMV plan. Those declarations were the principal means for Iraq to provide information regarding the use and any changes in the use of certain facilities, installations and sites and regarding the inventory and location of certain materials, equipment and isotopes. The most recent declarations were submitted in 1998 [YUN 1998, p. 265].

In the April report, IAEA noted that, in keeping with the safeguards agreement between Iraq and IAEA pursuant to the Treaty on the Non-Proliferation of Nuclear Weapons, adopted by the General Assembly in resolution 2373(XXII) [YUN 1968, p. 17], a five-person IAEA team carried out a physical inventory verification of the nuclear material in Iraq between 22 and 25 January 2000. The Agency inspectors were able to verify the presence of known nuclear material subject to safeguards, consisting of low enriched, natural and depleted uranium. Iraq provided the necessary cooperation for the inspection team to perform its activities effectively and efficiently, even though the inspection, planned for December 1999 [YUN 1999, p. 228], could take place only in January because of Iraq's delay in providing the necessary visas. The inspection had the limited objective of verifying the nuclear material in question and was not intended, nor could it serve, as a substitute for IAEA's activities under the relevant Council resolutions.

In October, IAEA noted that in May it had been able to complete the destruction, in Jordan, of a filament-winding machine and its associated spare parts and raw materials owned by Iraq. Procurement of that equipment and material had been initiated by Iraq in mid-1990 for use in its clandestine uranium enrichment gas centrifuge programme. IAEA coordinated its efforts with UNMOVIC. The Agency had refined the structure and content of its information system in the areas of computer support to inspections and analytical tools. An enhanced analysis of the available original Iraqi documentation had also continued, as well as an assessment of the results accumulated through the past inspection process. Those activities had confirmed the validity of the Agency's technically coherent picture of Iraq's past clandestine nuclear programme.

Iraq-Kuwait

POWs and Kuwaiti property

On 10 February [S/2000/112], the Secretary-General informed the Security Council that, in accordance with resolution 1284(1999) [YUN 1999, p. 230], he had appointed Yuli M. Vorontsov (Russian Federation) as the high-level Coordinator for compliance by Iraq with its obligations regarding the repatriation or return of all Kuwaiti and third-country nationals or their remains, as well as the return of all Kuwaiti property. The Council took note of the appointment on 14 February [S/2000/113].

Reports of Secretary-General (April, June, December). Pursuant to Council resolution 1284(1999), the Secretary-General submitted reports in April [S/2000/347 & Corr.1], June [S/2000/575] and December [S/2000/1197] on compliance by Iraq with its obligations regarding the repatriation or return of all Kuwaiti and third-country nationals or their remains, and on the return of all Kuwaiti property, including archives, seized by Iraq.

In April, the Secretary-General said the high-level Coordinator, at the initial stage of his efforts, would have the task of determining the factual up-to-date situation with the repatriation of Kuwaiti and third-country nationals and establishing working contacts with the whole range of parties that had dealt with the issue, while taking into account the recommendations of the 1999 panel on prisoners of war (POWs) and Kuwaiti property (the Amorim panel) [YUN 1999, p. 235]. The Coordinator's ultimate goal was to assist in closing the largest possible number of files.

The Coordinator, upon his arrival in New York in late March, held numerous meetings with various representatives of parties concerned with his mandated activities. He subsequently visited the headquarters of ICRC in Geneva, the Organization of the Islamic Conference (OIC) in Jeddah, Saudia Arabia, and the League of Arab States (LAS) in Cairo, Egypt. He also held high-level meetings with authorities in Kuwait, Saudi Arabia and Egypt, during which he emphasized the fact that the work of ascertaining the fate of the missing military personnel and civilians had been assigned to the Tripartite Commission. Established in 1991 under ICRC auspices, the Commission dealt with the question of persons still unaccounted for, and was made up of representatives of France, Iraq, Kuwait, Saudi Arabia, the United Kingdom and the United States. A Technical Subcommittee was established in 1994 to expedite the search for all persons for whom inquiry files had been opened. However, at the end of 1998, Iraq had decided not to participate in the Commission's work, arguing that it no longer held captive Kuwaiti prisoners in its territory and, thus, the issue had become one of missing persons, not POWs.

The activities of the Tripartite Commission and its Technical Subcommittee had resulted in the repatriation, with Iraq's participation, of some 6,000 Kuwaiti POWs through ICRC and other channels, but a significant number of people still remained unaccounted for. Though Iraq had not provided any information since 1998, it had submitted to ICRC requests to ascertain the fate and whereabouts of more than 1,000 Iraqis not accounted for after the withdrawal of Iraqi forces from Kuwait. In that connection, the Kuwaiti authorities informed the Coordinator that they had no Iraqi POWs on their territory except several common criminals of Iraqi origin. They also stated that they were prepared to allow Iraqi representatives, accompanied by ICRC and in the presence of observers from international organizations, to conduct search and identification operations inside Kuwait.

The Secretary-General observed that ICRC's independent dialogue with Iraq needed to proceed uninterrupted and that its principle of independence and confidentiality should be respected. Iraq's response to the issue of missing persons, as a purely humanitarian one, would become a yardstick by which the international community would measure Iraq's position on other outstanding problems. The Coordinator would continue to motivate the parties to cooperate in the framework of different existing mechanisms, taking into account the fact that the resolution of humanitarian issues could not wait for political movement on other outstanding matters.

In June, the Secretary-General described action taken by the United Nations since the end of the Gulf war on the return of Kuwaiti property, including archives, seized by Iraq. In 2000, the Coordinator, guided by the recommendations of the Amorim panel, conducted consultations with Kuwaiti officials, as well as with Security Council members, LAS and OIC. He noted, in particular, attention paid to the issue in the final document adopted by the Thirteenth Ministerial Conference of the Movement of Non-Aligned Countries (Cartagena, Colombia, 8-9 April) [A/54/917-S/2000/580]. The Secretary-General, in a meeting with Iraq's Minister for Foreign Affairs (Havana, Cuba, 13 April), urged Iraq, among other things, to cooperate on the return of Kuwaiti property and archives. The Iraqi interlocutors reconfirmed that the issue should be addressed under Council resolution 687(1991) [YUN 1991, p. 172].

On the basis of information provided by his contacts, the Coordinator concluded that Iraq had returned a substantial quantity of property over a nine-year period of time, though there remained many items that Iraq was under obligation to return to Kuwait. He also noted that it might never be possible to verify, with complete certainty, that all items in Iraq's possession had been returned, and that the continuing absence of a credible explanation from Iraq with regard to the missing property delayed the closure of the property issue.

The Secretary-General observed that, in order to minimize costs, he would consider asking the Commander of UNIKOM to assign an existing international staff member to help to facilitate the return of property.

In December, the Secretary-General, reporting on activities related to the repatriation of all Kuwaiti and third-country nationals or their remains, and the return of Kuwaiti property, said that in his meetings with dignitaries attending

the UN Millennium Summit in September (see p. 47) he repeatedly raised the issue and requested that all necessary assistance and cooperation be extended to the Coordinator. Iraq's Minister for Foreign Affairs reiterated that his country would not cooperate with anyone affiliated with Council resolution 1284(1999), which continued to be rejected by Iraq. However, before the Secretary-General attended the OIC summit meeting (Doha, Qatar, 12-13 November), the Permanent Representative of Iraq to the United Nations welcomed a comprehensive dialogue with the United Nations. At the OIC summit, the Secretary-General had several high-level exchanges on the issue of Kuwaiti missing persons. Many interlocutors referred to the meeting of the Foreign Ministers of the Gulf Cooperation Council (Jeddah, September), when they urged the Iraqi Government to respond to and cooperate with Council resolution 1284(1999), in particular on the issue of repatriation and return of Kuwaiti and Saudi nationals, as well as Kuwaiti property. In their final communiqué, participants in the summit called for the prompt resolution of the issue of Kuwaiti prisoners and missing persons, as well as the nationals of other countries, in collaboration with ICRC. They also called for cooperation on Iraq's proposals concerning missing Iraqi nationals under the auspices of ICRC.

The Secretary-General addressed the issue of missing persons during a meeting in New York on 31 August with the Speaker of the Kuwaiti Parliament. The Speaker stressed that his country considered that issue as entirely humanitarian, and therefore it should be separated from any other disputes relating to Iraq-Kuwait relations.

On the margins of the Millennium Summit, the high-level Coordinator had numerous discussions on the issue of Kuwaiti missing persons and property with a view to exploring new venues of cooperation. During the period under review, he also visited Kuwait and ICRC headquarters in Geneva. Despite numerous bilateral contacts between ICRC and the parties concerned, there had been no significant progress, except in the case of a missing Saudi pilot, whose remains had been retrieved by a joint Iraqi-Saudi operation. The Coordinator drew to ICRC's attention the fact that Iraqi officials had received assistance from UNIKOM in locating and accessing grave sites of Iraqi soldiers within the demilitarized zone.

Briefing the Security Council on 17 August, the Coordinator pointed to the intense exchanges on the issue of the missing persons between Kuwait and Iraq. In that context, some Council members observed that the international community should not be selective and that all missing persons, whether Kuwaitis, Iraqis or others, should be taken into account. The Coordinator, on that occasion, reiterated that his mandate was limited to Kuwaiti and third-country nationals. The Coordinator also maintained contacts with LAS and OIC, and visited the United Nations Compensation Commission (UNCC). He was informed that UNCC could do nothing for claimants seeking an order compelling the return of irreplaceable objects and other tangible properties stolen by Iraq during its 1990 occupation of Kuwait, since UNCC's mandate was to award monetary compensation for losses; it had no mechanism for requiring or enforcing specific performance. UNCC was also not in a position to consider claims for compensation for the families of the missing persons.

The Special Rapporteur of the Commission on Human Rights, having held discussions with Iraqi and Kuwaiti officials on the issue of missing persons, noted that Iraq was willing to extend its cooperation to ICRC and to have bilateral meetings with Kuwaiti representatives.

Regarding the return of Kuwaiti property, Iraq continued to maintain that it had returned a large part of the property found in Iraq and had expressed its readiness to return what it might find in the future. Kuwait maintained that there had been no progress on the priority issues, such as the return of the national archives, military equipment and museum items.

The Secretary-General observed that the Iraqi authorities continued to refuse cooperation with the Coordinator. However, he welcomed the fact that ICRC was continuing efforts to gather information on all missing persons through direct contacts with all parties. As Iraq claimed to seek a resolution to the issue of its own missing nationals, it was essential that it exercised an appropriate understanding of the position held by Kuwait and other countries concerned.

Communications. On 23 May [S/2000/478], Kuwait transmitted to the Secretary-General and the Security Council an OIC position paper concerning the issue of the Kuwaiti and third-country prisoners and missing persons in Iraq. The OIC Secretary-General, since assuming office in 1997, had called for sustained action to remedy the consequences of Iraq's invasion of Kuwait, foremost among them the matter of the Kuwaiti POWs and missing persons. All of the final communiqués and decisions adopted by successive ministerial conferences had called for the return of the Kuwaiti POWs and missing persons to their homeland and their families. OIC would continue to cooperate with the United Nations and to support the high-level Coordinator.

On 26 May [S/2000/502], in identical letters to the Secretary-General and the Security Council

President, Iraq said that, as a State member of OIC, it was unaware of the position paper that Kuwait claimed originated with OIC. In fact, Iraq stated that the submission by Kuwait of that unofficial and illegal paper represented a selective attempt to politicize the missing persons issue.

In identical letters of 21 June to the Secretary-General and the Council President [S/2000/622], Iraq submitted a 19 June letter from its Minister for Foreign Affairs to the OIC Secretary-General, seeking clarification of the facts concerning the alleged position paper transmitted by Kuwait. Iraq noted that OIC had provided verbal assurances that the paper was a set of talking points drawn up by an official of the OIC secretariat in connection with a visit by the OIC Secretary-General to Kuwait and that it had no official or legal standing. Iraq added that Kuwait's letter damaged the credibility of OIC, which was required to adopt a position of neutrality on issues that arose between two of its members.

In identical letters of 12 July to the Secretary-General and the Council President [S/2000/686], Kuwait transmitted the text of a resolution adopted by the Islamic Conference of Foreign Ministers at its twenty-seventh session (Kuala Lumpur, Malaysia, 27-30 June) entitled "The consequences of Iraqi aggression against the State of Kuwait and the necessity for Iraq to implement all the relevant Security Council resolutions". Kuwait claimed that the resolution was cogent proof of the falsehood of Iraq's allegations, as it confirmed that OIC was in full accord with all the points made in the position paper that Kuwait had circulated. The resolution, among other things, called on Iraq to resume full and effective cooperation with ICRC and with the Tripartite Commission in the context of discharging its obligations under Council resolution 1284(1999) [YUN 1999, p. 230] and reaffirmed the need for compliance with resolutions 686(1991) [YUN 1991, p. 171] and 687(1991) [ibid., p. 172] concerning the release of Kuwaiti and third-country POWs and the return of Kuwaiti property. It also emphasized that Iraq had to respect the security, territorial integrity and political independence of Kuwait.

In identical letters of 22 July to the Secretary-General and the Council President [S/2000/732], Iraq said that Kuwait's 12 July letter failed to mention the reservations expressed by certain OIC members, as well as the written reservations to the OIC resolution that Iraq asked to be included in the documents of the meeting. Iraq insisted that all POWs had been repatriated and that all Kuwaiti property in its possession had been returned. Iraq also highlighted a number of the resolution's provisions that affirmed respect for

Iraq's sovereignty and expressed sympathy for its people.

Related communications. In communications addressed to the Secretary-General and the Security Council President on 13 June [S/2000/569], 31 August [S/2000/847] and 4 October [S/2000/952], Kuwait detailed infiltrations by Iraqi citizens into Kuwaiti territory, movements in the demilitarized zone by Iraqi naval units and the assembly of 500 Iraqis near the border with Kuwait. On 9 August [S/2000/791], 18 September [S/2000/876] and 27 September [S/2000/918], Kuwait informed the Secretary-General and the Council President that senior Iraqi officials had made threatening statements against Kuwait and other countries in the region.

In 11 October [S/2000/982] and 27 October [S/2000/1047] letters to the Secretary-General, Iraq responded to Kuwait's allegations.

UN Iraq-Kuwait Observation Mission

The United Nations Iraq-Kuwait Observation Mission (UNIKOM), established by Security Council resolution 687(1991) [YUN 1991, p. 172], continued in 2000 to discharge its functions in accordance with its terms of reference, as expanded by resolution 806(1993) [YUN 1993, p. 406].

UNIKOM operations involved surveillance, control, investigation and liaison. Surveillance of the demilitarized zone (DMZ), an area about 200 to 240 kilometres long and extending 10 kilometres into Iraq and 5 kilometres into Kuwait, was based on ground and air patrols and observation points. Control operations included static checkpoints, random checks and maintenance of a mobile reserve force. For operational purposes, the DMZ was divided into the northern and southern sectors, with 10 and 7 patrol/observation bases, respectively. Investigation teams were stationed in those sectors and at UNIKOM headquarters. Continuous liaison was maintained with Iraqi and Kuwaiti authorities at all levels.

The military observers were responsible for patrol, observation, investigation and liaison activities. The infantry battalion, deployed at Camp Khor, Kuwait, at a company camp in Al-Abdali, at platoon camps in two DMZ sectors, and in the easternmost patrol/observation base on the DMZ's Iraqi side, conducted armed patrols within those areas and manned checkpoints at border-crossing sites, making random checks in cooperation with Iraqi and Kuwaiti liaison officers. It also provided security for UNIKOM personnel and installations.

UNIKOM maintained headquarters at Umm Qasr in Iraq, liaison offices in Baghdad and Kuwait City and a support centre at Camp Khor.

Reports of Secretary-General (March and September). UNIKOM's activities were described in two reports by the Secretary-General, covering the period 24 September 1999 to 30 March 2000 [S/2000/269] and 31 March to 21 September 2000 [S/2000/914].

The reports noted that the situation in the DMZ remained generally calm. However, there had been no UNIKOM flights over the Iraqi side of the DMZ since they were suspended in December 1998 [YUN 1998, p. 262], when Iraqi authorities informed UNIKOM that they could not guarantee the safety of such flights due to Iraq's conflict with the United States and the United Kingdom regarding the no-fly zones.

DMZ violations increased to 77 during the first period but dropped to 42 during the second period. Most of the ground violations occurred when Iraqi vehicles using the only hard-surface road along the border crossed in and out of Kuwaiti territory, while the maritime violations involved Iraqi boats observed in Kuwaiti territorial waters. The weapons violations consisted of incidents of single gunshots fired during the night. Most of the air violations were by aircraft generally flying too high to be identified. During the two reporting periods, UNIKOM received twelve official complaints, eight from Kuwait and four from Iraq. Following a lengthy period of preparation, the Khwar 'Abd Allah Waterway Monitoring Project commenced operation on 15 February, under the command of the Force Commander. Its area of responsibility covered the waterways and the land area patrolled by UNIKOM from a patrol and observation base on the Al Faw peninsula. It also had operational and logistical responsibility for three patrol and observation bases. UNIKOM continued to provide security and logistical support for ICRC's humanitarian activities.

The Secretary-General observed that UNIKOM received the cooperation of the Iraqi and Kuwaiti authorities in the performance of its tasks and recommended that it be maintained in view of its continued contribution to the maintenance of calm and stability in the DMZ.

SECURITY COUNCIL ACTION

The Security Council informed the Secretary-General on 5 April [S/2000/286] and on 5 October [S/2000/960] that, in the light of his reports, it concurred with his recommendation that UNIKOM be maintained. The Council would review the question again by 6 April 2001.

Composition

As at 31 August, UNIKOM, under the command of Major-General John A. Vize (Ireland), had an overall strength of 1,309, comprising 195 military observers from 32 Member States; an infantry battalion of 775 from Bangladesh; 133 support personnel, including a 50-member engineering unit and a 34-member logistic unit from Argentina, a helicopter unit of 35 from Bangladesh and a medical unit of 14 from Germany; plus a civilian staff of 206, of whom 52 were recruited internationally.

Financing

On 15 June [meeting 98], the General Assembly considered the Secretary-General's reports on the financial performance of UNIKOM for the period 1 July 1998 to 30 June 1999 [A/54/709] and its proposed budget for 1 July 2000 to 30 June 2001 [A/54/736], together with related report of ACABQ [A/54/841/Add.3]. On the recommendation of the Fifth Committee [A/54/510/Add.1], the Assembly adopted **resolution 54/18 B** without vote [agenda item 130 (a)].

Financing of the United Nations Iraq-Kuwait Observation Mission

The General Assembly,

Having considered the reports of the Secretary-General on the financing of the United Nations Iraq-Kuwait Observation Mission and the related reports of the Advisory Committee on Administrative and Budgetary Questions,

Recalling Security Council resolutions 687(1991) of 3 April 1991 and 689(1991) of 9 April 1991, by which the Council decided to establish the United Nations Iraq-Kuwait Observation Mission and to review the question of its termination or continuation every six months,

Recalling also its resolution 45/260 of 3 May 1991 on the financing of the Observation Mission and its subsequent resolutions and decisions thereon, the latest of which was resolution 53/229 of 8 June 1999,

Reaffirming that the costs of the Observation Mission that are not covered by voluntary contributions are expenses of the Organization to be borne by Member States in accordance with Article 17, paragraph 2, of the Charter of the United Nations,

Recalling its previous decisions regarding the fact that, in order to meet the expenditures caused by the Observation Mission, a different procedure is required from that applied to meet expenditures of the regular budget of the United Nations,

Taking into account the fact that the economically more developed countries are in a position to make relatively larger contributions and that the economically less developed countries have a relatively limited capacity to contribute towards such an operation,

Bearing in mind the special responsibilities of the States permanent members of the Security Council, as indicated in General Assembly resolution 1874(S-IV) of 27 June 1963, in the financing of such operations,

Expressing its appreciation for the substantial voluntary contributions made to the Observation Mission by the Government of Kuwait and the contributions of other Governments,

Mindful of the fact that it is essential to provide the Observation Mission with the necessary financial resources to enable it to fulfil its responsibilities under the relevant resolutions of the Security Council,

1. *Takes note* of the status of contributions to the United Nations Iraq-Kuwait Observation Mission as at 30 April 2000, including the contributions outstanding in the amount of 13.8 million United States dollars, representing some 5 per cent of the total assessed contributions from the inception of the Mission to the period ending 30 June 2000, notes that some 4 per cent of the Member States have paid their assessed contributions in full, and urges all other Member States concerned, in particular those in arrears, to ensure the payment of their outstanding assessed contributions;

2. *Expresses its continued appreciation* of the decision of the Government of Kuwait to defray two thirds of the cost of the Observation Mission, effective 1 November 1993;

3. *Expresses its appreciation* to those Member States which have paid their assessed contributions in full;

4. *Expresses concern* about the financial situation with regard to peacekeeping activities, in particular as regards the reimbursements to troop contributors that bear additional burdens owing to overdue payments by Member States of their assessments;

5. *Urges* all other Member States to make every possible effort to ensure payment of their assessed contributions to the Observation Mission in full and on time;

6. *Expresses concern* at the delay experienced by the Secretary-General in deploying and providing adequate resources to some recent peacekeeping missions, in particular those in Africa;

7. *Emphasizes* that all future and existing peacekeeping missions shall be given equal and non-discriminatory treatment in respect of financial and administrative arrangements;

8. *Also emphasizes* that all peacekeeping missions shall be provided with adequate resources for the effective and efficient discharge of their respective mandates;

9. *Requests* the Secretary-General to make the fullest possible use of facilities and equipment at the United Nations Logistics Base at Brindisi, Italy, in order to minimize the costs of procurement for the Observation Mission, and for this purpose requests the Secretary-General to speed up the implementation of the asset management system at all peacekeeping missions in accordance with General Assembly resolution 52/1 A of 15 October 1997;

10. *Endorses* the conclusions and recommendations contained in the report of the Advisory Committee on Administrative and Budgetary Questions, and requests the Secretary-General to ensure their full implementation;

11. *Requests* the Secretary-General to take all necessary action to ensure that the Observation Mission is administered with a maximum of efficiency and economy;

12. *Also requests* the Secretary-General, in order to reduce the cost of employing General Service staff, to continue efforts to recruit local staff for the Observation Mission against General Service posts, commensurate with the requirements of the Mission;

13. *Decides* to appropriate to the Special Account for the United Nations Iraq-Kuwait Observation Mission

the amount of 52,710,270 dollars gross (50,287,503 dollars net) for the maintenance of the Observation Mission for the period from 1 July 2000 to 30 June 2001, inclusive of the amount of 2,501,232 dollars gross (2,116,566 dollars net) for the support account for peacekeeping operations and the amount of 391,038 dollars gross (347,937 dollars net) for the United Nations Logistics Base, a two-thirds share of this amount, equivalent to 33,525,000 dollars, to be funded through voluntary contributions from the Government of Kuwait, subject to the review by the Security Council with regard to the question of termination or continuation of the Mission;

14. *Decides also,* as an ad hoc arrangement, taking into consideration the funding through voluntary contributions from the Government of Kuwait of the two-thirds share of the cost of the Observation Mission, equivalent to 33,525,000 dollars, to apportion among Member States the amount of 19,185,270 dollars gross (16,762,503 dollars net), representing one third of the cost of the maintenance of the Mission for the period from 1 July 2000 to 30 June 2001, the said amount to be apportioned at a monthly rate of 1,598,773 dollars gross (1,396,875 dollars net), in accordance with the composition of groups set out in paragraphs 3 and 4 of General Assembly resolution 43/232 of 1 March 1989, as adjusted by the Assembly in its resolutions 44/192 B of 21 December 1989, 45/269 of 27 August 1991, 46/198 A of 20 December 1991, 47/218 A of 23 December 1992, 49/249 A of 20 July 1995, 49/249 B of 14 September 1995, 50/224 of 11 April 1996, 51/218 A to C of 18 December 1996 and 52/230 of 31 March 1998 and its decisions 48/472 A of 23 December 1993, 50/451 B of 23 December 1995 and 54/456 to 54/458 of 23 December 1999, and taking into account the scale of assessments for the year 2000, as set out in its resolutions 52/215 A of 22 December 1997 and 54/237 A of 23 December 1999, and for the year 2001, subject to the review by the Security Council with regard to the question of termination or continuation of the Mission;

15. *Decides further* that, in accordance with the provisions of its resolution 973(X) of 15 December 1955, there shall be set off against the apportionment among Member States, as provided for in paragraph 14 above, their respective share in the Tax Equalization Fund of the estimated staff assessment income of 2,422,767 dollars approved for the Observation Mission for the period from 1 July 2000 to 30 June 2001;

16. *Decides* that, taking into consideration the funding through voluntary contributions from the Government of Kuwait of the two-thirds share of the cost of the Observation Mission, for Member States that have fulfilled their financial obligations to the Mission, there shall be set off against the apportionment, as provided for in paragraph 14 above, their respective share of the unencumbered balance of 894,967 dollars gross (643,967 dollars net), representing one third of the unencumbered balance of 2,182,900 dollars gross (1,931,900 dollars net) in respect of the period from 1 July 1998 to 30 June 1999;

17. *Decides also* that, for Member States that have not fulfilled their financial obligations to the Observation Mission, their share of the unencumbered balance of 894,967 dollars gross (643,967 dollars net) in respect of the period from 1 July 1998 to 30 June 1999 shall be set off against their outstanding obligations;

18. *Decides further* that two thirds of the net unencumbered balance of 1,931,900 dollars, equivalent to 1,287,933 dollars, shall be returned to the Government of Kuwait;

19. *Emphasizes* that no peacekeeping mission shall be financed by borrowing funds from other active peacekeeping missions;

20. *Encourages* the Secretary-General to continue to take additional measures to ensure the safety and security of all personnel under the auspices of the United Nations participating in the Observation Mission;

21. *Invites* voluntary contributions to the Observation Mission in cash and in the form of services and supplies acceptable to the Secretary-General, to be administered, as appropriate, in accordance with the procedure and practices established by the General Assembly;

22. *Decides* to include in the provisional agenda of its fifty-fifth session, under the item entitled "Financing of the activities arising from Security Council resolution 687(1991)", the sub-item entitled "United Nations Iraq-Kuwait Observation Mission".

At its resumed fifty-fourth session, the Assembly also considered the Secretary-General's report on the results of efforts to recover overpayment of mission subsistence allowance in UNIKOM [A/54/873], submitted in response to resolution 54/18 A [YUN 1999, p. 240], together with the Board of Auditors' report on the special audit of UNIKOM [A/54/869]. On the Fifth Committee's recommendation [A/54/510/Add.1], and having heard the related oral report of ACABQ's Chairman, the Assembly, on 15 June, decided to revert to the question of the payment of mission subsistence allowance in UNIKOM during the main part of its fifty-fifth session (**decision 54/483**).

On 23 December, the Assembly decided that the agenda item on the financing of the activities arising from Security Council resolution 687(1991) would remain for consideration during its resumed fifty-fifth (2001) session (**decision 55/458**) and that the Fifth Committee should continue consideration of the item at that session (**decision 55/455**).

Arms and related sanctions

The Security Council's reviews of the sanctions provisions against Iraq for the purposes of determining whether to reduce or lift the prohibitions against it imposed under resolution 687(1991) [YUN 1991, p. 172] remained suspended in 2000, in accordance with resolution 1194(1998) [YUN 1998, p. 257]. As it later reaffirmed in resolution 1205(1998) [ibid., p. 258], the Council would act in accordance with the relevant provisions of resolution 687(1991) on the duration of the prohibitions referred to in that resolution.

Sanctions Committee activities

The Security Council Committee established by resolution 661(1990) [YUN 1990, p. 192] (Sanctions Committee for Iraq), in its annual report [S/2001/738], described its activities from 21 November 1999 to 30 November 2000. In addition to its implementation activities under Council resolutions 986(1995) [YUN 1995, p. 475] and 1175(1998) [YUN 1998, p. 274] relating to the humanitarian programme for the Iraqi people (see p. 302), the Committee processed 5,257 notifications and applications from States and international organizations to send humanitarian goods to Iraq under resolutions 661(1990) and 687(1991). Some 2,052 of those requests, with an estimated value of $6,494,407,577 were approved; 288, valued at $681,654,599, were placed on hold for further information or clarification; 2,733, valued at $13,157,809,466, were blocked; and 24, valued at $11,926,797, were withdrawn or annulled.

Pursuant to resolution 1284(1999) [YUN 1999, p. 230], the Secretary-General submitted to the Security Council some proposed arrangements concerning financial procedures to facilitate the participation of Iraqi pilgrims in the hajj. Those arrangements were discussed and agreed by the Council, but no agreement was reached with Iraq.

The Committee considered a request from Jordan to authorize regular flights to Baghdad, but was not able to reach a consensus on granting approval. It agreed, however, that it would not refrain from considering ad hoc flights requests separately. The Committee also held a number of consultations at the expert level to discuss proposals by France and the United States on flight-related issues. The Chairman decided that he would continue to circulate communications on flights under the no-objection procedure pending an agreement on new procedures.

With regard to financial matters, the Committee discussed a request from LAS pertaining to the release of frozen funds and decided to gather further information on the matter. It did not reach consensus on an Indian request to establish a line of credit to Iraq. Concerning a request for the release of funds of a Jordanian company, the Committee responded that it was not in a position to agree to the request since investments in Iraq were prohibited, as were the release of frozen Iraqi funds. In connection with the proceeds of illegal Iraqi oil exports that had not been transferred to the UN escrow account under resolution 778(1992) [YUN 1992, p. 320], the Committee sent a letter to all Gulf States reminding them of their responsibilities. The Committee also decided that the UN Treasurer was authorized to open a UN Iraq account in euros, and requested an in-depth report within three months, including the possible costs and benefits for the oil-for-food programme and other financial and administrative implications of the payment for Iraqi oil in euros.

Following a request by Qatar to introduce a ferry service to transport pilgrims, the Committee decided to ask Qatar for further information. It also noted that it was not in a position to approve a request by the United Arab Emirates to transport passenger cars to Iraq. The Committee discussed a report by the independent inspection agents (Cotecna) who had observed that cargo was being transported to Iraq on a United Arab Emirates passenger ferry, and agreed to send a letter to the United Arab Emirates as well as to Bahrain.

The Committee did not grant Turkey's request, first introduced in 1996, to resume the import of petroleum and petroleum products from Iraq for domestic purposes. At an inter-agency meeting (New York, October), UN agencies briefed the Committee on their activities in Iraq. The Committee agreed in principle to the 2000 aerial pesticide campaign of FAO, provided the campaign complied with procedures established for that purpose and the related dual-use items to be shipped to Iraq were submitted for the Committee's consideration on a case-by-case basis.

In addition, the Committee considered a communication from the United States concerning alleged illicit export of petroleum and petroleum-derived products by Iraq through the Persian Gulf. However, no consensus emerged on how to proceed with the issue. It also decided to keep the issue of oil smuggling under review after it had received notification, by the Coordinator of the Multinational Interception Force, that there had been an increase in smuggling activities in the Gulf region during the previous year. The Committee sent letters to the Gulf States, soliciting their assistance in the prevention of further smuggling activities. After receiving a briefing from the OIP Executive Director on monitoring arrangements under the oil-for-food programme, the Committee stressed the need to improve those arrangements and called for a qualitative and quantitative increase in monitoring in the hope that such action would help reduce the number of holds placed on humanitarian supplies to Iraq.

During the year, the Committee issued four reports on the implementation of the arms and related sanctions against Iraq, in accordance with the guidelines approved by Council resolution 700(1991) [YUN 1991, p. 198] for facilitating full international implementation of resolution 687 (1991). The reports were transmitted to the

Council on 31 January [S/2000/72], 28 April [S/2000/365], 27 July [S/2000/748] and 25 October [S/2000/1033]. Each report indicated that no State had brought to the Committee's attention any information relating to possible violations of the arms and related sanctions against Iraq committed by other States or foreign nationals; no State or international organization had consulted the Committee on whether certain items fell within the provisions of paragraph 24 of resolution 687(1991), or on cases relating to dual-use or multiple-use items; and no international organization had reported any relevant information requested under the guidelines.

Oil-for-food programme

Pursuant to Security Council resolution 1284(1999) [YUN 1999, p. 230], the Secretary-General reported in January and March on the implementation of certain provisions of that resolution, which dealt with, among other things, the sale and export of petroleum and petroleum products by Iraq.

In accordance with Council resolutions 1281(1999) [YUN 1999, p. 250] and 1302(2000) (see p. 307), each extending for a 180-day period the provisions of resolution 986(1995) [YUN 1995, p. 475], which authorized States to import Iraqi petroleum and petroleum products as a temporary measure to finance a humanitarian programme to alleviate the adverse consequence of the sanctions regime on the Iraqi people (also known as the oil-for-food programme) [YUN 1996, p. 225], the Secretary-General and the Sanctions Committee for Iraq separately submitted a report 90 days after entry into force of each resolution and again before the end of the next 90 days. The 180-day periods under the first and second resolutions were extended, respectively, from 12 December 1999 to 8 June 2000 (phase VII) and from 9 June to 5 December (phase VIII).

The reports described progress in implementing the arrangements specified by the resolutions, taking account of the provisions of the 1996 Memorandum of Understanding between the UN Secretariat and the Government of Iraq [YUN 1996, p. 226] and the procedures established by the Sanctions Committee for the resolutions' implementation [ibid., p. 228]. They also described the distribution of humanitarian relief, on behalf of the Government, in the three northern governorates of Erbil, Dahuk and Sulaymaniyah under the United Nations Inter-Agency Humanitarian Programme, to complement government distribution in central and southern Iraq, thereby ensuring equitable distribution to all segments of the Iraqi population.

The provisions of resolution 986(1995) were extended for a further 180-day period beginning on 6 December by resolution 1330(2000) (see p. 310), inaugurating phase IX of the programme.

Report of Secretary-General (January). In response to resolution 1284(1999), the Secretary-General reported on the implementation of certain provisions of that resolution [S/2000/22]. In particular, he reviewed the sale and export of petroleum and petroleum products by Iraq; the UN accounts pertaining to the Iraq programme; the processing and approval of applications for contracts; observation and monitoring mechanisms; steps taken to maximize the effectiveness of the arrangements set out in resolution 986(1995); and progress on meeting the humanitarian needs of the Iraqi population.

Due to the numerous reports on the implementation of the humanitarian programme in Iraq that were being submitted to the Council and its Sanctions Committee within short time frames, the Secretary-General recommended a review in order to rationalize the number of reports. Accordingly, taking into account the number and schedule of the reports requested by resolution 1284(1999), the Secretary-General proposed to consolidate a number of reporting requirements under that resolution into one report to be submitted on 10 March.

On 28 January [S/2000/64], the Security Council endorsed the Secretary-General's proposal.

Hajj

Pursuant to resolution 1284(1999), the Secretary-General, in a 24 February letter to the Security Council President [S/2000/166], proposed arrangements to provide for reasonable expenses related to the hajj to be met by funds in the escrow account established by resolution 986(1995). According to Iraq, under the quota for the hajj established by OIC, the total number of pilgrims was 24,700. As Iraq indicated that $2,000 was required per pilgrim, the total amount needed to cover the hajj for Iraq would be $49.4 million. On 1 March [S/2000/167], the Council authorized the Secretary-General to proceed with the arrangements outlined in his letter.

By a 2 March letter to the Council President [S/2000/175], the Secretary-General submitted copies of correspondence between the OIP Executive Director and the Permanent Representative of Iraq to the United Nations pertaining to the hajj. Iraq said that the response to its request came after a considerable delay and there was no longer any time to study any proposal. The pilgrimage season had in fact already begun, and the few Iraqi pilgrims with material means had already arrived at the Holy Place in Saudi Arabia.

Programme review

On 10 March [S/2000/208], the Secretary-General reported to the Security Council on progress made in meeting the humanitarian needs of the Iraqi people and on the revenues necessary to meet those needs, including recommendations on necessary additions to the allocations for oil spare parts and equipment, on the basis of a comprehensive survey of the condition of the Iraqi oil production sector. In preparing the report, OIP undertook an inter-agency review of the humanitarian programme established by Council resolution 986(1995) [YUN 1995, p. 475]. It also reviewed the system of contracting, application processing, obtaining approval by the Sanctions Committee, procurement and shipment, as well as the timely distribution of humanitarian supplies within Iraq—a complex, interdependent chain of activities involving the Sanctions Committee, the Government of Iraq and other Member States, the UN Secretariat and the agencies and programmes concerned, as well as private firms and financial institutions. In addition, the report examined the extent to which the recommendations contained in the Secretary-General's 1998 supplementary report [YUN 1998, p. 270] had been implemented. It also identified additional measures aimed at increasing the effectiveness of the programme, with a view to achieving substantial improvement in both the health and nutritional status of the population and to address the deterioration of the social services infrastructure.

The six-part report also included the results of a comprehensive survey by a group of experts on Iraq's existing oil production and export capacity (see p. 304), as requested in Council resolution 1284(1999), and a 90-day report of phase VII (see p. 305), pursuant to Council resolution 1281 (1999) [YUN 1999, p. 250]. The Council had endorsed the Secretary-General's proposal to consolidate a number of reporting requirements under those resolutions into one report (see p. 302).

The Secretary-General observed that, despite difficulties and shortcomings, the programme had provided substantial assistance in all sectors to address pressing humanitarian needs affecting the lives of the Iraqi people. However, improvements in the humanitarian situation had been below expectations. The effectiveness of the programme had suffered considerably, not only because of shortfalls in the funding level, but also because of the very large number of applications placed on hold, in particular those concerning electricity, water and sanitation, transport and telecommunications, which impacted all sectors. The total value of applications placed on hold as at 31 January 2000 was over $1.5 billion. The Secretary-General said that a determined effort had to be made by all parties to collaborate effectively with a view to making further improvements in the programme's implementation. In that regard, he had directed OIP to review further the information requirements of the Sanctions Committee in respect of applications placed on hold. He also directed OIP to identify ways in which the observation mechanism could more effectively track and enhance observation procedures for items of special interest to the Committee.

The Secretary-General noted that some recommendations contained in his 1998 supplementary report remained to be addressed and called on Iraq to take action in that regard. Furthermore, he recommended that the Sanctions Committee should further improve its procedures with a view to expediting the approval of applications; identify with greater clarity the reasons for which applications had been placed on hold so that OIP could provide all available information to facilitate the lifting of such holds; streamline the processes by which such holds could be lifted; renew its efforts to reach consensus on the proposal submitted by OIP in 1999 to improve the current reimbursement system [YUN 1999, p. 242]; review further the options contained in OIP's 1999 paper concerning payment clauses for the 53 per cent account (the account for the 15 central and southern governorates); and address the difficulties encountered in the appointment of additional oil overseers. The Secretary-General also expressed the hope that the Council would find a way to overcome the impediments that continued to prevent Iraqi pilgrims from performing the hajj.

Allocation for oil-production equipment

Communication from Secretary-General. In response to resolution 1281(1999) [YUN 1999, p. 250], the Secretary-General submitted to the Council on 14 January a detailed list of parts and equipment needed to enable Iraq to increase the export of petroleum and petroleum products [S/2000/26]. An expert from Saybolt Nederland BV visited Iraq from 15 to 21 December 1999 to review the situation on the ground and, in consultation with the Government, to prepare the list of spare parts and equipment.

The Secretary-General noted that there had been continuing deterioration of the oil facilities in Iraq, which had been adversely affecting the safety of workers in the oil fields and causing serious environmental damage, as well as damaging oil wells. The deterioration could also cause a breakdown in Iraq's oil production and export capacity, which would have serious repercussions on the implementation of the humanitarian programme. Accordingly, he reiterated his October 1999 recommendation [YUN 1999, p. 248] that the Council approve Iraq's request to increase by $300 million the allocation for oil spare parts and equipment, bringing the total allocation to $600 million under phase VI. The Secretary-General also noted that the funds for such an increase were available.

For phase VII, Iraq had proposed an allocation of $600 million for oil spare parts and equipment, which was twice the amount approved by the Council in resolution 1281(1999). According to the Saybolt expert, the proposed allocation was a reasonable one. The Secretary-General would keep the matter under review and await the report of the group of six experts that he was dispatching to Iraq from 16 to 31 January to survey the conditions of the Iraqi oil production sector.

Report of Secretary-General (March). As requested in Security Council resolution 1284 (1999), the Secretary-General formed a six-member group of experts, including oil industry experts, to report on Iraq's existing petroleum production and export capacity and on the options for involving foreign oil companies in Iraq's oil sector, including investments. On 10 March, the Secretary-General submitted a report on the group's findings and made recommendations to the Council on necessary additions to the allocation for oil spare parts and equipment [S/2000/208]. The report also reviewed humanitarian needs (see p. 303).

The group, which visited Iraq from 16 to 31 January, said that the Iraqi oil industry continued to be in a lamentable state. It was apparent that the decline in the condition of all sectors of the industry continued, and was accelerating in some cases. That trend would continue, and the ability of the Iraqi oil industry to sustain the current reduced production levels would be seriously compromised unless effective action was taken immediately to reverse the situation. Exports had declined from the 2.2 million barrels per day achieved in phase VI and would probably be sustained at a level of only 1.9 million barrels per day in phase VII. The group of experts estimated that a further production (and therefore export) decline of 5 to 15 per cent would occur unless the delivery of spare parts and equipment was accelerated, and that the spare parts and equipment that had arrived were insufficient to sustain production. The value of investment required to repair the Iraqi oil industry was much greater than the value of investments discussed

under phases IV to VII, and would inevitably increase if essential repairs and maintenance were further delayed.

Taking into account the production required for local consumption needs from 1991 to 1996 and production since 1996 under the humanitarian programme, the Iraqi oil industry had produced some 5,000 million barrels of oil with virtually no investment in infrastructure repairs or maintenance. The result had been a massive decline in the condition, effectiveness and efficiency of that infrastructure, coupled with appalling safety conditions and significant environmental damage. In the ensuing period, oil-bearing structures in Iraq had suffered short-term damage, which was considered to be reparable, subject to the expeditious arrival of the necessary spare parts and equipment. Increasingly, however, damage to those structures had become more long-term in nature, resulting in irreversible damage to oilfields and the permanent loss of production and export capacity. Since the initiation of the oil spare parts and equipment programme in phase IV (at a level based on the need to maximize the funds for the humanitarian programme), the price of oil had more than doubled. The increase in income could therefore continue to support the current level of humanitarian programmes, or indeed an increased level, while concurrently allowing a greater allocation for spare parts and equipment, which was needed to support the export of crude oil on which the humanitarian programme depended. In the view of the expert group, it was a logical investment, especially given the volatility of oil prices. At the very least, therefore, the allocation of funds under phases VI and VII at the level of $600 million per phase was urgently required if production levels were to be sustained at, or even near, current levels and in order to offset permanent damage to oil-bearing structures in Iraq.

The Secretary-General recommended that the Security Council approve his 14 January request (see p. 303) to increase the allocations for phases VI and VII to $600 million each. Raising the level of allocations alone was not sufficient, however. A special effort had to be made to approve most expeditiously the applications for oil spare parts and equipment. The total value of applications placed on hold as at 31 January 2000 was $291 million, more than half of the total of $506 million approved.

Security Council consideration. The Security Council, on 24 March, discussed the situation between Iraq and Kuwait [meeting 4120]. Reporting on the humanitarian programme, the Secretary-General said that the rise in the price of oil had greatly increased the value of oil exports, with the result that a much larger income was available for the programme. However, Iraq's oil industry was hampered by a lack of spare parts and equipment. He had therefore recommended a significant increase in the allocation of resources for the purchase of spare parts. He also noted that many of the holds on contract applications imposed by the Sanctions Committee had a negative impact on the programme and on efforts to rehabilitate Iraq's infrastructure. Consequently, there was a need for a mechanism to review those holds. The Secretary-General observed that the humanitarian situation in Iraq posed a serious moral dilemma for the United Nations, which was in danger of losing the argument about who was responsible for the situation: President Saddam Hussein or the United Nations. Even if the oil-for-food programme was implemented perfectly, it might still prove insufficient to satisfy the population's needs.

The Russian Federation said that a significant improvement in the humanitarian and socioeconomic situation was impossible under the sanctions regime. The solution was to suspend sanctions in conjunction with a resumption of disarmament monitoring.

The United States insisted that sanctions were essential as long as there remained unanswered questions about Iraq's nuclear, chemical and biological weapons and the missiles to deliver them. The oil-for-food programme would never supplant the responsibilities of the Government of Iraq to provide for the needs of its people.

SECURITY COUNCIL ACTION

On 31 March [meeting 4123], the Security Council unanimously adopted **resolution 1293(2000)**. The draft [S/2000/266] was prepared in consultations among Council members.

The Security Council,
Recalling its relevant resolutions, in particular resolutions 986(1995) of 14 April 1995, 1111(1997) of 4 June 1997, 1129(1997) of 12 September 1997, 1143(1997) of 4 December 1997, 1153(1998) of 20 February 1998, 1175(1998) of 19 June 1998, 1210(1998) of 24 November 1998, 1242(1999) of 21 May 1999, 1266(1999) of 4 October 1999, 1275(1999) of 19 November 1999, 1280(1999) of 3 December 1999, 1281(1999) of 10 December 1999, and 1284(1999) of 17 December 1999,
Welcoming the report of the Secretary-General of 10 March 2000, in particular his recommendation on additions to the current allocation for oil spare parts and equipment pursuant to paragraph 28 of resolution 1284(1999),
Acting under Chapter VII of the Charter of the United Nations,
1. *Decides,* pursuant to paragraphs 28 and 29 of resolution 1284(1999), that from the funds in the escrow account produced pursuant to resolutions 1242(1999) and 1281(1999) up to a total of 600 million

United States dollars may be used to meet any reasonable expenses, other than expenses payable in Iraq, that follow directly from the contracts approved in accordance with paragraph 2 of resolution 1175(1998), and expresses its intention to consider favourably the renewal of this provision;
2. *Expresses its willingness* to consider expeditiously other recommendations contained in the report of the Secretary-General of 10 March 2000, and the provisions of section C of resolution 1284(1999);
3. *Decides* to remain seized of the matter.

Phase VII

On 12 January [S/2000/18], the Secretary-General informed the Security Council that he had approved the distribution plan for the purchase of humanitarian supplies during phase VII. The plan, submitted by Iraq, proposed spending over $3.5 billion dollars on food, medicine, education and infrastructure and included $600 million on oil industry spare parts and equipment. Approval was given on the understanding that the implementation would be governed by Council resolutions 986(1995) [YUN 1995, p. 475], 1281(1999) [YUN 1999, p. 250] and 1284(1999) [ibid., p. 230] and the 1996 Memorandum of Understanding between the UN Secretariat and Iraq [YUN 1996, p. 226], and would be without prejudice to the Sanctions Committee procedures.

By a 12 June letter [S/2000/565], the Secretary-General informed the Council President that he had approved the proposals made by Iraq for the inclusion of a housing sector as part IX of the distribution plans for phases VI and VII.

Reports of Secretary-General (March and June). Pursuant to resolution 1281(1999), the Secretary-General issued two progress reports covering the two 90-day periods under phase VII, which began on 12 December 1999. The reports, issued on 10 March (see p. 304) and 1 June [S/2000/520], provided information on all implementation aspects up to 31 January and 30 April, respectively.

Both reports reviewed revenue generation and status of the oil industry; monitoring activities; and the effectiveness, equitability and adequacy of the programme implementation in central and southern Iraq, as well as in the three northern governorates of Dahuk, Erbil and Sulaymaniyah, by focusing on food, health, agriculture, water and sanitation, education, electricity and telecommunications investments and projects.

In his March report, the Secretary-General recommended a series of actions for Iraq and the Sanctions Committee. He also recommended to the Council that it consider forgoing the requirement for a 90-day report on the implementation of the programme, given the amount of weekly and monthly status reports submitted to the Sanctions Committee and the Council.

In his June report, the Secretary-General welcomed steps taken by Iraq in requesting increased food basket items, and noted that it was essential that applications for contracts relating to distribution systems be approved by the Sanctions Committee most expeditiously. Also, the contracts aimed at the rehabilitation of the infrastructure in the electricity, water and sanitation sectors had to be approved without delay. In addition, he recommended that Iraq should increase the level of resources allocated to the education sector. The Secretary-General welcomed ongoing efforts by the Sanctions Committee to improve its procedures and define more specifically its information requirements, which had allowed for a significant number of contracts previously on hold to be approved.

The Secretary-General noted that the Sanctions Committee, as called for in resolution 1284(1999), had endorsed the appointment of a group of experts to approve speedily contracts for oil spare parts and equipment, according to lists of parts and equipment approved by the Committee for each individual project. He urged the Committee to approve most expeditiously the lists of oil spare parts and equipment to be submitted by OIP to the Committee for approval in the first week of June, in order to allow the group of experts to start its work as soon as possible. He also noted that the number of applications on hold remained excessive; as at 31 May 2000 they had reached 582, with a total value of $341 million. The Secretary-General recommended that the Council consider adding a further $300 million to the allocation for oil spare parts and equipment for phase VIII, following the $300 million allocation for phases VI and VII by resolution 1293(2000) (see p. 305). He also recommended that the Council consider authorizing the Committee to review and approve OIP requests for the use of funds in excess of requirements in earlier phases to fund humanitarian requirements under subsequent phases, in order to achieve greater utilization of available resources. The Secretary-General expressed concern over the restrictive practices imposed by Iraq on the allocation of travel permits and escorts, which had affected the unrestricted freedom of movement of UN observers. He requested Iraq to make the necessary adjustments.

The total amount of funds made available for the implementation and operation of the programme from December 1996 to 30 April 2000 was $16.676 billion. The total value of supplies that had been delivered to Iraq was $8.071 billion—including over 14 million of tons of food

basket items valued at $4.8 billion and health supplies worth just under $900 million. Additional approved supplies with a total value of $2.7 billion were awaiting delivery. Annex I to the report, which gave the status of the UN Iraq Account established under resolution 986(1995), recorded that, by 30 April, $4,606.1 million had been deposited into the account for phase VII, bringing the total oil sale since the inception of the programme to $25,341.9 million.

Communication from Secretary-General. On 30 June [S/2000/645], the Secretary-General informed the Council that, although phases I and II of the humanitarian programme were closed, $5.1 million and $2 million, respectively, remained available for the purchase of humanitarian supplies. Those funds could address phases IV and V, for which there was a revenue shortfall of $0.5 billion. Accordingly, he requested to know whether the Council would consider authorizing the Sanctions Committee to review and approve OIP requests for the use of funds in excess of requirements in earlier phases to fund humanitarian supplies under subsequent phases, as he had recommended in his June report (see above).

On 10 July [S/2000/663], the Council informed the Secretary-General that it concurred with his recommendation.

Communication. Commenting on the Secretary-General's June report, Iraq, in a 9 July letter [S/2000/668], said that it lacked, among other things, an objective approach to evaluating the repercussions of the implementation of the oil-for-food programme on the humanitarian situation in Iraq. It also ignored the cumulative impact of the sanctions on all the economic, social, cultural, educational and even psychological aspects of life for the Iraqi people.

Sanctions Committee reports (March and June). The Sanctions Committee reports for the first and second 90-day periods of phase VII were transmitted to the Council on 22 March [S/2000/242] and 5 June [S/2000/536], respectively. They noted that the export of petroleum from Iraq had proceeded smoothly, with excellent cooperation among the oil overseer, the independent inspection agents (contracted through Saybolt Nederland BV), Iraq's State Oil Marketing Organization and the national oil purchasers. The overseer continued to advise the Committee on oil pricing mechanisms, oil contract approval and modification, management of the revenue objective and other pertinent questions related to export and monitoring. The overseer also continued to work closely with the Saybolt inspection agents to ensure the effective monitoring of the relevant oil installations and oil liftings. For the fourth consecutive year, the overseer and the inspection agents had received Iraq's full cooperation. The reports noted that, since 1 July 1999, there had been only one oil overseer and that the Committee was committed to finding a viable solution to that matter as soon as possible.

Applications received as at 31 May for the export of humanitarian supplies to Iraq totalled 1,853. Of the 1,620 circulated to the Committee, 1,215 were found eligible for payment from the UN Iraq Account, in the amount of approximately $2.24 billion. Consignments of humanitarian supplies from previous phases confirmed as having arrived in Iraq in total or in partial shipments totalled 4,360 in the first half of phase VII and 5,621 in the second half.

Since the Council's authorization for export to Iraq of oil-production parts and equipment by resolution 1175(1998) [YUN 1998, p. 274] up to 31 May 2000, the number of applications to ship such items had reached 2,526, with a value of $1,378.3 million. Of those, 199 were returned for clarification, 69 were cancelled, 8 were under review by customs experts and 2,184 were circulated to the Committee. Of the latter, 1,651, valued at $832.9 million, were approved; 517, valued at $315.6 million, were placed on hold; and 16 were pending under the no-objection procedure. As at 25 May, 627 full or partial shipments of parts and equipment, worth $287.2 million, had arrived in Iraq.

Issues considered by the Committee included the humanitarian situation in Iraq, the monitoring undertaken by Saybolt and the UN observation mechanism, as well as the matter of applications placed on hold. It also received briefings from representatives of WHO, FAO, the UN Compensation Commission and the UN Department of Management. An appendix to the June report detailed the procedures to be employed for the implementation of paragraph 18 of resolution 1284(1999), which called for the appointment of a group of experts, including independent inspection agents appointed by the Secretary-General, to approve contracts for the parts and equipment necessary to enable Iraq to increase its exports of petroleum and petroleum products.

Communications. A number of communications on various subjects were received from Iraq during phase VII. In letters between 4 January and 28 April [S/2000/2, S/2000/35, S/2000/142, S/2000/360], Iraq alleged that the United States, with United Kingdom support, was obstructing implementation of the 1996 Memorandum of Understanding and the oil-for-food programme by using a number of illegal stratagems, including abuse of its membership of the Sanctions Committee, thus placing on hold contracts for the export to Iraq of humanitarian goods.

In letters addressed to the Security Council President, dated 5 January [S/2000/7] and 10 April [S/2000/302], Iraq, in order to meet the payment of the arrears in its contribution to international organizations, requested the Council to approve the allocation of $24 million from the Iraq Account, and specifically the 53 per cent and 13 per cent (for the three northern governorates) accounts, and/or from the 2.2 per cent account allocated to the administrative and operational expenses of the Iraq programme.

By a 22 May letter to the Secretary-General [S/2000/467], Iraq requested that the sum of $10 million be allocated for the purchase of equipment for the printing of Iraqi currency under the procurement and distribution plans for phases V, VI and VII, and noted that the UN Secretariat was continuing to ignore that request.

SECURITY COUNCIL ACTION

On 8 June [meeting 4152], the Security Council unanimously adopted **resolution 1302(2000)**. The draft [S/2000/544] was submitted by France and the United Kingdom.

The Security Council,

Recalling its relevant resolutions, in particular resolutions 986(1995) of 14 April 1995, 1111(1997) of 4 June 1997, 1129(1997) of 12 September 1997, 1143(1997) of 4 December 1997, 1153(1998) of 20 February 1998, 1175(1998) of 19 June 1998, 1210(1998) of 24 November 1998, 1242(1999) of 21 May 1999, 1266(1999) of 4 October 1999, 1275(1999) of 19 November 1999, 1280(1999) of 3 December 1999, 1281(1999) of 10 December 1999, 1284(1999) of 17 December 1999 and 1293(2000) of 31 March 2000,

Convinced of the need as a temporary measure to continue to provide for the humanitarian needs of the Iraqi people until the fulfilment by the Government of Iraq of the relevant resolutions, including notably resolution 687(1991) of 3 April 1991, allows the Council to take further action with regard to the prohibitions referred to in resolution 661(1990) of 6 August 1990, in accordance with the provisions of those resolutions,

Convinced also of the need for equitable distribution of humanitarian supplies to all segments of the Iraqi population throughout the country,

Determined to improve the humanitarian situation in Iraq,

Reaffirming the commitment of all Member States to the sovereignty and territorial integrity of Iraq,

Acting under Chapter VII of the Charter of the United Nations,

1. *Decides* that the provisions of resolution 986 (1995), except those contained in paragraphs 4, 11 and 12 and subject to paragraph 15 of resolution 1284 (1999), shall remain in force for a new period of 180 days beginning at 0001 hours eastern daylight time on 9 June 2000;

2. *Decides also* that from the sum produced from the import by States of petroleum and petroleum products

originating in Iraq, including financial and other essential transactions related thereto, in the 180-day period referred to in paragraph 1 above, the amounts recommended by the Secretary-General in his report of 1 February 1998 for the food/nutrition and health sectors should continue to be allocated on a priority basis in the context of the activities of the Secretariat, of which 13 per cent of the sum produced in the period referred to above shall be used for the purposes referred to in paragraph 8 *(b)* of resolution 986(1995);

3. *Requests* the Secretary-General to continue to take the actions necessary to ensure the effective and efficient implementation of the present resolution, and to continue to enhance as necessary the United Nations observation process in Iraq in such a way as to provide the required assurances to the Council that the goods produced in accordance with this resolution are distributed equitably and that all supplies authorized for procurement, including dual usage items and spare parts, are utilized for the purpose for which they have been authorized;

4. *Decides* to conduct a thorough review of all aspects of the implementation of the present resolution 90 days after the entry into force of paragraph 1 above and again prior to the end of the 180-day period, and expresses its intention, prior to the end of that period, to consider favourably renewal of the provisions of the present resolution as appropriate, provided that the reviews indicate that those provisions are being satisfactorily implemented;

5. *Requests* the Secretary-General to report to the Council 90 days after the entry into force of the present resolution on its implementation, and further requests the Secretary-General to report prior to the end of the 180-day period, on the basis of observations of United Nations personnel in Iraq, and of consultations with the Government of Iraq, on whether Iraq has ensured the equitable distribution of medicine, health supplies, foodstuffs, and materials and supplies for essential civilian needs, financed in accordance with paragraph 8 *(a)* of resolution 986(1995), including in his briefing and report any observations he may have on the adequacy of the revenues to meet the humanitarian needs of Iraq;

6. *Requests* the Security Council Committee established by resolution 661(1990), in close coordination with the Secretary-General, to report to the Council after the entry into force of paragraph 1 above and prior to the end of the 180-day period on the implementation of the arrangements in paragraphs 1, 2, 6, 8, 9 and 10 of resolution 986(1995);

7. *Requests* the Secretary-General to appoint, in consultation with the Committee established by resolution 661(1990), no later than 10 August 2000, the additional overseers necessary to approve petroleum and petroleum product export contracts in accordance with paragraph 1 of resolution 986(1995) and the procedures of the Committee established by resolution 661(1990);

8. *Requests* the Committee established by resolution 661(1990) to approve, after 30 days, on the basis of proposals from the Secretary-General, lists of basic water and sanitation supplies, decides, notwithstanding paragraph 3 of resolution 661(1990) and paragraph 20 of resolution 687(1991), that supplies of these items will not be submitted for approval of that Committee, except for items subject to the provisions of resolution 1051(1996) of 27 March 1996, and will be notified to the Secretary-General and financed in accordance with the provisions of paragraphs 8 *(a)* and 8 *(b)* of resolution 986(1995), and requests the Secretary-General to inform the Committee in a timely manner of all such notifications received and actions taken;

9. *Decides* that from the funds produced pursuant to the present resolution in the escrow account established by paragraph 7 of resolution 986(1995), up to a total of 600 million United States dollars may be used to meet any reasonable expenses, other than expenses payable in Iraq, that follow directly from the contracts approved in accordance with paragraph 2 of resolution 1175(1998) and paragraph 18 of resolution 1284(1999), and expresses its intention to consider favourably the renewal of this measure;

10. *Decides also* that the funds in the escrow account resulting from the suspension in accordance with paragraph 20 of resolution 1284(1999) shall be used for the purposes set out in paragraph 8 *(a)* of resolution 986(1995), and decides further that paragraph 20 of resolution 1284(1999) shall remain in force and shall apply to the new 180-day period referred to in paragraph 1 above and shall not be subject to further renewal;

11. *Welcomes* the efforts of the Committee established by resolution 661(1990) to review applications expeditiously, and encourages the Committee to make further efforts in that regard;

12. *Calls upon* the Government of Iraq to take all additional steps necessary to implement paragraph 27 of resolution 1284(1999), and further requests the Secretary-General regularly to review and report on the implementation of these measures;

13. *Requests* the Secretary-General to submit to the Committee established by resolution 661(1990) recommendations regarding the implementation of paragraphs 1 *(a)* and 6 of resolution 986(1995) to minimize the delay in the payment of the full amount of each purchase of Iraqi petroleum and petroleum products into the escrow account established by paragraph 7 of resolution 986(1995);

14. *Also requests* the Secretary-General to submit to the Committee established by resolution 661(1990) recommendations regarding the utilization of excess funds drawn from the account created by paragraph 8 *(d)* of resolution 986(1995), in particular for the purposes set out in paragraphs 8 *(a)* and 8 *(b)* of that resolution;

15. *Urges* all States, and in particular the Government of Iraq, to provide their full cooperation in the effective implementation of the present resolution;

16. *Appeals* to all States to continue to cooperate in the timely submission of applications and the expeditious issue of export licences, facilitating the transit of humanitarian supplies authorized by the Committee established by resolution 661(1990), and to take all other appropriate measures within their competence in order to ensure that urgently needed humanitarian supplies reach the Iraqi people as rapidly as possible;

17. *Stresses* the need to continue to ensure respect for the security and safety of all persons directly involved in the implementation of the present resolution in Iraq;

18. *Invites* the Secretary-General to appoint independent experts to prepare by 26 November 2000 a comprehensive report and analysis of the humanitarian situation in Iraq, including the current humanitarian needs arising from that situation and recommendations to meet those needs, within the framework of the existing resolutions;

19. *Decides* to remain seized of the matter.

The Secretary-General transmitted to the Council a 21 June exchange of letters [S/2000/618] between the UN Secretariat and Iraq extending, in the light of resolution 1302(2000), the provisions of the 1996 Memorandum of Understanding between them on the implementation of resolution 986(1995) for a new 180-day period.

On 10 August [S/2000/790], the Secretary-General informed the Council that he had appointed Michel Tellings (Netherlands) and Morten Buur-Jensen (Denmark) as oil overseers for the United Nations.

Phase VIII

Pursuant to paragraph 1 of Council resolution 1302(2000), the new 180-day extension (phase VIII) of the humanitarian programme established by resolution 986(1995) began on 9 June. The corresponding distribution plan was approved by the Secretary-General on 25 July [S/2000/733], on the understanding that its implementation would be governed by resolutions 986(1995), 1284(1999) and 1302(2000) and the 1996 Memorandum of Understanding between the UN Secretariat and Iraq, and without prejudice to Sanctions Committee procedures. The accompanying list of supplies and goods was made available to that Committee, which concluded that, based on the information provided in the annexes, no prohibited items could be identified.

Report of Secretary-General (September). On 8 September [S/2000/857], the Secretary-General submitted to the Security Council a report on the first 90-day period of phase VIII.

He observed that in many sectors, infrastructure remained heavily incapacitated despite the ordering by Iraq of essential inputs. Complementary items had been kept on hold long after the central items with which they were intended to be used had been delivered. That situation rendered the distribution of humanitarian aid and the amelioration of the overall situation more difficult and placed an additional strain on the already burdened population by delaying the arrival and use of many key supplies and equipment essential to all sectors. Despite commendable efforts to bring about a reduction in the number of contracts on hold, 647 contracts for humanitarian supplies, worth $1.5 billion, and 504 contracts for oil and spare parts, worth

$279 million, remained on hold as at 28 August. While the programme allowed for the importation of goods for infrastructure repair, it did not allow for financial investments in infrastructural rehabilitation projects. Hence, the impact of the imported goods under resolution 986(1995) was limited.

The Secretary-General welcomed measures taken by the Council to improve procedures to expedite notification of applications in the agriculture, food, nutrition, health, education, and water and sanitation sectors, as well as approval of contracts for oil and spare parts. He urged the expansion and extension of the lists and procedures involved to all remaining sectors in the distribution plan. A decision by the Sanctions Committee on the use of $52 million in unencumbered funds, available for alternative allocation, would be of significant assistance. He also welcomed the increases by Iraq in the allocation of funds in the distribution plan for food and health. The safety and security of UN personnel serving in Iraq was also of primary concern to the Secretary-General. He expressed deep concern at the killing of two FAO staff members and the injuring of eight others, including four UN staff, within the premises of the FAO office in Baghdad.

Communication from Secretary-General. On 3 October [S/2000/950], the Secretary-General expressed his concern that the total value of holds placed on applications for contracts submitted under the humanitarian programme exceeded $2 billion as at 27 September, involving a total of 1,204 applications. Furthermore, the list of oil spare parts and equipment related to phase VIII projects and the list of additional items for the agriculture sector, which were submitted by the UN Secretariat for approval to the Sanctions Committee on 8 August and 8 September, respectively, had been placed on hold. The Secretariat had also received an excessive number of applications that were either incomplete or awaiting additional technical information from the suppliers.

Report of Secretary-General (November). In a 29 November report on the second 90-day period of phase VIII [S/2000/1132], the Secretary-General gave an account of implementation activities up to 31 October. He stated that a total of $22.7 billion had been made available for the implementation of the programme—$18.7 billion for the centre and south and $4.4 billion for the three governorates, Dahuk, Erbil and Sulaymaniyah, where the United Nations implemented the programme on behalf of Iraq. Of the $16.22 billion worth of applications for contracts approved for the centre and south, supplies with a total value of $8.834 billion had been delivered. Additional quantities of supplies under approved applications, with an estimated value of $7.386 billion, were in the production and delivery pipeline.

Although locally produced food items had become increasingly available throughout the country, most Iraqis did not have the necessary purchasing power to buy them. The monthly food rations represented the largest proportion of their household income and, thus, they were obliged to either barter or sell items from the food basket in order to meet other essential needs. That was one of the factors that partly explained why the nutritional situation had not improved in line with the enhanced food basket. Moreover, the absence of normal economic activity had given rise to deep-seated poverty. The Secretary-General urged the Government of Iraq to ensure the distribution of the full food ration and to respond to the needs of internally displaced persons, particularly in the three northern governorates. Consideration could also be given to including in the next distribution plan provision of supplies in support of activities to meet the more specific needs of the poorest among the poor within the population.

The Secretary-General said that, with increasing funding for the humanitarian component of the programme, the time had come to review the validity of applying procedures and practices originally designed to cover food and medicine to a vastly more complex array of infrastructure and equipment. He had therefore directed the OIP Executive Director to initiate consultations with the Sanctions Committee in order to streamline and improve procedures governing the submission, processing and approval of applications. Despite all commendable efforts made, the volume of holds placed on applications had risen to $2.31 billion as at 31 October. That was one of the major factors impeding programme delivery in the centre and south. The Secretary-General also expressed concern regarding the large volume of incomplete or non-compliant applications submitted to the Secretariat, totalling over $850 million, which could not be processed until receipt of the information requested either from the suppliers or Iraq. In addition, he appealed to Iraq to expedite its contracting procedures and to ensure the timely submission of applications by its suppliers. He noted with concern that the project-based list of phase VIII oil spare parts and equipment submitted by the Secretariat to the Sanctions Committee on 8 August had remained on hold. Moreover, the absence of an appropriate cash component had increasingly hampered the implementation of the programme. The Secretary-General had directed the OIP Ex-

ecutive Director, together with the UN Humanitarian Coordinator for Iraq, to intensify efforts towards finding an appropriate mechanism acceptable to all concerned. He also appealed to the Council to direct its Sanctions Committee to review its work and procedures in order to avoid inordinate delays in resolving matters brought to its attention for action.

Communications. During phase VIII, a number of communications on various subjects were received from Iraq. In letters to the Secretary-General dated between 11 June and 7 November [S/2000/563, S/2000/1048, S/2000/1073], Iraq alleged that the United Kingdom and the United States, among other things, were obstructing the implementation of the oil-for-food programme and placing on hold contracts for the export to Iraq of humanitarian goods.

On 6 August [S/2000/781], Iraq noted that there had been no agreement among Security Council members on Iraq's proposal for paying its arrears in contributions to international organizations (see p. 307). The lack of agreement was due to United States opposition to the proposal.

On 7 August [S/2000/780], Iraq transmitted to the Council President the text of a resolution adopted on 7 June by the Council of Arab Economic Unity (Egypt, Iraq, Jordan, Libyan Arab Jamahiriya, Palestine, Sudan, Syrian Arab Republic and Yemen) at its seventy-first session in Cairo. The Council called for the lifting of the embargo imposed on Iraq, affirmed its rejection of the no-flight zones imposed on parts of Iraq, condemned military incursions into Iraq's territory and urged the Arab States to expand their trade with Iraq.

Phase IX

On 5 December [meeting 4241], the Security Council unanimously adopted **resolution 1330 (2000)**. The draft [S/2000/1149] was submitted by the United Kingdom.

The Security Council,

Recalling its relevant resolutions, in particular resolutions 986(1995) of 14 April 1995, 1111(1997) of 4 June 1997, 1129(1997) of 12 September 1997, 1143(1997) of 4 December 1997, 1153(1998) of 20 February 1998, 1175(1998) of 19 June 1998, 1210(1998) of 24 November 1998, 1242(1999) of 21 May 1999, 1266(1999) of 4 October 1999, 1275(1999) of 19 November 1999, 1280(1999) of 3 December 1999, 1281(1999) of 10 December 1999, 1284(1999) of 17 December 1999, 1293(2000) of 31 March 2000 and 1302(2000) of 8 June 2000,

Convinced of the need as a temporary measure to continue to provide for the humanitarian needs of the Iraqi people until the fulfilment by the Government of Iraq of the relevant resolutions, including notably resolution 687(1991) of 3 April 1991, allows the Council to take further action with regard to the prohibitions referred to in resolution 661(1990) of 6 August 1990, in accordance with the provisions of those resolutions,

Convinced also of the need for equitable distribution of humanitarian supplies to all segments of the Iraqi population throughout the country,

Determined to improve the humanitarian situation in Iraq,

Reaffirming the commitment of all Member States to the sovereignty and territorial integrity of Iraq,

Acting under Chapter VII of the Charter of the United Nations,

1. *Decides* that the provisions of resolution 986(1995), except those contained in paragraphs 4, 11 and 12 and subject to paragraph 15 of resolution 1284(1999), shall remain in force for a new period of 180 days beginning at 0001 hours eastern standard time on 6 December 2000;

2. *Decides also* that from the sum produced from the import by States of petroleum and petroleum products originating in Iraq, including financial and other essential transactions related thereto, in the 180-day period referred to in paragraph 1 above, the amounts recommended by the Secretary-General in his report of 1 February 1998 [S/1998/90] for the food/nutrition and health sectors should continue to be allocated on a priority basis in the context of the activities of the Secretariat, of which 13 per cent of the sum produced in the period referred to above shall be used for the purposes referred to in paragraph 8 *(b)* of resolution 986(1995);

3. *Requests* the Secretary-General to continue to take the actions necessary to ensure the effective and efficient implementation of this resolution, and to continue to enhance as necessary the United Nations observation process in Iraq including, within 90 days of the adoption of the present resolution, to complete the recruitment and placement in Iraq of a sufficient number of observers, in particular the recruitment of the number of observers agreed between the Secretary-General and the Government of Iraq, in such a way as to provide the required assurance to the Council that the goods produced in accordance with the present resolution are distributed equitably and that all supplies authorized for procurement, including dual usage items and spare parts, are utilized for the purpose for which they have been authorized, including in the housing sector and related infrastructure development;

4. *Decides* to conduct a thorough review of all aspects of the implementation of the present resolution 90 days after the entry into force of paragraph 1 above and again prior to the end of the 180-day period, and expresses its intention, prior to the end of the 180-day period, to consider favourably renewal of the provisions of the present resolution as appropriate, provided that the reports referred to in paragraphs 5 and 6 below indicate that those provisions are being satisfactorily implemented;

5. *Requests* the Secretary-General to provide a comprehensive report to the Council 90 days after the date of entry into force of the present resolution on its implementation and again at least one week prior to the end of the 180-day period, on the basis of observations of United Nations personnel in Iraq, and of consultations with the Government of Iraq, on whether Iraq has ensured the equitable distribution of medicine, health supplies, foodstuffs, and materials and supplies for essential civilian needs, financed in accordance with para-

graph 8 *(a)* of resolution 986(1995), including in his reports any observations he may have on the adequacy of the revenues to meet the humanitarian needs of Iraq;

6. *Requests* the Security Council Committee established by resolution 661(1990), in close consultation with the Secretary-General, to report to the Council 90 days after the entry into force of paragraph 1 above and prior to the end of the 180-day period on the implementation of the arrangements in paragraphs 1, 2, 6, 8, 9 and 10 of resolution 986(1995);

7. *Decides* that from the funds produced pursuant to this resolution in the escrow account established by paragraph 7 of resolution 986(1995), up to a total of 600 million United States dollars may be used to meet any reasonable expenses, other than expenses payable in Iraq, which follow directly from the contracts approved in accordance with paragraph 2 of resolution 1175(1998) and paragraph 18 of resolution 1284(1999), and expresses its intention to consider favourably the renewal of this measure;

8. *Expresses its readiness* to consider, in the light of the cooperation of the Government of Iraq in implementing all the resolutions of the Council, allowing a sum of 15 million United States dollars drawn from the escrow account to be used for the payment of the arrears in the contribution of Iraq to the budget of the United Nations, and considers that this sum should be transferred from the account created pursuant to paragraph 8 *(d)* of resolution 986(1995);

9. *Requests* the Secretary-General to take the necessary steps to transfer the excess funds drawn from the account created pursuant to paragraph 8 *(d)* of resolution 986(1995) for the purposes set out in paragraph 8 *(a)* of resolution 986(1995) in order to increase the funds available for humanitarian purchases, including as appropriate the purposes referred to in paragraph 24 of resolution 1284(1999);

10. *Directs* the Committee established by resolution 661(1990) to approve, on the basis of proposals from the Secretary-General, lists of basic electricity and housing supplies consistent with the priority given to the most vulnerable groups in Iraq, decides, notwithstanding paragraph 3 of resolution 661(1990) and paragraph 20 of resolution 687(1991), that supplies of these items will not be submitted for approval of that Committee, except for items subject to the provisions of resolution 1051(1996) of 27 March 1996, and will be notified to the Secretary-General and financed in accordance with the provisions of paragraphs 8 *(a)* and 8 *(b)* of resolution 986(1995), requests the Secretary-General to inform the Committee in a timely manner of all such notifications received and actions taken, and expresses its readiness to consider such action with regard to lists of further supplies, in particular in the transport and telecommunications sectors;

11. *Requests* the Secretary-General to expand and update, within 30 days of the adoption of the present resolution, the lists of humanitarian items submitted in accordance with paragraph 17 of resolution 1284(1999) and paragraph 8 of resolution 1302(2000), directs the Committee established by resolution 661(1990) to approve expeditiously the expanded lists, decides that supplies of these items will not be submitted for approval of the Committee established by resolution 661(1990), except for items subject to the provisions of resolution 1051(1996), and will be noti-

fied to the Secretary-General and financed in accordance with the provisions of paragraphs 8 *(a)* and 8 *(b)* of resolution 986(1995), and requests the Secretary-General to inform the Committee in a timely manner of all such notifications received and actions taken;

12. *Decides* that the effective deduction rate of the funds deposited in the escrow account established by resolution 986(1995) to be transferred to the Compensation Fund in the 180-day period shall be 25 per cent, decides further that the additional funds resulting from this decision will be deposited into the account established under paragraph 8 *(a)* of resolution 986(1995) to be used for strictly humanitarian projects to address the needs of the most vulnerable groups in Iraq as referred to in paragraph 126 of the report of the Secretary-General of 29 November 2000, requests the Secretary-General to report on the use of these funds in his reports referred to in paragraph 5 above, and expresses its intention to establish a mechanism to review, before the end of the 180-day period, the effective deduction rate of the funds deposited in the escrow account to be transferred to the Compensation Fund in future phases, taking into account the key elements of the humanitarian needs of the Iraqi people;

13. *Urges* the Committee established by resolution 661(1990) to review applications in an expeditious manner, to decrease the level of applications on hold and to continue to improve the approval process of applications, and, in this regard, stresses the importance of the full implementation of paragraph 3 above;

14. *Urges* all States submitting applications, all financial institutions, including the Central Bank of Iraq, and the Secretariat, to take steps to minimize the problems identified in the report of the Secretary-General of 29 November 2000 pursuant to paragraph 5 of resolution 1302(2000);

15. *Requests* the Secretary-General to make the necessary arrangements, subject to the approval of the Council, to allow funds deposited in the escrow account established by resolution 986(1995) to be used for the purchase of locally produced goods and to meet the local cost for essential civilian needs, which have been funded in accordance with the provisions of resolution 986(1995) and related resolutions, including, where appropriate, the cost of installation and training services, and further requests the Secretary-General to make the necessary arrangements, subject to the approval of the Council, to allow funds up to 600 million euros deposited in the escrow account established by resolution 986(1995) to be used for the cost of installation and maintenance, including training services, of the equipment and spare parts for the oil industry, which have been funded in accordance with the provisions of resolution 986(1995) and related resolutions, and calls upon the Government of Iraq to cooperate in the implementation of all such arrangements;

16. *Urges* all States, and in particular the Government of Iraq, to provide their full cooperation in the effective implementation of the present resolution;

17. *Calls upon* the Government of Iraq to take the remaining steps necessary to implement paragraph 27 of resolution 1284(1999), and further requests the Secretary-General to include in his reports under paragraph 5 above a review of the progress made by the Government of Iraq in the implementation of these measures;

18. *Requests* the Secretary-General to prepare a report as expeditiously as possible but no later than 31 March 2001 for the Committee established by resolution 661(1990) containing proposals for the use of additional export routes for petroleum and petroleum products, under appropriate conditions otherwise consistent with the purpose and provisions of resolution 986(1995) and related resolutions, and particularly addressing the possible pipelines that might be utilized as additional export routes;

19. *Reiterates* its request in paragraph 8 of resolution 1284(1999) to the Executive Chairman of the United Nations Monitoring, Verification and Inspection Commission and to the Director General of the International Atomic Energy Agency to complete by the end of this period the revision and updating of the lists of items and technology to which the import/export mechanism approved by resolution 1051(1996) applies;

20. *Stresses* the need to continue to ensure respect for the security and safety of all persons directly involved in the implementation of this resolution in Iraq, and calls upon the Government of Iraq to complete its investigation into the death of employees of the Food and Agriculture Organization and to forward it to the Council;

21. *Appeals* to all States to continue to cooperate in the timely submission of applications and the expeditious issue of export licences, facilitating the transit of humanitarian supplies authorized by the Committee established by resolution 661(1990), and to take all other appropriate measures within their competence in order to ensure that urgently needed humanitarian supplies reach the Iraqi people as rapidly as possible;

22. *Decides* to remain seized of the matter

In the light of the new 180-day extension of the humanitarian programme (phase IX) from 6 December, the UN Secretariat and Iraq, by a 6 December exchange of letters [S/2000/1178], agreed to extend for the same period the provisions of the 1996 Memorandum of Understanding between them on the implementation of Council resolution 986(1995).

Communications. On 7 December [S/2000/1166], Iraq brought to the attention of the Secretary-General the actions of UN agencies and offices involved in the electricity sector in Iraq's three northern governorates, which had approved economically and environmentally inappropriate projects in the area without consultation with Iraqi authorities.

By a 10 December letter to the Secretary-General [S/2000/1175], Iraq said, among other things, that resolution 1330(2000) clearly showed that some members of the Council wanted to maintain the embargo imposed on Iraq, instead of easing the restrictions on Iraq's right to dispose of its financial resources so as to use them in the interests of its people.

On 16 December [S/2000/1204], Iraq requested that all of the banking operations relating to revenues under the Memorandum of Understanding should be performed by more than one bank.

Bahrain transmitted to the Secretary-General the final communiqué adopted by the Supreme Council of the Gulf Cooperation Council at its twenty-first session (Manama, Bahrain, 30-31 December) [A/55/727-S/2001/5], as well as the Manama Declaration 2000. The Supreme Council, among other things, called on Iraq to discharge all of its obligations under the relevant Security Council resolutions and to resume cooperation with the United Nations in order to bring the outstanding issues relating to weapons of mass destruction and monitoring systems to a conclusion.

UN Compensation Commission and Fund

The United Nations Compensation Commission, established in 1991 [YUN 1991, p. 195] for the resolution and payment through the United Nations Compensation Fund, established at the same time, of claims against Iraq for losses and damage resulting from its 1990 invasion and occupation of Kuwait [YUN 1990, p. 189], continued in 2000 to expedite the prompt settlement of claims. The Commission was headquartered in Geneva, where its Governing Council held all of its sessions.

Governing Council. The Commission's Governing Council held four regular sessions during the year—the thirty-fifth (13-15 March) [S/2000/396], thirty-sixth (13-15 and 30 June) [S/2000/703], thirty-seventh (26-28 September) [S/2000/1057] and thirty-eighth (5-7 December) [S/2000/1249]—at which it considered the reports and recommendations of the Panels of Commissioners appointed to review specific instalments of various categories of claims. Each report described in detail the measures taken by the Panel to determine whether a given claim fell within the Commission's jurisdiction, to verify its validity, to evaluate compensable losses and to arrive at the compensation amounts to be recommended. The Governing Council also acted on the Executive Secretary's report submitted at each session, which, in addition to providing a summary of the previous period's activities, covered corrections to approved claim awards, claim withdrawals, the processing and payment of approved claims, the appointment of Commissioners, the 2000 progress report on the Commission's 1997-2003 work programme, and the review of the Commission's procedures.

In March, the Council considered Panel reports on specific instalments of corporate claims under category E, grouped as follows: one on oil sector claims (E1), one on non-Kuwaiti corporate claims (E2), three on non-Kuwaiti construction and engineering claims (E3), and four on Kuwaiti private sector claims (E4). Also discussed were several issues relating to the processing and payment of claims, including the mechanism for the third phase of payment. The Council recommended that a drafting group be established to prepare a draft decision concerning the details of the third phase of payment. In addition, it continued its consideration of the request of Yemen to accept the late filing of a category F government claim, in the light of further information provided by the Government of Yemen and the secretariat. While expressing sympathy for Yemen's circumstances, the Council was unable to accept the request for late filing.

Considered at the June session were four reports and recommendations made by the Panels in the D (individual claims for damages above $100,000), E1 (oil sector claims) and F1 (claims by Governments for losses related to departure and evacuation costs, and damage to physical property) categories. The Council approved the reports and recommendations concerning the D and F1 claims, and adjourned further consideration of the E1 claims until 30 June. On that date, the Council decided to postpone further consideration of the report until its thirty-seventh session, in an effort to reach consensus on its decision. The Council also adopted a decision concerning the priority of payment and payment mechanism for the third phase of payment. It decided that successful claimants in categories D, E and F would receive an initial amount of $5 million and subsequent payments of $10 million, in the order in which the claims had been approved. Newly approved claims would have priority in initial payment over subsequent payments to previously approved claims. Successful environmental monitoring and assessment claims were also accorded priority of payment in the above-mentioned amounts.

The September session examined seven reports and recommendations made by the Panels in the E1, E2, E3 and E4 categories of claims. It also considered a special report of the D1 Panel concerning 223 individual category A claims for departure from Iraq or Kuwait. With regard to the report on category E1 claims, which had been the subject of extensive discussions, the September session culminated in an agreement on three points, which allowed the Governing Council to proceed with the approval of the report and the recommendations by consensus. The Governing Council also examined the issue of overlapping business loss claims filed in categories C (damages up to $100,000), D and E4 by nationals of Jordan and Kuwait, and considered a request for the nullification of a previous withdrawal of a claim in category E. The Council decided that a withdrawn claim could not be reinstated or refiled. In the light of the Security Council agreement that required the review of the Compensation Commission's procedures, the Governing Council agreed to carry out such review before the end of the year.

The December session considered six reports and recommendations made by the Panels in the D and F2 (claims from the Government of Saudi Arabia) categories. The Council also reviewed the Commission's procedures and agreed by consensus on a number of conclusions and recommendations. The conclusions addressed the time allowed for the review of panels' reports, the transmission of claims files to Iraq and oral proceedings. It also considered the issue of providing technical assistance to Iraq and stated that it would consider further various proposals relating to such assistance, noting that some Council members indicated that such proposals should not relate to claims other than the F4 claims. The Council considered the issue of overlapping business loss claims filed in categories C, D and E4 by nationals of various countries, and heard a presentation on the status of the review of the F4 environmental claims. It also decided that a request by Iran for the late filing of category A claims could not be accepted.

Communications from Iraq. On 13 June [S/2000/572], Iraq drew the Secretary-General's attention to the fact that the Compensation Commission had deliberately concealed from Iraq documentation relating to claims, in violation of the proper legal procedures. Further, on 20 and 29 June [S/2000/609, S/2000/646], Iraq stated that the Commission had not provided details of claims for compensation from Turkey and the Syrian Arab Republic, respectively.

Other issues

Iraqi complaints

Reaffirming its absolute rejection of the northern and southern air exclusion (no-fly) zones imposed by the United States, Iraq reported regularly to the Secretary-General and the Security Council throughout 2000 on it. Iraq also alleged wanton military attacks by United States and British aircraft which had caused civilian deaths and injuries, as well as destruction of private and public property [S/2000/144, S/2000/159, S/2000/226, S/2000/260, S/2000/309, S/2000/473, S/2000/474, S/2000/806, S/2000/825, S/2000/1058]. In an October letter [S/2000/981], Iraq said that the United States and the United Kingdom and the countries that provided the logistic facilities for their aggression, namely Kuwait, Saudi Arabia and Turkey, should be made to bear full interna-

tional responsibility, including for the payment of compensation to Iraq.

During the year, Iraq also alleged violations of its territorial waters by Kuwait [S/2000/217, S/2000/340, S/2000/346, S/2000/355, S/2000/358, S/2000/405, S/2000/567, S/2000/570, S/2000/667, S/2000/798, S/2000/808, S/2000/1117], whose patrols increasingly subjected Iraqi fishing boats to armed aggressions. In a series of replies [S/2000/368, S/2000/556, S/2000/720, S/2000/972, S/2001/46], Kuwait described those allegations as fabrications. Iraq also alleged violations of its territorial waters and interceptions of Iraqi vessels by the United States [S/2000/354, S/2000/382, S/2000/1022, S/2000/1110].

On 2 April [S/2000/278], Iraq claimed that a Saudi patrol had fired a number of rounds at an Iraqi border observation post, which was denied by Saudi Arabia [S/2000/510].

Iraq submitted several reports [S/2000/327, S/2000/608, S/2000/840, S/2000/1013, S/2000/1203] concerning the finding and disposal of unexploded ordnance—left behind by what it called the 1991 30-Power aggression against it—which continued to be found in large quantities in the country.

Iraq also protested, throughout 2000, increasing land and air incursions and armed aggression in its northern territory by Turkey [S/2000/306, S/2000/353, S/2000/475, S/2000/546, S/2000/736, S/2000/750, S/2000/833].

In other communications, Iraq protested the illegal entry into northern Iraq, through Turkey, of a United States official accompanied by a Turkish delegation [S/2000/182]; provided documentation confirming the involvement of the United States in the financing of terrorist activities aimed at overthrowing the national regime in Iraq [S/2000/168, S/2000/687]; and submitted allegations of war crimes committed against Iraqi forces by the United States armed forces in 1991 [S/2000/669].

Tajikistan

Having completed its mandate, the United Nations Mission of Observers in Tajikistan (UN-MOT) withdrew from the country on 15 May, as scheduled. In their first multiparty elections, the people of Tajikistan went to the polls in February to fill the 63 seats in the Assembly of Representatives (lower house) and again in March to fill the 33 seats in the National Assembly (upper house). Presidential elections had taken place in 1999 [YUN 1999, p. 273].

The Joint Electoral Observation Mission (JEOM), which the United Nations and the Organization for Security and Cooperation in Europe (OSCE) deployed to Tajikistan to observe the elections, concluded that the February elections had not met minimum standards. On 27 April, Tajikistan's newly formed bicameral parliament convened its first joint session.

On 1 June, the Security Council noted the Secretary-General's intention to establish, for a limited time, a UN peace-building support office in Tajikistan to pursue the objectives of post-conflict peace-building and consolidation of peace.

UN Mission of Observers in Tajikistan

UNMOT, established by Security Council resolution 968(1994) [YUN 1994, p. 596], continued its work to promote peace and national reconciliation and to assist in the implementation of the 1997 General Agreement on the Establishment of Peace and National Accord in Tajikistan [YUN 1997, p. 264] until 15 May, when its mandate ended.

It also assisted JEOM by providing communications back-up and liaison with the local authorities on security matters.

In preparation for its withdrawal from Tajikistan, UNMOT closed all of its field stations and withdrew its personnel and equipment to Dushanbe by the end of April.

Composition

UNMOT continued to be headed by the Special Representative of the Secretary-General for Tajikistan, Ivo Petrov (Bulgaria); its military component continued under the command of the Chief Military Observer, Brigadier-General John Hvidegaard (Denmark). During the first few months of the year, the Mission was gradually withdrawn. The number of military observers, which stood at 37 in October 1999 [YUN 1999, p. 267], totalled 17 as at 30 April 2000.

Activities

During the year, the Secretary-General, in response to Security Council resolution 1274(1999) [YUN 1999, p. 274], submitted two reports updating the developments in Tajikistan and the activities of UNMOT.

Report of Secretary-General (March). In his 14 March report [S/2000/214], the Secretary-General informed the Security Council that the UN/OSCE JEOM, as recommended by the joint UN/OSCE assessment mission [YUN 1999, p. 274], arrived in Tajikistan in January and February to observe the country's first multiparty election. A total of 331 candidates were registered to contest

the 63 seats in the Assembly of Representatives. On polling day (27 February), JEOM deployed 86 short-term observers to some 300 of the 2,761 polling stations and also observed the counting of the votes and tabulation of the results. The following day, JEOM issued its preliminary findings and conclusions; it noted that the election had not met minimum standards and cited many weaknesses in the electoral legislation.

The Central Commission on Elections and Referenda (CCER), in the preliminary results of the first round of the election, announced that the ruling People's Democratic Party had won 33 seats, the Communist Party 7 and the Islamic Revival Party 2. Independent candidates won in eight constituencies, but two were declared invalid, requiring a new vote to be held at the end of April. In 12 constituencies where no candidate received a majority of the vote, a run-off election was held on 12 March. CCER announced that the ruling People's Democratic Party won in seven constituencies; in the remaining five, three went to independents and the results of the other two were unavailable at the time of the report.

Between 16 November 1999 and 5 February 2000, UNMOT carried out 34 visits to reintegrated units of former opposition fighters, either independently or together with members of the Commission on National Reconciliation (CNR) military subcommission and representatives of the Ministry of Defence, Ministry of the Interior or the State Border Protection Committee. Many units complained of non-payment of salaries, lack of food and equipment (including uniforms) and inadequate accommodation. They also complained that they had received no instructions, training or visits from their superior headquarters. Work in the job creation projects for former fighters in the Karategin valley, which was interrupted in November by the onset of winter, would be resumed in the spring.

The Secretary-General observed that after years of fighting, the Tajik parties had managed to overcome obstacles and put their country on the path to national reconciliation and democracy by holding the first multiparty parliamentary elections. He noted the important role that the United Nations played in the country's significant achievement. However, although there was cause for satisfaction at the overall success, there was no doubt that much remained to be done. He urged the international community to stay engaged and continue to provide assistance. He indicated his intention to withdraw UNMOT when its mandate expired in May, and promised to keep the Council informed about his consultations with Tajikistan about the possible future

UN role in the country's post-conflict, peace-building and consolidation period.

On 21 March [meeting 4116], following consultations among Security Council members, the President made statement **S/PRST/2000/9** on behalf of the Council:

The Security Council has considered the report of the Secretary-General of 14 March 2000 on the situation in Tajikistan, submitted pursuant to paragraph 12 of resolution 1274(1999) of 12 November 1999.

The Council welcomes decisive progress in the implementation of the General Agreement on the Establishment of Peace and National Accord in Tajikistan, signed in Moscow on 27 June 1997, achieved due to sequential and persistent efforts by the President of the Republic of Tajikistan and the leadership of the Commission on National Reconciliation.

The Council welcomes, in particular, the holding, on 27 February 2000, of the first multiparty and pluralistic parliamentary election in Tajikistan, in spite of serious problems and shortcomings, as noted by the Joint Electoral Observation Mission for Tajikistan. It notes that with the holding of these elections the transition period envisaged in the General Agreement is coming to a close. The Council acknowledges the significant achievement of the Tajik parties, which have managed to overcome many obstacles and to put their country on the path to peace, national reconciliation and democracy. It urges the Government and the Parliament of Tajikistan to work towards elections in the future that meet fully acceptable standards, as a means to consolidate peace.

The Council notes with satisfaction that the United Nations has played an important role in this success. It welcomes the United Nations Mission of Observers in Tajikistan, supported by the Contact Group of Guarantor States and International Organizations, the Mission of the Organization for Security and Cooperation in Europe and the collective peacekeeping forces of the Commonwealth of Independent States, being instrumental in assisting the parties in the implementation of the General Agreement.

The Council supports the intention of the Secretary-General to withdraw the Mission of Observers when its mandate expires on 15 May 2000. The Council expects that the Secretary-General will inform it of the outcome of his current consultations with the Government of Tajikistan on a role for the United Nations in the period of post-conflict peace-building and consolidation.

Report of Secretary-General (May). In his 5 May report [S/2000/387], the Secretary-General stated that the election to the 33-seat National Assembly was held on 23 March and, in accordance with the Constitution, 25 deputies were elected by local assemblies and 8 were appointed by the President. The by-elections for the remaining two seats in the Assembly of Representatives had still not taken place. On 27 April, the newly formed bicameral parliament convened its first joint session. CNR held its final session on 26 March, with both sides agreeing that its unfinished business would be addressed by appropriate government bodies. The Commission was formally dissolved by presidential decree as from 1 April.

Having held more than 130 meetings since it was established in 1997 [YUN 1997, p. 273], the Contact Group of Guarantor States and International Organizations—Afghanistan, Iran, Kazakhstan, Kyrgyzstan, Pakistan, the Russian Federation, Turkmenistan, Uzbekistan, OSCE and the Organization of the Islamic Conference—concluded its work of monitoring the implementation of the General Agreement [YUN 1997, p. 264] and providing expertise, consultation and good offices. In an 18 April statement, the Contact Group expressed its readiness to continue to support Tajikistan in its further efforts.

Since he was submitting his final report on UN-MOT, the Secretary-General reviewed the UN efforts relating to the situation in Tajikistan since 1993, when the Mission was established as a small political office in Dushanbe [YUN 1993, p. 514]. He stated that UN involvement in the peace process in Tajikistan had several characteristics that contributed to its overall positive outcome: early intervention by the United Nations in the conflict; sustained political support of the Security Council and interested Member States in the region; cooperation with other organizations, notably OSCE; effective crisis management; and, above all, the clear will of the Tajik people to end the war and pursue a political solution.

The Secretary-General stated that the reintegration of the opposition into the political life of Tajikistan was a big step along the path to peace and national reconciliation. Although the recent parliamentary elections had advanced the democratic process, they were, in the view of international observers, seriously flawed. Also, armed elements continued to operate outside the Government's control, contributing to insecurity, and daunting economic and social problems had to be addressed as a priority. The continued support of the international community in the post-conflict phase would be important for Tajikistan's ability to sustain, and build on, the achievements of the peace process. The Secretary-General intended to write to the Security Council shortly about the possible establishment of a post-conflict peace-building office.

On 12 May [meeting 4141], following consultations among Security Council members, the

President made statement **S/PRST/2000/17** on behalf of the Council:

The Security Council has considered the report of the Secretary-General of 5 May 2000 on the situation in Tajikistan.

The Council welcomes the success achieved in the peace process in Tajikistan with the completion of implementation of the main provisions of the General Agreement on the Establishment of Peace and National Accord in Tajikistan, signed in Moscow on 27 June 1997, under the auspices of the United Nations. It expresses its appreciation for the sequential and persistent efforts of the President of the Republic of Tajikistan and the leadership of the Commission on National Reconciliation in this regard. The Council acknowledges the significant achievement of the Tajik parties, which have managed to overcome many obstacles and to put their country on the path to peace, national reconciliation and democracy. It joins the Secretary-General in hoping that these achievements will be consolidated in the further strengthening of the institutions in the country, with a view to the democratic, economic and social development of Tajik society.

The Council notes with satisfaction that the United Nations has played a successful and important role in the peace process. It highly appreciates the efforts of the United Nations Mission of Observers in Tajikistan, supported by the Contact Group of Guarantor States and International Organizations, the Mission of the Organization for Security and Co-operation in Europe and the collective peacekeeping forces of the Commonwealth of Independent States, in assisting the parties in the implementation of the General Agreement.

The Council expresses its appreciation to the Russian Federation, the Islamic Republic of Iran and other interested Member States for their sustained political support for the peace efforts of the United Nations in Tajikistan, and for assisting the parties to maintain political dialogue and to overcome the crises in the peace process. It encourages the members of the former Contact Group to continue to support Tajikistan in its further efforts to consolidate peace, stability and democracy in the country.

The Council notes with satisfaction that the Mission of Observers maintained excellent relations with the collective peacekeeping forces and the Russian border forces, which contributed to the success of the Mission and helped to support the political process on the ground.

The Council reiterates its support for the intention of the Secretary-General to withdraw the Mission of Observers when its mandate expires on 15 May 2000. It pays tribute to all those who served in the Mission for the sake of peace in Tajikistan, and especially to those members of the Mission who gave their lives in the cause of peace.

The Council emphasizes that the continued support of the international community in the post-conflict phase will be crucial in allowing Tajikistan to sustain and build on the achievements of the peace process, and in helping it to lay a durable foundation for a better life for its people.

In this regard, the Council expresses its appreciation to the Secretary-General for his intention to inform the Council of the modalities of the establishment and functioning of a United Nations post-conflict peace-building office in Tajikistan, in order to consolidate peace and promote democracy. It encourages close cooperation between that office and the Mission of the Organization for Security and Co-operation in Europe, and other international agencies in Tajikistan. The Council also encourages Member States and others concerned to make voluntary contributions to support projects aimed at the social and economic rehabilitation of this country.

Financing

On 15 June [meeting 98], the General Assembly considered the Secretary-General's January report on UNMOT's financial performance from 1 July 1998 to 30 June 1999 [A/54/705], together with ACABQ's related reports [A/54/822, A/54/841]. On the recommendation of the Fifth Committee [A/54/903], the Assembly adopted **resolution 54/272** without vote [agenda item 141].

Financing of the United Nations Mission of Observers in Tajikistan

The General Assembly,

Having considered the report of the Secretary-General on the financing of the United Nations Mission of Observers in Tajikistan and the related reports of the Advisory Committee on Administrative and Budgetary Questions,

Recalling Security Council resolution 968(1994) of 16 December 1994, by which the Council established the United Nations Mission of Observers in Tajikistan, and the subsequent resolutions by which the Council extended the mandate of the Mission of Observers, the latest of which was resolution 1274(1999) of 12 November 1999,

Recalling also Security Council resolution 1138(1997) of 14 November 1997, by which the Council authorized the Secretary-General to expand the size of the Mission of Observers,

Recalling further its resolution 49/240 of 31 March 1995 on the financing of the Mission of Observers and its subsequent resolutions and decisions thereon, the latest of which was resolution 53/19 B of 8 June 1999,

Reaffirming that the costs of the Mission of Observers are expenses of the Organization to be borne by Member States in accordance with Article 17, paragraph 2, of the Charter of the United Nations,

Recalling its previous decisions regarding the fact that, in order to meet the expenditures caused by the Mission of Observers, a different procedure is required from that applied to meet expenditures of the regular budget of the United Nations,

Taking into account the fact that the economically more developed countries are in a position to make relatively larger contributions and that the economically less developed countries have a relatively limited capacity to contribute towards such an operation,

Bearing in mind the special responsibilities of the States permanent members of the Security Council, as indicated in General Assembly resolution 1874(S-IV) of 27 June 1963, in the financing of such operations,

Noting with appreciation that voluntary contributions have been made to the Mission of Observers,

Mindful of the fact that it is essential to provide the account of the Mission of Observers with the necessary financial resources to enable it to meet its outstanding liabilities,

1. *Takes note* of the status of contributions to the United Nations Mission of Observers in Tajikistan as at 30 April 2000, including the contributions outstanding in the amount of 4.5 million United States dollars, representing some 6.5 per cent of the total assessed contributions from the inception of the Mission of Observers to the period ending 15 May 2000, notes that some 34 per cent of the Member States have paid their assessed contributions in full, and urges all other Member States concerned, in particular those in arrears, to ensure payment of their outstanding assessed contributions;

2. *Expresses concern* about the financial situation with regard to peacekeeping activities, in particular as regards the reimbursements to troop contributors that bear additional burdens owing to overdue payments by Member States of their assessments;

3. *Expresses its appreciation* to those Member States which have paid their assessed contributions in full;

4. *Urges* all other Member States to make every possible effort to ensure payment of their assessed contributions to the Mission of Observers in full;

5. *Expresses concern* at the delay experienced by the Secretary-General in deploying and providing adequate resources to some recent peacekeeping missions, in particular those in Africa;

6. *Emphasizes* that all future and existing peacekeeping missions shall be given equal and non-discriminatory treatment in respect of financial and administrative arrangements;

7. *Also emphasizes* that all peacekeeping missions shall be provided with adequate resources for the effective and efficient discharge of their respective mandates;

8. *Endorses* the conclusions and recommendations contained in the report of the Advisory Committee on Administrative and Budgetary Questions, and requests the Secretary-General to ensure their full implementation;

9. *Decides* that Member States that have fulfilled their financial obligations to the Mission of Observers shall be credited their respective share of the unencumbered balance of 3,639,400 dollars gross (3,213,100 dollars net) in respect of the period from 1 July 1998 to 30 June 1999;

10. *Decides also* that, for Member States that have not fulfilled their financial obligations to the Mission of Observers, their share of the unencumbered balance of 3,639,400 dollars gross (3,213,100 dollars net) in respect of the period from 1 July 1998 to 30 June 1999 shall be set off against their outstanding obligations;

11. *Emphasizes* that no peacekeeping mission shall be financed by borrowing funds from other active peacekeeping missions;

12. *Encourages* the Secretary-General to continue to take additional measures to ensure the safety and security of all personnel under the auspices of the United Nations participating in the Mission of Observers;

13. *Decides* to include in the provisional agenda of its fifty-fifth session the item entitled "Financing of the United Nations Mission of Observers in Tajikistan".

On 23 December, the Assembly decided that the item on the financing of UNMOT would remain for consideration at the resumed fifty-fifth (2001) session (**decision 55/458**) and that the Fifth Committee would continue its consideration of the item at that session (**decision 55/455**).

UN Tajikistan Office of Peace-building

In a 26 May letter to the Security Council President [S/2000/518], the Secretary-General stated that, although the peace process in Tajikistan had brought about a restoration of normalcy to a large degree, the deep-seated roots of the civil conflict had not been fully addressed and the potential for renewed upheaval remained, owing to domestic factors and in view of the unstable situation in the region, notably in Afghanistan. As Tajikistan required continued support from the international community, the Secretary-General proposed that a UN peace-building support office be established, for a limited time, to pursue the objectives of post-conflict peace-building and consolidation of peace.

The office's mandate would be: to provide the political framework and leadership for post-conflict peace-building activities of the UN system in the country, including supporting the efforts of the Resident Coordinator and the UN system, including the Bretton Woods institutions, in promoting an integrated approach to the development and implementation of post-conflict peace-building programmes aimed at national reconstruction, economic recovery, poverty alleviation and good governance; to mobilize, in close cooperation with the UN country team, international support for the implementation of targeted programmes aimed at strengthening the rule of law, demobilization, voluntary arms collection and employment creation for former irregular fighters; to help in creating an enabling environment for consolidating peace, democracy and the rule of law; and to liaise with the Government, political parties and other representatives of civil society in broadening national consensus and reconciliation.

The Secretary-General recommended that the support office be headed by a representative of the Secretary-General and that it be established for an initial period of one year from 1 June.

On 1 June [S/2000/519], the Security Council informed the Secretary-General that his proposal to establish the office in Tajikistan had been brought to the attention of Council members, who took note of it with appreciation.

The United Nations Tajikistan Office of Peace-building (UNTOP) was established on 1 June. Ivo Petrov, the Secretary-General's former Special Representative for Tajikistan, was appointed as the Secretary-General's Representative in the country and as Head of UNTOP.

In **resolution 55/45** on emergency international assistance for peace, normalcy and rehabilitation in Tajikistan, the General Assembly welcomed the establishment of UNTOP.

Other issues

On 21 June [S/2000/630], the Council of Heads of State of the Commonwealth of Independent States adopted a decision to end the operations of the collective peacekeeping forces in Tajikistan, as requested by that country's President.

Other matters

Cambodia

During 2000, the United Nations continued its assistance to Cambodia with regard to establishing a court to try top Khmer Rouge leaders for crimes committed during the period of Democratic Kampuchea, including suggesting amendments to a draft law on the establishment of extraordinary chambers in the courts of Cambodia. At the end of the year, the draft law had not been adopted by the National Assembly.

(For the situation of human rights in Cambodia, see p. 624.)

Trial of Khmer Rouge leaders

In March and July, the United Nations Under-Secretary-General for Legal Affairs visited Cambodia to discuss with the Cambodian Task Force the draft articles of cooperation between the United Nations and the Government of Cambodia in the prosecution under Cambodian law of crimes committed during the period of Democratic Kampuchea. In 1999, the Cambodian Government had decided to bring the top Khmer Rouge leaders to justice before its own courts, rather than before an international court to be established for the purpose, as had been recommended by a Group of Experts that the Secretary-General had sent to Cambodia in 1998 [YUN 1999, p. 278]. The UN Secretariat team suggested amendments to the draft law on the establishment of extraordinary chambers in the courts of Cambodia for the prosecution of crimes committed during the period of Democratic Kampuchea, in order to ensure its conformity with the

articles of cooperation. By the end of the year, the draft law had not been adopted by the National Assembly.

In **resolution 55/95**, the General Assembly welcomed the successful conclusion of talks between the Government of Cambodia and the UN Secretariat on the question of the trial of the Khmer Rouge leaders most responsible for the most serious human rights violations, appealed strongly to the Government to ensure, including by facilitating the expedited completion of the necessary legislative process as soon as possible, that those leaders were brought to account in accordance with international standards of justice, fairness and due process of law, encouraged the Government to continue to cooperate with the United Nations on the issue, and welcomed the efforts of the Secretariat and the international community in assisting the Government to that end.

UNTAC financing and liquidation

On 23 December, the Assembly decided that the agenda item on the financing and liquidation of the United Nations Transitional Authority in Cambodia (UNTAC), which terminated in 1993 [YUN 1993, p. 371], would remain for consideration at its resumed fifty-fifth (2001) session (**decision 55/458**) and that the Fifth Committee should continue consideration of the item at that session (**decision 55/455**).

India-Pakistan

The United Nations Military Observer Group in India and Pakistan (UNMOGIP) continued in 2000 to monitor the situation in Jammu and Kashmir. As at 31 December, UNMOGIP had a strength of 46 military observers. UNMOGIP headquarters alternated between Srinagar, Kashmir, in the summer and Rawalpindi, Pakistan, in the winter. On 12 June [S/2000/573], the Secretary-General informed the Security Council of his intention to appoint Major-General Manuel Saavedra (Uruguay) as Chief Military Observer of UNMOGIP, replacing Major-General Joszef Bali (Hungary) who served in that position until 3 March. The Council took note of the Secretary-General's intention on 14 June [S/2000/574].

Communications. On 24 January [A/54/720-S/2000/49], Pakistan informed the Secretary-General that Indian forces had launched a premeditated attack against a small Pakistani post on the Pakistan side of the line of control. Two Pakistani soldiers lost their lives and five remained missing. In view of the increasingly dangerous situation, Pakistan sought the Secretary-

General's intercession in urging India to desist from provocative acts.

On 28 February [A/54/771-S/2000/162], Pakistan drew the Secretary-General's attention to a massacre of 14 civilians by Indian security forces in the Kotli sector of Azad Jammu and Kashmir. Pakistan stated that the assailants, dressed in military uniforms, had crossed the line of control from Indian-occupied Kashmir. Maintaining that it remained committed to a peaceful resolution of the core dispute of Jammu and Kashmir in accordance with the wishes of the Kashmiri people, Pakistan called on the international community to urge India to desist from such provocative acts.

On 4 May [S/2000/384], Pakistan apprised the Secretary-General of an artillery bombardment by the Indian army across the line of control that had resulted in the death of at least nine civilians.

On 4 December [A/55/670-S/2000/1158], Pakistan informed the Secretary-General of its new initiative to reduce tension along the line of control and promote a meaningful dialogue with India for the peaceful settlement of the Jammu and Kashmir dispute, with the participation of Kashmiris. The main elements were: with immediate effect, Pakistan's armed forces deployed along the line of control in Jammu and Kashmir would observe maximum restraint in order to strengthen and stabilize the ceasefire already being unilaterally implemented by Pakistan; Pakistan was prepared to enter into a meaningful dialogue with India to address the Jammu and Kashmir dispute; to enable the representatives of the Kashmiri people to participate in the dialogue, Pakistan had extended an invitation to the Executive Committee of the All Parties Hurriyat Conference for consultations to prepare the ground for a tripartite process of negotiations for a peaceful settlement of the dispute. Pakistan stated that India's announced suspension of military operations against the Kashmiri freedom fighters would be meaningful only if combined with a purposeful dialogue for the peaceful settlement of Jammu and Kashmir.

On 8 December, the EU welcomed India's decision to declare a unilateral ceasefire in Kashmir throughout Ramadan. It was also pleased to note Pakistan's statement that it would exercise maximum restraint along the line of control.

Iran-Iraq

Throughout 2000, Iran and Iraq continued to inform the Secretary-General of alleged repeated violations of their 1988 ceasefire agreement [YUN 1988, p. 193] and 1991 Tehran agreements [YUN 1991, p. 163] concerning the area of

separation between them. They also alleged cross-border attacks and terrorist activities in each other's territory.

In a series of notes verbales from 23 January to 22 November [S/2000/127, S/2000/128, S/2000/129, S/2000/164, S/2000/216, S/2000/271, S/2000/411, S/2000/912, S/2000/1036, S/2000/1170], and in a series of letters covering the period 16 August 1999 to 16 May 2000 [S/2000/361, S/2000/426, S/2000/589, S/2000/784, S/2000/1169, S/2001/28], Iran informed the Secretary-General of alleged ceasefire violations by Iraq and attacks by the alleged Iraq-based terrorist group known as Mujahedin Khalq Organization.

Between 7 February and 31 December, Iraq transmitted to the Secretary-General communications on alleged ceasefire violations by Iran [S/2000/93, S/2000/141, S/2000/258, S/2000/285, S/2000/328, S/2000/398, S/2000/528, S/2000/705, S/2000/896, S/2000/996, S/2000/1080, S/2001/12].

On 20 August [S/2000/821], Iraq drew the Secretary-General's attention to a press statement quoting officials of Iran and Kuwait implying their intention to reach an understanding on the delimitation of the continental shelf between the two countries. Iraq stated that any such delimitation should be agreed upon by all the States, including Iraq, that had political rights over the shelf for prospecting and exploiting natural resources.

Iran, on 26 December [S/2000/1243], stated that Iraq's assertion that agreement on delimitation should be made by all the States lacked legal basis.

Korea question

In June 2000, the two leaders of the Democratic People's Republic of Korea (DPRK) and the Republic of Korea held the inter-Korean summit in Pyongyang, DPRK, the first such meeting since the division of the peninsula in 1945. The summit produced a joint declaration based on three principles: independence, peaceful reunification and national unity.

The United States, on behalf of the Unified Command established pursuant to Security Council resolution 84(1950) [YUN 1950, p. 230], submitted to the Council on 6 November the report of the United Nations Command [YUN 1999, p. 276] concerning the maintenance in 1998 of the 1953 Armistice Agreement contained in General Assembly resolution 725(VIII) [YUN 1953, p. 136].

The DPRK's cooperation with IAEA in respect of its obligations under the nuclear safeguards agreement remained limited.

Summit meeting

The leaders of the DPRK and the Republic of Korea held an inter-Korean summit meeting in Pyongyang from 13 to 15 June. That historic meeting, the first of its kind since Korea's division, produced a joint declaration, the main elements of which dealt with reconciliation and eventual reunification; easing of tensions; reunion of divided families; exchanges in economic, social, cultural and other fields; and the establishment of liaison offices in each other's country.

On 1 August [A/55/219-S/2000/758], Japan forwarded to the Secretary-General a statement on the Korean peninsula that was adopted at the Kyushu-Okinawa summit meeting (Okinawa, 21-23 July) of the Group of Eight industrialized countries. The G-8 welcomed the inter-Korean summit; expressed the hope that the implementation of the joint declaration would usher in a new era in inter-Korean relations and reduce the tensions in the Korean peninsula. The G-8 strongly supported the Republic of Korea's engagement policy and welcomed the constructive attitude shown by the DPRK and took note of the reconfirmation of its moratorium on missile-launch.

On 6 September, the Co-Chairpersons of the Millennium Summit (see p. 47) issued a statement in which they welcomed the June summit meeting between the leaders of the DPRK and the Republic of Korea and their joint declaration as a major breakthrough in bringing peace, stability and reunification to the Korean peninsula. They encouraged the two parties to advance the dialogue so that it might eventually lead to the peaceful reunification of the peninsula, while contributing to the peace and security of the region and beyond [A/55/PV.4].

GENERAL ASSEMBLY ACTION

In accordance with a 6 October request from a group of Member States [A/55/236 & Add.1], the item "Peace, security and reunification on the Korean peninsula" was included in the agenda of the General Assembly's fifty-fifth session.

On 31 October [meeting 45], the Assembly adopted **resolution 55/11** [draft: A/55/L.14 & Add.1] without vote [agenda item 183].

Peace, security and reunification on the Korean peninsula

The General Assembly,

Reaffirming the purposes and principles embodied in the Charter of the United Nations regarding the maintenance of international peace and security,

Convinced that inter-Korean dialogue and co-operation are essential for consolidating peace and security on the Korean peninsula and also contribute to peace and stability in the region and beyond, in conformity with the purposes and principles embodied in the Charter,

Recognizing that the historic summit meeting, held in Pyongyang from 13 to 15 June 2000, between the leaders of the Democratic People's Republic of Korea and the Republic of Korea and their joint declaration represent a major breakthrough in inter-Korean relations and in realizing eventual peaceful reunification,

Commending the positive developments on the Korean peninsula taking place in the wake of the inter-Korean summit,

Recalling the statement welcoming the inter-Korean summit and the follow-up measures made on 6 September 2000 by the Co-Chairpersons of the Millennium Summit of the United Nations,

1. *Welcomes and supports* the inter-Korean summit and the joint declaration adopted on 15 June 2000 by the two leaders of the Democratic People's Republic of Korea and the Republic of Korea;

2. *Encourages* the Democratic People's Republic of Korea and the Republic of Korea to continue to implement fully and in good faith the joint declaration and other agreements reached between the two sides, thereby consolidating peace on the Korean peninsula and laying a solid foundation for peaceful reunification;

3. *Invites* Member States to support and assist, as appropriate, the process of inter-Korean dialogue, reconciliation and reunification so that it may contribute to peace and security on the Korean peninsula and in the world as a whole.

IAEA safeguards inspections

Pursuant to the agreement between IAEA and the DPRK for the application of safeguards in connection with the 1968 Treaty on the Non-Proliferation of Nuclear Weapons, adopted by the General Assembly in resolution 2373(XXII) [YUN 1968, p.17], which remained binding and in force since 1992 [YUN 1992, p. 73], IAEA continued to maintain an inspector presence in Nyongbyon to monitor the freeze of the DPRK's graphite moderated reactors instituted in 1994 [YUN 1994, p. 442]. The DPRK continued to accept IAEA's activities in that regard solely within the context of the 1994 Agreed Framework agreement between it and the United States [ibid.] and not under its safeguards agreement with the Agency [S/2001/107].

With regard to the preservation of information, IAEA inspectors had had access since February 2000 to records at facilities subject to and not subject to the freeze in order to identify, list and describe their contents. Although work on establishing a baseline of records continued, there was no progress on the preservation of information other than records, or on the methods to be used to preserve information.

Following the last round of technical talks in November, IAEA stated that the verification process would take three to four years to complete, reiterating that it would require the full co-operation of the DPRK.

In a 22 September resolution, the IAEA General Conference urged the DPRK to comply with its safeguards agreement, to cooperate fully and promptly with IAEA and to take all steps the Agency might deem necessary to preserve all information relevant to verifying the accuracy and completeness of the DPRK's initial report on the inventory of nuclear material subject to safeguards.

Papua New Guinea

During 2000, Bougainville, a province of Papua New Guinea, continued to implement the 1998 Lincoln Agreement on Peace, Security and Development on Bougainville (the Lincoln Agreement) [YUN 1998, p. 319] concluded between the Government of Papua New Guinea and the four Bougainville parties involved in the nine-year conflict that ended in the 1997 Burnham Truce [ibid.].

A UN presence in the form of the United Nations Political Office in Bougainville (UNPOB), requested under the terms of the Lincoln Agreement, continued to monitor and report on the Agreement's implementation by the parties and by the Peace Monitoring Group (Australia, Fiji, New Zealand and Vanuatu), which was also requested under the Agreement.

On 22 November [S/2000/1139], the Secretary-General informed the Security Council that he had received a note verbale from Papua New Guinea requesting that UNPOB's mandate, which was due to expire on 31 December, be extended by a further 12 months. The Bougainville parties to the Lincoln Agreement concurred with the request. Encouraged by the steady progress in the Bougainville peace process, the facilitating role of UNPOB and its contribution to a constructive engagement of the parties, the Secretary-General expressed his intention to extend the mandate for a further 12 months, so that UNPOB could continue to assist in the promotion of political dialogue among the parties, in an effort to move the peace process further, and plan and implement peace-building activities.

On 30 November [S/2000/1140], the Council took note of the Secretary-General's intention.

Communication. On 28 March [A/2000/265], Papua New Guinea transmitted to the Security Council the text of the Loloata Understanding on the Bougainville issue, which, at a historic meeting of all key leaders of Bougainville (Loloata Island and Port Moresby, 17-23 March), was signed by the Government of Papua New

Guinea and the Bougainville leaders, in the presence of the head of UNPOB and Ewan MacMillan, Chief Negotiator of the Peace Monitoring Group.

Under the terms of the Understanding, the parties: agreed to establish the Bougainville Interim Provincial Government afforded by laws of the National Court; noted that the Greenhouse Memorandum of 23 December 1999 provided for cooperation between the Bougainville Interim Provincial Government and the Bougainville People's Congress and Councils of Elders; stated that arrangements for an autonomous Bougainville Government would be provided within the Papua New Guinea Constitution; and the National Government of Papua New Guinea acknowledged the aspirations for a binding referendum on independence as called for by the Bougainville leaders.

Solomon Islands

In 2000, ethnic conflict in Solomon Islands reached a crisis point when an armed militia, the Malaita Eagle Force/Paramilitary Joint Operation, took control of the Government armoury on 5 June. That group then declared war against another militia, the Isatabu Freedom Movement, and placed the Prime Minister, Bartholomew Ulufa'alu, under house arrest. The Prime Minister subsequently resigned (28 June).

Communications. On 6 June [S/2000/578], the EU condemned the attempt to overthrow the Government, called for the release of Prime Minister Ulafa'alu and others and advocated strict respect for the democratic norms and procedures of the constitution.

On 10 November [S/2000/1088], Solomon Islands, having pursued a quest for a peaceful resolution to the crisis, forwarded to the Security Council President the Townsville Peace Agreement, concluded between the warring factions and the Solomon Islands Government (Townsville, Australia, 15 October).

SECURITY COUNCIL ACTION

On 16 November [meeting 4224], following consultations among Security Council members, the President made statement **S/PRST/2000/33** on behalf of the Council:

The Security Council strongly supports the Townsville Peace Agreement, concluded on 15 October 2000, for the cessation of hostilities between the Malaita Eagle Force and the Isatabu Freedom Movement and for the restoration of peace and ethnic harmony in Solomon Islands.

The Council encourages all parties to cooperate in promoting reconciliation, so that the objectives of the Townsville Peace Agreement can be met, and urges all parties to continue to cooperate in accordance with the Peace Agreement, namely, to restore and maintain peace and ethnic harmony, to renounce the use of armed force and violence, to settle their differences through consultation and peaceful negotiation and to confirm their respect for human rights and the rule of law.

The Council commends those countries in the region that have supported the resolution of the conflict, and welcomes the establishment, as outlined in the Townsville Peace Agreement, of the International Peace Monitoring Team composed of unarmed military personnel and civilian police from Australia and New Zealand, the mandate of which is based on annex II to the said Peace Agreement and agreed by the parties. It also encourages other nations, in particular those in the region, to participate and assist in the implementation of the Agreement.

United Arab Emirates–Iran

Greater Tunb, Lesser Tunb and Abu Musa

The Council of the League of Arab States, at two regular sessions (Beirut, Lebanon, 11-12 March; Cairo, Egypt, 3-4 September), adopted resolutions on Iran's occupation of the Arabian Gulf islands of Greater Tunb, Lesser Tunb and Abu Musa belonging to the United Arab Emirates [S/2000/281, S/2000/900]. The Council condemned Iran's violation of the sovereignty of the United Arab Emirates and called on the Iranian Government to put an end to its occupation of the three islands.

In a 7 September letter to the Secretary-General [A/55/365], Iran stated that the claims made against its territorial integrity were baseless and unacceptable.

The United Arab Emirates, on 20 December [S/2000/1222], requested that the Security Council retain on its 2001 agenda the item entitled "Letter dated 2 December 1971 from the Permanent Representatives of Algeria, the Libyan Arab Jamahiriya, the People's Democratic Republic of Yemen and Iraq to the United Nations addressed to the President of the Security Council" concerning the occupation by Iran of the three islands [YUN 1971, p. 209].

Chapter V

Europe and the Mediterranean

In 2000, prospects for achieving peace and security in Europe and the Mediterranean were not very encouraging as most of the major conflicts affecting the region were no nearer to a solution, particularly in the Balkans, which continued to defy the peacemaking efforts of the United Nations and the international community. However, there was hope that a new climate had been created with the election in September of the new President of the Federal Republic of Yugoslavia (FRY), Vojislav Kostunica, replacing Slobodan Milosevic, and the establishment of a new Government in Croatia. The election of the new President in FRY also raised hopes that the long-standing dispute regarding issues of succession related to the break-up of the former Socialist Federal Republic of Yugoslavia would soon be resolved. A first step in that regard was the admission of FRY to United Nations membership on 1 November.

Despite their declared willingness to resolve their dispute over the Prevlaka peninsula through bilateral negotiations, Croatia and FRY made no real progress in that regard. The fifth meeting on bilateral negotiations did not take place, with both sides continuing to blame each other for the delay. However, the Secretary-General observed that the political changes in the two countries might lead to the resumption of negotiations on Prevlaka.

In Bosnia and Herzegovina, the Peace Implementation Council, which continued to oversee and facilitate implementation of the 1995 General Framework Agreement for Peace in Bosnia and Herzegovina (also known as the Peace Agreement), noted the slow pace of implementation and, in order to accelerate it, set key strategic targets for the consolidation of State institutions, economic reform and refugee return. Municipal elections were held in April and a general election took place in November. The United Nations Mission in Bosnia and Herzegovina elaborated a comprehensive mandate implementation plan aimed at completing its core mandate by December 2002.

In 2000, the United Nations Interim Administration Mission in Kosovo (UNMIK) made significant progress in implementing the provisions of Security Council resolution 1244(1999) on the development of provisional institutions for democratic and autonomous self-government in the Kosovo province of FRY and in promoting the return of the territory to a viable administrative structure and economic and social recovery and reconstruction. As a first step towards a return to normalcy, municipal elections were successfully held on 28 October, paving the way for the establishment of functioning municipal assemblies in Kosovo. The political changes in Belgrade renewed hope for the constructive political dialogue on the future of Kosovo. Despite those positive developments, the Security Council remained concerned over the post-election violence, particularly the potentially explosive situation in the ground safety zone between Kosovo and Serbia proper. In a 19 December statement, the Council condemned the violence by Albanian extremist groups in southern Serbia and called for their dissolution. It called on UNMIK and the international security presence to continue to take all necessary efforts to address the problem.

With regard to Georgia, the Council, in November, noted with concern the continued failure of the parties to achieve a comprehensive settlement, including the political status of Abkhazia within the State of Georgia, and called on them to take immediate measures to move beyond the impasse. Efforts to reach a settlement of the armed conflict between Armenia and Azerbaijan over the Nagorny Karabakh region in Azerbaijan were also fruitless.

In the Mediterranean, despite the momentum generated by five rounds of proximity talks to resolve the Cyprus problem, meaningful negotiations on a permanent solution had yet to begin.

The former Yugoslavia

UN operations

The United Nations continued to work towards restoring peace and stability in the territories of the former Yugoslavia through its peacekeeping missions: the United Nations Mission in Bosnia and Herzegovina (UNMIBH); the United Nations Mission of Observers in Prevlaka (UN-MOP), which continued to monitor the demilitarization of the Prevlaka peninsula; and the United

Nations Interim Administration Mission in the FRY province of Kosovo (UNMIK), established to oversee the development of provisional democratic self-governing institutions. The Security Council extended UNMIBH's mandate, which included the International Police Task Force, until 21 June 2001, and that of UNMOP to 15 January 2001.

Financing

In March [A/54/803], the Secretary-General submitted to the General Assembly the financial performance report of the United Nations Protection Force (UNPROFOR), which ended in 1999, the United Nations Confidence Restoration Operation in Croatia (UNCRO), which ended in 1996, the United Nations Preventive Deployment Force (UNPREDEP)—known collectively as the United Nations Peace Forces (UNPF)—and UNPF headquarters (UNPF-HQ).

Requirements to meet the shortfall in resources for reimbursement of contingent-owned equipment totalled $138.5 million. In addition, funds were needed to settle outstanding government claims for which no obligations existed, as well as for death and disability claims, since all such obligated funds had been exhausted. Amounts owed to Governments in respect of all claims totalled $179.9 million. Since all those requirements could be met from unencumbered appropriations, the Secretary-General sought the Assembly's concurrence to retain that amount from the total appropriations balance of $304.2 million gross ($304.9 million net).

The recommendations of the Advisory Committee on Administrative and Budgetary Questions (ACABQ) on the Secretary-General's report were contained in an April report [A/54/835].

GENERAL ASSEMBLY ACTION

On 15 June [meeting 98], the General Assembly, on the recommendation of the Fifth (Administrative and Budgetary) Committee [A/54/900], adopted **resolution 54/269** without vote [agenda item 133].

Financing of the United Nations Protection Force, the United Nations Confidence Restoration Operation in Croatia, the United Nations Preventive Deployment Force and the United Nations Peace Forces headquarters

The General Assembly,

Having considered the report of the Secretary-General on the financing of the United Nations Protection Force, the United Nations Confidence Restoration Operation in Croatia, the United Nations Preventive Deployment Force and the United Nations Peace Forces headquarters and the related report of the Advisory Committee on Administrative and Budgetary Questions,

Recalling Security Council resolutions 727(1992) of 8 January 1992 and 740(1992) of 7 February 1992, in which the Council endorsed the sending of a group of military liaison officers to Yugoslavia to promote maintenance of the ceasefire,

Recalling also Security Council resolution 743(1992) of 21 February 1992, by which the Council established the United Nations Protection Force, and the subsequent resolutions by which the Council extended and expanded its mandate,

Recalling further Security Council resolution 981(1995) of 31 March 1995, by which the Council established the United Nations Confidence Restoration Operation in Croatia, to be known as UNCRO,

Recalling Security Council resolution 983(1995) of 31 March 1995, by which the Council decided that the United Nations Protection Force within the former Yugoslav Republic of Macedonia should be known as the United Nations Preventive Deployment Force,

Recalling also Security Council resolution 1025(1995) of 30 November 1995, in which the Council decided to terminate the mandate of the United Nations Confidence Restoration Operation in Croatia on 15 January 1996,

Recalling further Security Council resolution 1031(1995) of 15 December 1995, in which the Council decided to terminate the mandate of the United Nations Protection Force on the date on which the Secretary-General reported that the transfer of authority from the United Nations Protection Force to the Implementation Force had taken place,

Recalling the letter dated 1 February 1996 from the President of the Security Council to the Secretary-General informing him of the Council's concurrence in principle that the United Nations Preventive Deployment Force should become an independent mission,

Recalling also its resolution 46/233 of 19 March 1992 on the financing of the United Nations Protection Force and its subsequent resolutions and decisions thereon, the latest of which was decision 53/477 of 8 June 1999,

Reaffirming that the costs of the combined Forces are expenses of the Organization to be borne by Member States in accordance with Article 17, paragraph 2, of the Charter of the United Nations,

Recalling its previous decisions regarding the fact that, in order to meet the expenditures caused by the combined Forces, a different procedure is required from that applied to meet expenditures of the regular budget of the United Nations,

Taking into account the fact that the economically more developed countries are in a position to make relatively larger contributions and that the economically less developed countries have a relatively limited capacity to contribute towards such an operation,

Bearing in mind the special responsibilities of the States permanent members of the Security Council, as indicated in General Assembly resolution 1874(S-IV) of 27 June 1963, in the financing of such operations,

Noting with appreciation that voluntary contributions have been made to the combined Forces by certain Governments,

Mindful of the fact that it is essential to provide the combined Forces with the necessary financial resources to enable them to meet their outstanding liabilities,

1. *Takes note* of the status of contributions to the combined Forces as at 30 April 2000, including the contributions outstanding in the amount of 622.7 million United States dollars, representing 13 per cent of the total assessed contributions from the inception of the United Nations Protection Force to the period ending 30 June 1997, notes that some 49 per cent of the Member States have paid their assessed contributions in full, and urges all other Member States concerned, in particular those in arrears, to ensure payment of their outstanding assessed contributions;

2. *Expresses its appreciation* to those Member States which have paid their assessed contributions in full;

3. *Expresses concern* about the financial situation with regard to peacekeeping activities, in particular as regards the reimbursements to troop contributors that bear additional burdens owing to overdue payments by Member States of their assessments;

4. *Urges* all other Member States to make every possible effort to ensure payment of their assessed contributions to the combined Forces in full;

5. *Expresses concern* at the delay experienced by the Secretary-General in deploying and providing adequate resources to some recent peacekeeping missions, in particular those in Africa;

6. *Emphasizes* that all future and existing peacekeeping missions shall be given equal and non-discriminatory treatment in respect of financial and administrative arrangements;

7. *Also emphasizes* that all peacekeeping missions shall be provided with adequate resources for the effective and efficient discharge of their respective mandates;

8. *Endorses* the conclusions and recommendations contained in the report of the Advisory Committee on Administrative and Budgetary Questions, and requests the Secretary-General to ensure their full implementation;

9. *Authorizes* the Secretary-General to retain an amount of 1,193,000 dollars gross (963,300 dollars net) from the amount of 1,199,200 dollars gross (1,070,300 dollars net) concurred in by the Advisory Committee from the unencumbered balance of 3,467,200 dollars gross (4,094,200 dollars net) for the period from 1 July 1996 to 30 June 1997 to meet the cost of completing the liquidation of the mission;

10. *Also authorizes* the Secretary-General to retain an amount of 179,899,700 dollars gross and net from the balance of appropriations of 304,179,027 dollars gross (304,955,370 dollars net) to meet the cost of outstanding Government claims;

11. *Requests* the Secretary-General to present a more detailed explanation of the amounts required for reimbursement of contingent-owned equipment, including the impact of the retroactive application of the new procedures for contingent-owned equipment, in the context of the final report on the combined Forces, and to reconsider the question at its fifty-fifth session;

12. *Decides* to keep under review the amounts budgeted for reimbursement of contingent-owned equipment;

13. *Decides also* to suspend for the immediate future the provisions of regulations 4.3, 4.4 and 5.2 *(d)* of the financial regulations of the United Nations in respect

of the remaining surplus of 124,279,327 dollars gross (125,055,670 dollars net) in order to allow for reimbursements to troop contributors and in the light of the cash shortage of the combined Forces, and requests the Secretary-General to provide an updated report in one year;

14. *Emphasizes* that no peacekeeping mission shall be financed by borrowing funds from other active peacekeeping missions;

15. *Decides* to include in the provisional agenda of its fifty-fifth session the item entitled "Financing of the United Nations Protection Force, the United Nations Confidence Restoration Operation in Croatia, the United Nations Preventive Deployment Force and the United Nations Peace Forces headquarters".

On 23 December, the Assembly decided•that the item on the financing of UNPROFOR, UNCRO, UNPREDEP and UNPF-HQ would remain for consideration at the resumed fifty-fifth (2001) session (**decision 55/458**) and that the Fifth Committee should continue to consider the item at that session (**decision 55/455**).

(Details on the financing of the respective peacekeeping operations in the former Yugoslavia are described in the relevant sections below.)

UNTAES and UN Civilian Police Support Group

On 17 January, the Secretary-General submitted to the General Assembly the financial performance report of the Civilian Police Support Group from 1 July 1998 to 30 June 1999 [A/54/713]. Having terminated the mandate of the United Nations Transitional Administration for Eastern Slavonia, Baranja and Western Sirmium (UNTAES) on 15 January 1998 by resolution 1120(1997) [YUN 1997, p. 324], the Security Council, by resolution 1145(1997) [ibid., p. 332], established the Civilian Police Support Group for a single nine-month period ending on 15 October 1998.

Expenditures for the period covered totalled $6.6 million gross ($6.1 million net), resulting in an unencumbered balance of $877,160 gross ($894,960 net), which resulted mainly from staff vacancies, early repatriation of civilian police, the availability of some supplies from the UNTAES stock and the use of the mission's vehicles to transport equipment to the United Nations Logistics Base in Brindisi, Italy. The cost of completing the liquidation of UNTAES, as well as the final audit, could be met from the unencumbered balance, resulting in an adjusted unencumbered balance of $263,160 gross ($359,960 net).

On 3 April [A/54/823], ACABQ commented on the Secretary-General's report.

GENERAL ASSEMBLY ACTION

On 15 June [meeting 98], the General Assembly, on the recommendation of the Fifth Committee

[A/54/905], adopted **resolution 54/274** without vote [agenda item 145].

Financing of the Civilian Police Support Group

The General Assembly,

Having considered the report of the Secretary-General on the financing of the Civilian Police Support Group and the related reports of the Advisory Committee on Administrative and Budgetary Questions,

Recalling Security Council resolution 1037(1996) of 15 January 1996, by which the Council established the United Nations Transitional Administration for Eastern Slavonia, Baranja and Western Sirmium for an initial period of twelve months, and resolution 1145(1997) of 19 December 1997, in which the Council noted the termination of the Transitional Administration on 15 January 1998 and established, with effect from 16 January 1998, the Civilian Police Support Group for a single period of up to nine months,

Recalling also its decision 50/481 of 11 April 1996 on the financing of the Transitional Administration and its subsequent resolutions thereon, the latest of which was resolution 53/234 of 8 June 1999,

Reaffirming that the costs of the Transitional Administration and the Support Group are expenses of the Organization to be borne by Member States in accordance with Article 17, paragraph 2, of the Charter of the United Nations,

Recalling its previous decisions regarding the fact that, in order to meet the expenditures caused by the Transitional Administration and the Support Group, a different procedure is required from that applied to meet expenditures of the regular budget of the United Nations,

Taking into account the fact that the economically more developed countries are in a position to make relatively larger contributions and that the economically less developed countries have a relatively limited capacity to contribute towards such an operation,

Bearing in mind the special responsibilities of the States permanent members of the Security Council, as indicated in General Assembly resolution 1874(S-IV) of 27 June 1963, in the financing of such operations,

Noting with appreciation that voluntary contributions have been made to the Transitional Administration,

Mindful of the fact that it is essential to provide the account of the missions with the necessary financial resources to enable them to meet their outstanding liabilities,

1. *Takes note* of the status of contributions to the United Nations Transitional Administration for Eastern Slavonia, Baranja and Western Sirmium and the Civilian Police Support Group as at 30 April 2000, including the contributions outstanding in the amount of 29.8 million United States dollars, representing 7 per cent of the total assessed contributions from the inception of the Transitional Administration to the period ending 30 June 1999, notes that some 29 per cent of the Member States have paid their assessed contributions in full, and urges all other Member States concerned, in particular those in arrears, to ensure payment of their outstanding assessed contributions;

2. *Expresses its appreciation* to those Member States which have paid their assessed contributions in full;

3. *Expresses concern* about the financial situation with regard to peacekeeping activities, in particular as regards the reimbursements to troop contributors that bear additional burdens owing to overdue payments by Member States of their assessments;

4. *Urges* all other Member States to make every possible effort to ensure payment of their assessed contributions to the missions in full;

5. *Expresses concern* at the delay experienced by the Secretary-General in deploying and providing adequate resources to some recent peacekeeping missions, in particular those in Africa;

6. *Emphasizes* that all future and existing peacekeeping missions shall be given equal and non-discriminatory treatment in respect of financial and administrative arrangements;

7. *Also emphasizes* that all peacekeeping missions shall be provided with adequate resources for the effective and efficient discharge of their respective mandates;

8. *Endorses* the conclusions and recommendations contained in the report of the Advisory Committee on Administrative and Budgetary Questions;

9. *Decides* that Member States that have fulfilled their financial obligations to the Transitional Administration and the Support Group shall be credited their respective share of the remaining unencumbered balance of 601,200 dollars gross (541,500 dollars net) in respect of the period ending 30 June 1998 and of the unencumbered balance of 263,160 dollars gross (359,960 dollars net) in respect of the period ending 30 June 1999;

10. *Decides also* that, for Member States that have not fulfilled their obligations to the Transitional Administration and the Support Group, their share of the remaining unencumbered balance of 601,200 dollars gross (541,500 dollars net) in respect of the period ending 30 June 1998 and of the unencumbered balance of 263,160 dollars gross (359,960 dollars net) in respect of the period ending 30 June 1999 shall be set off against their outstanding obligations;

11. *Emphasizes* that no peacekeeping mission shall be financed by borrowing funds from other active peacekeeping missions;

12. *Decides* to include in the provisional agenda of its fifty-fifth session the item entitled "Financing of the United Nations Transitional Administration for Eastern Slavonia, Baranja and Western Sirmium and the Civilian Police Support Group".

On 23 December, the Assembly decided that the item on the financing of UNTAES and the Civilian Police Support Group would remain for consideration at the resumed fifty-fifth (2001) session (**decision 55/458**) and that the Fifth Committee should continue to consider the item at that session (**decision 55/455**).

UNPREDEP

On 7 February, the Secretary-General submitted to the General Assembly the financial performance report of the United Nations Preventive Deployment Force (UNPREDEP) covering 1 July 1998 to 30 June 1999 [A/54/740]. The mandate of UNPREDEP, which operated within the former Yugoslav Republic of Macedonia (FYROM), terminated on 28 February 1999 [YUN 1999, p. 370]. Expenditures for the period totalled $41.9 million gross ($40.9 million net), resulting in an unencumbered balance of $1.2 million gross ($1.1 million net), resulting mainly from lower costs of troop rotation and rapid liquidation of the mission during the period from March to June 1999. However, an amount of $904,000, which was not obligated for troop rotation, was still required.

On 3 April [A/54/824], ACABQ commented on the Secretary-General's report.

GENERAL ASSEMBLY ACTION

On 15 June [meeting 98], the General Assembly, on the recommendation of the Fifth Committee [A/54/906], adopted **resolution 54/275** without vote [agenda item 146].

Financing of the United Nations Preventive Deployment Force

The General Assembly,

Having considered the report of the Secretary-General on the financing of the United Nations Preventive Deployment Force and the related reports of the Advisory Committee on Administrative and Budgetary Questions,

Recalling Security Council resolutions 983(1995) of 31 March 1995, by which the Council decided that the United Nations Protection Force within the former Yugoslav Republic of Macedonia should be known as the United Nations Preventive Deployment Force, and 1186(1998) of 21 July 1998, by which the Council extended the mandate of the Force until 28 February 1999,

Recalling also its decision 50/481 of 11 April 1996 on the financing of the Force and its subsequent resolutions thereon, the latest of which was resolution 53/20 B of 8 June 1999,

Reaffirming that the costs of the Force are expenses of the Organization to be borne by Member States in accordance with Article 17, paragraph 2, of the Charter of the United Nations,

Recalling its previous decisions regarding the fact that, in order to meet the expenditures caused by the Force, a different procedure is required from that applied to meet expenditures of the regular budget of the United Nations,

Taking into account the fact that the economically more developed countries are in a position to make relatively larger contributions and that the economically less developed countries have a relatively limited capacity to contribute towards such an operation,

Bearing in mind the special responsibilities of the States permanent members of the Security Council, as indicated in General Assembly resolution 1874(S-IV) of 27 June 1963, in the financing of such operations,

Noting with appreciation that voluntary contributions have been made to the Force by certain Governments,

Mindful of the fact that it is essential to provide the account of the Force with the necessary financial resources to enable it to meet its outstanding liabilities,

1. *Takes note* of the status of contributions to the United Nations Preventive Deployment Force as at 30 April 2000, including the contributions outstanding in the amount of 10.8 million United States dollars, representing 8 per cent of the total assessed contributions from the inception of the Force to the period ending 30 June 1999, notes that some 42 per cent of the Member States have paid their assessed contributions in full, and urges all other Member States concerned, in particular those in arrears, to ensure payment of their outstanding assessed contributions;

2. *Expresses its appreciation* to those Member States which have paid their assessed contributions in full;

3. *Expresses concern* about the financial situation with regard to peacekeeping activities, in particular as regards the reimbursements to troop contributors that bear additional burdens owing to overdue payments by Member States of their assessments;

4. *Urges* all other Member States to make every possible effort to ensure payment of their assessed contributions to the Force in full;

5. *Expresses concern* at the delay experienced by the Secretary-General in deploying and providing adequate resources to some recent peacekeeping missions, in particular those in Africa;

6. *Emphasizes* that all future and existing peacekeeping missions shall be given equal and non-discriminatory treatment in respect of financial and administrative arrangements;

7. *Also emphasizes* that all peacekeeping missions shall be provided with adequate resources for the effective and efficient discharge of their respective mandates;

8. *Endorses* the conclusions and recommendations contained in the report of the Advisory Committee on Administrative and Budgetary Questions, and requests the Secretary-General to ensure their full implementation;

9. *Authorizes* the Secretary-General to retain the amount of 904,000 dollars from the unencumbered balance of 1,161,700 dollars gross (1,104,300 dollars net) in respect of the period from 1 July 1998 to 30 June 1999 to cover the costs of outstanding claims from a Government for the rotation of its troops during the prior period;

10. *Decides* that Member States that have fulfilled their financial obligations to the Force shall be credited their respective share of the remaining unencumbered balance of 257,700 dollars gross (200,300 dollars net) in respect of the period ending 30 June 1999;

11. *Decides also* that, for Member States that have not fulfilled their obligations to the Force, their share of the remaining unencumbered balance of 257,700 dollars gross (200,300 dollars net) in respect of the period ending 30 June 1999 shall be set off against their outstanding obligations;

12. *Emphasizes* that no peacekeeping mission shall be financed by borrowing funds from other active peacekeeping missions;

13. *Decides* to include in the provisional agenda of its fifty-fifth session the item entitled "Financing of the United Nations Preventive Deployment Force".

In September [A/55/390], the Secretary-General submitted details of the final disposition of UNPREDEP's assets, with an inventory value as at 1 March of some $20.2 million, 46 per cent of which had been transferred to other peace-keeping operations or to the United Nations Logistics Base.

On 23 December, the Assembly decided that the item on the financing of UNPREDEP would remain for consideration at the resumed fifty-fifth (2001) session (**decision 55/458**) and that the Fifth Committee would continue to consider the item at that session (**decision 55/455**).

State succession issues

On 3 February [A/54/742], four of the five successor States of the former Socialist Federal Republic of Yugoslavia (SFRY) (Bosnia and Herzegovina, Croatia, Slovenia and FYROM) drew the attention of the General Assembly President to the draft resolution [A/54/L.62] on the issue of succession [YUN 1999, p. 306], consideration of which had been postponed pending further consultations. The four States stated that they would continue to work with interested delegations to ensure full implementation of relevant Assembly resolutions, in particular resolution 47/1 [YUN 1992, p. 139], and underlined the importance of the principle of equality of all five successor States to SFRY.

In a 10 February letter [S/2000/109] to the Security Council President, the four States reconfirmed their readiness, in view of the expressed readiness of FRY, to resume negotiations to solve promptly the issue on the basis of the equality of all five successor States. The four States affirmed that settlement of the issue would contribute to political stabilization, economic cooperation and the improvement of relations.

On 25 April [S/2000/348], FRY transmitted to the Council President a copy of a letter from the head of its delegation to the negotiations of the Peace Implementation Council (PIC) (see p. 331) to the Negotiations Mediator, Sir Arthur Watts. The head of the delegation indicated that he had been informed that, at the PIC meeting (Sarajevo, Bosnia and Herzegovina, 4 April), discussion of the continuation of work on succession issues was avoided. Despite the fact that all involved were interested in negotiations, PIC had demonstrated a surprising lack of interest and had blocked the negotiations for more than a year without any explanation, taking upon itself prerogatives that it was not entitled to per se, nor were they established by the agreement. The only rational explanation for such conduct was that succession issues had assumed a political character, with all its implications at the current juncture of international relations. Although he could not advise as to the current position of the Yugoslav Government

on the standstill in the negotiations, he was certain that it insisted on the continuation of the negotiations on the basis of the Mediator's last proposal.

On 24 May [A/54/881], FRY said that statements made by Bosnia and Herzegovina, Croatia and Slovenia in the Assembly's Fifth Committee concerning FRY's status in the United Nations were unfounded and tendentious. FRY repeated its previous arguments in connection with the issue [YUN 1999, p. 305] and stated that the contention that FRY's status in the United Nations was linked with, and contingent upon, the solution of the succession issues of the former SFRY was unfounded and aimed at confusing Member States. FRY's status should be resolved in accordance with the Charter and relevant UN rules, while the succession issues of the division of assets and liabilities of the former SFRY were subject to negotiations between it and the other former Yugoslav republics based on international law, leading to solutions acceptable by all.

The Presidents of Bosnia and Herzegovina, Croatia, Slovenia and FYROM, in a joint statement forwarded to the Secretary-General and the Security Council President on 21 September [A/55/411, S/2000/897], said that, at a meeting held during the course of the Millennium Summit (see p. 47), they had discussed the succession to the former SFRY and had confirmed their common position in that regard. They underlined the importance of the consistent implementation of all the international community's decisions related to the succession that confirmed the legal equality of all the successors, and agreed that the existing illegal practice in the United Nations be discontinued. The four States would continue to ensure equal treatment of all of the successor States in international organizations and emphasized that FRY had to complete the procedure for admission to those organizations, as the others had done. They agreed to seek the support of the European Union (EU), the United States and other UN Member States to achieve their aims in relation to succession. The Presidents also agreed that, following democratic changes in FRY, they would advocate the lifting of sanctions and the swift admission of FRY to the United Nations and other international organizations, when and if that State so requested.

On 24 September, Vojislav Kostunica was elected President of FRY, replacing Slobodan Milosevic. The new Government dropped any claim to being the sole successor State to SFRY and was recognized by the international community.

On 27 October [A/55/528-S/2000/1043], FRY submitted to the Secretary-General its application for admission to membership of the United

Nations. On 1 November (**resolution 55/12**), the General Assembly, on the recommendation of the Security Council, admitted FRY to UN membership (see p. 1365).

Prevlaka peninsula

The United Nations continued in 2000 to assist Croatia and FRY in their efforts to arrive at a permanent solution to the disputed issue of the Prevlaka peninsula. The United Nations Mission of Observers in Prevlaka (UNMOP) continued to monitor the demilitarization of the peninsula and neighbouring areas in Croatia and FRY. The Security Council renewed its mandate until 15 January 2001.

During the year, despite the declared willingness of Croatia and FRY to resolve their dispute through bilateral negotiations, in accordance with the Agreement on Normalization of Relations between them, signed in Belgrade in 1996 [YUN 1996, p. 340], no progress was made in that regard. Their positions regarding the options for confidence-building, proposed by the Secretariat in 1999 [YUN 1999, p. 312], remained far apart. The fifth meeting on bilateral negotiations did not take place, and both sides continued to blame each other for the delay in restarting those negotiations. However, in December, the Secretary-General observed that the change in the FRY Presidency and elections to the Serbian Parliament, as well as the establishment of the new Government in Croatia, gave hope that a climate conducive to the resumption of negotiations was being created.

On the ground, the Secretary-General reported that the situation in the UN-controlled zones remained calm and free from any significant incidents.

Bilateral negotiations

On 10 January [S/2000/8], Croatia, in a letter to the Security Council President, summarized its position, contained in earlier submissions to the Council, on the disputed issue of the Prevlaka peninsula. It indicated that, as long as the Yugoslav side refused to honour its obligations and persisted in its quest to alter existing international borders between Croatia and FRY, Croatia had no justifiable basis on which to proceed with bilateral negotiations on a permanent solution of the security issue of Prevlaka. Croatia stood ready to engage in serious negotiations on the future bilateral security regime for Prevlaka and the neighbouring areas of Dubrovnik and the Bay of Kotor, starting from full respect for the existing, internationally recognized Croatian border. Croatia noted that the absence of the

Montenegrin representatives from the Yugoslav delegation rendered the legitimacy of any outcome doubtful. Moreover, several policy and legal measures taken by the international community against high-level Yugoslav federal officials in the past months compounded the problems in case of the resumption of bilateral negotiations.

On 8 February [S/2000/95], FRY forwarded to the Council President a memorandum on the facts, testifying that the Prevlaka peninsula was an integral part of FRY. Croatia rejected that assertion on 3 March [S/2000/180].

On 6 March [S/2000/268], FRY proposed that negotiations should continue based on a mutually agreed agenda, which could include the presentation of their respective positions concerning the arguments on which both sides based their perceptions of the extension of the State border, including the questions of the 1992 map, signed by the then FRY President and the Head of the General Staff of the Yugoslav Army, and the authenticity of the signatures of those individuals.

Reporting on 29 March [S/2000/268] on the status of bilateral negotiations between FRY and Croatia, as requested by Security Council resolution 1285(2000) of 13 January (see p. 332), FRY said that no meeting had taken place since March 1999 [YUN 1999, p. 307], as Croatia had failed to convene the fifth meeting. FRY reiterated its readiness to resume negotiations and engage in substantive discussions of the arguments the two sides had exchanged after four rounds of negotiations and referred to its 6 March proposals (see above). FRY was of the opinion that serious negotiations could be possible only through direct dialogue during meetings of delegations rather than by letters.

Referring to the special emphasis placed on confidence-building measures in resolution 1258(2000) and in the Secretary-General's last report on UNMOP [YUN 1999, p. 312], FRY considered them unacceptable in the Blue Zone (UN-controlled zone). The measures would amount to a revision of the concept of the Blue Zone, which did not allow the authorities and citizens of the two sides in the Zone, would imply movement of civilians in the Zone and the legalization of the border crossing at Kobila, and would legalize the presence of Croatians in the Zone and exonerate Croatia from the continued violation of the Blue Zone regime. There were no civilians who for "legitimate business" should be allowed in the Zone pending a solution of the disputed issue of Prevlaka. The two parties had committed themselves, in the Agreement on Normalization of Relations between them [YUN 1996, p. 340], to respect the existing regime established through UN monitoring, pending an agreement on Prevlaka, so that any unilateral request to change that provision constituted a violation of it.

Croatia responded on 5 April [S/2000/289] that confirmation of the authenticity of the 1992 map and signatures by UN officials involved in negotiations at the time could avert FRY from its ongoing insistence on framing the Prevlaka issue as a territorial dispute and would jump-start the negotiations. Croatia reiterated its request that the United Nations make inquiries with its former officials and confirm the authenticity of the map and signatures. Croatia stated that FRY's rejection of the Secretary-General's confidence-building measures had not come as a surprise, since FRY had continuously avoided the 1992 [YUN 1992, p. 343] and 1996 [YUN 1996, p. 340] agreements, particularly those parts relating to normalizing traffic and establishing joint customs controls at the border crossing points. The Secretary-General's proposal to allow limited civilian access to the Blue Zone served as a reminder of the mutually assumed legal obligations of the two countries. It was Croatia's view that the Secretary-General's recognition of the legitimate interests of the local population might contribute to the stability and normalization of the area.

The Secretary-General, reporting to the Security Council on UNMOP [S/2000/647], said that, on 10 April, Croatia invited representatives of FRY to attend a fifth round of discussions in Croatia at a date to be determined.

FRY, on 16 June [S/2000/602], in response to Croatia's 5 April letter, contended that there were differences in the interpretation of the rule of *uti possidetis*, which both sides had accepted, manifested in their separate perception of the extension of the border in the disputed area. The Croatian side invoked geographic maps as the sole piece of evidence, while the Yugoslav side invoked the federal laws of SFRY and republican laws, which delineated the exercise of authority in the disputed area. FRY annexed to the communication an 8 June letter from the head of its delegation to the negotiations, in which he acknowledged receipt of Croatia's confirmation of the holding of the fifth meeting at a date to be agreed through diplomatic channels and proposed the agenda item "Manner of the establishment of the border considering the application of the rule *uti possidetis*".

In a further communication [S/2000/954] submitted to the Secretary-General in October, FRY stated that the situation regarding bilateral negotiations remained unchanged as the Croatian side, for a year and a half, had persisted in its refusal to convene the fifth meeting. The FRY head

of delegation had pointed out in August that the negotiations between the two delegations could not be substituted for correspondence and the Yugoslav side could not accept an agenda for the next meeting, proposed by the head of the Croatian delegation in July, that prejudged the solution of the disputed issue of Prevlaka to the detriment of the Yugoslav side. FRY had proposed that the method for establishing the border be considered at the next meeting in view of the application of the rule of *uti possidetis* on which both sides had agreed. There were, however, differences in the perception of the application of that rule that needed to be resolved by negotiations. The agenda proposed by the Yugoslav side did not prejudge the outcome of the negotiations. Its basic positions on the solution of the issue remained the same and it reiterated its readiness to continue the bilateral negotiations.

The Secretary-General, in a December report on UNMOP [S/2000/1251], observed that regional developments and a movement towards stabilization of the political situation, in particular in FRY, had given rise to the hope that a climate conducive to the resumption of negotiations was being created. In FRY, the change in the Presidency was followed by elections to the Serbian Parliament and the new leadership was consolidating its position. In Croatia, the Government sworn into office a year earlier was well established. In the light of those developments and his meetings with the Croatian President and the Yugoslav Foreign Minister, the Secretary-General trusted that both sides would be able to resume negotiations in the near future and find ways to bridge their differences on the disputed Prevlaka issue.

UN Mission of Observers in Prevlaka (UNMOP)

The United Nations Mission of Observers in Prevlaka, which became a separate mission in 1996 [YUN 1996, p. 330], continued in 2000 to monitor the demilitarization of the disputed Prevlaka peninsula and the neighbouring areas in Croatia and FRY. The Mission, which comprised 27 military observers under the command of Chief Military Observer Colonel Graeme Williams (New Zealand), also held regular meetings with local authorities and maintained contact with authorities in Belgrade and Zagreb. UNMOP's area of responsibility consisted of two UN-designated zones: a demilitarized zone (DMZ) (Yellow Zone) and a UN-controlled zone (Blue Zone).

The Security Council twice extended UNMOP's mandate during the year, to 15 July 2000 and to 15 January 2001.

Although an independent mission, UNMOP was treated for administrative and budgetary purposes as part of UNMIBH. (For details on the financing of UNMOP, see p. 346.)

(For details on the financing of UNMOP, see p. 346.)

SECURITY COUNCIL ACTION (January)

On 13 January [meeting 4088], the Security Council, having considered the Secretary-General's December 1999 report on UNMOP [YUN 1999, p. 312], unanimously adopted **resolution 1285(2000)**. The draft [S/2000/10] was submitted by Canada, France, Germany, Italy, the Netherlands, the Russian Federation, the United Kingdom and the United States.

The Security Council,

Recalling all its relevant resolutions, in particular resolutions 779(1992) of 6 October 1992, 981(1995) of 31 March 1995, 1147(1998) of 13 January 1998, 1183(1998) of 15 July 1998, 1222(1999) of 15 January 1999 and 1252(1999) of 15 July 1999,

Having considered the report of the Secretary-General of 31 December 1999 on the United Nations Mission of Observers in Prevlaka,

Recalling the letter dated 24 December 1999 from the Chargé d'affaires a.i. of the Permanent Mission of the Federal Republic of Yugoslavia addressed to the Secretary-General and the letter dated 10 January 2000 from the Permanent Representative of Croatia to the United Nations addressed to the President of the Security Council, concerning the disputed issue of Prevlaka,

Reaffirming once again its commitment to the independence, sovereignty and territorial integrity of the Republic of Croatia within its internationally recognized borders,

Noting once again the Joint Declaration signed at Geneva on 30 September 1992 by the Presidents of the Republic of Croatia and the Federal Republic of Yugoslavia, in particular articles 1 and 3, the latter reaffirming their agreement concerning the demilitarization of the Prevlaka peninsula,

Reiterating its concern about violations of the demilitarization regime, including limitations placed on the free movement of United Nations military observers, while noting some positive development in those fields as outlined in the report of the Secretary-General,

Noting with satisfaction that the opening of crossing points between Croatia and the Federal Republic of Yugoslavia (Montenegro) in the demilitarized zone continues to facilitate civilian and commercial traffic in both directions without security incidents and continues to represent a significant confidence-building measure in the normalization of relations between the two parties, and urging the parties to utilize these openings as a basis for further confidence-building measures to achieve the normalization of relations between them,

Reiterating its serious concerns about the lack of substantive progress towards a settlement of the disputed issue of Prevlaka in the continuing bilateral negotiations between the parties pursuant to the Agreement on Normalization of Relations between the Republic of Croatia and the Federal Republic of Yugoslavia of 23 August 1996, and calling for the resumption of discussions,

Reiterating its call upon the parties urgently to put in place a comprehensive demining programme,

Commending the role played by the United Nations Mission of Observers in Prevlaka, and noting that the presence of the United Nations military observers continues to be essential to maintain conditions that are conducive to a negotiated settlement of the disputed issue of Prevlaka,

1. *Authorizes* the United Nations military observers to continue monitoring the demilitarization of the Prevlaka peninsula, in accordance with resolutions 779(1992) and 981(1995) and paragraphs 19 and 20 of the report of the Secretary-General of 13 December 1995, until 15 July 2000;

2. *Reiterates its calls* upon the parties to cease all violations of the demilitarization regime in the United Nations designated zones, to take steps further to reduce tension and to improve safety and security in the area, to cooperate fully with the United Nations military observers and to ensure their safety and full and unrestricted freedom of movement;

3. *Notes with satisfaction* that, pursuant to its request in resolution 1252(1999), the parties have been provided with recommendations and options to develop confidence-building measures, encourages the parties to take concrete steps to implement such recommendations and options with a view to, inter alia, further facilitating the freedom of movement of the civilian population, and requests the Secretary-General to report on the matter by 15 April 2000;

4. *Urges once again* that the parties abide by their mutual commitments and implement fully the Agreement on Normalization of Relations between the Republic of Croatia and the Federal Republic of Yugoslavia, and stresses in particular the urgent need for them to fulfil rapidly and in good faith their commitment to reach a negotiated resolution of the disputed issue of Prevlaka in accordance with article 4 of the Agreement;

5. *Requests* the parties to continue to report at least bimonthly to the Secretary-General on the status of their bilateral negotiations;

6. *Requests* the United Nations military observers and the multinational Stabilization Force authorized by the Council in resolution 1088(1996) of 12 December 1996 and extended by resolution 1247(1999) of 18 June 1999 to cooperate fully with each other;

7. *Decides* to remain seized of the matter.

Report of Secretary-General (April). The Secretary-General, in an April report on UNMOP [S/2000/305], stated that the situation remained stable and calm, with both sides continuing to respect the DMZ. However, on 7 March, elements of the newly formed Montenegrin Special Police were observed conducting training exercises within the zone. They remained there, bolstering the Border Police presence. In the UN-controlled zone, the long-standing violations of the security regime remained unchanged with police from both sides maintaining positions there. On two occasions, Croatian buses carrying local schoolchildren were observed in the zone. In January, in the context of the Croatian presidential election campaign, several senior Croatian political figures entered the zone.

Concerning the confidence-building measures conveyed to the parties by the Secretariat in 1999 [YUN 1999, p. 312], preliminary consultations on the options presented continued, including on the commencement of demarcation of the border, the regularization of the crossing point at Debeli Brijeg, the introduction of a limited access regime for local civilians in the UN-controlled zone and the replacement of the crossing point at Cape Kobila by alternative arrangements worked out under the controlled access regime. The parties favoured some elements of the options package but rejected others, reflecting their overall views in the dispute. Their positions on the package remained far apart.

Communications. On 16 June [S/2000/602], FRY advised the Security Council President of a number of long-standing violations of the security regime in the Blue Zone by Croatia, including the installation of a telephone booth at Cape Kobila border crossing, which it demanded be removed and the border crossing closed until a solution to the disputed issue of Prevlaka was found. Noting that the Council, in resolution 1285(2000), had called for an end to the violations of the demilitarization regime in the Blue Zone, while the Secretary-General had described the presence of civilians there as a violation of the agreed security regime, FRY called for strict implementation of the decisions and positions of the Council and the Secretary-General.

On 30 June [S/2000/642], the Foreign Ministers of Croatia and the FRY Republic of Montenegro, in a joint communiqué, expressed their continued support for full demilitarization on both sides of the border in the Prevlaka peninsula as a means of reducing tensions and stabilizing the entire area. The opening of the border crossings Debeli Brijeg and Konfin had resulted in demonstrable confidence-building among the local population on both sides of the border and provided an impetus for the renewed commercial and other ties between Croatia and Montenegro. Complete demining and unhindered civilian access throughout the entire Prevlaka range and the opportunity to use the natural resources would further strengthen stability and confidence, restart the tourist economy and thus constitute another step towards full normalization of relations.

Croatia and Montenegro considered UNMOP's mandate to be successful and remained confident that substantial reduction of its personnel should be able to start in the nearest possible future, consistent with the increased development of mutual trust and the willingness of Croatia and Montenegro to take responsibility for the security of the area.

Report of Secretary-General (July). The Secretary-General, in his July report on UNMOP [S/2000/647], said that neither Croatia nor FRY had put in place a comprehensive demining programme in the UNMOP area of responsibility. As a result, the situation of identified minefields remained unchanged. He also reported a significant increase in the number of Montenegrin Special Police in the DMZ, which did not constitute a violation of the security regime. In June, a Yugoslav army truck armed with a machine gun and carrying some 20 soldiers was observed within the DMZ. The violations of the security regime in the UN-controlled zone remained unchanged.

The Secretary-General observed that UNMOP's efforts to convince the parties to devise means for implementing the confidence-building measures proposed by the Secretariat had not been successful and the positions of the parties in that regard continued to reflect their differing interpretations of the Prevlaka dispute. Against that background, Croatia's invitation to FRY to attend the fifth round of negotiations and FRY's acceptance was a positive development. However, because of the still unsettled general political circumstances in the area, expectations for substantive progress remained limited. To maintain the conditions of stability that were essential to any meaningful progress towards a political settlement, the Secretary-General recommended that UNMOP's mandate be extended until 15 January 2001.

That recommendation was supported by FRY in a 6 July letter to the Council President [S/2000/653].

SECURITY COUNCIL ACTION (July)

On 13 July [meeting 4170], the Security Council unanimously adopted **resolution 1307(2000)**. The draft [S/2000/681] was prepared in consultations among Council members.

The Security Council,

Recalling all its relevant resolutions, in particular resolutions 779(1992) of 6 October 1992, 981(1995) of 31 March 1995, 1147(1998) of 13 January 1998, 1183(1998) of 15 July 1998, 1222(1999) of 15 January 1999, 1252(1999) of 15 July 1999 and 1285(2000) of 13 January 2000,

Having considered the report of the Secretary-General of 3 July 2000 on the United Nations Mission of Observers in Prevlaka,

Recalling the letter dated 5 April 2000 from the Permanent Representative of Croatia to the United Nations addressed to the Secretary-General and the letter dated 16 June 2000 from the Chargé d'affaires a.i. of the Permanent Mission of the Federal Republic of Yugoslavia addressed to the President of the Security Council, concerning the disputed issue of Prevlaka,

Reaffirming once again its commitment to independence, sovereignty and territorial integrity of the Republic of Croatia within its internationally recognized borders,

Noting once again the Joint Declaration signed at Geneva on 30 September 1992 by the Presidents of the Republic of Croatia and the Federal Republic of Yugoslavia, in particular articles 1 and 3, the latter reaffirming their agreement concerning the demilitarization of the Prevlaka peninsula,

Noting with satisfaction that the overall situation in the area of responsibility of the Mission has remained stable and calm,

Reiterating its concern about continuing violations of the demilitarization regime, including limitations placed on the free movement of United Nations military observers,

Noting with satisfaction that the opening of crossing points between Croatia and the Federal Republic of Yugoslavia (Montenegro) in the demilitarized zone continues to facilitate civilian and commercial traffic in both directions without security incidents and continues to represent a significant confidence-building measure in the normalization of relations between the two parties, and urging the parties to utilize these openings as a basis for further confidence-building measures to achieve the normalization of relations between them,

Reiterating its serious concerns about the lack of substantive progress towards a settlement of the disputed issue of Prevlaka in the continuing bilateral negotiations between the parties pursuant to the Agreement on Normalization of Relations between the Republic of Croatia and the Federal Republic of Yugoslavia of 23 August 1996, noting positive developments in this regard, and calling for the resumption of discussions,

Expressing its concern over the delay in putting in place a comprehensive demining programme by the parties,

Commending the role played by the Mission, and noting that the presence of the United Nations military observers continues to be essential to maintaining conditions that are conducive to a negotiated settlement of the disputed issue of Prevlaka,

Recalling the relevant principles contained in the Convention on the Safety of United Nations and Associated Personnel of 9 December 1994 and the statement by its President of 9 February 2000,

Welcoming and encouraging efforts by the United Nations to sensitize peacekeeping personnel in the prevention and control of HIV/AIDS and other communicable diseases in all its peacekeeping operations,

1. *Authorizes* the United Nations military observers to continue monitoring the demilitarization of the Prevlaka peninsula, in accordance with resolutions 779(1992) and 981(1995) and paragraphs 19 and 20 of the report of the Secretary-General of 13 December 1995, until 15 January 2001;

2. *Reiterates its call* upon the parties to cease all violations of the demilitarized regime in the United Nations designated zones, to take steps further to reduce tension and to improve safety and security in the area, to cooperate fully with the United Nations military observers and to ensure their safety and full and unrestricted freedom of movement;

3. *Notes with concern* the lack of progress by the parties in devising means of implementing the recommendations and options to develop confidence-building measures with which they were provided pursuant to its request in resolution 1252(1999), encourages the parties to take concrete steps to implement such recommendations and options with a view to, inter alia, further facilitating the freedom of movement of the civilian population, and requests the Secretary-General to report on the matter by 15 October 2000;

4. *Urges once again* that the parties abide by their mutual commitments and implement fully the Agreement on Normalization of Relations between the Republic of Croatia and the Federal Republic of Yugoslavia, and stresses in particular the urgent need for them to fulfil rapidly and in good faith their commitment to reach a negotiated resolution of the disputed issue of Prevlaka in accordance with article 4 of the Agreement;

5. *Requests* the parties to continue to report at least bi-monthly to the Secretary-General on the status of their bilateral negotiations;

6. *Reiterates its call* upon the parties to put a comprehensive demining programme in place in the identified minefields in the area of responsibility of the United Nations Mission of Observers in Prevlaka;

7. *Requests* the United Nations military observers and the multinational Stabilization Force authorized by the Council in resolution 1088(1996) of 12 December 1996 and extended by resolution 1305(2000) of 21 June 2000 to cooperate fully with each other;

8. *Decides* to remain seized of the matter.

Communications. On 17 July [S/2000/702], FRY, in response to Council resolution 1307(2000), said that the provision of the resolution relative to the border crossings containing a reference to Montenegro by the name of Yugoslavia was not acceptable and attempted to circumvent the fact that the issue could be resolved only with FRY as a sovereign State. Under its constitution, border crossings and relations with sovereign States fell within the exclusive competence of the FRY authorities. The opening of border crossings without FRY's agreement was contrary to international law and the relevant domestic laws and FRY could not accept the support provided to the undertaking in the resolution.

On 4 September [S/2000/858], FRY said that implementation of the Agreement on Normalization of Relations [YUN 1996, p. 340] had stagnated for more than a year due to Croatia's passive attitude and lack of cooperation. Croatia had unilaterally discontinued negotiations on the issue of missing persons and, from March 1999 to July 2000, despite several Yugoslav initiatives, had not called a meeting between the FRY Commission for humanitarian issues and missing persons and Croatia's Commission for detained and missing persons. Croatia continued to obstruct implementation of the 1998 agreement between the Ministers for Foreign Affairs of the two sides on the exchange of all detainees. The recent release of five Serbs was not satisfactory and FRY expected that all persons covered by that agreement would be released. In addition, Croatia did not accept a FRY proposal to hold a meeting, at the end of June in Belgrade, of the Joint Yugoslav-Croatian Commission for the implementation of article 7 of the Agreement on Normalization of Relations, which concerned the return of refugees and restitution of their property. It was also delaying the continuation of work of the Commissions for the resolution of the question of Prevlaka. While the Commissions had not met for more than a year, Croatia had held talks with Montenegro and border crossings between Croatia and FRY had been illegally opened on a part of the FRY-Croatian border in Montenegro, violating the border regime between the two countries. Moreover, Croatia had avoided the talks on the establishment of the borderline between the two countries on the Danube. It slowly and inadequately fulfilled its obligations under the Basic Agreement on the Region of Eastern Slavonia, Baranja and Western Sirmium [YUN 1995, p. 587] and the letter of intent concerning the unimpeded and free return of expelled and displaced Serbs, protection of human rights and security of all Serbs living in the area, restitution of property and compensation for seized, destroyed or damaged property.

Croatia had unilaterally joined separate negotiations with Montenegro, a federal unit of FRY, in flagrant violation of the Agreement on Normalization of Relations. FRY expressed its concern over the continued violations, delays and avoidance to carry out further scheduled and agreed activities and steps in the implementation of that Agreement and called on Croatia to respect the process of normalization of relations with FRY on the basis of the Agreement.

Report of Secretary-General (October). In October [S/2000/976], the Secretary-General reported no significant change in the overall situation in the UNMOP area of responsibility. On 23 September, the eve of FRY's elections, seven Yugoslav army officers were observed in Herceg Novi, guarding a municipal building in the DMZ. On the same day, the Montenegrin police deployed an anti-aircraft weapon at Debeli Brijeg on the border between Croatia and FRY, also in the DMZ. The Yugoslav Army personnel were withdrawn on 24 September but the heavy weapon remained in place. In the UN-controlled zone, the presence of unmanned checkpoints of Croatia and FRY for the purpose of operating a crossing regime at Cape Kobila continued to violate the security regime. On 26 August, the Croatian President and an official party entered the zone without prior authorization, constituting

the highest level of violation the zone had recorded since 1992.

The Secretary-General observed that, although the UN-controlled zones remained demilitarized and free of significant incidents, and despite the prevailing calm on the ground, there was still no movement towards a political settlement. Consultations on the confidence-building measures had not been followed by significant progress.

Communication. On 22 December [S/2000/1235], FRY said that it appreciated UNMOP's contribution to the maintenance of stability and security in Prevlaka thus far and its presence continued to be necessary to strengthen confidence and create conditions for finding an acceptable solution to the question. The major democratic changes that had taken place in FRY and the establishment of a new Government in Croatia would make it possible to step up the solution of the question of Prevlaka in a mutually acceptable way. FRY, therefore, invited Croatia to engage, as soon as possible, in concrete negotiations in the spirit of the current democratic changes in an attempt to solve the question of Prevlaka in good faith. As those negotiations would take some time, FRY expected that the Council would extend UNMOP's mandate until 15 July 2001.

Report of Secretary-General (December). In his December report on UNMOP [S/2000/1251], the Secretary-General said that Croatia's invitation in April to FRY to attend a fifth round of negotiations, together with FRY's acceptance, had not been followed so far by a meeting of the negotiating teams. Continued long-standing violations of the established security regime did not facilitate the establishment of mutual confidence. For that reason, the restrictions of movement imposed on UNMOP military observers on the Croatian side of the DMZ should be lifted. In the UN-controlled zone, the Montenegrin and Croatian police presence should be withdrawn and the violation of the security regime through continued operation of the checkpoints at Cape Kobila should be resolved. The Secretary-General recommended that UNMOP's mandate be extended until 15 July 2001.

Bosnia and Herzegovina

The United Nations continued to support efforts towards the full implementation of the 1995 General Framework Agreement for Peace in Bosnia and Herzegovina (the Peace Agreement) [YUN 1995, p. 544] through the Office of the High

Representative responsible for the Agreement's civil aspects [YUN 1996, p. 293] and the United Nations Mission in Bosnia and Herzegovina (UN-MIBH) [ibid., p. 294], the key components of which were the International Police Task Force (IPTF) and the Mine Action Centre (MAC). Both those entities worked in cooperation with the multinational Stabilization Force (SFOR), led by the North Atlantic Treaty Organization (NATO), which was responsible for the Agreements's military aspects.

The Peace Implementation Council (PIC), which continued to oversee and facilitate the Agreement's implementation, met in May to review progress in that regard. It issued a Declaration (see p. 338), in which it noted the slow pace of implementation and agreed on steps to accelerate it by setting key strategic targets for the consolidation of State institutions, economic reform and refugee return. Municipal elections were held in April and a general election in November.

UNMIBH elaborated a comprehensive mandate implementation plan aimed at completing its core mandate by December 2002. The Security Council extended the UNMIBH mandate until July 2001.

Implementation of Peace Agreement

Communications. On 28 January [S/2000/77], Bosnia and Herzegovina transmitted to the Security Council President the 25 January statement of the Secretary-General's Special Representative and Coordinator of United Nations Operations in Bosnia and Herzegovina, Jacques Paul Klein, before the Council of Europe on the subject of Bosnia and Herzegovina's admission to membership of that Council.

The Special Representative argued that real progress had been made in Bosnia and Herzegovina, although much more needed to be achieved for peace implementation to be self-sustaining. Five years after the conclusion of the Peace Agreement, the construction of the State of Bosnia and Herzegovina was still dogged by two major impediments: the building of a State identity and the continued domination of the political process by wartime leaders and recently enriched elites. Accession to the Council of Europe would promote State identity through a sense of belonging to a common value system based on respect for individual freedoms, rule of law and participatory government. It would enable Bosnia and Herzegovina to be confident in its relations with its neighbours and to fulfil its promise of being the most multi-ethnic democratic country in the Balkans. While Bosnia and Herzegovina still had a distance to go in fully meeting European stand-

ards, to deny accession would only reward those who caused its misfortunes. The dramatic change in Zagreb (Croatia), the expansion of the EU, and the strategic position of Bosnia and Herzegovina in the vision for a strong Europe argued for accession to be given.

Bosnia and Herzegovina, in agreeing with the Special Representative's overriding theme, said, in its letter of transmittal, that the longer the position of Bosnia and Herzegovina in relevant established institutions was blocked from without, the more that would encourage forces within the country not to fulfil commitments for membership.

On 9 February [S/2000/108], Bosnia and Herzegovina transmitted to the Secretary-General a proposal from the Co-Chairman of its Council of Ministers with respect to the Peace Agreement, entitled "Memorandum on Change". Though not a proposal of the Government, Bosnia and Herzegovina said that the proposal reflected the disappointment with the progress and development of the peace process. The Co-Chairman argued that the limited effects of the Peace Agreement and the fundamental changes in circumstances since its adoption pointed to the need to review the entire project, to remedy certain structural defects and to redefine the tactics for implementation. That was necessary to ensure the mass, rapid and secure return of refugees; to overcome the extended constitutional crisis; to define a well-thought-out strategy for the country's economic development; and to find solutions to the issue of the organization of the military. All those changes could be achieved in a relatively short period if the international community concentrated its efforts and made use of the resources at its disposal. Agreement could be reached within the framework of countries signatory to the Peace Agreement, with commitment on the part of PIC and a further expansion of the authority of the High Representative.

On 29 February [A/54/777-S/2000/170], Bosnia and Herzegovina forwarded to the Secretary-General the text of the "Position of the Croat Leadership regarding the process of deconstituization of Croats in Bosnia and Herzegovina." According to the leadership of the Croat community in Bosnia and Herzegovina, since the signing of the Peace Agreement, the international community, instead of upgrading the rights and powers of the Croat community and making it a more equal partner of the Serbs and Bosniacs in the building of a common State, had limited them and, in fact, deconstituted the Croats, further alienating them. Therefore, Croat support for the Federation and a unified State had declined dramatically. Among the grievances cited were limits on the powers of the cantons in areas such as education, language, media, policing and the use of symbols; efforts to "unitarize" and centralize the Federation, especially in judicial and internal affairs, and outvoting the Croat members of the Federation Government and its deputies in the House of Representatives on questions of vital national interest; the process, at the State level, towards eliminating the principle of consensus and parity in the common institutions of Bosnia and Herzegovina, which would lead to a one-party State; and the issue of the constituent right of the Croats to elect their own officials, or to be represented by persons of their own choosing. The Croat leadership in Bosnia and Herzegovina continued to believe that the international community should assist it in finding ways to enfranchise the Croatian community and to harmonize the Peace Agreement in terms of standardizing institutions for all three communities so that the Croats could also develop a stake in Bosnia and Herzegovina as the other two communities already had. If the situation was not reversed, the Croat leadership and people in Bosnia and Herzegovina reserved their right to decide unilaterally what modalities to pursue to protect their rights as a sovereign and constituent people under the Constitution.

On 22 March [S/2000/248], Ante Jelavic, Member of the Presidency of Bosnia and Herzegovina, referring to the International Tribunal for the Former Yugoslavia (ICTY) (see PART FOUR, Chapter II) and its role in the success or failure of the Peace Agreement, stated that, as the Tribunal entered its eighth year, it was time to review its work. Issues such as its most recent judgement, the lack of progress regarding the Srebrenica case (see p. 353), the make-up of indictments and the imprisoned, as well as the Tribunal's competence over individual versus institutional responsibility should be of particular concern. Mr. Jelavic proposed that the Security Council consider whether the time was appropriate to undertake that review and appoint a commission to recommend possible changes. The Council should also review the establishment of a new body to address appeals and the issue of proper defence of the accused. Those issues represented a stumbling block to the peace process in Bosnia and Herzegovina and the region and required the Council's immediate attention.

On 5 April [S/2000/290], the FRY Federal Minister for Foreign Affairs condemned the 3 April arrest by SFOR of Momcilo Krajisnik (see p. 1221), the Speaker of the Republika Srpska Parliament and a member of Bosnia and Herzegovina's collective Presidency. He contended that some of the Tribunal's activities violated the Peace Agreement, the UN Charter, the Universal Declaration of Human Rights and international law and brought into question peace and security in Bosnia and Herzegovina and the region. The Federal Minister called for the abolition of ICTY and that its records be forwarded to the regular courts of UN Member States to be acted upon in accordance with their internal laws.

On 4 May [S/2000/381], Bosnia and Herzegovina said that it would like to encourage a debate within the Council and the adoption of standards of protocol in dealing with individuals who denied ICTY's authority, and by extension the Council and the United Nations as a whole. It set out norms of protocol and behaviour that could be considered.

Implementation of New York Declaration

On 6 March [S/2000/211], Bosnia and Herzegovina submitted the report of its Presidency on the implementation of the New York Declaration, adopted in November 1999 [YUN 1999, p. 314]. The Presidency reported that it had passed the draft Law on Border Service, but the Parliament failed to do likewise, obliging the High Representative to impose it. The training of future border staff was running as envisaged. The first Border Service unit was formed and would assume duties in March. In February, the Presidency appointed the Director and Deputy Director of the Border Service and requested the Service to present a plan for harmonizing its organization and structure. It established the secretariat of the Presidency and adopted the Book of Rules of the Organization and the Job Classification in the secretariat and appointed its senior staff. The filling of other vacancies was in progress. The Presidency harmonized the new structure of the Council of Ministers, adopted the budget for Bosnia and Herzegovina's institutions, and determined foundations for the Electoral Law, which was being discussed in Parliament.

A decision was taken to accede to the Regional Centre South-East Europe Cooperative Initiative for the struggle against international crime and to sign the civic-legal convention of the Council of Europe for the struggle against corruption. A central database within the Ministry of Civil Affairs and Communications was in its final stage of establishment and changes to the Law on Passports had been forwarded to the Parliament. The Presidency appointed those members of the Committee for the Implementation of the Return Programme nominated by the Council of Ministers and entity Governments. The Committee met on 23 February and prepared a report on the situation regarding the return of refugees and internally displaced persons, which was submitted to the Security Council.

Security Council consideration. On 9 May [S/PV.4136], the Security Council met to consider the situation in Bosnia and Herzegovina. The High Representative, Wolfgang Petritsch (Austria), told the Council that time was running out for international engagement in Bosnia and Herzegovina and donor fatigue had set in. The $5.1 billion, four-year reconstruction aid package was all spoken for and SFOR had reduced its troop numbers by nearly a third. It was therefore necessary to focus on economic reform, acceleration of the return of refugees and displaced persons, and the consolidation of institutions, especially those at the State level.

On the economic front, the country was still far too dependent on international aid; to have any hope of a secure future, the economy had to become self-sustaining fast. Domestic and foreign investments were needed. However, the country's industry was still geared to the old command economy model. The Government's urgent task was to create an enabling environment for investors and to encourage small and medium-sized enterprises. The lack of a reliable banking system was another important obstacle to private investment, closely connected to the payment bureaux system. The numerous private banks were too small to provide the working capital necessary to kick-start enterprise. Overhauling the banking sector should encourage the participation of foreign banks and thus the necessary injection of capital. The process of privatization was in its first stage and the opening of the books of big State-sector companies to independent audit prior to evaluation had met with fierce political resistance.

As to the return of refugees and displaced persons, there had been twice as many returns so far in 2000 as in the same period in 1999 and that trend was likely to continue.

Concerning the consolidation of common institutions, the rule of law at the State and entity levels was actively being promoted and there was a major public affairs campaign to promote respect for property rights as part of efforts to accelerate returns. However, the High Representative reported that, despite the Presidency's pledge before the Council in the New York Declaration to establish the State Border Service, it had failed to do so, forcing him to impose it. Although the Presidency passed the draft election law to the Parliament as promised, its members stood by as the draft law was voted down. The New York Declaration also committed the Presidency to resolving the institutional crisis concerning the State Council of Ministers. Its mem-

bers failed to meet the deadline for agreement on a new arrangement to replace the policy of rotating the chairmanship of the Council of Ministers, as a result of which that common institution fell into abeyance in February. The new law proposed by the Presidency still followed old patterns of ethnic parity and rotation. The ethnic agenda had once again taken precedence over what was best for the people of Bosnia and Herzegovina. All those actions confirmed that the leaders of Bosnia and Herzegovina were still far from ready to take responsibility for their country.

The High Representative said that the establishment of the concept of ownership was starting to take root, as demonstrated by the result of the municipal elections held across the country on 8 April. He was encouraged by that development, as political pluralism was a sure sign that democracy in Bosnia and Herzegovina was maturing. While the nationalist parties were still strong, their grip was weakening. The reform of the media, the professionalization of the police and the insistence on economic reform were steadily eroding their source of power. The High Representative declared that it was imperative to persevere in Bosnia and Herzegovina, because if the project there failed, ethnically pure mini-States were likely to dominate South-East Europe in the twenty-first century.

Declaration of Peace Implementation Council

The Peace Implementation Council (PIC) and the leaders of Bosnia and Herzegovina met in Brussels, Belgium, on 23 and 24 May to review progress in implementing the Peace Agreement [YUN 1995, p. 544] and to set priorities for a new accelerated phase of peace implementation.

In its 25 May declaration [S/2000/586], PIC underscored that much had been accomplished and the building of the State of Bosnia and Herzegovina had begun. In particular, the security situation had stabilized, major reconstruction had been completed, the return of refugees and displaced persons was accelerating, the Brcko District was established and political pluralism was gaining strength. However, PIC was dissatisfied with the slow pace of domestic peace implementation since its Madrid meeting [YUN 1998, p. 329]. PIC urged the High Representative to ensure full and accelerated implementation in all sectors of civilian implementation, including removing obstacles to economic reform.

PIC agreed on steps to accelerate implementation of the Peace Agreement in the period up to the next scheduled presidential elections in 2002, focusing on deepening economic reform and creating the conditions for market-driven economic growth; accelerating the return of displaced persons and refugees; and fostering functional and democratically accountable common institutions supported by an effective merit-based civil service and a sound financial basis. PIC reaffirmed its commitment to Bosnia and Herzegovina integrating into European structures. It would continue to assist the country through a civilian and military presence and believed that SFOR's current level of active engagement was essential to successful peace implementation. PIC expected Bosnia and Herzegovina and relevant countries to cooperate with ICTY to bring to justice all political or military leaders indicted for war crimes.

The Council, urging donors to condition assistance on the implementation of concrete and specific reforms, cited a number of them, including: the creation of a single economic space; enabling private sector growth; expeditious and transparent privatization; and anti-corruption measures. PIC urged the authorities to collaborate closely with international financial institutions and other donors in the design and implementation of economic reforms.

PIC noted the significant progress made concerning the return of displaced persons and refugees but that the clear will of citizens to return was not matched by authorities at all levels. The slow progress in urban returns reflected the unwillingness by all sides to implement property legislation and enforce the legal rights of all citizens. The High Representative was urged to take action against prominent Bosnians who continued to occupy contested property. The Council endorsed the Reconstruction and Return Task Force programme to accelerate the pace of return.

As to the goal of fostering and consolidating institutions, PIC noted that many public institutions, particularly State institutions, continued to fail, due to the lack of political will on the part of the ruling political parties and the existence of parallel institutions. It supported the High Representative's efforts to empower State institutions and requested the donor community to funnel its assistance through those institutions. The Presidency and the Parliamentary Assembly should re-establish the Council of Ministers and assure adequate funding for State-level ministries.

Noting the limited progress in judicial reform, PIC called for a truly independent and impartial judiciary. In that regard, it considered the strengthening of the Constitutional Court and the establishment of a State court to be major priorities.

PIC requested the Bosnia and Herzegovina authorities, in collaboration with UNMIBH, to ac-

celerate deployment of the State Border Service and insisted that they complete the police restructuring process without delay. It endorsed the merger of the Human Rights Chamber with the Constitutional Court.

PIC also endorsed the holding of general elections in November, to be supervised by the Organization for Security and Cooperation in Europe (OSCE). It requested OSCE to incorporate the provisions of the draft Election Law in the "provisional rules and regulations" as the basis for conducting those elections. The Council urged Bosnia and Herzegovina to put its intelligence services under democratic control and to consolidate them, and develop the Standing Committee on Military Matters into a State defence structure so that it could develop and oversee a common security policy. It welcomed the commitment to further reduce military expenditure by 15 per cent in 2000.

Appended to the declaration was a list of issues on which PIC demanded prompt action and which would be reflected in the strategy and programming of the donor community: the economy, return issues, institutions, exhumations, military issues, public security, the media, sport and education. Bosnia and Herzegovina would present reports to the PIC Steering Board every six months on the implementation of the programme set out in the declaration and the appendix, the first of which would be in October.

Prior to the PIC meeting, the EU, in a 22 May statement [S/2000/486], said that the programme presented by PIC would empower the people of Bosnia and Herzegovina to seize the opportunities open to those in a modern European State, and to choose the path of prosperity and democratic freedoms.

In communications of 20 and 23 May [S/2000/458, S/2000/472], FRY condemned the failure of the EU Presidency to extend an invitation to it to participate in the PIC ministerial meeting and requested an urgent meeting of the Security Council to consider the matter.

Civilian aspects

The civilian aspects of the 1995 Peace Agreement [YUN 1995, p. 544] entailed a wide range of activities, including humanitarian aid, infrastructure rehabilitation, establishment of political and constitutional institutions, promotion of respect for human rights and the holding of free and fair elections. The High Representative, who chaired the PIC Steering Board and other key implementation bodies, was the final authority with regard to implementing the civilian aspects. UNMIBH, which comprised a UN civilian office, IPTF and MAC, reported to the Secretary-General through his Special Representative and Coordinator of United Nations Operations in Bosnia and Herzegovina, Jacques Paul Klein (United States).

Reports of High Representative. The High Representative, Wolfgang Petritsch (Austria), reported on the implementation process during the year, covering the periods from October 1999 to mid-April 2000 [S/2000/376] and mid-April to October 2000 [S/2000/999]. A later report [S/2001/219] covered activities during the remainder of the year. He described progress in the civilian implementation of the Peace Agreement, which he had been mandated to monitor, mobilize and coordinate. (For details, see below under specific subjects.)

UN Mission in Bosnia and Herzegovina (UNMIBH)

Report of Secretary-General (March). On 15 March [S/2000/215], the Secretary-General, reporting on UNMIBH activities in police restructuring, said that data collection and initial screening for the Law Enforcement Personnel Registry had proceeded quickly. On 1 March, over 5,500 officers had registered and 3,300 had been pre-screened, of whom only 120 did not meet required minimum standards. Steady progress was also being made in changing the composition of the police force to better reflect the multi-ethnic character of the communities it served. Over 320 minority police officers were attending courses or had already graduated from police academies in both Bosnia and Herzegovina entities. Graduates of the first multi-ethnic classes were completing field training before permanent deployment. The third multi-ethnic police academy class in Republika Srpska began in February. On 1 March, UNMIBH established the inter-entity Ministerial Consultative Meeting on Police Matters to facilitate inter-entity law enforcement agreements and establish procedures for recruitment and voluntary redeployment of minority officers. UNMIBH also initiated a police commissioner programme aimed at instituting a single chain of command in the cantonal police forces under a professional and independent police commissioner, selected on merit rather than ethnicity and insulated from political influences. That was intended to help remove political control and parallel chains of command in the Federation's police structures, a serious problem in ethnically mixed cantons. Both the Sarajevo Canton and the Federation Ministry of the Interior had begun the process of creating such posts.

In terms of the integration of the specialized police forces, in January, the Federal Ministry of the Interior finalized the restructuring of the Anti-Terrorist Unit, proportionally staffed by Croats and Bosniacs. In Republika Srpska, eligible members of the former Police Anti-Terrorist Brigade had started training for entry into the new specialized force. When fully staffed, IPTF co-locators would be appointed and the force transferred from SFOR supervision to civilian control. In February, UNMIBH organized the first meeting of commanders and deputy commanders of all cantonal specialized police units, at which Bosniacs and Croats agreed on improved operational cooperation and joint exercises. Those units would eventually replace international intervention in riot control and in case of serious threat to public security. UNMIBH was assisting in drafting amendments to the Federation Court Police Law and related rules and regulations for the establishment of court police.

UNMIBH faced severe obstruction and delay in integrating Bosniac and Croat police officers in Canton 7 (Herzegovina-Neretva) and in establishing the State Border Service. In Mostar, senior Croat authorities refused to allow Bosniac officers to work in the Croat-controlled western part of the city in the same building as their Croat counterparts. Local Croat obstruction affected all aspects of the international community's work in that canton. There had been only minimal achievements in technical aspects of integration of the cantonal Ministry of the Interior.

Concerning the State Border Service Law, which the High Representative imposed on 13 January, the Joint Presidency had accepted UNMIBH's draft organizational structure, the three-phase implementation plan and the deployment of the first operational support team at Sarajevo airport to prepare the police there for transition to the State Border Service.

The reform of the police continued. As at 1 March, 643 IPTF officers were fully co-located at 204 local police locations and 52 police stations were staffed on a 24-hour basis. The co-location programme had already produced tangible results, such as improved response of local police to IPTF advice and interventions and increased awareness among the local population of the presence of international monitors, which had resulted in increased complaints against the police and other ministerial organizations.

Random IPTF inspections of police stations continued to reveal instances of non-compliance with its policies, particularly the continued presence of mono-ethnic intelligence agencies inside multi-ethnic police buildings. During a 9 February weapons inspection of the Glamoc police station, the Canton 10 Ministry of Interior building and the Livno police station, IPFT discovered an intelligence-gathering complex and confiscated unauthorized weapons, explosives and eavesdropping equipment.

In terms of police training, UNMIBH had shifted its advanced training activities towards the training of local police trainers. Its human rights office continued to conduct independent investigations of alleged human rights abuses by local police officers and to monitor investigations by local law enforcement in crucial cases. Breaches of human rights by seven police officials in the Federation led to their decertification on 14 January.

UNMIBH released three public reports with specific recommendations to improve judicial practice and procedure: the report on arrest warrants, amnesty and trials in absentia resulted in the adoption of remedial measures in the cantonal and municipal courts in Sarajevo; the interim report on delays in detention led to the development of a methodology for countrywide follow-up of its recommendations in that regard; and the summary of conclusions of conferences on judicial independence led the Ministry of Justice in Canton 9 (Sarajevo) to separate the Ministry's budget from that for judicial institutions. UNMIBH intended to use the Canton 9 budget as a model for judicial reform throughout the country.

The Secretary-General observed that those developments demonstrated that, while tangible progress was possible, it required intensive, coordinated and robust international engagement. Progress had been made in police restructuring, but there were many areas where UNMIBH had to work with other members of the international community to achieve common goals in areas of shared responsibility. At a time of increasing calls on limited resources, it was essential that all international organizations involved in peace implementation in Bosnia and Herzegovina redouble their efforts to make timely progress.

Security Council consideration (March). The Security Council, on 22 March [S/PV.4117 & Corr.1], considered the Secretary-General's report on UNMIBH. The Council President, summarizing the debate, said that Council members welcomed the 6 March report of the Joint Presidency of Bosnia and Herzegovina (see p. 337) concerning the implementation of the New York Declaration and urged all parties to redouble their efforts to implement the outstanding commitments. Council members also urged those concerned to ensure without further delay the integration of the Ministry of the Interior, as well as the chain of command and communications system of the po-

lice throughout the Federation, and in particular in Mostar. The Council also urged the parties, in particular the Republika Srpska authorities, to increase the number of minority police officers, in accordance with their obligations.

Report of Secretary-General (June). In June [S/2000/529], the Secretary-General reported that, since 1 March, an additional 4,000 police officers had been registered, bringing the total near to the 20,000 ceiling. Of those registered, 2,295 had been authorized to exercise police powers, 2,600 were provisionally authorized, pending background checks, and the remainder were still in the pre-screening stage. On 15 May, UNMIBH issued comprehensive policy instructions to regulate all aspects of recruitment for the local police forces and authorization to exercise police powers. Progress continued in the recruitment and selection of minority cadets for police academies in both entities. A total of 393 minority police officers (203 in the Federation and 190 in Republika Srpska) were attending or had graduated from the two police academies. The Republika Srpska academy was preparing procedures for the selection and testing of cadets for the fourth class, scheduled for September. Under the auspices of the Ministerial Consultative Meeting on Police Matters, an agreement on the voluntary deployment of serving police officers wishing to return to their former place of employment was signed on 12 May by both entities. UNMIBH was identifying housing and other requirements for a target group of 200 such officers to be deployed between the entities in 2000.

Despite those efforts, progress in the representation of minorities in the local police was unsatisfactory. In the Federation, there was no significant recruitment of minority police other than cadets, and only about 600 of the Federation's 11,500 officers were minorities. The situation was even more disappointing in Republika Srpska, where there were currently only 57 minority police officers in a force of approximately 8,500.

In the area of police reform, the institution of the police commissioner programme continued. UNMIBH and the Ministry of the Interior of Canton 9 (Sarajevo) had agreed on a job description and selection and review procedures, as well as on the structural changes necessary in the Ministry. Preparations for political and legal implementation were ongoing. Discussions on a similar position in the Federation Ministry of the Interior were at an advanced stage. In an effort to integrate parallel police structures in the Croat-dominated Canton 7 (Herzegovina-Neretva), the Cantonal Assembly endorsed, on 18 May, an UNMIBH-brokered agreement on a permanent solution and interim measures for the immediate integration of the divided Ministry of the Interior, enabling Bosniacs to work with their Croat counterparts in west Mostar for the first time since the war. Another significant development was the appointment of judges from different ethnicities to the nine new municipal courts, making it possible to recommence the processing of long-delayed criminal cases. In Bosniac majority cantons, the contracts of 40 police officers were terminated by the new Minister of the Interior on grounds of fraud. UNMIBH worked closely with the new authorities to secure important changes in senior police management.

In Republika Srpska, spontaneous minority returns were beginning, but were not being encouraged or supported. Evictions of "double occupants" in towns were exceedingly slow and little progress was seen following the March agreement between Republika Srpska and Croatia to begin cross-border refugee returns within three months.

With regard to human rights, UNMIBH and the International Organization for Migration (IOM) assisted in 43 cases involving 185 foreign nationals brought into the country for the purpose of forced prostitution. UNMIBH completed a comprehensive report on trafficking in human beings in cooperation with the Office of the United Nations High Commissioner for Human Rights (OHCHR). It also broadened its approach from investigating individual cases to improving the institutional integrity of the police forces. To support minority returns, UNMIBH adopted a stricter policy on local police illegally occupying residential premises, involving loss of authorization to exercise police powers.

The judicial system assessment programme, established in 1998 [YUN 1998, p. 342] and scheduled to conclude in December 2000, found that the entire judiciary was, to a greater or lesser degree, politically, professionally and structurally dysfunctional throughout Bosnia and Herzegovina. The programme, which had created a working relationship with the judiciary and local officials, advised the judiciary on a daily basis, produced more than a dozen reports on different aspects of the judicial system, including recommendations for legislative, structural and political reform, monitored cases and worked with IPTF on joint police/judiciary issues. It also played a crucial role in creating the legal framework for the judicial review of all judges and prosecutors. The Secretary-General's Special Representative was in discussion with the High Representative to find a way to hand over the programme's work to either the Council of Europe, the Office of the High Representative itself or an appropriate UN agency, with UNMIBH retaining

appropriate expertise to assist and advise IPTF in its work.

The Secretary-General observed that the recent achievements required consolidation, and UNMIBH should address core mandate areas where little progress was possible in the past, such as minority police recruitment and finding adequate housing for returning minorities, including police officers. UNMIBH would have to monitor police performance closely, especially with regard to the ethnic minority population. To provide more focus to its work, UNMIBH was preparing a strategic and operational framework for the fulfilment of its core mandate by December 2002, which would identify specific achievable goals to complete its mission, the programmes and modalities to achieve them and a time line for the completion of each programme. The process would involve the continuous review of resource levels and progressive resource reallocation and reduction as programme objectives were met. Consideration would be given to follow-up arrangements once the core mandate was implemented.

The Secretary-General recommended that the Security Council extend UNMIBH's mandate until 21 June 2001.

SECURITY COUNCIL ACTION (June)

On 21 June [meeting 4162], the Security Council adopted **resolution 1305(2000)** by vote (14-0-1). The draft [S/2000/591] was submitted by Canada, France, Germany, Italy, the Netherlands, the United Kingdom and the United States.

The Security Council,

Recalling all its relevant resolutions concerning the conflicts in the former Yugoslavia, including resolutions 1031(1995) of 15 December 1995, 1035(1995) of 21 December 1995, 1088(1996) of 12 December 1996, 1144(1997) of 19 December 1997, 1168(1998) of 21 May 1998, 1174(1998) of 15 June 1998, 1184(1998) of 16 July 1998 and 1247(1999) of 18 June 1999,

Reaffirming its commitment to a political settlement of the conflicts in the former Yugoslavia, preserving the sovereignty and territorial integrity of all States there within their internationally recognized borders,

Underlining its commitment to supporting the implementation of the General Framework Agreement for Peace in Bosnia and Herzegovina and the annexes thereto (collectively the "Peace Agreement"),

Emphasizing its appreciation to the High Representative for the Implementation of the Peace Agreement on Bosnia and Herzegovina, the Commander and personnel of the multinational Stabilization Force, the Special Representative of the Secretary-General and the personnel of the United Nations Mission in Bosnia and Herzegovina, including the Commissioner and personnel of the International Police Task Force, the Organization for Security and Cooperation in Europe, and the personnel of other international organizations and agencies in Bosnia and Herzegovina for their contributions to the implementation of the Peace Agreement,

Noting that the States in the region must play a constructive role in the successful development of the peace process in Bosnia and Herzegovina, and noting especially the obligations of the Republic of Croatia and the Federal Republic of Yugoslavia in this regard as signatories to the Peace Agreement,

Welcoming, in this regard, the recent positive steps taken by the Republic of Croatia to strengthen its bilateral relations with Bosnia and Herzegovina, as well as its increasing cooperation with all relevant international organizations in implementing the Peace Agreement,

Emphasizing that a comprehensive and coordinated return of refugees and displaced persons throughout the region continues to be crucial to lasting peace,

Taking note of the declaration of the ministerial meeting of the Peace Implementation Council held in Brussels on 23 and 24 May 2000 and the conclusions of its previous meetings,

Taking note also of the reports of the High Representative, including his latest report of 3 May 2000,

Having considered the report of the Secretary-General of 2 June 2000, and noting that the judicial system assessment programme of the Mission will be concluded by December 2000,

Determining that the situation in the region continues to constitute a threat to international peace and security,

Determined to promote the peaceful resolution of the conflicts in accordance with the purposes and principles of the Charter of the United Nations,

Recalling the relevant principles contained in the Convention on the Safety of United Nations and Associated Personnel of 9 December 1994 and the statement by its President of 9 February 2000,

Welcoming and encouraging efforts by the United Nations to sensitize peacekeeping personnel in the prevention and control of HIV/AIDS and other communicable diseases in all its peacekeeping operations,

Acting under Chapter VII of the Charter,

I

1. *Reaffirms once again its support* for the General Framework Agreement for Peace in Bosnia and Herzegovina and the annexes thereto (collectively the "Peace Agreement"), as well as for the Dayton Agreement on Implementing the Federation of Bosnia and Herzegovina of 10 November 1995, calls upon the parties to comply strictly with their obligations under those Agreements, and expresses its intention to keep the implementation of the Peace Agreement and the situation in Bosnia and Herzegovina under review;

2. *Reiterates* that the primary responsibility for the further successful implementation of the Peace Agreement lies with the authorities in Bosnia and Herzegovina themselves and that the continued willingness of the international community and major donors to assume the political, military and economic burden of implementation and reconstruction efforts will be determined by the compliance and active participation by all the authorities in Bosnia and Herzegovina in implementing the Peace Agreement and rebuilding a civil society, in particular in full cooperation with the International Tribunal for the Prosecution of Persons Responsible for Serious Violations of International Humanitarian Law Committed in the Territory of the Former Yugoslavia since 1991, in strengthening joint institutions and in facilitating returns of refugees and displaced persons;

3. *Reminds* the parties once again that, in accordance with the Peace Agreement, they have committed themselves to cooperate fully with all entities involved in the implementation of this peace settlement, as described in the Peace Agreement, or which are otherwise authorized by the Security Council, including the International Tribunal for the Former Yugoslavia, as it carries out its responsibilities for dispensing justice impartially, and underlines the fact that full cooperation by States and entities with the International Tribunal includes, inter alia, the surrender for trial of all persons indicted by the Tribunal and provision of information to assist in Tribunal investigations;

4. *Emphasizes its full support* for the continued role of the High Representative for the Implementation of the Peace Agreement on Bosnia and Herzegovina in monitoring the implementation of the Peace Agreement and giving guidance to and coordinating the activities of the civilian organizations and agencies involved in assisting the parties to implement the Peace Agreement, and reaffirms that the High Representative is the final authority in theatre regarding the interpretation of annex 10 on civilian implementation of the Peace Agreement and that in case of dispute he may give his interpretation and make recommendations, and make binding decisions as he judges necessary on issues as elaborated by the Peace Implementation Council in Bonn on 9 and 10 December 1997;

5. *Expresses its support* for the declaration of the ministerial meeting of the Peace Implementation Council held in Brussels on 23 and 24 May 2000;

6. *Recognizes* that the parties have authorized the multinational force referred to in paragraph 10 below to take such actions as required, including the use of necessary force, to ensure compliance with annex 1-A of the Peace Agreement;

7. *Reaffirms its intention* to keep the situation in Bosnia and Herzegovina under close review, taking into account the reports submitted pursuant to paragraphs 18 and 25 below, and any recommendations those reports might include, and its readiness to consider the imposition of measures if any party fails significantly to meet its obligations under the Peace Agreement;

II

8. *Pays tribute* to those Member States which participated in the multinational Stabilization Force established in accordance with resolution 1088(1996), and welcomes their willingness to assist the parties to the Peace Agreement by continuing to deploy a multinational Stabilization Force;

9. *Notes* the support of the parties to the Peace Agreement for the continuation of the Stabilization Force, set out in the declaration of the ministerial meeting of the Peace Implementation Council in Madrid on 16 December 1998;

10. *Authorizes* the Member States acting through or in cooperation with the organization referred to in annex 1-A of the Peace Agreement to continue for a further planned period of twelve months the Stabilization Force as established in accordance with resolution

1088(1996) under unified command and control in order to fulfil the role specified in annexes 1-A and 2 of the Peace Agreement, and expresses its intention to review the situation with a view to extending this authorization further as necessary in the light of developments in the implementation of the Peace Agreement and the situation in Bosnia and Herzegovina;

11. *Also authorizes* the Member States acting under paragraph 10 above to take all necessary measures to effect the implementation of and to ensure compliance with annex 1-A of the Peace Agreement, stresses that the parties shall continue to be held equally responsible for compliance with that annex and shall be equally subject to such enforcement action by the Stabilization Force as may be necessary to ensure implementation of that annex and the protection of the Force, and notes that the parties have consented to the Force taking such measures;

12. *Authorizes* Member States to take all necessary measures, at the request of the Stabilization Force, either in defence of the Force or to assist the Force in carrying out its mission, and recognizes the right of the Force to take all necessary measures to defend itself from attack or threat of attack;

13. *Authorizes* the Member States acting under paragraph 10 above, in accordance with annex 1-A of the Peace Agreement, to take all necessary measures to ensure compliance with the rules and procedures established by the Commander of the Stabilization Force, governing command and control of airspace over Bosnia and Herzegovina with respect to all civilian and military air traffic;

14. *Requests* the authorities in Bosnia and Herzegovina to cooperate with the Commander of the Stabilization Force to ensure the effective management of the airports of Bosnia and Herzegovina, in the light of the responsibilities conferred on the Force by annex 1-A of the Peace Agreement with regard to the airspace of Bosnia and Herzegovina;

15. *Demands* that the parties respect the security and freedom of movement of the Stabilization Force and of other international personnel;

16. *Invites* all States, in particular those in the region, to continue to provide appropriate support and facilities, including transit facilities, for the Member States acting under paragraph 10 above;

17. *Recalls* all the agreements concerning the status of forces as referred to in appendix B to annex 1-A of the Peace Agreement, and reminds the parties of their obligation to continue to comply therewith;

18. *Requests* the Member States acting through or in cooperation with the organization referred to in annex 1-A of the Peace Agreement to continue to report to the Council, through the appropriate channels and at least at monthly intervals;

* *

Reaffirming the legal basis in the Charter of the United Nations on which the International Police Task Force was given its mandate in resolution 1035(1995),

III

19. *Decides* to extend the mandate of the United Nations Mission in Bosnia and Herzegovina, which includes the International Police Task Force, for an additional period terminating on 21 June 2001, and also decides that the Task Force shall continue to be entrusted with the tasks set out in annex 11 of the Peace Agreement, including the tasks referred to in the conclusions of the London, Bonn, Luxembourg, Madrid and Brussels Peace Implementation Conferences and agreed by the authorities in Bosnia and Herzegovina;

20. *Requests* the Secretary-General to keep the Council regularly informed and to report at least every six months on the implementation of the mandate of the Mission as a whole;

21. *Reiterates* that the successful implementation of the tasks of the International Police Task Force rests on the quality, experience and professional skills of its personnel, and once again urges Member States, with the support of the Secretary-General, to ensure the provision of such qualified personnel;

22. *Reaffirms* the responsibility of the parties to cooperate fully with, and to instruct their respective responsible officials and authorities to provide their full support to, the International Police Task Force on all relevant matters;

23. *Reiterates its call* upon all concerned to ensure the closest possible coordination between the High Representative, the Stabilization Force, the Mission and the relevant civilian organizations and agencies so as to ensure the successful implementation of the Peace Agreement and of the priority objectives of the civilian consolidation plan, as well as the security of International Police Task Force personnel;

24. *Urges* Member States, in response to demonstrable progress by the parties in restructuring their law enforcement institutions, to intensify their efforts to provide, on a voluntary-funded basis and in coordination with the International Police Task Force, training, equipment and related assistance for local police forces in Bosnia and Herzegovina;

25. *Requests* the Secretary-General to continue to submit to the Council reports from the High Representative, in accordance with annex 10 of the Peace Agreement and the conclusions of the Peace Implementation Conference held in London on 4 and 5 December 1996, and later Peace Implementation Conferences, on the implementation of the Peace Agreement and in particular on compliance by the parties with their commitments under that Agreement;

26. *Decides* to remain seized of the matter.

VOTE ON RESOLUTION 1305(2000):

In favour: Argentina, Bangladesh, Canada, China, France, Jamaica, Malaysia, Mali, Namibia, Netherlands, Tunisia, Ukraine, United Kingdom, United States.
Against: None.
Abstaining: Russian Federation.

Speaking before the vote, the Russian Federation said that, although it agreed with the general thrust of the draft resolution, it could not support it, particularly paragraph 5, by which the Council would express support for the declaration of the May PIC meeting in Brussels (see p. 338). The Russian Federation did not participate in that meeting since FRY, one of the signatories to the Peace Agreement, was not allowed to work in that forum. The Russian Federation opposed attempts to oust FRY from all multilateral mechanisms. The policy of further isolating FRY and enforcing a blockade against it reflected the desire of certain individual States unilaterally to undo the Council's decisions. Moreover, it had serious problems with the provision extending UNMIBH's reporting period from three to six months, since it would weaken the Council's oversight of the Bosnian settlement process.

Security Council consideration (August). At a 15 August meeting [S/PV.4188], the Council received a briefing from the Under-Secretary-General for Peacekeeping Operations in which he focused on police restructuring and reform and strengthening of common institutions in Bosnia and Herzegovina. He reported that IPTF had reduced the allowed maximum police strength in the Federation to 10,600 because of the opening of the State Border Service and reduced needs in some of the smaller Federation cantons. The registration of police officers continued and UNMIBH was on track to conclude the full registration by mid-December.

With regard to inter-entity police cooperation and the strengthening of common institutions, a major initiative was taken on 27 June with the establishment of Joint Entity Task Forces on Illegal Immigration and Organized Crime through the Ministerial Consultative Meeting on Police Matters. The Doboj Public Security Centre in Republika Srpska and the Canton 2 (Posavina) Ministry of the Interior in the Federation cooperated in breaking up a group involved in drug smuggling and the production of counterfeit deutsche marks. In the Federation, Croat and Bosniac officers were cooperating with the Mostar police in carrying out the joint investigation and subsequent arrest of a group producing counterfeit passports.

A significant step towards building State institutions was the inauguration of the State Border Service entry point at the Sarajevo airport on 6 June. In late July and early August, the Service opened three additional crossing points at Doljani/Metkovic, formerly controlled by the Croatian police; at Izacic, formerly controlled by Bosniac police; and at Zvornik, formerly controlled by Serb police. There were currently 358 officers assigned to the Service.

The return of minority refugees and displaced persons continued to show progress, including to former hard-line areas in Republika Srpska, with 300 Bosnian families having returned to the Prijedor, Doboj, Visegrad and Foca municipalities. Over the past six months, the Office of the United Nations High Commissioner for Refugees (UNHCR) had registered over 19,500 minority internally displaced persons and refugees re-

turning, compared to just over 2,000 registered for the same period in 1999.

Report of Secretary-General (November). In his November report on UNMIBH [S/2000/1137], the Secretary-General said that the comprehensive Mandate Implementation Plan developed by UNMIBH, which aimed to provide a clear focus for fulfilling the mandate by the end of 2002, divided the Mission's work into six core programmes: police reforms; police restructuring; police and criminal justice cooperation; institution-building and inter-police force cooperation; public awareness; and general support for the participation of Bosnia and Herzegovina in the UN system, in particular in UN peace operations. The programmes addressed the three levels of law enforcement: the individual police officer, organizational structures of police forces and the required support for democratic policing in society at large. The Plan would assist UNMIBH in evaluating progress and reviewing internal resource allocation and resource levels.

An initial survey indicated that UNMIBH had made considerable progress in the past 18 months in establishing the Brcko District police force and in providing basic training for local police officers. At the same time, IPTF's average strength had fallen from 1,959 during 1998/99 to 1,709 as at 30 June. UNMIBH believed that a force of 1,850 IPTF officers was a realistic figure for the 2001/02 period.

On police reform, the Secretary-General reported that 6,200 of the 20,120 personnel registered as at 20 November had been provisionally authorized to exercise police powers and had received UNMIBH identification cards. In phase 2 of the project, UNMIBH would conduct detailed checks of wartime background and other character-related issues to weed out individuals suspected of war crimes or other offences before granting final certification. Over 300 police had vacated illegally occupied properties. While that addressed the legal problem, it opened that of finding permanent housing solutions for thousands of displaced police officers.

In terms of police restructuring, UNMIBH had determined the maximum strength and targeted ethnic composition of local police forces, taking into account the transfer of border functions from ministries of the interior to the State Border Service. The total number of police in Bosnia and Herzegovina might not exceed 18,438, comprising 7,835 in Republika Srpska and 10,603 in the Federation. Those levels were subject to further review.

Under the police commissioner project, legislation had been passed in Canton 9 (Sarajevo) and an independent selection and review board formed to review the 18 applications received. In Cantons 1, 5 and 6, political consensus had been reached and new posts were being established. The next priority was to extend the project to Republika Srpska. Substantial progress was also made with regard to the UNMIBH voluntary redeployment initiative, which commenced in May. Some 250 officers had applied for redeployment, of whom 30 had been successfully placed.

The absence of mechanisms to protect judges and witnesses remained a major impediment to establishing the rule of law, especially since police operations against organized crime and corruption had become more effective. UNMIBH had made little progress in securing funding to establish a dedicated court police service. Other options were therefore being reviewed, including the use of regular police. UNMIBH was working with local authorities and the judiciary in three cantons to develop an operational plan, as well as budgetary requirements for establishing such a service. If funding was not available, UNMIBH would review the entire project and seek alternative means of providing court and judicial security.

The Secretary-General stated that the lack of local and international funding had made it impossible to expand the State Border Service beyond the four border entry points. Current funding levels were barely sufficient to meet salaries and local operational costs, and the planned deployment of a further eight Service units before the end of the year was doubtful and might not be even possible in 2001 owing to the dire financial situation of the entity and State budgets. He reported also that, since the inauguration of that Service in June, the magnitude of illegal migration through Bosnia and Herzegovina to Western Europe had become apparent. In addition, the past months had witnessed a dramatic increase in the number of women victims of trafficking seeking UNMIBH assistance. He was concerned that, owing to a lack of funding, IOM was substantially reducing operations in that area, exposing victims to further risk following their release from local police custody. To address those problems and encourage inter-entity law enforcement cooperation, a Cooperative Law Enforcement Arrangement on Illegal Immigration and Organized Crime, signed on 26 September, had established a Joint Entity Task Force to exchange intelligence information, coordinate plans to stem the flow of illegal migrants and pursue criminal elements involved in human trafficking. The Task Force would also assist the Brcko Supervisor in closing the so-called "Arizona Market", a long-standing hotbed of criminal activity. The ministers of the interior of both entities had

agreed to seek entity approval to request the State authorities to establish a centralized information-gathering mechanism to combat illegal activities.

In his concluding observations, the Secretary-General said that meeting UNMIBH's timetable to complete its core mandate by December 2002 would depend on the provision by international donors of the necessary financial resources. The voluntary redeployment programme for minority police officers was nearly stalled because of insufficient funding, and local funding for the State Border Service was barely sufficient to pay salary and operating costs. The International Monetary Fund doubted that the State budget for 2001 would be able to meet even those costs for the full year. The Secretary-General appealed to Member States to contribute generously to UNMIBH priority projects and to the Trust Fund for the Police Assistance Programme in Bosnia and Herzegovina.

Later developments. In a later report [S/2001/571 & Corr.1], the Secretary-General indicated that UNMIBH's judicial system assessment programme was dissolved on 1 December and its functions subsumed into the Independent Judicial Commission established within the Office of the High Representative, which had been given the mandate for judicial reform in Bosnia and Herzegovina. UNMIBH retained a small Criminal Justice Advisory Unit to support IPTF on criminal procedure and the criminal justice process, advising on the structure and functioning of the judiciary, acting as a liaison between IPTF and judicial officials and the courts and encouraging cooperation between the police, prosecutors and the courts.

UNMIBH financing

In January, the Secretary-General submitted to the General Assembly the UNMIBH financial performance report for the period 1 July 1998 to 30 June 1999 [A/54/697] and the proposed budget of $153,588,000 gross ($145,543,200 net) for the maintenance of the Mission, including UNMOP (see p. 331) and the United Nations liaison offices in Belgrade and Zagreb for the period 1 July 2000 to 30 June 2001 [A/54/712]. ACABQ's comments and recommendations with regard to those reports were submitted in April [A/54/841/Add.6]. The Assembly also considered the report of the Office of Internal Oversight Services on the investigation into allegations of fraud in travel at UNMIBH [YUN 1999, p. 321].

GENERAL ASSEMBLY ACTION

On 15 June [meeting 98], the General Assembly, on the recommendation of the Fifth Committee

[A/54/904], adopted **resolution 54/273** without vote [agenda item 144].

Financing of the United Nations Mission in Bosnia and Herzegovina

The General Assembly,

Having considered the reports of the Secretary-General on the financing of the United Nations Mission in Bosnia and Herzegovina and the related reports of the Advisory Committee on Administrative and Budgetary Questions,

Having considered also the report of the Office of Internal Oversight Services on the investigation into allegations of fraud in travel at the United Nations Mission in Bosnia and Herzegovina,

Recalling Security Council resolution 1035(1995) of 21 December 1995, by which the Council established the United Nations Mission in Bosnia and Herzegovina for an initial period of one year, and Council resolution 1247(1999) of 18 June 1999, by which the Council extended the mandate of the Mission until 21 June 2000,

Recalling also Security Council resolution 1285(2000) of 13 January 2000, in which the Council authorized the United Nations military observers to continue to monitor the demilitarization of the Prevlaka peninsula until 15 July 2000,

Recalling further its decision 50/481 of 11 April 1996 on the financing of the Mission and its subsequent resolutions and decisions thereon, the latest of which was resolution 53/233 of 8 June 1999,

Reaffirming that the costs of the Mission are expenses of the Organization to be borne by Member States in accordance with Article 17, paragraph 2, of the Charter of the United Nations,

Recalling its previous decisions regarding the fact that, in order to meet the expenditures caused by the Mission, a different procedure is required from that applied to meet expenditures of the regular budget of the United Nations,

Taking into account the fact that the economically more developed countries are in a position to make relatively larger contributions and that the economically less developed countries have a relatively limited capacity to contribute towards such an operation,

Bearing in mind the special responsibilities of the States permanent members of the Security Council, as indicated in General Assembly resolution 1874(S-IV) of 27 June 1963, in the financing of such operations,

Noting with appreciation that voluntary contributions have been made to the Mission,

Mindful of the fact that it is essential to provide the Mission with the necessary financial resources to enable it to fulfil its responsibilities under the relevant resolutions of the Security Council,

1. *Takes note* of the status of contributions to the United Nations Mission in Bosnia and Herzegovina as at 30 April 2000, including the contributions outstanding in the amount of 53.6 million United States dollars, representing 8 per cent of the total assessed contributions from the inception of the Mission to the period ending 21 June 2000, notes that some 41 per cent of the Member States have paid their assessed contributions in full, and urges all other Member States concerned, in particular those in arrears, to ensure the payment of their outstanding assessed contributions;

2. *Expresses its appreciation* to those Member States which have paid their assessed contributions in full;

3. *Urges* all other Member States to make every possible effort to ensure payment of their assessed contributions to the Mission in full and on time;

4. *Expresses concern* at the delay experienced by the Secretary-General in deploying and providing adequate resources to some recent peacekeeping missions, in particular those in Africa;

5. *Emphasizes* that all future and existing peacekeeping missions shall be given equal and non-discriminatory treatment in respect of financial and administrative arrangements;

6. *Also emphasizes* that all peacekeeping missions shall be provided with adequate resources for the effective and efficient discharge of their respective mandates;

7. *Requests* the Secretary-General to make the fullest possible use of facilities and equipment at the United Nations Logistics Base at Brindisi, Italy, in order to minimize the costs of procurement for the Mission, and for this purpose requests the Secretary-General to speed up the implementation of the asset management system at all peacekeeping missions in accordance with General Assembly resolution 52/1 A of 15 October 1997;

8. *Endorses* the conclusions and recommendations contained in the report of the Advisory Committee on Administrative and Budgetary Questions, and requests the Secretary-General to ensure their full implementation;

9. *Takes note* of the report of the Office of Internal Oversight Services on the investigation into allegations of fraud in travel at the United Nations Mission in Bosnia and Herzegovina;

10. *Requests* the Secretary-General to take all necessary action to ensure that the Mission is administered with a maximum of efficiency and economy;

11. *Also requests* the Secretary-General, in order to reduce the cost of employing General Service staff, to continue efforts to recruit local staff for the Mission against General Service posts, commensurate with the requirements of the Mission;

12. *Decides* to appropriate the amount of 158,707,667 dollars gross (149,375,001 dollars net) for the maintenance of the Mission for the period from 1 July 2000 to 30 June 2001, inclusive of the amount of 7,530,382 dollars gross (6,372,279 dollars net) for the support account for peacekeeping operations and the amount of 1,177,285 dollars gross (1,047,522 dollars net) for the United Nations Logistics Base, to be apportioned, as an ad hoc arrangement, among Member States at a monthly rate of 13,225,639 dollars gross (12,447,917 dollars net) in accordance with the composition of groups set out in paragraphs 3 and 4 of General Assembly resolution 43/232 of 1 March 1989, as adjusted by the Assembly in its resolutions 44/192 B of 21 December 1989, 45/269 of 27 August 1991, 46/198 A of 20 December 1991, 47/218 A of 23 December 1992, 49/249 A of 20 July 1995, 49/249 B of 14 September 1995, 50/224 of 11 April 1996, 51/218 A to C of 18 December 1996 and 52/230 of 31 March 1998 and its decisions 48/472 A of 23 December 1993, 50/451 B of 23 December 1995 and 54/456 to 54/458 of 23 December 1999, and taking into account the scale of assessments for the year 2000, as set out in its resolutions 52/215 A of 22 December 1997 and 54/237 A of 23 De-

cember 1999, and for the year 2001, subject to the decision of the Security Council to extend the Mission beyond 30 June 2000;

13. *Decides also* that, in accordance with the provisions of its resolution 973(X) of 15 December 1955, there shall be set off against the apportionment among Member States, as provided for in paragraph 12 above, their respective share in the Tax Equalization Fund of the estimated staff assessment income of 9,332,666 dollars approved for the Mission for the period from 1 July 2000 to 30 June 2001;

14. *Decides further* that, for Member States that have fulfilled their financial obligations to the Mission, there shall be set off against the apportionment, as provided for in paragraph 12 above, their respective share of the unencumbered balance of 19,642,720 dollars gross (17,805,020 dollars net) in respect of the period ending 30 June 1999;

15. *Decides* that, for Member States that have not fulfilled their financial obligations to the Mission, their share of the unencumbered balance of 19,642,720 dollars gross (17,805,020 dollars net) in respect of the period ending 30 June 1999 shall be set off against their outstanding obligations;

16. *Emphasizes* that no peacekeeping mission shall be financed by borrowing funds from other active peacekeeping missions;

17. *Encourages* the Secretary-General to continue to take additional measures to ensure the safety and security of all personnel under the auspices of the United Nations participating in the Mission;

18. *Invites* voluntary contributions to the Mission in cash and in the form of services and supplies acceptable to the Secretary-General, to be administered, as appropriate, in accordance with the procedure and practices established by the General Assembly;

19. *Decides* to include in the provisional agenda of its fifty-fifth session the item entitled "Financing of the United Nations Mission in Bosnia and Herzegovina".

On 23 December, the Assembly decided that the agenda item on the financing of UNMIBH should remain for consideration at its resumed fifty-fifth (2001) session (**decision 55/458**) and that the Fifth Committee should continue consideration of the item at that session (**decision 55/455**).

International Police Task Force (IPTF)

During 2000, the authorized strength of UNMIBH's International Police Task Force remained at 2,057. Owing to continued requirements in the Kosovo province of FRY and elsewhere, the actual strength as at December stood below that number, at 1,808. UNMIBH assessed that a strength of 1,850 officers would be realistic for the 2001/02 period.

In February, General Vincent Coeurderoy (France) was appointed to succeed Detlef Buwitt (Germany) as Commissioner of IPTF [S/2000/117, S/2000/118].

IPTF continued to assist in the restructuring and reform of the police services in the Federa-

tion and to monitor local police. Together with more specialized monitoring, such as co-location and support for local investigations, basic monitoring continued to be the core task of the majority of officers. As at 1 March, 643 IPTF officers were fully co-located at 204 local police locations. Full co-location was completed in all Brcko District police stations on 25 May. IPTF levels in that district were being reviewed so that they could be adjusted in accordance with progress made and officers redeployed to other high-priority regions. IPTF continued its training and certification programmes and the random inspection of police stations.

Civil affairs

In October [S/2000/999], the High Representative reported that the Council of Ministers was finally instituted. The new Law on the Council of Ministers was adopted on 13 April but it was not until 6 June that the Bosnia and Herzegovina House of Representatives approved Spasoje Tusevljak as Chair of the Council. On 22 June, the House approved the Ministers and Deputy Ministers nominated by the Chair. The Council had met regularly since its establishment and had adopted proposed legislation related to the State treasury, travel documents and political party financing. Three new Ministries (the Ministry of the Treasury for the Institutions of Bosnia and Herzegovina, the Ministry for European Integration and the Ministry for Human Rights and Refugees) were established.

However, overall progress in strengthening State institutions remained slow. Frequent delays in decision-making resulted in a serious backlog of legislation to be adopted, further hampering the work of the Bosnia and Herzegovina Parliamentary Assembly. The lack of commitment among politicians to strengthen the State continued to block the effective functioning of common institutions. Pending the adoption of a State-level Civil Service law, the High Representative had insisted on competitive recruitment of civil servants to new Ministries. The Ministry of European Integration had set a good example in that regard.

The Bosnia and Herzegovina Presidency had reached agreement on a number of areas, had ratified several agreements and treaties and agreed to the Rule Book on Internal Organization of the Auditing Office for Bosnia and Herzegovina Institutions. However, there was little or no progress in other areas. The Presidency secretariat had not been fully established and the High Representative was not satisfied with the method of staff recruitment. Important decisions continued to require the constant application of pressure from the international community due to the lack of dialogue and constructive engagement in decision-making among the three Presidency members, who continued to act and take decisions along strict ethnic lines. In July, the Chair of the Presidency, Alija Izetbegovic, announced his resignation, to take effect at the end of his term on 12 October.

The Parliamentary Assembly had adopted its 2000 work plan, as well as laws on party financing, the Council of Ministers and succession. The latter law contradicted the Constitution and the High Representative had decided to impose amendments so that the most important institutions served the interests of the citizens and not those of the ruling nationalistic elite. The Assembly also adopted the Law on State Treasury but failed to adopt the Law on Travel Documents, which had to be imposed by the High Representative in order to provide for a single national passport. The Office of the High Representative strengthened basic civil information management by establishing on 28 June the Central Registry of Passports in the Ministry of Civil Affairs and Communications. Legal working groups were also established to finalize the draft laws on identification cards, unique citizen number and residency. A joint working group of the Ministry of Civil Affairs and Communications/entity Ministry of the Interior was drafting State-level laws on data protection and mandatory data exchange to create protections for the first post-war citizens register.

The 1 July decision of the Bosnia and Herzegovina Constitutional Court on the Constituent Peoples' Case that no ethnic group constituent on the territory of Bosnia and Herzegovina should be excluded for exercising its rights in the entities was the most debated and sometimes contested juridical and political issue. In Republika Srpska, the decision was seen as politically motivated, while in the Federation it was welcomed by most political parties.

The High Representative reported that he had dismissed 21 public officials for serious and persistent obstruction of the Peace Agreement; 19 of those officials were to be barred from holding any public elected and appointed office.

Elections

The High Representative reported in May [S/2000/376] that Bosnia and Herzegovina had held its second municipal elections on 8 April without significant incident or disruption. They were the first to be held under the new Provisional Election Commission rules. Participation was high (around 66 per cent), with a higher turnout in Republika Srpska, despite calls by na-

tionalist Serb radicals for a boycott. Although party pluralism improved, nationalist parties continued to dominate in predominantly Croat or Serb municipalities. The multi-ethnic Social Democratic Party (SDP) gained significant ground against the main Bosniac nationalist party, the Party of Democratic Action (SDA) in the Bosniac-majority areas of the Federation. The main Croat party, the nationalist Croat Democratic Community (HDZ), retained most of its municipal seats. In Republika Srpska, the results were mixed, with the nationalist Serb Democratic Party retaining most of the municipalities it controlled, while the moderate forces made limited advances and a new party successfully made its appearance.

General elections were held on 11 November for the Bosnia and Herzegovina House of Representatives, the Federation and Republika Srpska parliaments, the Republika Srpska President and Vice-President, and Cantonal Assemblies in the Federation and the Srebrenica municipality. Supervised by OSCE, the elections were generally judged to be free and fair, except for the action by HDZ, which organized a "referendum" on election day. Voter turnout was estimated at 70 per cent, higher than that in the April municipal elections, although it varied from region to region. At the State level and in the Federation, moderate non-nationalist parties, which had formed a post-election coalition named "Alliance for Change", had made important gains. The multiethnic SDP polled well, but not as well as hoped, and smaller parties, such as the Party of Democratic Progress and the Party for Bosnia and Herzegovina, also gained ground. The Croat opposition parties—the New Croat Initiative and the Croatian Peasants Party of Bosnia and Herzegovina—survived. Overall the election results confirmed the pluralist nature of the political landscape and a continuation of growing support for more moderate political parties.

Republika Srpska issues

The High Representative reported during 2000 on issues related specifically to Republika Srpska, the entity of the Republic of Bosnia and Herzegovina where primarily Bosnian Serbs resided. In May [S/2000/376], he indicated that the ruling Sloga coalition (the three Serb government parties) had come under considerable pressure as a result of internal and external disaffection. The Socialist Party of Republika Srpska (SPRS) withdrew from Sloga, with its anti-government faction forming the new Democratic Socialist Party. Nevertheless, Prime Minister Dodik had withstood those repeated attacks on his authority. Vice President Mirko Sarovic of the

Serb Democratic Party (SDS) attempted to assume the Presidency of Republika Srpska.

In October [S/2000/999], the High Representative said that, in recent months, the political climate had deteriorated, almost short of collapse, with indications that FRY played a significant role. That crisis required frequent interventions by his Office to make sure that the entity parliament passed important legislation to provide visible support for the Government. With the growing economic problems in the entity, the cleavage among and within the Sloga parties after the municipal elections resulted in a split within two of the three coalition partners. As a result of those defections, Sloga was unable to prevent the most radical nationalist parties from challenging the Dodik Government in the entity parliament. On 7 September, Prime Minister Dodik lost a confidence vote. The High Representative urged the Government to stay in office until the elections in November (see p. 349). Following the elections, a new entity parliament was constituted by the end of the year. The SDS leadership, including Republika Srpska's newly elected President, Mr. Sarovic, issued a 12 December statement endorsing the Peace Agreement and all PIC documents and expressing the party's readiness to cooperate immediately with the international community at all levels, including ICTY.

Brcko District

On 8 March, the Brcko District was officially proclaimed, with the appointment of the interim government and District Assembly selected by the Supervisor based on professional credentials. Little progress was made on the privatization of State-owned enterprises. The Supervisor was working with the German Development Agency to establish an expedited privatization programme for the District. All elements of the Bosnia and Herzegovina army and police were removed from within the boundaries of the pre-war Brcko municipality and entity armed forces located there would either be disbanded or relocated under the directives issued by SFOR and in compliance with the provisions of the Brcko Final Award [YUN 1999, p. 324]. The tri-ethnic 320-strong Brcko District Police Service was fully restructured and integrated.

In October [S/2000/999], the High Representative reported that the multi-ethnic government and Assembly were in place and fully operational. The Assembly had already adopted 10 District laws and others were being prepared. In education, a school opened with multi-ethnic staff and pupils and would serve as a model for the rest of the District. Returns were moving forward; it was estimated that, since April, a little over 1,300 properties had been reinstated. By the end of the year [S/2001/219], over 5,000 minority returns were reported. Following an inter-entity meeting on 19 September, with the participation of the Brcko District Government, various working groups were created to tackle cooperation and participation of the entities' governments in the development of the Brcko District on crucial issues such as returns and reconstruction, revenues, pensions, health care and other social programmes and economic development.

Returns

Approximately 67,000 minority returns were registered in 2000 compared with 41,000 in 1999. The actual number was even greater than the registered figures showed, as individuals of all ethnic groups were spontaneously exercising their choice to return. Further, returns in 2000 were no longer limited to a few areas and took place all across Bosnia and Herzegovina, including Srebrenica. However, the High Representative said that that progress highlighted the need for targeted programmes to ensure that past and future returns were sustainable. Access to personal documents, employment, quality education, pensions and utilities remained a problem in many areas. The Return and Restitution Task Force and the Economic Task Force were working with donors and community leaders to develop economic opportunities to maintain the momentum on returns.

Human rights

In May [S/2000/376], the High Representative reported continued improvements in the implementation of the decisions of the Human Rights Chamber, recommendations of the Ombudsperson and those of the Commission for Real Property Claims of Displaced Persons (CRPC). Compensation awards issued by the Chamber in both entities had been almost paid in full. However, property-related matters continued to be among the most difficult to implement. Property decisions were generally only implemented with strong international pressure and there was no indication that the Governments had taken steps to prevent property-related violations of the European Convention on Human Rights and other international human rights instruments.

The draft Ombuds-Institution legislation was adopted by the Federation House of Representatives, although progress in the House of Peoples was slow. At the State level, it was with the appropriate Minister. Republika Srpska adopted its Ombudsman legislation in February and Ombudsmen were appointed in mid-November, taking up their duties in Banja Luka and four field offices (Prijedor, Doboj, Foca and Bijelina). On 10 November, Bosnia and Herzegovina, the Federation and Republika Srpska signed agreements providing for the continued operation of the Bosnia and Herzegovina Ombudsman, the Human Rights Chamber and CRPC, until at least 31 December 2003. The Mostar "Liska Street" incident of February 1997 [YUN 1997, p. 307] was being investigated by Mostar judicial authorities as recommended in the special report of the Ombudsman of Bosnia and Herzegovina.

Continued difficulties were anticipated in the implementation of the human rights institutions' decisions requiring the eviction of current occupants of previously abandoned accommodation. In addition, Republika Srpska had not complied with the order of the Human Rights Chamber to provide all available information on the Father Matanovic case, involving the disappearance of a priest and his family near the end of the war. Following repeated interventions by the High Representative, Banja Luka authorities, in November, gave an "urban permit" to reconstruct the former Ferhadija mosque, as required by a decision of the Human Rights Chamber. A building permit was expected to follow the submission of building plans.

The Republika Srpska Labour Law entered into force on 16 November, offering rights that were harmonized with those of Federation law. On the initiative of OHCHR, the Council of Ministers, on 2 December, decided to establish a Working Group to Combat Trafficking in Human Beings.

Judicial reform

The High Representative reported in May [S/2000/376] that the priorities outlined in the Comprehensive Judicial Reform Strategy [YUN 1999, p. 326] were being implemented. Notably, the goal of creating an independent and impartial judiciary was advancing considerably by the completion of laws regulating the selection and dismissal of judges and prosecutors. The Federation House of Representatives passed the Law on Judicial and Prosecutorial Service, and Republika Srpska, the Law on Courts and Court Service. However, those laws remained to be passed by the domestic bodies. The High Representative had emphasized the implementation of the imposed amendments to the Federation Law on the Supreme Court and the Law on the Federation Prosecutor's Office, creating a trial chamber within the Supreme Court for certain "federal crimes" with an inter-ethnic dimension. Cases primarily relating to drug trafficking had already

been sent from the cantons to the new chamber and his Office continued to support full funding by the Federation Government. The High Representative continued to promote the establishment of a nationwide structure for judicial training. A Joint Advisory Board linking relevant officials from both entities was formed in February and his Office had taken the lead in bringing together those parties in Government and the international community whose cooperation was essential to achieve that goal.

In Republika Srpska, the High Judicial Council and the High Prosecutorial Council, established in accordance with the Law on Courts and Court Service, had begun their work, providing for a non-politicized mechanism for the appointment, discipline and dismissal of judges and prosecutors. The Councils, under international oversight, would conduct an extraordinary review to scrutinize all sitting judges and prosecutors to make sure they met basic standards of education and training and had proven capable of independently and impartially performing their functions. Under a similar legal structure, the Federation and cantonal judicial commissions had commenced their judicial reviews.

The Coordinating Board for education of judges and prosecutors had been established to draft the Law on Judges and Prosecutors Institute in both entities. To promote a coherent, consolidated approach to the issues of judicial reform and the promotion of the rule of law, the High Representative established on 1 December the Independent Judicial Commission (IJC). IJC would be the focal point for international assistance to judicial reform initiatives, assist in the identification and design of specific programmes, monitor the status of the judicial system and support domestic training organizations. It would operate independently, reporting to the High Representative, and was expected to be operational by January 2001.

The Herzegovina-Neretva Cantonal Court, with panels consisting of representatives of all three peoples presiding, had begun to try war crime cases on Bosnian soil.

Economic reform and reconstruction

The May PIC meeting in Brussels (see p. 338) had put economic reform at the centre of the international community's strategy for Bosnia and Herzegovina, the objective being to deepen that reform and create conditions for self-sustaining market-driven economic growth. The strategy was aimed at creating a single economic space, enabling private sector growth and fostering privatization. To create a single economic space, significant steps were taken, which either had been or were expected to be completed before the end of the year. They included an agreed law on the Bosnia and Herzegovina Chamber of Commerce and a draft Law on Statistics, which were ready for parliamentary procedure; banks from one entity being able to open branches in the other without having to satisfy capital requirements requested of foreign banks; ongoing tax harmonization and the establishment of a working group to review double taxation cases; and approval of the State Treasury Law. The Bosnia and Herzegovina Treasury was already set up and the nomination of supreme auditors was under way.

Concerning private sector growth, several new initiatives were creating a more favourable environment for enterprises in Bosnia and Herzegovina. To facilitate clear ownership titles, the base of any market economy, a working group on a new law on land registry and cadastres, attended by both entities, would be preparing the necessary by-laws by the end of the year. Further progress was achieved in preparing a full set of laws in standardization, metrology and intellectual property. The final draft of a new obligation law was expected to be ready by mid-2001.

As to privatization, international standard tender regulations had been approved. The International Advisory Group for banking sector issues was focusing on a unified approach to bank privatization and reform, effective regulation and supervision, and deposit insurance. On 23 May, the High Representative issued a decision amending banking laws in both entities, providing protection for bank supervisors, examiners and officials of the banking agencies from personal liability arising from the normal performance of their duties. The Federation amended the Law on Deposit Insurance in April, providing a proper legal framework for setting up a system to improve security for deposits. Republika Srpska was to harmonize its Law on Deposit Insurance shortly and the international community was ready to provide considerable funds and technical assistance for deposit insurance. To reduce the risks for domestic and foreign direct investors participating in privatization and to remove obstacles to economic growth, the High Representative issued a decision protecting buyers of privatized assets from restitutions in kind without preventing claimants from seeking legal recourse.

In other areas, the entity Governments created, in March, the new joint Bosnia and Herzegovina Road Infrastructure Public Corporation. The Commission on Public Corporations recommended the establishment of three further joint public corporations for natural gas transmission, broadcasting transmission infrastructure and power transmission. In the energy sector, the Office of the High Representative, in cooperation with the World Bank and other international agencies, was developing and promoting a package of measures that included creating an independent regulatory commission for the energy market, an open privatization process that would attract foreign investors and establishing a joint, high-voltage transmission company. The new telephone numbering plan for Bosnia and Herzegovina had been successfully implemented and interconnection agreements signed. A new policy for the telecommunications sector was developed, which foresaw the liberalization of the telecom market, except for international telephone services. Measures to strengthen the role and capability of the Telecommunication Regulatory Authority were also under way.

Media issues

Efforts to reform the public broadcasting sector had resulted in encouraging progress. In February, the illegal broadcasts of HDZ-controlled Erotel TV were halted. The management of Radio and Television of Bosnia and Herzegovina (RTVBIH) was replaced by the Public Broadcasting Service Board of Governors, and a new Director and a Deputy Director of Federation Radio Television were appointed. The property of the old broadcaster (RTVBIH) was being assessed with a view to apportioning it to the national Public Broadcasting System (PBS) and Federation Radio Television and to extracting the transmission system for use by a nationwide transmission company, TRANSCO.

Given the failure of the Republika Srpska Government and National Assembly to adopt adequate public broadcasting legislation, the High Representative appointed a more diverse Board of Governors for Radio-Television Republika Srpska (RTRS) and assigned to it preparation of a draft law on public broadcasting for the entity. The Government pledged to create a new subscription-fee arrangement eliminating excessive service charges. However, the financial situation of RTRS remained critical with little action by the Republika Srpska Government to alleviate the situation.

A draft Freedom of Information Law, prepared by an expert group in coordination with OSCE and the Office of the High Representative, was adopted for discussion in both houses of the Bosnia and Herzegovina Parliament. Another expert group was preparing a draft Defamation Law.

The Independent Media Commission (IMC) was working to evolve into a Telecommunications Regulatory Agency of Bosnia and Herzegovina.

From 1 June, all heads of department posts were held by Bosnia and Herzegovina nationals; the remaining international members were reduced to three and shifted to advisory roles. IMC was preparing to issue long-term licences that would require broadcasters to meet international norms. It was also working to ensure development of a fully coordinated frequency plan and better population coverage for the national broadcasters. It had launched the Advertising and Sponsorship Code and helped in the establishment of the Bosnia and Herzegovina Press Council.

The High Representative, in order to implement the reform of the public broadcasting sector, issued on 23 October his second decision on restructuring the Public Broadcasting System, placing emphasis on ensuring that the three main public broadcasters, PBS, Federation Radio Television and RTRS, were economically viable, transparently financed and professionally run. The new system took into account the mutual interests of those broadcasting companies, which would remain independent, but would work together to improve the public service in both entities and across the whole of Bosnia and Herzegovina.

Srebrenica

On 13 July [meeting 4169], following consultations among Security Council members, the President made statement **S/PRST/2000/23** in commemoration of the tragic events in Srebrenica five years earlier [YUN 1995, p. 529]:

> Five years after the fall of Srebrenica in Bosnia and Herzegovina, the Security Council pays tribute to the victims of one of the worst civilian massacres in Europe since the end of the Second World War. In the week after the fall of Srebrenica, a United Nations designated safe area, thousands of innocent civilians were murdered, and thousands of others forcibly relocated as a result of the policy of ethnic cleansing.
>
> The tragic events at Srebrenica must not be forgotten. The Council regrets the deplorable events and recalls its resolve to ensure that justice is carried out fully through the work of the International Tribunal for the Prosecution of Persons Responsible for Serious Violations of International Humanitarian Law Committed in the Territory of the Former Yugoslavia since 1991, and that such crimes are not repeated in the future. The Council stresses the importance that lessons be learned and acknowledges the report of the Secretary-General on Srebrenica [YUN 1999, p. 327]. The Council reiterates its commitment to the full implementation of the Dayton-Paris Peace Agreement and to the establishment of multi-ethnic democracy and the rule of law throughout the territory of the former Yugoslavia.

> I invite the members of the Council to stand and observe a minute of silence in honour of the victims of the Srebrenica massacre.

In an 18 July letter [S/2000/709], FRY said that the Council President's statement was not founded on facts and material evidence and was part of the long propaganda campaign carried out by countries opposed to the stabilization of the situation in Bosnia and Herzegovina in an effort to undermine and revise the Peace Agreement and destabilize the entire region. The statement was also a function of the continued political pressure being brought to bear on Republika Srpska, FRY and the Serbian people in general.

The High Representative reported that, on 25 October [S/2001/219], he had issued a decision on the location of a cemetery and memorial site for the victims of the Srebrenica massacre to help Bosnia and Herzegovina come to terms with its past. The allocated land was in Potocari near Srebrenica. A plan was being developed to implement that decision, as was an inter-agency plan to create conditions for sustainable return to Srebrenica.

The Secretary-General, in his November report on UNMIBH [S/2000/1137], said that the legacy of Srebrenica continued to be of deep concern. The High Representative had exercised his authority to end the stalemate over the location of a permanent burial site for the remains of the victims and a memorial, and had established a trust fund for that purpose. That had helped to clear the way for concerted efforts at reconciliation, as well as to address the many problems of the families of victims wishing to return and the situation of displaced local Serb residents wishing to reclaim their own homes elsewhere or to remain in the area. The Secretary-General had requested his Special Representative to examine ways in which the United Nations, with other principal organizations, could play a special role in helping the people of Srebrenica.

GENERAL ASSEMBLY ACTION

On 14 November [meeting 61], the General Assembly adopted **resolution 55/24** [draft: A/55/L.31 & Add.1] without vote [agenda item 45].

The situation in Bosnia and Herzegovina

The General Assembly,

Recalling its resolutions 46/242 of 25 August 1992, 47/1 of 22 September 1992, 47/121 of 18 December 1992, 48/88 of 20 December 1993, 49/10 of 3 November 1994, 51/203 of 17 December 1996, 52/150 of 15 December 1997, 53/35 of 30 November 1998, 54/119 of 16 December 1999 and all relevant resolutions of the Security Council regarding the situation in Bosnia and Herzegovina,

Reaffirming its support for the independence, sovereignty, legal continuity and territorial integrity of Bosnia and Herzegovina, within its internationally recognized borders,

Reaffirming its support also for the equality of the three constituent peoples and others in Bosnia and Herzegovina as a united country, with two multi-ethnic entities,

Welcoming the General Framework Agreement for Peace in Bosnia and Herzegovina and the annexes thereto (collectively the "Peace Agreement"), signed in Paris on 14 December 1995,

Welcoming also the accomplishments achieved in implementation of the Peace Agreement, including the stabilization of the security situation, major reconstruction, the acceleration of the return of refugees and internally displaced persons, including to minority areas, the establishment of the Brcko District and the strengthening of political pluralism,

Welcoming further the efforts for the respect, promotion and protection of human rights and the strengthening of the rule of law in all of Bosnia and Herzegovina and for the development of the common institutions that will ensure that Bosnia and Herzegovina functions as an integrated modern State, accountable to its citizens,

Supporting those institutions and organizations of Bosnia and Herzegovina that are engaged in the implementation of the Peace Agreement and the process of reconciliation and reintegration, and noting, however, the slow progress in the development of efficient common institutions of Bosnia and Herzegovina,

Concerned by the continuing obstructions faced by refugees and displaced persons wishing to return to their pre-war homes, in particular in areas where they would be an ethnic minority, emphasizing the need for an unreserved commitment by all political authorities, including at the entity and local levels, also emphasizing the need for all parties and the relevant States and international organizations to create the conditions necessary to facilitate a secure and dignified return, particularly in urban areas such as Sarajevo, Banja Luka and Mostar, and stressing the need for a regional approach to the issue of refugees and displaced persons,

Supporting fully the efforts of the International Tribunal for the Prosecution of Persons Responsible for Serious Violations of International Humanitarian Law Committed in the Territory of the Former Yugoslavia since 1991, stressing the importance and urgency of the work of the International Tribunal as an element of the process of reconciliation and as a factor contributing to the maintenance of international peace and security in Bosnia and Herzegovina and in the region as a whole, demanding that States and parties to the Peace Agreement meet their obligations to cooperate fully with the Tribunal, as required by Security Council resolutions 827(1993) of 25 May 1993, 1022(1995) of 22 November 1995 and 1207(1998) of 17 November 1998, including with respect to surrendering persons sought by the Tribunal, and welcoming the efforts to secure compliance with the orders of the Tribunal, consistent with the Security Council mandate,

Noting improved cooperation between the International Tribunal and the States and entities in the region, as stated in the seventh annual report of the Tribunal, also noting that a number of individuals named in public indictments still remain at large, calling upon all the States and entities in the region to continue to improve cooperation and to comply fully with their obligations, and welcoming the efforts of the High Representative for the Implementation of the Peace Agreement on Bosnia and Herzegovina and the Commander of the multinational Stabilization Force in implementing the provisions of the Peace Agreement,

Welcoming the mutual recognition among all the successor States of the former Socialist Federal Republic of Yugoslavia within their internationally recognized borders, and stressing the importance of full normalization of relations among those States, including the unconditional establishment of diplomatic relations in accordance with the Peace Agreement and the settlement of all issues relating to the succession of the former Yugoslavia on the basis of the legal equality of all five successor States, in order to contribute to the achievement of lasting peace and stability in the area,

Noting the significant improvement of relations between Bosnia and Herzegovina and the Republic of Croatia following the elections held in Croatia in January 2000,

Welcoming the important political change following the recent elections in the Federal Republic of Yugoslavia, and noting the significance of this change for the region as a whole,

Welcoming also the successful summit meeting of heads of State and Government to launch the Stability Pact for South-Eastern Europe in Sarajevo on 29 and 30 July 1999, and stressing that the Stability Pact offers a broad regional framework for further progress in Bosnia and Herzegovina,

Noting that democratization in the region will enhance the prospects for a lasting peace and help to guarantee full respect for human rights in Bosnia and Herzegovina and in the region,

Stressing the importance of full respect for human rights and fundamental freedoms for the success of the peace efforts for the region, and calling upon the Governments and authorities in the region, as well as the relevant international organizations, to facilitate such full respect,

Concerned about the plight of thousands of families of missing persons in Bosnia and Herzegovina, and supporting fully the efforts of the International Commission on Missing Persons to resolve the fate of the missing persons,

Reaffirming the importance of the early adoption of a permanent electoral law, consistent, inter alia, with the ruling of the Constitutional Court on the equality of the three constituent peoples throughout the territory of Bosnia and Herzegovina, calling upon the Parliamentary Assembly elected in November to adopt this law expeditiously, noting that such adoption is a prerequisite of membership of the Council of Europe, and reaffirming the importance of genuine democratic representation of all three constituent peoples in all common institutions,

Stressing the importance of faster integration of the countries of the region into the political and economic mainstream of Europe, on the basis of individual merits and achievements, also stressing in particular the positive impact that the early admission to the Council of Europe could have on Bosnia and Herzegovina and the region in search of sustainable economic and political stability, and noting the importance of Bosnia and Herzegovina establishing its place in Euro-Atlantic institutions,

Noting the positive impact of the five pledging conferences, held on 21 December 1995, 13 and 14 April 1996, 25 July 1997, 8 and 9 May 1998 and 30 May 1999 and chaired by the World Bank and the European Union, on the peace process and reintegration of the country as well as the reconstruction effort, stressing the importance and urgency of providing the financial assistance and technical cooperation pledged for reconstruction efforts, and stressing the role of economic revitalization in the process of reconciliation, in the improvement of living conditions and in the maintenance of a durable peace in Bosnia and Herzegovina and in the region,

Stressing that the provision of reconstruction aid and financial assistance is conditional upon the parties meeting their obligations under the Peace Agreement,

Recognizing the importance of demining for the normalization of life and for the return of refugees and internally displaced persons,

Welcoming the achievements, and encouraging further efforts at reducing the military assets in line with the Agreement on Subregional Arms Control,

Noting with appreciation that Bosnia and Herzegovina is beginning to participate in the peacekeeping operations of the United Nations,

Welcoming the important efforts of the European Union to promote reform and stability through its stabilization and association process, and recognizing the work of the European Union and other donors in providing humanitarian and economic assistance for reconstruction,

1. *Expresses its full support* for the General Framework Agreement for Peace in Bosnia and Herzegovina and the annexes thereto (collectively the "Peace Agreement"), which constitute the key mechanism for the achievement of a durable and just peace in Bosnia and Herzegovina, leading to stability and cooperation in the region and the reintegration of Bosnia and Herzegovina at all levels;

2. *Reaffirms its support* for the New York Declaration, adopted on 15 November 1999, in which the Joint Presidency of Bosnia and Herzegovina agreed to important steps for moving forward the process of fully implementing the Peace Agreement, notes that the progress of its implementation has been slow, and urges the parties to take the additional steps necessary to comply with all of its aspects;

3. *Notes* the progress that has been made towards the implementation of the Peace Agreement, and reiterates its demands for the full, comprehensive and consistent implementation thereof;

4. *Supports fully* the efforts of the High Representative for the Implementation of the Peace Agreement on Bosnia and Herzegovina, in accordance with the Peace Agreement and subsequent Peace Implementation Council declarations, and calls upon all parties to cooperate fully and in good faith with him;

5. *Stresses* the importance for the peace process in Bosnia and Herzegovina and the region as a whole of the activities related to the Stability Pact for South-Eastern Europe launched in Sarajevo, and urges the authorities of Bosnia and Herzegovina to take concrete steps to play an active role in it;

6. *Welcomes* the Zagreb summit to be held on 24 November 2000;

7. *Notes* the progress achieved with the concept of "ownership" as presented by the High Representative, also notes the continuing need for the High Representative to use fully the authority of his office to deal with obstructionists, and stresses the need for the political leaders to assume more responsibility in the process of the implementation of the Peace Agreement;

8. *Recognizes* that the role of the international community remains essential, welcomes the readiness of the international community to continue its efforts towards a self-sustaining peace, and recalls that the responsibility for consolidating peace and security primarily lies with the authorities of Bosnia and Herzegovina;

9. *Welcomes* the ruling of the Constitutional Court of Bosnia and Herzegovina on the equality of all three constituent peoples throughout the territory of Bosnia and Herzegovina, urges the entity parliaments and cantonal assemblies to implement it accordingly, and also urges the Constitutional Court to rule further on the status of those other than the three constituent peoples;

10. *Also welcomes* the vital contribution of the multinational Stabilization Force in providing a secure environment for the implementation of civilian aspects of the Peace Agreement, calls for the fullest cooperation by all parties in this regard, expresses its full support for the efforts of the United Nations International Police Task Force in carrying out its mandate, and commends its efforts in the establishment of the rule of law in Bosnia and Herzegovina;

11. *Underlines* the fact that the assistance provided by the international community remains strictly conditional upon compliance with the Peace Agreement and subsequent obligations, including in particular cooperation with the International Tribunal for the Prosecution of Persons Responsible for Serious Violations of International Humanitarian Law Committed in the Territory of the Former Yugoslavia since 1991 and facilitation of the return of refugees and displaced persons;

12. *Insists* upon the need to surrender all indictees to the International Tribunal for trial, notes that the Tribunal has the authority to address individual responsibility for the perpetration of the crime of genocide, crimes against humanity and other serious violations of international humanitarian law in Bosnia and Herzegovina, and demands that all the parties fulfil their obligations to hand over to the Tribunal all indicted persons in territories under their control and otherwise to comply fully with the orders of the Tribunal and to cooperate with the work of the Tribunal, including with exhumations and other investigative acts, in accordance with article 29 of the statute of the Tribunal, with all relevant Security Council resolutions and in accordance with the relevant provisions of the Peace Agreement, in particular the Constitution of Bosnia and Herzegovina;

13. *Welcomes* the support given by Member States so far, and urges Member States, taking into account the orders and requests of the International Tribunal, to offer the Tribunal their full support, including financial support, in order to ensure the achievement of the purpose of the Tribunal, and to carry out their obliga-

tions under the statute of the Tribunal and all relevant Security Council resolutions;

14. *Reaffirms once again* the right of refugees and displaced persons to return voluntarily to their homes of origin in secure and dignified conditions in accordance with the Peace Agreement, in particular annex 7 thereof, and the realization of the same in cooperation with the Office of the United Nations High Commissioner for Refugees and host countries, calls upon all parties to improve substantially their cooperation with the international community at the State, entity and local levels, in order to establish immediately the conditions necessary for the return of refugees and displaced persons to their homes and for the freedom of movement and communication of all the citizens of Bosnia and Herzegovina, encourages the relevant international organizations to enhance the conditions to facilitate both spontaneous and organized return, in accordance with relevant provisions of the Peace Agreement, in particular the Constitution of Bosnia and Herzegovina, and welcomes continued and new efforts by the United Nations agencies, the European Union, bilateral and other donors and intergovernmental and non-governmental organizations to establish and implement projects designed to facilitate the accelerated voluntary and orderly return of refugees and displaced persons to all regions of Bosnia and Herzegovina, including projects that would help to create a safe and secure environment with increased economic opportunity;

15. *Encourages* the acceleration of the peaceful, orderly and phased return of refugees and displaced persons, including in areas where they would be the ethnic minority, strongly condemns all acts of intimidation, violence and killings, including those acts designed to discourage the voluntary return of refugees and displaced persons, and demands that such acts be investigated and prosecuted;

16. *Welcomes* the report of the Panel on United Nations Peace Operations, and takes note of the recommendations stemming from and relevant to the report of the Secretary-General pursuant to General Assembly resolution 53/35 on the fall of Srebrenica;

17. *Reaffirms* the previous conclusions of the Peace Implementation Council on the importance of reform of the media in Bosnia and Herzegovina, reiterates its support for the decision of the High Representative of 30 July 1999 on the restructuring of the public broadcasting system in Bosnia and Herzegovina, notes that its implementation remains behind schedule, and calls upon the authorities of Bosnia and Herzegovina to implement that decision in full;

18. *Stresses* the importance of establishing, strengthening and expanding throughout all of Bosnia and Herzegovina free and pluralistic media, deplores any action that seeks to intimidate or restrict the freedom of the media, and condemns violent acts of intimidation against journalists;

19. *Reaffirms once again its support* for the principle that all statements and commitments made under duress, particularly those regarding land and property, are wholly null and void, in accordance with the relevant provisions of the Peace Agreement, and in that regard supports the effective engagement of the Commission for Real Property Claims of Displaced Persons and Refugees, and calls upon all sides to implement the property laws imposed on 27 October 1999, in particular by evicting illegal occupants from the homes of returning refugees, and to ensure respect for individual rights to return and the establishment of the rule of law;

20. *Emphasizes* the importance of economic revitalization and reconstruction for the successful consolidation of the peace process in Bosnia and Herzegovina, recognizes the important contribution of the international community in this regard, and invites it to continue its efforts;

21. *Notes* that corruption and the lack of transparency seriously hamper the economic development of Bosnia and Herzegovina, emphasizes the importance of combating corruption, welcomes the important contribution made in this regard by the Customs and Fiscal Assistance Office, and expresses its full support for the efforts of the Government of Bosnia and Herzegovina and its local bodies and of others that are supportive in this regard;

22. *Supports* the efforts by the High Representative and the Commander of the multinational Stabilization Force, in accordance with the Peace Agreement and subsequent Peace Implementation Council declarations, to weaken the continued political and economic influence of remaining parallel nationalist structures obstructing the peace implementation;

23. *Stresses* the need for a more comprehensive approach to implementing economic reforms, and underlines the fact that a self-sustainable, market-oriented economy operating in a single economic space, expeditious and transparent privatization, improved banking and capital markets, reformed financial systems, the provision of adequate social protection and the adoption by both entities of a law on pension reforms that meet sound economic standards are crucial for achieving lasting peace and stability in Bosnia and Herzegovina;

24. *Welcomes* the proclamation of the Brcko District and the appointment of an interim government and District Assembly, expresses its support for implementation of the final arbitration award in accordance with the Peace Agreement, and stresses that the obligation to cooperate fully with the Supervisor for Brcko is an essential obligation for both of the entities;

25. *Also welcomes* the Mostar Document adopted on 12 July 2000 by the representatives of the city of Mostar and its six city municipalities under the auspices of the European Union, and calls for its implementation;

26. *Notes* that the pledged reduction of 15 per cent in the military assets of each entity was achieved in 1999, urges the authorities of Bosnia and Herzegovina to fulfil their commitment to a further 15 per cent reduction in 2000 in the areas of military budgets, personnel, equipment and structure, and encourages the authorities of Bosnia and Herzegovina to redefine their defence policies with particular reference to ensuring that the size and structure of the military is affordable, that it is consistent with the legitimate security needs of Bosnia and Herzegovina and contributes to regional security;

27. *Stresses* the need for timely information about the level of cooperation and compliance with the International Tribunal and its orders, the status and programme for the return of refugees and displaced persons to and within Bosnia and Herzegovina and the

status and implementation of the Agreement on Subregional Arms Control;

28. *Welcomes* the establishment of the Missing Persons Institute on 15 August 2000 in Sarajevo by the International Commission on Missing Persons, and supports the programmes put in place to resolve the continuing problem of missing persons within five to seven years;

29. *Also welcomes* the efforts of international regional organizations, Member States and non-governmental organizations, including through the Board of Donors, and the Slovenian International Trust Fund for Demining and Mine Victims Assistance in Bosnia and Herzegovina, and invites Member States to continue to support the mine-action activities in Bosnia and Herzegovina;

30. *Commends* the efforts of the international community, including the Council of Europe, the European Union, the European Community Monitoring Mission, the European Bank for Reconstruction and Development, the International Committee of the Red Cross, the International Monetary Fund, the multinational Stabilization Force, non-governmental organizations, the Organization of the Islamic Conference, the Islamic Development Bank, the Islamic Chamber of Commerce and Industry, the Organization for Security and Cooperation in Europe, the Peace Implementation Council and the World Bank, in their roles in the implementation of the Peace Agreement;

31. *Commends*, in particular, the efforts of the International Tribunal, the Office of the High Representative for the Implementation of the Peace Agreement on Bosnia and Herzegovina, the Office of the Special Rapporteur of the Commission on Human Rights on the situation of human rights in the territory of the former Yugoslavia, the Office of the United Nations High Commissioner for Refugees, the Office of the United Nations High Commissioner for Human Rights, the United Nations International Police Task Force, the United Nations Mission in Bosnia and Herzegovina, the United Nations Development Programme and the other United Nations agencies in the peace process, and encourages their further engagement in the peace process in Bosnia and Herzegovina;

32. *Decides* to include in the provisional agenda of its fifty-sixth session the item entitled "The situation in Bosnia and Herzegovina".

On 23 December, the Assembly decided that the item on the situation in Bosnia and Herzegovina would remain for consideration during its resumed fifty-fifth (2001) session (**decision 55/458**).

Military aspects of Agreement

Stabilization Force

During 2000, the NATO Secretary-General reported 10 times to the Security Council, in accordance with resolution 1088(1996) [YUN 1996, p. 310], on the activities of the multinational Stabilization Force (SFOR), also known as Operation Joint Guard [S/2000/46, S/2000/190, S/2000/297,

S/2000/399, S/2000/555, S/2000/690, S/2000/792, S/2000/872, S/2000/967, S/2000/1164]. The strength of the Force, which operated under NATO's leadership, fell from approximately 24,000 at the beginning of the year to 22,000 in December. The troops, which were deployed in Bosnia and Herzegovina and Croatia, were contributed by all NATO members and 15 non-NATO countries. The Security Council, by **resolution 1305(2000)** of 21 June, authorized the continuation of SFOR for a further period of 12 months (see p. 342).

During the year, SFOR continued to conduct surveillance and reconnaissance by ground and air patrols, and to monitor entity compliance with Council resolution 1160(1998) [YUN 1998, p. 369], prohibiting the transport of weapons and the movement of controlled petroleum products into FRY. It also supported IPTF by providing security for its inspection of local police stations and in conducting prison inspections, and provided assistance to international institutions in Bosnia and Herzegovina, including the Office of the High Representative. SFOR maintained a safe environment for and assisted OSCE in its supervision of the 11 November elections, delivered ballots to counting centres and assisted civil authorities in ensuring a safe and secure environment following the announcement of the results.

On 3 April, the meeting of the Standing Committee on Military Matters (SCMM) addressed the further reduction by 15 per cent of the entity armed forces (EAF) by the end of 2000. That planned reduction followed the 15 per cent reduction achieved at the end of 1999. At its 8 December meeting, SCMM decided that the target date for the completion of the 15 per cent reduction of EAF could slip from 31 December 2000 to 31 January 2001. SFOR would begin the development of a joint SFOR-EAF training and exercise plan in 2001. SCMM also agreed on plans for the expansion of its secretariat and indicated that it would consider the draft defence policy for Bosnia and Herzegovina and the future EAF restructuring in January 2001.

Communications. FRY, in letters of 31 May [S/2000/509] and 6 September [S/2000/852], protested the violation of its airspace by SFOR military aircraft and helicopters, stating that it would no longer tolerate such action. On 20 September [S/2000/884], FRY requested an explanation for the continued monitoring of the movement of controlled petroleum products into FRY. The Security Council had terminated sanctions against it by resolution 1074(1996) [YUN 1996, p. 316], and resolution 1088(1996) [ibid., p. 310], by which SFOR was established, contained no sanctions monitoring provisions.

Federal Republic of Yugoslavia

In 2000, the United Nations Interim Administration Mission in Kosovo (UNMIK), in implementation of Security Council resolution 1244(1999), made significant progress towards developing provisional institutions for democratic and autonomous self-government in the Kosovo province of the Federal Republic of Yugoslavia (FRY), promoting the return of the territory to a viable administrative structure and economic and social recovery and reconstruction. Nevertheless, the continuing violence in the province, mostly against Kosovo Serbs, and the slow pace in implementing some of the resolution's political provisions, especially with regard to the process of reconciliation and return of refugees and displaced persons, led the Council to send a mission to Kosovo in April to assess the situation there and look for ways to enhance support for implementation of the resolution.

As a first step towards a return to normalcy, municipal elections were successfully held on 28 October, despite the non-participation of the Kosovo Serb community, paving the way for the establishment of functioning municipal assemblies in Kosovo.

At the same time, relations between the FRY federal Government and the Republic of Montenegro deteriorated as that Republic asserted control over its own affairs in the face of a deepening constitutional crisis. That crisis was avoided following the election on 24 September of a new federal President, Vojislav Kostunica. The political changes in Belgrade renewed hope for the constructive political dialogue on the future of Kosovo.

Despite those positive developments, the Council remained concerned over the post-election violence, particularly the potentially explosive situation in the ground safety zone between Kosovo and Serbia proper. In a 19 December statement, the Council condemned the violent action by Albanian extremist groups in southern Serbia and called for their dissolution. It called on UNMIK and the international security presence to continue to make all necessary efforts to address the problem.

Situation in Kosovo

Implementation of resolution 1244(1999)

In 2000, the United Nations continued to work towards the full implementation of Security Council resolution 1244(1999) [YUN 1999, p. 353],

which set out the modalities for a political solution to the crisis in the Kosovo province of FRY. The civilian aspects of that solution were being implemented by UNMIK and the military aspects by the international security presence (KFOR), also known as Operation Joint Guardian.

During the year, the Council received a number of communications from FRY conveying its assessment of the status of implementation of resolution 1244(1999) and recommendations for action by the Council to address the situation.

Communications. On 10 January [S/2000/19], FRY listed a number of violations of resolution 1244(1999) by the Secretary-General's Special Representative, KFOR and UNMIK, which it demanded that the Council address in order to have the situation in Kosovo and Metohija restored to its prior state. On 14 January [S/2000/25], FRY listed crimes committed on 29 December 1999 and 11 January 2000, which, it said, provided telling evidence that the terrorists of the so-called Kosovo Liberation Army (KLA) continued to kill and ethnically cleanse non-Albanians. On 19 January [S/2000/41], FRY called for an urgent meeting of the Security Council, since none of its requests regarding illegal acts by KFOR and UNMIK had been acted upon. It asserted that, because of the failure to implement, and/or an arbitrary interpretation of their mandate established by resolution 1244(1999), KFOR and UNMIK and the Special Representative and Head of UNMIK, in particular, bore direct responsibility for the current situation in the province, characterized by lawlessness, chaos, massive crime, destruction and usurpation of public and private property and everyday terror, killings, kidnappings and ethnic cleansing of Serbs and other non-Albanians. Since 12 June 1999, over 350,000 people, mostly Serbs and Montenegrins, but also Roma, Muslims, Turks, Goranci and others, had been driven out of Kosovo and Metohija. A total of 793 persons had been killed, 611 wounded and 688 abducted.

On 25 January [S/2000/51], FRY drew the Council President's attention to the inauguration of the so-called Kosovo Protection Corps (KPC), which it claimed amounted to an attempt to legalize the terrorist separatist KLA, and its drive to impose itself as a security factor. FRY requested that the crimes committed by members of KLA, now KPC, be condemned and that the organization be fully demilitarized and disarmed, its structures disbanded and its leaders, who were guilty of crimes against non-Albanians, brought to justice.

Regarding further complaints of violations of and failure to implement resolution 1244(1999), FRY, on 11 February [S/2000/110], stated that the escalation of ethnic Albanian terrorism was evidenced by the upsurge in the number of terrorist attacks committed recently, including the shelling of the Serbian village of Gorazdevac on 7 January and the mortar attack on a UNHCR bus ferrying Serbs on 2 February, among others (see below). Those atrocities had shattered the trust of the Serbian community in the ability of the international presences to provide protection mandated by resolution 1244(1999). Ethnic Albanian terrorists were also responsible for destroying more than 50,000 homes and wiping out the Serbian historical heritage in Kosovo and Metohija, and more than 350,000 Serbs, Montenegrins, Roma, Muslims, Turks, Goranci and other non-Albanians had been ethnically cleansed. FRY said that the Secretary-General's Special Representative had illegally established the so-called Interim Administration Council, a de facto provincial "Government", composed exclusively of Albanians, mostly KLA leaders and Albanian separatist parties, in an attempt to legalize an ethnically pure Kosovo and Metohija and sever its ties with Serbia and FRY.

FRY demanded that the Council take the most energetic steps to implement resolution 1244 (1999) and redress the current situation, including by rescinding the illegal regulations of the Special Representative and bringing back the functioning of State and public services in accordance with the laws of Serbia and FRY. It also demanded that the Yugoslav border, customs and passport control authorities return to the Yugoslav international borders in Kosovo and Metohija.

Those demands and others were formally compiled in memorandums forwarded to the Council President on 2 March [S/2000/176] and 3 April [S/2000/284], in which FRY also provided its own assessment of current developments in Kosovo and Metohija. Appended to the memorandum of 3 April was a list of terrorist acts and other violations of resolution 1244(1999) reportedly committed between 10 June 1999 and 30 March 2000.

FRY contended that the 10-month-long international security and civilian presence in the southern Serb province was devastating. By their overall conduct, KFOR and UNMIK had confirmed that the presence of international forces under UN auspices was a complete fiasco. The Security Council bore primary responsibility for the tragic consequences, since it failed to take measures to ensure strict implementation of resolution 1244(1999) and related documents. There was no longer an excuse for the further stay of the mission of the international community, which should be ended as soon as possible. FRY expected that its previous initiative for a

Council mission to visit the country and see first-hand the dramatic developments in the southern Serb province would be implemented in the near future.

On 10 March [S/2000/206], FRY expressed its displeasure at a statement made by the Secretary-General at a 7 March press conference to the effect that he would provide a basis for discussing the issue of the autonomy of Kosovo and Metohija in the Security Council in support of his Special Representative's contention that it was necessary to open the question of the political future of that Serbian province. FRY protested the Secretary-General's announced intention of introducing the question of autonomy in the Council.

Mitrovica incident

The Secretary-General, in his March report on UNMIK [S/2000/177], informed the Security Council that, on 2 February, a clearly marked UNHCR humanitarian shuttle bus carrying 49 Kosovo Serb passengers and escorted by two KFOR vehicles was targeted by a rocket, resulting in two persons being killed and three injured. Following the attack, violence broke out in northern Mitrovica on 3 and 4 February, resulting in eight deaths and at least 20 to 30 persons seriously injured, the displacement of over 1,650 Kosovo Albanians from northern Mitrovica and the reduction of the number of Kosovo Serbs in the southern part of the city to just 20 individuals, the majority of whom were living at a monastery under KFOR protection. Some 5,000 Kosovo Serbs remained in isolated enclaves in the southern outskirts of the city, as well as some 2,000 Kosovo Albanians in the northern outskirts. UNMIK and non-governmental organizations (NGOs) were also affected by the violence, and international and local staff had to be relocated. Nine vehicles belonging to UNMIK, UNHCR, OSCE and international NGOs were burned or looted. The International Committee of the Red Cross (ICRC) office was burned and several NGO offices and one KFOR office were looted.

Following a period of tense calm, violence again broke out in Mitrovica on 13 and 14 February. On 13 February, a grenade attack against a Bosniac cafe in northern Mitrovica injured seven persons. Shortly thereafter, snipers firing from apartment buildings at KFOR positions on the ground seriously wounded two KFOR soldiers. One suspected sniper was killed and another wounded, both Kosovo Albanians. A total of 46 persons, the majority of whom were Kosovo Albanians, were taken into custody. On 21 February, a public march of Kosovo Albanians from Pristina to Mitrovica also led to a confrontation with KFOR forces. To improve security in Mitrovica, the KFOR Commander launched Operation Ibar on 20 February, during which part of the city was cordoned off and buildings searched.

Communications. In bringing those incidents to the attention of the Security Council President on 3, 13 and 21 February [S/2000/86, S/2000/111, S/2000/140], FRY said that it was obvious that a concentrated attack had been planned to drive Serbs, Montenegrins, Goranci, Slav Muslims and Turks out of Kosovska Mitrovica, the only remaining multi-ethnic and multi-religious community in Kosovo and Metohija, and complete the process of ethnic cleansing of non-Albanians living in isolated enclaves. It accused UNMIK and KFOR of not doing anything to put an end to ethnic Albanian terror and vandalism and of complicity in those practices. FRY said that it found the Secretary-General's reaction to the attack on the UNHCR bus unacceptable, as he did not condemn the rampant terrorism. It warned the Council that failure to confront the security situation in Kosovo and Metohija would cause an escalation of terrorism throughout the region and result in the destabilization of the Balkans and South-East Europe. It called for an urgent meeting of the Council and for action to put an end to ongoing and future attacks of armed ethnic Albanian terrorists on the unprotected Serbian population.

The EU, on 23 February [S/2000/158], expressed concern over the events in Mitrovica and reiterated its strong condemnation of all acts of violence and public disturbance. It reaffirmed its support for the efforts of UNMIK and KFOR in the implementation of resolution 1244(1999) and warned that defiance and threats to the international presence in Kosovo would not be tolerated.

On 28 February [S/2000/156], FRY protested the most recent attacks by ethnic Albanian terrorist separatists, in which a Yugoslav police officer and a physician were killed and three police officers and another physician wounded. On 8 March [S/2000/199], it said that the escalation of violence by ethnic Albanian terrorists against Serbs in Kosovska Mitrovica was further evidence that the terrorist-separatist KLA had not been disarmed and continued its attempts to drive all Serbs and other non-Albanians out of Kosovo and Metohija. It asked the Council to take urgent measures to protect them in accordance with resolution 1244(1999).

On 15 March [S/2000/219], FRY protested KFOR's establishment of an extended security zone in northern Kosovska Mitrovica in the town quarter called Bosnjacka mahala. It said that 16 Serb civilians were injured, two seriously, when they were assailed with stun grenades and tear gas as they gathered around the so-called Mali most (Little

Bridge). By those actions, KFOR continued to assist ethnic Albanian terrorists in putting pressure on the Serbian population to move out of Kosovo and Metohija, with the aim of ethnically cleansing it. FRY expected the Council to ensure minimum security and relatively normal living conditions to the Serbian population in Kosovska Mitrovica, the last Serb refuge in Kosovo and Metohija. On 22 March [S/2000/244], FRY indicated that a railway bridge at Zvecan, near Kosovska Mitrovica, an area inhabited almost exclusively by Serbs, was dynamited on the night of 21/22 March. Other acts of violence in Orahovac and Gnjilane were brought to the Council's attention on 29 March [S/2000/270] and 12 April [S/2000/310].

Between April and September, FRY transmitted numerous letters to the Security Council President describing other instances of violent acts against Kosovo Serbs and other non-Albanian minorities [S/2000/332, S/2000/342, S/2000/357, S/2000/374, S/2000/388, S/2000/497, S/2000/508, S/2000/526, S/2000/531, S/2000/543, S/2000/588, S/2000/613, S/2000/636, S/2000/675, S/2000/708, S/2000/815, S/2000/830, S/2000/843, S/2000/877].

Special Security Council briefing

On 28 February [S/PV.4105], Carl Bildt, Special Envoy of the Secretary-General for the Balkans, briefed the Security Council on the situation in the region. He said that, although the war in Kosovo ended with Council resolution 1244(1999), and with a military-technical agreement, there was no proper peace agreement, a key factor that made UNMIK's task so demanding and difficult. Since the core issues of the conflict concerning the long-term position of Kosovo were not settled, it had made it much more difficult to move towards stability for the region as a whole and there were too many expectations and fears generated by those unresolved issues.

The starting points for a settlement in Kosovo were: the Council's support for the search for a regional settlement, including dialogue within the Council on the shape of such a settlement; the States of the region actively participating, including not only Belgrade and the political representatives of the Kosovo Albanians but the leaders of FYROM and Albania; a true deal had to meet the minimum demands of everyone but the maximum demands of no one, as was the case of the Peace Agreement for Bosnia and Herzegovina [YUN 1995, p. 544]; and, most difficult, the agreement had to be set within the context of a wider arrangement for the region as a whole, and preferably within the wider European context.

However, the situation was handicapped by the regime in Belgrade, as the indictment of its key political and military leaders for crimes against humanity de facto excommunicated them from any dialogue or diplomatic contact. In addition, there was the situation between Serbia and Montenegro (see p. 381), which were headed on a collision course as long as there was no change in the regime in Belgrade. The confrontation between Montenegro and Serbia was a confrontation over the future of FRY and had obvious implications for the implementation of resolution 1244(1999).

The Special Envoy said the tensions along the fault lines between those wider interests could be seen on a daily basis in Mitrovica in northern Kosovo. One should not pretend not to recognize those extremist groups or individuals on both sides who were determined to exploit those tensions, be they in northern Kosovo, Serbia or FYROM. There was a clash between the forces of integration and those of disintegration in the region.

Security Council mission to Kosovo

Concerned about obstacles to the implementation of resolution 1244(1999) [YUN 1999, p. 353], the Security Council, on 14 April [S/2000/320], accepted the invitation of the Special Representative and Head of UNMIK and decided to send a mission to Kosovo. The mission, which comprised the Ambassadors of Argentina, Bangladesh (head of mission), Canada, China, France, Jamaica, Malaysia, the Russian Federation and Ukraine, visited Kosovo from 27 to 29 April. Its objectives were to look for ways to enhance support for the implementation of resolution 1244(1999); to observe UNMIK's operations and activities and gain a greater understanding of the situation on the ground in order to comprehend better the difficult challenges UNMIK faced; to convey a strong message to all concerned on the need to reject violence, ensure public safety and order, promote stability, safety and security, support the full and effective implementation of resolution 1244(1999), and fully cooperate with UNMIK to that end; and to review implementation of prohibitions imposed by Council resolution 1160(1998) [YUN 1998, p. 369].

On 7 April [S/2000/303], FRY said that it attached great importance to the envisaged visit, which it saw as an expression of the Council's readiness and openness to familiarize itself in greater detail with the situation in Kosovo and Metohija and to halt the ongoing violations of resolution 1244(1999). It undertook to assist and cooperate with the mission in fulfilling its mandate.

Report of mission. During its visit to Kosovo [S/2000/363], the mission consulted with a wide range of representatives at all levels and from all communities. It found that UNMIK had made significant progress in implementing resolution 1244(1999) but its full and effective implementation required sustained effort by UNMIK and KFOR, the full participation of local communities and support by the international community. All ethnic communities expressed a desire to live in peace together but were still deeply divided and the healing would require a long time. Despite improvement in the overall level of violence and criminality, attacks against minorities continued and special protection measures had to be constantly maintained, making KFOR's continued assistance and joint security operations with UNMIK police vital.

Inadequate physical, social and economic security remained a major concern. Lack of freedom of movement, access to education, health care, social services and employment hampered the return of internally displaced persons, primarily Serbs and Roma, and impeded the integration of ethnic minorities into public life.

There had been some positive signs of reconciliation but the painful issues of missing persons and detainees, continuing violence, and the return of internally displaced persons and refugees continued to be major impediments in that regard and undermined efforts to create a climate of tolerance and security. The mission noted the strong support of the different ethnic communities for the appointment of a special envoy for detainees and missing persons.

The recent participation of the Serbs as observers in the Joint Interim Administrative Structures, including the Kosovo Transitional Council and the Interim Administrative Council, was encouraging and hopefully would lead to their full participation and a larger representation of non-Albanians in the Structures. Bosniac and Roma representatives, however, had yet to join the Transitional Council.

The mission noted that a major effort by the international presences and long-term nurturing would be necessary to achieve progress in reconciliation. Nonetheless, several examples of more positive relations between communities were observed at the local level, where discussions were less politically charged and focused on practical modes of cooperation. The mission welcomed the renewal of contacts between leaders of both communities in Mitrovica, and believed that joint community-based programmes had a potential for confidence-building and reconciliation.

The lack of an effective and unbiased rule of law was a recurring theme at many of the mission's meetings. UNMIK's intention to recruit international judges and prosecutors and their staff to work with local counterparts would be critical in redressing the perceived culture of impunity undermining the judicial system. To increase the judiciary's effectiveness, substantial voluntary assistance, in both personnel and material resources, was required. Regarding the lack of sufficient policing resources, UNMIK should continue accelerating its training programmes for the Kosovo Police Service (KPS). The multi-ethnic and gender-sensitive KPS development programme and the OSCE-led Kosovo Police School should serve as models for future institutions in Kosovo. The mission was appreciative of the fact that human rights education and AIDS awareness were part of UNMIK's police curriculum.

While noting the serious staffing constraints UNMIK faced in civil administration and police, the mission recognized the significant imbalance in wages between its locally recruited civil service staff and the rest of the Kosovo population and felt that both issues should be pursued through the appropriate General Assembly process.

To ensure an organized, expeditious and sustainable return, significant resources would be required to create appropriate conditions for the returnees by increasing Kosovo's absorbing capacity.

The mission stated that it was unfortunate that all factions of the Kosovo Serb community had chosen not to participate in the civil and voter registration processes, due to the lack of physical security and freedom of movement. Substantial efforts by UNMIK and KFOR, with strong support from the international community, were essential to encourage and create the conditions for Serb participation, including those displaced outside Kosovo.

The mission noted UNMIK's intention to continue working to establish a joint committee to enhance dialogue with FRY authorities, and KFOR's regular contact with them on military issues within the framework of the Joint Implementation Committee. It was cognizant of the imperative for UNMIK to foster economic recovery as a means of underpinning confidence-building and reconciliation efforts at the local level and welcomed the deployment of EU economic reconstruction representatives at the municipal level. It supported UNMIK's view that UNMIK should guide economic investment priorities to ensure maximum effectiveness of donated funds. Property issues, however, remained unresolved and could potentially undermine international efforts aimed at Kosovo's economic recovery and even peace initiatives.

The mission felt that detailed information on KFOR's activities in the implementation of resolution 1160(1998) should be provided to the Committee established for that purpose.

Emphasizing that UNMIK had been deployed for only some 10 months, the mission stated that

expectations for its achievements should be realistic. Reconciliation was a protracted process, and the international community had to be patient and persistent. UNMIK and KFOR had made significant progress in implementing their mandates and should be commended. The mission noted the enormity of the task facing UNMIK, and commended, in particular, its efforts in capacity- and institution-building. Further efforts to ensure full implementation of resolution 1244 (1999) remained a high priority of the Council.

In presenting the report to the Council on 11 May [S/PV.4138], the head of the mission said that in its interaction with the ethnic communities the mission sensed a clear desire of people to live together in peace and engage in economic reconstruction and the restitution of law and order. Its strong message to those communities to reject all violence was taken seriously, with the full understanding that a multi-ethnic society represented the best hope for the people of Kosovo.

The mission recognized the shortage in meeting the staffing requirements for civil administration and the civilian police as a serious constraint for UNMIK's operations and asked the Secretariat and contributing countries to take steps in that regard with seriousness and urgency.

Communications. In a 12 May letter [S/2000/429], FRY said that the Council's mission was the important initial step to obtain first-hand knowledge of the dramatic situation brought about by systematic violations of resolution 1244(1999). Regrettably, the violations were not reflected in the mission's report, which, in part, diverted attention from the true problems and even glossed over the policy and behaviour of UNMIK and KFOR and, in particular, the Secretary-General's Special Representative. The report was silent about daily instances of terrorism and the responsibility for rampant crime and lawlessness, but was loud in endorsing views that set very strict conditions for and prevented the return of expelled Serbs, Muslims, Roma, Goranci, Turks and other non-Albanians. Notwithstanding its shortcomings, the mission's report had borne out the validity of FRY's warnings that, even 11 months after the adoption of resolution 1244 (1999), UNMIK and KFOR had not fulfilled a single obligation entrusted to them. FRY reiterated its readiness to conclude an agreement on the status and cooperation with those missions, including the establishment of a joint coordination committee.

FRY, on 12 May [S/2000/428], 7 June [S/2000/547], 23 August [S/2000/829] and 26 September [S/2000/905], forwarded to the Council President further memorandums containing its position on the implementation of resolution 1244(1999) and violations of it, as well as an overview of terrorist and other acts of violence.

On 8 June [S/2000/553], FRY declared null and void all acts and decisions taken by the Special Representative. It called on the Council to put an end to his activities, withdraw UNMIK and KFOR from Kosovo and take measures to ensure the full and consistent implementation of resolution 1244(1999). It asked the Council to consider those demands and provide an answer at its 9 June meeting (see p. 365).

UN Interim Administration Mission in Kosovo

Special Representative and Head of UNMIK. During 2000, Bernard Kouchner (France) continued as the Secretary-General's Special Representative and Head of UNMIK. On 8 December [S/2000/1179], the Secretary-General informed the Security Council of his intention to appoint Hans Haekkerup (Denmark) to replace Mr. Kouchner. The Council took note of that intention on 12 December [S/2000/1180].

Communication. On 6 January [S/2000/6], FRY said that the Secretary-General's December 1999 report on UNMIK [YUN 1999, p. 361] gave cause for concern because of the contradiction between the claim that UNMIK had made progress and the facts presented in the report testifying that the Serbs and other non-Albanians were threatened and their human rights were being violated. Those facts corroborated FRY's position that the security situation in Kosovo and Metohija was difficult, compounded by gross violations of human rights by the so-called KLA, the abuse of juveniles and the presence of organized crime. The provisions of Security Council resolution 1244(1999) continued to be violated. In particular, FRY's sovereignty and territorial integrity were not being abided by; conditions were not being created for normal life; violence continued unabated, particularly against non-Albanians; public law and order were non-existent; no proper border-monitoring activities had been established; the provisions on the return of an agreed number of Yugoslav Army and Serbian police personnel had not been implemented; and no secure environment had been created for the return of refugees and internally displaced persons. The report failed to assess blame for the situation and identify perpetrators or to propose measures to deal with it.

Report of Secretary-General (March). The Secretary-General, in his March report on UNMIK [S/2000/177], stated that the three major Kosovo Albanian rival political parties (the Democratic League of Kosovo (LDK) of Ibrahim

Rugova, the party coalition of United Democratic Movement of Rexhep Qosja and the Party for Democratic Progress of Kosovo (PPDK) of Hashim Thaci) had begun to work together in a new cooperative relationship in the Interim Administrative Council (IAC) and the Joint Interim Administrative Structure (JIAS). On the other hand, the Kosovo Serb political landscape remained diversified and dominated by divisions among three major political forces: the moderate Kosovo Serb National Council (SNC), mainly in the Pristina and the Gnjilane regions, and headed by Bishop Artemije and Momcilo Trajkovic; the SNC Mitrovica, led by Oliver Ivanovic and Vuko Antonijevic; and the pro-Belgrade Serb National Assembly led by Veljko Odalovic.

IAC met on average twice a week and had become involved in substantive issues, such as the events in Mitrovica (see p. 359) and draft regulations for municipal elections. Its work was hampered in February by friction linked to the dissolution of the parties' respective parallel structures and funds controlled by them. More recently, IAC members had exercised constructive political leadership. To ensure the participation of Kosovo Serb representatives in JIAS, an agreement in principle was reached between UNMIK and the Kosovo SNC on the need to enhance security, increase UNMIK's presence in Serbpopulated areas and ensure greater access of the Serb population to essential public services. However, persisting political divisions within the Serb community and the deterioration of the security situation in Mitrovica hampered efforts to secure their participation in JIAS and finalization of the agreement. The UNMIK Task Force charged with developing a strategy to implement JIAS had, with IAC, identified 20 departments needed to administer Kosovo, each codirected by an international and a local co-head. To date, 14 Kosovo and 16 international co-heads had been appointed, including three women.

Regarding the formation of municipal structures, by the end of February, 27 municipal councils and 12 administrative boards had been established. UNMIK administrators were continuing consultations to finalize the remaining municipal councils and administrative boards and to overcome disagreement among the various Kosovo Albanian political parties over the distribution of representatives. The limited participation of minorities within municipal structures remained a matter of concern and had been hampered by the withdrawal of their support in protest against ethnically motivated violence.

On 31 January, in accordance with the JIAS agreement [YUN 1999, p. 361], all parallel Kosovo Albanian bodies declared that they had ceased to exist and the so-called "ministries" of the self-proclaimed "Interim Government" officially stopped their work on that date. That was confirmed on 2 February by Dr. Rugova, the LDK President, and by Bujar Bukoshi, the "Prime Minister" of the parallel "Government". The integration of those structures into JIAS was smooth and UNMIK and KFOR had established monitoring mechanisms, especially of the former parallel law enforcement structures.

The Kosovo Transitional Council (KTC) was enlarged from 12 to 35 members on 9 February to better reflect Kosovo's pluralistic composition. The advisory bodies established by UNMIK, through which the local population and leadership were able to participate in the interim administration, were to be dissolved or absorbed into JIAS. UNMIK maintained channels of communication with the FRY Government, which also established the Committee for Cooperation with UNMIK in Pristina, with sub-offices in the Mitrovica and Gnjilane regions. Cooperation also took place through the Joint Implementation Committee established within the framework of the military-technical agreement [YUN 1999, p. 356]. Cooperation focused on humanitarian assistance to the Kosovo Serb community.

With the exception of events in Mitrovica, violent crime in Kosovo continued to follow a slow downward trend. However, an upsurge in grenade and arson attacks against Kosovo Serb enclaves was noted. In addition, on 26 February, a prominent Kosovo Serb medical doctor was killed in Gnjilane, and a Russian Federation KFOR soldier, who was shot in Srbica on 29 February, died from his wounds. Cross-boundary incursions by Yugoslav police were also reported in the Gnjilane region. International patrols along Kosovo's eastern boundary with Serbia had been stepped up and permanent boundary checkpoints established. KFOR and UNMIK reported seeing armed Albanians in military uniforms in the area of Dobrosin.

The Kosovo Protection Corps (KPC) was formally established on 21 January, with the appointment by the Special Representative of 46 KPC leaders. KPC's strength as at 25 February stood at 544 persons, out of a total authorized strength of 5,052. UNMIK regional administrators had begun identifying humanitarian and public works projects for KPC, and the first training courses for KPC personnel had begun. Minority communities had expressed concern about KPC with regard to its creation and composition, as well as the proposed location of KPC buildings, the alleged involvement of enrolled or aspiring KPC members in illegal law enforcement activi-

ties, their participation in political rallies and other incidents of ethnic intolerance.

Report of Secretary-General (June). In June [S/2000/538], the Secretary-General reported that, on 2 April, SNC Gracanica joined JIAS as an observer for an initial period of three months but listed additional conditions to be met before it joined as a full member. One Kosovo Serb represented the community in IAC and four in KTC, while two others were appointed as co-heads for the Departments of Agriculture and of Labour and Employment.

The trend towards pluralism within the Kosovo Albanian political landscape continued, with an increased number of political parties growing out of the former KLA. Altogether, some 30 Kosovo Albanian parties were active within the province. The Bosniac community was represented by three parties, and the Kosovo Turkish community fielded two.

On 11 April, for the first time, IAC held its meetings with both the Kosovo Serb and Kosovo Albanian representatives. IAC endorsed key regulations, including those establishing the JIAS departments, implementing the tax administration and creating the Central Election Commission, the Civil Registry and the Victim Recovery and Identification Commission, and addressed substantive issues, including the Kosovo consolidated budget, local administration, reconstruction, health, education, utilities and private sector development. It had also become increasingly vocal and active in promoting tolerance between ethnic communities and in condemning violence.

On 12 April, four Kosovo Serb representatives from SNC Gracanica returned to KTC as observers and two representatives of the Bosniac community rejoined on 3 May. On 17 May, a representative of the Roma community attended KTC for the first time. Consultations to nominate a second Kosovo Turkish representative continued. However, the representative of the Albanian party, the National Movement for the Liberation of Kosovo, resigned from that body on 10 May, protesting that UNMIK and the international community were not doing enough to solve the issue of Kosovo Albanian missing persons and detainees in Serbia proper. The expanded KTC focused on missing persons and detainees, civil registration, security, education, the judicial system, private sector development and the registration of political parties. On 10 May, it endorsed a statement on tolerance, condemning the crimes that took place in Kosovo before, during and after the recent conflict and urging all inhabitants of Kosovo to refrain from violence. It also called on the federal authorities to hand over all Kosovo Albanians and members of other Kosovo communities in prison in Serbia proper. Four KTC working groups were set up on tolerance and protection of local communities; detainees and missing persons; economic affairs and public utilities; and education. They formed another practical link between JIAS and the local population. The Working Group on Detainees and Missing Persons had begun to compile the information available on such persons of all ethnic communities.

Progress was also made in the establishment of municipal bodies. As at 29 May, a total of 27 out of 30 municipal councils had been established, as well as 27 out of 30 municipal administrative boards that managed the municipal services departments. All municipal councils and administrative boards had ad interim status in view of the upcoming municipal elections (see p. 367).

In keeping with UNMIK's mandate to organize and oversee the development of provisional institutions for democratic and autonomous self-government pending a political settlement, the Special Representative informed the Security Council on 6 March that he would develop a "contract" on self-government (see p. 367), which would build on existing joint bodies of JIAS, including IAC, and KTC. An important step would be the October municipal elections.

To advance meaningful dialogue with FRY, UNMIK suggested the establishment of a permanent joint consultative committee, which would deal with transboundary issues.

Although the general security situation in Kosovo had not changed significantly, in southern Serbia proper a series of violent incidents in the first quarter of the year gave rise to concern over the situation and its likely impact on Kosovo (see below).

Communications. On 15 June [S/2000/595], FRY commented that the Secretary-General's June report was selective in reflecting UNMIK's "successes" and biased in its appraisal of the situation, in particular the security situation. The report was characterized by generalization of the problems facing the Serbian population and showed an absence of criticism and condemnation of those responsible for the violence against Serbs. The situation in southern Serbia was raised without authority so as to project a picture of an alleged threat to Kosovo and Metohija. Calling on Member States to contribute to the release of Albanians detained in Serbia was an invitation to interference in its internal affairs, while no mention was made of Serbs detained in labour camps by ethnic Albanian terrorists. No firm evidence was given to corroborate the claims of mass graves, and scant attention was accorded to the return of 350,000 Serb refugees and other non-

Albanians, for whom UNMIK and KFOR had failed to create the conditions for safe return.

On 22 August [S/2000/824], the Russian Federation said that the Head of UNMIK and the KFOR Commander had unilaterally adopted a 17 August joint declaration on the status of UNMIK and KFOR and their personnel in Kosovo, which amounted to a de facto self-proclamation of such status without any form of agreement with the Yugoslav authorities. The generally recognized practice of deploying peacekeeping operations required the signing of appropriate agreements with the host country, in that case FRY, which had repeated its readiness to begin consultations on the status of international presences in Kosovo. Moscow believed that the so-called "document" adopted by them was dangerous and harmful and ran counter to the provisions of resolution 1244(1999) on FRY's sovereignty and territorial integrity.

Security Council consideration. During the Security Council's consideration of the Secretary-General's June report on 9 June [S/PV.4153], the Special Representative said that progress had been made in the 12 months since UNMIK started its operations in Kosovo. The job of implementing resolution 1244(1999) was a complex one. UNMIK had to provide an interim administration and establish provisional institutions for democratic and autonomous governance. That was being accomplished in four phases: the emergency phase, during which it had to deal with refugees; the demilitarization phase, which, while imperfect, met with some degree of success; the establishment of a political administration; and the elections, for which preparations were being made. Despite UNMIK's successes, there were many negative aspects and challenges relating to the departure of the non-Albanian population and particularly the precarious security situation for that population. In addition, the interim status of Kosovo and the ambiguities in resolution 1244(1999) had to be dealt with, especially providing an explanation on the meaning of "substantial autonomy". The United Nations was not in Kosovo for 12 months or 24 months; it would undoubtedly be there for a significant number of years.

The Council President informed the Council that, on 8 June, he had received a delegation of Serbs from Kosovo, which shared with him the difficulties that community was encountering, particularly violence. The decision of some Serbs in Kosovo to participate in the joint administration structures had entailed personal risks to them and was fraught with considerable sacrifices. However, those sacrifices had not been rewarded by improvement in the fate of the community and their participation in the joint structures had become difficult to justify. The delegation wished the international community to indicate that it would no longer tolerate violence against the Serb population and that the perpetrators should be brought to justice. Specific measures were necessary, including additional forces to ensure security in the Serb enclaves. The Serb community should also have its own information media, the border with Albania should be better controlled and voter registration should be carried out on a stricter basis.

The Council continued to consider the situation in Kosovo on 13 July [S/PV.4171], 24 August [S/PV.4190] and 27 September [S/PV.4200].

Following the 13 July meeting, FRY, on 18 July [S/2000/710], expressed its disappointment that, during the debate, there was no clear condemnation of the ethnic cleansing and terror against the Serbs, Turks, Roma, Muslims and other non-Albanians in Kosovo and Metohija. The situation called for vigorous measures to eradicate terrorism, organized crime and the systematic violation of resolution 1244(1999). In a later communication [S/2000/859], FRY complained about the non-implementation of the provisions of resolution 1244(1999) relating to the return of an agreed number of Yugoslav and Serbian military and police personnel to Kosovo and Metohija, despite several requests to UNMIK and KFOR in that regard. The deterioration in the overall situation in Kosovo and Metohija bore witness to the need for a speedy deployment of those personnel. FRY had therefore established a combined detachment for special purposes, the Kosovo and Metohija Detachment of Peace, ready to be deployed there. That would help implement key provisions of resolution 1244(1999) and create a secure environment for all residents of Kosovo and Metohija.

On 10 August [A/56/2], the Council members authorized the President to make a press statement expressing their concern over FRY's disregard for international obligations with regard to the arrest and detention of two British, two Canadian and four Netherlands citizens. Council members urged FRY authorities to fulfil all of the requirements of the relevant provisions of international law without delay.

Report of Secretary-General (September). In September [S/2000/878], the Secretary-General reported that UNMIK had made substantial progress in consolidating the participation of moderate Kosovo Serb elements in the joint interim administration. SNC Gracanica, which had temporarily suspended its participation in both IAC and KTC at the beginning of June, lifted that suspension on 25 June following initiatives by the in-

ternational community to encourage it to rejoin, including direct meetings between members of the Security Council and an SNC Gracanica delegation in New York. In addition, the Special Representative signed a Joint Understanding with Bishop Artemije of SNC Gracanica, outlining steps to enhance security and access to services for the Kosovo Serb population. Since then, SNC Gracanica representatives had played an increasingly constructive role in IAC and KTC, a position unanimously supported by its general membership in early August.

While the Understanding was well received by the Kosovo Serb community, Kosovo Albanian leaders feared that it would devolve elements of governance and delegate security powers to the Kosovo Serb population. Provisions in the regulation on self-government of municipalities, which called for the establishment of local community offices—a mechanism designed to improve minority access to municipal services—were criticized on similar grounds. That concern over potential divisions of the province culminated in the walk-out of Hashim Thaci and his party, PPDK, from IAC and KTC. Local co-heads of administrative departments nominated by PPDK also suspended their work. Following intensive efforts by UNMIK, the draft regulation was endorsed by IAC on 11 July, and PPDK resumed its participation in both bodies shortly thereafter.

Despite tension over the signing of the Understanding, encouraging signs of inter-ethnic political dialogue emerged. From 21 to 23 July, 40 representatives of Kosovo Serb and Albanian communities met in Airlie, Virginia, United States, at a conference convened by the United States Institute of Peace. The conference produced the unanimously supported Airlie Declaration, in which all participants agreed that building democracy in Kosovo was of the highest priority and that free elections were a key element in the process. The Declaration also recognized the fundamental right of all Kosovo residents to return to the province and that the cultivation of a strong and vibrant multi-ethnic civil society was essential for Kosovo's future. The conference participants also committed themselves to a "pact against violence" to promote tolerance, prevent negative exploitation of ethnic issues and enable physical integration and political participation by all residents of the province. The IAC and KTC representatives expressed strong support for the Airlie Declaration, and discussions were taking place on how to transform it into concrete initiatives.

As part of the continued development of Kosovo's provisional institutions, the Special Representative presented his initial concept of a "pact" for Kosovo society, formerly referred to as the "contract", and which would involve elaboration of a legal framework for substantial autonomy and community protection during the interim administrative period but would not address the issue of Kosovo's final status. It would include mechanisms to protect the rights of Kosovo's various ethnic communities and the establishment of Kosovo-wide institutions for genuine self-government. The first element of the pact, the regulation on self-government of municipalities (regulation 2000/45), which the Special Representative signed on 11 August, determined the nature and competencies of the municipalities, their elected and administrative bodies, and their relations with the central authorities. Most of the document's provisions would enter into force after the 28 October municipal elections, when municipalities would be delegated responsibilities in areas such as education, housing, primary health care and other social services. Funding for the municipalities would come from the central authority and local sources, but they would be allowed to generate revenue through licences, fees and fines. The regulation also included measures to ensure the non-discriminatory provision of municipal services and fair representation of minority communities within the municipal structures. As part of that effort, UNMIK had established local community offices in all but seven of Kosovo's municipalities.

UNMIK continued to strengthen ongoing and regular contacts with FRY, which focused on a number of issues, including the civil registration process, the upcoming municipal elections, the security of the Kosovo Serb community, returnees, detainees and missing persons. It also concluded a memorandum of understanding with FYROM on 30 June to improve cooperation between the two customs services, coordinate and harmonize customs procedures, expedite the flow of passengers and cargo, and normalize trade.

One of UNMIK's main concerns in the pre-election period was the rise in politically motivated violence, particularly against LDK members. Initiatives to address that threat included the establishment of an Information Coordination Group and an Operational Task Force to identify trends and implement security strategies to respond to and deter political violence. The Task Force developed procedures to provide security support to at-risk candidates and for major events during the election campaign period. Incidents of civil unrest occurred in various Kosovo Serb communities across the province; attacks against those communities in Gnjilane and Prizren were followed by attacks against UNMIK

and KFOR personnel. KFOR discovered two concrete bunkers filled with a large cache of weapons and a training site near Klecka village in the central Drenica Valley on 15 June, and another substantial cache on 18 June. According to documents found at the site, the weapons belonged to the former KLA. Activities related to the FRY elections on 24 September were a potential source of concern.

Municipal elections

UNMIK, in accordance with its mandate as set out in Security Council resolution 1244(1999), and in cooperation with OSCE, conducted municipal elections throughout Kosovo on 28 October, as part of the political transition process. During the year, a large part of its activities were focused on putting in place measures to implement that mandate, in the face of increasing political violence within Kosovo and objections from FRY.

On 28 April [S/2000/372], FRY, in a position paper on the holding of elections in Kosovo, said that free, democratic and fair elections, including voter registration, could be carried out only if the necessary conditions were established and implementation of resolution 1244(1999) was achieved. That implied that basic elements of a political settlement for Kosovo and Metohija should be reached in accordance with that resolution.

In conditions of continued terror, ethnic cleansing of Serbs and other non-Albanians, the lack of conditions for the return of more than 350,000 expelled persons and the illegal presence of 250,000 foreign nationals, preconditions did not exist for the registration of the population in preparation for elections. FRY could not be a front to legalize activities contrary to resolution 1244(1999); therefore, any registration of the population of the province not carried out on the basis of the laws of FRY and Serbia could not be legal or binding.

In June [S/2000/538], the Secretary-General reported that UNMIK had begun the process of political party registration, in accordance with UNMIK regulation 2000/16, and political party certification. Party supporter lists had been issued to some 30 parties, which were collecting the necessary signatures for registration and certification. The scale and complexity of election preparations led, in April, to the establishment of the Political Party Consultative Forum to keep all parties informed of decisions of the Central Election Commission regarding the electoral process. Political party training activities were also held around Kosovo to address such issues as public and media relations, the basic principles of party organization and platform development. Particular attention was paid to including Serbs and other ethnic minority parties in those activities. UNMIK also continued to work with international and local women's groups to promote the participation of women voters in the municipal elections and to encourage female candidates to run for office.

On 14 August [S/2000/800], FRY, drawing attention to the announcement by the Special Representative that local elections would be held in Kosovo and Metohija on 28 October, said that holding those elections amounted to a fait accompli, support for ethnic Albanian separatism and terrorism, did not contribute to achieving a peaceful solution and could lead to the destabilization of Kosovo and the entire region. The fallacy of such a policy had been pointed out also by other important international actors, including some permanent members of the Security Council.

In September [S/2000/878], the Secretary-General reported that his Special Representative had signed two regulations establishing the legal foundations of the municipal elections. The first (regulation 2000/39 of 8 July) established that a proportional representation system with open lists would be used. It was supported by all parties except PPDK. The first term of office would be for two years and parties were to submit candidate lists on which at least 30 per cent of the first 15 candidates had to be women. The second regulation (2000/43 of 27 July) determined the names and boundaries of Kosovo's 30 municipalities. The Central Election Commission had adopted electoral rules to govern key elements of the election process. Procedures to prevent voter fraud and ensure secrecy of balloting and security in voting centres were already adopted. The Commission certified 19 political parties, 2 coalitions, 3 citizens' initiatives and 15 independent candidates. The Secretary-General said that the first phase of the civil registration process was successfully completed on a timely basis, with some 90 per cent of the Albanian population participating. Despite UNMIK's efforts to ensure that the registration was simple and safe, widespread intimidation by hard-line Kosovo Serb elements dissuaded the majority of Serbs from participating in the process. In addition, Kosovo Turkish participation was limited because of ongoing division within that community over demands regarding the status of the Turkish language and dissatisfaction with the representation of their community. Some elements of the Kosovo Turkish leadership repeatedly rejected UNMIK proposals designed to ensure the full use of the Turkish language in municipalities where that

community resided and continued to demand the adoption of Turkish as a third national language.

To heighten the level of dialogue between UNMIK and the local population, the Special Representative launched a public outreach campaign, including "town hall" meetings, in which he urged participation in the elections and called for tolerance among ethnic communities.

On 4 October [S/2000/964], Turkey informed the Secretary-General that the Turkish minority, owing to the delay in the preparation of documents to reflect the understanding reached between the Turkish community representatives and UNMIK, were not able to complete their registration, and hence could not take part in the local elections in Kosovo. However, remarks made by UN representatives on the issue during the Security Council briefings on Kosovo on 24 August and 27 September did not fully reflect the real nature of the question, nor did the comments in the Secretary-General's September report (see above). Turkey clarified that the insistence of the Turkish community in Kosovo was to preserve their legitimate and acquired rights and was not an excessive drive by some splinter group. The Turkish community wanted those rights to be well and properly secured and for the Turkish language to have equal status with Albanian and Serbian, as stipulated in the 1974 Constitution. Thus, the comments on the "non-participation" of the Turkish community in the local elections were likely to cause confusion in the minds of the international community about the legitimate demands of the Kosovo Turks. Attached to Turkey's letter was a 15 September letter from the Special Representative containing the text, resulting from discussions held in August, entitled "To the Turkish Community", which outlined the main principles and ideas, as well as operational steps, that UNMIK would develop to guarantee the rights of the Turkish community in Kosovo.

On 27 October [S/2000/1039], FRY again expressed concern over the holding of the elections the next day and repeated its earlier reasons why the conditions for a free expression of will and democratic, free and fair elections had not been created. Holding elections, it said, where no security and freedom of movement existed for members of all ethnic communities led to the conclusion that the elections would be a competition of political parties of the Albanian ethnic community alone.

In December [S/2000/1196], the Secretary-General reported that municipal elections were held on 28 October in 30 municipal assemblies throughout Kosovo. Turnout was massive (79 per cent of the electorate), but Kosovo Serbs did not participate and voter turnout for Roma and Turks was low to negligible. On 7 November, the Special Representative certified the election results, except in the three northern Kosovo Serb majority municipalities of Leposavic, Zubin Potok and Zvecan, where voter turnout was negligible. In the 27 municipalities where the results were certified, LDK won in 21 municipalities, with approximately 58 per cent of the vote, and PPDK in six municipalities, mainly in the Drenica Valley, with 27 per cent. The Alliance for the Future of Kosovo got 8 per cent of the vote, while the rest of the parties obtained less than 1 per cent. A number of parties and other organizations that obtained elected seats in the municipal assemblies requested seats in KTC, arguing that the electoral results proved their popular support. UNMIK intended to expand KTC's membership to reflect Kosovo's political, religious and ethnic diversity.

Security Council consideration. During the Security Council's consideration of the situation in Kosovo on 16 November [S/PV.4225], the Special Representative observed that the municipal elections were a technical success and a victory for the burgeoning democracy, especially taking into account the context in which they took place and everything that had occurred over the past 17 months. He referred to his political plan for substantial autonomy, the "pact" (see p. 366), and advised that the process of defining that substantial autonomy and developing institutions of self-government, as set down in resolution 1244 (1999), should be hastened. That was more urgent following the municipal elections. Action should be taken to organize elections throughout Kosovo, most likely to elect a Parliament. He therefore proposed that general elections be held, possibly in the spring of 2001. A working group, involving the Group of Eight industrialized countries, the United Nations and the Contact Group, had been established to consider a possible provisional constitution.

In response to a question, the Special Representative said that he was of the opinion that, although the return of a limited number of FRY armed forces was provided for in resolution 1244(1999), he did not think that that was currently possible and the issue needed to be addressed through negotiations.

Report of Secretary-General (December). In December [S/2000/1196], the Secretary-General reported that, following the successful 28 October municipal elections, major progress was made in establishing functioning municipal assemblies. On 11 November, more than 800 members of the new assemblies took their oath of office and se-

lected their Presidents and Deputy Presidents. To ensure that all of Kosovo's communities were represented in the new municipal structures, the Special Representative appointed representatives of minority communities to elected assemblies in areas where they lived, mainly Kosovo Turks, Bosniacs, Roma, Ashkalija and Egyptians. The integration of Kosovo Serb appointees into the 27 elected municipal assemblies was slower, owing to demands from some of their leaders that they be allowed to set up their own municipal structures separate and apart from the elected assemblies. That issue proved particularly contentious in Mitrovica and Strepce, where Kosovo Serbs refused to participate in the elected assemblies altogether. However, UNMIK appointed assemblies in the three northern municipalities of Leposavic, Zubin Potok and Zvecan, where the results of the elections were not certified. The assemblies consisted of 18 seats, two of which were reserved for Kosovo Albanians, which remained vacant in both Zvecan and Leposavic, as their leaders showed little interest in identifying potential appointees.

The changes in the Government in Belgrade at the beginning of October (see p. 384) had influenced Kosovo's political life. While Kosovo Albanian leaders welcomed those changes, they were sceptical as to whether that alone would place FRY and its Republic of Serbia on the path to true democracy. They were also concerned about a perceived shift in the attention and priorities of the international community within the region, and at the prospect of increased competition for international political and financial support. In addition, Kosovo Albanian leaders perceived President Kostunica's victory as a threat to their aspirations for independence for the province.

In the Kosovo Serb community, SNC Gracanica viewed those changes as having created the conditions for a constructive political dialogue on Kosovo's future and continued to support UNMIK. For their part, the representatives of SNC Mitrovica expressed optimism that changes in Belgrade would trigger a process through which Kosovo could be reintegrated into Serbia proper and indicated a willingness to improve its relations with UNMIK, but shied away from joining KTC in the immediate future. In general, with their attention focused on Belgrade, Kosovo Serb political groups had not articulated a clear policy on a number of critical issues, including future participation of Kosovo Serbs in JIAS. Nevertheless, a more constructive attitude towards UNMIK was increasingly evident.

UNMIK continued to place primary emphasis on combating politically motivated violence. A Political Violence Task Force, staffed by UNMIK

Political Violence Task Force, staffed by UNMIK police and KFOR, established a Kosovo-wide network of officials to coordinate activities between them at the local, regional and central levels. The Task Force worked with the Information Coordination Group. The pre-election period saw a significant drop in the level of politically motivated violence. In the post-election period, however, the number of attacks returned to a level comparable to that of mid-summer.

Joint security operations between UNMIK police and KFOR became a cornerstone of their military and civilian law enforcement mandates. In a pre-emptive joint operation late in September, three Kosovo Serb males were arrested in Gracanica and a significant quantity of weapons and bomb-making equipment was discovered. On 14 October, UNMIK police and KFOR conducted a joint operation in Pristina where 27 Kosovo Albanians were arrested, three of whom were suspects in major crimes, 17 weapons were seized and $50,000 in cash was confiscated. On 17 November, a major operation against trafficking in illegal weapons and drugs was organized in Kosovo Polje, with five major arrests made of persons allegedly involved in the trafficking of women. A similar operation carried out in Pristina on 18 November resulted in the arrest of six persons.

Later developments. In a later report on UNMIK [S/2001/218], the Secretary-General indicated that a pattern of threats and violence emerged in December. Mitrovica city remained tense and the region had seen several outbreaks of violent public disorder in both Kosovo Serb and Kosovo Albanian areas. Riots and vandalism in Leposavic and Zubin Potok in December appeared to have been organized to destabilize the area before the 23 December Serbian parliamentary elections.

UNMIK regulations

Pursuant to resolution 1244(1999) [YUN 1999, p. 353], the Secretary-General submitted to the Security Council, in March [S/2000/177/Add.1,2], the texts of regulations 1999/24-27, 2000/1-5 and 2000/6-17 issued by the Special Representative. In May [S/2000/177/Add.3], he submitted the texts of regulations 2000/18-27 and, in June [S/2000/538/Add.1], the texts of regulations 2000/28-37. The texts of regulations 2000/38-49 were submitted in September [S/2000/878/Add.1] and those of regulations 2000/50-61 were transmitted in December [S/2000/1196/Add.1].

On 9 February [S/2000/102], FRY declared that the UNMIK draft regulation entitled "Privileges and immunities accorded to foreign government liaison offices in Kosovo" violated its sovereignty and territorial integrity, which were guaranteed by Council resolution 1244(1999). In that regard, on 16 February [S/2000/132], FRY said that the Special Representative's intention to allow Albania to open a representative office in the Serbian province of FRY would further encourage ethnic Albanian separatism, serve to promote the idea of a Greater Albania and destabilize the region. It said that representative offices of foreign and/or international organizations might be opened in the territory of FRY with the agreement and approval of that country's Government. On 1 August, it again protested over regulation 2000/42 concerning the establishment and functioning of those liaison offices [S/2000/757].

In other communications, FRY protested the issuance of travel documents to residents of the Serbian province of Kosovo [S/2000/178] and UNMIK's decision to issue postage stamps for the resumption of postal traffic in Kosovo and Metohija [S/2000/336]. It expressed concern over regulation 2000/18 of 29 March on issuing personal documents, primarily passports and identity cards, to residents of Kosovo and Metohija [S/2000/337]. In that regard, the EU issued a statement on 3 May [S/2000/403] welcoming that regulation and encouraging its member States and those States neighbouring Kosovo to recognize the travel documents.

UNMIK police

At the end of 2000, UNMIK's police strength stood at 4,411 from 53 countries, out of an authorized strength of 4,718, deployed in the Pristina, Mitrovica, Prizren, Gnjilane and Pec regions, and with the UNMIK border police, special police units, at the main headquarters, the Kosovo Police Service (KPS) development centre and the internal training centre.

UNMIK police had full responsibility for executive law enforcement in the Pristina and Prizren regions, as well as at the Pristina airport's international border crossing point, and investigative authority in the Gnjilane and Mitrovica regions, the Pec municipality and the international border crossing points of Djeneral Jankovic (Blace) and Globocica. They continued to run the Pristina and Mitrovica detention facilities, to develop and implement joint security operations with KFOR, including vehicle and foot patrols, weapons and ordnance searches and to build up a joint operations centre. UNMIK police carried out investigation, patrolling and public order functions, border policing and traffic control, and worked towards the development of professional capacities to counter organized crime affecting the Kosovo region through the establishment of a comprehensive criminal intelligence structure. They were responsible for establishing KPS, the future police in Kosovo. Training provided by the OSCE-run KPS school was coordinated with the UNMIK police field training programme. By December, of the 3,500 KPS cadets envisioned for training by January 2001, 2,516 had graduated from the KPS school and were deployed with UNMIK police field training officers throughout Kosovo.

UNMIK police developed a Special Security Task Force charged with designing measures to combat ethnically targeted violence, particularly the threat facing the Kosovo Serb community. It worked closely with KFOR to enhance joint security operations, including building a "partnership for security" at the local community and neighbourhood levels, and in educating the local population about crime prevention and general security practices. The Task Force also worked to strengthen information-sharing with local residents and develop recommendations for preventive investigation and enforcement measures. UNMIK police provided protection for at-risk persons, including international judges and prosecutors, key UNMIK partners within the minority communities, visiting dignitaries and other high-profile individuals.

UNMIK financing

The Secretary-General submitted in March [A/54/807 & Corr.1] the proposed budget for the maintenance of UNMIK for the period 1 July 2000 to 30 June 2001 in the amount of $461,380,600 gross ($434,981,000 net), which ACABQ considered in March and April [A/54/841, A/54/842]. ACABQ recommended that UNMIK's requirements be re-examined in September and that the General Assembly authorize commitment with assessment of $220 million gross to allow UNMIK to continue its activities to 31 December 2000. It also recommended that authority be granted to enter into contractural arrangements for staff for up to one year and that the Secretary-General be allowed to redeploy posts among various offices of the Mission.

GENERAL ASSEMBLY ACTION (June)

On 15 June [meeting 98], the General Assembly, on the recommendation of the Fifth Committee [A/54/674/Add.1], adopted **resolution 54/245 B** without vote [agenda item 166].

Financing of the United Nations Interim Administration Mission in Kosovo

The General Assembly,

Having considered the report of the Secretary-General on the financing of the United Nations Interim Administration Mission in Kosovo and the related reports of the Advisory Committee on Administrative and Budgetary Questions,

Bearing in mind Security Council resolution 1244(1999) of 10 June 1999 regarding the establishment of the United Nations Interim Administration Mission in Kosovo,

Recalling its resolutions 53/241 of 28 July 1999 and 54/245 A of 23 December 1999 on the financing of the Mission,

Acknowledging the complexity of the Mission,

Reaffirming that the costs of the Mission are expenses of the Organization to be borne by Member States in accordance with Article 17, paragraph 2, of the Charter of the United Nations,

Recalling its previous decisions regarding the fact that, in order to meet the expenditures caused by the Mission, a different procedure is required from that applied to meet expenditures of the regular budget of the United Nations,

Taking into account the fact that the economically more developed countries are in a position to make relatively larger contributions and that the economically less developed countries have a relatively limited capacity to contribute towards such an operation,

Bearing in mind the special responsibilities of the States permanent members of the Security Council, as indicated in General Assembly resolution 1874(S-IV) of 27 June 1963, in the financing of such operations,

Noting with appreciation that voluntary contributions have been made to the Mission by certain Governments,

Mindful of the fact that it is essential to provide the Mission with the necessary financial resources to enable it to fulfil its responsibilities under the relevant resolution of the Security Council,

Recalling its resolutions 51/243 of 15 September 1997 and 52/234 of 26 June 1998,

1. *Takes note* of the status of contributions to the United Nations Interim Administration Mission in Kosovo as at 30 April 2000, including the contributions outstanding in the amount of 105.5 million United States dollars, representing 25 per cent of the total assessed contributions, notes that some 23 per cent of the Member States have paid their assessed contributions in full, and urges all other Member States concerned, in particular those in arrears, to ensure payment of their outstanding assessed contributions;

2. *Expresses its appreciation* to those Member States which have paid their assessed contributions in full;

3. *Expresses concern* about the financial situation with regard to peacekeeping activities, in particular as regards the reimbursements to troop contributors that bear additional burdens owing to overdue payments by Member States of their assessments;

4. *Urges* all other Member States to make every possible effort to ensure payment of their assessed contributions to the Mission in full and on time;

5. *Expresses concern* at the delay experienced by the Secretary-General in deploying and providing adequate resources to some recent peacekeeping missions, in particular those in Africa;

6. *Emphasizes* that all future and existing peacekeeping missions shall be given equal and non-discriminatory treatment in respect of financial and administrative arrangements;

7. *Also emphasizes* that all peacekeeping missions shall be provided with adequate resources for the effective and efficient discharge of their respective mandates;

8. *Reiterates its request* to the Secretary-General to make the fullest possible use of facilities and equipment at the United Nations Logistics Base at Brindisi, Italy, in order to minimize the costs of procurement for the Mission, and for this purpose requests the Secretary-General to speed up the implementation of the asset management system at all peacekeeping missions in accordance with General Assembly resolution 52/1 A of 15 October 1997;

9. *Endorses* the conclusions and recommendations contained in the report of the Advisory Committee on Administrative and Budgetary Questions;

10. *Requests* the Secretary-General to take all necessary action to ensure that the Mission is administered with a maximum of efficiency and economy;

11. *Also requests* the Secretary-General, in order to reduce the cost of employing General Service staff, to continue efforts to recruit local staff for the Mission against General Service posts, commensurate with the requirements of the Mission;

12. *Authorizes* the Secretary-General to enter into commitments in an amount not exceeding 220 million dollars gross (207,407,400 dollars net) for the operation of the Mission for the period from 1 July to 31 December 2000;

13. *Decides*, as an ad hoc arrangement, to apportion the amount of 220 million dollars gross (207,407,400 dollars net) for the period from 1 July to 31 December 2000 among Member States in accordance with the composition of groups set out in paragraphs 3 and 4 of General Assembly resolution 43/232 of 1 March 1989, as adjusted by the Assembly in its resolutions 44/192 B of 21 December 1989, 45/269 of 27 August 1991, 46/198 A of 20 December 1991, 47/218 A of 23 December 1992, 49/249 A of 20 July 1995, 49/249 B of 14 September 1995, 50/224 of 11 April 1996, 51/218 A to C of 18 December 1996 and 52/230 of 31 March 1998 and its decisions 48/472 A of 23 December 1993, 50/451 B of 23 December 1995 and 54/456 to 54/458 of 23 December 1999, and taking into account the scale of assessments for the year 2000, as set out in its resolutions 52/215 A of 22 December 1997 and 54/237 A of 23 December 1999;

14. *Decides also* that, in accordance with the provisions of its resolution 973(X) of 15 December 1955, there shall be set off against the apportionment among Member States, as provided for in paragraph 13 above, their respective share in the Tax Equalization Fund of the estimated staff assessment income of 12,592,600 dollars approved for the Mission for the period from 1 July to 31 December 2000;

15. *Emphasizes* that no peacekeeping mission shall be financed by borrowing funds from other active peacekeeping missions;

16. *Encourages* the Secretary-General to continue to take additional measures to ensure the safety and security of all personnel under the auspices of the United Nations participating in the Mission;

17. *Invites* voluntary contributions to the Mission in cash and in the form of services and supplies acceptable to the Secretary-General, to be administered, as ap-

propriate, in accordance with the procedure and practices established by the General Assembly;

18. *Decides* to include in the provisional agenda of its fifty-fifth session the item entitled "Financing of the United Nations Interim Administration Mission in Kosovo".

The Secretary-General resubmitted the UNMIK budget proposal for the period 1 July 2000 to 30 June 2001 in October [A/55/477] in the amount of $474,401,800 gross ($446,239,700 net). In November [A/55/624], ACABQ recommended that the Assembly appropriate for the maintenance of UNMIK an amount of $450 million, reflecting a reduction of some 5 per cent from the proposed amount, inclusive of the $220 million already authorized by resolution 54/245 B.

GENERAL ASSEMBLY ACTION (December)

On 23 December [meeting 89], the General Assembly, on the recommendation of the Fifth Committee [A/55/663], adopted **resolution 55/227 A** without vote [agenda item 133].

Financing of the United Nations Interim Administration Mission in Kosovo

The General Assembly,

Having considered the report of the Secretary-General on the financing of the United Nations Interim Administration Mission in Kosovo and the related report of the Advisory Committee on Administrative and Budgetary Questions,

Bearing in mind Security Council resolution 1244(1999) of 10 June 1999 regarding the establishment of the United Nations Interim Administration Mission in Kosovo,

Recalling its resolution 53/241 of 28 July 1999 on the financing of the Mission and its subsequent resolutions thereon, the latest of which was resolution 54/245 B of 15 June 2000,

Acknowledging the complexity of the Mission,

Reaffirming that the costs of the Mission are expenses of the Organization to be borne by Member States in accordance with Article 17, paragraph 2, of the Charter of the United Nations,

Recalling its previous decisions regarding the fact that, in order to meet the expenditures caused by the Mission, a different procedure is required from that applied to meet expenditures of the regular budget of the United Nations,

Taking into account the fact that the economically more developed countries are in a position to make relatively larger contributions and that the economically less developed countries have a relatively limited capacity to contribute towards such operations,

Bearing in mind the special responsibilities of the States permanent members of the Security Council, as indicated in General Assembly resolution 1874(S-IV) of 27 June 1963, in the financing of such operations,

Noting with appreciation that voluntary contributions have been made to the Mission by certain Governments,

Mindful of the fact that it is essential to provide the Mission with the necessary financial resources to enable it to fulfil its responsibilities under the relevant resolution of the Security Council,

1. *Takes note* of the status of contributions to the United Nations Interim Administration Mission in Kosovo as at 31 October 2000, including the contributions outstanding in the amount of 125 million United States dollars, representing 20 per cent of the total assessed contributions from the inception of the Mission to the period ending 31 December 2000, notes that some 19 per cent of the Member States have paid their assessed contributions in full, and urges all other Member States concerned, in particular those in arrears, to ensure payment of their outstanding assessed contributions;

2. *Expresses its appreciation* to those Member States which have paid their assessed contributions in full;

3. *Expresses concern* about the financial situation with regard to peacekeeping activities, in particular as regards the reimbursements to troop contributors that bear additional burdens owing to overdue payments by Member States of their assessments;

4. *Urges* all other Member States to make every possible effort to ensure payment of their assessed contributions to the Mission in full and on time;

5. *Expresses concern* at the delay experienced by the Secretary-General in deploying and providing adequate resources to some recent peacekeeping missions, in particular those in Africa;

6. *Emphasizes* that all future and existing peacekeeping missions shall be given equal and non-discriminatory treatment in respect of financial and administrative arrangements;

7. *Also emphasizes* that all peacekeeping missions shall be provided with adequate resources for the effective and efficient discharge of their respective mandates;

8. *Reiterates its request* to the Secretary-General to make the fullest possible use of facilities and equipment at the United Nations Logistics Base at Brindisi, Italy, in order to minimize the costs of procurement for the Mission, and for this purpose requests the Secretary-General to speed up the implementation of the asset management system at all peacekeeping missions in accordance with its resolution 52/1 A of 15 October 1997;

9. *Endorses* the conclusions and recommendations contained in the report of the Advisory Committee on Administrative and Budgetary Questions;

10. *Notes* the increase in the number of high-level posts, and requests the Secretary-General to review this matter and to report thereon in the context of his next budget presentation;

11. *Requests* the Secretary-General to provide information, in the context of future budget submissions, on the level of interaction between the International Tribunal for the Prosecution of Persons Responsible for Serious Violations of International Humanitarian Law Committed in the Territory of the Former Yugoslavia since 1991 and the Mission;

12. *Also requests* the Secretary-General to include in future budget submissions information on the guidelines applied to determine the financing through assessed contributions and other sources of income;

13. *Further requests* the Secretary-General to take all necessary action to ensure that the Mission is administered with a maximum of efficiency and economy;

14. *Requests* the Secretary-General, in order to reduce the cost of employing General Service staff, to continue efforts to recruit local staff for the Mission against General Service posts, commensurate with the requirements of the Mission;

15. *Decides* to appropriate the amount of 450 million dollars gross (422,053,500 dollars net) for the maintenance of the Mission for the period from 1 July 2000 to 30 June 2001, inclusive of the amount of 220 million dollars gross (207,407,400 dollars net) authorized by the General Assembly in its resolution 54/245 B;

16. *Decides also*, as an ad hoc arrangement, and taking into account the amount of 220 million dollars gross (207,407,400 dollars net) already apportioned in accordance with its resolution 54/245 B for the period from 1 July to 31 December 2000, to apportion the additional amount of 230 million dollars gross (214,646,100 dollars net) for the period from 1 January to 30 June 2001 among Member States in accordance with the composition of groups set out in paragraphs 3 and 4 of General Assembly resolution 43/232 of 1 March 1989, as adjusted by the Assembly in its resolutions 44/192 B of 21 December 1989, 45/269 of 27 August 1991, 46/198 A of 20 December 1991, 47/218 A of 23 December 1992, 49/249 A of 20 July 1995, 49/249 B of 14 September 1995, 50/224 of 11 April 1996, 51/218 A to C of 18 December 1996, 52/230 of 31 March 1998 and 55/236 of 23 December 2000 and its decisions 48/472 A of 23 December 1993, 50/451 B of 23 December 1995 and 54/456 to 54/458 of 23 December 1999, and taking into account the scale of assessments for the year 2001, as set out in its resolution 55/5 B of 23 December 2000;

17. *Decides further* that, in accordance with the provisions of its resolution 973(X) of 15 December 1955, there shall be set off against the apportionment among Member States, as provided for in paragraph 16 above, their respective share in the Tax Equalization Fund of the estimated additional staff assessment income of 15,353,900 dollars approved for the Mission for the period from 1 January to 30 June 2001;

18. *Emphasizes* that no peacekeeping mission shall be financed by borrowing funds from other active peacekeeping missions;

19. *Encourages* the Secretary-General to continue to take additional measures to ensure the safety and security of all personnel under the auspices of the United Nations participating in the Mission;

20. *Invites* voluntary contributions to the Mission in cash and in the form of services and supplies acceptable to the Secretary-General, to be administered, as appropriate, in accordance with the procedure and practices established by the General Assembly;

21. *Decides* to keep under review during its fifty-fifth session the item entitled "Financing of the United Nations Interim Administration Mission in Kosovo".

On 23 December, the Assembly decided that the item on UNMIK financing would remain for consideration at its resumed fifty-fifth (2001) session (**decision 55/458**) and that the Fifth Committee would consider the item at that session (**decision 55/455**).

Protection of minorities and human rights

One of UNMIK's major preoccupations was the continued widespread harassment, attack, murder and forcible eviction of non-Albanian minorities across the province of Kosovo. The attack on the UNHCR bus on 2 February (see p. 359), one of eight bus lines that shuttled minorities living in isolated communities, caused the UNHCR bus line programme to be temporarily suspended and was a serious setback to UNMIK efforts to promote freedom of movement and protect minorities. The poor security conditions and the consequent restrictions on freedom of movement led to difficulties for minority populations in gaining access to basic public services and were determining factors in the departure of Kosovo Serbs and other non-Albanian groups from Kosovo. The Kosovo Albanian minority in northern Mitrovica was subjected to similar problems, particularly since the violence of 3 February, which led to the departure or forcible expulsion of some 1,650 Kosovo Albanians from their homes. Many Kosovo Serbs and Roma lived under heavy KFOR guard or in mono-ethnic enclaves. In life-threatening situations or particularly vulnerable circumstances, UNHCR resorted to assisting minorities wishing to depart to Serbia and to Montenegro.

The inter-agency Ad Hoc Task Force on Minorities continued to work towards enhancing the physical protection and freedom of movement of minority populations and to engage in longer-term confidence-building measures. Measures undertaken by the Task Force had led to an improvement in living conditions and the situation of minority groups around the province. Those measures included targeted deployment of KFOR and UNMIK police officers to protect those most at risk; installation of enhanced physical security measures in minorities' homes; improved freedom of movement through the eight KFOR-escorted UNHCR bus lines between minority enclaves and an UNMIK train service between Kosovo Polje and the Mitrovica region; a targeted distribution network to enhance access to health care and food; and the provision of satellite and mobile phones to isolated minority communities. Confidence-building measures, such as facilitating contact between community leaders, were also under way.

UNMIK promoted inter-community dialogue through a series of round-table discussions. At such a meeting on 12 April, Kosovo Albanian and other minority leaders met for the first time and adopted a declaration recognizing the Roma communities as an integral part of Kosovo society and agreeing to draft a platform for action to solve the problems of Roma, Ashkalija and Egyptians, which was endorsed by IAC and KTC. UNHCR facilitated two visits by Kosovo Albanian political leaders to Kosovo Roma and Ashkalija communities in June and August, designed to demonstrate the commitment of Kosovo Albanian leaders to inter-ethnic tolerance, non-discrimination and the return of displaced persons.

The Special Representative launched a new initiative to improve conditions and services for Kosovo's non-Serb minority communities, which envisaged special support programmes in areas such as health, education, social welfare and public services. He had also intensified direct contacts with those communities in support of the initiative.

Violations of human rights continued to be of serious concern to UNMIK. Problems surrounding residential property, incidents of illegal evictions and construction continued to be reported. UNMIK police confirmed that trafficking in persons was a growing and serious problem in Kosovo. A regulation designed to ensure adequate legal and other protection to victims was under review. A safe house for victims of trafficking had been set up to provide them with physical assistance until they were repatriated to their country of origin. As at September, 65 females had received assistance. Some enrolled or self-proclaimed KPC members had been accused of human rights violations and illegal police activities, the collection of illegal taxes from businesses and participating in demonstrations, sometimes in the guise of crowd control.

The criminal justice system remained ill-equipped to provide adequate redress for human rights violations. The irregular conduct of some criminal trials involving members of ethnic minorities had highlighted the need to ensure the impartiality of the courts and the equal treatment of all defendants. Although the issue of delays in the court system was being addressed, defendants continued to face lengthy pre-trial detention and difficulties in gaining timely access to review mechanisms. Problems related to access to and effectiveness of counsel affected the quality of representation. The court system also suffered from inconsistencies in the approach to the applicable law and from lack of understanding of relevant international human rights laws.

UNMIK's efforts to create mechanisms for ensuring respect for human rights took a step forward with the establishment of the ombudsperson institution on 21 November. The ombudsperson would investigate and mediate complaints from individuals, groups and organizations regarding human rights violations and other abuses of power by authorities.

Some 800 Kosovo Albanians were being held in prisons in Serbia proper and, according to ICRC, 3,476 cases of missing persons from Kosovo remained unresolved, of whom some 600 were ethnic Serbs and Roma. UNMIK established a Bureau for Detainees and Missing Persons in October to coordinate the activities of the principal agencies involved in those issues. To facilitate the Bureau's work, two resource centres were opened, one in Pristina and the other in Gracanica.

The issue of Kosovo Albanian detainees in Serbia proper was highlighted following riots in prisons throughout Serbia. Concern for their safety during those riots led to marches and hunger strikes throughout Kosovo and a general strike on 14 November. UNMIK officials met with FRY and Serbian officials in Pristina on 15 November, which led to concrete initiatives concerning the welfare and safety of detainees. FRY also provided the first official list of Kosovo Albanian detainees in its prisons and informed UNMIK that an amnesty law covering political prisoners detained in Serbia proper would be presented to FRY's parliament as soon as possible.

Communications. On 16 March [S/2000/222], FRY informed the Security Council that, as at 9 March, 1,330 persons, relocated from Kosovo and Metohija, were in Serbia's penal-correctional institutions.

On 17 and 26 April [S/2000/325, S/2000/352], FRY brought to the attention of the Security Council President the fate of 43 Serbs, who, it said, were detained arbitrarily and without legal grounds by KFOR and UNMIK in Kosovska Mitrovica, 37 of whom were on hunger strike, protesting the endless postponement of their cases. FRY said it was a blatant violation of basic human rights and a breach of judicial procedure. FRY informed the Council President of the deterioration of the detainees' health in a letter of 10 May [S/2000/407]. It called on him to use his influence to put an end to their suffering and forestall tragic consequences. FRY also drew attention to the case of Serb national Miroljub Momcilovic and his two sons, who had been detained at Camp Bondsteel, the military base of the United States KFOR contingent, since 10 July 1999, charged with murdering an ethnic Albanian [S/2000/737].

In another complaint [S/2000/272], FRY protested the violence committed by members of KFOR and UNMIK against residents of Lepine, which, it said, was telling evidence of their reprehensible attitude towards the Serbian community. It was necessary to conduct a thorough investigation and punish those responsible. FRY also protested the systematic and deliberate harassment of diplomatic representatives accredited to Belgrade [S/2000/887].

In February, FRY forwarded to the Council President its positions and comments on the OSCE report entitled "Kosovo/Kossova as Seen, as Told", on the situation of human rights in Kosovo and Metohija from October 1998 to October 1999 [S/2000/103]. It described the report as being one-sided and its publication as an abuse of that organization as an instrument for political purposes.

Establishment of the judicial system and the rule of law

UNMIK accorded priority attention to the establishment of an effective judicial and penal management system. The Secretary-General reported in June [S/2000/538] that, despite the appointment of more than 400 judges, prosecutors and lay judges and the increased capacity of the courts, the unwillingness of witnesses to testify and the ethnic bias and risk of intimidation of some judicial personnel hampered the administration of justice. Of the appointed judges, prosecutors and lay judges, only 46 were non-ethnic Kosovo Albanians and 7 of those were Kosovo Serbs. Since the swearing in of the appointees in January and February, a total of 116 trials had been conducted in Kosovo's district courts: 31 in Gnjilane, 26 in Pristina, 21 in Pec, 32 in Prizren and 6 in Mitrovica.

To build public confidence in the judicial system, UNMIK planned to take immediate measures, in particular the appointment of international judges and prosecutors throughout Kosovo. Preparations were under way to establish a Kosovo war and ethnic crimes court, which was a factor in the re-establishment of the rule of law, in consolidating peace through justice and in paving the way towards reconciliation.

The Kosovo Judicial Institute began functioning during the first week of March and conducted induction seminars for judges and prosecutors in all five regions of Kosovo. The Institute was preparing two round-table seminars, one on the collaboration between the police and the courts during the investigative stage and the other on juvenile justice.

On 9 August, the Special Representative appointed an additional 136 local professional judges, including 16 from non-Albanian ethnic groups and 24 women. The new appointments brought the judicial personnel in Kosovo to the level sufficient to meet the demand facing the court system. A total of 56 courts and 13 prosecutors' offices were staffed. Seven international judges and three international prosecutors were appointed to the Kosovo district courts and there were plans to have as many as 12 such judges and five prosecutors. Refurbishment of judicial establishments was ongoing under a capital project to improve those facilities. The increased human and material resources resulted in greater levels of activity.

UNMIK, with assistance from the Council of Europe, organized training seminars for local judges and prosecutors on the European Convention on Human Rights and Fundamental Freedoms. In June, it opened the Kosovo Law Centre, an NGO, which served as a research centre and publishing house for the legal community and housed a library of legal and human rights documents.

On 17 October, OSCE published its six-month review of Kosovo's criminal justice system, which found that, although substantial progress had been made in 2000 in establishing a functioning justice system, significant problems remained. They included a lack of clarity among local judges as to whether international human rights standards were the supreme law in Kosovo, continued application of laws that could be in breach of international standards, and evidence of bias on the part of the local judiciary against minorities. In response, the UNMIK Department of Justice established a joint working group with OSCE to study the report and develop ways to implement its recommendations.

Returns

During 2000, over 104,000 Kosovo Albanians returned to the province, including 12,500 forced returns. As at September, more than 880,000 persons had returned to Kosovo since June 1999. Most of the returns were conducted in an organized manner with the assistance of UNHCR and the International Organization for Migration. While the voluntary returns were ongoing, forced returns started at the end of March. At the Intergovernmental Consultations on Asylum and Migration (Geneva, March), UNMIK and UNHCR urged host Governments to ensure orderly, humane and phased returns. UNMIK also urged that they establish a clear policy for returns on a voluntary basis. Fearing the destabilizing effect of uncontrolled large-scale returns, the Special Representative issued an open letter on 13 April, appealing to host countries to minimize the practice of forced returns and to participate actively with UNMIK in the reception of returnees to Kosovo.

A Joint Committee on Returns for Kosovo Serbs was established on 2 May to explore prospects for the safe, orderly and sustainable return of those displaced Kosovo Serbs wishing to go back to their homes and to coordinate efforts and initiatives in that regard. The Steering Committee of the Joint Committee conducted assessments

of potential return locations throughout the province. UNHCR organized a go-and-see visit for displaced Serbs to five villages in Osojane. In a meeting with the FRY Minister for Refugees in August, the UNHCR Special Envoy for FRY stressed that it was not possible to promote returns until conditions for a safe, dignified and sustainable return were in place. The Envoy and the new FRY President Kostunica agreed in mid-November on the need to find a balance between hope and caution with respect to Kosovo Serb returns. However, as there were some small-scale spontaneous returns to a number of existing Serb communities, a system was put in place to track those returns so that assistance could be delivered. As many as 2,000 Kosovo Serbs might have returned to their places of origin over the course of the year.

Sectoral developments

UNMIK made considerable progress in establishing normality and improving the living conditions of the Kosovo population. By 8 February, some 90 per cent of the $29.6 million pledged to the UNMIK Trust Fund had been received. The Fund was used to finance quick-impact projects, including the payment of stipends to Kosovo civil servants and a winterization programme. "Kosovo: Reconstruction 2000", a comprehensive public reconstruction and investment programme, was presented to donors to better target resources in support of UNMIK's priorities for reconstruction. Donors pledged a total of 2.6 billion deutsche mark (DM). A number of high-priority needs remained without funding, including rehabilitation of the courts, schools, hospitals and other public buildings; the development of multiple solid waste disposal facilities and environmental clean-up; and the development of local human resources.

The Central Housing Committee was established as the coordinating board for housing reconstruction, and UNMIK and its partners had agreed on a common approach to reconstruction to maximize the impact of available aid and to ensure fair and transparent distribution. Coordination structures were also being established at the local level. Some 20,000 houses were rebuilt during the year for vulnerable families whose houses had been damaged or destroyed during the conflict. A similar number had been rebuilt by the local population themselves. The new public reconstruction and investment programme 2001-2003 would outline a medium-term road map for donors, refining and building on priorities set in "Kosovo: Reconstruction 2000".

In other sectoral areas, a health facility master plan to guide donors and NGOs in the reconstruction of health-care facilities had been prepared. A $3 million World Bank–funded project was initiated to design a strategy for health-care financing, strengthen the capacity of the health insurance fund, prepare an implementation plan for restructuring the health sector and monitor the impact of social reforms. Significant progress was made in refurbishing and re-equipping health-care institutions throughout Kosovo, including the construction of three mental health centres.

UNMIK, with international agencies, donors and local participants, initiated the formulation of a blueprint for the education system in Kosovo. The World Bank sponsored a project at Pristina University, which included the formulation of new statutes, the introduction of a modern management system and the establishment of a programme for the certification of physicians and lawyers. Some 1.8 million textbooks were printed and distributed to students of all ethnic groups after being screened for content. A school rehabilitation and reconstruction cell was established to oversee the building and rehabilitation of schools.

Efforts to rehabilitate and improve the transport and infrastructure sector had intensified. Eleven projects in various regions had been initiated on facilitating and managing urban traffic, maintaining streets and installing traffic signs and signals. Major road repair and rehabilitation works were undertaken throughout Kosovo, as well as repair to damaged bridges. Significant progress was also made in upgrading Pristina airport.

UNMIK, together with the Food and Agriculture Organization of the United Nations and the World Bank, was making vigorous efforts to revitalize agricultural activity. A $25 million World Bank–funded project to relaunch farming activities and reorganize veterinary services was initiated. The EU was committing DM 20 million to agricultural projects in 2000.

The development of a non-politicized and efficient civil service for Kosovo remained one of UNMIK's important objectives. Progress was made in developing a professional local civil service at the central and municipal levels. A significant achievement was the smooth transition from the system of stipend payments to salary payments for all public employees paid from the Kosovo consolidated fund. The Institute for Civil Administration, the official training body for the public sector, was formally opened on 20 September.

To encourage the restart of economic activity, manage existing assets and attract new investment, a private sector development strategy was finalized. It included a transparent process to determine ownership of commercial assets and property and to pay fair compensation. To foster the development of the private sector, regulations covering business organizations, foreign investment, sales contracts and secured transactions were to be issued by the end of the year. A regulation on bankruptcy was also in preparation. Extensive efforts to assist the courts to deal with those new regulations and to develop the necessary administrative procedures and registries to implement them were under way. Steps were taken to commercialize viable socially owned enterprises and teams were established to help them attract foreign investment partners and bring them under private management. A programme of technical assistance for small and medium-sized private enterprises was launched to help them draw up business plans, assist with financing and improve management. In addition, a women's business association assisted women to identify and develop opportunities in the private sector.

On 14 August, UNMIK assumed responsibility for and subsequently shut down the Zvecan lead smelter in the Mitrovica region, which was part of the Trepca mining complex. The smelter's operation had resulted in a major health hazard. Clean-up operations were under way and medical facilities had been set up to test levels of lead in the blood of workers and the local population. An initial inspection of the smelter indicated widespread neglect and poor safety and environmental standards. UNMIK administrators would repair or replace safety and production equipment throughout the facility. As part of that effort, up to 2,000 local Trepca workers would be employed over the next year. Most of the $16 million required for Trepca's renovation had already been raised.

Communications. FRY, on 19 July [S/2000/716], requested an urgent meeting of the Security Council to consider UNMIK's intention to take over the metallurgical section of Trepca and the threatened use of force to do so. It said that the question of the ownership of the corporation was complex, with a number of private entities laying claim to it, and should be resolved by an arbitration tribunal or competent court. The takeover would have serious reverberations for the ethnic cleansing of Serbs in Mitrovica, all the more so as the section was a key source of income for the Serbian population of the town. On 14 August [S/2000/801] and 12 September [S/2000/866], FRY lodged a strong protest over the armed attack on and takeover of Trepca by KFOR. It demanded that the Council condemn the takeover and restore the status quo ante so that Trepca and its employees could continue normal work. On 14 September [S/2000/871], FRY advised that over 60,000 litres of sulphuric acid had been released into the Ibar River from a Trepca battery plant. The disaster was illustrative of the tragic consequences of the seizure of Trepca. FRY had requested the United Nations Environment Programme to help relieve the consequences of the disaster and called for the reinstatement of the Trepca management and employees.

International security presence (KFOR)

During the year, the Secretary-General submitted to the Security Council, in accordance with resolution 1244(1999) [YUN 1999, p. 353], reports on the activities of KFOR, also known as Operation Joint Guardian, covering the period 24 November 1999 to 22 November 2000 [S/2000/50, S/2000/152, S/2000/235, S/2000/318, S/2000/489, S/2000/634, S/2000/814, S/2000/891, S/2000/1024, S/2000/1120, S/2000/1246]. Later reports covered activities in the remainder of the year [S/2001/52, S/2001/205]. As at 10 December, the Force, which operated under NATO leadership, comprised 44,000 troops from all the NATO countries, as well as from non-NATO countries. On 18 April, Lieutenant-General Juan Ortuño assumed command of KFOR from General Klaus Reinhardt; on 16 October, Lieutenant-General Carlo Cabigiosu succeeded Lieutenant-General Ortuño.

KFOR continued to uncover and confiscate caches of weapons, ammunition and explosives during house searches and at traffic control checkpoints. Among the most significant finds were the discovery on 10 May near Glogovac of 2 sagger missiles, 20 rocket-propelled grenade warheads, 7 grenade launchers, a machine gun and ammunition. Most explosives recovered were destroyed in situ. Confiscated weapons were being destroyed as part of the commercial destruction programme.

KFOR continued to work closely with the United Nations Mine Action Coordination Centre and other demining organizations in Kosovo, focusing on the eradication of cluster-bomb units, with ordnance disposal teams destroying bomblets marked during the winter. The Force provided appropriate control of Kosovo's internal and external borders and recognized crossing points, and tightened control of the provincial borders and boundaries to prevent extremists based in Kosovo from operating elsewhere. All but two of the recognized crossing points within each Multinational Brigade into the ground safety zone (see below) had been closed. Although those measures generally appeared to have been effective, KFOR noted a number of incidents relating to illegal border crossings. KFOR also supported UNMIK at all levels of the civilian administration. In March, they established a systematic framework to identify, coordinate and supervise the Kosovo Protection Corps (KPC), established in 1999 [YUN 1999, p. 366]. They also continued to ensure KPC's adherence to its civilian mandate. KFOR worked, at the district level, with the appointed civil administrators and provided personnel liaison with UNMIK civil administration officers in each district. KFOR continued to provide humanitarian assistance to international organizations and NGOs throughout Kosovo on a daily basis and on request, with a focus on the distribution of stoves, firewood, fuel, water, shelter kits and construction material. Troops also supported the food distribution efforts of international organizations, protected and escorted refugees and internally displaced persons and assisted NGOs in providing humanitarian aid to remote and isolated minorities and with a spring/summer housing and school construction programme.

Communications. In February [S/2000/139] and May [S/2000/425], FRY complained about violations of its airspace by NATO and SFOR.

Situation in the ground safety zone

In July [S/2000/744], FRY brought to the Security Council's attention the security situation in the ground safety zone (GSZ), the buffer zone that extended 5 kilometres beyond the Kosovo and Metohija administrative border into the rest of FRY, which was seriously threatened by persistent attacks on civilians and police by Albanian terrorists infiltrating from Kosovo and Metohija and often from Albania. Those attacks intensified in June and July, in particular. Heavy weapons were used ever more frequently and more ruthlessly. It was evident that their aim was to destabilize the GSZ. Failure of the international presences to take action had emboldened Albanian terrorists and accounted for the tragic loss of lives and extensive material damage. FRY called on the Council to condemn the attacks and to take effective measures to put an end to them and prevent their spread outside Kosovo and Metohija.

The Secretary-General, in December [S/2000/1196], said that on 22 November the house of the senior FRY representative in Kosovo, Ambassador Vucikevic of the FRY liaison committee with UNMIK, was fire-bombed, resulting in the death of a Serb security guard and injury to three other persons. The following day, a senior LDK politician was murdered in central Pristina. In mid-November, three Serb police officers were killed in the GSZ.

On 22 November [meeting 4232], following consultations among Security Council members, the President made statement **S/PRST/2000/35** on behalf of the Council:

> The Security Council expresses its shock at, and strongly condemns, the criminal attacks perpetrated on the home of the head of the liaison committee of the Federal Republic of Yugoslavia in Pristina on 22 November 2000, as well as on Serbian policemen in the south of Serbia on 21 November 2000, both of which resulted in several deaths and injuries.
>
> The Council calls for an immediate and full investigation to bring the perpetrators to justice.
>
> Fully aware of all the measures already taken to provide security for all inhabitants of that region, the Council calls upon the Kosovo Force and the United Nations Interim Administration Mission in Kosovo to continue to make all necessary efforts, including along the ground safety zone, to prevent further attacks.
>
> The Council demands that all those concerned refrain from any act of violence, in particular against ethnic minorities, and cooperate with the Force and the Mission.
>
> The Council will continue to follow the matter closely.

Communications. On 27 November [S/2000/1147], the EU condemned the attacks on the Yugoslav representative in Pristina and on the three Serb policemen, which it said were a reminder to the international community that extremist forces, bent on preventing coexistence between communities, were determined to continue their activities against Kosovo Serbs, in spite of resolution 1244(1999), the results of the 28 October municipal elections in Kosovo and the democratic change in FRY since the elections on 24 September.

On the same date [S/2000/1123], FRY President Kostunica warned of the deteriorating situation in the Presevo Valley in the GSZ inside Serbia proper. He said that KFOR and UNMIK had allowed the crossing of large groups of armed Albanian paramilitaries into the zone, forcing lightly armed local police to leave their checkpoints. He hoped the Security Council would act promptly to address the situation and assured it that FRY police and military would not enter the GSZ to fight the terrorists. However, viable conditions for the return of local police to the zone had to be created as soon as possible.

On 6 December [S/2000/1160], FRY said that it had taken urgent diplomatic steps to calm the situation in the GSZ, requesting UNMIK and KFOR to take appropriate measures. However, no measures were being taken to compel the infiltrated armed groups to withdraw and disarm without delay. According to reports, over 1,000 terrorists from Kosovo and Metohija were still in the GSZ,

from where they threatened the security of citizens and major routes in southern Serbia, cutting off communications of some tens of thousands of Serbs with other parts of Serbia. Considering the gravity of the situation, FRY requested the Council urgently to consider the question again, condemn the terrorist acts of the Albanian extremists and ask KFOR and UNMIK to take effective measures to compel them to withdraw and to have the GSZ fully respected. The request for an urgent meeting of the Council was reiterated by President Kostunica on 13 December [S/2000/1184].

FRY, in a Declaration on the Principles of the Protection of the National and State Interests of the Federal Republic of Yugoslavia [S/2000/1219], adopted by the FRY Government and the interim Government of Serbia at their joint session in Bujanovac on 16 December and submitted for adoption to the Federal Assembly, requested the Council to set the shortest deadline and take measures for an urgent withdrawal of Albanian terrorists from the GSZ. Otherwise it would invoke its legal and legitimate right to solve that problem by itself by resorting to all internationally allowed measures to combat terrorism.

Report of Secretary-General. The Secretary-General, in his 15 December report on UNMIK [S/2000/1196], confirmed that there was an escalation of armed confrontation in mid-November between Serbian security forces and the self-styled Liberation Army of Presevo, Medvedja and Bujanovac (UCPMB) in the GSZ. Initially limited to harassing fire against the Serbian police, the attacks increased in size, duration, sophistication and aggressiveness. On 23 November, three Serb police were killed in attacks some 5 kilometres south-west of Bujanovac, triggering an influx of almost 5,000 displaced persons from the GSZ and other locations into Kosovo.

UNHCR had reported that the internally displaced persons had fled out of fear of being caught between firing lines, and of a general concern about the build-up of police and military forces in Presevo Valley. While ethnic Albanian representatives claimed not to be disturbed by local police from southern Serbia proper, they indicated that the presence of security forces previously stationed in Kosovo served as a major source of intimidation. KFOR responded to armed activity in Presevo Valley, including by mounting successful operations to interdict UCPMB operations financially and logistically. It garnered support among key Kosovo Albanian leaders, encouraging them to exert their influence to moderate the activities of the Albanian extremists. By the beginning of December, the situation had begun to calm, with some 2,000 internally displaced persons returning to their homes.

In early December, the Special Envoy of UNHCR travelled to Belgrade and southern Serbia proper to assess the humanitarian situation. Government officials in Belgrade with whom the Special Envoy met were eager to find a solution to the problem in the Presevo Valley and were committed to the return of internally displaced persons to their homes. They acknowledged that ethnic Albanians had been the victims of social and institutional discrimination and accepted that confidence-building measures, such as the inclusion of Albanians in the local police force and increased representation in political structures, would go a long way towards decreasing tensions and longer-term stability in the region.

SECURITY COUNCIL ACTION (December)

The Security Council met on 19 December [meeting 4249] to consider the Secretary-General's December report on UNMIK [S/2000/1196]. On the same day [meeting 4250], following consultations among its members, the President made statement **S/PRST/2000/40** on behalf of the Council:

The Security Council welcomes the briefing by Mr. Hédi Annabi on 19 December and the presence of the Minister for Foreign Affairs of the Federal Republic of Yugoslavia at the meeting.

The Council expresses its grave concern at the situation in certain municipalities in southern Serbia, Federal Republic of Yugoslavia, and particularly in the ground safety zone, as defined in the military-technical Agreement referred to in annex II to resolution 1244(1999) of 10 June 1999. It strongly condemns the violent action by ethnic Albanian extremist groups in southern Serbia, and calls for an immediate and complete cessation of violence in this area. The Council reiterates its resolution 1244 (1999) in its entirety.

The Council calls for the dissolution of ethnic Albanian extremist groups. The Council also calls for the immediate withdrawal from the area, and in particular from the ground safety zone, of all non-residents engaged in extremist activities.

The Council welcomes the start of a dialogue between the Serbian and Yugoslav authorities and representatives of the affected communities which could facilitate a lasting settlement to the problem.

In this regard, the Council welcomes the commitment of the Yugoslav authorities to work towards a peaceful settlement, based on democratic principles, and to respect the provisions of resolution 1244 (1999) and the military-technical Agreement, as expressed in the letter dated 13 December 2000 from the President of the Federal Republic of Yugoslavia to the President of the Security Council.

The Council welcomes specific measures taken by the international security presence to address the problem, including increased surveillance of the border, confiscation of weapons and the disruption of identified and illegal activity within Kosovo in the vicinity of the eastern administrative boundary. It welcomes the constructive dialogue between the Kosovo Force and the Yugoslav and Serbian authorities, including through the Joint Implementation Commission. The Council calls upon the Kosovo Force and the United Nations Interim Administration Mission in Kosovo to continue to make all necessary efforts to address the problem. The Council also calls on Kosovo Albanian leaders to contribute to the stability of the situation.

The Council welcomes the detailed public statement by the Secretary-General of the North Atlantic Treaty Organization of 29 November 2000, and the strong message which this sent to extremist groups in the Presevo-Medvedja-Bujanovac area.

The Council will remain actively seized of the matter.

Sanctions against FRY

Sanctions Committee activities

On 27 June [S/2000/633], the Security Council Committee established pursuant to resolution 1160(1998) [YUN 1998, p. 369], which imposed an arms embargo on FRY, transmitted to the Council President a report covering its work from 1 January to 31 December 1999. During that period, the Committee had received only one reply (Oman) on measures that States had been requested to institute in meeting their obligations in respect of the prohibitions imposed by the resolution. The Committee had brought to the attention of Bosnia and Herzegovina that it was the only country bordering FRY that had not reported on steps taken to give effect to those prohibitions. It did not approve a request from Bulgaria for the shipment of industrial explosives to FRY, and ruled that the matter of the export of ammunition for M84 tanks from FRY to Kuwait under a 1989 contract did not fall within its mandate. The Committee reminded Albania, as a neighbour of FRY, that it had an important role in ensuring implementation of resolution 1160(1998), in particular the provision requiring States to prevent the sale or supply to FRY, including Kosovo, by their nationals or from their territories, of arms and related materiel and spare parts, and to prevent arming and training for terrorist activities there. The Committee requested the Secretary-General to forward its invitation to UNMIK and KFOR to consider arrangements that would allow them to report on possible violations of the prohibitions.

At several meetings, the Committee considered reports on violations of the prohibitions established by resolutions 1160(1998) and 1199 (1998) [YUN 1998, p. 377]. OSCE had indicated that smuggling from Albania to Kosovo continued.

The Committee reported that its work continued to be affected by the absence of an effective monitoring mechanism and the lack of information on possible violations. The information provided by the Secretariat from public sources on possible violations did not often allow the Committee to forward information to Member States enabling them to launch investigations on possible violations. With a view to assisting and encouraging Governments to implement the arms embargo and other prohibitions, the Committee was contemplating sending a mission to the region, headed by its Chairman.

In a report covering its work from 1 January to 31 December 2000 [S/2001/102], the Committee indicated that it had received no replies concerning measures that States had been requested to institute in meeting their obligations under paragraph 12 of resolution 1160(1998). The Committee approved, under the no-objection procedure, three requests from the United Kingdom for approval to transfer demining equipment to humanitarian demining organizations working for UNMIK in Kosovo.

On 20 June, the Committee drew the Secretary-General's attention to the section of the report of the Council mission to Kosovo on the implementation of resolution 1244(1999) [S/2000/363] (see p. 361). The mission had been requested, among other actions, to review ongoing implementation of the prohibitions imposed by resolution 1160(1998). The mission highlighted the discussions it had held with KFOR on strengthening the monitoring of the arms embargo. The Committee supported the findings contained in the mission's report, in particular that detailed information on KFOR activities in the implementation of resolution 1160(1998) should be provided to the Committee by the NATO Secretary-General on a regular basis.

The UN Department for Disarmament Affairs, replying to a Committee request for advice, said that the spare parts for MI-8 helicopters, reportedly detained on a Bulgarian lorry for lack of a special export permit, could be used for both military and civilian purposes. The Committee received information from FYROM on two incidents of arms trafficking on its territory, and raised no objection to a request from Bulgaria for approval to export the chemical substance pentaerythritol tetranitrate to FRY to be used in the manufacture of medications.

On 5 June, FYROM informed the Committee of violations of the prohibitions under resolution 1160(1998) and of that country's actions to prevent arms trafficking in its territory. The Committee also received several reports on KFOR activities and reports on activities of the Stabilization Force in Bosnia and Herzegovina. Both reported no violations.

EU sanctions

On 31 July [S/2000/753], FRY drew the attention of the Security Council President to the lack of legal basis for the EU sanctions imposed on it and the damage they had caused to the economy and society. Imposed since 1998, those sanctions were without legal grounding in any UN document, violated several provisions of the UN Charter and were contrary to the goals of the International Covenant on Economic, Social and Cultural Rights, adopted by the General Assembly in resolution 2200 A (XXI) [YUN 1966, p. 419].

A 30 June EU decision strengthened financial sanctions against FRY. The list of 190 firms in FRY that were allowed transactions with partners in EU member States constituted a flagrant violation of the rights of free movement of goods and capital, discriminated against economic subjects in FRY and violated the rights to life, to work, to development and to education, as well as the right to association of economic and social factors in a sovereign European country. The EU sanctions stopped and hindered FRY's stable and dynamic economic development, caused a rise in unemployment and the standard of living of the population to fall and affected neighbouring countries and all of South-Eastern Europe. FRY called on the Council to declare them illegal and propose that they be lifted urgently. FRY reserved the right to protect its interests and to request material and other indemnity from the EU in court.

On 20 September [S/2000/885], FRY drew attention to the announcement by the EU and the United States that they were ready to lift sanctions on FRY if its voters elected the opposition candidate in the 24 September presidential elections.

The EU announced the lifting of all sanctions against FRY, including the oil and air embargoes, on 11 October, following the presidential elections (see p. 384).

Internal and external conflict

Relations with Montenegro

Slovenia transmitted to the Security Council President on 21 June [S/2000/611] a non-paper entitled "Montenegro and the Balkan crisis", prepared by the Government of the FRY Republic of Montenegro and submitted in the context of the Council's debate on the situation in the Balkans on 23 June. Slovenia said, in its letter of transmittal, that it believed the document could usefully contribute to the understanding of that situation by the general membership of the United Nations.

In the non-paper, Montenegro declared that the policy of destruction, autocracy, confrontation with the international community and self-isolation of the Belgrade leadership was not reconcilable with the democratic choice of the citizens of Montenegro. That leadership was also using all methods to destabilize Montenegro and undermine its choice. Montenegro and the international community were facing the possibility of a new crisis breaking out. It remained committed and open to cooperation with Serbia, which it had offered as a basis for new relations, full equality of the two States and the creation of a common framework for the citizens of the two countries. Montenegro stated that peace, stability and prosperity of the former Yugoslavia and the Balkans depended on establishing new democratic relations in Serbia by organizing free and fair elections; strengthening the political-diplomatic isolation of the current policy and regime in Serbia; and creation of international support to Montenegro in its commitment to democracy, transformation of its economy and integration into all European and international processes. The Government of Montenegro did not accept the leadership of Serbia and its political and diplomatic representatives and services to be the representatives of the policy and interests of Montenegro.

FRY, on 24 June [S/2000/625], protesting the circulation of Montenegro's non-paper, said that it was unacceptable and contrary to the Charter and international law to allow a part of a sovereign country to communicate with the Council. Slovenia's request for the text to be circulated was a direct interference in FRY's internal affairs, which was a dangerous provocation for peace and security in the region and beyond. It was unacceptable for Slovenia to figure as a "representative" of Montenegro, which was an equal federal unit of FRY.

Security Council consideration (23 June). On 22 June [S/2000/617], FRY informed the Security Council President that certain persons would be attending the Council's meeting on 23 June, claiming to represent Montenegro. Considering that Montenegro was part of FRY, allowing any other persons to represent a part of a sovereign territory violated FRY's Constitution and the Charter and was in breach of international law, the Vienna Convention on Diplomatic Relations [YUN 1961, p. 512] and the Agreement between the United Nations and the United States of America regarding the Headquarters of the United Nations [YUN 1947-48, p. 199]. FRY asked the Council to reject the dangerous precedent and protect the Council's integrity and the Charter.

During the Council's 23 June meeting [S/PV.4164], the President stated that, since it was not possible to reach an understanding in prior consultations, the Council would have to decide on whether to invite the Secretary-General's Special Envoy for the Balkans to participate in the debate. It would also have to decide on requests from a number of Member States and the EU to participate under either rule 37 or rule 39 of the Council's provisional rules of procedure, and on a similar request from Vladislav Jovanovic, FRY Chargé d'affaires, which referred to neither rule.

The Council, by a vote of 4 in favour, 10 against and 1 abstention, did not adopt a Russian Federation proposal that a single decision be taken on all the requests, considered as a whole. By the no-objection procedure, it invited those Member States that had requested to participate, the Special Envoy for the Balkans and the EU Secretary-General to participate. By a vote of 4 in favour, 7 against and 4 abstentions, Mr. Jovanovic's request was not approved.

Following the vote, China expressed regret regarding the Council's decision. It said that FRY was an important country of the Balkan region and a party to the Dayton-Paris Peace Agreement [YUN 1995, p. 544]. It did not matter whether or not one agreed with FRY's policy; excluding FRY and not allowing it to speak would not solve the Balkan problem. The Council should not deprive a sovereign State of its right to state its position when it wanted to do so.

Argentina said that its abstention did not imply support for, endorsement of or sympathy for the Belgrade regime, but it had serious doubts regarding the underlying reasons for denying Mr. Jovanovic's participation in the debate.

The Russian Federation said that a very dangerous precedent was being created when States that were unpalatable for political reasons were excluded from participation in the work of the United Nations. The Council meeting on the Balkans without FRY's full participation lost its practical meaning.

On 23 June [S/2000/621], FRY, in protesting the Council's decision, said that, as a country situated in the Balkans, a signatory and a guarantor of the Peace Agreement, as well as a country with whose agreement the international civil and military presences had been deployed in its territory, FRY had more right than any other country to participate in the meeting. The rejection of its request was discriminatory and contrary to the principles of the Charter.

The Special Envoy for the Balkans, briefing the Council, said he believed that the most pressing issue in the region was the question of the future of FRY. There could not be self-sustaining stability in the region if there was not self-sustaining stability in its different parts. In that respect, the situation in FRY gave cause for concern. In his opinion, Yugoslavia's current structures were unsustainable, primarily due to the acute constitutional crisis between the Republic of Montenegro and the federal authorities in Belgrade, where the federal institutions had been grossly misused to exclude the representatives of the elected authorities of Montenegro. They were on a slow but steady collision course. He believed that it was important that the elected authorities in Montenegro be supported in their efforts to pave the way for the new deal they were seeking. Added to that acute constitutional crisis was the unresolved issue of the future status of Kosovo. Although on paper still an integral part of the Republic of Serbia, the reality was different. He failed to see any circumstances under which a peace agreement would not have to include a clear constitutional separation between the two.

The search for peace was handicapped by the fact that key persons in public positions in FRY were refusing to respect indictments that had been issued by ICTY. That situation was dangerous for FRY and the wider region. It was important to recall that, in the Dayton-Paris Peace Agreement, FRY subscribed to the position that persons indicted by the Tribunal and not cooperating with it could not hold public office. What was being demanded of them was no more than what they themselves had previously agreed to demand of others as part of the search for peace in the region, and the sooner the authorities there saw the logic of that, the sooner all could work together to create self-sustaining structures within FRY's borders and as part of the search for self-sustaining stability in the region as a whole.

Communications. On 11 July [S/2000/679], Slovenia forwarded to the Security Council President the text of an 8 July resolution adopted by the Parliament of the FRY Republic of Montenegro on the protection of rights and interests of Montenegro and its citizens. By that resolution, the Parliament declared its intention not to recognize any legal or political act passed by the federal legislative, executive and judicial authorities without participation of its own representatives, or any amendments to the FRY Constitution adopted by the federal Parliament against the majority will of the citizens of Montenegro. The Parliament called on the citizens of Montenegro and Serbia, as well as the international community, to help find peaceful solutions to the problems between Montenegro and the State authorities.

On 18 July [S/2000/724], FRY called the resolution a gross interference in its internal affairs. Slovenia had no right to circulate Montenegro's paper as a Council document. FRY called on the Council to reject the document as it contravened Council procedures and practice.

Earlier, on 11 July [S/2000/749], the Presidents of Croatia, the Czech Republic and Slovenia, in a joint statement following their meeting in Dubrovnik, Croatia, on 10 and 11 July, expressed their disquiet over the latest developments in FRY, especially the constitutional changes adopted by the Yugoslav Parliament, which jeopardized democracy, discriminated between the subjects of the Federation and rejected internationally respected principles. They held that, although the objective of those changes was to abolish the standing of Montenegro, they might in reality lead to FRY's dissolution. The international community should do its utmost to protect the human, civic and constitutional rights of FRY citizens and those of Montenegro, and prevent the current situation from evolving into a new wave of violence. They would deem unacceptable any power-based or confrontational solution the Belgrade regime might seek.

On 13 July [S/2000/692], Slovenia forwarded to the Council President a letter from the Minister for Foreign Affairs of Montenegro regarding Montenegro's representation in international relations and an aide-memoire on Montenegro's history, which further clarified some of Montenegro's views on the problem expressed in its earlier document (see p. 381). The aide-memoire said that the authorities in Serbia had never accepted the outcome of the 1997 and 1998 presidential elections in Montenegro and had obstructed the formation of common federal State bodies based on the majority will of the citizens of Montenegro. Instead, they appointed their partisan and political sympathizers, who were the opposition in Montenegro, to be Montenegro's representatives to the federal bodies. Since then, Montenegro had no access to the federal authorities, did not participate in their work and did not recognize their legitimacy. Montenegro gave examples of how the federal authorities had been used against it with a view to its economic and general exhaustion, political destabilization and the toppling of the democratically elected government. They included the removal of legal Montenegrin authorities from all institutions of the federal State and the work of those bodies, including in defence, internal and foreign affairs, finances, foreign trade, customs and the central bank, and the imposition of a comprehensive blockage of the overall payment operations and commodity trade with Montenegro for several months. Montenegro had therefore assumed control of the activities in foreign trade and import and export of goods and services, insurance and investment guarantees, production cooperation and joint ventures, the tax system, customs, border control, and monetary operations by legalizing the deutsche mark as parallel legal tender, together with the dinar.

On 27 July [S/2000/745], Serbia's Ministries of Finance and Justice issued a notification that all sales contracts concluded anywhere between Albanians and displaced Serbs and Montenegrins and members of other national communities after 10 June 1999 and relating to immovable property in Kosovo and Metohija were invalid.

FRY relations with other States

On 25 February [S/2000/154], FRY drew the attention of the Security Council President to the negotiations between UNMIK and FYROM concerning a memorandum on the construction of border infrastructure and customs cooperation at the Yugoslav-FYROM border. Stating that UNMIK was not authorized to enter into agreements with neighbouring States without its consent, FRY said that it would consider null and void any agreement reached by UNMIK in contravention of its authority changing the nature of border crossings between the two countries.

FYROM, for its part, drew attention on 8 June [S/2000/552] to several incidents at the FYROM border with the Kosovo province of FRY, which, it said, risked endangering the security situation in the region. The two most serious were the abduction on 2 April of four FYROM Army soldiers who were held for 24 hours before being released and the wounding by sniper shots coming from Kosovo of two soldiers on 5 June. The Government had requested an urgent investigation and the taking of immediate measures to identify and apprehend the perpetrators of those terrorist acts. It said that such incidents, most likely connected to the growing organized crime in Kosovo, presented a threat to FYROM's stability and that of neighbouring countries and could undermine joint efforts for stabilizing and promoting security in the region, particularly in Kosovo.

FRY protested on 25 May the visit of the Albanian President to Kosovo and Metohija [S/2000/490]. According to media reports, he had called on Kosovo and Metohija Albanians to work towards the creation of a "Greater Albania" that would include, in addition to the Serbian province and Albania, parts of FRY's Republic of Montenegro and FYROM. The illegal visit of the highest-ranking Albanian official to a sovereign

territory without prior agreement of its Government was contrary to international law and violated FRY's sovereignty and territorial integrity and resolution 1244(1999). FRY accused UNMIK, by failing to prevent that illegal act, of aligning itself with and giving UN approval to those who committed terror and crimes against the Serbs and other non-Albanians, and asked the Council to condemn the practice of illegal visits.

On 2 August [S/2000/765], FRY protested the establishment, on 24 July, of the Albanian liaison office in Pristina. It repeated its request for the Council to annul UNMIK's decision to allow Albania to establish the liaison office to serve the goals of furthering Albania's illegitimate and hostile claims against FRY. FRY reiterated its protest and request on 6 October [S/2000/965], citing reports that the "mission" would be further strengthened and transformed into a diplomatic representative office, which would render an inter-State character to Albania/Kosovo relations.

On 25 September [A/55/421], FRY drew the Secretary-General's attention to the statement made by the Albanian Minister for Foreign Affairs on 16 September to the fifty-fifth session of the General Assembly, which, it said, was illustrative of the persistence of Albania's policy of interference in FRY's internal affairs, paternalism in its relations with the ethnic Albanian minority in FRY and the territorial aspirations towards parts of FRY.

In other communications, FRY protested the visit of the Bulgarian Prime Minister, Ivan Kostov, to the Bulgarian units within KFOR on 19 March [S/2000/246]; the visit of Queen Rania of Jordan to Kosovo and Metohija on 27 March without its approval [S/2000/314]; the UNMIK initiative to host a conference on traffic corridors of the Balkans in Skopje, FYROM, in April, to which the "territory of Kosovo" was to be invited [S/2000/313]; and the UNMIK practice of flying Albanian flags on UN buildings in Kosovo and Metohija, despite its protests [S/2000/331]. FRY brought to the Council President's attention on 19 May [S/2000/457] UNMIK's intention to conclude an agreement with the Red Crescent of Saudi Arabia on the construction of a cultural centre near an Orthodox cemetery in Pristina.

Change of Government

On 7 October, Vojislav Kostunica, who was elected President of FRY on 24 September, took office. He replaced Slobodan Milosevic, who had been charged with crimes against humanity by ICTY in 1999 [YUN 1999, p. 1214]. The new Government, which was formed on 4 November, dropped any claim to being the sole successor

State of the former Socialist Federal Republic of Yugoslavia (which dissolved in 1992), and was recognized by the international community.

Communications. In a 3 March statement [S/2000/196], the EU expressed concern about the continued violations by Serbian authorities of the right of free expression of opinion. It stated that public threats against the independent media showed that the regime pursued an arbitrary and discriminatory policy to clamp down on independent voices, as demonstrated by the indictment of Dusan Mihajlovic, President of the New Democracy Party, for allegedly spreading false information and disrupting law and order. The EU stated that the Serbian people should be allowed to freely express their political will. On 10 May [S/2000/438], the EU said that it was disturbed by the intensification of repression against democratic forces, civil society and independent media in Serbia. The measures taken by FRY authorities to prevent a lawful and democratic rally in Pozarevac on 9 May was one more denial of democracy and a violation of the right to freedom of expression. The EU also condemned the recent arbitrary arrests of politicians, journalists and students and reiterated its support for the struggle of the Serbian people for freedom and democracy.

On 18 and 22 May [S/2000/463, S/2000/485], the EU condemned the takeover of Belgrade's independent television station, Studio B, on 17 May, and the simultaneous actions against Radio B292, Radio Index, the daily newspaper *Blic*, and TV Mladenovac. That action, following continuing mass arrests and detention of opposition representatives and student leaders, heavy punishment of independent media, repression of journalists and obstacles to public rallies of the democratic forces, was the latest in a series of repressive actions by the Milosevic regime. Increasing repression by that regime was leading FRY into a position of greater distance from free and democratic Europe, increasing its isolation and running against the wishes of the Serbian people. FRY remained the only South-Eastern European State still isolated from the mainstream of Europe, and President Milosevic's regime alone was responsible for that situation.

On 20 September [S/2000/885], FRY drew the attention of the Security Council President to the announcement by the EU and the United States that they were ready to lift sanctions on FRY if its voters elected the opposition candidate at the 24 September presidential elections. In addition, the United States and some EU member States continued to finance the activities of a number of political organizations and media in FRY and had substantially increased funding during the election campaign. Those actions, designed to swing the will of its electorate, constituted a flagrant violation of the Charter, relevant OSCE documents and international law and was condemned by the FRY Government. Those countries had encroached upon the inalienable right of Yugoslav voters to elect their own legitimate representatives and violated General Assembly resolution 54/168 [YUN 1999, p. 632] regarding respect for the principles of national sovereignty and non-interference in the internal affairs of States in their electoral processes. FRY requested the Council to consider the issue at its next meeting.

FRY also lodged a protest on 18 September [A/55/395-S/2000/880] regarding the establishment on 15 August of a "United States Bureau for Yugoslavia" in Budapest, Hungary, to assist the opposition in FRY and Serbia to swing the will of the people in the forthcoming elections, to establish and fund pro–United States and pro-NATO organizations in FRY, and to finance opposition parties and the so-called independent media. Hungary's consent to the opening of the "Bureau" and the use of Hungarian territory against a third country were unprecedented in international relations. FRY protested United States activities from Hungary and other countries, aimed at overt interference in FRY's internal affairs, destabilization of the country and the violation of its sovereignty and territorial integrity. It expected the Council to condemn that behaviour and to call on the United States to respect the Charter, United States international obligations and international law. FRY further elaborated those views and observations in a memorandum of 5 October [S/2000/961] regarding the elections in FRY in September-October. It also accused NATO countries, the EU and other European States of exerting political, psychological and military pressures, of subversive activities and of funding the opposition.

EU statement. On 11 October [A/55/486-S/2000/991], the EU welcomed the election of Mr. Kostunica as FRY's new President. It said that the people of FRY had chosen democracy and Europe. As a result, the EU decided to lift all sanctions imposed on the country since 1998, with the exception of the provisions affecting former President Milosevic and those associated with him. The EU also decided to lift the oil and air embargoes immediately and to allow FRY to benefit from the Community Assistance to Reconstruction, Development and Stabilization programme. The activities of the European Agency for Reconstruction would also be extended to FRY.

Among other initiatives, the EU Finance Ministers would examine, in consultation with international financial institutions, the conditions for integrating FRY into the international financial community as rapidly as possible. The Council of the EU had asked the European Commission and the World Bank, under the aegis of the Steering Committee for the Balkans, to be jointly responsible for evaluating FRY's needs and for coordinating economic and financial assistance to it.

Each of the 15 EU member States expressed its desire to re-establish or to normalize diplomatic relations with FRY and hoped that FRY would start a reconciliation process with its neighbours and re-establish relationships of trust and cooperation. The EU would help meet those objectives as far as it was able.

Georgia

At the end of 2000, there was still no breakthrough in efforts to reach a political settlement of the Abkhaz/Georgian conflict. During the year, the Secretary-General's Special Representative, the Russian Federation, in its capacity as facilitator, the Group of Friends of the Secretary-General (France, Germany, the Russian Federation, the United Kingdom and the United States) and OSCE worked with the Georgian and Abkhaz sides to reinvigorate the peace process and engage in bilateral discussions on specific related issues. Through those efforts, three meetings of the Coordinating Council were held during the year, at which agreement was reached on revitalizing the Council's working groups on security, on refugees and internally displaced persons and on social and economic questions. The Special Representative continued to refine the draft document "Basic principles for the distribution of constitutional competences between Tbilisi and Sukhumi" but the Group of Friends of the Secretary-General could not arrive at a shared position on the draft proposal.

Meanwhile, to address the deteriorating security situation in the zone of conflict, the parties signed a 3 May Protocol on the stabilization of the situation in the security zone. They also reached decisions on accelerating work on the draft protocol on the return of refugees to the Gali district and measures for economic rehabilitation, and the agreement on peace and guarantees for the non-resumption of hostilities. Special efforts were also made to improve confidence-building measures.

The Security Council, in November, noted with concern the continued failure of the parties to achieve a comprehensive settlement, including the political status of Abkhazia within the State of Georgia, and called on them to take immediate measures to move beyond the impasse and to spare no effort to achieve progress without further delay.

UN Observer Mission in Georgia

The United Nations Observer Mission in Georgia (UNOMIG), established by Security Council resolution 858(1993) [YUN 1993, p. 509], continued to monitor and verify compliance with the 1994 Agreement on a Ceasefire and Separation of Forces (Moscow Agreement) [YUN 1994, p. 583] and to fulfil other tasks as mandated by resolution 937(1994) [ibid., p. 584]. The Mission operated in close collaboration with the collective peacekeeping force of the Commonwealth of Independent States (CIS) that had been in the zone of conflict, at the request of the parties, since 1994 [ibid., p. 583]. The Council extended the Mission's mandate twice during the year, the first time until 31 July 2000 and the second until 31 January 2001.

UNOMIG's main headquarters was located in Sukhumi (Abkhazia, Georgia), with administrative headquarters in Pitsunda, a liaison office in the Georgian capital of Tbilisi and team bases and a sector headquarters in each of the Gali and Zugdidi sectors. A team base in the Kodori Valley was manned by observers operating from Sukhumi. UNOMIG, as at October 2000, had a strength of 103 military observers.

The Mission was headed by Dieter Boden (Germany). Major-General Anis Ahmed Bajwa (Pakistan) succeeded Major-General Tariq Waseem Ghazi (Pakistan) as UNOMIG's Chief Military Observer in mid-January [S/2000/15, S/2000/16].

Activities

Report of Secretary-General (January). The Secretary-General, in response to resolution 1255(1999) [YUN 1999, p. 380], submitted a January report [S/2000/39] on the situation in Abkhazia, Georgia, including UNOMIG operations. He stated that, since assuming his duties in November 1999, his Special Representative had met with Georgia's President, Eduard Shevardnadze, Abkhaz leader Vladislav Ardzinba, other representatives of both sides, the Russian Federation, in its capacity as facilitator, OSCE and members of the Group of Friends of the Secretary-General. The negotiating process resumed on 18 and 19 January, with the convening of the ninth session of the Coordinating Council of the Georgian and Abkhaz sides in Tbilisi, after a nine-month hiatus. The session, organized around small bilateral working groups, reached agreement on the protocol establishing a mechanism for joint investigation of violations of the Moscow Agreement and other violent incidents in the zone of conflict; the disinterring and reburial of Georgian remains buried near Sukhumi and assistance from the Georgian side in locating the buried remains of Abkhaz killed during the war; and further steps for the rehabilitation and use of the Inguri dam and power station. They also agreed to renew negotiations on a draft document on peace and the non-resumption of hostilities, and requested the Special Representative to carry out preparatory work for a third meeting on confidence-building measures. In parallel to those talks, the Special Representative called for work to proceed on issues relating to a comprehensive settlement of the conflict. Pursuant to Security Council resolution 1255(1999), a draft document entitled "Basic principles for the distribution of constitutional competences between Tbilisi and Sukhumi" was submitted for comments to the Russian Federation, OSCE and the Friends of the Secretary-General. Although the Abkhaz side had so far been reluctant to discuss that subject, the Secretary-General envisaged that ways of moving the issue forward would be explored at a later stage.

The Secretary-General reported that the situation in the UNOMIG area of responsibility remained calm but unstable and there were no serious violations of the Moscow Agreement. Two violent incidents in January, the detonation of a mine by a civilian bus and the abduction of two UNOMIG observers (who were subsequently released unharmed), created serious concern about security in the area and hindered UN and NGO activities. Meanwhile, despite the lack of proper security conditions for returning refugees and internally displaced persons, and the lack of agreement on that issue, a process of administrative and economic normalization was under way in the Gali district, affecting positively the lives of its residents, who were showing signs of optimism for a better future.

The Secretary-General observed that the critical issue of the return of refugees and internally displaced persons needed to be addressed urgently. He called on the two sides and the international community to find a formula for their return. Since negotiations on earlier draft documents addressing the issue had reached a standstill, he urged the two sides to put forward and implement new approaches to resolving the problem of displacement, including the revival of Working Group II of the Coordinating Council. The Secretary-General recommended that the Security Council extend UNOMIG's mandate until 31 July 2000.

Communication. On 26 January [S/2000/52], the Russian Federation informed the Council President that the CIS Council of Heads of State had decided to extend the presence of its collective peacekeeping force in Abkhazia, Georgia, for a further six months and to continue as soon as possible the consultations on ensuring implementation of previous decisions of the Council of Heads of State, particularly with respect to the expansion of the security zone and elaboration of a procedure for its implementation.

SECURITY COUNCIL ACTION (January)

On 31 January [meeting 4094], the Security Council unanimously adopted **resolution 1287(2000)**. The draft [S/2000/56] was prepared in consultations among Council members.

The Security Council,

Recalling all its relevant resolutions, in particular resolution 1255(1999) of 30 July 1999, and the statement by its President of 12 November 1999,

Having considered the report of the Secretary-General of 19 January 2000,

Recalling the conclusions of the summits of the Organization for Security and Cooperation in Europe, held in Lisbon in December 1996 and in Istanbul on 18 and 19 November 1999, regarding the situation in Abkhazia, Georgia,

Stressing that the lack of progress on key issues of a comprehensive settlement of the conflict in Abkhazia, Georgia, is unacceptable,

Welcoming the results of the ninth session of the Coordinating Council of the Georgian and Abkhaz sides held under the chairmanship of the Special Representative of the Secretary-General with the participation of the Russian Federation, in its capacity as facilitator, as well as of the Group of Friends of the Secretary-General and of the Organization for Security and Cooperation in Europe, in Tbilisi on 18 and 19 January 2000, in particular the signing by the parties of the Protocol establishing a mechanism for joint investigation of violations of the Agreement on a Ceasefire and Separation of Forces, signed in Moscow on 14 May 1994, and other violent incidents in the conflict zone, and their decision to renew negotiations under United Nations auspices and with the facilitation of the Russian Federation on the draft agreement on peace and guarantees for the prevention of armed confrontations and on the preparation of a draft of a new protocol on the return of refugees to the Gali region and measures to restore the economy,

Welcoming the decision on further measures for the settlement of the conflict in Abkhazia, Georgia, adopted by the Council of Heads of State of the Commonwealth of Independent States on 30 December 1999,

Deeply concerned that, although currently calm, the general situation in the conflict zone remains volatile,

Welcoming and encouraging efforts by the United Nations to sensitize peacekeeping personnel in the prevention and control of HIV/AIDS and other communicable diseases in all its peacekeeping operations,

Recalling the relevant principles contained in the Convention on the Safety of United Nations and Associated Personnel of 9 December 1994,

Welcoming the important contributions that the United Nations Observer Mission in Georgia and the collective peacekeeping force of the Commonwealth of Independent States continue to make in stabilizing the situation in the conflict zone, noting that the working relationship between the Mission and the collective peacekeeping force has been good at all levels, and stressing the importance of continuing and increasing close cooperation and coordination between them in the performance of their respective mandates,

1. *Welcomes* the report of the Secretary-General of 19 January 2000;

2. *Encourages* the parties to seize the opportunity of the appointment of a new Special Representative of the Secretary-General to renew their commitment to the peace process;

3. *Strongly supports* the sustained efforts of the Secretary-General and his Special Representative with the assistance of the Russian Federation, in its capacity as facilitator, as well as of the Group of Friends of the Secretary-General and of the Organization for Security and Cooperation in Europe, to promote the stabilization of the situation and the achievement of a comprehensive political settlement, which includes a settlement on the political status of Abkhazia within the State of Georgia;

4. *Reiterates its call* for the parties to the conflict to deepen their commitment to the United Nations–led peace process, continue to expand their dialogue, and display without delay the necessary will to achieve substantial results on the key issues of the negotiations, in particular on the distribution of constitutional competences between Tbilisi and Sukhumi as part of a comprehensive settlement, with full respect for the sovereignty and territorial integrity of Georgia within its internationally recognized borders;

5. *Reiterates* that it considers unacceptable and illegitimate the holding of self-styled elections and referendum in Abkhazia, Georgia;

6. *Calls upon* the parties to continue to enhance their efforts to implement fully the confidence-building measures on which they agreed at the Athens and Istanbul meetings of 16 to 18 October 1998 and 7 to 9 June 1999 respectively, and recalls the invitation of the Government of Ukraine to host a third meeting aimed at building confidence, improving security and developing cooperation between the parties;

7. *Reaffirms* the necessity for the parties strictly to respect human rights, and supports the efforts of the Secretary-General to find ways to improve their observance as an integral part of the work towards a comprehensive political settlement;

8. *Reaffirms also* the unacceptability of the demographic changes resulting from the conflict and the imprescriptible right of all refugees and displaced persons affected by the conflict to return to their homes in secure conditions, in accordance with international law and as set out in the Quadripartite Agreement on the Voluntary Return of Refugees and Displaced Persons, of 4 April 1994, and calls upon the parties to address this issue urgently by agreeing and implementing effective measures to guarantee the security of those who exercise their unconditional right to return, including those who have already returned;

9. *Demands* that both sides observe strictly the Agreement on a Ceasefire and Separation of Forces;

10. *Welcomes* the fact that the United Nations Observer Mission in Georgia is keeping its security arrangements under constant review in order to ensure the highest possible level of security for its staff;

11. *Decides* to extend the mandate of the Mission for a new period terminating on 31 July 2000, subject to a review by the Council of the mandate of the Mission in the event of any changes that may be made in the mandate or in the presence of the collective peacekeeping force of the Commonwealth of Independent States, and expresses its intention to conduct a thorough review of the operation at the end of its current mandate, in the light of steps taken by the parties to achieve a comprehensive settlement;

12. *Requests* the Secretary-General to continue to keep the Council regularly informed and to report three months from the date of the adoption of the present resolution on the situation in Abkhazia, Georgia;

13. *Decides* to remain actively seized of the matter.

Report of Secretary-General (April). In his April report on the situation in Abkhazia, Georgia [S/2000/345], the Secretary-General said that, accompanied by his Special Representative, he had visited Moscow from 27 to 29 January and discussed the Abkhaz/Georgian peace process with the Russian Federation Acting President, Vladimir Putin, and other officials. The Special Representative also continued consultations and preparatory work within the framework of the UN-led Geneva peace process. At the same time, work continued on the distribution of constitutional competences between Tbilisi and Sukhumi. A revised draft paper on that issue was distributed in mid-March to the Russian Federation and members of the Group of Friends of the Secretary-General, incorporating their comments on the original draft. Further discussions were continuing on finalizing the draft with a view to submitting it to the two sides in the near future. The Abkhaz side had indicated its interest in not being excluded from those discussions, though its basic position on the question of the status of those negotiations had not changed. In February and in April, the Abkhaz leader drew the Secretary-General's attention to some legal aspects related to the settlement of the conflict and asserted that, during the negotiations, the UN position had departed from principles agreed on in earlier signed documents. The Under-Secretary-General for Political Affairs, replying on the Secretary-General's behalf, stressed that the United Nations had consistently maintained that a comprehensive settlement had to be based on the principles of full respect for the sovereignty and territorial integrity of Georgia and the right of all refugees and internally displaced persons to a safe, secure and voluntary return to Abkhazia within Georgia.

To alleviate the deteriorating security situation, the Special Representative, at the request of the leaders of the two sides, convened a meeting in Sukhumi on 3 February between the State Minister of Georgia and the de facto "Prime Minister" of Abkhazia, with the participation of the Commander of the CIS peacekeeping force. The meeting resulted in the signing of a Protocol on a series of concrete measures to improve the situation. Discussions at a further meeting between the two sides in Sukhumi on 27 and 28 February focused on the non-use of force, the return of refugees and internally displaced persons to the Gali district and economic rehabilitation measures, based on two draft texts entitled "Agreement on peace and guarantees for the prevention of armed confrontation" and "Protocol on the return of refugees to the Gali district and measures for economic rehabilitation". The two sides clarified their views, produced new working drafts of both documents and agreed to continue bilateral consultations. On 26 March, the Georgian press agency Caucasus Press and Abkhaz counterparts reached agreements on bilateral cooperation in information.

UNOMIG continued its daily ground patrols from Sukhumi and the two sector headquarters in Gali and Zugdidi, as well as weekly helicopter patrols of its area of responsibility, except in the upper Kodori Valley, where the Georgian authorities had been unable to provide security guarantees for UNOMIG to carry out its observation mandate there and to bring to justice the perpetrators of the October 1999 hostage-taking incident [YUN 1999, p. 382]. Since its establishment in January, the Joint Investigation Group had taken up five new investigations and 14 investigations begun earlier continued. By emphasizing transparency in investigations and allowing personal contacts at the working level, the Group had reduced mistrust and tension on the ground and had itself become a valuable element of improved security, despite the still unresolved issue of the status of the Georgian representatives in the Group.

The Secretary-General reported that tensions reached a peak on 25 January, when two Abkhaz militiamen were killed in an ambush near Dikazurga in the Gali district. Three Abkhaz men, reportedly linked to organized crime, were also killed and two Abkhaz who survived the shooting were taken into custody by Georgian law enforcement personnel. Demonstrations in the aftermath of those incidents created tension and raised fears of retaliatory measures. Those events occurred against a background of tit-for-tat abductions on both sides of the ceasefire line. Implementation of the 3 February Protocol to address the situation (see above) resulted in the release of one abductee by the Abkhaz side, but the process broke down because of Georgia's declared inability to implement some of the Protocol's provisions within the established time frame. Further exchanges between the two sides eventually took place on 29 March, following mediation efforts by the Special Representative and the Chief Military Observer. The successful exchange noticeably improved mutual confidence in the conflict zone and decreased tensions. However, in April, two serious ambush attacks against Abkhaz law enforcement personnel in the lower Gali district, in which eight militiamen were killed and seven wounded, sharply heightened tensions and fears of retaliation. At the urging of the Special Representative and the Chief Military Observer, the two sides engaged in direct bilateral communications to discuss the matter.

UNOMIG's efforts to implement the 3 February Protocol had met with mixed results, since the verification of the numbers of security personnel on both sides of the ceasefire line and their reduction, in accordance with pre-established ceilings, were hampered by sometimes imprecise information from local commanders and by discrepancies in figures. In terms of the withdrawal of illegal armed groups from the security and restricted weapons zones, UNOMIG had deployed the necessary observation and reporting mechanism but had no mandate to actually remove such groups.

With regard to the humanitarian situation, the activities of the humanitarian community remained limited in the Gali district and failed to meet required needs. International aid agencies continued to find it difficult to assist returnees because of the security conditions. Looting associated with criminal activities compelled agencies at times to deliver humanitarian assistance under the armed protection of the CIS peacekeeping force. In the absence of security guarantees, agencies were reluctant to undertake programmes to encourage returns. Georgia, the United Nations Development Programme (UNDP), UNHCR, the World Bank and the United Nations Office for the Coordination of Humanitarian Affairs developed a new approach to assist internally displaced persons, which recognized their right to be treated in the same manner as all Georgian citizens and favoured giving them the opportunity to build skills and a level of self-reliance that would enable them to reintegrate into society. President Shevardnadze established a commission to facilitate the elaboration of the new approach in conjunction with UN agencies and the World Bank. Preliminary pledges to the Self-Reliance Pilot Fund, established under the new approach to finance innovative projects to contribute to the self-sufficiency of internally displaced persons, totalled over $1 million.

The United Nations Human Rights Office in Abkhazia, Georgia, continued to monitor the human rights situation in the region. Most of the cases of human rights violations related to property rights and residence permits; pension entitlements and humanitarian allowances; robberies; and harassment in the workplace or in the neighbourhood on ethnic or gender grounds.

SECURITY COUNCIL ACTION (May)

On 11 May [meeting 4137], following consultations among Security Council members, the President made statement **S/PRST/2000/16** on behalf of the Council:

The Security Council has considered the report of the Secretary-General of 24 April 2000 concerning the situation in Abkhazia, Georgia.

The Council welcomes the efforts by the Special Representative of the Secretary-General to enhance contacts at all levels between the Georgian and Abkhaz sides, and calls upon the parties to continue to expand such contacts. It supports the appeal by the Secretary-General to both sides to make more active use of the Coordinating Council machinery, and actively to consider the paper prepared by the Special Representative concerning the implementation of the agreed confidence-building measures. In this context, the Council recalls with appreciation the invitation of the Government of Ukraine to host a meeting in Yalta.

The Council believes that resolution of issues related to the improvement of the humanitarian situation, to socio-economic development and to ensuring stability in the conflict zone would facilitate the peace process. In this regard, it calls upon the parties to finalize their work on and to sign a draft agreement on peace and guarantees for the prevention of armed confrontation and a draft protocol on the return of refugees to the Gali region and measures for economic rehabilitation.

The Council notes with deep concern the continued failure of the parties to achieve a comprehensive political settlement, which includes a settlement on the political status of Abkhazia within the State of Georgia. It also notes the adverse impact that this failure has on the humanitarian situation, economic development and stability in the region. It calls upon the parties to display the political will required for a breakthrough and to spare no efforts in order to achieve substantive progress without further delay. In this regard, it joins the Secretary-General in encouraging the parties to be ready to consider proposals, based on the Council decisions, to be presented in due course by the Special Representative on the question of the distribution of constitutional competences between Tbilisi and Sukhumi.

The Council strongly reaffirms the imprescriptible right of all refugees and internally displaced persons directly affected by the conflict to return to their homes in secure and dignified conditions. It calls upon the parties to agree upon and to take, in the nearest future, concrete steps towards implementing effective measures to guarantee the security of those who exercise their unconditional right to return, including those who have already returned. In particular, the undefined and insecure status of spontaneous returnees to the Gali district is a matter that must be addressed urgently. The Council encourages the Abkhaz side to continue the process of improvement of security conditions for returnees, which, the Secretary-General notes, may be beginning in the Gali region.

The Council encourages the Special Representative, in this context, to continue his efforts, in close cooperation with the Russian Federation, in its capacity as facilitator, the Group of Friends of the Secretary-General and the Organization for Security and Cooperation in Europe.

The Council expresses its appreciation for the measures undertaken by the Government of Georgia, the United Nations Development Programme, the Office of the United Nations High Commissioner for Refugees and the Office for the Coordination of Humanitarian Affairs and the World Bank, in order to improve the situation of those refugees and internally displaced persons who have not been in a position to exercise their right of return, to develop their skills and to increase their self-reliance.

The Council notes that the situation on the ground in the area of responsibility of the United Nations Observer Mission in Georgia has remained generally calm although unstable during the reporting period. It welcomes all the efforts that have been undertaken, in particular by the Special Representative, with a view to alleviating tensions and increasing confidence between the parties. It regrets that the Protocol of 3 February 2000 has not been implemented in full and, in particular, that the withdrawal of illegal armed groups has not been brought about. It is concerned at the tension created by recent attacks against Abkhaz militiamen. It deplores these attacks and the high level of criminal activity in the conflict zone, as well as acts of violence against Mission personnel and members of their families. In this context, the Council recalls the relevant principles contained in the Convention on the Safety of United Nations and Associated Personnel of 9 December 1994 and the statement by its President of 9 February 2000. It calls upon the parties to refrain from any actions which could increase tensions on the ground and to ensure the safety of Mission personnel.

The Council welcomes the important contribution that the Mission and the collective peacekeeping force of the Commonwealth of Independent States continue to make in stabilizing the situation in the conflict zone, notes that the working relationship between the Mission and the collective peacekeeping force has been good at all levels, and stresses the importance of continuing and increasing close cooperation and coordination between them in the performance of their respective mandates.

Communications. Georgia, on 15 June [S/2000/594], expressed concern over the intensified violence in Abkhazia, Georgia. It contended that the Abkhaz regime had not spared efforts to legalize the forcibly changed demographic situation as a consequence of the ethnic cleansing, and was creating unbearable living conditions for the Georgian returnees in the Gali district. Moreover, threats to repeat the Gali events of May 1998 [YUN 1998, p. 394] had become a common denominator of the developments in the region.

Georgia declared that it would make all efforts to promote security in the zone of conflict and achieve a comprehensive resolution. In that respect, it attached great importance to the document on the distribution of constitutional competences between the central authorities of Georgia and the authorities of Abkhazia, Georgia, drafted by the United Nations and the Group of Friends of the Secretary-General. Implementation of the UNDP economic rehabilitation programme for the region, which was equally important for the settlement of the conflict, would start as soon as the political status of Abkhazia within Georgia was determined.

Georgia reaffirmed the unacceptability of violence directed at undermining the process of peaceful resolution and condemned the tensions in the zone of conflict stemming from the failure of the Abkhaz side to meet its obligations under the peace process and Security Council resolutions. It called on the Secretary-General, his Special Representative, the Security Council, the Group of Friends of the Secretary-General, the Russian Federation and UN specialized agencies to intensify their efforts in the Gali district to ensure security, as well as full implementation of Council resolutions.

On 26 June [S/2000/629], the Russian Federation informed the Council President that the CIS Council of Heads of State, on 21 June, had decided to extend the stay of the collective peacekeeping force until 31 December 2000.

Report of Secretary-General (July). The Secretary-General reported in July [S/2000/697] that his Special Representative had continued consultations with all parties concerned but progress was slow, mainly owing to a lack of effort by the two sides to achieve tangible results. Delays were also caused by the reshuffling of key players in the Government of Georgia following the re-election on 9 April of President Shevardnadze. On 4 July, the President named the newly appointed State Minister as head of the Georgian delegation to the Coordinating Council and created the new post of Minister for Special Assignments, with direct responsibility for conflict settlement in Georgia.

The Special Representative continued to work closely with the Group of Friends to refine further the draft document on the distribution of competences between Tbilisi and Sukhumi and discussed the issue with the Russian Federation in Moscow on 9 and 10 May. A 25 May version of the draft document was circulated among the Group of Friends in the expectation that it might serve in the near future as a basis on which to open a political dialogue between the Georgian and Abkhaz sides. However, differences of views had since arisen among the Group of Friends themselves concerning both content and strategy, and strong concerted efforts were urgently needed to produce a coordinated draft and approach. Meanwhile, the Georgian side continued to express its eagerness to commence negotiations on Abkhazia's future status on the basis of the document. The Abkhaz side, however, maintained that it would not engage in a dialogue with the Georgian side on the issue but did not wish to be left out of the debate completely. In consultations with the Special Representative, it renewed its interest in the convening of a conference of experts to discuss legal aspects of the conflict.

On 3 May, the Special Representative chaired a high-level emergency meeting of both sides to address the rapidly deteriorating security situation on the ground in the wake of the killing of some 12 members of the Abkhaz militia in a series of ambushes in the Gali district. Following the meeting, a draft Protocol on the stabilization of the situation in the security zone was produced, which provided for the monitoring by UNOMIG and the CIS peacekeeping force of an agreed ceiling in the number of armed law enforcement personnel stationed in the security zone, and for the creation of a new structure of increased cooperation by the two sides in the fight against crime.

On 11 July, the Special Representative convened the tenth session of the Coordinating Council in Sukhumi, at which the Protocol was signed. The Council decided that Working Group I on security issues should meet monthly to monitor its implementation and that the two sides would accelerate work on the draft Protocol on the return of refugees to the Gali district and measures for economic rehabilitation and the agreement on peace and guarantees for the non-resumption of hostilities, which had been discussed intermittently since 1998. The Council took note of the Special Representative's suggestions to improve implementation of confidence-building measures, including the creation of a database of existing projects.

A number of confidence-building projects were carried out. Of particular significance was the agreement reached in June that books and materials pertaining to Abkhazia, Georgia, would be sought among Georgian holdings and given to the Abkhaz side as a partial replacement for the Abkhaz Archives destroyed during the 1992-1993 war. The first presentation of such materials was made by the Georgian side during the 11 July session of the Coordinating Council and further cooperation in that area was planned.

The Joint Fact-finding Group established on 19 January continued to meet weekly. While the Abkhaz side formally refused to work with the Georgian representatives, all of whom were members of the Abkhaz "government-in-exile", there was satisfactory cooperation on the ground with local officials from Zugdidi representing the Georgian side. UNOMIG successfully introduced the concept of "quick reaction investigators", military observers posted in both sectors whose task was to go to the scene of an incident as quickly as possible after it occurred to record evidence before it was lost or contaminated.

The general situation in the conflict zone remained relatively calm although unstable, with peaks in tension in April and in the days leading up to the Georgian National Day on 26 May. The tension was defused due to the efforts of the two sides and to preventive measures taken by UNOMIG, including active liaison at every level and nearly doubling of the regular air and ground patrolling, thus creating a far more visible presence and providing the ability to dispel rumours through accurate reporting.

There was one confirmed violation of the Moscow Agreement on 12 June, when a UNOMIG helicopter patrol spotted an armoured vehicle at an Abkhaz observation post within the restricted weapons zone. The armoured vehicle, which had apparently been deployed in response to an armed attack on the post several days earlier, was withdrawn to a heavy weapons storage site. There were few exchanges of fire across the ceasefire line, but a number of ambushes were carried out in which 25 people were killed.

Endemic crime throughout the area remained a serious problem. Organized crime, particularly smuggling, was growing in scope and profitability, and there were indications that it was reaching into institutions on both sides.

The spring and summer seasons had brought local residents displaced from the Gali district back home to farm their land; up to 80 per cent of the pre-war population was reported to have returned. Funding for schools in the Gali district had increased slightly, including allocation of funds in the Georgian budget. There were also signs that the Abkhaz authorities were taking a more pragmatic and flexible view on the use of the Georgian language in Gali district schools attended by Mingrelian children.

The security and safety of its personnel remained the highest priority for UNOMIG. On 17 April, the father of a UNOMIG interpreter was shot dead during a robbery attempt in Gali town, on 26 April, the home of another UNOMIG interpreter was looted and, on 15 June, a group of armed men opened fire on the vehicles of a UNOMIG ground patrol in the lower Gali area. On 1 June, in the Kodori Valley, a UNOMIG foot patrol was taken hostage. They were released unharmed on 5 June, following consultations by the Special Representative with all the parties concerned. After the incident, the Special Representative reminded Georgia of the international community's expectation that the perpetrators would be brought to justice and UNOMIG would be provided with the security it required to implement its mandate in the Kodori Valley. UNOMIG patrols to the upper Kodori Valley remained suspended.

In June, an International Monetary Fund (IMF) mission visited Georgia to assist in developing a financial programme for the year 2000 and in outlining the macroeconomic programme for 2001. During the mission, it was agreed that adjustment efforts by Georgia were needed to create conditions to allow the resumption of the suspended IMF programme, including revising its budget and establishing a track record in implementing the budget and other financial policies by the end of November, implementation of measures to tackle problems of governance and corruption and elaboration of a poverty-reduction strategy. With support from the United Nations, the World Bank and IMF, the Government had started to prepare a comprehensive strategy to reduce poverty.

The Secretary-General said that, despite the slow progress, UNOMIG continued to play an essential role in the search for a peaceful solution to the Abkhaz/Georgian conflict through its sustained efforts to further the peace process. It remained a central element in efforts to stabilize the situation. He therefore recommended that the Council extend the UNOMIG mandate until 31 January 2001.

Communication. In a 25 July communiqué [S/2000/742], the Russian Federation rejected as groundless and detrimental to Russian-Georgian relations remarks made by the head of the Georgian delegation to an Economic and Social Council meeting to the effect that the Russian Federation was involved in the outbreak of the Abkhaz/Georgian conflict and that Russian peacekeepers deployed in the zone of separation were not carrying out their mission effectively.

The Russian Federation recalled that it was the only country to send peacekeepers, who at times laid down their lives to prevent new outbreaks of violence between the sides. The fact that the conflict between Tbilisi and Sukhumi had not been settled was evidence that the sides themselves had not done everything to restore lost confidence and convince each other of the desirability and possibility of living in one common home.

SECURITY COUNCIL ACTION (July)

On 28 July [meeting 4179], the Security Council unanimously adopted **resolution 1311(2000)**. The draft [S/2000/743] was prepared in consultations among Council members.

The Security Council,

Recalling all its relevant resolutions, in particular resolution 1287(2000) of 31 January 2000, and the statement by its President of 11 May 2000, as well as resolution 1308(2000) of 17 July 2000,

Having considered the report of the Secretary-General of 21 July 2000,

Recalling the conclusions of the summits of the Organization for Security and Cooperation in Europe, held in Lisbon in December 1996 and in Istanbul on 18 and 19 November 1999, regarding the situation in Abkhazia, Georgia,

Stressing that the lack of progress on key issues of a comprehensive settlement of the conflict in Abkhazia, Georgia, is unacceptable,

Recalling that, according to its statute, the Coordinating Council of the Georgian and Abkhaz sides should meet every two months, and welcoming, in this regard, the resumption of its work,

Welcoming the results of the tenth session of the Coordinating Council in Sukhumi on 11 July 2000, in particular the signing by the two sides, the Special Representative of the Secretary-General and the Commander of the collective peacekeeping force of the Commonwealth of Independent States of the Protocol related to the stabilization of the situation in the security zone, and the decision that the two sides would accelerate work on the draft protocol on the return of refugees to the Gali region and measures for economic rehabilitation and on the draft agreement on peace and guarantees for the prevention for the non-resumption of hostilities,

Deeply concerned that, although currently relatively calm, the general situation in the conflict zone remains unstable,

Recalling the relevant principles contained in the Convention on the Safety of United Nations and Associated Personnel of 9 December 1994,

Welcoming the important contributions that the United Nations Observer Mission in Georgia and the collective peacekeeping force continue to make in stabilizing the situation in the conflict zone, noting that the working relationship between the Mission and the collective peacekeeping force has been excellent at all levels, stressing the importance of continuing and increasing close cooperation and coordination between them in the performance of their respective mandates, and welcoming also the decision on the extension of the stay of the collective peacekeeping force in the conflict zone in Abkhazia, Georgia, adopted by the Council of Heads of State of the Commonwealth of Independent States on 21 June 2000,

1. *Welcomes* the report of the Secretary-General of 21 July 2000;

2. *Strongly supports* the sustained efforts of the Secretary-General and his Special Representative with the assistance of the Russian Federation, in its capacity as facilitator, as well as of the Group of Friends of the Secretary-General and of the Organization for Security and Cooperation in Europe, to promote the stabilization of the situation and the achievement of a comprehensive political settlement, which includes a settlement on the political status of Abkhazia within the State of Georgia;

3. *Also strongly supports* the efforts of the Special Representative on the question of the distribution of competences between Tbilisi and Sukhumi, and, in particular, his intention to submit, in the near future, proposals to the parties as a basis for meaningful negotiations on that issue;

4. *Underlines* the responsibility of the parties to the conflict to engage in negotiations on the key outstanding issues in the United Nations–led peace process, including on the distribution of competences between Tbilisi and Sukhumi as part of a comprehensive settlement;

5. *Welcomes* the commitment of the parties not to use force for the resolution of any disputed questions, which must be addressed through negotiations and by peaceful means only, and to refrain from propaganda aimed at the resolution of the conflict by force;

6. *Calls upon* the parties to the conflict to implement earlier agreed confidence-building measures and develop further measures on the basis of the relevant document signed in Sukhumi on 11 July 2000, and recalls, in this context, the invitation of the Government of Ukraine to host, in Yalta, a third meeting aimed at building confidence, improving security and developing cooperation between the parties;

7. *Reaffirms* the unacceptability of the demographic changes resulting from the conflict and the imprescriptible right of all refugees and displaced persons affected by the conflict to return to their homes in secure and dignified conditions, in accordance with international law and as set out in the Quadripartite Agreement on the Voluntary Return of Refugees and Displaced Persons, of 4 April 1994, and calls upon the parties to address this issue urgently by agreeing upon and implementing effective measures to guarantee the security of those who exercise their unconditional right to return, including those who have already returned;

8. *Urges* the parties, in this context, to address urgently and in a concerted manner, as a first step, the undefined and insecure status of spontaneous returnees to the Gali district, including through the reestablishment of functioning local administrative structures in which the returnee population is appropriately represented;

9. *Welcomes* steps taken by the Government of Georgia, the United Nations Development Programme, the Office of the United Nations High Commissioner for Refugees, the Office for the Coordination of Humanitarian Affairs and the World Bank, aiming at ensuring

that the internally displaced persons enjoy their right to be treated in the same manner as all Georgian citizens with full respect, in principle and in practice, for their imprescriptible right to return to their homes in secure and dignified conditions;

10. *Deplores* all violent incidents, as well as the development of criminal activity, in the conflict zone, and calls upon the two sides to take urgent measures to cooperate with each other in the fight against crime of all sorts and in improving the work of their respective law enforcement organs;

11. *Demands* that both sides observe strictly the Agreement on a Ceasefire and Separation of Forces, signed in Moscow on 14 May 1994;

12. *Welcomes* the fact that the United Nations Observer Mission in Georgia is keeping its security arrangements under constant review in order to ensure the highest possible level of security for its staff;

13. *Decides* to extend the mandate of the Mission for a new period terminating on 31 January 2001, subject to a review by the Council of the mandate in the event of any changes that may be made in the mandate or in the presence of the collective peacekeeping force of the Commonwealth of Independent States, and expresses its intention to conduct a thorough review of the operation at the end of its current mandate, in the light of steps taken by the parties to achieve a comprehensive settlement;

14. *Requests* the Secretary-General to continue to keep the Council regularly informed and to report three months from the date of the adoption of the present resolution on the situation in Abkhazia, Georgia;

15. *Decides* to remain actively seized of the matter.

Report of Secretary-General (October). In October [S/2000/1023], the Secretary-General stated that he had discussed issues related to the comprehensive political settlement of the conflict in Abkhazia, Georgia, with President Shevardnadze in New York on 5 September. Meanwhile, his Special Representative, in continuing efforts to move the peace process forward, chaired a series of bilateral consultations on key aspects of the political settlement, confidence-building contacts between the two sides in a variety of fields and steps to reinvigorate the machinery of the Coordinating Council, including the Council's three working groups. That included the revival of Working Group I on security issues, which convened twice during the reporting period, as well as separate visits to Sukhumi for consultations with the Abkhaz side by the heads of UNHCR and UNDP in Georgia, as coordinators of Working Group II on refugees and internally displaced persons and of Working Group III on social and economic questions, respectively. Unfortunately, the efforts of the Group of Friends, including visits by the Special Representative to capitals, to arrive at a coordinated draft document on basic principles for the distribution of competences between Tbilisi and Sukhumi had not succeeded.

On 6 and 7 August in Tbilisi, and again on 20 August in Sukhumi, the Special Representative chaired consultations between the Georgian Minister for Special Affairs and the personal representative of Abkhaz leader Ardzinba on the basis of the 11 July Protocol (see p. 391). Although the Georgian side put forward new versions of the draft protocol on the return of refugees to the Gali district and measures for economic rehabilitation and the draft agreement on peace and guarantees for the prevention of hostilities, disagreement between the two sides persisted. The consultations also included broader discussions of central aspects of a comprehensive political settlement. On the basis of the 11 July Protocol, both sides submitted to the Special Representative proposals concerning further work in confidence-building measures, with a view to preparing for the third meeting on confidence-building measures to be convened in Yalta, Ukraine, in November.

The Special Representative and UNOMIG continued to provide good offices and substantial logistical support for a wide array of cooperation projects between the two sides. Georgia agreed to an Abkhaz request that the United Nations Educational, Scientific and Cultural Organization fund the renovation of cultural monuments in Abkhazia, Georgia. On 28 and 29 September in Sukhumi, the United Nations facilitated the first contact between Georgian and Abkhaz technical experts and their Russian colleagues on a solution to the problem of safe storage of radioactive materials located at the Physico-technical Institute in Sukhumi. On 5 and 6 October, a delegation from the European Commission visited the Inguri power station and dam to concretize plans for their repair. The Director of the Georgian National Library gathered further materials to present to the Abkhaz side; the third round of restoration of films shot during the last century in Abkhazia, Georgia, was completed, with financing from Germany. Many of those projects were also facilitated by the Georgian/Abkhaz Coordination Commission.

On 22 September, the Ministers of Education of the two sides met in Sukhumi to discuss cooperation in improving education in the Gali district and resolving the matter of the language of education used in schools. On 9 October, the Abkhaz de facto "Minister of Health" travelled to Tbilisi and met her counterpart to discuss potential collaboration.

After extensive consultations in the aftermath of the hostage-taking incidents in the upper Kodori Valley, Georgia assured UNOMIG in August that the necessary security conditions existed to resume helicopter patrolling of the valley. That development took place as the CIS peacekeeping force prepared to open a new checkpoint on the ceasefire line between the upper Kodori Valley and the Abkhaz-controlled lower part, which was expected to enhance general security in the area and improve freedom of movement for UNOMIG patrols.

On 20 August in Sukhumi, and on 4 October in Tbilisi, the Chief Military Observer chaired sessions of Working Group I of the Coordinating Council dealing with security issues, which focused on the implementation of the specific security agreements listed in the Protocol to the 3 May high-level meeting in Gali and on improving the functioning and efficacy of the Joint Fact-finding Group. Among the measures discussed, and later carried out on the ground, were the verification by UNOMIG and the CIS peace-keeping force of the strength of the respective security personnel of the two sides in the security zone and the establishment of better communications between the heads of Georgian and Abkhaz law enforcement agencies in the security zone.

Although attendance was sporadic, the Joint Fact-finding Group continued to convene weekly, despite rising frustration on all sides with the lack of progress on specific cases. On 22 September, the Special Representative and the Abkhaz de facto "Prime Minister" officially opened a bridge located along the main trunk road through the conflict zone, which had been renovated by UNOMIG. A number of road surface repairs and road reconstruction projects were also completed, and projects in the Kodori Valley and on the road leading to the Inguri hydroelectric power station were under way.

The Secretary-General concluded that the improvement in the security climate might be attributed in part to the reactivation of Working Group I and the increasing cooperation of the Georgian and Abkhaz sides in implementing agreements reached in the Coordinating Council. In the Gali sector, the usual summer lull in partisan and criminal activity had been particularly noticeable. However, the undercurrent of endemic lawlessness continued, and the hazelnut harvest was the trigger for a sudden rise in armed robberies, primarily in the Gali security zone. To improve the security climate, the Abkhaz administration of the Gali district increased militia patrolling and formed additional village guards, while the CIS peacekeeping force introduced daily armoured patrols to provide security and escort local residents bringing large quantities of hazelnuts to collection points. While those initiatives had some positive impact, they could not address the underlying reasons for the general climate of insecurity.

In the Zugdidi sector, the appearance of several notorious figures from the criminal and rebel underworlds gave rise to concern at the overall political and security climate in which UNOMIG was operating. On 12 September, Georgian police in Zugdidi arrested the leader of a partisan group (the so-called "Forest Brothers") and a reputed organized crime figure in the zone of conflict. Meanwhile, a leader of the group that took UNOMIG members hostage in Zugdidi in February 1998 made threatening demands to the Government of Georgia for the release from prison of some of his allies. On 15 August, a legal assistant to the United Nations Human Rights Office in Sukuhumi was shot and killed.

During the reporting period, the humanitarian situation in Abkhazia, Georgia, was exacerbated by the continued deterioration of the infrastructure, the lack of economic development and the precarious security situation. UNHCR, in consultations with the Georgian and Abkhaz sides, explored the possibility of reanimating Working Group II on refugees and internally displaced persons. In September, it conducted a preliminary assessment of needs among spontaneous returnees to the Gali district, and concluded that a limited resumption of protection monitoring had become necessary in view of the size of the returnee population.

The Secretary-General said that it was encouraging that the two sides had demonstrated a willingness to engage in talks on key aspects of a political settlement. However, the lack of progress in defining the status of Abkhazia within the State of Georgia was regrettable. He appealed to both sides to undertake immediate efforts to move beyond that impasse. Negotiations on the draft paper on basic principles for the distribution of competences between Tbilisi and Sukhumi should be the next step. In that context, it was imperative that the members of the Group of Friends reach as soon as possible a shared position on the draft paper, which took into account the Security Council's view that any solution to the conflict had to be based on the territorial integrity of Georgia.

SECURITY COUNCIL ACTION (November)

On 14 November [meeting 4221], following consultations among Security Council members, the President made statement **S/PRST/2000/32** on behalf of the Council:

> The Security Council has considered the report of the Secretary-General of 25 October 2000 concerning the situation in Abkhazia, Georgia.
>
> The Council welcomes the efforts by the Special Representative of the Secretary-General to enhance contacts at all levels between the Georgian and

Abkhaz sides, in close cooperation with the Russian Federation, in its capacity as facilitator, as well as the Group of Friends of the Secretary-General and the Organization for Security and Cooperation in Europe. It notes with appreciation the expansion of such contacts, which resulted recently in a series of meetings and steps towards the implementation of concrete cooperation projects between the two sides. It notes the holding of the eleventh session of the Co-ordinating Council and urges further reinvigoration of this mechanism. It welcomes the readiness of the Government of Ukraine to host the third meeting on confidence-building measures in Yalta at the end of November and notes the important contribution a successful conference held in a timely fashion would make to the peace process.

The Council notes with deep concern, however, the continued failure of the parties to achieve a comprehensive political settlement, which includes a settlement of the political status of Abkhazia within the State of Georgia. It calls upon the parties, in particular the Abkhaz side, to undertake immediate efforts to move beyond the impasse and urges them to spare no effort in order to achieve substantive progress without further delay. In this regard, it strongly supports the efforts of the Special Representative of the Secretary-General, undertaken with the support of the Group of Friends of the Secretary-General, to address the issue of the future constitutional status of Abkhazia and, in particular, his intention to submit, in the near future, a draft paper containing proposals to the parties on the question of the distribution of competences between Tbilisi and Sukhumi as a basis for meaningful negotiations on that issue.

The Council calls upon the parties to agree upon and to take, in the nearest future, concrete steps towards implementing effective measures to guarantee the security of the refugees and internally displaced persons who exercise their unconditional right to return to their homes. In particular, the undefined and insecure status of spontaneous returnees to the Gali district is a matter that must be addressed urgently. The Council therefore urges the parties to engage in genuine negotiations to resolve concrete aspects of the matter and not to link this issue to political matters. In this regard, it joins the Secretary-General in encouraging the Abkhaz side to muster the requisite political will to resolve the problem of Georgian language education in the schools of the district, as well as to find the resources that those schools need, which, the Secretary-General notes, may affect directly the magnitude of the seasonal migration in the area.

The Council welcomes the results achieved within the framework of the policy implemented by the Government of Georgia, the United Nations Development Programme, the Office of the United Nations High Commissioner for Refugees, the Office for the Coordination of Humanitarian Affairs and the World Bank, aimed at ensuring that the internally displaced persons enjoy their right to be treated in the same manner as all other Georgian citizens.

The Council notes that the situation on the ground in the area of responsibility of the United Nations Observer Mission in Georgia has remained generally calm although unstable during the reporting period. It welcomes all the efforts that have been undertaken, in particular by the Special Representative, with a view to alleviating tensions and increasing confidence between the parties. It urges the parties to cooperate closely in combating crime and improving the work of their respective law enforcement agencies.

The Council strongly condemns the murder of Mr. Zurab Achba, legal assistant to the United Nations Human Rights Office in Sukhumi, recalls the commitment of the Abkhaz side to keep the Mission fully informed on the course of the investigation into this crime, and urges the Abkhaz side to shed light on this matter. It also deplores abductions of United Nations and humanitarian personnel. In this context, the Council recalls the relevant principles contained in the Convention on the Safety of United Nations and Associated Personnel of 9 December 1994 and the statement by its President of 9 February 2000. It calls upon the parties to refrain from any actions that could increase tensions on the ground and to ensure the safety of Mission personnel.

The Council welcomes the contribution that the Mission and the collective peacekeeping force of the Commonwealth of Independent States continue to make in stabilizing the situation in the conflict zone, notes that the working relationship between the Mission and the collective peacekeeping force has remained close, and stresses the importance of continuing and increasing active cooperation and coordination between them in the performance of their respective mandates. It calls on the parties to observe their obligations to prevent acts that violate the Agreement on a Ceasefire and Separation of Forces, signed in Moscow on 14 May 1994, and could pose a threat to the life and security of personnel of the Mission, the collective peacekeeping force and other international personnel.

Communications. On 13 November [S/2000/1100], Georgia said that, on 8 and 9 November, the Abkhaz "military forces" reportedly conducted training exercises in the restricted weapon zone, employing heavy armaments and firing a number of missiles. The Abkhaz side impeded the international observers deployed in the conflict zone from surveying the restricted weapon zone and ignored their requests to meet with the "commanders of the units" participating in the exercises. During the military manoeuvres, the airspace of the territory was also closed. The Abkhaz side deliberately violated commitments undertaken in the 1994 Moscow Agreement [YUN 1994, p. 583], and the inaction of the CIS peacekeeping force was also alarming. The Georgian side condemned the exercises and called on the Abkhaz side to refrain from actions that undermined the results achieved in the process of conflict resolution.

On 7 December [S/2000/1163], Georgia protested the participation by the so-called "Ministers for Foreign Affairs" of Abkhazia and Tskhinvali, the separatist regions of Georgia, in the meeting of representatives of self-proclaimed republics on the territory of the former Soviet Union (Tiraspol, Moldova, 20-22 November).

The Russian Federation, in a 7 December statement [S/2000/1176], said it had introduced on 5 December a visa regime with Georgia; the situation remained calm at the crossing points on the Russian-Georgian border. The Russian side was taking all measures to reduce to a minimum any inconvenience and planned to propose to the Georgian side in the near future the opening of additional consular offices in Georgia. It was amazed at attempts to depict the Russian Federation's legitimate actions to ensure its security as interference in Georgia's internal affairs. Georgian leaders knew that the Russian Federation continued to respect Georgia's sovereignty and territorial integrity and favoured the development of good-neighbourly relations. The introduction of the visa regime in no way affected those fundamental principles.

In a 19 December statement [S/2000/1221], Georgia said that it had responded with understanding to the introduction of the visa regime, since it assumed that it was to be in full compliance with the norms of international law. Its initial protests were caused by the Russian Federation's violation of that principle, which was manifested in a simplified border crossing on some segments of the State border between Georgia and the Russian Federation, in particular those of the Abkhazia, Georgia, and Tskhinvali regions. If the true sense of the introduction of a visa regime was to prevent the movement of terrorists and their accomplices, then intensified control over border crossings should have been introduced specifically for the area where separatist regimes predominated. There were serious grounds for presuming that the unilateral introduction of a simplified border crossing on some segments of the State border between Georgia and the Russian Federation was an attempt to support separatist regimes.

Further report of Secretary-General. In a later report [S/2001/59], the Secretary-General stated that the eleventh session of the Coordinating Council was held on 24 October in Tbilisi. The Council confirmed the reactivation of Working Group I on security matters, whose recommendations were adopted. The Working Group subsequently held its sixth session on 13 December in Sukhumi, at which it reached agreement on the need to modify slightly the boundaries of the restricted weapon zone to exclude exercise areas used by the Georgian and Abkhaz sides, which were situated on the fringes of the zone. It also considered a proposal that a joint information

centre be established to collect and provide information on criminal activity in the zone of conflict. After an interruption of almost three years, Working Group III on social and economic questions held its third session on 5 December in Tbilisi, at which agreement was reached on a number of specific projects aimed at rehabilitating the communications systems in the zone of conflict and adjacent areas. Efforts were continuing on the convening of Working Group II on refugees.

From 14 to 18 November, the Assistant Secretary-General for Peacekeeping Operations visited the UNOMIG area of operations to review its work and the ongoing peace efforts. Under the aegis of the United Nations, a joint assessment mission, including OSCE, UNHCR, UNDP and the Council of Europe, was carried out in the Gali district between 20 and 24 November to evaluate conditions for the safe, secure and dignified return of refugees and displaced persons to the district. The mission, in its preliminary findings attached to the Secretary-General's report, recommended that the Special Representative explore the opening in Gali city of a branch office of the UN Human Rights Office; consider with the two sides how to improve law enforcement training and further integration of the local population in the law enforcement structures; seek broader cooperation between the law enforcement organs of both sides; and assist in finding a non-discriminatory solution to the question of the language of instruction in Gali district schools.

With regard to the situation on the ground, the Secretary-General reported that the most serious violation of the Moscow Agreement was an Abkhaz military exercise on 9 and 10 November at the training area near Ochamchira, involving the use of heavy weapons, during which UNIMOG and CIS peacekeepers were prohibited from flying over the area. In another violation, a detachment from the Abkhaz "armed forces" was deployed from 21 to 28 November in a village in the security zone. On 10 December, two UNOMIG vehicles, returning from a patrol in the lower Kodori Valley, were ambushed and two military observers abducted and moved to the upper part of the valley, which was under Georgian control. The officers were released on 13 December. The Special Representative reminded the Georgian side that no one had been brought to justice for previous deeds in the Kodori Valley and that climate of impunity could not be allowed to continue.

Financing

On 15 June [meeting 98], the General Assembly, having considered the Secretary-General's reports on UNOMIG's financial performance for the period 1 July 1998 to 30 June 1999 [A/54/721], the proposed budget for the Mission's maintenance for the period 1 July 2000 to 30 June 2001 [A/54/735] and ACABQ's comments and recommendations thereon [A/54/841 & Add.5], adopted without vote, on the recommendation of the Fifth Committee [A/54/902], **resolution 54/271** [agenda item 137].

Financing of the United Nations Observer Mission in Georgia

The General Assembly,

Having considered the reports of the Secretary-General on the financing of the United Nations Observer Mission in Georgia and the related reports of the Advisory Committee on Administrative and Budgetary Questions,

Recalling Security Council resolution 854(1993) of 6 August 1993, by which the Council approved the deployment of an advance team of up to ten United Nations military observers for a period of three months and the incorporation of the advance team into a United Nations observer mission if such a mission was formally established by the Council,

Recalling also Security Council resolution 858(1993) of 24 August 1993, by which the Council decided to establish the United Nations Observer Mission in Georgia, and the subsequent resolutions by which the Council extended the mandate of the Observer Mission, the latest of which was resolution 1287(2000) of 31 January 2000,

Recalling further its decision 48/475 A of 23 December 1993 on the financing of the Observer Mission and its subsequent resolutions and decisions thereon, the latest of which was resolution 53/232 of 8 June 1999,

Reaffirming that the costs of the Observer Mission are expenses of the Organization to be borne by Member States in accordance with Article 17, paragraph 2, of the Charter of the United Nations,

Recalling its previous decisions regarding the fact that, in order to meet the expenditures caused by the Observer Mission, a different procedure is required from that applied to meet expenditures of the regular budget of the United Nations,

Taking into account the fact that the economically more developed countries are in a position to make relatively larger contributions and that the economically less developed countries have a relatively limited capacity to contribute towards such an operation,

Bearing in mind the special responsibilities of the States permanent members of the Security Council, as indicated in General Assembly resolution 1874(S-IV) of 27 June 1963, in the financing of such operations,

Noting with appreciation that voluntary contributions have been made to the Observer Mission,

Mindful of the fact that it is essential to provide the Observer Mission with the necessary financial resources to enable it to fulfil its responsibilities under the relevant resolutions of the Security Council,

1. *Takes note* of the status of contributions to the United Nations Observer Mission in Georgia as at 30 April 2000, including the contributions outstanding in the amount of 11.6 million United States dollars, representing 10 per cent of the total assessed contributions

from the inception of the Observer Mission to the period ending 30 June 2000, notes that some 20 per cent of the Member States have paid their assessed contributions in full, and urges all other Member States concerned, in particular those in arrears, to ensure payment of their outstanding assessed contributions;

2. *Expresses its appreciation* to those Member States which have paid their assessed contributions in full;

3. *Urges* all other Member States to make every possible effort to ensure payment of their assessed contributions to the Observer Mission in full and on time;

4. *Expresses concern* at the delay experienced by the Secretary-General in deploying and providing adequate resources to some recent peacekeeping missions, in particular those in Africa;

5. *Emphasizes* that all future and existing peacekeeping missions shall be given equal and non-discriminatory treatment in respect of financial and administrative arrangements;

6. *Also emphasizes* that all peacekeeping missions shall be provided with adequate resources for the effective and efficient discharge of their respective mandates;

7. *Requests* the Secretary-General to make the fullest possible use of facilities and equipment at the United Nations Logistics Base at Brindisi, Italy, in order to minimize the costs of procurement for the Observer Mission, and for this purpose requests the Secretary-General to speed up the implementation of the asset management system at all peacekeeping missions in accordance with General Assembly resolution 52/1 A of 15 October 1997;

8. *Endorses* the conclusions and recommendations contained in the report of the Advisory Committee on Administrative and Budgetary Questions, and requests the Secretary-General to ensure their full implementation;

9. *Requests* the Secretary-General to take all necessary action to ensure that the Observer Mission is administered with a maximum of efficiency and economy;

10. *Also requests* the Secretary-General, in order to reduce the cost of employing General Service staff, to continue efforts to recruit local staff for the Observer Mission against General Service posts, commensurate with the requirements of the Mission;

11. *Decides,* as an ad hoc arrangement, to apportion the additional amount of 290,200 dollars gross (485,200 dollars net) already appropriated by the General Assembly in its resolution 53/232 in respect of the period ending 30 June 1998 among Member States in accordance with the composition of groups set out in paragraphs 3 and 4 of General Assembly resolution 43/232 of 1 March 1989, as adjusted by the Assembly in its resolutions 44/192 B of 21 December 1989, 45/269 of 27 August 1991, 46/198 A of 20 December 1991, 47/218 A of 23 December 1992, 49/249 A of 20 July 1995, 49/249 B of 14 September 1995, 50/224 of 11 April 1996, 51/218 A to C of 18 December 1996 and 52/230 of 31 March 1998 and its decisions 48/472 A of 23 December 1993, 50/451 B of 23 December 1995 and 54/456 to 54/458 of 23 December 1999, and taking into account the scale of assessments for the year 1998, as set out in its resolution 52/215 A of 22 December 1997;

12. *Decides also* that, in accordance with the provisions of its resolution 973(X) of 15 December 1955, the apportionment among Member States, as provided for in paragraph 11 above, shall take into consideration the decrease in their respective share in the Tax Equalization Fund of the estimated staff assessment income of 195,000 dollars approved for the Observer Mission for the period ending 30 June 1998;

13. *Decides further* to appropriate the amount of 1,076,720 dollars gross (1,073,320 dollars net) for the maintenance of the Observer Mission in respect of the period ending 30 June 1999, in addition to the amount of 19,439,280 dollars gross (18,452,580 dollars net) already appropriated under the terms of General Assembly resolution 52/242 of 26 June 1998 and inclusive of the amount of 1,076,720 dollars gross (1,073,320 dollars net) from the amount of 1,534,400 dollars gross (1,426,600 dollars net) authorized by the Advisory Committee under the terms of section IV of Assembly resolution 49/233 A of 23 December 1994;

14. *Decides,* as an ad hoc arrangement, to apportion among Member States the additional amount of 1,076,720 dollars gross (1,073,320 dollars net) for the maintenance of the Observer Mission in respect of the period ending 30 June 1999, in accordance with the scheme set out in the present resolution and taking into account the scale of assessments for the year 1999, as set out in its resolutions 52/215 A and 54/237 A of 23 December 1999;

15. *Decides also* that, in accordance with the provisions of its resolution 973(X), there shall be set off against the apportionment among Member States, as provided for in paragraph 14 above, their respective share in the Tax Equalization Fund of the estimated additional staff assessment income of 3,400 dollars approved for the Observer Mission in respect of the period ending 30 June 1999;

16. *Decides further* to appropriate to the Special Account for the United Nations Observer Mission in Georgia the amount of 30,048,197 dollars gross (28,295,699 dollars net) for the maintenance of the Observer Mission for the period from 1 July 2000 to 30 June 2001, inclusive of the amount of 1,425,532 dollars gross (1,206,299 dollars net) for the support account for peacekeeping operations and the amount of 222,865 dollars gross (198,300 dollars net) for the United Nations Logistics Base at Brindisi;

17. *Decides,* as an ad hoc arrangement, to apportion among Member States the amount of 2,504,016 dollars gross (2,357,975 dollars net) for the period from 1 to 31 July 2000 in accordance with the scheme set out in the present resolution and taking into account the scale of assessments for the year 2000, as set out in its resolutions 52/215 A and 54/237 A;

18. *Decides also* that, in accordance with the provisions of its resolution 973(X), there shall be set off against the apportionment among Member States, as provided for in paragraph 17 above, their respective share in the Tax Equalization Fund of the estimated staff assessment income of 146,041 dollars approved for the Observer Mission for the period from 1 to 31 July 2000;

19. *Decides further,* as an ad hoc arrangement, to apportion among Member States the amount of 27,544,181 dollars gross (25,937,724 dollars net) for the period from 1 August 2000 to 30 June 2001, at a monthly rate of 2,504,016 dollars gross (2,357,975 dollars net), in accordance with the scheme set out in the present resolution and taking into account the scale of assessments for the year 2000, as set out in its resolutions 52/215 A and 54/237 A, and for the year 2001, subject to the decision of the Security Council to extend the mandate of the Observer Mission beyond 31 July 2000;

20. *Decides* that, in accordance with the provisions of its resolution 973(X), there shall be set off against the apportionment among Member States, as provided for in paragraph 19 above, their respective share in the Tax Equalization Fund of the estimated staff assessment income of 1,606,457 dollars approved for the Observer Mission for the period from 1 August 2000 to 30 June 2001;

21. *Emphasizes* that no peacekeeping mission shall be financed by borrowing funds from other active peacekeeping missions;

22. *Encourages* the Secretary-General to continue to take additional measures to ensure the safety and security of all personnel under the auspices of the United Nations participating in the Observer Mission;

23. *Invites* voluntary contributions to the Observer Mission in cash and in the form of services and supplies acceptable to the Secretary-General, to be administered, as appropriate, in accordance with the procedure and practices established by the General Assembly;

24. *Decides* to include in the provisional agenda of its fifty-fifth session the item entitled "Financing of the United Nations Observer Mission in Georgia".

In December [A/55/682], the Secretary-General submitted the UNOMIG financial performance report for the period 1 July 1999 to 30 June 2000.

The Assembly, on 23 December, decided that the item on UNOMIG financing would remain for consideration at the resumed fifty-fifth (2001) session (**decision 55/458**) and that the item would be considered by the Fifth Committee at that session (**decision 55/455**).

Armenia-Azerbaijan

In 2000, Armenia and Azerbaijan made no progress in efforts to reach a settlement of the armed conflict between them, which had erupted in 1992 [YUN 1992, p. 388] over the Nagorny Karabakh region in Azerbaijan, despite the efforts of the Minsk Group of OSCE (France, the Russian Federation and the United States) to advance the peace process. Both sides addressed communications to the Secretary-General during the year regarding developments in the conflict. Nagorny Karabakh's communications were transmitted by Armenia.

Communications. In a 15 February statement [S/2000/138], Azerbaijan referred to press reports indicating that the "prime minister" of the so-called "Nagorny Karabakh republic" began a "business visit" on 11 February to several Western European countries, at the invitation of businessmen from Hungary, Italy and Switzerland. The visit was reportedly to encourage European companies to invest in Nagorny Karabakh's economy, present a programme for the development of the agro-industrial complex and mining industry and the promotion of tourism in Nagorny Karabakh, and to establish joint enterprises.

Azerbaijan stated that Armenia, which seized power in the Nagorny Karabakh region of Azerbaijan, and the illegitimate regime that it established some 10 years previously continued to dictate their will to the international community. Armenia had recently been attempting to strengthen its military occupation through economic means by announcing a Programme for the Rehabilitation and Development of Nagorny Karabakh and was seeking, through that "programme", to attract investors to the occupied territories.

Azerbaijan was interested in normalizing life in the region and in its comprehensive economic development but that would be possible only after a just and consistent settlement of the conflict between Armenia and Azerbaijan and complete agreement on peace. The World Bank, the EU and other influential international organizations had already expressed their readiness to invest in the region, but only after the consequences of the occupation had been eliminated and peace achieved.

Over the preceding year, there had been some prospects for a peaceful settlement. The Presidents of Azerbaijan and Armenia had held talks with a view to solving the problem through peaceful means and had decided at their last meeting in Davos, Switzerland, to continue those talks. In the circumstances, any cooperation with the illegitimate regime and the conduct in the Nagorny Karabakh region of any activities that contravened the laws of Azerbaijan would be a serious blow to the fragile peace that was being observed.

Azerbaijan viewed the establishment by any country or international economic and financial organizations of military, political or economic ties with the Nagorny Karabakh region of Azerbaijan before a peace agreement was reached as a violation of inter-State, intergovernmental and other bilateral agreements with Azerbaijan, and interference in its internal affairs. It called on all States and organizations not to undertake such measures.

In response, the "Ministry of Foreign Affairs of the Nagorno-Karabagh Republic", in a 15 March statement [S/2000/221] submitted to the Secretary-General by Armenia, said that Azerbaijan's 15 February statement could negatively influence the peacemaking process. Efforts had been made in the "Nagorno-Karabagh Republic" over the last year towards the maintenance of stability in the society, the consolidation of law and order and the creation of favourable conditions for the development of entrepreneurship, which had stimulated the serious interest of foreign financial and industrial circles. It was significant that no State, except Armenia and the United States, assisted the "Nagorno-Karabagh Republic" in resolving humanitarian problems.

Azerbaijan had for two years rejected the peace proposals put forward by the OSCE Minsk Group Co-Chairmen, which were the most acceptable compromise for settling the conflict. Azerbaijan's irreconcilable position disclosed that its real intentions were to isolate Nagorny Karabakh and preserve and aggravate the economic and humanitarian crisis with the aim of displacing the autochthonal Armenian population from the region.

The Nagorny Karabakh leadership wished to reassure international organizations and States interested in the quickest possible final settlement of the Karabakh conflict of its adherence to the principle of a political settlement and stressed that the constructive mood of its people was indisputable evidence of its aspirations for peace and stability.

On 17 April [S/2000/329], Azerbaijan, referring to the Nagorny Karabakh statement, reiterated that there was no such administrative-territorial entity as the "Nagorny Karabakh Republic". There was a Nagorny Karabakh region of the Republic of Azerbaijan, which was occupied by the armed forces of Armenia. The statement circulated by Armenia was misleading and showed that country's true intent to legitimize the occupation of an integral part of its country. None of the Security Council resolutions reaffirming Azerbaijan's sovereignty and territorial integrity and demanding the immediate, complete and unconditional withdrawal of the occupying forces had been implemented, which allowed the Armenian aggressors to feel comfortable and to continue their annexationist policy.

Azerbaijan informed the Secretary-General, in a 20 April statement [S/2000/371], of Armenian media reports that elections to the "Parliament" of the so-called "Nagorny Karabakh Republic" were scheduled for 18 June. The holding of those elections was completely illegal and a flagrant violation of international law. Azerbaijan would not recognize the results and it was certain that States and parliaments throughout the world would take the same position. It called on all international organizations, the United Nations, the Parliamentary Assembly of the Council of Europe, and States members of the OSCE Minsk Group and its Co-Chairmen to condemn the illegal elections and to use all possible means to avert that political farce and to refuse to recognize the results. Similar sentiments were expressed in a statement by the head of the Azerbaijan community of Nagorny Karabakh to the Co-Chairmen of the OSCE Minsk Group, transmitted to the Secretary-General by Azerbaijan in the same communication. The head of that community described the elections as nothing more than an artificial freezing of the forthcoming talks within the OSCE Minsk process. Those sentiments were echoed by Azerbaijan's Milli Mejlis (Parliament) in a 28 April statement [S/2000/390], in which it said that the holding of the illegal "elections" would have an adverse effect on the course of the peace talks and called on the Armenian community of Nagorny Karabakh to renounce those actions and put an end to the violations of Azerbaijan's Constitution. It called on the Armenian side to take a constructive position in the peace process and to refrain from actions that could complicate the OSCE Minsk Group talks.

On 2 May [S/2000/375 & Corr.1], Azerbaijan expressed concern over the command staff training carried out from 27 to 30 March between Russian Federation military personnel and the national army of Armenia at the Marshal Bagramyan military training ground in the Armavir district. It was also following with concern the situation arising out of the signing on 1 March of a protocol transferring the Russian military base from Kafan to Gyumri for a period of 25 years and the signing on 16 March of a treaty between Armenia and the Russian Federation on joint military responsibilities in anti-aircraft defence and on the military training of Armenian forces on Russian military training grounds. Azerbaijan called on the Russian Federation to suspend plans to expand and strengthen the military alliance between itself and Armenia until the conflict between Armenia and Azerbaijan over Nagorny Karabakh had been settled and to reconsider its position on that question.

On 9 October [S/2000/978], Azerbaijan characterized as a gross violation of its national legislation and of the norms and principles of international law, reports of the signing by Armenia and the "Nagorny Karabakh" occupation regime of a memorandum on mutual cooperation in various areas and on additions to the laws of that regime relating to "local self-government" and "administrative-territorial units". Azerbaijan did not recognize the legality of such decisions and

rejected actions that consolidated the consequences of Armenia's aggression against it.

In a 19 October statement [S/2000/1034], transmitted by Armenia, the "Nagorny Karabakh Ministry of Foreign Affairs" said that Azerbaijan's claims in its 9 October statement were gross interference in its internal affairs. It reminded Azerbaijan that, even in the Soviet period, questions regarding the administrative and territorial division of Nagorny Karabakh fell within the competence of its authorities. It drew the international community's attention to the fact that the actions of Azerbaijani officials ran counter to its stated readiness to establish peace and stability in the region and its policy aimed at disrupting the socio-economic development of Nagorny Karabakh was openly hostile.

Cyprus

United Nations efforts to achieve a resolution of the Cyprus problem gained momentum in 2000 as five rounds of the proximity talks, initiated by the Secretary-General in 1999 [YUN 1999, p. 389], were held and further sessions were scheduled. The talks were aimed at preparing the ground for meaningful negotiations leading to a comprehensive settlement of the Cyprus question. Increasing contacts between Greek and Turkish Cypriots, which were an important factor in improving the political climate on the island, continued during the year. That climate was further enhanced by the May decision of the Turkish Cypriot side to lift onerous measures affecting visits to Greek Cypriots and Maronites living in the north.

The United Nations Peacekeeping Force in Cyprus (UNFICYP) continued to assist in the restoration of normal conditions and in humanitarian functions. The Security Council twice extended its mandate, the second time until 15 June 2001.

By **decision 54/493** of 5 September, the General Assembly included in the draft agenda of its fifty-fifth session the item entitled "Question of Cyprus". On 23 December (**decision 55/458**), it decided that the item would remain for consideration during its resumed fifty-fifth (2001) session and that it would be considered by the Fifth Committee at that session (**decision 55/455**).

Incidents

Communications. Throughout 2000, the Secretary-General received numerous letters from the Government of Cyprus and from the Turkish Cypriot authorities containing charges and countercharges, protests and accusations and explanations of position. The letters from the "Turkish Republic of Northern Cyprus" were transmitted by Turkey.

In communications dated between 3 January and 18 December, Cyprus protested violations of its airspace and unauthorized intrusions into the flight information region of Nicosia by military aircraft of the Turkish Air Force and Turkey transmitted letters from the "Representative of the Turkish Republic of Northern Cyprus" refuting those allegations, stating that the flights took place within its sovereign airspace [A/54/698-S/2000/4, A/54/728-S/2000/66, A/54/743-S/2000/100, A/54/790-S/2000/204, A/54/816-S/2000/263, A/54/852-S/2000/370, A/54/892-S/2000/539, A/54/911-S/2000/551, A/54/937-S/2000/666, A/54/951-S/2000/755, A/54/955-S/2000/763, A/54/963-S/2000/813, A/55/454-S/2000/959, A/55/503-S/2000/1004, A/55/527-S/2000/1041, A/55/693-S/2000/1193, A/55/701-S/2000/1210].

In other letters communicated to the Secretary-General between 9 February and 7 December, the "Turkish Republic of Northern Cyprus" drew attention to a paper submitted by the "Greek Cypriot administration" and statements made by its representatives in several UN bodies, which the "Turkish Republic of Northern Cyprus" described as containing false allegations and misrepresentations of the Cyprus situation [A/54/747-E/2000/6, A/55/445-S/2000/940, A/55/539-S/2000/1064, A/55/627-S/2000/1094, A/55/646-S/2000/1115, A/55/672-S/2000/1161]. Also submitted to the Secretary-General was a letter from Cyprus [A/55/524-S/2000/1035] on its application for membership in the EU and the response of Turkey [A/55/547-S/2000/1075], which also transmitted the views of the "Turkish Republic of Northern Cyprus" on the subject.

Good offices mission

Proximity talks

Pursuant to Security Council resolution 1250(1999) [YUN 1999, p. 388], proximity talks continued in 2000 with the two Cyprus parties, led by Cyprus President Glafcos Clerides and Turkish Cypriot Leader Rauf R. Denktash, to prepare the ground for meaningful negotiations leading to a comprehensive settlement. The talks were facilitated on the Secretary-General's behalf by his Special Adviser on Cyprus, Alvaro de Soto. The first round of talks was held in 1999 [ibid., p. 389]. During 2000, five rounds of proximity talks took place: the second from 31 January to 8 February; the third from 5 to 12 July and the fourth from 24 July to 4 August, all in Geneva; the fifth was held

from 12 to 26 September in New York; and the sixth from 1 to 10 November, again in Geneva.

During informal consultations of the Security Council on 15 February [A/55/2], the Special Adviser briefed Council members on the results of the second round of proximity talks. Following those consultations, the Council President, in a statement to the press on behalf of the Council, said that negotiation of a comprehensive settlement in Cyprus was a matter that the Council continued to follow with the closest interest; it had stated repeatedly that the status quo in Cyprus was unacceptable. Council members commended the continuing commitment shown by the parties to the talks and the fact that they had been conducted in a positive atmosphere and without preconditions. They encouraged all concerned to continue their efforts towards a comprehensive settlement of the Cyprus question and looked forward to the resumption of the talks in New York on 23 May.

In May [S/2000/496], the Secretary-General reported that, following the second round of proximity talks, his Special Adviser met separately with the two leaders and visited Athens, Greece, and Ankara, Turkey, in connection with those talks. However, the third round of talks, scheduled for 23 May in New York, had to be put off for health reasons. Both leaders accepted the Secretary-General's invitation to meet in Geneva starting 5 July.

On 10 May [S/2000/431], the Secretary-General informed the Council President that, to give priority to the good offices effort under way, he had asked his Special Adviser to remain in New York for the time being.

On 13 July [A/54/938-S/2000/688], the "Turkish Republic of Northern Cyprus", in a letter transmitted to the Secretary-General by Turkey, complained that, while the third round of talks was being held in Geneva, Greek Cypriot rearmament activities continued, casting a shadow on the spirit and purpose of the talks, which were aimed at preparing the ground for meaningful negotiations to a peaceful settlement. It also drew attention to a 27 February statement by the Cypriot Defence Minister to the effect that the current process of proximity talks and the expected third round would not have an effect on their rearmament efforts. The "Turkish Republic of Northern Cyprus" believed that the Council should take note of those serious developments, which did not augur well for the success of the proximity talks, and urge the Greek side to stop its arming frenzy.

Cyprus, on 20 July [A/54/944-S/2000/711], recalled that the Special Envoy, on 12 July, the last day of the third round of the proximity talks, had reiterated an appeal on the Secretary-General's behalf to the two sides to play down the tone, size and content of the official rhetoric during the period between the last and the forthcoming round of talks. Cyprus drew attention to provocative actions by the Turkish side, which ignored the appeal, including violations of the airspace of the Republic of Cyprus and reinforcement of the Turkish occupying forces. Cyprus protested those actions and expressed the hope that the necessary positive attitude would be shown by Turkey so that the proximity talks in progress, as well as other efforts for finding a just and viable solution to the Cyprus problem, would not be adversely affected.

On 28 November [S/2000/1188], the Secretary-General, reporting to the Council on his good offices mission in Cyprus, stated that, in furtherance of the mission, which included consultations in the region, as well as with various capitals, the Special Adviser had been assisted by a small team of Secretariat and UNFICYP staff, a legal adviser and international consultants. The Secretary-General expected the mission to continue from January until at least June 2001, at which point resource requirements in support of that mandate could be incorporated into UNFICYP's budget, on which he would report separately. On 14 December [S/2000/1189], the Council took note of the contents of the Secretary-General's letter and his expectations regarding the continuation of his mission of good offices in Cyprus.

Goodwill measures

As indicated during the second round of proximity talks, the "Turkish Cypriot Republic of Northern Cyprus", in a 19 May communication [A/54/878-S/2000/462] transmitted by Turkey, announced a series of unilateral goodwill measures aimed at further enhancing the living standards of the Greek Cypriots and Maronites residing in the "Turkish Republic of Northern Cyprus". Those measures included reducing crossing fees; issuing permits for visits to close relatives for a reasonable period of time, with the possibility of extension for family, health or other extenuating circumstances; removal of the age restriction applied to Greek Cypriot students wishing to visit their families and who had yet to fulfil military service; the granting of permission to the spouse of a Greek Cypriot or Maronite residing in the North who married a Greek Cypriot or Maronite or any other third party national residing outside the "Turkish Republic of Northern Cyprus" to take up residency in the "Turkish Republic of Northen Cyprus"; ensuring the freedom of movement throughout the territory of the "Turk-

ish Republic of Northern Cyprus", on a par with its citizens; and allowing any Maronite or Greek Cypriot residing in the "Turkish Cypriot Republic of Northern Cyprus" to apply for citizenship.

UNFICYP

The United Nations Peacekeeping Force in Cyprus, established by Security Council resolution 186(1964) [YUN 1964, p. 165], continued in 2000 to monitor the ceasefire lines between the Turkish and Turkish Cypriot forces on the northern side and the Cypriot National Guard on the southern side; to maintain the military status quo and prevent a recurrence of fighting; and to undertake humanitarian and economic activities. In the absence of a formal ceasefire agreement, the military status quo, as recorded by UNFICYP in 1974, remained the standard by which the Force judged whether changes constituted violations of the status quo.

UNFICYP, under the overall authority of the Deputy Special Representative and Chief of Mission, continued to keep the area between the cesaefire lines, known as the buffer zone, under constant surveillance through a system of observation posts, and through air, vehicle and foot patrols.

During the year, Alvaro de Soto continued as the Secretary-General's Special Adviser on Cyprus. On 10 May [S/2000/431], the Secretary-General informed the Council of his intention to appoint Zbigniew Wlosowicz (Poland) as Acting Special Representative and Chief of Mission of UNFICYP as of 1 June; he would succeed James Holger, whose term came to an end on 31 May.

As at 31 December, UNFICYP, under the command of Major-General Victory Rana (Nepal), comprised 1,213 troops and 33 civilian police. The military personnel were from Argentina, Austria, Canada, Finland, Hungary, Ireland, the Netherlands, Slovenia and the United Kingdom. The Argentine contingent included soldiers from Brazil, Paraguay and Uruguay. The civilian police were from Australia and Ireland. The civilian component comprised 42 international and 147 local staff.

Activities

Report of Secretary-General (May). The Secretary-General, in his report covering developments and UNFICYP activities from 30 November 1999 to 31 May 2000 [S/2000/496 & Corr.1], said that the situation along the ceasefire lines remained stable, with a significant reduction in the overall number of incidents. Threats against UN soldiers on patrol remained a concern. Local restrictions by the National Guard on the freedom of movement of the United Nations in the area of the Kokkina pocket and Kato Pyrgos at the western end of the buffer zone had impeded access to a number of UN observation posts. Efforts continued to have those restrictions removed. Air violations of the UN buffer zone increased. In addition, National Guard personnel in military vehicles were observed in the zone on 4 April.

Contacts between Greek Cypriots and Turkish Cypriots on the island increased, most of them occurring with UNFICYP's help. For the first time in several years, two meetings took place between political party representatives from both sides. UNFICYP continued to support civilian activities in the buffer zone, including farming, industry and recreational activities. Regular contacts and cooperation continued with both sides to resolve questions concerning movement and access, shared resources, such as water, and proposed works in the buffer zone. UNFICYP also maintained liaison with the police on both sides and carried out humanitarian tasks. On 5 May, the Turkish Cypriot authorities announced measures to ease restrictions affecting movement between the two sides, which had been instituted in February 1998 [YUN 1998, p. 413]. UNFICYP helped to arrange several large pilgrimages of Greek Cypriots and Turkish Cypriots to their respective holy places.

After an interruption of more than three years, the Committee on Missing Persons in Cyprus met from November 1999 to January 2000 and discussed the possibility of resuming its investigative work.

The Secretary-General recommended that the Security Council extend UNFICYP's mandate for a further period of six months, until 15 December 2000.

SECURITY COUNCIL ACTION

On 14 June [meeting 4155], the Security Council unanimously adopted **resolution 1303(2000)**. The draft [S/2000/549] was prepared in consultations among Council members.

The Security Council,

Welcoming the report of the Secretary-General of 26 May 2000 on the United Nations operation in Cyprus, in particular the call to the parties to assess and address the humanitarian issue of missing persons with due urgency and seriousness,

Noting that the Government of Cyprus has agreed that in view of the prevailing conditions in the island it is necessary to keep the United Nations Peacekeeping Force in Cyprus beyond 15 June 2000,

Welcoming and encouraging efforts by the United Nations to sensitize peacekeeping personnel in the prevention and control of HIV/AIDS and other communicable diseases in all its peacekeeping operations,

1. *Reaffirms* all its relevant resolutions on Cyprus, in particular resolutions 1251(1999) of 29 June 1999 and 1283(1999) of 15 December 1999;

2. *Decides* to extend the mandate of the United Nations Peacekeeping Force in Cyprus for a further period ending 15 December 2000;

3. *Requests* the Secretary-General to submit a report by 1 December 2000 on the implementation of the present resolution;

4. *Decides* to remain actively seized of the matter.

Report of Secretary-General (December). In December [S/2000/1138], the Secretary-General reported no significant change in the military situation along the ceasefire lines. However, air violations of the buffer zone by Turkish military aircraft rose to 47, compared with 7 in the same period the previous year. In addition, on 22 October, Turkish military aircraft reportedly came within a little over three nautical miles offshore from the Paphos air base, causing a National Guard air defence element to lock on its radar. Air violations of the buffer zone by military and civilian aircraft from the other side decreased to 10, compared with 18 in the same period the previous year. On 30 June, the Turkish Cypriot authorities and Turkish forces instituted a number of measures against UNFICYP, the main one being the closure of all crossings of the Turkish forces' ceasefire line, except for the one at the former Ledra Palace Hotel in Nicosia. In conjunction with existing restrictions on its movement in the north, that measure would have completely isolated UN troops in three camps in the north and at Strovilia. Three additional crossing points were subsequently reopened to allow access to the camps from the south. The next day, the Turkish forces/Turkish Cypriot security forces moved forward of their ceasefire line at Strovilia and had since controlled UNFICYP's access to its post there. Since October, the Turkish forces had prevented UNFICYP from moving along the Famagusta-Dherinia road. The impact of those restrictions was significant: UNFICYP's operational effectiveness had suffered; response times had increased; and command, logistic and administrative movements had lengthened significantly. The Turkish Cypriot authorities also imposed mandatory additional insurance for UN vehicles, which had to be obtained from insurance companies in the north, and announced that they would require UNFICYP to pay for electricity and other utilities for its bases in the north.

UNFICYP continued to monitor the status quo in the fenced area of Varosha, which continued to change. There were frequent crossings of the maritime security line, the seaward extension of the median of the buffer zone, by Greek Cypriot fishing and tourist boats offshore from Dherinia, occasionally triggering warning shots from the Turkish forces. In the north-west, the Turkish forces' supply boats on their way to and from Kokkina crossed the line on a daily basis.

Contacts between Greek Cypriots and Turkish Cypriots continued to increase, including at large public events, such as the Festival of Mutual Understanding organized by political parties in September and the United Nations Day celebration in October. Other initiatives ranged from meetings of politicians, youth workshops and a summer school to forums for business representatives, media and teachers. Regarding the easing of certain restrictions on movement between the two sides, which the Turkish Cypriot authorities announced in May, although crossing fees had been reduced, Greek Cypriots seeking to extend their visits to relatives in the Karpas beyond three days had encountered obstacles. The Turkish Cypriot authorities had also been less forthcoming than in the past with respect to crossings arranged by UNFICYP for humanitarian reasons.

UNFICYP assisted various projects in the buffer zone with the cooperation of the local authorities from both sides. Progress was achieved on water supply matters, urban renovation work, use of farmland and roadways and other issues.

The Secretary-General recommended that UNFICYP's mandate be extended until 15 June 2001.

SECURITY COUNCIL ACTION

On 13 December [meeting 4246], the Security Council unanimously adopted **resolution 1331 (2000)**. The draft [S/2000/1177] was prepared in consultations among Council members.

The Security Council,

Welcoming the report of the Secretary-General of 1 December 2000 on the United Nations operation in Cyprus, in particular the call to the parties to assess and address the humanitarian issue of missing persons with due urgency and seriousness,

Noting that the Government of Cyprus has agreed that in view of the prevailing conditions in the island it is necessary to keep the United Nations Peacekeeping Force in Cyprus beyond 15 December 2000,

Welcoming and encouraging efforts by the United Nations to sensitize peacekeeping personnel in the prevention and control of HIV/AIDS and other communicable diseases in all its peacekeeping operations,

1. *Reaffirms* all its relevant resolutions on Cyprus, in particular resolution 1251(1999) of 29 June 1999 and subsequent resolutions;

2. *Decides* to extend the mandate of the United Nations Peacekeeping Force in Cyprus for a further period ending 15 June 2001;

3. *Requests* the Secretary-General to submit a report, by 1 June 2001, on the implementation of the present resolution;

4. *Urges* the Turkish Cypriot side and Turkish forces to rescind the restrictions imposed on 30 June 2000 on the operations of the United Nations Peacekeeping Force in Cyprus, and to restore the military status quo ante at Strovilia;

5. *Decides* to remain actively seized of the matter.

On 28 December [A/55/717-S/2000/1241], Turkey transmitted to the Secretary-General the views of Mr. Denktas regarding resolution 1331(2000). He complained that, while the resolution mentioned the consent of the "so-called" Government of Cyprus to the extension of UNFICYP's mandate, no mention was made of the consent of the Turkish Cypriot party. Mr. Denktas reminded the Secretary-General that UNFICYP's deployment in the territory of the "Turkish Republic of Northern Cyprus" was subject to the approval of its authorities and the continuation of UNFICYP's operations could be possible only with the cooperation of the authorities and on the basis of a properly authorized framework. It again stressed the necessity of concluding an agreement to put its relations with UNFICYP on a sound basis. Mr. Denktas added that the resolution contradicted the principle of the political equality of the two parties, as well as the political, legal and practical realities prevailing in Cyprus.

Financing

On 15 June [meeting 98], the General Assembly, having considered the Secretary-General's report on UNFICYP's financial performance for the period 1 July 1998 to 30 June 1999 [A/54/704], the proposed budget for UNFICYP's maintenance for the period 1 July 2000 to 30 June 2001 [A/54/729] and ACABQ's comments and recommendations [A/54/841 & Add.4], adopted, on the recommendation of the Fifth Committee [A/54/901], **resolution 54/270** without vote [agenda item 136].

Financing of the United Nations Peacekeeping Force in Cyprus

The General Assembly,

Having considered the reports of the Secretary-General on the financing of the United Nations Peacekeeping Force in Cyprus and the related reports of the Advisory Committee on Administrative and Budgetary Questions,

Recalling Security Council resolution 186(1964) of 4 March 1964, by which the Council established the United Nations Peacekeeping Force in Cyprus, and the subsequent resolutions by which the Council extended the mandate of the Force, the latest of which was resolution 1303(2000) of 14 June 2000,

Recalling also its resolution 53/231 of 8 June 1999 on the financing of the Force,

Reaffirming that the costs of the Force that are not covered by voluntary contributions are expenses of the Organization to be borne by Member States in accordance with Article 17, paragraph 2, of the Charter of the United Nations,

Noting with appreciation that voluntary contributions have been made to the Force by certain Governments,

Recalling its previous decisions regarding the fact that, in order to meet the expenditures caused by the Force, a different procedure is required from that applied to meet expenditures of the regular budget of the United Nations,

Taking into account the fact that the economically more developed countries are in a position to make relatively larger contributions and that the economically less developed countries have a relatively limited capacity to contribute towards such an operation,

Bearing in mind the special responsibilities of the States permanent members of the Security Council, as indicated in General Assembly resolution 1874(S-IV) of 27 June 1963, in the financing of such operations,

Expressing its appreciation to all those Member States and observer States which have made voluntary contributions to the Special Account established for the financing of the Force for the period prior to 16 June 1993,

Noting that voluntary contributions were insufficient to cover all the costs of the Force, including those incurred by troop-contributing Governments prior to 16 June 1993, and regretting the absence of an adequate response to appeals for voluntary contributions, including that contained in the letter dated 17 May 1994 from the Secretary-General to all Member States,

Mindful of the fact that it is essential to provide the Force with the necessary financial resources to enable it to fulfil its responsibilities under the relevant resolutions of the Security Council,

1. *Takes note* of the status of contributions to the United Nations Peacekeeping Force in Cyprus as at 30 April 2000, including the contributions outstanding in the amount of 17.7 million United States dollars, representing some 11.2 per cent of the total assessed contributions from 16 June 1993 to the period ending 15 June 2000, notes that some 22 per cent of the Member States have paid their assessed contributions in full, and urges all other Member States concerned, in particular those in arrears, to ensure payment of their outstanding assessed contributions;

2. *Expresses concern* about the financial situation with regard to peacekeeping activities, in particular as regards the reimbursements to troop contributors that bear additional burdens owing to overdue payments by Member States of their assessments;

3. *Expresses its appreciation* to those Member States which have paid their assessed contributions in full;

4. *Urges* all other Member States to make every possible effort to ensure payment of their assessed contributions to the Force in full and on time;

5. *Expresses concern* at the delay experienced by the Secretary-General in deploying and providing adequate resources to some recent peacekeeping missions, in particular those in Africa;

6. *Emphasizes* that all future and existing peacekeeping missions shall be given equal and non-discriminatory treatment in respect of financial and administrative arrangements;

7. *Also emphasizes* that all peacekeeping missions shall be provided with adequate resources for the effective and efficient discharge of their respective mandates;

8. *Requests* the Secretary-General to make the fullest possible use of facilities and equipment at the United Nations Logistics Base at Brindisi, Italy, in order to minimize the costs of procurement for the Force, and for this purpose requests the Secretary-General to speed up the implementation of the asset management system at all peacekeeping missions in accordance with General Assembly resolution 52/1 A of 15 October 1997;

9. *Endorses* the conclusions and recommendations contained in the report of the Advisory Committee on Administrative and Budgetary Questions, and requests the Secretary-General to ensure their full implementation;

10. *Requests* the Secretary-General to take all necessary action to ensure that the Force is administered with a maximum of efficiency and economy;

11. *Also requests* the Secretary-General, in order to reduce the cost of employing General Service staff, to continue efforts to recruit local staff for the Force against General Service posts, commensurate with the requirements of the Force;

12. *Decides* to appropriate to the Special Account for the United Nations Peacekeeping Force in Cyprus the amount of 43,422,065 dollars gross (41,404,128 dollars net) for the maintenance of the Force for the period from 1 July 2000 to 30 June 2001, inclusive of the amount of 2,060,180 dollars gross (1,743,344 dollars net) for the support account for peacekeeping operations, and the amount of 322,085 dollars gross (286,584 dollars net) for the United Nations Logistics Base;

13. *Decides also*, as an ad hoc arrangement, taking into consideration the funding through voluntary contributions of one third of the cost of the Force, equivalent to 13,801,375 dollars, by the Government of Cyprus and the annual pledge of 6.5 million dollars from the Government of Greece, to apportion among Member States the amount of 23,120,690 dollars gross (21,102,753 dollars net) for the period from 1 July 2000 to 30 June 2001, at a monthly rate of 1,926,724 dollars gross (1,758,563 dollars net), in accordance with the composition of groups set out in paragraphs 3 and 4 of General Assembly resolution 43/232 of 1 March 1989, as adjusted by the Assembly in its resolutions 44/192 B of 21 December 1989, 45/269 of 27 August 1991, 46/198 A of 20 December 1991, 47/218 A of 23 December 1992, 49/249 A of 20 July 1995, 49/249 B of 14 September 1995, 50/224 of 11 April 1996, 51/218 A to C of 18 December 1996 and 52/230 of 31 March 1998 and its decisions 48/472 A of 23 December 1993, 50/451 B of 23 December 1995 and 54/456 to 54/458 of 23 December 1999, and taking into account the scale of assessments for the year 2000, as set out in its resolutions 52/215 A of 22 December 1997 and 54/237 A of 23 December 1999, and for the year 2001, subject to the decision of the Security Council to extend the mandate of the Force;

14. *Decides further* that, in accordance with the provisions of its resolution 973(X) of 15 December 1955, there shall be set off against the apportionment among Member States, as provided for in paragraph 13 above, their respective share in the Tax Equalization Fund of the estimated staff assessment income of 2,017,937 dollars approved for the Force for the period from 1 July 2000 to 30 June 2001;

15. *Decides* that, for Member States that have fulfilled their financial obligations to the Force, there

shall be set off against the apportionment, as provided for in paragraph 13 above, their respective share of the unencumbered balance of 374,000 dollars gross (421,700 dollars net) in respect of the period from 1 July 1998 to 30 June 1999;

16. *Decides also* that, for Member States that have not fulfilled their financial obligations to the Force, their share of the unencumbered balance of 374,000 dollars gross (421,700 dollars net) in respect of the period from 1 July 1998 to 30 June 1999 shall be set off against their outstanding obligations;

17. *Decides further* to continue to maintain as separate the account established for the Force for the period prior to 16 June 1993, invites Member States to make voluntary contributions to that account, and requests the Secretary-General to continue his efforts in appealing for voluntary contributions to the account;

18. *Emphasizes* that no peacekeeping mission shall be financed by borrowing funds from other active peacekeeping missions;

19. *Encourages* the Secretary-General to continue to take additional measures to ensure the safety and security of all personnel under the auspices of the United Nations participating in the Force;

20. *Invites* voluntary contributions to the Force in cash and in the form of services and supplies acceptable to the Secretary-General, to be administered, as appropriate, in accordance with the procedure and practices established by the General Assembly;

21. *Decides* to include in the provisional agenda of its fifty-fifth session the item entitled "Financing of the United Nations Peacekeeping Force in Cyprus".

On 23 December, the Assembly decided that the item on UNFICYP's financing would remain for consideration at the resumed fifty-fifth (2001) session (**decision 55/458**) and that the Fifth Committee would continue consideration of the item at that session (**decision 55/455**).

Other issues

Cooperation with OSCE

In response to General Assembly resolution 54/117 [YUN 1999, p. 394], the Secretary-General submitted a June report [A/55/98], describing cooperation between the United Nations and the Organization for Security and Cooperation in Europe (OSCE).

During the year, a number of meetings took place between UN and OSCE officials in New York, Geneva and Vienna. Of particular note was the ninth high-level meeting of the United Nations-OSCE-Council of Europe tripartite process of informal consultations (Geneva, 24-25 February), which discussed peace and stability in South-Eastern Europe. The meeting was preceded by a target-oriented tripartite meeting on "Law enforcement, in particular the police: op-

erations in South-Eastern Europe". Such meetings demonstrated the continued relevance of the process of improving the complementarity of activities undertaken by participating organizations. The two organizations also continued to practise a division of labour based on their comparative advantages. UNDP's cooperation with OSCE, particularly with its Office for Democratic Institutions and Human Rights (ODIHR) and with the High Commissioner on National Minorities (HCNM), included a continuous exchange of information, publications and coordination of activities and organization of events, such as the workshop for ombudsmen and human rights institutions in Almaty, Kazakhstan. Other mutual activities included projects in human rights protection institutions, gender issues, civil society and the rule of law; joint assistance in the drafting of a law on ombudsman institutions in Central Asia; and coordination of assistance to institutions in Albania, Estonia and Georgia. OSCE and UNDP also provided support for the holding of elections. The Economic Commission for Europe (ECE) and OSCE member Governments had given a strong mandate to their respective organizations to foster cooperation in view of the challenges they both faced with regard to economic post-conflict reconstruction and the implementation of the Stability Pact in South-Eastern Europe [YUN 1999, p. 398]. The two organizations had begun to give more attention to economic and environmental factors and their security implications. The relationship between UNHCR and OSCE had developed into a comprehensive strategic partnership, focusing on the prevention of mass displacement, the recognition of the critical linkage between displacement and security and the need to address the human dimension of conflict resolution. Cooperation at headquarters level included consultations on operational design and policy development. However, the field-level UNHCR-OSCE partnership needed to be continuously refined and focused to minimize duplication while maximizing synergies.

The United Nations Children's Fund (UNICEF) and OSCE had a number of cooperative efforts under way in the Kosovo province of FRY, including the implementation of the UNICEF juvenile justice project and a number of complementary juvenile justice activities. The World Food Programme also maintained mutually beneficial cooperation with OSCE in Kosovo. In Albania, UNICEF and OSCE collaborated extensively on institution-building and on strengthening the rights of the child. The Office of the United Nations High Commissioner for Human Rights also maintained constructive contacts with OSCE through its field offices in Bosnia and Herzegovina, Croatia and Kosovo, consulting on a wide range of human rights issues. The bulk of cooperation between the Office for the Coordination of Humanitarian Affairs and OSCE took place in the context of UN operations in Georgia, Tajikistan and, to a more limited extent, the Russian Federation. They also cooperated on issues of mutual interest, such as attracting donor assistance to the region and regular liaison with de facto authorities in situ, aimed at facilitating the creation of humanitarian space within which agencies could operate.

GENERAL ASSEMBLY ACTION

On 19 December [meeting 86], the General Assembly adopted **resolution 55/179** [draft: A/55/L.69 & Add.1, amended by A/55/L.70], by recorded vote (147-1-0) [agenda item 29].

Cooperation between the United Nations and the Organization for Security and Cooperation in Europe

The General Assembly,

Recalling the framework for cooperation and coordination between the United Nations and the Conference on Security and Cooperation in Europe, signed on 26 May 1993, as well as its resolutions on cooperation between the two organizations,

Recalling also the principles embodied in the Helsinki Final Act and in the declaration at the 1992 Helsinki Summit by the heads of State or Government of the participating States of the Conference on Security and Cooperation in Europe of their understanding that the Conference is a regional arrangement in the sense of Chapter VIII of the Charter of the United Nations and as such provides an important link between European and global security,

Acknowledging the increasing contribution of the Organization for Security and Cooperation in Europe to the establishment and maintenance of international peace and security in its region through activities in early warning and preventive diplomacy, including through the activities of the High Commissioner on National Minorities, crisis management and post-conflict rehabilitation, as well as arms control and disarmament,

Recalling the Charter for European Security adopted at the Summit in Istanbul in November 1999, which reaffirms the Organization for Security and Cooperation in Europe as a primary organization for the peaceful settlement of disputes within its region and as a key instrument for early warning, conflict prevention, crisis management and post-conflict rehabilitation,

Recalling also the special ties between the Organization for Security and Cooperation in Europe and the Mediterranean Partners for Cooperation, as well as between that organization and the Asian Partners for Cooperation, Japan and the Republic of Korea, which have been further enhanced in 2000,

Underlining the continued importance of enhanced cooperation and coordination between the United Nations and the Organization for Security and Cooperation in Europe,

1. *Welcomes* the report of the Secretary-General;

2. *Notes with appreciation* the further improvement of cooperation and coordination between the United Nations and its agencies and the Organization for Security and Cooperation in Europe, including at the level of activities in the field;

3. *Welcomes,* in this context, the participation of the Deputy Secretary-General in the meeting of the Ministerial Council of the Organization for Security and Cooperation in Europe, which was held in Vienna in November 2000, and the participation of high-level United Nations representatives in meetings of the Organization for Security and Cooperation in Europe;

4. *Encourages* further efforts of the Organization for Security and Cooperation in Europe to foster security and stability in its region through early warning, conflict prevention, crisis management and post-conflict rehabilitation, as well as through continued promotion of democracy, the rule of law, human rights and fundamental freedoms;

5. *Also encourages* the intention of the Organization for Security and Cooperation in Europe to create an environment in which the dignity, well-being, safety and human rights of all people are ensured;

6. *Welcomes* the documents of the meeting of the Ministerial Council held in Vienna on enhancing the efforts of the Organization for Security and Cooperation in Europe to combat trafficking in human beings and on the illicit trafficking in and the destabilizing accumulation and uncontrolled spread of small arms and light weapons;

7. *Also welcomes* the continued close cooperation between the Organization for Security and Cooperation in Europe and the United Nations High Commissioner for Refugees and the United Nations High Commissioner for Human Rights;

8. *Further welcomes* the admission of the Federal Republic of Yugoslavia into the Organization for Security and Cooperation in Europe on 10 November 2000 after the vivid demonstration of the commitment of the people of the Federal Republic of Yugoslavia to democracy, and commends the Federal Republic of Yugoslavia for its commitment to the principles and standards of the Organization for Security and Cooperation in Europe and its readiness to cooperate with European institutions and with its neighbours offering new perspectives for peace and prosperity in South-Eastern Europe;

9. *Notes with appreciation* the readiness of the Organization for Security and Cooperation in Europe to assist the Yugoslav people to this end and the preparedness of the Yugoslav Government to have a presence of the Organization for Security and Cooperation in Europe in the country, and welcomes the steps undertaken by the Government to ensure an early amnesty for all political prisoners;

10. *Expresses its appreciation* for the contribution by the Organization for Security and Cooperation in Europe to the United Nations Interim Administration Mission in Kosovo in implementing Security Council resolution 1244(1999) of 10 June 1999, including the establishment, pursuant to that resolution, of the Organization for Security and Cooperation in Europe Mission in Kosovo as an essential part of the broader United Nations Interim Administration Mission in Kosovo, responsible for institution-building, including the training of a new Kosovo police service, judicial

personnel and civil administrators, the development of free media, democratization and governance, the organization and supervision of elections and the monitoring, protection and promotion of human rights, in cooperation with, inter alia, the United Nations High Commissioner for Human Rights, and stresses the commitment of the United Nations and the Organization for Security and Cooperation in Europe to the full implementation of resolution 1244(1999);

11. *Commends* the Organization for Security and Cooperation in Europe for its substantial role in the preparation and organization of the local elections in Kosovo in view of the consolidation of stability and prosperity in Kosovo on the basis of substantial autonomy, respecting the sovereignty and territorial integrity of the Federal Republic of Yugoslavia, pending a final settlement in accordance with resolution 1244(1999);

12. *Welcomes* the role of the Organization for Security and Cooperation in Europe in the General Framework Agreement for Peace in Bosnia and Herzegovina, initialled in Dayton, United States of America, on 21 November 1995, in particular in the fields of human rights and judicial and police reform, and commends the Organization for Security and Cooperation in Europe for its substantial role in the preparation and organization of elections in Bosnia and Herzegovina;

13. *Underlines* the importance of regional cooperation as a means of fostering good-neighbourly relations, stability and economic development, welcomes the implementation of the Stability Pact for South-Eastern Europe under the auspices of the Organization for Security and Cooperation in Europe as an important long-term and comprehensive initiative to promote good-neighbourly relations, stability and economic development, and also welcomes the commitment of participating States of the Organization for Security and Cooperation in Europe to contribute further to the goals of the Stability Pact;

14. *Welcomes* the work of the Organization for Security and Cooperation in Europe in assisting in the implementation of articles II and IV of annex 1-B to the General Framework Agreement and its contribution to the creation of a framework for peace and stability in South-Eastern Europe;

15. *Fully supports* the activities of the Organization for Security and Cooperation in Europe to achieve a peaceful solution to the conflict in and around the Nagorny-Karabakh region of the Republic of Azerbaijan, and welcomes cooperation between the United Nations and the Organization for Security and Cooperation in Europe in this regard;

16. *Welcomes,* in view of lack of progress in the peace process of the Nagorny-Karabakh conflict, the intention of the Co-Chairmen of the Minsk Group of the Organization for Security and Cooperation in Europe and the Personal Representative of the Chairperson-in-Office of the Organization for Security and Cooperation in Europe to intensify their efforts in fulfilling their mandates and to further an atmosphere of mutual trust between all parties to the conflict, also welcomes the direct dialogue between the Presidents of the Republic of Azerbaijan and the Republic of Armenia, and encourages them to continue their efforts in working with the Co-Chairmen of the Minsk Group to expedite agreements that would serve as a basis for the resumption of full-scale negotiations within the Group;

17. *Stresses* the importance of all parties doing their utmost to ensure that the ceasefire along the line of contact is strictly observed until a comprehensive agreement resolving the conflict is signed, and commends the efforts taken by the Co-Chairmen of the Minsk Group since the Istanbul Summit to diminish tensions in the region and to prepare, in coordination with the United Nations and other international agencies, support measures that would facilitate the implementation of a political settlement;

18. *Welcomes* efforts undertaken in 2000 to strengthen cooperation between the Organization for Security and Cooperation in Europe and the United Nations in Georgia, and with regard to Abkhazia, Georgia, welcomes the completion of the joint assessment mission to the Gali district in November 2000 to evaluate conditions for the return of refugees and internally displaced persons to their former places of permanent residence;

19. *Fully supports* the efforts of the Organization for Security and Cooperation in Europe aimed at achieving a settlement of the problems in the Transdniestrian region of the Republic of Moldova, recalls the commitment by the Russian Federation to complete the withdrawal of the Russian forces from the territory of the Republic of Moldova by the end of 2002, as agreed at the Istanbul Summit, and welcomes the willingness of the Organization for Security and Cooperation in Europe together with the Republic of Moldova to facilitate this process, within their respective abilities, by the agreed deadline;

20. *Welcomes* the establishment of enhanced dialogue between the Organization for Security and Cooperation in Europe and the Central Asian participating States and the readiness of that organization to contribute, inter alia, together with the United Nations, to strengthening cooperation in the region, as well as the commitment of that organization to promote democratic institutions and assist the Central Asian countries in addressing security issues, the problem of organized crime and economic and environmental concerns, and takes note in this respect of the international conference on enhancing security and stability in Central Asia, held in Tashkent on 19 and 20 October 2000, which was organized jointly by the Chair of the Organization for Security and Cooperation in Europe and the United Nations Office for Drug Control and Crime Prevention with the assistance of the Government of Uzbekistan;

21. *Also welcomes* the in-depth discussions on cooperation of the United Nations, the European Union and the Organization for Security and Cooperation in Europe with regard to interaction and complementarity of rapid response mechanisms at the meeting of the Ministerial Council held in Vienna, and requests the Secretary-General to continue exploring with the Chairman-in-Office and the Secretary-General of the Organization for Security and Cooperation in Europe possibilities for further enhancement of cooperation, information exchange and coordination between the United Nations and the Organization for Security and Cooperation in Europe;

22. *Further welcomes* the fact that Thailand has become a new Partner for Cooperation of the Organization for Security and Cooperation in Europe;

23. *Decides* to include in the provisional agenda of its fifty-sixth session the item entitled "Cooperation

between the United Nations and the Organization for Security and Cooperation in Europe", and requests the Secretary-General to submit to the General Assembly at its fifty-sixth session a report on cooperation between the United Nations and the Organization for Security and Cooperation in Europe in implementation of the present resolution.

RECORDED VOTE ON RESOLUTION 55/179:

In favour: Afghanistan, Algeria, Andorra, Angola, Argentina, Australia, Austria, Azerbaijan, Bahamas, Bahrain, Bangladesh, Barbados, Belgium, Belize, Benin, Bhutan, Bolivia, Bosnia and Herzegovina, Botswana, Brazil, Brunei Darussalam, Bulgaria, Burkina Faso, Cambodia, Cameroon, Canada, Cape Verde, Chad, Chile, China, Colombia, Congo, Costa Rica, Croatia, Cyprus, Czech Republic, Denmark, Djibouti, Dominican Republic, Ecuador, Egypt, El Salvador, Eritrea, Estonia, Ethiopia, Fiji, Finland, France, Gabon, Gambia, Georgia, Germany, Ghana, Greece, Grenada, Guatemala, Guyana, Haiti, Honduras, Hungary, Iceland, India, Indonesia, Iran, Ireland, Israel, Italy, Jamaica, Japan, Jordan, Kazakhstan, Kenya, Kuwait, Kyrgyzstan, Latvia, Lebanon, Libyan Arab Jamahiriya, Liechtenstein, Lithuania, Luxembourg, Madagascar, Malawi, Malaysia, Maldives, Malta, Mauritania, Mauritius, Mexico, Monaco, Mongolia, Morocco, Myanmar, Nepal, Netherlands, New Zealand, Nicaragua, Nigeria, Norway, Oman, Pakistan, Panama, Papua New Guinea, Paraguay, Peru, Philippines, Poland, Portugal, Qatar, Republic of Korea, Republic of Moldova, Romania, Russian Federation, Saint Lucia, San Marino, Saudi Arabia, Senegal, Sierra Leone, Singapore, Slovakia, Slovenia, South Africa, Spain, Sri Lanka, Sudan, Suriname, Swaziland, Sweden, Syrian Arab Republic, Thailand, The former Yugoslav Republic of Macedonia, Togo, Tonga, Trinidad and Tobago, Tunisia, Turkey, Uganda, Ukraine, United Arab Emirates, United Kingdom, United Republic of Tanzania, United States, Uruguay, Uzbekistan, Venezuela, Yemen, Yugoslavia, Zambia.

Against: Armenia.

Abstaining: None.

Before the adoption of the resolution, a recorded vote (62-1-65) was taken on an amendment, adding paragraph 15, introduced by Azerbaijan [A/55/L.70], stating specifically that Nagorny Karabakh was a region of Azerbaijan.

Cooperation with the Council of Europe

On 20 October [meeting 38], the General Assembly adopted **resolution 55/3** [draft: A/55/L.8 & Add.1] without vote [agenda item 170].

Cooperation between the United Nations and the Council of Europe

The General Assembly,

Recalling the Agreement between the Council of Europe and the Secretariat of the United Nations signed on 15 December 1951 and the Arrangement on Cooperation and Liaison between the secretariats of the United Nations and the Council of Europe of 19 November 1971,

Acknowledging the contribution of the Council of Europe to the protection and strengthening of democracy, human rights and fundamental freedoms and the rule of law on the European continent, including its activities against racism and intolerance, the promotion of gender equality, social development and a common cultural heritage,

Acknowledging also that, with its significant expertise in the field of human rights, democratic institutions and the rule of law, the Council of Europe is also promoting the prevention of conflict and long-term postconflict peace-building through political and institutional reform,

Stressing the importance of adherence to the standards and principles of the Council of Europe and its

contribution to the solution of conflicts throughout the whole of Europe,

1. *Notes with appreciation* the further improvement of cooperation and coordination between the United Nations and its agencies and the Council of Europe, both at the level of headquarters and in the field;

2. *Welcomes* the increasingly close cooperation between the Council of Europe, the Office of the United Nations High Commissioner for Refugees and the Office of the United Nations High Commissioner for Human Rights;

3. *Welcomes also* the close and fruitful cooperation between the Council of Europe and the International Law Commission of the United Nations, and the contribution of the Council of Europe to the United Nations Decade of International Law;

4. *Welcomes further* the contributions of the Council of Europe to the twenty-third and twenty-fourth special sessions of the General Assembly entitled, respectively, "Women 2000: gender equality, development and peace for the twenty-first century", which was held in New York from 5 to 9 June 2000, and "World Summit for Social Development and beyond: achieving social development for all in a globalizing world", which was held in Geneva from 26 to 30 June 2000;

5. *Expresses its appreciation* to the Council of Europe for its organization of the European Conference against Racism, which was held in Strasbourg, France, from 11 to 13 October 2000, in preparation for the World Conference against Racism, Racial Discrimination, Xenophobia and Related Intolerance, which will be held in Durban, South Africa, in 2001;

6. *Welcomes* the participation of the Council of Europe in the implementation of Security Council resolution 1244(1999) of 10 June 1999, in its cooperation with the United Nations Interim Administration Mission in Kosovo, notably with regard to the reform of the judiciary, the protection of minorities, property rights, registration and local democracy, as well as the observation of the electoral process in Kosovo, as requested by the United Nations;

7. *Welcomes also* the readiness of the Council of Europe to continue to fulfil the role assigned to it, under the General Framework Agreement for Peace in Bosnia and Herzegovina, with regard to the protection and promotion of human rights as well as in the field of judicial reform;

8. *Welcomes further* the major contribution of the Council of Europe to the Stability Pact for South-Eastern Europe, launched at the initiative of the European Union, and to the development of regional projects to support its aims;

9. *Welcomes* the active role of the Council of Europe in the tripartite meetings between the United Nations, the Organization for Security and Cooperation in Europe and the Council of Europe;

10. *Requests* the Secretary-General to continue exploring, with the Chairman of the Committee of Ministers and the Secretary-General of the Council of Europe, possibilities for further enhancement of cooperation, information exchange and coordination between the United Nations and the Council of Europe;

11. *Decides* to include in the provisional agenda of its fifty-sixth session the item entitled "Cooperation between the United Nations and the Council of Europe", and requests the Secretary-General to submit to the

General Assembly at its fifty-sixth session a report on co-operation between the United Nations and the Council of Europe in implementation of the present resolution.

Strengthening of security and cooperation in the Mediterranean region

In response to General Assembly resolution 54/59 [YUN 1999, p. 396], the Secretary-General submitted replies from Algeria, Jordan, Portugal, on behalf of the EU, Qatar and the Russian Federation [A/55/254] to his note verbale requesting their views on ways to strengthen security and cooperation in the Mediterranean region.

GENERAL ASSEMBLY ACTION

On 20 November [meeting 69], the General Assembly, on the recommendation of the First (Disarmament and International Security) Committee [A/55/564], adopted **resolution 55/38** without vote [agenda item 78].

Strengthening of security and cooperation in the Mediterranean region

The General Assembly,

Recalling its previous resolutions on the subject, including resolution 54/59 of 1 December 1999,

Reaffirming the primary role of the Mediterranean countries in strengthening and promoting peace, security and cooperation in the Mediterranean region,

Bearing in mind all the previous declarations and commitments, as well as all the initiatives taken by the riparian countries at the recent summits, ministerial meetings and various forums concerning the question of the Mediterranean region,

Recognizing the indivisible character of security in the Mediterranean and that the enhancement of cooperation among Mediterranean countries with a view to promoting the economic and social development of all peoples of the region will contribute significantly to stability, peace and security in the region,

Recognizing also the efforts made so far and the determination of the Mediterranean countries to intensify the process of dialogue and consultations with a view to resolving the problems existing in the Mediterranean region and to eliminating the causes of tension and the consequent threat to peace and security, and their growing awareness of the need for further joint efforts to strengthen economic, social, cultural and environmental cooperation in the region,

Recognizing further that prospects for closer Euro-Mediterranean cooperation in all spheres can be enhanced by positive developments worldwide, in particular in Europe, in the Maghreb and in the Middle East,

Reaffirming the responsibility of all States to contribute to the stability and prosperity of the Mediterranean region and their commitment to respecting the purposes and principles of the Charter of the United Nations, as well as the provisions of the Declaration on Principles of International Law concerning Friendly Relations and Cooperation among States in accordance with the Charter of the United Nations,

Noting the peace negotiations in the Middle East, which should be of a comprehensive nature and repre-sent an appropriate framework for the peaceful settlement of contentious issues in the region,

Expressing its concern at the persistent tension and continuing military activities in parts of the Mediterranean that hinder efforts to strengthen security and cooperation in the region,

Taking note of the report of the Secretary-General,

1. *Reaffirms* that security in the Mediterranean is closely linked to European security as well as to international peace and security;

2. *Expresses its satisfaction* at the continuing efforts by Mediterranean countries to contribute actively to the elimination of all causes of tension in the region and to the promotion of just and lasting solutions to the persistent problems of the region through peaceful means, thus ensuring the withdrawal of foreign forces of occupation and respecting the sovereignty, independence and territorial integrity of all countries of the Mediterranean and the right of peoples to self-determination, and therefore calls for full adherence to the principles of non-interference, non-intervention, non-use of force or threat of use of force and the inadmissibility of the acquisition of territory by force, in accordance with the Charter and the relevant resolutions of the United Nations;

3. *Commends* the Mediterranean countries for their efforts in meeting common challenges through coordinated overall responses, based on a spirit of multilateral partnership, towards the general objective of turning the Mediterranean basin into an area of dialogue, exchanges and cooperation, guaranteeing peace, stability and prosperity, and encourages them to strengthen such efforts through, inter alia, a lasting multilateral and action-oriented cooperative dialogue among States of the region;

4. *Recognizes* that the elimination of the economic and social disparities in levels of development and other obstacles, as well as respect and greater understanding among cultures, in the Mediterranean area will contribute to enhancing peace, security and cooperation among Mediterranean countries through the existing forums;

5. *Calls upon* all States of the Mediterranean region that have not yet done so to adhere to all the multilaterally negotiated legal instruments related to the field of disarmament and non-proliferation, thus creating the necessary conditions for strengthening peace and cooperation in the region;

6. *Encourages* all States of the region to favour the necessary conditions for strengthening the confidence-building measures among them by promoting genuine openness and transparency on all military matters, by participating, inter alia, in the United Nations system for the standardized reporting of military expenditures and by providing accurate data and information to the United Nations Register of Conventional Arms;

7. *Encourages* the Mediterranean countries to strengthen further their cooperation in combating terrorism in all its forms and manifestations, international crime and illicit arms transfers, and illicit drug production, consumption and trafficking, which pose a serious threat to peace, security and stability in the region and therefore to the improvement of the current political, economic and social situation and which jeopardize friendly relations among States, hinder the development of international cooperation and result

in the destruction of human rights, fundamental free-doms and the democratic basis of pluralistic society;

8. *Requests* the Secretary-General to submit a report on means to strengthen security and cooperation in the Mediterranean region;

9. *Decides* to include in the provisional agenda of its fifty-sixth session the item entitled "Strengthening of security and cooperation in the Mediterranean region".

Stability and development in South-Eastern Europe

On 12 February [A/54/755-S/2000/125], the Third Meeting of Heads of State and Government of South-East European Countries (Bucharest, Ro-mania) adopted the Bucharest Declaration, in which they recognized their countries' responsi-bility to work within the international commu-nity to develop a shared strategy for stability and growth in the region and to cooperate with each other and the international community to imple-ment that strategy. They expressed their appre-ciation to the EU for launching the Stability Pact for South-Eastern Europe [YUN 1999, p. 398] and appreciated the first practical steps taken to im-plement it. They looked forward to the Regional Financing Conference to give strong impetus to the Pact's implementation and reiterated their commitment to carrying out the reform pro-cesses endorsed by the Stability Pact.

The heads of State and Government signed a Charter on Good-Neighbourly Relations, Stabil-ity, Security and Cooperation in South-Eastern Europe [A/54/781], emphasizing their commit-ment to economic and democratic reforms. The Charter constituted a Code of Conduct for rela-tions among their countries and an action pro-gramme for future cooperation.

The Ministers for Foreign Affairs of the coun-tries participating in the South-East European Cooperation Process (SEECP), at their annual meeting (Ohrid, FYROM, 14 July) [A/55/165], un-derlined the need for accelerated and full imple-mentation of the Stability Pact for South-Eastern Europe as a prerequisite for political stability and wider democratization in the region. They wel-comed the progress in the realization of initia-tives and projects within the Pact, especially the Investment Compact and the Anti-Corruption Initiative.

The G-8 countries, in a statement on regional issues, adopted at the Kyushu-Okinawa Summit Meeting (Okinawa, Japan, 21-23 July) [A/55/220-S/2000/759], expressed their commitment to sup-porting peace, stability, foreign and national in-vestment and development in South-East Europe and welcomed the coordination provided by the Stability Pact, which was contributing to en-hanced regional political and economic coopera-

tion in South-Eastern Europe. They also sup-ported the projects being implemented within the framework of the Stability Pact by the World Bank, the European Commission, the European Investment Bank and the European Bank for Re-construction and Development.

Further support for the Stability Pact for South-Eastern Europe was expressed in the Za-greb Declaration [A/55/406-S/2000/892], adopted by the Parliamentary Summit of the countries participating in the Pact (Zagreb, Croatia, 11-13 September).

The Foreign Ministers of the States participat-ing in SEECP, meeting on 12 September in New York [A/C.1/55/4], agreed that the activities of the Process were in accordance with the commit-ments contained in the Millennium Declaration (see p. 49) for intensifying cooperation between the United Nations and regional agencies, insti-tutions and organizations to strengthen interna-tional peace and security.

On 25 October [A/55/522-S/2000/1028], the heads of State and Government of the countries partici-pating in SEECP, at an informal summit in Skopje, FYROM, discussed the ongoing process of the Sta-bility Pact for South-Eastern Europe and stated their strong commitment to its early implemen-tation and to the undertaking of joint activities. They believed that SEECP represented a solid ba-sis for strengthening cooperation in the region and expressed their commitment that it would as-sume a more important role in the future devel-opment of the region.

GENERAL ASSEMBLY ACTION

On 20 November [meeting 69], the General As-sembly, on the recommendation of the First Committee [A/55/552], adopted **resolution 55/27** without vote [agenda items 66 & 67].

Maintenance of international security— good-neighbourliness, stability and development in South-Eastern Europe

The General Assembly,

Recalling the purposes and principles of the Charter of the United Nations and the Final Act of the Confer-ence on Security and Cooperation in Europe, signed at Helsinki on 1 August 1975,

Recalling also the United Nations Millennium Decla-ration,

Welcoming the democratic changes in the Federal Re-public of Yugoslavia and their positive effects on the peace, stability and development of South-Eastern Europe,

Recalling its resolutions 48/84 B of 16 December 1993, 50/80 B of 12 December 1995, 51/55 of 10 De-cember 1996, 52/48 of 9 December 1997, 53/71 of 4 De-cember 1998 and 54/62 of 1 December 1999,

Recalling also the Stability Pact for South-Eastern Europe initiated by the European Union, adopted at Cologne, Germany, on 10 June 1999 and endorsed at the Sarajevo Summit of 30 July 1999, and stressing the crucial importance of its implementation,

Recalling further the Sarajevo Summit Declaration, in which the participants affirm their collective and individual readiness to give concrete meaning to the Stability Pact for South-Eastern Europe by promoting political and economic reforms, development and enhanced security in the region and also their commitment to make every effort to assist countries in the region in making speedy and measurable progress along this road,

Emphasizing the crucial importance of the full implementation of Security Council resolution 1244(1999) of 10 June 1999 on Kosovo, Federal Republic of Yugoslavia,

Noting the importance of the activities of the international organizations, such as the European Union, the Organization for Security and Cooperation in Europe, the Council of Europe, and the contribution of the Central European Initiative and the Black Sea Economic Cooperation for the implementation of the Stability Pact for South-Eastern Europe,

Noting also the importance of the Charter on Good-Neighbourly Relations, Stability, Security and Cooperation in South-Eastern Europe, signed by the States participating in the South-East European Cooperation Process at Bucharest on 12 February 2000, and the joint statement of the heads of State and Government adopted at Skopje on 25 October 2000,

Noting further the convening of the International Conference on War-Affected Children at Winnipeg, Canada, from 10 to 17 September 2000,

Emphasizing the importance of regional efforts in South-Eastern Europe on arms control, demining, disarmament and confidence-building measures, and concerned that, in spite of ongoing efforts, the illicit traffic in and circulation of small arms continue to persist,

Mindful of the importance of national and international activities by all relevant organizations aimed at the creation of peace, security, stability, democracy, cooperation, economic development, the observance of human rights and good-neighbourliness in South-Eastern Europe,

Affirming its determination that all nations should live together in peace with one another as good neighbours,

1. *Affirms* the urgency of consolidating South-Eastern Europe as a region of peace, security, stability, democracy, cooperation and economic development and for the promotion of good-neighbourliness and the observance of human rights, thus contributing to the maintenance of international peace and security and enhancing the prospects for sustained development and prosperity for all peoples in the region as an integral part of Europe;

2. *Calls upon* all participants in the Stability Pact for South-Eastern Europe, and all concerned international organizations, to support the efforts of South-Eastern European States to overcome the negative effects of the Kosovo crisis and other recent crises so as to enable them to pursue sustainable development and their integration into the European structures, and welcomes the results of the third meeting of the Working Table on Security Issues of the Stability Pact, held at Sofia on 4 and 5 October 2000;

3. *Encourages* all States to contribute to the full implementation of Security Council resolution 1244 (1999) on Kosovo, Federal Republic of Yugoslavia, and welcomes the efforts and supports the role of the United Nations Interim Administration Mission in Kosovo and the Kosovo Force in the implementation of their mandates under that resolution;

4. *Calls upon* all States, the relevant international organizations and competent organs of the United Nations to respect the principles of territorial integrity and sovereignty of all States and the inviolability of international borders, to continue to take measures in accordance with the Charter of the United Nations, as appropriate, to eliminate threats to international peace and security and to help to prevent conflicts which can lead to the violent disintegration of States;

5. *Stresses* the importance of good-neighbourliness and the development of friendly relations among States, and calls upon all States to resolve their disputes with other States by peaceful means, in accordance with the Charter of the United Nations;

6. *Urges* strengthening of the relations among the States of South-Eastern Europe on the basis of respect for international law and agreements, in accordance with the principles of good-neighbourliness and mutual respect;

7. *Stresses* the importance of regional efforts aimed at preventing conflicts that endanger the maintenance of international peace and security and, in this regard, notes with satisfaction the role of the Multinational Peace Force for South-Eastern Europe;

8. *Emphasizes* the importance of regional efforts in South-Eastern Europe for arms control, disarmament and confidence-building measures;

9. *Recognizes* the seriousness of the problem of anti-personnel mines in South-Eastern Europe and, in this context, welcomes the efforts of the international community in support of mine action and encourages States to join and support these efforts;

10. *Urges* all States to take effective measures against illicit traffic in and circulation of small arms and to help programmes and projects aimed at the safe destruction of surplus stocks of small arms and light weapons, and stresses the importance of closer cooperation among States, inter alia, in crime prevention, combating illicit trade of people, drug trafficking and money-laundering;

11. *Stresses* that closer engagement of the South-Eastern European States in furthering cooperation on the European continent will favourably influence the security, political and economic situation in the region, as well as good-neighbourly relations among the States;

12. *Calls upon* all States and the relevant international organizations to communicate to the Secretary-General their views on the subject of the present resolution;

13. *Decides* to include in the provisional agenda of its fifty-sixth session an item entitled "Maintenance of international security—good-neighbourliness, stability and development in South-Eastern Europe".

Chapter VI

Middle East

In 2000, the work of the United Nations in the Middle East was affected by two major events, one of which was positive—the complete withdrawal of Israeli forces from southern Lebanon in June. The other—the escalation of violence in the Occupied Palestinian Territory in late September—resulted in the breakdown of the peace process between Israel and the Palestine Liberation Organization (PLO). Despite that setback, the United Nations continued, through its peacekeeping operations, the good offices of the Secretary-General and programmes of economic, social and other forms of assistance, as well as active participation in multilateral negotiations, to support and promote peace and economic development in the region.

Throughout the year, the international community made strenuous efforts to break the stalemate in the Middle East peace process by building on the 1999 Sharm el-Sheikh (Egypt) Memorandum, signed by Israeli Prime Minister Ehud Barak and PLO Chairman Yasser Arafat. Although no comprehensive agreement between the two parties was reached at the July Middle East Peace Summit, held at Camp David, Maryland, under the auspices of United States President William J. Clinton, Prime Minister Barak and Chairman Arafat committed themselves to continue their efforts to conclude an agreement on permanent status issues.

The Palestinian intifada (uprising) erupted at the end of September following the visit of Israeli opposition leader Ariel Sharon to a holy Islamic site in the Old City of Jerusalem. In an effort to end the violence, high-level meetings took place in early October in Paris and Sharm el-Sheikh but no agreement was reached. In the face of the continuing crisis, President Clinton and President Hosni Mubarak of Egypt convened the Sharm el-Sheikh Middle East Peace Summit on 16 and 17 October, which produced understandings aimed at ending the confrontation and established a Fact-Finding Committee, chaired by former United States Senator George Mitchell, to investigate the causes of the violence. Nevertheless, the security situation deteriorated further at the end of the year, with hundreds of civilians, the majority Palestinians, either killed or injured.

Following the September uprising, the Security Council convened in a three-day emergency meeting. In a 7 October resolution, the Council called for the immediate cessation of violence and for Israel to abide by its obligations under the 1949 Geneva Convention relative to the Protection of Civilian Persons in Time of War (Fourth Geneva Convention). In December, a draft resolution, by which the Council would have expressed its determination to establish a UN observer force in the territories occupied by Israel, was not adopted as it did not obtain the required number of votes.

In October, the General Assembly resumed its tenth emergency special session, which first convened in 1997, to discuss the item "Illegal Israeli actions in the Occupied Palestinian Territory". It condemned the violence that erupted in late September and the excessive use of force by the Israeli forces against Palestinian civilians and, among other things, urged all parties concerned to implement the understandings reached at the Sharm el-Sheikh Summit.

In southern Lebanon, guns fell silent after more than two decades as the United Nations confirmed the withdrawal of Israeli troops from the area on 16 June 2000 in compliance with Security Council resolution 425(1978) [YUN 1978, p. 312]. An international boundary line between Israel and Lebanon, the so-called Blue Line, was established by the United Nations for the sole purpose of confirming the withdrawal. Although both parties undertook to respect that boundary, violations and attacks across the Blue Line occurred during the second half of the year. The Secretary-General visited regional leaders in June to discuss the situation. He also appointed Rolf G. Knuttson as his Personal Representative for southern Lebanon to coordinate UN activities in the area. The United Nations Interim Force in Lebanon (UNIFIL) pursued efforts to limit the conflict and protect inhabitants from its consequences and, following the Israeli withdrawal, was reinforced and redeployed in the vacated areas. Although the Lebanese Government re-established its effective authority in the area, Lebanese security forces did not operate close to the Blue Line, where control was left to the paramilitary group Hezbollah.

The mandates of UNIFIL and of the United Nations Disengagement Observer Force (UN-DOF) in the Golan Heights were extended twice during the year, and the United Nations Truce Supervision Organization (UNTSO) continued to assist both peacekeeping operations in their tasks.

The United Nations Relief and Works Agency for Palestine Refugees in the Near East (UNRWA), despite ongoing financial difficulties, continued to provide a wide-ranging programme of education, health, relief and social services to 3.7 million Palestinian refugees living both in and outside camps in the West Bank and the Gaza Strip, as well as in Jordan, Lebanon and the Syrian Arab Republic. Following the September escalation of violence, UNRWA launched an urgent appeal to fund a three-month contingency plan to buy food and medical supplies for Palestinian refugees.

During the year, the Special Committee to Investigate Israeli Practices Affecting the Human Rights of the Palestinian People and Other Arabs of the Occupied Territories reported to the Assembly on the situation in the West Bank, including East Jerusalem, the Gaza Strip and the Golan Heights. The Committee on the Exercise of the Inalienable Rights of the Palestinian People continued to mobilize international support for the Palestinians.

By **decision 55/431** of 14 December, the General Assembly deferred consideration of the agenda item "Armed Israeli aggression against the Iraqi nuclear installations and its grave consequences for the established international system concerning the peaceful use of nuclear energy, the non-proliferation of nuclear weapons and international peace and security" and included it in the provisional agenda of its fifty-sixth (2001) session. The item had been inscribed yearly on the Assembly's agenda since 1981, following the bombing by Israel of a nuclear research centre near Baghdad [YUN 1981, p. 275].

Peace process

Overall situation

During the first nine months of 2000, Israel and the PLO continued to implement the 1999 Sharm el-Sheikh Memorandum [YUN 1999, p. 401]. Actions included the further redeployment of Israeli troops from parts of the West Bank, an agreement on the release of Palestinian prisoners, the opening of a southern safe passage between the West Bank and the Gaza Strip and the resumption of negotiations on permanent status issues.

The resumed negotiations between Israel and the PLO took place in the United States in March/April at Bolling Air Force Base near Washington, D.C., and at the Middle East Peace Summit, held in July under the auspices of President William J. Clinton, at Camp David, Maryland. Although Israeli Prime Minister Ehud Barak and PLO Chairman Yasser Arafat failed to reach a comprehensive agreement, they committed themselves, in the trilateral statement made at the conclusion of the Summit, to continue their efforts to conclude an agreement on all permanent status issues as soon as possible.

The eruption of the Palestinian intifada (uprising) in protest over the visit of Israeli opposition leader Ariel Sharon, accompanied by Likud Knesset members and hundreds of security personnel and police, to the holy Islamic site of Al-Haram Al-Sharif (the Dome of the Rock) compound in the Old City of Jerusalem on 28 September marked the end of peace negotiations and the beginning of a spiral of violence, which had devastating effects on the security and economic situation of the Occupied Palestinian Territory.

In an effort to stop the violence, Chairman Arafat and Prime Minister Barak met in Paris on 4 October with United States Secretary of State Madeleine Albright, French President Jacques Chirac and the Secretary-General. A further meeting took place in Sharm el-Sheikh, Egypt, on 5 October but Prime Minister Barak did not attend. Following the adoption of a Security Council resolution on 7 October and in order to bring about an end to the crisis, President Clinton and Egyptian President Hosni Mubarak convened the Sharm el-Sheikh Middle East Peace Summit on 16 and 17 October, which was also attended by King Abdullah II of Jordan, Prime Minister Barak, Chairman Arafat, President Javier Solana of the European Union (EU) and the Secretary-General. The Summit produced understandings in three areas—security cooperation, establishment of a fact-finding committee and renewal of the peace process aimed at ending the confrontation and restoring calm in the region. The further escalation of violence following the Summit made the achievement of those objectives all but impossible, with the exception of the establishment in November of the Fact-Finding Committee, which was expected to report in 2001.

In a November report [A/55/639-S/2000/1113], the Secretary-General said that the quest for a lasting peace between Israel and the Palestinians reached a crucial stage at the Camp David Summit in July. Though an overall agreement was not reached, for the first time the most difficult issues were seriously addressed. However, following Mr. Sharon's visit to the Temple Mount/Al-Haram Al-Sharif in Jerusalem, protests and violence erupted in which more than 230 people were killed, the vast majority Palestinians. The crisis held the potential for further escalation with dangerous consequences for the entire Middle East. The Israelis and Palestinians had to live side by side with each other and had to reconcile their differences through dialogue and cooperation. The question was how to respond to the legitimate aspirations of the Palestinian people to personal dignity and national independence and to the legitimate security concerns of Israel.

In **resolution 55/55** of 1 December (see p. 440), the General Assembly noted the signing of the 1999 Sharm el-Sheikh Memorandum and continued to express its full support for the peace process, which began in Madrid in 1991 [YUN 1991, p. 221], the 1993 Declaration of Principles on Interim Self-Government Arrangements [YUN 1993, p. 521] and the 1995 Israeli-Palestinian Interim Agreement on the West Bank and the Gaza Strip [YUN 1995, p. 626]. However, the Assembly stressed its deep concern over the clashes between the Israeli forces and the Palestinian police in the Occupied Palestinian Territory since 28 September, which had resulted in a high number of deaths and injuries.

Committee on Palestinian Rights. In its annual report [A/55/35], the Committee on the Exercise of the Inalienable Rights of the Palestinian People (Committee on Palestinian Rights) expressed grave concern over the violent confrontations between Israeli security forces and Palestinians in the Old City of Jerusalem that had erupted on 28 September, and noted that excessive force had been used by the Israel Defence Forces (IDF) against the Palestinian protesters. The Committee reiterated that those events were a direct result of the policies and practices of the Israeli occupation and Israel's failure to respect its obligations under the Fourth Geneva Convention and the provisions of relevant Security Council and General Assembly resolutions. Israel's persistent refusal to live up to those principles, as well as the continued lack of progress in the peace negotiations, jeopardized the peace process and increased volatility in the region. The Committee viewed the understandings reached at Sharm el-Sheikh as a useful step towards halting the violence.

Occupied Palestinian Territory

Communications (16 March–7 September). On 16 March [A/54/799-S/2000/220], Israel informed the Secretary-General of anti-Israel and anti-Jewish incitement emanating from some Arab countries. The campaign did not refrain from advocating violence and the rhetoric had been unleashed by official organs, appearing in official and governmental media, including in countries party to peace negotiations with Israel.

Responding on 31 March [A/54/821-S/2000/276], the United Arab Emirates, as Chairman of the Arab Group for the month of March, said that Israel's statement deliberately overlooked the fact that the fundamental reason for the condemnation of Israel was the shelling and bombing of civilians in Lebanon and the consequent destruction of Lebanese infrastructure. Israel also sought to cloak its acts of aggression, as illustrated by the fact that occupation, the building of settlements, the expropriation of land, the attempted Judaization of Jerusalem and repressive practices against Arab citizens in the Occupied Palestinian Territory continued.

On 19 June [A/54/924-S/2000/600], the Permanent Observer of Palestine informed the Secretary-General that Israel's army chief of staff had verbally threatened to use extreme force against the Palestinian people. Such threats were not only inconsistent with the peace process, but also increased tension between the Palestinian and Israeli peoples.

By a 29 June follow-up letter [A/54/930-S/2000/637] to the Secretary-General and the Security Council President, the Permanent Observer said that unusual military movements and preparations were being carried out by the Israeli forces in the occupied Gaza Strip. Such preparations were related to the verbal threats of force made by Israeli officials.

On 30 June [A/54/932-S/2000/644], the Permanent Observer said that Israel's Attorney-General had stated that UN resolutions calling for the withdrawal of Israeli forces from the occupied territories were not applicable to the West Bank, including East Jerusalem and the Gaza Strip.

By a 7 September letter to the Secretary-General [A/55/378-S/2000/868], Malaysia transmitted the final communiqué and recommendations adopted by the Al-Quds Committee at its eighteenth session (Agadir, Morocco, 28 August). The Committee, among other things, supported Palestinian sovereignty over Al-Quds Al-Sharif (Jerusalem), including the Mosque of Al-Haram Al-Sharif and all other Christian and Islamic sanctuaries situated inside the city.

Escalation of violence

Communications (29 September–3 October). By a 29 September letter to the Secretary-General [A/55/432-S/2000/921], the Permanent Observer of

Palestine said that on 28 September Mr. Sharon, a member of the Israeli parliament and the leader of the Likud Party, led a group of parliamentarians in a provocative visit to Al-Haram Al-Sharif in Occupied East Jerusalem, in order to emphasize Israeli sovereignty over the place. Hundreds of Israeli security forces accompanied Mr. Sharon, which further aggravated tensions, leading to clashes between Palestinian civilians and Israeli soldiers. On 29 September, Israeli security forces stormed Al-Haram Al-Sharif using rubber bullets and live ammunition against the worshippers, killing five Palestinian civilians and wounding about 200 others. Clashes later spread to the rest of East Jerusalem, Bethlehem, Ramallah and Gaza.

By a 2 October follow-up letter to the Secretary-General and the Security Council President [A/55/437-S/2000/930], the Permanent Observer said that Israel had continued its campaign against the Palestinians. As at 1 October and since the visit to Al-Haram Al-Sharif by Mr. Sharon, Israeli soldiers had killed 28 Palestinians and injured at least 800 others. Israel had deployed snipers and used high-velocity ammunition, as well as anti-tank missiles, rockets, grenades and helicopter gunships. Israeli tanks had moved towards several Palestinian cities and some posts manned by Palestinian police. The Permanent Observer called for an immediate meeting of the Council to consider the situation.

In a 2 October letter to the Secretary-General [A/55/440-S/2000/936], the Chairman of the Committee on Palestinian Rights expressed concern at the continued confrontation in the Old City of Jerusalem and throughout the West Bank and Gaza. According to media reports, 40 Palestinians had died and 1,500 others had been wounded since 28 September. The Committee was of the view that the events of the past several days were a direct result of the policies and practices of the Israeli occupation; Israel continued to violate its obligations under the Fourth Geneva Convention and the provisions of Security Council and General Assembly resolutions.

Responding on 2 October [A/55/441-S/2000/937], Israel said that the events of 28 September on the Temple Mount represented a further escalation of Palestinian violence. Muslim worshippers hurled rocks at Jewish worshippers gathered at the Western Wall on the eve of the Jewish New Year, and then attempted to force their way out of the Temple Mount area and through the Mughrabim gate to the Western Wall plaza. At that point, Israeli forces were compelled to enter the area to push back the charging crowd. Since then, the Palestinian violence had continued unabated, and there had been numerous instances of live fire emanating from within protesting crowds. Israeli security personnel returned fire only when absolutely necessary and exercised all possible restraint in their efforts to restore calm and security. Israel stressed that the responsibility for the escalation lay with the Palestinian Authority (PA) because of, among other things, its incitement of the population through inflammatory rhetoric and calls to violence. Furthermore, PA policemen and security forces had taken an active role in the events, including the use of live ammunition against Israelis.

On 3 October [A/55/449-S/2000/956], Malaysia transmitted to the Secretary-General the statement adopted by the Islamic Group at the United Nations at its meeting on the situation in the Occupied Palestinian Territory, including the situation in Al-Quds Al-Sharif (New York, 2 October). The Islamic Group condemned the actions of the Israeli security forces against Palestinian civilians and called for the full respect of Jerusalem's Holy Places. It called on Israel to abide by its obligations under the Fourth Geneva Convention and relevant Council resolutions and supported the Palestinian and Arab request for an immediate meeting of the Council to consider the situation in Occupied East Jerusalem and the rest of the Occupied Palestinian Territory.

SECURITY COUNCIL CONSIDERATION (3-5 October)

At the request of Iraq [S/2000/928], Malaysia [S/2000/929, S/2000/935] and South Africa [S/2000/934], and that of 2 October from the Permanent Observer of Palestine (see above), the Security Council, on 3, 4 and 5 October [meeting 4204], discussed the situation in the Middle East, including the Palestinian question. With the Council's consent, the President invited, among others, Egypt and Israel, at their request, to participate in the discussion without the right to vote. The President also invited the Permanent Observer of Palestine to participate, at his own request [S/2000/938].

On 3 October, the Permanent Observer of Palestine said that Mr. Sharon's provocative visit to Al-Haram Al-Sharif and the subsequent Israeli forced entry into Al-Haram Al-Sharif resulted in a large number of injuries and touched off massive protests by Palestinian civilians throughout the Occupied Palestinian Territory. Israeli forces reacted by using considerable military power, including snipers, live ammunition, hand grenades, anti-tank missiles, helicopters and tanks. The Palestinian police, having witnessed firsthand the severity of the Israeli forces' attacks against Palestinian civilians, engaged in clashes with those forces. That exchange of fire did not change the basic nature of the events in question, which were in essence acts of oppression and brutality by Israel against Palestinians. In addition, Israeli Arabs, who had staged demonstrations inside Israel in solidarity with their brethren in the Palestinian territories, were killed and injured by Israeli forces. The Permanent Observer stated that the Council had to put an immediate end to Israel's brutal campaign and to its violation of international law.

Israel said that although some were inclined to assign exclusive responsibility to Israel for the latest acts of provocation, the reality was far less simplistic. The Palestinian escalation dated back to well before the Temple Mount disturbances, when, on 13 September, stones and Molotov cocktails were thrown at Israeli positions in the vicinity of the Netzarim junction in Gaza. That was followed by a number of increasingly violent attacks against Israeli security forces. The events on the Temple Mount escalated the violence even further. Israel was not faced with peaceful demonstrators but, rather, with a coordinated escalation of violent confrontation throughout the West Bank and Gaza. In a phenomenon that had become a commonplace occurrence, there had been numerous instances of live fire emanating from within rioting crowds. Israel stressed that the responsibility for the escalation of violence lay with the PA, not only because of its failure to take action to halt those events, but also because it incited the population through inflammatory rhetoric and calls to violence. Furthermore, PA security forces and paramilitary groups, such as Fatah's Tanzim, had taken a leading role in the events. Even more disturbing for Israel was the violation of signed agreements regarding the use of weapons by Palestinian policemen. Israel called on the PA to put an end to the use of gunfire by Palestinian police, to collect the illegal weapons in the hands of the Tanzim and to keep Palestinian protesters at a distance from Israeli positions.

The United States said that President Clinton and his administration were involved in ongoing consultations with the parties in a search for ways to end the violence. The parties were expected to meet on 4 October in Paris with the United States Secretary of State and on 5 October in Cairo, Egypt, with President Mubarak. As soon as conditions permitted, the United States would chair an Israeli-Palestinian meeting for the purpose of fact-finding.

France condemned the visit by Mr. Sharon on 28 September to the sacred site of the Mosque Plaza, undertaken for reasons of domestic politics and at the most sensitive time in the peace negotiations. It noted that at issue was the responsibility of those who were in charge of maintaining order and that the disproportionate use of armed force violated the Fourth Geneva Convention. Speaking on behalf of the EU, France stated that the EU supported the creation of an objective fact-finding international commission.

Malaysia, as Chairman of the Islamic Group, condemned the actions of the Israeli security forces against Palestinian civilians, as well as the visit of the Likud Party leader to Al-Haram Al-Sharif in disregard of the religious sensitivities of the Palestinians. His visit at a delicate juncture in the peace process was intended to provoke a Palestinian reaction. Malaysia called on the Israeli authorities to put an end to the high-handed actions of their security forces and to bring to justice those directly responsible for violence. It reaffirmed its position that a comprehensive, just and lasting peace could be achieved only with the complete withdrawal of Israel from all Arab and Palestinian land occupied since 1967, including Jerusalem and occupied Syrian Golan. It also stated that the establishment of an independent State of Palestine, with Jerusalem as its capital, along with the implementation of all international resolutions on the Palestinian issue, were the only guarantees for lasting peace between Israel and Palestine.

Egypt questioned the position of the Israeli Government, which, while claiming to be working towards peace, allowed Mr. Sharon to undertake the provocative visit to Al-Haram Al-Sharif. Egypt viewed that situation as an attempt to bring pressure to bear on the Palestinians with regard to the issue of sovereignty over Jerusalem's holy sites. In fact, Egypt said that the crux of the crisis remained the question of Jerusalem—East Jerusalem and the Old City in particular, which had been occupied by Israel since 1967. Egypt called on the Council, among other things, to take measures to guarantee the non-entry by the Israeli armed forces, including security and army troops, into the courtyard of Al-Haram Al-Sharif; to investigate the events that had occurred since 28 September; and to condemn Mr. Sharon's visit.

On 5 October, Israel said that, whatever its motives and implications, Mr. Sharon's visit was undertaken in full compliance with the principles of Israeli democracy, thus Prime Minister Barak could not impede Mr. Sharon's visit to the Temple Mount. In addition, it affirmed that the Temple Mount, sacred to Islam on the side where Al-Haram Al-Sharif was located, was equally sacred to Judaism for its ancient layers, on which Jewish identity and history were based. Only if the two sides were able to consider and accept each other's symbolic and political systems could peace be achieved.

The Permanent Observer of Palestine replied that violence continued in the occupied territories, despite the efforts deployed in Paris and in Sharm el-Sheikh. At the 4 October meeting in Paris, no agreement was reached because Israel rejected the idea of an international commission of inquiry. In addition, Prime Minister Barak did not go to Sharm el-Sheikh on 5 October, despite the fact that Chairman Arafat and the United States Secretary of State did attend. Therefore, the four-party meeting was not held. The Permanent Observer reaffirmed that Al-Haram Al-Sharif was part of East Jerusalem, which was part of the occupied Palestinian land. It belonged to the Muslims and had to be under Palestinian-Arab-Muslim sovereignty, and the Palestinian people would not accept any claim of Israeli sovereignty over that part. At the same time, the Palestinians were ready to accept the control of Israel over the Wailing Wall.

SECURITY COUNCIL ACTION (7 October)

On 7 October [meeting 4205], the Security Council adopted **resolution 1322(2000)** by vote (14-0-1). The draft text [S/2000/963] was submitted by Bangladesh, Jamaica, Malaysia, Mali, Namibia, Tunisia and Ukraine.

The Security Council,

Recalling its resolutions 476(1980) of 30 June 1980, 478(1980) of 20 August 1980, 672(1990) of 12 October 1990 and 1073(1996) of 28 September 1996, and all its other relevant resolutions,

Deeply concerned at the tragic events that have taken place since 28 September 2000, which have led to numerous deaths and injuries, mostly among Palestinians,

Reaffirming that a just and lasting solution to the Arab and Israeli conflict must be based on its resolutions 242(1967) of 22 November 1967 and 338(1973) of 22 October 1973, through an active negotiating process,

Expressing its support for the Middle East peace process and the efforts to reach a final settlement between the Israeli and Palestinian sides, and urging the two sides to cooperate in those efforts,

Reaffirming the need for full respect of the Holy Places of the City of Jerusalem by all, and condemning any behaviour to the contrary,

1. *Deplores* the provocation carried out at Haram Al-Sharif in Jerusalem on 28 September 2000, and the subsequent violence there and at other Holy Places, as well as in other areas throughout the territories occupied by Israel since 1967, resulting in over eighty Palestinian deaths and many other casualties;

2. *Condemns* acts of violence, especially the excessive use of force against Palestinians, resulting in injury and loss of human life;

3. *Calls upon* Israel, the occupying Power, to abide scrupulously by its legal obligations and its responsibilities under the Fourth Geneva Convention relative to the Protection of Civilian Persons in Time of War of 12 August 1949;

4. *Calls* for the immediate cessation of violence, and for all necessary steps to be taken to ensure that violence ceases, that new provocative actions are avoided, and that the situation returns to normality in a way that promotes the prospects for the Middle East peace process;

5. *Stresses* the importance of establishing a mechanism for a speedy and objective inquiry into the tragic events of the last few days with the aim of preventing their repetition, and welcomes any efforts in this regard;

6. *Calls* for the immediate resumption of negotiations within the Middle East peace process on its agreed basis with the aim of achieving an early final settlement between the Israeli and Palestinian sides;

7. *Invites* the Secretary-General to continue to follow the situation and to keep the Council informed;

8. *Decides* to follow the situation closely and to remain seized of the matter.

VOTE ON RESOLUTION 1322(2000):

In favour: Argentina, Bangladesh, Canada, China, France, Jamaica, Malaysia, Mali, Namibia, Netherlands, Russian Federation, Tunisia, Ukraine, United Kingdom.
Against: None.
Abstaining: United States.

Further developments

Communications (4-16 October). In a 4 October letter [A/55/450-S/2000/957], the Permanent Observer of Palestine said that Israeli security forces continued to increase their presence in the Occupied Palestinian Territory, including Jerusalem, had reoccupied parts of the area under Palestinian jurisdiction and had actually used tanks to fire against Palestinian targets.

On 7 October [A/55/460-S/2000/970], Israel said that during the course of rioting in the West Bank, the Jewish holy site of Joseph's Tomb became a target of gunfire and violent attacks by Palestinian civilians and by armed militia and members of the Palestinian police, which had led to the death of an Israeli police officer. With a view to reducing tension, an agreement was reached on 6 October, between IDF and the Palestinian police, whereby Israeli personnel on duty at the Tomb would be removed from the site as a temporary measure, while the PA was to ensure its continued protection and preservation. However, with the removal of the Israeli personnel, Palestinians entered the site, set the Tomb ablaze and commenced dismantling the structure.

In identical letters of 9 October to the Secretary-General and the Security Council President [A/55/466-S/2000/971], the Permanent Observer of Palestine said that Israel had effectively transformed Youssef's Tomb into a military post. Israeli security forces had killed 18 Palestinians there since 29 September, which explained why the population, enraged over the killings, destroyed the place after the withdrawal of the Israeli personnel. The Palestinian side had already taken action to repair the original part of the site and to provide for effective protection. The Observer pointed out that acts had been committed against Israeli Arabs in Israel itself, like the desecration of a mosque in Tiberias, Galilee, and that Israeli settlers had been committing crimes against Palestinians in the occupied territories.

In an 11 October letter [A/55/470-S/2000/980], Israel said that during the course of the violence and rioting in the West Bank and Gaza, the Palestinian leadership had continually violated the concept of peaceful resolution of disputes and had breached explicit agreement between the two sides in an effort to bring the peace process to a halt. Israel listed a number of violations committed by the PA, including incitement, incidents of mob violence, the release of convicted terrorists from prisons and the desecration of religious sites.

In identical letters of 12 October to the Secretary-General and the Council President [A/55/474-S/2000/984], the Permanent Observer of Palestine said that Israel had taken military actions that were tantamount to a declaration of war against the Palestinians. Israeli forces had dramatically increased their presence in the vicinities of Palestinian cities, and fired rockets from helicopter gunships and Israeli military ships to destroy several official PA locations in Ramallah and near Gaza City.

On the same day, in identical letters to the Secretary-General and the Council President [S/2000/985], Israel stated that two Israeli reserve soldiers were brutally murdered after they mistakenly entered the Palestinian town of Ramallah. The soldiers were brought by Palestinian police to the police headquarters, following which a Palestinian mob infiltrated the complex and killed them. In responding to that attack, Israel exercised restraint, taking care to prevent the loss of life as much as possible. In fact, in attacking the Palestinian police headquarters where the soldiers were murdered, IDF took steps to prevent damage to surrounding areas and provided advance warning to the PA to evacuate personnel from the building. Chairman Arafat had inaccurately labelled those retaliatory strikes as a declaration of war. Israel had no interest in declaring war on the Palestinian people and, in fact, was meeting its obligation under international law to maintain order in the area and to protect its citizens. In another development, the PA freed a number of Hamas prisoners who had been convicted in Palestinian courts of committing violent acts against Israelis. Members of Hamas and Islamic Jihad terrorist groups were invited to participate in a meeting of the Palestinian Cabinet, an act which legitimized their commitment to terrorism as an alternative to peaceful negotiations.

In three letters dated 10 October [A/55/483-S/2000/988, A/55/484-S/2000/989, A/55/485-S/2000/990], the EU expressed concern over the violent clashes in Jerusalem and in the occupied territories. It considered that the disproportionate recourse to force could only further aggravate the situation and supported the forming of an international commission to establish objectively what had actually happened since 28 September.

On 16 October [A/55/490-S/2000/993], the Permanent Observer of Palestine said that Israel had imposed a virtual siege on the entire Occupied Palestinian Territory, including Jerusalem. The siege included the shutting down of the airspace of Gaza International Airport, as well as the closure of other international crossing points.

Sharm el-Sheikh Summit

Presidents Clinton and Mubarak co-chaired a Middle East Peace Summit in Sharm el-Sheikh on 16 and 17 October. Participants included Jordanian King Abdullah II, Israeli Prime Minister Barak, PA Chairman Arafat, the Secretary-General of the United Nations and EU President Solana.

The primary objective of the Summit was to end the cycle of violence in order to resume the peace process. The leaders agreed on three steps to achieve that objective. First, both sides agreed to issue public statements unequivocally calling for an end to violence and to take immediate, concrete measures to end the confrontation, eliminate points of friction, ensure an end to violence and incitement, maintain calm and prevent a recurrence of recent events. To accomplish that, both sides would act immediately to return the situation to that which existed prior to the current crisis, in areas such as restoring law and order, redeploying forces, eliminating points of friction, enhancing security cooperation and ending the closure of, and reopening, the Gaza airport. The United States undertook to facilitate security cooperation between the parties as needed. Second, it was agreed that the United States would develop with the Israelis and the Palestinians, as well as in consultation with the UN Secretary-General, a committee to undertake fact-finding on the events since 28 September and to seek ways to prevent their recurrence. President Clinton would share the committee's report with the Secretary-General and the parties prior to publication. A final report would be submitted under the auspices of the President for publication. Third, it was agreed that, in order to address the underlying roots of the Israeli-Palestinian conflict, there had to be a pathway back to negotiations and a resumption of efforts to reach a permanent status agreement based on resolutions 242(1967) [YUN 1967, p. 257] and 338(1973) [YUN 1973, p. 213] and subsequent understandings. President Clinton announced that, towards that end, the leaders had agreed that the United States would consult with the parties within the next two weeks about how to move forward.

Communications (17-20 October). By a 17 October letter [A/55/501-S/2000/1001], the United States transmitted to the Secretary-General President Clinton's statement on the occasion of the conclusion of the Middle East Peace Summit at Sharm el-Sheikh, which detailed the three major agreements reached by the parties.

By a 20 October letter to the Secretary-General [A/55/508-S/2000/1007], Israel submitted an update regarding its compliance with the understandings reached at the Sharm el-Sheikh Summit, as well as an assessment of the situation on the ground. Israel noted that while it had immediately issued a public statement that unequivocally called for a complete end to all violence, as agreed at the Summit, it took the PA over 24 hours to reciprocate. During that time, Palestinian gunmen continued provoking Israel's security forces throughout the territories and in Jerusalem. That outbreak of violence was carried out by the Tanzim paramilitary armed group, sponsored by the Fatah organization. Israel said that it would fully cooperate with the fact-finding committee, and that IDF troops and armoured vehicles had been redeployed, the Gaza airport had been reopened and the closure within the territories had been removed, as agreed at the Summit.

Emergency special session

In accordance with General Assembly resolution ES-10/6 [YUN 1999, p. 402] and at the request of Iraq [A/ES-10/36], on behalf of the League of Arab States, supported by the Coordinating Bureau of the Movement of Non-Aligned Countries [A/ES-10/37], the tenth emergency special session of the Assembly resumed on 18 October to discuss "Illegal Israeli actions in Occupied East Jerusalem and the rest of the Occupied Palestinian Territory". The session was first convened in April 1997 [YUN 1997, p. 394] and resumed in July and November of that year, as well as in March 1998 [YUN 1998, p. 425] and February 1999 [YUN 1999, p. 402].

GENERAL ASSEMBLY ACTION

On 20 October [meeting 14], the General Assembly adopted **resolution ES-10/7** [draft: A/ES-10/L.6] by recorded vote (92-6-46) [agenda item 5].

Illegal Israeli actions in Occupied East Jerusalem and the rest of the Occupied Palestinian Territory

The General Assembly,

Reaffirming the resolutions of the tenth emergency special session and the necessity of full implementation of those resolutions,

Welcoming the adoption by the Security Council of resolution 1322(2000) of 7 October 2000, and stressing the urgent need for full compliance with the resolution,

Expressing its deep concern over the provocative visit to Al-Haram Al-Sharif on 28 September 2000, and the tragic events that followed in Occupied East Jerusalem and other places in the Occupied Palestinian Territory, which resulted in a high number of deaths and injuries mostly among Palestinian civilians,

Expressing its deep concern also over the clashes between the Israeli army and the Palestinian police and the casualties on both sides,

Reaffirming that a just and lasting solution to the Arab-Israeli conflict must be based on Security Council resolutions 242(1967) of 22 November 1967 and 338(1973) of 22 October 1973, through an active negotiation process which takes into account the right of security for all States in the region, as well as the legitimate rights of the Palestinian people, including their right to self-determination,

Expressing its support for the Middle East peace process and the efforts to reach a final settlement between the Israeli and the Palestinian sides, and urging the two sides to cooperate in these efforts,

Reaffirming the need for full respect by all for the Holy Places of Occupied East Jerusalem and condemning any behaviour to the contrary,

Reaffirming also the need for the full respect by all for the Holy Places in the rest of the Occupied Palestinian Territory, as well as in Israel, and condemning any behaviour to the contrary,

Determined to uphold the purposes and principles of the Charter of the United Nations, international humanitarian law, and all other instruments of international law, as well as relevant resolutions of the General Assembly and Security Council,

Reiterating the permanent responsibility of the United Nations towards the question of Palestine until it is solved in all its aspects,

Conscious of the serious dangers arising from persistent violations and grave breaches of the Fourth Geneva Convention relative to the Protection of Civilian Persons in Time of War, of 12 August 1949, and the responsibility arising therefrom,

Stressing the urgent need for providing protection for the Palestinian civilians in the Occupied Palestinian Territory,

Noting the convening on 15 July 1999 for the first time of the Conference of High Contracting Parties to the Fourth Geneva Convention on measures to enforce the Convention in the Occupied Palestinian Territory, including Jerusalem, at the United Nations Office at Geneva, and welcoming also the statement adopted by the participating High Contracting Parties,

1. *Condemns* the violence that took place on 28 September 2000 and the following days at Al-Haram Al-Sharif and other Holy Places in Jerusalem as well as other areas in the Occupied Palestinian Territory, resulting in the deaths of over 100 people, the vast major-

ity of whom were Palestinian civilians, and many other casualties;

2. *Condemns also* acts of violence, especially the excessive use of force by the Israeli forces against Palestinian civilians;

3. *Expresses support* for the understandings reached at the summit convened at Sharm el-Sheikh, Egypt, and urges all parties concerned to implement these understandings honestly and without delay;

4. *Demands* the immediate cessation of violence and the use of force, calls upon the parties to act immediately to reverse all measures taken in this regard since 28 September 2000 and acknowledges that necessary steps have been taken by the parties in this direction since the summit of Sharm el-Sheikh;

5. *Reiterates* that Israeli settlements in the Occupied Palestinian Territory, including Jerusalem, are illegal and are an obstacle to peace, and calls for the prevention of illegal acts of violence by Israeli settlers;

6. *Demands* that Israel, the occupying Power, abide scrupulously by its legal obligations and its responsibilities under the Fourth Geneva Convention relative to the Protection of Civilian Persons in Time of War, of 12 August 1949, which is applicable to all territories occupied by Israel since 1967;

7. *Strongly supports* the establishment of a mechanism of inquiry into the recent tragic events, with the aim of establishing all the precise facts and preventing the repetition of these events, and in this regard the understanding reached in Sharm el-Sheikh on a committee of fact-finding, and calls for its establishment without delay;

8. *Supports* the efforts of the Secretary-General, including his efforts for the establishment of the above-mentioned committee, and requests him to report to the Assembly on the progress made in these efforts;

9. *Calls upon* the members of the Security Council to closely follow the situation, including the implementation of Council resolution 1322(2000) of 7 October 2000, in fulfilment of the Council's primary responsibility for the maintenance of international peace and security;

10. *Invites* the depository of the Fourth Geneva Convention to consult on the development of the humanitarian situation in the field, in accordance with the statement adopted on 15 July 1999 by the above-mentioned Conference of High Contracting Parties to the Convention, with the aim of ensuring respect for the Convention in all circumstances in accordance with common article 1 of the four Conventions;

11. *Supports* the efforts towards the resumption of the Israeli-Palestinian negotiations within the Middle East peace process on its agreed basis, and calls for the speedy conclusion of the final settlement agreement between the two sides;

12. *Decides* to adjourn the tenth emergency special session temporarily and to authorize the President of the most current General Assembly to resume its meeting upon request by Member States.

RECORDED VOTE ON RESOLUTION ES-10/7:

In favour: Algeria, Andorra, Argentina, Armenia, Austria, Azerbaijan, Bahrain, Bangladesh, Belgium, Belize, Bolivia, Bosnia and Herzegovina, Botswana, Brazil, Brunei Darussalam, Burkina Faso, Cape Verde, Chile, China, Colombia, Côte d'Ivoire, Cuba, Cyprus, Democratic People's Republic of Korea, Djibouti, Ecuador, Egypt, Ethiopia, Finland, France, Gambia, Ghana, Greece, Guinea, Guyana, India, Indonesia, Iran, Ireland, Jamaica, Jordan, Kuwait, Lao People's Democratic Republic, Lebanon,

Libyan Arab Jamahiriya, Luxembourg, Madagascar, Malaysia, Maldives, Mali, Malta, Mauritius, Mexico, Monaco, Mongolia, Morocco, Mozambique, Myanmar, Namibia, Nepal, Oman, Pakistan, Paraguay, Peru, Philippines, Portugal, Qatar, Republic of Korea, Russian Federation, Saudi Arabia, Senegal, Singapore, South Africa, Spain, Sri Lanka, Sudan, Suriname, Swaziland, Syrian Arab Republic, Thailand, Togo, Tunisia, Turkey, Ukraine, United Arab Emirates, United Republic of Tanzania, Uruguay, Venezuela, Viet Nam, Yemen, Zambia, Zimbabwe.

Against: Israel, Marshall Islands, Micronesia, Nauru, Tuvalu, United States.

Abstaining: Albania, Antigua and Barbuda, Australia, Barbados, Benin, Bulgaria, Cameroon, Canada, Costa Rica, Croatia, Czech Republic, Denmark, Dominican Republic, El Salvador, Estonia, Fiji, Germany, Grenada, Guatemala, Haiti, Hungary, Iceland, Italy, Japan, Kazakhstan, Kenya, Kyrgyzstan, Latvia, Liechtenstein, Lithuania, Netherlands, New Zealand, Nicaragua, Norway, Poland, Romania, Saint Vincent and the Grenadines, Samoa, San Marino, Sierra Leone, Slovakia, Slovenia, Sweden, The former Yugoslav Republic of Macedonia, Tonga, United Kingdom.

Speaking before the vote [A/ES-10/PV.13], the Permanent Observer of Palestine said that in response to the Palestinian protest over Mr. Sharon's visit to Al-Haram Al-Sharif and the storming of Al-Haram by IDF, Israel had used its war machine to launch a bloody campaign of repression, which caused many civilian deaths, including many children, and also imposed severe restrictions on the movement of persons and goods. A number of Palestinian cities and villages had been placed under siege by Israeli forces. Contrary to Israel's allegations, there had not been any large-scale exchanges of fire between the Palestinian police and Israeli forces. The Observer condemned the damage caused by Palestinian civilians to Joseph's Tomb near Nablus, and the killing of two Israeli soldiers at the police station in Ramallah. Palestinian authorities had issued instructions to repair Joseph's Tomb and to apprehend those who had committed the killing. Nevertheless, those issues and others could not change the real nature of what was happening—namely, the excessive and unjustifiable use of force by Israel against the Palestinians, a people that expressed their anger and frustration because of the occupation. Despite the adoption of resolution 1322(2000), the situation on the ground had not changed, and Israel had failed to comply with any of its provisions. Israel had in fact escalated the level of violence by shelling, on 12 October, some Palestinian locations in Ramallah and Gaza, which was tantamount to a declaration of war against the Palestinian people. A new attempt to rescue the situation and to revive the peace process was made by the convening of the Sharm el-Sheikh Summit on 16 and 17 October. The Observer welcomed the participation of the Secretary-General at the Summit, as well as all the efforts he made during his visit to the region. It was hoped that the United Nations would participate in the mechanism of inquiry into what happened, as called for in resolution 1322 (2000) and as agreed upon by the parties in Sharm el-Sheikh. The Observer said that the speedy establishment and immediate work of that committee of inquiry would be effective in ending the situation created since 28 September.

Israel expressed the hope that the statement made in Sharm el-Sheikh would succeed in restoring calm and quiet to the region, but noted that the deliberations of the Assembly's special session threatened, and were contrary to, the spirit of that declaration and had the potential to aggravate and disrupt efforts to bring an end to the violence. The killing of the two Israeli reserve soldiers inside the Palestinian police headquarters in Ramallah was not the first instance in which official PA organs had tolerated, encouraged or even directly engaged in violent actions against Israelis. In fact, Palestinian policemen, security personnel and armed militias had participated in many clashes with Israeli soldiers and civilians. In particular, Israel referred to the attack and dismantling of Joseph's Tomb, a site holy to both Jews and Muslims, by Palestinian civilians and police. The PA, rather than using its position to prevent violence and urge restraint, had allowed its official television and radio to be used for purposes of incitement, calling on its people to carry out attacks on Israeli citizens. The PA had also freed terrorist prisoners who had been convicted in Palestinian courts of committing violent acts against Israelis. Allegations that Israel used excessive force in confrontations with the Palestinians were unfounded. Israel had permitted, and would continue to permit, the passage of humanitarian aid to Palestinians in the territories. Its actions were intended not to harm but to maintain order in the area, and were in full accordance with international law. Only a negotiated solution, arrived at in an atmosphere free from violence, could put a permanent end to bloodshed and unrest in the Middle East. Israel called on Chairman Arafat to order his security forces and his people to stop the confrontations and the provocations, to disarm the militias as he had previously agreed, and to re-arrest members of Hamas and other terrorist organizations who were still at large. Israel was opposed to the draft resolution because, apart from being one-sided, unfair and biased, it demanded the unilateral condemnation of Israel. The text as it stood did not mention Palestinian excesses of any kind. Palestinians and Israelis had to rely on their own resources and on mutual assistance rather than on a draft resolution that was a repository of indignation for some and of bitterness for others.

The Chairman of the Committee on Palestinian Rights said that deadly violence had been raging in all Palestinian areas since Mr. Sharon's visit to Al-Haram Al-Sharif. In the ensuing clashes, more than 110 people, mostly Palestinians, were killed and some 3,000 injured. IDF re-

acted to the demonstrations with disproportionate force, often making use of metal bullets, live ammunition and tanks. Another disturbing development involved armed Jewish settlers, authorized to move within the towns and villages controlled by the PA, and able to use their firearms. To compound the situation, the Israelis proceeded to seal off Palestinian territory, immobilizing almost 3 million inhabitants and preventing them from working. The Committee welcomed all the efforts by the international community to bring an end to the violence, in particular the Sharm el-Sheikh Summit. For its part, the Committee, at a meeting on 10 October, adopted a declaration in which it reaffirmed that the United Nations had to continue to shoulder its permanent responsibility regarding all aspects of the question of Palestine, including Jerusalem, until that issue was resolved in a satisfactory manner.

The Secretary-General said that he had just returned from the Middle East region where he met with the principal players, attended the Sharm el-Sheikh Summit, and visited Lebanon to discuss regional issues and the capture of three Israeli soldiers from the Shaba area of the occupied Golan. His main purpose was to try to help the Israelis and Palestinians to resolve the crisis that had developed since 28 September by reaching an agreement with the following elements: disengagement, an end to violence and a return to normalcy; a resumption of the peace process; and the establishment of a mechanism to inquire into recent events and ways of avoiding a recurrence. Throughout his visit, the situation on the ground in Jerusalem, the West Bank and Gaza was extremely tense. While he was in the region, more than 50 Palestinians were killed and two Israeli reservists were lynched in Ramallah. That was the backdrop against which his peace efforts were set. The situation had, in his view, reached the brink of the abyss. His primary objective was therefore to get the two principal players, Prime Minister Barak and Chairman Arafat, to address public appeals to their respective populations for calm, and to ask them to indicate some specific measures that they were prepared to take in order to de-escalate the tension. Unfortunately, it became apparent that the rapidly deteriorating situation on the ground and the consequent hardening of public opinion on both sides had made it impossible for both leaders to make conciliatory statements. Despite initial reluctance to attend the Sharm el-Sheikh Summit, especially on the part of Chairman Arafat, both parties agreed to attend and reached agreement on three main objectives (see p. 420). The Secretary-General said that the Sharm el-Sheikh agreements were a vital first step back from the brink and towards a resumption of the peace process. It was essential that they should be faithfully implemented in their entirety by both sides. Both parties needed to demonstrate good faith—above all by their actions.

Communications (23 October–24 November). On 23 October [A/55/513-S/2000/1010], Egypt transmitted to the Secretary-General the final communiqué of the Extraordinary Arab Summit (Cairo, 21-22 October). The Arab leaders held Israel responsible for returning the region to tension and violence as a result of its practices, assaults and blockade of the Palestinian people in violation of its obligations as the occupying Power under the terms of the Fourth Geneva Convention. They affirmed that the Palestinian uprising had broken out as a result of the maintenance and perpetuation of the occupation and because of Israel's encroachment on Al-Haram Al-Sharif and other Holy Places in the occupied territories. In response to a proposal by Saudi Arabia, the Arab leaders decided to establish two funds. The Al-Aqsa Fund would be allocated a sum of $800 million to fund projects designed to preserve the Arab and Islamic identity of Jerusalem and prevent its loss and to enable the Palestinian people to disengage from their subordination to the Israeli economy. The Al-Quds Intifada Fund would have a capital of $200 million to be disbursed to the families of Palestinians who had fallen in the intifada and to provide for the care and education of their children. The Arab leaders called for the formation, within the framework of the United Nations, of an impartial international commission of inquiry to report to the Security Council and the Commission on Human Rights on the causes of and responsibility for the deterioration in the occupied territories and the acts committed by Israel against Palestinian, Lebanese and other Arab residents. They called on the Council and the General Assembly to provide protection to the Palestinian people under Israeli occupation by considering the establishment of a force or an international presence for that purpose. Since the halt in the peace process caused by Israel's policy and practices made talk of a common future in the region untimely, the leaders decided not to resume or participate in any official or informal activity in the multilateral framework, to suspend all measures and activities for regional economic cooperation with Israel, and to link their resumption to the attainment of tangible progress towards a comprehensive peace on all tracks of the peace process.

In a series of communications dated between 23 and 30 October [A/ES-10/39-S/2000/1015, A/ES-10/40-S/2000/1025, A/ES-10/41-S/2000/1046], the Permanent Observer of Palestine said that Israel continued its terror campaign and the imposition of restrictive blockades on the movement of persons and goods into, out of and throughout the occupied territories and, once again, had shut down the Gaza airport. He called on the Council to convene a meeting to consider the situation in the region and to establish a UN protection force for the occupied territories, including Jerusalem.

On 25 October [S/2000/1027], Iraq, in its capacity as Chairman of the Arab Group for October, requested a meeting of the Council to consider the situation in the Occupied Palestinian Territory and the establishment of a UN protection force.

In a 2 November letter to the Secretary-General [A/55/540-S/2000/1065], Israel said that on that day a car bomb exploded near the marketplace of Mahane Yehuda, killing two civilians and injuring several others. The Islamic Jihad claimed responsibility for the attack. Israel held the PA responsible as it had released Hamas and Islamic Jihad prisoners in recent weeks. The attack occurred less than 24 hours after an agreement was reached between Chairman Arafat and Israel's Minister for Regional Cooperation, Shimon Peres, to resume security cooperation and take steps to implement the provisions of the Sharm el-Sheik understanding.

In a series of communications dated between 6 and 20 November [A/ES-10/42-S/2000/1068, A/ES-10/43-S/2000/1078, A/ES-10/44-S/2000/1093, A/ES-10/45-S/2000/1104, A/ES-10/46-S/2000/1107], the Permanent Observer of Palestine informed the Secretary-General and the Security Council President that Israeli forces continued to kill and injure Palestinian civilians and had intensified measures to ensure the total isolation of Palestinian cities throughout the occupied territory. On 20 November, Israel launched massive bombardments of Gaza City and other locations in the Gaza Strip. Some Israeli missiles hit locations of the PA and caused injury to approximately 50 Palestinians.

On 20 November [A/55/634-S/2000/1108], Israel said that three Palestinian terrorists had carried out an attack on a bus carrying children and their chaperones near Kfar Darom, south of Gaza, killing two civilians and injuring 10 others, including children as young as seven. Israel held the PA responsible for the attack, which served as proof of Chairman Arafat's lack of credibility in claiming to combat Palestinian violence.

In a 22 November letter to the Secretary-General [A/55/641-S/2000/1114], Israel said that on that day a bomb was detonated near a local bus in the town of Hadera, killing two Israeli civilians and wounding over 41 others.

Also on 22 November, in a letter to the Security Council President [S/2000/1111], Qatar, as Chairman of the Ninth Islamic Summit Conference, and in compliance with the final communiqué of the Summit at which a Ministerial Committee was formed, requested the Council to convene to discuss the situation in the Middle East, including the Palestinian question. On 24 November [S/2000/1112], Malaysia, as a member of the delegation of the Ministerial Committee of the Organization of the Islamic Conference (OIC), supported Qatar's request.

SECURITY COUNCIL CONSIDERATION (22 November)

At the request of the Libyan Arab Jamahiriya [S/2000/1109], the Security Council, on 22 November, discussed the situation in the Middle East, including the Palestinian question [meeting 4231]. With the Council's consent, the Council President invited, among others, Israel, the Libyan Arab Jamahiriya and South Africa, at their request, to participate in the discussion without the right to vote. The President also invited the Permanent Observer of Palestine to participate, at his request [S/2000/112]. The 22 November meeting was preceded on 10 November by private meetings with Chairman Arafat [meeting 4217] and the representative of Israel [meeting 4218].

The Permanent Observer of Palestine said that, since 29 September, Israel had made excessive, disproportionate and indiscriminate use of its war machine, causing the death and injury of many Palestinians, as well as the destruction of infrastructure. Those actions had been accompanied by a stalemate in the peace process imposed by Israel's Government. Israeli policies and practices stemmed from the presence of Israeli occupiers and the policy of settlement—a policy that had continued even after the beginning of the peace process. Since 25 October, the Palestinians had been requesting the establishment of a UN observer force. At his private meeting with the Council on 10 November, Chairman Arafat requested 2,000 military observers who would operate under the UN emblem, auspices and supervision. Their only objective would be to ensure the safety and security of Palestinian civilians. Israel's approval was not a prerequisite for the Council measures to be enacted, said the Observer, as the Council was not dealing with a domestic situation of one Member State, but with a Member State that the Council had recognized as an occupying Power. The Council agreed to entrust the Secretary-General with conducting the necessary consultations on that issue.

Israel said that the situation in Israel and the Palestinian territories continued to deteriorate. Points of friction that had previously been localized and contained in certain areas had spread, engulfing the streets of Jerusalem and other Israeli towns and cities. A car bomb that had exploded on that day in the city of Hadera, causing the deaths of two Israeli citizens and injuries to 41, was the result of the release of prisoners from PA jails. Despite that attack and others against Israelis, the international community had failed to condemn Palestinian actions, thus encouraging the Palestinians to continue along a violent route. Moreover, the international community had not called for the establishment of a commission of inquiry to investigate Palestinian wrongdoing. In calling for the deployment of a UN protection force, the Palestinians were seeking to depart from bilateral negotiations and to pursue their goals unilaterally. An international force was not needed to stop the violence, nor was it clear that such a force would even be successful. The direct way to end the bloodshed was for the international community to call on the Palestinian leadership to exert every effort to stop the violence, the rioting, the use of live ammunition, the use of machine guns, the sending of children to the front and the use of terror against civilians.

The United States said that the violence in the Middle East had escalated again with the bombing of another busload of Israeli citizens, while a number of Palestinians were killed by IDF in circumstances that were still unclear. In consultation with the Secretary-General, the United States had worked towards establishing the Fact-Finding Committee agreed to at Sharm el-Sheikh (see p. 420). Former United States Senator George Mitchell, the Committee's Chairman, had met with the Secretary-General on 9 November and had outlined the Committee's mandate, which was to investigate the recent violence with the objective of preventing its recurrence. The Committee was to meet at the end of November in New York. The United States added that the United Nations, instead of lending support for efforts undertaken at Sharm el-Sheikh, had taken actions that undermined bilateral efforts at reaching peace. The Economic and Social Council had endorsed a resolution condemning Israel and calling for the creation of an inquiry commission and the dispatch of rapporteurs (see p. 434), an unnecessary measure that was supported by less than half the Council membership. Regarding a UN observer or military presence in the region, the United States said that the proposal required the agreement of the parties to the conflict.

The Libyan Arab Jamahiriya, on behalf of the Arab Group, called for an international observer force to protect the Palestinian people in the occupied territories; for the establishment of a fact-finding mission to inquire into all acts of violence perpetrated against the Palestinians, whose conclusions should be submitted to the International Criminal Court; and for the relevant Security Council resolutions to be implemented.

South Africa, on behalf of the Non-Aligned Movement, called on Israel to stop subjecting Palestinian civilians to collective punishment. The question of Palestine constituted the nucleus of the Middle East conflict and the achievement of the inalienable right of the Palestinian people to self-determination and to an independent State, with East Jerusalem as its capital, was pivotal to the achievement of a sustainable peace. The condition of land for peace was essential if meaningful progress in the peace process was to be attained, and negotiations towards final status issues had to be in accordance with the relevant UN resolutions and international legitimacy.

In response to statements made, Israel said that Prime Minister Barak had committed himself at the July Camp David Summit (see p. 415) to an innovative peace policy. Through a negotiated solution at the Summit, Chairman Arafat could have given rise to a Palestinian State and to the beginning of true reconciliation between the two peoples; instead, he had opted to achieve his political ends through violence.

The Permanent Observer of Palestine replied that it was Prime Minister Barak who had brought the situation to the brink of catastrophe, and that the occupation of Palestinian land and the violation of international law on the part of Israel were the real causes for the escalation of violence.

Communications (24 November–13 December). In a series of letters dated between 24 November and 13 December [A/ES/10/47-S/2000/1116, A/ES-10/48-A/2000/1129, A/ES-10/49-S/2000/1154, A/ES-10/50-S/2000/1173, A/ES/10/51-S/2000/1185], the Permanent Observer of Palestine stated that the killing and injuring of Palestinians by Israeli forces continued; he submitted lists of the names of those killed.

In identical letters of 26 November to the Secretary-General and the Security Council President [S/2000/1119], Iraq requested the Council to allocate to the Palestinian people part of the oil-export revenue governed by the Memorandum of Understanding signed by Iraq and the UN Secretariat on 20 May 1996 [YUN 1996, p. 226], in order to support the Palestinians in defence of their land. In a series of subsequent communica-

tions [S/2000/1174, S/2000/1216, S/2000/1217, S/2000/1218], Iraq requested that a billion euros from its oil-export revenues be allocated to the Palestinian people. On 4 December [S/2000/1152], Tunisia called on the Council to pay particular and benevolent attention to Iraq's request.

On 6 December [S/2000/1159], South Africa, as Chairman of the Coordinating Bureau of the Movement of Non-Aligned Countries, called on the Council to consider the adoption of a draft resolution prepared by the Movement's Security Council caucus pertaining to the deployment of a UN observer force in the Occupied Palestinian Territory (see below).

SECURITY COUNCIL CONSIDERATION (18 December)

On 18 December [meeting 4248], the Security Council discussed the situation in the Middle East, including the Palestine question, and considered the text of a draft resolution [S/2000/1171] submitted by Bangladesh, Jamaica, Malaysia, Mali, Namibia and Tunisia. By that draft, the Council would have expressed its determination to establish a UN force of military and police observers to be dispatched throughout the territories occupied by Israel since 1967, with the aim of contributing to the implementation of the Sharm el-Sheikh agreements, the cessation of violence and the enhancement of the safety and security of Palestinian civilians.

With the Council's consent, the Council President invited the Permanent Observer of Palestine, at his own request [S/2000/1206], to participate in the discussion. The President also invited Israel to participate without the right to vote.

On 27 November, the Council had held private meetings on the subject with the Ministerial Committee of OIC [meeting 4233] and with the representative of Israel [meeting 4234].

Speaking before the vote, Israel said that it was opposed to the draft resolution, but not to some form of international presence, provided it was established within the context of a comprehensive bilateral agreement, as that had always been the accepted sequence. An international presence had to be used to cement an agreement and not as an alternative to one. Sending a UN force into the region had the potential to escalate the violence as it would send a message to the Palestinians that there was no need to negotiate or coordinate with Israel and no need to compromise. Furthermore, international intervention did not appear necessary; Chairman Arafat had the ability to protect the lives of his people by relinquishing the path of confrontation, disarming the militias and controlling Hamas and Islamic Jihad groups, all of which he had already committed himself to do. Israel assured the Council that the violence would cease if the PA was to take those steps. The draft resolution was a recipe for long-term instability in the region, and Israel therefore urged the members of the Council not to support it.

Namibia, speaking on behalf of the members of the Non-Aligned Movement and Ukraine, said that the violence continued and the Council had not taken any action to address the situation. It was in that regard that the Movement's caucus had proposed the establishment of a protection force for Palestinian civilians in the occupied territories. The Movement did not believe that the consent of the parties was required to establish the force, but it agreed that their cooperation was needed.

France said that, together with the United Kingdom, it had argued in favour of an agreement on creating an observer mission. But France considered that it was not the most suitable time for adopting the draft resolution, in the light of ongoing efforts by the Secretary-General and the resumption of bilateral negotiations.

Speaking after the Council's vote (8-0-7) on the draft resolution, which was not adopted because it did not obtain the required number of votes, the United States said that the Council had acted wisely; if there had been a chance for the draft resolution to be adopted, the United States would have cast a veto. The United States supported the renewal of negotiations and dialogue, but was against action that did not advance the cause of peace. Negotiations would resume the following day, 19 December, in Washington, D.C., between the Israeli and Palestinian delegations.

The Permanent Observer of Palestine expressed his regret that the draft resolution had not been adopted. The Palestinian people and the Arab countries, as well as the members of OIC and the Non-Aligned Movement, had requested adequate protection for the Palestinian people through the establishment of a UN observer force. Negotiations scheduled for the next day should not have precluded action in the Council, and the Palestinians would not accept Israel's approval as a precondition for the Council's assumption of its responsibilities. The Permanent Observer said that the defeat of the draft resolution had only one explanation—the position of the United States, which was openly linked to that of Israel, and the pressure exerted by the United States on all the other members of the Council. The Council's action had persuaded the Palestinians and other Arabs that they could not rely on the Council.

Communications (19-28 December). In letters dated 19 [A/ES-10/52-S/2000/1215] and 28 [A/ES-10/53-S/2000/1247] December, the Permanent Observer of Palestine said that the killing and injuring of Palestinians by Israeli forces continued, and submitted lists of names of those killed.

On 21 December [A/55/716-S/2000/1236], Qatar transmitted to the Secretary-General the documents of the ninth session of the Islamic Summit Conference, Session of Peace and Development (Doha, Qatar, 12-14 November), which the Secretary-General attended. The documents included the text of the final communiqué; the Declaration of the Summit on the Al-Aqsa intifada—Palestinian independence intifada, the Doha Declaration and resolutions. The Conference, among other things, reiterated the necessity to put an end to all Israeli settlement activities; requested the Council to set up an international commission of inquiry to investigate Israeli actions; called on Member States to sever relations with Israel; reaffirmed the immutable responsibility of the United Nations towards the question of Palestine; and called on all States to recognize the State of Palestine with Al-Quds Al-Sharif as its capital.

On 28 December [A/55/719-S/2000/1252], Israel said that on that day two bombs exploded in a bus in Tel Aviv, injuring 12 people. It was the latest in a string of such attacks. Despite various agreements calling for an end to violence and the resumption of security cooperation between the sides, the PA had failed to call for an end to the violence and to reincarcerate released terrorist prisoners—steps that could have prevented those attacks.

Special Committee on Israeli Practices. In its thirty-second report [A/55/453], the Special Committee to Investigate Israeli Practices Affecting the Human Rights of the Palestinian People and Other Arabs of the Occupied Territories (Special Committee on Israeli Practices) stated that the confiscation of Palestinian-owned land, as well as Israeli settlement activity, continued. Unofficial estimates placed the percentage of the West Bank land that had been confiscated at 41 per cent in 1984 and 73 per cent in 1998. Since the 1995 Israeli-Palestinian Interim Agreement on the West Bank and the Gaza Strip [YUN 1995, p. 626], confiscation had continued at a rate of about 37 square kilometres (0.6 per cent of the West Bank) a year. The number of Israeli settlements in the Gaza Strip totalled 19, some of which were inhabited by no more than 10 people, while the total population of those settlements was about 5,000 settlers. The settlements were located in the most strategic areas of the Gaza Strip and included within their territories the most fertile land and most important water sources in the area. The election of a new Government in Israel in May

1999 had not changed the situation. In fact, in October 1999, the Israeli Ministerial Committee on Settlements adopted a proposal by the Minister of Housing to establish 2,600 settlement units in the West Bank.

Report of Secretary-General. On 4 August [A/55/263], the Secretary-General informed the Assembly that Israel had not replied to his July request for information on steps taken or envisaged to implement the relevant provisions of resolution 54/78 [YUN 1999, p. 407], demanding that Israel, among other things, cease all construction of new settlements in the Occupied Palestinian Territory, including Jerusalem.

GENERAL ASSEMBLY ACTION

On 8 December [meeting 83], the General Assembly, on the recommendation of the Fourth (Special Political and Decolonization) Committee [A/55/571], adopted **resolution 55/132** by recorded vote (152-4) [agenda item 85].

Israeli settlements in the Occupied Palestinian Territory, including Jerusalem, and the occupied Syrian Golan

The General Assembly,

Guided by the principles of the Charter of the United Nations, and affirming the inadmissibility of the acquisition of territory by force,

Recalling its relevant resolutions, including those adopted at its tenth emergency special session, as well as relevant Security Council resolutions, including resolutions 242(1967) of 22 November 1967, 446(1979) of 22 March 1979, 465(1980) of 1 March 1980 and 497(1981) of 17 December 1981,

Reaffirming the applicability of the Geneva Convention relative to the Protection of Civilian Persons in Time of War, of 12 August 1949, to the Occupied Palestinian Territory, including Jerusalem, and to the occupied Syrian Golan,

Aware of the Middle East peace process started at Madrid and the agreements reached between the parties, in particular the Declaration of Principles on Interim Self-Government Arrangements of 13 September 1993, and the subsequent implementation agreements,

Expressing grave concern about the continuation by Israel of settlement activities, including the ongoing construction of the settlement in Jabal Abu-Ghneim, in violation of international humanitarian law, relevant United Nations resolutions and the agreements reached between the parties,

Taking into consideration the detrimental impact of Israeli settlement policies, decisions and activities on the Middle East peace process,

Gravely concerned in particular about the dangerous situation resulting from actions taken by the illegal armed Israeli settlers in the occupied territory, as illustrated by the massacre of Palestinian worshippers by an illegal Israeli settler in Al-Khalil on 25 February 1994, and during recent weeks,

Taking note of the report of the Secretary-General,

1. *Reaffirms* that Israeli settlements in the Palestinian territory, including Jerusalem, and in the occupied

Syrian Golan are illegal and an obstacle to peace and economic and social development;

2. *Calls upon* Israel to accept the de jure applicability of the Geneva Convention relative to the Protection of Civilian Persons in Time of War, of 12 August 1949, to the Occupied Palestinian Territory, including Jerusalem, and to the occupied Syrian Golan and to abide scrupulously by the provisions of the Convention, in particular article 49;

3. *Demands* complete cessation of the construction of the settlement in Jabal Abu-Ghneim and of all Israeli settlement activities in the Occupied Palestinian Territory, including Jerusalem, and in the occupied Syrian Golan;

4. *Stresses* the need for full implementation of Security Council resolution 904(1994) of 18 March 1994, in which, among other things, the Council called upon Israel, the occupying Power, to continue to take and implement measures, including, inter alia, confiscation of arms, with the aim of preventing illegal acts of violence by Israeli settlers, and called for measures to be taken to guarantee the safety and protection of the Palestinian civilians in the occupied territory;

5. *Reiterates its call* for the prevention of illegal acts of violence by Israeli settlers, particularly in the light of recent developments;

6. *Requests* the Secretary-General to report to the General Assembly at its fifty-sixth session on the implementation of the present resolution.

RECORDED VOTE ON RESOLUTION 55/132:

In favour: Afghanistan, Algeria, Andorra, Antigua and Barbuda, Argentina, Armenia, Australia, Austria, Azerbaijan, Bahamas, Bahrain, Bangladesh, Barbados, Belarus, Belgium, Belize, Benin, Bhutan, Bolivia, Botswana, Brazil, Brunei Darussalam, Bulgaria, Burkina Faso, Burundi, Cambodia, Canada, Cape Verde, Chad, Chile, China, Colombia, Comoros, Costa Rica, Côte d'Ivoire, Croatia, Cuba, Cyprus, Czech Republic, Democratic People's Republic of Korea, Denmark, Djibouti, Dominican Republic, Ecuador, Egypt, El Salvador, Eritrea, Estonia, Ethiopia, Fiji, Finland, France, Gabon, Georgia, Germany, Ghana, Greece, Grenada, Guatemala, Guinea, Guyana, Haiti, Honduras, Hungary, Iceland, India, Indonesia, Iran, Ireland, Italy, Jamaica, Japan, Jordan, Kazakhstan, Kenya, Kuwait, Kyrgyzstan, Lao People's Democratic Republic, Latvia, Lebanon, Libyan Arab Jamahiriya, Liechtenstein, Lithuania, Luxembourg, Madagascar, Malaysia, Maldives, Mali, Malta, Mauritania, Mauritius, Mexico, Monaco, Mongolia, Morocco, Mozambique, Myanmar, Namibia, Nepal, Netherlands, New Zealand, Nicaragua, Nigeria, Norway, Oman, Pakistan, Panama, Papua New Guinea, Paraguay, Peru, Philippines, Poland, Portugal, Qatar, Republic of Korea, Republic of Moldova, Romania, Russian Federation, Saint Lucia, Samoa, San Marino, Saudi Arabia, Senegal, Singapore, Slovakia, Slovenia, Solomon Islands, South Africa, Spain, Sri Lanka, Sudan, Swaziland, Sweden, Syrian Arab Republic, Thailand, The former Yugoslav Republic of Macedonia, Togo, Tunisia, Turkey, Uganda, Ukraine, United Arab Emirates, United Kingdom, United Republic of Tanzania, Uruguay, Vanuatu, Venezuela, Viet Nam, Yemen, Yugoslavia, Zambia, Zimbabwe.

Against: Israel, Marshall Islands, Micronesia, United States.

Jerusalem

East Jerusalem, where most of the city's Arab inhabitants lived, remained one of the most sensitive issues in the Middle East peace process and a focal point of concern for the United Nations in 2000. The visit on 28 September by Mr. Sharon, leader of the opposition Likud Party in Israel, to the holy Islamic site of Al-Haram Al-Sharif in Jerusalem and the subsequent escalation of violence led to the convening of a three-day Security Council emergency meeting and to the resumption of the General Assembly's tenth emergency special session (see pp. 417 and 421).

Special Committee on Israeli Practices. In its annual report [A/55/453], the Special Committee on Israeli Practices described restrictions imposed by Israeli authorities on Jerusalem's Palestinian population and Israeli violations of their human rights.

The general situation with respect to housing seemed to have remained very much as it had been in previous years. The Special Committee was informed that Israel was investing a large amount of resources in building Jewish neighbourhoods in East Jerusalem while curtailing Palestinian development, the Palestinian population being viewed as a demographic threat to Israeli control of the city. Over a third of East Jerusalem lacked town-planning schemes, which made construction impossible, and those planning schemes that existed defined vast land tracts as green area, where building was forbidden. While some green areas were designed to protect the environment, others held land in reserve for the Jewish population, as in the case of the Jabal Abu-Ghneim, which, although originally defined as a green area, was later rezoned for residential construction of the Jewish neighbourhood of Har Homa. Palestinian building was only allowed in 7 per cent of East Jerusalem, and already-existing Palestinian neighbourhoods comprised most of that area. Israel had succeeded in creating an enormous Jewish population in East Jerusalem while reducing the Palestinian population. Israeli policies had created a housing shortage in Palestinian neighbourhoods and exacerbated overcrowding by denying building permits. The housing shortage among Palestinians in Jerusalem exceeded 20,000 housing units. In addition, land owned by an absentee was not given a building permit. That was a particularly harsh situation in East Jerusalem, where the term absentee included those with West Bank resident status.

Transfer of diplomatic missions

Report of Secretary-General. On 2 November [A/55/538], the Secretary-General reported that four Member States, including Israel, had replied to his request for information on steps taken or envisaged to implement General Assembly resolution 54/37 [YUN 1999, p. 409], which addressed the transfer by some States of their diplomatic missions to Jerusalem in violation of Security Council resolution 478(1980) [YUN 1980, p. 426] and called on them to abide by the relevant UN resolutions. Israel said that the one-sided approach reflected in those resolutions threatened to prejudge the outcome of bilateral negotiations between the parties concerned and undermined

the prospects of achieving a just and lasting peace settlement based on directly negotiated and mutually agreed solutions.

Committee on Palestinian Rights. In its annual report [A/55/35], the Committee on Palestinian Rights said that Israel's settlement policy and actions continued to damage the peace process. According to figures from Israel's Ministry of Construction and Housing, construction in settlements increased by 96 per cent in the first half of 2000. In fact, work began on 1,067 residential units in the first six months of the year (860 of which were located in settlements in the Jerusalem district), compared to 545 during the same period in 1999. In particular, the Committee was appalled by the intensified construction at the Jabal Abu-Ghneim and Ras al-Amud neighbourhoods of East Jerusalem. The Committee also stressed the inadmissibility and illegality of the Israeli policy of revoking the residency rights of Palestinian Jerusalemites. Although the Israeli Minister of the Interior declared the cessation of the revocation-of-residency policy in October 1999, no clear procedures had been introduced regarding the new policy, and the rules applied by the Ministry officials in East Jerusalem remained unclear.

GENERAL ASSEMBLY ACTION

On 1 December [meeting 78], the General Assembly adopted **resolution 55/50** [draft: A/55/L.49 & Add.1] by recorded vote (145-1-5) [agenda item 40].

Jerusalem

The General Assembly,

Recalling its resolutions 36/120 E of 10 December 1981, 37/123 C of 16 December 1982, 38/180 C of 19 December 1983, 39/146 C of 14 December 1984, 40/168 C of 16 December 1985, 41/162 C of 4 December 1986, 42/209 D of 11 December 1987, 43/54 C of 6 December 1988, 44/40 C of 4 December 1989, 45/83 C of 13 December 1990, 46/82 B of 16 December 1991, 47/63 B of 11 December 1992, 48/59 A of 14 December 1993, 49/87 A of 16 December 1994, 50/22 A of 4 December 1995, 51/27 of 4 December 1996, 52/53 of 9 December 1997, 53/37 of 2 December 1998 and 54/37 of 1 December 1999, in which it, inter alia, determined that all legislative and administrative measures and actions taken by Israel, the occupying Power, which have altered or purported to alter the character and status of the Holy City of Jerusalem, in particular the so-called "Basic Law" on Jerusalem and the proclamation of Jerusalem as the capital of Israel, were null and void and must be rescinded forthwith,

Recalling also Security Council resolution 478(1980) of 20 August 1980, in which the Council, inter alia, decided not to recognize the "Basic Law" and called upon those States which had established diplomatic missions in Jerusalem to withdraw such missions from the Holy City,

Having considered the report of the Secretary-General,

1. *Determines* that the decision of Israel to impose its laws, jurisdiction and administration on the Holy City of Jerusalem is illegal and therefore null and void and has no validity whatsoever;

2. *Deplores* the transfer by some States of their diplomatic missions to Jerusalem in violation of Security Council resolution 478(1980) and their refusal to comply with the provisions of that resolution;

3. *Calls once more upon* those States to abide by the provisions of the relevant United Nations resolutions, in conformity with the Charter of the United Nations;

4. *Requests* the Secretary-General to report to the General Assembly at its fifty-sixth session on the implementation of the present resolution.

RECORDED VOTE ON RESOLUTION 55/50:

In favour: Afghanistan, Algeria, Andorra, Antigua and Barbuda, Argentina, Armenia, Australia, Austria, Azerbaijan, Bahamas, Bahrain, Bangladesh, Barbados, Belarus, Belgium, Bolivia, Bosnia and Herzegovina, Botswana, Brazil, Brunei Darussalam, Bulgaria, Burkina Faso, Burundi, Cambodia, Canada, Chad, Chile, China, Colombia, Comoros, Croatia, Cuba, Cyprus, Czech Republic, Democratic People's Republic of Korea, Denmark, Djibouti, Dominican Republic, Ecuador, Egypt, Eritrea, Estonia, Ethiopia, Fiji, Finland, France, Gabon, Gambia, Georgia, Germany, Ghana, Greece, Grenada, Guatemala, Guinea, Guyana, Honduras, Hungary, Iceland, India, Indonesia, Iran, Ireland, Italy, Japan, Jordan, Kazakhstan, Kenya, Kuwait, Kyrgyzstan, Lao People's Democratic Republic, Latvia, Lebanon, Libyan Arab Jamahiriya, Liechtenstein, Lithuania, Luxembourg, Madagascar, Malaysia, Maldives, Mali, Malta, Mauritius, Mexico, Monaco, Mongolia, Morocco, Mozambique, Myanmar, Namibia, Nepal, Netherlands, New Zealand, Nicaragua, Nigeria, Norway, Oman, Pakistan, Panama, Paraguay, Peru, Philippines, Poland, Portugal, Qatar, Republic of Korea, Republic of Moldova, Romania, Russian Federation, Saint Lucia, Samoa, San Marino, Saudi Arabia, Senegal, Sierra Leone, Singapore, Slovakia, Slovenia, Solomon Islands, South Africa, Spain, Sri Lanka, Sudan, Swaziland, Sweden, Syrian Arab Republic, Tajikistan, Thailand, The former Yugoslav Republic of Macedonia, Togo, Trinidad and Tobago, Tunisia, Turkey, Uganda, Ukraine, United Arab Emirates, United Kingdom, United Republic of Tanzania, Uruguay, Venezuela, Viet Nam, Yemen, Yugoslavia, Zambia, Zimbabwe.

Against: Israel.

Abstaining: Angola, Marshall Islands, Micronesia, Nauru, United States.

Economic and social situation

A June report on the economic and social repercussions of the Israeli occupation on the living conditions of Palestinians in the occupied territory, including Jerusalem, and of the Arab population of the occupied Syrian Golan [A/55/84-E/2000/16] was prepared by the Economic and Social Commission for Western Asia (ESCWA), in accordance with Economic and Social Council resolution 1999/53 [YUN 1999, p. 410] and General Assembly resolution 54/230 [ibid., p. 411]; it covered the period since ESCWA's previous report [ibid., p. 409].

The report stated that the delays in implementing the agreements reached between Israel and the PLO, together with Israeli practices, particularly the settlement expansion and the closure of passage routes from areas controlled by the PA to Israel, continued to aggravate the Palestinians' living conditions. Approximately 200,000 Israelis resided in East Jerusalem and 7,000 settlers lived in 16 settlements in Gaza. In the Golan Heights, 17,000 settlers resided in 33 settlements. By the end of 2000, more than 400,000 Israelis would be living in over 200 communities established since 1967 in the Occupied Palestinian

Territory. In East Jerusalem, Israel had expropriated more than 5,845 acres of mostly Palestinian-owned land—one third of East Jerusalem—for the construction of 10 Israeli settlement neighbourhoods. The number of Palestinians holding Jerusalem identity documents issued by Israel was generally believed to number almost 200,000, putting the Palestinian percentage of the entire city at 30 per cent. Investigations undertaken by Palestinian officials suggested that the number of Palestinians actually residing in the city was half that number. According to a study by the Badil Resource Centre for Palestinian Refugee Rights, 8 per cent of Jerusalem residents were forced to leave Jerusalem and reside in the West Bank every year owing to Israeli discriminatory measures in the city. The revocation of residency rights of Palestinians in Jerusalem continued to be a problem, while requests of those who had appealed in the past to register births and marriages went unfulfilled, forcing many Arabs (estimated at some 30,000) to live in East Jerusalem without identity cards.

The Israeli occupation was affecting and undermining the supply of drinking water to Palestinians, as Israel controlled permits for drinking water networks and for drilling wells. In addition, Palestinians were faced with the growing problem of water waste coming from Israeli settlements.

Israel's control of the Occupied Palestinian Territory also had negative repercussions on the environment. Approximately 260 Israeli-owned industrial concerns existed in the West Bank, located either in Israeli-operated industrial zones or inside settlements. Environmental regulations on soil, air and water quality, and restrictions on industrial development were generally less comprehensive and much less assiduously enforced in the occupied territory compared with in Israel itself.

The Israeli occupation had inhibited investment and growth due to the continued ambiguity of the legal and political situation. There was no basic investment code nor a settled legal code in the areas controlled by the PA. In nominal terms, Palestinian registered exports to Israel amounted to $222.6 million, while registered imports from Israel totalled $843.5 million in the first half of 1999. Beginning in March 2000, Israel imposed a number of restrictions on Palestinian economic transactions, including suspending the "convoy system", which allowed vehicles from Gaza to pass through Israeli territory under military escort for the purpose of export and import. Restrictions on the movement of goods contributed to a further decline in economic growth.

Israeli settlement expansion in the Golan Heights continued, while employment opportunities and access to education for the Arab population remained limited.

ECONOMIC AND SOCIAL COUNCIL ACTION

On 28 July [meeting 45], the Economic and Social Council adopted **resolution 2000/31** [draft: E/2000/L.16] by recorded vote (41-1-1) [agenda item 11].

Economic and social repercussions of the Israeli occupation on the living conditions of the Palestinian people in the occupied Palestinian territory, including Jerusalem, and the Arab population in the occupied Syrian Golan

The Economic and Social Council,

Recalling General Assembly resolution 54/230 of 22 December 1999,

Recalling also its resolution 1999/53 of 29 July 1999,

Guided by the principles of the Charter of the United Nations, affirming the inadmissibility of the acquisition of territory by force, and recalling relevant Security Council resolutions, including resolutions 242(1967) of 22 November 1967, 465(1980) of 1 March 1980 and 497(1981) of 17 December 1981,

Reaffirming the applicability of the Geneva Convention relative to the Protection of Civilian Persons in Time of War, of 12 August 1949, to the Occupied Palestinian Territory, including Jerusalem, and other Arab territories occupied by Israel since 1967,

Stressing the importance of the revival of the Middle East peace process on the basis of Security Council resolutions 242(1967), 338(1973) of 22 October 1973 and 425(1978) of 19 March 1978, and the principle of land for peace as well as the full and timely implementation of the agreements reached between the Government of Israel and the Palestine Liberation Organization, the representative of the Palestinian people,

Reaffirming the principle of the permanent sovereignty of peoples under foreign occupation over their natural resources,

Convinced that the Israeli occupation impedes efforts to achieve sustainable development and a sound economic environment in the Occupied Palestinian Territory, including Jerusalem, and the occupied Syrian Golan,

Gravely concerned about the deterioration of economic and living conditions of the Palestinian people in the Occupied Palestinian Territory, including Jerusalem, and of the Arab population of the occupied Syrian Golan, and the exploitation by Israel, the occupying Power, of their natural resources,

Aware of the important work being done by the United Nations and the specialized agencies in support of the economic and social development of the Palestinian people,

Conscious of the urgent need for the development of the economic and social infrastructure of the Occupied Palestinian Territory, including Jerusalem, and for the improvement of the living conditions of the Palestinian people as a key element of a lasting peace and stability,

1. *Stresses* the need to preserve the territorial integrity of all of the Occupied Palestinian Territory and to guarantee the freedom of movement of persons and goods in the territory, including the removal of restrictions on going into and from East Jerusalem, and the freedom of movement to and from the outside world;

2. *Also stresses* the vital importance of the construction and operation of the seaport in Gaza and safe passage to the economic and social development of the Palestinian people;

3. *Calls upon* Israel, the occupying Power, to cease its measures against the Palestinian people, in particular the closure of the Occupied Palestinian Territory, the enforced isolation of Palestinian towns, the destruction of homes and the isolation of Jerusalem;

4. *Reaffirms* the inalienable right of the Palestinian people and the Arab population of the occupied Syrian Golan to all their natural and economic resources, and calls upon Israel, the occupying Power, not to exploit, endanger or cause loss or depletion of these resources;

5. *Also reaffirms* that Israeli settlements in the Occupied Palestinian Territory, including Jerusalem, and the occupied Syrian Golan, are illegal and an obstacle to economic and social development;

6. *Stresses* the importance of the work of the organizations and agencies of the United Nations, and of the United Nations Special Coordinator for the Middle East Peace Process and Personal Representative of the Secretary-General to the Palestine Liberation Organization and the Palestinian Authority;

7. *Urges* Member States to encourage private foreign investment in the Occupied Palestinian Territory, including Jerusalem, in infrastructure, job-creation projects and social development, in order to alleviate the hardship of the Palestinian people and improve living conditions;

8. *Requests* the Secretary-General to submit to the General Assembly at its fifty-sixth session, through the Economic and Social Council, a report on the implementation of the present resolution and to continue to include, in the report of the Special Coordinator, an update on the living conditions of the Palestinian people, in collaboration with relevant United Nations agencies;

9. *Decides* to include the item entitled "Economic and social repercussions of the Israeli occupation on the living conditions of the Palestinian people in the Occupied Palestinian Territory, including Jerusalem, and the Arab population in the occupied Syrian Golan" in the agenda of its substantive session of 2001.

RECORDED VOTE ON RESOLUTION 2000/31:

In favour: Algeria, Angola, Austria, Bahrain, Belarus, Belgium, Bolivia, Brazil, Bulgaria, Burkina Faso, Canada, China, Colombia, Cuba, Czech Republic, Denmark, Fiji, France, Germany, Greece, India, Indonesia, Italy, Japan, Mexico, Morocco, New Zealand, Norway, Oman, Pakistan, Poland, Portugal, Russian Federation, Saint Lucia, Saudi Arabia, Sudan, Suriname, Syrian Arab Republic, United Kingdom, Venezuela, Viet Nam.
Against: United States.
Abstaining: Croatia.

By **decision 2000/293** of the same date, the Council took note of the ESCWA report.

GENERAL ASSEMBLY ACTION

On 20 December [meeting 87], the General Assembly, on the recommendation of the Second (Economic and Financial) Committee [A/55/585], adopted **resolution 55/209** by recorded vote (147-2-3) [agenda item 98].

Permanent sovereignty of the Palestinian people in the Occupied Palestinian Territory, including Jerusalem, and of the Arab population in the occupied Syrian Golan over their natural resources

The General Assembly,

Recalling its resolution 54/230 of 22 December 1999, and taking note of Economic and Social Council resolution 2000/31 of 28 July 2000,

Reaffirming the principle of the permanent sovereignty of peoples under foreign occupation over their natural resources,

Guided by the principles of the Charter of the United Nations, affirming the inadmissibility of the acquisition of territory by force, and recalling the relevant Security Council resolutions, including resolutions 242(1967) of 22 November 1967, 465(1980) of 1 March 1980 and 497(1981) of 17 December 1981,

Reaffirming the applicability of the Geneva Convention relative to the Protection of Civilian Persons in Time of War, of 12 August 1949, to the Occupied Palestinian Territory, including Jerusalem, and other Arab territories occupied by Israel since 1967,

Expressing its concern at the exploitation by Israel, the occupying Power, of the natural resources of the Occupied Palestinian Territory, including Jerusalem, and other Arab territories occupied by Israel since 1967,

Aware of the additional detrimental economic and social impact of the Israeli settlements on Palestinian and other Arab natural resources, especially the confiscation of land and the forced diversion of water resources,

Reaffirming the need for an immediate resumption of negotiations within the Middle East peace process, on the basis of Security Council resolutions 242(1967) of 22 November 1967 and 338(1973) of 22 October 1973, and the principle of land for peace, and for the achievement of a final settlement on all tracks,

1. *Takes note* of the report transmitted by the Secretary-General;

2. *Reaffirms* the inalienable rights of the Palestinian people and the population of the occupied Syrian Golan over their natural resources, including land and water;

3. *Calls upon* Israel, the occupying Power, not to exploit, to cause loss or depletion of or to endanger the natural resources in the Occupied Palestinian Territory, including Jerusalem, and in the occupied Syrian Golan;

4. *Recognizes* the right of the Palestinian people to claim restitution as a result of any exploitation, loss or depletion of, or danger to, their natural resources, and expresses the hope that this issue will be dealt with in the framework of the final status negotiations between the Palestinian and Israeli sides;

5. *Requests* the Secretary-General to report to it at its fifty-sixth session on the implementation of the present resolution, and decides to include in the agenda of its fifty-sixth session the item entitled "Permanent sovereignty of the Palestinian people in the Occupied Palestinian Territory, including Jerusalem, and of the Arab population in the occupied Syrian Golan over their natural resources".

RECORDED VOTE ON RESOLUTION 55/209:

In favour: Afghanistan, Algeria, Andorra, Angola, Argentina, Armenia, Australia, Austria, Azerbaijan, Bahamas, Bahrain, Bangladesh, Barbados, Belarus, Belgium, Belize, Benin, Bolivia, Botswana, Brazil, Brunei Darussalam, Bulgaria, Burkina Faso, Burundi, Cambodia, Canada, Cape Verde, Chad, Chile, China, Colombia, Côte d'Ivoire, Croatia, Cuba, Cyprus, Czech Republic, Democratic People's Republic of Korea, Denmark, Djibouti, Dominican Republic, Ecuador, Egypt, Eritrea, Estonia, Ethiopia, Finland, France, Gabon, Gambia, Georgia, Germany, Ghana, Greece, Grenada, Guinea, Guyana, Haiti, Honduras, Hungary, Iceland, India, Indonesia, Iran, Ireland, Italy, Jamaica, Japan, Jordan, Kenya, Kuwait, Kyrgyzstan, Lao People's Democratic Republic, Latvia, Lebanon, Lesotho, Libyan Arab Jamahiriya, Liechtenstein, Lithuania, Luxembourg, Madagascar, Malawi, Malaysia, Maldives, Malta, Mauritania, Mauritius, Mexico, Monaco, Mongolia, Morocco, Mozambique, Myanmar, Namibia, Nepal, Netherlands, New Zealand, Nigeria, Norway, Oman, Pakistan, Panama, Papua New Guinea, Paraguay, Peru, Philippines, Poland, Portugal, Qatar, Republic of Korea, Romania, Russian Federation, Rwanda, Samoa, San Marino, Saudi Arabia, Senegal, Singapore, Slovakia, Slovenia, Solomon Islands, South Africa, Spain, Sri Lanka, Sudan, Swaziland, Sweden, Syrian Arab Republic, Tajikistan, Thailand, The former Yugoslav Republic of Macedonia, Togo, Trinidad and Tobago, Tunisia, Turkey, Uganda, Ukraine, United Arab Emirates, United Kingdom, United Republic of Tanzania, Uruguay, Uzbekistan, Venezuela, Viet Nam, Yemen, Yugoslavia, Zambia, Zimbabwe.

Against: Israel, United States.

Abstaining: Fiji, Marshall Islands, Nauru.

Other aspects

Special Committee on Israeli Practices. On 5 October, the Special Committee on Israeli Practices reported for the thirty-second time to the General Assembly on events in the territories it considered to be occupied—the Golan Heights, the West Bank, including East Jerusalem, and the Gaza Strip [A/55/453].

In addition to that annual report, the Special Committee, in response to a request by the Assembly in resolution 54/76 [YUN 1999, p. 414], submitted two periodic reports in 2000, one covering the period from 21 August 1999 to 29 February 2000 [A/55/373] and the other covering the period from 1 March to 31 July 2000 [A/55/373/Add.1]. The three reports contained information obtained from the Arab and Israeli press; testimony from persons from the occupied territories; and communications and reports from Governments, organizations and individuals. The Committee benefited from the cooperation of Egypt, Jordan, the Syrian Arab Republic, Palestinian representatives, the UN resident coordinator/United Nations Development Programme (UNDP) Resident Representative in Syria, and representatives from the International Labour Organization. As in the past, the Committee received no response from Israel to its request for cooperation and was unable to obtain access to the occupied territories, which had been the case since 1968, when the Committee was established [YUN 1968, p. 556]. However, the Special Committee was pleased that a number of Israeli nationals working in the field of human rights appeared before the Committee to speak about their work with Palestinians.

The Special Committee was informed that restrictions in the occupied territories of Gaza, the West Bank and East Jerusalem, with respect to land, housing and water, severely affected the

Palestinians, and the confiscation of Palestinian-owned land continued, as well as the establishment of new and expansion of existing settlements. Demolition of Palestinian houses had also continued throughout the period under review. The building of bypass roads to ensure the safety of the Israeli settlers in the West Bank often resulted in confiscation of land and house demolition.

The extremely sensitive and tense relations between settlers and Palestinians—one of the most unfortunate consequences of the occupation—reached higher levels of intensity and violence in times of crisis. The condition of those relations was caused by the confiscation of land, the uprooting of olive trees, the scarcity of water and the privileged position Israeli settlements had with respect to water, the fact that settlers carried arms and lived in barrier-enclosed areas, and the support provided by Israeli authorities and their army.

As Israeli settlements in the occupied territories were usually located on hilltops, spring water used by Palestinians had often been polluted by sewage water from the settlements or army centres. In addition, factories and industrial centres established within the settlements were trying to pump their wastes into adjacent Palestinian areas, without taking into consideration the consequences on the environment and on the Palestinians living nearby. Many of those factories had been established in Israeli settlements because they were not able to obtain permission to operate in Israel, due to their harmful impact on the environment and the threat they posed to the health of the population.

The permanent state of closure of the occupied territories continued to be applied and the movement of the population within the territories continued to be regulated by the Israeli authorities. Access to Israel and movement between the occupied territories were blocked during Jewish holidays and when security incidents occurred in Israel. A new development regarding the freedom of movement was the construction of a checkpoint near Bethlehem, which would de facto separate the northern part of the West Bank from the southern part. Furthermore, Israel had imposed restrictions on movement between areas that were under the PA's rule.

A positive development was the decline in the number of Palestinian administrative detainees. At the beginning of 1999, about 100 Palestinian detainees were under administrative detention in Israeli prisons; at the end of 1999, that number had been reduced to 14. Amendments were also introduced to the law governing administrative detention, making it possible, during the first 10 days of administrative detention, to bring the detainee before a committee under a military judge in order to ascertain whether the order, or the time period of the detention, was legal. However, the Israeli intelligence service did not respect the committee's decisions and could override the decisions of judges concerning extensions of detention. It was estimated that some 1,500 Palestinian detainees were held in Israeli jails, some of whom were not allowed to receive family visits for periods of up to a year. In 1999, the Israeli prison administration had adopted measures against Palestinian lawyers members of the Palestinian Union of Lawyers. Their visits to clients had to be in the presence of an Israeli policeman who listened in on the conversation. Although that measure contravened all laws governing legal representation, Israeli authorities argued that Palestinian lawyers did not have the right to defend before Israeli courts and therefore should be considered as family members visiting the detainee.

In September 1999, the Israeli Supreme Court of Justice ruled that the interrogation methods used by the General Security Service (GSS) were illegal and forbidden. It stated, however, that if the State wished to enable GSS investigators to use physical means of interrogation, it should seek the enactment of legislation for that purpose. Thus, the decision banned the practices because of the lack of a legal text that could be invoked. The Special Committee was informed that, following that decision, there had been continuous efforts to enact legislation to allow physical force to be used during interrogations, and the Israeli Government had pledged to confer immunity on investigators who used torture.

Administrative security measures hampered the development of industrial and commercial activities by Palestinian employers. The Israeli authorities continued to impede the movement of trucks carrying Palestinian goods and products, resulting in products being spoiled owing to long periods spent at checkpoints. Driven by the need to earn a decent income or even to find a job, a large number of Palestinian workers in the occupied territories had turned to the Israeli labour market. However, Palestinian workers continued to be humiliated at Israeli checkpoints; on some occasions, workers had also been arrested. In Gaza, Palestinian fishermen were allowed to fish only within a perimeter of 20 nautical miles out to sea and, among other restrictions, were not allowed to sell their products in the West Bank or in Israel. The Israelis had also hampered the work of Palestinian journalists by limiting their freedom of movement or preventing them from disseminating information inside or outside the occupied territories.

The Special Committee visited the Syrian Arab Republic and reported on the Israeli-occupied Syrian Golan Heights (for details, see p. 477).

The Special Committee observed that the Israeli authorities had put in place a comprehensive and elaborate system of laws and regulations that affected all aspects of the lives of the Palestinian and Syrian peoples in the occupied territories. The rigorous implementation of laws and regulations and administrative measures created a sense of fear and despondency among the inhabitants. Bitterness at their treatment by the authorities and the sense of dispossession, hopelessness and despair of the people in the occupied territories, caused to a large extent by lack of progress in the peace process and a lack of tangible benefits for the Palestinians, made the situation in the region one of the greatest urgency. The Committee called on the United Nations High Commissioner for Human Rights, in consultation with the Secretary-General, to establish a system of continuous communication with the Israeli authorities with a view to improving the difficult circumstances under which the Palestinian and Syrian peoples of the occupied territories lived.

In a later report [A/56/428], the Committee presented updated information on the human rights situation in the occupied territories during the last five months of 2000, providing details on restrictions relating to land, housing and water, as well as those affecting movement of Palestinians within and between the occupied territories, and the manner of implementation of restrictions and their economic, social and cultural effects on the Palestinian population. Information was provided on the escalation of violence in the occupied territories following the 28 September visit by Mr. Sharon to the Temple Mount. Also included was information on the occupied Syrian Arab Golan.

Report of Secretary-General. On 4 August [A/55/264], the Secretary-General informed the Assembly that Israel had not replied to his July request for information on steps taken or envisaged to implement Assembly resolution 54/79 [YUN 1999, p. 413] demanding that Israel, among other things, cease all practices and actions that violated the human rights of the Palestinian people and accelerate the release of all remaining Palestinians arbitrarily detained or imprisoned.

Commission on Human Rights. In October, the Commission on Human Rights held a special session on grave and massive violations of the human rights of the Palestinian people by Israel and adopted a resolution on the subject (see

p. 776). By **decision 2000/311** of 22 November, the Economic and Social Council endorsed the Commission's decisions to establish a human rights inquiry commission to gather and compile information on Israel's human rights violations in the occupied Palestinian territories; to request the High Commissioner for Human Rights to undertake an urgent visit to the territories; and to request rapporteurs, the Representative of the Secretary-General on internally displaced persons and the Working Group on Enforced or Involuntary Disappearances to carry out immediate missions to the territories.

The High Commissioner for Human Rights undertook a visit to the Middle East in November (see p. 776).

GENERAL ASSEMBLY ACTION

On 8 December [meeting 83], following consideration of the Special Committee's annual and periodic reports and five reports of the Secretary-General on specific aspects of the situation in the occupied territories [A/55/261-265], the General Assembly, on the recommendation of the Fourth Committee [A/55/571], adopted **resolution 55/133** by recorded vote (150-3-1) [agenda item 85].

Israeli practices affecting the human rights of the Palestinian people in the Occupied Palestinian Territory, including Jerusalem

The General Assembly,

Recalling its relevant resolutions, including those adopted at its tenth emergency special session, and the resolutions of the Commission on Human Rights,

Bearing in mind the relevant resolutions of the Security Council, the most recent of which are resolutions 904(1994) of 18 March 1994, 1073(1996) of 28 September 1996 and 1322(2000) of 7 October 2000,

Having considered the reports of the Special Committee to Investigate Israeli Practices Affecting the Human Rights of the Palestinian People and Other Arabs of the Occupied Territories and the reports of the Secretary-General,

Aware of the responsibility of the international community to promote human rights and ensure respect for international law,

Reaffirming the principle of the inadmissibility of the acquisition of territory by force,

Reaffirming also the applicability of the Geneva Convention relative to the Protection of Civilian Persons in Time of War, of 12 August 1949, to the Occupied Palestinian Territory, including Jerusalem, and other Arab territories occupied by Israel since 1967,

Stressing the need for compliance with the Israeli-Palestinian agreements reached within the context of the Middle East peace process,

Noting the withdrawal of the Israeli army, which took place in the Gaza Strip and the Jericho area, and the subsequent Israeli redeployments in accordance with the agreements reached between the parties, and noting that the third agreed-upon phase of redeployment has not been implemented,

Concerned about the continuing violation of the human rights of the Palestinian people by Israel, the occupying Power, including the use of collective punishment, closure of areas, annexation and establishment of settlements and the continuing actions by it designed to change the legal status, geographical nature and demographic composition of the Occupied Palestinian Territory, including Jerusalem,

Deeply concerned by the tragic events that have occurred since 28 September 2000 and have led to numerous deaths and injuries, mostly among Palestinians,

Gravely concerned about the severe restrictions on the movement of Palestinian persons and goods,

Expressing support for the understandings reached at the summit convened at Sharm el-Sheikh, Egypt, and urging all parties concerned to implement those understandings honestly and without delay,

Convinced of the positive impact of a temporary international or foreign presence in the Occupied Palestinian Territory for the safety and protection of the Palestinian people,

Expressing its appreciation to the countries that participated in the Temporary International Presence in Hebron for their positive contribution,

Convinced of the need for the full implementation of Security Council resolutions 904(1994), 1073(1996) and 1322(2000),

1. *Determines* that all measures and actions taken by Israel, the occupying Power, in the Occupied Palestinian Territory, including Jerusalem, in violation of the relevant provisions of the Geneva Convention relative to the Protection of Civilian Persons in Time of War, of 12 August 1949, and contrary to the relevant resolutions of the Security Council, are illegal and have no validity and that such measures should cease immediately;

2. *Condemns* acts of violence, especially the excessive use of force against Palestinian civilians, resulting in injury and loss of human life;

3. *Demands* that Israel, the occupying Power, cease all practices and actions which violate the human rights of the Palestinian people;

4. *Stresses* the need to preserve the territorial integrity of all the Occupied Palestinian Territory and to guarantee the freedom of movement of persons and goods within the Palestinian territory, including the removal of restrictions on movement into and from East Jerusalem, and the freedom of movement to and from the outside world;

5. *Calls upon* Israel, the occupying Power, to accelerate the release of all remaining Palestinians arbitrarily detained or imprisoned, in line with agreements reached;

6. *Calls* for complete respect by Israel, the occupying Power, of all fundamental freedoms of the Palestinian people;

7. *Requests* the Secretary-General to report to the General Assembly at its fifty-sixth session on the implementation of the present resolution.

RECORDED VOTE ON RESOLUTION 55/133:

In favour: Afghanistan, Algeria, Andorra, Antigua and Barbuda, Argentina, Armenia, Australia, Austria, Azerbaijan, Bahamas, Bahrain, Bangladesh, Barbados, Belarus, Belgium, Belize, Benin, Bhutan, Bolivia, Botswana, Brazil, Brunei Darussalam, Bulgaria, Burkina Faso, Burundi, Cambodia, Canada, Cape Verde, Chad, Chile, China, Colombia, Comoros, Côte d'Ivoire, Croatia, Cuba, Cyprus, Czech Republic, Democratic People's

Republic of Korea, Denmark, Djibouti, Dominican Republic, Ecuador, Egypt, El Salvador, Eritrea, Estonia, Ethiopia, Fiji, Finland, France, Gabon, Georgia, Germany, Ghana, Greece, Grenada, Guatemala, Guinea, Guyana, Haiti, Honduras, Hungary, Iceland, India, Indonesia, Iran, Ireland, Italy, Jamaica, Japan, Jordan, Kenya, Kuwait, Kyrgyzstan, Lao People's Democratic Republic, Latvia, Lebanon, Libyan Arab Jamahiriya, Liechtenstein, Lithuania, Luxembourg, Madagascar, Malaysia, Maldives, Mali, Malta, Mauritania, Mauritius, Mexico, Monaco, Mongolia, Morocco, Mozambique, Myanmar, Namibia, Nepal, Netherlands, New Zealand, Nicaragua, Nigeria, Norway, Oman, Pakistan, Panama, Papua New Guinea, Paraguay, Peru, Philippines, Poland, Portugal, Qatar, Republic of Korea, Republic of Moldova, Romania, Russian Federation, Saint Lucia, Samoa, San Marino, Saudi Arabia, Senegal, Singapore, Slovakia, Slovenia, Solomon Islands, South Africa, Spain, Sri Lanka, Sudan, Swaziland, Sweden, Syrian Arab Republic, Thailand, The former Yugoslav Republic of Macedonia, Togo, Tunisia, Turkey, Uganda, Ukraine, United Arab Emirates, United Kingdom, United Republic of Tanzania, Uruguay, Vanuatu, Venezuela, Viet Nam, Yemen, Yugoslavia, Zambia, Zimbabwe.

Against: Israel, Marshall Islands, United States.

Abstaining: Micronesia.

By **resolution 55/87** of 4 December, the Assembly reaffirmed the right of the Palestinian people to self-determination, including their right to a State, and urged all States, as well as UN specialized agencies and organizations, to continue to support the Palestinian people in their quest for self-determination (see p. 662).

Work of Special Committee

In an August report [A/55/261], the Secretary-General stated that all necessary facilities were provided to the Special Committee on Israeli Practices, as requested in General Assembly resolution 54/76 [YUN 1999, p. 414]. Arrangements were made for it to meet in March, May and August, and a field mission was carried out to Egypt, Jordan and the Syrian Arab Republic in May. Two periodic reports [A/55/373 & Add.1] and the thirty-second annual report of the Special Committee [A/55/453] were circulated to Member States. The UN Department of Public Information continued to provide press coverage of Special Committee meetings and to disseminate information materials on its activities (see p. 446).

GENERAL ASSEMBLY ACTION

On 8 December [meeting 83], the General Assembly, on the recommendation of the Fourth Committee [A/55/571], adopted **resolution 55/130** by recorded vote (91-2-61) [agenda item 85].

Work of the Special Committee to Investigate Israeli Practices Affecting the Human Rights of the Palestinian People and Other Arabs of the Occupied Territories

The General Assembly,

Guided by the purposes and principles of the Charter of the United Nations,

Guided also by the principles of international humanitarian law, in particular the Geneva Convention relative to the Protection of Civilian Persons in Time of War, of 12 August 1949, as well as international standards of human rights, in particular the Universal Declaration of Human Rights and the International Covenants on Human Rights,

Recalling its relevant resolutions, including resolution 2443(XXIII) of 19 December 1968, and relevant resolutions of the Commission on Human Rights,

Recalling also relevant resolutions of the Security Council,

Aware of the lasting impact of the uprising (intifada) of the Palestinian people,

Convinced that occupation itself represents a gross violation of human rights,

Gravely concerned about the recent tragic events that have taken place since 28 September 2000, including the excessive use of force by the Israeli occupying forces against Palestinian civilians, resulting in numerous deaths and injuries,

Having considered the reports of the Special Committee to Investigate Israeli Practices Affecting the Human Rights of the Palestinian People and Other Arabs of the Occupied Territories and the relevant reports of the Secretary-General,

Recalling the signing of the Declaration of Principles on Interim Self-Government Arrangements by the Government of Israel and the Palestine Liberation Organization in Washington, D.C., on 13 September 1993, as well as the subsequent implementation agreements, including the Israeli-Palestinian Interim Agreement on the West Bank and the Gaza Strip signed in Washington, D.C., on 28 September 1995, and the signing of the Sharm el-Sheikh Memorandum on 4 September 1999,

Expressing the hope that, with the progress of the peace process, the Israeli occupation will be brought to an end and therefore violation of the human rights of the Palestinian people will cease,

1. *Commends* the Special Committee to Investigate Israeli Practices Affecting the Human Rights of the Palestinian People and Other Arabs of the Occupied Territories for its efforts in performing the tasks assigned to it by the General Assembly and for its impartiality;

2. *Demands* that Israel cooperate with the Special Committee in implementing its mandate;

3. *Deplores* those policies and practices of Israel which violate the human rights of the Palestinian people and other Arabs of the occupied territories, as reflected in the reports of the Special Committee covering the reporting period;

4. *Expresses grave concern* about the situation in the Occupied Palestinian Territory, including Jerusalem, as a result of Israeli practices and measures, and especially condemns the excessive use of force in the past few weeks which has resulted in more than one hundred and sixty Palestinian deaths and thousands of injuries;

5. *Requests* the Special Committee, pending complete termination of the Israeli occupation, to continue to investigate Israeli policies and practices in the Occupied Palestinian Territory, including Jerusalem, and other Arab territories occupied by Israel since 1967, especially Israeli lack of compliance with the provisions of the Geneva Convention relative to the Protection of Civilian Persons in Time of War, of 12 August 1949, and to consult, as appropriate, with the International Committee of the Red Cross according to its regulations in order to ensure that the welfare and human rights of the peoples of the occupied territories are safeguarded and to report to the Secretary-General as soon as possible and whenever the need arises thereafter;

6. *Also requests* the Special Committee to submit regularly to the Secretary-General periodic reports on the current situation in the Occupied Palestinian Territory, including Jerusalem;

7. *Further requests* the Special Committee to continue to investigate the treatment of prisoners in the Occupied Palestinian Territory, including Jerusalem, and other Arab territories occupied by Israel since 1967;

8. *Requests* the Secretary-General:

(a) To provide the Special Committee with all necessary facilities, including those required for its visits to the occupied territories, so that it may investigate the Israeli policies and practices referred to in the present resolution;

(b) To continue to make available such additional staff as may be necessary to assist the Special Committee in the performance of its tasks;

(c) To circulate regularly to Member States the periodic reports mentioned in paragraph 6 above;

(d) To ensure the widest circulation of the reports of the Special Committee and of information regarding its activities and findings, by all means available, through the Department of Public Information of the Secretariat and, where necessary, to reprint those reports of the Special Committee that are no longer available;

(e) To report to the General Assembly at its fifty-sixth session on the tasks entrusted to him in the present resolution;

9. *Decides* to include in the provisional agenda of its fifty-sixth session the item entitled "Report of the Special Committee to Investigate Israeli Practices Affecting the Human Rights of the Palestinian People and Other Arabs of the Occupied Territories".

RECORDED VOTE ON RESOLUTION 55/130:

In favour: Afghanistan, Algeria, Antigua and Barbuda, Azerbaijan, Bahrain, Bangladesh, Barbados, Belarus, Belize, Benin, Bhutan, Bolivia, Botswana, Brazil, Brunei Darussalam, Burkina Faso, Burundi, Cambodia, Cape Verde, Chad, Chile, China, Colombia, Comoros, Côte d'Ivoire, Cuba, Cyprus, Democratic People's Republic of Korea, Djibouti, Ecuador, Egypt, Eritrea, Gabon, Ghana, Grenada, Guinea, Guyana, Haiti, India, Indonesia, Iran, Jordan, Kenya, Kuwait, Lao People's Democratic Republic, Lebanon, Libyan Arab Jamahiriya, Madagascar, Malaysia, Maldives, Mali, Malta, Mauritania, Mauritius, Mexico, Morocco, Mozambique, Myanmar, Namibia, Nepal, Nigeria, Oman, Pakistan, Panama, Papua New Guinea, Paraguay, Philippines, Qatar, Saint Lucia, Saudi Arabia, Senegal, Singapore, South Africa, Sri Lanka, Sudan, Swaziland, Syrian Arab Republic, Thailand, Togo, Tunisia, Turkey, Uganda, United Arab Emirates, United Republic of Tanzania, Uruguay, Vanuatu, Venezuela, Viet Nam, Yemen, Zambia, Zimbabwe.

Against: Israel, United States.

Abstaining: Andorra, Argentina, Armenia, Australia, Austria, Belgium, Bulgaria, Canada, Croatia, Czech Republic, Denmark, Dominican Republic, Estonia, Ethiopia, Fiji, Finland, France, Georgia, Germany, Greece, Guatemala, Honduras, Hungary, Iceland, Ireland, Italy, Jamaica, Japan, Kazakhstan, Kyrgyzstan, Latvia, Liechtenstein, Lithuania, Luxembourg, Marshall Islands, Micronesia, Monaco, Nauru, Netherlands, New Zealand, Nicaragua, Norway, Peru, Poland, Portugal, Republic of Korea, Republic of Moldova, Romania, Russian Federation, Samoa, San Marino, Slovakia, Slovenia, Solomon Islands, Spain, Sweden, The former Yugoslav Republic of Macedonia, Tonga, Ukraine, United Kingdom, Yugoslavia.

Fourth Geneva Convention

Report of Secretary-General. In August [A/55/262], the Secretary-General informed the General Assembly that Israel had not replied to his July request for information on steps taken or envisaged to implement Assembly resolution 54/77 [YUN 1999, p. 416] demanding that Israel accept the de jure applicability of the 1949 Geneva Convention relative to the Protection of Civilian Persons in Time of War in the Occupied Palestinian Territory, including Jerusalem, and that it comply scrupulously with its provisions. Also in July, the Secretary-General noted, he had drawn the attention of all States parties to the Convention to paragraph 3 of resolution 54/77 calling on them to exert all efforts to ensure respect by Israel for the Convention's provisions.

The high contracting parties to the Fourth Geneva Convention had reaffirmed the applicability of the Convention to the Occupied Palestinian Territory at their meeting in 1999 [YUN 1999, p. 415].

GENERAL ASSEMBLY ACTION

On 8 December [meeting 83], the General Assembly, on the recommendation of the Fourth Committee [A/55/571], adopted **resolution 55/131** by recorded vote (152-2-2) [agenda item 85].

Applicability of the Geneva Convention relative to the Protection of Civilian Persons in Time of War, of 12 August 1949, to the Occupied Palestinian Territory, including Jerusalem, and the other occupied Arab territories

The General Assembly,

Bearing in mind the relevant resolutions of the Security Council,

Recalling its relevant resolutions,

Having considered the reports of the Special Committee to Investigate Israeli Practices Affecting the Human Rights of the Palestinian People and Other Arabs of the Occupied Territories, and the relevant reports of the Secretary-General,

Considering that the promotion of respect for the obligations arising from the Charter of the United Nations and other instruments and rules of international law is among the basic purposes and principles of the United Nations,

Noting the convening of the meeting of experts of the high contracting parties to the Geneva Convention relative to the Protection of Civilian Persons in Time of War, of 12 August 1949, in Geneva from 27 to 29 October 1998, at the initiative of the Government of Switzerland in its capacity as the depositary of the Convention, concerning general problems of application of the Convention in general and, in particular, in occupied territories,

Noting also the convening for the first time, on 15 July 1999, of a Conference of High Contracting Parties to the Fourth Geneva Convention, as recommended by the General Assembly in its resolution ES-10/6 of 9 February 1999, on measures to enforce the Convention in the Occupied Palestinian Territory, including Jerusalem, and to ensure respect thereof in accordance with article 1 common to the four Geneva Conventions, and aware of the statement adopted by the Conference,

Stressing that Israel, the occupying Power, should comply strictly with its obligations under international law,

1. *Reaffirms* that the Geneva Convention relative to the Protection of Civilian Persons in Time of War, of 12 August 1949, is applicable to the Occupied Palestinian Territory, including Jerusalem, and other Arab territories occupied by Israel since 1967;

2. *Demands* that Israel accept the de jure applicability of the Convention in the Occupied Palestinian Territory, including Jerusalem, and other Arab territories occupied by Israel since 1967, and that it comply scrupulously with the provisions of the Convention;

3. *Calls upon* all States parties to the Convention, in accordance with article 1 common to the four Geneva Conventions, to exert all efforts in order to ensure respect for its provisions by Israel, the occupying Power, in the Occupied Palestinian Territory, including Jerusalem, and other Arab territories occupied by Israel since 1967;

4. *Reiterates* the need for speedy implementation of the recommendations contained in its resolutions ES-10/3 of 15 July 1997, ES-10/4 of 13 November 1997, ES-10/5 of 17 March 1998, ES-10/6 of 9 February 1999 and ES-10/7 of 20 October 2000 with regard to ensuring respect by Israel, the occupying Power, for the provisions of the Convention;

5. *Requests* the Secretary-General to report to the General Assembly at its fifty-sixth session on the implementation of the present resolution.

RECORDED VOTE ON RESOLUTION 55/131:

In favour: Afghanistan, Algeria, Andorra, Antigua and Barbuda, Argentina, Armenia, Australia, Austria, Azerbaijan, Bahamas, Bahrain, Bangladesh, Barbados, Belarus, Belgium, Belize, Benin, Bhutan, Bolivia, Botswana, Brazil, Brunei Darussalam, Bulgaria, Burkina Faso, Burundi, Cambodia, Canada, Cape Verde, Chad, Chile, China, Colombia, Comoros, Côte d'Ivoire, Croatia, Cuba, Cyprus, Czech Republic, Democratic People's Republic of Korea, Denmark, Djibouti, Dominican Republic, Ecuador, Egypt, El Salvador, Eritrea, Estonia, Ethiopia, Fiji, Finland, France, Gabon, Georgia, Germany, Ghana, Greece, Grenada, Guatemala, Guinea, Guyana, Haiti, Honduras, Hungary, Iceland, India, Indonesia, Iran, Ireland, Italy, Jamaica, Japan, Jordan, Kenya, Kuwait, Kyrgyzstan, Lao People's Democratic Republic, Latvia, Lebanon, Libyan Arab Jamahiriya, Liechtenstein, Lithuania, Luxembourg, Madagascar, Malaysia, Maldives, Mali, Malta, Mauritania, Mauritius, Mexico, Monaco, Mongolia, Morocco, Mozambique, Myanmar, Namibia, Nauru, Nepal, Netherlands, New Zealand, Nicaragua, Nigeria, Norway, Oman, Pakistan, Panama, Papua New Guinea, Paraguay, Peru, Philippines, Poland, Portugal, Qatar, Republic of Korea, Republic of Moldova, Romania, Russian Federation, Saint Lucia, Samoa, San Marino, Saudi Arabia, Senegal, Singapore, Slovakia, Slovenia, Solomon Islands, South Africa, Spain, Sri Lanka, Sudan, Swaziland, Sweden, Syrian Arab Republic, Thailand, The former Yugoslav Republic of Macedonia, Togo, Tonga, Tunisia, Turkey, Uganda, Ukraine, United Arab Emirates, United Kingdom, United Republic of Tanzania, Uruguay, Vanuatu, Venezuela, Viet Nam, Yemen, Yugoslavia, Zambia and Zimbabwe.

Against: Israel, United States.

Abstaining: Marshall Islands, Micronesia.

Palestinian women

The Secretary-General, in a report [E/CN.6/2000/2] to the Commission on the Status of Women on follow-up to and progress in the implementation of the Beijing Declaration and Platform for Action [YUN 1995, p. 1170], reviewed, in response to Economic and Social Council resolution 1999/15 [YUN 1999, p. 418], the situation of Palestinian women and described assistance provided by UN organizations during the period September 1998 to September 1999. He stated that the overall improvement of the economic performance in the West Bank and Gaza since 1997 had led to an increase in employment and higher household incomes in the occupied territories. Although women's unemployment rate in 1998 declined by 21.3 per cent, to 16.9 per cent, women's wages remained consistently below those of men. An increase in household income in 1998 was due to a real increase in average wages, and household expenditures declinèd by 2.1 per cent during the same period. Also in 1998, income and productivity were enhanced by fewer comprehensive and internal closure days in the West Bank and Gaza. The expansion of existing Israeli settlements and the building of new ones, as well as the construction of bypass roads, continued to affect the socio-economic life of Palestinians. Cases of confrontations between Palestinian women and Israeli settlers were reported.

Organizational mechanisms had been created to fulfil the goals of the Beijing Platform for Action. At the governmental level, a coordination framework (the Interministerial Coordination Committee) was formed of representatives from the women's affairs departments in ministries and State institutions with a view to promoting the national status of Palestinian women. According to the PA, activities were undertaken in accordance with the Platform with particular emphasis on the eight priority areas. Traditions notwithstanding, the gender concept was currently accepted in Palestinian society and the stereotypical image of women had begun to change. More education and employment were available for women, and their capacity to work and participate in the production and use of modern technologies was expected to grow.

The UN system continued to support Palestinian women and sought to maintain a gender perspective in its assistance programmes and funds. That assistance ranged across areas such as education, income-generation activities, capacity-building and institution-building. The Office of the United Nations High Commissioner for Human Rights supported the establishment of a Women's Human Rights Unit in a local non-governmental organization (NGO) and assisted legislators and civil society organizations in a review of personal status legislation. It also participated in the United Nations Gender Task Force, which organized a campaign on the prevention of violence against women. ESCWA provided, among other things, technical assistance and advisory services to the National Committee for Palestinian Women for Follow-up to Beijing in preparation of the Palestinian national report on implementation of the Platform for Action. In 1998, the World Food Programme began a two-

year project that supported the social safety net programme of the Ministry of Social Affairs, addressing the urgent food security needs of poor households.

The United Nations Relief and Works Agency for Palestinian Refugees in the Near East (UNRWA) assisted Palestinian women within the context of its regular programmes. In the education programme, women accounted for 62 per cent of all trainees enrolled in technical/semi-professional courses in 1998/99. UNRWA provided expanded maternal and child health care and family planning services to Palestinian refugees, in recognition of the fact that the burden of child and reproductive ill-health fell overwhelmingly on women. With women of reproductive age and children comprising two thirds of the 3.6 million registered Palestinian refugees, that investment in maternal and child health was key for socio-economic development. Also, more than 50 per cent of UNRWA's special hardship case families, who received direct food and material assistance from the Agency, were headed by women. During the period under review, a total of 20,534 participants benefited from programme activities, such as lectures on health and civil society, childcare, and computer and language skills. During 1998/99, UNRWA's Income Generation Programme granted loans valued at $1.67 million to 2,612 women who supported 13,060 dependants. A total of 1,526 women benefited from the UNRWA Poverty Alleviation Programme, which provided small amounts of credit for income-generation projects.

UNDP completed a project to support women's departments within various ministries to promote gender equality. Activities included a poverty alleviation project within the Ministry of Social Affairs to support deprived families and groups and a one-year pilot project, the Rural Girls Development Project, in three centres in the West Bank and Gaza.

The Secretary-General observed that, in spite of considerable efforts on the part of the PA, civil society and UN organizations to improve the economic and social conditions of Palestinian women, their situation still required special attention. Their status and living conditions were closely linked to the progress of the peace process. Women in the occupied territories continued to be affected in an adverse manner by a variety of measures, such as closures and settlement activities. The mainstreaming of a gender perspective into nation-building programmes and the full and equal participation of Palestinian women were critical to the sustainable outcome of the peace. The UN system would continue to assist Palestinian women to increase their capabilities to participate fully and equally in the peace process and to build and develop Palestinian society.

ECONOMIC AND SOCIAL COUNCIL ACTION

On 28 July [meeting 45], the Economic and Social Council, on the recommendation of the Commission on the Status of Women [E/2000/27], adopted **resolution 2000/23** by recorded vote (42-1-2) [agenda item 14 (a)].

Situation of and assistance to Palestinian women

The Economic and Social Council,

Having considered with appreciation the section concerning the situation of Palestinian women and assistance provided by organizations of the United Nations system of the report of the Secretary-General on follow-up to and implementation of the Beijing Declaration and Platform for Action adopted at the Fourth World Conference on Women,

Recalling the Nairobi Forward-looking Strategies for the Advancement of Women, in particular paragraph 260 concerning Palestinian women and children, and the Beijing Platform for Action,

Recalling also its resolution 1999/15 of 28 July 1999 and other relevant United Nations resolutions,

Recalling further the Declaration on the Elimination of Violence against Women as it concerns the protection of civilian populations,

Stressing the need for full implementation of the Memorandum signed at Sharm el-Sheikh, Egypt, on 4 September 1999 and full compliance with the existing agreements, as well as the need for the conclusion of the final settlement by the agreed time of September 2000,

Concerned about the continuing difficult situation of Palestinian women in the Occupied Palestinian Territory, including Jerusalem, and about the severe consequences of continuous illegal Israeli settlement activities, as well as the harsh economic conditions and other consequences for the situation of Palestinian women and their families resulting from the frequent closures and isolation of the occupied territory,

1. *Calls upon* the concerned parties, as well as the entire international community, to exert all the necessary efforts to ensure the continuity and success of the peace process and its conclusion by the agreed time of September 2000 and the achievement of tangible progress in the improvement of the situation of Palestinian women and their families;

2. *Reaffirms* that the Israeli occupation remains a major obstacle for Palestinian women with regard to their advancement, self-reliance and integration in the development planning of their society;

3. *Demands* that Israel, the occupying Power, comply fully with the provisions and principles of the Universal Declaration of Human Rights, the Regulations annexed to The Hague Convention IV, of 18 October 1907 and the Geneva Convention relative to the Protection of Civilian Persons in Time of War, of 12 August 1949, in order to protect the rights of Palestinian women and their families;

4. *Calls upon* Israel to facilitate the return of all refugees and displaced Palestinian women and children to their homes and properties, in compliance with the relevant United Nations resolutions;

5. *Urges* Member States, financial organizations of the United Nations system, non-governmental organizations and other relevant institutions to intensify their efforts to provide financial and technical assistance to Palestinian women, especially during the transitional period;

6. *Requests* the Commission on the Status of Women to continue to monitor and take action with regard to the implementation of the Nairobi Forward-looking Strategies for the Advancement of Women, in particular paragraph 260 concerning Palestinian women and children, and the Beijing Platform for Action;

7. *Requests* the Secretary-General to continue to review the situation and to assist Palestinian women by all available means, and to submit to the Commission on the Status of Women at its forty-fifth session a report on the progress made in the implementation of the present resolution.

RECORDED VOTE ON RESOLUTION 2000/23:

In favour: Algeria, Angola, Austria, Bahrain, Belarus, Belgium, Bolivia, Brazil, Bulgaria, Burkina Faso, China, Colombia, Costa Rica, Croatia, Cuba, Czech Republic, Denmark, Fiji, France, Germany, Greece, India, Indonesia, Italy, Japan, Mexico, Morocco, New Zealand, Oman, Pakistan, Poland, Portugal, Russian Federation, Rwanda, Saint Lucia, Saudi Arabia, Sudan, Suriname, Syrian Arab Republic, United Kingdom, Venezuela, Viet Nam.

Against: United States.

Abstaining: Canada, Norway.

Issues related to Palestine

General aspects

The General Assembly again considered the question of Palestine in 2000. Having discussed the annual report of the Committee on the Exercise of the Inalienable Rights of the Palestinian People (Committee on Palestinian Rights) [A/55/35], the Assembly adopted four resolutions, reaffirming, among other things, the necessity of achieving a peaceful settlement of the Palestine question—the core of the Arab-Israeli conflict—and stressing the need for the realization of the inalienable rights of the Palestinians, primarily the right to self-determination, for Israeli withdrawal from the Palestinian territory occupied since 1967 and for resolving the problem of the Palestine refugees.

In commemoration of the International Day of Solidarity with the Palestinian People, celebrated annually on 29 November, in accordance with Assembly resolution 32/40 B [YUN 1977, p. 304], the Committee held a solemn meeting and other activities. Under the Committee's auspices, an exhibit entitled "The Land" was presented by the Permanent Observer Mission of Palestine.

Report of Secretary-General. In a November report on the question of Palestine [A/55/639-S/2000/1113], the Secretary-General made observations on the Middle East peace process (see p. 415).

By a 9 August note verbale, the Secretary-General sought the positions of the Governments of Egypt, Israel, Jordan, Lebanon and the Syrian Arab Republic, as well as the PLO, regarding steps taken by them to implement the relevant provisions of resolution 54/42 [YUN 1999, p. 420]. As at 16 November, only Israel and the PLO had responded.

Israel said that it viewed the resolution as unbalanced and an undue interference in the Israeli-Palestinian bilateral negotiations. Since both Israeli and Palestinian leaders had agreed that their differences would be resolved only by good-faith negotiations, the one-sided approach reflected in the resolution threatened to prejudge the outcome of that process. A comprehensive solution to the conflict could be based only on directly negotiated and mutually agreed solutions.

The Permanent Observer of Palestine said that the resolution provided support for the peace process and implementation of the agreements reached between the two sides, and also provided the basis for the just settlement of the Palestine question. The resolution also emphasized the importance of a more active and expanded role for the United Nations in that process. As such, the resolution should serve as an acceptable basis for all parties to work on those issues. The Permanent Observer stated that Israel had failed to implement most of the overdue provisions and commitments agreed upon in the 1999 Sharm el-Sheikh Memorandum [YUN 1999, p. 401], including the third redeployment of its occupying forces, the release of Palestinian prisoners and the return of Palestinian displaced persons. It had also failed to adhere to the agreed timetable. The optimistic expectations for a positive change in the status of the peace process in the Middle East and the conclusion of a final settlement between the Palestinian and Israeli sides had not been fulfilled. Instead, the region had witnessed a dramatic deterioration of the situation and an unprecedented level of aggression against the Palestinian people since the 28 September visit by Ariel Sharon to Al-Haram Al-Sharif.

The Secretary-General visited the region in October and attended the Sharm el-Sheikh Summit (see p. 420). Of the three major understandings reached at the Summit (security cooperation, establishment of a fact-finding committee, renewal of the peace process), progress had been made only in relation to the establishment of the committee. On 7 November, United States President William J. Clinton announced the membership of the Fact-Finding Committee, chaired by former United States Senator George Mitchell, which was developed with the parties and in consultation with the Secretary-General. The Secretary-General remained concerned that the other understandings remained unimplemented and stressed that the full and good-faith implementation of those understandings was vital to restore calm and to create the right atmosphere for the resumption of peace talks. In his view, there was no alternative to a return to the negotiating table. He also participated in the Summit of the Organization of the Islamic Conference (OIC) (see p. 427), where he discussed the crisis in the Middle East with heads of State and Foreign Ministers. All of them expressed grave concern at the situation and many deplored the excessive use of force by Israel.

The crisis in the region had led to a serious deterioration of the humanitarian and economic situation in the Occupied Palestinian Territory. In order to improve the coordination of the UN humanitarian assistance to the Palestinians, a task force had been established, chaired by the UN Special Coordinator in Gaza. Also, UNRWA had launched an urgent appeal for $39 million to fund a three-month contingency plan to buy food and medical supplies. As the Assembly had underscored on many occasions, achieving a final and peaceful settlement of the question of Palestine was imperative for the attainment of a comprehensive and lasting peace in the Middle East. The Secretary-General hoped that there would also be movement on the Syrian and Lebanese tracks so that peace, security and stability could be achieved on the basis of Security Council resolutions 242(1967) [YUN 1967, p. 257] and 338(1973) [YUN 1973, p. 213].

GENERAL ASSEMBLY ACTION

On 1 December [meeting 78], the General Assembly adopted **resolution 55/55** [draft: A/55/L.48 & Add.1] by recorded vote (149-2-3) [agenda item 41].

Peaceful settlement of the question of Palestine
The General Assembly,

Recalling its relevant resolutions, including resolutions adopted at the tenth emergency special session,

Recalling also the relevant Security Council resolutions, including resolutions 242(1967) of 22 November 1967 and 338(1973) of 22 October 1973,

Aware that it has been more than fifty years since the adoption of resolution 181(II) of 29 November 1947 and thirty-three years since the occupation of Palestinian territory, including Jerusalem, in 1967,

Having considered the report of the Secretary-General submitted pursuant to the request made in its resolution 54/42 of 1 December 1999,

Reaffirming the permanent responsibility of the United Nations with regard to the question of Palestine until the question is resolved in all its aspects,

Convinced that achieving a final and peaceful settlement of the question of Palestine, the core of the Arab-Israeli conflict, is imperative for the attainment of a comprehensive and lasting peace in the Middle East,

Aware that the principle of equal rights and self-determination of peoples is among the purposes and principles embodied in the Charter of the United Nations,

Affirming the principle of the inadmissibility of the acquisition of territory by war,

Affirming also the illegality of the Israeli settlements in the territory occupied since 1967 and of Israeli actions aimed at changing the status of Jerusalem,

Affirming once again the right of all States in the region to live in peace within secure and internationally recognized borders,

Recalling the mutual recognition between the Government of the State of Israel and the Palestine Liberation Organization, the representative of the Palestinian people, and the signing by the two parties of the Declaration of Principles on Interim Self-Government Arrangements in Washington, D.C., on 13 September 1993, as well as the subsequent implementation agreements, including the Israeli-Palestinian Interim Agreement on the West Bank and the Gaza Strip, signed in Washington, D.C., on 28 September 1995,

Recalling also the withdrawal of the Israeli army, which took place in the Gaza Strip and the Jericho area in 1995 in accordance with the agreements reached by the parties, and the initiation of the Palestinian Authority in those areas, as well as the subsequent redeployments of the Israeli army in the rest of the West Bank,

Noting with satisfaction the successful holding of the first Palestinian general elections,

Noting the signing of the Memorandum at Sharm el-Sheikh, Egypt, on 4 September 1999,

Noting the appointment by the Secretary-General of the United Nations Special Coordinator for the Middle East Peace Process and Personal Representative of the Secretary-General to the Palestine Liberation Organization and the Palestinian Authority, and its positive contribution,

Welcoming the convening of the Conference to Support Middle East Peace in Washington, D.C., on 1 October 1993, as well as all follow-up meetings and the international mechanisms established to provide assistance to the Palestinian people, including the donor meeting held in Tokyo on 15 October 1999,

Expressing its deep concern over the tragic events in Occupied East Jerusalem and the Occupied Palestinian Territory since 28 September 2000, which have resulted in a high number of deaths and injuries, mostly among Palestinian civilians, and concerned also about the clashes between the Israeli armed forces and the Palestinian police and the casualties on both sides,

Expressing its deep concern also over the serious deterioration of the situation in the Occupied Palestinian Territory, including Jerusalem, and the difficulties facing the Middle East peace process,

1. *Reaffirms* the necessity of achieving a peaceful settlement of the question of Palestine, the core of the Arab-Israeli conflict, in all its aspects;

2. *Expresses its full support* for the ongoing peace process which began in Madrid and the Declaration of Principles on Interim Self-Government Arrangements of 1993, as well as the subsequent implementation agreements, including the Israeli-Palestinian Interim Agreement on the West Bank and the Gaza Strip of 1995 and the Sharm el-Sheikh Memorandum of 1999, and expresses the hope that the process will lead to the establishment of a comprehensive, just and lasting peace in the Middle East;

3. *Stresses* the necessity for commitment to the principle of land for peace and the implementation of Security Council resolutions 242(1967) and 338(1973), which form the basis of the Middle East peace process, and the need for the immediate and scrupulous implementation of the agreements reached between the parties, including the redeployment of the Israeli forces from the West Bank, and calls for the speedy conclusion of the final settlement agreement between the two sides;

4. *Calls upon* the concerned parties, the co-sponsors of the peace process and other interested parties, as well as the entire international community to exert all the necessary efforts and initiatives to reverse immediately all measures taken on the ground since 28 September 2000, in implementation of the Sharm el-Sheikh understandings and in order to ensure a successful and speedy conclusion of the peace process;

5. *Stresses* the need for:

(a) The realization of the inalienable rights of the Palestinian people, primarily the right to self-determination;

(b) The withdrawal of Israel from the Palestinian territory occupied since 1967;

6. *Also stresses* the need for resolving the problem of the Palestine refugees in conformity with its resolution 194(III) of 11 December 1948;

7. *Urges* Member States to expedite the provision of economic and technical assistance to the Palestinian people during this critical period;

8. *Emphasizes* the importance for the United Nations to play a more active and expanded role in the current peace process and in the implementation of the Declaration of Principles;

9. *Requests* the Secretary-General to continue his efforts with the parties concerned, and in consultation with the Security Council, for the promotion of peace in the region and to submit progress reports on developments in this matter.

RECORDED VOTE ON RESOLUTION 55/55:

In favour: Afghanistan, Algeria, Andorra, Antigua and Barbuda, Argentina, Armenia, Australia, Austria, Azerbaijan, Bahamas, Bahrain, Bangladesh, Barbados, Belarus, Belgium, Bolivia, Bosnia and Herzegovina, Botswana, Brazil, Brunei Darussalam, Bulgaria, Burkina Faso, Burundi, Cambodia, Cameroon, Canada, Cape Verde, Chad, Chile, China, Colombia, Comoros, Costa Rica, Croatia, Cuba, Cyprus, Czech Republic, Democratic People's Republic of Korea, Denmark, Djibouti, Dominican Republic, Ecuador, Egypt, El Salvador, Eritrea, Estonia, Ethiopia, Fiji, Finland, France, Gabon, Gambia, Georgia, Germany, Ghana, Greece, Grenada, Guatemala, Guinea, Guyana, Honduras, Hungary, Iceland, India, Indonesia, Ireland, Italy, Japan, Jordan, Kenya, Kuwait, Kyrgyzstan, Lao People's Democratic Republic, Latvia, Lebanon, Libyan Arab Jamahiriya, Liechtenstein, Lithuania, Luxembourg, Madagascar, Malaysia, Maldives, Mali, Malta, Mauritania, Mauritius, Mexico, Monaco, Mongolia, Morocco, Mozambique, Myanmar, Namibia, Nepal, Netherlands, New Zealand, Nicaragua, Nigeria, Norway, Oman, Pakistan, Panama, Papua New Guinea, Paraguay, Peru,

Philippines, Poland, Portugal, Qatar, Republic of Korea, Republic of Moldova, Romania, Russian Federation, Saint Lucia, Samoa, San Marino, Saudi Arabia, Senegal, Sierra Leone, Singapore, Slovakia, Slovenia, Solomon Islands, South Africa, Spain, Sri Lanka, Sudan, Swaziland, Sweden, Syrian Arab Republic, Tajikistan, Thailand, The former Yugoslav Republic of Macedonia, Togo, Trinidad and Tobago, Tunisia, Turkey, Uganda, Ukraine, United Arab Emirates, United Kingdom, United Republic of Tanzania, Uruguay, Venezuela, Viet Nam, Yemen, Yugoslavia, Zambia, Zimbabwe.

Against: Israel, United States.

Abstaining: Marshall Islands, Micronesia, Nauru.

Speaking before the vote, the United States said that the draft resolution presented the position of only one party to the negotiations—a position that was unacceptable to the other party. Direct negotiations between the parties had yielded significant progress and the draft resolution could only complicate efforts to achieve a settlement.

Israel stated that all diplomatic breakthroughs in the Middle East were arrived at exclusively through direct negotiations between the parties. The draft resolution sought to predetermine the issues to be resolved by those negotiations, violated existing agreements and undermined the foundations of the peace process.

Speaking after the vote, the Permanent Observer of Palestine said that the resolution was of great importance to the Middle East region and to the Palestinian people, and affirmed the responsibility of the United Nations vis-à-vis the question of Palestine.

By **decision 55/458** of 23 December, the Assembly decided that the agenda items entitled "Question of Palestine" and "The situation in the Middle East" would remain for consideration during its resumed fifty-fifth (2001) session.

Committee on Palestinian Rights

As mandated by General Assembly resolution 54/39 [YUN 1999, p. 424], the Committee on the Exercise of the Inalienable Rights of the Palestinian People continued to review the situation relating to the Palestine question, reported on it and made suggestions to the Assembly or the Security Council.

The Committee's Bureau continued its consultations with NGO representatives on the future shape of cooperation with civil society during the course of the UN seminar on prospects for Palestinian economic development and the Middle East peace process, held in Cairo, Egypt, in June 2000 (see p. 448). The Bureau urged NGOs to focus their initiatives on the most crucial issues at stake and to mobilize solidarity movements in support of Palestine refugees.

The Committee continued to follow the Palestine-related activities of intergovernmental bodies, such as the Organization of African Unity, the Movement of Non-Aligned Countries and the Group of 77 developing countries, and, through its Chairman, participated in a number of high-level meetings of those bodies. Through its Bureau, the Committee continued to cooperate on the question of Palestine with the EU. The Committee took part in the United Nations Asian Meeting on the Question of Palestine (Hanoi, Viet Nam, 1-3 March). The Hanoi Declaration, the meeting's final document, supported the right of the Palestinians to self-determination and the establishment of an independent and sovereign Palestinian State.

In cooperation with OIC and the League of Arab States, the Committee organized the International Conference on Palestine Refugees (Paris, 26-27 April). The Conference stressed that the social and economic conditions of some 3.7 million Palestine refugees required urgent intervention on the part of the international community. It stated that the multilateral track of negotiations remained an essential part of the peace process and reaffirmed the inalienable right of the Palestinian people to return to their land and property. Immediately following the Conference, the United Nations NGO Meeting on Palestine Refugees was convened (Paris, 28 April). Issues discussed included the role of NGOs in promoting a just settlement of the Palestine refugee problem, the experience of NGOs in delivering basic social services to refugee communities and promoting stronger support to UNRWA.

The Committee sponsored the United Nations International Meeting in Support of a Peaceful Settlement of the Question of Palestine and the Establishment of Peace in the Middle East (Athens, Greece, 23-24 May). The Final Statement called on the parties concerned to achieve interim and final settlement agreements, and noted that the Israeli-Palestinian negotiations had been offset on a number of occasions by Israeli actions and statements, incompatible with the spirit and letter of the peace process.

In its annual report to the Assembly [A/55/35] covering the period from 12 November 1999 to 10 October 2000, the Committee said that it had observed with hope a series of actions taken on the ground in implementation of the 1999 Sharm el-Sheikh Memorandum [YUN 1999, p. 401]. They included the further redeployment of Israeli troops from parts of the West Bank, the agreement on the release of Palestinian prisoners, the opening of a southern safe passage between the West Bank and the Gaza Strip and the resumption of negotiations on permanent status issues. The Committee welcomed the signing, on 7 June, of the Israeli-Palestinian agreement on the implementation of economic issues, as well as the agreement concerning the Gaza seaport, signed on 20 September. It supported the September 2000 Palestinian Central Council decisions to postpone the establishment of a Palestinian State and on steps to be taken in preparation for statehood, including the completion of work on the constitutional declaration and laws for presidential and parliamentary elections, and the submission of an application by Palestine for membership in the United Nations. The Committee welcomed the negotiations on permanent status issues conducted in March/April 2000 at Bolling Air Force Base near Washington, D.C., and the intense discussions at the Middle East Peace Summit, held in July at Camp David, Maryland (see p. 415). The Committee was of the view that with the meetings at Camp David the Israeli-Palestinian negotiations had reached a high-water mark. It was troubled, therefore, by the failure of the parties to bridge the gaps in their positions and reach a comprehensive agreement. It welcomed, however, the final trilateral statement made at the conclusion of the Summit, in which both parties committed themselves to continue their efforts to conclude an agreement on all permanent status issues as soon as possible. The Committee observed with much concern, however, the failure to create the necessary momentum for the conclusion of a final agreement on 15 September 2000, as stipulated by the provisions of the Sharm el-Sheikh Memorandum. In that regard, the Committee noted the determined effort of the United States President to re-engage the two sides on specific elements of the final settlement, in particular on the question of Jerusalem, in the course of the meetings held on the sidelines of the United Nations Millennium Summit in September 2000. Despite that optimism, the confrontation and escalation of violence that developed following Mr. Sharon's visit to Al-Haram Al-Sharif on 28 September placed the peace process in considerable jeopardy and led to increased volatility on the ground.

The Committee was alarmed by the fact that the Israeli settlement drive in the course of the year under review had been as vigorous as it had been in previous years. In July, Israel's Ministry of the Interior announced that the number of settlers in the occupied West Bank and Gaza Strip had risen in the past year by 13,600 to some 200,000. The Committee reiterated its concern over the provocative and often violent actions of extremist settlers occupying Palestinian land, erecting makeshift houses and engaging in violent confrontations with Palestinians. During the year, settlers were collecting donations in Israel and abroad to purchase special military and rescue equipment. According to the Council of Jewish Communities in Judea, Samaria and Gaza, the equipment was purchased in coordination with the Israel Defence Forces.

The Committee expressed concern that, although a number of Palestinian prisoners had been released, some 1,650 of them still remained imprisoned in Israel. It was especially alarmed by, among other things, reports of administrative detention of Palestinians without charge or trial; overcrowded confinement conditions; solitary confinement as a means of severe punishment; inadequate medical care; and deprivation of basic facilities, such as a place to practise religion.

The Palestinian economy remained beset by a number of restrictions on Palestinian economic transactions, limited passage between the West Bank and Gaza, and persistent unemployment. There was also a pressing need to improve the physical underdeveloped infrastructure, including water, energy, transportation and the sewage system. The Committee stressed the urgency of assisting the Palestinian people in meeting their social and economic development needs.

The Committee, in its conclusions and recommendations, said that illegal "facts on the ground" continued to be created in violation of the inalienable rights of the Palestinian people, jeopardizing the possibility of making tangible progress in the peace negotiations. The Committee considered it unacceptable that, on the threshold of the third millennium, the Palestinian people were still carrying the heavy weight of occupation. A core issue in the permanent status negotiations was the question of Jerusalem, which, according to the Committee, should be resolved based on Council resolution 242(1967) [YUN 1967, p. 257] and other relevant UN resolutions, the exercise by the Palestinian people of their inalienable rights, and with due regard to the universal spiritual meaning of Jerusalem for all humankind. Among other permanent status issues, the question of Palestine refugees remained a difficult one. Generations of Palestinians had grown up as refugees, living in dismal conditions in refugee camps or under occupation, many away from their homeland, denied their natural right to self-determination, with bleak economic prospects, their freedom of movement restricted, their hopes for a better future dependent on the outside world. If that problem was not resolved with due care and in accordance with international law, the potential for peace and stability in the region would be seriously jeopardized. The Committee reiterated that the solution to the problem should be based on Assembly resolution 194(III) [YUN 1948-49, p. 174]. In addition, the illegal settlements in the Occupied Palestinian Territory since 1967 had changed the geography of the area and had devastated the livelihood of individual Palestinian households and the Palestinian economy in general.

The Committee strongly believed that the United Nations should continue to exercise its permanent responsibility towards all aspects of the question of Palestine until it was resolved in a satisfactory manner, in conformity with relevant UN resolutions and international legitimacy, and until the inalienable rights of the Palestinian people were fully realized. The Committee shared the view that the work carried out by UNRWA should be continued and supported the view that the reactivation of the work of the United Nations Conciliation Commission for Palestine (UNCCP), established by Assembly resolution 194(III), and the use of the Commission's records related to land ownership in Palestine should be considered. The Committee planned to continue to review and assess its programme of activities with a view to making it more focused and responsive to developments in the peace process and on the ground.

GENERAL ASSEMBLY ACTION

On 1 December [meeting 78], the General Assembly adopted **resolution 55/52** [draft: A/55/L.45 & Add.1] by recorded vote (106-2-48) [agenda item 41].

Committee on the Exercise of the Inalienable Rights of the Palestinian People

The General Assembly,

Recalling its resolutions 181(II) of 29 November 1947, 194(III) of 11 December 1948, 3236(XXIX) of 22 November 1974, 3375(XXX) and 3376(XXX) of 10 November 1975, 31/20 of 24 November 1976, 32/40 A of 2 December 1977, 33/28 A and B of 7 December 1978, 34/65 A of 29 November 1979 and 34/65 C of 12 December 1979, ES-7/2 of 29 July 1980, 35/169 A and C of 15 December 1980, 36/120 A and C of 10 December 1981, ES-7/4 of 28 April 1982, 37/86 A of 10 December 1982, 38/58 A of 13 December 1983, 39/49 A of 11 December 1984, 40/96 A of 12 December 1985, 41/43 A of 2 December 1986, 42/66 A of 2 December 1987, 43/175 A of 15 December 1988, 44/41 A of 6 December 1989, 45/67 A of 6 December 1990, 46/74 A of 11 December 1991, 47/64 A of 11 December 1992, 48/158 A of 20 December 1993, 49/62 A of 14 December 1994, 50/84 A of 15 December 1995, 51/23 of 4 December 1996, 52/49 of 9 December 1997, 53/39 of 2 December 1998 and 54/39 of 1 December 1999,

Having considered the report of the Committee on the Exercise of the Inalienable Rights of the Palestinian People,

Recalling the signing of the Declaration of Principles on Interim Self-Government Arrangements, including its Annexes and Agreed Minutes, by the Government of the State of Israel and the Palestine Liberation Organization, the representative of the Palestinian people, in Washington, D.C., on 13 September 1993, as well as the subsequent implementation agreements, in particular the Israeli-Palestinian Interim Agreement on the West Bank and the Gaza Strip, signed in Washington, D.C., on 28 September 1995, and the Memorandum signed at Sharm el-Sheikh, Egypt, on 4 September 1999,

Reaffirming that the United Nations has a permanent responsibility with respect to the question of Palestine until the question is resolved in all its aspects in a satisfactory manner in accordance with international legitimacy,

1. *Expresses its appreciation* to the Committee on the Exercise of the Inalienable Rights of the Palestinian People for its efforts in performing the tasks assigned to it by the General Assembly;

2. *Considers* that the Committee can continue to make a valuable and positive contribution to international efforts to promote the Middle East peace process and the full implementation of the agreements reached and to mobilize international support for and assistance to the Palestinian people during the transitional period;

3. *Endorses* the conclusions and recommendations of the Committee contained in chapter VII of its report;

4. *Requests* the Committee to continue to keep under review the situation relating to the question of Palestine and to report and make suggestions to the General Assembly or the Security Council, as appropriate;

5. *Authorizes* the Committee to continue to exert all efforts to promote the exercise of the inalienable rights of the Palestinian people, to make such adjustments in its approved programme of work as it may consider appropriate and necessary in the light of developments, to give special emphasis to the need to mobilize support and assistance for the Palestinian people and to report thereon to the General Assembly at its fifty-sixth session and thereafter;

6. *Requests* the Committee to continue to extend its cooperation and support to Palestinian and other non-governmental organizations in order to mobilize international solidarity and support for the achievement by the Palestinian people of its inalienable rights and for a peaceful settlement of the question of Palestine, and to involve additional non-governmental organizations in its work;

7. *Requests* the United Nations Conciliation Commission for Palestine, established under General Assembly resolution 194(III), and other United Nations bodies associated with the question of Palestine to continue to cooperate fully with the Committee, and expresses appreciation for the cooperation between the Commission and the Committee with regard to the modernization and preservation of the records of the Commission;

8. *Requests* the Secretary-General to circulate the report of the Committee to all the competent bodies of the United Nations, and urges them to take the necessary action, as appropriate;

9. *Also requests* the Secretary-General to continue to provide the Committee with all the necessary facilities for the performance of its tasks.

RECORDED VOTE ON RESOLUTION 55/52:

In favour: Afghanistan, Algeria, Antigua and Barbuda, Azerbaijan, Bahamas, Bahrain, Bangladesh, Barbados, Belarus, Bolivia, Bosnia and Herzegovina, Botswana, Brazil, Brunei Darussalam, Burkina Faso, Burundi, Cambodia, Cape Verde, Chad, Chile, China, Colombia, Comoros, Costa Rica, Cuba, Cyprus, Democratic People's Republic of Korea, Djibouti, Dominican

Republic, Ecuador, Egypt, El Salvador, Eritrea, Ethiopia, Fiji, Gabon, Gambia, Ghana, Grenada, Guatemala, Guinea, Guinea, Guyana, Honduras, India, Indonesia, Iran, Jordan, Kenya, Kuwait, Kyrgyzstan, Lao People's Democratic Republic, Lebanon, Libyan Arab Jamahiriya, Madagascar, Malaysia, Maldives, Mali, Malta, Mauritania, Mauritius, Mexico, Mongolia, Morocco, Mozambique, Myanmar, Namibia, Nauru, Nepal, Nicaragua, Nigeria, Oman, Pakistan, Panama, Papua New Guinea, Paraguay, Peru, Philippines, Qatar, Republic of Korea, Saint Lucia, Saudi Arabia, Senegal, Sierra Leone, Singapore, Solomon Islands, South Africa, Sri Lanka, Sudan, Swaziland, Syrian Arab Republic, Tajikistan, Thailand, Togo, Trinidad and Tobago, Tunisia, Turkey, Uganda, Ukraine, United Arab Emirates, United Republic of Tanzania, Uruguay, Venezuela, Viet Nam, Yemen, Zambia, Zimbabwe.

Against: Israel, United States.

Abstaining: Andorra, Argentina, Armenia, Australia, Austria, Belgium, Bulgaria, Canada, Croatia, Czech Republic, Denmark, Estonia, Finland, France, Georgia, Germany, Greece, Hungary, Iceland, Ireland, Italy, Japan, Kazakhstan, Latvia, Liechtenstein, Lithuania, Luxembourg, Marshall Islands, Micronesia, Monaco, Netherlands, New Zealand, Norway, Poland, Portugal, Republic of Moldova, Romania, Russian Federation, Samoa, San Marino, Slovakia, Slovenia, Spain, Sweden, The former Yugoslav Republic of Macedonia, Tonga, United Kingdom, Yugoslavia.

Speaking before the vote, Israel said that the Committee on Palestinian Rights, since its inception, had obstructed dialogue and understanding through a preset, one-sided portrayal of the Arab-Israeli situation.

Speaking after the vote, the Permanent Observer of Palestine said that the resolution affirmed the responsibility of the United Nations vis-à-vis the question of Palestine, including through the Committee on Palestinian Rights.

Division for Palestinian Rights

Under the guidance of the Committee on Palestinian Rights, the Division for Palestinian Rights of the UN Secretariat continued to function as a centre of research, monitoring, preparation of studies, and collection and dissemination of information on all issues related to the Palestine question. The Division continued to respond to requests for information and to prepare and disseminate the following publications: a monthly bulletin covering action by the Committee, UN bodies and agencies, and intergovernmental organizations concerned with Palestine; a monthly chronology of events relating to the question of Palestine, based on media reports and other sources; reports of meetings organized under the auspices of the Committee; a special bulletin on the observance of the International Day of Solidarity with the Palestinian People (29 November); and an annual compilation of relevant General Assembly and Security Council resolutions, decisions and statements.

The Committee, in its annual report [A/55/35], noted that the Division continued to develop the electronic United Nations Information System on the Question of Palestine (UNISPAL), as mandated by Assembly resolution 46/74 B [YUN 1991, p. 228]. The Division completed the coordination and supervision of the electronic conversion by a contractor of the records of UNCCP, in accordance with Assembly resolution 51/129 [YUN 1996, p. 423].

The Division maintained the Internet web site entitled "NGO Network on the Question of Palestine" and, in consultation with NGOs, developed it into a permanent tool of mutual information and cooperation between the Committee on Palestinian Rights and civil society. The Division also continued to issue its periodic newsletter entitled *NGO Action News* covering the activities of civil society on the various aspects of the question of Palestine.

The Committee requested the Division to continue its publications programme and other activities, including the updating of UNISPAL on a day-to-day basis and the completion of work on UNISPAL's collection of documents previously unavailable in machine-readable form.

GENERAL ASSEMBLY ACTION

On 1 December [meeting 78], the General Assembly adopted **resolution 55/53** [draft: A/55/L.46 & Add.1] by recorded vote (107-2-48) [agenda item 41].

Division for Palestinian Rights of the Secretariat

The General Assembly,

Having considered the report of the Committee on the Exercise of the Inalienable Rights of the Palestinian People,

Taking note in particular of the relevant information contained in chapter V.B of that report,

Recalling its resolutions 32/40 B of 2 December 1977, 33/28 C of 7 December 1978, 34/65 D of 12 December 1979, 35/169 D of 15 December 1980, 36/120 B of 10 December 1981, 37/86 B of 10 December 1982, 38/58 B of 13 December 1983, 39/49 B of 11 December 1984, 40/96 B of 12 December 1985, 41/43 B of 2 December 1986, 42/66 B of 2 December 1987, 43/175 B of 15 December 1988, 44/41 B of 6 December 1989, 45/67 B of 6 December 1990, 46/74 B of 11 December 1991, 47/64 B of 11 December 1992, 48/158 B of 20 December 1993, 49/62 B of 14 December 1994, 50/84 B of 15 December 1995, 51/24 of 4 December 1996, 52/50 of 9 December 1997, 53/40 of 2 December 1998 and 54/40 of 1 December 1999,

1. *Notes with appreciation* the action taken by the Secretary-General in compliance with its resolution 54/40;

2. *Considers* that the Division for Palestinian Rights of the Secretariat continues to make a useful and constructive contribution;

3. *Requests* the Secretary-General to continue to provide the Division with the necessary resources and to ensure that it continues to carry out its programme of work as detailed in the relevant earlier resolutions, in consultation with the Committee on the Exercise of the Inalienable Rights of the Palestinian People and under its guidance, including, in particular, the organization of meetings in various regions with the participation of all sectors of the international community, the further development and expansion of the documents collection of the United Nations Information System on the Question of Palestine, the preparation and widest pos-

sible dissemination of publications and information materials on various aspects of the question of Palestine, and the provision of the annual training programme for staff of the Palestinian Authority;

4. *Also requests* the Secretary-General to ensure the continued cooperation of the Department of Public Information and other units of the Secretariat in enabling the Division to perform its tasks and in covering adequately the various aspects of the question of Palestine;

5. *Invites* all Governments and organizations to extend their cooperation to the Committee and the Division in the performance of their tasks;

6. *Notes with appreciation* the action taken by Member States to observe annually on 29 November the International Day of Solidarity with the Palestinian People, requests them to continue to give the widest possible publicity to the observance, and requests the Committee and the Division to continue to organize, as part of the observance of the Day of Solidarity, an annual exhibit on Palestinian rights in cooperation with the Permanent Observer Mission of Palestine to the United Nations.

RECORDED VOTE ON RESOLUTION 55/53:

In favour: Afghanistan, Algeria, Antigua and Barbuda, Azerbaijan, Bahamas, Bahrain, Bangladesh, Barbados, Belarus, Bolivia, Bosnia and Herzegovina, Botswana, Brazil, Brunei Darussalam, Burkina Faso, Burundi, Cambodia, Cameroon, Cape Verde, Chad, Chile, China, Colombia, Comoros, Costa Rica, Cuba, Cyprus, Democratic People's Republic of Korea, Djibouti, Dominican Republic, Ecuador, Egypt, El Salvador, Eritrea, Ethiopia, Fiji, Gabon, Gambia, Ghana, Grenada, Guatemala, Guinea, Guyana, Honduras, India, Indonesia, Iran, Jordan, Kenya, Kuwait, Kyrgyzstan, Lao People's Democratic Republic, Lebanon, Libyan Arab Jamahiriya, Madagascar, Malaysia, Maldives, Mali, Malta, Mauritania, Mauritius, Mexico, Mongolia, Morocco, Mozambique, Myanmar, Namibia, Nauru, Nepal, Nicaragua, Nigeria, Oman, Pakistan, Panama, Papua New Guinea, Paraguay, Peru, Philippines, Qatar, Republic of Korea, Saint Lucia, Saudi Arabia, Senegal, Sierra Leone, Singapore, Solomon Islands, South Africa, Sri Lanka, Sudan, Swaziland, Syrian Arab Republic, Tajikistan, Thailand, Togo, Trinidad and Tobago, Tunisia, Turkey, Uganda, Ukraine, United Arab Emirates, United Republic of Tanzania, Uruguay, Venezuela, Viet Nam, Yemen, Zambia, Zimbabwe.

Against: Israel, United States.

Abstaining: Andorra, Argentina, Armenia, Australia, Austria, Belgium, Bulgaria, Canada, Croatia, Czech Republic, Denmark, Estonia, Finland, France, Georgia, Germany, Greece, Hungary, Iceland, Ireland, Italy, Japan, Kazakhstan, Latvia, Liechtenstein, Lithuania, Luxembourg, Marshall Islands, Micronesia, Monaco, Netherlands, New Zealand, Norway, Poland, Portugal, Republic of Moldova, Romania, Russian Federation, Samoa, San Marino, Slovakia, Slovenia, Spain, Sweden, The former Yugoslav Republic of Macedonia, Tonga, United Kingdom, Yugoslavia.

Special information programme

As requested in General Assembly resolution 54/41 [YUN 1999, p. 426], the UN Department of Public Information (DPI) in 2000 continued its special information programme on the question of Palestine, which included the organization of its annual training programme for Palestinian broadcasters and journalists and the production of an exhibit entitled "The United Nations and the Question of Palestine".

DPI provided press coverage of all meetings held at UN Headquarters, including those of the Committee on Palestinian Rights, as well as coverage of conferences and meetings held elsewhere under the auspices of the Committee. The quarterly publication *UN Chronicle* continued to cover the Palestine question and regularly re-

ported on peacekeeping operations in the Middle East. The Radio News Unit covered aspects of the Palestine question and related issues in its news and current affairs programmes in various languages for regional and worldwide dissemination.

As in previous years, a major focus of the United Nations information centres was the promotion of the International Day of Solidarity with the Palestinian People through extensive print and electronic media coverage. Throughout the year, many UNICs dealt with the Palestine question and organized special outreach activities related to the issue.

GENERAL ASSEMBLY ACTION

On 1 December [meeting 78], the General Assembly adopted **resolution 55/54** [draft: A/55/L.47 & Add.1] by recorded vote (151-2-2) [agenda item 41].

Special information programme on the question of Palestine of the Department of Public Information of the Secretariat

The General Assembly,

Having considered the report of the Committee on the Exercise of the Inalienable Rights of the Palestinian People,

Taking note in particular of the information contained in chapter VI of that report,

Recalling its resolution 54/41 of 1 December 1999,

Convinced that the worldwide dissemination of accurate and comprehensive information and the role of non-governmental organizations and institutions remain of vital importance in heightening awareness of and support for the inalienable rights of the Palestinian people,

Aware of the Declaration of Principles on Interim Self-Government Arrangements signed by the Government of the State of Israel and the Palestine Liberation Organization in Washington, D.C., on 13 September 1993, and of the subsequent implementation agreements, in particular the Israeli-Palestinian Interim Agreement on the West Bank and the Gaza Strip signed in Washington, D.C., on 28 September 1995, and the Sharm el-Sheikh Memorandum of 4 September 1999, and their positive implications,

1. *Notes with appreciation* the action taken by the Department of Public Information of the Secretariat in compliance with resolution 54/41;

2. *Considers* that the special information programme on the question of Palestine of the Department is very useful in raising the awareness of the international community concerning the question of Palestine and the situation in the Middle East in general, including the achievements of the peace process, and that the programme is contributing effectively to an atmosphere conducive to dialogue and supportive of the peace process;

3. *Requests* the Department, in full cooperation and coordination with the Committee on the Exercise of the Inalienable Rights of the Palestinian People, to continue, with the necessary flexibility as may be required by developments affecting the question of Pal-

estine, its special information programme for the biennium 2000-2001, in particular:

(a) To disseminate information on all the activities of the United Nations system relating to the question of Palestine, including reports on the work carried out by the relevant United Nations organizations;

(b) To continue to issue and update publications on the various aspects of the question of Palestine in all fields, including materials concerning the recent developments in that regard, in particular the prospects for peace;

(c) To expand its collection of audio-visual material on the question of Palestine and to continue the production of such material, including the updating of the exhibit in the Secretariat;

(d) To organize and promote fact-finding news missions for journalists to the area, including the territories under the jurisdiction of the Palestinian Authority and the occupied territories;

(e) To organize international, regional and national seminars or encounters for journalists, aiming in particular at sensitizing public opinion to the question of Palestine;

(f) To continue to provide assistance to the Palestinian people in the field of media development, in particular to strengthen the training programme for Palestinian broadcasters and journalists initiated in 1995;

4. *Requests* the Department of Public Information to promote the Bethlehem 2000 Project, within existing resources and until the Bethlehem 2000 commemoration comes to a close, including the preparation and dissemination of publications, audio-visual material and further development of the "Bethlehem 2000" site on the United Nations Internet home page.

RECORDED VOTE ON RESOLUTION 55/54:

In favour: Afghanistan, Algeria, Andorra, Antigua and Barbuda, Argentina, Australia, Austria, Azerbaijan, Bahamas, Bahrain, Bangladesh, Barbados, Belarus, Belgium, Bolivia, Bosnia and Herzegovina, Botswana, Brazil, Brunei Darussalam, Bulgaria, Burkina Faso, Burundi, Cambodia, Cameroon, Canada, Cape Verde, Chad, Chile, China, Colombia, Comoros, Costa Rica, Croatia, Cuba, Cyprus, Czech Republic, Democratic People's Republic of Korea, Denmark, Djibouti, Dominican Republic, Ecuador, Egypt, El Salvador, Eritrea, Estonia, Ethiopia, Fiji, Finland, France, Gabon, Gambia, Georgia, Germany, Ghana, Greece, Grenada, Guatemala, Guinea, Guyana, Honduras, Hungary, Iceland, India, Indonesia, Iran, Ireland, Italy, Japan, Jordan, Kazakhstan, Kenya, Kuwait, Kyrgyzstan, Lao People's Democratic Republic, Latvia, Lebanon, Libyan Arab Jamahiriya, Liechtenstein, Lithuania, Luxembourg, Madagascar, Malaysia, Maldives, Mali, Malta, Mauritania, Mauritius, Mexico, Monaco, Mongolia, Morocco, Mozambique, Myanmar, Namibia, Nauru, Nepal, Netherlands, New Zealand, Nicaragua, Nigeria, Norway, Oman, Pakistan, Panama, Papua New Guinea, Paraguay, Peru, Philippines, Poland, Portugal, Qatar, Republic of Korea, Republic of Moldova, Romania, Russian Federation, Saint Lucia, Samoa, San Marino, Saudi Arabia, Senegal, Sierra Leone, Singapore, Slovakia, Slovenia, Solomon Islands, South Africa, Spain, Sri Lanka, Sudan, Swaziland, Sweden, Syrian Arab Republic, Tajikistan, Thailand, The former Yugoslav Republic of Macedonia, Togo, Trinidad and Tobago, Tunisia, Turkey, Uganda, Ukraine, United Arab Emirates, United Kingdom, United Republic of Tanzania, Uruguay, Venezuela, Viet Nam, Yemen, Yugoslavia, Zambia, Zimbabwe.

Against: Israel, United States.

Abstaining: Marshall Islands, Micronesia.

Assistance to Palestinians

UN activities

Report of Secretary-General. In a July report [A/55/137-E/2000/95], the Secretary-General described UN assistance to the Palestinian people between May 1999 and May 2000, assessed ongoing programmes and needs still unmet and presented proposals for additional assistance.

Throughout the reporting period, the UN Special Coordinator for the Middle East Peace Process and Personal Representative of the Secretary-General to the PLO and the Palestinian Authority (PA), Terje Roed-Larsen, continued to ensure better coordination between the relevant institutions of the PA and UN agencies, as well as the donor community, and monitored and documented economic and social conditions in the Occupied Palestinian Territory. He was also responsible for coordinating UN development assistance related to the peace process in Jordan, Lebanon and the Syrian Arab Republic, which included anticipating and strengthening the foundations of development cooperation. The sixth annual UN inter-agency meeting (14-15 June 2000) focused on further deepening cooperation between the resident and non-resident UN agencies and PA representatives.

The Secretary-General said that although, overall, progress continued to be made in meeting some of the urgent and most significant priorities that confronted the Palestinian people, additional support was necessary to address basic human needs. Technical and financial support was also required to improve the physical environment and infrastructure, including water, energy and transportation, and institutions and human resources had to be strengthened to cope with those challenges. The PA, with some support from the United Nations and other international partners, had undertaken institutional, economic and financial reforms, which would also benefit from assistance to ensure their implementation and impact. Institutional mechanisms that had been established to facilitate dialogue and coordination between the PA and donors were working well, and were supported by the Office of the UN Special Coordinator, in collaboration with the World Bank and other UN agencies.

UN organizations and specialized agencies continued to play a significant role in support of the Palestinian people. The UN development system worked as a complement and supplement to other international partners and had implemented sizeable multilateral and bilateral assistance. UNRWA and UNDP administered special, large-scale programmes. Other UN funds, agencies and programmes contributed to socioeconomic development priorities.

It was evident that many needs had been met and, due largely to the strengthening of the PA's capacity for planning and policy-making, the Palestinian Development Plan had been increasingly employed to influence the direction of donor assistance. The Plan represented the PA's commitment to develop national capacity in medium-term development planning and in the implementation of development projects. The Plan was reinforced in 2000 by the publication of the One-Year Action Plan, which provided a ranking of projects for the year according to national priority. Many UN agencies had contributed expertise to the PA to help with sectoral policies and strategies, needs assessments and programme formulation. Nevertheless, lack of sufficient assistance in certain priority sectors/subsectors had left the planned development process lagging in crucial areas. In the process of development cooperation, the coverage of priority needs should continue to be examined: in monetary terms, in terms of whether or not the funds available were being well targeted to the real needs spelled out by the PA, and in terms of information exchange and cooperation between donors, to foster complementarity and avoid overlap. Therefore, continued coordination between the PA and the donor community, and within the donor community itself, was vital if Palestinian development was to evolve and attain its intended objectives.

Progress in the development of the Occupied Palestinian Territory had been facilitated by the assistance provided by the international community with a total of approximately $2.75 billion having been distributed between 1993 and 1999. At the same time, the Secretary-General expressed concern about the declining trend of both new commitments and disbursements for development cooperation.

Seminar on assistance to Palestinian people. By a 3 July letter [A/55/144-E/2000/87], the Chairman of the Committee on Palestinian Rights transmitted to the Secretary-General the report of the seminar on prospects for Palestinian economic development and the Middle East peace process (Cairo, 20-21 June). The seminar provided the framework for a discussion on the state of the Palestinian economy, the factors that affected it and its future prospects. It also heightened awareness and promoted support for the Bethlehem 2000 Project (see p. 1040) The seminar was attended by donor and other Governments, intergovernmental organizations, UN agencies, PA officials and NGOs active in the field, as well as experts.

GENERAL ASSEMBLY ACTION

On 14 December [meeting 85], the General Assembly adopted **resolution 55/173** [draft: A/55/L.63 & Add.1] without vote [agenda item 20 (c)].

Assistance to the Palestinian people

The General Assembly,

Recalling its resolution 54/116 of 15 December 1999,

Recalling also previous resolutions on the question,

Welcoming the signing of the Declaration of Principles on Interim Self-Government Arrangements in Washington, D.C., on 13 September 1993, between the Government of the State of Israel and the Palestine Liberation Organization, the representative of the Palestinian people, as well as the signing of the subsequent implementation agreements, including the Israeli-Palestinian Interim Agreement on the West Bank and the Gaza Strip, in Washington, D.C., on 28 September 1995, and the signing of the Sharm el-Sheikh Memorandum on 4 September 1999,

Gravely concerned about the difficult economic and employment conditions facing the Palestinian people throughout the occupied territory,

Conscious of the urgent need for improvement in the economic and social infrastructure of the occupied territory and the living conditions of the Palestinian people,

Aware that development is difficult under occupation and best promoted in circumstances of peace and stability,

Noting the great economic and social challenges facing the Palestinian people and their leadership,

Conscious of the urgent necessity for international assistance to the Palestinian people, taking into account the Palestinian priorities,

Noting the convening of the United Nations seminar on assistance to the Palestinian people, entitled "Prospects for Palestinian economic development and the Middle East peace process", held in Cairo on 20 and 21 June 2000,

Stressing the need for the full engagement of the United Nations in the process of building Palestinian institutions and in providing broad assistance to the Palestinian people, including assistance in the fields of elections, police training and public administration,

Noting the appointment by the Secretary-General of the United Nations Special Coordinator for the Middle East Peace Process and Personal Representative of the Secretary-General to the Palestine Liberation Organization and the Palestinian Authority,

Welcoming the results of the Conference to Support Middle East Peace, convened in Washington, D.C., on 1 October 1993, and the establishment of the Ad Hoc Liaison Committee and the work being done by the World Bank as its secretariat, as well as the establishment of the Consultative Group,

Welcoming also the work of the Joint Liaison Committee, which provides a forum in which economic policy and practical matters related to donor assistance are discussed with the Palestinian Authority,

Welcoming further the results of the Ministerial Conference to Support Middle East Peace and Development, held in Washington, D.C., on 30 November 1998, and expressing appreciation for the pledges of the international donor community,

Welcoming the meeting of the Consultative Group in Frankfurt, Germany, on 4 and 5 February 1999, in particular the pledges of the international donor community and the presentation of the Palestinian Development Plan for the years 1999-2003,

Welcoming also the meeting of the Ad Hoc Liaison Committee held in Lisbon on 7 and 8 June 2000,

Having considered the report of the Secretary-General,

Expressing grave concern over the continuation of the recent tragic and violent events that have led to many deaths and injuries,

1. *Takes note* of the report of the Secretary-General;

2. *Expresses its appreciation* to the Secretary-General for his rapid response and efforts regarding assistance to the Palestinian people;

3. *Expresses its appreciation* to the Member States, United Nations bodies and intergovernmental, regional and non-governmental organizations that have provided and continue to provide assistance to the Palestinian people;

4. *Stresses* the importance of the work of the United Nations Special Coordinator for the Middle East Peace Process and Personal Representative of the Secretary-General to the Palestine Liberation Organization and the Palestinian Authority and of the steps taken under the auspices of the Secretary-General to ensure the achievement of a coordinated mechanism for United Nations activities throughout the occupied territories;

5. *Urges* Member States, international financial institutions of the United Nations system, intergovernmental and non-governmental organizations and regional and interregional organizations to extend, as rapidly and as generously as possible, economic and social assistance to the Palestinian people, in close cooperation with the Palestine Liberation Organization and through official Palestinian institutions;

6. *Calls upon* relevant organizations and agencies of the United Nations system to intensify their assistance in response to the urgent needs of the Palestinian people in accordance with Palestinian priorities set forth by the Palestinian Authority, with emphasis on national execution and capacity-building;

7. *Urges* Member States to open their markets to exports of Palestinian products on the most favourable terms, consistent with appropriate trading rules, and to implement fully existing trade and cooperation agreements;

8. *Calls upon* the international donor community to expedite the delivery of pledged assistance to the Palestinian people to meet their urgent needs;

9. *Stresses* in this context the importance of ensuring the free passage of aid to the Palestinian people and the free movement of persons and goods;

10. *Urges* the international donor community, United Nations agencies and organizations and non-governmental organizations to extend as rapidly as possible emergency economic and humanitarian assistance to the Palestinian people to counter the impact of the current crisis;

11. *Stresses* the need to implement the Paris Protocol on Economic Relations of 29 April 1994, fifth annex to the Israeli-Palestinian Interim Agreement on the West Bank and the Gaza Strip, in particular with regard to the full and prompt clearance of Palestinian indirect tax revenues;

12. *Suggests* the convening in 2001 of a United Nations–sponsored seminar on assistance to the Palestinian people;

13. *Requests* the Secretary-General to submit a report to the General Assembly at its fifty-sixth session, through the Economic and Social Council, on the implementation of the present resolution, containing:

(*a*) An assessment of the assistance actually received by the Palestinian people;

(*b*) An assessment of the needs still unmet and specific proposals for responding effectively to them;

14. *Decides* to include in the provisional agenda of its fifty-sixth session, under the item entitled "Strengthening of the coordination of humanitarian and disaster relief assistance of the United Nations, including special economic assistance", the sub-item entitled "Assistance to the Palestinian people".

UNRWA

In 2000, the United Nations Relief and Works Agency for Palestine Refugees in the Near East, in its fifty-first year of operation, continued to provide vital education, health and relief and social services to a growing refugee population, despite a critical budget deficit and cash-flow crisis.

On 30 June, 3.7 million refugees were registered with UNRWA, an increase of 3.1 per cent over the 1999 figure of 3.62 million. The largest refugee population was registered in Jordan (42 per cent of the Agency-wide total), followed by the Gaza Strip (22 per cent), the West Bank (15.6 per cent), the Syrian Arab Republic (10.3 per cent) and Lebanon (10.1 per cent). Of the registered population, 36.5 per cent were aged 15 or under and about one third lived in 59 refugee camps, while the remainder resided in towns and villages.

In his annual report on the work of the Agency (1 July 1999–30 June 2000) [A/55/13], the UNRWA Commissioner-General said that the Agency's performance during the reporting period was satisfactory, given the constraints on funding. In general, UNRWA managed to maintain the standard of its education and health services, although staff and infrastructure were increasingly under pressure, with unacceptably high teacher/student and doctor/patient ratios, overcrowding in clinics and classrooms and a shortage of funds to carry out essential maintenance.

The Agency continued to seek greater efficiency through an internal restructuring and reform programme. Donor funding was used to continue technical assistance in three areas: reform of the Agency's financial systems; improving educational planning mechanisms; and improving procurement policies and procedures. By mid-2000, the Agency had selected a new financial system, which was intended to be operational by mid-2001.

Palestine refugees remained anxious about their future status. UNRWA's continuing financial difficulties were interpreted by some as politically motivated, signalling a weakening in the international community's commitment to the refugee issue. The withdrawal of Israeli forces from southern Lebanon in May (see p. 461) was welcomed in the region and led to a period of relative calm.

The strife that broke out in late September following the visit of Mr. Sharon to the Temple Mount/Al-Haram Al-Sharif in Jerusalem undermined several years of economic progress and infrastructure development, with profound effects on the refugees in terms of lives, livelihoods and shelter lost. UNRWA launched a flash emergency appeal on 4 October for $4.83 million, concentrating on the provision of medical supplies. That was followed by the first consolidated emergency appeal on 8 November for $39.1 million to provide refugees with food and cash assistance, among other forms of aid, for the period from December 2000 through February 2001.

OIOS report. The General Assembly had before it a report by the Office of Internal Oversight Services (OIOS) on the investigation into the UNRWA field office in Lebanon [A/54/367]. The Office had investigated allegations of financial impropriety, the embezzlement of medical supplies and bribery by construction contractors. With regard to the bribery allegations, OIOS found them to be unsubstantiated but made recommendations for improving UNRWA tendering procedures to reduce the risk of fraud and suspicion of corruption. The allegations of financial impropriety and embezzlement of medical supplies were found to be without merit.

By **resolution 54/257** of 7 April, the Assembly took note of the OIOS report.

Advisory Commission. By a 28 September letter to the Commissioner-General, which he included in his report [A/55/13], the Advisory Commission of UNRWA recognized that the Agency's services to the refugees over the past 50 years had contributed to their socio-economic well-being and, thus, to stability in the region, and in that light recognized the need to mobilize an adequate level of resources for the Agency's core budget. It noted with appreciation the new format of the Agency's budget that had been welcomed by the Advisory Committee on Administrative and Budgetary Questions (ACABQ). The Commission noted with concern the imminent cash crisis that UNRWA was facing and called on donors to provide adequate, predictable and early payments to alleviate that situation. It welcomed UNRWA's efforts to improve the efficiency, productivity and effectiveness of its programmes, as well as the introduction of new administrative reform measures. It noted with concern the difficulties faced by the Agency due to the restrictions imposed by the Israeli authorities and called for measures to remove them.

Peace Implementation Programme

In its seventh year of operation, UNRWA's Peace Implementation Programme (PIP) remained the main channel for extrabudgetary funding of activities associated with the Agency's education, health and relief and social services programmes, as well as income generation. Since its inception in October 1993 [YUN 1993, p. 569], PIP had improved the refugees' overall living conditions, created employment opportunities and developed infrastructure. Following the adoption of the 2000-2001 programme-based biennium budget, which divided the Agency's budget into regular budget and projects budget sections, all new non-core contributions were credited to the projects budget. A new "Projects 2000-2002" programme was introduced in January 2000 to track all contributions to the biennium projects budget.

Between mid-1999 and mid-2000, with PIP funding, UNRWA completed the construction of 12 schools, 32 additional classrooms, one vocational education room, two water reservoirs and eight latrine units, a polyclinic, a health centre and the upgrading of a second, the expansion of a mother and child health centre, and a youth activities centre. PIP funds also enabled the Agency to rehabilitate 154 shelters of special hardship families. Several elements of the environmental health scheme in the Gaza Strip were completed, while some other components were still ongoing. Camp infrastructure projects ongoing at mid-2000 included the construction of a public health laboratory in the West Bank; the construction of several schools and additional classrooms Agency-wide; a women's programme centre and two community rehabilitation centres; and a major sewerage and drainage project for eight refugee camps in Lebanon. Other PIP activities included a slow learners' programme in Jordan; the integration of visually impaired children into the regular school system; and care for the destitute aged. PIP also helped to sustain regular Agency programmes by funding the running costs of two health centres in Gaza, the cost of university scholarships for refugee students and the procurement of medical supplies. Further funding went into the upgrading of facilities and courses at several of the Agency's vocational training centres. Cash expenditure under PIP amounted to $25.8 million during the reporting period, not including expenditures on the European Gaza Hospital.

UNRWA received $8.1 million in pledges and contributions for PIP projects during the reporting period. Of the new funding, $5.8 million went to projects in the education sector, while $0.9 million was allocated for the health sector and $1.4 million for the relief and social services sector. No funding was received for income-generation activities.

Lebanon appeal

Most of the over 370,000 registered Palestine refugees in Lebanon continued to face deplorable living conditions and depended almost entirely on UNRWA for basic services. By mid-2000, the Agency had received $9.2 million of the $11 million sought in additional contributions under the special emergency appeal, launched in 1997 to support essential health, education, relief and social services activities for Palestine refugees in Lebanon. Completed projects included the construction of a secondary school and a computer laboratory and the procurement of textbooks required under the new curriculum.

Major service areas

UNRWA continued to provide educational, health, and relief and social services to, and carried out income-generation activities for, Palestinian refugees throughout the occupied territories.

During the 1999/2000 school year, the 637 UNRWA schools across the region accommodated 466,955 pupils, most of whom were in elementary and preparatory cycles, apart from 1,696 students at the three Agency secondary schools in Lebanon. Total enrolment increased by 2.1 per cent, or 9,606 pupils, over the 1998/99 school year. The Jordan and Gaza fields each accounted for approximately one third of total Agency pupil enrolment, while the other three fields (Lebanon, Syria, West Bank) together accounted for the remaining third. UNRWA's school system continued to maintain full gender equity, with 50 per cent of pupils being female. The education programme, which was run in cooperation with the United Nations Educational, Scientific and Cultural Organization (UNESCO), remained the largest single area of UNRWA activity, with the 14,485 education personnel representing 66 per cent of all Agency staff. The proposed education budget for the 2000-2001 biennium was established at $328.3 million for regular programmes, or 54 per cent of UNRWA's regular budget for the period. The policy of operating schools on a double-shift basis (housing two schools in a single building) continued due to financial constraints and steadily rising student enrolment. Also due to financial constraints, the Agency remained unable to carry out the extension of the basic education cycle in the West Bank and Gaza from 9 to 10 years, which widened the gap between the Agency's and the host authorities' education systems. In June

2000, the Agency began a donor-funded project aimed at strengthening and supporting UNRWA's efforts to promote concepts and principles of basic human rights, raise awareness of the importance of tolerance and train Palestine refugee children and youth in non-violent means of conflict resolution. Total enrolment in the eight UNRWA vocational and technical training centres was 4,635 in the 1999/2000 school year, a decrease of 20 over the previous year. Overall, women accounted for 31.7 per cent of all trainees. UNRWA also provided placement and career guidance and continued with project funding to support some scholars until they graduated. In coordination with a United Kingdom consultancy team and senior education staff at both headquarters (Amman, Jordan) and in the field, a five-year development plan (2000-2004) was completed, covering educational planning, staff and management development, vocational and technical education, education management information system, personnel and finance.

UNRWA's health-care programme remained focused on comprehensive primary health care, including a full range of maternal and child health and family planning services; school health services, health education and promotion activities; outpatient medical care services; prevention and control of communicable and non-communicable diseases; and specialist care with emphasis on gynaecology and obstetrics, paediatrics and cardiology. Dental and basic support services, such as radiology and laboratory facilities, were also provided. Services were delivered through a network of 123 primary health-care facilities located in and outside refugee camps. UNRWA participated in two rounds of national immunization campaigns for the eradication of poliomyelitis in the context of a World Health Organization (WHO) regional strategy. Funding shortfalls continued to threaten the sustainability of hospitalization services, making the effective management of scarce resources a top priority. The Agency continued to emphasize the development of human resources for health through basic, inservice and postgraduate training as a key element to improve the quality of care. Approximately 1.2 million Palestine refugees in 59 official camps in the five fields of operation, representing 32 per cent of the total registered population, benefited from environmental health services provided by UNRWA, including sewage disposal, provision of safe drinking water, collection and disposal of refuse, and control of insect and rodent infestation. The proposed health budget for the 2000-2001 biennium was established at $107.7 million under the regular programme, representing 17.6 per cent of the Agency's total operating budget. UNRWA continued its cooperation with the PA, the EU and other UN agencies.

The relief and social services programme supported those Palestine refugees who were unable to meet basic needs for food, shelter and other essentials. It also maintained records on Palestine refugees in order to determine eligibility for all UNRWA services. Further progress was made on the unified registration system, which aimed to integrate two existing computerized databases—the registration database and the socioeconomic database—with the family files archives. The principal means of assistance to special hardship case (SHC) families were food support, shelter rehabilitation, selective cash assistance, hospitalization subsidies and preferential access to UNRWA training centres. The number of refugees in households that met the eligibility criteria—no male adult medically fit to earn an income and no other identifiable means of financial support above a defined threshold—increased by 3.5 per cent, from 200,078 at 30 June 1999 to 207,150 at 30 June 2000. The percentage of refugees enrolled in the programme was highest in Lebanon (10.8 per cent) and the Gaza Strip (8.6 per cent) and lowest in Jordan (2.6 per cent). The regular budget allocation for selective cash assistance, which was frozen in August 1997, was partially reinstated in January 2000. During the first half of 2000, small grants averaging $140 were provided on a case-by-case basis to 1,766 SHC families facing emergency situations. UNRWA also rehabilitated a total of 217 shelters of SHC families, as compared to 1,305 in the previous reporting period. The poverty alleviation programme continued to address poverty at the micro level. Most loans under the group guaranteed lending schemes and to SHC families were for between $500 and $10,000. UNRWA-sponsored centres within the refugee camps, or community-based organizations (CBOs), increased from 131 at mid-1999 to 133 at mid-2000, with a total of 71 women's programme centres, 27 youth activity centres and 35 community rehabilitation centres for the physically and mentally challenged. CBOs offered social development activities, including skills-training opportunities for women and disabled people. UNRWA's role in the implementation of social services programmes continued to evolve from that of service provider to that of facilitator, with emphasis on a community development approach that promoted, among other things, participation, self-reliance, revenue generation, and implementation and management skills. The proposed 2000-2001 budget of the relief and social services programme was $62.4 million for regular pro-

grammes, representing just over 10 per cent of UNRWA's total regular budget.

UNRWA's income-generation programme supported small and microenterprises within the refugee community by providing technical assistance, as well as capital investment and working capital loans through field-based revolving loan funds. The programme's objective was to create employment, generate income, reduce poverty and empower refugees, particularly women, through socio-economic growth. During the reporting period, the programme provided 10,875 loans worth $13.2 million to Palestinian-owned enterprises. UNRWA's income-generation activities continued to be concentrated in the Gaza Strip, although the programme in the West Bank was rapidly reducing the outreach gap between the two programmes. The programme targeted formal business enterprises that had the capacity to create jobs for the unemployed and the informal and microenterprises that could generate income for poor families. Although no additional capital funds were received during the reporting period, the number of loans disbursed increased from 7,014, valued at $8.33 million during the previous reporting period, to 8,135 valued at $10.2 million during 1999/2000. The Gaza income-generation programme was composed of four subprogrammes, three of which provided credit to various target groups and the fourth provided business training services. The microenterprise credit (MEC) subprogramme targeted working capital loans to the more than 20,000 microenterprises operating in Gaza. The solidarity group lending subprogramme also provided short-term working capital loans, but they were targeted at women working in microenterprises or women microenterprise owners. The small-scale enterprise subprogramme provided both working capital and capital investment loans to new and established businesses in the industry and service sectors to promote job creation, exports and import substitution. The small and microenterprise training subprogramme provided non-financial services to the business community and encouraged entrepreneurship through business training. The MEC subprogramme in the West Bank was the fastest growing of UNRWA's credit subprogrammes. In the second half of 2000, UNRWA formally changed the name of its income-generation programme in the West Bank and the Gaza Strip to the microfinance and microenterprise programme.

GENERAL ASSEMBLY ACTION

On 8 December [meeting 83], the General Assembly, on the recommendation of the Fourth Committee [A/55/570], adopted **resolution 55/123** by recorded vote (156-1-3) [agenda item 84].

Assistance to Palestine refugees

The General Assembly,

Recalling its resolution 54/69 of 6 December 1999 and all its previous resolutions on the question, including resolution 194(III) of 11 December 1948,

Taking note of the report of the Commissioner-General of the United Nations Relief and Works Agency for Palestine Refugees in the Near East covering the period from 1 July 1999 to 30 June 2000,

Stressing the importance of the Middle East peace process,

Welcoming the signature in Washington, D.C., on 13 September 1993 by the Government of the State of Israel and the Palestine Liberation Organization, the representative of the people of Palestine, of the Declaration of Principles on Interim Self-Government Arrangements and the subsequent implementation agreements,

Aware that the Multilateral Working Group on Refugees of the Middle East peace process has an important role to play in the peace process,

1. *Notes with regret* that repatriation or compensation of the refugees, as provided for in paragraph 11 of its resolution 194(III), has not yet been effected and that, therefore, the situation of the refugees continues to be a matter of concern;

2. *Also notes with regret* that the United Nations Conciliation Commission for Palestine has been unable to find a means of achieving progress in the implementation of paragraph 11 of General Assembly resolution 194(III), and requests the Commission to exert continued efforts towards the implementation of that paragraph and to report to the Assembly as appropriate, but no later than 1 September 2001;

3. *Expresses its thanks* to the Commissioner-General and to all the staff of the United Nations Relief and Works Agency for Palestine Refugees in the Near East, recognizing that the Agency is doing all it can within the limits of available resources, and also expresses its thanks to the specialized agencies and to private organizations for their valuable work in assisting refugees;

4. *Notes* the significant success of the Peace Implementation Programme of the Agency since the signing of the Declaration of Principles on Interim Self-Government Arrangements, and stresses the importance that contributions to this Programme not be at the expense of the General Fund;

5. *Welcomes* the increased cooperation between the Agency and international and regional organizations, States and relevant agencies and non-governmental organizations, which is essential to enhancing the contributions of the Agency towards improved conditions for the refugees and thereby the social stability of the occupied territory;

6. *Urges* all Member States to extend and expedite aid and assistance with a view to the economic and social development of the Palestinian people and the occupied territory;

7. *Reiterates its deep concern* regarding the persisting critical financial situation of the Agency, as outlined in the report of the Commissioner-General;

8. *Commends* the efforts of the Commissioner-General to move towards budgetary transparency and internal efficiency, and welcomes in this respect the new, unified budget structure for the biennium 2000-2001, which can contribute significantly to improved budgetary transparency of the Agency;

9. *Welcomes* the consultative process between the Agency, host Governments, the Palestinian Authority and donors on management reforms;

10. *Notes with profound concern* that the continuing shortfall in the finances of the Agency has a significant negative influence on the living conditions of the Palestine refugees most in need and that it therefore has possible consequences for the peace process;

11. *Calls upon* all donors, as a matter of urgency, to make the most generous efforts possible to meet the anticipated needs of the Agency, including the remaining costs of moving the headquarters to Gaza, encourages contributing Governments to contribute regularly and to consider increasing their regular contributions, and urges non-contributing Governments to contribute.

RECORDED VOTE ON RESOLUTION 55/123:

In favour: Afghanistan, Algeria, Andorra, Angola, Antigua and Barbuda, Argentina, Armenia, Australia, Austria, Azerbaijan, Bahamas, Bahrain, Bangladesh, Barbados, Belarus, Belgium, Belize, Benin, Bhutan, Bolivia, Botswana, Brazil, Brunei Darussalam, Bulgaria, Burkina Faso, Burundi, Cambodia, Cameroon, Canada, Cape Verde, Chad, Chile, China, Colombia, Comoros, Costa Rica, Côte d'Ivoire, Croatia, Cuba, Cyprus, Czech Republic, Democratic People's Republic of Korea, Denmark, Djibouti, Dominican Republic, Ecuador, Egypt, El Salvador, Eritrea, Estonia, Ethiopia, Fiji, Finland, France, Gabon, Georgia, Germany, Ghana, Greece, Grenada, Guatemala, Guinea, Guyana, Haiti, Honduras, Hungary, Iceland, India, Indonesia, Iran, Ireland, Italy, Jamaica, Japan, Jordan, Kazakhstan, Kenya, Kuwait, Kyrgyzstan, Lao People's Democratic Republic, Latvia, Lebanon, Libyan Arab Jamahiriya, Liechtenstein, Lithuania, Luxembourg, Madagascar, Malaysia, Maldives, Mali, Malta, Mauritania, Mauritius, Mexico, Monaco, Mongolia, Morocco, Mozambique, Myanmar, Namibia, Nauru, Nepal, Netherlands, New Zealand, Nicaragua, Nigeria, Norway, Oman, Pakistan, Panama, Papua New Guinea, Paraguay, Peru, Philippines, Poland, Portugal, Qatar, Republic of Moldova, Romania, Russian Federation, Saint Lucia, Samoa, San Marino, Saudi Arabia, Senegal, Sierra Leone, Singapore, Slovakia, Slovenia, Solomon Islands, South Africa, Spain, Sri Lanka, Sudan, Swaziland, Sweden, Syrian Arab Republic, Thailand, The former Yugoslav Republic of Macedonia, Togo, Tonga, Tunisia, Turkey, Uganda, Ukraine, United Arab Emirates, United Kingdom, United Republic of Tanzania, Uruguay, Vanuatu, Venezuela, Viet Nam, Yemen, Yugoslavia, Zambia, Zimbabwe.

Against: Israel.

Abstaining: Marshall Islands, Micronesia, United States.

The Assembly, on the same date [meeting 83] and also on the Fourth Committee's recommendation [A/55/570], adopted **resolution 55/127** by recorded vote (157-2-2) [agenda item 84].

Operations of the United Nations Relief and Works Agency for Palestine Refugees in the Near East

The General Assembly,

Recalling its resolutions 194(III) of 11 December 1948, 212(III) of 19 November 1948, 302(IV) of 8 December 1949 and all subsequent related resolutions,

Recalling also the relevant Security Council resolutions,

Having considered the report of the Commissioner-General of the United Nations Relief and Works Agency for Palestine Refugees in the Near East covering the period from 1 July 1999 to 30 June 2000,

Taking note of the letter dated 28 September 2000 from the Chairman of the Advisory Commission of the United Nations Relief and Works Agency for Palestine Refugees in the Near East addressed to the

Commissioner-General, contained in the report of the Commissioner-General,

Having considered the reports of the Secretary-General submitted in pursuance of its resolutions 48/40 E, 48/40 H and 48/40 J of 10 December 1993 and 49/35 C of 9 December 1994,

Recalling Articles 100, 104 and 105 of the Charter of the United Nations and the Convention on the Privileges and Immunities of the United Nations,

Affirming the applicability of the Geneva Convention relative to the Protection of Civilian Persons in Time of War, of 12 August 1949, to the Palestinian territory occupied since 1967, including Jerusalem,

Aware of the fact that Palestine refugees have, for over five decades, lost their homes, lands and means of livelihood,

Also aware of the continuing needs of Palestine refugees throughout the Occupied Palestinian Territory and in the other fields of operation, namely, in Lebanon, Jordan and the Syrian Arab Republic,

Further aware of the valuable work done by the refugee affairs officers of the Agency in providing protection to the Palestinian people, in particular Palestine refugees,

Gravely concerned about the increased suffering of the Palestine refugees, including loss of life and injury, during the recent tragic events in the Occupied Palestinian Territory, including Jerusalem,

Deeply concerned about the continuing critical financial situation of the Agency and its effect on the continuity of provision of necessary Agency services to the Palestine refugees, including the emergency-related programmes,

Aware of the work of the Peace Implementation Programme of the Agency,

Recalling the signing in Washington, D.C., on 13 September 1993 of the Declaration of Principles on Interim Self-Government Arrangements by the Government of the State of Israel and the Palestine Liberation Organization, and the subsequent implementation agreements,

Taking note of the agreement reached on 24 June 1994, embodied in an exchange of letters between the Agency and the Palestine Liberation Organization,

Aware of the establishment of a working relationship between the Advisory Commission of the Agency and the Palestine Liberation Organization in accordance with General Assembly decision 48/417 of 10 December 1993,

1. *Expresses its appreciation* to the Commissioner-General of the United Nations Relief and Works Agency for Palestine Refugees in the Near East, as well as to all the staff of the Agency, for their tireless efforts and valuable work;

2. *Also expresses its appreciation* to the Advisory Commission of the Agency, and requests it to continue its efforts and to keep the General Assembly informed of its activities, including the full implementation of decision 48/417;

3. *Takes note* of the functioning of the headquarters of the Agency in Gaza City on the basis of the Headquarters Agreement between the Agency and the Palestinian Authority;

4. *Acknowledges* the support of the host Governments and the Palestine Liberation Organization for the Agency in the discharge of its duties;

5. *Calls upon* Israel, the occupying Power, to accept the de jure applicability of the Geneva Convention relative to the Protection of Civilian Persons in Time of War, of 12 August 1949, and to abide scrupulously by its provisions;

6. *Also calls upon* Israel to abide by Articles 100, 104 and 105 of the Charter of the United Nations and the Convention on the Privileges and Immunities of the United Nations with regard to the safety of the personnel of the Agency and the protection of its institutions and the safeguarding of the security of the facilities of the Agency in the Occupied Palestinian Territory, including Jerusalem;

7. *Further calls upon* Israel to particularly cease obstructing the movement of the personnel, vehicles and supplies of the Agency, which has a detrimental impact on the Agency's operations;

8. *Calls once again upon* the Government of Israel to compensate the Agency for damages to its property and facilities resulting from actions by the Israeli side;

9. *Requests* the Commissioner-General to proceed with the issuance of identification cards for Palestine refugees and their descendants in the Occupied Palestinian Territory;

10. *Notes* that the new context created by the signing of the Declaration of Principles on Interim Self-Government Arrangements by the Government of the State of Israel and the Palestine Liberation Organization and subsequent implementation agreements has had major consequences for the activities of the Agency, which is henceforth called upon, in close cooperation with the United Nations Special Coordinator for the Middle East Peace Process and Personal Representative of the Secretary-General to the Palestine Liberation Organization and the Palestinian Authority, the specialized agencies and the World Bank, to continue to contribute towards the development of economic and social stability in the occupied territory;

11. *Notes also* that the functioning of the Agency remains essential in all fields of operation;

12. *Notes further* the significant success of the Peace Implementation Programme of the Agency;

13. *Expresses concern* about those remaining austerity measures due to the financial crisis, which have affected the quality and level of some of the services of the Agency;

14. *Reiterates its request* to the Commissioner-General to proceed with the modernization of the archives of the Agency;

15. *Urges* all States, specialized agencies and non-governmental organizations to continue and to increase their contributions to the Agency so as to ease current financial constraints and to support the Agency in maintaining the provision of the most basic and effective assistance to the Palestine refugees.

RECORDED VOTE ON RESOLUTION 55/127:

In favour: Afghanistan, Algeria, Andorra, Angola, Antigua and Barbuda, Argentina, Armenia, Australia, Austria, Azerbaijan, Bahamas, Bahrain, Bangladesh, Barbados, Belarus, Belgium, Belize, Benin, Bhutan, Bolivia, Botswana, Brazil, Brunei Darussalam, Bulgaria, Burkina Faso, Burundi, Cambodia, Cameroon, Canada, Cape Verde, Chad, Chile, China, Colombia, Comoros, Costa Rica, Côte d'Ivoire, Croatia, Cuba, Cyprus, Czech Republic, Democratic People's Republic of Korea, Denmark, Djibouti, Dominican Republic, Ecuador, Egypt, El Salvador, Eritrea, Estonia, Ethiopia, Fiji, Finland, France, Gabon, Georgia, Germany, Ghana, Greece, Grenada, Guatemala, Guinea, Guyana, Haiti, Honduras, Hungary, Iceland, India, Indonesia, Iran, Ireland, Italy, Jamaica, Japan, Jordan, Kazakhstan, Kenya, Kuwait, Kyrgyzstan, Lao People's Democratic Republic, Latvia, Lebanon, Libyan

Arab Jamahiriya, Liechtenstein, Lithuania, Luxembourg, Madagascar, Malaysia, Maldives, Mali, Malta, Mauritania, Mauritius, Mexico, Monaco, Mongolia, Morocco, Mozambique, Myanmar, Namibia, Nauru, Nepal, Netherlands, New Zealand, Nicaragua, Nigeria, Norway, Oman, Pakistan, Panama, Papua New Guinea, Paraguay, Peru, Philippines, Poland, Portugal, Qatar, Republic of Korea, Republic of Moldova, Romania, Russian Federation, Saint Lucia, Samoa, San Marino, Saudi Arabia, Senegal, Sierra Leone, Singapore, Slovakia, Slovenia, Solomon Islands, South Africa, Spain, Sri Lanka, Sudan, Swaziland, Sweden, Syrian Arab Republic, Thailand, The former Yugoslav Republic of Macedonia, Togo, Tonga, Tunisia, Turkey, Uganda, Ukraine, United Arab Emirates, United Kingdom, United Republic of Tanzania, Uruguay, Vanuatu, Venezuela, Viet Nam, Yemen, Yugoslavia, Zambia, Zimbabwe.

Against: Israel, United States.

Abstaining: Marshall Islands, Micronesia.

By **decision 55/458** of 23 December, the Assembly decided that the item "United Nations Relief and Works Agency for Palestine Refugees in the Near East" would remain for consideration during its resumed fifty-fifth (2001) session.

UNRWA financing

In 2000, UNRWA continued to face a difficult financial situation, characterized by large funding shortfalls in the regular budget, depleted working capital and cash reserves, and cumulative deficits in certain project accounts. The structural deficit—representing the inability of income to keep pace with needs arising from natural growth in the refugee population and inflation, which increased the cost of maintaining a constant level of services—remained a problem. However, through a combination of ad hoc additional donor contributions and prudent financial management, UNRWA was making some progress in reducing the deficit. Nevertheless, a budget deficit was expected by the end of 2000 unless additional contributions were made during the year.

At mid-2000, the cash position remained extremely weak, forcing the Agency to live from hand to mouth in terms of balancing incoming funds and outgoing payments. Expected cash expenditure in the regular programme was $280.4 million, as against expected cash income of $250 million. Working capital, defined as the difference between assets and liabilities in the regular budget for the calendar year, was for all practical purposes non-existent, making UNRWA vulnerable to any change in expected income or expenditure. Estimates indicated that the Agency's regular budget for 2000 would face a deficit of $30.4 million by year's end.

The Agency's biennium budget for 2000-2001 [A/54/13/Add.1] was well received by donors and ACABQ for the clarity of its presentation and objectives. A new preparation process and format sought to enhance the budget's usefulness as a planning, management and fund-raising tool. By mid-2000, an Agency-wide exercise was under way to monitor expenditure against budget proposals.

Working Group. The Working Group on the Financing of UNRWA held two meetings in 2000, on 11 September and 6 October. In its report to the General Assembly [A/55/456], the Working Group said that the critical financial situation of 1999 had continued in 2000. In 1999, UNRWA received income of $260.7 million against a cash budget of $322.1 million, leaving a deficit of some $61.4 million. In cash terms, the Agency ended the year with a balance of $14 million in its General Fund, although that amount included $12 million advanced from year 2000 pledges in order to enable the Agency to meet its December payroll.

Deficits in the cash budgets for previous years had been covered out of working capital, a reserve that had been virtually depleted by the beginning of 1999. At the end of 1999, outstanding and unpaid pledges amounted to $36.9 million: $12.7 million pertaining to the regular budget and $24.2 million to project funding. Further strain was exerted by the non-reimbursement by the PA of the value-added tax that the Agency had paid in the course of its operations in Gaza and the West Bank, which totalled some $18.5 million as at June 2000. In addition, some $4.5 million for port charges remained to be recovered. There also was a shortfall in funding for the European Gaza Hospital, and a deficit of $5.2 million in the account set up to fund the costs of transferring UNRWA headquarters from Vienna to Gaza and Amman.

The Working Group noted that UNRWA had made significant progress towards eliminating the structural deficit problem that plagued the Agency in previous years, in particular through the use of contract teachers, reductions in international staffing and other reforms. Nevertheless, it expressed alarm that austerity measures continued to prevent UNRWA's programmes from expanding at a rate commensurate with the growth in the refugee population.

The Working Group stressed that UNRWA services had to be viewed as the minimum required to enable the refugees to lead decent human lives. Any further reduction in those services would not only deprive the refugees of the minimum level of support to which they were entitled, but could also have a destabilizing effect on the entire region. The Group urged Governments to continue contributing generously and to consider additional contributions to finance deficit amounts so that services could continue uninterrupted.

GENERAL ASSEMBLY ACTION

On 8 December [meeting 83], the General Assembly, on the recommendation of the Fourth

Committee [A/55/570], adopted **resolution 55/124** without vote [agenda item 84].

Working Group on the Financing of the United Nations Relief and Works Agency for Palestine Refugees in the Near East

The General Assembly,

Recalling its resolutions 2656(XXV) of 7 December 1970, 2728(XXV) of 15 December 1970, 2791(XXVI) of 6 December 1971, 54/70 of 6 December 1999 and the previous resolutions on this question,

Recalling also its decision 36/462 of 16 March 1982, by which it took note of the special report of the Working Group on the Financing of the United Nations Relief and Works Agency for Palestine Refugees in the Near East,

Having considered the report of the Working Group,

Taking into account the report of the Commissioner-General of the United Nations Relief and Works Agency for Palestine Refugees in the Near East covering the period from 1 July 1999 to 30 June 2000,

Deeply concerned about the continuing financial situation of the Agency, which has affected and affects the continuation of the provision of necessary Agency services to Palestine refugees, including the emergency-related programmes,

Emphasizing the continuing need for extraordinary efforts in order to maintain, at least at the current minimum level, the activities of the Agency, as well as to enable the Agency to carry out essential construction,

1. *Commends* the Working Group on the Financing of the United Nations Relief and Works Agency for Palestine Refugees in the Near East for its efforts to assist in ensuring the financial security of the Agency;

2. *Takes note with approval* of the report of the Working Group;

3. *Requests* the Working Group to continue its efforts, in cooperation with the Secretary-General and the Commissioner-General, to find a solution to the financial situation of the Agency;

4. *Welcomes* the new, unified budget structure for the biennium 2000-2001, which can contribute significantly to improved budgetary transparency of the Agency;

5. *Requests* the Secretary-General to provide the necessary services and assistance to the Working Group for the conduct of its work.

Displaced persons

In a September report [A/55/391] on compliance with General Assembly resolution 54/71 [YUN 1999, p. 438], which called for the accelerated return of all persons displaced as a result of the June 1967 and subsequent hostilities to their homes or former places of residence in the territories occupied by Israel since 1967, the Secretary-General said that since UNRWA was not involved in arrangements for the return of either refugees or displaced persons not registered with it, the Agency's information was based on requests by returning registered refugees for the transfer of their entitlements to their areas of return. Displaced refugees known by UNRWA to

have returned to the West Bank and Gaza Strip since 1967 numbered 19,876. Records indicated that, between 1 July 1999 and 30 June 2000, 1,278 refugees had returned to the West Bank and 218 to Gaza. Some of the refugees might not have been displaced in 1967, but might be family members of a displaced registered refugee whom they either had accompanied on return or had joined later.

GENERAL ASSEMBLY ACTION

On 8 December [meeting 83], the General Assembly, on the recommendation of the Fourth Committee [A/55/570], adopted **resolution 55/125** by recorded vote (156-2-2) [agenda item 84].

Persons displaced as a result of the June 1967 and subsequent hostilities

The General Assembly,

Recalling its resolutions 2252(ES-V) of 4 July 1967, 2341 B (XXII) of 19 December 1967 and all subsequent related resolutions,

Recalling also Security Council resolutions 237(1967) of 14 June 1967 and 259(1968) of 27 September 1968,

Taking note of the report of the Secretary-General submitted in pursuance of its resolution 54/71 of 6 December 1999,

Taking note also of the report of the Commissioner-General of the United Nations Relief and Works Agency for Palestine Refugees in the Near East covering the period from 1 July 1999 to 30 June 2000,

Concerned about the continuing human suffering resulting from the June 1967 and subsequent hostilities,

Taking note of the relevant provisions of the Declaration of Principles on Interim Self-Government Arrangements, signed in Washington, D.C., on 13 September 1993 by the Government of the State of Israel and the Palestine Liberation Organization, with regard to the modalities for the admission of persons displaced in 1967, and concerned that the process agreed upon has not yet been effected,

1. *Reaffirms* the right of all persons displaced as a result of the June 1967 and subsequent hostilities to return to their homes or former places of residence in the territories occupied by Israel since 1967;

2. *Expresses concern* that the mechanism agreed upon by the parties in article XII of the Declaration of Principles on Interim Self-Government Arrangements on the return of displaced persons has not been effected, and expresses the hope for an accelerated return of displaced persons;

3. *Endorses,* in the meanwhile, the efforts of the Commissioner-General of the United Nations Relief and Works Agency for Palestine Refugees in the Near East to continue to provide humanitarian assistance, as far as practicable, on an emergency basis, and as a temporary measure, to persons in the area who are currently displaced and in serious need of continued assistance as a result of the June 1967 and subsequent hostilities;

4. *Strongly appeals* to all Governments and to organizations and individuals to contribute generously to the Agency and to the other intergovernmental and non-

governmental organizations concerned for the above-mentioned purposes;

5. *Requests* the Secretary-General, after consulting with the Commissioner-General, to report to the General Assembly before its fifty-sixth session on the progress made with regard to the implementation of the present resolution.

RECORDED VOTE ON RESOLUTION 55/125:

In favour: Algeria, Andorra, Angola, Antigua and Barbuda, Argentina, Armenia, Australia, Austria, Azerbaijan, Bahamas, Bahrain, Bangladesh, Barbados, Belarus, Belgium, Belize, Benin, Bhutan, Bolivia, Botswana, Brazil, Brunei Darussalam, Bulgaria, Burkina Faso, Burundi, Cambodia, Cameroon, Canada, Cape Verde, Chad, Chile, China, Colombia, Comoros, Costa Rica, Côte d'Ivoire, Croatia, Cuba, Cyprus, Czech Republic, Democratic People's Republic of Korea, Denmark, Djibouti, Dominican Republic, Ecuador, Egypt, El Salvador, Eritrea, Estonia, Ethiopia, Fiji, Finland, France, Gabon, Georgia, Germany, Ghana, Greece, Grenada, Guatemala, Guinea, Guyana, Haiti, Honduras, Hungary, Iceland, India, Indonesia, Iran, Ireland, Italy, Jamaica, Japan, Jordan, Kazakhstan, Kenya, Kuwait, Kyrgyzstan, Lao People's Democratic Republic, Latvia, Lebanon, Libyan Arab Jamahiriya, Liechtenstein, Lithuania, Luxembourg, Madagascar, Malaysia, Maldives, Mali, Malta, Mauritania, Mauritius, Mexico, Monaco, Mongolia, Morocco, Mozambique, Myanmar, Namibia, Nauru, Nepal, Netherlands, New Zealand, Nicaragua, Nigeria, Norway, Oman, Pakistan, Panama, Papua New Guinea, Paraguay, Peru, Philippines, Poland, Portugal, Qatar, Republic of Korea, Republic of Moldova, Romania, Russian Federation, Saint Lucia, Samoa, San Marino, Saudi Arabia, Senegal, Sierra Leone, Singapore, Slovakia, Slovenia, Solomon Islands, South Africa, Spain, Sri Lanka, Sudan, Swaziland, Sweden, Syrian Arab Republic, Thailand, The former Yugoslav Republic of Macedonia, Togo, Tonga, Tunisia, Turkey, Uganda, Ukraine, United Arab Emirates, United Kingdom, United Republic of Tanzania, Uruguay, Vanuatu, Venezuela, Viet Nam, Yemen, Yugoslavia, Zambia, Zimbabwe.

Against: Israel, United States.

Abstaining: Marshall Islands, Micronesia.

Education, training and scholarships

In a September report [A/55/402], the Secretary-General transmitted responses to the General Assembly's appeal in resolution 54/72 [YUN 1999, p. 439] for States, specialized agencies and NGOs to augment special allocations for scholarships and grants to Palestine refugees, for which UNRWA acted as recipient and trustee.

In the 2000 fiscal year, Japan awarded 12 fellowships to Palestine refugees who were employed by UNRWA as vocational training staff at the eight vocational training centres in the Agency's area of operations. In 1999, owing to the cancellation of the portion of the university scholarship fund for secondary school graduates financed from UNRWA's General Fund budget and the fact that financing was not forthcoming from donors to fund the subprogramme, UNRWA's Education Department used funds already available from the Japanese contribution, as well as from contributions made by Switzerland, to finance the studies of some students through their graduation. UNESCO granted 25 scholarships to Palestinian students in 1999/2000, while WHO provided 55 fellowships/study tours for qualified Palestinian candidates. The United World Colleges offered one scholarship for 1998/99 and one for 1999/2000.

GENERAL ASSEMBLY ACTION

On 8 December [meeting 83], the General Assembly, on the recommendation of the Fourth Committee [A/55/570], adopted **resolution 55/126** by recorded vote (160-0-1) [agenda item 84].

Offers by Member States of grants and scholarships for higher education, including vocational training, for Palestine refugees

The General Assembly,

Recalling its resolution 212(III) of 19 November 1948 on assistance to Palestine refugees,

Recalling also its resolutions 35/13 B of 3 November 1980, 36/146 H of 16 December 1981, 37/120 D of 16 December 1982, 38/83 D of 15 December 1983, 39/99 D of 14 December 1984, 40/165 D of 16 December 1985, 41/69 D of 3 December 1986, 42/69 D of 2 December 1987, 43/57 D of 6 December 1988, 44/47 D of 8 December 1989, 45/73 D of 11 December 1990, 46/46 D of 9 December 1991, 47/69 D of 14 December 1992, 48/40 D of 10 December 1993, 49/35 D of 9 December 1994, 50/28 D of 6 December 1995, 51/127 of 13 December 1996, 52/60 of 10 December 1997, 53/49 of 3 December 1998 and 54/72 of 6 December 1999,

Cognizant of the fact that Palestine refugees have, for the last five decades, lost their homes, lands and means of livelihood,

Having considered the report of the Secretary-General,

Having also considered the report of the Commissioner-General of the United Nations Relief and Works Agency for Palestine Refugees in the Near East covering the period from 1 July 1999 to 30 June 2000,

1. *Urges* all States to respond to the appeal in its resolution 32/90 F of 13 December 1977 and reiterated in subsequent relevant resolutions in a manner commensurate with the needs of Palestine refugees for higher education, including vocational training;

2. *Strongly appeals* to all States, specialized agencies and non-governmental organizations to augment the special allocations for grants and scholarships to Palestine refugees, in addition to their contributions to the regular budget of the United Nations Relief and Works Agency for Palestine Refugees in the Near East;

3. *Expresses its appreciation* to all Governments, specialized agencies and non-governmental organizations that responded favourably to its resolutions on this question;

4. *Invites* the relevant specialized agencies and other organizations of the United Nations system to continue, within their respective spheres of competence, to extend assistance for higher education to Palestine refugee students;

5. *Appeals* to all States, specialized agencies and the United Nations University to contribute generously to the Palestinian universities in the Palestinian territory occupied by Israel since 1967, including, in due course, the proposed University of Jerusalem "Al-Quds" for Palestine refugees;

6. *Appeals* to all States, specialized agencies and other international bodies to contribute towards the establishment of vocational training centres for Palestine refugees;

7. *Requests* the Agency to act as the recipient and trustee for the special allocations for grants and scholarships and to award them to qualified Palestine refugee candidates;

8. *Requests* the Secretary-General to report to the General Assembly at its fifty-sixth session on the implementation of the present resolution.

In favour: Afghanistan, Algeria, Andorra, Angola, Antigua and Barbuda, Argentina, Armenia, Australia, Austria, Azerbaijan, Bahamas, Bahrain, Bangladesh, Barbados, Belarus, Belgium, Belize, Benin, Bhutan, Bolivia, Botswana, Brazil, Brunei Darussalam, Bulgaria, Burkina Faso, Burundi, Cambodia, Cameroon, Canada, Cape Verde, Chad, Chile, China, Colombia, Comoros, Costa Rica, Côte d'Ivoire, Croatia, Cuba, Cyprus, Czech Republic, Democratic People's Republic of Korea, Denmark, Djibouti, Dominican Republic, Ecuador, Egypt, El Salvador, Eritrea, Estonia, Ethiopia, Fiji, Finland, France, Gabon, Georgia, Germany, Ghana, Greece, Grenada, Guatemala, Guinea, Guyana, Haiti, Honduras, Hungary, Iceland, India, Indonesia, Iran, Ireland, Italy, Jamaica, Japan, Jordan, Kazakhstan, Kenya, Kuwait, Kyrgyzstan, Lao People's Democratic Republic, Latvia, Lebanon, Libyan Arab Jamahiriya, Liechtenstein, Lithuania, Luxembourg, Madagascar, Malaysia, Maldives, Mali, Malta, Marshall Islands, Mauritania, Mauritius, Mexico, Micronesia, Monaco, Mongolia, Morocco, Mozambique, Myanmar, Namibia, Nauru, Nepal, Netherlands, New Zealand, Nicaragua, Nigeria, Norway, Oman, Pakistan, Panama, Papua New Guinea, Paraguay, Peru, Philippines, Poland, Portugal, Qatar, Republic of Korea, Republic of Moldova, Romania, Russian Federation, Saint Lucia, Samoa, San Marino, Saudi Arabia, Senegal, Sierra Leone, Singapore, Slovakia, Slovenia, Solomon Islands, South Africa, Spain, Sri Lanka, Sudan, Swaziland, Sweden, Syrian Arab Republic, Thailand, The former Yugoslav Republic of Macedonia, Togo, Tonga, Tunisia, Turkey, Uganda, Ukraine, United Arab Emirates, United Kingdom, United Republic of Tanzania, United States, Uruguay, Vanuatu, Venezuela, Viet Nam, Yemen, Yugoslavia, Zambia, Zimbabwe.

Against: None.

Abstaining: Israel.

Proposed University of Jerusalem "Al-Quds"

In response to General Assembly resolution 54/75 [YUN 1999, p. 440], the Secretary-General submitted a September report on the proposal to establish a university for Palestine refugees in Jerusalem [A/55/425]. First mentioned by the Assembly in resolution 35/13 B [YUN 1980, p. 443], the issue had been the subject of annual reports by the Secretary-General.

To assist in the preparation of a feasibility study and at the Secretary-General's request, the Rector of the United Nations University again asked expert Mihaly Simai to visit the area and meet with Israeli officials. In response to the Secretary-General's note verbale of 8 August, requesting Israel to facilitate the visit, Israel, in a 6 September reply, stated that it had consistently voted against the resolution on the proposed university and that its position remained unchanged. It charged that the resolution's sponsors sought to exploit higher education for political purposes extraneous to genuine academic pursuits. Accordingly, Israel was of the opinion that the proposed visit would serve no useful purpose. The Secretary-General reported that it had not been possible to complete the study as planned.

GENERAL ASSEMBLY ACTION

On 8 December [meeting 83], the General Assembly, on the recommendation of the Fourth Committee [A/55/570], adopted **resolution 55/129** by recorded vote (156-2-2) [agenda item 84].

University of Jerusalem "Al-Quds" for Palestine refugees

The General Assembly,

Recalling its resolutions 36/146 G of 16 December 1981, 37/120 C of 16 December 1982, 38/83 K of 15 December 1983, 39/99 K of 14 December 1984, 40/165 D

and K of 16 December 1985, 41/69 K of 3 December 1986, 42/69 K of 2 December 1987, 43/57 J of 6 December 1988, 44/47 J of 8 December 1989, 45/73 J of 11 December 1990, 46/46 J of 9 December 1991, 47/69 J of 14 December 1992, 48/40 I of 10 December 1993, 49/35 G of 9 December 1994, 50/28 G of 6 December 1995, 51/130 of 13 December 1996, 52/63 of 10 December 1997, 53/52 of 3 December 1998 and 54/75 of 6 December 1999,

Having considered the report of the Secretary-General,

Having also considered the report of the Commissioner-General of the United Nations Relief and Works Agency for Palestine Refugees in the Near East covering the period from 1 July 1999 to 30 June 2000,

1. *Emphasizes* the need for strengthening the educational system in the Palestinian territory occupied by Israel since 5 June 1967, including Jerusalem, and specifically the need for the establishment of the proposed university;

2. *Requests* the Secretary-General to continue to take all necessary measures for establishing the University of Jerusalem "Al-Quds", in accordance with General Assembly resolution 35/13 B of 3 November 1980, giving due consideration to the recommendations consistent with the provisions of that resolution;

3. *Calls once more upon* Israel, the occupying Power, to cooperate in the implementation of the present resolution and to remove the hindrances that it has put in the way of establishing the University of Jerusalem "Al-Quds";

4. *Requests* the Secretary-General to report to the General Assembly at its fifty-sixth session on the progress made in the implementation of the present resolution.

In favour: Afghanistan, Algeria, Andorra, Angola, Antigua and Barbuda, Argentina, Armenia, Australia, Austria, Azerbaijan, Bahamas, Bahrain, Bangladesh, Barbados, Belarus, Belgium, Belize, Benin, Bhutan, Bolivia, Botswana, Brazil, Brunei Darussalam, Bulgaria, Burkina Faso, Burundi, Cambodia, Cameroon, Canada, Cape Verde, Chad, Chile, China, Colombia, Comoros, Côte d'Ivoire, Croatia, Cuba, Cyprus, Czech Republic, Democratic People's Republic of Korea, Denmark, Djibouti, Dominican Republic, Ecuador, Egypt, El Salvador, Eritrea, Estonia, Ethiopia, Fiji, Finland, France, Gabon, Georgia, Germany, Ghana, Greece, Grenada, Guatemala, Guinea, Guyana, Haiti, Honduras, Hungary, Iceland, India, Indonesia, Iran, Ireland, Italy, Jamaica, Japan, Jordan, Kazakhstan, Kenya, Kuwait, Kyrgyzstan, Lao People's Democratic Republic, Latvia, Lebanon, Libyan Arab Jamahiriya, Liechtenstein, Lithuania, Luxembourg, Madagascar, Malaysia, Maldives, Mali, Malta, Marshall Islands, Mauritania, Mauritius, Mexico, Monaco, Mongolia, Morocco, Mozambique, Myanmar, Namibia, Nepal, Netherlands, New Zealand, Nicaragua, Nigeria, Norway, Oman, Pakistan, Panama, Papua New Guinea, Paraguay, Peru, Philippines, Poland, Portugal, Qatar, Republic of Korea, Republic of Moldova, Romania, Russian Federation, Saint Lucia, Samoa, San Marino, Saudi Arabia, Senegal, Sierra Leone, Singapore, Slovakia, Slovenia, Solomon Islands, South Africa, Spain, Sri Lanka, Sudan, Swaziland, Sweden, Syrian Arab Republic, Thailand, The former Yugoslav Republic of Macedonia, Togo, Tonga, Tunisia, Turkey, Uganda, Ukraine, United Arab Emirates, United Kingdom, United Republic of Tanzania, Uruguay, Vanuatu, Venezuela, Viet Nam, Yemen, Yugoslavia, Zambia, Zimbabwe.

Against: Israel, United States.

Abstaining: Micronesia, Nauru.

Property rights

In response to General Assembly resolution 54/74 [YUN 1999, p. 441], the Secretary-General submitted a September report [A/55/428] on steps taken to protect and administer Arab property, assets and property rights in Israel and to establish a fund for income derived therefrom, on behalf of the rightful owners. He indicated that he had transmitted the resolution to Israel and all other Member States, requesting information on any steps taken or envisaged with regard to its implementation.

In a 6 September reply, reproduced in the report, Israel stated that its position on the resolutions on Palestine refugees had been set forth in successive annual replies, the latest of which had been included in the Secretary-General's 1999 report on the subject [YUN 1999, p. 441]. Israel regretted that the resolutions regarding UNRWA remained rife with political issues irrelevant to the Agency's work and detached from the reality in the area. While Israel believed that UNRWA could play an important role in promoting the social and economic advancement foreseen in agreements between Israel and the Palestinians, it called on the Assembly to consolidate the resolutions on UNRWA into one directly related to the Agency's humanitarian tasks. No replies were received from other Member States.

Report of Conciliation Commission. The United Nations Conciliation Commission for Palestine, in its fifty-fourth report covering the period from 1 September 1999 to 31 August 2000 [A/55/329], noted that, pursuant to Assembly resolution 51/129 [YUN 1996, p. 423], the project to preserve and modernize its records was completed.

GENERAL ASSEMBLY ACTION

On 8 December [meeting 83], the General Assembly, on the recommendation of the Fourth Committee [A/55/570], adopted **resolution 55/128** by recorded vote (156-2-2) [agenda item 84].

Palestine refugees' properties and their revenues

The General Assembly,

Recalling its resolutions 194(III) of 11 December 1948, 36/146 C of 16 December 1981 and all its subsequent resolutions on the question,

Taking note of the report of the Secretary-General submitted in pursuance of its resolution 54/74 of 6 December 1999,

Taking note also of the report of the United Nations Conciliation Commission for Palestine for the period from 1 September 1999 to 31 August 2000,

Recalling that the Universal Declaration of Human Rights and the principles of international law uphold the principle that no one shall be arbitrarily deprived of his or her property,

Recalling in particular its resolution 394(V) of 14 December 1950, in which it directed the Conciliation Commission, in consultation with the parties concerned, to prescribe measures for the protection of the rights, property and interests of the Palestine Arab refugees,

Noting the completion of the programme of identification and evaluation of Arab property, as announced by the Conciliation Commission in its twenty-second progress report, and the fact that the Land Office had a schedule of Arab owners and file of documents defin-

ing the location, area and other particulars of Arab property,

Recalling that, in the framework of the Middle East peace process, the Palestine Liberation Organization and the Government of Israel agreed, in the Declaration of Principles on Interim Self-Government Arrangements of 13 September 1993, to commence negotiations on permanent status issues, including the important issue of the refugees,

1. *Reaffirms* that the Palestine Arab refugees are entitled to their property and to the income derived therefrom, in conformity with the principles of justice and equity;

2. *Requests* the Secretary-General to take all appropriate steps, in consultation with the United Nations Conciliation Commission for Palestine, for the protection of Arab property, assets and property rights in Israel;

3. *Expresses its appreciation* for the work done to preserve and modernize the existing records of the Commission;

4. *Calls once more upon* Israel to render all facilities and assistance to the Secretary-General in the implementation of the present resolution;

5. *Calls upon* all the parties concerned to provide the Secretary-General with any pertinent information in their possession concerning Arab property, assets and property rights in Israel that would assist him in the implementation of the present resolution;

6. *Urges* the Palestinian and Israeli sides, as agreed between them, to deal with the important issue of Palestine refugees' properties and their revenues in the framework of the final status negotiations of the Middle East peace process;

7. *Requests* the Secretary-General to report to the General Assembly at its fifty-sixth session on the implementation of the present resolution.

RECORDED VOTE ON RESOLUTION 55/128:

In favour: Afghanistan, Algeria, Andorra, Angola, Antigua and Barbuda, Argentina, Armenia, Australia, Austria, Azerbaijan, Bahamas, Bahrain, Bangladesh, Barbados, Belarus, Belgium, Belize, Benin, Bhutan, Bolivia, Botswana, Brazil, Brunei Darussalam, Bulgaria, Burkina Faso, Burundi, Cambodia, Cameroon, Canada, Cape Verde, Chad, Chile, China, Colombia, Comoros, Costa Rica, Côte d'Ivoire, Croatia, Cuba, Cyprus, Czech Republic, Democratic People's Republic of Korea, Denmark, Djibouti, Dominican Republic, Ecuador, Egypt, El Salvador, Eritrea, Estonia, Ethiopia, Fiji, Finland, France, Gabon, Georgia, Germany, Ghana, Greece, Grenada, Guatemala, Guinea, Guyana, Haiti, Honduras, Hungary, Iceland, India, Indonesia, Iran, Ireland, Italy, Jamaica, Japan, Jordan, Kazakhstan, Kenya, Kuwait, Kyrgyzstan, Lao People's Democratic Republic, Latvia, Lebanon, Libyan Arab Jamahiriya, Liechtenstein, Lithuania, Luxembourg, Madagascar, Malaysia, Maldives, Mali, Malta, Mauritania, Mauritius, Mexico, Monaco, Mongolia, Morocco, Mozambique, Myanmar, Namibia, Nauru, Nepal, Netherlands, New Zealand, Nicaragua, Nigeria, Norway, Oman, Pakistan, Panama, Papua New Guinea, Paraguay, Peru, Philippines, Poland, Portugal, Qatar, Republic of Korea, Republic of Moldova, Romania, Russian Federation, Saint Lucia, Samoa, San Marino, Saudi Arabia, Senegal, Singapore, Slovakia, Slovenia, Solomon Islands, South Africa, Spain, Sri Lanka, Sudan, Swaziland, Sweden, Syrian Arab Republic, Thailand, The former Yugoslav Republic of Macedonia, Togo, Tonga, Tunisia, Turkey, Uganda, Ukraine, United Arab Emirates, United Kingdom, United Republic of Tanzania, Uruguay, Vanuatu, Venezuela, Viet Nam, Yemen, Yugoslavia, Zambia, Zimbabwe.

Against: Israel, United States.

Abstaining: Marshall Islands, Micronesia.

Peacekeeping operations

In 2000, the United Nations Truce Supervision Organization (UNTSO), originally set up to monitor the ceasefire called for by the Security Council in resolution S/801 of 29 May 1948 [YUN 1947-48, p. 427] in newly partitioned Palestine, continued its work. UNTSO's unarmed military observers fulfilled changing mandates—from supervising the original four armistice agreements between Israel and its neighbours (Egypt, Jordan, Lebanon and the Syrian Arab Republic) to observing and monitoring other ceasefires, as well as performing a number of additional tasks. During the year, UNTSO personnel worked with the two remaining UN peacekeeping forces in the Middle East—the United Nations Disengagement Observer Force (UNDOF) in the Golan Heights and the United Nations Interim Force in Lebanon (UNIFIL).

On 13 March [S/2000/223], the Secretary-General informed the Council of his intention to appoint Major-General Franco Ganguzza (Italy) as the new Chief of Staff of UNTSO, replacing Major-General Timothy Roger Ford (Australia). On 17 March [S/2000/224], the Council took note of the appointment.

Lebanon

The United Nations confirmed the withdrawal of Israeli forces from southern Lebanon as at 16 June 2000, in compliance with Security Council resolution 425(1978) [YUN 1978, p. 312]. Both Lebanon and Israel undertook to respect the line of withdrawal—the so-called Blue Line—identified by the United Nations on the ground. Nevertheless, numerous violations and attacks across the line by both sides occurred throughout the second half of the year.

In August, the Secretary-General appointed Rolf G. Knuttson as his Personal Representative for southern Lebanon, responsible for coordinating UN activities in the area. Mr. Knuttson completed his assignment in mid-December. Staffan de Mistura was named to succeed him in January 2001.

In a series of monthly communications [A/54/703-S/2000/11, A/54/756-S/2000/126, A/54/786-S/2000/193, A/54/843-S/2000/299, A/54/871-S/2000/447, A/54/928-S/2000/626, A/54/961-S/2000/794, A/55/678-S/2000/1172, A/55/707-S/2000/1223, A/55/721-S/2000/1258], Lebanon detailed Israeli attacks on southern Lebanon and the Western Bekaa, as well as Israel's violations of Lebanese sovereignty.

Communications (25 January–3 March). On 25 January [A/54/723-S/2000/55], Israel informed the Secretary-General that Lebanon continued to openly support a terror campaign against a neighbouring State, while endorsing opposition to any peace agreement. Lebanon also refused to respond to Israel's repeated invitations to negotiate a solution to restore peace and security along their common border. In addition, organizations operating on Lebanese soil practised terrorist operations against Israel, and Lebanon took no action to prevent or restrain them. Lebanon's policies left Israel with no alternative but to exercise its sovereign right of self-defence in accordance with international law.

In a 31 January letter to the Secretary-General [A/54/731-S/2000/71], Lebanon said that Israel, after it had announced that it wished to withdraw from Lebanon, had directed its army to engage in actions that could result in the redrawing of Lebanon's southern boundaries.

On 8 February [A/54/741-S/2000/94], Lebanon informed the Secretary-General that Israeli aircraft had that day carried out a series of attacks against electric power stations in three Lebanese cities, including Beirut. Those attacks followed the escalation of Israeli aggression in southern Lebanon.

Responding on 9 February [A/54/745-S/2000/99], Israel said that it was its intention to pull its troops from the security zone by the end of July 2000, preferably within the framework of an agreement. Contrary to the Lebanese allegations, the Israeli army was not engaged in any activity aimed at redrawing the boundaries between Israel and Lebanon; its activities in the area were part of the preparations for pulling troops out, pending a decision of the Israeli Government.

On the same day [A/54/744-S/2000/98], Israel said that it had witnessed an escalation of attacks launched by Hezbollah from villages in Lebanon, which resulted in the killing of six Israeli soldiers and the wounding of 12 others. No restraining action had been undertaken by either the Lebanese or the Syrian Government. Against that background, the Israeli air force carried out strikes against a Hezbollah arms depot and three infrastructure targets. Since Hezbollah command posts and other terrorist targets were located within Lebanese villages, Israel had chosen not to strike at those targets in order to curtail injury to civilians. Israel said that it would continue to defend and protect residents of northern Israel and would take all necessary measures to strike at terrorists and those who supported them. At the same time, the negotiations between Israel and the Syrian Arab Republic were in a state of uncertainty. Israel expected Syria to exert restraint upon the Hezbollah and its aggression.

Responding on 14 February [A/54/753-S/2000/121], the Syrian Arab Republic said that Israel's letter characterized the actions of the Lebanese national resistance as terrorism that had to be curbed by the Lebanese and Syrian Governments. Israel sought to ignore the fact that resistance to foreign occupation was a legitimate right enshrined in international covenants and exercised by the peoples of the world throughout history. The international community addressed the volatile situation in southern Lebanon and for that purpose established a group to monitor the understanding of April 1996 between Israel and Lebanon [YUN 1996, p. 428]. Syria, which was a member of the monitoring group, together with France, Israel, Lebanon and the United States, continued to support the understanding and held Israel responsible for impeding the work of the group.

In a 9 February statement [S/2000/114], the EU said that it was concerned by the escalation of hostilities in southern Lebanon. It noted that in response to attacks on its forces, Israel had launched air attacks against the Lebanese infrastructure. In that context, the EU recalled that the April 1996 understanding aimed, in particular, at protecting civilians from attack. The EU called on all sides to show restraint and to observe the terms of the ceasefire understanding of April 1996; it also called for the early convening of the monitoring group to secure a de-escalation of tension and prevent further violations of the understanding.

On 18 February [A/54/759-S/2000/135], Lebanon said that while international efforts were being made to secure the resumption of the meetings of the monitoring group, Israel had decided to escalate the situation with the announcement that an Israeli ministerial troika, headed by Prime Minister Barak, had been given the authority to decide on strikes against Lebanese civilians and Lebanon's infrastructure.

Responding on 29 February [A/54/772-S/2000/163], Israel said Lebanon's letters obscured the fact that the continuation of violence in southern Lebanon was the direct result of the policies of the Lebanese and Syrian Governments in supporting and encouraging terrorism by Hezbollah and other organizations. In its campaign against Israel, Hezbollah had resorted to using civilian areas to provide a human shield for its terrorist activity. Lebanese sovereignty as a whole was undermined by the fact that Syrian forces were deployed and active inside its borders, using Hezbollah as a proxy, and thereby perpetuating a conflict that sabotaged the chances for bringing peace to the area.

By a 3 March letter to the Secretary-General [A/54/783-S/2000/184], Burkina Faso, as Chairman of the Islamic Group, submitted the text of a statement adopted by the Group at its meeting concerning the Israeli attacks against Lebanon (New York, 3 March). The Group expressed grave concern over the attacks, reiterated its soli-

darity with the Government and people of Lebanon in their struggle for the liberation of the southern part of their country and the Western Bekaa, and reaffirmed Lebanon's right to resist the occupation in accordance with the Charter of the United Nations and its relevant resolutions and international law and norms.

Israel's withdrawal from Lebanon

On 6 April [S/2000/294], the Secretary-General informed the Security Council of his meeting in Geneva on 4 April with David Levy, Foreign Minister of Israel, who reaffirmed his Government's decision to withdraw Israeli troops from southern Lebanon in accordance with Council resolution 425(1978) [YUN 1978, p. 312], fully and without conditions. The withdrawal would be implemented in a continuous operation, "in one go", by the end of July 2000 and Israel would cooperate fully with the United Nations throughout the process. The Secretary-General stressed that cooperation by all parties concerned would be needed in order to avoid any deterioration of the situation during the withdrawal.

On 17 April [S/2000/322], the Secretary-General transmitted to the President of the Security Council the formal notification by Foreign Minister Levy of Israel's decision to withdraw its forces from Lebanon by July 2000. The Secretary-General initiated preparations to enable the United Nations to carry out its responsibilities under Council resolutions 425(1978) and 426(1978) [YUN 1978, p. 312]. He also intended to consult with the parties and interested Member States, including those contributing troops to UNIFIL. Towards that end, he requested his Special Envoy, Terje Roed-Larsen, to travel to the region for consultations.

SECURITY COUNCIL ACTION (April)

On 20 April [meeting 4131], the President of the Security Council made statement **S/PRST/2000/13** on behalf of the Council members:

The Security Council welcomes the letter from the Secretary-General to its President dated 6 April and the letter dated 17 April 2000, which includes notification of the decision of the Government of Israel, as stated in the letter also dated 17 April 2000 from the Minister for Foreign Affairs of Israel to the Secretary-General, to withdraw its forces present in Lebanon in full accordance with resolutions 425(1978) and 426(1978) of 19 March 1978 and its intention to cooperate fully with the United Nations in the implementation of its decision.

The Council endorses the decision of the Secretary-General to initiate preparations to enable the United Nations to carry out its responsibilities under resolutions 425(1978) and 426(1978), as described in his letter dated 17 April 2000.

The Council shares the view expressed by the Secretary-General in his letter dated 6 April 2000 that cooperation by all parties concerned will be required in order to avoid a deterioration of the situation. It welcomes his decision to send his Special Envoy to the region as soon as practicable and encourages all parties to cooperate fully in the complete implementation of resolutions 425(1978) and 426(1978).

The Council looks forward to the Secretary-General reporting back as soon as possible on relevant developments, including the outcome of the consultations with the parties and all interested Member States and those contributing troops to the United Nations Interim Force in Lebanon, and his conclusions and recommendations regarding the plans and requirements for implementation of resolutions 425(1978) and 426(1978) and all other relevant resolutions.

The Council stresses the importance of, and the need for, achieving a comprehensive, just and lasting peace in the Middle East, based on all relevant Council resolutions, including resolutions 242(1967) of 22 November 1967 and 338(1973) of 22 October 1973.

Report of Secretary-General (May). In May [S/2000/460], the Secretary-General submitted to the Security Council a report on his conclusions and recommendations regarding the plans and requirements for the implementation of resolutions 425(1978) and 426(1978) and all other relevant resolutions. The Special Envoy, together with the UNIFIL Commander and a team of experts, travelled to the region from 26 April to 9 May and reviewed with the Governments of Israel and Lebanon and other concerned Member States in the region, including Egypt, Jordan and the Syrian Arab Republic, the requirements established under those resolutions for their full implementation.

The Secretary-General said that for the practical purpose of confirming the Israeli withdrawal, the United Nations needed to identify a line to be adopted conforming to the internationally recognized boundaries of Lebanon based on the best available cartographic material. The United Nations stressed in its consultations with all parties that it was not seeking to establish an international border, as that was a matter for States to undertake in accordance with international law and practice. Rather, it was requesting the help of the parties and others in the purely technical exercise of identifying a line for the purpose of confirming compliance with resolution 425(1978).

The international boundary between Israel and Lebanon was established pursuant to the 1923 Agreement between France and the United Kingdom entitled "Boundary Line between Syria and Palestine from the Mediterranean to El Hamme". Concerning the portion of Lebanon's border that it shared with the Syrian Arab Republic relevant to the Israeli withdrawal, there seemed to be no official record of a formal international boundary agreement between Lebanon and Syria that could easily establish the demarcation line. On 4 May, Lebanon informed the Secretary-General's Special Envoy that certain farmlands in the Shab'a area located outside UNIFIL's zone of operation as defined since 1978 would be claimed by Lebanon in the context of Israel's withdrawal. Lebanon subsequently provided the United Nations with title deeds of Lebanese ownership of farmlands in that area, as well as with documentation that indicated that Lebanese governmental and religious institutions had enjoyed, at various points in time, jurisdiction over those farmlands. Lebanon also informed the United Nations of a joint understanding between Lebanon and Syria that the farmlands were Lebanese. In May, the United Nations received documentation and a map, dated 1966, from the Lebanese Government [A/54/870-S/2000/443 & Add.1,2], which reflected Lebanon's position that those farmlands were located inside its territory. However, the United Nations possessed 10 other maps issued after 1966 by various Lebanese government institutions that placed the farmlands inside Syrian territory. On the basis of the 1974 Agreement on Disengagement between Israeli and Syrian forces of and its Protocol concerning UNDOF [YUN 1974, p. 198], the Shab'a farmlands fell within the scope of UNDOF's area of operations. It followed that in adopting resolutions 425(1978) and 426(1978), the Security Council could not have included as part of UNIFIL's area of operations a zone that had already formed part of UNDOF's area of operations. It was worth noting that, notwithstanding the conflicting evidence, those farmlands were in the area occupied by Israel since 1967 and were therefore subject to resolutions 242(1967) and 338(1973) calling for an Israeli withdrawal from occupied territory.

In the light of all the documents in UN possession, the Secretary-General recommended that a viable solution, which was without prejudice to the positions of Lebanon and Syria concerning their international boundaries, would be to proceed on the basis of the line separating the areas of operation of UNIFIL and UNDOF along the relevant portions of the Lebanese-Syrian boundary. The adoption of that line by the United Nations for the practical purpose of confirming the Israeli withdrawal from Lebanon was without prejudice to any internationally recognized border agreement that Lebanon and Syria might wish to conclude in the future, stressed the Secretary-General. The UNIFIL-UNDOF line coincided with the border line most commonly found on maps issued by the Government of Lebanon and had also been accepted by Lebanon for 22 years in the context of the UNIFIL area of operations. In addition, that same line was approved by Israel and Syria in their 1974 Disengagement Agreement and had thus defined the UNDOF area of operations for 26 years. Finally, that line would not prejudice the existing areas of operation of UNIFIL and UNDOF as approved by the Council.

The Secretary-General defined the main requirements that Israel would have to meet in order for the United Nations to confirm that the Israeli withdrawal had been completed in full compliance with relevant Council resolutions. They included the withdrawal of Israel's military and civilian personnel from Lebanon; the dismantling by Israel of the South Lebanon Army (SLA) command structure, the cessation of logistical support and supplies from Israel to SLA and the removal of its heavy weapons; and the handing over of prisoners in Al-Khiam detention centre. The full cooperation of Israel would also be required in identifying the withdrawal line.

From Lebanon, the Secretary-General requested full cooperation in the process of identifying, on the ground, the line to be used for the purpose of confirming the Israeli withdrawal. The return of effective Lebanese authority over the area would require decisive action by the Government of Lebanon to resume public services, as well as law and order functions, in order to resume its responsibility for providing for security and safety throughout the area. From Syria, the United Nations would require full cooperation on all relevant matters, including in identifying on the ground that portion of the Lebanese-Syrian boundary necessary to confirm the withdrawal. Lebanese and other armed groups in Lebanon, and Member States having influence over them, had to provide their cooperation and support to UNIFIL. The Secretary-General emphasized that before, during and after the withdrawal, all interested parties should exercise maximum restraint both in their actions and in their public statements. In that connection, the security of UN personnel was a central concern.

For the purpose of confirming the withdrawal, UNIFIL would dispatch verification teams protected by infantry detachments in armoured vehicles and supported by helicopters. The teams would also be accompanied by engineers to deal with unexploded ordnance and mines in the area. The Secretary-General welcomed the commitment given by Israel to provide detailed information on the location of mines. The verification teams would move throughout the area to con-

firm whether the positions held by Israeli forces and SLA had been vacated and whether Israel had withdrawn its military forces and civilians from Lebanon.

Before the reinforcement and redeployment of UNIFIL, the Secretary-General would confirm to the Council that a full Israeli withdrawal had taken place in fulfilment of the relevant resolutions. Following the redeployment, UNIFIL's area of operations would include the area between the eastern and western parts of its current area of deployment and the stretch of land along the international boundary. UNIFIL would use its best efforts to help prevent recurrence of fighting and to create conditions for the restoration of effective Lebanese authority in that area. As soon as the United Nations had confirmed that the Israeli withdrawal had been completed, the Government of Lebanon should resume the normal responsibilities of a State throughout the area. The Government had informed the United Nations that it would re-establish local civilian administration functions, which would include the assumption of law and order responsibilities through the re-establishment of civilian police forces. The United Nations could not assume law and order functions that were properly the responsibility of the Government. The Lebanese armed forces had to ensure that all national territory fell under the effective authority of the Government. With those actions taken, UNIFIL would complete its mission in Lebanon, said the Secretary-General. The Government of Lebanon had assured the United Nations that in re-establishing its authority in the area previously controlled by Israel and SLA, it would treat the inhabitants of the formerly occupied zone as equal citizens of Lebanon, in accordance with Lebanese law and in respect for the principles of the rule of law and international human rights standards. The Lebanese Government, together with UNDP, had developed a plan for the reconstruction of southern Lebanon. The United Nations would give its full support to that plan and called on donor countries to help Lebanon through the provision of necessary financial and technical assistance. The Secretary-General envisaged an increase in the civilian staff of UNIFIL to facilitate that work.

In order to carry out its responsibilities under resolution 425(1978) and taking into account the additional territory that UNIFIL would have to cover following the Israeli withdrawal, UNIFIL would require phased reinforcement. To enable the Force to carry out its tasks related to confirmation of Israeli withdrawal, the existing six infantry battalions were being increased and provided with additional armoured personnel carriers. UNIFIL would also require two additional helicopters with their crews and a number of engineer detachments specialized in explosive ordnance disposal, mine reconnaissance and mine-clearing operations. Additional logistics capability would also be required to support that increase. The total troop strength for carrying out the tasks related to confirming the withdrawal would thus increase from the current level of 4,513 to approximately 5,600. Once the withdrawal was confirmed and if the security situation permitted, UNIFIL would have to be immediately reinforced with two mechanized infantry battalions, and the engineer component of the Force would have to be increased to regimental level. Monitoring equipment, including that for airspace and territorial waters, would also be required at that time. With those reinforcements, the strength of UNIFIL would be brought to a total of eight battalions plus appropriate support units, or approximately 7,935 peacekeepers. Owing to constraints of time, the troop reinforcements would be required to possess a high degree of self-sufficiency and the capability to deploy to the mission area using their own national assets.

The Secretary-General said that if the Council agreed with his recommendations, the Special Envoy and his team would then return to the region to pursue the implementation of the plan outlined in his report.

SECURITY COUNCIL ACTION (May)

On 23 May [meeting 4146], the President of the Council made statement **S/PRST/2000/18** on behalf of the Council members:

The Security Council welcomes and strongly endorses the report of the Secretary-General of 22 May 2000. The Council stresses again the importance of, and the need for, achieving a comprehensive, just and lasting peace in the Middle East, based on all its relevant resolutions, including resolutions 242(1967) of 22 November 1967 and 338(1973) of 22 October 1973.

The Council welcomes the intention of the Secretary-General to take all necessary measures to enable the United Nations Interim Force in Lebanon to confirm that a complete withdrawal of Israeli forces from Lebanon has taken place in compliance with resolution 425(1978), and to take all necessary steps in order to deal with any eventuality, bearing in mind that the cooperation of all parties will be essential. The Council welcomes the intention of the Secretary-General to report on the withdrawal of Israeli forces from Lebanon, in accordance with resolution 425(1978).

The Council fully endorses the requirements put forward by the Secretary-General for confirming the compliance of all parties concerned with resolution 425(1978), calls upon all parties concerned to cooperate fully in implementing the recommendations of the Secretary-General, and requests the Secretary-General to report on their fulfilment of the requirements when he reports on the withdrawal.

The Council calls upon the States and other parties concerned to exercise utmost restraint and to cooperate with the Force and the United Nations to ensure the full implementation of resolutions 425 (1978) and 426(1978). The Council shares the view of the Secretary-General that it is crucial that the States and other parties concerned do their part to calm the situation, ensure the safety of the civilian population, and cooperate fully with the United Nations in its efforts to stabilize the situation, restore international peace and security, and assist the Government of Lebanon in ensuring the return of its effective authority in the area following confirmation of withdrawal.

The Council welcomes the decision of the Secretary-General to send his Special Envoy back to the region immediately to ensure that the requirements put forward by the Secretary-General are met and to ensure the commitment of all the parties concerned to cooperate fully with the United Nations in the complete implementation of resolutions 425 (1978) and 426(1978).

The Council takes this opportunity to express its appreciation and its full support for the continuing efforts of the Secretary-General, his Special Envoy to the region and his staff. It commends the troops of the Force and troop-contributing countries for their commitment to the cause of international peace and security under difficult circumstances. The Council stresses its concern that all the parties concerned cooperate with the United Nations, and recalls the relevant principles contained in the Convention on the Safety of United Nations and Associated Personnel of 9 December 1994.

Communications (22 May–19 June). On 22 May [A/54/880-S/2000/465], Lebanon informed the Secretary-General that Israeli helicopters and tanks had opened fire on Lebanese civilians who were returning to inspect their homes after the withdrawal of Israeli forces from certain villages in south Lebanon. Preliminary reports indicated that six persons were killed and 22 injured.

Responding on 31 May [A/54/890-S/2000/512], Israel said that IDF had completed the withdrawal from southern Lebanon swiftly and with maximum restraint, despite efforts by terrorists to provoke a confrontation. The only instances in which force was used occurred when lives were at risk, and even then in a manner designed to avoid further casualties. Israel called on Lebanon to fulfil its responsibility of ensuring peace and security within its borders.

On 9 June [A/54/914-S/2000/564], the President of Lebanon, Émile Lahoud, drew the Secretary-General's attention to a number of issues pertaining to the UN delimitation of the boundary lines between Lebanon and Israel, as well as between Lebanon and Syria. In particular, President Lahoud said that some discrepancies had emerged between the boundary lines defined in the Secretary-General's 22 May report and statements made by UN representatives during meetings with Lebanese authorities. In addition, President Lahoud called for the immediate release of Lebanese detainees held in Israeli prisons and raised the issue of the diversion of water from Lebanese territory.

On 14 June [S/2000/598], the Secretary-General informed the President of the Security Council that Ukraine had offered an engineering battalion and Sweden a unit specialized in the destruction of explosives and ammunition as part of the reinforcements needed by UNIFIL to perform its functions after the withdrawal of Israeli forces from Lebanon. He proposed that Ukraine and Sweden be added to the list of States providing contingents to UNIFIL. On 19 June [S/2000/599], the Council took note of the Secretary-General's proposal.

Report of Secretary-General (June). In a June report [S/2000/590 & Corr.1], the Secretary-General informed the Security Council that Israel had met the requirements defined in his report of 22 May and, therefore, he confirmed that Israeli forces had withdrawn from Lebanon as at 16 June, in compliance with resolution 425(1978).

On the return of the Secretary-General's Special Envoy and his team to Lebanon on 24 May, the question of translating the boundary line identified by the United Nations from a map to a line on the ground was discussed with the parties. Notwithstanding reservations of both Israel and Lebanon about the withdrawal line, both countries confirmed that identifying that line was solely the responsibility of the United Nations and that they would respect it. On 16 June, UNIFIL confirmed that Israeli forces had withdrawn; that SLA was disbanded, and thus supply lines no longer existed; Israel's heavy weapons were removed or destroyed or were in the hands of the Lebanese Government; and detainees were no longer held at the Al-Khiam prison, which was opened by the local inhabitants on 22 May. The Lebanese Government cooperated with the United Nations in the implementation of the report of 22 May and had moved quickly to reestablish its effective authority in the area through the deployment of security forces; no acts of vengeance against the inhabitants of southern Lebanon were reported by UNIFIL following the withdrawal of Israeli forces. On 12 June, Lebanon informed the United Nations that it would send a composite unit composed of army and internal security personnel to be based in Marjayoun. Although the Government had not yet deployed the armed forces throughout southern Lebanon, it had stated that it would consider doing so as soon as the Secretary-General had confirmed Israel's withdrawal. The Syrian Government was very cooperative throughout the latest mission of the Special Envoy, as were other interested Member States in the region and elsewhere.

The Secretary-General described the military and security situation in the former Israeli-controlled area as calm and relatively stable, despite a number of shooting incidents. The Lebanese authorities had restricted passage to the border in order to avoid further incidents. The presence of armed elements was steadily decreasing throughout the region and their checkpoints were being removed. UNIFIL maintained a visible presence by means of proactive patrolling, which had a very useful and calming effect on the security situation, and it provided humanitarian assistance throughout the area.

The Secretary-General said that the first phase of UNIFIL's reinforcement was currently under way; he expected that the Force would reach the level of 5,600 troops in early July. However, he stressed that no firm commitments had been made for the further reinforcement with two mechanized infantry battalions, as requested in his 22 May report, and, therefore, he was not in a position to state when they would be available and deployed. In the meantime, UNIFIL would use its available resources to extend its deployment in those areas that it did not cover. To that end, the Force would establish patrol bases in a number of locations, set up temporary observation posts as appropriate and undertake active patrolling throughout those areas, as well as continue to provide humanitarian assistance to the local population. UNIFIL would use its best efforts to help prevent the recurrence of fighting and to create the conditions for the restoration of effective Lebanese authority in that area.

SECURITY COUNCIL ACTION (June)

On 18 June [meeting 4160], the President of the Council made statement **S/PRST/2000/21** on behalf of the Council members:

The Security Council welcomes the report of the Secretary-General of 16 June 2000 and endorses the work done by the United Nations as mandated by the Council, as well as the conclusion of the Secretary-General that, as of 16 June 2000, Israel has withdrawn its forces from Lebanon in accordance with resolution 425(1978) of 19 March 1978 and met the requirements defined in the report of the Secretary-General of 22 May 2000. In this regard, the Council notes that Israel and Lebanon have confirmed to the Secretary-General, as stated in his report of 16 June 2000, that identifying the withdrawal line was solely the responsibility of the United Nations and that they would respect the line as identified. It notes with serious concern reports of violations that have occurred since 16 June 2000 and calls upon the parties to respect the line identified by the United Nations.

The Council welcomes the steps already taken by the parties to implement the recommendations of the Secretary-General contained in his report of 22 May 2000.

The Council calls upon all parties concerned to continue to cooperate fully with the United Nations and the United Nations Interim Force in Lebanon and to exercise utmost restraint. The Council re-emphasizes the need for strict respect for the territorial integrity, sovereignty and political independence of Lebanon within its internationally recognized boundaries.

The Council, recalling its resolutions 425(1978) and 426(1978) of 19 March 1978, calls upon the Government of Lebanon to ensure the restoration of its effective authority and presence in the south. The Council notes that the United Nations cannot assume law and order functions, which are properly the responsibility of the Government of Lebanon. In this regard, the Council welcomes the first steps taken by the Government of Lebanon and calls upon it to proceed with the deployment of the Lebanese Armed Forces as soon as possible, with the assistance of the Force, in the Lebanese territory recently vacated by Israel.

The Council welcomes the measures taken by the Secretary-General and the troop-contributing countries relating to augmentation of the Force, in accordance with paragraph 32 of the report of the Secretary-General of 22 May 2000. The Council stresses that the redeployment of the Force should be conducted in coordination with the Government of Lebanon and with the Lebanese Armed Forces, as stated in paragraph 21 of the report of the Secretary-General of 16 June 2000. In that context, the Council invites the Secretary-General to report back on the measures taken to that effect and those taken by the Government of Lebanon to restore its effective authority in the area, in accordance with resolutions 425(1978) and 426(1978). The Council looks forward to the completion of the mandate of the Force and will review, by 31 July 2000, the need to extend its present mandate, taking into account the report of the Secretary-General on the implementation of resolutions 425(1978) and 426(1978), including the actions taken by the Government of Lebanon to restore its effective authority in the area.

The Council expresses its appreciation and full support for the continuing efforts of the Secretary-General, his Special Envoy to the region, the Chief Cartographer, and their staff. It commends the troops of the Force and the troop-contributing countries for their commitment to the cause of international peace and security under difficult circumstances. The Council calls upon all parties concerned to continue to cooperate with the United Nations, and reiterates the relevant principles contained in the Convention on the Safety of United Nations and Associated Personnel of 9 December 1994.

The Council stresses again the importance of, and the need for, achieving a comprehensive, just and lasting peace in the Middle East, based on all its relevant resolutions, including resolutions 242(1967) of 22 November 1967 and 338(1973) of 22 October 1973.

Communications (24 June–31 December). On 24 June [A/54/927-S/2000/624], Lebanon said that Israeli troops had opened fire that day on a Jordanian trade union delegation that was visiting the Lebanese border, wounding four of its members.

Responding on 29 June [A/54/931-S/2000/638], Israel said that Lebanon had refused to fulfil its responsibilities under resolution 425(1978) and to establish its effective authority in southern Lebanon. As a result, the area was witnessing an escalating wave of violence on the Lebanese side of the border, directed against Israel. On 24 June, when dozens of Lebanese hurled stones and objects at passing Israelis and two individuals from the Lebanese side actually infiltrated into Israel, Israeli soldiers were faced with no alternative but to use force to stop the intruders. Israel called on the Lebanese Government to take all necessary steps to prevent the continued flare-ups, infiltrations and provocations.

In a series of communications between 6 July and 23 October [A/54/936-S/2000/661, A/54/939-S/2000/689, A/54/957-S/2000/769, S/2000/805, S/2000/1002, S/2000/1011], Israel detailed Lebanese territorial encroachments on Israeli territory, as well as hostile acts committed from the Lebanese side of the border against Israelis. The violations included the forced abduction of three Israeli soldiers and an Israeli businessman.

Responding on 24 October [S/2000/1020] to Israel's 7 October letter [S/2000/969] stating that Lebanon and the Syrian Arab Republic were directly responsible for acts of aggression at the border between Israel and Lebanon, Syria said that it held Israel directly responsible for the escalation of the situation in the Middle East. It cited Israel's persistence in ignoring the resolutions of international legitimacy, its failure to complete its withdrawal from south Lebanon, including the Shab'a farmlands, and its continued occupation of Arab lands seized in June 1967.

In a series of communications between 2 and 26 November [S/2000/1066, S/2000/1071, S/2000/1087, S/2000/1102, S/2000/1118], Lebanon transmitted details of Israeli violations of Lebanese territorial boundaries. In addition, Lebanon said that on 26 November the Israeli army fired 90 artillery shells on the Kfar Shuba area and carried out an aerial attack on the hills in the same region.

In two separate letters [S/2000/1121, S/2000/1145], Israel responded to the Lebanese allegations. In particular, it noted that on 26 November a roadside charge was detonated against an Israeli patrol by terrorists who had infiltrated from Lebanon, killing an Israeli soldier and wounding two others.

On 31 December [S/2001/1], Lebanon said that on 30 December an Israeli patrol opened fire and killed a Lebanese citizen inside Lebanon's territory.

UNIFIL

The Security Council twice extended the mandate of the United Nations Interim Force in Lebanon in 2000, in January and July, each time for a six-month period.

UNIFIL, which was established by Council resolution 425(1978) following Israel's invasion of Lebanon [YUN 1978, p. 296], was originally entrusted with confirming the withdrawal of Israeli forces, restoring international peace and security, and assisting the Lebanese Government in ensuring the return of its effective authority in southern Lebanon. Following a second Israeli invasion in 1982 [YUN 1982, p. 428], the Council, in resolution 511(1982) [ibid., p. 450], authorized the Force to carry out, in addition to its original mandate, the interim task of providing protection and humanitarian assistance to the local population, while maintaining its positions in the area of deployment.

The Force headquarters, based predominantly in Naqoura, provided command and control, as well as liaison with Lebanon and Israel, UNDOF, UNTSO and a number of NGOs.

Composition and deployment

As at 30 December 2000, UNIFIL comprised 5,800 troops from Fiji (594), Finland (645), France (254), Ghana (787), India (791), Ireland (609), Italy (68), Nepal (723), Poland (633) and Ukraine (650). The Swedish component (45) left on 27 December, as planned. The Force was assisted in its task by 51 military observers of UNTSO. In addition, UNIFIL employed 480 civilian staff, of whom 130 were recruited internationally and 350 locally. Major-General Seth Kofi Obeng (Ghana) continued as Force Commander.

Since the establishment of UNIFIL, 235 members of the Force had lost their lives: 78 as a result of firings or bomb explosions, 99 in accidents and 58 from other causes. A total of 344 were wounded by shooting or by mine or bomb explosions.

Activities

Report of Secretary-General (January). In a report on developments from 16 July 1999 to 15 January 2000 in the UNIFIL area of operations [S/2000/28], the Secretary-General said that fighting continued in southern Lebanon and the situation remained volatile, although the level of hostility was somewhat reduced and civilian casualties decreased. Negotiations between Israel and the Syrian Arab Republic, as brokered by the United States, had resumed. He reaffirmed his belief that UNIFIL's contribution to stability and the protection it provided to the population of the area remained important. Therefore, he recommended that the Force's mandate be extended for another six months, until 31 July 2000, as requested by Lebanon on 28 December 1999 [S/1999/1284].

SECURITY COUNCIL ACTION (January)

On 31 January [meeting 4095], the Security Council unanimously adopted **resolution 1288(2000)**. The draft text [S/2000/57] was prepared in consultations among Council members.

The Security Council,

Recalling its resolutions 425(1978) and 426(1978) of 19 March 1978, 501(1982) of 25 February 1982, 508(1982) of 5 June 1982, 509(1982) of 6 June 1982 and 520(1982) of 17 September 1982, as well as its resolutions on the situation in Lebanon,

Recalling also the relevant principles contained in the Convention on the Safety of United Nations and Associated Personnel of 9 December 1994,

Having studied the report of the Secretary-General of 17 January 2000 on the United Nations Interim Force in Lebanon, and taking note of the observations expressed and the commitments mentioned therein,

Welcoming and encouraging efforts by the United Nations to sensitize peacekeeping personnel in the prevention and control of HIV/AIDS and other communicable diseases in all its peacekeeping operations,

Taking note of the letter dated 28 December 1999 from the Permanent Representative of Lebanon to the United Nations addressed to the Secretary-General,

Responding to the request of the Government of Lebanon,

1. *Decides* to extend the present mandate of the United Nations Interim Force in Lebanon for a further period of six months, that is until 31 July 2000;

2. *Reiterates its strong support* for the territorial integrity, sovereignty and political independence of Lebanon within its internationally recognized boundaries;

3. *Re-emphasizes* the terms of reference and general guidelines of the Force as stated in the report of the Secretary-General of 19 March 1978, approved by resolution 426(1978), and calls upon all parties concerned to cooperate fully with the Force for the full implementation of its mandate;

4. *Condemns* all acts of violence committed in particular against the Force, and urges the parties to put an end to them;

5. *Reiterates* that the Force should fully implement its mandate as defined in resolutions 425(1978), 426(1978), and all other relevant resolutions;

6. *Encourages* further efficiency and savings provided they do not affect the operational capacity of the Force;

7. *Requests* the Secretary-General to continue consultations with the Government of Lebanon and other parties directly concerned with the implementation of the present resolution and to report to the Council thereon.

At the same meeting, the Council President made statement **S/PRST/2000/3** on behalf of the Council:

The Security Council has noted with appreciation the report of the Secretary-General of 17 January 2000 on the United Nations Interim Force in Lebanon, submitted in conformity with resolution 1254(1999) of 30 July 1999.

The Council reaffirms its commitment to the full sovereignty, political independence, territorial integrity and national unity of Lebanon within its internationally recognized boundaries. In this context, the Council asserts that all States shall refrain from the threat or use of force against the territorial integrity or political independence of any State, or in any manner inconsistent with the purposes of the United Nations.

As the Council extends the mandate of the Force for a further interim period on the basis of resolution 425(1978), the Council again stresses the urgent need for the implementation of that resolution in all its respects. It reiterates its full support for the Taif Agreement of 22 October 1989 and for the continued efforts of the Lebanese Government to consolidate peace, national unity and security in the country, while successfully carrying out the reconstruction process. The Council commends the Lebanese Government for its successful effort to extend its authority in the south of the country in full coordination with the Force.

The Council expresses its concern over the continuing violence in southern Lebanon, regrets the loss of civilian life, and urges all parties to exercise restraint.

The Council takes this opportunity to express its appreciation for the continuing efforts of the Secretary-General and his staff in this regard. The Council notes with deep concern the high level of casualties the Force has suffered and pays a special tribute to all those who gave their lives while serving in the Force. It commends the troops of the Force and troop-contributing countries for their sacrifices and commitment to the cause of international peace and security under difficult circumstances.

Report of Secretary-General (July). In a report on developments from 17 January to 17 July [S/2000/718], the Secretary-General said that after more than two decades the guns had fallen silent in southern Lebanon. The Israeli forces had left the area, their local Lebanese auxiliary had been disbanded and the risks inherent in such a withdrawal did not, for the most part, materialize. He noted, in particular, that the fighters of the Lebanese resistance conducted themselves in a controlled manner that deserved to be acknowledged; no acts of vengeance had taken place as

they reclaimed the region vacated by the Israeli forces. The Lebanese authorities had assured his Special Envoy that those who cooperated with Israel during the years they lived under its control would be treated in accordance with the rule of law. Both sides, despite their misgivings, had undertaken to respect the line of withdrawal identified by the United Nations on the ground.

From 17 to 23 June, the Secretary-General visited the Middle East, including Egypt, Iran, Israel, Jordan, Lebanon and the Syrian Arab Republic. He also visited Morocco, where he met King Mohammed V of Morocco and Crown Prince Abdullah of Saudi Arabia. The implementation of resolution 425(1978) was the principal topic of discussion at those meetings.

Following the verification of the Israeli withdrawal, UNIFIL confirmed a number of violations pertaining to the crossing of the withdrawal line by Israeli forces. Lebanon stated that it would consent to UNIFIL deployment in the vacated areas only after the Israeli violations had been corrected. For its part, Israel had committed itself to the removal of all Israeli violations by the end of July. At the time of reporting, Israeli authorities had corrected all but two of the violations identified by UNIFIL.

Since the end of May, the situation in the area of operation had remained generally calm. Signs of tensions had been reported between members of the militia groups Hezbollah and Amal over the elections that were to be held in Lebanon at the end of August or early September 2000. The Lebanese army, gendarmerie and police established checkpoints in the vacated area, controlling movement, maintaining law and order and retrieving heavy weapons abandoned by IDF and their Lebanese auxiliary. UNIFIL patrolled the area and, together with the Lebanese authorities, provided humanitarian assistance by supplying water, medical treatment and food to needy families.

The situation had been calm along the withdrawal line, except for sporadic incidents. UNIFIL monitored that line for possible violations on a daily basis by means of ground and air patrols. The Force's liaison arrangements provided a constant link with IDF's Chief of Operations and the Director of Lebanese General Security, as well as with the normal chain of command on each side. Armed elements continued to maintain a presence in the area and on a number of occasions had not allowed UNIFIL patrols to continue. The Lebanese authorities had promised that such incidents would stop.

The reintegration of the relatively underdeveloped area vacated by Israel imposed a heavy burden on the Lebanese economy. UNDP had been leading the efforts of the UN system in working with the Lebanese authorities on a programme for the development and rehabilitation of the area, with emphasis on rebuilding infrastructure, loans to small enterprises, vocational training and reactivating the municipalities. Immediate needs included the provision of drinking water to villages that used to be supplied from Israel, the rehabilitation of medical services, electricity and sewage systems, housing and road networks. The clearing of mines and unexploded ordnance was an urgent task. IDF had provided UNIFIL with maps of mined areas known to them, but the majority remained unmarked. In June, the Force established a regional mine action coordination cell to conduct mine awareness educational activities.

The Secretary-General said that the first phase of UNIFIL's reinforcement, required to carry out its tasks under resolutions 425(1978) and 426 (1978), was under way. In June, UNIFIL's mine-clearance capacity was reinforced with two units from Sweden and Ukraine. In addition, an engineer battalion of 600 all ranks from Ukraine would arrive by the end of July. Finland was providing an additional 64 armoured personnel carriers, of which 42 had arrived in theatre. The units from Finland, Ghana, Ireland and Nepal had been reinforced; Fiji and India had also undertaken to reinforce their units. Two additional helicopters from Italy were expected to arrive by the end of July. The United Nations had yet to receive commitments for the additional two infantry battalions that would meet the requirements set by the Secretary-General in his May report (see p. 462), namely a high degree of self-sufficiency and the capability to deploy to the mission area using national assets. In the absence of those reinforcements, the Force Commander had devised a deployment plan using existing resources and reinforcements to cover the area vacated by IDF, through a combination of mobile patrols, patrol bases and temporary observation posts. Five Force members had lost their lives during the reporting period.

The Secretary-General planned to submit to the General Assembly, during its fifty-fifth (2000) regular session, the revised budget proposals for UNIFIL, since the Assembly's appropriation of $146.8 million gross for the Force's maintenance for the period 1 July 2000 to 30 June 2001 (resolution 54/267 below) did not take into account the additional requirements needed by UNIFIL to carry out its responsibilities under resolutions 425(1978) and 426(1978). In the interim, ACABQ had concurred with the use of the approved initial 12-month budget for the

Force for the period from 1 July 2000 to 30 June 2001 to meet the cost of the most immediate operational requirements. As at 30 June 2000, unpaid assessments to the Special Account for UNIFIL for the period from the inception of the Force to 30 June 2000 amounted to $117.8 million.

While an enormous improvement compared to the past, the situation in the Israel-Lebanon sector fell well short of peace and the potential for serious incidents persisted. The Secretary-General stressed that both sides should maintain effective liaison with UNIFIL and take prompt action to rectify any violations or incidents brought to their attention. Therefore, he recommended that the Force's mandate be extended for another six months, until 31 January 2001, as requested by Lebanon on 11 July [S/2000/674], on the understanding that UNIFIL would be enabled to deploy and function throughout its area of operation and that the Lebanese authorities would strengthen their own presence in the area by deploying additional troops and internal security forces. Since there was a good chance of achieving the objectives of resolution 425(1978) and for the Force to complete the tasks originally assigned to it, the Secretary-General planned to report to the Council at the end of October 2000 so that it might review developments and consider any steps it might wish to take, in the light of the progress achieved in the restoration of the effective authority of the Government of Lebanon in the area. In that regard, it was essential that the redeployment of UNIFIL be closely coordinated with the Lebanese forces. Member States were encouraged to cooperate with Lebanese authorities and UN agencies and programmes in support of the reconstruction and development of southern Lebanon. In addition, in order to help coordinate UN activities in the area, the Secretary-General planned to appoint a senior official as his personal representative for southern Lebanon, who would work closely with the Special Envoy.

Communication (24 July). By a 24 July letter [S/2000/731] to the President of the Security Council, the Secretary-General said that the Israeli authorities had removed all violations of the line of withdrawal. Further, in a meeting with the Special Envoy, Lebanon's President Lahoud and Prime Minister Salim Hoss gave their consent to the full deployment of UNIFIL. The Force's deployment would take place on 26 July and was to be immediately followed by the deployment of the composite Lebanese unit referred to in the Secretary-General's June report (see p. 465).

On 27 July [meeting 4177], the Security Council unanimously adopted **resolution 1310(2000)**. The draft [S/2000/741] was prepared in consultations among Council members.

The Security Council,

Recalling its resolutions 425(1978) and 426(1978) of 19 March 1978, 501(1982) of 25 February 1982, 508(1982) of 5 June 1982, 509(1982) of 6 June 1982 and 520(1982) of 17 September 1982, as well as its resolutions on the situation in Lebanon and its resolution 1308(2000) of 17 July 2000,

Recalling also the statements by its President of 20 April, 23 May and 18 June 2000 on the situation in Lebanon, in particular its endorsement of the work done by the United Nations as mandated by the Council including the conclusion of the Secretary-General that, as of 16 June 2000, Israel had withdrawn its forces from Lebanon in accordance with resolution 425(1978) and met the requirements defined in the report of the Secretary-General of 22 May 2000,

Welcoming the report of the Secretary-General of 20 July 2000 on the United Nations Interim Force in Lebanon and its observations and recommendations mentioned therein,

Emphasizing the interim nature of the Force,

Recalling the relevant principles contained in the Convention on the Safety of United Nations and Associated Personnel of 9 December 1994,

Responding to the request of the Government of Lebanon, as stated in the letter dated 11 July 2000 from the Permanent Representative of Lebanon to the United Nations addressed to the Secretary-General,

1. *Endorses* the understanding, expressed in the report of the Secretary-General of 20 July 2000, that the United Nations Interim Force in Lebanon will deploy and function fully throughout its area of operations and that the Government of Lebanon will strengthen its presence in that area, by deploying additional troops and internal security forces;

2. *Decides*, in this context, to extend the present mandate of the Force for a further period of six months, until 31 January 2001;

3. *Reiterates its strong support* for the territorial integrity, sovereignty and political independence of Lebanon within its internationally recognized boundaries;

4. *Welcomes* the statement in the letter dated 24 July 2000 from the Secretary-General to the President of the Security Council that, as of that date, the Government of Israel had removed all violations of the withdrawal line;

5. *Calls upon* the parties to respect that line, to exercise utmost restraint and to cooperate fully with the United Nations and with the Force;

6. *Calls upon* the Government of Lebanon to ensure the restoration of its effective authority and presence in the south, in particular to proceed with a significant deployment of the Lebanese Armed Forces as soon as possible;

7. *Welcomes* the establishment of checkpoints by the Government of Lebanon in the vacated area, and encourages the Government of Lebanon to ensure a calm environment throughout the south, including through the control of all checkpoints;

8. *Welcomes also* the measures taken by the Secretary-General and the troop-contributing countries regarding military personnel of the Force and their deployment, as agreed to in the above-mentioned statements by its President, and reaffirms that the expected redeployment of the Force should be conducted in coordination with the Government of Lebanon and the Lebanese Armed Forces;

9. *Re-emphasizes* the terms of reference and general guidelines of the Force as stated in the report of the Secretary-General of 19 March 1978, approved by resolution 426(1978);

10. *Requests* the Secretary-General to continue consultations with the Government of Lebanon and other parties directly concerned on the implementation of the present resolution and to report to the Security Council thereon;

11. *Looks forward* to the early fulfilment of the mandate of the Force;

12. *Welcomes* the intention of the Secretary-General to submit to the Council, by 31 October 2000, a report on progress towards achieving the objectives of resolution 425(1978) and towards completion by the Force of the tasks originally assigned to it, and requests the Secretary-General to include in this report recommendations on the tasks that could be carried out by the United Nations Truce Supervision Organization;

13. *Decides* to review the situation, by early November 2000, and to consider any steps it deems appropriate regarding the Force, on the basis of this report, the extent of the deployment of the Force and the actions taken by the Government of Lebanon to restore its effective authority and presence in the area, in particular through a significant deployment of the Lebanese Armed Forces;

14. *Stresses* the importance of, and the need of achieving, a comprehensive, just and lasting peace in the Middle East, based on all relevant resolutions including its resolutions 242(1967) of 22 November 1967 and 338(1973) of 22 October 1973.

Communications (4-8 August). On 4 August [S/2000/778], the Secretary-General informed the Security Council of his intention to appoint Rolf G. Knuttson (Sweden) as his Personal Representative for Southern Lebanon. He would take up his assignment in Beirut as soon as possible for an initial period of six months. On 8 August [S/2000/779], the Council took note of the Secretary-General's decision.

Report of Secretary-General (October). In October [S/2000/1049], the Secretary-General submitted to the Security Council an interim report on UNIFIL. He said that from the end of July until early October, the situation in the UNIFIL area of operations had remained calm, except for numerous minor violations of the line of withdrawal, the so-called Blue Line. Those violations were attributable mainly to Israeli construction of new military positions and fencing along the line; they were corrected in each case after intervention by UNIFIL. Minor Lebanese violations also took place. Two serious incidents occurred on 7 October. In the context of the tension in the occupied territories and Israel, about 500 Palestinians and supporters approached the line to demonstrate against Israel. As they attempted to cross the fence, Israeli troops opened fire, killing three and injuring 20. In the other incident, Hezbollah launched an attack across the Blue Line and took three Israeli soldiers prisoner. Hezbollah stated that its operation had been planned for some time in order to obtain the release of 19 Lebanese prisoners who were still held by Israel. The Secretary-General, who had been pursuing the question of those prisoners with the Israeli authorities, remained ready to work with the Governments of Israel and Lebanon with a view to resolving that matter.

Lebanese administrators, police, security and army personnel were carrying out their functions throughout the area and their presence and activities continued to grow. They re-established local administration in the villages and had made progress in reintegrating the communications, infrastructure, health and welfare systems with the rest of the country. In late August, the former Israeli-controlled area participated for the first time since 1972 in a parliamentary election. However, near the Blue Line the authorities had, in effect, left control to Hezbollah. Its members worked in civilian attire and were normally unarmed. They maintained good discipline and were under effective command and control. They monitored the Blue Line, maintained public order and, in some villages, provided social, medical and educational services. On several occasions, Hezbollah personnel restricted UNIFIL's freedom of movement. Two serious incidents took place in October when Hezbollah forced UNIFIL personnel at gunpoint to hand over vehicles and military hardware they had found on the terrain. Lebanon had taken the position that, so long as there was no comprehensive peace with Israel, the army would not act as a border guard for Israel and would not be deployed to the border.

UNIFIL monitored the area through ground and air patrols and a network of observation posts. It acted to correct violations by raising them with the side concerned and used its best efforts, through continuous, close liaison with both sides, to prevent friction and limit incidents. By early August, the Force had redeployed southwards and up to the Blue Line. The redeployment proceeded smoothly, and the Lebanese authorities assisted in securing land and premises for new positions. In order to free the capacity needed for the move south, UNIFIL vacated an area in the rear and handed it over to the Lebanese authorities. However, UNIFIL had not been able to persuade the Lebanese authorities to assume their full responsibilities along the Blue Line. UNIFIL also assisted in demining activities and set up an information management system for mine action. In Tyre, Lebanon, a regional mine action cell was established with the help of the United Nations Mine Action Service, which cooperated closely with the Lebanese national demining office.

UNDP continued to lead the efforts of the UN system in working with the Lebanese Government on a plan of action for the development and rehabilitation of the area vacated by Israel. In that regard, UNDP cooperated closely with the UN Special Coordinator, who led the efforts at the international level with the EU and the World Bank, and with the Secretary-General's Personal Representative. On 27 and 28 September, UNDP organized in Beirut a conference of NGOs, funded by the Italian Government.

The Secretary-General observed that, while much remained to be done to restore the full range of government services to a standard comparable to that in the rest of Lebanon, there had been tangible progress in that direction. The sequence of steps foreseen in resolution 425(1978) was clear and logical: the Israeli forces had to withdraw, there had to be no further hostilities, and the effective authority of the Lebanese Government had to be restored. Thereafter, Israel and Lebanon were to be fully responsible for preventing any hostile acts from their respective territory against that of their neighbour.

The Secretary-General believed that the time had come to establish the state of affairs envisaged in the resolution. That required, first and foremost, that the Lebanese Government should take effective control of the whole area vacated by Israel and assume its full international responsibilities, including putting an end to the dangerous provocations that had continued on the Blue Line. The Secretary-General had discussed those matters with the President and Prime Minister of Lebanon during his visit to Beirut in June. He had also discussed Lebanon's need for international assistance to address long-standing problems, in particular the reintegration of the area that had been occupied by Israel. He appealed to donors to help Lebanon meet urgent needs for relief and economic revival in the south, pending the holding of a full-fledged donor conference. The Secretary-General added that his interim report was being written at a time of high tension in Arab-Israeli relations and continuing confrontations in the Occupied Palestinian Territory. Under the circumstances, he deemed it prudent not to submit suggestions for the reconfiguration of the UN presence in south Lebanon, as requested by resolution 1310(2000). He proposed to address that subject in the report to be submitted prior to the expiration of UNIFIL's mandate.

Further developments

In a report on developments during the second half of 2000 [S/2001/66], the Secretary-General noted that the general situation in south Lebanon had remained calm and orderly and minor violations had been quickly corrected. However, reckless behaviour by Lebanese demonstrators on the Blue Line continued, drawing at times an overly harsh response from Israeli soldiers. The greatest cause of concern, however, were the attacks across the Blue Line in the Shab'a farms area, which were deliberate acts in direct breach of the Security Council's decisions. In November, Lebanon asserted that the Blue Line was not valid in the Shab'a farms area, which had been left outside the Blue Line, and claimed the right to use every means, including force, against the Israeli forces occupying it.

The overall security situation in UNIFIL's area of operation had remained good and showed further improvement since October. Those residents who had left the area during the Israeli occupation continued to return, and members of the former de facto forces and their families, about 1,600 in all, had returned to Lebanon. As before, the Lebanese army and security forces did not operate close to the Blue Line, where control was left to Hezbollah. UNIFIL continued to assist the civilian population in the form of medical care, water projects, equipment or services for schools and orphanages, and supplies of social services to the needy. The large number of mines and unexploded ordnance remained a matter of concern. Since July, a total of five persons had died and 26 were injured as a result of exploding mines and ordnance. UNDP continued its support to the Lebanese Council for Development and Reconstruction for a programme of socio-economic rehabilitation and development in southern Lebanon.

Communications (6 December). On 6 December [S/2000/1167], the Secretary-General informed the Security Council of his intention to appoint Staffan de Mistura (Sweden) as his Personal Representative for Southern Lebanon, who would be succeeding Mr. Knutsson. On 8 December [S/2000/1168], the Council took note of the Secretary-General's decision.

Financing

Reports of Secretary-General and ACABQ (January-April). In a January report [A/54/708], the Secretary-General submitted the financial performance report of UNIFIL for the period 1 July 1998 to 30 June 1999. Expenditures for the period totalled $134,655,200 gross ($131,048,500 net), resulting in an unencumbered balance of $8,329,300 gross ($8,084,600 net), compared to the amount appropriated for the maintenance of UNIFIL by the General Assembly in resolution 52/237 [YUN 1998, p. 478]. The unencumbered balance was due largely to actual troop strength being lower than budgeted; a high vacancy rate for civilian staff caused by the temporary assignment of experienced UNIFIL international staff to assist in other peacekeeping missions; savings under purchase of vehicles because of better unit cost rates; and receipt of other vehicles, equipment and supplies from the UN Logistics Base in Brindisi, Italy, and other peacekeeping missions, which reduced budgeted expenditures.

Also in January [A/54/724], the Secretary-General submitted the proposed budget for UNIFIL for the period 1 July 2000 to 30 June 2001, in the amount of $139,547,600 gross ($135,721,900 net), inclusive of $180,000 of budgeted voluntary contributions.

The comments and recommendations of ACABQ were contained in an April report [A/54/841/Add.2].

GENERAL ASSEMBLY ACTION

On 15 June [meeting 98], the General Assembly, on the recommendation of the Fifth (Administrative and Budgetary) Committee [A/54/897], adopted **resolution 54/267** by recorded vote (110-2) [agenda item 128 (b)].

Financing of the United Nations Interim Force in Lebanon

The General Assembly,

Reaffirming its resolutions 51/233 of 13 June 1997, 52/237 of 26 June 1998 and 53/227 of 8 June 1999,

Having considered the reports of the Secretary-General on the financing of the United Nations Interim Force in Lebanon and the related reports of the Advisory Committee on Administrative and Budgetary Questions,

Bearing in mind Security Council resolution 425(1978) of 19 March 1978, by which the Council established the United Nations Interim Force in Lebanon, and the subsequent resolutions by which the Council extended the mandate of the Force, the latest of which was resolution 1288(2000) of 31 January 2000,

Recalling its resolution S-8/2 of 21 April 1978 on the financing of the Force and its subsequent resolutions thereon, the latest of which was resolution 53/227,

Reaffirming that the costs of the Force are expenses of the Organization to be borne by Member States in accordance with Article 17, paragraph 2, of the Charter of the United Nations,

Recalling its previous decisions regarding the fact that, in order to meet the expenditures caused by the Force, a different procedure is required from that applied to meet expenditures of the regular budget of the United Nations,

Taking into account the fact that the economically more developed countries are in a position to make relatively larger contributions and that the economically less developed countries have a relatively limited capacity to contribute towards such an operation,

Bearing in mind the special responsibilities of the States permanent members of the Security Council, as indicated in General Assembly resolution 1874(S-IV) of 27 June 1963, in the financing of such operations,

Noting with appreciation that voluntary contributions have been made to the Force,

Mindful of the fact that it is essential to provide the Force with the necessary financial resources to enable it to fulfil its responsibilities under the relevant resolutions of the Security Council,

Concerned that the Secretary-General continues to face difficulties in meeting the obligations of the Force on a current basis, including reimbursement to current and former troop-contributing States,

Concerned also that the surplus balances in the Special Account for the United Nations Interim Force in Lebanon have been used to meet expenses of the Force in order to compensate for the lack of income resulting from non-payment and late payment by Member States of their contributions,

1. *Takes note* of the status of contributions to the United Nations Interim Force in Lebanon as at 30 April 2000, including the contributions outstanding in the amount of 122.5 million United States dollars, representing some 4 per cent of the total assessed contributions from the inception of the Force to the period ending 30 June 2000, notes that some 18 per cent of the Member States have paid their assessed contributions in full, and urges all other Member States concerned, in particular those in arrears, to ensure payment of their outstanding assessed contributions;

2. *Expresses its deep concern* that Israel did not comply with General Assembly resolutions 51/233, 52/237 and 53/227;

3. *Stresses once again* that Israel should strictly abide by General Assembly resolutions 51/233, 52/237 and 53/227;

4. *Expresses its appreciation* to those Member States which have paid their assessed contributions in full;

5. *Expresses concern* about the financial situation with regard to peacekeeping activities, in particular as regards the reimbursements to troop contributors that bear additional burdens owing to overdue payments by Member States of their assessments;

6. *Urges* all other Member States to make every possible effort to ensure payment of their assessed contributions to the Force in full and on time;

7. *Expresses concern* at the delay experienced by the Secretary-General in deploying and providing adequate resources to some recent peacekeeping missions, in particular those in Africa;

8. *Emphasizes* that all future and existing peacekeeping missions shall be given equal and non-discriminatory treatment in respect of financial and administrative arrangements;

9. *Also emphasizes* that all peacekeeping missions shall be provided with adequate resources for the effective and efficient discharge of their respective mandates;

10. *Requests* the Secretary-General to make the fullest possible use of facilities and equipment at the United Nations Logistics Base at Brindisi, Italy, in order to minimize the costs of procurement for the Force, and for this purpose requests the Secretary-General to speed up the implementation of the asset management system at all peacekeeping missions in accordance with General Assembly resolution 52/1 A of 15 October 1997;

11. *Endorses* the conclusions and recommendations contained in the report of the Advisory Committee on Administrative and Budgetary Questions, and requests the Secretary-General to ensure their full implementation;

12. *Requests* the Secretary-General to take all necessary action to ensure that the Force is administered with a maximum of efficiency and economy;

13. *Also requests* the Secretary-General, in order to reduce the cost of employing General Service staff, to continue efforts to recruit local staff for the Force against General Service posts, commensurate with the requirements of the Force;

14. *Reiterates its request* to the Secretary-General to take the necessary measures to ensure the full implementation of paragraph 8 of General Assembly resolution 51/233, paragraph 5 of resolution 52/237 and paragraph 11 of resolution 53/227, stresses once again that Israel shall pay the amount of 1,284,633 dollars resulting from the incident at Qana on 18 April 1996, and requests the Secretary-General to report on this matter to the Assembly at its fifty-fifth session;

15. *Decides* to appropriate to the Special Account for the United Nations Interim Force in Lebanon the amount of 146,833,694 dollars gross (141,889,841 dollars net) for the maintenance of the Force for the period from 1 July 2000 to 30 June 2001, inclusive of the amount of 6,967,059 dollars gross (5,895,590 dollars net) for the support account for peacekeeping operations and the amount of 1,089,216 dollars gross (969,161 dollars net) for the United Nations Logistics Base;

16. *Decides also*, as an ad hoc arrangement, to apportion among Member States the amount of 12,236,141 dollars gross (11,824,153 dollars net) for the period from 1 to 31 July 2000, in accordance with the composition of groups set out in paragraphs 3 and 4 of General Assembly resolution 43/232 of 1 March 1989, as adjusted by the Assembly in its resolutions 44/192 B of 21 December 1989, 45/269 of 27 August 1991, 46/198 A of 20 December 1991, 47/218 A of 23 December 1992, 49/249 A of 20 July 1995, 49/249 B of 14 September 1995, 50/224 of 11 April 1996, 51/218 A to C of 18 December 1996 and 52/230 of 31 March 1998 and its decisions 48/472 A of 23 December 1993, 50/451 B of 23 December 1995 and 54/456 to 54/458 of 23 December 1999, and taking into account the scale of assessments for the year 2000, as set out in its resolutions 52/215 A of 22 December 1997 and 54/237 A of 23 December 1999;

17. *Decides further* that, in accordance with the provisions of its resolution 973(X) of 15 December 1955, there shall be set off against the apportionment among Member States, as provided for in paragraph 16 above, their respective share in the Tax Equalization Fund of the estimated staff assessment income of 411,988 dol-

lars approved for the Force for the period from 1 to 31 July 2000;

18. *Decides* that, for Member States that have fulfilled their financial obligations to the Force, there shall be set off against the apportionment, as provided for in paragraph 16 above, their respective share of the unencumbered balance of 8,329,300 dollars gross (8,084,600 dollars net) in respect of the period from 1 July 1998 to 30 June 1999;

19. *Decides also* that, for Member States that have not fulfilled their financial obligations to the Force, their share of the unencumbered balance of 8,329,300 dollars gross (8,084,600 dollars net) in respect of the period from 1 July 1998 to 30 June 1999 shall be set off against their outstanding obligations;

20. *Decides further,* as an ad hoc arrangement, to apportion among Member States the amount of 134,597,553 dollars gross (130,065,688 dollars net) for the period from 1 August 2000 to 30 June 2001, at a monthly rate of 12,236,141 dollars gross (11,824,153 dollars net), in accordance with the scheme set out in the present resolution, and taking into account the scale of assessments for the year 2000, as set out in its resolutions 52/215 A and 54/237 A, and for the year 2001, subject to the decision of the Security Council to extend the mandate of the Force beyond 31 July 2000;

21. *Decides* that, in accordance with the provisions of its resolution 973(X), there shall be set off against the apportionment among Member States, as provided for in paragraph 20 above, their respective share in the Tax Equalization Fund of the estimated staff assessment income of 4,531,864 dollars approved for the Force for the period from 1 August 2000 to 30 June 2001;

22. *Emphasizes* that no peacekeeping mission shall be financed by borrowing funds from other active peacekeeping missions;

23. *Encourages* the Secretary-General to continue to take additional measures to ensure the safety and security of all personnel under the auspices of the United Nations participating in the Force;

24. *Invites* voluntary contributions to the Force in cash and in the form of services and supplies acceptable to the Secretary-General, to be administered, as appropriate, in accordance with the procedure and practices established by the General Assembly;

25. *Decides* to include in the provisional agenda of its fifty-fifth session, under the item entitled "Financing of the United Nations peacekeeping forces in the Middle East", the sub-item entitled "United Nations Interim Force in Lebanon".

RECORDED VOTE ON RESOLUTION 54/267:

In favour: Algeria, Andorra, Angola, Antigua and Barbuda, Argentina, Armenia, Australia, Austria, Azerbaijan, Bahrain, Bangladesh, Barbados, Belgium, Benin, Bolivia, Brazil, Bulgaria, Burkina Faso, Cambodia, Canada, Chile, China, Colombia, Costa Rica, Côte d'Ivoire, Croatia, Cuba, Cyprus, Czech Republic, Democratic People's Republic of Korea, Denmark, Egypt, Estonia, Ethiopia, Finland, France, Gabon, Germany, Ghana, Greece, Guatemala, Hungary, Iceland, India, Indonesia, Ireland, Italy, Jamaica, Japan, Jordan, Kenya, Kuwait, Lao People's Democratic Republic, Latvia, Lebanon, Libyan Arab Jamahiriya, Liechtenstein, Lithuania, Luxembourg, Malaysia, Maldives, Malta, Mauritius, Mexico, Monaco, Morocco, Myanmar, Namibia, Nepal, Netherlands, New Zealand, Nicaragua, Nigeria, Norway, Oman, Pakistan, Panama, Paraguay, Philippines, Poland, Portugal, Qatar, Republic of Korea, Romania, Russian Federation, San Marino, Saudi Arabia, Singapore, Syrian Arab Republic, Thailand, The former Yugoslav Republic of Macedonia, Tonga, Tunisia, Turkey, Uganda, Ukraine, United Kingdom, United Republic of Tanzania, Uruguay, Venezuela, Viet Nam, Zambia, Zimbabwe.

Against: Israel, United States.

The Assembly and the Committee each had adopted the first preambular paragraph and operative paragraphs 2, 3 and 14 by a single recorded vote of, respectively, 64 to 2, with 43 abstentions, and 59 to 2, with 40 abstentions.

Speaking before the vote in the Assembly, Israel said that it was forced to vote against the resolution because it singled out and faulted Israel unfairly and entirely for the April 1996 incident at Qana, Lebanon [YUN 1996, p. 429], which was initiated by a terrorist group using human shields. Moreover, Israel noted that it was the only time a draft resolution called for one particular party to pay damages for the property of UN peacekeepers as a result of a clash.

Speaking after the vote, Lebanon said that the resolution confirmed that it was the responsibility of the occupying State—Israel—to assume full responsibility for its acts of aggression against Lebanon, especially since the aggression was deliberate and directed against the United Nations.

Reports of Secretary-General and ACABQ (October). In a 13 October report [A/55/482], the Secretary-General submitted the revised budget of UNIFIL for the period 1 July 2000 to 30 June 2001, which amounted to $225,715,700 gross ($221,506,300 net), inclusive of budgeted voluntary contributions in kind amounting to $180,000. The new budget incorporated additional requirements for the expansion of the Force as proposed in the Secretary-General's May report (see p. 462).

The comments and recommendations of ACABQ were contained in a 24 October report [A/55/516].

GENERAL ASSEMBLY ACTION

On 19 December [meeting 86], the General Assembly, on the recommendation of the Fifth Committee [A/55/681], adopted **resolution 55/180 A** by recorded vote (140-3) [agenda item 138 (*b*)].

Financing of the United Nations Interim Force in Lebanon

The General Assembly,

Having considered the report of the Secretary-General on the financing of the United Nations Interim Force in Lebanon and the related report of the Advisory Committee on Administrative and Budgetary Questions,

Bearing in mind Security Council resolution 425 (1978) of 19 March 1978, by which the Council established the United Nations Interim Force in Lebanon, and the subsequent resolutions by which the Council extended the mandate of the Force, the latest of which was resolution 1310(2000) of 27 July 2000,

Recalling its resolution S-8/2 of 21 April 1978 on the financing of the Force and its subsequent resolutions thereon, the latest of which was resolution 54/267 of 15 June 2000,

Reaffirming its resolutions 51/233 of 13 June 1997, 52/237 of 26 June 1998, 53/227 of 8 June 1999 and 54/267,

Reaffirming also that the costs of the Force are expenses of the Organization to be borne by Member Sates in accordance with Article 17, paragraph 2, of the Charter of the United Nations,

Recalling its previous decisions regarding the fact that, in order to meet the expenditures caused by the Force, a different procedure is required from that applied to meet expenditures of the regular budget of the United Nations,

Taking into account the fact that the economically more developed countries are in a position to make relatively larger contributions and that the economically less developed countries have a relatively limited capacity to contribute towards such operations,

Bearing in mind the special responsibilities of the States permanent members of the Security Council, as indicated in General Assembly resolution 1874(S-IV) of 27 June 1963, in the financing of such operations,

Noting with appreciation that voluntary contributions have been made to the Force,

Mindful of the fact that it is essential to provide the Force with the necessary financial resources to enable it to fulfil its responsibilities under the relevant resolutions of the Security Council,

Concerned that the Secretary-General continues to face difficulties in meeting the obligations of the Force on a current basis, including reimbursement to current and former troop-contributing States,

Concerned also that the surplus balances in the Special Account for the United Nations Interim Force in Lebanon have been used to meet expenses of the Force in order to compensate for the lack of income resulting from non-payment and late payment by Member States of their contributions,

1. *Takes note* of the status of contributions to the United Nations Interim Force in Lebanon as at 31 October 2000, including the contributions outstanding in the amount of 139.4 million United States dollars, representing some 3.9 per cent of the total assessed contributions from the inception of the Force to the period ending 31 December 2000, notes that some 21 per cent of the Member States have paid their assessed contributions in full, and urges all other Member States concerned, in particular those in arrears, to ensure the payment of their outstanding assessed contributions;

2. *Express its deep concern* that Israel did not comply with its resolutions 51/233, 52/237, 53/227 and 54/267;

3. *Stresses once again* that Israel should strictly abide by its resolutions 51/233, 52/237, 53/227 and 54/267;

4. *Expresses its appreciation* to those Member States which have paid their assessed contributions in full;

5. *Expresses concern* about the financial situation with regard to peacekeeping activities, in particular as regards the reimbursements to troop contributors that bear additional burdens owing to overdue payments by Member States of their assessments;

6. *Urges* all other Member States to make every possible effort to ensure payment of their assessed contributions to the Force in full and on time;

7. *Expresses concern* at the delay experienced by the Secretary-General in deploying and providing adequate resources to some recent peacekeeping missions, in particular those in Africa;

8. *Emphasizes* that all future and existing peacekeeping missions shall be given equal and non-discriminatory treatment in respect of financial and administrative arrangements;

9. *Also emphasizes* that all peacekeeping missions shall be provided with adequate resources for the effective and efficient discharge of their respective mandates;

10. *Requests* the Secretary-General to make the fullest possible use of facilities and equipment at the United Nations Logistics Base at Brindisi, Italy, in order to minimize the costs of procurement for the Force, and for this purpose requests the Secretary-General to speed up the implementation of the asset management system at all peacekeeping missions in accordance with its resolution 52/1 A of 15 October 1997;

11. *Endorses* the conclusions and recommendations contained in the report of the Advisory Committee on Administrative and Budgetary Questions;

12. *Requests* the Secretary-General to take all necessary action to ensure that the Force is administered with a maximum of efficiency and economy;

13. *Also requests* the Secretary-General, in order to reduce the cost of employing General Service staff, to continue efforts to recruit local staff for the Force against General Service posts, commensurate with the requirements of the Force;

14. *Reiterates its request* to the Secretary-General to take the necessary measures to ensure the full implementation of paragraph 8 of its resolution 51/233, paragraph 5 of its resolution 52/237, paragraph 11 of its resolution 53/227 and paragraph 14 of its resolution 54/267, stresses once again that Israel shall pay the amount of 1,284,633 dollars resulting from the incident at Qana on 18 April 1996, and requests the Secretary-General to report on this matter to the Assembly at its resumed fifty-fifth session;

15. *Decides* to appropriate to the Special Account for the United Nations Interim Force in Lebanon the amount of 86,758,400 dollars gross (86,301,300 dollars net) for the expansion of the Force for the period from 1 July 2000 to 30 June 2001, in addition to the amount of 146,833,694 dollars gross (141,889,841 dollars net) already appropriated by the Assembly in its resolution 54/267;

16. *Decides also*, as an ad hoc arrangement, taking into account the amount of 85,652,987 dollars gross (82,769,071 dollars net) already apportioned in accordance with its resolution 54/267 for the period from 1 July 2000 to 31 January 2001, to apportion among Member States the additional amount of 50,609,069 dollars gross (50,342,425 dollars net), in accordance with the composition of groups set out in paragraphs 3 and 4 of its resolution 43/232 of 1 March 1989, as adjusted by the Assembly in its resolutions 44/192 B of 21 December 1989, 45/269 of 27 August 1991, 46/198 A of 20 December 1991, 47/218 A of 23 December 1992, 49/249 A of 20 July 1995, 49/249 B of 14 September 1995, 50/224 of 11 April 1996, 51/218 A to C of 18 December 1996 and 52/230 of 31 March 1998 and its decisions 48/472 A of 23 December 1993, 50/451 B of 23 December 1995 and 54/456 to 54/458 of 23 December 1999, the scale of assessments for the year 2000 to be applied against a portion thereof, that is, 43,379,202 dol-

lars gross (43,150,650 dollars net), which is the amount pertaining to the period ending 31 December 2000, and the scale of assessments for the year 2001, to be applied against the balance, that is, 7,229,867 dollars gross (7,191,775 dollars net) for the period from 1 to 31 January 2001;

17. *Decides further* that, in accordance with the provisions of its resolution 973(X) of 15 December 1955, there shall be set off against the apportionment among Member States, as provided for in paragraph 16 above, their respective share in the Tax Equalization Fund of the estimated additional staff assessment income of 266,644 dollars approved for the Force for the period from 1 July 2000 to 31 January 2001, 228,552 dollars being the amount pertaining to the period ending 31 December 2000 and the balance, that is, 38,092 dollars, pertaining to the period from 1 to 31 January 2001;

18. *Decides*, as an ad hoc arrangement, and taking into account the amount of 61,180,707 dollars gross (59,120,770 dollars net) already apportioned in accordance with its resolution 54/267 for the period from 1 February to 30 June 2001, to apportion among Member States the additional amount of 36,149,331 dollars gross (35,958,875 dollars net), at a monthly rate of 7,229,867 dollars gross (7,191,775 dollars net), in accordance with the scheme set out in the present resolution, taking into account the scale of assessments for the year 2001, subject to the decision of the Security Council to extend the mandate of the Force beyond 31 January 2001;

19. *Decides also* that, in accordance with the provisions of its resolution 973(X), there shall be set off against the apportionment among Member States, as provided for in paragraph 18 above, their respective share in the Tax Equalization Fund of the estimated additional staff assessment income of 190,456 dollars approved for the Force for the period from 1 February to 30 June 2001;

20. *Emphasizes* that no peacekeeping mission shall be financed by borrowing funds from other active peacekeeping missions;

21. *Encourages* the Secretary-General to continue to take additional measures to ensure the safety and security of all personnel under the auspices of the United Nations participating in the Force;

22. *Invites* voluntary contributions to the Force in cash and in the form of services and supplies acceptable to the Secretary-General, to be administered, as appropriate, in accordance with the procedure and practices established by the General Assembly;

23. *Decides* to keep under review during its fifty-fifth session, under the item entitled "Financing of the United Nations peacekeeping forces in the Middle East", the sub-item entitled "United Nations Interim Force in Lebanon".

RECORDED VOTE ON RESOLUTION 55/180 A:

In favour: Algeria, Andorra, Angola, Argentina, Armenia, Australia, Austria, Azerbaijan, Bahamas, Bahrain, Bangladesh, Barbados, Belarus, Belgium, Belize, Benin, Bhutan, Bolivia, Botswana, Brazil, Brunei Darussalam, Bulgaria, Burkina Faso, Cambodia, Cameroon, Canada, Chad, Chile, China, Colombia, Comoros, Costa Rica, Croatia, Cuba, Cyprus, Czech Republic, Democratic People's Republic of Korea, Denmark, Djibouti, Dominican Republic, Ecuador, Egypt, El Salvador, Eritrea, Ethiopia, Fiji, Finland, France, Gabon, Gambia, Georgia, Germany, Ghana, Greece, Grenada, Guyana, Haiti, Honduras, Hungary, Iceland, India, Indonesia, Ireland, Italy, Jamaica, Japan, Jordan, Kenya, Kuwait, Lao People's Democratic Republic, Latvia, Lebanon, Libyan Arab Jamahiriya, Liechtenstein, Lithuania, Luxembourg, Madagascar, Malawi, Malaysia, Maldives, Malta, Mauritania, Mauritius,

Mexico, Monaco, Mongolia, Morocco, Myanmar, Nepal, Netherlands, New Zealand, Nicaragua, Nigeria, Norway, Oman, Pakistan, Panama, Papua New Guinea, Paraguay, Peru, Philippines, Poland, Portugal, Qatar, Republic of Korea, Romania, Russian Federation, Saint Lucia, Saudi Arabia, Senegal, Sierra Leone, Singapore, Slovakia, Slovenia, South Africa, Spain, Sri Lanka, Sudan, Suriname, Swaziland, Sweden, Syrian Arab Republic, Thailand, The former Yugoslav Republic of Macedonia, Togo, Tonga, Trinidad and Tobago, Tunisia, Turkey, Uganda, Ukraine, United Arab Emirates, United Kingdom, United Republic of Tanzania, Uruguay, Venezuela, Viet Nam, Yemen, Yugoslavia, Zambia.

Against: Israel, Marshall Islands, United States.

The Assembly and the Committee each had adopted the fourth preambular paragraph and operative paragraphs 2, 3 and 14 by a single recorded vote of, respectively, 85 to 3, with 47 abstentions, and 68 to 3, with 35 abstentions.

Speaking before the vote, Israel recalled the established practice that resolutions relating to budgetary questions were to be adopted by consensus. Due to the introduction of political elements in the resolution, that practice had been broken. The decision to place on Israel alone the burden of the cost of the damage resulting from the Qana incident was an unprecedented and one-sided initiative. Israel supported funding of UN peacekeeping operations but because of the fourth preambular paragraph and operative paragraphs 2, 3 and 14 it would vote against the draft resolution.

Speaking after the vote, Egypt, on behalf of the Arab Group, said that it supported the resolution because the sanctity of the principle of maintaining the security and safety of peacekeeping personnel was the cornerstone of the funding of peacekeeping operations. Any hesitation in the implementation of that principle would send the wrong message to States that violated UN resolutions and would allow them to circumvent their responsibility for the safety and security of UN peacekeeping personnel. The Arab Group expressed concern vis-à-vis Israel's disregard of the Secretary-General's letters, in which he sought reimbursement of the costs incurred as a result of Israel's attack on the UN compound in Qana. That sum had been recorded as a debit in UNI-FIL's Special Account.

By **decision 55/455** of 23 December, the Assembly decided that the Fifth Committee should continue consideration of UNIFIL's financing at the resumed fifty-fifth (2001) session.

Syrian Arab Republic

In 2000, the General Assembly again called for Israel's withdrawal from the Golan Heights in the Syrian Arab Republic, which it had occupied since 1967. The area was effectively annexed by Israel when it extended its laws, jurisdiction and administration to the territory towards the end of 1981 [YUN 1981, p. 309].

Israeli policies and measures affecting the human rights of the population in the Golan Heights and other occupied territories were monitored by the Special Committee to Investigate Israeli Practices Affecting the Human Rights of the Palestinian People and Other Arabs of the Occupied Territories (Committee on Israeli Practices) and were the subject of resolutions adopted by the Commission on Human Rights (see PART TWO, Chapter III) and the Assembly.

Special Committee on Israeli Practices. In its annual report [A/55/453], the Committee on Israeli Practices stated that it had visited Damascus and the Quneitra province, which bordered the occupied area, where it received information from witnesses on the current situation in the Syrian Arab Golan. The Committee was informed that there had been no change in Israeli policy regarding the occupied Golan, that the number of settlers had increased and that existing settlements had been expanded during the period under review, though no new ones were established. The human rights situation also did not improve. Relations between the settlers and the Arab population of the occupied Golan were tense and often of a violent nature. The attention of the Committee was drawn to the fact that all settlers were armed, while the Arab inhabitants were not allowed to carry weapons.

The Committee received information on the widespread nature of the consequences of the occupation: the intention of the Israeli authorities to increase the number of settlers, persistent Judaization of life in the occupied Golan and falsification of history at the expense of the Arab population. The economic constraints exercised by Israel were reflected in the lack of equal employment opportunities, heavy taxes, fixed low prices imposed on apples, the main agricultural produce, arbitrary arrest and detention and inadequate health care. In addition, the uprooting of trees, burning of forests, chemical residue from Israeli factories and waste from settlements had caused environmental deterioration. Settlers competed with Syrians in economic terms in the area of agriculture, the principal activity of the Arab population. The competition was rendered more uneven by the restricted access of the Syrian inhabitants to water compared with the settlers.

The separation of families who lived on either side of the valley constituting the demarcation line remained one of the principal negative impacts of the Israeli occupation of the Syrian Golan. However, a positive development was the issuance by the Israeli authorities of permits for Syrians from the occupied Golan to travel to Jordan for five days to meet their family and relatives living in the Syrian Arab Republic. The Committee called on the United Nations High Commissioner for Human Rights, in consultation with the Secretary-General, to establish a system of communication with the Israeli authorities with a view, among other things, to permit long-separated families in the Occupied Palestinian Territory and in the Syrian Golan to meet freely and often.

Reports of Secretary-General. On 4 August [A/55/265], the Secretary-General reported that no reply had been received from Israel to his July request for information on steps taken or envisaged to implement General Assembly resolution 54/80 [YUN 1999, p. 451], which called on Israel to desist from changing the physical character, demographic composition, institutional structure and legal status of the Golan, and from its repressive measures against the population.

By a 2 November report [A/55/538], the Secretary-General transmitted replies received from four Member States, including Israel, in response to his request for information on steps taken or envisaged to implement Assembly resolutions 54/38 [YUN 1999, p. 450], which dealt with Israeli policies in the Syrian territory occupied since 1967, and 54/37 [YUN 1999, p. 409] on the transfer by some States of their diplomatic missions to Jerusalem (see p. 429).

GENERAL ASSEMBLY ACTION

On 1 December [meeting 78], the General Assembly adopted **resolution 55/51** [draft: A/55/L.50 & Add.1] by recorded vote (96-2-55) [agenda item 40].

The Syrian Golan

The General Assembly,

Having considered the item entitled "The situation in the Middle East",

Taking note of the report of the Secretary-General,

Recalling Security Council resolution 497(1981) of 17 December 1981,

Reaffirming the fundamental principle of the inadmissibility of the acquisition of territory by force, in accordance with international law and the Charter of the United Nations,

Reaffirming once more the applicability of the Geneva Convention relative to the Protection of Civilian Persons in Time of War, of 12 August 1949, to the occupied Syrian Golan,

Deeply concerned that Israel has not withdrawn from the Syrian Golan, which has been under occupation since 1967, contrary to the relevant Security Council and General Assembly resolutions,

Stressing the illegality of the Israeli settlement construction and activities in the occupied Syrian Golan since 1967,

Noting with satisfaction the convening in Madrid on 30 October 1991 of the Peace Conference on the Middle East, on the basis of Security Council resolutions 242(1967) of 22 November 1967, 338(1973) of 22 October 1973 and 425(1978) of 19 March 1978 and the formula of land for peace,

Expressing grave concern over the halt in the peace process on the Syrian track, and expressing the hope that peace talks will soon resume from the point they had reached,

1. *Declares* that Israel has failed so far to comply with Security Council resolution 497(1981);

2. *Also declares* that the Israeli decision of 14 December 1981 to impose its laws, jurisdiction and administration on the occupied Syrian Golan is null and void and has no validity whatsoever, as confirmed by the Security Council in its resolution 497(1981), and calls upon Israel to rescind it;

3. *Reaffirms its determination* that all relevant provisions of the Regulations annexed to the Hague Convention of 1907, and the Geneva Convention relative to the Protection of Civilian Persons in Time of War, of 12 August 1949, continue to apply to the Syrian territory occupied by Israel since 1967, and calls upon the parties thereto to respect and ensure respect for their obligations under those instruments in all circumstances;

4. *Determines once more* that the continued occupation of the Syrian Golan and its de facto annexation constitute a stumbling block in the way of achieving a just, comprehensive and lasting peace in the region;

5. *Calls upon* Israel to resume the talks on the Syrian and Lebanese tracks and to respect the commitments and undertakings reached during the previous talks;

6. *Demands once more* that Israel withdraw from all the occupied Syrian Golan to the line of 4 June 1967 in implementation of the relevant Security Council resolutions;

7. *Calls upon* all the parties concerned, the co-sponsors of the peace process and the entire international community to exert all the necessary efforts to ensure the resumption of the peace process and its success by implementing Security Council resolutions 242(1967) and 338(1973);

8. *Requests* the Secretary-General to report to the General Assembly at its fifty-sixth session on the implementation of the present resolution.

RECORDED VOTE ON RESOLUTION 55/51:

In favour: Afghanistan, Algeria, Antigua and Barbuda, Argentina, Armenia, Bahamas, Bahrain, Bangladesh, Barbados, Belarus, Bolivia, Bosnia and Herzegovina, Botswana, Brunei Darussalam, Burkina Faso, Burundi, Cambodia, Chad, Chile, China, Colombia, Comoros, Costa Rica, Cuba, Cyprus, Democratic People's Republic of Korea, Djibouti, Dominican Republic, Ecuador, Egypt, El Salvador, Eritrea, Ethiopia, Fiji, Gabon, Gambia, Ghana, Grenada, Guatemala, Guinea, Guyana, Honduras, India, Indonesia, Iran, Jordan, Kuwait, Kyrgyzstan, Lao People's Democratic Republic, Lebanon, Libyan Arab Jamahiriya, Madagascar, Malaysia, Maldives, Mali, Malta, Mauritius, Mexico, Mongolia, Morocco, Mozambique, Myanmar, Namibia, Nepal, Nicaragua, Nigeria, Oman, Pakistan, Panama, Philippines, Qatar, Russian Federation, Saint Lucia, Saudi Arabia, Senegal, Sierra Leone, Singapore, South Africa, Sri Lanka, Sudan, Swaziland, Syrian Arab Republic, Tajikistan, Thailand, Togo, Trinidad and Tobago, Tunisia, Turkey, Uganda, United Arab Emirates, United Republic of Tanzania, Venezuela, Viet Nam, Yemen, Zambia, Zimbabwe.

Against: Israel, United States.

Abstaining: Andorra, Angola, Australia, Austria, Belgium, Brazil, Bulgaria, Canada, Croatia, Czech Republic, Denmark, Estonia, Finland, France, Georgia, Germany, Greece, Hungary, Iceland, Ireland, Italy, Japan, Kazakhstan, Kenya, Latvia, Liechtenstein, Lithuania, Luxembourg, Marshall Islands, Micronesia, Monaco, Nauru, Netherlands, New Zealand, Norway, Paraguay, Peru, Poland, Portugal, Republic of Korea, Republic of Moldova, Romania, Samoa, San Marino, Slovakia, Slovenia, Solomon Islands, Spain, Sweden, The former Yugoslav Republic of Macedonia, Tonga, Ukraine, United Kingdom, Uruguay, Yugoslavia.

On 8 December [meeting 83], the Assembly, under the agenda item on the report of the Committee on Israeli Practices and on the Fourth Committee's recommendation [A/55/571], adopted **resolution 55/134** by recorded vote (150-1-4) [agenda item 85].

The occupied Syrian Golan

The General Assembly,

Having considered the reports of the Special Committee to Investigate Israeli Practices Affecting the Human Rights of the Palestinian People and Other Arabs of the Occupied Territories,

Deeply concerned that the Syrian Golan occupied since 1967 has been under continued Israeli military occupation,

Recalling Security Council resolution 497(1981) of 17 December 1981,

Recalling also its previous relevant resolutions, the last of which was resolution 54/80 of 6 December 1999,

Having considered the report of the Secretary-General submitted in pursuance of resolution 54/80,

Recalling its previous relevant resolutions in which, inter alia, it called upon Israel to put an end to its occupation of the Arab territories,

Reaffirming once more the illegality of the decision of 14 December 1981 taken by Israel to impose its laws, jurisdiction and administration on the occupied Syrian Golan, which has resulted in the effective annexation of that territory,

Reaffirming that the acquisition of territory by force is inadmissible under international law, including the Charter of the United Nations,

Reaffirming also the applicability of the Geneva Convention relative to the Protection of Civilian Persons in Time of War, of 12 August 1949, to the occupied Syrian Golan,

Bearing in mind Security Council resolution 237(1967) of 14 June 1967,

Welcoming the convening at Madrid of the Peace Conference on the Middle East on the basis of Security Council resolutions 242(1967) of 22 November 1967 and 338(1973) of 22 October 1973 aimed at the realization of a just, comprehensive and lasting peace, and expressing grave concern about the stalling of the peace process on all tracks,

1. *Calls upon* Israel, the occupying Power, to comply with the relevant resolutions on the occupied Syrian Golan, in particular Security Council resolution 497(1981), in which the Council, inter alia, decided that the Israeli decision to impose its laws, jurisdiction and administration on the occupied Syrian Golan was null and void and without international legal effect, and demanded that Israel, the occupying Power, rescind forthwith its decision;

2. *Also calls upon* Israel to desist from changing the physical character, demographic composition, institutional structure and legal status of the occupied Syrian Golan and in particular to desist from the establishment of settlements;

3. *Determines* that all legislative and administrative measures and actions taken or to be taken by Israel, the occupying Power, that purport to alter the character and legal status of the occupied Syrian Golan are null and void, constitute a flagrant violation of interna-

tional law and of the Geneva Convention relative to the Protection of Civilian Persons in Time of War, of 12 August 1949, and have no legal effect;

4. *Calls upon* Israel to desist from imposing Israeli citizenship and Israeli identity cards on the Syrian citizens in the occupied Syrian Golan and from repressive measures against the population of the occupied Syrian Golan;

5. *Deplores* the violations by Israel of the Geneva Convention relative to the Protection of Civilian Persons in Time of War, of 12 August 1949;

6. *Calls once again upon* Member States not to recognize any of the legislative or administrative measures and actions referred to above;

7. *Requests* the Secretary-General to report to the General Assembly at its fifty-sixth session on the implementation of the present resolution.

RECORDED VOTE ON RESOLUTION 55/134:

In favour: Afghanistan, Algeria, Andorra, Antigua and Barbuda, Argentina, Armenia, Australia, Austria, Bahamas, Bahrain, Bangladesh, Barbados, Belarus, Belgium, Belize, Benin, Bhutan, Bolivia, Botswana, Brazil, Brunei Darussalam, Bulgaria, Burkina Faso, Burundi, Cambodia, Canada, Cape Verde, Chad, Chile, China, Colombia, Comoros, Costa Rica, Côte d'Ivoire, Croatia, Cuba, Cyprus, Czech Republic, Democratic People's Republic of Korea, Denmark, Djibouti, Dominican Republic, Ecuador, Egypt, El Salvador, Eritrea, Estonia, Ethiopia, Fiji, Finland, France, Gabon, Georgia, Germany, Ghana, Greece, Grenada, Guatemala, Guinea, Guyana, Haiti, Honduras, Hungary, Iceland, India, Indonesia, Iran, Ireland, Italy, Jamaica, Japan, Jordan, Kenya, Kuwait, Kyrgyzstan, Lao People's Democratic Republic, Latvia, Lebanon, Libyan Arab Jamahiriya, Liechtenstein, Lithuania, Luxembourg, Madagascar, Malaysia, Maldives, Mali, Malta, Mauritania, Mauritius, Mexico, Monaco, Mongolia, Morocco, Mozambique, Myanmar, Namibia, Nepal, Netherlands, New Zealand, Nicaragua, Nigeria, Norway, Oman, Pakistan, Panama, Papua New Guinea, Paraguay, Peru, Philippines, Poland, Portugal, Qatar, Republic of Korea, Republic of Moldova, Romania, Russian Federation, Saint Lucia, Samoa, San Marino, Saudi Arabia, Senegal, Singapore, Slovakia, Slovenia, Solomon Islands, South Africa, Spain, Sri Lanka, Sudan, Swaziland, Sweden, Syrian Arab Republic, Thailand, The former Yugoslav Republic of Macedonia, Togo, Tunisia, Turkey, Uganda, Ukraine, United Arab Emirates, United Kingdom, United Republic of Tanzania, Uruguay, Vanuatu, Venezuela, Viet Nam, Yemen, Yugoslavia, Zambia, Zimbabwe.

Against: Israel.

Abstaining: Marshall Islands, Micronesia, Nauru, United States.

UNDOF

The mandate of the United Nations Disengagement Observer Force, established by Security Council resolution 350(1974) [YUN 1974, p. 205] to supervise the observance of the ceasefire between Israel and the Syrian Arab Republic in the Golan Heights area and ensuring the separation of their forces, was renewed twice in 2000, in May and November, each time for a six-month period.

UNDOF maintained an area of separation, which was some 80 kilometres long and varied in width between approximately 10 kilometres in the centre to less than 1 kilometre in the extreme south. The area of separation was inhabited and policed by the Syrian authorities, and no military forces other than UNDOF were permitted within it.

Composition and deployment

As at 30 October 2000, UNDOF comprised 1,039 troops from Austria (369), Canada (188), Japan (30), Poland (359) and Slovakia (93). It was as-

sisted by 78 UNTSO military observers. Major-General Bo Wranker (Sweden) became Force Commander on 14 August, taking over from Major-General Cameron Ross (Canada), who completed his tour of duty on 7 July. The Secretary-General informed the Security Council on 6 July [S/2000/664] of his intention to appoint General Wranker; the Council took note of that intention on 10 July [S/2000/665]. The Force was entirely deployed within and close to the area of separation, with two base camps, 44 permanently manned positions and 11 observation posts. UNDOF's headquarters was located at Camp Faouar and an office was maintained in Damascus.

The Austrian battalion, which included a Slovak company, was deployed in the northern part of the area of separation, and the Polish battalion was deployed in the southern part. Both battalions conducted mine-clearing operations. The Canadian and Japanese logistic units, based in Camp Ziouani, with a detachment in Camp Faouar, performed second-line general transport tasks, rotation transport, control and management of goods received by the Force and maintenance of heavy equipment.

Activities

UNDOF continued in 2000 to supervise the area of separation between Israeli and Syrian troops in the Golan Heights, to ensure that no military forces of either party were deployed there, by means of fixed positions and patrols. The Force, accompanied by liaison officers from the party concerned, carried out fortnightly inspections of armament and force levels in the areas of limitation. As in the past, both sides denied inspection teams access to some of their positions and imposed some restrictions on the Force's freedom of movement.

UNDOF assisted the International Committee of the Red Cross with facilities for mail and the passage of persons through the area of separation. Within the means available, medical treatment was provided to the local population on request.

Reports of Secretary-General. The Secretary-General reported to the Security Council on UNDOF activities between 16 November 1999 and 19 May 2000 [S/2000/459] and between 23 May and 21 November 2000 [S/2000/1103]. Both reports noted that UNDOF continued to perform its functions effectively, with the cooperation of the parties. In general, the ceasefire in the Israel-Syria sector was maintained without serious incident, and the UNDOF area of operation remained calm. Minefields, especially in the area of separation, continued to be a concern. In consultation with

Syrian authorities, UNDOF instituted a minefield security and maintenance programme in the area of separation to identify and mark all minefields.

The Secretary-General observed that, despite the quiet in the Israel-Syria sector, the situation in the Middle East continued to be potentially dangerous and was likely to remain so unless and until a comprehensive settlement covering all aspects of the Middle East problem could be reached. He hoped for determined efforts by all concerned to tackle the problem in all its aspects, with a view to arriving at a just and durable peace settlement, as called for by Council resolution 338(1973) [YUN 1973, p. 213]. Stating that he considered the Force's continued presence in the area to be essential, the Secretary-General, with the agreement of both Syria and Israel, recommended that UNDOF's mandate be extended for a further six months, until 30 November 2000 in the first instance and 31 May 2001 in the second.

SECURITY COUNCIL ACTION

On 31 May [meeting 4148], the Security Council unanimously adopted **resolution 1300(2000)**. The draft [S/2000/482] was prepared during consultations among Council members.

The Security Council,

Having considered the report of the Secretary-General of 22 May 2000 on the United Nations Disengagement Observer Force,

Welcoming and encouraging efforts by the United Nations to sensitize peacekeeping personnel in the prevention and control of HIV/AIDS and other communicable diseases,

Decides:

(*a*) To call upon the parties concerned to implement immediately Security Council resolution 338(1973) of 22 October 1973;

(*b*) To renew the mandate of the United Nations Disengagement Observer Force for another period of six months, that is, until 30 November 2000;

(*c*) To request the Secretary-General to submit, at the end of this period, a report on the development in the situation and the measures taken to implement resolution 338(1973).

On 27 November [meeting 4235], the Council unanimously adopted **resolution 1328(2000)**. The draft [S/2000/1124] was prepared during consultations.

The Security Council,

Having considered the report of the Secretary-General of 17 November 2000 on the United Nations Disengagement Observer Force, and reaffirming Security Council resolution 1308(2000) of 17 July 2000,

1. *Calls upon* the parties concerned to implement immediately its resolution 338 (1973) of 22 October 1973;

2. *Decides* to renew the mandate of the United Nations Disengagement Observer Force for another period of six months, that is, until 31 May 2001;

3. *Requests* the Secretary-General to submit, at the end of this period, a report on the development in the situation and the measures taken to implement resolution 338(1973).

After the adoption of each resolution, the President made statements **S/PRST/2000/19** [meeting 4148] and **S/PRST/2000/36** [meeting 4235] on behalf of the Council:

In connection with the resolution just adopted on the renewal of the mandate of the United Nations Disengagement Observer Force, I have been authorized to make the following complementary statement on behalf of the Security Council:

"As is known, the report of the Secretary-General on the United Nations Disengagement Observer Force states, in paragraph 11: 'Despite the present quiet in the Israeli-Syrian sector, the situation in the Middle East continues to be potentially dangerous and is likely to remain so, unless and until a comprehensive settlement covering all aspects of the Middle East problem can be reached.' That statement of the Secretary-General reflects the view of the Security Council."

Financing

Reports of Secretary-General and ACABQ. On 14 January, the Secretary-General presented a report on UNDOF's financial performance for the period 1 July 1998 to 30 June 1999 [A/54/707 & Corr.1]. On 1 February, he also submitted UNDOF's proposed budget for the period 1 July 2000 to 30 June 2001 [A/54/732], totalling $34,946,700 gross ($34,195,300 net), which reflected a 5.1 per cent increase in gross terms compared with the resources approved for the preceding 12 months.

ACABQ's comments and recommendations on the two reports were contained in an April report to the Assembly [A/54/841/Add.1].

GENERAL ASSEMBLY ACTION

On 15 June [meeting 98], the General Assembly, on the recommendation of the Fifth Committee [A/54/896], adopted **resolution 54/266** without vote [agenda item 128 (*a*)].

Financing of the United Nations Disengagement Observer Force

The General Assembly,

Having considered the reports of the Secretary-General on the financing of the United Nations Disengagement Observer Force and the related reports of the Advisory Committee on Administrative and Budgetary Questions,

Recalling Security Council resolution 350(1974) of 31 May 1974, by which the Council established the United Nations Disengagement Observer Force, and the subsequent resolutions by which the Council extended the mandate of the Force, the latest of which was resolution 1300(2000) of 31 May 2000,

Recalling also its resolution 3211 B (XXIX) of 29 November 1974 on the financing of the United Nations

Emergency Force and of the United Nations Disengagement Observer Force, and its subsequent resolutions thereon, the latest of which was resolution 53/226 of 8 June 1999,

Reaffirming that the costs of the United Nations Disengagement Observer Force are expenses of the Organization to be borne by Member States in accordance with Article 17, paragraph 2, of the Charter of the United Nations,

Recalling its previous decisions regarding the fact that, in order to meet the expenditures caused by the Force, a different procedure is required from that applied to meet expenditures of the regular budget of the United Nations,

Taking into account the fact that the economically more developed countries are in a position to make relatively larger contributions and that the economically less developed countries have a relatively limited capacity to contribute towards such an operation,

Bearing in mind the special responsibilities of the States permanent members of the Security Council, as indicated in General Assembly resolution 1874(S-IV) of 27 June 1963, in the financing of such operations,

Noting with appreciation that voluntary contributions have been made to the Force,

Mindful of the fact that it is essential to provide the Force with the necessary financial resources to enable it to fulfil its responsibilities under the relevant resolutions of the Security Council,

Concerned that the surplus balances in the Special Account for the United Nations Disengagement Observer Force have been used to meet expenses of the Force in order to compensate for the lack of income resulting from non-payment and late payment by Member States of their contributions,

Bearing in mind the reported hardships incurred by the local staff upon relocation of the headquarters of the Force from Damascus to Camp Faouar,

1. *Notes* that some of the concerns regarding the improvement of the working conditions of the local staff in the United Nations Disengagement Observer Force have been addressed;

2. *Requests* the Secretary-General to continue the process of improving the working conditions of the local staff, including by making allowance for difficulties resulting from the relocation of the headquarters of the Force from Damascus to Camp Faouar, through mutual and fruitful dialogue;

3. *Takes note* of the status of contributions to the Force as at 30 April 2000, including the contributions outstanding in the amount of 17 million United States dollars, representing some 1.4 per cent of the total assessed contributions from the inception of the Force to the period ending 31 May 2000, notes that some 24 per cent of the Member States have paid their assessed contributions in full, and urges all other Member States concerned, in particular those in arrears, to ensure payment of their outstanding assessed contributions;

4. *Expresses its appreciation* to those Member States which have paid their assessed contributions in full;

5. *Expresses concern* about the financial situation with regard to peacekeeping activities, in particular as regards the reimbursements to troop contributors that bear additional burdens owing to overdue payments by Member States of their assessments;

6. *Urges* all other Member States to make every possible effort to ensure payment of their assessed contributions to the Force in full and on time;

7. *Expresses concern* at the delay experienced by the Secretary-General in deploying and providing adequate resources to some recent peacekeeping missions, in particular those in Africa;

8. *Emphasizes* that all future and existing peacekeeping missions shall be given equal and non-discriminatory treatment in respect of financial and administrative arrangements;

9. *Also emphasizes* that all peacekeeping missions shall be provided with adequate resources for the effective and efficient discharge of their respective mandates;

10. *Requests* the Secretary-General to make the fullest possible use of facilities and equipment at the United Nations Logistics Base at Brindisi, Italy, in order to minimize the costs of procurement for the Force, and for this purpose requests the Secretary-General to speed up the implementation of the asset management system at all peacekeeping missions in accordance with General Assembly resolution 52/1 A of 15 October 1997;

11. *Endorses* the conclusions and recommendations contained in the report of the Advisory Committee on Administrative and Budgetary Questions, and requests the Secretary-General to ensure their full implementation;

12. *Requests* the Secretary-General to take all necessary action to ensure that the Force is administered with a maximum of efficiency and economy;

13. *Also requests* the Secretary-General, in order to reduce the cost of employing General Service staff, to continue efforts to recruit local staff for the Force against General Service posts, commensurate with the requirements of the Force;

14. *Decides* to appropriate to the Special Account for the United Nations Disengagement Observer Force the amount of 36,975,496 dollars gross (35,924,037 dollars net) for the maintenance of the Force for the period from 1 July 2000 to 30 June 2001, inclusive of the amount of 1,754,501 dollars gross (1,484,675 dollars net) for the support account for peacekeeping operations and the amount of 274,295 dollars gross (244,062 dollars net) for the United Nations Logistics Base;

15. *Decides also*, as an ad hoc arrangement, to apportion among Member States the amount of 36,975,496 dollars gross (35,924,037 dollars net) for the period from 1 July 2000 to 30 June 2001, at a monthly rate of 3,081,291 dollars gross (2,993,670 dollars net), in accordance with the composition of groups set out in paragraphs 3 and 4 of General Assembly resolution 43/232 of 1 March 1989, as adjusted by the Assembly in its resolutions 44/192 B of 21 December 1989, 45/269 of 27 August 1991, 46/198 A of 20 December 1991, 47/218 A of 23 December 1992, 49/249 A of 20 July 1995, 49/249 B of 14 September 1995, 50/224 of 11 April 1996, 51/218 A to C of 18 December 1996 and 52/230 of 31 March 1998 and its decisions 48/472 A of 23 December 1993, 50/451 B of 23 December 1995 and 54/456 to 54/458 of 23 December 1999, and taking into account the scale of assessments for the year 2000, as set out in its resolutions 52/215 A of 22 December 1997 and 54/237 A of 23 December 1999, and for the

year 2001, subject to the decision of the Security Council to extend the mandate of the Force;

16. *Decides further* that, in accordance with the provisions of its resolution 973(X) of 15 December 1955, there shall be set off against the apportionment among Member States, as provided for in paragraph 15 above, their respective share in the Tax Equalization Fund of the estimated staff assessment income of 1,051,459 dollars approved for the Force for the period from 1 July 2000 to 30 June 2001;

17. *Decides* that, for Member States that have fulfilled their financial obligations to the Force, there shall be set off against the apportionment, as provided for in paragraph 15 above, their respective share in the unencumbered balance of 1,737,600 dollars gross (1,590,300 dollars net) in respect of the period from 1 July 1998 to 30 June 1999;

18. *Decides also* that, for Member States that have not fulfilled their financial obligations to the Force, their share of the unencumbered balance of 1,737,600 dollars gross (1,590,300 dollars net) in respect of the period from 1 July 1998 to 30 June 1999 shall be set off against their outstanding obligations;

19. *Decides further,* pursuant to the provisions of paragraph 13 of its resolution 53/226, to credit back to Member States the amount of 4,022,162 dollars during the fifth-fourth session of the General Assembly, according to the procedures set out in paragraphs 15 to 18 above, the net surplus balance of 8,022,162 dollars held in the suspense account for the Force;

20. *Emphasizes* that no peacekeeping mission shall be financed by borrowing funds from other active peacekeeping missions;

21. *Encourages* the Secretary-General to continue to take additional measures to ensure the safety and security of all personnel under the auspices of the United Nations participating in the Force;

22. *Invites* voluntary contributions to the Force in cash and in the form of services and supplies acceptable to the Secretary-General, to be administered, as appropriate, in accordance with the procedure and practices established by the General Assembly;

23. *Decides* to include in the provisional agenda of its fifty-fifth session, under the item entitled "Financing of the United Nations peacekeeping forces in the Middle East", the sub-item entitled "United Nations Disengagement Observer Force".

On 23 December, the Assembly decided that the Fifth Committee would continue consideration of the item on the financing of UNDOF at the resumed fifty-fifth (2001) session (**decision 55/455**).

By **decision 55/458** of the same date, the Assembly decided that the agenda item "Financing of the United Nations peacekeeping forces in the Middle East" would remain for consideration during the resumed fifty-fifth session.

Chapter VII

Disarmament

In 2000, differences among Member States persisted on various disarmament issues. The Conference on Disarmament remained unable to take any action on the agenda items during its 2000 session due to continuing disagreement on what would constitute a balanced programme of work, especially regarding nuclear disarmament and the prevention of an arms race in outer space. The Disarmament Commission, in view of its inability to achieve consensus between 1997 and 1999 on the agenda and objectives of a fourth special session of the General Assembly devoted to disarmament, considered in 2000 ways and means to achieve nuclear disarmament and practical confidence-building measures in the field of conventional arms. On the positive side, the 2000 Review Conference of the Parties to the 1968 Treaty on the Non-Proliferation of Nuclear Weapons broke new ground by identifying practical steps for the systematic pursuit of global nuclear disarmament. Those steps included the unequivocal commitment by nuclear-weapon States, for the first time, to the total elimination of their nuclear arsenals.

At the bilateral level, the Russian Federation ratified the 1993 Treaty with the United States on the Further Reduction and Limitation of Strategic Offensive Arms (START II) and its related 1997 agreements on anti-missile defence. During the year, the two parties held further discussions on START III and issues relating to the 1972 Anti-Ballistic Missile Treaty.

In May, the Secretary-General and the Executive Secretary of the Preparatory Commission for the Comprehensive Nuclear-Test-Ban Treaty Organization signed an agreement to regulate the relationship between the two organizations, establishing a formal working relationship between them. Following a request of the majority of ratifying States party to the 1996 Comprehensive Nuclear-Test-Ban Treaty, the Secretary-General decided to convene a second conference in 2001 to facilitate the Treaty's entry into force.

The Ad Hoc Group of the States Parties to the 1971 Convention on the Prohibition of the Development, Production and Stockpiling of Bacteriological (Biological) and Toxin Weapons and on Their Destruction continued efforts to strengthen the Convention through the development of a protocol on verification and confidence-building measures. The Organization for the Prohibition of Chemical Weapons continued efforts to achieve the objective and purpose of the 1993 Convention on the Prohibition of the Development, Production, Stockpiling and Use of Chemical Weapons and on Their Destruction.

The Preparatory Committee for the 2001 UN Conference on the Illicit Trade in Small Arms and Light Weapons in All Its Aspects held its first session in February/March in New York, during which views on the work of the Conference were expressed at the national, subregional and regional levels. In March, the Security Council recognized that effective action to curb the illegal flow of small arms into areas of conflict could contribute to the success of disarmament. The United Nations Register of Conventional Arms and the standardized instrument of international reporting of military expenditures continued to contribute to building transparency in military matters.

Regarding anti-personnel mines, the Second Meeting of the States Parties to the 1997 Convention on the Prohibition of the Use, Stockpiling, Production and Transfer of Anti-personnel Mines and on Their Destruction took place in September, and the States parties to the 1996 amended Protocol on the Use of Mines, Booby Traps and Other Devices (Protocol II) to the 1980 Convention on Prohibitions or Restrictions on the Use of Certain Conventional Weapons Which May Be Deemed to Be Excessively Injurious or to Have Indiscriminate Effects held their Second Annual Conference in December.

UN role in disarmament

UN machinery

Disarmament issues before the United Nations in 2000 were addressed mainly through the General Assembly and its First (Disarmament and International Security) Committee, the Disarmament Commission (a deliberative body) and the Conference on Disarmament (a multilateral negotiating forum which met in Geneva).

The Department for Disarmament Affairs (DDA) of the UN Secretariat continued to support the work of Member States and treaty bodies, to service the Advisory Board on Disarmament Matters and to administer the UN disarmament fellowship programme.

On 23 December, the General Assembly decided that the item entitled "General and complete disarmament" would remain for consideration at its resumed fifty-fifth (2001) session (**decision 55/458**).

UN Millennium Assembly

The Secretary-General, in his March report to the Millennium Assembly [A/54/2000] (see p. 55), noted that small arms and light weapons and nuclear weapons were of special concern. Pointing out that there was still no global non-proliferation regime to limit the spread of small arms, he urged serious action by Member States to curtail the illicit traffic in those weapons. Regarding nuclear weapons, the Secretary-General proposed a major international conference that would help identify ways of eliminating them.

In August [A/54/959], the Secretariat transmitted the final document of the Millennium Forum (see p. 66), urging the United Nations and interested Governments to draft a proposal for global disarmament for discussion in a fourth special session of the General Assembly on disarmament, specifically aimed at, among other measures, abolishing nuclear weapons.

Fourth special session devoted to disarmament

Pursuant to General Assembly resolution 54/54 U [YUN 1999, p. 457], the Secretary-General, in a July report with later addendum [A/55/130 & Add.1], presented the views of three Member States on the objectives, agenda and timing of the fourth special session of the Assembly devoted to disarmament.

The Assembly had decided, by resolution 51/45 C [YUN 1996, p. 447], to convene the special session in 1999, subject to the emergence of a consensus on its agenda and objectives.

GENERAL ASSEMBLY ACTION

On 20 November [meeting 69], the General Assembly, on the recommendation of the First Committee [A/55/559], adopted **resolution 55/33 M** without vote [agenda item 73 (v)].

Convening of the fourth special session of the General Assembly devoted to disarmament

The General Assembly,

Recalling its resolutions 49/75 I of 15 December 1994, 50/70 F of 12 December 1995, 51/45 C of 10 December 1996, 52/38 F of 9 December 1997, 53/77 AA of 4 December 1998 and 54/54 U of 1 December 1999,

Recalling also that, there being a consensus to do so in each case, three special sessions of the General Assem-

bly devoted to disarmament were held in 1978, 1982 and 1988, respectively,

Bearing in mind the Final Document of the Tenth Special Session of the General Assembly, adopted by consensus at the first special session devoted to disarmament, which included the Declaration, the Programme of Action and the Machinery for disarmament,

Bearing in mind also the objective of general and complete disarmament under effective international control,

Taking note of paragraph 145 of the Final Document of the Twelfth Conference of Heads of State or Government of Non-Aligned Countries, held at Durban, South Africa, from 29 August to 3 September 1998, which supported the convening of the fourth special session of the General Assembly devoted to disarmament, which would offer an opportunity to review, from a perspective more in tune with the current international situation, the most critical aspects of the process of disarmament and to mobilize the international community and public opinion in favour of the elimination of nuclear and other weapons of mass destruction and of the control and reduction of conventional weapons,

Taking note also of the report of the 1999 substantive session of the Disarmament Commission and of the fact that no consensus was reached on the item entitled "Fourth special session of the General Assembly devoted to disarmament",

Desiring to build upon the substantive exchange of views on the fourth special session of the General Assembly devoted to disarmament during the 1999 substantive session of the Disarmament Commission,

Reiterating its conviction that a special session of the General Assembly devoted to disarmament can set the future course of action in the field of disarmament, arms control and related international security matters,

Emphasizing the importance of multilateralism in the process of disarmament, arms control and related international security matters,

Noting that, with the recent accomplishments made by the international community in the field of weapons of mass destruction as well as conventional arms, the following years would be opportune for the international community to start the process of reviewing the state of affairs in the entire field of disarmament and arms control in the post-cold-war era,

Taking note of the report of the Secretary-General regarding the views of States Members of the United Nations on the objectives, agenda and timing of the fourth special session of the General Assembly devoted to disarmament,

1. *Decides,* subject to the emergence of a consensus on its objectives and agenda, to convene the fourth special session of the General Assembly devoted to disarmament;

2. *Requests* the Secretary-General to seek the views of States Members of the United Nations on the objectives, agenda and timing of the special session and to report to the General Assembly at its fifty-sixth session;

3. *Decides* to include in the provisional agenda of its fifty-sixth session the item entitled "Convening of the fourth special session of the General Assembly devoted to disarmament".

Disarmament Commission

The Disarmament Commission, composed of all UN Member States, held five plenary meetings in 2000 (New York, 26 June–7 July) [A/55/42] and organizational meetings on 15 February, 26 June and 1 December.

In 2000, the Commission considered ways and means to achieve nuclear disarmament (see p. 490), and practical confidence-building measures in the field of conventional arms (see p. 523). The Commission adopted consensus texts on those topics following consideration of the items by its working groups.

GENERAL ASSEMBLY ACTION

On 20 November [meeting 69], the General Assembly, on the recommendation of the First Committee [A/55/561], adopted **resolution 55/35 C** without vote [agenda item 75 (a)].

Report of the Disarmament Commission

The General Assembly,

Having considered the report of the Disarmament Commission,

Recalling its resolutions 47/54 A of 9 December 1992, 47/54 G of 8 April 1993, 48/77 A of 16 December 1993, 49/77 A of 15 December 1994, 50/72 D of 12 December 1995, 51/47 B of 10 December 1996, 52/40 B of 9 December 1997, 53/79 A of 4 December 1998 and 54/56 A of 1 December 1999,

Considering the role that the Disarmament Commission has been called upon to play and the contribution that it should make in examining and submitting recommendations on various problems in the field of disarmament and in the promotion of the implementation of the relevant decisions adopted by the General Assembly at its tenth special session,

Bearing in mind its decision 52/492 of 8 September 1998,

1. *Takes note* of the report of the Disarmament Commission;

2. *Reaffirms* the importance of further enhancing dialogue and cooperation among the First Committee, the Disarmament Commission and the Conference on Disarmament;

3. *Also reaffirms* the role of the Disarmament Commission as the specialized, deliberative body within the United Nations multilateral disarmament machinery that allows for in-depth deliberations on specific disarmament issues, leading to the submission of concrete recommendations on those issues;

4. *Requests* the Disarmament Commission to continue its work in accordance with its mandate, as set forth in paragraph 118 of the Final Document of the Tenth Special Session of the General Assembly, and with paragraph 3 of Assembly resolution 37/78 H of 9 December 1982, and to that end to make every effort to achieve specific recommendations on the items of its agenda, taking into account the adopted "Ways and means to enhance the functioning of the Disarmament Commission";

5. *Recommends* that the Disarmament Commission, at its 2000 organizational session, adopt the following items for consideration at its 2001 substantive session:

(a) Ways and means to achieve nuclear disarmament;

(b) Practical confidence-building measures in the field of conventional arms;

6. *Requests* the Disarmament Commission to meet for a period not exceeding three weeks during 2001 and to submit a substantive report to the General Assembly at its fifty-sixth session;

7. *Requests* the Secretary-General to transmit to the Disarmament Commission the annual report of the Conference on Disarmament, together with all the official records of the fifty-fifth session of the General Assembly relating to disarmament matters, and to render all assistance that the Commission may require for implementing the present resolution;

8. *Also requests* the Secretary-General to ensure the full provision to the Disarmament Commission and its subsidiary bodies of interpretation and translation facilities in the official languages and to assign, as a matter of priority, all the necessary resources and services, including verbatim records, to that end;

9. *Decides* to include in the provisional agenda of its fifty-sixth session the item entitled "Report of the Disarmament Commission".

Conference on Disarmament

The Conference on Disarmament, a multilateral negotiating body, held a three-part session in Geneva in 2000 (17 January–24 March, 22 May–7 July and 7 August–22 September) [A/55/27].

The Conference considered the cessation of the nuclear arms race and nuclear disarmament; prevention of nuclear war; prevention of an arms race in outer space; effective international arrangements to assure non-nuclear-weapon States against the use or threat of use of nuclear weapons; new types of weapons of mass destruction and new systems of such weapons; radiological weapons; a comprehensive programme of disarmament; and transparency in armaments.

During the session, successive Presidents of the Conference held intensive consultations with a view to reaching consensus on the programme of work, especially on nuclear disarmament and prevention of an arms race in outer space. At the end of their respective terms of office, two Presidents submitted proposals for the programme of work [CD/1620, CD/1624]. The second, by Celso Amorim (Brazil), which was widely recognized as a basis for further consultations, envisaged the establishment of ad hoc committees with non-negotiating mandates on both issues. In order to secure the agreement of States that had advocated negotiating mandates for either or both ad hoc committees, the Amorim proposal suggested that their establishment be accompanied by a presidential declaration, which, stressing the negotiating character of the Conference and the necessity of understanding the mandates and work of the subsidiary bodies in that light, left open the possibility of reconsidering the mandates of the ad hoc committees if developments in the international strategic scene affecting the security interests of Conference members warranted it.

While several States had submitted proposals, none of them achieved consensus. Thus, the Conference asked its President and the incoming President to hold consultations during the intersessional period and to make recommendations that could help work begin early in 2001.

GENERAL ASSEMBLY ACTION

On 20 November [meeting 69], the General Assembly, on the recommendation of the First Committee [A/55/561], adopted **resolution 55/35 B** without vote [agenda item 75 (b)].

Report of the Conference on Disarmament

The General Assembly,

Having considered the report of the Conference on Disarmament,

Convinced that the Conference on Disarmament, as the single multilateral disarmament negotiating forum of the international community, has the primary role in substantive negotiations on priority questions of disarmament,

Recognizing the need to conduct multilateral negotiations with the aim of reaching concrete agreements,

Recalling, in this respect, that the Conference has a number of urgent and important issues for negotiation,

1. _Reaffirms_ the role of the Conference on Disarmament as the single multilateral disarmament negotiating forum of the international community;

2. _Urges_ the Conference to fulfil that role in the light of the evolving international situation, with a view to making early substantive progress on priority items on its agenda;

3. _Welcomes_ the strong collective interest of the Conference in commencing substantive work as soon as possible during its 2001 session;

4. _Also welcomes_ the decision of the Conference to request its President to conduct jointly with the incoming President intensive consultations during the intersessional period in order to try to achieve this goal, as expressed in paragraph 35 of the report of the Conference;

5. _Encourages_ the Conference to continue the ongoing review of its membership, agenda and methods of work;

6. _Requests_ the Secretary-General to continue to ensure the provision to the Conference of adequate administrative, substantive and conference support services;

7. _Requests_ the Conference to submit a report on its work to the General Assembly at its fifty-sixth session;

8. _Decides_ to include in the provisional agenda of its fifty-sixth session the item entitled "Report of the Conference on Disarmament".

Multilateral disarmament agreements

As at 31 December 2000, the following numbers of States had become parties to the multilateral agreements listed below (in chronological order, with the years in which they were initially signed or opened for signature).

(Geneva) Protocol for the Prohibition of the Use in War of Asphyxiating, Poisonous or Other Gases, and of Bacteriological Methods of Warfare (1925): 132 parties

The Antarctic Treaty (1959): 44 parties

Treaty Banning Nuclear Weapon Tests in the Atmosphere, in Outer Space and under Water (1963): 124 parties

Treaty on Principles Governing the Activities of States in the Exploration and Use of Outer Space, including the Moon and Other Celestial Bodies (1967) [YUN 1966, p. 41, GA res. 2222(XXI), annex]: 97 parties

Treaty for the Prohibition of Nuclear Weapons in Latin America and the Caribbean (Treaty of Tlatelolco) (1967): 38 parties

Treaty on the Non-Proliferation of Nuclear Weapons (1968) [YUN 1968, p. 17, GA res. 2373(XXII), annex]: 187 parties

Treaty on the Prohibition of the Emplacement of Nuclear Weapons and Other Weapons of Mass Destruction on the Seabed and the Ocean Floor and in the Subsoil Thereof (1971) [YUN 1970, p. 18, GA res. 2660(XXV), annex]: 92 parties

Convention on the Prohibition of the Development, Production and Stockpiling of Bacteriological (Biological) and Toxin Weapons and on Their Destruction (1972) [YUN 1971, p. 19, GA res. 2826(XXVI), annex]: 143 parties

Convention on the Prohibition of Military or Any Other Hostile Use of Environmental Modification Techniques (1977) [YUN 1976, p. 45, GA res. 31/72, annex]: 66 parties

Agreement Governing the Activities of States on the Moon and Other Celestial Bodies (1979) [YUN 1979, p. 111, GA res. 34/68, annex]: 9 parties

Convention on Prohibitions or Restrictions on the Use of Certain Conventional Weapons Which May Be Deemed to Be Excessively Injurious or to Have Indiscriminate Effects (1981): 84 parties

South Pacific Nuclear-Free Zone Treaty (Treaty of Rarotonga) (1985): 17 parties

Treaty on Conventional Armed Forces in Europe (CFE Treaty) (1990): 30 parties

Treaty on Open Skies (1992): 24 parties

Convention on the Prohibition of the Development, Production, Stockpiling and Use of Chemical Weapons and on Their Destruction (1993): 141 parties

Treaty on the South-East Asia Nuclear-Weapon-Free Zone (Bangkok Treaty) (1995): 9 parties

African Nuclear-Weapon-Free Zone Treaty (Pelindaba Treaty) (1996): 16 parties

Comprehensive Nuclear-Test-Ban Treaty (1996): 69 parties

Inter-American Convention against the Illicit Manufacturing of and Trafficking in Firearms,

Ammunition, Explosives, and Other Related Materials (1997): 10 parties

Convention on the Prohibition of the Use, Stockpiling, Production and Transfer of Anti-personnel Mines and on Their Destruction (Mine-Ban Convention, formerly known as Ottawa Convention) (1997): 109 parties

Inter-American Convention on Transparency in Conventional Weapons Acquisitions (1999): 1 party

Agreement on Adaptation of the CFE Treaty (1999): 1 party

[*United Nations Disarmament Yearbook*, vol. 25: *2000*, Sales No. E.01.IX.1]

Nuclear disarmament

Non-Proliferation Treaty

In 2000, the number of States parties to the 1968 Treaty on the Non-Proliferation of Nuclear Weapons (NPT), adopted by the General Assembly in resolution 2373(XXII) [YUN 1968, p. 17], remained at 187. NPT entered into force on 5 March 1970.

NPT Review Conference

The 2000 Review Conference of the Parties to the Treaty on the Non-Proliferation of Nuclear Weapons (New York, 24 April–19 May) [NPT/CONF.2000/28 (Parts I-III)] was held to review the Treaty's operation, as provided for in article VIII, paragraph 3, and taking into account the decisions of the 1995 Review and Extension Conference [YUN 1995, p. 189], which extended NPT indefinitely, strengthened its review process and provided for further review conferences at five-year intervals. Previous quinquennial review conferences had been held in 1975 [YUN 1975, p. 27], 1980 [YUN 1980, p. 51], 1985 [YUN 1985, p. 56], 1990 [YUN 1990, p. 50] and 1995 [YUN 1995, p. 189].

The Preparatory Committee for the 2000 Conference had met in 1997 [YUN 1997, p. 478], 1998 [YUN 1998, p. 509] and 1999 [YUN 1999, p. 473].

States parties participating in the Conference numbered 158. Representatives of the United Nations and the International Atomic Energy Agency (IAEA) also participated, as well as a number of non–States parties, intergovernmental organizations and agencies, research institutes and non-governmental organizations (NGOs).

The Conference established three Main Committees, a Drafting Committee and a Credentials Committee. Substantive issues were discussed largely by the Main Committees, including a re-

view of the implementation of the Treaty's provisions on nuclear non-proliferation, disarmament and international security, including the security of non-nuclear-weapon States; nuclear-weapon-free zones; nuclear safeguards; and the peaceful uses of nuclear energy.

On 19 May, the Conference adopted by consensus a Final Document, which reaffirmed the central role of NPT in ongoing global efforts to strengthen nuclear non-proliferation and disarmament, and reflected consensus language dealing with all major aspects of NPT. The Final Document incorporated a set of practical steps for efforts to implement article VI (cessation of the nuclear arms race and disarmament). The most significant of those steps was the unequivocal commitment by nuclear-weapon States, for the first time, to totally eliminate their nuclear arsenals.

GENERAL ASSEMBLY ACTION

On 20 November [meeting 69], the General Assembly, on the recommendation of the First Committee [A/55/559], adopted **resolution 55/33 D** by recorded vote (163-1-3) [agenda item 73].

2000 Review Conference of the Parties to the Treaty on the Non-Proliferation of Nuclear Weapons

The General Assembly,

Recalling the decision on strengthening the review process for the Treaty on the Non-Proliferation of Nuclear Weapons of the 1995 Review and Extension Conference of the Parties to the Treaty, in which it was agreed that Review Conferences should continue to be held every five years and that, accordingly, the next Review Conference should be held in the year 2000,

Recalling also its resolutions 50/70 Q of 12 December 1995 and 51/45 A of 10 December 1996,

Recalling further that the parties to the Treaty on the Non-Proliferation of Nuclear Weapons met in New York from 24 April to 19 May 2000 to review the operation of the Treaty, as provided for in its article VIII, paragraph 3, taking into account the decisions and the resolution adopted by the 1995 Review and Extension Conference,

Welcomes the adoption by consensus on 19 May 2000 of the Final Document of the 2000 Review Conference of the Parties to the Treaty on the Non-Proliferation of Nuclear Weapons, including in particular the documents entitled "Review of the operation of the Treaty, taking into account the decisions and the resolution adopted by the 1995 Review and Extension Conference" and "Improving the effectiveness of the strengthened review process for the Treaty".

RECORDED VOTE ON RESOLUTION 55/33 D:

In favour: Albania, Algeria, Andorra, Angola, Antigua and Barbuda, Argentina, Armenia, Australia, Austria, Azerbaijan, Bahamas, Bahrain, Bangladesh, Barbados, Belarus, Belgium, Belize, Benin, Bhutan, Bolivia, Bosnia and Herzegovina, Botswana, Brazil, Brunei Darussalam, Bulgaria, Burkina Faso, Burundi, Cambodia, Cameroon, Canada, Cape Verde, Chile, China, Colombia, Costa Rica, Côte d'Ivoire, Croatia, Cyprus, Czech Republic, Denmark, Djibouti, Dominican Republic, Ecuador, Egypt, El Salvador, Equatorial Guinea, Eritrea, Estonia, Ethiopia, Fiji, Finland, France, Gabon, Gambia, Georgia, Germany, Ghana, Greece, Grenada, Guatemala, Guinea, Guyana, Haiti, Honduras, Hungary, Iceland, Indonesia, Iran, Ireland, Italy,

Jamaica, Japan, Jordan, Kazakhstan, Kenya, Kuwait, Kyrgyzstan, Lao People's Democratic Republic, Latvia, Lebanon, Lesotho, Libyan Arab Jamahiriya, Liechtenstein, Lithuania, Luxembourg, Madagascar, Malawi, Malaysia, Maldives, Mali, Malta, Marshall Islands, Mauritius, Mexico, Micronesia, Monaco, Mongolia, Morocco, Mozambique, Myanmar, Namibia, Nauru, Nepal, Netherlands, New Zealand, Nicaragua, Nigeria, Norway, Oman, Panama, Papua New Guinea, Paraguay, Peru, Philippines, Poland, Portugal, Qatar, Republic of Korea, Republic of Moldova, Romania, Russian Federation, Saint Lucia, Saint Vincent and the Grenadines, Samoa, San Marino, Saudi Arabia, Senegal, Sierra Leone, Singapore, Slovakia, Slovenia, Solomon Islands, South Africa, Spain, Sri Lanka, Sudan, Suriname, Swaziland, Sweden, Syrian Arab Republic, Tajikistan, Thailand, The former Yugoslav Republic of Macedonia, Togo, Tonga, Trinidad and Tobago, Tunisia, Turkey, Turkmenistan, Uganda, Ukraine, United Arab Emirates, United Kingdom, United Republic of Tanzania, United States, Uruguay, Uzbekistan, Vanuatu, Venezuela, Viet Nam, Yemen, Zambia, Zimbabwe.

Against: India.

Abstaining: Cuba, Israel, Pakistan.

Conference on Disarmament

In 2000, disagreements over the mandate of a potential subsidiary body to deal with nuclear disarmament prevented the Conference on Disarmament from undertaking any substantive work on that issue, despite possible compromises put forward by two Presidents of the Conference (see p. 485).

Progress was also blocked because some States of the Movement of Non-Aligned Countries insisted on linking nuclear disarmament to the negotiation of a treaty for the prohibition of the production of fissile material for military purposes and the prevention of an arms race in outer space, to which other delegations disagreed.

Differences were exacerbated by conflicting positions in the controversy over missile-related issues, with regard to the 1972 Anti-Ballistic Missile (ABM) Treaty (see p. 498), which intensified during the year.

Fissile material

During the year, the Conference on Disarmament was not able to establish the ad hoc committee on the prohibition of the production of fissile material for nuclear weapons or other explosive devices due to the persisting impasse regarding the adoption of a comprehensive programme of work (see p. 485). Calls from Eastern and Western European countries for work to begin on the issue were resisted by the non-aligned countries, which insisted that the programme of work should be adopted as a whole, and should include other States' priorities as well.

The 2000 NPT Review Conference had urged the Conference on Disarmament to agree on a work programme under which it should commence immediate negotiations on a non-discriminatory, multilateral and internationally and effectively verifiable treaty banning the production of fissile material for nuclear weapons and other nuclear explosive devices, with a view to concluding negotiations within five years.

The General Assembly, in 2000, returned to the question of the establishment of an ad hoc committee to negotiate a treaty banning the production of fissile material for nuclear weapons and other nuclear explosive devices, which it had previously considered in resolutions 48/75 L [YUN 1993, p. 118] and 53/77 I [YUN 1998, p. 493].

GENERAL ASSEMBLY ACTION

On 20 November [meeting 69], the General Assembly, on the recommendation of the First Committee [A/55/559], adopted **resolution 55/33 Y** without vote [agenda item 73].

The Conference on Disarmament decision (CD/1547) of 11 August 1998 to establish, under item 1 of its agenda entitled "Cessation of the nuclear arms race and nuclear disarmament", an ad hoc committee to negotiate, on the basis of the report of the Special Coordinator (CD/1299) and the mandate contained therein, a non-discriminatory, multilateral and internationally and effectively verifiable treaty banning the production of fissile material for nuclear weapons or other nuclear explosive devices

The General Assembly,

Recalling its resolutions 48/75 L of 16 December 1993 and 53/77 I of 4 December 1998,

Convinced that a non-discriminatory, multilateral and internationally and effectively verifiable treaty banning the production of fissile material for nuclear weapons or other nuclear explosive devices would be a significant contribution to nuclear disarmament and nuclear non-proliferation,

Recalling the 1998 report of the Conference on Disarmament, in which, inter alia, the Conference records that, in proceeding to take a decision on this matter, that decision is without prejudice to any further decisions on the establishment of further subsidiary bodies under agenda item 1 and that intensive consultations will be pursued to seek the views of the members of the Conference on Disarmament on appropriate methods and approaches for dealing with agenda item 1, taking into consideration all proposals and views in that respect,

1. *Recalls* the decision by the Conference on Disarmament to establish, under item 1 of its agenda entitled "Cessation of the nuclear arms race and nuclear disarmament", an ad hoc committee which shall negotiate, on the basis of the report of the Special Coordinator and the mandate contained therein, a non-discriminatory, multilateral and internationally and effectively verifiable treaty banning the production of fissile material for nuclear weapons or other nuclear explosive devices;

2. *Urges* the Conference on Disarmament to agree on a programme of work that includes the immediate commencement of negotiations on such a treaty.

Security assurances

The Conference on Disarmament addressed the issue of security assurances for non-nuclear-weapon States against the use or threat of use of nuclear weapons in the context of the development of its programme of work. All proposals in that regard concurred with the establishment of an ad hoc committee to negotiate with a view to reaching agreement on effective international arrangements to assure non-nuclear-weapon States against the use or threat of use of nuclear weapons. However, the ad hoc committee was not established due to the lack of consensus on a comprehensive programme of work (see p. 485), which had also prevented action on the issue in 1999 [YUN 1999, p. 460].

GENERAL ASSEMBLY ACTION

On 20 November [meeting 69], the General Assembly, on the recommendation of the First Committee [A/55/557], adopted **resolution 55/31** by recorded vote (111-0-54) [agenda item 71].

Conclusion of effective international arrangements to assure non-nuclear-weapon States against the use or threat of use of nuclear weapons

The General Assembly,

Bearing in mind the need to allay the legitimate concern of the States of the world with regard to ensuring lasting security for their peoples,

Convinced that nuclear weapons pose the greatest threat to mankind and to the survival of civilization,

Welcoming the progress achieved in recent years in both nuclear and conventional disarmament,

Noting that, despite recent progress in the field of nuclear disarmament, further efforts are necessary towards the achievement of general and complete disarmament under effective international control,

Convinced that nuclear disarmament and the complete elimination of nuclear weapons are essential to remove the danger of nuclear war,

Determined to abide strictly by the relevant provisions of the Charter of the United Nations on the non-use of force or threat of force,

Recognizing that the independence, territorial integrity and sovereignty of non-nuclear-weapon States need to be safeguarded against the use or threat of use of force, including the use or threat of use of nuclear weapons,

Considering that, until nuclear disarmament is achieved on a universal basis, it is imperative for the international community to develop effective measures and arrangements to ensure the security of non-nuclear-weapon States against the use or threat of use of nuclear weapons from any quarter,

Recognizing that effective measures and arrangements to assure non-nuclear-weapon States against the use or threat of use of nuclear weapons can contribute positively to the prevention of the spread of nuclear weapons,

Bearing in mind paragraph 59 of the Final Document of the Tenth Special Session of the General Assembly, the first special session devoted to disarmament, in which it urged the nuclear-weapon States to pursue efforts to conclude, as appropriate, effective arrangements to assure non-nuclear-weapon States against the use or threat of use of nuclear weapons, and desirous of promoting the implementation of the relevant provisions of the Final Document,

Recalling the relevant parts of the special report of the Committee on Disarmament[a] submitted to the General Assembly at its twelfth special session, the second special session devoted to disarmament, and of the special report of the Conference on Disarmament submitted to the Assembly at its fifteenth special session, the third special session devoted to disarmament, as well as the report of the Conference on its 1992 session,

Recalling also paragraph 12 of the Declaration of the 1980s as the Second Disarmament Decade, contained in the annex to its resolution 35/46 of 3 December 1980, which states, inter alia, that all efforts should be exerted by the Committee on Disarmament urgently to negotiate with a view to reaching agreement on effective international arrangements to assure non-nuclear-weapon States against the use or threat of use of nuclear weapons,

Noting the in-depth negotiations undertaken in the Conference on Disarmament and its Ad Hoc Committee on Effective International Arrangements to Assure Non-Nuclear-Weapon States against the Use or Threat of Use of Nuclear Weapons, with a view to reaching agreement on this question,

Taking note of the proposals submitted under the item in the Conference on Disarmament, including the drafts of an international convention,

Taking note also of the relevant decision of the Twelfth Conference of Heads of State or Government of Non-Aligned Countries, held at Durban, South Africa, from 29 August to 3 September 1998, as well as the relevant recommendations of the Organization of the Islamic Conference,

Taking note further of the unilateral declarations made by all the nuclear-weapon States on their policies of non-use or non-threat of use of nuclear weapons against the non-nuclear-weapon States,

Noting the support expressed in the Conference on Disarmament and in the General Assembly for the elaboration of an international convention to assure non-nuclear-weapon States against the use or threat of use of nuclear weapons, as well as the difficulties pointed out in evolving a common approach acceptable to all,

Taking note of Security Council resolution 984(1995) of 11 April 1995 and the views expressed on it,

Recalling its relevant resolutions adopted in previous years, in particular resolutions 45/54 of 4 December 1990, 46/32 of 6 December 1991, 47/50 of 9 December 1992, 48/73 of 16 December 1993, 49/73 of 15 December 1994, 50/68 of 12 December 1995, 51/43 of 10 December 1996, 52/36 of 9 December 1997, 53/75 of 4 December 1998 and 54/52 of 1 December 1999,

1. *Reaffirms* the urgent need to reach an early agreement on effective international arrangements to assure non-nuclear-weapon States against the use or threat of use of nuclear weapons;

2. *Notes with satisfaction* that in the Conference on Disarmament there is no objection, in principle, to the idea of an international convention to assure non-nuclear-weapon States against the use or threat of use of nuclear weapons, although the difficulties with regard to evolving a common approach acceptable to all have also been pointed out;

3. *Appeals* to all States, especially the nuclear-weapon States, to work actively towards an early agreement on a common approach and, in particular, on a

common formula that could be included in an international instrument of a legally binding character;

4. *Recommends* that further intensive efforts be devoted to the search for such a common approach or common formula and that the various alternative approaches, including, in particular, those considered in the Conference on Disarmament, be further explored in order to overcome the difficulties;

5. *Recommends also* that the Conference on Disarmament actively continue intensive negotiations with a view to reaching early agreement and concluding effective international arrangements to assure the non-nuclear-weapon States against the use or threat of use of nuclear weapons, taking into account the widespread support for the conclusion of an international convention and giving consideration to any other proposals designed to secure the same objective;

6. *Decides* to include in the provisional agenda of its fifty-sixth session the item entitled "Conclusion of effective international arrangements to assure non-nuclear-weapon States against the use or threat of use of nuclear weapons".

ᵃRedesignated the Conference on Disarmament as from 7 February 1984.

RECORDED VOTE ON RESOLUTION 55/31:

In favour: Algeria, Angola, Antigua and Barbuda, Armenia, Azerbaijan, Bahamas, Bahrain, Bangladesh, Barbados, Belarus, Belize, Benin, Bhutan, Botswana, Brazil, Brunei Darussalam, Burkina Faso, Burundi, Cambodia, Cameroon, Cape Verde, Chile, China, Colombia, Costa Rica, Côte d'Ivoire, Cuba, Democratic People's Republic of Korea, Djibouti, Dominican Republic, Ecuador, Egypt, El Salvador, Equatorial Guinea, Eritrea, Ethiopia, Fiji, Gabon, Ghana, Grenada, Guatemala, Guinea, Guyana, Haiti, Honduras, India, Indonesia, Iran, Jamaica, Japan, Jordan, Kazakhstan, Kenya, Kuwait, Kyrgyzstan, Lao People's Democratic Republic, Lebanon, Lesotho, Libyan Arab Jamahiriya, Madagascar, Malawi, Malaysia, Maldives, Mali, Mauritius, Mexico, Mongolia, Morocco, Mozambique, Myanmar, Namibia, Nauru, Nepal, Nicaragua, Nigeria, Oman, Pakistan, Panama, Papua New Guinea, Paraguay, Peru, Philippines, Qatar, Saint Lucia, Saint Vincent and the Grenadines, Samoa, Saudi Arabia, Senegal, Sierra Leone, Singapore, Solomon Islands, Sri Lanka, Sudan, Swaziland, Syrian Arab Republic, Tajikistan, Thailand, Togo, Trinidad and Tobago, Tunisia, Turkmenistan, Uganda, Ukraine, United Arab Emirates, United Republic of Tanzania, Uruguay, Uzbekistan, Venezuela, Viet Nam, Yemen, Zambia.

Against: None.

Abstaining: Albania, Andorra, Argentina, Australia, Austria, Belgium, Bolivia, Bosnia and Herzegovina, Bulgaria, Canada, Croatia, Cyprus, Czech Republic, Denmark, Estonia, Finland, France, Georgia, Germany, Greece, Hungary, Iceland, Ireland, Israel, Italy, Latvia, Liechtenstein, Lithuania, Luxembourg, Malta, Marshall Islands, Micronesia, Monaco, Netherlands, New Zealand, Norway, Poland, Portugal, Republic of Korea, Republic of Moldova, Romania, Russian Federation, San Marino, Slovakia, Slovenia, South Africa, Spain, Sweden, The former Yugoslav Republic of Macedonia, Tonga, Turkey, United Kingdom, United States, Vanuatu.

Disarmament Commission

In July [A/55/42], Working Group I of the Disarmament Commission considered the Chairman's working paper on ways and means to achieve nuclear disarmament. Following discussions on elements contained in the paper and proposals made by delegations, the Group adopted by consensus its report on the item, annexed to which was the Chairman's paper.

The Chairman's paper discussed the interrelationship between nuclear disarmament and international peace and security, existing mechanisms dealing with nuclear disarmament, and ways and means to achieve nuclear disarmament.

It reviewed achievements, current developments and emerging initiatives. The Chairman's conclusions and recommendations were to be finalized in future sessions of the Working Group.

START and other bilateral agreements and unilateral measures

The United States and the Russian Federation continued to implement the 1991 Treaty on the Reduction and Limitation of Strategic Offensive Arms (START I) [YUN 1991, p. 34], which entered into force on 5 December 1994 [YUN 1994, p. 145], by reducing their nuclear arms stockpiles.

A major development in 2000 was the approval by the Russian Duma, on 14 April [A/55/64], of the ratification of the 1993 START II Treaty [YUN 1993, p. 117], and of related 1997 agreements on antimissile defence. On 4 May, Russia enacted legislation to implement the Treaty. Although the United States had ratified START II in 1996 [YUN 1996, p. 465], the Treaty would enter into force only after its 1997 Protocol was also ratified, shifting the deadline for reductions from January 2003 to 31 December 2007.

During the year, further discussions on START III and issues relating to the 1972 ABM Treaty took place between the Russian Federation and the United States. However, no progress was reported, especially on resolving the contentious issues of the announced intention in 1999 [YUN 1999, p. 469] of the United States to develop a national missile defence (NMD) system, as well as its efforts to amend the ABM Treaty. There were also no major breakthroughs on those issues during a summit meeting (Moscow, 3-4 June) [A/55/87, CD/1617] between Acting President Vladimir V. Putin of the Russian Federation and President William J. Clinton of the United States. Nonetheless, the two States issued a Joint Statement on Principles of Strategic Stability, in which they agreed to maintain strategic nuclear stability and reaffirmed their commitment to strengthening the ABM Treaty as a cornerstone of that stability. They also announced their intention to intensify discussions on START III. The summit also produced agreements on the management and disposal of weapons-grade plutonium and on the establishment of a joint centre for the exchange of data (JDEC) from early warning systems and notifications of missile launches. As a follow-up to JDEC, on 16 December [A/55/807], both parties signed a Memorandum of Understanding in Brussels on notifications of missile launches.

A proposal put forward on 24 May by United States presidential candidate George W. Bush called for a broader missile defence system that would protect the United States and its allies, while also calling for a significant cut in the United States nuclear arsenal. On 13 November, President Putin proposed that the Russian Federation and the United States could each reduce their respective nuclear warheads to 1,500 by 2008.

Communications. In March [A/54/794-S/2000/210], New Zealand transmitted a resolution on nuclear disarmament adopted by its Parliament, calling on Member States to conclude negotiations leading to nuclear disarmament.

On 6 June [A/54/917-S/2000/580], South Africa, as Chairman of the Coordinating Bureau of the Movement of Non-Aligned Countries, transmitted the final document of the Thirteenth Ministerial Conference of the Movement of Non-Aligned Countries (Cartagena, Colombia, 8-9 April). The Ministers, among other things, called for an international conference to arrive at an agreement on a phased programme for the complete elimination of all nuclear weapons.

In June [A/55/93], the Russian Federation transmitted a statement by the heads of State of the Commonwealth of Independent States on maintaining strategic stability, adopted at a meeting of the Council of Heads of State of the Commonwealth (Moscow, 21 June). Welcoming the ratification by the Russian Federation of START II (see p. 490), the heads of State declared their commitment to strengthening strategic stability and international security.

In September [A/C.1/55/3], the Foreign Ministers of the New Agenda Coalition Countries (Brazil, Egypt, Ireland, Mexico, New Zealand, South Africa, Sweden) transmitted the text of a communiqué on their joint initiative "Towards a nuclear-weapon-free world: the need for a new agenda". They stressed that the total elimination of nuclear weapons must be achieved through accelerated negotiations on all fronts.

Reports of Secretary-General. In August [A/55/217], the Secretary-General described action taken to implement General Assembly resolution 54/54 G [YUN 1999, p. 466], entitled "Towards a nuclear-weapon-free world: the need for a new agenda".

The Secretary-General said that despite some progress in bilateral and unilateral nuclear weapons reduction, the international community remained deeply concerned at the persisting risk posed to humanity by the possible use of nuclear weapons. He recalled that his March report to the Millennium Assembly [A/54/2000] (see p. 55) stressed the need for reaffirmation of political commitment to reduce the dangers posed by nuclear weapons and their further proliferation. The Secretary-General noted the adoption of the Final Document of the 2000 NPT Review Conference, particularly the steps to implement article VI (see p. 487).

The report contained the views of IAEA, the South Pacific Forum secretariat, as depositary of the 1985 South Pacific Nuclear-Free Zone Treaty, the provisional technical secretariat of the Preparatory Commission for the Comprehensive Nuclear-Test-Ban Treaty Organization and Thailand, as depositary of the 1995 Treaty on the South-East Asia Nuclear-Weapon-Free Zone.

Also in August [A/55/324], the Secretary-General, pursuant to General Assembly resolution 54/54 K [YUN 1999, p. 468], presented the views of the Advisory Board on Disarmament Matters (see p. 536) regarding measures that would significantly reduce the risk of nuclear war. There was broad agreement that emphasis should be placed on de-alerting nuclear weapons, reviewing nuclear doctrines, eliminating tactical nuclear weapons and creating a climate for implementing nuclear disarmament. Other measures received varying degrees of support.

In response to General Assembly resolution 54/54 P [YUN 1999, p. 464], the Secretary-General, on 3 October [A/55/444], stated that despite some progress towards the reduction of nuclear weapons, the time factor was crucial when addressing the risk that nuclear weapons still posed. He noted the outcome of the 2000 NPT Review Conference, particularly the commitment of nuclear-weapon States to totally eliminate their nuclear arsenals, as well as the commitment of Member States to strive for the elimination of weapons of mass destruction, as expressed in the United Nations Millennium Declaration (see p. 49). The Secretary-General remained concerned, however, that the efforts of the Conference on Disarmament to make progress on nuclear disarmament and other issues had been frustrated by a lack of consensus.

GENERAL ASSEMBLY ACTION

On 20 November [meeting 69], the General Assembly, on the recommendation of the First Committee [A/55/559], adopted a series of resolutions related to nuclear disarmament.

The Assembly adopted **resolution 55/33 R** by recorded vote (155-1-12) [agenda item 73].

A path to the total elimination of nuclear weapons
The General Assembly,

Recalling its resolutions 49/75 H of 15 December 1994, 50/70 C of 12 December 1995, 51/45 G of 10 December 1996, 52/38 K of 9 December 1997, 53/77 U of 4 December 1998 and 54/54 D of 1 December 1999,

Recognizing that the enhancement of international peace and security and the promotion of nuclear disarmament mutually complement and strengthen each other,

Reaffirming the crucial importance of the Treaty on the Non-Proliferation of Nuclear Weapons as the cornerstone of the international regime for nuclear non-proliferation and as an essential foundation for the pursuit of nuclear disarmament,

Recalling the progress made by the nuclear-weapon States in the reduction of their nuclear weapons unilaterally or through negotiation, and the efforts made towards nuclear disarmament and non-proliferation by the international community,

Reaffirming the conviction that further advancement in nuclear disarmament will contribute to consolidating the international regime for nuclear non-proliferation, ensuring international peace and security,

Bearing in mind the recent nuclear tests, as well as the regional situations, which pose a challenge to international efforts to strengthen the global regime for non-proliferation of nuclear weapons,

Taking note of the report of the Tokyo Forum for Nuclear Non-Proliferation and Disarmament, bearing in mind the various views of Member States on the report,

Welcoming the successful adoption of the Final Document of the 2000 Review Conference of the Parties to the Treaty on the Non-Proliferation of Nuclear Weapons, which contains, inter alia, an unequivocal undertaking by the nuclear-weapon States to accomplish the total elimination of their nuclear arsenals, leading to nuclear disarmament to which all States parties are committed under article VI of the Treaty on the Non-Proliferation of Nuclear Weapons,

1. *Reaffirms* the importance of achieving the universality of the Treaty on the Non-Proliferation of Nuclear Weapons, and calls upon States not parties to the Treaty to accede to it as non-nuclear-weapon States without delay and without conditions;

2. *Also reaffirms* the importance for all States parties to the Treaty on the Non-Proliferation of Nuclear Weapons, to fulfil their obligations under the Treaty;

3. *Stresses* the central importance of taking the following practical steps for the systematic and progressive efforts to implement article VI of the Treaty on the Non-Proliferation of Nuclear Weapons, and paragraphs 3 and 4 *(c)* of the decision on principles and objectives for nuclear non-proliferation and disarmament of the 1995 Review and Extension Conference of the Parties to the Treaty:

(a) The early signature and ratification of the Comprehensive Nuclear-Test-Ban Treaty by all States, especially by those States whose ratification is required for its entry into force, with a view to its early entry into force before 2003, as well as a moratorium on nuclear-weapon-test explosions or any other nuclear explosions pending its entry into force;

(b) The immediate commencement of negotiations in the Conference on Disarmament and the conclusion as early as possible before 2005 of a non-discriminatory, multilateral and internationally and effectively verifiable treaty banning the production of fissile material for nuclear weapons or other nuclear explosive devices, in accordance with the report of the Special Coordinator of 1995 and the mandate contained therein, taking into consideration both nuclear disarmament and non-proliferation objectives and, pending its entry into force, a moratorium on the production of fissile material for nuclear weapons;

(c) The establishment of an appropriate subsidiary body of the Conference on Disarmament in the context of establishing a programme of work, with a mandate to deal with nuclear disarmament;

(d) The inclusion of the principle of irreversibility to apply to nuclear disarmament, nuclear and other related arms control and reduction measures;

(e) The early entry into force and full implementation of the Treaty on Further Reduction and Limitation of Strategic Offensive Arms (START II) and the conclusion of START III as soon as possible, while preserving and strengthening the Treaty on the Limitation of Anti-Ballistic Missile Systems of 26 May 1972 between the United States of America and the Union of Soviet Socialist Republics as a cornerstone of strategic stability and as a basis for further reductions of strategic offensive weapons, in accordance with its provisions;

(f) Steps by all nuclear-weapon States leading to nuclear disarmament in a way that promotes international stability, and based on the principle of undiminished security for all:

(i) Further efforts by all nuclear-weapon States to continue to reduce their nuclear arsenals, unilaterally or through negotiation;

(ii) Increased transparency by the nuclear-weapon States with regard to their nuclear weapons capabilities and the implementation of agreements pursuant to article VI of the Treaty on the Non-Proliferation of Nuclear Weapons and as voluntary confidence-building measures to support further progress in nuclear disarmament;

(iii) The further reduction of non-strategic nuclear weapons, based on unilateral initiatives and as an integral part of the nuclear arms reduction and disarmament process;

(iv) Concrete agreed measures to reduce further the operational status of nuclear weapons systems;

(v) A diminishing role for nuclear weapons in security policies so as to minimize the risk that these weapons will ever be used and to facilitate the process of their total elimination;

(vi) The engagement, as soon as appropriate, of all nuclear-weapon States in the process leading to the total elimination of their nuclear weapons;

4. *Recognizes* that the realization of a world free of nuclear weapons will require further steps by the nuclear-weapon States, including:

(a) The continuation of the nuclear disarmament process beyond START III;

(b) Deeper reductions by all nuclear-weapon States, unilaterally or through negotiation, in nuclear weapons in the process of working towards their elimination;

5. *Invites* the nuclear-weapon States to keep the States Members of the United Nations duly informed of the progress or efforts made towards nuclear disarmament;

6. *Welcomes* the ongoing efforts in the dismantlement of nuclear weapons, notes the importance of the safe and effective management of the resultant fissile materials and calls for arrangements by all nuclear-weapon States to place, as soon as practicable, the fissile material designated by each of them as no longer required for military purposes under the International

Atomic Energy Agency or other relevant international verification and arrangements for the disposition of such material for peaceful purposes in order to ensure that such material remains permanently outside military programmes;

7. *Stresses* the importance of further development of the verification capabilities, including International Atomic Energy Agency safeguards, that will be required to provide assurance of compliance with nuclear disarmament agreements for the achievement and maintenance of a nuclear-weapon-free world;

8. *Calls upon* all States to redouble their efforts to prevent the proliferation of nuclear and other weapons of mass destruction, including their means of delivery, confirming and strengthening, if necessary, their policies not to transfer equipment, materials or technology that could contribute to the proliferation of those weapons;

9. *Also calls upon* all States to maintain the highest possible standards of security, safe custody, effective control and physical protection of all materials that could contribute to the proliferation of weapons of mass destruction;

10. *Stresses* the importance of the Model Protocol Additional to the Agreement(s) between State(s) and the International Atomic Energy Agency for the Application of Safeguards with a view to enhancing nuclear non-proliferation, and encourages all States which have not done so to conclude an additional protocol with the International Atomic Energy Agency as soon as possible;

11. *Welcomes* the adoption by the General Conference of the International Atomic Energy Agency on 22 September 2000 of resolution GC(44)/RES/19, which contains elements of a plan of action to promote and facilitate the conclusion and entry into force of safeguards agreements and additional protocols, and calls for the early and full implementation of that resolution;

12. *Encourages* the constructive role played by civil society in promoting nuclear non-proliferation and nuclear disarmament.

RECORDED VOTE ON RESOLUTION 55/33 R:

In favour: Albania, Algeria, Andorra, Angola, Antigua and Barbuda, Argentina, Armenia, Australia, Austria, Azerbaijan, Bahamas, Bahrain, Bangladesh, Barbados, Belarus, Belgium, Belize, Benin, Bolivia, Bosnia and Herzegovina, Botswana, Brazil, Brunei Darussalam, Bulgaria, Burkina Faso, Burundi, Cambodia, Cameroon, Canada, Cape Verde, Chile, Colombia, Costa Rica, Côte d'Ivoire, Croatia, Cyprus, Czech Republic, Denmark, Djibouti, Dominican Republic, Ecuador, El Salvador, Equatorial Guinea, Eritrea, Estonia, Ethiopia, Fiji, Finland, Gabon, Gambia, Georgia, Germany, Ghana, Greece, Grenada, Guatemala, Guinea, Guyana, Haiti, Honduras, Hungary, Iceland, Indonesia, Iran, Ireland, Italy, Jamaica, Japan, Jordan, Kazakhstan, Kenya, Kuwait, Kyrgyzstan, Lao People's Democratic Republic, Latvia, Lebanon, Lesotho, Libyan Arab Jamahiriya, Liechtenstein, Lithuania, Luxembourg, Madagascar, Malawi, Malaysia, Maldives, Mali, Malta, Marshall Islands, Mexico, Micronesia, Mongolia, Morocco, Mozambique, Namibia, Nauru, Nepal, Netherlands, New Zealand, Nicaragua, Nigeria, Norway, Oman, Panama, Papua New Guinea, Paraguay, Peru, Philippines, Poland, Portugal, Qatar, Republic of Korea, Republic of Moldova, Romania, Saint Kitts and Nevis, Saint Lucia, Saint Vincent and the Grenadines, Samoa, San Marino, Saudi Arabia, Senegal, Sierra Leone, Singapore, Slovakia, Slovenia, Solomon Islands, South Africa, Spain, Sri Lanka, Sudan, Suriname, Swaziland, Sweden, Syrian Arab Republic, Tajikistan, Thailand, The former Yugoslav Republic of Macedonia, Togo, Tonga, Trinidad and Tobago, Tunisia, Turkey, Turkmenistan, Uganda, Ukraine, United Arab Emirates, United Kingdom, United Republic of Tanzania, United States, Uruguay, Uzbekistan, Vanuatu, Venezuela, Viet Nam, Zambia, Zimbabwe.

Against: India.

Abstaining: Bhutan, China, Cuba, Democratic People's Republic of Korea, Egypt, France, Israel, Mauritius, Monaco, Myanmar, Pakistan, Russian Federation.

In the First Committee, paragraph 8 was adopted by a recorded vote of 137 to 2, with 11 abstentions. The text as a whole was adopted by a recorded vote of 144 to 1, with 12 abstentions. The General Assembly retained paragraph 8 by a recorded vote of 150 to 2, with 10 abstentions.

Resolution 55/33 T was adopted by recorded vote (109-39-20) [agenda item 73 *(q)*].

Nuclear disarmament

The General Assembly,

Recalling its resolution 49/75 E of 15 December 1994 on a step-by-step reduction of the nuclear threat, and its resolutions 50/70 P of 12 December 1995, 51/45 O of 10 December 1996, 52/38 L of 9 December 1997, 53/77 X of 4 December 1998 and 54/54 P of 1 December 1999 on nuclear disarmament,

Reaffirming the commitment of the international community to the goal of the total elimination of nuclear weapons and the establishment of a nuclear-weapon-free world,

Bearing in mind that the Convention on the Prohibition of the Development, Production and Stockpiling of Bacteriological (Biological) and Toxin Weapons and on Their Destruction of 1972 and the Convention on the Prohibition of the Development, Production, Stockpiling and Use of Chemical Weapons and on Their Destruction of 1993 have already established legal regimes on the complete prohibition of biological and chemical weapons, respectively, and determined to achieve a nuclear weapons convention on the prohibition of the development, testing, production, stockpiling, loan, transfer, use and threat of use of nuclear weapons and on their destruction, and to conclude such an international convention at an early date,

Recognizing that there now exist conditions for the establishment of a world free of nuclear weapons,

Bearing in mind paragraph 50 of the Final Document of the Tenth Special Session of the General Assembly, the first special session devoted to disarmament, calling for the urgent negotiation of agreements for the cessation of the qualitative improvement and development of nuclear-weapon systems, and for a comprehensive and phased programme with agreed time frames, wherever feasible, for the progressive and balanced reduction of nuclear weapons and their means of delivery, leading to their ultimate and complete elimination at the earliest possible time,

Noting the reiteration by the States parties to the Treaty on the Non-Proliferation of Nuclear Weapons of their conviction that the Treaty is a cornerstone of nuclear non-proliferation and nuclear disarmament and the reaffirmation by the States parties of the importance of the decision on strengthening the review process for the Treaty, the decision on principles and objectives for nuclear non-proliferation and disarmament, the decision on the extension of the Treaty and the resolution on the Middle East, adopted by the 1995 Review and Extension Conference of the Parties to the Treaty on the Non-Proliferation of Nuclear Weapons,

Reiterating the highest priority accorded to nuclear disarmament in the Final Document of the Tenth Special Session of the General Assembly and by the international community,

Recognizing that the Comprehensive Nuclear-Test-Ban Treaty and any proposed treaty on fissile material for nuclear weapons or other nuclear explosive devices must constitute disarmament measures, and not only non-proliferation measures,

Welcoming the entry into force of the Treaty on the Reduction and Limitation of Strategic Offensive Arms (START I), to which Belarus, Kazakhstan, the Russian Federation, Ukraine and the United States of America are States parties,

Welcoming also the ratification of the Treaty on Further Reduction and Limitation of Strategic Offensive Arms (START II) by the Russian Federation, and looking forward to its early entry into force and its full implementation and to an early commencement of START III negotiations,

Noting with appreciation the unilateral measures by the nuclear-weapon States for nuclear arms limitation, and encouraging them to take further such measures,

Recognizing the complementarity of bilateral, plurilateral and multilateral negotiations on nuclear disarmament, and that bilateral negotiations can never replace multilateral negotiations in this respect,

Noting the support expressed in the Conference on Disarmament and in the General Assembly for the elaboration of an international convention to assure non-nuclear-weapon States against the use or threat of use of nuclear weapons, and the multilateral efforts in the Conference on Disarmament to reach agreement on such an international convention at an early date,

Recalling the advisory opinion of the International Court of Justice on the *Legality of the Threat or Use of Nuclear Weapons*, issued on 8 July 1996, and welcoming the unanimous reaffirmation by all Judges of the Court that there exists an obligation for all States to pursue in good faith and bring to a conclusion negotiations leading to nuclear disarmament in all its aspects under strict and effective international control,

Mindful of paragraph 114 and other relevant recommendations in the Final Document of the Twelfth Conference of Heads of State or Government of Non-Aligned Countries, held at Durban, South Africa, from 29 August to 3 September 1998, calling upon the Conference on Disarmament to establish, on a priority basis, an ad hoc committee to commence negotiations in 1998 on a phased programme of nuclear disarmament and for the eventual elimination of nuclear weapons with a specified framework of time,

Recalling paragraph 72 of the final document of the Thirteenth Ministerial Conference of the Movement of Non-Aligned Countries, held at Cartagena, Colombia, on 8 and 9 April 2000,

1. *Recognizes* that, in view of recent political developments, the time is now opportune for all the nuclear-weapon States to take effective disarmament measures with a view to the elimination of these weapons;

2. *Also recognizes* that there is a genuine need to diminish the role of nuclear weapons in security policies to minimize the risk that these weapons will ever be used and to facilitate the process of their total elimination;

3. *Urges* the nuclear-weapon States to stop immediately the qualitative improvement, development, pro-

duction and stockpiling of nuclear warheads and their delivery systems;

4. *Also urges* the nuclear-weapon States, as an interim measure, to de-alert and deactivate immediately their nuclear weapons and to take other concrete measures to reduce further the operational status of their nuclear weapon systems;

5. *Reiterates its call upon* the nuclear-weapon States to undertake the step-by-step reduction of the nuclear threat and to carry out effective nuclear disarmament measures with a view to the total elimination of these weapons;

6. *Calls upon* the nuclear-weapon States, pending the achievement of the total elimination of nuclear weapons, to agree on an internationally and legally binding instrument on the joint undertaking not to be the first to use nuclear weapons, and calls upon all States to conclude an internationally and legally binding instrument on security assurances of non-use and non-threat of use of nuclear weapons against non-nuclear-weapon States;

7. *Urges* the nuclear-weapon States to commence plurilateral negotiations among themselves at an appropriate stage on further deep reductions of nuclear weapons as an effective measure of nuclear disarmament;

8. *Underlines* the importance of applying the principle of irreversibility to the process of nuclear disarmament, nuclear and other related arms control and reduction measures;

9. *Welcomes* the positive outcome of the 2000 Review Conference of the Parties to the Treaty on the Non-Proliferation of Nuclear Weapons and the unequivocal undertaking by the nuclear-weapon States, in the Final Document of the Review Conference, to accomplish the total elimination of their nuclear arsenals leading to nuclear disarmament, to which all States parties are committed under article VI of the Treaty, and the reaffirmation by the States parties that the total elimination of nuclear weapons is the only absolute guarantee against the use or threat of use of nuclear weapons, and calls for the full and effective implementation of the steps set out in the Final Document;

10. *Calls* for the immediate commencement of negotiations in the Conference on Disarmament, on a non-discriminatory, multilateral and internationally and effectively verifiable treaty banning the production of fissile material for nuclear weapons or other nuclear explosive devices on the basis of the report of the Special Coordinator and the mandate contained therein;

11. *Urges* the Conference on Disarmament to agree on a programme of work which includes the immediate commencement of negotiations on such a treaty with a view to their conclusion within five years;

12. *Calls* for the conclusion of an international legal instrument or instruments on adequate security assurances to non-nuclear-weapon States;

13. *Calls also* for the early entry into force and strict observance of the Comprehensive Nuclear-Test-Ban Treaty;

14. *Expresses its regret* that the Conference on Disarmament was unable to establish an ad hoc committee on nuclear disarmament at its 2000 session, as called for in General Assembly resolution 54/54 P;

15. *Reiterates its call upon* the Conference on Disarmament to establish, on a priority basis, an ad hoc com-

mittee to deal with nuclear disarmament early in 2001 and to commence negotiations on a phased programme of nuclear disarmament leading to the eventual elimination of nuclear weapons;

16. *Calls* for the convening of an international conference on nuclear disarmament in all its aspects at an early date to identify and deal with concrete measures of nuclear disarmament;

17. *Requests* the Secretary-General to submit to the General Assembly at its fifty-sixth session a report on the implementation of the present resolution;

18. *Decides* to include in the provisional agenda of its fifty-sixth session the item entitled "Nuclear disarmament".

RECORDED VOTE ON RESOLUTION 55/33 T:

In favour: Algeria, Angola, Antigua and Barbuda, Bahamas, Bahrain, Bangladesh, Barbados, Belarus, Belize, Benin, Bhutan, Bolivia, Botswana, Brazil, Brunei Darussalam, Burkina Faso, Burundi, Cambodia, Cameroon, Cape Verde, Chile, China, Colombia, Costa Rica, Côte d'Ivoire, Cuba, Democratic People's Republic of Korea, Djibouti, Dominican Republic, Ecuador, Egypt, El Salvador, Equatorial Guinea, Eritrea, Ethiopia, Fiji, Gabon, Gambia, Ghana, Grenada, Guatemala, Guinea, Guyana, Haiti, Honduras, Indonesia, Iran, Jamaica, Jordan, Kenya, Kuwait, Lao People's Democratic Republic, Lebanon, Lesotho, Libyan Arab Jamahiriya, Madagascar, Malawi, Malaysia, Maldives, Mali, Marshall Islands, Mauritius, Mexico, Mongolia, Morocco, Mozambique, Myanmar, Namibia, Nauru, Nepal, New Zealand, Nicaragua, Nigeria, Oman, Panama, Papua New Guinea, Paraguay, Peru, Philippines, Qatar, Saint Kitts and Nevis, Saint Lucia, Saint Vincent and the Grenadines, Samoa, Saudi Arabia, Senegal, Sierra Leone, Singapore, Solomon Islands, South Africa, Sri Lanka, Sudan, Suriname, Swaziland, Syrian Arab Republic, Thailand, Togo, Tonga, Trinidad and Tobago, Tunisia, Uganda, United Republic of Tanzania, Uruguay, Vanuatu, Venezuela, Viet Nam, Yemen, Zambia, Zimbabwe.

Against: Albania, Andorra, Australia, Austria, Belgium, Bosnia and Herzegovina, Bulgaria, Canada, Croatia, Czech Republic, Denmark, Estonia, Finland, France, Germany, Greece, Hungary, Iceland, Italy, Latvia, Liechtenstein, Lithuania, Luxembourg, Malta, Micronesia, Monaco, Netherlands, Norway, Poland, Portugal, Republic of Moldova, Romania, Slovakia, Slovenia, Spain, The former Yugoslav Republic of Macedonia, Turkey, United Kingdom, United States.

Abstaining: Argentina, Armenia, Azerbaijan, Cyprus, Georgia, India, Ireland, Israel, Japan, Kazakhstan, Kyrgyzstan, Pakistan, Republic of Korea, Russian Federation, San Marino, Sweden, Tajikistan, Ukraine, United Arab Emirates, Uzbekistan.

In the First Committee, paragraph 9 was adopted by a recorded vote of 139 to 2, with 16 abstentions. The draft as a whole was adopted by a recorded vote of 99 to 39, with 17 abstentions. The Assembly retained the paragraph by a recorded vote of 150 to 2, with 15 abstentions.

The Assembly adopted **resolution 55/33 C** by recorded vote (154-3-8) [agenda item 73 *(i)*].

Towards a nuclear-weapon-free world: the need for a new agenda

The General Assembly,

Noting its resolutions 53/77 Y of 4 December 1998 and 54/54 G of 1 December 1999,

Expressing its deep concern at the continued risk for humanity represented by the possibility that nuclear weapons could be used,

Noting the advisory opinion of the International Court of Justice, on the *Legality of the Threat or Use of Nuclear Weapons,* issued at The Hague on 8 July 1996,

Noting also that three States continue to operate unsafeguarded nuclear facilities and have not acceded to the Treaty on the Non-Proliferation of Nuclear Weapons, and concerned at the continued retention of the nuclear-weapons option by those three States,

Declaring that nuclear test explosions carried out in 1998 by two of the States that have not renounced the nuclear-weapons option do not in any way confer a nuclear-weapon State status or any special status whatsoever,

Noting that, despite achievements in bilateral and unilateral arms reductions, the total number of nuclear weapons deployed and stockpiled still amount to many thousands,

Welcoming the significant progress achieved in nuclear weapon reductions made unilaterally or bilaterally under the Strategic Arms Reduction Treaty (START) process, as a step towards nuclear disarmament,

Welcoming also the ratification of the Treaty on Further Reduction and Limitation of Strategic Offensive Arms (START II) by the Russian Federation as an important step in the efforts to reduce strategic offensive weapons, and noting that completion of ratification of START II by the United States of America remains a priority,

Concerned that negotiations on nuclear arms reductions are not actively under way,

Welcoming the significant unilateral reduction measures taken by other nuclear-weapon States, including the closing down and dismantling of nuclear-weapon-related facilities,

Welcoming also the efforts of several States to cooperate in making nuclear disarmament measures irreversible, in particular through the adoption of initiatives on the verification, management and disposition of fissile material declared excess to military purposes,

Noting the declaration by the nuclear-weapon States that none of their nuclear weapons are targeted at any State,

Underlining the necessity of strict compliance by all parties with their obligations under the Treaty on the Non-Proliferation of Nuclear Weapons,

Noting the United Nations Millennium Declaration, in which the heads of State and Government resolved to strive for the elimination of weapons of mass destruction, in particular nuclear weapons, and to keep all options open for achieving this aim, including the possibility of convening an international conference to identify ways of eliminating nuclear dangers,

Welcoming the Final Document of the 2000 Review Conference of the Parties to the Treaty on the Non-Proliferation of Nuclear Weapons,

Taking into consideration the unequivocal undertaking by the nuclear-weapon States, in the Final Document of the 2000 Review Conference of the Parties to the Treaty on the Non-Proliferation of Nuclear Weapons, to accomplish the total elimination of their nuclear arsenals leading to nuclear disarmament, to which all States parties to the Treaty are committed under article VI of the Treaty,

Underlining the need for action to achieve a world free from nuclear weapons,

Determined to pursue practical steps for systematic and progressive efforts to implement article VI of the Treaty on the Non-Proliferation of Nuclear Weapons and paragraphs 3 and 4 *(c)* of the decision on principles and objectives for nuclear non-proliferation and disarmament of the 1995 Review and Extension Conference of the Parties to the Treaty,

1. *Agrees* on the importance and urgency of signatures and ratifications, without delay and without conditions and in accordance with constitutional processes, to achieve the early entry into force of the Comprehensive Nuclear-Test-Ban Treaty;

2. *Calls* for the upholding of a moratorium on nuclear-weapon-test explosions or any other nuclear explosions pending entry into force of the above-mentioned Treaty;

3. *Agrees* on the necessity for negotiations in the Conference on Disarmament on a non-discriminatory, multilateral and internationally and effectively verifiable treaty banning the production of fissile material for nuclear weapons or other nuclear explosive devices, in accordance with the report of the Special Coordinator of 1995 and the mandate contained therein, taking into consideration both nuclear disarmament and nuclear non-proliferation objectives, and urges the Conference on Disarmament to agree on a programme of work which includes the immediate commencement of negotiations on such a treaty, with a view to their conclusion within five years;

4. *Agrees also* on the necessity of establishing within the context of the Conference on Disarmament an appropriate subsidiary body with a mandate to deal with nuclear disarmament, and urges the Conference to agree on a programme of work which includes the immediate establishment of such a body;

5. *Calls* for the principle of irreversibility to apply to nuclear disarmament, nuclear and other related arms control and reduction measures;

6. *Calls also* for the early entry into force and full implementation of the Treaty on Further Reduction and Limitation of Strategic Offensive Arms (START II) and the conclusion of START III as soon as possible, while preserving and strengthening the Treaty on the Limitation of Anti-Ballistic Missile Systems as a cornerstone of strategic stability and as a basis for further reductions of strategic offensive weapons, in accordance with the provisions of that Treaty;

7. *Calls further* for the completion and implementation of the Trilateral Initiative between the United States of America, the Russian Federation and the International Atomic Energy Agency;

8. *Calls* for steps to be taken by all nuclear-weapon States that would lead to nuclear disarmament in a way that promotes international stability and, based upon the principle of undiminished security for all, for:

(*a*) Further efforts to be made by the nuclear-weapon States to reduce their nuclear arsenals unilaterally;

(*b*) Increased transparency by the nuclear-weapon States with regard to nuclear weapons capabilities, and the implementation of agreements pursuant to article VI of the Treaty on the Non-Proliferation of Nuclear Weapons and as a voluntary confidence-building measure to support further progress in nuclear disarmament;

(*c*) The further reduction of non-strategic nuclear weapons, based on unilateral initiatives and as an integral part of the nuclear arms reduction and disarmament process;

(*d*) Concrete agreed measures to reduce further the operational status of nuclear weapons systems;

(*e*) A diminishing role for nuclear weapons in security policies so as to minimize the risk that these weapons will ever be used and to facilitate the process of their total elimination;

(*f*) The engagement, as soon as appropriate, of all the nuclear-weapon States in the process leading to the total elimination of their nuclear weapons;

9. *Calls also* for arrangements by all nuclear-weapon States to place, as soon as practicable, the fissile material designated by each of them as no longer required for military purposes under International Atomic Energy Agency or other relevant international verification and arrangements for the disposition of such material for peaceful purposes in order to ensure that such material remains permanently outside military programmes;

10. *Reaffirms* that the ultimate objective of the efforts of States in the disarmament process is general and complete disarmament under effective international control;

11. *Calls* for regular reports, within the framework of the strengthened review process for the Treaty on the Non-Proliferation of Nuclear Weapons, by all States parties on the implementation of article VI of the Treaty and paragraph 4 (*c*) of the decision on principles and objectives for nuclear non-proliferation and disarmament of the 1995 Review and Extension Conference of the Parties to the Treaty, and, in this regard, recalls the advisory opinion of the International Court of Justice of 8 July 1996;

12. *Agrees* to pursue the further development of the verification capabilities that will be required to provide assurance of compliance with nuclear disarmament agreements for the achievement and maintenance of a nuclear-weapon-free world;

13. *Calls upon* all States not yet party to the Treaty on the Non-Proliferation of Nuclear Weapons to accede to the Treaty as non-nuclear-weapon States, promptly and without condition, in particular those States that operate unsafeguarded nuclear facilities, and also calls upon those States to bring into force the required comprehensive safeguards agreements, together with additional protocols, consistent with the Model Protocol Additional to the Agreement(s) between State(s) and the International Atomic Energy Agency for the Application of Safeguards approved by the Board of Governors of the International Atomic Energy Agency on 15 May 1997, for ensuring nuclear non-proliferation, and to reverse clearly and urgently any policies to pursue any nuclear weapons development or deployment and refrain from any action that could undermine regional and international peace and security and the efforts of the international community towards nuclear disarmament and the prevention of nuclear weapons proliferation;

14. *Calls upon* those States that have not yet done so to conclude full-scope safeguards agreements with the International Atomic Energy Agency and to conclude additional protocols to their safeguards agreements on the basis of the Model Protocol;

15. *Notes* the paramount importance of effective physical protection of all nuclear material, and calls upon all States to maintain the highest possible standards of security and physical protection of nuclear materials;

16. *Notes also* that the 2000 Review Conference of the Parties to the Treaty on the Non-Proliferation of Nuclear Weapons agreed that legally binding security

assurances by the five nuclear-weapon States to the non-nuclear-weapon States parties to the Treaty strengthen the nuclear non-proliferation regime, and that it called upon the Preparatory Committee to make recommendations on this issue to the 2005 Review Conference;

17. *Reaffirms* the conviction that the establishment of internationally recognized nuclear-weapon-free zones on the basis of arrangements freely arrived at among the States of the region concerned enhances global and regional peace and security, strengthens the nuclear non-proliferation regime and contributes towards realizing the objective of nuclear disarmament, and supports proposals for the establishment of nuclear-weapon-free zones where they do not yet exist, such as in the Middle East and South Asia;

18. *Affirms* that a nuclear-weapon-free world will ultimately require the underpinning of a universal and multilaterally negotiated legally binding instrument or a framework encompassing a mutually reinforcing set of instruments;

19. *Acknowledges* the report of the Secretary-General on the implementation of General Assembly resolution 54/54 G, and requests him, within existing resources, to prepare a report on the implementation of the present resolution;

20. *Decides* to include in the provisional agenda of its fifty-sixth session the item entitled "Towards a nuclear-weapon-free world: the need for a new agenda", and to review the implementation of the present resolution at that session.

RECORDED VOTE ON RESOLUTION 55/33 C:

In favour: Albania, Algeria, Andorra, Angola, Antigua and Barbuda, Argentina, Armenia, Australia, Austria, Azerbaijan, Bahamas, Bahrain, Bangladesh, Barbados, Belarus, Belgium, Belize, Benin, Bolivia, Bosnia and Herzegovina, Botswana, Brazil, Brunei Darussalam, Bulgaria, Burkina Faso, Burundi, Cambodia, Cameroon, Canada, Cape Verde, Chile, China, Colombia, Costa Rica, Côte d'Ivoire, Croatia, Cuba, Cyprus, Czech Republic, Denmark, Djibouti, Dominican Republic, Ecuador, Egypt, El Salvador, Equatorial Guinea, Eritrea, Estonia, Ethiopia, Fiji, Finland, Gabon, Gambia, Georgia, Germany, Ghana, Greece, Grenada, Guatemala, Guinea, Guyana, Haiti, Hungary, Iceland, Indonesia, Iran, Ireland, Italy, Jamaica, Japan, Jordan, Kazakhstan, Kenya, Kuwait, Lao People's Democratic Republic, Latvia, Lebanon, Lesotho, Libyan Arab Jamahiriya, Liechtenstein, Lithuania, Luxembourg, Madagascar, Malawi, Malaysia, Maldives, Mali, Malta, Marshall Islands, Mexico, Micronesia, Mongolia, Morocco, Mozambique, Myanmar, Namibia, Nauru, Nepal, Netherlands, New Zealand, Nicaragua, Nigeria, Norway, Oman, Panama, Papua New Guinea, Paraguay, Peru, Philippines, Poland, Portugal, Qatar, Republic of Korea, Republic of Moldova, Romania, Saint Lucia, Saint Vincent and the Grenadines, Samoa, San Marino, Saudi Arabia, Senegal, Sierra Leone, Singapore, Slovakia, Slovenia, Solomon Islands, South Africa, Spain, Sri Lanka, Sudan, Suriname, Swaziland, Sweden, Syrian Arab Republic, Thailand, The former Yugoslav Republic of Macedonia, Togo, Tonga, Trinidad and Tobago, Tunisia, Turkey, Uganda, Ukraine, United Arab Emirates, United Kingdom, United Republic of Tanzania, United States, Uruguay, Vanuatu, Venezuela, Viet Nam, Yemen, Zambia, Zimbabwe.

Against: India, Israel, Pakistan.

Abstaining: Bhutan, France, Kyrgyzstan, Mauritius, Monaco, Russian Federation, Tajikistan, Uzbekistan.

In the First Committee, preambular paragraph 15 and paragraph 16 were adopted by recorded votes of 151 to 3, with 1 abstention, and 151 to none, with 4 abstentions, respectively. The text as a whole was adopted by a recorded vote of 146 to 3, with 8 abstentions. The Assembly retained the paragraphs by recorded votes of 160 to 3, with 1 abstention, and 161 to none, with 4 abstentions, respectively.

Resolution 55/33 N was adopted by recorded vote (110-45-14) [agenda item 73 *(m)*].

Reducing nuclear danger

The General Assembly,

Bearing in mind that the use of nuclear weapons poses the most serious threat to mankind and to the survival of civilization,

Reaffirming that any use or threat of use of nuclear weapons would constitute a violation of the Charter of the United Nations,

Convinced that the proliferation of nuclear weapons in all its aspects would seriously enhance the danger of nuclear war,

Convinced also that nuclear disarmament and the complete elimination of nuclear weapons are essential to remove the danger of nuclear war,

Considering that, until nuclear weapons cease to exist, it is imperative on the part of the nuclear-weapon States to adopt measures that assure non-nuclear-weapon States against the use or threat of use of nuclear weapons,

Considering also that the hair-trigger alert of nuclear weapons carries unacceptable risks of unintentional or accidental use of nuclear weapons, which would have catastrophic consequences for all mankind,

Emphasizing the imperative need to adopt measures to avoid accidental, unauthorized or unexplained incidents arising from computer anomaly or other technical malfunctions,

Conscious that limited steps relating to detargeting have been taken by the nuclear-weapon States and that further practical, realistic and mutually reinforcing steps are necessary to contribute to the improvement in the international climate for negotiations leading to the elimination of nuclear weapons,

Mindful that reduction of tensions brought about by a change in nuclear doctrines would positively impact on international peace and security and improve the conditions for the further reduction and the elimination of nuclear weapons,

Reiterating the highest priority accorded to nuclear disarmament in the Final Document of the Tenth Special Session of the General Assembly and by the international community,

Recalling that in the advisory opinion of the International Court of Justice on the *Legality of the Threat or Use of Nuclear Weapons* it is stated that there exists an obligation for all States to pursue in good faith and bring to a conclusion negotiations leading to nuclear disarmament in all its aspects under strict and effective international control,

Welcoming the call in the United Nations Millennium Declaration to seek to eliminate the dangers posed by weapons of mass destruction and the resolve to strive for the elimination of weapons of mass destruction, particularly nuclear weapons, including the possibility of convening an international conference to identify ways of eliminating nuclear dangers,

1. *Calls* for a review of nuclear doctrines and, in this context, immediate and urgent steps to reduce the risks of unintentional and accidental use of nuclear weapons;

2. *Requests* the five nuclear-weapon States to take measures towards the implementation of paragraph 1 of the present resolution;

3. *Calls upon* Member States to take the necessary measures to prevent the proliferation of nuclear weapons in all its aspects and to promote nuclear disarmament, with the objective of eliminating nuclear weapons;

4. *Takes note* of the report prepared by the Advisory Board on Disarmament Matters and submitted by the Secretary-General in pursuance of paragraph 4 of General Assembly resolution 54/54 K of 1 December 1999, including the need for the Board to continue its discussions on the subject;

5. *Requests* the Secretary-General, within existing resources, to continue to seek inputs from the Advisory Board on Disarmament Matters on information with regard to specific measures that would significantly reduce the risk of nuclear war, including the proposal contained in the United Nations Millennium Declaration for convening an international conference to identify ways of eliminating nuclear dangers, and to report thereon to the General Assembly at its fifty-sixth session;

6. *Decides* to include in the provisional agenda of the fifty-sixth session the item entitled "Reducing nuclear danger".

RECORDED VOTE ON RESOLUTION 55/33 N:

In favour: Algeria, Angola, Antigua and Barbuda, Azerbaijan, Bahamas, Bahrain, Bangladesh, Barbados, Belarus, Belize, Benin, Bhutan, Bolivia, Botswana, Brunei Darussalam, Burkina Faso, Burundi, Cambodia, Cameroon, Cape Verde, Chile, Colombia, Costa Rica, Côte d'Ivoire, Cuba, Democratic People's Republic of Korea, Djibouti, Dominican Republic, Ecuador, Egypt, El Salvador, Equatorial Guinea, Eritrea, Ethiopia, Fiji, Gabon, Gambia, Ghana, Grenada, Guatemala, Guinea, Guyana, Haiti, Honduras, India, Indonesia, Iran, Jamaica, Jordan, Kenya, Kuwait, Lao People's Democratic Republic, Lebanon, Lesotho, Libyan Arab Jamahiriya, Madagascar, Malawi, Malaysia, Maldives, Mali, Marshall Islands, Mauritius, Mexico, Mongolia, Morocco, Mozambique, Myanmar, Namibia, Nauru, Nepal, Nicaragua, Nigeria, Oman, Pakistan, Panama, Papua New Guinea, Peru, Philippines, Qatar, Saint Kitts and Nevis, Saint Lucia, Saint Vincent and the Grenadines, Samoa, Saudi Arabia, Senegal, Sierra Leone, Singapore, Solomon Islands, South Africa, Sri Lanka, Sudan, Suriname, Swaziland, Syrian Arab Republic, Thailand, Togo, Tonga, Trinidad and Tobago, Tunisia, Turkmenistan, Uganda, United Arab Emirates, United Republic of Tanzania, Uruguay, Vanuatu, Venezuela, Viet Nam, Yemen, Zambia, Zimbabwe.

Against: Albania, Andorra, Australia, Austria, Belgium, Bosnia and Herzegovina, Bulgaria, Canada, Croatia, Cyprus, Czech Republic, Denmark, Estonia, Finland, France, Germany, Greece, Hungary, Iceland, Ireland, Italy, Latvia, Liechtenstein, Lithuania, Luxembourg, Malta, Micronesia, Monaco, Netherlands, New Zealand, Norway, Poland, Portugal, Republic of Moldova, Romania, Russian Federation, San Marino, Slovakia, Slovenia, Spain, Sweden, The former Yugoslav Republic of Macedonia, Turkey, United Kingdom, United States.

Abstaining: Argentina, Armenia, Brazil, China, Georgia, Israel, Japan, Kazakhstan, Kyrgyzstan, Paraguay, Republic of Korea, Tajikistan, Ukraine, Uzbekistan.

ABM Treaty and other missile issues

Missile defence issues and the status of the ABM Treaty, especially regarding the United States announcement in 1999 [YUN 1999, p. 469] of its plans to develop an NMD system, remained an issue of major international concern. The Russian Federation held an international experts meeting (Moscow, 16 March) to exchange views on its proposal to create a global control system for the non-proliferation of missiles and missile technology. Following the meeting, President Putin proposed that the North Atlantic Treaty Organization (NATO), Europe and Russia establish a joint anti-missile shield against missile threats from certain States. He believed that the

shield could replace the NMD system. The United States viewed the proposal only as a possible complement to its own NMD plans.

The Ministers for Foreign Affairs of China, Kazakhstan, Kyrgyzstan, the Russian Federation and Tajikistan adopted the Dushanbe Declaration (Dushanbe, Tajikistan, July) [A/55/133-S/2000/682], by which they declared that the deployment of closed bloc-based anti-ballistic missile defence systems in Asia and the Pacific might upset the stability and security of the region.

On 18 July [A/55/276, CD/1622], China and the Russian Federation issued a joint statement on anti-missile defence, calling for the gradual establishment of a global system for monitoring the non-proliferation of missiles and missile technology.

Although the United States held several rounds of discussions on missile issues with the Democratic People's Republic of Korea (DPRK), particularly concerning the DPRK's ballistic missile programme and related issues, there were no major breakthroughs. As further steps to develop an NMD system, the United States conducted a second and third missile interceptor test on 18 January and 7 July, respectively. In September [CD/1625], President Clinton reaffirmed the commitment of the United States to develop the system, but also announced that due to insufficient technical information, he would leave the decision for deployment to the next Administration.

On 12 October [A/C.1/55/8], the Russian Federation stated that the September statement [CD/1625] asserted that the Joint Statement on Principles of Strategic Stability between Russia and the United States [CD/1617] (see p. 490) contained a provision on the need to address the threat of the proliferation of weapons of mass destruction, missiles and missile technologies, "including through consideration of changes to the ABM Treaty". Russia stated that the Joint Statement contained no such provision, nor did any other document adopted jointly.

On 6 September in New York [CD/1626], Presidents Putin and Clinton issued a joint statement on a strategic stability cooperation initiative, in which they agreed to enhance strategic stability, to counter the proliferation of weapons of mass destruction, missiles and related technology, and to strengthen the ABM Treaty. In November [A/55/625], while acknowledging changes in the international strategic environment, President Putin said those changes could be dealt with, and missile proliferation counteracted, without exceeding the limits of the ABM Treaty.

Report of Secretary-General. In a July report with later addendum [A/55/116 & Add.1], the Secretary-General presented the views of seven

Member States on the issue of missiles in all its aspects, as requested by the General Assembly in resolution 54/54 F [YUN 1999, p. 470].

GENERAL ASSEMBLY ACTION

On 20 November [meeting 69], the General Assembly, on the recommendation of the First Committee [A/55/559], adopted **resolution 55/33 A** by recorded vote (97-0-65) [agenda item 73 *(h)*].

Missiles

The General Assembly,

Recalling its resolution 54/54 F of 1 December 1999,

Reaffirming the role of the United Nations in the field of arms regulation and disarmament and the commitment of Member States to take concrete steps to strengthen that role,

Realizing the need to promote regional and international peace and security in a world free from the scourge of war and the burden of armaments,

Convinced of the need for a comprehensive approach towards missiles, in a balanced and non-discriminatory manner, as a contribution to international peace and security,

Bearing in mind that the security concerns of Member States at the international and regional levels should be taken into consideration in addressing the issue of missiles,

Underlining the complexities involved in considering the issue of missiles in the conventional context,

Expressing its support for the international efforts against the development and proliferation of all weapons of mass destruction,

1. *Takes note with appreciation* of the report of the Secretary-General, submitted pursuant to resolution 54/54 F,

2. *Requests* the Secretary-General further to seek the views of Member States on the issue of missiles in all its aspects and to submit a report to the General Assembly at its fifty-sixth session;

3. *Also requests* the Secretary-General, with the assistance of a panel of governmental experts to be established in 2001 on the basis of equitable geographical distribution, to prepare a report for the consideration of the General Assembly at its fifty-seventh session on the issue of missiles in all its aspects;

4. *Decides* to include in the provisional agenda of its fifty-sixth session the item entitled "Missiles".

RECORDED VOTE ON RESOLUTION 55/33 A:

In favour: Algeria, Angola, Antigua and Barbuda, Bahamas, Bahrain, Bangladesh, Barbados, Belarus, Belize, Benin, Bhutan, Botswana, Brunei Darussalam, Burkina Faso, Burundi, Cambodia, Cameroon, Cape Verde, Chile, China, Colombia, Costa Rica, Côte d'Ivoire, Cuba, Dominican Republic, Ecuador, Egypt, El Salvador, Equatorial Guinea, Ethiopia, Fiji, Gabon, Ghana, Grenada, Guinea, Guyana, Haiti, Honduras, India, Indonesia, Iran, Jamaica, Jordan, Kazakhstan, Kenya, Kuwait, Kyrgyzstan, Lao People's Democratic Republic, Lesotho, Libyan Arab Jamahiriya, Madagascar, Malawi, Malaysia, Maldives, Mali, Mauritius, Mexico, Mongolia, Morocco, Mozambique, Myanmar, Namibia, Nepal, Nicaragua, Nigeria, Oman, Pakistan, Panama, Papua New Guinea, Peru, Philippines, Qatar, Russian Federation, Saint Lucia, Saudi Arabia, Senegal, Sierra Leone, South Africa, Sri Lanka, Sudan, Suriname, Swaziland, Tajikistan, Thailand, Togo, Tonga, Trinidad and Tobago, Tunisia, Turkmenistan, Uganda, United Arab Emirates, United Republic of Tanzania, Venezuela, Viet Nam, Yemen, Zambia, Zimbabwe.

Against: None.

Abstaining: Albania, Andorra, Argentina, Armenia, Australia, Austria, Azerbaijan, Belgium, Bolivia, Bosnia and Herzegovina, Brazil, Bulgaria, Canada, Croatia, Cyprus, Czech Republic, Denmark, Djibouti, Eritrea, Estonia, Finland, France, Georgia, Germany, Greece, Guatemala, Hungary, Iceland, Ireland, Israel, Italy, Japan, Latvia, Liechtenstein, Lithuania, Luxembourg, Malta, Marshall Islands, Micronesia, Monaco, Nauru, Netherlands, New Zealand, Norway, Paraguay, Poland, Portugal, Republic of Korea, Republic of Moldova, Romania, Samoa, San Marino, Singapore, Slovakia, Slovenia, Solomon Islands, Spain, Sweden, The former Yugoslav Republic of Macedonia, Turkey, Ukraine, United Kingdom, United States, Uruguay, Vanuatu.

On the same date [meeting 69], the Assembly, also on the recommendation of the First Committee [A/55/559], adopted **resolution 55/33 B** by recorded vote (88-5-66) [agenda item 73 *(e)*].

Preservation of and compliance with the Treaty on the Limitation of Anti-Ballistic Missile Systems

The General Assembly,

Recalling resolutions 50/60 of 12 December 1995 and 52/30 of 9 December 1997 on compliance with arms limitation and disarmament and non-proliferation agreements and its resolution 54/54 A of 1 December 1999 on preservation of and compliance with the Treaty on the Limitation of Anti-Ballistic Missile Systems,

Recognizing the historical role of the Treaty on the Limitation of Anti-Ballistic Missile Systems of 26 May 1972 between the United States of America and the Union of Soviet Socialist Republics as a cornerstone for maintaining global peace and security and strategic stability, and reaffirming its continued validity and relevance, especially in the current international situation,

Stressing the paramount importance of full and strict compliance with the Treaty by the parties,

Recalling that the provisions of the Treaty are intended as a contribution to the creation of more favourable conditions for further negotiations on limiting strategic arms,

Mindful of the obligations of the parties to the Treaty under article VI of the Treaty on the Non-Proliferation of Nuclear Weapons,

Concerned that the implementation of any measures undermining the purposes and provisions of the Treaty affects not only the security interests of the parties, but also those of the whole international community,

Recalling the widespread concern about the proliferation of weapons of mass destruction and their means of delivery,

1. *Calls* for continued efforts to strengthen the Treaty on the Limitation of Anti-Ballistic Missile Systems and to preserve its integrity and validity so that it remains a cornerstone in maintaining global strategic stability and world peace and in promoting further strategic nuclear arms reductions;

2. *Calls also* for renewed efforts by each of the States parties to preserve and strengthen the Treaty through full and strict compliance;

3. *Calls upon* the parties to the Treaty, in accordance with their obligations under the Treaty, to limit the deployment of anti-ballistic missile systems, to refrain from the deployment of anti-ballistic missile systems for the defence of the territory of their country, not to provide a base for such a defence and not to transfer to other States or deploy outside their national territory anti-ballistic missile systems or their components limited by the Treaty;

4. *Considers* that the implementation of any measure undermining the purposes and the provisions of the Treaty also undermines global strategic stability and world peace and the promotion of further strategic nuclear arms reductions;

5. *Urges* all Member States to support efforts aimed at stemming the proliferation of weapons of mass destruction and their means of delivery;

6. *Supports* further efforts by the international community, in the light of emerging developments, towards safeguarding the inviolability and integrity of the Treaty, which is in the strongest interest of the international community;

7. *Welcomes* the decision taken by the United States of America on 1 September 2000 not to authorize deployment of a national missile defence at this time, and considers that it constitutes a positive step for the preservation of strategic stability and security;

8. *Decides* to include in the provisional agenda of its fifty-sixth session the item entitled "Preservation of and compliance with the Treaty on the Limitation of Anti-Ballistic Missile Systems".

RECORDED VOTE ON RESOLUTION 55/33 B:

In favour: Algeria, Angola, Antigua and Barbuda, Armenia, Azerbaijan, Bangladesh, Barbados, Belarus, Belize, Benin, Bhutan, Botswana, Brunei Darussalam, Burkina Faso, Burundi, Cambodia, Cameroon, Cape Verde, China, Colombia, Côte d'Ivoire, Cuba, Cyprus, Democratic People's Republic of Korea, Ecuador, Egypt, Equatorial Guinea, Ethiopia, Fiji, France, Gabon, Grenada, Guinea, Guyana, Haiti, India, Indonesia, Iran, Ireland, Jamaica, Kazakhstan, Kenya, Kiribati, Kyrgyzstan, Lao People's Democratic Republic, Lebanon, Libyan Arab Jamahiriya, Madagascar, Malawi, Malaysia, Mali, Mexico, Monaco, Mongolia, Mozambique, Myanmar, Namibia, Nepal, Oman, Pakistan, Panama, Papua New Guinea, Republic of Moldova, Russian Federation, Saint Lucia, Saint Vincent and the Grenadines, Senegal, Sierra Leone, Singapore, South Africa, Sri Lanka, Sudan, Suriname, Swaziland, Syrian Arab Republic, Tajikistan, Thailand, Togo, Tonga, Turkmenistan, Uganda, Ukraine, United Republic of Tanzania, Vanuatu, Viet Nam, Yemen, Zambia, Zimbabwe.

Against: Albania, Honduras, Israel, Micronesia, United States.

Abstaining: Andorra, Argentina, Australia, Austria, Bahamas, Bahrain, Belgium, Bolivia, Bosnia and Herzegovina, Brazil, Bulgaria, Canada, Chile, Costa Rica, Croatia, Czech Republic, Denmark, Djibouti, Dominican Republic, Eritrea, Estonia, Finland, Georgia, Germany, Ghana, Greece, Guatemala, Hungary, Iceland, Italy, Japan, Latvia, Lesotho, Liechtenstein, Lithuania, Luxembourg, Malta, Marshall Islands, Mauritius, Morocco, Nauru, Netherlands, New Zealand, Nicaragua, Nigeria, Norway, Paraguay, Peru, Philippines, Poland, Portugal, Republic of Korea, Romania, Samoa, San Marino, Slovakia, Slovenia, Solomon Islands, Spain, Sweden, The former Yugoslav Republic of Macedonia, Trinidad and Tobago, Turkey, United Kingdom, Uruguay, Venezuela.

Comprehensive Nuclear-Test-Ban Treaty

Status

As at 31 December, 160 States had signed the 1996 Comprehensive Nuclear-Test-Ban Treaty (CTBT), adopted by General Assembly resolution 50/245 [YUN 1996, p. 454], and 69 had ratified it.

During the year, the Treaty was ratified by Bangladesh, Belarus, Cambodia, Chile, Gabon, Iceland, Kenya, Kiribati, the Lao People's Democratic Republic, Lithuania, Maldives, Morocco, Nicaragua, Portugal, the Russian Federation, the former Yugoslav Republic of Macedonia, Turkey and the United Arab Emirates.

In accordance with article XIV, CTBT was to enter into force 180 days after the 44 States pos-

sessing nuclear reactors, listed in annex 2 to the Treaty, had deposited their instruments of ratification. By year's end, 30 of those States had ratified the Treaty.

Following the request of a majority of ratifying States, the Secretary-General, as depositary, decided to convene a second conference in September 2001 to facilitate CTBT's entry into force. The first such conference was held in 1999 [YUN 1999, p. 471].

Communications. The Russian Federation transmitted a statement of 18 May [A/55/79] regarding its ratification of the Treaty.

The Secretary-General transmitted a decision of 23 August [A/55/336] adopted by the Preparatory Commission for the CTBT Organization calling upon all States that had not signed or ratified the Treaty to do so.

Nuclear testing

Regarding the joint Kazakhstan–United States Omega-3 calibration experiment, Kazakhstan stated that, on 29 July [A/55/255], the last tunnel at the Semipalatinsk former test site was destroyed by 100 metric tons of granulated trytol. The explosion was also used to check and calibrate the international monitoring system (see p. 501) for nuclear tests under CTBT.

GENERAL ASSEMBLY ACTION

On 20 November [meeting 69], the General Assembly, on the recommendation of the First Committee [A/55/567], adopted **resolution 55/41** by recorded vote (161-0-6) [agenda item 81].

Comprehensive Nuclear-Test-Ban Treaty

The General Assembly,

Recalling that the Comprehensive Nuclear-Test-Ban Treaty was adopted by its resolution 50/245 of 10 September 1996 and opened for signature on 24 September 1996,

Noting that, in its resolution 54/63 of 1 December 1999, it decided to include in the provisional agenda of its fifty-fifth session the item entitled "Comprehensive Nuclear-Test-Ban Treaty",

Encouraged by the signing of the Treaty by one hundred and sixty States, including forty-one of the forty-four needed for its entry into force, and welcoming the ratification of sixty-five States, including thirty of the forty-four needed for its entry into force,

Recalling its endorsement, in resolution 54/63, of the Final Declaration of the Conference on Facilitating the Entry into Force of the Comprehensive Nuclear-Test-Ban Treaty, held at Vienna from 6 to 8 October 1999 to promote the entry into force of the Treaty at the earliest possible date,

1. *Stresses* the importance and urgency of signature and ratification, without delay and without conditions and in accordance with constitutional processes, to achieve the early entry into force of the Comprehensive Nuclear-Test-Ban Treaty;

2. *Welcomes* the contributions by the States signatories to the work of the Preparatory Commission for the Comprehensive Nuclear-Test-Ban Treaty Organization, in particular to its efforts to ensure that the Treaty's verification regime will be capable of meeting the verification requirements of the Treaty upon its entry into force, in accordance with article IV of the Treaty;

3. *Urges* States to maintain their moratoria on nuclear weapons test explosions or any other nuclear explosions, pending the entry into force of the Treaty;

4. *Calls upon* all States that have not yet signed the Treaty to sign and ratify it as soon as possible and to refrain from acts that would defeat its object and purpose in the meanwhile;

5. *Calls upon* all States that have signed but not yet ratified the Treaty, in particular those whose ratification is needed for its entry into force, to accelerate their ratification processes with a view to their early successful conclusion;

6. *Urges* all States to remain seized of the issue at the highest political level;

7. *Decides* to include in the provisional agenda of its fifty-sixth session the item entitled "Comprehensive Nuclear-Test-Ban Treaty".

RECORDED VOTE ON RESOLUTION 55/41:

In favour: Albania, Algeria, Andorra, Angola, Antigua and Barbuda, Argentina, Armenia, Australia, Austria, Azerbaijan, Bahamas, Bahrain, Bangladesh, Barbados, Belarus, Belgium, Belize, Benin, Bolivia, Bosnia and Herzegovina, Botswana, Brazil, Brunei Darussalam, Bulgaria, Burkina Faso, Burundi, Cambodia, Cameroon, Canada, Cape Verde, Chile, China, Colombia, Comoros, Costa Rica, Côte d'Ivoire, Croatia, Cuba, Cyprus, Czech Republic, Denmark, Djibouti, Dominican Republic, Ecuador, Egypt, El Salvador, Equatorial Guinea, Eritrea, Estonia, Ethiopia, Fiji, Finland, France, Gabon, Gambia, Georgia, Germany, Ghana, Greece, Grenada, Guatemala, Guinea, Guyana, Haiti, Honduras, Hungary, Iceland, Indonesia, Iran, Ireland, Israel, Italy, Jamaica, Japan, Jordan, Kazakhstan, Kenya, Kuwait, Kyrgyzstan, Lao People's Democratic Republic, Latvia, Lesotho, Liechtenstein, Lithuania, Luxembourg, Madagascar, Malawi, Malaysia, Maldives, Mali, Malta, Marshall Islands, Mexico, Micronesia, Monaco, Mongolia, Morocco, Mozambique, Myanmar, Namibia, Nauru, Nepal, Netherlands, New Zealand, Nicaragua, Nigeria, Norway, Oman, Pakistan, Panama, Papua New Guinea, Paraguay, Peru, Philippines, Poland, Portugal, Qatar, Republic of Korea, Republic of Moldova, Romania, Russian Federation, Saint Kitts and Nevis, Saint Lucia, Saint Vincent and the Grenadines, Samoa, San Marino, Saudi Arabia, Senegal, Sierra Leone, Singapore, Slovakia, Slovenia, South Africa, Spain, Sri Lanka, Sudan, Suriname, Swaziland, Sweden, Tajikistan, Thailand, The former Yugoslav Republic of Macedonia, Togo, Tonga, Trinidad and Tobago, Tunisia, Turkey, Turkmenistan, Uganda, Ukraine, United Arab Emirates, United Kingdom, United States, Uruguay, Uzbekistan, Vanuatu, Venezuela, Viet Nam, Yemen, Zambia, Zimbabwe.

Against: None.

Abstaining: Bhutan, India, Libyan Arab Jamahiriya, Mauritius, Syrian Arab Republic, United Republic of Tanzania.

Preparatory Commission for the CTBT Organization

The Preparatory Commission for the Comprehensive Nuclear-Test-Ban Treaty Organization, established in 1996 [YUN 1996, p. 452], continued efforts towards setting up the Treaty's verification regime. Work progressed on building the global network of some 321 technical stations for the International Monitoring System (IMS) [YUN 1999, p. 472], designed to track and detect nuclear explosions prohibited by CTBT via a global satellite communications system to the International Data Center (IDC) in Vienna. About 60 per cent of the site surveys for finding suitable locations

for the stations were completed, with some 20 per cent of the stations fully installed. Since February, IDC had been sending IMS data and IDC products on a test basis to about 40 States parties to CTBT.

The Commission held its eleventh (2-5 May) [CTBT/PC-11/1], twelfth (22-24 August) [CTBT/PC-12/1] and thirteenth (20-21 November) [CTBT/PC-13/1 & Corr.1] sessions, all in Vienna, to consider the draft relationship agreement between the United Nations and the Commission, as well as to discuss organizational, budgetary and other matters.

In May, the Commission approved the draft agreement, which established a formal relationship between the two organizations, under which they would cooperate closely on matters of mutual interest. The Agreement was signed by the Secretary-General and the Commission's Executive Secretary on 26 May [A/54/884] and entered into force in June following approval by the General Assembly (see below). In other action, the Commission adopted a budget of $83.49 million for 2001, of which approximately half was earmarked for the global network of stations for IMS. The remainder would be used to develop IDC, the global communications infrastructure, and procedures and guidelines to support on-site inspection once the Treaty entered into force.

In October [A/55/433], the Secretary-General transmitted the report of the Executive Secretary covering 1999, in accordance with article IV, paragraph 1, of the Agreement, under which the Executive Secretary also addressed the General Assembly in October [A/55/PV.44].

By **decision 54/501** of 5 September, the General Assembly, on the recommendation of Austria [A/54/966], decided to include in the draft agenda of its fifty-fifth (2000) session the item on cooperation between the United Nations and the Preparatory Commission for CTBT. By **decision 55/408** of 30 October, the Assembly decided to include the item in the provisional agenda of its fifty-sixth (2001) session.

GENERAL ASSEMBLY ACTION

On 15 June [meeting 98], the General Assembly adopted **resolution 54/280** [draft: A/54/L.86 & Add.1] without vote [agenda item 167].

Agreement to regulate the relationship between the United Nations and the Preparatory Commission for the Comprehensive Nuclear-Test-Ban Treaty Organization

The General Assembly,

Recalling its resolution 54/65 of 6 December 1999, in which it invited the Secretary-General to take the appropriate steps to conclude, with the Executive Secretary of the Preparatory Commission for the Comprehensive Nuclear-Test-Ban Treaty Organization, an agreement to regulate the relationship between the United Nations and the Preparatory Commission, to be submitted to the General Assembly for its approval,

Noting the decision of the Preparatory Commission of 5 May 2000 to approve the Agreement to Regulate the Relationship between the United Nations and the Preparatory Commission for the Comprehensive Nuclear-Test-Ban Treaty Organization,

Having considered the Agreement to Regulate the Relationship between the United Nations and the Preparatory Commission for the Comprehensive Nuclear-Test-Ban Treaty Organization,

Approves the Agreement, the text of which is annexed to the present resolution.

ANNEX
Agreement to Regulate the Relationship between the United Nations and the Preparatory Commission for the Comprehensive Nuclear-Test-Ban Treaty Organization

The United Nations and the Preparatory Commission for the Comprehensive Nuclear-Test-Ban Treaty Organization,

Bearing in mind the relevant provisions of the Charter of the United Nations (hereinafter the "Charter") and of the Comprehensive Nuclear-Test-Ban Treaty (hereinafter the "Treaty"),

Bearing in mind also resolution CTBT/MSS/RES/1 of 19 November 1996 of the Meeting of States Signatories to the Treaty (hereinafter the "Resolution") establishing the Preparatory Commission for the Comprehensive Nuclear-Test-Ban Treaty Organization (hereinafter the "Commission"),

Recalling that in accordance with the Charter, the United Nations is the principal organization dealing with matters relating to the maintenance of international peace and security and acts as a centre for harmonizing the actions of nations in the attainment of goals set out in the Charter,

Recalling also the relevant provisions of the Treaty which provide for cooperation between the United Nations and the Comprehensive Nuclear-Test-Ban Treaty Organization,

Noting that, pursuant to the Resolution, the Commission was established for the purpose of carrying out the necessary preparations for the effective implementation of the Treaty,

Acknowledging that the activities of the Commission performed pursuant to the Treaty and the Resolution will contribute to the realization of the purposes and principles embodied in the Charter,

Desiring to make provision for a mutually beneficial relationship whereby the discharge of their respective responsibilities may be facilitated,

Noting that General Assembly resolution 54/65 of 6 December 1999 and the decision of the Commission of 29 April 1999 call for the conclusion of an agreement to regulate the relationship between the United Nations and the Commission,

Have agreed as follows:

Article I

General

1. The United Nations recognizes the Commission as an entity in working relationship with the United Nations as defined by the present Agreement, which, by virtue of the Resolution, has standing as an international organization, authority to negotiate and enter into agreements and such other legal capacity as is necessary for the exercise of its functions and the fulfilment of its purposes.

2. The Commission recognizes the responsibilities of the United Nations under the Charter, in particular, in the fields of international peace and security and economic and social, cultural and humanitarian development, protection and preservation of the environment and peaceful settlement of disputes.

3. The Commission undertakes to conduct its activities in accordance with the purposes and principles embodied in the Charter and with due regard to the policies of the United Nations furthering the said purposes and principles.

Article II

Cooperation and coordination

1. The United Nations and the Commission, recognizing the need to work jointly to achieve their common objectives, and with a view to facilitating the effective exercise of their responsibilities, agree to cooperate closely and to consult and to maintain a close working relationship on matters of mutual interest and concern. To that end, the United Nations and the Commission shall cooperate with each other in accordance with the provisions of their respective constituent instruments.

2. In view of the responsibilities of the Commission under the Resolution, the United Nations and the Commission shall, in particular, cooperate in the implementation of the following provisions of the Treaty:

(*a*) Paragraph 13 of article II of the Treaty, related to the convening by the Secretary-General of the United Nations, as the depositary of the Treaty, of the initial session of the Conference of the States Parties to the Treaty;

(*b*) Article XIV of the Treaty, related to the convening by the depositary, upon the request of a majority of States that have already deposited their instruments of ratification, of Conferences to consider and decide by consensus what measures consistent with international law may be taken to accelerate the ratification process in order to facilitate the early entry into force of the Treaty.

3. The Commission shall, within its competence and in accordance with the provisions of the Treaty, cooperate with the United Nations by providing to it at its request such information and assistance as may be required in the exercise of its responsibilities under the Charter. In case confidential information is provided, the United Nations shall preserve the confidential character of that information.

4. The United Nations and the Commission recognize the necessity of achieving, where applicable, effective coordination of the activities and services of the United Nations and the Commission with a view to avoiding unnecessary duplication of such activities and services, particularly with respect to common services at the Vienna International Centre.

5. The Secretariat of the United Nations and the provisional technical secretariat of the Commission shall maintain a close working relationship on issues of mutual concern in accordance with such arrangements as may be agreed from time to time.

6. The Secretary-General of the United Nations and the Executive Secretary of the Commission shall consult from time to time regarding their respective re-

sponsibilities and, in particular, regarding such administrative arrangements as may be necessary to enable the United Nations and the Commission effectively to carry out their functions and to ensure effective cooperation and liaison between the Secretariat of the United Nations and the provisional technical secretariat of the Commission.

Article III

Reciprocal representation

1. The Secretary-General of the United Nations, or his representative, shall be entitled to attend and participate without vote in sessions of the Commission and, subject to the rules of procedure and practice of the bodies concerned, in meetings of such other bodies as may be convened by the Commission, whenever matters of interest to the United Nations are under consideration.

2. The Executive Secretary of the Commission shall be entitled to attend plenary meetings of the General Assembly for the purposes of consultation. The Executive Secretary shall be entitled to attend and participate without vote in meetings of the Committees of the General Assembly and, subject to the rules of procedure and practice of the bodies concerned, in meetings of subsidiary bodies of the General Assembly and the Committees concerning matters of interest to the Commission. Whenever other principal organs of the United Nations consider matters which are of relevance to the activities of the Commission, at the invitation of that organ, the Executive Secretary may attend its meetings to supply it with information or give it other assistance with regard to matters within the competence of the Commission. The Executive Secretary may, for the purposes of the present paragraph, designate any person as his representative.

3. Written statements presented by the United Nations to the Commission for distribution shall be transmitted by the provisional technical secretariat of the Commission to all members of the appropriate organ or organs of the Commission. Written statements presented by the Commission to the United Nations for distribution shall be transmitted by the Secretariat of the United Nations to all members of the appropriate organ or organs of the United Nations.

Article IV

Reporting

1. The Commission shall, within its competence and in accordance with the provisions of the Treaty, keep the United Nations informed of its activities, and may submit through the Secretary-General of the United Nations reports thereon on a regular or ad hoc basis to the principal organs of the United Nations concerned.

2. Should the Secretary-General of the United Nations report to the United Nations on the common activities of the United Nations and the Commission or on the development of relations between them, any such report shall be promptly transmitted by the Secretary-General to the Commission.

3. Should the Executive Secretary of the Commission report to the Commission on the common activities of the Commission and the United Nations or on the development of relations between them, any such report shall be promptly transmitted by the Executive Secretary to the United Nations.

Article V

Resolutions of the United Nations

The Secretary-General of the United Nations shall transmit to the Executive Secretary of the Commission resolutions adopted by the principal organs of the United Nations pertaining to issues relevant to the Treaty and the Resolution. Upon receipt thereof, the Executive Secretary shall bring the resolutions concerned to the attention of the Commission and report back to the United Nations on any action taken by the Commission, as appropriate.

Article VI

Agenda items

1. The United Nations may propose agenda items for consideration by the Commission. In such cases, the United Nations shall notify the Executive Secretary of the Commission of the agenda item or items concerned, and the Executive Secretary, in accordance with his authority and the relevant rules of procedure, shall bring any such agenda item or items to the attention of the Commission.

2. The Commission may propose agenda items for consideration by the United Nations. In such cases, the Commission shall notify the Secretary-General of the United Nations of the agenda item or items concerned, and the Secretary-General shall, in accordance with his authority and the relevant rules of procedure, bring any such item or items to the attention of the principal organs of the United Nations concerned.

Article VII

Exchange of information and documents

1. The United Nations and the Commission shall arrange for the exchange of information, publications and documents of mutual interest.

2. In fulfilment of the responsibilities entrusted to him under article XVI of the Treaty and in the light of the responsibilities of the Commission under paragraph 18 of the Resolution, the Secretary-General of the United Nations shall transmit to the Commission copies of communications received by the Secretary-General as depositary of the Treaty.

3. The Commission shall, to the extent practicable, furnish special studies or information requested by the United Nations. The submission of such studies and information shall be subject to conditions set forth in article XII of the present Agreement.

4. The United Nations shall likewise, to the extent practicable, furnish the Commission, upon its request, with special studies or information relating to matters within the competence of the Commission. The submission of such studies and information shall be subject to conditions set forth in article XII of the present Agreement.

5. The United Nations and the Commission shall make every effort to achieve maximum cooperation with a view to avoiding undesirable duplication in the collection, analysis, publication and dissemination of information related to matters of mutual interest. They shall strive to combine, where appropriate, their efforts to secure the greatest possible usefulness and utilization of such information and to minimize the burdens placed on Governments and other international organizations from which such information may be collected.

Article VIII

International Court of Justice

The Commission agrees, subject to such arrangements as it may make for the safeguarding of confidential information, to furnish any information which may be requested by the International Court of Justice in accordance with the Statute of the Court.

Article IX

United Nations laissez-passer

The United Nations recognizes that due to the special nature and universality of the work of the Commission, as defined in the Resolution, officials of the Commission shall, in accordance with such special arrangements as may be concluded between the Secretary-General of the United Nations and the Executive Secretary of the Commission, be entitled to use the laissez-passer of the United Nations as a valid travel document where such use is recognized by States in the instruments or arrangements defining the privileges and immunities of the Commission.

Article X

Personnel arrangements

1. The United Nations and the Commission agree to consult whenever necessary concerning matters of common interest relating to the terms and conditions of employment of staff.

2. The United Nations and the Commission agree to cooperate regarding the exchange of personnel, bearing in mind the nationality of States signatories of the Treaty, and to determine conditions of such cooperation in supplementary arrangements to be concluded for that purpose in accordance with article XV of the present Agreement.

Article XI

Budgetary and financial matters

1. The Commission recognizes the desirability of establishing budgetary and financial cooperation with the United Nations in order that the Commission may benefit from the experience of the United Nations in this field and to ensure, as far as may be practicable, the consistency of the administrative operation of the two organizations in the field.

2. Subject to the provision of article XII of the present Agreement, the United Nations may arrange for studies to be undertaken concerning budgetary and financial matters of interest to the Commission with a view, as far as may be practicable, to achieving coordination and securing consistency in such matters.

3. The Commission agrees to follow, as far as may be practicable and appropriate, the standard budgetary and financial practices and forms used by the United Nations.

Article XII

Costs and expenses

The costs and expenses resulting from any cooperation or the provision of services pursuant to the present Agreement shall be subject to separate arrangements between the United Nations and the Commission.

Article XIII

Protection of confidentiality

Subject to the provisions of paragraphs 1 and 3 of article II, nothing in the present Agreement shall be so construed as to require either the United Nations or the Commission to provide any material, data and information the furnishing of which could, in its judgement, require it to violate its policy regarding the confidentiality of such information.

Article XIV

Registration

Either the United Nations or the Commission may register the present Agreement with the United Nations.

Article XV

Implementation of the Agreement

The Secretary-General of the United Nations and the Executive Secretary of the Commission may enter into such supplementary arrangements for the implementation of the present Agreement as may be found desirable.

Article XVI

Amendments

The present Agreement may be amended by mutual consent between the United Nations and the Commission. Any amendment, once agreed upon, shall enter into force upon its approval by the General Assembly of the United Nations and the Commission.

Article XVII

Entry into force

The present Agreement shall enter into force upon its approval by the General Assembly of the United Nations and the Commission.

IN WITNESS WHEREOF the undersigned, being duly authorized representatives of the United Nations and the Preparatory Commission for the Comprehensive Nuclear-Test-Ban Treaty Organization, have signed the present Agreement.

SIGNED this 26th day of May in the year two thousand in New York in two originals in the English language.

For the United Nations:
(*Signed*) Kofi A. ANNAN
Secretary-General

For the Preparatory Commission for
the Comprehensive Nuclear-Test-
Ban Treaty Organization:
(*Signed*) Wolfgang HOFFMANN
Executive Secretary

IAEA safeguards

As at 31 December, the Model Protocol Additional to Safeguards Agreements strengthening IAEA's safeguards regime, approved by the IAEA Board of Governors in 1997 [YUN 1997, p. 486], had been signed by 57 States, including the 5 nuclear-weapon States, and was in force or being provisionally applied in 19 States.

The IAEA General Conference [GC(44)/RES/19] once again requested all concerned States and other parties to safeguards agreements that had not done so to sign additional protocols promptly. Those that had signed were requested to bring the protocols into force or provisionally apply them, while Member States were asked to consider a plan of action to facilitate the protocols' application.

During the year, IAEA was not able to implement its mandate with regard to Iraq under the relevant Security Council resolutions, having had to withdraw its inspectors in 1998 [YUN 1998, p. 258]. Thus, IAEA was not in a position to provide any assurances that Iraq was in compliance with its obligations under those resolutions. In the absence of any Council-mandated activities, IAEA conducted a physical inventory verification in January related to the 1999 programme under the safeguards agreement between Iraq and IAEA pursuant to NPT. Agency inspectors verified the presence of nuclear material under safeguards at the Tuwaitha storage facility (see also p. 294).

Regarding the implementation of the agreement between IAEA and the DPRK for the application of safeguards under NPT, the Director General stated in September that the Agency remained unable to verify fully that all nuclear material subject to safeguards in the DPRK had been declared to IAEA. On 22 September [GC(44)/RES/26], the General Conference expressed continuing concern about the lack of cooperation by the DPRK, urging it to cooperate fully and promptly (see also p. 321).

Middle East

In 2000, the General Assembly (see below) and the IAEA General Conference [GC(44)/RES/28] took action regarding the risk of nuclear proliferation in the Middle East. While the Assembly called on the non-party in the region to accede to NPT and to place all its nuclear facilities under IAEA safeguards, IAEA reaffirmed the need for all States in the Middle East to accept the application of full-scope Agency safeguards and to adhere to international non-proliferation regimes, including NPT.

Pursuant to Assembly resolution 54/57 [YUN 1999, p. 474], the Secretary-General reported in October [A/55/448] that, apart from the IAEA resolution on the application of IAEA safeguards in the Middle East, he had not received any additional information since his 1999 report on the subject [YUN 1999, p. 474]. The IAEA resolution was annexed to the Secretary-General's report.

GENERAL ASSEMBLY ACTION

On 20 November [meeting 69], the General Assembly, on the recommendation of the First

Committee [A/55/562], adopted **resolution 55/36** by recorded vote (157-3-8) [agenda item 76].

The risk of nuclear proliferation
in the Middle East

The General Assembly,

Bearing in mind its relevant resolutions,

Taking note of the relevant resolutions adopted by the General Conference of the International Atomic Energy Agency, the latest of which is resolution GC(44)/RES/28, adopted on 22 September 2000,

Cognizant that the proliferation of nuclear weapons in the region of the Middle East would pose a serious threat to international peace and security,

Mindful of the immediate need for placing all nuclear facilities in the region of the Middle East under full-scope safeguards of the International Atomic Energy Agency,

Recalling the decision on principles and objectives for nuclear non-proliferation and disarmament adopted by the 1995 Review and Extension Conference of the Parties to the Treaty on the Non-Proliferation of Nuclear Weapons of 11 May 1995, in which the Conference urged universal adherence to the Treaty as an urgent priority and called upon all States not yet parties to the Treaty to accede to it at the earliest date, particularly those States that operate unsafeguarded nuclear facilities,

Recognizing with satisfaction that, in the Final Document of the 2000 Review Conference of the Parties to the Treaty on the Non-Proliferation of Nuclear Weapons, the Conference undertook to make determined efforts towards the achievement of the goal of universality of the Treaty on the Non-Proliferation of Nuclear Weapons, and called upon those remaining States not parties to the Treaty to accede to it, thereby accepting an international legally binding commitment not to acquire nuclear weapons or nuclear explosive devices and to accept International Atomic Energy Agency safeguards on all their nuclear activities, and underlined the necessity of universal adherence to the Treaty and of strict compliance by all parties with their obligations under the Treaty,

Recalling the resolution on the Middle East adopted by the 1995 Review and Extension Conference of the Parties to the Treaty on the Non-Proliferation of Nuclear Weapons on 11 May 1995, in which the Conference noted with concern the continued existence in the Middle East of unsafeguarded nuclear facilities, reaffirmed the importance of the early realization of universal adherence to the Treaty and called upon all States in the Middle East that had not yet done so, without exception, to accede to the Treaty as soon as possible and to place all their nuclear facilities under full-scope International Atomic Energy Agency safeguards,

Noting that Israel remains the only State in the Middle East that has not yet become party to the Treaty on the Non-Proliferation of Nuclear Weapons,

Concerned about the threats posed by the proliferation of nuclear weapons to the security and stability of the Middle East region,

Stressing the importance of taking confidence-building measures, in particular the establishment of a nuclear-weapon-free zone in the Middle East, in order to enhance peace and security in the region and to consolidate the global non-proliferation regime,

Emphasizing the need for all parties directly concerned to consider seriously taking the practical and urgent steps required for the implementation of the proposal to establish a nuclear-weapon-free zone in the region of the Middle East in accordance with the relevant resolutions of the General Assembly and, as a means of promoting this objective, inviting the countries concerned to adhere to the Treaty on the Non-Proliferation of Nuclear Weapons, and pending the establishment of the zone, to agree to place all their nuclear activities under International Atomic Energy Agency safeguards,

Noting that one hundred and sixty States have signed the Comprehensive Nuclear-Test-Ban Treaty, including a number of States in the region,

1. *Welcomes* the conclusions on the Middle East of the 2000 Review Conference of the Parties to the Treaty on the Non-Proliferation of Nuclear Weapons;

2. *Reaffirms* the importance of Israel's accession to the Treaty on the Non-Proliferation of Nuclear Weapons and placement of all its nuclear facilities under comprehensive International Atomic Energy Agency safeguards, in realizing the goal of universal adherence to the Treaty in the Middle East;

3. *Calls upon* that State to accede to the Treaty on the Non-Proliferation of Nuclear Weapons without further delay and not to develop, produce, test or otherwise acquire nuclear weapons, and to renounce possession of nuclear weapons, and to place all its unsafeguarded nuclear facilities under full-scope International Atomic Energy Agency safeguards as an important confidence-building measure among all States of the region and as a step towards enhancing peace and security;

4. *Requests* the Secretary-General to report to the General Assembly at its fifty-sixth session on the implementation of the present resolution;

5. *Decides* to include in the provisional agenda of its fifty-sixth session the item entitled "The risk of nuclear proliferation in the Middle East".

RECORDED VOTE ON RESOLUTION 55/36:

In favour: Albania, Algeria, Andorra, Angola, Antigua and Barbuda, Argentina, Armenia, Austria, Azerbaijan, Bahamas, Bahrain, Bangladesh, Barbados, Belarus, Belgium, Belize, Benin, Bhutan, Bolivia, Bosnia and Herzegovina, Botswana, Brazil, Brunei Darussalam, Bulgaria, Burkina Faso, Burundi, Cambodia, Cape Verde, Chile, China, Colombia, Comoros, Costa Rica, Côte d'Ivoire, Croatia, Cuba, Cyprus, Czech Republic, Democratic People's Republic of Korea, Denmark, Djibouti, Dominican Republic, Ecuador, Egypt, El Salvador, Equatorial Guinea, Eritrea, Estonia, Fiji, Finland, France, Gabon, Gambia, Georgia, Germany, Ghana, Greece, Grenada, Guatemala, Guinea, Guyana, Haiti, Honduras, Hungary, Iceland, Indonesia, Iran, Ireland, Italy, Jamaica, Japan, Jordan, Kazakhstan, Kenya, Kuwait, Kyrgyzstan, Lao People's Democratic Republic, Latvia, Lebanon, Lesotho, Libyan Arab Jamahiriya, Liechtenstein, Lithuania, Luxembourg, Madagascar, Malawi, Malaysia, Maldives, Mali, Malta, Mauritius, Mexico, Monaco, Mongolia, Morocco, Mozambique, Myanmar, Namibia, Nauru, Nepal, Netherlands, New Zealand, Nicaragua, Nigeria, Norway, Oman, Pakistan, Panama, Papua New Guinea, Paraguay, Peru, Philippines, Poland, Portugal, Qatar, Republic of Korea, Republic of Moldova, Romania, Russian Federation, Saint Kitts and Nevis, Saint Lucia, Saint Vincent and the Grenadines, Samoa, San Marino, Saudi Arabia, Senegal, Sierra Leone, Slovakia, Slovenia, South Africa, Spain, Sri Lanka, Sudan, Suriname, Swaziland, Sweden, Syrian Arab Republic, Tajikistan, Thailand, The former Yugoslav Republic of Macedonia, Togo, Tunisia, Turkey, Turkmenistan, Uganda, Ukraine, United Arab Emirates, United Kingdom, United Republic of Tanzania, Uruguay, Uzbekistan, Vanuatu, Venezuela, Viet Nam, Yemen, Zambia, Zimbabwe.

Against: Israel, Micronesia, United States.

Abstaining: Australia, Canada, Ethiopia, India, Marshall Islands, Singapore, Tonga, Trinidad and Tobago.

The First Committee adopted paragraph 6 by a recorded vote of 138 to 2, with 5 abstentions, as did the Assembly by 158 to 2, with 5 abstentions.

Prohibition of use of nuclear weapons

In 2000, the Conference on Disarmament was not able to undertake negotiations on a convention on the prohibition of the use of nuclear weapons, as called for in General Assembly resolution 54/55 D [YUN 1999, p. 474].

GENERAL ASSEMBLY ACTION

On 20 November [meeting 69], the General Assembly, on the recommendation of the First Committee [A/55/560], adopted **resolution 55/34 G** by recorded vote (109-43-16) [agenda item 74 *(d)*].

Convention on the Prohibition of the Use of Nuclear Weapons

The General Assembly,

Convinced that the use of nuclear weapons poses the most serious threat to the survival of mankind,

Bearing in mind the advisory opinion of the International Court of Justice of 8 July 1996 on the *Legality of the Threat or Use of Nuclear Weapons,*

Convinced that a multilateral, universal and binding agreement prohibiting the use or threat of use of nuclear weapons would contribute to the elimination of the nuclear threat and to the climate for negotiations leading to the ultimate elimination of nuclear weapons, thereby strengthening international peace and security,

Conscious that some steps taken by the Russian Federation and the United States of America towards a reduction of their nuclear weapons and the improvement in the international climate can contribute towards the goal of the complete elimination of nuclear weapons,

Recalling that, in paragraph 58 of the Final Document of the Tenth Special Session of the General Assembly, it is stated that all States should actively participate in efforts to bring about conditions in international relations among States in which a code of peaceful conduct of nations in international affairs could be agreed upon and that would preclude the use or threat of use of nuclear weapons,

Reaffirming that any use of nuclear weapons would be a violation of the Charter of the United Nations and a crime against humanity, as declared in its resolutions 1653(XVI) of 24 November 1961, 33/71 B of 14 December 1978, 34/83 G of 11 December 1979, 35/152 D of 12 December 1980 and 36/92 I of 9 December 1981,

Determined to achieve an international convention prohibiting the development, production, stockpiling and use of nuclear weapons, leading to their ultimate destruction,

Stressing that an international convention on the prohibition of the use of nuclear weapons would be an important step in a phased programme towards the complete elimination of nuclear weapons, with a specified framework of time,

Noting with regret that the Conference on Disarmament, during its 2000 session, was unable to undertake negotiations on this subject as called for in General Assembly resolution 54/55 D of 1 December 1999,

1. *Reiterates its request* to the Conference on Disarmament to commence negotiations in order to reach agreement on an international convention prohibiting the use or threat of use of nuclear weapons under any circumstances;

2. *Requests* the Conference on Disarmament to report to the General Assembly on the results of those negotiations.

RECORDED VOTE ON RESOLUTION 55/34 G:

In favour: Algeria, Angola, Antigua and Barbuda, Bahamas, Bahrain, Bangladesh, Barbados, Belarus, Belize, Benin, Bhutan, Bolivia, Botswana, Brazil, Brunei Darussalam, Burkina Faso, Burundi, Cambodia, Cameroon, Cape Verde, Chile, Colombia, Comoros, Costa Rica, Côte d'Ivoire, Cuba, Democratic People's Republic of Korea, Djibouti, Dominican Republic, Ecuador, Egypt, El Salvador, Equatorial Guinea, Eritrea, Ethiopia, Fiji, Gabon, Gambia, Ghana, Grenada, Guatemala, Guinea, Guyana, Haiti, Honduras, India, Indonesia, Iran, Jamaica, Jordan, Kenya, Kuwait, Lao People's Democratic Republic, Lebanon, Lesotho, Libyan Arab Jamahiriya, Madagascar, Malawi, Malaysia, Maldives, Mali, Marshall Islands, Mauritius, Mexico, Mongolia, Morocco, Mozambique, Myanmar, Namibia, Nauru, Nepal, Nicaragua, Nigeria, Oman, Pakistan, Panama, Papua New Guinea, Paraguay, Peru, Philippines, Qatar, Saint Kitts and Nevis, Saint Lucia, Saint Vincent and the Grenadines, Samoa, Saudi Arabia, Senegal, Sierra Leone, Singapore, South Africa, Sri Lanka, Sudan, Suriname, Swaziland, Syrian Arab Republic, Thailand, Togo, Tonga, Trinidad and Tobago, Tunisia, Uganda, United Republic of Tanzania, Uruguay, Vanuatu, Venezuela, Viet Nam, Yemen, Zambia, Zimbabwe.

Against: Albania, Andorra, Australia, Austria, Belgium, Bosnia and Herzegovina, Bulgaria, Canada, Croatia, Czech Republic, Denmark, Estonia, Finland, France, Germany, Greece, Hungary, Iceland, Ireland, Italy, Latvia, Liechtenstein, Lithuania, Luxembourg, Malta, Micronesia, Monaco, Netherlands, New Zealand, Norway, Poland, Portugal, Republic of Moldova, Romania, San Marino, Slovakia, Slovenia, Spain, Sweden, The former Yugoslav Republic of Macedonia, Turkey, United Kingdom, United States.

Abstaining: Argentina, Armenia, Azerbaijan, China, Cyprus, Georgia, Israel, Japan, Kazakhstan, Kyrgyzstan, Republic of Korea, Russian Federation, Tajikistan, Turkmenistan, Ukraine, Uzbekistan.

Advisory opinion of International Court of Justice

Pursuant to General Assembly resolution 54/54 Q [YUN 1999, p. 475] on the advisory opinion of the International Court of Justice that the threat or use of nuclear weapons was contrary to the UN Charter [YUN 1996, p. 461], the Secretary-General presented information received from Cuba, Iraq, New Zealand and Qatar on measures they had taken to implement the resolution and nuclear disarmament [A/55/131 & Add.1]. On 27 November [A/55/647], Saudi Arabia, referring to the information from Iraq, dissociated itself from Iraq's claim that it had participated in the alleged use of force against Iraq in the no-flight zones. In addition, there was no supporting evidence regarding Iraq's claim that the United States had extensively used depleted-uranium munitions against Iraq in 1991.

GENERAL ASSEMBLY ACTION

On 20 November [meeting 69], the General Assembly, on the recommendation of the First Committee [A/55/559], adopted **resolution 55/33 X** by recorded vote (119-28-22) [agenda item 73 (r)].

Follow-up to the advisory opinion of the International Court of Justice on the
Legality of the Threat or Use of Nuclear Weapons
The General Assembly,

Recalling its resolutions 49/75 K of 15 December 1994, 51/45 M of 10 December 1996, 52/38 O of 9 December 1997, 53/77 W of 4 December 1998 and 54/54 Q of 1 December 1999,

Convinced that the continuing existence of nuclear weapons poses a threat to all humanity and that their use would have catastrophic consequences for all life on Earth, and recognizing that the only defence against a nuclear catastrophe is the total elimination of nuclear weapons and the certainty that they will never be produced again,

Reaffirming the commitment of the international community to the goal of the total elimination of nuclear weapons and the creation of a nuclear-weapon-free world,

Mindful of the solemn obligations of States parties, undertaken in article VI of the Treaty on the Non-Proliferation of Nuclear Weapons, particularly to pursue negotiations in good faith on effective measures relating to cessation of the nuclear arms race at an early date and to nuclear disarmament,

Recalling the principles and objectives for nuclear non-proliferation and disarmament adopted at the 1995 Review and Extension Conference of the Parties to the Treaty on the Non-Proliferation of Nuclear Weapons,

Welcoming the unequivocal undertaking by the nuclear-weapon States to accomplish the total elimination of their nuclear arsenals leading to nuclear disarmament,

Recalling the adoption of the Comprehensive Nuclear-Test-Ban Treaty in its resolution 50/245 of 10 September 1996, and expressing its satisfaction at the increasing number of States that have signed and ratified the Treaty,

Recognizing with satisfaction that the Antarctic Treaty and the treaties of Tlatelolco, Rarotonga, Bangkok and Pelindaba are gradually freeing the entire southern hemisphere and adjacent areas covered by those treaties from nuclear weapons,

Noting the efforts by the States possessing the largest inventories of nuclear weapons to reduce their stockpiles of such weapons through bilateral agreements or arrangements and unilateral decisions, and calling for the intensification of such efforts to accelerate the significant reduction of nuclear-weapon arsenals,

Recognizing the need for a multilaterally negotiated and legally binding instrument to assure non-nuclear-weapon States against the threat or use of nuclear weapons,

Reaffirming the central role of the Conference on Disarmament as the single multilateral disarmament negotiating forum, and regretting the lack of progress in disarmament negotiations, particularly nuclear disarmament, in the Conference on Disarmament during its 2000 session,

Emphasizing the need for the Conference on Disarmament to commence negotiations on a phased programme for the complete elimination of nuclear weapons with a specified framework of time,

Desiring to achieve the objective of a legally binding prohibition of the development, production, testing, deployment, stockpiling, threat or use of nuclear weapons and their destruction under effective international control,

Recalling the advisory opinion of the International Court of Justice on the *Legality of the Threat or Use of Nuclear Weapons*, issued on 8 July 1996,

Taking note of the relevant portions of the note by the Secretary-General relating to the implementation of resolution 54/54 Q,

1. *Underlines once again* the unanimous conclusion of the International Court of Justice that there exists an obligation to pursue in good faith and bring to a conclusion negotiations leading to nuclear disarmament in all its aspects under strict and effective international control;

2. *Calls once again upon* all States immediately to fulfil that obligation by commencing multilateral negotiations in 2001 leading to an early conclusion of a convention prohibiting the development, production, testing, deployment, stockpiling, transfer, threat or use of nuclear weapons and providing for their elimination;

3. *Requests* all States to inform the Secretary-General of the efforts and measures they have taken on the implementation of the present resolution and nuclear disarmament, and requests the Secretary-General to apprise the General Assembly of that information at its fifty-sixth session;

4. *Decides* to include in the provisional agenda of its fifty-sixth session the item entitled "Follow-up to the advisory opinion of the International Court of Justice on the *Legality of the Threat or Use of Nuclear Weapons*".

RECORDED VOTE ON RESOLUTION 55/33 X:

In favour: Algeria, Angola, Antigua and Barbuda, Argentina, Bahamas, Bahrain, Bangladesh, Barbados, Belarus, Belize, Benin, Bhutan, Bolivia, Botswana, Brazil, Brunei Darussalam, Burkina Faso, Burundi, Cambodia, Cameroon, Cape Verde, Chile, China, Colombia, Comoros, Costa Rica, Côte d'Ivoire, Cuba, Democratic People's Republic of Korea, Djibouti, Dominican Republic, Ecuador, Egypt, El Salvador, Equatorial Guinea, Eritrea, Ethiopia, Fiji, Gabon, Gambia, Ghana, Grenada, Guatemala, Guinea, Guyana, Haiti, Honduras, India, Indonesia, Iran, Ireland, Jamaica, Jordan, Kenya, Kuwait, Lao People's Democratic Republic, Lebanon, Lesotho, Libyan Arab Jamahiriya, Madagascar, Malawi, Malaysia, Maldives, Mali, Malta, Marshall Islands, Mauritius, Mexico, Mongolia, Morocco, Mozambique, Myanmar, Namibia, Nauru, Nepal, New Zealand, Nicaragua, Nigeria, Oman, Pakistan, Panama, Papua New Guinea, Paraguay, Peru, Philippines, Qatar, Saint Kitts and Nevis, Saint Lucia, Saint Vincent and the Grenadines, Samoa, San Marino, Saudi Arabia, Senegal, Sierra Leone, Singapore, Solomon Islands, South Africa, Sri Lanka, Sudan, Suriname, Swaziland, Sweden, Syrian Arab Republic, Thailand, Togo, Tonga, Trinidad and Tobago, Tunisia, Uganda, Ukraine, United Arab Emirates, United Republic of Tanzania, Uruguay, Vanuatu, Venezuela, Viet Nam, Yemen, Zambia, Zimbabwe.

Against: Andorra, Belgium, Bulgaria, Czech Republic, Denmark, France, Germany, Greece, Hungary, Iceland, Israel, Italy, Latvia, Lithuania, Luxembourg, Monaco, Netherlands, Norway, Poland, Portugal, Romania, Russian Federation, Slovakia, Slovenia, Spain, Turkey, United Kingdom, United States.

Abstaining: Albania, Armenia, Australia, Austria, Azerbaijan, Bosnia and Herzegovina, Canada, Croatia, Cyprus, Estonia, Finland, Georgia, Japan, Kazakhstan, Kyrgyzstan, Liechtenstein, Republic of Korea, Republic of Moldova, Tajikistan, The former Yugoslav Republic of Macedonia, Turkmenistan, Uzbekistan.

The First Committee adopted paragraph 1 by a separate recorded vote of 150 to 4, with 1 abstention, while the text as a whole was adopted by a recorded vote of 109 to 27, with 21 abstentions. The General Assembly retained the paragraph by a recorded vote of 162 to 4, with 1 abstention.

Nuclear-weapon-free zones

Africa

As at 31 December, 16 States had ratified the African Nuclear-Weapon-Free Zone Treaty (Treaty of Pelindaba) [YUN 1995, p. 203], which was opened for signature in 1996 [YUN 1996, p. 486]. China and France had ratified Protocols I and II thereto and France had also ratified Protocol III.

The Russian Federation, the United Kingdom and the United States had signed Protocols I and II. The Treaty had 55 signatories.

Asia

Central Asia

Negotiations on drafting the text of the treaty for a nuclear-weapon-free zone in Central Asia continued in 2000. The UN-sponsored Expert Group, consisting of experts from each of the five States in the region (Kazakhstan, Kyrgyzstan, Tajikistan, Turkmenistan, Uzbekistan), held a meeting (Sapporo, Japan, 2-5 April), at which it made substantial progress and accepted almost all the draft provisions on an *ad credendum* basis (as an article of faith).

GENERAL ASSEMBLY ACTION

On 20 November [meeting 69], the General Assembly, on the recommendation of the First Committee [A/55/559], adopted **resolution 55/33 W** without vote [agenda item 73 *(b)*].

Establishment of a nuclear-weapon-free zone in Central Asia

The General Assembly,

Recalling its resolutions 52/38 S of 9 December 1997 and 53/77 A of 4 December 1998 and its decision 54/417 of 1 December 1999,

Recalling also paragraphs 60, 61, 62 and 64 of the Final Document of the Tenth Special Session of the General Assembly and the provisions of the Treaty on the Non-Proliferation of Nuclear Weapons, and recalling further the relevant paragraphs of the Final Document of the 2000 Review Conference of the Parties to the Treaty on the Non-Proliferation of Nuclear Weapons and of the report of its Main Committee II related to the establishment of a nuclear-weapon-free zone in Central Asia,

Convinced that the establishment of nuclear-weapon-free zones is conducive to the achievement of general and complete disarmament,

Emphasizing the importance of internationally recognized agreements on the establishment of nuclear-weapon-free zones in various parts of the world and on the strengthening of the non-proliferation regime,

Welcoming the adoption by the Disarmament Commission at its 1999 substantive session of principles and guidelines for the establishment of nuclear-weapon-free zones on the basis of arrangements freely arrived at among the States of the region concerned,

Believing that the establishment of a nuclear-weapon-free zone in Central Asia on the basis of arrangements freely arrived at among the States of the region and bearing in mind the specific characteristics of the region, can enhance the security of the States involved and strengthen global and regional peace and security,

Recalling the Almaty Declaration of the heads of State of the Central Asian States of 28 February 1997 on the establishment of a nuclear-weapon-free zone in Central Asia, the statement issued at Tashkent on 15

September 1997 by the Ministers for Foreign Affairs of Kazakhstan, Kyrgyzstan, Tajikistan, Turkmenistan and Uzbekistan on the establishment of a nuclear-weapon-free zone in Central Asia and the Communiqué of the Consultative Meeting of Experts of the Central Asian Countries, the Nuclear-Weapon States and the United Nations, held at Bishkek on 9 and 10 July 1998, on the elaboration of acceptable ways and means of establishing a nuclear-weapon-free zone in Central Asia,

Reaffirming the universally recognized role of the United Nations in the establishment of nuclear-weapon-free zones,

1. *Notes with appreciation* the support of all States for the initiative to establish a nuclear-weapon-free zone in Central Asia;

2. *Welcomes* the desire of all five States of the Central Asian region to finalize work on the establishment of a nuclear-weapon-free zone in Central Asia and the concrete steps that they have taken to that end to prepare the legal groundwork for the initiative and the progress that they have achieved in this regard;

3. *Calls upon* all five Central Asian States to continue their dialogue with the five nuclear-weapon States on the establishment of a nuclear-weapon-free zone in Central Asia;

4. *Requests* the Secretary-General, within existing resources, to continue to provide assistance to the Central Asian States in the elaboration of an agreement on the establishment of a nuclear-weapon-free zone in Central Asia;

5. *Decides* to continue its consideration of the question of the establishment of a nuclear-weapon-free zone in Central Asia at its fifty-sixth session under the agenda item entitled "General and complete disarmament".

Mongolia

Mongolia transmitted a law defining and regulating its nuclear-weapon-free status, adopted by its parliament on 3 February [A/55/56-S/2000/160], as well as a related resolution of the same date.

In July [A/55/166], the Secretary-General, pursuant to General Assembly resolution 53/77 D [YUN 1998, p. 515], reported on UN assistance accorded to Mongolia, as well as action taken by the country to promote its nuclear-weapon-free status. In October [A/55/530-S/2000/1052], the five nuclear-weapon States issued a joint statement reaffirming their commitment to Mongolia's nuclear-weapon-free status and their respective unilateral negative security assurances to the country. They also reaffirmed their commitment to seek immediate Security Council action to assist Mongolia if it became a victim of aggression. On 16 October [A/55/491-S/2000/994], Mongolia, referring to the joint statement, said it represented an important step towards institutionalizing its nuclear-weapon-free status at the international level.

On 20 November [meeting 69], the General Assembly, on the recommendation of the First Committee [A/55/559], adopted **resolution 55/33 S** without vote [agenda item 73 (c)].

Mongolia's international security and nuclear-weapon-free status

The General Assembly,

Recalling its resolution 53/77 D of 4 December 1998,

Recalling also the purposes and principles of the Charter of the United Nations as well as the Declaration on Principles of International Law concerning Friendly Relations and Cooperation among States in accordance with the Charter of the United Nations,

Bearing in mind its resolution 49/31 of 9 December 1994 on the protection and security of small States,

Proceeding from the fact that nuclear-weapon-free status is one of the means of ensuring the national security of States,

Convinced that the internationally recognized status of Mongolia will contribute to enhancing stability and confidence-building in the region as well as promote Mongolia's security by strengthening its independence, sovereignty and territorial integrity, the inviolability of its borders and the preservation of its ecological balance,

Welcoming the measures taken to implement resolution 53/77 D at the national and international levels,

Recalling that in the Final Document of the 2000 Review Conference of the Parties to the Treaty on the Non-Proliferation of Nuclear Weapons, held at Headquarters from 24 April to 19 May 2000, the Conference welcomed the declaration by Mongolia of its nuclear-weapon-free status and took note of the adoption by the Mongolian parliament of legislation defining and regulating that status,

Taking note of the efforts undertaken by the five nuclear-weapon States and Mongolia to implement the provisions of the resolution concerning Mongolia's nuclear-weapon-free status,

Taking note also of the joint statement of the five nuclear-weapon States made on 5 October 2000 on security assurances in connection with Mongolia's nuclear-weapon-free status, including their commitment to Mongolia to cooperate in the implementation of General Assembly resolution 53/77 D with respect to Mongolia's nuclear-weapon-free status, in accordance with the principles of the Charter,

Noting that the joint statement has been transmitted to the Security Council by the five nuclear-weapon States,

Welcoming Mongolia's active and positive role in developing peaceful, friendly and mutually beneficial relations with the States of the region and other States,

Having considered the report of the Secretary-General on the implementation of resolution 53/77 D,

1. *Takes note* of the report of the Secretary-General on the implementation of resolution 53/77 D entitled "Mongolia's international security and nuclear-weapon-free status";

2. *Takes note also* of the adoption by the Mongolian parliament of legislation defining and regulating its nuclear-weapon-free status as a concrete step towards promoting the aims of nuclear non-proliferation;

3. *Welcomes* the joint statement of the five nuclear-weapon States providing security assurances to Mongolia in connection with its nuclear-weapon-free status as a contribution to implementing resolution 53/77 D;

4. *Endorses and supports* Mongolia's good-neighbourly and balanced relationship with its neighbours as an important element of strengthening regional peace, security and stability;

5. *Invites* Member States to continue to cooperate with Mongolia in taking the necessary measures to consolidate and strengthen Mongolia's independence, sovereignty and territorial integrity, the inviolability of its borders, its economic security, its ecological balance and its nuclear-weapon-free status, as well as its independent foreign policy;

6. *Appeals* to the Member States of the Asia and Pacific region to support Mongolia's efforts to join the relevant regional security and economic arrangements;

7. *Requests* the Secretary-General and relevant United Nations bodies to continue to provide assistance to Mongolia in taking the necessary measures mentioned in paragraph 5 above;

8. *Requests* the Secretary-General to report to the General Assembly at its fifty-seventh session on the implementation of the present resolution;

9. *Decides* to include in the provisional agenda of its fifty-seventh session the item entitled "Mongolia's international security and nuclear-weapon-free status".

South-East Asia

Regarding the Treaty on the South-East Asia Nuclear-Weapon-Free Zone (Bangkok Treaty), which opened for signature in 1995 [YUN 1995, p. 207] and entered into force in 1997 [YUN 1997, p. 495], States parties continued to focus on negotiations with the nuclear-weapon States regarding the accession of the latter to the Treaty's Protocol. The executing organs of the Treaty, the Commission and Executive Committee, were established and began their work and undertook consultations with IAEA. With no new ratifications, the number of States that had ratified the Treaty remained at nine.

Latin America and the Caribbean

GENERAL ASSEMBLY ACTION

On 20 November [meeting 69], the General Assembly, on the recommendation of the First Committee [A/55/565], adopted **resolution 55/39** without vote [agenda item 79].

Consolidation of the regime established by the Treaty for the Prohibition of Nuclear Weapons in Latin America and the Caribbean (Treaty of Tlatelolco)

The General Assembly,

Recalling that, in its resolution 1911(XVIII) of 27 November 1963, it expressed the hope that the States of Latin America would take appropriate measures to conclude a treaty that would prohibit nuclear weapons in Latin America,

Recalling also that, in the same resolution, it voiced its confidence that, once such a treaty was concluded, all States, and in particular the nuclear-weapon States, would lend it their full cooperation for the effective realization of its peaceful aims,

Considering that, in its resolution 2028(XX) of 19 November 1965, it established the principle of an acceptable balance of mutual responsibilities and obligations between nuclear-weapon States and those that do not possess such weapons,

Recalling that the Treaty for the Prohibition of Nuclear Weapons in Latin America and the Caribbean (Treaty of Tlatelolco) was opened for signature at Mexico City on 14 February 1967,

Noting with satisfaction the holding on 14 February 1997 of the eleventh special session of the General Conference of the Agency for the Prohibition of Nuclear Weapons in Latin America and the Caribbean in commemoration of the thirtieth anniversary of the opening for signature of the Treaty of Tlatelolco,

Recalling that, in its preamble, the Treaty of Tlatelolco states that military denuclearized zones are not an end in themselves but rather a means for achieving general and complete disarmament at a later stage,

Recalling also that, in its resolution 2286(XXII) of 5 December 1967, it welcomed with special satisfaction the Treaty of Tlatelolco as an event of historic significance in the efforts to prevent the proliferation of nuclear weapons and to promote international peace and security,

Recalling further that in 1990, 1991 and 1992 the General Conference of the Agency for the Prohibition of Nuclear Weapons in Latin America and the Caribbean approved and opened for signature a set of amendments to the Treaty of Tlatelolco, with the aim of enabling the full entry into force of that instrument,

Recalling resolution C/E/RES.27 of the Council of the Agency for the Prohibition of Nuclear Weapons in Latin America and the Caribbean, in which the Council called for the promotion of cooperation and consultations with other nuclear-weapon-free zones,

Noting with satisfaction that the Treaty of Tlatelolco is now in force for thirty-two sovereign States of the region,

Also noting with satisfaction that on 8 November 1999 Nicaragua deposited its instrument of ratification of the amendment to the Treaty of Tlatelolco approved by the General Conference of the Agency for the Prohibition of Nuclear Weapons in Latin America and the Caribbean in its resolution 290(E-VII) of 26 August 1992; that on 8 August 2000 Panama deposited its instrument of accession to the amendments to the Treaty of Tlatelolco approved by the General Conference in its resolutions 267(E-V) of 3 July 1990, 268(XII) of 10 May 1991 and 290(E-VII); and that on 30 August 2000 Ecuador deposited its instrument of ratification of the amendments to the Treaty of Tlatelolco approved by the General Conference in its resolutions 268(XII) and 290(E-VII),

Further noting with satisfaction that the amended Treaty of Tlatelolco is fully in force for Argentina, Barbados, Brazil, Chile, Colombia, Costa Rica, Ecuador, Guyana, Jamaica, Mexico, Panama, Paraguay, Peru, Suriname, Uruguay and Venezuela,

1. *Welcomes* the concrete steps taken by some countries of the region during the past year for the consolidation of the regime of military denuclearization established by the Treaty for the Prohibition of Nuclear Weapons in Latin America and the Caribbean (Treaty of Tlatelolco);

2. *Urges* the countries of the region that have not yet done so to deposit their instruments of ratification of the amendments to the Treaty of Tlatelolco approved by the General Conference of the Agency for the Prohibition of Nuclear Weapons in Latin America and the Caribbean in its resolutions 267(E-V), 268(XII) and 290(E-VII);

3. *Decides* to include in the provisional agenda of its fifty-sixth session the item entitled "Consolidation of the regime established by the Treaty for the Prohibition of Nuclear Weapons in Latin America and the Caribbean (Treaty of Tlatelolco)".

Middle East

In response to General Assembly resolution 54/51 on the establishment of a nuclear-weapon-free zone in the Middle East [YUN 1999, p. 479], the Secretary-General, in September [A/55/388], reported on the implementation of the resolution. He noted that at a meeting of the Multilateral Steering Group of the Middle East Peace Process (Moscow, February), the participating Foreign Ministers emphasized the importance of reaching an agreed comprehensive agenda for the multilateral Working Group on Arms Control and Regional Security. The Secretary-General believed that the Working Group could be useful as a forum for discussing the establishment of a nuclear-weapon-free zone and reaffirmed the readiness of the United Nations to assist in that regard. He observed that the establishment of a nuclear-weapon-free zone received attention at the 2000 NPT Review Conference (see p. 487), particularly the implementation of the resolution adopted at the 1995 NPT Review and Extension Conference calling on States in the region to accede to NPT [YUN 1995, p. 189]. The report included the views of Egypt, Qatar and the Russian Federation on the establishment of a nuclear-weapon-free zone in the region.

GENERAL ASSEMBLY ACTION

On 20 November [meeting 69], the General Assembly, on the recommendation of the First Committee [A/55/556], adopted **resolution 55/30** without vote [agenda item 70].

Establishment of a nuclear-weapon-free zone in the region of the Middle East

The General Assembly,

Recalling its resolutions 3263(XXIX) of 9 December 1974, 3474(XXX) of 11 December 1975, 31/71 of 10 December 1976, 32/82 of 12 December 1977, 33/64 of 14 December 1978, 34/77 of 11 December 1979, 35/147 of 12 December 1980, 36/87 A and B of 9 December 1981,

37/75 of 9 December 1982, 38/64 of 15 December 1983, 39/54 of 12 December 1984, 40/82 of 12 December 1985, 41/48 of 3 December 1986, 42/28 of 30 November 1987, 43/65 of 7 December 1988, 44/108 of 15 December 1989, 45/52 of 4 December 1990, 46/30 of 6 December 1991, 47/48 of 9 December 1992, 48/71 of 16 December 1993, 49/71 of 15 December 1994, 50/66 of 12 December 1995, 51/41 of 10 December 1996, 52/34 of 9 December 1997, 53/74 of 4 December 1998 and 54/51 of 1 December 1999 on the establishment of a nuclear-weapon-free zone in the region of the Middle East,

Recalling also the recommendations for the establishment of such a zone in the Middle East consistent with paragraphs 60 to 63, and in particular paragraph 63 (*d*), of the Final Document of the Tenth Special Session of the General Assembly,

Emphasizing the basic provisions of the above-mentioned resolutions, which call upon all parties directly concerned to consider taking the practical and urgent steps required for the implementation of the proposal to establish a nuclear-weapon-free zone in the region of the Middle East and, pending and during the establishment of such a zone, to declare solemnly that they will refrain, on a reciprocal basis, from producing, acquiring or in any other way possessing nuclear weapons and nuclear explosive devices and from permitting the stationing of nuclear weapons on their territory by any third party, to agree to place their nuclear facilities under International Atomic Energy Agency safeguards and to declare their support for the establishment of the zone and to deposit such declarations with the Security Council for consideration, as appropriate,

Reaffirming the inalienable right of all States to acquire and develop nuclear energy for peaceful purposes,

Emphasizing the need for appropriate measures on the question of the prohibition of military attacks on nuclear facilities,

Bearing in mind the consensus reached by the General Assembly since its thirty-fifth session that the establishment of a nuclear-weapon-free zone in the Middle East would greatly enhance international peace and security,

Desirous of building on that consensus so that substantial progress can be made towards establishing a nuclear-weapon-free zone in the Middle East,

Welcoming all initiatives leading to general and complete disarmament, including in the region of the Middle East, and in particular on the establishment therein of a zone free of weapons of mass destruction, including nuclear weapons,

Noting the peace negotiations in the Middle East, which should be of a comprehensive nature and represent an appropriate framework for the peaceful settlement of contentious issues in the region,

Recognizing the importance of credible regional security, including the establishment of a mutually verifiable nuclear-weapon-free zone,

Emphasizing the essential role of the United Nations in the establishment of a mutually verifiable nuclear-weapon-free zone,

Having examined the report of the Secretary-General on the implementation of resolution 54/51,

1. *Urges* all parties directly concerned to consider seriously taking the practical and urgent steps required

for the implementation of the proposal to establish a nuclear-weapon-free zone in the region of the Middle East in accordance with the relevant resolutions of the General Assembly, and, as a means of promoting this objective, invites the countries concerned to adhere to the Treaty on the Non-Proliferation of Nuclear Weapons;

2. *Calls upon* all countries of the region that have not done so, pending the establishment of the zone, to agree to place all their nuclear activities under International Atomic Energy Agency safeguards;

3. *Takes note* of resolution GC(44)/RES/28, adopted on 22 September 2000 by the General Conference of the International Atomic Energy Agency at its forty-fourth regular session, concerning the application of Agency safeguards in the Middle East;

4. *Notes* the importance of the ongoing bilateral Middle East peace negotiations and the activities of the multilateral Working Group on Arms Control and Regional Security in promoting mutual confidence and security in the Middle East, including the establishment of a nuclear-weapon-free zone;

5. *Invites* all countries of the region, pending the establishment of a nuclear-weapon-free zone in the region of the Middle East, to declare their support for establishing such a zone, consistent with paragraph 63 *(d)* of the Final Document of the Tenth Special Session of the General Assembly, and to deposit those declarations with the Security Council;

6. *Also invites* those countries, pending the establishment of the zone, not to develop, produce, test or otherwise acquire nuclear weapons or permit the stationing on their territories, or territories under their control, of nuclear weapons or nuclear explosive devices;

7. *Invites* the nuclear-weapon States and all other States to render their assistance in the establishment of the zone and at the same time to refrain from any action that runs counter to both the letter and the spirit of the present resolution;

8. *Takes note* of the report of the Secretary-General;

9. *Invites* all parties to consider the appropriate means that may contribute towards the goal of general and complete disarmament and the establishment of a zone free of weapons of mass destruction in the region of the Middle East;

10. *Requests* the Secretary-General to continue to pursue consultations with the States of the region and other concerned States, in accordance with paragraph 7 of resolution 46/30 and taking into account the evolving situation in the region, and to seek from those States their views on the measures outlined in chapters III and IV of the study annexed to his report or other relevant measures, in order to move towards the establishment of a nuclear-weapon-free zone in the Middle East;

11. *Also requests* the Secretary-General to submit to the General Assembly at its fifty-sixth session a report on the implementation of the present resolution;

12. *Decides* to include in the provisional agenda of its fifty-sixth session the item entitled "Establishment of a nuclear-weapon-free zone in the region of the Middle East".

South Pacific

In October [A/55/536], New Zealand transmitted a communiqué issued by the heads of State and Government of the 16-member Pacific Island Forum, formerly the South Pacific Forum, at its thirty-first meeting (Tarawa, Kiribati, 27-30 October). The Forum considered a range of key issues of concern to the region and, while noting that there had been no new signatures or ratifications to the 1985 South Pacific Nuclear-Free-Zone Treaty (Treaty of Rarotonga) [YUN 1985, p. 58], called on the United States to ratify the relevant Protocols to the Treaty. Tonga's ratification, in December, brought the number of parties to the Treaty to 17. China and the Russian Federation had ratified Protocols 2 and 3, and France and the United Kingdom had ratified all three Protocols.

Under Protocol 1, the States internationally responsible for territories situated within the zone would undertake to apply the relevant prohibitions of the Treaty to those territories; under Protocol 2, the five nuclear-weapon States would provide security assurances to parties or to territories within the same zone; and under Protocol 3, the five would not carry out nuclear tests in the zone.

Southern hemisphere and adjacent areas

On 20 November [meeting 69], the General Assembly, on the recommendation of the First Committee [A/55/559], adopted **resolution 55/33 I** by recorded vote (159-4-5) [agenda item 73 *(n)*].

Nuclear-weapon-free southern hemisphere and adjacent areas

The General Assembly,

Recalling its resolutions 51/45 B of 10 December 1996, 52/38 N of 9 December 1997, 53/77 Q of 4 December 1998 and 54/54 L of 1 December 1999,

Welcoming the adoption by the Disarmament Commission at its 1999 substantive session of a text entitled "Establishment of nuclear-weapon-free zones on the basis of arrangements freely arrived at among the States of the region concerned",

Determined to pursue the total elimination of nuclear weapons,

Determined also to continue to contribute to the prevention of the proliferation of nuclear weapons in all its aspects and to the process of general and complete disarmament under strict and effective international control, in particular in the field of nuclear weapons and other weapons of mass destruction, with a view to strengthening international peace and security, in accordance with the purposes and principles of the Charter of the United Nations,

Recalling the provisions on nuclear-weapon-free zones of the Final Document of the Tenth Special Session of the General Assembly, the first special session devoted to disarmament,

Stressing the importance of the treaties of Tlatelolco, Rarotonga, Bangkok and Pelindaba, establishing nuclear-weapon-free zones, as well as the Antarctic Treaty, to, inter alia, achieve a world entirely free of nuclear weapons,

Underlining the value of enhancing cooperation among the nuclear-weapon-free zone treaty members by means of mechanisms such as joint meetings of States parties, signatories and observers to those treaties,

Recalling the applicable principles and rules of international law relating to the freedom of the high seas and the rights of passage through maritime space, including those of the United Nations Convention on the Law of the Sea,

1. *Welcomes* the continued contribution that the Antarctic Treaty and the treaties of Tlatelolco, Rarotonga, Bangkok and Pelindaba are making towards freeing the southern hemisphere and adjacent areas covered by those treaties from nuclear weapons;

2. *Calls* for the ratification of the treaties of Tlatelolco, Rarotonga, Bangkok and Pelindaba by all States of the region concerned, and calls upon all concerned States to continue to work together in order to facilitate adherence to the protocols to nuclear-weapon-free zone treaties by all relevant States that have not yet done so;

3. *Welcomes* the steps taken to conclude further nuclear-weapon-free zone treaties on the basis of arrangements freely arrived at among the States of the region concerned, and calls upon all States to consider all relevant proposals, including those reflected in its resolutions on the establishment of nuclear-weapon-free zones in the Middle East and South Asia;

4. *Convinced* of the important role of nuclear-weapon-free zones in strengthening the nuclear non-proliferation regime and in extending the areas of the world that are nuclear-weapon-free, and, with particular reference to the responsibilities of the nuclear-weapon States, calls upon all States to support the process of nuclear disarmament and to work for the total elimination of all nuclear weapons;

5. *Calls upon* the States parties and signatories to the treaties of Tlatelolco, Rarotonga, Bangkok and Pelindaba, in order to pursue the common goals envisaged in those treaties and to promote the nuclear-weapon-free status of the southern hemisphere and adjacent areas, to explore and implement further ways and means of cooperation among themselves and their treaty agencies;

6. *Welcomes* the vigorous efforts being made among States parties and signatories to those treaties to promote their common objectives, and considers that an international conference of States parties and signatories to the nuclear-weapon-free zone treaties might be held to support the common goals envisaged in those treaties;

7. *Encourages* the competent authorities of the nuclear-weapon-free zone treaties to provide assistance to the States parties and signatories to such treaties so as to facilitate the accomplishment of these goals;

8. *Decides* to include in the provisional agenda of its fifty-sixth session the item entitled "Nuclear-weapon-free southern hemisphere and adjacent areas".

RECORDED VOTE ON RESOLUTION 55/33 I:

In favour: Albania, Algeria, Angola, Antigua and Barbuda, Argentina, Armenia, Australia, Austria, Azerbaijan, Bahamas, Bahrain, Bangladesh, Barbados, Belarus, Belgium, Belize, Benin, Bhutan, Bolivia, Bosnia and Herzegovina, Botswana, Brazil, Brunei Darussalam, Bulgaria, Burkina Faso, Burundi, Cambodia, Cameroon, Canada, Cape Verde, Chile, China, Colombia, Costa Rica, Côte d'Ivoire, Croatia, Cuba, Cyprus, Czech Republic, Democratic People's Republic of Korea, Denmark, Djibouti, Dominican Republic, Ecuador, Egypt, El Salvador, Equatorial Guinea, Eritrea, Estonia, Ethiopia, Fiji, Finland, Gabon, Gambia, Georgia, Germany, Ghana, Greece, Grenada, Guatemala, Guinea, Guyana, Haiti, Honduras, Hungary, Iceland, Indonesia, Iran, Ireland, Italy, Jamaica, Japan, Jordan, Kazakhstan, Kenya, Kuwait, Kyrgyzstan, Lao People's Democratic Republic, Latvia, Lebanon, Lesotho, Libyan Arab Jamahiriya, Liechtenstein, Lithuania, Luxembourg, Madagascar, Malawi, Malaysia, Maldives, Mali, Malta, Marshall Islands, Mauritius, Mexico, Mongolia, Morocco, Mozambique, Myanmar, Namibia, Nauru, Nepal, Netherlands, New Zealand, Nicaragua, Nigeria, Norway, Oman, Pakistan, Panama, Papua New Guinea, Paraguay, Peru, Philippines, Poland, Portugal, Qatar, Republic of Korea, Republic of Moldova, Romania, Saint Kitts and Nevis, Saint Lucia, Saint Vincent and the Grenadines, Samoa, San Marino, Saudi Arabia, Senegal, Sierra Leone, Singapore, Slovakia, Slovenia, Solomon Islands, South Africa, Sri Lanka, Sudan, Suriname, Swaziland, Sweden, Syrian Arab Republic, Tajikistan, Thailand, The former Yugoslav Republic of Macedonia, Togo, Tonga, Trinidad and Tobago, Tunisia, Turkey, Turkmenistan, Uganda, Ukraine, United Arab Emirates, United Republic of Tanzania, Uruguay, Uzbekistan, Vanuatu, Venezuela, Viet Nam, Yemen, Zambia, Zimbabwe.

Against: France, Monaco, United Kingdom, United States.

Abstaining: Andorra, India, Israel, Russian Federation, Spain.

The First Committee adopted paragraph 3 and its last three words, "and South Asia", by two separate recorded votes of 138 to 1, with 9 abstentions, and 134 to 1, with 10 abstentions, respectively. The Assembly also retained paragraph 3 and the last three words by recorded votes of 155 to 1, with 9 abstentions, and 152 to 1, with 10 abstentions, respectively.

Bacteriological (biological) and chemical weapons

Bacteriological (biological) weapons

Efforts continued in 2000 to strengthen the Convention on the Prohibition of the Development, Production and Stockpiling of Bacteriological (Biological) and Toxin Weapons and on Their Destruction (BWC), adopted by the General Assembly in resolution 2826(XXVI) [YUN 1971, p. 19]. The Ad Hoc Group of the States Parties to the Convention attempted to achieve that goal through the development of a protocol on verification and confidence-building measures. Members of the Group, including the three depositary States (Russian Federation, United Kingdom, United States), undertook their sixth year of negotiations on the protocol and reaffirmed their determination to end the negotiations before the Convention's fifth review conference in 2001. Similar commitments were made by the leaders of the Group of 8 (G-8) major industrialized countries, in their G-8 Communiqué "Okinawa 2000" [A/55/257-S/2000/766], and by Presidents Vladimir V. Putin of the Russian Federation and William J. Clinton of the United States, in their joint statement on the strategic stability cooperation initiative [A/C.1/55/9] (see p. 498). However, obstacles still remained at year's end.

Ad Hoc Group

The Ad Hoc Group of the States Parties to BWC held its eighteenth (17 January–4 February) [BWC/AD HOC GROUP/50], nineteenth (13-31 March) [BWC/AD HOC GROUP/51], twentieth (10 July–4 August) [BWC/AD HOC GROUP/52] and twenty-first (20 November–8 December) [BWC/AD HOC GROUP/54] sessions in 2000, all in Geneva.

The Group continued to consider elements of the rolling text of a future draft protocol on verification and confidence-building relating to the preamble; general provisions; definitions of terms and objective criteria; measures to promote compliance; confidentiality issues; national implementation and assistance; measures related to article X of the Convention (scientific and technological exchange and technical cooperation); investigations; legal issues; and the seat of the organization. The work continued to be conducted under the guidance of the Chairman and Friends of the Chair. As at previous sessions, the results of discussions were incorporated in the rolling text, with brackets reflecting sections on which agreement was not yet possible. Textual proposals were annexed to the rolling text.

In August, the Chairman reported some progress in the negotiations on investigations and cooperation, with less progress on compliance measures. In December, the rolling text comprised a preamble, 23 articles, 6 annexes that provided detailed procedures on the implementation of the protocol, and 8 appendices. The Group decided that it would hold three sessions in 2001.

Parallel to their efforts to develop a verification mechanism, States parties continued their information exchange in the agreed framework of politically binding confidence-building measures, exchanging information on, among other things, relevant research centres and laboratories; national biological defence research and development programmes; outbreaks of infectious diseases and similar occurrences caused by toxins; relevant legislation, regulations and other measures; past activities in offensive and/or defensive biological research and development programmes; and vaccine production facilities. In 2000, 36 States parties submitted reports to the United Nations.

GENERAL ASSEMBLY ACTION

On 20 November [meeting 69], the General Assembly, on the recommendation of the First Committee [A/55/566], adopted **resolution 55/40** without vote [agenda item 80].

Convention on the Prohibition of the Development, Production and Stockpiling of Bacteriological (Biological) and Toxin Weapons and on Their Destruction

The General Assembly,

Recalling its previous resolutions relating to the complete and effective prohibition of bacteriological (biological) and toxin weapons and to their destruction,

Noting with satisfaction that there are one hundred and forty-three States parties to the Convention on the Prohibition of the Development, Production and Stockpiling of Bacteriological (Biological) and Toxin Weapons and on Their Destruction, including all of the permanent members of the Security Council,

Bearing in mind its call upon all States parties to the Convention to participate in the implementation of the recommendations of the Review Conferences, including the exchange of information and data agreed to in the Final Declaration of the Third Review Conference of the Parties to the Convention on the Prohibition of the Development, Production and Stockpiling of Bacteriological (Biological) and Toxin Weapons and on Their Destruction, and to provide such information and data in conformity with standardized procedure to the Secretary-General on an annual basis and no later than 15 April,

Recalling the provisions of the Convention related to scientific and technological cooperation and the related provisions of the final report of the Ad Hoc Group of Governmental Experts to Identify and Examine Potential Verification Measures from a Scientific and Technical Standpoint, the final report of the Special Conference of the States Parties to the Convention held from 19 to 30 September 1994, and the final documents of the Review Conferences,

Welcoming the reaffirmation made in the Final Declaration of the Fourth Review Conference that under all circumstances the use of bacteriological (biological) and toxin weapons and their development, production and stockpiling are effectively prohibited under article I of the Convention,

Recalling its resolution 49/86, adopted without a vote on 15 December 1994, in which it welcomed the final report of the Special Conference of the States Parties to the Convention, adopted by consensus on 30 September 1994, in which the States parties agreed to establish an ad hoc group, open to all States parties, whose objective should be to consider appropriate measures, including possible verification measures, and draft proposals to strengthen the Convention, to be included, as appropriate, in a legally binding instrument to be submitted for the consideration of the States parties,

1. *Notes with satisfaction* the increase in the number of States parties to the Convention on the Prohibition of the Development, Production and Stockpiling of Bacteriological (Biological) and Toxin Weapons and on Their Destruction, reaffirms the call upon all signatory States that have not yet ratified the Convention to do so without delay, and calls upon those States that have not signed the Convention to become parties thereto at an early date, thus contributing to the achievement of universal adherence to the Convention;

2. *Welcomes* the information and data provided to date, and reiterates its call upon all States parties to the Convention to participate in the exchange of informa-

tion and data agreed to in the Final Declaration of the Third Review Conference of the Parties to the Convention;

3. *Welcomes also* the progress achieved so far in the negotiation of a protocol to strengthen the Convention, and reaffirms the decision of the Fourth Review Conference of the Parties to the Convention urging the conclusion of the negotiations by the Ad Hoc Group of Governmental Experts to Identify and Examine Potential Verification Measures from a Scientific and Technical Standpoint as soon as possible before the commencement of the Fifth Review Conference and urging it to submit its report, which shall be adopted by consensus, to the States parties for consideration at a Special Conference;

4. *Calls upon* all States parties, in this context, to accelerate the negotiations, and to redouble their efforts within the Ad Hoc Group to formulate an efficient, cost-effective and practical regime and to seek early resolution of the outstanding issues through renewed flexibility in order to complete the protocol in accordance with the decision of the Fourth Review Conference;

5. *Notes* that, at the request of the States parties, the Fifth Review Conference of the Parties to the Convention will be held at Geneva from 19 November to 7 December 2001, and that, after appropriate consultation, a Preparatory Committee for that Conference, open to all States parties to the Convention, was established and will meet at Geneva from 25 to 27 April 2001;

6. *Requests* the Secretary-General to continue to render the necessary assistance to the depositary Governments of the Convention, to provide such services as may be required for the implementation of the decisions and recommendations of the Review Conferences, as well as the decisions contained in the final report of the 1994 Special Conference of the States Parties to the Convention, including all necessary assistance to the Ad Hoc Group and the Special Conference, which is to consider the report of the Ad Hoc Group, in accordance with its mandate, as confirmed by the Fourth Review Conference, and to render the necessary assistance and to provide such services as may be required for the Fifth Review Conference and the preparations for it;

7. *Decides* to include in the provisional agenda of its fifty-sixth session the item entitled "Convention on the Prohibition of the Development, Production and Stockpiling of Bacteriological (Biological) and Toxin Weapons and on Their Destruction".

1925 Geneva Protocol

In response to General Assembly resolution 53/77 L [YUN 1998, p. 521], the Secretary-General reported in July [A/55/115 & Add.1] that France, as the depositary of the Protocol for the Prohibition of the Use in War of Asphyxiating, Poisonous or Other Gases, and of Bacteriological Methods of Warfare (the 1925 Geneva Protocol), had received notice of two withdrawals of reservations (Canada and Estonia) since the Assembly's adoption of the resolution in 1998.

On 20 November [meeting 69], the General Assembly, on the recommendation of the First Committee [A/55/559], adopted **resolution 55/33 J** by recorded vote (163-0-5) [agenda item 73 *(d)*].

Measures to uphold the authority of the 1925 Geneva Protocol

The General Assembly,

Recalling its previous resolutions on the subject, in particular resolution 53/77 L of 4 December 1998,

Determined to act with a view to achieving effective progress towards general and complete disarmament under strict and effective international control,

Recalling the long-standing determination of the international community to achieve the effective prohibition of the development, production, stockpiling and use of chemical and biological weapons as well as the continuing support for measures to uphold the authority of the Protocol for the Prohibition of the Use in War of Asphyxiating, Poisonous or Other Gases, and of Bacteriological Methods of Warfare, signed at Geneva on 17 June 1925, as expressed by consensus in many previous resolutions,

Welcoming the end of the cold war, the ensuing easing of international tension and the strengthening of trust between States,

Welcoming also the initiatives by some States parties to withdraw their reservations to the 1925 Geneva Protocol,

1. *Renews its previous call* to all States to observe strictly the principles and objectives of the Protocol for the Prohibition of the Use in War of Asphyxiating, Poisonous or Other Gases, and of Bacteriological Methods of Warfare, signed at Geneva on 17 June 1925, and reaffirms the vital necessity of upholding its provisions;

2. *Notes with appreciation* the recent withdrawal of reservations by two State parties to the Geneva Protocol;

3. *Calls upon* those States that continue to maintain reservations to the 1925 Geneva Protocol to withdraw those reservations;

4. *Requests* the Secretary-General to submit to the General Assembly at its fifty-seventh session a report on the implementation of the present resolution.

RECORDED VOTE ON RESOLUTION 55/33 J:

In favour: Albania, Algeria, Andorra, Angola, Antigua and Barbuda, Argentina, Armenia, Australia, Austria, Azerbaijan, Bahamas, Bahrain, Bangladesh, Barbados, Belarus, Belgium, Belize, Benin, Bhutan, Bolivia, Bosnia and Herzegovina, Botswana, Brazil, Brunei Darussalam, Bulgaria, Burkina Faso, Burundi, Cambodia, Cameroon, Canada, Cape Verde, Chile, China, Colombia, Costa Rica, Côte d'Ivoire, Croatia, Cuba, Cyprus, Czech Republic, Democratic People's Republic of Korea, Denmark, Djibouti, Dominican Republic, Ecuador, Egypt, El Salvador, Equatorial Guinea, Eritrea, Estonia, Ethiopia, Fiji, Finland, France, Gabon, Gambia, Georgia, Germany, Ghana, Greece, Grenada, Guatemala, Guinea, Guyana, Haiti, Honduras, Hungary, Iceland, India, Indonesia, Iran, Ireland, Italy, Jamaica, Japan, Jordan, Kazakhstan, Kenya, Kuwait, Kyrgyzstan, Lao People's Democratic Republic, Latvia, Lebanon, Lesotho, Libyan Arab Jamahiriya, Liechtenstein, Lithuania, Luxembourg, Madagascar, Malawi, Malaysia, Maldives, Mali, Malta, Mauritius, Mexico, Monaco, Mongolia, Morocco, Mozambique, Myanmar, Namibia, Nauru, Nepal, Netherlands, New Zealand, Nigeria, Norway, Oman, Pakistan, Panama, Papua New Guinea, Paraguay, Peru, Philippines, Poland, Portugal, Qatar, Republic of Moldova, Romania, Russian Federation, Saint Kitts and Nevis, Saint Lucia, Saint Vincent and the Grenadines, Samoa, San Marino, Saudi Arabia, Senegal, Sierra Leone, Singapore, Slovakia, Slovenia, Solomon Islands, South Africa, Spain, Sri Lanka, Sudan, Suriname, Swaziland, Sweden, Syrian Arab Republic, Tajikistan, Thailand, The former Yugoslav Republic of Macedonia, Togo, Tonga, Trinidad and Tobago, Tunisia, Turkey, Turkmenistan, Uganda, Ukraine, United Arab Emirates, United Kingdom, United Republic of Tanzania, Uruguay, Uzbekistan, Vanuatu, Venezuela, Viet Nam, Yemen, Zambia, Zimbabwe.

Against: None.

Abstaining: Israel, Marshall Islands, Micronesia, Republic of Korea, United States.

Chemical weapons

Chemical weapons convention

In 2000, Azerbaijan, Colombia, Eritrea, Gabon, Jamaica, Kazakhstan, Kiribati, Malaysia, Mozambique, the United Arab Emirates, Yemen and Yugoslavia ratified or acceded to the Convention on the Prohibition of the Development, Production, Stockpiling and Use of Chemical Weapons and on Their Destruction, bringing the total number of States parties to 141. The number of signatories stood at 165. The Convention was adopted by the Conference on Disarmament in 1992 [YUN 1992, p. 65] and entered into force in 1997 [YUN 1997, p. 499].

At the fifth session of the Conference of the States Parties to the Convention (see below), the Director-General of the Organization for the Prohibition of Chemical Weapons (OPCW) noted that all States parties had submitted their initial declarations, as required under the Convention. (Under article III of the Convention, a State party was obligated to declare, 30 days after entry into force, whether or not chemical weapons or facilities existed on its territory, and to report on plans to destroy or convert existing chemical weapons and related facilities and on related laboratories and equipment that could be used to make chemical weapons. A State party was also obliged to declare all riot control agents.)

Organization for the Prohibition of Chemical Weapons

In 2000, the fifth session of the Conference of the States Parties (The Hague, Netherlands, 15-19 May) [OPCW, C-V/6] adopted the 2001 OPCW programme and budget, as well as a decision regarding the model agreement for chemical weapons destruction facilities and a recommendation on ensuring the universality of the Convention. Other decisions related to national implementation measures, requests to use chemical weapons production facilities for purposes not prohibited under the Convention, privileges and immunities agreements, and the request of the Russian Federation for an extension of its obligation to meet the first intermediate deadline for the destruction of its chemical weapons stockpiles.

Regarding inspections, at year's end OPCW had conducted more than 300 inspections in 45 States parties and extended inspection activities to 14 new States parties. In addition, one half of the 61

production plants declared by 11 States parties had been destroyed or converted to peaceful purposes, and 7 per cent of the world's declared stockpile of 70,000 tons of chemical agents and 15 per cent of the 8.4 million chemical munitions covered by the Convention had been destroyed.

In October, the relationship agreement for close cooperation on matters of mutual interest between the United Nations and OPCW was signed, and would be implemented provisionally until its adoption in 2001 by the Conference of the States Parties to OPCW and the General Assembly.

The OPCW Executive Council considered a wide range of issues at its eighteenth (15-18 February), nineteenth (3-7 April), twentieth (27-28 June), twenty-first (3-6 October) and twenty-second (5-8 December) sessions. Among other matters, it discussed issues relating to the practical elimination of chemical weapons stockpiles, including the destruction of production plants and the Convention's inspection regime.

On 23 December, the General Assembly decided that the item on cooperation between the United Nations and OPCW would remain for consideration at its resumed fifty-fifth (2001) session (**decision 55/458**).

GENERAL ASSEMBLY ACTION

On 20 November [meeting 69], the General Assembly, on the recommendation of the First Committee [A/55/559], adopted **resolution 55/33 H** without vote [agenda item 73 *(g)*].

Implementation of the Convention on the Prohibition of the Development, Production, Stockpiling and Use of Chemical Weapons and on Their Destruction

The General Assembly,

Recalling its previous resolutions on the subject of chemical weapons, in particular resolution 54/54 E of 1 December 1999, adopted without a vote, in which it noted with appreciation the ongoing work to achieve the objective and purpose of the Convention on the Prohibition of the Development, Production, Stockpiling and Use of Chemical Weapons and on Their Destruction,

Determined to achieve the effective prohibition of the development, production, acquisition, transfer, stockpiling and use of chemical weapons and their destruction,

Noting with satisfaction that since the adoption of resolution 54/54 E, fourteen additional States have ratified or acceded to the Convention, bringing the total number of States parties to the Convention to one hundred and forty,

1. *Emphasizes* the necessity of universal adherence to the Convention on the Prohibition of the Development, Production, Stockpiling and Use of Chemical Weapons and on Their Destruction, and calls upon all States that have not yet done so to become parties to the Convention without delay;

2. *Notes with appreciation* the ongoing work of the Organization for the Prohibition of Chemical Weapons

to achieve the objective and purpose of the Convention, to ensure the full implementation of its provisions, including those for international verification of compliance with it, and to provide a forum for consultation and cooperation among States parties;

3. *Stresses* the importance of the Organization for the Prohibition of Chemical Weapons in verifying compliance with the provisions of the Convention as well as in promoting the timely and efficient accomplishment of all its objectives;

4. *Also stresses* the vital importance of full and effective implementation of and compliance with all provisions of the Convention;

5. *Urges* all States parties to the Convention to meet in full and on time their obligations under the Convention and to support the Organization for the Prohibition of Chemical Weapons in its implementation activities;

6. *Stresses* the importance to the Convention that all possessors of chemical weapons, chemical weapons production facilities or chemical weapons development facilities, including previously declared possessor States, should be among the States parties to the Convention, and welcomes progress to that end;

7. *Welcomes* the cooperation between the United Nations and the Organization for the Prohibition of Chemical Weapons and the signature of the Relationship Agreement between the United Nations and the Organization, in accordance with the provisions of the Convention;

8. *Decides* to include in the provisional agenda of its fifty-sixth session the item entitled "Implementation of the Convention on the Prohibition of the Development, Production, Stockpiling and Use of Chemical Weapons and on Their Destruction".

Conventional weapons

In 2000, the United Nations, in collaboration with other international organizations, and at the request of the States concerned, continued to assist States in curbing the illicit traffic in small arms and collecting them. On 23 March [S/PRST/2000/10], the Security Council President stated that the Council recognized that effective action to curb the illegal flow of small arms and light weapons could contribute to the success of programmes for disarmament, demobilization and reintegration of ex-combatants in areas of conflict.

Although the Register of Conventional Arms remained the most well-known instrument of transparency for conventional weapons and the number of replies received for 1999 had increased, differences persisted among Member States regarding the Register's future development. In 2000, the expert group on the Register could not agree on expanding its scope to include data on military holdings and procurement through national production, on the same basis as data on transfers (see p. 524). The level of participation of Member States in the standardized reporting instrument for military expenditures remained low, while the upward trend in military expenditures reported in 1999 [YUN 1999, p. 486] seemed to persist.

Efforts continued to further strengthen the two legal instruments dealing with anti-personnel mines. The Second Meeting of the States Parties to the 1997 Convention on the Prohibition of the Use, Stockpiling, Production and Transfer of Anti-personnel Mines and on Their Destruction [YUN 1997, p. 503] took place (Geneva, 11-15 September), as did the Second Annual Conference of the States Parties to Amended Protocol II to the 1980 Convention on Prohibitions or Restrictions on the Use of Certain Conventional Weapons Which May Be Deemed to Be Excessively Injurious or to Have Indiscriminate Effects [YUN 1980, p. 76] (Geneva, 11-13 December).

Small arms

Reports of Secretary-General. In a July report with later addendum [A/55/189 & Add.1], the Secretary-General presented the views of six States on the 1999 report of the Group of Governmental Experts on Small Arms [YUN 1999, p. 486], pursuant to General Assembly resolution 54/54 V [ibid., p. 487].

In accordance with Security Council presidential statement S/PRST/1999/28 [YUN 1999, p. 48], the Secretary-General, in November [S/2000/1092], reported on the methods of destruction of small arms, light weapons, ammunition and explosives. The report, prepared with the assistance of governmental experts and in collaboration with relevant UN bodies, highlighted the advantages and disadvantages of various practical destruction methods available and their environmental impact, and was intended to provide guidance for the production of a reference manual. Technical experts had recommended the preparation of a UN reference manual for use in the field, emphasizing planning, management and supervision, as well as military/civilian manuals to deal with methods of destruction.

Expert meetings. The Group of Governmental Experts on Small Arms, established pursuant to General Assembly resolution 54/54 V [YUN 1999, p. 487], proceeded with preparing a report on the feasibility of restricting the manufacture and trade of small arms and light weapons to the manufacturers and dealers authorized by States. The Group held two sessions (New York, 14-19 May and 10-14 July), as well as an informal workshop (Sofia, Bulgaria, 17-19 October).

Communication. In November [A/55/631], Mali, on behalf of an eminent persons group, transmitted a document on the role of a small arms control regime in stemming small arms and light weapons proliferation (Rocard-Konaré report).

Illicit traffic

Reports of Secretary-General. Pursuant to General Assembly resolution 54/54 J [YUN 1999, p. 491], the Secretary-General, in August [A/55/216], outlined activities taken by the United Nations, as well as regional and subregional initiatives, to assist States to curb the illicit traffic in small arms and to collect them. He described requests for assistance, and the UN response thereto, from Albania, the Congo, Guinea-Bissau, the Niger and Sierra Leone.

In response to Assembly resolution 54/54 R [YUN 1999, p. 490], the Secretary-General, in an August report with later addendum [A/55/323 & Add.1], provided an overview of his broad-based consultations on illicit trafficking in small arms. He presented the outcome of meetings convened under UN auspices, as well as those convened by regional and subregional organizations and by States or groups of States. Annexed to the report were views on illicit traffic submitted by 10 States, in addition to France and Portugal on behalf of the European Union (EU), a description of activities taken by civil society, and a questionnaire prepared by the UN Department for Disarmament Affairs (DDA) that was transmitted to regional groups and organizations, research institutes and NGOs.

Other action. Ministers for Foreign Affairs attending the Great Lakes Region and the Horn of Africa Conference on the Proliferation of Small Arms (Nairobi, Kenya, 12-15 March) [A/54/860-S/2000/385] adopted the Nairobi Declaration on the Problem of the Proliferation of Illicit Small Arms and Light Weapons in the Great Lakes Region and the Horn of Africa. The Declaration called on States to strengthen subregional co-operation among police, intelligence, customs and border control officials to combat the illicit circulation and trafficking in small arms and light weapons. The Assembly of Heads of State and Government of the Organization of African Unity (OAU), at its thirty-sixth ordinary session (Lomé, Togo, 10-12 July) [A/55/286], affirmed that the uncontrolled spread of arms and light weapons, as well as the problem of landmines, posed a threat to peace and security in Africa. The G-8 Foreign Ministers (Miyazaki, Japan, 13 July) [A/55/161- S/2000/714], in the Miyazaki Initiatives for Conflict Prevention, expressed support for national, regional and international efforts to ensure that transfers of small arms were carried out

responsibly and legally. OAU member States appealed to suppliers to limit the arms trade to Governments and licensed agents identified in the Bamako Declaration on an African Common Position on the Illicit Proliferation, Circulation and Trafficking of Small Arms and Light Weapons (Bamako, Mali, 30 November-1 December) [A/CONF.192/PC/23].

(See also p. 527.)

Preparatory Committee for 2001 Conference

The Preparatory Committee for the 2001 UN Conference on the Illicit Trade in Small Arms and Light Weapons in All Its Aspects, established by General Assembly resolution 54/54 V [YUN 1999, p. 487], at its first session (New York, 28 February-3 March) [A/CONF.192/PC/9], decided to hold its second session from 8 to 19 January 2001, in New York, and its third from 19 to 30 March 2001. It decided to continue its consideration of recommendations to the Conference on all relevant matters, including the objective, a draft agenda, draft rules of procedure and draft final documents, but deferred any decision on the date and venue of the Conference to the Assembly's fifty-fifth (2000) session.

By **decision 55/415** of 20 November, the Assembly decided to convene the Conference from 9 to 20 July 2001, in New York, and the Preparatory Committee's third session from 19 to 30 March 2001. It decided to include the item entitled "Small arms" in the provisional agenda of its fifty-sixth (2001) session.

The Committee considered views on a final document for the Conference submitted by Canada [A/CONF.192/PC/14], China [A/CONF.192/PC/13], France and Switzerland [A/CONF.192/PC/7, A/CONF.192/PC/25], Japan [A/CONF.192/PC/22], South Africa [A/CONF.192/PC/5] and Switzerland [A/CONF.192/PC/16]. Proposals on various items were put forth by Algeria [A/CONF.192/PC/17], Canada [A/CONF.192/PC/15], the EU [A/CONF.192/PC/6], France on behalf of the EU [A/CONF.192/PC/18] and Indonesia on behalf of the Movement of Non-Aligned Countries [A/CONF.192/PC/8].

Documents transmitted by States included, in February, by Algeria [A/CONF.192/PC/2], a 1999 OAU decision [YUN 1999, p. 486] and, by Portugal on behalf of the EU [A/CONF.192/PC/3], the EU Programme for Preventing and Combating Illicit Trafficking in Conventional Arms and the EU Code of Conduct on Arms Exports; in June, by Portugal on behalf of the EU and the United States [A/CONF.192/PC/10], the United States-EU Statement of Common Principles and Action Plan on Small Arms and Light Weapons and, by Portugal on behalf of the EU [A/CONF.192/PC/11], a Canada-EU statement on small arms and light weapons; in July, by the United States [A/CONF.192/PC/12], the United States Comprehensive Initiative on Small Arms and Illicit Trafficking; and, in December, by Austria [A/CONF.192/PC/20], a document on small arms and light weapons adopted by the Organization for Security and Cooperation in Europe (OSCE) and, by France on behalf of the EU [A/CONF.192/PC/21], the text of a plan of action to prevent, combat and eradicate the illicit trade in small arms and light weapons in all its aspects.

In October [A/CONF.192/PC/24], the Pacific Island Forum countries transmitted information regarding their agreement to develop model legislation to facilitate implementation and enforcement of the common approach to weapons control contained in the Nadi Framework, which covered non-firearm weapons as well as firearms.

Brazil transmitted the Brasília Declaration adopted by the Latin American and Caribbean Regional Preparatory Meeting for the Conference (Brasília, 22-24 November) [A/55/679, A/CONF.192/PC/19].

The study completed by the Group of Governmental Experts on Small Arms [YUN 1999, p. 486] was to be submitted as a background document for the Conference.

Report of Secretary-General. In a February report with later addenda [A/54/260 & Add.1-3], the Secretary-General, in response to General Assembly resolutions 53/77 E [YUN 1998, p. 525] and 54/54 V [YUN 1999, p. 487], presented the views of five Member States on the objective, scope, agenda and venue of and preparatory work for the Conference.

GENERAL ASSEMBLY ACTION

On 20 November [meeting 69], the General Assembly, on the recommendation of the First Committee [A/55/559], adopted **resolution 55/33 Q** without vote [agenda item 73 (s)].

Illicit traffic in small arms and light weapons
The General Assembly,
Recalling its resolution 54/54 R of 1 December 1999,
Expressing its appreciation to the Secretary-General for his report,
Recognizing the human suffering caused by illicit trafficking in small arms and that Governments bear the responsibility of intensifying their efforts by developing an understanding of the issues and practical ways of addressing the problem,
Bearing in mind the interface among violence, criminality, drug trafficking, the illicit trade in diamonds, terrorism and illicit trafficking in small arms and light weapons,
Stressing the importance of the efforts to elaborate an international convention against transnational organized crime, including a protocol to combat the illicit manufacturing of and illicit trafficking in firearms, their parts and components and ammunition, within the framework of the Commission on Crime Prevention and Criminal Justice,

Convinced of the importance of national, regional and international measures to combat illicit trafficking in and illicit circulation of small arms and light weapons, including those suited to indigenous regional approaches,

Welcoming, in this regard, the decision by the Council of Ministers of the Organization of African Unity, to convene an African ministerial conference on the illicit proliferation, circulation and trafficking of small arms and light weapons at Bamako in November 2000, the establishment of the Consultative Committee by the States parties to the Inter-American Convention against the Illicit Manufacturing of and Trafficking in Firearms, Ammunition, Explosives and Other Related Materials, the decision by the Council of Ministers of the Southern African Development Community to conclude its negotiations on a protocol on the control of firearms, ammunition and other related materials in the region of the Southern African Development Community, the decision by the States members of the Economic Community of West African States to implement their Declaration of a Moratorium on the Importation, Exportation and Manufacture of Small Arms and Light Weapons in West Africa, and the adoption by the European Union of the Programme for Preventing and Combating Illicit Trafficking in Conventional Arms and the other initiatives it has taken, such as the Joint Action on Small Arms that has been endorsed by several Member States not members of the European Union,

Noting, in this regard, the commitments made by the Foreign Ministers of the Group of Eight industrialized countries, contained in the Miyazaki Initiatives for Conflict Prevention, the Foreign Ministers of the Euro-Atlantic Partnership Council, the members of the Stability Pact for South-Eastern Europe in the Joint Declaration on Responsible Arms Transfers, the members of the Organization for Security and Cooperation in Europe at the Istanbul Summit, the members of the South Pacific Forum in the Nadi Framework of principles, and by participants in the Great Lakes Region and Horn of Africa Conference on the Proliferation of Small Arms in the Nairobi Declaration on the Problem of the Proliferation of Illicit Small Arms and Light Weapons in the Great Lakes Region and the Horn of Africa,

Noting also that several regional and subregional workshops, seminars and conferences were held and that individual States have undertaken initiatives to promote measures to combat illicit trafficking in and illicit circulation of small arms and light weapons,

Welcoming the assistance provided by States in support of bilateral, regional and multilateral initiatives aimed at addressing illicit trafficking in small arms and light weapons and, in this regard, welcoming also the establishment of the United Nations Development Programme Trust Fund for Support to Prevention and Reduction of the Proliferation of Small Arms, the United Nations Trust Fund for the Consolidation of Peace through Practical Disarmament Measures and the United Nations Global and Regional Disarmament Trust Fund,

Welcoming also the preparatory process for the 2001 United Nations Conference on the Illicit Trade in Small Arms and Light Weapons in All Its Aspects, bearing in mind the recommendations made by the Secretary-General in his report on small arms, prepared with the assistance of the Group of Governmental Experts on Small Arms, as well as the views of Member States on the objectives, scope, agenda, dates and venue of the Conference,

Recalling the presidential statement issued by the Security Council on 24 September 1999 and the request of the Council therein to the Secretary-General to develop, with the assistance of technical experts and the support of Member States, a reference manual for use in the field on ecologically safe methods of weapons, ammunition and explosives destruction in order better to enable Member States to ensure the disposal of weapons, ammunition and explosives voluntarily surrendered by civilians or retrieved from former combatants,

Considering that the United Nations could, through a coordinated approach, collect, share and disseminate information to Member States on useful and successful practices to prevent the illicit trafficking in small arms and light weapons, and mindful of the role of the mechanism for coordinating action on small arms in this regard,

Recalling that the United Nations Regional Centre for Peace and Disarmament in Africa and the United Nations Regional Centre for Peace, Disarmament and Development in Latin America and the Caribbean, respectively, held workshops on illicit trafficking in small arms at Lomé and Lima in 1999, and noting with appreciation the regional seminar held at Jakarta on 3 and 4 May 2000 under the auspices of the United Nations Regional Centre for Peace and Disarmament in Asia and the Pacific,

Mindful of the impact of surplus small arms and light weapons on the illicit trade in these weapons, and welcoming the practical measures taken by States to destroy surplus weapons and confiscated or collected weapons, in accordance with the recommendations of the Secretary-General in his report on small arms,

1. *Requests* the Secretary-General to continue his broad-based consultations, within available financial resources and with any other assistance provided by States in a position to do so, and to provide the 2001 United Nations Conference on the Illicit Trade in Small Arms and Light Weapons in All Its Aspects with information on the magnitude and scope of illicit trafficking in small arms and light weapons, measures to combat illicit trafficking in and circulation of small arms and light weapons, and the role of the United Nations in collecting, collating, sharing and disseminating information on illicit trafficking in small arms and light weapons;

2. *Encourages* States to promote regional and subregional initiatives and requests the Secretary-General, within available financial resources, and those States in a position to do so, to assist States in undertaking such initiatives to address the illicit trafficking in small arms and light weapons in affected regions, and invites the Secretary-General to utilize these initiatives as part of his consultations;

3. *Encourages also* States in a position to do so to take appropriate national measures to destroy surplus, confiscated or collected small arms and light weapons, and to provide, on a voluntary basis, information to the Secretary-General on the types and quantities of arms destroyed as well as the methods of their destruction,

and requests the Secretary-General to circulate this information annually to all States;

4. *Invites* States in a position to do so to continue to provide assistance, bilaterally, regionally and through multilateral channels, such as the United Nations, in support of measures associated with combating illicit trafficking in small arms and light weapons, including assistance, in response to requests by States, in collecting and destroying surplus, confiscated or collected small arms and light weapons;

5. *Invites* the Secretary-General to provide advisory and financial assistance, within available financial resources and with any other assistance provided by States in a position to do so, in response to requests by States, in support of measures associated with combating illicit trafficking in small arms and light weapons, including assistance in collecting and destroying surplus, confiscated or collected small arms and light weapons;

6. *Requests* the Secretary-General to report to the General Assembly at its fifty-sixth session on the implementation of the present resolution;

7. *Decides* to include in the provisional agenda of its fifty-sixth session an item entitled "Illicit trafficking in small arms and light weapons".

Also on 20 November [meeting 69], the Assembly, on the recommendation of the First Committee [A/55/559], adopted **resolution 55/33 F** without vote [agenda item 73 (l)].

Assistance to States for curbing the illicit traffic in small arms and collecting them

The General Assembly,

Considering that the proliferation, illicit circulation of and traffic in small arms constitute an impediment to development, and a threat to populations and to national and regional security and are a factor contributing to the destabilization of States,

Gravely concerned at the extent of the proliferation, illicit circulation of and traffic in small arms in the States of the Saharo-Sahelian subregion,

Welcoming the conclusions of the United Nations advisory missions sent to the affected countries of the subregion by the Secretary-General to study the best way of curbing the illicit circulation of small arms and collecting them,

Welcoming also the designation of the Department for Disarmament Affairs of the Secretariat as the coordination centre for all United Nations activities concerning small arms,

Thanking the Secretary-General for his report on the causes of conflict and the promotion of durable peace and sustainable development in Africa, and bearing in mind the statement on small arms made by the President of the Security Council on 24 September 1999,

Welcoming the recommendations made at the meetings of the States of the subregion held at Banjul, Algiers, Bamako, Yamoussoukro and Niamey to establish close regional cooperation with a view to strengthening security,

Welcoming also the initiative taken by the Economic Community of West African States concerning the declaration of a moratorium on the importation, exportation and manufacture of small arms and light weapons in West Africa,

Recalling the Algiers Declaration adopted by the Assembly of Heads of State and Government of the Organization of African Unity at its thirty-fifth ordinary session, held at Algiers from 12 to 14 July 1999, and bearing in mind the report of the Secretary-General of the Organization of African Unity on the proliferation, illicit circulation of and traffic in small arms,

Emphasizing the need to advance efforts towards wider cooperation and better coordination in the struggle against the stockpiling, proliferation and widespread use of small arms, inter alia, through the common understanding reached at the meeting on small arms held at Oslo on 13 and 14 July 1998 and the Brussels Call for Action adopted by the International Conference on Sustainable Disarmament for Sustainable Development, held at Brussels on 12 and 13 October 1998, as adopted in document A/53/681, paragraph 4,

1. *Welcomes with satisfaction* the Declaration of the Ministerial Conference on Security, Stability, Development and Cooperation in Africa, held at Abuja on 8 and 9 May 2000, encourages the Secretary-General to continue his efforts, in the context of the implementation of General Assembly resolution 49/75 G of 15 December 1994 and of the recommendations of the United Nations advisory missions, to curb the illicit circulation of small arms and to collect such arms in the affected States that so request, with the support of the United Nations Regional Centre for Peace and Disarmament in Africa and in close cooperation with the Organization of African Unity;

2. *Encourages* the setting up in the countries in the Saharo-Sahelian subregion of national commissions against the proliferation of small arms, and invites the international community to support as far as possible the smooth functioning of the national commissions where they have been set up;

3. *Welcomes* the Declaration of a Moratorium on the Importation, Exportation and Manufacture of Small Arms and Light Weapons in West Africa, adopted by the heads of State and Government of the Economic Community of West African States at Abuja on 31 October 1998, and urges the international community to give its support to the implementation of the moratorium;

4. *Recommends* the involvement of organizations and associations of civil society in efforts to combat the illicit circulation of small arms in the context of the national commissions and their participation in the implementation of the moratorium on the importation, exportation and manufacture of small arms;

5. *Takes note* of the conclusions of the meeting of Ministers for Foreign Affairs of the Economic Community of West African States, held at Bamako on 24 and 25 March 1999, on the modalities for the implementation of the Programme for Coordination and Assistance for Security and Development, and welcomes the adoption by the meeting of a plan of action;

6. *Expresses its full support* for the appeal launched by the Assembly of Heads of State and Government of the Organization of African Unity at its thirty-fifth ordinary session for a coordinated African approach, under the auspices of the Organization of African Unity, to the problems posed by the proliferation, illicit circulation of and traffic in small arms, bearing in mind the experiences and activities of the various regions in this regard;

7. *Encourages* cooperation among State bodies, international organizations and civil society in combating the illicit circulation of small arms and supporting operations at the subregional level;

8. *Expresses its full support* for the convening of a United Nations conference on the illicit trade in small arms and light weapons in all its aspects in June/July 2001, in accordance with General Assembly resolution 54/54 V of 15 December 1999;

9. *Requests* the Secretary-General to continue to examine the question and to submit to the General Assembly at its fifty-sixth session a report on the implementation of the present resolution;

10. *Decides* to include in the provisional agenda of its fifty-sixth session the item entitled "Assistance to States for curbing the illicit traffic in small arms and collecting them".

Convention on excessively injurious conventional weapons and Protocols

In response to General Assembly resolution 54/58 [YUN 1999, p. 492], the Secretary-General reported on the status, as at 31 May 2000 [A/55/97], of the 1980 Convention on Prohibitions or Restrictions on the Use of Certain Conventional Weapons Which May Be Deemed to Be Excessively Injurious or to Have Indiscriminate Effects and its three annexed Protocols [YUN 1980, p. 76]: on Non-Detectable Fragments (Protocol I); on Prohibitions or Restrictions on the Use of Mines, Booby Traps and Other Devices, as amended on 3 May 1996 (Protocol II) [YUN 1996, p. 484]; and on Prohibitions or Restrictions on the Use of Incendiary Weapons (Protocol III); as well as the 1995 Protocol on Blinding Laser Weapons (Protocol IV) [YUN 1995, p. 221], which had taken effect on 30 July 1998 [YUN 1998, p. 530].

The accession of Bangladesh, Colombia, El Salvador, Estonia, Lesotho, Maldives, Moldova and Seychelles and the ratification of Nicaragua in 2000 brought the number of States parties to the Convention as at 31 December to 84.

Pursuant to resolution 53/81 and based on the decisions and recommendations of the First Annual Conference of the States Parties to Amended Protocol II in 1999 [YUN 1999, p. 492], the Second Annual Conference met in Geneva from 11 to 13 December [CCW/AP.II/CONF.2/1].

The Conference had before it 29 national annual reports, containing data on dissemination of information on the Protocol to armed forces and civilians; mine clearance and rehabilitation programmes; steps taken to meet technical requirements of the Protocol and any other relevant information pertaining thereto; legislation related to the Protocol; measures taken on international technical information exchange, on international cooperation on mine clearance, and on technical cooperation and assistance; and other relevant matters. On 13 December, the Conference issued a declaration urging all States that had not done so to accede to amended Protocol II as soon as possible. It also recommended that the Secretary-General, as depositary, and the President of the Conference exercise their authority to achieve the goal of universality of the Protocol. In accordance with General Assembly resolution 55/37 (see below), the Conference decided to convene the Third Annual Conference on 10 December 2001, in Geneva.

2001 second review conference

In accordance with a decision of the First Review Conference of the States Parties to the Convention in 1996 [YUN 1996, p. 484] to convene a further conference five years after the entry into force of the amendments it had adopted, but not later than 2001, the Preparatory Committee for the Second Review Conference held its first session (Geneva, 14 December) [CCW/CONF.II/PC.1/1].

The Committee reviewed the operation and status of the Convention and its Protocols, and considered related proposals. After addressing, among other things, the organization of work of the review conference and its subsidiary bodies, the Committee agreed that more consultations were needed and deferred decisions on those matters to its second session in April 2001. Noting the recommendation of General Assembly resolution 55/37 (see below), the Committee scheduled the review conference from 11 to 21 December 2001, in Geneva.

GENERAL ASSEMBLY ACTION

On 20 November [meeting 69], the General Assembly, on the recommendation of the First Committee [A/55/563], adopted **resolution 55/37** without vote [agenda item 77].

Convention on Prohibitions or Restrictions on the Use of Certain Conventional Weapons Which May Be Deemed to Be Excessively Injurious or to Have Indiscriminate Effects

The General Assembly,

Recalling its resolution 54/58 of 1 December 1999 and previous resolutions referring to the Convention on Prohibitions or Restrictions on the Use of Certain Conventional Weapons Which May Be Deemed to Be Excessively Injurious or to Have Indiscriminate Effects,

Recalling with satisfaction the adoption, on 10 October 1980, of the Convention, together with the Protocol on Non-Detectable Fragments (Protocol I), the Protocol on Prohibitions or Restrictions on the Use of Mines, Booby Traps and Other Devices (Protocol II) and the Protocol on Prohibitions or Restrictions on the Use of Incendiary Weapons (Protocol III), which entered into force on 2 December 1983,

Also recalling with satisfaction the adoption by the Review Conference of the States Parties to the Convention on Prohibitions or Restrictions on the Use of Certain Conventional Weapons Which May Be Deemed to Be Excessively Injurious or to Have Indiscriminate Effects, on 13 October 1995 of the Protocol on Blinding Laser Weapons (Protocol IV), and on 3 May 1996 of the amended Protocol on Prohibitions or Restrictions on the Use of Mines, Booby Traps and Other Devices (Protocol II),

Recalling that the States parties at the Review Conference declared their commitment to keeping the provisions of Protocol II under review in order to ensure that the concerns regarding the weapons it covers are addressed, and that they would encourage the efforts of the United Nations and other organizations to address all problems of landmines,

Recalling also the role played by the International Committee of the Red Cross in the elaboration of the Convention and the Protocols thereto,

Welcoming the additional ratifications and acceptances of or accessions to the Convention, as well as the ratifications and acceptances of or accessions to amended Protocol II and Protocol IV,

Noting that, in conformity with article 8 of the Convention, conferences may be convened to examine amendments to the Convention or to any of the Protocols thereto, to examine additional protocols concerning other categories of conventional weapons not covered by existing Protocols or to review the scope and application of the Convention and the Protocols thereto and to examine any proposed amendments or additional protocols,

Noting also that, in accordance with article 13 of amended Protocol II, a conference of States parties to that Protocol shall be held annually for the purpose of consultations and cooperation on all issues in relation to the Protocol,

Noting further that the provisional rules of procedure of the First Annual Conference of the States Parties to Amended Protocol II provide for the invitation of States not parties to the Protocol, the International Committee of the Red Cross and interested non-governmental organizations to take part in the Conference,

Welcoming the results of the First Annual Conference of States Parties to Amended Protocol II, held at Geneva from 15 to 17 December 1999,

Commending the efforts of the Secretary-General and the President of the Conference towards the promotion of the goal of universality of amended Protocol II,

Welcoming the holding of an informal meeting of experts of the States parties to amended Protocol II and other interested States at Geneva on 31 May and 2 June 2000, which provided for structured discussion on several items under amended Protocol II,

1. *Calls upon* all States that have not yet done so to take all measures to become parties, as soon as possible, to the Convention on Prohibitions or Restrictions on the Use of Certain Conventional Weapons Which May Be Deemed to Be Excessively Injurious or to Have Indiscriminate Effects and the Protocols thereto, in particular the amended Protocol on Prohibitions or Restrictions on the Use of Mines, Booby Traps and Other Devices (Protocol II), with a view to achieving the widest possible adherence to this instrument at an early date, and calls upon successor States to take appropriate measures so that ultimately adherence to these instruments will be universal;

2. *Calls upon* States parties to the Convention that have not yet done so to express their consent to be bound by the Protocols to the Convention;

3. *Welcomes* the convening, from 11 to 13 December 2000, of the Second Annual Conference of States Parties to Amended Protocol II, in accordance with article 13 thereof, and calls upon all States parties to amended Protocol II to address at that meeting, inter alia, the issue of holding the third annual conference in 2001;

4. *Recalls* the decision of the States parties to the Convention to convene the next review conference no later than 2001, preceded by a preparatory committee, and recommends that the review conference be held at Geneva in December 2001;

5. *Welcomes* the convening of the first session of the Preparatory Committee for the Second Review Conference at Geneva on 14 December 2000, and decides to convene the second session from 2 to 6 April 2001 and the third session from 24 to 28 September 2001;

6. *Notes* that, in conformity with article 8 of the Convention, the next review conference may consider any proposal for amendments to the Convention or the Protocols thereto as well as any proposal for additional protocols relating to other categories of conventional weapons not covered by existing Protocols to the Convention;

7. *Requests* the Secretary-General to render the necessary assistance and to provide such services, including summary records, as may be required for the Second Review Conference of the States Parties to the Convention and the Preparatory Committee for the Second Review Conference;

8. *Also requests* the Secretary-General, in his capacity as depositary of the Convention and the Protocols thereto, to continue to inform the General Assembly periodically of ratifications and acceptances of and accessions to the Convention and the Protocols thereto;

9. *Decides* to include in the provisional agenda of its fifty-sixth session the item entitled "Convention on Prohibitions or Restrictions on the Use of Certain Conventional Weapons Which May Be Deemed to Be Excessively Injurious or to Have Indiscriminate Effects".

Practical disarmament

The Group of Interested States, established in 1998 [YUN 1998, p. 531] to examine and support concrete projects of practical disarmament, met four times in 2000 (10 February, 6 June, 11 September, 12 December) to discuss practical disarmament measures in Albania, the Congo and the Niger (see p. 518). Working closely with the United Nations Development Programme (UNDP) and DDA, the Group explored the use of the United Nations Trust Fund for the Consolidation of Peace through Practical Measures, also established in 1998 [ibid.], to support weapons collection and destruction programmes in those countries.

Disarmament Commission action. In 2000 [A/55/42], the Disarmament Commission allocated to Working Group II the item entitled "Practical confidence-building measures in the field of conventional arms". On 6 July, the Working Group adopted its report by consensus.

On 20 November [meeting 69], the General Assembly, on the recommendation of the First Committee [A/55/559], adopted **resolution 55/33 G** without vote [agenda item 73 (j)].

Consolidation of peace through practical disarmament measures

The General Assembly,

Recalling its resolutions 51/45 N of 10 December 1996, 52/38 G of 9 December 1997, 53/77 M of 4 December 1998 and 54/54 H of 1 December 1999,

Convinced that a comprehensive and integrated approach towards certain practical disarmament measures, such as arms control, particularly with regard to small arms and light weapons, confidence-building measures, demobilization and reintegration of former combatants, demining and conversion, often is a prerequisite to maintaining and consolidating peace and security and thus provides a basis for effective rehabilitation and social and economic development in areas that have suffered from conflict,

Noting with satisfaction that the international community is more than ever aware of the importance of such practical disarmament measures, especially with regard to the growing problems arising from the excessive and destabilizing accumulation and proliferation of small arms and light weapons, which pose a threat to peace and security and reduce the prospects for economic development in many regions, particularly in post-conflict situations,

Stressing that further efforts are needed in order to develop and effectively implement programmes of practical disarmament in affected areas,

Taking note of the report of the Secretary-General prepared with the assistance of the Group of Governmental Experts on Small Arms, and in particular the recommendations contained therein, as an important contribution to the consolidation of the peace process through practical disarmament measures,

Taking into account the deliberations at the 2000 substantive session of the Disarmament Commission in Working Group II on agenda item 5, entitled "Practical confidence-building measures in the field of conventional arms", and encouraging the Disarmament Commission to continue its efforts aimed at the identification of such measures,

1. *Stresses,* in the context of the present resolution, the particular relevance of the "Guidelines on conventional arms control/limitation and disarmament, with particular emphasis on consolidation of peace in the context of General Assembly resolution 51/45 N", adopted by the Disarmament Commission by consensus at its 1999 substantive session;

2. *Takes note* of the report of the Secretary-General on the consolidation of peace through practical disarmament measures, submitted pursuant to resolution 51/45 N, and once again encourages Member States, as well as regional arrangements and agencies, to lend their support to the implementation of the recommendations contained therein;

3. *Welcomes* the activities undertaken by the group of interested States that was formed in New York in March 1998, and invites the group to continue to analyse lessons learned from previous disarmament and peace-building projects, as well as to promote new prac-

tical disarmament measures to consolidate peace, especially as undertaken or designed by affected States themselves;

4. *Encourages* Member States, including the group of interested States, to lend their support to the Secretary-General in responding to requests by Member States to collect and destroy small arms and light weapons in post-conflict situations;

5. *Decides* to include in the provisional agenda of its fifty-sixth session the item entitled "Consolidation of peace through practical disarmament measures".

Transparency

Conference on Disarmament. In 2000, the issue of transparency in armaments was considered during plenary meetings of the Conference on Disarmament [A/55/27], mainly in connection with efforts to find a comprehensive agreement on the establishment of subsidiary bodies on the agenda items. The two main proposals in that regard [CD/1620, CD/1624] envisaged the appointment of a special coordinator to seek the views of Conference members on the most appropriate way to deal with transparency, which could not be done due to the lack of consensus on a comprehensive programme of work (see p. 485).

UN Register of Conventional Arms

In response to General Assembly resolution 54/54 O [YUN 1999, p. 496], the Secretary-General submitted the eighth annual report on the United Nations Register on Conventional Arms [A/55/299 & Corr.1 & Add.1-6], which was established in 1992 [YUN 1992, p. 75] to enhance levels of transparency on arms transfers.

The report presented information provided by 96 Governments on imports and exports during the 1999 calender year in the seven categories of conventional arms (battle tanks, armoured combat vehicles, large-calibre artillery systems, attack helicopters, combat aircraft, warships, and missiles and missile launchers). Governments also provided information on procurement from national production and military holdings. The report indicated a slight increase in the number of submissions.

Group of Governmental Experts

In response to General Assembly resolution 54/54 O [YUN 1999, p. 496], the Secretary-General, in August [A/55/281], reported on the continuing operations of the Register and its further development, with data provided from the Group of Governmental Experts, which had held three sessions between March and August (New York). Regarding further development, the Group considered expanding the scope of the Register to include data on military holdings and procurement through national production on the same basis as data on transfers, and to add a new category to include weapons of mass destruction. The question of the relationship between existing categories and possible new categories of equipment of conventional arms, including light weapons and small arms, was discussed, as was the way that relationship could be of relevance to the purpose of the Register. The Group made a series of recommendations to Member States and to the Assembly.

GENERAL ASSEMBLY ACTION

On 20 November [meeting 69], the General Assembly, on the recommendation of the First Committee [A/55/559], adopted **resolution 55/33 U** by recorded vote (149-0-16) [agenda item 73 *(k)*].

Transparency in armaments

The General Assembly,

Recalling its resolutions 46/36 L of 9 December 1991, 47/52 L of 15 December 1992, 48/75 E of 16 December 1993, 49/75 C of 15 December 1994, 50/70 D of 12 December 1995, 51/45 H of 10 December 1996, 52/38 R of 9 December 1997, 53/77 V of 4 December 1998 and 54/54 O of 1 December 1999 entitled "Transparency in armaments",

Continuing to take the view that an enhanced level of transparency in armaments contributes greatly to confidence-building and security among States and that the establishment of the United Nations Register of Conventional Arms constitutes an important step forward in the promotion of transparency in military matters,

Welcoming the consolidated report of the Secretary-General on the Register, which includes the returns of Member States for 1999,

Welcoming also the response of Member States to the request contained in paragraphs 9 and 10 of resolution 46/36 L to provide data on their imports and exports of arms, as well as available background information regarding their military holdings, procurement through national production and relevant policies,

Welcoming further the report of the Secretary-General on the continuing operation of the Register and its further development,

Stressing that the continuing operation of the Register and its further development should be reviewed in order to secure a Register that is capable of attracting the widest possible participation,

1. *Reaffirms* its determination to ensure the effective operation of the United Nations Register of Conventional Arms, as provided for in paragraphs 7 to 10 of resolution 46/36 L;

2. *Endorses* the report of the Secretary-General on the continuing operation of the Register and its further development and the recommendations contained therein;

3. *Calls upon* Member States, with a view to achieving universal participation, to provide the Secretary-General by 31 May annually with the requested data and information for the Register, including nil reports if appropriate, on the basis of resolutions 46/36 L and

47/52 L, the recommendations contained in paragraph 64 of the 1997 report of the Secretary-General on the continuing operation of the Register and its further development and the recommendations contained in paragraph 94 of the 2000 report of the Secretary-General and the appendices and annexes thereto;

4. *Invites* Member States in a position to do so, pending further development of the Register, to provide additional information on procurement from national production and military holdings and to make use of the "Remarks" column in the standardized reporting form to provide additional information such as types or models;

5. *Reaffirms* its decision, with a view to further development of the Register, to keep the scope of and participation in the Register under review and, to that end:

(a) Recalls its request to Member States to provide the Secretary-General with their views on the continuing operation of the Register and its further development and on transparency measures related to weapons of mass destruction;

(b) Requests the Secretary-General, with the assistance of a group of governmental experts to be convened in 2003, on the basis of equitable geographical representation, to prepare a report on the continuing operation of the Register and its further development, taking into account the work of the Conference on Disarmament, the views expressed by Member States and the reports of the Secretary-General on the continuing operation of the Register and its further development, with a view to a decision at its fifty-eighth session;

6. *Requests* the Secretary-General to implement the recommendations in his 2000 report on the continuing operation of the Register and its further development and to ensure that sufficient resources are made available for the Secretariat to operate and maintain the Register;

7. *Invites* the Conference on Disarmament to consider continuing its work undertaken in the field of transparency in armaments;

8. *Reiterates its call upon* all Member States to cooperate at the regional and subregional levels, taking fully into account the specific conditions prevailing in the region or subregion, with a view to enhancing and coordinating international efforts aimed at increased openness and transparency in armaments;

9. *Requests* the Secretary-General to report to the General Assembly at its fifty-sixth session on progress made in implementing the present resolution;

10. *Decides* to include in the provisional agenda of its fifty-sixth session the item entitled "Transparency in armaments".

RECORDED VOTE ON RESOLUTION 55/33 U:

In favour: Albania, Andorra, Angola, Antigua and Barbuda, Argentina, Armenia, Australia, Austria, Azerbaijan, Bahamas, Bangladesh, Barbados, Belarus, Belgium, Belize, Benin, Bhutan, Bolivia, Bosnia and Herzegovina, Botswana, Brazil, Brunei Darussalam, Bulgaria, Burkina Faso, Burundi, Cambodia, Cameroon, Canada, Cape Verde, Chile, Colombia, Comoros, Costa Rica, Côte d'Ivoire, Croatia, Cuba, Cyprus, Czech Republic, Denmark, Djibouti, Dominican Republic, Ecuador, El Salvador, Equatorial Guinea, Eritrea, Estonia, Ethiopia, Fiji, Finland, France, Gabon, Gambia, Georgia, Germany, Ghana, Greece, Grenada, Guatemala, Guinea, Guyana, Haiti, Honduras, Hungary, Iceland, India, Indonesia, Ireland, Israel, Italy, Jamaica, Japan, Kazakhstan, Kenya, Kuwait, Kyrgyzstan, Latvia, Lebanon, Lesotho, Liechtenstein, Lithuania, Luxembourg, Madagascar, Malawi, Malaysia, Maldives, Mali, Malta, Marshall Islands, Mauritius, Micronesia, Monaco, Mongolia, Mozambique, Namibia, Nauru, Nepal, Netherlands, New Zealand, Nicaragua, Nigeria, Norway, Panama, Papua New Guinea, Paraguay, Peru, Philippines, Poland, Portugal, Qatar, Republic of Korea, Republic of Moldova, Romania, Russian Federation, Saint Kitts and Nevis, Saint Lucia, Saint Vincent and the Grenadines, Samoa, San Marino, Senegal, Sierra Leone, Singapore, Slovakia, Slovenia, Solomon Islands, South Africa, Spain, Sri Lanka, Suriname, Swaziland, Sweden, Thailand, The former Yugoslav Republic of Macedonia, Togo, Tonga, Trinidad and Tobago, Turkey, Turkmenistan, Uganda, Ukraine, United Kingdom, United Republic of Tanzania, United States, Uruguay, Uzbekistan, Vanuatu, Venezuela, Zambia, Zimbabwe.

Against: None.

Abstaining: Algeria, Bahrain, China, Democratic People's Republic of Korea, Egypt, Iran, Jordan, Libyan Arab Jamahiriya, Mexico, Morocco, Myanmar, Pakistan, Saudi Arabia, Syrian Arab Republic, Tunisia, United Arab Emirates.

The First Committee adopted the fifth preambular paragraph and paragraphs 2, 5 (b) and 7 by separate recorded votes of 134 to 2, with 12 abstentions, 136 to 3, with 11 abstentions, 135 to 3, with 12 abstentions, and 132 to none, with 16 abstentions, respectively. The Assembly retained the paragraphs by recorded votes of 149 to 2, with 10 abstentions, 147 to 3, with 11 abstentions, 147 to 3, with 13 abstentions, and 144 to none, with 17 abstentions, respectively.

Transparency of military expenditures

In response to General Assembly resolution 54/43 [YUN 1999, p. 497], the Secretary-General, in September [A/55/272], presented information received from 32 Member States on military expenditures for the latest fiscal year for which data were available. The reporting instrument used was that recommended by the Assembly in resolution 35/142 B [YUN 1980, p. 88].

Also in accordance with resolution 54/43, DDA organized an informal meeting on 10 October to enhance familiarity with the UN standardized instrument for reporting military expenditures and to discuss significant developments regarding transparency and other related matters.

The Assembly, in **decision 55/414** of 20 November, took note of the report of the First Committee [A/55/551] on the reduction of military budgets.

Anti-personnel mines

1997 Convention

The number of States parties to the Convention on the Prohibition of the Use, Stockpiling, Production and Transfer of Anti-personnel Mines and on Their Destruction (Mine-Ban Convention), which was adopted in 1997 [YUN 1997, p. 503] and entered into force in 1999 [YUN 1999, p. 498], totalled 109 as at 31 December. During the year, 18 States ratified or acceded to the Convention.

Pursuant to General Assembly resolution 54/54 B [YUN 1999, p. 499], the Second Meeting of the States Parties to the Convention was convened in Geneva from 11 to 15 September [APLC/MSP. 2/2000/1].

The Meeting reviewed the status and operation of the Convention and held consultations on international cooperation and assistance on mine clearance, victim assistance, socio-economic reintegration and mine awareness, the destruction of stockpiled anti-personnel mines, and the development of technologies for mine action. It adopted the President's Action Programme, which provided a summary of concrete initiatives and activities that flowed from the work of the five Standing Committees of Experts (SCEs), as well as other initiatives that had been announced since the conclusion of the work of the SCEs or during the Second Meeting. The States parties attending the Meeting adopted a declaration, reaffirming their commitment to eradicating anti-personnel mines, and calling on those who continued to use those weapons, as well as those who developed, acquired, stockpiled and transferred them, to join in the task.

The SCE on the general status and operation of the Convention noted that there was no evidence of either production or transfer of anti-personnel mines from States parties and that the number of countries producing mines, including non-States parties, had decreased from 55 to 16. Regarding the destruction of stockpiles, it noted that 25 States parties had completed the destruction process, in another 24 the process was under way, but in 17 it had not yet begun. The Committee was informed that there had been new mine victims in more than 70 countries since the Convention entered into force, and that 88 countries were considered to be mine-affected.

The SCE on victim assistance, socio-economic reintegration and mine awareness made progress regarding the development of a strategic, comprehensive and integrated approach to victim assistance.

The Third Meeting of the States Parties was scheduled for September 2001 in Managua, Nicaragua.

GENERAL ASSEMBLY ACTION

On 20 November [meeting 69], the General Assembly, on the recommendation of the First Committee [A/55/559], adopted **resolution 55/33 V** by recorded vote (143-0-22) [agenda item 73 *(f)*].

Implementation of the Convention on the Prohibition of the Use, Stockpiling, Production and Transfer of Anti-personnel Mines and on Their Destruction

The General Assembly,

Recalling its resolution 54/54 B of 1 December 1999,

Reaffirming its determination to put an end to the suffering and casualties caused by anti-personnel mines, which kill or maim hundreds of people every week, mostly innocent and defenceless civilians and especially children, obstruct economic development and reconstruction, inhibit the repatriation of refugees and internally displaced persons, and have other severe consequences for years after emplacement,

Believing it necessary to do the utmost to contribute in an efficient and coordinated manner to facing the challenge of removing anti-personnel mines placed throughout the world, and to assure their destruction,

Wishing to do the utmost in ensuring assistance for the care and rehabilitation, including the social and economic reintegration, of mine victims,

Welcoming the entry into force on 1 March 1999 of the Convention on the Prohibition of the Use, Stockpiling, Production and Transfer of Anti-personnel Mines and on Their Destruction, and noting with satisfaction the work undertaken to implement the Convention and the substantial progress made towards addressing the global landmine problem,

Recalling the First Meeting of the States Parties to the Convention, held at Maputo from 3 to 7 May 1999, and the reaffirmation made in the Maputo Declaration of a commitment to the total eradication of anti-personnel mines,

Recalling also the Second Meeting of States Parties to the Convention, held at Geneva from 11 to 15 September 2000, and the Declaration of the Second Meeting of States Parties reaffirming the commitment to implement completely and fully all provisions of the Convention,

Noting with satisfaction that additional States have ratified or acceded to the Convention, bringing the total number of States that have formally accepted the obligations of the Convention to one hundred and eight,

Emphasizing the desirability of attracting the adherence of all States to the Convention, and determined to work strenuously towards the promotion of its universalization,

Noting with regret that anti-personnel mines continue to be used in conflicts around the world, causing human suffering and impeding post-conflict development,

1. *Invites* all States that have not signed the Convention on the Prohibition of the Use, Stockpiling, Production and Transfer of Anti-personnel Mines and on Their Destruction to accede to it without delay;

2. *Urges* all States that have signed but not ratified the Convention to ratify it without delay;

3. *Stresses* the importance of the full and effective implementation of, and compliance with, the Convention;

4. *Urges* all States parties to provide the Secretary-General with complete and timely information, as required in article 7 of the Convention, in order to promote transparency and compliance with the Convention;

5. *Invites* all States that have not ratified the Convention or acceded to it to provide, on a voluntary basis, information to make global mine action efforts more effective;

6. *Renews its call upon* all States and other relevant parties to work together to promote, support and advance the care, rehabilitation and social and economic reintegration of mine victims, mine awareness programmes, and the removal of anti-personnel mines placed throughout the world and the assurance of their destruction;

7. *Invites and encourages* all interested States, the United Nations, other relevant international organizations or institutions, regional organizations, the Inter-

national Committee of the Red Cross and relevant non-governmental organizations to participate in the programme of intersessional work established at the First Meeting of States Parties to the Convention and further developed at the Second Meeting of States Parties to the Convention;

8. *Welcomes* the generous offer of the Government of Nicaragua to host the Third Meeting of States Parties to the Convention;

9. *Requests* the Secretary-General, in accordance with article 11, paragraph 2, of the Convention, to undertake the preparations necessary to convene the Third Meeting of States Parties to the Convention at Managua, from 18 to 21 September 2001, and, on behalf of States parties and in accordance with article 11, paragraph 4, of the Convention, to invite States not parties to the Convention, as well as the United Nations, other relevant international organizations or institutions, regional organizations, the International Committee of the Red Cross and relevant non-governmental organizations to attend the Meeting as observers;

10. *Decides* to include in the provisional agenda of its fifty-sixth session the item entitled "Implementation of the Convention on the Prohibition of the Use, Stockpiling, Production and Transfer of Anti-personnel Mines and on Their Destruction".

RECORDED VOTE ON RESOLUTION 55/33 V:

In favour: Albania, Algeria, Andorra, Angola, Antigua and Barbuda, Argentina, Armenia, Australia, Austria, Bahamas, Bahrain, Bangladesh, Barbados, Belarus, Belgium, Belize, Benin, Bhutan, Bolivia, Bosnia and Herzegovina, Botswana, Brazil, Brunei Darussalam, Bulgaria, Burkina Faso, Burundi, Cambodia, Cameroon, Canada, Cape Verde, Chile, Colombia, Comoros, Costa Rica, Côte d'Ivoire, Croatia, Cyprus, Czech Republic, Denmark, Djibouti, Dominican Republic, Ecuador, El Salvador, Equatorial Guinea, Eritrea, Estonia, Ethiopia, Fiji, Finland, France, Gabon, Gambia, Georgia, Germany, Ghana, Greece, Grenada, Guatemala, Guinea, Guyana, Haiti, Honduras, Hungary, Iceland, Indonesia, Ireland, Italy, Jamaica, Japan, Jordan, Kenya, Latvia, Lesotho, Liechtenstein, Lithuania, Luxembourg, Madagascar, Malawi, Malaysia, Maldives, Mali, Malta, Mauritius, Mexico, Monaco, Mongolia, Mozambique, Namibia, Nauru, Nepal, Netherlands, New Zealand, Nicaragua, Nigeria, Norway, Oman, Panama, Papua New Guinea, Paraguay, Peru, Philippines, Poland, Portugal, Qatar, Republic of Moldova, Romania, Saint Kitts and Nevis, Saint Lucia, Saint Vincent and the Grenadines, Samoa, San Marino, Senegal, Sierra Leone, Singapore, Slovakia, Slovenia, Solomon Islands, South Africa, Spain, Sri Lanka, Sudan, Suriname, Swaziland, Sweden, Thailand, The former Yugoslav Republic of Macedonia, Togo, Tonga, Trinidad and Tobago, Tunisia, Turkey, Turkmenistan, Uganda, Ukraine, United Arab Emirates, United Kingdom, United Republic of Tanzania, Uruguay, Vanuatu, Venezuela, Yemen, Zambia, Zimbabwe.

Against: None.

Abstaining: Azerbaijan, China, Cuba, Egypt, India, Iran, Israel, Kazakhstan, Kyrgyzstan, Lebanon, Libyan Arab Jamahiriya, Marshall Islands, Micronesia, Morocco, Myanmar, Pakistan, Republic of Korea, Russian Federation, Syrian Arab Republic, United States, Uzbekistan, Viet Nam.

Regional and other approaches to disarmament

Africa

OAU, with the support and collaboration of the Institute of Security Studies (Pretoria) and the UN Regional Centre for Peace and Disarmament in Africa (see p. 538) and the assistance of the Eminent Persons Group on Curbing Illicit Trafficking in Small Arms and Light Weapons, con-

vened the first continental meeting of African experts on small arms and light weapons (Addis Ababa, 17-19 May) [A/55/323], which considered, among other things, common elements that might increase the capacity of existing institutional arrangements to address illicit proliferation, circulation and trafficking in small arms. At the thirty-sixth ordinary session of the OAU Assembly of Heads of State and Government (Lomé, Togo, 10-12 July) [A/55/286], member States adopted the Lomé Declaration, which contained a plan of action for ending the illicit proliferation and trafficking in small arms and light weapons that had played a major role in perpetuating conflicts on the continent.

In 2000, guidelines were finalized for national commissions on proliferation of small arms, to be established in all countries of the Economic Community of West African States (ECOWAS) in support of its 1998 moratorium on the importation, exportation and manufacture of small arms and light weapons [YUN 1998, p. 537]. The first ministerial meeting between the EU and ECOWAS (Abuja, Nigeria, 16 October) discussed cooperation on the ECOWAS moratorium, among other things. ECOWAS continued its efforts at conflict prevention and management in West Africa, and, at the Fifth Ministerial Meeting of its Mediation and Security Council (Bamako, Mali, 12-13 December), participants considered country situations.

During the year, member States of the Southern African Development Community (SADC) were in the process of negotiating a protocol on the control of firearms, ammunition and other related materials in the region. In December [A/55/696-S/2000/1200], the United States and SADC member States issued the joint United States–SADC Declaration on United Nations Sanctions and Restraint in Sale and Transfers of Conventional Arms to Regions of Conflict in Africa, which urged States, particularly suppliers, to observe UN arms embargoes, to exercise restraint in the sale and transfer of those weapons to areas of conflict on the continent and to adopt national controls over surplus stocks.

(See also p. 518 for regional activities related to small arms.)

Standing Advisory Committee

In response to General Assembly resolution 54/55 A [YUN 1999, p. 501], the Secretary-General, in July [A/55/170], described the activities of the United Nations Standing Advisory Committee on Security Questions in Central Africa. In response to a 1999 decision [YUN 1999, p. 501] to incorporate the Council for Peace and Security in Central Africa (COPAX) into the Economic

Community of Central African States (ECCAS), the Committee had decided to convene jointly with ECCAS a meeting (Malabo, Equatorial Guinea, 14-17 February 2000), which drafted the Protocol on the Council for Peace and Security in Central Africa and the Mutual Assistance Pact between the member States of ECCAS. ECCAS members adopted the two documents (Malabo, 24 February) and committed themselves to speedy ratification in order to allow their entry into force as quickly as possible. At its thirteenth ministerial meeting (N'Djamena, Chad, 2-6 May) [A/54/889-S/2000/506], the Committee, to accelerate the process of rendering COPAX operational, decided to convene a meeting of experts to consider the proposed legislative mandates of the COPAX structures, which included the early-warning mechanism, the Central African Multinational Force and the Defence Commission for the Central African countries. However, the meeting was held under ECCAS auspices (Malabo, 19-22 June).

During its fourteenth ministerial meeting (Bujumbura, Burundi, 17-18 August) [A/55/505-S/2000/1005], the Committee reviewed developments related to COPAX, as well as the implementation of the recommendations of the 1999 subregional conference on the proliferation of and illicit traffic in small arms in Central Africa [YUN 1999, p. 501].

GENERAL ASSEMBLY ACTION

On 20 November [meeting 69], the General Assembly, on the recommendation of the First Committee [A/55/560], adopted **resolution 55/34 B** without vote [agenda item 74 *(a)*].

Regional confidence-building measures: activities of the United Nations Standing Advisory Committee on Security Questions in Central Africa

The General Assembly,

Bearing in mind the purposes and principles of the United Nations and its primary responsibility for the maintenance of international peace and security in accordance with the Charter of the United Nations,

Recalling its resolutions 43/78 H and 43/85 of 7 December 1988, 44/21 of 15 November 1989, 45/58 M of 4 December 1990, 46/37 B of 6 December 1991, 47/53 F of 15 December 1992, 48/76 A of 16 December 1993, 49/76 C of 15 December 1994, 50/71 B of 12 December 1995, 51/46 C of 10 December 1996, 52/39 B of 9 December 1997, 53/78 A of 4 December 1998 and 54/55 A of 1 December 1999,

Considering the importance and effectiveness of confidence-building measures taken at the initiative and with the participation of all States concerned and taking into account the specific characteristics of each region, since such measures can contribute to regional stability and to international security,

Convinced that the resources released by disarmament, including regional disarmament, can be devoted to economic and social development and to the protec-

tion of the environment for the benefit of all peoples, in particular those of the developing countries,

Recalling the guidelines for general and complete disarmament adopted at its tenth special session, the first special session devoted to disarmament,

Convinced that development can be achieved only in a climate of peace, security and mutual confidence both within and among States,

Bearing in mind the establishment by the Secretary-General on 28 May 1992 of the United Nations Standing Advisory Committee on Security Questions in Central Africa, the purpose of which is to encourage arms limitation, disarmament, non-proliferation and development in the subregion,

Recalling the Brazzaville Declaration on Cooperation for Peace and Security in Central Africa, the Bata Declaration for the Promotion of Lasting Democracy, Peace and Development in Central Africa, and the Yaoundé Declaration on Peace, Security and Stability in Central Africa,

Bearing in mind resolutions 1196(1998) and 1197(1998), adopted by the Security Council on 16 and 18 September 1998 respectively, following its consideration of the report of the Secretary-General on the causes of conflict and the promotion of durable peace and sustainable development in Africa,

Emphasizing the need to strengthen the capacity for conflict prevention and peacekeeping in Africa,

Recalling the decision of the fourth ministerial meeting of the Standing Advisory Committee in favour of establishing, under the auspices of the United Nations High Commissioner for Human Rights, a subregional centre for human rights and democracy in Central Africa,

1. *Takes note* of the report of the Secretary-General on regional confidence-building measures, which deals with the activities of the United Nations Standing Advisory Committee on Security Questions in Central Africa in the period since the adoption by the General Assembly of resolution 54/55 A;

2. *Reaffirms its support* for efforts aimed at promoting confidence-building measures at regional and sub-regional levels in order to ease tensions and conflicts in Central Africa and to further peace, stability and sustainable development in the subregion;

3. *Also reaffirms its support* for the programme of work of the Standing Advisory Committee adopted at the organizational meeting of the Committee, held at Yaoundé from 27 to 31 July 1992;

4. *Notes with satisfaction* the progress made by the States members of the Standing Advisory Committee in implementing the programme of activities for the period 1999-2000, in particular by:

(a) Holding the Subregional Conference on the Proliferation of and Illicit Traffic in Small Arms in Central Africa at N'Djamena from 25 to 27 October 1999;

(b) Holding the twelfth ministerial meeting of the Standing Advisory Committee at N'Djamena from 27 to 30 October 1999;

(c) Holding a meeting of experts of the countries of the subregion to draft the Protocol on the Council for Peace and Security in Central Africa and the Mutual Assistance Pact between countries of Central Africa at Malabo from 14 to 17 February 2000;

(d) Holding the thirteenth ministerial meeting of the Standing Advisory Committee at N'Djamena from 2 to 6 May 2000;

(e) Holding the Subregional Conference on the Question of Refugees and Internally Displaced Persons in Central Africa at Bujumbura from 14 to 16 August 2000;

(f) Holding the fourteenth ministerial meeting of the Standing Advisory Committee at Bujumbura from 17 to 19 August 2000;

5. *Emphasizes* the importance of providing the States members of the Standing Advisory Committee with the essential support they need to carry out the full programme of activities which they adopted at their ministerial meetings;

6. *Welcomes* the creation of a mechanism for the promotion, maintenance and consolidation of peace and security in Central Africa, to be known as the Council for Peace and Security in Central Africa, by the summit Conference of Heads of State and Government of the Central African countries, held at Yaoundé on 25 February 1999, and requests the Secretary-General to give his full support to the effective realization of that important mechanism;

7. *Emphasizes* the need to make the early-warning mechanism in Central Africa operational so that it will serve, on the one hand, as an instrument for analysing and monitoring political situations in the States members of the Standing Advisory Committee with a view to preventing the outbreak of future armed conflicts and, on the other hand, as a technical body through which the member States will carry out the programme of work of the Committee, adopted at its organizational meeting held at Yaoundé in 1992, and requests the Secretary-General to provide it with the assistance necessary for it to function properly;

8. *Requests* the Secretary-General and the United Nations High Commissioner for Human Rights to continue to lend all their support to the effective establishment and smooth functioning of the Subregional Centre for Human Rights and Democracy in Central Africa;

9. *Requests* the Secretary-General, pursuant to Security Council resolution 1197(1998), to provide the States members of the Standing Advisory Committee with the necessary support for the implementation and smooth functioning of the early-warning mechanism and the Council for Peace and Security in Central Africa;

10. *Also requests* the Secretary-General to support the establishment of a network of parliamentarians with a view to the creation of a subregional parliament in Central Africa;

11. *Requests* the Secretary-General and the Office of the United Nations High Commissioner for Refugees to continue to provide increased assistance to the countries of Central Africa for coping with the problems of refugees in their territories;

12. *Welcomes with satisfaction* the decision taken by the Standing Advisory Committee at its fourteenth ministerial meeting to organize a subregional conference on the protection of women and children in armed conflicts, and requests the Secretary-General to lend all the necessary support for the holding of the conference;

13. *Thanks* the Secretary-General for having established the Trust Fund for the United Nations Standing Advisory Committee on Security Questions in Central Africa;

14. *Appeals* to Member States and to governmental and non-governmental organizations to make additional voluntary contributions to the Trust Fund for the implementation of the programme of work of the Standing Advisory Committee;

15. *Requests* the Secretary-General to continue to provide the States members of the Standing Advisory Committee with assistance to ensure that they are able to carry on their efforts;

16. *Also requests* the Secretary-General to submit to the General Assembly at its fifty-sixth session a report on the implementation of the present resolution;

17. *Decides* to include in the provisional agenda of its fifty-sixth session the item entitled "Regional confidence-building measures: activities of the United Nations Standing Advisory Committee on Security Questions in Central Africa".

Asia and the Pacific

The Association of South-East Asian Nations (ASEAN), its Regional Forum (ARF) and the Council for Security Cooperation in the Asia Pacific addressed issues related to security, regional stability and confidence-building. The UN Regional Centre for Peace and Disarmament in Asia and the Pacific also contributed to security and stability in the region through its activities (see p. 539).

Foreign Ministers taking part in the thirty-third ASEAN ministerial meeting (Bangkok, 24-25 July) and the seventh meeting of ARF (Bangkok, 27 July) emphasized the importance of confidence-building measures and agreed that such efforts should be intensified. While confidence-building measures remained the primary focus of ARF, they believed that advances could be made to develop measures for preventive diplomacy. In that context, the Foreign Ministers commended the ARF intersessional support group (Singapore, 5-6 April), which had considered preventive diplomacy.

A number of other meetings concerning small arms issues were held at the regional, governmental and non-governmental levels, including a regional seminar (Jakarta, Indonesia, 3-4 May) and two conferences (Kandalama, Sri Lanka, 20-23 June; Kandy, Sri Lanka, 23-25 June), both of which emphasized the importance of cooperation and information exchange in combating the problem of illicit trafficking and proliferation of small arms in the region.

On 5 September in Tokyo [A/55/462-S/2000/974], the Russian Federation and Japan, in a joint statement on cooperation, accorded priority to contributing constructively to confidence-enhancement and stability in the Asia-Pacific region. The Russian Federation and Mongolia, on 14 November in Ulaanbaatar [A/55/644], in the Ulaanbaatar Declaration, expressed their intention to contribute to ARF and to join forces against illicit trafficking in arms and other security threats in the region.

Europe

Major security concerns in Europe related to developments in the Balkans, particularly the Kosovo province of the Federal Republic of Yugoslavia (FRY) (see p. 358), which led to the proliferation of small arms and light weapons in the region.

NATO continued its activities through various bodies and through the NATO-Russian Permanent Joint Council and the Euro-Atlantic Partnership Council, both established in 1997 [YUN 1997, pp. 518 & 519]. Under OSCE, work proceeded on the 1995 General Framework Agreement for Peace in Bosnia and Herzegovina (the Peace Agreement) [YUN 1995, p. 544]. The States parties to the 1996 Agreement on Regional Arms Control [YUN 1996, p. 493], signed by Bosnia and Herzegovina, Croatia, FRY, the Federation of Bosnia and Herzegovina and Republika Srpska, continued to destroy surplus weapons, despite FRY's temporary suspension of its participation in the Peace Agreement owing to the escalation of violence in Kosovo.

States participating in the negotiations on regional stability in South-Eastern Europe continued to consider confidence- and security-building measures and initiated discussions on information exchange on military forces. The EU and the United States (Queluz, Portugal, 31 May) stated that they remained committed to the goals of the 1999 Stability Pact for South-Eastern Europe [YUN 1999, p. 397], designed to foster cooperation among countries of the region towards long-term stability, security and economic reconstruction and development of the region.

States parties to the 1990 Treaty on Conventional Armed Forces in Europe [YUN 1990, p. 79] continued to implement the Treaty's provisions, as well as the Vienna Document 1999 on the Negotiations on Confidence- and Security-Building Measures [YUN 1999, p. 503], which entered into force on 1 January 2000. A series of conferences and workshops relating to small arms were held under the auspices of the Stability Pact for South-Eastern Europe (Ljubljana, Slovenia, 27 January) and the South-East European Cooperation Process (Ohrid, The former Yugoslav Republic of Macedonia, 14 July) [A/55/323, p. 12].

Latin America

The Organization of American States (OAS) continued to be involved in disarmament and security matters in the region, especially in promoting and implementing mine clearance and transparency in conventional weapons and in curbing illicit manufacturing and trafficking in firearms. At its June meeting (San José, Costa Rica, 3-5 June) the OAS General Assembly adopted a number of resolutions relating to those issues.

With regard to mine action, OAS, Argentina and Canada, in cooperation with the UN Mine Action Service and the UN Regional Centre for Peace, Disarmament and Development in Latin America and the Caribbean (see p. 540), organized a regional seminar on the destruction of stockpiled anti-personnel mines (Buenos Aires, November). The seminar was conceived as a practical exercise to assist Latin American parties to the Mine-Ban Convention (see p. 525) in fulfilling their legal obligations to destroy all stocks within four years of the Treaty's entry into force, which had occurred on 1 March 1999 [YUN 1999, p. 498].

GENERAL ASSEMBLY ACTION

On 20 November [meeting 69], the General Assembly, on the recommendation of the First Committee [A/55/559], adopted **resolution 55/33 O** without vote [agenda item 73 *(p)*].

Regional disarmament

The General Assembly,

Recalling its resolutions 45/58 P of 4 December 1990, 46/36 I of 6 December 1991, 47/52 J of 9 December 1992, 48/75 I of 16 December 1993, 49/75 N of 15 December 1994, 50/70 K of 12 December 1995, 51/45 K of 10 December 1996, 52/38 P of 9 December 1997, 53/77 O of 4 December 1998 and 54/54 N of 1 December 1999 on regional disarmament,

Believing that the efforts of the international community to move towards the ideal of general and complete disarmament are guided by the inherent human desire for genuine peace and security, the elimination of the danger of war and the release of economic, intellectual and other resources for peaceful pursuits,

Affirming the abiding commitment of all States to the purposes and principles enshrined in the Charter of the United Nations in the conduct of their international relations,

Noting that essential guidelines for progress towards general and complete disarmament were adopted at the tenth special session of the General Assembly,

Taking note of the guidelines and recommendations for regional approaches to disarmament within the context of global security adopted by the Disarmament Commission at its 1993 substantive session,

Welcoming the prospects of genuine progress in the field of disarmament engendered in recent years as a result of negotiations between the two super-Powers,

Taking note of the recent proposals for disarmament at the regional and subregional levels,

Recognizing the importance of confidence-building measures for regional and international peace and security,

Convinced that endeavours by countries to promote regional disarmament, taking into account the specific characteristics of each region and in accordance with the principle of undiminished security at the lowest level of armaments, would enhance the security of all States and would thus contribute to international peace and security by reducing the risk of regional conflicts,

1. *Stresses* that sustained efforts are needed, within the framework of the Conference on Disarmament and under the umbrella of the United Nations, to make progress on the entire range of disarmament issues;

2. *Affirms* that global and regional approaches to disarmament complement each other and should therefore be pursued simultaneously to promote regional and international peace and security;

3. *Calls upon* States to conclude agreements, wherever possible, for nuclear non-proliferation, disarmament and confidence-building measures at the regional and subregional levels;

4. *Welcomes* the initiatives towards disarmament, nuclear non-proliferation and security undertaken by some countries at the regional and subregional levels;

5. *Supports and encourages* efforts aimed at promoting confidence-building measures at the regional and subregional levels in order to ease regional tensions and to further disarmament and nuclear non-proliferation measures at the regional and subregional levels;

6. *Decides* to include in the provisional agenda of its fifty-sixth session the item entitled "Regional disarmament".

Also on 20 November [meeting 69], on the recommendation of the First Committee [A/55/559], the General Assembly adopted **resolution 55/33 P** by recorded vote (163-1-1) [agenda item 73 (*o*)].

Conventional arms control at the regional and subregional levels

The General Assembly,

Recalling its resolutions 48/75 J of 16 December 1993, 49/75 O of 15 December 1994, 50/70 L of 12 December 1995, 51/45 Q of 10 December 1996, 52/38 Q of 9 December 1997, 53/77 P of 4 December 1998 and 54/54 M of 1 December 1999,

Recognizing the crucial role of conventional arms control in promoting regional and international peace and security,

Convinced that conventional arms control needs to be pursued primarily in the regional and subregional contexts since most threats to peace and security in the post-cold-war era arise mainly among States located in the same region or subregion,

Aware that the preservation of a balance in the defence capabilities of States at the lowest level of armaments would contribute to peace and stability and should be a prime objective of conventional arms control,

Desirous of promoting agreements to strengthen regional peace and security at the lowest possible level of armaments and military forces,

Noting with particular interest the initiatives taken in this regard in different regions of the world, in particular the commencement of consultations among a number of Latin American countries and the proposals for conventional arms control made in the context of South Asia, and recognizing, in the context of this subject, the relevance and value of the Treaty on Conventional Armed Forces in Europe, which is a cornerstone of European security,

Believing that militarily significant States and States with larger military capabilities have a special responsibility in promoting such agreements for regional security,

Believing also that an important objective of conventional arms control in regions of tension should be to prevent the possibility of military attack launched by surprise and to avoid aggression,

1. *Decides* to give urgent consideration to the issues involved in conventional arms control at the regional and subregional levels;

2. *Requests* the Conference on Disarmament, as a first step, to consider the formulation of principles that can serve as a framework for regional agreements on conventional arms control, and looks forward to a report of the Conference on this subject;

3. *Decides* to include in the provisional agenda of its fifty-sixth session the item entitled "Conventional arms control at the regional and subregional levels".

RECORDED VOTE ON RESOLUTION 55/33 P:

In favour: Albania, Algeria, Andorra, Angola, Antigua and Barbuda, Argentina, Armenia, Australia, Austria, Azerbaijan, Bahamas, Bahrain, Bangladesh, Barbados, Belarus, Belgium, Belize, Benin, Bolivia, Bosnia and Herzegovina, Botswana, Brazil, Brunei Darussalam, Bulgaria, Burkina Faso, Burundi, Cambodia, Cameroon, Canada, Cape Verde, Chile, China, Colombia, Costa Rica, Côte d'Ivoire, Croatia, Cyprus, Czech Republic, Denmark, Djibouti, Dominican Republic, Ecuador, Egypt, El Salvador, Equatorial Guinea, Eritrea, Estonia, Ethiopia, Fiji, Finland, France, Gabon, Gambia, Georgia, Germany, Ghana, Greece, Grenada, Guatemala, Guinea, Guyana, Haiti, Honduras, Hungary, Iceland, Indonesia, Iran, Ireland, Israel, Italy, Jamaica, Japan, Jordan, Kazakhstan, Kenya, Kuwait, Kyrgyzstan, Latvia, Lebanon, Lesotho, Libyan Arab Jamahiriya, Liechtenstein, Lithuania, Luxembourg, Madagascar, Malawi, Malaysia, Maldives, Mali, Malta, Marshall Islands, Mauritius, Mexico, Micronesia, Monaco, Mongolia, Morocco, Mozambique, Myanmar, Namibia, Nauru, Nepal, Netherlands, New Zealand, Nicaragua, Nigeria, Norway, Oman, Pakistan, Panama, Papua New Guinea, Paraguay, Peru, Philippines, Poland, Portugal, Qatar, Republic of Korea, Republic of Moldova, Romania, Russian Federation, Saint Kitts and Nevis, Saint Lucia, Saint Vincent and the Grenadines, Samoa, San Marino, Saudi Arabia, Senegal, Sierra Leone, Singapore, Slovakia, Slovenia, Solomon Islands, South Africa, Spain, Sri Lanka, Sudan, Suriname, Swaziland, Sweden, Syrian Arab Republic, Tajikistan, Thailand, The former Yugoslav Republic of Macedonia, Togo, Tonga, Trinidad and Tobago, Tunisia, Turkey, Turkmenistan, Uganda, Ukraine, United Arab Emirates, United Kingdom, United Republic of Tanzania, United States, Uruguay, Uzbekistan, Vanuatu, Venezuela, Yemen, Zambia, Zimbabwe.

Against: India.

Abstaining: Bhutan.

Other disarmament issues

Prevention of an arms race in outer space

In 2000, the Conference on Disarmament did not establish an ad hoc committee on the prevention of an arms race in outer space. However, many delegations raised the issue of the militarization of outer space, especially in connection with ongoing plans by the United States to develop a national missile defence system (see p. 490).

On 20 November [meeting 69], the General Assembly, on the recommendation of the First Committee [A/55/558], adopted **resolution 55/32** by recorded vote (163-0-3) [agenda item 72].

Prevention of an arms race in outer space

The General Assembly,

Recognizing the common interest of all mankind in the exploration and use of outer space for peaceful purposes,

Reaffirming the will of all States that the exploration and use of outer space, including the Moon and other celestial bodies, shall be for peaceful purposes and shall be carried out for the benefit and in the interest of all countries, irrespective of their degree of economic or scientific development,

Reaffirming also the provisions of articles III and IV of the Treaty on Principles Governing the Activities of States in the Exploration and Use of Outer Space, including the Moon and Other Celestial Bodies,

Recalling the obligation of all States to observe the provisions of the Charter of the United Nations regarding the use or threat of use of force in their international relations, including in their space activities,

Reaffirming paragraph 80 of the Final Document of the Tenth Special Session of the General Assembly, in which it is stated that in order to prevent an arms race in outer space further measures should be taken and appropriate international negotiations held in accordance with the spirit of the Treaty,

Recalling its previous resolutions on this issue, and taking note of the proposals submitted to the General Assembly at its tenth special session and at its regular sessions, and of the recommendations made to the competent organs of the United Nations and to the Conference on Disarmament,

Recognizing that prevention of an arms race in outer space would avert a grave danger for international peace and security,

Emphasizing the paramount importance of strict compliance with existing arms limitation and disarmament agreements relevant to outer space, including bilateral agreements, and with the existing legal regime concerning the use of outer space,

Considering that wide participation in the legal regime applicable to outer space could contribute to enhancing its effectiveness,

Noting that the Ad Hoc Committee on the Prevention of an Arms Race in Outer Space, taking into account its previous efforts since its establishment in 1985 and seeking to enhance its functioning in qualitative terms, continued the examination and identification of various issues, existing agreements and existing proposals, as well as future initiatives relevant to the prevention of an arms race in outer space, and that this contributed to a better understanding of a number of problems and to a clearer perception of the various positions,

Noting also that there were no objections in principle in the Conference on Disarmament to the re-establishment of the Ad Hoc Committee, subject to re-examination of the mandate contained in the decision of the Conference on Disarmament of 13 February 1992,

Emphasizing the mutually complementary nature of bilateral and multilateral efforts in the field of preventing an arms race in outer space, and hoping that concrete results will emerge from those efforts as soon as possible,

Convinced that further measures should be examined in the search for effective and verifiable bilateral and multilateral agreements in order to prevent an arms race in outer space, including the weaponization of outer space,

Stressing that the growing use of outer space increases the need for greater transparency and better information on the part of the international community,

Recalling in this context its previous resolutions, in particular resolutions 45/55 B of 4 December 1990, 47/51 of 9 December 1992 and 48/74 A of 16 December 1993, in which, inter alia, it reaffirmed the importance of confidence-building measures as means conducive to ensuring the attainment of the objective of the prevention of an arms race in outer space,

Conscious of the benefits of confidence- and security-building measures in the military field,

Recognizing that negotiations for the conclusion of an international agreement or agreements to prevent an arms race in outer space remain a priority task of the Ad Hoc Committee and that the concrete proposals on confidence-building measures could form an integral part of such agreements,

1. *Reaffirms* the importance and urgency of preventing an arms race in outer space and the readiness of all States to contribute to that common objective, in conformity with the provisions of the Treaty on Principles Governing the Activities of States in the Exploration and Use of Outer Space, including the Moon and Other Celestial Bodies;

2. *Reaffirms its recognition,* as stated in the report of the Ad Hoc Committee on the Prevention of an Arms Race in Outer Space, that the legal regime applicable to outer space by itself does not guarantee the prevention of an arms race in outer space, that this legal regime plays a significant role in the prevention of an arms race in that environment, that there is a need to consolidate and reinforce that regime and enhance its effectiveness, and that it is important to comply strictly with existing agreements, both bilateral and multilateral;

3. *Emphasizes* the necessity of further measures with appropriate and effective provisions for verification to prevent an arms race in outer space;

4. *Calls upon* all States, in particular those with major space capabilities, to contribute actively to the objective of the peaceful use of outer space and of the prevention of an arms race in outer space and to refrain from actions contrary to that objective and to the relevant existing treaties in the interest of maintaining international peace and security and promoting international cooperation;

5. *Reiterates* that the Conference on Disarmament, as the single multilateral disarmament negotiating forum, has the primary role in the negotiation of a multilateral agreement or agreements, as appropriate, on the prevention of an arms race in outer space in all its aspects;

6. *Invites* the Conference on Disarmament to complete the examination and updating of the mandate contained in its decision of 13 February 1992, and to establish an ad hoc committee as early as possible during the 2001 session of the Conference;

7. *Recognizes,* in this respect, the growing convergence of views on the elaboration of measures de-

signed to strengthen transparency, confidence and security in the peaceful uses of outer space;

8. *Urges* States conducting activities in outer space, as well as States interested in conducting such activities, to keep the Conference on Disarmament informed of the progress of bilateral and multilateral negotiations on the matter, if any, so as to facilitate its work;

9. *Decides* to include in the provisional agenda of its fifty-sixth session the item entitled "Prevention of an arms race in outer space".

RECORDED VOTE ON RESOLUTION 55/32:

In favour: Albania, Algeria, Andorra, Angola, Antigua and Barbuda, Argentina, Armenia, Australia, Austria, Azerbaijan, Bahamas, Bahrain, Bangladesh, Barbados, Belarus, Belgium, Belize, Benin, Bhutan, Bolivia, Bosnia and Herzegovina, Botswana, Brazil, Brunei Darussalam, Bulgaria, Burkina Faso, Burundi, Cambodia, Cameroon, Canada, Cape Verde, Chile, China, Colombia, Costa Rica, Côte d'Ivoire, Croatia, Cuba, Cyprus, Czech Republic, Democratic People's Republic of Korea, Denmark, Djibouti, Dominican Republic, Ecuador, Egypt, El Salvador, Equatorial Guinea, Eritrea, Estonia, Ethiopia, Fiji, Finland, France, Gabon, Georgia, Germany, Ghana, Greece, Grenada, Guatemala, Guinea, Guyana, Haiti, Honduras, Hungary, Iceland, India, Indonesia, Iran, Ireland, Italy, Jamaica, Japan, Jordan, Kazakhstan, Kenya, Kuwait, Kyrgyzstan, Lao People's Democratic Republic, Latvia, Lebanon, Lesotho, Libyan Arab Jamahiriya, Liechtenstein, Lithuania, Luxembourg, Madagascar, Malawi, Malaysia, Maldives, Mali, Malta, Marshall Islands, Mauritius, Mexico, Monaco, Mongolia, Morocco, Mozambique, Myanmar, Namibia, Nauru, Nepal, Netherlands, New Zealand, Nicaragua, Nigeria, Norway, Oman, Pakistan, Panama, Papua New Guinea, Paraguay, Peru, Philippines, Poland, Portugal, Qatar, Republic of Korea, Republic of Moldova, Romania, Russian Federation, Saint Lucia, Saint Vincent and the Grenadines, Samoa, San Marino, Saudi Arabia, Senegal, Sierra Leone, Singapore, Slovakia, Slovenia, Solomon Islands, South Africa, Spain, Sri Lanka, Sudan, Swaziland, Sweden, Syrian Arab Republic, Tajikistan, Thailand, The former Yugoslav Republic of Macedonia, Togo, Tonga, Trinidad and Tobago, Tunisia, Turkey, Turkmenistan, Uganda, Ukraine, United Arab Emirates, United Kingdom, United Republic of Tanzania, Uruguay, Uzbekistan, Vanuatu, Venezuela, Viet Nam, Yemen, Zambia, Zimbabwe.

Against: None.

Abstaining: Israel, Micronesia, United States.

Disarmament and development

In response to General Assembly resolution 54/54 T [YUN 1999, p. 507], the Secretary-General, in August [A/55/258], described activities to implement the action programme adopted at the 1987 International Conference on the Relationship between Disarmament and Development [YUN 1987, p. 83]. In that context, he referred to panel discussions, meetings and expert consultations organized by the Steering Group on Disarmament and Development, established in 1999 [YUN 1999, p. 506].

The UN Department for Disarmament Affairs (DDA) continued its cooperation with UNDP on the disarmament and development approach, reflected in the weapons-for-development programmes pursued to combat the proliferation of small arms and light weapons. In July, DDA began consultations with independent experts, to seek their views on the changing paradigm of disarmament and development.

Annexed to the report was the view of one State (Colombia) on the implementation of the 1987 action programme, pursuant to resolution 54/54 T.

On 20 November [meeting 69], the General Assembly, on the recommendation of the First Committee [A/55/559], adopted **resolution 55/33 L** without vote [agenda item 73 (u)].

Relationship between disarmament and development

The General Assembly,

Recalling the provisions of the Final Document of the Tenth Special Session of the General Assembly concerning the relationship between disarmament and development,

Recalling also the adoption on 11 September 1987 of the Final Document of the International Conference on the Relationship between Disarmament and Development,

Recalling further its resolutions 49/75 J of 15 December 1994, 50/70 G of 12 December 1995, 51/45 D of 10 December 1996, 52/38 D of 9 December 1997, 53/77 K of 4 December 1998 and 54/54 T of 1 December 1999,

Bearing in mind the Final Document of the Twelfth Conference of Heads of State or Government of Non-Aligned Countries, held at Durban, South Africa, from 29 August to 3 September 1998, and the final document of the Thirteenth Ministerial Conference of the Movement of Non-Aligned Countries, held at Cartagena, Colombia, on 8 and 9 April 2000,

Welcoming the different activities organized by the high-level Steering Group on Disarmament and Development, as contained in the report of the Secretary-General,

Stressing the growing importance of the symbiotic relationship between disarmament and development in current international relations,

1. *Calls upon* the high-level Steering Group on Disarmament and Development to strengthen and enhance its programme of activities, in accordance with the mandate set out in the action programme adopted at the International Conference on the Relationship between Disarmament and Development;

2. *Urges* the international community to devote part of the resources made available by the implementation of disarmament and arms limitation agreements to economic and social development, with a view to reducing the ever-widening gap between developed and developing countries;

3. *Invites* all Member States to communicate to the Secretary-General, by 15 April 2001, their views and proposals for the implementation of the action programme adopted at the International Conference on the Relationship between Disarmament and Development, as well as any other views and proposals with a view to achieving the goals of the action programme, within the framework of current international relations;

4. *Requests* the Secretary-General to continue to take action, through appropriate organs and within available resources, for the implementation of the action programme adopted at the International Conference;

5. *Also requests* the Secretary-General to submit a report to the General Assembly at its fifty-sixth session;

6. *Decides* to include in the provisional agenda of its fifty-sixth session the item entitled "Relationship between disarmament and development".

Arms limitation and disarmament agreements

Pursuant to General Assembly resolution 54/54 S [YUN 1999, p. 508], the Secretary-General submitted a July report [A/55/129] containing information from two Member States on measures they had taken to ensure the application of scientific and technological progress in the context of international security, disarmament and related areas, without detriment to the environment or to its effective contribution to attaining sustainable development.

GENERAL ASSEMBLY ACTION

On 20 November [meeting 69], the General Assembly, on the recommendation of the First Committee [A/55/559], adopted **resolution 55/33 K** by recorded vote (165-0-4) [agenda item 73 _(t)_].

Observance of environmental norms in the drafting and implementation of agreements on disarmament and arms control

The General Assembly,

Recalling its resolutions 50/70 M of 12 December 1995, 51/45 E of 10 December 1996, 52/38 E of 9 December 1997, 53/77 J of 4 December 1998 and 54/54 S of 1 December 1999,

Emphasizing the importance of the observance of environmental norms in the preparation and implementation of disarmament and arms limitation agreements,

Recognizing that it is necessary to take duly into account the agreements adopted at the United Nations Conference on Environment and Development, as well as prior relevant agreements, in the drafting and implementation of agreements on disarmament and arms limitation,

Mindful of the detrimental environmental effects of the use of nuclear weapons,

1. _Reaffirms_ that international disarmament forums should take fully into account the relevant environmental norms in negotiating treaties and agreements on disarmament and arms limitation and that all States, through their actions, should fully contribute to ensuring compliance with the aforementioned norms in the implementation of treaties and conventions to which they are parties;

2. _Calls upon_ States to adopt unilateral, bilateral, regional and multilateral measures so as to contribute to ensuring the application of scientific and technological progress in the framework of international security, disarmament and other related spheres, without detriment to the environment or to its effective contribution to attaining sustainable development;

3. _Welcomes_ the information provided by Member States on the implementation of the measures they have adopted to promote the objectives envisaged in the present resolution;

4. _Invites_ all Member States to communicate to the Secretary-General information on the measures they have adopted to promote the objectives envisaged in the present resolution, and requests the Secretary-General to submit a report containing this information to the General Assembly at its fifty-sixth session;

5. _Decides_ to include in the provisional agenda of its fifty-sixth session the item entitled "Observance of environmental norms in the drafting and implementation of agreements on disarmament and arms control".

RECORDED VOTE ON RESOLUTION 55/33 K:

In favour: Albania, Algeria, Andorra, Angola, Antigua and Barbuda, Argentina, Armenia, Australia, Austria, Azerbaijan, Bahamas, Bahrain, Bangladesh, Barbados, Belarus, Belgium, Belize, Benin, Bhutan, Bolivia, Bosnia and Herzegovina, Botswana, Brazil, Brunei Darussalam, Bulgaria, Burkina Faso, Burundi, Cambodia, Cameroon, Canada, Cape Verde, Chile, China, Colombia, Costa Rica, Côte d'Ivoire, Croatia, Cuba, Cyprus, Czech Republic, Democratic People's Republic of Korea, Denmark, Djibouti, Dominican Republic, Ecuador, Egypt, El Salvador, Equatorial Guinea, Eritrea, Estonia, Ethiopia, Fiji, Finland, Gabon, Gambia, Georgia, Germany, Ghana, Greece, Grenada, Guatemala, Guinea, Guyana, Haiti, Honduras, Hungary, Iceland, India, Indonesia, Iran, Ireland, Italy, Jamaica, Japan, Jordan, Kazakhstan, Kenya, Kuwait, Kyrgyzstan, Lao People's Democratic Republic, Latvia, Lebanon, Lesotho, Libyan Arab Jamahiriya, Liechtenstein, Lithuania, Luxembourg, Madagascar, Malawi, Malaysia, Maldives, Mali, Malta, Marshall Islands, Mauritius, Mexico, Micronesia, Monaco, Mongolia, Morocco, Mozambique, Myanmar, Namibia, Nauru, Nepal, Netherlands, New Zealand, Nicaragua, Nigeria, Norway, Oman, Pakistan, Panama, Papua New Guinea, Paraguay, Peru, Philippines, Poland, Portugal, Qatar, Republic of Korea, Republic of Moldova, Romania, Russian Federation, Saint Kitts and Nevis, Saint Lucia, Saint Vincent and the Grenadines, Samoa, San Marino, Saudi Arabia, Senegal, Sierra Leone, Singapore, Slovakia, Slovenia, Solomon Islands, South Africa, Spain, Sri Lanka, Sudan, Suriname, Swaziland, Sweden, Syrian Arab Republic, Tajikistan, Thailand, The former Yugoslav Republic of Macedonia, Togo, Tonga, Trinidad and Tobago, Tunisia, Turkey, Turkmenistan, Uganda, Ukraine, United Arab Emirates, United Republic of Tanzania, Uruguay, Uzbekistan, Vanuatu, Venezuela, Viet Nam, Yemen, Zambia, Zimbabwe.

Against: None.

Abstaining: France, Israel, United Kingdom, United States.

Studies, information and training

Disarmament studies programme

The Group of Experts on the continuing operation of the UN Register of Conventional Arms and its further development, appointed by the Secretary-General pursuant to General Assembly resolution 54/54 O [YUN 1999, p. 496], completed and submitted its report [A/55/281] in August (see p. 524). The Group of Governmental Experts on Small Arms, appointed by the Secretary-General in response to Assembly resolution 54/54 V [YUN 1999, p. 487], also met during the year (see p. 517).

In 2000, the Assembly, in **resolution 55/33 A**, requested the Secretary-General to prepare a report on the issue of missiles in all its aspects for consideration in 2002. By **resolution 55/33 E**, the Assembly requested the Secretary-General to prepare, with the assistance of governmental experts, a study on disarmament and non-proliferation education.

GENERAL ASSEMBLY ACTION

On 20 November [meeting 69], the General Assembly, on the recommendation of the First Committee [A/55/559], adopted **resolution 55/33 E** without vote [agenda item 73].

United Nations study on disarmament and non-proliferation education

The General Assembly,

Desirous of stressing the urgency of promoting concerted international efforts at disarmament and non-proliferation, especially in the field of nuclear weapons and other weapons of mass destruction and their delivery systems, with a view to strengthening international security and enhancing sustainable economic and social development,

Conscious of the need, more than a decade after the end of the cold war and at the start of the twenty-first century, to combat the negative effects of cultures of violence and complacency in the face of current dangers in this field through long-term programmes of education and training,

1. *Requests* the Secretary-General to prepare, with the assistance of a group of qualified governmental experts, a study on disarmament and non-proliferation, that would have the following aims:

(a) To define contemporary disarmament and non-proliferation education and training, taking into account the need to promote a culture of non-violence and peace;

(b) To assess the current situation of disarmament and non-proliferation education and training at the primary, secondary, university and postgraduate levels of education, in all regions of the world;

(c) To recommend ways to promote education and training in disarmament and non-proliferation at all levels of formal and informal education, in particular the training of educators, parliamentarians, municipal leaders, military officers and government officials;

(d) To examine ways to utilize more fully evolving pedagogic methods, particularly the revolution in information and communications technology, including distance learning, to enhance efforts in disarmament education and training at all levels, in the developed and the developing world;

(e) To recommend ways in which organizations of the United Nations system with special competence in disarmament or education or both can harmonize and coordinate their efforts in disarmament and non-proliferation education;

(f) To devise ways to introduce disarmament and non-proliferation education into post-conflict situations as a contribution to peace-building;

and considers that the group of experts should invite representatives of organizations of the United Nations system with special competence in disarmament or education or both to participate in its work, and should also invite university educators, disarmament and peace-related institutes and non-governmental organizations that have special qualifications in education and training or in the field of disarmament and non-proliferation to make written and oral presentations to it;

2. *Also requests* the Secretary-General to report to the General Assembly at its fifty-seventh session on this question.

Disarmament Information Programme

In response to General Assembly resolution 53/78 E [YUN 1998, p. 548], the Secretary-General, in July [A/55/128], submitted a report on the performance of the Disarmament Information Programme from July 1998 to June 2000 and on activities planned for the next two years. The report described the activities of the UN Department for Disarmament Affairs (DDA) and efforts of the UN Department of Public Information to publicize arms limitation and disarmament. Activities, which focused on weapons of mass destruction, especially nuclear weapons, and conventional weapons, particularly small arms and light weapons, included publications, web-site access, exhibits, cooperation with civil society, training programmes, symposiums, radio broadcasts, video products and press briefings. United Nations information centres, services and offices produced or translated and disseminated information material, launched initiatives, and organized or supported local, regional and international meetings on disarmament.

In an August addendum [A/58/128/Add.1], the Secretary-General reported on the status of the Voluntary Trust Fund for the Disarmament Information Programme, which supported DDA information and outreach activities. At the end of the 1998-1999 biennium, the Fund's available balance totalled $487,012.

GENERAL ASSEMBLY ACTION

On 20 November [meeting 69], the General Assembly, on the recommendation of the First Committee [A/55/560], adopted **resolution 55/34 A** without vote [agenda item 74 *(g)*].

United Nations Disarmament Information Programme

The General Assembly,

Recalling its decision taken in 1982 at its twelfth special session, the second special session devoted to disarmament, by which the World Disarmament Campaign was launched,

Bearing in mind its resolution 47/53 D of 9 December 1992, in which it decided, inter alia, that the World Disarmament Campaign should be known thereafter as the "United Nations Disarmament Information Programme" and the World Disarmament Campaign Voluntary Trust Fund as the "Voluntary Trust Fund for the United Nations Disarmament Information Programme",

Recalling its resolutions 49/76 A of 15 December 1994, 51/46 A of 10 December 1996 and 53/78 E of 4 December 1998,

Welcoming the report of the Secretary-General on the United Nations Disarmament Information Programme,

1. *Takes note with appreciation* of the report of the Secretary-General on the United Nations Disarmament Information Programme;

2. *Commends* the Secretary-General for his efforts to make effective use of the limited resources available to him in disseminating as widely as possible, including by electronic means, information on arms limitation and disarmament to Governments, the media, non-

governmental organizations, educational communities and research institutes, and in carrying out a seminar and conference programme;

3. *Stresses* the importance of the Programme, as a significant instrument in enabling all Member States to participate fully in the deliberations and negotiations on disarmament in the various United Nations bodies, and in assisting them in complying with treaties, as required, and in contributing to agreed mechanisms for transparency;

4. *Notes with appreciation* the cooperation of the Department of Public Information of the Secretariat and its information centres in pursuit of the objectives of the Programme;

5. *Recommends* that the Programme focus its efforts:

(a) To inform, to educate and to generate public understanding of the importance of multilateral action and support for it, including action by the United Nations and the Conference on Disarmament, in the field of arms limitation and disarmament, in a factual, balanced and objective manner, and, inter alia, to continue to publish in all official languages *The United Nations Disarmament Yearbook*, periodic hard copy and regular electronic updates of the *Status of Multilateral Arms Regulation and Disarmament Agreements* and ad hoc publications in hard copy and electronic form;

(b) To continue to coordinate, produce and manage the disarmament Internet web site as a part of the United Nations web site with a view to maintaining an updated source of accessible information, and, within available resources, to produce versions of the site in as many official languages as feasible;

(c) To continue to intensify United Nations interaction with the public, principally non-governmental organizations and research institutes, to help further an informed debate on topical issues of arms limitation, disarmament and security;

(d) To continue to organize discussions on topics of interest in the field of arms limitation and disarmament with a view to broadening understanding and facilitating an exchange of views and information among Member States and civil society;

6. *Emphasizes* the importance of contributions to the Voluntary Trust Fund for the United Nations Disarmament Information Programme to sustain a strong outreach programme, and invites all Member States to make contributions to the Fund;

7. *Commends* the Secretary-General for supporting the efforts of universities, other academic institutions and non-governmental organizations active in the education field in widening the worldwide availability of disarmament education, invites him to continue to support and cooperate with educational institutions and non-governmental organizations engaged in such efforts, without cost to the regular budget to the United Nations, and takes note of the proposal made by the Advisory Board on Disarmament Matters in July 2000 for a study on disarmament and non-proliferation education;

8. *Requests* the Secretary-General to submit to the General Assembly at its fifty-seventh session a report covering both the implementation of the activities of the Programme by the United Nations system during the two previous years and the activities of the Programme contemplated by the system for the following two years;

9. *Decides* to include in the provisional agenda of its fifty-seventh session the item entitled "United Nations Disarmament Information Programme".

Advisory Board on Disarmament Matters

The Advisory Board on Disarmament Matters, which advised the Secretary-General on the disarmament studies programme and implementation of the Disarmament Information Programme and served as the Board of Trustees of the United Nations Institute for Disarmament Research (UNIDIR) (see below), held its thirty-fourth and thirty-fifth sessions (New York, 31 January–2 February; Geneva, 5-7 July) [A/55/349].

At the first session, the Board recommended that a study be commissioned on disarmament and non-proliferation education and training, with the view to combating governmental and public complacency regarding threats to international security, such as an enhanced emphasis on nuclear weapons in military doctrines, missile proliferation and possible deployment of national missile defence systems. It considered the issue of small arms proliferation in the light of the 2001 UN Conference on small arms (see p. 518), and identified a triple-track approach to the Conference: global consciousness-raising, the creation of international norms, and regional and subregional initiatives.

In July, the Board examined the question of the revolution in military affairs and agreed to study the issue further. Under its future work programme, the Board proposed to consider, among other issues, measures to reduce the risk of nuclear war significantly, pursuant to General Assembly resolution 54/54 K [YUN 1999, p. 468], and a review of its mandated function to advise the Secretary-General on the implementation of the Disarmament Information Programme.

UN Institute for Disarmament Research

The Secretary-General transmitted to the General Assembly the report of the UNIDIR Director covering the period from July 1999 to June 2000, as well as the report of the UNIDIR Board of Trustees on the proposed 2000-2001 programme of work [A/55/267].

The Institute's research activities continued to focus on global security, regional security and human security. The report highlighted UNIDIR's cooperation with research institutes, DDA and other UN system agencies, and contained a list of publications issued during the reporting period.

The Board of Trustees recommended a subvention of $213,000 from the UN regular budget for 2001, which was approved by the Assembly on 23 December (**resolution 55/238, section VI**), on the understanding that no additional appropriation would be required under section 4, Disarmament, of the proposed programme budget for the 2000-2001 biennium.

GENERAL ASSEMBLY ACTION

On 20 November [meeting 69], the General Assembly, on the recommendation of the First Committee [A/55/561], adopted resolution **55/35 A** without vote [agenda item 75 (d)].

Twentieth anniversary of the United Nations Institute for Disarmament Research

The General Assembly,

Recalling its resolution 34/83 M of 11 December 1979, in which it requested the Secretary-General to establish the United Nations Institute for Disarmament Research on the basis of the recommendations contained in the report of the Secretary-General,

Reaffirming its resolution 39/148 H of 17 December 1984, in which it approved the statute of the United Nations Institute for Disarmament Research, renewed the invitation to Governments to consider making voluntary contributions to the Institute and requested the Secretary-General to continue to give the Institute administrative and other support,

Recalling its resolution 45/62 G of 4 December 1990 adopted on the occasion of the tenth anniversary of the Institute,

Considering the continuing need for the international community to have access to independent and in-depth research on security issues and prospects for disarmament, taking note of the report of the Office of Internal Oversight Services on the in-depth evaluation of the disarmament programme, in which the Office indicated the erosion of the value of the United Nations subvention to the Institute in real terms and recommended the development of proposals for alleviating difficulties regarding the current financial and organizational arrangements adopted in implementation of the statute of the Institute and that those proposals should be submitted to the General Assembly for consideration at its fifty-fifth session, and having considered the annual report of the Director of the Institute and report of the Advisory Board on Disarmament Matters in its capacity as the Board of Trustees of the Institute, in which hope was expressed that the United Nations subvention to the Institute would be restored to its pre-1996 level and adjusted for inflation,

1. *Welcomes* the twentieth anniversary of the establishment of the United Nations Institute for Disarmament Research;

2. *Recognizes* the importance and high quality of the work of the Institute;

3. *Reiterates its conviction* that the Institute should continue to conduct independent research on problems relating to disarmament and security and to undertake specialized research requiring a high degree of expertise;

4. *Requests* all Member States to consider making financial contributions to the Institute in order to ensure its viability and the quality of its work over the long term;

5. *Recommends* that the Secretary-General seek ways to increase the funding of the Institute, within existing resources.

Disarmament fellowship, training and advisory services

In 2000 [A/55/152 & Corr.1], 28 fellows participated in the UN disarmament fellowship, training and advisory services programme. The programme, which began in Geneva on 4 September and ended in New York on 3 November, included a study session in Geneva; study trips to Austria, The Hague (Netherlands), Germany and Japan; and a study session at Headquarters.

GENERAL ASSEMBLY ACTION

On 20 November [meeting 69], the General Assembly, on the recommendation of the First Committee [A/55/560], adopted **resolution 55/34 C** without vote [agenda item 74(h)].

United Nations disarmament fellowship, training and advisory services

The General Assembly,

Having considered the report of the Secretary-General on the United Nations disarmament fellowship, training and advisory services programme,

Recalling its decision, contained in paragraph 108 of the Final Document of the Tenth Special Session of the General Assembly, the first special session devoted to disarmament, to establish a programme of fellowships on disarmament, as well as its decisions contained in annex IV to the Concluding Document of the Twelfth Special Session of the General Assembly, the second special session devoted to disarmament, in which it decided, inter alia, to continue the programme,

Noting with satisfaction that the programme has already trained an appreciable number of public officials selected from geographical regions represented in the United Nations system, most of whom are now in positions of responsibility in the field of disarmament affairs in their respective countries or Governments,

Recalling all the annual resolutions on the matter since the thirty-seventh session of the General Assembly, in 1982, including resolution 50/71 A of 12 December 1995,

Noting with satisfaction that the programme as designed continues to enable an increasing number of public officials, in particular from the developing countries, to acquire more expertise in the sphere of disarmament,

Believing that the forms of assistance available to Member States, in particular to developing countries, under the programme will enhance the capabilities of their officials to follow ongoing deliberations and negotiations on disarmament, both bilateral and multilateral,

1. *Reaffirms* its decisions contained in annex IV to the Concluding Document of the Twelfth Special Session of the General Assembly and the report of the Secretary-General approved by the Assembly in its resolution 33/71 E of 14 December 1978;

2. *Expresses its appreciation* to the Governments of Germany and Japan for inviting the 1999 and 2000 fel-

lows to study selected activities in the field of disarmament, and to the Government of the United States of America for having organized in 1999 a specific study programme in the field of disarmament thereby contributing to the fulfilment of the overall objectives of the programme;

3. *Expresses its appreciation also* to the International Atomic Energy Agency, the Organization for the Prohibition of Chemical Weapons, the Preparatory Commission for the Comprehensive Nuclear-Test-Ban Treaty Organization and the Monterey Institute of International Studies for having organized specific study programmes in the field of disarmament in their respective areas of competence, thereby contributing to the objectives of the programme;

4. *Commends* the Secretary-General for the diligence with which the programme has continued to be carried out;

5. *Requests* the Secretary-General to continue to implement annually the Geneva-based programme within existing resources and to report thereon to the General Assembly at its fifty-seventh session;

6. *Decides* to include in the provisional agenda of its fifty-seventh session the item entitled "United Nations disarmament fellowship, training and advisory services".

Regional centres for peace and disarmament

GENERAL ASSEMBLY ACTION

On 20 November [meeting 69], the General Assembly, on the recommendation of the First Committee [A/55/560], adopted **resolution 55/34 F** without vote [agenda item 74 *(e)*].

United Nations regional centres for peace and disarmament

The General Assembly,

Recalling its resolution 54/55 E of 1 December 1999 regarding the maintenance and revitalization of the three United Nations regional centres for peace and disarmament,

Recalling also the reports of the Secretary-General on the United Nations Regional Centre for Peace and Disarmament in Africa, the United Nations Regional Centre for Peace and Disarmament in Asia and the Pacific and the United Nations Regional Centre for Peace, Disarmament and Development in Latin America and the Caribbean,

Reaffirming its decision, taken in 1982 at its twelfth special session, to establish the United Nations Disarmament Information Programme, the purpose of which is to inform, educate and generate public understanding and support for the objectives of the United Nations in the field of arms control and disarmament,

Bearing in mind its resolutions 40/151 G of 16 December 1985, 41/60 J of 3 December 1986, 42/39 D of 30 November 1987 and 44/117 F of 15 December 1989 on the regional centres for peace and disarmament in Nepal, Peru and Togo,

Recognizing that the changes that have taken place in the world have created new opportunities as well as posed new challenges for the pursuit of disarmament and, in this regard, bearing in mind that the regional centres for peace and disarmament can contribute sub-

stantially to understanding and cooperation among the States in each particular region in the areas of peace, disarmament and development,

Noting that in paragraph 146 of the Final Document of the Twelfth Conference of Heads of State or Government of Non-Aligned Countries, held at Durban, South Africa, from 29 August to 3 September 1998, the heads of State or Government welcomed the decision adopted by the General Assembly on maintaining and revitalizing the three regional centres for peace and disarmament in Nepal, Peru and Togo,

1. *Reiterates* the importance of the United Nations activities at the regional level to increase the stability and security of its Member States, which could be promoted in a substantive manner by the maintenance and revitalization of the three regional centres for peace and disarmament;

2. *Reaffirms* that, in order to achieve positive results, it is useful for the three regional centres to carry out dissemination and educational programmes that promote regional peace and security aimed at changing basic attitudes with respect to peace and security and disarmament so as to support the achievement of the purposes and principles of the United Nations;

3. *Appeals* to Member States in each region and those that are able to do so, as well as to international governmental and non-governmental organizations and foundations, to make voluntary contributions to the regional centres in their respective regions to strengthen their programmes of activities and implementation;

4. *Requests* the Secretary-General to provide all necessary support, within existing resources, to the regional centres in carrying out their programmes of activities;

5. *Decides* to include in the provisional agenda of its fifty-sixth session the item entitled "United Nations regional centres for peace and disarmament".

Africa

Pursuant to General Assembly resolution 54/55 B [YUN 1999, p. 512], the Secretary-General described the activities of the United Nations Regional Centre for Peace and Disarmament in Africa [A/55/171], covering the period from September 1999 to July 2000. The Centre was established in Lomé, Togo, in 1986 [YUN 1986, p. 85].

The Secretary-General reported that the Centre continued its revitalization process in the priority areas endorsed in 1999 by the Group of African States at the United Nations [YUN 1999, p. 511], which included support for peace initiatives in Africa; arms control and disarmament; and information, research and publications.

During the reporting period, the Centre participated in activities that supported the implementation of the ECOWAS Declaration of a Moratorium on the Importation, Exportation and Manufacture of Small Arms and Light Weapons in West Africa, adopted in 1998 [YUN 1998, p. 537], and facilitated weapons collection exercises in Togo.

The Centre assisted the UN Peace-building Support Office in Guinea-Bissau in promoting the collection, neutralization and destruction of small arms in the country. It provided support to a conference (Niamey, Niger, March) to sensitize civil society on weapons proliferation in the Niger; to regional meetings, also in March, in preparation for the 2001 UN Conference on small arms (see p. 518); and to the West African Conference on Child Soldiers (Accra, Ghana, 27-28 April).

In July, the Centre initiated assessment missions to the Central African subregion to develop a "disarmament for development" programme.

GENERAL ASSEMBLY ACTION

On 20 November [meeting 69], the General Assembly, on the recommendation of the First Committee [A/55/560], adopted **resolution 55/34 D** without vote [agenda item 74 (b)].

United Nations Regional Centre for Peace and Disarmament in Africa

The General Assembly,

Mindful of the provisions of Article 11, paragraph 1, of the Charter of the United Nations stipulating that a function of the General Assembly is to consider the general principles of cooperation in the maintenance of international peace and security, including the principles governing disarmament and arms limitation,

Recalling its resolutions 40/151 G of 16 December 1985, 41/60 D of 3 December 1986, 42/39 J of 30 November 1987 and 43/76 D of 7 December 1988 on the United Nations Regional Centre for Peace and Disarmament in Africa, and its resolutions 46/36 F of 6 December 1991 and 47/52 G of 9 December 1992 on regional disarmament, including confidence-building measures,

Recalling also its resolutions 48/76 E of 16 December 1993, 49/76 D of 15 December 1994, 50/71 C of 12 December 1995, 51/46 E of 10 December 1996, 52/220 of 22 December 1997, 53/78 C of 4 December 1998 and 54/55 B of 1 December 1999,

Aware of the widespread support for the revitalization of the Regional Centre and the important role that the Centre can play in the present context in promoting confidence-building and arms-limitation measures at the regional level, thereby promoting progress in the area of sustainable development,

Taking into account the report of the Secretary-General on the causes of conflict and the promotion of durable peace and sustainable development in Africa,

Bearing in mind the efforts undertaken in the framework of the revitalization of the activities of the Regional Centre for the mobilization of the resources necessary for its operational costs,

Taking into account the need to establish close cooperation between the Regional Centre and the Mechanism for Conflict Prevention, Management and Resolution of the Organization of African Unity, in conformity with the relevant decision adopted by the Assembly of Heads of State and Government of the Organization of African Unity at its thirty-fifth ordinary session, held at Algiers from 12 to 14 July 1999,

1. *Takes note* of the report of the Secretary-General, and commends the activities carried out by the United Nations Regional Centre for Peace and Disarmament in Africa, in particular in support of the efforts made by the African States in the areas of peace and security;

2. *Reaffirms* its strong support for the revitalization of the Regional Centre, and emphasizes the need to provide it with resources to enable it to strengthen its activities and carry out its programmes;

3. *Appeals once again* to all States, as well as to international governmental and non-governmental organizations and the foundations, to make voluntary contributions in order to strengthen the programmes and activities of the Regional Centre and facilitate their implementation;

4. *Requests* the Secretary-General to continue to provide all necessary support, within existing resources, to the Regional Centre for better achievements and results;

5. *Also requests* the Secretary-General to facilitate the establishment of close cooperation between the Regional Centre and the Organization of African Unity, in particular in the area of peace, security and development, and to continue to assist the Director of the Regional Centre in his efforts to stabilize the financial situation of the Centre and revitalize its activities;

6. *Further requests* the Secretary-General to report to the General Assembly at its fifty-sixth session on the implementation of the present resolution;

7. *Decides* to include in the provisional agenda of its fifty-sixth session the item entitled "United Nations Regional Centre for Peace and Disarmament in Africa".

Asia and the Pacific

As requested by the General Assembly in resolution 54/55 C [YUN 1999, p. 513], the Secretary-General reported in July on the activities of the United Nations Regional Centre for Peace and Disarmament in Asia and the Pacific from August 1999 to July 2000 [A/55/181]. The Centre was inaugurated in Kathmandu, Nepal, in 1989 [YUN 1989, p. 88].

During the reporting period, the Centre organized the twelfth regional disarmament meeting in the Asia and Pacific region (Kathmandu, 15-17 February 2000) on issues relating to strategic stability, nuclear non-proliferation and disarmament, with a focus on measures and strategies towards a world free of nuclear weapons. The fourth and fifth (Sapporo, Japan, 5-8 October 1999; 2-5 April 2000) UN-sponsored expert group meetings to assist the five Central Asian States in drafting a treaty to establish a nuclear-weapon-free zone in Central Asia (see p. 508) were organized by the Centre. A regional seminar (Jakarta, Indonesia, 4 May 2000), held with the assistance of DDA, identified common concerns relating to problems from trafficking in small arms and light weapons.

Owing to the lack of sufficient extrabudgetary resources to finance the physical establishment and operation of the Centre in Kathmandu, the Director continued to operate from Headquarters.

On 20 November [meeting 69], the General Assembly, on the recommendation of the First Committee [A/55/560], adopted **resolution 55/34 H** without vote [agenda item 74 (c)].

United Nations Regional Centre for Peace and Disarmament in Asia and the Pacific

The General Assembly,

Recalling its resolutions 42/39 D of 30 November 1987 and 44/117 F of 15 December 1989, by which it established the United Nations Regional Centre for Peace and Disarmament in Asia and renamed it the United Nations Regional Centre for Peace and Disarmament in Asia and the Pacific, with headquarters in Kathmandu and with the mandate of providing, on request, substantive support for the initiatives and other activities mutually agreed upon by the Member States of the Asia-Pacific region for the implementation of measures for peace and disarmament, through appropriate utilization of available resources,

Welcoming the report of the Secretary-General, in which he expresses his belief that the mandate of the Regional Centre remains valid and that the Centre could be a useful instrument for fostering a climate of cooperation in the post-cold-war era,

Noting that trends in the post-cold-war era have emphasized the function of the Regional Centre in assisting Member States as they deal with new security concerns and disarmament issues emerging in the region,

Commending the useful activities carried out by the Regional Centre in encouraging regional and subregional dialogue for the enhancement of openness, transparency and confidence-building, as well as the promotion of disarmament and security through the organization of regional meetings, which has come to be widely known within the Asia-Pacific region as the "Kathmandu process",

Expressing its appreciation to the Regional Centre for its organization of the twelfth regional disarmament meeting in Asia and the Pacific, held at Kathmandu from 15 to 17 February 2000, the United Nations Conference on Disarmament Issues, held at Akita, Japan, from 22 to 25 August 2000, and the regional seminar on illicit trafficking in small arms and light weapons, held at Jakarta on 3 and 4 May 2000,

Welcoming the idea of the possible creation of an educational and training programme for peace and disarmament in Asia and the Pacific for young people with different backgrounds, to be financed from voluntary contributions,

Noting the important role of the Regional Centre in assisting region-specific initiatives of Member States, including its assistance in the work related to the establishment of a nuclear-weapon-free zone in Central Asia,

Appreciating highly the important role that Nepal has played as the host nation of the headquarters of the Regional Centre,

1. *Reaffirms* its strong support for the forthcoming operation and further strengthening of the United Nations Regional Centre for Peace and Disarmament in Asia and the Pacific;

2. *Underlines* the importance of the Kathmandu process as a powerful vehicle for the development of the practice of region-wide security and disarmament dialogue;

3. *Expresses its appreciation* for the continuing political support and financial contributions to the Regional Centre, which are essential for its continued operation;

4. *Appeals* to Member States, in particular those within the Asia-Pacific region, as well as to international governmental and non-governmental organizations and foundations, to make voluntary contributions, the only resources of the Regional Centre, to strengthen the programme of activities of the Centre and the implementation thereof;

5. *Requests* the Secretary-General, taking note of paragraph 6 of General Assembly resolution 49/76 D of 15 December 1994, to provide the Regional Centre with the necessary support, within existing resources, in carrying out its programme of activities;

6. *Expresses its appreciation* for the generous offer of His Majesty's Government of Nepal to bear the operational cost of the Centre for it to function from Kathmandu;

7. *Requests* the Secretary-General to expedite his ongoing consultations with other concerned Member States and interested organizations, and urges him to conclude them by 31 July 2001 to assess the possibility of enabling the Centre to operate effectively from Kathmandu as soon as possible;

8. *Requests* the Secretary-General to report to the General Assembly at its fifty-sixth session on the implementation of the present resolution;

9. *Decides* to include in the provisional agenda of its fifty-sixth session the item entitled "United Nations Regional Centre for Peace and Disarmament in Asia and the Pacific".

Latin America and the Caribbean

As requested by the General Assembly in resolution 54/55 F [YUN 1999, p. 514], the Secretary-General reported in July on the activities of the United Nations Regional Centre for Peace, Disarmament and Development in Latin America and the Caribbean from August 1999 to July 2000 [A/55/169]. The Centre was inaugurated in Lima, Peru, in 1987 [YUN 1987, p. 88].

The Secretary-General reported that activities in the period under review related to: firearms, ammunition and explosives; conventional arms and peace operations; nuclear disarmament issues; UN system activities; and information and public events.

Several activities were carried out under the "Regional clearing house on firearms, ammunition and explosives" project, an initiative intended to serve as a tool for nurturing national and regional expertise in the area of practical disarmament, through workshops, training courses and preventive programmes. In that regard, two awareness-building workshops (Lima, 23-24

November 1999; Fort-de-France, Martinique, 23-24 May 2000) were held in cooperation with the Inter-American Drug Abuse Control Commission, and focused on the import, export and in-transit movement of firearms, their parts and ammunition in the region.

Under conventional arms and peace operations, the Centre organized a workshop (Lima, 19 May 2000) on the military perspective of regional security: consultations with Lima military attachés, which discussed, among other things, the Centre's mandate, the role of the United Nations in enhancing regional security and cooperation in peace operations. The Centre helped organize a seminar on the destruction of stockpiles of anti-personnel mines (Buenos Aires, Argentina) and provided support to the regional preparatory meeting for the 2001 UN Conference on small arms (Brasília, Brazil) (see p. 518).

At the end of the 1998-1999 biennium, the balance of the Trust Fund for the Centre totalled $132,678.

GENERAL ASSEMBLY ACTION

On 20 November [meeting 69], the General Assembly, on the recommendation of the First Committee [A/55/560], adopted **resolution 55/34 E** without vote [agenda item 74 (*f*)].

United Nations Regional Centre for Peace, Disarmament and Development in Latin America and the Caribbean

The General Assembly,

Recalling its resolutions 41/60 J of 3 December 1986, 42/39 K of 30 November 1987 and 43/76 H of 7 December 1988 on the United Nations Regional Centre for Peace, Disarmament and Development in Latin America and the Caribbean, with headquarters in Lima,

Recalling also its resolutions 46/37 F of 9 December 1991, 48/76 E of 16 December 1993, 49/76 D of 15 December 1994, 50/71 C of 12 December 1995, 52/220 of 22 December 1997 and 53/78 F of 4 December 1998,

Recalling especially its resolution 54/55 F of 1 December 1999, in which it welcomed the revitalization of the Regional Centre, the efforts made by the Government of Peru to that end and the appointment of the Director of the Centre by the Secretary-General,

Welcoming the report of the Secretary-General, which concludes that the Regional Centre has launched projects aimed at furthering the understanding of the relationship between security and development, enhanced the role of the United Nations as a regional catalyst for activities on peace and disarmament

and acted as a politically neutral platform for discussions on security and development issues,

Noting that security and disarmament issues have always been recognized as significant topics in Latin America and the Caribbean, the first inhabited region in the world to be declared a nuclear-weapon-free zone,

Bearing in mind the important role that the Regional Centre can play in promoting confidence-building measures, arms control and limitation, disarmament and development at the regional level,

Also bearing in mind the importance of information, research, education and training for peace, disarmament and development in order to achieve understanding and cooperation among States,

Recognizing the need to provide the three United Nations regional centres for peace and disarmament with sufficient financial resources for the planning and implementation of their programmes of activities,

1. *Reiterates* its strong support for the role of the United Nations Regional Centre for Peace, Disarmament and Development in Latin America and the Caribbean in the promotion of activities of the United Nations at the regional level to strengthen peace, stability, security and development among its Member States;

2. *Expresses its satisfaction* with the vast range of activities carried out by the Regional Centre in the last year;

3. *Expresses its appreciation* for the political support and financial contributions to the Regional Centre, which are essential for its continued operation;

4. *Invites* all States of the region to take part in the activities of the Regional Centre, proposing items for inclusion in its agenda, making greater and better use of the Centre's potential to meet the current challenges facing the international community and with a view to fulfilling the aims of the Charter of the United Nations in the fields of peace, disarmament and development;

5. *Appeals* to Member States, in particular the States of the Latin American and Caribbean region, and to international governmental and non-governmental organizations and to foundations, to make voluntary contributions to strengthen the Regional Centre, its programme of activities and the implementation thereof;

6. *Requests* the Secretary-General to provide the Regional Centre with all necessary support within existing resources, so that it may carry out its programme of activities and achieve better results;

7. *Also requests* the Secretary-General to report to the General Assembly at its fifty-sixth session on the implementation of the present resolution;

8. *Decides* to include in the provisional agenda of its fifty-sixth session the item entitled "United Nations Regional Centre for Peace, Disarmament and Development in Latin America and the Caribbean".

Chapter VIII

Other political and security questions

United Nations consideration of other political and security questions in 2000 included the Organization's activities to support new or restored democracies, the promotion of self-determination of the remaining Non-Self-Governing Territories, and the peaceful uses of outer space.

The Fourth International Conference of New or Restored Democracies was held in Cotonou, Benin, in December. The Conference adopted the Cotonou Declaration, by which the participants undertook to foster a culture of peace and of democracy in all its dimensions, with full respect for human rights, and to create conditions conducive to sustainable development. To implement those undertakings, the Conference urged that the follow-up mechanism established by the Third (1997) Conference be strengthened and that the Secretary-General designate a focal point in the Organization to support government efforts and provide assistance to the follow-up mechanism for the Fourth Conference.

The Special Committee on the Situation with regard to the Implementation of the Declaration on the Granting of Independence to Colonial Countries and Peoples continued to review progress in implementing the 1960 Declaration, particularly the exercise of self-determination by the remaining Non-Self-Governing Territories. In December, the General Assembly observed the fortieth anniversary of the adoption of that Declaration, reviewed the achievements of the first International Decade for the Eradication of Colonialism (1990-2000), which ended during the year, and declared the period 2001-2010 as the Second International Decade for the Eradication of Colonialism.

The United Nations continued to adopt measures to reorient its public information and communications policies to better disseminate information on the work of the Organization and a unified message of its continuing relevance. To that end, it worked to expand its use of up-to-date technology and to improve coordination of the UN system's information and communications activities.

Also in December, the Assembly noted the plan of action to implement the recommendations of the Third (1999) United Nations Conference on the Exploration and Peaceful Uses of Outer Space and requested the Secretary-General to implement that plan.

The Assembly further adopted a resolution on the role of science and technology in the context of international security and disarmament and another on developments in information and telecommunications in the context of international security.

General aspects of international security

Support for democracies

Reports of Secretary-General. In response to General Assembly resolution 54/36 [YUN 1999, p. 516], the Secretary-General submitted two reports in October on UN support for the efforts of Governments to promote and consolidate new or restored democracies. The first report [A/55/489] described the activities of the follow-up mechanism to the Third (1997) International Conference of New or Restored Democracies on Democracy and Development [YUN 1997, p. 530]. That mechanism, comprising participants from interested countries, the UN system, academia and non-governmental organizations (NGOs), met in June in New York under Romania's chairmanship to review preparations for the forthcoming Fourth International Conference (see p. 544) and discuss UN system democratization activities and the Secretary-General's March note verbale to Member States (see p. 543) requesting comments on the review and on the suggestions in his 1999 report on new or restored democracies [YUN 1999, p. 515]. Ongoing preparatory activities included: a forum for youth and another for civil society; specific regional conferences or seminars on lessons learned about democratic transition in various parts of the world; and setting the agenda of the Conference, in order to arrive at its objectives of identifying the best practices in building democracy and human rights, defining an analytical framework showing, through case studies, the interdependence among peace, security, development and democracy, and illustrating the implications of the democratic process for sustainable development.

The report examined the interlinkages among the key concepts of good governance, human rights, sustainable development and peace. It pointed out that, in the light of increased recognition by the UN system of the importance of strengthening democratic institutions and improving governance, already 50 per cent of United Nations Development Programme (UNDP) resources had been allocated to programmes promoting political, economic and social governance. The United Nations itself was currently supporting initiatives that promoted policy dialogue to widen development choices; strengthened the capacities of key democratic governing institutions for people-centred development; promoted decentralization for stronger local governance and community empowerment; and increased efficiency and accountability in the public sector. The developing countries were requesting more services, however, for the furtherance of good governance as a tool for achieving human development goals. To foster a culture of human rights, the UN treaty-based human rights system provided the normative foundation for implementing and monitoring human rights in all countries. The Office of the United Nations High Commissioner for Human Rights could provide advisory services and technical assistance to conduct educational campaigns and to prepare reports under the core human rights treaties.

Also examined were insights for democratization gained from UN experience in electoral assistance, which suggested several areas for further work that would contribute to a broader framework for UN assistance to the democratization process, most critically in the expansion of the rule of law.

The Secretary-General concluded his report by repeating the main thrust of what he called the "forward-looking" recommendations of the International Institute for Democracy and Electoral Assistance, which had emerged from its two seminars (Stockholm, Sweden, February and June) on UN assistance in the democratization process. Those recommendations called on the United Nations to: adopt a learning approach; develop a "democracy database" and strategic partnerships; involve local political, social and communal actors; develop integrated programmes; design common country strategies and ensure continuous assessments; develop a roster of experts, avoiding mainly Western or "Westernized" experts; establish a strategic Secretariat unit to provide an "overall picture"; and improve coordination and information sharing.

The Secretary-General believed that the Institute's suggestions deserved the international community's serious consideration, noting, however, that their implementation necessitated more

resources than were currently available from UN regular and extrabudgetary sources. He said the UN system stood ready to see democracy-building and democratization assistance placed among its foremost priorities, but for that to happen, it needed the political, administrative and financial support of all Member States.

In his second October report [A/55/520], the Secretary-General indicated that, to date, Cuba, Germany, Japan, Romania and San Marino had replied to his March note verbale communicating their views on the review contained in his 1999 report [YUN 1999, p. 515] and on their experiences and "lessons learned" as new, restored or established democracies and/or as donors supporting democratic institutions.

GENERAL ASSEMBLY ACTION

On 27 November [meeting 71], the General Assembly adopted **resolution 55/43** without vote [draft: A/55/L.32/Rev.1 & Add.1] [agenda item 39].

Support by the United Nations system of the efforts of Governments to promote and consolidate new or restored democracies

The General Assembly,

Bearing in mind the indissoluble links between the principles enshrined in the Universal Declaration of Human Rights and the foundations of any democratic society,

Recalling the United Nations Millennium Declaration adopted by heads of State and Government on 8 September 2000, in particular paragraphs 6 and 24,

Recalling also the Manila Declaration adopted by the First International Conference of New or Restored Democracies in June 1988,

Considering the major changes taking place on the international scene and the aspirations of all peoples for an international order based on the principles enshrined in the Charter of the United Nations, including the promotion and encouragement of respect for human rights and fundamental freedoms for all and other important principles, such as respect for the equal rights and self-determination of peoples, peace, democracy, justice, equality, the rule of law, pluralism, development, better standards of living and solidarity,

Recalling its resolution 49/30 of 7 December 1994 in which it recognized the importance of the Managua Declaration and Plan of Action adopted by the Second International Conference of New or Restored Democracies in July 1994, as well as its resolutions 50/133 of 20 December 1995, 51/31 of 6 December 1996, 52/18 of 21 November 1997, 53/31 of 23 November 1998 and 54/36 of 29 November 1999,

Recalling also the document entitled "Progress Review and Recommendations", adopted by the Third International Conference of New or Restored Democracies on Democracy and Development, held in Bucharest from 2 to 4 September 1997, in which guidelines, principles and recommendations were addressed to Governments, civil society, the private sector, donor countries and the international community,

Taking note with satisfaction of the seminars, workshops and conferences on democratization and good governance organized in 2000, as well as those held under the auspices of the International Conference of New or Restored Democracies,

Taking note of the views of Member States expressed in the debate on this question at its forty-ninth, fiftieth, fifty-first, fifty-second, fifty-third, fifty-fourth and fifty-fifth sessions,

Bearing in mind that the activities of the United Nations carried out in support of the efforts of Governments to promote and consolidate democracy are undertaken in accordance with the Charter of the United Nations and only at the specific request of the Member States concerned,

Bearing in mind also that democracy, development and respect for all human rights and fundamental freedoms are interdependent and mutually reinforcing and that democracy is based on the freely expressed will of the people to determine their own political, economic, social and cultural systems and on their full participation in all aspects of their lives,

Noting that a considerable number of societies have recently undertaken significant efforts to achieve their social, political and economic goals through democratization and the reform of their economies, pursuits that are deserving of the support and recognition of the international community,

Noting with satisfaction that the Fourth International Conference of New or Restored Democracies will be held in Cotonou, Benin, from 4 to 6 December 2000,

Stressing the importance of support by Member States, the United Nations system, the specialized agencies and other intergovernmental organizations for the holding of the Fourth International Conference of New or Restored Democracies,

Having considered the report of the Secretary-General,

1. *Takes note* of the report of the Secretary-General, and invites Member States to consider the proposals contained therein;

2. *Commends* the Secretary-General, and through him the United Nations system, for the activities undertaken at the request of Governments to support the efforts to consolidate democracy and for his contribution to the preparatory process and success of the Fourth International Conference of New or Restored Democracies;

3. *Welcomes* the work carried out by the follow-up mechanism to the Third International Conference of New or Restored Democracies on Democracy and Development;

4. *Invites* the Secretary-General, Member States, the relevant specialized agencies, programmes, funds and other bodies of the United Nations system, as well as other intergovernmental organizations, to collaborate in the holding of the Fourth International Conference of New or Restored Democracies;

5. *Recognizes* that the Organization has an important role to play in providing timely, appropriate and coherent support to the efforts of Governments to achieve democratization within the context of their development efforts;

6. *Stresses* that activities undertaken by the Organization must be in accordance with the Charter of the United Nations;

7. *Encourages* the Secretary-General to continue to improve the capacity of the Organization to respond effectively to the requests of Member States through co-herent, adequate support of their efforts to achieve the goals of good governance and democratization;

8. *Encourages* Member States to promote democratization and to make additional efforts to identify possible steps to support the efforts of Governments to promote and consolidate new or restored democracies;

9. *Requests* the Secretary-General to submit a report to the General Assembly at its fifty-sixth session on the implementation of the present resolution;

10. *Decides* to include in the provisional agenda of its fifty-sixth session the item entitled "Support by the United Nations system of the efforts of Governments to promote and consolidate new or restored democracies".

On 4 December, the Assembly, in **resolution 55/96**, bearing in mind Commission on Human Rights resolution 2000/47 of 25 April [E/2000/23 & Corr.1], called on States to consolidate democracy by promoting pluralism, the protection of all human rights and fundamental freedoms, maximizing the participation of individuals in decision-making and the development of effective public institutions, including an independent judiciary, accountable legislature and public service and an electoral system that ensured periodic, free and fair elections.

Fourth International Conference

The Fourth International Conference of New or Restored Democracies was held in Cotonou, Benin, from 4 to 6 December [A/55/889]. Organized and hosted by Benin with UNDP assistance, the Conference held a general debate on: the best practices for strengthening democracy; conflict prevention, management and settlement in ways to preserve democracy; maximization of participation by youth and women in democratization; and obstacles to the consolidation of democracy. Parallel thematic debates were held on democracy in relation to good governance and development, and on the question of conflict prevention, management and resolution in Africa. The Conference concluded with the adoption of the Cotonou Declaration on peace, security, democracy and development.

In the Declaration, the participants, reaffirming the significant contribution of disarmament and arms control to international peace and security, undertook to promote a culture of peace within their respective countries. They pledged to consolidate democracy through political pluralism, greater citizen participation in decision-making, particularly by women and minorities, good governance and efforts to fight corruption. They further pledged to guarantee the rule of law and separation of constitutional powers and to contribute to the emergence of a free civil society, as well as to promote a culture of democracy in all its dimensions, with full respect for human rights.

Other undertakings concerned the creation of conditions conducive to sustainable development, primarily through the eradication of poverty and endemic diseases, such as HIV/AIDS and malaria; promotion of gender equality and women's economic independence; prioritizing protection of the rights, development and survival of the child; and support for initiatives for external debt relief or cancellation and efforts to find lasting solutions to the debt burden of new or restored democracies.

To enable the implementation of the foregoing undertakings, the participants urged the expansion of the services and other support activities of the UN system, other international organizations and NGOs, and called for more substantial development assistance from States and international financial institutions. They also recommended a series of actions to be taken by civil society organizations, the private sector, donor countries and the UN system. Finally, they called on the Secretary-General to designate a focal point within the UN system to support efforts to consolidate democracy and provide assistance to the follow-up mechanism for the Fourth International Conference.

Regional aspects of international peace and security

South Atlantic

As requested in General Assembly resolution 54/35 [YUN 1999, p. 517], the Secretary-General submitted an October report on the zone of peace and cooperation of the South Atlantic [A/55/476], declared in 1986 to promote cooperation among States of the region in the political, economic, scientific, technical, cultural and other fields [YUN 1986, p. 369]. The Secretary-General stated that, as at 10 October, one Government and eight UN organizations and bodies had responded to his request for views on the implementation of the declaration's objectives.

Nigeria transmitted to the Assembly the Declaration and the Havana Programme of Action adopted by the South Summit of the Group of 77 (Havana, Cuba, 12-14 April) [A/55/74].

GENERAL ASSEMBLY ACTION

On 29 November [meeting 74], the General Assembly adopted **resolution 55/49** [draft: A/55/L.39] by recorded vote (119-0-1) [agenda item 38].

Zone of peace and cooperation of the South Atlantic

The General Assembly,

Recalling its resolution 41/11 of 27 October 1986, in which it solemnly declared the Atlantic Ocean, in the region between Africa and South America, a zone of peace and cooperation of the South Atlantic,

Recalling also its subsequent resolutions on the matter, including resolution 45/36 of 27 November 1990, in which it reaffirmed the determination of the States of the zone to enhance and accelerate their cooperation in the political, economic, scientific, cultural and other spheres,

Reaffirming that the questions of peace and security and those of development are interrelated and inseparable and that cooperation for peace and development among States of the region will promote the objectives of the zone of peace and cooperation of the South Atlantic,

Aware of the importance that the States of the zone attach to the protection of the environment of the region, and recognizing the threat that pollution from any source poses to the marine and coastal environment, its ecological balance and its resources,

1. *Reaffirms* the importance of the purposes and objectives of the zone of peace and cooperation of the South Atlantic as a basis for the promotion of cooperation among the countries of the region;

2. *Calls upon* all States to cooperate in the promotion of the objectives established in the declaration of the zone of peace and cooperation of the South Atlantic and to refrain from any action inconsistent with those objectives and with the Charter of the United Nations and relevant resolutions of the Organization, in particular actions that may create or aggravate situations of tension and potential conflict in the region;

3. *Takes note* of the report of the Secretary-General submitted in accordance with its resolution 54/35 of 24 November 1999;

4. *Recalls* the agreement reached at the third meeting of the States members of the zone, held in Brasilia in 1994, to encourage democracy and political pluralism and, in accordance with the Vienna Declaration and Programme of Action adopted by the World Conference on Human Rights on 25 June 1993, to promote and defend all human rights and fundamental freedoms and to cooperate towards the achievement of those goals;

5. *Welcomes with satisfaction* the holding of the fifth meeting of the States members of the zone in Buenos Aires, on 21 and 22 October 1998, and takes note of the Final Declaration and Plan of Action adopted at the meeting;

6. *Welcomes* the progress towards the full entry into force of the Treaty for the Prohibition of Nuclear Weapons in Latin America and the Caribbean (Treaty of Tlatelolco) and of the African Nuclear-Weapon-Free Zone Treaty (Treaty of Pelindaba);

7. *Also welcomes* the entry into force of the Inter-American Convention against the Illicit Manufacturing of and Trafficking in Firearms, Ammunition, Explosives and Other Related Materials, adopted in November 1997, and the adoption of the Inter-American Convention on Transparency in Conventional Weapons Acquisitions by the Organization of American States in June 1999;

8. *Further welcomes* the decision on the illicit proliferation, circulation and trafficking of small arms and light weapons taken by the Assembly of Heads of State and Government of the Organization of African Unity at its thirty-fifth ordinary session, held in Algiers in July

1999, as well as the decisions on the prevention and combating of illicit trafficking in small arms and related crimes taken by the Council of the Southern African Development Community at its nineteenth Summit of Heads of State or Government, held in Maputo in August 1999, and the initiatives taken by States members of the Economic Community of West African States to conclude their agreement on a moratorium on the importing, exporting and manufacture of light weapons;

9. *Underlines* the fact that sustainable peace and security in Sierra Leone can only be achieved through the fulfilment of the broad objectives of the Peace Agreement signed in Lomé on 7 July 1999, including full disarmament, demobilization and reintegration, the legitimate exploitation of natural resources of Sierra Leone for the benefit of its people, full respect for the human rights of all, national reconciliation, effective action on the issues of impunity and accountability, the full extension of the authority of the State of Sierra Leone, and a free and inclusive democratic process leading to elections;

10. *Reaffirms* the sovereignty, territorial integrity and political independence of the Democratic Republic of the Congo and of all States in the region, and calls upon all the parties to the conflict to cease the hostilities and to fulfil their obligations under the Ceasefire Agreement signed in Lusaka;

11. *Also reaffirms* the importance for Member States to contribute by all means at their disposal to an effective and lasting peace in Angola, and in that context reiterates that the primary cause of the present situation in Angola is the failure of the National Union for the Total Independence of Angola, under the leadership of Jonas Savimbi, to comply with its obligations under the Peace Accords, the Lusaka Protocol and relevant Security Council resolutions;

12. *Views with concern* the humanitarian effects on the civilian population of the present situation in Angola, commends in this regard the efforts of Member States, including the Government of Angola, and humanitarian organizations in rendering humanitarian assistance to Angola, and urges them to continue to provide and to increase such assistance;

13. *Welcomes* the return to constitutional and democratic order in Guinea-Bissau following the holding of free and fair presidential and legislative elections on 16 January 2000, and calls upon the international community and the Government of Guinea-Bissau to support the economic reconstruction of Guinea-Bissau and promote the consolidation of democracy there;

14. *Affirms* the importance of the South Atlantic to global maritime and commercial transactions and its determination to preserve the region for all peaceful purposes and activities protected by international law, in particular the United Nations Convention on the Law of the Sea;

15. *Calls upon* Member States to continue their efforts towards the achievement of appropriate regulation of maritime transport of radioactive and toxic wastes, taking into account the interests of coastal States and in accordance with the United Nations Convention on the Law of the Sea and the regulations of the International Maritime Organization and the International Atomic Energy Agency;

16. *Views with concern* the increase in drug trafficking and related crimes, including drug abuse, and calls upon the international community and the States members of the zone to promote regional and international cooperation to combat all aspects of the problem of drugs and related offences;

17. *Recognizes*, in the light of the number, magnitude and complexity of natural disasters and other emergencies, the need to strengthen the coordination of humanitarian assistance by States members of the zone, so as to ensure a timely and effective response;

18. *Welcomes* the offer by Benin to host the sixth meeting of the States members of the zone;

19. *Requests* the relevant organizations, organs and bodies of the United Nations system to render all appropriate assistance that States members of the zone may seek in their joint efforts to implement the declaration of the zone of peace and cooperation of the South Atlantic;

20. *Requests* the Secretary-General to keep the implementation of resolution 41/11 and subsequent resolutions on the matter under review and to submit a report to the General Assembly at its fifty-sixth session, taking into account, inter alia, the views expressed by Member States;

21. *Decides* to include in the provisional agenda of its fifty-sixth session the item entitled "Zone of peace and cooperation of the South Atlantic".

RECORDED VOTE ON RESOLUTION 55/49:

In favour: Afghanistan, Algeria, Andorra, Angola, Argentina, Armenia, Australia, Azerbaijan, Bahamas, Bahrain, Bangladesh, Barbados, Belarus, Belgium, Benin, Bolivia, Brazil, Brunei Darussalam, Bulgaria, Burkina Faso, Burundi, Cameroon, Canada, Cape Verde, Chile, China, Colombia, Comoros, Congo, Costa Rica, Croatia, Cuba, Cyprus, Czech Republic, Denmark, Ecuador, El Salvador, Ethiopia, Finland, France, Gabon, Gambia, Georgia, Germany, Ghana, Greece, Grenada, Guatemala, Guinea, Guyana, Haiti, Honduras, Hungary, Iceland, India, Iran, Ireland, Israel, Italy, Japan, Kazakhstan, Kuwait, Kyrgyzstan, Lao People's Democratic Republic, Latvia, Libyan Arab Jamahiriya, Liechtenstein, Lithuania, Luxembourg, Malaysia, Maldives, Mali, Malta, Marshall Islands, Mexico, Monaco, Mongolia, Morocco, Mozambique, Myanmar, Namibia, Nauru, Netherlands, New Zealand, Norway, Oman, Pakistan, Panama, Paraguay, Peru, Poland, Portugal, Qatar, Republic of Moldova, Romania, San Marino, Senegal, Sierra Leone, Singapore, Slovakia, Slovenia, South Africa, Spain, Sri Lanka, Sudan, Sweden, Thailand, The former Yugoslav Republic of Macedonia, Togo, Tonga, Tunisia, Turkey, Ukraine, United Arab Emirates, United Kingdom, United Republic of Tanzania, Uruguay, Venezuela, Zambia.

Against: None.

Abstaining: United States.

Decolonization

The General Assembly's Special Committee on the Situation with regard to the Implementation of the Declaration on the Granting of Independence to Colonial Countries and Peoples (Special Committee on decolonization) held its annual session in New York in two parts—18 February, 24 and 28 March and 25 April for the first part, and from 5 to 20 July for the second. It considered various aspects of the implementation of the 1960 Declaration, adopted by the Assembly in resolution 1514(XV) [YUN 1960, p. 49], including general decolonization issues and the situation of individual Non-Self-Governing Territories (NSGTs). Pursuant to Assembly resolution 54/91 [YUN 1999, p. 523], the Special Committee transmitted to the Assembly the report on its 2000 activities [A/55/23].

Decade for the Eradication of Colonialism

Fortieth anniversary

The Chairman of the Special Committee on decolonization, in a 28 August letter to the Secretary-General [A/55/337], noted that the year 2000 marked the fortieth anniversary of the 1960 Declaration on the Granting of Independence to Colonial Countries and Peoples and, in accordance with the recommendation of the Special Committee's Pacific regional seminar (see p. 548), proposed that the General Assembly devote a plenary meeting to observe the anniversary. By **decision 55/410** of 14 November, the Assembly took note of the letter and decided to hold a plenary meeting for that purpose during the main part of its fifty-fifth (2000) session.

The observance took place on 8 December [meeting 83]. In his message to the Assembly on that occasion, the Secretary-General said that not only was the Declaration an expression of support by the majority of Member States for the liberation struggle of colonial territories, but it had also become a forceful tool with which to spur the implementation of the provisions on NSGTs in the Charter of the United Nations. While there was cause for celebration, there was also a need for awareness of the challenges ahead, as the United Nations faced the task of completing the implementation of the Declaration and of all the Organization's relevant resolutions on decolonization in the remaining NSGTs. The Secretary-General appealed to the administering Powers concerned to assist the Special Committee in the discharge of its mandate.

End of first International Decade

The Secretary-General, in response to General Assembly resolution 46/181 [YUN 1991, p. 777], submitted in October a final report [A/55/497] on the achievements of the International Decade for the Eradication of Colonialism (1990-2000), declared by the Assembly in resolution 43/47 [YUN 1988, p. 734].

In pointing to a number of notable decolonization events that had taken place during the Decade, the Secretary-General observed that the task of eradicating colonialism remained unfinished and required further concerted and determined efforts. There were still peoples, mostly in the small island NSGTs in the Pacific and the Caribbean, who had been unable to exercise their right to self-determination in accordance with Assembly resolution 1524(XV) [YUN 1960, p. 49] and other

relevant resolutions. Those Territories often faced problems stemming from their small size and population, geographical remoteness, limited natural resources and vulnerability to environmental change and natural disasters.

It was encouraging that, during the Decade, there had emerged a new international awareness of the unique development needs of the small island NSGTs. Some specialized agencies and regional commissions had exerted significant efforts to facilitate NSGT participation in their bodies as observers or associate members. Other positive developments included the critical review of the Special Committee's work to improve the effective discharge of its mandate, and to strengthen the mechanisms for consultation with the administering Powers so as to advance the implementation of the Declaration in the Territories under their administration. The establishment of a generic work plan to be applied to each Territory on a case-by-case basis and the informal meetings with the administering Powers on American Samoa and Pitcairn were steps in the right direction. The Secretary-General encouraged the administering Powers to continue to cooperate fully with the Committee and stressed the importance of continuous consultation with the peoples of those Territories to ascertain their wishes on their future.

The Secretary-General concluded that, while progress might have been limited during the Decade, it had provided a framework for concerted international action for the eradication of colonialism and served as a measure of what remained to be done. The trends described pointed to encouraging signs for the future.

Second International Decade for the Eradication of Colonialism

As indicated by the Secretary-General's foregoing October report [A/55/497], the Special Committee on decolonization, in its examination of the first International Decade's achievements, took account of the proposal by the Movement of Non-Aligned Countries at its Thirteenth Ministerial Conference (Cartagena, Colombia, 8-9 April) [A/54/917-S/2000/580] for the declaration of a new decade, to commence in 2001. That proposal was subsequently endorsed by the Pacific regional seminar (see p. 548), which also stressed the need to formulate an updated action plan for the eradication of colonialism, focusing on the self-determination of NSGTs, with the continued use of regional seminars as a means of hearing the views of the peoples concerned.

The Special Committee [A/55/23], having reviewed progress in the implementation of the plan of action for the first Decade [YUN 1991, p. 777] and having noted with concern that implementation could not be completed by the end of 2000 as envisaged, recommended a draft resolution for adoption by the General Assembly by which, among other things, it would declare the period 2001-2010 the Second International Decade for the Eradication of Colonialism (see below).

GENERAL ASSEMBLY ACTION

On 8 December [meeting 83], the General Assembly, on the recommendation of the Special Committee on decolonization [A/55/23], adopted **resolution 55/146** by recorded vote (125-2-30) [agenda item 18].

Second International Decade for the Eradication of Colonialism

The General Assembly,

Recalling that 2000 marks the fortieth anniversary of the Declaration on the Granting of Independence to Colonial Countries and Peoples,

Recalling also its resolution 43/47 of 22 November 1988, by which the General Assembly declared the period 1990-2000 as the International Decade for the Eradication of Colonialism, and recalling further resolution 46/181 of 19 December 1991, by which it adopted a plan of action for the Decade,

Bearing in mind the related recommendations of the Thirteenth Ministerial Conference of the Movement of Non-Aligned Countries, held in Cartagena, Colombia, on 8 and 9 April 2000, which proposed, inter alia, the declaration of a new decade for the elimination of colonialism, and which supported the effective implementation of the related plan of action,

Bearing in mind also the endorsement of the proposed declaration of a new decade for the eradication of colonialism by the participants in the Pacific regional seminar organized by the Special Committee on the Situation with regard to the Implementation of the Declaration on the Granting of Independence to Colonial Countries and Peoples to review the political, economic and social conditions in the small island Non-Self-Governing Territories, held in Majuro, Marshall Islands, from 16 to 18 May 2000,

Taking into account its resolution 54/90 A of 6 December 1999, in which it noted with concern that the plan of action for the International Decade could not be concluded by 2000,

Guided by the fundamental and universal principles enshrined in the Charter of the United Nations, the Universal Declaration of Human Rights and the International Covenant on Civil and Political Rights,

Having examined the relevant reports of the Secretary-General concerning the implementation of the plan of action for the International Decade,

Taking into account the important contribution of the United Nations in the field of decolonization, in particular through the Special Committee,

1. *Declares* the period 2001-2010 the Second International Decade for the Eradication of Colonialism;

2. *Calls upon* Member States to redouble their efforts to implement the plan of action, as contained in the annex to the report of the Secretary-General, updated where necessary, to serve as the plan of action for the Second International Decade;

3. *Calls upon* the administering Powers to cooperate fully with the Special Committee on the Situation with regard to the Implementation of the Declaration on the Granting of Independence to Colonial Countries and Peoples to develop a constructive programme of work on a case-by-case basis for the Non-Self-Governing Territories to facilitate the implementation of the mandate of the Special Committee and the relevant resolutions of the United Nations on decolonization, including resolutions on specific Territories;

4. *Invites* Member States, specialized agencies and other organizations of the United Nations system, and other governmental and non-governmental organizations, actively to support and participate in the implementation of the plan of action during the Second International Decade;

5. *Requests* the Secretary-General to provide the necessary resources for the successful implementation of the plan of action;

6. *Also requests* the Secretary-General to report to the General Assembly at its sixty-fifth session on the implementation of the present resolution.

RECORDED VOTE ON RESOLUTION 55/146:

In favour: Algeria, Andorra, Antigua and Barbuda, Argentina, Armenia, Australia, Azerbaijan, Bahamas, Bahrain, Bangladesh, Barbados, Belarus, Belize, Benin, Bhutan, Bolivia, Botswana, Brazil, Brunei Darussalam, Burkina Faso, Burundi, Cambodia, Cameroon, Canada, Cape Verde, Chad, Chile, China, Colombia, Comoros, Costa Rica, Côte d'Ivoire, Cuba, Cyprus, Democratic People's Republic of Korea, Djibouti, Dominican Republic, Ecuador, Egypt, El Salvador, Eritrea, Ethiopia, Fiji, Gabon, Ghana, Grenada, Guatemala, Guinea, Guyana, Haiti, Honduras, India, Indonesia, Iran, Ireland, Jamaica, Japan, Jordan, Kenya, Kuwait, Kyrgyzstan, Lao People's Democratic Republic, Lebanon, Libyan Arab Jamahiriya, Liechtenstein, Madagascar, Malaysia, Maldives, Mali, Malta, Marshall Islands, Mauritania, Mauritius, Mexico, Mongolia, Morocco, Mozambique, Myanmar, Namibia, Nauru, Nepal, New Zealand, Nicaragua, Nigeria, Oman, Pakistan, Panama, Papua New Guinea, Paraguay, Peru, Philippines, Portugal, Qatar, Republic of Korea, Republic of Moldova, Russian Federation, Saint Lucia, Samoa, San Marino, Saudi Arabia, Senegal, Sierra Leone, Singapore, Solomon Islands, South Africa, Spain, Sri Lanka, Sudan, Swaziland, Syrian Arab Republic, Thailand, Togo, Tonga, Tunisia, Uganda, Ukraine, United Arab Emirates, United Republic of Tanzania, Uruguay, Vanuatu, Venezuela, Viet Nam, Yemen, Zambia, Zimbabwe.

Against: United Kingdom, United States.

Abstaining: Austria, Belgium, Bulgaria, Croatia, Czech Republic, Denmark, Estonia, Finland, France, Georgia, Germany, Greece, Hungary, Iceland, Israel, Italy, Latvia, Lithuania, Luxembourg, Micronesia, Monaco, Netherlands, Norway, Poland, Romania, Slovakia, Slovenia, Sweden, The former Yugoslav Republic of Macedonia, Turkey.

The United Kingdom stated that there was scant evidence that the activities of the first Decade were of any great benefit to the interests of the peoples of NSGTs, which were more likely to be furthered through informal dialogue between the administering Powers and the Special Committee. No plan of action for the Second Decade had been submitted, and the United Kingdom could not support a request either for resources for unspecified activities, or to renew activities that had failed to achieve their objectives.

Pacific regional seminar

As part of its activities to implement the action plan of the first International Decade, the Special Committee on decolonization [A/55/23] organized a Pacific regional seminar (Majuro, Marshall Islands, 16-18 May) to review the political, economic and social conditions in the small island NSGTs.

The seminar concluded that, throughout the Decade, such regional seminars had served as effective forums for discussing the concerns of NSGTs and for presenting their views and recommendations to the Special Committee. Implementation of the 1960 Declaration on the Granting of Independence to Colonial Countries and Peoples [YUN 1960, p. 49] was not complete as long as there remained NSGTs that had yet to exercise their right to self-determination, whose specific characteristics should in no way prevent their populations from exercising that right.

In addition to recommending measures to bring NSGTs closer to the exercise of self-determination, the seminar called for closer cooperation between the Special Committee and the Economic and Social Council to promote increased UN economic and social assistance to NSGTs, which should be given access to relevant UN programmes in furtherance of capacity-building; preparation of a report by the Secretary-General to the General Assembly on the implementation of its decolonization resolutions since the declaration of the first International Decade; organization of commemorative activities by the Special Committee for the fortieth anniversary of the 1960 Declaration and the final year of the first Decade, including a solemn Assembly meeting; use of the newly established decolonization web page by the Secretariat's Department of Political Affairs (DPA) and Department of Public Information (DPI) to intensify information dissemination on UN decolonization activities so as to raise awareness of the political rights of NSGTs and options for determining their political status; and UN supervision of acts of self-determination in the NSGTs, which should be eligible for assistance from the Electoral Assistance Division of DPA.

The seminar also endorsed the proclamation of a Second Decade for the Eradication of Colonialism (see p. 547) and stressed the need for an updated action plan for the purpose.

GENERAL ASSEMBLY ACTION

On 8 December [meeting 83], the General Assembly adopted **resolution 55/147** [draft: A/55/L.58 & Add.1] by recorded vote (138-2-18) [agenda item 18].

Implementation of the Declaration on the Granting of Independence to Colonial Countries and Peoples

The General Assembly,

Having examined the report of the Special Committee on the Situation with regard to the Implementation of the Declaration on the Granting of Independence to Colonial Countries and Peoples,

Recalling its resolution 1514(XV) of 14 December 1960, containing the Declaration on the Granting of Independence to Colonial Countries and Peoples, and all its subsequent resolutions concerning the implementation of the Declaration, most recently resolution 54/91 of 6 December 1999, as well as the relevant resolutions of the Security Council,

Bearing in mind the end of the first International Decade for the Eradication of Colonialism, and the declaration of the period 2001-2010 as the Second International Decade for the Eradication of Colonialism, and that it is necessary to examine ways to ascertain the wishes of the peoples of the Non-Self-Governing Territories on the basis of resolution 1514(XV) and other relevant resolutions on decolonization,

Recognizing that the eradication of colonialism has been one of the priorities of the Organization and continues to be one of its priorities for the decade that begins in 2001,

Reconfirming the need to take measures to eliminate colonialism before 2010, as called for in its resolution 55/146 of 8 December 2000,

Reiterating its conviction of the need for the eradication of colonialism, as well as of racial discrimination and violations of basic human rights,

Noting with satisfaction the achievements of the Special Committee in contributing to the effective and complete implementation of the Declaration and other relevant resolutions of the United Nations on decolonization,

Stressing the importance of the participation of the administering Powers in the work of the Special Committee,

Noting with concern that the non-participation of certain administering Powers has adversely affected the implementation of the mandate and work of the Special Committee,

Noting with satisfaction the cooperation and active participation of some administering Powers in the work of the Special Committee,

Noting that the other administering Powers have now agreed to work informally with the Special Committee,

Taking note of the consultations and agreements between the parties concerned in some Non-Self-Governing Territories and the action taken by the Secretary-General in relation to certain Non-Self-Governing Territories,

Aware of the pressing need of newly independent and emerging States for assistance from the United Nations and its system of organizations in the economic, social and other fields,

Aware also of the pressing need of many of the remaining Non-Self-Governing Territories, including in particular small island Territories, for economic, social and other assistance from the United Nations and the organizations of its system,

Taking special note of the fact that the Special Committee held a Pacific regional seminar to review the situation in the small island Non-Self-Governing Territories, particularly their political evolution towards self-determination for the year 2000 and beyond, in Majuro, Marshall Islands, from 16 to 18 May 2000,

1. *Reaffirms* its resolution 1514(XV) and all other resolutions and decisions on decolonization, including its resolution 55/146, in which it declares the period 2001-2010 the Second International Decade for the

Eradication of Colonialism, and calls upon the administering Powers, in accordance with those resolutions, to take all necessary steps to enable the peoples of the Non-Self-Governing Territories concerned to exercise fully as soon as possible their right to self-determination, including independence;

2. *Takes note* of the report of the Secretary-General on the International Decade for the Eradication of Colonialism;

3. *Reaffirms once again* that the existence of colonialism in any form or manifestation, including economic exploitation, is incompatible with the Charter of the United Nations, the Declaration on the Granting of Independence to Colonial Countries and Peoples and the Universal Declaration of Human Rights;

4. *Reaffirms its determination* to continue to take all steps necessary to bring about the complete and speedy eradication of colonialism and the faithful observance by all States of the relevant provisions of the Charter of the United Nations, the Declaration on the Granting of Independence to Colonial Countries and Peoples and the Universal Declaration of Human Rights;

5. *Affirms once again its support* for the aspirations of the peoples under colonial rule to exercise their right to self-determination, including independence, in accordance with relevant resolutions of the United Nations on decolonization;

6. *Approves* the report of the Special Committee on the Situation with regard to the Implementation of the Declaration on the Granting of Independence to Colonial Countries and Peoples covering its work during 2000, including the programme of work envisaged for 2001;

7. *Calls upon* the administering Powers to cooperate fully with the Special Committee to finalize before the end of 2001 a constructive programme of work on a case-by-case basis for the Non-Self-Governing Territories to facilitate the implementation of the mandate of the Special Committee and the relevant resolutions on decolonization, including resolutions on specific Territories;

8. *Requests* the Special Committee to continue to seek suitable means for the immediate and full implementation of the Declaration and to carry out those actions approved by the General Assembly regarding the International Decade for the Eradication of Colonialism and the Second International Decade in all Territories that have not yet exercised their right to self-determination, including independence, and in particular:

(*a*) To formulate specific proposals to bring about an end to colonialism and to report thereon to the General Assembly at its fifty-sixth session;

(*b*) To continue to examine the implementation by Member States of resolution 1514(XV) and other relevant resolutions on decolonization;

(*c*) To continue to pay special attention to the small Territories, including through the dispatch of visiting missions, and to recommend to the General Assembly the most suitable steps to be taken to enable the populations of those Territories to exercise their right to self-determination, including independence;

(*d*) To finalize before the end of 2001 a constructive programme of work on a case-by-case basis for the Non-Self-Governing Territories to facilitate the implementation of the mandate of the Special Committee

and the relevant resolutions on decolonization, including resolutions on specific Territories;

(*e*) To take all necessary steps to enlist worldwide support among Governments, as well as national and international organizations, for the achievement of the objectives of the Declaration and the implementation of the relevant resolutions of the United Nations;

(*f*) To conduct seminars, as appropriate, for the purpose of receiving and disseminating information on the work of the Special Committee, and to facilitate participation by the peoples of the Non-Self-Governing Territories in those seminars;

(*g*) To observe annually the Week of Solidarity with the Peoples of Non-Self-Governing Territories;

9. *Calls upon* all States, in particular the administering Powers, as well as the specialized agencies and other organizations of the United Nations system, to give effect within their respective spheres of competence to the recommendations of the Special Committee for the implementation of the Declaration and other relevant resolutions of the United Nations;

10. *Calls upon* the administering Powers to ensure that all economic activities in the Non-Self-Governing Territories under their administration do not adversely affect the interests of the peoples but instead promote development, and to assist them in the exercise of their right to self-determination;

11. *Urges* the administering Powers concerned to take effective measures to safeguard and guarantee the inalienable rights of the peoples of the Non-Self-Governing Territories to their natural resources, including land, and to establish and maintain control over the future development of those resources, and requests the administering Powers to take all necessary steps to protect the property rights of the peoples of those Territories;

12. *Reiterates* that military activities and arrangements by administering Powers in the Non-Self-Governing Territories under their administration should not run counter to the rights and interests of the peoples of the Territories concerned, especially their right to self-determination, including independence, calls upon the administering Powers concerned to terminate such activities and to eliminate the remaining military bases in compliance with the relevant resolutions of the General Assembly, and also calls upon the administering Powers to promote alternative sources of livelihood for the peoples of the Territories concerned;

13. *Urges* all States, directly and through their action in the specialized agencies and other organizations of the United Nations system, to provide moral and material assistance to the peoples of the Non-Self-Governing Territories, and requests that the administering Powers take steps to enlist and make effective use of all possible assistance, on both a bilateral and a multilateral basis, in the strengthening of the economies of those Territories;

14. *Reaffirms* that the United Nations visiting missions to the Territories are an effective means of ascertaining the situation in the Territories, as well as the wishes and aspirations of their inhabitants, and calls upon the administering Powers to continue to cooperate with the Special Committee in the discharge of its mandate and to facilitate visiting missions to the Territories;

15. *Calls upon* the administering Powers that have not participated formally in the work of the Special Committee to do so at its session in 2001;

16. *Requests* the Secretary-General, the specialized agencies and other organizations of the United Nations system to provide economic, social and other assistance to the Non-Self-Governing Territories and to continue to do so, as appropriate, after they exercise their right to self-determination, including independence;

17. *Requests* the Secretary-General to provide the Special Committee with the facilities and services required for the implementation of the present resolution, as well as of the other resolutions and decisions on decolonization adopted by the General Assembly and the Special Committee.

RECORDED VOTE ON RESOLUTION 55/147:

In favour: Algeria, Andorra, Antigua and Barbuda, Argentina, Armenia, Australia, Austria, Azerbaijan, Bahamas, Bahrain, Bangladesh, Barbados, Belarus, Belize, Benin, Bhutan, Bolivia, Botswana, Brazil, Brunei Darussalam, Bulgaria, Burkina Faso, Burundi, Cambodia, Cameroon, Canada, Cape Verde, Chad, Chile, China, Colombia, Comoros, Costa Rica, Côte d'Ivoire, Cuba, Cyprus, Czech Republic, Democratic People's Republic of Korea, Denmark, Djibouti, Dominican Republic, Ecuador, Egypt, El Salvador, Eritrea, Ethiopia, Fiji, Gabon, Ghana, Greece, Grenada, Guatemala, Guinea, Guyana, Haiti, Honduras, Iceland, India, Indonesia, Iran, Ireland, Italy, Jamaica, Japan, Jordan, Kenya, Kuwait, Kyrgyzstan, Lao People's Democratic Republic, Lebanon, Libyan Arab Jamahiriya, Liechtenstein, Madagascar, Malaysia, Maldives, Mali, Malta, Marshall Islands, Mauritania, Mauritius, Mexico, Mongolia, Morocco, Mozambique, Myanmar, Namibia, Nauru, Nepal, New Zealand, Nicaragua, Nigeria, Norway, Oman, Pakistan, Panama, Papua New Guinea, Paraguay, Peru, Philippines, Poland, Portugal, Qatar, Republic of Moldova, Romania, Russian Federation, Saint Lucia, Samoa, San Marino, Saudi Arabia, Senegal, Sierra Leone, Singapore, Slovakia, Slovenia, Solomon Islands, South Africa, Spain, Sri Lanka, Sudan, Swaziland, Sweden, Syrian Arab Republic, Thailand, The former Yugoslav Republic of Macedonia, Togo, Tonga, Tunisia, Uganda, Ukraine, United Arab Emirates, United Republic of Tanzania, Uruguay, Vanuatu, Venezuela, Viet Nam, Yemen, Zambia, Zimbabwe.

Against: United Kingdom, United States.

Abstentions: Belgium, Croatia, Estonia, Finland, France, Georgia, Germany, Hungary, Israel, Kazakhstan, Latvia, Lithuania, Luxembourg, Micronesia, Monaco, Netherlands, Republic of Korea, Turkey.

Implementation by international organizations

As requested by the General Assembly in resolution 54/85 [YUN 1999, p. 527] on the implementation of the 1960 Declaration on decolonization, the Secretary-General reported in May [A/55/72 & Corr.1] that he had brought that resolution to the attention of the specialized agencies and other bodies of the UN system, as well as of international institutions associated with the United Nations, with a request for information on their implementation activities in support of NSGTs. Replies were subsequently received from the United Nations Conference on Trade and Development, UNDP, the United Nations Environment Programme and the Organization of African Unity, and were summarized in a June report [E/2000/68].

ECONOMIC AND SOCIAL COUNCIL ACTION

On 28 July [meeting 45], the Economic and Social Council adopted **resolution 2000/30** [draft: E/2000/L.17] by recorded vote (27-0-18) [agenda item 9].

Implementation of the Declaration on the Granting of Independence to Colonial Countries and Peoples by the specialized agencies and the international institutions associated with the United Nations

The Economic and Social Council,

Having examined the report of the Secretary-General and the information submitted by the specialized agencies and other organizations of the United Nations system on their activities with regard to the implementation of the Declaration on the Granting of Independence to Colonial Countries and Peoples,

Having heard the statement by the representative of the Special Committee on the Situation with regard to the Implementation of the Declaration on the Granting of Independence to Colonial Countries and Peoples,

Recalling General Assembly resolutions 1514(XV) of 14 December 1960 and 1541(XV) of 15 December 1960, the resolutions of the Special Committee and other relevant resolutions and decisions, including in particular Economic and Social Council resolution 1999/52 of 29 July 1999,

Bearing in mind the relevant provisions of the final documents of the successive Conferences of Heads of State or Government of Non-Aligned Countries and of the resolutions adopted by the Assembly of Heads of State and Government of the Organization of African Unity, the South Pacific Forum and the Caribbean Community,

Conscious of the need to facilitate the implementation of the Declaration,

Welcoming the current participation in the capacity of observer of those Non-Self-Governing Territories that are associate members of the regional commissions in United Nations world conferences in the economic and social sphere, subject to the rules of procedure of the General Assembly and in accordance with relevant United Nations resolutions and decisions, including resolutions and decisions of the Assembly and the Special Committee on specific Territories, and in the twenty-third special session of the Assembly, entitled "Women 2000: gender equality, development and peace for the twenty-first century", held in New York from 5 to 10 June 2000, and the twenty-fourth special session of the Assembly, entitled "World Summit for Social Development and beyond: achieving social development for all in a globalizing world", held at Geneva from 26 June to 1 July 2000,

Noting that the large majority of the remaining Non-Self-Governing Territories are small island Territories,

Welcoming the assistance extended to Non-Self-Governing Territories by certain specialized agencies and other organizations of the United Nations system, in particular the United Nations Development Programme,

Stressing that, because the development options of the small island Non-Self-Governing Territories are limited, there are special challenges to planning for and implementing sustainable development and that those Territories will be constrained in meeting the challenges without the continued cooperation and assistance of the specialized agencies and other organizations of the United Nations system,

Stressing also the importance of securing the necessary resources for funding expanded assistance programmes for the peoples concerned and the need to enlist the support of all major funding institutions within the United Nations system in that regard,

Reaffirming the mandates of the specialized agencies and other organizations of the United Nations system to take all appropriate measures, within their respective spheres of competence, to ensure the full implementation of General Assembly resolution 1514(XV) and other relevant resolutions,

Expressing its appreciation to the Organization of African Unity, the South Pacific Forum, the Caribbean Community and other regional organizations for the continued cooperation and assistance they have extended to the specialized agencies and other organizations of the United Nations system in this regard,

Expressing its conviction that closer contacts and consultations between and among the specialized agencies and other organizations of the United Nations system and regional organizations help to facilitate the effective formulation of programmes of assistance to the peoples concerned,

Mindful of the imperative need to keep under continuous review the activities of the specialized agencies and other organizations of the United Nations system in the implementation of the various United Nations decisions relating to decolonization,

Bearing in mind the extremely fragile economies of the small island Non-Self-Governing Territories and their vulnerability to natural disasters, such as hurricanes, cyclones and sea-level rise, and recalling the relevant resolutions of the General Assembly,

Recalling General Assembly resolution 54/85 of 6 December 1999 entitled "Implementation of the Declaration on the Granting of Independence to Colonial Countries and Peoples by the specialized agencies and the international institutions associated with the United Nations",

1. *Takes note* of the information submitted by the specialized agencies and other organizations of the United Nations system on their activities with regard to the implementation of the Declaration on the Granting of Independence to Colonial Countries and Peoples, and endorses the observations and suggestions arising therefrom;

2. *Also takes note* of the report of the Secretary-General;

3. *Recommends* that all States intensify their efforts in the specialized agencies and other organizations of the United Nations system to ensure the full and effective implementation of the Declaration, contained in General Assembly resolution 1514(XV), and other relevant resolutions of the United Nations;

4. *Reaffirms* that the specialized agencies and other organizations and institutions of the United Nations system should continue to be guided by the relevant resolutions of the United Nations in their efforts to contribute to the implementation of the Declaration and all other relevant General Assembly resolutions;

5. *Also reaffirms* that the recognition by the General Assembly, the Security Council and other United Nations organs of the legitimacy of the aspirations of the peoples of the Non-Self-Governing Territories to exercise their right to self-determination entails, as a corollary, the extension of all appropriate assistance to those peoples;

6. *Expresses its appreciation* to those specialized agencies and other organizations of the United Nations system that have continued to cooperate with the United Nations and the regional and subregional organizations in the implementation of General Assembly resolution 1514(XV) and other relevant resolutions of the United Nations, and requests all the specialized agencies and other organizations of the United Nations system to implement the relevant provisions of those resolutions;

7. *Requests* the specialized agencies and other organizations of the United Nations system and international and regional organizations to examine and review conditions in each Territory so as to take appropriate measures to accelerate progress in the economic and social sectors of the Territories;

8. *Requests* the specialized agencies and the international institutions associated with the United Nations and regional organizations to strengthen existing measures of support and formulate appropriate programmes of assistance to the remaining Non-Self-Governing Territories, within the framework of their respective mandates, in order to accelerate progress in the economic and social sectors of those Territories;

9. *Recommends* that the executive heads of the specialized agencies and other organizations of the United Nations system formulate, with the active cooperation of the regional organizations concerned, concrete proposals for the full implementation of the relevant resolutions of the United Nations and submit the proposals to their governing and legislative organs;

10. *Also recommends* that the specialized agencies and other organizations of the United Nations system continue to review, at the regular meetings of their governing bodies, the implementation of General Assembly resolution 1514(XV) and other relevant resolutions of the United Nations;

11. *Welcomes* the continuing initiative exercised by the United Nations Development Programme in maintaining close liaison among the specialized agencies and other organizations of the United Nations system and in providing assistance to the peoples of the Non-Self-Governing Territories;

12. *Encourages* Non-Self-Governing Territories to take steps to establish and/or strengthen disaster preparedness and management institutions and policies;

13. *Requests* the administering Powers concerned to facilitate, when appropriate, the participation of appointed and elected representatives of Non-Self-Governing Territories in the relevant meetings and conferences of the specialized agencies and other organizations of the United Nations system, in accordance with relevant United Nations resolutions and decisions, including resolutions and decisions of the General Assembly and the Special Committee on the Situation with regard to the Implementation of the Declaration on the Granting of Independence to Colonial Countries and Peoples on specific Territories, so that the Territories may benefit from the related activities of those agencies and organizations;

14. *Recommends* that all Governments intensify their efforts in the specialized agencies and other organizations of the United Nations system of which they are members to accord priority to the question of providing assistance to the peoples of the Non-Self-Governing Territories;

15. *Draws the attention* of the Special Committee to the present resolution and to the discussion held on the subject at the substantive session of 2000 of the Council;

16. *Welcomes* the adoption by the Economic Commission for Latin America and the Caribbean of resolution 574(XXVII) of 16 May 1998 calling for the necessary mechanisms for its associate members, including small island Non-Self-Governing Territories, to participate in the special sessions of the General Assembly, subject to the rules of procedure of the Assembly, to review and assess the implementation of the plans of action of those United Nations world conferences in which the Territories originally participated in the capacity of observer, and in the work of the Council and its subsidiary bodies;

17. *Also welcomes* the adoption by the General Assembly of its resolution 54/85, in which, inter alia, the Assembly recalled its resolution 53/189 of 15 December 1998, in which, inter alia, it had called for the participation of associate members of regional economic commissions in its special session on small island developing States, subject to the rules of procedure of the Assembly, and in the preparatory process thereof, in the same capacity of observer that had held for their participation in the Global Conference on the Sustainable Development of Small Island Developing States, held at Bridgetown from 25 April to 6 May 1994;

18. *Requests* the President of the Council to continue to maintain close contact on these matters with the Chairman of the Special Committee, and to report thereon to the Council;

19. *Requests* the Secretary-General to follow the implementation of the present resolution, paying particular attention to cooperation and integration arrangements for maximizing the efficiency of the assistance activities undertaken by various organizations of the United Nations system, and to report thereon to the Council at its substantive session of 2001;

20. *Decides* to keep these questions under continuous review.

RECORDED VOTE ON RESOLUTION 2000/30:

In favour: Algeria, Angola, Bahrain, Belarus, Benin, Bolivia, Brazil, Burkina Faso, China, Colombia, Costa Rica, Cuba, Fiji, Indonesia, Mexico, Morocco, New Zealand, Oman, Pakistan, Rwanda, Saint Lucia, Saudi Arabia, Sudan, Suriname, Syrian Arab Republic, Venezuela, Viet Nam.
Against: None.
Abstaining: Austria, Belgium, Bulgaria, Canada, Croatia, Czech Republic, Denmark, France, Germany, Greece, Italy, Japan, Norway, Poland, Portugal, Russian Federation, United Kingdom, United States.

GENERAL ASSEMBLY ACTION

On 8 December [meeting 83], the General Assembly, on the recommendation of the Fourth (Special Political and Decolonization) Committee [A/55/576], adopted **resolution 55/139** by recorded vote (109-0-50) [agenda items 90 & 12].

Implementation of the Declaration on the Granting of Independence to Colonial Countries and Peoples by the specialized agencies and the international institutions associated with the United Nations

The General Assembly,

Having considered the item entitled "Implementation of the Declaration on the Granting of Independence to Colonial Countries and Peoples by the specialized agencies and the international institutions associated with the United Nations",

Having also considered the report of the Secretary-General on the item,

Having examined the chapter of the report of the Special Committee on the Situation with regard to the Implementation of the Declaration on the Granting of Independence to Colonial Countries and Peoples relating to the item,

Recalling its resolutions 1514(XV) of 14 December 1960 and 1541(XV) of 15 December 1960 and the resolutions of the Special Committee, as well as other relevant resolutions and decisions, including in particular Economic and Social Council resolution 1999/52 of 29 July 1999,

Bearing in mind the relevant provisions of the final documents of the successive Conferences of Heads of State or Government of Non-Aligned Countries and of the resolutions adopted by the Assembly of Heads of State and Government of the Organization of African Unity, the Pacific Islands Forum and the Caribbean Community,

Conscious of the need to facilitate the implementation of the Declaration on the Granting of Independence to Colonial Countries and Peoples, contained in resolution 1514(XV),

Noting that the large majority of the remaining Non-Self-Governing Territories are small island Territories,

Welcoming the assistance extended to Non-Self-Governing Territories by certain specialized agencies and other organizations of the United Nations system, in particular the United Nations Development Programme,

Also welcoming the current participation in the capacity of observer of those Non-Self-Governing Territories that are associate members of regional commissions in the world conferences in the economic and social sphere, subject to the rules of procedure of the General Assembly and in accordance with relevant United Nations resolutions and decisions, including resolutions and decisions of the Assembly and the Special Committee on specific Territories, and in the special session of the General Assembly on the overall review and appraisal of the implementation of the Programme of Action of the International Conference on Population and Development, held at Headquarters from 30 June to 2 July 1999,

Noting that only some specialized agencies and other organizations of the United Nations system have been involved in providing assistance to Non-Self-Governing Territories,

Stressing that, because the development options of the small island Non-Self-Governing Territories are limited, there are special challenges to planning for and implementing sustainable development and that those Territories will be constrained in meeting the challenges without the continued cooperation and assistance of the specialized agencies and other organizations of the United Nations system,

Stressing also the importance of securing the necessary resources for funding expanded assistance programmes for the peoples concerned and the need to enlist the support of all major funding institutions within the United Nations system in that regard,

Reaffirming the mandates of the specialized agencies and other organizations of the United Nations system to take all appropriate measures, within their respective spheres of competence, to ensure the full implementation of General Assembly resolution 1514(XV) and other relevant resolutions,

Expressing its appreciation to the Organization of African Unity, the Pacific Islands Forum, the Caribbean Community and other regional organizations for the continued cooperation and assistance they have extended to the specialized agencies and other organizations of the United Nations system in this regard,

Expressing its conviction that closer contacts and consultations between and among the specialized agencies and other organizations of the United Nations system and regional organizations help to facilitate the effective formulation of assistance programmes to the peoples concerned,

Mindful of the imperative need to keep under continuous review the activities of the specialized agencies and other organizations of the United Nations system in the implementation of the various United Nations decisions relating to decolonization,

Bearing in mind the extremely fragile economies of the small island Non-Self-Governing Territories and their vulnerability to natural disasters, such as hurricanes, cyclones and sea-level rise, and recalling its relevant resolutions,

Recalling its resolution 54/85 of 6 December 1999 on the implementation of the Declaration by the specialized agencies and the international institutions associated with the United Nations,

1. *Takes note* of the report of the Secretary-General;

2. *Recommends* that all States intensify their efforts in the specialized agencies and other organizations of the United Nations system to ensure the full and effective implementation of the Declaration on the Granting of Independence to Colonial Countries and Peoples, contained in General Assembly resolution 1514(XV), and other relevant resolutions of the United Nations;

3. *Reaffirms* that the specialized agencies and other organizations and institutions of the United Nations system should continue to be guided by the relevant resolutions of the United Nations in their efforts to contribute to the implementation of the Declaration and all other relevant General Assembly resolutions;

4. *Reaffirms also* that the recognition by the General Assembly, the Security Council and other United Nations organs of the legitimacy of the aspirations of the peoples of the Non-Self-Governing Territories to exercise their right to self-determination entails, as a corollary, the extension of all appropriate assistance to those peoples;

5. *Expresses its appreciation* to those specialized agencies and other organizations of the United Nations system that have continued to cooperate with the United Nations and the regional and subregional organizations in the implementation of General Assembly resolution 1514(XV) and other relevant resolutions of the United Nations, and requests all the specialized agencies and other organizations of the United Nations system to implement the relevant provisions of those resolutions;

6. *Requests* the specialized agencies and other organizations of the United Nations system and international and regional organizations to examine and review conditions in each Territory so as to take appropriate measures to accelerate progress in the economic and social sectors of the Territories;

7. *Urges* those specialized agencies and organizations of the United Nations system that have not yet provided assistance to Non-Self-Governing Territories to do so as soon as possible;

8. *Requests* the specialized agencies and other organizations and institutions of the United Nations system and regional organizations to strengthen existing measures of support and formulate appropriate programmes of assistance to the remaining Non-Self-Governing Territories, within the framework of their respective mandates, in order to accelerate progress in the economic and social sectors of those Territories;

9. *Requests* the specialized agencies and other organizations of the United Nations system concerned to provide information on:

(a) Environmental problems facing the Non-Self-Governing Territories;

(b) The impact of natural disasters, such as hurricanes and volcanic eruptions, and other environmental problems, such as beach and coastal erosion and droughts, on those Territories;

(c) Ways and means to assist the Territories to fight drug trafficking, money-laundering and other illegal and criminal activities;

(d) The illegal exploitation of the marine resources of the Territories and the need to utilize those resources for the benefit of the peoples of the Territories;

10. *Recommends* that the executive heads of the specialized agencies and other organizations of the United Nations system formulate, with the active cooperation of the regional organizations concerned, concrete proposals for the full implementation of the relevant resolutions of the United Nations and submit the proposals to their governing and legislative organs;

11. *Also recommends* that the specialized agencies and other organizations of the United Nations system continue to review at the regular meetings of their governing bodies the implementation of General Assembly resolution 1514(XV) and other relevant resolutions of the United Nations;

12. *Welcomes* the continuing initiative exercised by the United Nations Development Programme in maintaining close liaison among the specialized agencies and other organizations of the United Nations system and in providing assistance to the peoples of the Non-Self-Governing Territories;

13. *Encourages* Non-Self-Governing Territories to take steps to establish and/or strengthen disaster preparedness and management institutions and policies;

14. *Requests* the administering Powers concerned to facilitate, when appropriate, the participation of appointed and elected representatives of Non-Self-Governing Territories in the relevant meetings and conferences of the specialized agencies and other organizations of the United Nations system, in accordance with relevant United Nations resolutions and decisions, including resolutions and decisions of the General Assembly and the Special Committee on the Situation with regard to the Implementation of the Declaration on the Granting of Independence to Colonial Countries and Peoples on specific Territories, so that the Territories may benefit from the related activities of those agencies and organizations;

15. *Recommends* that all Governments intensify their efforts in the specialized agencies and other organizations of the United Nations system of which they are

members to accord priority to the question of providing assistance to the peoples of the Non-Self-Governing Territories;

16. *Requests* the Secretary-General to continue to assist the specialized agencies and other organizations of the United Nations system in working out appropriate measures for implementing the relevant resolutions of the United Nations and to prepare for submission to the relevant bodies, with the assistance of those agencies and organizations, a report on the action taken in implementation of the relevant resolutions, including the present resolution, since the circulation of his previous report;

17. *Commends* the Economic and Social Council for its debate and resolution on this question, and requests it to continue to consider, in consultation with the Special Committee, appropriate measures for coordination of the policies and activities of the specialized agencies and other organizations of the United Nations system in implementing the relevant resolutions of the General Assembly;

18. *Requests* the specialized agencies to report periodically to the Secretary-General on the implementation of the present resolution;

19. *Requests* the Secretary-General to transmit the present resolution to the governing bodies of the appropriate specialized agencies and international institutions associated with the United Nations so that those bodies may take the necessary measures to implement it, and also requests the Secretary-General to report to the General Assembly at its fifty-sixth session on the implementation of the present resolution;

20. *Requests* the Special Committee to continue to examine the question and to report thereon to the General Assembly at its fifty-sixth session.

RECORDED VOTE ON RESOLUTION 55/139:

In favour: Algeria, Antigua and Barbuda, Argentina, Armenia, Australia, Azerbaijan, Bahamas, Bahrain, Bangladesh, Barbados, Belarus, Belize, Benin, Bhutan, Bolivia, Botswana, Brazil, Brunei Darussalam, Burkina Faso, Burundi, Cambodia, Cameroon, Cape Verde, Chad, Chile, China, Colombia, Comoros, Costa Rica, Côte d'Ivoire, Cuba, Democratic People's Republic of Korea, Djibouti, Dominican Republic, Ecuador, Egypt, El Salvador, Eritrea, Ethiopia, Fiji, Gabon, Ghana, Grenada, Guatemala, Guinea, Guyana, Haiti, Honduras, India, Indonesia, Iran, Jamaica, Jordan, Kenya, Kuwait, Lao People's Democratic Republic, Lebanon, Libyan Arab Jamahiriya, Madagascar, Malaysia, Maldives, Mali, Mauritania, Mauritius, Mexico, Mongolia, Morocco, Mozambique, Myanmar, Namibia, Nauru, Nepal, New Zealand, Nicaragua, Nigeria, Oman, Pakistan, Panama, Papua New Guinea, Paraguay, Peru, Philippines, Qatar, Saint Lucia, Samoa, Saudi Arabia, Senegal, Sierra Leone, Singapore, Solomon Islands, South Africa, Sri Lanka, Sudan, Swaziland, Syrian Arab Republic, Thailand, Togo, Tonga, Tunisia, Uganda, United Arab Emirates, United Republic of Tanzania, Uruguay, Vanuatu, Venezuela, Viet Nam, Yemen, Zambia, Zimbabwe.

Against: None.

Abstaining: Andorra, Austria, Belgium, Bulgaria, Canada, Croatia, Cyprus, Czech Republic, Denmark, Estonia, Finland, France, Georgia, Germany, Greece, Hungary, Iceland, Ireland, Israel, Italy, Japan, Kazakhstan, Kyrgyzstan, Latvia, Liechtenstein, Lithuania, Luxembourg, Malta, Marshall Islands, Micronesia, Monaco, Netherlands, Norway, Poland, Portugal, Republic of Korea, Republic of Moldova, Romania, Russian Federation, San Marino, Slovakia, Slovenia, Spain, Sweden, The former Yugoslav Republic of Macedonia, Turkey, Ukraine, United Kingdom, United States, Yugoslavia.

Military activities and arrangements in colonial countries

The Special Committee on decolonization considered military activities and arrangements by colonial Powers in Territories under their administration. It had before it Secretariat working papers containing, among other things, information on military activities and arrangements in Bermuda, Guam and the United States Virgin Islands [A/AC.109/2000/13, A/AC.109/2000/6, A/AC.109/2000/17 & Corr.1]. On 17 July, it recommended a draft decision for adoption by the General Assembly (see below).

GENERAL ASSEMBLY ACTION

In December, the General Assembly, on the recommendation of the Fourth Committee [A/55/575], adopted **decision 55/426** by recorded vote (100-47-5) [agenda items 89 & 18].

Military activities and arrangements by colonial Powers in Territories under their administration

At its 83rd plenary meeting, on 8 December 2000, the General Assembly, on the recommendation of the Special Political and Decolonization Committee (Fourth Committee), adopted the following text by a recorded vote of 100 to 47, with 5 abstentions:

"1. The General Assembly, having considered the chapter of the report of the Special Committee on the Situation with regard to the Implementation of the Declaration on the Granting of Independence to Colonial Countries and Peoples relating to an item on the agenda of the Special Committee entitled 'Military activities and arrangements by colonial Powers in Territories under their administration', and recalling its resolution 1514(XV) of 14 December 1960 and all other relevant resolutions and decisions of the United Nations relating to military activities in colonial and Non-Self-Governing Territories, reaffirms its strong conviction that military bases and installations in the Territories concerned could constitute an obstacle to the exercise by the people of those Territories of their right to self-determination, and reiterates its strong views that existing bases and installations, which are impeding the implementation of the Declaration on the Granting of Independence to Colonial Countries and Peoples, should be withdrawn.

"2. Aware of the presence of such bases and installations in some of those Territories, the General Assembly urges the administering Powers concerned to continue to take all necessary measures not to involve those Territories in any offensive acts or interference against other States.

"3. The General Assembly reiterates its concern that military activities and arrangements by colonial Powers in Territories under their administration might run counter to the rights and interests of the colonial peoples concerned, especially their right to self-determination and independence. The Assembly once again calls upon the administering Powers concerned to terminate such activities and to eliminate such military bases in compliance with its relevant resolutions. Alternative sources of livelihood for the peoples of the Non-Self-Governing Territories should be provided.

"4. The General Assembly reiterates that the colonial and Non-Self-Governing Territories and areas adjacent thereto should not be used for nuclear testing, dumping of nuclear wastes or deployment of nuclear or other weapons of mass destruction.

"5. The General Assembly deplores the continued alienation of land in colonial and Non-Self-Governing Territories, particularly in the small island Territories of the Pacific and Caribbean regions, for military installations. The large-scale utilization of local resources for this purpose could adversely affect the economic development of the Territories concerned.

"6. The General Assembly takes note of the decision of some of the administering Powers to close or downsize some of those military bases in the Non-Self-Governing Territories.

"7. The General Assembly requests the Secretary-General to continue to inform world public opinion of those military activities and arrangements in colonial and Non-Self-Governing Territories which constitute an obstacle to the implementation of the Declaration on the Granting of Independence to Colonial Countries and Peoples.

"8. The General Assembly requests the Special Committee on the Situation with regard to the Implementation of the Declaration on the Granting of Independence to Colonial Countries and Peoples to continue to examine this question and to report thereon to the Assembly at its fifty-sixth session."

RECORDED VOTE ON DECISION 55/426:

In favour: Algeria, Antigua and Barbuda, Argentina, Bahamas, Bahrain, Bangladesh, Barbados, Belarus, Benin, Bhutan, Bolivia, Botswana, Brazil, Brunei Darussalam, Burkina Faso, Burundi, Cambodia, Cameroon, Cape Verde, Chad, Chile, China, Colombia, Comoros, Costa Rica, Côte d'Ivoire, Cuba, Democratic People's Republic of Korea, Djibouti, Ecuador, Egypt, El Salvador, Eritrea, Ethiopia, Fiji, Gabon, Ghana, Grenada, Guatemala, Guinea, Guyana, Haiti, Honduras, India, Indonesia, Iran, Jamaica, Jordan, Kenya, Kuwait, Lao People's Democratic Republic, Lebanon, Libyan Arab Jamahiriya, Madagascar, Malaysia, Maldives, Mali, Marshall Islands, Mauritania, Mauritius, Mexico, Mongolia, Mozambique, Myanmar, Namibia, Nauru, Nepal, Nicaragua, Nigeria, Oman, Pakistan, Panama, Papua New Guinea, Paraguay, Peru, Philippines, Qatar, Saint Lucia, Saudi Arabia, Senegal, Singapore, Solomon Islands, South Africa, Sri Lanka, Sudan, Swaziland, Syrian Arab Republic, Thailand, Togo, Tunisia, Uganda, United Arab Emirates, United Republic of Tanzania, Uruguay, Vanuatu, Venezuela, Viet Nam, Yemen, Zambia, Zimbabwe.

Against: Andorra, Armenia, Australia, Austria, Belgium, Bulgaria, Canada, Croatia, Czech Republic, Denmark, Dominican Republic, Estonia, Finland, France, Germany, Greece, Hungary, Iceland, Ireland, Israel, Italy, Japan, Latvia, Liechtenstein, Lithuania, Luxembourg, Malta, Monaco, Netherlands, New Zealand, Norway, Poland, Portugal, Republic of Korea, Republic of Moldova, Romania, Russian Federation, San Marino, Slovakia, Slovenia, Spain, Sweden, The former Yugoslav Republic of Macedonia, Turkey, Ukraine, United Kingdom, United States.

Abstaining: Cyprus, Georgia, Micronesia, Samoa, Tonga.

Economic and other activities affecting the interests of NSGTs

The Special Committee on decolonization continued consideration of economic and other activities affecting the interests of the peoples of NSGTs. It had before it Secretariat working papers containing, among other things, information on economic conditions, with particular reference to foreign economic activities in Bermuda, the British Virgin Islands, the Cayman Islands and the United States Virgin Islands [A/AC.109/2000/13, A/AC.109/2000/18, A/AC.109/2000/14, A/AC.109/2000/17 & Corr.1].

On 8 December [meeting 83], the General Assembly, on the recommendation of the Fourth Committee [A/55/575], adopted **resolution 55/138** by recorded vote (151-2-5) [agenda items 89 & 18].

Economic and other activities which affect the interests of the peoples of the Non-Self-Governing Territories

The General Assembly,

Having considered the item entitled "Economic and other activities which affect the interests of the peoples of the Non-Self-Governing Territories",

Having examined the chapter of the report of the Special Committee on the Situation with regard to the Implementation of the Declaration on the Granting of Independence to Colonial Countries and Peoples relating to the item,

Recalling its resolution 1514(XV) of 14 December 1960, as well as all other relevant resolutions, including, in particular, resolution 46/181 of 19 December 1991,

Reaffirming the solemn obligation of the administering Powers under the Charter of the United Nations to promote the political, economic, social and educational advancement of the inhabitants of the Territories under their administration and to protect the human and natural resources of those Territories against abuses,

Reaffirming also that any economic or other activity that has a negative impact on the interests of the peoples of the Non-Self-Governing Territories and on the exercise of their right to self-determination in conformity with the Charter of the United Nations and General Assembly resolution 1514(XV) is contrary to the purposes and principles of the Charter,

Reaffirming further that the natural resources are the heritage of the peoples of the Non-Self-Governing Territories, including the indigenous populations,

Aware of the special circumstances of the geographical location, size and economic conditions of each Territory, and bearing in mind the need to promote the economic stability, diversification and strengthening of the economy of each Territory,

Conscious of the particular vulnerability of the small Territories to natural disasters and environmental degradation,

Conscious also that foreign economic investment, when done in collaboration with the peoples of the Non-Self-Governing Territories and in accordance with their wishes, could make a valid contribution to the socio-economic development of the Territories and could also make a valid contribution to the exercise of their right to self-determination,

Concerned about any activities aimed at exploiting the natural and human resources of the Non-Self-Governing Territories to the detriment of the interests of the inhabitants of those Territories,

Bearing in mind the relevant provisions of the final documents of the successive Conferences of Heads of State or Government of Non-Aligned Countries and of the resolutions adopted by the Assembly of Heads of State and Government of the Organization of African Unity, the Pacific Islands Forum and the Caribbean Community,

1. *Reaffirms* the right of peoples of Non-Self-Governing Territories to self-determination in conformity with the Charter of the United Nations and with General Assembly resolution 1514(XV), containing the Declaration on the Granting of Independence to Colonial Countries and Peoples, as well as their right to the enjoyment of their natural resources and their right to dispose of those resources in their best interest;

2. *Affirms* the value of foreign economic investment undertaken in collaboration with the peoples of the Non-Self-Governing Territories and in accordance with their wishes in order to make a valid contribution to the socio-economic development of the Territories;

3. *Reaffirms* the responsibility of the administering Powers under the Charter to promote the political, economic, social and educational advancement of the Non-Self-Governing Territories, and reaffirms the legitimate rights of their peoples over their natural resources;

4. *Reaffirms its concern* about any activities aimed at the exploitation of the natural resources that are the heritage of the peoples of the Non-Self-Governing Territories, including the indigenous populations, in the Caribbean, the Pacific and other regions, as well as their human resources, to the detriment of their interests, and in such a way as to deprive them of their right to dispose of those resources;

5. *Affirms* the need to avoid any economic and other activities which adversely affect the interests of the peoples of the Non-Self-Governing Territories;

6. *Calls once again upon* all Governments that have not yet done so to take, in accordance with the relevant provisions of General Assembly resolution 2621(XXV) of 12 October 1970, legislative, administrative or other measures in respect of their nationals and the bodies corporate under their jurisdiction that own and operate enterprises in the Non-Self-Governing Territories that are detrimental to the interests of the inhabitants of those Territories, in order to put an end to such enterprises;

7. *Reiterates* that the damaging exploitation and plundering of the marine and other natural resources of the Non-Self-Governing Territories, in violation of the relevant resolutions of the United Nations, is a threat to the integrity and prosperity of those Territories;

8. *Invites* all Governments and organizations of the United Nations system to take all possible measures to ensure that the permanent sovereignty of the peoples of the Non-Self-Governing Territories over their natural resources is fully respected and safeguarded;

9. *Urges* the administering Powers concerned to take effective measures to safeguard and guarantee the inalienable right of the peoples of the Non-Self-Governing Territories to their natural resources and to establish and maintain control over the future development of those resources, and requests the administering Powers to take all necessary steps to protect the property rights of the peoples of those Territories;

10. *Calls upon* the administering Powers concerned to ensure that no discriminatory working conditions prevail in the Territories under their administration and to promote in each Territory a fair system of wages applicable to all the inhabitants without any discrimination;

11. *Requests* the Secretary-General to continue, through all means at his disposal, to inform world public opinion of any activity that affects the exercise of the right of the peoples of the Non-Self-Governing Territories to self-determination in conformity with the Charter and General Assembly resolution 1514(XV);

12. *Appeals* to the mass media, trade unions and non-governmental organizations, as well as individuals, to continue their efforts to promote the economic well-being of the peoples of the Non-Self-Governing Territories;

13. *Decides* to follow the situation in the Non-Self-Governing Territories so as to ensure that all economic activities in those Territories are aimed at strengthening and diversifying their economies in the interest of their peoples, including the indigenous populations, and at promoting the economic and financial viability of those Territories;

14. *Requests* the Special Committee on the Situation with regard to the Implementation of the Declaration on the Granting of Independence to Colonial Countries and Peoples to continue to examine this question and to report thereon to the General Assembly at its fifty-sixth session.

RECORDED VOTE ON RESOLUTION 55/138:

In favour: Algeria, Andorra, Antigua and Barbuda, Argentina, Armenia, Australia, Austria, Azerbaijan, Bahamas, Bahrain, Bangladesh, Barbados, Belarus, Belgium, Belize, Benin, Bhutan, Bolivia, Botswana, Brazil, Brunei Darussalam, Bulgaria, Burkina Faso, Burundi, Cambodia, Cameroon, Canada, Cape Verde, Chad, Chile, China, Colombia, Comoros, Costa Rica, Côte d'Ivoire, Cuba, Cyprus, Czech Republic, Democratic People's Republic of Korea, Denmark, Djibouti, Dominican Republic, Ecuador, Egypt, El Salvador, Eritrea, Estonia, Ethiopia, Fiji, Finland, Gabon, Germany, Ghana, Greece, Grenada, Guatemala, Guinea, Guyana, Haiti, Honduras, Hungary, Iceland, India, Indonesia, Iran, Ireland, Italy, Jamaica, Japan, Jordan, Kazakhstan, Kenya, Kuwait, Kyrgyzstan, Lao People's Democratic Republic, Latvia, Lebanon, Libyan Arab Jamahiriya, Liechtenstein, Lithuania, Luxembourg, Madagascar, Malaysia, Maldives, Mali, Malta, Marshall Islands, Mauritania, Mauritius, Mexico, Monaco, Mongolia, Mozambique, Myanmar, Namibia, Nauru, Nepal, Netherlands, New Zealand, Nicaragua, Nigeria, Norway, Oman, Pakistan, Panama, Papua New Guinea, Paraguay, Peru, Philippines, Poland, Portugal, Qatar, Republic of Korea, Republic of Moldova, Romania, Russian Federation, Saint Lucia, Samoa, San Marino, Saudi Arabia, Senegal, Sierra Leone, Singapore, Slovakia, Slovenia, Solomon Islands, South Africa, Spain, Sri Lanka, Sudan, Swaziland, Sweden, Syrian Arab Republic, Thailand, The former Yugoslav Republic of Macedonia, Togo, Tonga, Tunisia, Turkey, Uganda, Ukraine, United Arab Emirates, United Republic of Tanzania, Uruguay, Vanuatu, Venezuela, Viet Nam, Yemen, Yugoslavia, Zambia, Zimbabwe.

Against: Israel, United States.

Abstaining: Croatia, France, Georgia, Micronesia, United Kingdom.

Dissemination of information

The Special Committee on decolonization held consultations in July with representatives of DPA and DPI on the dissemination of information on decolonization. The Committee, having considered the report of DPI on its publicity activities on decolonization [A/AC.109/2000/19], recommended a draft resolution for adoption by the General Assembly (see below).

GENERAL ASSEMBLY ACTION

On 8 December [meeting 83], the General Assembly, on the recommendation of the Special Committee on decolonization [A/55/23], adopted **resolution 55/145** by recorded vote (153-2-3) [agenda item 18].

Dissemination of information on decolonization

The General Assembly,

Having examined the chapter of the report of the Special Committee on the Situation with regard to the Implementation of the Declaration on the Granting of Independence to Colonial Countries and Peoples relating to the dissemination of information on decolonization and publicity for the work of the United Nations in the field of decolonization,

Recalling its resolution 1514(XV) of 14 December 1960, containing the Declaration on the Granting of Independence to Colonial Countries and Peoples, and other resolutions and decisions of the United Nations concerning the dissemination of information on decolonization, in particular resolution 54/92 of 6 December 1999,

Recognizing the need for flexible, practical and innovative approaches towards reviewing the options of self-determination for the peoples of the Non-Self-Governing Territories with a view to achieving complete decolonization by 2000,

Reiterating the importance of dissemination of information as an instrument for furthering the aims of the Declaration, and mindful of the role of world public opinion in effectively assisting the peoples of the Non-Self-Governing Territories to achieve self-determination,

Recognizing the role played by the administering Powers in transmitting information to the Secretary-General in accordance with the terms of Article 73 *e* of the Charter of the United Nations,

Aware of the role of non-governmental organizations in the dissemination of information on decolonization,

1. *Approves* the activities in the field of dissemination of information on decolonization undertaken by the Department of Public Information and the Department of Political Affairs of the Secretariat;

2. *Considers it important* to continue its efforts to ensure the widest possible dissemination of information on decolonization, with particular emphasis on the options of self-determination available for the peoples of the Non-Self-Governing Territories;

3. *Requests* the Department of Political Affairs and the Department of Public Information to take into account the suggestions of the Special Committee on the Situation with regard to the Implementation of the Declaration on the Granting of Independence to Colonial Countries and Peoples to continue their efforts to take measures through all the media available, including publications, radio and television, as well as the Internet, to give publicity to the work of the United Nations in the field of decolonization and, inter alia:

(*a*) To continue to collect, prepare and disseminate, particularly to the Territories, basic material on the issue of self-determination of the peoples of the Non-Self-Governing Territories;

(*b*) To seek the full cooperation of the administering Powers in the discharge of the tasks referred to above;

(*c*) To maintain a working relationship with the appropriate regional and intergovernmental organizations, particularly in the Pacific and Caribbean regions, by holding periodic consultations and exchanging information;

(*d*) To encourage the involvement of non-governmental organizations in the dissemination of information on decolonization;

(*e*) To report to the Special Committee on measures taken in the implementation of the present resolution;

4. *Requests* all States, including the administering Powers, to continue to extend their cooperation in the dissemination of information referred to in paragraph 2 above;

5. *Requests* the Special Committee to follow the implementation of the present resolution and to report thereon to the General Assembly at its fifty-sixth session.

RECORDED VOTE ON RESOLUTION 55/145:

In favour: Afghanistan, Algeria, Andorra, Antigua and Barbuda, Argentina, Armenia, Australia, Austria, Azerbaijan, Bahamas, Bahrain, Bangladesh, Barbados, Belarus, Belgium, Belize, Benin, Bhutan, Bolivia, Botswana, Brazil, Brunei Darussalam, Bulgaria, Burkina Faso, Burundi, Cambodia, Cameroon, Canada, Cape Verde, Chad, Chile, China, Colombia, Comoros, Costa Rica, Côte d'Ivoire, Croatia, Cuba, Cyprus, Czech Republic, Democratic People's Republic of Korea, Denmark, Djibouti, Dominican Republic, Ecuador, Egypt, El Salvador, Eritrea, Estonia, Ethiopia, Fiji, Finland, Gabon, Georgia, Germany, Ghana, Greece, Grenada, Guatemala, Guinea, Guyana, Haiti, Honduras, Hungary, Iceland, India, Indonesia, Iran, Ireland, Italy, Jamaica, Japan, Jordan, Kazakhstan, Kenya, Kuwait, Kyrgyzstan, Lao People's Democratic Republic, Latvia, Lebanon, Libyan Arab Jamahiriya, Liechtenstein, Lithuania, Luxembourg, Madagascar, Malaysia, Maldives, Mali, Malta, Marshall Islands, Mauritania, Mauritius, Mexico, Monaco, Mongolia, Mozambique, Myanmar, Namibia, Nauru, Nepal, Netherlands, New Zealand, Nicaragua, Nigeria, Norway, Oman, Pakistan, Panama, Papua New Guinea, Paraguay, Peru, Philippines, Poland, Portugal, Qatar, Republic of Korea, Republic of Moldova, Romania, Russian Federation, Saint Lucia, Samoa, San Marino, Saudi Arabia, Senegal, Sierra Leone, Singapore, Slovakia, Slovenia, Solomon Islands, South Africa, Spain, Sri Lanka, Sudan, Swaziland, Sweden, Syrian Arab Republic, Thailand, The former Yugoslav Republic of Macedonia, Togo, Tonga, Tunisia, Turkey, Uganda, Ukraine, United Arab Emirates, United Republic of Tanzania, Uruguay, Vanuatu, Venezuela, Viet Nam, Yemen, Zambia, Zimbabwe.

Against: United Kingdom, United States.

Abstaining: France, Israel, Micronesia.

Information on Territories

In response to General Assembly resolution 54/83 [YUN 1999, p. 532], the Secretary-General submitted a May report [A/55/77] showing the dates on which information on economic, social and educational conditions in NSGTs was transmitted to him from 1998 to 2000, under article 73 *e* of the United Nations Charter. The report was later updated by an addendum [A/55/77/Add.1].

GENERAL ASSEMBLY ACTION

On 8 December [meeting 83], the General Assembly, on the recommendation of the Fourth Committee [A/55/574], adopted **resolution 55/137** by recorded vote (153-0-5) [agenda item 88].

Information from Non-Self-Governing Territories transmitted under Article 73 *e* of the Charter of the United Nations

The General Assembly,

Having examined the chapter of the report of the Special Committee on the Situation with regard to the Implementation of the Declaration on the Granting of Independence to Colonial Countries and Peoples relating to the information from Non-Self-Governing Territories transmitted under Article 73 *e* of the Charter of the United Nations and the action taken by the Special Committee in respect of that information,

Having also examined the report of the Secretary-General,

Recalling its resolution 1970(XVIII) of 16 December 1963, in which it requested the Special Committee to study the information transmitted to the Secretary-General in accordance with Article 73 *e* of the Charter of the United Nations and to take such information fully into account in examining the situation with regard to the implementation of the Declaration on the Granting of Independence to Colonial Countries and Peoples, contained in General Assembly resolution 1514(XV) of 14 December 1960,

Recalling also its resolution 54/83 of 6 December 1999, in which it requested the Special Committee to continue to discharge the functions entrusted to it under resolution 1970(XVIII),

Stressing the importance of timely transmission by the administering Powers of adequate information under Article 73 *e* of the Charter, in particular in relation to the preparation by the Secretariat of the working papers on the Territories concerned,

1. *Approves* the chapter of the report of the Special Committee on the Situation with regard to the Implementation of the Declaration on the Granting of Independence to Colonial Countries and Peoples relating to the information from Non-Self-Governing Territories transmitted under Article 73 *e* of the Charter of the United Nations;

2. *Reaffirms* that, in the absence of a decision by the General Assembly itself that a Non-Self-Governing Territory has attained a full measure of self-government in terms of Chapter XI of the Charter, the administering Power concerned should continue to transmit information under Article 73 *e* of the Charter with respect to that Territory;

3. *Requests* the administering Powers concerned to transmit or continue to transmit to the Secretary-General the information prescribed in Article 73 *e* of the Charter, as well as the fullest possible information on political and constitutional developments in the Territories concerned, within a maximum period of six months following the expiration of the administrative year in those Territories;

4. *Requests* the Secretary-General to continue to ensure that adequate information is drawn from all available published sources in connection with the preparation of the working papers relating to the Territories concerned;

5. *Requests* the Special Committee to continue to discharge the functions entrusted to it under resolution 1970(XVIII), in accordance with established procedures, and to report thereon to the General Assembly at its fifty-sixth session.

RECORDED VOTE ON RESOLUTION 55/137:

In favour: Afghanistan, Algeria, Andorra, Antigua and Barbuda, Argentina, Armenia, Australia, Austria, Azerbaijan, Bahamas, Bahrain, Bangladesh, Barbados, Belarus, Belgium, Belize, Benin, Bhutan, Bolivia, Botswana, Brazil, Brunei Darussalam, Bulgaria, Burkina Faso, Burundi, Cambodia, Cameroon, Canada, Cape Verde, Chad, Chile, China, Colombia, Comoros, Costa Rica, Côte d'Ivoire, Croatia, Cuba, Cyprus, Czech Republic, Democratic People's Republic of Korea, Denmark, Djibouti, Dominican Republic, Ecuador, Egypt, El Salvador, Eritrea, Estonia, Ethiopia, Fiji, Finland, Gabon, Georgia, Germany, Ghana, Greece, Grenada, Guatemala, Guinea, Guyana, Haiti, Honduras, Hungary, Iceland, India, Indonesia, Iran, Ireland, Italy, Jamaica, Japan, Jordan, Kazakhstan, Kenya, Kuwait, Kyrgyzstan, Lao People's Democratic Republic, Latvia, Lebanon, Libyan Arab Jamahiriya, Liechtenstein, Lithuania, Luxembourg, Madagascar, Malaysia, Maldives, Mali, Malta, Marshall Islands, Mauritania, Mauritius, Mexico, Mongolia, Mozambique, Myanmar, Namibia, Nauru, Nepal, Netherlands, New Zealand, Nicaragua, Nigeria, Norway, Oman, Pakistan, Panama, Papua New Guinea, Paraguay, Peru, Philippines, Poland, Portugal, Qatar, Republic of Korea, Republic of Moldova, Romania, Russian Federation,

Saint Lucia, Samoa, San Marino, Saudi Arabia, Senegal, Sierra Leone, Singapore, Slovakia, Slovenia, Solomon Islands, South Africa, Spain, Sri Lanka, Sudan, Swaziland, Sweden, Syrian Arab Republic, Thailand, The former Yugoslav Republic of Macedonia, Togo, Tonga, Tunisia, Turkey, Uganda, Ukraine, United Arab Emirates, United Republic of Tanzania, Uruguay, Vanuatu, Venezuela, Viet Nam, Yemen, Yugoslavia, Zambia, Zimbabwe.

Against: None.

Abstaining: France, Israel, Micronesia, United Kingdom, United States.

Study and training

In response to General Assembly resolution 54/86 [YUN 1999, p. 533], the Secretary-General reported on offers by the following Member States of study and training scholarships for inhabitants of NSGTs during the period 13 August 1999 to 31 May 2000: Argentina, Australia, the Czech Republic, Malaysia and Qatar [A/55/81 & Add.1]. Forty-eight Member States and one non-member State had made similar offers over the years.

GENERAL ASSEMBLY ACTION

On 8 December [meeting 83], the General Assembly, on the recommendation of the Fourth Committee [A/55/577], adopted **resolution 55/140** without vote [agenda item 91].

Offers by Member States of study and training facilities for inhabitants of Non-Self-Governing Territories

The General Assembly,

Recalling its resolution 54/86 of 6 December 1999,

Having examined the report of the Secretary-General on offers by Member States of study and training facilities for inhabitants of Non-Self-Governing Territories, prepared pursuant to its resolution 845(IX) of 22 November 1954,

Conscious of the importance of promoting the educational advancement of the inhabitants of Non-Self-Governing Territories,

Strongly convinced that the continuation and expansion of offers of scholarships is essential in order to meet the increasing need of students from Non-Self-Governing Territories for educational and training assistance, and considering that students in those Territories should be encouraged to avail themselves of such offers,

1. *Takes note* of the report of the Secretary-General;

2. *Expresses its appreciation* to those Member States that have made scholarships available to the inhabitants of Non-Self-Governing Territories;

3. *Invites* all States to make or continue to make generous offers of study and training facilities to the inhabitants of those Territories that have not yet attained self-government or independence and, wherever possible, to provide travel funds to prospective students;

4. *Urges* the administering Powers to take effective measures to ensure the widespread and continuous dissemination in the Territories under their administration of information relating to offers of study and training facilities made by States and to provide all the necessary facilities to enable students to avail themselves of such offers;

5. *Requests* the Secretary-General to report to the General Assembly at its fifty-sixth session on the implementation of the present resolution;

6. *Draws the attention* of the Special Committee on the Situation with regard to the Implementation of the Declaration on the Granting of Independence to Colonial Countries and Peoples to the present resolution.

Visiting missions

In July, the Special Committee on decolonization considered the question of sending visiting missions to NSGTs [A/55/23]. It adopted a resolution by which it stressed the need for the periodic dispatch of such missions to help expedite the full implementation of the 1960 Declaration on decolonization, called on the administering Powers to receive those missions in the Territories under their administration, and asked its Chairman to enter into consultations with the administering Power of Guam to facilitate a mission to that Territory.

Subsequently, in two draft resolutions it recommended for adoption by the General Assembly, the Committee endorsed a number of conclusions and recommendations on the questions of Tokelau (see p. 563) and of the 11 island NSGTs (see p. 565).

Puerto Rico

In accordance with the 1998 decision of the Special Committee on decolonization concerning self-determination and independence for Puerto Rico [YUN 1998, p. 570], the Committee's Rapporteur, in a June report [A/AC.109/2000/L.3], described recent political developments and United States military and crime prevention activities in Puerto Rico, UN action and the views of the parties concerned on the question of Puerto Rico's political status.

Based on its usual practice, the Committee acceded to requests for hearings from representatives of a number of organizations, who presented their views on 12 July [A/55/23]. Subsequently, the Committee adopted a resolution without vote that reaffirmed the inalienable right of the people of Puerto Rico to self-determination and independence, expressed the hope that the United States would assume its responsibility to expedite a process towards the full exercise of that right, and requested the Rapporteur to report in 2001 on the resolution's implementation.

Territories under review

East Timor

On 5 July, the Special Committee on decolonization considered the issue of East Timor [A/55/23]. Before it was a June working paper mainly summarizing 1999 political developments in East Timor, together with related UN action in that Territory [A/AC.109/2000/12]. It further provided information on the creation of the National Consultative Council of East Timor as the primary mechanism for East Timorese representatives to participate in the decision-making process, and on the Secretary-General's visit to East Timor in February 2000 for meetings with the United Nations Transitional Administration in East Timor and local political leaders, as well as to Indonesia for meetings with President Abdurrahman Wahid and other government officials.

The Committee granted requests for hearings from a number of NGOs and heard a statement by Indonesia. It took account of the 27 June briefing of the Security Council by the Special Representative of the Secretary-General and Transitional Administrator for East Timor [meeting 4165], during which he stated that elections and, possibly, independence would take place in 2001, at some point between 30 August and December, depending on the attainment of the key benchmarks requested to be developed by the Secretary-General during his February visit to East Timor.

(For other political and security developments and human rights issues relating to East Timor, see PART ONE, Chapter IV, and PART TWO, Chapter III, respectively.)

Falkland Islands (Malvinas)

The Special Committee on decolonization considered the question of the Falkland Islands (Malvinas) on 11 July [A/55/23], when it examined a Secretariat working paper on constitutional and political developments and on the economic, social and educational conditions in that Territory [A/AC.109/2000/11 & Corr.1].

The paper reproduced a 3 January press communiqué from Argentina [A/54/701], reiterating its determination to recover the full exercise of sovereign power over the territory and maritime areas of the Malvinas by peaceful settlement and declaring its intention to continue dialogue with the United Kingdom to consolidate mutual trust and bilateral cooperation. Argentina believed that resumption of negotiations on the question of sovereignty would help to create a favourable framework for achieving a just and definitive settlement of their dispute. Also reproduced was the 23 March reply of the United Kingdom [A/54/811], stating it had no doubt about its sovereignty over the Falkland Islands and South Georgia and the South Sandwich Islands; it rejected Argentina's claims to sovereignty over those islands and the surrounding maritime areas and that the islands were under illegal occupation by the United Kingdom.

The Special Committee concluded its consideration of the question by adopting a resolution requesting Argentina and the United Kingdom to consolidate the current process of dialogue and cooperation through the resumption of negotiations in order to find, as soon as possible, a peaceful solution to their sovereignty dispute.

The President of Argentina, in concluding his statement before the Millennium Summit on 7 September [meeting 6] (see p. 47), noted that the United Nations, through several resolutions, had made similar requests of Argentina and the United Kingdom to end a colonial situation imposed by force in 1833. The United Kingdom replied [A/55/550] that it was pleased at the continued strengthening of bilateral relations with Argentina, as demonstrated by their 1999 joint statement [YUN 1999, p. 536]. However, the United Kingdom had a duty to respect and defend the right to self-determination of the people of the Falkland Islands, whose representatives had, on 11 July 2000, asked the Special Committee to recognize that they, like any other democratic people, were entitled to exercise that right, reiterating that they wanted to remain British and did not want to be part of Argentina. The United Kingdom remained committed to the joint statement despite its differences with Argentina on the subject of sovereignty. It was confident that both countries could build on that agreement in the spirit of reconciliation, cooperation and mutual interest.

By **decision 55/411** of 20 November, the Assembly deferred consideration of the item on the Falkland Islands (Malvinas) and included it in the provisional agenda of its fifty-sixth (2001) session.

Gibraltar

The Special Committee on decolonization took up the question of Gibraltar on 5 July [A/55/23]. Before it was a Secretariat working paper describing political developments and the economic, social and educational conditions in that Territory [A/AC.109/2000/10], and setting forth the positions of the United Kingdom (the administering Power), Gibraltar and Spain concerning Gibraltar's future status. The paper noted that, on 19 April, Spain and the United Kingdom successfully concluded discussions to resolve difficulties relating to Gibraltar authorities in the context of European Union and European Community instruments and related treaties. They also agreed that those arrangements did not imply any change in their respective positions on the question of Gibraltar or on the limits of that territory.

After hearing statements by Spain, the Chief Minister of Gibraltar and the Leader of the Opposition, the Special Committee decided to continue consideration of the question in 2001.

GENERAL ASSEMBLY ACTION

In December, the General Assembly, on the recommendation of the Fourth Committee [A/55/578], adopted **decision 55/427** without vote [agenda item 18].

Question of Gibraltar

At its 83rd plenary meeting, on 8 December 2000, the General Assembly, on the recommendation of the Special Political and Decolonization Committee (Fourth Committee), adopted the following text:

"The General Assembly, recalling its decision 54/423 of 6 December 1999, and recalling at the same time that the statement agreed to by the Governments of Spain and the United Kingdom of Great Britain and Northern Ireland at Brussels on 27 November 1984 stipulates, inter alia, the following:

'The establishment of a negotiating process aimed at overcoming all the differences between them over Gibraltar and at promoting cooperation on a mutually beneficial basis on economic, cultural, touristic, aviation, military and environmental matters. Both sides accept that the issues of sovereignty will be discussed in that process. The British Government will fully maintain its commitment to honour the wishes of the people of Gibraltar as set out in the preamble of the 1969 Constitution',

takes note of the fact that, as part of this process, the Ministers for Foreign Affairs of Spain and the United Kingdom of Great Britain and Northern Ireland hold annual meetings alternately in each capital, the most recent of which was held in London on 10 December 1997, and urges both Governments to continue their negotiations with the object of reaching a definitive solution to the problem of Gibraltar in the light of relevant resolutions of the General Assembly and in the spirit of the Charter of the United Nations."

On 18 December [S/2000/1205], Spain drew attention to the summary report of the exploratory hearing on Sierra Leone diamonds (see p. 204), containing references to Gibraltar as a country. Spain wished to make clear that Gibraltar was an NSGT administered by the United Kingdom, which was subject to the decolonization process and over which Spain maintained a claim of sovereignty.

New Caledonia

The Special Committee on decolonization considered the question of New Caledonia on 10 and 12 July [A/55/23]. It had before it a Secretariat working paper describing political and economic developments in that Territory [A/AC.109/2000/4].

In accordance with the 1998 Nouméa Accord on the Territory's future status [YUN 1998, p. 574], the transfer of powers from France (the administering Power) began in 2000 and was to end in 15 to 20 years, when the Territory would opt for either full independence or a form of associated statehood. New Caledonia's Economic and Social Council, composed of 39 members, of whom 28 represented professional organizations, labour unions and associations, was formally established on 2 February.

Ratification of the 1999 constitutional amendment on voter eligibility [YUN 1999, p. 538] by a special session of the French Congress (a joint sitting of the National Assembly and Senate), scheduled for 24 January 2000, had been postponed. The Front de libération nationale kanake socialiste (FLNKS) reiterated that the amendment was a key point of the Nouméa Accord and asked that a new date be set for the session.

In February, France announced that it was proceeding with a 1999 agreement [ibid.] to divest some of its Eramet holdings and to transfer them to a public organization to be formed by New Caledonia's three provinces. Forty per cent of the transferred assets would go to each of the North and South provinces and the remaining 20 per cent to the Loyalty Islands.

A later Secretariat working paper [A/AC.109/2001/14] reported that, in July, elections were repeated in the Loyalty Islands after the French State Council ruled that there had been irregularities during the 1999 elections [YUN 1999, p. 538]. The results confirmed the majority held by FLNKS in the Loyalty Islands provincial assembly.

The opposing positions of the Rassemblement pour la Calédonie dans la République (RPCR) and FLNKS over their interpretation of the concept of "collegiality" in government matters remained in place throughout the year. On 2 May, representatives of both parties met with the French Secretary of State for Overseas Territories for the first meeting of the Committee of Signatories of the Nouméa Accord. While both delegations expressed satisfaction at the establishment of new institutions, each restated their differing understanding of the idea of collegial government. The meeting also discussed the need to agree on general policy and the application of the Nouméa Accord provisions and the 1999 organic law on Kanak identity and culture; training policies for secondary school students and establishment of the new "cadres avenir" (managers of the future) project; external relations; and the drafting of a special agreement on the status of people from Wallis and Futuna living in New Caledonia. The meeting also agreed on the importance of developing trade and other relations within the Pacific region and decided to establish a steering group on external relations to coordinate action by the State, New Caledonia and the provinces.

GENERAL ASSEMBLY ACTION

On 8 December [meeting 83], the General Assembly, on the recommendation of the Fourth Committee [A/55/578], adopted **resolution 55/142** without vote [agenda item 18].

Question of New Caledonia

The General Assembly,

Having considered the question of New Caledonia,

Having examined the chapter of the report of the Special Committee on the Situation with regard to the Implementation of the Declaration on the Granting of Independence to Colonial Countries and Peoples relating to New Caledonia,

Reaffirming the right of peoples to self-determination as enshrined in the Charter of the United Nations,

Recalling its resolutions 1514(XV) of 14 December 1960 and 1541(XV) of 15 December 1960,

Noting the importance of the positive measures being pursued in New Caledonia by the French authorities, in cooperation with all sectors of the population, to promote political, economic and social development in the Territory, including measures in the area of environmental protection and action with respect to drug abuse and trafficking, in order to provide a framework for its peaceful progress to self-determination,

Noting also, in this context, the importance of equitable economic and social development as well as continued dialogue among the parties involved in New Caledonia in the preparation of an act of self-determination of New Caledonia,

Noting with satisfaction the intensification of contacts between New Caledonia and neighbouring countries of the South Pacific region,

1. *Welcomes* the significant developments that have taken place in New Caledonia as exemplified by the signing of the Nouméa Accord of 5 May 1998 between the representatives of New Caledonia and the Government of France;

2. *Urges* all the parties involved, in the interest of all the people of New Caledonia, to maintain, in the framework of the Nouméa Accord, their dialogue in a spirit of harmony;

3. *Notes* the relevant provisions of the Nouméa Accord aimed at taking more broadly into account the Kanak identity in the political and social organization of New Caledonia, and also those provisions of the Accord relating to control of immigration and protection of local employment;

4. *Also notes* the relevant provisions of the Nouméa Accord to the effect that New Caledonia may become a member or associate member of certain international organizations, such as international organizations in the Pacific region, the United Nations, the United Nations Educational, Scientific and Cultural Organization and the International Labour Organization, according to their regulations;

5. *Further notes* the agreement between the signatories of the Nouméa Accord that the progress made in

the emancipation process shall be brought to the attention of the United Nations;

6. *Welcomes* the fact that the administering Power invited to New Caledonia, at the time the new institutions were established, a mission of information that comprised representatives of countries of the Pacific region;

7. *Calls upon* the administering Power to transmit information regarding the political, economic and social situation of New Caledonia to the Secretary-General;

8. *Invites* all the parties involved to continue promoting a framework for the peaceful progress of the Territory towards an act of self-determination in which all options are open and which would safeguard the rights of all New Caledonians according to the letter and the spirit of the Nouméa Accord, which is based on the principle that it is for the populations of New Caledonia to choose how to control their destiny;

9. *Welcomes* measures that have been taken to strengthen and diversify the New Caledonian economy in all fields, and encourages further such measures in accordance with the spirit of the Matignon and Nouméa Accords;

10. *Also welcomes* the importance attached by the parties to the Matignon and Nouméa Accords to greater progress in housing, employment, training, education and health care in New Caledonia;

11. *Acknowledges* the contribution of the Melanesian Cultural Centre to the protection of the indigenous culture of New Caledonia;

12. *Notes* the positive initiatives aimed at protecting the natural environment of New Caledonia, notably the "Zonéco" operation designed to map and evaluate marine resources within the economic zone of New Caledonia, including preliminary studies relating to hydrocarbons;

13. *Acknowledges* the close links between New Caledonia and the peoples of the South Pacific and the positive actions being taken by the French and territorial authorities to facilitate the further development of those links, including the development of closer relations with the countries members of the Pacific Islands Forum;

14. *Welcomes*, in this regard, the accession by New Caledonia to the status of observer in the Pacific Islands Forum, continuing high-level visits to New Caledonia by delegations from countries of the Pacific region and high-level visits by delegations from New Caledonia to countries members of the Pacific Islands Forum;

15. *Decides* to keep under continuous review the process unfolding in New Caledonia as a result of the signing of the Nouméa Accord;

16. *Requests* the Special Committee on the Situation with regard to the Implementation of the Declaration on the Granting of Independence to Colonial Countries and Peoples to continue to examine the question and to report thereon to the General Assembly at its fifty-sixth session.

Tokelau

The Special Committee on decolonization considered, on 10 and 12 July, the question of Tokelau (the three small atolls of Nukunonu, Fakaofo and Atafu in the South Pacific), administered by New Zealand [A/55/23]. A Secretariat working paper detailed progress in the Territory's constitutional and political developments, as well as economic and social conditions, and set out the positions of the administering Power and the people of Tokelau concerning the future status of the Territory [A/AC.109/2000/5].

According to the administering Power, the organs of national self-government had progressively been given functions and powers previously exercised by New Zealand and there was a growing readiness by Tokelau's traditional leaders to join in the building of new structures to meet the Territory's needs. At meetings held with traditional leaders in the week of 6 March, senior elected leaders expressed readiness to embark fully on the Modern House of Tokelau project [YUN 1998, p. 575]. The 2000-2001 Plan of Action, undertaken in collaboration with New Zealand, aimed to integrate traditional decision-making processes with modern advice; set out the benefits; describe the programme and resources required to build the Modern House, indicating funding sources (New Zealand and UNDP) within the 2000-2001 budget; show how the delivery of public services could be changed by redistributing the workforce among the three Taupulega (Councils of Elders) and the nation; enhance public understanding of the work of the General Fono's (the national representative body of Tokelau) Special Constitution Committee to advance the goal of self-government; and underline the scope for each atoll to proceed in ways to reflect its different characteristics.

New Zealand currently had legislation in place to enable responsibility for the Tokelau Public Service to be passed from the State Services Commission in New Zealand to Tokelau, the timing to be set by mutual agreement as soon as the Territory had established a suitable employment framework, but not later then 30 June 2001.

A later Secretariat working paper [A/AC.109/2001/5] reported that the Modern House project was being overseen by a Joint Committee on management structure comprising Tokelau's six senior elected leaders, the Public Service Commissioner and the Administrator. A transition team of Tokelau heads of departments and a number of New Zealand–based specialists was also set up to provide, among other things, project oversight, management, coordination, planning and evaluation. In September, a discussion document was presented to the three Taupulega and the Tokelauans, who endorsed the key point that the Taupulega, the traditional foundation of the nation, should be the basis of a future Government. In November, the Joint Committee agreed on a programme that involved good governance, including a governance framework, constitutional development, management and operational structures and employer responsibility; capacity development, including the review of national and village administrations, development of a management support training workshop, identification of training needs and development of appropriate programmes; the "Friends of Tokelau", an organization to link outside individuals and organizations into Tokelau's development; and sustainable national and village development plans. The General Fono endorsed a Joint Committee statement noting the readiness of the three villages to embark on the Modern House project, Nukunonu's wish to start immediately, and the Committee's request that the transition team proceed, recognizing the needs of each village and the adjustments required to accomplish the Modern House. In December, UNDP sponsored a workshop on management support training to provide training in project planning and management, writing skills and financial management, and to assess further training needs.

GENERAL ASSEMBLY ACTION

On 8 December [meeting 83], the General Assembly, on the recommendation of the Fourth Committee [A/55/578], adopted **resolution 55/143** without vote [agenda item 18].

Question of Tokelau

The General Assembly,

Having considered the question of Tokelau,

Having examined the chapter of the report of the Special Committee on the Situation with regard to the Implementation of the Declaration on the Granting of Independence to Colonial Countries and Peoples relating to the question of Tokelau,

Recalling the solemn declaration on the future status of Tokelau, delivered by the *Ulu-o-Tokelau* (the highest authority on Tokelau) on 30 July 1994, that an act of self-determination in Tokelau is now under active consideration, together with the constitution of a self-governing Tokelau, and that the present preference of Tokelau is for a status of free association with New Zealand,

Recalling also its resolution 1514(XV) of 14 December 1960, containing the Declaration on the Granting of Independence to Colonial Countries and Peoples, and all resolutions and decisions of the United Nations relating to Non-Self-Governing Territories, in particular General Assembly resolution 54/89 of 6 December 1999,

Recalling further the emphasis placed in the solemn declaration on the terms of Tokelau's intended free association relationship with New Zealand, including the expectation that the form of help that Tokelau could continue to expect from New Zealand in promoting the well-being of its people, besides its external interests, would be clearly established in the framework of that relationship,

Noting with appreciation the continuing exemplary cooperation of New Zealand as the administering Power

with regard to the work of the Special Committee relating to Tokelau and its readiness to permit access by United Nations visiting missions to the Territory,

Noting also with appreciation the collaborative contribution to the development of Tokelau by New Zealand and the specialized agencies and other organizations of the United Nations system, in particular the United Nations Development Programme and the International Telecommunication Union,

Recalling the dispatch in 1994 of a United Nations visiting mission to Tokelau,

Noting that, as a small island Territory, Tokelau exemplifies the situation of most remaining Non-Self-Governing Territories,

Noting also that, as a case study pointing to successful decolonization, Tokelau has wider significance for the United Nations as it seeks to complete its work in decolonization,

1. *Notes* that Tokelau remains firmly committed to the development of self-government and to an act of self-determination that would result in Tokelau assuming a status in accordance with the options on future status for Non-Self-Governing Territories contained in principle VI of the annex to General Assembly resolution 1541(XV) of 15 December 1960;

2. *Also notes* the desire of Tokelau to move at its own pace towards an act of self-determination;

3. *Further notes* the inauguration in 1999 of a national Government based on village elections by universal adult suffrage;

4. *Acknowledges* the participation of the *Ulu-o-Tokelau* in the Pacific regional seminar, held at Majuro, from 16 to 18 May 2000, and his account of how the Modern House of Tokelau project, in both its governance and its economic development dimensions, is seen by Tokelauans as the means to achieving its act of self-determination;

5. *Welcomes* the statement of the Council of Faipule of July 2000 that, following consultations in each village and a meeting of the General Fono in June 2000, full and overwhelming support has been given to the implementation of the project;

6. *Notes* the confirmation by the Council of Faipule that in the twelve months from July 2000 there will be significant movement in implementing the project, in conjunction with New Zealand;

7. *Acknowledges* that New Zealand has committed substantial additional funding to the project in 2000-2001, and its intention to collaborate with Tokelau in ways that can produce a significant momentum;

8. *Notes* the changes being made in arrangements for the delivery of public services, within an environment in which the institution of the village is truly recognized as the foundation of the nation, and the expectation that the New Zealand State Services Commissioner may be able to withdraw from his role as employer of the Tokelau Public Service at a time to be set by mutual agreement when Tokelau has established a suitable local employment framework;

9. *Also notes* that the constitution of a self-governing Tokelau will continue to develop as a part and as a consequence of the building of the Modern House of Tokelau, and that both have national and international importance for Tokelau;

10. *Acknowledges* Tokelau's need for reassurance, given that local resources cannot adequately cover the

material side of self-determination, and the ongoing responsibility of Tokelau's external partners to assist Tokelau in balancing its desire to be self-reliant to the greatest extent possible with its need for external assistance;

11. *Notes* the special challenge inherent in the situation of Tokelau, among the smallest of the small Territories, and how a Territory's exercise of its inalienable right to self-determination may be brought closer, as in the case of Tokelau, by the meeting of that challenge in innovative ways;

12. *Welcomes* the assurance of the Government of New Zealand that it will meet its obligations to the United Nations with respect to Tokelau and abide by the freely expressed wishes of the people of Tokelau with regard to their future status;

13. *Calls upon* the administering Power and United Nations agencies to continue their assistance to Tokelau, as it further develops its economy and governance structures within the context of its ongoing constitutional evolution;

14. *Requests* the Special Committee on the Situation with regard to the Implementation of the Declaration on the Granting of Independence to Colonial Countries and Peoples to continue to examine the question and to report thereon to the General Assembly at its fifty-sixth session.

Western Sahara

The Special Committee on decolonization considered the question of Western Sahara on 5 July [A/55/23]. A Secretariat working paper [A/AC.109/2000/7 & Corr.1] provided details on the Secretary-General's good offices with the parties concerned and action taken by the Security Council and the General Assembly (see also PART ONE, Chapter II). The Special Committee transmitted the relevant documentation to the Assembly's fifty-fifth (2000) session to facilitate the Fourth Committee's consideration of the question. The Secretary-General's report was submitted to the Assembly in August [A/55/303].

Island Territories

The Special Committee on decolonization [A/55/23] considered working papers prepared by the Secretariat on American Samoa [A/AC.109/2000/3], Anguilla [A/AC.109/2000/15], Bermuda [A/AC.109/2000/13], the British Virgin Islands [A/AC.109/2000/18], the Cayman Islands [A/AC.109/2000/14], Guam [A/AC.109/2000/6], Montserrat [A/AC.109/2000/9], Pitcairn [A/AC.109/2000/2], St. Helena [A/AC.109/2000/8], the Turks and Caicos Islands [A/AC.109/2000/16] and the United States Virgin Islands [A/AC.109/2000/17 & Corr.1], describing political developments and economic and social conditions in each of those 11 island Territories. On 20 July, the Committee approved a two-part consolidated draft resolution recommended for adoption by the General Assembly (see below).

GENERAL ASSEMBLY ACTION

On 8 December [meeting 83], the General Assembly, on the recommendation of the Fourth Committee [A/55/578], adopted **resolutions 55/144 A** and **B** without vote [agenda item 18].

Questions of American Samoa, Anguilla, Bermuda, the British Virgin Islands, the Cayman Islands, Guam, Montserrat, Pitcairn, St. Helena, the Turks and Caicos Islands and the United States Virgin Islands

A
General

The General Assembly,

Having considered the questions of American Samoa, Anguilla, Bermuda, the British Virgin Islands, the Cayman Islands, Guam, Montserrat, Pitcairn, St. Helena, the Turks and Caicos Islands and the United States Virgin Islands, hereinafter referred to as "the Territories",

Having examined the relevant chapter of the report of the Special Committee on the Situation with regard to the Implementation of the Declaration on the Granting of Independence to Colonial Countries and Peoples,

Recalling its resolution 1514(XV) of 14 December 1960, containing the Declaration on the Granting of Independence to Colonial Countries and Peoples, and all resolutions and decisions of the United Nations relating to those Territories, including, in particular, the resolutions adopted by the General Assembly at its fifty-fourth session on the individual Territories covered by the present resolution,

Recognizing that the specific characteristics and the sentiments of the peoples of the Territories require flexible, practical and innovative approaches to the options of self-determination, without any prejudice to territorial size, geographical location, size of population or natural resources,

Recalling its resolution 1541(XV) of 15 December 1960, containing the principles that should guide Member States in determining whether or not an obligation exists to transmit the information called for under Article 73 *e* of the Charter of the United Nations,

Expressing its concern that even forty years after the adoption of the Declaration there still remain a number of Non-Self-Governing Territories,

Acknowledging the significant achievements by the international community towards the eradication of colonialism in accordance with the Declaration, and conscious of the importance of continuing effective implementation of the Declaration, taking into account the target set by the United Nations to eradicate colonialism by the year 2000 and the plan of action for the International Decade for the Eradication of Colonialism,

Noting the positive constitutional developments in some Non-Self-Governing Territories about which the Special Committee has received information, while also acknowledging the need for recognition to be given to expressions of self-determination by the peoples of the Territories consistent with practice under the Charter,

Recognizing that in the decolonization process there is no alternative to the principle of self-determination as enunciated by the General Assembly in its resolutions 1514(XV), 1541(XV) and other resolutions,

Welcoming the stated position of the Government of the United Kingdom of Great Britain and Northern Ireland that it continues to take seriously its obligations under the Charter to develop self-government in the dependent Territories and, in cooperation with the locally elected Governments, to ensure that their constitutional frameworks continue to meet the wishes of the people, and the emphasis that it is ultimately for the peoples of the Territories to decide their future status,

Welcoming also the stated position of the Government of the United States of America that it supports fully the principles of decolonization and takes seriously its obligations under the Charter to promote to the utmost the well-being of the inhabitants of the Territories under United States administration,

Aware of the special circumstances of the geographical location and economic conditions of each Territory, and bearing in mind the necessity of promoting economic stability and diversifying and strengthening further the economies of the respective Territories as a matter of priority,

Conscious of the particular vulnerability of the Territories to natural disasters and environmental degradation and, in this connection, bearing in mind Agenda 21, the Yokohama Strategy for a Safer World: Guidelines for Natural Disaster Prevention, Preparedness and Mitigation, containing the Principles, the Strategy and the Plan of Action, the Programme of Action for the Sustainable Development of Small Island Developing States and other relevant world conferences,

Aware of the usefulness both to the Territories and to the Special Committee of the participation of appointed and elected representatives of the Territories in the work of the Special Committee,

Convinced that the wishes and aspirations of the peoples of the Territories should continue to guide the development of their future political status and that referendums, free and fair elections and other forms of popular consultation play an important role in ascertaining the wishes and aspirations of the people,

Convinced also that any negotiations to determine the status of a Territory must not be held without the active involvement and participation of the people of that Territory,

Recognizing that all available options for self-determination of the Territories are valid as long as they are in accordance with the freely expressed wishes of the peoples concerned and in conformity with the clearly defined principles contained in resolutions 1514(XV), 1541(XV) and other resolutions of the General Assembly,

Mindful that United Nations visiting missions provide an effective means of ascertaining the situation in the Territories, and considering that the possibility of sending further visiting missions to the Territories at an appropriate time and in consultation with the administering Powers should be kept under review,

Noting that the Special Committee held a Pacific regional seminar at Majuro from 16 to 18 May 2000 to hear the views of the representatives of the Territories, as well as Governments and organizations in the region, in order to review the political, economic and social conditions in the Territories,

Mindful that, in order for the Special Committee to enhance its understanding of the political status of the peoples of the Territories and to fulfil its mandate effectively, it is important for it to be apprised by the administering Powers and to receive information from other appropriate sources, including the representatives of the Territories, concerning the wishes and aspirations of the peoples of the Territories,

Mindful also in this connection that the Special Committee regards the holding of regional seminars in the Caribbean and Pacific regions and at Headquarters and other venues, with the active participation of representatives of the Non-Self-Governing Territories, as a helpful means to fulfil its mandate, while recognizing the need for reviewing the role of those seminars in the context of a United Nations programme for ascertaining the political status of the Territories,

Mindful further that some Territories have not had any United Nations visiting mission for a long period of time and that no such visiting missions have been sent to some of the Territories,

Noting with appreciation the contribution to the development of some Territories by specialized agencies and other organizations of the United Nations system, in particular the United Nations Development Programme, and regional institutions such as the Caribbean Development Bank,

Noting that some territorial Governments have made efforts towards achieving the highest standards of financial supervision, but that some others have been listed by the Organisation for Economic Cooperation and Development as having met the criteria of the Organisation defining a tax haven, and noting that some territorial Governments have expressed concern about insufficient dialogue between them and the Organisation,

Noting also the ongoing efforts of the Special Committee in carrying out a critical review of its work with the aim of making appropriate and constructive recommendations and decisions to attain its objectives in accordance with its mandate,

1. *Reaffirms* the inalienable right of the peoples of the Territories to self-determination, including, if they so wish, independence, in conformity with the Charter of the United Nations and with General Assembly resolution 1514(XV), containing the Declaration on the Granting of Independence to Colonial Countries and Peoples;

2. *Reaffirms also* that it is ultimately for the peoples of the Territories themselves to determine freely their future political status in accordance with the relevant provisions of the Charter, the Declaration and the relevant resolutions of the General Assembly, and in that connection calls upon the administering Powers, in cooperation with the territorial Governments, to facilitate programmes of political education in the Territories in order to foster an awareness among the people of their right to self-determination in conformity with the legitimate political status options, based on the principles clearly defined in General Assembly resolution 1541(XV);

3. *Requests* the administering Powers to transmit to the Secretary-General information called for under Article 73 *e* of the Charter and other updated information and reports, including reports on the wishes and aspirations of the peoples of the Territories regarding

their future political status as expressed in fair and free referendums and other forms of popular consultation, as well as the results of any informed and democratic processes consistent with practice under the Charter that indicate the clear and freely expressed wish of the people to change the existing status of the Territories;

4. *Stresses* the importance for the Special Committee on the Situation with regard to the Implementation of the Declaration on the Granting of Independence to Colonial Countries and Peoples to be apprised of the views and wishes of the peoples of the Territories and to enhance its understanding of their conditions;

5. *Reaffirms* that United Nations visiting missions to the Territories at an appropriate time and in consultation with the administering Powers are an effective means of ascertaining the situation in the Territories, and requests the administering Powers and the elected representatives of the peoples of the Territories to assist the Special Committee in this regard;

6. *Reaffirms also* the responsibility of the administering Powers under the Charter to promote the economic and social development and to preserve the cultural identity of the Territories, and recommends that priority continue to be given, in consultation with the territorial Governments concerned, to the strengthening and diversification of their respective economies;

7. *Requests* the administering Powers, in consultation with the peoples of the Territories, to take all necessary measures to protect and conserve the environment of the Territories under their administration against any environmental degradation, and requests the specialized agencies concerned to continue to monitor environmental conditions in those Territories;

8. *Calls upon* the administering Powers, in cooperation with the respective territorial Governments, to continue to take all necessary measures to counter problems related to drug trafficking, money-laundering and other offences;

9. *Notes with concern* that the plan of action for the International Decade for the Eradication of Colonialism cannot be concluded by the year 2000;

10. *Calls upon* the administering Powers to enter into constructive dialogue with the Special Committee before the fifty-sixth session of the General Assembly to develop a framework for the implementation of the provisions of Article 73 *e* of the Charter and the Declaration on the Granting of Independence to Colonial Countries and Peoples for the period beyond 2000;

11. *Notes* the particular circumstances that prevail in the Territories concerned, and encourages the political evolution in them towards self-determination;

12. *Urges* Member States to contribute to the efforts of the United Nations to usher in the twenty-first century in a world free of colonialism, and calls upon them to continue to give their full support to the Special Committee in its endeavours towards that noble goal;

13. *Invites* the specialized agencies and other organizations of the United Nations system to initiate or to continue to take all necessary measures to accelerate progress in the social and economic life of the Territories, and calls for closer cooperation between the Special Committee and the Economic and Social Council in the furtherance of the provision of assistance to the Territories;

14. *Takes note* of statements made by the elected representatives of the Territories concerned emphasizing their willingness to cooperate with all international efforts aimed at preventing abuse of the international financial system and to promote regulatory environments with highly selective licensing procedures, robust supervisory practices and well-established anti-money-laundering regimes;

15. *Calls* for an enhanced and constructive dialogue between the Organisation for Economic Cooperation and Development and the concerned territorial Governments with a view to bringing about the changes needed to meet the highest standards of transparency and information exchange in order to facilitate the removal of those Non-Self-Governing Territories from the list of jurisdictions classified as tax havens, and requests the administering Power to assist those Territories in resolving this matter;

16. *Requests* the Secretary-General to report to the General Assembly on the implementation of resolutions concerning decolonization adopted since the declaration of the International Decade for the Eradication of Colonialism;

17. *Requests* the Special Committee to continue to examine the question of the small Territories and to report thereon to the General Assembly at its fifty-sixth session with recommendations on appropriate ways to assist the peoples of the Territories in exercising their right to self-determination.

B
Individual territories
The General Assembly,
Referring to resolution A above,

1. *American Samoa*
Taking note of the report by the administering Power that most American Samoan leaders express satisfaction with the island's present relationship with the United States of America,

Taking note with interest of the statement made and the information on the political and economic situation in American Samoa provided by the Governor of American Samoa to the Pacific regional seminar held at Nadi, Fiji, from 16 to 18 June 1998,

Noting that the territorial Government continues to have significant financial, budgetary and internal control problems and that the Territory's deficit and financial condition are compounded by the high demand for government services from the rapidly growing population, a limited economic and tax base and recent natural disasters,

Noting also that the Territory, similar to isolated communities with limited funds, continues to experience a lack of adequate medical and other infrastructural facilities,

Aware of the efforts of the territorial Government to control and reduce expenditures while continuing its programme of expanding and diversifying the local economy,

1. *Requests* the administering Power, bearing in mind the views of the people of the Territory ascertained through a democratic process, to keep the Secretary-General informed of the wishes and aspirations of the people regarding their future political status;

2. *Calls upon* the administering Power to continue to assist the territorial Government in the economic and social development of the Territory, including measures to rebuild financial management capabilities and strengthen other functions of the territorial Government;

3. *Welcomes* the invitation extended by the Governor of American Samoa to the Special Committee on the Situation with regard to the Implementation of the Declaration on the Granting of Independence to Colonial Countries and Peoples to send a visiting mission to the Territory;

II. *Anguilla*

Conscious of the commitment of both the Government of Anguilla and the administering Power to a new and closer policy of dialogue and partnership through the Strategic Country Programme 2000-2003,

Aware of the efforts of the Government of Anguilla to continue to develop the Territory as a viable and well-regulated offshore financial centre for investors by enacting modern company and trust laws, as well as partnership and insurance legislation, and computerizing the company registry system,

Noting the need for continued cooperation between the administering Power and the territorial Government in tackling the problems of drug trafficking and money-laundering,

Noting also that general elections were held on 3 March 2000, resulting in a new coalition government in the House of Assembly,

1. *Requests* the administering Power, bearing in mind the views of the people of the Territory ascertained through a democratic process, to keep the Secretary-General informed of the wishes and aspirations of the people regarding their future political status;

2. *Calls upon* the administering Power and all States, organizations and United Nations agencies to continue to assist the Territory in its social and economic development;

3. *Welcomes* the country cooperation framework of the United Nations Development Programme for the period 1997-1999 currently being implemented following consultations with the territorial Government and key development partners in the United Nations system and the donor community;

4. *Also welcomes* the assessment by the United Nations Development Programme that the Territory has made considerable progress in the domain of sustainable human development and in its sound management and preservation of the environment, which has been incorporated into the National Tourism Plan;

5. *Further welcomes* the assessment by the Caribbean Development Bank in its 1999 report on the Territory that, despite economic contraction in the first quarter, the economy rebounded to reach 6 per cent growth during 1999;

III. *Bermuda*

Noting the results of the independence referendum held on 16 August 1995, and conscious of the different viewpoints of the political parties of the Territory on the future status of the Territory,

Noting also the functioning of the democratic process and the smooth transition of government in November 1998,

Noting further the comments made by the administering Power in its recently published White Paper on Partnership for Progress and Prosperity: Britain and the Overseas Territories,

1. *Requests* the administering Power, bearing in mind the views of the people of the Territory ascertained through a democratic process, to keep the Secretary-General informed of the wishes and aspirations of the people regarding their future political status;

2. *Calls upon* the administering Power to continue to work with the Territory for its socio-economic development;

3. *Requests* the administering Power to elaborate, in consultation with the territorial Government, programmes specifically intended to alleviate the economic, social and environmental consequences of the closure of the military bases and installations of the United States of America in the Territory;

IV. *British Virgin Islands*

Noting the completion of a constitutional review in the Territory and the coming into force of the amended Constitution, and noting also the results of the general elections held on 17 May 1999,

Noting also the results of the constitutional review of 1993-1994, which made it clear that a prerequisite to independence must be a constitutionally expressed wish by the people as a result of a referendum,

Taking note of the statement made in 1995 by the Chief Minister of the British Virgin Islands that the Territory was ready for constitutional and political advancement towards full internal self-government and that the administering Power should assist through the gradual transfer of power to elected territorial representatives,

Noting that the Territory is emerging as one of the world's leading offshore financial centres,

Noting also the need for continued cooperation between the administering Power and the territorial Government in countering drug trafficking and money-laundering,

Noting further that the Territory commemorated its annual British Virgin Islands–United States Virgin Islands Friendship Day on 27 May 2000 in official ceremonies in Tortola,

1. *Requests* the administering Power, bearing in mind the views of the people of the Territory ascertained through a democratic process, to keep the Secretary-General informed of the wishes and aspirations of the people regarding their future political status;

2. *Requests* the administering Power, the specialized agencies and other organizations of the United Nations system and all financial institutions to continue to provide assistance to the Territory for socio-economic development and the development of human resources, bearing in mind the vulnerability of the Territory to external factors;

3. *Welcomes* the assessment by the Caribbean Development Bank in its 1999 report that the Territory enjoyed continued expansion of the financial services sector and tourism industries, and also welcomes the provision to the Territory of 21.1 million United States dollars in technical assistance loans by the Bank, in-

cluding 19.9 million dollars to assist with the financing of the Beef Island Airport;

V. *Cayman Islands*

Noting the constitutional review of 1992-1993, according to which the population of the Cayman Islands expressed the sentiment that the existing relations with the United Kingdom of Great Britain and Northern Ireland should be maintained and that the current status of the Territory should not be altered,

Aware that the Territory has one of the highest per capita incomes in the region, a stable political climate and virtually no unemployment,

Noting the actions taken by the territorial Government to implement its localization programme to promote increased participation by the local population in the decision-making process in the Cayman Islands,

Noting with concern the vulnerability of the Territory to drug trafficking, money-laundering and related activities,

Noting the measures taken by the authorities to deal with those problems,

Noting also that the Territory has emerged as one of the world's leading offshore financial centres,

Noting further the approval by the Cayman Islands Legislative Assembly of the Territory's Vision 2008 Development Plan, which aims to promote development that is consistent with the aims and values of Caymanian society,

1. *Requests* the administering Power, bearing in mind the views of the people of the Territory ascertained through a democratic process, to keep the Secretary-General informed of the wishes and aspirations of the people regarding their future political status;

2. *Requests* the administering Power, the specialized agencies and other organizations of the United Nations system to continue to provide the territorial Government with all required expertise to enable it to achieve its socio-economic aims;

3. *Calls upon* the administering Power and the territorial Government to continue to cooperate to counter problems related to money-laundering, smuggling of funds and other related crimes, as well as drug trafficking;

4. *Requests* the administering Power, in consultation with the territorial Government, to continue to facilitate the expansion of the current programme of securing employment for the local population, in particular at the decision-making level;

5. *Welcomes* the implementation of the country cooperation framework of the United Nations Development Programme for the Territory, which is designed to ascertain national development priorities and need for United Nations assistance;

VI. *Guam*

Recalling that, in the referendum held in 1987, the registered and eligible voters of Guam endorsed a draft Guam Commonwealth Act that would establish a new framework for relations between the Territory and the administering Power, providing for a greater measure of internal self-government for Guam and recognition of the right of the Chamorro people of Guam to self-determination for the Territory,

Recalling also its resolution 1514(XV) of 14 December 1960, containing the Declaration on the Granting of Independence to Colonial Countries and Peoples, and all resolutions and decisions of the United Nations relating to Non-Self-Governing Territories, in particular General Assembly resolutions 54/90 A and B of 6 December 1999,

Recalling further the requests by the elected representatives and non-governmental organizations of the Territory that Guam not be removed from the list of Non-Self-Governing Territories with which the Special Committee on the Situation with regard to the Implementation of the Declaration on the Granting of Independence to Colonial Countries and Peoples is concerned, pending the self-determination of the Chamorro people and taking into account their legitimate rights and interests,

Aware that negotiations between the administering Power and the territorial Government on the draft Guam Commonwealth Act are no longer continuing and that Guam has established a process for a self-determination vote by the eligible Chamorro voters,

Cognizant that the administering Power continues to implement its programme of transferring surplus federal land to the Government of Guam,

Noting that the people of the Territory have called for reform in the programme of the administering Power with respect to the thorough, unconditional and expeditious transfer of land property to the people of Guam,

Conscious that immigration into Guam has resulted in the indigenous Chamorros becoming a minority in their homeland,

Aware of the potential for diversifying and developing the economy of Guam through commercial fishing and agriculture and other viable activities,

Noting the proposed closing and realigning of four United States Navy installations on Guam and the request for the establishment of a transition period to develop some of the closed facilities as commercial enterprises,

Recalling the dispatch in 1979 of a United Nations visiting mission to the Territory, and noting the recommendation of the 1996 Pacific regional seminar for sending a visiting mission to Guam,

Noting with interest the statements made and the information on the political and economic situation in Guam provided by the representatives of the Territory to the Pacific regional seminar, held at Majuro from 16 to 18 May 2000,

1. *Requests* the administering Power to work with Guam's Commission on Decolonization for the Implementation and Exercise of Chamorro Self-Determination with a view to facilitating the decolonization of Guam and to keep the Secretary-General informed of progress to that end;

2. *Calls upon* the administering Power to take into consideration the expressed will of the Chamorro people as supported by Guam voters in the referendum of 1987 and as provided for in Guam law, encourages the administering Power and the territorial Government of Guam to enter into negotiations on the matter, and requests the administering Power to inform the Secretary-General of progress to that end;

3. *Requests* the administering Power to continue to assist the elected territorial Government in achieving its political, economic and social goals;

4. *Also requests* the administering Power, in co-operation with the territorial Government, to continue to transfer land to the original landowners of the Territory;

5. *Further requests* the administering Power to continue to recognize and respect the political rights and the cultural and ethnic identity of the Chamorro people of Guam, and to take all necessary measures to respond to the concerns of the territorial Government with regard to the question of immigration;

6. *Requests* the administering Power to cooperate in establishing programmes specifically intended to promote the sustainable development of economic activities and enterprises, noting the special role of the Chamorro people in the development of Guam;

7. *Also requests* the administering Power to continue to support appropriate measures by the territorial Government aimed at promoting growth in commercial fishing and agricultural and other viable activities;

VII. *Montserrat*

Taking note with interest of the statements made and the information on the political and economic situation in Montserrat provided by the elected representatives of the Territory to the Caribbean regional seminar, held at Castries, from 25 to 27 May 1999,

Taking note of the statement made by the Chief Minister of Montserrat on 22 May 1998 on the occasion of the observance of the Week of Solidarity with the Peoples of All Colonial Territories Fighting for Freedom, Independence and Human Rights,

Noting that the last visiting mission to the Territory was dispatched in 1982,

Noting also the functioning of a democratic process in Montserrat and that general elections were held in the Territory in November 1996,

Taking note of the reported statement of the Chief Minister that his preference was for independence within a political union with the Organization of Eastern Caribbean States and that self-reliance was more of a priority than independence,

Noting with concern the dire consequences of the eruptions of the Montsoufriere volcano, which led to the evacuation of three quarters of the population of the Territory to safe areas of the island and to areas outside the Territory, in particular Antigua and Barbuda and the United Kingdom of Great Britain and Northern Ireland, and which continue to have a negative impact upon the economy of the island,

Noting the efforts of the administering Power and the territorial Government to meet the emergency situation caused by the volcanic eruptions, including the implementation of a wide range of contingency measures for both the private and the public sectors in Montserrat,

Noting also the coordinated response measures taken by the United Nations Development Programme and the assistance of the United Nations disaster management team,

Noting with concern that a number of the inhabitants of the Territory continue to live in shelters because of volcanic activity,

1. *Requests* the administering Power, bearing in mind the views of the people of the Territory ascertained through a democratic process, to keep the Secretary-General informed of the wishes and aspirations of the people regarding their future political status;

2. *Calls upon* the administering Power, the specialized agencies and other organizations of the United Nations system, as well as regional and other organizations, to continue to provide urgent emergency assistance to the Territory in alleviating the consequences of the volcanic eruptions;

3. *Welcomes* the support of the Caribbean Community in the construction of housing in the safe zone to alleviate a shortage caused by the environmental and human crisis of the eruptions of the Montsoufriere volcano, as well as the material and financial support of the international community to help alleviate the suffering caused by the crisis;

VIII. *Pitcairn*

Taking into account the unique nature of Pitcairn in terms of population and area,

Expressing its satisfaction with the continued economic and social advancement of the Territory, as well as with the improvement of its communications with the outside world and its management plan to address conservation issues,

1. *Requests* the administering Power, bearing in mind the views of the people of the Territory ascertained through a democratic process, to keep the Secretary-General informed of the wishes and aspirations of the people regarding their future political status;

2. *Also requests* the administering Power to continue its assistance for the improvement of the economic, social, educational and other conditions of the population of the Territory;

3. *Calls upon* the administering Power to continue its discussions with the representatives of Pitcairn on how best to support their economic security;

IX. *St. Helena*

Taking into account the unique character of St. Helena, its population and its natural resources,

Noting that the Commission of Inquiry into the Constitution appointed at the request of the Legislative Council of St. Helena reported its recommendations in March 1999, and that the Legislative Council is currently considering the recommendations,

Also noting the administering Power's commitment to consider carefully suggestions for specific proposals for constitutional change from the territorial Governments, as stated in its White Paper on Partnership for Progress and Prosperity: Britain and the Overseas Territories,

Welcoming the participation of an expert from the Legislative Council of St. Helena for the first time in the Pacific regional seminar, held at Majuro from 16 to 18 May 2000,

Aware of the establishment by the territorial Government of the Development Agency in 1995 to encourage private sector commercial development on the island,

Also aware of the efforts of the administering Power and the territorial authorities to improve the socio-economic conditions of the population of St. Helena, in particular in the spheres of food production, continuing high unemployment and limited transport and communications, and calls for continuing negotiations to allow access to Ascension Island by civilian charter flights,

Noting with concern the problem of unemployment on the island, and noting the joint action of the administering Power and the territorial Government to deal with it,

1. *Notes* that the administering Power has taken note of various statements made by members of the Legislative Council of St. Helena about the Constitution and is prepared to discuss them further with the people of St. Helena;

2. *Requests* the administering Power, bearing in mind the views of the people of the Territory ascertained through a democratic process, to keep the Secretary-General informed of the wishes and aspirations of the people regarding their future political status;

3. *Requests* the administering Power and relevant regional and international organizations to continue to support the efforts of the territorial Government to address the socio-economic development challenges, including high unemployment and the problems of limited transport and communications;

X. *Turks and Caicos Islands*

Taking note with interest of the statements made and the information on the political and economic situation in the Turks and Caicos Islands provided by the Cabinet Minister as well as a member of the legislature from the opposition of the Territory to the Caribbean regional seminar, held at St. John's, from 21 to 23 May 1997,

Noting that the People's Democratic Movement was elected to power in the Legislative Council elections held in March 1999,

Also noting the efforts by the territorial Government to strengthen financial management in the public sector, including efforts to increase revenue,

Noting with concern the vulnerability of the Territory to drug trafficking and related activities, as well as its problems caused by illegal immigration,

Noting the need for continued cooperation between the administering Power and the territorial Government in countering drug trafficking and money-laundering,

Welcoming the assessment by the Caribbean Development Bank in its 1999 report that the economic performance of the Territory remained strong, with an increase in gross domestic product estimated at 8.7 per cent, reflecting strong growth in the tourism and construction sectors,

1. *Requests* the administering Power, bearing in mind the views of the people of the Territory ascertained through a democratic process, to keep the Secretary-General informed of the wishes and aspirations of the people regarding their future political status;

2. *Invites* the administering Power to take fully into account the wishes and interests of the Government and the people of the Turks and Caicos Islands in the governance of the Territory;

3. *Calls upon* the administering Power and the relevant regional and international organizations to continue to provide assistance for the improvement of the economic, social, educational and other conditions of the population of the Territory;

4. *Calls upon* the administering Power and the territorial Government to continue to cooperate in countering problems related to money-laundering, smuggling of funds and other related crimes, as well as drug trafficking;

5. *Welcomes* the assessment by the Caribbean Development Bank in its 1999 report that the economy continued to expand with considerable output and low inflation;

6. *Also welcomes* the first country cooperation framework approved by the United Nations Development Programme for the period 1998-2002, which should, inter alia, assist in the development of a national integrated development plan that will put into place procedures for determining the national development priorities over ten years, with the focus of attention on health, population, education, tourism and economic and social development;

7. *Takes note* of the statement made by the elected Chief Minister in May 2000 that the Territory was in the process of developing diversified resource mobilization strategies, including joint ventures with the private sector, and that external assistance would be welcomed as part of that process;

XI. *United States Virgin Islands*

Taking note with interest of the statements made and the information provided by the representative of the Governor of the Territory to the Pacific regional seminar, held at Majuro from 16 to 18 May 2000,

Noting that although 80.4 per cent of the 27.5 per cent of the electorate that voted in the referendum on the political status of the Territory held on 11 October 1993 supported the existing territorial status arrangements with the administering Power, the law required the participation of 50 per cent of the registered voters for the results to be declared legally binding and therefore the status was left undecided,

Noting also the continuing interest of the territorial Government in seeking associate membership in the Organization of Eastern Caribbean States and observer status in the Caribbean Community and the Association of Caribbean States,

Noting further the necessity of further diversifying the economy of the Territory,

Noting the efforts of the territorial Government to promote the Territory as an offshore financial services centre,

Noting with satisfaction the interest of the Territory in joining the United Nations International Drug Control Programme as a full participant,

Recalling the dispatch in 1977 of a United Nations visiting mission to the Territory,

Noting that the Territory commemorated its annual British Virgin Islands–United States Virgin Islands Friendship Day on 27 May 2000 in official ceremonies in Tortola,

1. *Requests* the administering Power, bearing in mind the views of the people of the Territory ascertained through a democratic process, to keep the Secretary-General informed of the wishes and aspirations of the people regarding their future political status;

2. *Also requests* the administering Power to continue to assist the territorial Government in achieving its political, economic and social goals;

3. *Further requests* the administering Power to facilitate the participation of the Territory, as appropriate,

in various organizations, in particular the Organization of Eastern Caribbean States, the Caribbean Community and the Association of Caribbean States;

4. *Expresses concern* that the Territory, which is already heavily indebted, had to borrow 21 million United States dollars from a commercial bank to carry out its year 2000 computer compliance programme, and calls for the United Nations year 2000 programme to be made available to the Non-Self-Governing Territories;

5. *Notes* that the general elections held in the Territory in November 1998 resulted in the orderly transfer of power;

6. *Expresses concern* that the territorial Government is facing severe fiscal problems, which has resulted in an accumulated debt of more than one billion dollars;

7. *Welcomes* the measures being taken by the newly elected territorial Government in addressing the crisis, including the adoption of a five-year operating and strategic financial plan, and calls upon the administering Power to provide every assistance required by the Territory to alleviate the fiscal crisis, including, inter alia, the provision of debt relief and loans;

8. *Notes* that the 1994 report of the United States Virgin Islands Commission on Status and Federal Relations concluded that, owing to the insufficient level of voter participation, the results of the 1993 referendum were declared legally null and void.

Information

UN public information

The General Assembly's 95-member Committee on Information, at its twenty-second session, held in New York from 1 to 12 May [A/55/21], continued to consider UN information policies and activities and to evaluate and follow up efforts made and progress achieved in information and communications. The Committee had before it reports on the reorientation of UN activities in public information and communications, a case-by-case review of the integration of UN information centres with UNDP field offices, and guidelines for the functioning of those centres and the allocation of resources to them. It also considered a progress report on the pilot project for the development of an international radio broadcasting capacity for the United Nations, the multilingual development, maintenance and enrichment of UN web sites, the section of the proposed 2002-2005 medium-term plan relating to public information, the 1999 activities of the Joint United Nations Information Committee in 1999 and the millennium promotional campaign.

By **decision 55/425** of 8 December, the Assembly increased the Committee's membership from 95 to 97.

Reorientation of information and communications activities

Pursuant to General Assembly resolution 54/82 B [YUN 1999, p. 552], the Secretary-General submitted to the Committee on Information a March report [A/AC.198/2000/2] emphasizing recent measures to develop further the conceptual framework and operational priorities for the reorientation of the Organization's communications and information policies, as presented to the Committee in 1998 [YUN 1998, p. 583]. To translate those priorities into an operational framework, the Department of Public Information (DPI) was taking new intiatives and making progress in the key areas of policy and strategic direction, the Internet and new technology, media access, radio and television programming, information activities in the field, development of thematic programmes, building global partnerships, and enhancing publications and library resources.

In all of its activities and materials, DPI continued to develop a unified message of the continuing relevance of the United Nations. In that regard, it implemented the millennium promotional campaign leading up to the Millennium Summit and Assembly (see p. 47) under the title "The United Nations Works".

The United Nations was rapidly expanding its multimedia presence on the Internet. DPI worked to improve the UN web sites, making them more user-friendly and avoiding duplication. It also coordinated and chaired the interdepartmental group on Internet matters. The Publications Board was to issue guidelines for Internet publishing.

A key component of the reorientation strategy was the creation of a new, integrated, fully fledged UN news service, cutting across all media and delivering a regionally oriented daily package of news directly to the media worldwide. DPI established a daily news service on the UN web site to facilitate reporting on the United Nations around the world. Efforts were also under way to integrate news stories directly from UN field offices into the UN news service. The enhanced United Nations News Centre site provided a one-site access to all significant UN system news sites and to audio-visual services and online magazines. The news service, available in English and French, would increasingly combine text-based audio and visual material in its dissemination of news on the Web. DPI would shortly launch a more proactive electronic mail/facsimile-based version that would go directly to media news desks around the world, as well as to other important target audiences, providing news "alerts" of breaking stories and upcoming events and links to further information sources.

DPI continued its coordinated placement of Op-Ed articles and other materials by UN officials. Research was under way to explore the possibility of developing a pool of field "stringer" correspondents for radio, print, photography and television so that timely and relevant raw materials might be gathered to enrich UN news stories.

DPI was also undertaking a comprehensive review of its radio and television operations, key to which would be the utilization of new communications technology to take advantage of the speed and cost-effectiveness offered by the growing convergence of radio, television and Internet media. A team of consultants was to review DPI's medium- and long-term technology needs in that regard, focusing on strengthening the ability to reach broadcast news media with useful materials. A synergetic, integrated multimedia approach was being formulated, paying particular attention to how best to use the Internet to reinforce traditional radio and television and to channel to it radio and television contents.

United Nations Radio continued to use new technology to expand its news-gathering and dissemination capacity. It was studying programme reorientation and streamlining in an effort to establish a daily news operation; it created a news development group to look into all aspects of that project, including promotion, monitoring and feedback mechanisms.

DPI proceeded with the preparations for a pilot project on the development of an international radio broadcasting capacity for the United Nations (see below). It was also investigating new ways to provide greater public access to UN-produced television material. Efforts were under way to introduce UN video stories in several languages onto the UN web sites. United Nations Television was increasing its output of live feeds and other easy-to-assemble raw materials for use by redisseminators. DPI planned to develop an integrated digital photo management system, which would also streamline photo production procedures. A study would shortly be undertaken on ways to deploy public information technology rapidly to new peacekeeping and humanitarian missions.

As part of the reorientation process, DPI strengthened its cooperation with Secretariat departments and other entities to convey the UN message more effectively. In developing strategies and planning steps for practical implementation of public information and communications campaigns in thematic areas, DPI would be guided by the new millennium promotional campaign.

DPI continued to attach great importance to its traditional print publications. Its magazine *UN Chronicle* expanded the use of colour illustrations, in line with its extended use of human interest stories and in-depth articles on specific issues and themes relevant to the Organization's goals; many of them were written by prominent personalities, leading experts and representatives of international agencies and NGOs. *Africa Recovery* continued to be the unique source of sustained coverage of UN system activities in Africa. Technological innovation was greatly helping the *Yearbook of the United Nations* to shorten the time lag between the end of the year covered and the publication date. *Development Business* continued to forge strong partnerships with international financial and other institutions to expand its services to the growing international business community. It was currently engaged in aggressive promotional campaigns to ensure greater participation in global business opportunities by both industrialized and developing countries.

The Dag Hammarskjöld Library continued to place emphasis on Web-related activities, digitization of UN documents, inter-agency resource sharing, training programmes for permanent missions to the United Nations and for Secretariat and depository library staff, and the creation of multilingual reference tools.

UN international radio broadcasting capacity

The Committee on Information had before it an April progress report by the Secretary-General, submitted pursuant to General Assembly resolution 54/82 B [YUN 1999, p. 552], on the implementation of the pilot project for the development of an international radio broadcasting capacity for the United Nations [A/AC.198/2000/6]. He indicated that two surveys were conducted, one in 1999 by DPI and the other in 2000 by an independent consultant, the results of which suggested that there was sufficient interest in the project to take it further. The surveys provided a good foundation to build on, to ensure that the pilot project's development was based on an understanding of the needs of individual radio stations in different regions. Steps were being taken to contact those major national broadcasters that had not responded to the second survey with the aim of developing an enhanced broadcasting relationship with them through the project.

The survey also revealed that airtime availability for the pilot project differed markedly by region, suggesting that consideration should be given to developing the project in progressive stages. Further steps should be taken to encourage additional national broadcasting organizations to support the project by providing airtime or satellite distributions, which would help overcome the difficulty of servicing a large number of small stations with fragmented audiences. It was suggested that the pilot project held less interest for the major broadcasters, which had correspondents stationed at the United Nations or already had good access to sources of UN information. In view of the survey results, DPI was considering ways to effectively allocate resources to ensure global dissemination of daily radio news from the United Nations through the project, which meant focusing on key markets and underserved regions.

DPI received limited responses to its request to Member States for contributions towards the implementation of the project in the form of airtime or cash contributions to a trust fund. A total of 114 radio stations and networks in 58 countries had expressed interest in participating in the pilot project by making available a daily segment of airtime on their transmission facilities for UN radio broadcasts. Since none offered any financial contribution or commitment, DPI was obliged to redeploy $1,760,300 from its approved 2000-2001 programme budget for the project's implementation but would continue to seek extrabudgetary support.

In a later report [A/AC.198/2001/7], the Secretary-General informed the Committee that DPI launched the pilot project on 28 August, targeting audiences in Africa, Asia, Europe and Latin America and the Caribbean, in time for the Millennium Summit (see p. 47). Arrangements were made with several communications service distributors to provide short-wave transmissions to Africa and the Middle East in Arabic, English and French, as well as with satellite service providers to transmit the programming to the Caribbean region. In addition, DPI ensured the establishment of an effective and multi-pronged delivery system, since distribution needs varied from one region to another. Other options for broadcasters included analogue telephone feeds, digital telephone systems lines and electronic file transfer.

DPI activities

In his October report on questions relating to information [A/55/452], the Secretary-General noted that DPI continued to strengthen the communications function within the United Nations and in its field offices in order to build broad-based global support for the Organization's work. It also continued to strengthen its coordination, management and policy guidance of the UN web site. In June, the Publications Board approved the Internet publishing guidelines, which provided for a Working Group on Internet Matters to help the Board better coordinate and enhance Internet publishing. DPI also initiated web site traffic analysis to reveal detailed usage patterns. A new design was launched in September allowing for easier navigation and better access.

General public information activities to the media included those carried out by the Office of the Spokesman for the Secretary-General, which continued to inform the accredited press, delegations and the public at large on the broad scope of UN activities and to utilize Internet technology to expand the audience for its products. New sections of its web page widened coverage of the Secretary-General's activities, including "The Secretary-General: off the cuff", introduced in January to allow electronic access to the Secretary-General's media encounters and press conferences.

DPI made important strides to better serve the global news media through intensified use of new communications technology, live radio and television/video feeds to broadcasters, as well as increased outreach to journalists. To help bridge the gap between developed and developing countries in their ability to access UN news and other information material immediately, DPI embarked on a project to create direct links to journalists worldwide by alerting them via electronic mail to new developments emanating from the United Nations. In addition, the Web-based United Nations News Centre provided news updates throughout the day. In a related activity, DPI was executing a pilot project to enable United Nations Radio to produce and deliver to radio stations around the globe daily 15-minute news bulletins in all six UN official languages (see p. 573). United Nations Television covered and distributed an increased number of live events at UN Headquarters, making available ready-for-television footage packages on key occasions as part of DPI's overall information strategy.

DPI continued to develop innovative ways to communicate with its 1,600 associated NGOs, including the introduction of a series of communications workshops to assist them in creating an informed understanding of the Organization's work; to reach out to young people by strengthening partnerships with educational and other NGOs and sponsoring teachers' workshops, programmes for students and projects over the Internet, often linked to specific observances; and to build partnerships through co-sponsorships of special events and programmes within the UN system and with civil society.

In addition, DPI continued to promote its thematic information programmes, including mobilization of public opinion in support of issues addressed in the follow-up to UN global conferences on development held during the 1990s, priority issues on the UN agenda, including the promotion of information technology for development, human rights, in particular the issue of racism, and peace and security.

Library services

The Dag Hammarskjöld Library continued to move in the direction of a virtual library, focusing on the delivery of electronic information, support for multilingualism and outreach to depository libraries. The Library's Internet presence was increasing and its web page was now available in Spanish. The *United Nations Documentation Research Guide* was currently available in English, French and Russian and work on its translation into the remaining official languages was well advanced. The Library also made substantial progress in translating the *United Nations Bibliographic Information System Thesaurus* into Arabic, Chinese and Russian. A software package that would permit full *Thesaurus* capability simultaneously in all scripts was being sought.

To strengthen UN connection to civil society partners, the Library enhanced its outreach programme for depository libraries through increased training and dissemination activities. The range of the *News Updates* service for depository libraries broadened substantially and the feedback to the expanded service was positive. The Library also established an additional outreach programme for depository libraries, consisting of the full-text transmission of selected materials in the official languages. A key initiative to improve and expand DPI's cartographic and geographic services was the formal establishment in March of the United Nations Geographic Information Working Group to coordinate activities and formulate UN system policies on geographic information. One of its principal objectives was to develop and maintain a common UN geographic database.

UN information centres

The United Nations information centres (UNICs) continued to demonstrate their strength as the local voice of the United Nations. They were increasingly active in placing Op-Ed articles by senior UN officials in leading newspapers and in responding to media queries. They recorded a significant growth in demand for information on social issues and actively publicized the Secretary-General's millennium message and his millennium report (see p. 55). Their technical ca-

pabilities continued to be enhanced through DPI's provision of equipment and training.

At its 2000 session, the Committee on Information considered the Secretary-General's report on the findings of a case-by-case review of UNICs integrated with UNDP field offices [A/AC.198/2000/3]. Each of the 14 host countries had been asked to rate its centre's performance in respect of the stated objectives of presenting a more unified UN image and of enhancing information activities, and to propose improvements. All 14 responded that the centres had fulfilled the first objective and most were satisfied with their efforts as to the second, including their proactive information initiatives. Most further praised the services provided by the UNIC reference libraries. Of the two countries that observed a decline in service, one attributed it to the UN financial crisis, the other to the integration exercise itself.

In their comments on improvements of the overall functioning of the centres, the respondents suggested that the centres be provided with more resources, in particular staff specializing in public information and communications, and that the centres' support to depository libraries, as well as their relationship with the host countries' public and private institutions, be strengthened.

In the meantime, DPI, in cooperation with UNDP, launched several initiatives to improve overall cooperation and the performance of the integrated UNICs, including regular meetings of a DPI/UNDP working group to strengthen partnership and address specific issues; formulation of terms of reference for a review mission to visit a representative number of integrated centres to evaluate performance and assist in resolving outstanding issues; and drafting of guidelines for the integrated centres' operational framework [A/AC.198/2000/4]. Directors of the centres, in response to a request for their comments and suggestions on the integration exercise, indicated that additional staffing, financing and training would help meet enhanced information targets and goals.

The Secretary-General said he remained confident that the integrated centres would meet their public information goals and their host countries' expectations. In that regard, DPI and UNDP would continue to work together to improve the overall effectiveness of those centres.

In February [A/AC.198/2000/5], the Secretary-General reported on the allocation of resources for the UN regular budget and a breakdown of host government assistance to UNICs in 1999.

Development of UN web sites

In response to General Assembly resolution 54/82 B [YUN 1999, p. 552], the Secretary-General reported in April on the multilingual development, maintenance and enrichment of UN web sites [A/AC.198/2000/7-A/AC.172/2000/4]. He said that the further development, coordination, production and management of information content on those sites would require a substantial increase in the level of investment, as would the upgrading of the related technical infrastructure, due primarily to the need to: increase the timely dissemination of information and data to a wider and rapidly growing audience; effect cost savings by limiting hard-copy distribution, and/or by shifting printing to the end-user; present constantly updated information; and promote, through the Internet, education and public understanding of the United Nations and of the issues before it.

The first task would be to rationalize the structure of the sites, requiring a feasibility study on their complete redesign and restructuring, including the refocusing of their multilingual aspects, together with the necessary hardware and connectivity requirements and the time frame for implementation, with particular attention to enhancing the search facility to cover all official languages. It would delineate the comprehensive resource investments essential for achieving that objective across the entire web-site operation. The study, to be conducted by outside industry experts, was estimated to cost $100,000, which was not included in the 2000-2001 programme budget.

Beforehand, however, a sound foundation for ensuring the ongoing regular maintenance of UN web sites needed to be established on the basis of resource requirements set out in proposal C of the options outlined by the Secretary-General in 1999 [YUN 1999, p. 550]. Without that administrative and budgetary support, the minimum necessary for the continuation of the current level of that activity, the desired objective of narrowing the differences among the web sites in all official languages, with the eventual achievement of parity, would not be attained. Those resource requirements pertained only to DPI and did not include either the infrastructure and technical support requirements for the Information Technology Services Division of the Department of Management or resources for the provision of content in other languages.

The Secretary-General observed that the current level of web-site operation had been accomplished primarily through temporary and ad hoc arrangements, using temporary assistance funds and a realignment of activities. The situation argued for a more coordinated approach. DPI, in undertaking the responsibility for the web sites across the Secretariat, as well as for some of the offices away from Headquarters, had taken on additional unforeseen tasks for which there was no budgetary allocation and had almost solely borne the associated costs. It was currently looking into ways of enhancing cooperation with content-providing departments, while minimizing such costs.

The Secretary-General concluded that Internet activity needed to be considered as an integral part of the Organization's work programme and would be included in a regular subprogramme of the 2002-2005 medium-term plan (see p. 577), as well as in the budget proposals for DPI for the 2002-2003 biennium. It was essential for each content-providing office to include Web-specific content in its regular programme activity and accordingly make provisions for its budget and for technological infrastructure support.

Since Member States had indicated that website activities should not be seen as replacing traditional means of communication, a realistic and cost-effective action plan to meet the requirement of linguistic parity would need to be developed.

JUNIC

At its twenty-sixth session (Geneva, 11-13 July) [ACC/2000/11], the Joint United Nations Information Committee (JUNIC), the inter-agency Administrative Committee on Coordination (ACC) body on information activities within the UN system, discussed the UN millennium promotional campaign [A/AC.198/2000/10] and supported the concept of "The United Nations Works" campaign as a way to reach out to global audiences with a positive message about the United Nations. It suggested that a component of the campaign be used to educate and motivate UN staff in the spirt of fostering a "culture of communications". It proposed that ACC endorse the campaign as a system-wide initiative, to be coordinated by DPI as the lead agency. JUNIC also discussed communications strategies for UN system media relations. It agreed on the need to develop an action plan for communications training of staff at all levels to enable them to better communicate the UN message to the media at Headquarters and in the field.

Regarding system-wide cooperation in television, JUNIC examined the issue of editorial control of programming produced or aired by outside broadcasters on the basis of footage or feature stories originating from the Organization and agreed that it might be better for the Organization to relinquish editorial control over such programming. Co-productions with major broadcasters were identified as another effective means of presenting UN stories and issues to the global public. Such contacts, it was stressed, should be established through editorial and co-production departments of major broadcasters to guarantee airtime. JUNIC identified the understanding of rights management issues as an important element of partnerships with broadcasting organizations.

JUNIC discussed the work of the Non-Governmental Liaison Service and noted that the number of sponsoring agencies had increased and that the Service had achieved greater financial stability. In other action, it agreed that the *JUNIC Information Exchange Bulletin* would continue to be coordinated by its secretariat and posted on the WebBoard, which would be used also to post a calendar of upcoming communications activities. Other features would be added gradually to meet the changing needs of JUNIC members and take advantage of technological improvements. JUNIC decided to devote more time at its future sessions to broad-based communications management issues and to establish a discussion group on information technology on the WebBoard. It agreed to hold a one-day meeting to examine recent developments in information technology and their system-wide application, and agreed to discuss in 2001 Internet and multimedia matters, as well as the communications aspects of the UN fight against AIDS.

The Secretary-General's report on the 1999 activities of JUNIC [A/AC.198/2000/9] was submitted to the May 2000 session of the Committee on Information.

Proposed 2002-2005
medium-term plan in public information

The Secretary-General, in a March note [A/AC.198/2000/8], transmitted the draft 2002-2005 medium-term plan for programme 23 (Public information), whose overall purpose was to increase awareness and understanding of the work and purposes of the United Nations, highlighting issues of concern to the international community, including those addressed by major international conferences and General Assembly special sessions.

The programme strategy was based on the premise that public information and communications should be placed at the heart of the strategic management of the United Nations and that a culture of communications should permeate all levels of the Organization. To project an image of the Organization as an open and transparent

public institution, emphasis would be placed on the continuing development of that culture. Partnerships would be strengthened at Headquarters and in the field to enable DPI to define the themes to be highlighted during the period of the medium-term plan and to coordinate the Organization's public information activities with a view to presenting a unified image. Information and communications plans and campaigns would be implemented in collaboration with departments and offices to publicize the Organization's work in their respective sectors. Cooperation among organizations of the UN system would also be strengthened and cooperation and partnerships with redisseminators pursued at all levels. The various elements of the system would work together in a more news-centred, media-friendly multimedia operation, providing information directly to international news editors in all Member States, including through the network of UNICs, services and offices worldwide.

Increased use would be made of the latest technology, in both the traditional and electronic media, including the Internet, to deliver news directly and instantaneously to the media worldwide. Particular attention would be given to tailoring the news disseminated to different regions, bearing in mind their technological capacity. Every effort would be made to ensure that publications and other information services of the Secretariat, including the UN web site, contained comprehensive, objective and equitable information about the issues before the Organization.

GENERAL ASSEMBLY ACTION

On 8 December [meeting 83], the General Assembly, on the recommendation of the Fourth Committee [A/55/573], adopted **resolutions 55/136 A and B** without vote [agenda item 87].

Questions relating to information

A
Information in the service of humanity
The General Assembly,

Taking note of the comprehensive and important report of the Committee on Information,

Also taking note of the report of the Secretary-General on questions relating to information,

Urges all countries, organizations of the United Nations system as a whole and all others concerned, reaffirming their commitment to the principles of the Charter of the United Nations and to the principles of freedom of the press and freedom of information, as well as to those of the independence, pluralism and diversity of the media, deeply concerned by the disparities existing between developed and developing countries and the consequences of every kind arising from those disparities that affect the capability of the public, private or other media and individuals in developing countries to disseminate information and communicate their views and their cultural and ethical values through endogenous cultural production, as well as to ensure the diversity of sources and their free access to information, and recognizing the call in this context for what in the United Nations and at various international forums has been termed "a new world information and communication order, seen as an evolving and continuous process":

(*a*) To cooperate and interact with a view to reducing existing disparities in information flows at all levels by increasing assistance for the development of communication infrastructures and capabilities in developing countries, with due regard for their needs and the priorities attached to such areas by those countries, and in order to enable them and the public, private or other media in developing countries to develop their own information and communication policies freely and independently and increase the participation of media and individuals in the communication process, and to ensure a free flow of information at all levels;

(*b*) To ensure for journalists the free and effective performance of their professional tasks and condemn resolutely all attacks against them;

(*c*) To provide support for the continuation and strengthening of practical training programmes for broadcasters and journalists from public, private and other media in developing countries;

(*d*) To enhance regional efforts and cooperation among developing countries, as well as cooperation between developed and developing countries, to strengthen communication capacities and to improve the media infrastructure and communication technology in the developing countries, especially in the areas of training and dissemination of information;

(*e*) To aim at, in addition to bilateral cooperation, providing all possible support and assistance to the developing countries and their media, public, private or other, with due regard to their interests and needs in the field of information and to action already adopted within the United Nations system, including:

(i) The development of the human and technical resources that are indispensable for the improvement of information and communication systems in developing countries and support for the continuation and strengthening of practical training programmes, such as those already operating under both public and private auspices throughout the developing world;

(ii) The creation of conditions that will enable developing countries and their media, public, private or other, to have, by using their national and regional resources, the communication technology suited to their national needs, as well as the necessary programme material, especially for radio and television broadcasting;

(iii) Assistance in establishing and promoting telecommunication links at the subregional, regional and interregional levels, especially among developing countries;

(iv) The facilitation, as appropriate, of access by the developing countries to advanced communication technology available on the open market;

(*f*) To provide full support for the International Programme for the Development of Communication

of the United Nations Educational, Scientific and Cultural Organization, which should support both public and private media.

B
**United Nations public information
policies and activities**

The General Assembly,

Reiterating its decision to consolidate the role of the Committee on Information as its main subsidiary body mandated to make recommendations to it relating to the work of the Department of Public Information of the Secretariat,

Concurring with the view of the Secretary-General that public information and communications should be placed at the heart of the strategic management of the United Nations, and that a culture of communications should permeate all levels of the Organization, as a means of fully informing the peoples of the world of the aims and activities of the United Nations,

1. *Reaffirms* its resolution 13(I) of 13 February 1946, in which it established the Department of Public Information of the Secretariat;

2. *Expresses its concern* that the gap in the information and communication technologies between the developed and the developing countries has continued to widen and that most developing countries are not benefiting from the present information and technology revolution, and, in this regard, underlines the necessity of rectifying the imbalances of the global information and technology revolution in order to make it more just, equitable and effective;

3. *Welcomes* Liberia and Mozambique to membership in the Committee on Information;

4. *Calls upon* the Secretary-General, in respect of the public information policies and activities of the United Nations, to continue to implement fully the recommendations contained in paragraph 2 of its resolution 48/44 B of 10 December 1993 and other mandates as established by the General Assembly;

5. *Takes note* of the report of the Secretary-General on the reorientation of United Nations activities in the field of public information and communications, and encourages him to continue the reorientation exercise, while stressing the need to take into account the views of Member States, and requests him to report thereon to the Committee on Information at its twenty-third session;

6. *Welcomes* the initiatives that have been taken by the Department of Public Information to strengthen the public information system of the United Nations, and, in this regard, stresses the importance of a coherent and results-oriented approach being undertaken by the United Nations, the specialized agencies and the programmes and funds of the United Nations system involved in public information activities and the provision of resources for their implementation;

7. *Emphasizes* that, through its reorientation, the Department of Public Information should maintain and improve its activities in the areas of special interest to developing countries and, where appropriate, other countries with special needs, including countries in transition, and that such reorientation should contribute to bridging the existing gap between the developing and the developed countries in the crucial field of public information and communications;

8. *Takes note* of the note by the Secretary-General on programme 23 (Public information) of the proposed medium-term plan for the period 2002-2005, and, emphasizing that the implementation of the broad objectives outlined in the proposal should be in accordance with the objectives set forth in relevant General Assembly resolutions regarding questions relating to information, requests the Secretary-General to proceed with the submission of the proposal to the Committee for Programme and Coordination for consideration, taking into account the amendments made by the Committee on Information at its twenty-second session, in accordance with section I of Assembly resolution 53/207 of 18 December 1998;

9. *Requests* the Secretary-General to focus, in particular, on educational institutions as key and indispensable partners of the United Nations in its efforts fully to inform the peoples of the world of its aims and activities;

10. *Encourages* the Secretary-General to strengthen further consultative arrangements between the Department of Public Information and other substantive departments of the Secretariat, in particular those dealing with development issues;

11. *Reaffirms* that United Nations information centres should continue to publicize United Nations activities and accomplishments in the areas of economic and social development, poverty eradication, debt relief, health, education, elimination of illiteracy, women's rights, children's rights, the plight of children in armed conflict, the sexual exploitation of children, the eradication of drug trafficking and environmental issues, as well as other issues of relevance;

12. *Welcomes* the contribution of the Department of Public Information to the efforts of the Secretary-General in closing the digital divide as a means of spurring economic growth and as a response to the continuing gulf between developed and developing countries, and, in this context, requests the Department further to enhance its role;

13. *Recalls* its resolution 54/113 of 10 December 1999 concerning the proclamation of 2001 as the United Nations Year of Dialogue among Civilizations, and encourages the Secretary-General to strengthen the public information capacity of the Department of Public Information with a view to disseminating information on and drawing international attention to the dialogue among civilizations and the impact it could have on promoting mutual understanding, tolerance, peaceful coexistence and international cooperation;

14. *Welcomes* the decision taken by the Department of Public Information to launch a new web site to publicize the United Nations Year of Dialogue among Civilizations, and requests the Secretary-General to continue to implement the promotional campaign to ensure that the Year enjoys the broadest international support and to report thereon and also on all follow-up activities in this respect to the Committee on Information at its twenty-third session;

15. *Recalls* its resolutions 53/202 of 17 December 1998 and 54/254 of 15 March 2000, concerning the designation of the fifty-fifth session of the General Assembly as the Millennium Assembly of the United Nations and the convening, as an integral part of the Millennium Assembly, of the Millennium Summit of the United Nations, takes note of the report of the Secretary-General on the millennium promotional campaign, and encourages him to continue to implement effective public information programmes in this regard so as to ensure that the outcome of the Summit is widely disseminated and enjoys broad international support;

16. *Appreciates and encourages* the efforts of the Department of Public Information in disseminating information to Member States regarding the promotion of women's rights and gender equality;

17. *Takes note with appreciation* of the efforts of the Secretary-General to strengthen the public information capacity of the Department of Public Information for the formation and day-to-day functioning of the information components of peacekeeping and other field operations of the United Nations, and requests the Secretariat to continue to ensure the involvement of the Department from the planning stage of such future operations through interdepartmental consultations and coordination with other substantive departments of the Secretariat;

18. *Stresses* the importance of enhancing the public information capacity of the Department of Public Information in the field of peacekeeping operations and its role in the selection process of spokespersons for United Nations peacekeeping operations or missions, and, in this regard, encourages the Department to second spokespersons who have the necessary skills for fulfilling the tasks of the operations or missions;

19. *Emphasizes* that all publications of the Department of Public Information, in accordance with existing mandates, should fulfil an identifiable need, should not duplicate other publications of the United Nations system and should be produced in a cost-effective manner;

20. *Takes note* of the continuing efforts of the Secretary-General to make the Dag Hammarskjöld Library a virtual library with world outreach, making United Nations information and other acquired materials accessible electronically to a growing number of readers and users, and, at the same time, requests him to enrich the stock of books and journals in the Library, including publications on peace and security and development-related issues, to ensure that it continues to be a broadly accessible resource for information about the United Nations and its activities;

21. *Welcomes* the development of the United Nations News Service by the Department of Public Information, and requests the Secretary-General to continue to exert all efforts to ensure that publications and other information services of the Secretariat, including the United Nations web site and the United Nations News Service, contain comprehensive, objective and equitable information about the issues before the Organization and that they maintain editorial independence, impartiality, accuracy and full consistency with resolutions and decisions of the General Assembly;

22. *Takes note* of the efforts of the Secretary-General in ensuring access for the representatives of Member States to the briefings organized at Headquarters by the Office of the Spokesman for the Secretary-General and in ensuring wider outreach of the outcome of such briefings, and requests him to consider taking further measures in this regard;

23. *Requests* the Secretary-General to ensure that information presented to the media is made available to delegations fully and in a timely fashion;

24. *Reaffirms* the importance attached by Member States to the role of United Nations information centres and information components in effectively and comprehensively disseminating information in all parts of the world, in particular in developing countries and countries in transition, and especially in those countries where there is need for a better understanding of United Nations activities;

25. *Also reaffirms* the importance of all United Nations information centres meeting the primary objectives outlined by the Committee on Information in its report on its ninth session;

26. *Emphasizes* that resources should be commensurate with the mandated programmes and activities of the United Nations information centres to ensure their full and effective implementation, expresses deep disappointment at the reduction of more than 40 per cent in the staffing of the information centres between the early and closing years of the last decade, and, in this context, acknowledges the generous contributions by several host Governments, as well as the partnership with the United Nations Development Programme and other United Nations system and local partners, to maintain the present level of operations of the information centres;

27. *Takes note* of the reports of the Secretary-General on the United Nations information centres and requests him to continue, if feasible and on a case-by-case basis, the integration policy in a cost-effective manner, taking into account the views of the host countries to ensure that the information functions and the autonomy of United Nations information centres are not adversely affected, to meet the policy's stated objective of improving the provision of information by the United Nations, and, in this regard, requests him to continue his efforts to address the problems that affect the centres;

28. *Also takes note* of the report of the Secretary-General on the integration of United Nations information centres with field offices of the United Nations Development Programme, requests him to implement the views and opinions of the host Governments concerned, as expressed in their replies to the questionnaire provided by the Secretariat, and also requests him to report to the Committee on Information at its twenty-third session on the steps taken in this regard;

29. *Further takes note* of the report of the Secretary-General on the guidelines for the functioning of the United Nations information centres integrated with the field offices of the United Nations Development Programme;

30. *Reaffirms* the role of the General Assembly in relation to the opening of new United Nations information centres, invites the Secretary-General to make such recommendations as he may consider necessary regarding the establishment and location of such centres, and, in this regard, welcomes the requests by Croatia, Gabon, Guinea, Haiti, Jamaica and Kyrgyzstan for information centres or information components;

31. *Stresses* the need to revitalize the centres that are currently not operational, for which requests have already been made by the countries concerned;

32. *Recalls* its resolution 54/82 B of 6 December 1999, in which it requested the Secretary-General to continue to study ways and means of rationalizing and effecting equitable disbursement of available resources to United Nations information centres, notes with great concern the existing imbalance in the available resources to the information centres in developing and developed countries and that, given the importance of this matter, more information is needed, and requests the Secretary-General to examine the situation thoroughly, taking into account all relevant factors, and to report thereon to the Committee on Information at its twenty-third session;

33. *Requests* the Secretary-General to look into the possibility of appointing directors to those United Nations information centres that are not yet integrated and are under the temporary management of offices of the United Nations Development Programme to ensure the autonomous status of the centres;

34. *Welcomes* the action taken by some Member States with regard to providing financial and material support to United Nations information centres in their respective capitals, and invites the Secretary-General, through the Department of Public Information, to consult Member States, where appropriate, on the possibility of providing the information centres with additional voluntary support on a national basis, bearing in mind that such support should not be a substitute for the full allocation of financial requirements for the United Nations information centres in the context of the programme budget of the United Nations;

35. *Recognizes* the continuing enhanced cooperation between the Department of Public Information and the University for Peace in Costa Rica as a focal point for promoting United Nations activities and disseminating United Nations information materials, and requests the Secretary-General to report on those activities;

36. *Expresses its full support* for wide, accurate, equal and prompt coverage of United Nations activities through the continuation and improvement of United Nations press releases, which should bring out the intergovernmental aspect of the Organization's work and deliberations, stresses the importance of having these press releases issued in all official languages of the United Nations, and requests other relevant bodies of the General Assembly to give due consideration to this matter;

37. *Stresses* that radio is one of the most cost-effective and far-reaching media available to the Department of Public Information and an important instrument in United Nations activities, such as development and peacekeeping, in accordance with General Assembly resolution 48/44 B;

38. *Encourages* an increase in the number of programmes of United Nations Radio, in all available languages, on the United Nations web site;

39. *Takes note* of the efforts under way by the Department of Public Information to disseminate programmes directly to broadcasting stations all over the world in the six official languages, and, in that regard, stresses the need for impartiality and objectivity concerning information activities of the United Nations;

40. *Encourages* the Department of Public Information to continue to include in its radio and television

programming specific programmes addressing the needs of developing nations;

41. *Requests* the Secretary-General to implement fully the recommendations contained in paragraph 9 of General Assembly resolution 38/82 B of 15 December 1983 with regard to the introduction of full programming in French and Creole in the work programme of the Caribbean Unit of United Nations Radio;

42. *Welcomes* the progress report of the Secretary-General on the implementation of the pilot project for the development of an international radio broadcasting capacity for the United Nations and the redeployment of the necessary resources for this purpose;

43. *Requests* the Secretary-General to submit to the Committee on Information at its twenty-third session a progress report on the results of the implementation of the pilot project, and declares its intention to examine before the end of 2001 and upon submission by the Secretary-General of his report, the final report on the results of the project with a view to taking a decision on the matter during its fifty-sixth session;

44. *Urges* the Secretary-General to maintain and strengthen the managerial capacity, staff resources, programme output and means of delivery of United Nations Radio in the six official languages and, if feasible, in other languages, in order to ensure the success of the radio pilot project and, to this end, enhance coordination with the United Nations News Centre and the United Nations information centres, as well as the cooperation with national and international radio organizations in Member States;

45. *Underlines* the continuing importance of using traditional and mass media channels to disseminate information on the United Nations, and encourages the Secretary-General, through the Department of Public Information, to continue to take full advantage of recent developments in information technologies, including the Internet, in order to improve, in a cost-effective manner, the dissemination of information on the United Nations, in accordance with the priorities established by the General Assembly and taking into account the linguistic diversity of the Organization;

46. *Takes note* of the efforts by some United Nations information centres to establish their own web pages in local languages, and, in this respect, encourages the Department of Public Information to provide resources and technical facilities, in particular to United Nations information centres whose web pages are not yet operational, to develop web pages in the respective local languages in their host countries;

47. *Encourages* the Department of Public Information to continue its efforts to coordinate and rationalize the content of web pages of United Nations information centres using the same language in order to enhance the information services with a view to avoiding overlap and repetition;

48. *Takes note* of the report of the Secretary-General on the multilingual development, maintenance and enrichment of United Nations web sites, encourages the Secretary-General to continue his efforts to develop and enhance the United Nations web sites in all the official languages of the Organization, and requests him to continue to develop proposals for consideration by the Committee on Information at its twenty-third session, keeping in mind the building of modular parity,

which should ultimately lead to achieving full parity among the official languages of the United Nations;

49. *Requests* the Secretary-General to include in his report, in accordance with paragraph 48 above, guidelines for content planning and publication on the United Nations web sites;

50. *Stresses* the importance of access to the United Nations treaty collection and the United Nations parliamentary documentation for the public, and commends the Secretary-General on his initiative to make parliamentary documentation of the Organization available through the United Nations web site in all the official languages;

51. *Expresses its appreciation* to the Department of Public Information for conducting the ongoing programme for broadcasters and journalists from developing countries and countries in transition, and calls for its further expansion so as to include a larger number of trainees from those countries;

52. *Acknowledges* the important work carried out by the United Nations Educational, Scientific and Cultural Organization and its collaboration with news agencies and broadcasting organizations in developing countries in disseminating information on priority issues;

53. *Requests* the Department of Public Information to continue to ensure the greatest possible access for United Nations guided tours and to ensure that displays in public areas are kept as informative, up-to-date, relevant and technologically innovative as possible;

54. *Recalls* its resolutions concerning the consequences of the Chernobyl disaster, in particular resolutions 51/138 B of 13 December 1996 and 52/172 of 16 December 1997, and encourages the Department of Public Information, in cooperation with the countries concerned and with the relevant organizations and bodies of the United Nations system, to continue to take appropriate measures to enhance world public awareness of the consequences of that disaster;

55. *Also recalls* its resolution 53/1 H of 16 November 1998, concerning international cooperation and coordination for the human and ecological rehabilitation of the Semipalatinsk region of Kazakhstan, which has been affected by nuclear tests, and encourages the Department of Public Information, in cooperation with relevant organizations and bodies of the United Nations system, to take appropriate measures to enhance world public awareness of the problems and needs of the Semipalatinsk region;

56. *Further recalls* its resolutions 53/59 B of 3 December 1998 and 54/82 B, and urges the Department of Public Information to take the necessary measures, through the provision of relevant and objective information, towards achieving the major objectives set forth in the report of the Secretary-General on the causes of conflict and the promotion of durable peace and sustainable development in Africa, and to publicize the activities of the open-ended working group established for that purpose;

57. *Requests* the Secretary-General to report to the Committee on Information at its twenty-third session and to the General Assembly at its fifty-sixth session on the activities of the Department of Public Information and on the implementation of the recommendations contained in the present resolution;

58. *Requests* the Committee on Information to report to the General Assembly at its fifty-sixth session;

59. *Decides* to include in the provisional agenda of its fifty-sixth session the item entitled "Questions relating to information".

Information and communications in the context of international security

Pursuant to General Assembly resolution 54/49 [YUN 1999, p. 555], the Secretary-General, in a July report with later addendum [A/55/140 & Add.1], transmitted the views of four Member States on the general appreciation of the issues of international security; the definition of basic notions related to information security, including unauthorized interference with or the misuse of information and telecommunications systems and information resources; and the advisability of developing international principles to enhance the security of global information and telecommunications systems and help combat information terrorism and criminality.

GENERAL ASSEMBLY ACTION

On 20 November [meeting 69], the General Assembly, on the recommendation of the First (Disarmament and International Security) Committee [A/55/554], adopted **resolution 55/28** without vote [agenda item 68].

Developments in the field of information and telecommunications in the context of international security

The General Assembly,

Recalling its resolutions 53/70 of 4 December 1998 and 54/49 of 1 December 1999,

Recalling also its resolutions on the role of science and technology in the context of international security, in which, inter alia, it recognized that scientific and technological developments could have both civilian and military applications and that progress in science and technology for civilian applications needed to be maintained and encouraged,

Noting that considerable progress has been achieved in developing and applying the latest information technologies and means of telecommunication,

Affirming that it sees in this process the broadest positive opportunities for the further development of civilization, the expansion of opportunities for cooperation for the common good of all States, the enhancement of the creative potential of mankind and additional improvements in the circulation of information in the global community,

Recalling in this connection the approaches and principles outlined at the Information Society and Development Conference, held at Midrand, South Africa, from 13 to 15 May 1996,

Bearing in mind the results of the Ministerial Conference on Terrorism, held in Paris on 30 July 1996, and the recommendations it made,

Noting that the dissemination and use of information technologies and means affect the interests of the entire international community and that optimum effectiveness is enhanced by broad international cooperation,

Expressing concern that these technologies and means can potentially be used for purposes that are inconsistent with the objectives of maintaining international stability and security and may adversely affect the security of States in both civil and military fields,

Noting the contribution of those Member States that have submitted their assessments on issues of information security to the Secretary-General pursuant to paragraphs 1 to 3 of resolutions 53/70 and 54/49,

Taking note of the reports of the Secretary-General containing those assessments,

Welcoming the initiative taken by the Secretariat and the United Nations Institute for Disarmament Research in convening an international meeting of experts at Geneva in August 1999 on developments in the field of information and telecommunications in the context of international security, as well as its results,

Considering that the assessments of the Member States contained in the reports of the Secretary-General and the international meeting of experts have contributed to a better understanding of the substance of issues of international information security and related notions,

1. *Calls upon* Member States to promote further at multilateral levels the consideration of existing and potential threats in the field of information security, as well as possible measures to limit the threats emerging in this field;

2. *Considers* that the purpose of such measures could be served through the examination of relevant international concepts aimed at strengthening the security of global information and telecommunications systems;

3. *Invites* all Member States to continue to inform the Secretary-General of their views and assessments on the following questions:

(*a*) General appreciation of the issues of information security;

(*b*) Definition of basic notions related to information security, including unauthorized interference with or misuse of information and telecommunications systems and information resources;

(*c*) The content of the concepts mentioned in paragraph 2 of the present resolution;

4. *Requests* the Secretary-General to submit a report based on replies received from Member States to the General Assembly at its fifty-sixth session;

5. *Decides* to include in the provisional agenda of its fifty-sixth session the item entitled "Developments in the field of information and telecommunications in the context of international security".

Role of science and technology in the context of international security and disarmament

GENERAL ASSEMBLY ACTION

On 20 November [meeting 69], the General Assembly, on the recommendation of the First Committee [A/55/555], adopted **resolution 55/29** by recorded vote (97-46-21) [agenda item 69].

Role of science and technology in the context of international security and disarmament

The General Assembly,

Recognizing that scientific and technological developments can have both civilian and military applications and that progress in science and technology for civilian applications needs to be maintained and encouraged,

Concerned that military applications of scientific and technological developments can contribute significantly to the improvement and upgrading of advanced weapon systems and, in particular, weapons of mass destruction,

Aware of the need to follow closely the scientific and technological developments that may have a negative impact on international security and disarmament, and to channel scientific and technological developments for beneficial purposes,

Cognizant that the international transfers of dual-use as well as high-technology products, services and know-how for peaceful purposes are important for the economic and social development of States,

Also cognizant of the need to regulate such transfers of dual-use goods and technologies and high technology with military applications through multilaterally negotiated, universally applicable, non-discriminatory guidelines,

Expressing concern about the growing proliferation of ad hoc and exclusive export control regimes and arrangements for dual-use goods and technologies, which tend to impede the economic and social development of developing countries,

Recalling that in the Final Document of the Twelfth Conference of Heads of State or Government of Non-Aligned Countries, held at Durban, South Africa, from 29 August to 3 September 1998, it was noted with concern that undue restrictions on exports to developing countries of material, equipment and technology for peaceful purposes persist,

Emphasizing that internationally negotiated guidelines for the transfer of high technology with military applications should take into account the legitimate defence requirements of all States and the requirements for the maintenance of international peace and security, while ensuring that access to high-technology products and services and know-how for peaceful purposes is not denied,

1. *Affirms* that scientific and technological progress should be used for the benefit of all mankind to promote the sustainable economic and social development of all States and to safeguard international security and that international cooperation in the use of science and technology through the transfer and exchange of technological know-how for peaceful purposes should be promoted;

2. *Invites* Member States to undertake additional efforts to apply science and technology for disarmament-related purposes and to make disarmament-related technologies available to interested States;

3. *Urges* Member States to undertake multilateral negotiations with the participation of all interested States in order to establish universally acceptable, non-discriminatory guidelines for international transfers of dual-use goods and technologies and high technology with military applications;

4. *Encourages* United Nations bodies to contribute, within existing mandates, to promoting the application of science and technology for peaceful purposes;

5. *Decides* to include in the provisional agenda of its fifty-sixth session the item entitled "Role of science and technology in the context of international security and disarmament".

RECORDED VOTE ON RESOLUTION 55/29:

In favour: Algeria, Angola, Antigua and Barbuda, Bahamas, Bahrain, Bangladesh, Barbados, Belarus, Belize, Benin, Bhutan, Bolivia, Botswana, Brunei Darussalam, Burkina Faso, Burundi, Cambodia, Cameroon, Cape Verde, Chile, China, Colombia, Costa Rica, Côte d'Ivoire, Cuba, Democratic People's Republic of Korea, Djibouti, Dominican Republic, Ecuador, Egypt, El Salvador, Equatorial Guinea, Eritrea, Ethiopia, Fiji, Gabon, Ghana, Grenada, Guatemala, Guinea, Guyana, Haiti, Honduras, India, Indonesia, Iran, Jamaica, Jordan, Kenya, Kuwait, Lao People's Democratic Republic, Lebanon, Lesotho, Libyan Arab Jamahiriya, Madagascar, Malawi, Malaysia, Maldives, Mali, Mauritius, Mexico, Mongolia, Morocco, Mozambique, Myanmar, Namibia, Nauru, Nepal, Nicaragua, Nigeria, Oman, Pakistan, Panama, Papua New Guinea, Peru, Philippines, Qatar, Saint Lucia, Saudi Arabia, Senegal, Sierra Leone, Singapore, Sri Lanka, Sudan, Swaziland, Syrian Arab Republic, Thailand, Togo, Trinidad and Tobago, Tunisia, Uganda, United Arab Emirates, United Republic of Tanzania, Venezuela, Viet Nam, Yemen, Zambia.

Against: Albania, Andorra, Australia, Austria, Belgium, Bosnia and Herzegovina, Bulgaria, Canada, Croatia, Cyprus, Czech Republic, Denmark, Estonia, Finland, France, Germany, Greece, Hungary, Iceland, Ireland, Israel, Italy, Latvia, Liechtenstein, Lithuania, Luxembourg, Malta, Marshall Islands, Micronesia, Monaco, Netherlands, New Zealand, Norway, Poland, Portugal, Republic of Moldova, Romania, San Marino, Slovakia, Slovenia, Spain, Sweden, The former Yugoslav Republic of Macedonia, Turkey, United Kingdom, United States.

Abstaining: Argentina, Armenia, Azerbaijan, Brazil, Georgia, Japan, Kazakhstan, Kyrgyzstan, Paraguay, Republic of Korea, Russian Federation, Samoa, Solomon Islands, South Africa, Tajikistan, Tonga, Turkmenistan, Ukraine, Uruguay, Uzbekistan, Vanuatu.

Peaceful uses of outer space

In 2000, the Committee on the Peaceful Uses of Outer Space (Committee on Outer Space), at its forty-third session (Vienna, 7-16 June) [A/55/20], discussed ways to maintain outer space for peaceful purposes and the spin-off benefits of space technology. It also reviewed the work of its two subcommittees, one concerned with scientific and technical issues and the other with legal questions. In December, the General Assembly endorsed the recommendations of the Committee for its future work, including those made by its subcommittees.

Implementation of UNISPACE-III recommendations

Pursuant to resolution 54/68 [YUN 1999, p. 557], by which the General Assembly endorsed "The Space Millennium: Vienna Declaration on Space and Human Development", adopted by the Third United Nations Conference on the Exploration and Peaceful Uses of Outer Space (UNISPACE III) [ibid., p. 556], the Secretary-General, in a May note [A/AC.105/L.224], submitted the action plan proposed by the Office for Outer Space

Affairs to implement the UNISPACE III recommendations.

The plan proposed initiatives to strengthen the role of the Committee on Outer Space and its subcommittees in the formulation of policy and the implementation of international cooperation in space initiatives, as well as the capacity-building activities of the United Nations Programme on Space Applications, including ways to increase synergy among the Programme's major components. To support the work of the Committee and its subcommittees, the plan proposed activities to promote the use of space science and technology within the UN system and to enhance further system-wide coordination of space-related activities, as well as new initiatives to increase the awareness of the general public and young people on the benefits of space activities and to encourage space-related industry and NGOs to play a larger role in promoting the peaceful uses of outer space. Also proposed was a set of measures to implement those recommendations not included in the programme budget for the 2000-2001 biennium.

The Committee on Outer Space, at its June session [A/55/20], endorsed the action plan proposed by the Office for Outer Space Affairs and agreed that the Scientific and Technical Subcommittee should be assigned the task of reaching a consensus on the implementation of the UNISPACE III recommendations and their associated work plans and of reporting thereon yearly. The Committee took note of the International Astronautical Federation's initiative and other initiatives to engage non-governmental entities in the implementation of selected recommendations; it agreed that those initiatives should be reviewed by the Subcommittee in 2001.

The Committee selected several priority projects from among those identified in the action plan and recommended their inclusion in the Secretary-General's letter to Member States inviting voluntary contributions to the Trust Fund for the United Nations Programme on Space Applications.

Report of Secretary-General. In response to General Assembly resolution 54/68 [YUN 1999, p. 557], the Secretary-General reported in July [A/55/153] on action taken by the Committee on Outer Space at its June session to implement the UNISPACE III recommendations, the strategy pursued by the Programme on Space Applications, including the Programme's reorientation following UNISPACE III, developments in inter-agency cooperation, and enhancement of the International Space Information Service.

Scientific and Technical Subcommittee

The Scientific and Technical Subcommittee of the Committee on Outer Space, at its thirty-seventh session (Vienna, 7-18 February) [A/AC.105/736], considered the United Nations Programme on Space Applications and the coordination of space activities within the UN system following UNISPACE III.

The Subcommittee also dealt with matters related to remote sensing of the Earth by satellites, including applications for developing countries and monitoring of the Earth's environment; the use of nuclear power sources in outer space; international cooperation in human space flight, presentations on new launch systems and ventures; space debris; and the examination of the physical nature and technical attributes of the geostationary orbit and of its utilization and applications.

United Nations
Programme on Space Applications

The United Nations Programme on Space Applications, as mandated by General Assembly resolution 37/90 [YUN 1982, p. 163], continued to focus on developing indigenous capability at the local level in space science and technology through long-range training fellowships, technical advisory services, regional and international training courses and conferences; acquiring and disseminating space-related information; and promoting cooperation between developed and developing countries.

The United Nations Expert on Space Applications, in his January 2001 report to the Subcommittee [A/AC.105/750] pursuant to Assembly resolution 45/72 [YUN 1990, p. 99], said the Programme in 2000 organized regional workshops on the use of space technology in disaster management, in particular for the benefit of developing countries. The objectives of the workshops were to increase awareness of the potential benefits and cost-effectiveness of using space technologies, to determine the types of information and communications needed in managing specific disasters and to develop a plan of action leading to pilot projects that incorporated and tested the use of space tools in disaster management.

The Programme focused on the establishment of regional centres for space science and technology education in developing countries and a Network of Space Science and Technology Education and Research Institutions for Central Eastern and South-Eastern Europe. In July, the Office for Outer Space Affairs invited the regional centres and the Network to provide reports, including information regarding their main objectives and programmes.

The Programme held eight training courses, workshops and conferences in 2000. Under its long-term fellowship programmes for in-depth training, three research fellowships were tenable in 2000 at the European Space Agency (ESA) facilities in Italy. ESA further offered five fellowships for 2001-2002. Under the short-term training programmes, China offered seven one-month fellowship awards tenable in July/August 2000. In addition, various technical advisory services and activities promoting regional cooperation were provided under the Programme.

Earlier, the Subcommittee, in examining the January 2000 report of the Expert on Space Applications [A/AC.105/730], continued to express concern over the limited financial resources available for the Programme and appealed to Member States for voluntary contributions. It noted that the Programme had achieved much with limited resources and agreed that there was no need for radical changes; however, the Programme could be reoriented to better assist developing countries and countries with economies in transition in participating in and benefiting from the implementation of the UNISPACE III recommendations. The emphasis should be on identifying priority areas, optimizing the relationship between the various types of Programme activities, strengthening partnerships and increasing the financial and in-kind resources for carrying out the Programme's mandate.

The Assembly, in **resolution 55/122** (see p. 587), endorsed the United Nations Programme on Space Applications, as proposed by the Expert on Space Applications.

Cooperation

The Inter-Agency Meeting on Outer Space Activities, at its twentieth session (Vienna, 2-4 February) [A/AC.105/727], discussed coordination of plans and programmes in the practical application of space technology and related areas. It reviewed cooperation within the UN system in remote sensing and related geographic information systems, the enhancement of that cooperation through the use of advanced information technologies, and the UNISPACE III action plan and implementation of follow-up activities.

The Meeting stressed that the safety of radioactive and nuclear power sources in outer space should not be treated in isolation from the existing international regime on radiation and nuclear safety and requested the Office for Outer Space Affairs to bring to the Scientific and Technical Subcommittee's attention its view that the Working Group on the Use of Nuclear Power

Sources in Outer Space should take that regime into account. It recommended that the Subcommittee, in conducting its work on the use of nuclear power sources in outer space, should enhance the involvement of the International Atomic Energy Agency and take into account the work of the United Nations Scientific Committee on the Effects of Atomic Radiation and the International Commission on Radiological Protection. The Meeting agreed to provide input into the work of the Commission on Sustainable Development and contribute to any future review of Agenda 21 of the 1992 United Nations Conference on Environment and Development [YUN 1992, p, 672].

In reviewing the UNISPACE III action plan, the Inter-Agency Meeting agreed that it was difficult to identify bodies responsible for space-related activities of some UN system organizations and that no such bodies existed for certain organizations. It felt that the recommendation to establish an ad hoc intergovernmental advisory group should be reformulated and that the Committee on Outer Space, in reviewing UNISPACE III recommendations, should establish a working group to examine the matter and the system-wide coordination of outer space activities, taking into account the Secretary-General's report on the subject. The working group, once established, should be apprised of the working methods of UN system organizations that undertook space-related activities and the Meeting's work should be brought more prominently to the attention of heads of UN system organizations.

The Committee on Outer Space [A/55/20] noted the report of the Inter-Agency Meeting and the Secretary-General's report on the coordination of outer space activities within the UN system: programme of work for 2000 and 2001 and future years [A/AC.105/726].

Other related documents submitted to the Committee were Secretariat notes [A/AC.105/729/ Add.1,2, A/AC.105/752] containing information received from a total of 15 Member States on their space activities, including information on national and international space programmes, as well as on spin-off benefits of space activities and other topics.

Scientific and technical issues

In 2000, the Scientific and Technical Subcommittee [A/AC.105/736] emphasized the importance of providing non-discriminatory access to state-of-the-art remote sensing data and to derived information at reasonable cost, as well as of building capacity in the adoption and use of remote sensing technology, in particular to meet the needs of developing countries. It also emphasized the importance of remote sensing systems for advancing sustainable development, including monitoring of the Earth's environment. It agreed that revision of the 1992 Principles Relevant to the Use of Nuclear Power Sources in Outer Space, adopted by General Assembly resolution 47/68 [YUN 1992, p. 116], was currently not warranted. Until a firm scientific and technical consensus had been reached on such revision, it would be inappropriate to pass on the topic to the Legal Subcommittee.

Concerning space debris, the Subcommittee agreed that: international cooperation was needed to expand strategies to minimize the potential impact of space debris on future space missions; Member States should pay more attention to the problem of collisions of space objects, including those with nuclear power sources on board, with space debris and to other aspects of space debris; and national research on space debris should continue, with Member States and international organizations making available the results of that research, including information on effective practices to minimize the creation of space debris. It noted the 1999 Secretariat report on the disposal of satellites in geosynchronous orbit [YUN 1999, p. 559]. The Subcommittee further noted that International Telecommunication Union (ITU) standards and Inter-Agency Space Debris Coordination Committee recommendations regarding the disposal of spacecraft in geostationary orbit had been recently developed and were not mandatory; that even self-imposed guidelines were not being followed in some cases due to technical and managerial problems; and that more research would be needed to understand fully the space debris environment near the geostationary orbit.

The Committee on Outer Space [A/55/20] agreed with the Subcommittee concerning the revision of the 1992 Principles and that States making use of nuclear power sources should conduct their activities in accordance with those Principles. It also agreed that the Subcommittee and the Working Group should continue to receive the widest input on matters affecting the use of nuclear power sources in outer space and any contribution related to improving the scope and application of the Principles. Member States should continue to be invited to report regularly to the Secretary-General on national and international research on the subject. Further studies should be conducted on the collision of orbiting space objects, with nuclear power sources on board, with space debris.

The Committee endorsed the Subcommittee's conclusions regarding space debris and sug-

gested that the Secretariat prepare a sample index to the United Nations Register of Objects Launched into Outer Space for the Subcommittee's 2001 session.

In response to the Committee's request that Member States report on national and international research on the safety of space objects with nuclear power sources, the Secretariat, in a November note [A/AC.105/751], submitted the replies received from three Member States and one international organization on the subject.

Legal Subcommittee

The Legal Subcommittee, at its thirty-ninth session (Vienna, 27 March–6 April) [A/AC.105/738], considered, through its working group, the definition and delimitation of outer space and the character and utilization of the geostationary orbit, including ways to ensure its rational and equitable use, without prejudice to ITU's role. The Subcommittee adopted the finalized version of a conference room paper by France and other sponsors, entitled "Some aspects concerning the use of the geostationary orbit", and endorsed the report of the working group.

A working group established by the Subcommittee continued to review the status of the international legal instruments governing outer space: the 1966 Treaty on Principles Governing the Activities of States in the Exploration and Use of Outer Space, including the Moon and Other Celestial Bodies, adopted by the General Assembly in resolution 2222(XXI) [YUN 1966, p. 41]; the 1967 Agreement on the Rescue of Astronauts, the Return of Astronauts and the Return of Objects Launched into Outer Space, adopted in resolution 2345(XXII) [YUN 1967, p. 33]; the 1971 Convention on International Liability for Damage Caused by Space Objects, contained in resolution 2777(XXVI) [YUN 1971, p. 52]; the 1974 Convention on Registration of Objects Launched into Outer Space, contained in resolution 3235(XXIX) [YUN 1974, p. 63]; and the 1979 Agreement Governing the Activities of States on the Moon and Other Celestial Bodies, contained in resolution 34/68 [YUN 1979, p. 111].

The working group recommended a series of measures to achieve the fullest adherence to the five instruments: States not parties to them should be invited to consider ratifying or acceding to them; States should be invited to consider making a declaration, in accordance with Assembly resolution 2777(XXVI), thereby binding themselves on a reciprocal basis to the decisions of the Claims Commission, established in the event of a dispute in terms of the provisions of the 1971 Convention; and the issue of the strict compliance by States with the provisions of instruments governing outer space to which they were currently parties should be examined further to identify measures to encourage full compliance.

The Legal Subcommittee, recalling its 1999 decision [YUN, 1999, p. 560] to suspend consideration of the 1992 Principles Relevant to the Use of Nuclear Power Sources in Outer Space [YUN 1992, p. 116] pending the results of deliberations in the Scientific and Technical Subcommittee, agreed to suspend its working group on the subject.

The Subcommittee, in its review of the concept of the "launching State", through its working group established for that purpose, requested the Secretariat to prepare a paper setting out the key elements of national space legislation that, in its judgement, illustrated how States were implementing their responsibilities to authorize and provide continuing supervision of non-governmental entities in outer space. It should include information on State practice drawn from, among other sources, the special presentations on new launch systems and ventures at the Subcommittee's current session.

GENERAL ASSEMBLY ACTION

On 8 December [meeting 83], the General Assembly, on the recommendation of the Fourth Committee [A/55/569], adopted **resolution 55/122** without vote [agenda item 83].

International cooperation in the peaceful uses of outer space

The General Assembly,

Recalling its resolutions 51/122 of 13 December 1996 and 54/67 and 54/68 of 6 December 1999,

Deeply convinced of the common interest of mankind in promoting and expanding the exploration and use of outer space for peaceful purposes and in continuing efforts to extend to all States the benefits derived therefrom, and also of the importance of international cooperation in this field, for which the United Nations should continue to provide a focal point,

Reaffirming the importance of international cooperation in developing the rule of law, including the relevant norms of space law and their important role in international cooperation for the exploration and use of outer space for peaceful purposes, and of the widest possible adherence to international treaties that promote the peaceful uses of outer space,

Seriously concerned about the possibility of an arms race in outer space,

Recognizing that all States, in particular those with major space capabilities, should contribute actively to the goal of preventing an arms race in outer space as an essential condition for the promotion of international cooperation in the exploration and use of outer space for peaceful purposes,

Considering that space debris is an issue of concern to all nations,

Noting the progress achieved in the further development of peaceful space exploration and applications as well as in various national and cooperative space projects, which contributes to international cooperation, and the importance of further international cooperation in this field,

Convinced of the importance of the recommendations contained in the resolution entitled "The Space Millennium: Vienna Declaration on Space and Human Development", adopted by the Third United Nations Conference on the Exploration and Peaceful Uses of Outer Space (UNISPACE III), held at Vienna from 19 to 30 July 1999,

Taking note of the report of the Secretary-General on the implementation of the recommendations of UNISPACE III,

Convinced that the use of space science and technology and their applications in such areas as telemedicine, tele-education and Earth observation contribute to achieving the objectives of the global conferences of the United Nations that address various aspects of economic, social and cultural development,

Having considered the report of the Committee on the Peaceful Uses of Outer Space on the work of its forty-third session,

1. *Endorses* the report of the Committee on the Peaceful Uses of Outer Space on the work of its forty-third session;

2. *Encourages* States that have not yet become parties to the international treaties governing the uses of outer space to give consideration to ratifying those treaties or acceding to them;

3. *Notes* that, at its thirty-ninth session, the Legal Subcommittee of the Committee on the Peaceful Uses of Outer Space continued its work, as mandated by the General Assembly in its resolution 54/67;

4. *Notes with satisfaction* the agreement reached by the Legal Subcommittee on the question of the character and utilization of the geostationary orbit and the subsequent endorsement of that agreement by the Committee;

5. *Endorses* the recommendation of the Committee that the Legal Subcommittee, at its fortieth session, taking into account the concerns of all countries, in particular those of developing countries:

 (a) Consider the following as regular agenda items:

 (i) General exchange of views;

 (ii) Status and application of the five United Nations treaties on outer space;

 (iii) Information on the activities of international organizations relating to space law;

 (iv) Matters relating to the definition and delimitation of outer space and the character and utilization of the geostationary orbit, including consideration of ways and means to ensure the rational and equitable use of the geostationary orbit without prejudice to the role of the International Telecommunication Union;

 (b) Consider the following single issues/items for discussion:

 (i) Review and possible revision of the Principles Relevant to the Use of Nuclear Power Sources in Outer Space;

 (ii) The draft convention of the International Institute for the Unification of Private Law on international interests in mobile equipment and the preliminary draft protocol thereto on matters specific to space property;

(c) Continue its review of the concept of the "launching State", in accordance with the work plan adopted by the Committee;

6. *Notes* that the Legal Subcommittee, at its fortieth session, will submit its proposals to the Committee for new items to be considered by the Subcommittee at its forty-first session, in 2002;

7. *Notes also* that, in the context of paragraph 5 *(a)* (iv) above, and in accordance with the agreement referred to in paragraph 4 above, the Legal Subcommittee will reconvene its working group on the item only to consider matters relating to the definition and delimitation of outer space;

8. *Notes further* that, in the context of paragraph 5 *(c)* above, the Legal Subcommittee will reconvene its working group to consider the item;

9. *Takes note* of the agreement reached by the Committee at its fortieth session on the composition of the bureaux of the Committee and its subsidiary bodies for the second term starting in 2000, in the context of the implementation of the measures relating to the working methods of those bodies, which were endorsed by the General Assembly in paragraph 11 of its resolution 52/56 of 10 December 1997;

10. *Notes with satisfaction* that consensus decisions were reached on the composition of the bureaux for the second term, and agrees that, in accordance with those consensus decisions, the Scientific and Technical Subcommittee and the Legal Subcommittee of the Committee should elect their chairmen for the second term at the beginning of their thirty-eighth and fortieth sessions respectively;

11. *Notes* that, in accordance with the measures relating to the working methods of the Committee and its subsidiary bodies, mentioned in paragraph 9 above, consultations will be held among the regional groups at the forty-fourth session of the Committee to determine which group will be responsible for which office for the third term, starting in 2003;

12. *Notes* that the Scientific and Technical Subcommittee, at its thirty-seventh session, continued its work as mandated by the General Assembly in its resolution 54/67;

13. *Notes with satisfaction* that the Scientific and Technical Subcommittee at its thirty-seventh session continued to consider, on a priority basis, the agenda item on space debris;

14. *Agrees* that the Scientific and Technical Subcommittee should assess the effectiveness of existing space debris mitigation practices and the extent to which they are being implemented and that efforts to model and characterize the debris environment should continue;

15. *Endorses* the recommendation of the Committee that the Scientific and Technical Subcommittee, at its thirty-eighth session, taking into account the concerns of all countries, in particular those of developing countries:

(a) Consider the following items:

(i) General exchange of views and introduction to reports submitted on national activities;

(ii) United Nations Programme on Space Applications, following the Third United Nations Conference on the Exploration and Peaceful Uses of Outer Space (UNISPACE III);

(iii) Matters relating to remote sensing of the Earth by satellite, including applications for developing countries and monitoring of the Earth's environment;

(b) Consider the following items in accordance with the work plans adopted by the Committee at its forty-third session:

(i) Use of nuclear power sources in outer space;

(ii) Means and mechanisms for strengthening inter-agency cooperation and increasing the use of space applications and services within and among entities of the United Nations system;

(iii) Implementation of an integrated, space-based global natural disaster management system;

(c) Consider the following single issues/items for discussion:

(i) Space debris, on a priority basis, consistent with paragraph 370 of the report of UNISPACE III;

(ii) Examination of the physical nature and technical attributes of the geostationary orbit and of its utilization and applications, including, inter alia, in the field of space communications, as well as other questions relating to developments in space communications, taking particular account of the needs and interests of developing countries;

(iii) Government and private activities to promote education in space science and engineering;

16. *Notes* that the Scientific and Technical Subcommittee at its thirty-eighth session will submit its proposal to the Committee for a draft provisional agenda for the thirty-ninth session of the Subcommittee, in 2002;

17. *Endorses* the recommendation of the Committee that the Committee on Space Research and the International Astronautical Federation, in liaison with Member States, be invited to arrange a symposium on the theme "Terrestrial hazards from outer space objects and phenomena", with as wide a participation as possible, to be held during the first week of the thirty-eighth session of the Scientific and Technical Subcommittee;

18. *Notes with satisfaction* that an industry symposium, with the participation of Member States, on emerging applications of global navigation satellite systems in improving the productivity of national and regional infrastructure will be organized during the thirty-eighth session of the Scientific and Technical Subcommittee;

19. *Agrees* that, in the context of paragraphs 15 *(a)* (ii) and 16 above, the Scientific and Technical Subcommittee at its thirty-eighth session should reconvene its Working Group of the Whole and that the Subcommittee should consider, through the Working Group of the Whole, the implementation of the recommendations of UNISPACE III;

20. *Also agrees* that, in the context of paragraph 15 *(b)* (i) above, the Scientific and Technical Subcommittee at its thirty-eighth session should reconvene its Working Group on the Use of Nuclear Power Sources in Outer Space;

21. *Encourages* all the organs, organizations and programmes of the United Nations system to contribute to the work of the Scientific and Technical Subcommittee in the context of paragraph 15 *(b)* (ii) above by, inter alia, providing the Subcommittee with appropriate in-

formation in response to the list of questions approved by the Committee at its forty-third session;

22. *Agrees* that, in the context of paragraph 15 *(c)* (i) above, the Scientific and Technical Subcommittee at its thirty-eighth session should conduct its work in accordance with the agreement of the Committee at its forty-third session;

23. *Endorses* the United Nations Programme on Space Applications for 2001, as proposed to the Committee by the United Nations Expert on Space Applications;

24. *Notes with satisfaction* that, in accordance with paragraph 30 of General Assembly resolution 50/27 of 6 December 1995, the African regional centres for space science and technology education, in the French language and in the English language, located in Morocco and Nigeria respectively, began their first educational activities in April 2000, that the Centre for Space Science and Technology Education in Asia and the Pacific continued its education programme in 2000 and that progress has been achieved in furthering the goals of the Network of Space Science and Technology Education and Research Institutions for Central, Eastern and South-Eastern Europe and in establishing regional centres for space science and technology education in the other regions;

25. *Also notes with satisfaction* that Member States concerned in Asia and the Pacific are holding further consultations, with the assistance of the Office for Outer Space Affairs, with a view to making the Centre for Space Science and Technology Education in Asia and the Pacific grow into a network of nodes;

26. *Recognizes* the usefulness and significance of the space conferences of the Americas for the Latin American countries, encourages the convening of a Fourth Space Conference of the Americas, and also encourages other regions to convene periodically regional conferences with a view to achieving convergence of positions on issues of common concern in the field of the peaceful uses of outer space among States Members of the United Nations;

27. *Urges* all Governments, organs, organizations and programmes within the United Nations system as well as intergovernmental and non-governmental entities conducting space-related activities to take the action necessary for the effective implementation of the recommendations of UNISPACE III, in particular its resolution entitled "The Space Millennium: Vienna Declaration on Space and Human Development", and requests the Secretary-General to report to the General Assembly at its fifty-sixth session on the implementation of the recommendations of UNISPACE III;

28. *Notes* that, pursuant to paragraph 11 of General Assembly resolution 54/68, the Office for Outer Space Affairs had submitted to the Committee for its review at its forty-third session a plan of action to implement the recommendations of UNISPACE III;

29. *Requests* the Secretary-General to begin implementing those measures and activities that are contained in the above-mentioned plan of action and are currently within the programme of work of the Office for Outer Space Affairs, based on the recommendations of UNISPACE III, and to ensure the full implementation of the plan with the necessary resources in 2002;

30. *Agrees* that the Committee should include in the agendas of its forty-fourth to forty-seventh sessions, in 2001, 2002, 2003 and 2004, an item on the implementation of the recommendations of UNISPACE III;

31. *Requests* the Committee to prepare a report under the agenda item on the implementation of the recommendations of UNISPACE III for submission to the General Assembly in order for the Assembly to review and appraise, at its fifty-ninth session, in 2004, in accordance with paragraph 16 of General Assembly resolution 54/68, the implementation of the outcome of UNISPACE III and to consider further actions and initiatives;

32. *Encourages* all Member States to contribute to the Trust Fund for the United Nations Programme on Space Applications to support activities to implement the recommendations of UNISPACE III, in particular the priority project proposals as recommended by the Committee at its forty-third session;

33. *Notes with satisfaction* that, in connection with paragraph 7 of General Assembly resolution 54/68, special events of the United Nations were held at Headquarters and at the United Nations Office at Vienna on 4 October 2000 to launch the first World Space Week and that other events were also held by interested Member States to celebrate World Space Week, and requests the Secretary-General to invite Member States, intergovernmental and non-governmental organizations as well as space-related industries to make voluntary contributions to support activities to celebrate World Space Week;

34. *Recommends* that more attention be paid to all matters relating to the protection and the preservation of the outer space environment, especially those potentially affecting the Earth's environment;

35. *Considers* that it is essential that Member States pay more attention to the problem of collisions of space objects, including those with nuclear power sources, with space debris, and other aspects of space debris, calls for the continuation of national research on this question, for the development of improved technology for the monitoring of space debris and for the compilation and dissemination of data on space debris, also considers that, to the extent possible, information thereon should be provided to the Scientific and Technical Subcommittee, and agrees that international cooperation is needed to expand appropriate and affordable strategies to minimize the impact of space debris on future space missions;

36. *Urges* all States, in particular those with major space capabilities, to contribute actively to the goal of preventing an arms race in outer space as an essential condition for the promotion of international cooperation in the exploration and use of outer space for peaceful purposes;

37. *Emphasizes* the need to increase the benefits of space technology and its applications and to contribute to the orderly growth of space activities favourable to sustained economic growth and sustainable development in all countries, including mitigation of the consequences of disasters, in particular in the developing countries;

38. *Agrees* that the benefits of space technology and its applications should be prominently brought to the attention of conferences organized within the United Nations system to address global issues relating to social, economic and cultural development and that the use of space technology should be promoted towards

achieving the objectives of those conferences and implementing the United Nations Millennium Declaration;

39. *Takes note* of the interest of certain countries, including Saudi Arabia and Slovakia, that submitted requests to become members of the Committee, as well as the requests of those countries that have been sharing seats on a rotating basis, namely, Cuba, Malaysia, Peru and the Republic of Korea, to have that practice terminated and to become full members, and requests the Committee to include in the agenda of its forty-fourth session an item on the enlargement of its membership to consider including as full members those countries requesting membership;

40. *Encourages* Member States to hold informal consultations on the enlargement of membership of the Committee during the thirty-eighth session of the Scientific and Technical Subcommittee and, if necessary, during the fortieth session of the Legal Subcommittee, with a view to reaching a consensus agreement on the matter at the forty-fourth session of the Committee;

41. *Requests* the Committee to continue to consider, as a matter of priority, ways and means of maintaining outer space for peaceful purposes and to report thereon to the Assembly at its fifty-sixth session;

42. *Also requests* the Committee to continue to consider, at its forty-fourth session, its agenda item entitled "Spin-off benefits of space technology: review of current status";

43. *Agrees* that a symposium on the theme "The human dimension in space science and technology applications" should be organized during the forty-fourth session of the Committee;

44. *Invites* the Committee to expand the scope of international cooperation relating to the social, economic, ethical and human dimension in space science and technology applications;

45. *Requests* the specialized agencies and other international organizations to continue and, where appropriate, enhance their cooperation with the Committee and to provide it with progress reports on their work relating to the peaceful uses of outer space;

46. *Requests* the Committee to continue its work, in accordance with the present resolution, to consider, as appropriate, new projects in outer space activities and to submit a report to the General Assembly at its fifty-sixth session, including its views on which subjects should be studied in the future;

47. *Also requests* the Committee to consider and identify new mechanisms of international cooperation in the peaceful uses of outer space, in accordance with the preamble to the present resolution.

Effects of atomic radiation

The United Nations Scientific Committee on the Effects of Atomic Radiation held its forty-ninth session in Vienna from 2 to 11 May [A/55/46]. The Committee, responding to General Assembly resolution 54/66 [YUN 1999, p. 563], continued to review problems in the field of radiation. It summarized developments in radiation science in the years leading up to the new millennium. It examined the effects and levels of radiation exposure, the radiological consequences of the Chernobyl accident (see PART THREE, Chapter III), sources of radiation exposure, including natural, man-made, medical and occupational exposures, and comparisons of exposures. It also considered radiation-associated cancer.

The Committee proposed a renewed programme of work to fulfil its obligations to the Assembly.

GENERAL ASSEMBLY ACTION

On 8 December [meeting 83], the General Assembly, on the recommendation of the Fourth Committee [A/55/568], adopted **resolution 55/121** without vote [agenda item 82].

Effects of atomic radiation

The General Assembly,

Recalling its resolution 913(X) of 3 December 1955, by which it established the United Nations Scientific Committee on the Effects of Atomic Radiation, and its subsequent resolutions on the subject, including resolution 54/66 of 6 December 1999, in which, inter alia, it requested the Scientific Committee to continue its work,

Taking note with appreciation of the work of the United Nations Scientific Committee on the Effects of Atomic Radiation and of the release of its extensive report,

Reaffirming the desirability of the Scientific Committee continuing its work,

Concerned about the potentially harmful effects on present and future generations resulting from the levels of radiation to which mankind and the environment are exposed,

Noting the views expressed by Member States at its fifty-fifth session with regard to the work of the Scientific Committee,

Conscious of the continuing need to examine and compile information about atomic and ionizing radiation and to analyse its effects on mankind and the environment,

1. *Commends* the United Nations Scientific Committee on the Effects of Atomic Radiation for the valuable contribution it has been making in the course of the past forty-five years, since its inception, to wider knowledge and understanding of the levels, effects and risks of ionizing radiation, and for fulfilling its original mandate with scientific authority and independence of judgement;

2. *Takes note with appreciation* of the work of the Scientific Committee and of the release of its extensive report, entitled *Sources and Effects of Ionizing Radiation: United Nations Scientific Committee on the Effects of Atomic Radiation—Report to the General Assembly, with Scientific Annexes,* which provides the scientific and world community with the Committee's latest evaluations of the sources and effects of ionizing radiation on human beings and their environment;

3. *Reaffirms* the decision to maintain the present functions and independent role of the Scientific Committee, including its present reporting arrangements;

4. *Requests* the Scientific Committee to continue its work, including its important activities to increase knowledge of the levels, effects and risks of ionizing radiation from all sources, and invites the Scientific Committee to submit its programme of work to the General Assembly;

5. *Endorses* the intentions and plans of the Scientific Committee for its future activities of scientific review and assessment on behalf of the General Assembly;

6. *Requests* the Scientific Committee to continue at its next session the review of the important problems in the field of ionizing radiation and to report thereon to the General Assembly at its fifty-sixth session;

7. *Requests* the United Nations Environment Programme to continue providing support for the effective conduct of the work of the Scientific Committee and for the dissemination of its findings to the General Assembly, the scientific community and the public;

8. *Expresses its appreciation* for the assistance rendered to the Scientific Committee by Member States, the specialized agencies, the International Atomic Energy Agency and non-governmental organizations, and invites them to increase their cooperation in this field;

9. *Invites* the Scientific Committee to continue its consultations with scientists and experts from interested Member States in the process of preparing its future scientific reports;

10. *Welcomes*, in this context, the readiness of Member States to provide the Scientific Committee with relevant information on the effects of ionizing radiation in affected areas, and invites the Scientific Committee to analyse and give due consideration to such information, particularly in the light of its own findings;

11. *Invites* Member States, the organizations of the United Nations system and non-governmental organizations concerned to provide further relevant data about doses, effects and risks from various sources of radiation, which would greatly help in the preparation of future reports of the Scientific Committee to the General Assembly.

PART TWO

Human rights

Chapter I

Promotion of human rights

United Nations efforts to promote human rights continued in 2000 through the Commission on Human Rights and its subsidiary body, the Subcommission on the Promotion and Protection of Human Rights. The Office of the United Nations High Commissioner for Human Rights continued its human rights coordination and implementation activities, and provided advisory services and technical cooperation.

Human rights instruments and their monitoring bodies promoted civil, political, economic, social and cultural rights, and aimed to eliminate racial discrimination and discrimination against women, to protect children and to end the practice of torture and other cruel, inhuman or degrading treatment or punishment.

In May, the General Assembly adopted an optional protocol to the Convention on the Rights of the Child on involvement of children in armed conflict, as well as an optional protocol to that Convention on the sale of children, child prostitution and child pornography.

The international community observed the International Year for the Culture of Peace, proclaimed by the General Assembly in 1997.

UN machinery

Commission on Human Rights

The Commission on Human Rights held its fifty-sixth session in Geneva from 20 March to 28 April [E/2000/23 & Corr.1], during which it adopted 87 resolutions and 13 decisions. The Commission recommended four draft resolutions and 49 draft decisions for adoption by the Economic and Social Council. On 28 April [dec. 2000/113], the Commission decided to include in its report to the Council the administrative and programme budget implications of the resolutions and decisions adopted. On 28 July, the Council took note of the Commission's report (**decision 2000/289**). In October, the Commission held a special session on grave and massive violations of the human rights of the Palestinian people by Israel [E/2000/112 & Add.1] (see p. 776). It also held a special debate on poverty and human rights [E/CN.4/2000/SR.41 & 42].

On 21 March [dec. 2000/101], the Commission invited special representatives, special rapporteurs, chairpersons and chairpersons-rapporteurs of various working groups and experts to participate in its meetings.

Regarding enhancing the effectiveness of the Commission's mechanisms, pursuant to a 1999 Subcommission request [YUN 1999, p. 567], the Secretary-General submitted, in February, financial data relating to meeting costs for the Commission, the Subcommission on the Promotion and Protection of Human Rights, the Human Rights Committee and the Committee on the Rights of the Child [E/CN.4/2000/114]. The Working Group on Enhancing the Effectiveness of the Mechanisms of the Commission on Human Rights, established in 1999 [YUN 1999, p. 567], adopted its report by consensus [E/CN.4/2000/112], following meetings in 1999 [YUN 1999, p. 568], on 18 and 19 January and from 7 to 11 February 2000. The Commission Chairperson, on 22 March, outlined the logistics of consideration of the Group's report [E/2000/23]. On 26 April [dec. 2000/109], the Commission decided to approve and implement the report and emphasized its importance and relevance. It also decided to facilitate the report's implementation, to transmit to the Economic and Social Council for approval a draft resolution on the procedure for dealing with communications concerning violations of human rights and fundamental freedoms, established by Council resolution 1503(XLVIII) [YUN 1970, p. 530] (the 1503 procedure), and a draft decision on enhancing the effectiveness of the Commission's mechanisms. Pending the Council's adoption of the draft on the 1503 procedure, the Commission, on 26 April [dec. 2000/110], decided that communications and replies thereto, on which the Subcommission in 1999 had decided to defer action to its next session, should be referred back to the Working Group on Communications, to be examined at its next annual session, following the Subcommission's 2000 session, to determine whether they should be brought to the attention of the Working Group on Situations, in accordance with the draft resolution.

ECONOMIC AND SOCIAL COUNCIL ACTION

On 16 June [meeting 10], the Economic and Social Council adopted **resolution 2000/3** [draft: E/2000/L.5] without vote [agenda item 2].

Procedure for dealing with communications concerning human rights

The Economic and Social Council,

Recalling its resolution 728 F (XXVIII) of 30 July 1959 concerning the handling of communications concerning human rights and its decision 79(LVIII) of 6 May 1975 relating thereto,

Recalling also its resolution 1235(XLII) of 6 June 1967 authorizing the Commission on Human Rights to examine information relevant to gross violations of human rights and fundamental freedoms, its resolution 1503(XLVIII) of 27 May 1970 establishing a procedure for dealing with communications relating to violations of human rights and fundamental freedoms and its resolution 1990/41 of 25 May 1990 concerning the establishment, composition and designation of the members of the Working Group on Situations of the Commission,

Recalling further resolution 1(XXIV) of the Subcommission on Prevention of Discrimination and Protection of Minorities (now the Subcommission on the Promotion and Protection of Human Rights) of 13 August 1971 concerning criteria for the admissibility of communications, as well as Subcommission resolution 2(XXIV) of 16 August 1971 concerning the establishment, composition and designation of the members of the Working Group on Communications,

Recalling Commission on Human Rights decisions 3(XXX) of 6 March 1974, 5(XXXIV) of 3 March 1978 and 9(XXXVI) of 7 March 1980, all aimed at facilitating government participation and cooperation under the procedure, and decision 3(XXXIV) of 3 March 1978 inviting the Chairman-Rapporteur of the Working Group on Communications to be present during the deliberations of the Commission on that item,

Taking note of Commission on Human Rights decision 2000/109 of 26 April 2000, in which the Commission, inter alia, approved the recommendations of its inter-sessional open-ended Working Group on Enhancing the Effectiveness of the Mechanisms of the Commission on Human Rights concerning the review of the procedure governed by Council resolution 1503(XLVIII) and related resolutions and decisions,

1. *Endorses* Commission on Human Rights decision 2000/109 insofar as it concerns the review of the procedure governed by Council resolution 1503(XLVIII) and related resolutions and decisions;

2. *Decides,* accordingly, that the Working Group on Communications designated in conformity with paragraph 37 of the report of the inter-sessional open-ended Working Group on Enhancing the Effectiveness of the Mechanisms of the Commission on Human Rights shall henceforth meet annually for two weeks, immediately following the annual session of the Subcommission on the Promotion and Protection of Human Rights, to examine the communications received under Council resolution 728 F (XXVIII) that have been transmitted to the Governments concerned not later than twelve weeks prior to the meeting of the Working Group on Communications, and any government replies relating thereto, in conformity with the criteria for the admissibility of communications contained in resolution 1(XXIV) of the Subcommission, with a view to bringing to the attention of the Working Group on Situations any particular situations which appear to reveal a consistent pattern of gross and reliably attested violations of human rights and fundamental freedoms;

3. *Requests* the Secretary-General, with the approval of the Chairman-Rapporteur of the Working Group on Communications, to screen out manifestly ill-founded communications in the preparation of the monthly confidential summaries of communications (confidential lists of communications) communicated to the members of the Working Group, it being understood that communications screened out would not be transmitted to the Governments concerned for reply;

4. *Calls upon* the Secretary-General to inform the countries concerned, immediately after the conclusion of the meeting of the Working Group on Communications, of the actions taken in regard to them;

5. *Entrusts* to the Working Group on Situations designated in conformity with paragraph 40 of the report of the inter-sessional open-ended Working Group on Enhancing the Effectiveness of the Mechanisms of the Commission on Human Rights, which shall meet annually for one week not less than one month prior to the annual session of the Commission, the role of examining the confidential report and recommendations of the Working Group on Communications and determining whether or not to refer a particular situation thus brought before it to the Commission, as well as of examining the particular situations kept under review by the Commission under the procedure, and, accordingly, of submitting to the Commission a confidential report identifying the main issues of concern, normally together with a draft resolution or draft decision recommending the action to be taken by the Commission in respect of the situations referred to it;

6. *Requests* the Secretary-General to make the confidential files available, at least one week in advance of the first closed meeting, to all members of the Commission on Human Rights;

7. *Authorizes* the Commission on Human Rights, as it deems appropriate, to consider the particular situations placed before it by the Working Group on Situations, as well as the situations kept under review, in two separate closed meetings, employing the following modalities:

(*a*) At the first closed meeting, each country concerned would be invited to make opening presentations; a discussion would then follow between members of the Commission and the Government concerned, based on the contents of confidential files and the report of the Working Group on Situations;

(*b*) In the interim between the first and second closed meetings, any member or members of the Commission could submit an alternative or an amendment to any texts forwarded by the Working Group on Situations; any such draft texts would be circulated confidentially by the secretariat, in accordance with the rules of procedure of the functional commissions of the Council, in advance of the second closed meeting;

(*c*) At the second closed meeting, members of the Commission would discuss and take action on the draft resolutions or decisions; a representative or representatives of the Governments concerned would have the right to be present during the adoption of the final resolution or decision taken in regard to the human rights situation in that country; as has been the established practice, the Chairperson of the Commission would subsequently announce in a public meeting which countries had been examined under the 1503 procedure, as well as the names of countries no longer being dealt with under the procedure; the 1503 dossiers would remain confidential, except where the Government concerned has indicated the wish that they become public;

(*d*) In accordance with the established practice, the action taken in respect of a particular situation should be one of the following options:

(i) To discontinue consideration of the matter when further consideration or action is not warranted;

(ii) To keep the situation under review in the light of any further information received from the Government concerned and any further information which may reach the Commission under the 1503 procedure;

(iii) To keep the situation under review and to appoint an independent expert;

(iv) To discontinue consideration of the matter under the confidential procedure governed by Council resolution 1503(XLVIII) in order to take up consideration of the same matter under the public procedure governed by Council resolution 1235(XLII);

8. *Decides* that the provisions of Council resolution 1503(XLVIII) and related resolutions and decisions not affected by the present reorganization of work shall remain in force, including:

(*a*) Provisions relating to the duties and responsibilities of the Secretary-General, it being understood that, in respect of the handling of communications and government replies relating thereto, the duties and responsibilities are as follows:

(i) The compilation, as before, of monthly confidential summaries of incoming communications concerning alleged violations of human rights; the identity of authors may be deleted upon request;

(ii) The transmittal of a copy of each summarized communication, in the language received, to the Government concerned for reply, without divulging the identity of the author if he or she so requests;

(iii) Acknowledging the receipt of communications to their authors;

(iv) The reproduction and circulation to the members of the Commission on Human Rights, as before, of the replies received from Governments;

(*b*) Provisions aimed at facilitating government cooperation and participation in the procedure, including the provisions of Commission decision 3(XXX), now to be applied following the meetings of the Working Group on Communications;

9. *Also decides* that all actions envisaged in the implementation of the present resolution by the Working Group on Communications, the Working Group on Situations and the Commission on Human Rights shall remain confidential until such time as the Commission may decide to make recommendations to the Council;

10. *Further decides* that the procedure as amended may continue to be referred to as the 1503 procedure.

On 28 July, the Council, on the recommendation of the Commission on Human Rights [E/2000/23 & Corr.1], adopted **decision 2000/284** without vote [agenda item 14 (*g*)].

Enhancing the effectiveness of the mechanisms of the Commission on Human Rights

At its 45th plenary meeting, on 28 July 2000, the Economic and Social Council, taking note of Commission on Human Rights decision 2000/109 of 26 April 2000, by which the Commission decided to approve and implement comprehensively and in its entirety the report of the inter-sessional open-ended Working Group on Enhancing the Effectiveness of the Mechanisms of the Commission on Human Rights, endorsed the following specific decisions of the Commission:

(*a*) To merge the mandates of the independent expert on the effects of structural adjustment policies on economic, social and cultural rights and the Special Rapporteur on the effects of foreign debt on the full enjoyment of economic, social and cultural rights, thus creating a post of independent expert on the effects of structural adjustment policies and foreign debt on the full enjoyment of all human rights, particularly economic, social and cultural rights;

(*b*) To establish a time-limit of two terms of three years for membership of special procedures working groups, as well as for special rapporteurs, whose position in relation to time-limits is covered by the statement made by the Chairperson of the Commission on 29 April 1999. In the case of the Working Group on Arbitrary Detention and the Working Group on Enforced or Involuntary Disappearances, as a transitional measure, turnover of membership in both groups shall be accomplished incrementally over a three-year period. In order to provide the appropriate continuity during this transitional period, two members shall be replaced in year one, two in year two and one in year three;

(*c*) To reduce the duration of the annual meeting of the Working Group on Contemporary Forms of Slavery of the Subcommission on the Promotion and Protection of Human Rights to five working days from the present eight days;

(*d*) To request the Chairperson of the Commission to convene a one-day informal meeting of the Commission in late September each year to facilitate exchange of information in advance of the consideration of the item on human rights by the General Assembly. Such a meeting shall be convened for the first time in September 2000;

(*e*) That the annual session of the Subcommission on the Promotion and Protection of Human Rights shall, from this year, be of three weeks' duration;

(*f*) That chairpersons of standard-setting working groups shall, if the working group considers it appropriate and in consultation with the Office of the United Nations High Commissioner for Human Rights, be provided with the necessary financial assistance to undertake informal consultations during the inter-sessional period with a view to advancing progress in respect of the working group's mandate.

On 14 August [dec. 2000/105], the Subcommission on the Promotion and Protection of Human Rights, with the object of implementing Commission decision 2000/109 (see p. 595), decided to include on an experimental basis in its annual report an overview of its discussions on human rights violations. The Subcommission, on 18 August, revised its decision and asked the Commission's advice as to how it could best inform the Commission of its deliberations under the item on human rights violations.

Pursuant to Commission decision 2000/109, the Commission Chairperson held a one-day informal meeting of the Commission on 15 September [E/CN.4/IM/2000/1] to facilitate exchange of information in advance of the General Assembly.

Organization of work in 2001

On 26 April [dec. 2000/111], the Commission decided that its fifty-seventh session should take place from 19 March to 27 April 2001. The Economic and Social Council approved that decision on 28 July (decision 2000/285).

Also on 26 April [dec. 2000/112], the Commission recommended that the Council authorize 30 fully serviced additional meetings, to be used only if necessary, for the Commission's 2001 session, and requested the Chairperson of that session to make every effort to organize its work within the times normally allotted. By decision 2000/286 of 28 July, the Council authorized the additional meetings and approved the Commission's request to its Chairperson.

Thematic procedures

A meeting of the special rapporteurs/representatives, experts and chairpersons of working groups of the special procedures of the Commission and of the advisory services programme was held in 2000 (see p. 623).

Commission action. On 27 April [res. 2000/86], the Commission asked the thematic special rapporteurs, representatives, experts and working groups to make recommendations to prevent human rights violations; follow progress made by Governments; continue close cooperation with relevant treaty bodies and country rapporteurs; include in their reports information provided by Governments on follow-up action, as well as their own observations thereon; include in their reports gender-disaggregated data and address human rights violations directed against women, or to which women were particularly vulnerable; and address human rights violations directed against children, or to which children were particularly vulnerable, and include age-disaggregated data. The Commission requested them to include in their reports comments on problems of responsiveness and the result of analyses, and suggestions as to areas where Governments might re-

quest assistance through the programme of advisory services administered by the Office of the United Nations High Commissioner for Human Rights (OHCHR). The Secretary-General was asked to convene periodic meetings of thematic special rapporteurs, representatives, experts and chairpersons of working groups and treaty bodies to enable them to exchange views, cooperate and coordinate more closely and make recommendations. He should issue annually their conclusions and recommendations; present annually a list of all persons currently constituting the thematic and country procedures; and ensure the availability of resources to implement all thematic mandates.

The Commission's requests to the Secretary-General to convene periodic meetings and to ensure the availability of resources were approved by the Economic and Social Council by decision 2000/281 of 28 July.

Subcommission on the Promotion and Protection of Human Rights

2000 session

The Subcommission on the Promotion and Protection of Human Rights, at its fifty-second session (Geneva, 31 July–18 August) [E/CN.4/2001/2], adopted 27 resolutions and 20 decisions, and recommended 14 draft decisions for adoption by the Commission.

The Subcommission approved the composition of its working groups for 2001 [dec. 2000/119], took note of items proposed by the Bureau for the Subcommission's draft provisional agenda for 2001 [dec. 2000/120] and asked its Chairperson to submit a written report to the Commission in 2001 regarding significant aspects of the Subcommission's work [dec. 2000/106]. It expressed concern that the reduction in length of its annual session would adversely affect the effectiveness of the sessional working group on the administration of justice [res. 2000/5].

The Subcommission adjourned until 2001 the debates on State cooperation with UN human rights mechanisms [dec. 2000/117] and on the adverse effects on human rights of the proliferation and transfer of small arms and light weapons [dec. 2000/118].

Report of Subcommission Chairperson. The Commission considered a January report [E/CN.4/2000/87], submitted in response to its 1999 request [YUN 1999, p. 568] and prepared by the Subcommission's 1999 Chairperson, Ribot Hatano (Japan), describing various aspects of the Subcommission's work, including its methods of work, the rationalization of its work, and studies, reports and new subjects. The report contained an evaluation of the Subcommission's work in 1999.

Commission action. On 26 April [res. 2000/83], the Commission decided to consider the Subcommission's work in 2001.

Office of the High Commissioner for Human Rights

Reports of High Commissioner. In her annual report to the Commission [E/CN.4/2000/12], the United Nations High Commissioner for Human Rights, Mary Robinson (Ireland), discussed the prevention of human rights violations. She stated that the evolution of a human rights situation was often a barometer of conflict, which she believed would assist the Security Council in its efforts to prevent conflicts. Preventive measures currently in use included urgent appeals by special rapporteurs and thematic mechanisms; requests by treaty bodies for emergency reports; the urgent discussion of situations in such bodies as the Committee on the Elimination of Racial Discrimination; the indication of interim measures of protection under petition procedures for which treaty bodies were responsible; the urgent dispatch of personal envoys of the Secretary-General, the High Commissioner or other organizations, as well as human rights and humanitarian observers or fact-finders; the establishment of international courts; and proposals to establish a rapid reaction force. It was the High Commissioner's intention to strengthen those activities and to seek the assistance of partners to maintain a list of eminent persons who could offer their good offices to defuse situations where gross violations of human rights appeared imminent; develop a capacity for the rapid dispatch of human rights and humanitarian observers or fact-finders in situations of need; dispatch personal envoys of the High Commissioner to incipient crisis situations; and submit urgent reports to the Bureau of the Commission and to the Secretary-General, requesting that he make them available to Council members.

In an addendum to her annual report [E/CN.4/2000/12/Add.1], the High Commissioner described activities taken to promote tolerance and pluralism, pursuant to a 1998 Commission request [YUN 1998, p. 653]; provided an assessment of OHCHR field presences, as requested in 1999 [YUN 1999, p. 570]; and described OHCHR efforts to promote democracy, also in response to a 1999 request [ibid., p. 630].

In a June report [E/2000/83], the High Commissioner described action taken by human rights mechanisms regarding racism, racial discrimination, xenophobia and related intolerance (see p. 640), social development and women's human rights and national institutions for the promotion and protection of human rights (see p. 636). On 28 July, the Economic and Social Council took note of that report (**decision 2000/289**).

In an August report [A/55/36], the High Commissioner invited the General Assembly to outline new strategies for the more effective protection of human rights, particularly to consider steps to prevent gross violations of human rights and for the integration of human rights and development, as well as of human rights in efforts for the maintenance of international peace and security and for the implementation of the right to development. She drew the Assembly's attention to new foundations that had been developed for more effective human rights protection and, regarding the prevention of human rights violations, updated the human rights situations in Chechnya (Russian Federation), East Timor and Sierra Leone. A review of developments in areas of structural significance included human rights and development; human rights and social strategies; women's human rights; human rights issues at the Millennium Assembly of the United Nations (2000); and perspectives on the 2001 World Conference against Racism, Racial Discrimination, Xenophobia and Related Intolerance (see p. 641). In an annex to the report, the High Commissioner discussed the international human rights treaty system. She urged universal ratification, accompanied by the strengthening and rationalization of the treaty system, better integration of treaty-body jurisprudence into UN activities, and expansion and improvement in Secretariat servicing. It was critical, she said, to allocate adequate resources for the servicing of the treaty bodies.

On 4 December, the General Assembly took note of the report of the Third (Social, Humanitarian and Cultural) Committee [A/55/602/Add.5] pertaining to the August report of the High Commissioner (**decision 55/422**).

Commission action. On 7 April [res. 2000/1], the Commission called on the High Commissioner to continue to emphasize the promotion and protection of economic, social and cultural rights and encouraged her to continue to strengthen her relationship with the relevant UN bodies, funds and specialized agencies. It also called on her to continue to strengthen the management of her Office and to improve OHCHR's responsiveness in all priority areas, especially economic, social and cultural rights. The High Commissioner was asked to submit information pursuant to the Commission's resolution in her annual report to the Commission. The Commission recommended that the Economic and Social Council and the General Assembly provide OHCHR with means commensurate to its increasing tasks, as well as more resources for special rapporteurs. By **decision 2000/244** of 28 July, the Council endorsed the Commission's recommendation.

On 25 April [E/2000/23 & Corr.1], the Commission adopted by consensus a statement of its Chairperson, reaffirming its appeal to the Council and the Assembly for additional resources. On 28 July, the Council, taking note of the statement, approved the Commission's recommendation to the Council regarding the allocation of additional resources (**decision 2000/287**).

Annual Appeal 2000

The Annual Appeal 2000, launched by the High Commissioner, sought $53.1 million in voluntary contributions for support to national human rights institutions and to develop regional strategies with partners in the five UN regional groups established by the General Assembly (Africa, Asia, Latin America and the Caribbean, Western Europe and other States, Eastern Europe) to promote and protect human rights through national capacity-building, national plans of action, the ratification and implementation of international conventions and the pursuit of regional cooperation. As at 31 October, $36 million had been received.

Commission action. On 7 April [res. 2000/1], the Commission welcomed the Annual Appeal 2000 and asked the High Commissioner to inform Member States on all aspects of follow-up to, and preparation of, annual appeals. It noted the High Commissioner's request that voluntary contributions should be unearmarked and asked Governments to take account of her request. The High Commissioner was asked to submit information pursuant to the resolution in her annual report to the Commission.

OIOS audit

In response to General Assembly resolution 54/244 [YUN 1999, p. 1274], the Secretary-General, in April [A/54/836], transmitted a report of the Office of Internal Oversight Services (OIOS) on the audit of the OHCHR Human Rights Field Operation in Rwanda (HRFOR), which was established in 1994 [YUN 1994, p. 1071] and had closed in 1998 [YUN 1998, p. 736]. The audit, carried out at OHCHR's request, covered the period September 1998 to February 1999.

The audit determined that HRFOR's internal controls relating to finance, personnel, procurement and property management either were not in place or did not function effectively. There

were also serious breakdowns in communications and cooperation between the field and headquarters. Based on the audit results, OHCHR recognized that it needed to change the administration of its field operations to improve management accountability. OIOS made a series of recommendations and, although HRFOR had already closed, OIOS expressed the view that OHCHR had benefited from the lessons learned and the related recommendations. Annexed to the report were the observations of OHCHR.

The General Assembly, on 15 June (**decision 54/462 B**), deferred consideration of the report until its fifty-fifth session. On 23 December (**decision 55/458**), it decided that the agenda items under which the report was submitted remained for consideration at the resumed fifty-fifth (2001) session.

Composition of staff

Report of High Commissioner. As requested by the Commission in 1999 [YUN 1999, p. 570], the High Commissioner, in February [E/CN.4/2000/104], submitted a report on the composition of OHCHR staff reflecting grade, nationality and gender as at 31 December 1999.

Commission action. On 26 April [res. 2000/73], by a roll-call vote of 35 to 17, with 1 abstention, the Commission requested the Secretary-General to ensure that particular attention was paid to recruiting personnel from developing countries for existing vacancies and additional OHCHR posts to ensure an equitable geographical distribution, giving priority to high-level and Professional posts and the recruitment of women. It asked the High Commissioner to report in 2001.

Strengthening action to promote human rights

Report of Secretary-General. In response to General Assembly resolution 54/174 [YUN 1999, p. 571], the Secretary-General, in an August report with later addenda [A/55/213 & Add.1,2], summarized replies received from five Member States in response to his request for information on proposals for strengthening UN action in human rights, through the promotion of international cooperation based on the principles of non-selectivity, impartiality and objectivity.

GENERAL ASSEMBLY ACTION

On 4 December [meeting 81], the General Assembly, on the recommendation of the Third Committee [A/55/602/Add.2 & Corr.1], adopted **resolution 55/104** without vote [agenda item 114 (b)].

Strengthening United Nations action in the field of human rights through the promotion of international cooperation and the importance of non-selectivity, impartiality and objectivity

The General Assembly,

Bearing in mind that among the purposes of the United Nations are those of developing friendly relations among nations based on respect for the principle of equal rights and self-determination of peoples and taking other appropriate measures to strengthen universal peace, as well as achieving international cooperation in solving international problems of an economic, social, cultural or humanitarian character and in promoting and encouraging respect for human rights and fundamental freedoms for all without distinction as to race, sex, language or religion,

Desirous of achieving further progress in international cooperation in promoting and encouraging respect for human rights and fundamental freedoms,

Considering that such international cooperation should be based on the principles embodied in international law, especially the Charter of the United Nations, as well as the Universal Declaration of Human Rights, the International Covenants on Human Rights and other relevant instruments,

Deeply convinced that United Nations action in this field should be based not only on a profound understanding of the broad range of problems existing in all societies but also on full respect for the political, economic and social realities of each of them, in strict compliance with the purposes and principles of the Charter and for the basic purpose of promoting and encouraging respect for human rights and fundamental freedoms through international cooperation,

Recalling its previous resolutions in this regard,

Reaffirming the importance of ensuring the universality, objectivity and non-selectivity of the consideration of human rights issues, as affirmed in the Vienna Declaration and Programme of Action, adopted by the World Conference on Human Rights on 25 June 1993,

Affirming the importance of the objectivity, independence and discretion of the special rapporteurs and representatives on thematic issues and on countries, as well as of the members of the working groups, in carrying out their mandates,

Underlining the obligation that Governments have to promote and protect human rights and to carry out the responsibilities that they have undertaken under international law, especially the Charter, as well as various international instruments in the field of human rights,

1. *Reiterates* that, by virtue of the principle of equal rights and self-determination of peoples enshrined in the Charter of the United Nations, all peoples have the right freely to determine, without external interference, their political status and to pursue their economic, social and cultural development, and that every State has the duty to respect that right within the provisions of the Charter, including respect for territorial integrity;

2. *Reaffirms* that it is a purpose of the United Nations and the task of all Member States, in cooperation with the Organization, to promote and encourage respect for human rights and fundamental freedoms and to remain vigilant with regard to violations of human rights wherever they occur;

3. *Calls upon* all Member States to base their activities for the promotion and protection of human rights, including the development of further international cooperation in this field, on the Charter of the United Nations, the Universal Declaration of Human Rights, the International Covenant on Economic, Social and Cultural Rights, the International Covenant on Civil and Political Rights and other relevant international instruments, and to refrain from activities that are inconsistent with that international framework;

4. *Considers* that international cooperation in this field should make an effective and practical contribution to the urgent task of preventing mass and flagrant violations of human rights and fundamental freedoms for all and to the strengthening of international peace and security;

5. *Reaffirms* that the promotion, protection and full realization of all human rights and fundamental freedoms, as a legitimate concern of the world community, should be guided by the principles of non-selectivity, impartiality and objectivity and should not be used for political ends;

6. *Requests* all human rights bodies within the United Nations system, as well as the special rapporteurs and representatives, independent experts and working groups, to take duly into account the contents of the present resolution in carrying out their mandates;

7. *Expresses its conviction* that an unbiased and fair approach to human rights issues contributes to the promotion of international cooperation as well as to the effective promotion, protection and realization of human rights and fundamental freedoms;

8. *Stresses,* in this context, the continuing need for impartial and objective information on the political, economic and social situations and events of all countries;

9. *Invites* Member States to consider adopting, as appropriate, within the framework of their respective legal systems and in accordance with their obligations under international law, especially the Charter, and international human rights instruments, the measures that they may deem appropriate to achieve further progress in international cooperation in promoting and encouraging respect for human rights and fundamental freedoms;

10. *Requests* the Commission on Human Rights to take duly into account the present resolution and to consider further proposals for the strengthening of United Nations action in the field of human rights through the promotion of international cooperation and the importance of non-selectivity, impartiality and objectivity;

11. *Takes note* of the report of the Secretary-General, and requests the Secretary-General to invite Member States to present practical proposals and ideas that would contribute to the strengthening of United Nations action in the field of human rights, through the promotion of international cooperation based on the principles of non-selectivity, impartiality and objectivity, and to submit a comprehensive report on this question to the General Assembly at its fifty-sixth session;

12. *Decides* to consider this matter at its fifty-sixth session under the item entitled "Human rights questions".

By **decision 55/458** of 23 December, the Assembly decided that human rights questions remained for consideration during its resumed fifty-fifth (2001) session.

International cooperation and promotion of dialogue

Commission action. On 26 April [res. 2000/70], the Commission considered that international cooperation in human rights should contribute to preventing violations of human rights and fundamental freedoms. It reaffirmed that the promotion, protection and full realization of all human rights and fundamental freedoms should be guided by the principles of universality, non-selectivity, objectivity and transparency.

Subcommission action. On 18 August [res. 2000/22], the Subcommission, reiterating its commitment to international cooperation in human rights, invited governmental and non-governmental observers of the Subcommission to carry out constructive dialogue and consultations based on equality and mutual respect. It endorsed the cooperative approach in search of common understanding and reasonable accommodation of divergent views.

GENERAL ASSEMBLY ACTION

On 4 December [meeting 81], the General Assembly, on the recommendation of the Third Committee [A/55/602/Add.2 & Corr.1], adopted **resolution 55/109** without vote [agenda item 114 (b)].

Enhancement of international cooperation in the field of human rights

The General Assembly,

Recalling its resolution 54/181 of 17 December 1999, taking note of Commission on Human Rights resolution 2000/70 of 26 April 2000 on the enhancement of international cooperation in the field of human rights, and recalling also Assembly resolution 54/113 of 10 December 1999 on the United Nations Year of Dialogue among Civilizations,

Reaffirming its commitment to promoting international cooperation, as set forth in the Charter of the United Nations, in particular Article 1, paragraph 3, as well as relevant provisions of the Vienna Declaration and Programme of Action adopted by the World Conference on Human Rights on 25 June 1993, for enhancing genuine cooperation among Member States in the field of human rights,

Recognizing that the enhancement of international cooperation in the field of human rights is essential for the full achievement of the purposes of the United Nations, including the effective promotion and protection of all human rights,

Recognizing also the importance of ensuring the universality, objectivity and non-selectivity of the consideration of human rights issues, and underlining the importance of the promotion of dialogue on human rights issues,

Reaffirming that dialogue among religions, cultures and civilizations in the field of human rights could contribute greatly to the enhancement of international cooperation in this field,

Emphasizing the need for further progress in the promotion and encouragement of respect for human rights and fundamental freedoms through, in particular, international cooperation,

Underlining the fact that mutual understanding, dialogue, cooperation, transparency and confidence-building are important elements in all the activities for the promotion and protection of human rights,

Recalling the adoption of resolution 1999/25 of 26 August 1999, entitled "Promotion of dialogue on human rights issues", by the Subcommission on the Promotion and Protection of Human Rights at its fifty-first session, and noting its consideration of the question of a dialogue among civilizations at its fifty-second session,

1. *Reaffirms* that it is one of the purposes of the United Nations and the responsibility of all Member States to promote, protect and encourage respect for human rights and fundamental freedoms through, inter alia, international cooperation;

2. *Considers* that international cooperation in this field, in conformity with the purposes and principles set out in the Charter of the United Nations and international law, should make an effective and practical contribution to the urgent task of preventing violations of human rights and of fundamental freedoms for all;

3. *Reaffirms* that the promotion, protection and full realization of all human rights and fundamental freedoms should be guided by the principles of universality, non-selectivity, objectivity and transparency, in a manner consistent with the purposes and principles set out in the Charter;

4. *Calls upon* Member States, specialized agencies and intergovernmental organizations to continue to carry out a constructive dialogue and consultations for the enhancement of understanding and the promotion and protection of all human rights and fundamental freedoms, and encourages non-governmental organizations to contribute actively to this endeavour;

5. *Invites* States and relevant United Nations human rights mechanisms and procedures to continue to pay attention to the importance of mutual cooperation, understanding and dialogue in ensuring the promotion and protection of all human rights;

6. *Decides* to continue its consideration of this question at its fifty-sixth session.

On the same date, the Assembly, also on the recommendation of the Third Committee [A/55/602/Add.2 & Corr.1], adopted **resolution 55/101** by recorded vote (104-52-15) [agenda item 114 (b)].

Respect for the purposes and principles contained in the Charter of the United Nations to achieve international cooperation in promoting and encouraging respect for human rights and for fundamental freedoms and in solving international problems of a humanitarian character

The General Assembly,

Recalling that, in accordance with Article 56 of the Charter of the United Nations, all Member States have pledged themselves to take joint and separate action in cooperation with the Organization for the achievement of the purposes set forth in Article 55, including universal respect for and observance of human rights and fundamental freedoms for all without distinction as to race, sex, language or religion,

Recalling also the Preamble to the Charter, in particular the determination to reaffirm faith in fundamental human rights, in the dignity and worth of the human person and in the equal rights of men and women and of nations large and small,

Reaffirming that the promotion and protection of all human rights and fundamental freedoms must be considered a priority objective of the United Nations in accordance with its purposes and principles, in particular the purpose of international cooperation, and that, within the framework of these purposes and principles, the promotion and protection of all human rights are a legitimate concern of the international community,

Considering the major changes taking place on the international scene and the aspirations of all peoples to an international order based on the principles enshrined in the Charter, including promoting and encouraging respect for human rights and fundamental freedoms for all and respect for the principle of equal rights and self-determination of peoples, peace, democracy, justice, equality, rule of law, pluralism, development, better standards of living and solidarity,

Recognizing that the international community should devise ways and means to remove current obstacles and meet the challenges to the full realization of all human rights and to prevent the continuation of human rights violations resulting therefrom throughout the world, as well as continue to pay attention to the importance of mutual cooperation, understanding and dialogue in ensuring the promotion and protection of all human rights,

Reaffirming that the enhancement of international cooperation in the field of human rights is essential for the full achievement of the purposes of the United Nations and that human rights and fundamental freedoms are the birthright of all human beings, the protection and promotion of such rights and freedoms being the first responsibility of Governments,

Reaffirming also that all human rights are universal, indivisible, interdependent and interrelated and that the international community must treat human rights globally in a fair and equal manner, on the same footing and with the same emphasis,

Reaffirming further the various articles of the Charter setting out the respective powers and functions of the General Assembly, the Security Council and the Economic and Social Council, as the paramount framework for the achievement of the purposes of the United Nations,

Reaffirming the commitment of all States to fulfil their obligations under other important instruments of international law, in particular those of international human rights and humanitarian law,

Taking into account that, in accordance with Article 103 of the Charter, in the event of a conflict between the obligations of the Members of the United Nations under the Charter and their obligations under any other international agreement, their obligations under the Charter shall prevail,

1. *Affirms* the solemn commitment of all States to enhance international cooperation in the field of human rights and in the solution to international problems of a humanitarian character in full compliance with the Charter of the United Nations, inter alia, by the strict observance of all the purposes and principles set forth in Articles 1 and 2 thereof;

2. *Stresses* the vital role of the work of United Nations and regional arrangements, acting consistently with the purposes and principles enshrined in the Charter, in promoting and encouraging respect for human rights and fundamental freedoms, as well as in solving international problems of a humanitarian character, and affirms that all States in these activities must fully comply with the principles set forth in Article 2 of the Charter, in particular respecting the sovereign equality of all States and refraining from the threat or use of force against the territorial integrity or political independence of any State, or acting in any other manner inconsistent with the purposes of the United Nations;

3. *Reaffirms* that the United Nations shall promote universal respect for and observance of, human rights and fundamental freedoms for all without distinction as to race, sex, language or religion;

4. *Calls upon* all States to cooperate fully, through constructive dialogue, in order to ensure the promotion and protection of all human rights for all and in promoting peaceful solutions to international problems of a humanitarian character and, in their actions towards that purpose, to comply strictly with the principles and norms of international law, inter alia, by fully respecting international human rights and humanitarian law;

5. *Requests* the Secretary-General to bring the present resolution to the attention of Member States, organs, bodies and other components of the United Nations system, and intergovernmental and nongovernmental organizations and to disseminate it on the widest possible basis;

6. *Decides* to consider this question at its fifty-sixth session under the item entitled "Human rights questions".

RECORDED VOTE ON RESOLUTION 55/101:

In favour: Afghanistan, Algeria, Angola, Antigua and Barbuda, Azerbaijan, Bahamas, Bahrain, Bangladesh, Barbados, Belarus, Belize, Benin, Bhutan, Bolivia, Botswana, Brunei Darussalam, Burkina Faso, Burundi, Cambodia, Cameroon, Chad, China, Colombia, Comoros, Congo, Costa Rica, Côte d'Ivoire, Cuba, Democratic People's Republic of Korea, Democratic Republic of the Congo, Djibouti, Dominica, Dominican Republic, Ecuador, Egypt, El Salvador, Eritrea, Ethiopia, Fiji, Gabon, Gambia, Ghana, Grenada, Guinea, Guyana, Haiti, Honduras, India, Indonesia, Iran, Jamaica, Jordan, Kazakhstan, Kenya, Kuwait, Kyrgyzstan, Lao People's Democratic Republic, Lebanon, Lesotho, Libyan Arab Jamahiriya, Madagascar, Malawi, Malaysia, Maldives, Mali, Mauritania, Mauritius, Mexico, Mozambique, Myanmar, Namibia, Nepal, Nigeria, Oman, Pakistan, Panama, Papua New Guinea, Qatar, Russian Federation, Rwanda, Saint Kitts and Nevis, Saint Lucia, Saint Vincent and the Grenadines, Saudi Arabia, Senegal, Sierra Leone, Solomon Islands, Sri Lanka, Sudan, Suriname, Swaziland, Syrian Arab Republic, Togo, Trinidad and Tobago, Tunisia, Uganda, United Arab Emirates, United Republic of Tanzania, Vanuatu, Venezuela, Viet Nam, Yemen, Zambia, Zimbabwe.

Against: Albania, Andorra, Armenia, Australia, Austria, Belgium, Bulgaria, Canada, Croatia, Cyprus, Czech Republic, Denmark, Estonia, Finland, France, Georgia, Germany, Greece, Hungary, Iceland, Ireland, Israel, Italy, Japan, Latvia, Liechtenstein, Lithuania, Luxembourg, Malta, Marshall Islands, Micronesia, Monaco, Netherlands, New Zealand, Norway, Palau, Poland, Portugal, Republic of Korea, Republic of Moldova, Romania, Samoa, San Marino, Slovakia, Slovenia, Spain, Sweden, The former Yugoslav Republic of Macedonia, Turkey, Ukraine, United Kingdom, United States.

Abstaining: Argentina, Brazil, Cape Verde, Chile, Guatemala, Nauru, Nicaragua, Paraguay, Peru, Philippines, Sao Tome and Principe, Singapore, South Africa, Thailand, Uruguay.

Right to promote and protect human rights

In response to a 1999 Commission request [YUN 1999, p. 572], the Secretary-General, in January [E/CN.4/2000/95], summarized the views of Governments, specialized agencies and intergovernmental and non-governmental organizations (NGOs) regarding the implementation of the 1998 Declaration on the Right and Responsibility of Individuals, Groups and Organs of Society to Promote and Protect Universally Recognized Human Rights and Fundamental Freedoms, adopted by the General Assembly in resolution 53/144 [YUN 1998, p. 608].

The Secretary-General presented possible ways to implement the Declaration, including its wide distribution; incorporating the monitoring of its implementation into existing UN mandates; the establishment by the Commission of a new mandate on human rights defenders to examine and respond more systematically to situations in which the rights and freedoms of human rights defenders were placed at risk; and the effective promotion and implementation of the Declaration by all Member States. He stated that OHCHR was preparing a fact sheet on human rights defenders for wide distribution.

Human rights defenders

Commission action. On 26 April [res. 2000/61], the Commission, by a roll-call vote of 50 to none, with 3 abstentions, calling on States to promote and give effect to the Declaration, asked the Secretary-General to appoint, for three years, a special representative to report on the situation of human rights defenders and on possible means to enhance their protection in full compliance with the Declaration. The Commission outlined the activities of the special representative. It asked the Secretary-General to assist the special representative and requested the special representative to report annually to the Commission and the General Assembly and to suggest ways to better enable him/her to carry out activities.

ECONOMIC AND SOCIAL COUNCIL ACTION

On 16 June, the Economic and Social Council, on the recommendation of the Commission on Human Rights [E/2000/23 & Corr.1], adopted **decision 2000/220** by recorded vote (29-2-11) [agenda item 2].

Human rights defenders

At its 10th plenary meeting, on 16 June 2000, the Economic and Social Council, taking note of Commission on Human Rights resolution 2000/61 of 26 April 2000, endorsed the Commission's decision to request the Secretary-General to appoint, for a period of three years, a special representative who shall report on the situation of human rights defenders in all parts of the

world and on possible means to enhance their protection; the main activities of the special representative shall be:

(a) To seek, receive, examine and respond to information on the situation and the rights of anyone, acting individually or in association with others, to promote and protect human rights and fundamental freedoms;

(b) To establish cooperation and conduct dialogue with Governments and other interested actors on the promotion and effective implementation of the Universal Declaration of Human Rights;

(c) To recommend effective strategies better to protect human rights defenders and follow up on these recommendations.

RECORDED VOTE ON DECISION 2000/220:

In favour: Austria, Belgium, Brazil, Bulgaria, Canada, Colombia, Costa Rica, Croatia, Czech Republic, Denmark, Fiji, France, Germany, Greece, India, Indonesia, Italy, Japan, Mexico, New Zealand, Norway, Pakistan, Poland, Portugal, Saudi Arabia, Suriname, United Kingdom, United States, Venezuela.

Against: Cuba, Syrian Arab Republic.

Abstaining: Algeria, Angola, Bahrain, Belarus, Burkina Faso, Cameroon, China, Oman, Russian Federation, Sudan, Viet Nam.

In August, Hina Jilani (Pakistan) was appointed Special Representative of the Secretary-General.

Report of High Commissioner. In response to a 1999 Subcommission resolution [YUN 1999, p. 688], the High Commissioner, in a June report [E/CN.4/Sub.2/2000/5], summarized correspondence she had had with the Governments concerned to ascertain information about the security situation of 11 human rights defenders.

Report of Secretary-General. Pursuant to General Assembly resolution 54/170 [YUN 1999, p. 573], the Secretary-General, in August [A/55/292], presented proposals that might contribute to further implementation of the 1998 Declaration. He described the role and risks of human rights defenders and UN action to support Governments and civil society in creating the necessary conditions for their work.

GENERAL ASSEMBLY ACTION

On 4 December [meeting 81], the General Assembly, on the recommendation of the Third Committee [A/55/602/Add.2 & Corr.1], adopted **resolution 55/98** without vote [agenda item 114 *(b)*].

Declaration on the Right and Responsibility of Individuals, Groups and Organs of Society to Promote and Protect Universally Recognized Human Rights and Fundamental Freedoms

The General Assembly,

Recalling its resolution 53/144 of 9 December 1998, by which it adopted by consensus the Declaration on the Right and Responsibility of Individuals, Groups and Organs of Society to Promote and Protect Universally Recognized Human Rights and Fundamental Freedoms, which is annexed to that resolution,

Reiterating the importance of the Declaration and its promotion and implementation,

Taking note of the decision of the Commission on Human Rights in its resolution 2000/61 of 26 April 2000 to request the Secretary-General to appoint, for a period of three years, a special representative who shall report on the situation of human rights defenders in all parts of the world and on possible means to enhance their protection in full compliance with the Declaration,

Welcoming the appointment by the Secretary-General of a special representative on human rights defenders,

Noting with deep concern that, in many countries, persons and organizations engaged in promoting and defending human rights and fundamental freedoms are facing threats, harassment and insecurity as a result of those activities,

1. *Calls upon* all States to promote and give effect to the Declaration on the Right and Responsibility of Individuals, Groups and Organs of Society to Promote and Protect Universally Recognized Human Rights and Fundamental Freedoms;

2. *Invites* all Governments to cooperate with and assist the Special Representative of the Secretary-General on human rights defenders in fulfilling her mandate;

3. *Requests* all concerned United Nations agencies and organizations, within their mandates, to provide all possible assistance and support to the Special Representative in the implementation of her programme of activities;

4. *Takes note* of the report of the Secretary-General on human rights defenders;

5. *Invites* the Commission on Human Rights to consider, at its fifty-seventh session, the report to be prepared by the Special Representative pursuant to Commission resolution 2000/61;

6. *Decides* to consider this question at its fifty-sixth session, under the item entitled "Human rights questions".

Human rights and human responsibilities

By a roll-call vote of 22 to 21, with 10 abstentions, the Commission, on 26 April [res. 2000/63], stressing the urgent need to give practical effect to the specific responsibilities defined in human rights instruments, asked the Subcommission to undertake a study on human rights and human responsibilities; it should submit an interim study in 2001 and a complete study in 2002.

On 18 August [dec. 2000/111], the Subcommission, by a roll-call vote of 14 to 4, with 5 abstentions, appointed Miguel Alfonso Martínez (Cuba) to undertake the study and asked the Commission in 2001 to recommend that the Economic and Social Council authorize him to do so and to submit a preliminary report in 2002 and a final report in 2003.

Other aspects

Good governance

Commission action. By a roll-call vote of 50 to none, with 2 abstentions, the Commission, on 26 April [res. 2000/64], asked the High Commissioner to invite States to provide examples of effective activities in strengthening good governance practices for the promotion of human rights at the national level, including activities in the context of development cooperation between States, for inclusion in a compilation of practices that could be consulted by interested States.

Note by Secretariat. A note by the Secretariat [E/CN.4/2001/117] stated that, in response to Commission resolution 2000/64, as at 7 December, nine States had provided practical examples of activities that had been effective in strengthening good governance.

Human rights instruments

General aspects

In 2000, seven UN human rights instruments were in force that required monitoring of their implementation by expert bodies. The instruments and their treaty bodies were: the 1965 International Convention on the Elimination of All Forms of Racial Discrimination [YUN 1965, p. 440, GA res. 2106 A (XX)] (Committee on the Elimination of Racial Discrimination (CERD)); the 1966 International Covenant on Civil and Political Rights [YUN 1966, p. 423, GA res. 2200 A (XXI)] (Human Rights Committee); the 1966 International Covenant on Economic, Social and Cultural Rights [ibid., p. 419, GA res. 2200 A (XXI)] (Committee on Economic, Social and Cultural Rights); the 1973 International Convention on the Suppression and Punishment of the Crime of Apartheid [YUN 1973, p. 103, GA res. 3068(XXVIII)] (Group of Three, suspended in 1995) [YUN 1995, p. 693]; the 1979 Convention on the Elimination of All Forms of Discrimination against Women [YUN 1979, p. 895, GA res. 34/180] (Committee on the Elimination of Discrimination against Women (CEDAW)); the 1984 Convention against Torture and Other Cruel, Inhuman or Degrading Treatment or Punishment [YUN 1984, p. 813, GA res. 39/46] (Committee against Torture); and the 1989 Convention on the Rights of the Child [YUN 1989, p. 560, GA res. 44/25] (Committee on the Rights of the Child).

On 18 August [res. 2000/27], the Subcommission recommended that the Commission consider the implications of withdrawal from, or limitation of the scope of, international treaty obligations at its next session. It decided to consider the question in 2001.

Human rights treaty bodies

Reports of Secretary-General. In a January report with later addendum [E/CN.4/2000/98 &

Add.1], the Secretary-General summarized comments received on the recommendations of the independent expert on enhancing the long-term effectiveness of the UN human rights treaty system, contained in the expert's final report [YUN 1997, p. 593], and gave his own views on the legal, administrative and other implications of the recommendations. In accordance with General Assembly resolution 53/138 [YUN 1998, p. 612], the Secretary-General, in August [A/55/313], stated that consultations with Governments, UN bodies, specialized agencies, NGOs and interested persons on the final report were held and a report thereon was submitted to the Commission (see above). On 4 December, the Assembly took note of the Secretary-General's note (**decision 55/420**).

The Secretary-General, also in January [E/CN.4/2000/106], reported on the effective functioning of human rights mechanisms. The report outlined measures taken to ensure financing and adequate staff and information resources for the treaty bodies. It also described assistance provided to States parties regarding the preparation of their reports and the publication status in all official UN languages of the *Manual on Human Rights Reporting* [Sales No. E.GV.97.0.16]. In August [A/55/278], the Secretary-General updated information contained in his January report.

In response to Assembly resolution 49/178 [YUN 1994, p. 1060], the Secretary-General transmitted the report of the persons chairing the human rights treaty bodies on their twelfth meeting (Geneva, 5-8 June) [A/55/206]. The three plans of action for strengthening the implementation of the International Covenant on Civil and Political Rights, the International Convention on the Elimination of All Forms of Racial Discrimination and the Convention against Torture and Other Cruel, Inhuman or Degrading Treatment or Punishment; the Convention on the Rights of the Child; and the International Covenant on Economic, Social and Cultural Rights had been converted into projects that were harmonized as part of a consolidated Annual Appeal by the High Commissioner to donors for extrabudgetary contributions (see p. 600). The Secretariat updated the chairpersons on efforts to develop human rights indicators and the Special Adviser of the High Commissioner briefed them on regional strategies on the new OHCHR regional approaches for the promotion and protection of human rights. The chairpersons updated each other on their treaty bodies' contributions to the 2001 World Conference against Racism, Racial Discrimination, Xenophobia and Related Intolerance (see p. 641). On 7 June, a joint meeting was held between the chairpersons and the special rapporteurs and representatives, experts and chairpersons of working groups of the special procedures system of the Commission and of the advisory services programme. The meeting identified areas of common concern, including the need to improve the exchange of information between the treaty bodies and the special procedures mandates; an exchange of best practices in the follow-up to concluding observations, decisions and opinions on individual cases and recommendations made by special rapporteurs that would be beneficial to both sets of mechanisms; and the possibility of joint or coordinated contributions to the 2001 World Conference.

The chairpersons agreed on the need to harmonize practices regarding the examination of States parties' reports, welcomed the organization of a workshop in 2001 to develop indicators on the right to education and recommended that they should be granted formal status within the Economic and Social Council.

The chairpersons had before them a report of the Secretary-General updating the status of the human rights instruments and the general situation of overdue reports as at 15 March [HRI/MC/2000/2]. A note by the Secretariat contained a compilation of the general comments or general recommendations adopted by the Committee on Economic, Social and Cultural Rights, the Human Rights Committee, CERD, CEDAW and the Committee against Torture [HRI/GEN/1/Rev.4]. During the year, OHCHR produced a document outlining the reporting history of States parties to the principal international human rights instruments as at 31 March [HRI/GEN/4].

Commission action. On 26 April [res. 2000/75], the Commission urged States parties to identify proposals to improve the functioning of the treaty bodies and to meet their reporting obligations. States parties that had not submitted their initial reports were invited to avail themselves of technical assistance to do so. Chairpersons of the treaty bodies were encouraged to pursue the reform process aimed at improving the effective implementation of human rights instruments. The Commission asked the Secretary-General to report in 2002 on measures taken to implement its resolution and on measures to ensure financing and adequate staff and information resources for the effective operation of the treaty bodies.

GENERAL ASSEMBLY ACTION

On 4 December [meeting 81], the General Assembly, on the recommendation of the Third Committee [A/55/602/Add.1], adopted **resolution 55/90** without vote [agenda item 114 (a)].

Effective implementation of international instruments on human rights, including reporting obligations under international instruments on human rights

The General Assembly,

Recalling its resolution 53/138 of 9 December 1998, as well as other relevant resolutions, and taking note of Commission on Human Rights resolution 2000/75 of 26 April 2000,

Recalling also the relevant paragraphs of the Vienna Declaration and Programme of Action, adopted by the World Conference on Human Rights on 25 June 1993,

Reaffirming that the full and effective implementation of United Nations human rights instruments is of major importance to the efforts of the Organization, pursuant to the Charter of the United Nations and the Universal Declaration of Human Rights, to promote universal respect for and observance of human rights and fundamental freedoms,

Considering that the effective functioning of the human rights treaty bodies established pursuant to United Nations human rights instruments is indispensable for the full and effective implementation of such instruments,

Conscious of the importance of coordination of the human rights promotion and protection activities of the United Nations bodies active in the field of human rights,

Recalling that the effectiveness of the human rights treaty bodies in encouraging the realization by States parties of their obligations under United Nations human rights instruments requires constructive dialogue aimed at assisting States parties in identifying solutions to human rights problems, which should be based on the reporting process supplemented by information from all relevant sources, which should be shared with all interested parties,

Recalling also the initiatives taken by a number of human rights treaty bodies to elaborate early warning measures and urgent procedures, within their mandates, with a view to preventing the occurrence or recurrence of serious human rights violations,

Reaffirming its responsibility for the effective functioning of human rights treaty bodies, and reaffirming also the importance of:

(*a*) Promoting the effective functioning of the periodic reporting by States parties to those instruments,

(*b*) Securing sufficient financial, human and information resources for the Office of the United Nations High Commissioner for Human Rights to enable the human rights treaty bodies to carry out their mandates effectively, including in regard to their ability to work in the applicable working languages,

(*c*) Promoting greater efficiency and effectiveness through better coordination of the activities of the United Nations bodies active in the field of human rights, taking into account the need to avoid unnecessary duplication and overlapping of their mandates and tasks,

(*d*) Addressing questions of both reporting obligations and financial implications when elaborating any further instruments on human rights,

Taking note of the report of the Secretary-General,

1. *Welcomes* the submission of the reports of the persons chairing the human rights treaty bodies on their eleventh and twelfth meetings, held at Geneva from 31 May to 4 June 1999 and 5 to 8 June 2000, respectively, and takes note of their conclusions and recommendations;

2. *Encourages* each treaty body to continue to give careful consideration to the relevant conclusions and recommendations contained in the reports of the persons chairing the human rights treaty bodies, and in this context also encourages enhanced cooperation and coordination between the treaty bodies;

3. *Welcomes* the initiative of the persons chairing the human rights treaty bodies of inviting representatives of Member States to participate in a dialogue within the framework of their meetings, and encourages them to continue this practice in the future;

4. *Also welcomes* the comments by Governments, United Nations bodies and specialized agencies, nongovernmental organizations and interested persons on the final report of the independent expert on enhancing the long-term effectiveness of the United Nations human rights treaty system and the report of the Secretary-General thereon;

5. *Emphasizes* the need to ensure financing and adequate staff and information resources for the operations of the human rights treaty bodies, and with this in mind:

(*a*) Reiterates its request to the Secretary-General to provide adequate resources in respect of each human rights treaty body, while making the most efficient use of existing resources, in order to give the human rights treaty bodies adequate administrative support and better access to technical expertise and relevant information;

(*b*) Calls upon the Secretary-General to seek, in the next biennium, the resources within the regular budget of the United Nations necessary to give the human rights treaty bodies adequate administrative support and better access to technical expertise and relevant information without diverting resources from the development programmes and activities of the United Nations;

(*c*) Welcomes the plans of action prepared by the United Nations High Commissioner for Human Rights to enhance the resources available to all the human rights treaty bodies and thereby strengthen the implementation of the human rights treaties, and encourages all Governments, United Nations bodies and specialized agencies, non-governmental organizations and interested persons to consider contributing to the appeal for extrabudgetary resources for the treaty bodies made by the High Commissioner until the regular budget funding meets their needs;

6. *Encourages* ongoing efforts to identify measures for more effective implementation of the United Nations human rights instruments;

7. *Takes note* of the measures taken by each of the human rights treaty bodies to improve their functioning, as reflected in their respective annual reports, and encourages continuing efforts by the treaty bodies and the Secretary-General to assist States parties in meeting their reporting obligations and to reduce the backlog in the consideration of reports by the treaty bodies;

8. *Welcomes* the continuing efforts by the human rights treaty bodies and the Secretary-General aimed at streamlining, rationalizing, rendering more transparent and otherwise improving reporting procedures, and encourages the Secretary-General, the treaty bod-

ies and the persons chairing the treaty bodies at their next meeting to continue to examine ways of reducing the duplication of reporting required under the different instruments, without impairing the quality of reporting, and of generally reducing the reporting burden on States parties, including through an ongoing examination of proposals for reports focused on a limited range of issues, the harmonization of the general guidelines regarding the form and content of reports, the possibility of consolidating overdue reports, the timing of consideration of reports and the methods of work of the treaty bodies;

9. *Calls upon* the Secretary-General to complete as soon as possible the detailed analytical study comparing the provisions of the International Covenant on Economic, Social and Cultural Rights, the International Covenant on Civil and Political Rights, the International Convention on the Elimination of All Forms of Racial Discrimination, the Convention on the Elimination of All Forms of Discrimination against Women, the Convention on the Rights of the Child and the Convention against Torture and Other Cruel, Inhuman or Degrading Treatment or Punishment, which is being prepared with a view to identifying duplication of reporting required under those instruments;

10. *Urges* States parties to contribute, individually and through meetings of States parties, to identifying practical proposals and ideas for improving the functioning of the human rights treaty bodies;

11. *Welcomes* the publication of the revised *Manual on Human Rights Reporting*, and encourages the updating of the *Manual* to reflect new developments in the field of human rights, including the adoption of new instruments;

12. *Underlines* the importance of providing technical assistance to a State, upon its request, in the process of ratifying human rights instruments and in the preparation of its initial and subsequent reports;

13. *Welcomes* the work done by the Secretary-General to compile in a single volume all the general guidelines regarding the form and content of reports to be submitted by States parties that have been issued by the human rights treaty bodies, and encourages the Secretary-General also to compile the rules of procedure for the treaty bodies;

14. *Reiterates its concern* about the persistent backlog of reports on the implementation by States parties of certain United Nations instruments on human rights and about delays in the consideration of reports of the human rights treaty bodies;

15. *Also reiterates its concern* about the large number of overdue reports, and again urges States parties to make every effort to meet their reporting obligations;

16. *Urges* all States parties whose reports have been examined by human rights treaty bodies to provide adequate follow-up to the observations and final comments of the treaty bodies on their reports;

17. *Encourages* the human rights treaty bodies to continue to identify specific possibilities for technical assistance, to be provided at the request of the State concerned, in the regular course of their work of reviewing the periodic reports of States parties, and encourages States parties to consider carefully the concluding observations of the treaty bodies in identifying their needs for technical assistance;

18. *Urges* each State party to translate, publish and make widely available in its territory the full text of the concluding observations on its reports to the human rights treaty bodies;

19. *Welcomes* the contribution to the work of the human rights treaty bodies made by the specialized agencies and other United Nations bodies, and encourages the specialized agencies and other United Nations bodies, the Commission on Human Rights, including its special procedures, and the Subcommission on the Promotion and Protection of Human Rights, the Office of the United Nations High Commissioner for Human Rights and the persons chairing the human rights treaty bodies to continue to explore specific measures to intensify this cooperation between them and to improve communication and information flow in order to improve further the quality of their work, including by avoiding unnecessary duplication;

20. *Recognizes* the important role played by non-governmental organizations in all parts of the world in the effective implementation of all human rights instruments, and encourages the exchange of information between the human rights treaty bodies and such organizations;

21. *Recalls*, with regard to the election of the members of the human rights treaty bodies, the importance of giving consideration to equitable geographical distribution and gender balance of the membership and to the representation of the principal legal systems and of bearing in mind that the members shall be elected and shall serve in their personal capacity and shall be of high moral character, acknowledged independence and recognized competence in the field of human rights, and encourages States parties, individually and through meetings of States parties, to consider how to give better effect to these principles;

22. *Takes note* of the discussion of the payment of honorariums to the members of the human rights treaty bodies included in the report of the Secretary-General, and of other work being done by the Secretary-General on this subject, and encourages Member States to consider possible follow-up;

23. *Encourages* the Economic and Social Council, as well as its functional commissions and their subsidiary bodies, other United Nations bodies and the specialized agencies to consider the feasibility of participation by representatives of the human rights treaty bodies in their meetings;

24. *Welcomes* the continuing emphasis by the persons chairing the human rights treaty bodies on closely monitoring the enjoyment of the human rights of women within their mandates;

25. *Also welcomes* the contributions of the human rights treaty bodies, within their mandates, to the prevention of violations of human rights, in the context of their consideration of reports submitted under their respective treaties;

26. *Invites* the Secretary-General to submit the reports of the persons chairing the human rights treaty bodies on their periodic meetings to the General Assembly at its fifty-seventh session;

27. *Requests* the Secretary-General to report to the General Assembly at its fifty-seventh session on measures taken to implement the present resolution, on obstacles to its implementation and on measures taken or planned to ensure financing and adequate staff and in-

formation resources for the effective operation of the human rights treaty bodies;

28. *Decides* to continue to give priority consideration at its fifty-seventh session to the conclusions and recommendations of the periodic meetings of the persons chairing the human rights treaty bodies, in the light of the deliberations of the Commission on Human Rights, under the item entitled "Human rights questions".

Reservations to human rights treaties

Commission action. On 26 April [dec. 2000/108], the Commission, taking note of a 1999 Subcommission resolution and a working paper submitted by Françoise Hampson (United Kingdom) [YUN 1999, p. 574], requested the Subcommission to ask her to submit in 2000 revised terms of reference for her proposed study on reservations to human rights treaties, further clarifying how the study would complement work already under way on such reservations, in particular by the International Law Commission (ILC).

Note by Secretariat. A July note by the Secretariat [E/CN.4/Sub.2/2000/32] stated that Ms. Hampson had not prepared the document requested by the Commission.

Subcommission action. On 18 August [res. 2000/26], the Subcommission appointed Ms. Hampson as Special Rapporteur to prepare a comprehensive study on reservations to human rights treaties, involving the examination of the actual reservations and interpretative declarations made to human rights treaties in the light of the legal regime applicable to reservations and interpretative declarations. A preliminary report was called for in 2001, a progress report in 2002 and a final report in 2003. The Subcommission asked the Secretary-General to assist the Special Rapporteur, who would seek the advice and cooperation of the ILC Special Rapporteur and of the relevant treaty bodies. The Subcommission requested the authorization of a meeting between its Special Rapporteur, the ILC Special Rapporteur and the chairpersons of the relevant treaty bodies or their nominees, when ILC and the Subcommission were in session.

States not parties to 1966 Covenants

Desiring to provide States that had not ratified the 1966 International Covenants on Human Rights (see below and next page) with assistance in the promotion and observance of the human rights and fundamental freedoms proclaimed in the 1948 Universal Declaration of Human Rights, adopted by the General Assembly in resolution 217 A (III) [YUN 1948-49, p. 535], the Subcommission, on 18 August [res. 2000/23], asked the High Commissioner to convene a seminar of States not parties to the Covenants, before the Subcommission's 2001 session or as soon as possible, with a view to examining obstacles to ratification of those Covenants and ways of surmounting them. In preparation for that seminar, it requested OHCHR to seek the views of States and NGOs concerned, and to gather information regarding obstacles to the enjoyment of the human rights and fundamental freedoms embodied in the Declaration and obstacles to ratification of the Covenants and the measures taken by States to remove them. The seminar should define areas of UN assistance that might be useful for States concerned and adopt specific recommendations on the provision of assistance to those States in meeting their needs. It should also formulate agreed recommendations concerning the creation of a permanent or temporary mechanism for encouraging efforts by States to observe the human rights and fundamental freedoms contained in the Declaration and for encouraging their ratification of the Covenants.

Covenant on Civil and Political Rights and Optional Protocols

Accessions and ratifications

As at 31 December 2000, parties to the International Covenant on Civil and Political Rights and the Optional Protocol thereto, adopted by the General Assembly in resolution 2200 A (XXI) [YUN 1966, p. 423], totalled 147 and 98 States, respectively. During the year, Bangladesh, Botswana and Ghana became parties to the Covenant; Cape Verde, Guatemala and Lesotho acceded to the Optional Protocol and Ghana ratified it.

In 2000, Cape Verde, Monaco and Turkmenistan acceded to the Second Optional Protocol, aiming at the abolition of the death penalty—adopted by the Assembly in resolution 44/128 [YUN 1989, p. 484]—bringing the total number of States parties to 44 at year's end.

On 26 April [res. 2000/67], the Commission asked the Secretary-General to report in 2001 and 2002 on the status of the Covenant and the Optional Protocols.

The Secretary-General reported on the status of the Covenant and its Optional Protocols as at 15 November [E/CN.4/2001/87] and provided the status of withdrawals and reservations [E/CN.4/2000/96].

Implementation

Monitoring body. The Human Rights Committee, established under article 28 of the Covenant, held three sessions in 2000: its sixty-eighth from 13 to 31 March in New York, and its sixty-ninth from 10 to 28 July [A/55/40, vol. I] and seventieth from 16 October to 3 November [A/56/40, vol. I], both in Geneva.

In 2000, the Committee considered reports from 13 States—Argentina, Australia, Congo, Denmark, Gabon, Guyana, Ireland, Kuwait, Kyrgyzstan, Mongolia, Peru, Trinidad and Tobago, United Kingdom (Crown Dependencies of Jersey, Guernsey and the Isle of Man)—under article 40 of the Covenant. It adopted views on communications from individuals claiming that their rights under the Covenant had been violated, and decided that other such communications were inadmissible. Those views and decisions were annexed to the Committee's reports [A/55/40, vol. II; A/56/40 vol. II].

On 29 March, the Committee adopted General Comment No. 28, updating its general comment adopted in 1981 [YUN 1981, p. 890] on article 3 of the Covenant concerning equality of rights between men and women. A June report of the Secretary-General [E/2000/76] contained General Comment Nos. 27 [YUN 1999, p. 575] and 28.

The twentieth meeting of States parties to the Covenant met in New York on 14 September [CCPR/SP/57] to elect nine members of the Committee to replace those whose terms were due to expire on 31 December [CCPR/SP/56 & Add.1-4].

The Commission, on 17 April [res. 2000/14], invited the Committee to contribute to the preparatory process for the 2001 World Conference against Racism, Racial Discrimination, Xenophobia and Related Intolerance (see p. 641). The resulting document was annexed to the Committee's report [A/56/40, vol. I].

On 26 April [res. 2000/67], the Commission asked the Secretary-General to ensure that OHCHR assisted the Committee.

Covenant on Economic, Social and Cultural Rights

Accessions and ratifications

As at 31 December 2000, the International Covenant on Economic, Social and Cultural Rights, adopted by the General Assembly in resolution 2200 A (XXI) [YUN 1966, p. 419], had 143 States parties. During the year, Ghana ratified the Covenant.

On 26 April [res. 2000/67], the Commission asked the Secretary-General to report in 2001 and 2002 on the status of the Covenant.

The Secretary-General reported on the status of the Covenant as at 15 November [E/CN.4/2001/87] and provided the status of withdrawals and reservations [E/CN.4/2000/96].

Draft optional protocol

Report of High Commissioner. In January [E/CN.4/2000/49], the High Commissioner presented the views of six States on a draft optional protocol that would allow the consideration of communications in relation to the Covenant and summarized options regarding the draft.

Commission action. On 17 April [res. 2000/9], the Commission asked the High Commissioner to invite States, international organizations and NGOs that had not done so to submit their comments on the draft optional protocol, as well as to invite States to submit their comments on the options relating to the proposal for a draft optional protocol, contained in her report (see above), or to propose any other option that would be conducive to a substantive dialogue.

Subcommission action. On 17 August [res. 2000/9], the Subcommission suggested that the Commission establish an open-ended working group to study further a draft optional protocol. It asked the High Commissioner to organize an expert meeting on a draft optional protocol and to report thereon in 2001.

Implementation

Monitoring body. The Committee on Economic, Social and Cultural Rights held its twenty-second (25 April–12 May), twenty-third (extraordinary) (14 August–1 September) and twenty-fourth (13 November–1 December) sessions, all in Geneva [E/2001/22]. The Committee's extraordinary session was used entirely for the consideration of States parties' reports in order to reduce the backlog of reports. The pre-sessional, five-member working group of the Committee met in Geneva for five days prior to each session to identify issues that might most usefully be discussed with representatives of reporting States.

The Economic and Social Council, by **decision 2000/289** of 28 July, took note of the Committee's report on its twentieth and twenty-first sessions, held in 1999 [YUN 1999, p. 575].

In 2000, the Committee examined reports under articles 16 and 17 of the Covenant submitted by Australia, Belgium, the Congo, Egypt, Finland, Georgia, Italy, Jordan, Kyrgyzstan, Mongolia, Morocco, Portugal, the Sudan and the Federal Republic of Yugoslavia (FRY). In addition, the Committee considered the state of implementation of recommendations it had made in 1998 regarding Israel and Nigeria [YUN 1998, p. 617].

On 27 November, the Committee held a day of general discussion on the right of everyone to benefit from the protection of the moral and material interests resulting from any scientific, literary or artistic production of which he/she was the author, organized in cooperation with the World Intellectual Property Organization.

The Committee adopted General Comment No. 14 on the right to the highest attainable standard of health.

As its contribution to the World Conference against Racism, Racial Discrimination, Xenophobia and Related Intolerance (see p. 641), the Committee decided to submit its General Comment Nos. 11 on plans of action for primary education and 13 on the right to education [YUN 1999, p. 575].

On 26 April [res. 2000/67], the Commission asked the Secretary-General to ensure that OHCHR assisted the Committee.

Convention against racial discrimination

Accessions and ratifications

As at 31 December 2000, there were 157 parties to the International Convention on the Elimination of All Forms of Racial Discrimination, adopted by the General Assembly in resolution 2106 A (XX) [YUN 1965, p. 440]. Ireland and Liechtenstein became parties during the year.

On 17 April [res. 2000/14], the Commission appealed to States that had not done so to consider ratifying or acceding to the Convention, and to States parties to consider making the declaration provided for in article 14 of the Convention (see below).

The Secretary-General reported on the status of the Convention as at 30 June [A/55/203].

Implementation

Monitoring body. The Committee on the Elimination of Racial Discrimination (CERD), set up under article 8 of the Convention, held its fifty-sixth and fifty-seventh sessions, both in Geneva, from 6 to 24 March and from 31 July to 25 August, respectively [A/55/18].

The Committee considered reports, comments and information submitted by 24 States parties—Australia, Bahrain, Czech Republic, Denmark, Estonia, Finland, France, Ghana, Holy See, Lesotho, Malta, Mauritius, Nepal, Netherlands, Norway, Rwanda, Slovakia, Slovenia, Spain, Sweden, Tonga, United Kingdom, Uzbekistan, Zimbabwe—on measures they had taken to implement the Convention and summarized its members' views on each country report and the statements made by the States parties concerned.

In conformity with article 14 of the Convention, CERD considered communications from individuals or groups of individuals claiming viola-

tion of their rights under the Convention by a State party recognizing CERD's competence to receive and consider such communications. Thirty States parties (Algeria, Australia, Bulgaria, Chile, Costa Rica, Cyprus, Denmark, Ecuador, Finland, France, Hungary, Iceland, Italy, Luxembourg, Malta, Netherlands, Norway, Peru, Poland, Portugal, Republic of Korea, Russian Federation, Senegal, Slovakia, South Africa, Spain, Sweden, The former Yugoslav Republic of Macedonia (FYROM), Ukraine, Uruguay) had declared such recognition.

Under article 15, the Committee was empowered to consider copies of petitions, reports and other information relating to Trust and Non-Self-Governing Territories. CERD noted that it had been difficult to fulfil its functions under article 15 as the documents did not include copies of petitions and contained scant information directly related to the Convention's principles and objectives. The Committee asked that the appropriate information be furnished.

In March, the Committee adopted general recommendations XXV (on gender-related dimensions of racial discrimination), XXVI (on article 6—the right to seek just and adequate reparation or satisfaction for damage suffered as a result of racial discrimination) and XXVII (on discrimination against Roma).

The Committee asked the General Assembly to implement its March decision to hold its fifty-eighth session in New York from 8 to 26 January 2001. An October addendum to the Committee's report [A/55/18/Add.1] contained the programme budget implications of the decision. By **decision 55/419** of 4 December, the Assembly decided to refer the decision back to CERD for further consideration and consultation with States parties.

Reporting on the financial situation of the Committee [A/55/266], the Secretary-General stated that, as at 30 June, the total outstanding in arrears amounted to $173,572.

As at 31 December, 30 States parties had accepted an amendment to the Convention regarding the financing of CERD [YUN 1992, p. 714]. The amendment was to enter into force when accepted by a two-thirds majority of States parties.

GENERAL ASSEMBLY ACTION

On 4 December [meeting 81], the General Assembly, on the recommendation of the Third Committee [A/55/600], adopted **resolution 55/81** without vote [agenda item 112].

International Convention on the Elimination of All Forms of Racial Discrimination

The General Assembly,

Recalling its previous resolutions concerning the reports of the Committee on the Elimination of Racial

Discrimination and its resolutions on the status of the International Convention on the Elimination of All Forms of Racial Discrimination, most recently resolution 53/131 of 9 December 1998,

Bearing in mind the Vienna Declaration and Programme of Action adopted by the World Conference on Human Rights on 25 June 1993, in particular section II.B of the Declaration, relating to equality, dignity and tolerance,

Reiterating the need to intensify the struggle to eliminate all forms of racial discrimination throughout the world, especially its most brutal forms,

Recalling its resolution 52/111 of 12 December 1997, in which it decided to convene the World Conference against Racism, Racial Discrimination, Xenophobia and Related Intolerance no later than 2001,

Recalling also its resolution 53/132 of 9 December 1998, in which it decided to observe 2001 as the International Year of Mobilization against Racism, Racial Discrimination, Xenophobia and Related Intolerance,

Taking note of Commission on Human Rights resolution 2000/14 of 17 April 2000 on racism, racial discrimination, xenophobia and related intolerance,

Reiterating the importance of the Convention, which is one of the most widely accepted human rights instruments adopted under the auspices of the United Nations,

Stressing the importance of achieving universal ratification of the Convention, which will contribute to the fight against racism and racial discrimination,

Mindful of the importance of the contributions of the Committee to the effective implementation of the Convention and to the efforts of the United Nations to combat racism and all other forms of discrimination based on race, colour, descent or national or ethnic origin,

Noting that the reports submitted by States parties under the Convention contain, inter alia, information about the causes of, as well as measures to combat, contemporary forms of racism, racial discrimination, xenophobia and related intolerance,

Emphasizing the obligation of all States parties to the Convention to take legislative, judicial and other measures in order to secure full implementation of the provisions of the Convention,

Recalling its resolution 47/111 of 16 December 1992, in which it welcomed the decision, taken on 15 January 1992 by the Fourteenth Meeting of States Parties to the International Convention on the Elimination of All Forms of Racial Discrimination, to amend paragraph 6 of article 8 of the Convention and to add a new paragraph, as paragraph 7 of article 8, with a view to providing for the financing of the Committee from the regular budget of the United Nations, and reiterating its deep concern that the amendment to the Convention has not yet entered into force,

Stressing the importance of enabling the Committee to function smoothly and to have all necessary facilities for the effective performance of its functions under the Convention,

I

Reports of the Committee on the Elimination of Racial Discrimination

1. *Takes note* of the reports of the Committee on the Elimination of Racial Discrimination on its fifty-fourth and fifty-fifth and its fifty-sixth and fifty-seventh sessions;

2. *Commends* the Committee for its continuing efforts to contribute to the effective implementation of the International Convention on the Elimination of All Forms of Racial Discrimination, especially the examination of reports under article 9 and action on communications under article 14 of the Convention, which contribute to the fight against racism, racial discrimination, xenophobia and related intolerance;

3. *Calls upon* States parties to fulfil their obligation, under paragraph 1 of article 9 of the Convention, to submit their periodic reports on measures taken to implement the Convention in due time;

4. *Expresses its concern* at the fact that a great number of reports are overdue and continue to be overdue, in particular initial reports, which constitutes an obstacle to the full implementation of the Convention;

5. *Encourages* States parties to the Convention whose reports are seriously overdue to avail themselves of the advisory services and technical assistance that the Office of the United Nations High Commissioner for Human Rights can provide, upon their request, for the preparation of the reports;

6. *Commends* the Committee for its continuing contribution to the prevention of racial discrimination, and welcomes its relevant action thereon;

7. *Encourages* the Committee to continue to contribute fully to the implementation of the Third Decade to Combat Racism and Racial Discrimination and its revised Programme of Action, including by continuing to cooperate and exchange information with United Nations bodies and mechanisms and intergovernmental organizations, in particular with the Subcommission on the Promotion and Protection of Human Rights and with the Special Rapporteur of the Commission on Human Rights on contemporary forms of racism, racial discrimination, xenophobia and related intolerance, as well as with non-governmental organizations;

8. *Encourages* States parties to continue to include a gender perspective in their reports to the Committee, and invites the Committee to take into account a gender perspective in the implementation of its mandate;

9. *Takes note with interest* of the contributions by the Committee to the preparatory process for the World Conference against Racism, Racial Discrimination, Xenophobia and Related Intolerance, including undertaking a series of studies, making suggestions for the agenda and draft programme of action of the World Conference, and preparing an assessment of the best practices of States parties in combating racial discrimination;

10. *Invites* the Committee to continue to participate actively in the preparatory process for the World Conference and at the Conference itself;

11. *Encourages* all States, relevant United Nations bodies, international and regional organizations and non-governmental organizations to draw attention to the Convention and to the work of the Committee during the information and awareness-raising campaign for the World Conference and the International Year of Mobilization against Racism, Racial Discrimination, Xenophobia and Related Intolerance;

II
Financial situation of the Committee on the Elimination of Racial Discrimination

1. *Takes note* of the report of the Secretary-General on the financial situation of the Committee on the Elimination of Racial Discrimination;

2. *Expresses its profound concern* about the fact that a number of States parties to the International Convention on the Elimination of All Forms of Racial Discrimination have still not fulfilled their financial obligations, as shown in the report of the Secretary-General, and strongly appeals to all States parties that are in arrears to fulfil their outstanding financial obligations under article 8, paragraph 6, of the Convention;

3. *Strongly urges* States parties to the Convention to accelerate their domestic ratification procedures with regard to the amendment to the Convention concerning the financing of the Committee and to notify the Secretary-General expeditiously in writing of their agreement to the amendment, as decided upon at the Fourteenth Meeting of States Parties to the International Convention on the Elimination of All Forms of Racial Discrimination on 15 January 1992, endorsed by the General Assembly in its resolution 47/111 and further reiterated at the Sixteenth Meeting of States Parties on 16 January 1996;

4. *Requests* the Secretary-General to continue to ensure adequate financial arrangements and to provide the necessary support, including an adequate level of Secretariat assistance, in order to ensure the functioning of the Committee and to enable it to cope with its increasing amount of work;

5. *Also requests* the Secretary-General to invite those States parties to the Convention that are in arrears to pay the amounts in arrears, and to report thereon to the General Assembly at its fifty-seventh session;

III
Status of the International Convention on the Elimination of All Forms of Racial Discrimination

1. *Takes note* of the report of the Secretary-General on the status of the International Convention on the Elimination of All Forms of Racial Discrimination;

2. *Expresses its satisfaction* at the number of States that have ratified the Convention or acceded thereto, which now stands at one hundred and fifty-six;

3. *Reaffirms once again its conviction* that ratification of or accession to the Convention on a universal basis and the implementation of its provisions are necessary for the realization of the objectives of the Third Decade to Combat Racism and Racial Discrimination and for action beyond the Decade;

4. *Urges* all States that have not yet become parties to the Convention to ratify it or accede thereto as soon as possible, bearing in mind the World Conference against Racism, Racial Discrimination, Xenophobia and Related Intolerance, to be held in South Africa, from 31 August to 7 September 2001;

5. *Urges* States to limit the extent of any reservation they lodge to the Convention and to formulate any reservation as precisely and as narrowly as possible in order to ensure that no reservation is incompatible with the object and purpose of the Convention or otherwise contrary to international treaty law, to review their reservations on a regular basis with a view to withdrawing them, and to withdraw reservations that are contrary to the object and purpose of the Convention or that are otherwise incompatible with international treaty law;

6. *Requests* the States parties to the Convention that have not yet done so to consider the possibility of making the declaration provided for in article 14 of the Convention;

7. *Decides* to consider, at its fifty-seventh session, under the item entitled "Elimination of racism and racial discrimination", the reports of the Committee on the Elimination of Racial Discrimination on its fifty-eighth and fifty-ninth and its sixtieth and sixty-first sessions, the report of the Secretary-General on the financial situation of the Committee and the report of the Secretary-General on the status of the Convention.

Convention against torture

Accessions and ratifications

As at 31 December 2000, 123 States were parties to the 1984 Convention against Torture and Other Cruel, Inhuman or Degrading Treatment or Punishment, adopted by the General Assembly in resolution 39/46 [YUN 1984, p. 813]. During the year, Botswana, Gabon, Ghana, Lebanon and Qatar became parties. Forty-three parties had made the required declarations under articles 21 and 22 (under which a party recognized the competence of the Committee against Torture to receive and consider communications to the effect that a party claimed that another was not fulfilling its obligations under the Convention, and to receive communications from or on behalf of individuals who claimed to be victims of a violation of the Convention by a State party) and three had made the declaration under article 21 only. Amendments to articles 17 and 18, adopted in 1992 [YUN 1992, p. 735], had been accepted by 23 States parties as at year's end.

On 20 April [res. 2000/43], the Commission invited all ratifying or acceding States and those that had not done so to make the declaration provided for in articles 21 and 22 and to consider withdrawing their reservations to article 20. It asked the Secretary-General to continue to report annually on the status of the Convention.

The Secretary-General reported on the status of the Convention as at 1 July [A/55/208] and 15 November [E/CN.4/2001/58]. On 4 December, the Assembly took note of the former report (**decision 55/420**).

The Assembly, in **resolution 55/89**, urged States that had not done so to become parties to the Convention and invited those becoming parties and those that were parties but had not done so to make the declarations provided for in articles 21 and 22 and to consider withdrawing reservations to article 20.

Draft optional protocol

Commission action. On 20 April [res. 2000/35], the Commission asked the working group on the draft optional protocol to the Convention (intended to establish a preventive system of regular visits to places of detention) to meet prior to the Commission's 2001 session to complete the final and substantive text. The Secretary-General was asked to transmit the report of the working group to Governments, specialized agencies, chairpersons of human rights treaty bodies, intergovernmental organizations and NGOs and to invite them to submit their comments to the group. He should invite them, as well as the Chairperson of the Committee against Torture and the Special Rapporteur on the question of torture, to participate in working group activities.

On 28 July, the Economic and Social Council authorized the group to meet for two weeks and encouraged the group's Chairperson/Rapporteur to facilitate the completion of a consolidated text (**decision 2000/262**).

Implementation

Monitoring body. The Committee against Torture, established as a monitoring body under the Convention, held its twenty-fourth and twenty-fifth sessions in Geneva from 1 to 19 May [A/55/44] and from 13 to 24 November [A/56/44], respectively. Under article 19, it considered reports submitted by Armenia, Australia, Belarus, Cameroon, Canada, China, El Salvador, Guatemala, the Netherlands, Paraguay, Poland, Portugal, Slovenia and the United States.

The Committee held four closed meetings in May and three in November, during which, in accordance with article 20, it studied confidential information that appeared to contain well-founded indications that torture was systematically practised in a State party to the Convention. Under article 22, the Committee considered communications submitted by individuals who claimed that their rights, as enumerated in the Convention, had been violated by a State party and who had exhausted all available domestic remedies.

The Committee's contribution to the preparatory process for the World Conference against Racism, Racial Discrimination, Xenophobia and Related Intolerance (see p. 641) was annexed to its report [A/56/44].

Convention on elimination of discrimination against women and optional protocol

On 4 December, the General Assembly, in **resolution 55/70**, urged States that had not ratified or acceded to the 1979 Convention on the Elimination of All Forms of Discrimination against Women to do so. It also urged them to become parties to the Optional Protocol.

(For details on the status of the Convention and on the Optional Protocol, see p. 1123.)

Convention on the Rights of the Child

Accessions and ratifications

As at 31 December 2000, there continued to be 191 States parties to the 1989 Convention on the Rights of the Child, adopted by the General Assembly in resolution 44/25 [YUN 1989, p. 560].

The Secretary-General reported on the status of the Convention as at 5 July [A/55/201] and 27 November [E/CN.4/2001/74]. On 4 December, the Assembly took note of the former report (**decision 55/418**).

An amendment to the Convention to expand the membership of the Committee on the Rights of the Child (CRC) from 10 to 18, approved by the Assembly in resolution 50/155 [YUN 1995, p. 706], had been accepted by 96 States parties in 2000. The amendment required acceptance by a two-thirds majority to enter into force.

On 27 April [res. 2000/85], the Commission urged States that had not done so to sign and ratify or accede to the Convention. It called on States parties to implement the Convention and to accept the amendment to expand CRC membership. The Commission asked the Secretary-General to assist the Committee; the Economic and Social Council endorsed that request on 28 July (**decision 2000/280**).

Implementation

Monitoring body. In 2000, CRC held its twenty-third (10-28 January) [CRC/C/94], twenty-fourth (15 May–2 June) [CRC/C/97] and twenty-fifth (18 September–6 October) [CRC/C/100] sessions, all in Geneva. Each session was preceded by a pre-sessional working group, which reviewed State party reports and identified the main questions to be discussed with reporting States. It also provided an opportunity to consider technical assistance and international cooperation.

Under article 44 of the Convention, CRC considered initial reports from 26 States parties: Armenia, Burundi, Cambodia, Central African Republic, Colombia, Comoros, Costa Rica, Djibouti, Finland, Georgia, Grenada, India, Iran, Jordan, Kyrgyzstan, Malta, Marshall Islands, Norway, Peru, Sierra Leone, Slovakia, South Africa, Suriname, Tajikistan, FYROM and United Kingdom (Isle of Man and Overseas Territories).

In September, the Committee devoted its day of general discussion to violence suffered by children living in institutions managed, licensed or supervised by the State, and in the context of law and public order concerns.

CRC reports on its eighteenth to twenty-third sessions were issued in a consolidated report [A/55/41].

Children in armed conflict

Working group activities. The working group on a draft optional protocol to the Convention on the Rights of the Child on the involvement of children in armed conflict adopted the draft at its sixth session (Geneva, 10-21 January and 23 March) [E/CN.4/2000/74]. The draft text was annexed to the group's report.

Commission action. On 26 April [res. 2000/59], the Commission adopted the draft optional protocol and called on States parties to the Convention to sign and ratify or accede to the optional protocol, following its adoption by the General Assembly. It recommended that the optional protocol be opened for signature and ratification or accession at the Assembly's special session on women from 5 to 9 June in New York (see p. 1082) and thereafter at UN Headquarters.

Also on 26 April [E/2000/42/Add.1], the Commission Chairperson transmitted the text of the draft optional protocol to the Economic and Social Council.

(For further information on children in armed conflict, see p. 722.)

Sale of children, child prostitution and child pornography

Working group activities. The working group for the elaboration of a draft optional protocol to the Convention on the Rights of the Child on the sale of children, child prostitution and child pornography adopted the draft at its sixth session (Geneva, 24 January–4 February and 23 March) [E/CN.4/2000/75]. The draft optional protocol was annexed to the group's report.

Commission action. On 26 April [res. 2000/59], the Commission adopted the draft optional protocol and called on States parties to the Convention to sign and ratify or accede to the optional protocol, following its adoption by the General Assembly. It recommended that the optional protocol be opened for signature and ratification or accession at the Assembly's special session on women and thereafter at UN Headquarters.

Also on 26 April [E/2000/42/Add.1], the Commission Chairperson transmitted the text of the draft optional protocol to the Economic and Social Council.

(For further information on the sale of children, child prostitution and child pornography, see p. 720.)

ECONOMIC AND SOCIAL COUNCIL ACTION

On 10 May [meeting 8], the Economic and Social Council, on the recommendation of the Commission on Human Rights [E/2000/23 & Corr.1], adopted **resolution 2000/2** without vote [agenda item 2].

Question of draft optional protocols to the Convention on the Rights of the Child on the involvement of children in armed conflict and on the sale of children, child prostitution and child pornography

The Economic and Social Council,

Taking note of Commission on Human Rights resolution 2000/59 of 26 April 2000, including the annexes thereto, in which the Commission approved the texts of the two draft optional protocols to the Convention on the Rights of the Child on the involvement of children in armed conflict and on the sale of children, child prostitution and child pornography,

1. *Expresses its appreciation* to the Commission on Human Rights for finalizing the two draft optional protocols to the Convention on the Rights of the Child on the involvement of children in armed conflict and on the sale of children, child prostitution and child pornography;

2. *Approves* the two draft optional protocols set out below;

3. *Recommends* that the two optional protocols, after adoption by the General Assembly, be open for early signature and ratification or accession at the special session of the General Assembly entitled "Women 2000: gender equality, development and peace for the twenty-first century", to be convened from 5 to 9 June 2000 in New York, and thereafter at United Nations Headquarters, including at the special session of the General Assembly entitled "World Summit for Social Development and beyond: achieving social development for all in a globalizing world", to be convened from 26 to 30 June 2000 in Geneva, and at the Millennium Summit of the United Nations, to be convened from 6 to 8 September 2000, in New York;

4. *Recommends* to the General Assembly the adoption of the following draft resolution:

[For text, see General Assembly resolution 54/263 below.]

GENERAL ASSEMBLY ACTION

On 25 May [meeting 97], the General Assembly, on the recommendation of the Economic and Social Council [A/54/L.84], adopted **resolution 54/263** without vote [agenda item 116 (a)].

Optional protocols to the Convention on the Rights of the Child on the involvement of children in armed conflict and on the sale of children, child prostitution and child pornography

The General Assembly,

Recalling all its previous resolutions on the rights of the child, in particular its resolution 54/149 of 17 December 1999, in which it strongly supported the work of the open-ended inter-sessional working groups and urged them to finalize their work before the tenth anniversary of the entry into force of the Convention on the Rights of the Child,

Expressing its appreciation to the Commission on Human Rights for having finalized the texts of the two optional protocols to the Convention on the Rights of the Child on the involvement of children in armed conflict and on the sale of children, child prostitution and child pornography,

Conscious of the tenth anniversaries, in the year 2000, of the World Summit for Children and the entry into force of the Convention on the Rights of the Child and of the symbolic and practical importance of the adoption of the two optional protocols to the Convention on the Rights of the Child before the special session of the General Assembly for the follow-up to the World Summit for Children, to be convened in 2001,

Adhering to the principle that the best interests of the child are to be a primary consideration in all actions concerning children,

Reaffirming its commitment to strive for the promotion and protection of the rights of the child in all avenues of life,

Recognizing that the adoption and implementation of the two optional protocols will make a substantial contribution to the promotion and protection of the rights of the child,

1. *Adopts and opens for signature, ratification and accession* the two optional protocols to the Convention on the Rights of the Child on the involvement of children in armed conflict and on the sale of children, child prostitution and child pornography, the texts of which are annexed to the present resolution;

2. *Invites* all States that have signed, ratified or acceded to the Convention on the Rights of the Child to sign and ratify or accede to the annexed optional protocols as soon as possible in order to facilitate their early entry into force;

3. *Decides* that the two optional protocols to the Convention on the Rights of the Child will be opened for signature at the special session of the General Assembly, entitled "Women 2000: gender equality, development and peace for the twenty-first century", to be convened from 5 to 9 June 2000 in New York, and thereafter at United Nations Headquarters, at the special session of the General Assembly, entitled "World Summit for Social Development and beyond: achieving social development for all in a globalizing world", to be convened from 26 to 30 June 2000 in Geneva, and at the Millennium Summit of the United Nations, to be convened from 6 to 8 September 2000 in New York;

4. *Requests* the Secretary-General to include information on the status of the two optional protocols in his report to the General Assembly on the status of the Convention on the Rights of the Child.

ANNEX I
Optional Protocol to the Convention on the Rights of the Child on the involvement of children in armed conflict

The States Parties to the present Protocol,

Encouraged by the overwhelming support for the Convention on the Rights of the Child, demonstrating the widespread commitment that exists to strive for the promotion and protection of the rights of the child,

Reaffirming that the rights of children require special protection, and calling for continuous improvement of the situation of children without distinction, as well as

for their development and education in conditions of peace and security,

Disturbed by the harmful and widespread impact of armed conflict on children and the long-term consequences this has for durable peace, security and development,

Condemning the targeting of children in situations of armed conflict and direct attacks on objects protected under international law, including places generally having a significant presence of children, such as schools and hospitals,

Noting the adoption of the Statute of the International Criminal Court and, in particular, its inclusion as a war crime of conscripting or enlisting children under the age of 15 years or using them to participate actively in hostilities in both international and non-international armed conflicts,

Considering, therefore, that to strengthen further the implementation of rights recognized in the Convention on the Rights of the Child there is a need to increase the protection of children from involvement in armed conflict,

Noting that article 1 of the Convention on the Rights of the Child specifies that, for the purposes of that Convention, a child means every human being below the age of 18 years unless, under the law applicable to the child, majority is attained earlier,

Convinced that an optional protocol to the Convention raising the age of possible recruitment of persons into armed forces and their participation in hostilities will contribute effectively to the implementation of the principle that the best interests of the child are to be a primary consideration in all actions concerning children,

Noting that the twenty-sixth international Conference of the Red Cross and Red Crescent in December 1995 recommended, inter alia, that parties to conflict take every feasible step to ensure that children under the age of 18 years do not take part in hostilities,

Welcoming the unanimous adoption, in June 1999, of International Labour Organization Convention No. 182 on the Prohibition and Immediate Action for the Elimination of the Worst Forms of Child Labour, which prohibits, inter alia, forced or compulsory recruitment of children for use in armed conflict,

Condemning with the gravest concern the recruitment, training and use within and across national borders of children in hostilities by armed groups distinct from the armed forces of a State, and recognizing the responsibility of those who recruit, train and use children in this regard,

Recalling the obligation of each party to an armed conflict to abide by the provisions of international humanitarian law,

Stressing that this Protocol is without prejudice to the purposes and principles contained in the Charter of the United Nations, including Article 51, and relevant norms of humanitarian law,

Bearing in mind that conditions of peace and security based on full respect of the purposes and principles contained in the Charter and observance of applicable human rights instruments are indispensable for the full protection of children, in particular during armed conflicts and foreign occupation,

Recognizing the special needs of those children who are particularly vulnerable to recruitment or use in hostilities contrary to this Protocol owing to their economic or social status or gender,

Mindful of the necessity of taking into consideration the economic, social and political root causes of the involvement of children in armed conflicts,

Convinced of the need to strengthen international cooperation in the implementation of this Protocol, as well as the physical and psychosocial rehabilitation and social reintegration of children who are victims of armed conflict,

Encouraging the participation of the community and, in particular, children and child victims in the dissemination of informational and educational programmes concerning the implementation of the Protocol,

Have agreed as follows:

Article 1

States Parties shall take all feasible measures to ensure that members of their armed forces who have not attained the age of 18 years do not take a direct part in hostilities.

Article 2

States Parties shall ensure that persons who have not attained the age of 18 years are not compulsorily recruited into their armed forces.

Article 3

1. States Parties shall raise the minimum age for the voluntary recruitment of persons into their national armed forces from that set out in article 38, paragraph 3, of the Convention on the Rights of the Child, taking account of the principles contained in that article and recognizing that under the Convention persons under 18 are entitled to special protection.

2. Each State Party shall deposit a binding declaration upon ratification of or accession to this Protocol that sets forth the minimum age at which it will permit voluntary recruitment into its national armed forces and a description of the safeguards that it has adopted to ensure that such recruitment is not forced or coerced.

3. States Parties that permit voluntary recruitment into their national armed forces under the age of 18 shall maintain safeguards to ensure, as a minimum, that:

(*a*) Such recruitment is genuinely voluntary;

(*b*) Such recruitment is done with the informed consent of the person's parents or legal guardians;

(*c*) Such persons are fully informed of the duties involved in such military service;

(*d*) Such persons provide reliable proof of age prior to acceptance into national military service.

4. Each State Party may strengthen its declaration at any time by notification to that effect addressed to the Secretary-General of the United Nations, who shall inform all States Parties. Such notification shall take effect on the date on which it is received by the Secretary-General.

5. The requirement to raise the age in paragraph 1 of the present article does not apply to schools operated by or under the control of the armed forces of the States Parties, in keeping with articles 28 and 29 of the Convention on the Rights of the Child.

Article 4

1. Armed groups that are distinct from the armed forces of a State should not, under any circumstances, recruit or use in hostilities persons under the age of 18 years.

2. States Parties shall take all feasible measures to prevent such recruitment and use, including the adoption of legal measures necessary to prohibit and criminalize such practices.

3. The application of the present article under this Protocol shall not affect the legal status of any party to an armed conflict.

Article 5

Nothing in the present Protocol shall be construed as precluding provisions in the law of a State Party or in international instruments and international humanitarian law that are more conducive to the realization of the rights of the child.

Article 6

1. Each State Party shall take all necessary legal, administrative and other measures to ensure the effective implementation and enforcement of the provisions of this Protocol within its jurisdiction.

2. States Parties undertake to make the principles and provisions of the present Protocol widely known and promoted by appropriate means, to adults and children alike.

3. States Parties shall take all feasible measures to ensure that persons within their jurisdiction recruited or used in hostilities contrary to this Protocol are demobilized or otherwise released from service. States Parties shall, when necessary, accord to these persons all appropriate assistance for their physical and psychological recovery and their social reintegration.

Article 7

1. States Parties shall cooperate in the implementation of the present Protocol, including in the prevention of any activity contrary to the Protocol and in the rehabilitation and social reintegration of persons who are victims of acts contrary to this Protocol, including through technical cooperation and financial assistance. Such assistance and cooperation will be undertaken in consultation with concerned States Parties and relevant international organizations.

2. States Parties in a position to do so shall provide such assistance through existing multilateral, bilateral or other programmes, or, inter alia, through a voluntary fund established in accordance with the rules of the General Assembly.

Article 8

1. Each State Party shall submit, within two years following the entry into force of the Protocol for that State Party, a report to the Committee on the Rights of the Child providing comprehensive information on the measures it has taken to implement the provisions of the Protocol, including the measures taken to implement the provisions on participation and recruitment.

2. Following the submission of the comprehensive report, each State Party shall include in the reports they submit to the Committee on the Rights of the Child, in accordance with article 44 of the Convention, any further information with respect to the implementation of the Protocol. Other States Parties to the Protocol shall submit a report every five years.

3. The Committee on the Rights of the Child may request from States Parties further information relevant to the implementation of this Protocol.

Article 9

1. The present Protocol is open for signature by any State that is a party to the Convention or has signed it.

2. The present Protocol is subject to ratification and is open to accession by any State. Instruments of ratification or accession shall be deposited with the Secretary-General of the United Nations.

3. The Secretary-General, in his capacity as depositary of the Convention and the Protocol, shall inform all States Parties to the Convention and all States that have signed the Convention of each instrument of declaration pursuant to article 13.

Article 10

1. The present Protocol shall enter into force three months after the deposit of the tenth instrument of ratification or accession.

2. For each State ratifying the present Protocol or acceding to it after its entry into force, the present Protocol shall enter into force one month after the date of the deposit of its own instrument of ratification or accession.

Article 11

1. Any State Party may denounce the present Protocol at any time by written notification to the Secretary-General of the United Nations, who shall thereafter inform the other States Parties to the Convention and all States that have signed the Convention. The denunciation shall take effect one year after the date of receipt of the notification by the Secretary-General. If, however, on the expiry of that year the denouncing State Party is engaged in armed conflict, the denunciation shall not take effect before the end of the armed conflict.

2. Such a denunciation shall not have the effect of releasing the State Party from its obligations under the present Protocol in regard to any act that occurs prior to the date on which the denunciation becomes effective. Nor shall such a denunciation prejudice in any way the continued consideration of any matter that is already under consideration by the Committee prior to the date on which the denunciation becomes effective.

Article 12

1. Any State Party may propose an amendment and file it with the Secretary-General of the United Nations. The Secretary-General shall thereupon communicate the proposed amendment to States Parties, with a request that they indicate whether they favour a conference of States Parties for the purpose of considering and voting upon the proposals. In the event that, within four months from the date of such communication, at least one third of the States Parties favour such a conference, the Secretary-General shall convene the conference under the auspices of the United Nations. Any amendment adopted by a majority of States Parties present and voting at the conference shall be submitted to the General Assembly for approval.

2. An amendment adopted in accordance with paragraph 1 of the present article shall enter into force when it has been approved by the General Assembly of the United Nations and accepted by a two-thirds majority of States Parties.

3. When an amendment enters into force, it shall be binding on those States Parties that have accepted it, other States Parties still being bound by the provisions of the present Protocol and any earlier amendments that they have accepted.

Article 13

1. The present Protocol, of which the Arabic, Chinese, English, French, Russian and Spanish texts are equally authentic, shall be deposited in the archives of the United Nations.

2. The Secretary-General of the United Nations shall transmit certified copies of the present Protocol to all States Parties to the Convention and all States that have signed the Convention.

ANNEX II
Optional Protocol to the Convention on the Rights of the Child on the sale of children, child prostitution and child pornography

The States Parties to the present Protocol,

Considering that, in order further to achieve the purposes of the Convention on the Rights of the Child and the implementation of its provisions, especially articles 1, 11, 21, 32, 33, 34, 35 and 36, it would be appropriate to extend the measures that States Parties should undertake in order to guarantee the protection of the child from the sale of children, child prostitution and child pornography,

Considering also that the Convention on the Rights of the Child recognizes the right of the child to be protected from economic exploitation and from performing any work that is likely to be hazardous or to interfere with the child's education, or to be harmful to the child's health or physical, mental, spiritual, moral or social development,

Gravely concerned at the significant and increasing international traffic of children for the purpose of the sale of children, child prostitution and child pornography,

Deeply concerned at the widespread and continuing practice of sex tourism, to which children are especially vulnerable, as it directly promotes the sale of children, child prostitution and child pornography,

Recognizing that a number of particularly vulnerable groups, including girl children, are at greater risk of sexual exploitation, and that girl children are disproportionately represented among the sexually exploited,

Concerned about the growing availability of child pornography on the Internet and other evolving technologies, and recalling the International Conference on Combating Child Pornography on the Internet (Vienna, 1999) and, in particular, its conclusion calling for the worldwide criminalization of the production, distribution, exportation, transmission, importation, intentional possession and advertising of child pornography, and stressing the importance of closer cooperation and partnership between Governments and the Internet industry,

Believing that the elimination of the sale of children, child prostitution and child pornography will be facilitated by adopting a holistic approach, addressing the contributing factors, including underdevelopment, poverty, economic disparities, inequitable socio-economic structure, dysfunctioning families, lack of education, urban-rural migration, gender discrimination, irresponsible adult sexual behaviour, harmful traditional practices, armed conflicts and trafficking of children,

Believing that efforts to raise public awareness are needed to reduce consumer demand for the sale of children, child prostitution and child pornography, and also believing in the importance of strengthening global partnership among all actors and of improving law enforcement at the national level,

Noting the provisions of international legal instruments relevant to the protection of children, including the Hague Convention on the Protection of Children and Cooperation with Respect to Inter-Country Adoption, the Hague Convention on the Civil Aspects of International Child Abduction, the Hague Convention on Jurisdiction, Applicable Law, Recognition, Enforcement and Cooperation in Respect of Parental Responsibility and Measures for the Protection of Children, and International Labour Organization Convention No. 182 on the Prohibition and Immediate Action for the Elimination of the Worst Forms of Child Labour,

Encouraged by the overwhelming support for the Convention on the Rights of the Child, demonstrating the widespread commitment that exists for the promotion and protection of the rights of the child,

Recognizing the importance of the implementation of the provisions of the Programme of Action for the Prevention of the Sale of Children, Child Prostitution and Child Pornography and the Declaration and Agenda for Action adopted at the World Congress against Commercial Sexual Exploitation of Children, held at Stockholm from 27 to 31 August 1996, and the other relevant decisions and recommendations of pertinent international bodies,

Taking due account of the importance of the traditions and cultural values of each people for the protection and harmonious development of the child,

Have agreed as follows:

Article 1

States Parties shall prohibit the sale of children, child prostitution and child pornography as provided for by the present Protocol.

Article 2

For the purpose of the present Protocol:

(a) Sale of children means any act or transaction whereby a child is transferred by any person or group of persons to another for remuneration or any other consideration;

(b) Child prostitution means the use of a child in sexual activities for remuneration or any other form of consideration;

(c) Child pornography means any representation, by whatever means, of a child engaged in real or simulated explicit sexual activities or any representation of the sexual parts of a child for primarily sexual purposes.

Article 3

1. Each State Party shall ensure that, as a minimum, the following acts and activities are fully covered under its criminal or penal law, whether these offences are committed domestically or transnationally or on an individual or organized basis:

(a) In the context of sale of children as defined in article 2:

  (i) The offering, delivering or accepting, by whatever means, a child for the purpose of:

    a. Sexual exploitation of the child;

    b. Transfer of organs of the child for profit;

    c. Engagement of the child in forced labour;

  (ii) Improperly inducing consent, as an intermediary, for the adoption of a child in violation of applicable international legal instruments on adoption;

(b) Offering, obtaining, procuring or providing a child for child prostitution, as defined in article 2;

(c) Producing, distributing, disseminating, importing, exporting, offering, selling or possessing for the above purposes child pornography as defined in article 2.

2. Subject to the provisions of a State Party's national law, the same shall apply to an attempt to commit any of these acts and to complicity or participation in any of these acts.

3. Each State Party shall make these offences punishable by appropriate penalties that take into account their grave nature.

4. Subject to the provisions of its national law, each State Party shall take measures, where appropriate, to establish the liability of legal persons for offences established in paragraph 1 of the present article. Subject to the legal principles of the State Party, this liability of legal persons may be criminal, civil or administrative.

5. States Parties shall take all appropriate legal and administrative measures to ensure that all persons involved in the adoption of a child act in conformity with applicable international legal instruments.

Article 4

1. Each State Party shall take such measures as may be necessary to establish its jurisdiction over the offences referred to in article 3, paragraph 1, when the offences are commited in its territory or on board a ship or aircraft registered in that State.

2. Each State Party may take such measures as may be necessary to establish its jurisdiction over the offences referred to in article 3, paragraph 1, in the following cases:

(a) When the alleged offender is a national of that State or a person who has his habitual residence in its territory;

(b) When the victim is a national of that State.

3. Each State Party shall also take such measures as may be necessary to establish its jurisdiction over the above-mentioned offences when the alleged offender is present in its territory and it does not extradite him or her to another State Party on the ground that the offence has been committed by one of its nationals.

4. This Protocol does not exclude any criminal jurisdiction exercised in accordance with internal law.

Article 5

1. The offences referred to in article 3, paragraph 1, shall be deemed to be included as extraditable offences in any extradition treaty existing between States Parties and shall be included as extraditable offences in every extradition treaty subsequently concluded between them, in accordance with the conditions set forth in those treaties.

2. If a State Party that makes extradition conditional on the existence of a treaty receives a request for extradition from another State Party with which it has no extradition treaty, it may consider this Protocol as a legal basis for extradition in respect of such offences. Extradition shall be subject to the conditions provided by the law of the requested State.

3. States Parties that do not make extradition conditional on the existence of a treaty shall recognize such offences as extraditable offences between themselves

subject to the conditions provided by the law of the requested State.

4. Such offences shall be treated, for the purpose of extradition between States Parties, as if they had been committed not only in the place in which they occurred but also in the territories of the States required to establish their jurisdiction in accordance with article 4.

5. If an extradition request is made with respect to an offence described in article 3, paragraph 1, and if the requested State Party does not or will not extradite on the basis of the nationality of the offender, that State shall take suitable measures to submit the case to its competent authorities for the purpose of prosecution.

Article 6

1. States Parties shall afford one another the greatest measure of assistance in connection with investigations or criminal or extradition proceedings brought in respect of the offences set forth in article 3, paragraph 1, including assistance in obtaining evidence at their disposal necessary for the proceedings.

2. States Parties shall carry out their obligations under paragraph 1 of the present article in conformity with any treaties or other arrangements on mutual legal assistance that may exist between them. In the absence of such treaties or arrangements, States Parties shall afford one another assistance in accordance with their domestic law.

Article 7

States Parties shall, subject to the provisions of their national law:

(a) Take measures to provide for the seizure and confiscation, as appropriate, of:

(i) Goods such as materials, assets and other instrumentalities used to commit or facilitate offences under the present protocol;

(ii) Proceeds derived from such offences;

(b) Execute requests from another State Party for seizure or confiscation of goods or proceeds referred to in subparagraph (a) (i);

(c) Take measures aimed at closing, on a temporary or definitive basis, premises used to commit such offences.

Article 8

1. States Parties shall adopt appropriate measures to protect the rights and interests of child victims of the practices prohibited under the present Protocol at all stages of the criminal justice process, in particular by:

(a) Recognizing the vulnerability of child victims and adapting procedures to recognize their special needs, including their special needs as witnesses;

(b) Informing child victims of their rights, their role and the scope, timing and progress of the proceedings and of the disposition of their cases;

(c) Allowing the views, needs and concerns of child victims to be presented and considered in proceedings where their personal interests are affected, in a manner consistent with the procedural rules of national law;

(d) Providing appropriate support services to child victims throughout the legal process;

(e) Protecting, as appropriate, the privacy and identity of child victims and taking measures in accordance with national law to avoid the inappropriate dissemination of information that could lead to the identification of child victims;

(f) Providing, in appropriate cases, for the safety of child victims, as well as that of their families and witnesses on their behalf, from intimidation and retaliation;

(g) Avoiding unnecessary delay in the disposition of cases and the execution of orders or decrees granting compensation to child victims.

2. States Parties shall ensure that uncertainty as to the actual age of the victim shall not prevent the initiation of criminal investigations, including investigations aimed at establishing the age of the victim.

3. States Parties shall ensure that, in the treatment by the criminal justice system of children who are victims of the offences described in the present Protocol, the best interest of the child shall be a primary consideration.

4. States Parties shall take measures to ensure appropriate training, in particular legal and psychological training, for the persons who work with victims of the offences prohibited under the present Protocol.

5. States Parties shall, in appropriate cases, adopt measures in order to protect the safety and integrity of those persons and/or organizations involved in the prevention and/or protection and rehabilitation of victims of such offences.

6. Nothing in the present article shall be construed as prejudicial to or inconsistent with the rights of the accused to a fair and impartial trial.

Article 9

1. States Parties shall adopt or strengthen, implement and disseminate laws, administrative measures, social policies and programmes to prevent the offences referred to in the present Protocol. Particular attention shall be given to protect children who are especially vulnerable to these practices.

2. States Parties shall promote awareness in the public at large, including children, through information by all appropriate means, education and training, about the preventive measures and harmful effects of the offences referred to in the present Protocol. In fulfilling their obligations under this article, States Parties shall encourage the participation of the community and, in particular, children and child victims, in such information and education and training programmes, including at the international level.

3. States Parties shall take all feasible measures with the aim of ensuring all appropriate assistance to victims of such offences, including their full social reintegration and their full physical and psychological recovery.

4. States Parties shall ensure that all child victims of the offences described in the present Protocol have access to adequate procedures to seek, without discrimination, compensation for damages from those legally responsible.

5. States Parties shall take appropriate measures aimed at effectively prohibiting the production and dissemination of material advertising the offences described in the present Protocol.

Article 10

1. States Parties shall take all necessary steps to strengthen international cooperation by multilateral, regional and bilateral arrangements for the prevention, detection, investigation, prosecution and punishment of those responsible for acts involving the sale of

children, child prostitution, child pornography and child sex tourism. States Parties shall also promote international cooperation and coordination between their authorities, national and international non-governmental organizations and international organizations.

2. States Parties shall promote international cooperation to assist child victims in their physical and psychological recovery, social reintegration and repatriation.

3. States Parties shall promote the strengthening of international cooperation in order to address the root causes, such as poverty and underdevelopment, contributing to the vulnerability of children to the sale of children, child prostitution, child pornography and child sex tourism.

4. States Parties in a position to do so shall provide financial, technical or other assistance through existing multilateral, regional, bilateral or other programmes.

Article 11

Nothing in the present Protocol shall affect any provisions that are more conducive to the realization of the rights of the child and that may be contained in:

(a) The law of a State Party;

(b) International law in force for that State.

Article 12

1. Each State Party shall submit, within two years following the entry into force of the Protocol for that State Party, a report to the Committee on the Rights of the Child providing comprehensive information on the measures it has taken to implement the provisions of the Protocol.

2. Following the submission of the comprehensive report, each State Party shall include in the reports they submit to the Committee on the Rights of the Child, in accordance with article 44 of the Convention, any further information with respect to the implementation of the Protocol. Other States Parties to the Protocol shall submit a report every five years.

3. The Committee on the Rights of the Child may request from States Parties further information relevant to the implementation of this Protocol.

Article 13

1. The present Protocol is open for signature by any State that is a party to the Convention or has signed it.

2. The present Protocol is subject to ratification and is open to accession by any State that is a party to the Convention or has signed it. Instruments of ratification or accession shall be deposited with the Secretary-General of the United Nations.

Article 14

1. The present Protocol shall enter into force three months after the deposit of the tenth instrument of ratification or accession.

2. For each State ratifying the present Protocol or acceding to it after its entry into force, the present Protocol shall enter into force one month after the date of the deposit of its own instrument of ratification or accession.

Article 15

1. Any State Party may denounce the present Protocol at any time by written notification to the Secretary-General of the United Nations, who shall thereafter in-

form the other States Parties to the Convention and all States that have signed the Convention. The denunciation shall take effect one year after the date of receipt of the notification by the Secretary-General of the United Nations.

2. Such a denunciation shall not have the effect of releasing the State Party from its obligations under this Protocol in regard to any offence that occurs prior to the date on which the denunciation becomes effective. Nor shall such a denunciation prejudice in any way the continued consideration of any matter that is already under consideration by the Committee prior to the date on which the denunciation becomes effective.

Article 16

1. Any State Party may propose an amendment and file it with the Secretary-General of the United Nations. The Secretary-General shall thereupon communicate the proposed amendment to States Parties, with a request that they indicate whether they favour a conference of States Parties for the purpose of considering and voting upon the proposals. In the event that, within four months from the date of such communication, at least one third of the States Parties favour such a conference, the Secretary-General shall convene the conference under the auspices of the United Nations. Any amendment adopted by a majority of States Parties present and voting at the conference shall be submitted to the General Assembly for approval.

2. An amendment adopted in accordance with paragraph 1 of the present article shall enter into force when it has been approved by the General Assembly of the United Nations and accepted by a two-thirds majority of States Parties.

3. When an amendment enters into force, it shall be binding on those States Parties that have accepted it, other States Parties still being bound by the provisions of the present Protocol and any earlier amendments that they have accepted.

Article 17

1. The present Protocol, of which the Arabic, Chinese, English, French, Russian and Spanish texts are equally authentic, shall be deposited in the archives of the United Nations.

2. The Secretary-General of the United Nations shall transmit certified copies of the present Protocol to all States Parties to the Convention and all States that have signed the Convention.

As at 31 December, the optional protocols on the involvement of children in armed conflict and on the sale of children, child prostitution and child pornography had 75 signatories and three parties (Bangladesh, Canada, Sri Lanka) and 69 signatories and one party (Bangladesh), respectively.

Convention on migrant workers

Accessions and ratifications

As at 31 December 2000, the International Convention on the Protection of the Rights of All Migrant Workers and Members of Their Families, adopted by the General Assembly in resolution 45/158 [YUN 1990, p. 594], had been ratified or acceded to by Azerbaijan, Bolivia, Bosnia and Herzegovina, Cape Verde, Colombia, Egypt, Ghana, Guinea, Mexico, Morocco, the Philippines, Senegal, Seychelles, Sri Lanka and Uganda, and signed by Bangladesh, Chile, the Comoros, Guatemala, Guinea-Bissau, Paraguay, Sao Tome and Principe, Sierra Leone, Tajikistan and Turkey. The Convention was to enter into force on the first day of the month following a period of three months after the date of deposit of the twentieth instrument of ratification or accession.

The Secretary-General reported on the status of the Convention as at 1 July [A/55/205] and 15 November [E/CN.4/2001/79].

Commission action. On 25 April [res. 2000/49], the Commission called on all Member States to sign and ratify or accede to the Convention as a matter of priority. It asked the Secretary-General to provide assistance to promote the Convention through the World Public Information Campaign on Human Rights, launched by the General Assembly in resolution 43/128 [YUN 1988, p. 539], and the human rights programme of advisory services, and to report in 2001 on the Convention's status and on Secretariat efforts to promote it and the protection of migrant workers' rights.

(For further information on migrant workers, see p. 651.)

GENERAL ASSEMBLY ACTION

On 4 December [meeting 81], the General Assembly, on the recommendation of the Third Committee [A/55/602/Add.1], adopted **resolution 55/88** without vote [agenda item 114 (a)].

International Convention on the Protection of the Rights of All Migrant Workers and Members of Their Families

The General Assembly,

Reaffirming once more the permanent validity of the principles and norms set forth in the basic instruments regarding the international protection of human rights, in particular the Universal Declaration of Human Rights, the International Covenants on Human Rights, the International Convention on the Elimination of All Forms of Racial Discrimination, the Convention on the Elimination of All Forms of Discrimination against Women and the Convention on the Rights of the Child,

Bearing in mind the principles and norms established within the framework of the International Labour Organization and the importance of the work done in connection with migrant workers and members of their families in other specialized agencies and in various organs of the United Nations,

Reiterating that, despite the existence of an already established body of principles and norms, there is a need to make further efforts to improve the situation and to guarantee respect for the human rights and dignity of all migrant workers and members of their families,

Aware of the situation of migrant workers and members of their families and the marked increase in migratory movements that has occurred, especially in certain parts of the world,

Considering that, in the Vienna Declaration and Programme of Action adopted by the World Conference on Human Rights on 25 June 1993, all States are urged to guarantee the protection of the human rights of all migrant workers and members of their families,

Underlining the importance of the creation and promotion of conditions to foster greater harmony and tolerance between migrant workers and the rest of the society of the State in which they reside, with the aim of eliminating the growing manifestations of racism and xenophobia perpetrated in segments of many societies by individuals or groups against migrant workers,

Recalling its resolution 45/158 of 18 December 1990, by which it adopted and opened for signature, ratification and accession the International Convention on the Protection of the Rights of All Migrant Workers and Members of Their Families,

Bearing in mind that, in the Vienna Declaration and Programme of Action, States are invited to consider the possibility of signing and ratifying the Convention at the earliest possible time,

1. *Expresses its deep concern* at the growing manifestations of racism, xenophobia and other forms of discrimination and inhuman or degrading treatment directed against migrant workers in different parts of the world;

2. *Welcomes* the signature or ratification of or accession to the International Convention on the Protection of the Rights of All Migrant Workers and Members of Their Families by some Member States;

3. *Calls upon* all Member States, in particular in view of the tenth anniversary of the adoption of the Convention, to consider signing and ratifying or acceding to the Convention as a matter of priority, expresses the hope that it will enter into force at an early date, and notes that, pursuant to article 87 of the Convention, only six ratifications or accessions are still needed for it to enter into force;

4. *Requests* the Secretary-General to provide all the facilities and assistance necessary for the promotion of the Convention through the World Public Information Campaign on Human Rights and the programme of advisory services in the field of human rights;

5. *Welcomes* the global campaign for the entry into force of the Convention, and invites the organizations and agencies of the United Nations system and intergovernmental and non-governmental organizations to intensify further their efforts with a view to disseminating information on and promoting understanding of the importance of the Convention;

6. *Also welcomes* the work of the Special Rapporteur on the human rights of migrants in relation to the Convention, and encourages her to continue in this endeavour;

7. *Takes note* of the report of the Secretary-General, and requests him to submit an updated report on the status of the Convention to the General Assembly at its fifty-sixth session;

8. *Decides* to consider the report of the Secretary-General at its fifty-sixth session under the sub-item entitled "Implementation of human rights instruments".

Convention on genocide

As at 31 December 2000, 132 States were parties to the 1948 Convention on the Prevention and Punishment of the Crime of Genocide, adopted by the General Assembly in resolution 260 A (III) [YUN 1948-49, p. 959]. In 2000, Guinea and Switzerland acceded to the Convention.

The Secretary-General reported on the status of the Convention as at 1 July [A/55/207]. On 4 December, the Assembly took note of the report (**decision 55/420**).

Convention against apartheid

As at 31 December 2000, there continued to be 101 States parties to the 1973 International Convention on the Suppression and Punishment of the Crime of Apartheid, adopted by the General Assembly in resolution 3068(XXVIII) [YUN 1973, p. 103].

The Commission on Human Rights in 1995 had suspended both consideration of the item on the Convention's implementation [YUN 1995, p. 790] and meetings of the Group of Three [ibid., p. 693], the Convention's monitoring body.

Other activities

Follow-up to 1993 World Conference

Report of High Commissioner. The Commission on Human Rights considered the High Commissioner's report [E/CN.4/2000/12 & Add.1] on follow-up to the World Conference on Human Rights [YUN 1993, p. 908]. She stated that, since the Conference, the Commission's special procedures mechanisms had been complemented by the establishment of field presences in a number of countries to assist host Governments to promote human rights, monitor human rights violations and help strengthen the rule of law. Among the countries hosting field presences were Angola, Burundi, Cambodia, Colombia, Georgia/Abkhazia, Sierra Leone and countries of the former Socialist Federal Republic of Yugoslavia. The number of human rights projects implemented through field activities had grown from one in 1992 to 26 in 1999. The High Commissioner gave an overview of field presences.

Annual meeting. The High Commissioner transmitted the report of the meeting of special rapporteurs/representatives, experts and chairpersons of working groups of the special procedures and advisory services programme of the Commission (Geneva, 5-9 June) [E/CN.4/2001/6], as called for in the Vienna Declaration and Programme of Action [YUN 1993, p. 908], adopted at the 1993 World Conference. Participants discussed capacity-building to improve the effectiveness of the special procedures system, support services, including the new thematic database within OHCHR (Human Rights Computerized Analysis Network Environment (HURICANE)), corporate responsibility for human rights violations, monitoring (special procedures) mechanisms and improving the work of special procedures mandates on human rights defenders. Participants met with NGO representatives to exchange views on the Commission's mechanisms and strengthening the special procedures system. The chairpersons of treaty bodies and the special rapporteurs/representatives, experts and chairpersons of working groups discussed possibilities for increased interaction between the treaty bodies and the special procedures mechanisms. The meeting adopted a set of conclusions and recommendations.

By **decision 55/421** of 4 December, the General Assembly took note of the Third Committee's report [A/55/602/Add.4] on follow-up to the Vienna Declaration and Programme of Action.

Advisory services and technical cooperation

In 2000 [E/CN.4/2001/104], the OHCHR technical cooperation programme supported countries in promoting and protecting all human rights, at their request, by incorporating international human rights standards in national laws, policies and practices and by building sustainable national capacities to implement those standards and ensure respect for human rights. Among the key result areas defined by OHCHR for 1999-2001 were national capacity-building to develop human rights strategies and structures; human rights education; the implementation of economic, social and cultural rights and the right to development; racism; the rights of indigenous people; trafficking of women and children, gender and women's human rights; the rights of the child; humanitarian law and human rights; and developing a policy for future human rights field activities and consolidating existing activities. Assistance was provided through expertise, advisory services, training courses, workshops and seminars, fellowships, grants and the provision of information and documentation.

During the year, 20 projects were completed, 41 were under way or approved and 14 were at the drafting stage. National technical cooperation field presences were operational in Chad, Ecuador, El Salvador, Guatemala, Indonesia, Madagascar, Mongolia, Somalia, South Africa and Palestine. The subregional office in Pretoria, South Africa, continued to implement and facilitate the implementation of activities at the regional level, as well as in various countries of the Southern African region. The following OHCHR field presences combined monitoring and technical cooperation mandates: Bosnia and Herzegovina, Burundi, Cambodia, Colombia, Croatia, the Democratic Republic of the Congo and FRY.

The programme cooperated with the United Nations Development Programme (UNDP) through the joint programme for human rights strengthening (HURIST), supporting the implementation of UNDP's policy on human rights. HURIST, which contributed to the international debate concerning the major areas of relevance for human rights and supported UNDP country offices, was active in Benin, Bolivia, Botswana, Brazil, Cambodia, Cape Verde, Côte d'Ivoire, the Dominican Republic, Egypt, Jordan, Kazakhstan, Lithuania, Malawi, Mauritania, Mongolia, Mozambique, Nepal, Nigeria, Somalia and Yemen. Another joint initiative, the Assisting Communities Together project, emphasized the role that civil society played in promoting and protecting human rights. OHCHR also cooperated with other UN agencies and programmes, as well as non-UN partners.

Activities were funded mainly by the Voluntary Fund for Technical Cooperation in the Field of Human Rights and partly by the UN regular budget. The Fund's Board, at its thirteenth and fourteenth sessions (19-21 June, 11-13 December), considered 15 new project proposals; reviewed five completed and evaluated projects; and examined the implementation status of four current projects. As at 31 October, the Fund's income amounted to $14.6 million and commitments totalled $6.7 million.

Commission action. On 26 April [res. 2000/80], the Commission asked the Secretary-General to assist the Board; to continue to ensure efficient management of the Fund, strict and transparent project management rules and periodic evaluations of its programme and projects; to arrange for information meetings open to all Member States and organizations directly involved; and to report in 2002.

Cambodia

Commission action. On 26 April [res. 2000/79], the Commission, expressing grave concern about human rights violations, noted some progress made by the Government of Cambodia. It wel-comed the adoption of a five-year action plan, as well as other measures, to improve the status of women, and the five-year national plan against child sexual exploitation. Noting with concern the continued problems related to the rule of law and the functioning of the judiciary, the Commission welcomed the Government's recent commitment to judicial reform. It also welcomed efforts to establish an independent national human rights commission and requested OHCHR to provide advice and technical assistance in that regard. The Secretary-General was asked to report in 2001; that request was approved by the Economic and Social Council on 28 July (**decision 2000/278**).

Report of Secretary-General. In August [A/55/291], the Secretary-General stated that the Under-Secretary-General for Legal Affairs visited Cambodia (16-22 March, 4-7 July) to hold discussions with the Cambodian Task Force on the draft articles of cooperation between the United Nations and the Government in the prosecution under Cambodian law of crimes committed during the period of Democratic Kampuchea and the scope of the court's jurisdiction and its chambers, a formula to settle disagreements between the co-prosecutors, the mutual obligations of the parties, financial mechanisms and the court's premises. The draft law on establishing extraordinary chambers in the courts of Cambodia to prosecute the crimes was pending before the Judicial Committee of the National Assembly. The Secretary-General reviewed the recommendations of his Special Representative for human rights in Cambodia [YUN 1999, p. 584] and the role and achievements of OHCHR from September 1999 to July 2000 in assisting the Government to strengthen democracy and establish the rule of law and respect for human rights.

Following the conclusion of the Special Representative's mandate on 31 December 1999, OHCHR/Cambodia continued to follow up on the implementation of his recommendations, as well as the efforts of the Government to investigate specific cases of serious human rights violations (see p. 625).

Report of Special Representative. The new Special Representative, Peter Leuprecht (Austria), appointed by the Secretary-General on 18 August, reported on his visit to Cambodia (26 November–2 December) [E/CN.4/2001/103]. The visit focused on the eradication of violence, the rule of law, domestic implementation of international human rights treaties to which Cambodia was a party, poverty issues and economic and social rights, and the situation of women and children.

The Special Representative recommended action against impunity, corruption and the lack of independence of the judiciary. He called for the application and enforcement of international human rights treaties through the legislative and judicial process, and serious efforts to improve conditions of detention. Resources devoted to the military should be reallocated to such areas as education, health and social services, and the gap between rich and poor should be narrowed. The Special Representative also called for respect for labour rights, the eradication of violence against women and of the exploitation of women and children, the promotion of human rights education, the protection of human rights defenders and respect for, and promotion and protection of, the human rights of minorities.

OHCHR/Cambodia

The Secretary-General reported in August [A/55/291] that OHCHR/Cambodia recorded during 2000 an increase in allegations of violations of labour rights and housing rights, curtailing of freedom of the press, expression and association, intolerance towards ethnic minorities and migrant workers, police violence during public demonstrations, trafficking of persons and cases of sexual exploitation of children and women. Allegations of illegal arrest and detention, excessive pre-trial detention, torture during arrest, prison conditions not in accordance with international standards, intimidation of human rights defenders, lack of independence of the judiciary, interference of the executive in the judiciary and some cases of political violence and intimidation were also reported. The office continued documenting and analysing patterns of human rights violations.

The previous memorandum of understanding between the Government and OHCHR/Cambodia expired on 28 February; the Government verbally agreed to extend it until March 2002 to enable the office to continue its operations and to maintain its technical cooperation programmes. OHCHR/Cambodia technical cooperation activities included assistance to develop the legal system, creating and strengthening national human rights institutions, training for government officials, support to human rights NGOs, assistance in human rights reporting obligations and implementation of treaty monitoring bodies' recommendations.

In a report covering the role and achievements of the office from August to November 2000 [E/CN.4/2001/102], the Secretary-General described the implementation of the technical cooperation programme.

Between 1 January and 31 October, the office received 240 allegations of human rights violations, including forced evictions, arbitrary confiscation of land and related intimidation, as well as cases of non-compliance with labour rights. Allegations of denial of medical assistance to victims in custody, discrimination against ethnic minorities, sexual exploitation of women and children, human trafficking and violence against women were also reported. In addition, the office received allegations of illegal arrest and detention, excessive pre-trial detention, police violence and excessive use of force, summary and extrajudicial execution, disappearance, mob killings, torture, political intimidation and violence against members of political parties, curtailment of freedom of association and expression, and intimidation of human rights defenders. During the period under review, OHCHR/Cambodia conducted training for some 1,450 police officials, 1,580 members of the armed forces and 110 gendarmes. It held a 15-week law drafting seminar, as well as two seminars for policy makers on their role in the law-making process and capacity-building programmes for judges, prosecutors, other court officials and lawyers on the application of human rights standards in the delivery of justice. Other areas of assistance included labour rights, the environment, trafficking in human beings and support to human rights NGOs.

GENERAL ASSEMBLY ACTION

On 4 December [meeting 81], the General Assembly, on the recommendation of the Third Committee [A/55/602/Add.2 & Corr.1], adopted **resolution 55/95** without vote [agenda item 114 *(b)*].

Situation of human rights in Cambodia

The General Assembly,

Guided by the purposes and principles embodied in the Charter of the United Nations, the Universal Declaration of Human Rights and the International Covenants on Human Rights,

Recalling the Agreement on a Comprehensive Political Settlement of the Cambodia Conflict, signed in Paris on 23 October 1991, including part III thereof, relating to human rights,

Recalling also its resolution 54/171 of 17 December 1999, taking note of Commission on Human Rights resolution 2000/79 of 26 April 2000, and recalling further previous relevant resolutions,

Recognizing that the tragic history of Cambodia requires special measures to ensure the protection of the human rights of all people in Cambodia and the non-return to the policies and practices of the past, as stipulated in the Agreement signed in Paris on 23 October 1991,

Desiring that the international community continue to respond positively to assist efforts to investigate the tragic history of Cambodia, including responsibility for past international crimes, such as acts of genocide and crimes against humanity during the regime of Democratic Kampuchea from 1975 to 1979,

Bearing in mind the request made in June 1997 by the Cambodian authorities for assistance in responding to past serious violations of Cambodian and international law, the letter dated 15 March 1999 from the Secretary-General to the President of the General Assembly and the President of the Security Council and the report of the Group of Experts appointed by the Secretary-General annexed thereto, and the discussions held between the Government of Cambodia and the United Nations Secretariat on standards and procedures for bringing to justice the Khmer Rouge leaders most responsible for the most serious violations of human rights in the years 1975-1979,

Recognizing the legitimate concern of the Government and people of Cambodia in the pursuit of internationally accepted principles of justice and of national reconciliation,

Recognizing also that accountability of individual perpetrators of grave human rights violations is one of the central elements of any effective remedy for victims of human rights violations and a key factor in ensuring a fair and equitable justice system and, ultimately, reconciliation and stability within a State,

Welcoming the continuing role of the United Nations High Commissioner for Human Rights in the promotion and protection of human rights in Cambodia,

1. *Requests* the Secretary-General, through his Special Representative for human rights in Cambodia, in collaboration with the office in Cambodia of the United Nations High Commissioner for Human Rights, to assist the Government of Cambodia in ensuring the protection of the human rights of all people in Cambodia and to ensure adequate resources for the continued functioning of the operational presence in Cambodia of the Office of the United Nations High Commissioner for Human Rights and to enable the Special Representative to continue to fulfil his tasks expeditiously;

2. *Takes note with appreciation* of the report of the Secretary-General concerning the situation of human rights in Cambodia;

3. *Requests* the Government of Cambodia and the office in Cambodia of the High Commissioner to exchange the memorandum of understanding for the extension of the mandate of the office after March 2000, and encourages the Government of Cambodia to continue to cooperate with the office;

4. *Commends and expresses its deep appreciation* for the work of the former Special Representative of the Secretary-General for human rights in Cambodia, Thomas Hammarberg, in promoting and protecting human rights in Cambodia;

5. *Welcomes* the appointment by the Secretary-General of Peter Leuprecht as his new Special Representative for human rights in Cambodia, and requests the Special Representative, in collaboration with the Office of the High Commissioner, to continue the work of his predecessors by evaluating the extent to which the recommendations in his forthcoming reports, and those contained in the reports of his predecessors, are followed up and implemented, while maintaining contact with the Government and people of Cambodia;

6. *Notes with concern* the continued problems related to the rule of law and the functioning of the judiciary,

including interference by the executive with the independence of the judiciary, inter alia, through rearrests, and welcomes statements by the Government committing itself to judicial reform, the work currently being done to prepare the laws and codes that are essential components of the basic legal framework, meetings of the Supreme Council of Magistracy and the establishment of the Council of Judicial Reform;

7. *Urges* the Government of Cambodia to continue to take the necessary measures to develop an independent, impartial and effective judicial system, including through the early adoption of the draft statute on magistrates, a penal code and a code on criminal procedures, and the reform of the administration of justice, and appeals to the international community to assist the Government to this end;

8. *Welcomes* the draft governance action plan prepared by the Government of Cambodia, encourages the early adoption and implementation thereof, and appeals to the international community to assist the Government in its efforts to implement the plan;

9. *Commends* the initial efforts of the Government of Cambodia with regard to the review and the stated commitment to the downsizing of the police and the military, urges the Government to take further measures to carry out effective reform aimed towards professional and impartial police and military forces, and invites the international community to continue to assist the Government to this end;

10. *Recognizes* the importance of human rights education and training in Cambodia, commends the efforts of the Government of Cambodia, the Office of the High Commissioner and civil society in this field, encourages further strengthening and wider dissemination of these programmes, and invites the international community to continue to assist these efforts;

11. *Commends* the vital and valuable role played by non-governmental organizations in Cambodia, inter alia, in the development of civil society, and encourages the Government of Cambodia to continue to work closely and cooperatively with non-governmental organizations in efforts to strengthen and uphold human rights in Cambodia;

12. *Notes with interest* the activities undertaken by the governmental Cambodian Human Rights Committee, the National Assembly Commission on Human Rights and Reception of Complaints and the Senate Commission on Human Rights and Reception of Complaints, and welcomes preliminary efforts to establish an independent national human rights commission, which should be based on the principles relating to the status of national institutions for the promotion and protection of human rights, known as the Paris principles, and requests the Office of the High Commissioner to continue to provide advice and technical assistance in these efforts;

13. *Expresses grave concern* about continued violations of human rights, including torture, extrajudicial killings, excessive pre-trial detention, violation of labour rights, illegal confiscation of land and forced relocation, as well as the apparent lack of protection from mob killings, as detailed in the report of the Special Representative to the Commission on Human Rights at its fifty-sixth session, and notes some progress made by the Government of Cambodia in addressing these issues;

14. *Expresses serious concern* about the continued prevalence of impunity in Cambodia, commends the initial commitment and efforts of the Government of Cambodia to tackle this question, and calls upon the Government to take further measures, as a matter of critical priority, to investigate urgently and prosecute, in accordance with due process of law and international human rights standards, all those who have perpetrated violations of human rights;

15. *Welcomes* the investigations into some cases of politically motivated violence, while remaining concerned at the continued reports of politically motivated violence and intimidation, and urges the Government of Cambodia to undertake further investigations in line with its stated commitments and to take appropriate measures to prevent politically motivated violence and intimidation in the future;

16. *Also welcomes* the commitment and efforts made by the Government of Cambodia with respect to tackling the question of human rights violations, and notes with interest the investigations undertaken by the governmental Cambodian Human Rights Committee and by the national police in order to bring to justice those responsible for such violations and to ensure security of persons and rights of association, assembly and expression;

17. *Reaffirms* that the most serious human rights violations in Cambodia in recent history have been committed by the Khmer Rouge, welcomes the final collapse of the Khmer Rouge, which has paved the way for the restoration of peace, stability and national reconciliation in Cambodia and the investigation and prosecution of the leaders of the Khmer Rouge, and notes with interest the progress made by the Government of Cambodia in bringing to justice the Khmer Rouge leaders most responsible for the most serious violations of human rights;

18. *Welcomes* the successful conclusion of the talks between the Government of Cambodia and the United Nations Secretariat on the question of the trial of the Khmer Rouge leaders who are most responsible for the most serious violations of human rights, appeals strongly to the Government to ensure, including by facilitating the expedited completion of the necessary legislative process as soon as possible, that those Khmer Rouge leaders are brought to account in accordance with international standards of justice, fairness and due process of law, encourages the Government to continue to cooperate with the United Nations on this issue, and welcomes the efforts of the Secretariat and the international community in assisting the Government to this end; .

19. *Takes note with interest* of the signing by Cambodia of the Rome Statute of the International Criminal Court;

20. *Reaffirms* the importance of the upcoming communal elections being conducted in a free and fair manner, takes note with interest of the draft legislation for preparing for communal elections, and urges the Government of Cambodia to continue to prepare for them accordingly;

21. *Welcomes* the initial progress made under the five-year action plan by the Government of Cambodia, in particular by the Ministry of Women's and Veterans' Affairs, to improve the status of women, and urges the Government to continue to take appropriate measures to eliminate all forms of discrimination against women, to combat violence against women in all its forms, including grave violations of the rights of women perpetrated by elements of law enforcement and armed forces personnel, and to take all steps to meet its obligations as a party to the Convention on the Elimination of All Forms of Discrimination against Women, including by seeking technical assistance;

22. *Calls upon* the Government of Cambodia to continue to take further measures to ensure adequate health conditions, with emphasis on ensuring such conditions for women and children and minority groups and on the problem of the human immunodeficiency virus/acquired immunodeficiency syndrome, and encourages the international community to continue to support the Government to this end;

23. *Commends* the continued efforts of the Government of Cambodia, together with non-governmental organizations, local authorities and United Nations bodies, to improve the quality of and access to education, calls for further measures to be taken in order to ensure the right of Cambodian children to education, especially at the primary level, in accordance with the Convention on the Rights of the Child, and requests the international community to provide assistance for the achievement of this goal;

24. *Welcomes* the signing of the United Nations inter-agency memorandum of understanding with the Ministry of the Interior on Law Enforcement against Sexual Exploitation of Children, and encourages the Government of Cambodia to ensure the necessary law enforcement and other measures to tackle the problem of child prostitution and trafficking in Cambodia;

25. *Notes with serious concern* the problem of child labour in its worst forms, calls upon the Government of Cambodia to ensure adequate health and safety conditions for children and to outlaw, in particular, the worst forms of child labour, invites the International Labour Organization to continue to extend the necessary assistance in this regard, and encourages the Government of Cambodia to consider ratifying the 1999 International Labour Organization Convention concerning the Prohibition and Immediate Action for the Elimination of the Worst Forms of Child Labour (Convention No. 182);

26. *Also notes with serious concern* the prison conditions in Cambodia, notes with interest some improvements in the prison system, commends the continued international assistance to improve the material conditions of detention, and calls upon the Government of Cambodia to take the further measures necessary to improve prison conditions, especially with regard to providing the minimum standard of food and health care and meeting the special needs of women and children, including by strengthening the coordinating role of the Prison Health Department with the Ministry of Health, provincial authorities and non-governmental organizations working in this field;

27. *Urges* an end to racial violence against and vilification of ethnic minorities, including the ethnic Vietnamese, and also urges the Government of Cambodia to take all steps to prevent such violence, as well as to meet its obligations as a party to the International Convention on the Elimination of All Forms of Racial Discrimination, inter alia, by seeking technical assistance;

28. *Welcomes* the actions taken by the Government of Cambodia to combat illicit logging, which has seriously threatened the full enjoyment of economic, social and cultural rights by many Cambodians, including indigenous people, expects these efforts by the Government to continue, and welcomes the progress made on the drafting of the new law on land;

29. *Also welcomes* the consideration by the Committee on the Rights of the Child of the initial report of Cambodia submitted under the Convention on the Rights of the Child, asks the Government of Cambodia to follow up the recommendations made by the international human rights treaty bodies regarding the reports submitted by it, calls upon the Government to meet its reporting obligations under all other international human rights instruments, and requests the office in Cambodia of the High Commissioner to continue to provide assistance in this regard;

30. *Expresses grave concern* at the devastating consequences and destabilizing effects of the use of anti-personnel landmines on Cambodian society, encourages the Government of Cambodia to continue its support and efforts for the removal of those mines and for victim assistance and mine-awareness programmes, and commends donor countries and other actors of the international community for their contributions and assistance to mine action;

31. *Expresses concern* about the large number of small arms in society and commends the efforts of the Government of Cambodia to control the spread of weapons;

32. *Notes with appreciation* the use by the Secretary-General of the United Nations Trust Fund for a Human Rights Education Programme in Cambodia to finance the programme of activities of the office in Cambodia of the High Commissioner, as defined in resolutions of the General Assembly and the Commission on Human Rights, and invites Governments, intergovernmental and non-governmental organizations, foundations and individuals to consider contributing to the Trust Fund;

33. *Requests* the Secretary-General to report to the General Assembly at its fifty-sixth session on the role and achievements of the Office of the High Commissioner in assisting the Government and people of Cambodia in the promotion and protection of human rights and on the recommendations made by the Special Representative on matters within his mandate;

34. *Decides* to continue its consideration of the situation of human rights in Cambodia at its fifty-sixth session under the item entitled "Human rights questions".

Chad

A March progress report by the High Commissioner [E/CN.4/2000/107] stated that the technical cooperation project on human rights and governance between Chad and UNDP [YUN 1999, p. 587] started in February 2000. The project aimed to strengthen the operational capacities of Chad's National Commission on Human Rights and support for the recently established Conseil constitutionnel and Supreme Court. The project was expected to be completed by July 2001.

Croatia

By a roll-call vote of 44 to 1, with 8 abstentions, the Commission, on 18 April [res. 2000/26], welcomed the agreement between Croatia and the High Commissioner on technical cooperation and assistance programmes [YUN 1999, p. 587].

Haiti

Commission action. On 26 April [res. 2000/78], the Commission deplored an increase of violent acts in Haiti and urged the Haitian authorities and political leaders to cooperate in ending them. The Government was called on to investigate politically motivated crimes and prosecute perpetrators, take action to eliminate human rights violations, ensure due process and continue structural reforms in the police and judicial system and improvement of the prison sector. Regretting the delay of the parliamentary elections foreseen for 19 March, the Commission urgently called on the Government to hold free, fair and prompt elections.

The Commission invited the Secretary-General and Haiti to contribute to the strengthening of the Office for the Protection of Citizens, including through regional representation, incorporating a gender perspective, and through the establishment of a technical cooperation programme, in collaboration with OHCHR and the International Civilian Support Mission in Haiti (MICAH) (see p. 251), and encouraged the international community to assist in that effort.

The independent expert was requested to report to the General Assembly in 2000 and to the Commission in 2001. The High Commissioner was asked to assist him. Those requests were approved by the Economic and Social Council on 28 July (**decision 2000/277**).

Reports of independent expert. In 2000, the independent expert, Adama Dieng (Senegal), visited Haiti from 27 July to 8 August [A/55/335] and from 13 to 20 December [E/CN.4/2001/106]. He also visited Port-au-Prince from 25 to 29 September [ibid.], at the invitation of MICAH and the Haitian Ministry of Justice, to contribute to the first conference on reform of the justice system.

The expert's first mission took place at a time of tension between Haiti and the international community as a result of the manner in which the elections of 21 May were conducted (see p. 251). Whatever the outcome of the electoral crisis, people had gained awareness of the importance of having a voter registration card. It was essential for the political leaders to make a commitment to strengthen the culture of democracy. Within the schools, civic education was reintegrated as education for citizenship. The curriculum was launched in April with a teacher training session.

Following his second visit, the expert remained convinced that the political polarization in the country was responsible for daily violence, which was worsened by the abject poverty of the most disadvantaged classes. Haiti's greatest ill was the lack of rigorous law enforcement. There was an urgent need to defuse the tension and find a solution that ensured the rule of law and was consistent with the aspirations of the Haitian people. Recommendations to the Government addressed the police forces, the judicial system, the management of the National Prison Authority, ratification of human rights instruments, support to the Judges School and the Office of the Ombudsman, respect for freedom of opinion, expression, association, assembly and peaceful demonstration and the successful completion of the Raboteau massacre trial, at which former members of the Haitian armed forces and the Front pour l'avancement et le progrès Haitien were found guilty. Recommendations to the international community included the provision of technical cooperation and assistance programmes, and cooperation with the Haitian authorities to arrest and extradite those convicted in absentia at the Raboteau trial. The expert recommended that the United Nations emphasize capacity-building to strengthen democratic values by holding a symposium on the culture of democracy. OHCHR should ensure support for the Office of the Ombudsman and human rights NGOs, and should undertake a programme of technical cooperation and assistance. The United Nations should donate some of MICAH's vehicles, computers and printers to the Public Prosecutor's Office and the offices of examining magistrates, and OHCHR and UNDP should set up a project for technical cooperation on human rights with other UN agencies associated in its implementation.

GENERAL ASSEMBLY ACTION

On 4 December [meeting 81], the General Assembly, on the recommendation of the Third Committee [A/55/602/Add.3], adopted **resolution 55/118** without vote [agenda item 114 (c)].

Situation of human rights in Haiti

The General Assembly,

Guided by the principles embodied in the Charter of the United Nations, the Universal Declaration of Human Rights and the International Covenants on Human Rights and other international human rights instruments, including the Convention on the Elimination of All Forms of Discrimination against Women,

Recalling its resolution 54/187 of 17 December 1999, and taking note of Commission on Human Rights reso-

lution 2000/78 of 26 April 2000 and Economic and Social Council decision 2000/277 of 28 July 2000,

Taking note of the report of the independent expert of the Commission on Human Rights on the situation of human rights in Haiti, Adama Dieng,

Bearing in mind the report of the Secretary-General on the International Civilian Support Mission in Haiti, and considering the statement by the President of the Security Council of 15 March 2000,

Taking note of the report on the visit to Haiti of the Special Rapporteur of the Commission on Human Rights on violence against women, its causes and consequences, and encouraging the Government of Haiti to follow up actively the recommendations contained therein,

Recognizing the interdependent relations and mutual reinforcement between democracy, development and respect for human rights and fundamental freedoms and the commitment of the international community to supporting, strengthening and promoting this principle,

Noting the establishment of the International Civilian Support Mission in Haiti with the mandate to support the democratization process and assist the Haitian authorities with the development of democratic institutions; to assist the Haitian authorities in the reform and the strengthening of the Haitian system of justice, including its penal institutions, and to promote the Office of the Ombudsman; to support the efforts of the Government of Haiti to professionalize the Haitian National Police through a special training and technical assistance programme and to help the Government to coordinate bilateral and multilateral aid in this area; to support the efforts of the Government of Haiti aimed at the full observance of human rights and fundamental freedoms; and to provide technical assistance for the organization of democratic elections and to collaborate with the Government of Haiti in the coordination of bilateral and multilateral assistance,

Commending the work of the Organization of American States in Haiti, in particular the efforts to promote a dialogue among Haitian political actors and civil society groups following the legislative elections held on 21 May 2000,

Expressing concern at the fact that no solution has yet been found with regard to the deficiencies of the elections of 21 May 2000, most notably those identified by national and international observers and by the electoral observation mission of the Organization of American States,

Underlining the importance of the legitimate election of parliament for the institution of democracy, for the rule of law and for the progress of civil, political, social, economic and cultural rights in favour of all Haitians,

Noting with satisfaction the efforts made by the Haitian authorities in the fight against impunity, which resulted in the convictions of the police officers responsible for the Carrefour-Feuilles massacre and the opening of the trial relating to the Raboteau massacre,

Deploring the increasing difficulties met by the press in expressing itself freely since the serious incidents of April 2000,

Recalling the statements made by the Haitian authorities to the effect that the Government remains committed to upholding human rights, and encouraging further actions to improve the promotion, defence and guarantee of those rights,

Underlining the need for the Provisional Electoral Council to be fully representative of the Haitian political scene, including the opposition, impartial, neutral and effective in the preparations for, and during, the forthcoming presidential and senatorial elections,

1. *Expresses its gratitude* to the Secretary-General, his Representative for Haiti and the independent expert of the Commission on Human Rights on the situation of human rights in Haiti for their continuing efforts in favour of the consolidation of democratic institutions in Haiti and respect for human rights in that country;

2. *Commends* the United Nations Civilian Police Mission in Haiti for its training and supervising of the Haitian National Police, and the International Civilian Mission in Haiti for monitoring the situation of human rights and for its activities in support of democratic institutions, the mandates of which Missions concluded on 15 March 2000, opening the way for the International Civilian Support Mission in Haiti, with its mandate to consolidate and build on the results obtained in this regard;

3. *Stresses* the need for the Haitian National Police to continue to undertake more effective efforts to improve its performance through, inter alia, technical assistance, training and education, in order to function efficiently, within a framework of respect for human rights, to curb the alarming increase in insecurity in the country;

4. *Renews its invitation* to the Government of Haiti to ratify, as soon as possible, the International Covenant on Economic, Social and Cultural Rights, the Convention against Torture and Other Cruel, Inhuman or Degrading Treatment or Punishment and the Optional Protocols to the International Covenant on Civil and Political Rights;

5. *Requests* all interested Governments to make available to the Government of Haiti information and documentation to enable it to prosecute the perpetrators of human rights violations, in order to reinforce the efforts already made by the Haitian authorities to fight against impunity and to facilitate the reconciliation process;

6. *Calls upon* the Government of Haiti to continue structural reforms in the police and the judicial system and the improvement of the prison sector, to investigate properly politically motivated crimes and to prosecute the perpetrators of such crimes in accordance with Haitian law, to take vigorous action to eliminate any continuing human rights violations, including illegal arrests and detentions and the detention by authorities of individuals in violation of court orders for their release, and to ensure due process, including reasonable time frames;

7. *Reaffirms* the importance, for combating impunity and for the realization of a genuine and effective process of transition and national reconciliation, of investigations undertaken by the National Commission for Truth and Justice, and encourages the Government of Haiti to continue legal proceedings against perpetrators of human rights violations identified by the National Commission and to create effective facilities for providing support to the victims, in particular women, children and members of their families;

8. *Welcomes* the decision of the Permanent Council of the Organization of American States to the effect that that Organization, acting in conjunction with the Caribbean Community and other political actors and civil society groups, should give support to the Government of Haiti and all other actors involved in order to identify, as soon as possible, any options and make recommendations for resolving the difficulties resulting from the conflicting interpretations of the electoral law, and expresses the hope that that will result in concrete corrective actions by the Government of Haiti and other authorities and continue to strengthen the democratic process in that country;

9. *Notes with interest* the forthcoming presidential elections and elections for the renewal of one third of the Senate, and urges the Government of Haiti and other authorities to ensure the necessary guarantees for holding those elections in a transparent, secure and credible environment in agreement with Haiti's political actors and civil society groups, inter alia, by restoring the credibility of the Provisional Electoral Council, and through a true dialogue, with the support of the international community, including the Organization of American States;

10. *Recalls with appreciation* the initiative of the Government of Haiti, in collaboration with the international community and women's groups, to adopt measures to promote the human rights of women and to fight against the violence of which they are victims, through the training of judicial staff and the dissemination of information on the rights of women at all levels of the education system, and encourages Haiti to continue these efforts;

11. *Encourages* the Government of Haiti further to promote the rights of children, in particular their right to education;

12. *Invites* the international community, including the Bretton Woods institutions, to consider, when conditions permit, continuing its involvement in the reconstruction and development of Haiti;

13. *Encourages* the Government of Haiti to contribute to the strengthening of the Office for the Protection of Citizens, inter alia, through regional representation as appropriate, incorporating a gender perspective, and through the establishment of a programme of technical cooperation, in close collaboration with, and with the assistance of, the Office of the United Nations High Commissioner for Human Rights and the International Civilian Support Mission in Haiti;

14. *Decides* to continue its consideration of the situation of human rights and fundamental freedoms in Haiti at its fifty-sixth session.

(See also p. 249.)

Somalia

Commission action. On 26 April [res. 2000/81], the Commission, condemning widespread violations and abuses of human rights and humanitarian law, urged all parties in Somalia to respect human rights and international humanitarian law pertaining to internal armed conflicts, to support the re-establishment of the rule of law and to protect UN personnel, humanitarian relief workers and representatives of NGOs and of the media. All parties to the conflict were called on to respond positively to peace initiatives. The international community was asked to provide continuing and increased assistance in response to UN appeals for relief, rehabilitation and reconstruction efforts (see p. 859) and to support OHCHR activities concerning Somalia.

The High Commissioner was asked to provide for the translation of the Commission's resolution into the local language for dissemination within Somalia through the human rights officer for Somalia based in Nairobi, Kenya. The Commission extended the independent expert's mandate for an additional year and asked her to report in 2001 and the Secretary-General to assist her. On 28 July, the Economic and Social Council endorsed the extension of the expert's mandate and approved the Commission's requests to the High Commissioner and to the Secretary-General (**decision 2000/279**).

Secretariat note. A note by the Secretariat [E/CN.4/2001/105] stated that the independent expert on the situation of human rights in Somalia resigned on 10 September.

The note described the political situation in the country (see p. 215), as well as human rights developments. The peace initiative in the country sparked vigorous political activism that led to a sharp polarization of those for it and those against it. Most of the human rights violations that occurred stemmed from that polarization. In north-west Somalia, attacks against humanitarian aid workers and UN staff continued to be a source of concern. The north-eastern part of the country witnessed violations of the right to demonstrate peacefully, fighting between sub-clans and a rise in attacks against aid workers and agencies. Militia attacks occurred in southern Somalia, and attacks against aid workers and agencies were exceptionally numerous. Central Somalia, especially the town of Merka, remained off limits to the UN community for much of the year, making it impossible to monitor human rights developments; attacks against aid workers and installations continued unabated. Lawlessness continued in the city of Mogadishu, where aid workers, their premises and other properties were routinely attacked.

The most recent OHCHR project for Somalia addressed the mainstreaming of human rights in the programmes and projects of the United Nations Country Team members by the Senior Human Rights Adviser working directly under the auspices of the Resident/Humanitarian Coordinator, and the provision of technical advice to UNDP in its law and governance programmes and projects in general and the Somali Civil Protection Programme in particular. The High Commissioner and the Resident/Humanitarian Coordinator signed the project document in December.

Human rights education

Commission action. On 26 April [res. 2000/71], the Commission urged Governments, intergovernmental organizations and NGOs to contribute to the mid-term global evaluation of progress made towards the achievement of the objectives of the United Nations Decade for Human Rights Education (1995-2004), proclaimed by the General Assembly in resolution 49/184 [YUN 1994, p. 1039]. It urged Governments to contribute further to the implementation of the Plan of Action for the Decade and encouraged OHCHR to further develop its web site, particularly regarding the dissemination of human rights education materials and tools.

The Commission asked the High Commissioner to continue to implement and expand the Assisting Communities Together project and to consider other ways to support human rights education activities. It requested the human rights treaty bodies to adopt a general comment on human rights education and to emphasize the obligations of States parties in human rights education and information. The Secretary-General was asked to submit the recommendations of the mid-term global evaluation report (see below).

Report of High Commissioner. By a September note [A/55/360], the Secretary-General transmitted the report of the High Commissioner on the mid-term global evaluation of the progress made towards the achievement of the Decade's objectives.

In Africa, some Governments had created new structures or assigned the task of initiating or supporting national programmes on human rights education to existing governmental agencies. Four national committees for the Decade were established while, in other countries, ministries of justice or of human rights dealt with activities related to the Decade. Governmental respondents reported that the pre-school to secondary-level curricula incorporated the teaching of human rights, but few universities had human rights courses. While police, the armed forces, prison officials, members of the judiciary and foreign service personnel had some human rights training, pre-service programmes for those groups and for health officials, immigration officials and journalists were rare.

In the Americas, very few Governments had established national committees for human rights education. Many countries were reforming the school curricula and had introduced human rights into the formal education system. Few efforts were aimed at institutionalizing human rights pre-service and in-service training for professionals.

Four countries in Asia and the Pacific had established national committees for human rights education, while others had designated ministries of justice, ministries of education and national human rights institutions as lead agencies for the Decade. Regarding formal education, discussions on human rights were integrated into social studies, geography, history, language or subjects on life experience. A number of countries were working on the inclusion of human rights education in schools. Universities in several countries included human rights in their syllabuses.

Fewer than one third of the 43 respondent Governments in Europe had national committees for human rights education. Only one Government reported integrated human rights at the pre-school, primary and secondary levels, while most Governments indicated such integration at some levels, mostly primary and secondary. Moreover, the responses indicated that human rights education was rarely imparted during every year of primary and secondary schooling, but was targeted at specific age groups.

The report analysed the responses by intergovernmental organizations, including the contribution of the United Nations, and by NGOs.

The High Commissioner made recommendations on the content of human rights education, programmes on human rights education, evaluation, research and monitoring, and mass media and freedom of information. Other recommendations addressed the obligations of States, a UN system-wide response to the Decade, regional cooperation and national and local actors.

GENERAL ASSEMBLY ACTION

On 4 December [meeting 81], the General Assembly, on the recommendation of the Third Committee [A/55/602/Add.2 & Corr.1], adopted **resolution 55/94** without vote [agenda item 114 (*b*)].

United Nations Decade for Human Rights Education, 1995-2004, and public information activities in the field of human rights

The General Assembly,

Guided by the fundamental and universal principles enshrined in the Charter of the United Nations and the Universal Declaration of Human Rights,

Reaffirming article 26 of the Declaration, which states that "education shall be directed to the full devel-opment of the human personality and to the strengthening of respect for human rights and fundamental freedoms",

Recalling the provisions of other international human rights instruments, including article 13 of the International Covenant on Economic, Social and Cultural Rights, article 10 of the Convention on the Elimination of All Forms of Discrimination against Women, article 7 of the International Convention on the Elimination of All Forms of Racial Discrimination, article 29 of the Convention on the Rights of the Child, article 10 of the Convention against Torture and Other Cruel, Inhuman or Degrading Treatment or Punishment and paragraphs 78 to 82 of the Vienna Declaration and Programme of Action adopted by the World Conference on Human Rights on 25 June 1993, which reflect the aims of article 26 of the Universal Declaration of Human Rights,

Recalling the relevant resolutions adopted by the General Assembly and the Commission on Human Rights concerning the United Nations Decade for Human Rights Education, 1995-2004, public information activities in the field of human rights, including the World Public Information Campaign on Human Rights and the implementation of and follow-up to the Vienna Declaration and Programme of Action, the project of the United Nations Educational, Scientific and Cultural Organization entitled "Towards a culture of peace", and the Dakar Framework for Action adopted at the World Education Forum, which, inter alia, reconfirmed the mandated role of the United Nations Educational, Scientific and Cultural Organization of coordinating Education For All partners and maintaining their collective momentum within the process of securing quality basic education,

Believing that the World Public Information Campaign is a valuable complement to the activities of the United Nations aimed at the further promotion and protection of human rights, and recalling the importance attached by the World Conference on Human Rights to human rights education and information,

Believing also that human rights education constitutes an important vehicle for the elimination of gender-based discrimination and for ensuring equal opportunities through the promotion and protection of the human rights of women,

Convinced that every woman, man and child, in order to realize their full human potential, must be made aware of all their human rights and fundamental freedoms,

Convinced also that human rights education should involve more than the provision of information and should constitute a comprehensive, lifelong process by which people at all levels of development and in all societies learn respect for the dignity of others and the means and methods of ensuring that respect in all societies,

Recognizing that human rights education and information are essential to the realization of human rights and fundamental freedoms and that carefully designed training, dissemination and information programmes can have a catalytic effect on national, regional and international initiatives to promote and protect human rights and prevent human rights violations,

Convinced that human rights education and information contribute to a holistic concept of development consistent with the dignity of women and men of all ages, which takes into account particularly vulnerable segments of society such as children, young persons, older persons, indigenous people, minorities, the rural and urban poor, migrant workers, refugees, persons with the human immunodeficiency virus/acquired immunodeficiency syndrome and disabled persons,

Taking into account the efforts to promote human rights education made by educators and non-governmental organizations in all parts of the world, as well as by intergovernmental organizations, including the Office of the United Nations High Commissioner for Human Rights, the United Nations Educational, Scientific and Cultural Organization, the International Labour Organization, the United Nations Children's Fund and the United Nations Development Programme,

Recognizing the invaluable and creative role that non-governmental and community-based organizations can play in disseminating public information and engaging in human rights education, especially at the grass-roots level and in remote and rural communities,

Aware of the potential supportive role of the private sector in implementing at all levels of society the Plan of Action for the United Nations Decade for Human Rights Education, 1995-2004, and the World Public Information Campaign, through creative initiatives and financial support for governmental and non-governmental activities,

Convinced that the effectiveness of existing human rights education and public information activities would be enhanced by better coordination and cooperation at the national, regional and international levels,

Recalling that it is within the responsibility of the United Nations High Commissioner for Human Rights to coordinate relevant United Nations education and public information programmes in the field of human rights,

Noting with appreciation the increased efforts undertaken so far by the Office of the High Commissioner to disseminate human rights information through its web site and its publications and external relations programmes,

Welcoming the initiative of the Office of the High Commissioner to develop further the project entitled "Assisting Communities Together", launched in 1998, supported by voluntary funds and designed to provide small grants to grass-roots and local organizations carrying out practical human rights activities,

Recalling that, according to the Plan of Action, in 2000 a mid-term global evaluation of progress made towards the achievement of the objectives of the Decade shall be undertaken by the Office of the High Commissioner, in cooperation with all other principal actors in the Decade,

Acknowledging with appreciation the mid-term global evaluation undertaken from April to August 2000 by the Office of the High Commissioner, which included the launching of a worldwide survey, the organization of an online forum, the convening of an expert meeting and the preparation of the High Commissioner's mid-term evaluation report,

1. *Takes note with appreciation* of the report of the United Nations High Commissioner for Human Rights on the mid-term global evaluation of the progress made towards the achievement of the objectives of the United Nations Decade for Human Rights Education, 1995-2004, which contains an analysis of available information on the progress made in the first five years of the Decade at the national, regional and international levels and recommendations for action during the remaining years of the Decade;

2. *Welcomes* the steps taken by Governments and intergovernmental and non-governmental organizations to implement the Plan of Action for the United Nations Decade for Human Rights Education, 1995-2004, and to develop public information activities in the field of human rights, as indicated in the report of the High Commissioner on the mid-term global evaluation;

3. *Urges* all Governments to contribute further to the implementation of the Plan of Action, in particular by encouraging the establishment, in accordance with national conditions, of broadly representative national committees for human rights education responsible for the development of comprehensive, effective and sustainable national plans of action for human rights education and information, taking into consideration the guidelines for national plans of action for human rights education developed by the Office of the United Nations High Commissioner for Human Rights within the framework of the Decade;

4. *Urges* Governments to encourage, support and involve national and local non-governmental and community-based organizations in the implementation of their national plans of action;

5. *Encourages* Governments to consider, within the national plans of action mentioned in paragraphs 3 and 4 above, the establishment of public access human rights resource and training centres capable of engaging in research, the gender-sensitive training of trainers, the preparation, collection, translation and dissemination of human rights education and training materials, the organization of courses, conferences, workshops and public information campaigns and assistance in the implementation of internationally sponsored technical cooperation projects for human rights education and public information;

6. *Encourages* States, where such national public access human rights resource and training centres exist, to strengthen their capacity to support human rights education and public information programmes at the international, regional, national and local levels;

7. *Calls upon* Governments, in accordance with national conditions, to accord priority to the dissemination, in the relevant national and local languages, of the Universal Declaration of Human Rights, the International Covenants on Human Rights and other human rights instruments, human rights materials and training manuals, as well as reports of States parties submitted under international human rights treaties, and to provide information and education in those languages on the practical ways in which national and international institutions and procedures may be utilized to ensure the effective implementation of those instruments;

8. *Encourages* Governments to support further, through voluntary contributions, the education and public information efforts undertaken by the Office of

the High Commissioner within the framework of the Plan of Action;

9. *Requests* the High Commissioner to continue to coordinate and harmonize human rights education and information strategies within the United Nations system, including the implementation of the Plan of Action, in cooperation, inter alia, with the United Nations Educational, Scientific and Cultural Organization, and to ensure maximum effectiveness and efficiency in the use, processing, management and distribution of human rights information and educational materials, including through electronic means;

10. *Encourages* Governments to contribute to the further development of the web site of the Office of the High Commissioner, in particular with respect to the dissemination of human rights education materials and tools, and to continue and expand the publications and external relations programmes of the Office;

11. *Encourages* the Office of the High Commissioner to continue to support national capacities for human rights education and information through its technical cooperation programme in the field of human rights, including the organization of training courses and the development of targeted training materials for professional audiences, as well as the dissemination of human rights information materials as a component of technical cooperation projects, and to continue to monitor developments in human rights education;

12. *Urges* the Department of Public Information of the Secretariat to continue to utilize United Nations information centres for the timely dissemination, within their designated areas of activity, of basic information, reference and audio-visual materials on human rights and fundamental freedoms, including the reports of States parties submitted under international human rights instruments and, to this end, to ensure that the information centres are supplied with adequate quantities of those materials;

13. *Stresses* the need for close collaboration between the Office of the High Commissioner and the Department of Public Information in the implementation of the Plan of Action and the World Public Information Campaign, and the need to harmonize their activities with those of other international organizations, such as the United Nations Educational, Scientific and Cultural Organization with regard to its project entitled "Towards a culture of peace" and the International Committee of the Red Cross and relevant non-governmental organizations with regard to the dissemination of information on international humanitarian law;

14. *Invites* the specialized agencies and relevant United Nations programmes and funds to continue to contribute, within their respective spheres of competence, to the implementation of the Plan of Action and the World Public Information Campaign and to cooperate and coordinate with each other and with the Office of the High Commissioner in that regard;

15. *Encourages* the relevant organs, bodies and agencies of the United Nations system, all human rights bodies of the United Nations system, including the Office of the United Nations High Commissioner for Human Rights and the Office of the United Nations High Commissioner for Refugees, to provide training in human rights for all United Nations personnel and officials;

16. *Encourages* the human rights treaty bodies, when examining reports of States parties, to place emphasis on the obligations of States parties in the area of human rights education and information and to reflect this emphasis in their concluding observations;

17. *Calls upon* international, regional and national non-governmental organizations and intergovernmental organizations, in particular those concerned with women, labour, development, food, housing, education, health care and the environment, as well as all other social justice groups, human rights advocates, educators, religious organizations and the media, to undertake specific activities of formal, non-formal and informal education, including cultural events, alone and in cooperation with the Office of the United Nations High Commissioner for Human Rights, in implementing the Plan of Action;

18. *Encourages* Governments, regional organizations and intergovernmental and non-governmental organizations to explore the potential support and contribution to human rights education of all relevant partners, including the private sector, development, trade and financial institutions and the media, and to seek their cooperation in the development of human rights education strategies;

19. *Encourages* regional organizations to develop strategies for the wider distribution of materials on human rights education through regional networks and to develop region-specific programmes to maximize the participation of national entities, whether governmental or non-governmental, in programmes on human rights education;

20. *Encourages* intergovernmental organizations to assist, upon request, collaboration between governmental institutions and non-governmental organizations at the national level;

21. *Requests* the Office of the High Commissioner to continue implementation of and to expand the "Assisting Communities Together" project and to consider other appropriate ways and means to support human rights education activities, including those undertaken by non-governmental organizations;

22. *Requests* the High Commissioner to bring the recommendations contained in the mid-term global evaluation report and the present resolution to the attention of all members of the international community and of intergovernmental and non-governmental organizations concerned with human rights education and public information, and to report to the General Assembly at its fifty-sixth session on the progress made towards the achievement of the objectives of the Decade under the item entitled "Human rights questions".

Culture of peace

Commission action. On 26 April [res. 2000/66], the Commission, welcoming the adoption, in General Assembly resolutions 53/243 A and B [YUN 1999, p. 593], of the Declaration and Programme of Action on a Culture of Peace and the Assembly's proclamation of the year 2000 as the International Year for the Culture of Peace in resolution 52/15 [YUN 1997, p. 622], invited States to promote a culture of peace. The Subcommission was requested to take into account and reflect in its deliberations the provisions of the Declaration and Programme of Action, as well as the contribution of the promotion, protection and realization of all human rights for the further development of a culture of peace. The Commission asked OHCHR to organize, provide the resources required for and coordinate, during the International Year, a panel/forum on a culture of peace, focusing on the contribution of the promotion, protection and realization of all human rights to the further development of a culture of peace (see below); on 28 July, the Economic and Social Council approved that request (**decision 2000/275**).

Report of OHCHR. In March [E/CN.4/2000/97/Add.1], OHCHR summarized the views of two States on the contribution of the promotion and protection of human rights to the further development of a culture of peace. Earlier views were presented in 1999 [YUN 1999, p. 593].

Expert Seminar. A note by the High Commissioner [E/CN.4/2001/120] transmitted the report of the Expert Seminar on Human Rights and Peace (Geneva, 8-9 December), as called for by the Commission in resolution 2000/66 (see above). The seminar was convened by OHCHR, in cooperation with the UN University for Peace (Costa Rica) and with the support of the Political Affairs Directorate of the Swiss Federal Department of Foreign Affairs, the Research Department of the Swedish International Development Cooperation Agency and the Bank of Sweden Tercentenary Foundation. The report of the Seminar took account of the presentations and discussions made at an intergovernmental forum on the contribution to a culture of peace of human rights education, convened by the High Commissioner on 11 December. Following their discussion of various aspects of human rights and peace, the 30 participants made proposals aimed at contributing to the prevention of conflicts, consolidation of peace processes and overcoming new forms of violence.

Communication. Bangladesh transmitted the Madrid Declaration, adopted at the International Conference on a Culture of Peace (Madrid, Spain, 11-13 December) [A/56/56]. The Declaration promoted action in the areas identified in the Programme of Action, including education, sustainable economic and social development, human rights and democracy, a gender perspective, democratic governance and the free flow of information and knowledge, among others.

Children and a culture of peace

A September report of the Secretary-General [A/55/377] on the International Decade for a Culture of Peace and Non-Violence for the Children of the World, 2001-2010, proclaimed by the General Assembly in resolution 53/25 [YUN 1998, p. 639], discussed how children might be the centre of actions for a culture of peace. It presented an organizational strategy to further develop the global movement for a culture of peace and a survey of the contributions made by the United Nations Educational, Scientific and Cultural Organization, the United Nations Children's Fund and other UN system entities.

GENERAL ASSEMBLY ACTION

On 29 November [meeting 74], the General Assembly adopted **resolution 55/47** [draft: A/55/L.43/Rev.1 & Add.1] without vote [agenda item 33].

International Decade for a Culture of Peace and Non-Violence for the Children of the World, 2001-2010

The General Assembly,

Bearing in mind the Charter of the United Nations, including the purposes and principles contained therein, and especially its dedication to saving succeeding generations from the scourge of war,

Recalling the Constitution of the United Nations Educational, Scientific and Cultural Organization, which states that, since wars begin in the minds of men, it is in the minds of men that the defences of peace must be constructed,

Recalling also its previous resolutions on a culture of peace, in particular resolution 52/15 of 20 November 1997 proclaiming 2000 as the International Year for the Culture of Peace, and resolution 53/25 of 10 November 1998 proclaiming the period 2001-2010 as the International Decade for a Culture of Peace and Non-Violence for the Children of the World,

Reaffirming the Declaration and Programme of Action on a Culture of Peace, recognizing that they serve, inter alia, as the basis for the observance of the Decade, and convinced that effective and successful observance of the Decade throughout the world will promote a culture of peace and non-violence that benefits humanity, in particular future generations,

Taking note of the report of the Secretary-General on the International Decade for a Culture of Peace and Non-Violence for the Children of the World,

Taking note also of Commission on Human Rights resolution 2000/66 of 26 April 2000, entitled "Towards a culture of peace",

Emphasizing the particular relevance of the special session of the General Assembly for follow-up to the World Summit for Children, to be held in New York in 2001, the World Conference against Racism, Racial Discrimination, Xenophobia and Related Intolerance, to be held in Durban, South Africa, in 2001, and the United Nations Decade for Human Rights Education, 1995-2004, for the International Decade for a Culture of Peace and Non-Violence for the Children of the World, 2001-2010,

Taking into account the Manifesto 2000 initiative of the United Nations Educational, Scientific and Cultural Organization promoting a culture of peace, which has so far received over sixty million signatures of endorsement throughout the world,

1. *Recognizes* that the objective of the International Decade for a Culture of Peace and Non-Violence for the Children of the World is to further strengthen the global movement for a culture of peace following the observance of the International Year for the Culture of Peace in 2000;

2. *Notes with satisfaction* the engagement of Member States, the United Nations system and civil society during the International Year for the Culture of Peace at the national, regional and global levels, and in this context recognizes the role of the United Nations Educational, Scientific and Cultural Organization as the focal point during the year;

3. *Invites* Member States to place greater emphasis on and expand their activities promoting a culture of peace and non-violence, in particular during the Decade, at the national, regional and international levels and to ensure that peace and non-violence is fostered at all levels;

4. *Welcomes* the establishment of national committees and national focal points in over one hundred and sixty countries in the context of the observance of the International Year for the Culture of Peace, stresses the importance of their continued close involvement in furthering the objectives of the Declaration and Programme of Action on a Culture of Peace and in the effective observance of the Decade, and encourages the establishment of such bodies in the remaining countries;

5. *Designates* the United Nations Educational, Scientific and Cultural Organization as the lead agency for the Decade with responsibility for coordinating the activities of the organizations of the United Nations system to promote a culture of peace, as well as liaison with the other organizations concerned in this matter;

6. *Recognizes* the important role of relevant United Nations bodies, in particular the United Nations Children's Fund and the University for Peace, in further promoting a culture of peace and non-violence, particularly by means of special activities during the Decade at national, regional and international levels;

7. *Requests* the United Nations Educational, Scientific and Cultural Organization to disseminate widely in various languages the Declaration and Programme of Action and related materials, in particular throughout the Decade;

8. *Calls upon* the relevant United Nations bodies, in particular the United Nations Educational, Scientific and Cultural Organization and the United Nations Children's Fund, to promote both formal and non-formal education at all levels that foster a culture of peace and non-violence;

9. *Invites* civil society at the local, regional and national levels to widen the scope of their activities to promote a culture of peace and non-violence, engaging in partnerships and sharing information, thus contributing to a global movement for a culture of peace, and encourages civil society, including non-governmental organizations, to further the objectives of the Decade by adopting their own programme of activities to complement the initiatives of Member States, the organiza-

tions of the United Nations system and other global and regional organizations;

10. *Stresses* the importance of the media and of new information and communications technology in further promoting a culture of peace and non-violence, especially among children and young people;

11. *Requests* the Secretary-General to submit to the General Assembly at its sixtieth session in 2005 a report on the observance of the Decade at its mid-point and on the implementation of the Declaration and Programme of Action, taking into account the views of Member States and in consultation with the United Nations Educational, Scientific and Cultural Organization, the United Nations Children's Fund and other relevant bodies of the United Nations system;

12. *Invites* civil society, including non-governmental organizations, to provide information to the Secretary-General on the observance of the Decade and the activities undertaken to promote a culture of peace and non-violence;

13. *Decides* to devote one day of plenary meetings at its sixtieth session to consideration of the item, including a review of the progress made in the implementation of the Declaration and Programme of Action, as well as the observance of the Decade at its mid-point, with the participation of all relevant actors, as appropriate;

14. *Requests* the Secretary-General to submit to the General Assembly at its fifty-sixth session a report on the implementation of the present resolution;

15. *Decides* to include in the provisional agenda of its fifty-sixth session the item entitled "Culture of peace".

National institutions and regional arrangements

National institutions for human rights promotion and protection

Report of Secretary-General. In December [E/CN.4/2001/99], the Secretary-General described OHCHR activities to strengthen national institutions and measures taken by Governments and national human rights institutions in those areas, as well as cooperation between UN human rights treaty bodies and national institutions. The report covered the period from 30 November 1999 to 30 November 2000.

OHCHR continued to implement its activities on national institutions, which included advisory missions by the High Commissioner's Special Adviser on National Institutions, Regional Arrangements and Preventive Strategies and/or staff members of the Office to Cambodia, Canada, Ecuador, Fiji, Guyana, Jamaica, Jordan, Kenya, Mexico, Nepal, New Zealand, the Philippines, Saint Lucia, Sierra Leone, South Africa, Sweden and Thailand. Advice concerning legislation to establish a national institution was provided by the Special Adviser to Cambodia, Guyana, Jamaica, Kenya, Nepal, the Republic of

Korea, Sierra Leone, Thailand and Trinidad and Tobago. Relevant technical cooperative activities continued in Bolivia, Ecuador, El Salvador, Georgia, Guatemala, Indonesia, Malawi, the Republic of Moldova, South Africa, Uganda and Palestine. Further consultations on cooperative agreements continued with established institutions in Colombia, Ecuador, Fiji, Indonesia, Malawi, Mexico, Rwanda and Sri Lanka.

At the international level, OHCHR supported the Fifth International Workshop of National Human Rights Institutions (Morocco, March). At the regional level, it supported the fifth annual meeting of the Asia-Pacific Forum of National Human Rights Institutions (Rotorua, New Zealand, 7-9 August). The Office attended the second Regional Meeting of National Institutions for the Promotion and Protection of Human Rights in the Americas and supported the fifth Annual Congress of the Iberoamerican Federation of Ombudsmen, both of which were held in Mexico in November. In May, the Office, together with the Asia-Pacific Forum of National Human Rights Institutions and the Fiji Human Rights Commission, organized the Regional Workshop on the Role of National Human Rights Institutions in Advancing the International Human Rights of Women. In November, OHCHR, in co-sponsorship with the Government of Canada and in collaboration with the Philippine Human Rights Commission and the Canadian Human Rights Foundation, conducted a workshop for national institutions and NGOs on economic, social and cultural rights.

Commission action. On 26 April [res. 2000/76], the Commission asked the Secretary-General to continue to provide assistance for holding Coordinating Committee meetings during its sessions. It also asked him to provide assistance for international and regional meetings of national institutions from within existing resources and the UN Voluntary Fund for Technical Cooperation in the Field of Human Rights (see p. 624). The Commission's requests were approved by the Economic and Social Council on 28 July (**decision 2000/276**).

The Secretary-General was asked to report in 2001.

Regional arrangements

Reports of Secretary-General. In response to General Assembly resolution 53/148 [YUN 1998, p. 641], the Secretary-General reported in August on OHCHR regional strategies and developments [A/55/279].

In Africa, OHCHR's programme was aimed at strengthening respect for human rights and the rule of law. In the Great Lakes region, the Office had field presences in Angola, Burundi and the Democratic Republic of the Congo. The High Commissioner visited the European Union (EU) secretariat in Brussels, Belgium, on 1 February to discuss cooperation; several meetings of OHCHR and EU representatives subsequently took place. The EU, OHCHR, the Council of Europe and the Organization for Security and Cooperation in Europe (OSCE) were working on an approach to provide training in human rights for international field missions. A joint mission to assess training needs was sent to Kosovo (FRY) in June. In Latin America and the Caribbean, the Office provided training in reporting obligations for Spanish-speaking countries. At the subregional level, it implemented initiatives in Central America and in the Andean subregion on the development of a judicial network, the training of officials in the administration of justice and the development of training methodologies.

In a later report [E/CN.4/2001/97], the Secretary-General stated that a subregional project for Southern Africa had been implemented. In 2000, the implementation of subregional strategies began for Central Africa, the Great Lakes region and West Africa. Subregional strategies were being prepared for East and North Africa. The High Commissioner inaugurated the Human Rights Documentation, Information and Training Centre (Rabat), a tripartite project supported by OHCHR, UNDP and Morocco. A human rights training course for senior command and staff officers from the Southern African Regional Police Chiefs Cooperation Organization was organized (Gaborone, Botswana, February). A regional expert seminar was held on the prevention of ethnic and racial conflicts (Addis Ababa, Ethiopia, 4-6 October). In April and November, OHCHR sent specialists to Albania to assist the OSCE mission in including a gender component in its training programme for national police. In December, an inter-agency meeting at the Council of Europe in Strasbourg, France, brought together UN and European partners to discuss the coordination of programmes in FRY. OHCHR, in collaboration with Chile, organized the Conference of the Americas (Santiago, 4-8 December) in preparation for the World Conference against Racism, Racial Discrimination, Xenophobia and Related Intolerance (see p. 641). The Office established relations with the Caribbean Ombudsman Association and supported its work and participation in various forums. It supported the second annual meeting of national institutions of the Americas and the Caribbean (Mexico City, 19-21 November).

(For information on Asia and the Pacific, see p. 639.)

GENERAL ASSEMBLY ACTION

On 4 December [meeting 81], the General Assembly, on the recommendation of the Third Committee [A/55/602/Add.2 & Corr.1], adopted **resolution 55/105** without vote [agenda item 114 (b)].

Regional arrangements for the promotion and protection of human rights

The General Assembly,

Recalling its resolution 32/127 of 16 December 1977 and all its subsequent resolutions concerning regional arrangements for the promotion and protection of human rights,

Recalling also Commission on Human Rights resolution 1993/51 of 9 March 1993 and its subsequent resolutions in this regard,

Bearing in mind the relevant resolutions of the Commission concerning advisory services and technical cooperation in the field of human rights, including its most recent on that subject, resolution 2000/80 of 26 April 2000,

Bearing in mind also the Vienna Declaration and Programme of Action, adopted by the World Conference on Human Rights on 25 June 1993, which reiterates, inter alia, the need to consider the possibility of establishing regional and subregional arrangements for the promotion and protection of human rights where they do not already exist,

Recalling that the World Conference recommended that more resources should be made available for the strengthening of regional arrangements for the promotion and protection of human rights under the programme of technical cooperation in the field of human rights of the Office of the United Nations High Commissioner for Human Rights,

Reaffirming that regional arrangements play a fundamental role in promoting and protecting human rights and should reinforce universal human rights standards, as contained in international human rights instruments, and their protection,

Noting the progress achieved so far in the promotion and protection of human rights at the regional level under the auspices of the United Nations, the specialized agencies and the regional intergovernmental organizations,

Considering that cooperation between the United Nations and regional arrangements in the field of human rights continues to be both substantive and supportive and that possibilities exist for increased cooperation,

1. *Takes note with satisfaction* of the report of the Secretary-General;

2. *Welcomes* the continuing cooperation and assistance of the Office of the United Nations High Commissioner for Human Rights in the further strengthening of the existing regional arrangements and regional machinery for the promotion and protection of human rights, in particular through technical cooperation which is aimed at national capacity-building, public information and education, with a view to exchanging information and experience in the field of human rights;

3. *Also welcomes*, in that respect, the close cooperation of the Office of the High Commissioner in the organization of regional and subregional training courses and workshops in the field of human rights, high-level governmental expert meetings and regional conferences of national human rights institutions, aimed at creating greater understanding in the regions of issues concerning the promotion and protection of human rights, improving procedures and examining the various systems for the promotion and protection of universally accepted human rights standards, and identifying obstacles to ratification of the principal international human rights treaties and strategies to overcome them;

4. *Recognizes*, therefore, that progress in promoting and protecting all human rights depends primarily on efforts made at the national and local levels and that the regional approach should imply intensive cooperation and coordination with all partners involved;

5. *Stresses* the importance of the programme of technical cooperation in the field of human rights, renews its appeal to all Governments to consider making use of the possibilities offered by the United Nations under this programme of organizing information or training courses at the national level for government personnel on the application of international human rights standards and the experience of relevant international bodies, and notes with satisfaction, in that respect, the establishment of technical cooperation projects with Governments of all regions;

6. *Welcomes* the growing exchanges between the United Nations and the bodies created by the United Nations in accordance with the treaties dealing with human rights, on the one hand, and regional intergovernmental organizations, such as the Council of Europe, the Organization for Security and Cooperation in Europe, the Inter-American Commission on Human Rights and the African Commission on Human and Peoples' Rights, on the other;

7. *Also welcomes* the appointment by the High Commissioner of four human rights personalities to serve as regional advisers, who will play a significant role in the promotion of human rights and human rights advocacy through the design of strategies and the development of partnerships for human rights, facilitate coordination of human rights technical cooperation in the region and assist regional cooperation at large, for example, among national institutions, parliamentary human rights bodies, bar associations and nongovernmental organizations;

8. *Recalls* in this regard the positive experience of the presence of the Office of the High Commissioner in southern Africa, which will serve as guidance in the development of the regional approach of the Office of the High Commissioner;

9. *Notes with interest* the programme for Africa of the Office of the High Commissioner and the objective of strengthening cooperation between the Office of the High Commissioner and the Organization of African Unity with a view to reviewing, on a regular basis, needs in the area of human rights in the various subregions;

10. *Also notes with interest* the further developments in the implementation of the Framework for Regional Technical Cooperation for the Asia-Pacific Region, which is enhancing technical cooperation in the promotion and protection of human rights in the region;

11. *Takes note with interest* of the Quito Framework for Technical Cooperation in the Field of Human Rights, which serves as a basis for the regional strategy of the Office of the High Commissioner and aims at

strengthening national capacities for the promotion of human rights in Latin America and the Caribbean;

12. *Welcomes* the continued cooperation between the Office of the High Commissioner and regional organizations in Europe and Central Asia, in particular in the development, as a priority, of a regional approach to preventing trafficking in persons;

13. *Invites* States in areas in which regional arrangements in the field of human rights do not yet exist to consider concluding agreements with a view to establishing, within their respective regions, suitable regional machinery for the promotion and protection of human rights;

14. *Requests* the Secretary-General, as foreseen in programme 19 (Human rights) of the medium-term plan for the period 1998-2001, to continue to strengthen exchanges between the United Nations and regional intergovernmental organizations dealing with human rights and to make available adequate resources from within the regular budget of technical cooperation to the activities of the Office of the High Commissioner to promote regional arrangements;

15. *Requests* the Commission on Human Rights to continue to pay special attention to the most appropriate ways of assisting, at their request, countries of the various regions under the programme of technical cooperation and to make, where necessary, relevant recommendations;

16. *Requests* the Secretary-General to submit to the General Assembly at its fifty-seventh session a report on the state of regional arrangements for the promotion and protection of human rights and to include therein the results of action taken in pursuance of the present resolution;

17. *Decides* to consider this question further at its fifty-seventh session.

Asia and the Pacific

In March [E/CN.4/2000/102], the Secretary-General reported on regional arrangements to promote and protect human rights in Asia and the Pacific. OHCHR organized the eighth workshop on regional arrangements for the promotion and protection of human rights in the Asian and Pacific region (Beijing, 1-3 March), which reviewed progress made since the last workshop, held in 1999 [YUN 1999, p. 600], in the four areas of the framework for regional technical cooperation (national plans of action for human rights promotion and protection and the strengthening of national capacities; human rights education; national institutions for the promotion and protection of human rights; and strategies for the realization of the right to development and economic, social and cultural rights). Other meetings held to discuss issues covered by the framework included the intersessional subregional workshop on national plans of action for human rights education (Tokyo, Japan, 17-19 January) and the intersessional workshop on the realization of the

right to development and economic, social and cultural rights (Sana'a, Yemen, 5-7 February).

In a later report [E/CN.4/2001/98], the Secretary-General gave details of other workshops held to address issues covered by the framework, including the intersessional subregional North-East Asia workshop on parliamentarians and human rights (Mongolia, 9-11 August), the fifth annual meeting of the Asia-Pacific Forum of National Human Rights Institutions (New Zealand, August), the workshop on the role of national human rights institutions in advancing the rights of women (Fiji, May) and the workshop on national institutions and economic, social and cultural rights (Philippines, November).

Commission action. On 26 April [res. 2000/74], the Commission encouraged Governments in the region to make use of UN facilities offered under the programme of human rights advisory services and technical cooperation to further strengthen national human rights capacities. The Secretary-General was asked to submit in 2001 a report containing the conclusions of the ninth workshop.

Cooperation with UN human rights bodies

The Commission on Human Rights examined a report of the Secretary-General containing allegations of intimidation and reprisals against private individuals and groups who sought to cooperate with the United Nations and with representatives of its human rights bodies [E/CN.4/2000/101].

Commission action. On 18 April [res. 2000/22], the Commission urged Governments to refrain from acts of intimidation or reprisal against persons who sought to cooperate or had cooperated with representatives of UN human rights bodies, or who had provided testimony or information to them; individuals who availed themselves of UN procedures and those who had provided legal assistance to them for that purpose; those who submitted communications under procedures established by human rights instruments; and relatives of victims of human rights violations. Representatives of UN human rights bodies and treaty bodies monitoring the observance of human rights were asked to help prevent the hampering of access to UN human rights procedures, to continue to take urgent steps to prevent the occurrence of intimidation or reprisal and to include in their reports references to allegations of intimidation or reprisal, as well as an account of action taken. The Secretary-General was asked to draw the Commission's resolution to the attention of UN human rights and treaty bodies and to report in 2001.

Chapter II

Protection of human rights

In 2000, the protection of human rights—civil and political, as well as economic, social and cultural—continued to be a major focus of UN activities.

In May, the Preparatory Committee for the World Conference against Racism, Racial Discrimination, Xenophobia and Related Intolerance decided that the Conference would take place from 31 August to 7 September 2001 in South Africa. The General Assembly, in December, reaffirmed the proclamation of the year 2001 as the International Year of Mobilization against Racism, Racial Discrimination, Xenophobia and Related Intolerance, which aimed at drawing attention to the objectives of the Conference. In other action, the Assembly proclaimed 18 December International Migrants Day. The General Conference of the United Nations Educational, Scientific and Cultural Organization proclaimed 23 August International Day for the Remembrance of the Slave Trade and Its Abolition.

As part of the twentieth anniversary observance of the 1981 Declaration on the Elimination of All Forms of Intolerance and of Discrimination Based on Religion or Belief, plans were made to convene an international conference on primary and secondary school education relating to freedom of religion and belief. In November, the Preparatory Committee for the conference adopted the first version of the draft final document. The conference was to take place in Madrid, Spain, in November 2001.

April and August resolutions of the Security Council condemned the deliberate targeting of civilians, other protected persons and children in situations of armed conflict.

In July, the Economic and Social Council established as a subsidiary organ a Permanent Forum on Indigenous Issues. The Forum would discuss indigenous issues within the Council's mandate relating to economic and social development, culture, the environment, education and health, and human rights.

Special rapporteurs, special representatives and independent experts of the Commission on Human Rights and its subsidiary body, the Subcommission on the Promotion and Protection of Human Rights, examined, among other issues,

allegations of torture; extralegal executions; impunity; mercenary activity; affirmative action; the rights of migrants; the independence of the judiciary; freedom of opinion and expression; freedom of religion or belief; human rights and terrorism; internally displaced persons; globalization and its impact on human rights; extreme poverty; illicit practices related to toxic and dangerous products and wastes; sexual violence during armed conflict; violence against women; the sale of children, child prostitution and child pornography; and the situation of children affected by armed conflict.

Working groups considered arbitrary detention, enforced or involuntary disappearances, minorities, the right to development, structural adjustment policies, contemporary forms of slavery and a draft declaration on the rights of indigenous peoples.

Racism and racial discrimination

Third Decade against racism

The General Assembly, in resolution 48/91 [YUN 1993, p. 853], had proclaimed the Third Decade to Combat Racism and Racial Discrimination (1993-2003) and adopted the Decade's Programme of Action. The Third Decade's goals and objectives were the same as those of the first Decade, which the Assembly had adopted in resolution 3057(XXVIII) [YUN 1973, p. 523]. The revised Programme of Action for the Third Decade was adopted by the Assembly in resolution 49/146 [YUN 1994, p. 988].

Implementation of Decade Programme

Commission action. On 17 April [E/2000/23 (res. 2000/14)], the Commission on Human Rights, regretting the lack of interest, support and financial resources for the Decade and Programme of Action and that few of the activities planned for 1994-1998 were carried out, recommended that the General Assembly ask the Secretary-General to assign high priority to the Programme's activities and earmark adequate resources to finance them. The Commission appealed to Governments, intergovernmental organizations, non-governmental organizations (NGOs) and individuals to contribute to the trust fund for the Programme for the Decade, and asked the Secretary-General to encourage contributions. It asked States to encourage the reporting of acts motivated by racism, racial discrimination, xenophobia or ethnic reasons and to give priority to education as the main means of preventing racism and racial discrimination.

Reports of Secretary-General. The Secretary-General, pursuant to General Assembly resolution 54/154 [YUN 1999, p. 605], submitted to the Economic and Social Council in June his annual report on implementation of the Programme of Action [E/2000/75]. He concluded that Member States and NGOs appeared to have mobilized themselves through the preparatory process for the 2001 World Conference against Racism, Racial Discrimination, Xenophobia and Related Intolerance (see below) to provide an impetus to the fight against racism and racial discrimination. Contributions made by UN bodies and specialized agencies to combat racism in all forms continued to reflect global and concerted efforts to address the issues and provide long-lasting solutions. Annexed to the report was a list of contributions received from Governments to the trust fund as at May 2000. On 28 July, the Council took note of the Secretary-General's report (**decision 2000/289**).

In an August report to the Assembly [A/55/285], the Secretary-General stated that, as requested by the Commission [YUN 1998, p. 645], the UN High Commissioner for Human Rights had oriented the activities of the Third Decade towards the preparation of the World Conference and would include the activities of the Decade's Programme of Action in her 2001 annual appeal. Further proposals to implement the Programme of Action would be considered after the Conference, in order to take into account its outcome and recommendations.

Subcommission action. On 11 August [E/CN.4/2001/2 (res. 2000/3)], the Subcommission on the Promotion and Protection of Human Rights, regretting the lack of interest, support and resources for the Decade and the Programme of Action, called on Governments, UN bodies and interested NGOs to contribute fully to the Programme's implementation.

World Conference

In accordance with General Assembly resolution 52/111 [YUN 1997, p. 629], the World Conference against Racism, Racial Discrimination, Xenophobia and Related Intolerance was scheduled to convene not later than 2001. The Conference would focus on practical measures to eradicate racism, including measures of prevention, education and protection and the provision of effective remedies. The High Commissioner for Human Rights was designated the Secretary-General of the Conference and the Commission on Human Rights served as its Preparatory Committee.

Report of Secretary-General. In response to General Assembly resolution 53/132 [YUN 1998, p. 646], the Secretary-General submitted an August report [A/55/285] on progress achieved in the preparatory process for the Conference.

At its first session (Geneva, 1-5 May) [A/55/307], the Preparatory Committee for the Conference decided that the Conference would take place from 31 August to 7 September 2001 and to accept the offer of South Africa to act as host [YUN 1999, p. 602]. It recommended that the Assembly establish an intersessional open-ended working group to meet in Geneva for five working days in January 2001 to develop the draft agenda, declaration and programme of action of the Conference. It also recommended that the Assembly authorize it to extend its second session, to be held in Geneva in May 2001, for up to five additional working days. The slogan for the Conference, "United to combat racism: equality, justice, dignity", was adopted.

The Secretary-General discussed documentation before the Committee regarding the expert seminar on racism, refugees and multi-ethnic States (Geneva, 6-8 December 1999) [A/CONF.189/PC.1/9]; the expert consultations to formulate recommendations on the Conference (Bellagio, Italy, 24-28 January 2000) [A/CONF.189/PC.1/10]; the expert seminar on remedies available to victims of racial discrimination, xenophobia and related intolerance and on good national practices in that field (Geneva, 16-18 February) [A/CONF.189/PC.1/8]; an analysis of replies from States, UN specialized agencies, intergovernmental organizations, NGOs and national institutions to a questionnaire prepared by the Office of the United Nations High Commissioner for Human Rights (OHCHR) on progress in the fight against racism [A/CONF.189/PC.1/3]; the Secretary-General's study on the effects of racial discrimination on the children of minorities and migrant workers in education, training and employment [A/CONF.189/PC.1/11]; consultations on the use of the Internet to incite racism and intolerance [A/CONF.189/PC.1/5]; and a note by the Secretariat on improving coordination between OHCHR and relevant organizations concerning action to combat racism and related intolerance [A/CONF.189/PC.1/4]. Proposals for the work of the Conference were submitted by the Subcommission on the Promotion and Protection of Human Rights [A/CONF.189/PC.1/13 & Add.1], while contributions to the preparatory process were received from the Committee on the Elimination of Racial Discrimination [A/CONF.189/ PC.1/12], the Committee on Economic, Social and Cultural Rights [A/CONF.189/PC.1/14] and the Committee on the Rights of the Child [A/CONF.189/ PC.1/15]. The Special Rapporteur on contemporary forms of racism, racial discrimination, xenophobia and related intolerance reported orally on the phenomenon, including political activities of extreme right-wing parties, racist violence against migrant workers, the dangers of xenophobic or racist groups, discrimination against Roma and the expansion of racist hate speeches through the Internet. The Special Rapporteur on religious intolerance reported on racial and religious discrimination [A/CONF.189/PC.1/7], and the Special Rapporteur on the human rights of migrants submitted a report on the human rights of migrant women [A/CONF.189/PC.1/19]. (See below for additional information on the preparatory process and p. 652 for Subcommission action on the Conference and migrant workers.)

The Secretary-General discussed the information campaign to sensitize public opinion about the Conference, coordination between OHCHR, UN bodies and the specialized agencies, and OHCHR's appointment of an NGO liaison officer.

Annexed to the report was the financial status as at July 2000 of the fund for voluntary contributions for the Conference, which amounted to $1.76 million.

Preparatory process

The Preparatory Committee for the Conference, in addition to the documents discussed in the Secretary-General's report (see p. 641), considered a note by him transmitting reviews and recommendations concerning the Conference received from specialized agencies, other international organizations, concerned UN bodies and regional organizations [A/CONF.189/PC.1/17]. The Committee also had before it the contributions of NGOs [A/CONF.189/PC.1/NGO/1-6].

Preparatory activities included the European Conference against Racism (Strasbourg, France, 11-13 October) [A/CONF.189/PC.2/6], which adopted a political declaration, and the Regional Conference of the Americas (Santiago, Chile, 5-7 December), which adopted a declaration and plan of action [A/CONF.189/PC.2/7]. Other regional meetings included the Central and Eastern European seminar of experts on the protection of minorities and other vulnerable groups and strengthening human rights capacity at the national level (Warsaw, Poland, 5-7 July) [A/CONF.189/ PC.2/2]; the Asian-Pacific seminar of

experts on migrants and trafficking in persons with particular reference to women and children (Bangkok, Thailand, 5-7 September) [A/CONF.189/ PC.2/3]; the seminar of experts on the prevention of ethnic and racial conflicts in Africa (Addis Ababa, Ethiopia, 4-6 October) [A/CONF.189/ PC.2/4]; the Latin American and Caribbean seminar of experts on economic, social and legal measures to combat racism with particular reference to vulnerable groups (Santiago, 25-27 October) [A/CONF.189/PC.2/5]; and the expert group meeting on gender and racial discrimination (Zagreb, Croatia, 21-24 November) [A/CONF.189/ PC.2/20]. Satellite meetings included the International Conference on Discrimination and Tolerance, organized by the Danish Centre for Human Rights (Copenhagen, Denmark, 7-9 May) [A/CONF.189/PC.2/Misc.1]; the International Youth Forum against Racism, organized by Canada (Hannover, Germany, 4-12 August) [A/CONF.189/ PC.2/Misc.2]; and the expert meeting on strengthening the implementation of the 1965 International Convention on the Elimination of All Forms of Racial Discrimination (see p. 611), convened by Minority Rights International in cooperation with OHCHR (Geneva, 5 August) [A/CONF.189/PC.2/Misc.3].

In August, the High Commissioner initiated the Visionary Declaration entitled "Tolerance and Diversity: A Vision for the Twenty-first Century", which was launched in New York on 5 September. Former South African President Nelson Mandela was the Patron of the Declaration. The first issue of the newsletter of the Conference secretariat, *Durban 2001: United against Racism*, was launched by the High Commissioner on 11 December, in commemoration of Human Rights Day. Other activities included preparation of flyers and brochures, a special event on 23 October which brought together Goodwill Ambassadors of various UN agencies and organizations, and a video conference hosted by international media and Spanish-speaking television networks (Santiago, 7 December).

Commission action. On 17 April [res. 2000/14], the Commission adopted a series of recommendations regarding the Conference, as well as requests to the Secretary-General, the High Commissioner, as Secretary-General of the Conference, and regional preparatory processes that were either approved or endorsed by the Economic and Social Council (see below).

ECONOMIC AND SOCIAL COUNCIL ACTION

On 28 July [meeting 45], the Economic and Social Council, on the recommendation of the Commission on Human Rights [E/2000/23 & Corr.1], adopted **resolution 2000/21** without vote [agenda item 14 *(g)*].

Racism, racial discrimination, xenophobia and related intolerance

The Economic and Social Council,

Taking note of Commission of Human Rights resolution 2000/14 of 17 April 2000,

1. *Approves* the Commission's recommendation that the General Assembly, through the Council, request the Secretary-General to assign high priority to the activities of the Programme of Action for the Third Decade to Combat Racism and Racial Discrimination and to earmark adequate resources to finance the activities of the Programme;

2. *Endorses* the Commission's decision to appoint an eleven-member Bureau for the two sessions of the Preparatory Committee for the World Conference against Racism, Racial Discrimination, Xenophobia and Related Intolerance, comprising two representatives per regional group and a representative of the host country as an ex-officio member, in order to ensure continuity and the adequate representation of all Member States;

3. *Approves* the Commission's requests to the United Nations High Commissioner for Human Rights:

(a) To continue and intensify, in her capacity as Secretary-General of the World Conference, the activities already initiated within the framework of the world information campaign with a view to mobilization and support for the objectives of the World Conference by all sectors of political, economic, social and cultural life, as well as other interested sectors;

(b) To undertake appropriate consultations with non-governmental organizations on the possibility that they might hold a forum before and partly during the World Conference and, insofar as possible, to provide them with technical assistance for that purpose;

4. *Also approves* the Commission's requests:

(a) To the Secretary-General, the United Nations specialized agencies and the regional economic commissions to provide financial and technical assistance for the organization of the regional preparatory meetings planned in the context of the World Conference;

(b) To the regional preparatory processes to identify trends, priorities and obstacles at the national and regional levels, to formulate specific recommendations for the action to be carried out in future to combat racism, racial discrimination, xenophobia and related intolerance and to submit to the Preparatory Committee, by its 2001 session at the latest, the conclusions of these regional preparatory processes;

(c) To the Secretary-General to submit a report to the Commission at its fifty-seventh session on the implementation of Commission resolution 2000/14 under the agenda item entitled "Racism, racial discrimination, xenophobia and all forms of discrimination";

5. *Further approves* the Commission's recommendations that:

(a) The World Conference adopt a declaration and a programme of action containing concrete and practical recommendations to combat racism, racial discrimination, xenophobia and related intolerance;

(b) The particular situation of children receive special attention during the preparations for and during the World Conference, especially in its outcome;

(c) The importance of adopting systematically a gender-based approach through the preparations for and in the outcome of the World Conference be stressed.

Subcommission action. On 11 August [res. 2000/3], the Subcommission suggested that the World Conference focus on, among other things, situations of racism and racial discrimination, xenophobia, related intolerance and ethnic conflict and other patterns of discrimination based on race, colour, social class, minority status, descent, national or ethnic origin or gender, as well as related topics. It recommended that the Conference define a global and system-wide strategy to combat racism and racial discrimination. The Subcommission recommended that the Special Rapporteur on contemporary forms of racism, racial discrimination, xenophobia and related intolerance (see p. 648) and the Special Rapporteur on the human rights of migrants (see p. 651) play an integral role in all Conference processes. The Secretary-General was asked to provide for the participation in the Preparatory Committee, as the Subcommission's representative, of Paulo Sérgio Pinheiro (Brazil), who had been asked in 1998 to prepare proposals for the Conference's work [YUN 1998, p. 646].

GENERAL ASSEMBLY ACTION

On 4 December [meeting 81], the General Assembly, on the recommendation of the Third (Social, Humanitarian and Cultural) Committee [A/55/600], adopted **resolution 55/84** without vote [agenda item 112].

Third Decade to Combat Racism and Racial Discrimination and the convening of the World Conference against Racism, Racial Discrimination, Xenophobia and Related Intolerance

The General Assembly,

Reaffirming its objectives, as set forth in the Charter of the United Nations, of achieving international cooperation in solving problems of an economic, social, cultural or humanitarian character and in promoting and encouraging respect for human rights and fundamental freedoms for all without distinction as to race, sex, language or religion,

Reaffirming also its firm determination and its commitment to eradicate totally and unconditionally racism in all its forms and racial discrimination and its conviction that racism and racial discrimination constitute a total negation of the purposes and principles of the Charter and the Universal Declaration of Human Rights,

Recalling the Universal Declaration of Human Rights, the International Convention on the Elimination of All Forms of Racial Discrimination and the Convention against Discrimination in Education adopted by the United Nations Educational, Scientific and Cultural Organization on 14 December 1960,

Noting the efforts of the Committee on the Elimination of Racial Discrimination since its establishment in 1970 to promote the implementation of the International Convention on the Elimination of All Forms of Racial Discrimination,

Recalling the outcome of the two World Conferences to Combat Racism and Racial Discrimination, held at Geneva in 1978 and in 1983,

Welcoming the outcome of the World Conference on Human Rights, held at Vienna from 14 to 25 June 1993, and, in particular, the attention given in the Vienna Declaration and Programme of Action to the elimination of racism, racial discrimination, xenophobia and other forms of intolerance,

Stressing the importance and sensitivity of the activities of the Special Rapporteur of the Commission on Human Rights on contemporary forms of racism, racial discrimination, xenophobia and related intolerance,

Recalling with satisfaction the proclamation, in resolution 48/91 of 20 December 1993, of the Third Decade to Combat Racism and Racial Discrimination, which began in 1993, and the adoption, in resolution 49/146 of 23 December 1994, of the revised Programme of Action for the Third Decade to Combat Racism and Racial Discrimination,

Noting with grave concern that, despite the efforts of the international community, the principal objectives of the two previous Decades have not been attained and that millions of human beings continue to the present day to be the victims of varied forms of racism and racial discrimination,

Noting with great concern that, despite the efforts undertaken by the international community at various levels, racism, racial discrimination, xenophobia and related forms of intolerance, ethnic antagonism and acts of violence are showing signs of increase in many parts of the world and that the number of associations established on the basis of racist and xenophobic platforms and charters is increasing, as reflected in the report of the Special Rapporteur,

Deeply concerned that, despite continuing efforts, contemporary forms of racism and racial discrimination, many forms of discrimination against, inter alia, blacks, Arabs, Muslims and Christians, xenophobia, Negrophobia, anti-Semitism and related intolerance persist or are even growing in magnitude, incessantly adopting new forms, including tendencies to establish policies based on racial, religious, ethnic, cultural and national superiority or exclusivity,

Noting with concern that racism, racial discrimination, xenophobia and related intolerance may be aggravated by, inter alia, inequitable distribution of wealth, marginalization and social exclusion,

Recognizing that the promotion of tolerance and respect for cultural diversity is an important factor, among others, in eliminating racism, racial discrimination, xenophobia and related intolerance,

Alarmed that technological developments in the field of communications, including the Internet, continue to be utilized by various groups engaged in violent activity to promote racist and xenophobic propaganda aimed at inciting racial hatred and to collect funds to sustain violent campaigns against multi-ethnic societies throughout the world,

Noting that the use of such technologies can also contribute to combating racism, racial discrimination, xenophobia and related intolerance,

Having considered the report submitted by the Secretary-General within the framework of the implementation of the Programme of Action,

Recalling its resolution 54/154 of 17 December 1999, in which it requested the Secretary-General to include in his report to the General Assembly at its fifty-fifth session concrete proposals on how to ensure the financial and personnel resources required for the implementation of the Programme of Action,

Recognizing the importance of strengthening national legislation and institutions for the promotion of racial harmony and for the effective enforcement of such legislation,

Remaining firmly convinced of the need to take more effective and sustained measures at the national and international levels for the elimination of all forms of racism and racial discrimination,

Deeply concerned that the phenomenon of racism and racial discrimination against migrant workers continues to increase, despite the efforts made by the international community to improve the protection of the human rights of migrant workers and members of their families,

Recalling the adoption at its forty-fifth session of the International Convention on the Protection of the Rights of All Migrant Workers and Members of Their Families,

Acknowledging that indigenous people are at times victims of particular forms of racism and racial discrimination,

Noting with concern the existence of multiple discrimination, in particular against women,

Stressing the importance of urgently eliminating growing and violent trends of racism and racial discrimination, and conscious that any form of impunity for crimes motivated by racist and xenophobic attitudes plays a role in weakening the rule of law and democracy and tends to encourage the recurrence of such crimes, and requires resolute action and cooperation for its eradication,

I

Implementation of the Programme of Action for the Third Decade to Combat Racism and Racial Discrimination and coordination of activities

1. *Welcomes* the report submitted by the Secretary-General;

2. *Reaffirms* that racism and racial discrimination are among the most serious violations of human rights in the contemporary world, and expresses its firm determination and its commitment to eradicate, by all available means, racism in all its forms and racial discrimination;

3. *Recognizes* that Governments implement and enforce appropriate and effective legislation to prevent acts of racism, racial discrimination, xenophobia and related intolerance, thereby contributing to the prevention of human rights violations;

4. *Urges* all Governments to take all necessary measures to combat new forms of racism, in particular by constantly adapting the means provided to combat them, especially in the legislative, judicial, administrative, educational and information fields;

5. *Calls upon* all States resolutely to bring to justice the perpetrators of crimes motivated by racism, and calls upon those that have not done so to consider including racist motivation as an aggravating factor for the purposes of sentencing;

6. *Requests* the United Nations High Commissioner for Human Rights to assign high priority to the follow-up to programmes and activities for combating racism and racial discrimination, consistent with the need to ensure the effective preparation of the World Conference against Racism, Racial Discrimination, Xenophobia and Related Intolerance;

7. *Requests* the Secretary-General in his reports on racism, racial discrimination, xenophobia and related intolerance to accord special attention to and provide information on the situation of migrant workers and members of their families in this regard;

8. *Calls upon* all Member States to consider signing and ratifying or acceding to the International Convention on the Protection of the Rights of All Migrant Workers and Members of Their Families as a matter of priority;

9. *Commends* all States that have ratified or acceded to the international instruments to combat racism and racial discrimination, especially the International Convention on the Elimination of All Forms of Racial Discrimination and the Convention against Discrimination in Education;

10. *Urges* all States that have not yet done so to become parties to the International Convention on the Elimination of All Forms of Racial Discrimination in order to achieve its universal ratification;

11. *Urges* States to limit the extent of any reservation that they lodge to the International Convention on the Elimination of All Forms of Racial Discrimination, to formulate any reservation as precisely and as narrowly as possible, to ensure that no reservations are incompatible with the objective and purpose of the Convention or otherwise incompatible with international treaty law, to review their reservations on a regular basis with a view to withdrawing them and to withdraw reservations that are contrary to the objective and purpose of the Convention or that are otherwise incompatible with international treaty law;

12. *Emphasizes* the importance of the full compliance of States parties with the obligations that they have accepted under the International Convention on the Elimination of All Forms of Racial Discrimination;

13. *Urges* all States parties to intensify efforts to meet the obligations that they have accepted under article 4 of the International Convention on the Elimination of All Forms of Racial Discrimination, with due regard to the principles contained in the Universal Declaration of Human Rights and to article 5 of the Convention, with respect to:

(a) Declaring an offence punishable by law any dissemination of ideas based on racial superiority or hatred, incitement to racial discrimination and all acts of violence or incitement to such acts against any race or group of persons of another colour or ethnic origin, and the provision of any assistance to racist activities, including the financing thereof;

(b) Declaring illegal and prohibited organizations and organized and all other propaganda activities that promote and incite racial discrimination, and recognizing participation in such organizations or activities as an offence punishable by law;

(c) Not permitting public authorities or public institutions, whether national or local, to promote or incite racial discrimination;

14. *Encourages* the mass media to promote ideas of tolerance and understanding among peoples and different cultures;

15. *Requests* the Secretary-General to continue to draw attention to the effects of racial discrimination on minorities and migrant workers and members of their families, especially children and women, in the fields of education, training and employment and to submit in his report specific recommendations for the implementation of measures to combat such discrimination;

16. *Recognizes* the need for adequate support and financial resources for the Third Decade to Combat Racism and Racial Discrimination and the Programme of Action for the Third Decade to Combat Racism and Racial Discrimination, and requests the Secretary-General to include in his report to the General Assembly at its fifty-sixth session concrete proposals on how to ensure the financial and personnel resources required for the implementation of the Programme of Action, including through the regular budget of the United Nations and extrabudgetary sources;

17. *Expresses its appreciation* to those that have made contributions to the Trust Fund for the Programme of Action for the Third Decade to Combat Racism and Racial Discrimination, strongly appeals to all Governments, intergovernmental and non-governmental organizations and individuals in a position to do so to contribute generously to the Fund, and to this end requests the Secretary-General to continue to establish the appropriate contacts and undertake the appropriate initiatives;

18. *Welcomes* the establishment of the racism project team in the Office of the United Nations High Commissioner for Human Rights with a view to coordinating all activities of the Third Decade;

19. *Urges* all Governments, the Secretary-General, United Nations bodies, the specialized agencies, intergovernmental organizations and relevant non-governmental organizations, in implementing the Programme of Action, to pay particular attention to the situation of indigenous people;

20. *Requests* States to consider the relevant decisions of the Economic and Social Council on the integrated follow-up to previous world conferences and the need to make optimum use of all available mechanisms in the struggle against racism;

21. *Strongly underlines* the importance of education as a significant means of preventing and eradicating racism and racial discrimination and of creating awareness of the principles of human rights, in particular among young people, and in this regard requests the United Nations Educational, Scientific and Cultural Organization to continue its work on the preparation and dissemination of teaching materials and teaching aids to promote teaching, training and educational activities on human rights and against racism and racial discrimination, with particular emphasis on activities at the primary and secondary levels of education;

22. *Considers* that, in order to attain the objectives of the Third Decade, all parts of the Programme of Action should be given equal attention;

23. *Requests* the Secretary-General to accord high priority to the activities of the Programme of Action and, in this regard, to ensure that the necessary financial resources are provided for the implementation of

the activities of the Third Decade during the biennium 2002-2003;

24. *Also requests* the Secretary-General to continue to submit each year to the Economic and Social Council a detailed report on all activities of United Nations bodies and the specialized agencies to combat racism and racial discrimination, containing an analysis of information received on such activities;

25. *Invites* the Secretary-General to submit to the General Assembly proposals which would assist in the full implementation of the Programme of Action;

26. *Reiterates its calls upon* all Governments, United Nations bodies, the specialized agencies, intergovernmental and regional organizations and interested non-governmental organizations to contribute fully to the effective implementation of the Programme of Action;

II
World Conference against Racism, Racial Discrimination, Xenophobia and Related Intolerance

1. *Recalls* its resolutions 52/111 of 12 December 1997 and 53/132 of 9 December 1998, in which it established that the Commission on Human Rights would act as the Preparatory Committee for the World Conference against Racism, Racial Discrimination, Xenophobia and Related Intolerance, and its resolution 54/154, and takes note of Commission on Human Rights resolution 2000/14 of 17 April 2000 and Economic and Social Council resolution 2000/21 of 28 July 2000;

2. *Welcomes* the slogan for the World Conference against Racism, Racial Discrimination, Xenophobia and Related Intolerance adopted by the Preparatory Committee, namely, "United to combat racism: equality, justice, dignity";

3. *Also welcomes* the report of the Special Rapporteur of the Commission on Human Rights on contemporary forms of racism, racial discrimination, xenophobia and related intolerence, and recommends that the Preparatory Committee for the World Conference give due consideration to the recommendations and suggestions contained therein;

4. *Requests* the Secretary-General to continue to ensure that adequate financial resources are made available for the preparatory process for the World Conference, including from the regular budget of the United Nations;

5. *Requests* the Secretary-General and the United Nations High Commissioner for Human Rights to continue to make every effort to ensure the mobilization of resources for the voluntary fund for the World Conference to cover the participation of the least developed countries in the preparatory process and in the Conference itself, and requests all Governments, international and non-governmental organizations and private individuals to contribute to the fund;

6. *Calls upon* the High Commissioner to help States and regional organizations, upon request, to convene and finalize inclusive national and regional meetings, in close consultation with the regional groups concerned, or to take other initiatives, including activities at the expert level, to prepare for the World Conference, and urges the specialized agencies and the regional commissions, in coordination with the High Commissioner, to contribute to the convening of regional preparatory meetings;

7. *Requests* the Secretary-General, the specialized agencies and the regional commissions to provide financial and technical assistance for the organization of the regional preparatory meetings planned in the context of the World Conference, and stresses that such assistance should be supplemented by voluntary contributions;

8. *Stresses* the importance of the widest possible participation of non-governmental organizations in the World Conference and the sessions of the Preparatory Committee, as well as in the regional meetings, regional expert seminars and other initiatives, including activities at the expert level, held in preparation for the World Conference;

9. *Decides* to convene the World Conference against Racism, Racial Discrimination, Xenophobia and Related Intolerance at Durban, South Africa, from 31 August to 7 September 2001;

10. *Welcomes* the holding by the Council of Europe of the regional preparatory meeting at Strasbourg, France, from 11 to 13 October 2000, and the offers made by the Governments of Chile, Senegal and the Islamic Republic of Iran to convene regional preparatory meetings, within the framework of the World Conference, at, respectively, Santiago, from 4 to 7 December 2000, Dakar, from 22 to 24 January 2001, and Tehran, from 19 to 21 February 2001;

11. *Requests* the High Commissioner:

(a) To help States, upon request, and regional organizations to convene national and regional meetings or to take other initiatives, including activities at the expert level, to prepare for the World Conference;

(b) To undertake appropriate consultations with non-governmental organizations on the possibility that they might hold a forum before and partly during the World Conference and, as far as possible, to provide them with technical assistance for that purpose;

(c) To continue fund-raising activities in order to increase the resources of the voluntary fund established specifically to cover all aspects of the preparatory process for the World Conference and the participation of non-governmental organizations, in particular those from developing countries, with special emphasis on those from least developed countries;

12. *Also requests* the High Commissioner, in her capacity as Secretary-General of the World Conference, to continue and intensify the activities already initiated within the framework of the world information campaign with a view to ensuring mobilization and support for the objectives of the World Conference by all sectors of political, economic, social and cultural life, as well as other interested sectors, to inform the Preparatory Committee of developments in this regard and to assist the Preparatory Committee in:

(a) Reviewing the political, historical, economic, social, cultural and any other factors leading to racism, racial discrimination, xenophobia and related intolerance with a view to reaching a better understanding of and appraising these problems;

(b) Reviewing progress made in the fight against racism, racial discrimination, xenophobia and related intolerance, in particular since the adoption of the Universal Declaration of Human Rights, and reappraising the obstacles to further progress in the field and ways in which to overcome them;

(*c*) Considering ways and means to better the application of existing standards and the implementation of existing instruments to combat racism, racial discrimination, xenophobia and related intolerance;

(*d*) Increasing the level of awareness about the scourges of racism and racial discrimination, xenophobia and related intolerance;

(*e*) Formulating concrete recommendations on ways in which to increase the effectiveness of the activities and mechanisms of the United Nations through programmes aimed at combating racism, racial discrimination, xenophobia and related intolerance;

(*f*) Formulating concrete recommendations to further action-oriented national, regional and international measures to combat all forms of racism, racial discrimination, xenophobia and related intolerance;

13. *Requests* the regional preparatory processes to identify trends, priorities and obstacles at the national and regional levels, and to formulate specific recommendations for the action to be carried out in the future to combat racism, racial discrimination, xenophobia and related intolerance;

14. *Calls upon* the regional preparatory meetings to submit to the Preparatory Committee, at its second session, through the High Commissioner, reports on the results of their deliberations, with concrete and pragmatic recommendations aimed at combating racism, racial discrimination, xenophobia and related intolerance, which will be duly reflected in the texts of the draft final documents of the World Conference, to be prepared by the Committee;

15. *Invites* Governments to promote the participation of national institutions and local non-governmental organizations in the preparations for the World Conference and in the regional meetings and to organize debates in national parliaments on the objectives of the World Conference;

16. *Encourages* all parliaments to participate actively in the preparation of the World Conference, and requests the High Commissioner to explore ways and means of effectively involving parliaments through the relevant international organizations;

17. *Reiterates* that the World Conference should be action-oriented and should adopt a declaration and a programme of action containing concrete and practical recommendations to combat racism, racial discrimination, xenophobia and related intolerance;

18. *Stresses* the importance of systematically taking a gender perspective into account throughout the preparations for and in the outcome of the World Conference;

19. *Recommends* that the particular situation of children and young people should receive special attention during the preparations for and during the World Conference, especially in its outcome;

20. *Encourages* Governments, to that end and to ensure further the engagement of young people on the broader issues of racism, racial discrimination, xenophobia and related intolerance, to include youth delegates in their official delegations to the World Conference and its preparatory processes;

21. *Recommends* that special attention be accorded, during the preparations for and during the World Conference, especially in its outcome, to the particular situation of migrants;

22. *Also recommends* that the particular situation of indigenous people receive special attention during the

preparations for and during the World Conference, especially in its outcome, and encourages Member States to facilitate the participation of their indigenous people, inter alia, by considering including representatives of indigenous people in their delegations;

23. *Welcomes* the report of the Commission on Human Rights acting as the Preparatory Committee for the World Conference against Racism, Racial Discrimination, Xenophobia and Related Intolerance on its first session, and requests the Preparatory Committee to develop in a comprehensive manner the provisional agenda, the draft declaration and the draft programme of action of the World Conference, taking into account the themes as adopted and all outstanding issues from its first session as covered in the report, as well as the contributions of all of the regional preparatory processes and other relevant initiatives;

24. *Decides* to establish an inter-sessional working group which will meet for five working days to develop further the draft agenda, the draft declaration and the draft programme of action of the World Conference;

25. *Also decides* to authorize the Preparatory Committee to extend its second session for up to five working days;

26. *Appeals* to Member States to contribute generously to the voluntary fund for the World Conference to cover the preparatory process and the Conference and the participation of non-governmental organizations from developing countries;

27. *Requests* Governments, the specialized agencies, other international organizations, concerned United Nations bodies, regional organizations, non-governmental organizations, the Committee on the Elimination of Racial Discrimination, the Special Rapporteur of the Commission on Human Rights on contemporary forms of racism, racial discrimination, xenophobia and related intolerance, the Special Rapporteur of the Commission on Human Rights on the human rights of migrants and other human rights mechanisms to participate actively in the preparatory process with a view to ensuring the success of the World Conference and to coordinate their activities in this regard with the assistance of the High Commissioner;

28. *Calls upon* States and regional organizations to continue the process of convening inclusive national and regional meetings or taking other initiatives, such as public information campaigns, to raise awareness of the World Conference as part of the preparations for the Conference;

III

Proclamation of 2001 as the International Year of Mobilization against Racism, Racial Discrimination, Xenophobia and Related Intolerance

1. *Strongly reaffirms* the proclamation of 2001 as the International Year of Mobilization against Racism, Racial Discrimination, Xenophobia and Related Intolerance, and in this context calls upon Governments, all relevant entities of the United Nations system and non-governmental organizations to observe the International Year in a suitable manner, including by means of programmes of action;

2. *Emphasizes* that the activities to be implemented within the framework of the International Year should be directed towards the preparation of the World Conference and the realization of its objectives;

IV
General

Decides to keep the item entitled "Elimination of racism and racial discrimination" on its agenda and to consider it as a matter of high priority at its fifty-sixth session.

On 23 December, the Assembly decided that the item on the elimination of racism and racial discrimination should remain for consideration during its resumed fifty-fifth (2001) session (**decision 55/458**).

Contemporary forms of racism

Reports of Special Rapporteur. In February [E/CN.4/2000/16], the Special Rapporteur on contemporary forms of racism, racial discrimination, xenophobia and related intolerance, Maurice Glèlè-Ahanhanzo (Benin), summarized information he had received regarding discrimination against blacks and against Roma asylum-seekers in Europe, as well as trends in anti-Semitism worldwide. The report contained replies to allegations of racism, racial discrimination and xenophobia transmitted to six Governments by the Special Rapporteur in 1996, 1998 and 1999. In his conclusions and recommendations, he observed that manifestations of racism, racial discrimination and related intolerance were continually occurring in different regions. He considered that the Commission, in cooperation with the Governments concerned, should pay particular attention to the Roma in order to secure their integration in the countries where they lived, emphasizing teaching and vocational training and the development of awareness of differences and of tolerance among the majority population groups. (For Subcommission action on the human rights of the Roma, see p. 657.) The Special Rapporteur remained concerned at the discriminatory manner in which the death penalty was applied in the United States.

In response to General Assembly resolution 54/153 [YUN 1999, p. 610], the Secretary-General transmitted, in August [A/55/304], a report of the Special Rapporteur describing his activities, trends in contemporary manifestations of racism and its related forms, measures taken by Governments and action by civil society. The Special Rapporteur concluded that there had been a resurgence of racist violence, mainly as a result of renewed activities of far-right, neo-Nazi and skinhead organizations; the Internet continued to be the preferred medium for incitement to racial hatred and dissemination of racist and xenophobic ideas; and increasingly commonplace racism could be uncovered when detection mechanisms, such as a toll-free number, were introduced. He

recommended the holding of international consultations at the governmental level with a view to regulating Internet use for racist purposes, and supporting initiatives that used the Internet to create and develop a culture centred on respect for the human person without distinction. The Assembly should continue to mobilize public opinion against racism, racial discrimination and xenophobia and make Member States and various organizations aware of the importance of the 2001 World Conference.

Commission action. On 17 April [res. 2000/14], the Commission asked the Special Rapporteur to examine the issue of political platforms that promoted or incited racial discrimination, to submit recommendations in 2001 to the Preparatory Committee for the Conference, and to continue his exchange of views with Member States and the UN system. Governments thus far visited were asked to implement the Special Rapporteur's recommendations, and he was asked to include that information in his 2001 report. The High Commissioner was urged to assist the countries visited by the Special Rapporteur, at their request, to implement his recommendations. She was asked to conduct research and hold consultations on Internet use to incite racial hatred, racist propaganda and xenophobia, to study ways of promoting international cooperation thereon and to draw up a programme of human rights education and exchanges over the Internet on the struggle against racism, xenophobia and anti-Semitism.

The Commission, on 20 April [res. 2000/40], invited its mechanisms and the treaty bodies, particularly the Special Rapporteur, to pay special attention to human rights violations stemming from the rise of racism and xenophobia, especially as regards their incompatibility with democracy. It invited the High Commissioner to report in 2001 on the implementation of its resolution. States were urged to promote tolerance and to fight against racism and related intolerance as a way to strengthen democracy and transparent and accountable governance.

GENERAL ASSEMBLY ACTION

On 4 December [meeting 81], the General Assembly, on the recommendation of the Third Committee [A/55/600], adopted **resolution 55/82** without vote [agenda item 112].

Measures to be taken against political platforms and activities based on doctrines of superiority which are based on racial discrimination or ethnic exclusiveness and xenophobia, including, in particular, neo-Nazism

The General Assembly,

Recalling that the United Nations emerged from the struggle against nazism, fascism, aggression and foreign occupation, and that the people expressed their resolve in the Charter of the United Nations to save succeeding generations from the scourge of war,

Aware of the determination proclaimed by the peoples of the world in the Charter to reaffirm faith in fundamental human rights, in the dignity and worth of the human person, in the equal rights of men and women and of nations large and small and to promote social progress and better standards of life in larger freedom,

Convinced that any doctrine of superiority based on racial differentiation is scientifically false, morally condemnable, socially unjust and dangerous, and that there is no justification for racial discrimination, in theory or in practice, anywhere,

Noting with appreciation the efforts undertaken by various regional organizations against political platforms and activities based on doctrines of superiority which are based on racial discrimination or ethnic exclusiveness and xenophobia, including, in particular, neo-Nazism,

Noting with regret that in the contemporary world there continue to exist various manifestations of neo-Nazi activities, as well as other political platforms and activities based on doctrines of superiority which are based on racial discrimination or ethnic exclusiveness and xenophobia, which entail contempt for the individual or a denial of the intrinsic dignity and equality of all human beings and of equality of opportunity in the civil, political, economic and social and cultural spheres and in social justice,

Deeply alarmed at the recent intensification of activities of neo-Nazi groups and organizations,

Noting with concern the widening use by such groups and organizations of the opportunities provided by scientific and technological progress, including the Internet global computer network, to promote racist and xenophobic propaganda aimed at inciting racial hatred and to collect funds to sustain violent campaigns against multi-ethnic societies throughout the world,

Noting that the use of such technologies can also contribute to combating racism, racial discrimination, xenophobia and related intolerance,

Expressing its serious concern at the rise in many parts of the world of doctrines based on racial discrimination or ethnic exclusiveness and at the growing coordination of activities based on such doctrines in society at large,

Recalling its resolutions 2331(XXII) of 18 December 1967, 2545(XXIV) of 11 December 1969, 35/200 of 15 December 1980, 36/162 of 16 December 1981, 37/179 of 17 December 1982, 38/99 of 16 December 1983, 39/114 of 14 December 1984, 41/160 of 4 December 1986 and 43/150 of 8 December 1988,

Recalling also Commission on Human Rights resolutions 1983/28 of 7 March 1983, 1984/42 of 12 March 1984, 1985/31 of 13 March 1985, 1986/61 of 13 March 1986, 1988/63 of 10 March 1988 and 1990/46 of 6 March 1990,

Taking into consideration the report of the Special Rapporteur of the Commission on Human Rights on contemporary forms of racism, racial discrimination, xenophobia and related intolerance,

Welcoming the convening of the World Conference against Racism, Racial Discrimination, Xenophobia and Related Intolerance in Durban, South Africa, from 31 August to 7 September 2001,

1. *Again resolutely condemns* political platforms and activities based on doctrines of superiority which are based on racial discrimination or ethnic exclusiveness and xenophobia, including, in particular, neo-Nazism, which entail abuse of human rights and fundamental freedoms;

2. *Expresses its determination* to resist such political platforms and activities which can undermine the enjoyment of human rights and fundamental freedoms and of equality of opportunity;

3. *Urges* States to take all available measures in accordance with their obligations under international human rights instruments to combat political platforms and activities based on doctrines of superiority which are based on racial discrimination or ethnic exclusiveness and xenophobia, including, in particular, neo-Nazism;

4. *Calls upon* all Governments to promote and encourage, especially among young people, respect for human rights and fundamental freedoms, as well as to promote awareness of and oppose political platforms and activities based on doctrines of superiority which are based on racial discrimination or ethnic exclusiveness and xenophobia, including, in particular, neo-Nazism;

5. *Urges* all States to consider the adoption, as a matter of high priority, of appropriate measures to eradicate activities that lead to violence and condemn any dissemination of ideas based on doctrines of superiority which are based on racial discrimination or ethnic exclusiveness and xenophobia, including, in particular, neo-Nazism, consistent with their national legal systems and in accordance with the provisions of the Universal Declaration of Human Rights, the International Covenants on Human Rights and the International Convention on the Elimination of All Forms of Racial Discrimination;

6. *Requests* the Secretary-General to include in his report to the World Conference against Racism, Racial Discrimination, Xenophobia and Related Intolerance information on the measures taken by Member States against political platforms and activities based on doctrines of superiority which are based on racial discrimination or ethnic exclusiveness and xenophobia, including, in particular, neo-Nazism.

On the same date [meeting 81], the Assembly, as recommended by the Third Committee [A/55/600], adopted **resolution 55/83** without vote [agenda item 112].

Measures to combat contemporary forms of racism and racial discrimination, xenophobia and related intolerance

The General Assembly,

Recalling its resolution 54/153 of 17 December 1999, and taking note of Commission on Human Rights resolution 2000/14 of 17 April 2000,

Stressing that the Vienna Declaration and Programme of Action adopted by the World Conference on Human Rights on 25 June 1993 attaches importance to the elimination of racism, racial discrimination, xenophobia and other forms of intolerance,

Convinced that racism, as one of the exclusionist phenomena plaguing many societies, requires resolute action and cooperation for its eradication,

Having examined the report of the Special Rapporteur of the Commission on Human Rights on contemporary forms of racism, racial discrimination, xenophobia and related intolerance, including its conclusions and recommendations,

Deeply concerned that, despite continued efforts, racism, racial discrimination, xenophobia and related intolerance and acts of violence persist and even grow in magnitude, incessantly adopting new forms, including tendencies to establish policies based on racial, religious, ethnic, cultural and national superiority or exclusivity,

Particularly alarmed at the increase in racist violence in many parts of the world, inter alia, as a result of resurgent activities of associations established on the basis of racist and xenophobic platforms and charters, as reflected in the report of the Special Rapporteur, and at the persisting use of those platforms and charters to promote or incite racist ideologies,

Deeply concerned that those advocating racism and racial discrimination misuse new communication technologies, including the Internet, to disseminate their repugnant views,

Noting that the use of such technologies can also contribute to combating racism, racial discrimination, xenophobia and related intolerance,

Conscious of the fundamental difference between, on the one hand, racism and racial discrimination as governmental policy or resulting from official doctrines of racial superiority or exclusivity and, on the other hand, other manifestations of racism, racial discrimination, xenophobia and related intolerance that are increasingly visible in segments of many societies and are perpetrated by individuals or groups, some of which manifestations are directed against migrant workers and members of their families,

Reaffirming, in this regard, the responsibility of Governments for safeguarding and protecting the rights of individuals within their jurisdiction against crimes perpetrated by racist or xenophobic individuals or groups,

Recognizing both the challenges and the opportunities in combating racism, racial discrimination, xenophobia and related intolerance in an increasingly globalized world,

Noting with concern that racism, racial discrimination, xenophobia and related intolerance may be aggravated by, inter alia, inequitable distribution of wealth, marginalization and social exclusion,

Deeply concerned that racism and racial discrimination against migrant workers continue to increase despite the efforts undertaken by the international community to protect the human rights of migrant workers and members of their families,

Noting that the Committee on the Elimination of Racial Discrimination, in its general recommendation XV(42) of 17 March 1993 concerning article 4 of the International Convention on the Elimination of All Forms of Racial Discrimination, holds that the prohibition of the dissemination of ideas based on racial superiority or racial hatred is compatible with the right to freedom of opinion and expression as outlined in article 19 of the Universal Declaration of Human Rights and in article 5 of the Convention,

Noting also that the reports that the States parties submit under the Convention contain, inter alia, information about the causes of, as well as measures to combat, contemporary forms of racism, racial discrimination, xenophobia and related intolerance,

Noting with concern the existence of multiple discrimination, in particular against women,

Particularly alarmed at the rise of racist and xenophobic ideas in political circles, in the sphere of public opinion and in society at large,

Noting with appreciation that the Special Rapporteur will continue to pay attention to the rise of racist and xenophobic ideas in political circles, in the sphere of public opinion and in society at large,

Underlining the importance of urgently eliminating growing and violent trends of racism and racial discrimination, and conscious that any form of impunity for crimes motivated by racist and xenophobic attitudes plays a role in weakening the rule of law and democracy and tends to encourage the recurrence of such crimes, and requires resolute action and cooperation for its eradication,

Recognizing that failure to combat racial discrimination and xenophobia, especially by public authorities and politicians, is a factor encouraging their perpetuation in society,

Emphasizing the importance of creating conditions that foster greater harmony and tolerance within societies,

1. *Reaffirms* the proclamation of 2001 as the International Year of Mobilization against Racism, Racial Discrimination, Xenophobia and Related Intolerance;

2. *Calls upon* the relevant United Nations bodies, Member States and intergovernmental and non-governmental organizations to carry out, promote and disseminate activities and action within the framework of the commemorative year in order to strengthen its impact and ensure its success, in particular the outcome of the World Conference against Racism, Racial Discrimination, Xenophobia and Related Intolerance;

3. *Expresses its full support and appreciation* for the work of the Special Rapporteur of the Commission on Human Rights on contemporary forms of racism, racial discrimination, xenophobia and related intolerance, encourages its continuation, and takes note with appreciation of the report of the Special Rapporteur;

4. *Requests* the Special Rapporteur to continue his exchange of views with Member States, United Nations organs and the specialized agencies, other relevant mechanisms and non-governmental organizations in order to further their effectiveness and mutual cooperation;

5. *Endorses* the request by the Commission on Human Rights to the Special Rapporteur to examine the issue of political platforms which promote or incite racial discrimination and the violation of human rights and to submit recommendations thereon to the Preparatory Committee for the World Conference at its second session;

6. *Welcomes* the recommendation of the Special Rapporteur on the need to hold international consultations at the governmental level with a view to combating the misuse of the Internet for racist purposes, and stresses the importance of international law enforcement cooperation in this area;

7. *Commends* the Committee on the Elimination of Racial Discrimination for its role in the effective implementation of the International Convention on the

Elimination of All Forms of Racial Discrimination, which contributes to the fight against contemporary forms of racism, racial discrimination, xenophobia and related intolerance;

8. *Reaffirms* that acts of violence against others stemming from racism do not constitute expressions of opinion but rather offences;

9. *Declares* that racism and racial discrimination are among the most serious violations of human rights in the contemporary world and must be combated by all available means;

10. *Expresses its profound concern* about and unequivocal condemnation of all forms of racism, racial discrimination, xenophobia and related intolerance, in particular all racist violence, including related acts of random and indiscriminate violence;

11. *Also expresses its profound concern* about and unequivocal condemnation of all forms of racism and racial discrimination, including propaganda, activities and organizations based on doctrines of superiority of one race or group of persons that attempt to justify or promote racism and racial discrimination in any form;

12. *Further expresses its profound concern* about and condemnation of manifestations of racism, racial discrimination, xenophobia and related intolerance against, and stereotyping of, migrant workers and members of their families, persons belonging to minorities and members of vulnerable groups in many societies;

13. *Notes with great concern* that, despite the efforts undertaken by the international community at various levels, racism, racial discrimination, xenophobia and other related forms of intolerance, ethnic antagonism and acts of violence are showing signs of increase in many parts of the world, and that the number of associations established on the basis of racist and xenophobic charters is increasing, as reflected in the report of the Special Rapporteur;

14. *Encourages* all States to include in their educational curricula and social programmes at all levels, as appropriate, knowledge of and tolerance and respect for foreign cultures, peoples and countries;

15. *Recognizes* that the increasing gravity of different manifestations of racism, racial discrimination and xenophobia in various parts of the world requires a more integrated and effective approach on the part of the relevant mechanisms of United Nations human rights machinery;

16. *Encourages* Governments to take appropriate measures to eradicate all forms of racism, racial discrimination, xenophobia and related intolerance;

17. *Calls upon* all States to review and, where necessary, revise their immigration policies with a view to eliminating all discriminatory policies and practices against migrants that are inconsistent with relevant international human rights instruments;

18. *Condemns* the misuse of print, audio-visual and electronic media and new communication technologies, including the Internet, to incite violence motivated by racial hatred;

19. *Recognizes* that Governments should implement and enforce appropriate and effective legislation to prevent acts of racism, racial discrimination, xenophobia and related intolerance, thereby contributing to the prevention of human rights violations;

20. *Calls upon* all Governments and intergovernmental organizations, with the assistance of non-governmental organizations, as appropriate, to continue to supply relevant information to the Special Rapporteur to enable him to fulfil his mandate;

21. *Commends* non-governmental organizations for the action that they have taken against racism and racial discrimination and for the continuous support and assistance that they have provided to the victims of racism and racial discrimination;

22. *Urges* all Governments to cooperate fully with the Special Rapporteur with a view to enabling him to fulfil his mandate, including the examination of incidents of contemporary forms of racism and racial discrimination, inter alia, against blacks, Arabs and Muslims, xenophobia, Negrophobia, anti-Semitism and related intolerance;

23. *Requests* the Secretary-General to provide the Special Rapporteur with all of the necessary human and financial assistance to carry out his mandate efficiently, effectively and expeditiously and to enable him to submit an interim report to the General Assembly at its fifty-sixth session.

Migrant workers

Reports of Special Rapporteur. The Special Rapporteur on the human rights of migrants, Gabriela Rodríguez Pizarro (Costa Rica), in her first report submitted in January [E/CN.4/2000/82], described her activities, outlined her plan of action for the three years of her mandate, considered the relevant legal framework of international instruments, and made observations on migrants needing protection and the obstacles to achieving full protection.

In her conclusions, the Special Rapporteur stated that the first challenge was to define a concept of migrant populations that would cover new situations and to translate that into definitions in the international instruments. The situations referred to were those in which a large number of persons found themselves after leaving their country of origin or even before they did so. Consideration of the limitations of international legislation was also necessary. The Special Rapporteur expressed deep concern over the problems faced by migrants, especially women migrants who had suffered from systematic gender-based violence (see p. 711) and who had been unable to receive a satisfactory response from the relevant authorities. Among her recommendations were the establishment of an interagency task force to assist her; the promotion of intersectoral cooperation; the promotion of existing standards and institutional arrangements to protect migrants; ratification of the International Convention on the Protection of the Rights of All Migrant Workers and Members of Their Families (see p. 621); government action to prevent trafficking in persons; and action to strengthen technical advisory services and training in international human rights instruments for civil servants and migration officials.

The Special Rapporteur visited Canada from 17 to 30 September at the invitation of the Government [E/CN.4/2001/83/Add.1]. She focused on the organization of migration in Canada, government measures to guarantee migrants' human rights, methods used to control so-called illegal migration, the reliability of investigations carried out by the authorities into the incidents considered, and measures adopted to prosecute persons responsible for the violation of the human rights of migrants.

The Special Rapporteur concluded that the greatest problem for Canada regarding immigration, in view of its regulated immigration system, was how to respond to people who arrived in Canada spontaneously. She appreciated Canada's good practices aimed at integrating migrants. Regarding detention centres, the Special Rapporteur had cases brought to her attention by migrants who had been detained for a long period. Although hygiene conditions in the centres were generally satisfactory, the Special Rapporteur was concerned at the treatment of detainees by security guards. The drafting of codes of conduct to regulate the centres was a positive development. A further concern was the lack of contact between detainees awaiting a decision on their case and their consular authorities. While noting a number of shortcomings in the realization of the rights of temporary agricultural workers, the Special Rapporteur asked that the Government take steps to prevent employer abuse. The Special Rapporteur made recommendations to the Government, civil society and migrants.

In response, Canada stated that guidelines for immigration detention stipulated that detention of asylum-seekers was an exceptional step and outlined cases when detention was applicable [E/CN.4/2001/141]. Under its new Immigration and Refugee Protection Act, the detention process would become more effective and transparent, and provide for a streamlined and more effective refugee determination process.

Report of Secretary-General. In response to General Assembly resolution 54/166 [YUN 1999, p. 613], the Secretary-General, in an August report with later addendum [A/55/275 & Add.1], summarized action taken by Governments to protect migrants' rights. On 4 December, the Assembly took note of the report (**decision 55/420**).

Commission action. On 25 April [res. 2000/48], the Commission asked the Special Rapporteur to request, receive and exchange information on violations of migrants' human rights from Governments, treaty bodies, UN bodies, specialized agencies, special rapporteurs, intergovernmental organizations and NGOs and to respond to such information. She was also asked to include in her work schedule a programme of visits for the next two years, to take into account bilateral and regional negotiations aimed at addressing the return and reinsertion of non-documented migrants or those in an irregular situation, and to report in 2001. The Secretary-General was asked to assist her. In accordance with the Commission's resolution, the Economic and Social Council, on 28 July, recommended that the General Assembly consider proclaiming 18 December as International Migrants Day. (**decision 2000/ 288**). (For General Assembly action, see p. 654.)

Subcommission action. On 11 August [res. 2000/2], the Subcommission asked the Preparatory Committee for the World Conference against Racism, Racial Discrimination, Xenophobia and Related Intolerance (see p. 641) to include a separate item on migrant workers in the Conference agenda. The Conference was requested to recommend to the Assembly that it proclaim 18 December of each year an international day of solidarity with migrant workers, and to propose ways of ending racist campaigns encouraging violence against migrant workers through the Internet, sections of the media and political activities.

GENERAL ASSEMBLY ACTION

On 4 December [meeting 81], the General Assembly, on the recommendation of the Third Committee [A/55/602/Add.2 & Corr.1], adopted **resolution 55/92** by recorded vote (165-0-8) [agenda item 114 (b)].

Protection of migrants

The General Assembly,

Recalling its resolution 54/166 of 17 December 1999,

Considering that the Universal Declaration of Human Rights proclaims that all human beings are born free and equal in dignity and rights and that everyone is entitled to all the rights and freedoms set out therein, without distinction of any kind, in particular as to race, colour or national origin,

Reaffirming the provisions concerning migrants adopted by the World Conference on Human Rights, the International Conference on Population and Development, the World Summit for Social Development and the Fourth World Conference on Women,

Bearing in mind the report of the Special Rapporteur of the Commission on Human Rights on the human rights of migrants,

Taking note of Commission on Human Rights resolution 2000/48 of 25 April 2000, on the human rights of migrants,

Recalling its resolution 40/144 of 13 December 1985, by which it approved the Declaration on the Human Rights of Individuals Who are not Nationals of the Country in which They Live,

Recognizing the positive contributions that migrants frequently make, including through their eventual integration into their host society,

Bearing in mind the situation of vulnerability in which migrants frequently find themselves, owing, inter alia, to their absence from their States of origin and to the difficulties they encounter because of differences of language, custom and culture, as well as the economic and social difficulties and obstacles for the return to their States of origin of migrants who are non-documented or in an irregular situation,

Bearing in mind also the need for a focused and consistent approach towards migrants as a specific vulnerable group, in particular migrant women and children,

Deeply concerned at the manifestations of violence, racism, xenophobia and other forms of discrimination and inhuman and degrading treatment against migrants, especially women and children, in different parts of the world,

Underlining the importance of the creation of conditions that foster greater harmony between migrant workers and the rest of the society of the States in which they reside, with the aim of eliminating the growing manifestations of racism and xenophobia perpetrated in segments of many societies by individuals or groups against migrants,

Encouraged by the increasing interest of the international community in the effective and full protection of the human rights of all migrants, and underlining the need to make further efforts to ensure respect for the human rights and fundamental freedoms of all migrants,

Taking note with appreciation of the recommendations on strengthening the promotion, protection and implementation of the human rights of migrants of the working group of intergovernmental experts on the human rights of migrants established by the Commission on Human Rights,

Noting the efforts made by States to penalize the international trafficking of migrants and to protect the victims of this illegal activity,

Taking note of the decisions of the relevant international juridical bodies on questions relating to migrants, in particular advisory opinion OC-16/99, issued by the Inter-American Court of Human Rights on 1 October 1999, regarding the right to information about consular assistance within the framework of due process guarantees,

1. *Welcomes* the renewed commitment made in the United Nations Millennium Declaration to take measures to ensure respect for and protection of human rights of migrants, migrant workers and their families, to eliminate the increasing acts of racism and xenophobia in many societies and to promote greater harmony and tolerance in all societies;

2. *Requests* all Member States, in conformity with their respective constitutional systems, effectively to promote and protect the human rights of all migrants, in conformity with the Universal Declaration of Human Rights and the international instruments to which they are party, which may include the International Covenants on Human Rights, the Convention against Torture and Other Cruel, Inhuman or Degrading Treatment or Punishment, the International Convention on the Elimination of All Forms of Racial Discrimination, the International Convention on the Protection of the Rights of All Migrant Workers and Members of Their Families, the Convention on the Elimination of All Forms of Discrimination against Women, the Convention on the Rights of the Child and other applicable international human rights instruments;

3. *Strongly condemns* all forms of racial discrimination and xenophobia with regard to access to employment, vocational training, housing, schooling, health services and social services, as well as services intended for use by the public, and welcomes the active role played by governmental and non-governmental organizations in combating racism and assisting individual victims of racist acts, including migrant victims;

4. *Calls upon* all States to review and, where necessary, revise immigration policies with a view to eliminating all discriminatory policies and practices against migrants and to provide specialized training for government policy-making and law enforcement, immigration and other concerned officials, thus underlining the importance of effective action to create conditions that foster greater harmony and tolerance within societies;

5. *Reiterates* the need for all States to protect fully the universally recognized human rights of migrants, especially women and children, regardless of their legal status, and to provide humane treatment, in particular with regard to assistance and protection, including those under the Vienna Convention on Consular Relations, regarding the right to receive consular assistance from the country of origin;

6. *Reaffirms* the responsibility of Governments to safeguard and protect the rights of migrants against illegal or violent acts, in particular acts of racial discrimination and crimes perpetrated with racist or xenophobic motivation by individuals or groups, and urges them to reinforce measures in this regard;

7. *Urges* all States to adopt effective measures to put an end to the arbitrary arrest and detention of migrants, including by individuals or groups;

8. *Requests* all Governments to cooperate fully with the Special Rapporteur of the Commission on Human Rights on the human rights of migrants in the performance of her mandated tasks and duties and to furnish all information requested, including by reacting promptly to her urgent appeals;

9. *Encourages* Member States that have not yet done so to enact domestic criminal legislation to combat international trafficking of migrants, which should take into account, in particular, trafficking that endangers the lives of migrants or includes different forms of servitude or exploitation, such as any form of debt bondage, sexual or labour exploitation, and to strengthen international cooperation to combat such trafficking;

10. *Welcomes* the recommendations of the Special Rapporteur that close links be established between her work and that of the Preparatory Committee for the World Conference against Racism, Racial Discrimination, Xenophobia and Related Intolerance, within the framework of the objectives of the Conference, and encourages her to assist in the identification of the main issues that the Conference should address;

11. *Calls upon* all States to protect the human rights of migrant children, in particular unaccompanied migrant children, ensuring that the best interests of the children are the paramount consideration, and encourages the relevant United Nations bodies, within the framework of their respective mandates, to pay special attention to the conditions of migrant children in all States and, where necessary, to put forward recommendations for strengthening their protection;

12. *Requests* the Secretary-General to submit to the General Assembly at its fifty-sixth session a report on the implementation of the present resolution under the sub-item entitled "Human rights questions, including alternative approaches for improving the effective enjoyment of human rights and fundamental freedoms".

RECORDED VOTE ON RESOLUTION 55/92:

In favour: Afghanistan, Albania, Algeria, Andorra, Angola, Antigua and Barbuda, Argentina, Armenia, Australia, Austria, Azerbaijan, Bahamas, Bangladesh, Barbados, Belarus, Belgium, Belize, Benin, Bhutan, Bolivia, Bosnia and Herzegovina, Botswana, Brazil, Brunei Darussalam, Bulgaria, Burkina Faso, Burundi, Cambodia, Cameroon, Canada, Cape Verde, Chad, Chile, China, Colombia, Comoros, Congo, Costa Rica, Côte d'Ivoire, Croatia, Cuba, Cyprus, Czech Republic, Democratic Republic of the Congo, Denmark, Djibouti, Dominica, Dominican Republic, Ecuador, Egypt, El Salvador, Eritrea, Estonia, Ethiopia, Fiji, Finland, France, Gabon, Gambia, Georgia, Germany, Ghana, Greece, Grenada, Guatemala, Guinea, Guyana, Haiti, Honduras, Hungary, Iceland, Indonesia, Iran, Ireland, Italy, Jamaica, Japan, Jordan, Kazakhstan, Kenya, Kuwait, Kyrgyzstan, Lao People's Democratic Republic, Latvia, Lebanon, Lesotho, Libyan Arab Jamahiriya, Liechtenstein, Lithuania, Luxembourg, Madagascar, Malawi, Maldives, Mali, Malta, Marshall Islands, Mauritania, Mauritius, Mexico, Monaco, Mongolia, Morocco, Mozambique, Namibia, Nauru, Nepal, Netherlands, New Zealand, Nicaragua, Nigeria, Norway, Oman, Panama, Papua New Guinea, Paraguay, Peru, Philippines, Poland, Portugal, Qatar, Republic of Korea, Republic of Moldova, Romania, Russian Federation, Rwanda, Saint Kitts and Nevis, Saint Lucia, Saint Vincent and the Grenadines, Samoa, San Marino, Sao Tome and Principe, Saudi Arabia, Senegal, Sierra Leone, Slovakia, Slovenia, Solomon Islands, South Africa, Spain, Sri Lanka, Sudan, Suriname, Swaziland, Sweden, Syrian Arab Republic, Tajikistan, Thailand, The former Yugoslav Republic of Macedonia, Togo, Trinidad and Tobago, Tunisia, Turkey, Uganda, Ukraine, United Arab Emirates, United Kingdom, United Republic of Tanzania, Uruguay, Vanuatu, Venezuela, Viet Nam, Yemen, Yugoslavia, Zambia, Zimbabwe.

Against: None.

Abstaining: India, Israel, Malaysia, Micronesia, Myanmar, Palau, Singapore, United States.

Also on 4 December [meeting 81], the Assembly, on the recommendation of the Third Committee [A/55/602/Add.2 & Corr.1], adopted **resolution 55/93** without vote [agenda item 114 *(b)*].

Proclamation of 18 December as International Migrants Day

The General Assembly,

Taking note of Economic and Social Council decision 2000/288 of 28 July 2000,

Considering that the Universal Declaration of Human Rights proclaims that all human beings are born free and equal in dignity and rights and that everyone is entitled to all the rights and freedoms set forth therein, without distinction of any kind, in particular as to race, colour or national origin,

Taking into account the large and increasing number of migrants in the world,

Encouraged by the increasing interest of the international community in the effective and full protection of the human rights of all migrants, and underlining the need to make further efforts to ensure respect for the human rights and fundamental freedoms of all migrants,

1. *Decides* to proclaim 18 December International Migrants Day;

2. *Invites* Member States, as well as intergovernmental and non-governmental organizations, to observe International Migrants Day, through, inter alia, the dissemination of information on the human rights and fundamental freedoms of migrants, the sharing of experience and the design of actions to ensure their protection;

3. *Requests* the Secretary-General to bring the present resolution to the attention of all Governments and appropriate intergovernmental and non-governmental organizations.

On the same date [meeting 81], the Assembly, also on the recommendation of the Third Committee [A/55/602/Add.2 & Corr.1], adopted **resolution 55/100** by recorded vote (106-1-67) [agenda item 114 *(b)*].

Respect for the right to universal freedom of travel and the vital importance of family reunification

The General Assembly,

Reaffirming that all human rights and fundamental freedoms are universal, indivisible, interdependent and interrelated,

Recalling the provisions of the Universal Declaration of Human Rights, as well as article 12 of the International Covenant on Civil and Political Rights,

Stressing that, as stated in the Programme of Action of the International Conference on Population and Development, family reunification of documented migrants is an important factor in international migration and that remittances by documented migrants to their countries of origin often constitute a very important source of foreign exchange and are instrumental in improving the well-being of relatives left behind,

Recalling its resolution 54/169 of 17 December 1999,

1. *Once again calls upon* all States to guarantee the universally recognized freedom of travel to all foreign nationals legally residing in their territory;

2. *Reaffirms* that all Governments, in particular those of receiving countries, must recognize the vital importance of family reunification and promote its incorporation into national legislation in order to ensure protection of the unity of families of documented migrants;

3. *Calls upon* all States to allow, in conformity with international legislation, the free flow of financial remittances by foreign nationals residing in their territory to their relatives in the country of origin;

4. *Also calls upon* all States to refrain from enacting, and to repeal if it already exists, legislation intended as a coercive measure that discriminates against individuals or groups of legal migrants by adversely affecting family reunification and the right to send financial remittance to relatives in the country of origin;

5. *Decides* to continue its consideration of this question at its fifty-seventh session under the item entitled "Human rights questions".

RECORDED VOTE ON RESOLUTION 55/100:

In favour: Afghanistan, Algeria, Angola, Antigua and Barbuda, Argentina, Armenia, Bahamas, Bangladesh, Barbados, Belarus, Belize, Benin, Bhutan, Bolivia, Botswana, Brazil, Burkina Faso, Burundi, Cambodia, Cameroon, Cape Verde, Chad, Chile, China, Comoros, Congo, Côte d'Ivoire, Cuba, Democratic People's Republic of Korea, Democratic Republic of the Congo, Dominica, Dominican Republic, Ecuador, Egypt, El Salvador, Eritrea, Ethiopia, Gabon, Gambia, Ghana, Grenada, Guatemala, Guinea, Guyana, Haiti, Honduras, India, Indonesia, Iran, Jamaica, Jordan, Kuwait, Lao People's Democratic Republic, Lebanon, Lesotho, Libyan Arab Jamahiriya, Madagascar, Malawi, Mali, Mauritania, Mauritius, Mexico, Morocco, Mozambique, Myanmar, Namibia, Nepal, Nicaragua, Nigeria, Oman, Pakistan, Panama, Papua New Guinea, Paraguay, Peru, Philippines, Qatar, Russian Federation, Rwanda, Saint Kitts and Nevis, Saint Lucia, Saint Vincent and the Grenadines, Sao Tome and Principe, Saudi Arabia, Senegal, Sierra Leone, Solomon Islands, Sri Lanka, Sudan, Suriname, Swaziland, Syrian Arab Republic, Togo, Trinidad and Tobago, Tunisia, Turkey, Uganda, United Arab Emirates, United Republic of Tanzania, Uruguay, Vanuatu, Venezuela, Viet Nam, Yemen, Zambia, Zimbabwe.

Against: United States.

Abstaining: Albania, Andorra, Australia, Austria, Azerbaijan, Bahrain, Belgium, Brunei Darussalam, Bulgaria, Canada, Colombia, Costa Rica, Croatia, Cyprus, Czech Republic, Denmark, Djibouti, Estonia, Fiji, Finland, France, Georgia, Germany, Greece, Hungary, Iceland, Ireland, Israel, Italy, Japan, Kazakhstan, Kenya, Kyrgyzstan, Latvia, Liechtenstein, Lithuania, Luxembourg, Malaysia, Maldives, Malta, Marshall Islands, Micronesia, Monaco, Mongolia, Nauru, Netherlands, New Zealand, Norway, Palau, Poland, Portugal, Republic of Korea, Republic of Moldova, Romania, Samoa, San Marino, Singapore, Slovakia, Slovenia, South Africa, Spain, Sweden, Thailand, The former Yugoslav Republic of Macedonia, Ukraine, United Kingdom, Uzbekistan.

Other forms of intolerance

Cultural prejudice

In response to General Assembly resolution 54/160 [YUN 1999, p. 615], the Secretary-General, in an August report with later addendum [A/55/296 & Add.1], summarized the views expressed by Governments, UN agencies and NGOs on human rights and cultural diversity. He concluded that the submissions highlighted the increasing need to emphasize the common core values shared by all cultures.

GENERAL ASSEMBLY ACTION

On 4 December [meeting 81], the General Assembly, on the recommendation of the Third Committee [A/55/602/Add.2 & Corr.1], adopted **resolution 55/91** without vote [agenda item 114 *(b)*].

Human rights and cultural diversity

The General Assembly,

Recalling the Universal Declaration of Human Rights and the International Covenant on Economic, Social and Cultural Rights, as well as other pertinent human rights instruments,

Noting that numerous instruments within the United Nations system promote cultural diversity, as well as the conservation and development of culture, in particular the Declaration of the Principles of International Culture Cooperation, proclaimed on 4 November 1966 by the General Conference of the United Nations Educational, Scientific and Cultural Organization at its fourteenth session,

Taking note of the report of the Secretary-General on human rights and cultural diversity,

Welcoming the proclamation of 2001 as the United Nations Year of Dialogue among Civilizations, in accordance with General Assembly resolution 53/22 of 4 November 1998,

Reaffirming that all human rights are universal, indivisible, interdependent and interrelated and that the international community must treat human rights globally in a fair and equal manner, on the same footing and with the same emphasis, and that, while the significance of national and regional particularities and various historical, cultural and religious backgrounds must be borne in mind, it is the duty of States, regardless of their political, economic and cultural systems, to promote and protect all human rights and fundamental freedoms,

Recognizing that cultural diversity and the pursuit of cultural development by all peoples and nations are a source of mutual enrichment for the cultural life of humankind,

Taking into account that a culture of peace actively fosters non-violence and respect for human rights and strengthens solidarity among peoples and nations and dialogue between cultures,

Recognizing that all cultures and civilizations share a common set of universal values,

Considering that tolerance of cultural, ethnic and religious diversities, as well as dialogue among and within civilizations, is essential for peace, understanding and friendship among individuals and people of different cultures and nations of the world, while manifestations of cultural prejudice, intolerance and xenophobia towards different cultures and religions generate hatred and violence among peoples and nations throughout the world,

Recognizing in each culture a dignity and value which deserves recognition, respect and preservation, and convinced that, in their rich variety and diversity, and in the reciprocal influences that they exert on one another, all cultures form part of the common heritage belonging to all humankind,

Convinced that the promotion of cultural pluralism and tolerance towards and dialogue among various cultures and civilizations would contribute to the efforts of all peoples and nations to enrich their cultures and traditions by engaging in a mutually beneficial exchange of knowledge and intellectual, moral and material achievements,

1. *Affirms* the importance for all peoples and nations to hold, develop and preserve their cultural heritage and traditions in a national and international atmosphere of peace, tolerance and mutual respect;

2. *Recognizes* the right of everyone to take part in cultural life and to enjoy the benefits of scientific progress and its applications;

3. *Affirms* that the international community should strive to respond to the challenges and opportunities posed by globalization in a manner that ensures respect for the cultural diversity of all;

4. *Also affirms* that inter-cultural dialogue essentially enriches the common understanding of human rights and that the benefits to be derived from the encouragement and development of international contacts and cooperation in the cultural fields are important;

5. *Recognizes* that respect for cultural diversity and the cultural rights of all enhances cultural pluralism, contributing to a wider exchange of knowledge and understanding of cultural background, advancing the application and enjoyment of universally accepted human rights throughout the world and fostering stable friendly relations among peoples and nations worldwide;

6. *Emphasizes* that the promotion of cultural pluralism and tolerance at the national and international levels is important for enhancing respect for cultural rights and cultural diversity;

7. *Also emphasizes* the fact that tolerance and respect for diversity facilitate the universal promotion and protection of human rights, including gender equality and the enjoyment of all human rights by all;

8. *Calls upon* States, international organizations and United Nations agencies, and invites civil society, including non-governmental organizations, to recognize and promote respect for cultural diversity for the purpose of advancing the objectives of peace, development and universally accepted human rights;

9. *Requests* the Secretary-General, in the light of the present resolution, to prepare a report on human rights and cultural diversity, taking into account the views of Member States, relevant United Nations agencies and non-governmental organizations, as well as the considerations in the present resolution regarding the recognition and importance of cultural diversity among all peoples and nations in the world, and to submit it to the General Assembly at its fifty-sixth session;

10. *Decides* to continue consideration of this question at its fifty-sixth session under the sub-item entitled "Human rights questions, including alternative approaches for improving the effective enjoyment of human rights and fundamental freedoms".

Discrimination against minorities

Commission action. On 25 April [res. 2000/52], the Commission urged States and the international community to promote and protect the rights of persons belonging to national or ethnic, religious and linguistic minorities, as set out in the 1992 Declaration on the Rights of Persons Belonging to National or Ethnic, Religious and Linguistic Minorities, adopted by the General Assembly in resolution 47/135 [YUN 1992, p. 722]. The Secretary-General was called on to make available, at the request of Governments, qualified expertise on minority issues. The High Commissioner was called on to promote the Declaration's implementation; to improve the cooperation of UN programmes and agencies dealing with minority issues; and to seek contributions to facilitate minority groups' participation in the Working Group on Minorities. OHCHR was requested to organize a seminar for international and regional organizations, treaty bodies and specialized agencies to discuss their work on the protection of minorities, improve coordination and seek ways of better protecting the rights of minorities. The Secretary-General was asked to report in 2001.

Working Group activities. The five-member Working Group on Minorities, at its sixth session (Geneva, 22-26 May) [E/CN.4/Sub.2/2000/27 & Corr.1], reviewed the promotion of the 1992 Declaration, examined possible solutions to problems involving minorities, including the promotion of mutual understanding between and among minorities and Governments, and recommended further measures to promote and protect the rights of minorities. Members also discussed the Group's future role.

The Working Group requested its Chairperson/Rapporteur to finalize the commentary on the Declaration and to ensure its publication in a future UN manual on minorities. The Group recommended holding a seminar in the Asia and Pacific region, one in the Americas focusing on the situation of Afro-Americans and another in Africa as a follow-up to the Group's seminar on multiculturalism in Africa: peaceful and other constructive arrangements between States and indigenous populations (Arusha, United Republic of Tanzania, 13-15 May). Other proposals included a voluntary fund for minority issues and further work on databases on minority protection. The Group called on the High Commissioner to organize a seminar for global and regional organizations, treaty bodies and specialized agencies to discuss their work on the protection of minorities, improve coordination and seek ways of better protecting the rights of persons belonging to minorities. On 28 July, the Economic and Social Council approved that request (**decision 2000/269**).

Subcommission action. On 17 August [res. 2000/16], the Subcommission recommended that the Commission ask Governments, intergovernmental organizations and NGOs to submit their views on the desirability of drafting a convention on the rights of persons belonging to minorities and on its content. It also recommended strengthening OHCHR to enable it to provide adequate services to the Working Group and to undertake relevant studies, evaluation and action. The Secretary-General was asked to invite UN bodies and regional organizations to provide information to the Working Group on their activities regarding minority protection.

Minorities and indigenous peoples

As requested by the Subcommission in 1999 [YUN 1999, p. 616], Erica-Irene Daes (Greece) and Asbjørn Eide (Norway) prepared, in July [E/CN.4/Sub.2/2000/10], a working paper on the relationship and distinction between the rights of persons belonging to minorities and those of indigenous peoples, for submission to the Working Group on Minorities, the Working Group on Indigenous Populations (see p. 726) and the Subcommission. Mr. Eide concluded that persons belonging to minorities often had several identities and participated actively in the common domain, while it was assumed that indigenous peoples participated less in the common domain. Indigenous rights tended to strengthen the separateness of a group from others in society. In the opinion of Ms. Daes, the main distinction in contemporary international law was with respect to internal self-determination: the right of a group to govern itself within recognized geographical areas, without State interference.

Roma

In response to a 1999 Subcommission request [YUN 1999, p. 616], Yeung Kam Yeung Sik Yuen (Mauritius) submitted, in June [E/CN.4/Sub.2/2000/28], a working paper on the human rights problems and protection of the Roma. Given the magnitude and complexity of Roma human rights problems, he found a need to initiate a study to identify why their problems were recurrent despite the fact that they had been living for several generations within the same countries, and to make recommendations to help solve their human rights problems.

Subcommission action. On 17 August [dec. 2000/109], the Subcommission endorsed the conclusions made in the working paper and proposed a draft text to the Commission recommending that the Economic and Social Council appoint Mr. Yeung Sik Yuen as Special Rapporteur to prepare the study.

Discrimination based on work and descent

On 11 August [res. 2000/4], the Subcommission decided to entrust Rajendra Kalidas Wimala Goonesekere (Sri Lanka) with preparing a working paper on discrimination based on work and descent, without financial implications, to identify communities in which such discrimination was experienced, to examine constitutional, legislative and administrative measures to abolish it, and to make recommendations on eliminating the discrimination.

Affirmative action

Report of Special Rapporteur. In accordance with a 1998 Subcommission resolution [YUN 1998, p. 652], the Special Rapporteur on the concept and practice of affirmative action, Marc Bossuyt (Belgium), reported in June [E/CN.4/Sub.2/2000/11 & Corr.1] that OHCHR had sent a questionnaire to Governments, international organizations and NGOs, inviting them to provide relevant national documentation on affirmative action. The Special Rapporteur described the concept of affirmative action in international law and the limits international law set on affirmative action measures.

Subcommission action. On 11 August [dec. 2000/104], the Subcommission asked the Secretary-General to remind Governments, international organizations and NGOs to respond to the questionnaire.

Right to nationality

In a January report with later addenda [E/CN.4/2000/56 & Add.1,2], the Secretary-General presented information received from six Governments on measures they had taken to prevent the arbitrary deprivation of nationality, as requested by the Commission in 1999 [YUN 1999, p. 611].

Rights of non-citizens

Commission action. On 25 April [dec. 2000/104], the Commission asked the Economic and Social Council to authorize the Subcommission to appoint a special rapporteur to prepare a study of the rights of non-citizens, based on a working paper by David Weissbrodt (United States) [YUN 1999, p. 611], as well as on comments made at the Subcommission's 1999 session, and to submit a preliminary report in 2001, a progress report in 2002 and a final report in 2003. The Council approved that request on 28 July (**decision 2000/283**).

Subcommission action. On 1 August [dec. 2000/103], the Subcommission appointed Mr. Weissbrodt as Special Rapporteur and asked him to submit reports as directed by the Commission. (See p. 690 for Subcommission action on the rights of non-citizens as asylum-seekers and refugees.)

Religious intolerance

Reports of Special Rapporteur. In a February report [E/CN.4/2000/65], the Special Rapporteur on religious intolerance, Abdelfattah Amor (Tunisia), summarized 93 communications, including two urgent appeals, sent by him to 55 States, as well as 23 replies received, regarding incidents and governmental action inconsistent with the provisions of the 1981 Declaration on the Elimination of All Forms of Intolerance and of Discrimination Based on Religion or Belief, contained in General Assembly resolution 36/55 [YUN 1981, p. 881]. In his conclusions, the Special Rapporteur noted the spread of religious extremism that affected most religions, including Islam, Hinduism and Judaism, and a general tendency to perpetuate policies, legislation and practices that affected freedom of religion and belief. Initiatives taken by the Special Rapporteur included efforts to create a compendium of national enactments relating to freedom of religion or belief; research on the status of women with regard to religion, on proselytism, freedom of religion and poverty, and on sects, new religious movements and religious communities; and plans to convene an international conference on school education in relation to freedom of religion and belief, tolerance and non-discrimination as part of the observance of the 1981 Declaration's twentieth anniversary. In a later report [E/CN.4/2001/63], the Special Rapporteur stated that the Preparatory Committee for the conference, at its first meeting (Geneva, 20-22 November), had adopted the first version of the draft final document. The conference was to take place in Madrid from 23 to 25 November 2001.

The Special Rapporteur visited Bangladesh (Dhaka and the Chittagong Hill Tracts in Rangamati) (15-24 May) [A/55/280/Add.2], where he focused on the legal aspects of freedom of religion or belief, on the influence of politics on those freedoms and on the status of women. Regarding the Chittagong Hill Tracts, the issue was the preservation of the identity of the indigenous peoples; that identity was mainly ethnic in nature, but also religious. The Special Rapporteur noted that Muslims, Hindus and Christians, who constituted 88.3, 10.5 and 0.3 per cent of the population, respectively, were distributed across the entire country, whereas Buddhists, constituting 0.6 per cent, lived mainly in the Chittagong Hill Tracts. Estimates indicated that ethnic communities accounted for 50 per cent of the population in that area, due to the large, mostly Muslim, Bengali community.

Following an examination of the legal aspects of freedom of religion or belief, the influence of the political sphere on freedom of religion or belief, the situation regarding religion or belief and the status of women, the Special Rapporteur concluded that constitutional measures guaranteed the freedom, in accordance with relevant international law, and also guaranteed the principle of non-discrimination, especially with respect to religion and gender. However, religious personal laws discriminated against women, and although efforts had been made to ensure equality for all, they had been limited. The Special Rapporteur considered that the State generally respected freedom of religion and belief, but there were problems in terms of the situation of religious and ethnic communities. The State appeared more sensitive to the interests of Muslims. Non-Muslims encountered obstacles in accessing public sector jobs and received weaker financial and educational support. That approach appeared to cause delays in implementing a 1997 peace accord in favour of the ethnic communities of the Chittagong Hill Tracts. The Special Rap-

porteur observed weakness in the State's efforts to combat religious extremism. He recommended protecting religion from political exploitation and that the State combat extremism, including the protection of mosques and madrasahs from extremist indoctrination. He proposed that the State implement a policy of prevention, especially through education, ensure that the media were open to the religious and ethnic pluralism of the country and be more aware of the legitimate claims of minorities and ethnic communities. The Special Rapporteur encouraged initiatives to establish a national commission for human rights and recommended that Bangladesh avail itself of the technical cooperation services of the Commission on Human Rights.

Commission action. On 20 April [res. 2000/33], the Commission condemned all forms of intolerance and discrimination based on religion or belief and urged States to: provide adequate constitutional and legal guarantees of freedom of thought, conscience, religion and belief; ensure that no one, because of religion or belief, was deprived of the right to life, liberty or security of person; combat hatred, intolerance and acts of violence, intimidation and coercion motivated by religious intolerance; recognize the right to worship or assemble in connection with a religion or belief and to establish and maintain places for those purposes; ensure that religious places were respected and protected; ensure that public officials respected different religions and beliefs; and promote tolerance through education and other means. The Commission decided to change the Special Rapporteur's title from Special Rapporteur on religious intolerance to Special Rapporteur on freedom of religion or belief. The Special Rapporteur was asked to submit an interim report to the General Assembly in 2000 (see p. 659) and a report to the Commission in 2001.

The Economic and Social Council, on 28 July (**decision 2000/261**), endorsed the Commission's decision to change the Special Rapporteur's title and approved the submission of the reports.

On 26 April [res. 2000/84], the Commission, expressing concern at negative stereotyping of religions and that Islam was frequently and wrongly associated with human rights violations and terrorism, urged States to combat hatred, discrimination, intolerance, acts of violence, intimidation and coercion motivated by religious intolerance. It called on the Special Rapporteur on religious intolerance and the Special Rapporteur on racism, racial discrimination, xenophobia and related intolerance to take account of the Commission's current resolution when reporting to it.

Interim report of Special Rapporteur. Pursuant to General Assembly resolution 54/159 [YUN 1999, p. 620], the Secretary-General, in September [A/55/280], transmitted the Special Rapporteur's interim report. The report covered 39 communications, including one urgent appeal, sent to 25 States, and contained the summaries of 19 replies. An analysis of the replies indicated an increase in religious extremism, whose primary victims were vulnerable groups, such as women and minorities. Apart from extremism, instances and situations of intolerance and discrimination against women and minorities were cited, and several communications dealt with defamation, which was often misused to censor the right to criticism and discussion of religion. The Special Rapporteur considered it essential that the Assembly, like the Commission, devote the fullest attention to religious extremism. He recommended that State intervention regarding religion or belief be limited to ensuring respect for the law, in conformity with international law. States had an obligation under international law to guarantee the right of minorities to freedom of religion within internationally agreed limits. He emphasized the urgency of preventing discrimination based on religion or belief.

The Special Rapporteur had submitted a contribution to the Preparatory Committee for the World Conference against Racism, Racial Discrimination, Xenophobia and Related Intolerance [A/CONF. 198/PC.1/7].

Communications. On 10 March [E/CN.4/2000/135], the Federal Republic of Yugoslavia (FRY) submitted allegations claiming maltreatment of clergy and destruction of religious buildings of the Serbian Orthodox Church in the Kosovo province of FRY and in Metohija.

On 4 December [A/55/665], the Russian Federation transmitted a statement made by participants in the Interreligious Peacemaking Forum (Moscow, 13-14 November), held under the patronage of the Patriarch of Moscow and All Russia, Alexy II, expressing alarm at manifestations of extremism and terrorism and attempts to justify them by means of religious rhetoric.

GENERAL ASSEMBLY ACTION

On 4 December [meeting 81], the General Assembly, on the recommendation of the Third Committee [A/55/602/Add.2 & Corr.1], adopted **resolution 55/97** without vote [agenda item 114 (b)].

Elimination of all forms of religious intolerance

The General Assembly,

Recalling that all States have pledged themselves, under the Charter of the United Nations, to promote and encourage universal respect for and observance of hu-

man rights and fundamental freedoms for all without distinction as to race, sex, language or religion,

Reaffirming that discrimination against human beings on the grounds of religion or belief constitutes an affront to human dignity and a disavowal of the principles of the Charter,

Recalling article 18 of the Universal Declaration of Human Rights, and article 18 of the International Covenant on Civil and Political Rights,

Reaffirming its resolution 36/55 of 25 November 1981, by which it proclaimed the Declaration on the Elimination of All Forms of Intolerance and of Discrimination Based on Religion or Belief, and the United Nations Millennium Declaration, in particular paragraph 4 thereof,

Emphasizing that the right to freedom of thought, conscience, religion and belief is far-reaching and profound and that it encompasses freedom of thought on all matters, personal conviction and the commitment to religion or belief, whether manifested individually or in community with others, and in public or private,

Reaffirming the call of the World Conference on Human Rights, held at Vienna from 14 to 25 June 1993, for all Governments to take all appropriate measures in compliance with their international obligations and with due regard to their respective legal systems to counter intolerance and related violence based on religion or belief, including practices of discrimination against women and the desecration of religious sites, recognizing that every individual has the right to freedom of thought, conscience, expression and religion,

Calling upon all Governments to cooperate with the Special Rapporteur of the Commission on Human Rights on religious intolerance to enable him to carry out his mandate fully,

Alarmed that serious instances of intolerance and discrimination on the grounds of religion or belief, including acts of violence, intimidation and coercion motivated by religious intolerance, occur in many parts of the world and threaten the enjoyment of human rights and fundamental freedoms,

Deeply concerned that, as reported by the Special Rapporteur, the rights violated on religious grounds include the right to life, the right to physical integrity and to liberty and security of person, the right to freedom of expression, the right not to be subjected to torture or other cruel, inhuman or degrading treatment or punishment and the right not to be arbitrarily arrested or detained,

Believing that further efforts are therefore required to promote and protect the right to freedom of thought, conscience, religion and belief and to eliminate all forms of hatred, intolerance and discrimination based on religion or belief,

1. *Reaffirms* that freedom of thought, conscience, religion and belief is a human right derived from the inherent dignity of the human person and guaranteed to all without discrimination;

2. *Urges* States to ensure that their constitutional and legal systems provide effective guarantees of freedom of thought, conscience, religion and belief, including the provision of effective remedies in cases in which the right to freedom of religion or belief is violated;

3. *Also urges* States to ensure, in particular, that no one within their jurisdiction is, because of his or her

religion or belief, deprived of the right to life or the right to liberty and security of person, or subjected to torture or arbitrary arrest or detention;

4. *Further urges* States, in conformity with international standards of human rights, to take all necessary action to prevent such instances, to take all appropriate measures to combat hatred, intolerance and acts of violence, intimidation and coercion motivated by religious intolerance and to encourage, through the educational system and by other means, understanding, tolerance and respect in matters relating to freedom of religion or belief;

5. *Emphasizes* that, as underlined by the Human Rights Committee, restrictions on the freedom to manifest religion or belief are permitted only if those limitations that are prescribed by law are necessary to protect public safety, order, health or morals, or the fundamental rights and freedoms of others, and are applied in a manner that does not vitiate the right to freedom of thought, conscience and religion;

6. *Urges* States to ensure that, in the course of their official duties, members of law enforcement bodies, civil servants, educators and other public officials respect different religions and beliefs and do not discriminate against persons professing other religions or beliefs;

7. *Calls upon* all States to recognize, as provided for in the Declaration on the Elimination of All Forms of Intolerance and of Discrimination Based on Religion or Belief, the right of all persons to worship or assemble in connection with a religion or belief and to establish and maintain places for those purposes;

8. *Expresses its grave concern* at any attack upon religious places, sites and shrines, and calls upon all States, in accordance with their national legislation and in conformity with international human rights standards, to exert their utmost efforts to ensure that such places, sites and shrines are fully respected and protected;

9. *Recognizes* that legislation alone is not enough to prevent violations of human rights, including the right to freedom of religion or belief, and that the exercise of tolerance and non-discrimination by persons and groups is necessary for the full realization of the aims of the Declaration;

10. *Takes note with appreciation* of the interim report of the Special Rapporteur of the Commission on Human Rights on religious intolerance, and encourages continued efforts on the part of the Special Rapporteur, who was appointed to examine incidents and governmental actions in all parts of the world that are incompatible with the provisions of the Declaration and to recommend remedial measures, as appropriate;

11. *Welcomes* the decision of the Commission on Human Rights in resolution 2000/33 of 20 April 2000 to change the title of the Special Rapporteur from Special Rapporteur on religious intolerance to Special Rapporteur on freedom of religion or belief;

12. *Takes note* of the study presented by the Special Rapporteur to the Preparatory Committee for the World Conference against Racism, Racial Discrimination, Xenophobia and Related Intolerance at its first session, and encourages the Special Rapporteur to continue to contribute to the preparations for the Conference, which is to be held at Durban, South Africa, in 2001, on matters relating to religious intolerance that have a bearing on the World Conference;

13. *Encourages* Governments to give serious consideration to inviting the Special Rapporteur to visit their countries so as to enable him to fulfil his mandate even more effectively;

14. *Welcomes* the initiatives of Governments and non-governmental organizations to collaborate with the Special Rapporteur, including by the convening of an international consultative conference on school education in relation to freedom of religion and belief, tolerance and non-discrimination, to be held at Madrid in November 2001, and encourages Governments, non-governmental organizations and other interested parties to participate actively in that conference;

15. *Encourages* Governments, when seeking the assistance of the United Nations Programme of Advisory Services and Technical Assistance in the Field of Human Rights, to consider, where appropriate, including requests for assistance for the promotion and protection of the right to freedom of thought, conscience and religion;

16. *Welcomes and encourages* the continuing efforts of non-governmental organizations and religious bodies and groups to promote the implementation and dissemination of the Declaration, and encourages their work in promoting freedom of religion or belief and in highlighting cases of religious intolerance, discrimination and persecution;

17. *Requests* the Commission on Human Rights to continue its consideration of measures for the implementation of the Declaration;

18. *Requests* the Special Rapporteur to submit an interim report to the General Assembly at its fifty-sixth session;

19. *Requests* the Secretary-General to ensure that the Special Rapporteur receives the resources necessary to enable him to discharge his mandate fully;

20. *Decides* to consider the question of the elimination of all forms of religious intolerance at its fifty-sixth session under the item entitled "Human rights questions".

Follow-up to UN Year for Tolerance

Report of UNESCO Director-General. In response to General Assembly resolution 53/151 [YUN 1998, p. 653], the Secretary-General, in August [A/55/338], transmitted a report of the Director-General of the United Nations Educational, Scientific and Cultural Organization (UNESCO) on the implementation of the Declaration of Principles on Tolerance and the Follow-up Plan of Action for the United Nations Year for Tolerance (1998-2000), adopted by UNESCO and observed in 1995 [YUN 1995, p. 1126]. The Director-General described activities carried out by UNESCO in the areas of awareness-raising and mobilization, and research, policies and standard-setting, in order to implement the Plan of Action, which aimed to educate, inform and empower individuals to assume the responsibilities of dialogue, mutual respect, toleration and non-violence, and to encourage pluralism and tolerance in the policies of Member States. He also described activities to observe the third (1998) and fourth (1999) International Day for Tolerance, as well as meetings and discussions held in 1999 and 2000 on the issue.

Commission action. On 25 April [res. 2000/50], the Commission, condemning all violent acts and activities that undermined tolerance and pluralism, called on the High Commissioner: to include in the OHCHR work programme the promotion of tolerance and to assist countries in their national programmes through its advisory services and technical cooperation programme; to undertake educational and public-awareness activities to promote tolerance and pluralism within the activities of the United Nations Decade for Human Rights Education (1995-2004) (see p. 631), the International Decade of the World's Indigenous People (1995-2004) (see p. 727) and the Third Decade to Combat Racism and Racial Discrimination (1993-2002) (see p. 640), and in the context of the 2001 World Conference against Racism, Racial Discrimination, Xenophobia and Related Intolerance (see p. 641) and the preparations for the twentieth anniversary of the Declaration on the Elimination of All Forms of Intolerance and of Discrimination Based on Religion or Belief (see p. 658); and to assist countries, upon request, to put in place safeguards to guarantee the enjoyment of all human rights by all segments of their population. The High Commissioner was called on to report to the Commission in 2002. The Commission's relevant mechanisms were called on to accord priority to promoting democracy, pluralism and tolerance, to study conditions that promoted intolerance and to identify principles and best practices to promote tolerance and pluralism.

Civil and political rights

Right to self-determination

In response to General Assembly resolution 54/155 [YUN 1999, p. 621], the Secretary-General, in July [A/55/176], summarized action taken by the Commission on Human Rights on the right of peoples to self-determination during the period April 1999 to June 2000. In September [A/55/176/Add.1], also in response to resolution 54/155, he summarized the views of three Member States on that right.

On 4 December [meeting 81], the General Assembly, on the recommendation of the Third Committee [A/55/601], adopted **resolution 55/85** without vote [agenda item 113].

Universal realization of the right of peoples to self-determination

The General Assembly,

Reaffirming the importance, for the effective guarantee and observance of human rights, of the universal realization of the right of peoples to self-determination enshrined in the Charter of the United Nations and embodied in the International Covenants on Human Rights, as well as in the Declaration on the Granting of Independence to Colonial Countries and Peoples contained in General Assembly resolution 1514(XV) of 14 December 1960,

Welcoming the progressive exercise of the right to self-determination by peoples under colonial, foreign or alien occupation and their emergence into sovereign statehood and independence,

Deeply concerned at the continuation of acts or threats of foreign military intervention and occupation that are threatening to suppress, or have already suppressed, the right to self-determination of sovereign peoples and nations,

Expressing grave concern that, as a consequence of the persistence of such actions, millions of people have been and are being uprooted from their homes as refugees and displaced persons, and emphasizing the urgent need for concerted international action to alleviate their condition,

Recalling the relevant resolutions regarding the violation of the right of peoples to self-determination and other human rights as a result of foreign military intervention, aggression and occupation adopted by the Commission on Human Rights at its fifty-sixth and previous sessions,

Reaffirming its previous resolutions on the universal realization of the right of peoples to self-determination, including resolution 54/155 of 17 December 1999,

Taking note of the report of the Secretary-General on the right of peoples to self-determination,

1. *Reaffirms* that the universal realization of the right of all peoples, including those under colonial, foreign and alien domination, to self-determination is a fundamental condition for the effective guarantee and observance of human rights and for the preservation and promotion of such rights;

2. *Declares its firm opposition* to acts of foreign military intervention, aggression and occupation, since these have resulted in the suppression of the right of peoples to self-determination and other human rights in certain parts of the world;

3. *Calls upon* those States responsible to cease immediately their military intervention in and occupation of foreign countries and territories and all acts of repression, discrimination, exploitation and maltreatment, in particular the brutal and inhuman methods reportedly employed for the execution of those acts against the peoples concerned;

4. *Deplores* the plight of millions of refugees and displaced persons who have been uprooted as a result

of the aforementioned acts, and reaffirms their right to return to their homes voluntarily in safety and honour;

5. *Requests* the Commission on Human Rights to continue to give special attention to the violation of human rights, especially the right to self-determination, resulting from foreign military intervention, aggression or occupation;

6. *Requests* the Secretary-General to report on this question to the General Assembly at its fifty-sixth session under the item entitled "Right of peoples to self-determination".

Rights of Palestinians

On 7 April [res. 2000/4], the Commission, by a roll-call vote of 44 to 1, with 6 abstentions, reaffirmed the permanent and unqualified Palestinian right to self-determination, including the option of a State. It requested the Secretary-General to transmit its resolution to Israel and all other Governments, to disseminate it as widely as possible, and to make available to the Commission, prior to its 2001 session, information pertaining to its implementation by the Government of Israel.

The Commission had before it a report of the Secretary-General [E/CN.4/2000/13] stating that he had received no reply to his request to Israel for information on the implementation of its 1999 resolution on the situation in occupied Palestine [YUN 1999, p. 622].

GENERAL ASSEMBLY ACTION

On 4 December [meeting 81], the General Assembly, on the recommendation of the Third Committee [A/55/601], adopted **resolution 55/87** by recorded vote (170-2-5) [agenda item 113].

The right of the Palestinian people to self-determination

The General Assembly,

Aware that the development of friendly relations among nations, based on respect for the principle of equal rights and self-determination of peoples, is among the purposes and principles of the United Nations, as defined in the Charter,

Recalling the International Covenants on Human Rights, the Universal Declaration of Human Rights, the Declaration on the Granting of Independence to Colonial Countries and Peoples and the Vienna Declaration and Programme of Action adopted by the World Conference on Human Rights on 25 June 1993,

Recalling also the Declaration on the Occasion of the Fiftieth Anniversary of the United Nations,

Recalling further the United Nations Millennium Declaration,

Expressing hope for an immediate resumption of negotiations within the Middle East peace process on its agreed basis and for the speedy achievement of a final settlement between the Palestinian and Israeli sides,

Affirming the right of all States in the region to live in peace within secure and internationally recognized borders,

1. *Reaffirms* the right of the Palestinian people to self-determination, including their right to a State;

2. *Expresses the hope* that the Palestinian people will soon be exercising their right to self-determination, which is not subject to any veto, in the current peace process;

3. *Urges* all States and the specialized agencies and the organizations of the United Nations system to continue to support and assist the Palestinian people in their quest for self-determination.

RECORDED VOTE ON RESOLUTION 55/87:

In favour: Afghanistan, Albania, Algeria, Andorra, Angola, Antigua and Barbuda, Argentina, Armenia, Australia, Austria, Azerbaijan, Bahamas, Bahrain, Bangladesh, Barbados, Belarus, Belgium, Belize, Benin, Bhutan, Bolivia, Bosnia and Herzegovina, Botswana, Brazil, Brunei Darussalam, Bulgaria, Burkina Faso, Burundi, Cambodia, Cameroon, Cape Verde, Chad, Chile, China, Colombia, Comoros, Congo, Costa Rica, Côte d'Ivoire, Croatia, Cuba, Cyprus, Czech Republic, Democratic People's Republic of Korea, Democratic Republic of the Congo, Denmark, Djibouti, Dominica, Dominican Republic, Ecuador, Egypt, El Salvador, Eritrea, Estonia, Ethiopia, Fiji, Finland, France, Gabon, Gambia, Georgia, Germany, Ghana, Greece, Grenada, Guatemala, Guinea, Guyana, Haiti, Honduras, Hungary, Iceland, India, Indonesia, Iran, Ireland, Italy, Jamaica, Japan, Jordan, Kazakhstan, Kenya, Kuwait, Kyrgyzstan, Lao People's Democratic Republic, Latvia, Lebanon, Lesotho, Libyan Arab Jamahiriya, Liechtenstein, Lithuania, Luxembourg, Malawi, Malaysia, Maldives, Mali, Malta, Mauritania, Mauritius, Mexico, Monaco, Mongolia, Morocco, Mozambique, Myanmar, Namibia, Nauru, Nepal, Netherlands, New Zealand, Nicaragua, Nigeria, Norway, Oman, Pakistan, Panama, Papua New Guinea, Paraguay, Peru, Philippines, Poland, Portugal, Qatar, Republic of Korea, Republic of Moldova, Romania, Russian Federation, Rwanda, Saint Kitts and Nevis, Saint Lucia, Saint Vincent and the Grenadines, Samoa, San Marino, Sao Tome and Principe, Saudi Arabia, Senegal, Sierra Leone, Singapore, Slovakia, Slovenia, Solomon Islands, South Africa, Spain, Sri Lanka, Sudan, Suriname, Swaziland, Sweden, Syrian Arab Republic, Tajikistan, Thailand, The former Yugoslav Republic of Macedonia, Togo, Trinidad and Tobago, Tunisia, Turkey, Uganda, Ukraine, United Arab Emirates, United Kingdom, United Republic of Tanzania, Uruguay, Uzbekistan, Vanuatu, Venezuela, Viet Nam, Yemen, Yugoslavia, Zambia, Zimbabwe.

Against: Israel, United States.

Abstaining: Canada, Marshall Islands, Micronesia, Palau, Tonga.

Western Sahara

On 7 April [res. 2000/2], the Commission, commending the Secretary-General and his Personal Envoy for the agreements on the settlement plan reached between Morocco and the Frente Popular para la Liberación de Saguia el-Hamra y de Río de Oro, called on the two parties to cooperate with them, as well as with the Secretary-General's Special Representative, in implementing the plan. It reaffirmed support for further efforts of the Secretary-General for the organization and supervision by the United Nations, in cooperation with the Organization of African Unity, of a referendum on self-determination of the people of Western Sahara (see p. 220).

Mercenaries

Commission action. On 7 April [res. 2000/3], the Commission, by a roll-call vote of 35 to 11, with 5 abstentions, decided to convene in 2000 a workshop on the traditional and new forms of mercenary activities as a means of violating human rights and impeding the exercise of the right of peoples to self-determination. The High Commissioner was asked to report on the workshop in 2001.

The Commission called on States that had not done so to consider signing or ratifying the International Convention against the Recruitment, Use, Financing and Training of Mercenaries, adopted by the General Assembly in resolution 44/34 [YUN 1989, p. 825]. The Special Rapporteur was asked to report in 2001. OHCHR was asked to publicize the adverse effects of mercenary activities on the right to self-determination and, when requested, to render advisory services to States that were so affected.

ECONOMIC AND SOCIAL COUNCIL ACTION

On 28 July, the Economic and Social Council, on the recommendation of the Commission on Human Rights [E/2000/23 & Corr.1], adopted **decision 2000/245** by recorded vote (29-9-9) [agenda item 14 *(g)*].

The use of mercenaries as a means of violating human rights and impeding the exercise of the right of peoples to self-determination
At its 45th plenary meeting, on 28 July 2000, the Economic and Social Council, taking note of Commission on Human Rights resolution 2000/3 of 7 April 2000, endorsed the Commission's decision, in accordance with the request of the General Assembly, to convene a workshop on the traditional and new forms of mercenary activities as a means of violating human rights and impeding the exercise of the right of peoples to self-determination before the fifty-fifth session of the Assembly, and its request to the United Nations High Commissioner for Human Rights to report on the outcome of the workshop to the Commission at its fifty-seventh session.

RECORDED VOTE ON DECISION 2000/245:

In favour: Algeria, Angola, Bahrain, Belarus, Bolivia, Brazil, Burkina Faso, Cameroon, China, Colombia, Comoros, Costa Rica, Cuba, Fiji, India, Indonesia, Mexico, Morocco, Oman, Pakistan, Russian Federation, Rwanda, Saint Lucia, Saudi Arabia, Sudan, Suriname, Syrian Arab Republic, Venezuela, Viet Nam.

Against: Canada, Czech Republic, Denmark, Germany, Japan, Norway, Poland, United Kingdom, United States.

Abstaining: Austria, Belgium, Bulgaria, Croatia, France, Greece, Italy, New Zealand, Portugal.

Reports of Special Rapporteur. In response to a 1999 Commission request [YUN 1999, p. 623], the Special Rapporteur on the question of the use of mercenaries, Enrique Bernales Ballesteros (Peru), submitted a report [E/CN.4/2000/14 & Corr.1]. He observed that mercenary activities continued through traditional measures of recruitment and in new forms, including recruitment by private companies offering military security services, which took part in armed conflicts by virtue of contracts signed with Governments. He intended to keep the question of private military security companies under review. The Special Rapporteur recommended that the Commission reiterate its call to Member States to ratify or accede to the International Convention against the Recruitment, Use, Financing and Training of Mercenaries, adopted by the General Assembly in resolution 44/34 [YUN 1989, p. 825] but not yet in force.

In response to Assembly resolution 54/151 [YUN 1999, p. 623], the Secretary-General, in August [A/55/334], transmitted a report by the Special Rapporteur, who summarized replies received from Member States in response to his request for information about mercenary activities, including legislation to outlaw them and information and views on private security service and military advice. He described mercenary activities in Africa, current mercenary activities and the status of the International Convention. He concluded that no significant progress had been observed in the reduction of mercenary activities. He suggested that the methods used to recruit mercenaries by private companies that offered security services and military assistance and advice should continue to be kept under review, as data indicated that, as a result of their activities, the supply of mercenaries had increased. Regarding Africa, in addition to the profit motive, the presence of mercenaries and their paymasters was intended to either control policy or play a political role that guaranteed access to Africa's natural resources, especially diamonds and oil; the Assembly should, in addition to condemning mercenary activities, declare its willingness to strengthen mechanisms to end the phenomenon and call for a system to protect Africa's natural resources. Other recommendations to the Assembly, including a legal definition of mercenaries and the publicizing of the adverse effects of mercenary activities, were incorporated in the resolution below.

GENERAL ASSEMBLY ACTION

On 4 December [meeting 81], the General Assembly, on the recommendation of the Third Committee [A/55/601], adopted **resolution 55/86** by recorded vote (119-19-35) [agenda item 113].

Use of mercenaries as a means of violating human rights and impeding the exercise of the right of peoples to self-determination
The General Assembly,

Recalling its resolution 54/151 of 17 December 1999, and taking note of Commission on Human Rights resolution 2000/3 of 7 April 2000,

Recalling also all of its relevant resolutions, in which, inter alia, it condemned any State that permitted or tolerated the recruitment, financing, training, assembly, transit and use of mercenaries with the objective of overthrowing the Governments of States Members of the United Nations, especially those of developing countries, and recalling further the relevant resolutions of the Security Council and the Organization of African Unity,

Reaffirming the purposes and principles enshrined in the Charter of the United Nations concerning the strict observance of the principles of sovereign equality, political independence, the territorial integrity of States, the non-use of force or of the threat of use of force in international relations and the self-determination of peoples,

Reaffirming also that, by virtue of the principle of self-determination, as developed in the Declaration on Principles of International Law concerning Friendly Relations and Cooperation among States in accordance with the Charter of the United Nations, all peoples have the right freely to determine, without external interference, their political status and to pursue their economic, social and cultural development and every State has the duty to respect this right in accordance with the provisions of the Charter,

Recognizing that mercenary activities continue to increase in many parts of the world and take on new forms, permitting mercenaries to operate in a better organized way, with increased pay, and that their numbers have grown and more persons are prepared to become mercenaries,

Alarmed and concerned about the danger that the activities of mercenaries constitute to peace and security in developing countries, in particular in Africa and in small States, and also elsewhere,

Deeply concerned about the loss of life, the substantial damage to property and the negative effects on the policy and economies of affected countries resulting from mercenary aggression and criminal activities,

Convinced that it is necessary for Member States to ratify the International Convention against the Recruitment, Use, Financing and Training of Mercenaries adopted by the General Assembly on 4 December 1989 and to develop and maintain international cooperation among States for the prevention, prosecution and punishment of mercenary activities,

Convinced also that, notwithstanding the way in which mercenaries or mercenary-related activities are used or the form that they take to acquire some semblance of legitimacy, they are a threat to peace, security and the self-determination of peoples and an obstacle to the enjoyment of human rights by peoples,

1. *Welcomes* the report of the Special Rapporteur of the Commission on Human Rights on the use of mercenaries as a means of violating human rights and impeding the exercise of the right of peoples to self-determination;

2. *Reaffirms* that the recruitment, use, financing and training of mercenaries are causes for grave concern to all States and violate the purposes and principles enshrined in the Charter of the United Nations;

3. *Recognizes* that armed conflict, terrorism, arms trafficking and covert operations by third Powers, inter alia, encourage the demand for mercenaries on the global market;

4. *Urges* all States to take the necessary steps and to exercise the utmost vigilance against the menace posed by the activities of mercenaries and to take the necessary legislative measures to ensure that their territories and other territories under their control, as well as their nationals, are not used for the recruitment, assembly, financing, training and transit of mercenaries for the planning of activities designed to destabilize or

overthrow the Government of any State or threaten the territorial integrity and political unity of sovereign States, or to promote secession or to fight the national liberation movements struggling against colonial or other forms of alien domination or occupation;

5. *Calls upon* all States that have not yet done so to consider signing or ratifying the International Convention against the Recruitment, Use, Financing and Training of Mercenaries;

6. *Welcomes* the cooperation extended by those countries that have received visits from the Special Rapporteur;

7. *Also welcomes* the adoption by some States of national legislation that restricts the recruitment, assembly, financing, training and transit of mercenaries;

8. *Invites* States to investigate the possibility of mercenary involvement whenever criminal acts of a terrorist nature occur;

9. *Requests* the Secretary-General to provide the Special Rapporteur with all the necessary assistance, both professional and financial;

10. *Recommends* that the Commission on Human Rights renew the mandate of the Special Rapporteur for a period of three years;

11. *Urges* all States to cooperate fully with the Special Rapporteur in the fulfilment of his mandate;

12. *Requests* the Office of the United Nations High Commissioner for Human Rights, as a matter of priority to be programmed in its immediate activities, to publicize the adverse effects of the activities of mercenaries on the right to self-determination and, when requested and where necessary, to render advisory services to States that are affected by the activities of mercenaries;

13. *Requests* the Secretary-General to invite Governments to make proposals towards a clearer legal definition of mercenaries, and in this regard strongly urges the United Nations High Commissioner for Human Rights to convene a workshop on the traditional and new forms of activities of mercenaries as a means of violating human rights and impeding the exercise of the right of peoples to self-determination before the fifty-seventh session of the Commission on Human Rights, so that a report on the outcome of the workshop may be submitted to the Commission at its fifty-seventh session;

14. *Requests* the Special Rapporteur to report his findings on the use of mercenaries to undermine the right of peoples to self-determination, with specific recommendations, to the General Assembly at its fifty-sixth session;

15. *Decides* to consider at its fifty-sixth session the question of the use of mercenaries as a means of violating human rights and impeding the exercise of the right of peoples to self-determination under the item entitled "Right of peoples to self-determination".

RECORDED VOTE ON RESOLUTION 55/86:

In favour: Algeria, Angola, Antigua and Barbuda, Argentina, Armenia, Azerbaijan, Bahamas, Bahrain, Bangladesh, Barbados, Belarus, Belize, Benin, Bhutan, Bolivia, Botswana, Brazil, Brunei Darussalam, Bulgaria, Burkina Faso, Burundi, Cambodia, Cameroon, Cape Verde, Chad, Chile, China, Colombia, Comoros, Congo, Costa Rica, Côte d'Ivoire, Cuba, Democratic People's Republic of Korea, Democratic Republic of the Congo, Djibouti, Dominica, Dominican Republic, Ecuador, Egypt, El Salvador, Eritrea, Ethiopia, Fiji, Gabon, Gambia, Ghana, Grenada, Guatemala, Guinea, Guyana, Haiti, Honduras, India, Indonesia, Iran, Jamaica, Jordan, Kenya, Kuwait, Kyrgyzstan, Lao People's Democratic Republic, Lebanon, Lesotho, Libyan Arab Jamahiriya, Madagascar, Malawi, Malaysia, Maldives, Mali, Mauritania, Mauritius, Mexico, Mongolia, Morocco, Mozambique, Myanmar, Namibia, Nauru, Nepal, Nicaragua, Nigeria, Oman, Pakistan, Panama, Papua New Guinea, Paraguay, Peru, Philippines, Qatar, Russian Federation, Saint Kitts and Nevis, Saint Lucia, Saint Vincent and the Grenadines, Samoa, Sao Tome and Principe, Saudi Arabia, Senegal, Singapore, Solomon Islands, South Africa, Sri Lanka, Sudan, Suriname, Swaziland, Syrian Arab Republic, Thailand, Togo, Trinidad and Tobago, Tunisia, United Arab Emirates, United Republic of Tanzania, Uruguay, Vanuatu, Venezuela, Viet Nam, Yemen, Zambia, Zimbabwe.

Against: Albania, Belgium, Canada, Czech Republic, Denmark, Finland, Germany, Hungary, Iceland, Japan, Luxembourg, Micronesia, Netherlands, Norway, Palau, Poland, Sweden, United Kingdom, United States.

Abstaining: Andorra, Australia, Austria, Croatia, Cyprus, Estonia, France, Georgia, Greece, Ireland, Israel, Italy, Kazakhstan, Latvia, Liechtenstein, Lithuania, Malta, Marshall Islands, Monaco, New Zealand, Portugal, Republic of Korea, Republic of Moldova, Romania, Rwanda, San Marino, Sierra Leone, Slovakia, Slovenia, Spain, The former Yugoslav Republic of Macedonia, Turkey, Uganda, Ukraine, Uzbekistan.

Administration of justice

Commission action. On 20 April [res. 2000/39], the Commission called on the Secretary-General and the High Commissioner to strengthen system-wide coordination in the administration of justice, particularly between UN programmes in human rights, crime prevention and criminal justice, and development. The Secretary-General was asked to report in 2002 on measures to implement international human rights standards in the administration of justice.

Subcommission action. On 1 August [dec. 2000/102], the Subcommission decided to establish a five-member sessional working group on the administration of justice. At its meetings on 3, 9 and 14 August [E/CN.4/Sub.2/2000/44], the working group considered the imposition of the death penalty; summary, arbitrary and other extrajudicial executions; privatization of prisons; improvement and efficiency of judicial instruments for the protection of human rights at the national level and their impact at the international level; the administration of justice through military tribunals and other exceptional jurisdictions; and domestic implementation in practice of the obligation to provide effective domestic remedies.

Compensation for victims

In response to a 1999 Commission request [YUN 1999, p. 625], the independent expert on the right to restitution, compensation and rehabilitation for victims of gross violations of human rights and fundamental freedoms, M. Cherif Bassiouni (Egypt/United States), submitted his final report in January [E/CN.4/2000/62], containing a revision of the basic principles and guidelines on that right. Previous versions of the guidelines were submitted in 1993 [YUN 1993, p. 962], 1996 [YUN 1996, p. 623] and 1997 [YUN 1997, p. 649].

Commission action. On 20 April [res. 2000/41], the Commission requested the Secretary-General to circulate to all Member States the text of the revised principles and guidelines. The

High Commissioner was asked to hold a consultative meeting in Geneva for interested Governments, intergovernmental organizations and NGOs, with a view to finalizing the principles and guidelines on the basis of the comments submitted.

Note by Secretariat. A December note by the Secretariat [E/CN.4/2001/61] stated that Member States had been requested to submit their comments on the basic principles and guidelines to OHCHR. As at 20 November, six replies had been received.

Rule of law

Pursuant to General Assembly resolution 53/142 [YUN 1998, p. 663], the Secretary-General, in July [A/55/177], described assistance provided by OHCHR as the focal point for coordinating system-wide attention to human rights, democracy and the rule of law. As at 30 April, of the 47 ongoing projects in the technical cooperation programme, at least 30 supported activities related to strengthening the rule of law. Assistance included support for: developing and implementing national plans of action; establishing and strengthening national institutions; constitutional and legislative reform, administration of justice, elections and national parliaments; training for police, armed forces and prison personnel; and the promotion of human rights education. In an effort to bridge the gap between the increasing number of requests for technical assistance and the limited resources available, the High Commissioner was making efforts to integrate human rights throughout the work of the UN system, thus involving UN partners in technical cooperation projects.

GENERAL ASSEMBLY ACTION

On 4 December [meeting 81], the General Assembly, on the recommendation of the Third Committee [A/55/602/Add.2 & Corr.1], adopted **resolution 55/99** without vote [agenda item 114 (b)].

Strengthening of the rule of law

The General Assembly,

Recalling that, by adopting the Universal Declaration of Human Rights fifty-two years ago, Member States pledged themselves to achieve, in cooperation with the United Nations, the promotion of universal respect for and observance of human rights and fundamental freedoms,

Firmly convinced that the rule of law is an essential factor in the protection of human rights, as stressed in the Declaration, and should continue to attract the attention of the international community,

Convinced that, through their own national legal and judicial systems, States must provide appropriate civil, criminal and administrative remedies for violations of human rights,

Recognizing the importance of the role that can be played by the Office of the United Nations High Commissioner for Human Rights in supporting national efforts to strengthen the institutions of the rule of law,

Bearing in mind that, in its resolution 48/141 of 20 December 1993, the General Assembly entrusted the United Nations High Commissioner for Human Rights with, inter alia, providing advisory services and technical and financial assistance in the field of human rights, enhancing international cooperation for the promotion and protection of all human rights and co-ordinating human rights activities throughout the United Nations system,

Recalling the recommendation of the World Conference on Human Rights, held at Vienna from 14 to 25 June 1993, that a comprehensive programme should be established within the United Nations with a view to helping States in the task of building and strengthening adequate national structures that have a direct impact on the overall observance of human rights and the maintenance of the rule of law,

Recalling also its resolution 53/142 of 9 December 1998 and Commission on Human Rights resolution 1999/74 of 28 April 1999,

1. *Welcomes* the report of the Secretary-General;

2. *Notes with appreciation* the increasing number of Member States seeking assistance in strengthening and consolidating the rule of law and the support provided to these States through the technical cooperation programme of the Office of the United Nations High Commissioner for Human Rights, as outlined in the above-mentioned report of the Secretary-General;

3. *Praises* the efforts made by the Office of the High Commissioner to accomplish its ever-increasing tasks with the limited financial and personnel resources at its disposal;

4. *Expresses its deep concern* at the scarcity of means at the disposal of the Office of the High Commissioner for the fulfilment of its tasks;

5. *Notes with concern* that the United Nations Programme of Advisory Services and Technical Assistance in the Field of Human Rights does not have sufficient funds to provide any substantial financial assistance to national projects that have a direct impact on the realization of human rights and the maintenance of the rule of law in countries that are committed to those ends but are lacking the necessary means and resources;

6. *Welcomes* the deepening of the ongoing co-operation between the Office of the High Commissioner and other relevant bodies and programmes of the United Nations system, with a view to enhancing system-wide coordination of assistance in human rights, democracy and the rule of law, and in this context notes the cooperation between the United Nations Development Programme and the Office of the High Commissioner in providing technical assistance, at the request of States, in the promotion of the rule of law;

7. *Affirms* that the Office of the High Commissioner remains the focal point for coordinating system-wide attention for human rights, democracy and the rule of law;

8. *Encourages* the United Nations High Commissioner for Human Rights to continue the dialogue between her Office and other organs and agencies of the United Nations system, taking into account the need to explore new synergies with a view to obtaining increased financial assistance for human rights and the

rule of law and to promoting inter-agency coordination, funding and allocation of responsibilities in order to improve efficiency and complementarity of action concerning, inter alia, assistance to States in strengthening the rule of law;

9. *Also encourages* the High Commissioner to continue to explore the possibility of further contact with and support from the international financial institutions, acting within their mandates, with a view to obtaining the technical and financial means to strengthen the capacity of the Office of the High Commissioner to provide assistance to national projects aiming at the realization of human rights and the maintenance of the rule of law;

10. *Requests* the High Commissioner to continue to accord high priority to the technical cooperation activities undertaken by her Office with regard to the rule of law and to continue to act as a catalyst in the system by, inter alia, helping other United Nations agencies and programmes, within their respective mandates, to include in their work, as appropriate, attention to institution-building in the area of the rule of law;

11. *Requests* the Secretary-General to submit a report to the General Assembly at its fifty-seventh session on the implementation of the present resolution and the above-mentioned recommendation of the World Conference on Human Rights.

Humanitarian standards

The Commission considered a report of the Secretary-General [E/CN.4/2000/94] containing information received from Governments, UN bodies and NGOs, in reply to the Commission's 1999 request [YUN 1999, p. 626], on fundamental standards of humanity applicable in all situations and consistent with international law.

Sweden, in cooperation with Denmark, Finland, Iceland and Norway, organized an expert meeting on fundamental standards of humanity (Stockholm, 22-24 February) [E/CN.4/2000/145]. The meeting concluded that the concept should be seen as a process towards increasing the protection of persons. Discussion should focus on the identification of fundamental standards of humanity, the problem of derogation, the problem of non-State actors, the need for a common strategy for universal ratification and strengthening the implementation of legal norms.

Commission action. On 26 April [res. 2000/69], the Commission asked the Secretary-General to report in 2001, and invited States, international organizations and NGOs to discuss the strengthening of protection of the individual in all situations, with a view to promoting the ongoing process with respect to fundamental standards of humanity.

Civilians in armed conflict

On 14 February [S/2000/119], the President of the Security Council informed the President of the General Assembly that, in accordance with

Council resolution 1265(1999) [YUN 1999, p. 649] on the protection of civilians in armed conflict, an informal working group of the Council was established. As some of the Secretary-General's recommendations in his 1999 report on the subject [ibid., p. 648] related to the Assembly, the report was issued as an Assembly document [A/54/619]. Members of the informal working group had suggested that four of those recommendations should be referred to the Assembly's Special Committee on Peacekeeping Operations (see p. 93 for further details). On 7 April [S/2000/298], the Assembly President transmitted to the Council President a reply from the Chairman of the Special Committee (see p. 93).

SECURITY COUNCIL ACTION

On 19 April [meeting 4130], the Security Council discussed the Secretary-General's 1999 report and unanimously adopted **resolution 1296(2000)**. The draft [S/2000/335] was prepared in consultations among Council members.

The Security Council,

Recalling its resolution 1265(1999) of 17 September 1999, the statement by its President of 12 February 1999 and other relevant resolutions and statements by its President,

Having considered the report of the Secretary-General of 8 September 1999 on the protection of civilians in armed conflict,

Expressing its appreciation to the informal working group established pursuant to resolution 1265(1999) for its work,

Expressing its regret that civilians account for the vast majority of casualties in armed conflicts and increasingly are targeted by combatants and armed elements, reaffirming its concern at the hardships borne by civilians during armed conflict, in particular as a result of acts of violence directed against them, especially women, children and other vulnerable groups, including refugees and internally displaced persons, and recognizing the consequent impact this has on durable peace, reconciliation and development,

Bearing in mind its primary responsibility under the Charter of the United Nations for the maintenance of international peace and security, and underlining the importance of taking measures aimed at conflict prevention and resolution,

Reaffirming its commitment to the purposes of the Charter as set out in Article 1, paragraphs 1 to 4, and to the principles of the Charter, as set out in Article 2, paragraphs 1 to 7, including its commitment to the principles of the political independence, sovereign equality and territorial integrity of all States, and to respect for the sovereignty of all States,

Underlining the need for all parties concerned to comply with the provisions of the Charter and with rules and principles of international law, in particular international humanitarian, human rights and refugee law, and to implement fully the relevant decisions of the Security Council,

1. *Emphasizes* the need, when considering ways to provide for the protection of civilians in armed conflict, to proceed on a case-by-case basis, taking into account the particular circumstances, and affirms its intention to take into account relevant recommendations contained in the report of the Secretary-General of 8 September 1999 when carrying out its work;

2. *Reaffirms its strong condemnation* of the deliberate targeting of civilians or other protected persons in situations of armed conflict, and calls upon all parties to put an end to such practices;

3. *Notes* that the overwhelming majority of internally displaced persons and other vulnerable groups in situations of armed conflict are civilians and, as such, are entitled to the protection afforded to civilians under existing international humanitarian law;

4. *Reaffirms* the importance of adopting a comprehensive approach to conflict prevention, invites Member States and the Secretary-General to bring to its attention any matter which in their opinion may threaten the maintenance of international peace and security, affirms in this regard its willingness to consider, in the light of its discussion of such matters, the establishment, in appropriate circumstances, of preventive missions, and recalls, in this regard, the statement by its President of 30 November 1999;

5. *Notes* that the deliberate targeting of civilian populations or other protected persons and the committing of systematic, flagrant and widespread violations of international humanitarian and human rights law in situations of armed conflict may constitute a threat to international peace and security, and in this regard reaffirms its readiness to consider such situations and, where necessary, to adopt appropriate steps;

6. *Invites* the Secretary-General to continue to refer to the Council relevant information and analysis where he believes that such information or analysis could contribute to the resolution of issues before it;

7. *Expresses its intention* to collaborate with representatives of the relevant regional and subregional organizations, where appropriate, in order further to improve opportunities for the resolution of armed conflicts and the protection of civilians in such conflict;

8. *Underlines* the importance of safe and unimpeded access of humanitarian personnel to civilians in armed conflicts, calls upon all parties concerned, including neighbouring States, to cooperate fully with the United Nations Humanitarian Coordinator and United Nations agencies in providing such access, invites States and the Secretary-General to bring to its attention information regarding the deliberate denial of such access in violation of international law, where such denial may constitute a threat to international peace and security, and in this regard expresses its willingness to consider such information and, when necessary, to adopt appropriate steps;

9. *Reaffirms its grave concern* at the harmful and widespread impact of armed conflict on civilians, including the particular impact that armed conflict has on women, children and other vulnerable groups, and further reaffirms in this regard the importance of fully addressing their special protection and assistance needs in the mandates of peacemaking, peacekeeping and peace-building operations;

10. *Expresses its intention*, where appropriate, to call upon the parties to a conflict to make special arrange-

ments to meet the protection and assistance requirements of women, children and other vulnerable
groups, including through the promotion of "days of
immunization" and other opportunities for the safe
and unhindered delivery of basic necessary services;

11. *Emphasizes* the importance for humanitarian organizations to uphold the principles of neutrality, impartiality and humanity in their humanitarian activities, and recalls in this regard the statement by its
President of 9 March 2000;

12. *Reiterates its call* to all parties concerned, including non-State parties, to ensure the safety, security and
freedom of movement of United Nations and associated personnel, as well as personnel of humanitarian
organizations, and recalls, in this regard, the statement
by its President of 9 February 2000;

13. *Affirms its intention* to ensure, where appropriate
and feasible, that peacekeeping missions are given suitable mandates and adequate resources to protect civilians under imminent threat of physical danger, including by strengthening the ability of the United Nations
to plan and rapidly deploy peacekeeping personnel, civilian police, civil administrators and humanitarian
personnel, utilizing the stand-by arrangements as appropriate;

14. *Invites* the Secretary-General to bring to its attention situations where refugees and internally displaced persons are vulnerable to the threat of harassment or where their camps are vulnerable to
infiltration by armed elements and where such situations may constitute a threat to international peace and
security, expresses, in this regard, its willingness to consider such situations and, where necessary, adopt appropriate steps to help to create a secure environment
for civilians endangered by conflicts, including by providing support to States concerned in this regard, and
recalls, in this regard, its resolution 1208(1998) of 19
November 1998;

15. *Indicates its willingness* to consider the appropriateness and feasibility of temporary security zones and
safe corridors for the protection of civilians and the delivery of assistance in situations characterized by the
threat of genocide, crimes against humanity and war
crimes against the civilian population;

16. *Affirms its intention* to include in the mandates of
United Nations peacekeeping operations, where appropriate and on a case-by-case basis, clear terms for activities related to the disarmament, demobilization and
reintegration of ex-combatants, including in particular
child soldiers, as well as for the safe and timely disposal
of surplus arms and ammunition, emphasizes the importance of incorporating such measures in specific
peace agreements, where appropriate and with the
consent of the parties, also emphasizes in this regard
the importance of adequate resources being made
available, and recalls the statement by its President of
23 March 2000;

17. *Reaffirms its condemnation* of all incitements to
violence against civilians in situations of armed conflict, also reaffirms the need to bring to justice individuals who incite or otherwise cause such violence, and
indicates its willingness, when authorizing missions, to
consider, where appropriate, steps in response to media broadcasts inciting genocide, crimes against humanity and serious violations of international humanitarian law;

18. *Affirms* that, where appropriate, United Nations
peacekeeping missions should include a mass-media
component that can disseminate information about international humanitarian law and human rights law,
including peace education and protection of children,
while also giving objective information about the activities of the United Nations, and further affirms that,
where appropriate, regional peacekeeping operations
should be encouraged to include such mass-media
components;

19. *Reiterates* the importance of compliance with
relevant provisions of international humanitarian,
human rights and refugee law and of providing appropriate training in such law, including child- and gender-
related provisions, as well as in negotiation and communications skills, cultural awareness, civil-military
coordination and sensitivity in the prevention of HIV/
AIDS and other communicable diseases, to personnel
involved in peacemaking, peacekeeping and peace-
building activities, requests the Secretary-General to
disseminate appropriate guidance and to ensure that
such United Nations personnel have the appropriate
training, and urges relevant Member States, as necessary and feasible, to disseminate appropriate instructions and to ensure that appropriate training is included in their programmes for personnel involved in
similar activities;

20. *Notes* the entry into force of the Convention on
the Prohibition of the Use, Stockpiling, Production
and Transfer of Anti-personnel Mines and on Their
Destruction of 1997 and the amended Protocol on Prohibitions or Restrictions on the Use of Mines, Booby
Traps and Other Devices (Protocol II), to the Convention on Prohibitions or Restrictions on the Use of Certain Conventional Weapons Which May Be Deemed to
Be Excessively Injurious or to Have Indiscriminate
Effects of 1980, recalls the relevant provisions contained therein, notes the beneficial impact that their
implementation will have on the safety of civilians and
encourages those in a position to do so to support humanitarian mine action, including by providing financial assistance to this end;

21. *Notes* that the excessive accumulation and destabilizing effect of small arms and light weapons pose a
considerable impediment to the provision of humanitarian assistance and have a potential to exacerbate and
prolong conflicts, endanger civilians and undermine
security and the confidence required for a return to
peace and stability;

22. *Recalls* the decision of the members of the
Council set out in the note by its President of 17 April
2000 to establish on a temporary basis an informal
working group of the Security Council on the general
issue of sanctions, and requests the informal working
group to consider the recommendations contained in
the report of the Secretary-General of 8 September
1999 relating to its mandate;

23. *Recalls* the letter from its President to the President of the General Assembly dated 14 February 2000,
takes note of the letter to its President from the President of the General Assembly dated 7 April 2000 transmitting a letter dated 1 April 2000 from the Chairman
of the Special Committee on Peacekeeping Operations, welcomes in this regard the work by the Committee with reference to the recommendations in the report of the Secretary-General of 8 September 1999

which relate to its mandate, and encourages the General Assembly to continue consideration of these aspects of the protection of civilians in armed conflict;

24. *Requests* the Secretary-General to continue to include in his written reports to the Council on matters of which it is seized, as appropriate, observations relating to the protection of civilians in armed conflict;

25. *Also requests* the Secretary-General to submit by 30 March 2001 his next report on the protection of civilians in armed conflict, with a view to requesting additional such reports in future, further requests the Secretary-General to include in this report any additional recommendations on ways the Council and other organs of the United Nations, acting within their sphere of responsibility, could further improve the protection of civilians in situations of armed conflict, and encourages the Secretary-General to consult the Inter-Agency Standing Committee in the preparation of the reports;

26. *Decides* to remain seized of the matter.

Security of UN staff

Note by Secretariat. The Commission considered a note by the Secretariat [E/CN.4/2000/100] that referred to its 1997 request [YUN 1997, p. 665] that the Secretary-General commission a study on the safety and security problems of UN and other personnel carrying out activities in UN operations. The note stated that the UN Security Coordinator informed the Secretariat that the General Assembly had requested a review of security arrangements to submit to the Millennium Assembly. The report was being prepared on an inter-agency basis to reflect the actual situation and would be provided to the Commission.

Report of Secretary-General. As the Commission had requested in 1998 [YUN 1998, p. 667], the Secretary-General, in January [E/CN.4/2000/99], summarized the comments of Governments, UN bodies and agencies and other organizations, and the Federation of International Civil Servants' Associations on the situation of UN and other personnel carrying out activities in fulfilment of a UN mandate who were imprisoned, missing or held in a country against their will, and on new cases that had been settled successfully.

Commission action. On 26 April [res. 2000/77], the Commission, calling on the UN system to report any incident involving the safety and security of staff to the UN Security Coordinator so that a comprehensive record might be maintained, asked States to consider signing and acceding to or ratifying the Convention on the Safety of United Nations and Associated Personnel, adopted by the General Assembly in resolution 49/59 [YUN 1994, p. 1289] (see p. 1345). Recalling its request to the Secretary-General to review security in UN operations and to develop safety and security measures, the Commission asked him to submit the results in 2002 and to report as well in 2002 on the situation of UN and associ-

ated personnel who were imprisoned, missing or held in a country against their will and on new cases that had been settled successfully.

Arbitrary detention

Commission action. On 20 April [res. 2000/36], the Commission requested the Governments concerned to take account of the views of the Working Group on Arbitrary Detention, to remedy the situation of persons arbitrarily deprived of their liberty and to pay attention to the Group's urgent appeals. It encouraged them to ensure that their legislation conformed with the relevant international standards and legal instruments and not to extend states of emergency beyond what was strictly required. The Secretary-General was asked to assist Governments, special rapporteurs and working groups to ensure promotion and observance of guarantees relating to states of emergency embodied in international instruments. The Commission decided to renew the Group's mandate for a three-year period, a decision endorsed by the Economic and Social Council on 28 July (**decision 2000/263**), and asked the Group to report in 2001.

Working Group activities. The Working Group on Arbitrary Detention held its twenty-seventh (15-19 May), twenty-eighth (11-15 September) and twenty-ninth (22 November-1 December) sessions in 2000 in Geneva [E/CN.4/2001/14]. During the year, the Working Group transmitted 34 communications concerning 94 new cases of alleged arbitrary detention to 20 Governments, of which 9 provided information. Of the 34 individual alleged cases of arbitrary detention, 24 were based on information submitted to the Group by NGOs and 10 by private sources. In 2000, the Group adopted 39 opinions regarding 115 persons in 21 countries. A description of the cases transmitted and the contents of the Governments' replies, as well as the complete text of 28 of the opinions, were contained in a separate report [E/CN.4/2001/14/Add.1]. The Group transmitted 107 urgent actions concerning 499 individuals to 45 Governments and the Palestinian Authority, of which 70 were issued jointly by the Group with other thematic or country mandates of the Commission. In 29 cases, the Governments concerned informed the Group that they had taken measures to remedy the victims' situation.

The Group, having learned of cases in which persons involved in environmental protection or the defence of human rights had been sentenced for divulging "State secrets", recommended that Governments ensure that any legislation concerning national security was not extended to cover the defence and protection of the environment or human rights. Noting that conscientious objection gave rise to repeated prosecutions and renewed sentences of deprivation of liberty, the Group recommended that States that had not done so ensure that conscientious objector status was recognized and attributed; pending the adoption of such measures, when de facto objectors were prosecuted, such prosecutions should not give rise to more than one conviction, in order to prevent the judicial system from being used to force conscientious objectors to change their convictions (see also p. 687). Regarding extradition measures, the Group recommended that Governments, in domestic law, set out the maximum permissible period of detention pending extradition of an individual to the requesting State. It also recommended that the requesting State, upon conviction and while imposing sentence on the extradited individual, take into account the period of detention served pending extradition. Annexed to the report were gender statistics regarding cases in which the Group adopted an opinion.

Impunity

Reports of Secretary-General. In response to a 1999 Commission request [YUN 1999, p. 627], the Secretary-General summarized replies from Governments, intergovernmental organizations and NGOs to a request for information on steps they had taken to combat impunity for human rights violations [E/CN.4/2000/90].

Also in response to a 1999 Commission request [YUN 1999, p. 627], the Secretary-General, in January [E/CN.4/2000/91], summarized information received from Governments and NGOs on the final report of the Special Rapporteur on the question of the impunity of perpetrators of violations of economic, social and cultural rights [YUN 1997, p. 655]. Proposals to combat impunity included the adoption of an optional protocol to the International Covenant on Economic, Social and Cultural Rights, adopted by the General Assembly in resolution 2200 A (XXI) [YUN 1966, p. 419], under which violations could be reported (see p. 610); the adoption of a declaration against violations of economic, social and cultural rights; and the reform of financial institutions, notably the International Monetary Fund and the World Bank.

Commission action. On 26 April [res. 2000/68], the Commission emphasized the importance of holding accountable perpetrators of violations of international human rights and humanitarian law and urged States to take action in accordance with due process of law. The Secretary-General was asked to seek the views of Governments, intergovernmental organizations and NGOs on the appointment of an independent expert to examine the issue of impunity, with a view to a decision

on the matter in 2001; to invite States to provide information on steps they had taken to combat impunity for human rights violations and on remedies available to the victims; and to collect the information and report thereon in 2001.

Subcommission action. On 18 August [res. 2000/24], the Subcommission, in a resolution on the role of universal or extraterritorial competence in preventing action against impunity, invited Governments to cooperate even when there was no treaty to facilitate dealing with proceedings initiated by victims acting either within the framework of universal competence as recognized in international law or under domestic law that had established an extraterritorial legal competence, in particular because of the nationality of the victim or of the perpetrator.

Independence of the judicial system

Reports of Special Rapporteur. In February, the Special Rapporteur on the independence of judges and lawyers, Param Cumaraswamy (Malaysia), submitted a report covering his activities in 1999 [E/CN.4/2000/61].

The Special Rapporteur transmitted 26 communications to 26 Governments and 11 urgent appeals to 9 States. Replies to communications were received from 16 countries and to urgent appeals from 5 countries. In order to avoid duplication of work, the Special Rapporteur joined with other special rapporteurs and working groups to transmit 18 urgent appeals to 12 countries. The report summarized the communications and urgent appeals, as well as replies received from Governments. The Special Rapporteur noted an increase in responses from Governments and in the number of urgent appeals submitted jointly by him. He urged the Commission to consider providing a monitoring mechanism to implement the Declaration on the Right and Responsibilities of Individuals, Groups and Organs of Society to Promote and Protect Universally Recognized Human Rights and Fundamental Freedoms, adopted by the General Assembly in resolution 53/144 [YUN 1998, p. 608] (see p. 604). He continued to be concerned over the possible proliferation of standards; unless standards were uniform and consistent there could be confusion. The Special Rapporteur called on Governments, national judiciaries, bar associations and NGOs to submit to him court judgements and legislation affecting the independence of the judiciary and the legal profession.

The Special Rapporteur visited South Africa (7-13 May) [E/CN.4/2001/65/Add.2] to examine the judicial system. He concluded that magistrates were not perceived to be independent, though there was no evidence of any interference in their adjudicative tasks. The Special Rapporteur welcomed the initiative of the Judicial Service Commission in collaborating with judges to draft legislation establishing a mechanism to deal with complaints against judges, as well as the agreement that there would be no punitive measures such as fines imposed on judges. While noting the negative attitude of some judges to the proposal for a unified judiciary, he welcomed the move towards an integrated legal profession. The minimum sentencing legislation, which impinged on international standards of judicial independence, was not as regimented in South Africa as that found in other jurisdictions. The appointment and subsequent extension of acting judges could adversely affect the independent character of tribunals. The Special Rapporteur regretted that many lawyers refused to provide legal aid services when the legal aid fees were reduced. He made recommendations regarding the independence of magistrates, the proposed complaints mechanism, minimum sentencing legislation, appointments of acting judges, the position of public prosecutors, legal aid, judicial training and continued legal education.

In Belarus (12-17 June) [E/CN.4/2001/65/Add.1], the Special Rapporteur examined the state of the administration of justice. He concluded that the manner in which executive power had been accumulated and concentrated in the President had resulted in authoritarian rule. Thus, the administration of justice, including the judiciary, the prosecutorial service and the legal profession, were undermined and not perceived as separate and independent. Executive control over the judiciary and repressive actions against independent judges appeared to produce indifference among many judges towards judicial independence. The Special Rapporteur expressed deep concern that the 1996 referendum on the Constitution had proceeded contrary to the rule of law and in violation of the independence of the judiciary. The procedure for appointing six of the Constitutional Court judges, which was within the sole discretion of the President, constituted a threat to the independence of the Court. The substantial number of inexperienced judges compounded the problems associated with a short initial tenure. In addition, the low salaries and the dependence of judges on the executive for promotions and the Presidential Administration compromised judges' ability to decide cases independently. The legal profession, including prosecutors, came under excessive executive control. Recommendations were made regarding the Constitution, the judiciary and the legal profession.

The Special Rapporteur's mission to Slovakia (27-29 November) [E/CN.4/2001/65/Add.3] was confined to the issue of whether the proposed removal by Parliament of the President of the Supreme Court, Stefan Harabin, at the behest of the Government, violated the constitutional, international and regional standards on judicial independence. The Special Rapporteur stated that the Government's allegations against Mr. Harabin, if proved, were sufficient misconduct for the removal of a judge from office; he added, however, that judges were entitled to due process of law if they were to be removed before the expiry of their term of office. Therefore, he was of the view that the Government's attempt to remove Mr. Harabin through the parliamentary process without due process violated international and regional standards to secure an independent judiciary. That action could be seen as politically motivated. The Government's haste in wanting to remove Mr. Harabin shortly before the coming into force of a constitutional amendment providing for an independent mechanism to appoint and remove judges further added to that perception.

Commission action. On 20 April [res. 2000/42], the Commission encouraged Governments that faced difficulties in guaranteeing the independence of judges and lawyers to consult and to consider the Special Rapporteur's services, for instance by inviting him to visit their country. The High Commissioner was asked to continue to provide technical assistance to train judges and lawyers and to associate the Special Rapporteur in the development of a manual on human rights training of judges and lawyers. The Commission decided to extend the Special Rapporteur's mandate for three years and asked him to report in 2001; the Secretary-General was asked to assist him.

The Commission's decision and its requests to the Special Rapporteur and the Secretary-General were endorsed by the Economic and Social Council on 28 July (**decision 2000/264**).

Juvenile justice

Report of Secretary-General. Pursuant to a 1998 Commission request [YUN 1998, p. 666], the Secretary-General, in a January report [E/CN.4/2000/54], discussed practical measures for the implementation of human rights international standards in the administration of justice, particularly juvenile justice, including the role of UN technical assistance. He observed that the technical assistance of OHCHR, the United Nations Children's Fund (UNICEF) and the United Nations Centre for International Crime Prevention helped States implement international standards through organizing programmes that related to law reform, training of personnel and institutional support and by preventing juvenile delinquency. The coordination panel on technical advice and assistance in juvenile justice provided an important tool to assist the implementing agencies in coordinating assistance.

Commission action. On 20 April [res. 2000/39], the Commission underlined that raising awareness of the specific situation of children and juveniles in the administration of justice and providing training in that field were crucial in strengthening the implementation of relevant standards. The Secretary-General was asked to make available to the Commission in 2002 his reports on the administration of juvenile justice, as well as on the activities of the coordination panel on technical advice and assistance in juvenile justice, submitted to the Commission on Crime Prevention and Criminal Justice. (See p. 673 for information on the imposition of the death penalty on juveniles.)

Capital punishment

Report of Secretary-General. Pursuant to a 1999 Commission request [YUN 1999, p. 628], the Secretary-General, in March [E/2000/3 & Corr.1], submitted his sixth quinquennial report on capital punishment and implementation of the safeguards guaranteeing protection of the rights of those facing the death penalty, covering the period 1994-1998. The report drew on current criminological research and the comments of specialized agencies, intergovernmental organizations, NGOs and States by means of a detailed questionnaire. Of the 45 countries that replied, 33 (73 per cent) were abolitionist. Nevertheless, only 39 per cent of all abolitionist countries replied. Of the 71 States that retained and enforced capital punishment at the end of 1999, only 6 (8.5 per cent) responded. Of the 38 de facto abolitionist countries, 6 (16 per cent) replied. More so than in the past, the Secretary-General relied on information derived from various other sources to ascertain the number of death sentences imposed and executions carried out during the period under review.

At the beginning of the quinquennial period, 56 countries and territories embraced total abolition of the death penalty; at the end, all but one of them remained abolitionist. In early 1994, 14 countries were abolitionist for ordinary offences only; five became abolitionist for all offences. Countries that were considered to be abolitionist de facto (they retained the death penalty for ordinary crimes but had not executed anyone in the last 10 years or more) numbered 30 at the beginning of 1994; by the end of 1998, two had become abolitionist for all offences, one had become abo-

litionist for ordinary offences and seven had resumed executions, thereby becoming retentionist. Thus, 20 of the 30 remained abolitionist de facto throughout the period. The number fell to 19 in 1999 when the Philippines resumed executions (in 2000, the Philippines declared a moratorium on executions [A/54/844]). From a variety of sources it was established that, at the beginning of 1994, 94 countries and territories retained the death penalty in their law and had enforced it. Of the 13 countries that were retentionist in 1994, all had become abolitionist and all but one for all crimes at the end of 1999; another 18 retentionist countries had become abolitionist de facto by the end of 1999. Thus, there were 63 countries and territories that did not change their death penalty status. However, six of them were believed not to have carried out executions between 1994 and 1999, leaving 55 retentionist countries that had carried out executions between 1994 and 1998. Over the period under review, figures available suggested that an estimated 23,000 persons were sentenced to death and some 13,500 judicially executed.

The report included information on the implementation of the safeguards guaranteeing protection of the rights of those facing the death penalty, adopted by the Economic and Social Council in resolution 1984/50 [YUN 1984, p. 709].

The Secretary-General concluded that the pace of the abolitionist movement showed no sign of faltering, with 17 countries abolishing the death penalty between 1994 and 1998; four more did so in 1999.

On 28 July, the Economic and Social Council took note of the report (**decision 2000/289**).

Commission action. By a roll-call vote of 27 to 13, with 12 abstentions, the Commission, on 26 April [res. 2000/65], called on States parties to the International Covenant on Civil and Political Rights, contained in General Assembly resolution 2200 A (XXI) [YUN 1966, p. 423], that had not done so to consider acceding to or ratifying the Second Optional Protocol thereto on the abolition of the death penalty, adopted by the Assembly in resolution 44/128 [YUN 1989, p. 484]. States that maintained the death penalty were called on to restrict the number of offences for which the death penalty might be imposed; to establish a moratorium on executions, with a view to completely abolishing the death penalty; and to make available to the public information on the imposition of the death penalty. States that had received an extradition request on a capital charge were asked to reserve the right to refuse extradition in the absence of assurances from the requesting State that capital punishment would not be carried out. The Secretary-General was asked to submit in 2001 a supplement to his quinquennial report.

Communication. On 26 April [E/CN.4/2000/162], Indonesia, also on behalf of 50 other States, dissociated itself from the Commission's resolution.

Juveniles

Report of Secretary-General. The Secretary-General's quinquennial report on capital punishment and implementation of the safeguards guaranteeing protection of the rights of those facing the death penalty [E/2000/3 & Corr.1] (see p. 672) stated that since 1994 several countries had brought themselves into line with the safeguard pertaining to persons under 18 years of age. Only one respondent country had a provision for imposing death sentences on persons of that age group, but had not imposed the sentence during the period of the survey.

Note by Secretariat. A June note by the Secretariat [E/CN.4/Sub.2/2000/6], noting a 1999 Subcommission resolution [YUN 1999, p. 628] requesting information on executions of juveniles carried out between the adoption of the resolution and the start of the Subcommisson's 2000 session, referred to the Secretary-General's sixth quinquennial report on capital punishment (see p. 672) and stated that the revised sixth survey of Governments, intergovernmental organizations and NGOs would include information on the execution of juveniles. A revised version of the report would be available by January 2001.

Subcommission action. On 17 August [res. 2000/17], the Subcommission, condemning the imposition and execution of the death penalty on those aged under 18 at the time of the offence, called on States that retained the death penalty for juvenile offenders to abolish it. It asked the Commission to reaffirm its resolution 2000/65 (see p. 672).

Forensic science

Report of OHCHR. In response to a 1998 Commission request [YUN 1998, p. 667], OHCHR, in a report on human rights and forensic science [E/CN.4/2000/57], presented a revised version of the cooperation service agreement regulating the use of forensic experts provided by either a Member State or an NGO. The report also contained the special service agreement on the obligations of the individual forensic expert working as a consultant to the United Nations. OHCHR noted that special rapporteurs continued to use or refer to the need for forensic specialists.

Commission action. On 20 April [res. 2000/32], the Commission recommended that the

Secretary-General establish procedures to evaluate the use of forensic expertise. It invited OHCHR and the UN Crime Prevention and Criminal Justice Division to consider revising the *Manual on the Effective Prevention and Investigation of Extralegal, Arbitrary and Summary Executions* [Sales No. E.91.IV.1], on standard procedures for post-mortem examinations. The Commission recommended that OHCHR encourage forensic experts to produce additional manuals concerned with examinations of living persons, and welcomed the Office's initiative to publish a manual on investigation and documentation of torture and other cruel, inhuman or degrading treatment or punishment. Another recommendation called for the Office to provide training in forensic activities relating to victims of human rights violations. OHCHR was asked to update the list of experts with biographical data and areas of expertise and to report in 2002.

Right to democracy

Report of High Commissioner. In her annual report to the Commission [E/CN.4/2000/12/Add.1], the High Commissioner, in February, discussed progress on the right to democracy, as requested in 1999 [YUN 1999, p. 630].

The High Commissioner stated that the promotion of the right to democracy was infused throughout the work of OHCHR. OHCHR continued to support new and restored democracies through the human rights machinery, particularly the Human Rights Committee (see p. 609) and the Committee on the Elimination of Racial Discrimination (see p. 611), and support for the Special Rapporteur on the independence of judges and lawyers (see p. 670), the Special Rapporteur on extrajudicial, summary or arbitrary executions (see p. 676) and the Working Group on Arbitrary Detention (see p. 669). The Office continued its programme of promoting and developing national human rights institutions (see p. 636). OHCHR technical cooperation programmes included modules covering the promotion of the right to democracy, and field representatives conducted activities related to its promotion.

Commission action. By a roll-call vote of 45 to none, with 8 abstentions, the Commission, on 25 April [res. 2000/47], called on States to consolidate democracy through the promotion of pluralism and the protection of human rights and fundamental freedoms; to strengthen the rule of law; to develop and maintain an electoral system that provided for genuine and periodic elections; to create and improve the legal system and mechanisms enabling the wide participation of civil society in the development of democracy; to strengthen democracy through good governance and promoting sustainable development; and to enhance social cohesion and solidarity. OHCHR and Commission and Subcommission mechanisms were asked to pay attention to those elements of democratic governance. The High Commissioner was asked to reflect progress on implementation of the Commission's resolution in her 2001 report.

Subcommission action. On 18 August [dec. 2000/116], the Subcommission, taking note of the Commission's resolution (see p. 673), entrusted Manuel Rodríguez-Cuadros (Peru) with preparing a working paper on the measures provided in international human rights instruments for the promotion and consolidation of democracy.

GENERAL ASSEMBLY ACTION

On 4 December [meeting 81], the General Assembly, on the recommendation of the Third Committee [A/55/602/Add.2 & Corr.1], adopted **resolution 55/96** by recorded vote (157-0-16) [agenda item 114 (b)].

Promoting and consolidating democracy

The General Assembly,

Reaffirming the purposes and principles of the Charter of the United Nations, and reaffirming also that everyone is entitled to all rights and freedoms without distinction of any kind, such as race, colour, sex, language, religion, political or other opinion, national or social origin, property, birth or other status, as set forth in the Universal Declaration of Human Rights,

Bearing in mind Commission on Human Rights resolutions 1999/57 of 27 April 1999 and 2000/47 of 25 April 2000,

Recognizing the indissoluble link between human rights as enshrined in the Universal Declaration of Human Rights and in the international human rights treaties and the foundation of any democratic society, and reaffirming the Vienna Declaration and Programme of Action adopted by the World Conference on Human Rights, which states that democracy, development and respect for human rights and fundamental freedoms are interdependent and mutually reinforcing,

Recalling that all peoples have the right to self-determination, by virtue of which they can freely determine their political status and freely pursue their economic, social and cultural development,

Recalling also that, in the Vienna Declaration and Programme of Action, the World Conference on Human Rights recommended that priority should be given to national and international action to promote democracy, development and human rights and that the international community should support the strengthening and promotion of democracy, development and respect for human rights and fundamental freedoms in the entire world,

Recalling further its resolutions 53/243 A and B of 13 September 1999, containing, respectively, the Declaration and the Programme of Action for a Culture of Peace,

Recognizing and respecting the rich and diverse nature of the community of the world's democracies, which arise out of all of the world's social, cultural and religious beliefs and traditions,

Recognizing that, while all democracies share common features, there is no one universal model of democracy,

Reaffirming its commitment to the process of democratization of States, and that democracy is based on the freely expressed will of the people to determine their own political, economic, social and cultural systems and their full participation in all aspects of their lives,

Reaffirming that good governance, as referred to in the United Nations Millennium Declaration, is among the indispensable factors for building and strengthening peaceful, prosperous and democratic societies,

Aware of the crucial importance of the active involvement and contribution of civil society in processes of governance that affect the lives of people,

Recalling commitments undertaken by Member States for the promotion of democracy and the rule of law, within the framework of the United Nations and other international organizations,

Welcoming measures, such as decision AHG/Dec.141(XXXV) adopted in 1999 by the Assembly of Heads of State and Government of the Organization of African Unity, resolution AG/RES.1080(XXI-091) adopted in 1991 by the General Assembly of the Organization of American States and the Moscow Document on the Human Dimension adopted in 1991 by the Conference on the Human Dimension of the Conference for Security and Cooperation in Europe, which commit Member States to taking certain steps in the event of an interruption of democratic government, as well as the Commonwealth Declaration adopted at the Commonwealth Heads of Government Meeting, held at Harare in 1991, which commits members to fundamental democratic principles,

Commending the wish of an increasing number of countries all over the world to devote their energy, means and political will to the building of democratic societies in which individuals have the opportunity to shape their own destiny,

Noting the initiatives taken by the countries that participated in the first, second and third International Conference of New or Restored Democracies, held, respectively, at Manila in June 1988, Managua in July 1994 and Bucharest in September 1997,

Noting also the ministerial conference entitled "Towards a Community of Democracies", hosted by the Government of Poland at Warsaw on 26 and 27 June 2000,

Noting further the Forum on Emerging Democracies, held at Sana'a from 27 to 30 June 1999,

Noting that the fourth International Conference of New or Restored Democracies is scheduled to be held at Cotonou, Benin, from 4 to 6 December 2000, and also noting the initiative of the Government of Mali to host, at Bamako from 1 to 3 November 2000, following the Moncton Declaration adopted in September 1999 at Moncton, Canada, by the Eighth Summit of la Francophonie, an international symposium at the ministerial level on the status of the practices of democracy, rights and freedoms in the French-speaking community,

1. *Calls upon* States to promote and consolidate democracy, inter alia, by:

(a) Promoting pluralism, the protection of all human rights and fundamental freedoms, maximizing the participation of individuals in decision-making and the development of effective public institutions, including an independent judiciary, accountable legislature and public service and an electoral system that ensures periodic, free and fair elections;

(b) Promoting, protecting and respecting all human rights, including the right to development, and fundamental freedoms, in particular:

(i) Freedom of thought, conscience, religion, belief, peaceful assembly and association, as well as freedom of expression, freedom of opinion, and free, independent and pluralistic media;

(ii) The rights of persons belonging to national, ethnic, religious or linguistic minorities, including the right freely to express, preserve and develop their identity without any discrimination and in full equality before the law;

(iii) The rights of indigenous people;

(iv) The rights of children, the elderly and persons with physical or mental disabilities;

(v) Actively promoting gender equality with the aim of achieving full equality between men and women;

(vi) Taking appropriate measures to eradicate all forms of racism and racial discrimination, xenophobia and related intolerance;

(vii) Considering becoming parties to international human rights instruments;

(viii) Fulfilling their obligations under the international human rights instruments to which they are parties;

(c) Strengthening the rule of law by:

(i) Ensuring equality before the law and equal protection under the law;

(ii) Ensuring the right to liberty and security of person, the right to equal access to justice, and the right to be brought promptly before a judge or other officer authorized by law to exercise judicial power in the case of detention with a view to avoiding arbitrary arrest;

(iii) Guaranteeing the right to a fair trial;

(iv) Ensuring due process of law and the right to be presumed innocent until proven guilty in a court of law;

(v) Promoting the independence and integrity of the judiciary and, by means of appropriate education, selection, support and allocation of resources, strengthening its capacity to render justice with fairness and efficiency, free from improper or corrupt outside influence;

(vi) Guaranteeing that all persons deprived of their liberty are treated with humanity and with respect for the inherent dignity of the human person;

(vii) Ensuring appropriate civil and administrative remedies and criminal sanctions for violations of human rights, as well as effective protection for human rights defenders;

(viii) Including human rights education in the training for civil servants and law enforcement and military personnel;

(ix) Ensuring that the military remains accountable to the democratically elected civilian government;

(d) Developing, nurturing and maintaining an electoral system that provides for the free and fair expression of the will of the people through genuine and periodic elections, in particular by:

(i) Guaranteeing that everyone can exercise his or her right to take part in the government of his or her country, directly or through freely chosen representatives;

(ii) Guaranteeing the right to vote freely and to be elected in a free and fair process at regular intervals, by universal and equal suffrage, conducted by secret ballot and with full respect for the right to freedom of association;

(iii) Taking measures, as appropriate, to address the representation of underrepresented segments of society;

(iv) Ensuring, through legislation, institutions and mechanisms, the freedom to form democratic political parties that can participate in elections, as well as the transparency and fairness of the electoral process, including through appropriate access under the law to funds and free, independent and pluralistic media;

(e) Creating and improving the legal framework and necessary mechanisms for enabling the wide participation of all members of civil society in the promotion and consolidation of democracy, by:

(i) Respecting the diversity of society by promoting associations, dialogue structures, mass media and their interaction as a means of strengthening and developing democracy;

(ii) Fostering, through education and other means, awareness and respect for democratic values;

(iii) Respecting the right to freedom of peaceful assembly and the exercise of the right freely to form, join and participate in non-governmental organizations or associations, including trade unions;

(iv) Guaranteeing mechanisms for consultations with and the contribution of civil society in processes of governance and encouraging cooperation between local authorities and non-governmental organizations;

(v) Providing or improving the legal and administrative framework for non-governmental, community-based and other civil society organizations;

(vi) Promoting civic education and education on human rights, inter alia, in cooperation with organizations of civil society;

(f) Strengthening democracy through good governance as referred to in the United Nations Millennium Declaration by, inter alia:

(i) Improving the transparency of public institutions and policy-making procedures and enhancing the accountability of public officials;

(ii) Taking legal, administrative and political measures against corruption, including by disclosing and investigating and punishing all those involved in acts of corruption and by criminalizing payment of commissions and bribes to public officials;

(iii) Bringing government closer to the people by appropriate levels of devolution;

(iv) Promoting the widest possible public access to information about the activities of national and local authorities, as well as ensuring access by all to administrative remedies, without discrimination;

(v) Fostering high levels of competence, ethics and professionalism within the civil service and its cooperation with the public, inter alia, by providing appropriate training for members of the civil service;

(g) Strengthening democracy by promoting sustainable development, in particular by:

(i) Taking effective measures aimed at the progressive realization of economic, social and cultural rights, such as the right to education and the right to a standard of living adequate for health and well-being, including food, clothing, housing, medical care and necessary social services, individually and through international cooperation;

(ii) Taking effective measures aimed at overcoming social inequalities and creating an environment that is conducive to development and to the elimination of poverty;

(iii) Promoting economic freedom and social development and pursuing active policies to provide opportunities for productive employment and sustainable livelihoods;

(iv) Ensuring equal access to economic opportunities and equal pay and other rewards for work of equal value;

(v) Creating a legal and regulatory framework with a view to promoting sustained economic growth and sustainable development;

(h) Enhancing social cohesion and solidarity by:

(i) Developing and strengthening, at the local and national levels, institutional and educational capabilities to resolve conflicts and disputes peacefully, including through mediation, and to prevent and eliminate the use of violence in addressing societal tensions and disagreements;

(ii) Improving social protection systems and ensuring access for all to basic social services;

(iii) Encouraging social dialogue and tripartite cooperation with respect to labour relations among government, trade unions and employer organizations, as reflected in the core Conventions of the International Labour Organization;

2. *Requests* the Secretary-General to disseminate the present resolution as widely as possible.

RECORDED VOTE ON RESOLUTION 55/96:

In favour: Afghanistan, Albania, Algeria, Andorra, Angola, Antigua and Barbuda, Argentina, Armenia, Australia, Austria, Azerbaijan, Bahamas, Bangladesh, Barbados, Belarus, Belgium, Belize, Benin, Bolivia, Bosnia and Herzegovina, Botswana, Brazil, Bulgaria, Burkina Faso, Burundi, Cambodia, Cameroon, Canada, Cape Verde, Chad, Chile, Colombia, Comoros, Congo, Costa Rica, Côte d'Ivoire, Croatia, Cyprus, Czech Republic, Denmark, Djibouti, Dominica, Dominican Republic, Ecuador, Egypt, El Salvador, Eritrea, Estonia, Ethiopia, Fiji, Finland, France, Gabon, Gambia, Georgia, Germany, Ghana, Greece, Grenada, Guatemala, Guinea, Guyana, Haiti, Hungary, Iceland, India, Indonesia, Iran, Ireland, Israel, Italy, Jamaica, Japan, Jordan, Kazakhstan, Kenya, Kuwait, Kyrgyzstan, Latvia, Lebanon, Lesotho, Liechtenstein, Lithuania, Luxembourg, Madagascar, Malawi, Malaysia, Mali, Malta, Marshall Islands, Mauritania, Mauritius, Mexico, Micronesia, Monaco, Mongolia, Morocco, Mozambique, Namibia, Nauru, Nepal, Netherlands, New Zealand, Nicaragua, Nigeria, Norway, Palau, Panama, Papua New Guinea, Paraguay, Peru, Philippines, Poland, Portugal, Republic of Korea, Republic of Moldova, Romania, Russian Federation, Rwanda, Saint Kitts and Nevis, Saint Lucia, Saint Vincent and the Grenadines, Samoa, San Marino, Sao Tome and Principe, Senegal, Sierra Leone, Singapore, Slovakia, Slovenia, Solomon Islands, South Africa, Spain, Sri Lanka, Sudan, Suriname, Sweden, Tajikistan, Thailand, The former Yugoslav Republic of Macedonia, Togo, Trinidad and Tobago, Tunisia, Turkey, Uganda, Ukraine, United Arab Emirates, United Kingdom, United Republic of Tanzania, United States, Uruguay, Vanuatu, Venezuela, Yemen, Yugoslavia, Zambia, Zimbabwe.

Against: None.

Abstaining: Bahrain, Bhutan, Brunei Darussalam, China, Cuba, Democratic Republic of the Congo, Honduras, Lao People's Democratic Republic, Libyan Arab Jamahiriya, Maldives, Myanmar, Oman, Qatar, Saudi Arabia, Swaziland, Viet Nam.

Other issues

Extralegal executions

Reports of Special Rapporteur. In January [E/CN.4/2000/3 & Add.1], the Special Rapporteur on extrajudicial, summary or arbitrary executions, Asma Jahangir (Pakistan), updated activities since the submission of her last report [YUN 1999, p. 633]. Between 1 November 1998 and 5 December 1999, the Special Rapporteur transmitted communications containing allegations regarding the violation of the right to life of more than 900 individuals to 39 Governments and the Palestinian Authority, as well as urgent appeals regarding 213 individuals and specific groups of persons to prevent imminent loss of life. The report summarized the cases transmitted to Governments and the replies received. The Special Rapporteur concluded that, during the period under review, extrajudicial, summary or arbitrary executions did not decrease. There were more reports of large-scale indiscriminate killings of women, children or elderly persons by Government-controlled security forces, paramilitary groups or non-State actors. She recommended a series of actions to Governments relating to capital punishment, death threats, deaths in custody, excessive use of force by law enforcement officials, violations of the right to life during armed conflict, the imminent expulsion of persons to countries where their lives were in danger, genocide, impunity, children in armed conflict, traditional practices regarding the right to life ("honour killings") and the right to life and sexual orientation.

Although the Special Rapporteur's visit to Nepal (5-14 February) [E/CN.4/2001/9/Add.2] was prompted by continuing reports of alleged extrajudicial killings of unarmed civilians in the context of the conflict between armed groups of the Communist Party of Nepal (Maoist) and the Nepal police, the allegations were not limited to areas affected by internal unrest. The Special Rapporteur expressed deep concern at reports that police officers had taken the law into their own hands and summarily executed suspects, under the pretext that they did not trust the judiciary to convict them. It appeared that the judiciary often found the investigative work of the police wanting, thus leaving judges unable to convict in cases brought before them. Those weaknesses in the police and the judiciary had resulted in gross injustices and in impunity. Among other things, she recommended establishing strong, independent and credible mechanisms to investigate and prosecute alleged human rights abuses attributed to the police and other State agents; upgrading hospital and forensic facilities to carry out post-mortems; government action to curb impunity; support to Nepal by the international community; training for the police and the judiciary; and maintaining the police and security forces under strict civilian control in order to ensure transparency and accountability.

In August [A/55/288], the Secretary-General transmitted the Special Rapporteur's interim report, as requested by the General Assembly in resolution 53/147 [YUN 1998, p. 672], covering activities from her appointment in 1998 to 1 July 2000. She regretted that many Governments had failed to respond to her urgent appeals requesting information on alleged violations of the right to life. She also regretted that most of her earlier recommendations remained valid in the absence of concrete action by Governments to implement them. The Special Rapporteur concluded that the global situation regarding respect for the right to life was bleak, found it unacceptable that some Governments insisted on defending or ignoring extrajudicial killings committed by their security forces, especially when confronted with armed opposition groups, and was concerned over the growing pessimism in countries where human rights violations occurred regularly and with impunity. She recommended establishing effective early warning and conflict prevention mechanisms, an independent judiciary and a moratorium on executions in countries that retained the death penalty, with a view to completely abolishing it.

Commission action. On 20 April [res. 2000/31], the Commission, strongly condemning extrajudicial, summary or arbitrary executions, demanded that Governments end the phenomenon in all its forms. The Commission asked the Special Rapporteur to continue examining situations of extrajudicial, summary or arbitrary executions and report annually; respond to information she received; enhance her dialogue with Governments and follow up on her recommendations after country visits; continue to pay special attention to extrajudicial, summary or arbitrary

executions of children and to related allegations concerning peaceful demonstrators or minorities; continue monitoring the implementation of international standards on safeguards and restrictions relating to capital punishment; and apply a gender perspective in her work. Governments were urged to assist the Special Rapporteur and to respond to her communications. The Secretary-General was asked to use his best endeavours in cases where the minimum standard of legal safeguards provided for in articles 6, 9, 14 and 15 of the International Covenant on Civil and Political Rights (see p. 609) appeared not to be respected and to continue to ensure that personnel specialized in human rights and humanitarian law issues formed part of UN missions, where appropriate, in order to deal with serious human rights violations, such as extrajudicial, summary or arbitrary executions.

GENERAL ASSEMBLY ACTION

On 4 December [meeting 81], the General Assembly, on the recommendation of the Third Committee [A/55/602/Add.2 & Corr.1], adopted **resolution 55/111** without vote [agenda item 114 (b)].

Extrajudicial, summary or arbitrary executions
The General Assembly,

Recalling the Universal Declaration of Human Rights, which guarantees the right to life, liberty and security of person, and the relevant provisions of the International Covenant on Civil and Political Rights,

Recalling also its resolutions 47/136 of 18 December 1992, 51/92 of 12 December 1996 and 53/147 of 9 December 1998, as well as Commission on Human Rights resolutions 1992/72 of 5 March 1992 and 1998/68 of 21 April 1998, and taking note of Commission resolution 2000/31 of 20 April 2000,

Recalling further Economic and Social Council resolution 1984/50 of 25 May 1984 and the safeguards guaranteeing protection of the rights of those facing the death penalty annexed thereto and Council resolution 1989/64 of 24 May 1989 on their implementation, as well as the Declaration of Basic Principles of Justice for Victims of Crime and Abuse of Power, adopted by the General Assembly in its resolution 40/34 of 29 November 1985,

Deeply alarmed at the persistence, on a large scale, of extrajudicial, summary or arbitrary executions in all parts of the world,

Dismayed that in a number of countries impunity, the negation of justice, continues to prevail and often remains the main cause of the continuing occurrence of extrajudicial, summary or arbitrary executions in those countries,

Recognizing the contribution of the establishment of the International Criminal Court with regard to ensuring effective prosecution concerning executions in serious violation of article 3 common to the four Geneva Conventions of 12 August 1949, without previous judgement pronounced by a regularly constituted court affording all judicial guarantees that are generally recognized as indispensable,

Convinced of the need for effective action to combat and eliminate the abhorrent practice of extrajudicial, summary or arbitrary executions, which represent a flagrant violation of the fundamental right to life,

1. *Strongly condemns once again* all the extrajudicial, summary or arbitrary executions that continue to take place throughout the world;

2. *Notes* that impunity continues to be a major cause of the perpetuation of violations of human rights, including extrajudicial, summary or arbitrary executions;

3. *Acknowledges* the historic significance of the adoption of the Rome Statute of the International Criminal Court, and the fact that a significant number of States have already signed and/or ratified the Statute, and calls upon all States to consider signing and ratifying the Statute;

4. *Demands* that all Governments ensure that the practice of extrajudicial, summary or arbitrary executions be brought to an end and that they take effective action to combat and eliminate the phenomenon in all its forms;

5. *Takes note* of the interim report of the Special Rapporteur of the Commission on Human Rights on extrajudicial, summary or arbitrary executions, including the attention given therein to various aspects and situations involving violations of the right to life by extrajudicial, summary or arbitrary executions;

6. *Reiterates* the obligation of all Governments to conduct exhaustive and impartial investigations into all suspected cases of extrajudicial, summary or arbitrary executions, to identify and bring to justice those responsible, while ensuring the right of every person to a fair and public hearing by a competent, independent and impartial tribunal established by law, to grant adequate compensation to the victims or their families and to adopt all necessary measures, including legal and judicial measures, in order to bring an end to impunity, to prevent the recurrence of such executions;

7. *Calls upon* Governments concerned to investigate promptly and thoroughly cases in various parts of the world of killings committed in the name of passion or in the name of honour, persons killed for reasons related to their peaceful activities as human rights defenders or as journalists, racially motivated violence leading to the death of the victim as well as other persons whose right to life has been violated, and to bring those responsible to justice before an independent and impartial judiciary, and to ensure that such killings are neither condoned nor sanctioned by government officials or personnel;

8. *Urges* Governments to undertake all necessary and possible measures to prevent loss of life, in particular that of children, during public demonstrations, internal and communal violence, civil unrest and public emergencies or armed conflict, and to ensure that the police and security forces receive thorough training in human rights matters, in particular with regard to restrictions on the use of force and firearms in the discharge of their functions;

9. *Stresses* the importance for States to take effective measures to end impunity with regard to extrajudicial, summary or arbitrary executions, inter alia, through the adoption of preventive measures, and calls upon Governments to ensure that such measures are included in post-conflict peace-building efforts;

10. *Encourages* the Special Rapporteur to continue, within the framework of her mandate, to collect information from all concerned and to seek the views and comments of Governments so as to be able to respond effectively to reliable information that comes before her and to follow up communications and country visits;

11. *Reaffirms* Economic and Social Council decision 1998/265 of 30 July 1998, in which the Council endorsed the decision of the Commission on Human Rights, in its resolution 1998/68, to extend the mandate of the Special Rapporteur for three years;

12. *Notes* the important role the Special Rapporteur has played in the elimination of extrajudicial, summary or arbitrary executions;

13. *Also notes* that the Commission, in its resolution 2000/31, requested the Special Rapporteur, in carrying out her mandate:

(*a*) To continue to examine situations of extrajudicial, summary or arbitrary executions and to submit her findings on an annual basis, together with conclusions and recommendations, to the Commission, as well as such other reports as the Special Rapporteur deems necessary in order to keep the Commission informed about serious situations of extrajudicial, summary or arbitrary executions that warrant its immediate attention;

(*b*) To respond effectively to information that comes before her, in particular when an extrajudicial, summary or arbitrary execution is imminent or seriously threatened or when such an execution has occurred;

(*c*) To enhance further her dialogue with Governments, as well as to follow up on recommendations made in reports after visits to particular countries;

(*d*) To continue to pay special attention to extrajudicial, summary or arbitrary executions of children and to allegations concerning violations of the right to life in the context of violence against participants in demonstrations and other peaceful public manifestations or against persons belonging to minorities;

(*e*) To pay special attention to extrajudicial, summary or arbitrary executions where the victims are individuals carrying out peaceful activities in defence of human rights and fundamental freedoms;

(*f*) To continue monitoring the implementation of existing international standards on safeguards and restrictions relating to the imposition of capital punishment, bearing in mind the comments made by the Human Rights Committee in its interpretation of article 6 of the International Covenant on Civil and Political Rights, as well as the Second Optional Protocol thereto;

(*g*) To apply a gender perspective in her work;

14. *Strongly urges* all Governments, in particular those that have not yet done so, to respond without undue delay to the communications and requests for information transmitted to them by the Special Rapporteur, and urges them and all others concerned to cooperate with and assist the Special Rapporteur so that she may carry out her mandate effectively, including, where appropriate, by issuing invitations to the Special Rapporteur when she so requests;

15. *Expresses its appreciation* to those Governments that have invited the Special Rapporteur to visit their countries, asks them to examine carefully the recommendations made by the Special Rapporteur and invites them to report to the Special Rapporteur on the

actions taken on those recommendations, and requests other Governments to cooperate in a similar way;

16. *Encourages* Governments, international organizations and non-governmental organizations to organize training programmes and to support projects with a view to training or educating military forces, law enforcement officers and government officials, as well as members of United Nations peacekeeping or observer missions, in human rights and humanitarian law issues connected with their work, and appeals to the international community to support endeavours to that end;

17. *Urges* the Special Rapporteur to continue to bring to the attention of the United Nations High Commissioner for Human Rights such situations of extrajudicial, summary or arbitrary executions as are of particularly serious concern to her or where early action might prevent further deterioration;

18. *Welcomes* the cooperation established between the Special Rapporteur and other United Nations mechanisms and procedures relating to human rights, as well as with medical and forensic experts, and encourages the Special Rapporteur to continue efforts in that regard;

19. *Calls upon* the Governments of all States in which the death penalty has not been abolished to comply with their obligations under relevant provisions of international human rights instruments, keeping in mind the safeguards and guarantees referred to in Economic and Social Council resolutions 1984/50 and 1989/64;

20. *Again requests* the Secretary-General to continue to use his best endeavours in cases where the minimum standard of legal safeguards provided for in articles 6, 9, 14 and 15 of the International Covenant on Civil and Political Rights appears not to have been respected;

21. *Requests* the Secretary-General to provide the Special Rapporteur with an adequate and stable level of human, financial and material resources to enable her to carry out her mandate effectively, including through country visits;

22. *Also requests* the Secretary-General to continue, in close collaboration with the United Nations High Commissioner for Human Rights, in conformity with the High Commissioner's mandate established by the General Assembly in its resolution 48/141 of 20 December 1993, to ensure that personnel specialized in human rights and humanitarian law issues form part of United Nations missions, where appropriate, in order to deal with serious violations of human rights, such as extrajudicial, summary or arbitrary executions;

23. *Requests* the Special Rapporteur to submit an interim report to the General Assembly at its fifty-seventh session on the situation worldwide in regard to extrajudicial, summary or arbitrary executions and her recommendations for more effective action to combat that phenomenon.

Disappearance of persons

Working Group on Enforced or Involuntary Disappearances

Commission action. On 20 April [res. 2000/37], the Commission, deeply concerned by the increase in enforced or involuntary disappearances and by reports concerning harassment, ill-treatment and intimidation of witnesses of disappearances or relatives of persons who had disappeared, urged Governments to cooperate with the Working Group on Enforced or Involuntary Disappearances. The Commission invited States to provide the Group with information on such disappearances and on giving effect to the Declaration on the Protection of All Persons from Enforced Disappearance, adopted by the General Assembly in resolution 47/133 [YUN 1992, p. 744]. The Group was asked to report in 2001. The Secretary-General was asked to inform the Group and the Commission of action he had taken to promote the Declaration. He was also requested to disseminate the draft international convention on the protection of all persons from enforced disappearance [YUN 1998, p. 662] and to ask States, international organizations and NGOs to submit their views on the draft and on whether a working group should consider it.

Working Group activities. The five-member Working Group on Enforced or Involuntary Disappearances held three sessions in 2000: its sixtieth in New York (24-27 April) and its sixty-first and sixty-second in Geneva (21-25 August and 15-24 November) [E/CN.4/2001/68]. In addition to its original mandate, which was to act as a channel of communication between families of disappeared persons and Governments concerned, with a view to ensuring that sufficiently documented individual cases were investigated, the Working Group provided assistance in the implementation by States of the 1992 Declaration and of the existing international rules. However, due to limitations in its resources and reporting requirements, the Group's report lacked some important information.

Cases under active consideration numbered 45,998 and countries with outstanding cases of alleged disappearance totalled 73. During the period under review, up to 24 November, the last day of the sixty-second session, the Group transmitted 487 new cases of disappearance to 29 countries, 120 of which allegedly occurred in 2000. The Group regretted that of the 24 countries with unclarified cases, the Governments of 17 countries did not communicate with the Group. The Group sent urgent action appeals to 20 Governments in respect of 95 cases.

The Group adopted general comments on the 1992 Declaration, as well as comments on the draft international convention on the protection of all persons from enforced disappearance. It stressed that impunity was one of the main causes of enforced disappearance and one of the major obstacles to clarifying past cases. In accordance with the Declaration, it was crucial that Governments take measures to prevent the occurrence of future disappearances. The Group stressed the need to continue to receive cooperation from concerned NGOs, and called on Governments to guarantee protection to them.

The report contained a separate opinion by a member of the Group objecting to the application of a 32-page limit on its report, as requested in General Assembly resolution 47/202 B [YUN 1992, p. 1083], as the report did not reflect the situation worldwide of enforced disappearances or the Group's efforts to clarify the fate of some 50,000 disappeared persons.

Report of Secretary-General. Pursuant to General Assembly resolution 53/150 [YUN 1998, p. 679], the Secretary-General, in August [A/55/289], described activities to disseminate the 1992 Declaration. The United Nations Department of Public Information (DPI) had distributed the text through UN information centres, to UN peace-keeping offices and to the specialized agencies, and had made it available to the general public and educational institutes, upon request. It was also available on the UN web site (www.un.org). DPI had also prepared background press releases and would produce media information packets and a background brochure on enforced disappearances. The Declaration had also been distributed by OHCHR field offices.

Subcommission action. On 17 August [res. 2000/18], the Subcommission recommended that the Commission establish an intersessional working group to consider the draft international convention on the protection of all persons from enforced disappearance, and urged the Commission to give priority to the draft convention.

GENERAL ASSEMBLY ACTION

On 4 December [meeting 81], the General Assembly, on the recommendation of the Third Committee [A/55/602/Add.2 & Corr.1], adopted **resolution 55/103** without vote [agenda item 114 (b)].

Question of enforced or involuntary disappearances

The General Assembly,

Guided by the purposes and principles set forth in the Charter of the United Nations, the Universal Declaration of Human Rights, the International Covenants on Human Rights and the other relevant international human rights instruments,

Recalling its resolution 33/173 of 20 December 1978 concerning disappeared persons and its previous resolutions on the question of enforced or involuntary disappearances, in particular resolution 53/150 of 9 December 1998,

Recalling also its resolution 47/133 of 18 December 1992 proclaiming the Declaration on the Protection of All Persons from Enforced Disappearance as a body of principles for all States,

Expressing concern that, according to the Working Group on Enforced or Involuntary Disappearances of the Commission on Human Rights, the practice of a number of States can run counter to the Declaration,

Deeply concerned, in particular, by the intensification of enforced disappearances in various regions of the world and by the growing number of reports concerning the harassment, ill-treatment and intimidation of witnesses of disappearances or relatives of persons who have disappeared,

Emphasizing that impunity with regard to enforced disappearances contributes to the perpetuation of this phenomenon and constitutes one of the obstacles to the elucidation of its manifestations,

Taking note with interest of the initiatives taken at the national and international levels in order to end impunity,

Bearing in mind Commission on Human Rights resolution 2000/37 of 20 April 2000,

Taking note of the transmission by the Subcommission on the Promotion and Protection of Human Rights to the Commission on Human Rights of a draft international convention on the protection of all persons from forced disappearance,

Convinced that further efforts are needed to promote wider awareness of and respect for the Declaration, and taking note in this regard of the report of the Secretary-General on the question of enforced or involuntary disappearances,

1. *Reaffirms* that any act of enforced disappearance is an offence to human dignity and a grave and flagrant violation of the human rights and fundamental freedoms proclaimed in the Universal Declaration of Human Rights and reaffirmed and developed in other international instruments in this field, as well as a violation of the rules of international law;

2. *Urges* all Governments to take appropriate legislative or other steps to prevent and suppress the practice of enforced disappearances, in keeping with the Declaration on the Protection of All Persons from Enforced Disappearance, and to take action to that end at the national and regional levels and in cooperation with the United Nations, including through the provision of technical assistance;

3. *Calls upon* Governments to take steps to ensure that, when a state of emergency is introduced, the protection of human rights is ensured, in particular as regards the prevention of enforced disappearances;

4. *Reminds* Governments that impunity with regard to enforced disappearances contributes to the perpetuation of this phenomenon and constitutes one of the obstacles to the elucidation of its manifestations, and in this respect also reminds them of the need to ensure that their competent authorities conduct prompt and impartial inquiries in all circumstances in which there is a reason to believe that an enforced disappearance has occurred in territory under their jurisdiction, and that, if allegations are confirmed, perpetrators should be prosecuted;

5. *Once again urges* the Governments concerned to take steps to protect the families of disappeared persons against any intimidation or ill-treatment to which they may be subjected;

6. *Encourages* States, as some have already done, to provide concrete information on measures taken to

give effect to the Declaration, as well as obstacles encountered;

7. *Requests* all States to consider the possibility of disseminating the text of the Declaration in their respective national languages and to facilitate its dissemination in local languages;

8. *Notes* the action taken by non-governmental organizations to encourage implementation of the Declaration, and invites them to continue to facilitate its dissemination and to contribute to the work of the Subcommission on the Promotion and Protection of Human Rights;

9. *Requests* the Working Group on Enforced or Involuntary Disappearances of the Commission on Human Rights, in the continued exercise of its mandate, to take into account the provisions of the Declaration and to modify its working methods, if necessary;

10. *Recalls* the importance of the Working Group, the primary role of which is, as described in its reports, to act as a channel of communication between the families of disappeared persons and the Governments concerned, with a view to ensuring that sufficiently documented and clearly identified individual cases are investigated, and to ascertain whether such information falls under its mandate and contains the required elements, and invites the Group to continue to seek the views and comments of all concerned, including Member States, in preparing its reports;

11. *Invites* the Working Group to identify obstacles to the realization of the provisions of the Declaration, to recommend ways of overcoming those obstacles and, in this regard, to continue a dialogue with Governments and relevant intergovernmental and nongovernmental organizations;

12. *Encourages* the Working Group to continue to consider the question of impunity, in the light of the relevant provisions of the Declaration and of the final reports submitted by the special rapporteurs appointed by the Subcommission;

13. *Requests* the Working Group to pay the utmost attention to cases of children subjected to enforced disappearance and children of disappeared persons and to cooperate closely with the Governments concerned to search for and identify those children;

14. *Appeals* to the Governments concerned, in particular those which have not yet replied to the communications transmitted by the Working Group, to cooperate fully with it and, in particular, to reply promptly to its requests for information so that, while respecting its working methods based on discretion, it may perform its strictly humanitarian role;

15. *Encourages* the Governments concerned to give serious consideration to inviting the Working Group to visit their countries so as to enable the Group to fulfil its mandate even more effectively;

16. *Expresses its profound thanks* to the many Governments that have cooperated with the Working Group and replied to its requests for information and to the Governments that have invited the Group to visit their countries, requests them to give all necessary attention to the recommendations of the Group, and invites them to inform the Group of any action they take on those recommendations;

17. *Calls upon* the Commission on Human Rights to continue to study this question as a matter of priority

and to take any steps it may deem necessary to the pursuit of the task of the Working Group and to the follow-up to its recommendations when it considers the report to be submitted by the Group to the Commission at its fifty-seventh session;

18. *Renews its requests* to the Secretary-General to continue to provide the Working Group with all of the facilities it requires to perform its functions, especially for carrying out missions and following them up;

19. *Requests* the Secretary-General to keep it informed of the steps he takes to secure the widespread dissemination and promotion of the Declaration;

20. *Also requests* the Secretary-General to submit to it at its fifty-seventh session a report on the steps taken to implement the present resolution;

21. *Decides* to consider the question of enforced disappearances, and in particular the implementation of the Declaration, at its fifty-seventh session under the sub-item entitled "Human rights questions, including alternative approaches for improving the effective enjoyment of human rights and fundamental freedoms".

Torture and cruel treatment

Reports of Special Rapporteur. In February [E/CN.4/2000/9], the Special Rapporteur on torture, Sir Nigel S. Rodley (United Kingdom), summarized his 1999 activities. He had sent 60 letters to 56 Governments on behalf of some 700 individuals and 32 groups involving about 3,000 persons. He also transmitted 144 urgent appeals to 51 countries on behalf of some 430 individuals (45 known to be minors and 35 known to be women), as well as 15 groups involving about 1,500 persons with regard to whom fears had been expressed that they might be subjected to torture. In addition, 26 Governments provided the Special Rapporteur with replies on 155 cases, whereas 24 did so regarding some 350 cases submitted in previous years. The Special Rapporteur provided brief summaries of general allegations and individual cases, as well as of the urgent appeals and government replies, and presented his observations where applicable. An addendum to the report contained an additional 20 replies received from Governments [E/CN.4/2000/9/Add.5].

In another addendum [E/CN.4/2000/9/Add.1], the Special Rapporteur reported on follow-up to his recommendations described in communications received from Governments between 6 December 1997 and 15 December 1999 regarding his visits to Colombia [YUN 1994, p. 1022], Chile [YUN 1995, p. 756], Venezuela [YUN 1996, p. 640] and Mexico [YUN 1997, p. 666].

The Special Rapporteur visited Brazil (20 August–12 September) [E/CN.4/2001/66/Add.2] to assess the extent of the practice of torture. He reported that torture and similar ill-treatment were widespread and systematic and found at all phases of detention. It mainly happened to poor, black common criminals involved in petty crime or small-scale drug distribution, and occurred in police stations and custodial institutions. The purposes ranged from obtaining information and confessions to financial extortion. The Special Rapporteur described conditions of detention in many places as subhuman. A culture of brutality and corruption was widespread, and the poor, usually black or mulatto or, in rural areas, indigenous, received the worst treatment. The Special Rapporteur observed that the 1997 Torture Law, which characterized torture as a serious crime, was virtually ignored. Free legal assistance was illusory for most of the 85 per cent of those who needed it, due to the limited number of public defenders. Some of the recommendations made to Brazil by the Special Rapporteur related to the abuse by police of the power of arrest, access to detainees by family members, detainees' rights to consult privately with a lawyer and the provision of free legal advice to the poor, the introduction of video- and audiotaping of proceedings in police interrogation rooms, unifying the police under civilian authority and civilian justice, installing a monitoring presence in all places of detention and training for police, detention personnel, public prosecutors and others involved in law enforcement. He urged the Government to consider inviting the Special Rapporteur on extrajudicial, summary or arbitrary executions to visit the country.

The Special Rapporteur visited Azerbaijan (7-15 May) [E/CN.4/2001/66/Add.1] to assess the situation regarding torture and ill-treatment. Based on testimony received, he concluded that the practice was widespread. He expressed concern that a person could be transferred from a remand centre back to police custody, albeit on the order of a prosecutor, thus enhancing the risk and fear of ill-treatment. Ill-treatment had been facilitated by the power of prosecutors to order detention in temporary detention facilities for up to 30 days. The Special Rapporteur recommended investigation of allegations of torture and ill-treatment by a body capable of prosecuting perpetrators; regular inspections of places of detention by prosecutors; a system of compensation for victims; public awareness campaigns on basic human rights; and improved legal aid services.

A note by the Secretariat [E/CN.4/2001/116] contained comments submitted by Cameroon regarding the Special Rapporteur's visit to the country in 1999 [YUN 1999, p. 636]. The note also drew attention to a statement by Cameroon before the Commission on 5 April [E/CN.4/2000/SR.27], following the Special Rapporteur's presentation of the report.

Commission action. On 20 April [res. 2000/43], the Commission, condemning all forms of torture as described in the Convention against Torture and Other Cruel, Inhuman or Degrading Treatment or Punishment, contained in General Assembly resolution 39/46 [YUN 1984, p. 813] (see p. 613), called on Governments to prohibit the practice and urged them to become parties to the Convention as a matter of priority. The Commission asked the Special Rapporteur to consider including information in his report on the follow-up by Governments to his recommendations, visits and communications and to submit an interim report (see below) to the Assembly in 2000 and a full report to the Commission in 2001.

The Economic and Social Council on 28 July approved the Commission's request to the Special Rapporteur to submit an interim and a full report (**decision 2000/265**).

Interim report. In August [A/55/290], the Secretary-General transmitted an interim report of the Special Rapporteur, pursuant to General Assembly resolution 54/156 [YUN 1999, p. 638]. The report covered issues of special concern to the Special Rapporteur, including gender-specific forms of torture, to which women were subjected, including rape, sexual abuse and harassment, virginity testing, forced abortion or forced miscarriage; children victims of torture or cruel, inhuman or degrading treatment or punishment; torture and human rights defenders; reparation for victims; and torture and poverty.

Voluntary Fund for torture victims

Commission action. On 20 April [res. 2000/43], the Commission appealed to Governments, organizations and individuals to contribute annually to the Voluntary Fund for Victims of Torture. It called on the Fund's Board of Trustees to present in 2001 an updated assessment of the global need for funding of rehabilitation services for torture victims and of lessons learned from the Fund's activities. The Secretary-General was asked to continue to include the Fund among the programmes receiving donations at the annual UN Pledging Conference for Development Activities, and to ensure adequate staffing and technical facilities for the UN bodies dealing with torture.

Reports of Secretary-General. In his annual report on the status of the Fund, submitted in July [A/55/178], the Secretary-General stated that contributions received between 17 May 1999 and 13 July 2000 totalled $7,567,853 from 34 countries. Contributions from two private individuals and the staff of the United Nations Office at Geneva totalled $13,567.

The Board of Trustees held its nineteenth session in Geneva (15-26 May). The total then available for grants to assist victims of torture amounted to some $7 million, of which $100,000 was earmarked for urgent assistance to victims in countries lacking appropriate treatment facilities and to assist victims of amputation and mutilation coming from Sierra Leone. A second category of grants, totalling $400,000, was set aside for organizations that might face financial difficulties prior to the Board's next session in 2001. During the year, $10.1 million was requested for 188 projects. Annexed to the report was a declaration on the International Day in Support of Victims of Torture, 26 June 2000, issued by the Committee against Torture, the Fund's Board of Trustees, the Special Rapporteur on torture and the High Commissioner.

On 4 December, the General Assembly took note of the Secretary-General's report (**decision 55/420**).

In a later report [E/CN.4/2001/59 & Corr.1], the Secretary-General stated that an additional $180,835 was received between 15 May and 15 December 2000 for allocation by the Board in 2001.

GENERAL ASSEMBLY ACTION

On 4 December [meeting 81], the General Assembly, on the recommendation of the Third Committee [A/55/602/Add.1], adopted **resolution 55/89** without vote [agenda item 114 (a)].

Torture and other cruel, inhuman or degrading treatment or punishment

The General Assembly,

Recalling article 5 of the Universal Declaration of Human Rights, article 7 of the International Covenant on Civil and Political Rights, the Declaration on the Protection of All Persons from Being Subjected to Torture and Other Cruel, Inhuman or Degrading Treatment or Punishment and its resolution 39/46 of 10 December 1984, by which it adopted and opened for signature, ratification and accession the Convention against Torture and Other Cruel, Inhuman or Degrading Treatment or Punishment, and all its subsequent relevant resolutions,

Recalling that freedom from torture is a right that must be protected under all circumstances, including in times of internal or international disturbance or armed conflict,

Recalling also that the World Conference on Human Rights, held at Vienna from 14 to 25 June 1993, firmly declared that efforts to eradicate torture should, first and foremost, be concentrated on prevention and called for the early adoption of an optional protocol to the Convention against Torture and Other Cruel, Inhuman or Degrading Treatment or Punishment, which is intended to establish a preventive system of regular visits to places of detention,

Urging all Governments to promote the speedy and full implementation of the Vienna Declaration and Programme of Action, adopted by the World Conference on Human Rights on 25 June 1993, in particular the section relating to freedom from torture, in which it is stated that States should abrogate legislation leading to impunity for those responsible for grave violations of human rights, such as torture, and prosecute such violations, thereby providing a firm basis for the rule of law,

Recalling its resolution 36/151 of 16 December 1981, in which it noted with deep concern that acts of torture took place in various countries, recognized the need to provide assistance to the victims in a purely humanitarian spirit and established the United Nations Voluntary Fund for Victims of Torture,

Recalling also the recommendation in the Vienna Declaration and Programme of Action that high priority should be given to providing the necessary resources to assist victims of torture and effective remedies for their physical, psychological and social rehabilitation, inter alia, through additional contributions to the Fund,

Noting with satisfaction the existence of a considerable international network of centres for the rehabilitation of victims of torture, which plays an important role in providing assistance to victims of torture, and the collaboration of the Fund with the centres,

Commending the persistent efforts by non-governmental organizations to combat torture and to alleviate the suffering of victims of torture,

Mindful of the proclamation by the General Assembly in its resolution 52/149 of 12 December 1997 of 26 June as the United Nations International Day in Support of Victims of Torture,

1. *Condemns* all forms of torture, including through intimidation, as described in article 1 of the Convention against Torture and Other Cruel, Inhuman or Degrading Treatment or Punishment;

2. *Stresses* that all allegations of torture or other cruel, inhuman or degrading treatment or punishment should be promptly and impartially examined by the competent national authority, that those who encourage, order, tolerate or perpetrate acts of torture must be held responsible and severely punished, including the officials in charge of the place of detention where the prohibited act is found to have taken place, and that national legal systems should ensure that the victims of such acts obtain redress and are awarded fair and adequate compensation and receive appropriate social and medical rehabilitation;

3. *Draws the attention* of Governments to the Principles on the Effective Investigation and Documentation of Torture and Other Cruel, Inhuman or Degrading Treatment or Punishment annexed to the present resolution, and strongly encourages Governments to reflect upon the Principles as a useful tool in efforts to combat torture;

4. *Notes with appreciation* that one hundred and twenty-two States have become parties to the Convention;

5. *Urges* all States that have not yet done so to become parties to the Convention as a matter of priority;

6. *Invites* all States ratifying or acceding to the Convention and those States that are parties to the Convention and have not yet done so to consider joining the States parties that have already made the declarations provided for in articles 21 and 22 of the Convention

and to consider the possibility of withdrawing their reservations to article 20;

7. *Urges* all States parties to the Convention to notify the Secretary-General of their acceptance of the amendments to articles 17 and 18 of the Convention as soon as possible;

8. *Urges* States parties to comply strictly with their obligations under the Convention, including their obligation to submit reports in accordance with article 19, in view of the high number of reports not submitted, and invites States parties to incorporate a gender perspective and information concerning children and juveniles when submitting reports to the Committee against Torture;

9. *Emphasizes* the obligation of States parties under article 10 of the Convention to ensure education and training for personnel who may be involved in the custody, interrogation or treatment of any individual subjected to any form of arrest, detention or imprisonment;

10. *Stresses*, in this context, that States must not punish personnel referred to in paragraph 9 above for not obeying orders to commit or conceal acts amounting to torture or other cruel, inhuman or degrading treatment or punishment;

11. *Welcomes* the work of the Committee, and takes note of the report of the Committee, submitted in accordance with article 24 of the Convention;

12. *Calls upon* the United Nations High Commissioner for Human Rights, in conformity with her mandate established in General Assembly resolution 48/141 of 20 December 1993, to continue to provide, at the request of Governments, advisory services for the preparation of national reports to the Committee and for the prevention of torture, as well as technical assistance in the development, production and distribution of teaching material for this purpose;

13. *Urges* States parties to take fully into account the conclusions and recommendations made by the Committee after its consideration of their reports;

14. *Urges* the inter-sessional open-ended working group of the Commission on Human Rights on the development of a draft optional protocol to the Convention against Torture and Other Cruel, Inhuman or Degrading Treatment or Punishment to complete as soon as possible a final text for submission to the General Assembly, through the Economic and Social Council, for consideration and adoption;

15. *Takes note with appreciation* of the interim report of the Special Rapporteur of the Commission on Human Rights on the question of torture and other cruel, inhuman or degrading treatment or punishment, describing the overall trends and developments with regard to his mandate, and encourages the Special Rapporteur to continue to include in his recommendations proposals on the prevention and investigation of torture;

16. *Invites* the Special Rapporteur to continue to examine questions of torture and other cruel, inhuman or degrading treatment or punishment directed against women, and conditions conducive to such torture, and to make appropriate recommendations for the prevention and redress of gender-specific forms of torture, including rape or any other form of sexual violence, and to exchange views with the Special Rapporteur of the Commission on Human Rights on violence against women, its causes and consequences, with a view to enhancing further their effectiveness and mutual cooperation;

17. *Also invites* the Special Rapporteur to continue to consider questions relating to the torture of children and conditions conducive to such torture and other cruel, inhuman or degrading treatment or punishment and to make appropriate recommendations for the prevention of such torture;

18. *Calls upon* all Governments to cooperate with and assist the Special Rapporteur in the performance of his task, in particular by supplying all necessary information requested by him, to react appropriately and expeditiously to his urgent appeals and to give serious consideration to his requests to visit their countries, and urges them to enter into a constructive dialogue with the Special Rapporteur with respect to the follow-up to his recommendations;

19. *Approves* the methods of work employed by the Special Rapporteur, in particular with regard to urgent appeals, reiterates the need for him to be able to respond effectively to credible and reliable information that comes before him, invites him to continue to seek the views and comments of all concerned, in particular Member States, and expresses its appreciation for the discreet and independent way in which he continues to carry out his work;

20. *Requests* the Special Rapporteur to continue to consider including in his report information on the follow-up by Governments to his recommendations, visits and communications, including progress made and problems encountered;

21. *Stresses* the need for the continued regular exchange of views between the Committee, the Special Rapporteur and other relevant United Nations mechanisms and bodies, as well as for the pursuance of cooperation with relevant United Nations programmes, notably the United Nations Crime Prevention and Criminal Justice Programme, with a view to enhancing further their effectiveness and cooperation on issues relating to torture, inter alia, by improving their coordination;

22. *Expresses its gratitude and appreciation* to the Governments, organizations and individuals that have already contributed to the United Nations Voluntary Fund for Victims of Torture;

23. *Stresses* the importance of the work of the Board of Trustees of the Fund, and appeals to all Governments and organizations to contribute annually to the Fund, preferably by 1 March before the annual meeting of the Board of Trustees, if possible with a substantial increase in the level of contributions, so that consideration may be given to the ever-increasing demand for assistance;

24. *Requests* the Secretary-General to transmit to all Governments the appeals of the General Assembly for contributions to the Fund and to continue to include the Fund on an annual basis among the programmes for which funds are pledged at the United Nations Pledging Conference for Development Activities;

25. *Also requests* the Secretary-General to assist the Board of Trustees of the Fund in its appeal for contributions and in its efforts to make better known the existence of the Fund and the financial means currently available to it, as well as in its assessment of the global need for international funding of rehabilitation serv-

ices for victims of torture and, in this effort, to make use of all existing possibilities, including the preparation, production and dissemination of information materials;

26. *Further requests* the Secretary-General to ensure the provision of adequate staff and facilities for the bodies and mechanisms involved in combating torture and assisting victims of torture, commensurate with the strong support expressed by Member States for combating torture and assisting victims of torture;

27. *Invites* donor countries and recipient countries to consider including in their bilateral programmes and projects relating to the training of armed forces, security forces, prison and police personnel, as well as health-care personnel, matters relating to the protection of human rights and the prevention of torture and to keep in mind a gender perspective;

28. *Calls upon* all Governments, the Office of the United Nations High Commissioner for Human Rights and other United Nations bodies and agencies, as well as relevant intergovernmental and non-governmental organizations, to commemorate, on 26 June, the United Nations International Day in Support of Victims of Torture;

29. *Requests* the Secretary-General to submit to the Commission on Human Rights at its fifty-seventh session and to the General Assembly at its fifty-sixth session a report on the status of the Convention against Torture and Other Cruel, Inhuman or Degrading Treatment or Punishment and a report on the operations of the United Nations Voluntary Fund for the Victims of Torture;

30. *Decides* to consider at its fifty-sixth session the reports of the Secretary-General, including the report on the United Nations Voluntary Fund for Victims of Torture, the report of the Committee against Torture and the interim report of the Special Rapporteur of the Commission on Human Rights on the question of torture and other cruel, inhuman or degrading treatment or punishment.

ANNEX
**Principles on the Effective Investigation and
Documentation of Torture and Other Cruel,
Inhuman or Degrading Treatment or Punishment**

1. The purposes of effective investigation and documentation of torture and other cruel, inhuman or degrading treatment or punishment (hereinafter "torture or other ill-treatment") include the following:

(*a*) Clarification of the facts and establishment and acknowledgement of individual and State responsibility for victims and their families;

(*b*) Identification of measures needed to prevent recurrence;

(*c*) Facilitation of prosecution and/or, as appropriate, disciplinary sanctions for those indicated by the investigation as being responsible and demonstration of the need for full reparation and redress from the State, including fair and adequate financial compensation and provision of the means for medical care and rehabilitation.

2. States shall ensure that complaints and reports of torture or ill-treatment are promptly and effectively investigated. Even in the absence of an express complaint, an investigation shall be undertaken if there are other indications that torture or ill-treatment might have occurred. The investigators, who shall be independent of the suspected perpetrators and the agency they serve, shall be competent and impartial. They shall have access to, or be empowered to commission investigations by, impartial medical or other experts. The methods used to carry out such investigations shall meet the highest professional standards and the findings shall be made public.

3. (*a*) The investigative authority shall have the power and obligation to obtain all the information necessary to the inquiry. The persons conducting the investigation shall have at their disposal all the necessary budgetary and technical resources for effective investigation. They shall also have the authority to oblige all those acting in an official capacity allegedly involved in torture or ill-treatment to appear and testify. The same shall apply to any witness. To this end, the investigative authority shall be entitled to issue summonses to witnesses, including any officials allegedly involved, and to demand the production of evidence.

(*b*) Alleged victims of torture or ill-treatment, witnesses, those conducting the investigation and their families shall be protected from violence, threats of violence or any other form of intimidation that may arise pursuant to the investigation. Those potentially implicated in torture or ill-treatment shall be removed from any position of control or power, whether direct or indirect, over complainants, witnesses and their families, as well as those conducting the investigation.

4. Alleged victims of torture or ill-treatment and their legal representatives shall be informed of, and have access to, any hearing, as well as to all information relevant to the investigation, and shall be entitled to present other evidence.

5. (*a*) In cases in which the established investigative procedures are inadequate because of insufficient expertise or suspected bias, or because of the apparent existence of a pattern of abuse or for other substantial reasons, States shall ensure that investigations are undertaken through an independent commission of inquiry or similar procedure. Members of such a commission shall be chosen for their recognized impartiality, competence and independence as individuals. In particular, they shall be independent of any suspected perpetrators and the institutions or agencies they may serve. The commission shall have the authority to obtain all information necessary to the inquiry and shall conduct the inquiry as provided for under these Principles.ª

(*b*) A written report, made within a reasonable time, shall include the scope of the inquiry, procedures and methods used to evaluate evidence as well as conclusions and recommendations based on findings of fact and on applicable law. Upon completion, the report shall be made public. It shall also describe in detail specific events that were found to have occurred and the evidence upon which such findings were based and list the names of witnesses who testified, with the exception of those whose identities have been withheld for their own protection. The State shall, within a reasonable period of time, reply to the report of the investigation and, as appropriate, indicate steps to be taken in response.

6. (*a*) Medical experts involved in the investigation of torture or ill-treatment shall behave at all times in conformity with the highest ethical standards and, in particular, shall obtain informed consent before any examination is undertaken. The examination must conform to established standards of medical practice.

In particular, examinations shall be conducted in private under the control of the medical expert and outside the presence of security agents and other government officials.

(b) The medical expert shall promptly prepare an accurate written report, which shall include at least the following:

   (i) Circumstances of the interview: name of the subject and name and affiliation of those present at the examination; exact time and date; location, nature and address of the institution (including, where appropriate, the room) where the examination is being conducted (e.g., detention centre, clinic or house); circumstances of the subject at the time of the examination (e.g., nature of any restraints on arrival or during the examination, presence of security forces during the examination, demeanour of those accompanying the prisoner or threatening statements to the examiner); and any other relevant factors;

   (ii) History: detailed record of the subject's story as given during the interview, including alleged methods of torture or ill-treatment, times when torture or ill-treatment is alleged to have occurred and all complaints of physical and psychological symptoms;

   (iii) Physical and psychological examination: record of all physical and psychological findings on clinical examination, including appropriate diagnostic tests and, where possible, colour photographs of all injuries;

   (iv) Opinion: interpretation as to the probable relationship of the physical and psychological findings to possible torture or ill-treatment. A recommendation for any necessary medical and psychological treatment and/or further examination shall be given;

   (v) Authorship: the report shall clearly identify those carrying out the examination and shall be signed.

(c) The report shall be confidential and communicated to the subject or his or her nominated representative. The views of the subject and his or her representative about the examination process shall be solicited and recorded in the report. It shall also be provided in writing, where appropriate, to the authority responsible for investigating the allegation of torture or ill-treatment. It is the responsibility of the State to ensure that it is delivered securely to these persons. The report shall not be made available to any other person, except with the consent of the subject or on the authorization of a court empowered to enforce such a transfer.

ªUnder certain circumstances, professional ethics may require information to be kept confidential. These requirements should be respected.

Freedom of opinion and expression

Reports of Special Rapporteur. In January [E/CN.4/2000/63], the Special Rapporteur on the promotion and protection of the right to freedom of opinion and expression, Abid Hussain (India), described his 1999 activities and summarized the texts of communications he had sent to 41 States and the Palestinian Authority and the replies thereto.

While noting a growing tide in favour of human rights, the Special Rapporteur also remarked that the rights to freedom of opinion, expression and information were violated, almost as a matter of routine, in States with widely different political systems and institutional frameworks for governance. He encouraged States that had not ratified the International Covenant on Civil and Political Rights and the International Covenant on Economic, Social and Cultural Rights, adopted by the General Assembly in resolution 2200 A (XXI) [YUN 1966, pp. 419 & 423], to do so. Governments were urged to ensure that press offences were not punishable by imprisonment, except in cases involving racist or discriminatory comments or calls to violence. They were also urged to remove formal and cultural obstacles to women's exercise of the right to freedom of expression, including the right to receive information. States were encouraged to ensure the full realization of the right to access to information.

·The Special Rapporteur visited Albania (29 May–2 June) [E/CN.4/2001/64/Add.1], where he observed that, although freedom of opinion and expression was widely apparent, the country still suffered from a general lack of a rights-oriented culture owing to many years of totalitarian rule and political isolation. True respect for the right required a change in social and cultural attitudes and practices, in addition to legislative reforms. A recently appointed Ombudsman should help to create a culture of democracy and human rights. Widespread criticism of the misuse of freedom by journalists and the unreliability of their work were described to the Special Rapporteur. Freedom of the media had been hindered to some extent by the restrictions on independent or opposition publications that resulted from financial and political pressure. The Special Rapporteur welcomed measures taken to promote and guarantee the right to freedom of opinion and expression of minorities, and noted that additional efforts were needed to make the media more sensitive to their needs. He recommended that the Government provide the ombudsman institution with adequate resources, invite the Special Rapporteurs on the independence of judges and lawyers and on violence against women to visit the country, amend the defamation provisions of the Penal Code so that the offence was no longer punishable by imprisonment and redefine the concept of a press offence, ensure the independence of the National Council for Radio and Televison and disseminate basic human rights instruments and information.

Albania, in its comments [E/CN.4/2001/138] on issues raised in the Special Rapporteur's report, emphasized that some of the recommendations had nothing to do with the current situation in the country.

In July [E/CN.4/2001/4], commenting on the Special Rapporteur's report on his visit to the country [YUN 1999, p. 641], Tunisia stated that the report did not reflect the true status of freedom of opinion and expression there, nor did it take into account the countless achievements resulting from reforms since the Constitution was amended in 1987.

Commission action. On 20 April [res. 2000/38], the Commission expressed concern at the detention, extrajudicial killing, persecution, harassment, threats, violence and discrimination directed at persons who exercised the right to freedom of opinion and expression and the rights to freedom of thought, conscience and religion, peaceful assembly and association and the right to take part in public affairs. It appealed to States to ensure respect and support for the rights of all persons who exercised those rights; to ensure non-discrimination against them; to cooperate with the Special Rapporteur; and to create an environment to promote and protect freedom of opinion and expression. The Special Rapporteur was asked to draw the attention of the High Commissioner to those situations which were of serious concern; in cooperation with the Special Rapporteur on violence against women, to pay particular attention to the situation of women and incidents of discrimination based on sex; to consider approaches taken to access information with a view to sharing best practices; to provide his views on the advantages and challenges of new information technologies; and to seek the views of Governments and others concerned. The Special Rapporteur was asked to report in 2001.

Conscientious objection

Report of Secretary-General. The Commission had before it a report of the Secretary-General [E/CN.4/2000/55] summarizing information received from 13 Governments on developments regarding the right of everyone to have conscientious objection to military service as a legitimate exercise of the right to freedom of thought, conscience and religion. The Secretary-General concluded that although most respondent countries recognized the right to conscientious objection to military service, not all of them accepted a general right to object—some restricted the basis to religious grounds only. Most countries provided some form of alternative service of a non-combative character, al-

though not always of a civilian character. Annexed to the report was the global status of conscientious objection to military service. A comparison with the information contained in the Secretary-General's previous report [YUN 1997, p. 648] indicated that the international situation regarding military service appeared to be static.

Commission action. On 20 April [res. 2000/34], the Commission called on States to review their laws and practices in relation to conscientious objection to military service and asked OHCHR to compile and analyse best practices in regard to the right to have conscientious objection to military service and to report thereon in 2002.

Communication. On 20 April [E/CN.4/2000/160], Singapore, also on behalf of 12 other States, dissociated itself from the Commission's resolution.

Terrorism

Commission action. By 27 votes to 13, with 12 abstentions, the Commission, on 20 April [res. 2000/30], condemning all acts, methods and practices of terrorism, urged States, in conformity with international law, to prevent, combat and eliminate terrorism. States were called on to enhance their cooperation with a view to bringing terrorists to justice and, in conformity with national and international law, to take appropriate measures before granting refugee status to ensure that an asylum-seeker had not participated in terrorist acts. The Commission urged relevant human rights mechanisms to address the consequences of the acts, methods and practices of terrorist groups. The Secretary-General was asked to collect information, including a compilation of studies and publications, on the implications of terrorism, as well as the effects of the fight against terrorism on the full enjoyment of human rights from relevant sources, and to make it available to concerned special rapporteurs and working groups. The Commission endorsed the Subcommission's 1999 request [YUN 1999, p. 642] to the Secretary-General to assist the Special Rapporteur.

ECONOMIC AND SOCIAL COUNCIL ACTION

On 28 July, the Economic and Social Council, on the recommendation of the Commission on Human Rights [E/2000/23 & Corr.1], adopted **decision 2000/260** by recorded vote (23-14-6) [agenda item 14 (g)].

Human rights and terrorism

At its 45th plenary meeting, on 28 July 2000, the Economic and Social Council, taking note of Commission on Human Rights resolution 2000/30 of 20 April 2000, approved the request of the Subcommission on the Promotion and Protection of Human Rights to the Secretary-General to give the Special Rapporteur on terrorism and human rights of the Subcommission all the assistance necessary so that she may hold consultations with the competent services and bodies of the United Nations system to complement her essential research and collect all the needed and up-to-date information and data for the preparation of her progress report.

RECORDED VOTE ON DECISION 2000/260:

In favour: Algeria, Angola, Bahrain, Belarus, Bolivia, Brazil, Burkina Faso, Cameroon, China, Colombia, Costa Rica, Cuba, Fiji, India, Indonesia, New Zealand, Oman, Pakistan, Russian Federation, Saudi Arabia, Sudan, Suriname, Viet Nam.

Against: Austria, Belgium, Bulgaria, Canada, Czech Republic, Denmark, France, Germany, Greece, Italy, Norway, Poland, Portugal, United Kingdom.

Abstaining: Croatia, Japan, Mexico, Syrian Arab Republic, United States, Venezuela.

Note by Secretariat. A June note by the Secretariat [E/CN.4/Sub.2/2000/31] stated that the Special Rapporteur on terrorism and human rights proposed to submit her progress report to the Subcommission in 2001, as it had not been possible to collect the data required in time to submit a report in 2000.

Subcommission action. On 18 August [dec. 2000/115], the Subcommission asked the Special Rapporteur to submit a progress report on her study in 2001. It asked the Secretary-General to transmit, as soon as possible, the preliminary report on terrorism and human rights [YUN 1999, p. 642] to Governments, specialized agencies and concerned intergovernmental organizations and NGOs for their comments; to make available to the Special Rapporteur all the information on the implications of terrorism, as well as the effects of the fight against terrorism, on the full enjoyment of human rights collected by him from all relevant sources; and to assist the Special Rapporteur.

Hostage-taking

On 20 April [res. 2000/29], the Commission, condemning hostage-taking, demanded the immediate and unconditional release of all hostages. States were called on to take measures to prevent, combat and punish hostage-taking, and thematic special rapporteurs and working groups were urged to address the consequences of such acts in their reports.

Freedom of movement

Mass exoduses

Report of High Commissioner. In response to a 1998 Commission request [YUN 1998, p. 674], the High Commissioner summarized information received from Governments, intergovernmental organizations, specialized agencies and NGOs on

measures they had taken to prevent violations and denials of human rights that led to and took place during mass exoduses and displacements [E/CN.4/2000/81]. In describing the relevant activities of OHCHR, the High Commissioner pointed to the complementarity between her mandate and that of the High Commissioner for Refugees and the importance of cooperation between them. She concluded that more focused attention was required on measures to prevent and redress the human rights violations causing and characterizing mass exoduses, as well as concrete action when such crises occurred. The further development of the Commission's mechanisms in that regard was critical, she stated.

Commission action. On 25 April [res. 2000/55], the Commission called on States to promote human rights and fundamental freedoms and to refrain from denying them to individuals because of nationality, ethnicity, race, gender, age, religion or language and thus contribute to addressing human rights situations that led to mass exoduses and displacements. The High Commissioner was asked to pay particular attention to human rights situations that caused or threatened to cause mass exoduses or displacements and to address such situations through promotion and protection measures, emergency preparedness and response mechanisms, early warning and information-sharing, technical advice and expertise and cooperation in countries of origin as well as host countries. She was also asked to report in 2003 on measures taken to implement the Commission's resolution, taking into account information provided by Governments, intergovernmental organizations, specialized agencies and NGOs.

Internally displaced persons

Reports of Secretary-General's Representative. In January [E/CN.4/2000/83], the Secretary-General's Representative, Francis M. Deng (Sudan), updated developments regarding the Guiding Principles on Internal Displacement [YUN 1998, p. 675] and efforts to develop an institutional framework for internally displaced persons. He discussed country visits as a way to focus on specific situations of internal displacement. The Representative presented areas where further research was needed, including addressing the problem of internal displacement in areas not under government control, the needs of internally displaced women and children, donor policies, and housing and property restitution for internally displaced persons.

The Representative visited Burundi (6-11 February) [E/CN.4/2001/5/Add.1], where the issue of regroupment (forced relocation) provided the main focus of the mission. Internal displacement affected 808,000 persons (12 per cent of the population), and over 500,000 Burundians were refugees outside the country. Internal displacement was largely the result of forced relocation, undertaken by the Government in response to the rebel attacks (see p. 143). The humanitarian consequences of regroupment had been grave; the authorities had not provided adequate assistance and protection, and although some international assistance reached the camps through NGOs, it was insufficient compared to the needs. There were also some camps that were inaccessible to the international community and thus had not received such assistance. The Representative recommended the cessation of regroupment, the dismantling of regroupment camps and the development of a strategy identifying the protection, assistance and reintegration needs of regrouped populations and returnees. He also made specific recommendations to the Government, the United Nations and donors.

In accordance with a 1999 Commission request [YUN 1999, p. 646], the Representative visited East Timor (26 February–1 March) [E/CN.4/2000/83/Add.3] to focus on the displacement that occurred in the lead-up to and following the popular consultation on autonomy in 1999 [YUN 1999, p. 280]. He examined issues of protection and assistance in all phases of displacement, including protection from arbitrary displacement, and protection and assistance during displacement and during return or resettlement and reintegration. The Representative concluded that, although the period of intense terror associated with the popular consultation had passed, durable solutions for the hundreds of thousands of persons displaced, within and outside the country, still needed to be found. Recommendations focused on the physical security of and international access to refugees in West Timor; voluntary and safe return or resettlement; the establishment of a judicial system and effective mechanisms of law and order; investigation and prosecution of violations of human rights and international humanitarian law and crimes against humanity; support for reconciliation efforts; reconstruction; support to women's groups; and greater involvement of the local community.

The Representative visited Georgia (13-17 May) [E/CN.4/2001/5/Add.4] to study the situation and the current conditions of internally displaced persons, and to understand the constraints impeding solutions for those displaced. He concluded that the population as a whole faced socioeconomic difficulties, but those displaced had additional disadvantages. In situations of protracted displacement, the vulnerabilities of the displaced risked being forgotten. The Representative recommended, among other things, disseminating the Guiding Principles to internally displaced persons, improving their living conditions, supporting programmes to address psychosocial needs, ending obstructions to the right to return in safety and dignity, giving special attention to the needs of women and ensuring the full rights of internally displaced persons as citizens.

In Armenia (18-19 May) [E/CN.4/2001/5/Add.3], the Representative studied and documented the situation of internal displacement. As in other cases in the region, a shared ethnic identity between the displaced and the authorities helped to explain why, in a situation of ethnic conflict, internally displaced persons were not associated by the authorities with the "enemy" and denied national protection and assistance on that basis. The number of persons uprooted in the country was comparatively small, and the nature of the displacement crisis was such that the affected areas were not in the centre of the area of conflict. There were no camps or other large concentrations of internally displaced persons, who instead had largely been taken in by relatives or friends or settled in small groups in temporary accommodation. In the light of the difficult economic situation of the country, the Government lacked the capacity to meet the needs of its internally displaced single-handedly without international support. The mission found that the lack of attention to those internally displaced was more due to oversight of their needs than a deliberate policy seeking their integration into society. Among the hardships faced were lack of shelter and access to land, psychological trauma, little engagement in economic activity and lack of government response to their needs. Among the Representative's recommendations were data collection on the situation, the recognition of internal displacement as a factor of vulnerability, safe access to land, comprehensive demining and mine-awareness, coordination of government policy on internal displacement and support for conflict resolution.

In Angola (31 October–9 November) [E/CN.4/2001/5/Add.5], the Representative noted that of a total population of some 12 million, there were an estimated 3.8 million internally displaced persons, of whom 2.6 million had become displaced since January 1998. He observed that some tangible improvements had been made regarding their situation and in the national and international response to the problem. He was encouraged by government measures to improve institutional arrangements and its coordination with the international community, particularly UN agencies. However, he found that coordination was often not effective on the ground and a number of serious humanitarian and protection concerns remained, particularly the lack of protection accorded to the security and human rights of those displaced and the civilian population. The Representative called for better coordination, increased access to populations in need, agreed criteria for targeting food distribution and increased engagement of the Government and donors in the humanitarian response.

Commission action. On 25 April [res. 2000/53], the Commission, stressing the need to strengthen inter-agency arrangements regarding internally displaced persons that were predictable, called on States to provide adequate resources for programmes to assist and protect internally displaced persons. It called on the High Commissioner to develop projects, in cooperation with others, to promote the human rights of internally displaced persons, as part of the programme of advisory services and technical cooperation (see p. 623), and to include in her annual report information on their implementation. The Secretary-General was asked to disseminate the Subcommission's 1998 resolution on housing and property restitution in the context of the return of refugees and internally displaced persons [YUN 1998, p. 675].

The Commission encouraged the Representative to seek the contribution of States, relevant organizations and institutions in order to put his work on a more stable basis. The Representative was asked to report to the General Assembly and the Commission and the Secretary-General was asked to assist him. Those requests were approved by the Economic and Social Council on 28 July (**decision 2000/270**).

Workshop. The Representative transmitted a summary report of the Regional Workshop on Internal Displacement in the South Caucasus (Tbilisi, Georgia, 10-12 May) [E/CN.4/2001/5/Add.2], organized by the Office for Democratic Institutions and Human Rights of the Organization for Security and Cooperation in Europe, the Brookings Institution Project on Internal Displacement and the Norwegian Refugee Council. Participants reviewed internal displacement in Armenia, Azerbaijan and Georgia, and emphasized the vulnerability and range of hardships internally displaced persons endured.

Subcommission action. By a vote of 11 to 9, with 1 abstention, the Subcommission, on 18 August [dec. 2000/113], adjourned the debate on a draft resolution on the right of return of displaced persons.

Right to asylum

The Subcommission, on 18 August [res. 2000/20], expressing concern that States' restrictive practices might create difficulties for people to gain protection in asylum States when escaping serious human rights violations in their own countries, urged States to respect the principle of non-refoulement within their obligations under the 1951 Convention relating to the Status of Refugees [YUN 1951, p. 520] and its 1967 Protocol [YUN 1967, p. 477] and other instruments. It also urged them to safeguard the right of everyone to seek and enjoy in other countries asylum from persecution and to ensure that refugees and asylum-seekers were treated with respect for their fundamental human rights. The Special Rapporteur on the rights of non-citizens (see p. 657), in consultation with the Office of the United Nations High Commissioner for Refugees (UNHCR) and OHCHR, was asked to examine the rights of non-citizens, with special attention to asylum-seekers and refugees, and to make recommendations for the Subcommission's work.

On the same date [res. 2000/21], the Subcommission recommended that where detention was employed, States, pursuant to the 1951 Convention, provide UNHCR with information on how detention policies and practices conformed to relevant international standards, including the Guidelines on Applicable Criteria and Standards relating to the Detention of Asylum-Seekers [http://www.unhcr.ch], adopted by UNHCR in 1999.

Smuggling and trafficking in persons

On 18 August [dec. 2000/110], the Subcommission decided to include in the provisional agenda of its 2001 session a sub-item entitled "Smuggling and trafficking in persons and the protection of their human rights" under the item "Freedom of movement: the right to leave any country, including one's own, and to return to one's own country, and the right to seek asylum from persecution". It asked the Secretary-General to submit a note on the subject in 2001.

Economic, social and cultural rights

Right to development

Reports of Secretary-General. As requested by the Commission on Human Rights in 1999 [YUN 1999, p. 652], the Secretary-General presented replies received from six Governments [E/CN.4/2000/19] in response to his request for information on follow-up to the Declaration on the Right to Development, adopted by the General Assembly in resolution 41/128 [YUN 1986, p. 717].

Pursuant to the Subcommission's 1999 request [YUN 1999, p. 652], the Secretary-General, in a June report with later addendum [E/CN.4/Sub.2/2000/14

& Add.1], described steps taken by UN bodies and agencies to promote international cooperation for the realization of the right to development in the context of the United Nations Decade for the Eradication of Poverty (1997-2006) (see p. 796).

In accordance with Assembly resolution 54/175 [YUN 1999, p. 652], the Secretary-General submitted, in August [A/55/283], a report on the right to development based on information received from four Governments and the United Nations Development Programme. On 4 December, the Assembly took note of the report (**decision 55/420**).

Reports of High Commissioner. In response to a 1999 Commission request [YUN 1999, p. 652], the United Nations High Commissioner for Human Rights described activities taken by her Office to implement the right to development [E/CN.4/2000/20]. She also provided information related to the implementation of General Assembly and Commission resolutions and inter-agency coordination within the UN system to implement relevant Commission resolutions.

In accordance with Assembly resolution 54/175, the Secretary-General transmitted, in August [A/55/302], a report of the High Commissioner containing an overview of OHCHR and other organizations and mechanisms concerned with the implementation of the right to development. OHCHR, together with the Government of Yemen, organized an Intersessional Workshop on Economic, Social and Cultural Rights and the Right to Development in the Asia-Pacific Region (Sana'a, 5-7 February). The Office was preparing a background note summarizing the existing material on the right to development. It provided support to the independent expert on the right to development and to the Chairperson of the open-ended working group on the right to development. In implementing resolution 54/175, the High Commissioner identified elements for a rights-based approach to development, and OHCHR prepared three background papers on the subject. The integration of elements of the right to development into the programmes and policies of development agencies as well as UN programmes was seen in OHCHR's contribution to the *Human Development Report 2000* [Sales No. E.00.III.B.8] and to the preparation of the common country assessment and the United Nations Development Assistance Framework process. In addition, the Office was involved in UN initiatives to provide human rights training and, as a member of the United Nations Development Group, helped to strengthen coherence of UN development activities. OHCHR encouraged a rights-based approach to the development and implementation of the Secretary-General's strategy to halve extreme poverty by 2015.

On 4 December, the General Assembly took note of the High Commissioner's report (**decision 55/420**).

Commission action. On 13 April [E/2000/23 (res. 2000/5)], the Commission, reaffirming the importance of the right to development for everyone, particularly in developing countries, urged States to eliminate obstacles to development by promoting and protecting economic, social, cultural, civil and political rights and by implementing development programmes and promoting international cooperation. The Commission welcomed the consensus on the need for the Working Group on the Right to Development to meet in two five-day sessions before the Commission's 2001 session. The Commission asked the High Commissioner to report annually, to provide interim reports to the Working Group and to make the reports available to the independent expert. The Secretary-General was asked to report to the General Assembly in 2000 and to the Commission in 2001, and to assist the Working Group and the independent expert.

On 28 July, the Economic and Social Council authorized the Working Group to meet as proposed, and approved the Commission's requests to the Secretary-General to submit reports (**decision 2000/246**).

Report of independent expert. In August [A/55/306], the Secretary-General transmitted to the General Assembly a report of the independent expert on the right to development, Arjun Sengupta (India), that outlined the current state of implementation of the right to development and set out guidelines for implementing the right. The expert stated that the realization of economic, social and cultural rights had to be based on coordinated actions in the form of a development plan aimed at growth of gross domestic product and other resources, as well as sustained improvement of social indicators related to the various rights. The plan would be based on decentralized decision-making with the participation and empowerment of the beneficiaries, and would have to be developed through consultation with civil society and the beneficiaries in a non-discriminatory and transparent manner.

Working group activities. The Commission's Open-ended Working Group on the Right to Development met for its resumed 1999 session on 24 February to elect its Chairperson [E/CN.4/2000/21].

At its first session in 2000 (Geneva, 18-22 September) [E/CN.4/2001/26], the Working Group examined the international economic order and the need for equity in economic and financial relations, particularly matters relating to market access for developing countries, as well as foreign debt servicing. It also considered ways to fight poverty and to promote access to education and health, and problems related to migration, racism and the standard of living. The Working Group highlighted the need to establish a balance between countries with regard to their access to technology and scientific knowledge, and the promotion of conditions needed for good governance and to fight against corruption. Also emphasized was the need to establish criteria and indicators in the context of the follow-up mechanisms on the right to development, and the development of an international compact for development, as proposed by the expert (see p. 691).

GENERAL ASSEMBLY ACTION

On 4 December [meeting 81], the General Assembly, on the recommendation of the Third Committee [A/55/602/Add.2 & Corr.1], adopted **resolution 55/108** without vote [agenda item 114 (b)].

The right to development

The General Assembly,

Guided by the Charter of the United Nations, expressing in particular the determination to promote social progress and better standards of life in larger freedom and to employ international machinery for the promotion of the economic and social advancement of all peoples,

Recalling that the Declaration on the Right to Development confirmed that the right to development is an inalienable human right and that equality of opportunity for development is a prerogative both of nations and of individuals who make up nations,

Noting that the World Conference on Human Rights, held at Vienna from 14 to 25 June 1993, reaffirmed the right to development as a universal and inalienable right and an integral part of all fundamental human rights,

Recognizing that the Declaration on the Right to Development constitutes an integral link between the Universal Declaration of Human Rights and the Vienna Declaration and Programme of Action adopted by the World Conference on Human Rights on 25 June 1993 through its elaboration of a holistic vision integrating economic, social and cultural rights with civil and political rights,

Expressing its concern that, more than fifty years after the adoption of the Universal Declaration of Human Rights, the unacceptable situation of absolute poverty, hunger, disease, lack of adequate shelter, illiteracy and hopelessness remains the lot of over one billion people,

Emphasizing that the promotion, protection and realization of the right to development are an integral part of the promotion and protection of all human rights,

Noting that the human person is the central subject of development and that development policy should therefore make the human being the main participant in and beneficiary of development,

Stressing the importance of creating an economic, political, social, cultural and legal environment that will enable people to achieve social development,

Affirming the need to apply a gender perspective in the implementation of the right to development, inter alia, by ensuring that women play an active role in the development process,

Emphasizing that the empowerment of women and their full participation on the basis of equality in all spheres of society is fundamental for development,

Underlining the fact that the realization of the right to development requires effective development policies at the national level, as well as equitable economic relations and a favourable economic environment at the international level,

Welcoming in this regard the adoption by the General Assembly of the Agenda for Development, which declares that development is one of the main priorities of the United Nations and which aims at invigorating a renewed and strengthened partnership for development, based on the imperatives of mutual benefits and genuine interdependence,

Noting with concern that the Declaration on the Right to Development is insufficiently disseminated and should be taken into account, as appropriate, in bilateral and multilateral cooperation programmes, national development strategies and policies and activities of international organizations,

Recalling the need for coordination and cooperation throughout the United Nations system for a more effective promotion and realization of the right to development,

Underlining the important role of the United Nations High Commissioner for Human Rights in the promotion and protection of the right to development, as mandated in paragraph 4 (c) of General Assembly resolution 48/141 of 20 December 1993,

Recalling its resolution 54/175 of 17 December 1999,

Taking note of Commission on Human Rights resolution 2000/5 of 13 April 2000,

Welcoming the report of the Intergovernmental Group of Experts on the Right to Development on its second session, including the proposed strategy contained therein, and welcoming in particular the recommendation that a follow-up mechanism should be established to ensure promotion and implementation of the Declaration on the Right to Development,

1. *Reaffirms* the importance of the right to development for every human person and all peoples in all countries, in particular the developing countries, as an integral part of their fundamental human rights, as well as the potential contribution that its realization could make to the full enjoyment of human rights and fundamental freedoms;

2. *Recognizes* that the passage of more than fifty years since the adoption of the Universal Declaration of Human Rights demands the strengthening of efforts to place all human rights and, in this context, the right to development in particular, at the top of the global agenda;

3. *Reiterates* that:

(a) The essence of the right to development is the principle that the human person is the central subject of development and that the right to life includes within it existence in human dignity with the minimum necessities of life;

(b) The existence of widespread absolute poverty inhibits the full and effective enjoyment of human rights and renders democracy and popular participation fragile;

(c) For peace and stability to endure, national action and international action and cooperation are required to promote a better life for all in larger freedom, a critical element of which is the eradication of poverty;

4. *Reaffirms* that democracy, development and respect for human rights and fundamental freedoms, including the right to development, are interdependent and mutually reinforcing, and in this context affirms that:

(a) The development experiences of countries reflect differences with regard to both progress and setbacks, and that the development spectrum has a wide range, not only between countries but also within countries;

(b) A number of developing countries have experienced rapid economic growth in the recent past and have become dynamic partners in the international economy;

(c) At the same time, the gap between developed and developing countries remains unacceptably wide and developing countries continue to face difficulties in participating in the globalization process, and many risk being marginalized and effectively excluded from its benefits;

(d) Democracy, which is spreading everywhere, has raised development expectations everywhere, that their non-fulfilment risks rekindling non-democratic forces, and that structural reforms that do not take social realities into account could destabilize democratization processes;

(e) Effective popular participation is an essential component of successful and lasting development;

(f) Democracy, respect for all human rights and fundamental freedoms, including the right to development, transparent and accountable governance and administration in all sectors of society, and effective participation by civil society are an essential part of the necessary foundations for the realization of social and people-centred sustainable development;

(g) The participation of developing countries in the international economic decision-making process needs to be broadened and strengthened;

5. *Urges* all States to eliminate all obstacles to development at all levels by pursuing the promotion and protection of economic, social, cultural, civil and political rights, implementing comprehensive development programmes at the national level, integrating those rights into development activities and promoting effective international cooperation;

6. *Reaffirms* that all human rights are universal, indivisible, interdependent and interrelated and that the universality, objectivity, impartiality and non-selectivity of the consideration of human rights issues must be ensured;

7. *Affirms* that international cooperation is acknowledged more than ever as a necessity deriving from recognized mutual interest and, therefore, that such cooperation should be strengthened in order to support the efforts of developing countries to solve their economic and social problems and to fulfil their obligations to promote and protect all human rights;

8. *Welcomes* the intention of the Secretary-General to give high priority to the right to development, and urges all States to promote further the right to development as a vital element in a balanced human rights programme;

9. *Also welcomes* the high priority assigned by the United Nations High Commissioner for Human Rights to activities relating to the right to development, and urges the Office of the High Commissioner to continue to implement Commission on Human Rights resolution 1998/72 of 22 April 1998;

10. *Further welcomes* Economic and Social Council decision 1998/269 of 30 July 1998 authorizing the establishment by the Commission on Human Rights of a follow-up mechanism, consisting of an open-ended working group on the right to development and an independent expert with a mandate to submit to the working group at each of its sessions a study on the current state of progress in the implementation of the right to development, as provided for in Commission resolution 1998/72;

11. *Welcomes* the holding at Geneva from 18 to 22 September 2000 of the first session of the Open-ended Working Group on the Right to Development under the chairmanship of Mr. M. S. Dembri (Algeria), and encourages the Working Group to proceed with its second session, scheduled for January 2001;

12. *Takes note* of the coordination mechanisms and initiatives within the United Nations system in which the Office of the United Nations High Commissioner for Human Rights participates to promote the implementation of the right to development;

13. *Also takes note* of the second report of the independent expert on the right to development, which focuses on poverty eradication as a priority area requiring attention in the realization of the right to development;

14. *Further takes note* of the *Human Development Report 2000*, of the United Nations Development Programme, and the *World Development Report 2000/2001: Attacking Poverty*, of the World Bank, which cover issues relevant to human rights and the right to development, and welcomes the participation in the Working Group of representatives of international financial institutions, as well as that of relevant United Nations specialized agencies, funds and programmes and non-governmental organizations, in accordance with relevant resolutions of the Economic and Social Council;

15. *Invites* the United Nations High Commissioner for Human Rights to submit a report to the Commission on Human Rights each year for the duration of the mechanism, to provide interim reports to the Working Group and to make those reports available to the independent expert, with each report covering:

(a) The activities of her Office relating to the implementation of the right to development, as contained in her mandate;

(b) The implementation of resolutions of the General Assembly and the Commission with regard to the right to development;

(c) Inter-agency coordination within the United Nations system for the implementation of relevant resolutions of the Commission in that regard;

16. *Urges* the United Nations system to continue to support the implementation of the recent resolutions of the Commission on Human Rights regarding the right to development;

17. *Calls upon* the Secretary-General to ensure that the Working Group and the independent expert receive all necessary assistance, in particular the staff and resources required to fulfil their mandates;

18. *Calls upon* the Working Group to take note of the deliberations on the right to development during the fifty-fifth session of the General Assembly and the fifty-sixth session of the Commission on Human Rights, and any other issue relevant to the right to development;

19. *Requests* the Secretary-General to submit to the General Assembly at its fifty-sixth session and to the Commission on Human Rights at its fifty-seventh session a comprehensive report on the implementation of the various provisions of the present resolution;

20. *Decides* to continue consideration of this question, as a matter of priority, at its fifty-sixth session.

Democratic and equitable international order

By a roll-call vote of 30 to 17, with 6 abstentions, the Commission, on 26 April [res. 2000/62], affirmed that a democratic and equitable international order fostered the full realization of all human rights for all and that it required the realization of a wide range of human rights. States were urged to continue their efforts, through enhanced international cooperation, to create a democratic and equitable international order. The Commission requested human rights treaty bodies, OHCHR and Commission and Subcommission mechanisms to contribute to implementation of the resolution. The Secretary-General was asked to bring the resolution to the attention of Member States, UN organs and bodies, intergovernmental organizations and NGOs and to disseminate it widely. The High Commissioner was asked to include in her annual report in 2001 information on progress made in implementing the resolution.

GENERAL ASSEMBLY ACTION

On 4 December [meeting 81], the General Assembly, on the recommendation of the Third Committee [A/55/602/Add.2 & Corr.1], adopted **resolution 55/107** by recorded vote (109-52-7) [agenda item 114 (b)].

Promotion of a democratic and equitable international order

The General Assembly,

Noting the adoption by the Commission on Human Rights of its resolution 2000/62 of 26 April 2000,

Reaffirming the commitment of all States to fulfil their obligations to promote universal respect for, and observance and protection of, all human rights and fundamental freedoms for all, in accordance with the Charter of the United Nations, other instruments relating to human rights and international law,

Affirming that the enhancement of international cooperation for the promotion and protection of all human rights should continue to be carried out in full conformity with the purposes and principles of the Charter and international law as set forth in Articles 1 and 2 of the Charter and, inter alia, with full respect for sovereignty, territorial integrity, political independence, the non-use of force or the threat of force in in-ternational relations and non-intervention in matters that are essentially within the domestic jurisdiction of any State,

Recalling the Preamble to the Charter, in particular the determination to reaffirm faith in fundamental human rights, in the dignity and worth of the human person, and in the equal rights of men and women and of nations large and small,

Reaffirming that everyone is entitled to a social and international order in which the rights and freedoms set forth in the Universal Declaration of Human Rights can be fully realized,

Reaffirming also the determination expressed in the Preamble to the Charter to save succeeding generations from the scourge of war, to establish conditions under which justice and respect for the obligations arising from treaties and other sources of international law can be maintained, to promote social progress and better standards of life in larger freedom, to practise tolerance and good-neighbourliness, and to employ international machinery for the promotion of the economic and social advancement of all peoples,

Considering the major changes taking place on the international scene and the aspirations of all peoples for an international order based on the principles enshrined in the Charter, including promoting and encouraging respect for human rights and fundamental freedoms for all and respect for the principle of equal rights and self-determination of peoples, peace, democracy, justice, equality, the rule of law, pluralism, development, better standards of living and solidarity,

Considering also that the Universal Declaration of Human Rights proclaims that all human beings are born free and equal in dignity and rights and that everyone is entitled to all the rights and freedoms set out therein, without distinction of any kind, such as race, colour, sex, language, religion, political or other opinion, national or social origin, property, birth or other status,

Reaffirming that democracy, development and respect for human rights and fundamental freedoms are interdependent and mutually reinforcing, and that democracy is based on the freely expressed will of the people to determine their own political, economic, social and cultural systems and their full participation in all aspects of their lives,

Emphasizing that democracy is not only a political concept but also has economic and social dimensions,

Recognizing that democracy, respect for all human rights, including the right to development, transparent and accountable governance and administration in all sectors of society, and effective participation by civil society are an essential part of the necessary foundations for the realization of social and people-centred sustainable development,

Underlining the fact that it is imperative for the international community to ensure that globalization becomes a positive force for all the world's people, and that only through broad and sustained efforts, based on common humanity in all its diversity, can globalization be made fully inclusive and equitable,

Stressing that efforts to make globalization fully inclusive and equitable must include policies and measures, at the global level, that correspond to the needs of developing countries and economies in transition and are formulated and implemented with their effective participation,

Resolved, on the eve of a new century and millennium, to take all measures within its power to secure a democratic and equitable international order,

1. *Affirms* that everyone is entitled to a democratic and equitable international order;

2. *Also affirms* that a democratic and equitable international order fosters the full respect for and realization of all human rights for all;

3. *Further affirms* that a democratic and equitable international order requires, inter alia, the realization of the following:

(a) The right of all peoples to self-determination, by virtue of which they can freely determine their political status and freely pursue their economic, social and cultural development;

(b) The right of peoples and nations to permanent sovereignty over their natural wealth and resources;

(c) The right of every human person and all peoples to development;

(d) The right of all peoples to peace;

(e) The promotion of an international economic order based on equal participation in the decision-making process, interdependence, mutual interest, solidarity and cooperation among all States;

(f) Solidarity, as a fundamental value, by virtue of which global challenges must be managed in a way that distributes costs and burdens fairly in accordance with basic principles of equity and social justice and ensures that those who suffer or who benefit the least receive help from those who benefit the most;

(g) The promotion and consolidation of transparent, democratic, just and accountable international institutions in all areas of cooperation, in particular through the implementation of the principles of full and equal participation in their respective decision-making mechanisms;

(h) The principle of equitable regional and gender-balanced representation in the composition of the staff of all bodies within the United Nations system;

(i) The promotion of a free, just, effective and balanced international information and communication order, based on international cooperation for the establishment of a new equilibrium and greater reciprocity in the international flow of information, in particular, correcting the inequalities in the flow of information to and from developing countries;

(j) The respect for cultural diversity and the cultural rights of all, since this enhances cultural pluralism, contributes to a wider exchange of knowledge and understanding of cultural backgrounds, advances the application and enjoyment of universally accepted human rights across the world and fosters stable, friendly relations among peoples and nations worldwide;

(k) The entitlement of every person and all peoples to a healthy environment;

(l) The promotion of equitable access to benefits from the international distribution of wealth through enhanced international cooperation, in particular in economic, commercial and financial international relations;

(m) The enjoyment by everyone of the common heritage of mankind;

4. *Stresses* the importance of preserving the rich and diverse nature of the international community of nations and peoples, as well as respect for national and regional particularities and various historical, cultural and religious backgrounds in the enhancement of international cooperation in the field of human rights;

5. *Also stresses* that all human rights are universal, indivisible, interdependent and interrelated and that the international community must treat human rights globally in a fair and equal manner, on the same footing and with the same emphasis, and reaffirms that, while the significance of national and regional particularities and various historical, cultural and religious backgrounds must be borne in mind, it is the duty of States, regardless of their political, economic and cultural systems, to promote and protect all human rights and fundamental freedoms;

6. *Reaffirms* that all States should promote the establishment, maintenance and strengthening of international peace and security and, to that end, should do their utmost to achieve general and complete disarmament under effective international control, as well as to ensure that the resources released by effective disarmament measures are used for comprehensive development, in particular that of the developing countries;

7. *Recalls* the proclamation by the General Assembly of the determination to work urgently for the establishment of a new international economic order based on equity, sovereign equality, interdependence, common interest and cooperation among all States, irrespective of their economic and social systems, which shall correct inequalities and redress existing injustices, make it possible to eliminate the widening gap between the developed and the developing countries and ensure steadily accelerating economic and social development and peace and justice for present and future generations;

8. *Reaffirms* that the international community should devise ways and means to remove the current obstacles and meet the challenges to the full realization of all human rights and to prevent the continuation of human rights violations resulting therefrom throughout the world;

9. *Urges* States to continue their efforts, through enhanced international cooperation, towards the promotion of a democratic and equitable international order;

10. *Requests* the Commission on Human Rights, the human rights treaty bodies, the Office of the United Nations High Commissioner for Human Rights, the mechanisms of the Commission on Human Rights and the Subcommission on the Promotion and Protection of Human Rights to pay due attention, within their respective mandates, to the present resolution and to make contributions for its implementation;

11. *Requests* the Secretary-General to bring the present resolution to the attention of Member States, United Nations organs, bodies and components, intergovernmental organizations, in particular the Bretton Woods institutions, and non-governmental organizations and to disseminate it on the widest possible basis;

12. *Decides* to continue consideration of the matter at its fifty-sixth session under the item entitled "Human rights questions".

RECORDED VOTE ON RESOLUTION 55/107:

In favour: Afghanistan, Algeria, Angola, Antigua and Barbuda, Armenia, Azerbaijan, Bahamas, Bahrain, Bangladesh, Barbados, Belarus, Belize, Benin, Bhutan, Bolivia, Botswana, Brazil, Brunei Darussalam, Burkina Faso, Burundi, Cambodia, Cameroon, Cape Verde, Chad, China, Colombia, Congo, Côte d'Ivoire, Cuba, Democratic People's Republic of Korea, Democratic Republic of the Congo, Djibouti, Dominica, Dominican Republic, Ecuador, Egypt, El Salvador, Eritrea, Ethiopia, Fiji, Gabon, Gambia, Ghana, Grenada, Guinea, Guyana, Haiti, Honduras, India, Indonesia, Iran, Jamaica, Jordan, Kazakhstan, Kenya, Kuwait, Kyrgyzstan, Lao People's Democratic Republic, Lebanon, Lesotho, Libyan Arab Jamahiriya, Madagascar, Malawi, Malaysia, Maldives, Mali, Mauritius, Mexico, Mongolia, Mozambique, Myanmar, Namibia, Nauru, Nepal, Nicaragua, Nigeria, Oman, Pakistan, Panama, Papua New Guinea, Philippines, Qatar, Russian Federation, Rwanda, Saint Kitts and Nevis, Saint Lucia, Saint Vincent and the Grenadines, Sao Tome and Principe, Sierra Leone, Singapore, Solomon Islands, Sri Lanka, Sudan, Suriname, Swaziland, Syrian Arab Republic, Thailand, Togo, Trinidad and Tobago, Tunisia, Uganda, United Republic of Tanzania, Uruguay, Vanuatu, Venezuela, Viet Nam, Yemen, Zambia, Zimbabwe.

Against: Albania, Andorra, Australia, Austria, Belgium, Bulgaria, Canada, Chile, Croatia, Cyprus, Czech Republic, Denmark, Estonia, Finland, France, Georgia, Germany, Greece, Hungary, Iceland, Ireland, Israel, Italy, Japan, Latvia, Liechtenstein, Lithuania, Luxembourg, Malta, Marshall Islands, Micronesia, Monaco, Netherlands, New Zealand, Norway, Palau, Poland, Portugal, Republic of Korea, Republic of Moldova, Romania, Samoa, San Marino, Slovakia, Slovenia, South Africa, Spain, Sweden, The former Yugoslav Republic of Macedonia, Ukraine, United Kingdom, United States.

Abstaining: Argentina, Costa Rica, Guatemala, Morocco, Paraguay, Peru, Senegal.

Globalization

Commission action. On 17 April [dec. 2000/102], the Commission, recalling its 1999 call for a study on globalization [YUN 1999, p. 655] and taking note of a 1999 Subcommission resolution [ibid.], endorsed the Subcommission's appointment of Joseph Oloka-Onyango (Uganda) and Deepika Udagama (Sri Lanka) as Special Rapporteurs to prepare a study on globalization and its impact on the full enjoyment of all human rights.

The Economic and Social Council approved the appointment of the Special Rapporteurs on 28 July (**decision 2000/282**).

Report of Special Rapporteurs. In June [E/CN.4/Sub.2/2000/13], the Special Rapporteurs, in their preliminary report on globalization and its impact on the full enjoyment of human rights, focused on the institutional framework that had been developed to pursue the essential goals of globalization, and examined the questions of equality and non-discrimination, particularly in relation to women. The Special Rapporteurs concluded that globalization had numerous implications for human rights promotion and protection. There was a dire need for human rights, emphasizing equality and non-discrimination, to be brought into the debate and policy considerations of those at the forefront of the drive for the increased globalization of contemporary society. Rules needed to be established to govern the international economy, specifically in relation to copyright violations, trade sanctions and protections for increased foreign investment. A more balanced approach was needed that ensured the integration of human rights principles into the rule-making processes from the outset. Further reviews of existing debt relief and poverty eradication measures should be undertaken from a human rights perspective. Women continued to be a grossly underrepresented group within in-

stitutions such as the World Trade Organization (WTO), the International Monetary Fund (IMF) and the World Bank. There was a need to engender the institutional frameworks within which the globalization processes were developed and to conduct gender-specific analyses of the impact of globalization in its trade, investment and financial aspects.

Report of Secretary-General. In response to General Assembly resolution 54/165 [YUN 1999, p. 655], the Secretary-General, in August [A/55/342], presented a preliminary report on globalization and human rights, based on reports of UN bodies and drawing on the proposals adopted by the Assembly's special session on social development (see p. 1012). The report discussed globalization issues and the relationship between the global economy and human rights. The Secretary-General concluded that, while globalization provided potential for protecting human rights through economic growth and greater interconnection between peoples and development, its benefits were not enjoyed evenly. It was difficult to assess the extent to which globalization led to or alleviated poverty. Poverty was both a cause and an effect of human rights abuses. By adopting a human rights approach, globalization could be examined in its civil, cultural, political, social and economic contexts so that the international community could meet its commitment to an international and social order conducive to respect for human rights.

GENERAL ASSEMBLY ACTION

On 4 December [meeting 81], the General Assembly, on the recommendation of the Third Committee [A/55/602/Add.2 & Corr.1], adopted **resolution 55/102** by recorded vote (112-46-15) [agenda item 114 (b)].

Globalization and its impact on the full enjoyment of all human rights

The General Assembly,

Guided by the purposes and principles of the Charter of the United Nations, and expressing in particular the need to achieve international cooperation in promoting and encouraging respect for human rights and fundamental freedoms for all without distinction,

Recalling the Universal Declaration of Human Rights, as well as the Vienna Declaration and Programme of Action adopted by the World Conference on Human Rights on 25 June 1993,

Recalling also the International Covenant on Civil and Political Rights and the International Covenant on Economic, Social and Cultural Rights,

Recalling further the Declaration on the Right to Development adopted by the General Assembly in its resolution 41/128 of 4 December 1986,

Recalling the United Nations Millennium Declaration and the outcome documents of the twenty-third and twenty-fourth special sessions of the General Assembly, held, respectively, in New York from 5 to 10 June 2000 and Geneva from 26 June to 1 July 2000,

Recognizing that all human rights are universal, indivisible, interdependent and interrelated and that the international community must treat human rights globally in a fair and equal manner, on the same footing and with the same emphasis,

Realizing that globalization affects all countries differently and makes them more exposed to external developments, positive as well as negative, including in the field of human rights,

Realizing also that globalization is not merely an economic process but also has social, political, environmental, cultural and legal dimensions which have an impact on the full enjoyment of all human rights,

Recognizing that multilateral mechanisms have a unique role to play in meeting the challenges and opportunities presented by globalization,

Expressing concern at the negative impact of international financial turbulence on social and economic development and on the full enjoyment of all human rights,

Deeply concerned that the widening gap between the developed and the developing countries, and within countries, has contributed, inter alia, to deepening poverty and has adversely affected the full enjoyment of all human rights, in particular in developing countries,

Noting that human beings strive for a world that is respectful of human rights and cultural diversity and that, in this regard, they work to ensure that all activities, including those affected by globalization, are consistent with those aims,

1. *Recognizes* that, while globalization, by its impact on, inter alia, the role of the State, may affect human rights, the promotion and protection of all human rights is first and foremost the responsibility of the State;

2. *Reaffirms* that narrowing the gap between rich and poor, both within and between countries, is an explicit goal at the national and international levels, as part of the effort to create an enabling environment for the full enjoyment of all human rights;

3. *Also reaffirms* the commitment to create an environment at both the national and global levels that is conducive to development and to the elimination of poverty through, inter alia, good governance within each country and at the international level, transparency in the financial, monetary and trading systems and commitment to an open, equitable, rule-based, predictable and non-discriminatory multilateral trading and financial system;

4. *Recognizes* that, while globalization offers great opportunities, its benefits are very unevenly shared and its costs are unevenly distributed, an aspect of the process that affects the full enjoyment of all human rights, in particular in developing countries;

5. *Also recognizes* that, only through broad and sustained efforts, including policies and measures at the global level to create a shared future based upon our common humanity in all its diversity, can globalization be made fully inclusive and equitable and have a human face, thus contributing to the full enjoyment of all human rights;

6. *Affirms* that globalization is a complex process of structural transformation, with numerous interdisci-

plinary aspects, which has an impact on the enjoyment of civil, political, economic, social and cultural rights, including the right to development;

7. *Also affirms* that the international community should strive to respond to the challenges and opportunities posed by globalization in a manner that ensures respect for the cultural diversity of all;

8. *Underlines*, therefore, the need to continue to analyse the consequences of globalization for the full enjoyment of all human rights;

9. *Takes note* of the preliminary report of the Secretary-General on globalization and its impact on the full enjoyment of all human rights, and requests the Secretary-General, taking into account the different views of Member States, to submit a comprehensive report on this subject to the General Assembly at its fifty-sixth session.

RECORDED VOTE ON RESOLUTION 55/102:

In favour: Algeria, Angola, Antigua and Barbuda, Azerbaijan, Bahamas, Bahrain, Bangladesh, Barbados, Belarus, Belize, Benin, Bhutan, Bolivia, Botswana, Brazil, Brunei Darussalam, Burkina Faso, Burundi, Cambodia, Cameroon, Cape Verde, Chad, China, Comoros, Congo, Côte d'Ivoire, Croatia, Cuba, Democratic People's Republic of Korea, Democratic Republic of the Congo, Djibouti, Dominica, Dominican Republic, Ecuador, Egypt, El Salvador, Eritrea, Ethiopia, Fiji, Gabon, Gambia, Ghana, Grenada, Guinea, Guyana, Haiti, Honduras, India, Indonesia, Iran, Jamaica, Jordan, Kazakhstan, Kenya, Kuwait, Kyrgyzstan, Lao People's Democratic Republic, Lebanon, Lesotho, Libyan Arab Jamahiriya, Madagascar, Malawi, Malaysia, Maldives, Mali, Mauritania, Mauritius, Mexico, Mongolia, Morocco, Mozambique, Myanmar, Namibia, Nauru, Nepal, Nicaragua, Nigeria, Oman, Pakistan, Panama, Papua New Guinea, Philippines, Qatar, Russian Federation, Rwanda, Saint Kitts and Nevis, Saint Lucia, Saint Vincent and the Grenadines, Samoa, Sao Tome and Principe, Saudi Arabia, Senegal, Sierra Leone, Solomon Islands, South Africa, Sri Lanka, Sudan, Suriname, Swaziland, Syrian Arab Republic, Togo, Trinidad and Tobago, Tunisia, Turkey, Uganda, United Republic of Tanzania, Vanuatu, Venezuela, Viet Nam, Yemen, Zambia, Zimbabwe.

Against: Albania, Andorra, Australia, Austria, Belgium, Bulgaria, Canada, Chile, Cyprus, Czech Republic, Denmark, Estonia, Finland, France, Georgia, Germany, Greece, Hungary, Iceland, Ireland, Israel, Italy, Japan, Latvia, Liechtenstein, Lithuania, Luxembourg, Malta, Marshall Islands, Monaco, Netherlands, New Zealand, Norway, Palau, Poland, Portugal, Romania, San Marino, Slovakia, Slovenia, Spain, Sweden, The former Yugoslav Republic of Macedonia, Ukraine, United Kingdom, United States.

Abstaining: Argentina, Armenia, Colombia, Costa Rica, Guatemala, Micronesia, Paraguay, Peru, Republic of Korea, Republic of Moldova, Singapore, Thailand, United Arab Emirates, Uruguay, Uzbekistan.

Intellectual property rights

On 17 August [E/CN.4/2001/2 (res. 2000/7)], the Subcommission affirmed that the right to protection of the moral and material interests resulting from any scientific, literary or artistic production of which one was the author was, in accordance with international human rights instruments, a human right subject to limitations in the public interest. Declaring that the implementation of the WTO Agreement on Trade-Related Aspects of Intellectual Property Rights (TRIPS) did not adequately reflect the fundamental nature and indivisibility of all human rights and that there were conflicts between the intellectual property rights embodied in the Agreement and international human rights law, the Subcommission reminded Governments of the primacy of human rights obligations over economic policies and agreements. The Special Rapporteurs on globalization (see p. 696) were asked to consider the human rights impact of the implementation of the TRIPS Agreement in their next report, and the High Commissioner was requested to analyse the human rights impacts of the Agreement. The Subcommission encouraged the Committee on Economic, Social and Cultural Rights to clarify the relationship between intellectual property rights and human rights, including through the drafting of a general comment. The Secretary-General was asked to report in 2001.

Structural adjustment policies

A January note by the Secretariat [E/CN.4/2000/51] stated that the Special Rapporteur on the effects of foreign debt, Reinaldo Figueredo (Venezuela), and the independent expert on the effects of structural adjustment policies on economic, social and cultural rights, Fantu Cheru (United States), having considered the related nature of those subjects, decided to submit a joint report, which was annexed to the note.

The authors analysed the enhanced Heavily Indebted Poor Countries Initiative and, while recognizing its limitations, concluded that its new emphasis on strengthening the link between debt relief and poverty reduction represented a tremendous step forward in the history of debt relief for poor countries. They focused on the need to link debt relief to three critical humanitarian emergencies that required an immediate response from the international community—the HIV/AIDS epidemic as a threat to Africa's development, the effects of hurricane Mitch on Honduras and Nicaragua, and the link between debt relief and implementation of the Worst Forms of Child Labour Convention, 1999 (No. 182), adopted by the International Labour Conference [YUN 1999, p. 1388]. Those topics were chosen, the authors said, because they were aimed at eradicating poverty in the poorest developing countries. The authors appealed to Member States, the Secretary-General and the High Commissioner to strengthen the responsiveness of OHCHR in the area of economic, social and cultural rights by strengthening the Office's internal research and analytical capacity, and its technical assistance support to countries in macroeconomic policy and trade and investment-related topics that had a direct bearing on human rights promotion and protection.

Working group activities. A March note by the Secretariat [E/CN.4/2000/53] stated that the third session of the open-ended working group on structural adjustment programmes and economic, social and cultural rights convened on 28 February. Following an adjournment to allow for consultations among regional coordinators, the working group resumed on 7 March. It agreed that the Commission be asked to extend its man-

date and authorize it to hold another two-week session between the Commission's 2000 and 2001 sessions.

Commission action. By a roll-call vote of 30 to 15, with 7 abstentions, the Commission, on 26 April [res. 2000/82], stressing the importance of implementing durable actions for alleviating the burdens of debt and debt service of developing countries with debt problems, considered that there was a need for a political dialogue between creditor and debtor countries within the UN system to find a solution to the problem. The Commission asked the High Commissioner to give particular attention to the problem of the debt burden of developing countries and to strengthen the responsiveness of her Office in the area of economic, social and cultural rights. The Commission took action regarding the work of the independent expert and of the working group, which were approved by the Economic and Social Council (see below).

ECONOMIC AND SOCIAL COUNCIL ACTION

On 16 June, the Economic and Social Council, on the recommendation of the Commission on Human Rights [E/2000/23 & Corr.1], adopted **decision 2000/221** by recorded vote (20-18-5) [agenda item 2].

Effects of structural adjustment policies and foreign debt on the full enjoyment of all human rights, particularly economic, social and cultural rights

At its 10th plenary meeting, on 16 June 2000, the Economic and Social Council, taking note of Commission on Human Rights resolution 2000/82 and decision 2000/109 of 26 April 2000, endorsed the Commission's decision to discontinue the mandates of the Special Rapporteur on the effects of foreign debt on the full enjoyment of economic, social and cultural rights and of the independent expert on the effects of structural adjustment policies on economic, social and cultural rights and to appoint, for a period of three years, Mr. Fantu Cheru as independent expert on the effects of structural adjustment policies and foreign debt on the full enjoyment of all human rights, particularly economic, social and cultural rights, and to request him to submit an analytical report to the Commission, on an annual basis, on the implementation of Commission resolution 2000/82, paying particular attention to:

(a) The effects of the foreign debt and the policies adopted to face them on the full enjoyment of all human rights, in particular economic, social and cultural rights in developing countries;

(b) Measures taken by Governments, the private sector and international financial institutions to alleviate such effects in developing countries, especially the poorest and heavily indebted countries;

(c) New developments, actions and initiatives being taken by international financial institutions, other United Nations bodies and intergovernmental and non-governmental organizations with respect to structural adjustment policies and human rights;

and to provide an advance copy of his annual report to the open-ended working group on structural adjustment programmes and economic, social and cultural rights in order to assist the group in the fulfilment of its mandate.

The Council also endorsed the Commission's request to the Secretary-General to provide the independent expert with all necessary assistance, in particular the staff and resources required to perform his functions.

The Council decided to authorize the working group on structural adjustment programmes and economic, social and cultural rights to meet for two weeks well in advance of, and at least four weeks prior to, the fifty-seventh session of the Commission with a mandate *(a)* to continue working on the elaboration of basic policy guidelines on structural adjustment programmes and economic, social and cultural rights which could serve as a basis for a continued dialogue between human rights bodies and international financial institutions and *(b)* to report to the Commission at its fifty-seventh session.

RECORDED VOTE ON DECISION 2000/221:

In favour: Algeria, Angola, Bahrain, Benin, Brazil, Burkina Faso, Cameroon, China, Cuba, Fiji, India, Indonesia, Oman, Pakistan, Saudi Arabia, Sudan, Suriname, Syrian Arab Republic, Venezuela, Viet Nam.

Against: Austria, Belgium, Bulgaria, Canada, Croatia, Czech Republic, Denmark, France, Germany, Greece, Italy, Japan, New Zealand, Norway, Poland, Portugal, United Kingdom, United States.

Abstaining: Belarus, Colombia, Costa Rica, Mexico, Russian Federation.

Prior to the text's adoption, it had been rejected by a recorded vote of 18 to 18, with 5 abstentions. However, the Council carried a motion to reconsider the draft by a recorded vote of 20 to 16, with 7 abstentions.

Social Forum

Commission action. On 26 April [dec. 2000/107], the Commission, taking note of a 1999 Subcommission resolution [YUN 1999, p. 657], endorsed the holding of a Social Forum during the Subcommission's 2000 session and decided that the Subcommission should further review its proposal to hold a forum on economic, social and cultural rights.

Subcommission action. On 17 August [res. 2000/6], the Subcommission decided to hold in Geneva a pre-sessional or intersessional forum on economic, social and cultural rights, to be known as the Social Forum, for three days, with the participation of 10 of its members. It asked the Commission and the Economic and Social Council to endorse the holding of the Forum.

Transnational corporations

The sessional working group on the working methods and activities of transnational corporations (TNCs), at its second session (Geneva, 1, 4 and 8 August) [E/CN.4/Sub.2/2000/12], discussed draft principles relating to the human rights conduct of companies. The aims of the draft princi-

ples were to help Governments identify legislation they should enact and enforcement mechanisms to ensure that the principles had a positive influence, to encourage companies to implement the principles and to lay the groundwork for the binding international standard-setting process. The group had before it working papers on the principles relating to the human rights conduct of companies, background information and a list of existing sources of international standards drawn on in the preparation of the draft principles. The group also considered the impact of TNCs on the enjoyment of civil, cultural, economic, political and social rights.

Coercive economic measures

Report of Secretary-General. In response to a 1999 Commission request [YUN 1999, p. 658], the Secretary-General submitted the views of five Governments on the implications and negative effects of unilateral coercive measures on their populations [E/CN.4/2000/46 & Add.1].

Commission action. By a roll-call vote of 36 to 9, with 7 abstentions, the Commission, on 17 April [res. 2000/11], called on States to avoid the unilateral imposition of economic coercive measures and the extraterritorial application of domestic laws that ran counter to the principles of free trade and hampered the development of developing countries. It requested the Secretary-General to bring the resolution to the attention of Member States and to seek their views and information on the effects of unilateral coercive measures on their populations and to report thereon in 2001.

Working paper. Pursuant to a 1999 Subcommission request [YUN 1999, p. 658], Marc Bossuyt (Belgium) submitted, in June [E/CN.4/Sub.2/2000/33], a working paper on the adverse consequences of economic sanctions on the enjoyment of human rights. He described various types of sanctions, including those pertaining to trade, finance, travel, the military, diplomacy and culture. A six-prong test was presented to evaluate sanctions that involved determining if the sanctions were imposed for valid reasons, targeted the proper parties, targeted the proper goods or objects, were reasonably time-limited, were effective and were free from protest arising from violations of the principles of humanity and the dictates of public conscience. Following a discussion of designing smarter sanctions, the paper presented case studies on sanctions regimes imposed on Burundi, Cuba and Iraq. In its conclusions, the paper asserted that any sanctions-imposing body should ensure that the sanctions regime passed the six-prong test prior to implementation. There were situations where a sanctions regime that might initially be deemed acceptable subsequently failed the test. Thus, sanctions should be reviewed periodically, at intervals not longer than every six months. Legal remedies should be available for victims of sanctions regimes that violated international law, if the imposer refused to alter them. Difficulties regarding remedies for civilians arose when the sanctions were imposed by the United Nations or by a regional body, as victims might not be able to file directly against the entity. For those entities, it was proposed that special mechanisms or procedures for relevant input from non-governmental sources regarding sanctions be established. The paper made a series of recommendations to UN bodies, NGOs and victims of sanctions.

Reports of Secretary-General. In July [A/55/ 214], the Secretary-General stated that, in accordance with General Assembly resolution 54/172 [YUN 1999, p. 658], he had requested information from Member States on human rights and unilateral coercive measures, for submission by 30 June. He had received no replies. In September [A/55/214/Add.1], he transmitted the replies of three States. On 4 December, the Assembly took note of the reports (**decision 55/420**).

Pursuant to Assembly resolution 53/10 [YUN 1998, p. 778] on the elimination of coercive economic measures as a means of political and economic compulsion, the Secretary-General, in an August report with later addenda [A/55/300 & Add.1-3], presented information received from 14 States on steps they had taken to implement the resolution.

Subcommission action. On 18 August [res. 2000/25], the Subcommission appealed to States to terminate all aspects of sanctions regimes that adversely affected human rights, that contravened international law or that conflicted with other international standards. It transmitted to the Commission the working paper on the adverse consequences of economic sanctions (see p. 699) and invited the Commission to recommend measures to avoid adverse consequences for human rights in imposing and maintaining economic sanctions.

The humanitarian consequences of sanctions, including embargoes, were addressed by the Subcommission on 11 August [res. 2000/1]. It urged the Commission to recommend that competent UN bodies implement the relevant provisions of human rights and international humanitarian law, and appealed to the Security Council to alleviate sanctions regimes so that civilian goods, particularly food and medical and pharmaceutical supplies, could be imported. The international community was encouraged to alleviate the suffering of people adversely affected by sanctions, par-

ticularly by facilitating the delivery of food and medical and pharmaceutical supplies and providing educational material for health-care professionals and educators.

GENERAL ASSEMBLY ACTION

On 4 December [meeting 81], the General Assembly, on the recommendation of the Third Committee [A/55/602/Add.2 & Corr.1], adopted **resolution 55/110** by recorded vote (117-49-6) [agenda item 114 *(b)*].

Human rights and unilateral coercive measures
The General Assembly,

Recalling its resolutions 51/103 of 12 December 1996, 52/120 of 12 December 1997, 53/141 of 9 December 1998 and 54/172 of 17 December 1999, as well as Commission on Human Rights resolution 1998/11 of 9 April 1998, and taking note of Commission resolution 2000/11 of 17 April 2000,

Reaffirming the pertinent principles and provisions contained in the Charter of Economic Rights and Duties of States proclaimed by the General Assembly in its resolution 3281(XXIX) of 12 December 1974, in particular article 32 thereof, in which it declared that no State may use or encourage the use of economic, political or any other type of measures to coerce another State in order to obtain from it the subordination of the exercise of its sovereign rights,

Taking note of the report submitted by the Secretary-General, pursuant to Commission on Human Rights resolution 1999/21 of 23 April 1999, and the report of the Secretary-General on the implementation of resolution 52/120,

Recognizing the universal, indivisible, interdependent and interrelated character of all human rights, and, in this regard, reaffirming the right to development as an integral part of all human rights,

Recalling that the World Conference on Human Rights, held at Vienna from 14 to 25 June 1993, called upon States to refrain from any unilateral coercive measure not in accordance with international law and the Charter of the United Nations that creates obstacles to trade relations among States and impedes the full realization of all human rights,

Bearing in mind all the references to this question in the Copenhagen Declaration on Social Development, adopted by the World Summit for Social Development on 12 March 1995, the Beijing Declaration and the Platform for Action, adopted by the Fourth World Conference on Women on 15 September 1995, and the Istanbul Declaration on Human Settlements and the Habitat Agenda, adopted by the second United Nations Conference on Human Settlements (Habitat II) on 14 June 1996,

Expressing its concern about the negative impact of unilateral coercive measures in the field of international relations, trade, investment and cooperation,

Deeply concerned that, despite the recommendations adopted on this question by the General Assembly and recent major United Nations conferences and contrary to general international law and the Charter of the United Nations, unilateral coercive measures continue to be promulgated and implemented with all their negative implications for the social-humanitarian activities and economic and social development of developing countries, including their extraterritorial effects, thereby creating additional obstacles to the full enjoyment of all human rights by peoples and individuals under the jurisdiction of other States,

Bearing in mind all the extraterritorial effects of any unilateral legislative, administrative and economic measures, policies and practices of a coercive nature against the development process and the enhancement of human rights in developing countries, which create obstacles to the full realization of all human rights,

Noting the continuing efforts of the Open-ended Working Group on the Right to Development of the Commission on Human Rights, and reaffirming in particular its criteria according to which unilateral coercive measures are one of the obstacles to the implementation of the Declaration on the Right to Development,

1. *Urges* all States to refrain from adopting or implementing any unilateral measures not in accordance with international law and the Charter of the United Nations, in particular those of a coercive nature with all their extraterritorial effects, which create obstacles to trade relations among States, thus impeding the full realization of the rights set forth in the Universal Declaration of Human Rights and other international human rights instruments, in particular the right of individuals and peoples to development;

2. *Invites* all States to consider adopting administrative or legislative measures, as appropriate, to counteract the extraterritorial application or effects of unilateral coercive measures;

3. *Rejects* unilateral coercive measures with all their extraterritorial effects as tools for political or economic pressure against any country, in particular against developing countries, because of their negative effects on the realization of all the human rights of vast sectors of their populations, in particular children, women and the elderly;

4. *Calls upon* Member States that have initiated such measures to commit themselves to their obligations and responsibilities arising from the international human rights instruments to which they are party by revoking such measures at the earliest time possible;

5. *Reaffirms*, in this context, the right of all peoples to self-determination, by virtue of which they freely determine their political status and freely pursue their economic, social and cultural development;

6. *Urges* the Commission on Human Rights to take fully into account the negative impact of unilateral coercive measures, including the enactment of national laws and their extraterritorial application, in its task concerning the implementation of the right to development;

7. *Requests* the United Nations High Commissioner for Human Rights, in discharging her functions relating to the promotion, realization and protection of the right to development and bearing in mind the continuing impact of unilateral coercive measures on the population of developing countries, to give priority to the present resolution in her annual report to the General Assembly;

8. *Requests* the Secretary-General to bring the present resolution to the attention of all Member States, to continue to collect their views and information on the implications and negative effects of unilateral coercive measures on their populations and to submit an analytical report thereon to the General Assembly at its fifty-sixth session, highlighting the practical and preventive measures in this respect;

9. *Decides* to examine this question on a priority basis at its fifty-sixth session under the sub-item entitled "Human rights questions, including alternative approaches for improving the effective enjoyment of human rights and fundamental freedoms".

RECORDED VOTE ON RESOLUTION 55/110:

In favour: Algeria, Angola, Antigua and Barbuda, Argentina, Armenia, Bahamas, Bahrain, Bangladesh, Barbados, Belarus, Belize, Benin, Bhutan, Bolivia, Botswana, Brazil, Brunei Darussalam, Burkina Faso, Burundi, Cambodia, Cameroon, Cape Verde, Chad, Chile, China, Colombia, Comoros, Congo, Costa Rica, Côte d'Ivoire, Cuba, Democratic People's Republic of Korea, Democratic Republic of the Congo, Djibouti, Dominica, Dominican Republic, Ecuador, Egypt, El Salvador, Eritrea, Ethiopia, Gabon, Gambia, Ghana, Grenada, Guatemala, Guinea, Guyana, Haiti, Honduras, India, Indonesia, Iran, Jamaica, Jordan, Kenya, Kyrgyzstan, Lao People's Democratic Republic, Lebanon, Lesotho, Libyan Arab Jamahiriya, Madagascar, Malawi, Malaysia, Mali, Mauritania, Mauritius, Mexico, Mongolia, Morocco, Mozambique, Myanmar, Namibia, Nauru, Nepal, Nicaragua, Nigeria, Oman, Pakistan, Panama, Papua New Guinea, Paraguay, Peru, Philippines, Qatar, Russian Federation, Rwanda, Saint Kitts and Nevis, Saint Lucia, Saint Vincent and the Grenadines, Samoa, Sao Tome and Principe, Saudi Arabia, Senegal, Sierra Leone, Singapore, Solomon Islands, South Africa, Sri Lanka, Sudan, Suriname, Swaziland, Syrian Arab Republic, Thailand, Togo, Trinidad and Tobago, Tunisia, Uganda, United Arab Emirates, United Republic of Tanzania, Uruguay, Vanuatu, Venezuela, Viet Nam, Yemen, Zambia, Zimbabwe.

Against: Albania, Andorra, Australia, Austria, Belgium, Bosnia and Herzegovina, Bulgaria, Canada, Croatia, Cyprus, Czech Republic, Denmark, Estonia, Finland, France, Georgia, Germany, Greece, Hungary, Iceland, Ireland, Israel, Italy, Japan, Latvia, Liechtenstein, Lithuania, Luxembourg, Malta, Marshall Islands, Micronesia, Monaco, Netherlands, New Zealand, Norway, Palau, Poland, Portugal, Republic of Moldova, Romania, San Marino, Slovakia, Slovenia, Spain, Sweden, The former Yugoslav Republic of Macedonia, Turkey, United Kingdom, United States.

Abstaining: Azerbaijan, Fiji, Kazakhstan, Republic of Korea, Ukraine, Uzbekistan.

Women and the right to development

A June note by the Secretariat [E/CN.4/Sub.2/ 2000/19], recalling a 1999 Subcommission request [YUN 1999, p. 659], stated that as at 25 May 2000 the Secretary-General was unable to provide information on women and the right to development, and that he would provide that information in 2001 in a comprehensive report on the right to development, in accordance with Commission resolution 2000/5 (see p. 695).

Extreme poverty

Report of independent expert. Pursuant to a 1999 Commission request [YUN 1999, p. 660], the independent expert on the question of human rights and extreme poverty, Anne-Marie Lizin (Belgium), reported in February [E/CN.4/2000/52], stressing the need to incorporate a human and social dimension in the globalization process in order to combat poverty. The report highlighted the activities of various development actors in combating extreme poverty. Special attention was paid to State practices and the activities of the UN system, the Bretton Woods institutions (the World Bank Group and the International Monetary Fund) and non-governmental agencies.

The expert stated that action in respect of certain essential needs—food, primary health care, primary education—would help launch an effective strategy for combating extreme poverty. The lack of political commitment remained a major obstacle in the struggle against extreme poverty. Some measures were also paralysed by the weakness of the State and its administrative and economic structures. The debt burden, armed conflicts, natural disasters and financial crises contributed to that weakness. Legislation guaranteeing a minimum income was one of the most effective weapons for fighting extreme poverty. The expert made a number of recommendations, including a proposal for a world alliance of development actors to fight against extreme poverty, more involvement of the Bretton Woods institutions, the incorporation of economic and social rights into national human rights institutions, decentralization and recognition of the role of local authorities, good governance, regularizing the situation of persons without documents, involving women in microcredit and special measures to help extremely poor women, and the adoption of a minimum guaranteed income and basic social security legislation.

Commission action. On 12 April [E/CN.4/2000/SR.41 & 42], the Commission held a special debate on poverty and the enjoyment of human rights.

On 17 April [res. 2000/12], the Commission, reaffirming that extreme poverty and exclusion from society constituted a violation of human dignity and that urgent action was required to eliminate them, called on the General Assembly, specialized agencies, UN bodies and intergovernmental organizations to take into account the contradiction between the existence of extreme poverty and exclusion from society, and the duty to guarantee enjoyment of human rights. States, intergovernmental organizations and NGOs were urged to take into account the links between human rights and extreme poverty, as well as efforts to empower people living in poverty to participate in decision-making processes on policies that affected them, and the United Nations was urged to strengthen poverty eradication as a priority throughout the system. The Commission decided to renew for a two-year period the mandate of the independent expert, who was asked to report in 2000 and 2001 and to make the reports available to the Commission for Social Development and the Commission on the Status of Women; and to contribute to the mid-term evaluation of the United Nations Decade for the Eradication of Poverty (1997-2006) (see p. 796), scheduled for 2002. The High Commissioner was asked to organize, before the Commission's

2001 session, a seminar to consider drafting a declaration on extreme poverty.

ECONOMIC AND SOCIAL COUNCIL ACTION

On 28 July, the Economic and Social Council, on the recommendation of the Commission on Human Rights [E/2000/23 & Corr.1], adopted **decision 2000/247** without vote [agenda item 14 *(g)*].

Human rights and extreme poverty

At its 45th plenary meeting, on 28 July 2000, the Economic and Social Council, taking note of Commission on Human Rights resolution 2000/12 of 17 April 2000, endorsed the Commission's decision to renew, for a period of two years, the mandate of the independent expert on the question of human rights and extreme poverty:

(a) To evaluate the relationship between the promotion and protection of human rights and the eradication of extreme poverty, including through the identification of national and international good practices;

(b) To hold consultations, including during her visits, with the poorest people and the communities in which they live, on means of developing their capacity to express their views and to organize themselves and to involve national human rights institutions in this exercise;

(c) To consider strategies to overcome extreme poverty and the social impact of those strategies;

(d) To continue her cooperation with the international financial institutions, with a view to identifying the best programmes for combating extreme poverty;

(e) To contribute to the mid-term evaluation of the first United Nations Decade for the Eradication of Poverty, scheduled for 2002;

(f) To report on her activities to the Commission on Human Rights at its fifty-seventh and fifty-eighth sessions and to make those reports available to the Commission for Social Development and the Commission on the Status of Women, as appropriate, for their sessions during the same years.

The Council approved the Commission's request to the United Nations High Commissioner for Human Rights to organize, before the fifty-seventh session of the Commission, a seminar to consider the need to develop a draft declaration on extreme poverty and, if appropriate, to identify its specific points.

The Council also approved the Commission's recommendation that, in view of the need to take into account work undertaken elsewhere, an invitation to this seminar should be extended to government representatives and experts of the United Nations specialized agencies, funds and programmes, the relevant functional commissions of the Council, the regional economic commissions, the international financial institutions, the Subcommission on the Promotion and Protection of Human Rights and interested non-governmental organizations.

GENERAL ASSEMBLY ACTION

On 4 December [meeting 81], the General Assembly, on the recommendation of the Third Committee [A/55/602/Add.2 & Corr.1], adopted **resolution 55/106** without vote [agenda item 114 *(b)*].

Human rights and extreme poverty

The General Assembly,

Reaffirming the Universal Declaration of Human Rights, the International Covenant on Civil and Political Rights, the International Covenant on Economic, Social and Cultural Rights, and other human rights instruments adopted by the United Nations,

Considering the relevant provisions of the Vienna Declaration and Programme of Action, adopted by the World Conference on Human Rights on 25 June 1993, and of the Copenhagen Declaration on Social Development and Programme of Action of the World Summit for Social Development, adopted by the World Summit on 12 March 1995, and the outcome document of the twenty-fourth special session of the General Assembly entitled "World Summit for Social Development and beyond: achieving social development for all in a globalizing world", adopted at Geneva on 1 July 2000,

Recalling its resolutions 47/196 of 22 December 1992, by which it declared 17 October the International Day for the Eradication of Poverty, 48/183 of 21 December 1993, by which it proclaimed 1996 the International Year for the Eradication of Poverty, 50/107 of 20 December 1995, by which it proclaimed the first United Nations Decade for the Eradication of Poverty (1997–2006), 51/97 of 12 December 1996 on human rights and extreme poverty, 52/193 of 18 December 1997, in which it emphasized the follow-up to the Decade, and 53/146 of 9 December 1998 on human rights and extreme poverty,

Recalling also its resolution 52/134 of 12 December 1997, in which it recognized that the enhancement of international cooperation in the field of human rights was essential for the understanding, promotion and protection of all human rights,

Recalling further its resolution 54/232 of 22 December 1999, in which it expressed its deep concern that the number of people living in extreme poverty continues to increase, with women and children constituting the majority and the most affected group,

Bearing in mind Commission on Human Rights resolutions 1992/11 of 21 February 1992, 1993/13 of 26 February 1993, 1994/12 of 25 February 1994, 1995/16 of 24 February 1995, 1996/10 of 11 April 1996, 1997/11 of 3 April 1997, 1998/25 of 17 April 1998, 1999/26 of 26 April 1999, and 2000/12 of 17 April 2000, as well as resolution 1996/23 of 29 August 1996 of the Sub-commission on Prevention of Discrimination and Protection of Minorities,

Recalling its resolution 47/134 of 18 December 1992, in which it reaffirmed that extreme poverty and exclusion from society constituted a violation of human dignity and stressed the need for a complete and in-depth study of extreme poverty, based on the experience and the thoughts of the poorest people,

Recognizing that the eradication of extreme poverty is a major challenge within the process of globalization and requires coordinated and continued policies through decisive national action and international cooperation,

Reaffirming that, as the existence of widespread extreme poverty inhibits the full and effective enjoyment of human rights and might, in some situations, constitute a threat to the right to life, its immediate alleviation and eventual eradication must remain a high priority for the international community,

Recalling the United Nations Millennium Declaration,

Taking note with satisfaction of the interim and progress reports submitted to the Commission on Human Rights by the independent expert on the question of human rights and extreme poverty and the recommendations contained therein,

1. *Reaffirms* that extreme poverty and exclusion from society constitute a violation of human dignity and that urgent national and international action is therefore required to eliminate them;

2. *Also reaffirms* that it is essential for States to foster participation by the poorest people in the decision-making process in the societies in which they live, in the promotion of human rights and in efforts to combat extreme poverty, and for people living in poverty and vulnerable groups to be empowered to organize themselves and to participate in all aspects of political, economic and social life, in particular the planning and implementation of policies that affect them, thus enabling them to become genuine partners in development;

3. *Emphasizes* that extreme poverty is a major issue to be addressed by Governments, civil society and the United Nations system, including international financial institutions, and in this context reaffirms that political commitment is a prerequisite for the eradication of poverty;

4. *Recognizes* that surmounting extreme poverty constitutes an essential means to the full enjoyment of political, civil, economic, social and cultural rights, and reaffirms the interrelationship among these goals;

5. *Reaffirms* that the existence of widespread absolute poverty inhibits the full and effective enjoyment of human rights and renders democracy and popular participation fragile;

6. *Also reaffirms* the commitments on development and poverty eradication contained in the United Nations Millennium Declaration;

7. *Invites* the United Nations High Commissioner for Human Rights, within the framework of the implementation of the United Nations Decade for the Eradication of Poverty, to continue to give appropriate attention to the question of human rights and extreme poverty;

8. *Notes with appreciation* the specific actions taken by the United Nations Children's Fund and the United Nations Educational, Scientific and Cultural Organization to mitigate the effects of extreme poverty on children and the efforts of the United Nations Development Programme to give priority to the search for some means of alleviating poverty within the framework of the relevant resolutions, and urges them to continue this work;

9. *Calls upon* States, United Nations bodies, in particular the Office of the United Nations High Commissioner for Human Rights and the United Nations Development Programme, intergovernmental organizations and non-governmental organizations to continue to give appropriate attention to the links between human rights and extreme poverty;

10. *Decides* to consider this question further at its fifty-seventh session under the sub-item entitled "Human rights questions, including alternative approaches for improving the effective enjoyment of human rights and fundamental freedoms".

Right to food

Report of High Commissioner. As requested by the Commission in 1999 [YUN 1999, p. 661], the High Commissioner, in a January report with later addendum [E/CN.4/2000/48 & Add.1], summarized the comments and suggestions received from Governments and UN bodies to implement the right to food, taking into account the second consultation on the right to adequate food [YUN 1998, p. 693]. She also described activities of the Subcommittee on Nutrition of the Administrative Committee on Coordination (ACC) (see p. 1172), an inter-agency mechanism for harmonizing nutrition policy, and of the Food and Agriculture Organization of the United Nations, including further progress made in the definition of the right to adequate food in international law and the updated study on the right to food [YUN 1999, p. 661]. Referring to General Comment No. 12 adopted by the Committee on Economic, Social and Cultural Rights regarding the right to food [ibid., p. 575], the High Commissioner stated that the implementation of the recommendations of the Comment should be prioritized.

Commission action. By a roll-call vote of 49 to 1, with 2 abstentions, the Commission, on 17 April [res. 2000/10], reaffirming that hunger constituted a violation of human dignity, considered it intolerable that some 825 million people did not have enough food to meet their basic nutritional needs. It recommended that the High Commissioner organize a third consultation on the right to food, with a focus on implementation mechanisms at the country level. It decided to appoint for a three-year period a special rapporteur on the right to food, who was to report in 2001. Governments, UN agencies, funds and programmes, treaty bodies and NGOs were requested to submit comments and suggestions on ways of realizing the right to food.

ECONOMIC AND SOCIAL COUNCIL ACTION

On 16 June, the Economic and Social Council, on the recommendation of the Commission on Human Rights [E/2000/L.5], adopted **decision 2000/219** by recorded vote (39-1-1) [agenda item 2].

The right to food

At its 10th plenary meeting, on 16 June 2000, the Economic and Social Council, taking note of Commission on Human Rights resolution 2000/10 of 17 April 2000, endorsed the Commission's decision, in order to respond fully to the necessity for an integrated and co-ordinated approach in the promotion and protection of the right to food, to appoint, for a period of three years, a special rapporteur whose mandate will focus on the right to food and who will accomplish the following main activities:

(a) Seek, receive and respond to information on all aspects of the realization of the right to food, including the urgent necessity of eradicating hunger;

(b) Establish cooperation with Governments, intergovernmental organizations, in particular the Food and Agriculture Organization of the United Nations, and non-governmental organizations on the promotion and effective implementation of the right to food, and make appropriate recommendations on the realization thereof, taking into consideration the work already done in this field throughout the United Nations system;

(c) Identify emerging issues related to the right to food worldwide.

The Council also endorsed the Commission's request to the Office of the United Nations High Commissioner for Human Rights to provide all necessary human and financial resources for the effective fulfilment of the mandate of the Special Rapporteur.

RECORDED VOTE ON DECISION 2000/219:

In favour: Algeria, Austria, Bahrain, Belarus, Belgium, Brazil, Bulgaria, Burkina Faso, Cameroon, Canada, China, Colombia, Costa Rica, Croatia, Cuba, Denmark, Fiji, France, Germany, Greece, India, Indonesia, Italy, Japan, Mexico, New Zealand, Norway, Oman, Pakistan, Poland, Portugal, Russian Federation, Saudi Arabia, Sudan, Suriname, Syrian Arab Republic, United Kingdom, Venezuela, Viet Nam.
Against: Czech Republic.
Abstaining: United States.

On 4 September, the Commission Chairman appointed Jean Ziegler (Switzerland) as Special Rapporteur.

Right to adequate housing

On 17 April [res. 2000/9], the Commission decided to appoint for a three-year period a special rapporteur on the right to adequate housing. The Economic and Social Council endorsed the Commission's decision on 16 June (**decision 2000/218**). On 4 September, the Commission Chairman appointed Miloon Kothari (India) as Special Rapporteur.

Women's right to property and adequate housing

On 17 April [res. 2000/13], the Commission, urging Governments to comply with their obligations and commitments concerning land tenure and the equal rights of women to own property and to an adequate standard of living, including adequate housing, recommended that they encourage financial lending institutions to ensure they did not discriminate against women. It invited the Secretary-General, as ACC Chairman, to encourage all UN bodies to undertake further initiatives promoting women's equal ownership of, access to and control over land and the equal rights to own property and to adequate housing, and to allocate further resources for studying the impact of complex emergency situations. OHCHR, UNHCR and relevant international organizations were asked to address discrimination against women with respect to land, property and adequate housing in their programmes and field activities.

Right to education

Report of Secretary-General. As requested by the Commission in 1999 [YUN 1999, p. 662], the Secretary-General reported on identifying progressive developmental benchmarks and indicators related to the right to education [E/CN.4/2000/47]. He suggested that the Commission sharpen practical approaches for the realization of economic, social and cultural rights, including the right to education. A possibility would be for the identification of indicators and benchmarks to create a positive impact on treaty recommendations. Equally, the mainstreaming of human rights within UN work would support the future integration of human rights treaty recommendations, including support for data collection, indicator disaggregation and benchmark-setting, into country programmes developed with Governments. The tasks of determining the core content of the right to education and identifying right-to-education indicators remained outstanding. The Special Rapporteur on the right to education was working on clarifying the content of the right to education, which would assist in identifying right-to-education indicators. The Secretary-General proposed that the Commission consider whether the method and approach on right-to-education indicators ought to be emulated for other economic and social rights, such as the rights to health and safe water.

Report of Special Rapporteur. The Special Rapporteur on the right to education, Katarina Tomasevski (Croatia), in a February report [E/CN.4/2000/6], focused on international cooperation from the viewpoint of financial obstacles to the realization of the right, especially at the level of primary education. She described the diminishing aid flows and the relative increase of aid for education, especially by multilateral agencies, and discussed the lack of coherence in international aid policies by highlighting the varying status of education, which was defined as a need or a right, subsumed under social development or poverty eradication. In a critique of the World Bank's recent education sector strategy, the Special Rapporteur pointed out discrepancies between the Bank's commitment to promoting basic education and to increasing its education lending, and discussed the need to apply pertinent international and domestic law. She continued to apply her 4-A scheme (availability, accessibility, acceptability and adaptability) to analyse governmental obligations corresponding to the

right to education. She examined State and non-State schools and the jurisprudence relating to State funding for private schools and also discussed school vouchers and school fees. The Special Rapporteur continued her approach to double mainstreaming (i.e., by merging human rights and gender throughout education). In her discussion of the human-capital approach, she stated that the approach moulded education solely towards economically relevant knowledge, skills and competence, to the detriment of human rights values. The Special Rapporteur stated that vast amounts of data in the field of education did not conform to the human rights approach to education, and the human rights community needed to design indicators regarding the right to education and human rights in education.

Commission action. On 17 April [res. 2000/9], the Commission, welcoming the convening of the World Education Forum (Dakar, Senegal, 26-28 April) (see p. 1081), asked the Special Rapporteur to continue her work and to identify ways to overcome obstacles in the realization of the right to education, notably through international cooperation. It asked the Special Rapporteur to report in 2001. The High Commissioner was asked to organize in 2001 a workshop to identify progressive developmental benchmarks and indicators related to the right to education. UNICEF and UNESCO were invited to develop a dialogue with the Special Rapporteur and to report to the Commission on their activities in promoting primary education, particularly for women and children, especially girls. The Secretary-General was asked to report in 2001.

Note by Secretariat. A July note by the Secretariat [E/CN.4/Sub.2/2000/15], recalling the Subcommission's 1999 request [YUN 1999, p. 662] to Mustapha Mehedi (Algeria) to prepare a final paper on the realization of the right to education, including education in human rights, stated that Mr. Mehedi was not nominated for re-election to the Subcommission and thus had ceased to be a member. It noted that as at mid-July the final paper had not been submitted.

Environmental and scientific concerns

Toxic wastes

Report of Special Rapporteur. In March [E/CN.4/2000/50], the Special Rapporteur on the adverse effects of the illicit movement and dumping of toxic and dangerous products and wastes on the enjoyment of human rights, Fatma-Zohra Ouhachi-Vesely (Algeria), described her activities and summarized comments she had received from six countries, as well as information submitted by concerned organizations. She reviewed and commented on three incidents of alleged toxic dumping and summarized replies from the Governments concerned. Information was provided on follow-up to her missions to Brazil, Costa Rica, Paraguay and South Africa [YUN 1998, p. 695]. The Special Rapporteur remarked on the absence of solutions to proven cases of illicit transfer of toxic products and regarding compensation for the victims and their families. The most alarming cases were related to the uncontrolled use of chemical substances, toxic agricultural products and persistent organic pollutants. She urged the Commission to consider the human rights aspects of problems that arose from the export of contaminated ships due for scrapping to developing countries.

Commission action. By a roll-call vote of 37 to 16, the Commission, on 26 April [res. 2000/72], reaffirming that illicit traffic and dumping of toxic and dangerous products and wastes constituted a serious threat to the human rights to life, health and a sound environment, urged Governments to take measures to prevent illegal trafficking. The Commission urged the Special Rapporteur to continue to study existing problems of and solutions to illicit trafficking, in particular in developing countries. She was asked to include in her 2001 report information on persons killed or injured in the developing countries through the illicit movement and dumping of toxic wastes; the question of impunity in those crimes; the question of rehabilitation of and assistance to victims; and the scope of national legislation in relation to transboundary movement and dumping of such products.

Water and sanitation services

Note by Secretariat. In a July note [E/CN.4/Sub.2/2000/16 & Corr.1], the Secretariat, recalling a 1999 Subcommission request [YUN 1999, p. 663] to El-Hadji Guissé (Senegal) to supplement his 1998 working paper on the right of access of everyone to drinking water supply and sanitation services [YUN 1998, p. 696], transmitted the new information reported by Mr. Guissé. Mr. Guissé described measures regarding the right to drinking water supply and sanitation services taken by Belgium, France and Spain and by the European Council on Environmental Law. He noted that the world already lacked water and, unless acceptable legal measures were taken to ensure sound management of that common asset, real conflicts would break out between and within societies. He recommended the submission of a preliminary report in 2001, a progress report in 2002 and a final report in 2003.

Subcommission action. On 17 August [res. 2000/8], the Subcommission recommended that the Commission authorize it to appoint Mr. Guissé as Special Rapporteur to conduct a study on the relationship between the enjoyment of economic, social and cultural rights and the promotion of the realization of the right to drinking water supply and sanitation. The Special Rapporteur was asked to define as accurately and as fully as possible the content of the right to water in relation to other human rights and to submit a preliminary report in 2001, a progress report in 2002 and a final report in 2003. The Secretary-General was requested to invite Governments, UN bodies, the specialized agencies and interested NGOs to provide the Special Rapporteur with information.

Slavery and related issues

Working Group activities. The five-member Working Group on Contemporary Forms of Slavery, at its twenty-fifth session (Geneva 14-23 June) [E/CN.4/Sub.2/2000/23], reviewed developments in contemporary forms of slavery and measures to prevent and repress all its forms, including the consideration of corruption and international debt as promoting factors of the phenomenon. It considered as a matter of priority the questions of bonded labour and debt bondage, as well as the issue of trafficking in persons and the exploitation of the prostitution of others. Other forms of exploitation examined were child labour, sexual exploitation, especially of children and domestic and migrant workers, the status of the slavery conventions, the activities of the United Nations Voluntary Trust Fund on Contemporary Forms of Slavery (see p. 708) and the Group's working methods.

The Group concluded that, despite the progress made in human rights protection and the preservation of human dignity, various forms of slavery still existed and new insidious forms were emerging. It made a series of recommendations on the issues it considered during the session.

Documents considered by the Group included May notes [E/CN.4/Sub.2/AC.2/2000/2, E/CN.4/Sub.2/AC.2/2000/3] by the Secretary-General updating the status of the slavery conventions (1956 Supplementary Convention on the Abolition of Slavery, the Slave Trade and Institutions and Practices Similar to Slavery [YUN 1956, p. 228] and the 1949 Convention for the Suppression of the Traffic in Persons and of the Exploitation of the Prostitution of Others, adopted by the General Assembly in resolution 317(IV) [YUN 1948-49, p. 613]); and a May report of the Secretary-General containing information on measures taken to prevent and repress all forms of slavery, as described by Governments, UN bodies, intergovernmental organizations and NGOs [E/CN.4/Sub.2/ AC.2/2000/4 & Add.1].

Working paper. In response to a 1999 Subcommission request [YUN 1999, p. 665], David Weissbrodt (United States) and Anti-Slavery International, in May, updated their 1999 review [ibid.] of existing treaty and customary law covering slavery-related practices and monitoring mechanisms [E/CN.4/Sub.2/2000/3]. The authors concluded that, in view of the fact that no international mechanism existed to monitor and enforce States' obligations to abolish slavery and related practices, the Working Group's mandate could be extended to include a review procedure. Alternatively, the Group could focus on thematic issues relevant to the prevention of slavery, or the Commission could transform the Working Group into a special rapporteur. The authors recommended the publication of their updated review.

In a May addendum to the report [E/CN.4/ Sub.2/2000/3/Add.1], the authors discussed various forms of slavery, including serfdom, forced labour, debt bondage, exploitation of migrant workers, trafficking in human beings, prostitution, forced marriage and the sale of wives, child labour and child servitude, apartheid and colonialism, trafficking in human organs and incest. They concluded that, as a number of slavery-like practices had evolved, proposals had been made to expand the definition of contemporary forms of slavery which could dilute efforts to eradicate the historical forms of slavery. Such proposals should be carefully scrutinized.

Subcommission action. On 18 August [res. 2000/19], the Subcommission addressed bonded labour and debt bondage; the United Nations Voluntary Trust Fund on Contemporary Forms of Slavery (see p. 708); the prevention of traffic in persons and exploitation of the prostitution of others; international cooperation for the prevention of illegal trafficking in persons, prostitution and the expansion of the world sex industry; the prevention of trans-border trafficking of children; misuse of the Internet for sexual exploitation; implementation of the slavery conventions; migrant workers; child domestic workers; child labour; forced labour; the sale of children, child prostitution and child pornography; and traffic in human organs and tissues.

The Subcommission invited Member States to provide information to the Working Group, in 2002, about measures taken to suppress or prevent debt bondage and to adopt national plans of action against trafficking in persons and exploi-

tation of prostitution. It requested OHCHR to design guidelines for national plans of action against trafficking. It called for cooperation among government and law enforcement bodies to combat trafficking for the prostitution of women and children, the globalization of that industry and the misuse of the Internet to promote sex trafficking, sex tourism, sexual violence and sexual exploitation. Condemning practices of unequal treatment of migrant workers and the denial of their human dignity, the Subcommission decided to continue to give special attention to their situation, particularly domestic workers. The Secretary-General was asked to invite States to inform the Working Group of measures adopted to implement several programmes of action and declarations on the issues of exploitation of child labour, prevention of the sale of children, child prostitution and child pornography, commercial sexual exploitation of children and other related developments, and to report to the Commission and the Subcommission in 2001. The Subcommission asked the Special Rapporteur on the sale of children, child prostitution and child pornography to continue to pay attention to issues relating to traffic, such as organ transplantation, disappearances, the purchase and sale of children, adoption for commercial purposes or exploitation, child prostitution and child pornography (see p. 721).

Traffic in human organs and tissue

The Commission had before it a Secretariat note [E/CN.4/2000/78] stating that pursuant to the Commission's 1999 request to the Secretary-General to continue to examine the reliability of allegations regarding the removal of organs and tissues of children and adults for commercial purposes [YUN 1999, p. 665], he had asked Governments and relevant UN agencies, as well as the International Criminal Police Organization, for information on the issue. As at 30 November 1999, no replies had been received.

Sexual exploitation during armed conflict

Report of Special Rapporteur. In June [E/CN.4/ Sub.2/2000/21], the Special Rapporteur on systematic rape, sexual slavery and slavery-like practices during periods of armed conflict, Gay J. McDougall (United States), updated her final report [YUN 1998, p. 698]. She reported that sexual violence continued to be used as a weapon of war, as evidenced in reports of sexual slavery and other forms of sexual violence, including rape, being used by all sides to the conflicts in Afghanistan, Burundi, Colombia, the Democratic Republic of the Congo, Liberia and Myanmar. Other States affected were Indonesia, Sierra Leone and Uganda, as well as the Kosovo province of the Federal Republic of Yugoslavia. She considered several aspects of the Statute of the International Criminal Court that represented the progressive development of international criminal law, particularly with respect to addressing gender-based crimes and sexual violence, and cited important developments in the ad hoc international criminal tribunals dealing with the former Yugoslavia and Rwanda (see PART FOUR, Chapter II). However, those international mechanisms would address only a small fraction of the violations that were being committed in contemporary armed conflicts; thus, it remained imperative that prosecution of such crimes take place at the national level. The right of victims to reparation had been developed in a revised set of basic principles and guidelines on the right to a remedy and reparation for victims of violations of international human rights and humanitarian law (see p. 665). Regarding developments concerning Japan's system of military sexual slavery during the Second World War [YUN 1996, p. 655], the atrocities committed against the so-called comfort women remained largely unremedied as there had been no reparation to the victims; thus, the Government had not fully discharged its obligations under international law. The Special Rapporteur noted efforts to redress abuses that took place in Europe during the Second World War, including trials of Nazi war criminals, agreements to compensate Holocaust victims whose assets were confiscated by the Nazis, and agreements to compensate victims of forced labour. Recommendations called for legislation at the national level, removal of gender bias in municipal law and procedure, protection for victims and witnesses, support services for victims, documentation with a view towards prosecution and action aimed at the cessation of hostilities.

Report of High Commissioner. In response to a 1999 Subcommission request [YUN 1999, p. 666], the High Commissioner, in June [E/CN.4/Sub.2/2000/20], described systematic rape, sexual slavery and slavery-like practices during specific conflict situations as reported by human rights treaty bodies, special rapporteurs and the Commission. The High Commissioner observed that the most recent conflicts had been the scene of brutal attacks against civilians, especially women and children. Sexual violence had been used systematically to terrorize civilians and destroy the social structure, family structure and pride of the enemy.

Subcommission action. On 17 August [res. 2000/13], the Subcommission called on the High Commissioner to report in 2001 on the issue of systematic rape, sexual slavery and slavery-like practices in situations of ongoing conflict.

1993 Programme of Action

In response to a 1997 Subcommission request [YUN 1997, p. 679], the Secretary-General, in May [E/CN.4/Sub.2/2000/22], presented information received from two Governments on action they had taken to implement the 1993 Programme of Action for the Elimination of the Exploitation of Child Labour [YUN 1993, p. 965]. A November note by the Secretary-General [E/CN.4/2001/77] drew the Commission's attention to the report.

Fund on slavery

Reports of Secretary-General. In March [E/CN.4/2000/80/Add.1], July [A/55/204] and December [E/CN.4/2001/82], the Secretary-General reported on the status of the United Nations Voluntary Trust Fund on Contemporary Forms of Slavery.

The Fund's Board of Trustees, at its fifth session (Geneva, 7-10 February), recommended 17 travel grants, amounting to $30,800, to enable NGO representatives to participate in the deliberations of the 2000 session of the Working Group on Contemporary Forms of Slavery (see p. 706), and 17 project grants amounting to $83,500. Taking into consideration the fact that requests received in 2000 amounted to some $700,000, the Board estimated that, in order to fulfil its mandate satisfactorily, the Fund would need $362,000 before its sixth session in January 2001. The Secretary-General reported that contributions available to the Board for grants in 2001 stood at $78,685 as at 23 November 2000, with pledges amounting to $54,112.

On 4 December, the General Assembly took note of the Secretary-General's July report (**decision 55/420**).

Subcommission action. On 17 August [res. 2000/12], the Subcommission emphasized the need for regular contributions to the Fund so that the Board of Trustees could recommend grants to assist representatives of organizations to participate in the Group's deliberations in 2001 and to finance NGO humanitarian assistance projects. It encouraged the Board to finance NGOs from all regions in order to provide the widest possible view of contemporary forms of slavery in the world.

Vulnerable groups

Women

Violence against women

Reports of Special Rapporteur. In February [E/CN.4/2000/68], the Special Rapporteur on violence against women, its causes and consequences, Radhika Coomaraswamy (Sri Lanka), highlighted women's movement, consensual and non-consensual, legal and illegal, for numerous reasons, including social, political, cultural and economic reasons. The element that distinguished trafficking from other forms of movement was its non-consensual nature. The Special Rapporteur emphasized the need in international law for a clear definition of trafficking, and provided a critique of the 1949 Convention for the Suppression of the Traffic in Persons and of the Exploitation of the Prostitution of Others, adopted by the General Assembly in resolution 317(IV) [YUN 1948-49, p. 613].

The report emphasized that movement and migration, coupled with Governments' reactions to and attempts to restrict those movements through immigration and emigration policies and the exploitation of such attempts by traffickers, placed women in situations in which they were unprotected or marginally protected by law. It highlighted the Special Rapporteur's concern about the link between protectionist, anti-immigration policies and the phenomenon of trafficking. Concern was also raised over the law and order approach that was overwhelmingly adopted by Governments to combat trafficking. Those approaches were often at odds with human rights protection and might create or exacerbate trafficking in women. The report affirmed that the lack of women's rights was the prime factor of both women's migration and trafficking. The failure of existing economic, political and social structures to provide equal and just opportunities for women to work had contributed to the feminization of poverty, which in turn had led to the feminization of migration, as women left their homes in search of viable economic options. Further, political instability, militarism, civil unrest, internal armed conflict and natural disasters also exacerbated women's vulnerability. The report stressed States' responsibility to prevent, investigate and punish acts of trafficking in women and provide protection to trafficked persons. The Special Rapporteur presented recommendations for action at the international and national levels. In an addendum to her report [E/CN.4/2000/68/Add.1], she stated that she had received 7 replies to the 18 communications she had transmitted to States regarding alleged violence against women.

A further addendum [E/CN.4/2000/68/Add.5] examined the relationship of economic and social policies to violence against women. The policies spanned from international economic strategies for globalization to national laws regulating inheritance. The Special Rapporteur observed that economic and social disparities could exacerbate the disparities between men and women and worsen women's situations. Macro-policies of States and Governments might result in human rights violations and violence, such as preventable malnutrition, preventable diseases or complications during pregnancy and childbirth resulting in death. Violence against women generally derived from the perceived inferiority of women and the unequal status granted by laws and societal norms. Recommendations were made at the international and national levels.

At the invitation of Bangladesh, India and Nepal, the Special Rapporteur visited those countries to study the issue of trafficking in women and girls (28 October–15 November) [E/CN.4/2001/73/Add.2]. The primary purpose of trafficking in the region was for forced prostitution, but girls, boys and women were also trafficked for domestic service, organ harvesting, forced begging, forced labour in sweatshops, work as camel jockeys or forced marriage. The lack of implementation of laws aimed at ending trafficking was reflected in the low conviction rates for perpetrators of violent crimes against women. In Bangladesh, according to the police, of some 7,000 cases of violence against women registered in the past year there were only 21 convictions, while 2,000 cases were being processed. In Nepal, police figures showed that of some 150 cases of trafficking offences during the past year, 55 per cent resulted in acquittals. There was a need, in terms of trafficking of women and girls from Nepal and Bangladesh to India, to collect data so as to ascertain the true scope of the problem; estimates varied from 10,000 to 25,000. For many countries, trafficking was considered an immigration problem and the campaign against trafficking was linked to the desire to close borders to people from other countries. The Special Rapporteur proposed that trafficking should be dealt with as a human rights issue. The South Asia Association for Regional Cooperation was preparing to adopt a convention for preventing and combating trafficking in women and children for prostitution, but the Special Rapporteur stated that a regional convention could not solve the problem without a regional monitoring mechanism, as well as regional cooperation among law enforcement officials. The Special Rapporteur expressed concern that legislation on trafficking as proposed in most countries in the region was unduly harsh and violated human rights law. Victims and women's groups in the three countries recounted many cases of police corruption. The Special Rapporteur received a mixed picture about the judiciary's role in fighting trafficking, especially in India as a receiving country. In all the countries, there were very few medical facilities available for AIDS patients, and AIDS education among the sex workers was also minimal owing to the ambiguous legal position of women.

In Bangladesh, one of the poorest countries, there was extensive trafficking, primarily to India, Pakistan and destinations within the country, largely for purposes of forced prostitution, although in some cases for labour servitude. Some children had reportedly been trafficked to the Middle East to work as camel jockeys. Although the Government had made efforts to improve the situation, including the enactment of laws to prohibit certain forms of discrimination against women, the Special Rapporteur was concerned about the introduction of new draconian laws and the application of the death penalty for a range of crimes against women, including trafficking, rape, acid throwing/burning and dowry violence. Police were aware of the problem of violence against women but most had not received training in handling such cases. The Government had set up women's police units to look into cases but the actual number of cases filed in court was extremely small. The Government had no special programmes relating to the social welfare of trafficked women.

Nepal was a primary sending country for the region, with India the main destination. It was estimated that 100,000 to 200,000 women from Nepal were engaged in exploitative situations of prostitution in India. Landlessness among women, unemployment and underemployment, poverty, widespread gender discrimination, religious and cultural sanctions for prostitution among certain groups and the growing acceptance of the inevitability of migration contributed to trafficking of women and children from the country. Discriminatory inheritance laws and citizenship laws were other factors. The Government had identified trafficking as one of its major priorities and had developed a national plan of action; however, it focused on the victim, awareness-raising, health and education and rescue and rehabilitation, but was not very concerned with traffickers, their prosecution and punishment. The Special Rapporteur was encouraged that the police at border posts seemed aware of the problem and were determined to deal with it. As in Bangladesh, rescue and social welfare for victims had been left to NGOs. International agencies in Nepal had been extremely active regarding trafficking.

India was a source, a transit point for persons trafficked to Pakistan and the Gulf States, and a destination for trafficked persons, and it remained the main receiving country in the region. Internal trafficking also occurred from the rural, economically depressed areas to the cities. The National Commission on Women was examining the possibility of replacing existing legislation with comprehensive trafficking prevention legislation. A manual for police training in the area of trafficking was being developed with the help of UNICEF. The Special Rapporteur questioned the use of government homes as a means of rehabilitating victims. Unlike other countries in the region, the United Nations in India did not have an integrated, coordinated strategy to address trafficking.

The Special Rapporteur presented recommendations for action at the international, national and regional levels.

Commission action. On 20 April [res. 2000/45], the Commission, condemning all acts of gender-based violence against women and violence occurring in the family, asked special rapporteurs, UN bodies, specialized agencies and intergovernmental organizations to consider violence against women in their respective mandates and to cooperate with the Special Rapporteur. States were called on to: ratify and implement relevant international human rights instruments; report on violence against women and measures taken to implement the 1993 Declaration on the Elimination of Violence against Women, adopted by the General Assembly in resolution 48/104 [YUN 1993, p. 1046], and the 1995 Beijing Platform for Action [YUN 1995, p. 1170]; condemn violence against women and not invoke custom, tradition or religion to avoid obligations to eliminate such violence; enact and reinforce or amend penal, civil, labour and administrative sanctions in domestic legislation to punish and redress the wrongs done to women and girls who were subjected to violence; conduct information campaigns about violence against women; establish relations with NGOs and community-based organizations to develop policies on violence against women; and create, improve or develop and fund training programmes for judicial, legal, medical, social, educational, police, correctional service, military, peacekeeping, humanitarian relief and immigration personnel in order to avoid the abuse of power leading to violence against women. The Commission asked Governments to support initiatives of women's organizations and NGOs to raise awareness of violence against women and to contribute to its elimination. The Commission decided to renew the Special Rapporteur's mandate for an additional three-year period, a decision endorsed by the Economic and Social Council on 28 July (**decision 2000/266**).

(For further information on trafficking in women, see below and p. 709.)

Women migrant workers

In response to its 1998 request [YUN 1998, p. 701], the Commission considered a report of the Secretary-General [E/CN.4/2000/76] containing information received from Governments, UN bodies, specialized agencies and intergovernmental organizations on measures they had taken to address violence against women migrant workers. Concluding that more extensive information was required on the situation of women migrant workers in order to identify concrete strategies, the Secretary-General called for additional attention at the national and international levels.

Commission action. On 25 April [res. 2000/54], the Commission called on Governments, if they had not done so, to set up penal sanctions to punish perpetrators of violence against women migrant workers, and to provide victims with assistance to allow them to be present during the judicial process, to safeguard their dignified return to the country of origin, and to establish reintegration and rehabilitation schemes for returning women migrant workers. States were invited to adopt legal measures against intermediaries who encouraged the clandestine movement of workers and who exploited women migrant workers. The Secretary-General was asked to report in 2002.

Traditional practices affecting the health of women and girls

Report of Special Rapporteur. In response to a 1999 Subcommission request [YUN 1999, p. 669], the Special Rapporteur on traditional practices affecting the health of women and the girl child, Halima Embarek Warzazi (Morocco), in a June report [E/CN.4/Sub.2/2000/17], reviewed the latest initiatives taken against the practice of female genital mutilation and other traditional practices. The Special Rapporteur welcomed the positive developments that had occurred in the struggle against some traditional practices, such as female genital mutilation, son preference, practices related to pregnancy, early marriage and the phenomenon of violence in the family. Nevertheless, despite the slow but steady progress in the campaign against female genital mutilation, the Special Rapporteur drew attention to the fact that many harmful traditional practices,

discriminatory attitudes and acts of violence existed and were not being dealt with as they should. The case of the crime of honour was an illustration of such violence exclusively affecting women and girls.

Subcommission action. On 17 August [res. 2000/10], the Subcommission appealed to States to intensify public awareness concerning the effects of all forms of harmful traditional practices and asked NGOs to study the various practices and ways to eradicate them and to inform the Special Rapporteur of any situation that merited the attention of the international community. It called on Governments to implement the 1994 Plan of Action on the practice [YUN 1994, p. 1123] and asked the Secretary-General to invite them to submit information regularly on the situation regarding those practices. The Subcommission proposed that three seminars be held, in Africa, Asia and Europe, to review progress achieved since 1985 and ways to overcome the obstacles encountered in implementing the Plan of Action. The Subcommission decided to extend the Special Rapporteur's mandate for a further two years and asked her to report in 2001 and 2002.

Traffic in women and girls

Report of Secretary-General. As requested by the Commission in 1999 [YUN 1999, p. 669], the Secretary-General, in January [E/CN.4/2000/66], described activities of the UN system and other international organizations to combat trafficking in women and girls. He stated that the root causes of trafficking were poverty, food scarcity, unemployment and indebtedness, violence against women, gender discrimination, the lack of appropriate legislation, lack of political will, public sector corruption, the growing feminization of labour migration on the one hand and increasingly restrictive immigration policies of recipient countries on the other, increased power and involvement of transnational criminal networks, the rapidly expanding global sex industry and the growing gap between rich and poor countries. Progress to eliminate the phenomenon and to protect the rights of trafficked persons could be made only by addressing those causes. It was important to ensure that human rights were integrated into analysis of the trafficking problem and the development of solutions. The integration of a human rights perspective into UN antitrafficking activities was an essential aspect of the broader commitment of the Organization to the integration of human rights throughout its work.

Commission action. On 20 April [res. 2000/44], the Commission called on Governments to criminalize trafficking in women and girls and to condemn and penalize offenders, urged them to address the root factors and encouraged them to conclude bilateral, subregional, regional and international agreements to address the problem. The Secretary-General was asked to report in 2001.

(See also p. 1117.)

Mainstreaming women's rights

Reports of Secretary-General. Pursuant to a 1999 Commission request [YUN 1999, p. 670], the Secretary-General reported on steps taken to integrate gender perspectives fully into the UN human rights system [E/CN.4/2000/67], particularly OHCHR, human rights treaty bodies, human rights mechanisms, UN bodies and specialized agencies. He recommended that Governments ratify the Convention on the Elimination of All Forms of Discrimination against Women, adopted by the General Assembly in resolution 34/180 [YUN 1979, p. 895], and the Convention on the Rights of the Child, adopted by the Assembly in resolution 44/25 [YUN 1989, p. 561]. The obligations of States to prevent and redress violations of women's rights needed further clarification. Progress had been made in implementing the recommendations of the expert group meeting on the development of guidelines for the integration of gender perspectives into human rights activities and programmes [YUN 1995, p. 767]. Guidelines that were still relevant were reproduced in the report and were updated to reflect changes in the UN structure.

In January [E/CN.4/2000/118-E/CN.6/2000/8], the Secretary-General presented the joint work plan of the United Nations Division for the Advancement of Women and OHCHR for 2000. It highlighted support for the work of treaty bodies and selected special mechanisms and cooperation between national machinery for the advancement of women and national human rights institutions. Cooperation between the Division and OHCHR would continue on the work of treaty bodies. The web sites of the Division (un.org/womenwatch/daw) and the Office (unhchr.ch) would be further improved to facilitate communication. The Division would continue to monitor progress in the work of treaty bodies in integrating a gender perspective and would provide gender-specific input for their work. Support would be provided for the work of the Commission's special rapporteurs on violence against women, as well as the Subcommission's experts on affirmative action and on reservations. Annexed to the report was an excerpt from the report of the 1999 workshop on gender integration into the human rights system [YUN 1999, p. 670].

In 2000, OHCHR collaborated with the Division in organizing an expert group meeting on the HIV/AIDS pandemic and its gender implications (Windhoek, Namibia, 13-17 November). OHCHR and the United Nations Development Fund for Women collaborated with the Division in organizing an expert group meeting on gender and racial discrimination (Zagreb, Croatia, 21-24 November).

Commission action. On 20 April [res. 2000/46], the Commission, emphasizing the need for further activities in the UN system to strengthen expertise concerning the equal status of human rights of women, asked the human rights treaty bodies, special procedures and other human rights mechanisms of the Commission and the Subcommission to take a gender perspective into account in implementing their mandates, and to include in their reports information on and qualitative analysis of women's and girls' human rights. It encouraged the treaty bodies to monitor more effectively the human rights of women in their activities, and reaffirmed their responsibility to integrate a gender perspective in their work. The Commission asked the Secretary-General to report in 2001 and decided to integrate a gender perspective into all of its agenda items. The Economic and Social Council endorsed that decision on 28 July (**decision 2000/267**).

The girl child

On 27 April [res. 2000/85], the Commission called on States to institute legal reforms to ensure girls' enjoyment of human rights and fundamental freedoms; to eliminate discrimination against girls and the root causes of son preference; to eradicate traditional or customary practices, particularly female genital mutilation, that were harmful to women and girls; and to enact and enforce laws to ensure that marriage was entered into only with the consent of the intending spouses, to enact and enforce laws concerning the minimum legal age for marriage, and to raise the minimum age for marriage where necessary.

(See also p. 1114.)

Women in Afghanistan

Commission action. On 18 April [res. 2000/18], the Commission, condemning the continuing grave human rights violations of women and girls in Afghanistan, particularly in Taliban-controlled areas, urged all Afghan parties, particularly the Taliban, to end those violations and to ensure: the repeal of legislative and other measures that discriminated against women and girls; women's participation in civil, cultural, economic, political and social life; respect for women's right to work; the right of women and girls to education without discrimination, the re-opening of schools and the admission of women and girls to all levels of education; respect for women's right to security of person and that those responsible for physical attacks on women were brought to justice; respect for women's freedom of movement; and equal access to facilities for physical and mental health. The Special Rapporteur on the situation of human rights in Afghanistan (see p. 750) was asked to continue to pay attention to the human rights of women and children and to apply a gender perspective in his 2001 report to the Commission.

Report of Secretary-General. The Secretary-General, in a July report on the situation of women and girls in Afghanistan [E/CN.4/Sub.2/2000/18], stated that their rights continued to be violated as a result of years of armed conflict, poverty and profound underdevelopment. There had been some easing of restrictions in some parts of the country, particularly in terms of women's and girls' access to health services, education and employment opportunities. The report examined areas of principal concern, including health, education, employment and freedom of movement. As there was little reporting and information on the situation in the territory controlled by the United Front, the Secretary-General called for strengthening the monitoring and evaluation of women's and girls' human rights promotion and protection in those areas. He described UN programmes and strategies.

The Secretary-General concluded that the situation of women and girls remained extremely serious; it was aggravated by the undeclared policy of gender discrimination. All Afghan parties, particularly the Taliban, should end the human rights violations and urgently ensure the elimination of discrimination against women; the participation of women in civil, cultural, economic, political and social life; respect for the right of women to work and reintegration in their employment; the right to education without discrimination; respect for women's right to security of person; respect for freedom of movement; and access to facilities necessary to protect their right to physical and mental health. The Secretary-General pointed to the need for the UN system in Afghanistan to reconsider its female recruitment policies and develop time-bound targets to employ more Professional internationally recruited women; give high priority to national female staff to enable them to perform their duties; and regulate, follow up and monitor Afghanistan's gradual relaxation of the mahatma edict for non-Afghan Muslim female staff—by issuing visas to non-Afghan Muslim women who were internationally recruited in the UN system.

Subcommission action. On 17 August [res. 2000/11], the Subcommission, condemning all forms of discrimination and violation affecting women and girls in the territories controlled by Afghan armed groups, considered it essential that the international community continue to follow closely their situation and bring the necessary pressure to bear so that all restrictions imposed on women were removed. It asked the Commission to insist that the Afghan armed groups abide by international human rights standards in relation to women, which entailed the repeal of all edicts and the end to all forms of discrimination based on sex. The Secretary-General was requested to make available all information compiled on the situation.

(See also p. 1120.)

Children

On 27 April, the Commission, in its resolution on the rights of the child [res. 2000/85], called on States to ensure the registration of all children immediately after birth, to respect the right of the child to preserve his or her identity and to ensure that a child would not be separated from his or her parents against their will, except when determined by competent authorities that such separation was necessary for the child's best interest. It urged Governments to protect children infected and/or affected by HIV/AIDS from all forms of discrimination, stigma, abuse and neglect, in particular in the access to and provision of health, education and social services. States were called on to promote children's right to education. The Commission asked all relevant human rights mechanisms to pay attention to the special situations of violence against children. It called on States to ensure the full and equal enjoyment of all human rights and fundamental freedoms by children with disabilities, and to protect the human rights of migrant children. They were also asked to devise economic and social solutions to the problems causing children to work and/or to live on the street, to increase protection of refugee and internally displaced children and to ensure that every child alleged to have or recognized as having infringed the penal law was treated in accordance with their obligations under the Convention on the Rights of the Child (see p. 614), adopted by General Assembly resolution 44/25 [YUN 1989, p. 561], and other international human rights instruments. States and other relevant actors were urged to promote the physical and psychological recovery and social reintegration of a child victim of any form of neglect, exploitation or abuse, torture or any other form of cruel, inhuman or degrading treatment or punishment, or armed conflicts. The Commission recommended that, within their mandates, relevant human rights mechanisms and entities of the UN system and specialized agencies take a child's rights perspective into account in implementing their mandates, and that they take into account the work of the Committee on the Rights of the Child (see p. 614). The Commission's recommendation was approved by the Economic and Social Council on 28 July (**decision 2000/280**). The Commission asked the Secretary-General to report in 2001.

Other aspects of the Commission's resolution—child labour, the prevention and eradication of the sale of children, child prostitution and child pornography, and protection of children affected by armed conflict—are covered below.

GENERAL ASSEMBLY ACTION

On 4 December [meeting 81], the General Assembly, on the recommendation of the Third Committee [A/55/598], adopted **resolution 55/79** without vote [agenda item 110].

The rights of the child

The General Assembly,

Recalling its resolutions 54/148 and 54/149 of 17 December 1999, and taking note of Commission on Human Rights resolution 2000/85 of 27 April 2000,

Bearing in mind the Convention on the Rights of the Child, emphasizing that the provisions of the Convention and other relevant human rights instruments must constitute the standard in the promotion and protection of the rights of the child, and reaffirming that the best interest of the child shall be the primary consideration in all actions concerning children,

Reaffirming the World Declaration on the Survival, Protection and Development of Children and the Plan of Action for Implementing the World Declaration on the Survival, Protection and Development of Children in the 1990s adopted by the World Summit for Children, held in New York on 29 and 30 September 1990, and the Vienna Declaration and Programme of Action adopted by the World Conference on Human Rights, held at Vienna from 14 to 25 June 1993, which, inter alia, states that national and international mechanisms and programmes for the defence and protection of children, in particular those in especially difficult circumstances, should be strengthened, including through effective measures to combat exploitation and abuse of children, such as female infanticide, harmful child labour, sale of children and organs, child prostitution and child pornography, and which reaffirms that all human rights and fundamental freedoms are universal,

Recalling its resolution 54/93 of 7 December 1999, by which it decided to convene a special session in September 2001 to follow up the World Summit for Children, and stressing the importance of addressing the rights and needs of the child in the preparatory process of the special session and the special session itself,

Profoundly concerned that the situation of girls and boys in many parts of the world remains critical as a result of the persistence of poverty, social inequality, inadequate social and economic conditions in an increasingly globalized world economy, pandemics, in particular human immunodeficiency virus/acquired immunodeficiency syndrome, natural disasters, armed conflict, displacement, exploitation, illiteracy, hunger, intolerance, discrimination and inadequate legal protection, and convinced that urgent and effective national and international action is called for,

Underlining the need for mainstreaming a gender perspective in all policies and programmes relating to children,

Recognizing the need for the realization of a standard of living adequate for the child's physical, mental, spiritual, moral and social development, the protection of the child from torture and other cruel, inhuman or degrading treatment or punishment, the provision of universal and equal access to primary education and the implementation of the commitments on the education of children contained in the United Nations Millennium Declaration,

Concerned at the number of illegal adoptions, of children growing up without parents and of child victims of family and social violence, neglect and abuse,

Welcoming the adoption of the Optional Protocols to the Convention on the Rights of the Child on the involvement of children in armed conflict and on the sale of children, child prostitution and child pornography,

Recognizing that partnership among Governments, international organizations and all sectors of civil society, in particular non-governmental organizations, is important to realizing the rights of the child,

Stressing the importance of integrating child-related issues into the work of the World Conference against Racism, Racial Discrimination, Xenophobia and Related Intolerance, the United Nations Conference on the Illicit Trade in Small Arms and Light Weapons in All Its Aspects and the special session of the General Assembly on the problem of human immunodeficiency virus/acquired immunodeficiency syndrome in all its aspects, to be held in 2001,

I
Implementation of the Convention on
the Rights of the Child

1. *Once again urges* the States that have not yet done so to sign and ratify or accede to the Convention on the Rights of the Child as a matter of priority with a view to reaching the goal of universal adherence as soon as possible;

2. *Invites* States to consider signing and ratifying the Optional Protocols to the Convention as a matter of priority with a view to their entry into force as soon as possible, bearing in mind the convening of the special session of the General Assembly to follow up the World Summit for Children in September 2001;

3. *Reiterates its concern* at the great number of reservations to the Convention, and urges States parties to withdraw reservations that are incompatible with the object and purpose of the Convention and to review on a regular basis any reservations with a view to withdrawing them;

4. *Calls upon* States parties to implement fully the Convention, stresses that the implementation of the

Convention contributes to the achievement of the goals of the World Summit for Children, and recommends that a thorough assessment of ten years of implementation of the Convention be an essential element in the preparation of the special session to follow up the Summit;

5. *Urges* States to assure the child who is capable of forming his or her own views the right to express those views freely in all matters that affect him or her, the views being given due weight in accordance with the age and maturity of the child, and in this regard to involve children and young people in their efforts to implement the goals of the Summit and the Convention, as well as in other programmes relating to children and young people, as appropriate;

6. *Calls upon* States parties to cooperate closely with the Committee on the Rights of the Child and to comply in a timely manner with their reporting obligations under the Convention, in accordance with the guidelines elaborated by the Committee, and encourages States parties to take into account the recommendations made by the Committee in the implementation of the provisions of the Convention;

7. *Requests* the Secretary-General to ensure the provision of appropriate staff and facilities for the effective and expeditious performance of the functions of the Committee, notes the temporary support given by the plan of action of the United Nations High Commissioner for Human Rights to strengthen the important role of the Committee in advancing the implementation of the Convention, and also requests the Secretary-General to make available information on the follow-up to the plan of action;

8. *Calls upon* States parties urgently to take appropriate measures so that acceptance of the amendment to paragraph 2 of article 43 of the Convention by a two-thirds majority of States parties can be reached as soon as possible in order for the amendment to enter into force, thus increasing the membership of the Committee from ten to eighteen experts, bearing in mind, inter alia, the additional workload of the Committee when the two Optional Protocols to the Convention enter into force;

9. *Invites* the Committee to continue to enhance its constructive dialogue with the States parties and its transparent and effective functioning;

10. *Recommends* that, within their mandates, all relevant human rights mechanisms and all other relevant organs and mechanisms of the United Nations system and the supervisory bodies of the specialized agencies pay attention to particular situations in which children are in danger and in which their rights are violated and that they take into account the work of the Committee, and encourages the further development of the rights-based approach adopted by the United Nations Children's Fund and further steps to increase system-wide coordination and inter-agency cooperation for the promotion and protection of the rights of the child;

11. *Encourages* the Committee, in monitoring the implementation of the Convention, to continue to pay attention to the needs of children in especially difficult circumstances;

12. *Urges* all States to assign priority to activities and programmes aimed at preventing the abuse of narcotic drugs, psychotropic substances and inhalants as well as preventing other addictions, in particular addiction to alcohol and tobacco, among children and young people, especially those in vulnerable situations, and urges all States to counter the use of children and young people in the illicit production of and trafficking in narcotic drugs and psychotropic substances;

13. *Reaffirms* the importance of ensuring adequate and systematic training in the rights of the child for professional groups working with and for children, including specialized judges, law enforcement officials, lawyers, social workers, medical doctors, health professionals and teachers, and of coordination among various governmental bodies involved in children's rights, and encourages States and relevant bodies and organizations of the United Nations system to continue to promote education and training in this regard;

14. *Encourages* Governments and relevant United Nations bodies, as well as relevant non-governmental organizations and child rights advocates, to contribute, as appropriate, to the web-based database launched by the United Nations Children's Fund so as to continue the provision of information on laws, structures, policies and processes adopted at the national level to translate the Convention into practice, and in this regard commends the Fund for its work to disseminate lessons learned in the implementation of the Convention;

II
Protection and promotion of the rights of children

Identity, family relations and birth registration

1. *Calls upon* all States to intensify efforts to ensure the registration of all children immediately after birth, including through the consideration of simplified, expeditious and effective procedures;

2. *Also calls upon* all States to undertake to respect the right of the child to preserve his or her identity, including nationality, name and family relations as recognized by law, without unlawful interference and, where a child is illegally deprived of some or all of the elements of his or her identity, to provide appropriate assistance and protection with a view to re-establishing speedily his or her identity;

3. *Urges* all States to ensure, as far as possible, the right of the child to know and be cared for by his or her parents;

4. *Also urges* all States to ensure that a child shall not be separated from his or her parents against their will, except when the competent authorities, subject to judicial review, determine, in accordance with applicable law and procedures, that such separation is necessary in the best interest of the child, and, where alternative care is necessary, to promote family and community-based care in preference to placement in institutions, recognizing that such determination may be necessary in a particular case, such as one involving abuse or neglect of the child by the parents or one in which the parents are living separately and a decision must be made as to the child's place of residence;

5. *Calls upon* States to take all necessary measures to ensure that the best interest of the child is the primary consideration in adoptions of children and to take all necessary measures to prevent and combat illegal adoptions and adoptions which do not follow the normal procedures;

6. *Also calls upon* States to take all necessary measures to address the problem of children growing up without parents, in particular orphaned children and

children who are victims of family and social violence, neglect and abuse;

Health

7. *Calls upon* all States and relevant bodies and organizations of the United Nations system, in particular the World Health Organization and the United Nations Children's Fund, to pay particular attention to the development of sustainable health systems and social services to ensure the effective prevention of diseases, malnutrition, disabilities and infant and child mortality, including through prenatal and post-natal health care, as well as the provision of necessary medical treatment and health care to all children, taking into consideration the special needs of young children and girls, including prevention of common infectious diseases, the special needs of adolescents, including those relating to reproductive and sexual health and threats from substance abuse and violence, and the particular needs of children living in poverty, children in situations of armed conflict and children in other vulnerable groups, and to strengthen ways of empowering families and communities;

8. *Calls upon* all States to adopt all necessary measures to ensure the full and equal enjoyment of all human rights and fundamental freedoms by children affected by disease and malnutrition, including protection from all forms of discrimination, abuse or neglect, in particular in the access to and provision of health care;

9. *Welcomes* the attention given by the Committee on the Rights of the Child to the realization of the highest attainable standards of health and access to health care and to the rights of children affected by human immunodeficiency virus/acquired immunodeficiency syndrome (HIV/AIDS);

10. *Urges* States to give particular emphasis to the prevention of HIV infection in young children and strengthen efforts to prevent adolescents and women from becoming HIV-infected, inter alia, by including HIV/AIDS prevention in educational curricula and educational programmes consistent with the epidemiology of the diseases in each State, and by supporting wide-scale voluntary HIV testing and counselling programmes for pregnant women, together with services for HIV-infected pregnant women to reduce the risk of transmitting the virus from HIV/AIDS-infected pregnant women to their children;

11. *Urges* all States to take all necessary measures to protect children infected and/or affected by HIV/AIDS from all forms of discrimination, stigma, abuse and neglect, in particular in the access to and provision of health, education and social services, with a view to the realization of their rights;

12. *Calls upon* the international community, relevant United Nations agencies, funds and programmes and intergovernmental and non-governmental organizations to intensify their support of national efforts against HIV/AIDS aimed at providing assistance to children infected or affected by the epidemic, including those orphaned as a result of the HIV/AIDS pandemic, focusing in particular on the worst-hit regions of Africa and areas in which the epidemic is severely setting back national development gains, calls upon them also to give importance to the treatment, care and support of children infected with HIV/AIDS, and invites them to consider further involving the private sector;

Education

13. *Calls upon* States to recognize the right to education on the basis of equal opportunity by making primary education compulsory and ensuring that all children have access to free and relevant primary education, as well as by making secondary education generally available and accessible to all, and in particular by the progressive introduction of free education;

14. *Reaffirms* the Dakar Framework for Action adopted at the World Education Forum and calls for its full implementation, and in this regard invites the United Nations Educational, Scientific and Cultural Organization to continue to implement its mandated role in coordinating Education for All partners and maintaining their collaborative momentum;

15. *Calls upon* all States to eliminate the gender gap in education, reaffirms the commitment contained in the United Nations Millennium Declaration to ensure equal access for girls and boys to all levels of education and the completion of a full course of primary schooling by children everywhere, boys and girls alike, by 2015, and in this regard encourages the implementation of the United Nations Girls' Education Initiative launched by the Secretary-General at the World Education Forum;

16. *Calls upon* States to ensure that emphasis is given to the qualitative aspects of education, that the education of the child is carried out, that States parties to the Convention on the Rights of the Child develop and implement programmes for the education of the child, in accordance with articles 28 and 29 of the Convention, and that education is directed, inter alia, to the development of respect for human rights and fundamental freedoms and to the preparation of the child for a responsible life in a free society in a spirit of understanding, peace, tolerance, gender equality and friendship among peoples, ethnic, national and religious groups and persons of indigenous origin, and to ensure that children, from an early age, benefit from education on values, attitudes, modes of behaviour and ways of life that will enable them to resolve any dispute peacefully and in a spirit of respect for human dignity and of tolerance and non-discrimination, bearing in mind the Declaration and Programme of Action on a Culture of Peace;

17. *Calls upon* all States to take all appropriate measures to prevent racist, discriminatory and xenophobic attitudes and behaviour by means of education, keeping in mind the important role that children have to play in changing such practices;

18. *Also calls upon* all States to remove educational disparities and make education accessible to children living in poverty, children living in remote areas, children with special educational needs, children affected by armed conflict and children requiring special protection, including refugee children, migrant children, street children, children deprived of their liberty, indigenous children and children belonging to minorities;

19. *Calls upon* States, educational institutions and the United Nations system, in particular the United Nations Children's Fund, the United Nations Development Fund for Women and the United Nations Educa-

tional, Scientific and Cultural Organization, to develop and implement gender-sensitive strategies to address the particular needs of the girl child in education;

Freedom from violence

20. *Reaffirms* the obligation of States to protect children from torture and other cruel, inhuman or degrading treatment or punishment;

21. *Calls upon* States to take all appropriate measures to prevent and protect children from all forms of violence, including physical, mental and sexual violence, torture, child abuse, abuse by police, other law enforcement authorities and employees and officials in detention centres or welfare institutions, including orphanages, and domestic violence;

22. *Also calls upon* States to investigate and submit cases of torture and other forms of violence against children to the competent authorities for the purpose of prosecution and to impose appropriate disciplinary or penal sanctions against those responsible for such practices;

23. *Requests* all relevant human rights mechanisms, in particular special rapporteurs and working groups, within their mandates, to pay attention to the special situations of violence against children, reflecting their experiences in the field;

24. *Takes note* of the general discussion on State violence against children held by the Committee on the Rights of the Child on 22 September 2000, as well as its recommendation to undertake a comprehensive study on the issue of violence against children, exploring its different forms and identifying its causes, its extent and its impact on children, and welcomes the forthcoming general discussion on violence suffered by children in schools and within the family to be held in September 2001;

III

Promotion and protection of the rights of children in particularly vulnerable situations and non-discrimination against children

Plight of children working and/or living on the streets

1. *Calls upon* Governments to seek comprehensive solutions to the problems that cause children to work and/or live on the streets and to implement appropriate programmes and policies for the protection and the rehabilitation and reintegration of those children, bearing in mind that such children are particularly vulnerable to all forms of violence, abuse, exploitation and neglect;

2. *Calls upon* all States to ensure that basic social services, notably education, are provided for children in order to divert them from and to address the economic imperatives that lead to involvement in harmful, exploitative and abusive activity;

3. *Strongly urges* all Governments to guarantee respect for all human rights and fundamental freedoms, in particular the right to life, to take urgent and effective measures to prevent the killing of children working and/or living on the streets, to combat torture and abusive treatment and violence against them and to bring the perpetrators to justice;

4. *Calls upon* all States to take the situation of children working and/or living on the streets into account when preparing reports for submission to the Committee on the Rights of the Child, and encourages the

Committee and other relevant bodies and organizations of the United Nations system, within their existing mandates, to pay increased attention to the question of children working and/or living on the streets;

5. *Calls upon* the international community to support, through effective international cooperation, including technical advice and assistance, the efforts of States to improve the situation of children working and/or living on the streets;

Refugee and internally displaced children

6. *Urges* Governments to improve the implementation of policies and programmes for the protection, care and well-being of refugee and internally displaced children and for the provision of basic social services, including access to education, with the necessary international cooperation, in particular with the Office of the United Nations High Commissioner for Refugees, the United Nations Children's Fund and the Representative of the Secretary-General on internally displaced persons, in accordance with the obligations of States under the Convention on the Rights of the Child;

7. *Calls upon* all States and other parties to armed conflict, as well as United Nations bodies and organizations, to give urgent attention, in terms of protection and assistance, to the fact that refugee and internally displaced children are particularly exposed to risks in connection with armed conflict, such as being forcibly recruited or subjected to sexual violence, abuse or exploitation;

8. *Expresses its deep concern* about the growing number of unaccompanied and/or separated refugee and internally displaced children, and calls upon all States and United Nations bodies and agencies and other relevant organizations to give priority to programmes for family tracing and reunification and to continue to monitor the care arrangements for unaccompanied and/or separated refugee and internally displaced children;

Children with disabilities

9. *Encourages* the working group on the rights of children with disabilities established pursuant to the decision of the Committee on the Rights of the Child to put into practice as soon as possible the recommendations arising from the day of general discussion on the rights of children with disabilities, held on 6 October 1997, including the drafting of a plan of action on children with disabilities, in close cooperation with the Special Rapporteur of the Commission for Social Development on Disability and other relevant parts of the United Nations system;

10. *Calls upon* all States to take all necessary measures to ensure the full and equal enjoyment of all human rights and fundamental freedoms by children with disabilities, and to develop and enforce legislation against their discrimination so as to ensure dignity, promote self-reliance and facilitate the child's active participation in the community, including effective access to educational and health services;

Migrant children

11. *Calls upon* States to protect all human rights of migrant children, in particular unaccompanied migrant children, and to ensure that the best interest of the child shall accordingly be a primary consideration, and encourages the Committee on the Rights of the Child, the United Nations Children's Fund and other

relevant United Nations bodies, within their respective mandates, to pay particular attention to the conditions of migrant children in all States and, as appropriate, to make recommendations to strengthen their protection;

12. *Also calls upon* States to cooperate fully with and to assist the Special Rapporteur of the Commission on Human Rights on the human rights of migrants in addressing the particularly vulnerable conditions of migrant children;

IV
Prevention and eradication of the sale of children and of their sexual exploitation and abuse, including child prostitution and child pornography

1. *Welcomes* the interim report of the Special Rapporteur of the Commission on Human Rights on the sale of children, child prostitution and child pornography, and expresses its support for her work;

2. *Requests* the Secretary-General to provide the Special Rapporteur with all necessary human and financial assistance to enable her to discharge her mandate fully;

3. *Calls upon* States to continue to cooperate with the Special Rapporteur and to give full consideration to all of her recommendations;

4. *Invites* further voluntary contributions through the Office of the United Nations High Commissioner for Human Rights and support for the work of the Special Rapporteur for the effective fulfilment of her mandate;

5. *Welcomes* the large number of signatories to the Optional Protocol to the Convention on the Rights of the Child on the sale of children, child prostitution and child pornography, and calls upon all States to consider signing and ratifying it as a matter of priority with a view to its entry into force as soon as possible, bearing in mind the convening of the special session of the General Assembly to follow up the World Summit for Children in September 2001;

6. *Reaffirms* the obligation of States parties to the Convention on the Rights of the Child to prevent the abduction of, the sale of or the trafficking in children for any purpose or in any form, including the transfer of the organs of the child for profit, and to protect children from all forms of sexual exploitation and abuse, in accordance with articles 35 and 34 of the Convention;

7. *Calls upon* States to take all appropriate steps to combat the misuse of new information and communication technologies, including the Internet, for trafficking in children and for purposes of all forms of sexual exploitation and abuse, in particular the sale of children, child prostitution and child pornography, and notes that the use of such technologies can also contribute to preventing and eradicating such phenomena;

8. *Also calls upon* States to criminalize and to penalize effectively all forms of sexual exploitation and abuse of children, including within the family or for commercial purposes, paedophilia, child pornography and child prostitution, including child sex tourism, while ensuring that the children who are victims of such practices are not penalized, and to take effective measures to ensure the prosecution of offenders, whether local or foreign, by the competent national authorities, either in the country of origin of the offender or in the country in which the abuse takes place, in accordance with due process of law;

9. *Calls upon* all Member States to take all necessary steps to strengthen international cooperation by means of multilateral, regional and bilateral arrangements for the prevention, detection, investigation, prosecution and punishment of those responsible for acts involving the sale of children, child prostitution, child pornography and child sex tourism, and in this regard calls upon Member States to promote international cooperation and coordination among their authorities, national and international non-governmental organizations and international organizations, as appropriate;

10. *Requests* States to increase cooperation and concerted action at the national, regional and international levels to prevent and dismantle networks that traffic in children;

11. *Stresses* the need to combat the existence of a market that encourages such criminal practices against children, including through preventive and enforcement measures that target customers or individuals who sexually exploit or abuse children;

12. *Calls upon* States to enact, enforce, review and revise, as appropriate, laws and to implement policies, programmes and practices to protect children from and to eliminate all forms of sexual exploitation and abuse, including commercial sexual exploitation, taking into account the particular problems posed by the use of the Internet in this regard;

13. *Encourages* Governments to facilitate the active participation of child victims of sexual exploitation and abuse in the development and implementation of strategies to protect children from sexual exploitation and abuse;

14. *Encourages* continued regional and interregional efforts, with the objective of identifying best practices and issues requiring particularly urgent action, and notes the convening of the Second World Congress against Commercial Sexual Exploitation of Children at Yokohama, Japan, from 17 to 20 December 2001, which is to be hosted by the Government of Japan in cooperation with the United Nations Children's Fund and which is aimed at reviewing progress in implementing the Declaration and Agenda for Action adopted by the World Congress against Commercial Sexual Exploitation of Children, held at Stockholm from 27 to 31 August 1996;

15. *Invites* States and relevant United Nations bodies and agencies to allocate appropriate resources for the rehabilitation of child victims of sexual exploitation and abuse and to take all appropriate measures to promote their full recovery and social reintegration;

V
Protection of children affected by armed conflict

1. *Welcomes* the report of the Special Representative of the Secretary-General on the impact of armed conflict on children, and takes note of the report of the Secretary-General on children and armed conflict;

2. *Expresses its support* for the work of the Special Representative in the fulfilment of his mandate, as established in paragraphs 35 to 37 of General Assembly resolution 51/77 of 12 December 1996, in particular in raising worldwide awareness and mobilizing official and public opinion for the protection of children af-

fected by armed conflict in order to promote respect for the rights and needs of children in conflict and post-conflict situations;

3. *Calls upon* the Secretary-General and all relevant parts of the United Nations system, including the Special Representative and the United Nations Children's Fund, to intensify further their efforts to continue to develop a concerted approach to the rights, protection and welfare of children affected by armed conflict, including, as appropriate, in the preparations for the field visits of the Special Representative and in the follow-up to such visits;

4. *Calls upon* all States and other parties concerned to continue to cooperate with the Special Representative in implementing the commitments that they have undertaken and to consider carefully all of the recommendations of the Special Representative and address the issues identified;

5. *Welcomes* the continued support for and voluntary contributions to the work of the Special Representative in the fulfilment of his mandate;

6. *Also welcomes* the large number of signatories to the Optional Protocol to the Convention on the Rights of the Child on the involvement of children in armed conflict, and calls upon all States to consider signing and ratifying it as a matter of priority with a view to its entry into force as soon as possible, bearing in mind the convening of the special session of the General Assembly to follow up the World Summit for Children in September 2001;

7. *Urges* all States and other parties to armed conflict to respect international humanitarian law and to put an end to any form of targeting of children and to attacking sites that usually have a significant presence of children, calls upon States parties to respect fully the provisions of the Geneva Conventions of 12 August 1949 and the Additional Protocols thereto, of 1977, and calls upon all parties to armed conflict to take all measures required to protect children from acts that constitute violations of international humanitarian law, including prosecution by States, within their national legal framework, of those responsible for such violations;

8. *Recognizes*, in this regard, the contribution of the establishment of the International Criminal Court to ending impunity for perpetrators of certain crimes committed against children, as defined in the Statute of the Court, which include those involving sexual violence or child soldiers, and thus to the prevention of such crimes;

9. *Stresses* the importance of all relevant United Nations actors in the field improving their reporting, within their respective mandates, concerning the situation of children affected by armed conflict and giving additional attention to this question;

10. *Condemns* the abduction of children in situations of armed conflict and into armed conflict, urges States, international organizations and other concerned parties to take all appropriate measures to secure the unconditional release, rehabilitation, reintegration and reunification with their families of all abducted children, and urges States to bring the perpetrators to justice;

11. *Calls upon* States to ensure that the adoption of children in situations of armed conflict is guided by the Convention on the Rights of the Child and that the best interest of the child is always envisaged as a paramount consideration;

12. *Urges* States and all other parties to armed conflict to end the use of children as soldiers, to ensure their demobilization and effective disarmament and to implement effective measures for their rehabilitation, physical and psychological recovery and reintegration into society, further encourages efforts by, inter alia, regional organizations, intergovernmental organizations and non-governmental organizations to bring an end to the use of children as soldiers in armed conflict, and emphasizes that no support shall be given to those who systematically abuse or violate the rights of children during armed conflicts;

13. *Underlines* the importance of including measures to ensure the rights of the child, inter alia, in the areas of health and nutrition, formal, informal or non-formal education, physical and psychological recovery and social reintegration, in emergency and other humanitarian assistance policies and programmes;

14. *Notes* the importance of the third open debate held in the Security Council, on 26 July 2000, on children and armed conflict and the undertaking provided by the Council to give special attention to the protection, welfare and rights of children when taking action aimed at maintaining peace and security, and reaffirms the essential role of the General Assembly and the Economic and Social Council in the promotion and protection of the rights and welfare of children;

15. *Calls upon* all parties to armed conflict to ensure the full, safe and unhindered access of humanitarian personnel and the delivery of humanitarian assistance to all children affected by armed conflict;

16. *Welcomes* agreed conclusions 1999/1 adopted by the Economic and Social Council on 23 July 1999, in which the Council, inter alia, calls for systematic, concerted and comprehensive inter-agency efforts on behalf of children, as well as adequate and sustainable resource allocation, to provide both immediate emergency assistance to and long-term measures for children throughout all the phases of an emergency;

17. *Urges* States to implement effective measures for the rehabilitation, physical and psychological recovery and reintegration into society of all child victims in cases of armed conflict, invites the international community to assist in this endeavour, and further emphasizes the importance of giving systematic consideration to the special needs and particular vulnerability of the girl child during conflicts and in post-conflict situations;

18. *Calls upon* States and relevant United Nations bodies to continue to support national and international mine-action efforts, including by means of financial contributions, mine-awareness programmes, victim assistance and child-centred rehabilitation, and welcomes the positive effects on children of concrete legislative measures with respect to anti-personnel mines;

19. *Invites* States, multilateral donors and the private sector to cooperate and to commit the resources necessary for the early development of new and more efficient mine-detection and mine-clearance technologies for assistance in mine action;

20. *Notes with concern* the impact of small arms and light weapons on children in situations of armed conflict, in particular as a result of their illicit production

and traffic, and calls upon States to address this problem, inter alia, during the United Nations Conference on the Illicit Trade in Small Arms and Light Weapons in All Its Aspects, to be held in 2001;

21. *Recommends* that, whenever sanctions are imposed, their impact on children be assessed and monitored and that humanitarian exemptions be child-focused and formulated with clear guidelines for their application;

22. *Calls upon* States, relevant United Nations bodies and agencies and regional organizations to integrate the rights of the child into all activities in conflict and post-conflict situations, including training programmes and emergency relief operations, country programmes and field operations aimed at promoting peace and preventing and resolving conflict, as well as the negotiation and implementation of peace agreements, and, given the long-term consequences for society, underlines the importance of including specific provisions for children, including resourcing, in peace agreements and in arrangements negotiated by parties;

23. *Calls upon* all States, in accordance with the norms of international humanitarian law, to integrate in the training and gender-sensitized education programmes of their armed forces, including those for peacekeeping, instruction on responsibilities towards the civilian population, in particular women and children;

24. *Calls upon* Member States, the United Nations system and non-governmental organizations to encourage the involvement of young people in activities concerning the protection of children affected by armed conflict, including programmes for reconciliation, peace consolidation, peace-building and children-to-children networks;

25. *Welcomes* the holding of the International Conference on War-Affected Children at Winnipeg, Canada, from 10 to 17 September 2000, and notes with appreciation the Winnipeg Agenda for War-Affected Children and efforts by regional organizations, in particular the Organization for Security and Cooperation in Europe, the European Union, the Economic Community of West African States, the Organization of American States and the Organization of African Unity, to include prominently the rights and protection of children affected by armed conflict in their policies and programmes;

VI

Progressive elimination of child labour

1. *Reaffirms* the right of the child to be protected from economic exploitation and from performing any work that is likely to be hazardous or to interfere with the child's education or to be harmful to the child's health or physical, mental, spiritual, moral or social development;

2. *Welcomes* the adoption by the International Labour Organization, at the eighty-seventh session of the International Labour Conference, held at Geneva from 1 to 17 June 1999, of the Convention concerning the Prohibition and Immediate Action for the Elimination of the Worst Forms of Child Labour (Convention No. 182), and calls upon all States to consider ratifying it;

3. *Calls upon* all States that have not yet done so to consider ratifying the conventions of the International Labour Organization relating to child labour, in particular the Convention concerning Forced or Compulsory Labour, 1930 (Convention No. 29) and the Convention concerning Minimum Age for Admission to Employment, 1973 (Convention No. 138), and to implement those conventions;

4. *Calls upon* all States to translate into concrete action their commitment to the progressive and effective elimination of child labour contrary to accepted international standards, and urges them, inter alia, to eliminate immediately the worst forms of child labour as set out in the 1999 International Labour Organization Convention No. 182;

5. *Also calls upon* all States to assess and examine systematically the magnitude, nature and causes of child labour and to elaborate and implement strategies for the elimination of child labour contrary to accepted international standards, giving special attention to specific dangers faced by girls, as well as to the rehabilitation and social reintegration of the children concerned;

6. *Recognizes* that primary education is one of the main instruments for reintegrating child workers, calls upon all States to recognize the right to education by making primary education compulsory and to ensure that all children have equal access to free primary education as a key strategy to prevent child labour, and recognizes, in particular, the important role of the United Nations Educational, Scientific and Cultural Organization and the United Nations Children's Fund in this regard;

7. *Calls upon* all States and the United Nations system to strengthen international cooperation as a means of assisting Governments in preventing or combating violations of the rights of the child and in attaining the objective of eliminating child labour contrary to accepted international standards;

8. *Calls upon* all States to strengthen cooperation and coordination at the national and international levels to address effectively the problem of child labour, in close cooperation with, inter alia, the International Labour Organization and the United Nations Children's Fund;

VII

Decides:

(a) To request the Secretary-General to submit to the General Assembly at its fifty-sixth session a report on the rights of the child containing information on the status of the Convention on the Rights of the Child and the problems addressed in the present resolution;

(b) To request the Special Representative of the Secretary-General on the impact of armed conflict on children to submit to the General Assembly and the Commission on Human Rights reports containing relevant information on the situation of children affected by armed conflict, bearing in mind existing mandates and reports of relevant bodies;

(c) To continue its consideration of this question at its fifty-sixth session under the item entitled "Promotion and protection of the rights of the child".

Sale of children, child prostitution and child pornography

Reports of Special Rapporteur. In response to a 1999 Commission request [YUN 1999, p. 672], the

Special Rapporteur on the sale of children, child prostitution and child pornography, Ofelia Calcetas-Santos (Philippines), in January [E/CN.4/2000/73], focused on the role of the family and the impact of domestic violence on the child. She described some international and country-specific developments relating to those issues, and the legal framework for the protection of children from all types of violence. After comparing the various forms of family violence, the Special Rapporteur noted certain factors linked to child abuse in the family, including a perception of power over the victim; a desire to compensate for low self-esteem; depression due to frustration and a general feeling of incompetence; a preconditioned attitude caused by a background of family abuse; drug, alcohol, substance and gambling addiction; cultural influence; a lack of awareness about children's rights; and conjugal difficulties. Evidence suggested an association, rather than a direct causal link, between childhood physical and sexual abuse, running away from home and subsequent involvement in prostitution. The Special Rapporteur recommended raising public awareness as to the harm of non-physical abuse; including sex education in schools; involving a range of professionals from various disciplines in conceptualizing programmes in order to ensure that the family was the primary caretaker of children; psychotherapy for sexually abused children; forums for children to be heard; and telephone hotlines for children to report abuse and consult a trained counsellor.

The Special Rapporteur visited Morocco (28 February–3 March) [E/CN.4/2001/78/Add.1] to study the issue of commercial sexual exploitation. The Special Rapporteur examined children in situations of economic exploitation, adoption, and trafficking and clandestine immigration, as well as prostitution, sex tourism and pornography. Of the three elements of the Special Rapporteur's mandate, child prostitution (boys and girls) was the most problematic and occurred in each of the five cities (Casablanca, Rabat, Meknès, Tangier, Marrakech) she visited. The widespread abuse of young girls working as household maids was also among the most serious problems. In most cases, the girls, 50 per cent of whom were below the age of 10, were sent by their families from rural areas to work as maids in houses in the cities. Morocco was facing the problem of clandestine emigration, attributable to globalization, which gave young people the perception of many opportunities in a more developed country. Child sex abuse was largely carried out by Moroccans and there were few reported cases where children had been used in prostitution for foreigners. Very few cases of child por-

nography were reported. The Special Rapporteur detected a genuine willingness on the part of the Government to confront the spread of child exploitation and to alleviate the suffering of children in situations of exploitation and abuse. She made recommendations regarding street children, the clandestine emigration of children, legislation, the situation of child maids, the prostitution of girls, response mechanisms to enable children to seek help, and drawing on the private sector for the protection of children and for the promotion and enhancement of their rights.

In the Russian Federation (Moscow and St. Petersburg, 2-11 October) [E/CN.4/2001/78/Add.2], the Special Rapporteur visited State institutions, including orphanages and medical centres, and met with UN agencies and other international organizations, academics and NGOs. In addition to the sale of children in the context of international adoption, child prostitution and child pornography, the Special Rapporteur considered the problem of child labour. In general, international adoption was not considered to be a common motive for trafficking. However, huge bribes were offered to judges and orphanages to speed up the adoption process, while the police had been reluctant to curtail such abuses. Legal staff attributed the growing number of children being adopted outside the country to the increasing involvement of middlemen, who were finding various ways to circumvent legal provisions. Prostitution was a widely developed business and, if the child was over 14, it was not considered a crime unless violence was involved.

The Special Rapporteur observed that the plight of social orphans—children without any effective caregivers in their lives—was particularly problematic. That phenomenon was largely attributed to extensive alcoholism among adults, which was also spreading among the younger population. The solution thus far had been to institutionalize the child, rather than confront the root problems. The lack of sex education in schools accounted for many cases of sexually transmitted diseases. The Government had tried to initiate a programme of sex education, but it was met with hostility by parents. Recommendations related to the allocation of resources to provide training in child rights, the establishment of special courts to deal with minors and their affairs, the creation of a position of children's ombudsman, greater use of foster parents, the development of networks of street educators to encourage children to leave the streets, mobilization of the media to address violence and pornography, the introduction of sex education in schools and apprenticeship programmes for youth.

Commission action. On 27 April [res. 2000/85], the Commission called on States to ensure the application of international standards concerning the prevention and the combat of trafficking and sale of children, child prostitution and child pornography, to take into account the problems posed by the use of the Internet in that regard, to enact, review and revise relevant laws, policies, programmes and practices, and to criminalize and penalize all forms of sexual exploitation and sexual abuse of children. The Commission asked that assistance be provided to the Special Rapporteur for her work and to enable her to submit an interim report to the General Assembly in 2000 and a report to the Commission in 2001. The Economic and Social Council endorsed the Commission's request on 28 July (**decision 2000/280**).

Interim report of Special Rapporteur. In response to the Commission's request, the Special Rapporteur submitted, in August [A/55/297], an interim report updating developments relating to her mandate and country-specific and regional developments.

(For information on the Optional Protocol to the Convention on the Rights of the Child on the sale of children, child prostitution and child pornography, see p. 615.)

Child labour

Commission action. On 27 April [res. 2000/85], the Commission called on States to eliminate child labour contrary to accepted international standards; ratify the conventions of the International Labour Organization (ILO) relating to child labour; examine and devise economic policies that addressed the problem; promote education as a key strategy to prevent child labour; and assess and examine the magnitude, nature and causes of child labour and develop strategies to eliminate the practice.

Children and armed conflict

Report of Special Representative. In response to General Assembly resolution 53/128 [YUN 1998, p. 712], the Secretary-General's Special Representative for Children and Armed Conflict, Olara A. Otunnu (Côte d'Ivoire), in February [E/CN.4/2000/71], provided an update on commitments to cease recruitment of children made to him during his field missions in 1998 [YUN 1998, p. 710] and 1999 [YUN 1999, p. 674]. The report supplemented the recommendations he had made in 1999. The Special Representative urged the international community to eliminate child soldiering by: advocating for 18 as the minimum age for participation in conflict; monitoring and compelling adherence by all parties in conflict to their commitments to protect children; mobilizing international pressure against warring parties that used children as combatants; addressing the political, social and economic factors that facilitated the exploitation of children as soldiers; and responding to the rehabilitation needs of ex–child soldiers.

Currently, there were over 300,000 young persons under the age of 18 taking part in hostilities in over 30 countries. The Special Representative advocated the integration of the protection and welfare of children into UN-mandated peace operations. In order to achieve that objective, he proposed including in the mandates of peacekeeping operations the protection and needs of children, instituting child protection advisers in relevant peacekeeping operations, and providing training on the rights and protection of children for peace operation personnel (see also p. 94).

Commission action. On 27 April [res. 2000/85], the Commission called on States and other parties to armed conflicts to respect international humanitarian law. States and relevant UN bodies and agencies and regional organizations were called on to integrate the rights of the child into all activities in conflict and post-conflict situations. The Commission recommended that the Special Representative and relevant UN entities continue to develop a concerted approach on the rights, protection and welfare of children affected by armed conflict, and to increase cooperation among their respective mandates and with NGOs, in the planning of field visits and follow-up to the Special Representative's recommendations.

The Economic and Social Council endorsed the Commission's recommendation on 28 July (**decision 2000/280**).

Report of Secretary-General. In accordance with Security Council resolution 1261(1999) [YUN 1999, p. 672], the Secretary-General, in July [A/55/163-S/2000/712], identified steps that were under way and others that could be taken by national, regional and international actors to fulfil collective responsibilities towards children in armed conflict. Among a wide-ranging series of recommendations, the Secretary-General called on Member States to ratify the Optional Protocol to the Convention on the Rights of the Child on the involvement of children in armed conflict (see p. 615), the Rome Statute of the International Criminal Court (see p. 1238) and ILO Convention No. 182 on the Worst Forms of Child Labour [YUN 1999, p. 1388], all of which contained provisions to protect children in situations of armed conflict. He proposed measures regarding the monitoring of and compliance with obligations and commitments, ensuring access to humanitarian assistance, curbing the illicit flow of small arms, ending the threat of landmines, protecting children from the impact of sanctions, improving the situation of uprooted and displaced children, respecting the rights and special needs of girls, protecting child soldiers and providing education, especially to adolescents, throughout and after periods of armed conflict.

The Secretary-General stated that the Council had adopted the proposal that child protection advisers be deployed with peacekeeping operations, and presented the terms of reference for those advisers (see p. 94). Two peacekeeping operations currently had child protection advisers on the ground; two were seconded from UNICEF and a third was previously with a UN peacekeeping operation. The Secretariat was working to ensure that peacekeeping personnel received training in international law, including child- and gender-related provisions. Post-conflict responses for children included psychosocial healing, strengthening norms and institutions to protect children's rights, reunification of children with their families and child-friendly spaces for development and protection. The Secretary-General concluded that more timely warning systems and better ongoing monitoring and reporting were needed to prevent the worst abuses. Should preventive steps fail, concerted efforts at the local, national, regional and global levels were needed to protect children. The United Nations would continue to seek closer cooperation and more regular consultations with regional and subregional organizations and arrangements concerning children's protection.

SECURITY COUNCIL ACTION

On 11 August [meeting 4185], the Security Council unanimously adopted **resolution 1314(2000)**. The draft [S/2000/787] was prepared during consultations among Council members.

The Security Council,

Recalling its resolution 1261(1999) of 25 August 1999,

Recalling also its resolutions 1265(1999) of 17 September 1999, 1296(2000) of 19 April 2000, 1306(2000) of 5 July 2000 and the statements by its President of 29 June 1998, 12 February, 8 July and 30 November 1999, and 20 July 2000,

Welcoming the adoption by the General Assembly, on 25 May 2000, of the Optional Protocol to the Convention on the Rights of the Child on the involvement of children in armed conflict,

Bearing in mind the purposes and principles of the Charter of the United Nations, and the primary responsibility of the Security Council for the maintenance of international peace and security,

Underlining the need for all parties concerned to comply with the provisions of the Charter and with the rules and principles of international law, in particular international humanitarian, human rights and refugee law, and to implement fully the relevant decisions of the Council, and recalling the relevant provisions on the protection of children contained in the International Labour Organization Convention on the Prohibition and Immediate Action for the Elimination of the Worst Forms of Child Labour (Convention No. 182), the Rome Statute of the International Criminal Court and the Convention on the Prohibition of the Use, Stockpiling, Production and Transfer of Anti-personnel Mines and on Their Destruction,

Noting the regional initiatives on war-affected children, including within the Organization for Security and Cooperation in Europe, the West African Conference on War-Affected Children, held in Accra, on 27 and 28 April 2000, and the forthcoming International Conference on War-Affected Children to be held in Winnipeg, Canada, from 10 to 17 September 2000,

Having considered the report of the Secretary-General of 19 July 2000 on the implementation of resolution 1261(1999) on children and armed conflict,

1. *Reaffirms its strong condemnation* of the deliberate targeting of children in situations of armed conflict and the harmful and widespread impact of armed conflict on children, as well as the long-term consequences this has for durable peace, security and development;

2. *Emphasizes* the responsibility of all States to put an end to impunity and to prosecute those responsible for genocide, crimes against humanity and war crimes, and, in this regard, stresses the need to exclude these, where feasible, from amnesty provisions and relevant legislation;

3. *Urges* all parties to armed conflict to respect fully international law applicable to the rights and protection of children in armed conflict, in particular the Geneva Conventions of 1949 and the obligations applicable to them under the Additional Protocols thereto, of 1977, the Convention on the Rights of the Child of 1989 and the Optional Protocol thereto, of 25 May 2000, and to bear in mind the relevant provisions of the Rome Statute of the International Criminal Court;

4. *Urges* Member States in a position to do so to sign and ratify the Optional Protocol to the Convention on the Rights of the Child on the involvement of children in armed conflict;

5. *Expresses support* for the ongoing work of the Special Representative of the Secretary-General for Children and Armed Conflict, the United Nations Children's Fund, the Office of the United Nations High Commissioner for Refugees, other parts of the United Nations system and other relevant international organizations dealing with children affected by armed conflict;

6. *Urges* Member States and parties to armed conflict to provide protection and assistance to refugees and internally displaced persons, as appropriate, the vast majority of whom are women and children;

7. *Calls upon* all parties to armed conflict to ensure the full, safe and unhindered access of humanitarian personnel and the delivery of humanitarian assistance to all children affected by armed conflict;

8. *Expresses its grave concern* at the linkage between the illicit trade in natural resources and armed con-

flict, as well as the linkage between the illicit trafficking in small arms and light weapons and armed conflict, which can prolong armed conflict and intensify its impact on children, and, in this regard, expresses its intention to consider taking appropriate steps, in accordance with the Charter of the United Nations;

9. *Notes* that the deliberate targeting of civilian populations or other protected persons, including children, and the commission of systematic, flagrant and widespread violations of international humanitarian and human rights law, including that relating to children, in situations of armed conflict may constitute a threat to international peace and security, and, in this regard, reaffirms its readiness to consider such situations and, where necessary, to adopt appropriate steps;

10. *Urges* all parties to abide by the concrete commitments they have made to the Special Representative of the Secretary-General for Children and Armed Conflict as well as relevant United Nations bodies to ensure the protection of children in situations of armed conflict;

11. *Requests* parties to armed conflict to include, where appropriate, provisions for the protection of children, including the disarmament, demobilization and reintegration of child combatants, in peace negotiations and in peace agreements, and for the involvement of children, where possible, in these processes;

12. *Reaffirms its readiness* to continue to include, where appropriate, child protection advisers in future peacekeeping operations;

13. *Underlines* the importance of giving consideration to the special needs and particular vulnerabilities of girls affected by armed conflict, including those heading households, orphaned, sexually exploited and used as combatants, and urges that their human rights, protection and welfare be incorporated in the development of policies and programmes, including those for prevention, disarmament, demobilization and reintegration;

14. *Reiterates* the importance of ensuring that children continue to have access to basic services during the conflict and post-conflict periods, including education and health care;

15. *Indicates its willingness*, when imposing measures under Article 41 of the Charter, to consider assessing the potential unintended consequences of sanctions on children and to take appropriate steps to minimize such consequences;

16. *Welcomes* recent initiatives by regional and subregional organizations and arrangements for the protection of children affected by armed conflict, and urges them:

(a) To consider establishing, within their secretariats, child protection units for the development and implementation of policies, activities and advocacy for the benefit of children affected by armed conflict, including children in the design and implementation of such policies and programmes where possible;

(b) To consider including child protection staff in their peace and field operations and providing training to members of their peace and field operations on the rights and protection of women and children;

(c) To undertake initiatives to curb the cross-border activities deleterious to children in times of armed conflict, such as the cross-border recruitment and abduc-

tion of children, the illicit movement of small arms and the illicit trade in natural resources;

(d) To allocate resources, as applicable, during policy and programme development for the benefit of children affected by armed conflict;

(e) To integrate a gender perspective into all policies, programmes and projects;

(f) To consider declaring regional initiatives towards full implementation of the prohibition of the use of child soldiers in violation of international law;

17. *Encourages* Member States, relevant parts of the United Nations system and regional organizations and arrangements to undertake efforts to obtain the release of children abducted during armed conflict, and their family reunification;

18. *Urges* Member States and relevant parts of the United Nations system to strengthen the capacities of national institutions and local civil society for ensuring the sustainability of local initiatives for the protection of children;

19. *Calls upon* Member States, relevant parts of the United Nations system, and civil society to encourage the involvement of young persons in programmes for peace consolidation and peace-building;

20. *Encourages* the Secretary-General to continue to include in his written reports to the Council on matters of which the Council is seized, as appropriate, observations relating to the protection of children in armed conflict;

21. *Requests* the Secretary-General to submit a report to the Council, by 31 July 2001, on the implementation of the present resolution and of resolution 1261 (1999);

22. *Decides* to remain actively seized of this matter.

International conference. The Agenda for War-Affected Children was negotiated and adopted by the 130 Governments attending the International Conference on War-Affected Children (Winnipeg, Canada, 10-17 September) [A/55/467-S/2000/973]. The Agenda called for political, moral, economic and social leadership to safeguard children and protect their rights in situations of armed conflict. It was necessary that States and other parties to armed conflict respect their obligations to children affected by conflict under international human rights and humanitarian law. Other measures called for included increased accountability and the end to impunity, the release of abducted children, prevention of the root causes of conflict, promotion of children's health and well-being, and concerted action over the long term for war-affected children.

Interim report of Special Representative. In response to General Assembly resolution 54/149 [YUN 1999, p. 676], the Special Representative, in an October report [A/55/442], assessed overall progress achieved during the course of his initial three-year mandate and outlined an agenda for future action. He also described country visits made by him or representatives of his Office. During his visit to Colombia (7-9 April), the Special Representative congratulated the Government on having discharged the final contingent of 950 soldiers under the age of 18 in December 1999. After another appeal from the Special Representative, the Revolutionary Armed Forces of Colombia (FARC) said in April that they had "committed an error" in recruiting youth under 15 and had repudiated the practice. The Special Representative called on FARC to demobilize those soldiers. His Office undertook a joint mission to East and West Timor (14-21 June) with the Japan Committee for UNICEF and its Goodwill Ambassador. Efforts had been made to protect children during the emergency and the ensuing reconstruction phases in East Timor (see p. 277). The Office made proposals aimed at ensuring that children's concerns were considered in policies and programmes. During his visit to Northern Ireland (26-28 June), the Special Representative appealed to political leaders to address the basic concerns of children, expressed support for the establishment of a body dedicated to promoting children's rights, and insisted that paramilitary organizations refrain from recruiting or using children in their organizations or involving them in violence. Punishment beatings should be halted, the Government should provide more support for families and parents affected by violence, and youth should be involved in the building and consolidation of peace. The Office participated in a workshop on the National Commission for War-Affected Children (16-18 August), convened by Sierra Leone with the support of the UNICEF country office and Canada. The workshop made recommendations regarding the structure, role and objectives of the National Commission and the procedures for its formal establishment, scheduled for 2001.

In future, the Special Representative intended to concentrate on building a global social and political movement of awareness, pressure and protection for children affected by armed conflict. The emphasis would be on consolidating progress achieved thus far, extending and deepening initiatives in priority areas, with a view to creating a critical and sustainable mass of activities and developing an era of application on the ground.

(For information on the Optional Protocol to the Convention on the Rights of the Child on the involvement of children in armed conflict, see p. 615.)

Abduction of children from northern Uganda

Report of Secretary-General. The Secretary-General, in response to the Commission's 1999 request [YUN 1999, p. 675], summarized information on the situation of children abducted from northern Uganda received from the Sudan, international organizations and NGOs [E/CN.4/2000/69]. The International Save the Children Alliance reported that there had been a great reduction in the number of incidents in 1999 and that children who had escaped or were rescued were taken to two rehabilitation centres in Gulu. According to the centres, up until the first quarter of 1999, a total of 5,837 children had been reintegrated since the beginning of the conflict into their communities after receiving medical treatment, counselling and education. Estimates as to the number of children believed to be in the southern Sudan camp of the Lord's Resistance Army (LRA), an armed opposition group, varied between 2,000 and 5,000. Many of the children had reportedly been killed either by their abductors or as a result of having been forced to participate in conflicts. The sexual exploitation of many of the abducted girls had reportedly led to the birth of some 200 babies.

Commission action. On 26 April [res. 2000/60], the Commission, condemning LRA for the abduction, torture, killing, rape, enslavement and forcible recruitment of children in northern Uganda, demanded an end to the abductions and called for the children's unconditional release and safe return. It asked the United Nations Voluntary Fund for Victims of Torture (see p. 682) to assist victims and their families. OHCHR was requested to assess the situation on the ground in the affected areas, including victims' needs, in consultation with relevant UN organizations and NGOs, and to report in 2001.

The Economic and Social Council approved the Commission's request to OHCHR on 28 July (**decision 2000/274**).

Indigenous populations

Commission action. On 25 April [res. 2000/56], the Commission recommended that the Economic and Social Council authorize the Subcommission's Working Group on Indigenous Populations to meet for five working days prior to the Subcommission's 2000 session. It welcomed the Group's proposal to highlight specific themes of the International Decade of the World's Indigenous People (1995-2004), proclaimed by the General Assembly in resolution 48/163 [YUN 1993, p. 865], in its future sessions, noting that in 2000 the Group would focus on the theme of indigenous children and youth. The Commission invited the Group to continue to consider ways in which the expertise of indigenous people could contribute to its work. The Secretary-General was asked to assist the Group and to transmit the Group's reports to Governments, organizations of indigenous people, intergovernmental organizations and NGOs for comments and suggestions.

On 28 July, the Council authorized the Working Group to meet for five days prior to the Subcommission's 2000 session and approved the Commission's request to the Secretary-General (**decision 2000/271**).

Working Group activities. The Working Group on Indigenous Populations held its eighteenth session (Geneva, 24-28 July) [E/CN.4/Sub.2/2000/24] to review developments pertaining to the promotion and protection of human rights and fundamental freedoms of indigenous peoples, and to give attention to the evolution of standards concerning their rights. In annotations to the provisional agenda [E/CN.4/Sub.2/AC.4/2000/1/Add.1], the Secretary-General presented background information on land issues, education and health; the International Decade of the World's Indigenous People (see p. 727); the 2001 World Conference against Racism, Racial Discrimination, Xenophobia and Related Intolerance (see p. 641); and standard-setting activities, including a review of indigenous peoples' relationship with natural resource, energy and mining companies, together with information received from an indigenous organization [E/CN.4/Sub.2/AC.4/2000/5]. Regarding the session's principal theme, indigenous children and youth, the Group considered a note by the Secretariat identifying issues related to the topic [E/CN.4/Sub.2/AC.4/2000/2]. In consultation with indigenous representatives, the following themes emerged: indigenous children in armed conflict; discrimination in health, the administration of justice and employment; education, including the loss of indigenous languages and culture; and child labour and sexual exploitation of indigenous children and youth. In related action, the first NGO workshop on indigenous children and youth (Geneva, 19-21 July) adopted a resolution, which was annexed to the Group's report. The Group recommended that OHCHR organize a second workshop in cooperation with UNICEF, indigenous organizations and child rights NGOs.

The Group decided to propose to the Commission and Subcommission that a world conference on indigenous issues be held during the last year of the Decade (2004) to evaluate the Decade's activities and consider future action. Further recommendations related to the Decade included a meeting or workshop in 2001 to evaluate progress and a seminar, organized by OHCHR, on legal instruments between indigenous peoples and States. The Group encouraged OHCHR, in collaboration with ILO, WTO and the United Nations Conference on Trade and Development, to organize a workshop on indigenous peoples, private sector natural resource, energy and mining companies, and human rights. It asked its Chairperson-Rapporteur to present a working paper on indigenous peoples and natural resource companies, with a view to developing model processes for the protection of indigenous peoples' cultural, social, economic and environmental rights. Regarding the World Conference against Racism, Racial Discrimination, Xenophobia and Related Intolerance, the Group recommended that a chapter in both the declaration and the programme of action of the Conference be dedicated to indigenous peoples. The theme "Indigenous peoples and their right to development, including their right to participate in development affecting them" was chosen as the main theme for the Group's session in 2001.

The Group's Chairperson-Rapporteur, Erica-Irene A. Daes (Greece), visited Mexico (28 January–14 February) [E/CN.4/Sub.2/2000/40], where she expressed concern over the militarization of indigenous areas and the increasing use of the military for police functions; reports that communities were deprived of their traditional lands and the fragmentation of indigenous lands; allegations of government interference, particularly in Chiapas and Guerrero, including the removal of indigenous authorities and their replacement by others selected by the Government, as well as the phenomenon of re-municipalization which appeared to undercut democratic processes; and the need for more resources in the area of health. The Chairperson commended efforts by the Government to facilitate education for indigenous peoples, among other things.

Workshop. In accordance with a 1998 Subcommission resolution [YUN 1998, p. 720], OHCHR, in cooperation with the United Nations Department of Public Information (DPI), organized a workshop on promoting the rights and cultures of indigenous peoples through the media (New York, 11-14 December) [E/CN.4/Sub.2/AC.4/2001/3]. The workshop underlined the importance of indigenous media as an indispensable tool to promote indigenous identity, language, culture, self-representation and collective and human rights, and as a vehicle for communicating international, regional and national issues to indigenous communities, as well as conveying community concerns to a wider public. Recommendations included strengthening the indigenous media, establishing an indigenous media agency, creating a UN web page on indigenous peoples and instituting training seminars for indigenous media to enable them to better use the global press.

Subcommission action. On 17 August [res. 2000/14], the Subcommission asked the Secretary-

General to transmit the Working Group's report on its 2000 session to the High Commissioner, indigenous organizations, Governments, intergovernmental organizations and NGOs concerned, as well as to thematic rapporteurs, special representatives, independent experts and working groups, and asked that it be made available to the Commission in 2001. It recommended that the Group, upon request, assist the working group to elaborate further the draft UN declaration on the rights of indigenous people (see p. 729), and adopt for its 2001 session the principal theme "Indigenous peoples and their right to development". The Commission was asked to invite Governments, intergovernmental organizations, indigenous organizations and NGOs to provide information and data, particularly on the principal theme. The High Commissioner was requested to encourage studies on the rights to food and adequate nutrition of indigenous peoples and indigenous peoples and poverty, and, in consultation with Governments, to organize meetings on indigenous issues. The Subcommission recommended that Ms. Daes prepare a second working paper on indigenous peoples and racism and racial discrimination for consideration at the second (2001) session of the Preparatory Committee for the World Conference against Racism, Racial Discrimination, Xenophobia and Related Intolerance. It asked Miguel Alfonso-Martínez (Cuba) to submit in 2001 a working paper on principles and guidelines for private sector energy and mining concerns that might affect indigenous lands. The Subcommission recommended that OHCHR organize a parallel activity on indigenous issues during the World Conference and that funds be set aside for that purpose, as well as for the participation of indigenous peoples at the Conference. The Commission was asked to consider appointing a special rapporteur on indigenous issues to request and receive information from Governments, indigenous peoples, intergovernmental organizations and NGOs relating to the recognition, promotion and protection of indigenous peoples' human rights. It was also asked to request the Economic and Social Council to authorize the Group to meet for five days prior to the Subcommission's 2001 session. The Secretary-General was requested to prepare an annotated agenda for that session.

Voluntary Fund for Indigenous Populations

A June note by the Secretariat [E/CN.4/Sub.2/ AC.4/2000/4] contained the recommendations adopted by the Board of Trustees of the United Nations Voluntary Fund for Indigenous Populations at its thirteenth session (Geneva, 10-12

April). The Board recommended travel grants for 66 representatives of indigenous communities and organizations to allow them to attend the Working Group on Indigenous Populations, for a total of some $163,000; travel grants to allow 29 representatives to attend the working group on the draft UN declaration on the rights of indigenous peoples, totalling some $102,200; and the allocation of sufficient funds, amounting to a minimum of $100,000, for grants to allow indigenous representatives to attend a possible new meeting on the permanent forum for indigenous peoples (see p. 730). The recommendations were approved by the High Commissioner on the Secretary-General's behalf on 13 April. Annexed to the report was a list of beneficiaries.

In July [A/55/202], the Secretary-General reported on activities of the Fund in 1999 [YUN 1999, p. 682] and early 2000. The Chairperson of the Board estimated that $600,000 would be necessary to cover expenditure for 2001.

International Decade of the World's Indigenous People

Commission action. On 25 April [res. 2000/56], the Commission invited the Working Group to continue its review of activities undertaken during the International Decade of the World's Indigenous People (1995-2004). The High Commissioner, in her capacity as coordinator of the Decade, was asked to update her annual report on activities within the UN system under the Decade's programme of activities. The Commission also asked her to ensure that the OHCHR indigenous people's unit was adequately staffed and resourced; it recommended that she give due regard to developing human rights training for indigenous people. It also recommended that the situation of indigenous people be taken into account in forthcoming relevant UN conferences.

UN financial and development institutions, operational programmes and specialized agencies were asked to give increased priority and resources to improve the conditions of indigenous people; launch special projects to strengthen their community-level initiatives, and facilitate the exchange of information and expertise among indigenous people and other relevant experts; and designate mechanisms to coordinate with OHCHR activities relating to the Decade.

Report of Secretary-General. In August [A/55/268], the Secretary-General summarized implementation of the programme of activities for the Decade undertaken by OHCHR up to mid-July (see also p. 728, under "Report of High Commissioner"). Under the indigenous fellowship programme, fellows from Bangladesh, Canada, Nepal and Rwanda had worked six months in the

Office. Efforts were being made to integrate indigenous issues into the OHCHR technical cooperation programmes and, in that regard, projects were ongoing in Bolivia, Ecuador and Guatemala. The Office observed the International Day of the World's Indigenous People on 27 July. An inter-agency consultation on indigenous peoples was held on 21 July. A seminar was held from 28 February to 1 March on draft principles and guidelines for the protection of the heritage of indigenous people.

Subcommission action. On 17 August [res. 2000/15], the Subcommission, welcoming the celebration of the International Day of the World's Indigenous People, recommended that it be held on the fourth day of the Working Group's session in 2001 to ensure as great a participation of indigenous peoples as possible. It also recommended that the coordinator of the Decade consider holding a fund-raising meeting to encourage financial contributions to the Voluntary Fund for the Decade (see below) and the UN Voluntary Fund for Indigenous Populations (see p. 727), as well as the appointment of qualified staff, including indigenous persons, to assist OHCHR in the indigenous programme, and to report thereon to the Subcommission and Working Group in 2001. Governments, intergovernmental organizations, NGOs and individuals were urged to contribute to the Voluntary Fund for the Decade and indigenous organizations were invited to do the same. The Subcommission recommended that the High Commissioner organize meetings and activities within the framework of the Decade to raise public awareness about indigenous issues; organize, not later than 2002, in collaboration with relevant organizations, a workshop on indigenous peoples, private sector natural resource, energy and mining companies and human rights; take action to promote the establishment, within the United Nations Office of Legal Affairs (OLA) (see below), of a database on national legislation on matters of relevance to indigenous peoples, and a compilation of treaties and agreements between States and indigenous peoples, as well as to establish, in coordination with DPI, a global public awareness programme on indigenous issues; and organize a seminar on legal instruments between States and indigenous peoples, to discuss possible follow-up to the study completed in 1999 [YUN 1999, p. 686]. The Commission was invited to recommend that the Economic and Social Council authorize the convening of a world conference on indigenous issues during the last year of the Decade (2004) to evaluate the Decade and consider future policies and programmes that would contribute to action by States to promote better relations between the indigenous and non-indigenous segments of their population.

OLA action. On 27 September [E/CN.4/Sub.2/2001/19], OHCHR transmitted a copy of Subcommission resolution 2000/15 to OLA, requesting its advice. OLA replied that it would not be for the Subcommission to establish new functions or mandates for OLA or any other Secretariat unit in the absence of a decision by the parent intergovernmental body, in this case the Economic and Social Council, as well as the consideration and approval of the financial implications of such a decision by the General Assembly. It stated that the establishment of the database would entail considerable resource requirements.

Report of High Commissioner. In December [E/CN.4/2001/84], the High Commissioner reviewed activities undertaken to implement the programme of activities for the Decade. OHCHR had implemented the Indigenous Fellowship Programme for four candidates from Bangladesh, Canada, Nepal and Rwanda (1 June–30 November) and had expanded the Programme, in collaboration with the Institute of Human Rights of the University of Deusto (Bilbao, Spain) to provide training for indigenous fellows from Latin America. Four fellows from Argentina, Chile, Colombia and Peru spent three months at the University, followed by two months at OHCHR. Two technical cooperation projects, in Guatemala and Mexico, incorporated a focus on indigenous issues. The High Commissioner also described the activities of the Voluntary Fund for the Decade (see below) and the Voluntary Fund for Indigenous Populations (see p. 727).

Voluntary Fund for International Decade

A June note by the Secretariat contained the report of the Advisory Group of the United Nations Voluntary Fund for the International Decade of the World's Indigenous People on its fifth session (Geneva, 13-14 April), including its recommendations for grants from the Fund that had been approved by the Coordinator of the Decade [E/CN.4/Sub.2/AC.4/2000/3]. The Group recommended that its next session be extended from two to three or four days, and that it should be scheduled prior to the Commission's consideration of indigenous populations. Contributions available to the Group as at 11 April totalled $308,928. The Advisory Group recommended 20 project grants, which were approved by the High Commissioner, for a total of some $175,000. Other recommended activities included a second workshop for journalists for an amount of $64,000; a subregional workshop on peaceful and constructive group accommodation in situations involving minorities and indigenous peoples, to be held in Kidal, Mali, in January 2001, for a maximum of $30,000; another subregional seminar in Africa for a maximum of $30,000; a workshop on indigenous children for experts and indigenous representatives for $23,000; the fifth session of the Advisory Group for some $6,000; and translation, editing and printing of the United Nations Guide for Indigenous Peoples for a maximum of $19,800.

The Advisory Group was of the view that, in order to fufil its mandate satisfactorily in 2001, the Fund needed some $470,000 before the beginning of the sixth (April 2001) session.

On 25 April [res. 2000/56], the Commission appealed to Governments, organizations and individuals to support the Decade by contributing to the Fund.

Draft declaration

Commission action. On 25 April [res. 2000/57], the Commission, recommending that the working group to elaborate a draft UN declaration on the rights of indigenous peoples meet for 10 working days prior to the Commission's 2001 session, asked the group to submit a progress report.

On 28 July, the Economic and Social Council authorized the working group to meet prior to the Commission's 2001 session **(decision 2000/272)**.

Subcommission action. On 17 August [res. 2000/15], the Subcommission recommended that, in accordance with General Assembly resolution 50/157 [YUN 1995, p. 772], the draft UN declaration on the rights of indigenous people be adopted as early as possible and not later than the end of the Decade. It appealed to participants in the intersessional working group and to others concerned to accelerate the preparation of the text.

Working group activities. The working group established to consider a draft declaration on the rights of indigenous peoples, at its sixth session (Geneva, 20 November–1 December) [E/CN.4/2001/85], focused on articles relating to the full and effective enjoyment of all human rights and fundamental freedoms, freedom from discrimination, future rights and actions contrary to the Charter of the United Nations. The report explained that there was no consensus on the term "indigenous peoples" at the working group; some States accepted it while others did not, in part because of the implications the term might have in international law, including with respect to self-determination and individual and collective rights. Annexed to the report were the proposals of States on those articles, as were proposals on the articles made by indigenous representatives and one NGO.

On 4 December [meeting 81], the General Assembly, on the recommendation of the Third Committee [A/55/599], adopted **resolution 55/80** without vote [agenda item 111].

International Decade of the World's Indigenous People

The General Assembly,

Recalling its resolution 54/150 of 17 December 1999 and previous resolutions on the International Decade of the World's Indigenous People,

Recalling also that the goal of the Decade is to strengthen international cooperation for the solution of problems faced by indigenous people in such areas as human rights, the environment, development, education and health and that the theme of the Decade is "Indigenous people: partnership in action",

Recognizing the importance of consultation and cooperation with indigenous people in planning and implementing the programme of activities for the International Decade of the World's Indigenous People, the need for adequate financial support from the international community, including support from within the United Nations system, and the need for adequate coordination and communication channels,

Urging all parties to continue to intensify their efforts to achieve the goals of the Decade,

1. *Takes note* of the report of the Secretary-General on the implementation of the programme of activities for the International Decade of the World's Indigenous People;

2. *Affirms its conviction* of the value and diversity of the cultures and forms of social organization of indigenous people and its conviction that the development of indigenous people within their countries will contribute to the socio-economic, cultural and environmental advancement of all the countries of the world;

3. *Emphasizes* the importance of strengthening the human and institutional capacity of indigenous people to develop their own solutions to their problems;

4. *Requests* the United Nations High Commissioner for Human Rights, as coordinator for the Decade:

(*a*) To continue to promote the objectives of the Decade, taking into account, in the fulfilment of her functions, the special concerns of the indigenous people;

(*b*) To give due regard to the dissemination, from within existing resources and voluntary contributions, of information on the situation, cultures, languages, rights and aspirations of indigenous people and, in that context, to consider the possibility of organizing projects, special events, exhibitions and other activities addressed to the public, in particular to young people;

(*c*) To submit, through the Secretary-General, an annual report to the General Assembly on the implementation of the programme of activities for the Decade;

5. *Reaffirms* the adoption of a declaration on the rights of indigenous people as a major objective of the Decade, and underlines the importance of effective participation by indigenous representatives in the open-ended inter-sessional working group of the Commission on Human Rights charged with developing a draft declaration on the rights of indigenous people,

established pursuant to Commission resolution
1995/32 of 3 March 1995;

6. *Welcomes* the decision of the Economic and Social
Council, in its resolution 2000/22 of 28 July 2000, to
establish a Permanent Forum on Indigenous Issues as a
subsidiary organ of the Council, thereby fulfilling an
important objective of the Decade, and encourages all
parties concerned to engage in the necessary preparations for the establishment of the Forum;

7. *Encourages* Governments to support the Decade
by:

(*a*) Preparing relevant programmes, plans and reports in relation to the Decade, in consultation with indigenous people;

(*b*) Seeking means, in consultation with indigenous
people, of giving indigenous people greater responsibility for their own affairs and an effective voice in decisions on matters that affect them;

(*c*) Establishing national committees or other
mechanisms involving indigenous people to ensure
that the objectives and activities of the Decade are
planned and implemented on the basis of full partnership with indigenous people;

(*d*) Contributing to the United Nations Trust Fund
for the International Decade of the World's Indigenous People;

(*e*) Contributing, together with other donors, to the
United Nations Voluntary Fund for Indigenous Populations in order to assist indigenous representatives in
participating in the Working Group on Indigenous
Populations of the Subcommission on the Promotion
and Protection of Human Rights and the open-ended
inter-sessional working group of the Commission on
Human Rights charged with elaborating a draft declaration on the rights of indigenous people;

(*f*) Considering contributing, as appropriate, to the
Fund for the Development of Indigenous Peoples in
Latin America and the Caribbean, in support of the
goals of the Decade;

(*g*) Identifying resources for activities designed to
implement the goals of the Decade, in cooperation
with indigenous people and intergovernmental and
non-governmental organizations;

8. *Invites* United Nations financial and development institutions, operational programmes and the
specialized agencies and secretariats, as well as other
regional and international organizations, in accordance with the existing procedures of their governing
bodies:

(*a*) To give increased priority and resources to improving the conditions of indigenous people, with particular emphasis on the needs of those people in developing countries, including through the preparation of
specific programmes of action for the implementation
of the goals of the Decade, within their areas of competence;

(*b*) To launch special projects, through appropriate
channels and in cooperation with indigenous people,
to strengthen their community-level initiatives and to
facilitate the exchange of information and expertise
among indigenous people and other relevant experts;

(*c*) To designate focal points for the coordination of
activities related to the Decade with the Office of the
United Nations High Commissioner for Human
Rights;

and commends those institutions, programmes, agencies and regional and international organizations that
have already done so;

9. *Recommends* that the Secretary-General ensure
coordinated follow-up to the recommendations concerning indigenous people of relevant United Nations
conferences, namely, the World Conference on Human
Rights, held at Vienna from 14 to 25 June 1993, the
United Nations Conference on Environment and Development, held at Rio de Janeiro, Brazil, from 3 to 14
June 1992, the International Conference on Population and Development, held at Cairo from 5 to 13 September 1994, the Fourth World Conference on Women,
held at Beijing from 4 to 15 September 1995, the World
Summit for Social Development, held at Copenhagen
from 6 to 12 March 1995, the second United Nations
Conference on Human Settlements (Habitat II), held
at Istanbul, Turkey, from 3 to 14 June 1996, and the
World Food Summit, held at Rome from 13 to 17 November 1996, and other relevant international conferences;

10. *Emphasizes* the importance of the participation
of indigenous people in United Nations world conferences and their national, regional and other preparatory processes, in particular the World Conference
against Racism, Racial Discrimination, Xenophobia
and Related Intolerance, to be held in South Africa in
2001, and encourages Member States to facilitate the
participation of their indigenous people, inter alia, by
considering including representatives of indigenous
people in their delegations;

11. *Requests* the United Nations High Commissioner for Human Rights to submit, through the
Secretary-General, a report on the implementation of
the programme of activities for the Decade to the General Assembly at its fifty-sixth session;

12. *Decides* to include in the provisional agenda of
its fifty-sixth session the item entitled "Programme of
activities of the International Decade of the World's Indigenous People".

Permanent forum for indigenous people

Working Group activities. Pursuant to a 1999
Commission resolution [YUN 1999, p. 685], the ad
hoc working group on a permanent forum for
indigenous people (Geneva, 14-23 February)
[E/CN.4/2000/86] considered proposals to establish the forum. The group discussed the forum's
mandate, terms of reference, membership and
participation, financial and secretariat implications, the UN body the forum would report to,
and its location and name, as well as other elements of a permanent forum. The group discussed the participation of indigenous people in
the work of the UN system, including the role
and function of the Working Group on Indigenous Populations and follow-up. It considered a
working paper on consultations held by the
Chairman-Rapporteur of its 1999 meeting
[E/CN.4/AC.47/2000/2] and information received
from one NGO [E/CN.4/AC.47/ 2000/3].

Commission action. On 27 April [res. 2000/87], the Commission, by a roll-call vote of 43 to none, with 9 abstentions, recommended a draft text to the Economic and Social Council.

ECONOMIC AND SOCIAL COUNCIL ACTION

On 28 July [meeting 45], the Economic and Social Council, on the recommendation of the Commission on Human Rights [E/2000/23 & Corr.1], adopted **resolution 2000/22** without vote [agenda item 14 (*g*)].

Establishment of a Permanent Forum on Indigenous Issues

The Economic and Social Council,

Recalling the provision contained in the final document of the World Conference on Human Rights, held in Vienna from 14 to 25 June 1993, according to which the establishment of a permanent forum for indigenous people within the United Nations system should be considered,

Recalling also that consideration of the establishment of a permanent forum is recognized as one of the important objectives of the programme of activities for the International Decade of the World's Indigenous People,

Noting the two workshops on the subject held under the auspices of the Commission on Human Rights in Copenhagen from 26 to 28 June 1995 and in Santiago from 30 June to 2 July 1997,

Recalling the report of the Secretary-General entitled "Review of the existing mechanisms, procedures and programmes within the United Nations concerning indigenous people", and noting in particular the striking absence of a mechanism to ensure coordination and regular exchange of information among interested parties—Governments, the United Nations and indigenous people—on an ongoing basis,

Taking into account the deliberations of the open-ended inter-sessional ad hoc working group on a permanent forum for indigenous people established pursuant to Commission on Human Rights resolutions 1998/20 of 9 April 1998 and 1999/52 of 27 April 1999 to consider the establishment of a permanent forum and to submit concrete proposals to that effect, as well as the consideration given to the subject at the fifty-sixth session of the Commission,

Wishing to finalize this project during the International Decade of the World's Indigenous People as one means of furthering the objectives of the Decade in partnership between Governments and indigenous people,

Stressing that the establishment of the permanent forum should lead to careful consideration of the future of the Working Group on Indigenous Populations of the Subcommission on the Promotion and Protection of Human Rights,

Bearing in mind the common resolve to promote peace and prosperity in accordance with the Charter of the United Nations, and recalling the functions and powers of the Council in that respect as contained in the Charter,

1. *Decides* to establish as a subsidiary organ of the Council a permanent forum on indigenous issues, consisting of sixteen members, eight members to be nominated by Governments and elected by the Council, and eight members to be appointed by the President of the Council following formal consultation with the Bureau and the regional groups through their coordinators, on the basis of broad consultations with indigenous organizations, taking into account the diversity and geographical distribution of the indigenous people of the world as well as the principles of transparency, representativity and equal opportunity for all indigenous people, including internal processes, when appropriate, and local indigenous consultation processes, with all members serving in their personal capacity as independent experts on indigenous issues for a period of three years with the possibility of re-election or reappointment for one further period; States, United Nations bodies and organs, intergovernmental organizations and non-governmental organizations in consultative status with the Council may participate as observers; organizations of indigenous people may equally participate as observers in accordance with the procedures which have been applied in the Working Group on Indigenous Populations of the Subcommission on the Promotion and Protection of Human Rights;

2. *Also decides* that the Permanent Forum on Indigenous Issues shall serve as an advisory body to the Council with a mandate to discuss indigenous issues within the mandate of the Council relating to economic and social development, culture, the environment, education, health and human rights; in so doing the Permanent Forum shall:

(*a*) Provide expert advice and recommendations on indigenous issues to the Council, as well as to programmes, funds and agencies of the United Nations, through the Council;

(*b*) Raise awareness and promote the integration and coordination of activities relating to indigenous issues within the United Nations system;

(*c*) Prepare and disseminate information on indigenous issues;

3. *Further decides* that the Permanent Forum shall apply the rules of procedure established for subsidiary organs of the Council as applicable, unless otherwise decided by the Council; the principle of consensus shall govern the work of the Permanent Forum;

4. *Decides* that the Permanent Forum shall hold an annual session of ten working days at the United Nations Office at Geneva or at United Nations Headquarters or at such other place as the Permanent Forum may decide in accordance with existing financial rules and regulations of the United Nations;

5. *Also decides* that the Permanent Forum shall submit an annual report to the Council on its activities, including any recommendations for approval; the report shall be distributed to the relevant United Nations organs, funds, programmes and agencies as a means, inter alia, of furthering the dialogue on indigenous issues within the United Nations system;

6. *Further decides* that the financing of the Permanent Forum shall be provided from within existing resources through the regular budget of the United Nations and its specialized agencies and through such voluntary contributions as may be donated;

7. *Decides* that, five years after its establishment, an evaluation of the functioning of the Permanent Forum, including the method for selection of its members, shall be carried out by the Council in the light of the experience gained;

8. *Also decides*, once the Permanent Forum has been established and has held its first annual session, to review, without prejudging any outcome, all existing mechanisms, procedures and programmes within the United Nations concerning indigenous issues, including the Working Group on Indigenous Populations of the Subcommission on the Promotion and Protection of Human Rights, with a view to rationalizing activities, avoiding duplication and overlap and promoting effectiveness.

Subcommission action. On 17 August [res. 2000/15], the Subcommission, taking note of the establishment of the Permanent Forum, noted the view expressed by many indigenous participants at the 2000 session of the Working Group on Indigenous Populations that the establishment of the Forum should not be construed as grounds for the abolition of the Working Group.

Indigenous land rights

Commission action. On 25 April [dec. 2000/106], the Commission, noting a 1999 Subcommission resolution [YUN 1999, p. 687], decided to approve the Subcommission's requests to the Secretary-General to transmit the second progress report on the working paper on indigenous people and their relationship to land [ibid.] to Governments, indigenous people, intergovernmental organizations and NGOs for their comments, data and suggestions, and to assist the Special Rapporteur to enable her to submit her final working paper in 2000.

Working paper of Special Rapporteur. In June [E/CN.4/Sub.2/2000/25], the Special Rapporteur on indigenous peoples and their relationship to land, Erica-Irene A. Daes (Greece), in her final working paper, stressed the need for a flexible approach to the consideration of that issue. She noted that dozens of countries had adopted constitutional and legislative measures recognizing the legal rights of indigenous peoples to their lands and resources, in various degrees, thereby demonstrating that such measures were consistent with domestic legal systems. The paper signalled the urgency of indigenous land issues. One of the most widespread contemporary problems was the failure of States to recognize the existence of indigenous land use, occupancy and ownership, and the failure to accord legal status to protect that use, occupancy or ownership. Another frequent complaint was the failure of States to demarcate indigenous lands, as was the failure of States to implement or enforce existing laws to protect indigenous lands and resources. Other significant problems were the removal and relocation of indigenous peoples; settlement programmes on indigenous lands; the practice of requiring that indigenous land be held in trust by the State; programmes that used indigenous lands as collateral for loans; adverse management of sacred and cultural sites by States; the failure of States and others to protect the environmental integrity of indigenous lands and resources; and failure to accord indigenous peoples an appropriate right to manage, use and control development of their lands and resources.

The Special Rapporteur recommended that States enact legislation to recognize, demarcate and protect indigenous peoples' lands and resources. Governments should renounce discriminatory legal doctrines and policies and adopt corrective legislation, constitutional reforms or corrective policies. They should provide measures to implement, amend and enforce land settlements and agreements, and for dispute resolution. The Permanent Forum should consider the creation of a fact-finding body to visit sites and report on particular indigenous land and resource issues; create an indigenous land and resource ombudsman or office to provide response, mediation and reconciliation services; create a complaint mechanism or procedure for human rights violations pertaining to indigenous land and resource situations; create a body with "peace-seeking" powers to investigate, recommend solutions, conciliate, mediate and otherwise assist in preventing or ending violence in situations regarding land rights; and create a procedure whereby countries would be called upon to make periodic reports regarding their progress in protecting the land and resource rights of indigenous peoples.

Subcommission action. On 17 August [dec. 2000/108], the Subcommission asked the Special Rapporteur to update her final working paper in 2001, based on comments made by Subcommission members and replies received from Governments and other reliable sources.

Indigenous heritage

In accordance with Economic and Social Council decision 1998/277 [YUN 1998, p. 723], a seminar was held (Geneva, 28 February–1 March) [E/CN.4/Sub.2/2000/26] to elaborate further the draft principles and guidelines for the protection of the heritage of indigenous people [YUN 1995, p. 780]. Participants endorsed the Special Rapporteur's recommendation that the report of the seminar and the revised draft principles and guidelines annexed thereto should be considered by the Subcommission, with the aim of transmitting them to the Commission in 2001.

Subcommission action. On 17 August [dec. 2000/107], the Subcommission decided to transmit to the Commission the revised draft principles and guidelines.

Persons with disabilities

On 25 April [res. 2000/51], the Commission, noting the work of the Special Rapporteur on disability of the Commission for Social Development (see p. 1035), invited him to address the Commission on Human Rights in 2002, and called on States to cooperate with the Special Rapporteur. Governments were urged to implement the Standard Rules on the Equalization of Opportunities for Persons with Disabilities, adopted by the General Assembly in resolution 48/96 [YUN 1993, p. 978]. The Secretary-General was asked to ensure support for the Long-term Strategy to Implement the World Programme of Action concerning Disabled Persons to the Year 2000 and Beyond [YUN 1995, p. 1256], to report biennially to the Assembly on progress made to ensure the full recognition and enjoyment of the human rights of persons with disabilities, and to make available to the Commission on Human Rights in 2001 the latest report of the Special Rapporteur on his monitoring of the Standard Rules. UN bodies and specialized agencies were asked to address the problems that existed in creating equal opportunities for persons with disabilities. The Commission recommended that OHCHR take account of information on legislation affecting the human rights of persons with disabilities that had been collected by the Special Rapporteur. The High Commissioner, in cooperation with the Special Rapporteur, was invited to examine measures to strengthen the protection and monitoring of the human rights of persons with disabilities and to solicit input and proposals from interested parties.

On 28 July, the Economic and Social Council approved the Commission's invitation to the Special Rapporteur to address the Commission and its request to the Secretary-General to report biennially (**decision 2000/268**).

Chapter III

Human rights violations

Alleged violations of human rights and international humanitarian law in a number of countries were examined in 2000 by the General Assembly, the Economic and Social Council, the Commission on Human Rights and its Subcommission on the Promotion and Protection of Human Rights, as well as by special rapporteurs, special representatives of the Secretary-General and independent experts appointed to examine the allegations. In October, the Commission held a special session on violations of the human rights of the Palestinian people by Israel.

General aspects

Under a procedure established by Economic and Social Council resolution 1503(XLVIII) [YUN 1970, p. 530] to deal with communications alleging denial or violation of human rights, the Working Group on Situations of the Commission on Human Rights, established by Council resolution 1990/41 [YUN 1990, p. 648], in closed session on 31 March, considered the human rights situations in Chile, the Congo, Kenya, Latvia, Uganda, the United Arab Emirates, Viet Nam, Yemen and Zimbabwe. The Commission discontinued consideration of the situations in Chile, the Congo, Kenya, Latvia, the United Arab Emirates, Viet Nam, Yemen and Zimbabwe.

On 18 August [E/CN.4/2001/2 (dec. 2000/114)], the Subcommission on the Promotion and Protection of Human Rights requested the Secretary-General to prepare a working document relating to mass and flagrant human rights violations that constituted crimes against humanity and that occurred during the colonial period, wars of conquest and slavery.

Africa

Burundi

Commission action. On 18 April [E/2000/23 (res. 2000/20)], the Commission on Human Rights appealed to all armed factions and other Burun-

dian political forces that had not done so to join the Arusha negotiation process (see p. 143), conclude a ceasefire as soon as possible and sign a peace agreement. It expressed deep concern at the violations of human rights and of international humanitarian law, particularly reports of massacres, enforced or involuntary disappearances, and arbitrary arrests and detention, and remained concerned at the ongoing violence and the security situation in parts of the country. Deploring the unacceptable living conditions in the regroupment camps and displaced persons sites, the Commission recommended that the Government and UN agencies and non-governmental organizations (NGOs) provide humanitarian assistance (see p. 858). The Commission requested the Government to end impunity and to foster a security environment conducive to the work of assistance organizations. The United Nations and the donor community were invited to augment the flow of humanitarian assistance, once a security environment existed. The Commission asked States not to allow their territories to be used as bases for incursions or attacks against another State.

The Commission decided to extend the Special Rapporteur's mandate for an additional year and asked her to submit an interim report to the General Assembly in 2000 and a report to the Commission in 2001, giving her work a gender-specific dimension. The Economic and Social Council endorsed the Commission's decision and its requests to the Special Rapporteur on 28 July (**decision 2000/253**).

Reports of Special Rapporteur. In September [A/55/358], Special Rapporteur Marie-Thérèse A. Keita-Bocoum (Côte d'Ivoire) submitted an interim report, covering the period from 15 April to 15 July, following her visit to Burundi (27 June–7 July).

The Special Rapporteur described the current political and economic and social situation and developments in the peace process (see p. 143). Although there had been no change in the human rights situation, the legal system had improved somewhat as a result of reforms. The situation around the capital and in some provinces was relatively calm as a result of the decline in mass killings and massacres. Elsewhere, the situation still gave cause for concern. The main human rights violations were violations of the right to life, including those attributed to State agents, rebel groups and unknown persons; the right to personal freedom and security; physical integrity, including torture and ill-treatment and rape; freedom of opinion and expression; the right of trade unions to function freely; the right to health; the right to education; and children's right to special aid and assistance. The situation of persons deprived of their liberty had improved since the beginning of the year as a result of judicial reforms, better conditions of detention in certain prisons and support by the Government, human rights associations and humanitarian organizations. Even so, irregularities persisted. Penitentiary establishments were still characterized by massive overcrowding, inadequate food, very poor health services and delays in processing the cases of detainees. In certain jail facilities of the police, public security police and judicial police of the prosecutors' offices, as well as in the *cachots* (communal detention centres) of communes and zones, cases of arbitrary detention, torture or abuse, malnutrition and starvation were found. Hygienic conditions in the *cachots* were appalling, with no water or ventilation. Secret detention centres in the communes, zones or camps and military posts also existed. The dismantling of camps allowed free movement, ease of access to humanitarian aid and the benefit of the solidarity of neighbours. At the time of the Special Rapporteur's visit, over 230,000 people had returned to their homes. In the camps that had not been dismantled, the situation remained intolerable, with harsh living conditions.

Appreciable progress had been made in the justice system since the inception on 1 January of the new Code of Criminal Procedure, particularly regarding respect for the legally permissible period of police custody and interrogations conducted by judicial police officers. Since the application of the new Code, arbitrary arrests had decreased and considerable work had been done to sort out detainees' files. The Legal Assistance Programme, operated by the Office of the United Nations High Commissioner for Human Rights (OHCHR), and the training courses for judges were still positively impacting the promotion and defence of human rights. Progress, however, remained hampered by many irregularities, inadequacies and violence that were aggravated by the war, extreme poverty and the excessive number of prisoners. Major problems remained in the slowness of the judiciary, the growing corruption of certain judges and political, social and cultural pressures.

The Special Rapporteur examined the situation of women, which, she said, was defined by poverty, an excessive burden of household duties and considerable dependence on the husband. It was also characterized by low levels of representation in decision-making, insufficient training and information, and a very low literacy rate. Violence against women was often physical, psychological and sexual. Their rights to inherit property and own land were also violated, consequences of polygamy and rape. The main obstacles to women's advancement were tradition and ignorance.

The Special Rapporteur called on parties to the conflict to participate in the Arusha negotiations (see p. 143), respect people's rights and observe international humanitarian law relating to the protection of children affected by armed conflict. She recommended that the Government continue efforts to lead Burundi towards a legally constituted State; reduce detention and ensure detainees access to family members, doctors and lawyers; combat enforced disappearances; improve the living conditions of refugees; change or enhance the view of women's roles; end discrimination against women and amend laws preventing them from owning or inheriting land, property or dwellings; develop a reliable health and social service system; devote attention to street and displaced children; and ensure the right to education. The international community was called on to develop socio-economic programmes and projects and secure the sustained flow of resources for reconstruction activities, establish and strengthen prevention, observation and monitoring mechanisms to avoid an escalation of the conflict, combat extreme poverty and social exclusion, strengthen humanitarian action and work more actively to combat HIV/AIDS.

In a later report [E/CN.4/2001/44], the Special Rapporteur updated developments since the signing of the Arusha Agreement on Peace and Reconciliation in Burundi on 28 August (see p. 146). Security in the country had improved due to cooperation between the army, the administration and the people. The forced regroupment camps in the province of Bujumbura-rural and the rest of the country had been permanently dismantled. However, the economic and social situation had been deteriorating constantly; the northern provinces were plagued by drought and famine. In the cities, the middle classes were becoming increasingly impoverished.

The human rights situation did not improve substantially. The main human rights violations concerned the right to life, to physical integrity and to personal freedom and security, freedom to choose one's residence, freedom of expression and economic, social and cultural rights. The Special Rapporteur observed that the people seemed hostage to the political establishment, which was experiencing some difficulties in resolving the question of leadership. Civilians were subjected to abusive treatment by the military and armed groups; they were forced to contribute to financing the war effort and made to perform forced labour. The situation had become more precarious, especially for those living in rural areas and the *collines*, giving rise to hunger, cold and disease. The army continued to become involved illegally in matters reserved for the justice system. Women, particularly those from rural areas, were the main victims of war, displacement and regroupment, yet were excluded from the peace process. The Special Rapporteur supported measures taken by the Ministry of Human Rights in favour of respect for and promotion of human rights. Parties to the conflict were urged to respect the right to life and end children's involvement in their fighting, end degrading and humiliating treatment, participate in negotiations and end political hostilities. Among other measures, the Government was called on to facilitate access for organizations and UN bodies to sites for displaced persons and to victims of the crisis, train legal professionals, set up halfway houses for children released from prison, enact a law for women on inheritance and marriage contracts, abolish the death penalty and increase support to judicial bodies.

Democratic Republic of the Congo

Commission action. On 18 April [res. 2000/15], the Commission welcomed the commitment by the Democratic Republic of the Congo (DRC) to cooperate with UN agencies and NGOs in ensuring the demobilization and reintegration of child soldiers; the general amnesty announced on 19 February by President Laurent Désiré Kabila, under which 200 persons accused, convicted or detained for crimes against State security had been released; the release and repatriation, carried out under the auspices of the International Committee of the Red Cross (ICRC) in the DRC, of persons at risk, mainly of Tutsi origin, and of prisoners of war; the setting up of a peace operation by the Security Council; and the Council's decision in **resolution 1291(2000)** to authorize the expansion of the United Nations Organization Mission in the DRC (MONUC) (see p. 123). The Commission expressed concern at the adverse impact of the conflict on the human rights situation; continuing violations of the Lusaka Ceasefire Agreement [YUN 1999, p. 87]; the situation of human rights, particularly in the east of

the country, and the continuing violations of human rights and international humanitarian law; the excessive accumulation and spread of small arms and light weapons and their illicit distribution; the harassment and persecution of human rights defenders and their organizations; the intimidation of church representatives and of civil society in the east; and the severe insecurity, which minimized the ability of humanitarian organizations to access affected populations. Parties were urged to implement fully the Lusaka Ceasefire Agreement and to protect human rights and respect international humanitarian law. The Government was called on to protect human rights, reform and restore the judicial system, end impunity, implement democratization, remove remaining restrictions on the activities of political parties and prepare to hold democratic, free and fair elections, ensure respect for freedom of opinion and expression, and cooperate with the International Criminal Tribunal for Rwanda (ICTR) (see p. 1225).

The Commission decided to extend the Special Rapporteur's mandate for an additional year and asked him to submit an interim report to the General Assembly in 2000 (see p. 737), to report to the Commission in 2001 and to maintain a gender perspective in seeking and analysing information. It also asked the Special Rapporteurs on the situation of human rights in the DRC and on extrajudicial, summary or arbitrary executions and a member of the Working Group on Enforced or Involuntary Disappearances to carry out, as soon as security considerations permitted and, where appropriate, in cooperation with the National Commission of Inquiry to investigate alleged human rights violations and breaches of international humanitarian law in the DRC between 1996 and 1997, a joint mission to investigate massacres carried out in the DRC, with a view to bringing to justice those responsible and to report to the Assembly in 2000 and to the Commission in 2001. The Commission asked the Secretary-General to assist the Special Rapporteur and the joint mission, the High Commissioner to provide technical expertise to the joint mission, and the international community to support the DRC human rights field office.

The Economic and Social Council endorsed the Commission's decisions and its requests to the Special Rapporteurs and Working Group member on 28 July **(decision 2000/248)**.

Note by Secretariat. An August note by the Secretariat [A/55/318] stated that the insecurity prevailing in the DRC in general and in the province of South Kivu in particular had prevented the deployment of the joint mission of inquiry.

Reports of Special Rapporteur. In September [A/55/403], the Secretary-General transmitted to the General Assembly the report of Special Rapporteur Roberto Garretón (Chile), based on his visit to the DRC (13-26 August). He noted the Government's request to the Secretary-General [S/2000/122] to investigate events in the locality of Ituri, as well as an investigation into allegations of the deaths of 15 women who were buried alive or burnt in Mwenga, situated in territory controlled by the Rassemblement congolais pour la démocratie (RCD). The Government and RCD had requested investigations into the Katogota massacre. Because of the prevailing insecurity and lack of financial resources, the investigations were still pending.

The Special Rapporteur described the various armed conflicts—the conflict between the Government and RCD, the conflict between the Government and the Mouvement de libération du Congo (MLC), clashes between Uganda and Rwanda in Kisangani, and tribal conflict between Balendu and Bahema. None of the parties to the conflicts fully respected the Lusaka Ceasefire Agreement. The conflicts, which involved at least seven national armies and many irregular armed groups, had destroyed the country, with more than half the population affected. All public moneys were diverted to the war effort. There had been terrible epidemics. Since the war made it impossible to cultivate the land, 17 per cent of the population, or some 14 million people, were affected by food insecurity. The number of *sheques* (street children) had risen alarmingly. More than 1.3 million people were internally displaced, many of whom were without assistance.

In the Government-controlled territory, the rights most affected were political rights, including the rights to participation, assembly, association and freedom of expression. In RCD- and RCD/Mouvement de libération (ML)–controlled territory, the rights most often violated were the right to life and physical integrity, without prejudice to political freedom. There was insufficient information on the MLC-controlled territory. Neither the Government nor RCD, RCD/ML or MLC had taken steps towards democracy. The Government maintained that it had not implemented the death penalty since February 2000. RCD, which had never done so, began to use the death penalty in 2000. The liberty of person was constantly violated, there was no freedom of expression and the right to due process was not respected by any of the parties. Torture, which was practised by all parties, resulted in death in many instances. In both Kinshasa and Goma, opposition members were prevented from leaving the country and from movement within it. The Gov-

ernment, with international assistance, had continued to protect people who looked like Tutsi in order to prevent reprisals against them, thereby disproving accusations of genocide. Religious persecution had been a constant. The situation of women and children continued to worsen, and although the Government and RCD had taken steps to demobilize children, neither MLC nor the Ugandan troops had done so.

The Special Rapporteur recommended that all parties implement fully the Lusaka Agreement, cooperate with MONUC and end impunity. He recommended that the Government establish an inter-Congolese dialogue; abolish the death penalty; eliminate the Military Court; free all political prisoners; cease pressure on or censorship of the press; demobilize child soldiers; restore relations with other States, intergovernmental organizations, the United Nations and the Organization of African Unity (OAU) and attend their conferences and meetings; implement a human rights action plan; and accord international human rights instruments precedence over national law and honour commitments made under them.

The Special Rapporteur proposed that RCD and other rebel groups cease all cooperation with foreign armies; avoid committing any act that implied the exercise of sovereignty over foreign armies; refrain from issuing fictitious accounts of atrocities committed by their troops and foreign allies and conduct objective investigations of allegations; free political prisoners; abolish the death penalty; cease to interpret acts of opposition as an alleged incitement to ethnic hatred; permit organizations of civil society to function freely; and demobilize child soldiers. Foreign armies occupying Congolese territory were urged to implement the Lusaka Agreement; refrain from reprisals; permit investigations of violations of human rights and international law; compensate victims; and return Congolese property that had been taken from the country since 1998. The United Nations should continue to support the peace process; pay attention to the human rights special rapporteurs; assist the mechanisms of the Commission on Human Rights; and establish an effective arms embargo on all countries involved in the conflict. He recommended that other organs of the international community support the peace process and make their voices heard regarding the massacres committed in the DRC.

In a later report [E/CN.4/2001/40], which covered incidents that occurred up to 11 December, the Special Rapporteur stated that the investigations into the events that occurred in the locality of Ituri were still pending. He described the various armed conflicts and political developments and democratization in the country. He recounted human rights violations similar to those in his September report (see p. 737) and observed that none of the parties to the conflicts were fully respecting the Lusaka Agreement. The sense of terror in RCD-controlled territories and the entire country's humiliation were still dramatically present. The Special Rapporteur reiterated his earlier recommendations. Annexed to the report were lists of international instruments to which the DRC was a party, armed conflicts taking place in the country, irregular armed groups involved in the armed conflicts and human rights violations committed in Government-controlled territory, as well as those that occurred in territory under the control of rebel movements, between 16 December 1999 and 11 December 2000.

(For political details, see p. 119.)

GENERAL ASSEMBLY ACTION

On 4 December [meeting 81], the General Assembly, on the recommendation of the Third (Social, Humanitarian and Cultural) Committee [A/55/602/Add.3], adopted **resolution 55/117** by recorded vote (102-2-63) [agenda item 114 (c)].

Situation of human rights in the Democratic Republic of the Congo

The General Assembly,

Reaffirming that all Member States have an obligation to promote and protect human rights and fundamental freedoms as stated in the Charter of the United Nations, the Universal Declaration of Human Rights, the International Covenants on Human Rights and other applicable human rights instruments,

Mindful that the Democratic Republic of the Congo is a party to the International Covenant on Civil and Political Rights, the International Covenant on Economic, Social and Cultural Rights, the Convention against Torture and Other Cruel, Inhuman or Degrading Treatment or Punishment, the Convention on the Elimination of All Forms of Discrimination against Women, the Geneva Conventions of 12 August 1949 for the protection of victims of war, the International Convention on the Elimination of All Forms of Racial Discrimination and the Convention on the Rights of the Child, as well as the African Charter on Human and Peoples' Rights,

Recalling its previous resolutions on this subject, including the most recent, resolution 54/179 of 17 December 1999, taking note of Commission on Human Rights resolution 2000/15 of 18 April 2000 and Security Council resolution 1304(2000) of 16 June 2000, and mindful of previous resolutions and presidential statements of the Security Council on the subject,

Recalling the Ceasefire Agreement signed at Lusaka and the Kampala disengagement plan,[a] the obligations of all signatories to those agreements and the obligations deriving from Security Council resolution 1304(2000),

Taking note of the outcome of the Extraordinary Summit of the Heads of State or Government of the Southern African Development Community, held at Maputo on 16 January 2000,[b] and of the holding of the summit meeting of the heads of State of Central Africa at Kinshasa on 27 October 2000,[c]

Concerned at all violations of human rights and international humanitarian law in the territory of the Democratic Republic of the Congo by parties to the conflict, as mentioned in the report of the Special Rapporteur of the Commission on Human Rights on the situation of human rights in the Democratic Republic of the Congo, including acts of and incitement to ethnic hatred and violence,

Recognizing that the promotion and the protection of human rights for all are essential for achieving stability and security in the region and will contribute to the creation of the environment necessary for cooperation among States in the region,

Taking into account the regional dimension of the human rights issues in the Great Lakes region, while underlining the primary responsibility of States for the promotion and protection of human rights, and stressing the importance of technical cooperation with a view to strengthening regional cooperation for the promotion and protection of human rights,

Recalling the decision of the Commission on Human Rights to request the Special Rapporteurs of the Commission on the situation of human rights in the Democratic Republic of the Congo and on extrajudicial, summary or arbitrary executions and a member of the Working Group on Enforced or Involuntary Disappearances to carry out a joint mission to the Democratic Republic of the Congo, and encouraging the mission to begin its work as soon as possible, with the cooperation of the Government and all other parties concerned,

Encouraging the Government of the Democratic Republic of the Congo to fulfil its earlier commitments, including to the United Nations High Commissioner for Human Rights, to restore and reform the judicial system, in accordance with the relevant international conventions, and noting in this regard the declared intention of the Government progressively to abolish the death penalty and to put an end to the trying of civilians by the Military Court,

1. *Welcomes:*

(*a*) The report of the Special Rapporteur of the Commission on Human Rights on the situation of human rights in the Democratic Republic of the Congo;

(*b*) The visit made to the country by the Special Rapporteur of the Commission on Human Rights on the situation of human rights in the Democratic Republic of the Congo at the invitation of the Government and the cooperation of the Government and of all Congolese parties to the Ceasefire Agreement signed at Lusaka in this regard;

(*c*) The visit made to the country by the United Nations High Commissioner for Human Rights from 1 to 3 October 2000;

(*d*) The activities of the human rights field office in the Democratic Republic of the Congo, and encourages the Government to continue to work in close cooperation with the office;

(*e*) The efforts of the Ministry of Human Rights of the Democratic Republic of the Congo to improve the human rights situation in the country and, in particular, the adoption in December 1999, in concert with non-governmental organizations, of the national action plan for the promotion and protection of human rights;

(f) The general amnesty ordered by President Kabila on 19 February 2000, as a timely and significant step towards reconciliation and towards preparation for the inter-Congolese dialogue called for in the Ceasefire Agreement, but deplores the fact that many other political prisoners continue to be detained and the arrests made since that date;

(g) The commitment by the Government of the Democratic Republic of the Congo to cooperate with the United Nations agencies and non-governmental organizations in ensuring the demobilization and reintegration of child soldiers and the holding at Kinshasa, on 10 December 1999, in cooperation with the United Nations Children's Fund, of the Forum on the Demobilization of Child Soldiers and the Protection of Human Rights, and measures of demobilization of children taken by the Government and by the Congolese Rally for Democracy, and encourages other parties to the conflict to do the same;

(h) The repatriation carried out under the auspices of the International Committee of the Red Cross in the Democratic Republic of the Congo, in conformity with international humanitarian law, of persons at risk because of their ethnic origin, but regrets, however, that the Government was apparently unable to provide adequate protection in the first place;

(i) The release of prisoners of war, and calls for the acceleration of exchanges of prisoners;

(j) The decision of the Security Council in its resolution 1291(2000) of 24 February 2000 to authorize the expansion of the United Nations Organization Mission in the Democratic Republic of the Congo;

(k) The work of the Special Envoy of the Secretary-General for the peace process in the Democratic Republic of the Congo;

(l) The appointment by the Secretary-General of the Special Representative for the Democratic Republic of the Congo;

2. *Expresses its concern* at:

(a) The adverse impact of the conflict on the situation of human rights and its severe consequences for the security and well-being of the civilian population throughout the territory of the Democratic Republic of the Congo;

(b) The continuing violations of the Ceasefire Agreement and the continuing use of hate speech;

(c) The preoccupying situation of human rights in the Democratic Republic of the Congo, in particular in the eastern part of the country, and the continuing violations of human rights and international humanitarian law committed throughout the territory of the Democratic Republic of the Congo, often with impunity, and, with that in view, condemns:

(i) The massacres of civilians perpetrated in the course of the conflict, which constitute a disproportionate response to attacks, in particular those occurring recently on the Lisenda-8 road and at Katogata, Kamanyola, Lurbarika, Luberezi, Ngenge, Kalehe, Kilambo, Cidaho, Uvira, Shabunda and Lusenda-Lubumba;

(ii) The fighting in Kisangani between Ugandan and Rwandan forces, most recently in May and June 2000, which resulted in many civilian victims;

(iii) The bombings of the hospital at Libenge and at Gemena and elsewhere, which affected civilian populations;

(iv) The conflicts between the Hema and Lendu ethnic groups in the eastern province, where thousands of Congolese have already been killed;

(v) The occurrence of cases of summary and arbitrary execution, disappearance, torture, beating, harassment, arbitrary arrest and detention without trial, including of journalists, opposition politicians and human rights defenders, reports of sexual violence against women and children, and the continuing recruitment and use of child soldiers, as well as, in the eastern part of the country in particular, reprisals against people who have cooperated with the United Nations mechanisms;

(vi) The trying of civilians and the imposition of the death penalty by the Military Court;

(d) The excessive accumulation and spread of small arms and light weapons and the illicit distribution, circulation and trafficking of arms in the region and their negative impact on human rights;

(e) The breaches of fundamental freedoms, such as freedom of expression, opinion, association and assembly, in the whole territory of the Democratic Republic of the Congo, in particular in the eastern part of the country;

(f) The acts of intimidation against representatives of the Churches and civil society, throughout the Congolese territory, as well as the killings of those persons in the eastern part of the country;

(g) The severe insecurity, which minimizes the ability of humanitarian organizations to secure access to affected populations;

(h) Reports of the illegal exploitation of natural resources and other forms of wealth of the Democratic Republic of the Congo;

3. *Urges* all parties to the conflict in the Democratic Republic of the Congo:

(a) To implement fully the provisions of the Ceasefire Agreement and to facilitate the re-establishment of the authority of the Government of the Democratic Republic of the Congo throughout the territory, as agreed in the inter-Congolese political negotiations provided for in the Ceasefire Agreement, and stresses, in the context of a lasting peaceful settlement, the need for the engagement of the Congolese in an all-inclusive process of political dialogue, with a view to achieving national reconciliation and the holding of democratic, free, transparent and fair elections;

(b) To cease all military activity in the Democratic Republic of the Congo, which breaches the ceasefire provided for in the Ceasefire Agreement and the Kampala disengagement plan;

(c) To protect human rights and to respect international humanitarian law, in particular, as applicable to them, the Geneva Conventions of 12 August 1949 for the protection of victims of war and the Additional Protocols thereto, of 1977, the Hague Convention respecting the Laws and Customs of War on Land of 18 October 1907, the Convention on the Prevention and

Punishment of the Crime of Genocide and other relevant provisions of international humanitarian, human rights and refugee law, and in particular to respect the rights of women and children and to ensure the safety of all civilians, including refugees and internally displaced persons within the territory of that country, regardless of their origin;

(d) To cease all forms of repression against people exercising their fundamental freedoms;

(e) To establish the conditions necessary for the safe and speedy deployment of the United Nations Organization Mission in the Democratic Republic of the Congo;

(f) To ensure the safety, security and freedom of movement of United Nations and associated personnel and humanitarian personnel within the Democratic Republic of the Congo and, in this regard, to ensure safe and unhindered access of humanitarian personnel to all affected populations throughout the territory of the Democratic Republic of the Congo;

(g) To put an immediate end to the use of child soldiers, which is in contravention of international human rights standards, and to demobilize them;

(h) To define and implement all necessary measures to create conditions conducive to the voluntary return, in safety and with dignity, of all refugees and displaced persons and to ensure their protection and fair and lawful treatment;

4. *Calls upon* the Government of the Democratic Republic of the Congo:

(a) To comply fully with its obligations under international human rights law and to promote and protect human rights and fundamental freedoms throughout its entire territory;

(b) To fulfil its responsibility to ensure the full protection of the human rights of the population in its territory, as well as to take a leading part in efforts to prevent conditions that might lead to further flows of internally displaced persons and refugees within the Democratic Republic of the Congo and across its border;

(c) To fulfil its commitment to reform and restore the judicial system, and, in particular, to reform military justice, and to stop using it to try civilians, in conformity with the provisions of the International Covenant on Civil and Political Rights;

(d) To ensure full respect for freedom of opinion and expression, including freedom of the press in relation to all types of mass media, as well as freedom of association and assembly;

(e) To remove the restrictions that still affect the work of non-governmental organizations and to promote human rights awareness, including by strengthening cooperation with civil society, including all human rights organizations;

(f) To implement fully its commitment to the democratization process, in particular the national dialogue, as stipulated in the Ceasefire Agreement, and to create, in this context, conditions that would allow for a democratization process that is genuine and all-inclusive and that fully reflects the aspirations of all people in the country, including by lifting restrictions on political parties and their activities and ensuring political pluralism, in order to lead the way for the holding of democratic, free and fair elections;

(g) To put an end to impunity and to fulfil its responsibility to ensure that those responsible for human rights violations and grave breaches of international humanitarian law are brought to justice;

(h) To cooperate fully with the International Criminal Tribunal for the Prosecution of Persons Responsible for Genocide and Other Serious Violations of International Humanitarian Law Committed in the Territory of Rwanda and Rwandan Citizens Responsible for Genocide and Other Such Violations Committed in the Territory of Neighbouring States between 1 January and 31 December 1994 in ensuring that all those responsible for the crime of genocide, crimes against humanity and other grave violations of human rights are brought to justice in accordance with international principles of due process;

(i) To work closely and strengthen further its cooperation with the human rights field office in the Democratic Republic of the Congo;

(j) To implement fully its commitment to cooperate with United Nations agencies and non-governmental organizations in ensuring the demobilization, rehabilitation and reintegration of child soldiers;

5. *Decides* to continue to examine the situation of human rights in the Democratic Republic of the Congo, and requests the Special Rapporteur to report to the General Assembly at its fifty-sixth session.

RECORDED VOTE ON RESOLUTION 55/117:

In favour: Afghanistan, Albania, Andorra, Argentina, Armenia, Australia, Austria, Azerbaijan, Bahamas, Barbados, Belarus, Belgium, Belize, Benin, Bolivia, Bosnia and Herzegovina, Brazil, Bulgaria, Canada, Chile, Colombia, Costa Rica, Croatia, Cyprus, Czech Republic, Denmark, Dominica, Dominican Republic, Ecuador, El Salvador, Estonia, Fiji, Finland, France, Georgia, Germany, Greece, Grenada, Guatemala, Guinea, Guyana, Haiti, Honduras, Hungary, Iceland, Ireland, Israel, Italy, Jamaica, Japan, Kazakhstan, Kuwait, Kyrgyzstan, Latvia, Liechtenstein, Lithuania, Luxembourg, Maldives, Malta, Marshall Islands, Mauritius, Mexico, Micronesia, Monaco, Mongolia, Nauru, Netherlands, New Zealand, Nicaragua, Norway, Palau, Panama, Papua New Guinea, Paraguay, Peru, Poland, Portugal, Republic of Korea, Republic of Moldova, Romania, Russian Federation, Samoa, San Marino, Slovakia, Slovenia, Solomon Islands, South Africa, Spain, Suriname, Sweden, Tajikistan, The former Yugoslav Republic of Macedonia, Trinidad and Tobago, Turkey, Ukraine, United Kingdom, United States, Uruguay, Uzbekistan, Vanuatu, Venezuela, Yugoslavia.

Against: Rwanda, Uganda.

Abstaining: Algeria, Angola, Antigua and Barbuda, Bahrain, Bangladesh, Bhutan, Botswana, Brunei Darussalam, Burkina Faso, Burundi, Cambodia, Cameroon, Cape Verde, Chad, China, Comoros, Congo, Côte d'Ivoire, Cuba, Democratic People's Republic of Korea, Democratic Republic of the Congo, Djibouti, Egypt, Eritrea, Ethiopia, Gambia, Ghana, India, Indonesia, Iran, Jordan, Kenya, Lao People's Democratic Republic, Lesotho, Libyan Arab Jamahiriya, Madagascar, Malawi, Malaysia, Mali, Mauritania, Morocco, Mozambique, Myanmar, Namibia, Nepal, Nigeria, Pakistan, Philippines, Qatar, Saint Lucia, Sao Tome and Principe, Senegal, Sierra Leone, Singapore, Sri Lanka, Sudan, Swaziland, Thailand, Togo, Tunisia, United Arab Emirates, United Republic of Tanzania, Zimbabwe.

---

[a]S/2000/330 & Corr.1.
[b]S/2000/36.
[c]S/2000/1050.

Equatorial Guinea

Commission action. On 18 April [res. 2000/19], the Commission encouraged the Government of Equatorial Guinea to comply with recommendations of the Commission and the Special Representative [YUN 1999, p. 694]. Welcoming the Government's intention to implement a national human rights action plan, the Commission encouraged the Government to discuss and to agree on means for its early implementation, together with a comprehensive technical assistance programme, with OHCHR. It called on the Government to ensure the independence of the National Commission on Human Rights and of the national electoral commission.

The Commission decided to renew the Special Representative's mandate for one year and asked him to report in 2001, applying a gender perspective. He was asked to verify that technical assistance provided to Equatorial Guinea supported its national plan of action on human rights. The Secretary-General was asked to assist him.

The Economic and Social Council endorsed the Commission's decision and its requests to the Special Representative on 28 July (**decision 2000/252**).

Report of Special Representative. Since he had not received replies from the Government of Equatorial Guinea to his requests to visit the country or for information, Special Representative Gustavo Gallón (Colombia) visited Spain (20-25 November) [E/CN.4/2001/38], where some 10 per cent of Equatorial Guinean citizens lived.

The Special Representative stated that the human rights situation in Equatorial Guinea did not improve during the year. His previous conclusions remained applicable [YUN 1999, p. 694]. There continued to be no sustained rule of law; rather, power was concentrated in the hands of the executive, which led to continued arbitrary detention and torture designed to prevent coup d'état attempts, or to prevent political parties or ethnic groups opposing the governing group from gaining power. The military and the governing party exercised various de facto and de jure powers to control the population, 65 per cent of which lacked the means to satisfy basic needs. Society as a whole was subjected to the constant presence of armed forces, which restricted the right to freedom of movement and exercised criminal jurisdiction over civilians. Legislation was not published regularly and there was no daily newspaper through which freedom of opinion might be exercised. Human rights organizations were not authorized to function, and there were no trade unions, except for a farmers' association. Women and children were the most seriously affected by discrimination, especially regarding education and health.

In 2000, technical assistance agreements between the Government and the European Commission, the United Nations Development Programme (UNDP) and the Government of Spain were concluded or were in their initial stages.

In November, the political opposition, gathered in Spain, handed the Special Representative a proposal inviting the Government to agree to arrangements which, with support by the international community, could ensure a transition to democracy, based on respect for human rights. The proposal merited consideration, said the Special Representative.

The Special Representative reiterated his previous recommendations [YUN 1999, p. 694] and added that the Government should be called on to end enforced disappearances and, to that end, to agree to organize a national register of detainees, open for consultation by anyone. It was also proposed that habeas corpus should be instituted and consideration be given to the engagement of a political dialogue outside the country between the Government and the opposition in exile to find ways to establish democracy and human rights. In view of the fact that the Government did not cooperate with the Special Representative's mandate in 2000, he recommended that the Commission appeal to the Government to take a position in conformity with its international obligations, and that the Commission arrange for the mechanisms to ensure that that was done.

Rwanda

Commission action. On 18 April [res. 2000/21], the Commission, while noting indications of improvement in the human rights situation in Rwanda, expressed concern at continued violations of human rights and international humanitarian law and urged the Government to continue to investigate and prosecute the violations. Welcoming the Government's efforts to build a State based on the rule of law and the guarantee of respect for human rights and fundamental freedoms, the Commission strongly condemned the crime of genocide and the crimes against humanity that were committed in Rwanda in 1994 and expressed concern that most of the perpetrators of genocide and other gross human rights violations continued to evade justice. It also expressed concern about the effectiveness of the ICTR witness protection programme and called for its improvement as a matter of urgency. The Commission encouraged the Government to support fully the National Human Rights Commission (NHRC) to enable it to investigate human rights violations and sensitize and train the population.

The Commission decided to extend the Special Representative's mandate for a further year and asked him to report to the General Assembly in 2000 (see p. 742) and to the Commission in 2001, and asked the High Commissioner to assist him. The Commission called for close consultations between the Special Representative, the Government, NHRC and other national institutions. The Economic and Social Council endorsed the Commission's decision and approved its requests to the Special Representative and the High Commissioner on 28 July (**decision 2000/254**).

Report of Special Representative. In August [A/55/269], the Secretary-General transmitted the report of Special Representative Michel Moussalli (Switzerland) based on his visits to Rwanda (January, March, June).

The Government was still professing its commitment to the ideals of participatory democracy, human rights, reconciliation and sustainable development, which showed in the continuing moral and material support accorded to NHRC and the National Unity and Reconciliation Commission (NURC). At the same time, some tensions had appeared in the population at large, reportedly due to the insufficiently explained personnel changes at or near the top of the political hierarchy, some apparently isolated and unexplained cases of assassinations of high-level officials, incidents of infiltration across the border with the DRC resulting in a number of deaths and the continued involvement of Rwanda in the DRC crisis (see p. 119) and its cost to the country. A drought had created severe food shortages in the eastern part of the country, and famine in some areas, resulting in internal displacement of populations in search of food. Another reported source of malaise was the significant number of cases of sexual abuse of children of both sexes, especially young girls, in some cases in the belief that a sexual relationship with a young girl would cure HIV/AIDS.

The Special Representative described security concerns in Kigali and its environs, and in the border areas, especially in north-west Rwanda, and new concerns related to the persecution of government opponents, the silencing of the press, the forced return of persons who had fled the country and the prevention of certain persons from fleeing abroad. He discussed cooperation with OHCHR, which had continued to improve. Expressing gratification at the progress made through NHRC, he was convinced that technical assistance would help it develop projects. In spite of the bold moves the Government had taken to reduce the prison population, the overall number of detainees had not declined. Conditions had worsened in the country's 154 *cachots,* which were meant to hold detainees for up to 48 hours, until they could be transferred to a prison. The Special Representative was distressed that prison conditions continued to violate the basic norms. Efforts to improve justice would enter a new phase with the introduction of the *gacaca,* a system of community justice for genocide suspects. Trials would take place in public before the entire community. Drawing on the recollections of the accused, the complainants and the villagers, the judges would compile a list of those who died in the genocide, and of those presumed responsible. The accused would be judged and sentenced. The Government established NURC, which, while focusing on creating a strong institutional foundation, had completed nationwide consultations, produced promotional material, organized reconciliation workshops and taken over the running of solidarity camps, and supported initiatives of other partners. In terms of economic and social rights, children had suffered terribly under the genocide and land and settlement issues were still outstanding. The Special Representative made a series of recommendations regarding prison and judicial reform; the media; children; human rights education; and NHRC. He made recommendations to the international community, bilateral donors, NGOs, the UN system, the High Commissioner, the Office of the United Nations High Commissioner for Refugees (UNHCR), UNDP and ICTR.

In a later report [E/CN.4/2001/45/Add.1 & Corr.1], the Special Representative, following his visit to Rwanda in October, observed that the national commissions had made progress since his last report. A programme of assistance and cooperation between OHCHR and NHRC, which started in November, aimed to facilitate the effective functioning of NHRC by improving its technical and substantive capacity. NHRC held human rights training and education programmes for police officers and senior non-commissioned officers in the army and for secondary school, university and health institute students. NURC was examining the link between justice and reconciliation, particularly how the *gacaca* justice system could promote reconciliation.

The Government had taken major steps towards decentralization and democracy. A new structure of territorial administration was introduced in December, which accelerated efforts to release detainees without files, to regularize files and to reduce the number of those held in communal *cachots* by transferring them to prisons. Large numbers of the population were still without shelter; thus, reintegration needs were not met. Land tenure needed to be resolved for reconciliation and sustainable development. Concerning a new law permitting women to own and inherit land, the Government began a nationwide information campaign to educate the population. The Special Representative expressed concern that many genocide survivors were still in dire need of assistance, and that many felt abandoned by the international community. He noted the growing number of new independent newspapers, but expressed concern that a weekly English newspaper had been harassed. Newspapers were printed in Uganda, as there was no local printing press. The draft press law was largely viewed by the media as a positive and balanced approach to media regulation. The first National Conference on the Rights of the Child was held in Kigali (14-18 August) and an inter-ministerial Task Force on the Rights of the Child had been established under the Ministry of Local Administration and Social Affairs.

(For political details, see p. 148.)

Sierra Leone

Commission action. On 18 April [res. 2000/24], the Commission, expressing concern regarding the continuing violations of human rights and humanitarian law committed in Sierra Leone, called on the Government to comply with its obligations to promote and protect human rights, to work closely in the human rights area with the United Nations Mission in Sierra Leone (UNAMSIL) and OHCHR and to prioritize the special needs of women and children. It welcomed steps taken by the Government and civil society to create a human rights infrastructure and the deployment of a child protection adviser with UNAMSIL to ensure the protection of children's rights. The Commission called on the Government to investigate reports of human rights abuses that had occurred since the signing of the Lomé Peace Agreement in 1999 [YUN 1999, p. 159] and to end impunity; the Secretary-General and the High Commissioner were asked to respond favourably to government requests for assistance with the investigation of abuses.

The Commission asked the High Commissioner and the international community to continue to assist the Government to establish and maintain an effective truth and reconciliation commission and national human rights commission. The Secretary-General, the High Commissioner and the international community were requested to assist the human rights section of UNAMSIL and, in consultation with the relevant UN agencies, assist the Government to address the country's human rights needs. The High Commissioner was asked to report to the General Assembly in 2000 and to the Commission in 2001.

On 28 July, the Economic and Social Council endorsed the Commission's requests to the High Commissioner and the international community to assist the Government and to the Secretary-General, the High Commissioner and the international community to assist the human rights section of UNAMSIL. It approved the Commission's requests to the High Commissioner to submit reports (**decision 2000/256**).

Reports of High Commissioner. In August [A/55/36], the High Commissioner noted that persistent fighting in Sierra Leone exacerbated the human rights violations that had characterized the conflict, among them extrajudicial executions, mutilations, torture, rape and sexual abuse, forced labour, abduction, forced recruitment and use of children, as well as women, as soldiers, wanton destruction and looting of civilian property, and massive internal displacement of persons. Regarding UNAMSIL, when the armed conflict resumed in May, a Sierra Leonean task force was established by OHCHR to support the Mission's human rights section in its response to the human rights–related aspects of the conflict. The poor security situation had so far delayed plans to deploy human rights officers throughout the country.

The High Commissioner in a later report [E/CN.4/2001/35], citing reports of the Secretary-General to the Security Council (see pp. 190-200), stated that the human rights situation in Sierra Leone remained grave. Arbitrary executions, rape, abduction and looting continued. The security situation remained a matter of serious concern. However, human rights assessment missions in Port Loko, Makeni, Magburaka, Kabala, Kenema and Daru found that the situation had improved due to the deployment of UN troops and military observers. The human rights situation in some parts of the country, especially areas not under government control, remained grave.

The human rights section of UNAMSIL, under the general guidance of OHCHR, identified human rights issues relevant to the humanitarian community and the UN agencies active in Sierra Leone. The section, in collaboration with UN agencies and NGOs, established a Sierra Leone human rights committee, which provided a forum for consultations and the exchange of ideas and information between human rights and humanitarian actors, and provided human rights training for law enforcement agencies, new UNAMSIL peacekeepers, military observers and civilian police. It provided support on the ground to the commitment of OHCHR to assist the establishment of a national human rights commission and a truth and reconciliation commission.

OHCHR provided technical assistance to the Government in drafting the Act to establish the Truth and Reconciliation Commission. According to the Act, the Commission should provide an impartial historical record of violations and abuses of human rights and international humanitarian law related to the conflict, address impunity and respond to the needs of victims. It should aim to promote healing and reconciliation and prevent a repetition of the violations and abuses. Accordingly, OHCHR had developed a project for the preparatory phase of the Commission. OHCHR and UNAMSIL jointly organized an international workshop on the Commission (Freetown, 16-17 November). Because of the renewal of hostilities in May, endeavours to establish the national human rights commission were temporarily suspended. The process resumed with the holding of the workshop on the establishment of that commission (15-16 December).

The High Commissioner concluded that the needs of Sierra Leone called for an enormous programme of international support and assistance. OHCHR would continue to assist in building national capacities in the areas of human rights, the rule of law and democracy. It would provide technical assistance for the establishment of the truth and reconciliation and national human rights commissions; capacity-building through training for law enforcement authorities; support for the local human rights community; and programmes to rehabilitate war victims, especially women and children.

(For political details, see p. 189.)

Sudan

Note by Secretariat. An April note by the Secretariat [E/CN.4/2000/36] summarized information contained in a draft report of Special Rapporteur Leonardo Franco (Argentina), who, owing to an emergency, had not been able to finalize his report to the Commission.

The Special Rapporteur visited the Sudan (19 February–3 March) to examine with the authorities the new Constitution and any new legislation adopted; to look into the implications of a recent declaration of a state of emergency; and to assess progress made by the recently established Committee for the Eradication of Abductions of Women and Children (CEAWC). In Khartoum, he observed signs of greater political dialogue and the enjoyment of a broader degree of the freedoms of expression, press and assembly, which was attributed to changes in the balance of power within the official party. Despite the new climate, the Special Rapporteur expressed concern that the official party continued to maintain unrelenting control over all segments of society and was reluctant to open its institutions to a greater degree of democratic participation; the independence of the judiciary was often undermined; executive action had no system of control; and the fundamental institutions and legal system remained basically unchanged. The Special Rap-

porteur continued to receive, although in declining numbers, allegations of cases of torture, arbitrary detention and other human rights abuses. Consistent and undisputed evidence indicated that the war was being conducted in disregard of human rights and humanitarian law principles, and that violations were perpetrated by all parties, the greater portion by the Government. He was convinced that the oil exploitation issue, in Western Upper Nile, lay at the heart of the conflict and had exacerbated the war. The Special Rapporteur recommended that the use of oil facilities for military purposes come to an end. During the mission, he received expressions of concern at the deterioration of the human rights situation in the Nuba Mountains as a result of action by the parties to the conflict.

The Special Rapporteur stated that the creation of CEAWC was a concrete indication of the political will of the Government to deal with abductions and noted the Committee's courage in helping victims of abduction and forced labour. He felt that CEAWC's work would benefit from a clear stand by government officials, openly supporting it, which had not been the case so far. He recommended the promotion of an agreement between the Government and OHCHR.

In April [E/CN.4/2000/149], the Sudan commented on the Special Rapporteur's report. Among other things, it stated that abduction was neither a government policy nor a war strategy, but an ongoing tribal practice, and confirmed that the airstrip of the petroleum companies had never been used for military operations and that it had signed an agreement with OHCHR on 29 March.

Commission action. On 18 April [res. 2000/27], by a vote of 28 to none, with 24 abstentions, the Commission welcomed the establishment in the Sudan of a Constitutional Court, the stipulation of basic human rights and freedoms in the Constitution, the creation of CEAWC, the release of political detainees, and efforts to improve freedom of expression, association, the press and assembly, to implement the right to education, and to address the problem of internally displaced persons. It expressed deep concern, however, at serious violations of human rights, fundamental freedoms and humanitarian law in the Sudan by all parties to the conflict. The parties were urged to respect and protect human rights, fundamental freedoms and international humanitarian law; stop the use of weapons; grant safe and unhindered access to international agencies and humanitarian organizations; cooperate with the peace efforts of the Intergovernmental Authority on Development; and not use children under the age of 18 as soldiers and refrain from forced conscription. The Commission called on the Government to comply with its obligations under international human rights instruments to which it was a party; ensure the rule of law; conform its national legislation with the instruments to which the Sudan was a party; end and prevent acts of torture and cruel, inhuman or degrading treatment and ensure that all accused persons were held in ordinary custody and received fair trials; improve the appeal procedures in the judiciary; investigate reports of the abduction of women and children; make further efforts to address the problem of internally displaced persons; end the aerial bombardment of civilians; ensure respect for freedom of opinion, expression, thought, conscience and religion, as well as freedom of association and assembly; and comply with the commitment made to the Special Representative of the Secretary-General for Children and Armed Conflict not to recruit children under the age of 18 as soldiers [YUN 1998, p. 711].

The Commission decided to extend the Special Rapporteur's mandate for an additional year and asked him to submit an interim report to the General Assembly in 2000 and to report to the Commission in 2001, applying a gender perspective. The Commission asked the Secretary-General to assist the Special Rapporteur. Noting the accord signed between the Government and OHCHR on 29 March, the Commission requested them to continue consultations to establish a permanent representation of the High Commissioner in the Sudan.

The Economic and Social Council endorsed the Commission's decision and its request to the Special Rapporteur on 28 July (**decision 2000/258**).

Interim report of Special Rapporteur. In September, the Secretary-General transmitted the Special Rapporteur's interim report [A/55/374].

Military hostilities had undergone a dramatic escalation, and parties to the conflict continued to commit ceasefire violations on an unprecedented level, taking a heavy toll on human life and causing much suffering, including greater forced displacement. The Government had continued its systematic policy of bombing civilians and civilian installations. Despite the existence of a more favourable political environment, the Special Rapporteur continued to receive reports of arbitrary execution, torture, arbitrary detention, attempts against the freedom of the press and other human rights violations. He stressed the need to guarantee the independence of the judiciary and to ensure the control of the security organs and the existence of a system of checks and balances. Although the state of emergency declared on 12 December 1999 had not been fol-

lowed by large-scale measures against human rights, patterns adversely affecting human rights continued; thus, the Special Rapporteur called on the Government to lift the state of emergency.

GENERAL ASSEMBLY ACTION

On 4 December [meeting 81], the General Assembly, on the recommendation of the Third Committee [A/55/602/Add.3], adopted **resolution 55/116** by recorded vote (85-32-49) [agenda item 114 (c)].

Situation of human rights in the Sudan

The General Assembly,

Reaffirming that all Member States have an obligation to promote and protect human rights and fundamental freedoms as stated in the Charter of the United Nations, the Universal Declaration of Human Rights, the International Covenants on Human Rights and other applicable human rights instruments and to fulfil the obligations that they have undertaken under the various international instruments in this field,

Mindful that the Sudan is a party to the International Covenant on Civil and Political Rights, the International Covenant on Economic, Social and Cultural Rights, the Convention on the Rights of the Child, the African Charter on Human and Peoples' Rights and the Geneva Conventions of 12 August 1949,

Recalling its previous resolutions on the situation of human rights in the Sudan, and taking note of Commission on Human Rights resolution 2000/27 of 18 April 2000,

Aware of the urgent need for the Government of the Sudan to implement effective additional measures in the field of human rights and humanitarian relief in order to protect the civilian population from the effects of armed conflicts,

Expressing its firm belief that progress towards a peaceful settlement of the conflict in southern Sudan within the peace initiative of the Intergovernmental Authority on Development will contribute greatly to the creation of a better environment to encourage respect for human rights in the Sudan,

Condemning the murder of four Sudanese relief workers in April 1999 while in the custody of the Sudan People's Liberation Army/Movement,

1. *Welcomes:*

(a) The interim report of the Special Rapporteur of the Commission on Human Rights on the situation of human rights in the Sudan;

(b) The visit by the Special Rapporteur to the Sudan in February and March 2000 at the invitation of the Government of the Sudan and the very good cooperation extended by the Government in this regard, as well as the stated willingness of the Government to continue to cooperate with the Special Rapporteur;

(c) The signing of the agreement of 29 March 2000 between the Government of the Sudan and the Office of the United Nations High Commissioner for Human Rights;

(d) The activities of the Committee for the Eradication of Abduction of Women and Children as a constructive response on the part of the Government of the Sudan, the cooperation extended to the Committee by the local communities and the support of the international community and non-governmental organizations;

(e) The expressed commitment of the Government of the Sudan to respect and promote human rights and the rule of law and its expressed commitment to a process of democratization with a view to establishing a representative and accountable government, reflecting the aspirations of the people of the Sudan;

(f) Recent additional efforts by the Government of the Sudan to improve freedom of expression, association, the press and assembly, in particular the adoption of the Political Organization Act of 2000, and the announcement relating to the creation of a high commission to review the law on public order;

(g) The stipulation of basic human rights and freedoms in the Constitution of the Sudan and the establishment of the Constitutional Court, which has been in operation since April 1999;

(h) The efforts to implement the right to education;

(i) The renewed invitation extended by the Government of the Sudan to the Special Rapporteur of the Commission on Human Rights on religious intolerance and the efforts of the Government of the Sudan to promulgate a new law on religious liberties and activities after an open and transparent process of consultation with high representatives of all religions;

(j) Leniency measures taken by the Government of the Sudan, which led to the release of a large number of imprisoned women;

(k) The release of political prisoners and the measures taken to allow the return of exiled opposition members;

(l) The recent shelter given by the Sudan to new groups of refugees;

(m) The commitments undertaken by the Sudan People's Liberation Army/Movement during the visit to Rumbek, southern Sudan, of the Executive Director of the United Nations Children's Fund, not to recruit into its armed forces children under the age of eighteen and to demobilize all child soldiers still remaining in the military and hand them over to the competent civil authorities for reintegration;

(n) The convening of the fourth meeting of the Technical Committee on Humanitarian Assistance at Geneva on 2 and 3 November 2000, attended by delegations of the Government of the Sudan, the Sudan People's Liberation Army/Movement and the United Nations, and its final communiqué;

(o) The repeated statements by the Government of the Sudan in favour of a global, lasting and effectively monitored ceasefire in southern Sudan;

2. *Expresses its deep concern:*

(a) At the impact of the current armed conflict, worsened by the breakdown of the ceasefire in June 2000 and by the upsurge of armed confrontations, on the situation of human rights and its adverse effects on the civilian population, in particular women and children, and the continuing serious violations of human rights and international humanitarian law by all parties, in particular:

  (i) The occurrence of cases of summary or arbitrary execution resulting from conflict between members of the armed forces and their allies and armed insurgent groups within the country, including the Sudan People's Liberation Army/Movement;

  (ii) The occurrence, within the framework of the conflict in southern Sudan, of cases of enforced or involuntary disappearance, the use of children as soldiers and combatants, forced conscription, forced displacement of populations, arbitrary detention, torture and ill-treatment of civilians;

  (iii) The abduction of women and children to be subjected to forced labour or similar conditions;

  (iv) The indiscriminate aerial bombardments, which seriously and recurrently affect civilian populations and installations, in particular the bombings of schools and hospitals, as well as the use of civilian premises for military purposes;

  (v) The use of weapons, including indiscriminate artillery shelling and landmines, against the civilian population;

  (vi) The conditions imposed by the Sudan People's Liberation Army/Movement on humanitarian organizations working in southern Sudan, which have seriously affected their safety and led to the withdrawal of many of them, with potentially grave consequences for the already endangered situation of thousands of people living in areas under its control;

  (vii) The difficulties encountered by United Nations and humanitarian staff in carrying out their mandate because of harassment, indiscriminate aerial bombings and the reopening of hostilities;

(b) At continuing violations of human rights in areas under the control of the Government of the Sudan, in particular:

  (i) Precarious conditions of detention, frequent use of torture, arbitrary detentions, interrogations, and violations of human rights by the security organs;

  (ii) Acts of intimidation and harassment against the civilian population;

  (iii) Restrictions on freedom of religion, as well as the obstacles remaining to the freedom of expression, association and peaceful assembly;

  (iv) Information that all means of avoiding the execution of severe, inhuman punishments have not been fully utilized;

3. *Urges* all parties to the continuing conflict in the Sudan:

(a) To work immediately to put in place a global, lasting and effectively monitored ceasefire as a first necessary step to a negotiated settlement to the conflict;

(b) To respect and protect human rights and fundamental freedoms, to respect fully international humanitarian law, thereby facilitating the voluntary return, repatriation and reintegration of refugees and internally displaced persons to their homes, and to ensure that those responsible for violations of human rights and international humanitarian law are brought to justice;

(c) To stop immediately the use of weapons, including indiscriminate artillery shelling and landmines, in particular by the Sudan People's Liberation Army/Movement, against the civilian population, which runs counter to principles of international humanitarian law;

(d) To stop attacks on sites that usually have a significant presence of children as well as during the

"days of tranquillity" which had been agreed upon for the purpose of ensuring peaceful polio vaccination campaigns;

(e) To stop immediately the use of civilian premises for military purposes, in particular by the Sudan People's Liberation Army/Movement, particularly sites that usually have a significant presence of children;

(f) To grant full, safe and unhindered access to international agencies and humanitarian organizations so as to facilitate by all means possible the delivery of humanitarian assistance, in conformity with international humanitarian law, to all civilians in need of protection and assistance, in particular in Bahr el-Ghazal, the Nuba Mountains, the Western Upper Nile and areas in need throughout the country, and to continue to cooperate in this regard with the Office for the Coordination of Humanitarian Affairs of the Secretariat and Operation Lifeline Sudan in the delivery of such assistance, and urges the Sudan People's Liberation Army/Movement to resume negotiations as soon as possible with a view to the withdrawal of the conditions imposed on the work of international agencies and humanitarian organizations;

(g) In particular the Sudan People's Liberation Army/Movement, not to misappropriate humanitarian assistance;

(h) To continue to cooperate with the peace efforts of the Intergovernmental Authority on Development, and, in this context, urges the Sudan People's Liberation Army/Movement to commit itself to a permanent ceasefire;

(i) Not to use or recruit children under the age of eighteen as soldiers, and urges the Sudan People's Liberation Army/Movement not to use or recruit children under the age of eighteen as soldiers and to refrain from the practice of forced conscription;

(j) To fulfil their commitments concerning the protection of children affected by war, including their commitments to cease the use of anti-personnel landmines, the abduction and exploitation of children and the recruitment of children by the Sudan People's Liberation Army/Movement as soldiers, to advance the demobilization and reintegration of child soldiers, and to ensure access to displaced and unaccompanied minors;

(k) To allow an independent investigation of the case of the four Sudanese nationals who were abducted on 18 February 1999 while travelling with a team from the International Committee of the Red Cross on a humanitarian mission and subsequently killed while in the custody of the Sudan People's Liberation Army/Movement, and urges the Sudan People's Liberation Army/Movement to return the bodies to their families;

4. *Calls upon* the Government of the Sudan:

(a) To comply fully with its obligations under the international human rights instruments to which the Sudan is a party and to promote and protect human rights and fundamental freedoms, as well as to respect its obligations under international humanitarian law;

(b) To strengthen its efforts to ensure the rule of law by bringing legislation into line with the Constitution and by the effective practice of law enforcement;

(c) To continue its efforts to bring its national legislation into conformity with the applicable international human rights instruments to which the Sudan is a party and to ensure that all individuals in its territory enjoy fully the rights recognized in those instruments;

(d) To take all effective measures to prevent and end all acts of torture and cruel, inhuman or degrading treatment, to ensure that all accused persons are held in ordinary custody and receive prompt, just and fair trials under internationally recognized standards, to investigate all reported human rights violations, including acts of torture, brought to its attention and to prosecute those responsible for the violations;

(e) To seriously consider ratifying, as a matter of priority, the Convention against Torture and Other Cruel, Inhuman or Degrading Treatment or Punishment;

(f) To make sure that all means of avoiding the execution of severe, inhuman punishments are fully utilized;

(g) To reinforce the action taken to prevent and stop abductions of women and children within the framework of the conflict in southern Sudan, to bring to trial any persons suspected of supporting or participating in such activities and not cooperating with the efforts of the Committee for the Eradication of Abduction of Women and Children in addressing and preventing those activities, to facilitate the safe return of affected children to their families as a matter of priority and to take further measures, in particular through the Committee, with which all concerned have the responsibility and the duty to cooperate;

(h) To stop definitively the indiscriminate aerial bombardment of civilian and humanitarian targets, which runs counter to fundamental principles of human rights and humanitarian law;

(i) To make further efforts to address effectively the growing problem of internally displaced persons, whose number has increased, including ensuring their right to effective protection and assistance;

(j) To continue to implement its commitment to the democratization process and the rule of law and to create, in this context, conditions that would allow for a democratization process that is genuine and wholly reflects the aspirations of the people of the country and ensures their full participation;

(k) To continue efforts to implement the commitment made to the Special Representative of the Secretary-General for Children and Armed Conflict not to recruit children under the age of eighteen as soldiers;

(l) To implement the Standard Minimum Rules for the Treatment of Prisoners and to raise the age of criminal responsibility for children in order to take into account the observations of the Committee on the Rights of the Child;

5. *Encourages* the Government of the Sudan to continue to pursue its dialogue with the Office of the United Nations High Commissioner for Human Rights on the basis of the agreement of 29 March 2000 between the Government and the High Commissioner, with a view to establishing a permanent representation of the High Commissioner;

6. *Encourages* the Office of the High Commissioner to continue to take into consideration requests for assistance by the Government of the Sudan, inter alia, with a view to establishing a permanent representation of the High Commissioner as a matter of priority;

7. *Calls upon* the international community to expand its support for activities, in particular those of the Committee for the Eradication of Abduction of Women and Children, aimed at improving respect for human rights and humanitarian law during the conflict;

8. *Decides* to continue its consideration of the situation of human rights in the Sudan at its fifty-sixth session, under the item entitled "Human rights questions", in the light of further elements provided by the Commission on Human Rights.

RECORDED VOTE ON RESOLUTION 55/116:

In favour: Albania, Andorra, Angola, Antigua and Barbuda, Argentina, Armenia, Australia, Austria, Bahamas, Barbados, Belgium, Belize, Bolivia, Brazil, Bulgaria, Canada, Chile, Colombia, Costa Rica, Croatia, Cyprus, Czech Republic, Denmark, Dominica, Dominican Republic, Ecuador, El Salvador, Estonia, Finland, France, Germany, Greece, Grenada, Guatemala, Guyana, Haiti, Hungary, Iceland, Ireland, Israel, Italy, Japan, Kazakhstan, Latvia, Liechtenstein, Lithuania, Luxembourg, Malta, Mauritius, Mexico, Monaco, Mongolia, Namibia, Nauru, Netherlands, New Zealand, Nicaragua, Norway, Panama, Papua New Guinea, Paraguay, Peru, Poland, Portugal, Republic of Korea, Republic of Moldova, Romania, Samoa, San Marino, Sao Tome and Principe, Slovakia, Slovenia, Solomon Islands, South Africa, Spain, Sweden, Tajikistan, The former Yugoslav Republic of Macedonia, Trinidad and Tobago, United Kingdom, Uruguay, Vanuatu, Venezuela, Yugoslavia, Zimbabwe.

Against: Algeria, Bahrain, Chad, China, Comoros, Cuba, Democratic People's Republic of Korea, Democratic Republic of the Congo, Djibouti, Egypt, Gambia, India, Indonesia, Iran, Jordan, Kuwait, Lao People's Democratic Republic, Lebanon, Libyan Arab Jamahiriya, Mauritania, Morocco, Myanmar, Oman, Pakistan, Qatar, Saudi Arabia, Sudan, Syrian Arab Republic, Togo, Tunisia, United Arab Emirates, Viet Nam.

Abstaining: Azerbaijan, Bangladesh, Belarus, Benin, Bhutan, Botswana, Brunei Darussalam, Burkina Faso, Burundi, Cambodia, Cameroon, Cape Verde, Congo, Côte d'Ivoire, Ethiopia, Fiji, Georgia, Ghana, Guinea, Honduras, Jamaica, Kenya, Lesotho, Madagascar, Malawi, Malaysia, Maldives, Mali, Marshall Islands, Micronesia, Mozambique, Nepal, Nigeria, Palau, Philippines, Russian Federation, Rwanda, Saint Lucia, Senegal, Sierra Leone, Singapore, Sri Lanka, Suriname, Swaziland, Thailand, Uganda, Ukraine, United Republic of Tanzania, United States.

On 28 December [E/CN.4/2001/28], Gerhart Baum (Germany) was appointed Special Rapporteur on the situation of human rights in the Sudan, following the resignation of Mr. Franco.

Togo

Note by Secretary-General. A July note by the Secretary-General [E/CN.4/Sub.2/2000/8], recalling Togo's agreement to the creation of an international commission of inquiry to verify the truth of an Amnesty International report alleging that hundreds of extrajudicial executions and other human rights violations had taken place in the country in 1998 [YUN 1999, p. 702], stated that on 7 June, the establishment of the three-member Commission, under the auspices of OAU and the United Nations, had been announced.

Commission of Inquiry. The International Commission of Inquiry for Togo held three meetings in Geneva (31 July–4 August, 18-22 September and 15-22 December) [E/CN.4/2001/134]. During those meetings, the Commission adopted its rules of procedure, exchanged views with several organizations and with permanent missions to the UN Office at Geneva, heard delegations of the Government of Togo and Amnesty International, and prepared for its field mission (Togo, 11-19 November and 4-12 December; Benin (Cotonou and the Mono region on the Togolese border), 19 November–2 December; and Ghana, 2-4 December). The field mission enabled the Commission to access information sources, collect testimony and documents concerning the allegations and conduct on-site visits.

Having rejected Amnesty International's allegations [YUN 1999, p. 702] as false, Togo brought judicial proceedings against the organization's Secretary-General and individuals suspected of having cooperated with its inquiry. The legal proceedings were suspended and protection guaranteed for potential Commission witnesses against any legal proceedings or reprisals subsequent to the field mission.

The Commission concluded that a systematic pattern of human rights violations existed in Togo in 1998 and was convinced that the allegations of extrajudicial executions should be given due consideration. In the main, those singled out for execution had been members of opposition parties, but in some cases persons arrested for offences under ordinary law had also been executed. Various accounts seemed to indicate that the perpetrators were associated with the security forces, the gendarmerie and the militias that operated in tandem with the authorities. In addition to extrajudicial, summary and arbitrary executions, they had engaged in torture and ill-treatment of detainees, and the rape and abduction of women. Armed militiamen closely linked to the authorities were said to rape rural women in the presence of their husbands and abduct women and hand them over to other men for payment. In the course of those night-time raids, the militiamen also robbed their victims. Although apprised of the allegations, the gendarmerie and the local authorities had been unable to stop the crimes. Regarding the establishment of responsibilities, the Commission was of the opinion that a judicial inquiry at the national level was the sole means of identifying the individuals responsible. As to allegations that bodies had been discovered by fishermen on the high seas, defined by them as an offshore area between 10 and 20 kilometres from the coast, a number of accounts substantiated the reports. However, the divergent estimates of the number of bodies seen by fishermen did not permit the Commission either to confirm or deny an exact number. Nor could it confirm or deny, on the basis of current information, allegations that aircraft had been used to dump bodies on the high seas.

The Commission recommended the publication of its report and the appointment of another team of experts to verify technical data concerning the operation of aircraft used by the Togolese armed forces, the computerized records of flights at the Lomé-Tonkoin airport in 1998, and the trajectories of bodies in the territorial sea adjacent to the coasts of Togo and Benin. It recommended that the OAU and UN Secretaries-General appoint a team of forensic scientists to exhume and examine bodies reportedly buried in Togo and Benin. Regarding the protection of witnesses who had cooperated in its inquiries, the Commission proposed that Member States and the relevant international organizations support OHCHR to enable it to follow up the situation of the witnesses. It recommended the appointment of a special rapporteur on the situation of human rights in Togo and suggested that the Special Rapporteurs of the Commission on Human Rights and the African Commission on Human and Peoples' Rights concerned, respectively, with extrajudicial, summary and arbitrary executions, torture and violence against women should visit Togo periodically. The Government of Togo was urged to begin, as soon as possible, a criminal inquiry through the establishment of a special team of judges, and adopt legislative and other measures to punish and prevent such violations.

Annexed to the Commission's report was a statement by the Subcommission Chairman made in 1999 [YUN 1999, p. 702] and the Commission's rules of procedure.

Americas

Colombia

Commission action. The Commission Chairperson, in a 28 April statement [E/2000/23], welcomed the willingness of the Government of Colombia to engage in constructive peace talks with the main guerrilla groups to achieve a sustainable peace, and the announcement of a promised integrated plan on human rights. Having taken note of the approval of the Military Penal Code reform bill by the Congress of Colombia, the Commission urged the Government to overcome constitutional impediments to its entry into force. The Commission strongly condemned all acts of terrorism and violation of international humanitarian law committed by guerrilla groups, deplored the persistence of worrying levels of impunity in cases of serious crimes, remained deeply concerned about the increase in the number of internally displaced persons and

noted with concern the effects of violence in the country, particularly those victimizing minority groups. It asked the High Commissioner to report in 2001.

Report of High Commissioner. A report of the High Commissioner, which was based on information collected by OHCHR in Bogotá, described the human rights situation in Colombia in 2000 [E/CN.4/2001/15]. The High Commissioner visited the country (3-4 December) to verify the human rights situation and to support the work and highlight the role of the Bogotá Office and its staff.

During the year, the Office received 1,017 complaints: 108 communications were sent to the authorities and 65 field visits were made by the Office to various parts of the country that were of special concern. The Office published an updated compilation of international human rights and humanitarian law recommendations applicable to the country and two further compilations were produced, one on international human rights and humanitarian law instruments and international criminal law, the other on international and national jurisprudence and doctrine. Regarding technical assistance and advisory services, the Office increased its dialogue and developed projects with institutions responsible for protecting and promoting human rights and with NGOs and academic institutions. The Office participated in seminars, forums, workshops and conferences and held two regional workshops with NGOs.

The human rights situation continued to deteriorate in 2000, with violations qualifying as grave, massive and systematic. The main rights affected were the right to life and the rights to inviolability, freedom and security of the person. Members of the paramilitary groups were the principal violators. Violations of the right to life took the form of massacres or individual, selective killings. Although a high percentage of the executions appeared to be politically motivated, in some cases the characteristic traits of the practice known as social cleansing were identifiable. The majority of the massacres were committed during paramilitary raids, many of which resulted in the forced displacement of local inhabitants. Reports were also received of extrajudicial executions, allegedly by members of the security forces. In some areas, paramilitaries systematically carried out social cleansing against prostitutes, homosexuals, criminals, drug addicts, street children and informal garbage collectors, among others. Threats received from paramilitary groups by human rights NGOs, judiciary officials, journalists, trade unionists, religious ministers, university professors and students were closely linked to violations of the right to life. Breaches of international humanitarian law were recurrent, massive and systematic, many of them forming part of a general assault on the population.

Regarding the Government's priorities, protection of human rights and compliance with international recommendations were neither accorded the importance nor pursued with the persistence or effectiveness that the situation required. In view of the Government's weak and inconsistent commitment to counter paramilitary groups, the phenomenon grew in extent and strength. Government instruments against the paramilitary groups had proved ineffective. The High Commissioner remained concerned at impunity, and the administration of justice was again affected by security conditions in which members of the judiciary performed their work; resource shortages; the weakening of institutions; and the lack of access to certain regions of the country. Human rights defenders continued to work under very difficult conditions. The High Commissioner was also concerned by the absence of effective State control of penal establishments, the lack of a comprehensive prison policy that safeguarded inmates' rights, the abuse of pre-trial detention and the limits on the exercise of habeas corpus. Forced displacement continued to increase and extend into new areas. Although noteworthy efforts were made to assist populations at risk and vulnerable groups, the Ministry of the Interior's Protection Programme suffered from financial, administrative and structural shortcomings. The State did not accord sufficient attention to economic, social and cultural rights. Violence against minors increased and women suffered from discrimination, domestic violence, sexual abuse and trafficking.

The High Commissioner recommended that the Government strengthen its cooperation with OHCHR; find a negotiated solution to the armed conflict; ensure the respect and guarantee of human rights; prevent human rights violations or infringement of international humanitarian law from being tried in military criminal courts; focus economic and social policies on the most disadvantaged; and guarantee human rights education. Colombia was urged to give effect to the enjoyment and exercise of fundamental rights and freedoms; cease impunity; adopt a crime policy in keeping with the principles of rights-based criminal law; combat paramilitarism and dismantle it; and combat inequality between men and women. Parties to the conflict were called on to abide strictly and unconditionally by the prin-

ciples and standards of international humanitarian law.

Communication. Commenting on the High Commissioner's report, Colombia charged, among other things, that it was unbalanced, went beyond OHCHR's terms of reference and ignored what had been accomplished despite the conflict [E/CN.4/2001/139].

Cuba

Commission action. On 18 April [res. 2000/25], by a roll-call vote of 21 to 18, with 14 abstentions, the Commission called on the Government of Cuba to ensure respect for human rights and fundamental freedoms. Noting certain measures taken to enhance freedom of religion, the Commission called on Cuban authorities to continue to take action in that regard and expressed the hope that further positive steps would be taken with regard to all human rights and fundamental freedoms. It expressed concern about the continued repression of political opposition members and about the detention of dissidents, including the members of the Internal Dissidence Working Group, and called on the Government to release those imprisoned for peacefully expressing their political, religious and social views and for exercising their rights to full and equal participation in public affairs. Cuba was called on to consider acceding to human rights instruments to which it was not a party, to open a dialogue with the political opposition and to cooperate with other mechanisms of the Commission. It recommended that the Government take advantage of the technical cooperation programmes of OHCHR.

Asia and the Pacific

Afghanistan

Commission action. On 18 April [res. 2000/18], the Commission, noting with deep concern the continuing pattern of human rights violations in Afghanistan, condemned the widespread violations and abuses of human rights and humanitarian law, the continuing grave human rights violations of women and girls, the frequent practice of arbitrary arrest and detention and of summary trials, which had resulted in summary executions, and recent violations by the Taliban in Kandahar of UN immunity. It urged all Afghan parties to respect the human rights and fundamental freedoms of all; cease hostilities; reaffirm publicly their commitment to international human rights and principles; protect civilians; provide effective remedies to victims of grave violations of human rights and accepted humanitarian rules and bring perpetrators to trial; fulfil their obligations regarding the safety of all personnel of diplomatic missions, the United Nations and other international organizations and NGOs; and repeal discriminatory legislation and other measures against women and girls. The Commission asked the parties to continue to cooperate with the Special Rapporteur. The Secretary-General was asked to ensure that the ongoing deployment of the civilian affairs observers in Afghanistan took place as soon as possible, security conditions permitting, and that gender issues were incorporated in their mission, and to ensure a gender perspective in the selection of the staff of the United Nations Special Mission to Afghanistan.

The Commission asked the High Commissioner to ensure a human rights presence to provide advice and human rights training to all Afghan parties, as well as to intergovernmental organizations and NGOs. It decided to extend the Special Rapporteur's mandate for another year, and asked him to report to the General Assembly in 2000 and to the Commission in 2001. The Secretary-General was asked to assist him and to consider his recommendations in developing UN activities in Afghanistan.

On 28 July, the Economic and Social Council approved the Commission's requests to the Secretary-General and the High Commissioner, and endorsed the Special Rapporteur's extension and the Commission's requests to him (**decision 2000/251**).

Reports of Special Rapporteur. Special Rapporteur Kamal Hossain (Bangladesh) visited Iran, where he interviewed Afghan refugees and met with high-ranking government officials [A/55/346].

The Special Rapporteur outlined developments from April to July aimed at promoting the peace process and described the resumption of the conflict from June to August as marked by fierce fighting and significant civilian displacement, noting that the combination of war, drought and displacement continued to take a terrible toll on Afghans and their livelihoods and there was an urgent need for humanitarian assistance (see pp. 271 and 864). Some 1.4 million Afghan refugees were in Iran and a similar number in Pakistan, even after the voluntary repatriation from both countries of a significant number (see p. 1162).

In July, reports were received of systematic human rights violations, including allegations of the summary execution of prisoners in Taliban-held areas in northern Afghanistan. The Special

Rapporteur obtained first-hand information regarding harsh conditions of detention, which also included the practice of torture. Afghanistan was one of the most heavily mined countries in the world. Landmines maimed and killed people but also denied people access to farmland, water, pasture, roads and buildings, said the Special Rapporteur. They were also an obstacle to post-conflict rehabilitation, the delivery of aid programmes, food security, sustainable livelihoods, and the return of refugees and internally displaced persons to their homes. On 5 August, gunmen shot and killed seven Afghans working in the western part of the country for the UN-supported mine-action agency. The Taliban militia, which controlled 90 per cent of Afghanistan, traded accusations with the opposition over who had carried out the killings. The Special Rapporteur described the impact of Taliban edicts and the existing legal regime on the human rights situation in Afghanistan. According to some reports, there had been some relaxation of the strict ban on female education imposed by previous edicts of the Taliban authorities. On 8 March, a formal public celebration of International Women's Day was held in Kabul. The statute on the activities of the United Nations in Afghanistan, promulgated by the Taliban around 15 August, introduced substantial restrictions on the UN and specialized agency operations that provided humanitarian, economic, rehabilitation and development assistance.

In a later report [E/CN.4/2001/43], the Special Rapporteur stated that an agreement signed by the Taliban and the United Front was the first time the two warring sides had committed themselves in writing to a process of dialogue, which would be held under the Secretary-General's good offices (see p. 266).

On 20 December, Hezb-e-Wahdat forces affiliated with the United Front took over an area in Bamian province (Yakawlang district) from the Taliban. Reliable sources reported widespread killings and displacement of innocent civilians. Of the estimated 90,000 inhabitants of Yakawlang district, approximately one third fled their homes.

The suffering of the Afghan people was compounded as the result of the country being used for various forms of cross-border criminal activity, including drug trafficking. Effective action was needed to prevent such activities. Regarding health, the impact of the ongoing conflict daily added victims, both through physical violence and mental stress. While some progress had been made in establishing community-based health and rehabilitation committees, activities were restricted to only some geographical regions and only a small proportion of the need even in the areas covered. Afghanistan had some of the worst education indicators in the world. Access was low at all levels, especially for girls but also for boys. The Taliban controlled all means of communication and had banned pictures. A number of positive developments signalled that severe restrictions on women's education and employment were slowly being reconsidered by the authorities. The level of vulnerability of rural areas remained of major concern. The impact of the war on the economic infrastructure had been devastating, transport and communication facilities were derelict and there were few job opportunities outside the subsistence economy on the one hand and the criminalized economy on the other. The report observed that there was strong consensus in Afghanistan on the need for the United Nations to upgrade and intensify its political engagement and peacemaking efforts.

(For political details, see p. 262.)

(For political details, see p. 262.)

GENERAL ASSEMBLY ACTION

On 4 December [meeting 81], the General Assembly, on the recommendation of the Third Committee [A/55/602/Add.3], adopted **resolution 55/119** without vote [agenda item 114 (c)].

Question of human rights in Afghanistan

The General Assembly,

Guided by the Charter of the United Nations, the Universal Declaration of Human Rights, the International Covenants on Human Rights and accepted humanitarian rules, as set out in the Geneva Conventions of 12 August 1949 and the Additional Protocols thereto, of 1977,

Reaffirming that all Member States have an obligation to promote and protect human rights and fundamental freedoms and to fulfil the obligations they have freely undertaken under the various international instruments,

Recalling that Afghanistan is a party to the Convention on the Prevention and Punishment of the Crime of Genocide, the International Covenant on Civil and Political Rights, the International Covenant on Economic, Social and Cultural Rights, the Convention against Torture and Other Cruel, Inhuman or Degrading Treatment or Punishment, the Convention on the Rights of the Child and the Geneva Convention relative to the Protection of Civilian Persons in Time of War and that it has signed the Convention on the Elimination of All Forms of Discrimination against Women,

Recalling also all its relevant resolutions, as well as the resolutions and presidential statements of the Security Council, the decisions of the Economic and Social Council, the resolutions and decisions of the Commission on Human Rights and the resolutions of the Commission on the Status of Women,

Recalling further that the United Nations continues to play its central and impartial role in international efforts towards a peaceful resolution of the Afghan conflict, and encouraging all efforts at the national, regional and international levels aimed at finding a solution to the continuing conflict through a broad-based dialogue involving all concerned actors,

Expressing deep concern at the lack of reconstruction in Afghanistan,

1. *Takes note with appreciation* of the interim report of the Special Rapporteur of the Commission on Human Rights on the situation of human rights in Afghanistan and of the conclusions and recommendations contained therein, and encourages the Special Rapporteur to continue to fulfil his mandate;

2. *Strongly condemns* the mass killings and systematic human rights violations perpetrated against civilians and prisoners of war, including in the areas of Mazar-e-Sharif and Bamian, and notes with alarm the resumption of the wider conflict by the Taliban during the past summer, especially in the Taloqan area, resulting in the massive, forced displacement of the civilian population, in particular of women and children;

3. *Condemns* the widespread violations and abuses of human rights and international humanitarian law, including the right to life, liberty and security of person, freedom from torture and from other forms of cruel, inhuman or degrading treatment or punishment, freedom of opinion, expression, religion, association and movement, the forced or compulsory recruitment of children for use in armed conflict and, in particular, the grave human rights violations committed against women and girls;

4. *Reiterates its condemnation* of the killings of Iranian diplomats and the correspondent of the Islamic Republic News Agency by the Taliban, which constituted flagrant violations of established international law, as well as the attacks on and killings of United Nations personnel in Taliban-held territories of Afghanistan, and calls upon the Taliban to fulfil their stated commitment to cooperate in urgent investigations of these heinous crimes with a view to bringing to justice those responsible;

5. *Notes with deep concern:*

(a) The persisting pattern of human rights violations in Afghanistan;

(b) The continuing and substantiated reports of human rights violations against women and girls, including all forms of discrimination against them, notably in areas under the control of the Taliban;

(c) The intensification of armed hostilities in Afghanistan and the complex nature of the conflict, including its ethnic, religious and political aspects, which have resulted in extensive human suffering and forced displacement, inter alia, on the grounds of ethnicity;

(d) The continued displacement of millions of Afghan refugees to the Islamic Republic of Iran, Pakistan, Tajikistan and other countries;

(e) The deliberate destruction of life-sustaining activities;

(f) The substantial restrictions introduced by the Taliban authorities on the operations of the United Nations and the specialized agencies that provide assistance in Afghanistan, and notes the negative impact that those restrictions have on providing women, children, in particular girls, and other most vulnerable groups with assistance;

6. *Also notes with deep concern* the sharp deterioration of the humanitarian situation in many areas of Afghanistan, including the Shamali Plains, the Panjshir Valley and the north-east, and calls for the full imple-

mentation of the agreement on the security of United Nations personnel in Afghanistan;

7. *Urges* all States to respect the sovereignty, independence, territorial integrity and national unity of Afghanistan, to refrain from interfering in its internal affairs and to end immediately the supply of arms, ammunition, military equipment, including fuel for military purposes where identifiable, training or any other military support, including the provision of foreign military personnel, to all parties to the conflict;

8. *Stresses* the need for national reconciliation and for the establishment of the rule of law, good governance and democracy in Afghanistan and, concurrently, the need for extensive rehabilitation and reconstruction;

9. *Urges* all the Afghan parties:

(a) To respect fully all human rights and fundamental freedoms, regardless of gender, ethnicity or religion, in accordance with international human rights instruments;

(b) To cease hostilities immediately, to work and cooperate fully with the Personal Representative of the Secretary-General for Afghanistan and the United Nations Special Mission to Afghanistan with a view to achieving a ceasefire and to implement the Tashkent Declaration on Fundamental Principles for a Peaceful Settlement of the Conflict in Afghanistan of 19 July 1999, thus laying the foundation for a comprehensive political solution leading to the voluntary return of displaced persons to their homes in safety and with dignity and to the establishment of a broad-based, multiethnic, fully representative Government through the full exercise of the Afghan people of the right to self-determination;

(c) To reaffirm publicly their commitment to international human rights and principles and to recognize, protect and promote all human rights and fundamental freedoms;

(d) To respect fully international humanitarian law, to protect civilians, to halt the use of weapons against the civilian population, to refrain from the wanton destruction of food crops and civilian property, in particular homes, to stop the laying of landmines, especially anti-personnel mines, to fulfil their duty to cooperate with the United Nations mine action programme and to protect its personnel, to prohibit conscripting or enlisting children or using them to participate in hostilities in violation of international law and to ensure the disarmament, demobilization and reintegration of children into society;

(e) To provide efficient and effective remedies to the victims of grave violations and abuses of human rights and of international humanitarian law and to bring the perpetrators to trial;

(f) To treat all suspects and convicted or detained persons in accordance with relevant international instruments and to refrain from arbitrary detention, including detention of civilian foreign nationals, and urges their captors to release them as well as non-criminal civilian prisoners;

10. *Demands* that all the Afghan parties fulfil their obligations regarding the safety of all personnel of diplomatic missions, the United Nations and other international organizations, as well as their premises in Afghanistan, and to cooperate fully and without discrimination on grounds of gender, nationality or religion with the United Nations and associated bodies and with other humanitarian organizations, agencies and non-governmental organizations;

11. *Urges* all the Afghan parties, in particular the Taliban, to bring to an end without delay all violations of the human rights of women and girls and to take urgent measures to ensure:

(a) The repeal of all legislative and other measures that discriminate against women and girls and those that impede the realization of all their human rights;

(b) The effective participation of women in civil, cultural, economic, political and social life throughout the country;

(c) Respect for the right of women to work and their reintegration into employment, including in the specialized agencies and human rights organizations;

(d) The equal right of women and girls to education without discrimination, the reopening of schools and the admission of women and girls to all levels of education;

(e) Respect for the equal right of women to security of person, and to ensure that those responsible for physical attacks on women are brought to justice;

(f) Respect for the freedom of movement of women;

(g) Respect for the effective and equal access of women and girls to the facilities necessary to protect their right to the highest attainable standard of physical and mental health;

12. *Takes note* of the report of the Special Rapporteur of the Commission on Human Rights on violence against women, its causes and consequences, on her mission to Afghanistan;

13. *Urges* all Afghan parties to respect all international human rights instruments, including the Convention on the Elimination of All Forms of Discrimination against Women, to bring to an end without delay all violations of the human rights of women and girls, to take urgent measures to ensure respect for all fundamental freedoms and to respect international humanitarian law with regard to the conduct of hostilities;

14. *Notes with appreciation* the activities carried out by the International Committee of the Red Cross, as well as by non-governmental organizations, throughout the territory of Afghanistan;

15. *Recalls* its invitation extended to the Secretary-General and the United Nations High Commissioner for Human Rights to proceed without delay to investigate fully reports of mass killings of prisoners of war and civilians, rape and cruel treatment in Afghanistan, expresses deep regret for the lack of cooperation by Afghan parties, calls upon the United Front and the Taliban to fulfil their stated commitment to cooperate with such investigations, and, noting the summary of the report on the investigations, expresses its deep regret to all the parties for the unsatisfactory results;

16. *Notes with grave concern* the recent reports of summary executions of prisoners in Taliban-held areas in the north of Afghanistan, which have been denied by the Taliban, and calls upon the Taliban to cooperate with the Special Rapporteur in fully investigating those allegations;

17. *Invites* the Secretary-General and the High Commissioner to ensure that the ongoing process of deployment of the civilian affairs observers in Afghanistan is completed as soon as possible and that gender is-

sues and the rights of children are fully taken into account in their mission;

18. *Appeals* to all States, organizations and programmes of the United Nations system, specialized agencies and other international organizations to provide humanitarian assistance to all in need, and urges all Afghan parties to ensure free, safe and unhindered access to all humanitarian personnel, as part of an overall effort to achieve peace;

19. *Expresses its deep concern* at reports of attacks on and looting of cultural artifacts in Afghanistan, emphasizes that all parties share the responsibility to protect their common heritage, and requests all Member States to take appropriate measures to prevent the looting of cultural artifacts and to ensure their return to Afghanistan;

20. *Urges* all the Afghan parties to extend their cooperation to the Commission on Human Rights and to all those special rapporteurs who are seeking invitations, and, in particular, calls upon the Taliban to accommodate the forthcoming visit of the Special Rapporteur of the Commission on Human Rights on the situation of human rights in Afghanistan;

21. *Requests* the Secretary-General to give all necessary assistance to the Special Rapporteur;

22. *Decides* to keep the situation of human rights in Afghanistan under consideration at its fifty-sixth session, in the light of additional elements provided by the Commission on Human Rights and the Economic and Social Council.

Cambodia

For information on the human rights situation in Cambodia, see p. 624.

China

On 18 April [E/2000/23], China made a motion that no action be taken on a draft text introduced in the Commission by the United States, which, among other things, called on China to ensure the observance of all human rights, improve the impartial administration of justice and the rule of law, release political prisoners, permit the peaceful exercise of the rights of freedom of religion or belief and of peaceful assembly, preserve and protect the cultural, ethnic, linguistic and religious identity of Tibetans and others, develop productive bilateral dialogues and cooperate with the Commission's thematic special rapporteurs and working groups. The motion was carried by a roll-call vote of 22 to 18, with 12 abstentions.

East Timor

International Commission of Inquiry. On 31 January [A/54/727-S/2000/65], the Secretary-General transmitted to the Security Council and General Assembly Presidents and to the Commission on Human Rights Chairperson Indonesia's response to the 1999 report of the International Commission of Inquiry (ICI) on East Timor [YUN 1999, p. 712]. Indonesia said that the report consisted of sweeping, uncorroborated allegations and was one-sided and selective in approach. In particular, it rejected the fact that the report held the Indonesian army responsible for the intimidation, terror, killings and other acts of violence in East Timor. Consequently, ICI's recommendation to establish an international human rights tribunal was totally unacceptable. Nevertheless, Indonesia considered it imperative that reports of human rights violations be investigated thoroughly; it had therefore established a National Commission of Inquiry on Human Rights Violations in East Timor, which had sent a fact-finding mission to the territory and had extended its cooperation to ICI.

On 18 February [S/2000/137], the Council informed the Secretary-General that it had taken note of the ICI report. It encouraged Indonesia to institute a swift, comprehensive, effective and transparent legal process in order to bring those responsible for human rights violations to justice, a key factor in ensuring reconciliation and stability in East Timor. It also reiterated its belief that the United Nations had a role to play in the process and encouraged the Secretary-General to consult with the Indonesian Government on any assistance it might need from the Organization in order to promote reconciliation and ensure future social and political stability.

Commission action. In a statement by its Chairperson, the Commission, on 25 April [E/2000/23], commending the enhancement of collaboration between the United Nations and the Government of Indonesia in human rights technical cooperation programmes, asked the High Commissioner to continue to provide assistance and advisory services in order to bring to justice the alleged perpetrators of violations of human rights and international humanitarian law in East Timor, including in the setting up of a special human rights court. It urged a rapid solution to the East Timorese refugee problem in West Timor and noted Indonesia's decision to set a deadline and take measures necessary for the refugees to express their choice freely. The Commission remained concerned at various obstacles to the voluntary repatriation of refugees, including intimidation and misinformation by remaining militias in refugee camps. The Government of Indonesia and the international community were asked to provide relief assistance to the refugees. The High Commissioner was asked to report to the General Assembly in 2000 (see next page) and to the Commission in 2001.

Reports of High Commissioner. In a March report [E/CN.4/2000/27], the High Commissioner stated that OHCHR was developing, with the Human Rights Office of the United Nations Transitional Administration in East Timor (UNTAET), technical cooperation programmes focusing on capacity-building and reconciliation and on ensuring the administration of justice and dealing with impunity. At the request of the Secretary-General's Special Representative, OHCHR was working with UNTAET to provide experts on truth commissions from three different countries to meet with various groups in East Timor to discuss the diverse forms truth commissions might take and examine how they functioned. The High Commissioner described action being taken by UNTAET to strengthen the capacity of East Timorese human rights organizations and associations. Developments relating to the individual accountability for human rights violations and bringing those responsible to justice included investigations into killings and rapes that occurred between January and October 1999; the establishment of a special panel to try crimes against humanity; efforts to put in place a forensic laboratory and mortuary; the pursuit of several different options for justice; the prospect of a truth commission; and the development of a position on justice and reconciliation.

In August [A/55/36], the High Commissioner noted that the Government of Indonesia had taken steps to investigate violations of human rights and international humanitarian law [YUN 1999, p. 707] and to bring those responsible to justice, including draft legislation to establish a human rights tribunal; the initiation of investigations into the East Timor violations; and the signing of a memorandum of understanding between Indonesia and UNTAET on cooperation in legal, judicial and human rights–related matters, dated 5 April. The High Commissioner had deployed a needs assessment mission to Indonesia (1-10 April) to develop a project of support to the administration of justice system for the prosecution of human rights violations. OHCHR conducted a preliminary mission to East Timor (13-15 April) to assess the manner in which it could respond to the needs of the UNTAET Human Rights Unit.

Following her visit to East Timor (5-7 August) and Indonesia (22-23 November) [E/CN.4/2001/37 & Corr.1], the High Commissioner updated information previously submitted. OHCHR was finalizing a human rights technical cooperation project with the UNTAET Human Rights Unit for implementation in 2001. An update of information from the Unit stated that, as at 14 December,

49 suspects were in pre-trial detention on suspicion of having committed serious crimes during 1999. The Serious Crimes Investigation Unit had reported that some five cases were being finalized. In addition, 11 indictments had been issued in relation to the murder of nine persons in Los Palos, and more indictments were being drafted and were expected to be issued in 2001. Trials before the Special Panel for Serious Crimes, to be composed of East Timorese and international judges, were expected to begin in 2001. Preparatory work to establish a commission for truth, reception and reconciliation was ongoing. The Human Rights Unit was involved in developing political institutions, the constitutional process, the institutions to protect human rights and an independent and strong civil society. Four district courts had been established in Dili, Baucau, Oecussi and Suai districts, and training of the judiciary was under way. The Human Rights Unit was also working with the Judicial Affairs Unit to develop a training programme for prison officials. UNTAET was planning to adopt regulations on the establishment of a defence force for East Timor, a law reform commission, a legal aid service and the administration of juvenile justice, and a press law. The Human Rights Unit had conducted activities to support the strengthening of civil society, particularly human rights organizations, and addressed the need for protection of particular vulnerable groups (ethnic and religious minorities), the security of East Timorese refugees returning from West Timor and violence against women.

(For political details, see p. 277.)

Iran

Commission action. On 18 April [res. 2000/28], the Commission, by a roll-call vote of 22 to 20, with 11 abstentions, welcomed the broad participation in parliamentary elections of 18 February, Iran's commitment to promote respect for the rule of law, progress in the area of freedom of expression, the invitation by Iran to the Working Group on Enforced or Involuntary Disappearances to visit the country, the visit to Iran of an OHCHR technical cooperation needs assessment mission, and progress made regarding the status of women in some areas. However, expressing concern at continuing human rights violations in Iran, the Commission called on the Government, among other things, to invite the Commission's Special Representative on human rights in Iran to visit the country; to continue efforts to consolidate respect for human rights and the rule of law and abide by its obligations under international human rights instruments; investigate suspicious deaths and killings of intellectuals and political activists and bring the perpetrators to justice; ensure that capital punishment would not be imposed for other than the most serious crimes; emancipate the Baha'is and other minority religious groups; end the use of torture; end discrimination against women; and make use of human rights technical cooperation programmes.

The Commission decided to extend the Special Representative's mandate for a further year and asked him to submit an interim report to the General Assembly in 2000 and to report to the Commission in 2001, keeping in mind a gender perspective. The Commission asked the Secretary-General to assist the Special Representative. The Economic and Social Council endorsed the Commission's decision and approved its requests to the Special Representative and the Secretary-General on 28 July (**decision 2000/259**).

Reports of Special Representative. In September [A/55/363], Special Representative Maurice Copithorne (Canada) reported on the human rights situation in Iran, covering the period from 1 January to 15 August, based on information received from the Government of Iran, other Governments, NGOs, individuals and international media.

The most dramatic development was the accelerating attack on the freedom of the press, which by the end of the period under review had led to the suppression of the entire reformist press and the imprisonment of many journalists. The economic situation of the poor and marginalized worsened. Iranians protested unemployment, inflation and inadequate services, as well as political issues, but paramilitary vigilantes often suppressed the demonstrations. The status of women remained largely unchanged, although there was the prospect that the new Majlis (consultative parliament) would raise the age of marriage to 14 for girls and 17 for boys and facilitate access to divorce. Prostitution was widespread among youth, mainly because of economic hardship and social alienation. In February, nine women were elected to the Majlis and the first woman was appointed governor of a district. A _fatwa_ was issued authorizing women to lead members of the same sex in prayers. There remained shadows over judiciary reform, one of them being the role of extrajudicial groups. Prisons were vastly overcrowded and executions remained suspiciously high. The evidence of the use of torture by law enforcement agencies, usually in illegal detention centres, was becoming a matter of public record. The murders and disappearances of intellectuals and political dissidents remained unsolved, and the status of ethnic and religious

minorities went unaddressed. Electoral democracy continued to grow, although major institutional obstacles to the exercise of the plenary powers by the legislature were coming to the fore. On balance, said the Special Representative, certain progress made had been overshadowed by backsliding in some areas and stagnation in others. Annexed to the report was information on the denial of fair trial and related rights in a case of Iranian Jews and Moslems in Shiraz, information on the situation of the Baha'is and correspondence between the Special Representative and the Government between January and July.

In a later report [E/CN.4/2001/39], the Special Representative stated that in the second half of the year the newly elected Majlis became the most active player in seeking to improve the status of women. Too often, however, the reform legislation passed by the Majlis was rejected by the Guardian Council, apparently because it was deemed to be "un-Islamic". In late August, the city of Khorramabad—the venue of a meeting of the main national students' reformist group—witnessed the largest outbreak of violence since July 1999 [YUN 1999, p. 713]. Two leading reformers who were invited to speak to the meeting were blockaded at the airport for six hours by vigilantes bused to the scene. Three days of clashes between students, vigilantes, police and other law enforcement agents ensued.

The problem of the lack of fair trial seemed to be widespread. Over the preceding year, the overcrowding in the prison system had become a major issue. A press account described them as "overcrowded dens of drug-taking, where the spread of infectious disease is rife". A continuing problem was the illegal detention centres—facilities run by government law enforcement agencies. The Special Representative was informed that the number of executions reported in the Iranian press during 2000 was about 200, with two other persons having been pardoned. Regarding torture, he noted a circular of the Head of the Judiciary to judges enumerating various types of conduct that would no longer be tolerated. Recognized minorities—Zoroastrians, Jews, Christians—despite having reserved seats in the Majlis and considerable freedom in their religious, educational and cultural activities, were monitored closely. There were indications that the Government might introduce some changes in the treatment of at least the recognized minorities. Concern about the human rights situation of the Baha'is remained on the Special Representative's agenda with reports of discrimination and persecution. He regularly received complaints from members of ethnic minority groups that were Sunni by religion.

Regarding democracy and civil society, the Majlis, in August, passed a bill that would bar police from entering universities without permission. Another initiative was the creation of a right of access for criminal suspects to a lawyer during all phases of investigation and interrogation. Unemployment was high and workers faced a variety of problems, such as non-payment of salaries. The enrolment rate in primary education had risen to 96 per cent at the national level; immunization rates were above 97 per cent; and infant mortality, under-five mortality and maternal mortality rates had fallen significantly. Other positive developments were the re-establishment of juvenile courts and an increase in the number of juvenile judges. As Iran remained a transit point for narcotics transported from Pakistan and Afghanistan to markets in Europe and the Persian Gulf countries, drugs continued to be a security and social problem for the Government.

The Special Representative urged the Government to achieve freedom of expression, expedite reform of the judiciary, and address the concerns of ethnic and religious minorities, inflation, unemployment and a general deterioration of the social infrastructure, and the problem of urban youth disillusionment and the resulting social crisis. The Special Representative, regretting that he was unable to visit Iran, called on the Government to return to full cooperation with the Commission. Annexed to the report was information on the situation of the Baha'is, and correspondence between the Special Representative and the Government between July and December.

GENERAL ASSEMBLY ACTION

On 4 December [meeting 81], the General Assembly, on the recommendation of the Third Committee [A/55/602/Add.3], adopted **resolution 55/114** by recorded vote (67-54-46) [agenda item 114 (c)].

Situation of human rights in the Islamic Republic of Iran

The General Assembly,

Guided by the Charter of the United Nations, the Universal Declaration of Human Rights, the International Covenants on Human Rights and other human rights instruments,

Reaffirming that all Member States have an obligation to promote and protect human rights and fundamental freedoms and to fulfil the obligations they have undertaken under the various international instruments in this field,

Mindful that the Islamic Republic of Iran is a party to the International Covenant on Civil and Political Rights, the International Covenant on Economic, Social and Cultural Rights, the International Convention on the Elimination of All Forms of Racial Discrimination and the Convention on the Rights of the Child,

Recalling its previous resolutions on the subject, the most recent of which is resolution 54/177 of 17 December 1999, and taking note of Commission on Human Rights resolution 2000/28 of 18 April 2000,

1. *Welcomes:*

(a) The interim report of the Special Representative of the Commission on Human Rights on the situation of human rights in the Islamic Republic of Iran;

(b) The broad participation in the parliamentary elections held during February and March 2000, which expressed the true commitment of the Iranian people to the democratic process in the Islamic Republic of Iran;

(c) The commitment made by the Government of the Islamic Republic of Iran to promote respect for the rule of law, including the elimination of arbitrary arrest and detention, and to reform the judicial and penitentiary system and bring it into line with international human rights standards in this field;

(d) The visit to the Islamic Republic of Iran of a technical cooperation needs assessment mission of the Office of the United Nations High Commissioner for Human Rights, and encourages the follow-up to that mission;

2. *Notes:*

(a) The provisions of the new code of penal procedure, which provide for the attendance of lawyers for all kinds of lawsuits, and the judiciary reform project, which aims, in particular, at re-establishing a distinction between the offices of the judge and the prosecutor;

(b) The legal changes recently put into effect within the Iranian judicial system by which members of religious minorities are no longer obliged to state their religion when applying for a marriage licence;

(c) Developments observed with regard to the status of women in areas such as education, training and health;

(d) The bill currently under consideration that aims at raising the age of marriage;

(e) The work of the Islamic Human Rights Commission on the human rights situation in the Islamic Republic of Iran and, in particular, its efforts to investigate illegal detentions and disappearances;

3. *Expresses its concern:*

(a) At the fact that, since 1996, no invitation has yet been extended by the Government of the Islamic Republic of Iran to the Special Representative to visit the country;

(b) At the deterioration of the situation with regard to freedom of opinion and expression, in particular at restrictions on the freedom of the press, judiciary suspension of numerous newspapers, prohibition of publications and the arrest of journalists, political activists and intellectuals on the basis of laws related to national security, which are used as a pretext to deny or restrict freedom of expression, opinion and thought;

(c) At the continuing violations of human rights in the Islamic Republic of Iran, in particular executions, in the apparent absence of respect for internationally recognized safeguards, and cases of torture and other cruel, inhuman or degrading treatment or punishment;

(d) At the failure to comply fully with international standards in the administration of justice and the absence of guarantees of due process of law and respect for internationally recognized legal safeguards, inter alia, with respect to persons belonging to religious minorities;

(e) At the discrimination against persons belonging to religious minorities, in particular the unabated pattern of persecution of the Baha'is, including the continuing detention and the sentencing to death of some of them;

(f) At the continuing discrimination, in law and in practice, against women, who still lack full and equal enjoyment of their human rights, as reported by the Special Representative;

4. *Calls upon* the Government of the Islamic Republic of Iran:

(a) To invite the Special Rapporteur of the Commission on Human Rights on religious intolerance to visit the country and to resume its full cooperation with him, in particular so that he may study the evolution of the human rights situation in the country, including through direct contacts with all sectors of society, and to make full use of technical cooperation programmes in the field of human rights;

(b) To give effect, in the near future, to its invitation to the Working Group on Enforced or Involuntary Disappearances to visit the Islamic Republic of Iran;

(c) To consolidate respect for human rights and the rule of law and to abide by its freely undertaken obligations under the International Covenants on Human Rights and under other international human rights instruments;

(d) To make efforts to ensure the full application of due process of law and fair and transparent procedures by the judiciary and, in this context, to ensure the respect for the rights of the defence and the equity of the verdicts in all instances, including for members of religious minority groups;

(e) To ensure that capital punishment will not be imposed for crimes other than the most serious and will not be pronounced in disregard of the provisions of the International Covenant on Civil and Political Rights and United Nations safeguards and to provide the Special Representative with relevant statistics on this matter;

(f) To accelerate the process of the investigation into the suspicious deaths and killings of intellectuals and political activists and to bring the alleged perpetrators to justice;

(g) To eliminate all forms of discrimination based on religious grounds or against persons belonging to minorities;

(h) To implement fully the conclusions and recommendations of the Special Representative with regard to religious intolerance relating to the Baha'is and other minority religious groups until they are completely emancipated;

(i) To take all necessary steps to end the use of torture and other forms of cruel, inhuman and degrading punishment, in particular the practice of amputation;

(j) To take further measures to promote full and equal enjoyment by women of their human rights;

5. *Decides* to continue the examination of the situation of human rights in the Islamic Republic of Iran, including the situation of minority groups such as the Baha'is, at its fifty-sixth session, under the item entitled "Human rights questions", in the light of additional elements provided by the Commission on Human Rights.

Iraq

Report of Special Rapporteur. In March [E/CN.4/2000/37], Special Rapporteur Andreas Mavrommatis (Cyprus), in view of the lateness of his appointment (December 1999) [YUN 1999, p. 716] and the fact that he had had little time to do anything beyond initial briefings, summarized his activities and initial observations on the human rights situation in Iraq. The conclusion he drew from his contacts during his first few months in office was that there was a grave humanitarian situation, given Iraq's shattered infrastructure and economy. It appeared that matters would improve if more attention were paid to improving infrastructure and accelerating the process of approval of contracts for the purchase of relevant supplies, he said.

Commission action. By a roll-call vote of 32 to none, with 21 abstentions, the Commission, on 18 April [res. 2000/17], strongly condemned the systematic, widespread and extremely grave violations of human rights and international humanitarian law by the Government of Iraq, its suppression of freedom of thought, expression, information, association, assembly and movement, widespread use of the death penalty, summary and arbitrary executions and widespread, systematic torture. It called on the Government to abide by its obligations under international human rights treaties and international humanitarian law; conform its military and security forces to standards of international law; cooperate with UN human rights mechanisms; establish independence of the judiciary and abrogate laws granting impunity; abrogate decrees that prescribed cruel and inhuman punishment or treatment; abrogate laws and procedures that penalized free expression; ensure free exercise of political opposition; cease repressive practices aimed at ethnic and religious groups; cooperate to resolve the fate of missing persons; cooperate with aid agencies and NGOs to provide humanitarian assistance; ensure equitable distribution of humanitarian supplies purchased with the proceeds from Iraqi oil; and cooperate in identifying minefields in the country.

The Commission decided to extend the Special Rapporteur's mandate for another year and asked him to submit an interim report to the General Assembly in 2000 and to report to the Commission in 2001, applying a gender perspective. The Secretary-General was asked to assist the Special Rapporteur and to approve the allocation of resources to send human rights monitors to locations that would facilitate improved information on the human rights situation in Iraq.

At Iraq's request, the Commission circulated a series of documents, including, in February, a study on the human rights consequences of the use of depleted uranium [E/CN.4/2000/121] and a document entitled "United States schemes to overthrow the system of government in Iraq in violation of international law and the Charter of the United Nations" [E/CN.4/2000/125], and, in March, studies on the economic embargo's effect on health [E/CN.4/2000/129] and on children and women [E/CN.4/2000/128].

ECONOMIC AND SOCIAL COUNCIL ACTION

On 28 July, the Economic and Social Council, on the recommendation of the Commission on Human Rights [E/2000/23 & Corr.1], adopted **decision 2000/250** by recorded vote (26-0-17) [agenda item 14 (g)].

Situation of human rights in Iraq

At its 45th plenary meeting, on 28 July 2000, the Economic and Social Council, taking note of Commission on Human Rights resolution 2000/17 of 18 April 2000, endorsed the Commission's decisions:

(a) To extend the mandate of the Special Rapporteur on the situation of human rights in Iraq, as contained in Commission resolution 1991/74 of 6 March 1991 and subsequent resolutions, for a further year, to request the Special Rapporteur to submit an interim report on the situation of human rights in Iraq to the General Assembly at its fifty-fifth session and to report to the Commission at its fifty-seventh session, and also to keep a gender perspective in mind when seeking and analysing information;

(b) To request the Secretary-General to continue to give all necessary assistance to the Special Rapporteur to enable him to discharge his mandate fully, and to approve the allocation of sufficient human and material resources for the sending of human rights monitors to such locations as would facilitate improved informa-

tion flow and assessment and help in the independent verification of reports on the situation of human rights in Iraq.

RECORDED VOTE ON DECISION 2000/250:

In favour: Angola, Austria, Belgium, Bolivia, Brazil, Bulgaria, Canada, Colombia, Costa Rica, Croatia, Czech Republic, Denmark, Fiji, France, Germany, Greece, Italy, Japan, Mexico, New Zealand, Norway, Poland, Portugal, Saudi Arabia, United Kingdom, United States.

Against: None.

Abstaining: Algeria, Bahrain, Belarus, Burkina Faso, China, Cuba, India, Indonesia, Morocco, Pakistan, Russian Federation, Saint Lucia, Sudan, Suriname, Syrian Arab Republic, Venezuela, Viet Nam.

Subcommission action. On 18 August [E/CN.4/2001/2 (dec. 2000/112)], the Subcommission appealed to the international community and to the Security Council for the embargo provisions affecting the humanitarian situation of the Iraqi population to be lifted and urged the international community and all Governments, including Iraq, to alleviate the suffering of Iraqis, particularly by facilitating the delivery of food, medical supplies and the wherewithal to meet their basic needs.

In other action, the Subcommission circulated a July study on environmental pollution resulting from the use of depleted uranium missiles [E/CN.4/Sub.2/2000/37], at Iraq's request, and an August aide-memoire from the United Kingdom and the United States regarding allegations by Iraq about the effects of sanctions on the country and about the actions of the two countries [E/CN.4/Sub.2/2000/45].

Report of Special Rapporteur. In August [A/55/294], the Special Rapporteur presented an interim report covering the period from 20 September 1999 to 20 June 2000, based on his visits to Kuwait (29 June–3 July) and London (11-15 July), as well as on information received from individuals, Iraqi opposition groups, Governments and UN agencies and programmes. The Government of Iraq had provided incomplete replies to a small number of cases, while no replies were provided to most of the specific allegations submitted by the Special Rapporteur.

It appeared that executions continued unabated during the period under review. The Government alleged that they were necessitated by the upsurge in crime and the considerable number of subversive acts. Information received from several sources indicated that Iraq allegedly staged car accidents resulting in the deaths of prominent religious or other local leaders and/or members of their families, as well as of members of the regime and individuals suspected of belonging to the opposition. There appeared to be alleged cases of arbitrary arrest and detention, as well as torture and ill-treatment of men and women. Prison conditions appeared to be grave.

Regarding the fate of Kuwaitis unaccounted for since Iraq's occupation of Kuwait, the Special

Rapporteur concluded that since the Government of Kuwait had devoted extraordinary efforts and resources to the cause and that sufficient material was produced to support the Kuwaiti claim that Iraq was in a position to clarify the fate of Kuwaitis unaccounted for, Iraq appeared to lack the political will to participate in the work and to examine cases before the Tripartite Commission and its Technical Subcommittee, established to facilitate work on the issue (see p. 295). Iraq alleged that there were some 1,250 missing Iraqi citizens in respect of whom evidence existed that they were seen alive in Kuwait following the war, allegations that Kuwait had dismissed as "mere afterthoughts".

In the Special Rapporteur's view, the most disturbing of recent complaints concerned harassment, intimidation and threats against the families of Iraqi opposition members residing abroad to induce them to stop their activities. During his visit to London, the Special Rapporteur heard allegations that non-Arab residents of the Kirkuk area—especially Kurds, Turkomen and Assyrians—were driven from their homes by the Government. On the one hand, the policy of "Arabization" was reported to be continuing and the Government reportedly maintained in force measures to that effect, such as the provision of grants and other incentives to Arabs to move to the Kirkuk area and legal impediments to the possession and transfer of property by non-Arabs. On the other hand, forced deportations of non-Arab families living in the area and confiscation of their property were also reported to continue on a large scale. Allegedly, those who refused to comply were subjected to intimidation, arrest, economic hardship through the revocation of ration cards and forced expulsion, and no compensation was provided for property loss.

The Special Rapporteur urged Iraq to review and revise laws regarding the death sentence and consider a moratorium on executions, rejoin the work of the Tripartite Commission and its Technical Subcommittee and examine files submitted by Kuwait, end harassment of families of people engaged in opposition activities abroad and practices against families of wanted or arrested Iraqi citizens and the widows and children of those executed, and accept and comply with the terms of all Security Council resolutions. The Government was invited to introduce democratic and political freedoms and end unlawful practices of arrest and torture.

Communications. On 2 November [A/C.3/55/5], Iraq transmitted its response to the Special Rapporteur's interim report. It stated that his information was gathered from countries known to adopt political positions hostile to Iraq and the sources were also hostile. Thus, the allegations and claims emanating from the sources and reflected in the report were false. Iraq claimed that the charges concerning arbitrary execution were overstated. Allegations regarding arbitrary arrest and detention were devoid of truth, as were allegations of the ill-treatment of prisoners. Iraq had the right to refuse to have anything to do with the Tripartite Commission as currently constituted. It continued to search and inquire for missing persons of all nationalities. Allegations of harassment of Iraqi opposition members were stories woven in the minds of those funded by the United States and other intelligence services. Additionally, Iraq presented comments on the Special Rapporteur's recommendations.

In a communication to the Chairperson of the Commission on Human Rights [E/CN.4/2001/150], Kuwait concurred with the Special Rapporteur's view regarding the fate of its missing nationals (see above).

Report of Special Rapporteur. In a report covering the period 14 August to 30 November [E/CN.4/2001/42], the Special Rapporteur stated that he had received noteworthy allegations of fresh or continuing violations during his visit to Iran (5-9 November), where he met with Iraqis who were allegedly expelled from Iraq in the early 1980s because they were of Iranian origin. They spoke about the current human rights situation in Iraq, particularly religious persecution or intolerance, missing persons and raids on villages resulting in loss of life and arrests. Some of them spoke about abject poverty, malnutrition and having to barter or sell their food rations, and infant mortality.

The Special Rapporteur continued to receive allegations of religious intolerance and persecution, extrajudicial, summary and arbitrary executions, and ill-treatment, psychological pressure and torture of suspects during questioning. Armed raids were still carried out by Iraqi security forces against villages in the south, with the intent of capturing armed guerrillas and army deserters, resulting in loss of life, property damage and searches and arrests without warrant. Information was received that men and women, including minors, were arrested and detained on suspicion of political or religious activities perceived as hostile to the regime, or because of family ties with opposition members, other activists and armed resisters. The main category of alleged violations that had continuing effects was that of disappearances. During the reporting period, the Special Rapporteur met with representatives of the Government of Kuwait and members of the National Committee for the Missing and Prisoners of War. Iraq continued not to attend meetings of the Tripartite Commission, and reiterated allegations that there were 1,250 of its citizens missing who were reportedly residing in Kuwait at the time of the occupation and were allegedly last seen in the hands of Kuwaiti forces or in Kuwaiti places of detention.

The Special Rapporteur urged the Government to respond positively to his request to visit the country, improve social, economic and cultural rights, approach the dialogue with the United Nations in a spirit of compromise, remove restrictions on the exercise of religious freedom, examine allegations of human rights violations, investigate allegations of unlawful arrest and torture and take remedial action, examine allegations of forced relocations, investigate the fate of all missing persons and join the work of the Tripartite Commission and its Technical Subcommittee. He called on the Government to ensure that unjustified or excessive force was not used against civilians and inhabited places, review and revise laws permitting the imposition of the death penalty and consider a moratorium on executions.

(For political details, see p. 292.)

GENERAL ASSEMBLY ACTION

On 4 December [meeting 81], the General Assembly, on the recommendation of the Third Committee [A/55/602/Add.3], adopted **resolution 55/115** by recorded vote (102-3-60) [agenda item 114 (c)].

Human rights situation in Iraq

The General Assembly,

Guided by the Charter of the United Nations, the Universal Declaration of Human Rights, the International Covenants on Human Rights and other human rights instruments,

Reaffirming that all Member States have an obligation to promote and protect human rights and fundamental freedoms and to fulfil the obligations they have undertaken under the various international instruments in this field,

Mindful that Iraq is a party to the International Covenants on Human Rights, other international human rights instruments and the Geneva Conventions of 12 August 1949 for the protection of victims of war,

Recalling its previous resolutions and those of the Commission on Human Rights on the subject, and taking note of the most recent, Commission resolution 2000/17 of 18 April 2000,

Recalling also Security Council resolution 686(1991) of 2 March 1991, in which the Council called upon Iraq to release all Kuwaitis and nationals of other States who might still be held in detention, Council resolution 687(1991) of 3 April 1991, Council resolution 688(1991) of 5 April 1991, in which the Council demanded an end to the repression of the Iraqi civilian population and insisted that Iraq cooperate with humanitarian organizations and that the human rights of all Iraqi citizens be respected, Council resolutions 986(1995) of 14 April 1995, 1111(1997) of 4 June 1997, 1129(1997) of 12 Sep-

tember 1997, 1143(1997) of 4 December 1997, 1153(1998) of 20 February 1998, 1175(1998) of 19 June 1998, 1210(1998) of 24 November 1998, 1242(1999) of 21 May 1999, 1266(1999) of 4 October 1999, 1281(1999) of 10 December 1999 and 1302(2000) of 8 June 2000, in which the Council authorized States to permit imports of Iraqi oil in order to allow Iraq to purchase humanitarian supplies, and Council resolution 1284(1999) of 17 December 1999, in which the Council, by means of a comprehensive approach to the situation in Iraq, inter alia, raised the ceiling for the allowable import of Iraqi oil in order to increase the amount of revenue available for the purchase of humanitarian supplies, laid down new provisions and procedures designed to improve the implementation of the humanitarian programme and to further achievements in meeting the humanitarian needs of the Iraqi population, and reiterated the obligation of Iraq to facilitate the repatriation of all Kuwaiti and third-country nationals referred to in paragraph 30 of Council resolution 687(1991),

Taking note of the concluding observations of the Human Rights Committee, the Committee on the Elimination of Racial Discrimination, the Committee on Economic, Social and Cultural Rights and the Committee on the Rights of the Child on the recent reports submitted to them by Iraq, in which these treaty-monitoring bodies point to a wide range of human rights problems and hold the view that the Government of Iraq remains bound by its treaty obligations, while pointing to the adverse effect of sanctions on the daily life of the population, in particular children,

Recalling the reports of the Secretary-General concerning the implementation of Security Council resolutions 986(1995), 1111(1997), 1143(1997), 1175(1998), 1210(1998) and 1242(1999), and taking note of the report of the Secretary-General on the implementation of Security Council resolution 1302(2000),

Reaffirming that it is the responsibility of the Government of Iraq to ensure the well-being of its entire population and the full enjoyment of all human rights and fundamental freedoms, concerned about the dire humanitarian situation in Iraq, which particularly affects certain vulnerable groups, including children, as stated in the reports of several United Nations human rights treaty bodies, and appealing to all concerned to fulfil their mutual obligations in the management of the humanitarian programme established by the Security Council in its resolution 986(1995),

1. *Welcomes* the report of the Special Rapporteur of the Commission on Human Rights on the situation of human rights in Iraq and the observations, conclusions and recommendations contained therein;

2. *Notes with dismay* that there has been no improvement in the situation of human rights in the country;

3. *Strongly condemns:*

(*a*) The systematic, widespread and extremely grave violations of human rights and of international humanitarian law by the Government of Iraq, resulting in an all-pervasive repression and oppression sustained by broad-based discrimination and widespread terror;

(*b*) The suppression of freedom of thought, expression, information, association, assembly and movement through fear of arrest, imprisonment, execution, expulsion, house demolition and other sanctions;

(*c*) The repression faced by any kind of opposition, in particular the harassment and intimidation of and threats against Iraqi opponents living abroad and members of their families;

(d) The widespread use of the death penalty in disregard of the provisions of the International Covenant on Civil and Political Rights and the United Nations safeguards;

(e) Summary and arbitrary executions, including political killings and the continuing so-called clean-out of prisons, as well as enforced or involuntary disappearances, routinely practised arbitrary arrests and detention and consistent and routine failure to respect due process and the rule of law;

(f) Widespread, systematic torture and the maintaining of decrees prescribing cruel and inhuman punishment as a penalty for offences;

4. *Calls upon* the Government of Iraq:

(a) To abide by its freely undertaken obligations under international human rights treaties and international humanitarian law and to respect and ensure the rights of all individuals, irrespective of their origin, ethnicity, gender or religion, within its territory and subject to its jurisdiction;

(b) To bring the actions of its military and security forces into conformity with the standards of international law, in particular those of the International Covenant on Civil and Political Rights;

(c) To cooperate with United Nations human rights mechanisms, in particular by inviting the Special Rapporteur to visit the country and allowing the stationing of human rights monitors throughout Iraq pursuant to the relevant resolutions of the General Assembly and the Commission on Human Rights;

(d) To establish the independence of the judiciary and abrogate all laws granting impunity to specified forces or persons killing or injuring individuals for any purpose beyond the administration of justice under the rule of law as prescribed by international standards;

(e) To abrogate all decrees that prescribe cruel and inhuman punishment or treatment, including mutilation, and to ensure that torture and cruel punishment and treatment no longer occur;

(f) To abrogate all laws and procedures, including Revolution Command Council Decree No. 840 of 4 November 1986, that penalize free expression, and to ensure that the genuine will of the people shall be the basis of the authority of the State;

(g) To ensure free exercise of political opposition and to prevent intimidation and repression of political opponents and their families;

(h) To respect the rights of all ethnic and religious groups and to cease immediately its repressive practices aimed at the Iraqi Kurds, Assyrians and Turkmen, in particular their deportation from the regions of Kirkuk and Khanaqin, and at the population of the southern marsh areas, where drainage projects have provoked environmental destruction and a deterioration of the situation of the civilian population, as well as to ensure the physical integrity of all citizens, including the Shi'a population, and to guarantee their freedoms;

(i) To cooperate with the Tripartite Commission and its Technical Subcommittee to establish the whereabouts and resolve the fate of the remaining several hundred missing persons, including prisoners of war, Kuwaiti nationals and third-country nationals, victims of the illegal Iraqi occupation of Kuwait, to cooperate with the Working Group on Enforced or Involuntary Disappearances of the Commission on Human Rights for that purpose, to cooperate with the high-level coordinator of the Secretary-General for Kuwaitis and third-country nationals and Kuwaiti property, to pay compensation to the families of those who died or disappeared in the custody of the Iraqi authorities, through the mechanism established by the Security Council in resolution 692(1991) of 20 May 1991, to release immediately all Kuwaitis and nationals of other States who may still be held in detention and inform families about the whereabouts of arrested persons, to provide information about death sentences imposed on prisoners of war and civilian detainees, and to issue death certificates for deceased prisoners of war and civilian detainees;

(j) To cooperate further with international aid agencies and non-governmental organizations in providing humanitarian assistance and monitoring in the northern and southern areas of the country;

(k) To continue to cooperate in the implementation of Security Council resolutions 986(1995), 1111(1997), 1143(1997), 1153(1998), 1210(1998), 1242(1999), 1266 (1999), 1281(1999) and 1302(2000), and to cooperate, together with all concerned, in the implementation of the sections on humanitarian questions of Council resolution 1284(1999), to ensure fully the timely and equitable distribution, without discrimination, to the Iraqi population, including the population in remote areas, of all humanitarian supplies purchased under the oil-for-humanitarian-goods programme, to address effectively the needs of vulnerable groups, including children, pregnant women, the disabled, the elderly and the mentally ill, among others, to facilitate the work of United Nations humanitarian personnel in Iraq by ensuring the free and unobstructed movement of observers throughout the country, as well as their free access, without any discrimination, to all the population, and to ensure that involuntarily displaced persons receive humanitarian assistance without the need to demonstrate that they have resided for six months at their places of temporary residence;

(l) To cooperate in the identification of minefields existing throughout Iraq with a view to facilitating their marking and eventual clearing;

5. *Requests* the Secretary-General to provide the Special Rapporteur with all necessary assistance in carrying out his mandate, and decides to continue the examination of the situation of human rights in Iraq at its fifty-sixth session, under the item entitled "Human rights questions", in the light of additional elements provided by the Commission on Human Rights.

RECORDED VOTE ON RESOLUTION 55/115:

In favour: Albania, Andorra, Angola, Argentina, Australia, Austria, Bahamas, Barbados, Belgium, Belize, Bhutan, Bolivia, Bosnia and Herzegovina, Botswana, Brazil, Bulgaria, Canada, Chile, Colombia, Comoros, Costa Rica, Côte d'Ivoire, Croatia, Cyprus, Czech Republic, Denmark, Dominica, Ecuador, El Salvador, Estonia, Ethiopia, Finland, France, Georgia, Germany, Greece, Grenada, Guatemala, Guyana, Haiti, Honduras, Hungary, Iceland, Ireland, Israel, Italy, Jamaica, Japan, Kazakhstan, Kuwait, Latvia, Lesotho, Liechtenstein, Lithuania, Luxembourg, Malawi, Maldives, Malta, Marshall Islands, Mauritius, Mexico, Micronesia, Monaco, Mongolia, Nauru, Netherlands, New Zealand, Nicaragua, Norway, Palau, Panama, Papua New Guinea, Paraguay, Peru, Poland, Portugal, Republic of Korea, Republic of Moldova, Romania, Samoa, San Marino, Sao Tome and Principe, Saudi Arabia, Senegal, Slovakia, Slovenia, Solomon Islands, South Africa, Spain, Suriname, Swaziland, Sweden, Tajikistan, The former Yugoslav Republic of

Macedonia, Trinidad and Tobago, Turkey, Ukraine, United Kingdom, United States, Uruguay, Uzbekistan, Vanuatu.

Against: Libyan Arab Jamahiriya, Mauritania, Sudan.

Abstentions: Algeria, Antigua and Barbuda, Armenia, Azerbaijan, Bahrain, Bangladesh, Belarus, Benin, Brunei Darussalam, Burkina Faso, Burundi, Cambodia, Cameroon, Cape Verde, Chad, China, Congo, Cuba, Democratic People's Republic of Korea, Democratic Republic of the Congo, Djibouti, Dominican Republic, Egypt, Eritrea, Fiji, Gambia, Ghana, Guinea, India, Indonesia, Jordan, Kenya, Kyrgyzstan, Lao People's Democratic Republic, Lebanon, Madagascar, Malaysia, Mozambique, Myanmar, Namibia, Nepal, Nigeria, Pakistan, Philippines, Qatar, Russian Federation, Rwanda, Saint Lucia, Sierra Leone, Singapore, Sri Lanka, Syrian Arab Republic, Thailand, Togo, Tunisia, Uganda, United Arab Emirates, United Republic of Tanzania, Venezuela, Viet Nam.

Myanmar

Report of Secretary-General. In response to General Assembly resolution 54/186 [YUN 1999, p. 719], the Secretary-General, in March [E/CN.4/2000/29], reported on consultations held in 1999 with the Government of Myanmar by his Special Envoy, Alvaro de Soto. The Secretary-General stated that he was in the process of replacing the Special Envoy, who had assumed new responsibilities.

Communication. On 17 March [E/CN.4/2000/137], Myanmar submitted to the Commission a memorandum concerning the human rights situation in the country, in the hope that Commission members would view the question from a more objective and balanced perspective.

Commission action. On 18 April [res. 2000/23], the Commission deplored the continued pattern of gross and systematic human rights violations in Myanmar; the lack of independence of the judiciary; widespread discrimination against minorities; violation of women's and children's human rights; the escalated persecution of democratic group activists; and severe restrictions on the freedoms of opinion, expression, assembly, association and movement. It called on Myanmar to establish a constructive dialogue with the UN system; to continue to cooperate with the Secretary-General or his representative; and to consider becoming a party to international human rights instruments. The Government was urged to cooperate with the Special Rapporteur and implement his recommendations; ensure full respect for human rights and fundamental freedoms; establish democracy; allow all citizens to participate freely in the political process; release political detainees; improve conditions of detention; ensure the well-being of all political leaders, including Aung San Suu Kyi; fulfil its obligations under the Convention on the Rights of the Child, adopted by General Assembly resolution 44/25 [YUN 1989, p. 561], and under the Convention on the Elimination of All Forms of Discrimination against Women, adopted by Assembly resolution 34/180 [YUN 1979, p. 895]; end forced labour; allow freedom of association;

cease laying landmines; end enforced displacement of persons; and end impunity.

The Commission asked the High Commissioner to cooperate with the Director-General of the International Labour Organization (ILO) with a view to identifying ways in which their offices might collaborate to improve the human rights situation in Myanmar and requested the Secretary-General to bring its resolution to the attention of the UN system.

The Commission decided to extend the Special Rapporteur's mandate for a further year and asked him to report to the Assembly in 2000 and to the Commission in 2001, keeping a gender perspective in mind; it also decided to ask the Secretary-General to assist the Special Rapporteur, to pursue efforts to ensure that the Special Rapporteur be authorized to visit Myanmar, and to continue his discussions with the Government and with anyone he might consider appropriate to assist in implementing Assembly resolution 54/186 [YUN 1999, p. 719], as well as its current resolution. The Economic and Social Council endorsed the Commission's decisions on 28 July (**decision 2000/255**).

Report of Special Rapporteur. In August [A/55/359], Special Rapporteur Rajsoomer Lallah (Mauritius) reported on the human rights situation in Myanmar as at 31 July, noting with deep concern the continued deterioration of the situation. He continued to receive persistent reports of government policies and directives aimed at the elimination of the National League for Democracy (NLD) through intimidation, threats, coercion and charges of a political character against its members, particularly since April. He had received reports of widespread and systematic torture and other forms of ill-treatment of detainees occurring in military intelligence centres and certain prisons. Allegations of arbitrary detention were also received. According to several reports, harsh conditions of detention existed in several prisons and other places of detention. ICRC continued to have access to jails, so-called "guest houses" and labour camps. The administration of justice was marked by legal and factual constraints inconsistent with judicial independence. Government policies regarding health still appeared indecisive and inadequate. Although nominally available to all, public education was costly in terms of school fees, books and classroom facilities. Moreover, widespread reports alleged that bribery was frequently required to be paid to school authorities. The obligation to suppress the use of forced or compulsory labour in Myanmar was violated in national law, as well as in actual practice, in a widespread and systematic manner, according to ILO. Thus, in June, considering that the situation had remained unchanged, the International Labour Conference resolved to take action to bring about Myanmar's compliance with ILO Convention No. 29 on forced labour [YUN 1999, p. 1388]. A series of measures would take effect on 30 November unless, before that date, the ILO Governing Body was satisfied that the intentions expressed by the Minister of Labour had been translated into a framework of legislative, executive and administrative measures. Vulnerable groups—women, children, displaced persons and refugees, ethnic minorities—suffered violations of their rights.

The Special Rapporteur encouraged the repeal of discriminatory provisions in the Citizenship Act, and the repeal of decrees and orders criminalizing the exercise of freedom of thought and expression, association and movement, and freedom to exercise political and democratic rights in accordance with international standards. He reiterated recommendations made in 1999 [YUN 1999, pp. 718 & 719].

Report of Secretary-General. The Secretary-General reported in October on the progress of discussions regarding the restoration of democracy in Myanmar [A/55/509]. In April, he appointed a new Special Envoy, Razali Ismail, who had visited the country (29 June–3 July) to build confidence with his interlocutors. The Special Envoy held consultations with government officials and with leaders of two political parties, NLD and the Shan Nationalities League for Democracy. During a second mission (9-12 October), he again held consultations, during what the Secretary-General called a setback in the atmosphere surrounding efforts for national reconciliation due to restrictions placed on the movement and access to the diplomatic corps imposed on Aung San Suu Kyi and other NLD leaders. Discussions focused on the need for national reconciliation, the practice of forced labour, the provision of UN humanitarian assistance and the issue of a visit of the Special Rapporteur. The Secretary-General welcomed the authorities' announcement that universities and colleges had been reopened for the first time in three years.

GENERAL ASSEMBLY ACTION

On 4 December [meeting 81], the General Assembly, on the recommendation of the Third Committee [A/55/602/Add.3], adopted **resolution 55/112** without vote [agenda item 114 *(c)*].

Situation of human rights in Myanmar

The General Assembly,

Reaffirming that all Member States have an obligation to promote and protect human rights and fundamental freedoms, as stated in the Charter of the United Nations and elaborated in the Universal Decla-

ration of Human Rights, the International Covenants on Human Rights and other applicable human rights instruments,

Aware that, in accordance with the Charter, the United Nations promotes and encourages respect for human rights and fundamental freedoms for all and that the Universal Declaration of Human Rights states that the will of the people shall be the basis of the authority of government, and therefore expressing its grave concern that the Government of Myanmar has still not implemented its commitment to take all necessary steps towards democracy in the light of the results of the elections held in 1990,

Recalling its resolution 54/186 of 17 December 1999 and Commission on Human Rights resolution 1992/58 of 3 March 1992, in which the Commission, inter alia, decided to nominate a special rapporteur with a given mandate, and taking note of Commission resolution 2000/23 of 18 April 2000, in which the Commission decided to extend for one year the mandate of its Special Rapporteur on the situation of human rights in Myanmar,

Recalling also the observation made by the Special Rapporteur that the absence of respect for the rights pertaining to democratic governance is at the root of all major violations of human rights in Myanmar,

Still gravely concerned at the deterioration of the human rights situation in Myanmar, especially the unabated suppression of the exercise of political rights and freedom of thought, expression, association and movement in Myanmar, as reported by the Special Rapporteur, and deeply concerned that new restrictions have been placed on Aung San Suu Kyi and other members of the National League for Democracy,

Also gravely concerned that the legal system is effectively used as an instrument of oppression and at the increasing intimidation and detention of lawyers,

Recognizing that the systematic violations of civil, political, economic, social and cultural rights by the Government of Myanmar have had a significant adverse effect on the health and welfare of the people of Myanmar,

Noting with interest the two recent visits to Myanmar by the Special Envoy of the Secretary-General and the cooperation extended by the Government of Myanmar in that regard,

Deeply regretting the failure of the Government of Myanmar to cooperate fully with the relevant United Nations mechanisms, in particular the Special Rapporteur, who still has not been invited to Myanmar, despite assurances by the Government of Myanmar in 1999 that it would seriously consider a visit,

1. *Expresses its appreciation* to the Special Rapporteur of the Commission on Human Rights on the situation of human rights in Myanmar for his interim report, and calls upon the Government of Myanmar to implement fully the recommendations made by the Special Rapporteur;

2. *Urges* the Government of Myanmar to cooperate fully and without further delay with the Special Rapporteur, and to allow him urgently, without preconditions, to conduct a field mission and to establish direct contacts with the Government and all other relevant sectors of society, thus enabling him fully to discharge his mandate;

3. *Notes with satisfaction* the continued cooperation with the International Committee of the Red Cross, allowing the Committee to communicate with and visit detainees in accordance with its modalities of work, and hopes that the programme will be pursued further;

4. *Deplores* the continued violations of human rights in Myanmar, including extrajudicial, summary or arbitrary executions, enforced disappearances, rape, torture, inhuman treatment, mass arrests, forced labour, including the use of children, forced relocation and denial of freedom of assembly, association, expression and movement, as reported by the Special Rapporteur;

5. *Expresses its grave concern* at the increasingly systematic policy of the Government of Myanmar to persecute the democratic opposition, members of the National League for Democracy, sympathizers and their families, and ethnic opposition parties, and at the use by the Government of intimidatory methods such as arbitrary arrest and detention and abuse of the legal system, including harsh long-term prison sentences, mass rallies and media campaigns, which have forced many to refrain from exercising their legitimate political rights;

6. *Urges* the Government of Myanmar to cease, without delay, all activities aimed at preventing the free exercise of internationally recognized human rights, including freedom of association, assembly, movement and speech, and in particular to remove all restrictions on the freedom of movement of Aung San Suu Kyi and other members of the National League for Democracy and on their freedom to communicate with the outside world;

7. *Strongly urges* the Government of Myanmar to release immediately and unconditionally detained political leaders and all political prisoners, including journalists, to ensure their physical integrity and to permit them to participate in the process of national reconciliation;

8. *Expresses its concern* that the composition and working procedures of the National Convention do not permit either Members of Parliament–elect or representatives of the ethnic minorities to express their views freely, and urges the Government of Myanmar to seek new and constructive ways to promote national reconciliation and to restore democracy, through, inter alia, the establishment of a time frame for action;

9. *Strongly urges* the Government of Myanmar, taking into account the assurances it has given on various occasions, to take all necessary steps towards the restoration of democracy, in accordance with the will of the people, as expressed in the democratic elections held in 1990 and, to that end, without delay, to engage in a substantive political dialogue with political leaders, including Aung San Suu Kyi, and representatives of ethnic groups, and, in that context, notes the existence of the committee representing the People's Parliament;

10. *Notes with grave concern* that the Government of Myanmar has failed to cease its widespread and systematic use of forced labour of its own people and to meet all three recommendations of the International Labour Organization on that issue; this failure has compelled the International Labour Organization to limit strictly further cooperation with the Government and has prompted the International Labour Conference to adopt, subject to certain conditions, a number of measures to secure compliance by the Government of Myanmar with the recommendations of the Commission of Inquiry established to examine the observance of International Labour Organization Convention No. 29 concerning forced or compulsory labour, of 1930;

11. *Notes* the recent visit by the technical cooperation mission of the International Labour Organization to Myanmar and the cooperation extended to the mission, while awaiting the results of the mission;

12. *Strongly urges* the Government of Myanmar to implement fully concrete legislative, executive and administrative measures to eradicate the practice of forced labour, in conformity with the relevant recommendations of the Commission of Inquiry;

13. *Welcomes* the reopening of most university courses, but remains concerned that the right to education continues to be a right that is exercised only by those willing to refrain from exercising their civil and political rights and concerned at the reduction in the length of the academic year, the division of the student population and its dispersal to distant campuses and the lack of adequate resources;

14. *Deplores* the continued violations of human rights, in particular those directed against persons belonging to ethnic and religious minorities, including summary executions, rape, torture, forced labour, forced portering, forced relocations, use of anti-personnel landmines, destruction of crops and fields and dispossession of land and property, which deprives those persons of all means of subsistence and results in large-scale displacement of persons and flows of refugees to neighbouring countries, with negative effects for those countries, and an increasing number of internally displaced persons;

15. *Urges* the Government of Myanmar to end the systematic enforced displacement of persons and other causes of refugee flows to neighbouring countries and to create conditions conducive to their voluntary return and full reintegration in conditions of safety and dignity and to allow the safe and unhindered access of humanitarian personnel to assist in the return and reintegration process;

16. *Deplores* the continued violations of the human rights of women, especially women who are refugees, are internally displaced or belong to ethnic minorities or the political opposition, in particular forced labour, trafficking, sexual violence and exploitation, including rape, as reported by the Special Rapporteur;

17. *Strongly urges* the Government of Myanmar to implement fully the recommendations made by the Committee on the Elimination of Discrimination against Women, in particular the request to prosecute and punish those who violate the human rights of women, and to carry out human rights education and gender-sensitization training, in particular for military personnel;

18. *Deplores* the recruitment of children as soldiers, in particular children belonging to ethnic minorities, and strongly urges the Government of Myanmar and all other parties to the hostilities in Myanmar to end the use of children as soldiers;

19. *Expresses its concern* at the growing incidence of human immunodeficiency virus/acquired immunodeficiency syndrome (HIV/AIDS) infection, and urges the Government of Myanmar urgently to address this issue, which will have a serious long-term impact on the de-

velopment of the country, and to ensure that the health system receives sufficient funding to enable health workers to meet the right of all people to the highest possible standard of health care;

20. *Expresses its grave concern* at the high rates of malnutrition among pre-school-aged children, which constitute serious violations of their rights to adequate food and the highest attainable standard of health and may have serious repercussions for the health and development of the affected children;

21. *Strongly urges* the Government of Myanmar to ensure full respect for all human rights and fundamental freedoms, including economic and social rights, and to fulfil its obligation to restore the independence of the judiciary and due process and to end the impunity of and bring to justice any perpetrators of human rights violations, including members of the military, and to investigate and prosecute alleged violations committed by government agents in all circumstances;

22. *Welcomes* the report of the Secretary-General on the visit of his Special Envoy to Myanmar, endorses the appeal of the Special Envoy for the initiation of a process of dialogue that would lead to national reconciliation, and supports his efforts to achieve such a dialogue;

23. *Requests* the Secretary-General to continue his discussions on the situation of human rights and the restoration of democracy with the Government of Myanmar, to submit additional reports to the General Assembly during its fifty-fifth session on the progress of those discussions, and to report to the Assembly at its fifty-sixth session and to the Commission on Human Rights at its fifty-seventh session on the progress made in the implementation of the present resolution;

24. *Decides* to continue its consideration of this question at its fifty-sixth session.

Europe

Belarus

Pursuant to the Subcommission Chairperson's 1999 statement on Belarus [YUN 1999, p. 721], which was based on information received from Belarus regarding steps that the Government was prepared to take to further promote and protect human rights, Belarus, in June [E/CN.4/Sub.2/2000/9], reported on measures it had taken to do so.

Cyprus

In response to a 1999 Commission request [YUN 1999, p. 721], the Secretary-General, in a February report on the human rights situation in Cyprus [E/CN.4/2000/26], described activities carried out under his good offices mission and by the United Nations Peacekeeping Force in Cyprus

and the Committee on Missing Persons in Cyprus (see pp. 402-404).

On 18 April [dec. 2000/103], the Commission decided to retain the item on its agenda, on the understanding that action required by its previous resolutions would continue to remain operative, including its request to the Secretary-General to report on their implementation.

The former Yugoslavia

Commission action. On 18 April [res. 2000/26], by a roll-call vote of 44 to 1, with 8 abstentions, the Commission noted that, while there had been significant positive developments on human rights in Croatia, Bosnia and Herzegovina (composed of the Federation of Bosnia and Herzegovina and Republika Srpska) had made limited improvement on human rights issues and the situation in the Federal Republic of Yugoslavia (FRY) remained a source of grave concern. The High Commissioner and the Secretary-General were requested, with the assistance of the international community, to develop early warning procedures to identify situations that could lead to conflict or humanitarian tragedy. The Commission recommended that Croatia be considered in 2001 under the agenda item on technical assistance and advisory services if progress on human rights and democratic principles continued.

Expressing grave concern at the ongoing serious human rights violations and the deteriorating human rights and humanitarian situation in FRY caused by the repressive policies and measures of the authorities, the Commission condemned the repression of the media, political opposition and NGOs, and the arbitrary administration of justice and application of the law. Noting with grave concern that Slobodan Milosevic and other senior leaders continued to maintain positions of power despite their indictment for war crimes and crimes against humanity [YUN 1999, p. 1214], and that FRY had repeatedly ignored the orders of the International Tribunal for the Former Yugoslavia (ICTY) to transfer indicted war criminals to The Hague and had not transferred any indictee since ICTY's inception in 1992, the Commission demanded that FRY cooperate with the Tribunal. It called on the authorities to respect human rights and fundamental freedoms; end torture and other cruel, inhuman or degrading treatment or punishment of detainees, and bring those responsible to justice; repeal repressive and discriminatory legislation on property rights, universities and the media, and apply other legislation without discrimination; respect the rights of minorities; return the armed and police forces to civil and democratic control; and account for and protect the humanitarian and legal rights of prisoners deprived of liberty and removed from the Kosovo province of FRY at the end of the conflict. The Commission called for information on the fate and the whereabouts of persons missing or unaccounted for.

Regarding Kosovo, the Commission condemned ethnic violence and intimidation by all parties and urged political leaders to cooperate fully with the United Nations Interim Administration Mission in Kosovo (UNMIK) and the international security presence in Kosovo (KFOR) in their efforts to strengthen law and security, to reject violence and to support only peaceful and democratic civil or political activity. The Commission stressed the need for an independent and impartial judiciary.

Welcoming the democratic election of a reform-oriented new Government in Croatia, steps to establish an independent media, undertake judicial reform and facilitate refugee returns, and the agreement between Croatia and the High Commissioner on technical cooperation and assistance programmes [YUN 1999, p. 587], the Commission called on the Government to sustain the progress.

Noting progress by Bosnia and Herzegovina in some areas in implementing the 1995 Peace Agreement [YUN 1995, p. 544], as well as some improvement in respect for human rights and some progress on refugee returns, the Commission strongly condemned the intimidation of and perpetuation of violence against minority refugees and internally displaced persons returning to their homes, the destruction of their homes and all other acts designed to discourage their voluntary return. It called on the authorities to facilitate returns, adopt an effective and fair election law, combat the growing problem of trafficking in persons, continue to improve police standards and ensure the establishment and functioning of an independent judiciary. All parties to the Peace Agreement were called on to cooperate with ICTY, and States and the Secretary-General were urged to support the Tribunal. All indicted persons were called on to surrender voluntarily to the Tribunal's custody.

The Commission decided to renew the Special Rapporteur's mandate for a further year and asked him to report to the General Assembly in 2000 and to the Commission in 2001; the Commission's decision and request were endorsed by the Economic and Social Council on 28 July (**decision 2000/257**).

Communications. On 17 April [E/CN.4/2000/157], FRY, commenting on the draft text of Commission resolution 2000/26, stated that the en-

tire text should be rejected for its highly politicized contents and for the absence of any reference to the real human rights problems in Kosovo and Metohija province. It presented amendments to the draft text.

During the year, FRY transmitted to the Commission and Subcommission communications on various subjects, including the humanitarian situation in the country, elections and the future political status of Kosovo and Metohija and people deprived of their liberty.

Reports of Special Rapporteur. In October [A/55/282], Special Rapporteur Jiri Dienstbier (Czech Republic) submitted a report on the human rights situation in Bosnia and Herzegovina, Croatia and FRY.

The Special Rapporteur visited Bosnia and Herzegovina (24-26 January and 11-15 June), where the political environment, lack of functioning institutions and a complicated constitutional and legal framework continued to impede any real change. He noted, however, that there was more reason for optimism than a year earlier. Over 1 million refugees and displaced persons were still waiting to return to their pre-war homes or for any other durable solution. Obstacles ranged from lack of adequate security to delays in property law implementation and lack of reconstruction assistance. Although some progress had been made in restoring property rights, the process was still moving too slowly. Also, discriminatory employment impacted the sustainability of returns. The major problem in education was the division of the system along ethnic lines. Progress was noted, though, in the removal of offensive and discriminatory material from textbooks. An uneven distribution of health care negatively affected the accessibility and cost of health services for all. Return-related incidents of violence continued to be reported in some areas and impunity persisted, with perpetrators in most cases not identified, arrested or prosecuted. The police forces remained overwhelmingly mono-ethnic and had unacceptably low numbers of female officers. Political interference in the work of police and the judiciary continued. The Special Rapporteur expressed serious concern that Bosnia and Herzegovina had emerged as a significant destination point for women trafficked from Eastern Europe. There was growing evidence that the country was serving for transit purposes and was becoming a country of origin. The Special Rapporteur noted a trend towards greater implementation of decisions of the Human Rights Chamber and the Ombudsperson, although implementation rates were still little better than 50 per cent. He recommended mainstreaming a gender perspective into all policies and programmes, improved and accelerated property-law implementation, the adoption of a law on labour relations with an anti-discrimination component in Republika Srpska, non-discrimination in health policy and practice, combating trafficking in persons and training for local and international police on human rights and on gender. The authorities were called on to implement the Declaration and Agreement on Education signed in May.

In reporting on human rights developments in Croatia from March to early July, the Special Rapporteur paid attention to the key issues of refugee returns, minority rights and war-crimes trials. He visited the country from 25 to 27 April.

Despite amendments to the Law on Reconstruction and adoption of amendments to the law on areas of special State concern, progress on returns had still been slow. War-crimes prosecutions of ethnic Serbs were ongoing, and the Special Rapporteur called attention to the lack of fairness in most of the proceedings, which were based on group indictments and failed to specify individual criminal acts; often, individuals belonging to groups were tried in absentia. The missing persons issue was a key factor in the peace and reconciliation process in Croatia and remained a pressing human rights concern. The Special Rapporteur expressed deep concern over Croatia's difficult financial situation and noted the dire need for investment to improve the standard of respect for social and economic rights and to implement measures to assist vulnerable groups. He noted government attempts to protect workers' rights better. Unemployment, estimated at between 18 and 20 per cent, was expected to grow due to bankruptcies. The Special Rapporteur commended the initiative of the State Commission for Gender Equality Issues to introduce legislative changes to better protect women and children. He also welcomed the signing on 6 June of an agreement on cooperation between the Government and the High Commissioner, setting out the legal status of OHCHR in Croatia, and commended the cooperation between the Government and the Office and the agreement between the Office and the city of Zagreb to establish a Human Rights Documentation Centre in government-provided premises. The Special Rapporteur concluded that, despite remarkable political changes, Croatia continued to fall short of meeting some of its human rights obligations. Recommendations included full use of the tripartite Croatian Economic and Social Council, revisions of labour and other legislation to improve the economic and social situation, resolution of cases of missing persons and the bringing of all perpetrators to justice.

The Special Rapporteur considered the human rights situation in FRY from March to mid-July, having visited the country twice. He observed that Serbia faced increasingly grave and violent violations of human rights and fundamental freedoms in the absence of the rule of law and due process. Serbian authorities used the legal and judicial systems to legitimize political repression and criminalize opposition activity, civil society and the expression of dissent. He noted with concern the mass detention of opposition party members and increasing violations of freedom of expression. There were violations of the rights to due process and to fair trial. Montenegro was facing many problems typical of a society in the initial stage of transition to democracy and a market economy.

With regard to Kosovo, the issue of missing persons and those deprived of liberty in connection with the crisis there (see p. 358) remained a serious obstacle to the resolution of tensions. Violence in the southern Serbian municipalities of Presevo, Bujanovac and Medvedja was increasing, including armed attacks on police checkpoints, arbitrary detentions, beatings, disappearances, kidnappings and other violence against Serb and Albanian civilians. Recommendations to FRY focused on ensuring the administration of justice; ending repression of the rights of political expression, freedom of association, independence of the media and related civil and political rights; ensuring the representation of minorities in government; and preventing torture and ill-treatment of detainees and bringing perpetrators to justice.

Regarding Kosovo, it was recommended that UNMIK ensure that all applicable laws complied with international human rights standards; expedite the appointment in Kosovo of the full contingent of planned international judges and prosecutors; redouble its efforts to train legal professionals; review a regulation on extension of periods of pre-trial detention to ensure conformity with international standards; and review regulations on the media to ensure that they conformed to international human rights standards and practices. KFOR was urged to review regulations, training programmes, codes of conduct and operational procedures for its personnel, and ensure that individuals detained by KFOR were treated in accordance with international standards. The Special Rapporteur recommended that the international community end sanctions and other forms of isolation of the people of FRY.

In a later report [E/CN.4/2001/47] covering events in the region from September to December, the Special Rapporteur observed that in Bosnia and Herzegovina there was little change or significant progress to report concerning respect for human rights and the rule of law. Compared to the dramatic changes in Croatia and FRY in 2000, change in Bosnia and Herzegovina was happening much more slowly. The main concern continued to be the return of refugees and displaced persons. Regarding trade in women and children for forced prostitution, the Council of Ministers had established a State-level working group to draw up a national plan of action.

The Special Rapporteur expressed continuing deep concern over the unequal application of the rule of law in Croatia and the politicization of local judiciaries, as demonstrated by the sharp escalation of arrests of Croatian citizens of Serb ethnicity on war-crimes charges. The arrests had a major impact on the return of refugees. The Special Rapporteur applauded the Government's commitment to respect the right of refugees and internally displaced persons to return to their homes, but noted that return continued to be obstructed in many ways. The central issue of property rights continued to slow the return process. He expressed support for the ongoing technical cooperation projects planned by OHCHR in 2001.

The last quarter of 2000 witnessed dramatic political changes in FRY, of which the most important, said the Special Rapporteur, was the 24 September presidential election in which the Democratic Opposition of Serbia candidate Vojislav Kostunica defeated Slobodan Milosevic and opened the door to a democratic transition (see p. 384). In Kosovo, UNMIK-supervised municipal elections (see p. 367) on 28 October resulted in moderate candidates being elected to a majority of local offices. Regarding Serbia (excluding Kosovo), the cases of many individuals arrested and subject to trial for political views during the Milosevic years remained unresolved, and hundreds of Kosovar Albanian political prisoners and thousands of Serbs who resisted service or deserted the security forces remained in prison or under threat of prosecution. In both Serbia and Montenegro, national minorities continued to suffer discrimination. Organized criminal activity, particularly trafficking in women, remained a serious problem. In Kosovo, violence against Serbs and other ethnic minorities continued to fuel tension, while political attacks and assassinations among Kosovo Albanians had increased since the municipal elections. The functioning of the judicial and prison systems remained far below acceptable international standards. FRY faced serious economic and humanitarian challenges. The Special Rapporteur urged the international community to redouble its efforts to ensure that humanitarian needs were met in the country.

GENERAL ASSEMBLY ACTION

On 4 December [meeting 81], the General Assembly, on the recommendation of the Third Committee [A/55/602/Add.3], adopted **resolution 55/113** without vote [agenda item 114 (c)].

Situation of human rights in parts of South-Eastern Europe

The General Assembly,

Bearing in mind all relevant resolutions on this subject, in particular Commission on Human Rights resolution 2000/26 of 18 April 2000, and all Security Council resolutions and presidential statements,

Guided by the purposes and principles of the Charter of the United Nations, the Universal Declaration of Human Rights, the International Covenants on Human Rights and other human rights instruments, the 1951 Convention relating to the Status of Refugees, the Geneva Conventions of 12 August 1949 for the protection of victims of war and the Additional Protocols thereto, of 1977,

Taking note of the principles and commitments undertaken by participating States of the Organization for Security and Cooperation in Europe,

Reaffirming the territorial integrity of all States in the region, within their internationally recognized borders, taking fully into account all relevant Security Council resolutions,

Expressing its full support for the General Framework Agreement for Peace in Bosnia and Herzegovina and the annexes thereto (collectively the "Peace Agreement"), which, inter alia, committed the parties in Bosnia and Herzegovina, the Republic of Croatia and the Federal Republic of Yugoslavia to respect human rights fully, in particular issues surrounding the return of refugees,

Expressing its support for the democratic forces and non-governmental organizations in the promotion and protection of human rights and in strengthening civil society, and noting in this regard the opportunities afforded by the Stability Pact for South-Eastern Europe, which was adopted at Cologne, Germany, on 10 June 1999,

Welcoming the admission of the Federal Republic of Yugoslavia into the framework of the Stability Pact for South-Eastern Europe at the extraordinary session of the Regional Table of the Pact, held at Bucharest on 26 October 2000,

Noting the importance of the respect for the rights of all persons belonging to minorities,

Welcoming all contributions of the Office of the High Representative, the Office of the United Nations High Commissioner for Human Rights, the Office of the United Nations High Commissioner for Refugees, the Special Rapporteur of the Commission on Human Rights and other entities of the United Nations, the Organization for Security and Cooperation in Europe, the Council of Europe, the European Community Monitoring Mission, Governments and intergovernmental and non-governmental organizations in the area in 2000,

Recalling Security Council resolutions 1160(1998) of 31 March 1998, 1199(1998) of 23 September 1998, 1203(1998) of 24 October 1998, 1239(1999) of 14 May 1999 and 1244(1999) of 10 June 1999, and the general principles annexed to that resolution, as well as the statement made on 24 March 1998 by the Chairman of the Commission on Human Rights at the fifty-fourth session of the Commission, Commission on Human Rights resolutions 1998/79 of 22 April 1998 and 1999/2 of 13 April 1999, and the report of the United Nations High Commissioner for Human Rights of 27 September 1999 on the situation of human rights in Kosovo,

Recalling also its condemnation of the Serbian military offensive against the civilian population of Kosovo, which resulted in war crimes and gross violations of international human rights and international humanitarian law being inflicted upon the Kosovars,

Condemning all violations of human rights in Kosovo, which have affected all ethnic groups in Kosovo, in particular the harassment and murder of ethnic Serb, Roma and other minorities of Kosovo by ethnic Albanian extremists,

Expressing concern that the entire population of Kosovo has been affected by the conflict there and its aftermath, and stressing that all of the national, ethnic, religious or linguistic minorities there must benefit from their full and equal rights, without discrimination,

Stressing, in this context, the importance of the International Tribunal for the Prosecution of Persons Responsible for Serious Violations of International Humanitarian Law Committed in the Territory of the Former Yugoslavia since 1991,

Distressed by the detention in Serbia of political prisoners of Kosovar Albanian or other origin, in violation of international human rights law and standards, but welcoming the pledge of authorities there to abide by international norms in carrying out judicial procedures in this and all other areas of judicial responsibility,

1. *Reiterates its call* for the full and consistent implementation of the General Framework Agreement for Peace in Bosnia and Herzegovina and the annexes thereto (collectively the "Peace Agreement") by all parties;

2. *Stresses* the crucial role of human rights in the successful implementation of the Peace Agreement, and underlines the obligations of all parties under the Peace Agreement to comply with international human rights law and to secure for all persons within their jurisdiction the highest level of international norms and standards of human rights and fundamental freedoms, including the rule of law and effective administration of justice at all levels of government, the freedom and independence of the media, freedom of expression, freedom of association, including with respect to political parties, freedom of religion and freedom of movement;

3. *Also stresses* the need for enhanced international efforts to foster and effect the prompt and voluntary return of displaced persons and refugees in safety and with dignity;

4. *Condemns* the growing problem of trafficking in women in the region, and calls upon all concerned authorities to combat actively this criminal practice;

5. *Urges* all States and parties to the Peace Agreement that have not done so to meet their obligations to cooperate fully with the International Tribunal for the Prosecution of Persons Responsible for Serious Violations of International Humanitarian Law Committed in the Territory of the Former Yugoslavia since 1991, as required by Security Council resolution 827(1993) of 25 May 1993 and all subsequent relevant resolutions, and in particular to comply with their obligations to arrest and transfer to the custody of the Tribunal those indicted persons present in their territories or under their control;

6. *Notes* that varying degrees of progress have been made in the human rights situation in all States and by all parties to the Peace Agreement, but that substantial efforts remain to be made in several areas;

7. *Reiterates its call* upon all States and parties to the Peace Agreement to ensure that the promotion and protection of human rights and effective, functioning democratic institutions will be central elements in developing civilian structures;

8. *Notes* the progress made by Bosnia and Herzegovina in the implementation of the Peace Agreement;

9. *Also notes* the progress made with regard to refugee returns in Bosnia and Herzegovina, while calling upon all authorities actively to support the return process for minority refugees and internally displaced persons, inter alia, through the eviction of illegal occupants of housing intended for internally displaced persons and refugees, in particular in areas of the Republika Srpska with a majority population of Bosnian Serbs and areas of the Federation of Bosnia and Herzegovina with a majority population of Bosnian Croats;

10. *Welcomes* the "Constituent Peoples" decision of the Constitutional Court of Bosnia and Herzegovina, which reflects the commitment of Bosnia and Herzegovina to meeting the highest standards of human rights and fundamental freedoms;

11. *Condemns* the harassment of returning minority refugees and internally displaced persons in Bosnia and Herzegovina, including the destruction of their homes, in particular in areas of the Republika Srpska with a majority population of Bosnian Serbs and areas of the Federation with a majority population of Bosnian Croats;

12. *Also condemns* recurrent instances of religious discrimination and the denial to religious minorities of their right to rebuild religious sites in Bosnia and Herzegovina, in particular in the territory of the Republika Srpska;

13. *Further condemns* the manipulation of the press by political parties and government officials, including the selective application of slander and tax laws to harass journalists and editors;

14. *Calls upon* all authorities in Bosnia and Herzegovina, in particular those within the Republika Srpska, to cooperate fully with the International Tribunal for the Former Yugoslavia;

15. *Calls upon* the authorities of Bosnia and Herzegovina, including those of the Republika Srpska and the Federation:

(*a*) To implement the decisions of the High Representative and to fulfil their obligations under the Peace Agreement and the declarations of the Peace Implementation Council;

(*b*) To implement the decisions of the Commission on Human Rights on Bosnia and Herzegovina, the Office of the Human Rights Ombudsman and the Human Rights Chamber, and the decisions of the Commission for Real Property Claims of Displaced Persons and Refugees;

(*c*) To establish a fully staffed and funded judiciary which effectively protects the rights of all citizens;

(*d*) To adopt an effective and fair election law, in cooperation with the Organization for Security and Cooperation in Europe;

(*e*) To implement fully all the provisions of the New York Declaration adopted on 15 November 1999;

(*f*) To support the work of the common institutions and implement fully the actions mandated by the Peace Implementation Council at its ministerial meeting held at Brussels on 23 and 24 May 2000;

16. *Welcomes* the political change following the recent elections in the Federal Republic of Yugoslavia, which shows the clear decision of the people to choose democracy, respect for human rights and integration into the international community over dictatorship and isolation, and looks forward to the new authorities ensuring respect for the rule of law and for the promotion and protection of human rights;

17. *Also welcomes* the admission of the Federal Republic of Yugoslavia to membership in the United Nations;

18. *Further welcomes* the commitment of, and encourages efforts by, the new democratic authorities of the Federal Republic of Yugoslavia to investigate past abuses of human rights, including violations of the human rights of ethnic groups in Kosovo, the repression and harassment of peaceful political activists, illegal and/or hidden detentions, and other violations of human rights and fundamental freedoms;

19. *Welcomes* the appointment by the United Nations High Commissioner for Human Rights of the Special Envoy on persons deprived of liberty in connection with the Kosovo crisis in the Federal Republic of Yugoslavia, and calls upon all authorities to cooperate with the Special Envoy;

20. *Also welcomes* the commitment of the new democratic authorities of the Federal Republic of Yugoslavia to promoting and protecting free and independent media, and looks forward to welcoming the repeal of any laws that hinder the full and free exercise of human rights and fundamental freedoms in the Federal Republic of Yugoslavia;

21. *Calls upon* all authorities of the Federal Republic of Yugoslavia to respect the rights of all persons belonging to any of its national or ethnic, religious and linguistic minorities;

22. *Welcomes* the commitment by the Federal Republic of Yugoslavia to implement fully and in good faith its obligations under the Peace Agreement and to abide by the terms of Security Council resolution 1244(1999), and calls upon the Federal Republic of Yugoslavia to cooperate with the Office of the United Nations High Commissioner for Refugees and other humanitarian organizations to alleviate the suffering of refugees and internally displaced persons, to protect them, and to assist their voluntary return to their homes in safety and with dignity;

23. *Encourages* States to consider providing additional voluntary contributions to support the new dem-

ocratic authorities so that they may meet the pressing human rights and humanitarian needs in the area;

24. *Calls upon* the authorities of the Federal Republic of Yugoslavia to comply with their obligation to cooperate fully with the International Tribunal for the Former Yugoslavia, and welcomes the announced reopening of the Office of the International Tribunal in Belgrade and the pledge of the authorities of the Federal Republic of Yugoslavia to cooperate with it;

25. *Underlines* the obligation of the authorities of the Federal Republic of Yugoslavia to abide by the terms of Council resolution 1244(1999) and the general principles on a political solution to the Kosovo crisis adopted on 6 May 1999 and annexed to that resolution;

26. *Reaffirms* that the human rights and humanitarian situation in Kosovo shall be addressed within the framework of a political solution based and built upon the general principles set out in the annex to Council resolution 1244(1999);

27. *Welcomes* the efforts of the United Nations Interim Administration Mission in Kosovo and the Kosovo Force, and calls upon all parties in Kosovo and the authorities of the Federal Republic of Yugoslavia to cooperate fully with the Mission and the Force in the fulfilment of their respective mandates;

28. *Encourages* States to consider providing additional voluntary contributions to support the Mission in meeting the pressing administrative, human rights and humanitarian needs in the area;

29. *Welcomes* the work in Kosovo of the Office of the United Nations High Commissioner for Human Rights and the Office of the United Nations High Commissioner for Refugees and the efforts of the Organization for Security and Cooperation in Europe;

30. *Recognizes* the strong efforts of the Mission, the United Nations civilian police and the Kosovo Police Service in developing and training the core of a multi-ethnic local police force throughout Kosovo;

31. *Calls upon* all parties in Kosovo to cooperate with the Mission to ensure full respect for all human rights and fundamental freedoms and democratic norms in Kosovo;

32. *Urges* all parties in Kosovo to support and strengthen a multi-ethnic society in Kosovo that respects the rights of all persons belonging to minorities and that includes them in all provisional and new civil administration institutions in Kosovo, and to support the Mission fully in this regard;

33. *Welcomes* the recent holding of peaceful municipal elections in Kosovo, which is a landmark in the democratic development of Kosovo and in the implementation of Council resolution 1244(1999), and commends in this regard the support by all parties of the efforts of the Mission;

34. *Commends* the Mission for its efforts to create an independent and impartial judiciary system in Kosovo, and urges all local Serb and Albanian leaders, and the leaders of other minorities in Kosovo, to take all steps necessary to support these efforts;

35. *Calls upon* all local Kosovar officials, ethnic representatives and all individuals to respect the right to freedom of opinion and expression for all points of view, the right to a free, independent media and the right to freedom of religion;

36. *Calls upon* the authorities in the Federal Republic of Yugoslavia, and the representatives of all ethnic groups in Kosovo, to condemn all acts of terrorism and forced evictions from homes or places of work of any resident of Kosovo, whatever the ethnic background of the victim and whoever the perpetrators, to refrain from all acts of violence and to use their influence and leadership to bring all parties to cooperate fully with the Force and the Mission in stopping these incidents and in bringing the perpetrators to justice;

37. *Stresses* the importance of the return of refugees and of all displaced persons, whatever their ethnic background, and expresses its concern about reports of continuing harassment or other impediments in this regard;

38. *Also stresses* the importance for, and the responsibility of, all parties in Kosovo to suppress all harassment of individuals or groups of any background and to create a secure environment that will offer to all those who wish to remain in Kosovo, irrespective of ethnic origin, a genuine possibility of doing so;

39. *Further stresses* the urgent need for all ethnic groups to cooperate with the Mission and the Force to rebuild and strengthen common institutions for all and to desist from creating any sort of parallel institutions;

40. *Calls upon* the authorities of the Federal Republic of Yugoslavia to release those persons detained and transferred from Kosovo to other parts of the Federal Republic of Yugoslavia, or to specify the charge under which each individual is detained and to afford them due process of law, and to guarantee their families and non-governmental organizations and international observers unimpeded and regular access to those who remain in detention, and, in this regard, welcomes as a first important step the release of the prominent human rights activist, Flora Brovina, and the release of twenty-three additional detainees;

41. *Calls upon* the authorities of the Federal Republic of Yugoslavia, and all local Kosovo ethnic Serb and Albanian leaders, to provide information on the fate and whereabouts of the high number of missing persons from Kosovo, and encourages the International Committee of the Red Cross, in this regard, to continue its clarification efforts, in cooperation with other organizations;

42. *Expresses its concern* about the forced ethnic division of any part of Kosovo as being contrary to Council resolution 1244(1999) and to the guiding principles of the Rambouillet accords, and stresses the need for all parties in Kosovo to take all necessary measures to prevent or reverse any action that de facto or de jure permits such ethnic cantonization;

43. *Condemns* all trafficking in women by any party in Kosovo, and calls upon the local authorities and the Mission to take all steps necessary to prevent and stop it;

44. *Requests* the Special Rapporteur of the Commission on Human Rights on the situation of human rights in Bosnia and Herzegovina, the Republic of Croatia and the Federal Republic of Yugoslavia to continue to monitor closely the situation of human rights in Kosovo, and to report his findings to the Commission at its fifty-seventh session and to the General Assembly at its fifty-sixth session;

45. *Decides* to continue its examination of this question at its fifty-sixth session under the item entitled "Human rights questions".

Russian Federation

Republic of Chechnya

Report of High Commissioner. On 5 April [E/CN.4/2000/SR.28], the High Commissioner reported orally to the Commission on her visit to the north Caucasus region of the Russian Federation (Ingushetia, Dagestan, Chechnya, 31 March–4 April). She also had a series of meetings in Moscow with international humananitarian organizations active in the north Caucasus and with Russian and international NGOs. Before travelling, she gave the Russian Government a list of some of the most serious allegations of human rights abuses in Chechnya.

From the Commission's perspective, the most pressing and immediate issue concerned the adequacy and credibility of the response by the Russian authorities to the scale of allegations of human rights violations in the region. Nine criminal prosecutions had been opened for offences against civilians. In her discussions in Moscow with the Minister for Foreign Affairs and other government members, the High Commissioner raised the possibility of establishing a broad-based, independent national commission of inquiry. Although she recognized the complexity of the situation, the High Commissioner believed that the primary responsibility for addressing human rights violations rested with the Russian authorities; she offered to send them models of national commissions of inquiry.

On 1 April, the High Commissioner travelled to Nazran, the capital of Ingushetia, where an estimated 213,000 internally displaced persons had fled. She heard testimony from witnesses of alleged mass killings, summary executions, rape, torture and pillage; those accounts bore out the seriousness of the alleged violations by the Russian military, militia and Ministry of the Interior forces in Chechnya. She visited Chechnya on 2 April, where she spoke to some of the remaining residents of Grozny, chiefly women and the elderly, who complained bitterly of the lack of food and miserable living conditions. They were also anxious about relatives who had been detained. The scale of destruction in Grozny was shocking, said the High Commissioner.

The High Commissioner welcomed the agreement of the Russian authorities to provide access by ICRC to places of detention in Chechnya. The Russian Minister for Foreign Affairs had invited her to return to Moscow, Chechnya and the north Caucasus later in the year to assess the situation.

Commission action. On 25 April [res. 2000/58], by a roll-call vote of 25 to 7, with 19 abstentions, the Commission called on all parties to the conflict in Chechnya to halt the hostilities and the indiscriminate use of force and to hold a political dialogue and negotiations to solve the crisis. The Russian Federation was called on to establish urgently a national, broad-based and independent commission of inquiry to investigate alleged human rights violations and breaches of international humanitarian law committed in Chechnya. It was also asked to disseminate, and ensure that the military had knowledge of, basic principles of human rights and international humanitarian law.

The Commission asked the Special Rapporteurs on the question of torture, on extrajudicial, summary or arbitrary executions, and on violence against women, the Special Representative of the Secretary-General for Children and Armed Conflict and the Representative on internally displaced persons to carry out missions to Chechnya and neighbouring republics and to report thereon to the Commission and the General Assembly. The High Commissioner was asked to facilitate their tasks and to consult with the Russian Federation to ensure the implementation of the current resolution. The High Commissioner was asked to report to the Commission in 2001 and to keep it and the Assembly informed on further developments.

ECONOMIC AND SOCIAL COUNCIL ACTION

On 28 July, the Economic and Social Council, on the recommendation of the Commission on Human Rights [E/2000/23 & Corr.1], adopted **decision 2000/273** by recorded vote (21-6-15) [agenda item 14 (g)].

Situation in the Republic of Chechnya of the Russian Federation

At its 45th plenary meeting, on 28 July 2000, the Economic and Social Council, taking note of Commission on Human Rights resolution 2000/58 of 25 April 2000, approved the Commission's request to the relevant special rapporteurs and working groups of the Commission, namely, the Special Rapporteur on the question of torture, the Special Rapporteur on extrajudicial, summary or arbitrary executions, the Special Rapporteur on violence against women, its causes and consequences, the Representative of the Secretary-General on internally displaced persons and the Special Representative of the Secretary-General for Children and Armed Conflict, to undertake missions to the Republic of Chechnya and neighbouring republics without delay and to submit reports to the Commission and to the General Assembly as soon as possible.

RECORDED VOTE ON DECISION 2000/273:

In favour: Austria, Belgium, Bulgaria, Canada, Costa Rica, Croatia, Czech Republic, Denmark, Fiji, France, Germany, Greece, Italy, New Zealand, Norway, Pakistan, Poland, Portugal, Saudi Arabia, United Kingdom, United States.

Against: Belarus, China, Cuba, India, Russian Federation, Viet Nam.

Abstaining: Algeria, Angola, Bahrain, Bolivia, Brazil, Burkina Faso, Colombia, Indonesia, Japan, Mexico, Saint Lucia, Sudan, Suriname, Syrian Arab Republic, Venezuela.

Middle East

Lebanon

Commission action. On 18 April [res. 2000/16], by a roll-call vote of 51 to 1, with 1 abstention, the Commission deplored continued Israeli violations of human rights in southern Lebanon and western Bekaa and called on Israel to end those practices. Israel was also called on to comply with the Geneva Conventions of 1949, particularly the Geneva Convention relative to the Protection of Civilian Persons in Time of War (Fourth Geneva Convention), and to release all Lebanese who had been imprisoned and held as hostages for bargaining purposes, as well as others arbitrarily detained in the occupied territories. The Commission asked the Secretary-General to bring its resolution to Israel's attention and to invite Israel to provide information on its implementation. He was asked to report to the General Assembly in 2000 and to the Commission in 2001.

ECONOMIC AND SOCIAL COUNCIL ACTION

On 28 July, the Economic and Social Council, on the recommendation of the Commission on Human Rights [E/2000/23 & Corr.1], adopted **decision 2000/249** by recorded vote (43-1) [agenda item 14 (g)].

Human rights situation in southern Lebanon and western Bekaa

At its 45th plenary meeting, on 28 July 2000, the Economic and Social Council, taking note of Commission on Human Rights resolution 2000/16 of 18 April 2000, approved the Commission's request to the Secretary-General:

(a) To bring Commission resolution 2000/16 to the attention of the Government of Israel and to invite it to provide information concerning the extent of its implementation thereof;

(b) To report to the General Assembly at its fifty-fifth session and to the Commission at its fifty-seventh session on the results of his efforts in this regard.

RECORDED VOTE ON DECISION 2000/249:

In favour: Algeria, Angola, Austria, Bahrain, Belarus, Belgium, Bolivia, Brazil, Bulgaria, Burkina Faso, Canada, China, Colombia, Costa Rica, Croatia, Cuba, Czech Republic, Denmark, Fiji, France, Germany, Greece, India, Indonesia, Italy, Japan, Mexico, Morocco, New Zealand, Norway, Oman, Pakistan, Poland, Portugal, Russian Federation, Saint Lucia, Saudi Arabia, Sudan, Suriname, Syrian Arab Republic, United Kingdom, Venezuela, Viet Nam.

Against: United States.

Reports of Secretary-General. In response to a 1999 Commission request [YUN 1999, p. 736], the Secretary-General stated that he had asked Israel for information on the extent of the implementation of the Commission's 1999 resolution on the situation of human rights in southern Lebanon and western Bekaa [ibid.], but had received no reply [E/CN.4/2000/28].

In September [A/55/400], the Secretary-General informed the General Assembly that he had asked Israel for information on the implementation of the Commission's 2000 resolution (see p. 773) and had received no reply.

Territories occupied by Israel

During the year, the question of human rights violations in the territories occupied by Israel as a result of the 1967 hostilities in the Middle East was again considered by the Commission on Human Rights. In addition to considering the matter at its fifty-sixth session in March/April, the Commission held a special session to discuss the matter in October following an escalation of violence. Political and other aspects were considered by the General Assembly, its Special Committee to Investigate Israeli Practices Affecting the Human Rights of the Palestinian People and Other Arabs of the Occupied Territories (Committee on Israeli Practices) and other bodies (see PART ONE, Chapter VI).

Reports of Secretary-General. Pursuant to a 1999 Commission resolution [YUN 1999, p. 738], the Secretary-General reported that he had brought that resolution, which concerned the occupied Syrian Golan, to the attention of all Governments, the Committee on Israeli Practices, the Committee on the Exercise of the Inalienable Rights of the Palestinian People (Committee on Palestinian Rights), the United Nations Relief and Works Agency for Palestine Refugees in the Near East (UNRWA), the specialized agencies, regional intergovernmental organizations and international humanitarian organizations [E/CN.4/2000/23]. The UN Department of Public Information provided press coverage for all meetings of the Committee on Israeli Practices and distributed information through documents, press releases, briefings and UN information centres and services.

Also in response to a 1999 Commission resolution [YUN 1999, p. 737], the Secretary-General stated that he had brought that resolution, dealing with violations of human rights in the occupied Arab territories, to the attention of the Government of Israel and all other Governments, the Committee on Israeli Practices and the Committee on Palestinian Rights, as well as to the attention of the

specialized agencies, UNRWA, regional intergovernmental organizations and international humanitarian organizations, requesting information pertaining to Israel's implementation of the resolution [E/CN.4/2000/22]. He had received no reply. By a March addendum to that report [E/CN.4/2000/22/Add.1], the Secretary-General transmitted a reply from the League of Arab States (LAS), which contained information on Israeli violations of Palestinian human rights in the occupied territories, on the suffering of the Lebanese from occupation and the Israeli aggression in southern Lebanon, and on Israeli practices affecting the human rights of Syrian citizens in the occupied territories.

The Secretary-General submitted to the Commission, in February, a list of all General Assembly and other reports issued since 30 April 1999 on the situation of the population living in the occupied Arab territories [E/CN.4/2000/24].

Report of Special Rapporteur. In March [E/CN.4/2000/25], Special Rapporteur Giorgio Giacomelli (Italy) discussed the human rights situation in the occupied Palestinian territories. The principal concerns included the right of return of persons residing in those territories; forced eviction of Palestinians; demolition of Palestinian homes; the implantation of Israeli settlers in the territories; practices that affected the natural environment of the occupied territories (degradation of the infrastructure, land confiscation, water depletion, uprooting of trees, dumping of toxic wastes and other pollution); closures of the occupied territories and their impact on the freedoms of movement, education, religion, expression and information; collective punishment; and discrimination against Palestinian workers. In addition, the Special Rapporteur discussed human rights violations against children, women and the family, violations of the rights of Palestinian prisoners and the application of double standards regarding the administration of justice. In East Jerusalem, where violations continued to be particularly intense, he pointed to the wholesale imposition of Israeli domestic law in the city, and the special discrimination practised by Israel's arbitrary denial and revocation of residency, which divided families. The Special Rapporteur recommended rigorous implementation of the relevant international norms, which implied the reversal of illegal trends, correction and, where appropriate, restitution.

Commission action. On 17 April [res. 2000/6], by a roll-call vote of 31 to 1, with 19 abstentions, the Commission condemned the continued human rights violations in the occupied Palestinian territories, and called on Israel to cease those acts immediately. Condemning the expropriation of Palestinian homes in Jerusalem, the revocation of identity cards, the imposition of exorbitant taxes aimed at forcing Palestinians out of Jerusalem and the use of torture against Palestinians during interrogation, the Commission called on Israel to end those practices. The Commission also called on Israel to cease its policy of enforcing collective punishments; desist from all forms of human rights violations in the Palestinian and other occupied Arab territories and respect the bases of international law, the principles of international humanitarian law and its international commitments and agreements; and withdraw from the Palestinian territories. The Secretary-General was asked to bring the Commission's resolution to the attention of the Government of Israel and all other Governments, competent UN organs, the specialized agencies, regional intergovernmental organizations and international humanitarian organizations, to disseminate it as widely as possible and to report in 2001 on its implementation by Israel. He was also asked to provide the Commission with all UN reports issued between its sessions that dealt with conditions in which the Palestinians were living under Israeli occupation.

Also on 17 April [res. 2000/7] and by the same roll-call vote, the Commission called on Israel to comply with UN resolutions on the occupied Syrian Golan and demanded that it rescind its decision to impose its laws, jurisdiction and administration on that occupied territory. It also called on Israel to desist from changing the physical character, demographic composition, institutional structure and legal status of the occupied Syrian Golan and to desist from imposing Israeli identity cards on Syrian citizens of the Syrian Golan and from its repressive measures against them. The Secretary-General was asked to bring the Commission's resolution to the attention of all Governments, UN organs, specialized agencies, regional intergovernmental organizations and international humanitarian organizations, to give the resolution wide publicity and to report in 2001.

On the same date [res. 2000/8], by a roll-call vote of 50 to 1, with 1 abstention, the Commission, expressing grave concern at Israeli settlement activities in the occupied Arab territories, including East Jerusalem, and condemning all acts of terrorism, called on all parties not to allow those acts to affect the ongoing peace process negatively. The Commission urged Israel to comply fully with the Commission's previous resolutions; to cease its policy of expanding the settlements and related activities in the occupied territories; and to forgo and prevent any new installation of settlers.

Communications. During the year, the Commission received a number of communications regarding the situation in the occupied Palestinian territories, including from LAS summarizing Israeli practices from January to July [E/CN.4/2001/108] and from Palestine describing violent acts by Israel and Jewish settlers [E/CN.4/2000/136, E/CN.4/2000/146, E/CN.4/2001/7, E/CN.4/2001/109-112, E/CN.4/2001/118]. It also received from Palestine a statistical table of the human and material losses from 29 February to 29 December [E/CN.4/2001/130].

The Commission on Human Rights held its fifth special session in Geneva from 17 to 19 October [E/2000/112 & Add.1] (see next page). The session was requested by Algeria [E/CN.4/S-5/2] on behalf of the Council of Arab Permanent Representatives, members of LAS, to discuss "the grave and massive violations of the human rights of the Palestinian people by the Israeli occupying Power".

Report of Special Rapporteur. The Commission had before it a report on Israel's violations of human rights in the Palestinian territories occupied since 1967 [E/CN.4/S-5/3] by the Special Rapporteur, who, in response to recent developments and the acute situation in the territories (see p. 416), had undertaken a mission to the region from 11 to 15 October.

He stated that the full range of human rights violations reported earlier (see p. 774) had remained constant. However, a number of violations from that spectrum had shown a dramatic upsurge since late September. The Special Rapporteur reported that Israel had dramatically escalated the use of lethal force against civilians, in response to demonstrations that began in Jerusalem and spread throughout the West Bank and Gaza Strip. Since 28 September, Israeli forces had killed at least 85 Palestinians, of whom more than 20 were under the age of 18, in the occupied Palestinian territories, and an estimated 2,000 to 3,700 were wounded. Israeli forces had obstructed, beaten and/or shot emergency medical personnel on duty, thus denying emergency medical aid to victims and wounding medical personnel. The level and number of casualties had strained local medical services beyond capacity. Israel's current closure of the occupied territories was characterized also by the sealing off of Palestinian populated areas, preventing free movement of people and material, and creating shortages and a sense of isolation. Freedom of movement was denied to businessmen and other professionals. Other economic losses included those resulting from the demolition of physical structures, including homes and apartments, the damaging and burning of vehicles, including ambulances, and vandalism of homes. The Special Rapporteur remained convinced that the current conflict had its roots in accumulated grievances and resentment at the continuing violations of human rights and humanitarian norms under Israeli occupation. He recommended that Israel issue orders to all its forces consistent with international humanitarian norms and that those orders be rigorously implemented. He supported the idea of establishing a mechanism for a speedy and objective inquiry into the ongoing crisis, and recommended establishing an observer and/or guarantor body to build up a sense of security and confidence on both sides.

Communication. On 19 October [E/CN.4/S-5/4], Israel stated that the Special Rapporteur's report was biased and selective. The allegations against Israel were unsubstantiated, the sources were never identified and those aspects that might have given a more balanced picture were ignored or otherwise curtailed. Attention should have been given to the continued Palestinian violations of written commitments, particularly to fighting terrorism and preventing incitement.

Commission action. On 19 October [E/2000/112 (res. S-5/1)], by a roll-call vote of 19 to 16, with 17 abstentions, the Commission strongly condemned the use of force by Israel against Palestinians, causing the death of 120 civilians, and called on Israel to end the use of force against unarmed civilians and to abide by its legal obligations under the Fourth Geneva Convention. It called on the international community to secure the cessation of violence by Israel and end the ongoing violations of the Palestinians' human rights.

The Commission decided to establish a human rights inquiry commission to gather information on violations of human rights that constituted grave breaches of humanitarian law by Israel. It further decided to request the High Commissioner to undertake an urgent visit to the occupied territories and to request several of the Commission's special rapporteurs, the Working Group on Enforced or Involuntary Disappearances and others to visit the occupied territories and to report to the Commission in 2001 and to the General Assembly in 2000. Those and other requests of the Commission were endorsed by the Economic and Social Council in the decision below.

ECONOMIC AND SOCIAL COUNCIL ACTION

On 22 November, the Economic and Social Council, on the recommendation of the Commission on Human Rights [E/2000/112 & Add.1], adopted **decision 2000/311** by recorded vote (21-19-11) [agenda item 14 *(g)*].

Grave and massive violations of the human rights of the Palestinian people by Israel

At its 48th plenary meeting, on 22 November 2000, the Economic and Social Council, taking note of Commission on Human Rights resolution S-5/1 of 19 October 2000, endorsed the Commission's decisions:

(a) To establish, on an urgent basis, a human rights inquiry commission, whose membership should be based on the principles of independence and objectivity, to gather and compile information on violations of human rights and acts that constituted grave breaches of international humanitarian law by the Israeli occupying Power in the occupied Palestinian territories and to provide the Commission with its conclusions and recommendations, with the aim of preventing the repetition of the recent human rights violations;

(b) To request the United Nations High Commissioner for Human Rights to undertake an urgent visit to the occupied Palestinian territories to take stock of the violations of the human rights of the Palestinian people by the Israeli occupying Power, to facilitate the activities of the mechanisms of the Commission in implementation of the present decision, to keep the Commission informed of developments and to report to the Commission at its fifty-seventh session and, on an interim basis, to the General Assembly at its fifty-fifth session;

(c) To request the Special Rapporteur on extrajudicial, summary or arbitrary executions, the Representative of the Secretary-General on internally displaced persons, the Special Rapporteur on the question of torture, the Special Rapporteur on violence against women, its causes and consequences, the Special Rapporteur on religious intolerance, the Special Rapporteur on contemporary forms of racism, racial discrimination, xenophobia and related intolerance, the Special Rapporteur on adequate housing as a component of the right to an adequate standard of living, and the Working Group on Enforced or Involuntary Disappearances to carry out immediate missions to the occupied Palestinian territories and to report the findings to the Commission at its fifty-seventh session and, on an interim basis, to the General Assembly at its fifty-fifth session.

Report of High Commissioner. In accordance with the Commission's request, as endorsed by the Economic and Social Council, the High Commissioner visited the occupied Palestinian territories, Israel, Egypt and Jordan (8-16 November) [E/CN.4/2001/114].

In the occupied Palestinian territories, the most persistent allegation brought to the High Commissioner's attention was the excessive use of force by Israeli security forces. The Minister of Health of the Palestinian Authority (PA) estimated that between 29 September and 9 November, some 6,958 persons (3,366 in the West Bank and 3,592 in the Gaza Strip) had been wounded and 1,016 Palestinians had been injured in Israel. Senior Israel Defence Forces (IDF) officers told the High Commissioner that the methods and weapons used were carefully calibrated according to the nature of the threat being faced and that live fire, whether from small arms or heavier weapons, had been directed only at those who had used firearms or petrol bombs in attacks against Israeli forces. The destruction of housing had left more than 1,000 children without homes, often in situations of food shortage and without access to medical care. Since the beginning of October, more than 40 schools had been closed or were unable to operate owing to curfews or closures. Many children suffered from psychological and social problems due to the current situation. Very serious allegations were made of attacks by Israeli security forces on medical personnel and ambulances. According to IDF, clearances and demolition of property had taken place as a matter of military necessity—meaning that compensation was not payable—because the structures or plantations had been used as cover by Palestinian gunmen. In response to the High Commissioner's call for lifting or easing the closures, which heavily restricted freedom of movement, IDF drew a link between the closures and the release in October by the PA of some 80 prisoners whom Israeli authorities considered a major security threat (see p. 420). Should the 80 prisoners be reincarcerated then the closures would be lifted the same day.

Since October, access to the Al-Aqsa Mosque had been denied to Muslims under the age of 45. Muslim and Christian leaders representing the Palestinian and Armenian communities in East Jerusalem wished to have full responsibility for their own holy places and complained of disrespectful behaviour by Israeli troops stationed at the holy sites. The Israeli authorities told the High Commissioner that the restrictions were necessary to prevent armed extremists from occupying the holy sites, which would necessitate an Israeli military response.

Some 128,000 Palestinian workers, normally employed in Israel, were barred from travelling to their workplaces due to closure. UN studies reported a 50 per cent reduction in normal economic activity within the territories. Access was a major preoccupation for all humanitarian organizations, affecting emergency evacuation of seriously injured civilians and the import of donations of humanitarian goods and equipment from abroad. The Ministry of Defence indicated that it was doing everything possible to facilitate humanitarian access.

Following her visits to Gaza, Hebron and Ramallah, the High Commissioner visited Israel where, among other things, she discussed with the Israeli authorities the use of force by IDF. IDF officers described as typical a situation that commenced with stone-throwing but quickly escalated into armed attacks. It was stated that out of 5,085 attacks on Israeli settlements, some 1,400 had involved live fire. According to IDF rules of engagement, attackers who used live ammunition could be shot by soldiers and sharpshooters deployed for that purpose. New weapons systems, they said, were being developed, which, IDF hoped, would be deployed to control crowds effectively at longer ranges with little or no risk of injury. The High Commissioner pursued with IDF the issue of how the use of lethal force was investigated, what punishments were available for improper or excessive use of such force, and how many investigations had been conducted to date and with what result.

Most of the Arab Israelis whom the High Commissioner met described their situation as one of exclusion, prejudice, official hostility and routine humiliation. Since 28 September, however, the threat of violence had become their primary concern. On 11 November, the Government of Israel decided to establish a State commission of inquiry to look into the clashes, since 29 September, between the security forces and Israeli citizens in which 13 Arabs were killed and hundreds of people injured. The Minister of Justice reiterated his commitment to establish a human rights commission and mentioned that research had been carried out on national human rights institutions. The High Commissioner offered the services of her Special Adviser on National Human Rights Institutions to assist the Government to establish a national commission.

In Egypt, the High Commissioner discussed with senior government officials and the LAS Secretary-General the human rights situation in the occupied Palestinian territories and the follow-up to the Commission's special session.

The High Commissioner was received in Jordan by His Royal Majesty King Abdullah II, who expressed deep concern about recent developments and said that Jordan was sparing no efforts to assist both parties in implementing decisions agreed upon in Sharm el-Sheikh in 1999 [YUN 1999, p. 401].

The High Commissioner recommended peaceful negotiation, exploring the feasibility of establishing an international monitoring presence and assistance by the international community through the task force established under the terms of the Sharm el-Sheikh Memorandum. She outlined specific steps to stop the escalation of violence. The High Commissioner would continue to assist the PA to build up its institutional capacity in the area of the rule of law, offer the services of her Special Adviser on National Human Rights Institutions to assist Israel, provide secretariat support to the Commission and its mechanisms to implement resolution S-5/1, be ready to facilitate dialogue between the human rights bodies of Israel and the PA, Palestinian and Israeli NGOs and other representatives of civil society, and urge the international community to support the work of UN agencies in the occupied Palestinian territories and to contribute to the various resource mobilization initiatives.

By a December note [A/55/684], the Secretary-General transmitted the High Commissioner's report to the General Assembly.

Communication. In identical reports to the Assembly [A/55/800] and to the Commission [E/CN.4/2001/133], Israel presented its views on the High Commissioner's report. It described what it claimed were the shortcomings of the report and presented its views on the current violence and Palestinian and Israeli policies and practices.

PART THREE

Economic and social questions

Chapter I

Development policy and international economic cooperation

Economic growth in 2000 was unexpectedly and unusually high and widespread. World output, which jumped to 4 per cent from 2.8 per cent in 1999, the strongest increase in more than a decade, was associated with double-digit growth in the volume of international trade. The developed economies, especially North America, were important sources of the strong performance. Although the economic situation of most developing countries also improved significantly, recovery from the setbacks of the financial crises of recent years remained incomplete. In many cases, employment and real wages had not returned to pre-crisis levels and broad negative social consequences persisted.

In action on development issues by UN bodies during the year, the challenges and opportunities of globalization were recognized, but concern was expressed about the exclusion of a large number of developing countries from the benefits of globalization and the growing income and technological gap, both between rich and poor countries and within countries. Those issues were also taken up by the Millennium Assembly (see p. 47) and the tenth session of the United Nations Conference on Trade and Development (see p. 890).

In July, ministers attending the high-level segment of the Economic and Social Council adopted a Declaration calling for action by Governments and the international community to improve the capacity of developing countries and economies in transition to participate in the emerging global knowledge-based economy in order to promote their economic and social development. Also in July, the Council recommended the creation of an information and communication technologies task force in order to formulate strategies for putting those technologies at the service of development. In a December resolution on the role of the United Nations in promoting development in the context of globalization and interdependence, the General Assembly encouraged the Secretary-General to continue consultations on establishing such a task force.

The Commission on Sustainable Development, at its April/May session, held a multi-stakeholder dialogue on agriculture and considered preparations for the 10-year review, to be held in 2002, of progress achieved in implementing Agenda 21, adopted in 1992 by the United Nations Conference on Environment and Development. The Committee for Development Policy, in April, carried out the triennial review of the list of least developed countries (LDCs), recommending that Senegal be added to and Maldives be graduated from the list. Preparations for the Third United Nations Conference on LDCs, to be held in 2001, were considered by the Assembly in December.

Other action by the Assembly on international economic cooperation included calling for the elimination of unilateral extraterritorial coercive economic measures, emphasizing the need for a favourable international and national environment for the industrialization of developing countries, calling on the UN system to continue to conduct analytical studies and provide advice and technical assistance to countries with economies in transition, requesting the Secretary-General to prepare for a second high-level dialogue on strengthening international economic cooperation for development through partnership and inviting the members of the UN system to reflect in their programmes measures for the implementation of the 1994 Programme of Action for the Sustainable Development of Small Island Developing States.

International economic relations

Development and international economic cooperation

A number of UN bodies addressed development and international economic cooperation issues during 2000, including the General Assembly and the Economic and Social Council.

On 14 December, the Assembly, by **decision 55/434**, deferred consideration of the launching of global negotiations on international economic cooperation for development and included the item in the provisional agenda of its fifty-sixth (2001) session.

On 20 December, the Assembly took note of the reports of the Second (Economic and Financial) Committee on its discussion of macro-economic policy questions [A/55/579] (**decision 55/437**) and of sustainable development and international economic cooperation [A/55/581] (**decision 55/440**). By **decision 55/458** of 23 December, the Assembly decided that the latter item would remain for consideration during its resumed fifty-fifth (2001) session.

Economic and Social Council consideration. On 18 April, the Economic and Social Council held its third special high-level meeting with the Bretton Woods institutions (the World Bank Group and the International Monetary Fund) [E/2000/79]. It considered a note by the Secretary-General identifying issues related to the reform of the global financial system and the fight against poverty in developing countries [E/2000/8] (see p. 906).

Promoting a new global human order

By a 5 May letter [A/55/74], Nigeria transmitted to the General Assembly the texts of the Declaration and the Havana Programme of Action adopted by the first South Summit (Havana, Cuba, 10-14 April). In the Declaration, the heads of State and Government of the member countries of the Group of 77 developing countries and China stressed the need for a new global human order aimed at reversing the growing disparities between rich and poor, both among and within countries, through the promotion of growth with equity, poverty eradication, expansion of productive employment and promotion of gender equality and social integration. Many of those objectives were included in the goals and targets of the Millennium Declaration (see p. 49).

GENERAL ASSEMBLY ACTION

On 29 November [meeting 74], the General Assembly adopted **resolution 55/48** [draft: A/55/L.15/Rev.2 & Add.1] without vote [agenda item 174].

The role of the United Nations in promoting a new global human order

The General Assembly,

Reaffirming the purposes and principles embodied in the Charter of the United Nations and the role of the United Nations in promoting international economic and social cooperation,

Recognizing that the well-being of people and the full development of their potential is the overall goal of sustainable development,

Deeply concerned about the growing disparities between rich and poor, both within and among countries, and about the adverse implications thereof for the promotion of human development throughout the world,

Determined to promote the economic and social advancement of all peoples, and convinced of the urgency of revitalizing international cooperation towards that end,

Emphasizing that countries are responsible for their development processes, and in this context stressing the responsibility of the international community, in partnership, to assist developing countries in their development efforts,

Reaffirming the United Nations Millennium Declaration of 8 September 2000, adopted by the heads of State and Government at the conclusion of the Millennium Summit of the United Nations, in particular the goals and targets agreed therein for promoting development and poverty eradication,

Taking note of the Declaration of the South Summit adopted in Havana on 14 April 2000, on, inter alia, the need for a new global human order aimed at reversing the growing disparities between rich and poor both among and within countries through the promotion of growth with equity, the eradication of poverty, the expansion of productive employment and the promotion of gender equality and social integration,

1. *Stresses* the need for a broad-based consensus for action within a comprehensive and holistic framework towards the achievement of the goals of development and poverty eradication involving all actors, namely Governments, the United Nations system and other international organizations, and relevant actors of civil society, including the private sector and non-governmental organizations;

2. *Notes with interest* the proposal regarding a new global human order;

3. *Requests* the Secretary-General to seek the views of Member States and of the agencies and organizations of the United Nations system on the promotion of a new global human order, and to prepare a report thereon for consideration by the General Assembly at its fifty-seventh session;

4. *Decides* to include in the agenda of its fifty-seventh session the item entitled "The role of the United Nations in promoting a new global human order".

Globalization and interdependence

During 2000, a number of UN bodies considered issues of globalization and interdependence, including the United Nations Conference on Trade and Development at its tenth session (UNCTAD X), which adopted the Bangkok Declaration and Plan of Action (see p. 891), and the General Assembly. The role of information technology in development in the context of globalization was discussed by the Committee for Development Policy and at the high-level segment of the Economic and Social Council (see p. 799).

Report of Secretary-General. In response to General Assembly resolution 54/231 [YUN 1999, p. 743], the Secretary-General submitted a September report on the role of the United Nations in promoting development in the context of globalization and interdependence [A/55/381]. The report focused on the need for the transfer of information and communication technologies (ICT) in the age of globalization, including issues related to such transfer to developing countries, and reviewed efforts undertaken by the UN system to enhance national ICT capacities. The report noted that the pivotal role of ICT in the emerging global knowledge-based economy was recognized in a series of documents, events and activities undertaken by the United Nations in 2000, including the Secretary-General's report "We the peoples: the role of the United Nations in the twenty-first century" [A/54/2000], submitted to the Millennium Assembly (see p. 55). Building on the proposals contained in the Ministerial Declaration adopted by the Economic and Social Council at its high-level segment (see p. 799), the Secretary-General presented a number of action-oriented recommendations regarding the role of the UN system in the transfer of ICT to developing countries. The suggestions included: providing advisory services on a number of ICT issues; strengthening collaboration among UN organizations in relation to ICT and establishing a system-wide inventory of the UN system's ICT activities; providing technical assistance to facilitate swifter diffusion of technological innovations; helping to generate reliable standardized and up-to-date statistical information on the impact of ICT on development; serving as a regional forum on ICT development and other regional activities; designing special programmes for the least developed countries (LDCs); upgrading the capabilities of UN organizations in using ICT for development; and taking steps to ensure dissemination of the UN system's wealth of knowledge and experience regarding the use of ICT for social and economic development, including creation of a web site on the Organization's ICT activities. A final section of the report, prepared by UNCTAD, addressed the promotion of policy coherence, complementarity and coordination in order to optimize the benefits of globalization.

GENERAL ASSEMBLY ACTION

On 20 December [meeting 87], the General Assembly, on the recommendation of the Second Committee [A/55/587], adopted **resolution 55/212** without vote [agenda item 100].

Role of the United Nations in promoting development in the context of globalization and interdependence

The General Assembly,

Recalling its resolutions 53/169 of 15 December 1998 and 54/231 of 22 December 1999,

Recalling also the United Nations Millennium Declaration adopted on 8 September 2000,

Taking note of the Plan of Action adopted by the United Nations Conference on Trade and Develop-

ment at its tenth session, held at Bangkok from 12 to 19 February 2000,

Taking note also of the Declaration and the Programme of Action adopted at the South Summit of the Group of 77, held at Havana from 10 to 14 April 2000,

Taking note further of the Ministerial Declaration of the high-level segment of the substantive session of 2000 of the Economic and Social Council, held in New York from 5 to 7 July 2000,

Taking note of Economic and Social Council resolution 2000/29 of 28 July 2000, in which the Council called for the establishment of a United Nations information and communication technologies task force,

Taking note also of the report of the Secretary-General,

Recognizing the challenges and opportunities of globalization and interdependence,

Expressing concern about the marginalization of a large number of developing countries from the benefits of globalization, the additional vulnerability of those developing countries that are integrating into the world economy and the general accentuation of the income and technological gap between developed and developing countries, as well as within countries,

Recognizing that globalization and interdependence are opening new opportunities through trade, investment and capital flows and advances in technology, including information technology, for the growth of the world economy, development and the improvement of living standards around the world, and recognizing also that some countries have made progress in successfully adapting to the changes and have benefited from globalization,

Recognizing also the importance of appropriate policy responses at the national level by all countries to the challenges of globalization, in particular by pursuing sound macroeconomic and social policies, noting the need for support from the international community for the efforts of the least developed countries, in particular, to improve their institutional and management capacities, and recognizing further that all countries should pursue policies conducive to economic growth and to promoting a favourable global economic environment,

Stressing that such national macroeconomic and social policies can yield better results with international support and with an enabling international economic environment,

Emphasizing the need to address those imbalances and asymmetries in international finance, trade, technology and investment patterns that have a negative impact on development prospects for developing countries, with a view to minimizing those impacts,

Noting with serious concern that a large number of developing countries have not yet been able to reap the full benefits of the existing multilateral trading system, and underlining the importance of promoting the integration of developing countries into the world economy so as to enable them to take the fullest possible advantage of the trading opportunities arising from globalization and liberalization,

Stressing that the process of reform for a strengthened and stable international financial architecture should be based on broad participation in a genuine multilateral approach, involving all members of the international community, to ensure that the diverse needs and interests of all countries are adequately represented,

Underlining the urgent need to mitigate the negative consequences of globalization and interdependence for all developing countries, including landlocked developing countries, small island developing States and, in particular, African countries and the least developed countries,

Reiterating that the United Nations, as a universal forum, is in a unique position to achieve international cooperation in addressing the challenges of promoting development in the context of globalization and interdependence, including, in particular, promoting a more equitable sharing of the benefits of globalization,

1. *Reaffirms* that the United Nations has a central role in promoting international cooperation for development and in promoting policy coherence on global development issues, including in the context of globalization and interdependence;

2. *Re-emphasizes* the urgency of coherent action by the United Nations, the Bretton Woods institutions and the World Trade Organization, as appropriate, along with the action of Governments, to promote equitable and broad sharing in the benefits of globalization, taking into account the specific vulnerabilities, concerns and needs of developing countries;

3. *Calls* for the effective addressing of globalization through, inter alia, making the decision-making process of international economic and financial policy more participatory, especially with regard to developing countries, the integrated consideration of trade, finance, investment, technology transfer and developmental issues by the relevant international institutions, the continuation of a wide range of reforms in the international financial system and further progress towards liberalization and enhanced market access in areas and for products of particular interest to developing countries, and, to this end, also calls for coherence and close cooperation among the United Nations, the Bretton Woods institutions and the World Trade Organization;

4. *Calls upon* all countries, in particular the major developed economies, to enhance coherence among their financial, investment, trade and development cooperation policies, with a view to enhancing the development prospects of developing countries;

5. *Stresses* the importance, at the national level, of maintaining sound macroeconomic policies and developing effective institutional and regulatory frameworks and human resources, so as to realize the mutually reinforcing objectives of poverty eradication and development, including through national poverty reduction strategies;

6. *Urges* the international community to promote international development cooperation aimed at enhancing growth, stability, equity and the participation of developing countries in the globalizing world economy;

7. *Encourages* developing countries to continue to pursue appropriate development policies to promote economic development and poverty eradication, and, in this regard, invites the international community to pursue strategies that support those policies through continued efforts to address the problems of market access, persistent external debt, transfer of resources, financial vulnerability and declining terms of trade;

8. *Strongly urges* the international community to take all necessary and appropriate measures, including support for structural and macroeconomic reform, foreign direct investment, enhanced official development assistance, the search for a durable solution to the external debt problem, market access, capacity-building and the dissemination of knowledge and technology, in order to achieve the sustainable development of Africa and to promote the participation of all African countries in the global economy;

9. *Reaffirms its resolve* to give greater opportunities to the private sector, non-governmental organizations and civil society in general to contribute to the realization of the goals and programmes of the United Nations and thereby to enhance opportunities and offset the negative economic and social consequences of globalization;

10. *Welcomes* the efforts of the United Nations Conference on Trade and Development and the International Trade Centre and other multilateral and bilateral efforts to help developing countries, including landlocked developing countries, small island developing States and, in particular, African countries and the least developed countries, in addressing their specific concerns within the globalizing economy, in particular through technology-related assistance in the fields of trade and policy, in the improvement of trade efficiency and policies and trade in services, and in electronic commerce;

11. *Stresses* the need for good governance within each country as well as at the international level;

12. *Emphasizes* the importance of recognizing and addressing the specific concerns of countries with economies in transition so as to help them to benefit from globalization, with a view to their full integration into the world economy;

13. *Emphasizes also* the technology-led dimension of globalization and the need to promote universal access to knowledge and information as well as the need to strive to bridge the digital divide and to bring information and communication technologies to the service of development and all the peoples of the world so as to enable the developing countries and the countries with economies in transition to benefit effectively from globalization by full and effective integration into the emerging global information network;

14. *Encourages* the Secretary-General, in this regard, to continue the ongoing consultations on the establishment of a United Nations information and communication technologies task force, and looks forward to the submission to the Economic and Social Council of the report requested by the Council in its resolution 2000/29;

15. *Requests* the Secretary-General to prepare, in close collaboration with the United Nations Conference on Trade and Development and other relevant organizations, an analytical report on the effect of increasing linkages and interdependencies among trade, finance, knowledge, technology and investment on growth and development in the context of globalization, containing action-oriented recommendations, including on appropriate development strategies at both the national and international levels, and to submit it to the General Assembly at its fifty-sixth session;

16. *Decides* to include in the provisional agenda of its fifty-sixth session the item entitled "Globalization and interdependence".

Development through partnership

On 21 December [meeting 88], the General Assembly adopted **resolution 55/215** [draft: A/55/L.71 & Add.1] without vote [agenda item 173].

Towards global partnerships

The General Assembly,

Reaffirming the central role of the United Nations, in particular the General Assembly, in the promotion of partnerships in the context of globalization,

Underlining the intergovernmental nature of the United Nations,

Recalling the priorities and objectives formulated in the United Nations Millennium Declaration, particularly in regard to developing strong partnerships in pursuit of development and poverty eradication,

Stressing that efforts to meet the challenges of globalization could benefit from enhanced cooperation between the United Nations and all relevant partners, in particular the private sector, in order to ensure that globalization becomes a positive force for all,

Taking into account ideas expressed in the report of the Secretary-General entitled "We the peoples: the role of the United Nations in the twenty-first century" of 27 March 2000 with regard to enhanced cooperation with the private sector,

1. *Stresses* the need for Member States further to discuss partnerships and consider, in appropriate intergovernmental consultations, ways and means to enhance cooperation between the United Nations and all relevant partners, inter alia, from the developing countries, to give them greater opportunities to contribute to the realization of the goals and programmes of the Organization;

2. *Requests* the Secretary-General in this regard to seek the views of all Member States on ways and means to enhance cooperation between the United Nations and all relevant partners, in particular the private sector;

3. *Invites* the Secretary-General also to seek the views of relevant partners, in particular the private sector, on how to enhance their cooperation with the United Nations;

4. *Requests* the Secretary-General to submit a comprehensive report on this matter, containing a compilation of views of Member States, views of other relevant partners, and his recommendations in this regard, for consideration by the General Assembly at its fifty-sixth session;

5. *Decides* to include in the agenda of its fifty-sixth session the item entitled "Towards global partnerships".

High-level dialogue (2001)

By a 30 June letter [A/54/952], the Chairman of the Second Committee reported to the President of the General Assembly on consultations held with Member States on 9 June regarding the date, modalities, nature of the outcome and fo-

cus of the discussions of the second high-level dialogue on strengthening international economic cooperation for development through partnership, to be held during the Assembly's fifty-sixth (2001) session with the theme "Responding to globalization: facilitating the integration of developing countries into the world economy in the twenty-first century". The first dialogue was held in 1998 [YUN 1998, p. 772]. By **decision 54/494** of 5 September, the Assembly took note of the letter.

Report of Secretary-General. In response to Assembly resolution 54/213 [YUN 1999, p. 742], the Secretary-General submitted an August report on the status of preparations for the second high-level dialogue [A/55/314]. Based on consultations with Member States, as well as recent experience in organizing high-level events, including the Millennium Summit, the Secretary-General made recommendations concerning the modalities, outcome, focus of discussions and next steps in preparing for the second high-level dialogue.

GENERAL ASSEMBLY ACTION

On 20 December [meeting 87], the General Assembly, on the recommendation of the Second Committee [A/55/581/Add.4], adopted **resolution 55/193** without vote [agenda item 94 (d)].

High-level dialogue on strengthening international economic cooperation for development through partnership

The General Assembly,

Recalling its resolutions 48/165 of 21 December 1993, 49/95 of 19 December 1994, 50/122 of 20 December 1995, 51/174 of 16 December 1996, 52/186 of 18 December 1997, 53/181 of 15 December 1998 and 54/213 of 22 December 1999,

Recalling also its resolution 55/2 of 8 September 2000, entitled "United Nations Millennium Declaration",

Recalling further the Agenda for Development and the relevant provisions on its follow-up and implementation, and the need to give impetus to international economic cooperation for development so as to follow up on the Agenda effectively,

Reaffirming the importance of continuing the dialogue to be conducted in response to the imperative of solidarity, mutual interests and benefits, genuine interdependence, shared responsibility and the partnership in promoting international economic cooperation for development,

Recognizing, in this context, the importance of an enabling environment and sound economic policy at both the national and the international levels,

Taking note of the need to ensure the integrated and coordinated follow-up and implementation by the United Nations system of the outcome of major United Nations conferences and summits,

Taking note also of the report of the Secretary-General entitled "Renewal of the dialogue on strengthening international economic cooperation for development through partnership", concerning the past experience of the high-level dialogue on strengthening international economic cooperation for development through partnership,

1. *Reaffirms* the importance of continued constructive dialogue and genuine partnership to promote further international economic cooperation for development in the twenty-first century;

2. *Reiterates* the overall theme adopted by the General Assembly in its resolution 54/213, namely, "Responding to globalization: facilitating the integration of developing countries into the world economy in the twenty-first century";

3. *Endorses* the agreement reached at the intergovernmental consultations, as contained in the report of the Secretary-General, whereby the two sub-themes of the second high-level dialogue would be *(a)* "Promoting the integration of developing countries into the world economy and generating new public and private financing resources to complement development efforts" and *(b)* "Enhancing the integration of developing countries in the emerging global information network, facilitating access to information and communication technology for developing countries", and decides that the high-level dialogue will be convened for two days immediately prior to the commencement of the general debate at the fifty-sixth session of the General Assembly, that the high-level dialogue shall consist of plenary meetings, ministerial round-table meetings and informal panels, with the participation of non-governmental actors, and that the final outcome of the dialogue will be a summary by the President, to be presented at the closure of the event;

4. *Requests* the President of the General Assembly to continue preparations for the second high-level dialogue, in close collaboration with Member States and taking into account the experience of the first high-level dialogue, as well as recent experience in the preparation and organization of high-level events;

5. *Requests* the Secretary-General, in close cooperation with Governments, all relevant parts of the United Nations system and other relevant stakeholders, to prepare for the second high-level dialogue, taking into account the results of major United Nations conferences and summits, General Assembly resolution 54/213, the outcome of the consultations held by the Chairman of the Second Committee, any further guidance provided by Member States and the outcome of the consideration of the relevant item by the General Assembly at its current session;

6. *Decides* to include in the provisional agenda of its fifty-sixth session, under the item entitled "Sustainable development and international economic cooperation", the sub-item entitled "High-level dialogue on strengthening international economic cooperation for development through partnership", and requests the Secretary-General to submit to it at that session a consolidated report on the implementation of the present resolution.

Implementation of the Declaration on International Economic Cooperation and the International Development Strategy

In response to General Assembly resolution 54/206 [YUN 1999, p. 745], the Secretary-General submitted a July report [A/55/209] on the implementation of the Declaration on International Economic Cooperation, in particular the Revitalization of Economic Growth and Development of the Developing Countries, adopted by the Assembly in resolution S-18/3 [YUN 1990, p. 337], and of the International Development Strategy for the Fourth United Nations Development Decade (the 1990s), adopted by the Assembly in resolution 45/199 [ibid., p. 343].

Progress was assessed in relation to six interrelated goals, singled out in the Strategy: economic growth in the developing countries; international financial matters, including foreign direct investment, debt and official development assistance; world trade; science and technology, industry and agriculture; human resources development, including education and health; and the situation of LDCs.

The report concluded that increasing globalization and liberalization had borne some fruit during the 1990s, with developing countries as a whole succeeding in improving their rate of growth over that of the 1980s. However, the economic improvements were not large enough to permit many developing countries, particularly the least developed, to make meaningful progress on the economic and social fronts. In particular, the weakest persons within a country, namely those who were unskilled or inadequately educated, and some women and children, were unable to enjoy economic improvements as much as had been hoped; in some instances, they were even further marginalized.

New international development strategy

Committee for Development Policy. In accordance with General Assembly resolution 54/206 [YUN 1999, p. 745], by which the Secretary-General was asked to draft, in collaboration with all concerned organizations of the UN system, in particular the Committee for Development Policy, a new international development strategy for the first decade of the new millennium, the Committee for Development Policy (New York, 3-7 April) [E/2000/33] discussed a range of issues relating to the purpose, thrust and content of an effective new strategy. A working group was established to formulate a set of commentaries for consideration by the Secretary-General, who was to submit the draft strategy to the Assembly, through the Economic and Social Council, at its fifty-fifth session. The Committee recognized that a new international development strategy had to be both comprehensive and balanced in order to respond to the needs of the new decade and be flexible enough to reflect the different constraints and opportunities of countries in very different circumstances and at different stages of development. It should be formulated so as to be readily monitored and assessed in order that progress could be measured and—where progress was found wanting—supplementary actions could be identified beyond what was formulated. The Committee stressed that formulation of a new strategy should be fully informed by a review of what was—and was not—achieved by prior UN development decades, and also that weaknesses and biases in the global system should be identified and addressed.

Report of Secretary-General. In response to General Assembly resolution 54/206, the Secretary-General submitted to the Economic and Social Council and the Assembly a report containing the draft international development strategy for the first decade of the new millennium [A/55/89-E/2000/80]. The draft, which drew on inputs from many parts of the UN system, aimed to give further impetus to international cooperation for development and to monitor long-term trends in the global economy. The draft focused on goals and desirable policy measures and actions and retained the quantifiable goals set by several major UN conferences for the year 2015.

The major challenges of the decade included development and peace; eradicating poverty and hunger; globalization and technological change; ensuring sustainable development; democracy, governance, the rule of law and human rights; promoting gender equality and the participation of women in development; addressing critical situations; and the international and national policy environment. Goals, policies and implementation measures were suggested in the areas of consolidation of peace; the eradication of poverty and hunger; economic development; social development; environmental protection and sustainable development; human settlements; human rights and governance; culture and development; and actions related to countries in special situations, including Africa and LDCs, small island developing States, landlocked developing countries, post-conflict countries and those with the highest prevalence of HIV/AIDS. The Secretary-General also suggested action for implementation of and follow-up to the strategy.

GENERAL ASSEMBLY ACTION

On 20 December [meeting 87], the General Assembly, on the recommendation of the Second Committee [A/55/581/Add.1], adopted **resolution 55/190** without vote [agenda item 94 *(a)*].

Implementation of the commitments and policies agreed upon in the Declaration on International Economic Cooperation, in particular the Revitalization of Economic Growth and Development of the Developing Countries, and implementation of the International Development Strategy for the Fourth United Nations Development Decade

The General Assembly,

Reaffirming the importance and continuing validity of the Declaration on International Economic Cooperation, in particular the Revitalization of Economic Growth and Development of the Developing Countries, contained in the annex to its resolution S-18/3 of 1 May 1990, and of the International Development Strategy for the Fourth United Nations Development Decade, contained in the annex to its resolution 45/199 of 21 December 1990,

Recalling the results of all the major United Nations conferences and summit meetings held since the beginning of the 1990s,

Reaffirming the United Nations Millennium Declaration, in particular the targets and commitments relating to development and poverty eradication,

Emphasizing the importance of the several other development-oriented meetings being convened under the auspices of the United Nations over the next two years, including the high-level international intergovernmental event on financing for development, the special session of the General Assembly to review and address the problem of human immunodeficiency virus/acquired immunodeficiency syndrome, the Third United Nations Conference on the Least Developed Countries, the special session of the General Assembly on children, the ten-year review of the implementation of the outcome of the United Nations Conference on Environment and Development, and the special session of the General Assembly for an overall review and appraisal of the implementation of the outcome of the United Nations Conference on Human Settlements (Habitat II),

Having considered the report of the Secretary-General, and the draft text of an international development strategy for the first decade of the new millennium, submitted by the Secretary-General,

1. *Expresses regret* that the consultations foreseen in resolution 54/206 of 22 December 1999 could not be held;

2. *Decides* to postpone the further development of a new international development strategy until after the aforementioned meetings have been held;

3. *Requests* the Secretary-General to provide the General Assembly at its fifty-seventh session with an overview of the challenges and constraints as well as progress made towards achieving the major development goals and objectives adopted by the United Nations during the decade of the 1990s;

4. *Decides* to include in the provisional agenda of its fifty-sixth session the sub-item entitled "Sustainable development and international economic cooperation: implementation of the commitments and policies agreed upon in the Declaration on International Economic Cooperation, in particular the Revitalization of Economic Growth and Development of the Developing Countries, and implementation of the International

Development Strategy for the Fourth United Nations Development Decade".

Industrial development

In response to General Assembly resolution 53/177 [YUN 1998, p. 777], the Secretary-General, in September [A/55/356], transmitted the report of the Director-General of the United Nations Industrial Development Organization (UNIDO) on efforts under way in the area of industrialization for development. UNIDO activities focused on supporting developing countries and economies in transition, particularly in Africa and LDCs, in adopting reforms to achieve competitiveness and a place in global markets. Those reforms were also designed to ensure that those countries experienced the social and economic benefits of globalization, rather than the downside in which wages decreased, working hours increased and the fruits of globalization were enjoyed only by a few.

By June 2000, UNIDO had 42 integrated programmes, based on specific cooperation requests, in the initial phase of implementation, valued at $280 million and covering time periods of three to four years. The organization also served as a global forum on industrial development issues and the challenges facing developing countries for Governments, representatives of industry from the public and private sectors, investors and others. UNIDO activities included a wide variety of seminars, workshops and expert group meetings related to industrial development and an active publications programme. System-wide cooperation with the UN system and other international organizations was another integral part of UNIDO's work.

In order to better respond to the needs of developing countries, UNIDO had been undergoing a major reform exercise since 1998, transforming its emphasis from headquarters-based operations to activities in the field. By the end of 1999, UNIDO had established 23 country offices and would establish nine regional centres by the end of 2000. Another important component of UNIDO's transformation was the grouping of services into 16 modules covering: industrial policy formulation and implementation; statistics and information networks; metrology, standardization, certification and accreditation; continuous improvement and quality management; investment and technology promotion; environmental policy framework; climate conventions and the 1997 Kyoto Protocol [YUN 1997, p. 1048]; energy efficiency and rural energy development (two modules); cleaner production; pollution control and waste management; the 1987 Mont-

real Protocol on Substances that Deplete the Ozone Layer [YUN 1987, p. 686]; small and medium-sized enterprise policy framework; policy for women's entrepreneurship development; entrepreneurship development; and upgrading agro-industries and related technical skills.

GENERAL ASSEMBLY ACTION

On 20 December [meeting 87], the General Assembly, on the recommendation of the Second Committee [A/55/580], adopted **resolution 55/187** without vote [agenda item 93].

Industrial development cooperation

The General Assembly,

Recalling its resolutions 46/151 of 18 December 1991, 49/108 of 19 December 1994, 51/170 of 16 December 1996 and 53/177 of 15 December 1998 on industrial development cooperation,

Recalling also the United Nations Millennium Declaration adopted by the heads of State and Government on 8 September 2000,

Recognizing the increasing role of the business community, including the private sector, in enhancing the dynamic process of the development of the industrial sector,

Recognizing also the importance of the transfer of technology to the developing countries as an effective means of international cooperation in the field of industrial development,

Taking note of the report of the Director-General of the United Nations Industrial Development Organization,

1. *Reiterates* that industrialization is a key element in the promotion of the sustainable development of developing countries, as well as in the creation of productive employment, eradication of poverty and facilitation of social integration, including the integration of women into the development process;

2. *Stresses* the importance of domestic industrial transformation in developing countries as a way of increasing the value added of their export earnings, so that they may benefit fully from the process of globalization and trade liberalization;

3. *Recognizes* the need for industry to play an enhanced role in fighting the marginalization of developing countries;

4. *Underlines* the importance of industrial development cooperation and a positive investment and business climate at the international, regional, subregional and national levels in promoting the expansion, diversification and modernization of productive capacities in developing countries and countries with economies in transition;

5. *Reaffirms* the need, within the existing service modules of the United Nations Industrial Development Organization, for initiatives stretching beyond those associated with economic adjustment and stabilization to support the survival and expansion of manufacturing activity in developing countries, especially in the least developed countries;

6. *Emphasizes* the necessity of a favourable international and national environment for the industrialization of developing countries, and urges all Governments to adopt and to implement development policies

and strategies that promote, within a framework of transparent and accountable industrialization policies, inter alia, enterprise development, foreign direct investment, technological adaptation and innovation, expanded access to markets and effective use of official development assistance to enable developing countries to enhance an environment that is attractive to investment so as to augment and supplement domestic resources for the expansion, diversification and modernization of their industrial production capacity in the context of an open, equitable, non-discriminatory, transparent, multilateral and rule-based international trading system;

7. *Acknowledges* the interlinkage of globalization and interdependence, and reiterates the importance of the transfer of technology to the developing countries as an effective means of international cooperation in the field of industrial development;

8. *Confirms* the contribution of industry to social development, especially in the context of the linkages between industry and agriculture, and notes that within the totality of these interlinkages, industry serves as a powerful source of the employment generation, income creation and social integration required for the eradication of poverty;

9. *Recognizes* the continuing use of official development assistance also for industrial development in the developing countries, and calls upon donor countries and recipient countries to continue to cooperate in their efforts to achieve greater efficiency and effectiveness of official development assistance resources devoted to industrial development cooperation;

10. *Emphasizes* the importance, for developing countries, of financing for industrial development, including market-based mechanisms and instruments as well as innovative funding modalities, such as co-financing schemes and trust funds, debt-equity swaps and, as appropriate, other debt relief measures and official development assistance specifically designed to strengthen the industrial capacities of developing countries through, inter alia, the facilitation of private capital flows, and, in this regard, requests relevant entities of the United Nations system, including the United Nations Industrial Development Organization and the United Nations Conference on Trade and Development, in the context of their strategic partnership, to support developing countries and countries with economies in transition in their efforts to mobilize resources for industrial development, especially by means of investment promotion activities, the development of small and medium-sized enterprises, an increase in the competitiveness of their exports, the encouragement of practices to promote employment in industries and various forms of business partnerships, such as industrial joint venture schemes, enterprise-to-enterprise cooperation and venture capital funds for industrial development;

11. *Reiterates* the importance of cooperation and co-ordination within the United Nations system in providing effective support for the sustainable industrial development of developing countries, calls upon the United Nations Industrial Development Organization to continue to carry out its central coordinating role within the United Nations system in that respect, and welcomes its efforts to strengthen its cooperation with the rest of the United Nations system at both the head-quarters and field levels by, inter alia, actively participating in the resident coordinator system, so as to enhance the effectiveness, relevance and development impact of such support;

12. *Calls upon* the international community and the relevant bodies and organizations of the United Nations system, in particular the United Nations Industrial Development Organization, to support the efforts of the developing countries to intensify and expand industrial cooperation among themselves with respect to, among other things, trade in manufactured products, industrial investments and business partnerships, and industrial technology and scientific exchanges;

13. *Requests* the United Nations Industrial Development Organization, in cooperation with the relevant organizations of the United Nations system, as appropriate, to continue to undertake an in-depth assessment, analysis and dissemination of best practices in the area of industrial policies and strategies and of lessons learned in industrial development, taking into account the effects of financial crises and the impact of globalization on the industrial structure of the developing countries, so as to support and boost South-South cooperation by providing practical insights and ideas for international industrial development cooperation and for economic and technical cooperation among developing countries;

14. *Emphasizes* the need for financial support to enable the United Nations Industrial Development Organization to implement its technical cooperation programmes and to strengthen its global forum activities, and, at the same time, strongly urges present and former member States to pay their assessed contributions in full, on time and without conditions;

15. *Welcomes* the structural transformation and revitalization of the United Nations Industrial Development Organization as well as its new approach in providing comprehensive and integrated services to its member States and the strengthening of its field representation, and requests it to continue to support the industrialization efforts of developing countries and to continue to accord priority to the needs of the least developed countries and countries in the African region;

16. *Also welcomes* the focus of the United Nations Industrial Development Organization both on the strengthening of industrial capacities and on cleaner and sustainable industrial development, in the context of its new programme orientation, as well as its cooperation with the relevant bodies and organizations of the United Nations system, in particular the United Nations Environment Programme;

17. *Requests* the Secretary-General to submit to the General Assembly at its fifty-seventh session a report on the implementation of the present resolution.

Coercive economic measures

In response to General Assembly resolution 53/10 [YUN 1998, p. 778], the Secretary-General submitted an August report with later addenda [A/55/300 & Add.1-3] containing replies received from 14 Governments in response to his request for information on the elimination of coercive economic measures as a means of political and economic compulsion.

On 26 October [meeting 41], the General Assembly adopted **resolution 55/6** [draft: A/55/L.9/Rev.1] by recorded vote (136-2-10) [agenda item 31].

Elimination of unilateral extraterritorial coercive economic measures as a means of political and economic compulsion

The General Assembly,

Guided by the principles embodied in the Charter of the United Nations, particularly those that call for the development of friendly relations among nations and the strengthening of cooperation in solving problems of an economic and social character,

Taking note of the opposition of the international community to unilateral extraterritorial coercive economic measures,

Recalling its resolutions in which it has called upon the international community to take urgent and effective steps to end unilateral extraterritorial coercive economic measures,

Gravely concerned over the continued application of unilateral extraterritorial coercive measures whose effects have an impact on the sovereignty of other States and the legitimate interests of their entities and individuals in violation of the norms of international law and the purposes and principles of the United Nations,

Believing that the prompt elimination of such measures would be consistent with the purposes and principles embodied in the Charter of the United Nations and the relevant provisions of the Agreement on the World Trade Organization,

Recalling its resolutions 51/22 of 27 November 1996 and 53/10 of 26 October 1998,

1. *Takes note* of the report of the Secretary-General on the implementation of resolution 53/10;

2. *Reaffirms* that all peoples have the right to self-determination and that by virtue of that right they freely determine their political status and freely pursue their economic, social and cultural development;

3. *Expresses its deep concern* at the negative impact of unilaterally imposed extraterritorial coercive economic measures on trade and financial and economic cooperation, including at the regional level, because they are contrary to the recognized principles of international law and pose serious obstacles to the freedom of trade and the free flow of capital at the regional and international levels;

4. *Reiterates its call* for the repeal of unilateral extraterritorial laws that impose coercive economic measures contrary to international law on corporations and nationals of other States;

5. *Again calls upon* all States not to recognize or apply unilateral extraterritorial coercive economic measures imposed by any State, which are contrary to recognized principles of international law;

6. *Requests* the Secretary-General to submit to the General Assembly at its fifty-seventh session a report on the implementation of the present resolution;

7. *Decides* to include in the provisional agenda of its fifty-seventh session an item entitled "Elimination of unilateral extraterritorial coercive economic measures as a means of political and economic compulsion".

RECORDED VOTE ON RESOLUTION 55/6:

In favour: Algeria, Andorra, Angola, Antigua and Barbuda, Argentina, Armenia, Austria, Azerbaijan, Bahamas, Bahrain, Bangladesh, Barbados, Belarus, Belgium, Belize, Benin, Bhutan, Bolivia, Botswana, Brazil, Brunei Darussalam, Bulgaria, Burkina Faso, Burundi, Cameroon, Cape Verde, Chad, Chile, China, Colombia, Comoros, Costa Rica, Croatia, Cuba, Cyprus, Czech Republic, Democratic People's Republic of Korea, Democratic Republic of the Congo, Denmark, Djibouti, Ecuador, Egypt, Estonia, Ethiopia, Finland, France, Gabon, Gambia, Germany, Ghana, Greece, Guatemala, Guinea, Guyana, Honduras, Hungary, Iceland, India, Indonesia, Iran, Ireland, Italy, Jamaica, Japan, Jordan, Kazakhstan, Kenya, Kuwait, Lao People's Democratic Republic, Lebanon, Lesotho, Libyan Arab Jamahiriya, Liechtenstein, Luxembourg, Madagascar, Malaysia, Mali, Malta, Mexico, Monaco, Mongolia, Morocco, Mozambique, Myanmar, Namibia, Nepal, Netherlands, Nigeria, Norway, Oman, Pakistan, Panama, Paraguay, Peru, Philippines, Poland, Portugal, Qatar, Republic of Moldova, Romania, Russian Federation, Saint Lucia, Samoa, San Marino, Sao Tome and Principe, Saudi Arabia, Senegal, Sierra Leone, Singapore, Slovakia, Slovenia, Solomon Islands, South Africa, Spain, Sri Lanka, Sudan, Swaziland, Sweden, Syrian Arab Republic, Tajikistan, Thailand, The former Yugoslav Republic of Macedonia, Togo, Tunisia, Turkey, Turkmenistan, Uganda, Ukraine, United Arab Emirates, United Kingdom, United Republic of Tanzania, Venezuela, Viet Nam, Yemen, Zambia, Zimbabwe.

Against: Israel, United States.

Abstaining: Albania, Australia, Canada, Dominican Republic, Kyrgyzstan, Nauru, New Zealand, Republic of Korea, Tonga, Uruguay.

Sustainable development

Commission on Sustainable Development

The Commission on Sustainable Development held the second part of its eighth session in New York from 24 April to 5 May [E/2000/29]; an organizational meeting had been held on 30 April 1999. The session included a multi-stakeholder dialogue on agriculture (see p. 791) and a high-level segment, which considered issues related to land and agriculture (see p. 791) and forests (see p. 979) and the status of preparations for the 10-year review of Agenda 21, adopted by the 1992 United Nations Conference on Environment and Development (UNCED) (see p. 792). The segment also addressed trade, finance and investment in relation to sustainable development and convened a panel on trade and indigenous people.

The Commission adopted decisions on: preparations for the 10-year review of Agenda 21 [dec. 8/1]; integrated planning and management of land resources [dec. 8/3]; agriculture [dec. 8/4]; financial resources [dec. 8/5]; economic growth, trade and investment [dec. 8/6]; the subprogramme on sustainable development of the draft UN medium-term plan for the period 2002-2005 [dec. 8/7]; matters related to the Commission's intersessional work [dec. 8/8]; the reports of the fourth session of the Intergovernmental Forum on Forests [dec. 8/2] (see p. 979) and of the first session of the Committee on Energy and Natural Resources for Development [dec. 8/9] [YUN 1999, p. 958]; and documents considered by the Commission at its eighth session [dec. 8/11].

By **decision 2000/215** of 3 May, the Economic and Social Council, pursuant to its decision 1996/302 [YUN 1996, p. 1367], approved the request of 15 non-governmental organizations (NGOs) that were on the Roster for the purposes of the work of the Commission to expand their participation into other fields of the Council. By **decision 2000/227** of 26 July, the Council took note of the Commission's report on its eighth session [E/2000/29] and approved the provisional agenda for the ninth (2001) session.

Agriculture and land management

The Commission's multi-stakeholder dialogue, which was held on 24 and 25 April and involved representatives of business and industry, workers and trade unions, farmers and NGOs, as well as representatives of indigenous people and scientists, discussed sustainable agriculture issues. It considered a note by the Secretary-General outlining the structure of the dialogue [E/CN.17/2000/3] and transmitting discussion papers contributed by the International Agri-Food Network, the International Federation of Agricultural Producers and Via Campesina, trade unions and NGOs [E/CN.17/2000/3/Add.1-4].

The Chairman's summary of the dialogue, which was contained in the Commission's report [E/2000/29], reflected issues raised, areas that would benefit from further dialogue and elaboration, and specific initiatives announced or proposed by the participants with regard to the following themes: choices in agricultural production techniques, consumption patterns and safety regulations—potentials and threats to sustainable agriculture; best practices in land resource management to achieve sustainable food cycles; knowledge for a sustainable food system—identifying and providing for education, training, knowledge-sharing and information needs; and globalization, trade liberalization and investment patterns—economic incentives and framework conditions to promote sustainable agriculture.

The Commission's high-level segment also discussed land and agriculture and had before it the report of the Intersessional Ad Hoc Working Group on Integrated Planning and Management of Land Resources; and on Agriculture (New York, 28 February–3 March) [E/CN.17/2000/11]. The Chairman's summary of the segment, which was addressed by government ministers and experts, was contained in the Commission's report [E/2000/29].

Agriculture was also the economic sector/major group discussed by the Commission, which had before it the documents prepared for the multi-stakeholder dialogue and for the high-level segment. In addition, it considered reports of the Secretary-General on sustainable agriculture and rural development: trends in national implementation [E/CN.17/2000/5 & Add.1] and on sustainable agriculture and rural development [E/CN.17/2000/7 & Add.1-3].

For its consideration of the sectoral theme of integrated planning and management of land resources, the Commission had before it a report of the Secretary-General on the subject [E/CN.17/2000/6 & Add.1-4] and the report of the Intersessional Ad Hoc Working Group [E/CN.17/2000/11].

In a 5 May decision [E/2000/29 (dec. 8/4)], the Commission, among priorities for action, encouraged Governments to complete the formulation and elaboration of national strategies for sustainable development by 2002 and to integrate agricultural production, food security and food safety as central elements in those strategies. It also identified areas for international cooperation, including trade, information exchange and dissemination and activities to be carried out by the United Nations and other relevant international organizations.

In a 5 May decision on integrated planning and management of land resources [dec. 8/3], the Commission stated that priority areas for future work on the issues should include prevention and/or mitigation of land degradation; access to land and security of tenure; critical sectors and issues: biodiversity, forests, drylands, rehabilitation of mining areas, mountain areas, wetlands and coastal zones, coral reefs, natural disasters, and rural-urban and land management interactions; access to information and stakeholder participation; international cooperation, including that for capacity-building, information-sharing and technology transfer; and minerals, metals and rehabilitation in the context of sustainable development.

Economic growth, trade and investment

For its discussion of the cross-sectoral theme of financial resources/trade and investment/economic growth, the Commission had before it reports of the Secretary-General on financial resources and mechanisms [E/CN.17/2000/2] and on economic growth, trade and investment [E/CN.17/2000/4], the summary of the Fifth Expert Group Meeting on Financial Issues of Agenda 21 (Nairobi, Kenya, 1-4 December 1999) [E/CN.17/2000/9] and the report of the Ad Hoc Intersessional Working Group on Financial Resources and Mechanisms and on Economic Growth, Trade and Investment (New York, 22-25 February 2000) [E/CN.17/2000/10].

The Commission's high-level session also discussed trade, finance and investment in relation to sustainable development and included a panel on trade and indigenous people.

In a 5 May decision [E/2000/29 (dec. 8/6)], the Commission stated that economic growth, trade and investment would be considered in 2002 as part of the 10-year review of progress achieved since UNCED. Priority areas for future work would include: promoting sustainable development through trade and economic growth; making trade and environment policies mutually supportive; promoting sustainable development through investment; and strengthening institutional cooperation, capacity-building and promoting partnerships. The Commission called for a balanced and integrated approach to trade and environment policies in pursuit of sustainable development, taking into account the economic, environmental and social aspects, as well as the different levels of development of countries, without undermining the open, equitable and non-discriminatory character of the multilateral trading system or creating disguised barriers to trade. An important challenge was to stimulate domestic investment and attract foreign direct investment for sustainable development in developing countries and economies in transition.

In a 5 May decision on financial resources [dec. 8/5], the Commission stated that, so far, the provision of resources required for the implementation of Agenda 21, particularly in developing countries, had fallen short of needs. It called for the urgent fulfilment of all financial commitments entered into under Agenda 21, noting that the cost of inaction could outweigh the financial costs of implementing Agenda 21. Priority areas for future work would include: mobilization of domestic financial resources for sustainable development; promotion of international cooperation and mobilization of international finance for sustainable development; strengthening of existing financial mechanisms and exploration of innovative ones; and improvement of institutional capacity and promotion of public/private partnerships.

Follow-up to UNCED and to nineteenth special session

In a March report on national reporting to the Commission on Sustainable Development [E/CN.17/2000/16], the Secretary-General noted that, by mid-March, 53 countries had submitted national reports on the implementation of Agenda 21 to the Commission's eighth (2000) session. The UN Secretariat was in the process of preparing guidelines for national reports to the ninth (2001) session and making preparations for national reporting for the 10-year review of Agenda 21 in 2002.

Report of Secretary-General. In a May report [A/55/78-E/2000/56], the Secretary-General reviewed work under way in the UN system to accelerate implementation of Agenda 21 and the Programme for the Further Implementation of

Agenda 21, adopted by the General Assembly at its nineteenth special session by resolution S/19-2 [YUN 1997, p. 792]. The obstacles identified in the Secretary-General's 1999 report on the subject [YUN 1999, p. 751]—including lack of financial resources, inadequate institutional capacity, cumbersome reporting and inconsistent decision-making by UN agencies—continued to hinder implementation, although progress had been achieved in some areas, especially inter-agency coordination. The Secretary-General recommended closer coordination of UN organizations at the regional and country levels and greater cooperation with regional bodies.

UNEP action. At its sixth special session (Malmö, Sweden, 29-31 May), the Governing Council of the United Nations Environment Programme (UNEP) adopted a decision [A/55/25 (dec. SS.VI/3)] by which it asked its Committee of Permanent Representatives to review UNEP activities to contribute to the implementation of Agenda 21 and the Programme for the Further Implementation of Agenda 21. To that end, the Executive Director was asked to prepare a report for consideration by the Committee to be distributed to all Governments for comments. He was also asked to submit a final version of that report to the General Assembly in 2000 and to the UNEP Governing Council at its twenty-first (2001) session.

In accordance with that request, the Secretary-General, in October [A/55/447 & Corr.1], transmitted the report of the UNEP Governing Council on UNEP's contribution to the implementation of Agenda 21 and the Programme for the Further Implementation of Agenda 21 (see also p. 969).

Preparations for 10-year review (2002)

Commission action. During the high-level segment of its eighth session, the Commission on Sustainable Development addressed preparations for the 10-year review in 2002 of the implementation of Agenda 21, which was adopted by UNCED in 1992 [YUN 1992, p. 672]. The first such review was carried out by the General Assembly at its nineteenth special session in 1997, when it adopted the Programme for the Further Implementation of Agenda 21. The Commission had before it a report of the Secretary-General [E/CN.17/2000/15] summarizing preliminary views and suggestions from Governments on preparations for the 10-year review, including views regarding the political level, venue, title, financing, goals, agenda and preparatory process of and participation in the 2002 event.

On 5 May [E/2000/29 (dec. 8/1)], the Commission underscored the political importance of the

10-year review and stressed that Agenda 21 should not be renegotiated. It recommended that the General Assembly at its fifty-fifth session consider organizing the 2002 event at summit level and convening it outside UN Headquarters, preferably in a developing country. It also recommended that meetings of the Commission's tenth (2002) session be transformed into an open-ended preparatory committee to undertake the comprehensive review and assessment of the implementation of Agenda 21 and other UNCED outcomes, including identifying constraints to and proposing specific time-bound measures for implementation. The Commission further recommended the establishment of a trust fund for voluntary donations in support of the preparatory process and invited the Assembly to decide on the agenda, main themes, timing, venue and other procedural matters related to the 2002 event.

UNEP action. The first Global Ministerial Environment Forum/sixth special session of the UNEP Governing Council was held in Malmö from 29 to 31 May [A/55/25] (see also p. 966).

On 31 May [dec. SS.VI/1], the Governing Council adopted the Malmö Ministerial Declaration, by which the Ministers of Environment and heads of delegation, having made a number of declarations with regard to the major environmental challenges of the twenty-first century, the private sector and the environment, civil society and the environment, and the 2002 review of UNCED, concluded that, with the unprecedented developments in production and information technologies and other factors, poverty could be decreased by half by 2015 without degrading the environment, environmental security through early warning could be ensured, environmental considerations could be better integrated into economic policy, legal instruments could be better coordinated and a vision of a world without slums could be realized. They committed themselves to realizing that common vision.

Report of Secretary-General. In a July report [A/55/120], the Secretary-General described action taken by the Commission on Sustainable Development and the UNEP Governing Council to ensure effective preparations for the 10-year review in 2002.

GENERAL ASSEMBLY ACTION

On 20 December [meeting 87], the General Assembly, on the recommendation of the Second Committee [A/55/582/Add.1], adopted **resolution 55/199** without vote [agenda item 95 *(a)*].

Ten-year review of progress achieved in the implementation of the outcome of the United Nations Conference on Environment and Development

The General Assembly,

Recalling the United Nations Conference on Environment and Development, held at Rio de Janeiro from 3 to 14 June 1992, and the nineteenth special session of the General Assembly for the purpose of an overall review and appraisal of the implementation of Agenda 21, held in New York from 23 to 28 June 1997,

Recalling also that Agenda 21 and the Rio Declaration on Environment and Development should constitute the framework within which the other results of the Conference are reviewed, and from within which new challenges and opportunities that have emerged since the Conference are addressed,

Recalling further its resolutions 53/188 of 15 December 1998 and 54/218 of 22 December 1999 on the implementation of and follow-up to the outcome of the Conference and the special session, as well as its resolution 55/2 of 8 September 2000,

Recalling Commission on Sustainable Development decision 8/1 on preparations for the ten-year review of progress achieved in the implementation of the outcome of the Conference,

Recalling also that chapter 33 of Agenda 21 identified the Global Environment Facility as one source of financing for the implementation of Agenda 21,

Recalling further the importance for developing countries of chapter 34 of Agenda 21,

Taking note with appreciation of the report of the Secretary-General on ensuring effective preparations for the ten-year review of progress achieved in the implementation of Agenda 21 and the Programme for the Further Implementation of Agenda 21,

Taking note with appreciation also of the Malmö Ministerial Declaration adopted by the Governing Council of the United Nations Environment Programme at its sixth special session,

Deeply concerned that, despite the many successful and continuing efforts of the international community since the United Nations Conference on the Human Environment, held at Stockholm from 5 to 16 June 1972, and the fact that some progress has been achieved, the environment and the natural resource base that support life on earth continue to deteriorate at an alarming rate,

Reaffirming the political importance of the forthcoming ten-year review of progress achieved since the United Nations Conference on Environment and Development, and stressing that the review should focus on the implementation of Agenda 21 and the other results of the Conference, as well as the Programme for the Further Implementation of Agenda 21 adopted by the General Assembly at its nineteenth special session,

Bearing in mind that the substantive activities of the review should take into account, as appropriate, the results relevant to sustainable development of other United Nations conferences and summits and their follow-up activities,

Bearing in mind also that national reports prepared by Governments since 1992 on national implementation of Agenda 21, to which major groups have contributed, could provide a fair basis for guiding national preparatory processes,

Reaffirming that Agenda 21 and the Rio Declaration on Environment and Development should not be renegotiated and that the review should identify measures for the further implementation of Agenda 21 and the other results of the Conference, including sources of funding,

1. *Decides* to organize the ten-year review of progress achieved in the implementation of the outcome of the United Nations Conference on Environment and Development in 2002 at the summit level to reinvigorate the global commitment to sustainable development, and accepts with gratitude the generous offer of the Government of South Africa to host the summit;

2. *Also decides* to call the summit the World Summit on Sustainable Development;

3. *Further decides* that the review should focus on the identification of accomplishments and areas where further efforts are needed to implement Agenda 21 and the other results of the Conference, and on action-oriented decisions in those areas, should address, within the framework of Agenda 21, new challenges and opportunities, and should result in renewed political commitment and support for sustainable development, consistent, inter alia, with the principle of common but differentiated responsibilities;

4. *Decides* that the Summit, including its preparatory process, should ensure a balance between economic development, social development and environmental protection, as these are interdependent and mutually reinforcing components of sustainable development;

5. *Stresses* the importance of early and effective preparations for the Summit and a comprehensive assessment of progress achieved in the implementation of Agenda 21 and the other results of the Conference to be carried out at the local, national, regional and international levels by Governments and the United Nations system so as to ensure high-quality inputs to the review process, and welcomes the preparatory activities carried out so far;

6. *Welcomes* the work undertaken at the regional level, in close collaboration with the respective regional commissions, to implement action programmes for sustainable development that could provide substantive inputs to the preparatory process and the Summit itself;

7. *Also welcomes* the work undertaken by the United Nations Secretariat in close cooperation with the United Nations Environment Programme, the United Nations Development Programme, the regional commissions and the secretariats of conventions related to the Conference, as well as other relevant organizations, agencies and programmes within and outside the United Nations system and international and regional financial institutions, including the Global Environment Facility, to support preparatory activities, in particular at the national and regional levels, in a coordinated and mutually reinforcing way;

8. *Further welcomes* the report of the Global Environment Facility to the General Assembly on its contributions to the implementation of Agenda 21, and notes the assistance provided by the Facility to the national implementation of Agenda 21;

9. *Welcomes* the decision of the Council of the Global Environment Facility at its last meeting, held from 1 to 3 November 2000, to request the Chief Executive Officer to explore the best options for enhancing the support of the Facility in assisting affected countries, especially those in Africa, in implementing the United Nations Convention to Combat Desertification in those Countries Experiencing Serious Drought and/or Desertification, particularly in Africa, taking into account the third replenishment;

10. *Also welcomes* the initiation of the third replenishment of the Global Environment Facility Trust Fund, invites all donor countries and other countries in a position to do so to make contributions to the third replenishment and ensure its successful conclusion, and invites the Facility to submit a report to the Summit on the status of the replenishment negotiations;

11. *Invites* relevant organizations and bodies of the United Nations and international financial institutions involved with the implementation of Agenda 21, including the United Nations Environment Programme, the United Nations Centre for Human Settlements (Habitat), the Global Environment Facility and the United Nations Development Programme, and of conventions related to the Conference, to participate fully in the ten-year review of progress achieved in the implementation of Agenda 21, including in the preparation of reports for submission to the Commission on Sustainable Development at its tenth session and the Summit, in order to reflect their experiences and the lessons learned and to provide ideas and proposals for the way forward for the further implementation of Agenda 21 in relevant areas;

12. *Encourages* effective contributions from, and the active participation of, all major groups, as identified in Agenda 21, at all stages of the preparatory process, in accordance with the rules and procedures of the Commission on Sustainable Development, as well as its established practices related to the participation and engagement of major groups;

13. *Decides* that the Commission on Sustainable Development at its tenth session shall meet as an open-ended Preparatory Committee that will provide for the full and effective participation of all States Members of the United Nations and members of the specialized agencies, as well as other participants in the Commission on Sustainable Development, in accordance with the rules of procedure of the functional commissions of the Economic and Social Council and the supplementary arrangements established for the Commission on Sustainable Development by the Council in its decisions 1993/215 of 12 February 1993 and 1995/201 of 8 February 1995;

14. *Invites* regional groups to nominate their candidates for the Bureau of the tenth session of the Commission on Sustainable Development by the end of 2000 so that they can be involved in its preparations in advance of the first session of the Preparatory Committee;

15. *Decides* that the Commission, acting as the Preparatory Committee, should:

(*a*) Undertake the comprehensive review and assessment of the implementation of Agenda 21 and the other results of the Conference on the basis of the results of national assessments and subregional and regional preparatory meetings, the documentation to be prepared by the Secretary-General in collaboration with the task managers, and other inputs from relevant international organizations, as well as on the basis of contributions from major groups;

(*b*) Identify major accomplishments and lessons learned in the implementation of Agenda 21;

(*c*) Identify major constraints hindering the implementation of Agenda 21, propose specific time-bound measures to be taken and institutional and financial requirements, and identify the sources of such support;

(*d*) Address new challenges and opportunities that have emerged since the Conference, within the framework of Agenda 21;

(*e*) Address ways of strengthening the institutional framework for sustainable development and evaluate and define the role and programme of work of the Commission on Sustainable Development;

(*f*) Consider and decide on accreditation for the participation in the preparatory process and the Summit of relevant non-governmental organizations that are not in consultative status with the Economic and Social Council;

(*g*) Propose a provisional agenda and possible main themes for the Summit based on the results of the preparatory activities carried out at the national, subregional, regional and international levels, taking into account also the input of major groups;

(*h*) Propose rules and procedures for the participation of representatives of major groups in the Summit, taking into account the rules and procedures applied at the Conference;

(*i*) Undertake any other functions that may be required by the preparatory process;

16. *Also decides* to hold, as recommended by the Commission on Sustainable Development in its decision 8/1, a three-day meeting of the tenth session of the Commission, so that the Commission can start its work as the Preparatory Committee for the Summit, and, in this context, invites the Commission to start its organizational work in order to do the following:

(*a*) Elect, from among all States, a Bureau composed of ten members, with two representatives from each of the geographical groups, one of whom would be elected Chairperson and the others Vice-Chairpersons, one of whom would also act as the Rapporteur;

(*b*) Consider progress in preparatory activities carried out at the local, national, subregional, regional and international levels, as well as by major groups;

(*c*) Decide, taking into account the provisions of paragraph 17 below, on the specific modalities of the future sessions of the Preparatory Committee;

(*d*) Consider a process for setting the agenda and determining possible main themes for the Summit in a timely manner;

17. *Further decides* that, in 2002, the Commission on Sustainable Development, acting as the Preparatory Committee for the Summit, shall hold three additional sessions, organized as follows:

(*a*) At its first and second sessions, to be held in January and March 2002, respectively, the Preparatory Committee shall undertake the comprehensive review and assessment of progress achieved in the implementation of Agenda 21 and the Programme for the Further Implementation of Agenda 21; at its second session, the Preparatory Committee shall agree on the text of a document containing the results of the review and

assessment, as well as conclusions and recommendations for further action;

(*b*) Drawing upon the agreed text of such a document, the Preparatory Committee at its third and final session, to be held at the ministerial level in May 2002, shall prepare a concise and focused document that should emphasize the need for a global partnership to achieve the objectives of sustainable development, reconfirm the need for an integrated and strategically focused approach to the implementation of Agenda 21, and address the main challenges and opportunities faced by the international community in this regard; the document submitted for further consideration and adoption by the Summit should reinvigorate, at the highest political level, the global commitment to a North/South partnership and a higher level of international solidarity and to the accelerated implementation of Agenda 21 and the promotion of sustainable development;

18. *Decides* to organize the third and final session of the Preparatory Committee at the ministerial level in Indonesia, and accepts with gratitude the generous offer of the Government of Indonesia to host it;

19. *Stresses* that the preparatory meetings and the Summit itself should be transparent and provide for effective participation and inputs from Governments and regional and international organizations, including financial institutions, and for contributions from and the active participation of major groups, as identified in Agenda 21;

20. *Welcomes* the establishment of a trust fund, urges international and bilateral donors and other countries in a position to do so to support the preparations for the ten-year review through voluntary contributions to the trust fund and to support the participation of representatives of developing countries in the regional and international preparatory process and the Summit itself, and encourages voluntary contributions to support the participation of major groups of developing countries in the regional and international preparatory processes and the Summit itself;

21. *Invites* the Secretary-General to submit a progress report on the state of preparations for the Summit for consideration by the General Assembly at its fifty-sixth session, taking into account, inter alia, the inputs of the various regional meetings;

22. *Decides* to include in the provisional agenda of its fifty-sixth session, under the item entitled "Environment and sustainable development", the sub-item entitled "Implementation of Agenda 21 and the Programme for the Further Implementation of Agenda 21".

Also on 20 December, in **resolution 55/200**, the Assembly requested the Secretary-General to provide the necessary resources from the regular budget to UNEP for the 2002-2003 biennium and to consider other ways to strengthen UNEP in view of the 10-year review of UNCED.

Inter-Agency Committee

The Inter-Agency Committee on Sustainable Development (IACSD) of the Administrative Committee on Coordination (ACC) met twice in 2000.

At its fifteenth meeting (New York, 24-25 January) [ACC/2000/1], the Committee addressed matters for consideration by ACC, including successor arrangements for the International Decade for Natural Disaster Reduction (1990s), matters related to the Environmental Management Group and preparations for the 10-year review of UNCED in 2002. It also addressed follow-up to meetings of ACC and the Economic and Social Council, and matters related to the work of the General Assembly and the Commission on Sustainable Development. In addition to considering the reports of the ACC Subcommittees on Water Resources and on Oceans and Coastal Areas, the Committee addressed the status of implementation of the Global Programme of Action for the Protection of the Marine Environment from Land-based Activities.

At its sixteenth meeting (Geneva, 18-19 September) [ACC/2000/12], IACSD again considered follow-up to meetings of intergovernmental bodies and reports of its subsidiary bodies, as well as preparations for the ninth (2001) session of the Commission on Sustainable Development and for the 10-year review of progress achieved since UNCED.

Eradication of poverty

In July, the Economic and Social Council adopted **resolution 2000/26** on the role of employment and work in poverty eradication, particularly in relation to the empowerment and advancement of women (see p. 1121).

UN Decade for Eradication of Poverty

In response to General Assembly resolution 54/232 [YUN 1999, p. 754], the Secretary-General submitted a September progress report [A/55/407] on implementation of the first United Nations Decade for the Eradication of Poverty (1997-2006), proclaimed by the Assembly in resolution 50/107 [YUN 1995, p. 844]. The report focused on progress achieved in global poverty reduction since the 1995 World Summit for Social Development [ibid., p. 1113], highlighting the need for more concerted and sustained efforts to eradicate poverty. The impact of globalization on the eradication of poverty was examined with particular reference to LDCs, which had so far not been able to take advantage of the opportunities offered by globalization. The report outlined a variety of possible actions, policies and measures that might be undertaken at the national and international levels to enable developing countries to better benefit from globalization and concluded with a summary of coordination at the intergov-

ernmental level and activities of the UN system in support of national efforts to eradicate poverty.

GENERAL ASSEMBLY ACTION

On 20 December [meeting 87], the General Assembly, on the recommendation of the Second Committee [A/55/586 & Corr.1], adopted **resolution 55/210** without vote [agenda item 99].

Implementation of the first United Nations Decade for the Eradication of Poverty (1997-2006), including the initiative to establish a world solidarity fund for poverty eradication

The General Assembly,

Recalling its resolution 47/196 of 22 December 1992, by which it established the International Day for the Eradication of Poverty, as well as its resolution 48/183 of 21 December 1993, by which it proclaimed 1996 the International Year for the Eradication of Poverty,

Recalling also its resolution 50/107 of 20 December 1995 on the observance of the International Year for the Eradication of Poverty and the proclamation of the first United Nations Decade for the Eradication of Poverty (1997-2006), as well as the declarations and programmes of action of the major United Nations conferences and summits of the 1990s as they relate to the eradication of poverty,

Expressing its deep concern that the number of people living in extreme poverty continues to increase, with women and children constituting the majority and the most affected group, in particular in African countries and the least developed countries,

Recognizing that, while the rate of poverty in some countries has been reduced, some developing countries and disadvantaged groups are being marginalized and others are at risk of being marginalized and effectively excluded from the benefits of globalization, resulting in increased income disparity among and within countries, thereby constraining efforts to eradicate poverty,

Also recognizing that for the poverty eradication strategy to be effective it is imperative for developing countries to be integrated into the world economy and equitably share the benefits of globalization,

Bearing in mind the Copenhagen Declaration on Social Development and the Programme of Action of the World Summit for Social Development, and the Political Declaration adopted by the General Assembly at its twenty-fourth special session, entitled "World Summit for Social Development and beyond: achieving social development for all in a globalizing world", held at Geneva from 26 to 30 June 2000, as well as the objectives of the World Food Summit, held at Rome from 13 to 17 November 1996,

Bearing in mind also the United Nations Millennium Declaration, adopted by heads of State and Government on the occasion of the Millennium Summit, particularly section III, "Development and poverty eradication", and its emphasis on solidarity as a fundamental value in international relations in the twenty-first century,

Recalling the commitment made by the heads of State and Government at the Millennium Summit to eradicate extreme poverty, in particular the commitment to halve, by 2015, the proportion of the world's people whose income is less than one dollar a day and the proportion of people who suffer from hunger,

Recognizing that, while it is the primary responsibility of States to attain social development, the international community should support the efforts of the developing countries to eradicate poverty and to ensure basic social protection,

Taking note of the report of the Secretary-General,

1. *Stresses* that the United Nations Decade for the Eradication of Poverty should contribute to achieving the targets of halving, by 2015, the proportion of the world's people whose income is less than one dollar a day and the proportion of people who suffer from hunger, through decisive national action and strengthened international cooperation;

2. *Calls* for strengthened efforts at all levels to implement fully and effectively the relevant resolutions and decisions of the United Nations and all agreements and commitments adopted at the major United Nations conferences and summits organized since 1990, as well as the United Nations Millennium Declaration, as they relate to the eradication of poverty, with a view to achieving tangible results;

3. *Stresses* the importance of tackling the root causes of poverty and the necessity of meeting the basic needs of all, and, in this context, emphasizes the fundamental role in the eradication of poverty of strong and sustained economic growth that favours the poor, creates substantive expansion in productive opportunities and employment, increases incomes, promotes equitable income distribution and minimizes environmental degradation;

4. *Reaffirms* that the causes of poverty should be addressed in an integrated way, taking into account the importance of sectoral strategies in such areas as education, development of human resources, health, human settlements, rural development, productive employment, population, environment, freshwater, food security and migration, and the specific needs of disadvantaged and vulnerable groups, in such a way as to increase opportunities and choices for people living in poverty and to enable them to build and to strengthen their assets so as to achieve social and economic development;

5. *Stresses* the importance of increasing access to and control by the poor over resources, including land, skills, knowledge, capital and social connections, and of improving access for all to basic social services;

6. *Recognizes* the importance of the adoption of appropriate policy responses to the challenges of globalization at the national level, in particular by pursuing sound and stable domestic policies, including sound macroeconomic and social policies, in order to realize the objective of the eradication of poverty;

7. *Reaffirms* that, within the context of overall action for the eradication of poverty, special attention should be given to the multidimensional nature of poverty and the national and international conditions and policies that are conducive to its eradication, fostering, inter alia, the social and economic integration of people living in poverty, thus empowering them to participate in decision-making with regard to the policies that affect them, the promotion and protection of all human rights and fundamental freedoms for all, including the right to development, bearing in mind the relationship between all human rights and development, and an efficient, transparent and accountable public service and administration;

8. *Also reaffirms*, as set out in the United Nations Millennium Declaration, that success in meeting the objectives of development and poverty eradication depends, inter alia, on good governance within each country; it also depends on good governance at the international level, on transparency in the financial, monetary and trading systems and on commitment to an open, equitable, rule-based, predictable and non-discriminatory multilateral trading and financial system;

9. *Calls upon* all countries to formulate and implement outcome-oriented national strategies and programmes, setting time-bound targets for poverty reduction, including the target of halving, by 2015, the proportion of people living in extreme poverty, which requires strengthening of national action and international cooperation;

10. *Urges* the strengthening of international assistance to developing countries in their efforts to alleviate poverty, including by creating an enabling environment that would facilitate the integration of developing countries into the world economy, improving their market access, facilitating the flow of financial resources and implementing fully and effectively all initiatives already launched regarding debt relief for developing countries, and emphasizes that the international community should consider further measures that would lead to effective, equitable, development-oriented and durable solutions to the external debt and debt-servicing problems of developing countries so that they can share equally in the benefits of globalization, cope with its negative effects, avoid being marginalized in the process of globalization and achieve full integration into the world economy;

11. *Reaffirms* that all Governments and the United Nations system should promote an active and visible policy of mainstreaming a gender perspective in all policies and programmes aimed at the eradication of poverty, at both the national and international levels, and encourages the use of gender analysis as a tool for the integration of a gender dimension into planning the implementation of policies, strategies and programmes for the eradication of poverty;

12. *Expresses its appreciation* to the developed countries that have agreed to and have reached the target of 0.7 per cent of their gross national product for overall official development assistance, and calls upon the developed countries that have not yet done so to strengthen their efforts to achieve the agreed target as soon as possible and, where agreed, within that target, to earmark 0.15 to 0.20 per cent of their gross national product for the least developed countries;

13. *Reaffirms* the role of United Nations funds and programmes, in particular the United Nations Development Programme, in assisting the national efforts of developing countries, including in the eradication of poverty, and the need for their funding in accordance with relevant resolutions of the United Nations;

14. *Welcomes favourably* the proposal submitted regarding the establishment of a world solidarity fund for poverty eradication, which will contribute to the eradication of poverty and the promotion of social and human development in the poorest regions of the

world, and requests the Secretary-General to undertake the necessary consultations with Member States and all relevant stakeholders on this issue, bearing in mind the voluntary nature of the contributions, and to report to the General Assembly at its fifty-sixth session;

15. *Emphasizes* the role of microcredit as an important anti-poverty tool that promotes the generation of production and self-employment and empowers people living in poverty, especially women, and therefore encourages Governments to adopt policies that support the development of microcredit institutions and their capacities, and calls upon the international community, in particular the relevant organs, organizations and bodies of the United Nations system and international and regional financial institutions involved in the eradication of poverty, to support and explore the incorporation of the microcredit approach into their programmes and the further development, as appropriate, of other microfinance instruments;

16. *Calls upon* the developed countries, by means of intensified and effective cooperation with developing countries, to promote capacity-building and facilitate access to and transfer of technologies and corresponding knowledge, in particular to developing countries, on favourable terms, including concessional and preferential terms, as mutually agreed, taking into account the need to protect intellectual property rights, as well as the special needs of developing countries, by identifying and implementing practical steps to ensure the achievement of progress in this regard and to assist developing countries in their efforts to eradicate poverty in an era influenced in large measure by technology;

17. *Emphasizes* the critical role of both formal and non-formal education, particularly basic education, and training, in particular for girls, in the empowerment of those living in poverty, and, in this context, welcomes the Dakar Framework for Action adopted at the World Education Forum, including the reconfirmation of the mandate of the United Nations Educational, Scientific and Cultural Organization to coordinate Education for All partners and maintain their collective momentum, and invites the organs and bodies of the United Nations system, in particular the United Nations Educational, Scientific and Cultural Organization and the United Nations Children's Fund, to promote the inclusion of education in anti-poverty strategies;

18. *Recalls* the commitments of the United Nations conferences and summits to eliminate gender disparity in primary and secondary education by 2005 and to promote universal primary education in all countries by 2015, and, in this regard, urges Member States to take immediate measures to remove obstacles to young girls' school attendance and to reduce drop-out rates;

19. *Welcomes* the efforts made by the United Nations system to assign priority to the eradication of poverty and to enhance coordination, and, in this regard, encourages the organizations of the United Nations system, including the Bretton Woods institutions, and other partners in development to continue to support all Member States in carrying forward their own strategy for the achievement of the objectives of the Decade;

20. *Reaffirms* the importance of agreeing on a mutual commitment of interested developed and developing country partners to allocate, on average, 20 per cent of official development assistance and 20 per cent of the national budget, respectively, to basic social programmes, and welcomes the efforts made to implement the 20/20 initiative, which emphasizes that promoting access for all to basic social services is essential for sustainable and equitable development and is an integral part of the strategy for the eradication of poverty;

21. *Recognizes* the devastating effect of the human immunodeficiency virus/acquired immunodeficiency syndrome (HIV/AIDS) epidemic on human development, economic growth and poverty reduction efforts in many countries, in particular African countries, and urges Governments and the international community to give urgent priority to the HIV/AIDS crisis, in particular addressing the special needs of developing countries by strengthening the relevant commitments through partnerships as agreed by the General Assembly at its twenty-fourth special session, and, in this regard, welcomes the convening of a special session of the General Assembly to review and address the problem of HIV/AIDS in all its aspects;

22. *Urges* the implementation of the enhanced programme of debt relief for the heavily indebted poor countries without delay and the cancellation of all official bilateral debts of those countries, in the context of poverty eradication, in return for their making demonstrable commitments to poverty reduction as part of their overall development strategy;

23. *Recognizes* the difficulties of heavily indebted middle-income developing countries in meeting their external debt and debt-servicing obligations, and notes the worsening situation in some of them in the context, inter alia, of greater liquidity constraints, which may require debt treatment through various national and international measures designed to assist those countries to make their debt burden sustainable in the long term and to combat poverty effectively;

24. *Encourages* the continuing examination in all relevant intergovernmental forums of ways and means to integrate poverty reduction objectives and strategies into discussions on international financial and development issues;

25. *Requests* the Secretary-General, in the context of the follow-up to the United Nations Millennium Declaration, to submit to it at its fifty-sixth session a comprehensive report containing an evaluation of progress made towards achieving the goals of the Decade, as well as in the achievement of the 2015 targets on poverty reduction, and recommendations for further action to achieve the 2015 targets, including the identification of resource requirements and possible sources of funding;

26. *Decides* to include in the provisional agenda of its fifty-sixth session the item entitled "Implementation of the first United Nations Decade for the Eradication of Poverty (1997-2006)".

Science and technology for development

The Commission on Science and Technology for Development did not meet in 2000. On 18 October, the Economic and Social Council, by **decision 2000/304**, decided that the Commission's fifth session would be convened in Geneva from 21 to 25 May 2001.

Science and technology issues were considered by the Council, the General Assembly and UNCTAD X (see p. 890).

Information and communication technologies

Committee for Development Policy. In accordance with Economic and Social Council resolution 1999/67 [YUN 1999, p. 766], the Committee for Development Policy, at its second session (New York, 3-7 April) [E/2000/33], considered the role of information technology (IT) in development. Following a review of the potential benefits and risks of IT, its production and application in developing countries and prospects for development, the Committee made recommendations for national and international action, including calls for strategies to create or enhance national information infrastructure and build human capacity for the IT age, and for international assistance to developing countries to ensure wide access to communication and information services and application of IT to solve pressing problems of human and economic development.

Economic and Social Council consideration. The Economic and Social Council, at the high-level segment (5-7 July) of its 2000 substantive session, addressed the theme of "Development and international cooperation in the twenty-first century: the role of information technology in the context of a knowledge-based global economy" pursuant to decision 1999/281 [YUN 1999, p. 743]. In addition to the report of the Committee for Development Policy on its second session, the Council had before it a report of the Secretary-General [E/2000/52], in which he explored the potential of information and communication technologies (ICTs) in advancing the process of development and optimizing the benefits of globalization. The Secretary-General stated that ICTs were central to the creation of a global knowledge-based economy and society and could play an important role in accelerating growth, eradicating poverty and promoting sustainable development in developing and transition economy countries and in facilitating beneficial integration into the global economy. At the same time, the experience of developed countries showed that indiscriminate investment in ICTs could lead to large-scale waste. The report outlined action required at the national level to maximize the potential of ICTs. It also discussed the kinds of strengthened international cooperation needed among Governments, the UN system and other international organizations, the private sector and civil society to support those national efforts.

Annexed to the report was a statement to the Council from ACC—finalized in accordance with the conclusions of ACC's first regular session of 2000 (Rome, Italy, 6-7 April) [ACC/2000/4]—by which the executive heads of the organizations and agencies of the UN system committed themselves to work, individually and collectively, towards making the goal of universal access to ICTs a reality. Other documents before the Council included the report of the high-level panel of experts on information and communication technology (New York, 17-20 April) [A/55/75-E/2000/55], convened as requested by the Assembly in resolution 54/231 [YUN 1999, p. 743], a compilation of contributions of the UN system to the Secretary-General's report to the high-level segment [E/2000/CRP.2] and contributions from the five regional commissions [E/2000/70, 71, 72, 73, 74].

On 7 July, the Council adopted a Ministerial Declaration by which ministers and heads of delegations attending the high-level segment recognized a wide consensus that ICTs were central to the creation of the emerging global knowledge-based economy and could play an important role in accelerating growth, promoting sustainable development and eradicating poverty in developing countries and economies in transition, and in facilitating their effective integration into the global economy [A/55/3/Rev.1].

The ministers recognized that consistent and coherent national and local actions were essential in order to make ICTs for development programmes effective and sustainable. National programmes should include: establishment of a legal and regulatory framework that fostered ICT development; development of the basic infrastructure for connectivity, including remote areas, and measures to bring down connectivity costs; application of ICT in schools, hospitals, libraries, government departments and other public institutions; policies to promote investment in ICTs; investment in human resource development; technical preparation of national manpower to administer information systems and develop sustainable ICT projects; promotion of the digital enhancement of already established mass media; strategies to link established technologies, such as radio, with new technologies, such as the Internet; and creation of technological incubators linked to universities and centres for research.

The ministers and heads of delegations stated that the UN system, in particular the Economic and Social Council, as well as partnerships involving Governments, development agencies, the private sector and other stakeholders, should also play a key role in promoting coherent efforts directed at expanding the development impact of ICTs. To that end, the Council's Working Group on Informatics was asked to make recommendations regarding the creation of an ICT task force.

The Secretary-General was requested to submit to the Council in 2001 a progress report on implementation of the Declaration.

ECONOMIC AND SOCIAL COUNCIL ACTION

On 28 July [meeting 45], the Economic and Social Council adopted **resolution 2000/29** [draft: E/2000/L.27] without vote [agenda item 7 *(e)*].

Information and communications technologies task force

The Economic and Social Council,

Recalling the Ministerial Declaration entitled "Development and international cooperation in the twenty-first century: the role of information technology in the context of a knowledge-based global economy", adopted on 7 July 2000 at the high-level segment of its substantive session of 2000,

Noting that several international initiatives are being taken to bridge the global digital divide and create digital opportunities, including the establishment of a Digital Opportunities Task Force (dot force) by the Summit of the Group of Eight nations held in Okinawa, Japan, from 21 to 23 July 2000,

1. *Endorses* the recommendations of the Ad Hoc Open-ended Working Group on Informatics as contained in the annex to the present resolution;

2. *Requests* the Secretary-General to submit a report to the Council on the implementation of the present resolution at a resumed substantive session of the Council for approval.

ANNEX
Recommendations of the Ad Hoc Open-ended Working Group on Informatics

1. The Ad Hoc Open-ended Working Group on Informatics recommends that an information and communications technologies task force be created with the objectives of providing overall leadership to the United Nations role in helping to formulate strategies for the development of information and communications technologies and putting those technologies at the service of development and, on the basis of consultations with all stakeholders and Member States, forging a strategic partnership between the United Nations system, private industry and financing trusts and foundations, donors, programme countries and other relevant stakeholders.

2. The Working Group recommends that the Secretary-General undertake consultations with all stakeholders and Member States regarding the composition, governance structure, mandate, terms of reference, secretarial support and project implementation arrangements of the task force and the trust fund, taking into account, inter alia, the following elements:

Mandate

The task force would:

—Serve as a mechanism to facilitate and promote collaborative initiatives, involving, as appropriate, public and private sectors, foundations and trusts, for the mobilization of resources and for the promotion and funding of information and communications technologies programmes and projects;

—Identify and mobilize new resources, public and private;

—Promote effective utilization of existing resources for information and communications technologies for development;

—Promote collaborative initiatives, at the request of and in consultation with programme countries, for information and communications technologies programmes and projects, including at the regional, subregional and national levels, taking into account the provisions of paragraphs 14 to 17 of the Ministerial Declaration entitled "Development and international cooperation in the twenty-first century: the role of information technology in the context of a knowledge-based global economy", adopted on 7 July 2000 at the high-level segment of the substantive session of 2000 of the Economic and Social Council;

—Facilitate the pooling of relevant experience of both developed and developing countries and lessons learned, in introducing and promoting information and communications technologies, in developing local content and using information and communications technologies for preserving and disseminating traditional knowledge, with a view to promoting North-South and South-South programme initiatives;

—Develop networking arrangements with other mechanisms and institutions, both public and private, engaged in information and communications technologies development activities with a view to promoting coherence and synergy and identifying joint programme initiatives;

—Administer the trust fund to be established and funded by all interested partners on the basis of voluntary contributions.

Composition, oversight and secretariat

—The composition of the task force should be balanced, in terms of partner representation (United Nations system, public and private sectors, foundations, trusts, developed and developing countries and countries with economies in transition), taking into account the need for geographical balance;

—The task force could be supported by a small secretariat on the basis of secondment from participants and funding by overhead support costs of the programmes and projects financed from the trust fund;

—The Secretary-General shall submit an annual report on the activities of the task force to the Council for its consideration.

Modalities of operation

—The modalities of operation of the task force should be simple, efficient, transparent and accountable.

GENERAL ASSEMBLY ACTION

Having considered a report of the Secretary-General on the role of the United Nations in promoting development in the context of globalization and interdependence [A/55/381], which paid particular attention to the pivotal role of ICT in the emerging global knowledge-based economy, the General Assembly adopted **resolution 55/212**, in which the Secretary-General was encouraged to continue consultations on establishing a UN information and communication technologies task force (see p. 783).

On 20 December (**decision 55/445**), the Assembly took note of the report of the high-level panel of experts on information and communication technology (see p. 799).

Coordination mechanisms

Report of Secretary-General. In response to General Assembly resolution 54/201 [YUN 1999, p. 761], the Secretary-General submitted to the Economic and Social Council and the Assembly a report, by the UNCTAD secretariat [A/55/96-E/2000/84], containing proposals for strengthening the coordination of mechanisms on the Commission on Science and Technology for Development within UNCTAD, in order to promote complementarity of activities within the UN system. In particular, the report recommended steps to be taken by the UNCTAD secretariat to create an electronic network relating to science and technology for development as a means to achieve coordination in the area of science and technology policy and programmes and to improve information sharing, knowledge diffusion and generation of ideas among UN agencies and other major players, including the private sector. The UNCTAD secretariat had already started the process of establishing such a network, which was expected to be operational by the end of 2000.

On 28 July, by **decision 2000/301**, the Economic and Social Council took note of the report.

Note by Secretariat. By a September note [A/55/413], the Secretariat drew attention to the report prepared by UNCTAD and noted that the follow-up to Assembly resolution 54/201 was also directly relevant to the Ministerial Declaration adopted at the high-level segment of the Economic and Social Council.

On 20 December (**decision 55/439**), the Assembly took note of the Secretariat's note.

GENERAL ASSEMBLY ACTION

On 20 December [meeting 87], the General Assembly, on the recommendation of the Second Committee [A/55/579/Add.4], adopted **resolution 55/185** without vote [agenda item 92 (d)].

Strengthening the coordination of the mechanisms on the Commission for Science and Technology for Development: promoting complementarity of activities in the area of new and innovative technologies within the United Nations system

The General Assembly,

Reaffirming its resolution 54/201 of 22 December 1999,

Taking note of the Ministerial Declaration entitled "Development and international cooperation in the twenty-first century: the role of information technol-

ogy in the context of a knowledge-based global economy", adopted by the Economic and Social Council during the high-level segment of its substantive session of 2000,

Taking note also of Economic and Social Council resolution 2000/29 of 28 July 2000 on the information and communication technologies task force,

Recognizing the role of the Commission on Science and Technology for Development in coordinating the activities of the United Nations system in the area of science and technology for development, noting the work being undertaken by the Commission in its work programme for Member States, especially the developing countries, and its work with some countries with economies in transition, emphasizing the importance of the activities that are to be pursued within the framework of the Commission, including a broad spectrum of new global challenges in science and technology, and encouraging support for those undertakings,

Cognizant of the role of the United Nations Conference on Trade and Development as the secretariat responsible for the substantive servicing of the Commission,

Taking note of the Plan of Action adopted by the United Nations Conference on Trade and Development at its tenth session, held at Bangkok from 12 to 19 February 2000, in which the Conference noted, inter alia, the growing technology gap between developed and developing countries, and stressed that actions were required by both developed and developing countries, among others, including the establishment of appropriate policy and legal frameworks, human resource development and the provision of technical assistance and, where possible, financial assistance and other incentives in order to narrow that gap and promote greater access, transfer and diffusion of technology to developing countries, in particular the least developed countries, as well as countries with economies in transition,

Recognizing the need to address the obstacles faced by developing countries in accessing new technologies, while taking into account the need to protect intellectual property rights and the special needs of developing countries,

Recognizing also the importance of establishing and strengthening partnership and networking among the public and private sectors and academic institutions of the South and the North to build and strengthen the technological capabilities and skills needed for developing countries to compete in the international markets,

Bearing in mind the cross-cutting nature of science and technology within the United Nations system and the need, inter alia, for effective policy guidance and better coordination,

Noting that the theme of the coordination segment of the substantive session of 2001 of the Economic and Social Council will be "The role of the United Nations in promoting development, particularly with respect to access to and transfer of knowledge and technology, especially information and communication technologies, inter alia, through partnerships with relevant stakeholders, including the private sector",

Recalling that the next biennial session of the Commission will be held in 2001,

Recognizing the need for adequate resources, including the provision of new and additional resources from all sources, to be devoted to fostering science and technology for development,

Recognizing also the need for strengthening the role of the Commission,

1. *Takes note* of the report of the Secretary-General on proposals for strengthening the coordination of the mechanisms on the Commission on Science and Technology for Development within the United Nations Conference on Trade and Development with the objective of promoting complementarity of activities within the United Nations system;

2. *Welcomes* the recommendations regarding the establishment of a knowledge and technology for development network contained in the report of the Secretary-General;

3. *Requests* the Commission to report on its biennial session, through the Economic and Social Council, to the General Assembly at its fifty-sixth session, in particular regarding proposals aimed at promoting complementarity of activities in the area of new and innovative technologies within the United Nations system;

4. *Calls upon* the Secretary-General to strengthen the Commission and its secretariat within the United Nations Conference on Trade and Development, by providing it with the necessary resources, in order to enable it to carry out better its mandate of assisting the developing countries with their national development efforts in the field of science and technology;

5. *Requests* the Secretary-General to submit to the General Assembly at its fifty-sixth session, through the Economic and Social Council, an analytical report on the progress made in the implementation of the present resolution, containing, in particular, concrete proposals for strengthening the critical role of the Commission in coordinating the activities of the United Nations system in support of the efforts of developing countries to obtain, effectively utilize and benefit from science and technology for their development;

6. *Decides* that, as from the fifty-sixth session of the General Assembly, the item entitled "Science and technology for development" will normally be included in its agenda on a biennial basis.

Economic and social trends

Economic surveys and trends

The *World Economic and Social Survey 2000* [Sales No. E.00.II.C.1], prepared in mid-2000 by the UN Department of Economic and Social Affairs (DESA), stated that the healing process in the global economy following the widespread economic setbacks of 1997-1998 gathered momentum in 1999 and was expected to broaden and deepen. Growth rates in all country groupings—developed countries, developing countries and economies in transition—increased in 1999 compared with 1998 and growth in world output was expected to accelerate to 3.5 per cent, the highest

rate since 1996. Although trade growth remained slow in early 1999, accelerating recovery in Asia and continued rapid growth in North America increased trade values and volumes during the second half of the year, and that accelerated in early 2000. Continuing economic expansion in the United States was an important factor in sustaining international trade and external demand for a number of economies. In spite of the acceleration in output and a sharp rise in oil prices, inflation worldwide remained under control.

Developing countries and economies in transition recovered more quickly than anticipated from the currency and financial crises of 1997-1998, with economic growth returning to the East Asian countries and the Brazilian and Russian recessions turning out to be shorter than forecast. Still, many countries failed to participate in the recovery or see their pace of economic expansion return to pre-crisis levels, and many of the social consequences of the crisis persisted, with unemployment and poverty levels remaining higher than they were a few years earlier. The number of developing countries that recorded falling per capita output in 1999 remained at 37 (out of the 95 regularly monitored) and the number of those countries that achieved sustained annual growth rates of 3 per cent—considered the minimum necessary to lead to long-term poverty reduction—declined from 24 in 1998 to 21 in 1999.

In developed countries, which led the global economic upturn with growth in gross domestic product (GDP) expected to be 3 per cent in 2000, up from 2.6 per cent in 1999, investment in information and communication technology (ICT) sectors, including personal computers, the Internet and telecommunications, was the most dynamic driving force of the upswing. That was particularly evident in North America, where the United States, in April 2000, recorded an unprecedented 109 months in a row of economic expansion combined with continuing low rates of inflation and low unemployment. Although that expansion was expected to continue in 2000 and 2001, there were several downside risks, including an increasing trade deficit and concerns about the overheating of the economy. As a result, monetary policy had been tightened, with other market economies following suit.

Growth in the developed countries of Europe was also robust in late 1999, driven by exports and strengthening domestic demand. For 2000, strong performances were expected in France, Spain and the United Kingdom, while there was sustained though moderate growth in Germany and Italy and some of the smaller economies of the region were expected to grow briskly. Employment growth throughout Western Europe was steady, and, in 1999, the unemployment rate dipped below 10 per cent for the first time since 1993. However, average annual rates of unemployment ranged from almost 16 per cent in Spain to about 2.5 per cent in Luxembourg.

In contrast, the Japanese economy remained sluggish as the Government's fiscal stimulus measures failed to put either private consumption or investment demand on a sustained path. Uncertainties related to the pace and depth of corporate restructuring, combined with the large and increasing public debt, contributed to the subdued outlook. Business investment began to pick up in mid-1999, but private consumption remained weak, as indicated by the falling retail sales for 36 months in a row by March 2000. In the other developed countries of Asia and the Pacific, Australia marked its eighth year of continuous GDP growth and New Zealand achieved a modest recovery from its mild recession.

For most developing countries, the economic outlook had become more optimistic, largely due to progress in domestic economic reforms and the improved international environment, including more favourable commodity prices and more stable global financial markets. GDP growth was expected to increase from 3.4 per cent in 1999 to 5.25 per cent in 2000 and 5.5 per cent in 2001, back to the rates of the pre-crisis period. Importantly, the world's two largest developing economies and those containing the largest number of the world's poor, China and India, were expected to sustain growth rates of 6 to 7 per cent in 2000 and 2001.

In South and East Asia, growth was expected to reach some 6.5 per cent in 2000-2001, compared with 6.2 per cent in 1999. Most crisis-affected East Asian economies had been recovering at a robust pace, led by the Republic of Korea, which recorded 10.7 per cent growth in 1999. Other economies in the region also performed well, with only Indonesia virtually stagnating in 1999 and yet to embark on a strong recovery path. The strength and pace of those recoveries stemmed from stimulatory domestic policies and improvements in international trade. Some of the economies were also positioning themselves to benefit from the ICT revolution, especially in semiconductors and broader computer hardware and software. India was among the best performers in South Asia. Favourable weather in the subregion led to increased agricultural output, which supported GDP growth in a number of countries, but pervasive political uncertainties in most countries weakened the effectiveness of government policies, increased fiscal expenditures and discouraged economic activity to varying degrees. China experienced a 7.1 per cent increase in GDP

growth in 1999. In the long run, however, China's economic prospects would rely on meeting the challenges of implementing structural adjustments necessary for the country's entry into the World Trade Organization and the continued reform of State-owned enterprises. Economic growth in the countries of West Asia decelerated sharply from 3.7 per cent in 1998 to 0.5 per cent in 1999. However, with oil production increasing, export markets continuing to recover and better weather leading to expanded agricultural output, regional growth, which continued to be heavily influenced by the Iraqi economy, was expected to reach 4 per cent in 2000.

In Latin America, growth stagnated in 1999, but was expected to rebound in 2000-2001. The region's performance—though dismal for many countries, particularly in South America—was better than earlier forecast because Brazil avoided a widely expected sharp contraction, while Mexico and most of the Central American and Caribbean economies grew relatively strongly. Severe recessions in several countries in South America, including Chile, Colombia, Ecuador and Venezuela, resulted in high levels of unemployment. On the other hand, inflation reached an annual average rate of 7.5 per cent for the region in 1999, the lowest in decades. Increasing exports and investment, especially in the main Latin American economies of Brazil, Chile and Mexico, were expected to set the pace of growth for the region, forecast at 3.75 per cent for 2000 and 4.25 per cent for 2001. However, regional growth could be restrained by slower recoveries in other economies, including Argentina, Colombia, Ecuador, Peru and Venezuela, due to high levels of unemployment, tight credit, fiscal retrenchment, political uncertainties and/ or social unrest.

Africa maintained a modest rate of growth in 1999, fed by exports and increased agricultural output, but economic performance varied widely from country to country. A surge in oil prices had benefited net fuel-exporting economies in the region but countries producing non-oil commodities faced less favourable conditions. Disciplined macroeconomic policies in a large number of countries contributed to stability but domestic demand was generally weak. GDP growth was expected to increase from 2.8 per cent in 1999 to 4.25 per cent in 2000 as domestic conditions improved and exports strengthened the recovery under way. Still, persistent conflicts and political instability, combined with the HIV/AIDS pandemic, continued to have an adverse impact on the long-term economic prospects of the region.

Boosted by increased exports, rising investment and more foreign capital inflows, a firm recovery was under way in the transition economies of Central Europe and the Baltic region. However, conditions in South-Eastern Europe remained subdued. The return of positive economic growth to the economies in transition in 1999 resulted from the unexpectedly quick recovery in the Commonwealth of Independent States (CIS) countries after the major crisis triggered by the collapse of the Russian rouble in mid-1998. Growth was expected to accelerate from 2.1 per cent in 1999 to 3.75 per cent in 2000, which was projected to be the first year since transformation started that all the transition economies would register positive GDP growth. Still, economic performance in Central and Eastern Europe continued to be uneven. The conflict in Kosovo imposed a heavy toll, particularly in South-Eastern Europe, and structural problems in some countries, especially the Czech Republic, Romania and Slovakia, constrained the region's recovery. In the CIS, particularly the three major economies of Kazakhstan, the Russian Federation and Ukraine, the recovery was expected to be sustained in 2000, but the presence of obsolete industry in those countries, combined with possible debt-servicing difficulties and the impact of the Chechnyan conflict in the Russian Federation, could fetter prospects for growth.

The *Trade and Development Report, 2000* [Sales No. E.00.II.D.19] observed that, despite a rapid recovery from the depressed conditions of 1998, external vulnerability was still a threat to growth prospects in the developing world. Concerted efforts by developing countries to become full participants in an increasingly interdependent global economy continued to be stymied by biases and asymmetries in the trading and financial system. There were too many exporters struggling to gain access to the markets of the rich countries, extreme price movements were affecting manufacturers, and trade imbalances among major industrial countries added to the anxieties of the developing world. Even after years of domestic reforms, developing countries were still dependent on highly volatile capital flows to support growth. Increased international cooperation and dialogue was needed to realize the full potential of new technologies to bridge the growing gap between rich and poor (see also PART THREE, Chapter IV).

Regarding the financial crisis and recovery in East Asia, the *Report* cautioned that, while the surprising speed of recovery in the region had been encouraging, there remained reasons for concern: first, recovery had been accompanied by only limited corporate restructuring and the health of the financial system continued to rely on public intervention in the credit mechanism; sec-

ond, exports were unlikely to continue at their recent pace, and public deficits and debt were on the rise in most countries seriously hit by the crisis; and third, the recovery had so far been supported by highly favourable conditions in the world economy, which were susceptible to change. A fundamental lesson of the financial crisis was that excessive reliance on foreign resources and markets left growth prospects vulnerable to external shocks. Greater attention needed to be paid to domestic sources of growth, such as rising wage shares and higher social spending.

According to a report on the world economic situation and prospects [Sales No. E.01.II.C.2], prepared jointly by DESA and UNCTAD, improvements in economic growth were widespread during 2000, but particularly marked in a number of developing countries and economies in transition. The vigorous performance was associated with an exceptional acceleration in the growth of international trade, but was also accompanied by a further widening in the external imbalances among the major economies. Per capita GDP increased in 121 countries in 2000, compared with 104 in 1999. Of those, 73 were developing countries compared to 60 the previous year. Just four countries (Côte d'Ivoire, the Democratic Republic of the Congo, the Republic of Moldova and Zimbabwe) experienced a decline in GDP, by far the lowest number in more than a decade. Once again, the economy of the United States surpassed forecasts by a wide margin, as did many other developed economies, including the countries of the European Union. Unemployment rates fell, generally to the lowest level in many years, though they remained above 10 per cent in France and Germany.

Economic growth in almost all countries with economies in transition was also generally better than had been anticipated and well above 1999 levels, with the CIS countries growing by 6 per cent in 2000, the best performance since transition began. The economic performance of developing countries improved significantly in 2000, with growth accelerating to 5.6 per cent from 3.5 per cent in 1999. However, progress varied widely among countries, with the poorest continuing to trail behind. Aggregate output rose at a sharply higher rate than in 1999 in all main developing country regions except Africa, where the improvement was modest and the growth rate low, particularly in the sub-Saharan region. The countries of East Asia were recovering much more quickly than expected from the financial crisis of the previous two years, with growth rates reaching 7 per cent in 2000, largely as a result of strong exports of ICT products and buoyant private consumption. Similarly, Brazil witnessed faster than expected export growth and improved credit conditions, which supported domestic demand and resulted in a strong and broad-based recovery that led the way for economic improvements throughout Latin America and the Caribbean, though some South American economies lagged behind.

Human Development Report 2000

The *Human Development Report 2000*, prepared by the United Nations Development Programme (UNDP), addressed the relationship between human rights and development, stressing that human rights were not a reward of development, but rather were critical to achieving it. The report examined many examples of egregious human rights violations across the world, with the aim of placing a human rights–based approach to human development and poverty eradication firmly on the global agenda. Sections of the *Report* dealt with struggles for human freedoms, including freedom from discrimination, want, fear and injustice and for realizing potential, participation, expression and association, and decent work; the link between human rights and democracy; how rights could empower people in the fight against poverty; using indicators for human rights accountability; and promoting rights in development.

The *Report* ranked 174 countries in its human development index by combining indicators of life expectancy, educational attainment and adjusted per capita income, among other factors. Of the 174 countries listed, 46 were in the high human development category, 93 were in the medium category and 35 were in the low category. Twenty countries had experienced reversals of human development since 1990 due to the HIV/AIDS pandemic (mostly in sub-Saharan Africa) or economic stagnation and conflict (especially in sub-Saharan Africa, Eastern Europe and the CIS). Substantial disparities in global human development persisted both within and between regions. The *Report* pointed out that two countries with similar levels of economic prosperity could have very different rankings in human development. Progress was most often determined by a country's ability to convert economic prosperity into better lives.

Development policy and public administration

Development policy

The Committee for Development Policy, at its second session (New York, 3-7 April) [E/2000/33],

discussed the role of information technology in development (see p. 799), made suggestions regarding the draft of a new international development strategy (see p. 786), and conducted the triennial review of the list of least developed countries (LDCs) (see p. 807). Regarding working methods and programme of work, the Committee proposed that special attention be given to: the concerns of LDCs, including the triennial review of the list and preparations for the Third United Nations Conference to be held in 2001; the sequencing of financial and trade policies by developing countries, taking into account their initial conditions and the opportunities and challenges offered by the global economy; securing sustainable development by improving institutional arrangements for meeting environmental and developmental vulnerabilities; and improving economic governance at the national, regional and international levels, as well as international economic cooperation more generally.

In July, the Economic and Social Council, in resolution 2000/34, took note of the Committee's report on its second session and welcomed the proposals regarding its future work programme (see p. 807).

Public administration

The fifteenth meeting of the Group of Experts on the United Nations Programme in Public Administration and Finance (New York, 8-12 May) [E/2000/66] was devoted to the theme "Globalization and the State". The Group of Experts deliberated and made a number of recommendations on the effects of globalization on the role and functioning of the State and its responses, institutional and managerial, to attain maximum benefits and minimal negative consequences of globalization. In relation to the marginalization effects of globalization, the process that affected national and global economic governance systems was addressed and a number of recommendations were made. The Group of Experts reviewed, commented and made recommendations on the public administration, finance and development subprogramme of the draft medium-term plan for 2002-2005, as well as the current programme budget for 2000-2001 and the next biennium's programme budget.

Other comments and recommendations concerned major undertakings by the Division for Public Economics and Public Administration of DESA and improvements in relationships with other UN funds and programmes, particularly UNDP, in the area of public administration and development.

In July, the Economic and Social Council adopted **decision 2000/231** without vote [agenda item 13 *(b)*].

Recommendations made by the Group of Experts on the United Nations Programme in Public Administration and Finance at its fifteenth meeting

At its 42nd plenary meeting, on 27 July 2000, the Economic and Social Council endorsed the following recommendations made by the Group of Experts on the United Nations Programme in Public Administration and Finance at its fifteenth meeting:

Recommendation 1

The Group of Experts on the United Nations Programme in Public Administration and Finance recommends that subprogramme 8 (Public administration, finance and development) of programme 7 (Economic and social affairs) of the proposed medium-term plan for the period 2002-2005 be adopted with the changes set out in the annex to the report of the Secretary-General on the work of the Group of Experts.

Recommendation 2

The Group of Experts recommends that its sixteenth meeting be held during the first quarter of the year 2002 and that the number of experts participating be maximized, possibly by shortening the meeting, in order to achieve a wider geographical representation.

Recommendation 3

The Group of Experts recommends the proclamation of a United Nations public service day to celebrate the value and the virtue of service to the community at the local, national and global levels, with prizes to be awarded by the Secretary-General for contributions made to the cause of enhancing the role, prestige and visibility of public service.

Recommendation 4

In view of the crucial importance of economic and social development issues relating to institutional and managerial development, the Group of Experts takes the view that its relations and interactions with such principal organs and intergovernmental bodies as the Economic and Social Council should be greatly reinforced and that the deliberations of the Council on matters concerning economic and social development could greatly benefit from the input of the Group of Experts. To make this more effective, it recommends that the Council review the status and reporting arrangements of the Group of Experts.

Recommendation 5

The Group of Experts recommends that the United Nations establish appropriate mechanisms to provide the opportunity for ministers and/or high-level officials of Member States responsible for public administration to meet periodically to discuss themes of common interest and exchange experiences.

Recommendation 6

The Group of Experts recommends that the Council, through its subsidiary bodies, undertake a comparative analysis of national economic governance systems and examine best practices in order to assist national strategies for efficient economic governance.

Recommendation 7

The Group of Experts recommends that the Council include in its agenda discussion on issues related to economic governance and provide policy guidance for the global economic governance regimes established for the different functional areas administered by the specialized agencies.

Recommendation 8

The Group of Experts recommends to the Council that serious consideration be given to expanding on the work already done by the African ministers of public service, and that consideration be given to drawing up a United Nations model charter of public service.

On 28 July, the Council took note of the report of the Group of Experts [E/2000/66] (**decision 2000/297**).

Developing countries and transition economies

Least developed countries

The Least Developed Countries 2000 Report [Sales No. E.00.II.D.21], issued by UNCTAD, assessed the main trends in the socio-economic development of LDCs during the 1990s and the challenges of financing LDC development, including aid, private capital flows and debt. As an input to the preparatory process for the Third United Nations Conference on LDCs, to be held in 2001, the *Report* addressed the scale of the development finance challenge in LDCs, the scope for meeting that challenge through domestic resource mobilization, and the constraints limiting LDCs' access to international capital markets and attractiveness for foreign direct investment. It contained constructive proposals for improving international cooperation for LDCs in the field of development finance in order to facilitate a progressive transition away from aid dependence.

The *Report* stated that, while the gap between the LDC growth rate and the growth rate of other developing countries narrowed during the 1990s, there were wide disparities among LDCs, ranging from greater than 2 per cent real GDP per capita growth per annum during 1990-1998 in 15 LDCs, including 7 in Asia, to stagnation or regression in 22 LDCs during the same period. Overall, growth during the 1990s was not high enough to make a significant dent in unacceptably high rates of poverty in most LDCs and the gap was widening between LDCs and other developing countries in the rates of social progress. At the same time, aid flows to LDCs had been declining, particularly since 1995. In real per capita terms, net official development assistance (ODA) to LDCs had fallen by 45 per cent since 1990, and was back to the levels of the early 1970s.

LDC list

The number of officially designated LDCs increased to 49 in 2000, when the Economic and Social Council endorsed the Committee for Development Policy's recommendation that Senegal be added to the list (see below). The full list of LDCs comprised: Afghanistan, Angola, Bangladesh, Benin, Bhutan, Burkina Faso, Burundi, Cambodia, Cape Verde, Central African Republic, Chad, Comoros, Democratic Republic of the Congo, Djibouti, Equatorial Guinea, Eritrea, Ethiopia, Gambia, Guinea, Guinea-Bissau, Haiti, Kiribati, Lao People's Democratic Republic, Lesotho, Liberia, Madagascar, Malawi, Maldives, Mali, Mauritania, Mozambique, Myanmar, Nepal, Niger, Rwanda, Samoa, Sao Tome and Principe, Senegal, Sierra Leone, Solomon Islands, Somalia, Sudan, Togo, Tuvalu, Uganda, United Republic of Tanzania, Vanuatu, Yemen, Zambia.

Triennial review

The Committee for Development Policy, which was responsible for adding countries to or graduating them from the LDC list, conducted the triennial review of the status of LDC designations at its second session in April [E/2000/33]. As requested by the Economic and Social Council in resolution 1999/67 [YUN 1999, p. 766], an expert group meeting of members of the Committee (the Expert Group Meeting on Testing and Simulations of the Economic Vulnerability Index) met in Paris from 29 February to 2 March. In its recommendations, which were annexed to the Committee's report, the Expert Group stated that a fuller incorporation of the concept of vulnerability through the economic vulnerability index, as recommended by the Committee in 1999 [ibid., p. 768], meant a significant improvement in capturing persistent structural difficulties associated with stagnating economic growth and slow poverty reduction.

Based on the Expert Group's proposals and its own review of the list, the Committee recommended that Senegal be added (subject to the Government's acceptance) and that Maldives be deleted, as it clearly met the provisions of a 1991 rule stating that a country qualified for graduation when it met two out of the three criteria (per capita GDP, augmented physical quality of life and economic vulnerability) for two consecutive triennial reviews. Two additional countries, the Congo and Ghana, met all three criteria for inclusion in the LDC list, but the Committee decided to review their situations further at the next

triennial review. Of the countries already designated as LDCs, 39 met all three criteria for inclusion; a further 3 (Bangladesh, Eritrea and Madagascar) were very low-income countries that had been shown to be, economically, only moderately exposed to external shocks; and the remaining 6 countries (Cape Verde, Equatorial Guinea, Liberia, Samoa, Tuvalu and Vanuatu) had levels of GDP per capita above those of the low-income category, but were retained on the LDC list because they remained handicapped by high levels of economic vulnerability or by low levels of human resource development.

The Committee proposed, prior to the next triennial review, to consider the treatment given to countries with large population size and to countries in transition, and to revisit the practice by which different rules and thresholds for inclusion in and graduation from the list of LDCs were applied, so as to ensure a measure of stability for the list and yet give equal treatment to countries in similar situations.

Communications. On 18 and 22 July, Maldives transmitted to the Economic and Social Council President a letter from its President [E/2000/97] and a letter from its Minister for Foreign Affairs [E/2000/104] expressing concern for, and outlining arguments against, the Committee for Development Policy's recommendation that Maldives be graduated from the LDC list.

ECONOMIC AND SOCIAL COUNCIL ACTION

On 28 July [meeting 45], the Economic and Social Council adopted **resolution 2000/34** [draft: E/2000/ L.29, orally corrected] without vote [agenda item 13 (a)].

Report of the Committee for Development Policy

The Economic and Social Council,

Recalling section B of annex I to its resolution 1998/46 of 31 July 1998, in which it decided that the Council should decide on an appropriate programme of work for the Committee for Development Policy,

Recalling also its resolution 1998/39 of 30 July 1998 on the status of the least developed countries, its resolution 1999/67 of 16 December 1999 on the report of the Committee and its decision 1999/290 of 26 October 1999 on the consideration of the graduation of the Maldives from the list of the least developed countries,

Recalling further General Assembly resolutions 46/206 of 20 December 1991 and 52/210 of 18 December 1997,

Taking note with appreciation of the presentation by the Chairman and other members of the Bureau of the Committee, and of the report of the Committee on its second session, including its analysis of the role of information technology and development and its suggestions regarding an international development strategy for the first decade of the new millennium,

Noting that the report requested from the Secretariat and the United Nations Conference on Trade and Development on the effective benefits derived by the least developed countries specifically on the basis of their inclusion in the list of the least developed countries and on the practical impact of the measures in favour of least developed countries has not yet been made available to the Committee,

Having considered the letter dated 14 July 2000 from the President of the Republic of Maldives addressed to the President of the Economic and Social Council,

Having considered also the memorandum dated 13 July 2000 submitted by the Government of the Republic of Maldives,

Taking note of section 7 of the report of the Expert Group Meeting on Testing and Simulations of the Economic Vulnerability Index, held in Paris from 29 February to 2 March 2000, which is annexed to the report of the Committee,

1.' _Endorses_ the recommendation of the Committee for Development Policy that Senegal be added to the list of the least developed countries, subject to the concurrence of the Government of Senegal;

2. _Decides_ to defer to its next substantive session the consideration of the recommendation to graduate the Maldives from the list of the least developed countries, and requests the Committee at its third session to re-examine its recommendation in this regard, taking into account, inter alia, the reports referred to in paragraphs 3 and 4 of the present resolution and the memorandum submitted by the Government of the Republic of Maldives;

3. _Requests_ the Secretary-General, in the context of the Committee's recommendation to graduate the Maldives, to report on the progress achieved in the implementation of paragraph 4 of General Assembly resolution 46/206, and to make recommendations on additional measures that can be taken to ensure a smooth transition from least developed country status for graduating countries;

4. _Looks forward_ to the report being prepared by the United Nations Conference on Trade and Development on the effective benefits derived by the least developed countries specifically on the basis of their inclusion in the list of the least developed countries and on the practical impact of the measures in favour of least developed countries, and requests the Conference to include in that report an assessment of the implications of graduation for the Maldives;

5. _Reiterates_ the importance of consulting with relevant Member States in the drawing up and use of country vulnerability profiles as well as the continuing need for transparency, objectivity and accuracy in these processes;

6. _Requests_ the United Nations Conference on Trade and Development to take into account the recommendations of the Expert Group on Testing and Simulations of the Economic Vulnerability Index on the format and content of future vulnerability profiles;

7. _Takes note with appreciation_ of the revised criteria for the identification of least developed countries presented by the Committee in its report, and requests the Committee to continue its work on the methodology to be used for the identification of the least developed countries, where appropriate in association with other international organizations working on environmental and economic vulnerability issues, and to report to the Council in 2002 on the criteria which it proposes to use

in the triennial review of the list of the least developed countries scheduled for 2003;

8. _Requests_ the Committee at its third session to examine and make recommendations regarding the theme chosen for the high-level segment of the substantive session of 2001 of the Council;

9. _Welcomes_ the proposals made by the Committee regarding its future programme of work;

10. _Invites_ the Chairman and, as necessary, other members of the Committee to continue the practice of reporting orally to the Council on the work of the Committee.

Programme of Action for the 1990s

In October, the UNCTAD Trade and Development Board (TDB) carried out the final review of progress in implementing the Programme of Action for the Least Developed Countries for the 1990s, adopted by the Second (1990) United Nations Conference on the Least Developed Countries (Paris Conference) [YUN 1990, p. 369] and endorsed by the General Assembly in resolution 45/206 [ibid., p. 373]. The background document was _The Least Developed Countries 2000 Report_ [Sales No. E.00.II.D.21] (see above). In agreed conclusions of 20 October [TD/B/47/11 (vol. I) (agreed conclusions 459(XLVII))], TDB recognized that implementation of the Programme of Action had fallen short of expectations. The socio-economic conditions in LDCs had continued to decline and the number of LDCs had increased during the decade, with only one LDC able to graduate from the list. The Board emphasized the importance of accelerating growth and sustainable development; promoting poverty eradication in LDCs; strengthening their productive and human capacities, especially in social sectors, such as education and health; transparent and accountable governance; structural reforms; and enhancing the beneficial integration of LDCs within the rapidly globalizing economy.

Third UN Conference on LDCs (2001)

Preparatory Committee. The Intergovernmental Preparatory Committee for the Third United Nations Conference on the Least Developed Countries (LDC-III), scheduled for 2001, held its first session in New York from 24 to 28 July [A/CONF.191/2]. The high-level Conference would assess the results of the Programme of Action for LDCs for the 1990s; review implementation of international support measures, particularly in the areas of ODA, debt, investment and trade; and consider adopting further measures for the sustainable development of LDCs and their integration into the world economy. The Preparatory Committee agreed on a draft agenda and rules of procedure for the Conference, and began the process of drafting a new programme of action, which would be finalized at the second preparatory session in April 2001.

The Committee had before it a note by the UNCTAD secretariat on past performance, challenges and the way forward for the sustainable development of LDCs and their beneficial integration into the global economy [A/CONF.191/ IPC/12]. The report outlined developments in the LDCs during the 1990s in several areas, including domestic resource mobilization, agriculture, manufacturing, mining, transport and communications, exports, supply capacity and competitiveness, social services delivery, gender and development in LDCs, and the environment. It also raised questions concerning the challenges currently faced by LDCs and suggested a framework for possible elements to be included in a new programme of action for LDCs.

The Committee also reviewed the preliminary findings [A/CONF.191/IPC/16] of a high-level panel to assess progress in national implementation of the Programme of Action and recommend ways to remedy its most critical weaknesses. A final meeting of the panel was scheduled for September. Regarding other Conference preparations, the Committee examined the results of the second and third inter-agency meetings (Geneva, 10 April; New York, 20 July) [A/CONF.191/IPC/9 & 15] and the second and third consultative forums (Geneva, 11 April; New York, 21 July) [A/CONF.191/ IPC/8 & 14] on the preparatory process, as well as the conclusions of three expert-level regional preparatory meetings, held in Addis Ababa, Ethiopia, for English-speaking African LDCs (27-29 March) [A/CONF.191/IPC/2], in Kathmandu, Nepal, for the Asian and Pacific LDCs (3-5 April) [A/CONF.191/IPC/3], and in Niamey, Niger, for French-speaking African LDCs (18-20 April) [A/CONF.191/IPC/4]. Country-level preparations, including national LDC action programmes, and the contributions of the UN system [A/CONF.191/ IPC/10] were also considered. In addition, the Committee had before it a progress report on the Integrated Framework for Trade-Related Technical Assistance to LDCs, undertaken jointly by six agencies: the International Monetary Fund (IMF), the International Trade Centre, UNCTAD, UNDP, the World Bank and the World Trade Organization (WTO) [A/CONF.191/ IPC/11].

Report of Secretary-General. In response to General Assembly resolution 54/235 [YUN 1999, p. 770], the Secretary-General submitted an August report on the state of preparations for the Third Conference [A/55/222]. He reviewed the first session of the Intergovernmental Preparatory Committee, as well as various other meetings and preparations undertaken at the regional and national levels. The report also addressed Conference promotion, resource mobilization and the participation of LDC representatives, NGOs and others.

TDB action. On 20 October [TD/B/47/11 (vol. I) (agreed conclusions 459(XLVII))], TDB requested that work on the preparation of the draft new programme of action commence immediately under the authority of the Chairman of the Preparatory Committee for LDC-III. In preparing the new programme of action, account should be taken of the views of the member States, particularly LDCs, the national programmes of action, the outcomes of major global summits and conferences, and ongoing processes within multilateral organizations, including the Bretton Woods institutions (the World Bank Group and IMF) and WTO. The Board emphasized the importance of an adaptable document that would include quantifiable, measurable and implementable targets based on international development targets. It was further emphasized that the preparation, implementation and follow-up of the programme of action should be undertaken with the active involvement of major multilateral organizations. The Board stressed the need for effective monitoring and follow-up to the implementation of the new programme of action.

Communication. By a 28 September letter [A/C.2/55/4], Bangladesh transmitted to the Secretary-General the text of the Declaration adopted by the Tenth Annual Ministerial Meeting of LDCs (New York, 18 September), which called on the UN system and other international organizations to participate fully in the formulation of the new programme of action and its implementation.

ACC action. The Administrative Committee on Coordination (ACC), at its second regular session of 2000 (New York, 27-28 October) [ACC/2000/20], adopted a statement on LDC-III, in which it declared the full commitment of the UN system to strongly support the Conference secretariat in the preparations.

GENERAL ASSEMBLY ACTION

On 20 December [meeting 87], the General Assembly, on the recommendation of the Second Committee [A/55/589], adopted **resolution 55/214** without vote [agenda item 102].

Third United Nations Conference on the Least Developed Countries

The General Assembly,

Recalling its resolution 52/187 of 18 December 1997, in which it decided to convene the Third United Nations Conference on the Least Developed Countries at a high level in 2001, as well as its resolutions 53/182 of 15 December 1998 and 54/235 of 23 December 1999,

Recalling also the United Nations Millennium Declaration adopted on 8 September 2000 by the heads of State and Government on the occasion of the Millennium Summit,

Taking note of the Declaration and the Programme of Action adopted at the South Summit of the Group of 77, held at Havana from 10 to 14 April 2000, the Declaration adopted by the Tenth Annual Ministerial Meeting of the Least Developed Countries, held in New York on 18 September 2000, and the Ministerial Statement adopted at the twenty-fourth annual meeting of the Ministers for Foreign Affairs of the Group of 77, held in New York on 15 September 2000,

Noting the progress made in the preparatory process for the Third United Nations Conference on the Least Developed Countries at the country, regional and global levels,

Taking note of the report of the Secretary-General on the status of preparations for the Conference, the report of the Intergovernmental Preparatory Committee for the Conference on its first session, held in New York from 24 to 28 July 2000, and the outcome of the forty-seventh session of the Trade and Development Board on the preparatory process of the Conference,

Taking note also of *The Least Developed Countries 2000 Report,*

1. *Recalls* that the Third United Nations Conference on the Least Developed Countries will convene from 14 to 20 May 2001 and will be hosted by the European Union at Brussels;

2. *Decides,* in the light of the recommendation of the Intergovernmental Preparatory Committee for the Conference at its first session, to convene, within existing resources, the second session of the Committee from 5 to 9 February 2001 in New York, at which the Committee will undertake the first formal reading of the draft programme of action and consider other relevant matters, while noting that the final session of the Committee will be held in New York from 2 to 6 April 2001;

3. *Requests* the Secretary-General of the United Nations to defray the cost of participation of two government representatives from each least developed country in the second and final sessions of the Preparatory Committee through the use of extrabudgetary resources, and also requests that the Bureau of the Preparatory Committee keep the matter under regular review on the basis of information provided by the Secretary-General of the Conference;

4. *Notes* that sufficient extrabudgetary resources will need to be mobilized to defray the cost of participation of the least developed countries in the third session of the Preparatory Committee, and, in this regard, invites additional contributions from multilateral and bilateral donors, and requests the Secretary-General of the Conference to seek funding from all possible sources for this purpose;

5. *Welcomes* the contributions already made by multilateral and bilateral donors for the participation of representatives from the least developed countries in the sessions of the Preparatory Committee and in the Conference;

6. *Emphasizes* the importance of the effective participation of all relevant stakeholders from the least developed countries and their development partners, as well as of the organizations and bodies of the United Nations system and other relevant multilateral organizations;

7. *Recognizes* the importance of the contribution of civil society actors at the Conference and its preparatory process, stresses, in this regard, the need for their active participation, including those from the least developed countries, and invites donors to make appropriate contributions for that purpose;

8. *Invites* the participation in the Conference and in its preparatory process of *(a)* the relevant non-governmental organizations that are in consultative status with the Economic and Social Council in accordance with Council resolution 1996/31 of 25 July 1996, *(b)* the non-governmental organizations that were accredited to the Second United Nations Conference on the Least Developed Countries, held from 3 to 14 September 1990 and *(c)* the non-governmental organizations that are in consultative status with the United Nations Conference on Trade and Development, decides that the accreditation of other interested civil society actors, in particular non-governmental organizations and the business sector, to the Conference and its preparatory process shall be considered by the Bureau of the Preparatory Committee on a no-objection basis before 31 January 2001 for final decision by the Committee at its second session, provided that requests for accreditation are submitted to the secretariat of the Conference before 15 January 2001 and are accompanied by the relevant information, and requests the Secretary-General of the Conference to inform the community of civil society actors appropriately about this accreditation process;

9. *Also invites* the Bureau of the Preparatory Committee to make recommendations for the consideration of Member States during the second session of the Committee as to the form of involvement of civil society actors in the final session of the Committee and at the Conference;

10. *Emphasizes* the importance of country-level preparations as a critical input to the preparatory process for the Conference and the implementation of and follow-up to its outcome;

11. *Requests* the Administrator of the United Nations Development Programme, in his capacity as convenor of the United Nations Development Group, to continue to ensure the full involvement of the United Nations resident coordinators and country teams in the least developed countries in the preparations for the Conference, in particular at the country level;

12. *Welcomes* the statement of the Administrative Committee on Coordination on the Conference, and calls upon the Secretary-General of the United Nations, in consultation with the Secretary-General of the Conference, to convene inter-agency consultations, within the context of the machinery of the Administrative Committee on Coordination, to ensure the full mobilization and coordination of all relevant organs, organizations and bodies of the United Nations system, as well as other relevant multilateral intergovernmental organizations, during the preparatory process for the Conference and the implementation of and follow-up to its outcome;

13. *Emphasizes* the importance of an effective arrangement for follow-up, review and monitoring of the new programme of action for the least developed countries, and requests the Secretary-General to recom-

mend to the General Assembly concrete steps in this regard;

14. *Stresses* that the intergovernmental follow-up, review and monitoring of the new programme of action should be undertaken in a more effective manner, with the participation of all relevant stakeholders, particularly the least developed countries, as well as with the involvement of concerned organizations and bodies of the United Nations system and other relevant multilateral intergovernmental organizations, and emphasizes the need to explore innovative approaches in this regard;

15. *Notes* the current level of regular budget resources available to the Office of the Special Coordinator for Least Developed, Landlocked and Island Developing Countries, and requests the Secretary-General to ensure that sufficient resources are made available throughout the remainder of the current biennium, through judicious management of the resources at his disposal, and to report on the matter at its fifty-sixth session;

16. *Requests* the Secretary-General to submit to it at its fifty-sixth session a report on the outcome of the Third United Nations Conference on the Least Developed Countries.

Resource requirements

In March [A/54/7/Add.13] and again in May [A/54/7/Add.14], the Advisory Committee on Administrative and Budgetary Questions considered two notes of the Secretary-General [A/C.5/54/50 & A/C.5/54/58] regarding the review of the resource requirements for the high-level intergovernmental event on financing for development (see p. 915) and LDC-III.

GENERAL ASSEMBLY ACTION

On 7 April [meeting 95], the General Assembly, on the recommendation of the Fifth (Administrative and Budgetary) Committee [A/54/691/Add.1], adopted **resolution 54/258 A** without vote [agenda item 121].

Review of resource requirements for the high-level international intergovernmental event on financing for development and the Third United Nations Conference on the Least Developed Countries

The General Assembly,

Having considered the note by the Secretary-General on the review of resource requirements for the high-level international intergovernmental event on financing for development and the Third United Nations Conference on the Least Developed Countries and the related report of the Advisory Committee on Administrative and Budgetary Questions,

1. *Takes note* of the note by the Secretary-General and the related report of the Advisory Committee on Administrative and Budgetary Questions;

2. *Reiterates* the provisions of section VI of its resolution 45/248 B of 21 December 1990, in which it reaffirmed that the Fifth Committee was the appropriate Main Committee of the General Assembly entrusted with responsibilities for administrative and budgetary

matters and also reaffirmed the role of the Advisory Committee;

3. *Reaffirms* section XIV of its resolution 54/251 of 23 December 1999, in which it decided that the special account would be maintained and the unspent balance retained until all the activities and programmes outlined in the report of the Secretary-General of 13 May 1998 and approved by the General Assembly in its resolution 53/3 of 12 October 1998 were completed;

4. *Notes with concern* that no extrabudgetary resources have been received to date in response to the note verbale of 14 February 2000 addressed to all States members of the United Nations Conference on Trade and Development, inviting them to consider providing, through voluntary contributions, resources to defray the costs of participation of government representatives in the meetings of the Intergovernmental Preparatory Committee for the Third United Nations Conference on the Least Developed Countries and the Conference itself;

5. *Requests* the Secretary-General to explore ways of providing the resource requirements for the high-level international intergovernmental event on financing for development and the Third United Nations Conference on the Least Developed Countries and to report to the General Assembly at the second part of its resumed fifty-fourth session.

On 15 June [meeting 98], the Assembly, on the recommendation of the Fifth Committee [A/54/691/Add.2], adopted **resolution 54/258 B** without vote [agenda item 121].

Review of resource requirements for the high-level international intergovernmental event on financing for development and the Third United Nations Conference on the Least Developed Countries

The General Assembly,

Having considered the note by the Secretary-General on the review of resource requirements for the high-level international intergovernmental event on financing for development and the Third United Nations Conference on the Least Developed Countries and the related report of the Advisory Committee on Administrative and Budgetary Questions,

I

1. *Welcomes* the fact that voluntary contributions for the financing of activities related to the first session of the Intergovernmental Preparatory Committee for the Third United Nations Conference on the Least Developed Countries have been pledged;

2. *Expresses appreciation* for the contributions and pledges received and, noting the current level of the resources in the Trust Fund for Least Developed Countries: Core Project, looks forward to the rapid disbursement of the funds being pledged;

3. *Decides,* as a precautionary measure, that should sufficient extrabudgetary resources not be immediately available for the financing of the first session of the Preparatory Committee, use would be made, on a provisional basis, of the contingency fund, on the understanding that the contingency fund would be replenished by those extrabudgetary resources as soon as they were available;

4. *Decides also* to revert to the question of the financing of the second session of the Preparatory Committee and the Conference itself at the fifty-fifth session of the General Assembly;

II

1. *Welcomes* the establishment of a Trust Fund for the Preparatory Committee for the high-level international intergovernmental event on financing for development;

2. *Decides* that the expenses related to the travel and subsistence of the members of the Bureau of the Preparatory Committee in relation to the consultations mandated in General Assembly resolution 54/279 of 15 June 2000 shall be met through the transfer, to the Trust Fund for the Preparatory Committee, of the balance available in the Trust Fund for the Participation of Least Developed Countries in Intergovernmental Meetings;

3. *Encourages* members of the Bureau to finance their own travel and subsistence where possible.

Economies in transition

In response to General Assembly resolution 53/179 [YUN 1998, p. 776], the Secretary-General submitted a July report [A/55/188] describing measures taken by organizations of the UN system in relation to the integration of the economies in transition into the world economy. Information was provided on, in particular, analytical activities, policy advice and technical assistance to the economies in transition especially with regard to the development of the necessary conditions for attracting foreign investment.

GENERAL ASSEMBLY ACTION

On 20 December [meeting 87], the General Assembly, on the recommendation of the Second Committee [A/55/581/Add.2], adopted **resolution 55/191** without vote [agenda item 94 *(b)*].

Integration of the economies in transition into the world economy

The General Assembly,

Reaffirming its resolutions 47/187 of 22 December 1992, 48/181 of 21 December 1993, 49/106 of 19 December 1994, 51/175 of 6 December 1996 and 53/179 of 15 December 1998,

Reaffirming also the need for the full integration of the countries with economies in transition into the world economy,

Taking note of the report of the Secretary-General,

Noting the progress made in those countries towards achieving macroeconomic and financial stability and economic growth in the course of structural reforms and the need to sustain those positive trends in the future,

Recognizing the difficulties faced by the countries with economies in transition in responding adequately to the challenges of globalization, including in the field of information and communication technologies, and the need to enhance their capacity to utilize effec-

tively the benefits and mitigate the negative implications of globalization,

Recognizing also the continuing need to ensure favourable conditions for market access of exports from countries with economies in transition, in accordance with multilateral trade agreements,

Recognizing further the important role foreign investment should play in those countries, and stressing the need to create an enabling environment to attract more foreign direct investment,

Noting the aspiration of the countries with economies in transition towards the further development of regional and interregional cooperation,

1. *Welcomes* the measures taken by the organizations of the United Nations system to implement General Assembly resolutions on the integration of the economies in transition into the world economy;

2. *Calls upon* the organizations of the United Nations system, including the Bretton Woods institutions, in collaboration with relevant non–United Nations multilateral and regional institutions, to continue to conduct analytical activities and provide policy advice and technical assistance to the Governments of the countries with economies in transition aimed at strengthening the social and political framework for completing market-oriented reforms with a view to sustaining the positive trends in the economic and social development of those countries, and, in this regard, emphasizes the importance of their further integration into the knowledge-based world economy through the effective utilization of information and communication technologies;

3. *Requests* the Secretary-General to submit to the General Assembly at its fifty-seventh session a report on the implementation of the present resolution with particular focus on an analysis that would determine the progress achieved in the integration of countries with economies in transition into the world economy.

Island developing countries

Implementation of Programme of Action

In response to General Assembly resolutions 54/224 [YUN 1999, p. 783] and 54/225 [ibid., p. 995], the Secretary-General submitted a July report [A/55/185] on progress in implementing the Programme of Action for the Sustainable Development of Small Island Developing States (SIDS), adopted in 1994 at the Global Conference on the subject [YUN 1994, p. 783], and on promoting an integrated management approach to the Caribbean Sea area in the context of sustainable development. The report was based on information provided by members of the UN system, regional organizations and Governments, especially in relation to the issues of climate change and sea-level rise; natural and environmental disasters; waste management; coastal and marine, freshwater, land, energy and biodiversity resources; tourism; national capacities; transport and communication; human resources development;

social and cultural development; and trade. Progress in the development of a vulnerability index specifically for SIDS, which would assist in identifying challenges to their sustainable development, was also reviewed.

With regard to promoting an integrated management approach to the Caribbean area, the report presented information received from UNDP, UNEP and the Caribbean Community.

The report concluded that there was scope for improving coordination among the UN agencies, the regional organizations and national Governments on tasks that were planned as well as ongoing.

Communication. By a 26 September letter [A/C.2/55/3], Samoa transmitted to the Secretary-General the report of the second Alliance of Small Island States workshop on climate change negotiations, management and strategy (Apia, Samoa, 26 July–4 August). Acknowledging that adaptation to the adverse effects of climate change remained the key challenge facing SIDS, participants made recommendations regarding national communications, capacity development, scientific research, land use and other mechanisms for developing common responses to that challenge.

GENERAL ASSEMBLY ACTION

On 20 December [meeting 87], the General Assembly, on the recommendation of the Second Committee [A/55/582/Add.4], adopted **resolution 55/202** without vote [agenda item 95 (d)].

Further implementation of the outcome of the Global Conference on the Sustainable Development of Small Island Developing States

The General Assembly,

Recalling its resolution 49/122 of 19 December 1994 on the Global Conference on the Sustainable Development of Small Island Developing States,

Recalling also its resolutions 51/183 of 16 December 1996, 52/202 of 18 December 1997, 53/189 of 15 December 1998 and 54/224 of 22 December 1999,

Recognizing that small island developing States, given their size, limited resources, geographic dispersion and, in most cases, isolation from markets, face special challenges and unique vulnerabilities of an environmental and economic nature in their efforts to achieve sustainable development and the need to enhance their capacity to effectively benefit from the opportunities presented by trade liberalization and globalization, while minimizing their negative impact on small island developing States,

Recalling the Declaration of Barbados and the Programme of Action for the Sustainable Development of Small Island Developing States of the Global Conference on the Sustainable Development of Small Island Developing States,

Recalling also the Declaration and review document adopted by the General Assembly at its twenty-second special session,

Having considered the report of the Secretary-General,

Having also considered the report of the United Nations Conference on Trade and Development on its tenth session,

Taking note of the report of the second Alliance of Small Island States workshop on climate change negotiations, management and strategy, which was held at Apia, Samoa, from 26 July to 4 August 2000,

Noting the significant efforts to implement the Programme of Action at the national, regional and international levels and the need for regional and global institutions to continue to supplement the efforts being made at the national level, including through effective financial support,

Acknowledging the efforts of small island developing States to convene, in cooperation with the Small Island Developing States Unit of the Department of Economic and Social Affairs of the Secretariat, a series of capacity-building workshops targeted at issues of specific relevance to small island developing States,

Welcoming the offer of the Government of Saint Kitts and Nevis to host the first Alliance of Small Island States workshop on the Cartegena Protocol on Biosafety in December 2000 and the offer of the Government of Cyprus to host the third Alliance of Small Island States workshop on climate change, energy and preparations for the ninth session of the Commission on Sustainable Development in January 2001,

Bearing in mind the continued need for the financing of projects that were presented within the context of the implementation of the Programme of Action, inter alia, at the meeting of representatives of donor countries and small island developing States held in New York from 24 to 26 February 1999,

Noting with appreciation the contribution by some donor countries towards further implementation of the Programme of Action, and underlining the need for those efforts to be intensified and supplemented by other donor countries and agencies,

Noting the work being undertaken by the Committee for Development Policy and other international organizations on a vulnerability index, which incorporates, inter alia, environmental and economic vulnerability factors,

1. *Reiterates* the urgent need for strong and effective implementation of the Programme of Action for the Sustainable Development of Small Island Developing States and of the Declaration and review document adopted by the General Assembly at its twenty-second special session;

2. *Welcomes* efforts at the national, subregional and regional levels to implement the Programme of Action;

3. *Invites* the relevant organs and agencies of the United Nations system and the regional commissions and organizations, within their respective mandates, to reflect measures for the implementation of the Programme of Action in their programmes;

4. *Invites* the relevant agencies within the United Nations system, in the preparation of the ten-year review of the progress achieved in the implementation of the outcome of the United Nations Conference on Environment and Development, to identify measures that would ensure the effective implementation of the Programme of Action;

5. *Calls upon* Member States, in particular the donor community, as well as the relevant organs and agencies of the United Nations system and the regional commissions and organizations, to support the efforts of small island developing States in the further implementation of the Programme of Action through, inter alia, the provision of adequate technical and financial resources, taking into account the Declaration and review document for further implementation and effective follow-up;

6. *Calls upon* the organizations of the United Nations system to assist small island developing States in their efforts to enhance their capacities to effectively utilize the benefits and mitigate the implications of globalization, including by bridging the digital divide and fostering digital opportunities in the field of information and communication technologies;

7. *Invites* all relevant stakeholders, nongovernmental organizations and the private sector to participate fully in the activities identified for the further implementation of and effective follow-up to the Programme of Action;

8. *Urges* all relevant organizations to finalize, as a matter of urgency, the work on the development of a vulnerability index;

9. *Welcomes* the strengthened Small Island Developing States Unit, and requests the Secretary-General to consider ways to further strengthen the Unit, inter alia, by establishing the Small Island Developing States Information Network within the Unit and by assisting small island developing States with, inter alia, project implementation advice and assistance in the identification of short and long-term capacity needs through coordination with regional and international institutions, and to make proposals in that regard;

10. *Welcomes* the contributions of Germany, Italy, Japan and Norway to the strengthening of the Small Island Developing States Unit, and encourages other Member States to make contributions, in particular, in support of the Small Island Developing States Information Network;

11. *Decides* to include in the provisional agenda of its fifty-sixth session, under the item entitled "Environment and sustainable development", the sub-item entitled "Further implementation of the Programme of Action for the Sustainable Development of Small Island Developing States";

12. *Requests* the Secretary-General to submit to the General Assembly at its fifty-sixth session a report on the implementation of the present resolution.

Chapter II

Operational activities for development

In 2000, the income of the United Nations Development Programme (UNDP), the central United Nations funding body for technical assistance to developing countries, totalled $2,554 million, as compared to $2,608 million in 1999. The total expenditure for all programme activities plus support costs also decreased, from $2,681 million in 1999 to $2,513 million in 2000.

Within the UN system as a whole, efforts were made by relevant bodies to implement all the elements of the General Assembly's 1998 resolution on a triennial policy review of operational activities for development. In July, the Economic and Social Council noted the progress made in implementing that resolution and requested the Secretary-General, in the context of the next triennial policy review in 2001, to report on, among other things, progress in implementing the multi-year funding framework, as part of efforts to reverse the declining trend in core resources and to establish a mechanism for more predictable funding.

On 11 September, the first Ministerial Meeting on UNDP was held to seek ways to boost recognition and support for it at the country level and in key international forums. Various options were put forward for rebuilding political support for UNDP.

UNDP continued its management and programme reforms in 2000. The reforms focused on performance and results and set a leaner staffing structure in place. In the results-oriented annual report for 2000, the first such report in the formal multi-year funding framework period, the Administrator analysed UNDP performance for each of the six goals—sustainable human development, poverty reduction, the environment, gender equality, special development situations and UNDP support to the United Nations.

The United Nations Office for Project Services (UNOPS) continued to operate under the self-financing principle, without assessed budget financing. The total value of the UNOPS project and loan portfolios amounted to $3.7 billion in 2000, comprising $1.5 billion in project value and $2.2 billion in loans under its supervision, primarily for the International Fund for Agricultural Development. Total delivery was $664 million, down from $764 million in 1999.

The United Nations Volunteers programme, administered by UNDP, grew for the fourth successive year, with some 4,800 volunteers carrying out nearly 5,200 assignments in 140 countries. During the year, the programme was evaluated and recommendations made concerning its future status and relations with UNDP. In November, the Secretary-General officially launched the International Year of Volunteers (2001) aimed at recognizing and promoting volunteerism, and in December the General Assembly called on States, organizations and the private sector to promote volunteer action in their own societies.

United Nations efforts to promote technical cooperation among developing countries (TCDC) were focused in UNDP's Special Unit for TCDC. Total core and non-core resources for TCDC amounted to $29.5 million for 1997-2000, and were allocated to building policy and institutional capacities, nurturing TCDC knowledge-networking, and forging partnerships for sustainable human development.

System-wide activities

Operational activities segment of the Economic and Social Council

The Economic and Social Council, at its 2000 substantive session (New York, 5-28 July, 18 October, 22 November), considered the question of operational activities of the United Nations for international development cooperation at meetings on 13, 14, 17, 18 and 28 July. A high-level meeting on operational activities was held on 17 and 18 July. On 13 July, the Council held an informal dialogue with the UN system country teams from Ghana and Madagascar, and, on 18 July, with the heads of UN funds and programmes. On 14, 17 and 18 July, the Council considered follow-up to policy recommendations of the Assembly and the Council, and the reports of the Executive Boards of UNDP/United Nations Population Fund (UNFPA), the United Nations Children's Fund (UNICEF) and the World Food Programme (WFP). The Council, on 17 July, held a panel discussion entitled "Celebration of 50 years of United Nations development cooperation".

Implementation of resolution 53/192

In May [E/2000/46/Add.1], the Secretary-General reported on progress in implementing General Assembly resolution 53/192 [YUN 1998, p. 802] on the triennial policy review of UN operational activities for development in the areas of impact evaluation; strategic frameworks and programming; harmonization of programming cycles; field-level coordination; country-level follow-up to global conferences and operational activities; gender and development; common premises and sharing of administrative services; the regional dimension; South-South cooperation; humanitarian assistance, peace-building and development; monitoring and evaluation; and capacity-building.

The Secretary-General stated that considerable progress had been achieved in implementing resolution 53/192 but more remained to be accomplished. In terms of evaluations of the impact of operational activities for development, out of the 24 planned evaluations under the current series to be completed in time for the 2001 triennial review, 2 had been completed, 4 initiated and activities for another 10 were ready, subject to financing.

Progress also continued in the operationalization of the common country assessment (CCA) and the United Nations Development Assistance Framework (UNDAF), designed to strengthen UN system coordination mechanisms at the programming level. Some 74 country teams were currently at various stages of the CCA/UNDAF process, based on the status of their harmonized programme cycles. However, while progress with the CCA/UNDAF process achieved so far was modifying the way the UN system collaborated at the country level, several challenges remained, including the substantive focus of the two instruments; the rationalization and simplification of relevant programming procedures; the monitoring of the UNDAF time line and its synchronization with the individual country programmes and projects derived from UNDAF; using CCA, originally conceived as a development tool, in crisis and post-conflict countries; further collaboration with the Bretton Woods institutions (the World Bank Group and the International Monetary Fund (IMF)); and the effective involvement of civil society and the private sector in policy debates generated by the CCA and UNDAF processes.

The harmonization of programming cycles presented several difficulties, since not all UN organizations worked on a country programme basis. A degree of flexibility was needed to harmonize the cycles of organizations that applied a country programme approach and those that followed a different approach. Partial harmonization of programme cycles in countries with a large representation of the UN development system also represented a continuing challenge to collaborative programming. Given the overall difficult progress in the harmonization of cycles, the United Nations Development Group (UNDG) had requested country teams to draw up local action plans with clear time frames. As a result, as at December 1999, 98 per cent of the countries qualifying for harmonization had done so, a 73 per cent increase since 1998, and 95 countries were expected to be harmonized by 2005. UNDG had put in place a monitoring mechanism to ensure that the progress would be maintained. The harmonization of programming cycles with national budgets or planning cycles was more complicated than originally expected.

Successful efforts at collaborative programming among several organizations had further energized field-level coordination. Arrangements to involve national partners were becoming more frequent and joint funding had increased significantly. Progress was also made in the coherence of many country teams and interest was growing among organizations with country representatives to advance both the work of the individual organization and the team effort of the resident coordinator system. However, because of reduced funds to support operational activities, country teams were facing severe cuts in programme activities. Other useful means of field-level coordination were the use of thematic groups and "retreats" to focus on specific concerns and review activities in progress, and expanded access to and use of information technology.

Both UNDAF and CCA had the potential of becoming the main instruments at the country level for a system-wide integrated follow-up to global conferences. Their further application was expected to be strengthened through the CCA indicator framework to reinforce the use and adaptation of conference indicators at the country level and help in the establishment of national data sets relevant to conference follow-up. Despite the progress made, a gap continued between conference outcomes and the objectives and priorities of UN system assistance programmes. Country-specific tools and advice, country-specific frameworks and models and appropriate baseline data needed further development, and, since most decision-making and funding continued on a sectoral basis, stronger linkages were needed between and among government units, civil society and international agencies. Two new major efforts to overcome that problem were the girls' education strategy and the poverty action strategy designed by UNDG and endorsed by the Consultative Committee on Programme and Operational Questions (CCPOQ) in March 2000 on behalf of the Administrative Committee on Coordination (ACC).

As part of UN system efforts to support and encourage gender mainstreaming, agencies had intensified efforts to ensure a gender perspective in their management strategies and operational activities. Progress was being made throughout the UN system to implement the critical areas of concern in the Beijing Platform for Action [YUN 1995, p. 1170]. In addition, the UNDG Subgroup on Gender had focused its efforts on the CCA and UNDAF guidelines, assuring a gender perspective in the text and indicators. The UN Department of Economic and Social Affairs, in collaboration with UNDP, carried out a major study assessing gender mainstreaming in governance and poverty eradication programmes in sub-Saharan Africa, and the UNDG Working Group on Girls' Education developed a comprehensive action strategy on girls' education, which was launched by the Secretary-General in April.

Several steps were under way to support the planning, implementation and oversight of the "United Nations House" programme. New guidelines on operational management of common services were being developed and additional guidance and support were being provided to the country teams. A consolidated common database and lease management maintenance software (Aperture) were completed to facilitate management of country office premises. The UNDG Management Group on Services and Premises was also developing guidance on common and shared services.

Regarding the involvement of the regional commissions in CCA and UNDAF, the physical distance between the commissions and the majority of the country offices in their respective region prevented the commissions from being actively involved in the CCA and UNDAF participatory working process. Resident coordinators needed to give special attention to involving the regional commissions and non-resident agencies in the preparation and implementation of CCA and UNDAF. The CCPOQ Working Group on the Resident Coordinator System had encouraged all parties to propose ways to improve collaboration.

UN system entities had done much in the past year to alleviate crisis and post-conflict situations. At the Headquarters level, the Inter-Agency Standing Committee (for humanitarian affairs) (IASC) (see p. 846) considered such issues as guidance to humanitarian/resident coordinators on internally displaced persons and linkages among humanitarian, peacekeeping and politi-

cal components of UN operations, especially in post-conflict situations. IASC also formed a UNDP-led reference group on post-conflict reintegration, which explored gaps and the factors compounding them and recommended several steps for United Nations action. UNDP was also redefining its role in crisis, post-conflict and recovery situations (see p. 823).

Concerning evaluation, there had been positive developments regarding follow-up to the General Assembly and the Economic and Social Council resolutions on the subject. However, the degree of implementation was at times uneven and a hindrance to effectiveness. One impact evaluation revealed that joint programme reviews and evaluations remained a rarity, resulting in programme-wide/country-level issues not being properly examined.

In capacity-building, there had been steady follow-up within the UN system. A guidance note on the subject was approved by CCPOQ in March on behalf of ACC. UNDP and UNICEF had been exploring the concept of capacity-building/capacity-building development, as well as methodologies and mechanisms for its planning and monitoring. However, the UN system, particularly the specialized agencies, continued to have difficulty in drawing lessons learned from their experience. The first impact evaluation suggested that it was important for all relevant UN system entities, as well as Member States, to evaluate their experience and current approaches, with a view to extracting the lessons learned and best practices.

ECONOMIC AND SOCIAL COUNCIL ACTION

On 28 July [meeting 44], the Economic and Social Council adopted **resolution 2000/20** [draft: E/2000/L.15] without vote [agenda item 3 *(a)* (iii)].

Progress in the implementation of General Assembly resolution 53/192 on the triennial policy review of operational activities for development of the United Nations system

The Economic and Social Council,

Recalling General Assembly resolution 53/192 of 15 December 1998 on the triennial policy review of operational activities for development of the United Nations system and Council resolution 1999/6 of 23 July 1999,

1. *Takes note* of the report of the Secretary-General on operational activities of the United Nations for international development cooperation and of the consolidated list of issues related to the coordination of operational activities;

2. *Reiterates* that the fundamental characteristics of the operational activities of the United Nations system should be, inter alia, their universal, voluntary and grant nature, their neutrality, impartiality and multilateralism and their ability to respond to the development needs of developing countries in a flexible manner, and that all operational activities must be

country-driven, in response to and in accordance with the national development plans, policies and priorities of the recipient Governments concerned;

3. *Notes* the progress achieved in simplification and harmonization of programming cycles and procedures, and calls on the funds and programmes and specialized agencies involved in the coordination efforts in the field to take further steps to enhance and ensure the sustainability of this process, in particular in the area of decentralization and financial management;

4. *Requests* the Secretary-General, as part of the preparation of the next triennial policy review of 2001, to assess, in full and close cooperation with programme countries, the extent to which such harmonization and simplification have benefited the programme countries, inter alia, through greater coordination and synergy in programme design and implementation, as well as the obstacles encountered, and to make appropriate recommendations for consideration at the next triennial comprehensive policy review of operational activities for development, utilizing, inter alia, the ongoing management process and an assessment, inter alia, of the joint mid-term review, joint evaluation and joint programme experiences, as appropriate;

5. *Emphasizes* that simplification and harmonization of procedures, in the context of decentralization of processes, as adopted by the executive boards of the United Nations funds and programmes, should be responsive to the needs of developing countries, while bearing in mind the impact of these procedures on the capacity of recipient countries to integrate the programmes of the United Nations system into the national development process;

6. *Stresses* the importance of ensuring full government participation in the formulation and the implementation of the common country assessment and the United Nations Development Assistance Framework, and urges the funds and programmes, in full and close consultation and cooperation with them, to continue to review these processes at the country level with a view to effecting streamlining and simplification so as to reduce the administrative and financial costs to the recipient Governments as well as to the United Nations system;

7. *Notes* the progress and the challenges with regard to the common country assessment and the United Nations Development Assistance Framework, as highlighted in the report of the Secretary-General, and encourages the funds and programmes to ensure that the United Nations Development Assistance Framework promotes a country-driven, collaborative and coherent response by the United Nations system so as to achieve a greater impact at the country level fully consistent with and in support of national priorities;

8. *Also notes* that coordination activities, though beneficial, represent transaction costs that are borne by both recipient countries and the organizations of the United Nations system, and emphasizes the need for their continuous evaluation and for an analysis and assessment of costs as compared with the total programme expenditures of operational activities for development, in order to ensure maximum efficiency and feasibility;

9. *Reaffirms* the importance of independent, transparent and impartial joint and periodic evaluations of operational activities at the country level, under the leadership of recipient Governments, and with the support of the resident coordinator system, to enhance their efficiency, effectiveness and impact;

10. *Notes* the preparations for the impact evaluation of operational activities, in particular of the United Nations Development Assistance Framework, as mandated in General Assembly resolution 53/192, as part of the preparations for the next triennial policy review;

11. *Invites* the funds, programmes and agencies of the United Nations system, with the full involvement of the recipient Government concerned in the process of such evaluation, to participate actively and to support the ongoing study by the Secretariat;

12. *Encourages* greater cooperation between the World Bank, the regional banks and all funds and programmes, with a view to achieving increased complementarity and better division of labour, as well as enhanced coherence in their sectoral activities, building on the existing arrangements and fully in accordance with the priorities of the recipient Government, and in this regard emphasizes the importance of ensuring, under the leadership of national Governments, greater consistency between the strategic frameworks developed by the United Nations funds, programmes and agencies and the Bretton Woods institutions;

13. *Notes* the ongoing dialogue of members of the United Nations Development Group with the Bretton Woods institutions, and encourages similar consultations with the World Trade Organization, fully recognizing the primary coordinating role of programme country Governments as well as the respective mandates of these institutions, and requests them to report to the Council on this dialogue at its next substantive session, especially in the context of preparations for the triennial policy review;

14. *Requests* the United Nations system to take further measures to improve the effective incorporation of technical cooperation among developing countries into their programmes and projects, and to intensify efforts towards mainstreaming the modality of technical cooperation among developing countries, inter alia, through support to the activities of the Special Unit for Technical Cooperation among Developing Countries, and encourages other relevant international institutions to take similar measures;

15. *Notes* that country-driven programming offers additional opportunities for greater use of the modalities of technical cooperation among developing countries by programme countries;

16. *Requests* the programmes and funds to submit to the Council, through their executive boards, information and analysis in respect of the extent to which cross-cutting themes and goals emerging from global conferences have been integrated into their programme priorities in a coherent manner, as well as in respect of specific steps taken to develop complementary and collaborative approaches with other United Nations organizations in promoting the implementation of global targets, to assist the Secretary-General in the preparation of his report to the General Assembly through the Council on this issue;

17. *Notes* the progress of the resident coordinator system in assisting Governments in their efforts towards an integrated and coordinated follow-up to global conferences, and encourages further work by

the country-level theme groups in addressing the areas highlighted by the Council;

18. *Encourages* the United Nations development system to strengthen efforts towards gender mainstreaming, empowerment of women and gender equality, in particular taking into account the outcomes of the twenty-third special session of the General Assembly, entitled "Women 2000: gender equality, development and peace for the twenty-first century", and the twenty-fourth special session of the Assembly, entitled "World Summit for Social Development and beyond: achieving social development for all in a globalizing world";

19. *Welcomes* in this context the ten-year United Nations Girls' Education Initiative launched by the Secretary-General at the World Education Forum, held in Dakar from 26 to 28 April 2000;

20. *Notes* the lessons learned by the programmes and funds in the implementation of their gender-balance policy, and calls for further efforts to retain women at mid-career and actively to promote their career advancement;

21. *Appreciates* the progress achieved so far in broadening the pool of resident coordinators and in improving the gender balance of resident coordinators, and invites the funds, programmes and agencies of the United Nations system to make further efforts to increase and monitor their nomination of qualified women candidates for the resident coordinator vacancies;

22. *Recommends* that the practice of holding joint meetings of the bureaux of the Executive Boards of the United Nations Development Programme/United Nations Population Fund, the United Nations Children's Fund and the World Food Programme be continued, with a view to improving the impact of these meetings, and in this regard requests the funds and programmes to examine the possibility of having joint reports prepared by their secretariats for these meetings, focused on some issues of specific joint interest, so as to ensure an effective follow-up of the resolutions of the Council and the General Assembly concerning the coordination of operational activities for development, and to report thereon to the Council at its substantive session of 2001;

23. *Underlines* the progress achieved in the coordination of operational activities for development, stresses the importance of continuing efforts for improving coordination based on a system-wide approach, and in this regard welcomes the recent initiatives taken by some specialized agencies to strengthen their participation in the internal coordination mechanisms, such as the United Nations Development Group and the Consultative Committee on Programme and Operational Questions;

24. *Requests* the Secretary General, in the context of the next triennial policy review, to report to the General Assembly at its fifty-sixth session on the impact of the United Nations Development Assistance Framework and progress in the implementation of the multi-year funding framework, as part of ongoing efforts to reverse the declining trend in core resources, and also on improving the efficiency and effectiveness of operational activities of the United Nations system, including recommendations for enhancing the impact of these processes, as well as for appropriate follow-up.

Coordination of operational activities

The Secretary-General, in response to Economic and Social Council resolution 1998/27 [YUN 1998, p. 811], reported in June on a number of issues related to the coordination of operational activities [E/2000/CRP.1]. He informed the Council that, within his reform programme and the provisions of the triennial comprehensive policy review of operational activities, UNDG, including its subsidiary bodies, had been consolidated. Specific progress had been achieved in the resident coordinator system in such areas as the selection process and the adoption of the ACC guidelines on the functioning of the system, but improving the performance appraisal system and the need to provide government inputs into the work of the thematic groups within the resident coordinator system required further attention. Although steady progress was achieved in the implementation of CCA and UNDAF, faster progress should be encouraged in developing individual UNDAFs to take full advantage of the projected harmonization of programme cycles. Other issues needing attention related to process and content, ensuring a more consistent level of quality in CCAs and UNDAFs and achieving greater involvement of non-resident agencies. As to the harmonization of programming periods and procedures, progress was made in joint mid-term reviews and the harmonization of programming instruments and periods. Further work was needed in country-programme and framework formats, the realignment of monitoring and evaluation stages, more uniform project implementation procedures, compatible information technology and databases on UN activities, common premises guidelines and harmonized security operations. Coordination by national authorities of the preparation processes of the new planning and programme instruments of the United Nations and the Bretton Woods institutions was crucial to avoid duplication of national and international efforts. Addressing the linkages between operational activities for development and special economic, humanitarian and disaster relief assistance was crucial at the intergovernmental and inter-agency levels because of the large number of countries in special circumstances, and all possible synergies between the Council's operational activities and humanitarian segments would be particularly important in that regard.

Simplification and harmonization of programming, operational and administrative procedures

In May [E/2000/46], the Secretary-General reported on the simplification and harmonization of programming, operational and administrative procedures. He stated that insufficient progress had been achieved because of the structure of the UN system and the creation of autonomous procedures, the diversity of programming procedures as a consequence of the diversity of mandates, institutional autonomy, the different analysis requirements to undertake programming, and different modalities in project execution of each organization. In particular, progress remained difficult at the country level.

Inter-agency initiatives for harmonization, through ACC and UNDG, were limited mostly to agreeing on common guidelines or defining a common understanding on a modality as guidance principles. However, there were problems in the implementation of common understandings on such topics as national execution and the programme approach because of differing modalities from agency to agency. UN country teams were sometimes unaware of the common definitions adopted at the inter-agency level at headquarters. Better results were obtained in implementing system-wide guidelines, but the actual translation of those guidelines and agreed concepts in alleviating the procedural burden was slow. Progress was achieved in harmonizing programme cycles, but consistent monitoring was required to ensure that those results were sustained. The CCA and UNDAF processes were expected to produce some visible benefits in the simplification and harmonization process at the level of individual organizations, but their synchronization with the preparation of individual country programmes required some vigilance. Budgetary, accounting, auditing and general financial practices represented an area where further steps might achieve cost reduction and higher productivity. Initiatives in the simplification and standardization of UN system reporting requirements, both financial and technical, had not been systematic and the results were often contradictory. Some progress was made in decentralization and delegation of authority, although it was uneven and affected decision-making at the country level.

Other areas where there was room for improvement included the development of common formats for project design and project documents, procurement, the development of computerization and the harmonization of management practices.

Funding UN system operational activities

Responding to General Assembly resolution 53/192 [YUN 1998, p. 802], the Secretary-General, in his main report on operational activities

[E/2000/46], provided an overview of the financial status of the UN funds and programmes, and assessed the impact of financial trends, as well as relevant decisions of the respective executive boards on funding arrangements.

He stated that combined total resources channelled annually through UN funds and programmes continued to increase and in 1999 stood at $5.13 billion, compared to $3.43 billion in 1990. However, total core resources, excluding WFP, had declined from $1.94 billion in 1994 to $1.56 billion in 1999. In UNDP, provisional data showed that for 1999 core resources amounted to $628 million, some $64 million or 8.5 per cent below the 1998 income figure of $746 million. For UNFPA, core resources declined from $305 million in 1995 to some $250 million in 1999, while contributions to UNICEF's core resources had stagnated, averaging around $542 million per year. Contributions to WFP had ranged, over the years, between $1 billion in 1990 and $1.56 billion in 1999.

The continuing decline or stagnation in core funds to UN funds and programmes to meet national demands and respond to global trends posed a serious challenge to their ability to undertake mandated tasks. The decline continued even as the funds and programmes had made great strides in structural reforms to address priority development policy issues with a more coordinated and effective approach. The factors cited for the continued decline related to the voluntary nature of core funding, an increased focus on humanitarian assistance, including specifically the need to find resources to sustain the international presence in such situations as in the Kosovo province of the Federal Republic of Yugoslavia (FRY) and East Timor, and the ever-increasing demands for other uses of grant multilateral official development assistance, such as the Heavily Indebted Poor Countries Initiative and the proposal for the establishment of broad open-ended global trust funds. In addition, the highly competitive international development cooperation environment needed to be changed. Also, the diversity of issues addressed by the UN development system made it difficult to provide crisp statements about achievements.

To restore growth and enhance predictability to the core resource base of UN funds and programmes, the UNDP/UNFPA and UNICEF Executive Boards had developed sustainable funding strategies, including the setting of annual funding targets and the establishment of multi-year funding frameworks for UNDP and UNFPA, and UNICEF's resource mobilization strategy. While it was too early to assess the full impact of the new funding arrangements, the initial pledges made in the first part of 2000 were disappointing in relation to set targets. The tendency for countries that made multi-year pledges in 1999 to use that as a minimal base for a further increase in 2000 was a positive trend and a manifestation of commitment to rebuilding the regular resource base. In reviewing those new funding arrangements, greater attention needed to be paid by the UNDP Executive Board and all Member States to finding ways to facilitate greater political will and commitment so that funding levels could quickly return to a pattern of growth.

Among his recommendations, the Secretary-General proposed that, since funding commitments to UN funds and programmes remained voluntary, Governments should be further encouraged to ensure that funding arrangements became predictable and relied on shared responsibility and inter-donor group pressure to ensure fair burden-sharing.

ECONOMIC AND SOCIAL COUNCIL ACTION

On 28 July [meeting 44], the Economic and Social Council adopted **resolution 2000/19** [draft: E/2000/L.14] without vote [agenda item 3 *(a)*].

Funding operational activities for development of the United Nations system

The Economic and Social Council,

Recalling General Assembly resolution 53/192 of 15 December 1998 on the triennial policy review of operational activities for development of the United Nations system and Council resolution 1999/6 of 23 July 1999,

1. *Takes note* of the report of the Secretary-General;

2. *Reiterates* that the fundamental characteristics of the operational activities of the United Nations system should be, inter alia, their universal, voluntary and grant nature, their neutrality, impartiality and multilateralism and their ability to respond to the development needs of developing countries in a flexible manner, and that all operational activities must be country-driven, in response to and in accordance with the national development plans, policies and priorities of the recipient Governments concerned;

3. *Stresses* the primary responsibility of national Governments for their country's development, and recognizes the importance of national ownership of development programmes;

4. *Recognizes* that operational activities are one of the major pillars of the United Nations and play a fundamental role in the creation of a more united, peaceful, and prosperous world;

5. *Strongly reaffirms* that the impact of operational activities for development of the United Nations system must be enhanced by, inter alia, a substantial increase in their funding on a predictable, continuous and assured basis, commensurate with the increasing needs of developing countries, as well as through the full implementation of General Assembly resolutions 47/199 of 22 December 1992, 48/162 of 20 December 1993, 50/120 of 20 December 1995 and 53/192 and the parts of resolution 52/12 B of 19 December 1997 relevant to operational activities for development;

6. *Reaffirms* the need for priority allocation of scarce grant resources to programmes and projects in low-income countries, in particular the least developed countries, and in this context expresses concern over any further decline in programme expenditures in those countries, and encourages all efforts to reverse this situation;

7. *Stresses* the need for a continuous overall improvement, within existing mandates, in the effectiveness, efficiency and impact of the United Nations system in delivering its development assistance, and welcomes the steps that have been taken to that end;

8. *Also stresses* in this regard the continued need for funds, programmes and agencies of the United Nations development system to continue to report on the overall results achieved to their executive boards or governing bodies and to the Council;

9. *Reaffirms* that core resources, because they are untied resources, are the bedrock of the operational activities of the United Nations system, and in this regard notes with serious concern the overall decline or stagnation in core resources available to many United Nations funds and programmes, in particular the United Nations Development Programme;

10. *Notes* the efforts of the Executive Boards and secretariats of the United Nations Development Programme/United Nations Population Fund and of the United Nations Children's Fund to establish multi-year funding frameworks that integrate programme objectives, resources, budgets and outcomes, with the objective of increasing core resources and enhancing their predictability, and in this regard invites them to continue to develop and refine the frameworks as a strategic resource management tool;

11. *Appreciates* in this context the efforts of countries, including donor and programme countries, which have increased or maintained their high level of contributions to the core resources of United Nations funds and programmes during 1999 and 2000 and also of those which have made multi-year pledges to core resources;

12. *Underlines* the need to avoid overdependence on a limited number of donors, emphasizes the importance of shared responsibility, taking into account established official development assistance targets, including targets established at the Second United Nations Conference on the Least Developed Countries, and calls on donors and other countries in a position to do so to increase their contributions to the core/ regular resources of United Nations funds and programmes;

13. *Notes* the increase in and the importance of non-core resources, including cost-sharing, trust funds and non-traditional sources of financing as a mechanism to enhance the capacity and to supplement the means of operational activities for development, contributing to an increase in total resources, even though unsatisfactory because the increase in non-core resources cannot compensate for the decline in the level of core resources;

14. *Also notes* in this context the contributions by private sources, which can supplement but cannot substitute for contributions by Governments, to finance or extend programmes implemented within existing guidelines of United Nations funds and programmes;

15. *Reaffirms* that South-South cooperation, including technical and economic cooperation among developing countries, offers viable opportunities for the development of developing countries, and in this context reiterates its request that the executive boards of the funds and programmes review, with a view to considering an increase, the allocation of resources for activities involving technical cooperation among developing countries;

16. *Requests* the Secretary General, in the context of the next triennial policy review, to report to the General Assembly at its fifty-sixth session, through the Economic and Social Council, on the progress in the implementation of the multi-year funding frameworks, as part of ongoing efforts to strengthen the strategic resource management in the funds and programmes and to reverse the declining trend in core resources.

Financing of operational activities in 1999

Expenditures of the UN system on operational activities, excluding loans and grants through the World Bank Group, reached $6 billion in 1999 [A/56/70/Add.1-E/2001/58/Add.1], the most recent year for which complete figures were available, compared with $5.3 billion in 1998 and $4.8 billion in 1997. Of the total amount, $2,044.1 million was distributed in development grants through UNDP or UNDP-administered funds, $1,429.8 million by WFP, $1,123.3 million by specialized agencies and other organizations from extrabudgetary sources, $817.9 million by UNICEF, $444 million by specialized agencies and other organizations from regular budgets (mainly the World Health Organization) and $187.1 million by UNFPA.

By region, 33.5 per cent of expenditures went to Africa, 27.7 per cent to Asia and the Pacific, 26.2 per cent to Latin America and the Caribbean, 7.1 per cent to Western Asia and 5.5 per cent to Europe.

Contributions from Governments and other sources for operational activities, excluding the International Fund for Agricultural Development (IFAD), totalled $6.9 billion in 1999, compared with $5.7 billion in 1998 and $5.4 billion in 1997.

The 2000 United Nations Pledging Conference for Development Activities (New York, 1-2 November) [A/CONF.193/3] heard the announcement of pledges by Governments to UN programmes and funds concerned with development. It noted that several Governments were not in a position to announce their contributions but proposed communicating the announcement of such contributions to the Secretary-General as soon as they were in a position to do so.

The Secretary-General provided a statement of contributions pledged or paid at the 1999 Pledging Conference, as at 30 June 2000, to 30 funds and programmes [A/CONF.190/2 & Corr.1].

The total amounted to some $1,127 million, with an estimated $536 million for UNDP.

Technical cooperation through UNDP

The UNDP Administrator, in his annual report covering 2000 [DP/2001/14 & Add.1-4], said that the year had seen a dramatic change in UNDP on both management and programme fronts, in fulfilment of his vision for the organization and in response to the new challenges and opportunities in global development. It was characterized by the coalescing of the international campaign to eradicate poverty, with a focus on promoting pro-poor growth and more inclusive globalization.

In 2000, the tone for UNDP was set by the ongoing implementation of the Administrator's Business Plans, 2000-2003 (see p. 831); the global development objectives and targets set by world leaders in the Millennium Declaration (see p. 49); and the outcome of the first Ministerial Meeting on UNDP, which boosted recognition and support for UNDP at the country level and in key international forums (see p. 836). Those events and the growing consensus underpinning them generated a challenging agenda for UNDP. In that context, UNDP was well positioned to play the role of a trusted partner, and much of the institutional change undertaken in 2000 was with that objective in mind.

The results were evidenced in the first results-oriented annual report [YUN 1999, p. 795], which marked a decisive step forward in the adoption of results-based management and led to the refinement of the strategic results framework (SRF), the development of a corporate database and intensive training for country office staff. UNDP continued its strong support to national poverty-reduction strategies, the development and implementation of which, as well as poverty monitoring, were largely successful and revealed the highest levels of outcome and output, particularly in sub-Saharan Africa. It published *Overcoming Human Poverty: UNDP Poverty Report 2000.* The *Human Development Report 2000* [Sales No. E.00.III.B.8] also presented the eradication of poverty not just as a goal but as a challenge for human rights. The year witnessed a dramatic progression in the national human development reports (NHDRs) programme, with the establishment of a support unit at headquarters and the preparation of a UNDP policy on NHDRs.

UNDP made efforts to expand democratic governance both within and between countries, particularly in such key areas as governing institutions, human rights, decentralization, public sector management and gender issues, by providing advice and technical support to authorities, civil society and communities of the poor. The provision of advisory services to legislative, electoral, justice and human rights institutions and processes remained important in 2000. UNDP also sought to build the gender dimension into its policies, programmes and management. It supported many Governments in the preparation of national reports for Beijing+5 (see p. 1082) and helped countries to ensure that the feminization of poverty and women's own coping strategies were taken fully into account in national poverty-reduction strategies.

Efforts to focus and improve UNDP activities in crisis and post-conflict environments were undertaken with renewed vigour in 2000. UNDP expanded activities in reintegration and recovery, peace-building, mine action, natural-disaster mitigation and related areas, and continued to support war-affected populations.

UNDP strengthened HIV/AIDS as one of its critical areas of support to developing countries, providing policy advice to Governments and civil society partners on ways to achieve a nationwide, effective response to the epidemic and assisting countries with capacity-building for planning and implementing those responses.

In partnership with the public and private sectors, UNDP worked on a comprehensive strategy and implementation package to help transform the growing digital divide into a digital opportunity, while addressing basic developmental needs. The Digital Opportunities Task Force, hosted jointly by UNDP and the World Bank, was launched in July. At the country level, UNDP launched the Global Network Readiness and Resource Initiative to assist countries in building national information infrastructure strategies.

Significant achievements were made in 2000 in energy and environment as UNDP played a leading role in coordinating environmental and energy programmes, and in the area of climate change it continued to support capacity-building efforts of developing countries.

To strengthen UNDP's policy capacity, an implementation plan for the new Bureau for Development Policy was approved in May to provide policy support in the field. The Bureau was reorganized through streamlining and rationalizing staff roles and redesigning staff responsibilities. In January, the new Bureau for Resources and Strategic Partnerships was created, bringing together responsibility for relations with the Executive Board, the UN system, civil society and the private sector, along with donor outreach and resource mobilization.

UNDP continued to cooperate with the UN system, especially at the country level, through its network of country offices and through the United Nations Volunteers programme, the World Bank, IMF, regional development banks, civil society and the private sector. The Division for Business Partnerships was created, as part of the Bureau for Resources and Strategic Partnerships, to develop UNDP strategy and guidelines for working with the business sector and support partnerships at the country, regional and global levels. A draft set of new corporate policies and guidelines was prepared during the year. UNDP also developed an aid coordination policy, ensuring that external resources were aligned with national priorities, and strengthened or created aid coordination mechanisms.

UNDP continued efforts to engender a new culture of performance in the organization. The Bureau of Management was created, bringing together the former Bureaux for Planning and Resources Management and for Finance and Administrative Services and including new divisions that better reflected its needs for improved cost efficiency, client service and accountability.

UNDP/UNFPA Executive Board

In 2000, the UNDP/UNFPA Executive Board held three regular sessions (New York, 24-28 and 31 January, 3-7 April and 25-29 September) and an annual session (Geneva, 13-23 June) [E/2000/35].

At the first regular session, the Board adopted six decisions, including one that gave an overview of the Board's action taken at the session [E/2000/35 (dec. 2000/6)]. Other decisions dealt with UNDP Business Plans for 2000-2003 (see p. 831); assistance to East Timor (see p. 836); UNDP regular funding and cash-flow management (see p. 835); and revision of the UNDP financial regulations and rules (see p. 838).

The Executive Board, at its second regular session, adopted four decisions, including an overview decision summarizing action it had taken at the session [dec. 2000/10]. In other decisions, the Board took action on UNFPA and the United Nations Development Fund for Women (see PART THREE, Chapters VIII and X, respectively).

At the annual session, the Board adopted seven decisions, including an overview decision [dec. 2000/17]. The others concerned UNFPA programmes, the United Nations Volunteers (see p. 843), the Administrator's 1999 report (see below) and the annual report of the Executive Director of UNOPS (see p. 840).

At the third regular session, the Board adopted seven decisions. One decision gave an overview of action taken at the session [dec. 2000/24]. By another, the Board encouraged UNDP to assist affected developing countries to implement the United Nations Convention to combat desertification at the national, subregional and regional levels (see p. 976). The others concerned UNFPA and UNOPS.

The Economic and Social Council, by **decision 2000/242** of 28 July, took note of the Board's report on its first regular session of 2000 [DP/2000/9], the decisions it adopted at its second regular session [DP/2000/19] and those adopted at its annual session [DP/2000/28].

UNDP/UNFPA reports

Annual reports

The Executive Board, on 23 June [dec. 2000/15], took note of the 1999 annual report of the Administrator [DP/2000/23 & Add.1-3].

By **decision 2000/242** of 28 July, the Economic and Social Council took note of the annual reports of the UNDP Administrator and the UNFPA Executive Director to the Council [E/2000/20].

Results-oriented annual report

The Administrator submitted the results-oriented annual report (ROAR) for 2000 [DP/2001/14/Add.1], the first within the formal multi-year funding framework period. It maintained the orientation of management for results, indicating the main features of performance (progress towards outcomes and the extent to which targets set for outputs were achieved), and pointed to issues requiring attention. The evolving methodology applied for 2000 enhanced transparency, accuracy and overall credibility of the analysis. It used an overall assessment of performance and in-depth analysis, with a parallel effort to corroborate the data reported in the ROAR with information available from independent sources.

As to the distribution of outcomes and outputs generated by the organization in 2000, the overall, strategy-setting and policy options, followed by capacity development, remained the main focus. The data also confirmed a strong UNDP presence at the level of strategy-setting and policy options, although they did not permit definitive conclusions about the pace and scale at which they might be changing.

Among its general findings, the report said that the ROAR data strongly suggested that there was considerable potential for UNDP to exercise leadership in key development processes and there had been notable advances in performance. NHDRs were completed or under way in 56 countries and were beginning to influence development policies and programmes. Assessment of the impact of liberalization and globalization on developing countries was expanded. Human rights had emerged, including political, social and economic dimensions, as a key focus in governance, with almost 40 per cent of country offices providing assistance for advocacy, awareness-raising, action planning and development of the underlying institutional framework. Poverty-reduction strategies had been formulated in 60 countries, with substantive engagement in the Poverty-Reduction Strategy Paper mechanism rising from 11 countries in 1999 to 24 in 2000. The country offices taking action on HIV/AIDS strategies had increased from 32 in 1999 to 55 in 2000, with good practices in advocacy, impact assessment and capacity development being pursued, particularly in Africa, Europe and the Commonwealth of Independent States (CIS). Advances were made to integrate environmentally sustainable development and the goals of the global conventions in planning. Progress was made in gender mainstreaming within governance, poverty reduction and HIV/AIDS interventions and through capacity development. In collaboration with other UN organizations, common country assessments (CCAs) were completed or drafted in 66 programme countries, United Nations Development Assistance Frameworks (UNDAFs) in 24 countries and joint programmes in 36 countries, and greater use was made of thematic groups.

In terms of the strategic results framework goals, in the area of governance, the policy and conceptual framework for mainstreaming human rights allowed UNDP to confront successfully the challenge of implementing a rights-based approach to programming and to adapt the focus of public sector management to meet capacity development needs. Good practices acquired through NHDRs provided a solid basis for linking analysis to action, and the strong demand for support in participatory governance indicated the potential for cross-cutting linkages with poverty reduction. That called for much higher levels of resource allocation than were currently available. In poverty reduction, opportunities increased at the policy level for dealing with pro-poor macroeconomic frameworks, target-setting, benchmarking and monitoring in relation to the poverty goal endorsed by the Millennium Declaration (see p. 49). Good practices in meeting the challenge HIV/AIDS posed to governance and poverty reduction should be synthesized to assist other regions and country offices to raise performance and become a key test of UNDP's ability to provide knowledge-driven advisory services in priority areas of country demand. An evaluation of the orientation and sustainability of UNDP activities addressing the asset base of the poor was timely. Poorly performing and increasingly marginal areas of work might have to be dropped and others developed.

Promoting environmentally sustainable development was one of UNDP's key strengths, allowing environmental concerns to be incorporated into poverty-reduction strategies. There was considerable scope for UNDP to address cross-border concerns, the follow-up to global commitments and the use, by programme countries, of the new mechanisms in such areas as climate change.

The expansion of UNDP's role in gender mainstreaming called for a reinforcement of its capacity in that area, as well as a major effort to bring together and share experiences and develop methods and tools for improved monitoring of performance. More effective partnerships with other UN partners were needed to build on the potential of complementary competencies.

In terms of support for the United Nations, support to programme countries with respect to the Millennium Declaration goals demanded a new impetus to UN reform, especially the resident coordinator system. A key task would be to employ CCA and UNDAF more systematically for integrated follow-up to conferences, definition of local targets linked to the Declaration's development goals and improvements in the benchmarking and monitoring of progress. The refocusing of thematic groups could be built upon to expand and accelerate collaborative action around the overall priority of poverty reduction. New tools, principally CCA and UNDAF and joint programming, would realize their full potential and take root in policy and practice only if they were made an integral part of the operations of UN specialized agencies, funds and programmes and were accompanied by a radical reduction in the complexity and duplication of operating policies and procedures across the UN system.

UNDP operational activities

Country programmes

The UNDP/UNFPA Executive Board, at its first regular session in January [dec. 2000/6], approved the first country cooperation framework (CCF) for Liberia and took note of the first extension of 26 CCFs and of one regional cooperation framework (Europe and CIS), as well as the first country review reports for Bangladesh, Botswana, China, Kazakhstan, Kyrgyzstan and Viet Nam.

At its second regular session in April, the Board, on the recommendation of the Administrator [DP/2000/12, DP/2000/16], authorized him to approve assistance to the Congo on a project-by-project basis for 2000-2001, and to Afghanistan on the same basis for 2000-2003 [dec. 2000/10]. It also approved second CCFs for Kazakhstan, Kyrgyzstan and Zimbabwe, took note of the first extension of CCFs for eight countries or territories, the first extension of the cooperation framework for technical cooperation among developing countries and the first regional cooperation framework for Latin America, and took note of the first country review reports for Cambodia, Uzbekistan and Zimbabwe.

In June, at its annual session [dec. 2000/17], the Board approved second CCFs for Azerbaijan, Iran, Romania and Turkmenistan and the extension of the first CCF for Brazil, and took note of the first extension of CCFs for Argentina, Chile and Uruguay.

The Board, at its third regular session in September [dec. 2000/24], approved second CCFs for Armenia, the Czech Republic, Hungary, Maldives, Poland, Slovakia, Slovenia, Uzbekistan and Viet Nam. It approved the second extension of the first CCF for Bulgaria and two-year extensions of first CCFs for El Salvador and Venezuela, and took note of first extensions for six other countries. The Board also took note of country review reports for Algeria, Guatemala, Poland and Uganda, and of reviews of regional cooperation frameworks for Africa, Asia and the Pacific, Europe and CIS, and Latin America and the Caribbean. The review of the first global cooperation framework was also noted. On the recommendation of the Administrator [DP/2000/40], the Board authorized him to approve projects for East Timor on a case-by-case basis for 2000-2002.

UNDP performance analysis by goal

The Administrator reported in his ROAR for 2000 [DP/2001/14/Add.1] on UNDP's performance in relation to its six goals: creating an enabling environment for sustainable human development (SHD); reduction of poverty; protection of the environment and use of natural resources; gender equality and the advancement of women; providing support to countries in special development situations; and providing support to UN activities.

Creating an enabling environment for SHD

The data in ROAR 2000, as in 1999, confirmed the importance of UNDP's work in advocacy for SHD, public sector management and support to governance institutions, as well as a growing emphasis on human rights. They also revealed increased evidence of the incorporation of SHD issues within governance initiatives and expanded support for local governance across all regions.

SHD received 42 per cent of programme resources ($684 million), both regular and other resources, representing the greatest share of total available resources.

Overall, 133 country offices (98 per cent of the total) reported under that goal. With regard to performance, positive change was reported for 54 per cent of outcomes, while annual targets were either fully or partially achieved for 92 per cent of outputs (73 per cent fully and 19 per cent partially). Performance in achieving output targets was higher than progress towards outcomes for all regions. Overall performance did not vary significantly across regions.

The results were mostly of an upstream nature, with 50 per cent of outcomes influencing strategy-setting and policy options, and an additional 38 per cent targeting capacity development. The report found substantial ongoing investment in promoting awareness of and policy dialogue on SHD, representing the second most reported strategic area of support in the SRF, across all regions, mainly by NHDRs. Human rights emerged as a key area of UNDP support to governance institutions. Decentralization was a stronger area of focus also, with 39 per cent of all country offices undertaking programmes to strengthen subnational capacity for participatory development planning and resource management. UNDP involvement in public sector management was extensive, focusing mainly on civil service reform. There was continued effort to incorporate poverty reduction, gender issues and participatory methods into governance programmes.

The spread and application of information and communication technology (ICT) were growing in all regions, mainly in strengthening capacity in governing institutions to use ICT for more effective delivery of public services.

The link between global, regional and country programmes remained weak, except in the area of local governance. In addition, regional cooperation received scant reporting at both outcome and output levels.

At the sub-goal level, there was support for policy-making and strategy-setting at the outcome and output levels, particularly in the use of NHDRs for promoting SHD. Support for analysis in globalization went beyond macrolevel considerations to examining the consequences for the poor. Emphasis was also placed on the impact of liberalization on society and the integration of pro-poor measures in national plans and policies.

An expanded number of initiatives supported private sector development.

Human rights activities were under way in some 50 country offices. The key features of work in that area included development of national human rights action plans by country offices in every region and providing assistance to human rights initiatives involving civic education, awareness-raising campaigns, strengthening or creation of ombudsman offices and extension of human rights institutions. Support was provided to parliaments and justice systems, including training parliamentary members and increasing parliaments' constituency relations and public accountability. Assistance would be provided from the global programme, which launched a $6 million programme in 2000 to strengthen parliaments. In the area of justice, mechanisms were established to increase access to legal services by the poor. Assistance was provided for the reform of justice systems, to improve court administration and case-flow management, computerization of caseloads, the training of judicial personnel and capacity development. A notable development was the establishment of a network of 350 civil society organizations working in the area of judicial reform. In terms of electoral assistance, support was aimed at ensuring transparency of electoral processes and their independent management.

Decentralization and empowerment of local organizations and the poor received great attention, with a wide variety of initiatives across all regions. UNDP assisted subnational authorities in formulating strategies and plans, and building capacities in resource mobilization, planning and service delivery, to empower communities for active participation in local-level decision-making. Support for public sector management resulted in positive change for 58 per cent of outcomes and annual targets achieved for 83 per cent of outputs. UNDP support focused on civil service reforms, including capacity development and initiatives to combat corruption, promote transparency and enhance public sector integrity, including the adoption of anti-corruption legislation. On a more limited scale, UNDP engaged in other areas, such as public sector financial management and aid coordination to strengthen nationally led mechanisms.

The ROAR indicated that, although there was a unique window for UNDP to support programme countries to manage national development and meet the challenge of globalization, there were areas of untapped potential. Those included further development of the NHDR; capacity development of partners to facilitate the integration of human rights within efforts to support SHD; focused assistance to build social capital by improving the ability of governance structures to mobilize the participation of stakeholders and build consensus among them on major development issues; expanded effort to exploit links between assistance for local governance and poverty reduction; support for public sector management to handle the challenges of globalization, such as effective regulation in a liberalized economic environment; and formulation and application of a clear strategy for e-governance that harnessed the potential of ICT.

Reduction of poverty

Support for poverty-reduction strategies and the monitoring of poverty were the main thrust of UNDP's efforts and produced the greatest changes in outcomes. Expenditure on poverty reduction accounted for 31 per cent of total resources ($512 million). Ninety per cent of UNDP country offices, 123 in all, reported on the goal of poverty reduction. Positive change was achieved for 60 per cent of outcomes but with significant regional variation. Over half of all outcomes supported by UNDP related to strategy-setting and policy options (53 per cent) and a further quarter addressed capacity development of institutions. Annual targets were either fully or partially achieved for 68 per cent of outputs. There was a greater cross-fertilization between governance and poverty programmes. The development of HIV/AIDS strategies received far greater priority in 2000, with 55 country offices reporting, up from 32 in 1999. UNDP's efforts were concentrated in the Africa region, as well as Europe and CIS. UNDP work on the asset base of the poor (such as that in microfinance, employment promotion and access to basic social services) was characterized by a range of interventions with varying prospects for generating significant results in poverty reduction, especially in terms of linkage to upstream policy change. In ICT, a new field for UNDP, the majority of results were still downstream in nature and did not capture a clear organizational niche. Progress was being made through public-private partnerships to increase access by the poor to ICT, but much remained to be done.

At the level of sub-goals, UNDP was concentrating its efforts on preparing and implementing poverty-reduction strategies by, among other things, making use of the Poverty Strategies Initiative within the global programme. It supported poverty-reduction strategies through advisory services, sectoral and thematic analyses, strengthening of monitoring capacity and playing a coordinating role in aligning donor resources more effectively. In Africa, its country

offices focused on national, as opposed to regional or sectoral, strategies, including Poverty-Reduction Strategy Papers (PRSPs). The country office focus was also at the national level in Latin America and the Caribbean, with activities concentrated on advocacy, preparing sectoral or thematic studies, monitoring, systematization of household surveys, analysis of the determinants of poverty and support to PRSP development. In Asia and the Pacific, greater emphasis was placed on monitoring poverty, while in the Arab States region, assistance focused on providing training, developing local and sectoral strategies or monitoring national strategies. In Europe and CIS, the focus was also on national-level strategies but at the initial stages of development.

In terms of HIV/AIDS, positive change reported for outcomes was relatively modest at 59 per cent, reflecting the difficulties of mobilizing an urgent, countrywide response to HIV/AIDS. There was a discernible upstream shift, focusing on the governance challenge, with a large increase in UNDP interventions assisting Governments in formulating national HIV/AIDS strategies, building national capacity to coordinate effective, multisectoral strategies, and supporting the creation of decentralized structures to manage local action plans. UNDP worked with the United Nations Volunteers (UNV) programme to combat the epidemic, particularly in Central and Southern Africa.

UNDP worked to support the access of the poor to productive assets, basic social services and technology, with positive change reported for close to 60 per cent of outcomes and annual targets achieving 70 per cent of outputs. Microfinance remained a major area of activity, with significant success in promoting policy, regulatory and institutional changes. Reporting by country offices on universal access to basic social services declined sharply (from 49 to 28). ICT was a new area reported on in 2000. Performance was encouraging, with positive change reported for 63 per cent of outcomes in the 24 countries reporting. Many of the results were, however, of a downstream nature.

Environmentally sustainable development

Under the goal of environmentally sustainable development, UNDP's cooperation was aimed at developing national strategic, policy, legal and regulatory frameworks; capacity development and the promotion of participatory processes; and follow-up and integration of global environmental issues into national development plans, policies and strategies. Expenditure on environmentally sustainable development accounted for 14 per cent ($251 million) of total resources. It remained the third most important goal for UNDP as a whole and for each of the five regions, with 119 country offices (87 per cent) reporting. Positive change was reported for 64 per cent of outcomes, while annual targets were either fully or partially achieved for 81 per cent of outputs (a figure that dropped to 64 per cent after adjusting for weak targets).

The findings under the goal suggested strong links between policy changes and capacity development for policy management. There was considerable investment in upstream results. The next step was for greater integration of environmental objectives into anti-poverty and development policies and programmes. Similarly, UNDP support to follow up global commitments indicated substantial scope for exploiting interlinkages or synergies between conventions. The data confirmed the importance of the Global Environment Facility (GEF) (see p. 970) in providing direction and resources for important components of the UNDP portfolio. In all regions, GEF-oriented programme development was critical in mobilizing significant non-core funding.

At the level of sub-goals, 42 country offices reported concerted efforts to incorporate the concept of environmentally sustainable development into national planning, with progress for almost two thirds of outcomes. Twenty-one reported a reinvigorated national commitment to Agenda 21 [YUN 1992, p. 672], including the implementation of national strategies by 2005. Progress was reported in drafting or amending national environmental action plans, in environmental management, energy, water and solid waste, and in the preparation of local action plans. Of some concern was the diminished emphasis during 2000 on the mobilization of domestic funding for environmental development activities. Building capacities of national as well as local institutions in sustainable environmental and energy management continued to be of major importance, with reporting by 37 country offices, especially in Africa and Asia and the Pacific, where three quarters of them reported progress in implementing capacity development programmes. UNDP cooperation was also focused on strengthening the capacities of newly established environmental ministries, agencies, coordinating bodies and environmental funds, such as those in Georgia, Guatemala, Haiti, Lebanon, Nepal, Paraguay and the Sudan.

At the downstream level, the sustainable management of natural resources and energy was primarily addressed through small-scale pilot activities, linked in many instances to public-private partnerships, mostly in Latin America and the Caribbean and in Asia and the Pacific. The UNDP/GEF Small Grants Programme proved to be an effective promoter of local-level income-generating opportunities linked with biodiversity and climate change and helped to establish community or non-governmental organization (NGO) networks on environmental issues. There was growing support of UNDP to programme countries on the follow-up and internalization of the goals of global environmental conventions through national action plans, strategies and programmes, particularly in biodiversity and climate change. Substantial progress was made in tackling the problem of ozone-layer depletion with the UNDP Montreal Protocol programme active in 73 countries. Country offices reported progress on the sensitization of national authorities to global environmental conventions through training programmes or the establishment of inter-ministerial groups, coordinating bodies and environmental units.

Gender equality and advancement of women

In 2000, UNDP efforts towards gender mainstreaming continued to focus on policy and planning, as well as capacity development. The delivery of programme resources under the goal was 1 per cent of total resources ($22 million). A total of 105 country offices (77 per cent) reported on the goal, with positive change for 77 per cent of outcomes, a relatively high rate compared to other goals. Those outcomes were mainly related to advocacy, networking and partnerships, capacity development of institutions, and strategy-setting and policy options. Annual targets were either fully or partially achieved for 74 per cent of outputs.

The data suggested progress in gender mainstreaming in UNDP cooperation, reflected by an increased demand for it in key areas of governance, poverty reduction and HIV/AIDS, capacity development across ministries, linking gender with other SRF goals and increased interventions in countries in special development situations, especially in post-conflict environments. Linkage and coherence in country-level activities improved and, in a substantial number of interventions, national action and implementation of international commitments were linked. Progress was also made in building linkages between country, regional and global programmes in the main strategic areas of the goal. The global gender programme focused on reinforcing corporate commitments and developed tools and methodologies to build capacities of country offices, strengthen the gender focal point network and develop a broad-based network of experts in the field through a consultative process involving 110 countries.

At the level of sub-goals, an increased number of countries reported on UNDP's role as a facilitator of participatory policy-formulation processes, as a source of support for national capacity development and as a promoter of advocacy work within civil society on a variety of gender-equality issues. In terms of tracking and measuring changes in the condition of women, the number of countries reporting decreased from 24 in 1999 to 12 in 2000. Work was concentrated mainly on preparing NHDRs and the training of staff in national statistical offices. Country offices and regional programmes supported government and NGO preparations for the twenty-third special session of the General Assembly on women (see PART THREE, Chapter X), through policy advice and technical cooperation and facilitating the participation of Governments and civil society in the session.

Special development situations

Under the special development situations (SDS) goal, UNDP assistance was most notable in natural-disaster mitigation, mine action and community-based recovery work. Country offices supported community-based activities in post-conflict situations, particularly in revitalizing local economies, rebuilding infrastructure and reintegrating war-affected populations. In terms of coverage, 54 country offices (40 per cent of the total) reported under the goal. As for performance, positive change was reported for 53 per cent of outcomes, with annual targets either fully or partially achieved for 89 per cent of outputs (or 69 per cent after adjusting for weak targets). Ten per cent, or $194 million, of total programme resources was devoted to the goal.

The thrust of UNDP's work in the area of reducing risk of disaster in programme countries was divided between capacity development to manage and reduce the risk of natural disasters (18 country offices) and policy development and advocacy on risk reduction. The two most common outcomes sought to integrate contemporary issues in disaster reduction in national and international disaster policy, and to expand national and regional access to approaches, methods and techniques for disaster reduction and recovery. Other outcomes focused on the establishment of early warning systems and support to UN system coordination in natural disaster response, recovery and reduction. UN disaster management teams successfully coordinated efforts to assist local authorities in planning responses to crises in the Dominican Republic, El Salvador and Indonesia. UNV made noteworthy contributions in that regard in India, Madagascar and Turkey on emergency preparedness or response, as well as awareness-raising and training on natural-disaster prevention. At the output level, progress was clustered on developing capacity for responding to disaster emergencies through the establishment of a government disaster-management focal point and response training, and data collection on local resources for disaster response and seismic hazards.

Under the sub-goal of conflict prevention, peace-building and recovery, the main area of support dealt with recovery processes at the community level. Particular emphasis was placed on re-establishing governing institutions. Specifically, the rule of law and justice institutions were supported by the majority (61 per cent) of country offices, through activities such as the training of judges and lawyers in substantive and procedural areas of law and the strengthening of democratic institutions, particularly in the Congo, East Timor, Guatemala, Haiti, the Lao People's Democratic Republic, Rwanda and Somalia.

In terms of coverage, 54 country offices (40 per cent of the total) reported under the SDS category. Positive change was reported for 53 per cent of outcomes, with annual targets either fully or partially achieved for 89 per cent of outputs.

UNDP support to the United Nations

Responding to the request that they all complete goal 6—UNDP support to the United Nations—were 125 country offices (or 92 per cent of the total). Performance was adequate at both outcome and output levels and positive change was reported for 54 per cent of outcomes with annual targets either fully or partially achieved for 57 per cent of outputs.

The key findings for the goal revealed that, in relation to follow-up to global conferences, country-level initiatives were collectively too varied and dispersed to achieve the critical mass necessary for worldwide impact. There was limited cross-regional evidence of either national-level target-setting or systematic monitoring of follow-up. Evidence on integrated follow-up to conferences was sparse and the degree of national ownership did not appear to be high overall.

Progress on UN reforms was mixed. On the one hand, both CCA and UNDAF were contributing to team-building and providing a platform for conference follow-up, while UNDAF in particular was being used as a springboard for joint programming. Data also pointed to increased restructuring, refocusing and utilization of thematic groups. In addition, there was a narrowing in the focus of UN system collaboration towards HIV/AIDS, gender issues and human rights. On the other hand, the uneven quality of CCAs and

UNDAFs was limiting the impact of those instruments, and the ability of UN organizations to tackle the issue was hampered by the lack of progress at headquarters on reducing procedural complexity.

The difference in emphasis between the two sub-goals—progress on the global agenda for development and operational activities for development—was mirrored by a divergence in performance, especially at the level of outcomes. Positive change was reported for less than half (44 per cent) for the first sub-goal, compared to 59 per cent for the second. At the output level, the performance rates dropped considerably (55 per cent and 53 per cent, respectively).

During the year, the most notable development at headquarters on follow-up to global conferences was the preparation by the United Nations Development Group (UNDG) of strategies relating to two critical issues: halving extreme poverty by 2015 and the promotion of girls' education, to be used in collaborative efforts with the UN system and in dialogue with development partners. Other developments included the adoption of a guidance note on the preparation of joint programmes/projects, elaboration of draft procedures for joint mid-term reviews of country programmes and UNDAFs, and the launch of DevLink, the UNDG web site to support UN country teams. With regard to administrative and management issues, progress was made on common services and premises with the publication of operational guidelines and the creation of a shared database, training for resident coordinators, team-building and preparation of a training module on poverty, continued development of the competency assessment programme, guidelines on gender balance and the system of performance appraisal, the launch of an inter-agency mobility programme and agreement on harmonized administrative procedures for national project personnel hired by various UN organizations.

The most dominant area of support at the country level was the resident coordinator system. Performance at both outcome and output levels was high. Positive change was reported for 64 per cent of all outcomes, while annual targets were either fully or partially achieved for 90 per cent of outputs, adjusted to 55 per cent to account for weak targets. Among the main efforts reported by country offices were mobilization of UN organizations around common positions on development issues as the springboard for advocacy with national and international partners; widespread application of the sequence in programmatic collaboration, starting with CCA and UNDAF and followed by joint programming; continued expansion and restructuring of the resident coordinator system machinery centred on the thematic groups; and adoption of common services, often in tandem with the creation of the United Nations House.

Programme planning and management

Reform measures

The UNDP Administrator, in a report outlining the implementation of the Secretary-General's reform measures [DP/2001/6], said that a review of ACC had led to the establishment of the High-Level Programme Committee (HLPC), which would have oversight of all programme and operational consultations under the ACC umbrella. However, he stressed that it was important that the inter-agency policy and procedural work on operational activities, which served to convert legislative mandates into actual operational policies, procedures and guidelines, continued while that new area of programme policy was dealt with. HLPC would rely on the Consultative Committee on Programme and Operational Questions (CCPOQ) and its Working Group on the Resident Coordinator System. As the subsidiary bodies of the new HLPC were reviewed and reformed, it was important that the work be given continuity in order for legislative mandates of the General Assembly and the Economic and Social Council on operational activities to be implemented. In addition, it was important that the bridge provided by the current mechanisms between the United Nations and the UN system as a whole be continued, particularly the resident coordinator system.

The Administrator also reported that the experience of UNDG with sunset clauses for its subsidiary bodies had proved positive in terms of simplifying the UNDG work processes and focusing staff time only on items of top priority.

In terms of funding and resources, UNDP made progress in implementing the multi-year funding framework. In particular, the first ROAR was well received by the Executive Board and the first Ministerial Meeting on UNDP was held with the objective of building further political support for UNDP (see p. 836). During 2000, efforts to strengthen the resident coordinator system included increasing the proportion of women and staff of other agencies as resident coordinators; improving the performance appraisal of resident coordinators and the selection process through the inter-agency advisory panel; training first-time resident coordinators and country teams; and improving the competency assessment model and the annual reporting by resident coordinators.

CCPOQ, at its sixteenth session (Geneva, 29 February–2 March) [ACC/2000/7], adopted, on behalf of ACC, guidelines and information for the resident coordinator system on the UN system and human rights.

UNDP Business Plans 2000-2003

In January, the Executive Board considered the UNDP Business Plans for 2000-2003 [YUN 1999, p. 802]. The Administrator, in introducing the Plans, stressed that UNDP was believed to be facing a funding crisis, but in reality it was a development crisis. The continued erosion of UNDP's funding base would greatly affect UN development activities, particularly in Africa, where UNDP would be spending less than 50 per cent of what it had spent five years previously. However, UNDP needed to show that it could perform and have an impact through its programmes, even with reduced resources. Through programme successes, the organization could attract more resources. In the light of the declining core resource base, UNDP had sought to organize and align its services, expertise and operations behind the priorities of programme countries. The organization could deliver advice, particularly in policy dialogue and institutional development. While driving its work upstream in response to programme country demand, UNDP was moving away from a small dispersed project portfolio towards projects that supported strategic advice for change.

In a 28 January decision [E/2000/35 (dec. 2000/1)], the Executive Board welcomed the Administrator's efforts to secure the future of UNDP as a leading UN development programme and affirmed its support for those efforts. It expressed concern at the decline in the level of core resources and called on the Administrator, in the context of the implementation of the Business Plans, to increase efforts to secure predictable funding for UNDP and to reach the agreed annual funding target of $1.1 billion in core resources. The Board noted that the Business Plans emphasized that UNDP operational activities should remain country-driven. Looking forward to the timely implementation of the Business Plans, the Board requested the Administrator to report on the Plans' evolution and implementation as part of the reporting cycle established under the multi-year funding framework.

Also on 28 January [dec. 2000/6], the Board took note of the report on the comprehensive assessment of the UNDP 2001 change management process [YUN 1999, p. 804].

UNDP role in post-conflict situations

Building on the UNDP Business Plans 2000-2003, the Administrator submitted a March report entitled "Meeting the challenge: the role of UNDP in crisis, post-conflict and recovery situations, 2000-2003" [DP/2000/18]. According to the Administrator, as the incidence of special development situations increased and the diversity of the underlying causes broadened, pressures had grown on UNDP and the world community to respond in a more effective and sustainable manner. UNDP had made considerable progress in reorganizing and redirecting its efforts and resources to act in those situations, by supporting and coordinating aid, instituting organizational, management and policy changes, and financing its operations in that area, using target for resource assignment from the core (TRAC) line 1.1.3, trust funds, cost-sharing and parallel financing generated within its frameworks or programmes. As at the end of February 2000, a total of $150 million had been assigned to 225 projects in 85 countries under TRAC line 1.1.3, 75 per cent of which ($113 million) was for complex development situations in 41 countries (category I), 9 per cent ($13 million) for immediate response to sudden crises in 68 countries (category II) and 16 per cent ($24 million) to capacity-building and prevention activities in 23 countries (category III). The resources were allocated to governance projects, general reintegration and reconstruction, mine action and demobilization, and the preparation of strategic frameworks.

Despite the steps taken by UNDP to address the underlying causes of special development situations, much still needed to be done. UNDP needed to improve its performance to make it a more predictable partner within the inter-agency framework, and its operations had to be made more coherent with its overall corporate goals. Additional extrabudgetary resources were required to consolidate and expand its programmes.

As a way forward, the Administrator proposed that UNDP focus on strengthening the resident/humanitarian coordinator system, expanding its partnerships with key organizations and agencies, improving preventive activities, consolidating activities both in post-conflict and post-disaster situations under sustainable recovery programmes and strengthening its own response capacities.

Also in March [DP/2000/14], the Administrator submitted an evaluation entitled "Sharing new ground in post-conflict situations: the role of UNDP in support of reintegration programmes". The evaluation team reviewed the adequacy of UNDP interventions and assessed the quality of its response to reintegration programmes in terms of being proactive or event/donor-driven, staffing and ability to form effective partnerships. The evaluation found many instances of successful programming by UNDP in its areas of intervention. It noted in particular the important role that area-based programmes had played in recovery and the significant technical assistance UNDP had provided to national demining efforts.

The team recommended that UNDP recognize post-conflict assistance as a major part of its mission and formulate an overall policy statement on its role in that area, and specifically in reintegration programmes; reassess the level of funding for special development situations; turn its Emergency Response Division into a strong technical resource unit and clarify the field backstopping responsibilities of the regional bureaux and the Division; concentrate its support to the reintegration of war-affected populations on restoring social and human capital through area-based approaches at the community level and not at the target-group level; devise a strategy to ensure greater use of NGOs and UNVs during post-conflict situations; and assign staff to country offices early on in complex emergencies to assist in infusing a development perspective into humanitarian assistance strategies and activities. The team also recommended that country offices develop special resource mobilization strategies for use during post-conflict periods, and that UNDP step up to the challenge of serving as manager of technical-level joint programming units.

The Executive Board, in April [dec. 2000/10], took note of the report on the role of UNDP in crisis, post-conflict and recovery situations, 2000-2003, and invited the Administrator to present in 2001 a further elaboration of UNDP's specific role in special development situations and plans for its further implementation after a full and wide-ranging consultation process. The Board also took note of the executive summary of the evaluation of UNDP's role in reintegration programmes.

Communication and advocacy strategy

During the Executive Board's June session [E/2000/35], the Director of the UNDP Communications Office gave an oral report on the UNDP communication strategy, aimed at mobilizing political and financial support for the organization. He said that a clear image of UNDP, differentiating it from other UN organizations, needed to be communicated to outside constituents. UNDP benefited from a global network of knowledge grounded in its field experience and access to a wide range of experts. Its mission of reducing poverty would be accomplished through its advice to Governments and institutions on meeting development challenges, working with partners

to mobilize talent and resources and playing an advocacy role through the *Human Development Report* and other mechanisms. The communication strategy would focus on issues related to information technology for development, sustainable trade, conflict prevention, post-crisis recovery, assistance to Governments, HIV/AIDS and UN coordination.

The Communications Office would market the plan. It intended to service UNDP country offices and headquarters through a strengthened media section at headquarters and in select cities in the field; a new Internet section that would tap web sites for media and advocacy outreach; the production of targeted and easy-to-read publications; private sector sponsorship of UNDP special events; and training.

On 23 June [dec. 2000/17], the Executive Board took note of the oral report on the communication and advocacy strategy.

Evaluation

The Administrator, in a July report on evaluation, covering the period from January 1999 to June 2000 [DP/2000/34], described evaluation activities that had contributed to increasing UNDP effectiveness.

Four strategic areas were highlighted: aligning monitoring and evaluation instruments with results-based management; strengthening substantive accountability; promoting organizational learning and partnerships; and a macro-level assessment of UNDP performance based on evaluation data. Considerable progress had been made in strengthening methodologies for results-based management and making it operational, managing the design of SRFs, working with country offices and contributing to the preparation of the first ROAR. Methodologies and tools for assessing impact at the country level and an evaluative research programme had been developed to promote stronger substantive accountability. That objective had been furthered by the systematic monitoring of evaluation compliance and by the promotion of evaluation plans as a real-time instrument for country-level substantive accountability.

The Evaluation Office, in overseeing the evaluation function of UNDP, had paid particular attention to assessing the extent to which evaluation recommendations had been followed up, and the mechanisms by which that was achieved. An upward trend was revealed in the achievement of immediate objectives, and the relevance of ownership, measured by the level of government support, in contributing towards that improvement.

The Executive Board, on 29 September [dec. 2000/24], took note of the evaluation report.

UNDP Funding

Multi-year funding framework

The Director of the Evaluation Office, in an oral report to the Executive Board in April on the emerging results of the multi-year funding framework (MYFF), which was introduced in 1999 [YUN 1999, p. 806], noted that the ROAR would be the next step in the implementation of the MYFF process. Key outcomes and outputs of all six MYFF goals would be included, with more detailed analysis of the three highlighted sub-goals for 1999: strengthening the capacity of key governance institutions for people-oriented development and fostering social cohesion; promoting poverty-focused development and reduced vulnerability; and providing effective and integrated follow-up to UN global conferences within the context of sustainable human development. Further action would include revising the SRF and employing it as a management tool, using the ROAR analysis as a basis for improving future performance, furthering the ROAR methodology's evolution, sharpening UNDP's comparative advantage and identifying and building on emerging products and services.

On 7 April [dec. 2000/10], the Executive Board took note of the oral report.

UNDP, in a July report on an updated resource allocation framework and the revised MYFF [DP/2000/31], focused on the main lessons with regard to the implementation of the MYFF through the SRF and ROAR instruments. The report warned that the current trend for core resources to stagnate risked jeopardizing UNDP's ability to meet fully the results envisaged under the MYFF. The approval of the four-year MYFF was a cornerstone in consolidating results-based management (RBM) in UNDP as a new approach to managing the delivery of results, and while it was premature to draw decisive lessons from the RBM experience, the formulation of the MYFF and the ROAR had pinpointed both clear successes and issues that required further attention and effort.

The corporate ROAR for 1999 [YUN 1999, p. 795] confirmed that UNDP's programme performance was, to a great extent, consonant with the intended results and outcomes of the MYFF. It did not suggest the need for a substantive revision of MYFF, but highlighted issues that needed to be addressed to place RBM firmly at the heart of UNDP management approaches. A number of those issues concerned aspects of the SRF/ROAR

methodology, which required further attention as part of a continuing, systematic effort to improve performance monitoring, and the SRF template needed to be simplified and updated to better reflect UNDP key results areas and policy focus. The information generated by the MYFF and the ROAR needed to be better organized through the integrated data management system. The link between the traditional classification of UNDP expenditures and the new SRF categories should be reviewed to strengthen the MYFF linkage between programme areas, results and financial resources.

At the country office level, there was a continuing need to ensure full alignment with other programme instruments, such as the CCF, the country office managment plan and UNDAF, to ensure clarity and coherence of purpose. UNDP was also reviewing links between key aspects in country SRFs and ROARs and performance accountability, particularly in terms of the UNDP resident representative.

At the end of the first year of the MYFF, the goal of increasing voluntary contributions had not been achieved. By contrast, trust funds/third-party cost-sharing and government cost-sharing continued to grow dynamically. The aggregate figures masked the serious financial crisis that UNDP was facing in its regular resource base, which represented only 28 per cent of total UNDP resources for 1999. Other resources could not substitute for a sufficient, predictable and sound base in regular funding. As a result, the Administrator expressed concern that the opportunity presented by RBM through the MYFF and its associated instruments could be undermined.

The Administrator believed that it would be premature to present an updated integrated resource framework (IRF), which linked activities, results and financial allocations, to the Executive Board at its current session, and he proposed to submit a revised IRF in conjunction with his biennial budget proposals in 2001.

In September [dec. 2000/24], the Board took note of the report and agreed to consider in 2001 a revised IRF in conjunction with the 2002-2003 biennial budget.

Successor programming arrangements

In February [DP/2000/17], the Administrator, in a report on successor programming arrangements, provided the revised and final TRAC earmarkings for 2001-2003. Final earmarkings were provided for total TRAC resources under lines 1.1.1 and 1.1.2 of the budget for that period, by region and category of country. The total final earmarkings for the period were $1,767.5 million, compared to the preliminary figure of $1,738.8 million, based on $3.3 billion in total resources for the period and excluding TRAC earmarkings for new net contributor countries. Of that amount, 88 per cent was allocated to low-income countries with a gross national product (GNP) per capita of $375 or less and 12 per cent for middle-income countries. By region, Africa would receive 48 per cent; Asia and the Pacific, 31 per cent; Arab States, 8 per cent; Europe and CIS, 8 per cent; and Latin America and the Caribbean, 5 per cent. Final earmarkings under line 1.1.1 were also provided for individual countries, grouped by region, and TRAC-1 earmarkings for new net contributor countries for 2001-2003 and reimbursable TRAC-1 for 2000.

In April [dec. 2000/10], the Executive Board took note of the report.

Financing

In his annual review of the financial situation for 2000 [DP/2001/22 & Add.1], the Administrator presented an overview of UNDP's financial status at the end of the year, as well as comparative figures for 1999.

The regular resources situation continued to present a major challenge for UNDP in meeting its MYFF goals. The continuing shortfall in voluntary contributions compared to the agreed targets led to the erosion of the amount of financial resources that programme countries received from UNDP through the TRAC system. Further, UNDP experienced significant cash-flow problems in terms of regular resources due to the irregular payment of contributions by some donors, necessitating the utilization of the operational reserve in eight months of the year, thus impeding UNDP's ability to manage its financial resources effectively. Third-party co-financing, on the other hand, had increased to 30 per cent of the aggregate income, and programme-country cost-sharing continued to represent a significant portion of the total income received.

Compared to 1999, total regular resources income decreased by 9.8 per cent to $649 million and total expenditure went down by 13.5 per cent to $702 million. Overall, there was a 29 per cent decline in the available resource balance. Voluntary contributions to the regular resources fell by 6.9 per cent, to $634 million. Contributions received from the top 15 non-programme country donors (Austria, Belgium, Canada, Denmark, Finland, France, Germany, Italy, Japan, Netherlands, Norway, Sweden, Switzerland, United Kingdom, United States) totalled $607 million, or 96 per cent of total resources. As at 31 December

ber 2000, some $25 million remained unpaid for 2000 and prior years.

Total expenditure under regular resources declined to $702 million from $811 million in 1999. Programme expenditures in 2000 fell to $378 million, compared to $490 million in 1999. Regular resources programme expenditure under national execution declined by 10 per cent, from $260 million to $233 million. In terms of percentage share of programme expenditure among regions, delivery dropped in the Africa region from $206 million in 1999 to $143 million, and in Asia and the Pacific, it fell from $145 million to $131 million. Expenditure in Eastern Europe and CIS remained steady at $41 million and in the Arab States it increased slightly from $25 million to $27 million. In Latin America and the Caribbean, regular resources expenditures amounted to $25 million, excluding the top five countries.

Programme support to implementing agents decreased to $42 million, compared to $51 million in 1999, as a result of the decrease in total delivery and the change in execution patterns.

As at 31 December, the balance of unexpended resources for regular resources activities was at its lowest level since 1984 at $76 million, a decline of 29 per cent from the 1999 figure of $107 million. The level of investments for regular resources increased by 58 per cent ($26 million) to $71.9 million, due mainly to the net reduction in advances to Governments.

For the other resource activities, which comprised mainly government and third-party cost-sharing, government cash-counterpart contributions, trust funds, management services agreements and the Junior Professional Officer programme, representing the bulk of all activities managed by UNDP, overall income remained stable at $1.8 billion. However, expenditure decreased by 4 per cent ($66 million). Contributions received totalled $1.69 billion, of which 56 per cent accounted for government cost-sharing. Third-party co-financing registered a marked increase, from $495 million in 1997 to $713 million in 2000.

In September [dec. 2000/24], the Executive Board took note of the UNDP annual review report on the financial situation for 1999 [YUN 1999, p. 809].

UNDP regular funding
and cash-flow management

In January [DP/2000/CRP.3], UNDP submitted a preliminary report on its regular funding and cash-flow management, which examined contributions payment performance and hedging activities in 1999. A more detailed review, covering contributions from all countries, was to be provided to the Executive Board in connection with the funding session to be held in April.

The Administrator reported that the overall experience in the payment of contributions in 1999 remained suboptimal. Of the 17 major donors that announced specific payment schedules for their 1999 voluntary contributions, with a combined value of $584 million, only 8 fully met the dates they had specified ($332 million), 4 countries ($127 million) effected payments within one month of the original dates, another 4 countries ($110 million) effected payments more than one month later and 1 country ($12 million) did not make any payment in 1999. The cash-flow contributions from major donors in 1999 did not keep pace with those of 1998. In November 1999, $157 million, or 22 per cent of 1999 pledges, remained unpaid, as compared to $18 million, or 2 per cent of 1998 pledges, a year earlier. Preliminary estimates indicated that UNDP had utilized up to $20 million from its operational reserve to meet its cash-flow needs through 30 November 1999. The cash-flow trend was particularly troublesome given the organization's commitment to and success in recent years in reducing its balance of liquid resources to a low level. Moreover, since a significant portion of 1999 pledged contributions was not received in accordance with the payment dates announced by donors, UNDP was only able to engage in hedging to the value of some $160 million in non-dollar denominated contributions. The total amounts hedged were affected by the lack of definitive information concerning amounts and/or payment schedules early in the year for several major contributors. The Administrator requested that all donors provide a set schedule of payments and ensure that it was honoured.

On 26 January [dec. 2000/3], the Executive Board noted the information presented by UNDP, the serious impact of delayed payments on cash-flow management and the importance of officially announcing regular resources contributions for 2000 as early in the year as possible. It supported the Administrator's recommendation for a comprehensive implementation of the elements of the UNDP funding strategy [YUN 1998, p. 825] concerning the announcement of pledges and adherence to a fixed payment schedule.

In March [DP/2000/CRP.6 & DP/2000/CRP.9/Rev.1], the Administrator reported on regular funding commitments and/or estimates for 2000 and onwards to UNDP and its associated funds and programmes. Estimates for the gross contributions to regular resources for 2000, using the UN official exchange rate as at 1 March 2000, were $682 million. Pledges for 2001 stood at $252 million. For 2000, 12 countries had increased their commitments by 20 per cent or more in the currency in which they pledged, 29 countries had pledged to retain their 1999 contribution levels, and a further nine programme countries had indicated their decision to resume payments to UNDP regular resources in 2000. However, it was of concern that six countries, including three members of the Development Assistance Committee of the Organisation for Economic Co-operation and Development, had announced reduced contributions. The report outlined the specific payment schedules for 2000 contributions provided to the secretariat on or before 28 March.

The Administrator said that, while the total amount of regular resources for 2000 was slightly below the level of the income received in 1999, it was estimated that by the end of the year, the downward trend would have stopped. While several programme countries were not in a position at the time of reporting to confirm their 2000 contributions to regular resources, a number of them had increased their contributions. The reversal of the downward trend by the end of 2000 was urgently required if progress was to be made towards the annual targets established by the MYFF. To rebuild the regular resource base, greater collective political commitment to increasing contributions should be developed. Since the voluntary nature of regular funding to UNDP continued to leave critical UN development activities particularly vulnerable to reductions, greater attention needed to be paid by the Executive Board to the collective MYFF targets agreed so that regular funding levels could quickly return to a pattern of growth. It was also important that in 2001 an even greater number of countries commit to the multi-year pledges. In terms of enhancing predictability, 16 Members had made indicative multi-year pledges. Given the strength of the United States dollar, it was important that those Member States that had not done so provide a schedule of payments at the second funding meeting so that UNDP could take financial decisions to protect the dollar value of the pledge. Given the continued critical situation regarding funding, the Board should review an updated regular resources situation for 2000 at its third regular session, in line with the MYFF discussion and the review of the overall financial situation, and request countries that were in a position to do so to supplement their 2000 contributions to UNDP.

In introducing the item on funding commitments to UNDP before the Executive Board in April, the Administrator pointed to five broad lessons of UNDP's current financial crisis: UNDP should remain firmly committed to its reform agenda, press ahead with new non-core strategies and partnerships, learn from the positive examples provided by the United Nations Volunteers programme and the United Nations Development Fund for Women, which had recorded increased contributions in 2000, reinforce political support for UNDP and translate political support into practical action. With regard to the last point, the Administrator emphasized the need for a more formalized transparent multi-year commitment from donors, and suggested establishing an International Development Association–like funding arrangement that would provide UNDP with a multi-year commitment that was predictable and ensured fair burden-sharing for donors. As a way forward, he proposed the holding of a ministerial-level meeting with the specific aim of debating and endorsing such a plan around the time of the General Assembly's Millennium Summit in September (see p. 47).

On 7 April [dec. 2000/10], the Executive Board took note of the report on regular funding commitments to UNDP and its associated programmes for 2000 and onwards. It also noted that the Administrator would consult with all partners to explore their interest in convening a ministerial-level meeting at the earliest appropriate date to address the organization's funding situation.

Ministerial Meeting on UNDP

The first Ministerial Meeting on UNDP was held in New York on 11 September. The purpose of the meeting was to consult Governments on the direction of the new UNDP and seek ways to boost recognition and support for it at the country level and in key international forums. The meeting, attended by ministers and representatives of 67 programme and donor countries, discussed support for the UN role in development and rebuilding political support for that mission; the new direction and reforms at UNDP; its comparative advantages and partnerships with developing countries; steps taken by UNDP to improve performance and deliver results; and the need to resolve UNDP's resource situation. It had before it a document entitled "Rebuilding support for United Nations development cooperation", containing a series of background notes on UNDP as the operational arm of the United Nations, building on results, UNDP and universality, UNDP's financial situation and UNDP's challenge ahead.

In his address to the meeting, the Secretary-General said that development had been one of the main tasks of the United Nations from the very beginning and UNDP was involved in that day-to-day work in individual countries. Being a universal network made its services uniquely valuable, since it was well placed to tell people what had worked in one country and what did not in another, problems that might arise with a particular policy and how to get around them. Through its country offices, it brought coherence to the work of the United Nations throughout the world and provided leadership to the different agencies; since not all agencies were represented in every country, UNDP's presence was even more important. UNDP was also best placed to take the lead in post-conflict peace-building, in cooperation with other UN agencies and the World Bank. UNDP was central to the whole UN mission, but it needed support and a sympathetic audience.

The Chairman, in his oral summary of the meeting [DP/2001/CRP.3], noted the endorsement of the Secretary-General's vision, outlined in his keynote address, of the UN role in development and the essential part played by UNDP, particularly in the light of the Millennium Declaration (see p. 49) and its emphasis on the continuing challenge of poverty eradication; and of the new direction of UNDP, as a poverty agency working in its areas of comparative advantage, including capacity-building in governance and policy, special development situations and new areas, such as information technology and the use of the Internet. He also noted the meeting's recognition of the value of UNDP's role as an advocate at global and national levels, including through the *Human Development Report* and its linkage to UNDP's universal presence, also serving the rest of the UN system; concerns that, while a universal UNDP was indispensable to the mandate of the United Nations itself, resource constraints presented a significant challenge to geographical coverage by the organization; the importance of UNDP's coordination role, as well as partnerships beyond the UN family; the importance of preserving the country-driven nature of UNDP programmes and of maintaining its capacity to respond to country priorities; recognition of the Administrator's commitment to results, internal reform and management performance and excellence at all levels; political and financial support for the reform process; and concern about the resource situation and the importance of rebuilding the core resource base.

The Chairman noted the various options put forward by ministers for rebuilding political support for UNDP, including advocacy for aid to development and to the United Nations, at the national level; options for UNDP to be considered in other international or regional forums; the proposal by a number of ministers to hold annual events similar to the 11 September 2000 meeting; ways for ministers to continue their involvement in the dialogue on UNDP and its future; means by which UNDP could communicate its improved performance from the field; and options for the role of the Executive Board.

The Executive Board, at its third regular session in September, discussed follow-up to the Ministerial Meeting. Suggestions were made that ministerial meetings be held every four years, in conjunction with the start of the new MYFFs, or in the context of UNDG meetings, or that the Bureau of the Board meet annually at the ministerial level until the funding crisis was resolved.

Audit reports

In January, the Executive Board considered the Administrator's updated report [DP/2000/6] on implementation of the recommendations of the Board of Auditors for the 1996-1997 biennium [YUN 1998, p. 1288], which provided a tabular summary of recommendations by area of audit, together with the status of follow-up action as at 30 September 1999 and target dates for implementation. The Administrator said that progress had already been made in many areas and efforts were being made to address outstanding issues.

On 28 January [dec. 2000/6], the Board took note of the Administrator's report.

In May [DP/2000/21 & Corr.1], the Administrator submitted a report on UNDP internal audit and oversight activities for 1999 provided by its Office of Audit and Performance Review (OAPR). During that year, OAPR produced 168 audit, investigation and related reports. In addition, 33 control self-assessment workshops were held, the results of 1,231 national execution audit reports were evaluated and feedback was provided to country offices.

OAPR conducted audits/reviews of headquarters units and corporate functions. Six reports were issued, containing 118 recommendations. Of those, 101 (86 per cent) were accepted by the auditees and had been or were being implemented. Two of the six reports included the special audits of change-management and information-systems expenditures prepared at the request of the Advisory Committee on Administrative and Budgetary Questions (ACABQ). Of the remaining four reports, two were audits/reviews of headquarters units and two were audits of corporate functions.

OAPR provided internal audit and related services to 64 of the 134 country offices. A total of 64 internal audit reports were issued, containing 2,297 recommendations. Of those, 88 per cent were accepted by auditees and the remaining 12

per cent were being pursued. As required under UNDP financial regulations, Governments submitted audited financial reports for nationally executed projects and programmes. In 1999, 1,352 reports were received from 108 countries, of which 1,231 were evaluated (from 104 countries), and the findings were reported to the country offices concerned. Significant improvement was noted in the number, timeliness and quality of audit reports received from country offices, as compared with the year before. However, a number of concerns remained, related to internal controls, project-management structure, financial monitoring, and procurement and equipment. The Office had 56 special audit and investigation cases active during the year, an increase of 6 per cent over 1998, 33 of which were still active at the end of 1999. The issues ranged from allegations of fraud and serious misconduct to inadequate performance and potential conflict of interest. Several cases were being dealt with in cooperation with the Office of Internal Oversight Services, including that of the Reserve for Field Accommodation, a case that involved legal action against two individuals.

On 23 June [dec. 2000/17], the Board took note of the Administrator's report.

2000-2001 budget update

In September, the Administrator, in an oral update on the budget for the 2000-2001 biennium, reported that total income for regular resources in 2000 was likely to amount to only $666 million, down from $681 million the previous year, due to a strong United States dollar. Cash-flow problems had necessitated a drawdown of close to $100 million from the operational reserve, although UNDP was in the process of replenishing it. UNDP would take steps to be financially prudent by reducing total expenditure by 8 per cent in 2000, remaining committed to a zero nominal growth budget for 2002-2003, unlocking $5 million in regular resources and shifting $20 million in regular and other non-core resources from headquarters to the field through the restructuring process. A target of a 15 per cent across-the-board cut in country offices' costs was set for 2001, due to the need to cap any increase in administrative costs so that 100 cents of every dollar of regular resources would go to programme rather than overhead costs. Part of the cut would generate extra savings for new investments, such as improving connectivity for country offices. Against that background, he had decided not to submit a revised budget for the 2000-2001 biennium.

On 29 September [dec. 2000/24], the Board took note of the oral update on the 2000-2001 budget.

Revision of Financial Regulations and Rules

The Executive Board in January considered the Administrator's report containing a comprehensive revision of UNDP Financial Regulations and Rules [YUN 1999, p. 811]; a comparative table [DP/2000/CRP.5] prepared by the United Nations Office of Legal Affairs (OLA), which contained a comparison of current UNDP Financial Regulations and Rules and the proposed new Financial Regulations and Rules, as well as relevant comments by OLA; and the comments and observations of ACABQ thereon [DP/2000/7]. ACABQ had recommended that the Administrator resubmit his proposed amendments in a format that would permit the easy identification of the proposed changes with precise and succinct explanations, indicating the reasons for the changes to each regulation.

In response to ACABQ's request, the Administrator, in January [DP/2000/CRP.4], submitted further clarifications to his proposed new Financial Regulations and Rules. While noting the difficulties and positions of ACABQ, he acknowledged that, because of their comprehensive nature touching many financial and technical issues relating to UNDP activities, the proposed revisions were not easily comparable to the current Regulations and Rules. The presentation as suggested by ACABQ would not facilitate an understanding of the rationale for the overall revision. Instead, he had chosen to present the proposed revisions and to circulate OLA's comprehensive comparative table. The Administrator also responded to ACABQ comments relating to a number of specific proposals. He underlined the implications any delays in approving the revised Financial Regulations and Rules would have for the implementation of a UNDP accountability framework, reiterating that the current Regulations and Rules were no longer adequate.

The Executive Board, on 28 January [dec. 2000/4], approved the proposed revised Financial Regulations with further amendments to eight of them, which were included in an annex to the decision, with the exception of regulations 16.03 regarding a limited authority for the Administrator to advance funds from regular resources prior to the receipt of anticipated contributions to other resources; 17.04 regarding authorization for the Administrator to select an intergovernmental or non-governmental organization as executing entity; 19.01 regarding an expanded grant modality; and 25.09 regarding authority for the Administrator to establish credit facilities. It requested the Administrator to present additional information on those issues, pending approval of which the current related Financial Regulations would remain in effect. He would also defer approval of the associated financial rules for the four proposed regulations. The Board requested the Administrator to keep the Financial Regulations under review and to submit to the Consultative Committee on Administrative Questions (Financial and Budgetary Questions) (CCAQ) of ACC the changes in terminology. It recommended that UNDP seek the views of CCAQ on any new proposed changes of terminology in the Financial Regulations and Rules, with a view towards harmonization. The Board called for informal consultations on any proposed change to ensure that the changes and their rationale were fully explained in a useful format.

Procurement

In September, the Executive Board considered the Administrator's report on the activities of the Inter-Agency Procurement Services Office (IAPSO) from June 1998 to June 2000 [DP/2000/33].

In addition to the information on 1998 and 1999 [YUN 1999, p. 811], the report also indicated that, in May 2000, IAPSO implemented the first phase of electronic commerce through its web site, enabling clients to request full quotations, including insurance, freight charges and handling fees. Automated quotations were provided by e-mail normally within 24 hours after review. That process was currently under review to ensure that eligible clients received fully automated quotations immediately. In the long term, IAPSO planned to enter fully into electronic commerce, involving both electronic ordering by IAPSO to suppliers and receiving electronic orders from eligible clients over the Internet. It also implemented a security package to provide enhanced security for electronic-commerce transactions. As an interim measure, electronic transactions would be backed up by hard-copy documentation to ensure that UNDP Financial Regulations and Rules were followed and that there was an adequate audit trail. IAPSO was also discussing expanding its web site for the dissemination of collective price agreements with other UN organizations and international finance institutions.

The annual statistical report, 1999 [DP/2000/32], issued in August 2000, covered procurement of goods and services, international project personnel, the UNV programme and fellowships, providing details on procurement by country of supply to the UN system. According to the information provided, total procurement by the UN system under all sources of funding during 1998 was $3 billion and the share of procurement from developing countries was 42 per cent. The percentage share of procurement from developing countries had been increasing steadily over the previous few years. Under UNDP funding, the corresponding figure for the share of procurement from developing countries was 85 per cent. At the time of the report, the collection of data for 1999 procurement was still in progress.

The Executive Board, on 29 September [dec. 2000/24], took note of the report on IAPSO activities and recommended that the Office continue to explore ways in which the expanded use of collective pricing agreements could be coordinated with other entities of the UN system.

Other technical cooperation

UN activities

The Department of Economic and Social Affairs (DESA), responsible for UN technical cooperation activities, had more than 1,100 technical cooperation projects under execution during 2000 in a dozen substantive sectors, with a total project expenditure of $72.5 million. Projects financed by UNDP represented $46.1 million; those by trust funds, $24.4 million; and, by UNFPA, $2 million.

On a geographical basis, the DESA-executed programme included expenditures of $29.3 million in the Middle East; $20.7 million in interregional and global programmes; $12.6 million in Africa; $7.6 million in Asia and the Pacific; $1.6 million in the Americas; and $0.7 million in Europe. Project delivery in the Middle East, which included expenditures of $21.5 million for the Iraq programme, was the largest, with a 40 per cent share of total delivery.

Distribution of expenditure by substantive sectors was as follows: energy, $28.1 million; Associate Expert programme, $13.7 million; economic policy, $11 million; public administration, $5.8 million; water, $5 million; social policy, $2.9 million; statistics, $2 million; infrastructure, $1.6 million; institutional support, $1 million; minerals, $0.6 million; public finance, $0.3 million; advancement of women, $0.3 million; and population, $0.2 million. Of the total delivery of $72.5 million, energy (including the Iraq programme) comprised 39 per cent; Associate Expert programme, 19 per cent; and economic policy, 15 per cent.

On a component basis, DESA's delivery in 2000 included $38 million for project personnel, $19.2 million for equipment, $10.5 million for subcontracts, $3.3 million for training and $1.5 million for miscellaneous expenses.

UN Office for Project Services

The United Nations Office for Project Services (UNOPS) continued to respond to specific and diverse demands for project services, operating in accordance with the self-financing principle with no assessed budget financing and executing programmes on behalf of UN organizations.

2000 activities

The UNOPS Executive Director, in his annual report to the Executive Board for 2000 [DP/2001/19], described activities and assessed performance compared to the targets set in the 2000-2001 UNOPS Business Plan.

The total value of the UNOPS project and loan portfolios amounted to $3.7 billion in 2000, comprising $1.5 billion in project value and $2.2 billion in loan value.

Total delivery was $664 million, 20 per cent below the target of $836 million, comprising $471 million in expenditure on project portfolio and $193 million in disbursement authorizations for the IFAD loan portfolio. The shortfall in UNOPS project delivery amounted to $119 million in 2000, owing to the unforeseen rephasing, reduction and cancellation of approved project budgets. Disbursements authorized by UNOPS under the IFAD loan portfolio ($193 million) were 22 per cent below the forecast of $246 million.

Total income was $48.5 million, $3.1 million or 6 per cent short of the target of $51.6 million, distributed as follows: $36.8 million from delivery of the project portfolio; $6.5 million from loan-administration and other services; and $5.2 million in other income. Income from sources other than UNDP rose to $16.5 million, or 34 per cent of the total UNOPS income.

Recurring administrative expenditure was $52.3 million, or $0.7 million above the projection of $51.6 million. Non-recurring administrative expenditure was $3 million, 97 per cent of the projection. Total expenditure was $6.8 million more than total income, a shortfall that would be met by a drawdown from the operational reserve in that amount.

In reviewing its activities, the Executive Director said that UNOPS had intensified efforts to diversify both its client base and the type of services it provided. In partnership with IFAD, it introduced new implementation concepts, such as new methods of channelling non-traditional rural microfinance in Bangladesh, Nepal and Uganda, and the establishment of financial instruments and institutions that focused exclusively on the rural poor, such as the discount funds for lending in Chile, Paraguay, the former Yugoslav Republic of Macedonia and Uruguay.

Work in countries in special circumstances included the management of the mine-action programme in northern Iraq and assisting in implementing programmes supporting internally displaced persons, a humanitarian information centre, and an urban water sanitation programme in Iraq. UNOPS began implementing a $17 million programme funded by the United Nations Environment Programme for the clean-up of environmental hot spots in four municipalities in Serbia (FRY). Its assistance provided to peacekeeping missions reached substantial levels in 2000. It implemented six projects for the United Nations Interim Administration Mission in Kosovo (UNMIK) (see PART ONE, Chapter V) worth $7 million and provided procurement and management services to the United Nations Transitional Administration in East Timor (see PART ONE, Chapter IV).

In the area of social accountability, UNOPS began to develop an independently audited and verified system to ensure quality in the workplace and worked with a not-for-profit organization in Brazil to promote business ethnics and social responsibility within the business community.

UNOPS released four of the nine volumes of its Operational Guide for the management of rehabilitation and social sustainability in societies affected by conflicts or natural disasters—an interagency effort coordinated by UNOPS. It provided procurement support services in developing countries and in countries in special circumstances. Procurement services supported post-conflict initiatives of UN organizations and missions, as well as projects in governance, public administration, capacity-building and economic and social development.

In the area of risk management, UNOPS offered a variety of contract tools, together with skills training. Specialized insurance arrangements and an operational reserve were maintained to protect against unavoidable risks. Support services were provided for procurement activities from the bidding process to contract disputes, trade advice and commercial practices.

Management advisory services were provided to the Economic and Social Commission for Asia and the Pacific to support its revitalization programme, management consultancy services to the International Atomic Energy Agency, and advisory services in support of UNMIK efforts in Kosovo to rehabilitate local administrative institutions, to WFP in Guatemala in the formulation of its country programme and to the Soros Foundation and the Centre for Legal Action and Human Rights. In 2000, the Executive Director introduced a new operational concept of partnerships with the private sector and with NGOs. Eleven partnerships were signed and work initiated on developing a dedicated partnership regime that would enable UNOPS to enter into non-commercial partnerships.

The UNDP/UNFPA Executive Board, on 23 June [E/2000/35 (dec. 2000/16)], took note of the Executive Director's report on UNOPS activities in 1999 [YUN 1999, p. 812], including operation in accordance with the self-financing principle in relation to recurring administrative expenditure. It requested the Management Coordination Committee to assist UNOPS and UNDP in overcoming difficulties relating to financial reporting and arrangements. The Board noted that a drawdown of $13.8 million from the UNOPS operational reserve was effected in 1999 to cover part of its non-recurring expenditure and requested the Executive Director to inform the Board regularly on the timing and means of reconstituting the operational reserve. It also noted with concern that the cost of relocating UNOPS headquarters had risen from $8.5 million to $14 million.

UNDP/UNOPS relationship

In March [DP/2000/13], the Administrator submitted to the Executive Board an evaluation of the relationship between UNDP and UNOPS, five years after they separated pursuant to General Assembly decision 48/501 [YUN 1994, p. 806]. The evaluation team also made recommendations on improving the working relationship between the two organizations. The evaluation found that cooperation between UNDP and UNOPS functioned well when there was a clear understanding of the respective roles and possible synergies, as well as effective personal relationships. In other cases, there was a lack of satisfaction on both sides with the performance of the other party. UNOPS continued to be heavily dependent on UNDP as a funding source for most of its business. However, their relations were largely characterized by mistrust and misunderstanding, due in part to the lack of a clear definition of their respective roles and responsibilities at the corporate level. The oversight and coordination mechanisms created had not functioned adequately and there were overlaps and competing competencies between the two institutions. Both had difficulty in recognizing each other's role—UNDP with regard to UNOPS as the major executing/implementing agent of the UN system and UNOPS with regard to UNDP as its major funding source. The budgetary cuts over the past 10 years had weakened the UNDP country office structure, which had led to reduced UNOPS participation in programme implementation. The performance of UNOPS in delivering its services was uneven, creating tension between the two institutions.

In terms of the future UNDP/UNOPS relationship, the evaluation recommended that UNOPS remain a separate and identifiable entity but that its relationship with UNDP be clearly defined. The team identified six main areas where action was urgently needed: defining the respective roles and responsibilities; institutional arrangements; fund-raising and business acquisition; execution modalities; financing principles for country offices; and administrative and management issues. It presented specific recommendations on each of those areas.

Also in March [DP/2000/CRP.8], UNOPS and UNDP submitted a joint review of the recommendations contained in the evaluation report, which were set out in two categories: those that were acceptable to both organizations and could be acted on immediately and those requiring further consultations, discussions and guidance from the Executive Board. Recommendations under the first category related to the status of UNOPS, instructions to resident representatives as representatives of UNOPS, the Users Advisory Group, the project-management matrix, financial reporting and administrative issues. The second category dealt with recommendations on delineation of responsibilities, the Management Coordination Committee, resource mobilization, execution modalities and financing principles for country offices.

On 7 April [dec. 2000/10], the Executive Board took note of the two reports and decided to revert to the item at its 2001 annual session.

On 23 June [dec. 2000/16], the Board emphasized the importance of follow-up of the evaluation report on the UNDP/UNOPS relationship and requested that a progress report be submitted later in the year on implementation of the recommendations.

In response, UNDP submitted, in July [DP/2000/35], a progress report on follow-up and a joint review of recommendations, which indicated the status of consultations between the two organizations. While some progress had been made in the first category of recommendations, considerable additional consultations between UNOPS and UNDP were required before progress could be made in the second category. In the first category, the two organizations had agreed that the current status of UNOPS should be maintained, with UNOPS having full responsibility for its internal management. The UNOPS Executive Director was preparing a letter to resident representatives, detailing their precise role as UNOPS representatives. The Users Advisory Group was to be maintained. A model project-management matrix had

been developed in order that the respective responsibilities of UNDP and UNOPS could be defined for each project. Efforts were also made to implement recommendations on financial reporting and administrative issues, particularly by implementing the Integrated Management Information System (IMIS). UNOPS had released the Operational Guide for implementing programmes designed for post-conflict situations, social sustainability and natural disasters. In addition, it was strengthening the management capacities of the decentralized offices.

On 28 September [dec. 2000/22], the Executive Board took note of the progress report, urged the Administrator and the Executive Director to ensure action on the outstanding recommendations as a matter of urgency and requested them to submit in 2001 a detailed report on progress achieved on all recommendations of the evaluation report.

Budget estimates

The Executive Director, in August [DP/2000/37 & Corr.1 & Add.1 & Add.1/Corr.1], issued revised 2000-2001 budget estimates for UNOPS, which proposed a decrease in total administrative expenditure from $113.8 million to $106.3 million, consisting of a decrease from $110.9 million to $103.2 million for recurring expenditures and an increase from $2.9 million to $3.1 million for non-recurring administrative expenditures. Those budget revisions were based on the targeted developments in the UNOPS project delivery and service portfolios detailed in the UNOPS 2000-2001 Business Plan.

In addition, as a flexibility provision necessitated by the variable nature of UNOPS activities, the Executive Director requested the authority to incur administrative expenditure in an amount not to exceed 5 per cent of the approved budget for the biennium when it was supported by unspent and/or projected income. The Executive Director also requested approval of the reclassification of two posts from the P-5 to the D-1 level.

ACABQ, in September [DP/2000/38], recommended that the Executive Board accept the Executive Director's proposals.

On 28 September [dec. 2000/20], the Executive Board approved the 2000-2001 revised budget estimates in the amount of $106.3 million, as well as the proposed staffing level and the reclassification of two posts from P-5 to D-1. It gave the Executive Director authority to incur expenditure, both personnel- and administrative-related, in an amount not exceeding 5 per cent of the budget estimates for the biennium in order to respond to unanticipated changes in business acquisition that were supported by unspent and/or projected income. The Executive Director was requested to work towards the replenishment of the operational reserve as a matter of urgency and to report in 2001 as part of the consolidated UNOPS report on the measures needed to restore the operational reserve to its prescribed level.

Audit reports

In May [DP/2000/26], the Executive Director provided an update on the implementation of the recommendations of the UN Board of Auditors contained in the UNOPS financial report and audited financial statements for 1996-1997, which had been covered in a first report in 1999 [YUN 1999, p. 815]. Action had been taken on recommendations on procurement, evaluation of international consultants and staff appraisal, year 2000 computer compliance and the reporting of fraud. Implementation of the recommendations relating to financial reporting was being postponed until later in 2000, due to the delay in getting complete data into IMIS.

Also in May [DP/2000/25/Add.1], the Executive Director issued his annual report on UNOPS internal audit and oversight activities. The oversight framework included an external audit performed by the UN Board of Auditors; an internal audit performed by the UNDP Office of Audit and Performance Review (OAPR); and internal management oversight.

OAPR conducted audits and management reviews of headquarters and field activities. In 1999, a total of 31 audit reports were issued, of which 16 contained a total of 248 recommendations. Of those recommendations, 89 were in finance, 31 in personnel, 47 in administration (including contracts and procurement), 37 in programme, 36 in management and 8 in policy. UNOPS agreed with 231 of the recommendations and provided its response on action taken or contemplated to implement them.

Major issues identified in the audit reports included the need to discontinue joint delegations to UNOPS project personnel and UNDP resident representatives and to review and revise chapter 30 (Delegation of authority) of the UNOPS Handbook. In the suspense and clearing accounts, items were identified that had been outstanding for several years. One of the main weaknesses identified in the audit of three field activities was that none of the units had a work plan or financial information for proper monitoring of projects, and one of them lacked terms of reference and was undertaking direct services outside of UNOPS Financial Regulations. Audits of imprest account operations identified some important issues that had organization-wide implications, including the need to ensure that those accounts

were immediately closed and/or transferred to UNOPS operational units or successor projects.

On 23 June [dec. 2000/17], the Executive Board took note of the Executive Director's report on the updated review of the implementation of the recommendations of the Board of Auditors and the UNOPS report on internal audit and oversight activities.

Personnel matters

The Executive Board, in June [dec. 2000/16], requested the Executive Director to report in September on steps taken to implement its 1999 decision on the appropriate authority and accountability for personnel matters [YUN 1999, p. 816] and to submit a detailed report in 2001 on the implementation of the delegation of authority. He was also asked to submit a new, justified proposal with regard to the upgrading of two existing posts from the P-5 to the D-1 level, and to review the procedures for approving the establishment of posts at the D-1 level, with a view to achieving a practice that was more consistent with the establishment of posts at all levels, up to and including the P-5 level.

In August [DP/2000/30], the Executive Director, reporting on those two personnel matters, stated that consultations between UNDP and UNOPS on the operational arrangements for implementation of the delegation of authority had sufficiently progressed to enable the UNDP Administrator to proceed with signing the delegation of authority. The two sides agreed that the overriding concern would be to ensure that UNOPS personnel were administered in the most cost-effective and efficient manner. The issuance of UNOPS letters of appointment would clarify further the accountability of the Executive Director in personnel matters. The Executive Director outlined the general provisions agreed on to govern the delegation of authority, and said that further agreements between UNDP and UNOPS would be concluded separately, specifying the UNDP services to be provided, together with associated charges based on identifiable workloads, and performance standards and time frames.

The Executive Director also described the rationale for the approval of the establishment of posts at the D-1 level and expressed his belief that he should be given the authority to establish such posts similar to his existing authority pertaining to the establishment of posts at the P-5 level and below. However, he proposed for the time being to continue the arrangement limiting his authority to establish posts at the P-5 level and below.

ACABQ, in its comments on the issue [DP/2000/38], noted that the steps taken by UNOPS to implement the Board's 1999 decision formed a sound basis for the implementation of the delegation of authority on personnel matters from the UNDP Administrator to the UNOPS Executive Director. ACABQ agreed with the view that a flexible post management system was essential to be responsive to changes in demand and project delivery and income. It was of the view that current procedures for establishing posts should be streamlined and recommended full delegation of authority to the Executive Director to cover all posts up to the D-2 category under the following conditions: posts up to the P-5 level would continue to be established by the Executive Director and approved ex post facto by the Executive Board following the current procedure; and posts at the D-1 and D-2 levels would also be established by the Executive Director, with prior ACABQ concurrence, on a temporary basis, pending approval of the budget by the Executive Board.

On 28 September [dec. 2000/20], the Executive Board approved the staffing level as proposed in the revised budget estimates for 2000-2001 (see p. 841), as well as the reclassification of two posts at the P-5 level to the D-1 level.

The following day [dec. 2000/21], the Board noted that the delegation of authority in personnel matters had been provided to the Executive Director by the UNDP Administrator and requested the Executive Director to report in 2001 on measures taken to ensure the proper discharge of the delegated authority and on the impact, if any, of the need for advance approval of the Board for establishing posts at the D-1 level and above.

UN Volunteers

UNV activities

The Administrator, in his annual report for 2000 [DP/2001/14], provided information on the United Nations Volunteers (UNV) programme, administered by UNDP. He reported that the number of volunteers grew from 4,383 in 1999 to 4,800 in 2000, comprising 157 nationalities serving in 140 countries. The number of assignments increased to 5,200 compared to 4,755 the previous year.

By programme area, UNV assignments supported activities in special development situations (34 per cent), sustainable human development (31 per cent), poverty eradication and sustainable livelihoods (17 per cent) and support to the United Nations (14 per cent). While the protection of the environment and the advancement of women formed, for the most part, an integral part of the work of UNVs in those programme areas, 4 per cent of assignments were directly related to environment and gender. Development cooperation activities thus remained the hallmark of UNV programme implementation in 2000. Particularly noteworthy was the operationalization of the United Nations Information Technology Services, which would link people through the Internet through a shared knowledge base; the expansion of activities to support community efforts in responding to the HIV/AIDS epidemic; and the extended involvement in confidence-building and peace promotion activities in countries emerging from internal conflict.

In a report on the review of the financial situation in 2000 [DP/2001/22], the Administrator stated that income recorded for 2000 decreased by $2.9 million or 13.6 per cent compared to 1999. Programme expenditure increased to $24.3 million in 2000 from $23.9 million in 1999. The balance of the reserve as at 31 December was $2.1 million.

In June [dec. 2000/14], the Executive Board, taking note of the Administrator's report on UNV activities in 1998-1999 [YUN 1999, p. 816], welcomed the use of the UNDP strategic results framework, including the way in which it encompassed UNV support to the UN system as a whole. The Board reaffirmed the importance and the value added of the UNV programme at the global, regional and national levels, and welcomed the programme's contribution to national capacity-building and sustainable development through the expanded mobilization of national UNVs. It supported the bridging role that UNVs could play in the transition from humanitarian assistance to reconstruction and rehabilitation and to longer-term sustainable development. In addition, the Board decided that the theme of the special event at its annual session in 2001 would be volunteering in the framework of the International Year of Volunteers and the thirtieth anniversary of the UNV programme.

International Year of Volunteers (2001)

In November, the Secretary-General officially launched the International Year of Volunteers [DP/2001/14]. UNV, the focal point for the Year, used the preparations for the Year as an opportunity not only to articulate its own core mandate and focus but also to confirm the relevance of the organization and of its operational activities on the ground.

At the request of the Preparatory Committee for the Special Session of the General Assembly on the Implementation of the Outcome of the World Summit for Social Development and Further Initiatives [YUN 1999, p. 1037], UNV, in February [A/AC.253/16/Add.7], issued a report on the role of volunteering in the promotion of social development. The report discussed the various forms of volunteering in different regional and national contexts, from self-help and participation to service provision and campaigning. It examined the benefits of volunteering, focusing on the three key priority areas of the Copenhagen Declaration on Social Development and Programme of Action [YUN 1995, p. 1114]—social integration, poverty alleviation and full employment—and focused on key issues in volunteering, including globalization and relations with the State and market. Recommendations were offered to Governments for strengthening and supporting volunteering.

The General Assembly, in **resolution S-24/2** of 1 July (see p. 1013), recommended the promotion of voluntarism as an additional mechanism in the promotion of social integration and invited the Commission for Social Development to consider the issue in 2001, the International Year of Volunteers.

ECONOMIC AND SOCIAL COUNCIL ACTION

On 28 July [meeting 45], the Economic and Social Council adopted **resolution 2000/25** [draft: E/2000/L.12] without vote [agenda item 14 *(b)*].

International Year of Volunteers
The Economic and Social Council

Recommends to the General Assembly the adoption of the following draft resolution:

[For text, see General Assembly resolution 55/57 below.]

GENERAL ASSEMBLY ACTION

On 4 December [meeting 81], the General Assembly, on the recommendation of the Third (Social, Humanitarian and Cultural) Committee [A/55/591], adopted **resolution 55/57** without vote [agenda item 103].

International Year of Volunteers
The General Assembly,

Recalling its resolution 52/17 of 20 November 1997, in which it proclaimed the year 2001 as the International Year of Volunteers, and also recalling Economic and Social Council resolution 1997/44 of 22 July 1997,

Recalling also the outcome document of the twenty-fourth special session of the General Assembly, entitled "World Summit for Social Development and beyond: achieving social development for all in a globalizing world", held at Geneva from 26 June to 1 July 2000, in which the General Assembly recommended the promotion of the involvement of volunteers in social development, inter alia, by encouraging Governments, taking into account the views of all actors, to develop comprehensive strategies and programmes by raising public awareness about the value and opportunities of voluntarism and by facilitating an enabling environment for individuals and other actors of civil society to engage in, and the private sector to support, voluntary activities,

Welcoming the decision of the Commission for Social Development, at its thirty-eighth session, to include the subject of volunteering in the provisional agenda for its thirty-ninth session,

Taking into account the valuable contribution of volunteering to both economic and social development,

Bearing in mind that volunteering is one of the important ways in which people participate in societal development,

1. *Welcomes* the activities undertaken by States, intergovernmental organizations, non-governmental organizations, community-based organizations and the United Nations system for the promotion of volunteerism and, specifically, in preparation for the observance of the International Year of Volunteers, and encourages them to continue their efforts;

2. *Calls upon* States to promote, especially during the Year, an environment conducive to the discussion, at the national and local levels, of the characteristics and trends of volunteer action in their own societies, including the major challenges which the Year can help to address, and to incorporate the subject of volunteering into high-level and other meetings and events during 2001;

3. *Invites* States to consider all means available for more people to become involved in voluntary action and to be drawn from a broader cross-section of society, especially from groups, including young people, older people and people with disabilities, in view of the benefits accruing to volunteers through volunteer action;

4. *Encourages* Governments, non-governmental organizations, the private sector, eminent persons and other relevant actors to take all possible measures to promote volunteer action, especially during the Year, in particular at the local level, and in cooperation with, inter alia, local authorities, community leaders, the media and schools;

5. *Encourages* organizations of the United Nations system to pay attention to the Year in their regular work and in their relevant meetings and to continue to collaborate with the United Nations Volunteers programme as focal point for the Year to ensure that the contributions of volunteers in their own areas of concern are fully recognized;

6. *Requests* the Commission for Social Development to make appropriate suggestions and recommendations to the General Assembly, through the Economic and Social Council, to further the contribution of volunteering to social development;

7. *Requests* the Secretary-General to submit his note transmitting the contribution of the United Nations Volunteers programme to the preparations for the twenty-fourth special session of the General Assembly, entitled "World Summit for Social Development and beyond: achieving social development for all in a globalizing world", as a document of the thirty-ninth session of the Commission for Social Development, and requests him, furthermore, to disseminate it widely within the United Nations system, including by making it available to the Commission on Human Settlements acting as the preparatory committee for the special session of the General Assembly for an overall review and appraisal of the Habitat Agenda, the preparatory committee for the special session of the General Assembly for follow-up to the World Summit for

Children, the preparatory committee for the World Conference against Racism, Racial Discrimination, Xenophobia and Related Intolerance and the Commission on the Status of Women at its forty-fifth session;

8. *Decides* that two plenary meetings of the fifty-sixth session of the General Assembly shall be devoted to volunteering, to coincide with the close of the International Year of Volunteers on 5 December 2001, and in this regard requests the Secretary-General to prepare a report on ways in which Governments and the United Nations system could support volunteering for discussion on that occasion;

9. *Requests* the Secretary-General to report to the General Assembly at its fifty-seventh session on the outcome of the International Year of Volunteers and its follow-up.

Economic and technical cooperation among developing countries

The UNDP Administrator, in response to the Executive Board's request [YUN 1999, p. 817], presented, in August [DP/2000/36], an assessment of the results of activities supported by the Special Unit for Technical Cooperation among Developing Countries (TCDC). The TCDC cooperation framework was designed to promote TCDC actively and to support sustainable human development (SHD) in such areas as poverty eradication; environment; production and employment; and trade, investment and macroeconomic management. Total core and non-core resources amounting to $29.5 million for 1997-2000 were allocated to three main activity clusters: building strategic policy and institutional capacities; nurturing TCDC knowledge-networking; and forging broad-based partnerships for SHD.

As part of the UNDP decentralization strategy, the Special Unit planned to redeploy two TCDC advisers to the field to work with the network of 50 policy specialists in the regions. The aim was to strengthen the field-based, action-oriented TCDC community, which would consist of TCDC-oriented networks; interested Southern experts, knowledge institutions and centres of excellence; selected intergovernmental, non-governmental, civil society and private sector organizations; developing country government focal points; interested donor agencies; and TCDC focal points within UNDP as well as the UN system. Thus, global support for multilateral TCDC could be significantly enhanced. Within that community, the Special Unit would remain the anchor of multilateral South-South cooperation. The new programme would concentrate on areas where the need for building policy and institutional capacities was greatest. The

TCDC programme would be geared to priority issues in the areas of trade and investment and macroeconomic management; social integration and transformation; science and technology for development; private sector development with emphasis on small and medium-sized enterprises; and environmental management.

Sub-strategies would be developed around the Unit's key functions, such as TCDC advocacy, policy dialogue, interregional networking, partnership-building and resource mobilization. A new TCDC cooperation framework would be submitted to the Executive Board in 2001.

The Executive Board considered the report on the Special Unit's activities and decided in September [dec. 2000/24] to resume its consideration in 2001.

UN Capital Development Fund

Contributions to the United Nations Capital Development Fund (UNCDF) regular resources amounted to $23.9 million in 2000, a 12.4 per cent decrease from 1999 contributions of $27.4 million [DP/2001/22]. Contributions received for trust fund activities totalled $2 million in 2000, compared to $2.1 million in 1999. Programme expenditure (including support costs paid to implementing agents) totalled $43.2 million. Total expenditure represented an overall project delivery of 84.6 per cent. UNCDF unexpended resources as at 31 December were $70.9 million ($86.9 million at the end of 1999), including $38 million in the operational reserve.

In his annual report for 2000 [DP/2001/14], the UNDP Administrator said that UNCDF had developed a strategy to build its complementarities with UNDP on substantive, administrative, operational and resource-mobilization issues. UNCDF had made some important breakthroughs affecting policy. UNCDF and UNDP had supported Cambodia in drafting the local commune administration and management law, based on the local-level planning system that UNCDF had been piloting in several provinces. In Malawi, it had helped the Government to formulate policy on fiscal decentralization and to ensure that resources would be available to match decentralized functions. UNCDF support to start-up microfinance operations in 2000 had indirectly given credit access to 3,600 poor clients in Malawi in just six months. By using UNCDF guarantee mechanisms, a new project in Madagascar had enabled four networks of microfinance institutions to access $1.8 million in bank loans.

Chapter III

Humanitarian and special economic assistance

In 2000, the United Nations, through the Office for the Coordination of Humanitarian Affairs (OCHA), continued to coordinate humanitarian action in partnership with national and international actors to alleviate human suffering in disasters and emergencies, promote preparedness and prevention, and facilitate sustainable solutions. OCHA's advocacy efforts aimed to help guarantee the protection of civilians in armed conflict and marshal the resources necessary for swift and vigorous humanitarian responses worldwide. Consolidated inter-agency appeals were launched or ongoing for Angola, the Democratic Republic of the Congo, the Democratic People's Republic of Korea, the Great Lakes region and Central Africa, the Maluku islands of Indonesia, Sierra Leone, Somalia, South-Eastern Europe, the Sudan and Tajikistan. The total sought for the appeals amounted to $1,922 million, of which $1,139 million was received, meeting 59.2 per cent of the requirements. In addition, an inter-agency appeal covering Afghanistan for 2000, which sought $220.8 million, received contributions totalling $106.8 million, or 48.38 per cent of the requirements.

During the year, OCHA reported contributions for natural disasters totalling $460.7 million for 45 situations in 35 countries.

In December, the General Assembly welcomed the closure of the nuclear power station in Chernobyl, Ukraine.

Humanitarian assistance

Coordination

Humanitarian affairs segment
of the Economic and Social Council

During the humanitarian affairs segment of the Economic and Social Council, held from 19 to 21 and on 28 July under the theme "Strengthening the coordination of humanitarian response and the role of technology in mitigating the effects of natural disasters and other humanitarian emergencies, including conflicts, with particular reference to the displacement of persons arising therefrom" (**decision 2000/206** of 4 Feb-

ruary), the Council considered special economic, humanitarian and disaster relief assistance. It also had before it, in addition to reports on individual States, a May report of the Secretary-General on strengthening coordination of UN emergency humanitarian assistance [A/55/82-E/2000/61], submitted pursuant to requests by the General Assembly in resolutions 54/30 [YUN 1999, p. 865] and 54/233 [ibid., p. 826] and by the Council in resolution 1995/56 [YUN 1995, p. 927]. The report covered the coordination of humanitarian assistance in 1999-2000 and the coordinated response of the Inter-Agency Standing Committee (IASC) to humanitarian emergencies, especially activities carried out in support of the Council's agreed conclusions 1999/1 [YUN 1999, p. 824]. It examined strengthening the coordination of humanitarian response and the actual and potential role of technology in mitigating the effects of natural disasters and other humanitarian emergencies, including conflicts, with particular reference to the displacement of persons.

During the period under review, the United Nations took steps to ensure a more coherent approach among the humanitarian, political and human rights components of the international response to crises, as recommended in agreed conclusions 1999/1. The approach was two-tiered, involving a partnership between the Security Council and the Economic and Social Council, in addition to the search for consistency among the political, humanitarian, development and human rights bodies of the UN system. That consistency had been achieved in East Timor and the Kosovo province of the Federal Republic of Yugoslavia. Regarding the importance of linking relief aid to sustainable development, as emphasized in the agreed conclusions, an IASC reference group had identified areas affecting post-conflict reintegration and rehabilitation operations, such as inadequate national capacities, the political priorities of bilateral donors, unsynchronized transitional funding, the planning and programming of transitional activities by agencies and inadequate efforts to reach agreements based on common strategic objectives. In April and May, missions to Azerbaijan, Bosnia and Herzegovina, the Congo and Somalia identified solutions to problems associated with post-conflict transitions and relief-to-development linkages. Also related to post-conflict efforts was the growing use by the Security Council of peace-building support offices, such as those in Guinea-Bissau and Liberia. IASC worked to strengthen legal and physical protection for civilians in situations of armed conflict and sought to tackle constraints to the delivery of humanitarian assistance. Inter-agency initiatives were taken to promote the rights and welfare of children in conflict situations, and to ensure that older persons were not marginalized in relief operations.

Regarding natural disasters, an IASC reference group was created to review assessment capacities, funding mechanisms, information-sharing, logistics and telecommunications. Efforts were under way to assist Governments in strengthening their early warning systems. A comparative country index of vulnerability and disaster risk was being prepared as part of a United Nations Development Programme (UNDP) initiative to develop a global disaster vulnerability report. An inter-agency initiative aimed to facilitate inter-agency collaboration in disaster reduction issues. UN disaster assessment and coordination teams were strengthened by including more participants from countries in regions likely to be affected by disasters.

During the period under review, humanitarian agencies were confronted with new or resurgent challenges. Emerging challenges in natural disasters and complex emergency responses were increasingly met by Member States through the peacetime uses of military capabilities. The UN Office for the Coordination of Humanitarian Affairs (OCHA) convened the Fribourg Forum (Fribourg, Switzerland, 15-16 June), an intergovernmental conference on cooperation and coordination in crisis management in Europe. Humanitarian agencies were increasingly recognizing the need to implement psychosocial assistance programmes in emergencies, although such assistance was not systematically included in relief programmes.

The situation of internally displaced persons was a focus of attention in 1999-2000 in countries such as Afghanistan, Angola, Burundi, Colombia and the Democratic Republic of the Congo. The Emergency Relief Coordinator (ERC) and IASC members developed new policies, training programmes and guidance material for humanitarian workers, as well as practical action to improve the quality and coverage of field operations. Estimates suggested that the number of persons displaced might total as many as 60 million. Of those, about 11.5 million were refugees (see p. 1145). Estimates were that at least 17 million and up to 25 million persons were displaced within the borders of their own countries as a re-sult of armed conflict or generalized violence. Approximately 30 million more persons were displaced as a result of natural, environmental or technological disasters. The United Nations sought to address the needs of displaced populations in over 20 major crisis situations. Arrangements for the effective coordination of the international response were reviewed and new institutional arrangements were endorsed by IASC in April, based on the premise that Governments were primarily responsible for displaced persons. However, in cases where government action was lacking or insufficient, humanitarian agencies were urged to cooperate with national and local authorities or other actors to support and supplement efforts on behalf of displaced persons. The IASC policy reaffirmed the coordinating responsibility of the ERC as the inter-agency focal point for internally displaced persons at the Headquarters level. At the country level, the IASC policy vested the overall responsibility for the response to needs of the internally displaced in the resident/humanitarian coordinator.

The Secretary-General observed that the number and range of organizations involved in the humanitarian response to crises was increasing, that the needs of people affected by the emergencies were rising and that the coordination challenge was growing as a result. He called for a renewed commitment by Member States to multilateral leadership of the international humanitarian response, provision of adequate resources to support that leadership and approval of effective administrative procedures to strengthen the coordination of humanitarian assistance. The Secretary-General made recommendations to the General Assembly and the Economic and Social Council regarding the coordinated response to natural disasters and complex emergencies, the protection of civilians in armed conflict, the role of technology in mitigating and responding to natural disasters and other emergencies and the coordinated response to crises of displacement.

Annexed to the report was a summary of activities taken to implement agreed conclusions 1999/1 and information on lessons learned from the flood response in Mozambique (see p. 885).

On 28 July, the Economic and Social Council took note of the Secretary-General's report and asked him to report in 2001 on further progress (**decision 2000/243**).

GENERAL ASSEMBLY ACTION

On 14 December [meeting 85], the General Assembly adopted **resolution 55/164** [draft: A/55/L.54 & Add.1] without vote [agenda item 20 (a)].

Strengthening of the coordination of emergency humanitarian assistance of the United Nations

The General Assembly,

Recalling its resolution 46/182 of 19 December 1991 and the guiding principles contained in the annex thereto, other relevant General Assembly and Economic and Social Council resolutions and agreed conclusions of the Council of 1998 and 1999,

Taking note of the report of the Secretary-General,

Welcoming the progress made by the Emergency Relief Coordinator and the Office for the Coordination of Humanitarian Affairs of the Secretariat in strengthening the coordination of humanitarian assistance of the United Nations,

Noting the efforts made by the Emergency Relief Coordinator and the members of the Inter-Agency Standing Committee to implement fully the recommendations set forth in agreed conclusions 1998/1 and 1999/1 of the Council,

1. *Welcomes* the holding of the third humanitarian affairs segment of the Economic and Social Council during its substantive session of 2000;

2. *Invites* the Economic and Social Council to continue to consider ways to further enhance the humanitarian affairs segment of future sessions of the Council;

3. *Emphasizes* the importance of discussion of humanitarian policies and activities in the General Assembly and the Economic and Social Council;

4. *Calls upon* relevant organizations of the United Nations system, other relevant international organizations, Governments and non-governmental organizations to cooperate with the Secretary-General and the Emergency Relief Coordinator to ensure timely implementation of and follow-up to agreed conclusions 1998/1 and 1999/1;

5. *Requests* the Secretary-General to report to the General Assembly at its fifty-sixth session, through the 2001 substantive session of the Economic and Social Council, on progress made in strengthening the coordination of emergency humanitarian assistance of the United Nations, including the implementation of and follow-up to agreed conclusions 1998/1 and 1999/1.

Also on 14 December [meeting 85], the Assembly adopted **resolution 55/163** [draft: A/55/L.38/Rev.1 & Add.1] without vote [agenda item 20 *(a)*].

International cooperation on humanitarian assistance in the field of natural disasters, from relief to development

The General Assembly,

Reaffirming its resolution 46/182 of 19 December 1991, which contains in its annex the guiding principles for the strengthening of the coordination of emergency humanitarian assistance of the United Nations system, and its resolutions 52/12 B of 19 December 1997 and 54/219 and 54/233 of 22 December 1999, and recalling agreed conclusions 1999/1 of the Economic and Social Council and Council resolution 1999/63 of 30 July 1999,

Taking note of the report of the Secretary-General on strengthening of the coordination of emergency humanitarian assistance of the United Nations,

Recognizing the importance of the principles of neutrality, humanity and impartiality for the provision of humanitarian assistance,

Emphasizing that the affected State has the primary responsibility in the initiation, organization, coordination and implementation of humanitarian assistance within its territory, and in the facilitation of the work of humanitarian organizations in mitigating the consequences of natural disasters,

Emphasizing also the responsibility of all States to undertake disaster preparedness and mitigation efforts in order to minimize the impact of natural disasters,

Emphasizing further, in this regard, the importance of international cooperation in support of the efforts of the affected State in dealing with natural disasters in all its phases,

Stressing the need to optimize and disseminate the listings of organizations of the United Nations system and other relevant humanitarian and scientific organizations, as well as the need to develop further a directory of the specialized national, regional and international institutions and agencies working in the field of international response to natural disasters, together with an inventory of national capacities, in order to lay the foundation for an efficient and effective use of resources available and collaborative efforts,

Noting the establishment of the secretariat of the International Strategy for Disaster Reduction and the need to strengthen cooperation and coordination among all relevant bodies of the United Nations system, within their respective mandates, in dealing with all phases of natural disasters,

1. *Expresses deep concern* at the increasing number and scale of natural disasters, resulting in massive losses of life and property worldwide, in particular in vulnerable societies lacking adequate capacity to mitigate effectively the long-term negative social, economic and environmental consequences of natural disaster;

2. *Stresses* that humanitarian assistance for natural disasters should be provided in accordance with and with due respect for the guiding principles contained in the annex to resolution 46/182 and should be determined on the basis of the human dimension and needs arising out of the particular natural disasters;

3. *Calls upon* all States to adopt, where required, and to continue to implement effectively necessary legislative and other appropriate measures to mitigate the effects of natural disasters, inter alia, by disaster prevention, including building regulations and appropriate land use, as well as disaster preparedness and capacity-building in disaster response, and requests the international community in this context to continue to assist developing countries, where appropriate;

4. *Stresses,* in this context, the importance of strengthening international cooperation in the provision of humanitarian assistance for all phases of a disaster, from relief and mitigation to development, including through the provision of adequate resources;

5. *Recognizes* that economic growth and sustainable development contribute to improving the capacity of States to mitigate, respond to and prepare for natural disasters;

6. *Stresses* the need to strengthen efforts at all levels, including at the domestic level, to improve natural disaster awareness, prevention, preparedness and mitiga-

tion, including early warning systems, as well as international cooperation in response to emergencies, from relief to rehabilitation, reconstruction and development, bearing in mind the overall negative impact of natural disasters, the resulting humanitarian need and requests from affected countries, as appropriate;

7. *Recognizes* efforts by the Under-Secretary-General for Humanitarian Affairs and Emergency Relief Coordinator, the members of the Inter-Agency Standing Committee and other members of the United Nations system in promoting preparedness for response at the national, regional and international levels and in strengthening the mobilization and coordination of humanitarian assistance of the United Nations system in the field of natural disasters, and in this context welcomes the expansion of the United Nations disaster assessment and coordination teams to include experts from all areas of the world;

8. *Notes* that the transition phase after natural disasters is often excessively long and characterized by a number of gaps and that Governments, in cooperation with relief agencies, as appropriate, when planning for meeting immediate needs, should place these needs in the perspective of sustainable development whenever such an approach is possible, and in this context takes note of the work of the United Nations disaster assessment and coordination teams;

9. *Encourages* enhanced cooperation among Governments, in particular through the United Nations and regional organizations, in order to strengthen early warning and preparedness mechanisms for natural disasters;

10. *Encourages* Governments, in particular through their disaster management or response agencies, as appropriate, relevant organizations of the United Nations system and non-governmental organizations, to continue to cooperate with the Secretary-General and the Under-Secretary-General for Humanitarian Affairs and Emergency Relief Coordinator to maximize the effectiveness of the international response to natural disasters, based, inter alia, on humanitarian need, from relief to development, and also to maximize the effectiveness of disaster preparedness and mitigation efforts at all levels;

11. *Encourages* further cooperation between the United Nations system and regional organizations in order to increase the capacity of those organizations to respond to natural disasters;

12. *Encourages* States that have not signed or ratified the Tampere Convention on the Provision of Telecommunication Resources for Disaster Mitigation and Relief Operations, adopted at Tampere, Finland, on 18 June 1998, to consider doing so;

13. *Stresses* the need for partnership among Governments of the affected countries, relevant humanitarian organizations and specialized companies to promote training in, access to and use of technologies to strengthen preparedness for and response to natural disasters and to enhance the transfer of current technologies and corresponding know-how, in particular to developing countries, on concessional and preferential terms, as mutually agreed;

14. *Encourages* the further use of space-based and ground-based remote-sensing technologies for the prevention, mitigation and management of natural disasters, where appropriate;

15. *Also encourages* in such operations the sharing of geographical data, including remotely sensed images and geographic information system and global positioning system data among Governments, space agencies and relevant international humanitarian organizations, as appropriate, and also notes in this context the work being done by the Global Disaster Information Network;

16. *Further encourages* compatibility and complementarity of telecommunications and other technological equipment required in humanitarian and disaster relief operations;

17. *Stresses* the need to ensure close links, as set out in resolution 54/219, between disaster prevention activities and the improvement of natural disaster preparedness and response;

18. *Encourages* Governments in natural-disaster-prone countries to establish, with the support of the international community, in particular the donors, national spatial information infrastructures relating to natural disaster preparedness, early warning, response and mitigation, including the necessary training of personnel;

19. *Encourages* innovative efforts that link various phases of international assistance, from relief to development, such as the joint Disaster Response and Recovery Mission undertaken by the Office for the Coordination of Humanitarian Affairs of the Secretariat, the United Nations Development Programme, the United Nations Children's Fund and the World Health Organization and Pan American Health Organization in all countries affected by hurricane Mitch, and reiterates the need to ensure adequate assessment of and follow-up to these approaches, with a view to further developing and applying them, as appropriate, in other natural disasters;

20. *Requests* the Secretary-General, in consultation with relevant bodies of the United Nations system, to prepare recommendations on how to improve the potential of the United Nations to mitigate natural disasters including, in particular, through the development of an inventory of the existing capacities at the national, regional and international levels;

21. *Notes* the submission by the Secretary-General of his note on enhancing the functioning and utilization of the Central Emergency Revolving Fund, pursuant to the request contained in resolutions 54/95 of 8 December 1999 and 54/233 for concrete proposals for enhancing the functioning and utilization of the Fund and the invitation to consider more active use of the Fund for timely and adequate natural disaster response, and decides to consider the note comprehensively at its fifty-sixth session;

22. *Requests* the Secretary-General to continue to consider innovative mechanisms to improve the international response to natural disasters, inter alia, by addressing any geographical and sectoral imbalances in such a response where they exist, as well as more effective use of national emergency response agencies, taking into account their comparative advantages and specializations, as well as existing arrangements, and to report thereon to the General Assembly at its fifty-sixth session under the item entitled "Strengthening of the coordination of humanitarian and disaster relief assistance of the United Nations, including special economic assistance", with a view, inter alia, to contribut-

ing towards the comprehensive report on the implementation of the International Strategy for Disaster Reduction, to be submitted to the Assembly at that session under the item entitled "Environment and sustainable development".

On 23 December, the Assembly decided that the item on strengthening coordination of UN humanitarian and disaster relief assistance, including special economic assistance, would remain for consideration at its resumed fifty-fifth (2001) session (**decision 55/458**).

UN and other humanitarian personnel

In an October report [A/55/494], the Secretary-General proposed measures to improve the existing security arrangements for UN personnel, including the appointment of a UN Security Coordinator (see p. 1346). He noted that the growing number of complex emergencies required the United Nations to provide assistance and protection in situations of armed conflict. The United Nations and other humanitarian organizations, as well as Member States, had a collective responsibility towards those who delivered assistance in high-risk environments.

On 9 February, the Security Council urged States and non-State parties to the Convention on the Safety of United Nations and Associated Personnel (see p. 1345) to respect fully the status of UN and associated personnel, and humanitarian personnel, and underlined the importance of unhindered access to populations in need (**S/PRST/2000/4**).

On 19 December, the General Assembly, in **resolution 55/175**, called on all Governments and parties in complex humanitarian emergencies to cooperate fully with the United Nations and other humanitarian agencies and organizations and to ensure the safe and unhindered access of their personnel to affected civilians, including refugees and internally displaced persons.

OCHA review

In accordance with General Assembly resolution 54/244 [YUN 1999, p. 1274], the Secretary-General, in March [E/AC.51/2000/5], submitted to the Committee for Programme and Coordination (CPC) the review by the Office of Internal Oversight Services (OIOS) of the implementation of CPC's 1997 recommendations on the in-depth evaluation of the Department of Humanitarian Affairs [YUN 1997, p. 897], renamed the Office for the Coordination of Humanitarian Affairs by the Assembly in resolution 52/12 B [ibid., p. 1392]. The report concluded that support to IASC had been enhanced, progress had been made to address gaps in the response to emergencies, and the mecha-

nisms to plan and monitor emergency assistance had been improved. However, efforts were still needed to make IASC more decision-oriented, to ensure stronger field coordination, to maintain close dialogue with activities other than humanitarian assistance and to promote rehabilitation programmes; OCHA and IASC had taken measures to address the difficulties. The rapid response to emergencies was hindered by the absence of special UN administrative and financial rules and procedures, suited to emergency situations. In a related matter, the IASC Steering Committee, proposed in 1997 [YUN 1997, p. 898] to enhance a rapid-response capacity to humanitarian emergencies, had not been established. An effective procedure for sharing lessons learned was still needed.

OIOS recommended that, pursuant to Assembly resolution 46/182 [YUN 1991, p. 421] and Economic and Social Council agreed conclusions 1998/1 [YUN 1998, p. 841], special emergency rules and procedures should be developed by year's end. The IASC Steering Committee, or a similar mechanism, should be established by the end of 2000, and the ERC should propose to IASC a procedure to ensure effective follow-up on lessons learned and best practices. The Secretary-General concurred with the recommendations.

CPC stressed the need to finalize the development of special emergency rules and procedures, which should be approved by the relevant intergovernmental bodies [A/55/16].

On 7 April, the General Assembly in **resolution 54/257** took note of the OIOS report on the 1999 review of OCHA [YUN 1999, p. 828] and the comments of the Joint Inspection Unit thereon [ibid]. It requested that, in future, the appropriate legislative mandates relating to OCHA's work be included in OIOS reports.

Resource mobilization

Central Emergency Revolving Fund

Pursuant to General Assembly resolution 54/95 [YUN 1999, p. 825], the Secretary-General, in November [A/55/649], submitted proposals to enhance the functioning and utilization of the Central Emergency Revolving Fund (CERF) as a cash-flow mechanism for the initial phase of humanitarian emergencies. Noting that the decline in CERF use had resulted from the availability within operational organizations of their own emergency funds and other sources of financing for such start-up requirements, the Secretary-General proposed that the level of the Fund be reduced from $50 million to $40 million. Should that proposal receive approval, the concurrence of CERF-contributing Member States would be sought to transfer $10 million to a trust fund for lifesaving assistance needs, particularly in Africa, which had received low funding and little attention. To ensure more efficient utilization of the Fund, the Secretary-General proposed expanding CERF operational guidelines, which currently provided only for funding of the initial phase of emergencies, to include humanitarian assistance resulting from natural disasters, humanitarian assistance for protracted emergencies and security arrangements for UN and associated personnel.

In 2000, the Fund granted 30 advances, amounting to $38.7 million.

Consolidated appeals

According to a May report of the Secretary-General [A/55/82-E/2000/61], a review of the consolidated appeal process, which facilitated the capacity of the UN system to meet its emergency resource requirements, was carried out between November 1999 and April 2000 by humanitarian coordinators, IASC and donors. Recommendations focused on increasing flexibility, improving financial tracking and impact analysis, and advocacy and marketing of appeals. Donors, meeting in Montreux, Switzerland, in March, agreed that more emphasis should be placed on the consolidated appeal process as a continuous year-round process of inter-agency coordination, and suggested that key components should include joint assessments, monitoring and results-based evaluation.

Contributions to the consolidated appeals process had fallen from $1.96 billion in 1994 to $1.2 billion in 2000, and the share of requirements met had declined from 80 per cent in 1994 to 59 per cent in 2000. In 2000, inter-agency consolidated appeals covered Afghanistan, Angola, Burundi, the Congo, the Democratic People's Republic of Korea, the Democratic Republic of the Congo, the Great Lakes region and Central Africa, Indonesia (Maluku crisis), Sierra Leone, Somalia, South-Eastern Europe, the Sudan, Tajikistan, Uganda and the United Republic of Tanzania. For the first time, the cost of security requirements was included in the consolidated appeals. In 2000, a total of $8.5 million in security requirements for 10 countries/regions was included. It was envisaged that all future appeals would contain a comprehensive account of the security arrangements proposed and their cost.

Mine clearance

In a November report [A/55/542], submitted in response to General Assembly resolution 54/191 [YUN 1999, p. 830], the Secretary-General presented information on various organizations involved in mine action.

In support of the United Nations Mine Action Service and its humanitarian partners, OCHA continued to make use of its field presence in complex emergency situations to ensure that the humanitarian aspects of landmines were addressed. OCHA Internet sites—ReliefWeb and Integrated Regional Information Network—produced analytical reports and articles that often contained information on countries affected by landmines. In the consolidated appeals for 2000, over $51 million had been requested for mine-action activities in six countries or regions, in support of UN agencies and their implementing partners. As at 27 September, only about $23 million had been secured.

In view of the increase in the number of countries and areas requiring assistance and the consequent need to spread a finite amount of resources and donor funds over a problem that had grown markedly, the Secretary-General proposed that the Mine Action Service should be firmly established as a core function of the Organization, with resources provided through assessed contributions. He reviewed mine-action programmes in Afghanistan, Angola, Azerbaijan, Bosnia and Herzegovina, Cambodia, Chad, Croatia, Eritrea and Ethiopia, Guinea-Bissau, Iraq, the Kosovo province of the Federal Republic of Yugoslavia, the Lao People's Democratic Republic, Mozambique, Somalia, southern Lebanon, Sri Lanka, the Sudan, Thailand and Yemen.

Annexed to the report was a table listing donor contributions totalling $68.6 million, as at 18 October, to the Voluntary Trust Fund for Assistance in Mine Action, established by the Assembly in resolution 49/215 [YUN 1994, p. 173] as the Voluntary Trust Fund for Assistance in Mine Clearance and renamed by the Assembly in resolution 53/26 [YUN 1998, p. 844].

GENERAL ASSEMBLY ACTION

On 6 December [meeting 82], the General Assembly adopted **resolution 55/120** [draft: A/55/L.44/Rev.2 & Corr.1] without vote [agenda item 47].

Assistance in mine action
The General Assembly,

Recalling its resolutions 48/7 of 19 October 1993, 49/215 of 23 December 1994, 50/82 of 14 December 1995, 51/149 of 13 December 1996 and 52/173 of 18 December 1997, on assistance in mine clearance, and its resolutions 53/26 of 17 November 1998 and 54/191 of

17 December 1999, on assistance in mine action, all adopted without a vote,

Considering mine action to be an important component of United Nations humanitarian and development activities,

Reaffirming its deep concern at the tremendous humanitarian and development problems caused by the presence of mines and other unexploded devices that constitute an obstacle to the return of refugees and other displaced persons, to humanitarian aid operations and to reconstruction and economic development, as well as to the restoration of normal social conditions, and that have serious and lasting social and economic consequences for the populations of mine-affected countries,

Bearing in mind the serious threat that mines and other unexploded devices pose to the safety, health and lives of local civilian populations, as well as of personnel participating in humanitarian, peacekeeping and rehabilitation programmes and operations,

Reiterating its dismay at the high number of victims of mines, especially among civilian populations, including women and children, and recalling in this context Commission on Human Rights resolutions 1995/79 of 8 March 1995, 1996/85 of 24 April 1996, 1997/78 of 18 April 1997, 1998/76 of 22 April 1998, 1999/80 of 28 April 1999 and 2000/85 of 27 April 2000, on the rights of the child, and resolutions 1996/27 of 19 April 1996, 1998/31 of 17 April 1998, 2000/51 of 25 April 2000 and decision 1997/107 of 11 April 1997, on the human rights of persons with disabilities,

Deeply alarmed by the number of mines that continue to be laid each year, as well as the presence of a large number of mines and other unexploded devices as a result of armed conflicts, and thus convinced of the necessity and urgency of a significant increase in mine-clearance efforts by the international community with a view to eliminating the threat of landmines to civilians as soon as possible,

Noting the decisions taken at the First Annual Conference of the States Parties to Amended Protocol II to the Convention on Prohibitions or Restrictions on the Use of Certain Conventional Weapons Which May Be Deemed to Be Excessively Injurious or to Have Indiscriminate Effects, held at Geneva from 15 to 17 December 1999, particularly with respect to Protocol II to the Convention, and the inclusion in Amended Protocol II of a number of provisions of importance for mine-clearance operations, notably the requirement of detectability,

Noting also the entry into force of Amended Protocol II to the Convention on 3 December 1998,

Recalling that the States parties at the Review Conference of the States Parties to the Convention declared their commitment to keep the provisions of the Protocol under review in order to ensure that the concerns regarding the weapons it covers are addressed, and that they would encourage the efforts of the United Nations and other organizations to address all problems related to landmines,

Noting that the Convention on the Prohibition of the Use, Stockpiling, Production and Transfer of Anti-personnel Mines and on Their Destruction entered into force on 1 March 1999 and that the Convention has been signed or acceded to by one hundred and thirty-nine States and ratified by one hundred and nine

States, noting also the conclusions of the Second Meeting of the States Parties to the Convention, held at Geneva from 11 to 15 September 2000, taking note of the reaffirmed commitments that were made, among other things, to provide assistance for mine clearance and rehabilitation, the social and economic reintegration of mine victims and mine-awareness programmes, and taking note also of the work of the inter-sessional programme established by States parties to the Convention,

Stressing the need to convince mine-affected States to halt new deployments of anti-personnel mines in order to ensure the effectiveness and efficiency of mine-clearance operations,

Recognizing the important role that the international community, in particular States involved in the deployment of mines, can play in assisting mine clearance in mine-affected countries by providing necessary maps and information and appropriate technical and material assistance to remove or otherwise render ineffective existing minefields, mines and booby traps,

Concerned about the limited availability of safe and cost-effective mine-detection and mine-clearance equipment, as well as the need for effective global coordination in research and development to improve the relevant technology, and conscious of the need to promote further and more rapid progress in this field and to foster international technical cooperation to this end,

Concerned also about the limited availability of the technical, material and financial resources needed to meet the cost associated with mine-clearance activities in mine-affected countries,

Recognizing that, in addition to the primary role of States, the United Nations has an important role to play in the field of assistance in mine action,

Reaffirming the need to reinforce international cooperation in the area of mine action and to devote the necessary resources to that end,

Concerned about the critical financial situation of the Mine Action Service of the Department of Peacekeeping Operations of the Secretariat,

Welcoming the mine-action coordination centres already established under the auspices of the United Nations, as well as the creation of international trust funds for mine clearance and mine assistance,

Noting with satisfaction the inclusion in the mandates of several peacekeeping operations of provisions relating to mine-action work carried out under the direction of the Department of Peacekeeping Operations, in the context of such operations,

Commending the action already taken by the United Nations system, donor and recipient Governments, the International Committee of the Red Cross and non-governmental organizations to coordinate their efforts and seek solutions to the problems related to the presence of mines and other unexploded devices, as well as their assistance to victims of mines,

Commending also the role of the Secretary-General in increasing public awareness of the problem of landmines,

1. *Welcomes* the report of the Secretary-General on the activities of the United Nations in assistance in mine action;

2. *Calls*, in particular, for the continuation of the efforts of the United Nations, with the assistance of

States and institutions as appropriate, to foster the establishment of mine-action capacities in countries where mines constitute a serious threat to the safety, health and lives of the local population or an impediment to social and economic development efforts at the national and local levels, emphasizes the importance of developing national mine-action capacities, and urges all Member States, in particular those that have the capacity to do so, to assist mine-affected countries in the establishment and development of national capacities in mine clearance, mine awareness and victim assistance;

3. *Invites* Member States to develop national programmes, in cooperation with the relevant bodies of the United Nations system where appropriate, to promote awareness of landmines, especially among women and children;

4. *Expresses its appreciation* to Governments, regional organizations and other donors for their financial and in-kind contributions to mine action, including contributions for emergency operations and for national capacity-building programmes;

5. *Appeals* to Governments, regional organizations and other donors to continue their support to mine action through further contributions, including contributions through the Voluntary Trust Fund for Assistance in Mine Action, to allow for the timely delivery of mine-action assistance in emergency situations;

6. *Encourages* all relevant multilateral and national programmes and bodies to include, in coordination with the United Nations, activities related to mine action in their humanitarian, rehabilitation, reconstruction and development assistance activities, where appropriate, bearing in mind the need to ensure national ownership, sustainability and capacity-building;

7. *Stresses* the importance of international support for emergency assistance to victims of mines and for the care and rehabilitation, and social and economic reintegration, of the victims, and also stresses that such assistance should be integrated into broader public health and socio-economic strategies;

8. *Encourages* Governments, relevant United Nations bodies and other donors to take further action to promote gender- and age-appropriate mine-awareness programmes, victim assistance and child-centred rehabilitation, thereby reducing the number of child victims and relieving their plight;

9. *Emphasizes again* the important role of the United Nations in the effective coordination of mine-action activities, including those by regional organizations, and especially the role of the Mine Action Service of the Department of Peacekeeping Operations of the Secretariat on the basis of the policy on mine action and effective coordination developed by the Secretary-General, and stresses the need for the continuous assessment by the General Assembly of the United Nations in this regard;

10. *Emphasizes* in this regard the role of the Mine Action Service as the focal point for mine action within the United Nations system and its ongoing collaboration with and coordination of all the mine-related activities of the United Nations agencies, funds and programmes;

11. *Encourages* the Secretary-General to develop further a comprehensive mine-action strategy, taking into consideration the impact of the landmine problem on rehabilitation, reconstruction and development, with a view to ensuring the effectiveness of assistance in mine action by the United Nations, emphasizes in this respect the importance of further multisectoral assessments and surveys, notes in this regard the ongoing development by the United Nations of standards and certification guidelines for such surveys, and emphasizes the need for an inclusive process to be followed in the development of such standards and guidelines;

12. *Emphasizes* in this respect the importance of developing a comprehensive information management system for mine action, under the overall coordination of the Mine Action Service and with the support of the Geneva International Centre for Humanitarian Demining, in order to facilitate the setting of priorities and the coordination of field activities;

13. *Welcomes* recent approaches with regard to the establishment of mine-action coordination centres, encourages the further establishment of such centres, especially in emergency situations, and also encourages States to support the activities of mine-action coordination centres and trust funds established to coordinate assistance in mine action under the auspices of the Mine Action Service;

14. *Encourages*, whenever appropriate, the use of the United Nations Office for Project Services by the United Nations, including in peacekeeping operations, in order to ensure the unity and continuity of implementation required for integrated mine-action programmes;

15. *Urges* Member States and regional, governmental and non-governmental organizations and foundations to continue to extend full assistance and cooperation to the Secretary-General and, in particular, to provide him with information and data, as well as other appropriate resources that could be useful in strengthening the coordination role of the United Nations in mine action, in particular in the fields of mine awareness, training, surveying, detection and clearance, scientific research on mine-detection and mine-clearance technology and information on and distribution of medical equipment and supplies;

16. *Emphasizes* in this regard the importance of recording the location of mines, of retaining all such records and making them available to concerned parties upon cessation of hostilities, and welcomes the strengthening of the relevant provisions in international law;

17. *Calls upon* Member States, especially those that have the capacity to do so, to provide the necessary information and technical, financial and material assistance, as appropriate, and to locate, remove, destroy or otherwise render ineffective minefields, mines, booby traps and other devices in accordance with international law, as soon as possible;

18. *Urges* Member States and regional, intergovernmental and non-governmental organizations and foundations that have the ability to do so to provide, as appropriate, technological assistance to mine-affected countries and to promote scientific research and development on humanitarian mine-action techniques and technology so that mine-action activities may be carried out more effectively at lower costs and through safer means and to promote international collaboration in this regard;

19. *Encourages* Member States and regional, inter-governmental and non-governmental organizations and foundations to continue to support ongoing activities to promote appropriate technology, as well as international operational and safety standards for humanitarian mine-action activities, and in this context welcomes the initiation of the revision of international mine-clearance standards and the development of guidelines for the use of mine-detection dogs and mechanical mine-clearance equipment, as well as the development of an international test and evaluation programme;

20. *Requests* the Secretary-General to submit to the General Assembly at its fifty-sixth session a comprehensive report on the United Nations mine-action policy, including the progress achieved on relevant issues outlined both in his previous reports to the Assembly on assistance in mine clearance and mine action and in the present resolution, as well as the progress made by the International Committee of the Red Cross and other international and regional organizations as well as national programmes, and on the operation of the Voluntary Trust Fund for Assistance in Mine Action and other mine-action programmes;

21. *Invites* the Secretary-General to study how to secure a more sound financial basis for the Mine Action Service and to present options to this effect to the General Assembly;

22. *Decides* to include in the provisional agenda of its fifty-sixth session the item entitled "Assistance in mine action".

New international humanitarian order

The Secretary-General, in a November report on the promotion of a new international humanitarian order [A/55/545], stated that, pursuant to General Assembly resolution 53/124 [YUN 1998, p. 846], he had asked States for information and expertise on humanitarian problems of special concern to them, in order to identify opportunities for future action. He suggested that in their replies they might wish to describe efforts they had taken to promote compliance with international humanitarian and human rights law and to confront situations in which those laws were violated. The report contained the reply of Bangladesh.

The Secretary-General had asked the Independent Bureau for Humanitarian Issues to conduct an in-depth study of the implementation of international humanitarian and human rights law at the field level in crisis situations, in consultation with OCHA. It was anticipated that the findings of the study would constitute the starting point for other initiatives to promote a culture of compliance. The Bureau appreciated the Secretary-General's efforts to make the discussion of the agenda item on a new international humanitarian order more issue-specific and suggested the creation of an expert group to analyse the replies of States and encourage those that had not responded to do so.

The Secretary-General suggested that the Assembly should make more effective use of the agenda item and focus on ways to promote a culture of compliance with international humanitarian and human rights law.

GENERAL ASSEMBLY ACTION

On 4 December [meeting 81], the General Assembly, on the recommendation of the Third (Social, Humanitarian and Cultural) Committee [A/55/597], adopted **resolution 55/73** without vote [agenda item 109].

New international humanitarian order

The General Assembly,

Recalling its resolution 53/124 of 9 December 1998 and other pertinent resolutions relating to the promotion of the new international humanitarian order and international cooperation in the humanitarian field,

Taking note of the report of the Secretary-General on the new international humanitarian order and his previous reports containing comments and views of Governments as well as of intergovernmental and non-governmental organizations,

Recalling its resolution 46/182 of 19 December 1991, pertaining to humanitarian assistance, and the annex thereto,

Bearing in mind the reports of the Secretary-General submitted in the context of the Millennium Summit of the United Nations,

Noting the importance of adherence to internationally accepted norms and principles as well as the need to promote, as required, national and international legislation to meet actual and potential humanitarian challenges,

Noting with deep concern the continuing trend of systematic violations of refugee law, international humanitarian law and human rights instruments, which can lead ultimately to emergency situations,

Noting with appreciation the increased attention of the Inter-Agency Standing Committee to addressing the security needs of personnel responding to these emergencies,

Noting with appreciation also the emphasis placed by the Secretary-General on promoting strict adherence to refugee law, international humanitarian law and human rights instruments,

Recognizing that the ultimate aim of all humanitarian assistance should be to save human lives and facilitate the transition, at the appropriate time, to rehabilitation and reconstruction and to facilitate local capacity-building and institution-building, as necessary, in the affected countries and regions,

Recognizing, in addition, the urgent need further to strengthen international cooperation and coordination in the humanitarian field,

1. *Notes* the Secretary-General's continuing support of efforts to promote a new international humanitarian order;

2. *Invites* the Secretary-General to continue to promote strict adherence to refugee law, international humanitarian law, human rights instruments and internationally accepted norms and principles in situations of armed conflict and complex emergencies;

3. *Urges* Governments, intergovernmental and non-governmental organizations and others concerned to extend cooperation and provide support to the efforts of the Secretary-General, inter alia, through the relevant United Nations agencies and organizational mechanisms set up to address the assistance and protection needs of victims of complex emergencies as well as the safety and security of United Nations and other humanitarian workers;

4. *Calls upon* all Governments and parties involved in complex humanitarian emergencies to ensure the safe and unhindered access of humanitarian personnel so as to allow them to perform efficiently their task of assisting the affected civilian populations;

5. *Invites* Governments to make available to the Secretary-General, on a voluntary basis, information and expertise on humanitarian problems of concern to them, in order to identify opportunities for future action;

6. *Invites* the Independent Bureau for Humanitarian Issues to continue and to strengthen further its activities, including cooperation with the Office for the Coordination of Humanitarian Affairs of the Secretariat and the other relevant bodies of the United Nations system;

7. *Requests* the Secretary-General to remain in contact with Governments and the relevant international and non-governmental organizations and to report to the General Assembly at its fifty-seventh session on the progress made concerning the promotion of a new international humanitarian order and compliance with refugee law, international humanitarian law and human rights instruments in armed conflicts and emergency situations.

Humanitarian aspects of peace and security

On 9 March [meeting 4110], following consultations among members, the Security Council President made statement **S/PRST/2000/7** on behalf of the Council:

The Security Council has considered the humanitarian aspects of issues before the Council.

The Council recalls its primary responsibility under the Charter of the United Nations for the maintenance of international peace and security, and reaffirms the purposes and principles of the Charter. The Council reaffirms also its commitment to the principles of the political independence, sovereign equality and territorial integrity of all States.

The Council recognizes the importance of the humanitarian dimension to the maintenance of international peace and security and to its consideration of humanitarian issues relating to the protection of all civilians and other non-combatants in situations of armed conflict. The Council recognizes that humanitarian crises can be both causes and consequences of conflicts and that they can affect the Council's efforts to prevent and end conflicts, and to deal with other threats to international peace and security.

The Council affirms that timely consideration of the following humanitarian issues contributes to preventing the escalation of conflicts and to maintaining international peace and security: access for United Nations and associated personnel, other humanitarian personnel and humanitarian supplies to the war-affected civilians; humanitarian components in peace agreements and peacekeeping operations; coordination between the Council and the relevant United Nations organs and agencies and regional bodies; and resource constraints.

The Council reaffirms its concern for the well-being and rights of war-affected civilians, and reiterates its call to all parties to a conflict to ensure safe and unimpeded access by humanitarian personnel to such civilians, in accordance with international law. The Council recognizes that the cooperation of all parties concerned is vital for effectiveness and safety in providing humanitarian assistance. In this regard, the Council reiterates its call for combatants to ensure the safety, security and freedom of movement of United Nations and associated personnel and humanitarian personnel. The Council stresses the importance of providing assistance to all those in need, with particular emphasis on women and children and other vulnerable groups affected by armed conflict, in accordance with the principle of impartiality.

The Council notes that full and timely support for humanitarian components can be critical in ensuring and enhancing the sustainability of any peace agreement and post-conflict peace-building. It emphasizes the importance of incorporating humanitarian elements in peace negotiations and agreements, including the issue of prisoners of war, detainees and missing persons and others protected by international humanitarian law. The Council invites the Secretary-General to encourage the early consideration of such humanitarian elements in peace negotiations sponsored or supported by the United Nations, as appropriate. In cases of peace negotiations sponsored or supported directly by Member States, the Council calls upon Member States to draw, as appropriate, upon the capacity of United Nations funds, programmes and specialized agencies as well as other relevant international humanitarian organizations and regional bodies.

The Council notes also that in some instances the integration of humanitarian components into peacekeeping operations would contribute effectively to the fulfilment of their mandate. In this regard, the Council notes the importance of adequate training for peacekeeping personnel in international humanitarian law and human rights and with regard to the special situations of women and children as well as vulnerable population groups. The Council notes with appreciation the inclusion of personnel to handle child protection issues in some recent peacekeeping operations, and encourages the inclusion of such personnel in future operations, particularly in the context of demobilization and reintegration of child soldiers and where there are a large number of displaced and other war-affected children. The Council welcomes and encourages efforts by the United Nations to sensitize peacekeeping personnel in the prevention and control of HIV/AIDS and other communicable diseases.

The Council underlines the importance of effective coordination among relevant United Nations organs and agencies, regional bodies, other intergovernmental and international organizations and other humanitarian actors in the field in situations of ongoing conflict and peace-building through, inter alia, the development of strategic frameworks, and expresses its willingness to consider ways to improve such coordination. In this regard, the Council notes the need for further improvement in communication, information flow and coordination between the peacekeeping, humanitarian and development aspects of United Nations action.

The Council recognizes the role played by international humanitarian organizations and non-governmental organizations in providing humanitarian assistance and alleviating the impact of humanitarian crises, and further recognizes the specific mandate of the International Committee of the Red Cross in this regard. It emphasizes that it is important for these organizations to uphold the principles of neutrality, impartiality and humanity in their humanitarian activities.

The Council notes with concern that inadequate financial support can undermine efforts to address human suffering in certain contexts. The Council recognizes the need for appropriate financial support for humanitarian activities, and calls for adequate funding of humanitarian activities, bilateral or otherwise, in particular in support of multilateral efforts. The Council notes the importance of early engagement and dispersal of funds from the international financial institutions. The Council notes also with satisfaction that its previous statements calling for full support for the United Nations consolidated appeals have had a positive impact, and expresses its willingness to continue to encourage a generous response to such appeals.

The Council encourages the Secretary-General to continue to include the humanitarian situation in his regular briefing to the Council on countries under review, as well as the funding status of the United Nations consolidated appeals, where appropriate. It further requests the Secretary-General to ensure that his regular country reports continue to include a substantive, analytical section on humanitarian issues and their impact on international efforts to implement activities mandated by the United Nations.

The Council will remain seized of the matter.

Humanitarian activities

Africa

Angola

The UN consolidated inter-agency appeal for Angola, launched in 2000, which initially sought $258.5 million for the period January to December 2000, was revised to $262 million in July. The donor community had covered 53.9 per cent, or $141.5 million, of the revised appeal.

Progress was made in 2000 in stabilizing the situation of the people of Angola. The number of newly displaced persons dropped from 1 mil-

lion in 1999 to 338,000 in 2000. Access to populations in need increased during the year, with the opening of at least six major road corridors. The extension of State administration to new areas also created opportunities for agencies to reach previously inaccessible groups, and opened the possibility of medium-scale resettlement and return. However, despite improved access, at the end of October an estimated 60 per cent of the areas hosting displaced populations were still without a humanitarian presence. Close to 10 per cent of the population (1.3 million) benefited from food assistance. The humanitarian operation was extensive, given the acute vulnerability among a large number of the population. About 4 million people, close to 25 per cent of the population, received some form of assistance during the year. A major development was the Government's increased commitment to humanitarian sectors through its national programme for emergency humanitarian assistance. In 2000, OCHA launched a UN consolidated inter-agency appeal covering January to December 2001 for a total of $202 million.

Comoros

Pursuant to General Assembly resolution 53/1 F [YUN 1998, p. 847], the Secretary-General, in a June report [A/55/92], assessed the efforts of the international community to assist the Comoros to achieve national reconstruction and sustainable development. The country was effectively divided in two, as the island of Anjouan continued to be administered and to function independently. The Secretary-General observed that the difficult political and economic context inherent in the separatist crisis that had undermined the Comoros since 1997, coupled with insufficient sources of financing and the political impasse, was helping to further tarnish the country's image. Thus, it had had difficulty getting its partners to support the choices it had made regarding development and public finance management, and convincing them of its current and future viability. Those factors, compounded by the international community's disapproval following the military coup d'état of April 1999 [YUN 1999, p. 189], had prompted most of the country's development partners—which traditionally provided more than 80 per cent of all official development assistance (ODA)—to withdraw or adopt a wait-and-see attitude. Relegation of the Antananarivo agreement—a proposal to establish the Union of the Comoros within which each island would enjoy broad autonomy in respect of decision-making and administration—to the back burner caused the country to miss the opportunity to hold a donors' round table. The political context had been marked by institutional instability and had not facilitated the introduction of a suitable framework for consultation to mobilize donors and maintain assistance at a level that would make it possible to attain the objectives of Assembly resolution 53/1 F. The current situation of the Comoros still justified retaining the resolution's content. The report suggested that the resolution should be referred to the Economic and Social Council with a view to initiating a reconstruction and rehabilitation programme.

Eritrea

In January, a UN country team appeal requested $42.8 million for January to December 2000 to assist war-affected people and drought victims in Eritrea. As the response to the appeal was modest, with only $16.8 million, or 39.2 per cent, funded by 1 July, and more than 1 million Eritreans had been displaced following the outbreak of a major round of fighting on 12 May, the appeal was revised to $87.4 million to cover July to December. As at 31 December, $58.1 million, or 66.5 per cent, of the requirements were met. In June, the Eritrean Relief and Refugee Commission issued an appeal for emergency humanitarian assistance to war and drought victims for a total of $183 million. The UN emergency appeal for the drought in the Horn of Africa sought $392.6 million, including $20 million earmarked for Eritrea (see p. 884).

Until May 2000, the war between Eritrea and Ethiopia was contained in Eritrea to a limited area, with some 270,000 internally displaced persons from the border areas. After 12 May, when hostilities resumed, there was a sudden and massive increase in the population of internally displaced persons, including evacuations from large regions in Eritrea that had contributed to 75 per cent of the country's agricultural production and had hosted 48 per cent of the total population. The Agreement on Cessation of Hostilities (see p. 173) of 18 June halted more than a month-long fierce fighting and triggered the first return movements of civilians to areas that were previously insecure and/or inaccessible. By the second half of the year, the most critical emergency phase had passed. On 12 December, the Algiers Peace Agreement (see p. 180) ended the two-year border war, which, coupled with the deployment of a UN peacekeeping force, improved prospects for return movements by internally displaced persons and refugees displaced from the border areas. At the same time, more than 200,000 internally displaced persons remained in camps and continued to require a broad range of humanitarian assistance, including food and non-food aid. Relief items and emergency services were required for internally displaced persons living outside camps until conditions allowed their return. Compounding the humanitarian implications of war was the drought that affected much of the Horn of Africa (see p. 884), making recovery difficult. OCHA launched a consolidated inter-agency appeal for a total of $157.5 million to cover January to December 2001.

Ethiopia

During 2000, three appeals were launched for Ethiopia by the UN country team. In January, an omnibus appeal covering January to December 2000 totalled $55.9 million, of which $51.5 million was received as at 31 December; in June, an updated drought appeal covered June to December, for a total of $190 million, of which $101.5 million was received; and an updated appeal for rehabilitation and recovery programmes for internally displaced persons was released in August for the period September to December amounting to $30.5 million, of which $4.6 million was received. In January, Ethiopia's Federal Disaster Prevention and Preparedness Commission launched its annual relief appeal, which sought $163.4 million. On 14 November, the Commission issued an appeal for relief assistance requirements for internally displaced people and deportees, amounting to $13.6 million.

As a result of poor rains and war in Ethiopia, the number of people requiring emergency assistance by July exceeded 10 million, or 15.7 per cent of the population. With better rains in pastoral areas and the highlands and an end to hostilities with Eritrea, there were signs of improvement. However, large numbers of people, including some 350,000 displaced by the conflict, continued to face an uncertain future. Although a major relief effort and fortuitous rains averted a looming famine, full recovery was expected to be a long process, especially in the pastoral areas where livestock herds had been devastated by drought. Given the vast needs in Ethiopia in relation to the region and in accordance with the recommendations of the Special Envoy for the Drought in the Greater Horn of Africa, the Office of the Regional Humanitarian Coordinator was established in Addis Ababa to help coordinate Ethiopia-specific responses, as well as cross-border issues. Following the signing of the Algiers Peace Agreement on 12 December (see p. 180), approval was given for a $400 million World Bank–supported emergency recovery programme. A UN consolidated inter-agency appeal for Ethiopia to cover January to December 2001 sought $203.3 million.

Great Lakes region and Central Africa

The UN consolidated inter-agency appeal for the Great Lakes region and Central Africa covering January to December 2000 required $292.1 million for the regional appeal, inclusive of all World Food Programme (WFP) requirements for country-specific appeals, and $129.9 million for Burundi, the Congo, the Democratic Republic of the Congo (DRC), Uganda and the United Republic of Tanzania. There was no appeal for Rwanda in 2000. Of the total requirement, amounting to $422 million, $243.9 million, or 57.8 per cent, was received as at October.

The humanitarian situation in the Great Lakes region and Central Africa continued to deteriorate and remained challenging for humanitarian organizations during 2000. Those most affected were caught up in the cycle of displacement, malnutrition, disease and insecurity. The lack of success in brokering peace and the ongoing conflicts in Burundi, the DRC and Uganda resulted in increased numbers of affected populations, internally, cross-border and outside the region. A UN consolidated inter-agency appeal covering January to December 2001 totalled $17.9 million.

Burundi

Despite progress on the political front, armed conflict continued to contribute to the deterioration of the humanitarian situation in Burundi throughout 2000. While the number of displaced persons decreased significantly, they remained as vulnerable as ever and had become more difficult to access because of the insecurity situation. The UN system was undertaking a national survey of internally displaced persons to assess their situation, basic needs and future plans. In November, OCHA launched a UN consolidated inter-agency appeal covering January to December 2001 for a total of $102 million.

Congo (Republic of the)

The UN consolidated inter-agency appeal for the Republic of the Congo, launched in 1999, which sought $17.1 million for January to December 2000, was revised to $28 million, of which $3.6 million, or 17.2 per cent, had been received.

Following the 1999 ceasefire, population return had accelerated and humanitarian access improved, including areas under the control of non-State actors. Support was required for communities and their returning members in their efforts to restore stability and security. The humanitarian community in the country had agreed on a series of priorities, including continuation of emergency relief combined with reintegration and rehabilitation, attaining full access to war-affected populations, ensuring that assistance met requirements in the northern regions of the country, and support for the peace process (see p. 120).

Uganda

In 2000, conflict and suffering continued in Uganda. The number of the affected population doubled from 690,000 to 1.2 million. Regional conflict and internal strife escalated, with the majority of refugees, displaced persons and drought victims lacking access to potable water, food, land, shelter, income and other basic rights. The consolidated inter-agency appeal for 2000 totalled $27.4 million, excluding WFP's budget of $39.6 million for Uganda, which was included in the Great Lakes regional appeal. By October, $16.3 million, or 59.5 per cent of the requirement, had been realized. Humanitarian activities were focused on fulfilling short-term relief needs at the expense of recovery and rehabilitation because of funding shortfalls.

In November, OCHA issued a UN consolidated inter-agency appeal seeking $78.7 million for January to December 2001.

United Republic of Tanzania

As a neighbour to conflicts and instability, the United Republic of Tanzania remained one of Africa's largest refugee-hosting countries. Ongoing civil and political unrest in Burundi and the DRC had hindered voluntary repatriation, causing increased refugee flows into Tanzania, with an estimated 484,000 refugee population as at the end of October. The Tanzanian population in the refugee-affected districts was about 1.2 million, and refugees thus comprised over one third of the districts' population. The long-term hosting of refugees had strained and negatively impacted the infrastructures and services available to the indigenous population, as well as to refugees. Other factors that affected the country, such as HIV/AIDS, malaria and natural disasters, had had a magnified impact on refugee-hosting regions.

In November, OCHA launched a UN consolidated inter-agency appeal totalling $110.4 million for January to December 2001.

Mozambique

In August [A/55/317], the Secretary-General reported on the economic and political recovery of Mozambique, following the 1992 General Peace Agreement [YUN 1992, p. 193]. Although recovery had been remarkable, the country's economy remained extremely fragile. Life had improved since the war, partly owing to favourable weather that contributed to increased agricultural production, but infrastructure remained weak. In

February, flooding set back farmers, fishermen and other small businesses in the southern part of the country (see p. 885). Mozambique continued to need high levels of international assistance to complete reconstruction and to end acute poverty. The Secretary-General reviewed political and economic developments, as well as action taken to reduce poverty and combat sexually transmitted diseases and HIV/AIDS. He presented an overview of UN system initiatives and updated activities regarding education, health, water and sanitation, governance, HIV/AIDS, gender issues, environment and natural resource management, disaster management, food security and demining.

GENERAL ASSEMBLY ACTION

On 14 December [meeting 85], the General Assembly adopted **resolution 55/167** [draft: A/55/L.53 & Add.1] without vote [agenda item 20 *(b)*].

Assistance to Mozambique

The General Assembly,

Recalling Security Council resolution 386(1976) of 17 March 1976,

Recalling also its relevant resolutions, in particular resolution 45/227 of 21 December 1990, 47/42 of 9 December 1992, 49/21 D of 20 December 1994, 51/30 D of 5 December 1996 and 53/1 G of 16 November 1998, in which it urged the international community to respond effectively and generously to the call for assistance to Mozambique,

Reaffirming the principles for humanitarian assistance contained in the annex to its resolution 46/182 of 19 December 1991,

Recalling its resolutions 48/7 of 19 October 1993, 49/215 of 23 December 1994, 50/82 of 14 December 1995, 51/149 of 13 December 1996 and 52/173 of 18 December 1997 on assistance in mine clearance, and stressing the need to foster the establishment of national mine-clearance capacity with a view to enabling the Government of Mozambique to deal more effectively with the adverse effects of those weapons within the framework of the efforts for national reconstruction,

Recalling also its resolution 54/96 L of 10 March 2000 on assistance to Mozambique following the devastating floods,

Deeply concerned at the unprecedented floods in Mozambique, which have resulted in tragic loss of human lives and extensive destruction of property and infrastructure,

Deeply concerned also at the impact of the disaster on the economic, social and humanitarian situation in Mozambique,

Recognizing that natural disasters constitute one of the major problems for the development of Mozambique,

Aware that, to prevent and manage natural disasters, strategies at local, national and regional levels are required, in addition to international assistance,

Bearing in mind the Paris Declaration and the Programme of Action for the Least Developed Countries for the 1990s, adopted by the Second United Nations Conference on the Least Developed Countries on 14

September 1990, and the mutual commitment entered into on that occasion,

Noting with appreciation the mobilization and allocation of resources by States, relevant organizations of the United Nations system and intergovernmental and non-governmental organizations to assist national efforts,

Noting with satisfaction the full support by the international community of the post-emergency reconstruction programme presented by the Government of Mozambique at the International Reconstruction Conference for Mozambique, organized by the United Nations Development Programme and the Government of Mozambique, which was held in Rome on 3 and 4 May 2000,

Having considered the report of the Secretary-General on assistance to Mozambique, and his report on assistance to Mozambique following the devastating floods,

1. *Takes note* of the report of the Secretary-General on assistance to Mozambique and his report on assistance to Mozambique following the devastating floods;

2. *Welcomes* the assistance rendered to Mozambique by various States, relevant organizations of the United Nations system, intergovernmental and non-governmental organizations and private individuals and groups to assist national development efforts, and their full support for the post-emergency reconstruction programme presented by the Government of Mozambique at the International Reconstruction Conference for Mozambique;

3. *Also welcomes* the progress made in the consolidation of a lasting peace and tranquillity, the enhancement of democracy and the promotion of national reconciliation in Mozambique;

4. *Notes* the importance of the International Reconstruction Conference for funding for the reconstruction programme, welcomes the pledges made by the development partners for the post-emergency programme, expresses its gratitude to the development partners that have already disbursed the pledged funds, and urges others to speed up the process;

5. *Requests* the Secretary-General to make all necessary arrangements to continue to mobilize and coordinate, with a view to supporting the efforts of the Government of Mozambique:

(a) Humanitarian assistance from the specialized agencies, organizations and bodies of the United Nations system;

(b) International assistance for the national reconstruction and development of Mozambique;

6. *Also requests* the Secretary-General to report to it, for consideration at its fifty-seventh session, under the item on strengthening of the coordination of humanitarian and disaster relief assistance of the United Nations, including special economic assistance, through the Economic and Social Council at the humanitarian segment of its substantive session in 2002, on the implementation of the present resolution.

Somalia

In a September report [A/55/415], submitted pursuant to General Assembly resolution 54/96 D [YUN 1999, p. 834], the Secretary-General reviewed the current situation in Somalia and the assistance provided to the country by the United Nations and its partners from August 1999 to July 2000. The Secretary-General reported that two countervailing forces characterized Somalia. On the one hand, commitment was shown to re-establishing the rule of law and promoting responsible public administration, while, on the other, there remained a lack of order and a potential for renewed violence, particularly in central and southern Somalia. It was essential to reduce malnutrition in southern Somalia through further emergency response activities. Emergency prevention activities would be enhanced, essential educational services would be extended and joint planning, implementation and monitoring of programmes with local authorities would be increased. The Secretary-General described three scenarios prepared by UN agencies to prioritize and coordinate action in preparation for possible crop failure or renewed conflict.

The UN consolidated inter-agency appeal, launched in November 1999, which initially solicited $124.3 million, was revised to $50.6 million in July. Of that amount, $30.2 million, or 71.5 per cent of requirements, was received. OCHA launched a UN consolidated inter-agency appeal for $129.6 million to cover the period January to December 2001.

Communication. The Sudan transmitted to the Secretary-General a resolution adopted by the Eighth Summit of Heads of State and Government of the Intergovernmental Authority on Development (Khartoum, 23 November) [A/55/772-S/2001/120] in support of assistance to Somalia for the realization of peace and national reconciliation and unity.

GENERAL ASSEMBLY ACTION

On 14 December [meeting 85], the General Assembly adopted **resolution 55/168** [draft: A/55/L.55/Rev.1 & Add.1] without vote [agenda item 20 *(b)*].

Assistance for humanitarian relief and the economic and social rehabilitation of Somalia

The General Assembly,

Recalling its resolutions 43/206 of 20 December 1988, 44/178 of 19 December 1989, 45/229 of 21 December 1990, 46/176 of 19 December 1991, 47/160 of 18 December 1992, 48/201 of 21 December 1993, 49/21 L of 20 December 1994, 50/58 G of 20 December 1995, 51/30 G of 13 December 1996, 52/169 L of 16 December 1997, 53/1 M of 8 December 1998 and 54/96 D of 8 December 1999 as well as the resolutions and decisions of the Economic and Social Council on emergency assistance to Somalia,

Recalling also Security Council resolution 733(1992) of 23 January 1992 and all subsequent relevant resolutions, in which the Council, inter alia, urged all parties, movements and factions in Somalia to facilitate the efforts of the United Nations, the specialized agencies and humanitarian organizations to provide urgent humanitarian assistance to the affected population in So-

malia, and reiterated the call for the full respect of the security and safety of the personnel of those organizations and guarantee of their complete freedom of movement in and around Mogadishu and other parts of Somalia,

Recalling further the statement by the President of the Security Council of 29 June 2000 in which, inter alia, the Security Council expressed its full support for the efforts exerted by the Intergovernmental Authority on Development to find a political solution to the situation in Somalia, underlined the importance of the widest participation of the representatives of all parts of Somali society, strongly urged representatives of all social and political forces of Somali society to participate actively, urged the warlords and faction leaders to desist from obstructing and undermining efforts to achieve peace, and also urged all States to stop providing those individuals with the means to carry on their destructive activities,

Noting the cooperation between the United Nations, the Organization of African Unity, the League of Arab States, the European Union, the Organization of the Islamic Conference, the countries members of the Intergovernmental Authority on Development and its Partners Forum, the Movement of Non-Aligned Countries and others in their efforts to resolve the humanitarian, security and political crisis in Somalia,

Noting with appreciation the continued efforts made by the Secretary-General to assist the Somali people in their efforts to promote peace, stability and national reconciliation,

Commending the initiative of the President of the Republic of Djibouti aiming at restoring peace and stability in Somalia, and noting with appreciation the efforts of the Government and people of Djibouti in hosting and facilitating the Somalia National Peace Conference, held in Arta, Republic of Djibouti,

Welcoming the outcome of the Arta peace process, led by Djibouti and sponsored by the Intergovernmental Authority on Development, which provides for the establishment of a transitional national parliament and the formation of a transitional national government,

Noting with appreciation that the mandate provided in the three-year transitional national charter emphasizes priorities, including reconciliation, demobilization of armed militia, restitution of properties to their lawful owners, holding of a national census, formulation of a new constitution, democratization, rehabilitation, recovery and reconstruction,

Welcoming the efforts of the transitional Government of Somalia to promote national reconciliation within Somalia, recognizing that progress has been achieved in some regions in re-establishing economic and administrative stability and encouraging the peaceful cooperation of all political groups with the new transitional Government towards this end,

Noting with concern that the lack of effective civil institutions in Somalia continues to impede sustained comprehensive development and that, while the environment has become more conducive to some reconstruction and development-oriented work in certain parts of the country, the humanitarian and security situation has remained fragile in other parts,

Reaffirming its support for the joint strategy for targeted assistance of the United Nations system that is focused on the rehabilitation and reconstruction of infrastructure and on sustainable community-based activities, as well as for the importance it attaches to the need for effective coordination and cooperation among the United Nations agencies and their partners,

Taking note of the report of the Secretary-General,

Deeply appreciative of the humanitarian assistance and rehabilitation support rendered by a number of States and relevant organizations to alleviate the hardship and suffering of the affected Somali population,

Recognizing that, while the humanitarian situation remains fragile in some parts of Somalia, there is a need to continue the ongoing rehabilitation and reconstruction process alongside the national reconciliation process, without prejudice to the provision of emergency relief assistance wherever and whenever required, as security allows,

Noting with appreciation that the prospects for humanitarian, rehabilitation and development activities have been more favourable in some parts of the country, owing to the formation of stronger administrative structures, the commitment shown to re-establishing the rule of law in general, and the leadership shown by some regional authorities and by civil society groups in attempting to establish an inclusive alternative to the faction-ridden past of Somalia,

Noting with appreciation also the efforts of the United Nations system aimed at working directly with Somali communities at the local level, whenever possible, and emphasizing the need for coordination with the transitional Government and with local and regional authorities,

Welcoming the continued focus of the United Nations, in partnership with Somali elders, other local leaders and skilled local counterparts at the grass-roots level and non-governmental organizations, on a programme of assistance, including both humanitarian and developmental approaches, given the varying conditions in different areas,

Re-emphasizing the importance of the further implementation of its resolution 47/160 to rehabilitate basic social and economic services at the local and regional levels throughout the country,

1. *Expresses its gratitude* to all States and the intergovernmental and non-governmental organizations that have responded to the appeals of the Secretary-General and others by extending assistance to Somalia;

2. *Expresses its appreciation* to the Secretary-General for his continued and tireless efforts to mobilize assistance to the Somali people;

3. *Welcomes* the ongoing efforts of the United Nations, the Organization of African Unity, the League of Arab States, the European Union, the Organization of the Islamic Conference, the countries members of the Intergovernmental Authority on Development and its Partners Forum, the Movement of Non-Aligned Countries and others to resolve the situation in Somalia;

4. *Also welcomes* the strategy of the United Nations focusing on the implementation of community-based interventions aimed at rebuilding local infrastructures and increasing the self-reliance of the local population, and the ongoing efforts by the United Nations agencies, their Somali counterparts and their partner organizations to establish and maintain close coordination and cooperation mechanisms available for the implementation of relief, rehabilitation and reconstruction programmes;

5. *Notes with appreciation* the holistic and prioritized approach of the United Nations system to addressing the continuing crisis in some parts of Somalia, while making long-term commitments to rehabilitation, recovery and development activities in more stable parts;

6. *Emphasizes* the principle that the Somali people have the primary responsibility for their own development and for the sustainability of rehabilitation and reconstruction assistance programmes, and reaffirms the importance it attaches to the creation of workable arrangements for collaboration between the United Nations system and its partner organizations and their Somali counterparts for the effective execution of rehabilitation and development activities in those parts of the country in which peace and security prevail;

7. *Urges* all States and intergovernmental and non-governmental organizations concerned to continue to implement further its resolution 47/160 in order to assist the Somali people in embarking on the rehabilitation of basic social and economic services, as well as institution-building aimed at the restoration of civil administration at all levels in all parts of the country in which peace and security prevail;

8. *Strongly urges* all political groups in Somalia, in particular those which have remained outside the Arta peace process, to participate in the ongoing peace process and to establish a constructive dialogue with the new transitional Government, in order to achieve national reconciliation that allows for transition from relief to reconstruction and development and preserves economic and administrative progress achieved in many regions;

9. *Calls upon* all parties, individual political leaders and factions in Somalia to respect fully the security and safety of personnel of the United Nations and the specialized agencies and of non-governmental organizations, and to guarantee their complete freedom of movement and safe access throughout Somalia;

10. *Calls upon* the Secretary-General to continue to mobilize international humanitarian, rehabilitation and reconstruction assistance for Somalia;

11. *Calls upon* the international community to provide continuing and increased assistance in response to the United Nations consolidated inter-agency appeal for relief, rehabilitation and reconstruction assistance for Somalia, covering the period from October 2000 to December 2001;

12. *Requests* the Secretary-General, in view of the critical situation in Somalia, to take all necessary measures for the implementation of the present resolution and to report thereon to the General Assembly at its fifty-sixth session.

Sudan

The UN consolidated inter-agency appeal for the Sudan, launched in 1999, which initially sought $125.6 million for January to December 2000, was revised to $131.5 million. The donor community covered 81.6 per cent, or $107.3 million.

Overall, most areas of the Sudan suffered from chronic structural underdevelopment, which was further compounded by ongoing conflict. People's livelihoods were directly affected in southern and eastern Sudan and indirectly in other areas as resources were diverted away from basic services and infrastructure. Violent conflict continued unabated around the oil fields in Unity State, Western Upper Nile, where the humanitarian situation remained critical. Humanitarian access to populations in the initial stages of displacement remained problematic due to insecurity and denial of access. Fighting continued in the Nuba Mountains, in parts of Bahr El Ghazal, Eastern Equatoria and Southern Blue Nile. In Bahr El Ghazal, the year was marked by the breakdown of the ceasefire in June and subsequent military activity by both sides to the conflict. Populations fleeing the conflict in Upper Nile and displaced in Bahr El Ghazal remained a priority. The humanitarian situation throughout most of the war-afflicted and other areas, except for Unity State, Southern Blue Nile and drought-affected Eastern Equatoria, had improved with better food security. Nevertheless, those gains remained very fragile, as no systematic and consistent longer-term building of local capacities for recovery could be undertaken due to funding restrictions.

In November, OCHA launched a UN consolidated inter-agency appeal covering January to December 2001 and totalling $194.2 million.

Communications. In March [A/54/818], the Sudan transmitted details of the detention, in February, by rebel militia at Fanjak district, Upper Nile State, of an aircraft of Operation Lifeline Sudan (OLS) Southern Sector. The WFP aircraft was used to transport three militia commanders from one area to another. The Sudan urged the United Nations to investigate the matter and to review OLS procedures and regulations in order to avoid a recurrence.

Also in March [A/54/789], the Sudan informed the Secretary-General that on 3 March the rebel movement expelled about 12 non-governmental organizations (NGOs), mainly from areas under the control of the Sudan People's Liberation Army (SPLA). SPLA had acted to repatriate over 200 NGO employees to Nairobi, Kenya. On 10 March [A/54/792-S/2000/209], Portugal transmitted a statement on humanitarian aid in southern Sudan issued by the Presidency of the European Union (EU), urging negotiations with NGOs with the aim of creating conditions for unhindered operations in accordance with international humanitarian law.

On 29 July [A/54/956], the Sudan called on the international community to condemn a 27 July attack by the rebel movement on a UN boat, during which a representative of the United Nations Children's Fund (UNICEF) sustained injuries. It announced that the SPLA attack on UN personnel and relief agencies in southern Sudan was in violation of the declared ceasefire.

West Africa

In 2000, the West African subregion, including Côte d'Ivoire, Guinea, Liberia and Sierra Leone, continued to experience escalating political and economic instability. By September, internal political disaffection and rebel incursions from Liberia and Sierra Leone heightened tensions in Guinea, leading to a campaign of terror and intimidation of Liberian and Sierra Leonean refugees there and to the internal displacement of Guinean citizens. Insecurity in the border areas between Guinea, Liberia and Sierra Leone caused further displacement of refugees. Prospects for peace in Sierra Leone were compromised by renewed hostilities and political inertia. Sporadic fighting, economic stagnation, a severe decline in international aid and the imposition of sanctions rendered the recovery process in Liberia close to collapse. A tense political and ethnic environment in Côte d'Ivoire continued to trigger the exodus of foreigners, mostly migrant workers from Burkina Faso and Mali.

OCHA launched a UN consolidated interagency appeal for West Africa, covering January to December 2001, for a total of $65 million. The appeal constituted a key complement to the appeal launched for Sierra Leone in November (see p. 864).

Liberia

In a June report on assistance for the rehabilitation and reconstruction of Liberia [A/55/90-E/2000/81], the Secretary-General said that the path to sustainable peace and recovery in the war-torn country remained uncertain, owing mainly to problems of governance and inadequate external support to the country's reconstruction programme. International assistance was geared towards building capacity for participatory and accountable governance and recreating a social safety net for the population. It also focused on rebuilding capacity for essential governmental operations, including the restoration of the effectiveness of the court system and confidence in the rule of law. The Secretary-General described UN assistance in the areas of governance, security and the rule of law; macroeconomic reform and stabilization; resettlement, repatriation and reintegration; health; education; community revival and restoration; food security; and gender concerns.

The Secretary-General said that an assessment mission jointly led by the World Bank and UNDP in

1999 had concluded that significant progress had been made in implementing the first phase of the Government's National Reconstruction Programme, presented in 1998 [YUN 1998, p. 850]. Some 90 per cent of the $230 million pledged in 1998 was being utilized. The overall security situation had improved and there were positive results from the resettlement of the conflict-affected population and rehabilitation of the war-ravaged social infrastructure. Progress had been made in stabilizing the macroeconomic environment through far-reaching monetary, fiscal and structural policy reforms. However, major infrastructures, such as the electricity grid, communications system and roads, remained dysfunctional, while the financial system and weak capacity in all sectors further constrained the recovery process.

The Secretary-General observed that the country's major challenge was consolidating the peace and addressing problems emanating from the conflict and the social disparity and ethnic divisions that fuelled the conflict. The presence of a large number of unemployed youth and former combatants in urban areas continued to threaten long-term stability, as did the economic base, which was at only one third of its pre-war level. The Secretary-General recommended that the General Assembly reaffirm resolution 53/1 I [YUN 1998, p. 850], which called for further support for rehabilitation and reconstruction in Liberia.

GENERAL ASSEMBLY ACTION

On 19 December [meeting 86], the General Assembly adopted **resolution 55/176** [draft: A/55/L.66 & Add.1] without vote [agenda item 120 (b)].

Assistance for the rehabilitation and reconstruction of Liberia

The General Assembly,

Recalling its resolutions 45/232 of 21 December 1990, 46/147 of 17 December 1991, 47/154 of 18 December 1992, 48/197 of 21 December 1993, 49/21 E of 20 December 1994, 50/58 A of 12 December 1995, 51/30 B of 5 December 1996, 52/169 E of 16 December 1997 and 53/1 I of 16 November 1998,

Having considered the report of the Secretary-General,

Commending the Economic Community of West African States and the United Nations for their collaborative efforts with the Government of Liberia in its peace-building objectives,

Realizing that the restoration of peace has not brought rapid and sustainable social and economic recovery, despite programmes initiated by the Government aimed at reconciliation and reconstruction,

1. *Expresses its gratitude* to all donor countries, the specialized agencies of the United Nations system, the European Union, the Bretton Woods institutions and non-governmental organizations for their participation in a joint mission held in Monrovia from 15 to 19 November 1999 to assess the National Reconstruction Programme and the use of donor funds committed at the 1998 Donors' Conference for the reconstruction of Liberia, and urges those that have not yet honoured their pledges and commitment to do so;

2. *Also expresses its gratitude* to all States and intergovernmental and non-governmental organizations for their assistance and support for the peace-building process in Liberia, and urges that such assistance be continued;

3. *Calls upon* all States and intergovernmental and non-governmental organizations to provide assistance to Liberia to facilitate the implementation of its National Reconstruction Programme submitted at the Donors' Conference;

4. *Urges* the Government of Liberia to provide an enabling environment for the promotion of socio-economic development and a culture of sustained peace in the country, including a commitment to upholding the rule of law, national reconciliation and human rights and to implementing ways and means of reducing tension and promoting sustainable and peaceful political development in the subregion;

5. *Urges* the United Nations system and all States, in working towards the reconstruction and development of Liberia, to direct their assistance to or through inter-governmental and non-governmental organizations;

6. *Renews its appeal* to the Government of Liberia to cooperate with the United Nations, the specialized agencies and other organizations in addressing the need for rehabilitation and reconstruction, and stresses the need for the Government of Liberia to assist and protect the civilian population, including refugees and internally displaced persons, regardless of their origin;

7. *Calls upon* all parties to respect fully the provisions of international humanitarian law and in this regard to ensure safe and unhindered access of humanitarian personnel to all affected populations throughout the territory of Liberia and the safety of United Nations and humanitarian personnel;

8. *Commends* the Secretary-General for his continuing efforts to mobilize international assistance for the development and reconstruction of Liberia, and requests him to continue his efforts to mobilize all possible assistance within the United Nations system to help in the reconstruction and development of Liberia, including the return and reintegration of refugees, displaced persons and demobilized soldiers;

9. *Requests* the Secretary-General to report to the General Assembly at its fifty-seventh session on the implementation of the present resolution;

10. *Decides* to consider at its fifty-seventh session the question of international assistance for the rehabilitation and reconstruction of Liberia.

Sierra Leone

The UN consolidated inter-agency appeal for Sierra Leone, launched in 1999, which initially sought $71 million for the period January to December 2000, was revised to $64.3 million in June. The donor community covered 67.6 per cent, or $43.5 million, of the revised appeal.

The security situation in Sierra Leone and the subregion remained precarious (see p. 189). Sporadic skirmishes between the main rebel group, the Revolutionary United Front (RUF), and the Civil Defence Forces continued in some areas. Interventions in small enclaves surrounded by RUF were intermittent and limited due to poor security and difficult road access. Reports from rebel-controlled areas, which comprised half the country, indicated severe food shortages and the rampant spread of disease. Subregional tensions between and within Sierra Leone, Guinea, Liberia and Côte d'Ivoire threatened to deteriorate into a large-scale complex emergency. In November, OCHA launched a UN consolidated interagency appeal for $78.1 million to cover January to December 2001.

Asia

Afghanistan

Despite efforts on several fronts, political resolution of the conflict in Afghanistan remained elusive (see p. 262). Sporadic fighting continued and the traditional intensification of fighting had occurred in the summer months in the north and central districts. Insecurity continued to constrain the provision of assistance. The economy continued to deteriorate, fostering poverty and unemployment. The firman (edict) restricting the employment of Afghan women in UN and NGO programmes, with the exception of the health sector, affected several thousand women who had been working throughout the assistance community. The extremely low level of precipitation had destroyed nearly all the rain-fed crops and decimated the livestock (see p. 271 for drought assistance).

In response to a consolidated appeal, launched in 1999 for $220.8 million to cover January to December 2000, the donor community contributed $106.8 million, or 48.38 per cent of the requirements.

A UN consolidated appeal covering 2001, which sought $229.2 million, was launched in November.

Pursuant to General Assembly resolution 54/189 B [YUN 1999, p. 838], the Secretary-General, in an August report [A/55/348] covering developments from 1 July 1999 to 30 June 2000, reviewed major humanitarian and socio-economic developments. He described assistance provided by the United Nations and its partners in the areas of food aid and food security, health, water and sanitation, education, mine action, food and agriculture, rural and urban rehabilitation, voluntary repatriation, drug control and human rights. The Secretary-General concluded that the combination of war, drought and displacement was likely to take a toll in the coming months. He noted that, apart from the humanitarian assistance, there were few responses to Afghanistan's huge rehabilitation and reconstruction needs.

GENERAL ASSEMBLY ACTION

On 19 December [meeting 86], the General Assembly adopted **resolution 55/174 B** [draft: A/55/L.62/Rev.1 & Add.1] without vote [agenda items 20 (d) & 46].

Emergency international assistance for peace, normalcy and reconstruction of war-stricken Afghanistan

The General Assembly,

Recalling its resolutions 51/195 A of 17 December 1996, 52/211 A of 19 December 1997, 53/203 B of 18 December 1998 and 54/189 B of 17 December 1999,

Expressing its grave concern about the continuation of the military confrontation in Afghanistan, threatening regional peace and security and causing massive loss of life and extensive human suffering, further destruction of property, serious damage to the economic and social infrastructure, refugee flows and other forcible displacements of large numbers of people, as well as the failure of all warring parties, in particular the Taliban, to stop the fighting,

Noting with deep concern the worst drought for decades, which affects large parts of Afghanistan and risks dramatically exacerbating the already fragile humanitarian situation,

Remaining deeply concerned about the problem of millions of anti-personnel landmines and unexploded ordnance as well as the continued laying of new anti-personnel landmines in Afghanistan, which continue to prevent many Afghan refugees and internally displaced persons from returning to their villages and working in their fields,

Noting with deep concern that the majority of the Afghan people are unable to enjoy fully their human rights and fundamental freedoms owing to the accumulated effects of warfare, further aggravated by ongoing fighting and destruction, in particular by the Taliban, searing poverty, profound underdevelopment, and the policies and practices of the authorities,

Expressing its grave concern at the serious violations of human rights and international humanitarian law, in particular by the Taliban, in Afghanistan and at the inadequacy of measures taken by the warring factions to reverse the situation,

Deeply concerned by the continuing and substantiated reports of violations of human rights, in particular of women and girls, including all forms of discrimination against them, notably in areas under the control of the Taliban,

Welcoming the ongoing work of gender and human rights advisers appointed by the United Nations, who form an integral part of the office of the United Nations resident and humanitarian coordinator in Afghanistan,

Taking note of the report of the Special Rapporteur of the Commission on Human Rights on violence against women, its causes and consequences,

Noting with alarm that the resumption of fighting by the Taliban during the past summer led to further displacement of civilian populations, especially in the provinces of Baghlan and Takhar,

Expressing its grave concern for the well-being of internally displaced persons and other vulnerable sections of the civilian population, who face a long winter possibly deprived of basic foods as a result of the drought and the recent fighting, as well as the repeated denial by the warring factions of adequate conditions for the delivery of aid by humanitarian organizations,

Affirming the urgent need to continue international humanitarian assistance to Afghanistan for the restoration of basic services, as well as the need for the conflicting parties to guarantee the safety and security of the personnel of all international organizations,

Welcoming the principle-centred approach towards humanitarian assistance and rehabilitation in Afghanistan, as outlined in the Strategic Framework for Afghanistan, and the consolidated appeals as tools to promote greater effectiveness and coherence in international aid programmes, and welcoming also the establishment of the independent strategic monitoring unit,

Deeply disturbed by the continuing security threat to United Nations personnel and other humanitarian personnel, including locally engaged staff, and by the fact that the authorities continue to limit their access to affected populations in certain areas,

Noting with deep concern the substantial restrictions introduced by the Taliban authorities on the operations of the United Nations and the specialized agencies and non-governmental organizations that provide humanitarian, economic rehabilitation and development assistance in Afghanistan, and noting in particular the negative impact these restrictions have on the provision of assistance to groups in need of special protection, especially women and children,

Noting with deep concern also that a significant number of Afghan refugees remain in neighbouring countries, as conditions in many parts of Afghanistan are currently not conducive to a safe and sustainable return, and acknowledging that those refugees constitute a continuing socio-economic burden for the host countries,

Expressing its gratitude to all Governments that have rendered assistance to Afghan refugees, in particular those of neighbouring countries that continue to host Afghan refugee populations, and at the same time again calling upon all parties to continue to honour their obligations for the protection of refugees and internally displaced persons and to allow international access for their protection and care,

Recognizing the need for continuing international assistance for the maintenance abroad and the voluntary repatriation and resettlement of refugees and internally displaced persons, and welcoming the voluntary return of refugees to rural districts in Afghanistan that are relatively stable and secure and not severely affected by the drought,

Expressing its appreciation to the United Nations system, and to all States and international and non-governmental organizations that have responded positively, and continue to respond, where conditions permit, to the humanitarian needs of Afghanistan, as well as to the Secretary-General for his efforts in mobilizing and coordinating the delivery of appropriate humanitarian assistance,

1. *Takes note* of the report of the Secretary-General, and endorses the observations contained therein;

2. *Stresses* that the responsibility for the humanitarian crisis lies with all warring parties, in particular with the Taliban;

3. *Strongly condemns* the resumption of major fighting by the Taliban during the past summer, especially in the Taloqan area and the Shomali Plains, resulting in further forcible displacement of civilian populations and destruction of infrastructure;

4. *Notes with alarm* numerous reports of the Taliban troops deliberately destroying, burning and looting homes and assets of civilians essential for their survival in the battle zones;

5. *Urges* all parties, in particular the Taliban, to end immediately all armed hostilities, and calls upon the leaders of all Afghan parties to place the highest priority on national reconciliation, acknowledging the desire of the Afghan people for rehabilitation, reconstruction and economic and social development;

6. *Calls upon* all relevant organizations of the United Nations system to continue to coordinate closely their humanitarian assistance to Afghanistan on the basis of the principles laid out in the Strategic Framework for Afghanistan, in particular to assure a consistent approach to the implementation of these principles, human rights and security, and appeals to donor countries as well as other humanitarian organizations to cooperate closely within the framework of the United Nations, taking into account the interagency consolidated appeal for emergency humanitarian and rehabilitation assistance to Afghanistan for 2001;

7. *Strongly condemns* the killing of seven Afghan employees of the United Nations–supported mine awareness programme by unidentified gunmen, as well as recent acts of violence and intimidation against United Nations personnel and offices;

8. *Urges* all Afghan parties, in particular the Taliban, to respect international humanitarian law, to ensure the safety, security and free movement of all United Nations and humanitarian personnel as well as their safe and unimpeded access to all affected populations, and to protect the property of the United Nations and of humanitarian organizations, including non-governmental organizations, so as to facilitate their work;

9. *Calls upon* the Taliban authorities to implement fully the Supplementary Protocol to the Memorandum of Understanding of 13 May 1998, signed by the United Nations and the Taliban, on the security of United Nations personnel in Afghanistan;

10. *Demands* that all Afghan parties cooperate fully with the United Nations and associated bodies as well as with other agencies and humanitarian organizations in their efforts to respond to the humanitarian needs of the people of Afghanistan;

11. *Condemns* all interference in the delivery of humanitarian relief supplies, and demands the secure and uninterrupted supply of humanitarian aid to all in need of it, especially in the Panjshir valley;

12. *Strongly condemns* substantial restrictions introduced by the Taliban authorities on the operations of the United Nations, in particular the recent decree of

law banning the employment of Afghan women in the United Nations and non-governmental programmes, except in the health sector;

13. *Calls upon* the Taliban authorities to cooperate fully and without discrimination on grounds of gender, nationality or religion with the United Nations and associated bodies and with other humanitarian organizations, agencies and non-governmental organizations;

14. *Denounces* the continuing discrimination against girls and women as well as ethnic and religious groups, including minorities, and other violations of human rights and international humanitarian law in Afghanistan, notably in areas under the control of the Taliban, notes with deep concern their adverse effects on international relief and reconstruction programmes in Afghanistan, and calls upon all parties within Afghanistan to respect fully the human rights and fundamental freedoms of all, regardless of gender, ethnicity or religion, in accordance with international human rights instruments, inter alia, the International Covenants on Human Rights, and to refrain from all attempts to single out minorities;

15. *Strongly urges* all the Afghan parties to end discriminatory policies and to recognize, protect and promote the equal rights and dignity of women and men, including their rights to full and equal participation in the life of the country, freedom of movement, access to education and health facilities, employment outside the home, personal security and freedom from intimidation and harassment, in particular with respect to the implications of discriminatory policies for the distribution of aid, notwithstanding some progress made with respect to access to education and health care for girls and women;

16. *Urges* all Afghan parties to prohibit conscripting or enlisting children or using them to participate in hostilities in violation of the provisions of the Optional Protocol to the Convention on the Rights of the Child on the involvement of children in armed conflict;

17. *Appeals* to all States and to the international community to ensure that all humanitarian assistance to the people of Afghanistan integrates a gender perspective, that it actively attempts to promote the participation of both women and men and that women benefit equally with men from such assistance;

18. *Expresses its appreciation* to those Governments that continue to host Afghan refugees, appeals to the Governments concerned to reaffirm their commitment to international refugee law on the rights of asylum and protection, and calls upon the international community to do likewise;

19. *Recognizes* the high number of refugees in neighbouring countries, and calls upon the international community to consider providing further assistance to Afghan refugees;

20. *Expresses concern* over the continued laying of anti-personnel landmines, which continues to take a heavy toll on civilians and seriously impedes the delivery of humanitarian assistance, and urges all Afghan parties to call a complete halt to the use of landmines, as well as to fulfil their duties to cooperate with the United Nations mine action programme and to protect their personnel;

21. *Urgently appeals* to all States, the United Nations system and international and non-governmental organizations to continue to provide, when conditions on the ground permit, all possible financial, technical and material assistance for the Afghan population, especially in the areas most affected by the drought, and the voluntary, safe and secure return of refugees and internally displaced persons;

22. *Calls upon* the international community to respond to the inter-agency consolidated appeal for emergency humanitarian and rehabilitation assistance for Afghanistan, launched by the Secretary-General on 29 November 2000 for the period from 1 January to 31 December 2001, bearing in mind the availability also of the Afghanistan Emergency Trust Fund;

23. *Requests* the Secretary-General to submit to the General Assembly at its fifty-sixth session a report on the actions taken pursuant to the present resolution;

24. *Decides* to include in the provisional agenda of its fifty-sixth session, under the cluster of items on coordination of humanitarian assistance, the sub-item entitled "Emergency international assistance for peace, normalcy and reconstruction of war-stricken Afghanistan".

East Timor

In response to General Assembly resolution 54/96 H [YUN 1999, p. 840], the Secretary-General, in September [A/55/418], reviewed humanitarian developments and sector requirements and assistance provided by the United Nations and its partners in East Timor, beginning with the last quarter of 1999.

The Secretary-General reported that, in recognition of the need to ensure the early phase-in of development activities, a joint assessment mission, comprising experts from UN agencies, the East Timorese community, donors, the European Commission, the Asian Development Bank and the International Monetary Fund (IMF) and led by the World Bank, took place from mid-October to mid-November 1999. The mission identified priority short-term reconstruction needs and provided estimates of external financing requirements. The mission's findings were presented at a donor conference convened under the auspices of the Government of Japan (Tokyo, 16-17 December 1999). The amount of external financing requirements presented for humanitarian, reconstruction and development activities for East Timor totalled $878.3 million over a three-year period. The total pledged at the conference was $522.4 million, of which $148.9 million was for humanitarian assistance and $373.4 million for development activities. A follow-up conference was organized on 22 and 23 June 2000, hosted by the Government of Portugal and co-chaired by the World Bank and the United Nations Transitional Administration in East Timor (UNTAET). Donors expressed support for the activities of the Trust Fund for East Timor, administered by the

World Bank, and endorsed a work programme for the period from July to December 2000.

In order to address emergency needs, the humanitarian community agreed on a series of common guidelines for priority intervention. The process was facilitated in the early stages of the humanitarian crisis by the Humanitarian Coordinator and OCHA. Subsequently, responsibility was transferred, effective 1 January 2000, to the UNTAET humanitarian assistance and emergency rehabilitation component.

The Secretary-General concluded that the engagement of the international community would be required to ensure that programmes continued to benefit the people of East Timor and to pave the way to self-reliance and sustainable development.

UNDP action. On 25 January [E/2000/35 (dec. 2000/2)], the Executive Board of UNDP/United Nations Population Fund approved the allocation of $5 million from the target for resource allocation from the core to meet immediate needs for assistance for 1999-2000 and the authority to make future allocations according to the formula applied to other programme countries.

GENERAL ASSEMBLY ACTION

On 14 December [meeting 85], the General Assembly adopted **resolution 55/172** [draft: A/55/L.65 & Add.1] without vote [agenda item 20 (b)].

Assistance for humanitarian relief, rehabilitation and development for East Timor

The General Assembly,

Recalling all of its relevant resolutions on the situation in East Timor, in particular resolutions 54/96 H of 15 December 1999 and 54/194 of 17 December 1999,

Recalling also its resolution 46/182 of 19 December 1991 and the guiding principles contained in the annex to that resolution,

Recalling further all of the relevant Security Council resolutions and decisions on the situation in East Timor, in particular resolutions 1272(1999) of 25 October 1999 and 1319(2000) of 8 September 2000,

Recalling the establishment by Security Council resolution 1272(1999) of the United Nations Transitional Administration in East Timor, whose mandate includes the coordination and delivery of humanitarian, rehabilitation and development assistance,

Welcoming the response of the United Nations, other intergovernmental organizations, Member States and non-governmental organizations, with the coordination of the Transitional Administration since 1 January 2000, and in cooperation with the East Timorese people, in terms of addressing the humanitarian relief, rehabilitation and development needs of East Timor,

Acknowledging the progress made in the transition from relief to development in East Timor and, in this regard, the important role played by the Transitional Administration in supporting the resilient and determined efforts of the East Timorese people themselves,

Welcoming the progress that has been made in alleviating the humanitarian assistance needs of East Timor, while noting continuing requirements for food and shelter assistance,

Welcoming also the efforts of the Government of Indonesia and relevant intergovernmental and non-governmental organizations in providing humanitarian assistance to the East Timorese refugees in the province of East Nusa Tenggara, West Timor, and in this respect recognizing the importance of the international community in assisting the efforts of the Government of Indonesia to implement resettlement and repatriation programmes of East Timorese refugees,

Emphasizing the need for continued international assistance to East Timor to support the transition from relief and rehabilitation to development, in preparation for independence, and recognizing the significant challenges that are to be faced in this regard, inter alia, in the education, health, agriculture and infrastructure sectors,

Deploring the killing of three personnel of the Office of the United Nations High Commissioner for Refugees at Atambua on 6 September 2000, which resulted in the withdrawal from West Timor of United Nations and other international humanitarian personnel, and welcoming in this respect the steps taken by the Government of Indonesia towards conducting a full-scale investigation, taking firm measures against those found guilty and ensuring a safe and secure environment,

1. *Takes note* of the report of the Secretary-General;
2. *Encourages* the United Nations, other intergovernmental organizations, Member States and non-governmental organizations, with the coordination of the United Nations Transitional Administration in East Timor, and in close consultation and cooperation with the East Timorese people, to continue to collaborate to address the remaining humanitarian relief needs of East Timor, and to support the transition from relief and rehabilitation to development in preparation for independence;
3. *Emphasizes* the importance of continuing close consultation with and participation of East Timorese institutions and civil society, including local non-governmental organizations, in the planning and delivery of humanitarian relief, rehabilitation and development assistance to East Timor;
4. *Welcomes* the establishment of the East Timor National Council as an interim step towards a democratic legislative institution as well as the appointment of a joint cabinet to increase Timorese participation in the Administration;
5. *Urges* United Nations organizations, the international community and non-governmental organizations to continue their efforts aimed at the enhanced ownership and participation of the East Timorese, known as "Timorization" in East Timor, of the social, economic and administrative infrastructure, and in this regard stresses the need for capacity-building, inter alia, in areas such as education, health, agriculture and rural development, the judiciary, governance and public administration, security and law and order;
6. *Commends* Member States for their prompt response to the United Nations consolidated inter-agency appeal for the East Timor crises, which was launched on 27 October 1999, and urges Member

States to fulfil their pledges to meet the external financing requirements for humanitarian relief, rehabilitation and development activities for East Timor;

7. *Welcomes* in this regard the convening of the Donors Meetings for East Timor in Tokyo on 16 and 17 December 1999, and in Lisbon on 22 and 23 June 2000, as well as the meeting in Brussels on 5 and 6 December 2000 which focused on the transition towards independence in East Timor in four key areas: political, public administration, public finances, and economic and social reconstruction;

8. *Encourages* continued international support in all sectors, including agriculture, infrastructure, health and education to assist the efforts of East Timor towards sustainable development, particularly in its transition to independence;

9. *Welcomes* the immediate response to food aid needs by the international community, urges it to continue to ensure food security for the remaining vulnerable groups in need, and calls upon the United Nations, other intergovernmental organizations, Member States and non-governmental organizations to assist the East Timorese in ensuring sustainable development in the areas of agriculture, livestock and fisheries;

10. *Recommends* that outstanding infrastructure needs remain an essential focus of international assistance in such areas as the reconstruction and rehabilitation of public buildings, educational facilities, roads and public services;

11. *Commends* the rapid international response in terms of providing health services to the general population, including the early deployment of immunization and disease prevention programmes, and reproductive health care and child nutrition programmes, while recognizing the need for further assistance to rebuild hospitals and for training health-care professionals;

12. *Welcomes* the ongoing reopening of schools, the supply and distribution of education materials, and teacher training, while emphasizing the need for capacity-building, particularly in the area of secondary and higher education, and for continued attention to the rehabilitation needs, including psychosocial support, of children affected by the violence;

13. *Stresses* the urgent need for sustained and enhanced efforts by the Government of Indonesia, the Transitional Administration and the international community effectively and comprehensively to resolve the question of the East Timorese refugees by the repatriation or resettlement of all those refugees, in conditions of safety and security at all stages, and based on their voluntary decisions, through the efforts of the Government of Indonesia to guarantee effective security in the West Timor camps, by the promotion of a credible and internationally observed registration process, and by the promotion of and support for reconciliation among all East Timorese;

14. *Acknowledges* the efforts of the Government of Indonesia, in cooperation with the Office of the United Nations High Commissioner for Refugees, the International Organization for Migration and other humanitarian organizations, to facilitate organized and spontaneous returns of East Timorese refugees from West Timor, including the repatriation of the former Indonesian military reservists known as Milsas,

and underscores the importance of continued international assistance to support the efforts of the Government of Indonesia and relevant organizations to meet the needs of East Timorese refugees in West Timor, inter alia, by assisting their voluntary repatriation or resettlement;

15. *Reaffirms* the need to ensure safe and unhindered access of humanitarian personnel and assistance to all those in need and to ensure the safety and security of all humanitarian personnel in West Timor, recognizes in this regard the steps taken and the efforts being made by the Government of Indonesia to implement Security Council resolution 1319(2000), such as the ongoing disarming and disbanding of the militias, the deploying of additional security apparatus and the bringing to justice of those found guilty, and calls upon the Government to continue to strengthen such efforts in full cooperation with Member States, the United Nations system and non-governmental organizations;

16. *Urges* the United Nations to continue to address the humanitarian, rehabilitation and development needs of East Timor;

17. *Requests* the Secretary-General to prepare a report on the implementation of the present resolution for consideration by the General Assembly at its fifty-sixth session.

Indonesia

Maluku

The conflict in Maluku between Muslim and Christian communities, which erupted in January 1999, cost thousands of lives and forced over 500,000 people to leave their homes. Some 215,000 displaced persons were reported in Maluku province and a further 207,000 in North Maluku, representing about 25 per cent of the population of the two provinces. Towards the latter part of the year, the region, made up of islands scattered across more than 1,200 square kilometres, had fewer clashes, yet tension persisted in many parts of the archipelago and few people felt secure enough to return to their homes. Many within the affected displaced population had been unable to support themselves and relied on outside assistance. In March, OCHA launched a UN consolidated inter-agency appeal totalling $14.1 million to cover 16 March to 30 September 2000, of which some $8.2 million, or 50 per cent, of requirements were met.

A further appeal, covering January to December 2001, sought $10.8 million for multisectoral activities.

West Timor

A UN consolidated inter-agency appeal that initially sought $28 million for West Timor from October 1999 to December 2000 was revised in June to $46.2 million, mainly to find durable solutions for East Timorese refugees in Indonesia, through either voluntary repatriation or local settlement in West Timor, or elsewhere in Indonesia, and to give increased aid to host communities in West Timor. As at 23 May, funds received totalled $21.1 million, or 45.7 per cent of requirements.

Kazakhstan

In a July report [A/55/212], the Secretary-General said that the international donor community had delivered humanitarian and development assistance to the affected population of the Semipalatinsk region, a former nuclear testing range in Kazakhstan (the Polygon), since the adoption of General Assembly resolutions 52/169 M [YUN 1997, p. 911] and 53/1 H [YUN 1998, p. 859], which called on the international community to contribute to the region's human and ecological rehabilitation and economic development.

The Tokyo International Conference on Semipalatinsk (Tokyo, 6-7 September 1999), jointly hosted by Japan and UNDP, aimed to raise awareness of the situation in the region and of the consequences of nuclear testing; appeal for further assistance; consider cooperation and coordination of the international community; and inform participants of the institutional arrangements of Kazakhstan to manage, coordinate, use and account for international assistance. An integrated Semipalatinsk Relief and Rehabilitation Programme, consisting of 38 impact-oriented actions for relief and rehabilitation in the areas of health, the environment and ecology, economic recovery, humanitarian issues, and information and advocacy, was distributed to the donor community prior to the Conference. The Conference pledged more than $20 million to assist the Programme.

GENERAL ASSEMBLY ACTION

On 27 November [meeting 71], the General Assembly adopted **resolution 55/44** [draft: A/55/L.16 & Add.1] without vote [agenda item 20 *(b)*].

International cooperation and coordination for the human and ecological rehabilitation and economic development of the Semipalatinsk region of Kazakhstan

The General Assembly,

Recalling its resolutions 52/169 M of 16 December 1997 and 53/1 H of 16 November 1998,

Welcoming the report of the Secretary-General,

Recognizing that the Semipalatinsk nuclear testing ground, inherited by Kazakhstan and closed in 1991, remains a matter of serious concern for the people and Government of Kazakhstan with regard to its consequences for the lives and health of the people, especially children and other vulnerable groups, as well as for the environment of the region,

Conscious that the international community should pay due attention to the issue of the human, ecological and socio-economic dimensions of the situation in the Semipalatinsk region,

Recognizing the need to coordinate national and international efforts aimed at the rehabilitation of the health of the affected population and the environment in this region,

Bearing in mind the need for know-how in minimizing and mitigating radiological, health, socio-economic, psychological and environmental problems in the Semipalatinsk region,

Recalling the Almaty Declaration of the heads of the Central Asian States of 28 February 1997, proclaiming 1998 as the Year of Environmental Protection in the region of Central Asia,

Taking into consideration the results of the international conference on the problems of the Semipalatinsk region, held in Tokyo in 1999, which have promoted the effectiveness of the assistance provided to the population of the region,

Recognizing the contribution of different organizations of the United Nations system, donor States, and intergovernmental and non-governmental organizations to humanitarian assistance and the implementation of the projects aimed at the rehabilitation of the region,

1. *Takes note* of the report of the Secretary-General and the information about the measures taken to solve the health, ecological, economic and humanitarian problems and to meet the needs of the Semipalatinsk region;

2. *Stresses* the need for continuing international attention and extra efforts in solving problems with regard to the Semipalatinsk region and its population;

3. *Urges* the international community to provide assistance in the formulation and implementation of special programmes and projects of treatment and care for the affected population in the Semipalatinsk region;

4. *Invites* all States, relevant multilateral financial organizations and other entities of the international community, including non-governmental organizations, to share their knowledge and experience in order to contribute to the human and ecological rehabilitation and economic development of the Semipalatinsk region;

5. *Invites* all Member States, in particular donor States, relevant organs and organizations of the United Nations system, including the funds and programmes, to participate in the rehabilitation of the Semipalatinsk region;

6. *Invites* the Secretary-General to pursue a consultative process, with the participation of interested States and relevant United Nations agencies, on modalities for mobilizing the necessary support to seek appropriate solutions to the problems and needs of the Semipalatinsk region, including those prioritized in the report of the Secretary-General;

7. *Calls upon* the Secretary-General to continue his efforts to enhance world public awareness of the problems and needs of the Semipalatinsk region;

8. *Requests* the Secretary-General to report to the General Assembly at its fifty-seventh session on progress made in the implementation of the present resolution under the item entitled "Strengthening of the coordination of humanitarian and disaster relief

assistance of the United Nations, including special economic assistance".

Tajikistan

Following the first multiparty parliamentary elections in Tajikistan (see p. 314), the country entered a new phase of nation-building, based on national reconciliation. However, those developments occurred against a backdrop of economic decline and infrastructure collapse that threatened to undermine further consolidation of the peace process. The overall situation worsened due to a severe drought that threatened the food security of more than a million people.

OCHA issued a UN consolidated inter-agency appeal that sought $34.8 million for January to December 2000, of which $27 million, or 77.6 per cent of requirements, was met by the donor community. In November, OCHA issued an inter-agency appeal covering January to December 2001 for a total of $82 million.

In response to General Assembly resolution 54/96 A [YUN 1999, p. 842], the Secretary-General, in August [A/55/347], described Tajikistan's current political and economic situation and humanitarian operations.

The Secretary-General observed that despite the conclusion of the peace process and improvement in the security environment, limited social and economic progress had been achieved. Access to food and basic social services had been further limited by deteriorating economic conditions and the prevailing drought. Humanitarian and rehabilitation assistance remained crucial, not only to sustain life but also to promote development and prevent renewed conflict. The UN team in the country was re-evaluating its activities to prepare a common strategy to support relief and recovery activities.

GENERAL ASSEMBLY ACTION

On 27 November [meeting 72], the General Assembly adopted **resolution 55/45** [draft: A/55/L.41 & Add.1] without vote [agenda item 20 *(b)*].

Emergency international assistance for peace, normalcy and rehabilitation in Tajikistan

The General Assembly,

Recalling its resolutions 51/30 J of 25 April 1997, 52/169 I of 16 December 1997, 53/1 K of 7 December 1998 and 54/96 A of 8 December 1999,

Recalling also Security Council resolutions 1113(1997) of 12 June 1997, 1128(1997) of 12 September 1997, 1138(1997) of 14 November 1997, 1167(1998) of 14 May 1998, 1206(1998) of 12 November 1998, 1240(1999) of 15 May 1999 and 1274(1999) of 12 November 1999, and the statements by the President of the Security Council of 21 March and 12 May 2000,

Having considered the report of the Secretary-General,

Welcoming the implementation of the main provisions of the General Agreement on the Establishment of Peace and National Accord in Tajikistan,

Recognizing with satisfaction that the United Nations has played a successful and important role in the peace process and was instrumental in assisting the negotiation and implementation processes conducted under its aegis, believing that the United Nations should continue the assistance to Tajikistan in post-conflict peace-building, and welcoming in this regard the establishment of the United Nations Tajikistan Office for Peace-building,

Noting with satisfaction the efforts of the United Nations Mission of Observers in Tajikistan, which should be regarded as a successful operation, supported by the Contact Group of Guarantor States and International Organizations, the Mission of the Organization for Security and Cooperation in Europe and the Collective Peacekeeping Forces of the Commonwealth of Independent States, in assisting the parties in the implementation of the General Agreement,

Noting that, despite the conclusion of the peace process and significant progress in the security environment, the humanitarian situation has not improved, owing to the severe economic deterioration and the prevailing drought, and that significant humanitarian needs continue to exist throughout Tajikistan,

Recognizing that until the economy is able to support the Tajik population, humanitarian operations will remain a critical factor in strengthening the achievements of the peace process in Tajikistan,

Expressing regret that, despite the importance of humanitarian operations for contributing to peace and stability, donor response to both the 1999 and the 2000 consolidated inter-agency appeals has been insufficient,

Stressing that international funding for humanitarian operations is particularly important since such operations remain the principal means by which hundreds of thousands of Tajiks meet their basic needs,

Noting with concern the lack of support for food assistance and health programmes, which aim to save lives and must receive immediate funding if social catastrophe is to be avoided in Tajikistan,

1. *Takes note* of the report of the Secretary-General, and endorses the observations and recommendations set out therein;

2. *Welcomes* the implementation of the main provisions of the General Agreement on the Establishment of Peace and National Accord in Tajikistan, and the end of the transition period;

3. *Also welcomes* the continued role of the United Nations in post-conflict peace-building in Tajikistan and the establishment of the United Nations Tajikistan Office for Peace-building;

4. *Stresses* that Tajikistan has entered a new phase of post-conflict peace-building, which requires continued international economic assistance;

5. *Recognizes* that humanitarian and rehabilitation assistance remains crucial, not only to sustain life but also to promote development and prevent renewed conflict;

6. *Welcomes with appreciation* the efforts undertaken by the Secretary-General in drawing the attention of the international community to the acute humanitarian problems of Tajikistan and in mobilizing assist-

ance for the post-conflict rehabilitation, recovery and reconstruction of the country;

7. *Expresses its appreciation* to the States, the United Nations, the World Bank and other intergovernmental organizations and all relevant humanitarian organizations, agencies and non-governmental organizations, including the International Committee of the Red Cross and the International Federation of Red Cross and Red Crescent Societies, that have responded and continue to respond positively to the humanitarian needs of Tajikistan;

8. *Encourages* Member States and others concerned to continue assistance to alleviate the urgent humanitarian needs of Tajikistan and to offer support to Tajikistan for the post-conflict rehabilitation and reconstruction of its economy;

9. *Warmly welcomes* the intention of the Secretary-General to continue the United Nations humanitarian programme in Tajikistan by issuing a consolidated inter-agency appeal for humanitarian assistance to Tajikistan for 2001, as a strategic document that will guide a gradual transition to a more development-oriented focus, and invites Member States to fund programmes included in the appeal;

10. *Calls upon* the Secretary-General to re-evaluate in 2001 all humanitarian assistance activities in Tajikistan with a view to addressing longer-term developmental issues;

11. *Stresses* the need to ensure the security and freedom of movement of humanitarian personnel, and of United Nations and associated personnel, as well as the safety and security of their premises, equipment and supplies;

12. *Requests* the Secretary-General to continue to give special attention, in the dialogue with the multilateral lending institutions, to the humanitarian implications of their adjustment programmes in Tajikistan;

13. *Also requests* the Secretary-General to continue to monitor the humanitarian situation in Tajikistan and to report to the General Assembly at its fifty-sixth session on the progress made in the implementation of the present resolution;

14. *Decides* to consider at its fifty-sixth session the question of the situation in Tajikistan under the item entitled "Strengthening of the coordination of humanitarian and disaster relief assistance of the United Nations, including special economic assistance".

Europe

Northern Caucasus (Russian Federation)

The flash appeal issued in 1999 for the northern Caucasus, which sought $16.2 million and covered 1 December 1999 to 29 February 2000, was revised to $51.6 million and extended to 31 December 2000. As at 10 October, the donor community had committed $40.4 million, or 78.3 per cent of the requirements.

The humanitarian consequences of the events in the northern Caucasus continued to affect the lives of some 330,000 internally displaced persons and up to 690,000 residents in the Republics of Chechnya and of Ingushetia. There was little

prospect for the return of the displaced population from Ingushetia to Chechnya during the 2000/01 winter. Assistance needs of the population in Chechnya remained largely unmet. On 16 August, the Russian Federation and the United Nations signed a memorandum of understanding, which established a firm basis for the United Nations to provide humanitarian assistance in the northern Caucasus.

In November, OCHA launched a UN consolidated inter-agency appeal for $44.9 million to cover programmes from 1 January to 31 December 2001.

South-Eastern Europe
(Albania and the former Yugoslavia)

The UN consolidated inter-agency appeal, issued in 1999 for South-Eastern Europe—Albania, Bosnia and Herzegovina, Croatia, the Federal Republic of Yugoslavia (FRY) and the former Yugoslav Republic of Macedonia (FYROM)—which sought $660 million to cover January to December 2000, was revised to $629 million, as the Office of the United Nations High Commissioner for Refugees (UNHCR) reduced its budget through prioritization. As at 31 October, $305.4 million, or 48.6 per cent of the requirements, had been committed. Resources were limited in 2000 due to reduced donor funding and the phasing out of bilateral actors.

Albania was transited by a large number of illegal migrants who might claim asylum and overburden the asylum system. Although some progress was made in disentangling asylum, trafficking and illegal economic migration, resources received were insufficient to meet the ongoing needs in the economically and security-troubled country. Assistance was needed to further institutional reform, curb illegal migration and trafficking, and extend international protection to those without Albanian citizenship. Bosnia and Herzegovina was affected negatively by the increased numbers of spontaneous minority returns, partly as a result of improved levels of implementation of property laws and the impact of underfunding the consolidated appeal for 2000, particularly programmes required to make such returns viable. A more favourable political situation and improved security conditions in Croatia facilitated the voluntary return of refugees and internally displaced persons, as well as support for peace-building and community reconciliation. Nevertheless, the funding shortfall affected the levels of protection and assistance provided, particularly to returnees in war-affected areas. In FRY, funding shortfalls forced many agencies to scale down their planned operations. Political constraints also limited the impact of the humanitarian operation (see also below). Repatriation of refugees continued but remained linked to the political and economic situation in Croatia and Bosnia and Herzegovina. On the whole, the objectives set for the Kosovo province of FRY were met. Programmes led to a sharp recovery in agricultural production, provided protection and relief for refugees, internally displaced persons and vulnerable returnees, and supported the rehabilitation of quality basic services in the education, health and social welfare sectors. In FYROM, host family fatigue increased towards the end of the year. Efforts were made to integrate vulnerable groups, but the remaining refugee population remained dependent on humanitarian organizations whose resources were limited.

In November, a UN consolidated inter-agency appeal sought $429 million for January to December 2001.

Federal Republic of Yugoslavia

Pursuant to General Assembly resolution 54/96 F [YUN 1999, p. 844], the Secretary-General, in September [A/55/416], reviewed humanitarian, socio-economic and human rights developments in FRY from 1 July 1999 to 30 June 2000. He described assistance provided by the United Nations and its partners.

Humanitarian efforts in FRY were carried out against a background of political complexities. Given Serbia's international isolation, assistance there had been limited to humanitarian aid. Montenegro was shifting to transitional initiatives. Although the international community had scored impressive achievements in Kosovo, the goal of promoting tolerance and peaceful coexistence among ethnic groups had proved elusive. The Secretary-General concluded that until the underlying political and economic problems could be resolved, the United Nations would continue efforts to address the urgent needs of affected populations.

GENERAL ASSEMBLY ACTION

On 14 December [meeting 85], the General Assembly adopted **resolution 55/169** [draft: A/55/L.57 & Add.1] without vote [agenda item 20 (b)].

Humanitarian assistance to the Federal Republic of Yugoslavia

The General Assembly,

Recalling its resolution 46/182 of 19 December 1991, and reaffirming that humanitarian assistance should be provided in accordance with the guiding principles contained in the annex to that resolution,

Recalling also its resolution 54/96 F of 15 December 1999,

Deeply appreciative of the humanitarian assistance and the rehabilitation support rendered by a number of States, in particular major contributors, interna-

tional agencies and organizations and non-governmental organizations to alleviate the humanitarian needs of the affected population in the Federal Republic of Yugoslavia, in particular emergency assistance packages provided by the European Union, participants in the FOCUS humanitarian relief initiative and other countries,

Deeply concerned about the continuing urgency of the humanitarian situation in the Federal Republic of Yugoslavia, aware of the magnitude of the humanitarian requirements of the country, and recognizing the need to ensure effective links between relief, rehabilitation, reconstruction and development of the Federal Republic of Yugoslavia,

Aware of the persisting gravity of the situation of socially and economically vulnerable segments of the population, including refugees and displaced persons, coupled with significantly decreased social services capacity, especially in the health sector,

Taking note of the report of the Secretary-General,

Taking note also of the report prepared by the Office for the Coordination of Humanitarian Affairs of the Secretariat in Belgrade entitled "Background on the Energy Sector in Serbia for Winter 2000-2001",

Recognizing the role of the United Nations in solving the humanitarian problems facing the Federal Republic of Yugoslavia and in coordinating the efforts of the international community to provide humanitarian assistance to the country,

Welcoming the admission of the Federal Republic of Yugoslavia to the Stability Pact for South-Eastern Europe on 26 October 2000,

Welcoming also the admission of the Federal Republic of Yugoslavia to membership in the United Nations on 1 November 2000,

1. *Calls upon* all States, regional organizations, intergovernmental and non-governmental organizations and other relevant bodies to provide humanitarian assistance to alleviate the humanitarian needs of the affected population in the Federal Republic of Yugoslavia, especially during the coming winter months, bearing in mind in particular the special situation of women, as well as children and other vulnerable groups;

2. *Also calls upon* all States, regional organizations, intergovernmental and non-governmental organizations and other relevant bodies to offer support to the Government of the Federal Republic of Yugoslavia in its efforts to ensure the transition from relief to the longer-term goals of rehabilitation, reconstruction and development of the country;

3. *Welcomes* the commitment of and encourages the Federal Republic of Yugoslavia to continue to cooperate with the United Nations system and humanitarian organizations to address the humanitarian needs of the affected population, including refugees and internally displaced persons, and urges the relevant authorities and the international community to support programmes to ensure that the humanitarian needs of refugees and internally displaced persons in the Federal Republic of Yugoslavia are met and to pursue durable solutions to their plight, in particular voluntary repatriation and reintegration, stresses the need to create conditions conducive to their safe return, and emphasizes in this regard the importance of regional cooperation in the search for solutions to the plight of refugees;

4. *Calls upon* the Secretary-General to continue to mobilize the timely provision of international humanitarian assistance to the Federal Republic of Yugoslavia;

5. *Emphasizes* the importance of strengthening the coordination of humanitarian assistance to the Federal Republic of Yugoslavia, inter alia, through the mechanisms of a consolidated inter-agency appeal, and recognizes in this regard especially the role of the Office for the Coordination of Humanitarian Affairs;

6. *Requests* the United Nations and the specialized agencies to continue their efforts to assess the humanitarian needs, in cooperation with the Government of the Federal Republic of Yugoslavia, relevant international and regional organizations and bodies and interested States, with a view to ensuring effective links between relief and longer-term assistance to the Federal Republic of Yugoslavia, taking into account the work already carried out in this field and the need to avoid duplication and the overlapping of efforts;

7. *Requests* the Secretary-General to submit to it at its fifty-sixth session, under the item entitled "Strengthening of the coordination of humanitarian and disaster relief assistance of the United Nations, including special economic assistance", a report on the implementation of the present resolution.

Special economic assistance

African economic recovery and development

During its discussion of the integrated and coordinated implementation of and follow-up to major UN conferences and summits, the Economic and Social Council, in July, considered a June report of the Secretary-General [E/2000/69] on the implementation of its agreed conclusions 1999/2 on the development of Africa [YUN 1999, p. 845].

Regarding consistency of coordination mechanisms, the report stated that the main modality for increased efficiency continued to be the promotion of coherent UN system support for countries in Africa, with a view to strengthening national capacity and supporting the integrated and coordinated follow-up to the major international conferences of the 1990s. The United Nations Development Group (UNDG) played an important role in that effort. Coordination mechanisms developed to harmonize development assistance provided by the UN system and interfaced with Governments included the resident coordinator system, the common country assessment, the United Nations Development Assistance Framework (UNDAF) and thematic groups. By the end of 2000, it was envisaged that 44 common country assessments and 19 UNDAFs would be completed in Africa.

With respect to country coverage, the cluster concept of the United Nations Special Initiative for the Implementation of the United Nations New Agenda for the Development of Africa in the 1990s (see p. 874), which assigned responsibility to agencies as either coordinating or cooperating agencies, provided an opportunity for effective coordination and coherence. In the education cluster, led by the World Bank, the United Nations Educational, Scientific and Cultural Organization (UNESCO) and UNICEF, a joint strategy for 16 low-enrolment countries had been developed and support for education sector development plans had been provided to Africa. In the cluster on harnessing information technology for development, national information and communication infrastructure plans had been approved in 10 countries, and 12 countries were in the process of preparing plans. A number of country teams had been working on coordinated responses to situations that fluctuated between crisis and development, or where the prospects of renewed crisis were considerable. Gender, reproductive health, HIV/AIDS, girls' education, poverty reduction, food security and disaster mitigation were examples of where collaboration crossed organizational boundaries to include different partners, various regions and a mixture of coordination instruments. Some agencies were working directly with regional and subregional organizations. Significant effort had been made to ensure the consistency of the various coordination mechanisms.

As to ownership of development assistance, the UN system, having established the common country assessment and UNDAF as coordination mechanisms, had started identifying the next wave of challenges, the most important of which was the need to continue efforts to ensure and improve government participation. Although it was too early to assess the impact of the two mechanisms, most country teams reported enhanced collaboration with local stakeholders, including Governments. While efforts to expand country ownership had increased, there was still much progress to be made, especially regarding the active participation of Governments in coordination meetings. The development of sector-wide approaches in Côte d'Ivoire, Ethiopia, Ghana and Uganda had fostered country ownership, with various partners supporting a single policy thrust as articulated by the Government. Weakness in institutional capacity and statistical data limitations were the main constraints to the full ownership of development assistance.

For the UN system, the framework for global coordination was the UN New Agenda for the Development of Africa in the 1990s, which addressed the priority areas critical to promoting recovery, growth and sustainable development. The 1998 report of the Secretary-General on the causes of conflict and the promotion of durable peace and sustainable development in Africa [YUN 1998, p. 66] and its follow-up by the UN system (see p. 116) was also a framework for addressing some of the key priority areas, with the goal of not just economic recovery and development but also a durable peace. The Office of the Special Coordinator for Africa and the Least Developed Countries of the Department of Economic and Social Affairs functioned as a point of coordination, and UNDG served to facilitate the coordination and harmonization of the various Africa initiatives to the extent that UNDAF and its coordination mechanisms integrated elements of the various programmes and initiatives of bilateral development agencies. The UN system continued to work with the regional and subregional organizations in defining common priorities at the policy and operational levels. Regarding a request contained in agreed conclusions 1999/2 to the Secretary-General to commission an independent evaluation of the New Agenda, the Office of the Special Coordinator, the Economic Commission for Africa and the Africa Recovery Unit of the Department of Public Information had jointly engaged in monitoring its implementation. The Office of the Special Coordinator was taking the lead in preparing a report on progress achieved in strengthening African capacity to coordinate international development assistance at the country level and at the subregional and regional levels, and in developing country-specific as well as comprehensive coordination mechanisms.

The report concluded that it was too early to assess UN reform in the area of coordination and harmonization, especially in Africa, but significant improvements had been made that had strengthened the overall contribution of the UN system to development in the region. Improved coordination frameworks had potential for the better management of programmes, but there was still a need to clarify and strengthen the links among them. The effects of the decline in core resources and its negative impact on human resources required to monitor programme implementation might undermine initial successes achieved thus far.

By **decision 2000/290** of 28 July, the Council took note of the Secretary-General's report.

New Agenda for the Development of Africa

The United Nations New Agenda for the Development of Africa in the 1990s, adopted by the General Assembly in resolution 46/151 [YUN 1991,

p. 402], continued to be implemented by the United Nations Conference on Trade and Development (UNCTAD), among others.

UNCTAD action. The twenty-fifth executive session of the UNCTAD Trade and Development Board (TDB) (Geneva, 22 September) [A/55/15 (Part III)] considered an August report by the UNCTAD Secretary-General [TD/B/EX(25)/2], containing an overview of UNCTAD research and analysis with regard to African development. The report summarized specific activities, including advisory services and technical cooperation, in each sector falling under UNCTAD's mandate. The UNCTAD Secretary-General noted that in the light of the Board's 1999 agreed conclusions [YUN 1999, p. 848], the UNCTAD secretariat had undertaken a study on capital flows and growth in Africa [UNCTAD/GDS/MDPB/7], which argued that growth in Africa continued to be too erratic and too slow to permit an increase in both living standards and domestic savings. The study discussed the policy approaches needed to ensure that aid was effectively translated into investment and growth, keeping in mind the policy mistakes made during the pre- and post-adjustment periods.

At its forty-seventh session (Geneva, 9-20 October) [A/55/15 (agreed conclusions 460(XLVII))], TDB stated that the average growth rate attained in the 1990s for Africa had been 2.4 per cent yearly, far below the average annual growth rate of at least 6 per cent, established as an objective of the New Agenda and needed to achieve sustained and sustainable economic growth and equitable development. It recommended increased foreign capital flows, both private and official, and institutional reforms to reverse capital flight. Foreign direct investment should be encouraged through the promotion of cooperation between industrialized countries and Africa, and efforts should be taken to mitigate the negative perception that prevented reforming countries from reaping the benefits of their efforts and to attract greater foreign capital flows. Concessionary resources akin to ODA were required to address the structural rigidities that constrained Africa's development effort, especially human resources capacities development and poverty alleviation, as well as the extension of physical infrastructure and production capacities. Efforts were needed to increase ODA and to maintain a substantial level of ODA flows to fill the investment gap; over the longer term, private capital flows and domestic savings should replace official financing, thereby reducing the aid dependence of African countries.

The Board noted that Africa's external debt had grown at a very high rate; the enhanced Heavily Indebted Poor Countries (HIPC) Initiative and the goal of bringing an additional 10

HIPCs to decision point by year's end were a welcome development. The Board observed that African countries needed to adopt policies to ensure the efficient use of existing and additional resources to develop human capital and social and physical infrastructure. The report on capital flows and growth in Africa (see p. 874) and a summary of the Board's discussions of the report should serve as an input to the preparatory process for the UN high-level international intergovernmental event on financing for development (see p. 915), as well as for the review of the New Agenda, scheduled for 2002.

Reports of Secretary-General. A September report of the Secretary-General [A/55/350], submitted in response to General Assembly resolution 51/32 [YUN 1996, p. 832], reviewed progress made by the UN system, as well as action taken by African States and donor countries, in implementing the recommendations of the 1996 midterm review [ibid., p. 829] of the UN New Agenda for the Development of Africa in the 1990s. The report updated a 1998 progress report [YUN 1998, p. 863].

A majority of African countries had made substantial progress in applying appropriate macroeconomic policies, promoting the private sector and intensifying the democratization process, yet more improvements were needed in those areas. Africa still lagged behind other developing regions in foreign direct investment, and recommendations on its debt problem had not been fully implemented despite various initiatives. Progress was limited in trade facilitation and market access, due largely to supply constraints, including lack of competitiveness of African products. Progress had been achieved in agriculture and food production, as well as in education, health, population, gender, environment and development. A number of factors continued to hinder the effective implementation of the recommendations of the mid-term review. African countries needed to increase their share in global trade and improve their domestic savings and investment through increased revenue mobilization and improved financial intermediation. The final review and appraisal of the New Agenda was scheduled for 2002.

An addendum to the Secretary-General's report [A/55/350/Add.1], on mobilization of additional resources for African development, noted that between 1992 and 1998 net aggregate resource flows to Africa were erratic, fluctuating from $22.2 billion in 1992 to a high of $28.2 billion in 1995, and thereafter declining to $23.4 billion in 1996. They increased to $26 billion in 1997, but declined steeply to $17.1 billion in 1998,

or by 22 per cent annually from 1995 to 1998. The report said that there were indications of some improvement in external resource flows to Africa in 1999.

GENERAL ASSEMBLY ACTION

On 21 December [meeting 88], the General Assembly adopted **resolution 55/216** [draft: A/55/L.68 & Add.1] without vote [agenda item 30].

Implementation of the United Nations New Agenda for the Development of Africa in the 1990s

The General Assembly,

Having considered the progress report of the Secretary-General on the implementation of the United Nations New Agenda for the Development of Africa in the 1990s, and its addendum on mobilization of additional resources for African development, a study on overall resource flows to Africa,

Recalling its resolution 46/151 of 18 December 1991, the annex to which contains the United Nations New Agenda for the Development of Africa in the 1990s, its resolutions 48/214 of 23 December 1993, 49/142 of 23 December 1994 and 53/90 of 7 December 1998 on the implementation of the New Agenda, as well as its resolution 51/32 of 6 December 1996 on the mid-term review of the implementation of the New Agenda,

Bearing in mind the report of the Secretary-General on the causes of conflict and the promotion of durable peace and sustainable development in Africa submitted to the Security Council and the General Assembly in 1998 and its resolution 54/234 of 22 December 1999 on the causes of conflict and the promotion of durable peace and sustainable development in Africa, as well as the recommendations of the Open-ended Ad Hoc Working Group on the Causes of Conflict and the Promotion of Durable Peace and Sustainable Development in Africa, established by the General Assembly to monitor the implementation of the recommendations contained in the report of the Secretary-General,

Recalling that, while the primary responsibility for the development of Africa remains with African countries, the international community has a stake in it and in supporting the efforts of those countries in that regard,

Welcoming recent efforts and initiatives of the United Nations on Africa, in particular, the meeting of the Security Council on human immunodeficiency virus/acquired immunodeficiency syndrome (HIV/AIDS) in Africa, held in January 2000, section VII of the United Nations Millennium Declaration on meeting the special needs of Africa, the high-level segment of the Economic and Social Council to be held in July 2001, as well as other events on development that will address issues of particular importance for Africa, such as the Third United Nations Conference on the Least Developed Countries to be hosted by the European Union in Brussels in May 2001, the special session of the General Assembly on HIV/AIDS scheduled for June 2001, the high-level international intergovernmental event on financing for development and the ten-year review of the United Nations Conference on Environment and Development,

Welcoming also the strong partnership between European Union and African countries through the Cairo

Declaration and Plan of Action,[a] as well as the Cotonou Agreement of 23 June 2000, with its financial commitments, between the members of the European Union and the African, Caribbean and Pacific Group of States, which is mainly composed of African countries,

Welcoming further the support by the international community, including the Beijing Declaration and Programme for China-Africa Cooperation in Economic and Social Development, adopted by the China-Africa Cooperation Forum on 12 October 2000, the United States of America Africa Growth and Opportunity Act, as well as the Ministerial Conference of the Tokyo International Conference on African Development on the follow-up of the implementation of the Tokyo Agenda for Action, scheduled for 2001 or early 2002,

Taking note with great concern of the debt burden of many African countries, as debt servicing continues to drain the limited resources for development,

Reaffirming the need for the integration of African countries into the international trading system by highlighting the importance of creating, at the national and international levels, an environment that is conducive to attracting foreign direct investment and promoting international trade as engines of growth and development,

Expressing its concern at the overall declining trends of resource flows to Africa, in particular the low levels of foreign direct investment and official development assistance, which have seriously constrained, among other things, the timely implementation of the New Agenda,

Recognizing the crucial need for a substantial increase in financial resource flows to Africa to support the implementation of development activities of African countries,

1. *Takes note with appreciation* of the progress report of the Secretary-General on the implementation of the United Nations New Agenda for the Development of Africa in the 1990s and its addendum on the mobilization of additional resources for African development, a study on overall resource flows to Africa;

2. *Recognizes and calls* for further broadening and strengthening of efforts by many African countries to enhance progress in areas covering economic reforms, including the putting in place of sound macroeconomic policies, promotion of the private sector, enhancement of the democratization process and strengthening of civil society and participatory, transparent and accountable governance and the rule of law, as well as increased attention to the human dimension, especially education, gender, population, health and south-south cooperation;

3. *Expresses its grave concern* at the limited progress in many other areas, such as poverty eradication, prevention and treatment of infectious diseases, such as malaria, tuberculosis and, in particular, the HIV/AIDS pandemic, the combating of drought and desertification, agriculture and food production, food security, infrastructure development, institutional capacity for regional cooperation and integration, environment and development and conflict prevention, management and resolution;

4. *Urges* the implementation of the enhanced programme of debt relief to heavily indebted poor countries without delay and the cancellation of all the official bilateral debt of those countries in the context of poverty eradication, in return for a demonstrable commitment by them to poverty reduction as part of their overall development strategy, and requests the support of the international community for debt relief for African countries in a comprehensive and effective manner;

5. *Stresses* the urgent need to facilitate the full integration of African countries into the world economy, and in this context calls for continued efforts to enhance market access for products of export interest to African economies and support for the efforts towards diversification and the building of supply capacity, and in this regard welcomes the efforts of the European Union and the United States, in particular through the Cotonou Agreement of the European Union and the African, Caribbean and Pacific Group of States and the United States Africa Growth and Opportunity Act;

6. *Expresses its appreciation* to the developed countries that have agreed to and have reached the target of 0.7 per cent of their gross national product for overall official development assistance, and calls upon the developed countries that have not yet done so to strengthen their efforts to achieve, as soon as possible, the agreed target of 0.7 per cent of their gross national product for overall official development assistance, taking into account the special development needs of the least developed countries in Africa;

7. *Urges* all States, international financial institutions, in particular the International Monetary Fund and the World Bank, multilateral organizations and development funds and programmes of the United Nations system, as well as intergovernmental and non-governmental organizations, to pursue with renewed vigour, and as a matter of urgency, the realization of the goals and objectives embodied in the New Agenda;

8. *Calls upon* the United Nations system, as well as other multilateral and bilateral development cooperation institutions, including international financial institutions, and non-governmental organizations, to ensure that development assistance activities in Africa are carried out in a more coordinated manner for greater efficiency, impact and tangible results under the leadership of recipient countries;

9. *Reaffirms* its resolution 51/32, recognizing the United Nations System-wide Special Initiative on Africa as an implementing arm of the New Agenda, and notes with satisfaction the progress achieved so far, and invites the Secretary-General to continue his efforts to strengthen this mechanism with a view to enabling it to advance coordination and harmonization of initiatives among development actors in Africa, and in this regard stresses the importance of establishing an integrated United Nations approach to Africa;

10. *Also reaffirms* its decision contained in resolution 51/32 to conduct in 2002 the final review and appraisal of the New Agenda in line with the provisions of section II, paragraph 43 *(e)*, of the annex to resolution 46/151;

11. *Invites* the Secretary-General to encourage the closer involvement of the Organization of African Unity in the implementation, follow-up and evaluation of the United Nations New Agenda for the Development of Africa in the 1990s and beyond, including the holding of the final review of the implementation of the New Agenda in 2002;

12. *Stresses* the importance, in preparation of the final review and appraisal of the New Agenda, of an independent and high-level quality evaluation;

13. *Reiterates*, in this regard, the importance of establishing a set of performance indicators to measure the progress made in the implementation of the New Agenda;

14. *Requests* the Secretary-General, taking into account these indicators, to submit an independent and objective evaluation of the New Agenda to the General Assembly not later than 31 May 2002;

15. *Reaffirms* its decision contained in resolution 54/234 to consider at its fifty-sixth session the modalities for undertaking the final review and appraisal of the New Agenda, taking into account the mid-term review of the New Agenda, agreed conclusions 1999/2 and decision 1999/270 adopted by the Economic and Social Council at its substantive session of 1999, and section VII of the United Nations Millennium Declaration.

ᵃA/54/855-E/2000/44.

UN System-wide Special Initiative on Africa

CPC action. In response to a 1999 request of the Committee for Programme and Coordination (CPC) [YUN 1999, p. 849], the Secretary-General submitted to CPC, at its fortieth session (New York, 5 June–1 July and 21-29 August) [A/55/16], a May report [E/AC.51/2000/6 & Corr.1] updating progress made in the implementation of the United Nations System-wide Special Initiative for the Implementation of the New Agenda for the period May 1999 to April 2000.

Further progress was recorded in governance, information technology, education, health, gender and population. Programmes relating to poverty reduction through employment and informal sector development, market access and trade opportunities, water, food security, environment and South-South cooperation had shown steady progress.

Pursuant to Economic and Social Council agreed conclusions 1999/2 [YUN 1999, p. 845] and a 1999 CPC request [ibid., p. 848], the Secretary-General presented a resource mobilization strategy, which would be discussed at the second annual regional consultation meeting of UN system organizations working in Africa (see below).

Improvements had been made regarding coordination at the country, subregional and regional levels.

Annexed to the report was the proposed resource mobilization strategy and information on action taken by the UN system in response to CPC recommendations made in 1998 [YUN 1998, p. 865] and 1999 [YUN 1999, p. 848]. The Secretary-General observed that much remained to be done to implement those recommendations.

On 22 June [A/55/16], CPC, expressing support for the resource mobilization strategy annexed to the Secretary-General's report, requested that an independent evaluation covering the five-year duration of the Special Initiative be carried out and submitted in 2001. The Committee reiterated the importance it attached to its 1998 recommendation that the various lead agencies be called upon, under the coordination of the Administrative Committee on Coordination (ACC) Steering Committee, to develop a common strategic framework for action.

Regional consultation. The second regional consultation of UN agencies working in Africa (Addis Ababa, Ethiopia, 26-27 June) stated that resource mobilization for Special Initiative activities was best addressed at the country level on the basis of country-owned sector-wide programmes.

Democratic Republic of the Congo

As the Democratic Republic of the Congo grappled with the third year of the war, the humanitarian crisis was growing throughout the country. The number of vulnerable people was estimated at 16 million, or about 33 per cent of the population, while 4.3 per cent of households faced chronic food insecurity. Health service provision halved and continued to dwindle. Access problems were encountered in government- and rebel-controlled areas. However, breakthroughs were made in Kasai, Northern Katanga, Equateur, Ituri and South Kivu.

A UN consolidated inter-agency appeal, covering January to December 2000, which had sought $71.4 million, was revised in July to $37 million. The decrease reflected the exclusion of WFP requirements that were included in the 2000 appeal for the Great Lakes region (see p. 858). Of the revised amount, $11.8 million, or 31.8 per cent of the requirements, was received. An inter-agency appeal for January to December 2001 sought $139.5 million.

Report of Secretary-General. Pursuant to General Assembly resolution 54/96 B [YUN 1999, p. 849], the Secretary-General, in August [A/55/319], described financial and material assistance provided by the UN system to the DRC in its economic recovery and reconstruction process.

Humanitarian activities constituted a major part of the activities undertaken by UN agencies, but support to development activities also continued. Aside from UNICEF, which had drawn up a country programme, all the other development agencies were executing interim programmes. UNHCR continued to carry out its assistance programmes for refugees in the reception zones. Interventions by UN agencies that had gone beyond emergency humanitarian assistance covered health, including the fight against AIDS, education, governance, management of development,

agriculture, rural development and environment, humanitarian needs, infrastructure and
employment/labour. However, their efforts were
handicapped by certain decisions of DRC authorities, particularly the monetary measures to fix
the exchange rate of the national currency.

Furthermore, ODA had been drastically reduced subsequent to the deteriorating relations
between the DRC and its major development partners since the beginning of the 1990s. Since certain partners of the DRC later stated that they
intended to resume their cooperation programmes, the various sectoral programmes formulated with the financial and technical support
of the specialized agencies would serve as supporting documents for meetings to mobilize resources and/or for dialogues. Only Belgium and
the EU had officially confirmed their decision to
resume unconditionally their structural cooperation with the DRC.

GENERAL ASSEMBLY ACTION

On 14 December [meeting 85], the General Assembly adopted **resolution 55/166** [draft: A/55/L.36
& Add.1] without vote [agenda item 20 *(b)*].

Special assistance for the economic recovery and reconstruction of the Democratic Republic of the Congo

The General Assembly,

Recalling its resolutions 52/169 A of 16 December
1997, 53/1 L of 7 December 1998 and 54/96 B of 8 December 1999,

Recalling also Security Council resolutions
1234(1999) of 9 April 1999, 1258(1999) of 6 August
1999, 1273(1999) of 5 November 1999, 1279(1999) of
30 November 1999, 1291(2000) of 24 February 2000,
1304(2000) of 16 June 2000, 1316(2000) of 23 August
2000 and 1323(2000) of 13 October 2000, the statement
adopted by the Council at its meeting of 7 September
2000, held at the level of heads of State and Government, and all previous statements by its President relating to the situation in the Democratic Republic of the
Congo,

Recalling further the Ceasefire Agreement signed in
Lusaka and the Kampala disengagement plan and the
obligations of all signatories to those agreements and
the obligations deriving from Security Council resolution 1304(2000),

Reaffirming the sovereignty, territorial integrity and
political independence of the Democratic Republic of
the Congo and all States in the region,

Alarmed at the plight of the civilian population
throughout the country, and calling for its protection,

Gravely concerned at the deteriorating economic and
social situation in the Democratic Republic of the
Congo, in particular in the eastern Congo, and at the
effect of the continued fighting on the inhabitants of
the country,

Expressing its deep concern at the dire consequences of
the conflict for the humanitarian and human rights
situation, as well as at the reports of the illegal exploitation of the natural resources of the Democratic Republic of the Congo,

Urging all parties to respect and protect human
rights and respect international humanitarian law, in
particular the Geneva Conventions of 1949 and the additional Protocols thereto, of 1977,

Deeply concerned about the continuing extensive destruction of life and property, as well as the severe damage to infrastructure and the environment suffered by
the Democratic Republic of the Congo,

Bearing in mind that the Democratic Republic of the
Congo also suffers from the problems encountered by a
country that has received thousands of refugees from
neighbouring countries,

Recalling that the Democratic Republic of the Congo
is a least developed country with severe economic and
social problems arising from its weak economic infrastructure and aggravated by the ongoing conflict,

Bearing in mind the close interrelationship between
ensuring peace and security and the ability of the
country to meet the humanitarian needs of its people
and to take effective steps towards the rapid revitalization of the economy, and reaffirming the urgent need
to assist the Democratic Republic of the Congo in the
rehabilitation and reconstruction of its damaged economy and in its efforts to restore basic services and the
infrastructure of the country,

1. *Takes note* of the report of the Secretary-General;

2. *Urges* all parties concerned in the region to cease
all military activity in the Democratic Republic of the
Congo which breaches the ceasefire provided for in the
Ceasefire Agreement signed in Lusaka and the Kampala disengagement plan and to implement fully those
agreements and create the conditions necessary for the
speedy and peaceful resolution of the crisis, and also
urges all parties to engage in a process of political dialogue and negotiation;

3. *Encourages* the Government of the Democratic
Republic of the Congo to pursue sound macroeconomic policies and to promote good governance
and the rule of law, and urges the Government to exert
all efforts for economic recovery and reconstruction
despite the ongoing armed conflict;

4. *Renews its invitation* to the Government of the
Democratic Republic of the Congo to cooperate with
the United Nations, the specialized agencies and other
organizations in addressing the need for rehabilitation
and reconstruction, and stresses the need for the Government to assist and protect the civilian population,
including refugees and internally displaced persons
within the territory of that country regardless of their
origin;

5. *Urges* all parties to respect fully the provisions of
international humanitarian law and, in this regard, to
ensure the safe and unhindered access of humanitarian personnel to all affected populations throughout
the territory of the Democratic Republic of the Congo
and the safety of United Nations and humanitarian
personnel;

6. *Renews its urgent appeal* to the executive boards of
the United Nations funds and programmes to continue
to keep under consideration the special needs of the
Democratic Republic of the Congo;

7. *Invites* Governments to continue to provide support to the Democratic Republic of the Congo;

8. *Requests* the Secretary-General:

(a) To continue to consult urgently with regional leaders, in coordination with the Secretary-General of the Organization of African Unity, about ways to bring about a peaceful and durable solution to the conflict;

(b) To continue to consult with regional leaders, in coordination with the Secretary-General of the Organization of African Unity, in order to convene, when appropriate, an international conference on peace, security and development in Central Africa and in the Great Lakes region, under the auspices of the United Nations and the Organization of African Unity, to address the problems of the region in a comprehensive manner;

(c) To keep under review the economic situation in the Democratic Republic of the Congo with a view to promoting participation in and support for a programme of financial and material assistance to the country to enable it to meet its urgent needs in terms of economic recovery and reconstruction;

(d) To submit to the General Assembly at its fifty-sixth session a report on the actions taken pursuant to the present resolution.

Other economic assistance

Central America

Nicaragua

In response to General Assembly resolution 53/1 D [YUN 1998, p. 869], the Secretary-General submitted a July report [A/55/125-E/2000/91] on efforts taken to assist Nicaragua to consolidate democracy, reintegrate ex-combatants and Nicaraguans in exile, establish a national disaster prevention, mitigation and response system and adopt a national policy on population. Strategies had been proposed to reduce environmental degradation. In April, a regional UNDP/United Nations Environment Programme (UNEP) project to establish a programme for the consolidation of the Mesoamerican biological corridor was initiated.

Haiti

In response to Economic and Social Council resolution 1999/11 [YUN 1999, p. 855], the Secretary-General submitted a June report [E/2000/63] on the development and implementation of a long-term programme of support for Haiti. The report covered progress achieved and constraints faced by the international community in that regard from August 1999 to May 2000.

The Secretary-General concluded that it remained difficult to lay out a precise timetable for the elaboration of a coherent long-term programme of support that would meet the approval and draw the active support of the international community, especially Haiti's key development partners. Nonetheless, the groundwork for the programme was being laid through the ongoing common country assessment, the planned formulation by the interim Government of a medium-term development strategy, and later a Poverty Reduction Strategy Paper with the support of the World Bank and IMF, and the formulation by the UN system in Haiti of an UNDAF in 2001.

A key requirement in the formulation of the international community's programme of support, as requested in resolution 1999/11, would be the availability of credible statistics on the social sectors. That information would provide a clearer picture of the social development constraints facing Haiti, as well as the baseline data needed by the Government to formulate, over the next two years, a long-term poverty-reduction strategy along the lines set out by IMF and the World Bank.

Annexed to the report was a table of external aid disbursements by donor from 1995 to 1998.

By **decision 2000/235** of 27 July, the Economic and Social Council took note of the Secretary-General's report and asked him to report at its next substantive session on steps taken by the Haitian Government, the UN system and the international community towards the development and implementation of a long-term programme of support for Haiti.

Third States affected by sanctions

A May note by the Secretariat [E/2000/45] stated that, pursuant to Economic and Social Council resolution 1999/59 [YUN 1999, p. 856] and General Assembly resolution 54/107 [ibid., p. 1252], the Secretary-General's report on the implementation of the provisions of the Charter of the United Nations related to assistance to third States affected by the application of sanctions [ibid.] would be available to the Council in 2000 (see also p. 1269).

ECONOMIC AND SOCIAL COUNCIL ACTION

On 28 July [meeting 45], the Economic and Social Council adopted **resolution 2000/32** [draft: E/2000/L.26] without vote [agenda item 13].

Assistance to third States affected by the application of sanctions

The Economic and Social Council,

Recalling its resolution 1999/59 of 30 July 1999,

Recalling also General Assembly resolution 54/107 of 9 December 1999 on the implementation of the provisions of the Charter of the United Nations related to assistance to third States affected by the application of sanctions,

Aware of the decision of the Security Council to establish on a temporary basis an informal working group of the Council to develop general recommendations on how to improve the effectiveness of United Nations sanctions, including, inter alia, the issues of unintended impacts of sanctions and assistance to Member States in implementing sanctions, as contained in the note by the President of the Security Council of 17 April 2000,

Taking note of the note by the Secretariat,

Taking note also of section VII, on assistance to countries invoking Article 50 of the Charter of the United Nations, of the annual overview report of the Administrative Committee on Coordination for 1999,

1. *Takes note* of the most recent report of the Secretary-General on the implementation of the provisions of the Charter of the United Nations related to assistance to third States affected by the application of sanctions, in particular sections IV and V thereof;

2. *Welcomes* the report of the Secretary-General containing a summary of the deliberations and main findings of the ad hoc expert group meeting on developing a methodology for assessing the consequences incurred by third States as a result of preventive or enforcement measures and on exploring innovative and practical measures of international assistance to the affected third States, and invites States and relevant international organizations within and outside the United Nations system which have not yet done so to provide their views regarding the report of the ad hoc expert group meeting;

3. *Reaffirms* the important role of the General Assembly, the Economic and Social Council and the Committee for Programme and Coordination in mobilizing and monitoring, as appropriate, the economic assistance efforts of the international community and the United Nations system to States confronted with special economic problems arising from the carrying out of preventive or enforcement measures imposed by the Security Council and, as appropriate, in identifying solutions to the special economic problems of those States;

4. *Decides* to continue consideration of this question, under the item entitled "Economic and environmental questions", taking into account the relevant decisions of the General Assembly and the Security Council.

States affected in the Balkans

In response to General Assembly resolution 54/96 G [YUN 1999, p. 857], the Secretary-General submitted a November report on economic assistance to States affected by the consequences of severing their economic relations with FRY [A/55/620 & Corr.1]. The report contained information provided by nine States and 19 organizations, programmes and funds of the UN system describing action they had taken to assist the affected States.

The Secretary-General concluded that because of the limited number of replies received from the affected States and the donor countries, it was not possible to make a conclusive assessment. However, recent assessments by international bodies active in the region indicated that the affected countries continued to face adjustment problems stemming from a range of factors, including the long-term consequences of

major systemic transformations, violent conflicts and economic sanctions. It was essential that those problems be addressed in the context of the ongoing reconstruction and rehabilitation effort, as well as through enhancing regional cooperation for stabilization, economic recovery and development in the Balkans. At the regional level, attention was needed in the areas of infrastructure reconstruction, including the resumption of navigation on the Danube, private sector development, trade integration, investment promotion and institutional capacity-building. To date, the reconstruction and stabilization process and regional cooperation programmes had yielded positive results in the most seriously affected countries.

The UN system continued to implement substantial programmes of financial and technical assistance. In response to the renewed appeals for special economic assistance, programmes had been enhanced with a view to providing support to economic recovery, structural adjustment and development. Within the framework of the reconstruction and recovery programme for the Kosovo province of FRY, a series of emergency measures and activities had been carried out to address the regional consequences of the Kosovo crisis as a result of economic and social constraints caused by large numbers of refugees and displaced persons, as well as by disruptions in trade, transport and foreign investment in the neighbouring and other affected countries. As most urgent requirements resulting from the Kosovo crisis had been met, the focus had shifted to addressing a variety of longer-term economic and social problems of the affected States.

GENERAL ASSEMBLY ACTION

On 14 December [meeting 85], the General Assembly adopted **resolution 55/170** [draft: A/55/L.59 & Add.1] without vote [agenda item 20 *(b)*].

Economic assistance to the Eastern European States affected by the developments in the Balkans

The General Assembly,

Recalling its resolution 54/96 G of 15 December 1999,

Recalling also the Stability Pact for South-Eastern Europe, adopted in Cologne, Germany, on 10 June 1999, and endorsed at the Sarajevo Summit of 30 July 1999, and emphasizing the crucial importance of its implementation,

Stressing the importance of the regional cooperation initiatives, assistance arrangements and organizations, such as the Process of Stability and Good-Neighbourliness in South-East Europe (Royaumont Initiative), the South-East European Cooperative Initiative, the South-East European Cooperation Process, the Central European Initiative, the Black Sea Economic Cooperation and the Danube Commission,

Noting the leading role played by the high-level steering group for South-Eastern Europe, under the joint chairmanship of the European Commission and the World Bank, in guiding the donor coordination process for the economic reconstruction, stabilization, reform and development of the region, in close cooperation with the Stability Pact for South-Eastern Europe,

Mindful of the positive results of the regional funding conference for South-Eastern Europe organized by the European Commission and the World Bank, held in Brussels on 29 and 30 March 2000, and of the progress achieved in mobilizing and coordinating support of the donor community and international financial institutions for reconstruction and development efforts in South-Eastern Europe,

Welcoming the democratic changes in the Federal Republic of Yugoslavia and their positive effects on peace, stability and development in South-Eastern Europe,

Taking note of the report of the Secretary-General on economic assistance to the Eastern European States affected by the developments in the Balkans and the conclusions contained therein,

1. *Expresses concern* at the persistence of special economic problems confronting the Eastern European States affected by the developments in the Balkans, in particular their impact on regional trade and economic relations and on the navigation along the Danube and on the Adriatic Sea;

2. *Welcomes* the support already provided by the international community, in particular by the European Union and other major donors, to the affected States to assist them in coping with their special economic problems during the transition period following the developments in the Balkans, as well as in the longer-term process of economic recovery, structural adjustment and development in the region;

3. *Stresses* the importance of the effective implementation of the Stability Pact for South-Eastern Europe, the objective of which is to strengthen countries in South-Eastern Europe in their efforts to foster peace, democracy, respect for human rights and economic prosperity, in order to achieve stability in the whole region, and welcomes its follow-up activities, aimed, inter alia, at economic reconstruction, development and cooperation, including economic cooperation in the region and between the region and the rest of Europe;

4. *Invites* all States and the relevant international organizations, both within and outside the United Nations system, in particular the international financial institutions, to continue to take into account the special needs and situations of the affected States in providing support and assistance to their efforts for economic recovery, structural adjustment and development;

5. *Emphasizes* the importance of a well-coordinated and timely donor response to the external funding requirements of the process for economic reconstruction, stabilization, reform and development in the Balkans, as well as financial support to other affected countries of Eastern Europe;

6. *Encourages* the affected States of the region to continue and enhance the process of multilateral regional cooperation in the fields of transport and infrastructure development, including the resumption of navigation on the Danube, as well as to foster conditions favourable to trade, investment and private sector development in all the countries of the region;

7. *Invites* the relevant international organizations to take appropriate steps, consistent with the principle of efficient and effective procurement and with the agreed measures for procurement reform, in order to broaden access for interested local and regional vendors and to facilitate their participation in the international assistance efforts for reconstruction, recovery and development of the region;

8. *Requests* the Secretary-General to report to the General Assembly at its fifty-sixth session on the implementation of the present resolution.

Disaster relief

In 2000, natural disasters were not confined to particular regions, nor did they discriminate between developed and developing countries. Forest fires raged for several weeks in the United States and floods caused devastation in several parts of Europe, notably in France, Italy, Switzerland and the United Kingdom. Developing countries were, however, much more severely affected, especially in terms of loss of lives and the percentage of economic losses in relation to their gross national product. Widespread drought in the Horn of Africa threatened 12.3 million people in many parts of the region, including Djibouti, Eritrea, Ethiopia, Kenya, Somalia, the Sudan and Uganda. Mozambique required emergency humanitarian assistance following severe flooding caused by heavy rains. Madagascar was struck by tropical cyclones Eline and Hudah. Zimbabwe was also hit by cyclone Eline, which flooded the main river basins. Severe drought in the first half of 2000 afflicted much of Central and Southern Asia, particularly Afghanistan, India, Iran, Pakistan, Tajikistan, Uzbekistan and the Caucasian countries of Armenia, Azerbaijan and Georgia. Cambodia was devastated by two major floods, affecting 2.2 million people. In the Democratic People's Republic of Korea, longer-term economic problems and continuing poor harvests had been further exacerbated by an ongoing series of natural disasters, namely, floods, drought and tropical storm damage. A severe monsoon season in Viet Nam affected more than 5 million people and claimed 370 lives. In Central America, hurricane Keith battered Belize, causing extensive flood damage along with associated health risks and economic setbacks.

During the year, the Office for the Coordination of Humanitarian Affairs (OCHA) reported contributions for natural disasters totalling $460.7 million for 45 situations in 35 countries.

Through its Disaster Response Branch (DRB), OCHA mobilized and coordinated assistance to 61 natural and environmental disasters. DRB disbursed emergency cash grants of $640,000 and channelled some $6.1 million in cash and in-kind contributions into emergency relief programmes. The Branch dispatched 11 United Nations Disaster Assessment and Coordination (UNDAC) missions to support the in-country disaster assessment and coordination mechanisms in the aftermath of disasters, and conducted UNDAC training in Europe, Latin America and Asia and the Pacific. DRB coordinated support programmes and advocated humanitarian needs resulting from the Chernobyl disaster (see p. 889), and concluded the divestiture of the OCHA warehouse in Pisa, Italy, which maintained a stock of donated disaster relief items, to WFP and the remaining stocks to the United Nations Logistics Base in Brindisi, Italy.

International Strategy for Disaster Reduction

The United Nations International Strategy for Disaster Reduction (UNISDR), adopted by the programme forum of the International Decade for Natural Disaster Reduction (1990-2000) (IDNDR) in 1999 [YUN 1999, p. 859] and endorsed by the General Assembly in resolution 54/219 [ibid., p. 861], built upon the experience of IDNDR, which was launched by the Assembly in resolution 44/236 [YUN 1989, p. 355]. The Strategy reflected a shift from the traditional emphasis on disaster response to disaster reduction. The inter-agency secretariat, which was established on 1 January, developed a framework for action to implement the Strategy, which sought to enable societies to become more resilient to the effects of natural hazards and related technological and environmental phenomena in order to reduce human, economic and social losses.

The UNISDR secretariat, which reported to the Under-Secretary-General for Humanitarian Affairs, was established to serve as the focal point within the UN system for the coordination of strategies and programmes for natural disaster reduction, and to ensure synergy between disaster reduction strategies and those in the socio-economic and humanitarian fields; to support the Inter-Agency Task Force for Disaster Reduction in the development of policies on natural disaster reduction; to promote a worldwide culture of reduction of the negative effects of natural hazards; to serve as an international clearing house for the dissemination and exchange of information and knowledge on disaster reduction strategies;

and to backstop the policy and advocacy activities of national committees for natural disaster reduction.

The secretariat organized the first meeting of the Inter-Agency Task Force for Disaster Reduction (Geneva, 27-28 April). The Task Force was composed of eight UN agencies (FAO, ITU, UNDP, UNESCO, UNEP, WFP, WMO, World Bank), seven regional bodies and eight representatives of civil society and NGOs; the membership would be rotated on a biennial basis. The Task Force identified focal areas for its work, including ecosystems management, land-use management and unplanned urban areas; advocacy, information, education and training; public awareness and commitment; raising political will and the profile of prevention; the social and health impact of disasters; capacity-building in developing countries; mainstreaming disaster reduction in sustainable development and in national planning; lessons learned for prevention from actual disasters; private and public sector partnerships; technological disasters; and the application of science and technology in disaster reduction. It established four working groups: working group 1, led by WMO, dealt with climate and disasters, particularly the El Niño/La Niña phenomenon (see p. 883); working group 2, led by UNEP, focused on early warning; working group 3, led by UNDP, dealt with risk vulnerability and impact assessment; and working group 4, which was established at its second meeting in October and led by the Global Fire Monitoring Centre located in Freiburg, Germany, dealt with wildfires.

During 2000, the secretariat produced studies and reports, such as the Risk Assessment Tools for Diagnosis of Urban Areas against Seismic Disasters methodology for seismic risk reduction strategies, and a report on the Usoi Landslide Dam and Lake Sarez in Tajikistan.

The Trust Fund for the International Decade for Natural Disaster Reduction was renamed the Trust Fund for the International Strategy for Disaster Reduction for the purpose of receiving voluntary contributions in support of the secretariat's activities. The Trust Fund had received contributions amounting to $2.2 million for the 2000-2001 biennium.

ACC action. In April [ACC/2000/4], ACC invited the Task Force to emphasize building and strengthening the capacities of disaster-prone countries through research and the training of experts.

In October [ACC/2000/20], the Committee observed that the Task Force might consider establishing a working group on science and technology. It was pointed out that the development aspects of the Strategy should be considered by the General Assembly's Second (Economic and Financial) Committee, whereas the relief, emergency and humanitarian aspects should be addressed by the Third (Social, Humanitarian and Cultural) Committee. It was observed that the UNISDR secretariat should maintain a distinct and multidisciplinary character under the joint ownership of ACC and that consultations were needed on issues of common interest to the concerned agencies and on the development of Task Force work plans. ACC asked the Task Force to continue to emphasize natural disaster monitoring, prediction, early warning and preparedness and the role of science and technology.

El Niño

In response to General Assembly resolution 54/220 [YUN 1999, p. 863], the Secretary-General submitted a June report on international cooperation to reduce the impact of the El Niño phenomenon [A/55/99-E/2000/86], a disruption of the ocean-atmosphere system in the tropical Pacific that had important consequences for weather and climate worldwide. The report reviewed the context of the El Niño phenomenon, ongoing activities and future arrangements regarding the Inter-Agency Task Force on El Niño, created under IDNDR.

A study on the prediction and amelioration of socio-economic impacts of the El Niño Southern Oscillation (ENSO) began in March for a duration of 18 months. The study, a collaborative effort of the Inter-American Development Bank and WMO, evaluated the existing institutional and technical forecasting capability in Latin America and the Caribbean, formulated project proposals and analysed the economic value of improved early warning systems.

The Secretary-General discussed the role of the working group on El Niño/La Niña established under the UNISDR Task Force for Disaster Reduction (see p. 882). He recommended that the working group assume the role of the former IDNDR Inter-Agency Task Force on El Niño and build on its outputs. He also proposed that UNISDR activity on ENSO be linked to other strategic platforms, such as the Climate Agenda and the United Nations Framework Convention on Climate Change [YUN 1992, p. 681], the Convention on Biological Diversity [ibid., p. 683] and the United Nations Convention to Combat Desertification in those Countries Experiencing Serious Drought and/or Desertification, particularly in Africa [YUN 1994, p. 944]. The Secretary-General advocated the convening of relevant workshops and forums and support to proposed regional ENSO centres.

Annexed to the report were country and agency reviews on the impact of the 1997/98 El Niño event.

In a later report [A/56/76-E/2001/54], the Secretary-General described a global review of regional outlook forums held in Pretoria, South Africa, in October. The review recognized the significant role the regional climate outlook forums had played in capacity-building and the links they had helped to develop between meteorologists and end-users of seasonal forecasts. It made recommendations to enhance the service provided by the forums in terms of regional issues, capacity-building, the delivery of products and other technical subjects.

ECONOMIC AND SOCIAL COUNCIL ACTION

On 28 July [meeting 45], the Economic and Social Council adopted **resolution 2000/33** [draft: E/2000/L.28] without vote [agenda item 13 (a)].

International cooperation to reduce the impact of the El Niño phenomenon

The Economic and Social Council,

Recalling General Assembly resolutions 52/200 of 18 December 1997, 53/185 of 15 December 1998, 54/219 and 54/220 of 22 December 1999 and Council resolutions 1999/46 of 28 July 1999 and 1999/63 of 30 July 1999,

Having considered the report of the Secretary-General,

Reiterating that the coordination function of the Council is to give guidance to its functional commissions on natural disaster reduction within the overall context of sustainable development strategies,

1. *Takes note with appreciation* of the conclusions and recommendations contained in the report of the Secretary-General, and expresses its willingness to study them;

2. *Welcomes* the steps taken to ensure the continuity of international cooperation to reduce the impact of the El Niño phenomenon within the International Strategy for Disaster Reduction;

3. *Notes with satisfaction* the establishment of the working group on El Niño/La Niña within the Inter-Agency Task Force for Disaster Reduction;

4. *Recognizes* the contribution to the research on the El Niño phenomenon made by existing institutions, including the International Research Institute for Climate Prediction, the Pan-American Health Organization and the International Federation of Red Cross and Red Crescent Societies;

5. *Invites* the international community to provide technical, financial and scientific cooperation for the prompt establishment of the international centre for research on El Niño in Guayaquil, Ecuador, as requested by the General Assembly in its resolution 54/220, and also invites the host country to facilitate the process of establishing the centre;

6. *Requests* the Secretary-General to continue the full implementation of General Assembly resolutions 52/200, 53/185, 54/219 and 54/220, and Council resolutions 1999/46 and 1999/63.

On 20 December [meeting 87], the General Assembly, on the recommendation of the Second Committee [A/55/582/Add.8], adopted **resolution 55/197** without vote [agenda item 95].

International cooperation to reduce the impact of the El Niño phenomenon

The General Assembly,

Recalling its resolutions 52/200 of 18 December 1997, 53/185 of 15 December 1998 and 54/220 of 22 December 1999 and Economic and Social Council resolutions 1999/46 of 28 July 1999 and 1999/63 of 30 July 1999, and taking note of Council resolution 2000/33 of 28 July 2000,

Having considered the report of the Secretary-General,

Reaffirming the importance of international cooperation for a better scientific understanding of the El Niño phenomenon and that international cooperation and solidarity with the affected countries are indispensable,

Reaffirming also the importance of developing strategies at the national, subregional, regional and international levels that aim to prevent, mitigate and rehabilitate the damage caused by natural disasters resulting from the El Niño phenomenon,

1. *Takes note with appreciation* of the conclusions and recommendations contained in the report of the Secretary-General;

2. *Also takes note with appreciation* of the measures adopted in order to ensure the continuity of international cooperation to reduce the impact of the El Niño phenomenon, within the framework of the International Strategy for Disaster Reduction, and reiterates its invitation to Member States, organs and organizations of the United Nations system, contained in paragraphs 7, 8 and 9 of its resolution 52/200;

3. *Welcomes* the establishment of the working group on the El Niño/La Niña phenomenon within the framework of the Inter-Agency Task Force for Disaster Reduction;

4. *Calls upon* the Secretary-General and the relevant United Nations organs, funds and programmes, in particular those taking part in the International Strategy for Disaster Reduction, and the international community to adopt, as appropriate, the necessary measures for the prompt establishment of the international centre for the study of the El Niño phenomenon at Guayaquil, Ecuador, and invites the international community to provide scientific, technical and financial assistance and cooperation for that purpose, in accordance with resolution 54/220;

5. *Invites* the Government of the host country to facilitate the process for the prompt establishment of the international centre for the study of the El Niño phenomenon;

6. *Requests* the Secretary-General to continue the full implementation of its resolutions 52/200, 53/185, 54/219 and 54/220 and Economic and Social Council resolutions 1999/46, 1999/63 and 2000/33;

7. *Also requests* the Secretary-General to report to the General Assembly at its fifty-sixth session, through the Economic and Social Council at its substantive session of 2001, on the implementation of the present resolution, under the item entitled "Environment and sustainable development".

Disaster assistance

Africa

Horn of Africa

In the Horn of Africa, including Djibouti, Eritrea, Ethiopia, Kenya, Somalia and the United Republic of Tanzania, poor and unreliable rainfalls during the preceding three years culminated in a serious drought in 2000, putting at risk the lives and livelihoods of nearly 16 million people. Small-scale movements of people took place during the first quarter of the year. Towards year's end, improvements in the drought situation occurred, particularly in Ethiopia and Somalia, and a large-scale famine was avoided.

OCHA launched a UN emergency appeal seeking $392.6 million to cover June to December 2000 for the first five countries. A further UN emergency consolidated appeal to cover January to December 2001 sought $352.9 million for emergency and recovery programmes.

Kenya

In 2000, the drought in Kenya unfolded against a backdrop of long-term economic decline that had had an impact on every sector. The most affected were populations in pastoral and agro-pastoral districts, where the nutritional status of children under five deteriorated significantly. By November, over 3.2 million people in 22 districts were receiving food assistance. Insecurity, particularly in the north, constrained humanitarian operations.

OCHA launched a UN inter-agency donor alert for the drought in Kenya for $146.3 million to cover June to December 2000. Of that amount, $121 million, or 82.74 per cent of the requirements, was received. A further appeal sought $122.7 million to cover January to December 2001.

Madagascar

Within a three-week period in February, Madagascar was struck by tropical cyclone Eline, followed by tropical storm Gloria. Furthermore, tropical cyclone Hudah struck in March with rare intensity in several districts that had already been battered by Gloria. The natural disasters crossed the island with strong winds, torrential flood-producing rains and landslides. The three cataclysms combined caused 222 deaths, affected 1.1 million people, left 295,613 persons in need of urgent assistance and damaged agricultural, health, educational and public infrastructures.

On 14 March [meeting 92], the General Assembly adopted **resolution 54/96 M** [draft: A/54/L.80 & Add.1] without vote [agenda item 20 *(b)*].

Assistance to Madagascar following the tropical cyclones

The General Assembly,

Gravely concerned about the extensive damage and the devastation caused by tropical cyclones Eline and Gloria and the floods that have struck Madagascar,

Noting with concern the destruction of thousands of homes and the damage to major sectors of the national infrastructure as well as the growing needs of hundreds of thousands of victims,

Noting also with concern that those natural disasters have been aggravated by various epidemics that have resulted in the loss of human lives,

Recognizing the efforts of the Government and the people of Madagascar to provide relief and emergency assistance to the victims of those disasters,

Noting that the determined efforts of the Government of Madagascar to promote economic growth and development are hindered by this kind of recurring natural disaster,

Aware that, to mitigate and to prevent the consequences of those disasters, international assistance is required, both for emergency relief and for rehabilitation and reconstruction of the infrastructure,

1. *Expresses its solidarity* with the Government and the people of Madagascar;

2. *Notes with satisfaction* the efforts of the Government and the people of Madagascar to provide rapid relief to the victims through their own means;

3. *Expresses its gratitude* to the international community, including organizations and bodies of the United Nations system, for the measures it has taken to support the efforts of the Government of Madagascar to carry out relief operations and to provide emergency assistance;

4. *Requests* all States and international organizations to provide additional emergency support to Madagascar, with a view to alleviating the economic and financial burden that the people of Madagascar will have to bear during the emergency period and in the subsequent process of rehabilitation;

5. *Requests* the Secretary-General to make all necessary arrangements to continue mobilizing and coordinating humanitarian assistance from the specialized agencies and other organizations and bodies of the United Nations system, with a view to supporting the efforts of the Government of Madagascar;

6. *Also requests* the Secretary-General, acting in conjunction with the relevant organizations and bodies of the United Nations system and in close cooperation with the government authorities, to assist the Government of Madagascar in effectively carrying out its rehabilitation efforts;

7. *Further requests* the Secretary-General to report to it at its fifty-fifth session, under the item on strengthening of the coordination of humanitarian and disaster relief assistance of the United Nations, including special economic assistance, through the Economic and Social Council at the humanitarian segment of its substantive session in 2000, on the implementation of the present resolution.

Report of Secretary-General. In July [A/55/124-E/2000/90], the Secretary-General reported that the most seriously affected regions in Madagascar were in isolated areas and inaccessible from Antananarivo, the capital. In the north-east, as only 28 per cent of the villages surveyed were accessible by road, large-scale deployment of aircraft was required, making the logistics of intervention difficult and costly. A UN system working group developed an intervention strategy comprising immediate emergency response to assist victims, a short-term response and a joint mechanism for responding to emergencies in general. The immediate response strategy was manifest in a flash appeal from UN agencies following cyclone Hudah, disseminated through OCHA, totalling $15.8 million. Short-term strategic responses consisted of a joint WFP/FAO mission, backed by the Ministry of Agriculture (25 April–12 May), to evaluate the crop year and balance sheet following the various climatic phenomena. The United Nations was also involved in the medium-term response, which included assistance to the Government in the formulation of a medium-term rehabilitation plan. The long-term support mechanism was based on institutional support provided by UNDP with a view to preparing national institutions to deal with emergency situations arising from natural disasters. UNDP made available to the Government's National Relief Council five national consultants and an international consultant responsible for guiding the process of drawing up a national strategy to prevent and manage natural disasters and risks, and the definition of a sustainable institutional management framework. The Government launched appeals in March and April, the first of which generated $3.5 million and the second, $15.6 million.

Mozambique

Beginning in December 1999, heavy rains fell over Mozambique, reaching unprecedented levels by the end of the month. In early February 2000, the Umbeluzi, Incomati and Limpopo rivers exceeded all known records and, on 25 February, when the river floods caused by cyclone Eline reached Mozambique, the central and southern provinces experienced the most extensive floods in more than 50 years. The floods affected 2 million people, or 12.1 per cent of the population, and impacted all sectors of the economy.

On 6 March, the Security Council President issued a press statement in which the Council called for all possible steps to avert a humanitarian crisis.

On 9 March, the Economic and Social Council authorized its President to transmit to the Government and people of Mozambique his statement on the devastation caused by the floods (decision 2000/212). The President stated that the Council called on Governments to continue and intensify relief efforts. It also called on the international community and the private sector to accelerate their efforts to provide relief and assistance.

On 10 March [meeting 91], the General Assembly adopted **resolution 54/96 L** [draft: A/54/L.79 & Add.1] without vote [agenda item 20 *(b)*].

Assistance to Mozambique following the devastating floods

The General Assembly,

Deeply concerned about the unprecedented floods in Mozambique, which have resulted in tragic loss of human lives and extensive destruction of property and infrastructure,

Also deeply concerned about the impact of the disaster on the economic, social and humanitarian situation in Mozambique,

Gravely concerned about the widespread destruction of crops, which may lead to food security problems and loss of income,

Disturbed by the resulting lack of clean water, shelter and health care and by the outbreak of diseases, particularly malaria and cholera,

Recognizing the efforts of the Government and the people of Mozambique to save lives and to alleviate the suffering of the flood victims,

Recognizing also that natural disasters constitute a major problem for development,

Aware that, to mitigate and to prevent the consequences of this disaster, international assistance is required, both for emergency relief and for rehabilitation and reconstruction of the infrastructure,

Noting the appeal to the international community made by the Government of Mozambique for emergency humanitarian aid and the need for assistance for the rehabilitation and reconstruction of the areas affected by the disaster,

Noting also the appeal made by the Secretary-General to the international community for aid and assistance to Mozambique in dealing with the effects of the floods,

Noting further the statement issued by the President of the Security Council on 6 March 2000 concerning the floods in Mozambique,

1. *Expresses its solidarity,* at this difficult time, with the Government and the people of Mozambique in their efforts to cope with the serious consequences of the disaster;

2. *Urges* the international community, the United Nations, the specialized agencies, international financial institutions and other bodies of the United Nations system as well as non-governmental organizations to respond urgently and to provide assistance to Mozambique in its relief, rehabilitation and reconstruction efforts and programmes following the disaster;

3. *Expresses its gratitude* to the Member States, international and non-governmental organizations and private individuals and groups that are providing emergency relief to Mozambique;

4. *Requests* the relevant organs and agencies of the United Nations system and other multilateral organizations to increase their support and assistance for the strengthening of the capacity for disaster preparedness of Mozambique;

5. *Requests* the Secretary-General to make all necessary arrangements to continue mobilizing and coordinating humanitarian assistance from the specialized agencies and other organizations and bodies of the United Nations system, with a view to supporting the efforts of the Government of Mozambique;

6. *Also requests* the Secretary-General to continue mobilizing and coordinating assistance for the required reconstruction and rehabilitation of the infrastructure in Mozambique and to meet other needs for the normalization of the life of citizens;

7. *Encourages* the holding of an international donors conference to assist Mozambique in its humanitarian relief, rehabilitation and reconstruction efforts;

8. *Requests* the Secretary-General to report to it at its fifty-fifth session, under the item on strengthening of the coordination of humanitarian and disaster relief assistance of the United Nations, including special economic assistance, through the Economic and Social Council at the humanitarian segment of its substantive session in 2000, on the collaborative efforts referred to in paragraphs 5 and 6 above and on the progress made in the relief, rehabilitation and reconstruction efforts of Mozambique.

Report of Secretary-General. In response to General Assembly resolution 54/96 L (see above), the Secretary-General submitted a July report [A/55/123-E/2000/89] on assistance to Mozambique following the devastating floods of February and March that had killed 699 persons, displaced an estimated 544,000 and affected 5 million. OCHA/UNDAC teams played a role in preparing two emergency appeals. On 23 February, the Government and UN entities appealed for some $60 million for 300,000 flood victims. The impact of cyclone Eline was such that $130 million was contributed by donors to the relief phase. The Government and UN entities launched a transitional appeal on 22 March for $100 million of additional emergency assistance from March to August 2000 to benefit more than 600,000 victims. The International Conference on the Reconstruction of Mozambique (Rome, Italy, 3-4 May), organized by UNDP and the Government, obtained pledges of $453 million.

The Secretary-General said that a number of points emerged as salient to the coordination process, and contributed to mitigating the fallout on the affected populations, including a government-led response, supported by the United Nations; rapid mobilization of resources by the UN system; a disaster management team in Maputo, comprising the country management team and technical focal points from each agency, established by the UN system; the use of international military forces coordinated by civilians and the United Nations in an unprecedented way; and the Secretary-General's appointment of his first-ever special humanitarian envoy for a natural disaster.

Zimbabwe

On 22 February, Zimbabwe was hit by tropical cyclone Eline, at a time when some parts of the country were experiencing life-threatening floods from the main river basins. Communications systems were destroyed and bridges were damaged and swept away, as were some dwellings. The disasters occurred during a period when Zimbabwe was experiencing a deep economic crisis.

Following a UN Disaster Management Team assessment, a UN inter-agency and NGO appeal for emergency relief was issued in March for $3.3 million to meet the needs of 96,000 people.

Asia

Cambodia

A UN inter-agency appeal for emergency relief and initial rehabilitation for Cambodia, totalling $10.7 million to cover 2 October 2000 to 31 March 2001, was launched in October following two major floods that struck in less than three months and affected more than 2.2 million people. The appeal aimed to facilitate the transition to longer-term rehabilitation and reconstruction and to bridge the gap until resources for rehabilitation/reconstruction could be mobilized.

Democratic People's Republic of Korea

In response to the UN consolidated inter-agency appeal for the Democratic People's Republic of Korea (DPRK), launched in 1999, which sought $331.7 million for January to December 2000, the donor community had committed $153.1 million, or 48.8 per cent of requirements.

In 2000, the harvest was one of the worst ever, resulting in severe shortages in the domestic food supply. The poor harvest was due to climatic conditions and the cumulative effect of underlying agriculture problems that had resulted in a food gap of some 1.9 metric tons. Although efforts were being made to revitalize the domestic food production sector, the beneficiary caseload continued to be large, with some 22 per cent of the DPRK's population of 22 million reliant on supplementary rations.

In November, OCHA presented a UN consolidated inter-agency appeal to the donor community of $384 million to cover requirements from January to December 2001.

Viet Nam

The unusually early monsoon season in Viet Nam caused unrelenting rains starting in July. Prolonged flooding affected more than 5 million people, claimed 370 lives and caused damage estimated at more than $251 million. Some 670,000 people either had been evacuated or were in need of urgent relocation. In October, the UN Disaster Management Team in Viet Nam launched a UN inter-agency appeal for emergency relief and initial rehabilitation for $9.4 million to cover the period from 20 October 2000 to 20 April 2001.

West Timor

On 18 May [S/2000/450], the Secretary-General informed the Security Council that Indonesia had requested assistance from the United Nations Transitional Administration in East Timor (UNTAET) to deal with an emergency in West Timor, caused by extensive flooding during which many had died and tens of thousands had been displaced. Among the dead were East Timorese refugees, most of them women and children. UNTAET had been requested to provide assistance in the form of two helicopters to evacuate flood victims and deliver relief supplies, initially for one week. The Secretary-General intended to accede to the request. On the same date [S/2000/451], the Council took note of the Secretary-General's proposal to accede to Indonesia's request.

Latin America and the Caribbean

Belize

Belize was battered by hurricane Keith from 1 to 3 October, causing extensive flood damage, along with associated health risks and economic setbacks. For weeks after the hurricane struck, the water levels continued to rise as persistent, heavy rains caused more flooding. Total damages were estimated at some $261.5 million. The UN Emergency Disaster Management Team coordinated the UN response from the capital of Belmopan.

The Government sought $17.1 million for the urgent reconstruction of houses that would benefit 4,500 persons. About half of the requirements had been met by the Inter-American Development Bank and the Belize Development Finance Corporation. OCHA sought the assistance of the international community for the remainder ($8.5 million).

GENERAL ASSEMBLY ACTION

On 14 December [meeting 85], the General Assembly adopted **resolution 55/165** [draft: A/55/L.35/Rev.1 & Add.1] without vote [agenda item 20 *(b)*].

Emergency assistance to Belize

The General Assembly,

Recalling its resolutions 42/169 of 11 December 1987, 43/202 of 20 December 1988, 44/236 of 22 December 1989, 45/185 of 21 December 1990, 46/149 of 18 December 1991, 46/182 of 19 December 1991, 48/188 of 21 December 1993 and 49/22 A of 2 December 1994,

Having been made aware of the extensive damage caused by powerful hurricane Keith during its landfall and passage through Belize from 1 to 3 October 2000,

Mindful of the human suffering caused by the displacement of thousands of people due to the loss of homes,

Aware of the devastating effect that the continuing emergency, due to flooding, is having on the infrastructure of the country, its agricultural and fisheries sectors and the delivery of health and social services,

Noting the enormous efforts required to alleviate the devastation caused by this natural disaster,

Cognizant of the efforts of the Government and people of Belize to relieve the suffering of the victims of hurricane Keith,

Conscious of the rapid response being made by the Government of Belize, the agencies and bodies of the United Nations system, international and regional agencies, non-governmental organizations and private individuals to provide relief,

Underlining the importance of efforts aimed at strengthening early warning, prevention and preparedness mechanisms for natural disasters and measures to strengthen capacity-building at the local, national and regional levels, with an emphasis on risk reduction,

Aware that the extent of the disaster and its medium-term and long-term effects will require, as a complement to the efforts being made by the Government and people of Belize, a demonstration of international solidarity and humanitarian concern to ensure broad multilateral cooperation in order to facilitate the transition from the immediate emergency situation in the affected areas to the process of reconstruction,

1. *Expresses its solidarity and support* to the Government and people of Belize;

2. *Expresses its appreciation* to all States of the international community, international agencies and non-governmental organizations that are providing emergency relief assistance to Belize;

3. *Urges* Member States, as a matter of urgency, to contribute generously to the relief, rehabilitation and reconstruction efforts of Belize;

4. *Requests* the Secretary-General, in collaboration with the international financial institutions, agencies and bodies of the United Nations system, to assist the Government of Belize in identifying medium-term and long-term needs and in mobilizing resources, as well as to help with the efforts towards rehabilitation and reconstruction of the affected areas in Belize;

5. *Encourages* the Government of Belize, in conjunction with relevant partners, further to develop strategies aimed at preventing and mitigating natural disasters;

6. *Requests* the Secretary-General to make all necessary arrangements to continue mobilizing and coordinating humanitarian assistance from the specialized agencies and other organizations and bodies of the United Nations system with a view to supporting the efforts of the Government of Belize.

Hurricanes Jose and Lenny

In an August report [A/55/333], the Secretary-General described the destruction caused by hurricanes Jose and Lenny, which struck several small island developing States and territories of the Eastern Caribbean in October and November 1999 [YUN 1999, p. 867]. The report gave details of the response of the international community and that of countries affected, as well as an assessment of efforts by the Governments of the region to deal with such occurrences.

Antigua and Barbuda was worst affected by hurricane Jose, with one fatality, confirmed injuries of 15 persons and more than 500 people forced to seek shelter. Extensive flooding in Saint Kitts and Nevis washed out several main roads. In Anguilla, damage was limited to beach erosion in the eastern and southern sections, as well as to damage to roads and electricity and telephone systems. No significant damage was reported in the British Virgin Islands and Montserrat, except for small landslides in the latter. Regarding hurricane Lenny, severe damage occurred in Antigua and Barbuda, Saint Martin and the United States Virgin Islands, particularly Saint Croix. On the island of Barbuda, 95 per cent of agriculture was destroyed and groundwater contamination occurred across the island. On Saint Kitts, over 200 families were left homeless, and extensive infrastructure damage affected ports, sea defences and coastal communities. The western coast of Dominica experienced economic damage as a result of the hurricane's effect on tourism and agriculture, and the housing stock underwent widespread damage and destruction. Much of the damage in several low-lying communities along the coast of Saint Vincent and the Grenadines was economic, with the road and port infrastructure heavily affected. Heavy winds caused storm surges in the tourism region of Saint Lucia, Soufrière, where scores of people were left homeless.

In all cases, initial damage assessments were made difficult owing to the heavy toll on roads, ports and bridges. Prior to the impact, all national authorities had responded to the various warnings by putting into effect the preliminary stages of national preparedness plans. Most had, however, moved swiftly to begin main road repairs and to clear debris to allow relief and damage assessment teams access to affected communities.

The Secretary-General concluded that higher levels of resources were required for more comprehensive planning and response capability on a regional basis. With the support of the Government of Italy, UNDP had launched a Caribbean disaster reduction initiative to strengthen the capacities of national Governments and mandated regional organizations in the English-, French-, Spanish- and Dutch-speaking Caribbean in order to mainstream disaster reduction into development and post-disaster recovery. UNDP was also committed to coordinating the recovery planning interventions on a regional basis.

Chernobyl closure

On 15 December [A/55/744], following an order of the President of Ukraine, the Chernobyl nuclear power station closed. In 1986, a nuclear reactor at Chernobyl had caused a massive humanitarian disaster [YUN 1986, p. 584].

GENERAL ASSEMBLY ACTION

On 14 December [meeting 85], the General Assembly adopted **resolution 55/171** [draft: A/55/L.60 & Add.1] without vote [agenda item 20 (b)].

Closure of the Chernobyl nuclear power plant
The General Assembly,

Recalling its resolutions 45/190 of 21 December 1990, 46/150 of 18 December 1991, 47/165 of 18 December 1992, 48/206 of 21 December 1993, 50/134 of 20 December 1995, 52/172 of 16 December 1997 and 54/97 of 8 December 1999,

Conscious of the long-term nature of the consequences of the disaster at the Chernobyl nuclear power plant, which was a major technological catastrophe in terms of its scope and created humanitarian, environmental, social, economic and health consequences in the affected countries,

Appreciative of the efforts made by the organizations of the United Nations system and Member States to mitigate and minimize the consequences of the Chernobyl disaster, in particular, the contributions of the members of the Group of Seven and the European Union and others to the Shelter Implementation Plan aimed at securing the environmental safety of the sarcophagus covering the destroyed Chernobyl reactor in accordance with the memorandum of understanding between the Governments of the members of the Group of Seven and the Commission of the European Communities and the Government of Ukraine,

Noting with concern the gravity of economic and social problems arising for Ukraine as a result of the closure of the Chernobyl nuclear power plant,

1. *Welcomes* the decision of Ukraine to close the Chernobyl nuclear power plant on 15 December 2000;

2. *Calls upon* the international community to continue to assist the Government of Ukraine in coping with the range of newly emerging economic and social problems arising as a result of the closure of the Chernobyl nuclear power plant;

3. *Invites* all States and the relevant international and non-governmental organizations to continue to provide support to Belarus, the Russian Federation and Ukraine, as the most affected countries, in mitigating and minimizing the consequences of the Chernobyl disaster.

Chapter IV

International trade, finance and transport

In 2000, the revival in international economic activity and trade, which began in the second half of 1999, continued. Exports and imports of all groups of countries increased at significantly faster rates and became more balanced among countries. The improvements in growth were particularly marked in a number of developing countries and economies in transition. In contrast with the expansion in trade, capital flows to developing countries declined.

In February, the tenth session of the United Nations Conference on Trade and Development (UNCTAD X), which had as its theme "Developing strategies in an increasingly interdependent world: applying the lessons of the past to make globalization an effective instrument for the development of all countries and all people", took place in Bangkok, Thailand. The Conference adopted the Bangkok Declaration, which reaffirmed UNCTAD as the focal point in the United Nations for the integrated treatment of development and the interrelated issues of trade, finance, investment, technology and sustainable development, and the Plan of Action, which harmonized UNCTAD's mandate with the new global economy and its challenges. In December, the General Assembly requested the Secretary-General to take measures to strengthen UNCTAD's management and enhance its programme delivery capacity and performance to enable it to implement the outcome of UNCTAD X. With regard to developments in the multilateral trading system, the Assembly recognized the need for expeditious and complete integration of developing countries and economies in transition into the international trading system, in full cognizance of the opportunities and challenges of globalization and liberalization. It also reiterated the importance of continued trade liberalization in developed and developing countries, including in sectors of export interest to developing countries.

In September, the Fourth United Nations Conference to Review All Aspects of the Set of Multilaterally Agreed Equitable Principles and Rules for the Control of Restrictive Business Practices considered major developments in the field of competition law and policy and requested UNCTAD to expand its technical co-

operation activities. In the area of commodities, the Assembly expressed concern at the declining terms of trade in most primary commodities and invited UNCTAD to assist developing countries in the financing of commodity diversification.

The Trade and Development Board, the governing body of UNCTAD, considered interdependence and global economic issues from a trade and development perspective, focusing on crisis and recovery in emerging markets. It also reviewed technical cooperation activities. The *Trade and Development Report, 2000*, produced by the UNCTAD secretariat, focused on the related issues of global economic growth and imbalances.

In action on financial issues, the Assembly stressed the importance of creating an enabling international economic environment through cooperative efforts by all countries and institutions to promote equitable development. Recognizing that development-oriented and durable solutions to external debt and debt-service burdens of developing countries could strengthen the global economy, the Assembly encouraged the international community to consider measures for countries with a high level of debt overhang to make their debt sustainable in the long term, and called for concerted action to address the debt problems of low- and middle-income developing countries. With regard to financing for development, the Assembly decided that the high-level international intergovernmental event on the subject would take place in 2002.

The International Trade Centre (ITC) focused on capacity-building to enhance international competitiveness and trade performance; during the year, more than 100 countries benefited from its support.

UNCTAD X

The tenth session of the United Nations Conference on Trade and Development, known as UNCTAD X, was held in Bangkok, Thailand, from 12 to 19 February [TD/390], in accordance with General Assembly resolutions 1995(XIX) [YUN 1964, p. 210] and 51/167 [YUN 1996, p. 847], with the unifying theme: "Development strategies in an increasingly interdependent world: applying the lessons of the past to make globalization an effective instrument for the development of all countries and all people". The Trade and Development Board (TDB) served as the preparatory committee for the Conference (see p. 892), which was attended by 158 member States of UNCTAD and representatives of UN specialized agencies, bodies and programmes, and intergovernmental and non-governmental organizations (NGOs). Palestine attended as an observer. At the special inaugural ceremony on 12 February, the Conference was addressed by Chuan Leekpai, Prime Minister of Thailand, by the Secretary-General of the United Nations and by Rubens Ricupero, Secretary-General of UNCTAD.

On 13 February, the Ministers of Trade of the Least Developed Countries (LDCs) discussed LDC-related issues and the preparatory process for the Third United Nations Conference on LDCs, to be held in 2001; a communiqué was adopted [TD/384 & Corr.1] and submitted to the Conference. A debate with heads of UN regional commissions took place on 14 February on the regional dimension of development and the impact of globalization on different regions in the wake of the recent financial crisis. In the course of the Conference, the following round tables were organized: High-level Round Table with Eminent Economists on Trade and Development Directions for the Twenty-first Century: the Academic Perspective; High-level Round Table with Heads of UN Agencies, Programmes and Related Institutions; and Round Table on the Human Dimension of Development: Empowering Entrepreneurs for the Twenty-first Century. At a special high-level event on 19 February, heads of State or Government discussed the main findings of the Conference.

The Conference had before it a report of the UNCTAD Secretary-General [TD/380], which discussed globalization and development: the sources of the present impasse; towards a new international commitment to growth and development: enhancing the governance of the globalizing world economy; UNCTAD: a knowledge-based institution at the service of development; and partnerships and effectiveness: increasing UNCTAD's impact on development.

The following parallel events were organized in connection with the Conference: NGO Plenary Caucus (7-8 February), which adopted a statement entitled "UNCTAD and Civil Society: Towards Our Common Goals" [TD/382]; Parliamentary Meeting (9-11 February), which adopted a Final Declaration [TD/383]; fifth Annual Conference of the World Association of Investment Promotion Agencies (9-11 February); South-South Trade Promotion Programme—Buyers/Sellers Meeting on Pharmaceuticals (12-13 February);

Symposium on Commodities and Development at the Turn of the Millennium (13 February); Special Round Table on Transnational Corporations (TNCs), Small and Medium-sized Enterprises (SMEs) and Development, Involving Federations, Organizations and Young Entrepreneurs (15 February); and the UNCTAD/UNDP Global Programme on Globalization, Liberalization and Sustainable Human Development (16 February). Other events included a one-day Symposium on Economic and Financial Recovery in Asia on 17 February.

Declaration and Plan of Action

On 19 February, the Conference adopted the Bangkok Declaration: Global Dialogue and Dynamic Engagement, which emphasized the need for increased policy coherence at the national and international levels, and reaffirmed UNCTAD as the focal point within the United Nations for the integrated treatment of development and the interrelated issues in the areas of trade, finance, investment, technology and sustainable development.

It also adopted a two-part Plan of Action [TD/386]. Part I addressed development strategies in an increasingly interdependent world: applying the lessons of the past to make globalization an effective instrument for the development of all countries and all people. It evaluated the developmental impact of globalization, and noted that, although globalization and interdependence had opened new opportunities through increased trade liberalization and advancement in technology, many developing countries, especially LDCs, had not increased their GDP per capita over the last three decades. It stated that development strategies promoted mainly by multilateral financial institutions should adapt to evolving global conditions, and the international community should elaborate strategies and policies to help developing countries to overcome any negative effect of globalization. Maximizing the benefits of globalization required sound domestic policies supported by an enabling global environment and international economic cooperation. The international community should address the imbalances in the international economy and the effects of volatility; and intensified international cooperation, in addition to national and regional efforts, would be essential to address effectively the domestic and external factors of underdevelopment. The Plan of Action also reviewed major international initiatives such as the Uruguay Round and the United Nations New Agenda for the Development of Africa in the 1990s (UN-NADAF), the Programme of Action for LDCs for the 1990s and debt relief developments. It proposed measures to be taken by the international community to ensure integration of developing countries into the world economy in the areas of finance and investment, international trade and other development-related issues. Part II of the Plan of Action examined UNCTAD's engagement in the areas of: globalization, interdependence and development; investment, enterprise and technology; international trade; service infrastructure for development and trade efficiency and human resources development; LDCs, landlocked developing countries and small island developing States; and technical cooperation. It stated that, to enhance the development opportunities offered by globalization, UNCTAD should act as a forum for intergovernmental discussions; undertake research, analysis and data collection; provide technical assistance tailored to the needs of developing countries; and continue to focus on four fields of activity: globalization and development; investment, enterprise development and technology; trade in goods and services and commodity issues; and services infrastructure for development and trade efficiency. UNCTAD should also pay special attention to the concerns of LDCs and further explore the role of economic cooperation among developing countries as an instrument to promote economic growth. The Plan of Action recommended that UNCTAD's existing capacity-building programme be strengthened by organizing for officials from developing countries and countries in transition, in cooperation with the UN Staff College, training courses on the international economic agenda. The courses could draw on UNCTAD's expertise and policy analysis work, with the support of an advisory body to be established by TDB.

Other action. In a 19 February statement [174(X)], the Conference paid tribute to the King of Thailand for his contribution to the cause of development. By a resolution of the same date [res. 175(X)], UNCTAD X expressed appreciation to the Government and the people of Thailand for the hospitality accorded to the Conference participants. In another 19 February resolution [res. 176(X)], the Conference approved the report of the Credentials Committee [TD/385].

Preparatory process for UNCTAD X

At the second part of its twenty-third executive session, on 27 January [A/55/15], TDB considered and took note of the pre-Conference text, as submitted by the Preparatory Committee of the Whole, and requested the TDB President to transmit it to the Conference. The Preparatory Committee had begun its work in 1999 [YUN 1999, p. 912]. The reports of a number of meetings held in 1999 in preparation for UNCTAD X [ibid.] were submitted to the Conference.

UNCTAD X follow-up

At its twenty-fourth executive session (Geneva, 24 March and 12 May) [A/55/15], TDB discussed the follow-up to the outcome of UNCTAD X, including action taken by the Working Party on the Medium-term Plan and the Programme Budget (see p. 922).

In **resolution 55/182** (see p. 895), the General Assembly, taking note of the outcome of UNCTAD X, requested the Secretary-General, in consultation with the UNCTAD Secretary-General, to take measures to strengthen the management and enhance the programme delivery capacity and performance of the UNCTAD secretariat in order to enable it to implement fully and effectively the outcome of the tenth session.

International trade

The *Trade and Development Report, 2000* [Sales No. E.00.II.D.19] observed that the revival in world trade in 1999, in the wake of the economic recovery in East Asia, was more evident in value than in volume on account of disparate movements in the prices of internationally traded goods and services in 1998 and 1999. With the major exception of the transition economies, there was a sharp turnaround in all regions, particularly in value terms, as price declines levelled off, and the return of financial stability in the crisis-stricken Asian economies led to a modest recovery in certain non-oil commodity prices of interest to developing countries.

The volume of world imports grew by some 5 per cent in 1999, an improvement that was due mainly to a recovery in developing countries and to sustained growth in developed countries; import volumes in the transition economies contracted by 10 per cent. Owing to statistical discrepancies, the rebound in world trade in 1999 was not reflected to the same extent in terms of the volume of exports, which, unlike imports, rose less than in 1998. The slowdown was accounted for by a contraction of exports in the transition economies, as well as slower export growth in developing countries. For developed countries as a whole, the export volume growth rate was maintained at the same level as in 1998. The dollar values of both world imports and exports increased, with the exception of the transition economies, where both fell. There was a relatively rapid increase in the value of imports in the

United States and a marked rebound for Japan and for developing Asia. Export earnings increased in all major economic regions except the European Union (EU) and the transition economies. Both world imports and exports showed smaller increases in value than in volume terms, on account of price declines. However, the discrepancy between volume and value figures was much narrower for 1999 than for 1998, suggesting that the downward trend in world prices had moderated.

The *World Economic and Social Survey 2000* [Sales No. E.00.II.C.1], prepared in mid-2000 by the UN Department of Economic and Social Affairs (DESA), stated that international trade recovered in 1999 from the slowdown of 1998. Trade growth was slow during the first half of the year, with significant declines in some regions, as many economies, especially in Asia and Latin America but also among the economies in transition, continued their post-crisis adjustment by cutting import demand. However, international trade revived strongly in the second half of the year, when an accelerating recovery in Asia and rapid growth in North America increased trade values and volumes, and became one of the more dynamic features of the world economy as it entered 2000. Although the rebound in trade was widespread, contrasting increases in export supplies and import demand at the national level left large trade imbalances in some countries, while reducing or eliminating external deficits and surpluses in others. Those changes in nominal trade balances were induced by significant changes in exchange rates and in relative prices of traded goods.

Preliminary estimates placed the total value of world merchandise trade in 1999 at over $5,500 billion, a 4.6 per cent increase over 1998. Much of that increase was attributable to soaring prices for petroleum. The volume of world merchandise trade increased considerably faster than in 1998. Export volume rose by 4.8 per cent measured in dollars, and by the end of the year it exceeded the rate of increase in gross world product (GWP). Reflecting the expansion of world merchandise trade volume, the ratio of world trade growth to world output growth rose.

There was a strong rebound in developing country trade as the value of exports from that group rose 8.3 per cent in 1999. The economies in transition also recorded an increase in the value of their exports, whereas the developed economies increased the value of their trade at a slower rate. For all developing countries taken together, over 80 per cent of the increase in export value was accounted for by an increase in export volume rather than export price. However, the

largest relative increase in the value of exports from developing countries was recorded by petroleum-exporting countries in Western Asia. Similarly, in Africa, the increase in export value outpaced the increase in volume. Over 70 per cent of the value of world imports was accounted for by demand originating in the developed market economies, where imports into North America and Japan grew at a pace of 11.8 per cent and 8.3 per cent, respectively. The United States continued to provide a major stimulus to the world economy as its foreign demand increased by almost 13 per cent from 1998. In contrast, the increase in import value by Western Europe was less than 2.5 per cent. The economies in transition recorded a surplus on their merchandise trade account, with a gain in export value and a lower value of imports. The reduction in import value was centred in the Commonwealth of Independent States (CIS), where both the value and the volume of imports declined by more than 20 per cent. The developing countries contributed to the growth of world import demand: at almost 6 per cent in value terms, imports rose faster than the world average and accounted for 30 per cent of the increment in import demand, which was especially strong in China and South and East Asia.

In a joint report on the world economic situation and prospects [Sales No. E.01.II.C.2] issued at the end of 2000 by DESA and UNCTAD, it was observed that the growth of international trade accelerated and broadened in 2000 from the uneven recovery of 1999. The volume of world merchandise imports surged almost 11 per cent in 2000. Import demand remained particularly robust in North America, strengthened among the developed economies and increased rapidly across the developing countries and the economies in transition. The rise was strong in Latin America and the Caribbean and in the Russian Federation, where imports had declined significantly in 1999, and in South and East Asia, where economic activity and international trade continued to recover from the effects of the financial crisis of 1997.

Report of Secretary-General. In response to General Assembly resolution 54/198 [YUN 1999, p. 875], the Secretary-General submitted a September report [A/55/396], prepared in collaboration with UNCTAD, on international trade and development. It discussed developments in the multilateral trading system and other issues raised in resolution 54/198, including: investment agreements; dispute settlement; the Third Conference on LDCs (2001); landlocked countries; small island developing States; Africa; debt; the volatility of short-term capital flows and effects of the financial crisis on the international trading system; and debt.

The report stated that the main developments in the multilateral trading system were related to the 1999 third World Trade Organization (WTO) Ministerial Conference [YUN 1999, p. 1422], which ended without launching new multilateral trade negotiations or agreeing to a future WTO work programme. From a development perspective, the most important policy challenge was how to strengthen orientations of the system to formulate effective and sustained responses to the concerns of developing countries. Based on the experiences of the first five years of WTO, developing countries insisted that the WTO agreements were unbalanced and offered inadequate benefits and opportunities to them. In particular, they called for: incorporation of the agricultural trade sector within normal WTO rules, while addressing the problems of predominantly agrarian and small island developing economies and net food-importing developing countries; developed countries to open their markets to the exports of developing countries and provide duty-free and quota-free access for the exports of LDCs, with future negotiations addressing the elimination of tariff peaks and tariff escalation and prevention of the abuse of measures such as anti-dumping, countervailing duties and safeguard actions, sanitary and phytosanitary regulations, technical barriers to trade and the use of voluntary export restraints; and a review and strengthening of special and differential treatment, giving special emphasis to capacity-building in developing countries and to measures taken by industrialized countries to transfer technology and know-how and invest in developing countries.

Addressing the outcome of UNCTAD X and its relevance for the WTO process, the Secretary-General said that the Plan of Action reflected the view that the international community should address the imbalances in the WTO agreements and the international economy as a whole and that new multilateral negotiations should enable developing countries to establish the infrastructure and other conditions necessary for the implementation of the agreements. It further stated that market access conditions for agricultural and industrial products of export interest to LDCs should be improved, and consideration should be given to the proposal for a commitment by developed countries to grant duty-free and quota-free market access for all exports originating in LDCs. Essentially, the Plan of Action set out the core elements of an agenda for the "development round". The Secretary-General added that the Bangkok Conference gave UNCTAD the mandate

to continue to assist developing countries in their positive agenda by providing the necessary technical and analytical inputs to their negotiating objectives, supporting their capacity-building process and providing a forum for the exchange of information.

With regard to the resumption of work in WTO, the Secretary-General stated that the export subsidies issue was a major concern of developing countries, in many of which the trade policy regime in the agricultural sector was more liberal than in developed countries where, in some of them, subsidization of agriculture continued to increase. The impact of agricultural reform on the net food-importing developing countries and LDCs needed to be addressed more vigorously. Classification of services was also subject to criticism. To achieve liberalization of one service sector meant that the regulatory framework of interrelated services also had to be adapted, hence the need to consider a so-called cluster of interrelated service sectors. The major concerns of many developing countries regarding the implementation of the WTO agreements were the lack of progress towards liberalization in sectors of interest to them; the imbalances between their rights and obligations under some of the agreements; and the conditions of market access. The implementation of the Agreement on Textiles and Clothing gave rise to many concerns. Although that sector accounted for about 20 per cent of developing countries' exports of manufactured products, the implementation of the Agreement failed to meet their expectations and, almost six years after its implementation, the committed progressive liberalization of quotas had not materialized.

The Secretary-General noted that the effectiveness of the generalized system of preferences (GSP) and other trade preferences in favour of developing countries was undermined by economic liberalization, the tightening of multilateral rules on waivers and the trend towards reciprocity in North/South trade relations. Since January 2000, international actions had been taken that underpinned the role of trade preferences and regional integration among developing countries. At UNCTAD X, States agreed to maintain the level of tariff-free or reduced-tariff access to markets through national GSP schemes for all beneficiaries, and that UNCTAD would devise mechanisms for advancing trade integration within regional integration arrangements of developing countries.

Communication. On 5 May [A/55/74], Nigeria transmitted to the General Assembly the Declaration and the Havana Programme of Action, adopted by the South Summit of the Group of 77 (developing countries) (Havana, Cuba, 10-14 April). At the first-ever South Summit, the Group of 77 and China emphasized that the process of globalization and interdependence should not be used to weaken or reinterpret the Charter of the United Nations, international law or sovereignty and sovereign equality of States, among other principles. They further emphasized that development was the best contribution to peace. The Havana Programme of Action covered globalization, knowledge and technology, South-South cooperation, North-South relations and institutional follow-up.

GENERAL ASSEMBLY ACTION

On 20 December [meeting 87], the General Assembly, on the recommendation of the Second (Economic and Financial) Committee [A/55/579/Add.1], adopted **resolution 55/182** without vote [agenda item 92 (a)].

International trade and development

The General Assembly,

Reaffirming its resolutions 50/95 and 50/98 of 20 December 1995, 51/167 of 16 December 1996, 52/182 of 18 December 1997, 53/170 of 15 December 1998 and 54/198 of 22 December 1999, as well as relevant international agreements concerning trade, economic growth and development,

Taking note of the outcome of the tenth session of the United Nations Conference on Trade and Development, held at Bangkok from 12 to 19 February 2000, specifically the Bangkok Declaration: global dialogue and dynamic engagement and the Plan of Action, which provide an important framework for promoting a partnership for growth and development,

Recalling the United Nations Millennium Declaration adopted by the heads of State and Government on 8 September 2000,

Taking note of the Declaration and the Programme of Action adopted by the South Summit of the Group of 77, held at Havana from 10 to 14 April 2000,

Emphasizing that a favourable and conducive international economic and financial environment and a positive investment climate are necessary for the growth of the world economy, including the creation of employment with equal opportunities for women and men, in particular for the growth and development of developing countries, and emphasizing also that each country is responsible for its own economic policies for sustainable development,

Noting the need for multilateral trade liberalization, and noting also that a large number of developing countries have assumed the rights and obligations of the World Trade Organization without being able to reap the full benefits of, and participate fully in, the multilateral trading system, and that there is a need for progress towards liberalization and enhanced market access, including in areas and products of particular interest to developing countries,

Noting also the importance of assisting developing countries in building their capacity, in accordance with their national priorities, to engage effectively in international trade,

Stressing that full and faithful implementation of the commitments and obligations in multilateral trade agreements is important to the equitable and sustainable development and stability of the world economy,

Strongly emphasizing the importance of providing all members of the World Trade Organization with the opportunity to engage fully and effectively in the process of multilateral trade negotiations and in other activities within the multilateral trading system in order to facilitate the attainment of balanced results with respect to the interests of all members,

Taking note of the report of the Trade and Development Board on its forty-seventh session, the report of the Secretary-General on international trade and development and on the developments in the multilateral trading system, and the report of the Secretary-General of the United Nations Conference on Trade and Development on the transit environment in the landlocked States in Central Asia and their transit developing neighbours,

Noting, in the context of international trade and development, the ongoing work of the Commonwealth Secretariat/World Bank Joint Task Force on Small States,

1. *Recognizes* the importance of the expansion of international trade as an engine of growth and development and, in this context, the need for expeditious and complete integration of developing countries and countries with economies in transition into the international trading system, in full cognizance of the opportunities and challenges of globalization and liberalization and taking into account the circumstances of individual countries, in particular the trade interests and development needs of developing countries;

2. *Renews its commitment* to uphold and strengthen an open, rule-based, equitable, secure, non-discriminatory, transparent and predictable multilateral trade system which contributes to the economic and social advancement of all countries and peoples, including equal opportunities for women and for men, by promoting the liberalization and expansion of trade, employment and stability and by providing a framework for the conduct of international trade relations;

3. *Expresses concern* at the declining terms of trade in most primary commodities, in particular for net exporters of such commodities, as well as the lack of progress in many developing countries in diversification, and, in this regard, strongly emphasizes the need for action at both the national and the international levels, inter alia, through improved market access conditions, addressing supply-side constraints and support for capacity-building, including in areas that actively involve women;

4. *Recognizes* that the substantial improvement of market access for exports of goods and services from developing countries through, inter alia, the reduction or removal of tariff and non-tariff barriers should be assigned high priority in multilateral trade negotiations;

5. *Urges* those countries that have announced market-access initiatives in favour of developing countries, in particular the least developed countries, and have not yet fulfilled them to expedite the implementation of those initiatives, and calls upon other countries

that have not yet done so to undertake similar initiatives;

6. *Deplores* any attempt to bypass or undermine multilaterally agreed procedures on the conduct of international trade by taking unilateral actions that are inconsistent with the multilateral trade rules and regulations, including those agreed upon in the Uruguay Round of multilateral trade negotiations;

7. *Expresses concern* about the proliferation of anti-dumping and countervailing measures, and stresses that they should not be used as protectionist measures;

8. *Reaffirms* the role of the United Nations Conference on Trade and Development as the focal point within the United Nations for the integrated treatment of development and related issues in the areas of trade, finance, technology, investment and sustainable development;

9. *Requests* the Secretary-General, in consultation with the Secretary-General of the United Nations Conference on Trade and Development and in line with the successful outcome of the tenth session of the United Nations Conference on Trade and Development, to take the necessary measures to strengthen the management and enhance the programme delivery capacity and performance of the secretariat of the United Nations Conference on Trade and Development in order to enable it to implement fully and effectively the outcome of its tenth session;

10. *Reiterates* the importance of continued trade liberalization in developed and developing countries, including in sectors of export interest to developing countries, through, inter alia:

(a) Substantial reductions of tariffs, the rolling back of tariff peaks and the removal of tariff escalation;

(b) The elimination of trade-distorting policies, protectionist practices and non-tariff barriers in international trade relations;

(c) Ensuring that resort to anti-dumping duties, countervailing duties, phytosanitary regulations and technical standards is subject to effective multilateral surveillance so that such measures respect and are consistent with multilateral trading rules and obligations and are not used for protectionist purposes;

(d) The improvement and renewal, by preference-giving countries, of their Generalized System of Preferences schemes with the objective of integrating developing countries, especially the least developed countries, into the international trading system and of finding ways and means to ensure more effective utilization of those schemes; and, in this context, reiterates its original principles, namely, non-discrimination, universality, burden-sharing and non-reciprocity;

11. *Also reiterates* that it is an ethical imperative for the international community to arrest and to reverse the marginalization of the least developed countries and to promote their expeditious integration into the world economy and that all countries should work together towards further enhancement of duty- and quota-free market access for exports from the least developed countries within the context of supporting their own efforts at capacity-building; recognizes that the full implementation of the Plan of Action for the Least Developed Countries adopted at the first Ministerial Conference of the World Trade Organization, held at Singapore from 9 to 13 December 1996, provides for further and expeditious progress towards duty-free imports from the least developed countries; invites the relevant international organizations to provide the enhanced technical assistance required to help to strengthen the supply and institutional capacity of the least developed countries so as to help them to take the fullest possible advantage of the trading opportunities that arise from globalization and liberalization, and, in this regard, reiterates the need for a speedy implementation of the Integrated Framework for Trade-related Technical Assistance to Least Developed Countries; takes note of the preparatory activities being undertaken for the Third United Nations Conference on the Least Developed Countries, to be held at Brussels in May 2001; and, in this connection, calls upon development partners, in particular industrialized countries, to make efforts towards the adoption of a policy of duty-and quota-free access for essentially all exports originating in the least developed countries;

12. *Notes* the need to better coordinate trade-related technical assistance and, in this regard, to implement the Integrated Framework for Trade-related Technical Assistance to Least Developed Countries in order to promote coordination among the six core agencies, bearing in mind that the resources made available should be utilized in line with their respective roles;

13. *Stresses* the urgent need to facilitate the integration of the countries of Africa into the world economy, and, in this context, takes note with appreciation of the action-oriented agenda for the development of Africa contained in the report of the Open-ended Ad Hoc Working Group on the Causes of Conflict and the Promotion of Durable Peace and Sustainable Development in Africa and the recommendations contained therein; calls for continued efforts to increase market access for products of export interest to African economies and support for their efforts to diversify and build supply capacity, and, in this context, requests the United Nations Conference on Trade and Development to continue to enhance its contribution to the United Nations New Agenda for the Development of Africa in the 1990s, taking into account the agreed conclusions of the Trade and Development Board on Africa; further encourages the Secretary-General of the United Nations to establish a new subprogramme on Africa, as agreed in the Plan of Action; and emphasizes the importance of increased inter-agency cooperation, which has proven its relevance through the joint integrated technical assistance programmes for selected least developed and other African countries;

14. *Requests* the Secretary-General to ensure the initiation by the United Nations Conference on Trade and Development, in the areas falling within its mandate, of the preparatory process for the final review and appraisal of the implementation of the New Agenda, to be held in 2002, in particular focusing on market access, diversification and supply capacity, resource flows and external debt, foreign direct and portfolio investment and access to technology, and, in this context, also requests the Secretary-General to submit a report, based on the recommendations of the Trade and Development Board on Africa, on measures taken in this regard, with a special emphasis on African trade issues, for the consideration of the General Assembly at its fifty-sixth session under the agenda item entitled "International trade and development";

15. *Stresses* the need to give special attention, within the context of international cooperation on trade and development issues, to the implementation of the many international development commitments geared to meeting the special development needs and problems of small island developing States and/or of landlocked developing countries and to recognize that those developing countries that provide transit services need adequate support for the maintenance and improvement of their transit infrastructure;

16. *Reiterates* the need for the United Nations Conference on Trade and Development to enhance its contribution to the implementation of the Programme of Action for the Sustainable Development of Small Island Developing States and the review document in addressing the specific concerns of small island developing States in their efforts aimed at diversification, capacity-building and benefiting from improved market access opportunities for their effective integration into the global economy;

17. *Also reiterates* the importance of the effective application by all members of the World Trade Organization of all provisions of the Final Act Embodying the Results of the Uruguay Round of Multilateral Trade Negotiations, taking into account the specific interests of developing countries, so as to maximize economic growth and development benefits for all, and the need to address implementation issues seriously, as well as to implement effectively all of the special provisions in the multilateral trade agreements and related ministerial decisions in favour of developing countries, in particular by making operational and ensuring fuller implementation of the previously agreed special and differential provisions, including the strengthening of these concepts, taking into account the changing realities of world trade and globalization, and urges Governments and concerned international organizations to apply effectively the Ministerial Decisions on Measures in Favour of Least Developed Countries and on Measures Concerning the Possible Negative Effects of the Reform Programme on Least Developed and Net Food-importing Developing Countries;

18. *Recognizes* the importance of increasing trade liberalization, in particular as regards areas and products of interest to developing countries, and that further liberalization should be sufficiently broad-based to respond to the range of interests and concerns of all members within the framework of the World Trade Organization, and, in this regard, welcomes the activities of the United Nations Conference on Trade and Development aimed at assisting developing countries in developing a positive agenda for future multilateral trade negotiations, and invites the secretariat of the Conference to continue to provide analytical support and technical assistance, including capacity-building activities, to those countries for their effective participation in the negotiations;

19. *Invites* members of the international community to consider the interests of non-members of the World Trade Organization in the context of trade liberalization;

20. *Invites* the international financial institutions to ensure that, in their development cooperation activities with developing countries, the obligations of the latter with regard to their development policies, strategies and programmes in trade and trade-related areas

are consistent with their commitments under the framework of rules agreed upon within the multilateral trading system;

21. *Emphasizes* the importance of the strengthening of, and the attainment of greater universality by, the international trading system and of accelerating the process directed towards accession to the World Trade Organization of developing countries and countries with economies in transition, also emphasizes the necessity for Governments that are members of the World Trade Organization and relevant international organizations to assist non-members of the World Trade Organization so as to facilitate their efforts with respect to accession in an expeditious and transparent manner, on the basis of undertaking balanced World Trade Organization rights and obligations, and further emphasizes the necessity for the United Nations Conference on Trade and Development and the World Trade Organization to provide technical assistance, within their mandates, that will contribute to the rapid and full integration of those countries into the multilateral trading system;

22. *Stresses* the need for improved measures to address the volatility of short-term capital flows as well as the effects of financial crises on the international trading system and the development prospects of developing countries and countries affected by such crises, emphasizing the fact that keeping all markets open and maintaining continued growth in world trade are key elements in overcoming such crises, and, in this context, rejects the use of any protectionist measures; also stresses, at a broader level, the need for greater coherence between the development objectives agreed to by the international community and the functioning of the international trading and financial system, and, in this context, calls for close cooperation between the members and observers of the organizations of the United Nations system and of the multilateral trade and financial institutions, with participation in accordance with their established rules, procedures and practices;

23. *Requests* the Secretary-General, in scheduling and organizing mandated events on trade and trade-related issues, to promote complementarity in the work of the relevant bodies of the United Nations system and with the work of other international organizations, as appropriate, bearing in mind the mandate of the United Nations Conference on Trade and Development;

24. *Recognizes* the importance of open regional economic integration in the creation of new opportunities for expanding trade and investment, stresses the importance of those initiatives being in conformity with the rules of the World Trade Organization, where applicable, and, bearing in mind the primacy of the multilateral trading system, affirms that regional trade agreements should be outward-oriented and supportive of the multilateral trading system, and, in this context, invites Governments and intergovernmental and multilateral institutions to continue to provide support for economic integration among developing countries and among countries with economies in transition;

25. *Requests* the secretariat of the United Nations Conference on Trade and Development to continue to identify and analyse the implications for development of issues relevant to investment and to identify ways and means of promoting foreign direct and portfolio

investment directed to all developing countries, taking into account their interests, in particular to those most in need, as well as to those countries with economies in transition with similar needs, and bearing in mind the work undertaken by other organizations, including the regional commissions;

26. *Emphasizes* the fact that, in line with Agenda 21 and the Rio Declaration on Environment and Development, Governments should have the objective of ensuring that trade and environmental policies are mutually supportive so as to achieve sustainable development, and also emphasizes that, in so doing, their environmental policies and measures with a potential trade impact should not be used for protectionist purposes;

27. *Reaffirms* the role of competition law and policy for sound economic development, takes note of the important and useful work of the United Nations Conference on Trade and Development in this field, and, in this regard, decides to convene in 2005 a fifth United Nations Conference to Review All Aspects of the Set of Multilaterally Agreed Equitable Principles and Rules for the Control of Restrictive Business Practices, under the auspices of the United Nations Conference on Trade and Development;

28. *Emphasizes* that the dispute settlement mechanism of the World Trade Organization is a key element with regard to the integrity and credibility of the multilateral trading system and the full realization of the benefits anticipated from the conclusion of the Uruguay Round of multilateral trade negotiations;

29. *Strongly emphasizes* the need for technical assistance, including legal assistance, to developing countries through, inter alia, the Advisory Centre on World Trade Organization Law and other mechanisms, to enable those countries to take the fullest possible advantage of the dispute settlement mechanism of the World Trade Organization, based on multilaterally agreed rules and regulations, and, in this context, also emphasizes that it is important for the United Nations Conference on Trade and Development to continue to strengthen its technical assistance to developing countries, in particular the least developed countries, landlocked developing countries and small island developing States in this area;

30. *Notes* the increasing importance and application of electronic commerce in international trade and the need to strengthen the capacities of developing countries to participate effectively in electronic commerce; urges the organizations of the United Nations system, within their mandates and in cooperation with other relevant bodies, with the participation of their secretariats and the States Members of the United Nations and observer States, the United Nations Conference on Trade and Development, the International Telecommunication Union, the International Trade Centre and the regional commissions, to continue to assist developing countries and countries with economies in transition; emphasizes in this regard the need for analysis of the fiscal, legal and regulatory aspects of electronic commerce, as well as its implications for the trade and development prospects of developing countries; and, in this connection, welcomes the Ministerial Declaration entitled "Development and international cooperation in the twenty-first century: the role of information technology in the context of a knowledge-based global economy" adopted by the Economic and Social Council during the high-level segment of the substantive session of 2000;

31. *Stresses* the importance of assisting developing countries and interested countries with economies in transition in improving the efficiency of trade-supporting services, inter alia, through the elimination of procedural barriers and by greater use of trade facilitating mechanisms, in particular in the areas of transport, customs, banking and insurance, and business information, especially in the case of small and medium-sized enterprises, and, in this respect, invites the United Nations Conference on Trade and Development, in accordance with its mandate and in collaboration with other relevant bodies of the United Nations, including the regional commissions, to continue to assist developing countries in those areas;

32. *Requests* the Secretary-General of the United Nations, in collaboration with the secretariat of the United Nations Conference on Trade and Development, to report to the General Assembly at its fifty-sixth session on the implementation of the present resolution and developments in the multilateral trading system.

Trade policy

Trade in goods and services, and commodities

The Commission on Trade in Goods and Services, and Commodities did not meet in 2000. Its fourth session took place in 1999 [YUN 1999, p. 878].

Subsidiary bodies. In accordance with the UNCTAD X Plan of Action [TD/386], expert meetings on a number of issues took place, all in Geneva. The Expert Meeting on the Impact of the Reform Process in Agriculture on LDCs and Net Food-importing Developing Countries (NFIDCs) and Ways to Address Their Concerns in Multilateral Trade Negotiations (24-26 July) [TD/B/COM.1/31] had before it an UNCTAD note on the subject [TD/B/COM.1/EM.11/2 & Corr.1]. The Meeting discussed actions under the Marrakesh Decision (a 1994 commitment by WTO member States to assist NFIDCs and LDCs should there be negative impacts resulting from the commitments on agriculture under the Uruguay Round); negotiations on the continuation of the reform process in agriculture; and other issues. The meeting recommended that UNCTAD and other international organizations should provide technical assistance and statistical and analytical background to developing countries in analysing information on agricultural trade policies and in negotiations on accession to WTO. UNCTAD should analyse the impact of the Agreement on Agriculture on LDCs, NFIDCs and small island developing countries in agricultural trade and develop a specific action plan and budget. It should also analyse ways to reduce the cost disadvantages in agricultural trade faced by the landlocked countries.

The Expert Meeting on National Experiences with Regulation and Liberalization: Examples in the Construction Services Sector and Its Contribution to the Development of Developing Countries (23-25 October) [TD/B/COM.1/32] had before it an UNCTAD note on the subject [TD/B/ COM.1/ EM.12/2]. The Meeting analysed domestic policy instruments and strategies aimed at building capacities in the construction services sector, and discussed action in international trade negotiations and by international financial agencies and donors. It recommended that UNCTAD promote continued dialogue in the area of construction services and noted that a model law for promoting the development of an efficient and competitive construction services sector might be needed. UNCTAD should support the participation of developing countries in multilateral trade negotiations and organize a follow-up meeting on construction services.

The Expert Meeting on Systems and National Experiences for the Protection of Traditional Knowledge, Innovations and Practices (30 October–1 November) [TD/B/COM.1/33] had before it an UNCTAD note on the subject [TD/B/ COM.1/ EM.13/2]. The Meeting discussed the role of traditional knowledge in several economic and other sectors and systems for its protection. It underlined the need to raise awareness of the role and value of traditional knowledge among local and indigenous communities, policy makers and other stakeholders, and recommended continued cooperation between intergovernmental organizations carrying out programmes on traditional knowledge. UNCTAD was requested to organize seminars and promote the implementation of national strategies to harness traditional knowledge for development and trade, and assist developing countries in exploring systems for protection of such knowledge.

The Expert Meeting on the Impact of Anti-Dumping and Countervailing Actions (4-6 December) [TD/B/COM.1/34] had before it an UNCTAD note on the subject [TD/B/COM.1/ EM.14/2]. The Meeting identified a number of issues relating to anti-dumping and countervailing measures that might be addressed in: future multilateral trade negotiations; the WTO Committee on Anti-Dumping Practices; the WTO dispute settlement mechanism; national policies of member States; and UNCTAD's future work and technical assistance activities.

UNCTAD/WTO study. In a joint January study on the post-Uruguay Round tariff environment for developing countries' exports: tariff peaks and tariff escalation [TD/B/COM.1/14/Rev.1], UNCTAD and WTO analysed the tariff situation that would prevail in a number of major developed and developing countries once all the Uruguay Round concessions had been implemented, taking account of the concessions granted by preference-giving countries under their GSP schemes. The study observed that problems of high tariffs and tariff escalation remained widespread for developing countries even after the Uruguay Round. Peak tariffs affected both agricultural and industrial products.

Interdependence and global economic issues

TDB, at its forty-seventh session (Geneva, 9-20 October) [A/55/15], considered interdependence and global economic issues from a trade and development perspective: crisis and recovery in emerging markets. While it was recognized that technological progress and the globalization of trade, finance and productive activity offered new opportunities for wealth creation under appropriate macroeconomic policies and with good governance, weaknesses in national policies and institutions could be punished more quickly and severely by international markets than in the past, even when there was no solid basis for a negative risk assessment. There was concern about the disparities in economic performance across and within regions and about the persistence of macroeconomic imbalances. Difficult policy choices were not restricted to developing countries; growth disparities within the industrialized world had resulted in trade imbalances, while technological and financial innovations had led to greater fragility of financial and trade flows. There was broad agreement that the recent rise in oil prices had added another element of fragility, and that oil-importing countries were in a particularly difficult situation and required compensatory financing through the multilateral financial institutions. Expanding trade opportunities and improving market access would help developing countries to become less dependent on capital inflows and hence less vulnerable to external shocks originating from international capital markets and policy shifts in the developed countries.

While increased private capital flows to developing countries might serve as a vehicle to accelerate development, international capital markets did not always allocate funds efficiently at the global level. There was a major role for national policies in crisis prevention and solution; good corporate governance, an appropriate maturity structure of external debt and an effective regulatory system for the domestic financial sector were stressed. Attention was drawn to the fact that, while much of the burden of the Asian crisis was borne by the public sector, the crisis had originated in the private sector. Consequently, more attention should be given to a prudential regulation and supervision of private capital flows.

The discussion also addressed the systemic factors behind the financial crises, and noted that greater stability of the international financial system required appropriate regulation of financial flows. Governance in the international monetary and financial system should be made more transparent and participatory, and greater regional monetary cooperation was considered useful to the prevention and management of currency crises, albeit through complementing existing multilateral arrangements. Emphasis was placed on the need for strengthened policy coordination among the major developed countries to avoid large fluctuation of the exchange rates among the three major currencies. The enhanced Heavily Indebted Poor Countries (HIPC) Initiative was welcomed, but it was made clear that the debt problem remained an obstacle to faster development, especially in LDCs. An acceleration of debt relief procedures and their extension to a greater number of poor countries, as well as renewed efforts on the part of donor countries to raise their official development assistance (ODA) to previously agreed targets, were considered necessary preconditions for a reduction of poverty and a narrowing of the income gap between North and South.

Trade promotion and facilitation

In 2000, UN bodies continued to assist developing countries to promote their exports and facilitate the movement of their goods in international commerce. The International Trade Centre was the main originator of technical cooperation projects in that area.

International Trade Centre

During 2000, the International Trade Centre (ITC), under the joint sponsorship of WTO and UNCTAD, focused on capacity-building to enhance international competitiveness and trade performance [ITC/AG(XXXIV)/185 & Add.1,2]. The Centre's goals during the year were to: facilitate the integration of developing/transition economy enterprises into the multilateral trading system; support national efforts to design and implement trade development strategies; streng then key trade support services, both public and private; improve export performance in sectors of critical importance and opportunity; and foster international competitiveness within the business community as a whole, and the small and medium-sized enterprise sector in particular. ITC maintained a pro-

gramme of applied research to develop a set of competitiveness-enhancement tools suitable for adaptation by local partners for use by local trade support institutions and enterprises. Several new tools emerged, and the number of national networks partnering with ITC increased. The Centre maintained its role as the principal source of specialized technical assistance in the competitive aspects of trade-related capacity-building. It intensified its coordination with the Joint ITC/UNCTAD/WTO Integrated Technical Assistance Programme in Selected Least Developed and Other African Countries (JITAP) and became increasingly engaged, at the field level, in trade development work related to the Integrated Framework for Trade-related Technical Assistance to LDCs (IF). During the year, a programme of specialized cooperation in opportunity identification, market development, institution-strengthening and enterprise assistance was maintained under various interregional, regional and national projects.

ITC increasingly broadened the reach of technical cooperation delivery: a total of 52 national, 15 regional and 22 interregional projects were under implementation, and more than 100 countries, including 27 LDCs, benefited from its support. In addition to JITAP, capacity-building in multilateral trading system issues was an area of concentration under a programme for the Arab States and the countries participating in World Tr@de Net. Capacity-building for trade support services reached critical mass in Central America, Romania, the United Republic of Tanzania and Viet Nam. Improved sectoral performance figured in a number of national programmes and under the ITC South-South trade promotion programme, which broadened its coverage to include Southern Africa subregional trade, intra-Arab trade, the Economic Cooperation Organization (ECO) region in Central Asia and the Greater Mekong region. Particular emphasis was placed on involving LDCs in ITC product networks and on supporting the process of formulating trade development strategies.

The Executive Forum on National Export Strategies (Montreux, Switzerland, 26-30 September) highlighted the theme "Export development in the digital economy". The Forum, which was attended by over 20 national teams, emerged as ITC's main vehicle for reviewing and assessing best practice in national export strategy management.

JAG action. The ITC Joint Advisory Group (JAG) held its thirty-third session in Geneva from 10 to 14 April [ITC/AG(XXXIII)/181]. JAG had before it reports on ITC activities in 1999 [YUN 1999, p. 880]; the evaluation of the ITC programme on trade information [ITC/AG(XXXIII)/177]; the ITC strategy for trade information services [ITC/AG (XXXIII)/178]; ITC's contribution to the medium-term plan of the United Nations for 2002-2005 [ITC/AG(XXXIII)/183]; and the report of the 1999 ITC technical meeting [YUN 1999, p. 880]. It also considered the report of the ITC Global Trust Fund's Consultative Committee [ITC/AG(XXXIII)/182].

The Group emphasized ITC's important role in complementing the work of UNCTAD and WTO by undertaking a range of operational activities to help businesses unpderstand the new multilateral trade rules, develop and implement new strategies and programmes for trade promotion and export development, and strengthen the competitiveness of enterprises. Representatives of developing countries and economies in transition testified to ITC's useful support of trade expansion programmes, and JAG expressed its appreciation for ITC's continuing efforts to expand assistance to LDCs and contribute to poverty alleviation through its Export-led Poverty Reduction Programme. ITC was encouraged to collaborate with other development partners, notably the United Nations Development Programme (UNDP) and the World Bank, in implementing the Programme. The Group expressed satisfaction with the Global Trust Fund, which continued to be an important funding mechanism for ITC and a successful example of cooperation addressing the needs of developing countries and economies in transition, particularly LDCs, in their integration in the multilateral trading system.

Pledges of trust fund contributions to ITC were announced by Canada, China, Denmark, France, India, Italy, the Netherlands, Norway, Sweden, Switzerland and Turkey. Pledges had been made earlier by Cyprus, the Islamic Development Bank and the Agence intergouvernementale de la Francophonie.

TDB, at its twenty-fifth executive session in September [A/55/15], took note of the JAG report.

Enterprise, business facilitation and development

The Commission on Enterprise, Business Facilitation and Development did not meet in 2000. Its fourth session took place in 1999 [YUN 1999, p. 881].

Subsidiary bodies. In accordance with the UNCTAD X Plan of Action [TD/386], three expert meetings took place in 2000, all in Geneva. The Expert Meeting on Electronic Commerce and Tourism (18-20 September) [TD/B/COM.3/30] discussed policies and strategies to be adopted by developing countries in order to increase

their participation in electronic commerce (e-commerce) in tourism, and the possible role of UNCTAD and other international organizations in realizing the development benefits of those policies and strategies. It had before it an UNCTAD secretariat report on the subject [TD/B/COM.3/EM.9/2]. In recommendations to Governments and enterprises, the Meeting stated that solutions for e-commerce in tourism should address broader issues of electronic commerce in general, and their effects on and benefits for development. E-tourism should be considered alongside a multisectoral strategy for improved Internet access and telecommunications infrastructure, and telecommunications and Internet services should be liberalized to attract new investment. The Meeting recommended that UNCTAD should analyse the effect of tourism-related e-commerce on development and support the development of sustainable e-tourism in developing countries.

The Expert Meeting on the Relationships between SMEs and TNCs to Ensure the Competitiveness of SMEs (27-29 November) [TD/B/COM.3/31] focused on government and corporate programmes to promote beneficial relationships between TNCs and SMEs. It had before it an UNCTAD secretariat paper on enhancing the competitiveness of SMEs through linkages [TD/B/COM.3/EM.11/2]. The experts discussed how globalization had changed the nature of TNCs' production and outsourcing networks, thereby promoting TNC-SME linkages; and how TNCs needed such linkages with SMEs to implement their global strategies. However, many SMEs missed opportunities for linkages because they could not meet international standards for production. The Meeting suggested that UNCTAD should continue its research to strengthen competitiveness by promoting linkages for interested Governments, TNCs, SMEs and support institutions.

The Expert Meeting on Human Resources Development and Training in Trade-supporting Services: Key to Growth with Special Potential for LDCs (13-15 December) [TD/B/COM.3/32] had before it an UNCTAD secretariat note on the subject [TD/B/COM.3/EM.10/2]. The Meeting made recommendations for action by countries and the international community to achieve and support the application of effective policies.

Restrictive business practices

Fourth Review Conference

In accordance with General Assembly resolution 52/182 [YUN 1997, p. 935], the Fourth United Nations Conference to Review All Aspects of the Set of Multilaterally Agreed Equitable Principles and Rules for the Control of Restrictive Business Practices was held in Geneva from 25 to 29 September [TD/RBP/CONF.5/16 & Corr.1]. The first conference to review the 1980 Set of Multilaterally Agreed Equitable Principles and Rules for the Control of Restrictive Business Practices (known as the Set) [YUN 1980, p. 626] was held in 1985 [YUN 1985, p. 563], the second in 1990 [YUN 1990, p. 464] and the third in 1995 [YUN 1995, p. 961]. The Conference had before it a note by the UNCTAD Secretary-General which reviewed application and implementation of the Set [TD/RBP/CONF.5/3] and considered major developments that had taken place at the national, regional and multilateral levels in the field of competition law and policy since the Third Review Conference. The Conference also considered UNCTAD secretariat reports on: experiences gained on international cooperation on competition policy issues and the mechanisms used [TD/RBP/CONF.5/4 & Corr.1]; technical assistance, advisory and training programmes on competition law and policy [TD/RBP/CONF.5/5 & Corr.1]; competition policy and the exercise of intellectual property rights [TD/RBP/CONF.5/6]; and continued work on the elaboration of a model law or laws on restrictive business practices [TD/RBP/CONF.5/7]. The Conference also had before it a number of declarations adopted at regional preparatory meetings [TD/RBP/CONF.5/8, TD/RBP/CONF.5/9, TD/RBP/CONF.5/11, TD/RBP/CONF.5/12, TD/RBP/CONF.5/13]; and the Declaration of the CIS Antimonopoly Authorities [TD/RBP/CONF.5/10].

By a 29 September resolution, the Conference called on member States to implement the Set's provisions; recommended that the General Assembly convene a Fifth Review Conference in 2005; requested UNCTAD to expand its technical cooperation activities; and invited member States to assist UNCTAD on a voluntary basis in its technical cooperation by providing experts, training facilities or resources. The Conference invited the Commission on Trade in Goods and Services, and Commodities to consider convening an expert meeting on consumer policy as a distinct body from the Intergovernmental Group of Experts on Competition Law and Policy; and decided that the Intergovernmental Group of Experts on Competition Law and Policy, at its 2001 session, would consider, for better implementation of the Set, cooperation regarding merger control, and the interface between competition policy and intellectual property rights. In the light of the UNCTAD X Plan of Action [TD/386], the Group of Experts should draw up its work plan to encompass institutional capacity-building; competition advocacy and educating the public;

studies on competition, competitiveness and development; and inputs to possible international agreements on competition.

TDB, at its forty-seventh session, in October [TD/B/47/11 (Vol.I & Corr.1)], was informed of the outcome of the Conference, and noted that the convening of an expert meeting on consumer policy would not be additional to the existing 10 UNCTAD expert meetings.

Commodities

The *Trade and Development Report, 2000* [Sales No. E.00.II.D.19] stated that in 1999 world commodity markets continued to suffer from the effects of the economic slowdown of 1998, which reduced demand and exerted a downward pressure on the prices of most commodities. By mid-1999, the downward trend in most prices levelled and prices increased moderately. However, they did not recover from the market slump in the aftermath of the Asian and Brazilian crises, which resulted in a decline in the commodity price index (excluding crude petroleum) of about 30 per cent. The widespread decline in non-oil commodity prices in both 1998 and 1999 reflected a combination of sluggish demand and ample supplies in almost all markets, as well as the continued effects of currency devaluation for important exporters and importers, most notably Brazil and the Russian Federation. The large devaluations in Brazil led to an increase in exports of sugar and coffee, whereas the devaluation of the Russian rouble reduced the demand for many imported commodities. At the same time as world demand for many non-oil commodities declined, due mainly to the sharp economic downturn experienced in most East Asian countries, technological advances enhanced productivity and reduced production costs, leading to an oversupply in commodity markets. Furthermore, novel applications of genetic engineering and biotechnology in agriculture, combined with favourable weather conditions, resulted in higher output of most agricultural products. Notwithstanding the improvement in the global economy in the second half of 1999, prices of non-oil primary commodities were on average well below the 1998 level. The fall was widespread, but the collapse in sugar and cocoa prices by 30 and 32 per cent, respectively, was particularly acute.

The key feature of the oil market in 1999 was the sharp rise in crude oil prices to unexpectedly high levels. They rebounded steadily throughout the year, so that prices averaged $17.5 a barrel for the year as a whole. The rally in oil prices in 1999 accounted for about $75 billion (some 40 per cent) of the increase in world merchandise exports. Oil prices rose sharply after both the producers of the Organization of Petroleum Exporting Countries (OPEC) and non-OPEC producers decided to cut output by 2.1 million barrels per day as of 1 April 1999. Following OPEC's decision in September 1999 to maintain supply limits until March 2000, prices continued to rise, reaching $27 a barrel in February 2000.

In a joint report on the world economic situation and prospects [Sales No. E.01.II.C.2], issued at the end of 2000 by DESA and UNCTAD, it was observed that the global economic recovery had given a stimulus to commodity demand in 2000. However, only a few commodities had benefited from the upturn and there were sharp divergences in the movements of prices of various groups of primary commodities. Prices for tropical beverages and vegetable products weakened further, those for food and agricultural raw materials firmed and those for minerals, metals and crude petroleum continued to surge. On average, the combined index of non-fuel commodity prices rose 4.5 per cent by the end of the third quarter of 2000 compared with the same quarter in 1999. In the petroleum sector, the price of a barrel of oil climbed steadily from a trough in February 1999 of $10 per barrel to a peak of $38 in September 2000.

UNCTAD report. In response to General Assembly resolution 53/174 [YUN 1998, p. 891], the Secretary-General submitted an August report [A/55/332], prepared by UNCTAD, on world commodity trends and prospects. The report stated that the importance of commodities in world trade was declining, and developing countries were losing their share in world commodity trade, even for their traditional export products. The loss was especially marked for African countries, LDCs and the African, Caribbean and Pacific group of countries. The extremely low prices for commodities aggravated the negative impact of the situation on the economies of commodity-dependent countries. Moreover, the margins between international prices for commodities and the final prices paid by consumers had widened, and a smaller proportion of the value of the final product went to the producing countries. The concentration on the demand side of world commodity markets continued, while State participation in developing countries' agricultural sectors was radically reduced, and purchasing firms with large financial resources had penetrated the marketing and production structures in developing countries.

The report reviewed recent developments in the world commodity economy and discussed changes in commodity market structures and re-cent developments in international cooperation on commodities. The report concluded that poverty-reduction efforts should attach due importance to commodity issues, and that the revival of international cooperation in commodities, within a new market-based framework, was called for. The key market access problems faced by commodity exporters should be addressed, with the elimination of tariff peaks and tariff escalation, placing agricultural commodities on the same footing as other products in the trading system and ending trade-distorting agricultural support measures by developed countries. Enhanced financial and technical assistance was also required for addressing supply-side constraints, which affected LDCs in particular. Support measures were also required for developing countries dependent on the imports of essential commodities. The report recommended that the activities of the Second Account of the Common Fund for Commodities should be expanded and increased funding made available to it to finance research and development and extension services in developing countries.

GENERAL ASSEMBLY ACTION

On 20 December [meeting 87], the General Assembly, on the recommendation of the Second Committee [A/55/579/Add.2], adopted **resolution 55/183** without vote [agenda item 92 (b)].

Commodities

The General Assembly,

Recalling its resolutions 45/200 of 21 December 1990, 47/185 of 22 December 1992, 48/214 of 23 December 1993, 51/169 of 16 December 1996 and 53/174 of 15 December 1998, and stressing the urgent need to ensure their full implementation,

Taking note of the outcome of the tenth session of the United Nations Conference on Trade and Development, held at Bangkok from 12 to 19 February 2000, and the Plan of Action adopted by the Conference,

Recalling the United Nations Millennium Declaration adopted by the heads of State and Government on 8 September 2000,

Taking note of the Declaration and the Programme of Action adopted by the South Summit of the Group of 77, held at Havana from 10 to 14 April 2000,

Taking note with concern of the report of the United Nations Conference on Trade and Development on the declining trend of most commodity prices,

Taking note of the report of the Trade and Development Board on its forty-seventh session, held at Geneva from 9 to 20 October 2000,

Recognizing that many developing countries, in particular African countries and the least developed countries, are highly dependent on the commodity sector, which still remains the principal source of export revenues and the primary source of the creation of employment, income-generation and domestic savings, as well as a driving force of investment and a contributor to economic growth and social development,

Expressing deep concern about the negative effects of unfavourable weather conditions on the supply side of most commodity-dependent countries and any continuing effects of the 1997-1998 financial crisis on the demand for commodities, as well as the continuing depressed levels of most commodity prices, which adversely affect the economic growth of commodity-dependent countries, especially in Africa and the least developed countries, as well as commodity-dependent small island developing States,

Concerned about the difficulties experienced by the developing countries in financing and implementing viable diversification programmes and in attaining access to markets for their commodities,

Emphasizing the necessity for a domestic industrial transformation of commodity production in the developing countries, in particular African countries and the least developed countries, with a view to enhancing productivity and stabilizing and increasing their export earnings, thus promoting the sustainable economic growth of developing countries and their integration into the global economy,

1. *Emphasizes* the need for the developing countries that are heavily dependent on primary commodities to continue to promote a domestic policy and an institutional environment that encourage diversification and liberalization of the trade and export sectors and enhance competitiveness;

2. *Expresses* the urgent need for supportive international policies and measures to improve the functioning of commodity markets through efficient and transparent price formation mechanisms, including commodity exchanges, and through the use of commodity price risk management instruments;

3. *Expresses concern* at the declining terms of trade in most primary commodities, in particular for net exporters of such commodities, as well as the lack of progress in many developing countries in achieving diversification, and, in this regard, strongly emphasizes the need for actions at both the national and international levels, inter alia, to improve market access conditions, address supply-side constraints and provide support for capacity-building, including in areas that actively involve women;

4. *Urges* the developed countries to continue to support the commodity diversification and liberalization efforts of commodity-dependent developing countries, especially in Africa and the least developed countries, as well as commodity-dependent small island developing States, in a spirit of common purpose and efficiency, inter alia, by providing technical and financial assistance for the preparatory phase of their commodity diversification programmes;

5. *Urges* producers and consumers of individual commodities to intensify their efforts to reinforce mutual cooperation and assistance;

6. *Reiterates* the importance of maximizing the contribution of the commodity sector to economic growth and sustainable development, while continuing with diversification efforts in developing countries, especially in commodity-dependent countries, and, in this respect, stresses that:

(*a*) International support for the efforts of developing countries in the industrial transformation of their commodities is required to increase their export revenues and improve their competitiveness with a view to facilitating their integration into the global economy;

(*b*) In the context of the process of trade liberalization, tariff peaks should be minimized and the use of trade-distorting policies and protectionist practices and non-tariff barriers should be eliminated as they have negative effects on the ability of developing countries to diversify their exports and undertake the required restructuring of their commodity sector and have an adverse impact on liberalization measures taken by commodity-dependent developing countries and their efforts to eliminate poverty;

(*c*) In line with Agenda 21 and the Rio Declaration on Environment and Development, Governments should make it their objective to ensure that trade and environmental policies are mutually supportive so as to achieve sustainable development; in so doing, their environmental policies and measures with a potential trade impact should not be used for protectionist purposes;

(*d*) In the light of the process of multilateral trade liberalization, which has led to the diminution of differentials accorded by preferred trade regimes, there is a need to take measures, as appropriate and consistent with international obligations, to address the diminution, in particular by strengthening technical assistance, by continuing to provide financial assistance to commodity-dependent developing countries and by addressing supply-side constraints faced by such countries, in order to improve the competitiveness of their commodity sectors and to overcome difficulties encountered in their diversification programmes;

(*e*) Timely and effective financial cooperation to facilitate the management by commodity-dependent countries of excessive fluctuations in commodity export earnings should be maintained and further pursued;

(*f*) Strengthening technical cooperation in the areas of transfer of new technologies and know-how in production processes and training for technical, managerial and commercial staff in developing countries is of paramount importance for quality improvements in the commodity sector;

(*g*) Expansion of South-South trade and investment in commodities enhances complementarities and offers opportunities for intersectoral linkages within and among exporting countries;

(*h*) There is a need to promote, expand and intensify research and development, to provide infrastructure and support services and to encourage investment, including joint ventures in developing countries engaged in the commodity and commodity-processing sectors;

7. *Encourages* the Common Fund for Commodities, in cooperation with the International Trade Centre, the United Nations Conference on Trade and Development and other relevant bodies, to continue to expand the activities of its Second Account with the necessary and effective support for research and development and extension services in developing countries, including adaptive research on production and processing aimed at smallholders and small-sized and medium-sized enterprises in developing countries, in order to widen the scope of activities and thus ensure the effective participation of all stakeholders;

8. *Invites* the United Nations Conference on Trade and Development, within its mandate, to provide assistance to developing countries in the financing of commodity diversification and to include issues related to commodities in the provision of analytical support and technical assistance to developing countries in their preparation for effective participation in multilateral trade negotiations and in formulating a positive agenda for future trade negotiations;

9. *Requests* the Secretary-General of the United Nations Conference on Trade and Development to report to the General Assembly at its fifty-seventh session on world commodity trends and prospects;

10. *Decides* to include in the provisional agenda of its fifty-seventh session, under the item entitled "Macroeconomic policy questions", the sub-item entitled "Commodities".

Individual commodities

Coffee. At its eighty-second session (London, 27-28 September), the International Coffee Council approved the International Coffee Agreement 2001. The Agreement was opened for signature at United Nations Headquarters in New York on 1 November 2000 and was to remain open until 25 September 2001. As at 31 December, Costa Rica had signed the Agreement.

Jute. The United Nations Conference on Jute and Jute Products, 2000 held its first session (Geneva, 27-31 March) [TD/JUTE.3/7] to prepare a successor agreement to the International Agreement on Jute and Jute Products, 1989 [YUN 1989, p. 373], which was due to expire on 11 April 2000. The Conference represented the culmination of a series of meetings held within the framework of the International Jute Organization (IJO) in Dhaka, Bangladesh, which led to a recognition that there was a continued need for international cooperation on jute, a commodity produced primarily by developing countries and providing employment to millions of people. Its production, however, was suffering from the competition with its synthetic substitutes and had been affected by price instability. At its second session (Dhaka, 6-8 April), the Conference established the text of the International Instrument of Cooperation in Jute and Jute Products, 2000 [TD/JUTE.3/7]. By an 8 April resolution [TD/JUTE.3/6], the Conference requested the Secretary-General to arrange for the Instrument to be open for signature at United Nations Headquarters in New York from 1 July 2000 to 30 June 2001.

Following the Conference, the EU, which accounted for about one third of IJO's financing, announced that it was unable to endorse the Instrument. Consequently, the Instrument was not deposited with the Secretary-General and IJO entered into a liquidation period.

Common Fund for Commodities

The 1980 Agreement Establishing the Common Fund for Commodities [YUN 1980, p. 621], a mechanism intended to stabilize the commodities market by helping to finance buffer stocks of specific commodities, as well as commodity development activities such as research and marketing, entered into force in 1989, and the Fund became operational later that year.

As at 31 December 2000, the number of parties to it remained at 106 States, plus the European Community (EC), the Common Market for Eastern and Southern Africa and the Organization of African Unity (OAU).

Finance

Financial policy

The *Trade and Development Report, 2000* [Sales No. E.00.II.D.19] stated that 1999 was less turbulent than 1998 for the currencies of major emerging market economies, whose currency regimes continued to span the spectrum from rigid pegs through various forms of managed floating to full flexibility; there was widespread easing of monetary conditions in those economies. Substantial movements in exchange rates were rare in East Asian countries but more frequent elsewhere.

The *World Economic and Social Survey 2000* [Sales No. E.00.II.C.1] noted that macroeconomic policy measures had been crucial in stimulating recovery from recent international financial crises and in deepening and broadening the recovery to include a growing number of countries. In certain developed economies, the combination of strong output growth with low inflation and unemployment suggested a decoupling of the links that had traditionally prevailed among those variables when the economic cycle matured and slack capacity began to be exhausted. That decoupling was most pronounced in the United States. In many emerging market economies, the international financial crises of the late 1990s prompted changes in the institutional framework for economic policy. Examples included changes in exchange-rate regimes, improvements in the rules and instruments for monetary policy, and reforms of banking and financial systems. Those and other changes altered the channels through which financial policies affected real economic sectors.

In a joint report on the world economic situation and prospects [Sales No. E.01.II.C.2], issued at the end of 2000 by DESA and UNCTAD, it was observed that central banks in many developed economies, which had begun tightening their monetary policies in mid-1999, continued to do so until mid-2000 when signs of moderation in the pace of global economic growth began to surface and some central banks held their policy interest rates steady. While some economies in transition, particularly the Czech Republic and Slovenia, moved towards a more neutral monetary policy in late 1999 and early 2000, most of them kept a relatively tight stance during the year. Developing countries followed diverse paths with their monetary policy in 2000. Despite higher oil prices and other supply shocks, as well as improved demand conditions in several countries, prudent macroeconomic policies kept inflation under control in most of them.

Financial flows

The *World Economic and Social Survey 2000* [Sales No. E.00.II.C.1] stated that net financial inflows to developing countries and transition economies in 1999 remained well below the levels of the pre-crisis 1990s, owing to subdued private flows and a sharp decline in official financing. By late 1999, however, investor sentiment towards emerging markets improved significantly, based on stronger economic performance and improved external balances of a growing number of countries. As a result, the cost of external credit fell and the flow of credit to emerging market economies began to rebound. However, countries that were on the sidelines as regards financial flows before the crisis remained so in 1999.

According to the *Trade and Development Report, 2000* [Sales No. E.00.II.D.19], net private capital flows to developing and transition economies increased in 1999, but only marginally from the levels of 1998, which represented a fall of more than 50 per cent from those of 1997, and reflected the aftermath of the financial crises in East Asia and the Russian Federation. That outcome was accompanied by a more stable environment for major financial indicators than that of the preceding two years. However, there were large regional differences: recovery was recorded for inflows into Asia, while in Latin America the inflow was substantially reduced. By contrast, the changes for economies in Europe and Africa were much more limited. There was also significant variation in the volatility of different categories of inflow: estimates of foreign direct investment (FDI) mostly showed either little change or rises in 1999, while those of debt securities and bank lending were subject to greater variation. Financial crises had a more limited impact on FDI than on other major categories of private financial flow to developing and transition economies. FDI was significantly

influenced by privatization and by the growing importance of cross-border merger and acquisition transitions. The rise in FDI in 1999 was associated with substantial receipts from privatization in Latin America and with asset sales in East Asia associated with bank and non-bank corporate restructuring and facilitated by the recent relaxation of restrictions on foreign investment. Net private capital inflows in the form of debt declined sharply, and net issues of international debt instruments by developing and transition economies fell slightly.

In a joint report on the world economic situation and prospects [Sales No. E.01.II.C.2], issued at the end of 2000 by DESA and UNCTAD, it was observed that net financial flows to developing and transition economies fell in 2000 to their lowest level in more than a decade, mainly owing to strong net outflows in the banking sector. Official flows increased moderately and there were higher, if small, net inflows of portfolio investment. FDI flows reached a record level in 2000, estimated at $1.1 trillion, 14 per cent higher than in 1999, but that increase was fully accounted for by flows to developed countries, with the surge in cross-border mergers and acquisitions serving as the driving force.

The *World Investment Report 2000* [Sales No. E.00.II.D.20], prepared by UNCTAD, focused on cross-border mergers and acquisitions and development.

International financial system

High-level meeting of Economic and Social Council and Bretton Woods institutions. In accordance with General Assembly resolution 54/197 [YUN 1999, p. 892] and Economic and Social Council **decision 2000/205** of 4 February, the third special high-level meeting between the Council and the Bretton Woods institutions (the World Bank Group and the International Monetary Fund (IMF)) took place in New York on 18 April [A/55/3/Rev.1]. The first two meetings were held in 1998 [YUN 1998, p. 898] and 1999 [YUN 1999, p. 890]. The meeting addressed the theme of strengthening international financial arrangements and eradicating poverty and had before it a note by the Secretary-General on the subject [E/2000/8], which identified a number of issues to be discussed in two major policy areas: reform of the global financial system and fighting poverty in developing countries.

In an informal summary of the high-level meeting [E/2000/79], the Secretariat summarized the salient points and main aspects of statements made and exchanges of views that took place and provided a synopsis of the dialogue, from which four main themes emerged: the state of the world economy, globalization and international trade; strengthening the global financial system; development and poverty reduction; and the institutional dimensions to promote faster economic growth and enhance international cooperation for development.

In concluding remarks, the Managing Director of the World Bank pointed to the increasing convergence of views of the United Nations and the Bretton Woods institutions on development and global financial system reform based on a common set of objectives. He noted that the poverty-reduction strategy papers endorsed by the World Bank and IMF, which were required to set the basis for concessional lending by those institutions, were important for the consideration of debt relief and poverty eradication. He also observed that funding the HIPC Initiative was a major challenge. Although $2.4 billion had been pledged, the overall debt relief provided amounted to $15 billion and was a crucial part of the process to move ahead. He hoped that the middle-income countries would not participate as beneficiaries of the HIPC Initiative but grow out of debt and preserve access to capital markets. The Acting Managing Director of IMF noted that for any country, trade liberalization was one of the best ways to integrate into the global economy. Regarding the HIPC Initiative, he stated that IMF had to take into account the social and budgetary implications of the policies to be implemented, and that countries' strategies were more important than the advice of IMF or the World Bank.

In his closing remarks, the President of the Council said that the meeting had stressed the need to take advantage of the easing of financial crises to push ahead in the consideration of further reforms to foster integration of the developing and transition economies into the global economy. He noted that the structure of international institutions was incomplete, particularly in involving developing and transition economies in drawing up prudential norms and standards. Although the meeting reconfirmed the critical role of the private sector in finance and entrepreneurship, Governments played a role that the private sector could not perform, in particular in fighting poverty and HIV/AIDS and more generally to work towards the goals of equity and fairness. Governments and multilateral institutions needed to work together to provide free market access to developing countries, particularly LDCs. Sound national policies supported by increased official development assistance (ODA) and strengthened debt relief were needed.

Report of Secretary-General. In response to General Assembly resolution 54/197 [YUN 1999, p. 892], the Secretary-General submitted a 27 July report entitled: "Towards a stable international financial system, responsive to the challenges of development, especially in the developing countries" [A/55/187]. The report summarized recent trends in global capital flows (see p. 906) and examined the main actions taken and concerns raised on policy in industrialized countries and the international economic environment, the reform of the international financial system and systemic reform and confidence-building at global and regional levels—issues addressed in resolution 54/197.

The Secretary-General stated that there appeared to be a widespread willingness among policy makers to consider and adopt significant changes in the international financial architecture. However, several proposals, all of which sought to build a strengthened and more stable financial system, responsive to the priorities of growth and to the promotion of economic and social equity, warranted further consideration by the international community. Those proposals fell into a number of key areas: crisis prevention; crisis resolution; and institutional structure. Noting that reform of the international monetary and financial system had reached the international political agenda, the Secretary-General observed that it was an extremely sensitive moment, as many Governments had deep interests at stake, as had the private sector around the world. Civil society had raised important political, ethical and developmental considerations. Therefore, the issue warranted discussion from multiple perspectives and in multiple forums, and since discussion was an essential part of consensus-building, it was best to include the views of all relevant stakeholders. The United Nations was a natural forum for such considerations, the Secretary-General said. In that regard, the agreement of Member States to include systemic issues in the preparatory process of the high-level international event on financing for development and the event itself, to be held in 2002 (see p. 915), provided an unique opportunity to bring the world's political decision makers together to reach a new understanding that could shape the future of financing for development.

In a 28 July addendum [A/55/187/Add.1], the Secretary-General discussed regional perspectives and developments with regard to the international financial system and provided the views of the executive secretaries of the regional commissions on the subject (see also p. 923). He stated that the Asian financial crisis and its contagion effect had generated an impetus in favour of fundamental reforms in the international financial architecture to improve the management of crises and prevent their recurrence. The crisis had also led to the recognition that there was an enormous discrepancy between the dynamic financial world and the institutions regulating it.

By a second addendum of 2 August [A/55/187/Add.2], the Secretary-General transmitted an UNCTAD note, which provided information on its work on the involvement of the private sector in the prevention and resolution of financial crises. The report stated that in past crisis situations, ad hoc bail-out operations by multilateral institutions had protected creditors from bearing the full risk of their lending decisions, putting the burden on debtors. The application of insolvency principles would help make the resolution of financial crises in developing countries more equitable, less costly and less time-consuming, and reduce the probability of their occurrence. An effective framework for greater private sector involvement would need to contain three key elements: provisions for an automatic standstill on debt servicing; maintaining the debtor's access to the working capital required for the continuation of its operations; and an arrangement for the reorganization of the debtor's assets and liabilities, aimed at sharing the adjustment burden between debtor and creditors as well as distributing equitably the costs among creditors.

Ministerial meeting. By a 17 July letter [A/55/158-E/2000/102], Japan transmitted to the Secretary-General the report of the Group of Seven (G-7) industrialized countries' major finance ministers to the heads of State and Government entitled "Strengthening the international financial architecture" (Fukuoka, Japan, 8 July).

GENERAL ASSEMBLY ACTION

On 20 December [meeting 87], the General Assembly, on the recommendation of the Second Committee [A/55/579/Add.5], adopted **resolution 55/186** without vote [agenda item 92 (e)].

Towards a strengthened and stable international financial architecture responsive to the priorities of growth and development, especially in developing countries, and to the promotion of economic and social equity

The General Assembly,

Recalling its resolution 54/197 of 22 December 1999, entitled "Towards a stable international financial system, responsive to the challenges of development, especially in the developing countries",

Recalling also the United Nations Millennium Declaration adopted by the heads of State and Government on 8 September 2000,

Taking note of the high-level regional meetings on financing for development held at Jakarta from 2 to 5 August 2000, Bogotá on 9 and 10 November 2000, Addis Ababa from 15 to 22 November 2000, Beirut on 23 and 24 November 2000 and Geneva on 6 and 7 December 2000, which addressed issues of, inter alia, domestic resources mobilization, external private flows, reform of the international financial architecture, regional cooperation and collaboration, innovative sources of financing and issues relating to the external sector, including official development assistance and trade, from the regional perspective, in order to contribute to the preparatory process for the high-level international intergovernmental event on financing for development,

Emphasizing the importance of mobilizing in a coherent manner all sources available for the provision of financing for development, inter alia, domestic resources, international private capital flows, official development assistance, market access for goods and services from developing countries and external debt relief, and emphasizing also the importance of utilizing those resources in an efficient way,

Expressing concern that net financial flows to developing countries continued in 1999 the contraction that had begun with the onset of the financial crisis in 1997, and regretting the continued marginalization of the least developed countries from private capital flows,

Emphasizing the importance of long-term investment flows, in particular foreign direct investment, in complementing the development efforts of all developing countries as well as economies in transition and the need for all countries to develop stable access to private capital and for regional and international cooperation to promote the mobilization of new and additional capital for development,

Concerned about the excessive volatility of speculative short-term capital flows and the contagion effects in financial markets in times of crisis,

Deeply concerned by the low levels of official development assistance,

Stressing the need for increased access to markets, in particular for goods and services that are of export interest to developing countries, inter alia, through multilateral trade negotiations,

Emphasizing the importance of finding a durable solution for those developing countries that have difficulties in meeting their external debt and debt-servicing obligations,

Encouraging the efforts to enhance the stabilizing role of regional and subregional financial institutions and arrangements in supporting the management of monetary and financial issues,

Underlining the urgent need to continue to work on a wide range of reforms for a strengthened and more stable international financial system with a view to enabling it to deal more effectively and in a timely manner with the new challenges of development in the context of global financial integration,

Stressing that the process of reform for a strengthened and stable international financial architecture should be based on broad participation in a genuine multilateral approach, involving all members of the international community, to ensure that the diverse needs and interests of all countries are adequately represented,

Reaffirming that the United Nations, in fulfilling its role in the promotion of development, in particular of developing countries, plays an important part in the international efforts to build up the necessary international consensus for the reforms needed for a strengthened and stable international financial system, taking into account the mandate of all relevant international institutions, especially the international financial institutions,

Noting that the high-level international intergovernmental event on financing for development will provide a unique opportunity to consider, in an integrated manner, all sources of financing for development, and mindful that in the United Nations Millennium Declaration the heads of State and Government decided to make every effort to ensure its success,

1. *Takes note with appreciation* of the report of the Secretary-General entitled "Towards a stable international financial system, responsive to the challenges of development, especially in the developing countries", the addendum thereto on regional perspectives and developments provided by the regional commissions and the addendum thereto provided by the United Nations Conference on Trade and Development on the work it has undertaken on the involvement of the private sector in the prevention and resolution of financial crises;

2. *Underlines* the utmost importance of implementing the resolve expressed in the United Nations Millennium Declaration to create an environment, at the national and global levels alike, that is conducive to development and to the elimination of poverty, inter alia, through good governance within each country, as well as good governance at the international level and transparency in the financial, monetary and trading systems;

3. *Also underlines* the utmost importance of implementing the commitment in the United Nations Millennium Declaration to an open, equitable, rule-based, predictable and non-discriminatory multilateral trading and financial system;

4. *Stresses* the special importance of creating an enabling international economic environment through strong cooperative efforts by all countries and institutions to promote equitable economic development in a world economy that benefits all people, and, in this context, invites developed countries, in particular major industrialized countries, which have significant weight in influencing world economic growth, when formulating their macroeconomic policies, to take into account their effects in terms of the external economic environment favourable to growth and development, in particular of developing countries;

5. *Also stresses* the special importance of creating an enabling domestic environment through, inter alia, the rule of law, capacity-building, including institutional capacity-building, and the implementation of appropriate economic and social policies, so that domestic and international resources may be effectively mobilized and used for development;

6. *Reiterates* the urgent need to accelerate the growth and development prospects of the least developed countries, which remain the poorest and most vulnerable of the international community, and calls upon development partners, in particular industrialized countries, to facilitate the financing of their development, inter alia, through public and private financial flows, increased official development assistance, strengthened debt relief, the adoption of a policy of duty- and quota-free access for essentially all of their exports and enhanced balance-of-payments support, and in this context welcomes the holding at Brussels in May 2001 of the Third United Nations Conference on the Least Developed Countries;

7. *Recognizes* the stability of the international financial system as an important global public good and a necessary condition for positive financial flows for development, and, in this context, calls upon all countries, including major industrialized countries, whose policies have significant impact on most economies, to adopt and to pursue policies that promote international financial stability and facilitate financial flows for development, and requests the Secretary-General, in collaboration with the United Nations Development Programme, to provide information to the General Assembly at its fifty-sixth session on the analysis it has undertaken of international financial stability as a global public good;

8. *Emphasizes,* in this regard, the need to continue national, regional and international efforts to promote international financial stability and, to this end, to improve surveillance, early warning, prevention and response capabilities for dealing with the emergence and spread of financial crises in a timely manner, taking a comprehensive and long-term perspective while remaining responsive to the challenges of development and the protection of the most vulnerable countries and social groups;

9. *Stresses* the importance of strong domestic institutions to promote financial stability for the achievement of growth and development, inter alia, through sound macroeconomic policies and policies aimed at strengthening the regulatory systems of the financial and banking sectors, including considering arrangements in destination and source countries to reduce the risks of excessive international financial volatility and measures to ensure orderly, gradual and well-sequenced capital-account liberalization processes, and invites in this connection all relevant international institutions to continue to provide, upon the request of concerned countries, policy advice and technical assistance so as to strengthen their capacity in the above-mentioned areas;

10. *Emphasizes* the importance of deepening the convergence of the efforts of all international institutions able to contribute to the strengthening of an international financial architecture responsive to the priorities of growth and development, especially in developing countries, and to the promotion of economic and social equity;

11. *Reiterates* the need for broadening and strengthening the participation of developing countries in the international economic decision-making process;

12. *Emphasizes* the importance of the improved participation of developing countries in the work of the international institutions dealing with the reform of the international financial architecture, in particular the International Monetary Fund, as well as in relevant norm-setting processes;

13. *Expresses the need* for multilateral surveillance by the International Monetary Fund and regional and subregional institutions of all countries in a symmetrical manner;

14. *Emphasizes* that the international financial institutions, in providing policy advice and supporting adjustment programmes, should ensure that they are sensitive to the specific circumstances and implementing capacities of concerned countries and to the special

needs of developing countries and should work towards the best possible outcomes in terms of growth and development, inter alia, through gender-sensitive employment and poverty eradication policies and strategies, and stresses the importance of national ownership of programmes supported by the International Monetary Fund for their sustained implementation;

15. *Encourages* the continuing efforts undertaken by the Bretton Woods institutions, the regional development banks and the International Labour Organization to help Governments to address the social consequences of crisis, and welcomes, in this regard, the commitments made by the General Assembly at its twenty-fourth special session on the implementation of the outcome of the World Summit for Social Development, to ensure that, when structural adjustment programmes are agreed to, they include social development goals, in particular those of eradicating poverty, promoting full and productive employment and enhancing social integration;

16. *Emphasizes* that the international financial institutions should, when invited by national Governments, provide assistance and advice, as appropriate, to the countries in their efforts to promote development and reduce poverty through national programmes, including, where relevant, nationally owned and developed poverty reduction strategy papers that integrate macroeconomic, structural and social policies;

17. *Underlines* the continuing importance of providing the international institutions, in particular the International Monetary Fund, with adequate resources to provide emergency financing in a timely and accessible manner to countries affected by financial crises, and notes the regional and subregional efforts to facilitate emergency financing in time of crisis;

18. *Welcomes* the progress made in developing early warning capacities to address in a timely manner the threat of financial crisis, and in this regard encourages the International Monetary Fund and other relevant international and regional institutions to continue their efforts to contribute to this process;

19. *Calls upon* the international community, in particular the World Bank and the regional development banks, and other relevant international and regional institutions, including the regional commissions, working with the private sector, to support the promotion of long-term private financial flows, especially foreign direct investments, inter alia, through enhanced technical cooperation, to all developing countries as well as economies in transition, in particular the least developed countries and other developing countries with special difficulties in attracting private financial flows, including those in Africa, as well as the small island developing countries, and, in this context, requests the United Nations Conference on Trade and Development to provide information to the General Assembly at its fifty-sixth session on the work it has undertaken on this matter;

20. *Reiterates its invitation* to the International Monetary Fund to facilitate the dialogue among relevant actors to consider the possibility of establishing regulatory frameworks for short-term capital flows and trade in currencies;

21. *Emphasizes* that it is important for sovereign risk assessments made by private sector agencies to be based on objective and transparent parameters;

22. *Reaffirms* the need to consider appropriate frameworks for the involvement of the private sector in the prevention and resolution of financial crises, including the need to implement and further refine the framework laid down by the International Monetary and Financial Committee at its meeting held on 16 April 2000, and underlines the importance of an equitable distribution of the cost of adjustments between the public and private sectors and among debtors, creditors and investors, concerning, inter alia, highly leveraged operations, as well as the consideration, in exceptional cases, of debt standstill arrangements;

23. *Emphasizes* the important supportive role that stronger regional and subregional financial institutions and arrangements can play in the reform of the international financial system and the enhancement of financing for development;

24. *Encourages* the deepening of the dialogue between the Economic and Social Council and the Bretton Woods institutions, and in this regard recommends that at their next high-level meeting they consider the modalities needed to consolidate further a broader global agenda for a strengthened and stable international financial system that is responsive to the priorities of growth and development, in particular of developing countries, and to the promotion of economic and social equity in the global economy;

25. *Requests* the Secretary-General to make the present resolution available to the Preparatory Committee for the High-level International Intergovernmental Event on Financing for Development, at its second substantive session, as an input for its work on the systemic issues contained in its preliminary substantive agenda;

26. *Also requests* the Secretary-General, in close cooperation with all relevant entities of the United Nations, including the United Nations Conference on Trade and Development and the regional commissions, within their respective mandates, and in consultation with the Bretton Woods institutions, and taking into account the progress made at the high-level international intergovernmental event on financing for development, to report to the General Assembly at its fifty-sixth session on the implementation of the present resolution under a sub-item entitled "International financial system and development", with an analysis of the current trend in global financial flows, including net transfer of resources between developed and developing countries, and recommendations to consolidate further a broader global agenda for a strengthened and stable international financial system that is responsive to the priorities of growth and development, in particular of developing countries, and to the promotion of economic and social equity in the global economy;

27. *Requests* the President of the General Assembly to present this resolution to the Board of Executive Directors of the World Bank and the Executive Board of the International Monetary Fund, before their joint annual spring meeting, in order to bring it to their attention as an input to their discussions on the matters addressed herein.

Debt problems of developing countries

In response to General Assembly resolution 54/202 [YUN 1999, p. 896], the Secretary-General submitted a September report on recent developments in the debt situation of developing countries [A/55/422]. He stated that an analysis of key debt indicators showed that external debt and debt-servicing problems were most severe and persistent in HIPCs, the target group of the HIPC Initiative. However, debt restructuring problems lingered in a number of other developing countries and countries in transition and they remained exposed to adverse developments in commodity prices, interest rates, exchange rates and private capital flows. Moreover, the debt-servicing capacity of some countries continued to be affected by war and natural disasters.

Discussing international debt problems and strategies, the Secretary-General stated that the total outstanding debt of developing countries and countries in transition showed little change in 1999. Their total debt at the end of the year was estimated at $2,554 billion, a slight increase over the end-1998 level. Long-term debt increased by $40 billion, while short-term debt fell slightly and represented 16 per cent of the total. The debt-service ratio remained broadly unchanged at about 18-19 per cent. The ratio of total outstanding debt to exports fell to 137 per cent; and that of debt to gross national product (GNP) decreased to below 42 per cent. Short-term debt corresponded to 53 per cent of the stock of foreign exchange reserves as compared with 59 per cent at the end of 1998. The distribution of debt among different regions remained the same as in 1998: East and South Asia, 33 per cent; Latin America, 31 per cent; Europe and Central Asia, 19 per cent; sub-Saharan Africa, 9 per cent; and the Middle East and North Africa, 8 per cent. Latin America had the highest ratio of debt service to exports, at about 35 per cent, while the highest debt-to-exports ratio, 225 per cent, was recorded by sub-Saharan Africa.

The report noted that by the end of 1999, little assistance had been delivered under the HIPC Initiative, which suffered from problems of underfunding, excessive conditionality, restrictions over eligibility, inadequate debt relief and cumbersome procedures. The HIPCs' total outstanding external debt increased by some $4.5 billion in 1999 to a level of $219 billion, and the ratio of debt to exports amounted to 389 per cent, more than twice that for developing countries as a whole and considerably above that of sub-Saharan Africa (including the region's HIPCs). There were 41 countries on the list of HIPCs—33 were in sub-Saharan Africa and 30 were classified as LDCs. Following the G-7 Cologne summit in June 1999 [YUN 1999, p. 896], deeper and broader relief was expected to be achieved through a lowering of debt sustainability targets, resulting in

an increased number of countries becoming eligible for HIPC assistance. A main innovation under the enhanced HIPC framework was the explicit link to poverty reduction. Up to the end of July 2000, nine countries had reached their decision points under the enhanced scheme: Bolivia, Mauritania and Uganda were declared eligible for additional relief in February, Mozambique and the United Republic of Tanzania followed in April, Senegal in June and Benin, Burkina Faso and Honduras in July. Also, in May, Sao Tome and Principe negotiated its first Paris Club (a group of creditor countries) agreement, a flow rescheduling in support of the country's new Poverty Reduction and Growth Facility arrangement with IMF. An important development in late 1999 and early 2000 was the commitment by an increasing number of creditor countries to grant even deeper debt relief. In April, G-7 finance ministers and central bank governors committed themselves to increasing debt reduction to 100 per cent of non-ODA claims treated within the Paris Club framework, a commitment reaffirmed by G-7 leaders at their Okinawa (Japan) summit in July. However, the G-8 meeting (Okinawa, 21-23 July) [A/55/257-S/2000/766] did not advance any major new debt initiative similar to the 1999 Cologne initiative [YUN 1999, p. 896]. The leaders did agree to push forward the HIPC Initiative to ensure that as many countries as possible reached their decision points. As of July, only a small number of countries were well advanced in the HIPC process, while others had not met the requirements for entering the process. The countries concerned were almost all LDCs suffering from civil conflict or severe governance problems, and were among the most indebted HIPCs.

As to non-HIPC debtors, the report noted that 18 LDCs were not included in the HIPC category and that some of them were considered severely or moderately indebted according to the World Bank classification. A number of special measures were devised for LDCs, such as the reliance mainly on grants in the provision of financing to them, and most donor countries also extended ODA debt cancellation to LDCs. However, their external debt burden had continued to grow over time.

The report also analysed conditions in markets for commercial debt; debt restructuring agreements; financial crises and debt in emerging markets; and issues in commercial debt workouts.

The Secretary-General concluded that, in order to remove the debt overhang of the world's poorest nations, an independent panel of experts not influenced by creditor interests should be established to assess debt sustainability, eligibility for debt reduction, the amount of debt reduction needed, conditionality and financing for HIPC and other debt-distressed low- and middle-income countries. There should also be a commitment on the part of creditors to implement any recommendation of that panel regarding the writing-off of unpayable debt. Moreover, HIPCs and other countries covered by the panel's recommendations should benefit from new aid resources in grant form or on highly concessional terms in order to avoid the renewed build-up of an unsustainable debt burden. There should also be an immediate suspension of the debt-service payments of all HIPCs, and that suspension should also be extended to non-HIPC countries declared eligible for debt relief by the proposed panel. Reform of the international strategy regarding the official debt of poor countries should also address the problems of debt-distressed low-income countries not eligible for the special treatment accorded to HIPCs. Further, it was necessary to recognize that countries seriously affected by war and natural disasters and facing problems of reconstruction and recovery required debt relief and urgent assistance regardless of their longer-term prospects and debt profiles. For commercial debt, establishing orderly and equitable work-out procedures with explicit responsibilities of creditors and debtors and well-defined roles for public and private sectors remained the most important step. Given the volatility of private capital flows and the increased frequency of liquidity problems in emerging markets, provision of international liquidity, as well as temporary standstills, should constitute an essential component of an effective international financial architecture.

GENERAL ASSEMBLY ACTION

On 20 December [meeting 87], the General Assembly, on the recommendation of the Second Committee [A/55/579/Add.3], adopted **resolution 55/184** without vote [agenda item 92 *(c)*].

Enhancing international cooperation towards a durable solution to the external debt problem of developing countries

The General Assembly,

Recalling its resolutions 51/164 of 16 December 1996, 52/185 of 18 December 1997, 53/175 of 15 December 1998 and 54/202 of 22 December 1999 on enhancing international cooperation towards a durable solution to the external debt problems of developing countries,

Taking note of the report of the Secretary-General on recent developments in the debt situation of developing countries,

Recalling the United Nations Millennium Declaration adopted by the heads of State and Government on 8 September 2000,

Noting with concern the continuing debt and debt-servicing problems of heavily indebted developing countries as constituting an element that adversely affects their development efforts and economic growth, and stressing the importance of alleviating once and for all, where applicable, their onerous debt and debt-service burden with the aim of attaining a sustainable level of debt and debt service,

Noting with great concern the continuing high debt burden borne by most African countries and the least developed countries, as exacerbated, inter alia, by the declining trend in commodity prices, and noting that the financial crisis has aggravated the debt-service burdens of many developing countries, including low- and middle-income countries, in particular in the context of meeting their international debt and debt-servicing obligations in a timely fashion despite serious external and domestic financial constraints,

Reaffirming the need to consider further measures, as appropriate, for dealing with the external debt and debt-servicing problems of developing countries in an effective, equitable and development-oriented manner, in order to help them to exit from the rescheduling process and unsustainable debt burdens, and welcoming the efforts already made in this regard,

Welcoming and emphasizing the importance of the efforts of debtor countries to pursue, despite the great social cost often involved, economic reforms and structural adjustment programmes that are aimed at achieving stability, raising domestic savings and investment, attaining competitiveness to take advantage of market access opportunities where available, reducing inflation, improving economic efficiency and addressing the social aspects of development, including the eradication of poverty and the development of social safety nets for the vulnerable and poorer strata of their populations, and encouraging them to continue in these efforts,

Recognizing that close attention should be paid to the impact of economic reforms on the poor and, in this context, that the country-owned poverty reduction strategy papers linked to the Heavily Indebted Poor Countries Initiative should contribute to poverty reduction,

Stressing the need for continuing global economic growth, equitable distribution of the opportunities and benefits of globalization and a continuing supportive international economic environment with regard to, inter alia, terms of trade, commodity prices, improved market access, trade practices, access to technology, exchange rates and international interest rates, and noting the continued need for resources for sustained economic growth and sustainable development of the developing countries, in accordance with the relevant General Assembly resolutions and the results of recent United Nations conferences,

Noting that mechanisms such as debt rescheduling and debt conversions alone are not sufficient to resolve all of the problems relating to long-term debt sustainability, and, in this connection, stressing the continuing need for sound macroeconomic policies as well as the need for full, swift and effective implementation of initiatives that will further assist developing countries, in particular the poorest and most heavily indebted countries, especially in Africa, in their efforts to improve their debt situation, in view of their continued very high levels of total debt stock and debt-service burdens,

Welcoming the enhanced Heavily Indebted Poor Countries Initiative, launched by the Group of Seven major industrialized countries at their meeting held at Cologne, Germany, from 18 to 20 June 1999, and the decisions on the enhanced initiative taken by the International Monetary Fund and the World Bank in October 1999 that are designed to provide deeper, broader and faster relief,

Welcoming also the actions taken by creditor countries within the framework of the Paris Club and by some creditor countries through the cancellation of bilateral debts, and urging all creditor countries to participate in efforts to remedy the external debt and debt-servicing problems of developing countries,

Welcoming further the adoption by the Executive Boards of the International Monetary Fund and the World Bank of a number of measures to speed up the implementation of the enhanced Heavily Indebted Poor Countries Initiative, including greater flexibility on track record with a focus on policy implementation, as well as the emphasis that the decision point may be reached and that debt relief may be provided before the finalization of full poverty reduction strategy papers, as long as interim poverty reduction strategy papers are agreed, and noting with appreciation their approval of proposals to streamline preliminary heavily indebted poor countries documents,

Recognizing that the full implementation of the enhanced Heavily Indebted Poor Countries Initiative will require substantial financial resources, and, in this regard, stressing the need for fair, equitable and transparent burden-sharing among the international public creditor community and other donor countries, and also stressing the need to fund adequately the Heavily Indebted Poor Countries Trust Fund and the Poverty Reduction and Growth Facility/Heavily Indebted Poor Countries Trust Fund, and, in this regard, welcoming the contributions and pledges made by donors to the trust funds,

Noting with concern that some highly indebted middle-income developing countries are facing serious difficulties in meeting their external debt-servicing obligations owing, inter alia, to liquidity constraints,

Stressing that the effective management of the debt of developing countries, including middle-income countries, is an important factor, among others, in their sustained economic growth and in the smooth functioning of the world economy,

Stressing also the importance of a sound enabling environment for effective debt management,

1. *Recognizes* that effective, equitable, development-oriented and durable solutions to the external debt and debt-service burdens of developing countries can contribute substantially to the strengthening of the global economy and to the efforts of developing countries to achieve sustained economic growth and sustainable development, in accordance with the relevant General Assembly resolutions and the results of recent global conferences;

2. *Reaffirms* the need, as expressed in the United Nations Millennium Declaration, for the international community to deal comprehensively and effectively with the debt problems of low- and middle-income developing countries, through various national and inter-

national measures designed to make their debt sustainable in the long term;

3. *Calls* for the full, speedy and effective implementation of the enhanced Heavily Indebted Poor Countries Initiative, and, in this regard, stresses the need for the donor community to provide the additional resources necessary to fulfil the future financial requirements of the Initiative, hence welcomes the agreement that financing for heavily indebted poor countries should be reviewed analytically and separately from International Development Association replenishment requirements but back to back with meetings for the thirteenth replenishment of the Association, and calls upon all donors to participate fully in this process;

4. *Calls upon* the heavily indebted poor countries to take, as soon as possible, the policy measures necessary to become eligible for the enhanced Heavily Indebted Poor Countries Initiative and to reach the decision point;

5. *Reiterates its call* upon industrialized countries, as expressed in the United Nations Millennium Declaration in the context of addressing the special needs of the least developed countries, to agree to cancel all bilateral official debts of the heavily indebted poor countries in return for their making demonstrable commitments to poverty reduction;

6. *Stresses* the importance of continuing to implement the enhanced Heavily Indebted Poor Countries Initiative flexibly, noting the provision of significant interim debt relief between the decision and completion points and taking due account of the policy performance of the countries concerned in a transparent manner and with the full involvement of the debtor countries, including for the setting of the floating completion point, and in this regard stresses the importance of country-owned poverty reduction strategy papers;

7. *Also stresses* the importance of continued flexibility with regard to the eligibility criteria for the enhanced Heavily Indebted Poor Countries Initiative, in particular for countries in post-conflict situations;

8. *Notes* that it is important for the International Monetary Fund and the World Bank to continue their efforts to strengthen the transparency and integrity of debt sustainability analysis, and also notes the importance of cooperation with debtor countries in order to obtain relevant information;

9. *Welcomes* the framework for strengthening the link between debt relief and poverty eradication, and stresses the need for its continued flexible implementation, recognizing that, while the poverty reduction strategy papers should be in place by the decision point, on a transitional basis the decision point could be reached with agreement on an interim poverty reduction strategy paper, but that in all cases demonstrable progress in implementing a poverty reduction strategy would be required by the completion point;

10. *Emphasizes* that poverty reduction programmes as linked to the implementation of the enhanced Heavily Indebted Poor Countries Initiative must be country-driven and in accordance with the priorities and programmes of countries eligible under the Initiative, and stresses the importance of a participatory process that involves civil society in this regard;

11. *Welcomes* the decision of those countries that have cancelled bilateral official debt, and urges credi-

tor countries that have not done so to consider the full cancellation and equivalent relief of the bilateral official debts of countries eligible under the Heavily Indebted Poor Countries Initiative and, as appropriate, action to address the needs of post-conflict countries, in particular those with protracted arrears, developing countries affected by serious natural disasters and poor countries with very low social and human development indicators, including the possibility of debt-relief measures, and stresses the importance of building coalitions with civil society organizations and non-governmental organizations in all countries to ensure in the shortest possible time the implementation of pronouncements of debt forgiveness;

12. *Notes* that the multilateral debt-relief funds can have a positive impact in assisting Governments in safeguarding or increasing expenditures on priority social sectors, and encourages donors and other countries in a position to do so to continue their efforts in this regard in the context of the enhanced Heavily Indebted Poor Countries Initiative;

13. *Emphasizes* the need to secure adequate funding for an overall financing plan for the enhanced Heavily Indebted Poor Countries Initiative, including in particular the Heavily Indebted Poor Countries Trust Fund and the Poverty Reduction and Growth Facility/Heavily Indebted Poor Countries Trust Fund in the context of fair, equitable and transparent burden-sharing;

14. *Stresses* the principle that funding of any debt relief should not affect adversely the support for other development activities in favour of developing countries, including the level of funding for United Nations funds and programmes; welcomes, in this regard, the decision of the Joint Ministerial Committee of the Boards of Governors of the World Bank and the International Monetary Fund on the Transfer of Real Resources to Developing Countries that financing of debt relief should not compromise the financing made available through concessional windows such as the International Development Association; and expresses its appreciation to those developed countries that have reached, gone beyond or recently made commitments towards reaching the agreed target for official development assistance of 0.7 per cent of their gross national product, and at the same time calls upon other developed countries to meet the target for official development assistance as soon as possible;

15. *Expresses its appreciation* for the action taken by creditor countries of the Paris Club with regard to the debts of developing countries that are affected by natural disasters, and, in this regard, reiterates the need for relief promises to be fulfilled within the shortest possible time frame in order to free the requisite resources for national reconstruction efforts;

16. *Encourages* the international creditor community to consider appropriate measures for countries with a very high level of debt overhang, including, in particular, the poorest African countries, in order to make an appropriate and consistent contribution to the common objective of debt sustainability;

17. *Recognizes* the difficulties of highly indebted middle-income developing countries and other highly indebted middle-income countries in meeting their external debt and debt-servicing obligations, and notes the serious situation in some of them in the context, in-

ter alia, of significant liquidity constraints, which may require debt treatment, including, as appropriate, debt-reduction measures;

18. *Calls* for concerted national and international action to address effectively the debt problems of middle-income developing countries with a view to resolving their potential long-term debt-sustainability problems through various debt-treatment measures, including, as appropriate, existing orderly mechanisms for debt reduction, and encourages all creditors, both public and private, and debtor countries to utilize to the fullest extent possible, where appropriate, the mechanisms for debt reduction;

19. *Recognizes* the need for countries, even when experiencing a debt problem, to continue to work with creditors in order to facilitate continued access to international capital markets, and, in the event that extraordinary circumstances preclude a country from temporarily meeting its debt-servicing commitments, urges creditors and Governments to work together in a transparent and timely fashion towards an orderly and equitable resolution of the repayment problem, including consideration of temporary debt standstill arrangements in exceptional cases;

20. *Notes* the importance of an orderly, gradual and well-sequenced liberalization of capital accounts to strengthen the ability of countries to sustain its consequences so as to mitigate the adverse impact of the volatility of short-term capital flows;

21. *Stresses* that debt relief should contribute to development objectives, including poverty reduction, and in this regard urges countries to direct those resources freed through debt relief, in particular through debt cancellation and reduction, towards these objectives;

22. *Notes* that debt relief alone will not lead to poverty reduction and economic growth, and, in this regard, emphasizes the need for an enabling environment, including sound economic management as well as an efficient, transparent and accountable public service and administration, and stresses the need to mobilize financial resources from all sources, in addition to debt-relief measures and continued concessional financial assistance, in particular to the least developed countries, in order to support their efforts for achieving economic growth and sustainable development;

23. *Underlines* the absolute importance of implementing the resolve expressed in the United Nations Millennium Declaration to create an environment, at the national and global levels alike, that is conducive to development and to the elimination of poverty, inter alia, through good governance within each country as well as good governance at the international level and transparency in the financial, monetary and trading systems;

24. *Stresses* the need to strengthen the institutional capacity of developing countries in debt management, calls upon the international community to support the efforts made towards this end, and, in this regard, stresses the importance of initiatives such as the Debt Management and Financial Analysis System and the debt-management capacity-building programme;

25. *Notes* the importance of providing adequate resources for debt-relief measures in the light of the difficulties that many developing countries, especially

those in Africa and the least developed countries, are facing with respect to mobilizing both domestic and external resources for their development, and, in accordance with the United Nations Millennium Declaration, calls for special measures to address the challenges of poverty eradication and sustainable development in Africa, including debt cancellation;

26. *Stresses* the importance for developing countries to continue their efforts to promote a favourable environment for attracting foreign investment, thereby promoting economic growth and sustainable development, so as to favour their exit from debt and debt-servicing problems, and also stresses the need for the international community to promote a conducive external environment through, inter alia, improved market access, efforts aimed at the stabilization of exchange rates and the effective stewardship of interest rates, increased resource flows, access to international financial markets, flow of financial resources and improved access to technology for developing countries;

27. *Calls upon* the international community, including the United Nations system, and invites the Bretton Woods institutions, as well as the private sector, to take appropriate measures and actions for the implementation of the commitments, agreements and decisions of the major United Nations conferences and summits on development organized since the beginning of the 1990s, as well as of the results of review processes, in particular those related to the question of the external debt problem of developing countries;

28. *Requests* the Secretary-General to report to the General Assembly at its fifty-sixth session on the implementation of the present resolution and to include in that report a comprehensive and substantive analysis of the external debt and debt-servicing problems of developing countries, including, inter alia, those resulting from global financial instability.

Financing for development

High-level intergovernmental event (2002)

Throughout 2000, meetings took place in preparation for the high-level intergovernmental event on financing for development. In December, the General Assembly decided that the event, originally planned for 2001, should be held in the first quarter of 2002 (**resolution 55/213**).

At its organizational session (see p. 916), the Preparatory Committee for the High-level International Intergovernmental Event on Financing for Development, in accordance with Assembly resolution 54/196 [YUN 1999, p. 900], undertook consultations with a number of stakeholders on the modalities of their participation in the preparations for the event and in the event itself. However, not all aspects of the consultation process could be covered within the time frame specified. In June, the Assembly considered the report of the Bureau of the Preparatory Committee on those modalities [A/AC.257/6].

On 15 June [meeting 98], the General Assembly adopted **resolution 54/279** without vote [agenda item 97 (a)]. The draft [A/54/L.82] was recommended by the Preparatory Committee for the High-level International Intergovernmental Event on Financing for Development [A/55/28].

Preparations for the substantive preparatory process and the high-level international intergovernmental event on financing for development

The General Assembly

1. *Welcomes* the report of the Bureau of the Preparatory Committee for the high-level international intergovernmental event on financing for development on modalities of the participation of all relevant stakeholders in the substantive preparatory process and the high-level intergovernmental event on financing for development;

2. *Approves:*

(a) The proposals contained in paragraph 7 of the report regarding modalities of the participation of the World Bank, and requests the Bureau to seek clarification on paragraph 7 (c) thereof, taking into account the views expressed in the Preparatory Committee;

(b) The recommendations regarding the participation of the Bretton Woods institutions and the World Trade Organization in the work of the Preparatory Committee, as contained in paragraph 10 of the report;

(c) The recommendations regarding the participation of intergovernmental organizations, the specialized agencies, the funds and programmes of the United Nations and other relevant official or quasi-official organizations, as contained in paragraph 13 of the report;

(d) Paragraph 11 of the report regarding the holding of regional consultative meetings during the second half of 2000 on substantive matters before the Preparatory Committee;

(e) The recommendations regarding the participation of non-governmental organizations and the business sector, as contained in paragraphs 14 to 19 of the report, and requests the Bureau to submit to the Preparatory Committee for its approval the applications for accreditation of those non-governmental organizations which do not already have consultative status with the Economic and Social Council;

3. *Requests* the Bureau, in connection with the modalities proposed by the World Bank, to convey to the Bank the desire of the Preparatory Committee that the Bank participate actively in the Preparatory Committee, to reinforce the impact of the cooperation envisaged under the proposed modalities;

4. *Also requests* the Bureau to continue consultations intensively with the institutional stakeholders indicated in paragraph 11 (e)(i) of General Assembly resolution 54/196 of 22 December 1999 on modalities of their participation and to report to the Preparatory Committee as soon as possible with proposals and recommendations thereon, as well as possible proposals and recommendations for additional modalities of the participation of the private sector;

5. *Further requests* the Bureau to make proposals and recommendations to the Preparatory Committee at its resumed organizational session on subparagraphs (a), (b), (c) and (g) of paragraph 11 of resolution 54/196,

taking into account discussions in the Preparatory Committee;

6. *Requests* the Bureau to make arrangements for open-ended informal consultations on subparagraph (*d*) of paragraph 11 of resolution 54/196 before the convening of the first substantive session, taking into account paragraph 3 of the resolution and the elements indicated in the report of the Ad Hoc Open-ended Working Group of the General Assembly on Financing for Development;

7. *Requests* the Secretary-General to assist in the implementation of the recommendations contained in the report of the Bureau, as approved by the Preparatory Committee and in the present resolution, and to continue to provide all needed support to the Preparatory Committee and to the Bureau, including arrangements to facilitate the travel of Bureau members to take part in consultations with the major institutional stakeholders;

8. *Reiterates its decision* that the first substantive session of the Preparatory Committee should be held beginning on 15 May 2000, at United Nations Headquarters;

9. *Decides* that the Preparatory Committee should hold its second substantive session, of two weeks' duration, in the first quarter of 2001 and its third substantive session, of two weeks' duration, in the second quarter of 2001, at Headquarters;

10. *Also decides* that the Preparatory Committee should suspend its resumed organizational session and reconvene it at the earliest possible date in order to complete its work.

Preparatory Committee. In accordance with General Assembly resolution 54/196 [YUN 1999, p. 900], the Preparatory Committee for the High-level International Intergovernmental Event on Financing for Development held its organizational and resumed organizational sessions in New York on 10 and 25 February, 27, 28 and 31 March and 30 May [A/55/28]. It had before it a number of documents dealing with the modalities of the participation of all relevant stakeholders in both the substantive preparatory process and the high-level intergovernmental event on financing for development [A/AC.257/1, A/AC.257/6] and with procedural matters [A/AC.257/4, A/AC.257/5, A/AC.257/8, A/AC.257/9].

In addition to recommending to the General Assembly the adoption of a draft resolution on the preparations for the substantive preparatory process and the high-level international intergovernmental event on financing for development, the Preparatory Committee adopted a decision by which it referred all outstanding issues to its first substantive session.

The Preparatory Committee held its first session in New York on 31 May and 2 June and resumed on 30 October and 16, 20 and 27 November [A/55/28]. The Committee had before it the list of NGOs recommended by its Bureau for accreditation [A/AC.257/10 & Add.1]. It recommended

to the General Assembly for adoption a draft resolution on further preparations for the substantive preparatory process and the high-level international intergovernmental event on financing for development. It brought to the Assembly's attention a decision on the same subject [dec.1/1], by which it adopted the preliminary agenda for the financing-for-development process, covering: mobilizing domestic financial resources for development; mobilizing international resources for development: FDI and other private flows; trade; increasing international financial cooperation for development through, inter alia, ODA; debt; and addressing systemic issues: enhancing the coherence and consistency of the international monetary, financial and trading systems in support of development. The Preparatory Committee also adopted decisions on accreditation of NGOs [dec. 1/2]; accreditation of additional NGOs [dec. 1/3]; and extension of the accreditation of NGOs [dec. 1/4].

Other preparatory meetings. In preparation for the high-level international intergovernmental event, five regional consultative meetings on financing for development took place: Asia and the Pacific (Jakarta, Indonesia, 2-5 August) [A/AC.257/13]; Latin America and the Caribbean (Bogotá, Colombia, 9-10 November) [A/AC.257/17]; Africa (Addis Ababa, Ethiopia, 15-17 November) [A/AC.257/14]; Western Asia (Beirut, Lebanon, 23-24 November) [A/AC.257/16]; and Europe (Geneva, 6-7 December) [A/AC.257/15].

In accordance with resolution 54/279 (see above), the Preparatory Committee held two sets of hearings, one with civil society organizations (New York, 6-7 November) [A/AC.257/18] and the other with the business community (New York, 11-12 December) [A/AC.257/19].

Report of Secretary-General. On 24 August, the Secretary-General submitted a report on high-level international intergovernmental consideration of financing for development [A/55/315]. The report, which complemented the report of the Preparatory Committee [A/55/28], focused on secretariat activities, specifically the status of secretariat cooperation with relevant stakeholders; preparation of the regional consultations; preparations for the hearings with civil society and the business community; and arrangements for secretariat support for the preparatory process, including the establishment of an extrabudgetary trust fund.

GENERAL ASSEMBLY ACTION

On 20 December [meeting 87], the General Assembly, on the recommendation of the Second Committee [A/55/588], adopted **resolution 55/213** without vote [agenda item 101].

**Preparations for the substantive preparatory process
and the high-level international intergovernmental event**

The General Assembly,

Taking note with appreciation of the report of the Preparatory Committee for the High-level International Intergovernmental Event on Financing for Development on its organizational and first sessions,

Welcoming the continuing progress made in the consultations with the major institutional stakeholders with regard to their involvement in the process of financing for development,

Encouraging Governments and all other relevant stakeholders to consider taking concrete initiatives in support of the financing for development preparatory process and the high-level international intergovernmental event, within the framework of its substantive agenda,

Welcoming the regional consultative meetings being held to provide the regional input to the financing for development process, and encouraging the deepening of regional efforts in support of the financing for development preparatory process and the high-level international intergovernmental event, within the framework of its substantive agenda,

Also welcoming the hearings held with civil society to support the financing for development process, looking forward to the contribution of the forthcoming hearings with the private sector, and encouraging the deepening of those efforts in support of the financing for development preparatory process and the high-level international intergovernmental event, within the framework of its substantive agenda,

Expressing its appreciation to Governments for the support they have provided to the trust fund for extra-budgetary contributions for the financing for development process,

1. *Decides* that the high-level international intergovernmental event should be scheduled for the first quarter of 2002, at a date to be agreed upon, and extends its invitation to interested countries to consider hosting or confirming existing offers to host the high-level international intergovernmental event;

2. *Also decides* that the Preparatory Committee should hold a final session from 14 to 25 January 2002, on the understanding that the second session will be held from 12 to 23 February 2001 and the third session from 30 April to 11 May 2001;

3. *Requests* the Secretary-General to address a letter to all Governments further sensitizing them to the high profile and high level of participation that the substantive preparatory process and the high-level international intergovernmental event on financing for development deserve.

On the same day, by **decision 55/446**, the Assembly took note of the Secretary-General's report on the high-level international intergovernmental consideration of financing for development.

Resource requirements

In March [A/54/7/Add.13] and again in May [A/54/7/Add.14], the Advisory Committee on Administrative and Budgetary Questions (ACABQ)

considered two notes of the Secretary-General [A/C.5/54/50 & A/C.5/54/58] regarding the review of the resource requirements for the high-level international intergovernmental event on financing for development and the Third United Nations Conference on LDCs (LDC-III) (see p. 808).

On 7 April, by **resolution 54/258 A**, the General Assembly requested the Secretary-General to explore ways of providing the resource requirements for the two meetings and to report to the Assembly at the second part of its resumed fifty-fourth session. On 15 June, the Assembly welcomed the establishment of a Trust Fund for the Preparatory Committee for the High-level International Intergovernmental Event on Financing for Development (**resolution 54/258 B**).

Investment, technology and related financial issues

The Commission on Investment, Technology and Related Financial Issues did not meet in 2000. Its fourth session took place in 1999 [YUN 1999, p. 902].

Subsidiary bodies. In accordance with the UNCTAD X Plan of Action [TD/386], two expert meetings took place in 2000. The Expert Meeting on Home Country Measures (Geneva, 8-10 November) [TD/B/COM.2/27] discussed national experiences and best practices in six broad categories of major types of existing home country measures used by both developed and developing countries to promote outward FDI, including transfer of technology. It had before it an UNCTAD secretariat note on the subject [TD/B/COM.2/EM.8/2]. Experts noted that home countries, including the private sector, should encourage FDI flows, particularly to and between developing countries, and especially to LDCs.

The Expert Meeting on Mergers and Acquisitions: Policies Aimed at Maximizing the Positive and Minimizing the Possible Negative Impact of International Investment (Geneva, 19-21 June) [TD/B/COM.2/26] discussed trends, motivations and performance of mergers and acquisitions and their impact on host-country development policy considerations and identified issues for further research. It had before it an UNCTAD secretariat note on the subject [TD/B/COM.2/EM.7/2 & Corr.1].

International standards of accounting and reporting

The Intergovernmental Working Group of Experts on International Standards of Accounting and Reporting (ISAR) held its seventeenth session in Geneva from 3 to 5 July [TD/B/COM.2/25]. It had before it an UNCTAD report on accounting by SMEs [TD/B/COM.2/ISAR/9].

In its agreed conclusions, the Group stressed the importance of SMEs to economic growth and development in both developed and developing countries. However, it noted that existing international and some national accounting and reporting requirements were intended primarily for large, listed companies, and identified obstacles that SMEs faced in maintaining financial records and accounts. ISAR agreed that each country should define different categories of SMEs in a manner appropriate to its needs and recommended that ad hoc expert consultations be held to consider an accounting and reporting framework appropriate for SMEs.

Taxation

On 6 June [E/2000/96], the Chairman of the Ad Hoc Group of Experts on International Cooperation in Tax Matters brought to the attention of the Economic and Social Council that the Steering Committee of the Group of Experts had met in New York from 12 to 14 April. Following the Group's adoption of the revised text of the United Nations Model Double Taxation Convention between Developed and Developing Countries at its ninth meeting [YUN 1999, p. 903], the Steering Committee had reviewed and consolidated editorial comments and suggestions elicited by the Secretary-General from members of the Group of Experts on the text of the Model Convention and concurred on its definitive text. The Group of Experts had noted that the Secretary-General therefore intended to publish the revised Model Convention.

ECONOMIC AND SOCIAL COUNCIL ACTION

On 27 July, the Economic and Social Council, on the recommendation of the Ad Hoc Group of Experts on International Cooperation in Tax Matters [E/1999/84 & Corr.1], adopted **decision 2000/232** without vote [agenda item 13 (g)].

Recommendations made by the Ad Hoc Group of Experts on International Cooperation in Tax Matters at its ninth meeting

At its 42nd plenary meeting, on 27 July 2000, the Economic and Social Council endorsed the following recommendations made by the Ad Hoc Group of Experts on International Cooperation in Tax Matters at its ninth meeting:

1. The Ad Hoc Group of Experts on International Cooperation in Tax Matters recommends that the Secretariat publish as soon as possible the United Nations Model Double Taxation Convention between Developed and Developing Countries. The Group of Experts also decides to keep the United Nations Model Double Taxation Convention under a biennial revision process.

2. The Group of Experts has suggested the following items for its review during its forthcoming meetings:
 (a) Transfer pricing:
 (i) Advance pricing agreements;
 (ii) Arbitration as a means of dispute resolution;
 (b) Innovative financial instruments;
 (c) Tax implications of electronic commerce, including the scope of the permanent establishment concept;
 (d) Exchange of information;
 (e) Mutual assistance in collection of tax debts;
 (f) Pensions;
 (g) Alternative dispute resolution procedure;
 (h) Tracking changes in the Model Tax Convention on Income and on Capital of the Organisation for Economic Cooperation and Development;
 (i) Examining the revisions of regional model conventions.

3. On the basis of the decision of the Group of Experts, the Council may wish to take note of the revised United Nations Model Double Taxation Convention between Developed and Developing Countries, and to approve the holding of the tenth meeting of the Group of Experts in the first half of 2001.

By **decision 2000/300** of 28 July, the Council took note of the Secretary-General's report on the ninth meeting of the Ad Hoc Group of Experts on International Cooperation in Tax Matters [YUN 1999, p. 904], taking into account the corrigendum to the report [E/1999/84/Corr.1] and the following text that was to be inserted after the word "Thereafter" in the third line of the corrigendum: "taking fully into account the fact that some Member States expressed the desire that the report should be as accurate as possible".

Transport

Maritime transport

The *Review of Maritime Transport 2000* [Sales No. E.00.II.D.34] stated that world seaborne trade recorded its fourteenth consecutive annual increase in 1999, reaching a record high of 5.23 billion tons. Annual growth, however, declined at a rate of 1.3 per cent, the lowest since 1987. Preliminary data available indicated that global maritime trade growth in 2000 was expected to be 2 per cent. Total maritime activities measured in ton-miles in global trade decreased to the minimal level of 21,480 billion ton-miles in 1999, compared to 21,492 billion ton-miles in 1998.

The world merchant fleet expanded to 799 million deadweight tons (dwt) at the end of 1999, representing a 1.3 per cent increase over 1998. The relatively low rate of fleet expansion reflected the balance between new-building deliveries of 40.5 million dwt, and tonnage broken up and lost of 30.7 million dwt, leaving a net gain of 9.8 million dwt. The developing countries' share of tonnage registered in major open-registry countries had increased slowly, reaching about one third in 1999. On the other hand, the developed market-economy countries' share had pursued a downward trend, representing about two thirds of the total tonnage registered in the major open-registry countries.

Transport of dangerous goods

The Committee of Experts on the Transport of Dangerous Goods held its twenty-first session in Geneva from 4 to 13 December [ST/SG/AC.10/27 & Add.1,2]. It had before it the reports of its Subcommittee of Experts on the Transport of Dangerous Goods on its sixteenth and seventeenth sessions, held in 1999 [YUN 1999, p. 905], and on its eighteenth session (Geneva, 3-12 July) [ST/SG/AC.10/C.3/36 & Add.1]. The Committee adopted a number of amendments to the Recommendations on the Transport of Dangerous Goods (Model Regulations) and to the Manual of Tests and Criteria, as proposed by its Subcommittee. It considered implementation of Economic and Social Council resolution 1999/62 [YUN 1999, p. 905], and discussed activities related to the implementation of Agenda 21, adopted by the 1992 United Nations Conference on Environment and Development [YUN 1992, p. 672], particularly on global harmonization of systems of classification and labelling of chemicals, health hazards and hazards to the environment, and implementation of Council resolution 1999/65 [YUN 1999, p. 906]. The Committee prepared a draft resolution for consideration by the Council in 2001.

UNCTAD institutional and organizational questions

UNCTAD programme

In 2000, TDB—the executive body of UNCTAD—held four sessions, all in Geneva: the second part of the twenty-third executive session (27 January), the twenty-fourth (24 March and 12 May) and the twenty-fifth (22 September) executive sessions, and the forty-seventh regular session (9-20 October) [A/55/15]. In January, the Board took note of the pre-Conference text for UNCTAD X as submitted by the Preparatory Committee of the Whole and requested the President of the Board to transmit it to the Conference (see p. 892). In March and May, the Board discussed

follow-up to the outcome of UNCTAD X; the outcome of the thirty-fifth session of the Working Party on the Medium-term Plan and the Programme Budget (see p. 922); the agenda items of the three TDB Commissions; and implementation of paragraph 166 of the Bangkok Plan of Action on the strengthening of UNCTAD's capacity-building programme. In September, TDB considered UNCTAD's contribution to the implementation of the United Nations New Agenda for the Development of Africa in the 1990s (NADAF)—UNCTAD's activities in favour of Africa (see p. 874); preparations for the forty-seventh session of TDB; the establishment of an Advisory Body on strengthening the capacity-building programme; and the report of the Joint Advisory Group on ITC on its thirty-third session (see p. 900).

In October, the Board discussed interdependence and global economic issues from a trade and development perspective: crisis and recovery in emerging markets (see p. 899). It adopted agreed conclusions on progress in implementing the Programme of Action for LDCs for the 1990s [agreed conclusions 459(XLVII)] (see p. 808); and on UNCTAD's contribution to the implementation of NADAF: capital flows and growth in Africa [460(XLVII)] (see p. 874). The Board adopted six decisions (see below): on technical cooperation activities of UNCTAD and their financing [dec. 461(XLVII)]; on financial sustainability of certain technical cooperation programmes and activities, pursuant to paragraph 164 (viii) of the UNCTAD X Plan of Action, in order to ensure sufficient funding [462(XLVII)]; on implementation of paragraph 166 of the UNCTAD X Plan of Action [463(XLVII)]; on the evaluation of technical cooperation programmes [464(XLVII)]; on financing of experts from developing countries and economies in transition when participating in UNCTAD meetings [465(XLVII)]; and on the establishment of an Advisory Body in accordance with paragraph 166 of the Bangkok Plan of Action [466(XLVII)]. It also took note of several reports and was informed of the outcome of the Fourth United Nations Conference to Review All Aspects of the Set of Multilaterally Agreed Equitable Principles and Rules for the Control of Restrictive Business Practices (see p. 901). The Board's one-day high-level segment (16 October) was devoted to regional integration and the global economy [TD/B/47/12].

By **decision 55/438** of 20 December, the General Assembly took note of TDB's report on its twenty-third, twenty-fourth and twenty-fifth executive sessions and on its forty-seventh session.

Technical cooperation activities

In a July report [TD/B/47/2 & Add.1,2], the UNCTAD Secretary-General gave an overview of technical cooperation activities in 1999, when UNCTAD's expenditures amounted to $25.4 million, an increase of some 16.5 per cent over the previous year. Of that amount, $16.9 million was from trust fund contributions, $6.5 million was financed by UNDP, and $2 million was from the regular programme of technical cooperation.

By region, approximately $5.3 million went to Africa, $4.6 million to Asia and the Pacific, $2.3 million to Europe, and $1.1 million to Latin America and the Caribbean. Some $12 million went to the interregional programme. The LDCs' share of technical cooperation expenditures in 1999 amounted to 40 per cent, up from 37.6 per cent in 1998.

By programme, the Division for Services Infrastructure for Development and Trade Efficiency accounted for 42 per cent of total expenditure. The Divisions on International Trade in Goods and Services, and Commodities, on Globalization and Development Strategies, and on Investment, Technology and Enterprise Development represented respectively 11.4, 13.9 and 15.5 per cent of total expenditure. The balance (17.2 per cent) was represented by the Office of the Special Coordinator for Least Developed, Landlocked and Island Developing Countries (3.7 per cent) and by activities reported for the secretariat as a whole (13.5 per cent).

As requested in the UNCTAD X Plan of Action [TD/386], the UNCTAD secretariat, in an August note [TD/B/47/8], submitted the indicative plan of technical cooperation programmes for 2001, including information on: ongoing projects that were expected to continue in 2001; projects proposed by the secretariat to implement the mandate of UNCTAD X as well as mandates given to UNCTAD by the General Assembly; and projects proposed as a result of specific requests received from beneficiaries. All projects included in the plan placed particular emphasis on capacity-building, in accordance with paragraph 166 of the Plan of Action.

In an October decision [A/55/15 (dec. 461(XLVII))], TDB requested the secretariat, in consultation with member States, to ensure a better relative balance in the share of technical cooperation activities of the various regions, and urged it to make maximum use of capacities from developing countries, including local and regional expertise; developing countries were encouraged to provide names of experts to the secretariat. The Board called on the secretariat to consider, in consultation with donors and beneficiaries, clus-

tering activities and formulating umbrella projects to enhance international coordination and cooperation among donors, to create economies of scale and support cooperation among developing countries at the subregional, regional and interregional levels. TDB expressed its appreciation for the secretariat's indicative plan for UNCTAD's technical cooperation for 2001, and for reissuance of that document in the light of the comments made by the Working Party on the Medium-term Plan and the Programme Budget at its thirty-sixth session (see p. 922).

Evaluations

In July, an independent evaluation team submitted an evaluation of the UNCTAD EMPRETEC programme [TD/B/WP/129], which provided developing countries with training in entrepreneurship. The programme's activities involved the delivery of seminars, the provision of advisory services and the development of national and international networks serving the needs of entrepreneurs. As at December 1999, EMPRETEC was fully active in 12 countries, with preliminary activities being initiated in 7 others. The evaluation stated that the training component of the programme needed adaptation, and made a number of recommendations to improve the programme's effectiveness in two broad areas: enhancing the substantive and operational sustainability of national programmes and promoting international networking.

A July progress report on implementation of the three-year Trade Point Programme strategy [TD/B/WP/128], approved in 1999 [YUN 1999, p. 911], stated that capacity development activities were hampered by the lack of extrabudgetary funding. Nevertheless, progress was achieved in empowering Trade Points and reducing their dependence on UNCTAD resources through regional cooperation and the strengthening of Trade Point forums. The report noted that the Global Trade Point Network (GTPNet) web site was renovated and its services enhanced. Options were presented for a suitable non-profit organization to manage the Electronic Trading Opportunities (ETO) system, and activities to be undertaken in line with the strategy were proposed.

With regard to implementation of the recommendations of the 1999 in-depth evaluation of the technical cooperation activities on competition law and policy [TD/B/WP/119 & Add.1], an August UNCTAD secretariat report [TD/B/WP/130] stated that a strategy had been developed that focused on: activities that were sustainable and could make an impact; alternative sources and ways of mobilizing human and financial resources; and the development of networking among high-level institutions in each country.

In an October decision on the evaluation of technical cooperation programmes [dec. 464 (XLVII)], TDB agreed with the recommendations contained in the evaluation of the EMPRETEC programme and urged the UNCTAD Secretary-General to implement them and report to the Working Party on the Medium-term Plan and the Programme Budget in 2001. It invited the secretariat to enhance the geographical coverage of EMPRETEC and to strengthen its cooperation with other organizations and entities dealing with entrepreneurship. The Board took note of the progress report on implementing the recommendations of the evaluation of the programme of technical cooperation activities on competition law and policy and invited the secretariat to continue the implementation. It also took note of the progress report on implementation of the Trade Point Programme strategy and requested the secretariat to proceed with the implementation in the time frame agreed. It encouraged donor countries to make available extrabudgetary resources for capacity-building projects aiming to achieve that objective, and requested the secretariat to report to the Working Party in 2001 on progress made. TDB also decided that an in-depth evaluation of the TRAINMAR (Training human resources in maritime management) programme should be considered by the Working Party in 2001.

Funding

In an October decision on the review of the financial sustainability of certain technical cooperation programmes and activities, pursuant to paragraph 164 (viii) of the UNCTAD X Plan of Action, in order to ensure sufficient funding [dec. 462(XLVII)], TDB recommended that the UNCTAD Secretary-General establish advisory groups for the Automated System for Customs Data (ASYCUDA), the Debt Management and Financial Analysis System (DMFAS) and the Advance Cargo Information System (ACIS) programmes, consider the establishment of a DMFAS trust fund in order to ensure the financial sustainability of the central operation of the DMFAS programme as well as the different options and modalities for such a trust fund, and report to the Working Party in 2001.

Training courses

A September note on strengthening UNCTAD's capacity-building programmes and activities [TD/B/WP/133] discussed implementation of paragraph 166 of the UNCTAD X Plan of Action, which called for a strengthening of UNCTAD's capacity-building activities, particularly through regular training courses on key trade and development issues, so as to better enable developing countries and interested countries with economies in transition to meet global economic and trade challenges. The note outlined activities designed to strengthen and deepen UNCTAD's capacity-building programmes.

In an October decision [dec. 463(XLVII)], TDB invited the UNCTAD Secretary-General to seek the necessary resources to prepare and deliver three training courses in 2001 by exploring a variety of funding arrangements, including the UN programme budget, voluntary contributions and a combination thereof. It reiterated the importance of an early and full implementation of paragraph 166 of the Plan of Action, and urged the UNCTAD Secretary-General to take all necessary measures to that end in the context of the preparation of the programme budget for 2002-2003.

In another October decision [dec. 466(XLVII)], TDB decided to review the arrangements for the implementation of the regular training courses provided for in paragraph 166 of the Plan of Action at its next regular (2001) session. It also decided to establish an Advisory Body to advise the UNCTAD Secretary-General on regular training, in accordance with paragraph 166. The draft terms of reference of the Advisory Body were annexed to the decision.

Participation of developing country experts in UNCTAD meetings

In a 17 August note on financing of experts from developing countries and economies in transition when participating in UNCTAD meetings [TD/B/WP/131], the UNCTAD secretariat stated that, at the time of reporting, two expert meetings had been held in 2000, in which 29 experts from developing countries participated: 11 from Africa, 8 from Asia and the Pacific and 10 from Latin America, of which 10 were from LDCs.

The unspent balance carried over to 2000 for the financing of experts' participation amounted to $587,712. The total cost of the participation of the experts in the two meetings was estimated at $102,421. The secretariat estimated that there would remain a balance at end-2000 of about $93,000 against the original provision established by the General Assembly in resolution 53/3 [YUN 1998, p. 912].

In an October decision [A/55/15 (dec. 465(XLVII))], TDB invited the UNCTAD Secretary-General to seek the necessary resources to finance the participation of experts from developing countries and economies in transition in UNCTAD expert meetings foreseen for 2001, including in the context of preparing the programme budget for 2002-2003.

Medium-term plan and programme budget

The UNCTAD Working Party on the Medium-term Plan and the Programme Budget held two sessions in 2000, both in Geneva.

At its thirty-fifth session (13 and 20-21 March, 17-19 April) [TD/B/47/3], the Working Party reviewed the draft UNCTAD section of the UN medium-term plan for the period 2002-2005 and adopted a decision in which it recommended to TDB the adoption of the text of the medium-term plan, as amended by the Working Party, for transmission to the appropriate authorities at United Nations Headquarters. It also recommended that TDB consider the proposal that the UNCTAD secretariat undertake an evaluation of its activities in accordance with the indicators of achievement set forth in the plan, and present it to member States for discussion. At its twenty-fourth executive session in March [TD/B/EX (24)/3], TDB endorsed the Working Party's decision, thereby adopting the draft medium-term plan, and agreed to consider the proposal on evaluation approved by the Working Party.

The Working Party also reviewed the UNCTAD programme of work for 2000-2001, which was revised in the light of the UNCTAD X outcome. In agreed conclusions, it concurred with the revised programme of work, to be forwarded to TDB for its endorsement. The Working Party requested that the UNCTAD Secretary-General submit detailed costed proposals on the implementation of paragraph 166 of the UNCTAD X Plan of Action for consideration at the thirty-sixth session of the Working Party, as well as proposals for an Advisory Body to be established by TDB (see p. 921). At its twenty-fourth executive session in May, TDB decided that, in 2002, it would conduct a mid-term review of UNCTAD's work, based on the indicators of achievement agreed to in the medium-term plan (2002-2005). In addition, it would review the functioning of the intergovernmental machinery on the basis of a March note by

the UNCTAD secretariat [TD/B/EX(24)/L.1]. TDB also endorsed the revised work programme and the related agreed conclusions.

At its thirty-sixth session (11-15 September) [TD/B/47/9], the Working Party considered progress reports on the implementation of a number of technical cooperation activities (see p. 920): the Trade Point Programme strategy [TD/B/WP/128]; the UNCTAD EMPRETEC programme [TD/B/WP/ 129]; technical cooperation activities on competition law and policy [TD/B/WP/130]; and UNCTAD's capacity-building programmes and activities [TD/B/WP/133]. Other reports before TDB (see above) were: a review of UNCTAD's technical cooperation activities and their financing [TD/B/ 47/2 & Add.1,2]; a note on financing of experts from developing countries and economies in transition when participating in UNCTAD meetings [TD/B/WP/131]; and the indicative plan of UNCTAD's technical cooperation for 2001 [TD/B/ 47/8]. The Working Party recommended five draft decisions on technical cooperation programmes for adoption by TDB. TDB adopted those decisions in October (see above).

OIOS investigations

On 7 April, by **resolution 54/257** on reports of the Office of Internal Oversight Services (OIOS), the General Assembly took note of the following OIOS reports that concerned UNCTAD: the investigation into allegations of theft of funds by an UNCTAD staff member (see p. 1318); the investigation into allegations concerning an electronic commerce project at UNCTAD [YUN 1999, p. 911]; and the review of the programme and administrative practices of the ITC secretariat [YUN 1997, p. 1400], and the comments of the Joint Inspection Unit thereon [YUN 1998, p. 1259], reaffirming that the merging of UNCTAD and ITC had not been approved by the pertinent legislative bodies.

By **decision 54/462 B** of 15 June, the Assembly deferred until its fifty-fifth session consideration of the note by the Secretary-General transmitting the OIOS report on allegations of theft of funds by an UNCTAD staff member.

Chapter V

Regional economic and social activities

In 2000, the five regional commissions continued to provide technical cooperation, including advisory services, to their member States, promote programmes and projects, and provide training to enhance national capacity-building in various sectors. Three of them held regular sessions during the year: the Economic Commission for Europe (ECE), the Economic and Social Commission for Asia and the Pacific (ESCAP) and the Economic Commission for Latin America and the Caribbean (ECLAC). The Economic Commission for Africa (ECA) and the Economic and Social Commission for Western Asia (ESCWA) did not meet in 2000; both were scheduled to meet in May 2001. The regional commissions organized follow-up activities to the UN conferences and summits held in the 1990s and held regional meetings in preparation for the General Assembly's special sessions on women and on social development, as well as for future international conferences.

In December, the Assembly invited the United Nations Conference on Trade and Development to elaborate a programme for improving the efficiency of the transit environment of the newly independent and developing landlocked States in Central Asia and their transit developing neighbours. The Economic and Social Council established the Statistical Conference of the Americas of ECLAC, proclaimed the years 2000-2009 as the Decade of Greater Mekong Subregion Development Cooperation, and endorsed the Delhi Declaration on Space Technology Applications in Asia and the Pacific for Improved Quality of Life in the New Millennium and the Strategy and Action Plan on Space Technology Applications for Sustainable Development in Asia and the Pacific for the New Millennium. It also amended the terms of reference of ESCAP to include and admit Georgia as a member.

Regional cooperation

Efforts continued in 2000 to further strengthen the regional commissions to achieve greater effectiveness and efficiency.

On 4 February (**decision 2000/207**), the Economic and Social Council decided that the theme at its 2000 substantive session for the item on regional cooperation would be "Follow-up to major United Nations conferences and summits: exchange of regional experiences".

Meetings of executive secretaries. The executive secretaries of the regional commissions met on 13 and 14 February in Bangkok, Thailand, and on 10 and 11 May, 24 July and 17 October in New York.

At their February meeting, they considered globalization, regionalism and development within the context of their participation in the tenth session of the United Nations Conference on Trade and Development (UNCTAD) (see p. 890). They considered regionalism as a step towards preparing countries and enterprises to face the challenges and risks of globalization and as an alternative for countries that perceived unfairness and asymmetries in the globalization programme promoted by the more developed countries. They were unanimous in underlining those asymmetries and the risk that they posed for development. They also discussed the relationship between the regional commissions and the Economic and Social Council, as well as ways to strengthen their contributions to the Council's policy review. The executive secretaries welcomed new modalities linking the commissions' activities with other UN entities in line with Council resolution 1998/46 [YUN 1998, p. 1262] on the commissions' dual role, but felt that there was additional scope for substantive interaction between the regional commissions and the Council at the intergovernmental level. In that regard, they suggested that the Secretary-General's report on regional cooperation focus more on policy issues at the regional level, including intergovernmental perspectives. The report should concentrate on new developments and significant initiatives undertaken, highlighting analytically the commissions' response to global mandates and other major issues of which the United Nations was seized. It would continue to update the Council on developments in interregional and inter-agency cooperation in response to regional priorities and draw the Council's attention to any significant initiatives undertaken with regional partners.

By **decision 2000/226** of 25 July, the Council endorsed those recommendations.

Review and reform of
the regional commissions

Reports of Secretary-General. In a May report [E/2000/10], the Secretary-General outlined steps taken by the regional commissions to implement the guidance given in Council resolution 1998/46 with respect to their dual role as UN outposts and the regional expression of the Organization. The report also discussed regional trends and activities, interregional cooperation, further measures undertaken by the commissions to achieve greater effectiveness and efficiency and the report of the executive secretaries (see p. 923).

In an addendum to his report [E/2000/10/Add.1], the Secretary-General reviewed cooperation between the regional commissions and other regional bodies in their respective regions. A second addendum examined the work of the regional commissions in normative and operational activities [E/2000/10/Add.2]. In a third addendum [E/2000/10/Add.3], the Secretary-General submitted the resolutions and decisions adopted at recent sessions of the regional commissions calling for action by the Council.

ECONOMIC AND SOCIAL COUNCIL ACTION

By **decision 2000/222** of 16 June, the Economic and Social Council agreed to circulate as official documents the reports of the regional commissions' meetings on the theme of the Council's high-level segment—"Development and international cooperation in the twenty-first century: the role of information technology in the context of a knowledge-based global economy" (see p. 799).

By **decision 2000/226** of 25 July, the Council took note of the Secretary-General's reports on regional cooperation (see above) and the summaries of the economic and social situation in Africa, 1999 [E/2000/12]; the economic survey of Europe, 1999 [E/2000/11]; the economic survey of Latin America and the Caribbean, 1999 [E/2000/14]; the economic and social survey of Asia and the Pacific, 2000 [E/2000/13]; and the survey of economic and social developments in the ESCWA region, 1999-2000 [E/2000/15].

The Council also adopted resolutions on amendment of the terms of reference of ESCAP to include Georgia in the geographical scope of the Commission and to admit it as a member (2000/4); the Decade of Greater Mekong Subregion Development Cooperation, 2000-2009 (2000/5); regional cooperation on space applications for sustainable development in Asia and the

Pacific (2000/6); the establishment of the Statistical Conference of the Americas of ECLAC (2000/7); and the place and date of ECLAC's twenty-ninth session (2000/8).

(The summaries of the surveys and the resolutions are covered in the relevant sections of this chapter.)

The General Assembly, in **resolution 54/257** of 7 April, took note of the report of the Office of Internal Oversight Services on the audits of the regional commissions [YUN 1998, p. 918].

Africa

The Economic Commission for Africa (ECA) did not hold a regular session in 2000. The thirty-fourth session of the Commission/twenty-fifth meeting of the Conference of Ministers/ninth session of the Conference of African Ministers of Finance was scheduled to be held in Algiers, Algeria, from 8 to 10 May 2001.

The eighth session of the Conference of African Ministers of Finance was held in Addis Ababa, Ethiopia, on 21 and 22 November 2000 to prepare African countries for the high-level international intergovernmental event on financing for development (see p. 915), to be held in 2002, and the Third United Nations Conference on the Least Developed Countries (LDCs) (see p. 808), to be held in 2001. The Conference adopted a resolution on the New Global Compact with Africa proposed by the ECA Executive Secretary, by which donor countries would invest resources through aid, debt relief and market access, while the African countries in turn would intensify political and economic reforms. The Conference also adopted statements on the high-level event on financing for development and on the Third Conference on LDCs (see p. 926).

The Conference of African Ministers of Finance was preceded by the Regional Consultative Meeting on Financing for Development in the African Region and Preparatory Meeting for the Third United Nations Conference on the Least Developed Countries (Addis Ababa, 15-17 November) [A/AC.257/14].

A meeting of the Ministerial Follow-up Committee of the Conference of Ministers responsible for economic and social development and planning (Abuja, Nigeria, 4-5 May) recommended that the pledging conference for the UN Trust Fund for African Development should take place in Addis Ababa to coincide with ECA's biennial session, starting in 2001, and endorsed the ECA medium-term plan 2002-2005.

An expert group meeting on Africa's development strategies was also held (Addis Ababa, 22-24 March), which took stock of the important aspects of the region's development agenda, economic reforms and policy, inequality, poverty, human and physical capital development, governance, conflicts and institutions, as well as structural transformation and industrial policy, and resource mobilization, savings and investment [ECA/ESPD/AD-HOC/EXP/04/2000].

Communications. On 3 February [S/2000/91], Mali transmitted the text of the Bamako Declaration on the acceleration of the integration process in West Africa, adopted by the ministerial meeting of the Economic Community of West African States (ECOWAS) and the West African Economic and Monetary Union (Bamako, 28-29 January).

On 27 April [A/54/855-E/2000/44], Algeria, Egypt and Portugal transmitted to the Secretary-General the Cairo Declaration and the Cairo Plan of Action adopted by the Africa-Europe Summit (Cairo, Egypt, 3-4 April), held under the aegis of the Organization of African Unity (OAU) and the European Union (EU).

On 16 December [S/2000/1201], Mali transmitted the final communiqué of the twenty-fourth session of the Authority of Heads of State and Government of ECOWAS (Bamako, 15-16 December).

Economic and social trends

Economic trends

Africa's economy grew at an estimated 3.5 per cent in 2000, compared with the 1999 figure of 3.2 per cent, according to the ECA summary of the economic and social situation in Africa [E/2001/13]. In sharp contrast to the experience in recent years, only one country (Zimbabwe) posted negative growth and no economy grew at a rate less than 1 per cent. In 21 countries, the growth rates ranged between 1 and 2.9 per cent, another 15 countries managed to grow within the range of 3 to 4.9 per cent and nine countries had growth rates between 5 and 6.9 per cent. However, only two countries (Equatorial Guinea, Libyan Arab Jamahiriya), as opposed to five in 1999, grew at or higher than 7 per cent in 2000. Growth in sub-Saharan Africa was relatively modest, increasing from 3 to 3.1 per cent.

At the subregional level, growth declined in East Africa from 4.1 to 3 per cent, with Ethiopia achieving the highest growth rate, 5 per cent, while the lowest, 1 per cent, was recorded in Bu-

rundi, the Comoros and Kenya. Likewise, growth in West Africa declined from a robust 3.7 per cent in 1999 to 2.8 per cent in 2000, mainly on account of the slowdown in Ghana and the below-average performance in Côte d'Ivoire. In contrast, North Africa boosted its growth from 2.6 per cent to 4.1 per cent and Southern Africa's growth doubled to 3 per cent, mainly due to the strong resurgence of the South African economy. Economic performance also improved in Central Africa, with growth increasing from 4 per cent to 4.5 per cent. The five largest economies in Africa (Algeria, Egypt, Morocco, Nigeria, South Africa) posted a growth rate of 3.2 per cent in 2000, compared to 2.8 per cent in 1999, while the 11 oil-exporting countries managed to push their growth to 4.4 per cent from 3.8 per cent in 1999 because of higher oil revenue. The African LDCs saw their growth shrink from 4.5 per cent in 1999 to 3.5 per cent in 2000, while the 15 landlocked countries were the hardest hit, with growth declining from 4.9 to 2.9 per cent.

At the sectoral level, there was significant recovery in agriculture, which registered a 3.6 per cent growth compared to 2.1 per cent in 1999. Despite that improvement, the region remained far short of satisfying its food needs. The industrial sector also showed a positive trend, particularly in the oil-exporting and North African countries, growing by 3.4 per cent compared to 2.8 per cent in 1999. The service sector continued its buoyant growth, with a 1-percentage-point increase to reach 4 per cent. Inflation measured 11 per cent, exceeding the 1999 level by 1 percentage point. Export volume increased by 8 per cent, while import volume rose by 5 per cent. The balance of trade registered export earnings of $131 billion during the year, 30 per cent higher than 1999. The value of imports was estimated at $117 billion. The balance on current account of the non-oil-exporting countries, however, further deteriorated. The trade balance was in deficit by $23 billion and the current account by $48 billion. External resource flows rose from $22 billion in 1999 to $23 billion in 2000. Foreign direct investment (FDI) amounted to about $6 billion, while transfers reached $8 billion. The volume of debt declined to $342 billion, compared to $359 billion in 1999, while debt servicing increased from $39.4 billion in 1999 to $43.4 billion in 2000.

Social trends

According to the summary of economic and social conditions in Africa, despite the slight progress worldwide in poverty reduction, the continent had the largest share of people living on less than $1 a day. The average income of the region's poor as a whole was only 83 cents per person per day. Africa also had the worst income distribution, with a Gini coefficient (measure of income equality) of 51 per cent. The mean share of the top 20 per cent of the population was about 48 per cent, an excess of 28 points.

The health status of the continent declined, largely due to the ravages of the HIV/AIDS epidemic. Some 25 million people, including more than 1 million children, were living with the disease, and at least 5 million people were newly infected with the virus in 2000. There were indications that the epidemic had spread out of control in Africa, where over 20 countries had a prevalence rate of 7 to 10 per cent or more. It was estimated that deaths due to HIV/AIDS in Africa would soon surpass 21 million.

Africa also faced the critical challenge of reducing widespread poverty while conserving the rich biodiversity and reducing environmental degradation. The quality and capacity of the soil to support productive agriculture were critical to sustainable development. Africa, however, was the victim of both endogenous and exogenous factors of environmental degradation, and, since agriculture would continue to play a leading role in generating incomes, providing food and industrial inputs and producing the bulk of exports, any credible attempt to reduce poverty, conserve biodiversity and reduce environmental degradation needed to focus on that sector. Moreover, Africa's population growth rate of about 3 per cent per annum was greater than the increase in food production of 2.5 per cent per annum, which called for new ways of improving and sustaining food production to move in tandem with the population growth rate.

Activities in 2000

ECA's activities in 2000 were undertaken through the following subprogrammes: facilitating economic and social policy analysis; ensuring food security and sustainable development; strengthening development management; harnessing information technology for development; promoting regional cooperation and integration; promoting the advancement of women; and promoting subregional activities for development.

Development policy and regional economic cooperation

African recovery and development

In 2000, ECA continued to monitor implementation of the United Nations New Agenda for the Development of Africa in the 1990s, adopted by the General Assembly in resolution 46/151 [YUN 1991, p. 402], and the United Nations System-wide Special Initiative on Africa, launched in 1996 [YUN 1996, p. 832] (see pp. 874 and 877, respectively). Activities undertaken in support of the New Agenda included follow-up conferences to review progress made in poverty reduction, employment generation and achieving social sector objectives in education, health and good governance. ECA helped African countries prepare for the Assembly's special session on the World Summit for Social Development (see p. 1012). In the context of capacity-building in Africa, ECA organized a regional conference (Addis Ababa, February), which examined the causes, trends, extent and implications of the brain-drain phenomenon for Africa's development and made recommendations for reversing it. In two follow-up meetings (Geneva, June; Dakar, Senegal, October), a draft programme document was finalized on the partnership for brain-drain reversal and capacity-building in Africa. Ad hoc experts' group meetings were held to review an ECA secretariat report on HIV/AIDS and education in Eastern and Southern Africa (Entebbe, Uganda, September), and to examine major trends in public sector policy reforms, identify impediments to their effective implementation and make recommendations for further reforms (Niamey, Niger, May). Other meetings organized by the secretariat included an expert group meeting in April on the development implications of civil conflicts in Africa, and a high-level seminar in November on external trade promotion and monitoring tools in Central Africa.

Other ECA activities in support of the New Agenda focused on building capacity through technical assistance to regional economic groupings. A major effort was launched to assess the continent's integration performance and to inform policy makers of the results to help them set policy. ECA facilitated consensus-building around common African positions in global negotiations and facilitated policy consensus in such key sectors as transportation and civil aviation.

In connection with the System-wide Special Initiative, the second regional consultation of UN agencies working in Africa (Addis Ababa, 26-27 June) reviewed activities and discussed work plans in the five priority areas of the Initiative (education, health, water, governance and information technology). It agreed to convene cluster meetings in those areas to refocus objectives through the collaborative action of the UN system and to set benchmarks to assess progress.

Third UN Conference on LDCs (2001)

As part of the preparation for the Third United Nations Conference on the Least Developed Countries, to be held in 2001 (see p. 808), the Conference of African Ministers of Finance (see p. 924) adopted a statement on the Conference, which called for a new approach to international development cooperation in support of the development of African LDCs. It noted that with 34 of the world's 49 LDCs in Africa, urgent action was required to avoid further marginalization of those countries in a globalizing world economy. The statement called for special measures to help the African LDCs in trade, finance and development and urged Africa's development partners to increase official development assistance and FDI, and to enhance the Heavily Indebted Poor Countries Initiative to benefit all African LDCs [YUN 1997, p. 950].

ECA and UNCTAD collaborated in organizing subregional preparatory meetings for anglophone and francophone African countries (Addis Ababa, 27-29 March, and Niamey, 18-20 April, respectively), in response to General Assembly resolution 54/235 [YUN 1999, p. 770].

Information technology

ECA carried out programmes to raise awareness about the importance of the information society and on the utilization of information and communication technology (ICT) to enhance the competitiveness of African economies. Its secretariat implemented activities in statistics, ICT, geoinformation and library services.

ECA organized an ad hoc expert group meeting (Addis Ababa, 6-10 November) to review a study on geoinformation, so as to raise awareness of the importance of geographic information in socio-economic development and identify mechanisms to facilitate spatial data collection, access and use.

The Commission provided technical support for building national capacity in ICT, including the elaboration of a medium-term programme in the Democratic Republic of the Congo, a statistical master plan in Mauritania, the design of a sectoral statistical information system in Rwanda and an integrated information system in Lesotho. ECA also helped the Port Management Association for Eastern and Southern Africa in surveying the statistical systems in ports, as well as in organizing an expert meeting on port statistics (Mombasa, Kenya, June). It assisted several countries to develop their national information and communication infrastructure policies and plans, and the Regional Centre for Mapping of Resources for Development in Nairobi, Kenya, in restructuring its programme. Among other capacity-building activities undertaken were a workshop on international, economic and social classifications (Addis Ababa, December) and

training workshops for francophone African countries on the implementation of the 1993 System of National Accounts (Addis Ababa, 20-24 March) and for anglophone African countries on household sector accounts (Addis Ababa, 20-24 November). A meeting of the Task Force of the Committee on African Statistical Development with consultants on the evaluation of the Addis Ababa Plan of Action for Statistical Development in Africa in the 1990s [YUN 1991, p. 304] met in Addis Ababa (6-10 March). The tenth meeting of the Coordinating Committee on African Statistical Development was also held in Addis Ababa (30 October–3 November).

The Scan-ICT project for building support for a phased development of a comprehensive African capacity for the collection and management of key information to support the growing investment in ICTs, as well as Africa's transition to an information society, was launched. An inaugural Scan-ICT methodology and work-plan workshop was held in November in Addis Ababa and a financing agreement signed between ECA and the EU.

Transportation and communications

ECA's secretariat carried out a number of programmes to promote the development of transportation and communications, including studies on the impact of improved rural transport on women, needs assessment for the modernization of rail track rolling stocks and telecommunications and signalling equipment in West and Central Africa. Other projects included a framework report for the development and implementation of transit agreements, privatization of ports and railways in selected African countries and a study assessing progress in the implementation of the Yamoussoukro Declaration on a new air transport policy [YUN 1988, p. 273]. The first meeting of the monitoring body of that Declaration, held in November, prepared guidelines for the Declaration's implementation. Evaluation continued of progress in the implementation of the programme for the Second Transport and Communications Decade in Africa, adopted by the Economic and Social Council in resolution 1991/83 [YUN 1991, p. 301]. The ECA secretariat organized an ad hoc expert group meeting on private sector participation in infrastructure development in Africa (Lusaka, Zambia, May) and a seminar on transport facilitation for Eastern Africa (Mombasa, Kenya, November).

Europe-Africa permanent link

The ECA and ECE Executive Secretaries, in their report on a Europe-Africa permanent link through the Strait of Gibraltar [E/2001/19], submitted by the Secretary-General pursuant to Economic and Social Council resolution 1999/37 [YUN 1999, p. 918], stated that the *Norskald 98/99* survey had demonstrated the need for surveys involving deeper drilling. Since one of the most important elements was the technological approach to the drilling system, two approaches were proposed in that regard. It was decided to postpone continuation of the investigations until a comparative independent study of drilling techniques had determined the most suitable technique for the surveys. The study, entitled "Evaluation of technological approaches to offshore geological coring in the Strait of Gibraltar", was conducted by a maritime classification society.

Activities in 2000 included a technical workshop on deep drilling in the Strait of Gibraltar (Rabat, Morocco, 9-10 March).

Energy and natural resources

ECA carried out several activities to strengthen regional and subregional cooperation in the development of mineral and energy resources. It organized an ad hoc expert group meeting on the subject (Douala, Cameroon, December). Several studies were prepared to define the role and framework for government/private sector participation in the minerals and energy sector in Africa. A paper on mineral resources development and alleviation of poverty in Africa was also prepared for a special conference of African Ministers of Energy and Mining (Ouagadougou, Burkina Faso, December).

Food security and sustainable development

ECA's work in ensuring food security and sustainable development was aimed at promoting better understanding and management of the interrelationships between food security, population and environmental sustainability. Its Food Security and Sustainable Development Division promoted environmentally sustainable development, including the development and utilization of modern science and technology for food security.

The Division, in collaboration with the United Nations Centre for Human Settlements, organized an African ministerial conference (Addis Ababa, 6-8 November) to review progress in the implementation of the Habitat Agenda, adopted at the 1996 United Nations Conference on Human Settlements [YUN 1996, p. 994]. The conference adopted a regional position for the General Assembly's special session on the review and appraisal of the implementation of the Habitat Agenda in 2001 (see p. 989). Other meetings organized during the year included the third meeting of the Advisory Board on Science and Technology (Addis Ababa, 2-4 October) and the second meeting of the Advisory Board on Population, Environment and Agriculture (Addis Ababa, 24-26 October). ECA offered policy and advisory services to member States and implemented capacity- and institution-building activities.

The African regional preparatory process for the World Summit on Sustainable Development began in January with the first high-level stakeholders meeting, jointly organized by ECA and the United Nations Environment Programme (UNEP) in Addis Ababa.

Development management

Activities organized in the area of development management were aimed at enhancing public sector management, private sector development and civil society participation in the governance and development process. A consultative meeting of parliamentarians and private sector officials (Addis Ababa, November) examined the concept and role of the State in the political and economic transition process in Africa, including the legislature's role in the design and implementation of policies that would promote broad-based, poverty-reducing growth and development. The meeting emphasized the need for African countries to strengthen the capacity of the State to discharge its legitimate functions.

In the area of governance, the secretariat fielded assessment missions to selected countries and was finalizing draft indicators to measure the state of governance. It also collaborated with the United Nations Development Programme (UNDP) in organizing the fourth African Governance Forum (Kampala, Uganda, September).

ECA activities supported private sector development to enhance the competitiveness of African economies. Two studies, one on support services for improving regional and global competitiveness of small and medium-scale enterprises (SMEs) and one on a strategic framework for designing and providing those services to enhance SMEs' regional and global competitiveness, were reviewed at an ad hoc expert group meeting (Mauritius, December). The meeting made recommendations for improving the operating environment for SMEs in Africa, including the regulatory and policy environment, facilitating access to credit, improving transport and communication infrastructure and developing human resources, support services institutions, technologies, quality control and markets.

ECA worked closely with UNCTAD and the African Capital Markets Forum to address the development of capital markets. It undertook needs assessment missions to Algeria, Egypt, Kenya, Malawi, Morocco, Tunisia, Uganda and the United Republic of Tanzania to identify their technical assistance needs in establishing capital markets. The secretariat also organized an Asia-Africa Summit (Kuala Lumpur, Malaysia, November) to promote cooperation between private sector entities in Africa and Asia.

Post-conflict reconstruction and development

ECA's work in peace-building helped create stable, enabling environments for peace in the region. Together with OAU, it facilitated the launching of the Conference on Security, Development and Cooperation in Africa (Abuja, Nigeria, May), whose main objective was to articulate principles to guide African countries in security issues, stability, economic development and co-operation. ECA organized the second consultative meeting (Conakry, Guinea, 23-24 March) on its Mano River Basin Initiative to promote subregional reconstruction and development in Guinea, Liberia and Sierra Leone.

To help policy makers appreciate the economic causes and consequences of conflicts, ECA organized an ad hoc expert group meeting (Addis Ababa, 7-8 April) on the development implications of civil conflicts. ECA developed indices of good governance to be published annually as the "African Governance Report". Issues to be dealt with included representation, institutional effectiveness and economic management capacities.

Integration of women in development

ECA activities under the subprogramme on the integration of women in development were directed at building the institutional and technical capacities of its member States to design and implement gender-sensitive policies and programmes. Its African Centre for Women assisted in improving the knowledge base on African women's issues through training, research, awareness raising and policy advisory work. The Centre launched a new annual publication, *African Women's Report*, which monitored and assessed the status of African women in socio-economic development. It also launched the first edition of a new CD-ROM on the status of women in Africa. Capacity-building support was provided to the African delegations attending the General Assembly special session on women (see p. 1082). Several workshops were organized to increase women's awareness of international and national human rights instruments to enable them to defend their rights and sensitize policy makers on mainstreaming gender in policies and programmes. ECA, in collaboration with the Afri-

can Women's Committee on Peace and Development and Femmes Solidarité Africa, organized a conference (Abuja, June) on mainstreaming a gender perspective into the peace-building process, particularly as it related to HIV/AIDS, health and education in refugee camps.

Subregional Development Centres

The five Subregional Development Centres, based in Central, East, North, Southern and West Africa, continued to enhance the Commission's outreach programmes with the various regional economic communities. The Centres promoted regional cooperation and integration by providing effective technical support and facilitated networking and information-sharing, dissemination of ECA policy recommendations and technical publications on regional cooperation and integration issues. They also engaged in advocacy and capacity-building by convening policy forums, seminars and training workshops, and providing technical advisory services.

Social development

ECA organized the second African Development Forum (Addis Ababa, 3-7 December) on the theme "AIDS: the greatest leadership challenge". The Forum highlighted the lack of political will and leadership to make HIV/AIDS a top priority on the development agenda. Participants called for comprehensive multisectoral plans to expand and deepen country-level programmes to combat the pandemic and create an enabling environment with prevention, care and mitigation programmes to protect Africa's future development prospects. The Forum adopted the Africa Consensus and Plan of Action, which called for leadership at all levels to overcome the continent-wide threat of HIV/AIDS and contained a commitment by African leaders to invest the necessary resources to fight the disease. The Forum led to the adoption of concrete actions by African Governments and their development partners to create multisectoral programmes and plans with country-level impact.

Programme, administration and organizational questions

ECA reform

As part of efforts to deepen its reform, ECA continued to implement measures to strengthen its programme delivery and management systems. During the year, it delegated authority to its Subregional Development Centres in human resources management. The Centres were empowered to handle their recruitment, placement and promotion of General Service staff members, recruitment of consultants and contractors, and processing of staff entitlements. To enhance its administrative processes further, the Commission adopted the Integrated Management Information System and installed the Very Small Aperture Terminal to improve electronic communication between ECA and its Subregional Development Centres, as well as its link with other parts of the UN system.

Asia and the Pacific

The Economic and Social Commission for Asia and the Pacific (ESCAP), at its fifty-sixth session (Bangkok, Thailand, 1-7 June) [E/2000/39], had as its theme "Development through globalization and partnership in the twenty-first century: an Asia-Pacific perspective for integrating developing countries and economies in transition into the international trading system on a fair and equitable basis". The Commission reviewed the implications of recent economic and social developments and emerging issues and developments at the regional level, including regional economic cooperation; environment and natural resources development; socio-economic measures to alleviate poverty in rural and urban areas; transport, communications, tourism and infrastructure development; statistics; and issues related to least developed, landlocked and island developing countries. In addition, it considered technical cooperation activities and programme and organizational questions.

The Commission decided that the theme for its 2001 session would be "Balanced development of urban and rural areas and regions within the countries of Asia and the Pacific".

Economic trends

According to the summary of the economic and social survey of Asia and the Pacific [E/2001/14], following the impressive recovery in 1999, economic performance strengthened further in 2000. The average growth rate of the developing economies of the region increased by 1 percentage point, while the developed economies improved their collective growth rate by 1.3 percentage points. As in 1999, both developing and developed economies achieved higher gross domestic product (GDP) growth in a lower inflationary environment, despite rising energy prices and weaker exchange rates in a number of

countries. All the main geographical subregions contributed to the higher GDP growth and enjoyed lower inflation, with the exception of the Pacific island economies, where collective GDP growth was negative in 2000. The most impressive subregion in terms of growth performance was South-East Asia. In East and North-East Asia deflation in 1999 was followed by modest inflation in 2000.

A favourable external environment, reflected in the buoyancy of world trade, combined with domestic measures to improve and sustain the momentum of growth in the region. The strong growth of world trade embodied a robust export performance by the ESCAP region, where the dynamism of intraregional and intra-industry trade revived almost to pre-crisis levels. Several economies in the region registered export growth of 20 per cent or more in value terms. The strong export growth was led by electronics and electronic components, of which the ESCAP region was a major supplier. Foreign capital flows to the ESCAP region rose marginally, while its share of flows to the developing economies nearly doubled, from 23 per cent in 1998 to 40 per cent in 2000, which aided the process of financial and corporate sector restructuring.

On the domestic side, declining interest rates and continuing fiscal stimulus supported output growth, while exchange-rate weakness and improved capacity utilization enhanced competitiveness and stimulated export growth. Furthermore, there was evidence that private domestic demand was beginning to play a greater role in the growth process than in 1999.

Policy issues

The principal policy challenge confronting the region was maintaining the momentum of growth in 2001 and beyond in the face of potential unfavourable developments in the external environment and within a framework of macroeconomic prudence.

At the national level, Governments needed to maintain a strong commitment to macroeconomic balance, streamline and rationalize public spending, improve revenue collection, enhance domestic savings, deepen and widen financial markets, and help domestic businesses through improved information on alternative markets and ways to diversify.

At the subregional level, Governments should consult more frequently on a wider range of policy questions, particularly on the implementation of regional trading arrangements and the maintenance of market access. An issue of particular concern was the problem of weak stock markets in the region. A related problem was the slow progress in many countries in financial and corporate restructuring, especially the difficultly of resolving non-performing loans in the banking systems of several countries. That restructuring needed to be accelerated with time-bound targets and relevant institutions and procedures, such as debt-recovery agencies and the strengthening of bankruptcy courts.

ESCAP, at its 2000 session, considered reports on the current economic situation in the region and related policy issues [E/ESCAP/1157] and on development through globalization and partnership in the twenty-first century: an Asia-Pacific perspective for integrating developing countries and economies in transition into the international trading system on a fair and equitable basis [E/ESCAP/1158].

The Commission noted that many ESCAP countries remained highly dependent on and vulnerable to the external environment and stressed the need for strengthening the preventive approach. It emphasized the urgency of integrating the developing countries at the regional and global levels through improvements in their technological levels, and for LDCs to move effectively in that direction. The Commission urged ESCAP to continue its technical assistance in private sector development and to promote foreign direct investment in disadvantaged economies in the region, paying particular attention to strengthening the legal and institutional framework of those economies. It also urged the secretariat to continue to act as the regional centre for the promotion of poverty eradication and to assist developing countries in integrating more effectively into the multilateral trading system, especially those seeking World Trade Organization (WTO) membership.

As requested in 1999 [YUN 1999, p. 925], the secretariat undertook research on economic and financial monitoring and surveillance in the ESCAP region, including a review of existing monitoring and early warning systems within different international bodies.

The Commission noted that there were several ongoing monitoring and surveillance initiatives in the region and that it was necessary to build on them, to identify the most appropriate mechanism applicable and to widen that coverage.

Activities in 2000

ESCAP activities in 2000 were carried out under six thematic subprogrammes: regional economic cooperation; environment and sustainable development; poverty alleviation through economic and social development; transport and communications; statistics; and least developed, landlocked and island developing countries.

Development policy and regional economic cooperation

ESCAP in 2000 had before it a report on the implementation of its 1999 resolution on economic and financial monitoring and surveillance [YUN 1999, p. 925], which contained the study on that subject [E/ESCAP/1162]; a note on emerging issues relevant to the subprogramme on regional economic cooperation [E/ESCAP/1161]; and the report of the eleventh meeting of the Steering Group of the Committee on Regional Economic Cooperation [YUN 1999, p. 926].

The study revealed significant scope for regional cooperation in the area. Recommendations for future action ranged from informal exchanges of experience within the region to the establishment of formal surveillance systems at the subregional level. The Commission took note of the study and endorsed the recommendations for action by ESCAP.

The Commission also endorsed the major recommendations, conclusions and decisions of the Steering Group. It noted that the 1997 economic crisis underscored the need to reform the international financial architecture and agreed that regional cooperation needed to be strengthened to avoid or minimize any future financial crisis. It requested the secretariat to study the development impact of regional trading arrangements on their members, the harmonization of standards and the role of developing countries in international standard-setting bodies, including a comparative analysis of rules of origin under various regional trading arrangements. The twelfth meeting of the Steering Group was held in Inchon City, Republic of Korea, from 25 to 27 October.

The Commission requested that the secretariat continue to accord high priority to its technical assistance activities in policy analysis related to regional and multilateral liberalization, WTO accession, and training on the implementation of WTO agreements. It reiterated the importance of trade facilitation and stressed the need for capacity-building in that area. The Commission noted the importance of information technology and electronic commerce as catalysts for the integration of developing countries, in particular Pacific island countries and landlocked countries, into the international trading system. In that regard, the Commission adopted a resolution on the Decade of Greater Mekong Subregion Development Cooperation, 2000-2009 [E/2000/39 (res. 56/1)].

On 25 July [meeting 39], the Economic and Social Council, on the recommendation of ESCAP [E./2000/10/Add.3], adopted **resolution 2000/5** without vote [agenda item 10].

Decade of Greater Mekong Subregion Development Cooperation, 2000-2009

The Economic and Social Council,

Recalling the responsibility of the Economic and Social Commission for Asia and the Pacific for initiating and participating in measures for facilitating concerted action for the economic reconstruction and development of Asia and the Pacific, and for raising the level of economic activity in Asia and the Pacific,

Noting the large membership and diverse needs of the region, and considering it essential for the secretariat of the Commission to sharpen the focus of its programme of work so as to support subregional initiatives and enhance the effectiveness and efficiency of programmes established at the subregional level,

Acknowledging the importance of having a concerted strategy and close coordination among member countries of the Commission region and the relevant development agencies, as well as the development frameworks concerned, to promote cooperation among the countries of the Greater Mekong subregion in enhancing economic and social development and poverty alleviation in the area,

Recognizing the need to strengthen the capacity of the countries in the Greater Mekong subregion as a means of helping to narrow the large development gap between countries in the region,

Noting with appreciation the contribution made by the secretariat to various development programmes in the Commission region, including the Greater Mekong subregion, and the high level of support extended to the secretariat in that endeavour by other concerned United Nations bodies and the specialized agencies,

Welcoming the statement of the Ninth Conference on the Programme of Economic Cooperation in the Greater Mekong Subregion, held in Manila on 13 January 2000, and in particular the determination expressed by the ministers to redouble their initiatives to accelerate, strengthen and extend regional cooperation within the subregion,

Noting with appreciation the continued financial support given by United Nations bodies, the specialized agencies and the Asian Development Bank to a number of development programmes for countries in the subregion under the Greater Mekong subregion framework, some of which have been undertaken in collaboration with the secretariat,

Recognizing the important role played by the Mekong River Commission, which is now implementing, through its secretariat, the Agreement on the Cooperation for the Sustainable Development of the Mekong River Basin of 5 April 1995, in pursuance of an economically and socially just and environmentally sound Mekong River basin,

1. _Calls upon_ the concerned regional members and associate members:

_(a)_ To reaffirm their commitment to the development programmes in the Greater Mekong subregion through existing bodies, including the Mekong River Commission;

_(b)_ To review jointly the existing development strategies with a view to developing a more concerted and rational approach that could respond effectively to the challenges of globalization while avoiding duplication of efforts in the development of the Greater Mekong subregion;

_(c)_ To continue to work closely together to ensure that development cooperation in the Greater Mekong subregion is being pursued in a complementary manner;

_(d)_ To formulate the development programmes in such a way that the private sector is encouraged to support them;

2. _Proclaims_ the Decade of Greater Mekong Subregion Development Cooperation, 2000-2009, in order to draw the attention of the international community to the intensification of economic and social development in the subregion and to encourage its support thereof;

3. _Requests_ the General Assembly to endorse the present resolution and to encourage, at the global level, support for its implementation;

4. _Urges_ member countries, and international and intergovernmental organizations and institutions, to strengthen cooperation with and assistance to Greater Mekong subregion development programmes;

5. _Encourages_ donor Governments and agencies, regional and international financial institutions, United Nations bodies and specialized agencies, nongovernmental organizations and the private sector to assist countries in the Greater Mekong subregion in their capacity-building to enable them to integrate effectively into the regional and global economy;

6. _Requests_ the Executive Secretary of the Economic and Social Commission for Asia and the Pacific:

_(a)_ To help to mobilize the necessary resources to provide technical assistance and assistance in other areas that may be deemed necessary, upon the request of various Greater Mekong subregion development frameworks, in particular in such key sectors as human resources development, trade and investment, transportation and communications, poverty alleviation and social development;

_(b)_ To call necessary meetings among the parties concerned to design a work programme for the development of the Greater Mekong subregion with the aim of achieving a tangible result in the given period;

7. _Also requests_ the Executive Secretary to monitor the overall programmes of various framework activities in order to report to the Commission at its annual sessions and to all concerned member countries, and to evaluate the implementation of the programmes every three years until the end of the Decade.

On 20 December, the General Assembly endorsed Council resolution 2000/5 (**decision 55/447**).

Least developed, landlocked and island developing countries

Special Body on Pacific Island Developing Countries

The Commission endorsed the recommendations in the report of the Special Body on Pacific Island Developing Countries on its sixth session (Bangkok, 30-31 May) [E/ESCAP/ 1184] on transport and tourism issues and on children's welfare issues in Pacific island countries, and recommended that ESCAP activities in those areas be extended to least developed and landlocked countries.

It urged the secretariat to strengthen the ESCAP Pacific Operations Centre, especially in development planning, economic policy, social development, transport, physical planning and water supply, small business development, trade policy and environmental and sustainable development. It suggested that ecotourism issues be included in the agenda of the seventh session of the Special Body.

In addition, the Commission, in a resolution on the promotion of a sustainable energy future for small island States [E/2000/39 (res. 56/4)], requested the ESCAP Executive Secretary to facilitate the exchange of experiences and information on the efficient use of energy and the enhanced application of renewable energy technologies for small island States; to convene an expert meeting to develop pilot and demonstration projects in small island States; to assist in securing the resources for the programme's implementation; to support national and subregional training and capacity-building initiatives for the promotion of renewable energy and its efficient use; and to report to the Special Body and the Commission in 2002.

Landlocked States in Central Asia

In August [A/55/320], the Secretary-General transmitted to the General Assembly the report of the UNCTAD Secretary-General on the transit environment in the landlocked States in Central Asia and their transit developing neighbours, in response to Assembly resolution 53/171 [YUN 1998, p. 932]. The report discussed the economic recovery and the emerging trade and transit patterns of Central Asia, including alternative transit transport corridors; physical infrastructure bottlenecks and developments to improve physical infrastructure; measures to overcome non-physical barriers to the available transit transport corridors; and a framework for better coordination and cooperation.

GENERAL ASSEMBLY ACTION

On 20 December [meeting 87], the General Assembly, on the recommendation of the Second (Economic and Financial) Committee [A/55/579/Add.1], adopted **resolution 55/181** without vote [agenda item 92 (a)].

Transit environment in the landlocked States in Central Asia and their transit developing neighbours

The General Assembly,

Recalling its resolutions 48/169 and 48/170 of 21 December 1993, 49/102 of 19 December 1994, 51/168 of 16 December 1996, 53/171 of 15 December 1998 and 55/2 of 8 September 2000,

Recalling also the Global Framework for Transit Transport Cooperation between Landlocked and Transit Developing Countries and the Donor Community and other relevant international legal instruments,

Recognizing that the overall socio-economic development efforts of the landlocked States in Central Asia, seeking to enter world markets through the establishment of a multicountry transit system, are impeded by a lack of territorial access to the sea and by remoteness and isolation from world markets as well as by a lack of adequate infrastructure in the transport sector in their transit developing neighbours owing to their economic problems,

Reaffirming that transit States, in the exercise of full sovereignty over their territory, have the right to take all measures necessary to ensure that the rights and facilities provided for landlocked States in no way infringe upon their legitimate interests,

Expressing its support for the current efforts being undertaken by the newly independent and developing landlocked States in Central Asia and their transit developing neighbours, through relevant multilateral, bilateral and regional arrangements, to address issues regarding the development of a viable transit infrastructure in the region,

Taking note of the report prepared by the secretariat of the United Nations Conference on Trade and Development on the transit environment in the landlocked States in Central Asia and their transit developing neighbours, and considering that the problems of transit transport facing the Central Asian region need to be seen against the backdrop of increased trade and capital flows and advancement in technology in the region,

Recognizing that, to be effective, a transit transport strategy for the newly independent and developing landlocked States in Central Asia and their transit developing neighbours should incorporate actions that address both the problems inherent in the use of existing transit routes and those associated with the early development and smooth functioning of new alternative routes, and welcoming in this context the further cooperation of landlocked States with all interested countries,

Noting that there have been a number of important developments at the subregional and regional levels, including the signing at Almaty, Kazakhstan, on 9 May 1998, of a transit transport framework agreement among States members of the Economic Cooperation Organization, the signing on 26 March 1998 by the heads of State of Kazakhstan, Kyrgyzstan, Tajikistan and Uzbekistan, the Economic Commission for Europe and the Economic and Social Commission for Asia and the Pacific of the Tashkent Declaration on the United Nations Special Programme for the Economies of Central Asia, the implementation of the expanded Transport Corridor-Europe-Caucasus-Asia programme and the signing on 8 September 1998 of the Baku Declaration,

Welcoming the presentation of the United Nations Special Programme for the Economies of Central Asia, held at Almaty, Kazakhstan, on 27 April 2000, the adoption of the concept of the Special Programme and the joint statement by the Governments of Kazakhstan, Kyrgyzstan and Tajikistan, the Economic Commission for Europe and the Economic and Social Commission for Asia and the Pacific,

Emphasizing once again the importance of strengthening international support measures to address further the problems of the newly independent and developing landlocked States in Central Asia and their transit developing neighbours,

1. *Notes with appreciation* the contribution of the United Nations Conference on Trade and Development to improving the efficiency of the transit transport system in the landlocked States in Central Asia and their transit developing neighbours;

2. *Invites* the Secretary-General of the United Nations Conference on Trade and Development and the Governments concerned, in cooperation with the United Nations Development Programme, the Economic and Social Commission for Asia and the Pacific, the Economic Commission for Europe and relevant regional and international organizations and in accordance with approved programme priorities and within existing financial resources, to continue to elaborate a programme for improving the efficiency of the current transit environment in the newly independent and developing landlocked States in Central Asia and their transit developing neighbours;

3. *Invites* the United Nations Conference on Trade and Development, in close cooperation with the regional commissions within their respective mandates and current resources, as well as with other relevant international organizations, to provide technical assistance and advisory services to the newly independent landlocked States in Central Asia and their transit developing neighbours, taking into account the relevant transit transport agreements;

4. *Invites* donor countries and multilateral financial and development institutions, within their mandates, to continue to provide the newly independent and developing landlocked States in Central Asia and their transit developing neighbours with appropriate financial and technical assistance for the improvement of the transit environment, including construction, maintenance and improvement of their transport, storage and other transit-related facilities and improved communications;

5. *Calls upon* the United Nations system to continue to study, within the scope of the implementation of the present resolution, possible ways of promoting more cooperative arrangements between the landlocked States in Central Asia and their transit developing neighbours, and to encourage a more active supportive role on the part of the donor community;

6. *Requests* the Secretary-General of the United Nations Conference on Trade and Development, in close cooperation with the regional commissions, to prepare a report on the implementation of the present resolution, to be submitted to the General Assembly at its fifty-eighth session.

Economic and technical cooperation

In 2000, ESCAP received $14.8 million for technical cooperation activities, of which $4.2 million came from within the UN system and $10.6 million came from donor and participating developing countries and other intergovern-mental and non-governmental organizations [E/2001/39].

Bilateral donors and participating developing countries had contributed a total of $9.6 million for the ESCAP technical cooperation programme and the regional institutions. Japan remained the largest bilateral donor, followed by Germany, the Netherlands and the Republic of Korea. Twenty developing countries and associated members also contributed to the ESCAP technical cooperation programme, the largest donor being China, followed by India. In addition to cash contributions, donors and developing members provided about 305 work-months of the services of experts on non-reimbursable loan, which had enhanced the implementation capacity of the secretariat's technical cooperation programme. The secretariat initiated the implementation of 69 technical assistance projects with a financial outlay of $6.5 million.

Technical cooperation among developing countries

In 2000 [E/ESCAP/1221], the secretariat implemented about 100 promotional activities related to technical cooperation among developing countries and economic cooperation among developing countries (TCDC/ECDC). It also promoted and facilitated the participation of approximately 82 officials in 43 operational TCDC activities, including training, seminars, study visits and workshops. During the year, the secretariat continued to sensitize TCDC focal points of selected least developed, landlocked and island developing countries, as well as economies in transition. It conducted a workshop on TCDC national focal points for selected LDCs and disadvantaged economies in transition (Hangzhou, China, 13-17 November), in cooperation with China's Ministry of Foreign Trade and Economic Cooperation. In that regard, the Commission stated that countries should be assisted in building up the capacities and capabilities of TCDC national focal points and urged ESCAP to mobilize resources for that purpose.

Transport, communications, tourism and infrastructure development

The Commission had before it the report of the Committee on Transport, Communications, Tourism and Infrastructure Development on its second session [YUN 1999, p. 928] and endorsed the recommendations contained therein.

The third session of the Committee (Bangkok, 15-17 November) [E/ESCAP/1212] reaffirmed its commitment to the New Delhi Action Plan on Infrastructure Development in Asia and the Pacific (1997-2006) [YUN 1995, p. 1012] and identified priority areas for integration into the Plan's next phase. It adopted recommendations for action in the water transport sector, including the review of national positions on the new round of General Agreement on Trade in Services negotiations on maritime transport services, and of the viability and business plans of the national flag fleet, the promotion of sharing experience in private sector participation in ports, and the identification of approaches to attract both domestic and foreign tonnage to register under the national flag. The Committee reiterated that priority should be given to multimodal transport and tourism in the ESCAP programme. It recommended that the secretariat support national efforts to implement the Plan of Action for Sustainable Tourism Development in the Asian and Pacific Region [YUN 1999, p. 929].

Infrastructure development

The Commission reiterated its support for the priority status of the Asian land transport infrastructure development (ALTID) project. It endorsed the main thrust areas in the implementation of the project as reflected in the report on the implementation of its 1996 resolution [YUN 1996, p. 898] on intra-Asia and Asia-Europe land bridges [E/ESCAP/1179], the completion of the formulation of the Asian Highway and Trans-Asian Railway networks covering the whole of Asia, and the operationalization and improvement of the efficiency of international land transport corridors. The Commission stressed the importance of early completion of the study on the Trans-Asian Railway in the Northern Europe/Russian Federation/Persian Gulf corridor and the second ALTID project assessment to be carried out in 2001.

The Commission had before it a report on the implementation of the New Delhi Action Plan on Infrastructure Development [E/ESCAP/1180]. It endorsed the recommendation of the Committee on Transport, Communications, Tourism and Infrastructure Development that progress on all 64 projects within phase I of the Action Plan's programme be evaluated to provide a basis for the formulation and prioritization of phase II activities. The Commission emphasized the need to incorporate demand-driven, results-oriented and cost-effective activities in phase II and reaffirmed that high priority should be given to inland water transport. It stressed the importance of involving all the concerned agencies in the formulation of phase II.

The Commission endorsed themes for a ministerial conference on infrastructure to be held in 2001: transport infrastructure and logistics; administration, restructuring and private sector participation in the transport sector; sustainable transport development; social issues in transport development; and regional and subregional cooperation in sustainable energy development. The Commission requested that the impact of the rapidly changing maritime environment and the importance of multimodal transport and logistics in globalization should be given priority in the work programme. It also requested that issues related to HIV/AIDS in the transport sector be dealt with by the Joint United Nations Programme on HIV/AIDS and the World Health Organization, with the support of ESCAP's Transport, Communications, Tourism and Infrastructure Development Division.

Tourism

The Commission reaffirmed that tourism should continue to be accorded high priority in the secretariat's programme of work. It requested the secretariat to intensify activities to promote cooperation in tourism education and to strengthen activities in ecotourism. The secretariat should organize a seminar on the development of Buddhist tourism circuits, promote beach tourism and strengthen activities to promote tourism development in the Greater Mekong subregion.

The Commission asked the secretariat to support activities related to universal access to transport and tourism facilities for people with disabilities and the elderly. In that respect, it took note of Indonesia's organization, in cooperation with ESCAP, of the Asia-Pacific Conference on Tourism for People with Disability (Bali, Indonesia, September).

Science and technology

The Governing Board of the Asian and Pacific Centre for Transfer of Technology (APCTT) held its fifteenth session in Bali on 29 and 30 November [E/ESCAP/1203].

In 2000, APCTT organized 46 technology transfer–related events, including training programmes, regional workshops, exhibitions, seminars and expert group meetings. It arranged 800 business meetings between prospective technology suppliers and technology seekers, and facilitated 270 technology transfer negotiations per month.

The Commission endorsed the report on the Governing Board's fourteenth session [YUN 1999, p. 929] and requested APCTT to assist developing countries through technology transfer mechanisms as well as human resources development and training programmes so that the requisite capacities could be created for the transfer and adoption of new and modern technologies, including managerial and technical expertise. It urged the Centre to enhance its activities to assist small and medium-sized enterprises of developing member States in utilizing information and communication technology as a strategic tool to improve the competitiveness and profitability of those enterprises. In addition, member countries were urged to provide institutional support for APCTT and to adhere to the formula for establishing an endowment fund.

Environment and sustainable development

The Commission endorsed the recommendations of the Committee on Environment and Natural Resources Development at its second session [YUN 1999, p. 930], especially the recommendation that the secretariat continue the integration of environmental considerations into economic policy-making processes and its work on the strategic environmental initiative. The secretariat was requested to facilitate greater capacity-building in that regard, to continue to implement, at the regional level, Agenda 21, adopted by the United Nations Conference on Environment and Development (UNCED) [YUN 1992, p. 672], and to strengthen the integration of environmental considerations into its overall programme of work.

The Fourth Ministerial Conference on Environment and Development in Asia and the Pacific (Kitakyushu, Japan, 31 August–5 September) [E/ESCAP/1205] adopted the Regional Action Programme for Environmentally Sound and Sustainable Development, 2001-2005, the Ministerial Declaration on Environment and Development, the Regional Message for the 10-year Review of the Implementation of the Outcome of UNCED and the Kitakyushu Initiative for a Clean Environment. They were to guide the ESCAP programme on environment and natural resources development, in particular the development of a Kitakyushu Initiative Network for a Clean Environment and the regional preparations for the 2002 World Summit on Sustainable Development (see p. 792).

The Commission endorsed the report of the Second Ministerial Conference on Space Applications for Sustainable Development in Asia and the Pacific [YUN 1999, p. 930] and the launching of the second phase of the Regional Space Applications Programme for Sustainable Development. The Commission adopted a resolution on regional cooperation on space applications for sustainable development in Asia and the Pacific [E/2000/39 (res. 56/3)].

On 25 July [meeting 39], the Economic and Social Council, on the recommendation of ESCAP [E/2000/10/Add.3], adopted **resolution 2000/6** without vote [agenda item 10].

Regional cooperation on space applications for sustainable development in Asia and the Pacific

The Economic and Social Council,

Recalling Economic and Social Commission for Asia and the Pacific resolution 51/11 of 1 May 1995 on regional cooperation on space applications for environment and sustainable development in Asia and the Pacific, in which the Commission endorsed the recommendations of the First Ministerial Conference on Space Applications for Development in Asia and the Pacific, held in Beijing on 23 and 24 September 1994, and the Beijing Declaration on Space Technology Applications for Environmentally Sound and Sustainable Development in Asia and the Pacific,

Recalling also General Assembly resolution 51/123 of 13 December 1996 on international cooperation in the peaceful uses of outer space, in which the Assembly, inter alia, emphasized the need to increase the benefits of space technology and its applications and to contribute to an orderly growth of space activities favourable to sustainable development,

Recalling further the recommendations of the Third United Nations Conference on the Exploration and Peaceful Uses of Outer Space (UNISPACE III),

Recalling the decision of the Commission at its fifty-fifth session in April 1999 to hold the Second Ministerial Conference on Space Applications for Sustainable Development in Asia and the Pacific in New Delhi from 15 to 20 November 1999,

Noting with satisfaction the success of the Second Ministerial Conference, which adopted the Delhi Declaration on Space Technology Applications in Asia and the Pacific for Improved Quality of Life in the New Millennium and the Strategy and Action Plan on Space Technology Applications for Sustainable Development in Asia and the Pacific for the New Millennium and launched the second phase of the Regional Space Applications Programme for Sustainable Development,

Reiterating the strong interest of members and associate members of the Commission in participating in the cooperative activities that will emerge from the second phase of the Programme and their commitment to contributing to those activities,

Recognizing the essential role of space technologies and their applications in environment and natural resources management, food security and agricultural systems, capacity-building, human resources development and education, poverty alleviation, natural disaster reduction, health care and hygiene, and sustainable development planning towards improving the quality of life,

Recalling the efforts of the Commission in promoting space applications for sustainable development in the region and its commitment to continuing to play a pivotal and catalytic role in that regard,

1. *Endorses* the recommendations of the Second Ministerial Conference on Space Applications for Sustainable Development in Asia and the Pacific, held in New Delhi from 15 to 20 November 1999;

2. *Also endorses* the Delhi Declaration on Space Technology Applications in Asia and the Pacific for Improved Quality of Life in the New Millennium and the Strategy and Action Plan on Space Technology Applications for Sustainable Development in Asia and the Pacific for the New Millennium;

3. *Calls* for the early implementation of the Delhi Declaration, the Strategy and Action Plan, and other recommendations of the Second Ministerial Conference;

4. *Encourages* all members and associate members of the Economic and Social Commission for Asia and the Pacific to participate actively in the second phase of the Regional Space Applications Programme for Sustainable Development and to initiate effective national implementation of the Strategy and Action Plan;

5. *Recommends* that the Intergovernmental Consultative Committee on the Regional Space Applications Programme for Sustainable Development, under the purview of the Committee on Environment and Natural Resources Development of the Commission, advise as appropriate on the implementation of the Programme, and invites members and associate members to enhance their representation on the Consultative Committee;

6. *Invites* all United Nations bodies and agencies concerned, and multilateral donors and international agencies, to provide technical and financial support for the implementation of the recommendations of the Second Ministerial Conference, the Delhi Declaration and the Strategy and Action Plan envisaged for the second phase of the Programme;

7. *Requests* the Executive Secretary of the Economic and Social Commission for Asia and the Pacific:

(a) To accord due priority to the activities proposed in the Strategy and Action Plan and to incorporate the Programme in the biennial programmes of work;

(b) To strengthen the capability of the secretariat of the Commission, subject to the availability of resources, to support the regional cooperative network towards successful implementation of the Strategy and Action Plan;

(c) To mobilize resources for technical cooperation activities in line with the recommendations of the Second Ministerial Conference, the Delhi Declaration and the Strategy and Action Plan;

(d) To report to the Commission at its fifty-ninth session on the implementation of these recommendations.

Natural resources development

Energy and mineral resources

Having considered a secretariat note on emerging issues and developments related to mineral supply and land-use planning for sustainable development [E/ESCAP/1168 & Corr.1], the Commission endorsed the general statements and conclusions regarding those issues and invited further secretariat initiatives, such as seminars, workshops and individual and group training courses focusing on specific themes, skills development and institution-building. The secretariat was to convene a meeting of heads of National Geological Surveys in the region to formulate a strategy for mutual cooperation in sustainable mineral supply and land-use planning. It was also to promote the use of geoscientific information in land-use and urban planning and to continue training activities to improve the presentation skills of National Geological Survey departments, such as the preparation of user-friendly thematic maps.

In the area of energy resources, the Commission convened a High-level Regional Meeting on Energy for Sustainable Development (Bali, 21-24 November) [E/ESCAP/1206], which adopted the Sustainable Energy Development Action Programme, Strategies and Implementation Modalities for the Asian and Pacific Region, 2001-2005, and the Bali Declaration on Asia-Pacific Perspectives on Energy and Sustainable Development, for submission to the Commission on Sustainable Development in 2001.

Water resources

In 2000, important achievements and progress were made by the Mekong River Commission (MRC), established in 1995 [YUN 1995, p. 1017]. Financial resources were successfully mobilized for the three MRC core programmes, on water utilization, the environment and basin development. Ten studies were completed in 2000 and MRC continued implementation of other projects and activities under its work programme, which had recently been reorganized to comprise three categories of activities: a core programme, a support programme and a sector programme.

The Commission considered the MRC report on its 1999 activities [E/ESCAP/1192].

Agriculture and development

The Commission had before it the report on the Regional Coordination Centre for Research and Development of Coarse Grains, Pulses, Roots and Tuber Crops in the Humid Tropics of Asia and the Pacific [E/ESCAP/1171], which summarized major developments in 1999 and presented activities planned for 2000 and beyond, as endorsed by its Governing Board. It also contained a review of the financial status of the Centre.

The Commission recommended that the Centre strengthen collaborative programmes for research and development, as well as human resources development and information services. It expressed concern over the continuing unstable condition of the Centre's institutional and programme support resources and urged a substantial increase in funding and early and timely allocation of funds, as well as the provision of the services of experts to ensure the effective implementation of programme activities. The ESCAP secretariat was asked to explore more funding sources to stabilize the Centre's financial situation.

The Commission noted the deliberations and recommendations of the nineteenth session of the Governing Body of the Regional Network for Agricultural Machinery (RNAM) [YUN 1999, p. 931]. It directed the secretariat to continue seeking extrabudgetary contributions for the programmes for 2000-2001 and approved the expansion of RNAM activities in post-harvest technologies and those designed to take advantage of leading-edge technologies. The Commission approved the Governing Body's recommendation that the new name for RNAM should be the Regional Network for Agricultural Engineering and Machinery (RNAEM).

The Governing Body of RNAEM, at its twentieth session [E/ESCAP/1204] (Rongcheng, China, 19-21 October), approved the extension of the project into its seventh phase, for the period 1999-2001.

Social development

The Commission considered the report of the Committee on Socio-economic Measures to Alleviate Poverty in Rural and Urban Areas on its second session [YUN 1999, p. 932], as well as a secretariat note on progress in implementing resolutions and decisions on the topic [E/ESCAP/1170].

The Commission noted that unemployment rates and the incidence of poverty remained relatively high in those countries adversely affected by the recent economic crisis. It said various targeted programmes by Governments and community-based organizations should be continued and strengthened, while more broad-based growth policies should be pursued for lower-income groups. The Commission stressed ways in which the secretariat could assist Governments to alleviate poverty, including monitoring socio-economic trends, conducting a regional study on national poverty alleviation programmes to document successful approaches, and bringing information on best practices and successful approaches to the attention of Governments. The secretariat was to carry out a regional assessment of social safety-net programmes and set priorities in its programme of work on poverty alleviation to enhance the impact of its activities.

Also before the Commission was a secretariat note on the empowerment of the rural poor through decentralization in poverty alleviation actions [E/ESCAP/1172]. The Commission noted re-

forms in a number of countries to alleviate rural poverty by improving governance through the devolution of authority and responsibility, but there had been no systematic documentation of lessons learned. It urged that the secretariat do more to learn from success cases and best practices and disseminate them more widely. It also urged the secretariat to undertake follow-up activities on interrelationships among governance, decentralization and rural poverty alleviation and the empowerment of the rural poor through decentralization, to assign priorities to its activities and to focus on population trends, rural development and the alleviation of poverty.

The Commission endorsed the report of the Senior Officials' Meeting on the Agenda for Action on Social Development in the ESCAP Region [YUN 1999, p. 931]. It expressed concern over the negative effects in many ESCAP countries of globalization and structural adjustment programmes that neglected to integrate social dimensions, and highlighted the need for a framework of principles and examples of good practice concerning social policy and social development that would promote a more humane and equitable development path that was more resilient to external shock. The Commission emphasized the need for targeted social protection and social justice measures for vulnerable groups, and the need for the effectiveness of social safety-net programmes as a poverty alleviation measure to be reviewed and strengthened.

At its third session (Bangkok, 6-8 December) [E/ESCAP/1208], the Committee on Socio-economic Measures to Alleviate Poverty in Rural and Urban Areas recommended that countries suffering from population pressure and high population growth should accelerate efforts to stabilize their populations using a holistic approach. Also, a High-level Regional Meeting for Asia and the Pacific in Preparation for Istanbul+5, which was to review and appraise the implementation of the Habitat Agenda, adopted by the United Nations Conference on Human Settlements (Habitat II) [YUN 1996, p. 992], was held in Hangzhou, China, from 19 to 23 October [E/ESCAP/1209].

Disabled persons

The Commission considered a secretariat note on equalization of opportunities and the inclusion of disabled persons in the development process [E/ESCAP/1176]. It endorsed the 107 strengthened targets for action on the implementation of the Agenda for Action for the Asian and Pacific Decade of Disabled Persons, 1993-2002 [YUN 1993, p. 621], as revised by the ESCAP forum on the subject [YUN 1999, p. 932]. It noted that those targets had been adopted by regional meetings on the education of disabled children and youth and equalization of opportunities for disabled persons. The Commission requested the secretariat to strengthen its assistance to ESCAP members in support of the targets.

International Year of Older Persons (1999)

The Commission endorsed the guidelines on the implementation of the Macao Plan of Action on Ageing for Asia and the Pacific [YUN 1998, p. 942], as contained in a secretariat note [E/ESCAP/1174], and emphasized the need to implement the Plan of Action in consonance with the guidelines. It asked the secretariat to continue providing technical assistance and support to implement the Plan at the national and regional levels and to organize more training activities and information exchange forums on issues relating to ageing.

The Commission noted the successful observance in the ESCAP region in 1999 of the International Year of Older Persons, proclaimed by the General Assembly in resolution 47/5 [YUN 1992, p. 889]. In a report on the observance of the Year and on progress in the implementation of the Macao Plan of Action [E/ESCAP/1175], it was indicated that national agencies and mechanisms on ageing, as well as national focal points, had been established in many countries of the region. The Commission asked the secretariat to play an active part in regional preparation for the Second World Assembly on Ageing in 2002 (see p. 1140).

Women in development

The Commission endorsed the report of the High-level Intergovernmental Meeting to Review Regional Implementation of the Beijing Platform for Action [YUN 1999, p. 933]. It urged the secretariat to strengthen activities in advancing the status of women. It noted the initiatives taken to promote the economic situation of women and recommended that target-oriented self-employment and income-generating projects should continue to be implemented for women in poverty, particularly displaced women, widows and female heads of household. The Commission noted that protection and respect of women's human rights were a concern in the region and that countries had adopted awareness-raising measures, provided greater legal protection for women against violence, and promoted their increased participation in the decision-making process. The Commission recommended that special attention be paid to the girl child and women in difficult circumstances and emphasized the need for cooperation and coordination in dealing with trafficking in women and children.

Human resources development

On 7 June [E/2000/39 (res. 56/2)], the Commission acknowledged the successful implementation of phases I, II and III of the Jakarta Plan of Action on Human Resources Development in the ESCAP Region, adopted by the Commission in 1988 [YUN 1988, p. 282] and revised in 1994 [YUN 1994, p. 715]. It called on ESCAP members and associate members to strengthen national policies to advance human resources development and to review human resources strategies with a view to developing new approaches to respond more effectively to the challenges and opportunities of globalization and a knowledge-based and information-based society. The Commission encouraged donors, regional and international financial institutions, UN bodies and specialized agencies, non-governmental organizations (NGOs) and the private sector to assist developing countries to develop their human resources and to build and strengthen national capacity. In its recommendations to the Executive Secretary, the Commission asked that priority be accorded to the implementation of phase IV (2001-2005) of the Jakarta Plan of Action, the focus of which should be on building a stronger foundation in the region in education, health and sustainable livelihoods.

Natural disasters

The Commission, having considered the report of the Typhoon Committee [E/ESCAP/1193], noted the important progress and achievements made in 1999 on meteorological observations, forecasts and warnings; hydrological components, including improvements in flood forecasts and warning, as well as storm surge forecasts; and natural disaster reduction. It took particular note of the increased importance attached by the Committee to addressing the impacts of water-related disasters, including an increase in research on and the improvement of forecasts.

The Commission also considered the report of the Panel on Tropical Cyclones [E/ESCAP/1194], including the recommendations adopted at its twenty-seventh session (Muscat, Oman, 29 February-6 March). The Commission urged donor countries and institutions, as well as the ESCAP secretariat, to support the work of the Panel. It noted that a trust fund had been established with the World Meteorological Organization for the activities of the Panel and encouraged Panel members and other ESCAP members to contribute to the fund.

Statistics

The Commission examined a secretariat note on emerging issues and developments in statistics [E/ESCAP/1181]. Recognizing that the secretariat's statistical activities had assisted in strengthening the statistical capabilities of the countries in the region, it suggested that advisory services and co-operation should be strengthened in areas identified by the Bureau of the Committee on Statistics. The Commission also recognized the urgent need to develop a sound conceptual and methodological framework for the measurement of electronic commerce and endorsed the suggestion of the Working Group of Statistical Experts that a discussion group on the subject should be formed to facilitate the sharing of experience and the establishment of uniform measurement tools. It suggested that ESCAP should continue to play a coordinating role in gender statistics in the region and to promote the exchange of experience among member countries. It also suggested that its Committee on Statistics contribute to the establishment of standards on urban and rural poverty measures and that ESCAP should play a coordinating role in improving environment statistics in the region.

The Commission had before it the report of the fifth session of the Governing Board of the Statistical Institute for Asia and the Pacific (SIAP) (Tokyo, 6-8 October 1999) [E/ESCAP/1182]. The Commission supported the Institute's 2000-2001 work programme, as well as the long-term (2000-2005) programme, and urged ESCAP members and associate members to support the further implementation of the programme. It requested SIAP to expand its training programme and strengthen training in information technology. The Commission noted that the overall cash contribution to SIAP had declined in the past two years.

The Commission considered a secretariat note on the year 2000 computer problem [E/ESCAP/1183] and decided that since the transition had been smoother than expected and interest in the problem had reduced, the second follow-up report requested for 2001 had become unnecessary.

The ESCAP Committee on Statistics held its twelfth session in Bangkok (29 November–1 December) [E/ESCAP/1214].

Programme and organizational questions

The Commission endorsed the ESCAP draft medium-term plan for 2002-2005 [E/ESCAP/1185/Rev.1] with some amendments. It recommended that ESCAP make continuous efforts towards capacity-building in the region and be more re-sponsive to the challenges and opportunities presented by globalization and the knowledge-based economy. It directed the secretariat to define more clearly expected accomplishments and programme indicators when formulating the 2002-2005 programme budgets.

The Commission considered a secretariat note on the implementation of the programme of work for the 1998-1999 biennium [E/ESCAP/1186 & Corr.1]. It noted that outputs and the level of programme implementation were satisfactory despite the reduced level of resources and the 15 per cent average vacancy rate in the Professional and higher categories. The Commission endorsed the programme of work for 2000-2001 and the proposed changes to that programme [E/ESCAP/1187]. It approved the tentative calendar of meetings and training programmes for the period April 2000 to March 2001 [E/ESCAP/1188] and adopted a resolution on the impending retirement of Adrianus Mooy, Executive Secretary of ESCAP [E/2000/39 (res. 56/5)].

ESCAP reform

The Commission had before it the Executive Secretary's report [E/ESCAP/1159] on the implementation of a 1997 Commission resolution on ESCAP reform [YUN 1997, p. 993]. The Commission noted the various constraints on the effective performance of its subsidiary structure, including the broad coverage of certain legislative committees which had led to less focused discussions. It recommended that deliberations focus more on the needs of member countries, and that coordination and synergy within the secretariat be improved.

Also before the Commission was the report of the Advisory Committee of Permanent Representatives and Other Representatives Designated by Members of the Commission (ACPR) and its Open-ended Informal Working Group [E/ESCAP/1195 & Add.1,2]; the latter had reconvened to assist ACPR in its work on ESCAP reform. The Commission endorsed the Working Group's proposals and urged that they be implemented as part of the reform process to strengthen ESCAP's core competence and its role in the region.

Admission of Georgia

The Commission endorsed the application of Georgia to become a member of ESCAP [E/ESCAP/1156] and approved a draft resolution for submission to the Economic and Social Council.

ECONOMIC AND SOCIAL COUNCIL ACTION

On 25 July [meeting 39], the Economic and Social Council, on the recommendation of ESCAP [E/2000/

10/Add.3], adopted **resolution 2000/4** without vote [agenda item 10].

Amendment of the terms of reference of the Economic and Social Commission for Asia and the Pacific: inclusion of Georgia in the geographical scope of the Commission and its admission as a member of the Commission

The Economic and Social Council,

Noting the recommendation of the Economic and Social Commission for Asia and the Pacific that Georgia be included in the geographical scope of the Commission and be admitted as a member of the Commission,

1. *Approves* the recommendation of the Economic and Social Commission for Asia and the Pacific that Georgia be included in the geographical scope of the Commission and admitted as a member of the Commission;

2. *Decides* to amend paragraphs 2 and 3 of the terms of reference of the Commission accordingly.

Change of spelling of Macau

By **decision 2000/210** of 4 February, the Economic and Social Council amended paragraphs 2 and 4 of ESCAP's terms of reference by changing the English-language spelling of "Macau, China" to "Macao, China".

Subregional activities

Cooperation between the United Nations and the Economic Cooperation Organization

In response to General Assembly resolution 54/100 [YUN 1999, p. 935], the Secretary-General reported in July on cooperation between the United Nations and the Economic Cooperation Organization (ECO) [A/55/122]. The report described the cooperative relationship of ECO with UNDP, UNCTAD, the United Nations Population Fund (UNFPA), the United Nations International Drug Control Programme, the Food and Agriculture Organization of the United Nations (FAO) and ESCAP.

GENERAL ASSEMBLY ACTION

On 21 November [meeting 70], the General Assembly adopted **resolution 55/42** [draft: A/55/L.22/Rev.1] without vote [agenda item 28].

Cooperation between the United Nations and the Economic Cooperation Organization

The General Assembly,

Recalling its resolution 48/2 of 13 October 1993, by which it granted observer status to the Economic Cooperation Organization,

Recalling also the resolutions previously adopted by the General Assembly on cooperation between the United Nations and the Economic Cooperation Organization, and inviting various specialized agencies and other organizations and programmes of the United Nations system and relevant international fi-

nancial institutions to join in their efforts towards implementation of economic programmes and projects of the Economic Cooperation Organization,

Bearing in mind the progress attained by the Economic Cooperation Organization in its reorganizational endeavours as well as in launching and implementing various regional development projects and programmes over the past decade,

Welcoming the endeavours of the Economic Cooperation Organization in regard to consolidating its ties with the United Nations system and with relevant international and regional organizations towards the furtherance of its objectives,

Taking note of the Tehran Declaration issued at the sixth summit meeting of the heads of State or Government of the States members of the Economic Cooperation Organization, held in Tehran on 10 June 2000,

Taking note with appreciation of the decision of the Economic Cooperation Organization at its sixth summit meeting to welcome the initiative of Mohammad Khatami, President of the Islamic Republic of Iran, on dialogue among civilizations, the United Nations having designated 2001 as the United Nations Year of Dialogue among Civilizations, in order to promote this concept through planning and implementation of appropriate cultural, educational and social activities in the regional and global context,

Recalling that one of the main objectives of the United Nations and the Economic Cooperation Organization is to promote international cooperation in solving international problems of an economic, social, cultural or humanitarian character,

Expressing grave concern over the human casualties caused by natural disasters and their devastating impact on the socio-economic situation of some States members of the Economic Cooperation Organization,

Noting with appreciation the decision of the Economic Cooperation Organization to hold ministerial-level meetings in the areas of energy, agriculture, industry and human development,

1. *Takes note with appreciation* of the report of the Secretary-General on the implementation of General Assembly resolution 54/100 of 9 December 1999, and expresses satisfaction at the enhanced pace of mutually beneficial interaction between the two organizations;

2. *Stresses* the importance of cooperation between the United Nations system and the Economic Cooperation Organization to address the challenges and opportunities of globalization in the region of the Economic Cooperation Organization by promoting the integration of States members of the Economic Cooperation Organization, as appropriate, into the world economy, particularly in areas of concern to States members of the Economic Cooperation Organization, inter alia, trade, finance and transfer of technology;

3. *Notes* the holding of ministerial-level meetings in the transport and communications sector and in commerce/foreign trade, which, inter alia, resulted in the adoption of annexes to the Economic Cooperation Organization Transit Transport Framework Agreement and a framework agreement on trade, respectively;

4. *Welcomes* the signing of a memorandum of understanding between the Economic Cooperation Organization and the United Nations Conference on Trade and Development in November 1999, and expresses the hope that their mutual cooperation will add

impetus to the ongoing trade/transit trade and transport arrangements in the region of the Economic Cooperation Organization;

5. *Notes with satisfaction* the increasing cooperation between the Economic Cooperation Organization and the World Trade Organization which has accorded observer status to the former, and the increasing involvement of the Economic Cooperation Organization in the relevant forums and ministerial conferences of the World Trade Organization, and also notes the holding of joint Economic Cooperation Organization and World Trade Organization seminars on trade negotiation simulation;

6. *Welcomes* the growing cooperation between the Economic Cooperation Organization and relevant international financial institutions, such as the World Bank and the Islamic Development Bank, in particular the financial assistance extended by the latter in the fields of transport, trade, energy and agriculture;

7. *Expresses satisfaction* at the regional arrangements made by the States members of the Economic Cooperation Organization for transporting the oil and gas of the region to different parts of the world;

8. *Welcomes* the holding of a joint Economic Cooperation Organization and United Nations Population Fund Conference on Expanding Contraceptive Choice and Improving Quality of Reproductive Health Programmes, held in Istanbul in May 2000, and calls upon the Fund and other relevant United Nations entities, in cooperation with the Economic Cooperation Organization, to continue activities in the field of public health and social development in the future;

9. *Notes* the increasing problem of the production, transit and abuse of narcotic drugs and their ill effects in the region, expresses its appreciation for the operations of the joint Economic Cooperation Organization and United Nations International Drug Control Programme project on a drug control coordination unit established within the secretariat of the Economic Cooperation Organization in July 1999, and calls upon the other international and regional organizations to assist, as appropriate, the Economic Cooperation Organization in its efforts against the drug menace in the region of that organization;

10. *Also notes* the expansion of cultural ties in the region under the aegis of the Cultural Institute of the Economic Cooperation Organization, and requests support for efforts to promote, and promote awareness of, the rich cultural and literary heritage of the region of the Economic Cooperation Organization through the launching of appropriate projects and programmes dealing with, inter alia, the issues regarding the initiative of President Khatami on dialogue among civilizations, with possible assistance from the United Nations Educational, Scientific and Cultural Organization and other relevant entities;

11. *Invites* the United Nations system, its relevant bodies and the international community to continue to provide technical assistance, as appropriate, to the States members of the Economic Cooperation Organization and its secretariat in strengthening their early warning system, preparedness, capacity for timely response and rehabilitation with a view to reducing the incidence of human casualties and mitigating the socio-economic impact of natural disasters;

12. *Requests* the Secretary-General to submit to the General Assembly at its fifty-sixth session a report on the implementation of the present resolution;

13. *Decides* to include in the provisional agenda of its fifty-sixth session the item entitled "Cooperation between the United Nations and the Economic Cooperation Organization".

Europe

The Economic Commission for Europe (ECE), at its fifty-fifth session (Geneva, 3-5 May) [E/2000/37], focused on increasing regional cooperation within the ECE region, its operational activities and a number of cross-sectoral concerns.

As called for in the Plan of Action on the Strengthening of Economic Cooperation in Europe [YUN 1997, p. 1002], the ECE secretariat organized a debate on the economic regeneration of South-East Europe. Discussions centred on supporting the transition process of the economies of South-East Europe using regional cooperation to overcome some of their key problems, and on whether strategies for economic policy and regional cooperation could ignore the political context.

The Commission reviewed ECE's operational activities and agreed that priority should continue to be given to requests for assistance from the most vulnerable transition economies, particularly those from the Commonwealth of Independent States (CIS) and the Balkan countries. It agreed that ways to strengthen the Coordinating Unit for Operational Activities should be explored and that the secretariat should evaluate operational projects to help it prioritize its work. The Commission encouraged countries to include ECE on their list of eligible institutions for funding and the secretariat to renew efforts to attract funds from public and private sources.

In the context of its consideration of cross-sectoral and intersectoral concerns, the Commission was updated on development with the participation of the chairpersons of the principal subsidiary bodies (PSBs). It agreed to initiate, on a regular basis, debates and possible action on cross-sectoral concerns and intersectoral issues. The Commission supported ECE involvement with the business community and agreed that such cooperation should continue along the lines suggested in a note by the Executive Secretary [E/ECE/1377]. It decided that the Group of Experts on the Programme of Work should take up the issues outlined in that paper and highlighted at the meeting, in particular the development of guidelines and procedures for facilitating public/private partnership. The PSBs were requested to examine issues, such as strengthening the involvement of small and medium-sized enterprises in ECE activities.

The Commission supported the conclusions agreed at the ECE regional preparatory meeting for the 2000 review of the implementation of the Beijing Platform for Action [YUN 1995, p. 1170], which constituted the region's input to the global review process (see p. 1082). As a follow-up to the International Year of Older Persons [YUN 1999, p. 1124], the Commission decided to convene a ministerial conference on ageing in Berlin, Germany, in September 2002.

The Commission agreed to look into the resource implications arising from ECE's contribution to global events and issues, including strengthening the Office of the Executive Secretary. Taking into account the limited resources available to the ECE secretariat, the Commission agreed that any new mandate should be supported by the necessary additional budgetary resources from the body delivering the mandate.

The Commission endorsed the recommendation of the Group of Experts on the Programme of Work [E/ECE/1380] that, in deciding that biennialization would currently not be in ECE's best interests, the Commission should request the Group to consider whether any improvements should be made to the format of the Commission's annual session; any recommendations arising from such deliberations should be submitted to an ad hoc informal meeting of the Commission.

Economic trends

According to the *Economic Survey of Europe, 2000* [Sales No. E.00.II.E.28], the strengthening of global economic activity in 1999 continued in the first half of 2000, as the international business cycle gained more momentum than was expected at the beginning of the year. That favourable performance was due largely to the continued rapid expansion of the United States economy, leading to a very strong growth in import demand and the strengthening of cyclical growth forces in developed and developing countries. The dynamism of the world economy also stimulated domestic activity in Western Europe and the transition economies of Central and Eastern Europe. As a result of closer economic linkages within the region, foreign trade also led to mutually reinforcing economic growth between Western and Eastern Europe. However, there were indications in the latter months of the year that the global business cycle had passed its peak, as evidenced by the further tightening of monetary policy in the United States and Western Europe during 2000 and the unexpectedly sharp and sustained rise in international oil prices.

Western Europe and North America

In the United States, economic activity continued to increase at a brisk rate in the first half of 2000 with demand outpacing supply, but it slowed down more abruptly than expected in the third quarter. Real GDP rose only 0.7 per cent, compared with 1.4 per cent in the preceding quarter. The cyclical downturn had already been signalled by the Purchasing Managers' Index, which fell below the threshold of 50 per cent in August and September, and the decline in the composite leading indicators since May and in capacity utilization rates in manufacturing in the third quarter. Export growth remained strong, but the growth of imports slowed down somewhat in the third quarter.

Inflation edged upwards in 2000, mainly because of higher energy prices. The annual inflation rate was 3.5 per cent in September, while core inflation was 2.6 per cent, compared with 1.9 per cent at the beginning of the year. Higher labour costs were offset by sizeable gains in productivity. Non-farm employment increased in the first two quarters and again in September, when the unemployment rate fell to a very low 3.9 per cent.

The current account deficit rose to $425 billion in the second quarter, corresponding to 4.3 per cent of GDP, compared to an average of 3.7 per cent of GDP in 1999. Tax revenues continued to outpace government expenditures, and the federal budget surplus rose by $100 billion to $237 billion, or just over 2 per cent of GDP in fiscal 2000. The target for the federal funds rate was raised by half a percentage point to 6.5 per cent in May. Since then, it had been left unchanged, reflecting the conviction that the economy was heading for a "soft landing". Short-term interest rates in the money market responded to that tightening of monetary policy and fell slightly in the third quarter.

In Western Europe, the business cycle maintained strong momentum in the first half of 2000. Real GDP during that period was 3.4 per cent higher than a year earlier, with exports of goods and services continuing to be the main sources of growth. Domestic demand remained strong in the first half of 2000, but its rate of expansion did not accelerate. Private consumption was supported by gains in aggregate real incomes associated with rising employment, but the growth of real disposable incomes was checked by the sharp rise in energy prices, which put some pressure on consumer prices. The relatively strong growth of domestic demand led to a considerable rise in imports. In 2000, price developments were strongly influenced by the large increase in crude oil prices, and the continuing decline of the euro placed further upward pressure on import prices; both factors accounted for much of the pronounced increases in aggregate import and producer prices. The average inflation rate for the first nine months of 2000 was 2.2 per cent, although in the euro area it ranged from 2.2 per cent in Austria to 5.5 per cent in Ireland. Employment was expected to increase by 1.6 per cent, the same as in 1999. Against the backdrop of favourable trends in output and employment, the rate of unemployment fell in all countries, averaging 9 per cent in the euro area and 8.3 per cent in the EU.

The European Central Bank raised the main refinancing rate from 3 per cent to 4.75 per cent between February and October to check the potential effects of rising energy prices on inflationary expectations and to arrest and reverse the weakening of the euro in foreign exchange markets. The tightening of monetary policy was reflected in higher interest rates in the money and capital markets and in the lending rates of banks to enterprises and households.

Eastern Europe, Baltic States and CIS

According to the summary [E/2001/12] of the *Economic Survey of Europe, 2000*, for the first time since the start of their economic and political transformation, the former centrally planned economies of Eastern Europe and the former Soviet Union were all growing in 2000: their aggregate GDP increased by 6 per cent, significantly more than the world economy as a whole. That was largely due to the strong recovery in the Russian Federation, where GDP increased by 7.7 per cent, the highest growth rate in more than 30 years. Output also recovered strongly in Eastern Europe and the Baltic States, their aggregate GDP increasing by 3.9 per cent and 4.8 per cent, respectively.

Those outcomes suggested that after 10 years of painful reforms, the prolonged and deep transformational recession in those economies had for the most part come to an end. However, for a number of countries the strong growth in 2000 represented only a meagre recovery after a long economic slump. On average, the CIS economies were still some 40 per cent below their GDP levels of 1989, and in a number of individual countries GDP in 2000 was less than half of what it was a decade earlier. Also, with the exception of a few Central European economies, domestic

demand generally remained weak despite moderate recovery in 2000.

In 2000, many transition economies benefited from strong and diversified demand in their major export markets, principally for manufactured goods but also for services and a wide range of primary commodities and semi-manufactures. In particular, the Eastern European and Baltic economies capitalized on the sharp rebound in Western European import demand, while the recovery in the Russian Federation stimulated exports from neighbouring CIS countries. In addition, the commodity-exporting countries, especially the oil and natural gas exporters in the CIS, benefited from the upsurge in world market prices, which led to a considerable improvement in their trade and current-account balances.

The EU, the main trading partner for all the Eastern European and Baltic economies, accounted for about two thirds of their exports and imports. The acceleration in the volume of Western European imports in 2000 was the major factor behind Central European and Baltic exports increasing by some 20 per cent in volume. That strong export performance made a major contribution to the recovery of output in Eastern Europe and the Baltic area. However, for most transition economies, the strong performance in 2000 underlined the considerable sensitivity of those economies to changes in the external environment, especially in the short run.

The average unemployment rate in Eastern Europe was still about 15 per cent and, despite the high rate of economic growth, enterprise restructuring was still releasing more labour than was being employed in new jobs.

Activities in 2000

Trade, industry and enterprise development

The Committee for Trade, Industry and Enterprise Development, at its fourth session (Geneva, 21-23 June) [ECE/TRADE/262], approved the change of name of the United Nations Centre for the Facilitation of Procedures and Practices for Administration, Commerce and Transport to the Centre for Trade Facilitation and Electronic Business. It also modified the Centre's mandate, terms of reference and procedures.

The Committee established a Working Party for Industry and Enterprise Development to assist in creating more favourable conditions for investment, industrial restructuring and enterprise development in transition economies. It adopted its 2000-2002 programme of work and approved the topic of the forum to be held in 2001, which would focus on the service sector in transition economies and its role in stimulating trade, innovation, investment and enterprise development. The Committee also established a task team to develop draft strategic policy objectives for it, to recommend changes in its terms of reference and to propose measures to implement those strategic objectives.

Transport

The Inland Transport Committee, at its sixty-second session (Geneva, 15-17 February) [ECE/TRANS/133 & Add.1], discussed various aspects of the transport situation in ECE member countries.

The Committee noted the report of the second session of the Joint Meeting on Transport and the Environment and endorsed the creation of an ad hoc expert group to assist the Joint Meeting, particularly in the identification of priorities for the effective implementation of the Programme of Joint Action, adopted at the 1997 Regional Conference on Transport and the Environment [YUN 1997, p. 1005], and in the preparation of the 2002 mid-term review, including an evaluation of its programme of work.

The Committee requested that sufficient resources be allocated for assisting countries with economies in transition from the ECE budget and through contributions from member States to the UN/ECE Trust Fund for Assistance to Countries in Transition.

The Committee approved the report of the Working Party on Road Traffic Safety on its thirty-second and thirty-third sessions. It noted that, following serious accidents in the Mont Blanc and Tauern tunnels, the question of safety in tunnels had been considered by the Working Party. It adopted a proposal to establish a multi-disciplinary group of experts on safety in tunnels.

The Committee noted that the European Agreement on Main Inland Waterways of International Importance had entered into force on 26 July 1999 and that 10 States were currently parties to it. It invited Governments that had not done so to accede to the Agreement as soon as possible to facilitate its implementation. The Committee endorsed four new resolutions adopted by the Working Party, amending the Recommendations on Technical Requirements for Inland Navigation Vessels and the European Code for Inland Waterways.

Energy

The Committee on Sustainable Energy, at its tenth session (Geneva, 31 October–2 November) [ECE/ENERGY/43], endorsed the decisions of the Task Force on the United Nations International

Framework Classification for Reserves/Resources: Solid Fuels and Mineral Commodities (UNFC) [YUN 1997, p. 1006] and noted progress in the implementation of UNFC in the solid fuels and mineral sectors in the ECE region, Asia and Latin America. It extended the trial period of application of UNFC to 31 December 2002 and requested the secretariat to revise the Project Plan of the Energy Efficiency 21 Project, 2000-2003.

In preparation for the 2001 session of the Commission on Sustainable Development (CSD-9), which was to address energy-related sustainability issues, the High-level Forum on Sustainable Energy in a Competitive Market: Forging Partnerships was held on 1 November in conjunction with the Committee's tenth session. The Committee adopted the "Contribution to CSD-9 on Sustainable Energy Development: A Regional Perspective—One More Step on the Path to a Sustainable Energy Future", and established a Task Force on Environment and Energy together with the Committee on Environmental Policy to develop guidelines for decision makers on reforming energy prices to promote sustainable energy development.

Agriculture

The Specialized Section on Standardization of Dry and Dried Produce (Fruit), at its forty-seventh session (Geneva, 19-22 June) [TRADE/WP.7/GE.2/2000/17], made corrections to the main text of the standard layout for dry and dried produce (fruit). The agreed text, indicating the changes, would be recommended to the Working Party on Standardization of Perishable Produce and Quality Development for adoption as the revised Standard Layout for Dry and Dried Produce (Fruit). It agreed to changes to the recommendation on in-shell hazelnuts and hazelnut kernels; it recommended the amended text to the Working Party for adoption as revised UN/ECE standards. It also recommended the extension of the recommendation on walnut kernels for one year and formed an informal working group to look at proposals concerning scuffing, crop year, mould and colour chart for walnut kernels.

In a joint session (Rome, Italy, 9-13 October) [ECE/TIM/95], the Timber Committee (fifty-eighth session) and the European Forestry Commission (thirtieth session) endorsed the general direction of ECE/FAO activities, reaffirming their core mandate to "monitor and analyse sustainable forest management in the region" and the similar role of FAO at the global level. The joint session also reviewed the markets for forest products in 2000 and prospects for 2001. It reviewed its activities and programme of work for 2001-2005, and agreed, in view of the imbalance between resources and aspirations, to undertake a review of the Committee's objectives, methods, resources and outputs to be completed before the 2001 ECE session.

Environment

The Committee on Environment Policy (seventh session, Geneva, 25-28 September) [ECE/CEP/74] discussed its substantive input to the fifth Ministerial Conference "Environment for Europe", to be held in 2002 in Kiev, Ukraine. It established an open-ended intergovernmental working group to prepare a legally binding instrument on pollutant release and transfer registers. The Committee welcomed a recommendation to the Meeting of the Parties to the Convention on Environmental Impact Assessment in a Transboundary Context to start the preparation of a protocol to the Convention on strategic environmental assessment.

The Committee supported the launching of negotiations for a joint protocol on civil liability to the Conventions on the Transboundary Effects of Industrial Accidents and on the Protection and Use of Transboundary Watercourses and International Lakes. An ad hoc working group on environmental monitoring was established and its terms of reference and work plan adopted. The Committee established a task force to draft guidelines on compliance with and enforcement of environmental legislation and adopted the recommendations for strengthening environmental policy and management in Armenia, Bulgaria, Kazakhstan and Kyrgyzstan.

The Executive Body for the Convention on Long-range Transboundary Air Pollution, at its eighteenth session (Geneva, 28 November-1 December) [ECE/EB.AIR/71], adopted the 2000 Review of Strategies and Policies for Air Pollution Abatement.

Human settlements

The Committee on Human Settlements (sixty-first session, Geneva, 18 and 20 September) [ECE/HBP/119] discussed the implementation of the ECE Strategy for a Sustainable Quality of Life in Human Settlements in the 21st Century and the Ministerial Declaration, adopted by the meeting of ECE Ministers of Housing and Spatial Planning (Geneva, 19 September) [ECE/HBP/119/Add.1], as the basis for its future programme of work to promote the sustainable development of human settlements, foster economic and social prosperity and support democratic governance in the ECE region.

The Committee decided that the Declaration and the Strategy constituted the ECE contribution to the special session of the General Assem-

bly in 2001 (Istanbul+5) on the review and appraisal of progress in the global implementation of the Habitat Agenda [YUN 1996, p. 994]. The Committee would consider the impact of the Strategy and the Declaration on its programme of work and on national programmes at its 2001 session and assess the implementation of them in five years.

The Committee adopted the report of the first session of the Working Party on Land Administration and confirmed the high priority of the country profile project on the housing sector and activities related to land registration and land markets, and approved the general outline and topics suggested for the Ninth (2002) Conference on Urban and Regional Research. It welcomed the report of the Housing and Urban Management Advisory Network and supported the project proposal for an ECE handbook on housing financing.

Statistics

The Conference of European Statisticians (forty-eighth session, Paris, 13-15 June) [ECE/CES/58] considered the implications of the meetings of its parent bodies—the May session of ECE and the February/March session of the UN Statistical Commission (see p. 1200). The Conference agreed to review the Integrated Presentation of international statistical work in the ECE region, especially quality assessments of statistics, harmonized consumer price indices and agriculture statistics. The Conference considered a proposal to convert the Integrated Presentation into a database, but noted that the secretariat did not have sufficient resources to look into that possibility on its own. It welcomed the offer of interested national statistical offices to assist the secretariat in that endeavour.

The Conference also discussed sustainable development indicators, international statistical work in South-East Europe and relations between official statisticians, NGOs and academics.

Operational activities

The Commission considered a note by the Executive Secretary [E/ECE/1376 & Add.1] on ECE operational activities.

A review by external auditors of the Coordinating Unit and the Regional Advisers, responsible for carrying out ECE operational activities, concluded that the objectives and impacts of the Unit and the Regional Advisory Programme were being compromised by weaknesses, such as a lack of strategic planning, insufficient extra-budgetary funding and no fund-raising strategy. Subsequently, the secretariat held extensive discussions on the goal of operational activities and on whether existing resources were being used in the best way to achieve maximum impact. In that context, it was proposed to continue giving high priority to requests from and for projects in CIS and Balkan countries. Close cooperation between ECE and other organizations and institutions in Europe could help to enhance ECE's profile, increase the effect of its programme delivery, mobilize resources and ensure their best use. It was felt that ECE should intensify its efforts to involve the UNDP resident coordinators more in its operational activities.

It was emphasized that ECE needed more extra-budgetary funding for operational activities. It was proposed that countries that did not have ECE on their list of eligible institutions for receiving funds for operational activities should include it. Better coordination of all operational activities and mechanisms for systematic feedback and evaluation were required. The secretariat requested member countries to reflect on the question of more predictable and sustained financing for operational activities and to provide constructive suggestions in that regard.

Intersectoral activities and cross-sectoral concerns

The Commission considered a note by the Executive Secretary on intersectoral activities and cross-sectoral concerns [E/ECE/1377], which reviewed ECE intersectoral activities, highlighting progress made on the follow-up to the Vienna Regional Conference on Transport and the Environment [YUN 1997, p. 1005] and to the London Charter on Transport, Environment and Health, adopted at the Third Ministerial Conference on Environment and Health (London, June 1999). Progress in ECE's relationship with the business community was also reviewed as one of the cross-sectoral concerns identified by the Plan of Action on the Strengthening of Economic Cooperation in Europe [ibid., p. 1002]. A number of issues relating to principles that should govern such cooperation, such as mutual benefits, promotion of the UN development agenda, prevention of unfair comparative advantage and equal access to ECE's public goods, were also raised.

UN restructuring and revitalization

As follow-up to Economic and Social Council resolution 1998/46 [YUN 1998, p. 1262] on further measures for the restructuring and revitalization of the United Nations in the economic, social and related fields, the Executive Secretary reported to the Commission [E/ECE/1378], describing ac-

tions that had been taken in response to the guidance provided by that resolution. He provided information on contributions made by ECE with respect to the process leading up to the 2000 review of the Beijing Platform for Action [YUN 1995, p. 1170]. He briefed the Commission on the contribution made by the ECE secretariat to UNCTAD X (see p. 890). He also discussed ECE's contribution to follow-up action to the International Year of Older Persons [YUN 1999, p. 1124].

Latin America and the Caribbean

At its twenty-eighth session (Mexico City, 3-7 April) [E/2000/40], the Economic Commission for Latin America and the Caribbean (ECLAC) focused its deliberations on ensuring equity for the region's citizenry in the context of the challenges posed by globalization. The Commission considered a main document, "Equity, Development and Citizenship" [LC/G.2071(SES.28/3) & Corr.1], which examined the question of equity, integrating macroeconomic and growth-related issues with principles of universality, solidarity and efficiency, and characterizing education and employment as essential to development in democratic societies capable of promoting ongoing progress towards the full exercise of citizens' rights.

The Commission adopted the Mexico resolution on equity, development and citizenship [E/2000/40 (res. 582(XXVIII))], in which it recognized that the development patterns and opportunities open to the region's inhabitants were influenced by worldwide economic, social and cultural processes deriving from economic globalization. It urged the secretariat to continue deepening its analysis of: social policy as an integrative force, based on institutions that gave priority consideration to the principles of universality, solidarity and efficiency in the design, financing, delivery and regulation of social services, while seeking the appropriate public/private mix; responsible macroeconomic policy based on a longer time horizon; the reinforcement of citizenship; the interrelationship between development agendas of the region's countries and policies associated with globalization processes; and the construction of a stable, predictable international financial system linked to social development.

The Commission also adopted resolutions on follow-up to the 1995-2001 regional programme of action for Latin American and Caribbean women [YUN 1994, p. 739]; priority lines of action for population and development for 2000-2002;

its programme of work for 2002-2003; the 2000-2002 calendar of conferences; the establishment of the Statistical Conference of the Americas; support for the work of the Latin American and Caribbean Institute for Economic and Social Planning; technical cooperation among developing countries and regions; the place and date of the next session; and the Caribbean Development and Cooperation Committee. (See below, under the respective sections.)

Economic trends

The 2000 summary of the economic survey of Latin America and the Caribbean [E/2001/15] stated that the recovery of Latin American and Caribbean economies, which began in the final quarter of 1998, continued during 2000. The performance of the region's two largest economies (Brazil and Mexico), in particular, enabled GDP to expand at an average annual rate of 4 per cent, compared to the 1998 rate of 2.3 per cent and just 0.3 per cent in 1999. All the countries, with the exception of Argentina and Uruguay, posted positive growth rates, with the highest recorded in Belize, Chile, Cuba, the Dominican Republic and Mexico,

High international growth rates boosted the region's exports, but commodity price trends were uneven, with petroleum soaring by 60 per cent, while prices of some agricultural products fell. Exports of goods and services rose by 19 per cent in value and imports climbed by 17 per cent.

In 2000, total capital inflows for the region were estimated at approximately $52 billion, compared to $40 billion in 1999, a reflection of the larger amounts of capital flowing into Brazil, which outweighed the decline in Argentina's inflows and outflows from Venezuela. Foreign direct investment continued to be the major source of capital inflows; bond issues were used for refinancing maturing debt obligations, while bank loans and investment in local exchanges contributed very little to total capital inflows. As the year progressed, macroeconomic policy was relaxed, especially in countries that allowed their currencies to float freely. Fiscal deficits declined from 3.1 per cent of GDP in 1999 to 2.4 per cent in 2000. Consumer prices improved with a regional average of 8.8 per cent for the entire year.

Over 80 per cent of the countries for which statistics were available had single-digit inflation rates. Inflation continued to subside in Venezuela, and Ecuador's recent dollarization policy had been bringing its inflation rate down. The labour market still posed the region's most serious problems. Although the upturn in GDP growth in 2000 slightly raised employment levels, it was insufficient to lower unemployment rates, which remained at an almost record high of about 9 per cent. In addition to other factors, the situation was linked to the lag in domestic demand. Meanwhile, wages increased by an average 1.5 per cent in the 10 countries that provided information.

External debt

In 2000, the disbursed external debt of the region was over $750 billion, reflecting a nominal decrease for the first time since 1988. While external debt levels in most of the countries did not vary, the countries posting a reduction included Brazil, Ecuador, Honduras and Mexico. There was an across-the-board improvement in the debt/export ratios during the year, and the regional coefficient fell from 217 per cent in 1999 to 180 per cent in 2000. However, a number of countries continued having high levels of indebtedness. The ratio between interest payments and exports diminished to 14.5 per cent. Bolivia, which had qualified for the Heavily Indebted Poor Countries Initiative in 1998, began to apply for the second phase of the scheme early in 2000. It stood to secure about $650 million in debt relief. Honduras could also benefit from the Initiative. Ecuador, which had suspended the servicing of its external debt in October 1999, signed an agreement with 98 per cent of its creditors by which its $6.4 billion eligible debt would be reduced by nearly 40 per cent. In September, Ecuador concluded a preliminary agreement with the Paris Club of creditor countries to restructure $880 million in bilateral debt.

Activities in 2000

Development policy and regional economic cooperation

In 2000, ECLAC combined activities deriving from its role as a forum for regional dialogue, facilitating the emergence of common regional positions that could contribute to the world debate on development issues, with normative activities, comprehensive analysis of development and public policy-making processes and other operational activities, such as technical assistance, specialist information provision and training.

It monitored national and regional economic and social developments and analysed national public policies to present a systematic analytical view of the situation of regional countries and an evaluation of the main tendencies in the region so future challenges could be identified. As a result, five annual reports, including the *Economic Survey of Latin America and the Caribbean* and the *Social Panorama of Latin America*, were published.

The Special Studies Unit of the Office of the Executive Secretary conducted a study on strengthening regional institutions for external financing in the region. It also organized a seminar on aspects of financing for development in the context of financial globalization (Santiago, Chile, 7 September). A joint workshop was organized with ESCAP (Bangkok, February) on the expansion of trade and investment relations between countries in Latin America and those in Asia and the Pacific, and a project was being prepared for closer cooperation between the two commissions with regard to small and medium-sized enterprises.

To assist countries in the region to prepare for the high-level international intergovernmental event on financing for development (see p. 915), the ECLAC secretariat organized the Latin American and Caribbean Regional Consultation on Financing for Development (Bogotá, Colombia, 9-10 November) [LC/G.2132(CONF.89/4)]. The Consultation formulated a statement, "Towards the international conference on financing for development", in which it identified a number of political considerations and concerns regarding financing for development from a regional perspective.

The Latin American and Caribbean Institute for Economic and Social Planning (ILPES) carried out activities related to the strategic management and reform of the State, regulation of public services, development and land-use management, national systems of public investment and basic planning functions. ILPES held 15 seminars, including one on basic planning functions for English-speaking Caribbean countries (Port of Spain, Trinidad and Tobago, 5-6 October) and another on basic planning functions and successful experiences (Havana, Cuba, 16-17 November).

The twentieth meeting of the Presiding Officers of the Regional Council for Planning of ILPES (Montevideo, Uruguay, 9 March) considered the Institute's activities and approved its work programme.

The Commission [res. 581(XXVIII)] took note of the resolutions emanating from that meeting and recommended that ILPES significantly expand its training activities, in collaboration with the Commission's various subregional offices and divisions and other international institutions. ILPES should focus its substantive work on analysis, prospective studies, coordination and evaluation of public management and investment and of territorially based and local development. The Commission also recommended that meetings of the Presiding Officers should be held within the framework of the Commission's session. It re-

quested the Executive Secretary to submit in 2002 a progress report on the integration and coordination of ILPES activities with those of the Commission.

Human settlements

The Latin American and Caribbean regional conference preparatory to the General Assembly's special session for an overall review and appraisal of the implementation of the Habitat Agenda, adopted at the United Nations Conference on Human Settlements (Habitat II) [YUN 1996, p. 992], was held in Santiago from 25 to 27 October [LC/G.2126(CONF.88/4)]. ECLAC presented a document entitled "From rapid urbanization to the consolidation of human settlements in Latin America and the Caribbean: a territorial perspective", which examined various aspects of the territorial, urban and housing situation in the region.

The conference adopted the Santiago Declaration on Human Settlements, which reaffirmed the validity and relevance of the Regional Plan of Action [YUN 1995, p. 1044]. The Declaration was considered an important instrument for moving forward regional cooperation and developing a consensus on urban issues. ECLAC was requested to pursue the design of indicators for implementing the Regional Plan of Action and the analysis of new challenges so as to keep it up to date as an instrument for the adoption of specific actions.

Social development and equity

The ECLAC secretariat convened the Second Regional Conference on Follow-up to the World Summit for Social Development (Santiago, 15-17 May) [LC/G.2108(CONF.87/4)], at which it presented a document entitled "The equity gap: a second appraisal", presenting analyses and proposals on qualitative aspects of growth, such as the relationship between growth and poverty, employment trends, and wages and productivity, social policy reform, sectoral activities and the status of integration in societies in the region.

The Conference adopted the Santiago Declaration, in which ECLAC member countries pointed to the contribution of the World Summit for Social Development [YUN 1995, p. 1113] to the reinforcement of many social policies applied in the countries of the region during the past five years and reaffirmed their commitment to achieving the objectives of the Copenhagen Declaration on Social Development and the Programme of Action of the World Summit.

The tenth Ibero-American Summit of Heads of State and Government (Panama City, 17-18 November) requested ECLAC to evaluate the situation of children and adolescents as a contribution to the adoption of a common approach by member countries of that forum at the General Assembly's special session for follow-up to the World Summit for Children in 2001. ECLAC, in support of the Office of the United Nations High Commissioner for Human Rights, prepared a study on ethnic and racial discrimination and xenophobia in Latin America and the Caribbean, which was presented at the regional seminar of experts for Latin America and the Caribbean on economic, social and legal measures to combat racism with particular reference to vulnerable groups (Santiago, 25-27 October) in preparation for the 2001 World Conference against Racism, Racial Discrimination, Xenophobia and Related Intolerance (see p. 641).

Population and development

The third meeting of the ECLAC sessional Ad Hoc Committee on Population and Development (Mexico City, 3-4 April) considered the topics of youth, population and development, and systems of indicators for monitoring and following up on the Programme of Action of the International Conference on Population and Development [YUN 1994, p. 955].

ECLAC, in collaboration with the International Organization for Migration, held a symposium on international migration in the Americas (San José, Costa Rica, 4-6 September), which examined migration trends and patterns in the Americas, the relationship between migration and development, governance of international migration and multilateral diplomacy, the economic and social importance of migration and human rights of migrants. The conclusions of the symposium were to provide an input to the plan of action to be formulated at the third Summit of the Americas, to be held in Quebec City, Canada, in 2001.

In a resolution on priority lines of action for population and development in 2000-2002 [res. 577(XXVIII)], the Commission decided that the Ad Hoc Committee should examine in 2002 the question of social vulnerability: population, household and communities, and that its secretariat should prepare documentation on the social vulnerability of small island developing States of the Caribbean, as well as of Belize, Guyana and Suriname.

The Commission instructed the Latin American and Caribbean Demographic Centre (CELADE) (ECLAC's Population Division) and the ECLAC subregional headquarters for the Caribbean to give priority to assisting countries in developing information systems with indicators to allow for adequate follow-up and appraisal of the implementation of the recommendations of the Programme of Action of the International Conference on Population and Development and the Regional Plan of Action [YUN 1994, p. 740].

CELADE and other relevant international agencies were asked to continue to support the countries of the region to prepare for their censuses and, in particular, to promote and facilitate the use and dissemination of census information in implementing the recommendations of international summit meetings. They were also asked to place priority on human resources training in population and development to enhance the countries' capacity to generate sociodemographic information and knowledge. The Commission requested countries in the region to allocate sufficient resources to strengthen the incorporation of population and development programmes in public policies that included poverty reduction, and that population and reproductive health issues should be more closely linked to social, environmental and cultural policies and promoted in reforms in the education and health-care sectors. It expressed concern over the continued reduction of international financial resources available to Latin America and the Caribbean for activities in population and development; it urged countries in the region and the Ad Hoc Committee to take steps to reverse that trend and the international community to increase its technical and financial assistance.

Integration of women in development

The eighth session of the Regional Conference on Women in Latin America and the Caribbean (Lima, Peru, 8-10 February) [LC/G.2087(CRM.8/6)] reviewed ECLAC activities and the status of gender equity, especially as it related to human rights and peace. The Conference adopted the Lima Consensus as the region's contribution to the General Assembly's special session on "Women 2000: gender equality, development and peace for the twenty-first century" (see p. 1082), and resolutions on the participation of associate members of regional commissions and NGOs in that special session, and on ECLAC activities relating to regional cooperation for gender mainstreaming.

Two meetings of the Presiding Officers of the Regional Conference were held (Lima, 7 February; Santiago, 13-15 September). At the ninth meeting of specialized agencies and other bodies of the UN system on the advancement of women in Latin America and the Caribbean (Santiago, 12 September) [LC/L.1467], participants agreed to strengthen inter-agency coordination forums at the regional and national levels and to request

ECLAC, UNDP, the United Nations Development Fund for Women and UNFPA to establish a working group to design a strategy to expedite incorporation of the gender perspective in UN system programmes. They also urged participating organizations to intensify efforts to open up opportunities for exchange with Caribbean countries.

In its resolution on follow-up to the Regional Programme of Action for the Women of Latin America and the Caribbean, 1995-2001 [YUN 1994, p. 739], the Commission approved the Lima Consensus as the region's contribution to the Assembly's special session on women and recommended that technical and financial resources be increased at all levels to accelerate the attainment of gender equity and the full integration of women in the development process, together with the full enjoyment of citizenship within the framework of sustainable development, social justice and democracy [res. 576(XXVIII)].

Information technology and development

The regional meeting on information technology for development (Florianopolis, Santa Catarina, Brazil, 20-21 June) [LC/L.1401] was held as a regional forum preparatory to the high-level segment of the Economic and Social Council (5-7 July) on development and international cooperation in the twenty-first century: the role of information technology in the context of a knowledge-based economy (see p. 799). The meeting adopted the Declaration of Florianopolis, in which Latin American and Caribbean countries shared the aspirations of becoming full-fledged members of the information society by the year 2005, and urged the Council to support developing countries in their efforts to design and implement programmes to ensure that the entire population had access to information and communications technology–related products and services, and to promote the growth of digital network infrastructure and research. The deliberations of the meeting were transmitted to the Council [E/2000/74].

On 20 November [A/55/636], Brazil transmitted to the General Assembly the Declaration of Itacuruçá, adopted at the 2000 info-ethics seminar of governmental experts from Latin America and the Caribbean (Rio de Janeiro, 26-27 October), which recommended creating a regional programme to provide for the continuity of efforts carried out by Latin American and Caribbean countries to insert themselves fully into the digital era.

Economic statistics and technical cooperation

The Commission approved the establishment of the Statistical Conference of the Americas as a subsidiary body of ECLAC and requested the Executive Secretary to submit the proposal to the relevant UN bodies for consideration [res. 580(XXVIII)].

ECONOMIC AND SOCIAL COUNCIL ACTION

On 25 July [meeting 39], the Economic and Social Council, on the recommendation of ECLAC [E/2000/10/Add.3], adopted **resolution 2000/7** without vote [agenda item 10].

Establishment of the Statistical Conference of the Americas of the Economic Commission for Latin America and the Caribbean

The Economic and Social Council,

Recalling the Buenos Aires Plan of Action for Promoting and Implementing Technical Cooperation among Developing Countries, which was endorsed by the General Assembly in its resolution 33/134 of 19 December 1978,

Bearing in mind the decisions adopted at the tenth session of the High-level Committee on the Review of Technical Cooperation among Developing Countries, held at United Nations Headquarters in New York from 5 to 9 May 1997, in particular section B of decision 10/1, on the review of the progress made in the implementation of the new directions strategy for technical cooperation among developing countries,

Considering that, insofar as technical cooperation in the field of statistics is concerned, the Economic Commission for Latin America and the Caribbean has been cooperating systematically to facilitate interinstitutional coordination among developed countries, international organizations and national statistical offices in member countries that carry out technical cooperation projects,

Bearing in mind, on the one hand, that since 1994, the Organization of American States has collaborated with the Commission in the organization of the Joint Organization of American States/Economic Commission for Latin America and the Caribbean Meeting on Statistical Matters and, on the other, that the Permanent Executive Committee of the Inter-American Council for Integral Development of the Organization of American States, in its resolution 34 of 8 October 1998, decided to put an end to the existence, within the Organization, of the Inter-American Statistical Conference, whose Permanent Executive Committee had been the counterpart to the Commission in the Agreement on Cooperation in Statistical Matters between the Organization and the Commission of 7 October 1993, and, moreover, that the Organization has asked its member countries to bring the coordination of statistical matters into a single entity within the framework of the Commission,

Bearing in mind also that the Commission has been including the Joint Organization of American States/Economic Commission for Latin America and the Caribbean Meeting on Statistical Matters in its programme of work, and that, therefore, the technical, operational and financial implications of establishing a Statistical Conference of the Americas of the Economic Commission for Latin America and the Caribbean as one of its subsidiary bodies can be dealt with by reallocating existing regular budgetary resources,

Considering that, by its resolution 34, the Permanent Executive Committee of the Inter-American Council for Integral Development entrusted the representatives of the statistical offices of Canada, Mexico and Peru and the secretariat of the Commission with the task of preparing a proposal on the organization and operation of the Statistical Conference of the Americas of the Economic Commission for Latin America and the Caribbean, the content of which was improved and approved by consensus at the Meeting of Directors of Statistics of the Americas, held at the headquarters of the Commission in Santiago from 24 to 26 March 1999,

Recalling resolution 489(PLEN.19) of the Committee of the Whole of the Economic Commission for Latin America and the Caribbean, on the intergovernmental structure and functions of the Commission, in which the Committee recommended that the current institutional structure of the Commission should be maintained, Commission resolution 553(XXVI) on the reform of the United Nations and its impact on the Commission, in which the Commission recommended that the current pattern of conferences of the Commission system should be continued, and Commission resolution 573(XXVII) on technical cooperation among developing countries and regions,

Having examined the proposal on the establishment of the Statistical Conference of the Americas of the Economic Commission for Latin America and the Caribbean, which is contained in the annex to the present resolution,

Considering, finally, the nature of and the objectives set forth in the proposal on the establishment of the Statistical Conference of the Americas of the Economic Commission for Latin America and the Caribbean,

1. *Approves* the proposal on the establishment, as one of the subsidiary bodies of the Economic Commission for Latin America and the Caribbean, of the Statistical Conference of the Americas of the Economic Commission for Latin America and the Caribbean, as set forth in the annex to the present resolution, with the observations and suggestions included in the report of the Commission on its twenty-eighth session;

2. *Requests* the Executive Secretary of the Economic Commission for Latin America and the Caribbean to submit for consideration by the relevant United Nations bodies such proposals as may be necessary for the establishment of the Statistical Conference of the Americas of the Economic Commission for Latin America and the Caribbean;

3. *Also requests* the Executive Secretary to report on the implementation of the present resolution at the twenty-ninth session of the Commission.

ANNEX
Establishment of the Statistical Conference of the Americas of the Economic Commission for Latin America and the Caribbean

I. Statistical Conference of the Americas of the Economic Commission for Latin America and the Caribbean

1. *Nature*

The Statistical Conference of the Americas of the Economic Commission for Latin America and the Caribbean shall be a subsidiary body of the Commission

that shall contribute to the progress of policies on statistics and statistical activities in the countries of the region.

2. *Objectives*

(a) To promote the development and improvement of national statistics and work to ensure that they are comparable internationally, bearing in mind the recommendations of the United Nations Statistical Commission, the specialized agencies and other relevant organizations;

(b) To promote international, regional and bilateral cooperation among national offices and international and regional agencies;

(c) To draw up a biennial programme of regional and international cooperation activities, to meet the demands of the countries of the region, subject to the availability of resources.

3. *Membership*

All countries that are members of the Economic Commission for Latin America and the Caribbean are members of the Conference.

4. *Meetings of the Conference*

The Conference shall hold its regular meetings every other year. The Conference may accept an invitation from a member Government to hold its regular meeting in its country.

5. *Membership of the Executive Committee*

The Conference shall elect an Executive Committee, in accordance with the regulations established by the Commission. The Chairperson of the Executive Committee shall also preside over the meetings of the Conference. The Executive Committee is empowered to convene a special meeting in the interval between regular meetings.

6. *Secretariat*

The secretariat of the Economic Commission for Latin America and the Caribbean shall serve as the secretariat of the Conference. The secretariat shall make available to the Conference such documents and facilities as have been approved by the Commission.

II. Executive Committee of the Conference

1. *Nature*

The Statistical Conference of the Americas of the Economic Commission for Latin America and the Caribbean shall set up an Executive Committee to support the Conference, as set forth in paragraph 4 below.

2. *Composition*

The Executive Committee shall be made up of a Chairperson and six members. Its members shall be elected from among the member countries of the Economic Commission for Latin America and the Caribbean. Special attention shall be paid to ensuring that the subregional groups of countries are represented on the Committee.

3. *Election of the Executive Committee and terms of office*

At the beginning of each Conference, the Chairperson of the Executive Committee, in consultation with the members of the Committee and of the Conference, shall draw up a proposal on the election of the new Committee.

The newly elected Executive Committee shall take up its duties once the regular meeting of the Conference at which it was elected has ended, and shall remain in office until the end of the next regular meeting.

The members of the Executive Committee, including the Chairperson, shall be elected by the Conference at its regular meeting for a term of two years.

The members of the Executive Committee may be re-elected for three successive terms. The Chairperson may not be re-elected in that office for a second consecutive term, but may be elected as a member of the Committee. Anyone who has been a member of the Committee for three successive terms may be elected again after two years have elapsed since the end of that person's last term of office.

4. *Duties*

The Executive Committee shall have the following duties:

(a) To carry out the tasks assigned to it by the Conference;

(b) To draw up, every two years, a biennial programme of activities of regional and international cooperation on statistical matters, to be submitted at the regular meeting of the Conference;

(c) To follow up the implementation of the agreements reached at the Conference and the tasks entrusted to it by the Conference, particularly the biennial programme of activities referred to in section I, paragraph 2 *(c)*, above;

(d) To decide on the documentation required for its meetings. As a general rule, no substantive discussion shall be initiated unless an appropriate document is available. The secretariat shall be responsible for facilitating compliance with this rule.

5. *Meetings*

The Executive Committee shall meet at least twice during the interval between regular meetings of the Conference. At the meeting preceding the Conference, it shall approve a biennial programme of activities of the Conference, which shall be presented at the regular meeting of the Conference.

The Executive Committee may invite to its meetings any countries or experts who can make a contribution to the fulfilment of its duties.

Technical cooperation and assistance

The Commission considered a report on ECLAC activities to promote and support technical cooperation among developing countries (TCDC) and regions during the 1998-1999 biennium [LC/G.2081(SES.28/13)].

In a resolution on TCDC [res. 583(XXVIII)], the Commission took note of the report and emphasized the need to strengthen the activities of regional Governments in enhancing the use of TCDC mechanisms and modalities in the priority areas of public economic and social development policy, and the need for more resources for development cooperation from developed countries and multilateral agencies. It set out actions the Executive Secretary should take towards that end, including intensifying the incorporation of TCDC modalities in the secretariat's work programme; holding consultations to identify priority areas for TCDC in member countries; underscoring the need for a new concept of co-

operation that emphasized the transfer of resources, and consulting with member States on new measurement criteria that took into account the increasing inequity in the region; broadening the dissemination of information on technical cooperation projects and activities to national focal points for development cooperation, with special emphasis on the use of global information networks; strengthening the exchange of experiences and best practices of countries in technical cooperation projects; and supporting training programmes that enabled countries of the region to make greater and better use of global cooperation funds and programmes.

Subregional activities

Caribbean

In 2000, the ECLAC subregional headquarters for the Caribbean—the secretariat of the Caribbean Development and Cooperation Committee (CDCC) (Port of Spain)—celebrated its twenty-fifth anniversary.

CDCC, at its eighteenth session (Port of Spain, 30 March–1 April), reviewed its programme of work for 1998-1999 and adopted the programme for 2002-2003. It adopted a resolution requesting a comprehensive review of its Constituent Declaration and Functions and Rules of Procedure. It also adopted resolutions on support for activities to implement the Programme of Action of the International Conference on Population and Development [YUN 1994, p. 955]; the work of the ECLAC subregional headquarters for the Caribbean; implementation of the Programme of Action for the Sustainable Development of Small Island Developing States [ibid., p. 783]; the importance of economic and social data in the planning and policy formulation process in CDCC member countries; activities to implement the Beijing Platform for Action [YUN 1995, p. 1170]; integrated management of the Caribbean Sea; and the 1975 Chaguaramas Declaration, which established the Caribbean Development and Cooperation Committee.

The Commission noted the report of CDCC's eighteenth session and endorsed the resolutions adopted [res. 585(XXVIII)].

Mexico and Central America

The ECLAC subregional headquarters in Mexico City placed emphasis on the review of structural reform policies, trends in foreign direct investment, social marginalization, the wider participation of women, economic integration and sectoral competitiveness. The main analysis activities carried out included a review of the economic situation in the 10 countries served by the subregional headquarters; the mobilization of resources to assess the economic, environmental and social consequences of natural disasters; the study "Desarrollo económico y social en la República Dominicana: los últimos 20 años y perspectivas para el siglo XXI"; the dissemination of the second and expanded edition of *The Cuban economy: structural reforms and economic performance in the 1990s*; and cooperation in the activities of the Panama-Puebla Plan, in particular the review of compatibility between the regional proposal for transformation and modernization of Central America and the "Mexico" chapter of the Plan, and support for the Meso-American initiatives and the 17 projects approved by the Presidents.

Programme and organizational questions

The Commission approved the draft programme of work of the ECLAC system [LC/G.2075 (SES.28/7)], including ILPES, for the 2002-2003 biennium [res. 578(XXVIII)]. Activities were proposed under 12 subprogrammes. The Commission requested the Ad Hoc Working Group, established pursuant to resolution 553(XXVI) [YUN 1996, p. 930], to continue to collaborate with the Executive Secretary in setting priorities for the programme of work and in the debate and analysis of strategic directions for future activities of the Commission, and called on the Executive Secretary to ensure that the member States of the Central American isthmus and the Caribbean participated meaningfully in all areas of the work programme. The Commission also approved the ECLAC calender of conferences [LC/G.2076 (SES.28/8)] for 2000-2002 [res. 579(XXVIII)].

Venue and date of
twenty-ninth session of ECLAC

On 25 July [meeting 39], the Economic and Social Council, acting on ECLAC's recommendation [E/2000/10/Add.3], adopted **resolution 2000/8** without vote [agenda item 10].

Place and date of the twenty-ninth session of the Economic Commission for Latin America and the Caribbean

The Economic and Social Council,

Bearing in mind paragraph 15 of the terms of reference of the Economic Commission for Latin America and the Caribbean and rules 1 and 2 of its rules of procedure,

Considering the invitation of the Government of Brazil to hold the twenty-ninth session of the Commission in that country,

1. *Expresses its gratitude* to the Government of Brazil for its generous invitation;

2. *Accepts* this invitation with pleasure;

3. *Approves* the holding of the twenty-ninth session of the Economic Commission for Latin America and the Caribbean during the first half of 2002.

Western Asia

The Economic and Social Commission for Western Asia (ESCWA) did not meet in 2000, nor did its Preparatory Committee.

The Commission's twenty-first session was to be held in Beirut, Lebanon, on 10 and 11 May 2001.

Economic and social trends

Economic trends

Economic growth, boosted by the oil sector, accelerated in the ESCWA region in 2000, according to the summary of the survey of economic and social developments in the region [E/2001/16]. The combined real GDP of ESCWA members, excluding Iraq, was estimated to have grown by 4.5 per cent, considerably higher than the 1.7 and 2.7 per cent registered in 1999 and 1998, respectively. For the majority of members, the acceleration was due to the surge in oil prices and revenues, but economic reform and liberalization policies pursued in the Gulf Cooperation Council (GCC) countries (Bahrain, Kuwait, Oman, Qatar, Saudi Arabia, United Arab Emirates) were also important.

Real GDP growth rates varied significantly between the GCC countries and those ESCWA members with more diversified economies (Egypt, Iraq, Jordan, Lebanon, Syrian Arab Republic, West Bank and Gaza Strip, Yemen), and among the members of each group. The combined real GDP growth rate for the GCC countries as a group was 5 per cent, while in the more diversified economies, excluding Iraq, it was 3.7 per cent.

Among the GCC countries, the highest economic growth rates in 2000 were registered in Qatar and the United Arab Emirates, and the lowest rates in Kuwait and Oman. Among ESCWA members with more diversified economies, Egypt, Jordan and Yemen achieved estimated real GDP growth rates of 3.2 per cent or higher, while the Syrian Arab Republic witnessed estimated real GDP growth of 2.5 per cent. Lebanon witnessed zero growth and real GDP was estimated to have declined by 3.5 per cent in the West Bank and Gaza Strip. As for Iraq, economic growth was estimated to have increased, owing mainly to higher oil production and revenues, but UN economic sanctions continued to depress economic conditions in the country.

For most of the ESCWA members with more diversified economies, labour-market conditions remained generally unfavourable for job-seekers. Developments in the labour markets in 2000 differed between the members with more diversified economies and the GCC countries, and among the members of each group. By far the most adverse developments in the labour market took place in the West Bank and Gaza Strip, as the closure of those areas by Israeli authorities resulted in instant additional unemployment of about 125,000 workers with jobs in Israel. The unemployment rate in the West Bank and Gaza Strip was 11 per cent during the first half of 2000; in the second half of the year, during border closures, the unemployment rate was estimated to have reached close to 30 per cent. In the GCC countries, expatriate workers accounted for a major share of the total labour force, ranging from about 33 per cent in Bahrain to almost 90 per cent in the United Arab Emirates.

Inflation rates remained low, with most ESCWA members having inflation rates of lower than 3 per cent. In the GCC countries, inflation rates ranged from 0.8 per cent in Bahrain to 2.6 per cent in Kuwait, according to preliminary estimates. Lebanon had the lowest inflation rate, negative 0.8 per cent, among the members with more diversified economies and in the region as a whole. Yemen and the West Bank and Gaza Strip had the highest inflation rates, estimated at 8.5 per cent and 8 per cent, respectively.

The jump in oil revenues during the second half of 2000 enabled most GCC countries to finance their projected 2000 fiscal year budget deficits. The considerably higher oil revenues allowed them not only to increase capital expenditures but also to reduce, or eliminate altogether, their respective budget deficits.

Oil

In 2000, the oil sector performed exceptionally well in most countries of the region. World oil prices surged by 58 per cent, and the region's oil production increased by 6.3 per cent and its oil revenues by 68.3 per cent to reach $163 billion in 2000. That was more than twice the 1998 level of $70 billion and 68.3 per cent larger than its 1999 level of $96.6 billion. The region's oil revenues in 2000 were at their highest level since 1981, when they totalled $171.6 billion. The combined oil revenues of the GCC countries amounted to $130 billion, an increase of $54 billion over the 1999 level. Saudi Arabia's oil revenues alone were estimated at $74.3 billion for 2000, which was about $31 billion more than the level for the preceding year.

Trade

The overall trade performance in 2000 was again driven by the performance of oil exports in the region. Exports of GCC countries were estimated to have increased by 56 per cent. Among the group of more diversified countries, the oil-exporting countries also registered high growth in their exports on account of high oil prices—39 per cent for Egypt, 22 per cent for the Syrian Arab Republic and 72 per cent for Yemen. Other more diversified countries, however, had a relatively weak export performance—7 per cent for Jordan and a low 3 per cent for Lebanon.

Intraregional exports increased by an estimated 2 per cent during the first two quarters of 2000. Among the GCC countries, the share of intraregional exports in total exports was highest for Bahrain, at 34 per cent, 15 per cent for Oman and 9 per cent for the United Arab Emirates. Among the more diversified economies, intraregional exports accounted for 40 per cent and 30 per cent of the exports of Lebanon and Jordan, respectively. Egypt had the highest level of exports to the region of all the more diversified countries ($459 million). The increase in oil prices and revenues led to increased economic growth and a rise in imports in the ESCWA region. The total imports of the ESCWA region (excluding Iraq and the West Bank and Gaza Strip) rose by 11 per cent in 2000. GCC countries registered a 12 per cent growth rate of imports between 1999 and 2000, except the United Arab Emirates and Oman, which registered much lower rates owing to relatively lower reliance on oil revenue. Imports of the more diversified economies grew at about 9 per cent between 1999 and 2000. However, imports to Lebanon came to a virtual halt during 2000 as the country was burdened by economic stagnation.

Social trends

The ESCWA region had undergone significant social and demographic change. Population growth and the resultant urbanization and migration in the region were posing serious challenges reflected in growing poverty, inadequate shelter, deterioration in the quality of education and health services, rising unemployment, migration and the brain drain. There were signs that certain population groups had been marginalized and that an invisible gender division of labour had emerged. There were also challenges posed by globalization and the revolution in communications technology.

Public expenditure on social support systems, particularly care for the elderly and disabled persons, was less than adequate in many countries of the region, while the role of the family and the community in providing services to their members in need was being emphasized. The family, as the primary form of "bonding social capital", was still a powerful and important cell for nurturing, education and caregiving. The demographic transformation in the ESCWA region indicated a rapid decline in children aged 0 to 14 and an increase in the proportion of the working-age group (25-64 years), accompanied by an increase in the relative weight of the elderly (65 years and over). Those demographic transformations were adding to the burden on the family of providing care for the elderly, particularly when family size was being reduced. That, compounded by other social transformations, had begun to reduce the family's capacity to provide proper care for the elderly and the needy in the ESCWA region.

The outlook for the future, both immediately and in the medium term, for most countries in the region did not indicate that the issue of building up social capital for institutionalizing participatory development would become the priority concern of planners and policy makers in the region.

Activities in 2000

During 2000, ESCWA activities under the 2000-2001 work programme [YUN 1999, p. 954] focused on regional follow-up to global conferences, environment, poverty, civil society institutions, gender, WTO and related concerns, globalization, electronic commerce and free trade in the region, as well as gender mainstreaming and human rights.

Economic development and cooperation

ESCWA published the *Survey of Economic and Social Developments in the ESCWA Region, 1999-2000* [Sales No. E.00.II.L.7], which monitored and analysed the region's macroeconomic policies and economic developments in 2000 and provided a forecast for 2001. It also underlined science and technology issues and gender-sensitive participatory development. The *Preliminary Overview of Economic Developments in the ESCWA Region in 2000* [E/ESCWA/ED/2000/5] provided the business community and policy makers with an early assessment of the region's economic performance and the direction of economic changes.

ESCWA undertook a study and convened an expert group meeting (Beirut, 8-10 November) to assess the electronic commerce environment in the region, discuss the constraints faced by companies in the use of e-commerce and the role of Governments in regulating and promoting it, and formulate policies and measures to enhance

its use. The "Comparative study on corporate tax: prospects for harmonization in the ESCWA region" was finalized. The Expert Panel on Information Technology and Development Priorities: Competing in a Knowledge-based Global Economy (Beirut, 15-16 May) provided input to the high-level segment of the substantive session of the Economic and Social Council on the role of information technology in the context of a knowledge-based global economy (see p. 799). It was followed by another expert group meeting on capacity-building initiatives for the twenty-first century in technology (Beirut, 1-3 November), which promoted capacity-building schemes in the region, including technology parks, technology incubators and high-technology clusters.

In agriculture, a study was issued on the harmonization of norms, standards and legal instruments for selected agricultural inputs. A workshop on capacity-building in on-farm water-use efficiency (Beirut, 13-23 November) was organized to increase awareness of the critical water situation, especially its availability for agricultural use; increase efficiency and productivity in water development and use; and identify methods of obtaining quantitative measurements of on-farm water-use efficiency and provide training on the use of those methods.

Transportation

ESCWA member countries considered the facilitation of transport and trade between them an important issue requiring regional cooperation if intraregional trade, which was currently severely limited, was to be increased. In that connection, an expert group meeting on coordination of transport policies to facilitate transboundary flows (Beirut, 26-28 September) assessed the impact of regional and international developments in the transport sector on ESCWA members and considered the role of each of the three elements involved in the development of an integrated transport system: a complementary transport network, a related transport data network and a methodological framework.

Statistics

Support continued for the implementation of the 1993 System of National Accounts (SNA) [YUN 1993, p. 1112]. A workshop on the links between the balance of payments and the 1993 SNA was organized in cooperation with the UN Statistics Division and the International Monetary Fund (Beirut, 27-29 June) to facilitate the exchange of experiences; update information in those two areas, especially with regard to the definitions, classifications and concepts associated with the

1993 SNA; and discuss methods of registering, evaluating and estimating accounts, in particular accounts of transactions with the rest of the world. *A Dictionary of National Accounts Terms* comprised complementary sections in English, French and Arabic and was prepared in cooperation with the Council of Arab Economic Unity of the League of Arab States.

Another workshop was organized on economically active population: employment, unemployment and underemployment (Cairo, 17-21 September) to provide training and upgrade specialists' information and skills in line with international guidelines for the measurement of various aspects of the economically active population. The Regional Meeting on Social Indicators within the Framework of the Implementation and Follow-up of Major United Nations Conferences and Summits in the Arab Countries (Muscat, Oman, 29 October–1 November) presented national efforts to harmonize basic indicators; exchanged views on ways of linking the common country assessment with policies for alleviating poverty and reducing unemployment; and assessed the progress made by national programmes in filling the gaps in data and information and improving their reliability and accuracy. Publications issued on statistical issues included the *Statistical Abstract of the ESCWA Region 2000* (No. 20), the *National Accounts Studies of the ESCWA Region* (No. 20), the *Bulletin on Vital Statistics in the ESCWA Region* (No. 3) and the *External Trade Bulletin of the ESCWA Region* (No. 10).

Natural resources, energy and environment

The Committee on Water Resources, at its fourth session (Beirut, 14-17 November), reviewed the work carried out by the Energy, Natural Resources and Environment Division during 1998-1999, examined the draft programme of work for the 2002-2003 biennium and reviewed the recommendations of expert group meetings held in 2000. An expert group meeting on implications of groundwater rehabilitation for water resources protection and conservation was held concurrently with the Committee session. The secretariat convened an expert group meeting on legal aspects of the management of shared water resources in the ESCWA region (Sharm el-Sheikh, Egypt, 8-11 June) to discuss the legal aspects of shared water resources and the impact of the Convention on the Law of the Non-navigational Uses of International Watercourses, adopted by the General Assembly in resolution 51/229 [YUN 1997, p. 1336].

An expert group meeting on disseminating renewable energy technologies in ESCWA member States (Beirut, 2-5 October) was convened to exchange views and experiences, including opportunities and challenges in the development of renewable energy (especially solar energy), regional and international initiatives and programmes for promoting its use, prospects for renewable energy electricity generation, and policies, regulations and financing mechanisms relating to renewable energy. The Seminar on the Initiation of the ESCWA Renewable Energy Promotion Mechanism (Beirut, 5 October) discussed the updated proposal for the Mechanism and the framework for renewable energy country profiles. By October 2000, 11 ESCWA members had agreed to participate in the Mechanism and had nominated concerned national authorities to represent them as national focal points.

Quality of life

The work of the Social Development Issues and Policies Division focused on building on earlier work relating to poverty alleviation, follow-up to global conferences, human resources development and marginalized groups. It issued studies on the role of microcredit in poverty alleviation: profile of the microcredit sector in Lebanon, and on female-headed households in selected conflict-stricken ESCWA areas: an exploratory survey for formulating poverty alleviation policies, covering Lebanon, the West Bank, the Gaza Strip and Yemen.

A round-table discussion was arranged on capacity-building of NGOs to follow up on the implementation of the recommendations of global conferences (Cairo, 19-21 September). Work continued on a local community development project aimed at mobilizing local capabilities and resources and promoting self-reliance. Under the project, workshops for training local community development workers were held in Jordan (15-26 July), the Syrian Arab Republic (29 July–9 August) and Lebanon (11-21 September).

An expert group meeting (Beirut, 25-26 October) was held on appropriate technologies for accessing population information in the ESCWA region. The Division completed No. 48 of the *Population Bulletin*, which focused on improving demographic analysis through increased attention to accuracy in reporting projections and census figures relating to fertility and death rates in Iraq and Kuwait.

A high-level Arab meeting for follow-up on the implementation of the Habitat Agenda (Istanbul+5) (Manama, Bahrain, 16-18 October) assessed urban development trends in the Arab countries since 1996, examined local and national urban development strategies and explored future prospects for housing and human settlements in the Arab countries. The meeting adopted the main rules and procedures for implementing the Habitat Agenda [YUN 1996, p. 994] in the Arab region, as well as the Manama Declaration on Cities and Human Settlements in the New Millennium.

An expert group meeting on the dynamics of sustainable social development: interlinkages with migration, poverty and urbanization (Beirut, 15-17 November) was organized to identify or provide the means for planning and monitoring urban development, designing integrated local development strategies and disseminating information on best practices in sustainable urban development.

Technical cooperation activities were carried out to assist disabled persons, including computer Braille and income-generating activities for blind persons in the West Bank and Gaza Strip. Two workshops were held to promote self-reliance, with emphasis on employment: one in Bourj al-Barajneh, Lebanon, focused on how to start small-scale businesses (10-27 July) and the other was on self-reliance and advocacy for disabled persons (25-29 September).

Gender issues were considered in a report "Gender and citizenship and the role of NGOs in conflict-stricken ESCWA member countries: case study of Lebanon". National workshops on the development of national gender statistics programmes in the Arab countries were held in Muscat (27-29 February), Algiers, Algeria (29-30 March), and Tunis, Tunisia (23-24 November).

Chapter VI

Energy, natural resources and cartography

The development and conservation of natural resources and energy were considered by several United Nations bodies in 2000, including the Committee on Energy and Natural Resources for Development, which discussed water and land management in the context of sustainable development and other water-resource issues. The Committee also made recommendations to the Economic and Social Council on energy-related matters.

In December, the General Assembly, in a resolution on the World Solar Programme 1996-2005, emphasized the need to intensify research and development in support of sustainable energy development and encouraged the Secretary-General to continue to mobilize technical assistance and funding for national and regional renewable energy projects.

The Fifteenth United Nations Regional Cartographic Conference for Asia and the Pacific was held in Kuala Lumpur, Malaysia, in April. The Conference's recommendations were endorsed by the Economic and Social Council in July. The Council also endorsed the recommendations of the United Nations Group of Experts on Geographical Names, which held its twentieth session in January.

Consideration of the report of the International Atomic Energy Agency, which was presented to the Assembly in November, was deferred to the resumed fifty-fifth session in 2001.

Energy and natural resources

The Committee on Energy and Natural Resources for Development held its second session in New York from 14 to 25 August [E/2000/32]. Two subgroups considered energy and water-resource issues.

The Committee recommended to the Economic and Social Council for adoption a draft resolution on case studies from Governments and international institutions on matters relating to integration of water and land management in the context of Agenda 21 for sustainable development and a draft decision on the report on its second session and the provisional agenda for its third (2001) session.

The Committee brought to the Council's attention decisions on the need to establish linkages between policy makers and professionals working on food security, water security and environmental security [E/2000/32 (dec. 2/1)], the water supply and sanitation subsector [dec. 2/2], strengthening and coordination of the activities of the UN system in the field of water resources [dec. 2/3], UN agency technical reports [dec. 2/4], priorities for action and assessment in water and related areas of Agenda 21 for the 10-year review of the implementation of the outcome of the 1992 United Nations Conference on Environment and Development [dec. 2/5], reconciliation of the incompatible interests of water use, land use and ecosystems [dec. 2/6], river basin management [dec. 2/7] and sustainable exploitation of mineral resources [dec. 2/8]. In addition, the Committee brought a number of recommendations on energy to the Council's attention.

The Council did not consider the Committee's report on its second session in 2000.

Energy

At the second session of the Committee on Energy and Natural Resources for Development [E/2000/32], the Subgroup on Energy considered a report on the follow-up to the first (1999) session of the Committee [E/C.14/2000/7] and the report of the Ad Hoc Open-ended Intergovernmental Group of Experts on Energy and Sustainable Development (see below), on which it based its discussion of the Committee's contribution to the ninth (2001) session of the Commission on Sustainable Development and its preparatory process.

For its review of salient trends, the Subgroup had before it reports on energy and the residential sector [E/C.14/2000/8]; renewable sources of energy, with emphasis on solar energy [E/C.14/2000/9]; financial mechanisms and economic instruments to speed up the investment in sustainable energy development [E/C.14/2000/4]; and coordination of energy activities within the UN system [E/C.14/2000/6]. The Committee, in a plenary meeting, considered a report of the Secretary-General on the status of hydroelectricity generation [E/C.14/2000/5].

The Subgroup also discussed progress made in preparing the *World Energy Assessment* [Sales No.

00.III.B.5], initiated by the United Nations Development Programme, the United Nations Department of Economic and Social Affairs and the World Energy Council and published later in 2000, and its implication for sustainable energy policy development. The Committee recommended to the Economic and Social Council that a mechanism be developed to update the *Assessment* regularly.

Contribution to CSD (ninth session). In accordance with Economic and Social Council resolution 1999/60 [YUN 1999, p. 959], the Ad Hoc Open-ended Intergovernmental Group of Experts on Energy and Sustainable Development, established to prepare for the ninth (2001) session of the Commission on Sustainable Development (CSD), held its first session in New York from 6 to 10 March [E/CN.17/2000/12]. The Group of Experts, having considered the Secretary-General's report on key issues of energy and sustainable development [E/CN.17/ESD/2000/3], identified the following as being of particular importance: accessibility of energy, energy efficiency, renewable energy, advanced fossil fuel technologies, nuclear energy technologies, rural energy, energy and transportation, technology transfer, capacity-building, mobilization of financial resources, and international and regional cooperation. The Expert Group recommended to CSD the agenda for its second session, to be held in 2001.

CSD, at its eighth session (New York, 24 April–5 May) (see p. 790), endorsed the agenda for the Group's second session [E/2000/29 (dec. 8/10)]. It also took note of the report of the Committee on Energy and Natural Resources for Development on its first (1999) [YUN 1999, p. 958] session [dec. 8/9].

On 25 August [E/2000/32], the Committee on Energy and Natural Resources for Development adopted recommendations concerning the key issues formulated by the Group of Experts; it also recommended the establishment of a task force on energy within the UN system.

In preparation for the 2001 sessions of CSD and the Group of Experts, a High-level Regional Meeting on Energy for Sustainable Development of the Economic and Social Commission for Asia and the Pacific was hosted by Indonesia (Bali, 23-24 November) [E/CN.17/2001/10].

The Global Forum on Sustainable Energy held its first meeting in Laxenburg, Austria, from 11 to 13 December [E/CN.17/2001/7].

World Solar Programme (1996-2005)

In response to General Assembly resolution 54/215 [YUN 1999, p. 960], the Secretary-General submitted a June report on the promotion of new and renewable sources of energy, including the implementation of the World Solar Programme 1996-2005 [A/55/91]. He stated that a number of countries had taken legislative action to promote renewable sources of energy in line with the recommendations contained in the 1996 Harare Declaration on Solar Energy and Sustainable Development.

The World Solar Commission and its General Secretariat (located in the United Nations Educational, Scientific and Cultural Organization (UNESCO)) continued to guide and coordinate a number of projects included in the Programme. Other areas of the UN system that were undertaking initiatives in new and renewable sources of energy included UNESCO, the UN Department of Economic and Social Affairs, the regional commissions, the Food and Agriculture Organization of the United Nations, the Global Environment Facility, the United Nations Environment Programme, the United Nations Industrial Development Organization, the World Bank and the World Meteorological Organization.

The Secretary-General concluded that the number and size of the activities being carried out demonstrated that there was an increasing interest worldwide in the use of renewable sources of energy and that progress had been achieved at the international, regional and national levels in the implementation of solar energy projects and programmes, including those of the World Solar Programme.

GENERAL ASSEMBLY ACTION

On 20 December [meeting 87], the General Assembly, on the recommendation of the Second (Economic and Financial) Committee [A/55/582/Add.6], adopted **resolution 55/205** without vote [agenda item 95 (*f*)].

World Solar Programme 1996-2005

The General Assembly,

Recalling its resolutions 53/7 of 16 October 1998 and 54/215 of 22 December 1999 on the World Solar Programme 1996-2005,

Recalling also resolution 14 concerning the World Solar Programme 1996-2005, adopted by the General Conference of the United Nations Educational, Scientific and Cultural Organization at its twenty-ninth session in November 1997,

Reaffirming that the convening at Harare on 16 and 17 September 1996 of the World Solar Summit, at which the Harare Declaration on Solar Energy and Sustainable Development was adopted and preparation of the World Solar Programme 1996-2005 approved, was a step in pursuance of the implementation of Agenda 21, which is a multifaceted and, at the same time, fundamental programme of action for achieving sustainable development,

Recalling resolution 19 adopted by the General Conference of the United Nations Educational, Scientific and Cultural Organization at its thirtieth session in November 1999, concerning the Global Renewable Energy Education and Training Programme 1996-2005, which constitutes one of the major programmes of universal value of the World Solar Programme 1996-2005,

Reiterating that mutually supportive efforts at the national and international levels are imperative in the pursuit of sustainable development, which includes the provision of financial resources and the transfer of technology for the application of cost-effective energy and the wider use of environment-friendly, renewable energies,

Acknowledging that the General Assembly continues to play an important role in promoting the World Solar Programme 1996-2005,

Acknowledging also that the Commission on Sustainable Development and the Economic and Social Council play a pivotal role as forums for the discussions on new and renewable sources of energy and sustainable development,

Expressing its appreciation of the continued efforts of the Secretary-General in bringing the World Solar Programme 1996-2005 to the attention of relevant sources of funding and technical assistance,

Calling for further action to ensure that the World Solar Programme 1996-2005 is fully integrated into the mainstream of the efforts of the United Nations system towards attaining the objective of sustainable development,

Emphasizing that the achievement of more substantive results in the implementation of the World Solar Programme 1996-2005 will require the active involvement of all concerned parties, including Governments, multilateral funding agencies and relevant bodies within the United Nations system,

1. *Takes note with appreciation* of the report of the Secretary-General on the promotion of new and renewable sources of energy, including the implementation of the World Solar Programmme 1996-2005;

2. *Notes with appreciation* the role that the World Solar Commission continues to play in the mobilization of international support and assistance for the implementation of many of the national high-priority projects on renewable sources of energy included in the World Solar Programme 1996-2005, many of which are being executed with national funding;

3. *Notes* that although significant financial support has been provided by some developed countries that are Members of the United Nations and some intergovernmental organizations, within and outside the United Nations system, in the implementation of the World Solar Programme 1996-2005, more action still needs to be taken in this regard;

4. *Invites* the international community to support, as appropriate, including by providing financial resources, the efforts of developing countries to move towards sustainable patterns of energy production and consumption;

5. *Recognizes* that rural energy services, including their financing, should be designed to maximize local ownership, as appropriate;

6. *Reiterates its call upon* all relevant funding institutions and bilateral and multilateral donors, as well as regional funding institutions and non-governmental organizations, to support, as appropriate, the efforts being made for the development of the renewable energy sector in developing countries on the basis of environment-friendly, renewable sources of energy of demonstrated viability, while taking fully into account the development structure of energy-based economies of developing countries, and to assist in the attainment of the levels of investment necessary to expand energy supplies beyond urban areas;

7. *Encourages* the Secretary-General to continue his efforts to promote the mobilization of adequate technical assistance and funding and to enhance the effectiveness and the full utilization of existing international funds for the effective implementation of national and regional high-priority projects in the area of renewable sources of energy;

8. *Emphasizes* the need to intensify research and development in support of sustainable energy development, which will require increased commitment on the part of all stakeholders, including Governments and the private sector, to deploy financial and manpower resources for accelerating research efforts;

9. *Recognizes* that the wider use of available renewable energy technologies requires the diffusion of available technologies on a global scale, including through North-South and South-South cooperation;

10. *Takes note* of the decision of the General Conference of the United Nations Educational, Scientific and Cultural Organization regarding the contribution of the Global Renewable Energy Education and Training Programme 1996-2005 in attaining the objective of sustainable development, and encourages the Director-General of the United Nations Educational, Scientific and Cultural Organization, in this context, to mobilize resources, both human and financial, as mandated, to ensure the effective implementation of the Programme and make efforts to promote public awareness in all Member States in this regard, with the support of international, regional and national institutions, both public and private;

11. *Invites* the Director-General of the United Nations Educational, Scientific and Cultural Organization to make effective the implementation of the Global Renewable Energy Education and Training Programme 1996-2005 in the different regions and to strengthen the implementation of its African chapter;

12. *Encourages* the Ad Hoc Inter-Agency Task Force on Energy to continue its efforts to ensure that the work of the World Solar Programme 1996-2005 is fully integrated into the mainstream of the efforts of the United Nations system to achieve the objectives of sustainable development and to coordinate the contributions of all relevant organizations of the United Nations system to the consideration of the theme of energy by the Commission on Sustainable Development at its ninth session, to be held in 2001, and at the ten-year review of progress achieved in the implementation of the outcome of the United Nations Conference on Environment and Development, to be held in 2002;

13. *Requests* the Secretary-General, in consultation with the United Nations Educational, Scientific and Cultural Organization and in cooperation with the United Nations Development Programme, the Global Environment Facility, the United Nations Environment Programme and other relevant organizations, to submit to the General Assembly at its fifty-sixth session a report on concrete action being taken for the promotion of new and renewable sources of energy, including

the effective implementation of, and mobilization of resources for, the World Solar Programme 1996-2005;

14. *Decides* to include in the provisional agenda of its fifty-sixth session, under the item entitled "Environment and sustainable development", the sub-item entitled "Promotion of new and renewable sources of energy, including the implementation of the World Solar Programme 1996-2005".

Nuclear energy

By an August note [A/55/284], the Secretary-General transmitted to the General Assembly the 1999 report of the International Atomic Energy Agency (IAEA). Presenting and updating the report in the Assembly on 6 November [A/55/PV.52], the IAEA Director General stated that in 1999 nuclear power supplied roughly one sixth of global electricity. Trends varied by region: some countries were phasing out nuclear power plants, while others had embarked on new construction or innovative research and development. While the future of nuclear power remained uncertain, it was clear that certain factors would be crucial to that future: the safety of facility operations; the demonstrated feasibility of safe and environmentally sound radioactive-waste disposal; the ability to make nuclear power economically competitive; the growing need for environmentally clean sources of energy; and public acceptance.

IAEA's role, said the Director General, was to help ensure that the nuclear power option remained open, a process that required, above all, developing innovative reactor and fuel cycle technologies. In that regard, IAEA intended to establish a task force to assess the technology and energy demands of prospective users.

Noting that a major part of the Agency's nuclear technology activities was related to applications other than electricity generation, the Director General described IAEA's work in the areas of food production, human health, water resources management, environmental protection and nuclear safeguards. He also discussed IAEA's inability to implement its nuclear inspection mandate in the Democratic People's Republic of Korea and in Iraq (see pp. 321, 293).

On 23 December, the General Assembly decided that the agenda item on the report of IAEA would remain for consideration at its resumed fifty-fifth (2001) session (**decision 55/458**).

Natural resources

Water resources

At the second session of the Committee on Energy and Natural Resources for Development [E/2000/32], the Subgroup on Water Resources reviewed reports of the Secretary-General on: progress made in providing safe water supply and sanitation for all during the 1990s [E/CN.17/2000/13], prepared for CSD's 2000 session (see p. 790); issues related to the spatial planning of land (including minerals) and water resources [E/C.14/2000/2]; and technical cooperation activities of the UN system in the field of water resources [E/CN.14/2000/10].

On 25 August, the Committee, on the Subgroup's recommendation, adopted decisions on the need to establish linkages between policy makers and professionals working on food security, water security and environmental security [E/2000/32 (dec. 2/1)]; the water supply and sanitation subsector [dec. 2/2]; strengthening and coordination of the activities of the UN system in the field of water resources [dec. 2/3]; UN agency technical reports [dec. 2/4]; priorities for action and assessment in water and related areas of Agenda 21 for the 10-year review of the implementation of the outcome of the 1992 United Nations Conference on Environment and Development (UNCED) [dec. 2/5]; reconciliation of the incompatible interests of water use, land use and ecosystems [dec. 2/6]; and river basin management [dec. 2/7].

Also on the recommendation of the Subgroup, the Committee recommended to the Economic and Social Council for adoption a draft resolution on case studies from Governments and international institutions on matters relating to integration of water and land management in the context of Agenda 21 for sustainable development, by which the Council would invite Governments and international organizations to make available for the 10-year review of the outcome of UNCED case studies carried out by them on river basin cooperation; the protection of catchment areas for the management of drinking water sources; community involvement in land and water resources management for agriculture; water supply in both rain-fed and irrigated areas; integrated land and water resources management; and impacts of management of water resources, both quality and quantity, on the economy of a country or region. The Economic and Social Council did not consider the Committee's report in 2000.

Water supply and sanitation

In response to General Assembly resolution 50/126 [YUN 1995, p. 1059], the Secretary-General submitted to CSD at its eighth session (see PART THREE, Chapter I) a report on progress made in providing safe water supply and sanitation for all during the 1990s [E/CN.17/2000/13], including proposals for action for the ensuing decade at the national and international levels. The report, which was based on information provided by the World Health Organization/United Nations Children's Fund joint monitoring programme and took into account the request made by the Economic and Social Council in resolution 1999/47 [YUN 1999, p. 964] for a number of issues to be included, was transmitted to the Council and the Assembly by an April note of the Secretary-General [A/55/65-E/2000/19].

The report stated that current estimates confirmed that in 2000 at least 1.1 billion people still lacked access to water supply and almost 2.5 billion to sanitation. Nevertheless, some progress had been achieved during the decade. According to a new methodology, approximately 4.9 billion people worldwide, representing about 81 per cent of the total population, currently had access to water supply, and 3.6 billion people, representing 59 per cent of the total population, had access to sanitation. However, in the developing regions the improvement was uneven between 1990 and 2000. In Africa, access to water supply rose from 52.3 per cent of the population to 60.7 per cent; in Asia, it rose from 74.8 per cent to 81.1 per cent; and in Latin America and the Caribbean, it rose from 80.6 per cent to 82.2 per cent. Access to sanitation over the same period rose from 56.8 per cent to 58.5 per cent of the population in Africa; from 36.4 per cent to 47.2 per cent in Asia; and from 64.9 per cent to 75.3 per cent in Latin America and the Caribbean. There was also a discrepancy between rural and urban areas, with access to water supply in urban areas in all three developing regions having fallen from 92.4 per cent in 1990 to 92.1 per cent in 2000; it had risen in rural areas from 60.7 per cent to 68.9 per cent. Access to sanitation over the same period rose from 70.8 per cent to 80 per cent in urban areas and from 26.1 per cent to 32.5 per cent in rural areas.

In view of the statistics, the report called for action on a broad front, starting with an assessment or update by Governments of their current situation, based on reliable data and on the establishment of time-bound ambitious but realistic targets.

On 28 July, the Economic and Social Council took note of the report (**decision 2000/298**); the General Assembly took note of it on 20 December (**decision 55/442**).

International Year of Freshwater (2003)

By a 17 April letter to the Secretary-General [A/55/60-E/2000/17], Tajikistan proposed that the General Assembly proclaim the year 2003 as the International Year of Freshwater, referring to the fact that the President of Tajikistan had made such a proposal in his statement to the

fifty-fourth (1999) session of the Assembly [A/54/PV.20].

On 20 December [meeting 87], the General Assembly, on the recommendation of the Second Committee [A/55/582/Add.8], adopted **resolution 55/196** without vote [agenda item 95].

International Year of Freshwater, 2003

The General Assembly,

Recalling the provisions of Agenda 21, the Programme for the Further Implementation of Agenda 21 adopted at its nineteenth special session and decisions of the Economic and Social Council and those of the Commission on Sustainable Development at its sixth session, relating to freshwater,

Recalling also Economic and Social Council resolution 1980/67 of 25 July 1980 on international years and anniversaries, in which the Council recognized the contribution that the celebration of international years could make to the furtherance of international co-operation and understanding,

Recalling further its resolution 53/199 of 15 December 1998 on the proclamation of international years,

Noting the ongoing work in the United Nations system and the work of other intergovernmental organizations on freshwater,

1. *Proclaims* the year 2003 as the International Year of Freshwater;

2. *Invites* the Subcommittee on Water Resources of the Administrative Committee on Coordination to serve as the coordinating entity for the Year and to develop relevant preliminary proposals for consideration by the General Assembly at its fifty-sixth session on possible activities, including possible sources of funding, that could take place at all levels, as appropriate;

3. *Calls upon* Member States, national and international organizations, major groups and the private sector to make voluntary contributions in accordance with the guidelines for international years and anniversaries;

4. *Encourages* all Member States, the United Nations system and all other actors to take advantage of the Year to increase awareness of the importance of freshwater and to promote action at the local, national, regional and international levels;

5. *Requests* the Secretary-General to submit to the General Assembly at its fifty-seventh session a progress report on the preparations for the International Year of Freshwater.

Inter-agency action

The Subcommittee on Water Resources of the Administrative Committee on Coordination (ACC), at its twenty-first session (Bangkok, Thailand, 16-20 October) [ACC/2000/18], discussed and brought to the attention of the Inter-Agency Committee on Sustainable Development (IACSD) (see PART THREE, Chapter I) matters relating to preparations for the 10-year review in 2002 of the UNCED process related to water resources; preparations for the World Water Development Report (to be issued in 2003) and the World Water Assessment Programme; follow-up to the review of the Subcommittee's methods of work; and arrangements for the Subcommittee's twenty-second (2001) session. Also discussed were the outcome of the eighth session of CSD (see PART THREE, Chapter I); regional activities; activities related to the reduction of arsenic in drinking water; water quality and waste-water initiatives; environmental sanitation initiatives; the outcome of the second session of the Committee on Energy and Natural Resources for Development (see p. 959); public information with particular reference to the 2001 World Day for Water (22 March); and other issues related to water supply and sanitation.

On 5 May [E/2000/29 (dec. 8/11)], CSD took note of a consultant's review of the ACC Subcommittee on Water Resources and the comments of IACSD thereon [E/CN.17/2000/18].

Land resources

By a 5 May decision on integrated planning and management of land resources [E/2000/29 (dec. 8/3)], CSD established priorities for future work in the area and urged Governments and the international community to take action with regard to prevention and/or mitigation of land degradation; access to land and security of tenure; critical sectors and issues; stakeholder participation; and international cooperation, including that for capacity-building, information-sharing and technology transfer (see also PART THREE, Chapters I and VII).

Mineral resources

During the second session of the Committee on Energy and Natural Resources for Development, a one-day panel discussion took place on minerals, metals and rehabilitation in the context of sustainable development. The discussion was jointly organized by the UN Department of Economic and Social Affairs and the International Council on Metals and the Environment as follow-up to CSD decision 8/3 (see above).

On 25 August, the Committee adopted a decision on the sustainable exploitation of mineral resources [E/2000/32 (dec. 2/8)], in which, taking note of CSD decision 8/3 and aware that mining investments had shifted significantly towards developing countries where they might not have had adequate regulatory frameworks for sustainable mining, it decided to examine, at its third (2001) session, the social, economic and environmental impacts of minerals extraction and metal production on integrated land and water management. It also decided to work towards formulating strategies for the rehabilitation of land and water degradation by mining operations.

Cartography

UN Regional Cartographic Conference for Asia and the Pacific

By **decision 2000/209** of 4 February, the Economic and Social Council accepted the Government of Malaysia's offer [E/2000/5] to host the Fifteenth United Nations Regional Cartographic Conference for Asia and the Pacific in Kuala Lumpur from 10 to 14 April 2000.

As recommended by the Fourteenth Conference in 1997 and endorsed by the Council in decision 1997/221 [YUN 1997, p. 1037], the Fifteenth Conference, which was held from 11 to 14 April, focused on the continued and strengthened contribution of surveying, mapping and charting to the implementation of Agenda 21, adopted by the 1992 United Nations Conference on Environment and Development [YUN 1992, p. 672]. The Conference's work was organized around five technical committees dealing with cadastral issues, regional geodetic infrastructure, fundamental data, development needs and geographical names.

The Conference adopted resolutions dealing with fundamental data; institutional strengthening, education and training; regional geodetic infrastructure; land administration for sustainable development; economic aspects of modern surveying, mapping, geospatial data infrastructure and land administration programmes; promotion of national and regional geographic names standardization programmes; and cooperation with the United Nations Geographic Database initiative. It also established the provisional agenda for the Sixteenth Conference. The texts of the resolutions and the provisional agenda were included in the report of the Conference [E/CONF.92/1].

By **decision 2000/229** of 26 July, the Economic and Social Council endorsed the recommendations of the Fifteenth Conference that the Sixteenth Conference be convened for five working days in mid-2003, with a primary focus on the continued and strengthened contribution of cartography and geographic information in support of the implementation of Agenda 21; and that the Secretary-General be requested to take measures to implement the other recommendations of the Fifteenth Conference. In particular, the United Nations should continue to support surveying, mapping and spatial data infrastructure activities in the Asia and Pacific region and continue to facilitate the participation of the least developed countries and the small island developing States of the region.

On 28 July, the Council took note of the report of the Secretary-General on the Fifteenth Conference [E/2000/48] (**decision 2000/299**).

Standardization of geographical names

At its twentieth session (New York, 17-28 January) [E/2000/49], the United Nations Group of Experts on Geographical Names considered the reports of linguistic/geographical divisions on their regions and on progress being made in the standardization of geographical names since the Seventh (1998) United Nations Conference on the Standardization of Geographical Names [YUN 1998, p. 978]. Six working groups reported and continued their activities in the areas of training courses in toponymy, toponymic data files and gazetteers, toponymic terminology, romanization systems, country names, and publicity and funding. The Group of Experts ascertained that the provisional agenda and rules of procedure were in place for the Eighth Conference, to be held in Berlin in 2002 in accordance with Economic and Social Council decision 1998/221 [ibid., p. 979]. It also prepared a provisional agenda for a proposed twenty-first session to be held in conjunction with the Eighth Conference.

By **decision 2000/230** of 26 July, the Council endorsed the recommendations of the Group of Experts that the twenty-first session of the Group be convened for two working days (26 August and 6 September 2002) in Berlin, in conjunction with the Eighth Conference, to facilitate and to follow up the work of the Conference; and that the Secretary-General be requested to take measures to implement that decision.

On 28 July, the Council took note of the report of the Secretary-General on the twentieth session of the Group of Experts [E/2000/49] (**decision 2000/299**).

Chapter VII

Environment and human settlements

In 2000, the United Nations and the international community continued efforts to protect the environment through legally binding instruments and the activities of the United Nations Environment Programme (UNEP).

The first Global Ministerial Environment Forum/sixth special session of the UNEP Governing Council (Malmö, Sweden, 29-31 May) adopted the Malmö Ministerial Declaration, which aimed at setting the environmental agenda for the twenty-first century. The Declaration provided input to the Millennium Summit in September (see p. 47) and to the 10-year review of the implementation of the outcome of the United Nations Conference on Environment and Development planned for 2002 (see p. 792), which together would set the global agenda for environment and sustainable development for the years ahead. In his report to the United Nations Millennium Summit (see p. 55), the Secretary-General called on Member States to become actively engaged in the Millennium Ecosystem Assessment—an international collaborative effort to evaluate the five major ecosystems (forests, freshwater systems, grasslands, coastal areas and agroecosystems). The Assessment, scheduled to be launched in June 2001, would provide parties to various international ecosystem conventions with access to the data needed to evaluate progress towards meeting convention goals.

Concerned about the need for conservation and sustainable development of forests, the Economic and Social Council established in October the United Nations Forum on Forests to promote policy development and dialogue among Governments, enhance programme coordination and strengthen political commitment in that area. The Global International Waters Assessment, inaugurated in 2000, was aimed at assessing international waters in 66 subregions, as well as the ecological status and the causes of environmental problems in those water areas. The first phase of the Global Programme of Action for the Protection of the Marine Environment from Land-based Activities was completed in 2000, including the preparation of 10 regional assessments and nine regional programmes.

The Conference of the Parties to the 1992 Convention on Biological Diversity (Montreal, 24-29 January) adopted the Cartagena Protocol on Biosafety. Upon entry into force, the Protocol would provide a framework for addressing environmental impacts of bioengineered products, referred to as living modified organisms, that crossed international borders. The Intergovernmental Negotiating Committee for an International Legally Binding Instrument for Implementing International Action on Certain Persistent Organic Pollutants met in March and December and approved the draft text of a legally binding instrument. The Conference of the Parties to the 1994 United Nations Convention to Combat Desertification in those Countries Experiencing Serious Drought and/or Desertification, particularly in Africa (Bonn, 11-22 December), approved a declaration on the commitments to enhance implementation of the Convention, stressing the need for special efforts to combat and prevent desertification and/or mitigate the effects of drought between 2001 and 2010.

The Commission on Human Settlements, at its first session (Nairobi, Kenya, 8-12 May), acting as the Preparatory Committee for the special (2001) session of the General Assembly for an overall review and appraisal of the implementation of the 1996 Habitat Agenda, adopted a series of resolutions on the review and appraisal process. It submitted two initiatives—the Global Campaign for Secure Tenure and the Global Campaign for Urban Governance—to operationalize its own role in assisting countries to implement the Habitat Agenda. In December, the General Assembly decided on the provisional agenda for the special session and that it would be held in June 2001 in New York.

Environment

UN Environment Programme

Ministerial Forum/Governing Council special session

The first annual Global Ministerial Environment Forum, also serving as the sixth special session of the Governing Council of the United Nations Environment Programme, was held (Malmö, Sweden, 29-31 May) [A/55/25], as called for by the General Assembly in resolution 53/242 [YUN 1999,

p. 975]. At the session, the Ministers of Environment and heads of delegation considered major environmental challenges in the new century, the private sector and the environment, and the responsibility and role of civil society regarding the environment in a globalized world, topics that were the subject of May discussion papers [UNEP/GCSS.VI/8] submitted by the UNEP Executive Director. The Forum adopted the Malmö Ministerial Declaration [A/55/25 (dec. SS.VI/1)] (see p. 968), aimed at setting the environmental agenda for the twenty-first century. The Declaration, which emphasized a major role for UNEP, provided a significant input to the Assembly's Millennium Summit in September (see p. 47) and would contribute to the 10-year review of the implementation of the outcome of the United Nations Conference on Environment and Development (UNCED) [YUN 1992, p. 670] in 2002 (see pp. 792 and 969), which together would set the global agenda for environment and sustainable development for the years ahead.

On 31 May [dec. SS.VI/4], the Governing Council decided to include in the agenda of its twenty-first (2001) session the item "Outcome of the first Global Ministerial Environment Forum", and asked its Bureau, in consultation with the Committee of Permanent Representatives and with the support of the Executive Director, to decide on the organizational aspects of the ministerial-level consultations at the second Forum, also serving as the twenty-first session of the Council, and to decide on the themes for the consultations.

The Committee of the Whole considered an April report of the Executive Director on the activities of UNEP [UNEP/GCSS.VI/6 & Add.1/Rev.1]; UNEP's contribution to the implementation of Agenda 21, adopted by UNCED [YUN 1992, p. 672], and the Programme for the Further Implementation of Agenda 21, contained in Assembly resolution S/19-2 [YUN 1997, p. 792]; and the provisional agenda of the second Global Ministerial Environment Forum/twenty-first session of the Governing Council.

Subsidiary body

The Bureau of the 36-member High-level Committee of Ministers and Officials of UNEP met (Geneva, 2 April) [UNEP/HLC/5/INF/1] to consider the Committee's role and mandate. The Bureau was of the view that the future of the Committee, having fulfilled its mandate to provide a political framework during the Governing Council's intersessional period, should be determined by the Council in 2001 and that the Committee itself should consider the issue. The Bu-

reau noted that in doing so the Council would benefit from the experience gained through the convening of the first Ministerial Forum/Sixth Special Session of the Council. The Bureau recommended the consideration of a high-level intergovernmental consultative mechanism during the intersessional period of the Council and the Forum, a mechanism that was flexible and based on equitable geographical representation. It also discussed the option of a consolidated/extended Bureau of the Governing Council, the Forum and the Committee of Permanent Representatives as a possible intersessional consultative mechanism. It entrusted the Executive Director to undertake consultations with Member States to facilitate a decision on the issue by the Council in 2001.

GENERAL ASSEMBLY ACTION

On 20 December [meeting 87], the General Assembly, on the recommendation of the Second (Economic and Financial) Committee [A/55/582/Add.1], adopted **resolution 55/200** without vote [agenda item 95 (a)].

Report of the Governing Council of the United Nations Environment Programme on its sixth special session

The General Assembly,

Recalling its resolution 2997(XXVII) of 15 December 1972, by which it decided to establish the Governing Council of the United Nations Environment Programme,

Recalling also its resolutions 54/216 of 22 December 1999 on the report of the Governing Council of the United Nations Environment Programme on its twentieth session and 53/242 of 28 July 1999 on the report of the Secretary-General on environment and human settlements,

Recalling further the Nairobi Declaration on the Role and Mandate of the United Nations Environment Programme, adopted by the Governing Council of the Programme at its nineteenth session,

Underlining the fact that the forthcoming ten-year review of progress achieved in the implementation of the outcome of the United Nations Conference on Environment and Development will provide the international community with a unique opportunity to take action to implement its commitments and to strengthen the international cooperation urgently required to address the challenges of sustainable development in the twenty-first century,

Reaffirming the role of the United Nations Environment Programme in the preparations for the ten-year review of progress achieved in the implementation of the outcome of the Conference, as reflected in the decisions taken by the Commission on Sustainable Development at its eighth session,

1. *Takes note with appreciation* of the report of the Governing Council of the United Nations Environment Programme on its sixth special session, takes note of the decisions contained therein as well as the consultations among member States in preparation for the twenty-first session, and, in this regard, also takes note

of the ongoing consultations contributing to the further elaboration and implementation of the water policy and strategy of the Programme;

2. *Welcomes* the convening of the First Global Ministerial Environment Forum, and, in this regard, expresses its deep appreciation to the Government of Sweden for the generous manner in which it hosted and provided facilities for the Forum, and takes note with appreciation of the Malmö Ministerial Declaration as one of the contributions to the Millennium Summit and to the preparations for the ten-year review of progress achieved in the implementation of the outcome of the United Nations Conference on Environment and Development;

3. *Stresses* the importance of the section of the United Nations Millennium Declaration on protecting our common environment, in which heads of State and Government reaffirmed the principles of sustainable development as set out in Agenda 21, and in particular resolved to adopt a new ethic of conservation and stewardship in all our environmental actions;

4. *Welcomes* the decision of the Governing Council on the contribution of the United Nations Environment Programme to the implementation of Agenda 21 and the Programme for the Further Implementation of Agenda 21;

5. *Stresses* that the United Nations Environment Programme, as the principal body in the field of the environment within the United Nations system, should continue to play an important role in the implementation of Agenda 21 and in the preparations for the ten-year review of progress achieved in the implementation of the outcome of the Conference;

6. *Underlines* the need for sufficient financial resources, on a stable and predictable basis, to ensure the full implementation of the mandate of the Programme, in particular with a view to ensuring its strong involvement in the preparatory process for the ten-year review of progress achieved in the implementation of the outcome of the Conference at its various levels, and in the implementation of the outcome of the review;

7. *Requests* the Secretary-General to provide the necessary resources from the regular budget of the United Nations to the United Nations Environment Programme for the biennium 2002-2003, in accordance with current budgetary practices, and to consider other ways to support the strengthening of the Programme in view of the ten-year review of progress achieved in the implementation of the outcome of the United Nations Conference on Environment and Development.

Malmö Ministerial Declaration

In the Malmö Ministerial Declaration, adopted on 31 May [dec. SS.VI/1], the Governing Council recognized the growing trends of environmental degradation that threatened the sustainability of the planet, despite the commitment of the international community to halt them. Underscoring an alarming discrepancy between commitments and action, it emphasized that goals and targets agreed by the international community in relation to sustainable develop-

ment should be implemented. The prevailing challenges appeared to be to ensure that actions were taken to implement the political and legal commitments entered into by the international community in a timely manner, and to ensure that the results of such actions reversed the current trend of environmental degradation.

The Declaration stressed the need to address the root causes of global environmental degradation embedded in social and economic problems such as pervasive poverty, unsustainable production and consumption patterns, inequity in distribution of wealth and the debt burden. It underlined that success in combating environmental degradation depended on the full participation of all actors in society and suggested measures to enhance collaboration with the private sector and civil society to address environmental issues.

UNEP activities

In an April report [UNEP/GCSS.VI/6], the Executive Director summarized the major activities undertaken by UNEP since the conclusion of the Governing Council's twentieth session in February 1999 [YUN 1999, p. 971].

UNEP concentrated on five priority areas: environmental information, assessment and research, including environmental emergency response capacity and strengthening UNEP early warning and assessment functions; enhanced coordination of environmental conventions and development of environmental policy instruments; freshwater; technology transfer and industry; and support to Africa. Activities in other areas of importance were described, including regional cooperation and representation, communication and public information, and the Global Environment Facility (GEF) (see p. 970).

The report contained information on the financial structure of UNEP. As at 31 March, the Environment Fund had received pledges of $12.8 million from 27 countries, of which 8 had paid a total of $3.6 million. Total contributions for 2000 were estimated at $49.3 million. For 2000-2001, it was estimated that UNEP would receive contributions to the Fund of some $98.7 million, and would have resources available for 2000-2001 of $124 million. For 2000, an allocation of $59.6 million was released by the Executive Director. Of that amount, $50 million was allocated to Fund programme activities, $2.5 million to the Fund programme reserve and $7.1 million to management and administration. UNEP administered 92 trust funds, of which 73 or $38.9 million directly supported UNEP's work programme. Another 19 trust funds supported conventions, protocols, regional seas action plans, the full Multilateral Fund, the United Nations Fund for International Partnership, funded by the United Nations Foundation (see p. 1328), and the GEF-funded trust fund. Their total expenditure amounted to $290.2 million, of which the Multi-lateral Fund alone accounted for $202.2 million (70 per cent) of the total expenditure. An addendum to the report [UNEP/GCSS.VI/6/Add.1/Rev.1] contained the UNEP water policy and strategy.

On 31 May [dec. SS.VI/2], the Governing Council, taking note of the report, asked the Executive Director to take into account comments made in the further development of the water policy and strategy and to take steps for its implementation and to report in 2001. It asked that future activity reports to the Council and the Committee of Permanent Representatives present a clear correlation between relevant decisions of the Council and other legislative bodies, activities and resources set aside, actual budget expenditure and qualitative evaluation of results achieved.

Agenda 21

In May [UNEP/GCSS.VI/7], the Executive Director reported to the Governing Council on the proposed process of preparation for the 10-year review of the implementation of the outcome of UNCED [YUN 1992, p. 670] in 2002. He stated that the Council might wish to consider means by which it would submit to the General Assembly its views on how UNEP activities were contributing to the implementation of Agenda 21, a global plan of action for sustainable development adopted at UNCED [ibid., p. 672], and the Programme for the Further Implementation of Agenda 21 contained in General Assembly resolution S-19/2 [YUN 1997, p. 792], as well as its views on UNEP's contribution to the preparatory process for the 10-year review.

The Governing Council, on 31 May [dec. SS.VI/3], requested the Committee of Permanent Representatives to review UNEP activities that contributed to the implementation of Agenda 21 and the Programme for its further implementation; called on the Executive Director to prepare a report to the Committee for distribution to Governments for their information and comments, and to ensure UNEP's contribution to the preparatory process for the 10-year review; further requested the Executive Director to submit a final report to the forthcoming Assembly session (see below); and asked him to report in 2001.

In October [A/55/447 & Corr.1], the Secretary-General transmitted to the Assembly the report of the Executive Director describing UNEP's contribution to the implementation of Agenda 21 and the Programme for its further implementation. The report traced the evolution of UNEP's

policy framework since UNCED in terms of the intergovernmental decisions and institutional reforms that had clarified, refined and strengthened UNEP's role and mandate, restructuring and thus positioning UNEP to catalyse and coordinate the UN system's response to the environmental dimension of Agenda 21. It presented UNEP's programme developments that had contributed to the implementation of Agenda 21 and the Programme for its further implementation, and addressed the issue of financing.

The report concluded that, despite considerable progress in the implementation of Agenda 21, the scale of current environmental and sustainable development problems required the mobilization of political will, as well as financial and technical resources, supported by strong and focused institutions that went beyond what was currently available.

GEF action. In response to General Assembly resolution 54/218 [YUN 1999, p. 751], the Secretary-General, in June [A/55/94], transmitted a report describing GEF contributions to Agenda 21. GEF provided funds for projects that addressed biodiversity, climate change, international waters and ozone depletion, and had impacts on cross-cutting issues, most notably land degradation. It encouraged approaches and policies that contributed to sustainable outcomes or promoted equitable results for all.

In December, the Assembly decided to organize in 2002 the 10-year review of progress achieved in implementing the outcome of UNCED at the summit level to reinvigorate the global commitment to sustainable development (**resolution 55/199**).

(See also p. 792.)

Coordination and cooperation

Environmental emergencies

A December report of the Executive Director [UNEP/GC.21/3/Add.1] regarding the joint project on environmental emergencies carried out by UNEP and the UN Office for the Coordination of Humanitarian Affairs (OCHA) (the joint UNEP/OCHA Environment Unit) contained a draft strategic framework on emergency prevention, preparedness, assessment, response and mitigation.

During the year, UNEP and OCHA sent an assessment mission to Hungary, Romania and Yugoslavia (26 February–5 March) to assess the environmental impacts of the spill of liquid and suspended waste containing cyanide and heavy metals from a gold mine in Baia Mare, Romania. Two workshops were organized (May and October) by UNEP on disaster prevention and preparedness in the mining industry. UNEP and the United Nations Centre for Human Settlements (UNCHS) developed a joint project on mitigation, management and control of floods in South Asia to promote technical cooperation in flood management among South Asian countries. Joint UNEP/UNCHS technical missions visited Venezuela (June) to identify areas for assistance in flood mitigation and management and Mozambique to assess the impact of floods in early 2000 on the environment and human settlements. On 15 March, UNEP released a report on the environmental impact of refugees in Guinea, produced in cooperation with UNCHS and the Office of the United Nations High Commissioner for Refugees, which analysed the environmental impact of the large influx of refugees in southern Guinea fleeing from conflicts in Liberia and Sierra Leone. From September to November, UNEP, in collaboration with Kenya, conducted a study on the drought in Kenya. The joint Unit also assisted Venezuela as a result of chemical contamination of a major port area (January), and Kosovo, following a major sulphuric acid spill from a battery factory (September) (see p. 378). The UNEP Awareness and Preparedness for Emergencies at Local Level (APELL) programme continued to contribute to raising public awareness of the need for emergency preparedness and the prevention and reduction of environmental emergencies and damage. APELL seminars were held in India, Jordan, Qatar, South Africa, Tunisia and the United Kingdom. The fourth meeting of the Advisory Group on Environmental Emergencies (Brussels, Belgium, 20-21 November) discussed cooperation between UNEP and OCHA and the work of the joint Unit.

Global Environment Facility

The Global Environment Facility (GEF), a joint programme of the United Nations Development Programme (UNDP), UNEP and the World Bank, was established in 1991 [YUN 1991, p. 505] to help solve global environmental problems. In a December note [UNEP/GC.21/INF/4], the secretariat provided an overview of the status of implementation of the Action Plan on Complementarity [YUN 1999, p. 977] between UNEP's GEF-related activities and its regular programme of work. It also presented an overview of UNEP's GEF-related activities during 1999-2000 and UNEP's contribution to GEF corporate activities.

The 1999-2000 activities brought the overall UNEP GEF-funded project portfolio to a total of $286 million, of which $119 million was approved by GEF for 1999-2000, representing a 42 per cent increase since 1998.

During the period, UNEP consolidated a portfolio of seven activities relating to persistent organic pollutants (POPs). The period also saw project development on flyway approaches to ecosystem conservation of habitats required by migratory species, the inauguration of the Global International Waters Assessment (see p. 982), the development of the prototype of the Millennium Ecosystem Assessment (see p. 977) and the implementation of activities under the UNEP GEF strategic partnership, a $2 million grant under which activities relating to environmental analyses, outreach to the scientific community and global environmental knowledge and data management were completed. In 2000, an increased emphasis was placed on actions in Africa in support of a special initiative on land and water. The Scientific and Technical Advisory Panel, for which UNEP provided secretariat support, provided strategic support for new areas of intervention, providing scientific and technical advice on issues ranging from biosafety and sustainable use to power sector reform.

Memorandums of understanding

In 2000 [UNEP/GC.21/INF/7], UNEP signed memorandums of understanding (MOUs) with UNCHS and the International Council for Local Environmental Initiatives (June) on cooperation in sustainable urban development and management, local governance and capacity-building; with the Asian Development Bank (September) to promote sustainable development and environmental management throughout the Asia and Pacific region in information management and monitoring of trends; with the Global Legislators Organization for Balanced Environment International (November) to promote, among parliamentarians, awareness on the state of the environment, emerging environmental issues of global significance and the environmental dimension of sustainable development; and with the World Bank (December) concerning areas of collaboration for activities related to POPs.

Environmental information

The UNEP global environmental information exchange network (INFOTERRA) representatives' meeting (Dublin, Ireland, 11-14 September) [UNEP/GC.21/INF/17] adopted the Dublin Declaration on Access to Environmental Information, by which they agreed to enhanced networking and coordinating mechanisms to strengthen partnerships, primarily in the form of consortia. National consortia would be established through MOUs between participating Governments and UNEP to provide an information flow between

UNEP and the Governments, and also among Governments. The consortia were called on to use Web-based technologies and establish protocols and standards for delivering the integrated information service. The enhanced global network would be renamed UNEP INFOTERRA.

UNEP secretariat

Follow-up to OIOS review

In response to General Assembly resolution 54/244 [YUN 1999, p. 1274], the Secretary-General transmitted a March report [A/54/817] of the Office of Internal Oversight Services (OIOS) on the follow-up to the 1996 review of the UNEP programme and administrative practices [YUN 1997, p. 1044]. OIOS concluded that UNEP had rebuilt its credibility by transforming UNEP into a viable organization with the authority and adequate, predictable resources to fulfil its mandates, as called for in the Nairobi Declaration on the Role and Mandate of UNEP [ibid., p. 1040]. However, there were lingering questions about the efficiency of the transfer of the United Nations Environment Fund management to the United Nations Office at Nairobi. The report contained recommendations, which included the operationalization of the new functional structure; the rationalization of the Executive Director's travel schedule; delegation of authority to senior managers; the alignment of programme planning with budgeting; and the institution of systematic feedback mechanisms to assess the relevance and usefulness of implemented programme outputs. OIOS proposed a further review in 2002. The Secretary-General concurred with the recommendations.

On 15 June, the Assembly decided to defer consideration of the OIOS report until its fifty-fifth session (**decision 54/462 B**).

Misdirection of contributions

Pursuant to General Assembly resolution 54/244 [YUN 1999, p. 1274], the Secretary-General transmitted, in September [A/55/353], an OIOS report on the investigation into 13 misdirected contributions made by Member States totalling $701,998.94 to the UNEP Trust Fund account. OIOS concluded that the contributions were misdirected in error to the account of a private individual. If the private individual had returned the funds deposited in error instead of spending them, the matter would not have been presented to OIOS. OIOS made several recommendations, with which the Secretary-General concurred.

On 23 December, the General Assembly took note of the report (**decision 55/453**).

International conventions and mechanisms

Implementation of conventions related to sustainable development

As requested by the Assembly in resolution 54/217 [YUN 1999, p. 983], the Secretary-General in September [A/55/357] provided an overview of actions taken by the convention secretariats and relevant organizations to maximize benefits from complementarities in implementing conventions related to environment and sustainable development. The report also brought to the Assembly's attention emerging issues of common concern for global and regional agreements, such as the critical cross-cutting issue of trade and environment, including the interface between, and implications of, trade regimes and negotiations in the context of the effective implementation of multilateral environmental agreements.

The report suggested that consideration should be given to undertaking a comprehensive integrated assessment of progress in implementing environmental and environment-related conventions on the occasion of the 10-year review of the implementation of Agenda 21 in 2002 (see p. 969).

GENERAL ASSEMBLY ACTION

On 20 December [meeting 87], the General Assembly, on the recommendation of the Second Committee [A/55/582/Add.8], adopted **resolution 55/198** without vote [agenda item 95].

Enhancing complementarities among international instruments related to environment and sustainable development

The General Assembly,

Recalling Agenda 21 and the Programme for the Further Implementation of Agenda 21 adopted at its nineteenth special session, and its resolutions 53/186 of 15 December 1998, 53/242 of 28 July 1999 and 54/217 of 22 December 1999,

Reaffirming the need, as stipulated in the Programme for the Further Implementation of Agenda 21, for greater coherence in various intergovernmental organizations and processes by means of better policy coordination at the intergovernmental level, as well as for continued and more concerted efforts to enhance collaboration among the secretariats of relevant decision-making bodies, within their respective mandates,

Emphasizing the need for the conferences of the parties and the secretariats of the environmental conventions to continue to pursue sustainable development objectives that are consistent with those conventions and with Agenda 21,

1. *Takes note* of the report of the Secretary-General on international institutional arrangements related to environment and sustainable development;

2. *Welcomes* the work undertaken by the secretariats of the instruments related to environment and sustainable development and other relevant organizations to implement resolution 54/217;

3. *Encourages* the conferences of the parties to, and the secretariats of, the United Nations Framework Convention on Climate Change, the Convention on Biological Diversity and the United Nations Convention to Combat Desertification in those Countries Experiencing Serious Drought and/or Desertification, particularly in Africa, and other international instruments related to environment and sustainable development, as well as relevant organizations, especially the United Nations Environment Programme, including, as appropriate, the involvement of the environmental management group, to continue their work for enhancing complementarities among them with full respect for the status of the secretariats of the conventions and the autonomous decision-making prerogatives of the conferences of the parties to the conventions concerned, and to strengthen cooperation with a view to facilitating progress in the implementation of those conventions at the international, regional and national levels and to report thereon to their respective conferences of the parties;

4. *Also encourages* the conferences of the parties, assisted by their secretariats, to coordinate the timing of their sessions and the sessions of their subsidiary bodies, taking into account the organization of work of the General Assembly and the Commission on Sustainable Development;

5. *Further encourages* the conferences of the parties to promote the streamlining of national reporting;

6. *Invites* the secretariats of the United Nations Framework Convention on Climate Change, the Convention on Biological Diversity and the United Nations Convention to Combat Desertification in those Countries Experiencing Serious Drought and/or Desertification, particularly in Africa, and other international instruments related to environment and sustainable development, as well as relevant organizations, to provide further information on their work to implement resolution 54/217 and other complementary activities in their contributions to the preparatory process for the review of the implementation of Agenda 21, to be carried out in 2002;

7. *Requests* the Secretary-General to take into account the above-mentioned work in the preparation of documentation and other preparatory activities for the review of the implementation of Agenda 21, to be carried out in 2002.

Climate change convention

As at 31 December, 186 States were parties to the United Nations Framework Convention on Climate Change, which was opened for signature in 1992 [YUN 1992, p. 681] and entered into force in 1994 [YUN 1994, p. 938]. During the year, Angola ratified the Convention, Botswana, Bosnia and Herzegovina, Equatorial Guinea and Kyrgyzstan acceded to it and Belarus approved it.

At year's end, there were 31 parties to the Kyoto Protocol to the Convention [YUN 1997, p. 1048]. During the year, Ecuador, Honduras, Mexico and Samoa ratified it, and Azerbaijan, Barbados, Equatorial Guinea, Guinea, Kiribati and Lesotho acceded to it.

Conference of Parties

On 25 November, the sixth session of the Conference of the Parties to the United Nations Framework Convention on Climate Change (The Hague, Netherlands, 13-25 November) [FCCC/CP/2000/5 & Add.1-3] suspended talks on making operational the 1997 Kyoto Protocol and strengthening financial and technical cooperation between developed and developing countries on climate-friendly policies and technologies.

The Conference made progress towards outlining a package of financial support and technology transfer to help developing countries contribute to global action on climate change. However, the key political issues, including an international emissions trading system, a clean development mechanism, the rules for counting emissions reductions from carbon sinks such as forests, and a compliance regime, could not be resolved. A compromise text was scheduled to be forwarded to a resumed sixth session to be held in 2001.

In other action, the Conference expressed solidarity with Southern African countries, particularly Mozambique, in view of the climate changes they were facing, and invited the Third (2001) UN Conference on the Least Developed Countries (see p. 808) to address matters relating to the specific concerns of the least developed countries arising from the adverse effects of climate change. The Conference took note of the GEF review of its climate change enabling activities.

The Subsidiary Body for Scientific and Technological Advice held its twelfth session (Bonn, Germany, 12-16 June) [FCCC/SBSTA/2000/5]. It also held the first (Lyon, France, 11-15 September) [FCCC/SBSTA/2000/10 & Add.1-4] and second (The Hague, 13-18 November) [FCCC/SBSTA/2000/14] parts of its thirteenth session. The Subsidiary Body for Implementation also held its twelfth session (Bonn, 12-16 June) [FCCC/SBI/2000/5] and the first (Lyon, 11-15 September) [FCCC/SBI/2000/10 & Add.1-4] and second (The Hague, 13-18 November) [FCCC/SBI/2000/17] parts of its thirteenth session.

GENERAL ASSEMBLY ACTION

On 20 December, the General Assembly, on the recommendation of the Second Committee [A/55/582/Add.7], adopted **decision 55/443** without vote [agenda item 95 (g)].

Protection of global climate for present and future generations of mankind

At its 87th plenary meeting, on 20 December 2000, the General Assembly, on the recommendation of the Second Committee, decided:

(a) To express its regret that negotiations could not be completed at the sixth session of the Conference of the Parties to the United Nations Framework Convention on Climate Change, held at The Hague from 13 to 25 November 2000, and to call upon all parties to intensify political consultations to reach a successful conclusion at a resumed session;

(b) To invite the Conference of the Parties at its seventh session to contribute to the preparation of the ten-year review of the progress achieved in the implementation of Agenda 21 and the Programme for the Further Implementation of Agenda 21, and to request the Executive Secretary of the United Nations Framework Convention on Climate Change to report to the Commission on Sustainable Development at its tenth session to this end;

(c) To request the Secretary-General to make the necessary provisions to include in the calendar of conferences and meetings for the biennium 2002-2003 those sessions of the Conference of the Parties and its subsidiary bodies that the Conference of the Parties may need to convene in that period;

(d) To request the Executive Secretary of the United Nations Framework Convention on Climate Change to report to the General Assembly at its fifty-sixth session on the work of the Conference of the Parties;

(e) To include in the provisional agenda of its fifty-sixth session the item entitled "Protection of global climate for present and future generations of mankind".

In related action on the same date, the Assembly took note of the Second Committee's main report [A/55/582] on environment and sustainable development (**decision 55/441**).

Vienna Convention and Montreal Protocol

As at 31 December, 175 States and the European Community (EC) were parties to the 1985 Vienna Convention for the Protection of the Ozone Layer [YUN 1985, p. 804], which entered into force in 1988 [YUN 1988, p. 810]. In 2000, Angola, Haiti and Kyrgyzstan acceded to the Convention.

Parties to the Montreal Protocol on Substances that Deplete the Ozone Layer, which was adopted in 1987 [YUN 1987, p. 686], numbered 174 States and the EC; to the 1990 Amendment to the Protocol, 143 and the EC; to the 1992 Amendment, 116 and the EC; to the 1997 Amendment, 49 and the EC; and to the 1999 Amendment, 2.

The Twelfth Meeting of Parties to the Montreal Protocol (Ouagadougou, Burkina Faso, 11-14 December) [UNEP/OzL.Pro.12/9] considered the possible adjustments of the hydrochlorofluorocarbon phase-out schedule for developing countries and adopted decisions on the transition to chlorofluorocarbon-free metered-dose inhalers, the disposal of controlled substances, methyl bromide production and illegal trade in ozone-depleting substances. It adopted the Ouagadougou Declaration, which was annexed to the Meeting's report.

Convention on air pollution

As at 31 December, 46 States and the EC were parties to the 1979 Convention on Long-Range Transboundary Air Pollution [YUN 1979, p. 710], which entered into force in 1983 [YUN 1983, p. 645]. Eight protocols to the Convention dealt with the programme for monitoring and evaluation of the pollutants in Europe (1984), the reduction of sulphur emissions or their transboundary fluxes by at least 30 per cent (1985), the control of emissions of nitrogen oxides or their transboundary fluxes (1988), the control of volatile organic compounds or their transboundary fluxes (1991), further reduction of sulphur emissions (1994), heavy metals (1998), POPs (1998) and the abatement of acidification, eutrophication and ground-level ozone (1999).

Convention on Biological Diversity

At year's end, the number of parties to the 1992 Convention on Biological Diversity [YUN 1992, p. 683], which entered into force in 1993 [YUN 1993, p. 810], rose to 179 States and the EC, with ratification during 2000 by Liberia, Malta and the United Arab Emirates and approval by Azerbaijan.

The resumed session of the first extraordinary meeting of the Conference of the Parties to the Convention (Montreal, Canada, 24-29 January) [UNEP/CBD/ExCOP/1/3] adopted the Cartagena Protocol on Biosafety, so named to honour Colombia, which had hosted the extraordinary meeting in 1999 [YUN 1999, p. 987]. Upon entry into force, the Protocol would provide a framework for addressing environmental impacts of bioengineered products, referred to as living modified organisms, that crossed international borders. It provided for an information-sharing mechanism so that countries could take informed decisions about the risks and benefits associated with transboundary movements of living modified organisms. The Protocol, which was open for signature in Nairobi from 15 to 26 May 2000 and in New York from 5 June 2000 to 4 June 2001, would enter into force 90 days following the fiftieth instrument of ratification, acceptance, approval or accession. As at 31 December, there were 81 signatories and two parties (Bulgaria and Trinidad and Tobago). The text of the Protocol was contained in the meeting's report.

The first meeting of the Intergovernmental Committee for the Cartagena Protocol (Montpellier, France, 11-15 December) [UNEP/CBD/ICCP/1/9 & Corr.1] considered the preparation for the first meeting of parties to the Protocol, as well as its future work. The Committee decided to hold its second meeting in October 2001.

The Subsidiary Body on Scientific, Technical and Technological Advice, at its fifth meeting (Montreal, 31 January–4 February) [UNEP/CBD/COP/5/3], developed recommendations for the Conference of the Parties to the Convention to consider.

The fifth meeting of the Conference of the Parties (Nairobi, 15-26 May) [UNEP/CBD/COP/5/23 & Corr.1] endorsed the work plan for the Intergovernmental Committee for the Cartagena Protocol. The Conference took action on the biological diversity of inland water ecosystems, marine and coastal biological diversity, forest biological diversity and agricultural biological diversity. It endorsed an ecosystem approach and operational guidance; urged parties, Governments and relevant organizations to apply the interim guiding principles for the prevention, introduction and mitigation of impacts of alien species, which were contained in the meeting's report; established a Global Taxonomy Initiative coordination mechanism; and decided to consider at its sixth meeting the establishment of a global strategy for plant conservation. The sixth meeting of the Conference of the Parties was scheduled to take place in The Hague in 2002.

In accordance with General Assembly resolutions 54/218 and 54/221 [YUN 1999, pp. 751 & 987], the Secretary-General transmitted, in August [A/55/211], a report of the Executive Secretary of the Convention describing the Convention's contribution to the implementation of Agenda 21 and the Programme for the Further Implementation of Agenda 21 (see pp. 969 and 792).

GENERAL ASSEMBLY ACTION

On 20 December [meeting 87], the General Assembly, on the recommendation of the Second Committee [A/55/582/Add.2], adopted **resolution 55/201** without vote [agenda item 95 *(b)*].

Convention on Biological Diversity

The General Assembly,

Recalling its resolution 54/221 of 22 December 1999 on the Convention on Biological Diversity and other relevant resolutions, including its resolution 49/119 of 19 December 1994, in which it proclaimed 29 December, the date of the entry into force of the Convention, the International Day for Biological Diversity,

Recalling also the provisions of the Convention on Biological Diversity,

Reaffirming that the conservation of biological diversity is a common concern of humankind,

Recalling that States have, in accordance with the Charter of the United Nations and the principles of international law, the sovereign right to exploit their own resources pursuant to their own environmental policies and the responsibility to ensure that activities within their jurisdiction or control do not cause damage to the environment of other States or of areas beyond the limits of national jurisdiction,

Recalling also Agenda 21, in particular its chapter 15 on the conservation of biological diversity, chapter 16 on the environmentally sound management of biotechnology and related chapters,

Having considered the report of the Executive Secretary of the Convention on Biological Diversity as submitted by the Secretary-General to the General Assembly at its fifty-fifth session,

Emphasizing the importance of public education and awareness for the implementation of the Convention at all levels,

Noting the recommendation of the Conference of the Parties to the Convention on Biological Diversity at its fifth meeting that the date of the International Day for Biological Diversity be changed to give it greater visibility,

Deeply concerned about the continuing loss of the world's biological diversity, and, on the basis of the provisions of the Convention, reaffirming the commitment to the conservation of biological diversity, the sustainable use of its components and the fair and equitable sharing of benefits arising out of the utilization of genetic resources, including by appropriate access to genetic resources and appropriate transfer of relevant technologies, taking into account all rights over those resources and technologies, and by appropriate funding,

Recognizing the contribution of indigenous and local communities embodying traditional lifestyles, and women within those communities, to the conservation and sustainable use of biological resources,

Noting the continuing dialogue in the Committee on Trade and Environment of the World Trade Organization on the provisions of the Agreement on Trade-related Aspects of Intellectual Property Rights,

Encouraged by the work carried out to date under the Convention, and satisfied that most States and one regional economic integration organization are parties to the Convention,

Recognizing the importance of the adoption by the Conference of the Parties, in its decision EM-I/3 of 29 January 2000, of the Cartagena Protocol on Biosafety to the Convention on Biological Diversity, and the subsequent signature of the Protocol by seventy-five parties to the Convention,

Expressing its appreciation to the Government of Kenya for hosting the fifth meeting of the Conference of the Parties, held at Nairobi from 15 to 26 May 2000,

Also expressing its appreciation to the Government of Spain for hosting the first meeting of the Ad Hoc Open-ended Inter-sessional Working Group on article 8 *(j)* of the Convention regarding the traditional knowledge, innovations and practices of indigenous and local communities, held at Seville from 27 to 31 March 2000,

Welcoming the generous offer of the Government of France, accepted by the Conference of the Parties at its fifth meeting, to host the first meeting of the Intergovernmental Committee for the Cartagena Protocol, held at Montpellier from 11 to 15 December 2000,

Welcoming also the generous offer of the Government of the Netherlands, accepted by the Conference of the Parties at its fifth meeting, to host the sixth meeting of the Conference of the Parties and the second meeting of the Intergovernmental Committee for the Cartagena Protocol, which will be held at The Hague from 8 to 26 April 2002,

Urging the parties to the Convention to undertake thorough preparations to advance progress at the sixth meeting of the Conference of the Parties,

Recalling its invitation to the Executive Secretary of the Convention to report to the General Assembly on the results of future meetings of the Conference of the Parties,

1. *Urges* Member States that have not joined the Convention on Biological Diversity to become parties to it, without further delay;

2. *Calls upon* Member States that are parties to the Convention to sign and ratify the Cartagena Protocol on Biosafety as soon as possible;

3. *Takes note* of the results of the fifth meeting of the Conference of the Parties to the Convention, held at Nairobi from 15 to 26 May 2000;

4. *Reaffirms* the importance of the decision of the Conference of the Parties on the adoption of its programme of work and the thematic approach to guide its work in the development of the Convention for the foreseeable future, including its in-depth consideration of ecosystems and other cross-cutting issues;

5. *Notes* the decision by the Conference of the Parties to undertake a limited number of pilot scientific assessments in preparation for the sixth meeting of the Conference of the Parties, to be involved in the proposed millennium ecosystem assessment, and its request to the Subsidiary Body on Scientific, Technical and Technological Advice to identify opportunities for collaboration;

6. *Stresses* the importance of capacity-building activities, especially in developing countries, for the implementation of the Convention and the Cartagena Protocol, particularly the development of systems to allow parties to implement the Convention and the Protocol, and encourages developed countries to provide adequate support for those activities;

7. *Urges* developed countries to facilitate the transfer of environmentally sound biotechnology for the effective implementation of the Cartagena Protocol, in accordance with relevant articles of the Convention and the Protocol;

8. *Decides* to proclaim 22 May, the date of the adoption of the text of the Convention, as the International Day for Biological Diversity henceforth;

9. *Reiterates its request* to the Secretary-General, the Executive Director of the United Nations Environment Programme and the Executive Secretary of the Convention to take all steps necessary to ensure the successful observance of the International Day for Biological Diversity;

10. *Welcomes* the decision of the Conference of the Parties to contribute to the ten-year review of the implementation of Agenda 21 and the Programme for the Further Implementation of Agenda 21, and decides to invite the Executive Secretary and, if appropriate, the President of the sixth meeting of the Conference of the Parties to report to it at its relevant session;

11. *Recognizes* the importance of the rapid development and implementation of the Strategic Plan for the Convention, and encourages States parties to provide to the Executive Secretary, in accordance with decision V/20 adopted by the Conference of the Parties, their detailed views on the matter as soon as possible;

12. *Welcomes* the collaborative work between the Convention and related conventions, in particular the Convention on Wetlands of International Importance especially as Waterfowl Habitat, adopted at Ramsar, Islamic Republic of Iran, on 2 February 1971;

13. *Also welcomes* the decision of the Conference of the Parties regarding its programme of work for forest biological diversity, and encourages the parties to cooperate with the United Nations Forum on Forests, in particular with regard to respecting, preserving and maintaining the knowledge, innovations and practices of indigenous and local communities embodying traditional lifestyles, in accordance with article 8 *(j)* and related provisions of the Convention;

14. *Takes note* of the fact that the provisions of the Agreement on Trade-related Aspects of Intellectual Property Rights and the Convention are interrelated, in particular with respect to intellectual property rights and relevant provisions of the Convention, and invites the World Trade Organization and the World Intellectual Property Organization, within their respective mandates, to explore this relationship, taking into account the ongoing work in other relevant forums and bearing in mind decision V/26 B of the Conference of the Parties;

15. *Encourages* Member States that are members of the World Trade Organization to support the request by the Executive Secretary for observer status at the meetings of the Council for the Agreement on Trade-related Aspects of Intellectual Property Rights and the Committee on Agriculture;

16. *Welcomes* the progress made in implementing cooperation with the secretariats of the United Nations Framework Convention on Climate Change and the United Nations Convention to Combat Desertification in those Countries Experiencing Serious Drought and/or Desertification, particularly in Africa, and encourages further cooperation;

17. *Stresses* the need to enhance complementarities between the Convention on Biological Diversity and the United Nations Framework Convention on Climate Change in order to ensure that their activities are mutually supportive;

18. *Invites* all funding institutions and bilateral and multilateral donors, as well as regional funding institutions and non-governmental organizations, to cooperate with the secretariat of the Convention on Biological Diversity in the implementation of the programme of work;

19. *Notes* the work of the Global Environment Facility in assisting developing countries and countries with economies in transition in the implementation of the Convention, and urges the Facility to enhance its support for the conservation and sustainable use of biodiversity within the context of national sustainable development, and, within its mandate, in identifying and coordinating additional financial resources from bilateral and international organizations as well as the private sector for this purpose;

20. *Welcomes* the initiatives of the Facility in the area of capacity development to assess the capacity-building needs and priorities of developing countries, relating to the conservation of biological diversity, and to develop a strategy and implement a multi-year plan for responding to such needs and priorities, and calls upon other multilateral and bilateral organizations to cooperate with the Facility in strengthening the capacity of developing countries for the conservation and management of biodiversity;

21. *Notes* the efforts that the Facility is making towards developing programmes for assisting developing countries in capacity-building activities relating to the Cartagena Protocol;

22. *Calls upon* States parties to the Convention to settle urgently any arrears and to pay their contributions

in full and in a timely manner so as to ensure continuity in the cash flows required to finance the ongoing work of the Conference of the Parties, the subsidiary bodies and the Convention secretariat;

23. *Invites* the Executive Secretary of the Convention to report to the General Assembly on the ongoing work regarding the Convention;

24. *Requests* the conferences of the parties to the multilateral environmental conventions to take into consideration the schedule of meetings of the General Assembly and the Commission on Sustainable Development when setting the dates of meetings of the conferences of the parties so as to ensure the adequate representation of developing countries at those meetings;

25. *Decides* to include in the provisional agenda of its fifty-sixth session the sub-item entitled "Convention on Biological Diversity".

Convention to combat desertification

In 2000, 12 additional States became parties to the 1994 United Nations Convention to Combat Desertification in those Countries Experiencing Serious Drought and/or Desertification, particularly in Africa [YUN 1994, p. 944], which entered into force in 1996 [YUN 1996, p. 958], bringing the number of parties to 172.

The Conference of the Parties, at its fourth session (Bonn, 11-22 December) [ICCD/COP(4)/11 & Add.1], approved a declaration on the commitments to enhance the implementation of the obligations of the Convention. The participants recognized the need to strengthen international cooperation to combat desertification and drought by identifying ways to promote and facilitate access to appropriate technology by affected country parties, and to provide financial resources. The Conference decided that its ad hoc working group would review and analyse national reports in order to propose concrete recommendations on further steps to implement the Convention. In 1999 and 2000, over 150 reports were submitted by the parties and subregional and regional institutions. Countries in Africa, Asia, Latin America and the Caribbean and the northern Mediterranean that had already adopted a national action programme to combat desertification illustrated initiatives taken, successes accomplished and problems encountered. The Conference adopted an additional implementation annex to the Convention for Central and Eastern European countries, as well as decisions on traditional knowledge, early warning systems, a dryland degradation assessment and millennium ecosystem assessment and administrative issues. The fifth meeting was scheduled to take place in September 2001 in Bonn.

The Committee on Science and Technology, a subsidiary body of the Conference (Bonn, 12-14 December), considered, among other things, reports on early warning systems [ICCD/COP(4)/

CST/4], traditional knowledge [ICCD/COP(4)/CST/2] and a survey and evaluation of existing networks, institutions, agencies and bodies [ICCD/COP(4)/CST/3 & Add.1].

Report of Secretary-General. As requested in General Assembly resolution 54/223 [YUN 1999, p. 989], the Secretary-General, in an August report [A/55/331], discussed the headquarters agreement for the Convention's secretariat in Bonn, the 2000-2001 programme budget, reports on and procedures for reviewing implementation of the Convention, the first review of the Global Mechanism, the Recife Initiative for a declaration on commitments under the Convention [YUN 1999, p. 989], an MOU between the Conference of the Parties and the International Fund for Agricultural Development, action by States and regional implementation.

UNDP action. On 29 September [E/2000/35 (dec. 2000/23)], the Executive Board of UNDP and the United Nations Population Fund asked UNDP to explore with the Convention's secretariat ways to support the ongoing national consultative processes of the Convention on partnership-building through the round-table mechanism. UNDP was encouraged to contribute to capacity-building and resource mobilization, particularly through its regional and national offices, with a view to assisting affected developing countries to implement the Convention at all levels. The UNDP Administrator was asked to report in 2001.

GENERAL ASSEMBLY ACTION

On 20 December [meeting 87], the General Assembly, on the recommendation of the Second Committee [A/55/582/Add.5], adopted **resolution 55/204** without vote [agenda item 95 *(e)*].

Implementation of the United Nations Convention to Combat Desertification in those Countries Experiencing Serious Drought and/or Desertification, particularly in Africa

The General Assembly,

Recalling its resolution 54/223 of 22 December 1999 and other relevant resolutions relating to the United Nations Convention to Combat Desertification in those Countries Experiencing Serious Drought and/or Desertification, particularly in Africa,

Noting with satisfaction that the third session of the Conference of the Parties to the Convention was held at Recife, Brazil, from 15 to 26 November 1999,

Expressing its deep appreciation to the Government of Brazil for the generous manner in which it hosted and provided facilities for the third session of the Conference of the Parties,

Acknowledging that desertification and drought are problems of a global dimension in that they affect all regions of the world and that joint action of the international community is needed to combat desertification and/or mitigate the effects of drought, including the integration of strategies for poverty eradication,

Having considered the report of the Secretary-General,

1. *Welcomes* the convening of the fourth session of the Conference of the Parties to the United Nations Convention to Combat Desertification in those Countries Experiencing Serious Drought and/or Desertification, particularly in Africa, at Bonn, Germany, from 11 to 22 December 2000;

2. *Also welcomes* the very large number of ratifications of the Convention, and calls upon all remaining countries that have not yet ratified or acceded to the Convention to do so as soon as possible;

3. *Further welcomes* the progress made in producing a draft additional regional implementation annex to the Convention for the countries of Central and Eastern Europe, and invites the Conference of the Parties to consider adopting it at its fourth session;

4. *Stresses* the importance of a coherent and timely implementation of the provisions of the Convention at all levels, including the general provisions and obligations of all States parties, in accordance with the provisions of part II of the Convention;

5. *Notes with satisfaction* the steps being taken by affected developing country parties to the Convention, with the assistance of international organizations and bilateral development partners, to implement the Convention, and the efforts being made to promote the participation of all actors of society in the elaboration of national action programmes to combat desertification, and in this regard encourages countries to cooperate at the subregional and regional levels, as appropriate;

6. *Welcomes* the strengthened cooperation between the secretariat of the Convention and the Global Mechanism, and encourages further efforts in this regard for the effective implementation of the Convention;

7. *Also welcomes* the financial support already provided on a voluntary basis by some countries, and urges Governments, the private sector and all relevant organizations, including non-governmental organizations, to make or continue to make voluntary contributions to the Global Mechanism to enable it to implement its mandate effectively and fully;

8. *Calls upon* the Global Environment Facility to continue to enhance, within its mandate, its ongoing support for land degradation activities in developing countries;

9. *Welcomes* the decision of the Council of the Global Environment Facility, at its meeting held from 1 to 3 November 2000, to request the Chief Executive Officer to explore the best options for enhancing the support of the Facility in assisting affected countries, especially those in Africa, in implementing the Convention, taking into account the third replenishment;

10. *Calls upon* the Global Environment Facility and its implementing agencies to strengthen their cooperation with the Global Mechanism and the secretariat of the Convention;

11. *Encourages* the parties to the Convention to provide the necessary support to the secretariat so as to enable it to discharge effectively its responsibilities to the Convention;

12. *Welcomes* decision 2000/23 of 29 September 2000 of the Executive Board of the United Nations Development Programme aimed at developing co-operation between the secretariat of the Convention and the United Nations Development Programme in order to mainstream activities to combat desertification at the national, subregional and regional levels;

13. *Urges* all parties to the Convention that have not yet done so to pay promptly and in full their contributions to the core budget of the Convention so as to ensure continuity in the cash flow required to finance the ongoing work of the Conference of the Parties, the subsidiary bodies, the secretariat and the Global Mechanism;

14. *Calls upon* Governments, multilateral financial institutions, regional development banks, regional economic integration organizations and all other interested organizations, as well as non-governmental organizations and the private sector, to contribute generously to the General Fund, the Supplementary Fund and the Special Fund, in accordance with the relevant paragraphs of the financial rules of the Conference of the Parties;

15. *Requests* the Secretary-General to make a provision in the proposed calendar of conferences and meetings for the biennium 2002-2003 for the sessions of the Conference of the Parties and its subsidiary bodies, including the sixth ordinary session of the Conference of the Parties and meetings of its subsidiary bodies;

16. *Invites* the Conference of the Parties to contribute towards the preparation of the ten-year review of progress achieved in the implementation of Agenda 21 and other outcomes of the United Nations Conference on Environment and Development, inter alia, by elaborating proposals, including options for funding, aimed at enhancing the implementation of the Convention at the national, subregional and regional levels, and requests the Executive Secretary to report to the Commission on Sustainable Development at its tenth session to this end;

17. *Requests* the Secretary-General to report to the General Assembly at its fifty-sixth session on the implementation of the present resolution, as well as on the outcome of the fourth session of the Conference of the Parties;

18. *Decides* to include in the provisional agenda of its fifty-sixth session the sub-item entitled "Implementation of the United Nations Convention to Combat Desertification in those Countries Experiencing Serious Drought and/or Desertification, particularly in Africa".

Environmental activities

Millennium Ecosystem Assessment

In his report to the United Nations Millennium Summit [A/54/2000] (see p. 55), the Secretary-General called on Member States to become actively engaged in and to help provide financial support for the Millennium Ecosystem Assessment—a proposed international collaborative effort to evaluate the state of the five major ecosystems (forests, freshwater systems, grasslands, coastal areas, agroecosystems). An initiative of the World Resources Institute, the World Bank, UNDP and UNEP, among others, the Assessment would provide parties to various international ecosystem conventions with access to the data needed to evaluate progress towards meeting convention goals. National Governments would gain access to information needed to meet reporting requirements under international conventions. The private sector would benefit by being able to make more informed forecasts. Civil society organizations would be able to access information needed to hold corporations and Governments accountable for meeting their environmental obligations.

The Assessment was scheduled to be launched on 5 June 2001 to coincide with the observance of World Environment Day.

The atmosphere

The second workshop of the Alliance of Small Island States on climate change negotiations, management and strategy was held (Apia, Samoa, 26 July–4 August) [A/C.2/55/3] in cooperation with the Division for Sustainable Development of the UN Department of Economic and Social Affairs.

On 16 September, UNEP marked the International Day for the Preservation of the Ozone Layer by calling on Governments, industries, non-governmental organizations (NGOs) and individuals to remain vigilant in their efforts to protect the ozone layer. Cities with high levels of ozone depletion—Ushuaia (Argentina), the world's southernmost city, and Sodankylä (Finland), the city closest to the Arctic—actively participated in the observance.

During a UNEP-facilitated meeting of 300 financial institutions, held in November through UNEP's Financial Initiatives Round Table, banks, the insurance sector and asset management companies, agreed to adjust their portfolios to favour investments that helped mitigate climate change.

Also in November, UNEP launched its Vital Climate Graphics, visual tools designed to help the public understand the concepts and threats of climate change.

Intergovernmental Panel on Climate Change

The Intergovernmental Panel on Climate Change (IPCC), at its sixteenth session (Montreal, 1-8 May), reviewed progress reports of its working groups for the third assessment report of policy-relevant scientific, technical and socio-economic dimensions of climate change. It approved the interim terms of reference of the IPCC Programme on National Greenhouse Gas Inventories.

During the year, the Panel issued special reports covering methodological and technological issues in technology transfer, emissions scenarios, and land use, land-use change and forestry.

Terrestrial ecosystems

Land degradation

The Commission on Sustainable Development, at its eighth session (New York, 24 April–5 May) [E/2000/29], considered several February reports by the Secretary-General regarding various aspects of land resources.

In a report on integrated planning and management of land resources [E/CN.17/2000/6], the Secretary-General observed that the magnitude of landscape changes through deforestation, expansion of agricultural land, urban and peri-urban growth, and unsustainable use of freshwater resources, as well as the increasing intensity of urbanization, and industrial and agricultural production, represented far-reaching environmental threats. Asia had the highest percentage of the world's degraded lands (38 per cent), followed by Africa (25 per cent), South America (12 per cent), Europe (11 per cent), North America (8 per cent) and Australia (5 per cent). The Secretary-General outlined priorities for future action, including action at the national level, a focus on "hot spots" or critical problems, organizing information on the current status and trends of land resources, and international cooperation.

A report on combating deforestation [E/CN.17/2000/6/Add.1] noted that the latest figures on forest cover indicated that between 1990 and 1995 the global area of forests decreased by 56.3 million hectares, the result of a loss of 65.1 million hectares in developing countries and an increase of 8.8 million hectares in developed countries. The many causes of forest degradation included overharvesting of industrial wood and fuelwood, overgrazing, fire and the effects of insect pests and diseases, storms and air pollution. The report outlined required action and options for international cooperation.

A further report of the Secretary-General [E/CN.17/2000/6/Add.2] reviewed progress in implementing chapter 12 of Agenda 21 (combating desertification and drought), in the context of integrated land resource planning and management, and focused on trends in achieving the objectives of the desertification Convention (see p. 976) regarding the sustainable management of drylands. At least one quarter of the total world land area, or 3.6 billion hectares, was affected by desertification.

The Secretary-General described progress made regarding sustainable mountain development [E/CN.17/2000/6/Add.3] at the national and regional levels and by inter-agency mechanisms, international and regional networking and financial mechanisms, and the planned observance of the International Year of Mountains (2002) (see p. 981). Emerging issues and priorities for action were conflict in mountain areas, highland/lowland interaction, policy mechanisms, planning and management at the national and local levels, natural hazards and risks, and funding.

A further report of the Secretary-General [E/CN.17/2000/6/Add.4] described progress in conserving biodiversity, with emphasis on landscape diversity, as an integral component of land resources. Planning strategies and policies were presented to address biodiversity and land resources management.

(See p. 790 for Commission action.)

Deforestation and forest degradation

Intergovernmental Forum on Forests

The Intergovernmental Forum on Forests (IFF), established in 1997 [YUN 1997, p. 1057] under the aegis of the Commission on Sustainable Development to work towards a legally binding instrument on the management, conservation and sustainable development of all types of forests, held its fourth session (New York, 31 January–11 February) [E/CN.17/2000/14]. In order to carry out its functions, IFF proposed that the Economic and Social Council and the General Assembly establish an intergovernmental body called the United Nations Forum on Forests (UNFF) open to all States.

On 28 July, the Council authorized the Chairman of the consultations on options for placing UNFF within the intergovernmental machinery of the UN system to continue consultations (**decision 2000/296**).

Commission action. The Commission on Sustainable Development in 2000 adopted a decision containing elements for UNFF [E/2000/29 (dec. 8/2)], which were incorporated in Economic and Social Council resolution 2000/35.

ECONOMIC AND SOCIAL COUNCIL ACTION

On 18 October [meeting 46], the Economic and Social Council adopted **resolution 2000/35** [draft: E/2000/L.32] without vote [agenda item 13 (a)].

Report on the fourth session of the Intergovernmental Forum on Forests

The Economic and Social Council,

Recalling its decision 1995/226 of 1 June 1995, approving the establishment of an ad hoc open-ended Intergovernmental Panel on Forests to pursue consensus and to formulate coordinated proposals for action towards the management, conservation and sustainable development of all types of forests,

Recalling also its resolution 1997/65 of 25 July 1997, approving the establishment of an ad hoc open-ended Intergovernmental Forum on Forests to continue the intergovernmental policy dialogue on forests and to promote and facilitate the implementation of the proposals for action of the Intergovernmental Panel on Forests,

Taking into account decision 8/2 adopted on 5 May 2000 by the Commission on Sustainable Development, in which the Commission welcomed the report of the Intergovernmental Forum on Forests on its fourth session and endorsed the conclusions and proposals for action contained therein, in particular regarding an international arrangement on forests,

1. *Decides* that the main objective of the international arrangement on forests is to promote the management, conservation and sustainable development of all types of forests and to strengthen long-term political commitment to this end. The purpose of such an international arrangement is to promote the implementation of internationally agreed actions on forests, at the national, regional and global levels, to provide a coherent, transparent and participatory global framework for policy implementation, coordination and development, and to carry out principal functions, based on the Rio Declaration on Environment and Development, the Non-legally Binding Authoritative Statement of Principles for a Global Consensus on the Management, Conservation and Sustainable Development of All Types of Forests (Forest Principles), chapter 11 of Agenda 21 and the outcomes of the Intergovernmental Panel on Forests/Intergovernmental Forum on Forests process, in a manner consistent with and complementary to existing international legally binding instruments relevant to forests;

2. *Also decides* that, to achieve the objective, the international arrangement on forests shall perform the following principal functions:

(a) Facilitate and promote the implementation of the Intergovernmental Panel on Forests/Intergovernmental Forum on Forests proposals for action as well as other actions which may be agreed upon, including through national forest programmes and other integrated programmes relevant to forests, catalyse, mobilize and generate financial resources, and mobilize and channel technical and scientific resources to this end, including by taking steps towards the broadening and development of mechanisms and/or further initiatives to enhance international cooperation;

(b) Provide a forum for continued policy development and dialogue among Governments, which would involve international organizations and other interested parties, including major groups, as identified in Agenda 21, to foster a common understanding on sustainable forest management and to address forest-related issues and emerging areas of priority concern in a holistic, comprehensive and integrated manner;

(c) Enhance cooperation as well as policy and programme coordination on forest-related issues among relevant international and regional organizations, institutions and instruments, as well as contribute to synergies among them, including coordination among donors;

(d) Foster international cooperation, including North-South and public-private partnerships, as well as cross-sectoral cooperation at the national, regional and global levels;

(e) Monitor and assess progress at the national, regional and global levels through reporting by Governments, as well as by international and regional organizations, institutions and instruments, and on this basis consider future actions needed;

(f) Strengthen political commitment to the management, conservation and sustainable development of all types of forests through ministerial engagement, the development of ways to liaise with the governing bodies of international and regional organizations, institutions and instruments, and the promotion of action-oriented dialogue and policy formulation related to forests;

3. *Further decides*, in order to achieve the objective and to carry out the functions outlined above:

(a) To establish an intergovernmental body called the United Nations Forum on Forests;

(b) To invite the executive heads of relevant organizations of the United Nations system and heads of other relevant international and regional organizations, institutions and instruments to form a collaborative partnership on forests to support the work of the Forum and to enhance cooperation and coordination among participants, and to call upon their governing bodies and their heads to support the activities of the collaborative partnership on forests to achieve the goals of the Forum;

(c) That the Forum shall, inter alia:

(i) Within five years, on the basis of the assessment referred to in paragraph 2 (e) above, consider, with a view to recommending to the Council, and through it to the General Assembly, the parameters of a mandate for developing a legal framework on all types of forests. This process could develop the financial provisions to implement any future agreed legal framework. The process could also consider recommendations made by the expert groups referred to in paragraph 4 (k) below on the establishment of mechanisms on finance, technology transfer and trade;

(ii) Take steps to devise approaches towards appropriate financial and technology transfer support to enable the implementation of sustainable forest management, as recommended under the Intergovernmental Panel on Forests/ Intergovernmental Forum on Forests process;

4. *Decides* to establish the Forum as a subsidiary body of the Council composed of all States Members of the United Nations and States members of the specialized agencies with full and equal participation, including voting rights, with the following working modalities:

(a) The Forum should be open to all States and should operate in a transparent and participatory manner. Relevant international and regional organizations, including regional economic integration organizations, institutions and instruments, as well as major groups, as identified in Agenda 21, should also be involved;

(b) The Forum shall operate under the rules of procedure of the functional commissions of the Council,

provided that this is not in contradiction with the present paragraph;

(c) The supplementary arrangements established by the Council for the Commission on Sustainable Development in Council decisions 1993/215 of 12 February 1993 and 1995/201 of 8 February 1995 shall also apply to the Forum. Within the rules of procedure, the work of the Forum should build upon the transparent and participatory practices established by the Commission, the Intergovernmental Panel on Forests and the Intergovernmental Forum on Forests;

(d) The Bureau of the Forum shall consist of one Chairperson and four Vice-Chairpersons, one of whom shall also act as Rapporteur, in accordance with the principle of equitable geographical distribution;

(e) The Forum shall report to the Council and through it to the General Assembly;

(f) The Forum shall seek ways and means of strengthening synergies and coordination in policy development and implementation of forest-related activities, inter alia, by making the reports of its sessions available to relevant United Nations bodies and other international forest-related organizations, instruments and intergovernmental processes;

(g) The Forum shall work on the basis of a multi-year programme of work, drawing on the elements reflected in the Rio Declaration on Environment and Development, the Forest Principles, chapter 11 of Agenda 21 and the Intergovernmental Panel on Forests/ Intergovernmental Forum on Forests proposals for action;

(h) The Forum should maintain close links with the Commission on Sustainable Development, inter alia, through the convening of joint bureau meetings, taking particular account of the importance of ensuring the coherence of its activities with the broader sustainable development agenda carried out by the Commission;

(i) The Forum may hold its sessions at venues other than United Nations Headquarters in accordance with established United Nations rules and practices;

(j) The Forum shall initially meet once a year for a period of up to two weeks, subject to the review referred to below. The Forum shall hold a high-level ministerial segment for two to three days, as required. The high-level segment could include a one-day policy dialogue with the heads of organizations participating in the collaborative partnership on forests, as well as other forest-related international and regional organizations, institutions and instruments. The Forum should ensure the opportunity to receive and consider inputs from representatives of major groups, as identified in Agenda 21, in particular through the organization of multi-stakeholder dialogues;

(k) The Forum may recommend, as appropriate, the convening of ad hoc expert groups of limited duration, involving experts from developed and developing countries, to provide scientific and technical advice as well as to consider mechanisms and strategies for the financing and transfer of environmentally sound technologies, and may encourage country-sponsored initiatives, such as international expert meetings;

5. *Recommends* that the General Assembly, taking into account its resolution 1798(XVII) of 11 December 1962, make the necessary provisions so that travel expenses for one representative of each of those member States of the Forum that is also a member State of the

Commission on Sustainable Development and is participating in a session of the Forum are paid from the regular budget of the United Nations;

6. *Invites* voluntary extrabudgetary contributions in support of the participation of representatives of developing countries that are not members of the Commission on Sustainable Development in sessions of the Forum and its subsidiary bodies;

7. *Decides* that the Forum shall:

(a) Hold a short organizational meeting, as soon as possible, for the purpose of electing its officers, determining the duration of their terms of office and considering all proposals and options on the location of the secretariat, in conjunction with four days of informal consultations regarding the draft multi-year programme of work;

(b) Hold its first substantive session in 2001 with the following provisional agenda:

1. Adoption of the multi-year programme of work.
2. Development of a plan of action for the implementation of the Intergovernmental Panel on Forests/Intergovernmental Forum on Forests proposals for action, which will address financial provisions.
3. Initiation of the work of the Forum with the collaborative partnership on forests.
4. Provisional agenda, date and venue for the second substantive session of the Forum in 2002.
5. Proposed venues of future sessions of the Forum;

8. *Recommends* that the collaborative partnership on forests build on a high-level, informal group, such as the Inter-Agency Task Force on Forests, which would receive guidance from the Forum, facilitate and promote coordinated and cooperative action, including joint programming and submission of coordinated proposals to their respective governing bodies, and facilitate donor coordination. Such a partnership would submit coordinated inputs and progress reports to the Forum, operate in an open, transparent and flexible manner, and undertake periodic reviews of its effectiveness;

9. *Also recommends* that the Forum complete its consideration of the issues noted in paragraph 3 *(c)* (ii) above as a matter of priority in the context of the multi-year programme of work;

10. *Requests* the Secretary-General to establish a compact secretariat, comprised of highly qualified staff, constituted in accordance with established rules and procedures of the United Nations and strengthened through staff from secretariats of international and regional organizations, institutions and instruments, to support the work described above. The secretariat should service the Forum and support the collaborative partnership on forests. It should also coordinate its activities with the secretariat of the Commission on Sustainable Development;

11. *Decides,* bearing in mind paragraph 10 above and unless otherwise decided at the intergovernmental level, that it would be preferable to have the secretariat located at United Nations Headquarters in New York. A recommendation for a final decision on this matter should be made at the first organizational meeting of the Forum, in early 2001, taking into consideration all proposals;

12. *Encourages* the executive heads of relevant organizations of the United Nations system and heads of other relevant international and regional organiza-

tions, institutions and instruments to support the secretariat of the Forum, including by seconding staff, as done during the Intergovernmental Panel on Forests/Intergovernmental Forum on Forests process;

13. *Recommends* that the funding for the functioning of the Forum and its secretariat be provided from the regular budget of the United Nations, within existing resources, resources of organizations participating in the partnership and extrabudgetary resources provided by interested donors. Specific modalities shall be determined by relevant bodies of the United Nations and the governing bodies of the other organizations concerned;

14. *Also recommends* that the General Assembly decide on the funding for the functioning of the Forum and its secretariat in accordance with the budget procedures established by the Assembly in its resolution 41/213 of 19 December 1986;

15. *Requests* the Secretary-General, in proposing future United Nations programme budgets, to include provisions for the Forum and its secretariat;

16. *Calls upon* interested donor Governments, financial institutions and other organizations to make voluntary financial contributions to a trust fund to be established in order to facilitate, in particular, an early start of the work of the Forum and its secretariat;

17. *Decides* that the international arrangement on forests shall be dynamic and shall adapt to evolving conditions and that the effectiveness of this arrangement shall be reviewed in five years, and also decides that the five-year review of this arrangement shall also address the institutional framework of the Forum, including its position within the United Nations system;

18. *Also decides* that the establishment of the United Nations Forum on Forests shall not be construed as constituting a precedent.

Central African forest ecosystems

In response to General Assembly resolution 54/214 [YUN 1999, p. 992], the Secretary-General, in June [A/55/95], presented examples of various activities by international organizations regarding the conservation and sustainable development of Central African forest ecosystems. The report also identified obstacles in the efforts towards sustainable forest management in the region. The Secretary-General observed that improvements had been achieved by individual countries, especially at the policy level. There was still a general sense that tropical forests were threatened and that unsustainable forest management practices were still widespread. Participation of civil society in forest management required strengthening, further attention needed to be accorded to biodiversity conservation and enhanced financial support was necessary. In addition, there was a need to step up strong measures against illegal operations, such as illegal logging and poaching.

International Year of Mountains (2002)

An August report of the Secretary-General [A/55/218], prepared by the Food and Agriculture

Organization of the United Nations (FAO), described preparations for the International Year of Mountains (2002), declared by the General Assembly in resolution 53/24 [YUN 1998, p. 994]. FAO had been designated the lead agency for the Year. The report also explored areas that required greater attention in preparing for the Year and covered the issue of mobilizing adequate funding.

GENERAL ASSEMBLY ACTION

On 20 December [meeting 87], the General Assembly, on the recommendation of the Second Committee [A/55/581/Add.6], adopted **resolution 55/189** without vote [agenda item 94].

Status of preparation for the International Year of Mountains, 2002

The General Assembly,

Recalling its resolution 53/24 of 10 November 1998 on the International Year of Mountains, 2002,

Recalling also the relevant provisions of Agenda 21, in particular chapter 13 concerning mountain ecosystems and their conservation and sustainable development,

Recalling further Economic and Social Council resolutions 1997/45 of 22 July 1997 and 1998/30 of 29 July 1998,

Recalling the report of the Secretary-General entitled "Coordination, programme and other questions: proclamation of an international year of mountains",

Taking note of the report of the Secretary-General on the status of preparations for the International Year of Mountains, 2002,

Noting with appreciation the work already undertaken to achieve sustainable mountain development by States, organizations of the United Nations system, in particular the Food and Agriculture Organization of the United Nations, and non-governmental organizations,

1. *Welcomes* the activities undertaken by States, United Nations organizations, in particular the Food and Agriculture Organization of the United Nations, and non-governmental organizations in preparation for the observance of the International Year of Mountains, and encourages them to continue their efforts;

2. *Encourages* all States, the United Nations system and all other actors to take advantage of the International Year of Mountains to ensure the present and future well-being of mountain communities by promoting conservation and sustainable development in mountain areas; to increase awareness and knowledge of mountain ecosystems, their dynamics and functioning, and their overriding importance in providing a number of crucial goods and services essential to the well-being of both rural and urban, highland and lowland people, in particular water supply, food security; and to promote and defend the cultural heritage of mountain communities and societies;

3. *Encourages* States and relevant United Nations funds and programmes, specialized agencies, non-governmental organizations and the private sector to support local, national and international programmes and projects for the International Year of Mountains, inter alia, through voluntary financial contributions;

4. *Requests* the Secretary-General to submit to the General Assembly at its fifty-seventh session an interim report on the activities of the International Year of Mountains and to report to the Assembly at its fifty-eighth session on the outcome of the Year and the further implementation of efforts to achieve sustainable mountain development, taking into account any relevant decisions adopted during the ten-year review of the implementation of the outcome of the United Nations Conference on Environment and Development in 2002.

Marine ecosystems

Oceans and seas

Global waters assessment

The Global International Waters Assessment, inaugurated in 2000, was aimed at assessing international waters and causes of environmental problems in 66 water regions and at focusing on the key issues facing the aquatic environment in transboundary waters. The programme, mainly funded by GEF, formed the assessment component of UNEP's new water policy and strategy.

Global Programme of Action

The first phase of the Global Programme of Action (GPA) for the Protection of the Marine Environment from Land-based Activities [YUN 1995, p. 1081] was completed in 2000, which included the preparation of 10 regional assessments and nine regional programmes of action on land-based activities. Those assessments were the basis of two global reports on the state of the marine environment and on land-based activities affecting the quality of the marine, coastal and freshwater environment. The activities of the GPA clearing house mechanism continued to expand with the development of the pollutant source categories of nodes by the relevant UN agencies and of regional prototype nodes in selected regions of the regional seas programme.

In response to a 1999 UNEP Governing Council request [YUN 1999, p. 996], an expert group meeting to prepare for the first intergovernmental GPA review in 2001 was held (The Hague, 26-28 April) [UNEP/GC.21/INF/9]. The experts agreed to focus the review on national and regional programmes of action; voluntary agreements involving the private and public sectors; capacity-building; financing; and monitoring progress and sharing experiences. The meeting of experts recommended that sewage, as one of the most important GPA components, should be assigned a priority for discussion at the 2001 review meeting and at a high-level segment on sewage.

Regional seas programme

The Executive Director, by a December note [UNEP/GC.21/INF/6], presented a progress report for 2000 on the regional seas programme, the central programme of UNEP, providing the major legal, administrative, substantive and financial framework for the implementation of Agenda 21, and its chapter on oceans in particular. The programme was based on periodically revised action plans adopted by high-level intergovernmental meetings and implemented, in most cases, within the framework of legally binding regional seas conventions and protocols. Currently, 15 regions were covered by adopted action plans, and 11 of the action plans were supported by regional seas conventions.

The Third Global Meeting of Regional Seas Conventions and Action Plans (Monaco, 6-10 November) [UNEP/GC.21/INF/14] discussed critical problems and issues facing regional seas conventions and action plans; strengthening links among regional seas conventions and action plans, and between seas conventions and chemicals-related conventions, as well as biodiversity-related conventions and agreements; GPA implementation; and oceans assessment and monitoring.

Pursuant to a 1999 Governing Council decision [YUN 1999, p. 997], the first meeting of high-level, Government-designated experts of the proposed north-east Pacific regional seas programme met (Panama City, 5-8 September) [UNEP/GC.21/INF/11] to negotiate a convention and action plan for the protection and sustainable development of that region. A major outcome of the meeting was initiating a process linking the region to the 2001 GPA review, culminating in a regional work programme for 2001-2006. A second meeting of experts was planned for March 2001 in Managua, Nicaragua.

GENERAL ASSEMBLY ACTION

On 20 December [meeting 87], the General Assembly, on the recommendation of the Second Committee [A/55/582/Add.4], adopted **resolution 55/203** without vote [agenda item 95 (d)].

Promoting an integrated management approach to the Caribbean Sea area in the context of sustainable development

The General Assembly,

Reaffirming the principles and commitments enshrined in the Rio Declaration on Environment and Development and the principles embodied in the Declaration of Barbados and the Programme of Action for the Sustainable Development of Small Island Developing States, as well as other relevant declarations and international instruments,

Recalling the Declaration and review document adopted by the General Assembly at its twenty-second special session,

Taking into account all other relevant resolutions adopted by the General Assembly, including resolution 54/225 of 22 December 1999,

Reaffirming the United Nations Convention on the Law of the Sea, and emphasizing the fundamental character of the Convention,

Conscious that the problems of ocean space are closely interrelated and that they need to be considered as a whole,

Recalling the Convention for the Protection and Development of the Marine Environment of the Wider Caribbean Region, signed at Cartagena de Indias, Colombia, on 24 March 1983, which contains the definition of the wider Caribbean region of which the Caribbean Sea is part,

Welcoming the adoption, on 16 October 1999 in Aruba, of the Protocol Concerning Pollution from Land-based Sources and Activities to the Convention for the Protection and Development of the Marine Environment of the Wider Caribbean Region,

Welcoming also the entry into force, on 18 June 2000, of the Protocol Concerning Specially Protected Areas and Wildlife to the Convention for the Protection and Development of the Marine Environment of the Wider Caribbean Region,

Recalling the relevant work done by the International Maritime Organization,

Considering that the Caribbean Sea area includes a large number of States, countries and territories, most of which are developing countries and small island developing States that are ecologically fragile, structurally weak and economically vulnerable and are also affected, inter alia, by their limited capacity, narrow resource base, need for financial resources, high levels of poverty and the resulting social problems and the challenges and opportunities of globalization and trade liberalization,

Recognizing that the Caribbean Sea has a unique biodiversity and highly fragile ecosystem,

Emphasizing that the Caribbean countries have a high degree of vulnerability occasioned by climate change and variability, associated phenomena, such as the rise in sea level, the El Niño/Southern Oscillation phenomenon and the increase in the frequency and intensity of natural disasters caused by hurricanes, floods and droughts, and that they are also subject to natural disasters, such as those caused by volcanoes, tsunamis and earthquakes,

Welcoming the establishment of the working group on the El Niño/La Niña phenomenon within the framework of the Inter-Agency Task Force for Disaster Reduction,

Bearing in mind the heavy reliance of most of the Caribbean economies on their coastal areas, as well as on the marine environment in general, to achieve their sustainable development needs and goals,

Recognizing the Caribbean Environment Outlook process currently being undertaken by the United Nations Environment Programme, and welcoming the support being provided by the Caribbean Environment Programme of the United Nations Environment Programme towards its implementation,

Acknowledging that the intensive use of the Caribbean Sea for maritime transport, as well as the considerable number and interlocking character of the maritime areas under national jurisdiction where Caribbean countries exercise their rights and duties under international law, present a challenge for the effective management of the resources,

Noting the problem of marine pollution caused, inter alia, by land-based sources and the continuing threat of pollution from ship-generated waste and sewage as well as from the accidental release of hazardous and noxious substances in the Caribbean Sea area,

Taking note of resolution GC(44)/RES/17 of 22 September 2000 of the General Conference of the International Atomic Energy Agency on safety of transport of radioactive materials,

Mindful of the diversity and dynamic interaction and competition among socio-economic activities for the use of the coastal areas and the marine environment and their resources,

Mindful also of the efforts of the Caribbean countries to address in a more holistic manner the sectoral issues relating to the management of the Caribbean Sea area and, in so doing, to promote an integrated management approach to the Caribbean Sea area in the context of sustainable development, through a regional cooperative effort among Caribbean countries,

Noting the efforts of the Caribbean countries, within the framework of the Association of Caribbean States, to develop further support for their concept of the Caribbean Sea as an area of special importance, in the context of sustainable development and in conformity with the relevant provisions of the United Nations Convention on the Law of the Sea,

Cognizant of the importance of the Caribbean Sea to present and future generations and its importance to the heritage, the continuing economic well-being and sustenance of people living in the area, and the urgent need for the countries of the region to take appropriate steps for its preservation and protection, with the support of the international community,

1. *Recognizes* the importance of adopting an integrated management approach to the Caribbean Sea area in the context of sustainable development;

2. *Encourages* the further promotion of an integrated management approach to the Caribbean Sea area in the context of sustainable development, in accordance with the recommendations contained in resolution 54/225, as well as the provisions of Agenda 21, the Programme of Action for the Sustainable Development of Small Island Developing States, the outcome of the twenty-second special session of the General Assembly and the work of the Commission on Sustainable Development, and in conformity with relevant international law, including the United Nations Convention on the Law of the Sea;

3. *Also encourages* the continued efforts of the Caribbean countries to develop further an integrated management approach to the Caribbean Sea area in the context of sustainable development and, in this regard, to continue to develop regional cooperation in the management of their ocean affairs in the context of sustainable development, to address such issues as land-based pollution, pollution from ships and the diversity and dynamic interaction of, and competition among, socio-economic activities for the use of the coastal areas and the marine environment and their resources;

4. *Calls upon* the United Nations system and the international community to assist Caribbean countries and their regional organizations in their efforts to ensure the protection of the Caribbean Sea from degradation as a result of pollution from ships, in particular through the illegal release of oil and other harmful substances, from illegal dumping or accidental release of hazardous waste, including radioactive materials, nuclear waste and dangerous chemicals, in violation of relevant international rules and standards, as well as pollution from land-based activities;

5. *Calls upon* all relevant States to take the necessary steps to bring into force, and to support the implementation of, the Protocol Concerning Pollution from Land-based Sources and Activities, in order to protect the marine environment of the Caribbean Sea from land-based pollution and degradation;

6. *Calls upon* all States to become contracting parties to relevant international agreements to promote the protection of the marine environment of the Caribbean Sea from pollution and degradation from ships;

7. *Invites* intergovernmental organizations within the United Nations system to continue efforts to assist Caribbean countries to become parties to the relevant conventions and protocols and to implement them effectively;

8. *Calls upon* the international community, the United Nations system and the multilateral financial institutions, including the Global Environment Facility, within its mandate, to support actively the abovementioned approach;

9. *Calls upon* Member States to improve as a matter of priority their emergency response capabilities and the containment of environmental damage, particularly in the Caribbean Sea, in the event of natural disasters or of an accident or incident relating to maritime navigation;

10. *Requests* the Secretary-General to report to it at its fifty-seventh session, under the sub-item entitled "Further implementation of the Programme of Action for the Sustainable Development of Small Island Developing States" of the item entitled "Environment and sustainable development", on the implementation of the present resolution, taking into account the views expressed by relevant regional organizations.

Living marine resources

Drift-net fishing, unauthorized fishing and fisheries by-catch and discards

In September [A/55/386], the Secretary-General presented information received from States, UN bodies, specialized agencies, intergovernmental and non-governmental organizations and regional and subregional fisheries organizations on efforts made to implement General Assembly resolution 53/33 [YUN 1998, p. 995] regarding the impact on the world's living marine resources by large-scale pelagic drift-net fishing, unauthorized fishing in zones of national jurisdiction, fisheries by-catch and discards. He also included information on their efforts to implement plans of action for the management of fishing capacity, for reducing incidental catch of seabirds in longline fisheries and for the conservation of sharks.

GENERAL ASSEMBLY ACTION

On 30 October [meeting 44], the General Assembly adopted **resolution 55/8** [draft: A/55/L.11 & Add.1] by recorded vote (103-0-44) [agenda item 34 (b)].

Large-scale pelagic drift-net fishing, unauthorized fishing in zones of national jurisdiction and on the high seas, fisheries by-catch and discards, and other developments

The General Assembly,

Reaffirming its resolutions 46/215 of 20 December 1991, 49/116 and 49/118 of 19 December 1994, 50/25 of 5 December 1995, 51/36 of 9 December 1996, 52/29 of 26 November 1997 and 53/33 of 24 November 1998, as well as other resolutions on large-scale pelagic drift-net fishing, unauthorized fishing in zones of national jurisdiction and on the high seas, fisheries by-catch and discards, and other developments,

Welcoming the Rome Declaration on the Implementation of the Code of Conduct for Responsible Fisheries adopted by the Ministerial Meeting on Fisheries of the Food and Agriculture Organization of the United Nations in March 1999,

Noting that the Code of Conduct for Responsible Fisheries sets out principles and global standards of behaviour for responsible practices to conserve, manage and develop fisheries, including guidelines for fishing on the high seas and in areas under the national jurisdiction of other States, and on fishing gear selectivity and practices, with the aim of reducing by-catch and discards,

Recognizing that coordination and cooperation at the global, regional, subregional as well as national levels in the areas, inter alia, of data collection, information-sharing, capacity-building and training are crucial for the conservation, management and sustainable development of marine living resources,

Noting the conclusion of negotiations to establish new regional organizations and arrangements in several heretofore unmanaged fisheries, in particular the Convention on the Conservation and Management of Highly Migratory Fish Stocks in the Western and Central Pacific Ocean and the Convention on the Conservation and Management of Fishery Resources in the South-east Atlantic Ocean, and highlighting that these agreements were concluded pursuant to the Agreement for the Implementation of the Provisions of the United Nations Convention on the Law of the Sea of 10 December 1982 relating to the Conservation and Management of Straddling Fish Stocks and Highly Migratory Fish Stocks,

Noting also the adoption by the States members of the Permanent Commission for the South Pacific of the Framework Agreement for the Conservation of Living Marine Resources in High Seas of the South-east Pacific,

Recognizing the importance of the Agreement for the Implementation of the Provisions of the United Nations Convention on the Law of the Sea of 10 December 1982 relating to the Conservation and Management of Straddling Fish Stocks and Highly Migratory Fish Stocks and the Agreement to Promote Compliance with International Conservation and Management Measures by Fishing Vessels on the High Seas, and noting with concern that neither of these agreements has yet entered into force,

Noting with satisfaction that the Committee on Fisheries of the Food and Agriculture Organization of the United Nations in February 1999 adopted international plans of action for the management of fishing capacity, for reducing the incidental catch of seabirds in longline fisheries and for the conservation and management of sharks,

Taking note with appreciation of the report of the Secretary-General, and emphasizing the useful role that the report plays in bringing together information relating to the sustainable development of the world's marine living resources provided by States, relevant international organizations, regional and subregional fisheries organizations and non-governmental organizations,

Noting with satisfaction that, while significant work remains to be done, interested parties have made real progress towards sustainable fisheries management,

Noting that while there has been generally a marked decrease in the reporting of large-scale pelagic drift-net fishing activities in most regions of the world's oceans and seas, large-scale pelagic drift-net fishing remains a threat to marine living resources in some areas,

Expressing its continuing concern that efforts should be made to ensure that the implementation of resolution 46/215 in some parts of the world does not result in the transfer to other parts of the world of drift-nets that contravene the resolution,

Noting with concern that unauthorized fishing in zones of national jurisdiction and on the high seas/illegal, unreported and unregulated fishing remains as one of the most severe problems currently affecting world fisheries and the sustainability of marine living resources, and noting also that unauthorized fishing in zones of national jurisdiction and on the high seas/illegal, unreported and unregulated fishing has a detrimental impact on the food security and the economies of many States, particularly developing States,

Noting the significance of the work being undertaken under the aegis of the Food and Agriculture Organization of the United Nations to develop a comprehensive international plan of action to prevent, deter and eliminate illegal, unreported and unregulated fishing, involving consideration of the range of possibilities for action in accordance with international law, and acknowledging the work done by certain regional fisheries organizations,

Welcoming the efforts in the Food and Agriculture Organization of the United Nations to address the causes of illegal, unreported and unregulated fishing, through a comprehensive and integrated approach which involves all relevant States and regional and subregional fisheries management organizations and arrangements in the deterrence of illegal, unreported and unregulated fishing which encourages all States to take measures, to the greatest extent possible, or to cooperate to ensure that their nationals, in accordance with article 117 of the United Nations Convention on the Law of the Sea, and vessels flying their flag do not support or engage in illegal, unreported and unregulated fishing,

Welcoming also the cooperation being undertaken with the International Labour Organization and other relevant international organizations in the joint Ad Hoc Working Group on combating illegal, unreported and unregulated fishing of the Food and Agriculture

Organization of the United Nations and the International Maritime Organization,

Recognizing the need for the International Maritime Organization, the Food and Agriculture Organization of the United Nations and regional and subregional fisheries management organizations and arrangements to address the issue of marine debris derived from land-based and ship-generated sources of pollution, including derelict fishing gear, which can cause mortality and habitat destruction of marine living resources,

Expressing concern at the significant level of by-catch and discards in several of the world's commercial fisheries, and recognizing that the development and use of selective, environmentally safe and cost-effective fishing gear and techniques will be important for reducing by-catch and discards,

Expressing concern also at the reports of continued loss of seabirds, particularly albatrosses, as a result of incidental mortality from longline fishing operations, and the loss of other marine species, including sharks and fin-fish species, as a result of incidental mortality, and noting the recent initiative to develop a convention for the protection of southern hemisphere albatrosses and petrels,

1. *Reaffirms* the importance it attaches to the long-term conservation, management and sustainable use of the marine living resources of the world's oceans and seas and the obligations of States to cooperate to this end, in accordance with international law, as reflected in the relevant provisions of the United Nations Convention on the Law of the Sea, in particular the provisions on cooperation set out in part V and part VII, section 2, of the Convention regarding straddling stocks, highly migratory species, marine mammals, anadromous stocks and marine living resources of the high seas;

2. *Also reaffirms* the importance it attaches to compliance with its resolutions 46/215, 49/116, 49/118, 50/25, 52/29 and 53/33, and urges States and other entities to enforce fully the measures recommended in those resolutions;

3. *Encourages* all States to implement directly or, as appropriate, through the relevant international, regional and subregional organizations and regional and subregional fisheries organizations and arrangements, the international plans of action of the Food and Agriculture Organization of the United Nations for reducing the incidental take of seabirds in longline fisheries, for the conservation and management of sharks and for the management of fishing capacity, since the state of progress in the implementation of all three plans will be reported to the Committee on Fisheries of the Food and Agriculture Organization of the United Nations at the twenty-fourth session of the Committee, to be held from 26 February to 2 March 2001;

4. *Takes note with satisfaction* of the activities of the Food and Agriculture Organization of the United Nations aimed at providing assistance to developing countries in upgrading their capabilities in monitoring, control and surveillance, through its Interregional Programme of Assistance to Developing Countries for the Implementation of the Code of Conduct for Responsible Fisheries;

5. *Also takes note with satisfaction* of the activities of the Food and Agriculture Organization of the United Nations, in cooperation with relevant United Nations agencies, in particular the United Nations Environment Programme and the Global Environment Facility, aimed at promoting the reduction of by-catch and discards in fisheries activities;

6. *Reiterates* the importance of continued or strengthened efforts by States directly or, as appropriate, through the relevant regional and subregional organizations, and by other international organizations, to make it a high priority to support, including through financial and/or technical assistance, with a particular emphasis on capacity-building, the efforts of developing States, in particular the least developed countries and the small island developing States, to achieve the goals and implement the actions called for in the present resolution, including to improve the monitoring and control of fishing activities and the enforcement of fishing regulations;

7. *Urges* States, relevant international organizations and regional and subregional fisheries management organizations and arrangements that have not done so to take action to reduce by-catch, fish discards and post-harvest losses, consistent with international law and relevant international instruments, including the Code of Conduct for Responsible Fisheries;

8. *Calls upon* States and other entities referred to in article 1, paragraph 2 *(b)*, of the Agreement for the Implementation of the Provisions of the United Nations Convention on the Law of the Sea of 10 December 1982 relating to the Conservation and Management of Straddling Fish Stocks and Highly Migratory Fish Stocks that have not done so to ratify or accede to the Agreement and to consider applying it provisionally;

9. *Calls upon* States and other entities referred to in article 10, paragraph 1, of the Agreement to Promote Compliance with International Conservation and Management Measures by Fishing Vessels on the High Seas that have not deposited instruments of acceptance of the Agreement to do so;

10. *Recalls* that Agenda 21, adopted at the United Nations Conference on Environment and Development, calls upon States to take effective action, consistent with international law, to deter reflagging of vessels by their nationals as a means of avoiding compliance with applicable conservation and management measures for fishing vessels on the high seas;

11. *Calls upon* States that have not done so to take measures to deter reflagging of fishing vessels flying their flag to avoid compliance with applicable obligations and to ensure that fishing vessels entitled to fly their flag do not fish in areas under the national jurisdiction of other States unless duly authorized by the authorities of the States concerned and in accordance with the conditions set out in the authorization, and that they do not fish on the high seas in contravention of the applicable conservation and management measures;

12. *Urges* States to continue the development of an international plan of action on illegal, unreported and unregulated fishing for the Food and Agriculture Organization of the United Nations, as a matter of priority, so that its Committee on Fisheries can be in a position to adopt elements for inclusion in a comprehensive and effective plan of action at its twenty-fourth session;

13. *Appeals* to States and regional fisheries organizations, including regional fisheries management bodies

and regional fisheries arrangements, to promote the application of the Code of Conduct for Responsible Fisheries within their areas of competence;

14. *Reaffirms* the rights and duties of coastal States to ensure proper conservation and management measures with respect to the living resources in zones under their national jurisdiction, in accordance with international law, as reflected in the United Nations Convention on the Law of the Sea;

15. *Invites* regional and subregional fisheries management organizations and arrangements to ensure that all States having a real interest in the fisheries concerned may become members of such organizations or participate in such arrangements;

16. *Encourages* the International Maritime Organization and other relevant agencies, organizations and States to continue working constructively with the Food and Agriculture Organization of the United Nations to combat unauthorized fishing in zones of national jurisdiction and on the high seas/illegal, unreported and unregulated fishing;

17. *Invites* the Food and Agriculture Organization of the United Nations to continue its cooperative arrangements with United Nations agencies on illegal, unreported and unregulated fishing and to report to the Secretary-General, for inclusion in his annual report on oceans and the law of the sea, on priorities for cooperation and coordination in this work;

18. *Affirms* the need to strengthen, where necessary, the international legal framework for intergovernmental cooperation in the management of fish stocks and in combating illegal, unreported and unregulated fishing, in a manner consistent with the United Nations Convention on the Law of the Sea and taking into account the Agreement for the Implementation of the Provisions of the United Nations Convention on the Law of the Sea of 10 December 1982 relating to the Conservation and Management of Straddling Fish Stocks and Highly Migratory Fish Stocks, and other relevant principles of international law;

19. *Also affirms* the central role that regional and subregional fisheries management organizations and arrangements have in intergovernmental cooperation to assess marine living resources within their competence, to manage their conservation and sustainable use and thus to promote food security and sustain the economic base of many States and communities, and further affirms that they also will play a key role in implementing applicable international law including, as appropriate, the United Nations Convention on the Law of the Sea, the Fish Stocks Agreement and the Compliance Agreement, and in promoting the application of the Code of Conduct for Responsible Fisheries;

20. *Calls upon* the Food and Agriculture Organization of the United Nations, the International Maritime Organization, regional and subregional fisheries management organizations and arrangements and other appropriate intergovernmental organizations to take up, as a matter of priority, the issue of marine debris as it relates to fisheries and, where appropriate, to promote better coordination and help States to implement fully relevant international agreements, including annex V to and the Guidelines of the International Convention for the Prevention of Pollution from Ships, 1973, as modified by the Protocol of 1978 relating thereto;

21. *Invites* all relevant parts of the United Nations system, international financial institutions and multilateral and bilateral donor agencies to take into account the importance of marine science, including the importance of protecting the ecosystem, and the precautionary approach, with the aim of providing support to subregional and regional organizations and arrangements and their member States, for sustainable fisheries management and conservation, and notes that, for developing countries, capacity-building is essential for the sustainable development of marine living resources;

22. *Recommends* that the biennial conference of regional and subregional fisheries management organizations and arrangements with the Food and Agriculture Organization of the United Nations consider measures to strengthen further the role of these organizations in all aspects of fisheries conservation and management;

23. *Also recommends* that the Food and Agriculture Organization of the United Nations consider inviting the intergovernmental organizations relevant to its work to join the biennial conference of regional fisheries organizations;

24. *Requests* the Secretary-General to bring the present resolution to the attention of all members of the international community, relevant intergovernmental organizations, the organizations and bodies of the United Nations system, regional and subregional fisheries management organizations and relevant nongovernmental organizations, and to invite them to provide the Secretary-General with information relevant to the implementation of the present resolution;

25. *Also requests* the Secretary-General to submit to the General Assembly at its fifty-seventh session a report on the implementation of the present resolution, including the status and implementation of the Agreement to Promote Compliance with International Conservation and Management Measures by Fishing Vessels on the High Seas, the implementation of the international plans of action for the management of fishing capacity, for reducing the incidental catch of seabirds in longline fisheries, and for the conservation and management of sharks, and efforts undertaken by the Food and Agriculture Organization of the United Nations to combat illegal, unreported and unregulated fishing, taking into account the information provided by States, relevant specialized agencies, in particular the Food and Agriculture Organization of the United Nations, and other appropriate organs, organizations and programmes of the United Nations system, regional and subregional organizations and arrangements and other relevant intergovernmental and nongovernmental organizations;

26. *Decides* to include in the provisional agenda of its fifty-seventh session, under the item entitled "Oceans and the law of the sea", a sub-item entitled "Large-scale pelagic drift-net fishing, unauthorized fishing in zones of national jurisdiction and on the high seas/illegal, unreported and unregulated fishing, fisheries by-catch and discards, and other developments".

RECORDED VOTE ON RESOLUTION 55/8:

In favour: Algeria, Angola, Antigua and Barbuda, Argentina, Armenia, Australia, Bahamas, Bahrain, Bangladesh, Barbados, Belarus, Belize, Bolivia, Brazil, Brunei Darussalam, Cambodia, Cameroon, Canada, Chile, China, Colombia, Costa Rica, Côte d'Ivoire, Cuba, Djibouti, Dominica, Dominican Republic, Ecuador, Egypt, El Salvador, Equatorial Guinea, Eritrea, Ethiopia, Fiji, Gambia, Ghana, Grenada, Guyana, Haiti, India, Indonesia,

Iran, Israel, Jamaica, Jordan, Kenya, Kuwait, Lao People's Democratic Republic, Lesotho, Libyan Arab Jamahiriya, Malawi, Malaysia, Maldives, Marshall Islands, Mauritius, Micronesia, Mongolia, Morocco, Mozambique, Myanmar, Namibia, Nauru, New Zealand, Nigeria, Norway, Oman, Pakistan, Panama, Papua New Guinea, Paraguay, Peru, Philippines, Qatar, Russian Federation, Saint Kitts and Nevis, Saint Lucia, Saint Vincent and the Grenadines, Samoa, Senegal, Sierra Leone, Singapore, Solomon Islands, South Africa, Sri Lanka, Sudan, Suriname, Tajikistan, Thailand, Togo, Tonga, Trinidad and Tobago, Tunisia, Uganda, Ukraine, United Arab Emirates, United Republic of Tanzania, United States, Uruguay, Venezuela, Viet Nam, Yemen, Zambia, Zimbabwe.

Against: None.

Abstaining: Andorra, Austria, Belgium, Bulgaria, Croatia, Cyprus, Czech Republic, Denmark, Estonia, Finland, France, Georgia, Germany, Greece, Guinea, Hungary, Iceland, Ireland, Italy, Japan, Kazakhstan, Latvia, Lebanon, Liechtenstein, Lithuania, Luxembourg, Malta, Mexico, Monaco, Nepal, Netherlands, Poland, Portugal, Republic of Korea, Republic of Moldova, Romania, San Marino, Slovakia, Slovenia, Spain, Sweden, The former Yugoslav Republic of Macedonia, Turkey, United Kingdom.

Conservation of wildlife

As at 31 December, the 1994 Lusaka Agreement on Cooperative Enforcement Operations Directed at Illegal Trade in Wild Fauna and Flora [YUN 1994, p. 951], which entered into force in 1996 [YUN 1996, p. 970], had been ratified or acceded to by six States (Congo, Kenya, Lesotho, Uganda, United Republic of Tanzania, Zambia). The Agreement aimed to reduce, and ultimately eliminate, illegal trafficking in African wildlife.

The third meeting of the Governing Council of the Parties to the Lusaka Agreement took place (Nairobi, 3-5 July) to review the status of implementation of the Agreement by the parties and the Lusaka Agreement Task Force, established to combat international syndicates smuggling wildlife in the region.

Protection against harmful products and wastes

Chemical safety

As at 31 December, 72 States and the EC had signed and 12 States (Bulgaria, Czech Republic, El Salvador, Guinea, Hungary, Kyrgyzstan, Netherlands, Oman, Panama, Saudi Arabia, Slovenia, Suriname) had ratified or acceded to the 1998 Rotterdam Convention on the Prior Informed Consent (PIC) Procedure for Certain Hazardous Chemicals and Pesticides in International Trade [YUN 1998, p. 997]. The Convention was to enter into force 90 days following the deposit of the fiftieth instrument of ratification.

The seventh session of the Intergovernmental Negotiating Committee (INC) for an International Legally Binding Instrument for the Application of the PIC Procedure (Geneva, 30 October–3 November) [UNEP/FAO/PIC/INC.7/15] reviewed proposals to place two additional pesticides, ethylene oxide and ethylene dichloride, on a list of hazardous chemicals that were subject to international controls. In other action, INC adopted a policy on contaminants. Other decisions dealt with approaches to consider certain contami-

nants, discontinuation of the interim PIC procedure, the site of the Convention's secretariat, an incident report form and the process of drafting decision guidance documents.

The 29-member Interim Chemical Review Committee, a subsidiary body established by INC in 1999 [YUN 1999, p. 997] to make recommendations on the inclusion of banned and severely restricted chemicals or hazardous pesticide formulations in the PIC procedure, held its first session (Geneva, 21-25 February) [UNEP/FAO/PIC/ICRC.1/6]. The Committee considered mechanisms for adding hazardous pesticides and industrial chemicals to the PIC procedure, as well as the addition of four pesticides to PIC (bromacil, ethylene dichloride, ethylene oxide, maleic hydrazide).

Persistent organic pollutants

The fourth session of the Intergovernmental Negotiating Committee for an International Legally Binding Instrument for Implementing International Action on Certain Persistent Organic Pollutants (POPs) (Bonn, 20-25 March) [UNEP/POPS/INC.4/5] considered individual draft articles. At the Committee's fifth session (Johannesburg, South Africa, 4-9 December) [UNEP/POPS/INC.5/7 & Corr.1], the legal drafting group made proposals for streamlining the successive drafts of the articles and annexes, which culminated in the approval of the draft articles. The Conference of Plenipotentiaries to adopt the Convention was planned for May 2001 in Sweden. The Committee agreed to name the text the "Stockholm Convention"; the draft text was appended to the Committee's report.

Hazardous wastes

As at 31 December 2000, the number of parties to the 1989 Basel Convention on the Control of Transboundary Movements of Hazardous Wastes and their Disposal [YUN 1989, p. 420], which entered into force in 1992 [YUN 1992, p. 685], rose to 142, with the accession of the Dominican Republic, Ethiopia, Kenya, Kiribati, Lesotho, Mali, Malta and Yugoslavia. The 1995 amendment to the Convention [YUN 1995, p. 1333], not yet in force, had been ratified, accepted or approved by 22 parties. The 1999 Basel Protocol on Liability and Compensation for Damage Resulting from Transboundary Movements of Hazardous Wastes and their Disposal [YUN 1999, p. 998], which opened for signature in Berne, Switzerland, from 6 to 17 March and in New York from 1 April to 10 December, had 13 signatories at year's end.

The Technical Working Group of the Convention held its sixteenth (Geneva, 3-5 April)

[UNEP/CHW/TWG/16/12] and seventeenth (Geneva, 9-11 October) [UNEP/CHW/TWG/17/15] sessions. In October, the Group, among other things, adopted the technical guidelines on preventing and monitoring illegal traffic of biomedical and health-care wastes and reviewed draft guidelines for the environmentally safe dismantling of ships.

A regional consultation to prepare African countries towards reduction of reliance on DDT for malaria control (Harare, Zimbabwe, 8-10 February) [UNEP/HW CONF.1/AFRICA/Session 6/3] and an Organisation for Economic Cooperation and Development/FAO/UNEP workshop on obsolete pesticides (Alexandria, Virginia, United States, 13-15 September) [UNEP/HW CONF.1/AFRICA/Background/2] were held within the context of the First Continental Conference for Africa on the Environmentally Sound Management of Unwanted Stockpiles of Hazardous Wastes and Their Prevention, to be held in January 2001 jointly by the Convention secretariat and Morocco.

Cleaner production

UNEP's Division of Technology, Industry and Economics continued efforts to work as a catalyst and encourage decision makers in government, industry and business to develop and adopt environmentally sound policies, strategies, practices and technologies. The implementation of a cleaner and safer production programme in all regions remained a priority. The sixth High-level Seminar on Cleaner Production (Montreal, 16-17 October), organized by UNEP to review and evaluate the status of cleaner production strategies worldwide, was followed by the International Pollution Prevention Summit (18-20 October), which aimed at expanding current understanding and implementation of pollution prevention. Another key event was the first Cleaner Production Round Table for Africa (Nairobi, 9-10 August), aimed at creating a mechanism for review, assessment and information exchange on cleaner production in Africa, and at linking cleaner production with sustainable consumption.

Other matters

Environmental law

In response to a 1999 Governing Council request [YUN 1999, p. 998], the Executive Director convened the Meeting of Senior Government Officials Expert in Environmental Law to Prepare a Programme for the Development and Periodic Review of Environmental Law for the First Decade of the Twenty-first Century (Nairobi, 23-27 October) [UNEP/Env.Law/4/4]. The officials adopted a draft UNEP strategic programme on

environmental law for the next decade (Montevideo Programme III), which was annexed to the meeting's report. The draft programme contained components to increase the effectiveness of environmental law in such areas as implementation, compliance and enforcement; capacity-building; prevention and mitigation of environmental damage; avoidance and settlement of international environmental disputes; development of international environmental law; harmonization and coordination; public participation; and information technology. The programme also considered the issues of freshwater resources, coastal and marine ecosystems, soils, forests, biological diversity, pollution prevention and control, production and consumption patterns, and environmental emergencies and natural disasters.

Global Compact

The Global Compact, which aimed to engage the business community in advancing basic values in human rights, labour and the environment, was officially launched on 26 July in New York. The Global Compact challenged corporations and business associations to support a set of core values within their sphere of influence. The environment-related principles, taken from the 1992 Rio Declaration on Environment and Development adopted by UNCED [YUN 1992, p. 670], required business to support a precautionary approach to environmental challenges, undertake initiatives to promote greater environmental responsibility and encourage the development and diffusion of environmentally friendly technologies.

Human settlements

Follow-up to the 1996 UN Conference on Human Settlements (Habitat II)

2001 General Assembly special session

Preparatory Committee

The Commission on Human Settlements, acting as the Preparatory Committee for the special (2001) session of the General Assembly for an overall review and appraisal of the implementation of the Habitat Agenda, adopted by the 1996 United Nations Conference on Human Settlements (Habitat II) [YUN 1996, p. 992], held its first session (Nairobi, Kenya, 8-12 May) [A/55/121]. It adopted a resolution regarding international cooperation and financial support for the preparatory activities and the special session, as well as a resolution on the role of local authorities in the preparatory process and at the special session. A resolution on the scope to be covered by the review and appraisal process requested the Executive Director of the United Nations Centre for Human Settlements (UNCHS) to report on the Advisory Committee of Local Authorities at the Preparatory Committee's second (2001) session and on the actions of the Global Campaign for Secure Tenure and the Global Campaign for Urban Governance (see p. 995) at the special session. Its secretariat was asked to prepare a draft declaration on human settlements in the new millennium. Other resolutions dealt with local, national and regional preparations, the outcome of the special session, and participation of youth in the review and appraisal of the implementation of the Habitat Agenda, proposing that the special session include a thematic focus on youth. In the provisional agenda for its second session, the Committee included a draft report on the overall review and appraisal of the implementation of the Habitat Agenda, based on information contained in national reports, and a draft declaration on cities and other human settlements in the new millennium.

A February note by the secretariat [HS/C/PC.1/5] contained a draft text of a declaration on the role and mandate of UNCHS. February reports of the Executive Director discussed the scope to be covered by the review and appraisal process [HS/C/PC.1/2], local, national and regional preparations for the special session [HS/C/PC.1/3], and the role of local authorities, other partners and relevant UN organizations and agencies in the review and appraisal process [HS/C/PC.1/4].

Regional meetings that reviewed implementation of the Habitat Agenda included a ministerial-level meeting of the Economic Commission for Europe (ECE), held together with the sixty-first session of the ECE Committee on Human Settlements (Geneva, 18-20 September) [HS/C/PC.2/2/Add.4 & Corr.1], which adopted the Ministerial Declaration towards a Sustainable Improvement in Living Conditions; a meeting for Western Asia, organized by UNCHS and the Economic and Social Commission for Western Asia (Manama, Bahrain, 16-18 October) [HS/C/PC.2/2/Add.6]; a meeting organized by the Economic and Social Commission for Asia and the Pacific and UNCHS, in collaboration with other organizations (Hangzhou, China, 19-23 October) [HS/C/PC.2/2/Add.3]; a meeting organized by the Economic Commission for Latin America and the Caribbean and UNCHS (Santiago, Chile,

25-27 October) [HS/C/PC.2/2/Add.5]; and a meeting of the Economic Commission for Africa (ECA), organized by ECA and UNCHS (Addis Ababa, Ethiopia, 6-8 November) [HS/C/PC.2/ 2/Add.2]. In December [HS/C/PC.2/2], the Executive Director issued a draft report on the overall review and appraisal of the implementation of the Habitat Agenda, which addressed the questions of constraints, priorities, strengthening of local authorities and the participation of the UN system, to be submitted to the Preparatory Committee.

Implementation

Report of Secretary-General. In response to Economic and Social Council decision 1999/281 [YUN 1999, p. 1347] and General Assembly resolution 54/208 [ibid., p. 1000], the Secretary-General, in June [A/55/83-E/2000/62], reported on the coordinated implementation by the UN system of the Habitat Agenda. He noted that further attention was required to strengthen the modalities of partnership between the UN system and its partners in civil society, particularly regarding mobilizing resources, promoting exchange of technology and access to information, raising the priority of adequate shelter and sustainable urban development in international cooperation and strengthening the strategic and operational partnerships with local authorities, NGOs, community-based organizations and the private sector. The Secretary-General discussed the Assembly's special session in terms of key commitments and strategies of the Habitat Agenda, presented guidelines for country reports, emphasized partnerships and the role of civil society, and presented various aspects of the role of the Commission on Human Settlements in monitoring and assessing progress made in implementing the Habitat Agenda goals.

The Committee of Local Authorities was established as an advisory body in January to strengthen the dialogue with local authorities involved in implementing the Habitat Agenda. It was expected to act as a think tank and as an early warning system on the future of cities. Regarding the coordinated implementation of the Habitat Agenda, a task manager system would address the gap in information and reporting within the UN system.

The UN system of organizations and agencies was called on to enhance its capacity for coordinated and complementary action and to make those efforts visible at regional, national and local levels. In addition, the Secretary-General presented recommendations to the Economic and Social Council aimed at the modalities of a UN-coordinated approach for implementing the Habitat Agenda, priorities for system-wide action and coordination of the UN system in preparing for the Assembly's special session.

The Council took note of the Secretary-General's report on 27 July (**decision 2000/234**).

Economic and Social Council action. In July, at its substantive session, the Economic and Social Council held a discussion on the coordinated implementation by the UN system of the Habitat Agenda. On 21 July [A/55/3/Rev.1 (agreed conclusions 2000/1)], the Council requested the relevant UN bodies and agencies, particularly the Executive Committee of the United Nations Development Group, to review the follow-up of their commitments on implementing the Habitat Agenda goals. Recalling General Assembly resolution 35/77 C [YUN 1980, p. 739], it asked the Secretary-General to review the matter of UNCHS participation in the work of the Administrative Committee on Coordination (ACC) and its subsidiary machinery, in the light of its role as focal point within the UN system on implementing the Habitat Agenda. ACC was invited to include in the agenda of its meetings issues relating to the implementation of the Habitat Agenda, and the Secretary-General was asked to organize regular briefings to inform Member States on ACC deliberations. The Council noted a proposal to merge existing initiatives into a streamlined Urban Forum, as well as the creation of the Advisory Committee of Local Authorities to advise the Executive Director on the role of local authorities in implementing the Habitat Agenda. The Secretary-General was asked to consider adopting a Habitat Agenda task manager system to facilitate coordinated implementation of the Habitat Agenda and to streamline reporting, to appoint a full-time UNCHS Executive Director and fill UNCHS vacancies for high-level positions, and to call on Member States to contribute financially to the secretariat to assist developing countries to participate in the special session and the preparatory process. Regional commissions were asked to facilitate the holding of regional meetings in preparation for the special session, and the international community, particularly developed countries, were asked to support the elaboration by developing countries of their national reports on the implementation of the Habitat Agenda.

Appointment. In July, the Secretary-General appointed Anna Kajumulo Tibaijuka (United Republic of Tanzania) as the Executive Director of UNCHS, with effect from 1 September.

Report of Executive Director. A report of the Executive Director [HS/C/PC.2/2/Add.1] stated that, by November, 69 national reports had been received by UNCHS, indicating that progress had been made towards most of the commitments in many countries but that more intensive action was needed in all areas. New housing and decentralization policies and strategies had been adopted or revised by several Governments, but implementation remained limited. Public-private partnerships, community-based approaches to shelter and sustainable urban development and stakeholder participation in local decision-making had increased, but more needed to be done in terms of resource allocation, capacity-building and empowerment to alleviate poverty and address shelter and sustainable human settlements.

Other action. At the first session of the Preparatory Committee, UNCHS submitted several new initiatives to operationalize its own role in assisting countries to implement the Habitat Agenda, such as the Global Campaign for Secure Tenure and the Global Campaign for Urban Governance, as well as the draft World Charter of Local Self-Government. The Global Campaign for Urban Governance (see p. 995), launched by UNCHS in 2000, aimed to improve the quality of life in urban areas, especially for the poor and marginalized, while the Global Campaign for Secure Tenure (see p. 995), also launched in 2000, offered viable policy options on tenure systems.

On 15 June, UNCHS organized an inter-agency meeting on the coordinated implementation of the Habitat Agenda by the UN system (New York). The coordination segment of the Economic and Social Council (New York, 10-12 July) considered prospects and specific action on the coordinated implementation by the UN system.

GENERAL ASSEMBLY ACTION

On 20 December [meeting 87], the General Assembly, on the recommendation of the Second Committee [A/55/581/Add.5], adopted **resolution 55/194** without vote [agenda item 94 (e)].

Scope to be covered by the special session of the General Assembly for an overall review and appraisal of the implementation of the outcome of the United Nations Conference on Human Settlements (Habitat II)

The General Assembly,

Recalling paragraph 218 of the Habitat Agenda and its resolutions 51/177 of 16 December 1996 on the implementation of the outcome of the United Nations Conference on Human Settlements (Habitat II) and 53/180 of 15 December 1998 in which it decided that its special session for an overall review and appraisal of the implementation of the outcome of the Conference would be held in June 2001 and that the Commission on Human Settlements should serve as the Preparatory Committee for the special session,

Taking into account its resolutions 54/208 and 54/209 of 22 December 1999 on the implementation of the outcome of the United Nations Conference on Human

Settlements (Habitat II) and on the follow-up to the Conference,

Bearing in mind Commission on Human Settlements resolutions 17/1 and 17/14 of 14 May 1999 on the follow-up to the United Nations Conference on Human Settlements (Habitat II) and on the preparations for the special session of the General Assembly for an overall review and appraisal of the implementation of the Habitat Agenda,

Taking note of the report of the Commission on Human Settlements acting as the Preparatory Committee for the special session, on its first substantive session, held at Nairobi from 8 to 12 May 2000,

Taking note also of the report of the Secretary-General on the coordinated implementation by the United Nations system of the Habitat Agenda,

I
Outcome of the special session of the General Assembly for an overall review and appraisal of the implementation of the Habitat Agenda

1. *Confirms* that the special session should result in:

(a) Reconfirmation of the goals and commitments of the Habitat Agenda and review of the status of implementation, including the identification of progress, gaps, obstacles and challenges;

(b) The setting of global priorities for future action;

2. *Emphasizes* the role of the Commission on Human Settlements, as a standing body of the Economic and Social Council, as a central monitoring and coordinating body within the United Nations system for the implementation of the Habitat Agenda;

3. *Also emphasizes* the existing role of the United Nations Centre for Human Settlements (Habitat) in supporting the implementation of the Habitat Agenda;

4. *Further emphasizes*, while recognizing that the implementation of the Habitat Agenda is the sovereign right and responsibility of each State, that international cooperation as stipulated in the Agenda remains an important component in the implementation of the Agenda;

II
Arrangements regarding participation of Habitat Agenda partners and observers in the special session

1. *Decides* that representatives of local authorities, non-governmental organizations and other Habitat Agenda partners may make statements in the Ad Hoc Committee of the Whole and in the thematic committee of the special session for an overall review and appraisal of the implementation of the outcome of the United Nations Conference on Human Settlements (Habitat II);

2. *Also decides* that, given the time available, a limited number of representatives of local authorities, non-governmental organizations and other Habitat Agenda partners may also make statements in the debate in plenary meeting, and requests the President of the General Assembly to submit the list of selected Habitat Agenda partners to the Member States in a timely manner for approval and to ensure that the selection of speakers is made on an equal and transparent basis, taking into account the geographical representation and diversity of Habitat Agenda partners;

3. *Further decides* that observers may make statements during the debate in plenary meeting in accordance with the rules and procedures of the General Assembly;

4. *Decides* that arrangements concerning the accreditation and participation of Habitat Agenda partners in the special session shall in no way create a precedent for other special sessions of the General Assembly;

III
Arrangements regarding accreditation of Habitat Agenda partners to the special session

1. *Decides* that accreditation to the special session shall be open to:

(a) Habitat Agenda partners that were accredited to the United Nations Conference on Human Settlements (Habitat II);

(b) Non-governmental organizations in consultative status with the Economic and Social Council, with the exception of those whose application for consultative status with the Council has been rejected or whose consultative status has been withdrawn or suspended;

2. *Also decides* that accreditation of other interested and relevant Habitat Agenda partners that were not accredited to the United Nations Conference on Human Settlements (Habitat II) should be considered by the Preparatory Committee, provided that those partners submit to the Committee composed of the Bureau of the Preparatory Committee and the Secretariat by 9 February 2001 an application for accreditation containing the following information:

(a) The purpose of the organization;

(b) Information identifying the programmes and activities of the organization in areas relevant to the subject of the special session and indicating in which country or countries they are carried out;

(c) Confirmation of the activities of the organization at the national, regional or international levels;

(d) Copies of annual or other reports of the organization, with financial statements and a list of financial sources and contributions, including governmental contributions;

(e) A list of the members of the governing body of the organization and their country of nationality;

(f) A description of the membership of the organization, indicating the total number of members, the names or organizations that are members and their geographical distribution;

(g) A copy of the constitution and/or by-laws of the organization;

and further decides that the Bureau of the Preparatory Committee should submit by 19 February 2001 to the Preparatory Committee at its second session a list of partners that have submitted their application containing information on each partner's competence and relevance to the subject of the special session, and that the Preparatory Committee at its second session shall decide on a no-objection basis regarding the accreditation of those partners;

3. *Requests* the Secretary-General to disseminate widely all available information on accreditation procedures for the special session;

4. *Decides* that the arrangements set out above concerning accreditation to the special session shall in no way create a precedent for other special sessions of the General Assembly;

IV
Action at the local, national and regional levels

1. *Calls upon* all States to strengthen broad-based, participatory, gender-balanced national habitat committees, or similar consultative mechanisms, to review and report on local and national plans of action and, through consultative mechanisms, to coordinate and support further the implementation of the Habitat Agenda at the local and national levels;

2. *Urges* States to focus their assessment and monitoring of the implementation of the Habitat Agenda at the local, national and regional levels on key commitments related to policies and methods of evaluation, and recommends that States identify best practices, including enabling policies, legislation and exemplary plans of action, in implementing the Habitat Agenda in a gender-sensitive way, that they promote research on low-cost building technology for affordable housing and that they support the transfer of all such knowledge to ensure sustainability;

3. *Confirms* that the special session should facilitate sharing views on local, national and regional experiences in the implementation of the Habitat Agenda;

V
Partnership and the role of civil society

1. *Encourages* Member States to integrate contributions made by different partner groups towards further implementation of the Habitat Agenda in their national reports and to consider the inclusion of partner groups in broad-based, gender-balanced national delegations;

2. *Requests* the Executive Director of the United Nations Centre for Human Settlements (Habitat) to report to the Preparatory Committee at its second session on the activities of the Advisory Committee of Local Authorities;

VI
Monitoring and assessment

1. *Encourages* Member States and Habitat Agenda partners to provide support for the preparation of the *Global Report on Human Settlements* and the *State of the World's Cities* report on a biennial basis so as to raise awareness of human settlements and to provide information on urban conditions and trends around the world;

2. *Recommends* that the Commission on Human Settlements pursue agreement by all Member States on a pool of common and easy-to-measure indicators applicable for national reporting and evaluation;

3. *Encourages* all relevant United Nations organizations and agencies and other development partners to support the efforts of national Governments to coordinate data collection and analysis and to develop a monitoring system at the local level on sustainable human settlements, with appropriate strengthening at all levels;

4. *Encourages* all Governments and partners to submit to the Secretariat examples of enabling urban policies and legislation relating to key items selected for country reporting to allow the Secretariat to combine best practices, enabling policies, legislation and action plans;

VII
International cooperation

1. *Requests* the Preparatory Committee, at its second session, to prepare a draft declaration on cities and other human settlements in the new millennium;

2. *Requests* the Executive Director of the United Nations Centre for Human Settlements (Habitat) to report to the special session on the implementation of the twin goals of the Habitat Agenda, namely, adequate shelter for all and sustainable human settlements development, as well as on the actions and achievements of the Global Campaign for Secure Tenure and the Global Campaign for Urban Governance;

3. *Calls upon* the international community to support developing countries in the preparatory process for the special session, the second session of the Preparatory Committee and the special session itself;

4. *Requests* the international community to support urban poverty eradication in developing countries as well as reconstruction programmes following conflicts and natural disasters in order to allow affected countries to implement the Habitat Agenda effectively.

Also on 20 December [meeting 87], the General Assembly, on the recommendation of the Second Committee [A/55/581/Add.5], adopted **resolution 55/195** without vote [agenda item 94 *(e)*].

Preparations for the special session of the General Assembly for an overall review and appraisal of the implementation of the outcome of the United Nations Conference on Human Settlements (Habitat II)

The General Assembly,

Recalling its resolutions 48/162 of 20 December 1993, 50/227 of 24 May 1996, 51/177 of 16 December 1996, 52/190 of 18 December 1997, 53/180 of 15 December 1998, 54/207 of 22 December 1999 and 54/209 of 22 December 1999,

Recalling also Economic and Social Council decision 1999/281 of 30 July 1999, and taking note of agreed conclusions 2000/1 of the Economic and Social Council concerning the implementation of the outcome of the United Nations Conference on Human Settlements (Habitat II) and the United Nations Millennium Declaration,

Acknowledging the efforts made to secure extrabudgetary resources to defray the costs of the participation of representatives of developing countries, in particular the least developed countries, in the sessions of the Preparatory Committee for the special session of the General Assembly for an overall review and appraisal of the implementation of the outcome of the United Nations Conference on Human Settlements (Habitat II) and the special session itself in June 2001, as requested in paragraph 14 of resolution 53/180, and noting with concern that the response has not been adequate,

Taking note of the report of the Commission on Human Settlements acting as the Preparatory Committee for the special session, on its first substantive session, held at Nairobi from 8 to 12 May 2000,

Taking note also of the report of the Secretary-General on the coordinated implementation by the United Nations system of the Habitat Agenda,

1. *Welcomes* the appointment of the new Executive Director of the United Nations Centre for Human Settlements (Habitat);

2. *Requests* the Secretary-General to consider further strengthening of the Centre through the provision of the requisite support and stable, adequate and predictable financial resources, including by proposing additional regular budget resources and sufficient human resources, as envisaged by the General Assembly in its resolutions 52/220 of 22 December 1997 and 53/242 of 28 July 1999, for the consideration of the Assembly, with due regard for proper United Nations budgetary procedures;

3. *Decides* that the special session shall be held from 6 to 8 June 2001 at United Nations Headquarters in New York;

4. *Also decides* that the special session shall have a plenary, an ad hoc committee of the whole and a thematic committee, the details of which shall be worked out by the Preparatory Committee at its second session;

5. *Further decides* that the provisional agenda shall include the following items:

(a) Review and appraisal of progress made in the implementation of the Habitat Agenda;

(b) Further actions and initiatives for overcoming obstacles to the implementation of the Habitat Agenda;

(c) A declaration on cities and other human settlements in the new millennium;

6. *Reiterates its invitation* to Member States to participate in the special session at the highest political level possible and, in the meantime, to continue to extend support to the preparatory process;

7. *Also reiterates its invitation* to States members of the specialized agencies of the United Nations that are not members of the United Nations, as well as Palestine, in their capacity as observers, to participate in the special session in accordance with the rules and procedures of the General Assembly;

8. *Invites* other entities having a standing invitation to participate in the United Nations as observers to participate in the special session in accordance with the rules and procedures of the General Assembly;

9. *Decides* to invite the footnoted associate members[a] of the regional commissions to participate as observers in the special session and its preparatory process, subject to the rules of the General Assembly;

10. *Requests* the Secretary-General to consider defraying the costs not covered by General Assembly resolution 1798(XVII) of 11 December 1962 of the participation of one governmental representative from each least developed country in the special session and the cost of their participation in the second session of the Preparatory Committee through the use of extrabudgetary resources and, in the event that those resources prove to be insufficient, requests the Secretary-General to seek extrabudgetary funding from all possible sources;

11. *Calls upon* all States in a position to do so to make voluntary financial contributions to the Secretariat to assist developing countries, in particular the least developed countries, and their civil society partners to prepare adequately for, and be fully involved in, the preparatory process and the special session itself;

12. *Reiterates its invitation* to all relevant organs, funds and programmes, as well as the agencies of the United Nations system, including the Bretton Woods institutions, to continue to contribute to and be actively involved in the preparatory process and the special session;

13. *Welcomes* the launching of the Cities Alliance initiative by the United Nations Centre for Human Settlements (Habitat) and the World Bank to implement effectively the Cities without Slums programme of action as part of the efforts to achieve the twin goals of the Habitat Agenda, namely, adequate shelter for all and sustainable human settlements development in an urbanizing world, requests the Executive Director of the Centre to take a leadership and coordinating role in this initiative, and urges the Cities Alliance to include national Governments of developing countries as well as relevant United Nations organizations and specialized agencies in this initiative;

14. *Requests* the Executive Director of the United Nations Centre for Human Settlements (Habitat) to report to the special session on the Cities Alliance initiative, including on its contribution to the implementation of the Habitat Agenda;

15. *Requests* the Preparatory Committee and the special session to take into account the outcome of the coordination segment of the Economic and Social Council on the implementation of the Habitat Agenda within the United Nations system;

16. *Requests* the Secretary-General to submit to it at its fifty-sixth session a report on the special session;

17. *Decides* to include in the provisional agenda of its fifty-sixth session an item entitled "Implementation of the Habitat Agenda and outcome of the special session of the General Assembly on this topic".

[a]American Samoa, Anguilla, Aruba, British Virgin Islands, Commonwealth of the Northern Mariana Islands, Cook Islands, French Polynesia, Guam, Montserrat, Netherlands Antilles, New Caledonia, Niue, Puerto Rico and United States Virgin Islands.

OIOS review of Habitat II

In accordance with General Assembly resolution 48/218 B [YUN 1994, p. 1362], the Secretary-General, in February [A/54/764], transmitted a report of the Office of Internal Oversight Services (OIOS) on the follow-up to the 1997 review of the programme and administrative practices of UNCHS [YUN 1997, p. 1098]. The report observed that the revitalization efforts, which began in 1998 [YUN 1998, p. 1023] and continued in 1999 [YUN 1999, p. 1003], had given new impetus to the Centre's future work, and much effort had resulted in a strategically focused draft work programme, and a streamlined organizational structure based on strategic goals, which provided for enhanced flexibility in implementing substantive activities.

The inspection observed advances in redefining the Centre's mission, in redesigning its work programme to concentrate resources on strategic goals and in aligning the new organizational and programmatic structures. OIOS noted encouraging signs of an emerging new work culture that placed a premium on initiative, creativity and flexibility. However, the administrative support necessary to sustain those efforts was weak. OIOS recommended that priority be given to financial and personnel management. The Centre, jointly with the United Nations Office at Nairobi, should continuously update, and energetically implement, concrete and detailed measures relative to financial and human resources management. The Secretary-General took note of the report's findings and concurred with the OIOS recommendations.

On 15 June, the General Assembly decided to defer consideration of the Secretary-General's report until its fifty-fifth session (**decision 54/462 B**).

In other action, on 7 April, the Assembly took note of the 1998 OIOS audit of Habitat II [YUN 1998, p. 1022] and of a 1997 OIOS report on an alleged conflict of interest in the Centre and the Joint Inspection Unit's comments thereon [A/52/339 & Add.1] (**resolution 54/257**).

Global Strategy for Shelter to the Year 2000

The implementation of the Global Strategy for Shelter to the Year 2000, adopted by the General Assembly in resolution 43/181 [YUN 1988, p. 478] and aimed at facilitating adequate shelter for all by the year 2000 with an operational focus on national action, had been incorporated in the implementation of the Habitat Agenda. Most countries had enhanced their national shelter strategies and had incorporated them into their national Habitat Agenda action plans. Progress was especially noticeable in policy formulation reflected in enabling and participatory strategies for shelter development, the facilitation of public-private partnerships and the progressive realization of housing rights. Despite that progress, the gap between policy formulation and actual implementation had widened in many developing countries. Progress in carrying out programmes to improve living and housing conditions of low-income groups had generally been slow and inadequate as compared to the growing magnitude of the problem. In view of the complexities of translating enabling policies into sustained housing delivery programmes, UNCHS had shifted its approach. With its new emphasis on establishing norms and standards in the shelter policy sector, the Centre launched the Global Campaign for Secure Tenure (see below), which was geared towards promoting secure land tenure conditions as a prerequisite for mobilizing a people-centred housing process.

UN Centre for Human Settlements

The UNCHS work programme for 2000 focused on two subprogrammes, corresponding to the two main action areas of the Habitat Agenda: adequate shelter for all and sustainable human settlements in an urbanizing world. An operationalized version of the work programme for the year, including the specific responsibilities and objectives of the Centre's new organizational units, was submitted to the Committee of Permanent Representatives. The revitalization of the Centre gained further momentum and a new organizational structure was implemented during the year.

The Centre took steps to build the profile of an advocacy agency and focused on maximizing its operational impact through the launching of global campaigns. Following consultations with partner groups and stakeholders from civil society, the Global Campaign for Secure Tenure was launched in various regions between July and October. The events demonstrated the new advocacy role of the Centre and created political space for dialogue with the organized urban poor and women's groups. UNCHS, as a first step in following up the events with slum-upgrading projects under the City Alliance facility, set up cooperation agreements with local federations of slum-dwellers to provide support to local action plans, combining normative and operational activities. International instruments on housing rights were being activated by formulating a normative framework on secure tenure as an entry point to the application of housing rights within the context of the rights to development.

In adopting the Habitat Agenda, Member States and their partners recognized the importance of good governance and committed themselves to enabling the practice of transparent, responsible, accountable, just, effective and efficient governance of towns, cities and metropolitan areas. In 2000, the Centre conceptualized and launched the Global Campaign for Urban Governance, which represented the Centre's key contribution to implementing the Habitat Agenda's goal of sustainable development in an urbanizing world. The objective of the Campaign was to increase the capacity of local governments and urban stakeholders to practise good governance. In that regard, the Centre drafted a declaration on norms of good governance to guide the implementation of activities under the Campaign. Consultations on the normative framework of the Campaign were held during a series of international and regional meetings on urban governance and urban development strategies. Together with the draft World Charter of Local Self-Government, the declaration on norms of good governance was a vehicle for global advocacy. Furthermore, the Campaign developed an approach to identifying, supporting and promoting "Illustrative Cities", those cities whose local government was committed to developing its governance, where there was a critical mass of urban governance practices promoted by the local authority, and where there was potential for Campaign partners to work with the city in improving governance and in developing a learning process.

The Cities Alliance, a joint initiative between the Centre, the World Bank and bilateral agencies, provided financial and technical assistance for activities in two thematic areas: city development strategies and improving slum upgrading. The "Cities without Slums" action plan, a component of the initiative, was mentioned in the Secretary-General's action plan on the work of the United Nations in the twenty-first century, adopted in September as part of the Millennium Declaration (see p. 49). In June, an agreement was reached between the stakeholders of the Cities Alliance on the core partnership between the World Bank and the UN system, represented by UNCHS.

Assessment missions were carried out in Latin American and Caribbean countries affected by natural disasters, which led to action plans for rehabilitating human settlements, as well as for mitigating the effects of future events. Follow-up projects were implemented directly by the relevant Governments or with the participation of other external support agencies. UNCHS carried out assessment and identification missions to Indonesia (forest fires), Turkey (seismic vulnerability reduction) and India (floods), which led to the development of technical recommendations and longer-term collaborative activities. The Centre collaborated with UNEP in supporting China's flood vulnerability reduction. In the Kosovo province of the Federal Republic of Yugoslavia, the Centre focused on providing technical assistance to rehabilitate the municipal administration; regularize housing and property rights; and restore property and land registries. UNCHS provided support to the United Nations Interim Administration Mission in Kosovo in establishing the Housing and Property Directorate and the Housing and Property Claims Commission, which were responsible for settling disputes on housing and property rights; the temporary allocation of vacant housing; and the provision of legal guidance on housing and property issues. In the countries of Central and Eastern Europe with economies in transition, there was major progress in capacity-building for better urban governance.

By the end of 2000, the Global Urban Observatory of the Centre was assisting two countries and eight cities in each region in capacity-building to strengthen urban indicators and the collection of city-specific information and analysis. More than 90 cities in 20 countries had designated urban observatories and were being given training on the use of indicators for policy development. The Observatory was working on an index or indices that could be used to track progress in poverty reduction, city investment potential and overall quality of urban life.

During the year 2000, the Global Parliamentarians for Habitat organized and held several national and regional meetings, culminating in the Third Global Forum of Parliamentarians (Manila, Philippines, 25-28 July), which adopted the Manila Declaration, endorsing the new strategic vision of UNCHS.

Cooperation with UNEP continued on city environmental profiles, demonstrations in broad-based urban environmental planning and management, and normative work on guidelines and tools, as well as joint efforts for environmentally sound human settlements technology under the joint Sustainable Cities Programme. The future of the Programme was unclear due to problems with funding.

During the year, the Centre developed a comprehensive regionalization strategy based on the premise that a regional presence was necessary to increase the policy and operational capacities of the Centre and that the regional presence should be financially affordable and sustainable. Currently, the Centre had regional offices in Nairobi, Kenya (for Africa and the Arab States), Fukuoka, Japan (for Asia and the Pacific), and Rio de Janeiro, Brazil (for Latin America and the Caribbean). Activities in Europe and Central Asia were managed from Nairobi.

UN Habitat and Human Settlements Foundation

Biennial financial audit

In July [A/55/5/Add.8], the UN Board of Auditors transmitted to the General Assembly the financial report and audited financial statements of the United Nations Habitat and Human Settlements Foundation for the 1998-1999 biennium. Expenditures in respect of project activities and programme support cost activities amounted to $18 million. The Board found that the Foundation did not fully comply with the UN System Accounting Standards insofar as it disclosed accounts receivable and accounts payable in net instead of gross terms. Expenditures exceeded allotment limits by a total of $1.3 million in respect of 11 trust funds and by $0.41 million in respect of three earmarked projects, indicating weak budgetary control and expenditure monitoring. In 12 of 28 cases, the Foundation did not select consultants on a competitive basis, contrary to the requirement of the comprehensive guidelines for the use of consultants. The Board made recommendations to improve compliance with the Accounting Standards, to strengthen the monitoring of expenditure and to improve the selection process for consultants.

Chapter VIII

Population

In 2000, with the world's population reaching 6.06 billion at mid-year, UN activities in the field of population were guided by the Programme of Action adopted at the 1994 International Conference on Population and Development (ICPD) and the key actions for the further implementation of the Programme of Action adopted at the twenty-first special session of the General Assembly in 1999.

A top priority for the United Nations Population Fund (UNFPA), the largest internationally funded source of population assistance and the lead UN organization for advancing the ICPD Programme of Action, was the development of a new global strategy for reproductive health commodity security. UNFPA also continued to mobilize human and financial resources to provide universal access to primary education and reproductive health care; to work with both men and women to break the vicious cycle of discrimination and gender-based violence; and to focus many of its projects on young people, who needed better information and services. The Fund further strengthened emergency reproductive health services in order to help millions of people fleeing armed conflict and natural disaster, and joined with partners to protect the health of mothers and decrease maternal mortality by expanding the availability and use of emergency obstetric care for complications of pregnancy and childbirth.

At its thirty-third session, the Commission on Population and Development considered the central theme of population, gender and development. It adopted a resolution on the subject, which was brought to the attention of the Economic and Social Council. The Commission considered the key actions for the implementation of the ICPD Programme of Action and discussed national experience in population matters. With regard to its future work, the Commission reaffirmed that "Population, environment and development" would be the special theme for 2001, and decided that future special themes would be "Reproductive rights and reproductive health" in 2002, and "Population, education and development" in 2003.

During the year, the United Nations Population Division continued to analyse demographic trends and population policies and to prepare and publish population estimates and projections.

Follow-up to the 1994 Conference on Population and Development

Implementation of the Programme of Action

Commission on Population and Development action. At its thirty-third session (New York, 27-30 March) [E/2000/25], the Commission on Population and Development had before it a report of the Secretary-General [E/CN.9/2000/2] on the twenty-first special session of the General Assembly, held in 1999 [YUN 1999, p. 1005], for the review and appraisal of the implementation of the Programme of Action of the 1994 International Conference on Population and Development (ICPD) [YUN 1994, p. 955]. The special session, known as ICPD+5, had, by resolution S-21/2 [YUN 1999, p. 1006], adopted key actions for the further implementation of the ICPD Progamme of Action. The report presented the major aspects and events of the review process and the key future actions adopted by the Assembly. It also highlighted some of the findings regarding progress in, and constraints on, the implementation of the Programme of Action.

With regard to the next steps to be taken, the report noted that ICPD+5 was widely regarded as a most successful endeavour, demonstrating the effectiveness of the United Nations in building global consensus through open and inclusive discussion. Although the progress of the first five years following ICPD provided an encouraging basis on which to build, formidable challenges remained. Foremost among them was the need to ensure the reproductive rights of individuals, especially women and girls, which was as pressing in 2000 as it was in 1994. Other areas to be addressed were the shortfall in funding to implement the Programme of Action; the need to enhance country capacity to meet ICPD goals; and the need to build partnerships among UN organizations and agencies. The report further noted the need to discuss possible options to mark the tenth anniversary, in 2004, of the adoption of the Progamme of Action.

On 30 March [E/2000/25 (dec. 2000/2)], the Commission took note of the Secretary-General's report.

UNFPA action. In response to a 1999 request of the Executive Board of the United Nations Development Programme (UNDP)/UNFPA [YUN 1999, p. 1019], the Fund presented to the Board's annual session in June a report on UNFPA's future programme directions in the light of the outcome of ICPD+5 [DP/FPA/2000/9]. In reflecting on its future role against the backdrop of progress made and challenges remaining, the Fund came to two main conclusions: that the three UNFPA core programme areas endorsed by the UNDP/UNFPA Executive Board in 1995 [YUN 1995, p. 1093] (reproductive health, including family planning and sexual health; population and development strategies; and advocacy) remained valid, although there was a need to sharpen the focus of the Fund's support; and there was a need to strengthen the interlinkages between the three core programme areas.

The Fund was also taking account of trends in global demographic and reproductive patterns, including a continuing decline in the age at menarche for girls and a gradual increase in the age at marriage, resulting in a longer period of time of sexual maturity for young people before marriage and family-building, thus increasing sexual health risks for adolescents. Also, decreasing family size and the condensation of childbearing into a shorter period resulted in a longer period of sexual but not reproductive activity that had implications for contraceptive needs and for other reproductive health issues, such as unwanted pregnancy, abortion and sexually transmitted diseases. Further, as mortality and fertility both continued to decline, population ageing and its social and economic consequences, already a concern in developed countries, were emerging in almost every developing country as well. Finally, high rates of urbanization, with their social and economic implications, were an increasing concern for many countries.

As the tasks set out in the Programme of Action, which were further elaborated in the ICPD+5 process, were clearly beyond the capacity of a single organization to achieve, UNFPA would continue to strengthen working arrangements both within and outside the UN system in order to assist countries in their efforts to achieve the ICPD goals.

On 16 June [E/2000/35 (dec. 2000/11)], the UNDP/UNFPA Executive Board endorsed the continuing use of the Fund's three core programme areas and emphasized that UNFPA support should be focused on meeting the priority needs as identified by programme countries within those areas. UNFPA was encouraged to fulfil its leadership role as an advocate at global and national levels for reproductive health, population and development issues, as well as actions agreed at ICPD and ICPD+5, and to help to ensure that ICPD goals and ICPD+5 benchmarks of particular concern to UNFPA were achieved. The Board endorsed the Fund's overall approach to collaboration and coordination within the UN system and with other stakeholders and organizations, and at the country level under the leadership of the concerned programme country Government. The Board noted with grave concern UNFPA's financial situation and the critical need for increased mobilization of resources, particularly from bilateral donors, the private sector, foundations and other appropriate sources.

Population, gender and development

In the context of follow-up to ICPD and ICPD+5, and as approved by the Economic and Social Council by decision 1999/224 [YUN 1999, p. 1032], the Commission on Population and Development's special theme at its 2000 session was "Population, gender and development". The Commission had before it a report of the Secretary-General on world population monitoring, 2000: population, gender and development [E/CN.9/2000/3], which provided a summary of selected aspects of the issue. It included a historical review of population and gender issues in the global agenda and provided recent information on such topics as family formation, health and mortality, including HIV/AIDS, ageing and internal and international migration.

Also before the Commission was a report of the Secretary-General on monitoring of population programmes: population, gender and development [E/CN.9/2000/4], which gave a broad overview of the range of activities that had been initiated towards the implementation of the outcome of ICPD in the population, gender and development field. It presented the strategies and approaches adopted by countries in response to the Programme of Action concerning gender in population and development and analysed the challenges and constraints encountered by countries in programme implementation and matters pertaining to resource mobilization within the area of gender, population and development.

By a 30 March resolution [E/2000/25 (res. 2000/1)], which it brought to the attention of the Economic and Social Council, the Commission requested the United Nations Population Division to continue to incorporate gender perspectives in all its research on population policies, levels and trends, including the analysis of demographic, social and economic data disaggregated by age and sex, so that Governments could benefit by achieving a better understanding of the relationships between population, gender and development in the global context and through inter-country comparisons. The Population Division was also requested to pay particular attention to the gender dynamics and demographic implications of the HIV/AIDS pandemic, infant, child and maternal mortality, and ageing of populations, and to improving the statistical description and analysis of the phenomena of all forms of discrimination and abuse against women and children, including sexual abuse, exploitation, trafficking and violence, as well as to the gender dimensions of migration.

Financial resources

In response to General Assembly resolutions 49/128 [YUN 1994, p. 963] and 50/124 [YUN 1995, p. 1094], the Secretary-General submitted to the Commission on Population and Development a report on the flow of financial resources for assisting in the implementation of the ICPD Programme of Action [E/CN.9/2000/5 & Corr.1]. He observed that international population assistance increased negligibly from $1.96 billion in 1997 to $2.06 billion in 1998. Although assistance remained virtually unchanged since 1996 at about $2 billion, the 1998 figures were positive in that they reversed the downward trend first observed in 1997. However, funding levels were only roughly 36 per cent of the $5.7 billion target agreed upon at ICPD as the international community's share in financing the Programme of Action.

The Secretary-General noted that the ICPD+5 process showed many encouraging signs of progress in advancing the Programme of Action. Country after country addressing the special session of the General Assembly had pointed out progress made, lessons learned, constraints encountered and further actions required to achieve full implementation of the ICPD goals. An important part of the review exercise was an analysis of actual funding for population programmes, as compared with resource targets contained in the Programme of Action. A lack of sufficient financial resources was cited as one of the chief constraints on full implementation of the Programme of Action. ICPD+5 had called on donor countries to intensify efforts to meet ICPD's $5.7 billion target in 2000, to reverse the current decline in overall official development assistance (ODA) and to strive to fulfil the agreed target of 0.7 per cent of gross national product for overall ODA as soon as possible. In view of limited

resources, donor countries, international agencies and recipient countries were also called on to strengthen their efforts and enhance their collaboration to avoid duplication, identify funding gaps and ensure that available funds were used as effectively and efficiently as possible.

UN Population Fund

In 2000, Dr. Nafis Sadik, Executive Director of UNFPA since 1987, indicated her intention to retire at the end of the year. On 26 September [E/2000/35 (dec. 2000/18)], the UNDP/UNFPA Executive Board, commending Dr. Sadik's visionary and courageous leadership of the Fund and recognizing her vital role as Secretary-General of ICPD, expressed its deep appreciation and gratitude for her effective management and distinguished leadership, for her accomplishments and for her deep commitment to population and development.

Thoraya Ahmed Obaid was appointed as the new Executive Director effective 1 January 2001.

2000 activities

In her annual report for 2000 [DP/FPA/2001/4 (Part I)] to the UNDP/UNFPA Executive Board, the UNFPA Executive Director stated that, as always, the major work of the Fund during the year was the implementation of the Board-approved country programmes. In 2000, 94 country programmes were being implemented, including two subregional programmes in Caribbean and Pacific island countries. During the year, some $134.2 million was spent on country programmes and the intercountry programme, which were carried out in the three core programme areas: reproductive health, including family planning and sexual health; population and development strategies; and advocacy. As in the past, the largest share of resources, 63.2 per cent, went to reproductive health activities. Of the world's regions, sub-Saharan Africa absorbed 35.5 per cent of programme assistance while Asia and the Pacific accounted for 31.9 per cent.

A major event during 2000 was the Executive Board's adoption of the first multi-year funding framework (MYFF) for UNFPA (see p. 1005), which was designed to strengthen the Fund's contribution to addressing the challenges faced by countries in implementing the ICPD Programme of Action and the key actions endorsed at ICPD+5 and to help secure increasing, predictable and stable financial resources to implement programmes. In order to achieve the goals and outputs specified in the MYFF results framework, the Fund continued efforts to strengthen results-based management through training, review of systems and tools and the use of such tools as the logical framework (logframe). One important challenge was to strengthen country-level data systems that would make it possible to track progress in UNFPA-supported country programmes and in meeting the ICPD goals and the ICPD+5 benchmarks.

In response to the HIV/AIDS pandemic, the Fund had mobilized resources to safeguard youth and intensify efforts to integrate AIDS prevention into reproductive health programmes. UNFPA's efforts to prevent the spread of HIV centred on advocacy campaigns; providing information and education to promote safer sexual behaviour; promoting voluntary counselling and testing; helping to ensure reproductive health commodity security, especially of condoms; and training service providers. The Fund received a $57 million grant in 2000 from the Bill and Melinda Gates Foundation to promote adolescent reproductive health with a focus on HIV/AIDS in four countries that had been greatly affected by the pandemic and had exhibited the political will necessary to combat it—Botswana, Ghana, Uganda and the United Republic of Tanzania. UNFPA increased advocacy in 2000 for greater involvement of men to help stem the AIDS epidemic and to boost gender equality, including the publication of a new booklet, "Partners for Change: Enlisting Men in HIV/AIDS Prevention". In December, the Fund organized a panel discussion on "Gender and HIV/AIDS", which was the most widely attended panel at the African Development Forum 2000 in Addis Ababa, Ethiopia. The five-day forum, attended by over 1,500 representatives of African Governments and civil society, was called to marshal a new level of political commitment and to develop more effective strategies for combating HIV/AIDS in Africa.

In addition, UNFPA's annual *State of World Population* report for 2000, "Lives Together, Worlds Apart: Men and Women in a Time of Change", focused on the negative impact of gender inequality, not only for individuals but also for national economic and social progress. On a policy level, UNFPA participated actively in the Beijing+5 meeting, the five-year follow-up to the Fourth World Conference on Women (see p. 1082).

A top priority for the Fund in 2000 was the development of a new global strategy for reproductive health commodity security. Without adequate supplies of condoms and other contraceptives, the world would not be able to meet the ICPD goal of universal access to repro-ductive health care by 2015. The strategy, which was formulated in response to the growing need in developing countries for contraceptives at a time of declining support from donors, was endorsed by Governments, UN agencies, the World Bank, non-governmental organizations (NGOs), foundations and the private sector.

A major contribution to UNFPA's efforts to respond quickly to urgent reproductive health needs in emergency situations was the provision of emergency reproductive health kits, containing equipment and supplies to deliver babies safely, provide emergency obstetric care, provide contraceptives, treat the consequences of miscarriage and prevent and treat sexually transmitted diseases.

An increasingly effective way for UNFPA to get its messages across was through the use of Goodwill Ambassadors who raised awareness of reproductive health needs in developing countries. In 2000, the Fund appointed two new Ambassadors—Miss Universe, Mpule Kwelagobe, and a prominent German television host, Alfred Biolek. In December, Ms. Kwelagobe toured her home country of Botswana to raise awareness of HIV/AIDS. In June, UNFPA brought all of its Goodwill Ambassadors together in Geneva to discuss future strategies and to coordinate outreach and advocacy efforts.

UNFPA's annual report for 2000 focused on the Fund's advocacy activities, concentrating on efforts made at the national level through its country programmes.

In another section of her annual report for 2000 [DP/FPA/2001/4 (Part III)], the Executive Director provided information on reproductive health commodity security; implementation of UNFPA country programmes in Algeria, China, Egypt, Nicaragua, Paraguay and Pacific island countries; and humanitarian assistance.

By **decision 2000/242** of 28 July, the Economic and Social Council took note of the annual reports of the UNDP Administrator and the UNFPA Executive Director to the Council [E/2000/20].

Sector-wide approaches

In response to a 1999 UNDP/UNFPA Executive Board request [YUN 1999, p. 1024], the Executive Director presented to the Board's April session a conference room paper on sector-wide approaches (SWAps) [DP/FPA/2000/CRP.3]. The report built on information presented in 1999 [YUN 1999, p. 1024], as well as on discussions with a broad range of concerned partners, notably programme countries, other UN agencies, the World Bank and civil society groups. It also drew on recent literature documenting the experience to date with SWAps, on available case studies and on the guidelines of other UN agencies.

UNFPA continued to take an active part in the planning and implementation stages of SWAPs, an essential quality of which was strong government ownership and broad political commitment. In both planning and implementation of SWAPs, the Fund played an important advocacy role to see that reproductive and sexual health and reproductive rights and population variables were included, as well as gender equity and equality and the empowerment of women, taking into account the ICPD Programme of Action and the outcome of ICPD+5.

The paper provided details of UNFPA participation in SWAps in Bangladesh, Ethiopia, Ghana, Mozambique, Uganda and the United Republic of Tanzania.

On 6 April [E/2000/35 (dec. 2000/8)], the Executive Board encouraged UNFPA to strengthen further its participation in the design and execution of SWAps in accordance with its mandate and comparative advantage, particularly regarding normative aspects, in the areas of reproductive health, including family planning and maternal and sexual health, and population and development strategies, and its comprehensive advocacy for gender equality and the empowerment of women. The Fund was also encouraged to play an advocacy role to ensure that reproductive health and rights and population variables were included in other relevant sectors. The Board urged UNFPA to pay increased attention to the HIV/AIDS epidemic in SWAps. It endorsed UNFPA participation in common-basket funding arrangements in SWAps where the Fund was satisfied that adequate monitoring, reporting and accounting mechanisms were in place. The Fund was asked to track carefully its involvement in SWAps, compiling lessons learned and good practices, including the impact UNFPA participation in common baskets had on the achievement of MYFF outputs, and to share that knowledge with the Executive Board and, where appropriate, with Governments, donors, partners in the UN system and civil society organizations. The Fund was further asked, in collaboration with United Nations Development Group partners, to ensure adequate staff training on SWAps to enable the full participation of UNFPA in the processes. The Board asked the Executive Director to keep UNFPA financial regulations under active review, taking into account any adjustment that might facilitate the Fund's full participation in SWAps and to present proposals on the issue in 2002 after submitting it to the Advisory Committee on Administrative and Budgetary Questions.

Reproductive health in emergency situations

In response to a 1999 UNDP/UNFPA Executive Board request [YUN 1999, p. 1025], the Executive Director submitted a May report on ensuring reproductive health in especially difficult circumstances: UNFPA programme experience and challenges [DP/FPA/2000/12]. She stated that UNFPA had become better equipped to deal with emergency situations. It had streamlined its programming in order to be able to respond to the increasing number of requests for emergency reproductive health and population assistance. The set of 12 types of pre-packaged emergency reproductive health kits (developed by the Inter-Agency Working Group and assembled by UNFPA) had been evaluated and improved and were in increasingly greater demand by other UN agencies and NGOs. With support from Belgium, a training programme had been started for UNFPA, other UN agencies, NGOs and national staff in the use of the guidelines found in the *Inter-Agency Field Manual.*

A review of best practices for provision of reproductive health for adolescent refugees and internally displaced persons was taking place. A roster of UNFPA staff with special expertise and emergency experience available for temporary redeployment had been developed, and discussions were under way concerning staffing needs for country offices in special situations. With support from the United Nations Foundation, the Fund had begun an evaluation of past experience in the provision of reproductive health services to refugee and displaced populations, as well as documentation of the reproductive health status and needs of forced migrants. Newly recruited UNFPA representatives were receiving briefings on UN emergency response and post-conflict rehabilitation modalities.

The greatest impediment to effective UNFPA response in emergencies were the financial constraints. In order to be able to respond quickly, UNFPA had to be able to access funds quickly in emergency situations. UNFPA proposed using a small amount, up to $1 million per year, for special circumstances, based on principles similar to such mechanisms as UNDP's TRAC 1.1.3, which earmarked 5 per cent of UNDP core resources to be available to countries in special development situations. UNFPA would continue to seek extra-budgetary resources for support of population and reproductive health in crisis situations, considering the $1 million of core resources as a leveraging base from which to build appeals. UNFPA would set clear criteria for access to such funding and would use the same financial and accounting procedures and oversight as for other programmes. The Executive Board would be provided with a detailed report on the use of the proposed fund after the first year, with an assessment of how well the mechanism had functioned during that period.

On 16 June [dec. 2000/13], the Executive Board encouraged UNFPA to provide appropriate and timely support in emergencies. It appealed to UNFPA to ensure close cooperation in the framework of the existing international coordination mechanisms and to incorporate reproductive health issues in a timely manner in health responses to emergencies. The Fund was encouraged to continue to seek extrabudgetary resources for support of population and reproductive health in emergencies, whenever possible through the UN consolidated appeals process. The Board urged Fund members to respond in a timely manner so that such appeals from UNFPA were adequately funded, and endorsed the use of up to $1 million of regular resources per year from the interregional programme for reproductive health needs in special circumstances as a leveraging base from which to build appeals for extrabudgetary resources. UNFPA was encouraged to evaluate its organizational capacity and systematize its responses to reproductive health needs in special circumstances, and to monitor and evaluate its overall performance in that regard. The Board requested the Executive Director to include in her annual report a summary of activities funded by those resources. Annexed to the decision was a set of criteria under which emergency funds could be accessed.

Country and intercountry programmes

UNFPA's provisional project expenditures for country and intercountry (regional and interregional) programmes in 2000 totalled $134.2 million, compared to $187.1 million in 1999, according to the Executive Director's statistical overview report covering 2000 [DP/FPA/2001/4 (Part I)/Add.1]. The 2000 figure included $117 million for country programmes and $17.2 million for intercountry programmes. In accordance with criteria defined by the UNDP/UNFPA Executive Board in 1996 [YUN 1996, p. 989], total expenditures in 2000 to those countries most in need amounted to $78.2 million, compared to $96 million in 1999.

In a report on the UNFPA intercountry programme, 2000-2003 [DP/FPA/2000/1], the Executive Director stated that the proposed programme was designed to produce the information, tools, strategies and approaches needed to help countries build their capacity to further implement the ICPD Programme of Action [YUN 1994, p. 956] and the ICPD+5 key future actions [YUN 1999, p. 1006]. The programme's fundamental premise was that certain needs of countries were more

effectively and efficiently addressed through regional and interregional initiatives; it established linkages between sectors and across regions.

The proposed programme reflected an almost 20 per cent reduction compared to the previous programme. The distribution of resources in the total amount of $160 million would be: $93 million for the interregional programme; $25 million for the regional programme for sub-Saharan Africa; $12 million for the Arab States and Europe; $17 million for Asia and the Pacific; and $13 million for Latin America and the Caribbean. Distribution by programme area would be: $76 million for reproductive health; $45 million for population and development strategies; and $39 million for advocacy.

An addendum to the report [DP/FPA/2000/1/Add.1] contained a review of the intercountry programme for 1996-1999.

By a 28 January decision [E/2000/35 (dec. 2000/6)], the Executive Board approved the intercountry programme, 2000-2003, and took note of the review of the intercountry programme, 1996-1999.

Africa. Provisional expenditures for UNFPA programmes in sub-Saharan Africa totalled $47.7 million in 2000, compared to $59.4 million in 1999. Most of the resources (61.9 per cent) went to reproductive health and family planning, followed by population and development strategies (29.6 per cent) and advocacy (5.7 per cent).

On 28 January [dec. 2000/6], the UNDP/UNFPA Executive Board approved assistance to the Niger and Zimbabwe.

Arab States and Europe. Provisional expenditures for UNFPA programmes in the Arab States and Europe totalled $17.4 million in 2000, compared to $26 million in 1999. Most of the resources (68.5 per cent) went to reproductive health and family planning, followed by population and development strategies (22 per cent) and advocacy (4.7 per cent).

Asia and the Pacific. Provisional expenditures for UNFPA programmes in Asia and the Pacific totalled $42.8 million in 2000, compared to $58.9 million in 1999. Most of the resources (71.1 per cent) went to reproductive health and family planning, followed by population and development strategies (18.1 per cent) and advocacy (7.6 per cent).

On 28 January [dec. 2000/6], the UNDP/UNFPA Executive Board approved the country programme for Iran; on 29 September [dec. 2000/24], it approved the country programmes for Cambodia and Viet Nam.

Latin America and the Carribean. Provisional expenditures for UNFPA programmes in Latin America and the Carribean totalled $15 million in 2000, compared to $19 million in 1999. Most of the resources (59.3 per cent) went to reproductive health and family planning, followed by population and development strategies (25.6 per cent) and advocacy (6.3 per cent).

Interregional programmes. Provisional expenditures for UNFPA's interregional and global programmes in 2000 totalled $11.3 million, compared to $23.8 million in 1999. Of the total, 35.8 per cent went to reproductive health and family planning, 34.2 per cent to advocacy, 26.5 per cent to population and development strategies and 3.5 per cent to multisectoral activities.

Reproductive health commodities

During 2000, the functions of the Global Initiative on Reproductive Health Commodity Management were taken over by UNFPA's new Commodity Management Unit to reflect the expanded scope of the work being undertaken to ensure reproductive health commodity security. That Unit, in close cooperation with the Fund's Procurement Section, also assumed the responsibility for the activities and management of the Global Contraceptive Commodity Programme [DP/FPA/2001/4 (Part III)].

With regard to national capacity-building, the Commodity Management Unit was continuing the Global Initiative's in-depth field studies in order to estimate short- and long-term contraceptive requirements, as well as condom needs to combat sexually transmitted diseases (STDs), including HIV; recommend measures to make good quality contraceptives more accessible; and review social marketing efforts and the roles of NGOs and the private sector. A list of all reproductive health commodities was being prepared in consultation with the World Health Organization. Important publications included: _Reproductive Health Commodity Security: Partnerships for Change, A Global Call for Action; Reproductive Health Commodity Security: Partnerships for Change, The UNFPA Strategy; Donor Support for Contraceptives and Logistics;_ and _The Role of the Logistics Manager in Contraceptive Procurement: A Checklist of Essential Actions._

With regard to advocacy and donor coordination, the Commodity Management Unit had prepared global projections of condom needs for the prevention of STDs, including HIV, and contraceptives for family planning programmes, which were being used as part of the effort to specify additional levels of commodity support (from donors and the Governments of programme countries) that were needed to meet the ICPD goals for 2015.

As to emphasizing sustainability and self-reliance in meeting reproductive health commodity needs, UNFPA continued its innovative private sector initiative, which focused on helping Governments work with the private sector and NGOs to expand access to affordably priced commercial products and services in developing countries. The goal of that approach, in which selected UNFPA field offices served as facilitators or brokers between Governments and the private sector to negotiate better prices for consumers, was to free up public sector resources to better serve the needs of those who could not afford to pay full prices for contraceptive products and services.

The Global Contraceptive Commodity Programme continued to provide essential buffer stocks of contraceptives and other reproductive health supplies to developing countries. In 2000, contraceptives and other reproductive health kits were sent to 35 destinations experiencing severe shortfalls, including Afghanistan, Angola, East Timor, Eritrea, Indonesia, Mongolia, Rwanda, Sierra Leone, the Sudan and the Federal Republic of Yugoslavia (Kosovo).

A major watershed was reached in September 2000 when UNFPA presented a global strategy for reproductive health commodity security to some 60 donors and technical agencies. Among the key points raised during the meeting were: the declining trend since 1996 in donor support for reproductive health commodities, in particular contraceptives; the consequences of contraceptive and condom shortfalls on women's reproductive health, including HIV infection, in developing countries; and the longer-term measures that should be undertaken at global and country levels to expand access to safe and affordable reproductive health commodities.

Financial and administrative questions

UNFPA's income from all sources totalled $410.8 million in 2000 compared with $325.6 million in 1999 [DP/FPA/2001/11]. That comprised $260.7 million of Regular Funds and $150.1 million from Other Funds. Expenditures totalled $211 million from Regular Funds and $66.8 million from Other Funds. Together with fund transfers of $3.5 million to Regular Funds and $8 million from Other Funds, that resulted in a net surplus of $53.2 million to Regular Funds and of $75.3 million to Other Funds. Of the $53.2 million surplus in Regular Funds, $28 million was required to replenish the operational reserve, and the remaining $25.2 million would be fully utilized in programme expenditures in 2001. Government contributions to Regular Funds in 2000 totalled $254.6 million, representing an increase of $9.4 million (4 per cent) over the previous year's total of $245.1 million.

In response to a 1998 UNDP/UNFPA Executive Board request [YUN 1998, p. 1014], the Executive Director submitted a report on administrative and operational support costs reimbursed to UNFPA [DP/FPA/2000/2]. In 1998, the Executive Board had accepted, as an interim measure, a proposed increase in those costs from 5 per cent to 7.5 per cent. The Executive Director reviewed the evolution of UNFPA support-cost arrangements, described the experiences of partner organizations within the United Nations, defined the major tasks that comprised administrative and operational support costs both at UNFPA headquarters and in the field, and provided a staff workload analysis quantifying the cost of UNFPA execution.

On 28 January [E/2000/35 (dec. 2000/6)], the Executive Board endorsed the standard rate of 7.5 per cent for reimbursement of administrative and operational support costs for UNFPA execution of co-financing trust fund activities.

Also before the Executive Board in January was a report of the Executive Director proposing revisions to the UNFPA Financial Regulations [DP/FPA/2000/3]. The revisions were the result of an overall review of the Financial Regulations as part of the development of a comprehensive UNFPA Policies and Procedures Manual and included an addition to the regulations as they pertained to procurement in order to reflect agreements reached by the Procurement Working Group established as part of the Secretary-General's reform programme.

On 28 January [dec. 2000/5], the Executive Board approved the revisions to the Financial Regulations and requested the Executive Director to keep them under active review.

Resource allocation

In response to a 1996 Executive Board request [YUN 1996, p. 989], the Executive Director submitted the first quinquennial review of the system for the allocation of UNFPA resources to country programmes [DP/FPA/2000/14]. The report, which included an assessment of the indicators used to establish the relative shares of resources for and nature of assistance provided to UNFPA programme countries, reviewed the experience of the preceding four years and examined progress made in implementing the resource allocation system since it began in 1996 [YUN 1996, p. 989]. Experience showed that the system had resulted in a marked increase in the overall share of resources going to those countries in greatest need of support. The system was within close reach of the target allocation percentages set by the Executive Board in 1996. The report also proposed an updating of the methodology for allocating UNFPA resources by incorporating new in-

terim benchmarks that constituted part of the key actions for the further implementation of the ICPD Programme of Action adopted by the General Assembly in resolution S-21/2 [YUN 1999, p. 1006]. The report recommended continuation of the basic framework and overall principles guiding the resource allocation system agreed to in 1996 with the addition of the ICPD+5 benchmarks.

On 28 September [E/2000/35 (dec. 2000/19)], the UNDP/UNFPA Executive Board endorsed the approach for resource allocation proposed by the Executive Director and decided that the updated system should take effect at the beginning of the new programme cycle for any given country; in case an upgrading country faced particularly adverse circumstances, its new resource allocation level would be implemented on a gradual basis. The Board reaffirmed the 1996 procedure for categorizing countries into Groups A, B and C [YUN 1996, p. 988] and approved the relative share of resources presented in the report. The Executive Director was asked to undertake a further quinquennial review of the resource allocation system, including an assessment of the indicators and their threshold levels, and to report in 2005.

Multi-year funding framework (MYFF)

In response to a 1999 UNDP/UNFPA Executive Board decision [YUN 1999, p. 1031], the Executive Director submitted the first UNFPA multi-year funding framework for 2000-2003 [DP/FPA/2000/6]. The MYFF integrated programme objectives, resources, budgets and outcomes, with the objective of increasing core resources. Regular monitoring and evaluation to determine the most effective programming and management strategies, and feeding that knowledge back into improving performance, were essential characteristics of the MYFF, which also included resource requirements to achieve the expected results. It was hoped that the MYFF's clear definition of organizational priorities, greater emphasis on organizational effectiveness and an improved tracking of and reporting on the Fund's performance would contribute to a more accurate determination of resource requirements and utilization and would encourage a more predictable and stable funding system.

On 7 April [E/2000/356 (dec. 2000/9)], the UNDP/UNFPA Executive Board requested the Executive Director to implement the MYFF, 2000-2003, and to provide annual updates on the development and refinement of the framework. The Board noted the funding scenarios as representing UNFPA resource mobilization targets and encouraged all countries in a position to do so to assist UNFPA to reach a total figure of regular and supplementary resources of $1,434 million for the period covered by the MYFF. The Executive Director was requested to present a detailed report in 2003 on the results achieved in the 2000-2003 MYFF cycle, lessons learned and their implications for priority-setting and formulation of the MYFF for the subsequent cycle, taking into account the need to harmonize UNDP/UNFPA/ United Nations Children's Fund reporting cycles.

Programming process

In response to a 1997 UNDP/UNFPA Executive Board request [YUN 1997, p. 1086], the Executive Director submitted a May report on the country-programming approval process [DP/FPA/2000/11], which provided an overview of the Fund's current programming process, delineated lessons learned, outlined progress made in relation to harmonization goals and presented conclusions and a recommendation.

In reviewing its programming process, UNFPA found many positive features as well as some areas that could be improved. The process provided Executive Board member countries with several opportunities to be involved at an early stage, particularly at the country level. However, those opportunities had not been fully utilized. UNFPA regularly informed member countries of its planned Country Population Assessments, but only a relatively small number of member countries provided inputs in response to those notifications, although representatives of member countries in-country were more likely to do so than were those from capitals. UNFPA proposed maintaining the current arrangements for approving country programmes as set forth by the Executive Board in 1997 [YUN 1997, p. 1086] and recommended some improvements.

On 16 June [E/2000/35 (dec. 2000/12)], the Executive Board welcomed progress towards the development of a more inclusive country programme preparation process with enhanced national ownership. It emphasized the need for further harmonization and standardization of programmes and programming procedures for all UN funds and programmes within the United Nations Development Group and also emphasized the need for such further harmonization efforts to provide the basis for a substantive, timely and joint oversight function of the respective Executive Boards. It requested UNFPA to propose to the other members of the Development Group the establishment of a working group with the objective of developing a common programme approval process. The Executive Board requested the Executive Director to report to it in 2001 on progress and future options in the programming process.

Technical Advisory Programme

In response to a 1999 Executive Board decision [YUN 1999, p. 1030], the Executive Director submitted a July progress report on implementation of Technical Advisory Programme (TAP) arrangements [DP/FPA/2000/16].

TAP, an inter-agency arrangement through which technical assistance was provided to countries in all three of the Fund's core programme areas (reproductive health, including family planning and sexual health; population and development strategies; and advocacy), was established in 1992 and had continued to evolve since then, in terms of both its substantive areas of focus and its structural arrangements. It had a two-tier arrangement: the first tier was composed of technical specialists assigned to eight multidisciplinary regional Country Technical Services Teams (CSTs); and the second tier was made up of Technical Advisory Services (TAS) specialists posted at the headquarters or regional offices of relevant UN agencies and regional commissions, and, in general, was organized to provide technical backstopping to CSTs.

Since its inception, TAP had developed in response to changing priorities, needs and circumstances. Following the adoption of the 1994 ICPD Programme of Action, the system was modified to support more effectively the reproductive health approach and to ensure mainstreaming of gender concerns and issues. More recently, the system had been revised to meet the need to strengthen monitoring and evaluation of UNFPA country programmes, to respond to the HIV/AIDS pandemic and to utilize new information technology more effectively. In addition, CST specialists were being given more opportunity to adopt a proactive approach with respect to country programme development, focus and management.

Attention was drawn to the fact that due to the decline in UNFPA's general resources in recent years, the number of TAS and CST positions had been reduced. In 1992, a total of 156 posts were authorized, including 40 TAS specialists. In 2000, the total number of authorized posts had declined to 130, with 18 TAS specialists. Because of time lags in filling vacant posts and budgetary constraints, approximately 20-25 per cent of the authorized posts were vacant at any one time.

UN Population Award

The 2000 United Nations Population Award was presented to Professor Ismail Awadallah Sallam in the individual category and the Fundación

Mexicana para la Planeación Familiar (Mexfam) in the institutional category. Professor Sallam was selected for his extensive contributions to the field of population, especially from the biomedical perspective, his long-term interest in preventive health care and making basic health care available to the poor and underserved populations of Egypt. Mexfam was selected as an innovator and leader of Mexican civil society in the fields of family planning and sexual and reproductive health. One of its new initiatives was in the area of a comprehensive programme for adolescent sexual health incorporating elements of peer training, community capacity-building, the development of age-appropriate health education materials and school-based workshops.

The award was established by the General Assembly in resolution 36/201 [YUN 1981, p. 792], to be presented annually to individuals or institutions for outstanding contributions to increased awareness of population problems and to their solutions. In September, the Secretary-General transmitted to the Assembly the report of the UNFPA Executive Director on the Population Award [A/55/419]. By **decision 55/448** of 20 December, the Assembly took note of the report.

Other population activities

Commission on Population and Development

The Commission on Population and Development, at its thirty-third session (New York, 27-30 March) [E/2000/25], considered as its central theme "Population, gender and development", which was discussed in the context of the follow-up to ICPD [YUN 1994, p. 955]. Documents before the Commission focusing on the theme of the session were reports of the Secretary-General on world population monitoring, 2000 [E/CN.9/2000/3], and on the monitoring of population programmes [E/CN.9/2000/4] (see p. 999). Other reports dealing with the ICPD follow-up were reports of the Secretary-General on the special session of the General Assembly for the review and appraisal of the ICPD Programme of Action [E/CN.9/2000/2] (see p. 998), and on the flow of financial resources for assisting in the implementation of the Programme of Action [E/CN.9/2000/5 & Corr.1] (see p. 1000). Also before the Commission was the Secretary-General's report on programme implementation and progress of work in the field of population in 1999 [E/CN.9/2000/6] [YUN 1999, p. 1032].

In addition to adopting a resolution on population, gender and development [E/2000/25 (res. 2000/1)] (see p. 999), the Commission recommended to the Economic and Social Council for adoption a draft decision on the report of the Commission on its thirty-third session and the provisional agenda for the thirty-fourth (2001) session. It also adopted a decision [dec. 2000/1] by which it reaffirmed that "Population, environment and development" should be the special theme for the Commission's thirty-fourth session and that the special themes for the thirty-fifth (2002) and thirty-sixth (2003) sessions should be, respectively, "Reproductive rights and reproductive health, with special reference to HIV/AIDS" and "Population, education and development". The UN Population Division was asked to give due attention to the impact of HIV/AIDS in the preparation of reports for the Commission's forthcoming theme sessions for the years 2001-2003. In another decision [dec. 2000/2], the Commission took note of all the documents before it, including a note by the Secretariat on the draft medium-term plan of the Population Division for the period 2002-2005 [E/CN.9/2000/CRP.2].

By **decision 2000/233** of 27 July, the Economic and Social Council took note of the report of the Commission on its thirty-third session and approved the provisional agenda and documentation for the thirty-fourth session. On 18 October, the Council decided that the Commission's thirty-fourth session should be held from 2 to 6 April 2001 (**decision 2000/305**).

In preparation for the thirty-fourth session, the Commission's Bureau held an intersessional meeting in Nairobi, Kenya, on 27 and 28 September [E/CN.9/2001/CRP.1].

2000 UN activities

In a report on programme implementation and progress of work of the UN Population Division in 2000 [E/CN.9/2001/5], the Secretary-General described the activities dealing with the analysis of demographic variables at the world level; world population estimates and projections; population policy and socio-economic development; monitoring, coordination and dissemination of population information; and technical cooperation in population.

The Population Division completed two databases: one on contraceptive use by country and by type of method and another on fertility by country. Two areas of ongoing study were the impact of AIDS on fertility and the effect of changing marital patterns on childbearing. In response to the AIDS epidemic and extensive AIDS-related information and educational activities carried out in many countries, sexual and childbearing behaviours had changed.

Work continued on a revision of the draft of the manual on the estimation of adult mortality. The manual presented census survival methods, methods utilizing intercensal deaths, estimations of adult deaths derived from the survivorship of parents, and estimations derived from the survivorship of siblings. Work had started on updating the database on infant and child mortality. Both revisions were expected to be ready in 2001.

With regard to international migration, the Population Division issued in March a working paper "Replacement migration: is it a solution to declining and ageing populations?", which examined in detail the cases of eight low-fertility countries (France, Germany, Italy, Japan, Republic of Korea, Russian Federation, United Kingdom, United States) and two regions (Europe, European Union). In each case, alternative scenarios for the period 1995-2000 were considered, highlighting the impact that various levels of immigration might have on population size and population ageing. The study found that the populations of most of the developed countries were projected to become smaller and older in the next half century as a result of low fertility and increased longevity. Population decline appeared certain in the absence of replacement migration. For the European Union, a continuation of the immigration levels observed in the 1990s would roughly suffice to prevent the total population from declining, while for Europe as a whole immigration would need to double. Work continued on the creation of a database on east-to-west migration in Europe, expected to become available in 2001, which would include immigration and emigration data covering the years since 1980, by country of origin and by country of destination, for the countries of Eastern Europe, the former USSR, the former Yugoslavia and Albania.

As a follow-up to that paper, the Population Division organized an expert group meeting on policy responses to population ageing and population decline (New York, 16-18 October). The experts reviewed the demographic prospects of each country and region for the next half century, identified the consequences of population decline and population ageing, and examined various policy options that Governments might adopt to cope with the unprecedented demographic challenges.

Work continued on the creation of a database on internal migration, starting with Latin America and the Caribbean, and Northern America. The database, which would become available in 2001, would include, for 51 countries and areas, information on migration over the past five years and lifetime migration, as available in each census. A report on the components of urban growth

in developing countries was completed and would be published in 2001. It presented, for 55 countries in the 1960s, 1970s and 1980s, estimates of the components of urban growth (natural growth and migration-reclassification). The main conclusion was that the major component of urban growth in most developing countries was not migration but natural increase.

As to world population estimates and projections, the third and last report in the series of publications related to the *1998 Revision* was issued under the title *World Population Prospects: The 1998 Revision: volume III, Analytical Report* [Sales No. E.99.XIII.10]. The report entitled *Long-Range World Population Projections: Based on the 1998 Revision* [Sales No. E.00.XIII.8] was also issued. It presented the results of long-range projections to 2150 for the major areas of the world. The long-range projections of fertility were made according to seven different scenarios. The results of the *2000 Revision* of population estimates and projections to 2050 had been compiled and volume I of *World Population Prospects: The 2000 Revision* had been issued as a working paper. The *2000 Revision* incorporated explicitly the impact of HIV/AIDS for over 40 countries and used a revised methodology to project the impact of the epidemic.

The results of the *1999 Revision of World Urbanization Prospects* were issued as a working paper. A full report, including an in-depth analysis of the *Revision* results, was completed and was awaiting publication. According to the *1999 Revision*, the proportion of people living in urban areas worldwide was expected to rise from 47 per cent in mid-2000 to 50 per cent in 2007 and to reach 60 per cent by 2030.

In the area of emerging issues in population policy, the ongoing project on abortion policies continued. During 2000, the first volume (vol. I, *Afghanistan to France*) of the three-volume series *Abortion Policies: A Global Review* was completed and submitted for publication. The second and third volumes (vol. II, *Gabon to Norway;* and vol. III, *Oman to Zimbabwe*) were also completed and were in the editing process. The publication aimed at providing objective information about the nature of abortion law and policy in all countries at the end of the twentieth century. For each country, there was a fact sheet containing information on the grounds on which abortions were performed, additional requirements and key indicators on reproductive health. Included in the background text was information on the social and political setting of changes in abortion laws and policies, the ways in which those laws and policies had been formulated and how they had evolved over time. Work continued on the database on population policies, which contained information on national population policies from all available sources, including the United Nations Population Inquiries. Preliminary work began on the eighth edition of the Population Policy Database, 2001.

The report *Charting the Progress of Populations*, published in January, grew out of the participation of the Population Division in activities aimed at ensuring a coordinated and system-wide implementation of the goals and commitments adopted by recent global conferences. It featured the 12 key statistical indicators which were chosen on the basis of their relevance to the goals adopted at the conferences. It provided updated data as well as an analytic summary of the information, showing how near or how far countries were from achieving the goals set out at the conferences with respect to the selected indicators in the areas of population and primary health care, including reproductive health; nutrition; basic education; safe water and sanitation; and shelter.

The Technical Meeting on Population Ageing and Living Arrangements of Older Persons (New York, 8-10 February) brought together experts from the different world regions to consider the most pressing issues concerning population ageing and the living arrangements of older persons, historical and cultural contexts, the social process through which living arrangements of older persons influenced the demand for formal and informal support systems, and how Governments responded to those perceived needs. Work was in progress on a publication tentatively entitled *Population Ageing in Numbers*, to be issued as a background document in advance of the Second World Assembly on Ageing in 2002.

A new wallchart, *Population, Environment and Development, 2001*, was linked to the topical theme of the Commission on Population and Development for 2001. The chart presented statistical data relating to countries' population size and growth, economic development and selected areas of environmental concern, including the supply of freshwater, deforestation, food and agriculture and greenhouse gas emissions.

During 2000, the Population Division prepared the latest edition of its annual report, *World Population Monitoring*, the theme of which was population, environment and development. The general trends of rapid population growth, sustained but uneven economic improvement and environmental change were widely acknowledged. However, the interrelationships between population size and growth, environmental change and development were not well understood. *World Population Monitoring* investigated what was known about those interrelationships,

analysing recent information and policy perspectives on the three factors.

During 2000, the Population Division developed its web site within the site of the Department of Economic and Social Affairs. The home page of the site provided an overview of activities and organizations in the UN system that were active in the population and development area and provided a link to the Population Division web site and the sites of other relevant UN entities.

During the year, the Population Division's Population Information Network (POPIN) continued to focus on increasing access to substantive population information at the interregional, regional and national levels. Global and regional commission POPIN web sites were updated and revised, and the POPIN Internet *Worldwide Directory of Population Institutions* was expanded. Global POPIN and the Association for Population/Family Planning Libraries and Information Centers launched a new series of guides to electronic resources—namely, *Getting Started: Selected Electronic Resources on HIV/AIDS*, the *Guide to Citation of Electronic Information, Copyright and Intellectual Property* and *Selected Electronic Training Resources on Population and Reproductive Health*.

POPIN was also active at the regional level. In Africa, the Economic Commission for Africa Food Security and Sustainable Development Division, which coordinated POPIN–Africa, updated its web site to include more links to African electronic population information resources, more full-text African publications on population issues, an electronic version of the second issue of *Africa's Population and Development Bulletin*, and a new version of the Population, Environment, Agriculture and Development computer software model. In Asia and the Pacific, global POPIN continued to provide technical support and assistance for the maintenance and updating of the web sites of the UNFPA country support teams for the South Pacific and Central and South Asia. The POPIN of the Economic and Social Commission for Asia and the Pacific (ESCAP) created electronic databases of population and family planning information and/or reproductive health indicators for a number of Asian countries. In the Arab States and Western Asia, the League of Arab States Population Research Unit web site was updated to include survey information from the Pan Arab Project for Child Development (PAPCHILD) Morocco Survey and the PAPCHILD Lebanese Survey. In Europe, the Economic Commission for Europe (ECE) Population Activities Unit, which coordinated POPIN–Europe, expanded its web site to offer comprehensive access to Fertility and Family Survey data and reports, and proceedings of other ECE meetings. The

Latin American and Caribbean Demographic Centre of the Economic Commission for Latin America and the Caribbean redesigned, updated and expanded its web site and assisted with the creation of two new POPIN–Latin America and the Caribbean sites at the Caja Costarricense de Seguro Social in Costa Rica and the Maestria en Demografia, Universidad Nacional de Cordoba, Argentina.

The Population Division continued to implement a programme of technical assistance to build capacity among population research centres in developing countries. It co-organized and participated in a training workshop for staff of institutions belonging to the Demoneta network of francophone population research centres in Western Africa, held in Niamey, Niger, in April, and assisted in the maintenance and continued development of the network's web site. In collaboration with ESCAP's Population and Rural and Urban Development Division, the Population Division organized a training workshop, "Advanced use of the Internet for population research", in Bangkok, Thailand, in December, for staff from eight population training and research centres in developing countries of the ESCAP region.

The Population Division initiated a programme of outreach to doctoral population students from developing countries, through which selected students were provided with the opportunity to participate in technical meetings organized by the Division and to receive additional training on the activities of the United Nations in the area of population. Three students (from Bolivia, India and Nepal) benefited from the programme in 2000, in connection with the Expert Group Meeting on Policy Responses to Population Ageing and Population Decline.

Demographics

The twenty-first session of the Subcommittee on Demographic Estimates and Projections of the Administrative Committee on Coordination (Geneva, 27-29 June) [ACC/2000/14] discussed the continuing collaboration in the preparation of demographic and sectoral estimates and projections in the UN system.

The Subcommittee agreed that it was essential to continue inter-agency coordination in the field of demographic and sectoral estimates and projections in order to strengthen the UN system database, maintain consistency in their coverage and timing, and ensure homogeneity in the presentation of results. The Subcommittee underscored the importance of that unique set of coordinated and consistent demographic and sectoral estimates and projections.

The Subcommittee was successful in establishing a schedule for the coordinated production and dissemination of the 2000 round of consistent demographic and sectoral estimates and projections, undertaken by the Population Division in cooperation with its partners.

The Subcommittee established a Task Force comprising the Food and Agriculture Organization of the United Nations, the International Labour Organization, the Institute for Statistics of the United Nations Educational, Scientific and Cultural Organization and the Population Division, in cooperation with the regional commissions, to devise a strategy for the development, documentation and exchange of methods to interpolate and extrapolate existing estimates and projections.

The Subcommittee requested that the International Tribunal for the Former Yugoslavia (see p. 1221) be invited to make a presentation on its work in the use of demographic information in war crime cases to the twenty-second (2002) session.

The Subcommittee also discussed the activities of the Population Division, the regional commissions and other Secretariat offices, the specialized agencies and other UN bodies.

Chapter IX

Social policy, crime prevention and human resource development

In 2000, the United Nations continued efforts to advance social, cultural and human resource development and to strengthen its crime prevention and criminal justice programme.

In June, the General Assembly held its twenty-fourth special session to review and appraise the implementation of the Copenhagen Declaration on Social Development and the Programme of Action, adopted at the 1995 World Summit for Social Development. The special session, entitled "World Summit for Social Development and beyond: achieving social development for all in a globalizing world", adopted further initiatives for social development, which reaffirmed the 1995 Copenhagen Declaration and established a broad framework for follow-up action by Governments, civil society and the international community.

The Commission for Social Development, at its February/March session, considered as its priority theme its contribution to the special session and adopted a set of agreed conclusions, which it transmitted to the Economic and Social Council and to the Preparatory Committee for the special session.

The Council, in other social development-related action, renewed until 2002 the mandate of the Special Rapporteur on disability of the Commission for Social Development, following a review of his report on the second monitoring period (1997-2000) of the implementation of the 1993 Standard Rules on the Equalization of Opportunities for Persons with Disabilities.

The Tenth United Nations Congress on the Prevention of Crime and the Treatment of Offenders, held in April, considered the state of crime and criminal justice worldwide; international cooperation in combating transnational crime; promoting the rule of law and strengthening the criminal justice system; new developments in effective crime prevention; and accountability and fairness in the justice process for offenders and victims. It adopted the Vienna Declaration on Crime and Justice: Meeting the Challenges of the Twenty-first Century, which was endorsed by the Assembly in December. The Ad Hoc Committee on the Elaboration of a Convention against Transnational Organized Crime

finalized the United Nations Convention against Transnational Organized Crime, as well as the Protocol to Prevent, Suppress and Punish Trafficking in Persons, Especially Women and Children and the Protocol against the Smuggling of Migrants by Land, Sea and Air. The Convention and related Protocols, which were adopted in November by the Assembly, were opened for signature from 12 to 15 December in Palermo, Italy, and thereafter in New York until 12 December 2002. Other crime-related issues addressed by the Assembly were the development of an international legal instrument against corruption, combating the criminal misuse of information technologies, and combating corrupt practices and illegal transfer of funds and repatriation of such funds to the countries of origin. The Commission on Crime Prevention and Criminal Justice held its ninth session in April.

Regarding cultural development, the Assembly took action relating to the United Nations Year of Dialogue among Civilizations, the Olympic Truce and the Bethlehem 2000 project.

Human resource development remained the focus of the United Nations Institute for Training and Research and the United Nations University.

Social policy and cultural issues

Social development

**Follow-up to 1995
World Summit for Social Development**

In 2000, the General Assembly held its twenty-fourth special session to review and appraise the implementation of the Copenhagen Declaration on Social Development and the Programme of Action, adopted at the 1995 World Summit for Social Development [YUN 1995, p. 1113]. Entitled "World Summit for Social Development and beyond: achieving social development for all in a globalizing world", the special session adopted further initiatives for social development (**resolution S-24/2**), which included a political declaration by Member States on how to promote social development in the context of globalization and a series of recommendations for further initiatives at the local, national, regional and international levels for the further implementation of the 10 commitments adopted at the 1995 Summit.

Twenty-fourth special session

The twenty-fourth special session of the General Assembly to review and appraise the implementation of the Copenhagen Declaration on Social Development and the Programme of Action [YUN 1995, p. 1114], adopted at the 1995 World Summit for Social Development, was held in Geneva from 26 June to 1 July [A/S-24/10]. The session was convened in accordance with Assembly resolution 50/161 [YUN 1995, p. 1122], subsequent to a recommendation of the Summit [ibid., p. 1118]. Participants at the session included delegations from 178 countries, 11 observers and representatives of 500 non-governmental organizations (NGOs).

Preparations for the session were made by the Preparatory Committee at its first [YUN 1999, p. 1037] and second sessions (see below).

In **resolution S-24/2** of 1 July (see p. 1013), the Assembly adopted proposals for further initiatives for social development, including poverty eradication, the promotion of full employment, social integration, respect for human dignity, and the attainment of the goals of universal and equitable access to quality education, the highest attainable standard of physical and mental health, and the access of all to primary health care. Other proposals emphasized acceleration of the economic, social and human resource development of Africa and the least developed countries (LDCs), structural adjustment programmes and cooperation through the United Nations and other multilateral institutions.

In other action, the Assembly approved the report of the Credentials Committee on 30 June (**resolution S-24/1**). Regarding procedural matters, the Assembly on 26 June appointed the members of the Credentials Committee (**decision S-24/11**); elected its President (**decision S-24/12**), Vice-Presidents (**decision S-24/13**), Chairpersons of the Main Committees (**decision S-24/14**) and officers of the Ad Hoc Committee of the Whole of the Twenty-fourth Special Session (**decision S-24/15**); made arrangements with regard to the organization of the session (**decision S-24/21**); and adopted the agenda for the special session (**decision S-24/22**). On 30 June, the Assembly decided that nine NGOs might make statements in the debate in plenary (**decision S-24/23**).

In his opening statement [A/S-24/PV.1], the Assembly President recalled that the signatories at the 1995 Summit had promised to establish time-bound targets to cut poverty, promote greater equality between women and men, achieve full employment and establish universal access to education and primary health care. Since then, some noticeable national efforts and programmes had been launched. However, overall, many developing countries had continued to fall behind. The most frequently cited indication that social development was not yet secure on the international agenda was the decline in official development assistance (ODA) that had continued since Copenhagen, where the goal of committing 0.7 per cent of gross national product for such assistance was reaffirmed. The current task was to build upon the strong foundation of consensus reached in Copenhagen and to uphold the social commitment expressed at the Summit.

Preparatory process

Preparatory Committee. The Preparatory Committee for the special session, established by General Assembly resolution 52/25 [YUN 1997, p. 1109] to consider and decide on the process to achieve the session's purpose, held its second session in New York from 3 to 14 April 2000 [A/S-24/2]. It held a resumed session on 20 and 22 June [A/S-24/2/Add.1,2], also in New York, to consider the draft final document. The Committee's first session took place in 1999 [YUN 1999, p. 1037].

In April, the Committee, in addition to taking action on various procedural matters, adopted a decision bringing to the Assembly's attention a series of documents it had considered, including review reports and proposals for further action and initiatives submitted by organs and specialized agencies of the UN system and other concerned organizations [A/AC.253/16 & Add.1-17]; reports of the Secretary-General on implementation of the outcome of the 1995 Summit [A/AC.253/13-E/CN.5/2000/2] (see p. 1013), progress achieved in implementing UN resolutions concerning the right self-determination [A/AC.253/17], the development of guidelines on the role and social responsibilities of the private sector [A/AC.253/21], acceleration of development in Africa and LDCs [A/AC.253/22], promoting social integration in post-conflict situations [A/AC.253/23], the impact of globalization on social development [A/AC.253/25], the social impact of economic measures taken in response to financial crises in developing countries [A/AC.253/27], and resources for social development: additional and innovative measures [A/AC.253/28]; and the reports of the seminar on values and market economies (Paris, 19-21 January) [A/AC.253/24], as well as of the 1999 symposiums on States, markets and social progress [YUN 1999, p. 1038] and on socio-economic policies during macroeconomic stabilization in countries with economies in transition [ibid.].

Commission for Social Development. At its thirty-eighth session (New York, 8-17 February) [E/2000/26 & Corr.1], the Commission for Social Development, the body responsible for Summit follow-up and implementation of the Copenhagen Declaration, considered as its priority theme the Commission's contribution to the overall review of the implementation of the Summit. On 28 February, the Economic and Social Council authorized the Commission to hold a resumed session on an exceptional basis, which took place on 14 and 17 March, to complete its work for the special session of the General Assembly (**decision 2000/211**). The Commission, on 17 March [res. 38/1], adopted a set of agreed conclusions on the review and appraisal of the implementation of the outcome of the 1995 World Summit and transmitted them to the Economic and Social Council and to the Preparatory Committee for the special session. The agreed conclusions addressed the themes of poverty eradication, full employment, social integration, Africa and LDCs, mobilization of resources for social development and capacity-building to implement social programmes.

The Commission had before it a comprehensive report of the Secretary-General on the implementation of the 1995 World Summit [A/AC.253/13-E/CN.5/2000/2], which highlighted national strategies and policies to implement the Summit outcome based on information contained in national submissions. It described the scope of regional and international cooperation for social development based on information received from regional commissions, specialized agencies, funds and programmes and other national and international bodies. A series of regional overviews and analyses evaluated the implementation of the Summit in the context of progress achieved, constraints encountered and lessons learned. An analytical overview and conclusions of the report were based on 11 cross-cutting issues (importance of rehabilitating the public sector; growth of inequality; informalization of employment; the working poor; making economic growth more employment-intensive; financing social protection; conflict, crises and social development; reversing the decline of ODA; debt reduction; globalization and liberalization; and local development and values in the global economy) arising from national reports and regional and global trends. Annexed to the report was a review of progress towards targets for 2000. The Commission took note of the Secretary-General's report [dec. 38/101], which was also submitted to the Preparatory Committee for the special session.

In other action related to the special session [dec. 38/101], the Commission took note of the report on the 1999 symposium on States, markets and social progress [YUN 1999, p. 1038].

Workshops. In May [A/S-24/5], Austria transmitted to the special session the outcome of workshops held during the Tenth United Nations Congress on the Prevention of Crime and the Treatment of Offenders (see p. 1040) relating to combating corruption and to community involvement in crime prevention.

GENERAL ASSEMBLY ACTION

On 1 July [meeting 10], the General Assembly, on the recommendation of the Ad Hoc Committee of the Whole [A/S-24/8/Rev.1], adopted **resolution S-24/2** without vote [agenda item 9].

Further initiatives for social development

The General Assembly

Adopts the proposals for further initiatives for social development annexed to the present resolution.

ANNEX
Further initiatives for social development

I. Political declaration

1. Five years have passed since the World Summit for Social Development, which marked the first time in history that heads of State and Government had gathered to recognize the significance of social development and human well-being for all and to give these goals the highest priority into the twenty-first century. The Copenhagen Declaration on Social Development and the Programme of Action of the World Summit for Social Development established a new consensus to place people at the centre of our concerns for sustainable development and pledged to eradicate poverty, promote full and productive employment, and foster social integration to achieve stable, safe and just societies for all.

2. We, the representatives of Governments, meeting at this special session of the General Assembly at Geneva to assess achievements and obstacles and to decide on further initiatives to accelerate social development for all, reaffirm our will and commitment to implement the Copenhagen Declaration and Programme of Action, including the strategies and agreed targets contained therein. The Copenhagen Declaration and Programme of Action will remain the basic framework for social development in the years to come.

3. Since the Summit, recognition of the imperative of social development requiring an enabling environment has spread and strengthened. Furthermore, there is a growing awareness of the positive impact of effective social policies on economic and social development. Our review and appraisal has shown that Governments, relevant international organizations as well as actors of civil society have made continued efforts to improve human well-being and eradicate poverty. However, further actions are needed for the full implementation of the Copenhagen Declaration and Programme of Action. It has also become clear that there is no single universal path to achieving social development and

that all have experience, knowledge and information worth sharing.

4. Globalization and continuing rapid technological advances offer unprecedented opportunities for social and economic development. At the same time, they continue to present serious challenges, including widespread financial crises, insecurity, poverty, exclusion and inequality within and among societies. Considerable obstacles to further integration and full participation in the global economy remain for developing countries, in particular the least developed countries, as well as for some countries with economies in transition. Unless the benefits of social and economic development are extended to all countries, a growing number of people in all countries and even entire regions will remain marginalized from the global economy. We must act now in order to overcome those obstacles affecting peoples and countries and to realize the full potential of opportunities presented for the benefit of all.

5. We therefore reiterate our determination and duty to eradicate poverty, promote full and productive employment, foster social integration and create an enabling environment for social development. The maintenance of peace and security within and among nations, democracy, the rule of law, the promotion and protection of all human rights and fundamental freedoms, including the right to development, effective, transparent and accountable governance, gender equality, full respect for fundamental principles and rights at work and the rights of migrant workers are some of the essential elements for the realization of social and people-centred sustainable development. Social development requires not only economic activity but also reduction in the inequality in the distribution of wealth and more equitable distribution of the benefits of economic growth within and among nations, including the realization of an open, equitable, secure, non-discriminatory, predictable, transparent and multilateral rule-based international trading system, maximizing opportunities and guaranteeing social justice, and recognizing the interrelationship between social development and economic growth.

6. Full and effective implementation of the Copenhagen Declaration and Programme of Action is necessary at all levels. We reaffirm that while social development is a national responsibility it cannot be successfully achieved without the collective commitment and efforts of the international community. We invite Governments, the United Nations and other relevant international organizations, within their respective mandates, to strengthen the quality and consistency of their support for sustainable development, in particular in Africa and the least developed countries, as well as in some countries with economies in transition, and to continue coordinating their efforts in this regard. We also invite them to develop coordinated and gender-sensitive social, economic and environmental approaches in order to close the gap between goals and achievements. This in turn requires not only renewed political will but also the mobilization and allocation of additional resources at both the national and international levels. In this connection, we will strive to fulfil the yet to be attained internationally agreed target of 0.7 per cent of gross national product of developed countries for overall official development assistance as soon as possible.

7. We recognize that excessive debt-servicing has severely constrained the capacity of many developing countries, as well as countries with economies in transition, to promote social development. We also recognize the efforts being made by indebted developing countries to fulfil their debt-servicing commitment despite the high social cost incurred. We reaffirm our pledge to find effective, equitable, development-oriented and durable solutions to the external debt and debt-servicing burdens of developing countries.

8. The fight against poverty requires the active participation of civil society and people living in poverty. We are convinced that universal access to high-quality education, including opportunities for the acquisition of skills required in the knowledge-based economy, health and other basic social services, and equal opportunities for active participation and sharing the benefits of the development process are essential for the achievement of the objectives of the Copenhagen Declaration and Programme of Action. Recognizing the primary responsibility of Governments in this regard, we acknowledge the importance of strengthening partnerships, as appropriate, among the public sector, the private sector and other relevant actors of civil society.

9. We reaffirm our pledge to place particular focus on, and give priority attention to, the fight against the worldwide conditions that pose severe threats to the health, safety, peace, security and well-being of our people. Among these conditions are: chronic hunger; malnutrition; illicit drug problems; organized crime; corruption; natural disasters; foreign occupation; armed conflicts; illicit arms trafficking; trafficking in persons; terrorism; intolerance and incitement to racial, ethnic, religious and other hatreds; xenophobia; and endemic, communicable and chronic diseases, in particular the human immunodeficiency virus/acquired immunodeficiency syndrome (HIV/AIDS), malaria and tuberculosis.

10. We reiterate our resolve to reinforce solidarity with people living in poverty and dedicate ourselves to strengthening policies and programmes to create inclusive, cohesive societies for all—women and men, children, young and older persons—particularly those who are vulnerable, disadvantaged and marginalized. We recognize that their special needs will require specific targeted measures to empower them to live more productive and fulfilling lives.

11. Enhanced international cooperation is essential to implement the Copenhagen Declaration and Programme of Action as well as the further actions and initiatives adopted at the current special session, and to address the challenges of globalization. We recognize the need to continue to work on a wide range of reforms for a strengthened and more stable international financial system, enabling it to deal more effectively and in a timely manner with new challenges of development. We acknowledge the need for a coordinated follow-up to all major conferences and summits by Governments, regional organizations and all the bodies and organizations of the United Nations system, within their respective mandates.

12. Determined to give new momentum to our collective efforts to improve the human condition, we here set out further initiatives for the full implementation of the Copenhagen Declaration and Programme of Action. At the dawn of the new millennium, aware of our

responsibilities towards future generations, we are strongly committed to social development, including social justice, for all in a globalizing world. We invite all people in all countries and in all walks of life, as well as the international community, to join in renewed dedication to our shared vision for a more just and equitable world.

II. Review and assessment of the implementation of the outcome of the World Summit for Social Development

1. One of the most important developments since the World Summit for Social Development in March 1995 is the increased priority which social development has been given in national and international policy objectives. The Summit also signified a recognition by States of the importance of making social improvement an integral part of development strategy at the national and international levels, as well as placing people at the centre of development efforts. The review and appraisal of the implementation of the outcome of the Summit shows that many new national policies and programmes have been initiated. The Summit has clearly also had an impact on the United Nations system, leading to a refocusing of its activities and galvanizing action. However, it is equally clear that national and international policy responses have been uneven. Despite some advances, there has been little progress in some key areas and regress is evident in others. As noted in one of the key issues of the analytical report of the Secretary-General, one major development since the Summit is that inequality within and among States continues to grow. Achieving the goals agreed upon at the Summit will require much stronger and more comprehensive action and new, innovative approaches (see sect. III below) by all actors, national and international, governmental and non-governmental, taking into account the outcomes of the relevant United Nations conferences and summits.

2. Since the Summit, globalization has presented new challenges for the fulfilment of the commitments made and the realization of the goals of the Summit. Globalization and interdependence have provided many beneficial opportunities but have also involved potential damage and costs. If anything, these forces have accelerated and often strained the capacity of Governments and the international community to manage them for the benefit of all. Economic growth has been impressive in some places and disappointing in others. Current patterns of globalization have contributed to a sense of insecurity as some countries, particularly developing countries, have been marginalized from the global economy. The growing interdependence of nations, which has caused economic shocks to be transmitted across national borders, as well as increased inequality, highlight weaknesses in current international and national institutional arrangements and economic and social policies, and reinforce the importance of strengthening them through appropriate reforms. There is wide recognition of the need for collective action to anticipate and offset the negative social and economic consequences of globalization and to maximize its benefits for all members of society, including those with special needs. For most developing countries, the terms of international trade have worsened and inflows of concessional financial resources have declined. The high debt burden has weakened the capacity of many Governments to service their increasing external debt and eroded resources available for social development. Inappropriate design of structural adjustment programmes has weakened the management capacity of public institutions as well as the ability of Governments to respond to the social development needs of the weak and vulnerable in society and to provide adequate social services.

3. Since the Summit, policies and programmes to achieve social development have been implemented within the context of national economic, political, social, legal, cultural and historical environments. There has been an increasing interest in strengthening an enabling environment for sustainable development through the interaction of economic and social development and environmental protection. However, these national environments have been increasingly affected by global influences and forces beyond the control of individual Governments. Serious impediments to social development, many of which were identified by the Summit, still persist, including chronic hunger; malnutrition; illicit drug problems; organized crime; corruption; foreign occupation; armed conflicts; illicit arms trafficking; terrorism; intolerance and incitement to racial, ethnic, religious and other hatreds; xenophobia; endemic, communicable and chronic diseases, in particular HIV/AIDS, malaria and tuberculosis; and economic sanctions and unilateral measures at variance with international law and the Charter of the United Nations.

4. The ultimate goals of development are to improve living conditions for people and to empower them to participate fully in the economic, political and social arenas. Some Governments, in partnership with other actors, have contributed to an enabling environment for social development through efforts to ensure democracy and transparency in decision-making; the rule of law; accountability of government institutions; empowerment of women; and gender equality. Efforts have also been made to promote peace and security; respect for all human rights and fundamental freedoms, including the right to development; and tolerance and respect for cultural and ethnic diversity. However, progress in all these areas has been uneven and requires further effort.

5. At the Summit, quantitative targets were adopted and reaffirmed in the areas of basic social services and official development assistance. Out of thirteen targets, for the following nine areas the target date set was the year 2000: education; adult illiteracy; improved access to safe water supply and sanitation; malnutrition among children under five years of age; maternal mortality; infant mortality and the under-five mortality; life expectancy; malaria mortality and morbidity; and affordable and adequate shelter for all. Available data indicate that progress in these areas remains unsatisfactory. In the field of education, for example, there are still twenty-nine countries which have enrolment rates of less than 50 per cent, instead of the target of 80 per cent of children attending primary school.

6. Gender mainstreaming is widely accepted, but in some parts of the world the implementation of this concept has often not started. In many countries, women continue to suffer from discrimination with regard to the full enjoyment of all human rights.

7. The compilation by national Governments of broad-based and disaggregated data, both qualitative and quantitative indicators, to evaluate progress in the areas covered by the targets, has presented an important challenge. In this regard, Governments may, as appropriate, seek assistance from international organizations. Since the Summit, efforts have been made to improve the quality, timeliness and country coverage of data.

8. Given the nature and the broad scope of many of the goals and targets set in Copenhagen and the inevitable lag between the initiation of policies and measurable results, a comprehensive evaluation of the impact of new policies and programmes will take time. However, it is possible to make the following early assessments.

Poverty eradication

9. One of the most significant outcomes of the World Summit for Social Development has been to place the goal of eradicating poverty at the centre of national and international policy agendas. At the international level, development targets adopted at Copenhagen have increasingly influenced the policies and planning of bilateral and multilateral development partners. Many Governments have set national poverty reduction targets and formulated poverty eradication plans and strategies, including by promoting employment and developing or reinforcing tools to evaluate progress. Some have further developed existing poverty eradication plans, programmes and measures. Microcredit and other financial instruments have received increasing attention as effective means of empowering the poor, and many countries have expanded access to such programmes. Many countries have achieved improvements in literacy, life expectancy, school enrolment and the availability of basic social services, and have enhanced social protection systems and reduced infant mortality. However, progress has been uneven, revealing continuing disparities in access to basic social services, including a lack of access to quality education. Of particular concern in this regard is the increasing feminization of poverty and the uneven access to education for girls. For example, while countries in East Asia and the Pacific have achieved enrolment rates similar to those in developed countries, almost one third of school-age children in Africa are still without access to any form of education. In South Asia, it is estimated that fifty million children are out of primary school. Also, enrolment rates in some economies in transition have been declining. Groups with special needs are also affected by social exclusion and by poverty in different manners. In many countries, there are insufficient measures for improving their situation.

10. Progress in eradicating poverty has been mixed. In many countries, the number of people living in poverty has increased since 1995. In many developing countries, social service provision has deteriorated, leaving many without access to basic social services. Lack of resources, inadequate levels of economic development and in most cases the worsening terms of international trade, as well as weak infrastructures and inefficient administrative systems, have all undermined measures to eradicate poverty. Demographic changes in many parts of the world have led to new challenges and caused new obstacles in eradicating poverty. In Africa and the least developed countries, economic growth has barely resumed. Also, in some countries with economies in transition, economic reform has been slow and social security arrangements have weakened. In several developed countries, economic growth and rising incomes have improved the living conditions of many people. In some developed countries, however, unemployment has contributed to situations of inequality, poverty and social exclusion. Countries affected by the recent international crises have experienced a sharp increase in poverty, especially among women and groups with special needs, and unemployment. Although there are now some signs that growth is resuming, the sharp reversal in this area has pushed back their progress in poverty reduction and employment by several years.

11. At the Summit and at the Fourth World Conference on Women held in Beijing, the international community recognized expressly that women and men experience poverty differently and unequally and become impoverished through different processes, and that if those differences are not taken into account the causes of poverty cannot be understood or dealt with by public actions. Persistent discrimination against women in the labour market, the existing gap in their wages, unequal access to productive resources and capital as well as education and training, and the sociocultural factors that continue to influence gender relations and preserve the existing discrimination against women continue to hinder women's economic empowerment and exacerbate the feminization of poverty. Equality between women and men is widely accepted as essential for social development, but its implementation, including by mainstreaming a gender perspective into all policies and programmes aimed at eradicating poverty and the empowerment of women, has been slow.

Full employment

12. While overall progress since the World Summit for Social Development in reducing unemployment has been slow and uneven, there has been increased attention by Governments as well as civil society, including the private sector, to the goal of full employment and to policies aimed at employment growth, as well as a renewed perception that full employment is a feasible goal. Employment promotion has increasingly been put at the centre of socio-economic development, in recognition of the central importance of employment to poverty eradication and social integration.

13. The international community has also recognized the need to promote employment that meets labour standards as defined by relevant International Labour Organization and other international instruments, including prohibitions on forced and child labour, guarantees of the rights of freedom of association and bargaining collectively, equal remuneration for men and women for work of equal value and non-discrimination in employment. This is reflected in the adoption of the International Labour Organization Declaration on Fundamental Principles and Rights at Work and its Follow-up, and in the unanimous adoption of International Labour Organization Convention No. 182 concerning the Prohibition and Immediate Action for the Elimination of the Worst Forms of Child

Labour. While some progress has been made in this respect, universal ratification of the relevant International Labour Organization conventions has not yet been achieved.

14. Many developed countries have strengthened their active employment promotion measures, including by the introduction of programmes to create jobs in social services and the provision of other public goods. These activities are sometimes relatively labour-intensive and also meet a growing demand for personal services, particularly for the elderly. In developing countries and those with economies in transition, labour-intensive public works programmes, in particular infrastructure investments in rural access roads, including farm-to-market roads, environmental rehabilitation, irrigation and urban regeneration schemes, have proven to be effective means of promoting employment and stimulating people-centred sustainable development. The important role of education and of vocational and skills development training at all levels in promoting employment, particularly in the long term, is increasingly recognized.

15. While in most countries the employment of women has increased steadily, gender inequalities, reflected in particular in the wage gap and a disproportionate share of family responsibilities, have remained obstacles to women's equal access to and participation in the labour market. Furthermore, in countries experiencing a lack of adequate employment and/or declining employment rates, women are often disproportionately affected and forced into the low-paid informal sector and out of social safety nets. In many parts of the world, this situation has also led to poverty and social exclusion, with inhuman consequences, such as forced prostitution, trafficking in women and children for the purposes of prostitution and sexual and other forms of exploitation, and the worst forms of child labour. At the same time, women's unpaid work remains unrecognized and unaccounted for in national accounts. To date, no universal measurement tools have been developed to evaluate women's unpaid work.

16. There has been an increase in casual and informal employment since the Summit. Casual employment arrangements have tended to spread in industrialized economies, with increasingly flexible labour markets and new mechanisms for subcontracting. In developing countries, the lack of growth of employment in the formal sector, among other factors, has led many people, especially women, into informal sector work and has increased migration to more attractive labour markets in other countries. While employment growth still remains the most effective means of reducing poverty, there appears to be a growing number of employed and underemployed persons, particularly women, with little employment security, low wages and low levels of social protection. In a number of countries, considerable attention has been focused on this issue in recent years, including the development of new initiatives. In some countries with economies in transition, there has been extensive growth of the shadow economy.

17. As a means of combating social exclusion, there have been efforts to integrate income support policies with active labour market policies for those marginalized from the labour market. It is increasingly being recognized that these policies are an important tool to reduce the dependency of individuals on social assistance and to reintegrate them into the world of work and into society.

18. In a number of countries, social dialogue among employers, employees and Governments has contributed to social and economic development.

Social integration

19. Social integration is a prerequisite for creating harmonious, peaceful and inclusive societies. Promotion and protection of all human rights and fundamental freedoms, promotion of a culture of peace, tolerance and non-violence, respect for cultural and religious diversity, elimination of all forms of discrimination, equal opportunities for access to productive resources and participatory governance are important for social integration. Governments have developed new policy instruments, set up institutional arrangements, strengthened participation and dialogue with all social actors, and launched programmes to foster social cohesion and solidarity. However, lack of access to education, the persistence of poverty and unemployment, and inequitable access to opportunities and resources have caused social exclusion and marginalization. A growing number of people are afflicted by poverty because of the inequitable distribution of opportunities, resources, incomes and access to employment and to social services. In many countries, there is a growing schism between those in high-quality, well-paid employment and those in poorly remunerated, insecure jobs with low levels of social protection. Owing to continued discrimination and exclusion, women and girls face particular disadvantages in this regard.

20. Governments have made progress in promoting more inclusive societies. The adoption of democratic forms of government by an increasing number of countries offers opportunities for all to participate in all spheres of public life. The devolution of political power, the decentralization of administration and the development of local and municipal authorities have sometimes contributed to the creation of inclusive and participatory societies. In some countries, there are also consultative arrangements that enable wider involvement in the planning and evaluation of policies. In those countries, Governments as well as civil society, including the private sector, are involved in these processes. An encouraging development has been the strengthening of civil society, including non-governmental organizations and volunteers. In many countries, this provides the means for people to work together through partnerships with Governments, thereby promoting and protecting common interests and complementing the action of the public sector. The promotion and protection of all human rights, including the right to development, is an important element in the promotion of social integration. In this context, it is noted that the overall level of ratification of international human rights instruments has increased considerably since the World Summit for Social Development; however, universal ratification has not yet been achieved.

21. Governments have implemented a wide range of policies and programmes to respond to the special needs of vulnerable and disadvantaged groups and to

strengthen their participation in development processes through the provision of, inter alia, social services, employment opportunities, credit, skill development and training. However, further efforts in this area are required.

22. The protection of immigrants and migrant workers required the adoption of a broad range of targeted policies. Governments were urged to ensure the protection of the human rights and dignity of migrants, irrespective of their legal status. Governments were also urged to intensify efforts to provide basic social services, facilitate family reunification of documented migrants, promote social and economic integration of documented migrants, and ensure their equal treatment before the law. There has not been enough accession and ratification of the International Convention on the Protection of the Rights of All Migrant Workers and Members of Their Families for it to come into force. Since the Summit, progress in implementing international instruments on the protection of migrants has been limited and problems concerning the violation of the human rights of migrants have persisted. In many parts of the world, migrants have been subjected to discrimination and documented migrants have not received adequate social protection.

23. Despite attempts to address the causes leading to and the pressures resulting from the movement of refugees and displaced persons, many countries, especially those hosting large refugee populations, have required international support to provide basic social services.

24. While there has been incremental but uneven movement towards equality and equity between women and men in all regions of the world, the fact remains that women are the most affected in times of crisis and economic restructuring. Whereas many countries have adopted national strategies on the implementation of the Beijing Declaration and Platform for Action, including general policy recommendations and specific plans of action, concrete progress in improving the status of women and promoting gender equality has been slow and uneven. All forms of violence against women and girls remain a persistent problem for all countries and create obstacles to social integration, hindering the advancement of gender equality and the full enjoyment of human rights by women.

25. There has been continued recognition that the family is the basic unit of society and that it plays a key role in social development and is a strong force of social cohesion and integration. In different cultural, political and social systems, various forms of the family exist.

26. The increase in violent conflicts, including those around issues of local autonomy and ethnic identity, as well as conflicts over the distribution of resources, have hampered social integration and diverted attention and resources from social and economic development to conflict management. This development has underlined the importance of social integration and access to basic social services as preventive measures against crises. Access to basic social services in conflict situations and social integration in post-conflict situations have also been underlined as important preventive tools.

27. The obstacles to the realization of the right of peoples to self-determination, in particular of peoples living under colonial or other forms of alien domination or foreign occupation, have continued to adversely affect the achievement of their social and economic development.

28. In some countries, social development is adversely affected by unilateral measures at variance with international law and the Charter of the United Nations that create obstacles to trade relations among States, impede the full realization of social and economic development and hinder the well-being of the population in the affected countries.

Africa and the least developed countries

29. At the World Summit for Social Development, Governments committed themselves to accelerating the economic, social and human resources development of Africa and the least developed countries. Many of the objectives undertaken at the Summit have yet to be fulfilled by the countries concerned and their international partners, although in this regard donors continue to support the efforts by Africa and the least developed countries.

30. The deteriorating social and economic condition of the least developed countries requires priority attention to the many international development commitments towards those countries which have not been met. Many least developed countries have seen their share of official development assistance decrease, and progress has not been achieved in fulfilling the agreed target of earmarking 0.15 to 0.20 per cent of gross national product as official development assistance for the least developed countries. Technical cooperation provided by the United Nations and its affiliated agencies has been cut back since the Summit.

31. African countries have made real efforts to implement the commitments made at Copenhagen, but internal and external constraints continue to make progress extremely difficult. The mobilization of resources at the national and international levels to accelerate the economic and social development of Africa and the least developed countries through a holistic approach is needed for the full implementation of the commitments. Equitable access to education and health services, income-earning opportunities, land, credit, infrastructure and technology, as well as official development assistance and debt reduction, are vital to social development in Africa and the least developed countries.

32. Social indicators in Africa show that the continent falls dramatically short of the targets set at the Summit five years ago. About 90 per cent of countries in sub-Saharan Africa will not meet the year 2000 goals on child mortality. Life expectancy remained lower than sixty years in forty-one of the fifty-three countries during the period 1995-2000. The HIV/AIDS pandemic is having severe social, economic, political and security impacts in some of the hardest hit countries.

33. Progress has been achieved in the development of democratic institutions in a number of countries. Further progress needs to be made in Africa and the least developed countries in strengthening institutions which are transparent and accountable in order to achieve faster economic and social development.

34. In a rapidly globalizing economic world, Africa continues to be marginalized. A persistent decline in the international terms of trade for commodities exported from African countries has reduced real national income and savings to finance investment. The external debt burden has drastically reduced resources available for social development. Furthermore, promises made to provide official development assistance to developing countries in general and the least developed countries in particular have not been fulfilled. More concerted efforts and an internationally enabling environment are necessary to integrate Africa as well as the least developed countries into the world economy.

Mobilization of resources for social development

35. The mobilization of domestic and international resources for social development is an essential component for the implementation of the commitments made at the World Summit for Social Development in Copenhagen. Since the Summit, reforms to promote the effective and efficient utilization of existing resources have received increasing attention. However, inadequate national revenue generation and collection, combined with new challenges regarding social services and social protection systems due, for instance, to demographic changes and other factors, jeopardize the financing of social services and social protection systems in many countries. New budgeting and accounting techniques have been adopted in several countries. The involvement and cooperation of local authorities, civil society and beneficiary communities have been found to be valuable in raising efficiency in the delivery of services.

36. In several countries and for various reasons, a shift has been occurring in the modalities for financing social protection away from universal, publicly provided coverage to income-based, targeted assistance. Among those reasons are stagnant or declining public revenues or the need to reduce fiscal deficits as well as changing priorities for public expenditures. Also, the need to create new employment opportunities and to provide incentives for the unemployed or underemployed and coverage for new social problems as well as to address the specific needs of disadvantaged and marginalized populations has motivated changes in social protection systems. In some countries, the principle of universal free provision of services, such as health care, education and water supply, has been replaced by user fees and privatization and by more targeted social service provision. However, in many countries, the impact of such measures, especially on the poor and vulnerable, remains to be seen.

37. Despite the renewed commitment at the Summit by donor countries to meet the agreed target of 0.7 per cent of their gross national product for official development assistance, overall official development assistance has continued to decline. Only four countries now meet the agreed target, with one more country about to reach it. In the meantime, the relative role of official development assistance within various forms of financing for development has also been declining. As a result of the Summit, however, earmarking of funds for social development has been formulated more explicitly in official development assistance policy. Official development assistance has been found to be more effective when countries are committed to growth-oriented strategies combined with poverty eradication goals and strategies. Poverty eradication through sustainable development is seen by most donor countries as the main objective of development cooperation. The Bretton Woods institutions have also begun to pay more focused attention to the social development dimension in their structural adjustment programmes and lending policies. This process is currently being further strengthened.

38. The 20/20 initiative has encouraged interested Governments and donors to increase the amount of resources earmarked for basic social services and to enhance equity and efficiency in their use. It has also emphasized the need for additional resources in order to pursue effectively the social development agenda, while highlighting the difficulties and limitations of many countries, in particular developing countries, in raising or reallocating domestic resources.

39. There is greater acceptance that the increasing debt burden faced by the most indebted developing countries is unsustainable and constitutes one of the principal obstacles to achieving progress in people-centred sustainable development and poverty eradication. For many developing countries, as well as countries with economies in transition, excessive debt servicing has severely constrained their capacity to promote social development and provide basic services. Although the Heavily Indebted Poor Countries Debt Initiative has the potential to reduce debt-servicing costs significantly for the countries it covers, the fact remains that it has so far benefited only a few of them. This initiative has recently been strengthened to provide faster, deeper and broader debt relief, in the context of poverty reduction strategies in which Governments and civil society cooperate to make commitments to utilize the financial benefits to alleviate poverty. A few lender countries have adopted bilateral debt-cancellation initiatives which go beyond the Heavily Indebted Poor Countries Debt Initiative.

40. Microcredit and other financial instruments provide financial and other services to people who are often overlooked by the traditional banking sector, thus trying to reach the poorest families. Women play a very important role in such initiatives. Experience shows that women are creditworthy and when they earn an income they are able to contribute more directly to the economy.

41. Since the Summit, the external debt problems of the middle-income developing countries have crippled their social development efforts. A need has arisen for concerted national and international action to address effectively the debt problems of middle-income developing countries with a view to resolving their potential long-term debt-sustainability problems.

Capacity-building to implement social policies and programmes

42. Capacity-building is an important means of creating a national political, socio-economic and legal environment conducive to development and social progress. Member States have taken a number of actions to enhance their capacities to achieve the goals of the World Summit for Social Development, including adopting long-term strategies for social development; conducting national assessments of their institutional

capacities; taking legislative action to create an enabling environment; establishing partnerships with civil society; involving people in the management of their local affairs; mainstreaming a gender perspective into policies and programmes; improving transparent and accountable governance; strengthening the implementation, monitoring and evaluation of social policies, programmes and projects; and providing technical cooperation. However, the years since the Summit have also been marked by growing constraints on the capacity for public action. In some countries, increased constraints, including fiscal and political ones on Governments, have resulted in a reduction of the programmes and activities of the State.

43. The State has an important role in the provision of basic social services. However, in several countries, the State is no longer the sole provider of social services but rather the enabler of an overall favourable environment for social development, with increased responsibility for ensuring equitable delivery of and access to quality social services. This development has increased the need for stronger public institutions to provide an effective framework to ensure an equitable provision of basic social services for all. It is also recognized that an effective and accountable public sector is vital to ensuring the provision of social services.

44. International cooperation has been a critical element in the efforts of Governments towards capacity-building for social development. Technical cooperation, including that provided by the United Nations, has been supportive of such efforts by Governments, although in many areas such cooperation should be strengthened and broadened.

III. Further actions and initiatives to implement the commitments made at the World Summit for Social Development

1. Governments should adopt an integrated focus in order to ensure that social development objectives are incorporated in all areas of governmental decision-making. In this connection, the General Assembly recommends taking the following further initiatives at the local, national, regional and international levels for the further implementation of the ten commitments adopted at the World Summit for Social Development as contained in the report of the Summit:

Commitment 1

To create an economic, political, social, cultural and legal environment that will enable people to achieve social development:

2. Governments, while designing and implementing their development policies, should ensure that people are placed at the centre of development. Therefore, people must have the right and the ability to participate fully in the social, economic and political life of their societies. Our global drive for social development and the recommendations for action contained in the present document are made in a spirit of consensus and international cooperation, in full conformity with the purposes and principles of the Charter of the United Nations, recognizing that the formulation and implementation of strategies, policies, programmes and actions for social development are the responsibility of each country and should take into account the diverse economic, social and environmental conditions in each

country, with full respect for the various religious and ethical values, cultural backgrounds and philosophical convictions of its people, and in conformity with all human rights and fundamental freedoms. In this context, international cooperation is essential for the full implementation of social development programmes and actions.

3. Make a renewed commitment to effective, transparent and accountable governance and democratic institutions that are responsive to the needs of people and enable them to take an active part in decision-making about priorities, policies and strategies.

4. Reaffirm the crucial role of Government in advancing people-centred sustainable development through actions to develop and maintain increased equality and equity, including gender equality; markets which function efficiently within a framework of ethical values; policies to eradicate poverty and enhance productive employment; universal and equal access to basic social services; social protection; and support for disadvantaged and vulnerable groups.

5. Reaffirm, promote and strive to ensure the realization of the rights set out in relevant international instruments and declarations, such as the Universal Declaration of Human Rights, the International Covenant on Economic, Social and Cultural Rights, and the Declaration on the Right to Development, including those relating to education, food, shelter, employment, health and information, particularly in order to assist people living in poverty and to ensure the strengthening of national and local institutions in charge of their implementation.

6. Urge the international community, particularly creditor and debtor countries and pertinent international financial institutions, to identify and implement development-oriented and durable solutions to external debt and debt-servicing problems of developing countries, which constitute an element affecting the development efforts and economic growth, inter alia, through debt relief, including the option of debt cancellation within the framework of official development assistance, and thereby strengthen the efforts of the Governments of such countries to attain the full realization of the economic, social and cultural rights of their people.

7. Enhance positive interaction among environmental, economic and social policies as also being essential for the successful attainment of Summit goals, by promoting the coordinated and simultaneous consideration of this objective in the process of policy formulation and recognizing continuously the impact of social, economic and financial policies on employment and sustainable livelihoods, poverty and social development.

8. Institute systems for ensuring the ex ante assessment and continuous monitoring of the social impact of economic policies at both the international and national levels, with a particular focus on the formulation of macroeconomic policies for dealing with financial crises and the design of economic reform programmes.

9. Develop national and, where appropriate, regional guidelines, taking into account broad definitions of productivity and efficiency, in order to undertake comprehensive assessments of the social and economic costs of unemployment and poverty to facili-

tate appropriate strategies for employment generation and poverty eradication.

10. Acknowledging that there is no single universal path to achieving social development, and recognizing the importance of Member States sharing information on their national experiences and best practices in social development on the basis of equality and mutual respect, request the Economic and Social Council to consider, through the Commission for Social Development, ways of sharing these experiences and practices to assist Member States in the development of policies to promote the goals of the Summit.

11. Strengthen the capacities of developing countries and countries with economies in transition to address the obstacles that hinder their participation in an increasingly globalized economy by:

(a) Stimulating and strengthening the industrialization process in developing countries;

(b) Facilitating the transfer to developing countries and countries with economies in transition of appropriate technology, know-how, knowledge and information, including for social development and capacity-building, complementing efforts of these countries in this regard through enhanced international cooperation, including technical cooperation and adequate financial resources;

(c) Increasing and improving access of products and services of developing countries to international markets through, inter alia, the negotiated reduction of tariff barriers and the elimination of non-tariff barriers, which unjustifiably hinder trade of developing countries, according to the multilateral trading system;

(d) Increasing and improving access of products and services of countries with economies in transition to international markets;

(e) Attaining, according to existing multilateral trading rules, greater universality of the multilateral trading system and accelerating the process directed towards the further accession to the World Trade Organization of developing countries and countries with economies in transition;

(f) Providing technical assistance bilaterally and through the auspices of the World Trade Organization, the United Nations Conference on Trade and Development, the International Trade Centre and other organizations to developing countries and countries with economies in transition for capacity-building and to address the ability to trade, as well as to participate effectively in international economic forums, and in international trade negotiations, including the dispute settlement mechanism of the World Trade Organization.

12. Take steps with a view to the avoidance of and refrain from any unilateral measure at variance with international law and the Charter of the United Nations that impedes the full achievement of economic and social development by the population of the affected countries, in particular women, children and persons with special needs, that hinders their well-being and that creates obstacles to the full enjoyment of their human rights, including the right of everyone to a standard of living adequate for their health and well-being and their right to food, medical care and the necessary social services. Ensure that food and medicine are not used as tools for political pressure.

13. Reduce negative impacts of international financial turbulence on social and economic development, inter alia, by:

(a) Improving preventive and other measures and early warning capabilities to address the excessive volatility of short-term capital flows, including consideration, inter alia, of a temporary debt standstill;

(b) Enhancing institutional capacities at the national and international levels to improve transparency of financial flows, and developing, strengthening and enforcing regulatory frameworks for monitoring operations, inter alia, to reduce the potential negative impact of financial operations;

(c) Where appropriate, establishing or strengthening at the regional level intergovernmental coordination mechanisms in economic, financial and social fields to promote economic and financial stability and social development at that level;

(d) Providing technical assistance to developing countries and countries with economies in transition to strengthen their domestic capital markets and to ensure their proper regulation by national Governments;

(e) Taking measures to protect basic social services, in particular education and health, in the policies and programmes adopted by countries when dealing with international financial crises;

(f) Acting to strengthen national institutions and consultative mechanisms for economic policy formulation, involving improved transparency and consultation with civil society;

(g) Encouraging international financial institutions and other related mechanisms to be vigilant about potential financial crises in countries, and assist countries in developing their capacities to forestall and mitigate crises with a view to providing a timely and effective response.

14. Ensure the effective involvement of developing countries and countries with economies in transition in the international economic decision-making process through, inter alia, greater participation in international economic forums, ensuring transparency and accountability of international financial institutions to accord a central position for social development in their policies and programmes.

15. Enhance development cooperation in order to augment the productive potential of people in developing countries and to build the capacity, among others, of the private sector to compete more effectively in the global marketplace in order to create the basis for generating greater resources for social development.

16. Support the Cologne initiative for the reduction of debt, particularly the speedy implementation of the enhanced Heavily Indebted Poor Countries Debt Initiative, and welcome commitments to ensure that additional financing is mobilized to fully fund debt relief to heavily indebted poor countries over the longer term and the provision that funds saved should be used to support anti-poverty programmes and social development.

17. Bearing in mind that corporations must abide by national legislation, encourage corporate social responsibility so that it contributes to social development goals, inter alia, by:

(a) Promoting increased corporate awareness of the interrelationship between social development and economic growth;

(b) Providing a legal, economic and social policy framework that is just and stable to support and stimulate private sector initiatives aimed at achieving these goals;

(c) Enhancing partnerships with business, trade unions and civil society at the national level in support of the goals of the Summit.

18. Take further effective measures to remove the obstacles to the realization of the right of peoples to self-determination, in particular peoples living under colonial and foreign occupation, which continue to adversely affect their economic and social development and are incompatible with the dignity and worth of the human person and must be combatted and eliminated.

19. Enhance international cooperation, including burden-sharing, and coordination of humanitarian assistance to countries affected by natural disasters and other humanitarian emergencies and post-conflict situations in ways that will be supportive of recovery and long-term development.

20. Create and improve conditions to allow for the voluntary repatriation of refugees in safety and dignity to their countries of origin, and the voluntary and safe return of internally displaced persons to their places of origin and their smooth reintegration into their societies.

21. Encourage relevant bodies of the United Nations system to address the issue of corruption which undermines the efforts made and efficient use of resources for social development, and in that context take note of the recommendation of the Commission on Crime Prevention and Criminal Justice that the General Assembly adopt a resolution to start the elaboration of an effective international legal instrument against corruption, and encourage relevant bodies of the United Nations system to give it serious consideration.

22. Encourage the ongoing work on a draft convention against transnational organized crime and the additional protocols thereto, with a view to the speedy finalization of this work.

23. Give proper consideration to urgent and effective measures regarding the issue of the social and humanitarian impact of sanctions, in particular on women and children, with a view to minimizing social and humanitarian effects of sanctions.

24. Support countries with economies in transition to establish effective regulatory environments, including adequate legal frameworks and institutions, to develop progressive and efficient tax systems to provide adequate resources for social development, and to better utilize existing material and labour resources, inter alia, by implementing measures to reduce the social costs of transition, in particular in order to reverse the trend of cuts in public spending for social services, and encouraging efforts to integrate non-governmental organizations, trade unions, employer organizations and other organizations of civil society into the operation of social policy.

Commitment 2

To eradicate poverty in the world, through decisive national actions and international cooperation, as an ethical, social, political and economic imperative of humankind:

25. Place poverty eradication at the centre of economic and social development and build consensus with all relevant actors at all levels on policies and strategies to reduce the proportion of people living in extreme poverty by one half by the year 2015 with a view to eradicating poverty.

26. Urge countries that have not yet done so to incorporate goals and targets for combating poverty into their national strategies for socio-economic development and to adjust their national strategies, as appropriate to the country context, by striving to establish or strengthen institutional mechanisms that ensure a multisectoral approach to poverty eradication, and enhancing the capacity of local government to address poverty while maintaining accountability, both to the central Government for funds allocated by it and to the constituents concerning the use of those funds.

27. In the context of comprehensive national strategies on poverty eradication, integrate policies at all levels, including economic and fiscal policies, capacity-building and institution-building, giving priority to investments in education and health, social protection and basic social services, in order to help to empower people living in poverty, by:

(a) Promoting coherence between national and international strategies and programmes to combat poverty at all levels;

(b) Assisting developing countries in improving capacities for poverty-related data collection and analysis, which is necessary for formulation of poverty reduction policies;

(c) Ensuring that macroeconomic policies reflect and fully integrate, inter alia, employment growth and poverty reduction goals;

(d) Encouraging Governments to re-evaluate, as appropriate, their national fiscal policies, including progressive tax mechanisms, with the aim of reducing income inequalities and promoting social equity;

(e) Restructuring public expenditure policies to make them more efficient, transparent and with clear lines of accountability to maximize their impact on poverty eradication;

(f) Improving access for people living in poverty to productive resources by implementing measures, such as skills training and microcredit schemes;

(g) Using employment policies, including self-employment, to reduce poverty;

(h) Encouraging the growth of small and medium-sized enterprises by formulating a consistent, long-term policy to support such enterprises, and by, inter alia, furthering access to capital and credit, promoting training opportunities and appropriate technology, reducing bureaucratic regulations, promoting gender equality and labour standards, and fostering improved access of small and medium-sized enterprises to contracts for infrastructure projects;

(i) Devising ways and means to allow for better acknowledgement of the nature of the informal sector so as to evaluate its share in the national economy and, where appropriate, to improve its productivity by increasing training and access to capital, including microcredit, to progressively improve working conditions through respect for basic workers' rights, to enhance social protection and to facilitate its eventual integration into the formal economy;

(j) Establishing, strengthening and expanding microcredit and other financial instruments adapted to the needs and potentials of marginalized people and vulnerable groups in order to make microcredit available to a greater number of people, particularly women, and disadvantaged groups, especially people living in poverty, and to make information and training on its effective operation and benefits widely available;

(*k*) Encouraging and facilitating the development of cooperatives, where appropriate;

(*l*) Encouraging sustainable rural development, especially in areas low in agricultural potential;

(*m*) Expanding advisory services and technical assistance in the areas of agriculture, including animal husbandry and fisheries, and promoting small businesses and self-employment for rural workers, in particular women, in the light of increasing rural poverty, landlessness and rural-urban migration, and, similarly, promoting industrialization in rural areas for employment generation;

(*n*) Developing and promoting institutional capacities (e.g., by management training);

(*o*) Ensuring a gender equality perspective at all levels and taking measures to counteract the feminization of poverty, keeping in mind the potential role of women and girls in poverty eradication;

(*p*) Promoting participatory poverty assessments as well as social impact assessments which include sex, age and relevant socio-economic categories, defining, inter alia, the extent and localization of poverty and the groups most severely affected, in order to design anti-poverty strategies;

(*q*) Targeting the special needs of vulnerable and disadvantaged groups;

(*r*) Supporting initiatives that help to empower people living in poverty, especially female heads of households, and promote their capacities for self-organization to enable them to better utilize available opportunities, basic social services and productive resources;

(*s*) Ensuring community participation in the formulation and implementation of poverty reduction strategies and programmes with a view to increasing people's self-reliance and promoting a holistic approach to the various needs of the people. Civil society can play an important role in cooperation with national Governments in planning, organizing and providing basic social services;

(*t*) Ensuring access for all to basic social services, even during financial crises;

(*u*) Using health policies as an instrument for poverty eradication, along the lines of the World Health Organization strategy on poverty and health, developing sustainable and effectively managed pro-poor health systems which focus on the major diseases and health problems affecting the poor, achieving greater equity in health financing, and also taking into account the provision of and universal access to high-quality primary health care throughout the life cycle, including sexual and reproductive health care, not later than 2015, as well as health education programmes, clean water and safe sanitation, nutrition, food security and immunization programmes;

(*v*) Encouraging decentralization in the delivery of basic social services as a means of responding more efficiently to the needs of the people.

28. Develop and implement sustainable pro-poor growth strategies that enhance the potential and increase the ability of women and men living in poverty to improve their lives; such strategies could include improving access to productive resources and microfinance and establishing programmes to raise productivity and improve knowledge, skills and capabilities.

29. Share best practices on how to establish or improve social protection systems covering risks that cannot be mastered by the beneficiaries themselves and trap people into poverty, ensuring access to social protection, including social safety nets, for people living in poverty, and promoting the role of systems of self-help and mutual benefits, including small, community-based innovative schemes, thereby supporting social cohesion and contributing to more universal and comprehensive systems of protection, taking into account country-specific circumstances, by:

(*a*) Exploring ways and means, supported by resources, including, as appropriate, through the reallocation of resources and financial assistance from donors, to develop social protection systems for vulnerable, unprotected and uninsured people, and in this context call upon the International Labour Organization and other relevant international organizations, within their mandates, to render technical assistance to developing countries and countries with economies in transition, upon their request;

(*b*) Developing, as required, new mechanisms to ensure the sustainability of these systems in the appropriate country context, especially that of ageing populations and increased unemployment.

30. Improve national capacity to address hunger, malnutrition and food insecurity at the household level, in cooperation with the World Food Programme, the Food and Agriculture Organization of the United Nations and other concerned agencies, in particular by recognizing and supporting women in their pivotal role in providing food security. In this regard, call upon Governments which have not done so to place food security as an essential element of their poverty eradication strategies and social policies.

31. Encourage international support to countries with economies in transition in order to assist them in:

(*a*) Combining universal coverage of social services, with targeted assistance to the most vulnerable groups to ease the pain of transition;

(*b*) Implementing policies to involve those individuals marginalized by the transition and to overcome exclusion and further deprivation;

(*c*) Maintaining adequate social programmes.

Commitment 3

To promote the goal of full employment as a basic priority of economic and social policies, and to enable all men and women to attain secure and sustainable livelihoods through freely chosen productive employment and work:

32. Reassess, as appropriate, their macroeconomic policies with the aim of greater employment generation and reduction in the poverty level while striving for and maintaining low inflation rates.

33. Create an enabling environment for social dialogue by ensuring effective representation and participation of workers' and employers' organizations in order to contribute to the development of policies for achieving broad-based social progress.

34. Expand opportunities for productive employment, including self-employment, with particular

focus on small and medium-sized enterprises, by investing in the development of human resources, entrepreneurship and employability, especially through education, vocational and management training, occupational safety and health, and by, inter alia, strengthening technical cooperation and cooperation with the private sector in this area.

35. Support the comprehensive International Labour Organization programme on decent work, which includes promoting equal opportunities for all women and men, including persons with disabilities, to obtain decent and productive work, with full respect for the basic rights of workers as defined by relevant International Labour Organization and other international instruments, including prohibitions on forced labour and child labour, safeguarding of the rights of freedom of association and collective bargaining, equal remuneration for women and men for work of equal value, and non-discrimination in employment, and improving social protection and promoting social dialogue.

36. Recognize the need to elaborate a coherent and coordinated international strategy on employment to increase opportunities for people to achieve sustainable livelihoods and gain access to employment, and in this connection support the convening of a world employment forum by the International Labour Organization in 2001.

37. Invite the International Labour Organization to facilitate a coordinated exchange of best practices in the field of employment policies to stimulate and expand employment generation, reduce unemployment, enhance the quality of work and improve labour-market and employment services.

38. Improve the quality of work and level of employment, inter alia, by:

(a) Making continued efforts towards ratifying—where they have not done so—and fully implementing the International Labour Organization conventions concerning basic rights of workers, namely, freedom of association and the effective recognition of the right to organize and bargain collectively, the elimination of all forms of forced or compulsory labour, the effective abolition of child labour and the elimination of discrimination in respect of employment and occupation;

(b) Strongly considering the ratification and full implementation of other International Labour Organization conventions concerning the employment rights of minors, women, youth, persons with disabilities, migrants and indigenous people;

(c) Respecting, promoting and realizing the principles contained in the International Labour Organization Declaration on Fundamental Principles and Rights at Work and its Follow-up;

(d) Supporting and participating in the global campaign for the immediate elimination of the worst forms of child labour, including by promoting universal ratification and implementation of International Labour Organization Convention No. 182 concerning the Prohibition and Immediate Action for the Elimination of the Worst Forms of Child Labour;

(e) Promoting safe and healthy settings at work in order to improve working conditions and to reduce the impact on individuals and health-care systems of occupational accidents and diseases.

39. Ensure effective and comprehensive action to eliminate harmful child labour, inter alia, by designing and implementing national plans of action; ensuring access to basic education; strengthening employment and income-earning opportunities for families of child workers; giving special attention to the girl child; promoting cooperation among Governments, employers' and workers' organizations, families of child workers and civil society; and stressing the need for close cooperation among the International Labour Organization, the United Nations Children's Fund, the World Bank and other relevant actors.

40. Call upon relevant organizations of the United Nations system to provide national Governments with technical assistance in a coordinated manner in order to help them in their efforts to promote social development and achieve the goals of poverty eradication, full employment and social integration, including gender equality.

41. Encourage the private sector to respect basic worker rights as reaffirmed in the International Labour Organization Declaration on the Fundamental Principles and Rights at Work and its Follow-up.

42. Improve methods for collection and analysis of basic employment data, disaggregated by, inter alia, age, sex and relevant socio-economic categories, as appropriate in the country context, including with regard to the informal, agricultural and service sectors and new forms of employment, and assess the feasibility of developing and improving mechanisms to measure unremunerated work.

43. Consider the possibility of a major event on the informal sector in the year 2002, to be organized by the International Labour Organization.

44. Invite the International Labour Organization to help Member States, upon their request, to extend a range of support measures to informal sector workers, including legal rights, social protection and access to credit.

45. Devise and strengthen the modalities of coverage of social protection systems, as appropriate, to meet the needs of people engaged in flexible forms of employment.

46. Wherever appropriate, adopt and/or strengthen legislation or other mechanisms for determining minimum wages.

47. Ensure that migrant workers benefit from the protection provided by relevant national and international instruments, take concrete and effective measures against the exploitation of migrant workers, and encourage all countries to consider the ratification and full implementation of the relevant international instruments on migrant workers, including the International Convention on the Protection of the Rights of All Migrant Workers and Members of their Families.

48. Undertake appropriate measures, in cooperation with employers' and workers' organizations, as well as other relevant actors of civil society, to address the specific employment issues of youth, ageing workers, persons with disabilities, single parents and long-term unemployed, with particular regard to women, including:

(a) Improving access to new technologies, vocational training and counselling, implementing programmes for job placement and facilitating the acquisition of work experience, including on-the-job training, as well as by the recognition of work experience acquired through voluntary activities and unpaid work;

(b) Promoting lifelong learning and access to labour market information, and tailoring programmes to meet the specific needs of those groups in the acquisition of skills required in the knowledge-based economy;

(c) Involving the private sector in skill training programmes;

(d) Adapting and improving access of youth to technical, secondary and higher education curricula, to meet the needs of a rapidly changing labour market, and easing transition between learning and work;

(e) Enabling older workers to remain and actively participate in working life.

49. Promote gender equality and eliminate gender discrimination in the labour market by:

(a) Promoting the principles of equal remuneration and the elimination of discrimination, and strongly considering ratifying International Labour Organization Conventions No. 100 concerning Equal Remuneration for Men and Women Workers for Work of Equal Value, and No. 111 concerning Discrimination in Respect of Employment and Occupation and fully implementing them once ratified;

(b) Ensuring the right to equal pay for equal work or work of equal value for women and men;

(c) Assisting women and men in reconciling employment and family responsibilities, inter alia, by flexible working arrangements, including parental voluntary part-time employment and work-sharing, as well as accessible and affordable quality child-care and dependant-care facilities, paying particular attention to the needs of single-parent households.

Commitment 4

To promote social integration by fostering societies that are stable, safe and just and that are based on the promotion and protection of all human rights, as well as on non-discrimination, tolerance, respect for diversity, equality of opportunity, solidarity, security and participation of all people, including disadvantaged and vulnerable groups and persons:

50. Strengthen mechanisms for the participation of all people, and promote cooperation and dialogue among all levels of government and civil society as contributions to social integration.

51. Strengthen support for civil society, including community organizations working with groups with special needs, and accelerate the implementation of United Nations instruments relating to those groups, encouraging sustained investment in social institutions and social capital and enhancing social networks, particularly with respect to people living in poverty and other marginalized groups.

52. Ensure an enabling environment for civil society organizations, inter alia, to facilitate their participation in the delivery of social services in a coordinated, democratic, transparent and accountable manner. Efforts should also be made to facilitate the contribution of civil society organizations, particularly from developing countries, to relevant international forums.

53. Promote the effective participation and contribution of disadvantaged and vulnerable groups and persons when drawing up legislation and programmes for poverty eradication and social inclusion.

54. Promote the contribution that voluntarism can make to the creation of caring societies as an additional mechanism in the promotion of social integration. The Commission for Social Development is invited to consider the issue in 2001, the International Year of Volunteers.

55. Promote the involvement of volunteers in social development, inter alia, by encouraging Governments, taking into account the views of all actors, to develop comprehensive strategies and programmes, by raising public awareness about the value and opportunities of voluntarism, and by facilitating an enabling environment for individuals and other actors of civil society to engage in voluntary activities and for the private sector to support such activities.

56. Recognize that the family is the basic unit of society and that it plays a key role in social development and is a strong force of social cohesion and integration. In different cultural, political and social systems, various forms of the family exist. Further recognize that equality and equity between women and men and respect for the rights of all family members are essential for family well-being and for society at large, and promote appropriate actions to meet the needs of families and their individual members, particularly in the areas of economic support and provision of social services. Greater attention should be paid to helping the family in its supporting, educating and nurturing roles, to the causes and consequences of family disintegration, and to the adoption of measures to reconcile work and family life for women and men.

57. Encourage the media, including via the Internet and other forms of information technology, to contribute to the promotion of social integration by adopting inclusive and participatory approaches in the production, dissemination and use of information, including by its accessibility to disadvantaged and marginalized groups.

58. While recognizing the positive role of the media and information technology, including the Internet, identify and take measures to counter the increasing dissemination of child pornography and other obscene materials, intolerance, including religious intolerance, hatred, racism, discrimination based on sex and age and the incitement to violence through the media and information technology, including the Internet.

59. Ensure that education at all levels promotes all human rights and fundamental freedoms, tolerance, peace, understanding of and respect for cultural diversity and solidarity in a globally interdependent world, as expressed in the Declaration and Programme of Action on a Culture of Peace, as well as in the context of the United Nations Year of Dialogue among Civilizations (2001), the United Nations Decade for Human Rights Education and the Third Decade to Combat Racism and Racial Discrimination.

60. Eliminate all forms of discrimination, including racial discrimination, xenophobia and related intolerance, and in this context support the implementation of the International Convention on the Elimination of All Forms of Racial Discrimination and the convening of the World Conference against Racism, Racial Discrimination, Xenophobia and Related Intolerance, to be held in South Africa in 2001.

61. Ensure continued and intensified action to combat all forms of gender-based violence, and recognize

that violence against women, whether in private or public life, both violates and impairs or nullifies the enjoyment by women of their human rights and fundamental freedoms.

62. Recognize the contribution of indigenous people to society, promote ways of giving them greater responsibility for their own affairs, inter alia, by:

(*a*) Seeking means of giving them effective voice in decisions directly affecting them;

(*b*) Encouraging United Nations agencies within their respective mandates to take effective programmatic measures for engaging indigenous people in matters relevant to their interests and concerns.

63. Encourage the ongoing work on a draft declaration on the rights of indigenous people with the aim of achieving completion prior to the conclusion of the International Decade on the World's Indigenous People in 2004, and support the establishment of a United Nations permanent forum to discuss indigenous issues, within the mandate of the Economic and Social Council, relating to economic and social development, culture, the environment, education, health and human rights.

64. Exchange views and information on national experience and best practices in designing and implementing policies and programmes on ageing, and in promoting full integration and continued participation of older persons in society as full actors in the development process, and in this context support the convening of the Second World Assembly on Ageing, to be held in Spain in the year 2002.

65. Support, on an urgent basis, research on the actual and projected situation of older persons, particularly in developing countries, especially on their productive role and contributions to development, in order to contribute significantly to the revision of the International Plan of Action on Ageing at the Second World Assembly on Ageing.

66. Expand the range of policies and measures, inter alia, by promoting the implementation of the Standard Rules on the Equalization of Opportunities for Persons with Disabilities, to empower persons with disabilities to play their full role in society. Special attention should be given to women and children with disabilities and to persons with developmental, mental and psychiatric disabilities.

67. Ensure access to employment for persons with disabilities through the organization and design of the workplace environment, and improve their employability through measures which enhance education and acquisition of skills, through rehabilitation within the community wherever possible and other direct measures, which may include incentives to enterprises to employ people with disabilities.

68. Intensify efforts to ensure the protection of the human rights and dignity of migrants irrespective of their legal status, the social and economic integration of documented migrants, the provision of effective protection for migrants, particularly by implementing the relevant provisions of the Vienna Convention on Consular Relations, the provision of basic social services, the facilitation of family reunification of documented migrants and their equal treatment under the law.

69. Promote measures, at the national and international levels, to prevent trafficking and illegal transport of migrants and trafficking in persons, particu-

larly women and children, for the purposes of prostitution, economic exploitation and any other form of exploitation, such as domestic servitude and bonded labour. Develop clear penalties for trafficking in persons and trafficking and illegal transport of migrants, backed by effective administrative procedures and laws, ensuring the punishment of those who have been convicted of such crimes.

70. Finalize as soon as possible the trafficking and smuggling protocols which are currently being negotiated in Vienna by the Ad Hoc Committee on the Elaboration of a Convention against Transnational Organized Crime.

71. Support the efforts of the United Nations International Drug Control Programme to implement its mandate, within the framework of international drug control treaties and the outcome of the twentieth special session of the General Assembly devoted to combating the world drug problem, in a balanced and comprehensive approach, which includes reducing demand, fighting trafficking and reducing the supply of narcotic drugs and psychotropic substances.

72. Recognize that stable, supportive and nurturing family relationships, supported by communities and, where available, professional services, can provide a vital shield against substance abuse, particularly among minors. Schools and the media, inter alia, through the use of information technologies, including the Internet, should be encouraged to provide young people with information on the dangers of substance abuse and addiction and on how to seek help.

73. Recognize that the consumption of tobacco and the abuse of alcohol, especially by young women and men, pose a major threat to health, and support the development in each country of comprehensive programmes to reduce the consumption of tobacco, exposure to environmental tobacco smoke and the abuse of alcohol.

74. Further strengthen the effectiveness of organizations and mechanisms working for the prevention and peaceful resolution of conflicts and to address their social roots and consequences.

75. Strengthen the capability of relevant United Nations bodies, within their respective mandates, to promote measures for social integration in their post-conflict management strategies and activities, including in their research, analyses, training and operational activities, so as to better address trauma recovery, rehabilitation, reconciliation and reconstruction in post-conflict situations, inter alia, by promoting participatory development initiatives. Greater attention should be given to children, including unaccompanied refugee minors, displaced children, children separated from their families, those acting as soldiers and those involved in armed conflicts.

Commitment 5

To promote full respect for human dignity and to achieve equality and equity between women and men, and to recognize and enhance the participation and leadership roles of women in political, civil, economic, social and cultural life and in development:

76. Promote the full enjoyment of all human rights and fundamental freedoms by all women and girls as one of the prerequisites of gender equality. Governments should ensure that the human rights of women

and girls are respected, protected and promoted through the development, implementation and effective enforcement of gender-sensitive policies and legislation.

77. The elimination of discrimination against women and their empowerment and full participation in all areas of life and at all levels should be priority objectives at the national as well as at the international levels and an intrinsic part of social development. Equitable social development requires full respect for human dignity, equality and equity between women and men, and the mainstreaming of gender considerations in all levels of policy-making and in the planning of programmes and projects. Despite some progress, gender mainstreaming is not yet universal, and gender-based inequality continues in many areas of most societies.

78. Take fully into account and implement the outcome of the twenty-third special session of the General Assembly entitled "Women 2000: gender equality, development and peace for the twenty-first century".

79. Ensure gender mainstreaming in the implementation of each of the further initiatives related to each of the commitments made at the World Summit for Social Development, considering the specific roles and needs of women in all areas of social development, inter alia, by evaluating the gender implications of proposals and taking action to correct situations in which women are disadvantaged. The use of positive or affirmative action and empowerment programmes is commended to both Governments and international organizations.

80. Strengthen national efforts, including with assistance from the international community, to promote the empowerment of women, inter alia, by:

(a) Closing the gender gap in primary and secondary education by 2005 and ensuring free compulsory and universal primary education for both girls and boys by 2015;

(b) Increasing the access of women and girls to all levels and forms of education;

(c) Achieving a 50 per cent improvement in levels of adult literacy by 2015, especially for women;

(d) Increasing the participation of women and bringing about a balanced representation of women and men in all sectors and occupations in the labour market and closing the gender gap in earnings;

(e) Ensuring the reduction of maternal morbidity and mortality as a health sector priority;

(f) Eliminating all forms of violence against women, in the domestic as well as in the public sphere;

(g) Promoting programmes to enable women and men to reconcile their work and family responsibilities and to encourage men to share equally with women household and child care responsibilities.

81. Promote international cooperation to support regional and national efforts in the development and use of gender-related analysis and statistics, inter alia, by providing national statistical offices, upon their request, with institutional and financial support in order to enable them to respond to requests for data disaggregated by sex and age for use by national Governments in the formulation of gender-sensitive statistical indicators for monitoring and policy and programme impact assessment, as well as to undertake regular strategic surveys.

82. Support Governments in their efforts to institute action-oriented programmes and measures to accelerate the full implementation of the Copenhagen Programme of Action and the Beijing Platform for Action, with time-bound targets and/or measurable goals and evaluation methods, including gender-impact assessments, with the full participation of women for measuring and analysing progress.

83. Consider signing and ratifying the Optional Protocol to the Convention on the Elimination of All Forms of Discrimination against Women.

84. Increased efforts are needed to provide equal access to education, health, and social services and to ensure the rights of women and girls to education and the enjoyment of the highest attainable standard of physical and mental health and well-being throughout the life cycle, as well as adequate, affordable and universally accessible health care and services, including as regards sexual and reproductive health, particularly in the face of the HIV/AIDS pandemic; they are also needed with regard to the growing proportion of older women.

85. Ensure that the reduction of maternal morbidity and mortality is a health sector priority and that women have ready access to essential obstetric care, well-equipped and adequately staffed maternal healthcare services, skilled attendants at delivery, emergency obstetric care, effective referral and transport to higher levels of care, when necessary, post-partum care and family planning, in order to, inter alia, promote safe motherhood, and give priority attention to measures to prevent, detect and treat breast, cervical and ovarian cancer and osteoporosis, and sexually transmitted infections, including HIV/AIDS.

Commitment 6

To promote and attain the goals of universal and equitable access to quality education, the highest attainable standard of physical and mental health, and the access of all to primary health care, making particular efforts to rectify inequalities relating to social conditions, without distinction as to race, national origin, gender, age or disability, respecting and promoting our common and particular cultures, striving to strengthen the role of culture in development, preserving the essential bases of people-centred sustainable development, and contributing to the full development of human resources and to social development, with the purpose of eradicating poverty, promoting full and productive employment and fostering social integration:

86. Recognize the primary responsibility of Governments for providing or ensuring access to basic social services for all; develop sustainable, pro-poor health and education systems by promoting community participation in planning and managing basic social services, including health promotion and disease prevention; and diversify approaches to meet local needs, to the extent possible, utilizing local skills and resources.

87. Ensure appropriate and effective expenditure of resources for universal access to basic education and primary health care, within the country context, in recognition of the positive impact this can have on economic and social development, with particular efforts

to target the special needs of vulnerable and disadvantaged groups.

88. Improve the performance of health-care systems, in particular at the primary health-care level, by broadening access to health care.

89. Make basic health services available to all members of society and, where appropriate, explore the possibility of promoting non-profit community-based health insurance programmes among possible methods to support the Government in the promotion of accessible primary health care for all.

90. Encourage new action at the international level, including examining the feasibility of proclaiming a United Nations literacy decade, to support national efforts to achieve universal access to basic education and primary health services for all by the year 2015.

91. Invite international organizations, in particular the international financial institutions, according to their mandates, to keep in mind the overall objective of facilitating long-term development to support national health and education programmes.

92. Reaffirm the Dakar Framework for Action on Education for All, adopted at the World Education Forum, held in Dakar from 26 to 28 April 2000, to develop or strengthen national strategies or action plans at the appropriate level to promote its goals: to ensure that by 2015 all children, particularly girls and children in difficult circumstances or with special needs, including children with disabilities, have access to and complete free and compulsory primary education of good quality; to improve early childhood care and education; to ensure access to appropriate learning, life skills and citizenship programmes; to achieve a 50 per cent improvement in levels of adult literacy; to improve the quality of education; and to take action to eliminate gender disparities and to ensure that girls and women have full and equal access to education.

93. Recognize that achieving education for all will require additional financial support by countries and increased development assistance and debt relief for education by bilateral and multilateral donors, estimated to cost on the order of $8 billion a year. It is therefore essential that new, concrete financial commitments be made by national Governments and also by bilateral and multilateral donors, including the World Bank and the regional development banks, by civil society and by foundations.

94. Take measures to better acknowledge and support the work of teachers and other educational personnel, including, where appropriate, improved compensation and benefits, relevant training and retraining programmes, human resource and career development strategies, and measures to encourage teachers' sustained contributions to quality education.

95. Encourage and assist developing countries and others in need in building capacities for secondary and tertiary education, as well as in training students in the skills and technologies necessary for effective participation in the modern, knowledge-based global economy, and promote international exchanges in the field of education so as to foster greater self-reliance in meeting the challenges of social and economic development and to increase sensitivity for and better understanding of all cultures and awareness of global issues.

96. Take all appropriate measures to ensure that infectious and parasitic diseases, such as malaria, tuberculosis, leprosy and schistosomiasis, neither continue to take their devastating toll nor impede economic and social progress; and strengthen national and international efforts to combat these diseases, inter alia, through capacity-building in the developing countries with the cooperation of the World Health Organization, including support for research centres.

97. Take multisectoral measures at the national level to enable all women and men, including young people, to protect themselves and others against, and be protected from, HIV infection in order to counteract the devastating impact of the epidemic on personal, social and economic development. It is particularly important to protect the dignity and the human rights of and improve the quality of life for people living with HIV/AIDS. Measures to enhance prevention and address the consequences of the transmission of HIV/AIDS and other sexually transmitted infections may include:

(a) Strengthening health-care services, including sexual and reproductive health;

(b) Strengthening information, education and communication campaigns to raise awareness of HIV/AIDS and to promote safe and responsible sexual behaviour, in full partnership with youth, parents, families, educators and health-care providers;

(c) Training health-care providers in all areas of prevention and control of HIV/AIDS and sexually transmitted infections, and giving special attention to the avoidance of contaminating equipment and blood products, the need to ensure a safe blood supply and the avoidance of reusing or sharing needles among injecting drug users;

(d) Developing and implementing strategies to prevent mother-to-child transmission;

(e) Promoting analyses of the political, cultural, social, economic and legal aspects of HIV/AIDS in order to develop strategies and measures to address the epidemic and its impact on national development;

(f) Providing social and educational support to communities, households, orphans and children affected by HIV/AIDS.

98. Strengthen political commitment and efforts at the international and national levels against HIV/AIDS, with a focus on developing countries and countries with economies in transition, through partnership among the Joint United Nations Programme on Human Immunodeficiency Virus/Acquired Immunodeficiency Syndrome (HIV/AIDS) and its co-sponsors, bilateral donors, Governments and non-governmental organizations, including youth organizations, and the private sector, based on a multisectoral approach encompassing, among other things, education and prevention programmes and services, care, including prenatal care, access to affordable medications and other pharmaceutical agents, and support for people living with HIV/AIDS, including home-based care, family planning programmes and the empowerment of women.

99. Provide support to countries with economies in transition to revitalize systems of primary health care and to promote more vigorous campaigns for health education and the promotion of healthy lifestyles.

100. Encourage, at all levels, arrangements and incentives to mobilize commercial enterprises, especially in pharmaceuticals, to invest in research aimed at finding remedies that can be provided at affordable prices for diseases that particularly afflict people in developing countries, and invite the World Health Organization to consider improving partnerships between the public and private sectors in the area of health research.

101. Recognize the right of everyone to the enjoyment of the highest attainable standards of physical and mental health as contained in relevant international human rights instruments as well as in the Constitution of the World Health Organization. Further recognize the critical importance of access to essential medicines at affordable prices. Acknowledge the contribution of intellectual property rights to promote further research, development and distribution of drugs, and the fact that these intellectual property rights should contribute to the mutual advantage of producers and users of technological knowledge and in a manner conducive to social and economic welfare. Agree that Member States may freely exercise, consistent with national laws and international agreements acceded to, in an unrestricted manner, the options available to them under international agreements to protect and advance access to life-saving, essential medicines.

102. Invite the World Health Organization, in collaboration with the United Nations Conference on Trade and Development, the World Trade Organization and other concerned agencies, to help to strengthen the capacities of the developing countries, particularly the least developed countries, to analyse the consequences of agreements on trade in health services for health equity and the ability to meet the health needs of people living in poverty, and to develop policies to ensure the promotion and protection of national health services.

103. Invite the World Health Organization to cooperate with Governments, at their request, and with international organizations, in monitoring and analysing the pharmaceutical and public health implications of relevant international agreements, including trade agreements, so that Governments can effectively assess and subsequently develop pharmaceutical and health policies and regulatory measures that address their concerns and priorities, and can maximize the positive and mitigate the negative impact of those agreements.

104. Invite the organizations of the United Nations system to cooperate with the World Health Organization to integrate the health dimension into their policies and programmes, in view of the close interdependence between health and other fields and the fact that solutions to good health may often be found outside of the health sector itself; such cooperation may build on initiatives undertaken in one or more of the following areas: health and employment, health and education, health and macroeconomic policy, health and environment, health and transport, health and nutrition, health and food security, health and housing, development of more equitable health financing systems, and trade in health goods and services.

105. Invite the United Nations system to support national efforts, where appropriate, to build on initiatives undertaken in one or more of the above-mentioned fields.

Commitment 7

To accelerate the economic, social and human resource development of Africa and the least developed countries:

106. Encourage concerted national and international efforts to promote an integrated approach to people-centred sustainable development.

107. Make concerted national and international efforts for promoting an enabling environment that will facilitate the integration of Africa and the least developed countries into the global economy and promote their participation in the multilateral trading system, inter alia, by:

(a) Implementing appropriate debt-relief initiatives that can lead to a sustainable solution to their debt burden;

(b) Improving market access for export products of Africa and the least developed countries, including through tariff- and quota-free treatment for essentially all products originating in least developed countries on as broad and liberal a basis as possible;

(c) Supporting programmes to assist them in taking full advantage of the multilateral trading regime, both on a bilateral basis and through multilateral efforts, inter alia, through the World Trade Organization, the International Trade Centre, United Nations Conference on Trade and Development and other relevant regional and subregional economic organizations;

(d) Pursuing structural adjustment programmes relevant to the needs of these countries by supporting growth-enhancing, poverty-reducing economic reforms;

(e) Supporting, inter alia, initiatives in the development of venture capital funds for investment in these countries in fields conducive to sustainable development.

108. Assist Governments in Africa and the least developed countries in enhancing the productive capacity and competitiveness of their countries through, inter alia, policies and programmes to support agricultural and industrial diversification, the establishment of cooperative business networks, public and private systems for sharing information, promoting technology and encouraging domestic and foreign investment, especially in the field of technology.

109. Call upon donor Governments and international organizations to encourage investment in critical infrastructure services, including reconstruction in post-conflict and natural disaster situations, and invite Governments in Africa and the least developed countries to utilize infrastructure investments to also promote employment.

110. Encourage interested Governments to consider the establishment of a world solidarity fund to be financed on a voluntary basis in order to contribute to the eradication of poverty and to promote social development in the poorest regions of the world.

111. Call upon the World Food Programme and other concerned agencies to strengthen food-for-work activities in low-income food-deficit countries, in particular in Africa, as an important measure to expand or rehabilitate needed community infrastructure, create employment and enhance household food security.

112. Strengthen support for South-South cooperation as a means to promote development in Af-

rica and the least developed countries by enhancing investment and transfer of appropriate technology through mutually agreed arrangements, as well as promoting regional human resource development and development of technology through, inter alia, technology-promotion centres.

113. Support increased efforts of Governments to promote and strengthen human-resource development in Africa and the least developed countries, in partnership with civil society, to achieve quality basic education for all, while at the same time continuing to invest in secondary and tertiary education, and with enhanced cooperation of the international community.

114. Support the efforts of Governments to allocate additional resources to education and the management capacities of the educational sector, and improve enrolment ratios, particularly for girls and women.

115. Support steps taken by Governments to encourage skilled and highly educated Africans to remain in the region and to utilize and further develop their skills.

116. Urge developed countries to strive to fulfil as soon as possible the agreed target of earmarking 0.15 to 0.20 per cent of gross national product as official development assistance for the least developed countries.

117. Accord priority to the least developed countries by the international community, including by United Nations funds and programmes, as well as international and regional financial institutions, in the allocation of resources on concessional terms for economic and social development.

118. Encourage the United Nations and its affiliated agencies to enhance the provision of technical cooperation to the least developed countries. In this context, call for the strengthening of the integrated framework for trade-related technical assistance to the least developed countries.

119. Encourage creditor countries to implement bilateral debt relief arrangements for the African and the least developed countries and stress that debt relief should contribute to national development objectives, including poverty eradication.

120. Give special attention to the least developed countries, in particular those in sub-Saharan Africa, in the implementation of the 20/20 initiative in cooperation with civil society in order to ensure access to basic social services for all.

121. Support the recommendations contained in the report of the Secretary-General and in that context await the outcome of the open-ended ad hoc working group on the causes of conflict and promotion of durable peace and sustainable development in Africa.

122. Encourage the twenty-five African countries most affected by HIV/AIDS to adopt time-bound targets for reducing infection levels, such as a target for reducing infection levels in young people by 25 per cent by 2005, and invite the Joint United Nations Programme on HIV/AIDS, in conjunction with its co-sponsoring agencies, to prepare and propose means for implementing a strategy for achieving this target.

123. Support African Governments in expanding and strengthening programmes related to young people and HIV/AIDS by developing a collective strategy with the donor community, international organizations and non-governmental organizations, facilitated by the establishment of national young people's task

forces, in order to ensure the necessary multisectoral response and the interventions to raise the awareness and address the needs of young people, as well as the needs of those living with HIV/AIDS and children orphaned by AIDS.

124. Invite the Joint United Nations Programme on HIV/AIDS and its co-sponsors, as part of the International Partnership Against AIDS in Africa, to support countries most affected by the HIV/AIDS pandemic, upon request, in their efforts:

(a) To allocate adequate resources, in particular financial resources, as well as wider access to quality medication by ensuring the provision and affordability of drugs, including a reliable distribution and delivery system; implementation of a strong generic drug policy; bulk purchasing; negotiation with pharmaceutical companies; appropriate financing systems; and encouragement of local manufacturing and import practices consistent with national laws and international agreements acceded to;

(b) To develop a strategy for resource mobilization for programmes on young people with their full involvement;

(c) To consolidate resources by creating or strengthening technical resource networks and identifying best practices at the country and regional levels;

(d) To develop a core set of indicators and tools to monitor implementation of youth programmes and progress towards achievement of the target to reduce infection levels in young people by 25 per cent by 2005.

125. Support African Governments and civil society organizations, inter alia, through the International Partnership Against AIDS in Africa and national programmes, in the provision of key services linked to social security, care and support, prevention and treatment of sexually transmitted infections, reduction of mother-to-child transmission, access to voluntary and confidential counselling and testing, and support of behavioural change and responsible sexual behaviour in order to scale up significantly efforts in Africa to curtail the spread of HIV, reduce the impact of HIV/AIDS and halt the further reversal of human, social and economic development.

126. Support and assist research and development centres in Africa and the least developed countries in the field of vaccines, medicine and public health, thereby strengthening training of medical personnel and counsellors, improving control and treatment of communicable and infectious diseases, such as HIV/AIDS, malaria and tuberculosis, as well as assisting in making vaccines and medicines for the control and treatment of these diseases widely available at affordable prices.

127. Encourage the international community to give its full support to an effective and successful outcome of the Third United Nations Conference on the Least Developed Countries to be held in Brussels in 2001.

Commitment 8

To ensure that when structural adjustment programmes are agreed to they include social development goals, in particular eradicating poverty, promoting full and productive employment and enhancing social integration:

128. Encourage international financial institutions and national Governments to adopt the principle of in-

tegration of social as well as economic aspects in the design of structural adjustment as well as reform programmes.

129. Adjustment programmes to address economic crises, including those negotiated between national Governments and the International Monetary Fund, should strive to ensure that this process does not lead to a severe drop in economic activity or sharp cuts in social spending.

130. Encourage Governments and international financial institutions to improve the ongoing dialogue on the design, implementation and reform of structural adjustment programmes, ensuring the full integration of social and economic frameworks for protecting social policies and programmes so that such programmes are genuinely nationally owned and driven; such dialogue would benefit from consultations by Governments with relevant actors and organizations of civil society. Encourage the international financial institutions to take into account the specific circumstances of countries concerned in providing support to their structural adjustment programmes.

131. Encourage the development of nationally owned poverty reduction strategies as a way to facilitate the dialogue of Governments with development partners and as a tool for the integration of social goals in national development strategies.

132. Design national policies, taking into account concerns of people living in poverty, by incorporating social development goals in the formulation of structural adjustment programmes, including poverty reduction strategies, in consultation with civil society, with a particular emphasis on:

(a) Designing economic policies for more equitable and enhanced access to income and resources to promote sustained economic growth and sustainable development, taking fully into account economic and social programmes aimed at poverty reduction;

(b) Protecting core social development expenditures identified by individual Governments from budgetary cuts, especially in times of crises, and encouraging international development banks to support national efforts in this regard;

(c) Ensuring that public services reach people living in poverty and vulnerable groups as a matter of priority, particularly through strengthening existing social programmes;

(d) Implementing adjustment and stabilization policies in ways that protect people living in poverty as well as vulnerable groups;

(e) Preserving and enhancing the social capital and strengthening the social fabric of society;

(f) Taking into account the evolving concept of poverty reduction strategy papers.

133. Ensure transparency and accountability by both Governments and international financial institutions for improved efficacy of structural adjustment programmes and fulfilment of social development goals.

134. Establish participatory mechanisms to undertake assessment of the social impact of structural adjustment programmes and reform packages before, during and after the implementation process with a view to mitigating their negative impact and developing policies to improve their positive impact on social development goals. Such assessments might involve

the support and cooperation of the United Nations system, including the Bretton Woods institutions, regional development banks and organizations of civil society.

135. Improve information-sharing and coordination between the Economic and Social Council and the relevant organizations of the United Nations system, including the Bretton Woods institutions, with a view to promoting social development and exploring ways and means to reduce the negative effects and improve the positive impact of structural adjustment programmes.

136. Ensure that gender issues are taken into account in the formulation and implementation of structural adjustment programmes.

Commitment 9
To increase significantly and/or utilize more efficiently the resources allocated to social development in order to achieve the goals of the Summit through national action and regional and international cooperation:

137. Recommend that the high-level intergovernmental event on financing for development, to be held in 2001, consider the mobilization of national and international resources for social development for the implementation of the Copenhagen Declaration and Programme of Action.

138. With the assistance of the international community, upon request, strengthen national information systems to produce reliable and disaggregated statistics on social development in order to assess the impact of social policies on economic and social development as well as to ensure that economic and social resources are used efficiently and effectively.

139. Undertake efforts to mobilize domestic resources for social development in accordance with national priorities and policies, inter alia, by:

(a) Reallocating public resources for investment in social development, inter alia, through the appropriate reduction of excessive military expenditures, including global military expenditures and the arms trade, and investments for arms production and acquisition, taking into consideration national security requirements;

(b) Endeavouring to enhance the cost-effectiveness of social spending;

(c) Strengthening mechanisms and policies to attract and manage private investment, thus freeing and also increasing public resources for social investments;

(d) Facilitating ways and means for the involvement and active partnership of civil society in the provision of social services.

140. Taking into account the challenges of globalization facing developing countries, support Governments, at their request, in the establishment of guidelines for policies aimed at generating domestic revenue to pay for social services, social protection and other social programmes, inter alia, by:

(a) Promoting equitable and progressive broadening of the tax base;

(b) Improving the efficiency of tax administration, including tax collection;

(c) Seeking new sources of revenue which simultaneously may discourage public bads;

(d) Undertaking various forms of public borrowing, including issuance of bonds and other financial instruments to finance capital works.

141. Promote, through national action, the mobilization of new and additional resources for social development, inter alia, by:

(a) Extending access to microcredit and other financial instruments to people living in poverty, particularly women;

(b) Supporting community participation in the planning, provision and maintenance of local infrastructure, through mechanisms such as community contracting of labour-based works;

(c) Improving and restructuring, as appropriate, national tax regimes and administration in order to establish an equitable and efficient system that supports social development policies and programmes and, inter alia, take measures to reduce tax evasion;

(d) Requesting the international community to support the efforts of all countries aimed at strengthening institutional capacity for preventing corruption, bribery, money-laundering and illegal transfer of funds, as well as repatriating these funds to their countries of origin.

142. Promote, through international action, the mobilization of new and additional resources for social development, inter alia, by:

(a) Developing appropriate means of international cooperation in tax matters;

(b) Exploring methods for dividing the liability of multinational corporations to pay taxes on profits among the various jurisdictions in which they operate;

(c) Exploring ways to combat the use of tax shelters and tax havens that undermine national tax systems;

(d) Improving the existing mechanisms for helping to stabilize commodity export earnings so as to respond to the real concerns of developing country producers, taking into account the fact that commodity price instability has remained extremely high, with declining trends for a number of commodities;

(e) Preventing tax avoidance and promoting treaties for avoiding double taxation;

(f) Exploring ways and means to increase and widen flows of public and private financial resources to developing countries, especially least developed countries;

(g) Conducting a rigorous analysis of advantages, disadvantages and other implications of proposals for developing new and innovative sources of funding, both public and private, for dedication to social development and poverty eradication programmes;

(h) Exploring ways and means of promoting the micro- and small enterprise sector whereby it becomes a possible vehicle for a new development model.

143. Urge international action to support national efforts to attract additional resources for social development, in several important areas:

(a) Encouraging creditor countries and institutions to take action to achieve rapid progress towards faster, broader and deeper debt relief as agreed under the enhanced Heavily Indebted Poor Countries Debt Initiative, which already considers increased flexibility with regard to eligibility criteria and through other means, to help to alleviate the debt burdens of those countries covered by the Initiative, stressing that debt relief should contribute to development objectives, including poverty reduction, and in this regard urging countries to direct those resources freed through debt relief, in particular through debt cancellation and reduction,

towards these objectives, consistent with General Assembly resolution 54/202 of 22 December 1999;

(b) Strengthening the institutional capacity of developing countries in debt management, calling upon the international community to support the efforts towards this end, and in this regard stressing the importance of such initiatives as the Debt Management and Financial Analysis System and the debt-management capacity-building programme;

(c) Calling for concerted national and international action to address effectively debt problems of low and middle-income developing countries with a view to resolving their potential long-term debt-sustainability problems through various debt-treatment measures, including, as appropriate, orderly mechanisms for debt reduction, and encouraging all creditor and debtor countries to utilize to the fullest extent possible, where appropriate, all existing mechanisms for debt reduction;

(d) Calling for continued international cooperation, including the reaffirmation to strive to fulfil the yet to be attained internationally agreed target of 0.7 per cent of the gross national product of developed countries for overall official development assistance as soon as possible, thereby increasing the flow of resources for social development;

(e) Encouraging donor and recipient countries, based on mutual agreement and commitment, to implement fully the 20/20 initiative, in line with the Oslo and Hanoi Consensus documents, to ensure universal access to basic social services;

(f) Providing concessional financing for social development programmes and projects to support the efforts of developing countries to achieve social development goals and targets;

(g) Providing landlocked countries and transit developing countries with appropriate technical and financial assistance in their efforts to implement the outcome of the Summit, particularly in addressing their special needs and problems;

(h) Implementing the commitments regarding the special needs and vulnerabilities of the small island developing States, in particular by providing effective means, including adequate, predictable, new and additional resources for social development programmes, in accordance with the Programme of Action for the Sustainable Development of Small Island Developing States and the results of the twenty-second special session of the General Assembly and on the basis of the relevant provisions of the Programme of Action.

144. Promote greater efficiency and effectiveness in the use of resources for social development.

145. Invite Governments to consider sector-wide approaches for the achievement of social development goals, in accordance with overall national development goals and priorities.

Commitment 10

To promote an improved and strengthened framework for international, regional and subregional cooperation for social development, in a spirit of partnership, through the United Nations and other multilateral institutions:

146. Develop, strengthen and make more effective indicators at the national level for assessing and guiding social development, in collaboration with research

institutions and civil society, as appropriate. These could include quantitative and qualitative indicators for assessing, inter alia, the social and gender impact of policies. Also develop and strengthen national information systems to produce reliable statistics on social and economic development. The relevant bodies of the United Nations and other relevant institutions should support, upon request, these national efforts.

147. Invite the Statistical Commission, with the assistance of the Statistics Division of the Department of Economic and Social Affairs of the Secretariat and in close cooperation with other relevant bodies of the United Nations system, including the Administrative Committee on Coordination, and, as appropriate, other relevant international organizations, to review, with a view to facilitating future consideration by the Economic and Social Council, the work undertaken in harmonizing and rationalizing basic indicators in the context of follow-up to United Nations conferences and summits, taking fully into account the decisions taken in other functional and regional commissions, and in that process to identify a limited number of common indicators from among those currently accepted and widely used by the States Members of the United Nations in order to lessen the data-provision burden on Member States, bearing in mind the work done so far in this area.

148. Strengthen cooperation at the regional level, which might include:

(a) Promoting dialogue among regional and subregional groups and organizations;

(b) Encouraging regional commissions to initiate or continue evaluation of the implementation of the Copenhagen Declaration and Programme of Action and the further initiatives contained in the present document;

(c) Encouraging the implementation of regional social development agendas where they exist; encouraging recipient countries, donor Governments and agencies and multilateral financial institutions to take greater account of the regional social development agenda of regional commissions and regional and subregional organizations, including in their funding policies and programmes.

149. Further strengthen the Economic and Social Council as the body primarily responsible for coordinating international action in follow-up to United Nations conferences and summits, which could include:

(a) Fostering a closer working relationship with the United Nations funds and programmes and the specialized agencies;

(b) Supporting continuing existing cooperation between the Economic and Social Council and the Bretton Woods institutions and joint meetings with the World Bank and the International Monetary Fund, so that the objectives and policy approaches of the United Nations conferences and summits are given due consideration by those institutions.

150. Promote South-South cooperation, particularly in terms of economic and technical cooperation, and support triangular mechanisms whereby donors would provide appropriate support.

151. Promote the full realization of the right to development and the elimination of obstacles to development through, inter alia, the implementation of the provisions of the Declaration on the Right to Development as reaffirmed by the Vienna Declaration and Programme of Action adopted by the World Conference on Human Rights on 25 June 1993.

152. Continue work on a wide range of reforms to create a strengthened and more stable international financial system, enabling it to deal more effectively and in a timely manner with the new challenges of development.

153. Consider the establishment, as appropriate, of national mechanisms, where they do not already exist, for the implementation of the Copenhagen Declaration and Programme of Action and the further initiatives contained in the present document.

154. Invite parliamentarians to continue to adopt legislative measures and to expand awareness-raising, necessary for implementing the commitments of the World Summit for Social Development and the further initiatives contained in the present document, and encourage the contribution of the Inter-Parliamentary Union in this effort.

155. Invite the Economic and Social Council to consolidate the ongoing initiatives and actions established in the Copenhagen Declaration and Programme of Action, the first United Nations Decade for the Eradication of Poverty (1997-2006) and the recommendations contained in the present document with a view to launching a global campaign to eradicate poverty.

156. Commit ourselves and encourage the United Nations system and all other relevant actors to take further determined sustained action to implement the commitments of the Copenhagen Declaration and Programme of Action and the results of the current special session of the General Assembly, entitled "World Summit for Social Development and beyond: achieving social development for all in a globalizing world", and request the Economic and Social Council to assess regularly, through the Commission for Social Development, the further implementation of the Copenhagen commitments and the outcome of the special session, not excluding the possibility of bringing together, at the appropriate time, all parties involved to evaluate progress and to consider new initiatives.

Outcome of special session

Report of Secretary-General. A September report of the Secretary-General on the twenty-fourth special session [A/55/344], prepared in response to General Assembly resolution 54/23 [YUN 1999, p. 1038], contained an analysis of the outcome document, particularly new initiatives regarding the role of Governments; the relationship between social policies and economic development; financial stability and international financial architecture; poverty eradication; employment; social integration; gender equality and mainstreaming; health and education for all; greater integration of developing countries, Africa and LDCs and those with economies in transition; debt relief; and resources for social development. It discussed further follow-up action by the UN system, particularly the Economic and Social Council, and presented an overview of the new initiatives.

On 29 November [meeting 74], the General Assembly adopted **resolution 55/46** [draft: A/55/L.40 & Add.1] without vote [agenda item 37].

Implementation of the outcome of the World Summit for Social Development and of the special session of the General Assembly in this regard

The General Assembly,

Recalling the World Summit for Social Development, held in Copenhagen from 6 to 12 March 1995, and the twenty-fourth special session of the General Assembly entitled "World Summit for Social Development and beyond: achieving social development for all in a globalizing world", held in Geneva from 26 June to 1 July 2000,

Stressing the importance of the outcome of the twenty-fourth special session of the General Assembly which reviewed and assessed the implementation of the Copenhagen Declaration on Social Development and the Programme of Action and adopted further actions and initiatives to implement the commitments made at the Summit,

Recalling the United Nations Millennium Declaration and the outcome of the twenty-third special session of the General Assembly entitled "Women 2000: Gender equality, development and peace for the twenty-first century",

1. *Reaffirms* the commitments made by heads of State and Government at the World Summit for Social Development, contained in the Copenhagen Declaration on Social Development and the Programme of Action, which established a new consensus to place people at the centre of the concerns for sustainable development and pledged to eradicate poverty, promote full and productive employment and foster social integration so as to achieve stable, safe and just societies for all, and the decisions on further action and initiatives to accelerate social development for all, adopted at the twenty-fourth special session of the General Assembly and contained in the further initiatives for social development;

2. *Also reaffirms* that the Copenhagen Declaration and the Programme of Action and the further initiatives for social development adopted at the twenty-fourth special session will constitute the basic framework for the further promotion of social development in the forthcoming years;

3. *Emphasizes* the vital importance of placing the goals of social development, as contained in the Copenhagen Declaration and the Programme of Action and in the outcome document of the twenty-fourth special session, at the centre of economic policy-making, including in policies that influence domestic and global market forces and the global economy;

4. *Invites* the Secretary-General, the Economic and Social Council, the Commission for Social Development, the regional commissions, the relevant agencies, funds and programmes of the United Nations system and other relevant intergovernmental forums, within their respective mandates, to take on a priority basis all steps necessary to ensure the effective implementation of all commitments and undertakings contained in the Copenhagen Declaration and the Programme of Action and in the outcome document of the twenty-fourth special session;

5. *Expresses its appreciation* to the Government and people of Switzerland for contributing to the successful outcome of the twenty-fourth special session;

6. *Takes note* of the report of the Secretary-General on the outcome of the twenty-fourth special session;

7. *Decides* to include in the provisional agenda of its fifty-sixth session an item entitled "Implementation of the outcome of the World Summit for Social Development and of the twenty-fourth special session of the General Assembly", and requests the Secretary-General to submit to the General Assembly at its fifty-sixth session a report on this question.

Commission for Social Development

The Commission for Social Development held its thirty-eighth session from 8 to 17 February and on 14 and 17 March in New York [E/2000/26 & Corr.1]. In addition to adopting a set of agreed conclusions on the review and appraisal of the implementation of the outcome of the 1995 World Summit for Social Development (see p. 1013), the Commission recommended to the Economic and Social Council the adoption of draft resolutions on further promotion of equalization of opportunities by, for and with persons with disabilities (see p. 1036) and follow-up to the 1999 International Year of Older Persons (see p. 1140).

In the context of preparations for the Commission's 2001 session, the Secretariat organized, in cooperation with Germany and South Africa, expert group meetings on the challenge of social protection in a globalizing world (Berlin, 10-12 October) and on traditional and modern schemes of social protection in the context of development (Cape Town, 30 October–1 November) [E/CN.5/2001/2]. The meetings aimed to explore the development of social protection systems for vulnerable and unprotected people, as well as to make suggestions on new mechanisms to ensure the sustainability of the systems in various country contexts.

On 27 July, the Economic and Social Council, taking note of the Commission's report on its thirty-eighth session, endorsed the Commission's resolutions and decisions and approved its provisional agenda and documentation for 2001 (**decision 2000/238**).

On 18 October, the Council decided to invite those NGOs accredited to the twenty-fourth special session of the General Assembly to attend the Commission's thirty-ninth (2001) session, provided that they had started the process of applying for consultative status (**decision 2000/310**).

2000 Report on the World Social Situation

An overview of the *2000 Report on the World Social Situation* [E/2000/9], presented by the Secretary-General in April, summarized global developments from a social perspective. It reviewed demographic and economic trends; societal changes affecting and affected by the situation of families, civil society and public institutions; trends in living conditions; contemporary social problems, such as discrimination, armed conflicts, violence, corruption and crime; and education, technology and information. The report identified developments that were expected to influence and shape society, radically affecting life in far-reaching and fundamental ways.

The report was to be issued as a sales publication in 2001.

On 28 July, the Economic and Social Council took note of the overview of the report (**decision 2000/289**).

UN Research Institute for Social Development

In 2000, the United Nations Research Institute for Social Development (UNRISD) continued to conduct research into the social dimensions of development. A November report of the UNRISD Board [E/CN.5/2001/3] described the Institute's activities, including participation in the twenty-fourth special session of the General Assembly (see p. 1012), for which UNRISD had produced the report *Visible Hands: Taking Responsibility for Social Development*, a synthesis of 40 commissioned papers that highlighted patterns of economic growth, liberalization and inequality which continued to obstruct progress. UNRISD commissioned papers and held a public workshop to coincide with the Assembly's special session on women (see p. 1082), and began a project to strengthen the empirical basis for the 2001 World Conference against Racism, Racial Discrimination, Xenophobia and Related Intolerance (see p. 641). A special initiative was begun on improving research and knowledge on social development within international organizations (Bellagio, Italy, November).

Research continued within six projects initiated during the previous biennium: information technologies and social development; gender, poverty and well-being; business responsibility for sustainable development; public sector reform and crisis-ridden States; grass-roots initiatives for land reform; and urban governance. In addition, four new projects initiated during 1999-2000 were under way on neo-liberalism and institutional reform in East Asia; social policy in a development context; technocratic policy-making and democratization; and HIV/AIDS and development.

Although it was part of the UN system, UNRISD activities were financed through voluntary contributions from Governments, international agencies and foundations.

Persons with disabilities

Report of Special Rapporteur. During the year, the Commission for Social Development considered the final report of its Special Rapporteur on disability, Bengt Lindqvist (Sweden) [E/CN.5/2000/3 & Corr.1], describing the second monitoring period (1997-2000) of implementation of the Standard Rules on the Equalization of Opportunities for Persons with Disabilities, contained in General Assembly resolution 48/96 [YUN 1993, p. 977]. During the period under review, the Special Rapporteur continued to advise Governments upon request, participate in seminars and conferences to discuss the practical implementation of the Rules, and study the implementation of the Rules worldwide through the use of surveys. He had visited countries in transition (Armenia, Bulgaria, Mongolia, Romania, Russian Federation), where he observed that they had not yet developed guidelines for a modern disability policy. In visits to developing countries (Chile, Costa Rica, Jordan, Thailand, Uruguay), he noted that programmes varied considerably. The Special Rapporteur reported on the results of the third global survey, conducted in collaboration with the World Health Organization (WHO), the body responsible for three of the Rules under preconditions for equal opportunity (medical care, rehabilitation, support services). The survey aimed to identify government policies regarding medical care, rehabilitation, support services and personnel training, as well as strategies adopted and problems encountered when working in the area of medical care and rehabilitation of persons with disabilities. The Special Rapporteur stated that a high proportion of Governments indicated the existence of medical services (99 countries of 104 responding), rehabilitation (73 of 102) and the provision of devices and equipment (87 of 96). He noted positive developments regarding children with disabilities and legislation, but more needed to be done, in particular to improve living conditions for girls and women with disabilities and for persons with developmental and psychiatric disabilities.

Report of Secretary-General. In a December interim report [E/CN.5/2001/7] on implementation of the World Programme of Action concerning Disabled Persons [YUN 1982, p. 981], the Secretary-General stated that in 2000 the Special Rapporteur had formulated a multi-year work programme and travelled, on request, to Belarus, Brazil, Bulgaria, Hungary, the Russian Federation and Uganda. He participated in the Nineteenth World Congress of Rehabilitation International (Rio de Janiero, Brazil, 25-29 August) and the Sixth Congress on the Inclusion of Children with Disabilities (Edmonton, Canada, 22-24 October), and organized an international seminar on human rights and disability (Stockholm, Sweden, 4-10 November).

Regarding activities under the African Decade of Disabled People (2000-2009), proclaimed by the Organization of African Unity, the UN Voluntary Fund on Disability supported an international workshop on environmental accessibility and universal design in developing countries (Providence, Rhode Island, United States, 14-18 June) and the Eastern Africa regional workshop on application of universal design concepts and principles and information technologies (Nairobi, 6-10 November). Within the context of the Asian and Pacific Decade of Disabled Persons (1993-2002), proclaimed in 1992 by the Economic and Social Commission for Asia and the Pacific [YUN 1992, p. 490], a series of regional and subregional technical meetings on accessibility focused on training related to barrier-free design.

The Secretary-General reported that, from 1 September 1999 to 31 October 2000, the UN Voluntary Fund on Disability provided $763,901 in grants to 26 disability-related projects. Annexed to the report was a description of the projects.

NGO Summit. The World NGO Summit on Disability (Beijing, 10-12 March) [A/54/861-E/2000/47, A/S-24/3] adopted the Beijing Declaration on the Rights of People with Disabilities in the New Century, which called for an initiative that would lead to the adoption of an international convention on the rights of all people with disabilities.

(For information on persons with disabilities and human rights, see p. 733.)

ECONOMIC AND SOCIAL COUNCIL ACTION

On 27 July [meeting 43], the Economic and Social Council, on the recommendation of the Commission for Social Development [E/2000/26 & Corr.1], adopted **resolution 2000/10** without vote [agenda item 14 (*b*)].

Further promotion of equalization of opportunities by, for and with persons with disabilities

The Economic and Social Council,

Recalling General Assembly resolution 37/52 of 3 December 1982, by which the Assembly adopted the World Programme of Action concerning Disabled Persons, resolution 48/96 of 20 December 1993, by which it adopted the Standard Rules on the Equalization of Opportunities for Persons with Disabilities, and resolutions 52/82 of 12 December 1997 and 54/121 of 17 December 1999,

Recalling also Economic and Social Council resolutions 1997/19 on equalization of opportunities for per-

sons with disabilities and 1997/20 on children with disabilities, of 21 July 1997, Commission on Human Rights resolution 1998/31 on the human rights of persons with disabilities of 17 April 1998 and other relevant resolutions of the General Assembly and the Economic and Social Council and its functional commissions,

Recalling further the purposes and principles of the Charter of the United Nations, and reaffirming the obligations contained in relevant human rights instruments, including the Convention on the Elimination of All Forms of Discrimination against Women and the Convention on the Rights of the Child,

Recalling the Copenhagen Declaration on Social Development and Programme of Action of the World Summit for Social Development, in which Governments are requested to promote the Standard Rules and to develop strategies for their implementation,

Reaffirming the outcomes of the major United Nations conferences and summits and their respective follow-up reviews, in particular as they pertain to the promotion of the rights and well-being of persons with disabilities on the basis of their full participation and equality,

Mindful of the need to adopt and implement effective strategies and policies to promote the rights and the full and effective participation of persons with disabilities in economic, social, cultural and political life, on the basis of equality, to achieve a society for all,

Noting with great concern that persons with disabilities in some circumstances are among the poorest of the poor and continue to be excluded from the benefits of development, such as education and access to gainful employment,

Noting with satisfaction that the Standard Rules play an important role in influencing the promotion, formulation and evaluation of policies, plans, programmes and actions at the national, regional and international levels to further the equalization of opportunities by, for and with persons with disabilities,

Acknowledging the active role played by non-governmental organizations, including organizations of persons with disabilities, in cooperation with Governments and relevant intergovernmental bodies and organizations, to promote awareness and support implementation and evaluation of the Standard Rules at the national, regional and international levels,

Recognizing that the United Nations Voluntary Fund on Disability has relied on a narrow donor base, and that a sustained and predictable financial basis for the execution of the World Programme of Action concerning Disabled Persons and the implementation of the Standard Rules needs a broadening of its donor base,

1. *Takes note with appreciation* of the valuable work done by the Special Rapporteur for monitoring the implementation of the Standard Rules on the Equalization of Opportunities for Persons with Disabilities of the Commission for Social Development, and welcomes his report on his second mission, 1997-2000;

2. *Also takes note with appreciation* of the important efforts of Governments as well as non-governmental organizations and academic institutions during the first and second missions of the Special Rapporteur to build capacities to implement the Standard Rules at the national, regional and interregional levels;

3. *Welcomes* the many initiatives and actions of Governments, relevant United Nations bodies and organi-

zations, including the Bretton Woods institutions, as well as non-governmental organizations to implement further the goal of full participation and equality for persons with disabilities in accordance with the Standard Rules;

4. *Urges* Governments, intergovernmental organizations as well as non-governmental organizations to take practical action to create greater awareness and support to implement further the Standard Rules, and to consider taking further initiatives, as appropriate, with special emphasis accorded, as noted in the report of the Special Rapporteur, to the human rights of persons with disabilities, children with disabilities and their families, gender aspects, in particular the issue of discrimination against women and girls with disabilities, and the situation of persons with developmental and psychiatric disabilities, with a focus on integrating such persons into society;

5. *Urges* the relevant bodies and organizations of the United Nations system, including relevant human rights treaty bodies, within their respective mandates, the regional commissions, intergovernmental organizations as well as non-governmental organizations to work closely with the programme on disability of the Division for Social Policy and Development of the Secretariat to promote the rights of persons with disabilities, including activities at the field level, by sharing knowledge, experiences, findings and recommendations concerning persons with disabilities;

6. *Encourages* the United Nations system, the Bretton Woods institutions and Governments to enhance cooperation, through appropriate mechanisms, with organizations of persons with disabilities or concerned with disability issues so as to implement the Standard Rules in an effective and coordinated manner;

7. *Decides* to renew the mandate of the Special Rapporteur for a further period through the year 2002 so that the results of his continued promotion and monitoring of the implementation of the Standard Rules, in accordance with section IV of the Standard Rules, will be available to the fourth quinquennial review and appraisal of the World Programme of Action concerning Disabled Persons, in accordance with General Assembly resolution 52/82, and to request the Special Rapporteur, assisted by the Secretariat and in consultation with his panel of experts, to prepare a report for submission to the Commission for Social Development at its fortieth session, in which he should, inter alia, present his views on further developing the proposals contained in his report on his second mission and on forms for complementing and developing the Standard Rules, and on ways to enhance the involvement of the relevant bodies and organizations of the United Nations system and relevant intergovernmental regional organizations regarding the implementation of the Standard Rules;

8. *Encourages* States parties to include in their reports to the relevant treaty bodies information on persons with disabilities, and reiterates its invitation to the Special Rapporteur and the relevant human rights treaty bodies, including the Committee on the Rights of the Child, within their respective mandates, to enhance their cooperation, as appropriate, to ensure that the rights of persons with disabilities are appropriately addressed;

9. *Requests* the Secretary-General to invite relevant organizations of the United Nations system to provide, upon request, advisory services to Governments, inter alia, on formulating and evaluating disability-sensitive policies and programmes, on reinforcing the disability dimension in mainstream technical cooperation activities, and for building national capacities and institutions to further equalization of opportunities in accordance with the Standard Rules, and to submit a report to the Commission at its fortieth session;

10. *Also requests* the Secretary-General to strengthen and improve mechanisms for consultation, exchange of information and coordination, as appropriate, and active participation of relevant United Nations bodies, specialized agencies and related organizations to implement further the Standard Rules, inter alia, within the framework of the Administrative Committee on Coordination;

11. *Urges* relevant bodies and organizations of the United Nations system to identify ways and means and to develop within their existing programmes support services and related initiatives to improve living conditions for persons with developmental and psychiatric disabilities, in particular women and children;

12. *Encourages* Governments, non-governmental organizations and the private sector to continue to contribute to the United Nations Voluntary Fund on Disability so that it is able to support on a predictable and sustained basis new and expanded initiatives at the regional, subregional and national levels to strengthen national capacities for equalization of opportunities by, for and with persons with disabilities, and the activities of the Special Rapporteur during his renewed mandate;

13. *Urges* Governments to observe the International Day of Disabled Persons, 3 December, as an opportunity for promoting the human rights of persons with disabilities and for raising awareness of their special needs with a view towards their full and effective participation in society;

14. *Encourages* international support for the African Decade of Disabled People during the years 2000-2009, to promote equalization of opportunities by, for and with persons with disabilities as well as to promote and protect their human rights.

Cultural development

Follow-up to 1998 intergovernmental conference

In response to General Assembly resolution 53/184 [YUN 1998, p. 1030], the Secretary-General, in August, transmitted a report of the Director-General of the United Nations Educational, Scientific and Cultural Organization (UNESCO) on cultural development [A/55/339], which described activities taken by Member States, international organizations and UNESCO to implement the Action Plan adopted by the 1998 Intergovernmental Conference on Cultural Policies for Development [YUN 1998, p. 1030].

On 20 December [meeting 87], on the recommendation of the Second (Economic and Financial) Committee [A/55/581/Add.3], the General Assembly adopted **resolution 55/192** without vote [agenda item 94 (c)].

Culture and development

The General Assembly,

Recalling its resolutions 41/187 of 8 December 1986, 46/158 of 19 December 1991, 51/179 of 16 December 1996, 52/197 of 18 December 1997 and 53/184 of 15 December 1998 on cultural development,

Encouraged by the positive international response to the results of the work of the World Commission on Culture and Development and of the Intergovernmental Conference on Cultural Policies for Development organized by the United Nations Educational, Scientific and Cultural Organization at Stockholm from 30 March to 2 April 1998,

Noting the steps taken by Member States, organizations of the United Nations system and nongovernmental organizations to implement the recommendations in the Action Plan on Cultural Policies for Development adopted at the Conference,

Bearing in mind the importance of cultural values and cultural diversity as elements of sustainable development,

Underlining the fact that tolerance and respect for cultural diversity and universal promotion and protection of human rights, including the right to development, are mutually supportive,

Emphasizing the need to enhance the potential of culture as a means of prosperity, sustainable development and global coexistence,

1. *Takes note* of the report of the Director-General of the United Nations Educational, Scientific and Cultural Organization;

2. *Invites* all Member States, intergovernmental bodies, organizations of the United Nations system and non-governmental organizations:

(*a*) To ensure, in cooperation with the United Nations Educational, Scientific and Cultural Organization, continuous and effective implementation of the Action Plan on Cultural Policies for Development;

(*b*) To intensify further their efforts to integrate cultural factors into their development programmes and projects, so as to ensure sustainable development that fully respects cultural diversity;

(*c*) To implement fully the Declaration and Programme of Action on a Culture of Peace adopted by the General Assembly on 13 September 1999;

(*d*) To commit themselves to promoting the dialogue among civilizations as an essential process for human development and mutual understanding and for strengthening international cooperation;

(*e*) To analyse the connection between culture and development and the elimination of poverty in the context of the first United Nations Decade for the Eradication of Poverty (1997-2006), as recommended in the Action Plan;

(*f*) To safeguard cultural and linguistic diversity in the context of globalization and to support action by the United Nations Educational, Scientific and Cultural Organization in this regard;

3. *Encourages* the United Nations Educational, Scientific and Cultural Organization to continue its work to promote a greater awareness of the crucial relationship between culture and development;

4. *Also encourages* the United Nations Educational, Scientific and Cultural Organization, in conjunction, as appropriate, with other relevant United Nations bodies and multilateral development institutions, to continue to provide support, upon request, to developing countries, in particular in national capacity-building, for the implementation of international cultural conventions, including conservation of heritage and protection of cultural property, and for the restitution of cultural property, in accordance with General Assembly resolution 54/190 of 17 December 1999, as well as support and opportunities for the promotion and enhancement of cultural goods and services and of cultural tourism respectful of the integrity of cultural and natural heritage;

5. *Requests* the Secretary-General, in consultation with the Director-General of the United Nations Educational, Scientific and Cultural Organization, to submit to the General Assembly at its fifty-seventh session a report on the implementation of the present resolution.

International Year of Dialogue among Civilizations (2001)

Pursuant to General Assembly resolution 54/113 [YUN 1999, p. 1044], the Secretary-General presented a November report [A/55/492/Rev.1], describing activities taken to implement the United Nations Year of Dialogue among Civilizations (2001), proclaimed by the Assembly in resolution 53/22 [YUN 1998, p. 1031]. A number of initiatives were launched to celebrate and defuse the fear of diversity and to underline the importance of inclusion. Governments, academic institutions and NGOs conducted seminars, debates and research. On 5 September, dialogue among civilizations was the subject of a meeting at the head-of-State level held at Headquarters. Reports on preparations for the Year received from Governments, UN bodies, specialized agencies and intergovernmental organizations were available for consultation in the UN Department of Economic and Social Affairs.

The Trust Fund established for the dialogue among civilizations had received limited contributions.

Communication. In October [A/55/455], Uzbekistan transmitted the text of the Declaration of the UNESCO International Congress on Inter-religious Dialogue and a Culture of Peace (Tashkent, 14-16 September).

On 13 November [meeting 60], the General Assembly adopted **resolution 55/23** [draft: A/55/L.30 & Add.1] without vote [agenda item 32].

United Nations Year of Dialogue among Civilizations

The General Assembly,

Recalling its resolutions 53/22 of 4 November 1998 and 54/113 of 10 December 1999 entitled "United Nations Year of Dialogue among Civilizations",

Reaffirming the purposes and principles embodied in the Charter of the United Nations, which, inter alia, call for collective effort to strengthen friendly relations among nations, remove threats to peace and foster international cooperation in resolving international issues of an economic, social, cultural and humanitarian character and in promoting and encouraging universal respect for human rights and fundamental freedoms for all,

Noting that civilizations are not confined to individual nation-States, but rather encompass different cultures within the same civilization, and reaffirming that civilizational achievements constitute the collective heritage of humankind, providing a source of inspiration and progress for humanity at large,

Bearing in mind the specificities of each civilization and the United Nations Millennium Declaration of 8 September 2000, which considers, inter alia, that tolerance is one of the fundamental values essential to international relations in the twenty-first century and should include the active promotion of a culture of peace and dialogue among civilizations, with human beings respecting one another, in all their diversity of belief, culture and language, neither fearing nor repressing differences within and between societies but cherishing them as a precious asset of humanity,

Noting that globalization brings greater interrelatedness among people and increased interaction among cultures and civilizations, and encouraged by the fact that the celebration of the United Nations Year of Dialogue among Civilizations, at the beginning of the twenty-first century, will provide the opportunity to emphasize that globalization not only is an economic, financial and technological process which could offer great benefit, but also constitutes a profoundly human challenge that invites us to embrace the interdependence of humankind and its rich cultural diversity,

Recognizing the diverse civilizational achievements of humankind, crystallizing cultural pluralism and creative human diversity,

Bearing in mind the valuable contribution that dialogue among civilizations can make to an improved awareness and understanding of the common values shared by all humankind,

Stressing the need for the universal protection and promotion of all human rights and fundamental freedoms, including the right of all peoples to self-determination, by virtue of which they freely determine their political status and freely pursue their economic, social and cultural development,

Underlining the fact that tolerance and respect for diversity and universal promotion and protection of human rights are mutually supportive, and recognizing that tolerance and respect for diversity effectively promote and are supported by, inter alia, the empowerment of women,

Emphasizing the need to acknowledge and respect the richness of all civilizations, to seek common grounds among and within civilizations in order to address threats to global peace and common challenges to human values and achievements, taking into consideration, inter alia, cooperation, partnership and inclusion,

Welcoming the collective endeavour of the international community to enhance understanding through constructive dialogue among civilizations,

Encouraged by the positive reception of Governments, international organizations, civil society organizations and international public opinion to the proclamation of the United Nations Year of Dialogue among Civilizations, and welcoming the initiatives undertaken by governmental and non-governmental actors to promote dialogue,

Expressing its firm determination to facilitate and promote dialogue among civilizations,

1. *Takes note with appreciation* of the report of the Secretary-General;

2. *Welcomes* the convening, at the level of heads of State, of a round table on dialogue among civilizations, organized by the Islamic Republic of Iran and the United Nations Educational, Scientific and Cultural Organization, held at United Nations Headquarters on 5 September 2000 and which further contributed to the promotion of dialogue among civilizations;

3. *Invites* Governments, the United Nations system, including the United Nations Educational, Scientific and Cultural Organization, and other relevant international and non-governmental organizations to continue and further intensify planning and organizing appropriate cultural, educational and social programmes to promote the concept of dialogue among civilizations, inter alia, through organizing conferences and seminars and disseminating information and scholarly material on the subject, and to inform the Secretary-General of their activities;

4. *Calls upon* Governments to encourage all members of society to take part in promoting dialogue among civilizations and provide them with an opportunity to make contributions to the United Nations Year of Dialogue among Civilizations;

5. *Encourages* all Governments to expand their educational curricula relative to the teaching of respect for various cultures and civilizations, human rights education, the teaching of languages, the history and philosophy of various civilizations as well as the exchange of knowledge, information and scholarships among Governments and civil society in order to promote a better understanding of all cultures and civilizations;

6. *Encourages* all Member States, regional and international organizations, civil society and non-governmental organizations to continue to develop appropriate initiatives at all levels to promote dialogue in all fields with a view to fostering mutual recognition and understanding among and within civilizations;

7. *Notes with interest* the activities undertaken and proposals made by Member States, the United Nations Educational, Scientific and Cultural Organization and international and regional organizations, including the Organization of the Islamic Conference and non-governmental organizations, for the preparation of the United Nations Year of Dialogue among Civilizations;

8. *Decides* to devote two days of plenary meetings at the fifty-sixth session of the General Assembly, on 3 and 4 December 2001, to the consideration of the item, including consideration of any follow-up measures, and commemoration of the United Nations Year of

Dialogue among Civilizations, and encourages Member States and observers to be represented at the highest possible political level;

9. *Invites* all Governments, funding institutions, civil society organizations and the private sector to consider contributing to the Trust Fund established by the Secretary-General in 1999 to promote dialogue among civilizations;

10. *Requests* the Secretary-General to continue to provide the necessary support for strengthening the activities pertaining to dialogue among civilizations;

11. *Also requests* the Secretary-General to submit to the General Assembly at its fifty-sixth session a substantive report on the prospect of dialogue among civilizations and the activities pertaining to the United Nations Year of Dialogue among Civilizations;

12. *Decides* to include in the provisional agenda of its fifty-sixth session the item entitled "United Nations Year of Dialogue among Civilizations".

Olympic Truce

On 1 September [A/54/971], the President of the General Assembly appealed to States to observe the Olympic Truce at the XXVII Olympic Games (Sydney, Australia, 15 September–1 October).

The General Assembly, on 5 September, took note of its President's appeal (**decision 54/487**).

Communication. On 5 September [A/54/972], Greece appealed for the observance of the Olympic Truce.

Bethlehem 2000

On 7 November [meeting 54], the General Assembly adopted **resolution 55/18** [draft: A/55/L.3 & Add.1] without vote [agenda item 36].

Bethlehem 2000

The General Assembly,

Recalling the fact that the Palestinian city of Bethlehem is the birthplace of Jesus Christ and one of the most historic and significant sites on earth,

Noting that the world is continuing to celebrate in Bethlehem, a city of peace, the onset of the new millennium in a global vision of hope for all peoples,

Stressing again the monumental importance of the event for the Palestinian people, for the peoples of the region and for the international community as a whole, as it comprises significant religious, historical and cultural dimensions,

Aware of the Bethlehem 2000 Project as a multifaceted undertaking for commemoration of the event, which began at Christmas, 1999, and will come to a close at Easter, 2001,

Aware also of the assistance needed with regard to the above-mentioned Project, and expressing appreciation for the steps already taken towards increasing the engagement and participation of the international community, including donor countries, and organizations of the United Nations system, in particular the United Nations Educational, Scientific and Cultural Organization, the United Nations Development Programme and the World Bank, as well as the European Commission, religious institutions and others,

Recalling the convening of the Bethlehem 2000 International Conference in Rome, on 18 and 19 February 1999, and its impact on the promotion of the Bethlehem 2000 Project and the mobilization of public awareness in all regions in support of this endeavour,

Welcoming the participation in the Bethlehem celebrations of several heads of State and Government and many other eminent personalities, including religious leaders, and expressing appreciation for the Palestinian preparations for this event,

Welcoming also the historic Jubilee 2000 pilgrimage of His Holiness Pope John Paul II to the Holy Land, his landmark visit to the holy sites in Bethlehem and the important message delivered by the Pontiff at Manger Square,

Expressing the need for immediate change in the situation on the ground in the vicinity of Bethlehem, especially with regard to ensuring freedom of movement,

Stressing the need for ensuring free and unhindered access to the holy places in Bethlehem to the faithful of all religions and the citizens of all nationalities,

Expressing the renewed hope for a successful outcome of the Middle East peace process and the achievement of a final settlement between the Palestinian and Israeli sides, so that the millennium may be celebrated in an atmosphere of peace and reconciliation,

1. *Welcomes* this global and historic celebration in Bethlehem and the onset of the third millennium as a symbol of the shared hope for peace among all peoples of the world;

2. *Expresses support* for the Bethlehem 2000 Project, and commends the efforts undertaken by the Palestinian Authority in this regard;

3. *Notes with appreciation* the worldwide support for the Bethlehem 2000 Project, and calls for sustained assistance and engagement by the international community as a whole, including private sector participation, in ensuring the success of the Project and of this monumental commemoration;

4. *Requests* the Secretary-General to continue to mobilize the pertinent organizations and agencies of the United Nations system to increase their efforts to ensure the successful completion of the Bethlehem 2000 Project;

5. *Decides* to conclude, at the current session, consideration by the General Assembly of the item entitled "Bethlehem 2000".

Crime prevention and criminal justice

Tenth UN Crime Congress

The Tenth United Nations Congress on the Prevention of Crime and the Treatment of Offenders, held in Vienna from 10 to 17 April [A/CONF.187/15], with a high-level segment on 14 and 15 April, adopted the Vienna Declaration on Crime and Justice: Meeting the Challenges of the Twenty-first Century. The Declaration was subsequently submitted to the General Assembly's millennium session, in accordance with Assembly resolution 54/125 [YUN 1999, p. 1050]. In other action, the Congress approved the report of the Credentials Committee.

The Congress, which was attended by 134 States, as well as observers from UN offices and organs and the specialized agencies, intergovernmental organizations, NGOs and over 300 experts, was held under the theme crime and justice: meeting the challenges of the twenty-first century. It considered five major topics with a corresponding working paper prepared by the Secretariat: the state of crime and criminal justice worldwide [A/CONF.187/5]; international cooperation in combating transnational crime: new challenges in the twenty-first century [A/CONF.187/6]; promoting the rule of law and strengthening the criminal justice system [A/CONF.187/3]; effective crime prevention: keeping pace with new developments [A/CONF.187/7]; and offenders and victims: accountability and fairness in the justice process [A/CONF.187/8]. During the Congress, workshops were convened on combating corruption [A/CONF.187/9]; crimes related to computer networks [A/CONF.187/10]; community involvement in crime prevention [A/CONF.187/11]; and women in the criminal justice system [A/CONF.187/12].

Penuell Mpapa Maduna, Minister of Justice of South Africa, was elected President of the Congress.

In opening remarks, the Deputy Secretary-General of the United Nations, on behalf of the Secretary-General, noted that unprecedented challenges posed by increasingly global criminal networks fostered the recognition that no country could cope with the growth of transnational crime on its own. She stressed that new forms of transnational crime undermined confidence in political institutions and affected the stability and prosperity of societies. Fighting crime should be part of a global effort to create a more peaceful and prosperous world.

Follow-up to the Tenth Congress

On 18 and 19 April, the Commission on Crime Prevention and Criminal Justice (see p. 1044) considered the report of the Tenth Congress and an April note by the Secretariat [E/CN.15/2000/6], recalling that the General Assembly, in resolution 54/125 [YUN 1999, p. 1050], had requested the Commission to give priority in 2000 to the conclusions and recommendations of the Tenth Congress, with a view to recommending, through the Economic and Social Council, follow-up by the Assembly at its fifty-fifth (2000) session. The Assembly had also asked the Congress to submit,

through the Commission and the Council, the Vienna Declaration to the Millennium Assembly.

Following deliberations, the Commission recommended to the Council two draft texts, which were adopted as resolutions 2000/11 and 2000/12.

ECONOMIC AND SOCIAL COUNCIL ACTION

On 27 July [meeting 43], the Economic and Social Council, on the recommendation of the Commission on Crime Prevention and Criminal Justice [E/2000/30], adopted **resolution 2000/11** without vote [agenda item 14 *(c)*].

Vienna Declaration on Crime and Justice: Meeting the Challenges of the Twenty-first Century

The Economic and Social Council

Recommends to the General Assembly the adoption of the following draft resolution:

[For text, see General Assembly resolution 55/59 below.]

GENERAL ASSEMBLY ACTION

On 4 December [meeting 81], the General Assembly, on the recommendation of the Third (Social, Humanitarian and Cultural) Committee [A/55/593], adopted **resolution 55/59** without vote [agenda item 105].

Vienna Declaration on Crime and Justice: Meeting the Challenges of the Twenty-first Century

The General Assembly,

Recalling that, in its resolution 54/125 of 17 December 1999, it requested the Tenth United Nations Congress on the Prevention of Crime and the Treatment of Offenders to submit, through the Commission on Crime Prevention and Criminal Justice and the Economic and Social Council, its declaration to the Millennium Assembly for consideration and action, and requested the Commission to give priority attention at its ninth session to the conclusions and recommendations of the Tenth Congress, with a view to recommending, through the Economic and Social Council, appropriate follow-up by the General Assembly at its fifty-fifth session,

Endorses the Vienna Declaration on Crime and Justice: Meeting the Challenges of the Twenty-first Century, adopted by the States Members of the United Nations and the other States participating in the high-level segment of the Tenth United Nations Congress on the Prevention of Crime and the Treatment of Offenders, as contained in the annex to the present resolution.

ANNEX
Vienna Declaration on Crime and Justice:
Meeting the Challenges of the Twenty-first Century

We the States Members of the United Nations,

Concerned about the impact on our societies of the commission of serious crimes of a global nature, and convinced of the need for bilateral, regional and international cooperation in crime prevention and criminal justice,

Concerned in particular about transnational organized crime and the relationships between its various forms,

Convinced that adequate prevention and rehabilitation programmes are fundamental to an effective crime control strategy and that such programmes should take into account social and economic factors that may make people more vulnerable to and likely to engage in criminal behaviour,

Stressing that a fair, responsible, ethical and efficient criminal justice system is an important factor in the promotion of economic and social development and of human security,

Aware of the promise of restorative approaches to justice that aim to reduce crime and promote the healing of victims, offenders and communities,

Having assembled at the Tenth United Nations Congress on the Prevention of Crime and the Treatment of Offenders in Vienna from 10 to 17 April 2000 to decide to take more effective concerted action, in a spirit of cooperation, to combat the world crime problem,

Declare as follows:

1. We note with appreciation the results of the regional preparatory meetings for the Tenth United Nations Congress on the Prevention of Crime and the Treatment of Offenders.

2. We reaffirm the goals of the United Nations in the field of crime prevention and criminal justice, specifically the reduction of criminality, more efficient and effective law enforcement and administration of justice, respect for human rights and fundamental freedoms, and promotion of the highest standards of fairness, humanity and professional conduct.

3. We emphasize the responsibility of each State to establish and maintain a fair, responsible, ethical and efficient criminal justice system.

4. We recognize the necessity of closer coordination and cooperation among States in combating the world crime problem, bearing in mind that action against it is a common and shared responsibility. In this regard, we acknowledge the need to develop and promote technical cooperation activities to assist States in their efforts to strengthen their domestic criminal justice systems and their capacity for international cooperation.

5. We shall accord high priority to the completion of the negotiation of the United Nations Convention against Transnational Organized Crime and the protocols thereto, taking into account the concerns of all States.

6. We support efforts to assist States in capacity-building, including in obtaining training and technical assistance and in developing legislation, regulations and expertise, with a view to facilitating the implementation of the Convention and the protocols thereto.

7. Consistent with the goals of the Convention and the protocols thereto, we shall endeavour:

(*a*) To incorporate a crime prevention component into national and international development strategies;

(*b*) To intensify bilateral and multilateral cooperation, including technical cooperation, in the areas to be covered by the Convention and the protocols thereto;

(*c*) To enhance donor cooperation in areas with crime prevention aspects;

(*d*) To strengthen the capability of the United Nations Centre for International Crime Prevention, as well as the United Nations Crime Prevention and Criminal Justice Programme network, to assist States, at their request, in building capacity in areas to be covered by the Convention and the protocols thereto.

8. We welcome the efforts being made by the United Nations Centre for International Crime Prevention to develop, in cooperation with the United Nations Interregional Crime and Justice Research Institute, a comprehensive global overview of organized crime as a reference tool and to assist Governments in policy and programme development.

9. We reaffirm our continued support for and commitment to the United Nations and to the United Nations Crime Prevention and Criminal Justice Programme, especially the Commission on Crime Prevention and Criminal Justice and the United Nations Centre for International Crime Prevention, the United Nations Interregional Crime and Justice Research Institute and the institutes of the Programme network, and resolve to strengthen the Programme further through sustained funding, as appropriate.

10. We undertake to strengthen international cooperation in order to create a conducive environment for the fight against organized crime, promoting growth and sustainable development and eradicating poverty and unemployment.

11. We commit ourselves to taking into account and addressing, within the United Nations Crime Prevention and Criminal Justice Programme, as well as within national crime prevention and criminal justice strategies, any disparate impact of programmes and policies on women and men.

12. We also commit ourselves to the development of action-oriented policy recommendations based on the special needs of women as criminal justice practitioners, victims, prisoners and offenders.

13. We emphasize that effective action for crime prevention and criminal justice requires the involvement, as partners and actors, of Governments, national, regional, interregional and international institutions, intergovernmental and non-governmental organizations and various segments of civil society, including the mass media and the private sector, as well as the recognition of their respective roles and contributions.

14. We commit ourselves to the development of more effective ways of collaborating with one another with a view to eradicating the scourge of trafficking in persons, especially women and children, and the smuggling of migrants. We shall also consider supporting the global programme against trafficking in persons developed by the United Nations Centre for International Crime Prevention and the United Nations Interregional Crime and Justice Research Institute, which is subject to close consultation with States and review by the Commission on Crime Prevention and Criminal Justice, and we establish 2005 as the target year for achieving a significant decrease in the incidence of those crimes worldwide and, where that is not attained, for assessing the actual implementation of the measures advocated.

15. We also commit ourselves to the enhancement of international cooperation and mutual legal assistance to curb illicit manufacturing of and trafficking in firearms, their parts and components and ammunition, and we establish 2005 as the target year for achieving a significant decrease in their incidence worldwide.

16. We further commit ourselves to taking enhanced international action against corruption, building on the United Nations Declaration against Corruption and Bribery in International Commercial Transactions, the International Code of Conduct for Public Officials, relevant regional conventions and regional and global forums. We stress the urgent need to develop an effective international legal instrument against corruption, independent of the United Nations Convention against Transnational Organized Crime, and we invite the Commission on Crime Prevention and Criminal Justice to request the Secretary-General to submit to it at its tenth session, in consultation with States, a thorough review and analysis of all relevant international instruments and recommendations as part of the preparatory work for the development of such an instrument. We shall consider supporting the global programme against corruption developed by the United Nations Centre for International Crime Prevention and the United Nations Interregional Crime and Justice Research Institute, which is subject to close consultation with States and review by the Commission on Crime Prevention and Criminal Justice.

17. We reaffirm that combating money-laundering and the criminal economy constitutes a major element of the strategies against organized crime, established as a principle in the Naples Political Declaration and Global Action Plan against Organized Transnational Crime, adopted by the World Ministerial Conference on Organized Transnational Crime, held at Naples, Italy, from 21 to 23 November 1994. We are convinced that the success of this action rests upon setting up broad regimes and coordinating appropriate mechanisms to combat the laundering of the proceeds of crime, including the provision of support to initiatives focusing on States and territories offering offshore financial services that allow the laundering of the proceeds of crime.

18. We decide to develop action-oriented policy recommendations on the prevention and control of computer-related crime, and we invite the Commission on Crime Prevention and Criminal Justice to undertake work in this regard, taking into account the ongoing work in other forums. We also commit ourselves to working towards enhancing our ability to prevent, investigate and prosecute high-technology and computer-related crime.

19. We note that acts of violence and terrorism continue to be of grave concern. In conformity with the Charter of the United Nations and taking into account all the relevant General Assembly resolutions, we shall together, in conjunction with our other efforts to prevent and to combat terrorism, take effective, resolute and speedy measures with respect to preventing and combating criminal activities carried out for the purpose of furthering terrorism in all its forms and manifestations. With this in view, we undertake to do our utmost to foster universal adherence to the international instruments concerned with the fight against terrorism.

20. We also note that racial discrimination, xenophobia and related forms of intolerance continue, and we recognize the importance of taking steps to incorporate into international crime prevention strategies and norms measures to prevent and combat crime associated with racism, racial discrimination, xenophobia and related forms of intolerance.

21. We affirm our determination to combat violence stemming from intolerance on the basis of ethnicity, and we resolve to make a strong contribution, in the area of crime prevention and criminal justice, to the planned World Conference against Racism, Racial Discrimination, Xenophobia and Related Intolerance.

22. We recognize that the United Nations standards and norms in crime prevention and criminal justice contribute to efforts to deal with crime effectively. We also recognize the importance of prison reform, the independence of the judiciary and the prosecution authorities, and the International Code of Conduct for Public Officials. We shall endeavour, as appropriate, to use and apply the United Nations standards and norms in crime prevention and criminal justice in national law and practice. We undertake to review relevant legislation and administrative procedures, as appropriate, with a view to providing the necessary education and training to the officials concerned and ensuring the necessary strengthening of institutions entrusted with the administration of criminal justice.

23. We also recognize the value of the model treaties on international cooperation in criminal matters as important tools for the development of international cooperation, and we invite the Commission on Crime Prevention and Criminal Justice to call upon the United Nations Centre for International Crime Prevention to update the *Compendium of United Nations Standards and Norms in Crime Prevention and Criminal Justice* in order to provide the most up-to-date versions of the model treaties to States seeking to utilize them.

24. We further recognize with great concern that juveniles in difficult circumstances are often at risk of becoming delinquent or easy candidates for recruitment by criminal groups, including groups involved in transnational organized crime, and we commit ourselves to undertaking countermeasures to prevent this growing phenomenon and to including, where necessary, provisions for juvenile justice in national development plans and international development strategies and to including the administration of juvenile justice in our funding policies for development cooperation.

25. We recognize that comprehensive crime prevention strategies at the international, national, regional and local levels must address the root causes and risk factors related to crime and victimization through social, economic, health, educational and justice policies. We urge the development of such strategies, aware of the proven success of prevention initiatives in numerous States and confident that crime can be reduced by applying and sharing our collective expertise.

26. We commit ourselves to according priority to containing the growth and overcrowding of pre-trial and detention prison populations, as appropriate, by promoting safe and effective alternatives to incarceration.

27. We decide to introduce, where appropriate, national, regional and international action plans in support of victims of crime, such as mechanisms for mediation and restorative justice, and we establish 2002 as a target date for States to review their relevant practices, to develop further victim support services and awareness campaigns on the rights of victims and to consider the establishment of funds for victims, in ad-

dition to developing and implementing witness protection policies.

28. We encourage the development of restorative justice policies, procedures and programmes that are respectful of the rights, needs and interests of victims, offenders, communities and all other parties.

29. We invite the Commission on Crime Prevention and Criminal Justice to design specific measures for the implementation of and follow-up to the commitments that we have undertaken in the present Declaration.

ECONOMIC AND SOCIAL COUNCIL ACTION

On 27 July [meeting 43], the Economic and Social Council, on the recommendation of the Commission on Crime Prevention and Criminal Justice [E/2000/30], adopted **resolution 2000/12** without vote [agenda item 14 *(c)*].

Follow-up to the Tenth United Nations Congress on the Prevention of Crime and the Treatment of Offenders

The Economic and Social Council

Recommends to the General Assembly the adoption of the following draft resolution:

[For text, see General Assembly resolution 55/60 below.]

GENERAL ASSEMBLY ACTION

On 4 December [meeting 81], the General Assembly, on the recommendation of the Third Committee [A/55/593], adopted **resolution 55/60** without vote [agenda item 105].

Follow-up to the Tenth United Nations Congress on the Prevention of Crime and the Treatment of Offenders

The General Assembly,

Recalling its resolution 54/125 of 17 December 1999,

Taking note with appreciation of the results of the Tenth United Nations Congress on the Prevention of Crime and the Treatment of Offenders, including the Vienna Declaration on Crime and Justice: Meeting the Challenges of the Twenty-first Century, adopted by the Tenth Congress during its high-level segment, which were considered by the Commission on Crime Prevention and Criminal Justice at its ninth session, held in Vienna from 18 to 20 April 2000,

1. *Urges* Governments, in their efforts to prevent and combat crime, especially transnational crime, and to maintain well-functioning criminal justice systems, to be guided by the results of the Tenth United Nations Congress on the Prevention of Crime and the Treatment of Offenders;

2. *Requests* the Commission on Crime Prevention and Criminal Justice to continue at its tenth session its consideration of the findings and recommendations embodied in the Vienna Declaration on Crime and Justice: Meeting the Challenges of the Twenty-first Century adopted by the Tenth Congress and, as appropriate, the report of the Tenth Congress, and to take appropriate action;

3. *Requests* the Secretary-General to prepare, in consultation with Member States, draft plans of action to include specific measures for the implementation of and follow-up to the commitments undertaken in the Declaration for consideration and action by the Commission at its tenth session.

Commission on Crime Prevention and Criminal Justice

The Commission on Crime Prevention and Criminal Justice, at its ninth session (Vienna, 18-20 April) [E/2000/30], recommended the adoption of three draft resolutions by the General Assembly, and two draft resolutions and one draft decision by the Economic and Social Council.

The Commission brought to the Council's attention its resolution on strategic management [res. 9/1], by which the Commission decided that the theme of its tenth (2001) session would be progress made in global action against corruption.

By **decision 2000/239** of 27 July, the Council took note of the report of the Commission on its ninth session and approved the provisional agenda and documentation for the tenth session.

Note by Secretariat. An April note by the Secretariat [E/2000/3] informed the Commission that the Secretary-General had issued his sixth quinquennial report on capital punishment and implementation of the safeguards guaranteeing protection of the rights of those facing the death penalty (see p. 672).

UN Crime Prevention and Criminal Justice Programme

A July report of the Secretary-General [A/55/119] provided an overview of progress made in implementing General Assembly resolution 54/131 [YUN 1999, p. 1052] on strengthening the UN Crime Prevention and Criminal Justice Programme. It updated information contained in a February report of the Executive Director of the Office for Drug Control and Crime Prevention [E/CN.15/2000/2].

The report noted that advances had been made in reinforcing reform measures to combat uncivil elements of society and achieve synergy in fighting crime and drug abuse. Further progress was made in strengthening the Programme's operations, particularly the global programmes against corruption, trafficking in human beings and transnational organized crime. Secretariat support for the programmes and for developing international legal instruments continued, and traditional crime and justice issues were addressed. Those measures had led to greater donor confidence, as evidenced through increased voluntary contributions to the UN Crime Prevention and Criminal Justice Fund, which in turn enabled the Programme to expand its operational activities.

The report described action taken at the Tenth Crime Congress (see p. 1040) and the Commission's ninth session (see above) and noted that significant progress had been achieved in drafting a Convention against Transnational Organized Crime and related Protocols (see p. 1048).

Regarding the technical cooperation activities of the Centre for International Crime Prevention, as at 30 June the total value of ongoing projects amounted to $5.4 million for: an assessment of corruption in Hungary; support to Lebanon's anti-corruption strategy and strengthening its legislative and institutional capacity for juvenile justice; assistance to the Philippines for coalitions against trafficking in human beings; the control and prevention of drugs and related organized crime in the Russian Federation; measures to counteract domestic violence and organized crime and for capacity-building in the area of youth justice in South Africa; preventing and controlling economic and financial crime in the former Yugoslav Republic of Macedonia; and a global programme relating to the UN transnational organized crime survey. Under the global programme against corruption, following assessment missions, pilot projects were being finalized for Benin, Nicaragua, Nigeria, South Africa and Uganda. An expert group meeting (Vienna, 13-14 April) reviewed and strengthened an anti-corruption tool kit. In collaboration with Transparency International, the Centre organized a meeting of chief justices on the global programme's component element of strengthening judicial integrity. The Centre advanced the implementation of the global programme against trafficking in human beings, in cooperation with the UN Interregional Crime and Justice Research Institute (UNICRI). Two missions were undertaken to Brazil in connection with a project to assess routes and methods used by organized crime groups to traffic human beings in the Latin American region. A project was being developed to assess trafficking flows and countermeasures in Benin, Nigeria and Togo and support government efforts to combat the disappearance of children believed to be sold by traffickers as slave labour. Progress was made in implementing the first phase of global studies on transnational organized crime, aimed at assessing transnational organized crime groups worldwide according to their level of danger. Information was collected on the most dangerous organized crime groups active in 12 countries (Australia, Canada, Colombia, Czech Republic, Germany, Italy, Japan, Netherlands, Russian Federation, South Africa, United Kingdom, United States) and one region (Caribbean). In cooperation with UNICRI, the Centre drew up a project aimed at analysing and assessing the threat posed by Nigerian criminal networks active in Côte d'Ivoire, Ghana, Nigeria and Senegal. Another project aimed at analysing and assessing transnational organized crime in Central Asia.

Projects outside the global programmes included a juvenile justice programme in Guatemala, a project to support the establishment of a unified data bank, and a project to assess the situation of and enhance cooperation in combating organized crime among countries of the Commonwealth of Independent States. A prison reform project was designed for the Caribbean region, as was a project on crime prevention in Senegal.

Contributions and pledges to the UN Crime Prevention and Criminal Justice Fund during 1999 and 2000, as at 30 June 2000, totalled $3.3 million and $1.6 million, respectively.

In an April report [A/55/6 (Prog. 12)], the Secretary-General discussed the proposed medium-term plan for 2002-2005 on crime prevention and criminal justice, noting that its overall objective was to strengthen international cooperation and assistance to Governments in tackling crime problems, particularly those posed by transnational organized crime, trafficking in persons, and economic and financial crime, including money-laundering, corruption and terrorism.

1998 OIOS report

On 7 April, on the recommendation of the Fifth (Administrative and Budgetary) Committee, the General Assembly adopted **resolution 54/257**, by which it took note of the 1998 report of the Office of Internal Oversight Services (OIOS) [YUN 1998, p. 1035] on the review of programme management in the Crime Prevention and Criminal Justice Division, which had become the Centre for International Crime Prevention. The Assembly reaffirmed that the discontinuation of mandates on crime prevention and criminal justice was within the prerogative of the pertinent legislative bodies.

GENERAL ASSEMBLY ACTION

On 4 December [meeting 81], the General Assembly, on the recommendation of the Third Committee [A/55/593], adopted **resolution 55/64** without vote [agenda item 105].

Strengthening of the United Nations Crime Prevention and Criminal Justice Programme, in particular its technical cooperation capacity

The General Assembly,

Recalling its resolution 46/152 of 18 December 1991 on the creation of an effective United Nations crime prevention and criminal justice programme, in which it approved the statement of principles and programme of action annexed to that resolution,

Emphasizing the role of the United Nations in the field of crime prevention and criminal justice, specifically the reduction of criminality, more efficient and effective law enforcement and administration of justice, respect for human rights and promotion of the highest standards of fairness, humanity and professional conduct,

Convinced of the desirability of closer coordination and cooperation among States in combating crime, including drug-related crimes such as money-laundering, illicit arms trade and terrorist crimes, bearing in mind the role that could be played by both the United Nations and regional organizations in this respect,

Recognizing the urgent need to increase technical cooperation activities to assist countries, in particular developing countries and countries with economies in transition, with their efforts in translating United Nations policy guidelines into practice,

Recognizing also the need to maintain a balance in the technical cooperation capacity of the United Nations Centre for International Crime Prevention of the United Nations Office for Drug Control and Crime Prevention between the immediate priority of the United Nations Convention against Transnational Organized Crime and the protocols thereto and other priorities identified by the Economic and Social Council,

Recalling its relevant resolutions in which it requested the Secretary-General, as a matter of urgency, to provide the United Nations Crime Prevention and Criminal Justice Programme with sufficient resources for the full implementation of its mandate, in conformity with the high priority attached to the Programme,

Bearing in mind the Vienna Declaration on Crime and Justice: Meeting the Challenges of the Twenty-first Century, which was adopted by the Tenth United Nations Congress on the Prevention of Crime and the Treatment of Offenders, and endorsed by the General Assembly in its resolution 55/59 of 4 December 2000, in which Member States renewed their commitment to combat organized crime in all its forms and manifestations and to promote crime prevention in all its areas,

Welcoming the successful completion of the work of the Ad Hoc Committee on the Elaboration of a Convention against Transnational Organized Crime, established by its resolution 53/111 of 9 December 1998, and the progress achieved in the elaboration of the three supplementary protocols, namely the Protocol against the Smuggling of Migrants by Land, Sea and Air, the Protocol against the Illicit Manufacturing of and Trafficking in Firearms, Their Parts and Components and Ammunition and the Protocol to Prevent, Suppress and Punish Trafficking in Persons, Especially Women and Children,

1. *Takes note with appreciation* of the report of the Secretary-General on the progress made in the implementation of General Assembly resolution 54/131 of 17 December 1999;

2. *Reaffirms* the importance of the United Nations Crime Prevention and Criminal Justice Programme in promoting effective action to strengthen international cooperation in crime prevention and criminal justice, in responding to the needs of the international community in the face of both national and transnational criminality and in assisting Member States in achieving the goals of preventing crime within and among States and improving the response to crime;

3. *Also reaffirms* the role of the United Nations Centre for International Crime Prevention in providing to Member States, upon request, technical cooperation, advisory services and other forms of assistance in the field of crime prevention and criminal justice, including in the area of prevention and control of organized crime;

4. *Notes* the programme of work of the Centre, including the three global programmes addressing, respectively, trafficking in human beings, corruption and organized crime, formulated on the basis of close consultations with Member States and review by the Commission on Crime Prevention and Criminal Justice, and calls upon the Secretary-General further to strengthen the Centre by providing it with the resources necessary for the full implementation of its mandate;

5. *Supports* the high priority given to technical cooperation and advisory services in the field of crime prevention and criminal justice, including in the area of prevention and control of transnational organized crime, and stresses the need to enhance the operational activities of the Centre to assist, in particular, developing countries and countries with economies in transition;

6. *Welcomes* the increased number of technical assistance projects in the field of juvenile justice, reflecting an increased awareness among Member States of the importance of juvenile justice reform in establishing and maintaining stable societies and the rule of law;

7. *Invites* all States to support, through voluntary contributions to the United Nations Crime Prevention and Criminal Justice Fund, the operational activities of the United Nations Crime Prevention and Criminal Justice Programme;

8. *Encourages* relevant programmes, funds and organizations of the United Nations system, in particular the United Nations Development Programme, international financial institutions, in particular the World Bank, and regional and national funding agencies to support the technical operational activities of the Centre;

9. *Urges* States and funding agencies to review, as appropriate, their funding policies for development assistance and to include a crime prevention and criminal justice component in such assistance;

10. *Welcomes* the efforts undertaken by the Commission on Crime Prevention and Criminal Justice to exercise more vigorously its mandated function of resource mobilization, and calls upon the Commission to strengthen further its activities in this direction;

11. *Expresses its appreciation* to non-governmental organizations and other relevant sectors of civil society for their support to the United Nations Crime Prevention and Criminal Justice Programme;

12. *Welcomes* the efforts of the Executive Director of the United Nations Office for Drug Control and Crime Prevention to enhance the synergies between the United Nations International Drug Control Programme and the United Nations Centre for International Crime Prevention, in conformity with the reform proposals of the Secretary-General;

13. *Requests* the Secretary-General to take all necessary measures to assist the Commission on Crime Pre-

vention and Criminal Justice, as the principal policy-making body in this field, in performing its activities, including cooperation and coordination with other relevant bodies, such as the Commission on Narcotic Drugs, the Commission on Human Rights, the Commission on the Status of Women and the Commission for Social Development;

14. *Invites* States to make adequate voluntary contributions to the United Nations Crime Prevention and Criminal Justice Fund in order to strengthen the capacity of the Centre to provide technical assistance to requesting States for the implementation of the commitments entered into at the Tenth United Nations Congress on the Prevention of Crime and the Treatment of Offenders and, in particular, to implement programmes designed to combat and prevent the trafficking in human beings, the smuggling of migrants and corruption, and to study and bring about action to combat and prevent transnational organized crime;

15. *Encourages* States to begin making adequate and regular voluntary contributions for the implementation of the United Nations Convention against Transnational Organized Crime and the protocols thereto, which will be open for signature in Palermo, Italy, on 12 December 2000, through the United Nations funding mechanism specifically designed for that purpose in the Convention;

16. *Requests* the Secretary-General to take all necessary measures and provide adequate support to the Centre during the biennium 2002-2003 so as to enable it to promote the speedy entry into force of the Convention and the protocols thereto;

17. *Welcomes* the decision of the Commission on Crime Prevention and Criminal Justice to mainstream a gender perspective into its activities and its request to the Secretariat that a gender perspective be integrated into all activities of the Centre;

18. *Requests* the Secretary-General to submit a report on the implementation of the present resolution to the General Assembly at its fifty-sixth session.

On 23 December, the Assembly decided that the agenda item on crime prevention and criminal justice would remain for consideration during its resumed fifty-fifth (2001) session (**decision 55/458**).

UN African crime prevention institute

In response to General Assembly resolution 54/130 [YUN 1999, p. 1056], the Secretary-General, in July [A/55/156], updated information on the activities, operations and funding of the African Institute for the Prevention of Crime and the Treatment of Offenders (UNAFRI).

UNAFRI implemented the final phase of a project on regional extradition and mutual legal assistance and undertook the second phase of a project on trafficking in firearms and ammunition in Africa. The Institute, in cooperation with other concerned agencies, was developing a programme to counter the proliferation of illicit small arms in Africa. Studies on penal reform continued, as did the development of strategies

to assist Governments in implementing UN standards and norms related to juvenile justice. A crime victimization survey continued to be implemented in cooperation with the University of South Africa, and a survey report on Lesotho was published.

Although UNAFRI continued to receive political support from its member States, the Governing Board, the General Assembly, the Commission and the Tenth Crime Congress, its financial situation remained precarious, constraining its capacity to deliver effective and comprehensive services to African countries. The sixth session of the Institute's Governing Board (Kampala, Uganda, 29-30 May) approved the proposed programme of work, including measures to address the serious financial situation. UNAFRI was directed to adopt innovative and attractive programmes designed as a package to enhance their market appeal. The Director was requested to undertake an evaluation of the Institute to serve as a basis for a review of its mission, functions, funding and support, and methods of work.

The Institute's total resources for 2000 amounted to $423,689, which came from member States' assessed contributions, a UN grant and specific project grants, and income received from the rental of parts of its premises and facilities, in addition to other sources. As at 30 June, member States' outstanding balances totalled some $2.5 million for the period 1989 to 2000. Contributions had been received from 15 members, while 13 had never paid.

GENERAL ASSEMBLY ACTION

On 4 December [meeting 81], the General Assembly, on the recommendation of the Third Committee [A/55/593], adopted **resolution 55/62** without vote [agenda item 105].

United Nations African Institute for the Prevention of Crime and the Treatment of Offenders

The General Assembly,

Recalling its resolution 54/130 of 17 December 1999 and all other relevant resolutions,

Taking note of the report of the Secretary-General,

Bearing in mind the urgent need to establish effective crime prevention strategies for Africa, as well as the importance of law enforcement agencies and the judiciary at the regional and subregional levels,

Noting that the financial situation of the United Nations African Institute for the Prevention of Crime and the Treatment of Offenders has greatly affected its capacity to deliver its services to African Member States in an effective and comprehensive manner,

1. *Commends* the United Nations African Institute for the Prevention of Crime and the Treatment of Offenders for its efforts to promote and coordinate regional technical cooperation activities related to crime prevention and criminal justice systems in Africa;

2. *Also commends* the Secretary-General for his efforts to mobilize the financial resources necessary to provide the Institute with the core professional staff required to enable it to function effectively in the fulfilment of its mandated obligations;

3. *Reiterates* the need to strengthen further the capacity of the Institute to support national mechanisms for crime prevention and criminal justice in African countries;

4. *Urges* the States members of the Institute to make every possible effort to meet their obligations to the Institute;

5. *Calls upon* all Member States and non-governmental organizations to adopt concrete practical measures to support the Institute in the development of the requisite capacity and implement its programmes and activities aimed at strengthening crime prevention and criminal justice systems in Africa;

6. *Requests* the Secretary-General to intensify efforts to mobilize all relevant entities of the United Nations system to provide the necessary financial and technical support to the Institute to enable it to fulfil its mandate;

7. *Also requests* the Secretary-General to deploy his efforts to mobilize the financial resources necessary to maintain the Institute with the core professional staff required to enable it to function effectively in the fulfilment of its mandated obligations;

8. *Calls upon* the United Nations Crime Prevention and Criminal Justice Programme and the United Nations International Drug Control Programme to work closely with the Institute;

9. *Requests* the Secretary-General to enhance the promotion of regional cooperation, coordination and collaboration in the fight against crime, especially in its transnational dimension, which cannot be dealt with adequately by national action alone;

10. *Also requests* the Secretary-General to make concrete proposals, including the provision of additional core professional staff, in order to strengthen the programmes and activities of the Institute and to report to the General Assembly at its fifty-sixth session on the implementation of the present resolution.

Transnational crime

Efforts were made in 2000 to complete the drafting of an international instrument against organized transnational crime, central to the implementation of the Naples Political Declaration and Global Action Plan against Organized Transnational Crime adopted by the 1994 World Ministerial Conference on Organized Transnational Crime [YUN 1994, p. 1160] and in accordance with General Assembly resolution 54/126 [YUN 1999, p. 1058]. To that end, the Ad Hoc Committee on the Elaboration of a Convention against Transnational Organized Crime finalized, in 2000, the Convention and two of the three supplementary legal instruments: the Protocol to Prevent, Suppress and Punish Trafficking in Persons, Especially Women and Children and the Protocol against the Smuggling of Migrants by Land, Sea

and Air. The Committee was unable to achieve consensus on the draft Protocol against the Illicit Manufacturing of and Trafficking in Firearms, Their Parts and Components and Ammunition.

International convention

In 2000, the Ad Hoc Committee on the Elaboration of a Convention against Transnational Organized Crime held five sessions in Vienna, during which it finalized the Convention and the draft Protocol against the Smuggling of Migrants by Land, Sea and Air, and the draft Protocol to Prevent, Suppress and Punish Trafficking in Persons, Especially Women and Children: 17-28 January [A/AC.254/25]; 21 February–3 March [A/AC.254/28]; 5-16 June [A/AC.254/31]; 17-28 July [A/AC.254/34]; and 2-29 October [A/AC.254/38]. The Ad Hoc Committee was unable to finalize the draft Protocol against the Illicit Manufacturing of and Trafficking in Firearms, Their Parts and Components and Ammunition, due to a lack of consensus. Many delegations emphasized the importance of finalizing the draft Protocol prior to the 2001 Conference on the Illicit Trade in Small Arms and Light Weapons in All its Aspects (see p. 518). The reports of the Ad Hoc Committee on its 1999 [YUN 1999, p. 1057] and 2000 sessions were summarized in a November report [A/55/383].

At a High-level Political Signing Conference in Palermo, Italy [A/CONF.195/2 & Corr.1], the Convention and its Protocols thereto were opened for signature from 12 to 15 December, and thereafter in New York until 12 December 2002. As at 31 December, 124 States had signed the Convention; 81, the Protocol on illegal trafficking in persons, especially women and children; and 78, the Protocol on smuggling migrants.

GENERAL ASSEMBLY ACTION

On 15 November [meeting 62], the General Assembly, on the recommendation of the Ad Hoc Committee on the Elaboration of a Convention against Transnational Organized Crime [A/55/383], adopted **resolution 55/25** without vote [agenda item 105].

United Nations Convention against Transnational Organized Crime

The General Assembly,

Recalling its resolution 53/111 of 9 December 1998, in which it decided to establish an open-ended intergovernmental ad hoc committee for the purpose of elaborating a comprehensive international convention against transnational organized crime and of discussing the elaboration, as appropriate, of international instruments addressing trafficking in women and children, combating the illicit manufacturing of and trafficking in firearms, their parts and components and ammunition, and illegal trafficking in and transporting of migrants, including by sea,

Recalling also its resolution 54/126 of 17 December 1999, in which it requested the Ad Hoc Committee on the Elaboration of a Convention against Transnational Organized Crime to continue its work, in accordance with resolutions 53/111 and 53/114 of 9 December 1998, and to intensify that work in order to complete it in 2000,

Recalling further its resolution 54/129 of 17 December 1999, in which it accepted with appreciation the offer of the Government of Italy to host a high-level political signing conference in Palermo for the purpose of signing the United Nations Convention against Transnational Organized Crime (Palermo Convention) and the protocols thereto, and requested the Secretary-General to schedule the conference for a period of up to one week before the end of the Millennium Assembly in 2000,

Expressing its appreciation to the Government of Poland for submitting to it at its fifty-first session a first draft United Nations convention against transnational organized crime and for hosting the meeting of the inter-sessional open-ended intergovernmental group of experts, established pursuant to resolution 52/85 of 12 December 1997, on the elaboration of a preliminary draft of a possible comprehensive international convention against transnational organized crime, held in Warsaw from 2 to 6 February 1998,

Expressing its appreciation to the Government of Argentina for hosting the informal preparatory meeting of the Ad Hoc Committee, held in Buenos Aires from 31 August to 4 September 1998,

Expressing its appreciation to the Government of Thailand for hosting the Asia-Pacific Ministerial Seminar on Building Capacities for Fighting Transnational Organized Crime, held in Bangkok on 20 and 21 March 2000,

Deeply concerned by the negative economic and social implications related to organized criminal activities, and convinced of the urgent need to strengthen cooperation to prevent and combat such activities more effectively at the national, regional and international levels,

Noting with deep concern the growing links between transnational organized crime and terrorist crimes, taking into account the Charter of the United Nations and the relevant resolutions of the General Assembly,

Determined to deny safe havens to those who engage in transnational organized crime by prosecuting their crimes wherever they occur and by cooperating at the international level,

Strongly convinced that the United Nations Convention against Transnational Organized Crime will constitute an effective tool and the necessary legal framework for international cooperation in combating, inter alia, such criminal activities as money-laundering, corruption, illicit trafficking in endangered species of wild flora and fauna, offences against cultural heritage and the growing links between transnational organized crime and terrorist crimes,

1. *Takes note* of the report of the Ad Hoc Committee on the Elaboration of a Convention against Transnational Organized Crime, which carried out its work at the headquarters of the United Nations Office for Drug Control and Crime Prevention in Vienna, and commends the Ad Hoc Committee for its work;

2. *Adopts* the United Nations Convention against Transnational Organized Crime and the Protocol to Prevent, Suppress and Punish Trafficking in Persons, Especially Women and Children, supplementing the United Nations Convention against Transnational Organized Crime, and the Protocol against the Smuggling of Migrants by Land, Sea and Air, supplementing the United Nations Convention against Transnational Organized Crime annexed to the present resolution, and opens them for signature at the High-level Political Signing Conference to be held in Palermo, Italy, from 12 to 15 December 2000 in accordance with resolution 54/129;

3. *Requests* the Secretary-General to prepare a comprehensive report on the High-level Political Signing Conference to be held in Palermo in accordance with resolution 54/129;

4. *Notes* that the Ad Hoc Committee has not yet completed its work on the draft Protocol against the Illicit Manufacturing of and Trafficking in Firearms, Their Parts and Components and Ammunition, supplementing the United Nations Convention against Transnational Organized Crime;

5. *Requests* the Ad Hoc Committee to continue its work in relation to this draft Protocol, in accordance with resolutions 53/111, 53/114 and 54/126, and to finalize such work as soon as possible;

6. *Calls upon* all States to recognize the links between transnational organized criminal activities and acts of terrorism, taking into account the relevant General Assembly resolutions, and to apply the United Nations Convention against Transnational Organized Crime in combating all forms of criminal activity, as provided therein;

7. *Recommends* that the Ad Hoc Committee established by the General Assembly in its resolution 51/210 of 17 December 1996, which is beginning its deliberations with a view to developing a comprehensive convention on international terrorism, pursuant to resolution 54/110 of 9 December 1999, should take into consideration the provisions of the United Nations Convention against Transnational Organized Crime;

8. *Urges* all States and regional economic organizations to sign and ratify the United Nations Convention against Transnational Organized Crime and the protocols thereto as soon as possible in order to ensure the speedy entry into force of the Convention and the protocols thereto;

9. *Decides* that, until the Conference of the Parties to the Convention established pursuant to the United Nations Convention against Transnational Organized Crime decides otherwise, the account referred to in article 30 of the Convention will be operated within the United Nations Crime Prevention and Criminal Justice Fund, and encourages Member States to begin making adequate voluntary contributions to the above-mentioned account for the provision to developing countries and countries with economies in transition of the technical assistance that they might require for implementation of the Convention and the protocols thereto, including for the preparatory measures needed for that implementation;

10. *Also decides* that the Ad Hoc Committee on the Elaboration of a Convention against Transnational Organized Crime will complete its tasks arising from the elaboration of the United Nations Convention against

Transnational Organized Crime by holding a meeting well before the convening of the first session of the Conference of the Parties to the Convention, in order to prepare the draft text of the rules of procedure for the Conference of the Parties and other rules and mechanisms described in article 32 of the Convention, which will be communicated to the Conference of the Parties at its first session for consideration and action;

11. _Requests_ the Secretary-General to designate the Centre for International Crime Prevention of the United Nations Office for Drug Control and Crime Prevention to serve as the secretariat for the Conference of the Parties to the Convention in accordance with article 33 of the Convention;

12. _Also requests_ the Secretary-General to provide the Centre for International Crime Prevention with the resources necessary to enable it to promote in an effective manner the expeditious entry into force of the United Nations Convention against Transnational Organized Crime and to discharge the functions of secretariat of the Conference of the Parties to the Convention, and to support the Ad Hoc Committee in its work pursuant to paragraph 10 above.

ANNEX I
United Nations Convention against
Transnational Organized Crime

Article 1
Statement of purpose

The purpose of this Convention is to promote cooperation to prevent and combat transnational organized crime more effectively.

Article 2
Use of terms

For the purposes of this Convention:

(a) "Organized criminal group" shall mean a structured group of three or more persons, existing for a period of time and acting in concert with the aim of committing one or more serious crimes or offences established in accordance with this Convention, in order to obtain, directly or indirectly, a financial or other material benefit;

(b) "Serious crime" shall mean conduct constituting an offence punishable by a maximum deprivation of liberty of at least four years or a more serious penalty;

(c) "Structured group" shall mean a group that is not randomly formed for the immediate commission of an offence and that does not need to have formally defined roles for its members, continuity of its membership or a developed structure;

(d) "Property" shall mean assets of every kind, whether corporeal or incorporeal, movable or immovable, tangible or intangible, and legal documents or instruments evidencing title to, or interest in, such assets;

(e) "Proceeds of crime" shall mean any property derived from or obtained, directly or indirectly, through the commission of an offence;

(f) "Freezing" or "seizure" shall mean temporarily prohibiting the transfer, conversion, disposition or movement of property or temporarily assuming custody or control of property on the basis of an order issued by a court or other competent authority;

(g) "Confiscation", which includes forfeiture where applicable, shall mean the permanent deprivation of property by order of a court or other competent authority;

(h) "Predicate offence" shall mean any offence as a result of which proceeds have been generated that may become the subject of an offence as defined in article 6 of this Convention;

(i) "Controlled delivery" shall mean the technique of allowing illicit or suspect consignments to pass out of, through or into the territory of one or more States, with the knowledge and under the supervision of their competent authorities, with a view to the investigation of an offence and the identification of persons involved in the commission of the offence;

(j) "Regional economic integration organization" shall mean an organization constituted by sovereign States of a given region, to which its member States have transferred competence in respect of matters governed by this Convention and which has been duly authorized, in accordance with its internal procedures, to sign, ratify, accept, approve or accede to it; references to "States Parties" under this Convention shall apply to such organizations within the limits of their competence.

Article 3
Scope of application

1. This Convention shall apply, except as otherwise stated herein, to the prevention, investigation and prosecution of:

(a) The offences established in accordance with articles 5, 6, 8 and 23 of this Convention; and

(b) Serious crime as defined in article 2 of this Convention;

where the offence is transnational in nature and involves an organized criminal group.

2. For the purpose of paragraph 1 of this article, an offence is transnational in nature if:

(a) It is committed in more than one State;

(b) It is committed in one State but a substantial part of its preparation, planning, direction or control takes place in another State;

(c) It is committed in one State but involves an organized criminal group that engages in criminal activities in more than one State; or

(d) It is committed in one State but has substantial effects in another State.

Article 4
Protection of sovereignty

1. States Parties shall carry out their obligations under this Convention in a manner consistent with the principles of sovereign equality and territorial integrity of States and that of non-intervention in the domestic affairs of other States.

2. Nothing in this Convention entitles a State Party to undertake in the territory of another State the exercise of jurisdiction and performance of functions that are reserved exclusively for the authorities of that other State by its domestic law.

Article 5
Criminalization of participation in an organized criminal group

1. Each State Party shall adopt such legislative and other measures as may be necessary to establish as criminal offences, when committed intentionally:

(a) Either or both of the following as criminal offences distinct from those involving the attempt or completion of the criminal activity:

(i) Agreeing with one or more other persons to commit a serious crime for a purpose relating directly or indirectly to the obtaining of a financial or other material benefit and, where required by domestic law, involving an act undertaken by one of the participants in furtherance of the agreement or involving an organized criminal group;

(ii) Conduct by a person who, with knowledge of either the aim and general criminal activity of an organized criminal group or its intention to commit the crimes in question, takes an active part in:

    a. Criminal activities of the organized criminal group;

    b. Other activities of the organized criminal group in the knowledge that his or her participation will contribute to the achievement of the above-described criminal aim;

(b) Organizing, directing, aiding, abetting, facilitating or counselling the commission of serious crime involving an organized criminal group.

2. The knowledge, intent, aim, purpose or agreement referred to in paragraph 1 of this article may be inferred from objective factual circumstances.

3. States Parties whose domestic law requires involvement of an organized criminal group for purposes of the offences established in accordance with paragraph 1 *(a)* (i) of this article shall ensure that their domestic law covers all serious crimes involving organized criminal groups. Such States Parties, as well as States Parties whose domestic law requires an act in furtherance of the agreement for purposes of the offences established in accordance with paragraph 1 *(a)* (i) of this article, shall so inform the Secretary-General of the United Nations at the time of their signature or of deposit of their instrument of ratification, acceptance or approval of or accession to this Convention.

Article 6
Criminalization of the laundering of proceeds of crime

1. Each State Party shall adopt, in accordance with fundamental principles of its domestic law, such legislative and other measures as may be necessary to establish as criminal offences, when committed intentionally:

(a) (i) The conversion or transfer of property, knowing that such property is the proceeds of crime, for the purpose of concealing or disguising the illicit origin of the property or of helping any person who is involved in the commission of the predicate offence to evade the legal consequences of his or her action;

    (ii) The concealment or disguise of the true nature, source, location, disposition, movement or ownership of or rights with respect to property, knowing that such property is the proceeds of crime;

(b) Subject to the basic concepts of its legal system:

    (i) The acquisition, possession or use of property, knowing, at the time of receipt, that such property is the proceeds of crime;

    (ii) Participation in, association with or conspiracy to commit, attempts to commit and aiding, abetting, facilitating and counselling the commission of any of the offences established in accordance with this article.

2. For purposes of implementing or applying paragraph 1 of this article:

(a) Each State Party shall seek to apply paragraph 1 of this article to the widest range of predicate offences;

(b) Each State Party shall include as predicate offences all serious crime as defined in article 2 of this Convention and the offences established in accordance with articles 5, 8 and 23 of this Convention. In the case of States Parties whose legislation sets out a list of specific predicate offences, they shall, at a minimum, include in such list a comprehensive range of offences associated with organized criminal groups;

(c) For the purposes of subparagraph *(b)*, predicate offences shall include offences committed both within and outside the jurisdiction of the State Party in question. However, offences committed outside the jurisdiction of a State Party shall constitute predicate offences only when the relevant conduct is a criminal offence under the domestic law of the State where it is committed and would be a criminal offence under the domestic law of the State Party implementing or applying this article had it been committed there;

(d) Each State Party shall furnish copies of its laws that give effect to this article and of any subsequent changes to such laws or a description thereof to the Secretary-General of the United Nations;

(e) If required by fundamental principles of the domestic law of a State Party, it may be provided that the offences set forth in paragraph 1 of this article do not apply to the persons who committed the predicate offence;

(f) Knowledge, intent or purpose required as an element of an offence set forth in paragraph 1 of this article may be inferred from objective factual circumstances.

Article 7
Measures to combat money-laundering

1. Each State Party:

(a) Shall institute a comprehensive domestic regulatory and supervisory regime for banks and non-bank financial institutions and, where appropriate, other bodies particularly susceptible to money-laundering, within its competence, in order to deter and detect all forms of money-laundering, which regime shall emphasize requirements for customer identification, record-keeping and the reporting of suspicious transactions;

(b) Shall, without prejudice to articles 18 and 27 of this Convention, ensure that administrative, regulatory, law enforcement and other authorities dedicated to combating money-laundering (including, where appropriate under domestic law, judicial authorities) have the ability to cooperate and exchange information at the national and international levels within the conditions prescribed by its domestic law and, to that end, shall consider the establishment of a financial intelligence unit to serve as a national centre for the collection, analysis and dissemination of information regarding potential money-laundering.

2. States Parties shall consider implementing feasible measures to detect and monitor the movement of cash and appropriate negotiable instruments across their borders, subject to safeguards to ensure proper use of information and without impeding in any way the movement of legitimate capital. Such measures

may include a requirement that individuals and businesses report the cross-border transfer of substantial quantities of cash and appropriate negotiable instruments.

3. In establishing a domestic regulatory and supervisory regime under the terms of this article, and without prejudice to any other article of this Convention, States Parties are called upon to use as a guideline the relevant initiatives of regional, interregional and multilateral organizations against money-laundering.

4. States Parties shall endeavour to develop and promote global, regional, subregional and bilateral cooperation among judicial, law enforcement and financial regulatory authorities in order to combat money-laundering.

Article 8
Criminalization of corruption

1. Each State Party shall adopt such legislative and other measures as may be necessary to establish as criminal offences, when committed intentionally:

(a) The promise, offering or giving to a public official, directly or indirectly, of an undue advantage, for the official himself or herself or another person or entity, in order that the official act or refrain from acting in the exercise of his or her official duties;

(b) The solicitation or acceptance by a public official, directly or indirectly, of an undue advantage, for the official himself or herself or another person or entity, in order that the official act or refrain from acting in the exercise of his or her official duties.

2. Each State Party shall consider adopting such legislative and other measures as may be necessary to establish as criminal offences conduct referred to in paragraph 1 of this article involving a foreign public official or international civil servant. Likewise, each State Party shall consider establishing as criminal offences other forms of corruption.

3. Each State Party shall also adopt such measures as may be necessary to establish as a criminal offence participation as an accomplice in an offence established in accordance with this article.

4. For the purposes of paragraph 1 of this article and article 9 of this Convention, "public official" shall mean a public official or a person who provides a public service as defined in the domestic law and as applied in the criminal law of the State Party in which the person in question performs that function.

Article 9
Measures against corruption

1. In addition to the measures set forth in article 8 of this Convention, each State Party shall, to the extent appropriate and consistent with its legal system, adopt legislative, administrative or other effective measures to promote integrity and to prevent, detect and punish the corruption of public officials.

2. Each State Party shall take measures to ensure effective action by its authorities in the prevention, detection and punishment of the corruption of public officials, including providing such authorities with adequate independence to deter the exertion of inappropriate influence on their actions.

Article 10
Liability of legal persons

1. Each State Party shall adopt such measures as may be necessary, consistent with its legal principles, to establish the liability of legal persons for participation in serious crimes involving an organized criminal group and for the offences established in accordance with articles 5, 6, 8 and 23 of this Convention.

2. Subject to the legal principles of the State Party, the liability of legal persons may be criminal, civil or administrative.

3. Such liability shall be without prejudice to the criminal liability of the natural persons who have committed the offences.

4. Each State Party shall, in particular, ensure that legal persons held liable in accordance with this article are subject to effective, proportionate and dissuasive criminal or non-criminal sanctions, including monetary sanctions.

Article 11
Prosecution, adjudication and sanctions

1. Each State Party shall make the commission of an offence established in accordance with articles 5, 6, 8 and 23 of this Convention liable to sanctions that take into account the gravity of that offence.

2. Each State Party shall endeavour to ensure that any discretionary legal powers under its domestic law relating to the prosecution of persons for offences covered by this Convention are exercised to maximize the effectiveness of law enforcement measures in respect of those offences and with due regard to the need to deter the commission of such offences.

3. In the case of offences established in accordance with articles 5, 6, 8 and 23 of this Convention, each State Party shall take appropriate measures, in accordance with its domestic law and with due regard to the rights of the defence, to seek to ensure that conditions imposed in connection with decisions on release pending trial or appeal take into consideration the need to ensure the presence of the defendant at subsequent criminal proceedings.

4. Each State Party shall ensure that its courts or other competent authorities bear in mind the grave nature of the offences covered by this Convention when considering the eventuality of early release or parole of persons convicted of such offences.

5. Each State Party shall, where appropriate, establish under its domestic law a long statute of limitations period in which to commence proceedings for any offence covered by this Convention and a longer period where the alleged offender has evaded the administration of justice.

6. Nothing contained in this Convention shall affect the principle that the description of the offences established in accordance with this Convention and of the applicable legal defences or other legal principles controlling the lawfulness of conduct is reserved to the domestic law of a State Party and that such offences shall be prosecuted and punished in accordance with that law.

Article 12
Confiscation and seizure

1. States Parties shall adopt, to the greatest extent possible within their domestic legal systems, such measures as may be necessary to enable confiscation of:

(a) Proceeds of crime derived from offences covered by this Convention or property the value of which corresponds to that of such proceeds;

(b) Property, equipment or other instrumentalities used in or destined for use in offences covered by this Convention.

2. States Parties shall adopt such measures as may be necessary to enable the identification, tracing, freezing or seizure of any item referred to in paragraph 1 of this article for the purpose of eventual confiscation.

3. If proceeds of crime have been transformed or converted, in part or in full, into other property, such property shall be liable to the measures referred to in this article instead of the proceeds.

4. If proceeds of crime have been intermingled with property acquired from legitimate sources, such property shall, without prejudice to any powers relating to freezing or seizure, be liable to confiscation up to the assessed value of the intermingled proceeds.

5. Income or other benefits derived from proceeds of crime, from property into which proceeds of crime have been transformed or converted or from property with which proceeds of crime have been intermingled shall also be liable to the measures referred to in this article, in the same manner and to the same extent as proceeds of crime.

6. For the purposes of this article and article 13 of this Convention, each State Party shall empower its courts or other competent authorities to order that bank, financial or commercial records be made available or be seized. States Parties shall not decline to act under the provisions of this paragraph on the ground of bank secrecy.

7. States Parties may consider the possibility of requiring that an offender demonstrate the lawful origin of alleged proceeds of crime or other property liable to confiscation, to the extent that such a requirement is consistent with the principles of their domestic law and with the nature of the judicial and other proceedings.

8. The provisions of this article shall not be construed to prejudice the rights of bona fide third parties.

9. Nothing contained in this article shall affect the principle that the measures to which it refers shall be defined and implemented in accordance with and subject to the provisions of the domestic law of a State Party.

Article 13
International cooperation for purposes of confiscation

1. A State Party that has received a request from another State Party having jurisdiction over an offence covered by this Convention for confiscation of proceeds of crime, property, equipment or other instrumentalities referred to in article 12, paragraph 1, of this Convention situated in its territory shall, to the greatest extent possible within its domestic legal system:

(a) Submit the request to its competent authorities for the purpose of obtaining an order of confiscation and, if such an order is granted, give effect to it; or

(b) Submit to its competent authorities, with a view to giving effect to it to the extent requested, an order of confiscation issued by a court in the territory of the requesting State Party in accordance with article 12, paragraph 1, of this Convention insofar as it relates to proceeds of crime, property, equipment or other instrumentalities referred to in article 12, paragraph 1, situated in the territory of the requested State Party.

2. Following a request made by another State Party having jurisdiction over an offence covered by this Convention, the requested State Party shall take measures to identify, trace and freeze or seize proceeds of crime, property, equipment or other instrumentalities referred to in article 12, paragraph 1, of this Convention for the purpose of eventual confiscation to be ordered either by the requesting State Party or, pursuant to a request under paragraph 1 of this article, by the requested State Party.

3. The provisions of article 18 of this Convention are applicable, mutatis mutandis, to this article. In addition to the information specified in article 18, paragraph 15, requests made pursuant to this article shall contain:

(a) In the case of a request pertaining to paragraph 1 *(a)* of this article, a description of the property to be confiscated and a statement of the facts relied upon by the requesting State Party sufficient to enable the requested State Party to seek the order under its domestic law;

(b) In the case of a request pertaining to paragraph 1 *(b)* of this article, a legally admissible copy of an order of confiscation upon which the request is based issued by the requesting State Party, a statement of the facts and information as to the extent to which execution of the order is requested;

(c) In the case of a request pertaining to paragraph 2 of this article, a statement of the facts relied upon by the requesting State Party and a description of the actions requested.

4. The decisions or actions provided for in paragraphs 1 and 2 of this article shall be taken by the requested State Party in accordance with and subject to the provisions of its domestic law and its procedural rules or any bilateral or multilateral treaty, agreement or arrangement to which it may be bound in relation to the requesting State Party.

5. Each State Party shall furnish copies of its laws and regulations that give effect to this article and of any subsequent changes to such laws and regulations or a description thereof to the Secretary-General of the United Nations.

6. If a State Party elects to make the taking of the measures referred to in paragraphs 1 and 2 of this article conditional on the existence of a relevant treaty, that State Party shall consider this Convention the necessary and sufficient treaty basis.

7. Cooperation under this article may be refused by a State Party if the offence to which the request relates is not an offence covered by this Convention.

8. The provisions of this article shall not be construed to prejudice the rights of bona fide third parties.

9. States Parties shall consider concluding bilateral or multilateral treaties, agreements or arrangements to enhance the effectiveness of international cooperation undertaken pursuant to this article.

Article 14
Disposal of confiscated proceeds of crime or property

1. Proceeds of crime or property confiscated by a State Party pursuant to articles 12 or 13, paragraph 1, of this Convention shall be disposed of by that State Party in accordance with its domestic law and administrative procedures.

2. When acting on the request made by another State Party in accordance with article 13 of this Convention, States Parties shall, to the extent permitted by domestic law and if so requested, give priority consideration to returning the confiscated proceeds of crime or property to the requesting State Party so that it can give compensation to the victims of the crime or return such proceeds of crime or property to their legitimate owners.

3. When acting on the request made by another State Party in accordance with articles 12 and 13 of this Convention, a State Party may give special consideration to concluding agreements or arrangements on:

(a) Contributing the value of such proceeds of crime or property or funds derived from the sale of such proceeds of crime or property or a part thereof to the account designated in accordance with article 30, paragraph 2 (c), of this Convention and to intergovernmental bodies specializing in the fight against organized crime;

(b) Sharing with other States Parties, on a regular or case-by-case basis, such proceeds of crime or property, or funds derived from the sale of such proceeds of crime or property, in accordance with its domestic law or administrative procedures.

Article 15
Jurisdiction

1. Each State Party shall adopt such measures as may be necessary to establish its jurisdiction over the offences established in accordance with articles 5, 6, 8 and 23 of this Convention when:

(a) The offence is committed in the territory of that State Party; or

(b) The offence is committed on board a vessel that is flying the flag of that State Party or an aircraft that is registered under the laws of that State Party at the time that the offence is committed.

2. Subject to article 4 of this Convention, a State Party may also establish its jurisdiction over any such offence when:

(a) The offence is committed against a national of that State Party;

(b) The offence is committed by a national of that State Party or a stateless person who has his or her habitual residence in its territory; or

(c) The offence is:

(i) One of those established in accordance with article 5, paragraph 1, of this Convention and is committed outside its territory with a view to the commission of a serious crime within its territory;

(ii) One of those established in accordance with article 6, paragraph 1 (b) (ii), of this Convention and is committed outside its territory with a view to the commission of an offence established in accordance with article 6, paragraph 1 (a) (i) or (ii) or (b) (i), of this Convention within its territory.

3. For the purposes of article 16, paragraph 10, of this Convention, each State Party shall adopt such measures as may be necessary to establish its jurisdiction over the offences covered by this Convention when the alleged offender is present in its territory and it does not extradite such person solely on the ground that he or she is one of its nationals.

4. Each State Party may also adopt such measures as may be necessary to establish its jurisdiction over the offences covered by this Convention when the alleged offender is present in its territory and it does not extradite him or her.

5. If a State Party exercising its jurisdiction under paragraph 1 or 2 of this article has been notified, or has otherwise learned, that one or more other States Parties are conducting an investigation, prosecution or judicial proceeding in respect of the same conduct, the competent authorities of those States Parties shall, as appropriate, consult one another with a view to coordinating their actions.

6. Without prejudice to norms of general international law, this Convention does not exclude the exercise of any criminal jurisdiction established by a State Party in accordance with its domestic law.

Article 16
Extradition

1. This article shall apply to the offences covered by this Convention or in cases where an offence referred to in article 3, paragraph 1 (a) or (b), involves an organized criminal group and the person who is the subject of the request for extradition is located in the territory of the requested State Party, provided that the offence for which extradition is sought is punishable under the domestic law of both the requesting State Party and the requested State Party.

2. If the request for extradition includes several separate serious crimes, some of which are not covered by this article, the requested State Party may apply this article also in respect of the latter offences.

3. Each of the offences to which this article applies shall be deemed to be included as an extraditable offence in any extradition treaty existing between States Parties. States Parties undertake to include such offences as extraditable offences in every extradition treaty to be concluded between them.

4. If a State Party that makes extradition conditional on the existence of a treaty receives a request for extradition from another State Party with which it has no extradition treaty, it may consider this Convention the legal basis for extradition in respect of any offence to which this article applies.

5. States Parties that make extradition conditional on the existence of a treaty shall:

(a) At the time of deposit of their instrument of ratification, acceptance, approval of or accession to this Convention, inform the Secretary-General of the United Nations whether they will take this Convention as the legal basis for cooperation on extradition with other States Parties to this Convention; and

(b) If they do not take this Convention as the legal basis for cooperation on extradition, seek, where appropriate, to conclude treaties on extradition with other States Parties to this Convention in order to implement this article.

6. States Parties that do not make extradition conditional on the existence of a treaty shall recognize offences to which this article applies as extraditable offences between themselves.

7. Extradition shall be subject to the conditions provided for by the domestic law of the requested State Party or by applicable extradition treaties, including, inter alia, conditions in relation to the minimum pen-

alty requirement for extradition and the grounds upon which the requested State Party may refuse extradition.

8. States Parties shall, subject to their domestic law, endeavour to expedite extradition procedures and to simplify evidentiary requirements relating thereto in respect of any offence to which this article applies.

9. Subject to the provisions of its domestic law and its extradition treaties, the requested State Party may, upon being satisfied that the circumstances so warrant and are urgent and at the request of the requesting State Party, take a person whose extradition is sought and who is present in its territory into custody or take other appropriate measures to ensure his or her presence at extradition proceedings.

10. A State Party in whose territory an alleged offender is found, if it does not extradite such person in respect of an offence to which this article applies solely on the ground that he or she is one of its nationals, shall, at the request of the State Party seeking extradition, be obliged to submit the case without undue delay to its competent authorities for the purpose of prosecution. Those authorities shall take their decision and conduct their proceedings in the same manner as in the case of any other offence of a grave nature under the domestic law of that State Party. The States Parties concerned shall cooperate with each other, in particular on procedural and evidentiary aspects, to ensure the efficiency of such prosecution.

11. Whenever a State Party is permitted under its domestic law to extradite or otherwise surrender one of its nationals only upon the condition that the person will be returned to that State Party to serve the sentence imposed as a result of the trial or proceedings for which the extradition or surrender of the person was sought and that State Party and the State Party seeking the extradition of the person agree with this option and other terms that they may deem appropriate, such conditional extradition or surrender shall be sufficient to discharge the obligation set forth in paragraph 10 of this article.

12. If extradition, sought for purposes of enforcing a sentence, is refused because the person sought is a national of the requested State Party, the requested Party shall, if its domestic law so permits and in conformity with the requirements of such law, upon application of the requesting Party, consider the enforcement of the sentence that has been imposed under the domestic law of the requesting Party or the remainder thereof.

13. Any person regarding whom proceedings are being carried out in connection with any of the offences to which this article applies shall be guaranteed fair treatment at all stages of the proceedings, including enjoyment of all the rights and guarantees provided by the domestic law of the State Party in the territory of which that person is present.

14. Nothing in this Convention shall be interpreted as imposing an obligation to extradite if the requested State Party has substantial grounds for believing that the request has been made for the purpose of prosecuting or punishing a person on account of that person's sex, race, religion, nationality, ethnic origin or political opinions or that compliance with the request would cause prejudice to that person's position for any one of these reasons.

15. States Parties may not refuse a request for extradition on the sole ground that the offence is also considered to involve fiscal matters.

16. Before refusing extradition, the requested State Party shall, where appropriate, consult with the requesting State Party to provide it with ample opportunity to present its opinions and to provide information relevant to its allegation.

17. States Parties shall seek to conclude bilateral and multilateral agreements or arrangements to carry out or to enhance the effectiveness of extradition.

Article 17
Transfer of sentenced persons

States Parties may consider entering into bilateral or multilateral agreements or arrangements on the transfer to their territory of persons sentenced to imprisonment or other forms of deprivation of liberty for offences covered by this Convention, in order that they may complete their sentences there.

Article 18
Mutual legal assistance

1. States Parties shall afford one another the widest measure of mutual legal assistance in investigations, prosecutions and judicial proceedings in relation to the offences covered by this Convention as provided for in article 3 and shall reciprocally extend to one another similar assistance where the requesting State Party has reasonable grounds to suspect that the offence referred to in article 3, paragraph 1 *(a)* or *(b)*, is transnational in nature, including that victims, witnesses, proceeds, instrumentalities or evidence of such offences are located in the requested State Party and that the offence involves an organized criminal group.

2. Mutual legal assistance shall be afforded to the fullest extent possible under relevant laws, treaties, agreements and arrangements of the requested State Party with respect to investigations, prosecutions and judicial proceedings in relation to the offences for which a legal person may be held liable in accordance with article 10 of this Convention in the requesting State Party.

3. Mutual legal assistance to be afforded in accordance with this article may be requested for any of the following purposes:

(a) Taking evidence or statements from persons;

(b) Effecting service of judicial documents;

(c) Executing searches and seizures, and freezing;

(d) Examining objects and sites;

(e) Providing information, evidentiary items and expert evaluations;

(f) Providing originals or certified copies of relevant documents and records, including government, bank, financial, corporate or business records;

(g) Identifying or tracing proceeds of crime, property, instrumentalities or other things for evidentiary purposes;

(h) Facilitating the voluntary appearance of persons in the requesting State Party;

(i) Any other type of assistance that is not contrary to the domestic law of the requested State Party.

4. Without prejudice to domestic law, the competent authorities of a State Party may, without prior request, transmit information relating to criminal matters to a competent authority in another State Party where they believe that such information could assist

the authority in undertaking or successfully concluding inquiries and criminal proceedings or could result in a request formulated by the latter State Party pursuant to this Convention.

5. The transmission of information pursuant to paragraph 4 of this article shall be without prejudice to inquiries and criminal proceedings in the State of the competent authorities providing the information. The competent authorities receiving the information shall comply with a request that said information remain confidential, even temporarily, or with restrictions on its use. However, this shall not prevent the receiving State Party from disclosing in its proceedings information that is exculpatory to an accused person. In such a case, the receiving State Party shall notify the transmitting State Party prior to the disclosure and, if so requested, consult with the transmitting State Party. If, in an exceptional case, advance notice is not possible, the receiving State Party shall inform the transmitting State Party of the disclosure without delay.

6. The provisions of this article shall not affect the obligations under any other treaty, bilateral or multilateral, that governs or will govern, in whole or in part, mutual legal assistance.

7. Paragraphs 9 to 29 of this article shall apply to requests made pursuant to this article if the States Parties in question are not bound by a treaty of mutual legal assistance. If those States Parties are bound by such a treaty, the corresponding provisions of that treaty shall apply unless the States Parties agree to apply paragraphs 9 to 29 of this article in lieu thereof. States Parties are strongly encouraged to apply these paragraphs if they facilitate cooperation.

8. States Parties shall not decline to render mutual legal assistance pursuant to this article on the ground of bank secrecy.

9. States Parties may decline to render mutual legal assistance pursuant to this article on the ground of absence of dual criminality. However, the requested State Party may, when it deems appropriate, provide assistance, to the extent it decides at its discretion, irrespective of whether the conduct would constitute an offence under the domestic law of the requested State Party.

10. A person who is being detained or is serving a sentence in the territory of one State Party whose presence in another State Party is requested for purposes of identification, testimony or otherwise providing assistance in obtaining evidence for investigations, prosecutions or judicial proceedings in relation to offences covered by this Convention may be transferred if the following conditions are met:

(a) The person freely gives his or her informed consent;

(b) The competent authorities of both States Parties agree, subject to such conditions as those States Parties may deem appropriate.

11. For the purposes of paragraph 10 of this article:

(a) The State Party to which the person is transferred shall have the authority and obligation to keep the person transferred in custody, unless otherwise requested or authorized by the State Party from which the person was transferred;

(b) The State Party to which the person is transferred shall without delay implement its obligation to return the person to the custody of the State Party from which the person was transferred as agreed beforehand, or as otherwise agreed, by the competent authorities of both States Parties;

(c) The State Party to which the person is transferred shall not require the State Party from which the person was transferred to initiate extradition proceedings for the return of the person;

(d) The person transferred shall receive credit for service of the sentence being served in the State from which he or she was transferred for time spent in the custody of the State Party to which he or she was transferred.

12. Unless the State Party from which a person is to be transferred in accordance with paragraphs 10 and 11 of this article so agrees, that person, whatever his or her nationality, shall not be prosecuted, detained, punished or subjected to any other restriction of his or her personal liberty in the territory of the State to which that person is transferred in respect of acts, omissions or convictions prior to his or her departure from the territory of the State from which he or she was transferred.

13. Each State Party shall designate a central authority that shall have the responsibility and power to receive requests for mutual legal assistance and either to execute them or to transmit them to the competent authorities for execution. Where a State Party has a special region or territory with a separate system of mutual legal assistance, it may designate a distinct central authority that shall have the same function for that region or territory. Central authorities shall ensure the speedy and proper execution or transmission of the requests received. Where the central authority transmits the request to a competent authority for execution, it shall encourage the speedy and proper execution of the request by the competent authority. The Secretary-General of the United Nations shall be notified of the central authority designated for this purpose at the time each State Party deposits its instrument of ratification, acceptance or approval of or accession to this Convention. Requests for mutual legal assistance and any communication related thereto shall be transmitted to the central authorities designated by the States Parties. This requirement shall be without prejudice to the right of a State Party to require that such requests and communications be addressed to it through diplomatic channels and, in urgent circumstances, where the States Parties agree, through the International Criminal Police Organization, if possible.

14. Requests shall be made in writing or, where possible, by any means capable of producing a written record, in a language acceptable to the requested State Party, under conditions allowing that State Party to establish authenticity. The Secretary-General of the United Nations shall be notified of the language or languages acceptable to each State Party at the time it deposits its instrument of ratification, acceptance or approval of or accession to this Convention. In urgent circumstances and where agreed by the States Parties, requests may be made orally, but shall be confirmed in writing forthwith.

15. A request for mutual legal assistance shall contain:

(a) The identity of the authority making the request;

(b) The subject matter and nature of the investigation, prosecution or judicial proceeding to which the request relates and the name and functions of the authority conducting the investigation, prosecution or judicial proceeding;

(c) A summary of the relevant facts, except in relation to requests for the purpose of service of judicial documents;

(d) A description of the assistance sought and details of any particular procedure that the requesting State Party wishes to be followed;

(e) Where possible, the identity, location and nationality of any person concerned; and

(f) The purpose for which the evidence, information or action is sought.

16. The requested State Party may request additional information when it appears necessary for the execution of the request in accordance with its domestic law or when it can facilitate such execution.

17. A request shall be executed in accordance with the domestic law of the requested State Party and, to the extent not contrary to the domestic law of the requested State Party and where possible, in accordance with the procedures specified in the request.

18. Wherever possible and consistent with fundamental principles of domestic law, when an individual is in the territory of a State Party and has to be heard as a witness or expert by the judicial authorities of another State Party, the first State Party may, at the request of the other, permit the hearing to take place by video conference if it is not possible or desirable for the individual in question to appear in person in the territory of the requesting State Party. States Parties may agree that the hearing shall be conducted by a judicial authority of the requesting State Party and attended by a judicial authority of the requested State Party.

19. The requesting State Party shall not transmit or use information or evidence furnished by the requested State Party for investigations, prosecutions or judicial proceedings other than those stated in the request without the prior consent of the requested State Party. Nothing in this paragraph shall prevent the requesting State Party from disclosing in its proceedings information or evidence that is exculpatory to an accused person. In the latter case, the requesting State Party shall notify the requested State Party prior to the disclosure and, if so requested, consult with the requested State Party. If, in an exceptional case, advance notice is not possible, the requesting State Party shall inform the requested State Party of the disclosure without delay.

20. The requesting State Party may require that the requested State Party keep confidential the fact and substance of the request, except to the extent necessary to execute the request. If the requested State Party cannot comply with the requirement of confidentiality, it shall promptly inform the requesting State Party.

21. Mutual legal assistance may be refused:

(a) If the request is not made in conformity with the provisions of this article;

(b) If the requested State Party considers that execution of the request is likely to prejudice its sovereignty, security, *ordre public* or other essential interests;

(c) If the authorities of the requested State Party would be prohibited by its domestic law from carrying out the action requested with regard to any similar offence, had it been subject to investigation, prosecution or judicial proceedings under their own jurisdiction;

(d) If it would be contrary to the legal system of the requested State Party relating to mutual legal assistance for the request to be granted.

22. States Parties may not refuse a request for mutual legal assistance on the sole ground that the offence is also considered to involve fiscal matters.

23. Reasons shall be given for any refusal of mutual legal assistance.

24. The requested State Party shall execute the request for mutual legal assistance as soon as possible and shall take as full account as possible of any deadlines suggested by the requesting State Party and for which reasons are given, preferably in the request. The requested State Party shall respond to reasonable requests by the requesting State Party on progress of its handling of the request. The requesting State Party shall promptly inform the requested State Party when the assistance sought is no longer required.

25. Mutual legal assistance may be postponed by the requested State Party on the ground that it interferes with an ongoing investigation, prosecution or judicial proceeding.

26. Before refusing a request pursuant to paragraph 21 of this article or postponing its execution pursuant to paragraph 25 of this article, the requested State Party shall consult with the requesting State Party to consider whether assistance may be granted subject to such terms and conditions as it deems necessary. If the requesting State Party accepts assistance subject to those conditions, it shall comply with the conditions.

27. Without prejudice to the application of paragraph 12 of this article, a witness, expert or other person who, at the request of the requesting State Party, consents to give evidence in a proceeding or to assist in an investigation, prosecution or judicial proceeding in the territory of the requesting State Party shall not be prosecuted, detained, punished or subjected to any other restriction of his or her personal liberty in that territory in respect of acts, omissions or convictions prior to his or her departure from the territory of the requested State Party. Such safe conduct shall cease when the witness, expert or other person having had, for a period of fifteen consecutive days or for any period agreed upon by the States Parties from the date on which he or she has been officially informed that his or her presence is no longer required by the judicial authorities, an opportunity of leaving, has nevertheless remained voluntarily in the territory of the requesting State Party or, having left it, has returned of his or her own free will.

28. The ordinary costs of executing a request shall be borne by the requested State Party, unless otherwise agreed by the States Parties concerned. If expenses of a substantial or extraordinary nature are or will be required to fulfil the request, the States Parties shall consult to determine the terms and conditions under which the request will be executed, as well as the manner in which the costs shall be borne.

29. The requested State Party:

(a) Shall provide to the requesting State Party copies of government records, documents or information in its possession that under its domestic law are available to the general public;

(b) May, at its discretion, provide to the requesting State Party in whole, in part or subject to such conditions as it deems appropriate, copies of any government records, documents or information in its possession that under its domestic law are not available to the general public.

30. States Parties shall consider, as may be necessary, the possibility of concluding bilateral or multilateral agreements or arrangements that would serve the purposes of, give practical effect to or enhance the provisions of this article.

Article 19
Joint investigations

States Parties shall consider concluding bilateral or multilateral agreements or arrangements whereby, in relation to matters that are the subject of investigations, prosecutions or judicial proceedings in one or more States, the competent authorities concerned may establish joint investigative bodies. In the absence of such agreements or arrangements, joint investigations may be undertaken by agreement on a case-by-case basis. The States Parties involved shall ensure that the sovereignty of the State Party in whose territory such investigation is to take place is fully respected.

Article 20
Special investigative techniques

1. If permitted by the basic principles of its domestic legal system, each State Party shall, within its possibilities and under the conditions prescribed by its domestic law, take the necessary measures to allow for the appropriate use of controlled delivery and, where it deems appropriate, for the use of other special investigative techniques, such as electronic or other forms of surveillance and undercover operations, by its competent authorities in its territory for the purpose of effectively combating organized crime.

2. For the purpose of investigating the offences covered by this Convention, States Parties are encouraged to conclude, when necessary, appropriate bilateral or multilateral agreements or arrangements for using such special investigative techniques in the context of cooperation at the international level. Such agreements or arrangements shall be concluded and implemented in full compliance with the principle of sovereign equality of States and shall be carried out strictly in accordance with the terms of those agreements or arrangements.

3. In the absence of an agreement or arrangement as set forth in paragraph 2 of this article, decisions to use such special investigative techniques at the international level shall be made on a case-by-case basis and may, when necessary, take into consideration financial arrangements and understandings with respect to the exercise of jurisdiction by the States Parties concerned.

4. Decisions to use controlled delivery at the international level may, with the consent of the States Parties concerned, include methods such as intercepting and allowing the goods to continue intact or be removed or replaced in whole or in part.

Article 21
Transfer of criminal proceedings

States Parties shall consider the possibility of transferring to one another proceedings for the prosecution of an offence covered by this Convention in cases where such transfer is considered to be in the interests of the proper administration of justice, in particular in cases where several jurisdictions are involved, with a view to concentrating the prosecution.

Article 22
Establishment of criminal record

Each State Party may adopt such legislative or other measures as may be necessary to take into consideration, under such terms as and for the purpose that it deems appropriate, any previous conviction in another State of an alleged offender for the purpose of using such information in criminal proceedings relating to an offence covered by this Convention.

Article 23
Criminalization of obstruction of justice

Each State Party shall adopt such legislative and other measures as may be necessary to establish as criminal offences, when committed intentionally:

(a) The use of physical force, threats or intimidation or the promise, offering or giving of an undue advantage to induce false testimony or to interfere in the giving of testimony or the production of evidence in a proceeding in relation to the commission of offences covered by this Convention;

(b) The use of physical force, threats or intimidation to interfere with the exercise of official duties by a justice or law enforcement official in relation to the commission of offences covered by this Convention. Nothing in this subparagraph shall prejudice the right of States Parties to have legislation that protects other categories of public officials.

Article 24
Protection of witnesses

1. Each State Party shall take appropriate measures within its means to provide effective protection from potential retaliation or intimidation for witnesses in criminal proceedings who give testimony concerning offences covered by this Convention and, as appropriate, for their relatives and other persons close to them.

2. The measures envisaged in paragraph 1 of this article may include, inter alia, without prejudice to the rights of the defendant, including the right to due process:

(a) Establishing procedures for the physical protection of such persons, such as, to the extent necessary and feasible, relocating them and permitting, where appropriate, non-disclosure or limitations on the disclosure of information concerning the identity and whereabouts of such persons;

(b) Providing evidentiary rules to permit witness testimony to be given in a manner that ensures the safety of the witness, such as permitting testimony to be given through the use of communications technology such as video links or other adequate means.

3. States Parties shall consider entering into agreements or arrangements with other States for the relocation of persons referred to in paragraph 1 of this article.

4. The provisions of this article shall also apply to victims insofar as they are witnesses.

Article 25
Assistance to and protection of victims

1. Each State Party shall take appropriate measures within its means to provide assistance and protection to victims of offences covered by this Convention, in particular in cases of threat of retaliation or intimidation.

2. Each State Party shall establish appropriate procedures to provide access to compensation and restitution for victims of offences covered by this Convention.

3. Each State Party shall, subject to its domestic law, enable views and concerns of victims to be presented and considered at appropriate stages of criminal proceedings against offenders in a manner not prejudicial to the rights of the defence.

Article 26
Measures to enhance cooperation with law enforcement authorities

1. Each State Party shall take appropriate measures to encourage persons who participate or who have participated in organized criminal groups:

(a) To supply information useful to competent authorities for investigative and evidentiary purposes on such matters as:

(i) The identity, nature, composition, structure, location or activities of organized criminal groups;

(ii) Links, including international links, with other organized criminal groups;

(iii) Offences that organized criminal groups have committed or may commit;

(b) To provide factual, concrete help to competent authorities that may contribute to depriving organized criminal groups of their resources or of the proceeds of crime.

2. Each State Party shall consider providing for the possibility, in appropriate cases, of mitigating punishment of an accused person who provides substantial cooperation in the investigation or prosecution of an offence covered by this Convention.

3. Each State Party shall consider providing for the possibility, in accordance with fundamental principles of its domestic law, of granting immunity from prosecution to a person who provides substantial cooperation in the investigation or prosecution of an offence covered by this Convention.

4. Protection of such persons shall be as provided for in article 24 of this Convention.

5. Where a person referred to in paragraph 1 of this article located in one State Party can provide substantial cooperation to the competent authorities of another State Party, the States Parties concerned may consider entering into agreements or arrangements, in accordance with their domestic law, concerning the potential provision by the other State Party of the treatment set forth in paragraphs 2 and 3 of this article.

Article 27
Law enforcement cooperation

1. States Parties shall cooperate closely with one another, consistent with their respective domestic legal and administrative systems, to enhance the effectiveness of law enforcement action to combat the offences covered by this Convention. Each State Party shall, in particular, adopt effective measures:

(a) To enhance and, where necessary, to establish channels of communication between their competent authorities, agencies and services in order to facilitate the secure and rapid exchange of information concerning all aspects of the offences covered by this Convention, including, if the States Parties concerned deem it appropriate, links with other criminal activities;

(b) To cooperate with other States Parties in conducting inquiries with respect to offences covered by this Convention concerning:

(i) The identity, whereabouts and activities of persons suspected of involvement in such offences or the location of other persons concerned;

(ii) The movement of proceeds of crime or property derived from the commission of such offences;

(iii) The movement of property, equipment or other instrumentalities used or intended for use in the commission of such offences;

(c) To provide, when appropriate, necessary items or quantities of substances for analytical or investigative purposes;

(d) To facilitate effective coordination between their competent authorities, agencies and services and to promote the exchange of personnel and other experts, including, subject to bilateral agreements or arrangements between the States Parties concerned, the posting of liaison officers;

(e) To exchange information with other States Parties on specific means and methods used by organized criminal groups, including, where applicable, routes and conveyances and the use of false identities, altered or false documents or other means of concealing their activities;

(f) To exchange information and coordinate administrative and other measures taken as appropriate for the purpose of early identification of the offences covered by this Convention.

2. With a view to giving effect to this Convention, States Parties shall consider entering into bilateral or multilateral agreements or arrangements on direct cooperation between their law enforcement agencies and, where such agreements or arrangements already exist, amending them. In the absence of such agreements or arrangements between the States Parties concerned, the Parties may consider this Convention as the basis for mutual law enforcement cooperation in respect of the offences covered by this Convention. Whenever appropriate, States Parties shall make full use of agreements or arrangements, including international or regional organizations, to enhance the cooperation between their law enforcement agencies.

3. States Parties shall endeavour to cooperate within their means to respond to transnational organized crime committed through the use of modern technology.

Article 28
Collection, exchange and analysis of information on the nature of organized crime

1. Each State Party shall consider analysing, in consultation with the scientific and academic communities, trends in organized crime in its territory, the circumstances in which organized crime operates, as well as the professional groups and technologies involved.

2. States Parties shall consider developing and sharing analytical expertise concerning organized criminal activities with each other and through international and regional organizations. For that purpose, common definitions, standards and methodologies should be developed and applied as appropriate.

3. Each State Party shall consider monitoring its policies and actual measures to combat organized crime and making assessments of their effectiveness and efficiency.

Article 29
Training and technical assistance

1. Each State Party shall, to the extent necessary, initiate, develop or improve specific training programmes for its law enforcement personnel, including prosecutors, investigating magistrates and customs personnel, and other personnel charged with the prevention, detection and control of the offences covered by this Convention. Such programmes may include secondments and exchanges of staff. Such programmes shall deal, in particular and to the extent permitted by domestic law, with the following:

(a) Methods used in the prevention, detection and control of the offences covered by this Convention;

(b) Routes and techniques used by persons suspected of involvement in offences covered by this Convention, including in transit States, and appropriate countermeasures;

(c) Monitoring of the movement of contraband;

(d) Detection and monitoring of the movements of proceeds of crime, property, equipment or other instrumentalities and methods used for the transfer, concealment or disguise of such proceeds, property, equipment or other instrumentalities, as well as methods used in combating money-laundering and other financial crimes;

(e) Collection of evidence;

(f) Control techniques in free trade zones and free ports;

(g) Modern law enforcement equipment and techniques, including electronic surveillance, controlled deliveries and undercover operations;

(h) Methods used in combating transnational organized crime committed through the use of computers, telecommunications networks or other forms of modern technology; and

(i) Methods used in the protection of victims and witnesses.

2. States Parties shall assist one another in planning and implementing research and training programmes designed to share expertise in the areas referred to in paragraph 1 of this article and to that end shall also, when appropriate, use regional and international conferences and seminars to promote cooperation and to stimulate discussion on problems of mutual concern, including the special problems and needs of transit States.

3. States Parties shall promote training and technical assistance that will facilitate extradition and mutual legal assistance. Such training and technical assistance may include language training, secondments and exchanges between personnel in central authorities or agencies with relevant responsibilities.

4. In the case of existing bilateral and multilateral agreements or arrangements, States Parties shall strengthen, to the extent necessary, efforts to maximize operational and training activities within international and regional organizations and within other relevant bilateral and multilateral agreements or arrangements.

Article 30
Other measures: implementation of the Convention through economic development and technical assistance

1. States Parties shall take measures conducive to the optimal implementation of this Convention to the extent possible, through international cooperation, taking into account the negative effects of organized crime on society in general, in particular on sustainable development.

2. States Parties shall make concrete efforts to the extent possible and in coordination with each other, as well as with international and regional organizations:

(a) To enhance their cooperation at various levels with developing countries, with a view to strengthening the capacity of the latter to prevent and combat transnational organized crime;

(b) To enhance financial and material assistance to support the efforts of developing countries to fight transnational organized crime effectively and to help them implement this Convention successfully;

(c) To provide technical assistance to developing countries and countries with economies in transition to assist them in meeting their needs for the implementation of this Convention. To that end, States Parties shall endeavour to make adequate and regular voluntary contributions to an account specifically designated for that purpose in a United Nations funding mechanism. States Parties may also give special consideration, in accordance with their domestic law and the provisions of this Convention, to contributing to the aforementioned account a percentage of the money or of the corresponding value of proceeds of crime or property confiscated in accordance with the provisions of this Convention;

(d) To encourage and persuade other States and financial institutions as appropriate to join them in efforts in accordance with this article, in particular by providing more training programmes and modern equipment to developing countries in order to assist them in achieving the objectives of this Convention.

3. To the extent possible, these measures shall be without prejudice to existing foreign assistance commitments or to other financial cooperation arrangements at the bilateral, regional or international level.

4. States Parties may conclude bilateral or multilateral agreements or arrangements on material and logistical assistance, taking into consideration the financial arrangements necessary for the means of international cooperation provided for by this Convention to be effective and for the prevention, detection and control of transnational organized crime.

Article 31
Prevention

1. States Parties shall endeavour to develop and evaluate national projects and to establish and promote best practices and policies aimed at the prevention of transnational organized crime.

2. States Parties shall endeavour, in accordance with fundamental principles of their domestic law, to reduce existing or future opportunities for organized criminal groups to participate in lawful markets with proceeds of crime, through appropriate legislative, administrative or other measures. These measures should focus on:

(a) The strengthening of cooperation between law enforcement agencies or prosecutors and relevant private entities, including industry;

(b) The promotion of the development of standards and procedures designed to safeguard the integrity of public and relevant private entities, as well as codes of conduct for relevant professions, in particular lawyers, notaries public, tax consultants and accountants;

(c) The prevention of the misuse by organized criminal groups of tender procedures conducted by public authorities and of subsidies and licences granted by public authorities for commercial activity;

(d) The prevention of the misuse of legal persons by organized criminal groups; such measures could include:

(i) The establishment of public records on legal and natural persons involved in the establishment, management and funding of legal persons;

(ii) The introduction of the possibility of disqualifying by court order or any appropriate means for a reasonable period of time persons convicted of offences covered by this Convention from acting as directors of legal persons incorporated within their jurisdiction;

(iii) The establishment of national records of persons disqualified from acting as directors of legal persons; and

(iv) The exchange of information contained in the records referred to in subparagraphs (d) (i) and (iii) of this paragraph with the competent authorities of other States Parties.

3. States Parties shall endeavour to promote the reintegration into society of persons convicted of offences covered by this Convention.

4. States Parties shall endeavour to evaluate periodically existing relevant legal instruments and administrative practices with a view to detecting their vulnerability to misuse by organized criminal groups.

5. States Parties shall endeavour to promote public awareness regarding the existence, causes and gravity of and the threat posed by transnational organized crime. Information may be disseminated where appropriate through the mass media and shall include measures to promote public participation in preventing and combating such crime.

6. Each State Party shall inform the Secretary-General of the United Nations of the name and address of the authority or authorities that can assist other States Parties in developing measures to prevent transnational organized crime.

7. States Parties shall, as appropriate, collaborate with each other and relevant international and regional organizations in promoting and developing the measures referred to in this article. This includes participation in international projects aimed at the prevention of transnational organized crime, for example by alleviating the circumstances that render socially marginalized groups vulnerable to the action of transnational organized crime.

Article 32
Conference of the Parties to the Convention

1. A Conference of the Parties to the Convention is hereby established to improve the capacity of States Parties to combat transnational organized crime and to promote and review the implementation of this Convention.

2. The Secretary-General of the United Nations shall convene the Conference of the Parties not later than one year following the entry into force of this Convention. The Conference of the Parties shall adopt rules of procedure and rules governing the activities set forth in paragraphs 3 and 4 of this article (including rules concerning payment of expenses incurred in carrying out those activities).

3. The Conference of the Parties shall agree upon mechanisms for achieving the objectives mentioned in paragraph 1 of this article, including:

(a) Facilitating activities by States Parties under articles 29, 30 and 31 of this Convention, including by encouraging the mobilization of voluntary contributions;

(b) Facilitating the exchange of information among States Parties on patterns and trends in transnational organized crime and on successful practices for combating it;

(c) Cooperating with relevant international and regional organizations and non-governmental organizations;

(d) Reviewing periodically the implementation of this Convention;

(e) Making recommendations to improve this Convention and its implementation.

4. For the purpose of paragraphs 3 (d) and (e) of this article, the Conference of the Parties shall acquire the necessary knowledge of the measures taken by States Parties in implementing this Convention and the difficulties encountered by them in doing so through information provided by them and through such supplemental review mechanisms as may be established by the Conference of the Parties.

5. Each State Party shall provide the Conference of the Parties with information on its programmes, plans and practices, as well as legislative and administrative measures to implement this Convention, as required by the Conference of the Parties.

Article 33
Secretariat

1. The Secretary-General of the United Nations shall provide the necessary secretariat services to the Conference of the Parties to the Convention.

2. The secretariat shall:

(a) Assist the Conference of the Parties in carrying out the activities set forth in article 32 of this Convention and make arrangements and provide the necessary services for the sessions of the Conference of the Parties;

(b) Upon request, assist States Parties in providing information to the Conference of the Parties as envisaged in article 32, paragraph 5, of this Convention; and

(c) Ensure the necessary coordination with the secretariats of relevant international and regional organizations.

Article 34
Implementation of the Convention

1. Each State Party shall take the necessary measures, including legislative and administrative measures, in accordance with fundamental principles of its domestic law, to ensure the implementation of its obligations under this Convention.

2. The offences established in accordance with articles 5, 6, 8 and 23 of this Convention shall be established in the domestic law of each State Party independently of the transnational nature or the involvement of an organized criminal group as described in article 3, paragraph 1, of this Convention, except to the

extent that article 5 of this Convention would require the involvement of an organized criminal group.

3. Each State Party may adopt more strict or severe measures than those provided for by this Convention for preventing and combating transnational organized crime.

Article 35
Settlement of disputes

1. States Parties shall endeavour to settle disputes concerning the interpretation or application of this Convention through negotiation.

2. Any dispute between two or more States Parties concerning the interpretation or application of this Convention that cannot be settled through negotiation within a reasonable time shall, at the request of one of those States Parties, be submitted to arbitration. If, six months after the date of the request for arbitration, those States Parties are unable to agree on the organization of the arbitration, any one of those States Parties may refer the dispute to the International Court of Justice by request in accordance with the Statute of the Court.

3. Each State Party may, at the time of signature, ratification, acceptance or approval of or accession to this Convention, declare that it does not consider itself bound by paragraph 2 of this article. The other States Parties shall not be bound by paragraph 2 of this article with respect to any State Party that has made such a reservation.

4. Any State Party that has made a reservation in accordance with paragraph 3 of this article may at any time withdraw that reservation by notification to the Secretary-General of the United Nations.

Article 36
Signature, ratification, acceptance, approval and accession

1. This Convention shall be open to all States for signature from 12 to 15 December 2000 in Palermo, Italy, and thereafter at United Nations Headquarters in New York until 12 December 2002.

2. This Convention shall also be open for signature by regional economic integration organizations provided that at least one member State of such organization has signed this Convention in accordance with paragraph 1 of this article.

3. This Convention is subject to ratification, acceptance or approval. Instruments of ratification, acceptance or approval shall be deposited with the Secretary-General of the United Nations. A regional economic integration organization may deposit its instrument of ratification, acceptance or approval if at least one of its member States has done likewise. In that instrument of ratification, acceptance or approval, such organization shall declare the extent of its competence with respect to the matters governed by this Convention. Such organization shall also inform the depositary of any relevant modification in the extent of its competence.

4. This Convention is open for accession by any State or any regional economic integration organization of which at least one member State is a Party to this Convention. Instruments of accession shall be deposited with the Secretary-General of the United Nations. At the time of its accession, a regional economic integration organization shall declare the extent of its competence with respect to matters governed by this Convention. Such organization shall also inform the

depositary of any relevant modification in the extent of its competence.

Article 37
Relation with protocols

1. This Convention may be supplemented by one or more protocols.

2. In order to become a Party to a protocol, a State or a regional economic integration organization must also be a Party to this Convention.

3. A State Party to this Convention is not bound by a protocol unless it becomes a Party to the protocol in accordance with the provisions thereof.

4. Any protocol to this Convention shall be interpreted together with this Convention, taking into account the purpose of that protocol.

Article 38
Entry into force

1. This Convention shall enter into force on the ninetieth day after the date of deposit of the fortieth instrument of ratification, acceptance, approval or accession. For the purpose of this paragraph, any instrument deposited by a regional economic integration organization shall not be counted as additional to those deposited by member States of such organization.

2. For each State or regional economic integration organization ratifying, accepting, approving or acceding to this Convention after the deposit of the fortieth instrument of such action, this Convention shall enter into force on the thirtieth day after the date of deposit by such State or organization of the relevant instrument.

Article 39
Amendment

1. After the expiry of five years from the entry into force of this Convention, a State Party may propose an amendment and file it with the Secretary-General of the United Nations, who shall thereupon communicate the proposed amendment to the States Parties and to the Conference of the Parties to the Convention for the purpose of considering and deciding on the proposal. The Conference of the Parties shall make every effort to achieve consensus on each amendment. If all efforts at consensus have been exhausted and no agreement has been reached, the amendment shall, as a last resort, require for its adoption a two-thirds majority vote of the States Parties present and voting at the meeting of the Conference of the Parties.

2. Regional economic integration organizations, in matters within their competence, shall exercise their right to vote under this article with a number of votes equal to the number of their member States that are Parties to this Convention. Such organizations shall not exercise their right to vote if their member States exercise theirs and vice versa.

3. An amendment adopted in accordance with paragraph 1 of this article is subject to ratification, acceptance or approval by States Parties.

4. An amendment adopted in accordance with paragraph 1 of this article shall enter into force in respect of a State Party ninety days after the date of the deposit with the Secretary-General of the United Nations of an instrument of ratification, acceptance or approval of such amendment.

5. When an amendment enters into force, it shall be binding on those States Parties which have expressed

their consent to be bound by it. Other States Parties shall still be bound by the provisions of this Convention and any earlier amendments that they have ratified, accepted or approved.

Article 40
Denunciation

1. A State Party may denounce this Convention by written notification to the Secretary-General of the United Nations. Such denunciation shall become effective one year after the date of receipt of the notification by the Secretary-General.

2. A regional economic integration organization shall cease to be a Party to this Convention when all of its member States have denounced it.

3. Denunciation of this Convention in accordance with paragraph 1 of this article shall entail the denunciation of any protocols thereto.

Article 41
Depositary and languages

1. The Secretary-General of the United Nations is designated depositary of this Convention.

2. The original of this Convention, of which the Arabic, Chinese, English, French, Russian and Spanish texts are equally authentic, shall be deposited with the Secretary-General of the United Nations.

IN WITNESS WHEREOF, the undersigned plenipotentiaries, being duly authorized thereto by their respective Governments, have signed this Convention.

ANNEX II
Protocol to Prevent, Suppress and Punish Trafficking in Persons, Especially Women and Children, supplementing the United Nations Convention against Transnational Organized Crime

Preamble

The States Parties to this Protocol,

Declaring that effective action to prevent and combat trafficking in persons, especially women and children, requires a comprehensive international approach in the countries of origin, transit and destination that includes measures to prevent such trafficking, to punish the traffickers and to protect the victims of such trafficking, including by protecting their internationally recognized human rights,

Taking into account the fact that, despite the existence of a variety of international instruments containing rules and practical measures to combat the exploitation of persons, especially women and children, there is no universal instrument that addresses all aspects of trafficking in persons,

Concerned that, in the absence of such an instrument, persons who are vulnerable to trafficking will not be sufficiently protected,

Recalling General Assembly resolution 53/111 of 9 December 1998, in which the Assembly decided to establish an open-ended intergovernmental ad hoc committee for the purpose of elaborating a comprehensive international convention against transnational organized crime and of discussing the elaboration of, inter alia, an international instrument addressing trafficking in women and children,

Convinced that supplementing the United Nations Convention against Transnational Organized Crime with an international instrument for the prevention, suppression and punishment of trafficking in persons, especially women and children, will be useful in preventing and combating that crime,

Have agreed as follows:

I. General provisions

Article 1
Relation with the United Nations Convention against Transnational Organized Crime

1. This Protocol supplements the United Nations Convention against Transnational Organized Crime. It shall be interpreted together with the Convention.

2. The provisions of the Convention shall apply, mutatis mutandis, to this Protocol unless otherwise provided herein.

3. The offences established in accordance with article 5 of this Protocol shall be regarded as offences established in accordance with the Convention.

Article 2
Statement of purpose

The purposes of this Protocol are:

(a) To prevent and combat trafficking in persons, paying particular attention to women and children;

(b) To protect and assist the victims of such trafficking, with full respect for their human rights; and

(c) To promote cooperation among States Parties in order to meet those objectives.

Article 3
Use of terms

For the purposes of this Protocol:

(a) "Trafficking in persons" shall mean the recruitment, transportation, transfer, harbouring or receipt of persons, by means of the threat or use of force or other forms of coercion, of abduction, of fraud, of deception, of the abuse of power or of a position of vulnerability or of the giving or receiving of payments or benefits to achieve the consent of a person having control over another person, for the purpose of exploitation. Exploitation shall include, at a minimum, the exploitation of the prostitution of others or other forms of sexual exploitation, forced labour or services, slavery or practices similar to slavery, servitude or the removal of organs;

(b) The consent of a victim of trafficking in persons to the intended exploitation set forth in subparagraph *(a)* of this article shall be irrelevant where any of the means set forth in subparagraph *(a)* have been used;

(c) The recruitment, transportation, transfer, harbouring or receipt of a child for the purpose of exploitation shall be considered "trafficking in persons" even if this does not involve any of the means set forth in subparagraph *(a)* of this article;

(d) "Child" shall mean any person under eighteen years of age.

Article 4
Scope of application

This Protocol shall apply, except as otherwise stated herein, to the prevention, investigation and prosecution of the offences established in accordance with article 5 of this Protocol, where those offences are transnational in nature and involve an organized criminal group, as well as to the protection of victims of such offences.

Article 5
Criminalization

1. Each State Party shall adopt such legislative and other measures as may be necessary to establish as criminal offences the conduct set forth in article 3 of this Protocol, when committed intentionally.

2. Each State Party shall also adopt such legislative and other measures as may be necessary to establish as criminal offences:

(a) Subject to the basic concepts of its legal system, attempting to commit an offence established in accordance with paragraph 1 of this article;

(b) Participating as an accomplice in an offence established in accordance with paragraph 1 of this article; and

(c) Organizing or directing other persons to commit an offence established in accordance with paragraph 1 of this article.

II. Protection of victims of trafficking in persons

Article 6
Assistance to and protection of victims of trafficking in persons

1. In appropriate cases and to the extent possible under its domestic law, each State Party shall protect the privacy and identity of victims of trafficking in persons, including, inter alia, by making legal proceedings relating to such trafficking confidential.

2. Each State Party shall ensure that its domestic legal or administrative system contains measures that provide to victims of trafficking in persons, in appropriate cases:

(a) Information on relevant court and administrative proceedings;

(b) Assistance to enable their views and concerns to be presented and considered at appropriate stages of criminal proceedings against offenders, in a manner not prejudicial to the rights of the defence.

3. Each State Party shall consider implementing measures to provide for the physical, psychological and social recovery of victims of trafficking in persons, including, in appropriate cases, in cooperation with non-governmental organizations, other relevant organizations and other elements of civil society, and, in particular, the provision of:

(a) Appropriate housing;

(b) Counselling and information, in particular as regards their legal rights, in a language that the victims of trafficking in persons can understand;

(c) Medical, psychological and material assistance; and

(d) Employment, educational and training opportunities.

4. Each State Party shall take into account, in applying the provisions of this article, the age, gender and special needs of victims of trafficking in persons, in particular the special needs of children, including appropriate housing, education and care.

5. Each State Party shall endeavour to provide for the physical safety of victims of trafficking in persons while they are within its territory.

6. Each State Party shall ensure that its domestic legal system contains measures that offer victims of trafficking in persons the possibility of obtaining compensation for damage suffered.

Article 7
Status of victims of trafficking in persons in receiving States

1. In addition to taking measures pursuant to article 6 of this Protocol, each State Party shall consider adopting legislative or other appropriate measures that permit victims of trafficking in persons to remain in its territory, temporarily or permanently, in appropriate cases.

2. In implementing the provision contained in paragraph 1 of this article, each State Party shall give appropriate consideration to humanitarian and compassionate factors.

Article 8
Repatriation of victims of trafficking in persons

1. The State Party of which a victim of trafficking in persons is a national or in which the person had the right of permanent residence at the time of entry into the territory of the receiving State Party shall facilitate and accept, with due regard for the safety of that person, the return of that person without undue or unreasonable delay.

2. When a State Party returns a victim of trafficking in persons to a State Party of which that person is a national or in which he or she had, at the time of entry into the territory of the receiving State Party, the right of permanent residence, such return shall be with due regard for the safety of that person and for the status of any legal proceedings related to the fact that the person is a victim of trafficking and shall preferably be voluntary.

3. At the request of a receiving State Party, a requested State Party shall, without undue or unreasonable delay, verify whether a person who is a victim of trafficking in persons is its national or had the right of permanent residence in its territory at the time of entry into the territory of the receiving State Party.

4. In order to facilitate the return of a victim of trafficking in persons who is without proper documentation, the State Party of which that person is a national or in which he or she had the right of permanent residence at the time of entry into the territory of the receiving State Party shall agree to issue, at the request of the receiving State Party, such travel documents or other authorization as may be necessary to enable the person to travel to and re-enter its territory.

5. This article shall be without prejudice to any right afforded to victims of trafficking in persons by any domestic law of the receiving State Party.

6. This article shall be without prejudice to any applicable bilateral or multilateral agreement or arrangement that governs, in whole or in part, the return of victims of trafficking in persons.

III. Prevention, cooperation and other measures

Article 9
Prevention of trafficking in persons

1. States Parties shall establish comprehensive policies, programmes and other measures:

(a) To prevent and combat trafficking in persons; and

(b) To protect victims of trafficking in persons, especially women and children, from revictimization.

2. States Parties shall endeavour to undertake measures such as research, information and mass media campaigns and social and economic initiatives to prevent and combat trafficking in persons.

3. Policies, programmes and other measures established in accordance with this article shall, as appropriate, include cooperation with non-governmental organizations, other relevant organizations and other elements of civil society.

4. States Parties shall take or strengthen measures, including through bilateral or multilateral cooperation, to alleviate the factors that make persons, especially women and children, vulnerable to trafficking, such as poverty, underdevelopment and lack of equal opportunity.

5. States Parties shall adopt or strengthen legislative or other measures, such as educational, social or cultural measures, including through bilateral and multilateral cooperation, to discourage the demand that fosters all forms of exploitation of persons, especially women and children, that leads to trafficking.

Article 10
Information exchange and training

1. Law enforcement, immigration or other relevant authorities of States Parties shall, as appropriate, cooperate with one another by exchanging information, in accordance with their domestic law, to enable them to determine:

(a) Whether individuals crossing or attempting to cross an international border with travel documents belonging to other persons or without travel documents are perpetrators or victims of trafficking in persons;

(b) The types of travel document that individuals have used or attempted to use to cross an international border for the purpose of trafficking in persons; and

(c) The means and methods used by organized criminal groups for the purpose of trafficking in persons, including the recruitment and transportation of victims, routes and links between and among individuals and groups engaged in such trafficking, and possible measures for detecting them.

2. States Parties shall provide or strengthen training for law enforcement, immigration and other relevant officials in the prevention of trafficking in persons. The training should focus on methods used in preventing such trafficking, prosecuting the traffickers and protecting the rights of the victims, including protecting the victims from the traffickers. The training should also take into account the need to consider human rights and child- and gender-sensitive issues and it should encourage cooperation with non-governmental organizations, other relevant organizations and other elements of civil society.

3. A State Party that receives information shall comply with any request by the State Party that transmitted the information that places restrictions on its use.

Article 11
Border measures

1. Without prejudice to international commitments in relation to the free movement of people, States Parties shall strengthen, to the extent possible, such border controls as may be necessary to prevent and detect trafficking in persons.

2. Each State Party shall adopt legislative or other appropriate measures to prevent, to the extent possible, means of transport operated by commercial carriers from being used in the commission of offences established in accordance with article 5 of this Protocol.

3. Where appropriate, and without prejudice to applicable international conventions, such measures shall include establishing the obligation of commercial carriers, including any transportation company or the owner or operator of any means of transport, to ascertain that all passengers are in possession of the travel documents required for entry into the receiving State.

4. Each State Party shall take the necessary measures, in accordance with its domestic law, to provide for sanctions in cases of violation of the obligation set forth in paragraph 3 of this article.

5. Each State Party shall consider taking measures that permit, in accordance with its domestic law, the denial of entry or revocation of visas of persons implicated in the commission of offences established in accordance with this Protocol.

6. Without prejudice to article 27 of the Convention, States Parties shall consider strengthening cooperation among border control agencies by, inter alia, establishing and maintaining direct channels of communication.

Article 12
Security and control of documents

Each State Party shall take such measures as may be necessary, within available means:

(a) To ensure that travel or identity documents issued by it are of such quality that they cannot easily be misused and cannot readily be falsified or unlawfully altered, replicated or issued; and

(b) To ensure the integrity and security of travel or identity documents issued by or on behalf of the State Party and to prevent their unlawful creation, issuance and use.

Article 13
Legitimacy and validity of documents

At the request of another State Party, a State Party shall, in accordance with its domestic law, verify within a reasonable time the legitimacy and validity of travel or identity documents issued or purported to have been issued in its name and suspected of being used for trafficking in persons.

IV. Final provisions

Article 14
Saving clause

1. Nothing in this Protocol shall affect the rights, obligations and responsibilities of States and individuals under international law, including international humanitarian law and international human rights law and, in particular, where applicable, the 1951 Convention and the 1967 Protocol relating to the Status of Refugees and the principle of non-refoulement as contained therein.

2. The measures set forth in this Protocol shall be interpreted and applied in a way that is not discriminatory to persons on the ground that they are victims of trafficking in persons. The interpretation and application of those measures shall be consistent with internationally recognized principles of non-discrimination.

Article 15
Settlement of disputes

1. States Parties shall endeavour to settle disputes concerning the interpretation or application of this Protocol through negotiation.

2. Any dispute between two or more States Parties concerning the interpretation or application of this Protocol that cannot be settled through negotiation within a reasonable time shall, at the request of one of those States Parties, be submitted to arbitration. If, six months after the date of the request for arbitration, those States Parties are unable to agree on the organization of the arbitration, any one of those States Parties may refer the dispute to the International Court of Justice by request in accordance with the Statute of the Court.

3. Each State Party may, at the time of signature, ratification, acceptance or approval of or accession to this Protocol, declare that it does not consider itself bound by paragraph 2 of this article. The other States Parties shall not be bound by paragraph 2 of this article with respect to any State Party that has made such a reservation.

4. Any State Party that has made a reservation in accordance with paragraph 3 of this article may at any time withdraw that reservation by notification to the Secretary-General of the United Nations.

Article 16
Signature, ratification, acceptance, approval and accession

1. This Protocol shall be open to all States for signature from 12 to 15 December 2000 in Palermo, Italy, and thereafter at United Nations Headquarters in New York until 12 December 2002.

2. This Protocol shall also be open for signature by regional economic integration organizations provided that at least one member State of such organization has signed this Protocol in accordance with paragraph 1 of this article.

3. This Protocol is subject to ratification, acceptance or approval. Instruments of ratification, acceptance or approval shall be deposited with the Secretary-General of the United Nations. A regional economic integration organization may deposit its instrument of ratification, acceptance or approval if at least one of its member States has done likewise. In that instrument of ratification, acceptance or approval, such organization shall declare the extent of its competence with respect to the matters governed by this Protocol. Such organization shall also inform the depositary of any relevant modification in the extent of its competence.

4. This Protocol is open for accession by any State or any regional economic integration organization of which at least one member State is a Party to this Protocol. Instruments of accession shall be deposited with the Secretary-General of the United Nations. At the time of its accession, a regional economic integration organization shall declare the extent of its competence with respect to matters governed by this Protocol. Such organization shall also inform the depositary of any relevant modification in the extent of its competence.

Article 17
Entry into force

1. This Protocol shall enter into force on the ninetieth day after the date of deposit of the fortieth instrument of ratification, acceptance, approval or accession, except that it shall not enter into force before the entry into force of the Convention. For the purpose of this paragraph, any instrument deposited by a regional economic integration organization shall not be counted as additional to those deposited by member States of such organization.

2. For each State or regional economic integration organization ratifying, accepting, approving or acceding to this Protocol after the deposit of the fortieth instrument of such action, this Protocol shall enter into force on the thirtieth day after the date of deposit by such State or organization of the relevant instrument or on the date this Protocol enters into force pursuant to paragraph 1 of this article, whichever is the later.

Article 18
Amendment

1. After the expiry of five years from the entry into force of this Protocol, a State Party to the Protocol may propose an amendment and file it with the Secretary-General of the United Nations, who shall thereupon communicate the proposed amendment to the States Parties and to the Conference of the Parties to the Convention for the purpose of considering and deciding on the proposal. The States Parties to this Protocol meeting at the Conference of the Parties shall make every effort to achieve consensus on each amendment. If all efforts at consensus have been exhausted and no agreement has been reached, the amendment shall, as a last resort, require for its adoption a two-thirds majority vote of the States Parties to this Protocol present and voting at the meeting of the Conference of the Parties.

2. Regional economic integration organizations, in matters within their competence, shall exercise their right to vote under this article with a number of votes equal to the number of their member States that are Parties to this Protocol. Such organizations shall not exercise their right to vote if their member States exercise theirs and vice versa.

3. An amendment adopted in accordance with paragraph 1 of this article is subject to ratification, acceptance or approval by States Parties.

4. An amendment adopted in accordance with paragraph 1 of this article shall enter into force in respect of a State Party ninety days after the date of the deposit with the Secretary-General of the United Nations of an instrument of ratification, acceptance or approval of such amendment.

5. When an amendment enters into force, it shall be binding on those States Parties which have expressed their consent to be bound by it. Other States Parties shall still be bound by the provisions of this Protocol and any earlier amendments that they have ratified, accepted or approved.

Article 19
Denunciation

1. A State Party may denounce this Protocol by written notification to the Secretary-General of the United Nations. Such denunciation shall become effective one year after the date of receipt of the notification by the Secretary-General.

2. A regional economic integration organization shall cease to be a Party to this Protocol when all of its member States have denounced it.

Article 20
Depositary and languages

1. The Secretary-General of the United Nations is designated depositary of this Protocol.

2. The original of this Protocol, of which the Arabic, Chinese, English, French, Russian and Spanish texts are equally authentic, shall be deposited with the Secretary-General of the United Nations.

IN WITNESS WHEREOF, the undersigned plenipotentiaries, being duly authorized thereto by their respective Governments, have signed this Protocol.

ANNEX III
Protocol against the Smuggling of Migrants by Land, Sea and Air, supplementing the United Nations Convention against Transnational Organized Crime

Preamble

The States Parties to this Protocol,

Declaring that effective action to prevent and combat the smuggling of migrants by land, sea and air requires a comprehensive international approach, including cooperation, the exchange of information and other appropriate measures, including socio-economic measures, at the national, regional and international levels,

Recalling General Assembly resolution 54/212 of 22 December 1999, in which the Assembly urged Member States and the United Nations system to strengthen international cooperation in the area of international migration and development in order to address the root causes of migration, especially those related to poverty, and to maximize the benefits of international migration to those concerned, and encouraged, where relevant, interregional, regional and subregional mechanisms to continue to address the question of migration and development,

Convinced of the need to provide migrants with humane treatment and full protection of their rights,

Taking into account the fact that, despite work undertaken in other international forums, there is no universal instrument that addresses all aspects of smuggling of migrants and other related issues,

Concerned at the significant increase in the activities of organized criminal groups in smuggling of migrants and other related criminal activities set forth in this Protocol, which bring great harm to the States concerned,

Also concerned that the smuggling of migrants can endanger the lives or security of the migrants involved,

Recalling General Assembly resolution 53/111 of 9 December 1998, in which the Assembly decided to establish an open-ended intergovernmental ad hoc committee for the purpose of elaborating a comprehensive international convention against transnational organized crime and of discussing the elaboration of, inter alia, an international instrument addressing illegal trafficking in and transporting of migrants, including by sea,

Convinced that supplementing the United Nations Convention against Transnational Organized Crime with an international instrument against the smuggling of migrants by land, sea and air will be useful in preventing and combating that crime,

Have agreed as follows:

I. General provisions

Article 1
Relation with the United Nations Convention against Transnational Organized Crime

1. This Protocol supplements the United Nations Convention against Transnational Organized Crime. It shall be interpreted together with the Convention.

2. The provisions of the Convention shall apply, mutatis mutandis, to this Protocol unless otherwise provided herein.

3. The offences established in accordance with article 6 of this Protocol shall be regarded as offences established in accordance with the Convention.

Article 2
Statement of purpose

The purpose of this Protocol is to prevent and combat the smuggling of migrants, as well as to promote cooperation among States Parties to that end, while protecting the rights of smuggled migrants.

Article 3
Use of terms

For the purposes of this Protocol:

(a) "Smuggling of migrants" shall mean the procurement, in order to obtain, directly or indirectly, a financial or other material benefit, of the illegal entry of a person into a State Party of which the person is not a national or a permanent resident;

(b) "Illegal entry" shall mean crossing borders without complying with the necessary requirements for legal entry into the receiving State;

(c) "Fraudulent travel or identity document" shall mean any travel or identity document:

(i) That has been falsely made or altered in some material way by anyone other than a person or agency lawfully authorized to make or issue the travel or identity document on behalf of a State; or

(ii) That has been improperly issued or obtained through misrepresentation, corruption or duress or in any other unlawful manner; or

(iii) That is being used by a person other than the rightful holder;

(d) "Vessel" shall mean any type of water craft, including non-displacement craft and seaplanes, used or capable of being used as a means of transportation on water, except a warship, naval auxiliary or other vessel owned or operated by a Government and used, for the time being, only on government non-commercial service.

Article 4
Scope of application

This Protocol shall apply, except as otherwise stated herein, to the prevention, investigation and prosecution of the offences established in accordance with article 6 of this Protocol, where the offences are transnational in nature and involve an organized criminal group, as well as to the protection of the rights of persons who have been the object of such offences.

Article 5
Criminal liability of migrants

Migrants shall not become liable to criminal prosecution under this Protocol for the fact of having been the object of conduct set forth in article 6 of this Protocol.

Article 6
Criminalization

1. Each State Party shall adopt such legislative and other measures as may be necessary to establish as criminal offences, when committed intentionally and in order to obtain, directly or indirectly, a financial or other material benefit:

(a) The smuggling of migrants;

(b) When committed for the purpose of enabling the smuggling of migrants:

(i) Producing a fraudulent travel or identity document;

(ii) Procuring, providing or possessing such a document;

(c) Enabling a person who is not a national or a permanent resident to remain in the State concerned without complying with the necessary requirements for legally remaining in the State by the means mentioned in subparagraph (b) of this paragraph or any other illegal means.

2. Each State Party shall also adopt such legislative and other measures as may be necessary to establish as criminal offences:

(a) Subject to the basic concepts of its legal system, attempting to commit an offence established in accordance with paragraph 1 of this article;

(b) Participating as an accomplice in an offence established in accordance with paragraph 1 (a), (b) (i) or (c) of this article and, subject to the basic concepts of its legal system, participating as an accomplice in an offence established in accordance with paragraph 1 (b) (ii) of this article;

(c) Organizing or directing other persons to commit an offence established in accordance with paragraph 1 of this article.

3. Each State Party shall adopt such legislative and other measures as may be necessary to establish as aggravating circumstances to the offences established in accordance with paragraph 1 (a), (b) (i) and (c) of this article and, subject to the basic concepts of its legal system, to the offences established in accordance with paragraph 2 (b) and (c) of this article, circumstances:

(a) That endanger, or are likely to endanger, the lives or safety of the migrants concerned; or

(b) That entail inhuman or degrading treatment, including for exploitation, of such migrants.

4. Nothing in this Protocol shall prevent a State Party from taking measures against a person whose conduct constitutes an offence under its domestic law.

II. Smuggling of migrants by sea

Article 7
Cooperation

States Parties shall cooperate to the fullest extent possible to prevent and suppress the smuggling of migrants by sea, in accordance with the international law of the sea.

Article 8
Measures against the smuggling of migrants by sea

1. A State Party that has reasonable grounds to suspect that a vessel that is flying its flag or claiming its registry, that is without nationality or that, though flying a foreign flag or refusing to show a flag, is in reality of the nationality of the State Party concerned is engaged in the smuggling of migrants by sea may request the assistance of other States Parties in suppressing the use of the vessel for that purpose. The States Parties so requested shall render such assistance to the extent possible within their means.

2. A State Party that has reasonable grounds to suspect that a vessel exercising freedom of navigation in accordance with international law and flying the flag or displaying the marks of registry of another State Party is engaged in the smuggling of migrants by sea may so notify the flag State, request confirmation of registry and, if confirmed, request authorization from the flag State to take appropriate measures with regard to that vessel. The flag State may authorize the requesting State, inter alia:

(a) To board the vessel;

(b) To search the vessel; and

(c) If evidence is found that the vessel is engaged in the smuggling of migrants by sea, to take appropriate measures with respect to the vessel and persons and cargo on board, as authorized by the flag State.

3. A State Party that has taken any measure in accordance with paragraph 2 of this article shall promptly inform the flag State concerned of the results of that measure.

4. A State Party shall respond expeditiously to a request from another State Party to determine whether a vessel that is claiming its registry or flying its flag is entitled to do so and to a request for authorization made in accordance with paragraph 2 of this article.

5. A flag State may, consistent with article 7 of this Protocol, subject its authorization to conditions to be agreed by it and the requesting State, including conditions relating to responsibility and the extent of effective measures to be taken. A State Party shall take no additional measures without the express authorization of the flag State, except those necessary to relieve imminent danger to the lives of persons or those which derive from relevant bilateral or multilateral agreements.

6. Each State Party shall designate an authority or, where necessary, authorities to receive and respond to requests for assistance, for confirmation of registry or of the right of a vessel to fly its flag and for authorization to take appropriate measures. Such designation shall be notified through the Secretary-General to all other States Parties within one month of the designation.

7. A State Party that has reasonable grounds to suspect that a vessel is engaged in the smuggling of migrants by sea and is without nationality or may be assimilated to a vessel without nationality may board and search the vessel. If evidence confirming the suspicion is found, that State Party shall take appropriate measures in accordance with relevant domestic and international law.

Article 9
Safeguard clauses

1. Where a State Party takes measures against a vessel in accordance with article 8 of this Protocol, it shall:

(a) Ensure the safety and humane treatment of the persons on board;

(b) Take due account of the need not to endanger the security of the vessel or its cargo;

(c) Take due account of the need not to prejudice the commercial or legal interests of the flag State or any other interested State;

(d) Ensure, within available means, that any measure taken with regard to the vessel is environmentally sound.

2. Where the grounds for measures taken pursuant to article 8 of this Protocol prove to be unfounded, the vessel shall be compensated for any loss or damage that may have been sustained, provided that the vessel has not committed any act justifying the measures taken.

3. Any measure taken, adopted or implemented in accordance with this chapter shall take due account of the need not to interfere with or to affect:

(*a*) The rights and obligations and the exercise of jurisdiction of coastal States in accordance with the international law of the sea; or

(*b*) The authority of the flag State to exercise jurisdiction and control in administrative, technical and social matters involving the vessel.

4. Any measure taken at sea pursuant to this chapter shall be carried out only by warships or military aircraft, or by other ships or aircraft clearly marked and identifiable as being on government service and authorized to that effect.

III. Prevention, cooperation and other measures

Article 10
Information

1. Without prejudice to articles 27 and 28 of the Convention, States Parties, in particular those with common borders or located on routes along which migrants are smuggled, shall, for the purpose of achieving the objectives of this Protocol, exchange among themselves, consistent with their respective domestic legal and administrative systems, relevant information on matters such as:

(*a*) Embarkation and destination points, as well as routes, carriers and means of transportation, known to be or suspected of being used by an organized criminal group engaged in conduct set forth in article 6 of this Protocol;

(*b*) The identity and methods of organizations or organized criminal groups known to be or suspected of being engaged in conduct set forth in article 6 of this Protocol;

(*c*) The authenticity and proper form of travel documents issued by a State Party and the theft or related misuse of blank travel or identity documents;

(*d*) Means and methods of concealment and transportation of persons, the unlawful alteration, reproduction or acquisition or other misuse of travel or identity documents used in conduct set forth in article 6 of this Protocol and ways of detecting them;

(*e*) Legislative experiences and practices and measures to prevent and combat the conduct set forth in article 6 of this Protocol; and

(*f*) Scientific and technological information useful to law enforcement, so as to enhance each other's ability to prevent, detect and investigate the conduct set forth in article 6 of this Protocol and to prosecute those involved.

2. A State Party that receives information shall comply with any request by the State Party that transmitted the information that places restrictions on its use.

Article 11
Border measures

1. Without prejudice to international commitments in relation to the free movement of people, States Parties shall strengthen, to the extent possible, such border controls as may be necessary to prevent and detect the smuggling of migrants.

2. Each State Party shall adopt legislative or other appropriate measures to prevent, to the extent possible, means of transport operated by commercial carriers from being used in the commission of the offence established in accordance with article 6, paragraph 1 (*a*), of this Protocol.

3. Where appropriate, and without prejudice to applicable international conventions, such measures shall include establishing the obligation of commercial carriers, including any transportation company or the owner or operator of any means of transport, to ascertain that all passengers are in possession of the travel documents required for entry into the receiving State.

4. Each State Party shall take the necessary measures, in accordance with its domestic law, to provide for sanctions in cases of violation of the obligation set forth in paragraph 3 of this article.

5. Each State Party shall consider taking measures that permit, in accordance with its domestic law, the denial of entry or revocation of visas of persons implicated in the commission of offences established in accordance with this Protocol.

6. Without prejudice to article 27 of the Convention, States Parties shall consider strengthening cooperation among border control agencies by, inter alia, establishing and maintaining direct channels of communication.

Article 12
Security and control of documents

Each State Party shall take such measures as may be necessary, within available means:

(*a*) To ensure that travel or identity documents issued by it are of such quality that they cannot easily be misused and cannot readily be falsified or unlawfully altered, replicated or issued; and

(*b*) To ensure the integrity and security of travel or identity documents issued by or on behalf of the State Party and to prevent their unlawful creation, issuance and use.

Article 13
Legitimacy and validity of documents

At the request of another State Party, a State Party shall, in accordance with its domestic law, verify within a reasonable time the legitimacy and validity of travel or identity documents issued or purported to have been issued in its name and suspected of being used for purposes of conduct set forth in article 6 of this Protocol.

Article 14
Training and technical cooperation

1. States Parties shall provide or strengthen specialized training for immigration and other relevant officials in preventing the conduct set forth in article 6 of this Protocol and in the humane treatment of migrants who have been the object of such conduct, while respecting their rights as set forth in this Protocol.

2. States Parties shall cooperate with each other and with competent international organizations, non-governmental organizations, other relevant organizations and other elements of civil society as appropriate to ensure that there is adequate personnel training in their territories to prevent, combat and eradicate the conduct set forth in article 6 of this Protocol and to protect the rights of migrants who have been the object of such conduct. Such training shall include:

(*a*) Improving the security and quality of travel documents;

(*b*) Recognizing and detecting fraudulent travel or identity documents;

(c) Gathering criminal intelligence, relating in particular to the identification of organized criminal groups known to be or suspected of being engaged in conduct set forth in article 6 of this Protocol, the methods used to transport smuggled migrants, the misuse of travel or identity documents for purposes of conduct set forth in article 6 and the means of concealment used in the smuggling of migrants;

(d) Improving procedures for detecting smuggled persons at conventional and non-conventional points of entry and exit; and

(e) The humane treatment of migrants and the protection of their rights as set forth in this Protocol.

3. States Parties with relevant expertise shall consider providing technical assistance to States that are frequently countries of origin or transit for persons who have been the object of conduct set forth in article 6 of this Protocol. States Parties shall make every effort to provide the necessary resources, such as vehicles, computer systems and document readers, to combat the conduct set forth in article 6.

Article 15
Other prevention measures

1. Each State Party shall take measures to ensure that it provides or strengthens information programmes to increase public awareness of the fact that the conduct set forth in article 6 of this Protocol is a criminal activity frequently perpetrated by organized criminal groups for profit and that it poses serious risks to the migrants concerned.

2. In accordance with article 31 of the Convention, States Parties shall cooperate in the field of public information for the purpose of preventing potential migrants from falling victim to organized criminal groups.

3. Each State Party shall promote or strengthen, as appropriate, development programmes and cooperation at the national, regional and international levels, taking into account the socio-economic realities of migration and paying special attention to economically and socially depressed areas, in order to combat the root socio-economic causes of the smuggling of migrants, such as poverty and underdevelopment.

Article 16
Protection and assistance measures

1. In implementing this Protocol, each State Party shall take, consistent with its obligations under international law, all appropriate measures, including legislation if necessary, to preserve and protect the rights of persons who have been the object of conduct set forth in article 6 of this Protocol as accorded under applicable international law, in particular the right to life and the right not to be subjected to torture or other cruel, inhuman or degrading treatment or punishment.

2. Each State Party shall take appropriate measures to afford migrants appropriate protection against violence that may be inflicted upon them, whether by individuals or groups, by reason of being the object of conduct set forth in article 6 of this Protocol.

3. Each State Party shall afford appropriate assistance to migrants whose lives or safety are endangered by reason of being the object of conduct set forth in article 6 of this Protocol.

4. In applying the provisions of this article, States Parties shall take into account the special needs of women and children.

5. In the case of the detention of a person who has been the object of conduct set forth in article 6 of this Protocol, each State Party shall comply with its obligations under the Vienna Convention on Consular Relations, where applicable, including that of informing the person concerned without delay about the provisions concerning notification to and communication with consular officers.

Article 17
Agreements and arrangements

States Parties shall consider the conclusion of bilateral or regional agreements or operational arrangements or understandings aimed at:

(a) Establishing the most appropriate and effective measures to prevent and combat the conduct set forth in article 6 of this Protocol; or

(b) Enhancing the provisions of this Protocol among themselves.

Article 18
Return of smuggled migrants

1. Each State Party agrees to facilitate and accept, without undue or unreasonable delay, the return of a person who has been the object of conduct set forth in article 6 of this Protocol and who is its national or who has the right of permanent residence in its territory at the time of return.

2. Each State Party shall consider the possibility of facilitating and accepting the return of a person who has been the object of conduct set forth in article 6 of this Protocol and who had the right of permanent residence in its territory at the time of entry into the receiving State in accordance with its domestic law.

3. At the request of the receiving State Party, a requested State Party shall, without undue or unreasonable delay, verify whether a person who has been the object of conduct set forth in article 6 of this Protocol is its national or has the right of permanent residence in its territory.

4. In order to facilitate the return of a person who has been the object of conduct set forth in article 6 of this Protocol and is without proper documentation, the State Party of which that person is a national or in which he or she has the right of permanent residence shall agree to issue, at the request of the receiving State Party, such travel documents or other authorization as may be necessary to enable the person to travel to and re-enter its territory.

5. Each State Party involved with the return of a person who has been the object of conduct set forth in article 6 of this Protocol shall take all appropriate measures to carry out the return in an orderly manner and with due regard for the safety and dignity of the person.

6. States Parties may cooperate with relevant international organizations in the implementation of this article.

7. This article shall be without prejudice to any right afforded to persons who have been the object of conduct set forth in article 6 of this Protocol by any domestic law of the receiving State Party.

8. This article shall not affect the obligations entered into under any other applicable treaty, bilateral

or multilateral, or any other applicable operational agreement or arrangement that governs, in whole or in part, the return of persons who have been the object of conduct set forth in article 6 of this Protocol.

IV. Final provisions

Article 19
Saving clause

1. Nothing in this Protocol shall affect the other rights, obligations and responsibilities of States and individuals under international law, including international humanitarian law and international human rights law and, in particular, where applicable, the 1951 Convention and the 1967 Protocol relating to the Status of Refugees and the principle of non-refoulement as contained therein.

2. The measures set forth in this Protocol shall be interpreted and applied in a way that is not discriminatory to persons on the ground that they are the object of conduct set forth in article 6 of this Protocol. The interpretation and application of those measures shall be consistent with internationally recognized principles of non-discrimination.

Article 20
Settlement of disputes

1. States Parties shall endeavour to settle disputes concerning the interpretation or application of this Protocol through negotiation.

2. Any dispute between two or more States Parties concerning the interpretation or application of this Protocol that cannot be settled through negotiation within a reasonable time shall, at the request of one of those States Parties, be submitted to arbitration. If, six months after the date of the request for arbitration, those States Parties are unable to agree on the organization of the arbitration, any one of those States Parties may refer the dispute to the International Court of Justice by request in accordance with the Statute of the Court.

3. Each State Party may, at the time of signature, ratification, acceptance or approval of or accession to this Protocol, declare that it does not consider itself bound by paragraph 2 of this article. The other States Parties shall not be bound by paragraph 2 of this article with respect to any State Party that has made such a reservation.

4. Any State Party that has made a reservation in accordance with paragraph 3 of this article may at any time withdraw that reservation by notification to the Secretary-General of the United Nations.

Article 21
Signature, ratification, acceptance, approval and accession

1. This Protocol shall be open to all States for signature from 12 to 15 December 2000 in Palermo, Italy, and thereafter at United Nations Headquarters in New York until 12 December 2002.

2. This Protocol shall also be open for signature by regional economic integration organizations provided that at least one member State of such organization has signed this Protocol in accordance with paragraph 1 of this article.

3. This Protocol is subject to ratification, acceptance or approval. Instruments of ratification, acceptance or approval shall be deposited with the Secretary-General of the United Nations. A regional economic integration organization may deposit its instrument of ratification, acceptance or approval if at least one of its member States has done likewise. In that instrument of ratification, acceptance or approval, such organization shall declare the extent of its competence with respect to the matters governed by this Protocol. Such organization shall also inform the depositary of any relevant modification in the extent of its competence.

4. This Protocol is open for accession by any State or any regional economic integration organization of which at least one member State is a Party to this Protocol. Instruments of accession shall be deposited with the Secretary-General of the United Nations. At the time of its accession, a regional economic integration organization shall declare the extent of its competence with respect to matters governed by this Protocol. Such organization shall also inform the depositary of any relevant modification in the extent of its competence.

Article 22
Entry into force

1. This Protocol shall enter into force on the ninetieth day after the date of deposit of the fortieth instrument of ratification, acceptance, approval or accession, except that it shall not enter into force before the entry into force of the Convention. For the purpose of this paragraph, any instrument deposited by a regional economic integration organization shall not be counted as additional to those deposited by member States of such organization.

2. For each State or regional economic integration organization ratifying, accepting, approving or acceding to this Protocol after the deposit of the fortieth instrument of such action, this Protocol shall enter into force on the thirtieth day after the date of deposit by such State or organization of the relevant instrument or on the date this Protocol enters into force pursuant to paragraph 1 of this article, whichever is the later.

Article 23
Amendment

1. After the expiry of five years from the entry into force of this Protocol, a State Party to the Protocol may propose an amendment and file it with the Secretary-General of the United Nations, who shall thereupon communicate the proposed amendment to the States Parties and to the Conference of the Parties to the Convention for the purpose of considering and deciding on the proposal. The States Parties to this Protocol meeting at the Conference of the Parties shall make every effort to achieve consensus on each amendment. If all efforts at consensus have been exhausted and no agreement has been reached, the amendment shall, as a last resort, require for its adoption a two-thirds majority vote of the States Parties to this Protocol present and voting at the meeting of the Conference of the Parties.

2. Regional economic integration organizations, in matters within their competence, shall exercise their right to vote under this article with a number of votes equal to the number of their member States that are Parties to this Protocol. Such organizations shall not exercise their right to vote if their member States exercise theirs and vice versa.

3. An amendment adopted in accordance with paragraph 1 of this article is subject to ratification, acceptance or approval by States Parties.

4. An amendment adopted in accordance with paragraph 1 of this article shall enter into force in respect of a State Party ninety days after the date of the deposit with the Secretary-General of the United Nations of an instrument of ratification, acceptance or approval of such amendment.

5. When an amendment enters into force, it shall be binding on those States Parties which have expressed their consent to be bound by it. Other States Parties shall still be bound by the provisions of this Protocol and any earlier amendments that they have ratified, accepted or approved.

Article 24
Denunciation

1. A State Party may denounce this Protocol by written notification to the Secretary-General of the United Nations. Such denunciation shall become effective one year after the date of receipt of the notification by the Secretary-General.

2. A regional economic integration organization shall cease to be a Party to this Protocol when all of its member States have denounced it.

Article 25
Depositary and languages

1. The Secretary-General of the United Nations is designated depositary of this Protocol.

2. The original of this Protocol, of which the Arabic, Chinese, English, French, Russian and Spanish texts are equally authentic, shall be deposited with the Secretary-General of the United Nations.

IN WITNESS WHEREOF, the undersigned plenipotentiaries, being duly authorized thereto by their respective Governments, have signed this Protocol.

Strategies for crime prevention

Corruption

In January [A/AC.254/25], the Ad Hoc Committee on the Elaboration of a Convention against Transnational Organized Crime (see p. 1048), in response to General Assembly resolution 54/128 [YUN 1999, p. 1062], discussed the desirability of an international legal instrument against corruption. The Committee was of the view that the legal instrument was desirable and that it should be independent of the United Nations Convention against Transnational Organized Crime (see p. 1050).

The Committee transmitted its views to the Commission on Crime Prevention and Criminal Justice, which drafted a resolution for the Assembly's adoption (see below).

ECONOMIC AND SOCIAL COUNCIL ACTION

On 27 July [meeting 43], the Economic and Social Council, on the recommendation of the Commission on Crime Prevention and Criminal Justice [E/2000/30], adopted **resolution 2000/13** without vote [agenda item 14 *(c)*].

An effective international legal instrument against corruption

The Economic and Social Council

Recommends to the General Assembly the adoption of the following draft resolution:

[For text, see General Assembly resolution 55/61 below.]

GENERAL ASSEMBLY ACTION

On 4 December [meeting 81], the General Assembly, on the recommendation of the Third Committee [A/55/593], adopted **resolution 55/61** without vote [agenda item 105].

An effective international legal instrument against corruption

The General Assembly,

Noting the corrosive effect that corruption has on democracy, development, the rule of law and economic activity,

Recalling its resolutions 53/111 of 9 December 1998, by which it established the Ad Hoc Committee on the Elaboration of a Convention against Transnational Organized Crime, and 54/126 of 17 December 1999, in which it requested the Ad Hoc Committee to complete its work in 2000,

Recalling also its resolution 54/128 of 17 December 1999, in which it requested the Ad Hoc Committee to explore the desirability of an international instrument against corruption, either ancillary to or independent of the United Nations Convention against Transnational Organized Crime,

Taking note of the report of the Ad Hoc Committee on its seventh session, during which it considered the implementation of resolution 54/128,

Recalling the debates and especially the statements made at the high-level segment and the results of the Tenth United Nations Congress on the Prevention of Crime and the Treatment of Offenders, in particular the Vienna Declaration on Crime and Justice: Meeting the Challenges of the Twenty-first Century,

Bearing in mind the need to prepare a broad instrument that takes into account existing international conventions against corruption,

1. *Recognizes* that an effective international legal instrument against corruption, independent of the United Nations Convention against Transnational Organized Crime, is desirable;

2. *Decides* to begin the elaboration of such an instrument in Vienna at the headquarters of the United Nations Centre for International Crime Prevention of the United Nations Office for Drug Control and Crime Prevention;

3. *Requests* the Secretary-General to prepare a report analysing all relevant international legal instruments, other documents and recommendations addressing corruption, considering, inter alia, obligations as regards criminalization of all forms of corruption and international cooperation, regulatory aspects of corruption and the relationship between corruption and money-laundering, and to submit it to the Commission on Crime Prevention and Criminal Justice at an inter-sessional meeting in order to allow Member States to provide comments to the Commission prior to its tenth session;

4. *Requests* the Commission, at its tenth session, to review and assess the report of the Secretary-General and, on that basis, to provide recommendations and guidance as to future work on the development of a legal instrument against corruption;

5. *Requests* the Secretary-General to convene, upon completion of the negotiation of the United Nations Convention against Transnational Organized Crime and the related protocols, an intergovernmental open-ended expert group to examine and prepare, on the basis of the report of the Secretary-General and of the recommendations of the Commission at its tenth session, draft terms of reference for the negotiation of the future legal instrument against corruption;

6. *Requests* the intergovernmental open-ended expert group to submit the draft terms of reference for the negotiation of the future legal instrument, through the Commission on Crime Prevention and Criminal Justice and the Economic and Social Council, to the General Assembly at its fifty-sixth session for adoption;

7. *Decides* to establish an ad hoc committee for the negotiation of such an instrument to start its work in Vienna as soon as the draft terms of reference for such negotiation are adopted;

8. *Invites* donor countries to assist the United Nations in ensuring the effective participation of developing countries, in particular least developed countries, in the work of the intergovernmental open-ended expert group and the ad hoc committee, including travel and local expenses;

9. *Requests* the Secretary-General to provide the Commission and the intergovernmental open-ended expert group with the required facilities and resources to support their work.

ANNEX
Indicative list of international legal instruments, documents and recommendations against corruption

(a) International Code of Conduct for Public Officials;

(b) United Nations Declaration against Corruption and Bribery in International Commercial Transactions;

(c) General Assembly resolution 54/128, in which the Assembly subscribed to the conclusions and recommendations of the Expert Group Meeting on Corruption and its Financial Channels, held in Paris from 30 March to 1 April 1999;

(d) Report of the Tenth United Nations Congress on the Prevention of Crime and the Treatment of Offenders;

(e) Inter-American Convention against Corruption adopted by the Organization of American States on 29 March 1996;

(f) Recommendation 32 of the Senior Experts Group on Transnational Organized Crime endorsed by the Political Group of Eight in Lyon, France, on 29 June 1996;

(g) The Twenty Guiding Principles for the Fight against Corruption adopted by the Committee of Ministers of the Council of Europe on 6 November 1997;

(h) Convention on Combating Bribery of Foreign Public Officials in International Business Transactions adopted by the Organisation for Economic Cooperation and Development on 21 November 1997;

(i) Agreement Establishing the Group of States against Corruption adopted by the Committee of Ministers of the Council of Europe on 1 May 1999, and the Criminal Law Convention on Corruption adopted by the Committee of Ministers of the Council of Europe on 4 November 1998;

(j) Joint Action on corruption in the private sector adopted by the Council of the European Union on 22 December 1998;

(k) Declarations made by the first Global Forum on Fighting Corruption, held in Washington, D.C., from 24 to 26 February 1999, and the second Global Forum, to be held in The Hague in 2001;

(l) Civil Law Convention on Corruption adopted by the Committee of Ministers of the Council of Europe on 9 September 1999;

(m) Model Code of Conduct for Public Officials adopted by the Committee of Ministers of the Council of Europe on 11 May 2000;

(n) Principles to Combat Corruption in African Countries of the Global Coalition for Africa;

(o) Conventions and related protocols of the European Union on corruption;

(p) Best practices such as those compiled by the Basel Committee on Banking Supervision, the Financial Action Task Force on Money-Laundering and the International Organization of Securities Commissions.

Corrupt practices and illegal transfer of funds

Pursuant to General Assembly resolutions 53/176 [YUN 1998, p. 1046] and 54/205 [YUN 1999, p. 1063], the Secretary-General, in September [A/55/405], submitted a report prepared by the United Nations Conference on Trade and Development, describing measures taken by 47 countries, as well as international organizations, groups of countries and NGOs, to give effect to Assembly resolutions aimed at preventing corrupt practices in international commercial transactions and the illegal transfer of funds.

GENERAL ASSEMBLY ACTION

On 20 December [meeting 87], on the recommendation of the Second Committee [A/55/580], the General Assembly adopted **resolution 55/188** without vote [agenda item 93].

Preventing and combating corrupt practices and illegal transfer of funds and repatriation of such funds to the countries of origin

The General Assembly,

Recalling its resolutions 53/176 of 15 December 1998 on action against corruption and bribery in international commercial transactions, 54/205 of 22 December 1999 on the prevention of corrupt practices and illegal transfer of funds and 55/61 of 4 December 2000 on an effective international legal instrument against corruption,

Concerned about the seriousness of problems posed by corruption, which may endanger the stability and security of societies, undermine the values of democracy and morality and jeopardize social, economic and political development,

Recognizing the importance of international cooperation and existing international and national laws for combating corruption in international commercial transactions,

Noting with appreciation the recent adoption of the United Nations Convention against Transnational Organized Crime and its two protocols,

Recognizing the important role of the business community, including, in particular, the private sector, in enhancing the dynamic process of the development of the agricultural, industrial and service sectors and the need to create an enabling environment at the national and international levels for business in order to facilitate economic growth and sustainable development of developing countries, most especially African countries, taking into account the development priorities of Governments,

Mindful of the very important role that the private sector can play in fostering economic growth and development and of the active involvement of the United Nations system in facilitating the constructive participation and orderly interaction of the private sector in the development process by embracing universal principles and norms, such as honesty, transparency and accountability,

Taking note of the report of the Secretary-General on the prevention of corrupt practices and illegal transfer of funds,

1. *Reiterates its condemnation* of corruption, bribery, money-laundering and the illegal transfer of funds;

2. *Calls* for further international and national measures to combat corrupt practices and bribery in international transactions and for international cooperation in support of those measures;

3. *Also calls* for, while recognizing the importance of national measures, increased international cooperation, inter alia, through the United Nations system, in regard to devising ways and means of preventing and addressing illegal transfers, as well as repatriating illegally transferred funds to the countries of origin, and calls upon all countries and entities concerned to cooperate in this regard;

4. *Requests* the international community to support the efforts of all countries to strengthen institutional capacity and regulatory frameworks for preventing corruption, bribery, money-laundering and illegal transfer of funds, as well as for the repatriation of those funds to the countries of origin;

5. *Reiterates its request* to the Secretary-General, as contained in resolution 55/61, to convene an intergovernmental open-ended expert group to examine and prepare, on the basis of the report of the Secretary-General and of recommendations of the Commission on Crime Prevention and Criminal Justice at its tenth session, draft terms of reference for the negotiation of the future legal instrument against corruption, and invites the expert group on the same basis to examine the question of illegally transferred funds and the repatriation of such funds to the countries of origin;

6. *Decides* to keep this matter under review, and, in this regard, requests the Secretary-General, in consultation with Member States and relevant bodies of the United Nations system, to prepare, without duplicating material contained in the report requested by the Assembly in resolution 55/61, an analytical report containing information on the progress made in the implementation of the present resolution and, bearing in mind resolution 54/205, concrete recommendations,

inter alia, with regard to the repatriation of illegally transferred funds to the countries of origin, and to submit the report to the General Assembly at its fifty-sixth session under the item entitled "Sectoral policy questions: business and development".

Criminal misuse of information technologies

GENERAL ASSEMBLY ACTION

On 4 December [meeting 81], the General Assembly, on the recommendation of the Third Committee [A/55/593], adopted **resolution 55/63** without vote [agenda item 105].

Combating the criminal misuse of information technologies

The General Assembly,

Recalling the United Nations Millennium Declaration, in which Member States resolved to ensure that the benefits of new technologies, especially information and communication technologies, in conformity with recommendations contained in the Ministerial Declaration of the high-level segment of the substantive session of 2000 of the Economic and Social Council, are available to all,

Recalling also its resolution 45/121 of 14 December 1990, in which it endorsed the recommendations of the Eighth United Nations Congress on the Prevention of Crime and the Treatment of Offenders, and noting in particular the resolution on computer-related crimes, in which the Eighth Congress called upon States to intensify their efforts to combat computer-related abuses more effectively,

Emphasizing the contributions that the United Nations, in particular the Commission on Crime Prevention and Criminal Justice, can make in the promotion of more efficient and effective law enforcement and administration of justice and of the highest standards of fairness and human dignity,

Recognizing that the free flow of information can promote economic and social development, education and democratic governance,

Noting significant advancements in the development and application of information technologies and means of telecommunication,

Expressing concern that technological advancements have created new possibilities for criminal activity, in particular the criminal misuse of information technologies,

Noting that reliance on information technologies, while it may vary from State to State, has resulted in a substantial increase in global cooperation and coordination, with the result that the criminal misuse of information technologies may have a grave impact on all States,

Recognizing that gaps in the access to and use of information technologies by States can diminish the effectiveness of international cooperation in combating the criminal misuse of information technologies, and noting the need to facilitate the transfer of information technologies, in particular to developing countries,

Noting the necessity of preventing the criminal misuse of information technologies,

Recognizing the need for cooperation between States and private industry in combating the criminal misuse of information technologies,

Underlining the need for enhanced coordination and cooperation among States in combating the criminal misuse of information technologies, and, in this context, stressing the role that can be played by both the United Nations and regional organizations,

Welcoming the work of the Tenth United Nations Congress on the Prevention of Crime and the Treatment of Offenders,

Noting the work of the Committee of Experts on Crime in Cyberspace of the Council of Europe on a draft convention on cybercrime, the principles agreed to by the Ministers of Justice and the Interior of the Group of Eight in Washington, D.C., on 10 December 1997, which were endorsed by the heads of State of the Group of Eight in Birmingham, United Kingdom of Great Britain and Northern Ireland, on 17 May 1998, the work of the Conference of the Group of Eight on a dialogue between government and industry on safety and confidence in cyberspace, held in Paris from 15 to 17 May 2000, and the recommendations approved on 3 March 2000 by the Third Meeting of Ministers of Justice or of Ministers or Attorneys General of the Americas, convened in San José, Costa Rica, from 1 to 3 March 2000 within the framework of the Organization of American States,

1. *Notes with appreciation* the efforts of the above-mentioned bodies to prevent the criminal misuse of information technologies, and also notes the value of, inter alia, the following measures to combat such misuse:

(*a*) States should ensure that their laws and practice eliminate safe havens for those who criminally misuse information technologies;

(*b*) Law enforcement cooperation in the investigation and prosecution of international cases of criminal misuse of information technologies should be coordinated among all concerned States;

(*c*) Information should be exchanged between States regarding the problems that they face in combating the criminal misuse of information technologies;

(*d*) Law enforcement personnel should be trained and equipped to address the criminal misuse of information technologies;

(*e*) Legal systems should protect the confidentiality, integrity and availability of data and computer systems from unauthorized impairment and ensure that criminal abuse is penalized;

(*f*) Legal systems should permit the preservation of and quick access to electronic data pertaining to particular criminal investigations;

(*g*) Mutual assistance regimes should ensure the timely investigation of the criminal misuse of information technologies and the timely gathering and exchange of evidence in such cases;

(*h*) The general public should be made aware of the need to prevent and combat the criminal misuse of information technologies;

(*i*) To the extent practicable, information technologies should be designed to help to prevent and detect criminal misuse, trace criminals and collect evidence;

(*j*) The fight against the criminal misuse of information technologies requires the development of solutions taking into account both the protection of individual freedoms and privacy and the preservation of the capacity of Governments to fight such criminal misuse;

2. *Invites* States to take into account the above-mentioned measures in their efforts to combat the criminal misuse of information technologies;

3. *Decides* to maintain the question of the criminal misuse of information technologies on the agenda of its fifty-sixth session, as part of the item entitled "Crime prevention and criminal justice".

UN standards and norms

Juvenile justice reform

In an April report on juvenile justice reform [E/CN.15/2000/5], prepared pursuant to Economic and Social Council resolutions 1997/30 [YUN 1997, p. 1158] and 1998/21 [YUN 1998, p. 1047], the Secretary-General analysed the roles, functions and activities of partners, including UN entities, within the parameters of relevant UN instruments and policies, particularly the 1989 Convention on the Rights of the Child, adopted by the General Assembly in resolution 44/25 [YUN 1989, p. 561]. The report contained information provided by the Office of the UN High Commissioner for Human Rights, the United Nations Children's Fund (UNICEF), the Committee on the Rights of the Child and WHO.

Noting that the standards originating in the United Nations were incorporated into the Convention on the Rights of the Child, the report described the activities of the Committee on the Rights of the Child (see p. 614), the Convention's monitoring body, and reviewed UN action with regard to standard-setting, monitoring and implementation of instruments and technical advisory services.

Non-binding instruments establishing and governing juvenile justice were described, including the United Nations Standard Minimum Rules for the Administration of Juvenile Justice (the Beijing Rules), adopted by the Assembly in resolution 40/33 [YUN 1985, p. 746]; the United Nations Guidelines for the Prevention of Juvenile Delinquency (the Riyadh Guidelines), adopted by the Assembly in resolution 45/112 [YUN 1990, p. 738]; and the United Nations Rules for the Protection of Juveniles Deprived of Their Liberty, adopted by the Assembly in resolution 45/113 [ibid., p. 743].

Restorative justice

In April [A/CONF.187/15], following a discussion on restorative justice, the Tenth United Nations Congress on the Prevention of Crime and the Treatment of Offenders concluded that restorative justice was desirable, as was quality control and evaluation of relevant initiatives. It was suggested that the Commission on Crime Prevention and Criminal Justice should be invited to formulate basic principles and standards to guide States in the fair and effective use of mediation and other processes of restorative justice.

On 27 July [meeting 43], the Economic and Social Council, on the recommendation of the Commission on Crime Prevention and Criminal Justice [E/2000/30], adopted **resolution 2000/14** without vote [agenda item 14 (c)].

Basic principles on the use of restorative justice programmes in criminal matters

The Economic and Social Council,

Recalling its resolution 1999/26 of 28 July 1999, entitled "Development and implementation of mediation and restorative justice measures in criminal justice", in which the Council requested the Commission on Crime Prevention and Criminal Justice to consider the desirability of formulating United Nations standards in the field of mediation and restorative justice,

Noting the discussions on restorative justice during the Tenth United Nations Congress on the Prevention of Crime and the Treatment of Offenders in relation to the agenda item entitled "Offenders and victims: accountability and fairness in the justice process",

Recognizing that the use of restorative justice measures does not prejudice the right of States to prosecute alleged offenders,

1. *Takes note* of the preliminary draft elements of a declaration of basic principles on the use of restorative justice programmes in criminal matters, annexed to the present resolution;

2. *Requests* the Secretary-General to seek comments from Member States and relevant intergovernmental and non-governmental organizations, as well as the institutes of the United Nations Crime Prevention and Criminal Justice Programme network, on the desirability and the means of establishing common principles on the use of restorative justice programmes in criminal matters, including the advisability of developing an instrument, such as the preliminary draft elements of a declaration annexed to the present resolution, and on the contents of this draft;

3. *Also requests* the Secretary-General to convene, subject to the availability of voluntary contributions, a meeting of experts selected on the basis of equitable geographical representation to review the comments received and to examine proposals for further action in relation to restorative justice, including mediation, as well as the possibility of developing an instrument such as a declaration of basic principles on the use of restorative justice programmes in criminal matters, taking into account the preliminary draft elements of a declaration annexed to the present resolution;

4. *Further requests* the Secretary-General to report to the Commission on Crime Prevention and Criminal Justice at its eleventh session on the comments received and the results of the meeting of experts;

5. *Invites* the Commission to take action at its eleventh session on the basis of the report of the Secretary-General;

6. *Calls upon* Member States, building on the results of the Tenth United Nations Congress on the Prevention of Crime and the Treatment of Offenders, to continue to exchange information on experiences in the implementation and evaluation of programmes for restorative justice, including mediation.

ANNEX
Preliminary draft elements of a declaration of basic principles on the use of restorative justice programmes in criminal matters

I. Definitions

1. "Restorative justice programme" means any programme that uses restorative processes or aims to achieve restorative outcomes.

2. "Restorative outcome" means an agreement reached as the result of a restorative process. Examples of restorative outcomes include restitution, community service and any other programme or response designed to achieve reparation for the victim and community and reintegration of the victim and/or the offender.

3. "Restorative process" means any process in which the victim, the offender and/or any other individuals or community members affected by a crime participate together actively in the resolution of matters arising from the crime, often with the help of a fair and impartial third party. Examples of restorative processes include mediation, conferencing and sentencing circles.

4. "Parties" means the victim, the offender and any other individuals or community members affected by a crime who may be involved in a restorative justice programme.

5. "Facilitator" means a fair and impartial third party whose role is to facilitate the participation of victims and offenders in an encounter programme.

II. Use of restorative justice programmes

6. Restorative justice programmes should be generally available at all stages of the criminal justice process.

7. Restorative processes should be used only with the free and voluntary consent of the parties. The parties should be able to withdraw such consent at any time during the process. Agreements should be arrived at voluntarily by the parties and should contain only reasonable and proportionate obligations.

8. All parties should normally acknowledge the basic facts of a case as a basis for participation in a restorative process. Participation should not be used as evidence of admission of guilt in subsequent legal proceedings.

9. Obvious disparities with respect to factors such as power imbalances and the age, maturity or intellectual capacity of the parties should be taken into consideration in referring a case to and in conducting a restorative process. Similarly, obvious threats to the safety of any of the parties should also be considered in referring a case to and in conducting a restorative process. The views of the parties themselves about the suitability of restorative processes or outcomes should be given great deference in this consideration.

10. Where restorative processes and/or outcomes are not possible, criminal justice officials should do all they can to encourage the offender to take responsibility vis-à-vis the victim and affected communities, and reintegration of the victim and/or offender into the community.

III. Operation of restorative justice programmes

11. Guidelines and standards should be established, with legislative authority when necessary, that govern the use of restorative justice programmes. Such guidelines and standards should address:

(a) The conditions for the referral of cases to restorative justice programmes;

(b) The handling of cases following a restorative process;

(c) The qualifications, training and assessment of facilitators;

(d) The administration of restorative justice programmes;

(e) Standards of competence and ethical rules governing the operation of restorative justice programmes.

12. Fundamental procedural safeguards should be applied to restorative justice programmes and in particular to restorative processes:

(a) The parties should have the right to legal advice before and after the restorative process and, where necessary, to translation and/or interpretation. Minors should, in addition, have the right to parental assistance;

(b) Before agreeing to participate in restorative processes, the parties should be fully informed of their rights, the nature of the process and the possible consequences of their decision;

(c) Neither the victim nor the offender should be induced by unfair means to participate in restorative processes or outcomes.

13. Discussions in restorative processes should be confidential and should not be disclosed subsequently, except with the agreement of the parties.

14. Judicial discharges based on agreements arising out of restorative justice programmes should have the same status as judicial decisions or judgements and should preclude prosecution in respect of the same facts *(non bis in idem)*.

15. Where no agreement can be made between the parties, the case should be referred back to the criminal justice authorities and a decision as to how to proceed should be taken without delay. Lack of agreement may not be used as justification for a more severe sentence in subsequent criminal justice proceedings.

16. Failure to implement an agreement made in the course of a restorative process should be referred back to the restorative programme or to the criminal justice authorities and a decision as to how to proceed should be taken without delay. Failure to implement the agreement may not be used as justification for a more severe sentence in subsequent criminal justice proceedings.

IV. Facilitators

17. Facilitators should be recruited from all sections of society and should generally possess good understanding of local cultures and communities. They should be able to demonstrate sound judgement and the interpersonal skills necessary for conducting restorative processes.

18. Facilitators should perform their duties in an impartial manner, based on the facts of the case and on the needs and wishes of the parties. They should always respect the dignity of the parties and ensure that the parties act with respect towards each other.

19. Facilitators should be responsible for providing a safe and appropriate environment for the restorative process. They should be sensitive to any vulnerability of the parties.

20. Facilitators should receive initial training before taking up facilitation duties and should also receive in-service training. The training should aim at providing skills in conflict resolution, taking into account the particular needs of victims and offenders, at providing basic knowledge of the criminal justice system and at providing a thorough knowledge of the operation of the restorative programme in which they will do their work.

V. Continuing development of restorative justice programmes

21. There should be regular consultation between criminal justice authorities and administrators of restorative justice programmes to develop a common understanding of restorative processes and outcomes, to increase the extent to which restorative programmes are used and to explore ways in which restorative approaches might be incorporated into criminal justice practices.

22. Member States should promote research on and evaluation of restorative justice programmes to assess the extent to which they result in restorative outcomes, serve as an alternative to the criminal justice process and provide positive outcomes for all parties.

23. Restorative justice processes may need to undergo change in concrete form over time. Member States should therefore encourage regular, rigorous evaluation and modification of such programmes in the light of the above definitions.

International fund

In accordance with Economic and Social Council resolution 1998/21 [YUN 1998, p. 1047], a working group of experts on the possible establishment of a fund for victims of crimes and abuse of power was convened in January.

The group endorsed the creation of such an international fund and suggested that it be used to support the development and/or strengthening of victim support services through technical assistance, develop measures for special victim types or groups, particularly with regard to transnational crime, and design international awareness-raising campaigns promoting victims' rights and effective crime prevention.

ECONOMIC AND SOCIAL COUNCIL ACTION

On 27 July [meeting 43], the Economic and Social Council, on the recommendation of the Commission on Crime Prevention and Criminal Justice [E/2000/30], adopted **resolution 2000/15** without vote [agenda item 14 (c)].

Implementation of the Declaration of Basic Principles of Justice for Victims of Crime and Abuse of Power

The Economic and Social Council,

Recognizing the importance of the Declaration of Basic Principles of Justice for Victims of Crime and Abuse of Power, adopted by the General Assembly in its resolution 40/34 of 29 November 1985, and the adoption of the Declaration as an important landmark in international efforts to improve the treatment of victims,

Bearing in mind that the General Assembly, in its resolution 40/34, called upon Member States to take the necessary steps to give effect to the provisions of the Declaration, and urged United Nations entities, other intergovernmental organizations and non-governmental organizations to cooperate in the implementation of those provisions,

Recalling its resolution 1998/21 of 28 July 1998, in which it requested the Secretary-General to seek the views of Member States regarding the desirability and feasibility of establishing an international fund for victims of crime and abuse of power and to convene a working group on this matter, consisting of Member States that expressed an interest in such a fund,

Recalling also the plan of action for the implementation of the Declaration of Basic Principles of Justice for Victims of Crime and Abuse of Power, annexed to its resolution 1998/21,

Deeply concerned about the continuing victimization by crime, especially organized crime, violence, terrorism and abuse of power, in particular of vulnerable individuals such as women and children, which exacts a vast human cost and impairs the quality of life in many parts of the world,

1. *Notes with appreciation* the work done by the working group of experts that met in January 2000 pursuant to resolution 1998/21;

2. *Takes note* of the finding of the working group of experts that there is a need to provide adequate assistance to initiatives in the area of victim care;

3. *Requests* the Secretary-General to prepare a report on possible ways and means of providing adequate assistance to initiatives in the area of victim care, taking into account, inter alia, the existing mechanisms providing such assistance and the report of the working group of experts, and to submit it to the Commission on Crime Prevention and Criminal Justice at its tenth session;

4. *Calls upon* the Secretary-General, Member States and intergovernmental and non-governmental organizations to continue to take the necessary steps to give effect to the provisions of the Declaration of Basic Principles of Justice for Victims of Crime and Abuse of Power in cooperation with United Nations entities and other intergovernmental and non-governmental organizations;

5. *Invites* the Commission on Crime Prevention and Criminal Justice to consider at its tenth session the report of the working group of experts and the report of the Secretary-General.

Human resource development

UN research and training institutes

UN Institute for Training and Research

Report of Executive Director. A report of the Executive Director of the United Nations Insti-

tute for Training and Research (UNITAR) [A/55/14], covering the period from 1 July 1998 to 30 June 2000, presented the accomplishments achieved during the Institute's restructuring period, as well as its current situation and future challenges. The report described the activities of UNITAR's training programme in multilateral diplomacy and international affairs management, and training and capacity-building programmes in social and economic development. Annexed to the report was a chronological list of training activities during the reporting period, statistical data on participation, a list of materials published during the reporting period and financial data.

Report of Secretary-General. A September report of the Secretary-General [A/55/510], prepared in accordance with General Assembly resolution 54/229 [YUN 1999, p. 1069], noted that UNITAR programmes had remained steady and sustained. Some 120 programmes, seminars and workshops had been organized throughout the world each year since 1996. Project delivery on a limited number of well-identified areas in which UNITAR had expertise and sound track records, introduced as part of the restructuring process, had continued. The network of partnership with national and regional academic and specialized centres had been expanded, particularly in Africa. Research on the design and development of new pedagogic methodologies was continued and efforts were made to develop distance learning, including e-training.

The Secretary-General said that UNITAR's financial situation had improved, but remained fragile. The funding of Special Purpose Grants was satisfactory but voluntary contributions to the General Fund remained insufficient. The Secretary-General discussed the provision of additional facilities to the Institute.

GENERAL ASSEMBLY ACTION

On 20 December [meeting 87], the General Assembly, on the recommendation of the Second Committee [A/55/584], adopted **resolution 55/208** without vote [agenda item 97].

United Nations Institute for Training and Research

The General Assembly,

Recalling its resolutions 49/125 of 19 December 1994, 50/121 of 20 December 1995, 51/188 of 16 December 1996, 52/206 of 18 December 1997, 53/195 of 15 December 1998 and 54/229 of 22 December 1999,

Having considered the reports of the Secretary-General and the Executive Director of the United Nations Institute for Training and Research,

Welcoming the efforts made towards consolidation of the restructuring process of the Institute and the recent progress made by the Institute in its various programmes and activities, including the improved cooperation that has been established with other organizations of the United Nations system and with regional and national institutions,

Expressing its appreciation to the Governments and private institutions that have made or pledged financial and other contributions to the Institute,

Noting that contributions to the General Fund have not increased and that the participation of the developed countries in training programmes in New York and Geneva is increasing,

Noting also that the bulk of the resources contributed to the Institute are directed to the Special Purpose Grants Fund rather than to the General Fund, and stressing the need to address that unbalanced situation,

Noting further that the Institute receives no subsidy from the United Nations regular budget, that it provides training programmes to all Member States free of charge and that similar United Nations institutions based at Geneva are not charged rent or maintenance costs,

Reiterating that training activities should be accorded a more visible and larger role in support of the management of international affairs and in the execution of the economic and social development programmes of the United Nations system,

1. *Reaffirms* the importance of a coordinated, United Nations system-wide approach to research and training based on an effective coherent strategy and an effective division of labour among the relevant institutions and bodies;

2. *Also reaffirms* the relevance of the United Nations Institute for Training and Research in view of the growing importance of training within the United Nations and the training requirements of States and the relevance of training-related research activities undertaken by the Institute within its mandate;

3. *Stresses* the need for the Institute to strengthen further its cooperation with other United Nations institutes and relevant national, regional and international institutes;

4. *Welcomes* the progress made in building partnerships between the Institute and other agencies and bodies of the United Nations system with respect to their training programmes, and, in this context, underlines the need to develop further and to expand the scope of these partnerships, in particular at the country level;

5. *Welcomes also* the decisions taken so far by the Secretary-General to ensure continuity in the management of the Institute and to consider the proper grade for the post of Executive Director;

6. *Requests* the Board of Trustees of the United Nations Institute for Training and Research to intensify its efforts to attract experts from developing countries and countries with economies in transition for the preparation of relevant training materials for the programmes and activities of the Institute, and stresses that the courses of the Institute should focus primarily on development issues;

7. *Renews its appeal* to all Governments, in particular those of developed countries, and to private institutions that have not yet contributed financially or otherwise to the Institute, to give it their generous financial and other support, and urges the States that have interrupted their voluntary contributions to consider re-

suming them in view of the successful restructuring and revitalization of the Institute;

8. *Calls upon* developed countries, which are increasingly participating in the training programmes conducted in New York and Geneva, to make contributions or consider increasing their contributions to the General Fund;

9. *Encourages* the Board of Trustees of the Institute to continue its efforts to resolve the critical financial situation of the Institute, in particular with a view to broadening its donor base and increasing the contributions made to the General Fund;

10. *Also encourages* the Board of Trustees to consider diversifying further the venues of the events organized by the Institute and to include the cities hosting regional commissions, in order to promote greater participation and reduce costs;

11. *Requests* the Secretary-General, in consultation with the Institute and United Nations funds and programmes, to continue to explore ways and means of systematically utilizing the Institute in the execution of training and capacity-building programmes for the economic and social development of developing countries;

12. *Notes with appreciation* the services rendered by the Executive Director of the Institute in the light of the challenges emanating from the increased responsibilities encountered by his office;

13. *Requests* the Secretary-General to consider reclassifying the rental rates and maintenance costs charged to the Institute with a view to alleviating its current financial difficulties, which are aggravated by the current practice of charging commercial rates, taking into account that other organizations affiliated with the United Nations enjoy such privileges;

14. *Also requests* the Secretary-General to report to it at its fifty-sixth session on the implementation of the present resolution.

On 23 December, the Assembly decided that the item on training and research would remain for consideration at its resumed fifty-fifth (2001) session **(decision 55/458)**.

United Nations University

In a September report [A/55/412], the Secretary-General, in response to General Assembly resolution 53/194 [YUN 1998, p. 1058], presented measures taken to improve interaction between the United Nations University (UNU) and the rest of the UN system. He observed that over the preceding year, UNU had continued to progress in developing closer relations with other UN entities. Under the UNU Council's four-year strategic plan (2000-2004), developed in consultation with UN organizations and agencies, ongoing projects and new initiatives would be structured within two broad programme areas: peace and governance, and environment and sustainable development.

The Secretary-General concluded that, in spite of the relatively modest level of funding,

UNU continued to expand its activities and programmes. UNU research findings had played an important role in policy formulation within the UN system. However, there was a need for better communication between UNU research producers and potential system-wide research consumers, an area partially addressed through a new dialogue process initiated in Geneva during 2000, which brought the two together to discuss enhanced collaboration.

GENERAL ASSEMBLY ACTION

On 20 December [meeting 87], the General Assembly, on the recommendation of the Second Committee [A/55/584], adopted **resolution 55/206** without vote [agenda item 97].

United Nations University

The General Assembly,

Reaffirming its previous resolutions on the United Nations University, including resolution 53/194 of 15 December 1998,

Having considered the report of the Council of the United Nations University, as presented by the Rector of the University on 31 October 2000, and the report of the Secretary-General,

Bearing in mind the need to continue to ensure a coordinated, system-wide approach to training and training-related research issues and to continue to pursue a coherent strategy for building on common fields of interest and complementarities among the various training and research institutions in the United Nations system,

Expressing its deep appreciation for the voluntary contributions made to date by Governments and other public and private entities in support of the University,

Noting with satisfaction that, since its creation twenty-five years ago, the University has developed a distinctive identity in the United Nations system and the international academic and scientific community,

1. *Welcomes* the adoption by the Governing Council of the United Nations University of the "Strategic Plan, 2000: Advancing Knowledge for Human Security and Development", which has a programmatic focus on research, policy studies, capacity-building and dissemination of information in the two thematic areas of peace and governance and environment and sustainable development, in line with the priority concerns of the United Nations;

2. *Takes note with appreciation* of the steps taken by the Council and the Rector of the University to promote the work and the visibility of the University, in particular among Member States, the United Nations and its agencies, through such measures as organizing a series of public forums for the purpose of disseminating the results of its research, and requests them to further intensify such efforts;

3. *Welcomes* the contribution made by the University to the work of the United Nations, both in intergovernmental processes, including United Nations global conferences, and in analytical work, and requests the Rector to intensify his efforts to extend the policy studies programme of the University;

4. *Emphasizes* the continuing need of the University to strengthen the capacity of scholarly and scientific institutions in developing countries by extending its capacity-building programmes and through innovative partnerships and networking, involving the United Nations system, academic entities, professional associations, private sector bodies and other elements of civil society that will bring additional input to the work of the University;

5. *Welcomes* the progress made by the University in improving interaction and communication between the University and the rest of the United Nations system, noted in the report of the Secretary-General, requests the Rector to intensify his efforts in this regard, and also requests the Secretary-General to encourage other bodies of the United Nations system to improve their interaction and communication with the University so that it may serve as a think tank for the system;

6. *Requests* the Secretary-General, in this connection, to continue his consideration of innovative measures to improve interaction and communication between the University and other relevant bodies of the United Nations system and, in the light of resolution 53/194, to ensure that the work of the University is taken into account in all relevant activities of the system so that the system may draw more extensively upon the work of the University, and to submit a report thereon to the Assembly at its fifty-seventh session;

7. *Welcomes* the progress made with regard to the participation of the University in the work of the Administrative Committee on Coordination, and encourages the University to play an active role in this regard in order to better understand and respond to the needs of the United Nations system as it carries out its work;

8. *Also welcomes* the initiative taken by the University, together with the United Nations Office at Geneva, in bringing together United Nations research entities, and invites the Secretary-General to use those annual meetings to develop greater synergy among them, and between them and other bodies of the United Nations system;

9. *Takes note* of the important ongoing cooperation between the University and the United Nations Educational, Scientific and Cultural Organization, in particular in the follow-up activities to the World Conference on Higher Education, held in Paris from 5 to 9 October 1998, the preparation of the *World Water Development Report* and the initiation of the programme on dialogue among civilizations;

10. *Recognizes* the importance of the creation of linkages, collaboration and cooperation with other research institutions and universities throughout the world, in particular in developing countries, in order to facilitate the exchange of information, experience and best practice so as to mainstream the perspective of developing countries in the activities of the University;

11. *Requests* the University to broaden the reach of its dissemination activities by using innovative methods, including new information and communication technologies, to ensure that the knowledge developed by the University is made available to all those to whom it may be of benefit;

12. *Requests* the Council and the Rector, taking into account the previous resolutions of the Assembly and the report of the Joint Inspection Unit on the University, to continue to make further efforts to ensure the

efficiency and cost-effectiveness of the activities of the University, as well as its financial transparency and accountability, to intensify efforts to augment its Endowment Fund and to find innovative ways to mobilize operating contributions and other programme and project support;

13. *Invites* the international community to make voluntary contributions to the University, including its research and training centres and programmes, and in particular to its Endowment Fund.

Education for all

The Education for All (EFA) 2000 Assessment—a detailed analysis of the state of basic education worldwide—which was launched in 1997 under the auspices of the EFA Forum [YUN 1997, p. 1181] to follow up the 1990 World Conference on Education for All [YUN 1990, p. 763], demonstrated significant progress in many countries. However, in 2000, more than 113 million children did not have access to primary education, 880 million adults were illiterate, gender discrimination con-

tinued to permeate education systems, and the quality of learning and the acquisition of human values and skills fell short of the aspirations and needs of individuals and societies.

The World Education Forum (Dakar, Senegal, 26-28 April), sponsored by the United Nations Development Programme, UNESCO, the United Nations Population Fund, UNICEF and the World Bank, was convened to assess progress towards education for all since the 1990 World Conference. At the opening of the Forum, the Secretary-General launched the 10-year United Nations Girls' Education Initiative. The Forum adopted the Dakar Framework for Action, Education for All: Meeting Our Collective Commitments, which reaffirmed the goal of education for all, committed participants to work towards specific educational goals by 2015 or earlier, and called for the development or strengthening of national action plans and the reinforcement of national, regional and international mechanisms.

Chapter X

Women

United Nations efforts to advance the status of women and ensure their rights in 2000 centred on implementation of the Beijing Declaration and Platform for Action, a comprehensive plan for women's empowerment based on the goals of equality, development and peace, which was adopted at the Fourth (1995) World Conference on Women. In June, the General Assembly held its twenty-third special session to review progress in implementing the 12 critical areas of concern outlined in the Platform for Action. The special session—known as Beijing+5 and entitled "Women 2000: gender equality, development and peace for the twenty-first century"—culminated in the adoption of a political declaration and an outcome document containing further actions and initiatives for overcoming obstacles to realizing the Platform's goals. Those documents reaffirmed the importance of gender mainstreaming in all areas and at all levels and the complementarity between mainstreaming and special activities targeting women.

In December, the Assembly addressed follow-up to the Fourth World Conference and the outcome of the special session, as well as issues related to the elimination of all forms of violence against women, including crimes committed in the name of honour, and the girl child.

In October, following discussions on the issue of women, peace and security, the Security Council adopted a resolution calling for measures to protect women and girls from gender-based violence during armed conflict. The Council also urged adoption of a gender perspective during the negotiation and implementation of peace agreements.

The Economic and Social Council adopted resolutions addressing the situation of women and girls in Afghanistan, Palestinian women, revitalization of the International Research and Training Institute for the Advancement of Women, and follow-up to the Council's 1999 high-level segment on the role of employment and work in poverty eradication: empowerment and advancement of women.

The Commission on the Status of Women took action with regard to the release of women and children taken hostage in armed conflicts and on issues related to women, the girl child and

HIV/AIDS. The Commission also acted as the preparatory committee for Beijing+5.

In June, the United Nations Development Fund for Women published the first *Progress of the World's Women 2000*, a new biennial report documenting advances and challenges with regard to improving women's economic, social and political status and securing their rights. The 2000 report charted progress made from the mid-1980s to the late 1990s, particularly in relation to the economic dimensions of gender equality and women's empowerment in the context of globalization.

The Committee on the Elimination of Discrimination against Women considered reports from 15 States parties to the 1979 Convention.

Follow-up to the Fourth World Conference on Women

Twenty-third special session (Beijing+ 5)

The General Assembly held its twenty-third special session from 5 to 10 June to appraise and assess implementation of the 1985 Nairobi Forward-looking Strategies for the Advancement of Women [YUN 1985, p. 940] and the Beijing Declaration and Platform for Action, adopted in 1995 by the Fourth World Conference on Women [YUN 1995, p. 1170]. The theme of the session was "Women 2000: gender equality, development and peace for the twenty-first century". Convened in accordance with resolution 52/100 [YUN 1997, p. 1188], the special session, also known as Beijing+5, culminated in the adoption of a political declaration and of further actions and initiatives to implement the Beijing Declaration and Platform for Action (the outcome document). The declaration reaffirmed the commitment of Governments to the goals and objectives of the Fourth World Conference and to implementation of the 12 critical areas of concern set forth in the Platform for Action: women and poverty; education and training of women; women and health; violence against women; women and armed conflict; women and the economy; women in power and decision-making; institutional mechanisms for the advancement of women; human rights of women;

women and the media; women and the environment; and the girl child.

The outcome document listed and described 199 actions to be taken at the national and international levels by Governments, the UN system, international and regional organizations, the private sector, non-governmental organizations (NGOs) and other actors of civil society. In particular, it called for action in the areas of education, social services and health; violence against women and girls; the persistent burden of poverty on women; natural disasters and environmental management; the development of strong, effective and accessible national machineries for the advancement of women; and the formulation of strategies to enable women and men to reconcile and equally share work and family responsibilities.

In addition to further action on the 12 critical areas of concern, the outcome document addressed issues that had become prominent since the convening of the Fourth World Conference: women's access to decision-making, particularly in peacekeeping processes; gender-sensitive approaches to HIV/AIDS and humanitarian crises; changing patterns of migratory flows; technologies; violence against women, including trafficking and in armed conflict; and the realization of women's full enjoyment of economic, social, cultural, civil and political rights. The document also proposed measures to address the challenges presented by globalization to implementation of the Beijing Declaration and Platform for Action.

Addressing the special session, which was attended by representatives of 178 Member States and a large number of international organizations and institutions, the Secretary-General focused on the importance of education, stressing that it was both the entry point into the global economy and the best defence against its pitfalls. Once educated and integrated into the workforce, women would have more choices and provide better nutrition, health care and education for their children.

In a decision on organizational arrangements for the session, the Assembly established an Ad Hoc Committee of the Whole to consider the question of the review and appraisal of progress made in the implementation of the 12 critical areas of concern in the Beijing Platform for Action and the question of further actions and initiatives for overcoming obstacles to its implementation (**decision S-23/21**). In other action, the Assembly appointed the members of the Credentials Committee (**decision S-23/11**); approved the report of the Credentials Committee (**resolution S-23/1**); elected the President of the Assembly (**decision S-23/12**); elected the Vice-Presidents of the Assembly (**decision S-23/13**); elected the Chairpersons of the Main Committees (**decision S-23/14**); and elected the officers of the Ad Hoc Committee (**decision S-23/15**) (see APPENDIX III for details). The Assembly also adopted the agenda for the special session (**decision S-23/22**) and decided that five NGOs might make statements in the debate in plenary (**decision S-23/23**).

Preparatory process

Preparatory committee. The Commission on the Status of Women, acting as the preparatory committee for the special session of the General Assembly, held its third session in New York from 3 to 17 March and on 20 April [A/S-23/2]; it held its resumed third session on 2 June [A/S-23/2/Add.1,2 (Parts I-IV) & Add.2/Corr.1] to complete negotiations on the draft political declaration, continue work on the proposed outcome document on further actions and initiatives for implementation of the Beijing Platform for Action and finalize organizational arrangements. A panel discussion entitled "Outlook on gender equality, development and peace beyond the year 2000" took place on 6 March.

On 15 March, the General Assembly, by **decisions 54/466 and 54/467**, decided, as recommended by the Commission acting as preparatory committee, on arrangements regarding the participation and accreditation of NGOs in the special session.

Reports of Secretary-General. The preparatory committee had before it a January report of the Secretary-General [E/CN.6/2000/PC/2 & Corr.1-3], which comprised a review and appraisal of progress made towards implementation of the Beijing Platform for Action nationally, regionally and internationally. The three-part report provided the background to the Beijing Conference, the intergovernmental process since Beijing and an overview of the major trends in implementation of the Platform for Action. It also analysed implementation in each critical area of concern and the institutional and financial arrangements called for in the Platform for Action. Part three of the report identified some of the political, economic, social and cultural changes noted in the Platform for Action that had become particularly pronounced in the five years since the Beijing Conference and that posed new challenges for the Platform's implementation. The overview of trends drew on responses from 133 Governments to a questionnaire prepared by the Secretariat in collaboration with the regional commissions. Those trends concerned changes in policy, legislation and institutions and programmes initiated by Governments to comply with the strategic objectives set forth in the 12 critical areas of concern of the Platform of Action.

In a January report on emerging issues affecting the situation of women [E/CN.6/2000/PC/4], submitted in response to General Assembly resolution 52/231 [YUN 1998, p. 1062], the Secretary-General presented material on further actions and initiatives for the preparation of the outlook beyond the year 2000, which was based on the results of an international workshop, "Beijing+5—Future Actions and Initiatives" (Beirut, Lebanon, 8-10 November 1999). The workshop assessed the impact of trends of global change since 1995 on gender equality, development and peace in terms of the implementation of the Platform and recommended measures to address the emerging challenges. Experts attending the workshop found that the 1995 World Conference had led to new legislation and an increased awareness of women's rights and gender equality, which had not been matched by significant changes in attitudes and practices in key areas. Women's participation in economic and political life at decision-making levels was stagnating; new perceptions of gender identities and roles were evolving at the margins rather than in the mainstream; and a gap persisted between legislation and enforcement, as demonstrated in the area of violence against women. Future actions and strategies needed to respond to new realities, including globalization. The workshop's action-oriented recommendations, which cut across the three themes of equality, development and peace and the 12 critical areas of concern, addressed attitudes and practices, governance, alliances and coalitions, social and economic justice, and peace-building.

Other reports. The preparatory committee also had before it a report on the mainstreaming of gender within UN projects and programmes [E/CN.6/2000/PC/3] and considered the results of five regional preparatory meetings [E/CN.6/2000/PC/6 & Add.1-5]: for Asia and the Pacific (Bangkok, Thailand, 26-29 October 1999); for Africa (Addis Ababa, Ethiopia, 22-26 November 1999); for Western Asia (Beirut, 12-15 December 1999); for Europe (Geneva, 19-21 January 2000); and for Latin America and the Caribbean (Lima, Peru, 8-10 February 2000). Additional documents before the special session included a statement submitted by the Administrative Committee on Coordination [A/S-23/8], expressing its commitment to and outlining actions for intensified action in support of accelerated implementation of the Platform for Action and gender mainstreaming.

On 10 June [meeting 10], the General Assembly, on the recommendation of the Ad Hoc Committee of the Whole [A/S-23/10/Rev.1], adopted **resolution S/23-2** without vote [agenda item 10].

Political declaration

The General Assembly

Adopts the political declaration annexed to the present resolution.

ANNEX
Political declaration

We the Governments participating in the special session of the General Assembly

1. *Reaffirm* our commitment to the goals and objectives contained in the Beijing Declaration and Platform for Action, adopted in 1995 at the Fourth World Conference on Women, and the Nairobi Forward-looking Strategies for the Advancement of Women to the year 2000 as the culmination of the United Nations Decade for Women, 1976 to 1985;

2. *Also reaffirm* our commitment to the implementation of the twelve critical areas of concern in the Beijing Platform for Action, which are women and poverty, education and training of women, women and health, violence against women, women and armed conflict, women and the economy, women in power and decision-making, institutional mechanisms for the advancement of women, human rights of women, women and the media, women and the environment, and the girl child; and call for the implementation of the agreed conclusions and resolutions on the follow-up to the Fourth World Conference on Women adopted by the Commission on the Status of Women since the fortieth session of the Commission;

3. *Recognize* that we have primary responsibility for the full implementation of the Nairobi Forward-looking Strategies for the Advancement of Women, the Beijing Declaration and Platform for Action and all the relevant commitments for the advancement of women, and, in this connection, call for continued international cooperation, including the reaffirmation to strive to fulfil the yet to be attained internationally agreed target of 0.7 per cent of the gross national product of developed countries for overall official development assistance as soon as possible;

4. *Welcome* the progress made thus far towards gender equality and the implementation of the Beijing Platform for Action and reaffirm our commitment to accelerate the achievement of universal ratification of the Convention on the Elimination of All Forms of Discrimination against Women and in this regard acknowledge the efforts at all levels of Governments, the United Nations system, and intergovernmental, other international and regional organizations and urge continued efforts for the full implementation of the Beijing Platform for Action;

5. *Recognize* the role and contribution of civil society, in particular non-governmental organizations and women's organizations, in the implementation of the Beijing Declaration and Platform for Action, and en-

courage their participation in further implementation and assessment processes;

6. *Emphasize* that men must involve themselves and take joint responsibility with women for the promotion of gender equality;

7. *Reaffirm* the importance of mainstreaming a gender perspective in the process of implementation of the outcome of other major United Nations conferences and summits and the need for a coordinated follow-up to all major conferences and summits by Governments, regional organizations, and all of the bodies and organizations of the United Nations system within their respective mandates.

We the Governments, at the beginning of the new millennium,

8. *Reaffirm* our commitment to overcoming obstacles encountered in the implementation of the Beijing Platform for Action and the Nairobi Forward-looking Strategies for the Advancement of Women and to strengthening and safeguarding a national and international enabling environment, and to this end pledge to undertake further action to ensure their full and accelerated implementation, inter alia, through the promotion and protection of all human rights and fundamental freedoms, mainstreaming a gender perspective into all policies and programmes and promoting full participation and empowerment of women and enhanced international cooperation for the full implementation of the Beijing Platform for Action;

9. *Agree* to assess regularly further implementation of the Beijing Platform for Action with a view to bringing together all parties involved in 2005 to assess progress and consider new initiatives, as appropriate, ten years after the adoption of the Beijing Platform for Action and twenty years after the adoption of the Nairobi Forward-looking Strategies for the Advancement of Women;

10. *Pledge* to ensure the realization of societies in which both women and men work together towards a world where every individual can enjoy equality, development and peace in the twenty-first century.

At the same meeting, the Assembly, on the recommendation of the Ad Hoc Committee of the Whole [A/S-23/10/Rev.1], adopted **resolution S-23/3** without vote [agenda item 10].

Further actions and initiatives to implement the Beijing Declaration and Platform for Action

The General Assembly

Adopts the further actions and initiatives to implement the Beijing Declaration and Platform for Action, annexed to the present resolution.

ANNEX
Further actions and initiatives to implement the Beijing Declaration and Platform for Action

I. Introduction

1. The Governments which came together at the special session of the General Assembly have reaffirmed their commitment to the goals and objectives contained in the Beijing Declaration and Platform for Action adopted at the Fourth World Conference on Women in 1995 as contained in the report of the Conference. The Beijing Declaration and Platform for Action set as goals gender equality, development and peace and constituted an agenda for the empowerment of women. The Governments reviewed and appraised progress and identified obstacles and current challenges in the implementation of the Platform for Action. They recognized that the goals set and commitments made in the Platform for Action have not been fully achieved and implemented, and have agreed upon further actions and initiatives at the local, national, regional and international levels to accelerate the implementation of the Platform for Action and to ensure that commitments for gender equality, development and peace are fully realized.

2. The Beijing Platform for Action identified twelve critical areas of concern for priority action to achieve the advancement and empowerment of women. The Commission on the Status of Women has reviewed progress in each of the twelve critical areas of concern and since 1996 has adopted agreed conclusions and recommendations for accelerated implementation. The Platform for Action, together with these agreed conclusions and recommendations, forms the basis for further progress towards the achievement of gender equality, development and peace in the twenty-first century.

3. The objective of the Platform for Action, which is in full conformity with the purposes and principles of the Charter of the United Nations and international law, is the empowerment of all women. The full realization of all human rights and fundamental freedoms of all women is essential for the empowerment of women. While the significance of national and regional particularities and various historical, cultural and religious backgrounds must be borne in mind, it is the duty of States, regardless of their political, economic and cultural systems, to promote and protect all human rights and fundamental freedoms. The implementation of the Platform for Action, including through national laws and the formulation of strategies, policies, programmes and development priorities, is the sovereign responsibility of each State, in conformity with all human rights and fundamental freedoms, and the significance of and full respect for various religious and ethical values, cultural backgrounds and philosophical convictions of individuals and their communities should contribute to the full enjoyment by women of their human rights and the achievement of equality, development and peace.

4. The Platform for Action emphasizes that women share common concerns that can only be addressed by working together and in partnership with men towards the common goal of gender equality around the world. It respects and values the full diversity of women's situations and conditions and recognizes that some women face particular barriers to their empowerment.

5. The Platform for Action recognizes that women face barriers to full equality and advancement because of such factors as their race, age, language, ethnicity, culture, religion or disability, because they are indigenous women or of other status. Many women encounter specific obstacles related to their family status, particularly as single parents, and to their socio-economic status, including their living conditions in rural, isolated or impoverished areas. Additional barriers also exist for refugee women, other displaced women, including internally displaced women, as well as for immigrant women and migrant women, including women

migrant workers. Many women are also particularly affected by environmental disasters, serious and infectious diseases and various forms of violence against women.

II. Achievements in and obstacles to the implementation of the twelve critical areas of concern of the Beijing Platform for Action

6. Assessment of achievements and obstacles must be made in relation to the commitments made in the Beijing Platform for Action and its twelve critical areas of concern, namely by looking into the actions taken and the results attained, as indicated in national reports, as well as by taking note of the reports of the Secretary-General and of the results, conclusions and agreements of the five regional meetings held in preparation for the special session of the General Assembly and other relevant sources. Such assessment shows that, even though significant positive developments can be identified, barriers remain and that the goals set and commitments made in Beijing need to be implemented further. The summary of achievements and of persistent or new obstacles can therefore constitute a global framework for the identification of further actions and initiatives to overcome obstacles and to achieve the full and accelerated implementation of the Platform for Action at all levels and in all areas.

A. Women and poverty

7. *Achievements.* Considerable progress has been achieved in increasing recognition of gender dimensions of poverty and in the recognition that gender equality is one of the factors of specific importance for eradicating poverty, particularly in relation to the feminization of poverty. Efforts have been made to integrate a gender perspective into poverty eradication policies and programmes by Governments, in cooperation with non-governmental organizations. Multilateral, international and regional financial institutions are also giving increased attention to the incorporation of a gender perspective into their policies. Progress has been made by pursuing a two-pronged approach of promoting employment and income-generating activities for women and providing access to basic social services, including education and health care. Microcredit and other financial instruments for women have emerged as a successful strategy for economic empowerment and have widened economic opportunities for some women living in poverty, in particular in rural areas. Policy development has taken account of the particular needs of female-headed households. Research has enhanced the understanding of the differing impacts of poverty on women and men and tools have been developed to assist with this assessment.

8. *Obstacles.* Many factors have contributed to widening economic inequality between women and men, including income inequality, unemployment and the deepening of poverty levels of the most vulnerable and marginalized groups. Debt burdens, excessive military spending, inconsistent with national security requirements, unilateral coercive measures at variance with international law and the Charter of the United Nations, armed conflict, foreign occupation, terrorism, low levels of official development assistance and the unfulfilled commitment to strive to fulfil the yet to be attained internationally agreed target of 0.7 per cent of the gross national product of developed countries for overall official development assistance and 0.15 to 0.2 per cent for the least developed countries, as well as the lack of efficient use of resources, among other factors, can constrain national efforts to combat poverty. In addition, gender inequalities and disparities in economic power-sharing, unequal distribution of unremunerated work between women and men, lack of technological and financial support for women's entrepreneurship, unequal access to, and control over, capital, particularly land and credit and access to labour markets, as well as all harmful traditional and customary practices, have constrained women's economic empowerment and exacerbated the feminization of poverty. Fundamental economic restructuring experienced by the countries with economies in transition has led to lack of resources for poverty-eradication programmes aimed at empowerment of women.

B. Education and training of women

9. *Achievements.* There is an increased awareness that education is one of the most valuable means of achieving gender equality and the empowerment of women. Progress was achieved in women's and girls' education and training at all levels, especially where there was sufficient political commitment and resource allocation. Measures were taken in all regions to initiate alternative education and training systems to reach women and girls in indigenous communities and other disadvantaged and marginalized groups to encourage them to pursue all fields of study, in particular non-traditional fields of study, and to remove gender biases from education and training.

10. *Obstacles.* In some countries, efforts to eradicate illiteracy and strengthen literacy among women and girls and to increase their access to all levels and types of education were constrained by the lack of resources and insufficient political will and commitment to improve educational infrastructure and undertake educational reforms; persisting gender discrimination and bias, including in teacher training; gender-based occupational stereotyping in schools, institutions of further education and communities; lack of childcare facilities; persistent use of gender stereotypes in educational materials; and insufficient attention paid to the link between women's enrolment in higher educational institutions and labour market dynamics. The remote location of some communities and, in some cases, inadequate salaries and benefits make attracting and retaining teaching professionals difficult and can result in lower quality education. Additionally, in a number of countries, economic, social and infrastructural barriers, as well as traditional discriminatory practices, have contributed to lower enrolment and retention rates for girls. Little progress has been made in eradicating illiteracy in some developing countries, aggravating women's inequality at the economic, social and political levels. In some of these countries, the inappropriate design and application of structural adjustment policies has had a particularly severe impact on the education sector since they resulted in declining investment in education infrastructure.

C. Women and health

11. *Achievements.* Programmes have been implemented to create awareness among policy makers and planners of the need for health programmes to cover

all aspects of women's health throughout women's life cycle, which have contributed to an increase in life expectancy in many countries. There is: increased attention to high mortality rates among women and girls as a result of malaria, tuberculosis, water-borne diseases, communicable and diarrhoeal diseases and malnutrition; increased attention to sexual and reproductive health and reproductive rights of women as contained in paragraphs 94 and 95 of the Platform for Action, as well as in some countries increased emphasis on implementing paragraph 96 of the Platform for Action; increased knowledge and use of family planning and contraceptive methods as well as increased awareness among men of their responsibility in family planning and contraceptive methods and their use; increased attention to sexually transmitted infections, including human immunodeficiency virus/acquired immunodeficiency syndrome (HIV/AIDS) among women and girls, and methods to protect against such infections; increased attention to breastfeeding, nutrition, infants' and mothers' health; the introduction of a gender perspective in health and health-related educational and physical activities, and gender-specific prevention and rehabilitation programmes on substance abuse, including tobacco, drugs and alcohol; increased attention to women's mental health, health conditions at work, environmental considerations and recognition of the specific health needs of older women. At its twenty-first special session, held in New York from 30 June to 2 July 1999, the General Assembly reviewed achievements and adopted key actions in the field of women's health for the further implementation of the Programme of Action of the International Conference on Population and Development.

12. *Obstacles.* Worldwide, the gap between and within rich and poor countries with respect to infant mortality and maternal mortality and morbidity rates, as well as with respect to measures addressing the health of women and girls, given their special vulnerability regarding sexually transmitted infections, including HIV/AIDS and other sexual and reproductive health problems, together with endemic, infectious and communicable diseases, such as malaria, tuberculosis, diarrhoeal and water-borne diseases and chronic non-transmissible diseases, remains unacceptable. In some countries, such endemic, infectious and communicable diseases continue to take a toll on women and girls. In other countries, non-communicable diseases, such as cardiopulmonary diseases, hypertension and degenerative diseases, remain among the major causes of mortality and morbidity among women. Despite progress in some countries, the rates of maternal mortality and morbidity remain unacceptably high in most countries. Investment in essential obstetric care remains insufficient in many countries. The absence of a holistic approach to health and health care for women and girls based on women's right to the enjoyment of the highest attainable standard of physical and mental health throughout the life cycle has constrained progress. Some women continue to encounter barriers to their right to the enjoyment of the highest attainable standard of physical and mental health. The predominant focus of health-care systems on treating illness rather than maintaining optimal health also prevents a holistic approach. There is, in some countries, insufficient attention to the role of social and economic determinants of health. A lack of access to clean water, adequate nutrition and safe sanitation, a lack of gender-specific health research and technology and insufficient gender sensitivity in the provision of health information and health care and health services, including those related to environmental and occupational health hazards, affect women in developing and developed countries. Poverty and the lack of development continue to affect the capacity of many developing countries to provide and expand quality health care. A shortage of financial and human resources, in particular in developing countries, as well as restructuring of the health sector and/or the increasing trend to privatization of health-care systems in some cases, has resulted in poor quality, reduced and insufficient health-care services, and has also led to less attention to the health of the most vulnerable groups of women. Such obstacles as unequal power relationships between women and men, in which women often do not have the power to insist on safe and responsible sex practices, and a lack of communication and understanding between men and women on women's health needs, inter alia, endanger women's health, particularly by increasing their susceptibility to sexually transmitted infections, including HIV/AIDS, and affect women's access to health care and education, especially in relation to prevention. Adolescents, particularly adolescent girls, continue to lack access to sexual and reproductive health information, education and services. Women who are recipients of health care are frequently not treated with respect nor guaranteed privacy and confidentiality, and do not receive full information about options and services available. In some cases, health services and workers still do not conform to human rights and to ethical, professional and gender-sensitive standards in the delivery of women's health services, nor do they ensure responsible, voluntary and informed consent. There continues to be a lack of information on availability of and access to appropriate, affordable, primary health-care services of high quality, including sexual and reproductive health care, insufficient attention to maternal and emergency obstetric care as well as a lack of prevention, screening and treatment for breast, cervical and ovarian cancers and osteoporosis. The testing and development of male contraceptives is still insufficient. While some measures have been taken in some countries, the actions set out in paragraphs 106 *(j)* and *(k)* of the Platform for Action regarding the health impact of unsafe abortion and the need to reduce the recourse to abortion have not been fully implemented. The rising incidence of tobacco use among women, particularly young women, has increased their risk of cancer and other serious diseases, as well as gender-specific risks from tobacco and environmental tobacco smoke.

D. Violence against women

13. *Achievements.* It is widely accepted that violence against women and girls, whether occurring in public or private life, is a human rights issue. It is accepted that violence against women, where perpetrated or condoned by the State or its agents, constitutes a human rights violation. It is also accepted that States have an obligation to exercise due diligence to prevent, investigate and punish acts of violence, whether those acts are

perpetrated by the State or by private persons, and provide protection to victims. There is increased awareness of and commitment to preventing and combating violence against women and girls, including domestic violence, which violates and impairs or nullifies the enjoyment of their human rights and fundamental freedoms, through, inter alia, improved legislation, policies and programmes. Governments have initiated policy reforms and mechanisms, such as interdepartmental committees, guidelines and protocols, national, multidisciplinary and coordinated programmes to address violence. Some Governments have also introduced or reformed laws to protect women and girls from all forms of violence and laws to prosecute the perpetrators. There is an increasing recognition at all levels that all forms of violence against women seriously affect their health. Health-care providers are seen to have a significant role to play in addressing this matter. Some progress has been made in the provision of services for abused women and children, including legal services, shelters, special health services and counselling, hotlines and police units with special training. Education for law enforcement personnel, members of the judiciary, health-care providers and welfare workers is being promoted. Educational materials for women and public awareness campaigns have been developed as well as research on the root causes of violence. Research into and specialized studies on gender roles are increasing, in particular on men's and boys' roles, and all forms of violence against women, as well as on the situation of and impact on children growing up in families where violence occurs. Successful cooperation has been achieved between governmental and non-governmental organizations in the field of preventing violence against women. The active support of civil society, in particular women's organizations and non-governmental organizations, has had an important role, inter alia, in promoting awareness-raising campaigns and in the provision of support services to women victims of violence. Efforts towards the eradication of harmful traditional practices, including female genital mutilation, which is a form of violence against women, have received national, regional and international policy support. Many Governments have introduced educational and outreach programmes, as well as legislative measures criminalizing these practices. In addition, this support includes the appointment of the Special Ambassador for the Elimination of Female Genital Mutilation by the United Nations Population Fund.

14. *Obstacles.* Women continue to be victims of various forms of violence. Inadequate understanding of the root causes of all forms of violence against women and girls hinders efforts to eliminate violence against women and girls. There is a lack of comprehensive programmes dealing with the perpetrators, including programmes, where appropriate, which would enable them to solve problems without violence. Inadequate data on violence further impedes informed policy-making and analysis. Sociocultural attitudes which are discriminatory and economic inequalities reinforce women's subordinate place in society. This makes women and girls vulnerable to many forms of violence, such as physical, sexual and psychological violence occurring in the family, including battering, sexual abuse

of female children in the household, dowry-related violence, marital rape, female genital mutilation and other traditional practices harmful to women, non-spousal violence and violence related to exploitation. In many countries, a coordinated multidisciplinary approach to responding to violence which includes the health system, the workplace, the media, the education system, as well as the justice system, is still limited. Domestic violence, including sexual violence in marriage, is still treated as a private matter in some countries. Insufficient awareness of the consequences of domestic violence, how to prevent it and the rights of victims still exists. Although improving, the legal and legislative measures, especially in the criminal justice area, to eliminate different forms of violence against women and children, including domestic violence and child pornography, are weak in many countries. Prevention strategies also remain fragmented and reactive and there is a lack of programmes on these issues. It is also noted that, in some countries, problems have arisen from the use of new information and communication technologies for trafficking in women and children and for purposes of all forms of economic and sexual exploitation.

E. Women and armed conflict

15. *Achievements.* There is a wider recognition that the destructive impact of armed conflict is different on women and men and that a gender-sensitive approach to the application of international human rights law and international humanitarian law is important. Steps have been taken at the national and international levels to address abuses against women, including increased attention to ending impunity for crimes against women in situations of armed conflict. The work of the International Tribunals for the former Yugoslavia and Rwanda has been an important contribution to address violence against women in the context of armed conflict. Also of historical significance is the adoption of the Rome Statute of the International Criminal Court, which provides that rape, sexual slavery, enforced prostitution, forced pregnancy, enforced sterilization and other forms of sexual violence are war crimes when committed in the context of armed conflict and also under defined circumstances, crimes against humanity. The contribution of women in the areas of peace-building, peacemaking and conflict resolution is being increasingly recognized. Education and training in non-violent conflict resolution have been introduced. Progress has been made in the dissemination and implementation of the guidelines for the protection of refugee women, and in addressing the needs of displaced women. Gender-based persecution has been accepted as a basis for refugee status in some countries. There is recognition by Governments, the international community and organizations, in particular the United Nations, that women and men experience humanitarian emergencies differently, and there is a need for a more holistic support for refugee and displaced women, including those who have suffered all forms of abuse, including gender-specific abuse, to ensure equal access to appropriate and adequate food and nutrition, clean water, safe sanitation, shelter, education, social and health services, including reproductive health care and maternity care. There is greater recognition of the need to integrate a gender

perspective in the planning, design and implementation of humanitarian assistance and to provide adequate resources. Humanitarian relief agencies and civil society, including non-governmental organizations, have played an increasingly important role in the provision of humanitarian assistance, as well as in the design, where appropriate, and implementation of programmes to address the needs of women and girls, including refugee and displaced women and girls in humanitarian emergencies, and in conflict and post-conflict situations.

16. *Obstacles.* Peace is inextricably linked to equality between women and men and development. Armed conflicts and conflicts of other types, wars of aggression, foreign occupation, colonial or other alien domination, as well as terrorism, continue to cause serious obstacles to the advancement of women. The targeting of civilians, including women and children, the displacement of people, and the recruitment of child soldiers in violation of national or international law, by State and/or non-State actors, which occur in armed conflicts, have had a particularly adverse impact on gender equality and women's human rights. Armed conflict creates or exacerbates the high level of female-headed households, which in many cases are living in poverty. The underrepresentation, at all levels, of women in decision-making positions, such as special envoys or special representatives of the Secretary-General, in peacekeeping, peace-building, post-conflict reconciliation and reconstruction, as well as lack of gender awareness in these areas, presents serious obstacles. There has been a failure to provide sufficient resources, to distribute adequately resources and to address the needs of increasing numbers of refugees, who are mostly women and children, particularly in developing countries hosting large numbers of refugees; international assistance has not kept pace with the increasing number of refugees. The growing number of internally displaced persons and the provision for their needs, in particular women and children, continue to represent a double burden to the affected countries and their financial resources. Inadequate training of personnel dealing with the needs of women in situations of armed conflict or as refugees, such as a shortage of specific programmes that address the healing of women from trauma and skills training, remains a problem.

17. Excessive military expenditures, including global military expenditures, trade in arms and investment for arms production, taking into consideration national security requirements, direct the possible allocation of funds away from social and economic development, in particular for the advancement of women. In several countries, economic sanctions have had social and humanitarian impacts on the civilian population, in particular women and children.

18. In some countries, the advancement of women is adversely affected by unilateral measures at variance with international law and the Charter of the United Nations that create obstacles to trade relations among States, impede the full realization of social and economic development and jeopardize the well-being of the population in the affected countries, with particular consequences for women and children.

19. In situations of armed conflict, there are continued violations of human rights of women, which are violations of fundamental principles of international human rights law and international humanitarian law. There has been an increase in all forms of violence against women, including sexual slavery, rape, systematic rape, sexual abuse and forced pregnancies, in situations of armed conflict. Displacement compounded by loss of home and property, poverty, family disintegration and separation and other consequences of armed conflict are severely affecting the populations, especially women and children. Girls are also abducted or recruited, in violation of international law, into situations of armed conflict, including as combatants, sexual slaves or providers of domestic services.

F. Women and the economy

20. *Achievements.* There is increased participation of women in the labour market and subsequent gain in economic autonomy. Some Governments have introduced a variety of measures that address women's economic and social rights, equal access to and control over economic resources and equality in employment. Other measures include the ratification of international labour conventions as well as enacting or strengthening legislation to make it compatible with these conventions. There is increased awareness of the need to reconcile employment and family responsibilities and of the positive effect of such measures as maternity and paternity leave and also parental leave, and child and family care services and benefits. Some Governments have made provisions to address discriminatory and abusive behaviour in the workplace and to prevent unhealthy working conditions, and have established funding mechanisms to promote women's roles in entrepreneurship, education and training, including scientific and technical skills and decision-making. Research has been conducted on barriers to economic empowerment faced by women, including the relationship between remunerated and unremunerated work, and tools are being developed to assist with this assessment.

21. *Obstacles.* The importance of a gender perspective in the development of macroeconomic policy is still not widely recognized. Many women still work in rural areas and the informal economy as subsistence producers, and in the service sector with low levels of income and little job and social security. Many women with comparable skills and experience are confronted with a gender wage gap and lag behind men in income and career mobility in the formal sector. Equal pay for women and men for equal work, or work of equal value, has not yet been fully realized. Gender discrimination in hiring and promotion and related to pregnancy, including through pregnancy testing, and sexual harassment in the workplace persist. In some countries, women's full and equal rights to own land and other property, including through the right to inheritance, is not recognized yet in national legislation. Progression in the professions, in most cases, is still more difficult for women, due to the lack of structures and measures that take into account maternity and family responsibilities. In some cases, persistent gender stereotyping has led to a lower status of male workers who are fathers and to insufficient encouragement for men to reconcile professional and family responsibilities. Lack of

family-friendly policies regarding the organization of work increases these difficulties. Effective implementation of legislation and practical support systems is still inadequate. The combination of remunerated work and caregiving within families, households and communities still leads to a disproportionate burden for women since there is insufficient sharing of tasks and responsibilities by men. It is still also women who perform the larger part of unremunerated work.

G. Women in power and decision-making

22. *Achievements.* There has been growing acceptance of the importance to society of the full participation of women in decision-making and power at all levels and in all forums, including the intergovernmental, governmental and non-governmental sectors. In some countries, women have also attained higher positions in these spheres. An increasing number of countries applied affirmative and positive action policies, including quota systems or voluntary agreements in some countries and measurable goals and targets, developed training programmes for women's leadership, and introduced measures to reconcile family and work responsibilities of both women and men. National mechanisms and machineries for the advancement of women as well as national and international networks of women politicians, parliamentarians, activists and professionals in various fields have been established or upgraded and strengthened.

23. *Obstacles.* Despite general acceptance of the need for a gender balance in decision-making bodies at all levels, a gap between de jure and de facto equality has persisted. Notwithstanding substantial improvement of de jure equality between women and men, the actual participation of women at the highest levels of national and international decision-making has not significantly changed since the time of the Fourth World Conference on Women in 1995, and gross underrepresentation of women in decision-making bodies in all areas, including politics, conflict prevention and resolution mechanisms, the economy, the environment and the media, hinders the inclusion of a gender perspective in these critical spheres of influence. Women continue to be underrepresented at the legislative, ministerial and sub-ministerial levels, as well as at the highest levels of the corporate sector and other economic and social institutions. Traditionally assigned gender roles limit women's choices in education and careers and compel women to assume the burden for household responsibilities. Initiatives and programmes aimed at women's increased participation in decision-making have been hindered by a lack of human and financial resources for training and advocacy for political careers; gender-sensitive attitudes towards women in society; awareness of women to engage in decision-making in some cases; accountability of elected officials and political parties for promoting gender equality and women's participation in public life; social awareness of the importance of balanced participation of women and men in decision-making; willingness on the part of men to share power; sufficient dialogue and cooperation with women's non-governmental organizations, along with organizational and political structures, which enable all women to participate in all spheres of political decision-making.

H. Institutional mechanisms for the advancement of women

24. *Achievements.* National machineries have been instituted or strengthened and recognized as the institutional base acting as catalysts for promoting gender equality, gender mainstreaming and monitoring of the implementation of the Platform for Action and in many instances of the Convention on the Elimination of All Forms of Discrimination against Women. In many countries, progress has been achieved in terms of the visibility, status, outreach and coordination of activities of these machineries. Gender mainstreaming has been widely acknowledged as a strategy to enhance the impact of policies to promote gender equality. The goal of the strategy is to incorporate a gender perspective in all legislation, policies, programmes and projects. These machineries, despite their limited financial resources, have made a significant contribution to the development of human resources in the field of gender studies and have also contributed to the growing efforts for the generation and dissemination of data disaggregated by sex and age, gender-sensitive research and documentation. Within the United Nations system, much progress has been made in the mainstreaming of a gender perspective, including through the development of tools and the creation of gender focal points.

25. *Obstacles.* In a number of countries, inadequate financial and human resources and a lack of political will and commitment are the main obstacles confronting national machineries. This is further exacerbated by insufficient understanding of gender equality and gender mainstreaming among government structures, as well as prevailing gender stereotypes, discriminatory attitudes, competing government priorities and, in some countries, unclear mandates, a marginalized location within the national government structures, lack of data disaggregated by sex and age in many areas and insufficiently applied methods for assessing progress, in addition to paucity of authority and insufficient links to civil society. The activities of the national machineries have been also hindered by structural and communication problems within and among government agencies.

I. Human rights of women

26. *Achievements.* Legal reforms have been undertaken to prohibit all forms of discrimination and discriminatory provisions have been eliminated in civil, penal and personal status law governing marriage and family relations, all forms of violence, women's property and ownership rights and women's political, work and employment rights. Steps have been taken to realize women's de facto enjoyment of their human rights through the creation of an enabling environment, including the adoption of policy measures, the improvement of enforcement and monitoring mechanisms and the implementation of legal literacy and awareness campaigns at all levels. The Convention on the Elimination of All Forms of Discrimination against Women has been ratified or acceded to by one hundred and sixty-five countries and its full implementation has been promoted by the Committee on the Elimination of Discrimination against Women. At its fifty-fourth session, the General Assembly adopted the Optional Protocol to the Convention, allowing women claiming to be victims of a violation of any of the rights set

forth in the Convention by a State party to submit their claims to the Committee on the Elimination of Discrimination against Women, to which non-governmental organizations contributed by raising awareness and generating support for its adoption. Women's non-governmental organizations have also contributed to raising awareness that women's rights are human rights. They also generated support for the inclusion of a gender perspective in the elaboration of the Rome Statute of the International Criminal Court. Progress has also been made to integrate the human rights of women and mainstream a gender perspective into the United Nations system, including into the work of the Office of the United Nations High Commissioner for Human Rights and of the Commission on Human Rights.

27. *Obstacles.* Gender discrimination and all other forms of discrimination, in particular racism, racial discrimination, xenophobia and related intolerance continue to cause threat to women's enjoyment of their human rights and fundamental freedoms. In situations of armed conflict and foreign occupation, human rights of women have been extensively violated. Even though a number of countries have ratified the Convention on the Elimination of All Forms of Discrimination against Women, the goal of universal ratification by the year 2000 has not been achieved, and there continue to be a large number of reservations to the Convention. While there is an increasing acceptance of gender equality, many countries have not yet implemented fully the provisions of the Convention. Discriminatory legislation as well as harmful traditional and customary practices and negative stereotyping of women and men still persist. Family, civil, penal, labour and commercial laws or codes, or administrative rules and regulations, still have not fully integrated a gender perspective. Legislative and regulatory gaps, as well as lack of implementation and enforcement of legislation and regulations, perpetuate de jure as well as de facto inequality and discrimination, and in a few cases, new laws discriminating against women have been introduced. In many countries, women have insufficient access to the law, resulting from illiteracy, lack of legal literacy, information and resources, insensitivity and gender bias, and lack of awareness of the human rights of women by law enforcement officials and the judiciary, who in many cases fail to respect the human rights of women and the dignity and worth of the human person. There is insufficient recognition of women's and girls' reproductive rights, as well as barriers to their full enjoyment of those rights, which embrace certain human rights as defined in paragraph 95 of the Beijing Platform for Action. Some women and girls continue to encounter barriers to justice and the enjoyment of their human rights because of such factors as their race, language, ethnicity, culture, religion, disability or socio-economic class or because they are indigenous people, migrants, including women migrant workers, displaced women or refugees.

J. Women and the media

28. *Achievements.* The establishment of local, national and international women's media networks has contributed to global information dissemination, exchange of views and support to women's groups active in media work. The development of information and communication technologies, especially the Internet, has provided improved communication opportunities for the empowerment of women and girls, which has enabled an increasing number of women to contribute to knowledge sharing, networking and electronic commerce activities. The number of women's media organizations and programmes has increased, facilitating the aims of increased participation and promotion of positive portrayals of women in the media. Progress has been made to combat negative images of women by establishing professional guidelines and voluntary codes of conduct, encouraging fair gender portrayal and the use of non-sexist language in media programmes.

29. *Obstacles.* Negative, violent and/or degrading images of women, including pornography and stereotyped portrayals, have increased in different forms using new communication technologies in some instances, and bias against women remains in the media. Poverty, the lack of access and opportunities, illiteracy, lack of computer literacy and language barriers, prevent some women from using the information and communication technologies, including the Internet. Development of and access to Internet infrastructure is limited, especially in developing countries and particularly for women.

K. Women and the environment

30. *Achievements.* Some national environment policies and programmes have incorporated gender perspectives. In recognition of the link between gender equality, poverty eradication, sustainable development and environment protection, Governments have included income-generating activities for women, as well as training in natural resource management and environmental protection in their development strategies. Projects have been launched to preserve and utilize women's traditional ecological knowledge, including the traditional ecological knowledge of indigenous women, in the management of natural resources and the preservation of biodiversity.

31. *Obstacles.* There is still a lack of public awareness about environmental risks faced by women and of the benefits of gender equality for promoting environmental protection. Women's limited access to technical skills, resources and information, in particular in developing countries, due to, inter alia, gender inequality, has impeded women's effective participation in decision-making, regarding the sustainable environment, including at the international level. Research, action, targeted strategies and public awareness remain limited regarding the differential impacts and implications of environmental problems for women and men. Real solutions to environmental problems, including environmental degradation, need to address the root causes of these problems, such as foreign occupation. Environmental policies and programmes lack a gender perspective and fail to take into account women's roles and contributions to environmental sustainability.

L. The girl child

32. *Achievements.* Some progress was made in primary and, to a lesser extent, secondary and tertiary education for girls, owing to the creation of a more gender-sensitive school environment, improved educational infrastructure, increased enrolment and retention, support mechanisms for pregnant adolescents and adolescent mothers, increased non-formal educa-

tion opportunities and enhanced attendance at science and technology classes. Increased attention was given to the health of the girl child, including the sexual and reproductive health of adolescents. An increasing number of countries introduced legislation to ban female genital mutilation and imposed heavier penalties on those involved in sexual abuse, trafficking and all other forms of exploitation of the girl child, including for commercial ends. A recent achievement has been the adoption of the optional protocols to the Convention on the Rights of the Child on involvement of children in armed conflict and on the sale of children, child prostitution and child pornography.

33. *Obstacles.* The persistence of poverty, discriminatory attitudes towards women and girls, negative cultural attitudes and practices against girls, as well as negative stereotyping of girls and boys, which limits girls' potential, and inadequate awareness of the specific situation of the girl child, child labour and the heavy burden of domestic responsibilities on girls, inadequate nutrition and access to health services, and lack of finance, which often prevent them from pursuing and completing their education and training, have contributed to a lack of opportunities and possibilities for girls to become confident and self-reliant, and independent adults. Poverty, lack of parental support and guidance, lack of information and education, abuse and all forms of exploitation of, and violence against, the girl child in many cases result in unwanted pregnancies and transmission of HIV, which may also lead to a restriction of educational opportunities. Programmes for the girl child were hindered by a lack of or an insufficient allocation of financial and human resources. There were few established national mechanisms to implement policies and programmes for the girl child and, in some cases, coordination among responsible institutions was insufficient. The increased awareness of the health needs, including the sexual and reproductive health needs, of adolescents has not yet resulted in sufficient provision of necessary information and services. Despite advances in legal protection, there is increased sexual abuse and sexual exploitation of the girl child. Adolescents continue to lack the education and service needed to enable them to deal in a positive and responsible way with their sexuality.

III. Current challenges affecting the full implementation of the Beijing Declaration and Platform for Action

34. The review and appraisal of the implementation of the Beijing Declaration and Platform for Action occurred in a rapidly changing global context. Since 1995, a number of issues have gained prominence and acquired new dimensions which pose additional challenges to the full and accelerated implementation of the Beijing Platform for Action and the realization of gender equality, development and peace by Governments, intergovernmental bodies, international organizations, the private sector and non-governmental organizations as appropriate. Continued political commitment to gender equality at all levels is needed for the full implementation of the Platform for Action.

35. Globalization has presented new challenges for the fulfilment of the commitments and the realization of the goals of the Fourth World Conference on Women. The globalization process has, in some coun-

tries, resulted in policy shifts in favour of more open trade and financial flows, privatization of State-owned enterprises and in many cases lower public spending, particularly on social services. This change has transformed patterns of production and accelerated technological advances in information and communication and affected the lives of women, both as workers and consumers. In a large number of countries, particularly in developing and least developed countries, these changes have also adversely impacted on the lives of women and have increased inequality. The gender impact of these changes has not been systematically evaluated. Globalization also has cultural, political and social impacts affecting cultural values, lifestyles and forms of communication as well as implications for the achievement of sustainable development. The benefits of the growing global economy have been unevenly distributed, leading to wider economic disparities, the feminization of poverty, increased gender inequality, including through often deteriorating work conditions and unsafe working environments, especially in the informal economy and rural areas. While globalization has brought greater economic opportunities and autonomy to some women, many others have been marginalized and deprived of the benefits of this process, owing to deepening inequalities among and within countries. Although in many countries the level of participation of women in the labour force has risen, in other cases the application of certain economic policies has had such a negative impact that increases in women's employment often have not been matched by improvements in wages, promotions and working conditions. In many cases, women continue to be employed in low-paid part-time and contract jobs marked by insecurity and by safety and health hazards. In many countries, women, especially new entrants into the labour market, continue to be among the first to lose jobs and the last to be rehired.

36. Increasing economic disparities among and within countries, coupled with a growing economic interdependence and dependence of States on external factors as well as financial crises have, in recent years, altered prospects for growth and caused economic instability in many countries, with a heavy impact on the lives of women. These difficulties have affected the ability of States to provide social protection and social security as well as funding for the implementation of the Platform for Action. Such difficulties are also reflected in the shift of the cost of social protection, social security and other welfare provisions from the public sector to the household. The decreasing levels of funding available through international cooperation has contributed to further marginalization of a large number of developing countries and countries with economies in transition within which women are among the poorest. The agreed target of 0.7 per cent of the gross national product of developed countries for overall official development assistance has not been achieved. These factors have contributed to the increasing feminization of poverty, which has undermined efforts to achieve gender equality. Limited funding at the State level makes it imperative that innovative approaches to the allocation of existing resources be employed, not only by Governments but also by non-governmental organizations and the private sector. One such innovation is the gender analysis of

public budgets, which is emerging as an important tool for determining the differential impact of expenditures on women and men to help ensure equitable use of existing resources. This analysis is crucial to promote gender equality.

37. The impact of globalization and structural adjustment programmes, the high costs of external debt servicing and declining terms of international trade in several developing countries have worsened the existing obstacles to development, aggravating the feminization of poverty. Negative consequences of structural adjustment programmes, stemming from inappropriate design and application, have continued to place a disproportionate burden on women, inter alia, through budget cuts in basic social services, including education and health.

38. There is a greater acceptance that the increasing debt burden faced by most developing countries is unsustainable and constitutes one of the principal obstacles to achieving progress in people-centred sustainable development and poverty eradication. For many developing countries, as well as countries with economies in transition, excessive debt servicing has severely constrained their capacity to promote social development and provide basic services and has affected full implementation of the Platform for Action.

39. In countries with economies in transition, women are bearing most of the hardships induced by the economic restructuring and are the first to lose jobs in times of recession. They are being squeezed out from fast-growth sectors. Loss of childcare facilities due to elimination or privatization of State work places, increased need for older care without the corresponding facilities and continuing inequality of access to training for finding re-employment and to productive assets for entering or expanding businesses are current challenges facing women in these countries.

40. Science and technology, as fundamental components of development, are transforming patterns of production, contributing to the creation of jobs and new job classifications, and ways of working, and contributing to the establishment of a knowledge-based society. Technological change can bring new opportunities for all women in all fields, if they have equal access and adequate training. Women should also be actively involved in the definition, design, development, implementation and gender impact evaluation of policies related to these changes. Many women worldwide are yet to use effectively these new communications technologies for networking, advocacy, exchange of information, business, education, media consultation and e-commerce initiatives. For instance, millions of the world's poorest women and men still do not have access to and benefits from science and technology and are currently excluded from this new field and the opportunities it presents.

41. The patterns of migratory flows of labour are changing. Women and girls are increasingly involved in internal, regional and international labour migration to pursue many occupations, mainly in farm labour, domestic work and some forms of entertainment work. While this situation increases their earning opportunities and self-reliance, it also exposes them, particularly the poor, uneducated, unskilled and/or undocumented migrants, to inadequate working conditions, increased health risk, the risk of trafficking, economic and sexual exploitation, racism, racial discrimination and xenophobia, and other forms of abuse, which impair their enjoyment of their human rights and, in some cases, constitute violations of human rights.

42. While recognizing that Governments have the primary responsibility to develop and implement policies to promote gender equality, partnerships between Governments and different actors of civil society are increasingly recognized as an important mechanism to achieve this goal. Additional innovative approaches can be further developed to foster this collaboration.

43. In some countries, current demographic trends show that lowered fertility rates, increased life expectancy and lower mortality rates have contributed to the ageing of the population, and increase in chronic health conditions has implications for health-care systems and spending, informal care systems and research. Given the gap between male and female life expectancy, the number of widows and older single women has increased considerably, often leading to their social isolation and other social challenges. Societies have much to gain from the knowledge and life experience of older women. On the other hand, the current generation of young people is the largest in history. Adolescent girls and young women have particular needs which will require increasing attention.

44. The rapid progression of the HIV/AIDS pandemic, particularly in the developing world, has had a devastating impact on women. Responsible behaviour and gender equality are among the important prerequisites for its prevention. There is also the need for more effective strategies to empower women to have control over and decide freely and responsibly on matters related to their sexuality, to protect themselves from high risk and irresponsible behaviour leading to sexually transmitted infections, including HIV/AIDS, and to promote responsible, safe and respectful behaviour by men and to also promote gender equality. HIV/AIDS is an urgent public health issue, is outstripping efforts to contain it and, in many countries, is reversing hard-won gains of development. The burden of care for people living with HIV/AIDS and for children orphaned by HIV/AIDS falls particularly on women as infrastructures are inadequate to respond to the challenges being posed. Women with HIV/AIDS often suffer from discrimination and stigma and are often victims of violence. Issues related to prevention, mother-to-child transmission of HIV, breastfeeding, information and education in particular of youth, curbing high-risk behaviour, intravenous drug users, support groups, counselling and voluntary testing, partner notification and provision and high cost of essential drugs have not been sufficiently addressed. There are positive signs in the fight against HIV/AIDS in some countries that behavioural changes have occurred among young people, and experience shows that educational programmes for young people can lead to a more positive view on gender relations and gender equality, delayed sexual initiation and reduced risk of sexually transmitted infections.

45. Growing drug and substance abuse among young women and girls, both in developed and developing countries, has raised the need for increased efforts towards demand reduction and fight against illicit production, supply and trafficking of narcotic drugs and psychotropic substances.

46. The increase in casualties and damage caused by natural disasters has raised awareness of the inefficiencies and inadequacies of the existing approaches and intervention methods in responding to such emergency situations, in which women, more often than men, are burdened with the responsibility of meeting the immediate daily needs of their families. This situation has raised awareness that a gender perspective must be incorporated whenever disaster prevention, mitigation and recovery strategies are being developed and implemented.

47. The changing context of gender relations, as well as the discussion on gender equality, has led to an increased reassessment of gender roles. This has further encouraged a discussion on the roles and responsibilities of women and men working together towards gender equality and the need for changing those stereotypical and traditional roles that limit women's full potential. There is a need for balanced participation between women and men in remunerated and unremunerated work. Failure to recognize and measure in quantitative terms unremunerated work of women, which is often not valued in national accounts, has meant that women's full contribution to social and economic development remains underestimated and undervalued. As long as there is insufficient sharing of tasks and responsibilities with men, the combination of remunerated work and caregiving will lead to the continued disproportionate burden for women in comparison to men.

IV. Actions and initiatives to overcome obstacles and to achieve the full and accelerated implementation of the Beijing Platform for Action

48. In view of the evaluation of progress made in the five years since the Fourth World Conference on Women in implementing the Beijing Declaration and Platform for Action, as contained in section II above, as well as the current challenges affecting its full realization, as outlined in section III above, Governments now recommit themselves to the Beijing Declaration and Platform for Action and also commit themselves to further actions and initiatives to overcome the obstacles and address the challenges. Governments, in taking continued and additional steps to achieve the goals of the Platform for Action, recognize that all human rights—civil, cultural, economic, political and social, including the right to development—are universal, indivisible, interdependent and interrelated, and are essential for realizing gender equality, development and peace in the twenty-first century.

49. Organizations of the United Nations system and the Bretton Woods institutions, as well as the World Trade Organization, other international and regional intergovernmental bodies, parliaments and civil society, including the private sector and non-governmental organizations, trade unions and other stakeholders, are called upon to support government efforts and, where appropriate, develop complementary programmes of their own to achieve full and effective implementation of the Platform for Action.

50. Governments and intergovernmental organizations recognize the contribution and complementary role of non-governmental organizations, with full respect for their autonomy, in ensuring the effective implementation of the Platform for Action, and should continue to strengthen partnerships with non-governmental organizations, particularly women's organizations, in contributing to the effective implementation of and follow-up to the Platform for Action.

51. Experience has shown that the goal of gender equality can be fully achieved only in the context of renewed relations among different stakeholders at all levels. The full, effective participation of women on the basis of equality in all spheres of society is necessary to contribute to this goal.

52. Achieving gender equality and empowerment of women requires redressing inequalities between women and men and girls and boys and ensuring their equal rights, responsibilities, opportunities and possibilities. Gender equality implies that women's needs, interests, concerns, experiences and priorities as well as men's are an integral dimension of the design, implementation, national monitoring, and follow-up and evaluation, including at the international level, of all actions in all areas.

53. By adopting the Platform for Action, Governments and the international community agreed to a common development agenda with gender equality and women's empowerment as underlying principles. The efforts towards ensuring women's participation in development have expanded and need to combine a focus on women's conditions and basic needs with a holistic approach based on equal rights and partnerships, promotion and protection of all human rights and fundamental freedoms. Policies and programmes should be formulated to achieve the goal of people-centred sustainable development, secure livelihoods and adequate social protection measures, including safety nets, strengthened support systems for families, equal access to and control over financial and economic resources, and to eliminate increasing and disproportionate poverty among women. All economic policies and institutions as well as those responsible for resource allocation should adopt a gender perspective to ensure that development dividends are shared on equal grounds.

54. Given the persistent and increasing burden of poverty on women in many countries, particularly in developing countries, it is essential to continue from a gender perspective to review, modify and implement integrated macroeconomic and social policies and programmes, including those related to structural adjustment and external debt problems, to ensure universal and equitable access to social services, in particular to education and affordable quality health-care services and equal access to and control over economic resources.

55. Increased efforts are needed to provide equal access to education, health and social services and to ensure women's and girls' rights to education and the enjoyment of the highest attainable standard of physical and mental health and well-being throughout the life cycle, as well as adequate, affordable and universally accessible health care and services, including sexual and reproductive health, particularly in the face of the HIV/AIDS pandemic; they are also necessary with regard to the growing proportion of older women.

56. Given that a majority of the world's women are subsistence producers and users of environmental resources, there is a need to recognize and integrate women's knowledge and priorities in the conservation and management of such resources to ensure their

sustainability. Programmes and infrastructures that are gender-sensitive are needed in order to respond effectively to disaster and emergency situations that threaten the environment, livelihood security, as well as the management of the basic requirements of daily life.

57. Sustaining the livelihoods of populations in States with limited or scarce resources, including small island developing States, is critically dependent on the preservation and protection of the environment. Women's customary knowledge, management and sustainable use of biodiversity should be recognized.

58. Political will and commitment at all levels are crucial to ensure mainstreaming of a gender perspective in the adoption and implementation of comprehensive and action-oriented policies in all areas. Policy commitments are essential for further developing the necessary framework which ensures women's equal access to and control over economic and financial resources, training, services and institutions as well as their participation in decision-making and management. Policy-making processes require the partnership of women and men at all levels. Men and boys should also be actively involved and encouraged in all efforts to achieve the goals of the Platform for Action and its implementation.

59. Violence against women and girls is a major obstacle to the achievement of the objectives of gender equality, development and peace. Violence against women both violates and impairs or nullifies the enjoyment by women of their human rights and fundamental freedoms. Gender-based violence, such as battering and other domestic violence, sexual abuse, sexual slavery and exploitation, international trafficking in women and children, forced prostitution and sexual harassment, as well as violence against women resulting from cultural prejudice, racism and racial discrimination, xenophobia, pornography, ethnic cleansing, armed conflict, foreign occupation, religious and anti-religious extremism and terrorism are incompatible with the dignity and worth of the human person and must be combated and eliminated.

60. Women play a critical role in the family. The family is the basic unit of society and is a strong force for social cohesion and integration and, as such, should be strengthened. The inadequate support to women and insufficient protection and support to their respective families affect society as a whole and undermine efforts to achieve gender equality. In different cultural, political and social systems, various forms of the family exist and the rights, capabilities and responsibilities of family members must be respected. Women's social and economic contributions to the welfare of the family and the social significance of maternity and paternity continue to be inadequately addressed. Motherhood and fatherhood and the role of parents and legal guardians in the family and in the upbringing of children and the importance of all family members to the family's well-being are also acknowledged and must not be a basis for discrimination. Women also continue to bear a disproportionate share of the household responsibilities and the care of children, the sick and the elderly. Such imbalance needs to be consistently addressed through appropriate policies and programmes, in particular those geared towards education, and through legislation where appropriate. In order to achieve full partnership, both in public and in private spheres, both women and men must be enabled to reconcile and share equally work responsibilities and family responsibilities.

61. Strong national machineries for the advancement of women and promotion of gender equality require political commitment at the highest level and all necessary human and financial resources to initiate, recommend and facilitate the development, adoption and monitoring of policies, legislation, programmes and capacity-building for the empowerment of women and to act as catalysts for open public dialogue on gender equality as a societal goal. This would enable them to promote the advancement of women and mainstream a gender perspective in policies and programmes in all areas, to play an advocacy role and to ensure equal access to all institutions and resources, as well as enhanced capacity-building for women in all sectors. Reforms to meet the challenges of the changing world are essential to ensure women's equal access to institutions and organizations. Institutional and conceptual changes are a strategic and important aspect of creating an enabling environment for the implementation of the Platform for Action.

62. Programme support to enhance women's opportunities, potentials and activities need to have a dual focus: on the one hand, programmes aimed at meeting the basic as well as the specific needs of women for capacity-building, organizational development and empowerment, and on the other, gender mainstreaming in all programme formulation and implementation activities. It is particularly important to expand into new areas of programming to advance gender equality in response to current challenges.

63. Girls and women of all ages with any form of disability are generally among the more vulnerable and marginalized of society. There is therefore need to take into account and to address their concerns in all policy-making and programming. Special measures are needed at all levels to integrate them into the mainstream of development.

64. Effective and coordinated plans and programmes for the full implementation of the Platform for Action require a clear knowledge of the situation of women and girls, clear research-based knowledge and data disaggregated by sex, short- and long-term time-bound targets and measurable goals, and follow-up mechanisms to assess progress. Efforts are needed to ensure capacity-building for all actors involved in the achievement of these goals. Efforts are also needed at the national level to increase transparency and accountability.

65. The realization and the achievement of the goals of gender equality, development and peace need to be supported by the allocation of necessary human, financial and material resources for specific and targeted activities to ensure gender equality at the local, national, regional and international levels as well as by enhanced and increased international cooperation. Explicit attention to these goals in the budgetary processes at the national, regional and international levels is essential.

A. Actions to be taken at the national level

By Governments:

66. (a) Set and encourage the use of explicit short- and long-term time-bound targets or measurable goals, including, where appropriate, quotas, to pro-

mote progress towards gender balance, including women's equal access to and full participation on a basis of equality with men in all areas and at all levels of public life, especially in decision- and policy-making positions, in political parties and political activities, in all government ministries and at key policy-making institutions, as well as in local development bodies and authorities;

(b) Address the barriers faced by women, particularly by indigenous and other marginalized women, in accessing and participating in politics and decision-making, including lack of training, women's double burden of paid and unpaid work, negative societal attitudes and stereotypes.

67. (a) Ensure policies that guarantee equal access to education and the elimination of gender disparities in education, including vocational training, science and technology and completion of basic education for girls, especially for those living in rural and deprived areas, and opportunities for continuing education at all levels for all women and girls;

(b) Support the implementation of plans and programmes of action to ensure quality education and improved enrolment retention rates for boys and girls and the elimination of gender discrimination and gender stereotypes in educational curricula and materials, as well as in the process of education;

(c) Accelerate action and strengthen political commitment to close the gender gap in primary and secondary education by 2005 and to ensure free compulsory and universal primary education for both girls and boys by 2015, as advocated by several global conferences, and eliminate policies that have been proven to worsen and perpetuate the gap;

(d) Develop a gender-sensitive curriculum from kindergarten to elementary schools to vocational training and universities in order to address gender stereotyping as one of the root causes of segregation in working life.

68. (a) Design and implement policies that promote and protect women's enjoyment of all human rights and fundamental freedoms and create an environment that does not tolerate violations of the rights of women and girls;

(b) Create and maintain a non-discriminatory and gender-sensitive legal environment by reviewing legislation with a view to striving to remove discriminatory provisions as soon as possible, preferably by 2005, and eliminating legislative gaps that leave women and girls without protection of their rights and without effective recourse against gender-based discrimination;

(c) Ratify the Convention on the Elimination of All Forms of Discrimination against Women, limit the extent of any reservations to it, and withdraw reservations that are contrary to the object and purpose of the Convention or otherwise incompatible with international treaty law;

(d) Consider signing and ratifying the Optional Protocol to the Convention on the Elimination of All Forms of Discrimination against Women;

(e) Consider signing and ratifying the Rome Statute of the International Criminal Court;

(f) Develop, review and implement laws and procedures to prohibit and eliminate all forms of discrimination against women and girls;

(g) Take measures, including programmes and policies, to ensure that maternity, motherhood and parenting and the role of women in procreation are not used as a basis for discrimination nor restrict the full participation of women in society;

(h) Ensure that national legislative and administrative reform processes, including those linked to land reform, decentralization and reorientation of the economy, promote women's rights, particularly those of rural women and women living in poverty, and take measures to promote and implement those rights through women's equal access to and control over economic resources, including land, property rights, right to inheritance, credit and traditional saving schemes, such as women's banks and cooperatives;

(i) Mainstream a gender perspective into national immigration and asylum policies, regulations and practices, as appropriate, in order to promote and protect the rights of all women, including the consideration of steps to recognize gender-related persecution and violence when assessing grounds for granting refugee status and asylum;

(j) Take all appropriate measures to eliminate discrimination and violence against women and girls by any person, organization or enterprise;

(k) Take necessary measures for the private sector and educational establishments to facilitate and strengthen compliance with non-discriminatory legislation.

69. (a) As a matter of priority, review and revise legislation, where appropriate, with a view to introducing effective legislation, including on violence against women, and take other necessary measures to ensure that all women and girls are protected against all forms of physical, psychological and sexual violence, and are provided recourse to justice;

(b) Prosecute the perpetrators of all forms of violence against women and girls and sentence them appropriately, and introduce actions aimed at helping and motivating perpetrators to break the cycle of violence and take measures to provide avenues for redress to victims;

(c) Treat all forms of violence against women and girls of all ages as a criminal offence punishable by law, including violence based on all forms of discrimination;

(d) Establish legislation and/or strengthen appropriate mechanisms to handle criminal matters relating to all forms of domestic violence, including marital rape and sexual abuse of women and girls, and ensure that such cases are brought to justice swiftly;

(e) Develop, adopt and fully implement laws and other measures, as appropriate, such as policies and educational programmes, to eradicate harmful customary or traditional practices, including female genital mutilation, early and forced marriage and so-called honour crimes, which are violations of the human rights of women and girls and obstacles to the full enjoyment by women of their human rights and fundamental freedoms, and intensify efforts, in cooperation with local women's groups, to raise collective and individual awareness on how these harmful traditional or customary practices violate women's human rights;

(f) Continue to undertake research to develop a better understanding of the root causes of all forms of violence against women in order to design programmes and take measures towards eliminating those forms of violence;

(g) Take measures to address through policies and programmes, racism and racially motivated violence against women and girls;

(h) Take concrete steps, as a priority and with their full and voluntary participation, to address the impact of violence on indigenous women in order to implement appropriate, effective programmes and services to eliminate all forms of violence;

(i) Promote women's and girls' mental well-being, integrate mental health services into primary health-care systems, develop gender-sensitive supportive programmes and train health workers to recognize gender-based violence and provide care for girls and women of all ages who have experienced any form of violence;

(j) Adopt and promote a holistic approach to respond to all forms of violence and abuse against girls and women of all ages, including girls and women with disabilities, as well as vulnerable and marginalized women and girls in order to address their diverse needs, including education, provision of appropriate health care and services and basic social services;

(k) Approve and promote a holistic approach to combat violence against women during all their life cycle and circumstances.

70. (a) Take appropriate measures to address the root factors, including external factors, that encourage trafficking in women and girls for prostitution and other forms of commercialized sex, forced marriages and forced labour in order to eliminate trafficking in women, including by strengthening existing legislations with a view to providing better protection of the rights of women and girls and to punishing the perpetrators, through both criminal and civil measures;

(b) Devise, enforce and strengthen effective measures to combat and eliminate all forms of trafficking in women and girls through a comprehensive anti-trafficking strategy consisting of, inter alia, legislative measures, prevention campaigns, information exchange, assistance and protection for and reintegration of the victims and prosecution of all the offenders involved, including intermediaries;

(c) Consider preventing, within the legal framework and in accordance with national policies, victims of trafficking, in particular women and girls, from being prosecuted for their illegal entry or residence, taking into account that they are victims of exploitation;

(d) Consider setting up or strengthening a national coordinating mechanism, for example, a national rapporteur or an inter-agency body, with the participation of civil society, including non-governmental organizations, to encourage the exchange of information and to report on data, root causes, factors and trends in violence against women, in particular trafficking;

(e) Provide protection and support to women and their respective families and develop and strengthen policies to support family security.

71. (a) Consider adopting, where appropriate, national legislation consistent with the Convention on Biological Diversity to protect the knowledge, innovations and practices of women in indigenous and local communities relating to traditional medicines, biodiversity and indigenous technologies;

(b) Adapt environmental and agricultural policies and mechanisms, when necessary, to incorporate a gender perspective, and in cooperation with civil society, support farmers, particularly women farmers and those living in rural areas, with education and training programmes.

72. (a) Adopt policies and implement measures to address, on a prioritized basis, the gender aspects of emerging and continued health challenges, such as malaria, tuberculosis, HIV/AIDS and other diseases having a disproportionate impact on women's health, including those resulting in the highest mortality and morbidity rates;

(b) Ensure that the reduction of maternal morbidity and mortality is a health sector priority and that women have ready access to essential obstetric care, well-equipped and adequately staffed maternal health-care services, skilled attendance at delivery, emergency obstetric care, effective referral and transport to higher levels of care when necessary, post-partum care and family planning in order to, inter alia, promote safe motherhood, and give priority attention to measures to prevent, detect and treat breast, cervical and ovarian cancer and osteoporosis, and sexually transmitted infections, including HIV/AIDS;

(c) Take measures to meet the unmet needs in good quality family planning services and in contraception, namely regarding the existing gap in services, supplies and use;

(d) Collect and disseminate updated and reliable data on mortality and morbidity of women and conduct further research regarding how social and economic factors affect the health of girls and women of all ages, as well as research about the provision of health-care services to girls and women and the patterns of use of such services and the value of disease prevention and health promotion programmes for women;

(e) Ensure universal and equal access for women and men throughout the lifecycle, to social services related to health care, including education, clean water and safe sanitation, nutrition, food security and health education programmes;

(f) Ensure the provision of safe working conditions for health-care workers;

(g) Adopt, enact, review and revise, where necessary or appropriate, and implement health legislation, policies and programmes, in consultation with women's organizations and other actors of civil society, and allocate the necessary budgetary resources to ensure the highest attainable standard of physical and mental health, so that all women have full and equal access to comprehensive, high-quality and affordable health care, information, education and services throughout their life cycle; reflect the new demands for service and care by women and girls as a result of the HIV/AIDS pandemic and new knowledge about women's needs for specific mental and occupation health programmes and for the ageing process; and protect and promote human rights by ensuring that all health services and workers conform to ethical, professional and gender-sensitive standards in the delivery of women's health services, including by establishing or strengthening, as appropriate, regulatory and enforcement mechanisms;

(h) Eliminate discrimination against all women and girls in the access to health information, education and health care and health services;

(i) Reproductive health is a state of complete physical, mental and social well-being, and not merely the absence of disease or infirmity, in all matters relating to the reproductive system and to its functions and processes. Reproductive health therefore implies that people are able to have a satisfying and safe sex life and that they have the capability to reproduce and the freedom to decide if, when and how often to do so. Implicit in this last condition is the right of men and women to be informed and to have access to safe, effective, affordable and acceptable methods of family planning of their choice, as well as other methods of their choice for regulation of fertility which are not against the law, and the right of access to appropriate health-care services that will enable women to go safely through pregnancy and childbirth and provide couples with the best chance of having a healthy infant. In line with the above definition of reproductive health, reproductive health care is defined as the constellation of methods, techniques and services that contribute to reproductive health and well-being by preventing and solving reproductive health problems. It also includes sexual health, the purpose of which is the enhancement of life and personal relations, and not merely counselling and care related to reproduction and sexually transmitted diseases;

(j) Given the above definition, reproductive rights embrace certain human rights that are already recognized in national laws, international human rights documents and other consensus documents. These rights rest on the recognition of the basic right of all couples and individuals to decide freely and responsibly the number, spacing and timing of their children and to have the information and means to do so, and the right to attain the highest standard of sexual and reproductive health. They also include their right to make decisions concerning reproduction free of discrimination, coercion and violence, as expressed in human rights documents. In the exercise of these rights, they should take into account the needs of their living and future children and their responsibilities towards the community. The promotion of the responsible exercise of these rights for all people should be the fundamental basis for government- and community-supported policies and programmes in the area of reproductive health, including family planning. As part of their commitment, full attention should be given to the promotion of mutually respectful and equitable gender relations and particularly to meeting the educational and service needs of adolescents to enable them to deal in a positive and responsible way with their sexuality. Reproductive health eludes many of the world's people because of such factors as inadequate levels of knowledge about human sexuality and inappropriate or poor-quality reproductive health information and services; the prevalence of high-risk sexual behaviour; discriminatory social practices; negative attitudes towards women and girls; and the limited power many women and girls have over their sexual and reproductive lives. In most countries, adolescents are particularly vulnerable because of their lack of information and access to relevant services. Older women and men have distinct reproductive and sexual health issues which are often inadequately addressed;

(k) The human rights of women include their right to have control over and decide freely and responsibly on matters related to their sexuality, including sexual and reproductive health, free of coercion, discrimination and violence. Equal relationships between women and men in matters of sexual relations and reproduction, including full respect for the integrity of the person, require mutual respect, consent and shared responsibility for sexual behaviour and its consequences;

(l) Design and implement programmes to encourage and enable men to adopt safe and responsible sexual and reproductive behaviour, and to use effectively methods to prevent unwanted pregnancies and sexually transmitted infections, including HIV/AIDS;

(m) Take all appropriate measures to eliminate harmful, medically unnecessary or coercive medical interventions as well as inappropriate medication and overmedication of women and ensure that all women are properly informed of their options, including likely benefits and potential side effects, by properly trained personnel;

(n) Adopt measures to ensure non-discrimination against and respect for the privacy of those living with HIV/AIDS and sexually transmitted infections, including women and young people, so that they are not denied the information needed to prevent further transmission of HIV/AIDS and sexually transmitted diseases and are able to access treatment and care services without fear of stigmatization, discrimination or violence;

(o) In the light of paragraph 8.25 of the Programme of Action of the International Conference on Population and Development, which states:

"In no case should abortion be promoted as a method of family planning. All Governments and relevant intergovernmental and non-governmental organizations are urged to strengthen their commitment to women's health, to deal with the health impact of unsafe abortion as a major public health concern and to reduce the recourse to abortion through expanded and improved family-planning services. Prevention of unwanted pregnancies must always be given the highest priority and every attempt should be made to eliminate the need for abortion. Women who have unwanted pregnancies should have ready access to reliable information and compassionate counselling. Any measures or changes related to abortion within the health system can only be determined at the national or local level according to the national legislative process. In circumstances where abortion is not against the law, such abortion should be safe. In all cases, women should have access to quality services for the management of complications arising from abortion. Post-abortion counselling, education and family-planning services should be offered promptly, which will also help to avoid repeat abortions.",

consider reviewing laws containing punitive measures against women who have undergone illegal abortions;

(p) Promote and improve comprehensive gender-specific tobacco prevention and control strategies for all women, particularly adolescent girls and pregnant women, which would include education, prevention and cessation programmes and services, and the reduction of people's exposure to environmental tobacco smoke, and support the development of the World Health Organization international framework convention on tobacco control;

(*q*) Promote or improve information programmes and measures including treatment for the elimination of the increasing substance abuse among women and adolescent girls, including information campaigns about the risks to health and other consequences and its impact on families.

73. (*a*) Mainstream a gender perspective into key macroeconomic and social development policies and national development programmes;

(*b*) Incorporate a gender perspective into the design, development, adoption and execution of all budgetary processes, as appropriate, in order to promote equitable, effective and appropriate resource allocation and establish adequate budgetary allocations to support gender equality and development programmes that enhance women's empowerment and develop the necessary analytical and methodological tools and mechanisms for monitoring and evaluation;

(*c*) Increase, as appropriate, and effectively utilize financial and other resources in the social sector, particularly in education and health, to achieve gender equality and women's empowerment as a central strategy for addressing development and poverty eradication;

(*d*) Strive to reduce the disproportionate number of women living in poverty, in particular rural women, by implementing national poverty eradication programmes with a focus on a gender perspective and the empowerment of women, including short- and long-term goals.

74. (*a*) Undertake socio-economic policies that promote sustainable development and support and ensure poverty eradication programmes, especially for women, by, inter alia, providing skills training, equal access to and control over resources, finance, credit, including microcredit, information and technology, and equal access to markets to benefit women of all ages, in particular those living in poverty and marginalized women, including rural women, indigenous women and female-headed households;

(*b*) Create and ensure access to social protection systems, taking into account the specific needs of all women living in poverty, demographic changes and changes in society, to provide safeguards against the uncertainties and changes in conditions of work associated with globalization, and strive to ensure that new, flexible and emerging forms of work are adequately covered by social protection;

(*c*) Continue to review, modify and implement macroeconomic and social policies and programmes, inter alia, through an analysis from a gender perspective of those related to structural adjustment and external debt problems, in order to ensure women's equal access to resources and universal access to basic social services.

75. Facilitate employment for women through, inter alia, promotion of adequate social protection, simplification of administrative procedures, removal of fiscal obstacles, where appropriate, and other measures, such as access to risk capital, credit schemes, microcredit and other funding, facilitating the establishment of microenterprises and small and medium-sized enterprises.

76. (*a*) Establish or reinforce existing institutional mechanisms at all levels to work with national machineries to strengthen societal support for gender equality, in cooperation with civil society, particularly women's non-governmental organizations;

(*b*) Take action at the highest levels for the continued advancement of women, in particular by strengthening national machineries to mainstream the gender perspective to accelerate the empowerment of women in all areas and to ensure commitment to gender equality policies;

(*c*) Provide national machineries with the necessary human and financial resources, including through exploring innovative funding schemes, so that gender mainstreaming is integrated into all policies, programmes and projects;

(*d*) Consider establishing effective commissions or other institutions to promote equal opportunities;

(*e*) Strengthen efforts to implement fully national action plans developed for the implementation of the Beijing Platform for Action and, when necessary, adjust or develop national plans for the future;

(*f*) Ensure that the design of all government information policies and strategies is gender-sensitive.

77. (*a*) Provide national statistical offices with institutional and financial support so that they may collect, compile and disseminate data disaggregated by sex, age and other factors, as appropriate, in formats that are accessible to the public and to policy makers for, inter alia, gender-based analysis, monitoring and impact assessment, and support new work to develop statistics and indicators, especially in areas where information is particularly lacking;

(*b*) Regularly compile and publish crime statistics, and monitor trends in law enforcement concerning violations of the rights of women and girls to increase awareness in order to develop more effective policies;

(*c*) Develop national capacity to undertake policy-oriented and gender-related research and impact studies by universities and national research/training institutes to enable gender-specific knowledge-based policy-making.

B. Further actions to be taken at the national level

By Governments, the private sector, non-governmental organizations and other actors of civil society:

78. (*a*) Encourage the creation of training and legal literacy programmes which build and support the capacities of women's organizations to advocate for women's and girls' human rights and fundamental freedoms;

(*b*) Encourage collaboration, where appropriate, among Governments, non-governmental organizations, grass-roots organizations and traditional and community leaders for the promotion and protection of all human rights and fundamental freedoms of women and girls, the dignity and worth of the human person and equal rights for women and men;

(*c*) Encourage cooperation between governmental authorities, parliamentarians and other relevant authorities and women's organizations, including non-governmental organizations, as appropriate, in ensuring that legislation is non-discriminatory;

(*d*) Provide gender-sensitive training to all actors, including police, prosecutors and the judiciary, in dealing with victims of violence, particularly women and girls, including sexual violence.

79. (*a*) Adopt a holistic approach to women's physical and mental health throughout the life cycle,

take further measures to redesign health information, services and training for health workers in order to make them gender-sensitive, promote gender balance at all levels of the health-care system, and reflect women's perspective and right to privacy, confidentiality, voluntary and informed consent;

(b) Reinforce efforts to ensure universal access to high quality primary health care throughout the life cycle, including sexual and reproductive health care, no later than 2015;

(c) Review and revise national policies, programmes and legislation to implement the key actions for the further implementation of the Programme of Action of the International Conference on Population and Development adopted by the General Assembly at its twenty-first special session, paying particular attention to achieving the specific benchmarks to reduce maternal mortality, to increase the proportion of births assisted by skilled attendants, to provide the widest achievable range of safe and effective family planning and contraceptive methods and to reduce young people's risk of HIV/AIDS;

(d) Strengthen measures to improve the nutritional status of all girls and women, recognizing the effects of severe and moderate malnutrition, the lifelong implications of nutrition and the link between mother and child health, by promoting and enhancing support for programmes to reduce malnutrition, such as school meal programmes, mother-child-nutrition programmes and micronutrient supplementation, giving special attention to bridging the gender gap in nutrition;

(e) Review with the full participation of women and monitor the impact of health-sector reform initiatives on women's health and their enjoyment of human rights, in particular with regard to rural and urban health service delivery to women living in poverty, and ensure that reforms secure full and equal access to available, affordable and high-quality health care and services for all women, taking into account the diverse needs of women;

(f) Design and implement programmes with the full involvement of adolescents, as appropriate, to provide them with education, information and appropriate, specific, user-friendly and accessible services, without discrimination, to address effectively their reproductive and sexual health needs, taking into account their right to privacy, confidentiality, respect and informed consent, and the responsibilities, rights and duties of parents and legal guardians to provide in a manner consistent with the evolving capacities of the child appropriate direction and guidance in the exercise by the child of the rights recognized in the Convention on the Rights of the Child, in conformity with the Convention on the Elimination of All Forms of Discrimination against Women and ensuring that in all actions concerning children, the best interests of the child are a primary consideration. These programmes should, inter alia, build adolescent girls' self-esteem and help them take responsibility for their own lives; promote gender equality and responsible sexual behaviour; raise awareness about, prevent and treat sexually transmitted infections, including HIV/AIDS, and sexual violence and abuse; and counsel adolescents on avoiding unwanted and early pregnancies;

(g) Design and implement programmes to provide social services and support to pregnant adolescents and adolescent mothers, in particular to enable them to continue and complete their education;

(h) Give particular attention to developing and improving access to improved and new technologies and to safe and affordable drugs and treatments to meet women's health needs, including cardiopulmonary diseases, hypertension, osteoporosis, breast, cervical and ovarian cancer and family planning and contraceptive methods, for both women and men.

80. Develop and use frameworks, guidelines and other practical tools and indicators to accelerate gender mainstreaming, including gender-based research, analytical tools and methodologies, training, case studies, statistics and information.

81. (a) Provide equal opportunities and favourable conditions for women of all ages and backgrounds on equal terms with men by encouraging their entry into politics and their participation at all levels;

(b) Encourage the nomination of more women candidates, inter alia, through political parties, quotas or measurable goals or other appropriate means for election to parliaments and other legislative structures, to increase their share and contribution in the formulation of public policy;

(c) Develop and maintain consultative processes and mechanisms, in partnership with women's organizations, including non-governmental organizations and community groups, to ensure that all women, with particular attention to those who face particular barriers to their participation in public life, are fully involved in and informed about decisions that impact their lives.

82. (a) Promote and protect the rights of women workers and take action to remove structural and legal barriers as well as stereotypical attitudes to gender equality at work, addressing, inter alia, gender bias in recruitment; working conditions; occupational segregation and harassment; discrimination in social protection benefits; women's occupational health and safety; unequal career opportunities and inadequate sharing, by men, of family responsibilities;

(b) Promote programmes to enable women and men to reconcile their work and family responsibilities and to encourage men to share equally with women household and childcare responsibilities;

(c) Develop or strengthen policies and programmes to support the multiple roles of women in contributing to the welfare of the family in its various forms, which acknowledge the social significance of maternity and motherhood, parenting, the role of parents and legal guardians in the upbringing of children and caring for other family members. Such policies and programmes should also promote shared responsibility of parents, women and men and society as a whole in this regard;

(d) Design, implement and promote family friendly policies and services, including affordable, accessible and quality care services for children and other dependants, parental and other leave schemes and campaigns to sensitize public opinion and other relevant actors on equal sharing of employment and family responsibilities between women and men;

(e) Develop policies and programmes to enhance the employability of women and their access to quality jobs, through improving access to formal, non-formal and vocational training, lifelong learning and retraining, long-distance education, including in information and communications technology and entrepreneurial skills, particularly in developing countries, to support women's empowerment in the different stages of their lives;

(f) Take action to increase women's participation and to bring about a balanced representation of women and men in all sectors and occupations in the labour market, inter alia, by encouraging the creation or expansion of institutional networks to support the career development and promotion of women;

(g) Develop and/or strengthen programmes and policies to support women entrepreneurs, including those engaged in new enterprises, through access to information, training, including vocational training, new technologies, networks, credit and financial services;

(h) Initiate positive steps to promote equal pay for equal work or work of equal value and to diminish differentials in incomes between women and men;

(i) Encourage and support the education of girls in science, mathematics, new technologies, including information technologies, and technical subjects, and encourage women, including through career advising, to seek employment in high-growth and high-wage sectors and jobs;

(j) Develop policies and implement programmes, particularly for men and boys, on changing stereotypical attitudes and behaviours concerning gender roles and responsibilities to promote gender equality and positive attitudes and behaviour;

(k) Strengthen gender-awareness campaigns and gender equality training among women and men, girls and boys to eliminate the persistence of harmful stereotypes;

(l) Analyse and respond, as necessary, to the major reasons why men and women may be affected differently by the process of job creation and retrenchment associated with economic transition and structural transformation of the economy, including globalization;

(m) Promote gender-sensitivity and social responsibility of the private sector, inter alia, through the management of work time and dissemination of gender-sensitive information and advocacy campaigns.

83. *(a)* Strengthen or establish, where appropriate, national collaborative and regular reporting mechanisms, with the participation of non-governmental organizations, especially women's organizations, to monitor progress in the implementation of national policies, programmes and benchmarks for achieving gender equality;

(b) Support the work of non-governmental organizations and community-based organizations in helping disadvantaged women, in particular rural women, in gaining access to financial institutions in establishing businesses and other sustainable means of livelihood;

(c) Take measures to enable all older women to be actively engaged in all aspects of life, as well as to assume a variety of roles in communities, public life and decision-making, and develop and implement policies and programmes to ensure their full enjoyment of human rights and quality of life, as well as to address their needs, with a view to contributing to the realization of a society for all ages;

(d) Design and implement policies and programmes to address fully specific needs of women and girls with disabilities, to ensure their equal access to education at all levels, including technical and vocational training and adequate rehabilitation programmes, health care and services and employment opportunities, to protect and promote their human rights and, where appropriate, to eliminate existing inequalities between women and men with disabilities.

C. Actions to be taken at the international level

By the United Nations system and international and regional organizations, as appropriate:

84. *(a)* Assist Governments, at their request, in building institutional capacity and developing national action plans or further implementing existing action plans for the implementation of the Platform for Action;

(b) Support non-governmental organizations, especially women's organizations, to build their capacity to advocate for, implement, assess and follow up the Platform for Action;

(c) Allocate sufficient resources to regional and national programmes to implement the Platform for Action in its twelve critical areas of concern;

(d) Assist Governments in countries with economies in transition to further develop and implement plans and programmes aimed at economic and political empowerment of women;

(e) Encourage the Economic and Social Council to request the regional commissions, within their respective mandates and resources, to build up a database to be updated regularly, in which all programmes and projects carried out in their respective regions by agencies or organizations of the United Nations system are listed, and to facilitate their dissemination, as well as the evaluation of their impact on the empowerment of women through the implementation of the Platform for Action.

85. *(a)* Continue to implement and evaluate and follow up the mandated work of the United Nations agencies, drawing on the full range of expertise available within the United Nations system, as well as agreed conclusions of the Economic and Social Council and other programmes and initiatives, to mainstream a gender perspective into all policies, programmes and planning of the United Nations system, including through the integrated and coordinated follow-up to all major United Nations conferences and summits, as well as to ensure the allocation of sufficient resources and maintenance of gender units and focal points to achieve this end;

(b) Assist countries, upon their request, in developing methods for and compiling statistics on the contributions of women and men to society and the economy, and the socio-economic situation of women and men, in particular in relation to poverty and paid and unpaid work in all sectors;

(c) Support national efforts, particularly in developing countries, for enlarged access to new information technology as part of the efforts to develop collaborative research, training and information dissemination, including through the Gender Awareness Information and Networking System developed by the International Research and Training Institute for the Advancement of Women, while at the same time supporting traditional methods of information dissemination, research and training;

(d) Ensure that all United Nations personnel and officials at Headquarters and in the field, especially in field operations, receive training in order to mainstream a gender perspective in their work, including gender impact analysis, and ensure appropriate follow-up to such training;

(e) Support the Commission on the Status of Women, within its mandate, in assessing and advancing the implementation of the Beijing Platform for Action and the follow-up thereto;

(f) Assist Governments, upon their request, in incorporating a gender perspective as a dimension of development into national development planning;

(g) Assist States parties, upon their request, in building capacity to implement the Convention on the Elimination of All Forms of Discrimination against Women, and in this regard encourage States parties to pay attention to the concluding comments as well as the general recommendations of the Committee on the Elimination of Discrimination against Women.

86. *(a)* Assist Governments, upon request, in developing gender-sensitive strategies for the delivery of assistance and, where appropriate, responses to humanitarian crises resulting from armed conflict and natural disasters;

(b) Ensure and support the full participation of women at all levels of decision-making and implementation in development activities and peace processes, including conflict prevention and resolution, post-conflict reconstruction, peacemaking, peacekeeping and peace-building, and in this regard, support the involvement of women's organizations, community-based organizations and non-governmental organizations;

(c) Encourage the involvement of women in decision-making at all levels and achieve gender balance in the appointment of women and men, with full respect for the principle of equitable geographical distribution, including, as special envoys and special representatives and in pursuing good offices on behalf of the Secretary-General, inter alia, in matters relating to peacekeeping, peace-building and in operational activities, including as resident coordinators;

(d) Provide gender-sensitive training to all actors, as appropriate, in peacekeeping missions in dealing with victims, particularly women and girls, of violence, including sexual violence;

(e) Take further effective measures to remove the obstacles to the realization of the right of peoples to self-determination, in particular peoples living under colonial and foreign occupation, that continue to adversely affect their economic and social development.

87. *(a)* Support activities aimed at the elimination of all forms of violence against women and girls, including by providing support for the activities of women's networks and organizations within the United Nations system;

(b) Consider launching an international "zero tolerance" campaign on violence against women.

88. Encourage the implementation of measures designed to achieve the goal of 50/50 gender balance in all posts, including at the Professional level and above, in particular at the higher levels in their secretariats, including in peacekeeping missions, peace negotiations and in all activities, and report thereon, as appropriate, and enhance management accountability mechanisms.

89. Take measures, with the full participation of women, to create, at all levels, an enabling environment conducive to the achievement and maintenance of world peace, for democracy and peaceful settlement of disputes, with full respect for the principles of sovereignty, territorial integrity and political independence of States and non-intervention in matters which are essentially within the jurisdiction of any State, in accordance with the Charter of the United Nations and international law, as well as the promotion and protection of all human rights, including the right to development, and fundamental freedoms.

D. Actions to be taken at the national and international levels

By Governments, regional and international organizations, including the United Nations system, and international financial institutions and other actors, as appropriate:

90. Take steps with a view to the avoidance of and refrain from any unilateral measure at variance with international law and the Charter of the United Nations that impedes the full achievement of economic and social development by the population of the affected countries, in particular women and children, that jeopardizes their well-being and that creates obstacles to the full enjoyment of their human rights, including the right of everyone to a standard of living adequate for their health and well-being and their right to food, medical care and the necessary social services. Ensure that food and medicine are not used as tools for political pressure.

91. Take urgent and effective measures in accordance with international law with a view to alleviating the negative impact of economic sanctions on women and children.

92. *(a)* Promote international cooperation to support regional and national efforts in the development and use of gender-related analysis and statistics by, inter alia, providing national statistical offices, upon their request, with institutional and financial support in order to enable them to respond to requests for data disaggregated by sex and age for use by national Governments in the formulation of gender-sensitive statistical indicators for monitoring and policy and programme impact assessments, as well as to undertake regular strategic surveys;

(b) Develop with the full participation of all countries an international consensus on indicators and ways to measure violence against women, and consider establishing a readily accessible database on statistics, legislation, training models, good practices, lessons learned and other resources with regard to all forms of violence against women, including women migrant workers;

(c) In partnership, as appropriate, with relevant institutions, promote, improve, systemize and fund the collection of data disaggregated by sex, age and other appropriate factors, on health and access to health services, including comprehensive information on the impact of HIV/AIDS on women, throughout the life cycle;

(d) Eliminate gender biases in bio-medical, clinical and social research, including by conducting voluntary clinical trials involving women, with due regard for their human rights, and in strict conformity with internationally accepted legal, ethical, medical, safety, and scientific standards, and gather, analyse and make

available to appropriate institutions and to end-users gender-specific information about dosage, side effects and effectiveness of drugs, including contraceptives and methods that protect against sexually transmitted infections.

93. (a) Develop and support the capacity of universities, national research and training institutes and other relevant research institutes to undertake gender-related and policy-oriented research in order to inform policy makers and to promote full implementation of the Platform for Action and the follow-up thereto;

(b) Develop a South-South cooperation programme with a view to assisting in the capacity-building of national machineries on women through, inter alia, the sharing of expertise, experiences and knowledge of national machineries on women's empowerment, gender issues and gender mainstreaming methodologies and approaches on the twelve critical areas of concern of the Platform for Action;

(c) Support Governments in their efforts to institute action-oriented programmes and measures to accelerate the full implementation of the Platform for Action, with time-bound targets and/or measurable goals and evaluation methods, including gender impact assessments, with full participation of women for measuring and analysing progress;

(d) Undertake appropriate data collection and research on indigenous women, with their full participation, in order to foster accessible, culturally and linguistically appropriate policies, programmes and services;

(e) Continue research on all current trends that may be creating new gender disparities in order to provide a basis for policy action.

94. (a) Take measures to develop and implement gender-sensitive programmes aimed at stimulating women's entrepreneurship and private initiative, and assist women-owned business in participating in and benefiting from, inter alia, international trade, technological innovation and investment;

(b) Respect, promote and realize the principles contained in the ILO Declaration on Fundamental Principles and Rights at Work and its Follow-up, and strongly consider ratification and full implementation of International Labour Organization conventions which are particularly relevant to ensuring women's rights at work;

(c) Encourage the strengthening of existing and emerging microcredit institutions and their capacity, including through the support of international financial institutions, so that credit and related services for self-employment and income-generating activities may be made available to an increasing number of people living in poverty, in particular women, and to further develop, where appropriate, other microfinance instruments;

(d) Reaffirm commitment to gender-sensitive development and support women's role in sustainable and ecologically sound consumption and production patterns and approaches to natural resource management;

(e) Adopt measures to ensure that the work of rural women, who continue to play a vital role in providing food security and nutrition and are engaged in agricultural production and enterprises related to farming, fishing and resource management and home-based work, especially in the informal sector, is recognized and valued in order to enhance their economic security, their access to and control over resources and credit schemes, services and benefits, and their empowerment.

95. (a) Encourage and implement curriculum changes in training for public officials to make them fully gender-sensitive;

(b) Strengthen and promote programmes to support the participation of young women in youth organizations and encourage dialogue among youth between and among developed and developing countries;

(c) Support national efforts to promote formal and non-formal education and mentoring programmes for women and girls in order to enable them to acquire knowledge, develop self-esteem and skills in leadership, advocacy and conflict resolution;

(d) Undertake comprehensive actions to provide skills training for women and girls at all levels, in order to eradicate poverty, in particular the feminization of poverty, through national and international efforts;

(e) With the full voluntary participation of indigenous women, develop and implement educational and training programmes that respect their history, culture, spirituality, languages and aspirations and ensure their access to all levels of formal and non-formal education, including higher education;

(f) Continue to support and strengthen national, regional and international adult literacy programmes with international cooperation in order to achieve a 50 per cent improvement in the levels of adult literacy by 2015, especially for women, and equitable access to basic and continuing education for all adults;

(g) Continue to examine the decline in enrolment rates and the increase in the drop-out rates of girls and boys at the primary and secondary education levels in some countries, and, with international cooperation, design appropriate national programmes to eliminate the root causes and support lifelong learning for women and girls, with a view to ensuring achievement of relevant international targets on education set by the relevant international conferences;

(h) Ensure equal opportunities for women and girls in cultural, recreational and sports activities, as well as in participation in athletics and physical activities at the national, regional and international levels, such as access, training, competition, remuneration and prizes;

(i) Continue to design efforts for the promotion of respect for cultural diversity and dialogue among and within civilizations in a manner which contributes to the implementation of the Platform for Action, which aims at the empowerment of women and the full realization of all human rights and fundamental freedoms for all women, and in a manner which ensures that gender equality and the full enjoyment of all human rights by women are not undermined;

(j) Apply and support positive measures to give all women, particularly indigenous women, equal access to capacity-building and training programmes to enhance their participation in decision-making in all fields and at all levels.

96. (a) Increase cooperation, policy responses, effective implementation of national legislation and other protective and preventive measures aimed at the elimination of violence against women and girls, especially all forms of commercial sexual exploitation, as well as economic exploitation, including trafficking in

women and children, female infanticide, crimes committed in the name of honour, crimes committed in the name of passion, racially motivated crimes, abduction and sale of children, dowry-related violence and deaths, acid attacks and harmful traditional or customary practices, such as female genital mutilation, early and forced marriages;

(b) Increase awareness and knowledge of the Rome Statute of the International Criminal Court, which affirms that rape, sexual slavery, enforced prostitution, forced pregnancy, enforced sterilization and other forms of sexual violence constitute war crimes and, in defined circumstances, crimes against humanity, with the aim of preventing such crimes from occurring, and take measures to support the prosecution of all persons responsible for such crimes and provide avenues for redress to victims; also increase awareness of the extent to which such crimes are used as a weapon of war;

(c) Provide support to non-governmental organizations, in collaboration with the United Nations system, inter alia, through regional and international cooperation, including women's organizations and community groups, in addressing all forms of violence against women and girls, including for programmes to combat race and ethnic-based violence against women and girls;

(d) Encourage and support public campaigns, as appropriate, to enhance public awareness of the unacceptability and social costs of violence against women, and undertake prevention activities to promote healthy and balanced relationships based on gender equality.

97. (a) Intensify cooperation between States of origin, transit and destination to prevent, suppress and punish trafficking in persons, especially women and children;

(b) Support the ongoing negotiations on a draft protocol to prevent, suppress and punish trafficking in persons, especially women and children, to supplement the draft United Nations Convention against Transnational Organized Crime;

(c) As appropriate, pursue and support national, regional and international strategies to reduce the risk to women and girls, including those who are refugees and displaced persons, as well as women migrant workers, of becoming victims of trafficking; strengthen national legislation by further defining the crime of trafficking in all its elements and by reinforcing the punishment accordingly; enact social and economic policies and programmes, as well as informational and awareness-raising initiatives, to prevent and combat trafficking in persons, especially women and children; prosecute perpetrators of trafficking; provide measures to support, assist and protect trafficked persons in their countries of origin and destination; and facilitate their return to and support their reintegration into their countries of origin.

98. (a) Improve knowledge and awareness of the remedies available for violations of women's human rights;

(b) Promote and protect the human rights of all migrant women and implement policies to address the specific needs of documented migrant women and, where necessary, tackle the existing inequalities between men and women migrants to ensure gender equality;

(c) Promote respect for the right of women and men to the freedom of thought, conscience and religion.

Recognize the central role that religion, spirituality and belief play in the lives of millions of women and men;

(d) Encourage, through the media and other means, a high awareness of the harmful effects of certain traditional or customary practices affecting the health of women, some of which increase their vulnerability to HIV/AIDS and other sexually transmitted infections, and intensify efforts to eliminate such practices;

(e) Take necessary measures to protect individuals, groups and organs of society engaged in promoting and protecting women's human rights;

(f) Encourage States parties to continue to include a gender perspective in their reports to the treaty bodies; also encourage these bodies to continue to take into account a gender perspective in the implementation of their mandates, taking into account the need to avoid unnecessary duplication and overlapping of their work; and further encourage human rights mechanisms to continue to take into account a gender perspective in their work;

(g) Support innovative programmes to empower older women to increase their contribution to and benefit from development and efforts to combat poverty.

99. (a) Promote comprehensive human rights education programmes, inter alia, in cooperation, where appropriate, with education and human rights institutions, the relevant actors of civil society, in particular non-governmental organizations and the media networks, to ensure widespread dissemination of information on human rights instruments, in particular those concerning the human rights of women and girls;

(b) Take measures through, inter alia, supporting and strengthening existing mechanisms entrusted with prosecuting perpetrators of violations of the human rights of women, to eliminate impunity;

(c) Take measures to eliminate violations of international law and the Charter of the United Nations. Many of these violations have a negative impact on the promotion and protection of the human rights of women;

(d) Address the root causes of armed conflict in a comprehensive and durable manner, as well as the differences in the impact of armed conflict on women and men, and take them into account in relevant policies and programmes in order to, inter alia, enhance the protection of civilians, particularly women and children;

(e) Ensure the release of hostages, particularly women and children, including those subsequently imprisoned, in armed conflict;

(f) Develop and support policies and programmes for the protection of children, especially girls, in hostilities, in order to prohibit their forced recruitment and use by all actors and to promote and/or strengthen mechanisms for their rehabilitation and reintegration, taking into account the specific experiences and needs of girls;

(g) Improve and strengthen the capacity of women affected by situations of armed conflict, including women refugees and displaced women, by, inter alia, involving them in the design and management of humanitarian activities so that they benefit from these activities on an equal basis with men;

(h) Invite the Office of the United Nations High Commissioner for Refugees, other relevant United Nations agencies, within their respective mandates, and other relevant humanitarian organizations as well as

Governments to continue to provide adequate support to countries hosting large numbers of refugees and those with displaced persons, in their efforts to provide protection and assistance, paying particular attention to the needs of refugees and other displaced women and children;

(*i*) Seek to ensure the full and equal participation of women in the promotion of peace, in particular through the full implementation of the Declaration and Programme of Action on a Culture of Peace;

(*j*) Provide support to and empower women who play an important role within their families as stabilizing factors in conflict and post-conflict situations;

(*k*) Strengthen efforts towards general and complete disarmament under strict and effective international control, based on the priorities established by the United Nations in the field of disarmament, so that released resources could be used for, inter alia, social and economic programmes which benefit women and girls;

(*l*) Explore new ways of generating new public and private financial resources, inter alia, through the appropriate reduction of excessive military expenditures and the arms trade and investment for arms production and acquisition, including global military expenditures, taking into consideration national security requirements, so as to permit the possible allocation of additional funds for social and economic development, inter alia, for the advancement of women;

(*m*) Take measures to ensure the protection of refugees, especially women and girls, and their access to and the provision of gender-sensitive appropriate basic social services, including education and health.

100. (*a*) Cooperate and work with private sector partners and media networks at the national and international levels to promote equal access for women and men as producers and consumers, particularly in the area of information and communications technologies, including through encouraging the media and the information industry consistent with freedom of expression to adopt, or develop further codes of conduct, professional guidelines and other self-regulatory guidelines to remove gender stereotypes and promote balanced portrayals of women and men;

(*b*) Develop programmes that support women's ability to create, access and promote networking, in particular through the use of new information and communications technology, including through the establishment and support of programmes to build the capacity of women's non-governmental organizations in this regard;

(*c*) Capitalize on the new information technologies, including the Internet, to improve the global sharing of information, research, strengths, lessons learned from women's experiences, including "Herstories" related to achieving gender equality, development and peace, and study other roles that these technologies can play towards that goal.

101. (*a*) Take effective measures to address the challenges of globalization, including through the enhanced and effective participation of developing countries in the international economic policy decision-making process, in order to, inter alia, guarantee the equal participation of women, in particular those from developing countries, in the process of macroeconomic decision-making;

(*b*) Take measures, with the full and effective participation of women, to ensure new approaches to international development cooperation, based on stability, growth and equity, with the enhanced and effective participation and the integration of developing countries in the globalizing world economy, geared towards poverty eradication and the reduction of gender-based inequality within the overall framework of achieving people-centred sustainable development;

(*c*) Design and strengthen poverty eradication strategies, with the full and effective participation of women, that reduce the feminization of poverty and enhance the capacity of women and empower them to meet the negative social and economic impacts of globalization;

(*d*) Intensify efforts to implement poverty eradication programmes and evaluate, with the participation of women, the extent to which these programmes have an impact on the empowerment of women living in poverty, in terms of access to quality training and education as well as physical and mental health care, employment, basic social services, inheritance and access to and control over land, housing, income, microcredit and other financial instruments and services, and introduce improvements to such programmes in the light of the above assessment;

(*e*) Recognizing the mutually reinforcing links between gender equality and poverty eradication, elaborate and implement, where appropriate, in consultation with civil society, comprehensive gender-sensitive poverty eradication strategies addressing social, structural and macroeconomic issues;

(*f*) Encourage the establishment, in partnership with private financial institutions, where appropriate, of "lending windows" and other accessible financial services with simplified procedures that are specifically designed to meet the savings, credit and insurance needs of all women;

(*g*) Undertake comprehensive actions to provide and support quality skills training for women and girls at all levels, on the basis of strategies developed with their full and effective participation, to achieve agreed targets to eradicate poverty, in particular the feminization of poverty, through national, regional and international efforts. National efforts need to be complemented by intensified regional and international cooperation in order to tackle the risks, overcome the challenges and ensure that opportunities created by globalization benefit women, particularly in developing countries;

(*h*) Establish, with the full and effective participation of women and in consultation with civil society, particularly non-governmental organizations, in a timely manner, social development funds, where appropriate, to alleviate the negative effects on women associated with structural adjustment programmes and trade liberalization and the disproportionate burden borne by women living in poverty;

(*i*) Identify and implement development-oriented and durable solutions which integrate a gender perspective to external debt and debt-servicing problems of developing countries, including least developed countries, inter alia, through debt relief, including the option of official development assistance debt cancellation, in order to help them to finance programmes and projects targeted at development, including the advancement of women;

(*j*) Support the Cologne initiative for the reduction of debt, particularly the speedy implementation of the enhanced Heavily Indebted Poor Countries Debt Initiative; ensure the provision of adequate funds for its implementation and implement the provision that funds saved should be used to support anti-poverty programmes that address gender dimensions;

(*k*) Promote and accelerate the implementation of the 20/20 initiative, which integrates a gender perspective to fully benefit all, particularly women and girls;

(*l*) Call for continued international cooperation, including the reaffirmation to strive to fulfil the yet to be attained internationally agreed target of 0.7 per cent of the gross national product of developed countries for overall official development assistance as soon as possible, thereby increasing the flow of resources for gender equality, development and peace;

(*m*) Facilitate the transfer to developing countries and countries with economies in transition of appropriate technology, particularly new and modern technology, and encourage efforts by the international community to eliminate restrictions on such transfers, as an effective means of complementing national efforts for further acceleration in achieving the goals of gender equality, development and peace;

(*n*) Recommend that the Preparatory Committee for the Millennium Assembly make an effort, within the context of gender mainstreaming in the United Nations system, to integrate a gender perspective in all activities and documents related to the Millennium Assembly and Summit, including in the consideration of poverty eradication;

(*o*) Create an enabling environment and design and implement policies that promote and protect the enjoyment of all human rights—civil, cultural, economic, political and social rights, including the right to development—and fundamental freedoms, as part of the efforts to achieve gender equality, development and peace.

102. (*a*) Create and strengthen an enabling environment, in accordance with national laws, to support the capacity of women's non-governmental organizations to mobilize resources to ensure the sustainability of their development activities;

(*b*) Encourage the establishment and strengthening of multi-stakeholder partnerships/cooperation at all levels among international and intergovernmental organizations, with relevant actors of civil society, including non-governmental organizations, the private sector and trade unions, and women's organizations and other non-governmental organizations, communications and media systems in support of the goals of the Fourth World Conference on Women;

(*c*) Encourage partnerships and cooperation among Governments, international organizations, in particular international financial institutions, and multilateral organizations, private sector institutions and civil society, including non-governmental organizations, especially women's and community-based organizations, to support poverty eradication initiatives focused on women and girls;

(*d*) Recognize the crucial role of and support women and women's non-governmental organizations and community-based organizations in the implemen-

tation of Agenda 21, by integrating a gender perspective in the formulation, design and implementation of sustainable environmental and resource management mechanisms, programmes and infrastructure.

103. (*a*) Promote programmes for healthy active ageing that stress the independence, equality, participation and security of older women and undertake gender-specific research and programmes to address their needs;

(*b*) As a matter of priority, especially in those countries most affected, and in partnership with nongovernmental organizations, wherever possible, intensify education, services and community-based mobilization strategies to protect women of all ages from HIV and other sexually transmitted infections, including through the development of safe, affordable, effective and easily accessible female-controlled methods, including such methods as microbicides and female condoms that protect against sexually transmitted infections and HIV/AIDS; voluntary and confidential HIV testing and counselling; the promotion of responsible sexual behaviour, including abstinence and condom use; and the development of vaccines, simple low-cost diagnosis and single dose treatments for sexually transmitted infections;

(*c*) Provide access to adequate and affordable treatment, monitoring and care for all people, especially women and girls, infected with sexually transmitted diseases or living with life-threatening diseases, including HIV/AIDS and associated opportunistic infections, such as tuberculosis. Provide other services, including adequate housing and social protection, including during pregnancy and breastfeeding; assist boys and girls orphaned as a result of the HIV/AIDS pandemic; and provide gender-sensitive support systems for women and other family members who are involved in caring for persons affected by serious health conditions, including HIV/AIDS;

(*d*) Take effective and expeditious measures to mobilize international and national public opinion concerning the effects of different dimensions of the world drug problem on women and girls and ensure that appropriate resources are provided to this end.

104. Encourage partnerships between Governments and non-governmental organizations in the implementation of commitments made at the Fourth World Conference on Women and at other United Nations world conferences and summits in order to promote gender equality, development and peace in the twenty-first century.

Implementation of Beijing Declaration and Platform for Action

Reports of Secretary-General. During 2000, the Secretary-General reported to each of the three intergovernmental bodies responsible for overseeing follow-up to the Fourth World Conference and implementation of the Beijing Declaration and Platform for Action—the Commission on the Status of Women, the Economic and Social Council and the General Assembly. Each of the annual reports provided information on progress made since the previous year that was most pertinent to the respective intergovernmental body, in order to facilitate its decision-making process.

The Commission on the Status of Women (New York, 28 February-2 March) had before it a report of the Secretary-General on follow-up to and implementation of the Beijing Declaration and Platform for Action [E/CN.6/2000/2], which emphasized efforts undertaken by the Secretariat in support of mainstreaming a gender perspective and follow-up activities, including those undertaken by NGOs, since his previous report [YUN 1999, p. 1078]. In addition, the report covered women, the girl child and HIV/AIDS, as well as the situation of Palestinian women and the release of women and children taken hostage in armed conflicts and imprisoned (see below). An addendum [E/CN.6/2000/2/Add.1] contained a joint work plan for the Office of the United Nations High Commissioner for Human Rights (OHCHR) and the UN Division for the Advancement of Women (DAW).

The Secretary-General's June report to the Economic and Social Council [E/2000/77] focused on facilitating the Council's coordination function, particularly with regard to developments related to implementation of the Beijing Declaration and Platform for Action in intergovernmental forums reporting to the Council, in the regional commissions and in the Inter-Agency Committee on Women and Gender Equality. By **decision 2000/289** of 28 July, the Council took note of the report.

On 11 August [A/55/293], the Secretary-General provided the General Assembly with updated information on implementation activities undertaken by intergovernmental bodies, organizations of the UN system and NGOs. He pointed out that the main priority of the UN system in that connection was the mainstreaming of a gender perspective into programmes and policies, and there had been increased cooperation within the system and with other international organizations and NGOs regarding gender programmes.

In a 30 August report [A/55/341], the Secretary-General, in response to Assembly resolution 54/141 [YUN 1999, p. 1078], provided an overview of the provisions and recommendations for action contained in the political declaration and outcome document adopted at the twenty-third special session. He focused on areas where the Beijing Platform for Action had been strengthened and reinforced; implementation measures for Governments, the UN system, NGOs and others; and recommendations that had immediate implications for action at the international level, including those requiring consideration by the Assembly at its fifty-fifth session.

Inter-agency action. The Inter-Agency Committee on Women and Gender Equality of the Administrative Committee on Coordination (ACC), at its fifth session (New York, 23-25 February) [ACC/2000/3], urged ACC to select, on a regular basis, gender-specific topics for consideration and to continue to highlight gender equality issues in its discussions. The Committee decided to expand its good practices initiative (in implementing the Beijing Platform for Action and gender mainstreaming), in particular to conduct a content analysis and to create an analytic framework to provide summaries of the work displayed on the WomenWatch web site, with the United Nations Development Fund for Women (UNIFEM) and the United Nations Development Programme (UNDP) as task managers. The Committee noted that the gender focal point study prepared by the United Nations Population Fund (UNFPA) had revealed discrepancies between entities' stated gender equality policies and goals and the institutional framework, technical expertise, support and human and financial resources allocated for their achievement. The Committee emphasized that the designation of gender focal points throughout the UN system had resulted in increased attention to gender equality issues and improved gender mainstreaming, despite some problems concerning seniority, resources and the multiple tasks assigned to the focal points.

Stressing that the WomenWatch web site was extremely valuable, the Committee welcomed its continuation beyond the General Assembly's special session, possibly with the inclusion of the database on gender training materials. The Committee also discussed gender mainstreaming in programme budgets; tools and indicators for gender impact analysis, monitoring and evaluation; mainstreaming a gender perspective in common country assessments (CCAs) and the United Nations Development Assistance Framework (UNDAF); and preparation of the system-wide medium-term plan for the advancement of women, 2002-2005, among other issues.

GENERAL ASSEMBLY ACTION

On 4 December [meeting 81], the General Assembly, on the recommendation of the Third (Social, Humanitarian and Cultural) Committee [A/55/596], adopted **resolution 55/71** without vote [agenda item 108].

Follow-up to the Fourth World Conference on Women and full implementation of the Beijing Declaration and Platform for Action and the outcome of the twenty-third special session of the General Assembly

The General Assembly,

Recalling its resolutions 50/203 of 22 December 1995, 51/69 of 12 December 1996, 52/100 of 12 December 1997, 53/120 of 9 December 1998 and 54/141 of 17 December 1999,

Welcoming the outcome of the twenty-third special session of the General Assembly, entitled "Women 2000: gender equality, development and peace for the twenty-first century", namely the "Political declaration" and "Further actions and initiatives to implement the Beijing Declaration and Platform for Action",

Stressing the importance of the outcome of the twenty-third special session, which has assessed the implementation of the Beijing Declaration and Platform for Action, identified obstacles and challenges thereto and proposed actions and initiatives to overcome them and achieve full and accelerated implementation,

Deeply convinced that the Beijing Declaration and Platform for Action and the outcome of the twenty-third special session are important contributions to the advancement of women worldwide in the achievement of gender equality and must be translated into effective action by all States, the United Nations system and other organizations concerned, as well as by non-governmental organizations,

Stressing the importance of strong, sustained political will and commitment at the national, regional and international levels in order to achieve full and accelerated implementation of the Beijing Declaration and Platform for Action and the outcome of the twenty-third special session,

Recognizing that the responsibility for the implementation of the Beijing Declaration and Platform for Action and the outcome of the twenty-third special session·rests primarily at the national level and that strengthened efforts are necessary in this respect, and reiterating that enhanced international cooperation is essential for the effective implementation of the Beijing Declaration and Platform for Action and the outcome of the twenty-third special session,

1. *Reaffirms* the commitments contained in the "Political declaration" and "Further actions and initiatives to implement the Beijing Declaration and Platform for Action", adopted by the General Assembly at its twenty-third special session, entitled "Women 2000: gender equality, development and peace for the twenty-first century";

2. *Takes note with appreciation* of the reports of the Secretary-General on the follow-up to the Fourth World Conference on Women and full implementation of the Beijing Declaration and Platform for Action and on the implementation of the outcome of the Fourth World Conference on Women and of the special session of the General Assembly entitled "Women 2000: gender equality, development and peace for the twenty-first century";

3. *Calls upon* Governments, the relevant entities of the United Nations system within their respective mandates and all other relevant actors of civil society, including non-governmental organizations, to take effective action to achieve full and effective implementation of the Beijing Declaration and Platform for Action and the outcome of the twenty-third special session, as elaborated in the above-mentioned documents;

4. *Calls upon* Governments, in collaboration with relevant actors of civil society, including non-governmental organizations, to facilitate the translation and dissemination of the outcome of the twenty-

third special session, as broadly and as accessibly as possible;

5. *Strongly encourages* Governments to continue to support the role and contribution of civil society, in particular non-governmental organizations and women's organizations, in the implementation of the Beijing Declaration and Platform for Action and the outcome of the twenty-third special session;

6. *Reaffirms further* its decision that the General Assembly, the Economic and Social Council and the Commission on the Status of Women, in accordance with their respective mandates and with General Assembly resolution 48/162 of 20 December 1993 and other relevant resolutions, constitute a three-tiered intergovernmental mechanism that plays the primary role in the overall policy-making and follow-up and in coordinating the implementation and monitoring of the Beijing Platform for Action and the outcome of the twenty-third special session;

7. *Invites* the Economic and Social Council to continue to promote a coordinated and integrated follow-up to and implementation of the outcomes of major United Nations conferences and summits and their reviews, and requests the Council to intensify further its efforts to ensure that gender mainstreaming is an integral part of all its activities concerning integrated and coordinated follow-up to United Nations conferences, building upon agreed conclusions 1997/2 adopted by the Council on 18 July 1997;

8. *Also invites* the Council to continue to further policy coordination and inter-agency cooperation towards the achievement of the objectives of the Beijing Platform for Action and the outcome of the twenty-third special session, including by considering the dedication of specific segments of the Council to the advancement of women and implementation of the above-mentioned documents and by mainstreaming a gender perspective in all its work;

9. *Encourages* the Council to request the regional commissions, within their respective mandates and resources, to build up a database, to be updated regularly, in which all programmes and projects carried out in their respective regions by agencies or organizations of the United Nations system are listed, and to facilitate their dissemination, as well as the evaluation of their impact on the empowerment of women through the implementation of the Beijing Platform for Action;

10. *Reaffirms* that the Commission on the Status of Women has a central role in assisting the Council in monitoring, assessing progress made in and accelerating, within the United Nations system, the implementation of the Beijing Platform for Action and the outcome of the twenty-third special session, and in advising the Council thereon;

11. *Notes* that, at its forty-fifth session, in 2001, the Commission will develop a new multi-year programme of work, and in this respect requests the Secretary-General to report to the Commission with recommendations for the effective implementation of the Beijing Platform for Action and the outcome of the twenty-third special session, including by enhancing the effectiveness of its work and its catalytic role in mainstreaming a gender perspective in United Nations activities;

12. *Recognizes* the importance attached to the regional and subregional monitoring of the global and regional platforms for action and of the implementa-

tion of the outcome of the twenty-third special session by regional commissions and other regional or sub-regional structures, within their mandates, in consultation with Governments, and calls for the promotion of further cooperation in that respect among Governments and, where appropriate, national machineries of the same region;

13. *Reaffirms* that, in order to implement the Beijing Platform for Action and the outcome of the twenty-third special session, adequate mobilization of resources at the national and international levels, as well as new and additional resources for the developing countries, in particular those in Africa and the least developed countries, from all available funding mechanisms, including multilateral, bilateral and private sources, will also be required;

14. *Recognizes* that the implementation of the Beijing Platform for Action and the outcome of the twenty-third special session in the countries with economies in transition requires continued national efforts and international cooperation and assistance;

15. *Reaffirms* that in order to implement the Beijing Platform for Action and the outcome of the twenty-third special session a reformulation of policies and reallocation of resources may be needed, but that some policy changes may not necessarily have financial implications;

16. *Also reaffirms* that in order to ensure the effective implementation of the strategic objectives of the Beijing Platform for Action and the outcome of the twenty-third special session, the United Nations system should promote an active and visible policy of mainstreaming a gender perspective, including through the work of the Special Adviser on Gender Issues and Advancement of Women and through the maintenance of gender units and focal points;

17. *Further reaffirms* that United Nations bodies that focus on gender issues, such as the United Nations Population Fund, the United Nations Development Fund for Women and the International Research and Training Institute for the Advancement of Women, have an important role to play in the implementation of the objectives of the Beijing Declaration and Platform for Action and the outcome of the twenty-third special session;

18. *Requests* the Secretary-General to submit a report to the General Assembly on the full range of tasks of the Division for the Advancement of Women of the Department of Economic and Social Affairs of the Secretariat, including those that might arise from the implementation of the outcome of the twenty-third special session and from the entry into force of the Optional Protocol to the Convention on the Elimination of All Forms of Discrimination against Women, with a view to ensuring that the Division can effectively fulfil its tasks;

19. *Also requests* the Secretary-General to ensure that all United Nations personnel and officials at Headquarters and in the field, especially in field operations, receive training so that they mainstream a gender perspective in their work, including gender impact analysis, and to ensure appropriate follow-up to such training;

20. *Requests* all bodies that deal with programme and budgetary matters, including the Committee for Programme and Coordination, to ensure that all programmes, medium-term plans and programme budgets visibly mainstream a gender perspective;

21. *Invites* States parties to the Convention on the Elimination of All Forms of Discrimination against Women to include information on measures taken to implement the outcome of the twenty-third special session, as well as the Beijing Platform for Action, in their reports to the Committee on the Elimination of Discrimination against Women under article 18 of the Convention;

22. *Requests* the Secretary-General to disseminate the outcome of the twenty-third special session as widely as possible in all official languages of the United Nations;

23. *Also requests* the Secretary-General to report annually to the General Assembly, the Economic and Social Council and the Commission on the Status of Women on follow-up to and progress in the implementation of the Beijing Declaration and Platform for Action and the outcome of the twenty-third special session;

24. *Decides* to include in the provisional agenda of its fifty-sixth session an item entitled "Implementation of the outcome of the Fourth World Conference on Women and of the twenty-third special session of the General Assembly, entitled 'Women 2000: gender equality, development and peace for the twenty-first century'".

Critical areas of concern

Violence against women

In February, the Secretary-General transmitted to the Commission on the Status of Women a UNIFEM report on its activities during the previous year to eliminate violence against women [E/CN.6/2000/6]. The Fund's inter-agency regional campaigns had raised public awareness at the community, national and regional levels on the issue of violence against women as a violation of human rights. New pilot initiatives addressing gender-based violence included establishment of zero-tolerance zones, community pacts to end violence, the appointment of regional rapporteurs on the issue, new forms of cooperation between police and women's crisis centres, municipality contests to showcase best strategies to end violence against women and innovative media initiatives.

Since beginning operations in 1997 [YUN 1997, p. 1193], the Trust Fund in Support of Actions to Eliminate Violence against Women had received over $4.3 million in contributions and funded 88 projects around the world, including 16 new projects selected for funding in 1999.

A UNIFEM global videoconference, broadcast to audiences in 20 countries on Women's Day (8 March) in 1999, highlighted successful strategies for addressing various forms of violence against women in different regions of the world, focusing in particular on domestic violence, including dowry-related violence and rape within marriage; threats to women's bodily integrity, such as female genital mutilation; violence against women in conflict situations; and economic violence, including trafficking in women and girls. More than 2,300 individuals and groups had taken part in a virtual working group, launched on the Internet during preparations for the videoconference to identify successful strategies around the world for combating violence against women and girls.

(For details of action on violence against women taken by the Commission on Human Rights, see p. 709.)

GENERAL ASSEMBLY ACTION

On 4 December [meeting 81], the General Assembly, on the recommendation of the Third Committee [A/55/595 & Corr.1,2], adopted **resolution 55/68** without vote [agenda item 107].

Elimination of all forms of violence against women, including crimes identified in the outcome document of the twenty-third special session of the General Assembly, entitled "Women 2000: gender equality, development and peace for the twenty-first century"

The General Assembly,

Recalling the purposes and principles of the Charter of the United Nations, which, inter alia, calls for international cooperation in promoting and encouraging respect for human rights and fundamental freedoms for all without distinction as to race, sex, language or religion,

Recalling also the Universal Declaration of Human Rights, the Declaration on the Elimination of Discrimination against Women, the Declaration on the Elimination of Violence against Women, the United Nations Declaration on the Elimination of All Forms of Racial Discrimination, the Beijing Declaration and Platform for Action adopted by the Fourth World Conference on Women, the Vienna Declaration and Programme of Action, adopted on 25 June 1993 by the World Conference on Human Rights, and the United Nations Millennium Declaration,

Reaffirming the obligations of all States to promote and protect human rights and fundamental freedoms, as enunciated in the Charter, and reaffirming also the obligations of States parties under international human rights instruments, in particular the International Covenant on Civil and Political Rights, the International Covenant on Economic, Social and Cultural Rights, the Convention on the Elimination of All Forms of Discrimination against Women, the International Convention on the Elimination of All Forms of Racial Discrimination, the Convention on the Rights of the Child, the Convention against Torture and Other Cruel, Inhuman or Degrading Treatment or Punishment and the International Convention on the Protection of the Rights of All Migrant Workers and Members of Their Families,

Reaffirming also the outcome document of the twenty-third special session of the General Assembly, entitled "Women 2000: gender equality, development and peace for the twenty-first century",

Reaffirming further the call for the elimination of violence against women and girls, especially all forms of commercial sexual exploitation as well as economic exploitation, including trafficking in women and children, female infanticide, crimes committed in the name of honour, crimes committed in the name of passion, racially motivated crimes, the abduction and sale of children, dowry-related violence and deaths, acid attacks and harmful traditional or customary practices, such as female genital mutilation and early and forced marriages,

Stressing the importance of the empowerment of women as a tool to eliminate all forms of violence against women, including crimes identified in the outcome document of the twenty-third special session,

1. *Expresses deep concern* at the persistence of various forms of violence and crimes against women in all parts of the world, especially all forms of commercial sexual exploitation as well as economic exploitation, including trafficking in women and children, female infanticide, crimes committed in the name of honour, crimes committed in the name of passion, racially motivated crimes, the abduction and sale of children, dowry-related violence and deaths, acid attacks and harmful traditional or customary practices, such as female genital mutilation and early and forced marriages;

2. *Stresses* that all forms of violence against women, including crimes identified in the outcome document of the twenty-third special session of the General Assembly, are obstacles to the advancement and empowerment of women, and reaffirms that violence against women both violates and impairs or nullifies the enjoyment by women of their human rights and fundamental freedoms;

3. *Also stresses* the need to treat all forms of violence against women and girls of all ages as a criminal offence punishable by law, including violence based on all forms of discrimination;

4. *Reaffirms* that there is increased awareness of and commitment to preventing and combating violence against women, including crimes identified in the outcome document of the twenty-third special session, and in this context welcomes various legal, administrative and other measures taken by Governments for their prevention and elimination, and calls for high priority to be attached to the further strengthening of such measures;

5. *Urges* Member States to strengthen awareness and preventive measures for the elimination of all forms of violence against women, whether occurring in public or private life, by encouraging and supporting public campaigns to enhance awareness about the unacceptability and the social costs of violence against women, inter alia, through educational and media campaigns in cooperation with educators, community leaders and the electronic and print media;

6. *Expresses its appreciation* of the work being done by non-governmental organizations, including women's organizations, community-based organizations and individuals, in raising awareness about the economic, social and psychological costs of all forms of violence against women, including crimes identified in the outcome document of the twenty-third special session, and in this regard encourages Governments to continue their support to the work of the non-governmental organizations in addressing this issue;

7. *Calls upon* States to fulfil their obligations under the relevant human rights instruments and implement the Beijing Platform for Action as well as the outcome document of the twenty-third special session;

8. *Encourages* States parties to include in their reports to the Committee on the Elimination of Discrimination against Women and other relevant treaty bodies, wherever possible, sex-disaggregated data and information on measures taken or initiated to eliminate all forms of violence against women, including crimes identified in the outcome document of the twenty-third special session;

9. *Urges* relevant entities of the United Nations system, within their mandates, to assist countries, upon their request, in their efforts aimed at preventing and eliminating all forms of violence against women, including crimes identified in the outcome document of the twenty-third special session, and in this regard expresses its appreciation of the work being done by the United Nations Population Fund, the United Nations Children's Fund and the United Nations Development Fund for Women and other relevant funds and programmes aimed at preventing and eliminating violence against women and girls;

10. *Invites* the Special Rapporteur of the Commission on Human Rights on violence against women, its causes and consequences, to further devote equal attention to all forms of violence against women, including crimes identified in the outcome document of the twenty-third special session, in her work and her reports, within her mandate, to the Commission on Human Rights and the General Assembly;

11. *Requests* the Secretary-General to submit a comprehensive report on this matter to the General Assembly at its fifty-seventh session.

Honour crimes

GENERAL ASSEMBLY ACTION

On 4 December [meeting 81], the General Assembly, on the recommendation of the Third Committee [A/55/595 & Corr.1,2], adopted **resolution 55/66** by a recorded vote of 146 to 1, with 26 abstentions [agenda item 107].

Working towards the elimination of crimes against women committed in the name of honour

The General Assembly,

Reaffirming the obligation of all States to promote and protect human rights and fundamental freedoms, as stated in the Charter of the United Nations, and reaffirming also their obligations under human rights instruments, in particular the Universal Declaration of Human Rights, the International Covenant on Economic, Social and Cultural Rights, the International Covenant on Civil and Political Rights, the Convention on the Elimination of All Forms of Discrimination against Women and the Convention on the Rights of the Child,

Bearing in mind the Declaration on the Elimination of Violence against Women, as well as the Beijing Declaration and Platform for Action adopted at the Fourth World Conference on Women, and recalling the outcome document of the twenty-third special session of the General Assembly, entitled "Women 2000: gender

equality, development and peace for the twenty-first century",

Bearing in mind also that crimes against women committed in the name of honour are a human rights issue and that States have an obligation to exercise due diligence to prevent, investigate and punish the perpetrators of such crimes and to provide protection to the victims, and that the failure to do so constitutes a human rights violation,

Aware that inadequate understanding of the root causes of all violence against women, including crimes committed in the name of honour, and inadequate data on such violence hinder informed policy analysis, at both the domestic and the international levels, and efforts to eliminate such violence,

Noting general recommendation 19 concerning violence against women adopted by the Committee on the Elimination of Discrimination against Women,

Noting also relevant paragraphs in recent reports of the Special Rapporteur of the Commission on Human Rights on violence against women, its causes and consequences, the Special Rapporteur of the Commission on Human Rights on extrajudicial, summary or arbitrary executions and the Special Rapporteur of the Commission on Human Rights on the independence of judges and lawyers, and of the Special Rapporteur of the Subcommission on the Promotion and Protection of Human Rights on traditional practices affecting the health of women and the girl child,

Bearing in mind relevant paragraphs in Commission on Human Rights resolutions 2000/31 and 2000/45, of 20 April 2000, as well as in resolution 2000/10 of 17 August 2000 of the Subcommission on the Promotion and Protection of Human Rights,

Emphasizing that the elimination of crimes against women committed in the name of honour requires greater efforts and commitment from Governments and the international community, inter alia, through international cooperation efforts, and civil society, including non-governmental and community organizations, and that fundamental changes in societal attitude are required, and underlining the importance of the empowerment of women as a tool,

1. *Expresses its concern* at the fact that women continue to be victims of various forms of violence, including those that are identified in the outcome document of the twenty-third special session of the General Assembly, entitled "Women 2000: gender equality, development and peace for the twenty-first century", and at the continuing occurrence in all regions of the world of such violence, including crimes against women committed in the name of honour, which take many different forms, and also expresses its concern at the fact that some perpetrators assume that they have some justification for committing such crimes;

2. *Welcomes* the activities of States aimed at the elimination of crimes against women committed in the name of honour, including the adoption of amendments to relevant national laws relating to such crimes, the effective implementation of such laws and national campaigns, all of which have already led to a decrease in the incidence of these crimes in some countries;

3. *Also welcomes* the efforts, such as concrete projects, undertaken by United Nations bodies, programmes and organizations, including the United Nations Population Fund, the United Nations Children's

Fund and the United Nations Development Fund for Women, to address the issue of crimes against women committed in the name of honour, and encourages them to coordinate their efforts, and further welcomes the work carried out by civil society, including non-governmental organizations, such as women's organizations, grass-roots movements and individuals, in raising awareness of such crimes and their harmful effects;

4. *Calls upon* all States:

(a) To implement their relevant obligations under international human rights law and to implement specific international commitments, inter alia, under the outcome document of the twenty-third special session of the General Assembly;

(b) To intensify efforts to prevent and eliminate crimes against women committed in the name of honour, which take many different forms, by using legislative, educational, social and other measures, including the dissemination of information, and to involve, among others, public opinion leaders, educators, religious leaders, chiefs, traditional leaders and the media in awareness-raising campaigns;

(c) To encourage, support and implement measures and programmes aimed at increasing the knowledge and the understanding of the causes and consequences of crimes against women committed in the name of honour, among those responsible for enforcing the law and implementing policies, such as police personnel, judicial workers and health personnel;

(d) To establish, strengthen or facilitate, where possible, support services to respond to the needs of actual and potential victims by, inter alia, providing for them the appropriate protection, safe shelter, counselling, legal aid, rehabilitation and reintegration into society;

(e) To create, strengthen or facilitate institutional mechanisms so that victims and others can report such crimes in a safe and confidential environment, and encourages States to gather and disseminate statistical information on the occurrence of such crimes;

5. *Invites* the international community, including United Nations bodies, programmes and organizations, inter alia, through the technical assistance and advisory services programmes of the United Nations Centre for International Crime Prevention, the Office of the United Nations High Commissioner for Human Rights and the United Nations Development Fund for Women, to support the efforts of all countries, at their request, aimed at strengthening institutional capacity for preventing crimes against women committed in the name of honour and at addressing their root causes;

6. *Encourages* the relevant human rights treaty bodies to continue to address this issue, where appropriate;

7. *Requests* the Secretary-General to submit to the General Assembly at its fifty-seventh session a report on the subject of the present resolution, including on initiatives taken by States to work towards the elimination of the crimes in question.

RECORDED VOTE ON RESOLUTION 55/66:

In favour: Afghanistan, Albania, Andorra, Angola, Antigua and Barbuda, Argentina, Armenia, Australia, Austria, Azerbaijan, Bahamas, Bangladesh, Barbados, Belarus, Belgium, Belize, Benin, Bhutan, Bolivia, Bosnia and Herzegovina, Botswana, Brazil, Bulgaria, Burkina Faso, Burundi, Cambodia, Canada, Cape Verde, Chad, Chile, Colombia, Congo, Costa Rica, Côte d'Ivoire, Croatia, Cuba, Cyprus, Czech Republic, Democratic Republic of the Congo, Denmark, Dominica, Dominican Republic, Ecuador, El Salvador, Eritrea, Estonia, Ethiopia, Fiji, Finland, France, Gambia, Georgia, Germany, Ghana, Greece, Grenada, Guatemala, Guinea, Guyana, Haiti, Honduras, Hungary, Iceland, India, Indonesia, Ireland, Israel, Italy, Jamaica, Japan, Kazakhstan, Kyrgyzstan, Lao People's Democratic Republic, Latvia, Liechtenstein, Lithuania, Luxembourg, Madagascar, Malawi, Mali, Malta, Marshall Islands, Mauritius, Mexico, Micronesia, Monaco, Mongolia, Mozambique, Namibia, Nauru, Nepal, Netherlands, New Zealand, Nicaragua, Norway, Palau, Panama, Papua New Guinea, Paraguay, Peru, Philippines, Poland, Portugal, Republic of Korea, Republic of Moldova, Romania, Rwanda, Saint Kitts and Nevis, Saint Lucia, Saint Vincent and the Grenadines, Samoa, San Marino, Sao Tome and Principe, Senegal, Singapore, Slovakia, Slovenia, Solomon Islands, South Africa, Spain, Sri Lanka, Suriname, Swaziland, Sweden, Tajikistan, Thailand, The former Yugoslav Republic of Macedonia, Togo, Trinidad and Tobago, Tunisia, Turkey, Turkmenistan, Uganda, Ukraine, United Kingdom, United Republic of Tanzania, United States, Uruguay, Uzbekistan, Vanuatu, Venezuela, Viet Nam, Yemen, Yugoslavia, Zambia, Zimbabwe.

Against: Lesotho.

Abstaining: Algeria, Bahrain, Brunei Darussalam, Cameroon, China, Comoros, Djibouti, Egypt, Iran, Jordan, Kenya, Kuwait, Libyan Arab Jamahiriya, Malaysia, Maldives, Myanmar, Nigeria, Oman, Pakistan, Qatar, Russian Federation, Saudi Arabia, Sierra Leone, Sudan, Syrian Arab Republic, United Arab Emirates.

Women migrant workers

In April, the Commission on Human Rights reviewed a follow-up report of the Secretary-General on violence against women migrant workers [E/CN.4/2000/76]. Summarizing measures taken by States, UN bodies, specialized agencies and intergovernmental organizations to address the issue, the Secretary-General concluded that more information was needed in order to identify concrete strategies (see also p. 711).

Women and children in armed conflict

In a report to the Commission on the Status of Women on follow-up to and implementation of the Beijing Platform for Action [E/CN.6/2000/2], the Secretary-General summarized replies received from six Governments and six entities of the UN system in response to his request for information on the release of women and children taken hostage in armed conflicts and imprisoned.

On 2 March [E/2000/27 (res. 44/1)], the Commission condemned violent acts in contravention of international humanitarian law against civilian women and children in areas of armed conflict and called for the immediate release of those imprisoned. All parties to armed conflicts were urged to respect the norms of international humanitarian law and to provide unimpeded access to humanitarian assistance for women and children. The Commission asked the Secretary-General and relevant international organizations to facilitate the release of imprisoned women and children. The Secretary-General was also asked to submit a report to the Commission in 2001.

Women, peace and security

On 8 March—International Women's Day—the Security Council President, in a statement to the press [SC/6816], said that the Council recognized that women and girls were particularly affected by the consequences of armed conflict and that women constituted the majority of the world's refugees and internally displaced persons. Also, although women had begun to play an important role in conflict resolution, peacekeeping and peace-building, they were still underrepresented in decision-making with regard to conflict. The statement called on all concerned to refrain from human rights abuses in conflict situations and welcomed the inclusion of all forms of sexual violence as a war crime in the Rome Statute of the International Criminal Court [YUN 1998, p. 1209]. It stressed the need for protection, assistance and training to refugee and displaced women and the importance of promoting gender mainstreaming in all policies and programmes while addressing conflicts.

Namibia, in a 14 July letter [A/55/138-S/2000/693], transmitted to the Secretary-General the Windhoek Declaration and the Namibia Plan of Action on Mainstreaming a Gender Perspective in Multidimensional Peace Support Operations, adopted at a seminar organized by the Department of Peacekeeping Operations and the Office of the Special Adviser on Gender Issues and Advancement of Women (Windhoek, 29-31 May). Those documents called for enhanced participation of women in peace support operations.

SECURITY COUNCIL ACTION

The issue of women and peace and security was considered by the Security Council on 24 and 25 October [meeting 4208]. On 31 October [meeting 4213], the Council unanimously adopted **resolution 1325(2000)**. The draft [S/2000/1044] was prepared in consultations among Council members.

The Security Council,

Recalling its resolutions 1261(1999) of 25 August 1999, 1265(1999) of 17 September 1999, 1296(2000) of 19 April 2000 and 1314(2000) of 11 August 2000, as well as relevant statements of its President, and recalling also the statement of its President to the press on the occasion of the United Nations Day for Women's Rights and International Peace (International Women's Day) of 8 March 2000,

Recalling also the commitments of the Beijing Declaration and Platform for Action as well as those contained in the outcome document of the twenty-third special session of the General Assembly entitled "Women 2000: gender equality, development and peace for the twenty-first century", in particular those concerning women and armed conflict,

Bearing in mind the purposes and principles of the Charter of the United Nations and the primary responsibility of the Security Council under the Charter for the maintenance of international peace and security,

Expressing concern that civilians, particularly women and children, account for the vast majority of those adversely affected by armed conflict, including as refugees and internally displaced persons, and are targeted increasingly by combatants and armed elements, and recognizing the consequent impact this has on durable peace and reconciliation,

Reaffirming the important role of women in the prevention and resolution of conflicts and in peacebuilding, and stressing the importance of their equal participation and full involvement in all efforts for the maintenance and promotion of peace and security, and the need to increase their role in decision-making with regard to conflict prevention and resolution,

Reaffirming also the need to implement fully international humanitarian and human rights law that protects the rights of women and girls during and after conflicts,

Emphasizing the need for all parties to ensure that mine clearance and mine awareness programmes take into account the special needs of women and girls,

Recognizing the urgent need to mainstream a gender perspective into peacekeeping operations, and in this regard noting the Windhoek Declaration and the Namibia Plan of Action on Mainstreaming a Gender Perspective in Multidimensional Peace Support Operations,

Recognizing also the importance of the recommendation contained in the statement by its President to the press on 8 March 2000 for specialized training for all peacekeeping personnel on the protection, special needs and human rights of women and children in conflict situations,

Recognizing further that an understanding of the impact of armed conflict on women and girls, effective institutional arrangements to guarantee their protection and full participation in the peace process can significantly contribute to the maintenance and promotion of international peace and security,

Noting the need to consolidate data on the impact of armed conflict on women and girls,

1. *Urges* Member States to ensure increased representation of women at all decision-making levels in national, regional and international institutions and mechanisms for the prevention, management, and resolution of conflict;

2. *Encourages* the Secretary-General to implement his strategic plan of action for the improvement of the status of women in the Secretariat (1995-2000), which calls for an increase in the participation of women at decision-making levels in conflict resolution and peace processes;

3. *Urges* the Secretary-General to appoint more women as special representatives and envoys to pursue good offices on his behalf, and in this regard calls on Member States to provide candidates to the Secretary-General, for inclusion in a regularly updated centralized roster;

4. *Also urges* the Secretary-General to seek to expand the role and contribution of women in United Nations field-based operations, and especially among military observers, civilian police, human rights and humanitarian personnel;

5. *Expresses its willingness* to incorporate a gender perspective into peacekeeping operations, and urges the Secretary-General to ensure that, where appropriate, field operations include a gender component;

6. *Requests* the Secretary-General to provide to Member States training guidelines and materials on the protection, rights and the particular needs of

women, as well as on the importance of involving women in all peacekeeping and peace-building measures, invites Member States to incorporate these elements as well as HIV/AIDS awareness training into their national training programmes for military and civilian police personnel in preparation for deployment, and also requests the Secretary-General to ensure that civilian personnel of peacekeeping operations receive similar training;

7. *Urges* Member States to increase their voluntary financial, technical and logistical support for gender-sensitive training efforts, including those undertaken by relevant funds and programmes, inter alia, the United Nations Development Fund for Women and the United Nations Children's Fund, and by the Office of the United Nations High Commissioner for Refugees and other relevant bodies;

8. *Calls upon* all actors involved, when negotiating and implementing peace agreements, to adopt a gender perspective, including:

(a) The special needs of women and girls during repatriation and resettlement, and for rehabilitation, reintegration and post-conflict reconstruction;

(b) Measures that support local women's peace initiatives and indigenous processes for conflict resolution, and that involve women in all of the implementation mechanisms of the peace agreements;

(c) Measures that ensure the protection of and respect for human rights of women and girls, particularly as they relate to the constitution, the electoral system, the police and the judiciary;

9. *Calls upon* all parties to armed conflict to respect fully international law applicable to the rights and protection of women and girls, especially as civilians, in particular the obligations applicable to them under the Geneva Conventions of 1949 and the Additional Protocols thereto of 1977, the 1951 Convention and the 1967 Protocol thereto, relating to the Status of Refugees, the 1979 Convention on the Elimination of All Forms of Discrimination against Women and the Optional Protocol thereto of 6 October 1999 and the Convention on the Rights of the Child of 1989 and the two Optional Protocols thereto of 25 May 2000, and to bear in mind the relevant provisions of the Rome Statute of the International Criminal Court;

10. *Also calls upon* all parties to armed conflict to take special measures to protect women and girls from gender-based violence, particularly rape and other forms of sexual abuse, and all other forms of violence in situations of armed conflict;

11. *Emphasizes* the responsibility of all States to put an end to impunity and to prosecute those responsible for genocide, crimes against humanity and war crimes, including those relating to sexual and other violence against women and girls, and in this regard stresses the need to exclude these crimes, where feasible, from amnesty provisions;

12. *Calls upon* all parties to armed conflict to respect the civilian and humanitarian character of refugee camps and settlements, and to take into account the particular needs of women and girls, including in their design, and recalls its resolutions 1208(1998) of 19 November 1998 and 1296(2000) of 19 April 2000;

13. *Encourages* all those involved in the planning for disarmament, demobilization and reintegration to consider the different needs of female and male ex-combatants and to take into account the needs of their dependants;

14. *Reaffirms its readiness*, whenever measures are adopted under Article 41 of the Charter of the United Nations, to give consideration to their potential impact on the civilian population, bearing in mind the special needs of women and girls, in order to consider appropriate humanitarian exemptions;

15. *Expresses its willingness* to ensure that Security Council missions take into account gender considerations and the rights of women, including through consultation with local and international women's groups;

16. *Invites* the Secretary-General to carry out a study on the impact of armed conflict on women and girls, the role of women in peace-building and the gender dimensions of peace processes and conflict resolution, and also invites him to submit a report to the Council on the results of this study and to make this available to all Member States;

17. *Requests* the Secretary-General, where appropriate, to include in his reporting to the Council progress on gender mainstreaming throughout peacekeeping missions and all other aspects relating to women and girls;

18. *Decides* to remain actively seized of the matter.

The girl child

GENERAL ASSEMBLY ACTION

On 4 December [meeting 81], the General Assembly, on the recommendation of the Third Committee [A/55/598], adopted **resolution 55/78** without vote [agenda item 110].

The girl child

The General Assembly,

Recalling its resolution 54/148 of 17 December 1999 and all previous relevant resolutions, including the agreed conclusions of the Commission on the Status of Women, in particular those relevant to the girl child,

Recalling also all relevant United Nations conferences and the Declaration and Agenda for Action adopted by the World Congress against Commercial Sexual Exploitation of Children, held at Stockholm from 27 to 31 August 1996, as well as the outcome documents of the recent five-year reviews of the implementation of the Programme of Action of the International Conference on Population and Development and the Programme of Action of the World Summit for Social Development,

Deeply concerned about discrimination against the girl child and the violation of the rights of the girl child, which often result in less access for girls to education, nutrition, physical and mental health care and in girls enjoying fewer of the rights, opportunities and benefits of childhood and adolescence than boys and often being subjected to various forms of cultural, social, sexual and economic exploitation and to violence and harmful practices, such as female infanticide, incest, early marriage, prenatal sex selection and female genital mutilation,

Recognizing the need to achieve gender equality so as to ensure a just and equitable world for girls,

Deeply concerned that, in situations of poverty, war and armed conflict, girl children are among the victims most affected and that thus their potential for full development is limited,

Concerned that the girl child has furthermore become a victim of sexually transmitted diseases and the human immunodeficiency virus, which affects the quality of her life and leaves her open to further discrimination,

Reaffirming the equal rights of women and men as enshrined, inter alia, in the Preamble to the Charter of the United Nations, the Convention on the Elimination of All Forms of Discrimination against Women and the Convention on the Rights of the Child,

Reaffirming also the political declaration and further actions and initiatives to implement the Beijing Declaration and Platform for Action, adopted by the General Assembly at its twenty-third special session, entitled "Women 2000: gender equality, development and peace for the twenty-first century",

Reaffirming further the Dakar Framework for Action adopted at the World Education Forum,

1. *Stresses* the need for full and urgent implementation of the rights of the girl child as guaranteed to her under all human rights instruments, including the Convention on the Rights of the Child and the Convention on the Elimination of All Forms of Discrimination against Women, as well as the need for universal ratification of those instruments;

2. *Urges* States to consider signing and ratifying the Optional Protocol to the Convention on the Elimination of All Forms of Discrimination against Women;

3. *Welcomes* the adoption of the Optional Protocols to the Convention on the Rights of the Child on the involvement of children in armed conflict and on the sale of children, child prostitution and child pornography, and invites States to consider signing and ratifying the Optional Protocols as a matter of priority with a view to their entry into force as soon as possible;

4. *Also welcomes* the United Nations Girls' Education Initiative launched by the Secretary-General at the World Education Forum;

5. *Urges* all Governments and the United Nations system to strengthen efforts bilaterally and with international organizations and private sector donors in order to achieve the goals of the World Education Forum, in particular that of eliminating gender disparities in primary and secondary education by 2005, and for the implementation of the United Nations Girls' Education Initiative as a means of reaching this goal, and reaffirms the commitment contained in the United Nations Millennium Declaration;

6. *Calls upon* all States to take measures to address the obstacles that continue to affect the achievement of the goals set forth in the Beijing Platform for Action, as contained in paragraph 33 of the further actions and initiatives to implement the Beijing Declaration and Platform for Action, where appropriate, including the strengthening of national mechanisms to implement policies and programmes for the girl child and, in some cases, to enhance coordination among responsible institutions for the realization of the human rights of girls, as indicated in the further actions and initiatives;

7. *Urges* all States to take all necessary measures and to institute legal reforms to ensure the full and equal enjoyment by the girl child of all human rights and fundamental freedoms, to take effective action against violations of those rights and freedoms and to base pro-grammes and policies for the girl child on the rights of the child;

8. *Urges* States to enact and enforce strictly laws to ensure that marriage is entered into only with the free and full consent of the intending spouses, to enact and enforce strictly laws concerning the minimum legal age of consent and the minimum age for marriage and to raise the minimum age for marriage where necessary;

9. *Urges* all States to fulfil their obligations under the Convention on the Rights of the Child and the Convention on the Elimination of All Forms of Discrimination against Women as well as the commitment to implement the Beijing Platform for Action;

10. *Also urges* all States to enact and enforce legislation to protect girls from all forms of violence, including female infanticide and prenatal sex selection, female genital mutilation, rape, domestic violence, incest, sexual abuse, sexual exploitation, child prostitution and child pornography, and to develop age-appropriate safe and confidential programmes and medical, social and psychological support services to assist girls who are subjected to violence;

11. *Calls upon* all States and international and non-governmental organizations, individually and collectively, to implement further the Beijing Platform for Action, in particular the strategic objectives relating to the girl child and including the further actions and initiatives to implement the Beijing Declaration and Platform for Action;

12. *Urges* States to take special measures for the protection of war-affected girls and in particular to protect them from sexually transmitted diseases, such as human immunodeficiency virus/acquired immunodeficiency syndrome, and gender-based violence, including rape and sexual abuse, torture, sexual exploitation, abduction and forced labour, paying special attention to refugee and displaced girls, and to take into account the special needs of the war-affected girl child in the delivery of humanitarian assistance and disarmament, demobilization and reintegration processes;

13. *Urges* all States and the international community to respect, protect and promote the rights of the child, taking into account the particular vulnerabilities of the girl child in pre-conflict, conflict and post-conflict situations, and calls for special initiatives designed to address all of the rights and needs of war-affected girls;

14. *Welcomes* the holding of the International Conference on War-Affected Children at Winnipeg, Canada, from 10 to 17 September 2000, and takes note with appreciation of the Winnipeg Agenda for War-Affected Children;

15. *Urges* States to formulate comprehensive, multi-disciplinary and coordinated national plans, programmes or strategies to eliminate all forms of violence against women and girls, which should be widely disseminated and should provide targets and time-tables for implementation, as well as effective domestic enforcement procedures through the establishment of monitoring mechanisms involving all parties concerned, including consultations with women's organizations, giving attention to the recommendations relating to the girl child of the Special Rapporteur of the Commission on Human Rights on violence against women, its causes and consequences;

16. *Calls upon* Governments, civil society, including the media, and non-governmental organizations to promote human rights education and the full respect for and enjoyment of the human rights of the girl child, inter alia, through the translation, production and dissemination of age-appropriate information material on those rights to all sectors of society, in particular to children;

17. *Requests* the Secretary-General, as Chairman of the Administrative Committee on Coordination, to ensure that all organizations and bodies of the United Nations system, individually and collectively, in particular the United Nations Children's Fund, the United Nations Educational, Scientific and Cultural Organization, the World Food Programme, the United Nations Population Fund, the United Nations Development Fund for Women, the World Health Organization, the United Nations Development Programme and the Office of the United Nations High Commissioner for Refugees, take into account the rights and the particular needs of the girl child in the country programme of cooperation in accordance with the national priorities, including through the United Nations Development Assistance Framework;

18. *Requests* all human rights treaty bodies, special procedures and other human rights mechanisms of the Commission on Human Rights and its Subcommission on the Promotion and Protection of Human Rights to adopt regularly and systematically a gender perspective in the implementation of their mandates and to include in their reports information on the qualitative analysis of violations of the human rights of women and girls, and encourages the strengthening of cooperation and coordination in that regard;

19. *Calls upon* States and international and non-governmental organizations to mobilize all necessary resources, support and efforts to realize the goals, strategic objectives and actions set out in the Beijing Platform for Action and the further actions and initiatives to implement the Beijing Declaration and Platform for Action;

20. *Stresses* the importance of a substantive assessment of the implementation of the Beijing Platform for Action with a life-cycle perspective so as to identify gaps and obstacles in the implementation process and to develop further actions for the achievement of the goals of the Platform;

21. *Welcomes* the convening of the Second World Congress against Commercial Sexual Exploitation of Children at Yokohama, Japan, from 17 to 20 December 2001, and invites Member States and observers to participate in the Congress;

22. *Encourages* the regional commissions and other regional organizations to carry out activities in support of the preparations for the Second World Congress;

23. *Requests* the Secretary-General to ensure that a gender perspective and the needs and rights of the girl child are integrated into the preparatory work for the special session of the General Assembly on the follow-up to the World Summit for Children in 2001, inter alia, by providing the General Assembly with a comprehensive report drawing on the experiences and outcomes of the five-year reviews of the International Conference on Population and Development, the Fourth World Conference on Women and the World Summit for Social Development, and the World Education Forum.

Women's health

HIV/AIDS

In his report to the Commission on the Status of Women on follow-up to the Beijing Declaration and Platform for Action [E/CN.6/2000/2], the Secretary-General described trends in HIV/AIDS infection of women and efforts by the UN system to address the gender dimension of the pandemic. The report noted that HIV/AIDS infection rates among women had risen steadily, with new information suggesting that there were significantly more women than men living with HIV infection in sub-Saharan Africa and that girls in Africa aged 15-19 were five or six times more likely to be HIV-positive than boys of the same age. Women tended to be infected at a younger age than men for biological and cultural reasons.

The Joint United Nations Programme on HIV/AIDS (UNAIDS) (see p. 1165) was increasingly addressing the gender dimension of the pandemic; gender-based differences were taken into account in risk- and vulnerability-reduction approaches, and UNAIDS was cooperating with women's networks that were undertaking advocacy and prevention measures and offered support to affected women. The Inter-Agency Working Group on Gender and AIDS continued to seek ways to incorporate gender into all the UN programmes and departments dealing with AIDS. UNIFEM, in collaboration with UNAIDS and UNFPA, supported a pilot initiative entitled "Gender-focused responses to address the challenges of HIV/AIDS".

Areas of particular concern identified by the Secretary-General included: promotion of female-controlled methods of prevention and vaccine development; mother-to-child transmission and care of children orphaned by AIDS; violence against women affecting the health of women and girls; sexual and reproductive health education for young people, particularly girls; and support for women living with HIV/AIDS. The report concluded that it was important to identify, promote and apply best practices in reducing the vulnerability of women and girls. A gender-based response to the HIV/AIDS epidemic required continued efforts, coordination and long-term commitment at the country, regional and global levels, giving priority to the UN-AIDS International Partnership against AIDS in Africa. Strategies needed to focus on improving women's control over their reproductive health because of evidence that infections of the reproductive tract and sexually transmitted diseases increased the risk of HIV transmission.

In March [E/2000/27 (dec. 44/2)], the Commission, concerned by the fact that women represented 46 per cent of all people over the age of 15 living with AIDS and 55 per cent of those infected in sub-Saharan Africa, called for effective prevention strategies and intensified support for national efforts against HIV/AIDS, especially in favour of women and girls in the worst-hit regions of Africa and where the epidemic was severely setting back national development gains. Governments were urged to create an environment of support for those infected with HIV, as well as for children orphaned by AIDS; to provide the legal framework that would protect their rights; to provide access to counselling services; and to adopt long-term, timely, coherent and integrated AIDS prevention policies. The Commission called on UNAIDS to assist Governments in determining the best policies and programmes to prevent women and girls from contracting HIV/AIDS, giving priority to African women and girls. It requested Governments to ensure that condoms and care for sexually transmitted diseases were available and affordable to women, and to provide health care for women with HIV.

The expert group meeting entitled "The HIV/AIDS pandemic and its gender implications" (Windhoek, 13-27 November) [EGM/HIV-AIDS/2000/Rep.1], organized by DAW, UNAIDS and the World Health Organization (WHO), considered the interlinkages among HIV/AIDS, gender, human rights and human security as an input for the Commission's consideration of the issue and for the special session of the General Assembly on HIV/AIDS, to be held in 2001. The meeting made recommendations for both short-term and long-term action and remarked that a lasting solution could not be found without political commitment, adequate resources, good governance and democratic participation.

Traffic in women and girls

In 2000, trafficking in women and girls was addressed by the General Assembly, in resolution 55/67 (below), and the Commission on Human Rights (see p. 711). The Commission on the Status of Women, acting as preparatory committee for the twenty-third special session of the Assembly, also addressed the issue in the context of its review and appraisal of implementation of the critical areas of concern contained in the Beijing Platform for Action.

Report of Secretary-General. In response to General Assembly resolution 53/116 [YUN 1998, p. 704], the Secretary-General submitted an August report [A/55/322] on steps taken in several

forums of the United Nations and other international bodies and at the regional and national levels to address trafficking in women and girls. The report concluded that although the actual incidence of trafficking remained unknown, it appeared to be a growing problem as a result of both the persistence of its root causes—poverty, discrimination and inequality—and the proliferation of trans-border organized crime networks. Priority should be given to strategies addressing the root causes and to the adoption of measures to discourage traffickers, the Secretary-General stated. At the same time, alternatives should be provided to women and girls who were vulnerable to traffickers and to the risks associated with informal migration.

Regional meeting. The Meeting of the Asian Regional Initiative against Trafficking in Persons, especially Women and Children (Manila, Philippines, 29-31 March) adopted a regional action plan, which the Philippines forwarded to the Secretary-General on 29 September [A/C.3/55/3].

On 4 December [meeting 81], the General Assembly, on the recommendation of the Third Committee [A/55/595 & Corr.1,2], adopted **resolution 55/67** without vote [agenda item 107].

Traffic in women and girls

The General Assembly,

Reaffirming the principles set forth in the Universal Declaration of Human Rights, the Convention on the Elimination of All Forms of Discrimination against Women, the International Covenants on Human Rights, the Convention against Torture and Other Cruel, Inhuman or Degrading Treatment or Punishment, the Convention on the Rights of the Child and the Declaration on the Elimination of Violence against Women,

Welcoming the adoption by the General Assembly of the two Optional Protocols to the Convention on the Rights of the Child, in particular the Optional Protocol on the sale of children, child prostitution and child pornography, and the increasing number of Member States that have signed and ratified these Optional Protocols,

Recalling all previous resolutions on the problem of the traffic in women and girls adopted by the General Assembly, the Commission on the Status of Women, the Commission on Human Rights and the Commission on Crime Prevention and Criminal Justice, as well as the Convention for the Suppression of the Traffic in Persons and of the Exploitation of the Prostitution of Others, as well as the conclusions on violence against women adopted on 13 March 1998 by the Commission on the Status of Women at its forty-second session and the recommendations of the Working Group on Contemporary Forms of Slavery adopted on 21 August 1998 by the Subcommission on Prevention of Discrimination and Protection of Minorities at its fiftieth session,

Reaffirming the provisions of the outcomes of the World Conference on Human Rights, held in Vienna from 14 to 25 June 1993, the International Conference on Population and Development, the World Summit for Social Development, the Fourth World Conference on Women, the twenty-third special session of the General Assembly, entitled "Women 2000: gender equality, development and peace for the twenty-first century", held in New York from 5 to 9 June 2000, and the twenty-fourth special session of the Assembly, entitled "World Summit for Social Development and beyond: achieving social development for all in a globalizing world", held in Geneva from 26 June to 1 July 2000, as well as the Ninth United Nations Congress on the Prevention of Crime and the Treatment of Offenders, held in Cairo from 29 April to 8 May 1995, and the Tenth Congress, pertaining to the traffic in women and girls,

Welcoming the inclusion of gender-related crimes in the Rome Statute of the International Criminal Court, adopted on 17 July 1998 by the United Nations Diplomatic Conference of Plenipotentiaries on the Establishment of an International Criminal Court,

Noting the work of the Ad Hoc Committee on the Elaboration of a Convention against Transnational Organized Crime, in particular the elaboration of the Protocol to Prevent, Suppress and Punish Trafficking in Persons, Especially Women and Children,

Reaffirming that sexual violence and trafficking in women and girls for purposes of economic exploitation, sexual exploitation through prostitution and other forms of sexual exploitation and contemporary forms of slavery are serious violations of human rights,

Seriously concerned at the increasing number of women and girl children, in particular from developing countries and from some countries with economies in transition, who are being trafficked to developed countries, as well as within and between regions and States, and acknowledging that the problem of trafficking also includes the victimizing of boys,

Welcoming bilateral and regional cooperation mechanisms and initiatives to address the problem of trafficking in women and girls,

Welcoming also the efforts of Governments and intergovernmental and non-governmental organizations participating in the meeting of the Asian Regional Initiative against Trafficking in Persons, Especially Women and Children, held in Manila from 29 to 31 March 2000, to develop a regional action plan against trafficking in persons, especially women and children,

Welcoming further the efforts of the European Union to develop a comprehensive European policy and programmes on trafficking in human beings, as expressed in the conclusions of the European Council at its meeting held in Tampere, Finland, on 15 and 16 October 1999, and the activities of the Council of Europe and of the Organization for Security and Cooperation in Europe in this field,

Acknowledging the work being done by intergovernmental and non-governmental organizations in compiling information on the scale and complexity of the problem of trafficking, in providing shelter for trafficked women and children and in effecting their voluntary repatriation to their countries of origin,

Recognizing that global efforts, including international cooperation and technical assistance programmes, to eradicate trafficking in persons, in particular women and children, demand strong political commitment by and the active cooperation of all Governments of countries of origin, transit and destination,

Deeply concerned about the unabated use of new information technologies, including the Internet, for purposes of prostitution, child pornography, paedophilia and any other forms of sexual exploitation of children, trafficking in women as brides and sex tourism,

Gravely concerned at the increasing activities of transnational criminal organizations and others that profit from international trafficking in women and children without regard to dangerous and inhumane conditions and in flagrant violation of domestic laws and international standards,

Stressing once again the need for Governments to provide standard humanitarian treatment to trafficked persons consistent with human rights standards,

1. *Takes note with appreciation* of the report of the Secretary-General on activities of United Nations bodies and other international organizations pertaining to the problem of trafficking in women and girls;

2. *Welcomes* the steps taken by human rights treaty bodies, the special rapporteurs and subsidiary bodies of the Commission on Human Rights, the Office of the United Nations High Commissioner for Human Rights, other United Nations bodies, and international, intergovernmental and governmental organizations, within their mandates, as well as non-governmental organizations, to address the problem of trafficking in women and girls, and encourages them to continue doing so and to share their knowledge and best practices as widely as possible;

3. *Urges* Governments to take appropriate measures to address the root factors, including external factors, that encourage trafficking in women and girls for prostitution and other forms of commercialized sex, forced marriages and forced labour, in order to eliminate trafficking in women, including by strengthening existing legislation with a view to providing better protection of the rights of women and girls and to punishing perpetrators, through both criminal and civil measures;

4. *Also urges* Governments to devise, enforce and strengthen effective measures to combat and eliminate all forms of trafficking in women and girls through a comprehensive anti-trafficking strategy consisting of, inter alia, legislative measures, prevention campaigns, information exchange, assistance and protection for and reintegration of the victims and prosecution of all the offenders involved, including intermediaries;

5. *Encourages* Member States to conclude bilateral, subregional, regional and international agreements, as well as undertake initiatives, including regional initiatives, to address the problem of trafficking in women and girls, such as the Action Plan for the Asia-Pacific region of the Asian Regional Initiative against Trafficking in Persons, Especially Women and Children, the European Union initiatives on a comprehensive European policy and programmes on trafficking in human beings as expressed in the conclusions of the European Council at its meeting held in Tampere, and the activities of the Council of Europe and of the Organization for Security and Cooperation in Europe in this field;

6. *Calls upon* all Governments to criminalize trafficking in women and children, in particular girls, in

all its forms, to condemn and penalize all those offenders involved, including intermediaries, whether their offence was committed in their own or in a foreign country, while ensuring that the victims of those practices are not penalized, and to penalize persons in authority found guilty of sexually assaulting victims of trafficking in their custody;

7. *Invites* Governments to consider setting up or strengthening a national coordinating mechanism, for example, a national rapporteur or an inter-agency body, with the participation of civil society, including non-governmental organizations, to encourage the exchange of information and to report on data, root causes, factors and trends in violence against women, in particular trafficking;

8. *Urges* concerned Governments, in cooperation with intergovernmental and non-governmental organizations, to support and allocate resources for programmes to strengthen preventive action, in particular education and campaigns to increase public awareness of the issue at the national and grass-roots levels;

9. *Calls upon* concerned Governments to allocate resources to provide comprehensive programmes designed to heal, rehabilitate and reintegrate into society and communities victims of trafficking, including through job training, legal assistance and health care, and by taking measures to cooperate with non-governmental organizations to provide for the social, medical and psychological care of the victims;

10. *Encourages* Governments, in cooperation with intergovernmental and non-governmental organizations, to undertake campaigns aimed at clarifying opportunities, limitations and rights in the event of migration so as to enable women to make informed decisions and to prevent them from becoming victims of trafficking;

11. *Also encourages* Governments to intensify collaboration with non-governmental organizations to develop and implement programmes for effective counselling, training and reintegration into society of victims of trafficking, and programmes that provide shelter and helplines to victims or potential victims;

12. *Invites* Governments to take steps, including witness protection programmes, to enable women who are victims of trafficking to make complaints to the police and to be available when required by the criminal justice system, and to ensure that during this time women have access to social, medical, financial and legal assistance, and protection, as appropriate;

13. *Also invites* Governments to consider preventing, within the legal framework and in accordance with national policies, victims of trafficking, in particular women and girls, from being prosecuted for their illegal entry or residence, taking into account that they are victims of exploitation;

14. *Further invites* Governments to encourage Internet service providers to adopt or strengthen self-regulatory measures to promote the responsible use of the Internet with a view to eliminating trafficking in women and children, in particular girls;

15. *Stresses* the need for a global approach to eradicate trafficking in women and children and the importance, in this regard, of systematic data collection and comprehensive studies, and encourages Governments to develop systematic data-collection methods and to update continuously information on trafficking in women and girls, including the analysis of the modus operandi of trafficking syndicates;

16. *Urges* Governments to strengthen national programmes to combat trafficking in women and girls through sustained bilateral, regional and international cooperation, taking into account innovative approaches and best practices, and invites Governments, United Nations bodies and organizations, intergovernmental and non-governmental organizations and the private sector to undertake collaborative and joint research and studies on trafficking in women and girls that can serve as a basis for policy formulation or change;

17. *Invites* Governments, once again, with the support of the United Nations, to formulate training manuals for law enforcement and medical personnel and judicial officers who handle cases of trafficked women and girls, taking into account current research and materials on traumatic stress and gender-sensitive counselling techniques, with a view to sensitizing them to the special needs of victims;

18. *Invites* State parties to the Convention on the Elimination of All Forms of Discrimination against Women, the Convention on the Rights of the Child and the International Covenants on Human Rights to include information and statistics on trafficking in women and girls as part of their national reports to their respective committees;

19. *Encourages* Governments as well as intergovernmental and non-governmental organizations, the human rights treaty bodies, the special rapporteurs, especially the Special Rapporteur of the Commission on Human Rights on violence against women, its causes and consequences, the Special Rapporteur of the Commission on Human Rights on the sale of children, child prostitution and child pornography and the Special Rapporteur of the Commission on Human Rights on the human rights of migrants, and subsidiary bodies of the Commission on Human Rights and other relevant United Nations bodies, within their respective mandates, to participate in and contribute to the work of the Working Group on Contemporary Forms of Slavery of the Subcommission on the Promotion and Protection of Human Rights at its twenty-sixth session, in 2001, which will focus on the issue of trafficking;

20. *Requests* the Secretary-General to compile, as reference and guidance, successful interventions and strategies in addressing the various dimensions of the problem of trafficking in women and children, in particular girls, based on reports, research and other materials from within the United Nations, including the United Nations Office for Drug Control and Crime Prevention, as well as from outside the United Nations, and to submit a report on the implementation of the present resolution to the General Assembly at its fifty-seventh session.

Palestinian women

In a report to the Commission on the Status of Women on follow-up to the Beijing Platform for Action [E/CN.6/2000/2], the Secretary-General described assistance provided by the UN system to Palestinian women, whose status and living conditions were closely linked with the progress of the peace process and whose lives continued to be adversely affected by a variety of measures, including closures and settlement activities. The Secretary-General concluded that the mainstreaming of a gender perspective into nation-building programmes and the full participation of Palestinian women were critical to sustainable peace in the region. To that end, UN organizations would continue to assist Palestinian women to participate fully in the peace process and to build Palestinian society.

On 28 July, the Economic and Social Council, in **resolution 2000/23**, asked the Commission to continue to monitor and take action regarding the situation of Palestinian women and children (see p. 439).

Women in Afghanistan

In April, the Commission on Human Rights took action on the grave human rights situation of women and girls in Afghanistan, and the Secretary-General reported in July on that issue (see p. 713).

ECONOMIC AND SOCIAL COUNCIL ACTION

On 27 July [meeting 43], the Economic and Social Council, on the recommendation of the Commission on the Status of Women [E/2000/27], adopted **resolution 2000/9** without vote [agenda item 14 (a)].

Situation of women and girls in Afghanistan

The Economic and Social Council,

Guided by the Charter of the United Nations, the Universal Declaration of Human Rights, the International Covenants on Human Rights, the Convention against Torture and Other Cruel, Inhuman or Degrading Treatment or Punishment, the Convention on the Elimination of All Forms of Discrimination against Women, the Convention on the Rights of the Child, the Declaration on the Elimination of Violence against Women, the Beijing Declaration and Platform for Action adopted by the Fourth World Conference on Women, and other instruments of human rights and international humanitarian law,

Recalling that Afghanistan is a party to the Convention on the Prevention and Punishment of the Crime of Genocide, the International Covenant on Civil and Political Rights, the International Covenant on Economic, Social and Cultural Rights, the Convention against Torture and Other Cruel, Inhuman or Degrading Treatment or Punishment, the Convention on the Rights of the Child and the Geneva Convention relative to the Protection of Civilian Persons in Time of War, and that it has signed the Convention on the Elimination of All Forms of Discrimination against Women,

Deeply concerned about the deteriorating economic and social conditions of women and girls in all areas of Afghanistan, in particular in areas under the control of the Taliban movement, as documented by the continued and substantiated reports of grave violations of the human rights of women and girls, including all forms of discrimination against them, such as restrictions on access to health care, to many levels and types of education, to employment outside the home and, at times, to humanitarian aid, as well as restrictions on their freedom of movement,

Welcoming the ongoing work of the Special Rapporteur of the Commission on Human Rights on the situation of human rights in Afghanistan, in particular his special focus on violations of the human rights of women and girls, especially in territories under the control of the Taliban faction,

Noting with concern the detrimental impact of these harmful conditions on the well-being of Afghan women and the children in their care,

Welcoming the United Nations Inter-Agency Gender Mission to Afghanistan in November 1997, conducted by the Special Adviser to the Secretary-General on Gender Issues and Advancement of Women, taking into account the report of the Mission, and hoping that the Mission will serve as a model for future efforts to address the gender dimension of crisis/conflict situations,

Expressing its appreciation for the international community's support of and solidarity with the women and girls of Afghanistan, being supportive of the women of Afghanistan who protest against violations of their human rights, and encouraging women and men worldwide to continue efforts to draw attention to their situation and to promote the immediate restoration of their ability to enjoy their human rights,

1. *Condemns* the continuing grave violations of the human rights of women and girls, including all forms of discrimination against them, in all areas of Afghanistan, in particular in areas under the control of the Taliban;

2. *Also condemns* the continued restrictions on the access of women to health care and the systematic violation of the human rights of women in Afghanistan, including the restrictions on access to education and to employment outside the home, freedom of movement and freedom from intimidation, harassment and violence, which has a serious detrimental effect on the well-being of Afghan women and the children in their care;

3. *Urges* the Taliban and other Afghan parties to recognize, protect, promote and act in accordance with all human rights and fundamental freedoms, regardless of gender, ethnicity or religion, in accordance with international human rights instruments, and to respect international humanitarian law;

4. *Urges* all the Afghan parties, in particular the Taliban, to bring to an end without delay all human rights violations against women and girls and to take urgent measures to ensure:

(a) The repeal of all legislative and other measures that discriminate against women and girls and those that impede the realization of all their human rights;

(b) The effective participation of women in civil, cultural, economic, political and social life throughout the country;

(c) Respect for the equal right of women to work and their reintegration in employment;

(d) The equal right of women and girls to education without discrimination, the reopening of schools and the admission of women and girls to all levels of education;

(e) Respect for the right of women to security of person, and that those responsible for physical attacks on women are brought to justice;

(f) Respect for freedom of movement for women;

(g) Respect for effective and equal access of women and girls to the facilities necessary to protect their right to the highest attainable standard of physical and mental health;

5. *Encourages* the continuing efforts of the United Nations, international and non-governmental organizations and donors to ensure that all United Nations-assisted programmes in Afghanistan are formulated and coordinated in such a way as to promote and ensure the participation of women in those programmes and that women benefit equally with men from such programmes;

6. *Appeals* to all States and to the international community to ensure that all humanitarian assistance to the people of Afghanistan, in conformity with the Strategic Framework for Afghanistan, is based on the principle of non-discrimination, integrates a gender perspective, and actively attempts to promote the participation of both women and men and to promote peace and respect for human rights and fundamental freedoms;

7. *Urges* States to continue to give special attention to the promotion and protection of the human rights of women in Afghanistan and to mainstream a gender perspective in all aspects of their policies and actions related to Afghanistan;

8. *Welcomes* the establishment of the positions of Gender Adviser and Human Rights Adviser at the United Nations Office of the Resident Coordinator for Afghanistan, in order to ensure more effective consideration and implementation of human rights and gender concerns in all United Nations programmes within Afghanistan, taking into account the recommendations contained in the report of the United Nations Inter-Agency Gender Mission to Afghanistan conducted by the Special Adviser to the Secretary-General on Gender Issues and Advancement of Women in November 1997;

9. *Takes note* of the report of the Special Rapporteur of the Commission on Human Rights on violence against women, its causes and consequences on her mission to Afghanistan from 1 to 13 September 1999;

10. *Urges* the Secretary-General to ensure that all United Nations activities in Afghanistan are carried out according to the principle of non-discrimination against women and girls, that a gender perspective and special attention to the human rights of women and girls are fully incorporated into the work of the Civil Affairs Unit established within the United Nations Special Mission to Afghanistan, including the training and selection of staff, and that efforts are made to enhance the role of women in preventive diplomacy, peacemaking and peacekeeping;

11. *Stresses* the importance of the Special Rapporteur of the Commission on Human Rights on the situation of human rights in Afghanistan giving special attention to the human rights of women and girls and fully incorporating a gender perspective in his work;

12. *Appeals* to States and the international community to implement the recommendations of the United Nations Inter-Agency Gender Mission to Afghanistan under the leadership of the Special Adviser to the Secretary-General on Gender Issues and Advancement of Women;

13. *Urges* all Afghan factions, in particular the Taliban, to ensure the safety and protection of all United Nations and humanitarian workers in Afghanistan and to allow them, regardless of gender, to carry out their work unhindered;

14. *Requests* the Secretary-General to continue to review the situation of women and girls in Afghanistan and to submit to the Commission on the Status of Women at its forty-fifth session a report on progress made in the implementation of the present resolution.

Women and development

In response to a 1999 Economic and Social Council ministerial communiqué [YUN 1999, p. 1096], the Secretary-General submitted a June report on the role of employment and work in poverty eradication: the empowerment and advancement of women [E/2000/64]. The report reviewed progress in implementing the communiqué's recommendations, based primarily on the relevant activities of the UN system conducted within the framework of the follow-up to the global conferences held in the 1990s and other major initiatives. National development experience relevant to implementation of recommendations was illustrated by examples from four countries. Among the challenges that had hampered implementation, the report noted, was that while equality between women and men was widely accepted as essential for economic and social development, the mainstreaming of a gender perspective into poverty eradication programmes and policies and for the empowerment of women had lagged behind. In most countries, the employment of women had increased significantly; however, gender inequalities, as reflected in the wage gap and a disproportionate share of family responsibilities, remained obstacles to women's equal access to and participation in the labour market. Women's participation in economic and political fields at the decision-making level was stagnating and their productive and creative potential was largely underutilized. Recommendations were made for further Council action. On 28 July, the Council, by **decision 2000/290**, took note of the report.

ECONOMIC AND SOCIAL COUNCIL ACTION

On 28 July [meeting 45], the Economic and Social Council adopted **resolution 2000/26** [draft: E/2000/L.25] without vote [agenda item 6].

The role of employment and work in poverty eradication: empowerment and advancement of women

The Economic and Social Council,

Recalling the ministerial communiqué on the theme "The role of employment and work in poverty eradication: empowerment and advancement of women", adopted on 7 July 1999 at the high-level segment of its substantive session of 1999,

Acknowledging the important outcomes of the twenty-third special session of the General Assembly, entitled "Women 2000: gender equality, development and peace for the twenty-first century", and of the twenty-fourth special session of the General Assembly, entitled "World Summit for Social Development and beyond: achieving social development for all in a globalizing world",

Recognizing the progress achieved in placing poverty eradication at the centre of national and international policy agendas and in formulating poverty eradication policies and strategies,

Recognizing also that considerable progress has been made in increasing recognition of gender dimensions of poverty and in the recognition that gender equality is one of the factors of specific importance for eradicating poverty, in particular in relation to the feminization of poverty,

Recognizing further that there has been increased attention to the goal of full employment and to policies aimed at employment growth,

Noting with concern the persistent problems in addressing the challenges of poverty eradication, gender inequalities, empowerment and advancement of women and employment, as reflected in the outcome documents of the recent five-year reviews of the Fourth World Conference on Women and the World Summit for Social Development,

1. *Reaffirms* the commitments and recommendations contained in its 1999 ministerial communiqué, and welcomes the outcome documents of the twenty-third and twenty-fourth special sessions of the General Assembly;

2. *Strongly encourages* Governments to pursue and strengthen their efforts to work towards achieving the goals of poverty eradication, full and productive employment and the empowerment and advancement of women by implementing the recommendations of the communiqué and the commitments that they undertook at the World Summit for Social Development, the Fourth World Conference on Women and their five-year reviews, and the other major conferences and summits of the 1990s, as well as at the World Education Forum;

3. *Reiterates* the call for the relevant organizations of the United Nations system and the international community to take consistent, coherent, coordinated and joint action in support of national efforts to eradicate poverty, with particular attention to employment creation and work and the empowerment and advancement of women;

4. *Welcomes* the commitment undertaken by the General Assembly at its twenty-fourth special session on the five-year review of the World Summit for Social Development to place poverty eradication at the centre of economic and social development and build consensus with all relevant actors at all levels on policies and strategies to reduce the proportion of people living in extreme poverty by one half by the year 2015, with a view to eradicating poverty;

5. *Reaffirms* the need for Governments and the international community, in the context of their efforts to achieve the empowerment and advancement of women, to address, as a matter of urgency, the chal-

lenges of poverty eradication and employment creation in a holistic manner, which includes alleviation of the negative effects on women associated with structural adjustment programmes and trade liberalization and of the disproportionate burden borne by women living in poverty, as well as the identification and implementation of development-oriented and durable solutions which integrate a gender perspective with regard to external debt and debt-servicing problems of developing countries, including least developed countries;

6. *Urges* all Member States to take measures, at the national and international levels, to promote the effective mobilization of resources in order to facilitate the full implementation of the recommendations of the 1999 ministerial communiqué and the outcomes of the twenty-third and twenty-fourth special sessions of the General Assembly, and urges donor countries to strive to fulfil the internationally agreed target, yet to be attained, of 0.7 per cent of their gross national product for overall official development assistance as soon as possible, and in this regard welcomes the efforts made by those donors that have reached and surpassed such targets;

7. *Urges* all States that have not yet ratified or acceded to the Convention on the Elimination of All Forms of Discrimination against Women to do so as soon as possible, urges all States parties to fulfil their obligations under the Convention, and invites all States to promote universal ratification and implementation of International Labour Organization Convention No. 182 concerning the Prohibition and Immediate Action for the Elimination of the Worst Forms of Child Labour, and to consider signing and ratifying or acceding to the International Convention on the Protection of the Rights of All Migrant Workers and Members of Their Families;

8. *Invites* States parties to the Convention on the Elimination of All Forms of Discrimination against Women to consider signing and ratifying or acceding to the Optional Protocol thereto;

9. *Encourages* Governments, international organizations and civil society, including non-governmental organizations, in particular women's organizations, the media and the private sector to interact further and establish partnerships within and across countries aimed at contributing to poverty eradication and the empowerment of women.

System-wide plan

The Commission on the Status of Women had before it the Secretary-General's January assessment of the implementation of the system-wide medium-term plan for the advancement of women, 1996-2001 [E/CN.6/2000/3]. The report summarized information provided by UN entities on their efforts to implement the plan in the areas of the gender mainstreaming strategy; gender units and gender focal points; mobilization and allocation of financial resources; human resources; and coordination. Among the obstacles encountered were lack of understanding of gender as a concept or the failure to perceive issues such as poverty, the environment or HIV/AIDS as having gender dimensions; lack of staff capacity to implement gender mainstreaming strategies or carry out gender analysis; inadequately defined management competencies for gender main-streaming; absence of strategic planning and channels of communication; and lack of staff confidence in their ability to incorporate gender concerns. Information on activities undertaken by the UN system in the 12 critical areas of concern of the Beijing Platform for Action was set out in an annex to the report.

By a June note [E/2000/78], the Secretary-General transmitted the January report to the Economic and Social Council.

The Council, by **decision 2000/289** of 28 July, took note of the Secretary-General's note.

Evaluation. In accordance with General Assembly resolution 54/255 [YUN 1999, p. 1274], the Office of Internal Oversight Services (OIOS) submitted to the Committee for Programme and Coordination (CPC), in March, an in-depth evaluation of the advancement of women programme [E/AC.51/2000/3]. Focusing mainly on the work of the Office of the Special Adviser on Gender Issues and DAW, the report assessed the following activities: servicing of intergovernmental bodies, in particular the Commission on the Status of Women, CEDAW, the Economic and Social Council and the Assembly; monitoring the implementation of the Beijing Platform for Action; gender mainstreaming; the status of women in the Secretariat; coordination; outreach; and gender advisory services and other activities. Recommendations were made with regard to enhancing the effectiveness of the reporting mechanism of the Convention on the Elimination of All Forms of Discrimination against Women; improving coordination within the Inter-Agency Committee on Women and Gender Equality, and between DAW and other UN programmes and entities; and enhancing outreach efforts through more effective marketing and distribution of DAW publications, improving the WomenWatch and DAW web sites, encouraging DAW staff to publish in professional journals, and improving collaboration with NGOs.

In June [A/55/16], CPC agreed on the continued importance and relevance of the advancement of women programme and endorsed many recommendations contained in the report, subject to certain observations.

UN machinery

Convention on elimination of discrimination against women

As at 31 December 2000, 166 States were parties to the 1979 Convention on the Elimination of All Forms of Discrimination against Women,

adopted by the General Assembly in resolution 34/180 [YUN 1979, p. 895]. During the year, Saudi Arabia acceded to the Convention. At year's end, 24 States parties had also accepted the amendment to article 20, paragraph 1, of the Convention in respect of the meeting time of CEDAW, which had been adopted by the States parties in 1995 [YUN 1995, p. 1178]. The amendment would enter into force when accepted by a two-thirds majority of States parties.

The Optional Protocol to the Convention, adopted by the Assembly in resolution 54/4 [YUN 1999, p. 1100], entered into force on 22 December. The Protocol, which entitled individuals or groups to submit directly to CEDAW complaints concerning alleged Convention violations and established procedures for inquiries into situations of grave or systematic violations of women's rights, had 15 States parties by the end of 2000.

The Secretary-General submitted his annual report to the Assembly on the status of the Convention as at 1 August [A/55/308].

Meeting of States parties. The eleventh meeting of States parties to the Convention (New York, 31 August) [CEDAW/SP/2000/6] reviewed reservations, declarations and objections of States parties to the Convention and notifications of withdrawals, as well as objections to State parties' reservations [CEDAW/SP/2000/2]. At the meeting, 11 members of CEDAW were elected to replace those whose terms were due to expire at the end of the year.

CEDAW

In 2000, the 23-member Committee on the Elimination of Discrimination against Women (CEDAW), established in 1982 [YUN 1982, p. 1149] to monitor compliance with the 1979 Convention, held two sessions in New York [A/55/38]. At its twenty-second session (17 January–4 February), CEDAW reviewed the initial or periodic reports of Belarus, Burkina Faso, the Democratic Republic of the Congo, Germany, India, Jordan, Luxembourg and Myanmar on measures they had taken to implement the Convention. It also considered a comparative analysis of the Optional Protocol with existing treaty-based communications and inquiry mechanisms [CEDAW/C/2000/I/5].

The Committee stated that the Convention and the monitoring process established under it would play a crucial role in achieving the goals of the Beijing Platform for Action and any fresh initiatives emerging from the twenty-third special session of the General Assembly. It adopted four decisions on reporting and other procedural matters.

At its twenty-third session (12-30 June), CEDAW reviewed the initial or periodic reports of Austria, Cameroon, Cuba, Iraq, Lithuania, the Republic of Moldova and Romania. The Committee decided to begin to prepare a general recommendation on article 4 of the Convention (on temporary special measures) with a general discussion in 2001. It adopted a suggestion requesting the Secretariat to explore the possibility of holding one of the CEDAW sessions in 2002 or 2003 outside UN Headquarters, in particular in the Asia-Pacific region, in order to facilitate consideration of reports of State parties from that region. Two other decisions on procedural matters were also adopted.

GENERAL ASSEMBLY ACTION

On 4 December [meeting 81], the General Assembly, on the recommendation of the Third Committee [A/55/595 & Corr.1,2], adopted **resolution 55/70** without vote [agenda item 107].

Convention on the Elimination of All Forms of Discrimination against Women

The General Assembly,

Recalling its resolutions 54/4 of 6 October 1999 and 54/137 of 17 December 1999,

Bearing in mind that one of the purposes of the United Nations, as stated in Articles 1 and 55 of the Charter, is to promote universal respect for human rights and fundamental freedoms for all without distinction of any kind, including distinction as to sex,

Affirming that women and men should participate equally in social, economic and political development, should contribute equally to such development and should share equally in improved conditions of life,

Recalling the Vienna Declaration and Programme of Action adopted by the World Conference on Human Rights on 25 June 1993, in which the Conference reaffirmed that the human rights of women and the girl child were an inalienable, integral and indivisible part of universal human rights,

Acknowledging the need for a comprehensive and integrated approach to the promotion and protection of the human rights of women, which includes the integration of the human rights of women into the mainstream of United Nations activities system-wide,

Welcoming the political declaration and the outcome document of the twenty-third special session of the General Assembly, entitled "Women 2000: gender equality, development and peace for the twenty-first century", in particular paragraph 68 *(c)* and *(d)* concerning the Convention on the Elimination of All Forms of Discrimination against Women and the Optional Protocol thereto,

Recalling that in the United Nations Millennium Declaration heads of State and Government resolved to implement the Convention on the Elimination of All Forms of Discrimination against Women,

Welcoming the progress made in the implementation of the Convention, but concerned about the remaining challenges,

Welcoming also the growing number of States parties to the Convention, which now stands at one hundred and sixty-six,

Welcoming further the adoption and opening for signature, ratification and accession of the Optional Protocol to the Convention on the Elimination of All Forms of Discrimination against Women, and the subsequent entry into force of the Optional Protocol, thereby fulfilling a goal of the Beijing Platform for Action,

Bearing in mind the recommendation of the Committee on the Elimination of Discrimination against Women that national reports should include information on the implementation of the Beijing Platform for Action, in accordance with paragraph 323 of the Platform,

Having considered the report of the Committee on its twenty-second and twenty-third sessions,

Expressing concern at the great number of reports that are overdue and that continue to be overdue, in particular initial reports, which constitutes an obstacle to the full implementation of the Convention,

1. *Welcomes* the report of the Secretary-General on the status of the Convention on the Elimination of All Forms of Discrimination against Women;

2. *Expresses disappointment* that universal ratification of the Convention has not been achieved by the year 2000, and urges all States that have not yet ratified or acceded to the Convention to do so;

3. *Emphasizes* the importance of full compliance by States parties with their obligations under the Convention;

4. *Welcomes* the fact that, as at 22 September 2000, ten States had become parties to the Optional Protocol to the Convention on the Elimination of All Forms of Discrimination against Women, thereby allowing it to enter into force on 22 December 2000;

5. *Urges* States parties to consider signing and ratifying the Optional Protocol;

6. *Notes* that some States parties have modified their reservations, expresses satisfaction that some reservations have been withdrawn, and urges States parties to limit the extent of any reservations they lodge to the Convention, to formulate any such reservations as precisely and as narrowly as possible, to ensure that no reservations are incompatible with the object and purpose of the Convention or otherwise incompatible with international treaty law, to review their reservations regularly with a view to withdrawing them and to withdraw reservations that are contrary to the object and purpose of the Convention or that are otherwise incompatible with international treaty law;

7. *Urges* States parties to the Convention to make every possible effort to submit their reports on the implementation of the Convention in accordance with article 18 thereof and with the guidelines provided by the Committee on the Elimination of Discrimination against Women and to cooperate fully with the Committee in the presentation of their reports;

8. *Encourages* the Secretariat to extend further technical assistance to States parties, upon their request, in the preparation of reports, in particular initial reports, and invites Governments to contribute to these efforts;

9. *Commends* the Committee on its contributions to the effective implementation of the Convention;

10. *Urges* States parties to the Convention to take appropriate measures so that acceptance of the amendment to article 20, paragraph 1, of the Convention by a two-thirds majority of States parties can be reached as soon as possible in order for the amendment to enter into force;

11. *Expresses its appreciation* for the additional meeting time that allows the Committee to hold two sessions annually, each session of three weeks' duration and each preceded by a pre-session working group of the Committee;

12. *Requests* the Secretary-General, in accordance with resolution 54/4, to provide the resources, including staff and facilities, necessary for the effective functioning of the Committee within its full mandate, in particular taking into account the entry into force of the Optional Protocol;

13. *Urges* Governments, agencies and organizations of the United Nations system and intergovernmental as well as non-governmental organizations to disseminate the Convention and the Optional Protocol thereto;

14. *Encourages* all relevant entities of the United Nations system, within their mandates, as well as Governments and intergovernmental and non-governmental organizations, as appropriate, to continue to assist States parties, upon their request, in implementing the Convention, and in this regard encourages States parties to pay attention to the concluding comments as well as the general recommendations of the Committee;

15. *Encourages* all relevant parts of the United Nations system to continue to build women's knowledge and understanding of and capacity to utilize human rights instruments, in particular the Convention and the Optional Protocol thereto;

16. *Welcomes* the submission of reports by the specialized agencies at the invitation of the Committee on the implementation of the Convention in areas falling within the scope of their activities and the contribution of non-governmental organizations to the work of the Committee, and encourages the agencies to continue to submit reports;

17. *Requests* the Secretary-General to submit to the General Assembly at its fifty-sixth session a report on the status of the Convention on the Elimination of All Forms of Discrimination against Women and the implementation of the present resolution.

Commission on the Status of Women

The Commission on the Status of Women, at its forty-fourth session (New York, 28 February–17 March) [E/2000/27], adopted two resolutions related to improving the status of women and ensuring their rights and one decision by which it took note of six documents it had considered. In addition, it recommended two draft resolutions and one decision for adoption by the Economic and Social Council. The Commission held its third and final session (7-17 March, 20 April and 2 June) [A/S-23/2 & Add.1,2] as preparatory committee for the General Assembly's special session in June to review implementation of the 1985 Nairobi Forward-looking Strategies for the Advancement of Women and the 1995 Beijing Platform for Action (see p. 1083). The Commission convened two panel discussions: one, during its regular session, on emerging issues, trends and approaches to issues affecting the situation of women or equality between women and men;

and another, during the preparatory session, on gender equality, development and peace beyond the year 2000. It considered a February note by the Secretariat [E/CN.6/2000/5] containing a summary of actions taken by the Commission to implement recommendations of the Economic and Social Council, in particular in the areas of restructuring and revitalization and follow-up to UN conferences and summits.

On 27 July, the Economic and Social Council, by **decision 2000/237**, took note of the Commission's report on its forty-fourth session and approved the provisional agenda and documentation for its forty-fifth (2001) session. On 18 October, the Council, by **decision 2000/310**, decided, on an exceptional basis and as an interim measure, to invite those NGOs accredited to the twenty-third and/or twenty-fourth special sessions of the General Assembly to attend the forty-fifth session of the Commission on the Status of Women, provided that they had applied for consultative status.

Communications on the status of women

At a closed meeting on 2 March [E/2000/27], the Commission took note of the report of the Working Group on Communications on the Status of Women, established in 1993 [YUN 1993, p. 1050] to consider ways of making the communications procedure more transparent and efficient. The Working Group considered 25 confidential communications and 4 non-confidential communications received directly by DAW and 44 confidential communications received by OHCHR. The Working Group expressed deep concern regarding the continuing grave violations of women's human rights, as well as persistent and pervasive discrimination. In particular, the Working Group was concerned at the abusive treatment of women, including torture, rape, custodial deaths, abduction, disappearances, arbitrary arrests, and harassment by security forces and other authorities, especially where separatist movements had been reported. Concern was also expressed about the targeting of civilians, especially women and children; the mistreatment of those who were internally displaced in conflict situations; discrimination against women in respect of their access to humanitarian aid; the failure of Governments to protect women and children, including ethnic and minority women, in times of political instability; discrimination against indigenous women and children; and harassment of human rights defenders and their families. The Working Group expressed concern that women and children continued to be the primary victims of armed conflicts. It was gravely concerned in one case by more than 8,000 allegations of gross violations of all the basic human rights of women, particularly degrading and inhuman punishment that included women being beaten, tortured, shot and burnt alive.

UN Development Fund for Women (UNIFEM)

The UN Development Fund for Women (UNIFEM) continued in 2000 [A/56/174] to focus on women's economic and political empowerment and on advocacy for gender equality and women's empowerment through multilateral policy dialogue, especially in three areas of immediate concern: strengthening women's economic capacity as entrepreneurs and producers, especially in the context of the new trade agenda and the emergence of new technologies; engendering governance and leadership to increase women's participation in the decision-making processes that shaped their lives; and promoting women's human rights to eliminate all forms of violence against women and transform development into a more peaceful, equitable and sustainable process. Those issues were addressed in relation to regional realities in Africa, Asia and the Pacific, Latin America and the Caribbean, Eastern Europe and the countries of the Commonwealth of Independent States.

During the year, UNIFEM approved 77 new projects and supported 159 ongoing initiatives around the world. Those activities aimed to link women's issues and concerns to national, regional and global agendas, by fostering collaboration and providing technical expertise on gender mainstreaming and women's empowerment strategies. For example, in relation to women's economic empowerment, UNIFEM supported situational analyses for the tourism industry in Jordan and hand-loomed textile businesses in the Lao People's Democratic Republic. To increase women's access to information communication technologies, UNIFEM provided training in e-commerce for small and medium-sized businesses owned by women in Albania, Ecuador, Nepal, the Philippines and Romania. The Fund continued to work with regional commissions to expand gender statistics and to bring women into multilateral trade negotiations and policy planning processes. Other activities involved providing assistance to women in conflict situations and supporting their participation in peace and reconstruction efforts, including in Burundi, Guatemala, Somalia and Uganda and in the Palestinian/Israeli conflict; and supporting women candidates for public office in Brazil, Ecuador, Fiji, the former Yugoslav Republic of Macedonia,

the Kosovo province of Yugoslavia, and the Pacific region.

In June, during the twenty-third special session of the General Assembly, UNIFEM launched a new biennial report, *Progress of the World's Women 2000*. Four other key publications were released by UNIFEM in 2000: *Women at the Peace Table—Making a Difference; With an End in Sight; Strategies from the UNIFEM Trust Fund to Eliminate Violence against Women;* and *The Impact of Armed Conflict on Children.*

UNIFEM's Trust Fund in Support of Actions to Eliminate Violence against Women funded 17 new projects in 2000, including educating the public and sensitizing law enforcement agents about domestic violence laws in the United Republic of Tanzania, addressing the problem of so-called honour killings in Jordan, building local capacity to protect women from trafficking and domestic violence in the Republic of Moldova, and training human rights lawyers on domestic violence issues in Peru. Since it began in 1997, the Trust Fund had granted more than $4 million to 105 projects in 65 countries.

Total contributions for UNIFEM increased by more than 20 per cent in 2000, to $29.41 million from $23.65 million in 1999. Governments provided $24.68 million, and cost-sharing and sub-trust fund contributions amounted to $7.6 million, an increase of 34 per cent over 1999.

In August [A/55/271], the Secretary-General transmitted to the General Assembly a report on UNIFEM's 1999 activities. The Assembly, by **decisions 55/416** and **55/444** of 4 and 20 December, respectively, took note of the report.

Strategy and business plan

In a February report [DP/2000/15 & Add.1], UNIFEM presented to the UNDP/UNFPA Executive Board its strategy and business plan for 2000-2003. Based on the results achieved, lessons learned and gaps remaining from the previous strategy and business plan (1997-1999) [YUN 1997, p. 1205], the new plan set forth the Fund's strategic objectives and activities, taking into account the UN reform programme and the five-year review of the Beijing Platform for Action, as well as the social, economic, political and cultural contexts that influenced efforts to achieve gender equality.

The Fund's activities would continue to focus on the three thematic areas identified in the previous plan—strengthening women's economic capacity; promoting women's human rights and the elimination of violence against women; and engendering governance and leadership. In particular, its work would be based on five objectives: to increase opportunities for women, especially those living in poverty, through focused programming in the thematic areas; to strengthen UN capacity to support women's empowerment and gender mainstreaming; to strengthen UNIFEM's effectiveness by incorporating the principles of a learning organization and building strategic partnerships that enhanced field-based operations; to ensure that UNIFEM's human resources and financial systems efficiently supported the Fund's goals and programmes; and to build a larger and more diversified resource base.

UNDP Executive Board action. On 6 April [E/2000/35 (dec. 2000/7)], the UNDP/UNFPA Executive Board endorsed the programme focus, strategies and targets set out in the UNIFEM strategy and business plan, 2000-2003. The Board recommended that the UNDP Administrator include UNIFEM among the organizations to which execution responsibility for UNDP projects and programmes could be entrusted. Member States were urged to contribute or increase their contributions to UNIFEM.

International Research and Training Institute (INSTRAW)

The Board of Trustees of the International Research and Training Institute for the Advancement of Women (INSTRAW) held its twentieth session at the Institute's headquarters in Santo Domingo, Dominican Republic, from 4 to 6 April [E/2000/58]. INSTRAW, an autonomous institution, undertook research and training programmes for the advancement and mobilization of women in development.

The Board approved the feasibility study on the Gender Awareness Information and Networking System (GAINS) and recommended that the Institute give priority to its implementation. It decided that INSTRAW should concentrate on launching GAINS and defer all thematic research projects, except for two that were near completion. To start the GAINS project, the Board asked for additional funds over the approved operational budget for 2000.

In a September report on INSTRAW activities [A/55/385], the Secretary-General said that, in the previous year, with minimal financial and staffing resources, the Institute had been able to begin the process of restructuring and revitalization; however, it had not received the funds required for long-term sustainability and to establish GAINS. In the absence of significant additional contributions, INSTRAW would run out of funds in early 2001 and would be closed.

INSTRAW restructuring

In response to Economic and Social Council resolution 1999/54 [YUN 1999, p. 1107], the INSTRAW Director submitted a May report on the implementation of revitalization measures [E/2000/59]. Steps taken included the appointment of a new director and development of a new vision and working method based on the GAINS system. A prototype GAINS web site had been developed, an independent feasibility study of GAINS had been carried out, and the system had been approved as the Institute's new working method by the INSTRAW Board of Trustees. However, the Director stated, resources available in the INSTRAW Trust Fund were not sufficient to cover the costs of implementing the initial phases of GAINS. If sufficient support to INSTRAW was not forthcoming in the next few months, all the revitalization efforts undertaken would not bear fruit and the Institute would continue to be threatened with pending closure.

The Council also had before it an executive summary of the independent feasibility study of GAINS [E/2000/98], according to which its objectives were to provide a system for researchers to collaborate and disseminate their work and for trainers to deliver training and capacity-building to women. GAINS services would include a comprehensive, searchable database on gender-related research and training, collaborative research and training, and capacity-building. The study concluded that putting INSTRAW's programme of collaborative research and training on women on the global electronic network was both technically feasible and essential. It estimated a start-up cost of $800,000 and recommended operationalizing GAINS by building the web site and deploying the tools in cooperation with partners at UNDP and in the industry.

ECONOMIC AND SOCIAL COUNCIL ACTION

On 28 July [meeting 45], the Economic and Social Council adopted **resolution 2000/24** [draft: E/2000/L.23] without vote [agenda item 14 (a)].

Revitalization and strengthening of the International Research and Training Institute for the Advancement of Women

The Economic and Social Council,

Recalling its resolution 1979/11 of 9 May 1979, in which it recommended that the International Research and Training Institute for the Advancement of Women be located in the Dominican Republic, a developing country,

Recalling also its resolution 1999/54 of 29 July 1999, in which it requested the Institute to adopt a new approach to research, training and communications through increased use of new information and communications technologies,

Recalling further the report of the Secretary-General on the activities of the Institute and General Assembly resolution 54/140 of 17 December 1999 on the revitalization and strengthening of the Institute,

Recalling the importance of information and communications technologies for the advancement of women and the role of the Gender Awareness Information and Networking System in gender research, training, information dissemination and networking, in particular for women in developing countries, while at the same time supporting traditional methods of information dissemination, research and training,

Taking note of paragraph 85 *(c)* of the outcome document of the twenty-third special session of the General Assembly, entitled "Women 2000: gender equality, development and peace for the twenty-first century", held in New York from 5 to 10 June 2000, which called for support for national efforts, particularly in developing countries, for enlarged access to new information technology as part of the efforts to develop collaborative research, training and information dissemination, including through the Gender Awareness Information and Networking System being developed by the Institute, while at the same time supporting traditional methods of information dissemination, research and training,

Stressing the need to rectify continuing anomalies noted in the report of the Joint Inspection Unit on an evaluation of the Institute,

1. *Takes note* of the report of the Board of Trustees of the International Research and Training Institute for the Advancement of Women on its twentieth session and of the recommendations and decisions contained therein;

2. *Also takes note* of the report of the Director of the International Research and Training Institute for the Advancement of Women;

3. *Commends* the Institute for undertaking important measures for its revitalization, in particular the development and launching of the prototype of the Gender Awareness Information and Networking System at the twenty-third special session of the General Assembly, entitled "Women 2000: gender equality, development and peace for the twenty-first century", and its presentation at the information technology exhibit held in this connection at the high-level segment of the Economic and Social Council from 5 to 7 July 2000;

4. *Acknowledges and appreciates* the support of those Governments and organizations that have contributed towards the revitalization efforts of the Institute and the preparation of the prototype of the Gender Awareness Information and Networking System;

5. *Expresses grave concern* that, despite these efforts, the level of contributions has not adequately increased to a level to enable the full implementation of the System nor the operational viability of the Institute beyond 31 December 2000;

6. *Urges* Member States to inform the Institute as soon as possible if contributions will be forthcoming in order for it to be able to plan its operations beyond 2000;

7. *Urges* the Institute, in order to improve its financial situation, to continue to explore new and innovative means of funding, and in this regard decides to amend article VI, paragraph 1, of the statute of the Institute, as follows:

"The activities of the Institute shall be funded by voluntary contributions from States, intergovernmental and non-governmental organizations, foundations, including the United Nations Foundation, private sources and other sources in accordance with article VII of the statute";

8. *Urges* the Secretary-General:

(a) To continue to invite Member States to contribute to the United Nations Trust Fund for the International Research and Training Institute for the Advancement of Women so that it can continue to fulfil its mandate beyond 2000;

(b) To encourage other relevant sources of funding within the United Nations, such as the United Nations Foundation, to contribute to the restructuring of the Institute;

9. *Requests* the Secretary-General to include in his report to the General Assembly at its fifty-fifth session information on:

(a) Progress made in securing an adequate financial base for the operational viability of the Institute beyond 2000;

(b) Progress made in addressing the administrative anomalies noted in the report of the Joint Inspection Unit;

10. *Also requests* the Secretary-General to report to the Council at its substantive session of 2001 on the implementation of the present resolution.

ACABQ report. In December [A/55/677], the Advisory Committee on Administrative and Budgetary Questions (ACABQ) reported that the level of contributions to the INSTRAW Trust Fund had continued to decrease rapidly, declining from $1.9 million in 1992 to $602,150 in 1999. So far in 2000, the Institute had received $388,489 in contributions, and unpaid pledges amounted to $144,950. Based on a statement submitted by the Secretary-General [A/C.5/55/26], which estimated INSTRAW's financial requirements for 2001 at $1.3 million, compared with projected contributions of $90,000, ACABQ stated that it would be for the General Assembly to indicate the level and manner in which assistance should be provided to meet the anticipated shortfall.

GENERAL ASSEMBLY ACTION

On 23 December, the General Assembly, on a one-time, exceptional and emergency basis, decided to advance INSTRAW up to $800,000 from the regular budget for 2001 pending receipt of voluntary contributions. If voluntary contributions were insufficient to meet 2001 requirements, the advance would be considered a one-time-only subvention and those resources would be reported in the context of the performance report on the 2000-2001 programme budget. The Assembly emphasized the need for the Institute to pursue, as a priority activity, the expansion of its donor base (**decision 55/457**).

Also on 23 December [meeting 89], the Assembly, on the recommendation of the Third Committee [A/55/595 & Corr.1,2], adopted **resolution 55/219** without vote [agenda item 107].

The critical situation of the International Research and Training Institute for the Advancement of Women

The General Assembly,

Recalling its resolution 54/140 of 17 December 1999, in which it, inter alia, took note with appreciation of the proposal for a new working method of the International Research and Training Institute for the Advancement of Women through the establishment of an electronic Gender Awareness Information and Networking System, and urged Member States and intergovernmental and non-governmental organizations to contribute or consider increasing their contributions to the United Nations Trust Fund for the International Research and Training Institute for the Advancement of Women,

Reiterating paragraph 85 *(c)* of the outcome document of the twenty-third special session of the General Assembly, entitled "Women 2000: gender equality, development and peace for the twenty-first century", which called for support for national efforts, particularly in developing countries, for enlarged access to new information technology as part of the efforts to develop collaborative research, training and information dissemination, including through the Gender Awareness Information and Networking System developed by the Institute, while at the same time supporting traditional methods of information dissemination, research and training,

Taking note of Economic and Social Council resolution 2000/24 of 28 July 2000, in which article VI, paragraph 1, of the statute of the Institute was amended with the aim of allowing the Institute to fund its activities on the basis of voluntary contributions from States, intergovernmental and non-governmental organizations, foundations, including the United Nations Foundation, private sources and other sources, in accordance with article VII of the statute,

1. *Takes note* of the report of the Secretary-General, which provides an overview of the current situation of the International Research and Training Institute for the Advancement of Women;

2. *Acknowledges with appreciation* that, despite severe limitations, and in compliance with the request of the General Assembly in its resolution 54/140, the Institute translated the Gender Awareness Information and Networking System into Spanish and is in the process of initiating translation into other official languages of the United Nations;

3. *Expresses its appreciation* for the current efforts being made by the Office of the Under-Secretary-General for Economic and Social Affairs and the Office of the Special Adviser on Gender Issues and Advancement of Women of the Secretariat for the revitalization of the Institute;

4. *Expresses grave concern* over the following matters:

(a) Despite the revitalization and fund-raising efforts undertaken by the Secretary-General and the Institute, contributions have not reached the level required to enable the Institute to operate beyond 31 December 2000;

(b) The lack of resources to ensure the future of the only research and training institute for the advancement of women within the United Nations system;

5. *Requests* the Secretary-General to report to the General Assembly during its fifty-fifth session on additional possibilities to support the Institute in fulfilling its personnel and administrative needs in conformity with article VII of its statute;

6. *Decides*, in view of the difficult financial situation of the Institute, to provide it with financial assistance on a non-recurrent basis, in a manner to be determined, in order to enable it to continue its activities throughout 2001;

7. *Expresses its appreciation* to those Member States and intergovernmental and non-governmental organizations that continue to contribute to and support the activities of the Institute;

8. *Urges* Member States and intergovernmental and non-governmental organizations to continue to contribute to or consider increasing their contributions to the United Nations Trust Fund for the International Research and Training Institute for the Advancement of Women to facilitate the ongoing programmes and activities of the Institute;

9. *Invites* the Institute to intensify its campaign to raise funds and attract support from, inter alia, private sector foundations and corporations for its activities;

10. *Requests* the Secretary-General to report to the General Assembly at its fifty-sixth session on the implementation of the present resolution and to include in his reports on the activities of the Institute detailed information on the financial flows of the Trust Fund and the utilization of the resources of the Institute, in keeping with similar reports on such institutes as the United Nations African Institute for the Prevention of Crime and the Treatment of Offenders.

Chapter XI

Children, youth and ageing persons

In 2000, the United Nations Children's Fund (UNICEF) continued efforts to improve the situation of children worldwide, especially through advocacy and alliance-building activities and programmes aimed at confronting major challenges affecting children's well-being, including poverty, armed conflict, HIV/AIDS and discrimination.

UNICEF continued to focus on follow-up to the 1990 World Summit for Children, which set comprehensive goals for child survival and development. During the year, national, regional and global end-decade reviews were prepared for the special session of the General Assembly in 2001 to assess progress towards World Summit goals and consider future action. Following the first substantive meeting of the Preparatory Committee for the special session (May/June), the Assembly, in November, decided that the special session would be convened from 19 to 21 September 2001.

UNICEF efforts towards child protection were supported in 2000 by the Security Council and the General Assembly. The Council adopted a resolution on the impact of armed conflict on children (see p. 723), by which it called for all parties to abide by commitments made to ensure the protection of children in situations of armed conflict, as well as for the disarmament and demobilization of child soldiers. The Assembly adopted two optional protocols to the Convention on the Rights of the Child, on the involvement of children in armed conflict, and on the sale of children, child prostitution and child pornography (see p. 615). The Commission on Human Rights and the Assembly also took action to protect children's rights, including meeting the needs of the girl child (see pp. 714 and 1114 respectively).

United Nations activities concerning young people continued to focus on accelerating implementation of the 1995 World Programme of Action for Youth to the Year 2000 and Beyond, based on the results of two high-level global meetings convened in Portugal in 1998: the first World Conference of Ministers Responsible for Youth, which adopted the Lisbon Declaration on Youth Policies and Programmes, and the third session of the World Youth Forum of the United Nations System, which approved the Braga Youth Action Plan.

As follow-up to the 1999 International Year of Older Persons, the General Assembly decided to convene the Second World Assembly on Ageing in Madrid, Spain, in April 2002, on the occasion of the twentieth anniversary of the first World Assembly (Vienna, 1982), which had adopted the International Plan of Action on Ageing. The Second World Assembly was expected to adopt a revised Plan of Action and a new long-term strategy on ageing.

Children

United Nations Children's Fund

UNICEF's annual flagship reports assessed the well-being of children: *The State of the World's Children 2000* noted that despite the many steps forward, a number of the goals of the 1990 World Summit for Children [YUN 1990, p. 797] remained out of reach for hundreds of millions of children; *The Progress of Nations 2000* chronicled progress, challenges and constraints regarding early childhood care, immunization and HIV/AIDS, as well as the plight of children who were not reachable, and presented statistical data on a number of social indicators, such as child mortality rates, maternal mortality, malnutrition, education and health.

In 2000, UNICEF's global advocacy, partnerships, programme activities, data collection and analysis, and management and operations were oriented towards achievement of the objectives of the 1998-2001 medium-term plan [YUN 1998, p. 1093], within the context of the end-decade goals of the 1990 World Summit for Children and the 1989 Convention on the Rights of the Child, adopted by the General Assembly in resolution 44/25 [YUN 1989, p. 560] (see p. 614). UNICEF also took steps to consolidate its rights-based approach. Activities at all levels focused on the end-decade review of the 1990 World Summit goals, preparations for the General Assembly special session on children in 2001, and the preparation of the medium-term strategic plan for 2002-2005.

Among the events and activities in 2000 that offered UNICEF special opportunities to promote the rights of children, and to build and sustain partnerships and alliances were the adoption, by General Assembly **resolution 54/263** (see p. 615), of two optional protocols to the Convention on the Rights of the Child on children in armed conflict and on the sale of children, child prostitution and child pornography; the adoption of International Labour Organization (ILO) Convention No. 182 on the elimination of the worst forms of child labour [YUN 1999, p. 1388]; Security Council resolutions on women and children in armed conflict (see pp. 723 and 1113); the Millennium Summit (see p. 47); the International Conference on War-Affected Children (see p. 724); and the World Education Forum (see p. 1081). In addition, a major step forward for the Global Movement for Children was made with the launch of the Leadership Initiative in May; UNICEF worked with partners in the Movement to develop a set of 10 imperatives for children. However, several setbacks and long-standing problems impeded progress for children, such as persistent poverty, the high debt burdens of developing countries, the HIV/AIDS pandemic, armed conflicts and natural disasters.

UNICEF cooperated with 162 countries, areas and territories during the year: 46 in sub-Saharan Africa; 35 in Latin America and the Caribbean; 34 in Asia; 20 in the Middle East and North Africa; and 27 in Central and Eastern Europe, the Commonwealth of Independent States (CIS) and the Baltic States.

Programme expenditures totalled $1,021 million in 2000, of which 40 per cent was spent on child health; 18 per cent on education; 12 per cent on hygiene, water and environmental sanitation; 9 per cent on community development and gender programmes; 8 per cent on child protection; 7 per cent on child nutrition; and 6 per cent on assessment, analysis and monitoring. In addition, $90 million was spent on management, administration, write-offs and other charges. UNICEF operations in 2000 were described in the *2001 UNICEF Annual Report* and the annual report of its Executive Director [E/ICEF/2001/4 (Parts I & II)].

The UNICEF Executive Board held its first regular session of 2000 (31 January–3 February), the annual session (22-25 May) and the second regular session (18-20 September), all in New York [E/2000/34/Rev.1]. During those sessions, the Board adopted 18 decisions.

The Economic and Social Council, in **decision 2000/242** of 28 July, took note of the Board's report on its first regular session; an extract from the report on its 2000 annual session [E/2000/L.8] listing various decisions adopted; and the annual report of the Executive Director covering 1999

[E/2000/7], which was transmitted in accordance with a February decision of the Board [E/2000/34/Rev.1 (dec. 2000/4)].

In September [dec. 2000/18], the Executive Board adopted the dates and programme of work for its 2001 sessions. The first regular session would be held from 22 to 26 January, the annual session from 4 to 8 June, and the second regular session from 4 to 7 September.

Programme policies

In decisions related to UNICEF's programme policies, the Executive Board encouraged Governments to ratify the two optional protocols to the 1989 Convention on the Rights of the Child and asked the Executive Director to support States' efforts to do so [dec. 2000/11]. The Board requested the Executive Director to continue cooperating with UN agencies and other partners to promote achievement of the 1990 World Summit goals and to prepare for the General Assembly's special session in 2001 [dec. 2000/9]. The Board took note [dec. 2000/5] of the recommendations of the second meeting of the World Health Organization (WHO)/UNICEF/United Nations Population Fund (UNFPA) Coordinating Committee on Health [YUN 1999, p. 1151]. It approved an extension of the programme of cooperation with Rotary International's PolioPlus programme (2001-2005), in addition to an extension of the Vaccine Independence Initiative (2001-2005) [dec. 2000/14]. It endorsed proposals regarding the timing of various elements of the multi-year funding framework [dec. 2000/3] and approved the 2000-2003 financial medium-term plan [dec. 2000/15]. The medium-term plan was a rolling four-year plan updated every two years [YUN 1998, p. 1093], except for the financial plan, which was updated annually.

Follow-up to 1990 World Summit for Children

In March [E/ICEF/2000/11], UNICEF submitted to the Executive Board its annual progress report on follow-up to the 1990 World Summit for Children [YUN 1990, p. 797], covering 1999. The report presented an overall assessment of global trends and outlined the processes established to prepare for the end-decade review in 2001 (see p. 1132), including national reviews and ongoing efforts to strengthen national capacities in the collection and use of data for monitoring progress towards the Summit goals.

The report stated that, while progress had been made on some of the goals, overall achievements fell short of the global targets set for the end of the decade. Key challenges remained in addressing underlying conditions that had had an impact on children and their families, including debt servicing, declining levels of development aid, armed conflicts, natural disasters and the HIV/AIDS pandemic. Regarding the major goals of the Summit, the under-five mortality rate (U5MR) had declined, but the pace of the decline was slowing. Lack of progress in the reduction of maternal mortality during the 1990s was due, among other factors, to the overall status of women and the lack of respect for their rights. WHO projections suggested that malnutrition rates in children under five had decreased from 32 per cent in 1990 to 27 per cent in 2000, representing only one third of the targeted reduction. However, significant progress was made for some micronutrient goals, particularly the provision of iodized salt and vitamin A supplements. Slow progress in education revealed the decisive impact of prevailing economic and social disparities on access to school, completion of basic education and learning achievement. The number of people lacking access to safe drinking water and sanitation remained virtually unchanged over the decade. Child protection had gained ground, particularly in the development of international standards related to child labour, the sale of children, child prostitution and child pornography, and children in armed conflict.

In May [dec. 2000/9], the Executive Board urged Governments to adopt appropriate measures to accelerate progress towards the end-decade goals, including allocating the maximum resources possible for action, and asked them to conduct national and subnational reviews of such progress. The Executive Director was asked to support the efforts of Governments and civil society to achieve the end-decade goals and to improve national capacities for monitoring progress. She was also asked to cooperate with UN agencies and other partners at the national and international levels to promote the achievement of Summit goals and in preparing for the special session of the General Assembly in 2001, to support the Secretary-General in preparations for his report on the end-decade review in 2001, and to report in 2001.

General Assembly special session (2001)

In May [dec. 2000/6], the Executive Board, having considered the activities and budget for UNICEF secretariat support to the General Assembly special session on the follow-up to the World Summit for Children in 2001, approved the request and allocated the funds for global advocacy for children's rights and for the special session ($2.02 million), civil society mobilization ($1.37 million), children and youth mobilization

($875,000), regional advocacy and mobilization ($690,000) and the substantive secretariat work ($450,000). The Executive Director was asked to provide an interim report on the use of the funds in 2001 and a final report in 2002.

A March report [E/ICEF/2000/AB/L.2] to the Executive Board, on the activities and budget for UNICEF as the substantive secretariat to the General Assembly special session on children in 2001 and additional events, outlined UNICEF's substantive and technical support to the special session's preparatory process. The Executive Director requested that the Board approve additional funds amounting to $5.4 million for 2000-2001 to cover the preparations.

Preparatory Committee. The Preparatory Committee for the special session, established by General Assembly resolution 54/93 [YUN 1999, p. 1113], held an organizational session on 7 and 8 February [A/55/43 (Part I)] and a substantive session from 30 May to 2 June [ibid. (Part II)], both in New York.

In February, the Committee considered a report of the Secretary-General [A/AC.256/2] containing proposals on the scope of the Committee's review and consideration of further initiatives, and on the role of the UN system and non-governmental organizations (NGOs) in the preparatory process. The Committee adopted decisions related to its substantive session, NGO participation in its work and arrangements for future sessions.

In May/June, the Committee adopted a decision proposing the dates and venue of the special session, adopted the provisional agenda for its second substantive session and decided on arrangements for NGO accreditation and participation of associate members of the regional commissions. It agreed to authorize its Bureau, with the support of the substantive secretariat, to prepare a draft outcome document.

The Committee had before it an April report of the UNICEF Executive Director on emerging issues for children in the twenty-first century [A/AC.256/3-E/ICEF/2000/13], which analysed progress since the 1990 World Summit and examined the major challenges remaining, including deepening poverty and greater inequality; proliferating conflict and violence; the spread of HIV/AIDS; and continuing discrimination, particularly against women and girls. Proposals for future action were also outlined. The Committee also considered the views of the UNICEF Executive Board [A/AC.256/6] on the report. It reviewed a May report of the Secretary-General updating progress in the preparatory process [A/AC.256/5].

Report of Secretary-General. In response to General Assembly resolution 54/93 [YUN 1999,

p. 1113], the Secretary-General, in September [A/55/429], reported on the state of preparations for the special session at the national, regional and global levels. The Secretary-General indicated that strong momentum was building for the special session. The report highlighted elements of the draft outcome document to be considered at the special session. It described action taken to facilitate the participation of key actors—Governments, NGOs, children and adolescents, the UN system—in the special session, as well as activities taken to support regional reviews of follow-up to the 1990 World Summit.

GENERAL ASSEMBLY ACTION

On 20 November [meeting 69], the General Assembly adopted **resolution 55/26** [draft: A/55/L.34/Rev.1] without vote [agenda item 42].

Preparations for the special session on children

The General Assembly,

Recalling its resolutions 45/217 of 21 December 1990, in which it welcomed the adoption by the World Summit for Children of the World Declaration on the Survival, Protection and Development of Children and Plan of Action for Implementing the World Declaration on the Survival, Protection and Development of Children in the 1990s, 51/186 of 16 December 1996, 53/193 of 15 December 1998 and 54/93 of 7 December 1999,

Bearing in mind the nearly universal ratification of the Convention on the Rights of the Child,

Recalling the United Nations Millennium Declaration and, in particular, the paragraphs relevant to the situation of children,

Taking note of the report of the Secretary-General on the state of the preparations for the special session of the General Assembly in 2001 for follow-up to the World Summit for Children,

Taking note also of the reports of the Preparatory Committee for the Special Session on its organizational and first substantive sessions and of the decisions contained therein,

1. *Reaffirms* the commitments adopted by the heads of State and Government at the World Summit for Children on 30 September 1990, as contained in the World Declaration on the Survival, Protection and Development of Children and Plan of Action for Implementing the World Declaration on the Survival, Protection and Development of Children in the 1990s, and their appeal to give every child a better future;

2. *Also reaffirms* that the special session of the General Assembly in 2001, while reviewing the achievements in the implementation and results of the World Declaration and Plan of Action, will make a renewed commitment and consider future action for children in the forthcoming decade;

3. *Stresses* that the implementation of the Convention on the Rights of the Child contributes to the achievement of the goals of the World Summit for Children, and recommends that a thorough assessment of the ten years of implementation of the Convention be an essential element in the preparations for the special session;

4. *Welcomes* the initiatives and actions taken by Governments and relevant organizations, in particular the United Nations Children's Fund, as well as regional and subregional organizations, to review the progress achieved since the World Summit for Children, and in this regard encourages appropriate national, regional and international preparatory activities with a view to contributing to the preparations for the special session and building partnerships for and with children;

5. *Requests* the Secretary-General, taking into account the national reports to be submitted by Member States, to submit to the General Assembly at its special session, through the Preparatory Committee for the Special Session, a review of the implementation and results of the World Declaration and Plan of Action, including appropriate recommendations for further actions, which also elaborates on the best practices noted and obstacles encountered in the implementation process, as well as on measures to overcome those obstacles;

6. *Reaffirms* the need for the full and effective participation of Member States, and in this regard reiterates its invitation to heads of State and Government to participate in the special session;

7. *Welcomes* the assignment by heads of State and Government of personal representatives to the Preparatory Committee, and reiterates the invitation to heads of State and Government who have not assigned personal representatives to consider doing so;

8. *Reiterates its invitation* to States members of the specialized agencies that are not Members of the United Nations to participate in the work of the special session, in the capacity of observers;

9. *Reaffirms* the important role of all relevant actors, including non-governmental organizations, in implementing the Plan of Action, and stresses the need for their active involvement in the preparatory process, including in the work of the Preparatory Committee, and at the special session, the modalities for which are being addressed by the Preparatory Committee;

10. *Reiterates* the importance of a participatory process at the national, regional and international levels with a view, inter alia, to establishing partnerships among a broad range of actors, including children and young people, in order to raise momentum for the rights and needs of children;

11. *Highlights* the important role of children and young people in this process, and in this regard encourages States to facilitate and promote their active contribution to the preparatory process, including in the work of the Preparatory Committee, and the special session;

12. *Urges* all relevant organizations and bodies of the United Nations system, including the funds and programmes, specialized agencies and the international financial institutions, actively to participate in the preparations for the special session;

13. *Reiterates its invitation* to the Committee on the Rights of the Child to provide its input to the preparatory process and at the special session;

14. *Reiterates its invitation also* to all relevant experts, including the Special Representative of the Secretary-General for Children and Armed Conflict and the Special Rapporteur of the Commission on Human Rights on the sale of children, child prostitution and child pornography, to participate in the preparatory process

and the special session, in accordance with the established practice;

15. *Decides* to convene the special session of the General Assembly for follow-up to the World Summit for Children from 19 to 21 September 2001, and to refer to it as the "special session on children";

16. *Decides also* to convene two substantive sessions of the Preparatory Committee in New York during 2001, one from 29 January to 2 February and the other from 11 to 15 June;

17. *Decides further* to invite the associate members of the regional commissions listed in the footnote to participate as observers in the special session and its preparatory process, subject to the rules of procedure of the General Assembly;

18. *Reaffirms* the importance of the full participation of the least developed countries in the special session and the preparations for the session, and in this regard expresses its appreciation to the Governments which have made financial contributions to the trust fund established by the Secretary-General for that purpose, and invites the Governments which have not yet contributed to do so;

19. *Expresses its appreciation* to the Governments which have made financial contributions towards the preparatory activities undertaken by the United Nations Children's Fund as the substantive secretariat of the special session, and encourages Governments which have not yet contributed to do so;

20. *Decides* to include in the provisional agenda of its fifty-sixth session an item entitled "Follow-up to the outcome of the special session on children".

On 23 December, the Assembly, by **decision 55/458**, decided that the agenda item on the special session would remain for consideration during its resumed fifty-fifth (2001) session.

Emergency assistance

A March report [E/ICEF/2000/12], prepared in response to a 1997 Executive Board request [YUN 1997, p. 1209], described UNICEF's role in unstable situations, such as armed conflict, disasters and violent situations. UNICEF implemented programme activities for children and women, emphasizing advocacy, assessment and coordination, and care and protection. In those efforts, UNICEF implemented an integrated approach in meeting the rights and needs of children and women in crisis, taking into account the relationships between physical and emotional security, social and cognitive development, and health and nutritional status. The approach highlighted UNICEF's commitment to providing support to children and women affected by unstable situations, through mutually reinforcing actions in the areas of humanitarian policy, global advocacy and humanitarian response.

The report reviewed UNICEF's initial response to the protection and care of children in unstable situations at the programme level, as well as the

implementation of core corporate commitments (CCCs) to ensure effective action at the outset of crises. The CCCs, which were identified at the Martigny Global Consultation, convened by UNICEF in 1998 to formulate recommendations to improve UNICEF responsiveness to children in unstable situations, covered rapid assessment, coordination, and programme and operational commitments. Since the Consultation, improvements had been made in coordinated action in support of children and women; assessment and vulnerability analysis; effective delivery of UNICEF CCCs and competencies to ensure life-saving support, in order to advocate and sustain support throughout the transition from relief to development; and planning, management and monitoring of programme responses to the rights and needs of children and women. Annexed to the report was a detailed description of the CCCs.

Maurice Pate Award

The Executive Director recommended that the Maurice Pate Award for 2000 be presented to an NGO, the Rural Family Support Organization (RUFAMSO) of Jamaica, and that $25,000 be allocated from general resources for that purpose. Established in 1966 [YUN 1966, p. 385], the Award was presented to RUFAMSO for advancing the survival, protection and development of young children and adolescents in Jamaica through a holistic and integrated programme of family support. On 25 May [dec. 2000/10], the Executive Board decided to present the Award to RUFAMSO and approved the allocation.

UNICEF programmes by region

During 2000, regional UNICEF expenditure in support of programmes totalled $1,021 million, of which $392 million (38 per cent) was spent for programmes in sub-Saharan Africa; $309 million (30 per cent) for programmes in Asia; $89 million (9 per cent) for programmes in Central and Eastern Europe, CIS and the Baltic States; $86 million (8 per cent) for programmes in the Middle East and North Africa; and $84 million (8 per cent) for programmes in the Americas and the Caribbean. In addition, $61 million (6 per cent) was spent for interregional programmes. Total programme expenditure represented an increase of 5 per cent over 1999.

As in previous years, the majority of UNICEF resources was spent in 63 low-income countries with a per capita gross national product of $785 or less. Those countries had a total child population of 1.3 billion, or about 69 per cent of all children worldwide, and received 67 per cent of programme expenditure, which was 1 per cent higher than in 1999. About 35 per cent of UNICEF programme expenditure went to countries where the U5MR was classified as very high or high.

Field visits

In March, members of the UNICEF Executive Board visited Ghana and Namibia to learn more about the strategies adopted by UNICEF offices in relation to basic service delivery, capacity-building and strengthening of ownership at the community level. The team found that the Governments of both countries had played a strong role in the coordination of activities in various sectors and in harmonizing the different types of support provided. Mid-term reviews of the two country programmes had resulted in changes that better adapted the programmes of the country offices to national priorities. In Ghana, UNICEF had responded to marked disparities in socio-economic indicators by geographically refocusing its programme to target the most disadvantaged and vulnerable groups; improve coverage and delivery of social services in the areas of health, education, water and sanitation, and household food security; and promote capacity-building in those sectors. In Namibia, where HIV/AIDS had become the primary cause of death, UNICEF had taken the lead within the UN system in advocating HIV/AIDS-related activities in the area of capacity-building and technical assistance and had included HIV/AIDS components in existing projects. Projects in both countries had been implemented in the context of a community-based approach to improve sustainability and ownership by local people. The team concluded that country programmes reflected the special situation of children in each country and the decentralized structure of UNICEF had proved to be very helpful in that regard. UNICEF was also a leading partner in key areas relating to children's rights and had been working effectively in the priority areas of early childhood care and adolescence.

A second delegation visited China from 19 March to 1 April, where it observed that the key problems in the UNICEF programming environment were related to problems of equity, quality and gender, as well as to the limitations of cost recovery in social services and the need to continue developing and refining social policies. Regarding equity, the Government was concerned about growing gaps in basic social services between the eastern and western parts of the country. Although remarkable achievements were noted in basic services, particularly education, the challenge was to upgrade their quality. Some pro-

gress was made regarding the status of women and girls, but gender imbalance persisted in the remote areas for various reasons, including old-age support and security concerns. Gender imbalance was particularly obvious in the area of basic education. As to the limitations of cost recovery in social services, the introduction of user fees could create a hardship for the poor or put the services out of their reach. The delegation observed the need for qualified and trained social workers as part of the development of social safety nets. Among emerging challenges were issues of social protection, HIV/AIDS and the continuing problem of rural water and sanitation.

The Executive Board, in May [dec. 2000/8], took note of the reports on the field visits.

UNICEF programmes by sector

The major share of UNICEF programme expenditure continued to be in the areas of health ($358 million or 35 per cent), basic education ($160 million or 16 per cent) and programme support ($136 million or 13 per cent). Significant shares also went to water and environmental sanitation ($104 million or 10 per cent), community development and gender programmes ($84 million or 8 per cent), child protection ($70 million or 7 per cent), nutrition ($58 million or 6 per cent) and programme assessment, evaluation and monitoring ($51 million or 5 per cent).

A total of $26.2 million was available to country programmes in 2000 from the global set-aside of 7 per cent of regular resources. Based on the criteria set out in a 1997 Executive Board decision establishing the set-aside [YUN 1997, p. 1220], allocations were made by the Executive Director for strategic programming efforts in support of programme priorities and for additional special needs. The largest portion of funds—38 per cent of the total—was spent on immunization programming, as was the case in 1999. The portion of the funds utilized to support AIDS-related programming increased to 23 per cent in 2000, compared with 11 per cent in 1999. In addition, 15 per cent of the global set-aside was used for malaria prevention and control while the remainder was earmarked for special purposes, including support for various programmes in East Timor (8 per cent), Bangladesh (2 per cent), Afghanistan (2 per cent) and Jamaica (1 per cent). Overall, 53 per cent of the set-aside was allocated to sub-Saharan Africa, and 26 per cent went to Asia.

Child and adolescent health

UNICEF activities to reduce childhood death and disease, improve early childhood care, reduce maternal mortality, prevent childhood disability and improve adolescent health continued to focus on achieving the targets and goals established at the 1990 World Summit for Children [YUN 1990, p. 797], including immunization, HIV/AIDS prevention, malaria control and nutritional support. In 2000, UNICEF, as a Board member of the Global Alliance for Vaccines and Immunization (GAVI), made key contributions to the GAVI goals of universal access to, and use of, immunization services and accelerated introduction of new and underused vaccines in the poorest countries. UNICEF remained the main vaccine supplier to developing countries, buying vaccines for 75 per cent of those children. UNICEF's Vaccine Independence Initiative aimed to help Governments build and sustain their own immunization programmes. Through the Initiative, Kazakhstan and Turkmenistan covered the costs of their children's vaccine needs for the first time in 2000. As a result of UNICEF partnerships, some 12 million women were immunized against tetanus, a disease that put them at risk of dying during or after childbirth; the number of measles cases in southern and central Iraq declined from 10,000 in 1999 to just 678 in 2000; and the lives of almost 1 million children might have been saved since 1998 by the distribution of vitamin A capsules, an increasingly common add-on to immunization campaigns.

Through the Global Polio Eradication Initiative, a campaign spearheaded by UNICEF, WHO, Rotary International, the United States Centers for Disease Control and national Governments, some 1 billion children had been vaccinated against polio in the past two years, placing the world on track for certification as polio-free by 2005. An unprecedented 550 million children under the age of five were immunized during 2000, including 76 million in West Africa. In October, 36 countries in Asia and the Western Pacific region were declared polio-free.

The Roll-Back Malaria Initiative, led by UNICEF, WHO, the United Nations Development Programme (UNDP) and the World Bank, promoted the distribution of bednets treated with insecticides and anti-malarial drugs in 37 countries. Within Africa, UNICEF procured more than 1 million bednets and helped to develop anti-malarial policies. Community-based health and nutrition programmes were being supported in some 70 countries.

During the year, early childhood care and development strategies succeeded in improving the practices of some 32,500 caregivers in Nepal, training 8,000 parents in Jordan and training counsellors and preparing national infant feeding policy guidelines in several countries in Eastern and Southern Africa. UNICEF supported sur-

veys on childhood disabilities in 10 countries, and continued to promote universal salt iodization to eliminate iodine deficiency disorders. In addition, landmine awareness efforts were supported in some 24 countries, including Azerbaijan, Cambodia, Eritrea and Lebanon, and the northern Caucasus.

As part of the Safe Motherhood Initiative and an alliance for women's reproductive health, UNICEF supported maternal health programmes in 111 countries and provided training for birth attendants in some 71 countries. The distribution of iron folate and other micronutrient supplements was supported in 59 countries and the fortification of commercial foods in 14 countries. However, the World Summit goal of reducing global low birth-weight rates to less than 10 per cent had proved to be one of the most difficult to achieve. Some of the constraints facing efforts were country-specific, such as resistance to supplementation or problems associated with monitoring weight within 24 hours of birth. More than 100 UNICEF country programmes included a focus on young people's health, development and participation, mostly through life skills and health education as well as the provision of youth-friendly health services. Much of UNICEF mobilization and communication efforts regarding HIV/AIDS focused on young people, with support provided in 2000 for innovative outreach programmes in Haiti and the United Republic of Tanzania. In addition, pilot programmes were initiated in several countries for the prevention of mother-to-child transmission of the virus.

Basic education

In 2000, school enrolment rates continued to increase, despite continuing challenges to the goals of improving access to and the quality of basic education, such as instability and crisis, the AIDS pandemic, persistent poverty, early marriage and a large number of working children. UNICEF assisted 390,000 more girls to enter school in Ethiopia, 130,000 more children (30 per cent girls) in Afghanistan and 11,500 children in Yemen. Some 12,000 working children were reintegrated into schools in Bolivia. In Egypt, retention rates to the fifth grade reached 95 per cent in UNICEF-supported community schools. About 10,000 schools in 46 countries improved the learning environment with UNICEF support, while almost 270,000 teachers and school principals participated in UNICEF-assisted training programmes. In Zambia, UNICEF helped set up 250 community schools for thousands of AIDS-orphaned and other vulnerable children; in Bangladesh, more than 200,000 urban working children were enrolled in learning centres supported by the Fund. As a result of the joint efforts of UNICEF, the World Food Programme, NGOs and other partners to rebuild East Timor's education system, some 95 per cent of school-age children were enrolled by mid-2000. In addition, UNICEF-supplied Schools-in-a-Box brought learning basics to 50,000 students.

UNICEF was asked to lead the 10-year Girls' Education Initiative of the United Nations, launched at the 2000 World Education Forum in Dakar (see p. 1081). During the year, an increase in girls' enrolment rates was reported in more than 20 countries. In Pakistan, some 4,500 girls aged 12 to 18 were trained as educators through UNICEF support and helped establish 950 home schools for children, mostly girls, in need of basic education or extra help. Some 10,000 schools in 46 countries improved the learning environment with UNICEF support, while almost 270,000 teachers and school principals participated in UNICEF-assisted training programmes.

Protection from armed conflict, exploitation and abuse

UNICEF continued to work with various partners to provide protection, relief and rehabilitation to young victims of war, abuse and all forms of violence. New child labour legislation or plans were introduced in some 20 countries, mostly in Latin America and the Caribbean. Efforts were also directed at promoting birth registration, which was increasingly recognized as having an important role in the realization of children's rights. During the year, UNICEF-supported campaigns resulted in the registration of more than 1 million births in Bangladesh and some 322,000 births in Ecuador.

UNICEF provided assistance to some 50 countries in order to ensure greater consistency of juvenile justice systems with the 1989 Convention on the Rights of the Child, adopted by the General Assembly in resolution 44/25 [YUN 1989, p. 560]. In 2000, juvenile justice laws were reformed in Lebanon; child and adolescent defence systems in Peru processed 120,000 cases of violation of children's rights; and UNICEF supported training of police, judges and social workers in Iran.

Humanitarian relief efforts—including rehabilitation of basic health care, education, nutrition, and water and sanitation systems, usually accompanied by major shipments of critically needed supplies—benefited children of displaced and returnee populations in the Congo, the Democratic Republic of the Congo, Eritrea and Sierra Leone, and the UN-administered Kosovo province of the Federal Republic of Yugoslavia, as well as victims of drought and floods in Ethiopia, Madagascar and Mozambique. UNICEF supported mine-awareness efforts in 24 countries during 2000.

UNICEF, in collaboration with NGOs and agencies of the UN system, supported the organization of special events on strategies for delaying marriage of girls; ending female genital mutilation; combating sexual exploitation of girls; and identifying the role of men as partners in ending violence. It supported the elimination of female genital mutilation in 16 countries, including Burkina Faso, Djibouti, Egypt, Ethiopia, Kenya, Mali and Senegal.

Prevention of gender discrimination

UNICEF continued to highlight activities aimed at eliminating gender inequalities in childhood, ending violence against women and girls and promoting their rights. Sensitization seminars were organized for nearly 90,000 women and their husbands in Bangladesh. Local leaders, child protection officers, law officers and children received gender and child rights training in 66 districts in Viet Nam; similar training was provided to 4,800 community leaders in Uganda and to 85,000 village government members in two states in India. In Peru, UNICEF supported an initiative aimed at breaking patterns of gender socialization and stereotyping at an early age and provided gender-sensitive parent education in Jamaica, Maldives, Mexico, Nepal, the Philippines and Viet Nam. UNICEF worked with local women activists, NGOs and other UN agencies to support innovative programmes against domestic violence in almost all regions. The Fund's advocacy efforts resulted in the declaration of honour killings as a criminal offence in Pakistan and the launch of campaigns against violence and abuse in Guyana and the Philippines.

Poverty reduction

The UNICEF strategy on poverty reduction asserted that it must begin with children to prevent lifelong damage. In 2000, UNICEF launched the booklet *Poverty Reduction Begins with Children* and organized panel discussions with ILO and the World Bank.

UNICEF continued as the lead agency for the 20/20 Initiative, endorsed by the 1995 World Summit for Social Development [YUN 1995, p. 1113]. The precepts of the 20/20 Initiative had become better known and understood, and the principle that it encapsulated—joint and equal partnership between donor and developing countries to accelerate improvements in human well-being and capacity—had gained legitimacy as an essential element in the overall strategy to reduce poverty.

Studies had been prepared in 40 countries to assess the percentage of social budgets and official development assistance allocated to basic social services.

In October, UNICEF collaborated with the World Bank on the Poverty Reduction Strategy Paper/Heavily Indebted Poor Countries (HIPC) Initiative. The enhanced HIPC Initiative had created an opportunity for policy dialogue and the potential for support of additional programmes benefiting children.

Organizational and administrative matters

UNICEF finances

In 2000, UNICEF income amounted to $1,139 million, which was $27 million higher than the $1,112 million estimated in the 2000 financial medium-term plan and $21 million more than 1999 income. UNICEF derived its income entirely from voluntary contributions, primarily from two sources: contributions of Governments and intergovernmental organizations (64 per cent ($725 million)); and non-governmental and private sector groups and individuals (32 per cent ($366 million)). Another 4 per cent ($48 million) came from other sources.

Budget appropriations

In January [dec. 2000/2], the Executive Board approved the allocation of additional regular resources totalling $9,967,000 to fund programmes in 10 countries as well as a one-year extension of country programmes for Egypt and for Malaysia, as recommended by the Executive Director [E/ICEF/2000/P/L.19].

In September [dec. 2000/12], the Board approved the Executive Director's recommendations for funding for 33 country programmes, one subregional programme for Palestinian children and women and four programmes with other resources only [E/ICEF/2000/P/L.27], amounting to the following respective amounts for regular resources and other resources for each region: Africa, $129.9 million and $282.3 million; Americas and the Caribbean, $9.3 million and $49.2 million; Asia, $221.6 million and $420.6 million; Central and Eastern Europe, CIS and the Baltic States, $11.3 million and $38 million; and the Middle East and North Africa, $10.8 million and $28.5 million. Also in September [dec. 2000/13], the Board approved the allocation of additional regular resources totalling $41.7 million for programmes in 21 countries, as recommended by the Executive Director [E/ICEF/2000/P/L.46].

On 19 September [dec. 2000/15], the Board approved the Executive Director's proposal regarding the 2000-2003 financial medium-term plan [E/ICEF/2000/AB/L.5 & Corr.1] as a framework of projections, including the preparation of up to $640 million in programme expenditures from regular resources to be submitted to the Board in 2001. The amount was subject to the availability of resources and to the condition that estimates of income and expenditure in the medium-term plan remained valid.

On the recommendation of the Executive Director [E/ICEF/2000/P/L.47], in September [dec. 2000/14], the Board approved a five-year extension (2001-2005) of the programme of cooperation with the PolioPlus Programme of Rotary International and an increase of $20 million in funding from other resources, subject to the availability of specific-purpose contributions from Rotary International. A five-year extension (2001-2005) of the Vaccine Independence Initiative was also approved, with an increase of $10 million from other resources, for a total of $20 million.

Audits

A July report of the Office of Internal Audit (OIA) [E/ICEF/2000/AB/L.7] summarized the results of audits completed in 1999. Consistent with the field-based emphasis of the UNICEF structure, the focus of OIA audit efforts in 1999 was directed towards the assessment of risks and controls in field offices. The report observed that overall control in almost all UNICEF field locations continued to be satisfactory, although some offices experienced transitional challenges in the introduction of the Programme Manager System and its reporting features. The Executive Board, on 20 September [dec. 2000/17], took note of the report.

Resource mobilization strategy

In response to a 1999 Executive Board decision [YUN 1999, p. 1120] requesting UNICEF to develop a multi-year funding framework (MYFF) that conceptually integrated organizational priorities and major areas of action, resources, budget and outcomes, the Executive Director submitted a report [E/ICEF/2000/5] describing the main building blocks of the MYFF in current practice and how they functioned. It presented an outline of the system UNICEF intended to build, including the actions planned or under way to strengthen each element of the MYFF, as well as the interlinkages among them. The report proposed possible changes in the timing of presentation of MYFF elements that called for the Board's first regular session to focus largely on the budget, financial resources and strategic issues in programme cooperation; the second regular session to focus on planning issues; and the annual session to consolidate all elements of reporting on results, including resource mobilization results, and provide opportunities to present and discuss policy issues.

In February [dec. 2000/3], the Board endorsed the proposed timing of the presentations of the various MYFF elements, with due regard for the extra provisions regarding proposed changes to the support budget. In that regard, the Board asked the Executive Director to submit the proposed modifications to the budget process to the Advisory Committee on Administrative and Budgetary Questions (ACABQ) prior to the Board's 2000 annual session (see below). The Board endorsed the proposal that the next medium-term strategic plan be presented in 2001 for a fixed period of four years (2002-2005); at that occasion, the timing of the presentation of the MYFF elements would also be reviewed. The Executive Director was asked to update the programmatic content of the medium-term strategic plan during the four-year period.

In accordance with decision 2000/3 (see above), the Executive Director submitted a March report [E/ICEF/2000/AB/L.3], proposing modifications to the budget process. Describing constraints in the existing process, she recommended that the biennial support budget be submitted to the first regular session of the first year of the biennium and that the Executive Director have the authority to manage the support management structure within the approved appropriation.

An April report of ACABQ [E/ICEF/2000/AB/L.4], noting that UNICEF did not have a mechanism to deal with unforeseen expenditures, recommended that the Executive Director examine the Fund's current practice and report to the Board through ACABQ on possible policy options. ACABQ also asked her to review all elements and components of the present planning, programming and budget process to identify areas that might be streamlined, as well as reported on less often.

In May [dec. 2000/7], the Board asked UNICEF to conduct consultations with its members and the Committee on Conferences with a view to enabling the Board to approve future biennial support budgets before the end of the preceding biennium, while maintaining the principle that the plan drove the budget. It decided that, within the approved support budget appropriations, the Executive Director had the authority to adjust the support management structure to meet programme and medium-term strategic plan priorities, with the proviso that the establishment of any post above the level of P-5 would require prior approval by the Board. Any changes in the support structure in terms of the grading and number of posts would be reported in the Executive Director's annual report to the Board.

Private Sector Division

In a financial report on the Private Sector Division (PSD) for the year ending 31 December 2000 [E/ICEF/2001/AB/L.6], UNICEF stated that the total net income from PSD activities for the year was $163.3 million for regular resources, compared to $202.9 million in 1999. That amount included $41.7 million from the sale of UNICEF greeting cards and other products, $154.1 million from private sector fund-raising activities, and an offset of $32.5 million for other charges and adjustments. In addition, $146.2 million ($153.5 million in 1999) was raised from private sector fund-raising activities that were earmarked for other resources. The net consolidated income, including both regular and other resources, totalled $309.5 million ($356.4 million in 1999).

The Executive Board, in January [dec. 2000/1], approved for 2000 budgeted expenditures of $93.1 million for the PSD work plan, as presented in the proposed budget [E/ICEF/2000/AB/L.1]. The Board authorized the Executive Director to incur expenditures as outlined in the proposed budget and to increase expenditures up to the proposed maximum ($95.1 million) should there be an apparent net proceeds increase from product sales and/or private sector fund-raising, and, accordingly, to reduce expenditures should the net proceeds decrease. She was also authorized to redeploy resources between the various budget lines up to 10 per cent of the amounts approved, and to spend additional funds between Board sessions, when necessary, up to the amount caused by currency fluctuations, to implement the 2000 work plan.

In related action, the Board approved the changes in posts with a net decrease of six posts, as indicated in the proposed budget; established the Nordic Investment Programme, which included four countries, with a budget of $4 million for 2000; authorized the Executive Director to incur expenditures in the 2000 fiscal period related to the cost of goods delivered for the 2001 fiscal year up to $37.6 million; and approved the PSD medium-term plan.

In September [dec. 2000/16], the Board took note of the PSD financial report and statements for the year ended 31 December 1999 [YUN 1999, p. 1120].

Coordinating Committee on Health

The second meeting of the WHO/UNICEF/UNFPA Coordinating Committee on Health (Geneva, 2-3 December 1999) [E/ICEF/2000/7] made recommendations related to improving the coverage, scope and quality of immunization services and enhancing follow-up to the 1994 International Conference on Population and Development [YUN 1994, p. 955], especially regarding maternal disease and death, adolescent health and development, mother-to-child transmission of HIV/AIDS and coordination of follow-up activities. The Committee also reviewed resolutions and decisions adopted by the governing bodies of the three organizations.

The Executive Board, on 3 February [dec. 2000/5], took note of the Committee's recommendations.

Youth

Implementation of the World
Programme of Action for Youth

In 2000, United Nations policies and programmes involving youth continued to focus on implementation of the 1995 World Programme of Action for Youth to the Year 2000 and Beyond, adopted by the General Assembly in resolution 50/81 [YUN 1995, p. 1211]. The Programme of Action addressed the problems faced by youth worldwide and outlined ways to enhance youth participation in national and international policy- and decision-making. The 1998 Lisbon Declaration on Youth Policies and Programmes, adopted at the first World Conference of Ministers Responsible for Youth [YUN 1998, p. 1103], outlined further policy commitments by Governments in the areas of national youth policy, participation, development, peace, education, employment, health and drug abuse. Just prior to the World Conference, the third session of the World Youth Forum of the United Nations System adopted the Braga (Portugal) Youth Action Plan, a set of goals and actions aimed at fostering youth participation for human development. The Plan and the outcomes of the World Conference were submitted to the Assembly in 1999.

Report of Secretary-General. The Commission for Social Development, at its thirty-eighth session (New York, 8-17 February, 14 and 17 March) [E/2000/26 & Corr.1], considered a report of the Secretary-General [A/AC.253/13-E/CN.5/2000/2] on the implementation of the outcome of the 1995 World Summit for Social Development [YUN 1995, p. 1114] that described action taken by Governments to integrate groups at risk of marginalization, including children and youth.

Based on reports received from 74 Governments, the report observed that although many countries had made progress in improving the situation of youth, much remained to be done. The social marginalization of youth was a problem of increasing severity in many countries. One important source was unemployment and barriers to entering the labour market. Persistent high unemployment among youth had led to exclusion and alienation from society and in some cases to increased crime, drug abuse and violence. There was an increased awareness among Governments of the need for comprehensive youth policies. Many Governments had formulated national plans of action for the integration of youth and increased youth employment. A large percentage of Member States had adopted cross-sectoral national youth policies and implemented national plans of action for youth. Other initiatives included programmes to facilitate transition from the educational system to the labour market, efforts to enhance youth entrepreneurship and self-employment, improved social services for youth, increased youth participation in public affairs and measures to combat and prevent illicit drug use among young people.

Ageing persons

Follow-up to 1999
International Year of Older Persons

Report of Secretary-General. At its thirty-eighth session (New York, 8-17 February, 14 and 17 March [E/2000/26 & Corr.1], the Commission for Social Development considered a report of the Secretary-General [E/CN.5/2000/4] on follow-up to the 1999 International Year of Older Persons [YUN 1999, p. 1124], designated by the General Assembly in a 1992 Proclamation on Ageing contained in resolution 47/5 [YUN 1992, p. 889]. The Year aimed to promote the United Nations Principles for Older Persons, adopted by the Assembly in resolution 46/91 [YUN 1991, p. 698].

The report presented possible options for the review and update of the International Plan of Action on Ageing, adopted by the 1982 World Assembly on Ageing [YUN 1982, p. 1184]. It summarized the views of States, organizations of the UN system and NGOs on the feasibility and desirability of convening a Second World Assembly on Ageing in 2002 and the development of a long-term strategy on ageing for the consideration of the Commission; the Assembly, in resolution 54/24 [YUN 1999, p. 1125], had entrusted the Commission with revising the Plan and developing the long-term strategy. The report contained a possible chronology of events leading to the proposed Second World Assembly.

The report concluded that there was broad support and interest among those countries expressing a view on convening a World Assembly in 2002. Various opinions were expressed regarding the revision, updating or adjusting of the 1982 International Plan of Action and the development of a long-term strategy on ageing. Initial draft texts would need to be submitted to the Commission in 2001, with a view to their being finalized in 2002. The Commission would need to make a decision on postponing the fifth review and appraisal of the Plan of Action, mandated to take place in 2001, and on a review of the global targets on ageing, should it decide to proceed with the revision of the Plan of Action.

Commission action. In February [E/2000/26 & Corr.1 (dec. 38/100)], the Commission for Social Development decided to establish a working group to meet in 2001 and 2002 to revise the 1982 International Plan of Action on Ageing and develop a long-term strategy on ageing for presentation to the Second World Assembly on Ageing. The Secretary-General was asked to present to the Commission in 2001 a first draft of a long-term strategy on ageing and a draft revised plan of action, as requested in resolution 54/24. The Economic and Social Council was requested to extend until 2002 the mandate of the Commission's consultative group for the preparation for the International Year of Older Persons, in order to serve as a forum for exchanging views on preparations for the Second World Assembly as a follow-up to the 1999 International Year. The Commission decided to postpone the fifth review and appraisal of the International Plan of Action until finalization of the activities for the revision of the Plan and the development of the long-term strategy.

ECONOMIC AND SOCIAL COUNCIL ACTION

On 3 May [meeting 7], the Economic and Social Council adopted **resolution 2000/1** [draft: E/2000/L.4] without vote [agenda item 2].

The Economic and Social Council

Recommends to the General Assembly the adoption of the following draft resolution:

[For text, see General Assembly resolution 54/262 below.]

GENERAL ASSEMBLY ACTION

On 25 May [meeting 97], the General Assembly adopted **resolution 54/262** [draft: A/54/L.85] without vote [agenda item 106].

Follow-up to the International Year of Older Persons: Second World Assembly on Ageing

The General Assembly,

Recalling the World Assembly on Ageing, held at Vienna in 1982, which adopted the International Plan of Action on Ageing,

Reaffirming the importance of the United Nations Principles for Older Persons, as adopted by its resolution 46/91 of 16 December 1991,

Recalling its resolution 54/24 of 10 November 1999 and previous resolutions on ageing and the International Year of Older Persons,

Acknowledging the initiatives undertaken and the momentum generated, at all levels, towards addressing the challenge of ageing and the concerns and contributions of ageing and older persons by the celebration of the International Year of Older Persons, and convinced of the necessity of ensuring an action-oriented follow-up to the International Year of Older Persons with a view to sustaining that momentum,

Recalling resolution 37/2 adopted by the Commission for Social Development at its thirty-seventh session,

Bearing in mind that, under its resolution 54/24, the General Assembly has entrusted the Commission for Social Development with the revision of the International Plan of Action on Ageing and the elaboration of a long-term strategy on ageing,

Recalling the offer made at the fifty-fourth session of the General Assembly by the Government of Spain to host a second World Assembly on Ageing in 2002,

1. *Decides* to convene the Second World Assembly on Ageing in 2002, on the occasion of the twentieth anniversary of the first World Assembly on Ageing held at Vienna, to be devoted to the overall review of the outcome of the first World Assembly, as well as to the adoption of a revised plan of action and a long-term strategy on ageing, encompassing its periodic reviews, in the context of a society for all ages;

2. *Stresses* that, in fulfilling these objectives, the Second World Assembly should give particular attention, inter alia, to:

(a) Action-oriented measures to be taken by societies in a comprehensive response to the current ageing processes, on the basis of the best practices and lessons learned during the International Year of Older Persons, and bearing in mind the social, cultural and economic realities of each society;

(b) Linkages between ageing and development, with particular attention to the needs and perspectives of developing countries;

(c) Measures to mainstream ageing within the context of current global development agendas;

(d) Appropriate forms of public and private partnership, including with non-governmental organizations, at all levels, for building societies for all ages;

(e) Measures to strengthen the solidarity between generations, keeping in mind the needs of both older and younger generations;

3. *Accepts* the offer of the Government of Spain to host the Second World Assembly on Ageing, and decides that the Second World Assembly shall be held in Spain in April 2002;

4. *Invites* all States Members of the United Nations, members of the specialized agencies and observers, as well as other intergovernmental organizations, in accordance with the established practice of the General Assembly, to participate at a high level in the Second World Assembly;

5. *Invites* non-governmental organizations in the field of ageing, as well as research institutions and representatives of the private sector, to participate in and

contribute to the Second World Assembly and its preparatory process, including organizing meetings and studies related to the themes of the Second World Assembly;

6. *Decides* that the Commission for Social Development shall serve as the preparatory committee for the Second World Assembly on Ageing and, as such, shall be open to the participation of all States Members of the United Nations, members of the specialized agencies and observers, in accordance with the established practice of the General Assembly;

7. *Requests* the Secretary-General to consult Governments, intergovernmental organizations and non-governmental organizations to elicit their views on progress in and obstacles to the implementation of the International Plan of Action on Ageing, as well as on priority issues to be addressed in a revised plan of action and a long-term strategy on ageing;

8. *Invites* the Secretary-General to establish a technical committee, funded through voluntary contributions, to assist him in the formulation of proposals to be submitted during the preparatory process to the Commission for Social Development;

9. *Stresses* that the technical committee should ensure, in its composition, an adequate geographical balance among its members, who will serve in a personal capacity, and the integration of multidisciplinary backgrounds, including perspectives from the research institutions, non-governmental organizations in the field of ageing, the private sector and older persons themselves;

10. *Requests* the Secretary-General to encourage the active participation of the United Nations programmes and funds and the specialized agencies and related organizations in the preparations for the Second World Assembly, *inter alia*, within the framework of the Administrative Committee on Coordination and its subsidiary machinery;

11. *Invites* all relevant organs of the United Nations system, including the regional commissions, funds and programmes, the specialized agencies and the Bretton Woods institutions, to participate in the Second World Assembly and its preparatory process;

12. *Encourages* Member States and other actors to support the preparatory activities by the Secretariat so as to ensure the quality of the outcome of the Second World Assembly and to provide voluntary contributions to the United Nations Trust Fund for Ageing in support of preparatory activities of the Second World Assembly, including the participation of least developed countries;

13. *Requests* the Secretary-General to report to the General Assembly at its fifty-fifth session on the implementation of the present resolution under the item devoted to social development.

Report of Secretary-General. In accordance with resolution 54/262 (see p. 1141), the Secretary-General, in a July report [A/55/167], reviewed activities and developments related to follow-up to the 1999 International Year of Older Persons, including initial preparations for the Second World Assembly on Ageing (2002).

The Secretary-General drew attention to two meetings held as follow-up activities. The Eco-

nomic Commission for Africa convened an expert group meeting on sustainable social structures in a society for all ages (Addis Ababa, Ethiopia, 2-5 May), and the first international conference on rural ageing (West Virginia, United States, June) was held on the theme "A global challenge". He described activities taken to implement the conceptual framework developed by the UN programme on ageing to facilitate exploration of a society for all ages, which was built on a four-dimensional framework, comprising the situation of older persons, lifelong individual development, multigenerational relationships and the interplay between population ageing and development.

The preparatory process leading up to the Second World Assembly, which would be devoted to a review of the first World Assembly, as well as the adoption of a revised plan of action and a long-term strategy on ageing, was under way. The Secretary-General observed that, while the essence of the 1982 Plan of Action remained useful, its content and policy recommendations were in need of a fresh and updated approach in order to contend with current demographic and socio-economic realities. The UN programme on ageing had initiated the revision process, beginning with the development and mailing of questionnaires to Member States, intergovernmental organizations, UN system members and NGOs. An analysis of the questionnaires would be submitted to the Commission for Social Development in 2001.

The first meeting of the Technical Committee for the Second World Assembly on Ageing (Frankfurt, Germany, 13-16 June), an expert group established by the Secretary-General, considered ways to ensure that ageing in developing countries was fully integrated into the revised Plan of Action; the possible format of the revised Plan; issues to be addressed; and implementation and monitoring, including follow-up measures. The Committee's second meeting (Dominican Republic, 24-27 October) focused on the main part of the new Plan of Action, involving priority directions with priority issues, including corresponding objectives and recommendations.

GENERAL ASSEMBLY ACTION

On 4 December [meeting 81], the General Assembly, on the recommendation of the Third Committee [A/55/592], adopted **resolution 55/58** without vote [agenda item 104].

Follow-up to the International Year of Older Persons: Second World Assembly on Ageing

The General Assembly,

Recalling its resolution 54/24 of 10 November 1999, and its resolution 54/262 of 25 May 2000, by which it decided to convene the Second World Assembly on Ageing, to be held in Spain in April 2002,

Taking note of Economic and Social Council resolution 2000/1 of 3 May 2000, as well as Commission for Social Development decision 38/100 of 17 February 2000,

Acknowledging the initiatives undertaken and the momentum generated, at all levels, towards addressing the challenges of the ageing of populations and the concerns and contributions of older persons by the celebration of the International Year of Older Persons,

Bearing in mind that, in its resolution 54/262, the General Assembly decided that the Commission for Social Development would serve as the preparatory committee for the Second World Assembly on Ageing,

Reiterating that the Second World Assembly on Ageing should give particular attention, inter alia, to linkages between ageing and development, with particular attention to the needs, priorities and perspectives of developing countries,

Reaffirming the necessity of ensuring that the Second World Assembly on Ageing will provide an action-oriented follow-up to the International Year of Older Persons, and recognizing the importance of an adequate preparatory process,

Reaffirming also that the revised plan of action and the long-term strategy on ageing will contain realistic financial recommendations for implementation,

Recognizing the continuing process of elaboration of the United Nations research agenda on ageing for the twenty-first century, which is aimed at providing a background for policy responses to ageing, in particular in developing countries,

1. *Takes note* of the report of the Secretary-General on the follow-up to the International Year of Older Persons;

2. *Decides* that the Second World Assembly on Ageing shall be held at Madrid from 8 to 12 April 2002;

3. *Invites* Member States, where appropriate, to consider extending the mandate of national committees or other mechanisms established on the occasion of the International Year of Older Persons in order to undertake national preparations for the Second World Assembly on Ageing, and also invites Member States currently without them to consider appropriate ways or mechanisms for their preparations for the Second World Assembly;

4. *Notes* the encouraging responses of Member States, United Nations entities and non-governmental organizations to the request by the Secretariat eliciting their views on the progress in and obstacles to the implementation of the International Plan of Action on Ageing, as well as on priority issues to be addressed in a revised plan of action, and encourages those that have not yet responded to consider doing so;

5. *Invites* the regional commissions to explore the feasibility of holding regional activities with Member States, non-governmental organizations and other relevant actors of civil society in their region, in preparation for and as follow-up to the Second World Assembly on Ageing;

6. *Invites* the Department of Public Information of the Secretariat to launch, in cooperation with the Department of Economic and Social Affairs of the Secretariat and the host country, an information campaign for the Second World Assembly on Ageing;

7. *Welcomes* the establishment by the United Nations programme on ageing of the Internet-accessible database on policies and programmes on ageing, and invites Member States and intergovernmental and non-governmental organizations to collaborate with the Secretariat in updating and maintaining the database through the provision of timely information;

8. *Requests* the Secretary-General to report to the General Assembly at its fifty-sixth session on the implementation of the present resolution.

Chapter XII

Refugees and displaced persons

In 2000, the Office of the United Nations High Commissioner for Refugees (UNHCR) provided assistance to 21.1 million persons throughout the world, a decrease from 22.3 million the previous year. More than half of those people (12.1 million) were refugees, 5.5 million were internally displaced persons, 900,000 were asylum-seekers, 800,000 had repatriated, and almost 1.7 million were in other special situations. While there were no new refugee emergencies on the scale experienced in the previous few years, UNHCR continued to face challenging refugee and forced displacement situations, often exacerbated by natural disasters.

African countries continued to host the largest number of refugees, representing almost a third of the worldwide total, with the main groups originating in Sierra Leone, 487,000; the Sudan, 468,000; Somalia, 452,000; Angola, more than 351,000; Eritrea, 346,000; and Burundi, 326,000. The United Republic of Tanzania hosted one of the largest caseloads on the continent, some 488,000 refugees. In January, the Security Council, in a statement on assistance to refugees in Africa, affirmed the need to ensure that both refugees and internally displaced persons in Africa received sufficient protection and assistance, taking into account the special difficulties in providing humanitarian assistance to internally displaced persons on that continent.

Protracted inter-ethnic tension and violence caused displacement of more than 200,000 non-Albanians from Kosovo province into other parts of the Federal Republic of Yugoslavia, which remained one of UNHCR's major concerns in Europe.

In Central and South-West Asia, renewed and continued fighting between warring factions in Afghanistan dampened hopes for finding a long-term political settlement and peace, a situation that was further compounded by the worst drought experienced in three decades. Thousands of Afghans were displaced internally and thousands more were forced to flee across the border into Iran and Pakistan, where the vast majority of the 2.6 million Afghan refugees were living. During 2000, UNHCR assisted 261,000 Afghans to return voluntarily to Afghanistan from those countries.

Staff safety remained a major concern for UNHCR as it faced restricted access to and lack of security in conflict-ridden areas in Africa, South-West and South-East Asia, the Balkans and Caucasus regions, and South America. During the year, three UNHCR staff members were killed in West Timor and one in Guinea, while carrying out their duties. In October, the UNHCR Executive Committee, noting the coming into force of the 1994 Convention on the Safety of United Nations and Associated Personnel, urged States to consider signing and ratifying that instrument. It also urged the conclusion of an optional protocol to the Convention, which would extend protection to all humanitarian personnel. In other action, the Executive Committee welcomed the UNHCR proposal for commencing global consultations with States aimed at revitalizing the international protection regime for refugees.

In October, the General Assembly elected Ruud Lubbers (Netherlands) as United Nations High Commissioner for Refugees for a three-year term beginning on 1 January 2001 to succeed Sadako Ogata (Japan), who had held the position for 10 years.

UNHCR observed its fiftieth anniversary in 2000. In December, the Assembly paid tribute to the work and dedication of UNHCR staff and reaffirmed its support for UNHCR activities on behalf of returnees, stateless persons and internally displaced persons. It decided that, as from 2001, 20 June would be celebrated as World Refugee Day.

Office of the United Nations High Commissioner for Refugees

Programme policy

Executive Committee action. At its fifty-first session (Geneva, 2-6 October) [A/55/12/Add.1], the Executive Committee of the UNHCR Programme welcomed the UNHCR proposal to commence global consultations on international protection with States to revitalize the international refugee protection regime and to discuss measures to ensure international protection, while taking account of the legitimate concerns of States, host communities and the international community. It affirmed that such a process, on the eve of the fiftieth anniversary of the 1951 Convention relating to the Status of Refugees [YUN 1951, p. 520], was important for promoting effective implementation of that Convention and its 1967 Protocol [YUN 1967, p. 477], while identifying approaches to new situations not covered by those instruments. The Committee encouraged UNHCR to seek practical responses, in cooperation with States and other relevant actors, to address current and future protection challenges.

For consideration of its annual theme "UNHCR@50: from response to solutions", the Committee had before it a millennium theme paper [A/AC.96/938], which retraced some of the main challenges of the past in chronological order and portrayed in broad terms the essential elements of the international community's response to the refugee problem. It also gave an overview of some of the current dilemmas and identified elements for solutions.

The Secretary-General, in a statement to the Committee in which he paid tribute to the commitment of High Commissioner Sadako Ogata, whose term of office would expire in December, called for support for the High Commissioner's legacy in three areas: strengthening the notion of asylum; a more timely, consistent and adequate system of funding for UNHCR's programmes; and action by States to ensure the safety of humanitarian workers.

Addressing the Committee, the High Commissioner outlined areas needing concrete action in the future. The High Commissioner noted that the refugee crisis in the Kosovo province of the Federal Republic of Yugoslavia (FRY) had revealed a critical need to review UNHCR's emergency mechanisms and response capacity. Consequently, based on the recommendations of an independent evaluation of UNHCR's response to that crisis, UNHCR had begun implementing a plan of action to increase its "surge capacity" through expanded standby arrangements, rosters of trained personnel ready for rapid deployment, and kits and packages designed to meet immediate security, logistics, telecommunications and accommodation needs in the field. In the area of staff safety, UNHCR was examining its security arrangements, including reassessing benchmarks for suspending operations, evacuating staff and the resumption of activities. In developing new approaches to complex forced population movements, UNHCR needed to address two key aspects: ensuring asylum for refugees and meeting the requirements of internally displaced people more effectively. The High

Commissioner also addressed the need to bridge the gap between humanitarian and development assistance in the transition from war to peace, and to promote coexistence in divided communities in post-conflict situations.

To meet those challenges, the High Commissioner emphasized that the Office should be managed, trained and equipped for a technologically advanced and globalized environment, taking advantage of the revolution in communications and information technology. Decentralization was crucial, especially in the area of financial and human resources management, and, in that regard, the process had already begun in Africa. Other areas that should be addressed were human resources, staff rotation policies and fund-raising. Raising funds had been a major activity for the High Commissioner, yet UNHCR remained an underfunded organization, while new emergencies had added $100 million to its requirements. UNHCR was reaching out to a new, wider circle of potential supporters among the private sector, the corporate world and the public at large. The budget had been repeatedly reduced during the year, resulting in diminished credibility of UNHCR and strained relations with refugees, Governments and its non-governmental organization (NGO) implementing partners.

By **decision 2000/289** of 28 July, the Economic and Social Council took note of the High Commissioner's report for 1999/2000 [E/2000/18 & Corr.1,2].

By **decision 55/417** of 4 December, the General Assembly took note of the High Commissioner's report for 1999 [YUN 1999, p. 1128].

Coordination of emergency humanitarian assistance

In 2000, UNHCR developed new partnerships, while reinforcing ongoing ones in efforts to increase resources reaching refugees and returnees [A/56/12]. Two memorandums of understanding (MOUs) on partnership arrangements were signed with the United Nations Volunteers (UNV) and with the League of Arab States. As a complement to its MOU with the International Organization for Migration (IOM), a joint "Guidance Note on Cooperation in the Transportation Sector" was issued in May.

UNHCR strengthened its collaboration with the World Bank through staff exchanges and joint initiatives under the terms of a Framework for Cooperation signed in 1998 [YUN 1998, p. 1108]. Joint projects were implemented in Sri Lanka and in countries in the southern Caucasus region, and a staff exchange agreement was activated between the two organizations. During the year, UNHCR also collaborated with the International Labour Organization (ILO) and held its annual high-level meeting with the International Committee of the Red Cross (ICRC), which discussed internally displaced persons and the situations in Angola, Colombia and Sri Lanka. UNHCR began a series of meetings with the International Federation of Red Cross and Red Crescent Societies (IFRC) on geographical and technical issues. UNHCR and IFRC also embarked on an NGO training programme on protection.

In terms of coordination within the UN system, UNHCR continued to participate in the Administrative Committee on Coordination (ACC), where, with the support of operational agencies, it ensured that staff safety and security remained high on the agenda, as well as in the Inter-Agency Standing Committee (IASC). Using tools such as the United Nations Development Assistance Framework (UNDAF) and the common country assessment (CCA), UNHCR was able to strengthen cooperation and coordination with other UN agencies.

During 2000, UNHCR entered into project agreements with 536 NGOs covering operational activities in favour of refugees and other populations of concern to UNHCR. It continued to promote the Partnership in Action (PARinAC) process, aimed at enhancing coordination of refugee activities. The process was introduced to NGOs from the five Central Asian republics, linking members of the Commonwealth of Independent States (CIS) to the more global UNHCR-NGO network. In the Balkans, UNHCR met in Sarajevo with 30 NGOs from Bosnia and Herzegovina, Croatia and FRY to discuss the return of refugees and internally displaced persons and linking those efforts to a broader international NGO network. Meetings were also held in the United Republic of Tanzania and Tunisia where a conference was held for UNHCR and NGO staff from North Africa, the Middle East and the Gulf States.

In October [A/55/12/Add.1], the Executive Committee, recognizing the importance of NGOs as partners in UNHCR's humanitarian work on behalf of refugees, extended their observer participation until the end of 2003, at which time it would be reviewed.

Evaluation and inspection activities

UNHCR, reporting on its evaluation activities in an August report [A/AC.96/935], stated that, with the establishment of the Evaluation and Policy Analysis Unit [YUN 1999, p. 1129], a new evaluation policy was introduced based on the principles of transparency, independence, consultation and relevance. As an initial step in its application, UNHCR declassified all previous evaluation reports and posted those issued during the past four years on its web

site. It also established an Evaluation Committee to guide the evaluation function and created individual steering committees for each evaluation project. Several initiatives were being undertaken to further enhance the evaluation function in UNHCR, including providing evaluation training, expanding the evaluation consultancy roster and finding ways to plan the work programme more systematically and to integrate evaluation findings more effectively into UNHCR's planning, programming and policy-making.

The major evaluation undertaken during the year was a review of UNHCR's emergency preparedness and response in the Kosovo refugee crisis, based on the findings of an independent team of experts. That evaluation played a major part in the formulation of UNHCR's plan of action to strengthen its emergency preparedness and response capacity. In the area of refugee security and protection, UNHCR undertook a study of violence in Kenya's refugee camps and an evaluation of its security measures in the United Republic of Tanzania. The Office began an evaluation of its policy for refugees in urban areas with reviews of its programmes in New Delhi, India; Cairo, Egypt; and Nairobi, Kenya. Other evaluations were initiated on the reintegration of returning refugees, refugee education, internally displaced persons, protracted situations of displacement, UNHCR's role in relation to statelessness and in strengthening national NGOs, and UNHCR training activities with implementation partners, among others.

As described by UNHCR in its annual report [A/56/12], real-time evaluation missions were undertaken to assess new emergency operations in Angola, Eritrea and the Sudan, while a beneficiary-based evaluation of the UNHCR programme was conducted in Guinea. The Office also joined the Office for the Coordination of Humanitarian Affairs (OCHA), the United Nations Children's Fund (UNICEF) and the World Food Programme (WFP) in commissioning an inter-agency evaluation of the UN humanitarian assistance programmes in Afghanistan, focusing on needs assessment and beneficiary identification.

On 4 December [meeting 81], the General Assembly, on the recommendation of the Third (Social, Humanitarian and Cultural) Committee [A/55/597], adopted **resolution 55/74** without vote [agenda item 109].

Office of the United Nations High Commissioner for Refugees

The General Assembly,

Having considered the report of the United Nations High Commissioner for Refugees on the activities of her Office and the report of the Executive Committee of the Programme of the United Nations High Commissioner for Refugees on the work of its fifty-first session and the conclusions and decisions contained therein,

Recalling its resolution 54/146 of 17 December 1999,

Commending the High Commissioner, her staff and their implementing partners for the competent, courageous and dedicated manner in which they discharge their responsibilities, paying tribute to those staff members whose lives have been endangered in the course of their duties, and strongly condemning the deaths and injuries and other forms of physical and psychological violence experienced by staff members as a consequence of generalized as well as targeted violence,

Expressing appreciation, in this year which marks the fiftieth anniversary of the Office of the United Nations High Commissioner for Refugees, for the work accomplished since its establishment in responding to the protection and assistance needs of refugees and in promoting durable solutions to their plight, and commending States for their cooperation and support,

1. *Endorses* the report of the Executive Committee of the Programme of the United Nations High Commissioner for Refugees on the work of its fifty-first session;

2. *Strongly reaffirms* the fundamental importance and the purely humanitarian and non-political character of the function of the Office of the United Nations High Commissioner for Refugees of providing international protection to refugees and seeking permanent solutions to the problem of refugees, and reiterates the need for Governments to continue to facilitate the effective exercise of this function;

3. *Expresses sincere appreciation and gratitude* to Sadako Ogata for her unrelenting efforts throughout her tenure as United Nations High Commissioner for Refugees to promote innovative humanitarian solutions to the refugee problem in various parts of the world, and for her inspiring example in performing her functions in an effective and dedicated manner;

4. *Reaffirms* that the 1951 Convention and the 1967 Protocol relating to the Status of Refugees remain the foundation of the international refugee regime and recognizes the importance of their full application by States parties, notes with satisfaction that one hundred and forty States are now parties to one instrument or to both, welcomes the fact that an intergovernmental event involving those States is planned on the occasion of the fiftieth anniversary of the Convention, and encourages the Office of the High Commissioner and States to strengthen their efforts to promote broader accession to those instruments and their full implementation;

5. *Notes* that fifty-two States are now parties to the 1954 Convention relating to the Status of Stateless Persons and that twenty-three States are parties to the 1961 Convention on the reduction of statelessness, and encourages the High Commissioner to continue her activities on behalf of stateless persons;

6. *Reaffirms* that, as set out in article 14 of the Universal Declaration of Human Rights, everyone has the right to seek and enjoy in other countries asylum from persecution, and calls upon all States to refrain from taking measures that jeopardize the institution of asylum, in particular by returning or expelling refugees or asylum-seekers contrary to international standards;

7. *Emphasizes* that the protection of refugees is primarily the responsibility of States, whose full and effective cooperation, action and political resolve are required to enable the Office of the High Commissioner to fulfil its mandated functions, welcomes the proposal of the Office of the High Commissioner to commence a process of global consultations on international protection, and requests a report thereon;

8. *Welcomes* measures taken by the Office of the High Commissioner to make protection effective, recognizing that international protection is a dynamic and action-oriented function, carried out in cooperation with States and other partners, inter alia, to promote and facilitate the admission, reception and treatment of refugees and to ensure protection-oriented solutions;

9. *Stresses* the importance of international solidarity, burden-sharing and international cooperation to share responsibilities and partnerships in reinforcing the international protection of refugees, urges all States and relevant non-governmental and other organizations, in conjunction with the Office of the High Commissioner, to cooperate and to mobilize resources with a view to reducing the heavy burden borne by States, in particular developing countries, that have received large numbers of asylum-seekers and refugees, and calls upon the Office of the High Commissioner to continue to play its catalytic role in mobilizing assistance from the international community to address the economic, environmental and social impact of large-scale refugee populations, especially in developing countries;

10. *Condemns* all acts that pose a threat to the personal security and well-being of refugees and asylum-seekers, such as refoulement, unlawful expulsion and physical attacks, and calls upon all States of refuge, in cooperation with international organizations where appropriate, to take all necessary measures to ensure respect for the principles of refugee protection, including the humane treatment of asylum-seekers;

11. *Urges* States to uphold the civilian and humanitarian character of refugee camps and settlements, inter alia, through effective measures to prevent the infiltration of armed elements, to identify and separate any such armed elements from refugee populations, to settle refugees in secure locations and to afford the Office of the High Commissioner and other appropriate humanitarian organizations prompt, unhindered and safe access to asylum-seekers, refugees and other persons of concern;

12. *Calls upon* States and all concerned parties to take urgently all possible measures to safeguard the physical security and property of the staff of the Office of the High Commissioner and other humanitarian personnel, to investigate fully any crime committed against them and to bring to justice persons responsible for such crimes;

13. *Encourages* the Office of the High Commissioner, in cooperation with host countries and in coordination with other relevant United Nations bodies, further to develop and integrate appropriate security arrangements in its operations, and to allocate adequate resources for the safety and security of its staff and the persons under its mandate;

14. *Notes* that the 1994 Convention on the Safety of United Nations and Associated Personnel is now in force, calls upon those States that have not yet done so to consider signing and ratifying the Convention, but notes in this regard that the Convention does not automatically apply to most humanitarian personnel, and therefore invites States to provide a timely response to the recommendation of the Secretary-General to extend the scope of legal protection to all United Nations and associated personnel through the development of a protocol to the 1994 Convention or by other appropriate means;

15. *Urges* all States and relevant organizations to support the High Commissioner's search for durable solutions to refugee problems, including voluntary repatriation, local integration and resettlement in a third country, as appropriate, reaffirms that voluntary repatriation is the preferred solution to refugee problems, and calls upon countries of origin, countries of asylum, the Office of the High Commissioner and the international community to act in a spirit of burden-sharing and partnership to enable refugees to exercise their right to return home in safety and with dignity;

16. *Calls upon* all States to promote conditions conducive to the voluntary repatriation of refugees in safety and with dignity, including conditions furthering reconciliation and long-term development in countries of return, and to support the sustainable reintegration of returnees by providing countries of origin with necessary rehabilitation and development assistance in conjunction, as appropriate, with the Office of the High Commissioner, relevant mechanisms, including those within the United Nations system, and development agencies;

17. *Reiterates* the right of all persons to return to their country of origin, emphasizes in this regard the obligation of all States to accept the return of their nationals, calls upon all States to facilitate the return of their nationals who have sought asylum and have been determined not to be in need of international protection, and affirms the need for the return of persons to be undertaken in a humane manner and with full respect for their human rights and dignity, irrespective of the status of the persons concerned;

18. *Acknowledges* the desirability of comprehensive approaches by the international community, notably at the regional level, to the problems of refugees and displaced persons, and notes in this regard that capacity-building in countries of origin and countries of asylum can play an important role in addressing the root causes of refugee flows, strengthening emergency preparedness and response, promoting and building peace, and developing regional standards for the protection of refugees;

19. *Urges* States, in cooperation with the Office of the High Commissioner and other relevant organizations, to explore and support fully capacity-building initiatives as part of a comprehensive approach to addressing refugee issues and to take necessary measures to promote sustainable development and to ensure the success of capacity-building activities, and reiterates that such initiatives may include those which strengthen legal and judicial institutions and civil society, those which promote services for refugees, the observance of human rights, the rule of law and accountability and those which enhance the capacity of States to fulfil

their responsibilities with respect to persons under the mandate of the Office of the High Commissioner;

20. *Reiterates its support* for the role of the Office of the High Commissioner in providing humanitarian assistance and protection to internally displaced persons on the basis of criteria enumerated in paragraph 16 of its resolution 53/125 of 9 December 1998, and underlines the continuing relevance of the Guiding Principles on Internal Displacement;

21. *Calls upon* States to adopt an approach that is sensitive to gender-related concerns and to ensure that women whose claims to refugee status are based upon a well-founded fear of persecution for reasons enumerated in the 1951 Convention and the 1967 Protocol, including persecution through sexual violence or other gender-related persecution, are recognized as refugees, and encourages the Office of the High Commissioner to continue and to strengthen its efforts for the protection of refugee women;

22. *Urges* States and relevant parties to respect and observe principles of international human rights and humanitarian and refugee law that are of particular relevance to safeguarding the rights of the child and adolescent refugees whose situation is particularly vulnerable to abuse, welcomes in this regard the adoption of the Optional Protocols to the Convention on the Rights of the Child on the involvement of children in armed conflict and on the sale of children, child prostitution and child pornography, and calls upon States to consider signing and ratifying them as a matter of priority;

23. *Underlines* the particular role of elderly refugees within the refugee family, welcomes the development by the Office of the High Commissioner of guidelines to address their special needs, and calls upon States and the Office of the High Commissioner to make renewed efforts to ensure that the rights, needs and dignity of elderly and disabled refugees are fully respected and that programmes are designed bearing in mind their special vulnerabilities;

24. *Recalls* that the family is the natural and fundamental group unit of society and that it is entitled to protection by society and the State, and calls upon States, working in close collaboration with the Office of the High Commissioner and other concerned organizations, to take measures to ensure that the refugee's family is protected, including through measures aimed at reuniting family members separated as a result of refugee flight;

25. *Calls upon* Governments and other donors to demonstrate their international solidarity and burden-sharing with countries of asylum, in particular developing countries, countries with economies in transition and countries with limited resources that, owing to their location, host large numbers of refugees and asylum-seekers, and urges Governments to respond promptly and adequately to the global appeal issued by the Office of the High Commissioner, presenting requirements under its annual programme budget, to support efforts to widen the donor base so as to achieve greater burden-sharing among donors and to assist the High Commissioner in securing additional and timely income from traditional governmental sources, other Governments and the private sector so as to ensure that the needs of persons under the mandate of the Office of the High Commissioner are fully met.

UNHCR fiftieth anniversary and World Refugee Day

In 2000, UNHCR commemorated its fiftieth anniversary. As a lasting legacy to that achievement, the High Commissioner announced that the independent Refugee Education Trust was being launched on 14 December to provide refugee adolescents in developing countries with opportunities for post-primary education.

The Executive Committee, in a decision on the anniversary and World Refugee Day [A/55/12/Add.1], forwarded to the General Assembly a draft resolution for adoption.

GENERAL ASSEMBLY ACTION

On 4 December [meeting 81], the General Assembly, on the recommendation of the Third Committee [A/55/597], adopted **resolution 55/76** without vote [agenda item 109].

Fiftieth anniversary of the Office of the United Nations High Commissioner for Refugees and World Refugee Day

The General Assembly

1. *Commends* the Office of the United Nations High Commissioner for Refugees for its leadership and coordination of international action for refugees, and acknowledges the tireless efforts of the Office of the High Commissioner to provide international protection and assistance to refugees and other persons of concern and to promote durable solutions for their problems during the past fifty years;

2. *Pays tribute* to the dedication of United Nations humanitarian workers and associated personnel, the staff of the Office of the High Commissioner in the field, including local staff, who risk their lives in the performance of their duties;

3. *Reaffirms its support* for the activities of the Office of the High Commissioner, in accordance with the relevant General Assembly resolutions, on behalf of returnees, stateless persons and internally displaced persons;

4. *Notes* the crucial role of partnerships with Governments and international, regional and non-governmental organizations, as well as of the participation of refugees in decisions that affect their lives;

5. *Recognizes* that, by virtue of its activities on behalf of refugees and other persons of concern, the Office of the High Commissioner also contributes to promoting the purposes and principles of the United Nations, in particular those related to peace, human rights and development;

6. *Notes* that 2001 marks the fiftieth anniversary of the 1951 Convention relating to the Status of Refugees, which sets out the fundamental concepts for international refugee protection;

7. *Also notes* that the Organization of African Unity has agreed that an international refugee day may coincide with Africa Refugee Day on 20 June;

8. *Decides* that, as from 2001, 20 June will be celebrated as World Refugee Day.

Enlargement of Executive Committee

ECONOMIC AND SOCIAL COUNCIL ACTION

On 28 July, the Economic and Social Council, by **decision 2000/302**, took note of Mexico's request [E/2000/92] for membership in the UNHCR Executive Committee and recommended that the General Assembly take a decision at its fifty-fifth (2000) session on the question of increasing the membership of the Executive Committee from 57 to 58 States.

GENERAL ASSEMBLY ACTION

On 4 December [meeting 81], the General Assembly, on the recommendation of the Third Committee [A/55/597], adopted **resolution 55/72** without vote [agenda item 109].

Enlargement of the Executive Committee of the Programme of the United Nations High Commissioner for Refugees

The General Assembly,

Taking note of Economic and Social Council decision 2000/302 of 28 July 2000 concerning the enlargement of the Executive Committee of the Programme of the United Nations High Commissioner for Refugees,

Taking note also of the request regarding the enlargement of the Executive Committee contained in the letter dated 11 July 2000 from the Permanent Representative of Mexico to the United Nations addressed to the Secretary-General,

1. *Decides* to increase the number of members of the Executive Committee of the Programme of the United Nations High Commissioner for Refugees from fifty-seven to fifty-eight States;

2. *Requests* the Economic and Social Council to elect the additional member at its resumed organizational session for 2001.

Financial and administrative questions

UNHCR's initial annual programme budget for 2000, presented for the first time under a single unified structure, was $933.5 million [A/56/12], revised later to $942.3 million. Of that amount, $824.7 million related to the annual programme budget, $6.8 million to Junior Professional Officers, $20.2 million to the UN regular budget and $90.6 million to supplementary programmes for Angola, East Timor, Eritrea, Sierra Leone and the northern Caucasus. Total income, including adjustments and prior-year cancellations, reached $786 million. Total expenditure amounted to $801.4 million, of which $707.5 million was from the annual programme budget. The latter figure was $117.2 million (or 14 per cent) less than the revised budget, as a result of actions taken in late 2000 to closely manage expenditure. UNHCR expenditure by region in 2000 was as follows: Africa, $285 million; Asia and the Pacific, $75.4 million; Europe, $229 million; the Americas and the Caribbean, $25 million; Central and South-West Asia, and North Africa and the Middle East, $73.4 million.

For 2001, the Executive Committee approved budgetary requirements of $898.5 million. By 31 December, total needs had increased to $953.7 million due to supplementary programmes for Angola, Eritrea and Sierra Leone. It approved the revised 2000 annual programme budget amounting to $824,740,973, which, together with the UN regular budget contribution of $20,191,400, provision for Junior Professional Officers of $6,826,400 and the needs for supplementary programmes, brought total requirements for the year to $942,346,173. The Committee requested the High Commissioner, within available resources, to respond flexibly and efficiently to needs currently under the 2001 budget and authorized her, in the case of additional emergency needs that could not be fully met from the Operational Reserve, to issue special appeals and create supplementary programmes.

Funding arrangements

The Executive Committee, in a decision on the pledging conference [A/55/12/Add.1], recalled the decision of the Standing Committee at its eighteenth meeting [A/AC.96/393] proposing an alternative pledging arrangement and reaffirmed the need to link more closely the procedures relating to the adoption of UNHCR's annual programme budget, the issue of the global appeal and the funding mechanism. It recommended a draft resolution to the General Assembly for adoption.

GENERAL ASSEMBLY ACTION

On 4 December [meeting 81], the General Assembly, on the recommendation of the Third Committee [A/55/597], adopted **resolution 55/75** without vote [agenda item 109].

Ad hoc Committee of the General Assembly for the announcement of voluntary contributions to the Programme of the United Nations High Commissioner for Refugees

The General Assembly,

Recalling its resolutions 1556 A (XV) of 18 December 1960 and 1729(XVI) of 20 December 1961 on the convening of an ad hoc Committee of the Whole, under the chairmanship of the President of the General Assembly, as soon as practicable after the opening of each regular session of the Assembly, for the purpose of announcing pledges of voluntary contributions to the refugee programmes for the following year,

Recalling also that the ad hoc Committee of the General Assembly for the announcement of voluntary contributions to the Programme of the United Nations High Commissioner for Refugees has been convened annually, under the chairmanship of the President of the General Assembly or his or her designated repre-

sentative, at United Nations Headquarters, immediately following the debate on the report of the High Commissioner in the Third Committee,

Noting that the General Assembly, in its resolution 54/146 of 17 December 1999, endorsed the presentation of a unified annual programme budget of the Office of the High Commissioner,

Noting also that financial requirements under the annual programme budget for the programmes of the Office of the High Commissioner are presented in the global appeal issued late in November or early in December each year at Geneva, forming the basis for pledges in response to the information provided in the global appeal,

Decides, in order to improve and rationalize the funding mechanism following the adoption of the annual programme budget, that the ad hoc Committee of the General Assembly may be convened as from 2001 at Geneva, the headquarters of the Office of the High Commissioner.

Accounts (1999)

The audited financial statements on voluntary funds administered by UNHCR for the year ending 31 December 1999 [A/55/5/Add.5] showed total expenditure of over $1,023 million and total income of $927 million, with a reserve balance of $145.1 million.

The Board of Auditors' main findings were that a decline in voluntary contributions from donor countries posed a liquidity risk for UNHCR; inadequate segregation of functions in field offices could not ensure checks and balances of responsibility; the asset tracking system had been inadequate to capture accurate and complete non-expendable property databases and had failed to support effective tracking and decentralized management of UNHCR assets; financial statements did not include comprehensive inventory lists and therefore did not reflect an accurate valuation of non-expendable property; of 13 implementing partners having $8.2 million in outstanding advances, 8 had not submitted final sub-project monitoring reports, which had delayed closure of the projects; and the required submission of audit certificates by implementing partners had reached the set target of 70 per cent.

The Board recommended that the Administration should improve presentation of non-expendable property in notes to the financial statements; ensure regular reconciliation of account balances between headquarters and field offices; strengthen proper monitoring and evaluation of programme implementation; and strictly adhere to UN accounting standards.

UNHCR, in September [A/AC.96/933/Add.1], reported on measures taken or proposed to respond to the recommendations of the Board of Auditors.

In an October report [A/55/487], the Advisory Committee on Administrative and Budgetary Questons (ACABQ) shared the concern of the Board of Auditors about UNHCR's financial situation. It commended the Office for steps taken to ensure accountability of implementing partners and hoped that, in view of resource constraints, UNHCR activities would be planned and implemented more efficiently, and greater financial control would be exercised over agency funds and operations. It urged UNHCR to address urgently the shortcomings identified by the Board regarding budgetary control, human resources, programme management and project implementation. Noting the abandonment of the asset management system, ACABQ requested comprehensive data on the implementation of all information technology projects, including costs.

The Executive Committee, in a decision on administrative, financial and programme matters [A/55/12/Add.1], requested to be kept regularly informed on measures taken to address the recommendations and observations raised by the Board of Auditors and ACABQ.

OIOS report

On 7 April, the General Assembly, in **resolution 54/257**, took note of the report of the Office of Internal Oversight Services (OIOS) on the 1998 review of the procurement of Lysol disinfectant by UNHCR [A/52/887]. That review determined that there was no evidence that UNHCR staff had acted negligently in the loss of $2.1 million.

Standing Committee

The Standing Committee held three meetings in 2000 (29 February–2 March [A/AC.96/929]; 5-7 July [A/AC.96/939]; 27-28 September [A/AC.96/943]). It considered programmes and funding for the near term, as well as UNHCR's medium-term plan for 2002-2005, and reviewed its programmes and activities in various regions. Other issues included programme/protection policy issues, such as safety and security of staff, and the civilian and humanitarian character of refugee camps and settlements and their security; the independent evaluation of UNHCR's response to the Kosovo emergency; international protection; and matters relevant to management, finance, oversight and human resources. Decisions were adopted on programme and funding, the medium-term plan, the new annual programme budget, and mobilizing resources for a unified budget: the pledging conference, as were conclusions on older refugees and on mainstreaming environmental concerns in refugee operations. The Committee recognized general principles

on resourcing UNHCR's unified budget. It endorsed UNCHR's policy on older refugees.

In October [A/55/12/Add.1], the Executive Committee requested UNHCR to include in the documentation for each item of the Standing Committee's 2001 programme of work the relevant audit and ACABQ recommendations, as well as information on steps taken to implement those recommendations and related Executive Committee decisions and conclusions. It authorized the Standing Committee to add items to or delete them from its intersessional programme of work, as appropriate. The items adopted for the 2001 programme of work were international protection; programme/protection policy; programme and funding; governance; coordination; and management, financial, oversight and human resources.

Safety of staff

In 2000, restricted access in conflict areas in various parts of the world inhibited UNHCR's ability to protect and provide relief to many affected populations and impacted the Office's own security, as was evidenced by the murder of three UNHCR staff members in West Timor and one in Guinea. In the aftermath of the killings and abductions of several staff members, UNHCR reassessed its safety and security preparedness and established a strategy to improve security.

On 8 September, the Security Council, in **resolution 1319(2000)** (see p. 283), welcomed Indonesia's intention to conduct a full-scale investigation into the killings in West Timor and to take firm action against those found guilty.

In an October decision on safety of staff of UNHCR and all other humanitarian personnel [A/55/12/Add.1], the Executive Committee urged States to safeguard the physical security of the staff of the United Nations and its agencies and of other humanitarian personnel, to ensure their safe and unhindered access to affected populations and to investigate fully any crimes committed against those persons and bring to justice those responsible. It noted that the 1994 Convention on the Safety of United Nations and Associated Personnel [YUN 1994, p. 1289] was in force and urged States to consider signing and ratifying that instrument. It also urged the conclusion of an optional protocol to the Convention, which would extend protection to all humanitarian personnel. The Committee encouraged UNHCR to further develop appropriate security arrangements in its operations and to allocate sufficient resources for the safety and security of its staff and its beneficiary populations.

Refugee protection and assistance

Protection issues

In the 2000 annual report [A/56/12], the High Commissioner said many States, often those with the most limited resources, continued to host large refugee populations on their territories. However, the quality of asylum had deteriorated in a number of countries due to economic and social difficulties of hosting such populations for extended periods, national security considerations, concern about the use of asylum procedures by illegal immigrants, and trafficking and smuggling of persons. While there was general tightening of borders around the world, regions faced different problems, such as politicization and militarization of refugee camps; security risks due to the presence of armed elements in camps and areas populated with refugees; forced conscription of refugees, often minors; trafficking of refugee women and their vulnerability to sexual violence; exploitation and abuse of refugee children; and forced repatriation despite the risks to returnees' safety.

A July note on international protection [A/AC.96/930] pointed out that the Office's international protection function had evolved over the past five decades from being a surrogate for consular and diplomatic protection to ensuring the basic rights of refugees and, increasingly, their physical safety and security. UNHCR had to contend with a rapidly changing and complex environment in which the political, security, economic and social costs of hosting refugees had affected States' willingness and capacity to receive refugees. Its protection function had come under increasing scrutiny and, in situations of large-scale influxes, international assistance to affected States had overshadowed issues of international protection, causing confusion over the relationship between protection and assistance. Additionally, because a plethora of varying notions of protection had emerged, there was a need to clarify its content. International protection encompassed activities covering both policy and operational concerns carried out in cooperation with States and other partners to enhance respect for the rights of refugees and to resolve their problems. The operational focus of UNHCR's international protection activities, coupled with the fact that UNHCR did not have to be invited to become involved in protection matters, had made UNHCR's mandate distinct within the international system. The note examined the Office's organizational practice regarding its four principal protection challenges: ensuring the availability and quality of asylum; revitalizing the refugee protection system; promoting durable solutions for protection and engaging in in-country protection activities; and fostering partnerships to support the international refugee protection system.

Regarding asylum, UNHCR activities were aimed at enhancing the capacity of States to receive and protect refugees; intervening with authorities; ensuring physical safety of refugees; prioritizing the protection needs of women, children, adolescents and the elderly; promoting national legislation and asylum procedures; and determining refugee status. In efforts to revitalize the protection system, UNHCR promoted international refugee law and standards, including through its global campaign to promote accession to international refugee instruments. The Office also explored new approaches to refugee protection, strengthened linkages with international human rights law and international humanitarian law, and encouraged consistency in regional approaches.

UNHCR's work in the field focused on establishing conditions for voluntary repatriation, an activity that retained a political nature, placing it beyond the Office's capabilities. According to the note, return had been used in certain countries as the sole vehicle to achieve ethnic integration and promote multi-ethnicity and, eventually, reconciliation. However, in the highly politicized context in which it often occurred, caution was necessary to ensure respect for protection standards. Other activities in that area included concluding voluntary repatriation agreements; monitoring treatment of returnees; maintaining a presence in the country of origin; assisting returnees, particularly women and children; local integration; and resettlement.

The Office strengthened its partnerships with States, intergovernmental and non-governmental organizations, judges, parliamentarians, journalists, the military and the corporate sector. It promoted collaboration on refugee protection through the "Reach Out" consultative process, initiated in 1998 to engage non-State actors in dialogues on the nature and dimensions of protection challenges, among other initiatives.

In an October conclusion on international protection [A/55/12/Add.1], the Executive Committee welcomed UNHCR's proposal to commence global consultations with States, involving refugee protection experts, NGOs and refugees, to revitalize the international protection regime and to discuss measures to ensure international protection for those who needed it. It also affirmed the importance of according priority attention to the protection needs of women, children, adolescents and the elderly in the planning and implementation of UNHCR's programmes and State policies.

International instruments

In 2000, Mexico and Trinidad and Tobago became parties to the 1951 Convention relating to the Status of Refugees [YUN 1951, p. 520] and its 1967 Protocol [YUN 1967, p. 477]. Swaziland also acceded to the 1951 Convention, bringing the number of States party to one or both instruments to 137. Guatemala, Lithuania, Mexico and Slovakia became parties to the 1954 Convention relating to the Status of Stateless Persons [YUN 1954, p. 416], raising the number of States parties to 53. With the accession of Slovakia and Tunisia, the number of States party to the 1961 Convention on the Reduction of Statelessness [YUN 1961, p. 533] reached 23.

Promotional activities

Global consultations

In July, UNHCR launched a process of global consultations on international protection to promote full and effective implementation of the 1951 Convention [YUN 1951, p. 520] and its 1967 Protocol [YUN 1967, p. 477] and to develop new approaches, tools and standards to ensure its continuing vitality and relevance. The consultations were designed along three parallel tracks. The first was to encourage reaffirmation of States parties' commitment to implementation of the Convention and its Protocol, and to promote further accessions. To that end, a major intergovernmental event to mark the fiftieth anniversary of the Convention was being organized by the Swiss Government and UNHCR, to be held in Geneva in December 2001. The second track would provide for the study of developments in refugee law and an examination of emerging issues through expert discussions on specific interpretive aspects of the Convention and its Protocol. The process would comprise four round tables, drawn from Governments, NGOs, academia, the judiciary and the legal profession. The third track would focus on protection policy issues, including those inadequately covered by the Convention. It was designed to foster common understanding of protection challenges and enhance cooperation to address them; to identify and promote practical responses to those challenges; and to develop new approaches, tools and standards. The discussions would take place within the framework of the Executive Committee in 2001 and 2002.

Assistance measures

The global population of concern to UNHCR decreased from 22.3 million in 1999 to 21.1 million in 2000. Those assisted included asylumseekers, refugees, returning refugees in the early stages of their reintegration, internally displaced persons and other people of concern, mainly victims of conflict. Although there was no massive repatriation on the scale of the 1999 Kosovo repatriation [YUN 1999, p. 1135], some 800,000 refugees returned home, often to situations of uncertainty or fragile peace. The Office also facilitated the resettlement of 40,000 refugees from first asylum countries. Although less frequently an option, local integration provided an opportunity for some groups of refugees to start new lives, particularly in West Africa and the Balkans region. However, solutions remained elusive for the majority of displaced persons, and some protracted situations spanned decades, as in the case of refugees from Afghanistan.

In 2000, UNHCR received a total of some $705.3 million in voluntary contributions towards its annual programme budget.

Refugees and the environment

In 2000, UNHCR's focus on environmental issues evolved in response to the changing needs of its operations in different countries and regions. Priority issues addressed included promoting and implementing UNHCR's environmental policy through practical field activities; designing and implementing an environmental assessment and monitoring programme; strengthening the education programme to raise environmental awareness; training in environmental management for UNHCR staff and implementing partners; and improving communications and outreach within and outside UNHCR.

The Office supported a number of model projects in Afghanistan, Rwanda, the Sudan and Zimbabwe. To raise awareness of environmental management, other initiatives included developing an educational booklet in Liberia, *Our Environment: Taking Care of Our Future*, in collaboration with the Environmental Foundation for Africa. UNHCR also worked with the United Nations Educational, Scientific and Cultural Organization (UNESCO) on environmental education projects in Djibouti, Ethiopia, Guinea, Kenya, the Sudan and Zambia, as well as with the United Nations Environment Programme (UNEP) on projects in Guinea and Kosovo, and in assessing the environmental impact of refugees in Albania and in the former Yugoslav Republic of Macedonia.

Refugee women

UNHCR's approach in addressing the rights and needs of refugee women was to continue efforts to incorporate a gender equality perspective in all its operational activities. Key objectives included the integration of gender analysis into UNHCR's policies, guidelines and key documents, as well as the evaluation of activities from a gender perspective; improvement of prevention of and response to sexual and gender-based violence; empowerment of refugee and returnee women to participate in peace-building; encouragement of dialogue with displaced women; and development of multisectoral regional and country-level gender networks. UNHCR disseminated a new policy directive, *Gender Based Persecution*, in 2000 and began developing a new Policy on Gender Equality for People of Concern to UNHCR. It also updated its *Policy on Refugee Women* and began a revision of the *Guidelines on the Protection of Refugee Women*. The Office facilitated a consultation between representatives of displaced women from Burundi, Colombia, Kosovo, Myanmar and Sierra Leone, and government and intergovernmental and nongovernmental organization representatives in October to maintain focus on those women's real needs and concerns.

Also in 2000, UNHCR funded the participation of Burundian refugee women in the Arusha peace talks for Burundi (see p. 146) and supported the creation of a network of women peace activists in West Africa. In addition, UNHCR continued to implement programmes to address sexual and gender-based violence.

Refugee children and adolescents

Some 10 million, approximately 45 per cent of all refugees and other persons of concern to UNHCR, were children and adolescents under 18 years. In 2000, UNHCR retained the issue of refugee children as a policy priority in terms of both international protection and assistance activities. It worked closely with the Office of the Special Representative of the Secretary-General for Children and Armed Conflict and with UNICEF. It also collaborated with the Geneva-based NGO subgroup on refugee children and children in armed conflict and maintained close association with the Action for the Rights of Children training and capacity-building programme. The focus throughout 2000 remained the review and revision of resource materials and regional follow-up activities. Five resource packs—Working with Children; Community Mobilization; Child Soldiers; Education; and Sexual and Reproductive Health—were completed and made available on UNHCR's web site. Other initiatives included workshops to train trainers in East and West Africa and in the Great Lakes region, an expansion of the regional scope of the project to Southern Africa and regional follow-up activities in Eastern Europe and West Africa.

Elderly refugees

UNHCR's policy on older refugees, calling for efforts to mainstream the policy priorities relating to the elderly, was endorsed by the Standing Committee in March [A/AC.96/929] and operationalized through integration into UNHCR programming and learning tools. During the year, all field offices received HelpAge International research and best practices, funded by UNHCR and the European Community Humanitarian Office, as well as the video *Hardship and Courage*, which described the situation of older refugees, internally displaced persons and returnees in Croatia, and a policy document on older refugees. The policy and examples of activities with older refugees in UNHCR operations were presented in the form of a brochure, *Older Refugees—A Resource for the Refugee Community*, which was disseminated to UNHCR offices and partners.

Refugees and HIV/AIDS

UNHCR, recognizing that conflicts, instability, food insecurity, poverty and deprivation offered fertile ground for the spread of HIV and AIDS, developed a strong partnership with the Joint United Nations Programme on HIV/AIDS (UNAIDS) and continued to rely on that agency's expertise and advocacy role in ensuring that refugees were included in existing assistance programmes. In 2000, UNHCR benefited from a grant from the United Nations Foundation—a public charity founded by Robert Edward Turner to manage his gift to the United Nations of some $1 billion—to strengthen reproductive health and HIV/AIDS activities for refugees. The focus of UNHCR's efforts was in Southern and East Africa.

Regional activities

Africa

Security Council consideration. The Security Council, on 13 January [meeting 4089], considered the agenda item "Promoting peace and security: humanitarian assistance to refugees in Africa".

Addressing the meeting, the High Commissioner said that in the last few years, the pattern of refugee crises, especially in Africa, had undergone significant changes. Although refugees continued to flee violence and conflict and to seek asylum in safer countries, they increasingly sought refuge in safer parts of their own countries. In Angola, almost 20 per cent of the population had fled, both outside and inside the country's borders. Hundreds of thousands of people at risk in war areas, such as Angola, Burundi, the Democratic Republic of the Congo, Sierra Leone and southern Sudan, the majority of them displaced, were currently not accessible to humanitarian organizations. Where such access was possible, it was often very dangerous. Asylum countries that had generously hosted refugees, such as Guinea and the United Republic of Tanzania, had paid a high price in terms of their security and socio-economic and natural environment. War-induced mass population movements had also contributed to the spread of conflicts, as in Central and West Africa. The High Commissioner said that there could be no solution to the refugee crisis if wars that forced people to flee did not stop. However, refugee crises could not be solved in a vacuum. The Council should seek more decisive measures to solve the problems of the indiscriminate struggle for resources, the uncontrolled flow of arms, the lack of a conflict resolution mechanism, and weak support in post-conflict situations.

The High Commissioner suggested the adoption of a comprehensive regional strategy to deal with the host of problems facing Africa. The Council should promote regional initiatives, following the model of the Stability Pact on South-Eastern Europe [YUN 1999, p. 398], that could involve States in the respective regions. It had an essential role to play in preventing, containing and resolving conflicts and, hence, refugee problems in Africa by taking clear, strong and united positions, supporting more decisively, rapidly and substantively the follow-up to peace agreements and promoting the mobilization of resources for reconstruction and peacebuilding.

The High Commissioner noted that resources provided to refugees in Africa, including food and other basic survival items, were far less than in other parts of the world. She hoped that the Council would prompt the international community to address seriously that grave imbalance in material assistance.

SECURITY COUNCIL ACTION

On 13 January [meeting 4089], the Security Council President, following consultations among Council members, made statement **S/PRST/ 2000/1** on behalf of the Council:

The Security Council recalls its previous statements concerning protection for humanitarian assistance to refugees and others in conflict situa-

tions, the situation in Africa, the protection of civilians in armed conflict, and the role of the Security Council in the prevention of armed conflicts. The Council further recalls its relevant resolutions, as well as relevant resolutions of the General Assembly.

Bearing in mind its primary responsibility under the Charter of the United Nations for the maintenance of international peace and security, the Council underlines the importance of taking measures aimed at conflict prevention and resolution in Africa. The Council stresses the need to address the root causes of armed conflict in a comprehensive manner in order to prevent those circumstances that lead to internal displacement and the outflow of refugees. The Council notes with concern that the majority of refugees, returnees, internally displaced persons and others affected by conflict are women and children, and stresses the need to intensify efforts to meet their special protection needs, including their vulnerability to violence, exploitation and disease, including HIV/AIDS. The Council underlines the obligation of all Member States to seek to settle their international disputes by peaceful means. The Council condemns deliberate targeting of civilians and practices of forced displacement. The Council reaffirms its commitment to the principles of political independence, sovereignty and territorial integrity of all States. The Council emphasizes that national authorities have the primary duty and responsibility to provide protection and humanitarian assistance to internally displaced persons within their jurisdiction. The Council reaffirms the obligation of States to prevent arbitrary displacement in situations of armed conflict, and reaffirms as well their responsibility to meet the protection and assistance needs of internally displaced persons within their jurisdiction.

The Council expresses its grave concern that alarmingly high numbers of refugees and internally displaced persons in Africa do not receive sufficient protection and assistance. In this context, the Council notes that refugees are protected under the 1951 United Nations Convention and the 1967 Protocol relating to the Status of Refugees, the 1969 Organization of African Unity Convention Governing the Specific Aspects of Refugee Problems in Africa, and other relevant initiatives in the region. The Council notes also that there is no comprehensive protection regime for internally displaced persons and that existing norms are not being fully implemented. The Council recognizes that large-scale human suffering as well as violations of human rights and humanitarian law are consequences of, and contributing factors to, instability and further conflict. In this regard, the Council affirms the need to ensure adequate protection and assistance both for refugees and for internally displaced persons, taking into account the special difficulties in the provision of humanitarian assistance to internally displaced persons in Africa.

The Council urges all parties concerned to comply strictly with their obligations under international humanitarian, human rights and refugee law, and emphasizes the need for better implementation of relevant norms with regard to internally displaced persons. The Council invites States that have not already done so to consider ratifying the relevant instruments of international humanitarian, human rights and refugee law. The Council takes note of the efforts made within the United Nations system aimed at promoting an effective collective response by the international community to situations of internal displacement. The Council calls upon States, in particular States with situations of internal displacement in Africa, to cooperate fully with such efforts. The Council notes further that the United Nations agencies and regional and non-governmental organizations, in cooperation with host Governments, are making use of the Guiding Principles on Internal Displacement, inter alia, in Africa.

The Council reaffirms the responsibility of States hosting refugees to ensure the security and the civilian and humanitarian character of refugee camps and settlements, in accordance with existing international standards and international humanitarian, human rights and refugee law. In this regard, the Council underlines the unacceptability of using refugees and other persons in refugee camps and settlements to achieve military purposes in the country of asylum or the country of origin.

The Council underlines the importance of safe and unhindered access, in accordance with international law, of humanitarian personnel to civilians in armed conflict, including refugees and internally displaced persons, and the protection of humanitarian assistance to them, and recalls the responsibility of all parties in conflict to ensure the safety and security of such personnel. The Council condemns recent acts of deliberate violence in Africa against humanitarian personnel.

The Council recognizes the extensive experience and burden of African States in hosting refugees and in dealing with the effects of refugee camps and settlements. The Council welcomes the efforts made to support the needs of refugees in Africa, in particular those of the Office of the United Nations High Commissioner for Refugees and the host countries. Noting with concern the shortfall in funding for programmes for refugees and internally displaced persons in Africa, the Council calls upon the international community to provide such programmes with the necessary financial resources, taking into account the substantial needs in Africa.

Report of Secretary-General. In an October report on assistance to refugees, returnees and displaced persons in Africa [A/55/471], submitted in accordance with resolution 54/147 [YUN 1999, p. 1141], the Secretary-General stated that, at midyear, UNHCR was assisting almost 6.3 million persons in that continent, nearly one third of the total number of refugees worldwide. The report noted that the main refugee groups continued to originate in Sierra Leone (487,200), the Sudan (467,700), Somalia (451,500), Angola (350,700), Eritrea (345,600) and Burundi (325,500). The tripartite agreement signed in April by Eritrea, the Sudan and UNHCR raised hopes that some 160,000 Eritrean refugees living in the Sudan for

the past 30 years would finally go home. However, with the resumption of hostilities between Eritrea and Ethiopia one month later, that did not happen.

In West Africa, security incidents in northern Liberia triggered the flight of more than 11,000 Sierra Leonean refugees further south in Liberia, while 8,000 Liberian refugees left their homes for Guinea. UNHCR and its non-governmental partners also had to leave the area. Since 1997, more than 356,000 Liberian refugees had returned home, either spontaneously or with assistance, and UNHCR was planning to complete the organized repatriation by the end of 2000. During the year, UNHCR continued preparations for the voluntary return of refugees to safe places in Sierra Leone and facilitated the return of some 1,200 Chadian refugees from Cameroon. Meanwhile, it continued humanitarian assistance activities in Gabon and Guinea.

In Central Africa, Sudanese refugees fled to Chad, and the civil wars in the Congo and in the Democratic Republic of the Congo (DRC) caused the flight of more refugees from those countries to the Central African Republic and Gabon. In the Great Lakes region, the DRC accommodated 300,000 refugees and 1.4 million displaced persons. UNHCR provided assistance to 180,000 refugees in the DRC from Angola, Burundi, the Congo, Rwanda, the Sudan and Uganda, as well as 300,000 displaced persons. Due to the ongoing unsettled situation in Burundi, refugees from that country continued to flee to the United Republic of Tanzania, which hosted one of the largest caseloads on the continent, some 488,000 refugees. UNHCR supported the Government in dealing with security issues in refugee-affected areas and surrounding villages, addressed sexual and gender-based violence and provided care and maintenance to the majority of refugees in that country. UNHCR monitored the situation in Rwanda and played a role in the reintegration of returnees. The Office contributed also to the drafting, translation and distribution of refugee legislation.

In East Africa and the Horn of Africa, strategies and solutions were developed to end protracted refugee programmes. Agreement was reached on arrangements to allow the repatriation beginning in March of some 3,700 Ethiopian refugees in the Sudan who had fled before 1991. In Somalia, an encouraging development was the resumed voluntary repatriation of Somali refugees from Ethiopia to north-west Somalia. By mid-2000, some 10,000 Somali refugees from camps in Ethiopia had been assisted to repatriate. The resumption of fighting between Eritrea and Ethiopia resulted in an influx of 90,000 Eritrean refugees into the Sudan, and some 750,000 people were displaced inside Eritrea. The signing of a tripartite agreement by UNHCR, Ethiopia and Kenya in June paved the way for the return of 5,000 Kenyan refugees who had been in southern Ethiopia since 1992.

In 2000, UNHCR assisted over 300,000 refugees and asylum-seekers in Southern Africa and 300,000 internally displaced persons in northern Angola. Developments in the Caprivi Strip of Namibia triggered an influx of asylum-seekers into Botswana, which was hosting 3,000 refugees, and UNHCR was working with the Botswana Refugee Advisory Committee to integrate some of the refugees locally. Meanwhile, Angolan refugees in Namibia had increased to over 20,580 persons who were provided with food, non-food items, medical and legal assistance, and shelter. In Zambia, which hosted over 218,000 refugees, UNHCR provided food aid to 60,000 and helped to establish a new camp to accommodate the ever-increasing refugee population, mostly from Angola and the DRC. UNHCR also assisted over 2,000 refugees in Malawi from different countries and close to 1,750 who had been affected by extensive flood damage in Mozambique. The Office provided basic assistance and legal protection to the 58,000 asylum-seekers in South Africa. It also carried out activities to promote refugee law and protection principles in Swaziland and Zimbabwe.

The Secretary-General noted that interagency cooperation had been important in providing assistance to refugees, returnees and displaced persons in Africa, although the ravages caused by the AIDS pandemic had added to the difficulties encountered. Such cooperation had been undertaken in the areas of relief assistance; access to populations of concern; coordinating resources; assisting and protecting children; post-conflict reconstruction; and internally displaced persons in Africa. Regional cooperation was strengthened with the Organization of African Unity (OAU) and the Intergovernmental Authority on Development, as well as with financial institutions, such as the African Development Bank. UNHCR and OAU organized a special meeting of technical experts and policy advisers on international refugee protection (Conakry, Guinea, 27-29 March), which formulated proposals for a comprehensive plan to help strengthen the implementation of the 1969 OAU Refugee Convention and the regime of international protection for asylum-seekers, refugees and returnees and to facilitate the search for durable solutions to refugee problems.

Concluding, the Secretary-General stated that rebuilding a peaceful society in Africa could not be achieved unless displaced persons and refugees successfully returned and reintegrated. Durable solutions could be found only if the alarming pattern of violence in the continent was reversed.

Report of High Commissioner. In the 2000 annual report [A/56/12], the High Commissioner, outlining UNHCR's regional activities in Africa, said that, following the assassination of a UNHCR staff member and the kidnapping of two others in Guinea in September and December, UN Security Phase IV was declared in all locations in that country, except Conakry and Kissidougou, further restricting UNHCR's protection and operational capacity. Responding to the evolving situation in West Africa, UNHCR adopted a regional strategy, establishing, among other initiatives, a subregional repatriation and reintegration cell in April, which contributed to the coordination of the Sierra Leonean and Liberian refugee situations and the reallocation of resources within the subregion. In Guinea, a three-pronged approach was used to provide emergency assistance to Sierra Leonean and Liberian refugees and internally displaced persons in south-east Guinea; to organize internal relocation to relatively safe areas, giving priority to 135,000 refugees stranded west of Gueckedou; and to facilitate repatriation and reintegration for Sierra Leonean refugees from Guinea and promote the same for Liberian refugees. In Southern Africa, UNHCR's overall objective in 2000 was to ensure that the 320,000 refugees in the region continued to enjoy the right to seek asylum and be treated in accordance with international protection standards.

By subregion, UNHCR assisted 1.6 million persons in Central and West Africa, which received almost $77 million in agency expenditure. In East Africa and the Horn of Africa and the Great Lakes region, $175.2 million was spent on more than 2.9 million persons of concern, while in Southern Africa, $32.8 million was spent on programmes assisting almost 600,000 refugees, internally displaced persons, asylum-seekers and returned refugees.

Communications. By a 3 August letter [A/55/286], Ghana transmitted the decisions adopted by the OAU Council of Ministers (Lomé, Togo, 6-8 July) and the declarations and decisions adopted by the Assembly of Heads of State and Government of OAU (10-12 July), which included a decision on the situation of refugees and displaced persons in Africa. The ministers endorsed the global implementation plan adopted by the OAU/UNHCR Special Meeting of Government and Non-Government Technical Experts (Conakry, Guinea, 27-29 March), as well as the recommendations of the sixth OAU/ICRC Seminar on International Humanitarian Law (Addis Ababa, Ethiopia, 15-16 May).

By an October letter [A/55/506-S/2000/1006], Burundi conveyed the report of the Subregional Conference on the Question of Refugees and Displaced Persons in Central Africa (Bujumbura, Burundi, 14-16 August), organized by the United Nations Standing Advisory Committee on Security Questions in Central Africa. The participants recommended measures to be taken at the national and subregional levels to find lasting solutions to the problems of refugees and displaced persons in Central Africa.

GENERAL ASSEMBLY ACTION

On 4 December [meeting 81], the General Assembly, on the recommendation of the Third Committee [A/55/597], adopted **resolution 55/77** without vote [agenda item 109].

Assistance to refugees, returnees and displaced persons in Africa

The General Assembly,

Recalling its resolution 54/147 of 17 December 1999,

Recalling also the provisions of its resolution 2312(XXII) of 14 December 1967, by which it adopted the Declaration on Territorial Asylum,

Recalling further the Organization of African Unity Convention governing the specific aspects of refugee problems in Africa of 1969 and the African Charter on Human and Peoples' Rights,

Recalling the Khartoum Declaration and the Recommendations on Refugees, Returnees and Internally Displaced Persons in Africa adopted by the Organization of African Unity at the ministerial meeting held at Khartoum on 13 and 14 December 1998,

Welcoming decision CM/Dec.531(LXXII) on the situation of refugees, returnees and displaced persons in Africa adopted by the Council of Ministers of the Organization of African Unity at its seventy-second ordinary session, held at Lomé from 6 to 8 July 2000,

Welcoming also the convening by the Organization of African Unity and the Office of the United Nations High Commissioner for Refugees of the Special Meeting of Governmental and Non-Governmental Technical Experts at Conakry from 27 to 29 March 2000, on the occasion of the thirtieth anniversary of the adoption of the Organization of African Unity Convention governing the specific aspects of refugee problems in Africa, commending the comprehensive implementation plan adopted by the Special Meeting, and noting its endorsement by the Council of Ministers of the Organization of African Unity at its seventy-second ordinary session,

Commending the First Ministerial Conference on Human Rights in Africa of the Organization of African Unity, held at Grand-Baie, Mauritius, from 12 to 16 April 1999, and recalling the attention paid to issues relevant to refugees and displaced persons in the Declaration and Plan of Action adopted by the Conference,

Recalling the sixth Seminar on International Humanitarian Law, convened by the Organization of African Unity and the International Committee of the Red Cross at Addis Ababa on 15 and 16 May 2000, and noting the endorsement of the recommendations of the Seminar by the Council of Ministers of the Organization of African Unity at its seventy-second ordinary session,

Recognizing the contributions made by African States to the development of regional standards for the protection of refugees and returnees, and noting with appreciation that countries of asylum are hosting refugees in a humanitarian spirit and in a spirit of African solidarity and brotherhood,

Recognizing also the need for States to address resolutely the root causes of forced displacement and to create conditions that facilitate durable solutions for refugees and displaced persons, and stressing in this regard the need for States to foster peace, stability and prosperity throughout the African continent,

Convinced of the need to strengthen the capacity of States to provide assistance and protection for refugees, returnees and displaced persons and of the need for the international community, within the context of burden-sharing, to increase its material, financial and technical assistance to the countries affected by refugees, returnees and displaced persons,

Acknowledging with appreciation that some assistance is already rendered by the international community to refugees, returnees and displaced persons and host countries in Africa,

Noting with great concern that, despite all the efforts deployed so far by the United Nations, the Organization of African Unity and others, the situation of refugees and displaced persons in Africa, especially in the West African and Great Lakes regions and in the Horn of Africa, remains precarious,

Stressing that the provision of relief and assistance to African refugees by the international community should be on an equitable, non-discriminatory basis,

Considering that, among refugees, returnees and internally displaced persons, women and children are the majority of the population affected by conflict and bear the brunt of atrocities and other consequences of conflict,

1. *Takes note* of the reports of the Secretary-General and the United Nations High Commissioner for Refugees;

2. *Notes with concern* that the declining socio-economic situation, compounded by political instability, internal strife, human rights violations and natural disasters, has led to increased numbers of refugees and displaced persons in some countries of Africa, and remains particularly concerned about the impact of large-scale refugee populations on the security, socio-economic situation and environment of countries of asylum;

3. *Recalls* the commemoration in 1999 of the thirtieth anniversary of the adoption of the Organization of African Unity Convention governing the specific aspects of refugee problems in Africa of 1969, and commends the convening by the Organization of African Unity and the Office of the United Nations High Commissioner for Refugees of the Special Meeting of Governmental and Non-Governmental Technical Experts at Conakry from 27 to 29 March 2000 to mark that anniversary;

4. *Encourages* African States to ensure the full implementation of and follow-up to the comprehensive

implementation plan adopted by the Special Meeting and endorsed by the Council of Ministers of the Organization of African Unity;

5. *Also encourages* African States to ensure the full implementation of and follow-up to the recommendations of the sixth Seminar on International Humanitarian Law, convened by the Organization of African Unity and the International Committee of the Red Cross at Addis Ababa on 15 and 16 May 2000;

6. *Calls upon* States and other parties to armed conflict to observe scrupulously the letter and the spirit of international humanitarian law, bearing in mind that armed conflict is one of the principal causes of forced displacement in Africa;

7. *Expresses its sincere appreciation and gratitude* to Sadako Ogata for her tireless efforts, throughout her tenure as United Nations High Commissioner for Refugees, to address the plight of refugees, returnees and displaced persons in Africa and for her inspiring example in performing her functions in an exemplary and dedicated manner;

8. *Expresses its gratitude and appreciation*, in this year which marks the fiftieth anniversary of the Office of the United Nations High Commissioner for Refugees, for the work accomplished since its establishment, with the support of the international community, in assisting African countries of asylum and responding to the needs of refugees, returnees and displaced persons in Africa for assistance and protection;

9. *Notes* the intergovernmental event planned in commemoration of the fiftieth anniversary of the adoption of the 1951 Convention relating to the Status of Refugees, in 2001, and encourages African States parties to the Convention to participate actively in the event;

10. *Reaffirms* that the 1951 Convention and the 1967 Protocol relating to the Status of Refugees, as complemented by the Organization of African Unity Convention of 1969, remain the foundation of the international refugee protection regime in Africa, encourages African States that have not yet done so to accede to those instruments, and calls upon States parties to the Conventions to reaffirm their commitment to their ideals and to respect and observe their provisions;

11. *Notes* the need for States to address the root causes of forced displacement in Africa, and calls upon African States, the international community and relevant United Nations organizations to take concrete action to meet the needs of refugees, returnees and displaced persons for protection and assistance and to contribute generously to national projects and programmes aimed at alleviating their plight;

12. *Also notes* the link, inter alia, between human rights violations, poverty, natural disasters and environmental degradation and population displacement, and calls for redoubled and concerted efforts by States, in collaboration with the Organization of African Unity, to promote and protect human rights for all and to address these problems;

13. *Encourages* the Office of the United Nations High Commissioner for Refugees to continue to cooperate with the Office of the United Nations High Commissioner for Human Rights and the African Commission on Human and Peoples' Rights, within their respective mandates, in the promotion and protection of the human rights and fundamental freedoms of refugees, returnees and displaced persons in Africa;

14. *Notes with appreciation* the ongoing mediation and conflict resolution efforts carried out by African States, the Organization of African Unity and subregional organizations, as well as the establishment of regional mechanisms for conflict prevention and resolution, and urges all relevant parties to address the humanitarian consequences of conflicts;

15. *Expresses its appreciation and strong support* for those African Governments and local populations that, in spite of the general deterioration of socio-economic and environmental conditions and overstretched national resources, continue to accept the additional burden imposed upon them by increasing numbers of refugees and displaced persons, in compliance with the relevant principles of asylum;

16. *Expresses its concern* about instances in which the fundamental principle of asylum is jeopardized by unlawful expulsion or refoulement or by threats to the life, physical security, integrity, dignity and well-being of refugees;

17. *Calls upon* States, in cooperation with international organizations, within their mandates, to take all necessary measures to ensure respect for the principles of refugee protection and, in particular, to ensure that the civilian and humanitarian nature of refugee camps is not compromised by the presence or the activities of armed elements;

18. *Notes* the proposal of the Office of the United Nations High Commissioner for Refugees to commence a process of global consultations on the international refugee protection regime, and in this context invites African States to participate actively in this process so as to bring their regional perspective to bear, thus ensuring that adequate attention is paid to concerns that are specific to Africa;

19. *Deplores* the deaths and injuries and other forms of violence sustained by staff members of the Office of the High Commissioner and urges States, parties to conflict and all other relevant actors to take all necessary measures to protect activities related to humanitarian assistance, to prevent attacks on and kidnapping of national and international humanitarian workers and to ensure their safety and security, calls upon States to investigate fully any crimes committed against humanitarian personnel and bring to justice persons responsible for such crimes, and calls upon organizations and aid workers to abide by the national laws and regulations of the countries in which they operate;

20. *Calls upon* the Office of the High Commissioner, the Organization of African Unity, subregional organizations and all African States, in conjunction with United Nations agencies, intergovernmental and non-governmental organizations and the international community, to strengthen and revitalize existing partnerships and forge new ones in support of the international refugee protection system;

21. *Calls upon* the Office of the High Commissioner, the international community and other concerned entities to intensify their support to African Governments through appropriate capacity-building activities, including training of relevant officers, disseminating information about refugee instruments and principles, providing financial, technical and advisory services to accelerate the enactment or amendment and imple-

mentation of legislation relating to refugees, strengthening emergency response and enhancing capacities for the coordination of humanitarian activities;

22. *Reaffirms* the right of return and also the principle of voluntary repatriation, appeals to countries of origin and countries of asylum to create conditions that are conducive to voluntary repatriation, and recognizes that, while voluntary repatriation remains the pre-eminent solution, local integration and third-country resettlement, as appropriate, are also viable options for dealing with the situation of African refugees who, owing to prevailing circumstances in their respective countries of origin, are unable to return home;

23. *Notes with satisfaction* the voluntary return of millions of refugees to their homelands following the successful repatriation and reintegration operations carried out by the Office of the High Commissioner, with the cooperation and collaboration of countries hosting refugees and countries of origin, and looks forward to other programmes to assist the voluntary repatriation and reintegration of all refugees in Africa;

24. *Reiterates* that the Plan of Action adopted by the Regional Conference on Assistance to Refugees, Returnees and Displaced Persons in the Great Lakes Region, held at Bujumbura from 15 to 17 February 1995, as endorsed by the General Assembly in its resolution 50/149 of 21 December 1995, continues to be a viable framework for the resolution of the refugee and humanitarian problems in that region;

25. *Appeals* to the international community to respond positively, in the spirit of solidarity and burden-sharing, to the third-country resettlement requests of African refugees, and notes with appreciation that some African countries have offered resettlement places for refugees;

26. *Welcomes* the programmes carried out by the Office of the High Commissioner with host Governments, the United Nations, non-governmental organizations and the international community to address the environmental impact of refugee populations;

27. *Calls upon* the international donor community to provide material and financial assistance for the implementation of programmes intended for the rehabilitation of the environment and infrastructure affected by refugees in countries of asylum;

28. *Expresses its concern* about the long stay of refugees in certain African countries, and calls upon the Office of the High Commissioner to keep its programmes under review, in conformity with its mandate in the host countries, taking into account the increasing needs of refugees;

29. *Emphasizes* the need for the Office of the High Commissioner to collate statistics, on a regular basis, on the number of refugees living outside refugee camps in certain African countries, with a view to evaluating and addressing the needs of those refugees;

30. *Urges* the international community, in a spirit of international solidarity and burden-sharing, to continue to fund generously the refugee programmes of the Office of the High Commissioner and, taking into account the substantially increased needs of programmes in Africa, to ensure that Africa receives a fair and equitable share of the resources designated for refugees;

31. *Requests* all Governments and intergovernmental and non-governmental organizations to pay particular attention to meeting the special needs of refugee women and children and displaced persons, including those with special protection needs;

32. *Calls upon* States and the Office of the High Commissioner to make renewed efforts to ensure that the rights, needs and dignity of elderly refugees are fully respected and addressed through appropriate programme activities;

33. *Invites* the Representative of the Secretary-General on internally displaced persons to continue his ongoing dialogue with Member States and the intergovernmental and non-governmental organizations concerned, in accordance with his mandate, and to include information thereon in his reports to the Commission on Human Rights and the General Assembly;

34. *Expresses grave concern* about the plight of internally displaced persons in Africa, calls upon States to take concrete action to pre-empt internal displacement and to meet the protection and assistance needs of internally displaced persons, recalls in this regard the Guiding Principles on Internal Displacement, and urges the international community, led by relevant United Nations organizations, to contribute generously to national projects and programmes aimed at alleviating the plight of internally displaced persons;

35. *Requests* the Secretary-General to submit a comprehensive report on assistance to refugees, returnees and displaced persons in Africa to the General Assembly at its fifty-sixth session, taking fully into account the efforts expended by countries of asylum, under the item entitled "Report of the United Nations High Commissioner for Refugees, questions relating to refugees, returnees and displaced persons and humanitarian questions", and to present an oral report to the Economic and Social Council at its substantive session of 2001.

The Americas

In 2000, UNHCR's primary operational challenge in South America continued to be the displacement caused by the internal conflict in Colombia and the consequent cross-border movements mainly into Ecuador, Panama and Venezuela. In response, the Office implemented an integrated regional strategy. It reinforced Ecuador's national asylum system, strengthened an emergency contingency plan, provided emergency assistance and supported initial repatriation movements. A tripartite mechanism between the Governments of Ecuador and Colombia and UNHCR was created to promote durable solutions. The Office also lobbied for the adoption of refugee legislation in Venezuela and the establishment of a formal eligibility mechanism. However, Venezuelan authorities reportedly returned more than 2,000 Colombians without granting them access to asylum procedures. In Panama, UNHCR provided emergency assistance to 1,100 Colombians under the special temporary protection mechanism established in Panama's refugee legislation. The Office also strengthened Colombia's national institutional framework for internally displaced persons and, at the regional level, reinforced its emergency response capacity, early warning and standard-setting, paying particular attention to displaced women and children.

In Southern South America, UNHCR promoted regional harmonization of refugee laws and asylum procedures using model refugee legislation for Southern Cone Common Market (MERCOSUR) countries. Among its activities in Central America, UNHCR helped strengthen protection networks. It completed a repatriation programme in Guatemala and closed its office there in December. Other subregional activities were implemented in Costa Rica and Mexico.

In Canada and the United States, UNHCR continued monitoring and advising agencies that implemented complex refugee and asylum systems. The Office also monitored the situation in the Caribbean, particularly regarding possible displacement from Haiti, developed contingency plans and promoted capacity-building efforts in the subregion.

Total UNHCR expenditure in the Americas and the Caribbean for the year was $24.6 million for a total population of concern numbering 1,620,784.

Asia and the Pacific and the Arab States

In 2000, total UNHCR expenditure for activities in Asia and the Pacific amounted to $75.4 million for a total population of concern of 1,753,830. For activities in Central Asia, South-West Asia, North Africa and the Middle East, expenditure totalled $73.5 million for a population of concern of 5,800,000.

South Asia

While the majority of refugees who had fled the Northern Rakhine State of Myanmar to Bangladesh had returned by 2000, procedural difficulties slowed the return of the remaining 21,500 refugees. Only 1,323 persons returned to Myanmar during the year. UNHCR discussed other possibilities with the Bangladesh Government for refugees who were unwilling or unable to return in the near future. In Myanmar, the Office assisted in reintegrating returnees to stabilize the situation of the Muslim population and reduce the likelihood of a renewed population outflow. UNHCR-funded assistance activities in Northern Rakhine State would be taken over by the United Nations Development Programme, but UNHCR would continue its field monitoring activities to address public policy and governance

issues affecting the 230,000 returnees from Bangladesh and the local population.

Some 170,000 persons in the Jaffna Peninsula of Sri Lanka were displaced because of the escalation of armed hostilities in the north of the country. UNHCR worked with the Government and others to ease the situation of 560,000 displaced persons. Although there were no large-scale movements of Sri Lankans to India, over 66,000 Sri Lankan refugees remained in India's Tamil Nadu State.

In December, Bhutan and Nepal resolved their differences over modalities for verifying the 97,500 Bhutanese refugees in Nepal. To facilitate the process, UNHCR provided technical expertise and financial support to Nepal and offered to do the same for Bhutan.

East Asia and the Pacific

In 2000, a regional emergency training centre on international humanitarian response (E-centre) was established by UNHCR in Japan to enhance the regional capacity to respond to emergency situations. In China, the Office encouraged naturalization of the majority of the 230,000 Vietnamese refugees who wanted to settle in that country and voluntary repatriation for a limited number who might wish to return. It continued to raise with China the situation of North Korean populations within its northern border provinces and sought access to those populations. UNHCR worked with Thailand on the admission of asylum-seekers from Myanmar into the 11 border camps, and cooperated with Mongolia in the areas of refugee law, capacity-building and refugee status determination. It phased out its reintegration assistance in north-west Cambodia in December and scaled down its activities in the Lao People's Democratic Republic.

Timor

The brutal murder in September of three UNHCR staff members in West Timor precipitated the imposition of UN Security Phase V, which precluded UNHCR from implementing direct protection activities. However, the Office pursued ad hoc repatriation operations beginning in November, allowing for the return of demobilized soldiers, ex–civil servants and other refugees to East Timor. To encourage the return of East Timorese from West Timor, UNHCR expanded basic assistance to returnees, initiated discussions with the United Nations Transitional Administration in East Timor (UNTAET) (see PART ONE, Chapter IV) on the prosecution of persons charged with committing various crimes before and during the 1999 referendum on independence, and proposed the expansion of "safe houses", which served as transit centres for returnees hesitant to return to their villages of origin immediately after arriving in East Timor. Meanwhile, UNHCR was involved with screening a number of asylum-seekers intercepted in Indonesian waters while trying to reach Australia.

Central Asia, South-West Asia, North Africa and the Middle East

Little progress was achieved in realizing durable solutions to the refugee situation in the region in 2000. Protracted conflicts were exacerbated in many cases by either political or natural constraints, creating more displacement and suffering. In Central Asia, the repatriation operation in Tajikistan was delayed when the Government suspended returnee movements following security incidents between returnees and local populations. In Kazakhstan, Kyrgyzstan, Tajikistan and Turkmenistan, UNHCR offices worked for the passage and implementation of refugee laws. Local settlement projects were implemented in Kyrgyzstan and Turkmenistan for the Tajiks of Kyrgyz and Turkmen ethnicity, respectively. In South-West Asia, the situation in Afghanistan was compounded by the worst drought experienced in three decades, displacing thousands of Afghans internally, as well as to Iran and Pakistan. While the majority of the 2.6 million Afghans remained in those countries, UNHCR succeeded in assisting some 261,000 to return voluntarily to Afghanistan.

In North Africa, UNHCR focused on enhancing its protection presence, promoting refugee law and assisting Governments to establish national asylum legislation and procedures. The lack of a breakthrough in the peace process in Western Sahara prevented implementation of the UN settlement plan, including the repatriation of 165,000 refugees from Algeria. UNHCR continued to provide assistance in the Tindouf refugee camps, in cooperation with other partners. In the Middle East, it assisted 130,000 refugees living in urban settings, as well as in small camps in Iraq, Saudi Arabia and the Syrian Arab Republic, and resettled 7,000 refugees from the region.

Europe

In 2000, UNHCR's expenditure for activities in Europe (excluding South-Eastern Europe) totalled $85.1 million for a population of concern numbering 5,148,062.

Western Europe

UNHCR's priority in the subregion in 2000 was maintaining and strengthening the quality of asylum. Its relations with European Union (EU) institutions intensified. In July, UNHCR and the European Commission signed an exchange of letters to reinforce cooperation on asylum and refugee matters, which led to formal strategic senior-level consultations, in addition to the day-to-day liaison and advocacy work of UNHCR Brussels. UNHCR also assisted Western European Governments in their adoption, implementation and amendment of national asylum legislation and policies.

Central Europe and the Baltic States

Central Europe and the Baltic States were in the process of developing functioning asylum legislation and systems, and UNHCR played a catalytic role in linking Governments and NGOs with Western European counterparts for capacity-building assistance. UNHCR offices in EU countries also participated in the EU's Poland/Hungary: Assistance for the Reconstruction of the Economy (PHARE) horizontal programme on asylum, which came to a close at the end of the year, by organizing meetings, workshops, and training and exchange programmes for governmental counterparts in cooperation with EU member States. Activities in the area of asylum institution- and capacity-building were being conducted through national action plans.

Eastern Europe

UNHCR assisted Governments in Eastern Europe to bridge the gap between legislation, in place in most countries, and its proper implementation, thus strengthening the quality of asylum. The Office also supported local NGOs in responding to the needs of asylum-seekers, refugees and displaced persons; assisted Governments to find sustainable solutions for displaced groups; and enhanced partnerships with the Council of Europe, the Organization for Security and Cooperation in Europe (OSCE) and others.

In the Caucasus, finding durable solutions to those displaced due to the conflict in Chechnya in the Russian Federation remained a key objective. Over 160,000 internally displaced persons in the neighbouring republic of Ingushetia received assistance for accommodation, water, sanitation and basic domestic needs. In Georgia, UNHCR provided limited assistance to about 7,000 Chechen refugees, although security conditions hampered monitoring. A small number of convoys carrying food and non-food relief items were sent into Chechnya, and UNHCR worked with the Academy of Science of the Russian Federation to develop a geographical database for better targeting of assistance.

Conference on refugees of CIS countries and neighbouring States

The formal follow-up process to the 1996 Regional Conference to Address the Problems of Refugees, Displaced Persons, Other Forms of Involuntary Displacement and Returnees in the Countries of the Commonwealth of Independent States and Relevant Neighbouring States (CIS Conference) [YUN 1996, p. 1117] ended in July. The Steering Group established to monitor implementation of the CIS Conference met on 13 and 14 July to review the achievements in the implementation of the Programme of Action [YUN 1996, p. 1118] adopted by the Conference and to take a decision on future activities. The Steering Group decided that the follow-up to the 1996 Conference would last for five years starting from 2000, and would focus on four thematic issues: assuring continued focus on groups of concern; migration management, including combating illegal/illicit migration and trafficking, particularly trafficking in women, and improving border management; sustaining the achievements and activities of NGOs and civil society and further promoting their participation; and implementing legislation and avoiding implementation gaps.

A work plan emphasizing protection matters was developed, focusing on building national asylum and migration management systems in the CIS countries in accordance with international standards, including the implementation of national refugee and citizenship legislation, reduction and avoidance of statelessness and support to NGOs and civil society development.

Executive Committee action. The Executive Committee endorsed the Steering Group's decision on the future of the follow-up action. It reaffirmed the continuing validity of the Programme of Action as the basis for future activities and stressed the necessity for joint efforts. The Committee called on Governments, which bore primary responsibility for addressing the acute problems of population displacement, to strengthen their commitment to implementing the Programme of Action to ensure more consistent and far-reaching progress. It urged the High Commissioner to further enhance relationships with other key actors, such as the European Commission and other human rights, development and financial institutions, and called on CIS countries to facilitate the formation and work of NGOs, to further strengthen cooperation with them and to increase their involvement in the follow-up activities.

Report of Secretary-General. The Secretary-General, in October [A/55/472], submitted a report on the follow-up to the Conference, in response to General Assembly resolution 54/144 [YUN 1999, p. 1146]. He said that the Conference process had considerably advanced several issues identified in the Programme of Action and had met its objectives. In addition, it had given impetus to the development of the NGO sector and civil society and forged vital partnerships.

UNHCR had contributed to the growing awareness of Governments in the region that refugees and asylum-seekers' problems needed to be addressed through effective legislative and institutional frameworks that were consistent with international standards. It continued to provide substantial humanitarian and integration assistance and played a key role in inter-agency efforts to assist internally displaced persons from Chechnya. It also contributed to finding solutions to problems of formerly deported Crimean Tartars, including their legal status. Other types of activities specifically generated by the CIS Conference process, such as legal assistance, capacity-building and training to help States strengthen implementation of the Programme of Action, had been gradually mainstreamed into UNHCR country operations. With the support of IOM, progress was made in establishing national migration management systems in 10 countries. The Office of the United Nations High Commissioner for Human Rights supported the Programme of Action through its technical cooperation programme aimed at establishing or strengthening human rights institutions.

By **decision 55/417** of 4 December, the General Assembly took note of the Secretary-General's report on follow-up to the CIS Conference.

South-Eastern Europe

Following a year dominated by massive population displacement caused by the conflict in the Kosovo province of FRY, hundreds of thousands of Kosovars were reintegrated into their home communities in 2000 as a result of the encouragement by the new FRY Government (see PART ONE, Chapter V) and a large-scale humanitarian relief effort. To facilitate assistance delivery and reconstruction, UNHCR developed a geographical database of the province using Geographical Information System technology. However, the fact that more than 220,000 non-Albanians from Kosovo remained in other parts of FRY was one of UNHCR's major concerns in the region. Inter-ethnic violence in southern Serbia and the former Yugoslav Republic of Macedonia (FYROM) caused more than a million people to remain displaced, with hundreds of thousands requiring support from the international community. The number of refugees and persons of concern to UNHCR in Albania and FYROM declined due to the large-scale repatriation to Kosovo, while tens of thousands of displaced persons and refugees, mainly from FRY, returned to Bosnia and Herzegovina and Croatia. Enforcement of property legislation in Bosnia and Herzegovina, combined with improved security conditions, led many displaced persons to return to areas to which minorities had not ventured since the end of the war. In Croatia, the new administration eliminated discriminatory elements of legislation governing reconstruction of property in an effort to encourage minority returns.

UNHCR, in efforts to assist countries faced with an increasing number of migrants and asylum-seekers transiting the region en route to Western Europe, initiated a region-wide initiative within the framework of the Stability Pact for South-Eastern Europe (see p. 412) to develop national asylum systems and improve countries' capacities to deal with the issue.

During 2000, UNHCR remained engaged in emergency preparedness response activities with regard to potential areas of population displacement in the region, such as Montenegro, Kosovo, southern Serbia and FYROM.

Total UNHCR expenditure in South-Eastern Europe for the year was $154 million for a population of concern numbering 1,698,342.

Chapter XIII

Health, food and nutrition

In 2000, the United Nations continued to take action to promote human health, coordinate food aid and food security and support research in nutrition.

The total number of people living with HIV/AIDS worldwide at the end of 2000 was 36.1 million, according to the Joint United Nations Programme on Human Immunodeficiency Virus/Acquired Immunodeficiency Syndrome (UNAIDS) and the World Health Organization (WHO). Some 5.3 million new infections and an estimated 3 million deaths due to the epidemic were recorded, representing the highest annual total of AIDS deaths ever. UNAIDS effectively promoted HIV/AIDS as a priority on national agendas and emphasized the importance of leadership in all sectors. It supported decentralized planning efforts at the district and community levels and promoted synergy with other multilateral and bilateral partners within the framework of national strategies.

In the Millennium Declaration adopted by the Millennium Summit of the United Nations, held in September, world leaders committed themselves to halting and beginning to reverse the spread of HIV/AIDS by 2015; providing special assistance to children orphaned by HIV/AIDS; and helping Africa build its capacity to tackle the spread of the HIV/AIDS pandemic and other infectious diseases. The General Assembly decided to convene a special session in June 2001 to review and address the problem of HIV/AIDS as a matter of urgency.

The United Nations continued to be concerned with tobacco and its ill effects. Based on current smoking trends, it was predicted that tobacco would be the leading cause of disease by the 2020s, resulting in about one in eight deaths, a proportion greater than from any other single cause. The Ad Hoc Inter-Agency Task Force on Tobacco Control, at its second session, decided that inter-agency partnerships should focus on the economics of tobacco control, including supply and production issues. In October, the Intergovernmental Negotiating Body on the WHO Framework Convention on Tobacco Control considered draft elements and provisional texts.

The World Food Programme—a joint undertaking of the United Nations and the Food and Agriculture Organization of the United Nations—provided food aid to 83 million people. Total quantities of food provided amounted to 3.5 million tons, an increase of 3 per cent over the previous year and the highest since the record high of 1992.

Health

AIDS prevention and control

The Joint United Nations Programme on Human Immunodeficiency Virus/Acquired Immunodeficiency Syndrome (UNAIDS), which became fully operational in 1996 [YUN 1996, p. 1121], continued to coordinate UN activities for AIDS prevention and control. The Programme, which served as the main advocate for global action on HIV/AIDS, had seven co-sponsors: the United Nations Development Programme (UNDP), the United Nations Children's Fund (UNICEF), the United Nations Educational, Scientific and Cultural Organization (UNESCO), the United Nations International Drug Control Programme (UNDCP), the United Nations Population Fund (UNFPA), the World Bank and the World Health Organization (WHO). UNAIDS was to lead, strengthen and support an expanded response to the epidemic, mainly through facilitation and coordination, best practice development and advocacy.

According to UNAIDS/WHO, provisional estimates indicated that 36.1 million people were living with HIV/AIDS worldwide at year's end, which was more than 50 per cent higher than projected in 1991 by the WHO Global Programme on AIDS. In 2000, some 5.3 million people were newly infected and about 3 million people died, representing the highest annual total of AIDS deaths ever recorded and bringing the total of deaths since the onset of the epidemic to 21.8 million. By year's end, the epidemic had left behind a cumulative total of 13.2 million AIDS orphans, defined as children who had lost their mother before reaching the age of 15.

In all parts of the world except sub-Saharan Africa, more men were HIV-infected and dying of AIDS than women. Altogether, an estimated 2.5 million men aged 15 to 49 became infected during 2000, bringing the number of adult males living with HIV or AIDS at year's end to 18.2 million. The year 2000 World AIDS Campaign focused on the difference men could make to curb HIV transmission, care for infected family members and look after orphans and other survivors of the epidemic.

According to a report of the UNAIDS Executive Director [E/2001/82], of the more than 36 million people living with HIV at the end of 2000, some 95 per cent were in the developing world. Sub-Saharan Africa continued to be the worst-hit region. Even though the number of new infections in some countries was stabilizing, in the eight African countries with HIV prevalence of at least 15 per cent, some one third of the current population of 15-year-olds were expected to die from AIDS. In the Caribbean region, AIDS was the primary cause of death among young men and women. Eastern Europe and Latin America saw steep rises of new infections. In Asia, some 7 million people were living with HIV. The disproportionate impact of HIV in minority communities and the risk of complacency were growing concerns in industrialized countries.

At the end of the year, 64 countries had completed national strategic plans on HIV/AIDS and 28 others were developing them. UNAIDS supported decentralized planning efforts at the district and community levels and promoted synergy with other multilateral and bilateral partners within the framework of national strategies. Although UNAIDS had limited capacity to keep up with governmental demands for support in preparing plans to expand access to care, it supported the development of 16 care plans during the year. In May, the Contact Group on Accelerating Access to Care and Treatment was set up as a forum for the exchange of information, views and strategic recommendations. Several UN resident coordinator reports for 2000 singled out the theme groups on HIV/AIDS as the most active and successful of all such system theme groups. Many groups had broadened the scope of their efforts, to include advocacy, resource mobilization, support for national programme development and facilitating exchanges of experiences within regions. Although the resources available for the support of national responses from the UNAIDS secretariat were very modest, they represented a significant proportion of the UNAIDS core biennial budget. In 2000, strategic planning development funds were renamed the Programme Acceleration Fund, which was intended to support designing and developing strategic plans, UN integrated work plans and grant or loan programmes addressing HIV/AIDS, including World Bank credits and debt relief programmes; filling funding gaps in existing UN system integrated work plans; and initiating major new and innovative priority activities identified through the strategic planning process.

The Programme Coordinating Board of UNAIDS, at its ninth meeting (Geneva, 25-26 May), endorsed the framework for the International Partnership against AIDS in Africa (IPAA), a broad coalition of actors—African Governments, UN organizations, donors, the private sector and the community sector—committed to reaching agreement on a "Framework for action" for a major intensification and mobilization to address the epidemic in Africa (see p. 1169). The Board made recommendations regarding prevention and access to care, and endorsed a process for developing a coordinated strategy in the education sector to support and strengthen regional and national responses to HIV/AIDS. At its tenth thematic meeting (Rio de Janeiro, Brazil, 14-15 December), the Board further discussed the Global Strategy for HIV/AIDS and took note of the progress on the development of the UN Strategic Plan for HIV/AIDS 2001-2005 and on the five-year evaluation of UNAIDS in 2001.

In the Millennium Declaration (General Assembly resolution 55/2) adopted by the Millennium Summit of the United Nations (see p. 47), held in September, world leaders committed themselves to halting and beginning to reverse the spread of HIV/AIDS by 2015, providing special assistance to children orphaned by HIV/AIDS and helping Africa build its capacity to tackle the spread of the HIV/AIDS pandemic and other infectious diseases. The decision by the Assembly to convene a special session to review and address the problem of HIV/AIDS as a matter of urgency was seen as a step in the realization of the commitments expressed in the Declaration.

ACC Subcommittee action. In September [ACC/2000/17], the Subcommittee on Drug Control of the Administrative Committee on Coordination (ACC) adopted a draft UN system position paper on preventing HIV transmission among drug abusers, prepared by UNDCP in collaboration with UNAIDS and WHO, which was to be submitted to the Consultative Committee on Programme and Operational Questions.

GENERAL ASSEMBLY ACTION

On 5 September [meeting 100], the General Assembly adopted **resolution 54/283** [draft: A/54/L.88/Rev.1 & Add.1] without vote [agenda item 176].

Review of the problem of human immunodeficiency virus/acquired immunodeficiency syndrome in all its aspects

The General Assembly,

Recalling its resolution 44/233 of 22 December 1989, Economic and Social Council resolution 1999/36 of 28 July 1999 and other relevant resolutions,

Noting with deep concern the accelerating spread of human immunodeficiency virus (HIV), which has already infected millions of people worldwide, and the resulting increase in cases of acquired immunodeficiency syndrome (AIDS),

Recognizing that no country in the world has been spared by the AIDS epidemic and that 90 per cent of the people living with HIV/AIDS live in the developing world, which has been very severely affected, particularly in Africa,

Mindful that the AIDS epidemic has become a development crisis in many countries, with devastating consequences for human, social and economic progress, and that the development gains of the past fifty years, including the increase in child survival and in life expectancy, are being reversed by the HIV/AIDS epidemic,

Alarmed that, despite all efforts, the HIV/AIDS epidemic is having a more severe impact than was originally projected, and recognizing that resources devoted to combating the epidemic at both national and international levels are not commensurate with the magnitude of the problem,

Commending the efforts by the Joint United Nations Programme on Human Immunodeficiency Virus/Acquired Immunodeficiency Syndrome to coordinate and intensify efforts to address HIV/AIDS in all appropriate forums,

Recognizing that the needs in countries addressing AIDS far outweigh both the human and the financial resources being made available and that high-level political commitment is critical to strengthen the response to the epidemic,

1. *Decides* to convene a special session of the General Assembly for a duration of three days to review and address the problem of HIV/AIDS in all its aspects and to coordinate and intensify international efforts to combat it, as soon as possible, preferably in May 2001 but not later than the end of its fifty-sixth session;

2. *Urges* Member States and observers to ensure their representation at the special session at a high political level;

3. *Decides* that the exact date of the special session, as well as the modalities, participation in and organization of the preparatory process and the special session, should be finalized, at the earliest opportunity, at its fifty-fifth session;

4. *Also decides* to include in the agenda of its fifty-fifth session the item entitled "Review of the problem of human immunodeficiency virus/acquired immunodeficiency syndrome in all its aspects".

By **decision 55/409** of 2 November, the Assembly took note of the report of the Fifth (Administrative and Budgetary) Committee [A/55/529] on programme budget implications of Assembly resolution 54/283.

On 3 November [meeting 51], the Assembly adopted **resolution 55/13** [draft: A/55/L.13 & Add.1] without vote [agenda item 179].

Review of the problem of human immunodeficiency virus/acquired immunodeficiency syndrome in all its aspects

The General Assembly,

Recalling its resolution 54/283 of 5 September 2000 and resolution 55/2 of 8 September 2000, entitled "United Nations Millennium Declaration", in particular paragraphs 19, 20 and 28 thereof, as well as other relevant resolutions, and taking note of Economic and Social Council resolution 1999/36 of 28 July 1999, as well as Security Council resolution 1308(2000) of 17 July 2000,

Recalling also the relevant provisions of the final document adopted at its twenty-first special session on 2 July 1999 on key actions for the further implementation of the Programme of Action of the International Conference on Population and Development, the final document adopted at its twenty-third special session on 10 June 2000 on further actions and initiatives to implement the Beijing Declaration and Platform for Action, and the final document adopted at its twenty-fourth special session on 1 July 2000 on further initiatives for social development,

Taking note of the statement of thirteen women Ministers for Foreign Affairs concerning the worldwide threat of the human immunodeficiency virus/acquired immunodeficiency syndrome (HIV/AIDS), issued on 12 September 2000 and the Ouagadougou Declaration adopted at the fifth Pan-African Conference of Red Cross and Red Crescent Societies, which was held at Ouagadougou from 21 to 25 September 2000,

1. *Decides* to convene, as a matter of urgency, a special session of the General Assembly, from 25 to 27 June 2001, to review and address the problem of human immunodeficiency virus/acquired immunodeficiency syndrome (HIV/AIDS) in all its aspects, as well as to secure a global commitment to enhancing coordination and the intensification of national, regional and international efforts to combat it in a comprehensive manner;

2. *Confirms* that the special session will be open for participation to all States Members of the United Nations and observers, in accordance with the established practice of the General Assembly, and urges Member States and observers to ensure their representation at the special session at the highest political level;

3. *Decides* to invite States members of the specialized agencies that are not members of the United Nations to participate in the work of the special session in the capacity of observers;

4. *Also decides* that the special session shall be composed of plenary meetings, as well as interactive round-table meetings, the organization, number and themes of which will be finalized during the preparatory process, to discuss, inter alia, issues such as HIV/AIDS in Africa, international funding and cooperation, the social and economic impact of the epidemic, human rights and AIDS, including reduction of the stigma related to AIDS, the gender-specific impacts of AIDS, especially on women and girls, HIV/AIDS prevention, including development of microbicides, improved access to care and treatment including drugs, protection and care of children affected by AIDS, in particular orphans, scientific research and vaccine development, expanded public/private sector partnerships and the building and strengthening of national capacities to combat HIV/AIDS, including the development of national action plans and their implementation, with each interactive meeting to be held in concurrence with a plenary meeting;

5. *Requests* the Secretary-General to make the necessary administrative arrangements towards the convening of the special session;

6. *Also requests* the Secretary-General to make available all necessary documentation in a timely manner for the special session;

7. *Encourages* all entities of the United Nations system, including programmes, funds, the specialized agencies and the regional commissions, to be involved actively in the preparatory activities and to participate at the highest level in the special session, including through presentations on best practices and different experiences in addressing the problem of HIV/AIDS, obstacles encountered and possible strategies for overcoming them, as well as further initiatives, methods, practical activities and specific measures to strengthen national, regional and international efforts and cooperation, taking into account the different ways of addressing the problem of HIV/AIDS;

8. *Decides* to convene, within the framework of the preparatory process for the special session, open-ended informal consultations of the plenary, chaired by the President of the General Assembly, to undertake, as appropriate, preparations for the special session, including elaboration of a draft declaration of commitment and other relevant documents for consideration during the special session, to further address the modalities and other organizational matters of the special session, with a view to submitting proposals for final decision by the Assembly, and to organize other relevant activities to contribute to the preparations for the special session, and invites the President of the General Assembly to appoint, in consultation with Member States, two facilitators to assist in carrying out these consultations with the effective participation of all countries;

9. *Requests* the Secretary-General, with the support of the Joint United Nations Programme on the human immunodeficiency virus/acquired immunodeficiency syndrome (HIV/AIDS), acting as the substantive secretariat of the special session, to provide substantive input to the preparatory process;

10. *Also requests* the Secretary-General to present, in a timely manner, in order to facilitate and focus the preparatory consultations, a comprehensive report describing both the status of the epidemic and the status and level of national, regional and international response and cooperation as well as other issues, including the developmental impact of the epidemic, its long-term social and economic manifestations, national achievements to date, best practices in prevention and care and identification of major gaps and challenges, taking into account all relevant information and inputs, including relevant findings from previous appropriate conferences;

11. *Encourages* regional bodies and organizations, as well as the regional commissions, to make available to the preparatory process and to the special session the outcomes of respective subregional, regional and global level initiatives addressing a range of HIV/AIDS issues;

12. *Recognizes* the importance of the contribution of civil society actors in the response to the epidemic at all levels, and in this regard underlines the need for the active involvement of civil society representatives in the preparatory process and the special session;

13. *Invites* to the special session and to the preparatory process activities, apart from the informal consultations of the General Assembly to which only Member States and observers are invited, in accordance with paragraph 14 below, non-governmental organizations which enjoy consultative status in accordance with Economic and Social Council resolution 1996/31 of 25 July 1996, or are members of the Programme Coordinating Board of the Joint United Nations Programme on HIV/AIDS, requests the Executive Director of the Joint Programme to prepare, not later than 15 February 2001, for consideration by Member States, on a non-objection basis during the preparatory process, for final decision by the Assembly, a list of other relevant civil society actors, in particular associations of people living with HIV/AIDS, non-governmental organizations and the business sector, including pharmaceutical companies, along with relevant background information to be made available to Member States, and invites those civil society actors to the special session and to the preparatory process activities for the special session, according to the modalities defined above;

14. *Invites*, in this context, the President of the General Assembly to make recommendations, for consideration by Member States during the preparatory process, for final decision by the Assembly as soon as possible, but not later than 2 March 2001, as to the form of the involvement of such civil society actors, in particular associations of people living with HIV/AIDS, non-governmental organizations and the business sector, including pharmaceutical companies, in the special session and, to the extent possible, in the preparatory process;

15. *Stresses* the importance of the full and active participation of all States, including the least developed countries, in the preparatory consultations in order to provide substantive input to the special session, invites Governments to make appropriate voluntary contributions to a trust fund to be established by the Secretary-General for that purpose, and requests the Secretary-General to make every effort to ensure mobilization of resources to the fund;

16. *Requests* the Secretary-General to ensure an effective and coordinated system-wide response to preparations for the special session and to carry out, particularly in the most affected countries, in cooperation with the Joint Programme, a comprehensive public information programme to raise global HIV/AIDS awareness while also building broad international support for the special session and its goals;

17. *Decides* that the provisions contained in paragraphs 8, 12, 13 and 14 above will in no way create a precedent for other special sessions of the General Assembly;

18. *Requests* the Secretary-General to bring the present resolution to the attention of all Governments, the relevant specialized agencies and programmes of the United Nations, international financial and trade institutions, other intergovernmental organizations, non-governmental organizations and other relevant civil society actors, as well as the business sector, including pharmaceutical companies;

19. *Decides* to include in the provisional agenda of its fifty-sixth session the item entitled "Review of the problem of human immunodeficiency virus/acquired immunodeficiency syndrome in all its aspects".

On 23 December, the Assembly, by **decision 55/458,** decided that the item on review of the HIV/AIDS problem would remain for consideration at its resumed fifty-fifth (2001) session.

AIDS in Africa

Security Council consideration (January). The Security Council, on 10 January [meeting 4087], held an open high-level debate to discuss for the first time the impact of AIDS on peace and security in Africa. In an opening statement, the Secretary-General remarked that nowhere else in the world had AIDS threatened economic, social and political stability on the scale that it had in Southern and Eastern Africa. In 1999, AIDS had killed about 10 times more people in Africa than had armed conflict. By overwhelming the continent's health services, by creating millions of orphans and by decimating health workers and teachers, AIDS was causing social and economic crises, which, in turn, threatened political stability and good governance. The breakdown of health and education services, obstruction of humanitarian assistance and displacement of entire populations all ensured further and faster spread of the epidemic on the continent. The fight against the disease in Africa was an immediate priority, said the Secretary-General. Council members and interested non-members focused on actions Member States and the international community might take to address the devastating impact of AIDS on Africa.

On 31 January [E/2000/4], the Security Council President informed the President of the Economic and Social Council that the Security Council had received a letter dated 21 January from the Executive Director of UNAIDS, outlining the follow-up actions UNAIDS planned to take to combat and control the spread of HIV/AIDS, as well as UNAIDS plans to coordinate with the Security Council. The Security Council wished to explore the possibility of further cooperative action with the Economic and Social Council.

In a 31 January letter to the General Assembly President [S/2000/75], the Security Council President said that, as a result of the 10 January meeting (see above) and further consultations, the Council recognized the negative impact of AIDS on peace and security in Africa, as well as worldwide, and considered that it was time the United Nations developed a comprehensive and effective agenda for action against the epidemic. Therefore, the Council suggested that the Assembly might wish to review the HIV/AIDS problem in all its aspects and propose new strategies, methods, practical activities and specific measures to strengthen international cooperation in addressing the problem.

Communications. On 10 January [S/2000/9], the President of Mali, in his capacity as Chairman of the Economic Community of West African States, called for increased commitment by the international community to intensify AIDS research, expand prevention and support the millions of persons affected by HIV/AIDS, particularly those in Africa.

On 18 January [S/2000/42], the President of Senegal described his country's initiatives regarding HIV/AIDS.

Report of Secretary-General. In his report to the Millennium Assembly [A/54/2000] (see p. 55), the Secretary-General, referring to the situation in Africa, noted that of nearly 36 million persons living with HIV/AIDS, more than 23 million were in sub-Saharan Africa. In the worst-hit cities of Southern Africa, 40 per cent of pregnant women were HIV-positive and more than 1 child in every 10 had already lost its mother to AIDS. It was estimated that by 2010 there would be 40 million orphans in sub-Saharan Africa, largely because of HIV/AIDS. The Government of Zimbabwe projected that HIV/AIDS would consume 60 per cent of the nation's health budget by 2005 and even that would be inadequate. AIDS was decimating the ranks of the skilled and educated during their prime years, with tragic implications for every affected country and the region. The report mentioned the effect of the severity of Africa's AIDS crisis on the region's economic difficulties.

Security Council consideration (July). On 5 July [S/2000/657], the Secretary-General conveyed to the Security Council a note from UNAIDS summarizing actions taken as follow-up to the Council's 10 January meeting. It outlined steps taken to intensify UN clearing house efforts on HIV/AIDS in Africa within the United Nations; efforts to address HIV/AIDS in emergencies, conflict situations and in the uniformed services in Africa; and progress made in developing IPAA (see p. 1166).

The Security Council, on 17 July [meeting 4172], focused on HIV/AIDS and international peacekeeping operations as part of its responsibility in maintaining international peace and security. The UNAIDS Executive Director reported that, regarding clearing house efforts on information on AIDS in Africa within the United Nations, one of the most comprehensive initiatives—the Country Response Monitoring Project—would provide easy access to the latest information through the World Wide Web. The IPAA framework had been endorsed by the Conference of African Ministers of Health (Ouagadougou, Burkina Faso, May) and the Organization of African Unity Summit of Heads of State or Government (Lomé, Togo, July). The most significant progress, however, was being made at the country level through, among other achievements, a successful round table in Malawi that had mobilized more than $100 million for AIDS in the country; the creation by the Government of special funds in Burkina Faso and Ghana; renewed community responses in Ethiopia; strategic plans in Mozambique; and the establishment of high-level national coordination councils in the United Republic of Tanzania and other countries. An Inter-Agency Standing Committee working group had endorsed an action plan that emphasized the importance of incorporating AIDS into humanitarian action and addressed the role of uniformed services and peacekeeping forces in the prevention and spread of AIDS; the epidemic's potential to contribute to social instability and emergency situations; and the need to ensure minimum standards of prevention and care before, during and immediately after conflicts or disasters occurred. Subsequently, the UNAIDS secretariat established a humanitarian coordination unit, and a number of countries, the majority in Africa, had been identified for the first phase of the effort. Talks were under way with the UN Department of Peacekeeping Operations to promote responsible behaviour among staff providing humanitarian aid and peacekeeping troops. Referring to the draft resolution before the Council, he noted that its emphasis on the uniformed services was significant.

At the end of the discussion, the Council adopted **resolution 1308(2000)** on the impact of HIV/AIDS on peace and security (see p. 82).

Tobacco or health

In response to Economic and Social Council resolution 1999/56 [YUN 1999, p. 1151], the Secretary-General, in a May report [E/2000/21], described progress made by the Ad Hoc Inter-Agency Task Force on Tobacco Control.

According to the report, an estimated 4 million deaths annually were caused by tobacco, and the figure was expected to rise to about 10 million in 2030. Based on current smoking trends, it was predicted that tobacco would be the leading cause of disease by the 2020s, resulting in about one in eight deaths, a proportion greater than from any other single cause. Of those deaths, 70 per cent would occur in developing countries. Half of all long-term smokers would eventually die from tobacco use, and of those, half would die during the productive middle age, losing from 20 to 25 years of life. Recent studies indicated that the tobacco epidemic showed a significant socio-economic gradient and, increasingly, tobacco use clustered in lower socio-economic groups.

Moreover, tobacco use among women, particularly young women, was increasing worldwide.

Effective demand reduction strategies included tax and price increases, advertising bans and counter-advertising, and nicotine replacement and other cessation therapies. Controls on smuggling were an effective supply-side intervention. Crop substitution was often proposed to reduce the tobacco supply, but there was scarcely any evidence that it was applied, as the incentives to grow tobacco were currently much greater than for other crops.

The Ad Hoc Inter-Agency Task Force on Tobacco Control, established in 1999 [YUN 1999, p. 1151], held its second session (Rome, 7 March) to consider specific strategies and projects for strengthening and extending inter-agency collaboration among Task Force member organizations. New inter-agency partnerships focusing on the economics of tobacco control, and supply and production issues, were initiated. The principal themes for future work by the Task Force related to dissemination of Task Force information to the country level; employment effects of tobacco control; effects of passive smoking; the framework convention on tobacco control (see below); risk-taking behaviour; trade and investment issues; and women and tobacco.

By **decision 2000/236** of 27 July, the Economic and Social Council requested the Secretary-General to report in 2002 on the continuing work of the Task Force.

Framework convention

In March, the working group on the WHO framework convention on tobacco control continued to lay the technical foundation for formal negotiations by the Intergovernmental Negotiating Body (INB). The working group, which was open to the participation of all WHO member States and regional economic integration organizations and observers, reached consensus on, among other things, focusing on the framework convention and its related protocols on demand reduction strategies; emphasizing evidence-based interventions; the necessity of an incremental, comprehensive approach to negotiating an international legal regime for tobacco; and emphasizing the importance of taking account of the social, economic and agricultural impacts of tobacco control, especially in developing countries. It agreed to a general architecture for the framework convention. A document before the group contained provisional texts of proposed draft elements for the convention. A further document explored the technical components of three possible protocols.

At its first session (Geneva, 16-21 October), INB, among other things, considered the proposed draft elements for the convention, taking into account the comments of the working group and of the WHO World Health Assembly. INB was scheduled to meet again in 2001.

Food and agriculture

Food aid

World Food Programme

In July, the Economic and Social Council examined two reports pertaining to the work of the World Food Programme (WFP) in 1999: the annual report of the Executive Director [E/2000/54] and a report of the WFP Executive Board containing an overview of activities in 1999 and the decisions and recommendations of its four 1999 sessions [E/2000/36]. The Council, by **decision 2000/242** of 28 July, took note of the two reports.

The WFP Executive Board [E/2001/36] decided on organizational and programme matters and approved a number of projects at its 2000 sessions, all held in Rome: first regular session (8-10 February), second regular session (17-19 May), annual session (22-25 May) and third regular session (23-26 October). In October, the Board adopted a resource mobilization strategy, which, among other things, called for the promotion of a broadened base of donor support. It stated that pledging conferences had outlived their usefulness and should not be convened and recommended hiring an experienced professional fund-raiser to achieve the full potential benefits from the private sector.

WFP activities

During 2000 [E/2001/47], WFP assisted 83 million people in 83 countries, of whom 36 million were victims of natural disasters, 7 million were victims of man-made disasters such as wars and civil unrest, 18 million were beneficiaries of protracted relief and recovery operations and 22 million people benefited from development programmes. Included among the beneficiaries were 18 million internally displaced persons in 32 countries and 3 million refugees in 25 countries. Assistance to victims of sudden natural disasters, which increased over the previous year by 20 per cent, and to victims of drought and crop failure, which increased by 12 per cent, accounted for one third of all WFP food aid. A range of scientific experts forecast that not only would the future bring more natural disasters, but their damage would be greater as people's vulnerability increased. Assistance to victims of conflict and civil unrest increased by 7 per cent compared with the year before and accounted for almost 50 per cent of WFP's total expenditures.

Total quantities of food provided amounted to 3.5 million tons—an increase of 3 per cent from 1999 and the highest since the record high of 1992. Of the total food provided, 649,000 tons was for development projects, 1,958,000 tons for emergency operations and 936,000 tons for protracted relief and recovery operations.

Global food aid deliveries amounted to 10.4 million tons, down some 27 per cent from 15 million tons delivered in 1999. Programme food aid provided bilaterally on a government-to-government basis decreased by 65 per cent, from 7.8 million to 2.9 million tons, which accounted for the decrease of global food aid deliveries in 2000. Nearly half of the food aid delivered in 2000 was emergency food aid provided as relief to people affected by man-made or natural emergency situations. Emergency food aid deliveries in 2000 increased by 16 per cent, while project food aid delivered increased only slightly, from 2.5 million to 2.7 million tons. Thus, targeted food aid, made up of project and emergency food aid, represented some 74 per cent of 2000 deliveries, compared with less than 50 per cent in 1999.

Sub-Saharan Africa received the largest share of WFP assistance, with 60.3 per cent of its operational expenditures spent in 40 countries; Asia received 26.6 per cent for 16 countries; Eastern Europe and the Commonwealth of Independent States, 7.1 per cent for 7 countries; the Middle East and North Africa, 3.4 per cent for 9 countries; and Latin America and the Caribbean, 3.1 per cent for 14 countries.

Administrative and financial matters

Resources and financing

WFP operational expenditure for 2000 amounted to $1,490 million for development and relief activities in the least developed countries and low-income, food-deficit countries. Contributions totalled $1,750 million, of which $226 million was contributed to development, $381 million to protracted relief and recovery operations, $1,070 million to emergency operations and $70 million was provided as "other contributions".

Food security

Follow-up to 1996 World Food Summit

The Food and Agriculture Organization of the United Nations (FAO) continued to implement the Plan of Action adopted at the 1996 World Food Summit [YUN 1996, p. 1129], in which the organization committed itself to assisting developing countries on trade issues, particularly in preparing for multilateral trade negotiations in agriculture, through studies, analyses and training. At the FAO Council meeting in November 2000, member countries endorsed a proposal to hold a "World Food Summit: five years later" from 5 to 9 November 2001 to review progress towards the Summit goal of reducing the number of hungry in the world from 800 million to 400 million by 2015. In 2000, the number of hungry people declined at the rate of only 8 million per year instead of the 20 million necessary to achieve Summit goals. Unless extra efforts were made to accelerate progress in the fight against hunger, those goals would not be achieved before 2030.

The State of Food and Agriculture 2000, an FAO publication, reflected on humankind's achievements and failures in fighting hunger and poverty over the past 50 years. Undernourishment, especially in populous countries in Asia, had diminished. Famine currently occurred only in exceptional cases, such as in war and conflict where suffering already existed from undernutrition and institutional capacity. On the other hand, the past 50 years had left a backlog of unresolved problems, new challenges, risks and uncertainties. More than 800 million people—13 per cent of the world's population—still lacked access to sufficient food and were therefore destined for short and unfulfilled lives. *The State of Food and Agriculture 2000* advocated ways out of the "poverty trap" in which Governments and institutional structures played a major role.

Nutrition

ACC activities

During its twenty-seventh session (Washington, D.C., 10-14 April) [ACC/2000/9], the ACC Subcommittee on Nutrition (ACC/SCN) reviewed reports of working groups on such questions as life-cycle consequences of foetal and infant malnutrition; micronutrients; breastfeeding and complementary feeding; nutrition in emergencies; nutrition, ethics and human rights; household food security; and nutrition of school-age children.

The Interim Steering Committee, established by the Subcommittee in 1999 [YUN 1999, p. 1154], had drawn up a draft ACC/SCN strategic plan containing proposals with respect to the structure and functioning of SCN. Several aspects of

the plan had been implemented and an assessment of effectiveness was proposed for 2003. As regards funding, the draft plan suggested that, in place of the voluntary nature of both core and programme funding, it would be desirable to establish a system of assessed contributions from UN agencies to the core budget. Currently, of the total programme budget of $1,077,000 for 2000-2001, donor commitments totalling $527,500 had been confirmed, leaving $549,500 to raise.

The Subcommittee was informed of the recent creation of the World Health Policy Forum, designed as a global membership network aimed at creating a context in which policy action plans addressing important public health issues could be developed and made to work. It was also informed of the release of the *Fourth Report on the World Nutrition Situation*, based on the theme "Nutrition throughout the life cycle". The report covered available indicators of nutritional status from foetal life to the elderly and stressed that nutrition was fundamental, nutrition failures were egregious, but rapid progress was possible.

The Subcommittee decided to establish two new working groups: one on nutrition and HIV/AIDS and the other on capacity-building in nutrition.

UNU activities

The United Nations University (UNU) continued its food and nutrition programme in 2000. The programme, undertaken in collaboration with WHO, UNICEF and FAO, addressed major nutrition concerns in developing countries. During 2000, it maintained six major global projects and a number of minor ones, and provided 15 fellowships for various kinds of advanced training. The topics of some of the projects under the programme were: international network of food data systems; international iron nutrition project; international dietary energy consultative group; multi-country growth reference study; global initiative for enhancing institutional capacity in food and nutrition; African leadership initiative (a joint project with the International Union of Nutritional Sciences); and harmonization of approaches for setting national dietary standards. The programme continued its quarterly publication of the *Food and Nutrition Bulletin* and the *Journal of Food Composition and Analysis*.

The priority in 2000 was to work more effectively in strengthening capacity in Africa; two workshops were held, in East and West Africa.

Within the framework of its "Food and Nutrition Programme for Human and Social Welfare", UNU supported three workshops in Africa and

Latin America. Those workshops provided potential leaders in nutrition with an opportunity for close interaction with senior nutrition leaders and for practical training in leadership, communication and management skills. In cooperation with the Humanity Development Library, UNU Press continued to expand the "Food and Nutrition Library" CD-ROM project. Designed as a cooperative project with numerous international and non-governmental organizations, such as WFP, FAO and the Peace Corps, the "Food and Nutrition Library" contained the full text of 260 publications and was available free of charge in developing countries.

Chapter XIV

International drug control

During 2000, the United Nations, through the Commission on Narcotic Drugs, the International Narcotics Control Board (INCB) and the United Nations International Drug Control Programme (UNDCP) of the Secretariat, continued to strengthen international cooperation and increase efforts to counter the world drug problem, in accordance with the obligations of States under the United Nations drug control conventions, and on the basis of the outcome of the General Assembly's twentieth special session, held in 1998. Activities focused mainly on implementation of the 1999 Action Plan for the Implementation of the Declaration on the Guiding Principles of Drug Demand Reduction, which served as a guide to Member States in adopting strategies and programmes for reducing illicit drug demand in order to achieve significant results by 2008.

UNDCP stimulated action at the national, regional and international levels through technical cooperation programmes and supported the international community in implementing the strategy agreed upon by the Assembly at its special session. It assisted States in complying with international treaties and supported national efforts and initiatives to reduce or eliminate illicit cultivation of narcotic crops through alternative development and to strengthen national capacities in demand reduction and institution-building.

The Commission on Narcotic Drugs—the main UN policy-making body dealing with drug control—addressed a number of issues and adopted resolutions on the reduction of the demand for illicit drugs, illicit drug trafficking and supply, and the implementation of international treaties. In July, the Economic and Social Council urged Governments to continue to contribute to maintaining a balance between the licit supply of and demand for opiate raw materials for medical and scientific needs, and to prevent illicit production or diversion of opiate raw materials to illicit channels. It also promoted the design of national and regional prevention programmes through an interdisciplinary approach.

INCB continued to oversee the implementation of the three major international drug control conventions, to analyse the drug situation worldwide and to draw Governments' attention to weaknesses in national control and treaty compliance. It examined the problem of the excessive use of controlled drugs in many developed countries and highlighted the scarce availability of narcotic drugs for medical needs in a number of developing countries.

Follow-up to the twentieth special session

In response to General Assembly resolution 54/132 [YUN 1999, p. 1157], the Secretary-General, in a July report [A/55/126], presented an overview of the implementation of the outcome of the twentieth special session of the General Assembly on the world drug problem, held in 1998 [YUN 1998, p. 1135], and of resolution 54/132, by which the Assembly adopted the Action Plan for the Implementation of the Declaration on the Guiding Principles of Drug Demand Reduction. The Guiding Principles were adopted at the special session [ibid., p. 1137]. The report reviewed 2003 and 2008 goals and targets, set by the special session; the role of the Commission on Narcotic Drugs; the Action Plan for implementing the Declaration on the principles; elimination of illicit cultivation of the opium poppy, coca bush and cannabis through alternative development; measures to promote judicial cooperation; the Action Plan against Illicit Manufacture, Trafficking and Abuse of Amphetamine-type Stimulants and their Precursors [YUN 1998, p. 1139]; control of precursors; countering money-laundering; and UNDCP as a catalyst for action by Member States and the UN system.

In December [E/CN.7/2001/2], the UNDCP Executive Director submitted his first biennial report on the implementation of the outcome of the special session. The report, prepared pursuant to Commission resolution 42/11 [YUN 1999, p. 1191], presented an analysis of the drug situation and described efforts by Governments to implement the action plans and measures adopted by the Assembly, drawing on information provided by Governments through biennial questionnaires. The report described the role of the Commission in the implementation process; reviewed global trends in drug abuse; and provided an overview of regional trends.

(For information on follow-up of activities in specific areas, see below.)

On 4 December [meeting 81], the General Assembly, on the recommendation of the Third (Social, Humanitarian and Cultural) Committee [A/55/594], adopted **resolution 55/65** without vote [agenda item 106].

International cooperation against the world drug problem

The General Assembly,

Recalling its resolutions 52/92 of 12 December 1997, 53/115 of 9 December 1998 and 54/132 of 17 December 1999,

Reaffirming its commitment to the outcome of the twentieth special session of the General Assembly devoted to countering the world drug problem together, held in New York from 8 to 10 June 1998, and welcoming the continued determination of Governments to overcome the world drug problem by a full and balanced application of national, regional and international strategies to reduce the demand for, production of and trafficking in illicit drugs, as reflected in the Political Declaration, the Action Plan for the Implementation of the Declaration on the Guiding Principles of Drug Demand Reduction and the measures to enhance international cooperation to counter the world drug problem,

Gravely concerned that, despite continued increased efforts by States, relevant international organizations, civil society and non-governmental organizations, the drug problem is still a challenge of a global dimension, which constitutes a serious threat to the health, safety and well-being of all mankind, in particular young people, in all countries, undermines development, including efforts to reduce poverty, socio-economic and political stability and democratic institutions, entails an increasing economic cost for Governments, also threatens the national security and sovereignty of States, as well as the dignity and hope of millions of people and their families, and causes irreparable loss of human lives,

Concerned that the demand for, production of and trafficking in illicit drugs and psychotropic substances continue to threaten seriously the socio-economic and political systems, stability, national security and sovereignty of many States, especially those involved in conflicts and wars, and that trafficking in drugs could make conflict resolution more difficult,

Deeply alarmed by the violence and economic power of criminal organizations and terrorist groups engaged in drug-trafficking activities and other criminal activities, such as money-laundering and illicit traffic in arms, precursors and essential chemicals, and by the increasing transnational links between them, and recognizing the need for international cooperation and implementation of effective strategies on the basis of the outcome of the twentieth special session of the General Assembly, which are essential to achieving results against all forms of transnational criminal activities,

Noting with grave concern the global increase in the use of minors in the illicit production of and trafficking in narcotic drugs and psychotropic substances, as well as in the number of children and young people starting to use drugs at an earlier age and in their access to substances not previously used,

Alarmed by the rapid and widespread increase in the illicit manufacture, trafficking and consumption, in particular by young people, of synthetic drugs in many countries and by the high probability that amphetamine-type stimulants, in particular methamphetamine and amphetamine, may become drugs of choice among abusers in the twenty-first century,

Deeply convinced that the special session made a significant contribution to a new comprehensive framework for international cooperation, based on an integrated and balanced approach with strategies, measures, methods, practical activities, goals and specific targets to be met, that all States, the United Nations system and other international organizations must implement them with concrete actions and that the international financial institutions, such as the World Bank, and the regional development banks should be invited to include action against the world drug problem in their programmes, taking into account the priorities of States,

Reaffirming the importance of the commitments of Member States in meeting the objectives targeted for 2003 and 2008, as set out in the Political Declaration adopted by the General Assembly at its twentieth special session, and welcoming the guidelines for reporting on the follow-up to the twentieth special session adopted by the Commission on Narcotic Drugs at its reconvened forty-second session,

Emphasizing the importance of the Action Plan for the Implementation of the Declaration on the Guiding Principles of Drug Demand Reduction, which introduces a global approach, recognizing a new balance between illicit supply and demand reduction, under the principle of shared responsibility, aims at preventing the use of drugs and at reducing the adverse consequences of drug abuse, ensuring that special attention is paid to vulnerable groups, in particular children and young people, and constitutes one of the pillars of the new global strategy, and reaffirming the need for demand reduction programmes,

Emphasizing equally the importance of supply reduction as an integral part of a balanced drug control strategy under the principles enshrined in the Action Plan on International Cooperation on the Eradication of Illicit Drug Crops and on Alternative Development, reaffirming the need for alternative development programmes that are sustainable, welcoming the achievements of some States on their way to eradicating illicit drug crops, and inviting all other States to make similar efforts,

Underlining the role of the Commission on Narcotic Drugs as the principal United Nations policy-making body on drug control issues, the leadership role and commendable work of the United Nations International Drug Control Programme as the main focus for concerted multilateral action and the important role of the International Narcotics Control Board as an independent monitoring authority, as set out in the international drug control treaties,

Recognizing the efforts of all countries, in particular those that produce narcotic drugs for scientific and medical purposes, and of the International Narcotics Control Board in preventing the diversion of such substances to illicit markets and in maintaining production at a level consistent with licit demand, in line with the Single Convention on Narcotic Drugs of 1961 and the Convention on Psychotropic Substances of 1971,

Recognizing also that the problem of the illicit production of and trafficking in narcotic drugs and psychotropic substances is often related to development problems and that those links and the promotion of the economic development of countries affected by the illicit drug trade require, within the context of shared responsibility, appropriate measures, including strengthened international cooperation in support of alternative and sustainable development activities, in the affected areas of those countries, that have as their objectives the reduction and elimination of illicit drug production,

Stressing that respect for all human rights is and must be an essential component of measures taken to address the drug problem,

Ensuring that women and men benefit equally, and without any discrimination, from strategies directed against the world drug problem, through their involvement in all stages of programmes and policy-making,

Recognizing that the use of the Internet poses new opportunities and challenges to international cooperation in countering drug abuse and illicit production and trafficking, and recognizing also the need for increased cooperation among States and the exchange of information, including with reference to national experiences, on how to counter the promotion of drug abuse and illicit drug trafficking through this instrument and on ways to use the Internet for information concerning drug demand reduction,

Convinced that civil society, including nongovernmental organizations and community-based organizations, should continue to play an active role and make an effective contribution to countering the world drug problem,

Acknowledging with appreciation the increased efforts and achievements of many States, relevant international organizations, civil society and non-governmental organizations in countering drug abuse and illicit production of and trafficking in drugs, and that international cooperation has shown that positive results can be achieved through sustained and collective efforts,

I
Respect for the principles enshrined in the Charter of the United Nations and international law in countering the world drug problem

1. *Reaffirms* that countering the world drug problem is a common and shared responsibility which must be addressed in a multilateral setting, requiring an integrated and balanced approach, and must be carried out in full conformity with the purposes and principles of the Charter of the United Nations and international law, and in particular with full respect for the sovereignty and territorial integrity of States, the principle of non-intervention in the internal affairs of States and all human rights and fundamental freedoms;

2. *Calls upon* all States to take further action to promote effective cooperation at the international and regional levels in the efforts to counter the world drug problem so as to contribute to a climate conducive to achieving that end, on the basis of the principles of equal rights and mutual respect;

3. *Urges* all States to ratify or accede to and implement all the provisions of the Single Convention on Narcotic Drugs of 1961 as amended by the 1972 Protocol, the Convention on Psychotropic Substances of 1971 and the United Nations Convention against Illicit Traffic in Narcotic Drugs and Psychotropic Substances of 1988;

II
International cooperation to counter the world drug problem

1. *Welcomes* the renewed commitment made in the United Nations Millennium Declaration to counter the world drug problem;

2. *Urges* competent authorities, at the international, regional and national levels, to implement the outcome of the twentieth special session, within the agreed time frames, in particular the high-priority practical measures at the international, regional or national level, as indicated in the Political Declaration, the Action Plan for the Implementation of the Declaration on the Guiding Principles of Drug Demand Reduction and the measures to enhance international cooperation to counter the world drug problem, including the Action Plan against Illicit Manufacture, Trafficking and Abuse of Amphetamine-type Stimulants and Their Precursors, the measures to prevent the illicit manufacture, import, export, trafficking, distribution and diversion of precursors used in the illicit manufacture of narcotic drugs and psychotropic substances, the measures to promote judicial cooperation, the measures to counter money-laundering and the Action Plan on International Cooperation on the Eradication of Illicit Drug Crops and on Alternative Development;

3. *Urges* all Member States to implement the Action Plan for the Implementation of the Declaration on the Guiding Principles of Drug Demand Reduction in their respective national, regional and international actions and to strengthen their national efforts to counter the abuse of illicit drugs among their population, in particular among children and young people;

4. *Recognizes* the role of the United Nations International Drug Control Programme in developing action-oriented strategies to assist Member States in the implementation of the Declaration, and requests the Executive Director of the United Nations International Drug Control Programme to report to the Commission on Narcotic Drugs at its forty-fourth session on the follow-up to the Action Plan;

5. *Reaffirms its resolve* to continue to strengthen the United Nations machinery for international drug control, in particular the United Nations International Drug Control Programme, and the International Narcotics Control Board in order to enable them to fulfil their mandates, bearing in mind the recommendations contained in Economic and Social Council resolution 1999/30 of 28 July 1999, and notes the measures taken by the Commission on Narcotic Drugs at its forty-third session aimed at the enhancement of its functioning;

6. *Renews its commitment* to further strengthening international cooperation and substantially increasing efforts to counter the world drug problem, in accordance with the obligations of States under the United Nations drug control conventions, on the basis of the general framework given by the Global Programme of

Action, and the outcome of the special session, and taking into account experience gained;

7. *Calls upon* all States to adopt effective measures, including national laws and regulations, to implement the mandates and recommendations of the Global Programme of Action and the outcome and the goals of the special session, within the agreed time frame, to strengthen national judicial systems and to carry out effective drug control activities in cooperation with other States in accordance with those international instruments;

8. *Calls upon* the relevant United Nations bodies, the specialized agencies, the international financial institutions and other concerned intergovernmental and international organizations, within their mandates, and all actors of civil society, notably nongovernmental organizations, community-based organizations, sports associations, the media and the private sector, to continue their close cooperation with Governments in their efforts to promote and implement the Global Programme of Action, the outcome of the special session and the Action Plan for the Implementation of the Declaration on the Guiding Principles of Drug Demand Reduction, including through public information campaigns, resorting, inter alia, where available, to the Internet;

9. *Urges* Governments, the relevant United Nations bodies, the specialized agencies and other international organizations to assist and support States, upon request, in particular developing countries in need of such assistance and support, with the aim of enhancing their capacity to counter illicit trafficking of narcotic drugs and psychotropic substances, taking into account national plans and initiatives, and emphasizes the importance of subregional, regional and international cooperation in countering illicit drug trafficking;

10. *Reaffirms* that preventing the diversion of chemicals from legitimate commerce to illicit drug manufacture is an essential component of a comprehensive strategy against drug abuse and trafficking, which requires the effective cooperation of exporting, importing and transit States, notes the progress made in developing practical guidelines to prevent such diversion of chemicals, including those of the International Narcotics Control Board and the recommendations on implementing article 12 of the 1988 Convention, and calls upon all States to adopt and implement measures to prevent the diversion of chemicals to illicit drug manufacture, in cooperation with competent international and regional bodies and, if necessary and to the extent possible, with the private sector in each State, in accordance with the objectives targeted for 2003 and 2008 in the Political Declaration and the resolution on the control of precursors adopted at the special session;

11. *Calls upon* States in which cultivation and production of illicit drug crops occur to establish or reinforce, where appropriate, national mechanisms to monitor and verify illicit crops, and requests the Executive Director of the United Nations International Drug Control Programme to report to the Commission on Narcotic Drugs at its forty-fourth session, in March 2001, on the follow-up to the Action Plan on International Cooperation on the Eradication of Illicit Drug Crops and on Alternative Development;

12. *Calls upon* all States to report biennially to the Commission on Narcotic Drugs on their efforts to meet the goals and targets for 2003 and 2008, as set out in the Political Declaration adopted at the special session, in accordance with the terms established in the guidelines adopted by the Commission on Narcotic Drugs at its reconvened forty-second session;

13. *Welcomes* the decision of the Commission on Narcotic Drugs to submit a report to the General Assembly in 2003 and 2008 on the progress achieved in meeting the goals and targets set out in the Political Declaration;

14. *Encourages* the Commission on Narcotic Drugs and the International Narcotics Control Board to continue their useful work on the control of precursors and other chemicals used in the illicit manufacture of narcotic drugs and psychotropic substances;

15. *Calls upon* the Commission on Narcotic Drugs to mainstream a gender perspective into all its policies, programmes and activities, and requests the Secretariat to integrate a gender perspective into all documentation prepared for the Commission;

16. *Recalls* the World Programme of Action for Youth to the Year 2000 and Beyond adopted by the General Assembly on 14 December 1995, notes with satisfaction the commitment of young people to a drug-free society made at various forums, and stresses the importance of young people continuing to contribute their experiences and to participate in the decision-making processes and, in particular, putting into effect the Action Plan for the Implementation of the Declaration on the Guiding Principles of Drug Demand Reduction;

17. *Urges* all States to assign priority to activities aimed at preventing drug and inhalant abuse among children and young people, inter alia, through the promotion of information and education programmes aimed at raising awareness of the risks of drug abuse with a view to giving effect to the Action Plan for the Implementation of the Declaration on the Guiding Principles of Drug Demand Reduction;

18. *Calls upon* States to adopt effective measures, including possible national legislative measures, and to enhance cooperation to stem the illicit trade in small arms, which, as a result of its close link to the illicit drug trade, is generating extremely high levels of crime and violence within the societies of some States, threatening the national security and the economies of those States;

19. *Welcomes* the elaboration of the United Nations Convention against Transnational Organized Crime, and notes the progress achieved in the elaboration of the three related international instruments, within the framework of the Ad Hoc Committee on the Elaboration of a Convention against Transnational Organized Crime;

20. *Acknowledges* the efforts made by Member States, the United Nations International Drug Control Programme and the United Nations system during the United Nations Decade against Drug Abuse, 1991–2000, under the theme "A global response to a global challenge";

III
Action by the United Nations system

1. *Reaffirms* the role of the Executive Director of the United Nations International Drug Control Pro-

gramme in coordinating and providing effective leadership for all United Nations drug control activities so as to increase cost-effectiveness and ensure coherence of action, as well as coordination, complementarity and non-duplication of such activities throughout the United Nations system;

2. *Emphasizes* that the multidimensional nature of the world drug problem calls for the promotion of integration and coordination of drug control activities throughout the United Nations system, including in the follow-up to major United Nations conferences;

3. *Invites* Governments and the United Nations International Drug Control Programme to attach high priority to the improvement of the coordination of United Nations activities related to the world drug problem so as to avoid duplication of such activities, strengthen efficiency and accomplish the goals approved by Governments;

4. *Urges* the specialized agencies, programmes and funds, including humanitarian organizations, and invites multilateral financial institutions, to include action against the world drug problem in their programming and planning processes in order to ensure that the integral and balanced strategy that emerged from the special session devoted to countering the world drug problem together is being addressed;

IV
United Nations International Drug Control Programme

1. *Welcomes* the efforts of the United Nations International Drug Control Programme to implement its mandate within the framework of the international drug control treaties, the Comprehensive Multidisciplinary Outline of Future Activities in Drug Abuse Control, the Global Programme of Action, the outcome of the special session of the General Assembly devoted to countering the world drug problem together and relevant consensus documents;

2. *Expresses its appreciation* to the Programme for the support provided to different States in meeting the objectives of the Global Programme of Action and of the special session, especially in cases where significant and anticipated progress was achieved regarding the objectives targeted for 2003 and 2008;

3. *Requests* the Programme to continue:

(a) To strengthen cooperation with Member States and with United Nations programmes, funds and relevant agencies, as well as relevant regional organizations and agencies and non-governmental organizations, and to provide, on request, assistance in implementing the outcome of the special session;

(b) To allocate, while keeping the balance between supply and demand reduction programmes, adequate resources to allow it to fulfil its role in the implementation of the Action Plan for the Implementation of the Declaration on the Guiding Principles of Drug Demand Reduction;

(c) To strengthen dialogue and cooperation with multilateral development banks and with international financial institutions so that they may undertake lending and programming activities related to drug control in interested and affected countries to implement the outcome of the special session, and to keep the Commission on Narcotic Drugs informed of further progress made in this area;

(d) To take into account the outcome of the special session, to include in its report on illicit traffic in drugs an updated, objective and comprehensive assessment of worldwide trends in illicit traffic and transit in narcotic drugs and psychotropic substances, including methods and routes used, and to recommend ways and means of improving the capacity of States along those routes to deal with all aspects of the drug problem;

(e) To publish the *World Drug Report*, with comprehensive and balanced information about the world drug problem, and to seek additional extrabudgetary resources for its publication in all official languages;

4. *Urges* all Governments to provide the fullest possible financial and political support to the Programme by widening its donor base and increasing voluntary contributions, in particular general-purpose contributions, to enable it to continue, expand and strengthen its operational and technical cooperation activities;

5. *Calls upon* the International Narcotics Control Board to increase efforts to implement all its mandates under international drug control conventions and to continue to cooperate with Governments, inter alia, by offering advice to Member States that request it;

6. *Notes* that the Board needs sufficient resources to carry out all its mandates, and therefore urges Member States to commit themselves in a common effort to assigning adequate and sufficient budgetary resources to the Board, in accordance with Economic and Social Council resolution 1996/20 of 23 July 1996, and emphasizes the need to maintain its capacity, inter alia, through the provision of appropriate means by the Secretary-General and adequate technical support by the Programme;

7. *Stresses* the importance of the meetings of Heads of National Drug Law Enforcement Agencies, in all regions of the world, and the Subcommission on Illicit Drug Traffic and Related Matters in the Near and Middle East of the Commission on Narcotic Drugs, and encourages them to continue to contribute to the strengthening of regional and international cooperation, taking into account the outcome of the special session;

8. *Takes note* of the report of the Secretary-General, and, taking into account the promotion of integrated reporting, requests the Secretary-General to submit to the General Assembly at its fifty-sixth session a comprehensive report on the implementation of the outcome of the twentieth special session, including on the Action Plan for the Implementation of the Declaration on the Guiding Principles of Drug Demand Reduction, and the present resolution.

Millennium Assembly and Summit

ECONOMIC AND SOCIAL COUNCIL ACTION

On 27 July [meeting 43], the Economic and Social Council, on the recommendation of the Commission on Narcotic Drugs [E/2000/28], adopted **resolution 2000/16** without vote [agenda item 14 (d)].

Inclusion of international drug control as a topic for the Millennium Assembly of the United Nations and the Millennium Summit of the United Nations

The Economic and Social Council,

Recalling that the General Assembly, at its twentieth special session, devoted to countering the world drug problem together, held in New York from 8 to 10 June

1998, reaffirmed the unwavering determination and commitment of Member States to overcoming the world drug problem through domestic and international strategies to reduce both the illicit supply of and the demand for drugs, and recognized that action against the world drug problem is a common and shared responsibility requiring an integrated and balanced approach with full respect for the sovereignty of States,

Recalling also that the General Assembly, in its resolution 53/202 of 17 December 1998, decided to designate its fifty-fifth session as "The Millennium Assembly of the United Nations" and to convene a Millennium Summit of the United Nations,

Noting that the Secretary-General, in response to the need to address persistent problems efficiently and effectively and to deal with the emerging trends and challenges of the future, identified drug control as one of the overall priorities of work for the United Nations in its medium-term plan for the period 1998-2001,

Noting with grave concern that the drug problem is a global challenge involving tens of millions of victims abusing drugs worldwide and causing massive social and health difficulties, as well as undermining economies,

Aware that drug trafficking and abuse have an impact on many key areas of United Nations activities,

Recognizing the need for Governments to implement comprehensive measures to follow up the work of the General Assembly at its twentieth special session and to monitor their implementation,

Emphasizing the important role of the international community in mobilizing efforts to give effect to its commitment to drug control as an integral part of the United Nations overall programme for the new millennium,

Noting the forthcoming publication of the new *World Drug Report*,

1. *Invites* the General Assembly to include the world drug problem as an item in the agenda of the Millennium Assembly of the United Nations and of the Millennium Summit of the United Nations to be held from 6 to 8 September 2000;

2. *Requests* the Executive Director of the United Nations International Drug Control Programme to inform the Secretary-General of the contents of the present resolution in the light of the preparations being undertaken for the Millennium Assembly of the United Nations and the Millennium Summit of the United Nations.

(For details of the Millennium Assembly and Summit, see p. 47.)

Conventions

In 2000, international efforts to control narcotic drugs were governed by three global conventions: the 1961 Single Convention on Narcotic Drugs [YUN 1961, p. 382], which, with some exceptions of detail, replaced earlier narcotics treaties and was amended in 1972 by a Protocol [YUN 1972, p. 397] intended to strengthen the role of INCB; the 1971 Convention on Psychotropic Substances [YUN 1971, p. 380]; and the 1988 United Nations Convention against Illicit Traffic in Narcotic Drugs and Psychotropic Substances [YUN 1988, p. 690].

As at 31 December 2000, 161 States were parties to the 1961 Convention, as amended by the 1972 Protocol. During the year, the Comoros, Georgia, Maldives and San Marino became parties.

The number of parties to the 1971 Convention stood at 167 as at 31 December 2000. The Comoros, Iran, Kenya, Maldives, San Marino and the United Republic of Tanzania became parties during the year.

At year's end, 158 States and the European Community were parties to the 1988 Convention. The Comoros, Estonia, Kuwait, Maldives and San Marino became parties in 2000.

Commission action. At its forty-third session in March [E/2000/28], the Commission on Narcotic Drugs reviewed implementation of the international drug control treaties. It had before it a note by the Secretariat on changes in substance control [YUN 1999, p. 1167] and the INCB report covering 1999 [ibid.]. The Commission emphasized the importance of achieving the objective that narcotic drugs and psychotropic substances should be available for legitimate medical and scientific purposes. With regard to implementation of article 12 of the 1988 Convention concerning the control of precursors, the Commission recognized the need to establish mechanisms for the rapid exchange of information on shipments of precursors, and welcomed the extension into its second phase of "Operation Purple", established in 1999 [YUN 1999, p. 1168] as a systematic international tracking programme for shipments of the precursor potassium permanganate. Since the Operation's inception on 1 April 1999, it had monitored 248 shipments of the substance and stopped or seized 32 of them as suspect and liable to diversion for illicit drug manufacture.

On 7 March [E/2000/28 (dec. 43/1)], the Commission decided to include norephedrine, as well as its salts and optical isomers, in Table I of the 1988 Convention.

On 15 March [res. 43/9], the Commission urged Governments to take measures to control potassium permanganate, in accordance with the measures to control chemical precursors adopted in General Assembly resolution S-20/4 B [YUN 1998, p. 1142], and called on them to consider participating in regional and multilateral activities such as "Operation Purple". It encouraged interested Governments, regional and international organizations and INCB to consider initiatives targeting acetic anhydride, identified for particular attention in the measures to control precursors set forth in resolution S-20/4 B.

On the same date [res. 43/10], the Commission adopted a resolution on the promotion of regional and international cooperation in the fight against the illicit manufacture, trafficking and consumption of synthetic drugs, in particular amphetamine-type stimulants. Welcoming the convening, as part of the anti-drug conferences (Tokyo, January) (see p. 1187), of the Conference on Amphetamine-type Stimulants in East and South-East Asia, the Commission called on Member States and relevant regional and international organizations to give synthetic drugs, particularly amphetamine-type stimulants, due priority in their policies and programmes, and to exchange information on ensuring rapid identification and assessment of new synthetic drugs and on models used to improve the flexibility of the process of scheduling pursuant to the Action Plan against Illicit Manufacture, Trafficking and Abuse of Amphetamine-type Stimulants and Their Precursors, adopted by the Assembly in resolution S-20/4 A [YUN 1998, p. 1139]. Member States were called on to enhance programmes, particularly those targeting youth; to facilitate information exchange on new synthetic drugs; and to strengthen cooperation against their illicit manufacture, trafficking and abuse. The Commission asked UNDCP to expand its regional projects related to synthetic drugs and their precursors and to develop new regional programmes; to assist Member States, upon their request, in establishing a regional system or mechanism, and enhancing those already established, to assess drug abuse trends, particularly synthetic drugs; and to assist Member States in facilitating information exchange on measures taken by Governments and regional and international organizations to counter problems associated with synthetic drugs, in order to promote international cooperation. The Commission decided to consider the matters reviewed in its resolution, based on a report to be prepared by UNDCP.

By another 15 March resolution [res. 43/11], the Commission requested INCB to examine provisions which, in the same way as those contained in the 1971 Convention, might facilitate and enhance security in cases involving travellers carrying medical preparations containing narcotic drugs.

INCB action. In its report covering 2000 [E/INCB/2000/1], INCB stated that the implementation of the provisions of both the 1961 and 1971 Conventions was a prerequisite for achieving the objectives of the 1988 Convention. It welcomed the fact that a growing number of States had taken steps to implement the 1988 Convention

and accede to it, and reiterated its requests to States that had not yet done so to accede to the 1988 Convention. The Board invited all metropolitan Governments that had not already done so to extend the territorial application of the 1988 Convention to their non-metropolitan territories; likewise, non-metropolitan territories were encouraged to implement article 12 of the Convention.

ECONOMIC AND SOCIAL COUNCIL ACTION

On 27 July [meeting 43], the Economic and Social Council, on the recommendation of the Commission on Narcotic Drugs [E/2000/28], adopted **resolution 2000/18** without vote [agenda item 14 (d)].

Demand for and supply of opiates for medical and scientific needs

The Economic and Social Council,

Recalling its resolution 1999/33 of 28 July 1999 and previous relevant resolutions,

Emphasizing that the need to balance the global licit supply of opiates against the legitimate demand for opiates for medical and scientific purposes is central to the international strategy and policy of drug control,

Noting the fundamental need for international cooperation and solidarity with the traditional supplier countries in drug control to ensure universal application of the provisions of the Single Convention on Narcotic Drugs of 1961,

Having considered the *Report of the International Narcotics Control Board for 1999,* in which the Board points out that in 1998 the current status of stocks of opiate raw materials and major opiates seemed to have improved, and that a balance between consumption and production of opiate raw materials was achieved as a result of the efforts made by the two traditional suppliers, India and Turkey, together with other producing countries,

Noting the importance of opiates in pain relief therapy as advocated by the World Health Organization,

1. *Urges* all Governments to continue to contribute to the maintenance of a balance between the licit supply of and demand for opiate raw materials for medical and scientific needs, the achievement of which would be facilitated by maintaining, insofar as their constitutional and legal systems permit, support to the traditional supplier countries, and to cooperate in preventing the proliferation of sources of production of opiate raw materials;

2. *Urges* Governments of all producing countries to adhere strictly to the provisions of the Single Convention on Narcotic Drugs of 1961, and to take effective measures to prevent illicit production or diversion of opiate raw materials to illicit channels, especially when increasing licit production;

3. *Urges* consumer countries to assess their licit needs for opiate raw materials realistically and to communicate those needs to the International Narcotics Control Board in order to ensure easy supply, and urges concerned producing countries and the Board to increase efforts to monitor the available supply and to ensure sufficient stocks of licit opiate raw materials;

4. *Requests* the Board to continue its efforts in monitoring the implementation of the relevant Economic

and Social Council resolutions in full compliance with the Single Convention on Narcotic Drugs of 1961;

5. *Commends* the Board for its efforts in monitoring the implementation of the relevant Council resolutions and, in particular:

(a) In urging the Governments concerned to adjust global production of opiate raw materials to a level corresponding to actual licit needs and to avoid unforeseen imbalances between licit supply of and demand for opiates caused by the exportation of products manufactured from seized and confiscated drugs;

(b) In inviting the Governments concerned to ensure that opiates imported into their countries for medical and scientific use do not originate from countries that transform seized and confiscated drugs into licit opiates;

(c) In arranging informal meetings, during sessions of the Commission on Narcotic Drugs, with the main States importing and producing opiate raw materials;

6. *Requests* the Secretary-General to transmit the text of the present resolution to all Governments for consideration and implementation.

International Narcotics Control Board

The 13-member International Narcotics Control Board held its sixty-eighth (15-26 May) and sixty-ninth (1-17 November) sessions, both in Vienna [E/INCB/2000/1].

In performing the functions assigned to it under the international conventions, the Board maintained a continuous dialogue with Governments. The statistical data and other information received from them were used in analyses of the licit manufacture of and trade in narcotic drugs and psychotropic substances worldwide, in order to identify whether Governments had enforced treaty provisions requiring them to limit to medical and scientific purposes the licit manufacture of, trade in and distribution and use of those substances. The international drug control treaties required the Board to report annually on the drug control situation worldwide, noting gaps and weaknesses in national control and in treaty compliance and making recommendations for improvements.

As the aim of the treaties was to prevent drug abuse and its associated problems, the special theme of the Board's report in 2000 focused on the prevention of drug use that had no medical or scientific legitimacy. The linchpin of prevention was to reduce drug availability for non-medical purposes by statutory regulation. However, according to the Board, that approach was insufficient on its own. The Board examined the excessive use of controlled drugs in several countries and discussed possible factors contributing to that situation. It examined ways to curb excessive drug consumption and outlined the responsibilities of health-care professionals, pharmaceutical companies, professional organizations, consumer associations, government and the public. Although the Board observed that the recent trend towards medicalizing social problems should be reversed, it stressed that the proper use of medicines should not be discouraged. In addition to educational programmes, preventive measures that were likely to be effective included reducing drug availability by law enforcement measures that entailed the application of penalties to deter those dealing in illicit drugs. Reducing the excess use of prescription drugs, however, depended more on educating doctors and other health-care professionals in rational prescribing.

The Board analysed the operation of the international drug control system and the major developments in drug abuse and trafficking worldwide. It contacted States that had extremely low consumption of, and estimates for, pain relief drugs to clarify the reasons and identify problems in ensuring the availability of narcotic drugs for medical purposes. The Governments concerned were invited to review the assessments of requirements for psychotropic substances established for their States, establish their own assessments as soon as possible and ensure that they were regularly updated. As a result of the worldwide application of the system of estimates and the import and export authorization system, no cases involving the diversion of narcotic drugs from licit international trade into the illicit traffic were detected, despite the large number of transactions involved. The Board noted, however, that the diversion of narcotic drugs from inadequately functioning domestic distribution channels continued to occur, and hoped that Governments concerned would take measures to prevent it.

In its conclusions and recommendations, the Board noted that its current review had shown that the excessive or inappropriate use of psychoactive substances, once they became strictly controlled, was often replaced by the use of less strictly controlled substitutes. The safest way for Governments to prevent the emergence of new problems was to react in a timely manner to avoid the potential for overconsumption of such drugs. The Board recommended that Governments closely supervise the supply and consumption of controlled drugs, explore ways for closer intergovernmental cooperation and develop intergovernmental arrangements and standards for application at the regional level. Developing countries should establish regulatory control over the national drug supply, seek bilateral and multilateral assistance, promote the manufacture and/or import of generic drug substitutions of good quality, and enlist the assistance of local pharmacies as a source of information. Smuggling of diverted pharmaceutical products containing psychotropic substances had become widespread, and the Board requested Governments to ensure exchange of information among their national authorities on seizures and illicit trafficking, and to provide information, training and technical means to customs officials. It called to Governments' attention the hazards of inadequately storing psychotropic substances seized after having been diverted from licit manufacture and trade. The diversion of precursors from licit trade for the illicit manufacture of narcotic drugs or psychotropic substances continued. In 2000, major drug manufacturing, exporting and importing countries continued to participate in "Operation Purple" to monitor potassium permanganate, a key chemical used in the illicit manufacture of cocaine. In order to initiate a comparable programme for acetic anhydride, used in illicit heroin manufacture, the Board convened an international meeting (Antalya, Turkey, October), which agreed to initiate "Operation Topaz" to prevent the diversion of that chemical from international trade, to intercept illicit consignments and to investigate seizures in order that the sources of the seized substance could be identified. Legal provisions regarding travellers under treatment involving the use of preparations containing narcotic drugs differed significantly from country to country. Thus, the Board recognized the need to establish provisions for carrying narcotic drugs similar to those for psychotropic substances as contained in the 1971 Convention. Expressing concern about the increasing use of the Internet to illicitly advertise and sell controlled substances and noting that national efforts had only a limited impact, the Board drew the attention of the Commission to the urgent need to further consider the problem. In view of the introduction of a new variety of opium poppy with a high thebaine content and the growing importance of thebaine as a raw material for the manufacture of opiates, the Board deemed it necessary to review the methodology used for the analysis of the global situation regarding the supply of and demand for opiates for medical purposes.

On 27 July, the Economic and Social Council, by **decision 2000/241**, took note of the INCB report for 1999 [Sales No. E.00.XI.1].

World drug situation

In its 2000 report [E/INCB/2000/1], INCB provided a regional analysis of world drug abuse trends and control efforts, so that Governments would be kept aware of situations that might endanger the objectives of international drug control treaties.

Africa

In most countries in Africa, drug abuse appeared to be rising. Cannabis remained the most widely grown and abused drug. Psychotropic substance abuse was widespread because of inadequate systems for licensing and inspecting trade in those substances, and heroin and cocaine abuse had become more widespread in urban areas. The rise of heroin injecting was of concern due to the high prevalence of HIV/AIDS in most parts of Africa. The lack of resources for drug control remained the main obstacle in the fight against illicit crop cultivation, drug production and trafficking in Africa.

Despite eradication efforts and significant seizures in some countries, the region remained a major supplier of cannabis. South Africa remained one of the world's largest producers of cannabis, most of which was sold on illicit markets in the country or in the subregion of Southern Africa, although the amount smuggled into Europe and the United States continued to increase. Despite law enforcement efforts and the strengthening of customs control, Morocco remained a major source of cannabis resin destined mainly for Western Europe. Significant cannabis cultivation was also reported in Western Africa.

The only confirmed report of opium poppy cultivation in Africa came from the Sinai peninsula in Egypt, where opium was abused but heroin was not manufactured. While the total amount of heroin seized in Africa remained small, heroin seizures increased, particularly in countries in Eastern and Western Africa, through which heroin, mainly from India, Pakistan and Thailand, was smuggled. Cocaine originating in South America and shipped mainly from Brazil transited countries in Western and Southern Africa on its way to Europe. Even though South Africa was only a transit point, the consumption of cocaine in its hard crystalline form, "crack", and in powder form increased in that country. Trafficking in and the abuse of psychotropic substances increased in Western and Central Africa and, along with narcotic drugs, continued to be available over the counter, due to the lack of control over pharmaceutical products. South Africa was thought to be the country with the world's largest prevalence of methaqualone abuse; the substance remained a problem in Eastern, Western and other parts of Southern Africa. When India ceased to be a major source of the substance, local illicit manufacture compensated for the loss, primarily in South Africa. Methylenedioxymethamphetamine (MDMA), commonly known as Ecstasy, was the most recent drug of abuse that appeared in the region; clandestine laboratories manufacturing MDMA and methamphetamine had been detected in South Africa. However, the bulk of MDMA abused in South Africa had been smuggled in from Europe, notably the Netherlands and the United Kingdom.

In September, the Board sent a mission to Senegal and to the United Republic of Tanzania and urged both Governments to strengthen their system of control. It welcomed the establishment of the Inter-Ministerial Anti-Drug Commission in Tanzania, which was to coordinate all drug control efforts in that country.

Many countries had updated their drug laws and policies. National drug control strategies had been adopted in Benin, Côte d'Ivoire, Guinea, Kenya and Togo and were being prepared in the Central African Republic, Madagascar and Tanzania. Mauritius developed legislation to enable it to become a party to the 1988 Convention; Ghana initiated drug prevention education in the curriculum of all secondary schools and teacher training colleges; Nigeria created committees on drugs and financial crime in its parliament; and South Africa established an asset forfeiture unit under the 1988 Prevention of Organized Crime Act.

Regionally, several Governments cooperated in the fight against drug trafficking through bilateral and international agreements. Kenya and Uganda had joint operations aimed at curbing cannabis trafficking along their common border; Egypt and Pakistan concluded a bilateral agreement on drug control cooperation; and Nigeria signed memorandums of understanding on drug control with Iran and the Russian Federation. The Organization of African Unity (OAU) convened a third expert group meeting on drug control (Algiers, February), to monitor the implementation of the OAU plan of action on the control of drug abuse and illicit trafficking in Africa. The first Africa-Europe summit (Cairo, Egypt, April), held under the aegis of OAU and the European Union (EU), resulted in a plan of action to, among other things, fight illicit drug trafficking. Subregional organizations, namely, the Common Market for Eastern and Southern Africa and the East African Community, developed a draft protocol on combating drug trafficking within Eastern Africa; and the Southern African Development Community's (SADC) regional drug control programme became operational. SADC activities included a project aimed at increasing drug awareness and involving the mass media in Southern Africa, a study to assess the needs of law enforcement agencies regarding information sharing and exchange on drug-related issues, and work towards enhancing coordination among national drug control bodies in the subregion. The first meeting of ministers of the interior and the third meeting of the committee of police chiefs in Eastern Africa (Khartoum, June), organized by the Sudan in collaboration with Interpol, decided to gather and share information on drug trafficking, and to hold regular meetings to discuss drug trafficking trends and operations aimed at countering the problem. A seminar was held, under the auspices of the Central Bank of West African States (Dakar, Senegal, July), to sensitize and inform national authorities and financial institutions throughout the subregion about money-laundering issues.

Americas

Central America and the Caribbean

In Central America and the Caribbean, the illicit cultivation of cannabis, mainly for domestic illicit markets, was widespread. Opium poppy cultivation was limited to Guatemala, where the area under cultivation had decreased only slightly. Most countries continued to experience problems involving the enforcement of prescription requirements for anxiolitics and, to a lesser extent, stimulants used as anorectics. Seizures of coca paste decreased in 1999 and the first half of 2000 in all countries in Central America, except Guatemala. Seizures of cocaine hydrochloride and "crack", however, continued to increase and were much higher in Nicaragua and Panama than the rest of the region. Belize was the only country in the subregion that did not report seizures of heroin. Weak institutional and political situations in some countries and the large number of political entities in the Caribbean posed challenges to the fight against illicit drug trafficking and abuse. Drug traffickers capitalized on those challenges, moving their operations to weaker jurisdictions and stockpiling illicit drugs in isolated locations. They also took advantage of the potential offered by the growing tourism industry, and the region's location between major drug-producing areas and significant illicit drug markets.

In Jamaica and Saint Vincent and the Grenadines, where the cultivation and abuse of cannabis had become socially acceptable and a major source of income, there was considerable illicit cultivation of cannabis, which was destined for illicit national and international markets. On several other islands, as well as in Central America, cannabis was cultivated mainly to be abused locally. Eradication efforts continued to be successful and large amounts were seized. In the region, information on illicit activities related to psychotropic substances was scarce. The manufacture of those substances appeared to be non-existent and the diversion of such substances from licit into illicit channels was rarely reported.

In Central America, the smuggling of drugs, mostly cocaine hydrochloride, coca paste (basuco) and "crack", by land continued unabated. It appeared that in Central America, ports on the Caribbean Sea and on the Pacific Ocean were increasingly used for the trans-shipment of illicit drugs. The spillover of that drug trafficking had a noticeable impact on the abuse of drugs, in particular cocaine and "crack". Private vessels, fishing boats, cruisers and pleasure ships were increasingly used in maritime drug trafficking.

Reliable data on levels of drug abuse in Central America and the Caribbean remained scarce. According to information furnished by Governments to the Inter-American Drug Abuse Commission (CICAD), the most common drug of first-time abuse was cannabis, and in Central America, also inhalants. In Costa Rica, "crack" ranked slightly above cannabis, while in Honduras, tranquillizers were more than twice as popular as cannabis as the drug of first-time abuse. In some parts of the Caribbean, the abuse of Ecstasy was detected.

Following a mission to El Salvador in July, the Board welcomed the adoption of new laws against money-laundering and the sale of glue and solvents, the establishment of a joint secretariat for the anti-narcotics trafficking commission and the anti-drugs commission, and nationwide drug abuse prevention initiatives. The Board also visited Honduras in July and welcomed the Government's efforts to enhance drug control. It remarked that the national anti-narcotics council should be strengthened, particularly regarding the handling of drug policy matters; coordination between law enforcement agencies and the health authorities on drug-related issues required improvement; and the Government needed to establish a regulatory mechanism and designate an agency responsible for precursor control. The Board stated that the Government's efforts should be complemented by financial and technical support from the international community.

The Board noted that, during 2000, Costa Rica, the Dominican Republic and Panama developed new national drug control plans; the financial investigation unit created by El Salvador became operational; and Antigua and Barbuda,

Barbados and Panama enacted legislation against money-laundering. The Board expressed concern about reports of money-laundering activities in Dominica, Saint Kitts and Nevis, and Saint Vincent and the Grenadines; and the political (see p. 249) and economic situation in Haiti, which had hindered the country's ability to combat drug abuse and illicit trafficking. Although Jamaica had enacted drug legislation and created a Port Security Corps to deal with seaport security, drug trafficking had increased significantly. In Saint Lucia, improvements in the police force resulted in increased eradication activities and more seizures. Transit trafficking in Cuba had led to increased availability of drugs in the country.

Regionally, the cooperative efforts of Central American Governments led to multilateral law enforcement operations, such as "Operation Central Skies", a United States counternarcotics aerial reconnaissance programme. In July, El Salvador reached an agreement with the United States on the establishment of a regional centre to combat illicit drug trafficking. In other initiatives, the Permanent Central American Commission for the Eradication of Illicit Production, Traffic, Consumption and Use of Drugs and Psychotropic Substances proposed to design a subregional plan of action; and El Salvador, Guatemala and Nicaragua pursued a tripartite agreement to combat smuggling in the Pacific basin of Central America. The Board noted the importance of regional and subregional initiatives in the Caribbean, such as the United Nations Offshore Forum (Cayman Islands, March); the third joint meeting (Barbados, May) of the Caribbean Drug Control Coordination Mechanism; and the chemical control workshop organized by CICAD for Caribbean countries (Barbados, October).

North America

Cannabis remained the most common drug of abuse in Canada, Mexico and the United States. The spread of high-content tetrahydrocannabinol (THC) cannabis in Canada and part of the United States was of major concern to law enforcement agencies. Illicit production in Canada was estimated at 800 tons, more than 60 per cent of which might have entered the illicit market in the United States. In the United States, cannabis was mainly smuggled into the country from Canada, Mexico and other countries in the region; however, much of the cannabis was illicitly grown by small-scale operators within the United States. Though efforts to eradicate cannabis had been made by law enforcement agencies in Canada, the impact of those efforts had been reduced by Canadian courts that gave lenient sentences to cannabis growers and couriers. While the overall level of cocaine abuse in the United States remained unchanged, the rate declined for adolescents, which was attributed to drug abuse education. Overall, heroin abuse declined. Although there were no recent statistics on drug abuse in Canada, surveys showed increased drug abuse among secondary school students. Cocaine abuse in Mexico remained at a much lower rate than in both Canada and the United States but appeared to be increasing. Methamphetamine abuse continued to be widespread in Canada and the United States, and Ecstasy from Western Europe was increasingly being abused by young people. Illicit methamphetamine manufacture continued in North America and increased in Canada, where law enforcement agencies uncovered a record number of clandestine laboratories. Gammahydroxybutyrate (GHB) abuse was spreading rapidly in the United States, which placed it on schedule I of the country's Controlled Substance Act.

Drug trafficking continued to increase in Canada. Besides cannabis and cocaine, the amount of heroin smuggled into the country increased. Canadian law enforcement agencies intercepted a consignment of heroin that weighed 156 kilograms, the largest heroin seizure ever made in the country. Mexico continued to be a major source of cannabis. Mexican drug trafficking groups were also involved in Ecstasy trafficking, exchanging cocaine from Latin America for Ecstasy manufactured in Europe. Cannabis, cocaine and heroin seized along the Mexico–United States border increased in 2000. As it became more difficult to smuggle drugs into the United States by air, South American traffickers turned to shipping cocaine and heroin by sea to Central America, and then smuggling the drugs into the United States by land.

In North America, the spread of information by the media on methods used to manufacture illicit drugs continued to be a concern, particularly in Canada and the United States. Messages about indoor cannabis cultivation and the manufacture of synthetic drugs, especially methamphetamine, were common on web sites.

Canada, Mexico and the United States continued cooperative efforts against drug abuse and illicit trafficking. Mexico and the United States, based on the 1997 Bi-national Drug Threat Assessment and the Alliance against Drugs, developed procedures to evaluate progress made under their respective national drug control strategies. Customs authorities of both countries signed an agreement to work more on various issues, including money-laundering and drug trafficking. Joint operations by their law enforcement authorities, especially the Mexican Navy

and the United States Coast Guard, resulted in increased cocaine seizures. Based on the Cross-Border Crime Forum established in 1997, Canada and the United States worked on a mechanism to enhance the sharing of intelligence and developing priorities for targeting criminal groups involved in drug trafficking. A subregional agreement to promote cooperation in demand reduction was approved at a summit of the Presidents of Mexico and the Central American countries. In June, China and the United States entered into an agreement to increase cooperation in the fight against drug-related crime, particularly by sharing evidence related to crime and drug trafficking. A multinational drug law enforcement operation led by the United States and joined by 25 countries in the Caribbean and South America resulted in the capture of thousands of suspected drug traffickers and the seizure of large amounts of illicit drugs.

The Board welcomed the comprehensive review of scientific evidence to assess the potential health benefits and risks of cannabis and its constituent cannabinoids, which was completed in 1999 by the Institute of Medicine in the United States. The study stated that smoking cannabis delivered harmful substances and that plants contained a variable mixture of biologically active compounds and could not provide a precisely defined drug effect. It concluded that, for those reasons, any medical future of cannabinoid drugs did not lie in smoked cannabis but in its isolated components, the cannabinoids and their synthetic derivatives. The Board encouraged further scientific research into the possible medical uses of cannabis.

South America

Cannabis remained the most common drug of abuse in South America, followed by cocaine and inhalants. In most South American countries, cocaine abuse continued to rise, while only in some did the abuse of cocaine base continue to increase. Heroin abuse remained negligible. Statistical data on the abuse of psychotropic substances in South America were rarely available. However, household surveys showed that in Bolivia and Peru the abuse of tranquillizers was widespread. Argentina reported seizures of lysergic acid diethylamide (LSD), and the seizure of Ecstasy became more common in several countries, as the drug had become fashionable among youth.

South America continued to be the sole source of illicitly manufactured cocaine hydrochloride, which was primarily smuggled into North America and, increasingly, into Europe. Despite significant reductions in illicit coca bush cultivation in Bolivia and Peru, the overall capacity of the region to manufacture cocaine hydrochloride was not significantly reduced. Judging by seizure and other data, illicit coca leaf production continued to increase in Colombia, especially in areas where illicit trafficking provided a considerable source of income for guerrillas and paramilitary and criminal groups. In 2000, record amounts of cocaine hydrochloride were seized in several countries. Drug trafficking methods varied, and it appeared that all countries were being used as trans-shipment points. In the northern part of the continent, large-scale trafficking in cocaine destined for North America and Europe was reported, while in the southern part, smaller quantities were smuggled by courier mostly into Europe. Most countries in South America were also the final destination of some of the smuggled cocaine.

Cannabis continued to be cultivated in South America, mainly for local consumption, although extensive cultivation for international trafficking took place in several countries. The Board noted the need for more reliable data on the extent of illicit cannabis cultivation in the region.

In Colombia, illicit opium poppy cultivation and heroin seizures increased. Seizure data from the United States showed that a significant part of its illicit heroin supply was from Colombia. Colombian heroin also appeared on illicit European markets. Brazil and Colombia had taken steps to monitor the movements of acetic anhydride to prevent it from being diverted for heroin manufacture.

The Board noted that, in 2000, coordinated law enforcement activities yielded positive results. Most Governments used the same method to collect and report to CICAD data on drug seizures and drug abuse, which facilitated evaluation of the development of trafficking in and abuse of drugs. Although in South America there had been numerous recent legal developments and policy initiatives to fight drug trafficking and related crime, the Board observed that difficulties in their implementation persisted, due to institutional, organizational, political and/or financial impediments.

The Board undertook missions to Paraguay and Uruguay in February. It welcomed the efforts of both countries in combating drug trafficking and related crime, and suggested that Paraguay take steps to improve its coordination and exchange of information with neighbouring countries. It proposed that Uruguay conduct drug abuse studies regularly using consistent methodology so that trends might be assessed better.

Asia

East and South-East Asia

The abuse of opiates was widespread in all countries in the Mekong area, particularly China, the Lao People's Democratic Republic, Myanmar and Viet Nam. Research findings showed that virtually all cases of HIV infection along a particular heroin trafficking route in South-East Asia involved the same subtype of the virus, HIV-1, suggesting that HIV infection was spreading together with the practice of injecting heroin. Heroin abuse appeared to be limited in other countries in East and South-East Asia, such as Japan, Mongolia, the Philippines and the Republic of Korea. China and Thailand were markets for methamphetamine illicitly manufactured in the Golden Triangle. The abuse of Ecstasy significantly increased among youth.

Myanmar continued to be the world's second largest source of heroin and opium. Illicit opium poppy cultivation occurred to a lesser extent in the Lao People's Democratic Republic and was minimal in Thailand and Viet Nam. Heroin manufactured in the Golden Triangle was smuggled into Yunnan Province of China and transported eastward to the coast and beyond, and through the Lao People's Democratic Republic and Viet Nam into the Guanxi Autonomous Region and Guangdong Province of China. Other transit routes brought heroin from the Golden Triangle to major cities on the South-East Asian peninsula, where it was sold on illicit markets or transported to other parts of the world.

Significant sources of illicitly cultivated cannabis destined for other countries included Cambodia, Indonesia, the Lao People's Democratic Republic and the Philippines. Australia continued to be one of the primary destinations of cannabis cultivated in the region.

Drug trafficking groups shifted their activities from the illicit trade in opiates to the illicit trade in stimulants, which had become increasingly profitable. Most countries reported increased seizures of methamphetamine in 2000. Cambodia and the Lao People's Democratic Republic saw an increase in abuse and seizures of stimulants, while in Singapore the abuse of ketamine by young people increased. Seizures and the number of abusers of Ecstasy rose in some countries.

Countries in East and South-East Asia continued to strengthen their national legislation and policies to deal more effectively with drug abuse and drug-related crime. China strengthened its monitoring of the domestic distribution of ephedrine, to prevent it from being diverted to clandestine methamphetamine laboratories; in

Indonesia, some 200 NGOs established a consortium to consolidate their resources to deal more effectively with drug abuse and illicit trafficking; the cabinet of Thailand endorsed a proposal by the National Narcotics Control Board for a comprehensive strategy to deal with the drug problem; and Viet Nam adopted comprehensive legislation on the control of narcotic drugs.

At the regional level, Japan organized four anti-drug conferences on operational drug law enforcement, maritime drug law, the collection and analysis of intelligence on illicit drug trafficking and amphetamine-type stimulants (Tokyo, January). As follow-up to the Association of South-East Asian Nations (ASEAN) ministerial meeting (Bangkok, Thailand, July), an international congress (Bangkok, October) endorsed a plan of action for ASEAN members and China that set targets and measures for them to become drug-free. In May, Thailand agreed to train officials in the Lao People's Democratic Republic and Myanmar in the use of remote-sensing technology to map areas under opium poppy cultivation. An agreement was signed between China and the United States, in June, to strengthen cooperation in curbing the flow of illicit drugs between China and Myanmar.

The Board undertook missions to the Philippines and the Republic of Korea in September. It noted the strict measures by the Philippines against all types of drug-related offences, including drug abuse, and the adoption of new legislation against money-laundering. It encouraged the Philippines to cooperate in drug profiling and other law enforcement efforts to prevent trafficking in methamphetamine, the abuse of which was increasing, and its precursors. The Republic of Korea, because of its law enforcement efforts and effective programmes to prevent drug abuse, had avoided almost all of the negative effects of developments in drug trafficking and abuse. While the abuse of stimulants had spread, drug abuse levels remained extremely low.

The Board reviewed progress made by Viet Nam on its 1997 recommendations [YUN 1997, p. 1274], and noted the establishment of a national coordinating body for drug control, efforts to control precursors, and improvements in the submission of data on licit activities related to narcotic drugs, psychotropic substances and precursors.

South Asia

Countries in South Asia experienced increased drug abuse. Heroin abuse rose in Bangladesh and Nepal and was widespread in India. The abuse of licitly manufactured narcotic drugs and psychotropic substances, particularly codeine-based cough syrups and benzodiazepines, continued to increase in Bangladesh, India and Nepal, mainly because of the lack of uniformity in monitoring compliance with prescription requirements.

Drug problems in South Asia related to its proximity to the main regions that produced opiates illicitly, namely West Asia, including Afghanistan, and East Asia, including Myanmar. South Asian countries became involved in supplying drugs, within and outside the region, for illicit purposes.

In addition to being cultivated illicitly, cannabis grew wild in nearly all countries in the region. Afghanistan, India and Nepal were regarded as major sources. Cannabis was sold locally and elsewhere within South Asia and continued to be smuggled out of the region into Europe and North America. Cannabis eradication campaigns were carried out regularly but did not reach all areas. The situation was further exacerbated by cross-border criminal activities, such as those by Indian smugglers who leased land from Nepalese to cultivate cannabis.

Licitly manufactured psychotropic substances, mainly diazepam and nitrazepam, continued to be smuggled out of India, not only into Nepal, but also into the Russian Federation and Central Asia. In India, efforts by the authorities resulted in a decline in the illicit manufacture of methaqualome (Mandrax), which was being smuggled into South Africa and Nepal; the seizure of methamphetamine of Indian origin, at the border of Myanmar; and a decline in the diversion and smuggling of buprenorphine. As the border between India and Myanmar could become a major illicit drug-producing area, the Board welcomed India's intention to establish a drug profiling programme to collect and examine seized methamphetamine and ephedrine samples from the area and to investigate intelligence obtained on drug-trafficking routes and the precursors required for illicit drug manufacture.

Heroin seizures indicated that Afghanistan and Myanmar were the major sources of heroin smuggled through the region and of that destined for illicit markets in Bangladesh, India and Sri Lanka. While traditionally India was used as a transit country, recently clandestine heroin laboratories were detected and destroyed in the country. Drug seizures and drug-related arrests revealed that multinational drug-trafficking groups were operating in South Asia and that West Africans were involved in smuggling heroin out of India into Africa and Europe.

Initiatives taken by India to counter the drug problem were a national survey on the extent, patterns and trends of drug abuse, the adoption of a community-based multidisciplinary approach in programmes to reduce illicit drug demand and a study to identify illicit opium poppy cultivation sites in Arunchal Pradesh. Bangladesh reviewed its Narcotics Control Act to bring it into line with international and regional drug control conventions. In Sri Lanka, a system for monitoring drug abuse began in hospitals.

Bilateral efforts to combat drug trafficking included meetings between authorities in India and Myanmar to facilitate the exchange of intelligence, and high-level talks between India and Pakistan on drug law enforcement and operational matters. India entered into legal arrangements with countries in and outside the region to improve cooperation aimed at reducing the illicit demand for drugs and preventing drug trafficking.

West Asia

Cannabis continued to be the most widely abused substance in West Asia. Heroin addiction rates in Iran and Pakistan appeared to be among the world's highest. The abuse of stimulants, mainly methcathinone and other amphetamine-type stimulants, occurred in Central Asia. In Afghanistan and Pakistan, the abuse of benzodiazepines in the form of pharmaceutical tablets was widespread. Benzodiazepine abuse was increasing in Turkey. Cocaine abuse in the region remained negligible.

In Afghanistan and, to a lesser extent, in Pakistan, where huge quantities of cannabis were illicitly cultivated or grew wild, no eradication efforts were reported. Cannabis resin from those countries was smuggled into West Asia and Europe. In March, the Taliban banned the collection of taxes on cannabis resin and destroyed 4,500 kilograms of the substance, but those efforts had a limited impact. Cannabis was also illicitly cultivated and grew wild in Kazakhstan and, to a lesser degree, in Kyrgyzstan.

The annual opium poppy survey in Afghanistan for 2000, conducted by the UN Office of Drug Control and Crime Prevention, estimated the total opium harvest at 3,300 tons, which was 28 per cent less than the previous crop year, following bad weather conditions and the reduction of the area under cultivation. In April, the Taliban began an opium poppy eradication campaign, but the overall impact on cultivation remained limited. The Taliban issued a decree in July banning opium poppy cultivation. Pakistan's goal of a zero-poppy harvest in 2000 was not achieved. Illicit opium poppy cultivation was limited in Central Asia, where eradication campaigns were conducted annually.

In March, the Taliban destroyed 350 kilograms of heroin; however, it appeared that opiates were sold freely throughout Afghanistan. The huge increase in heroin seizures in West Asia indicated that heroin processing in Afghanistan had increased substantially in the past two years. Heroin processing had disappeared in Pakistan. In Iran and Turkey, morphine seizures remained constant, and some heroin laboratories had moved from Turkey to Azerbaijan. Iran accounted for 80 per cent of the world's total amount of opium seized and 90 per cent of the total amount of morphine seized. In Pakistan, the amount of opiates seized since mid-1999 had increased and seizures of cocaine were reported for the first time. Weak border control between Afghanistan and Tajikistan and between Turkmenistan and Uzbekistan and rugged terrain posed obstacles to effective control of drug trafficking from Afghanistan.

Significant seizures of Ecstasy were reported in Israel and of amphetamines in Saudi Arabia.

Pakistan planned to amend legislation so that law enforcement agencies might utilize assets confiscated from drug criminals, and so that assessments of money-laundering might be made. It intended to complement those steps by establishing special courts in five major cities and to continue to upgrade its judicial system. The Board encouraged the Government to provide resources to reduce illicit drug demand. Activities of the newly established Drug Control Agency of Tajikistan had led to significant seizures. In Kazakhstan, a drug control agency was established in February. Azerbaijan had recently created a national committee on drug control. The fourteenth conference of heads of Arab drug control agencies (Tunis, July) discussed a draft model law to combat money-laundering.

The Board urged the Governments of the region to continue to assess the nature and extent of drug abuse in their countries. It expressed concern about the lack of adequate treatment centres in West Asian countries most affected by drug abuse and at ineffective measures against money-laundering.

Regarding regional cooperation, the "six plus two" group (China, Iran, Pakistan, Tajikistan, Turkmenistan and Uzbekistan, plus the Russian Federation and the United States) met to address the drug-related issues in a coordinated manner, with a view to eliminating illicit drug production in and smuggling out of Afghanistan, through a comprehensive and balanced subregional plan. It adopted a comprehensive action plan in September to deal with the illicit drug supply and demand in the subregion. The Board also noted the establishment, in June, of the Turkish International Academy against Drugs and Organized Crime, which would train law enforcement personnel in States members of the Economic Cooperation Organization. Agreements were reached by law enforcement agencies from Iran and Pakistan to assist their counterparts in the territory ruled by the Taliban. An international conference on enhancing security and stability in Central Asia (Tashkent, Uzbekistan, October) was held to develop an integrated approach to countering drug trafficking, organized crime and terrorism in the region. A subregional seminar was held (Abu Dhabi, United Arab Emirates, May) on the prevention of money-laundering.

Following a mission to Lebanon, the Board expressed regret that the Government had shown no intention of lifting bank secrecy on drug traffickers, which had made it impossible to confiscate their assets and to investigate money-laundering. It called on Lebanon to withdraw its reservation to the 1988 Convention against drug trafficking regarding the provisions on money-laundering.

Europe

While cannabis abuse remained stable in most countries in Europe, the availability and abuse of synthetic drugs and cocaine continued to rise. In many countries, the prevalence of the abuse of amphetamine-type stimulants was second only to that of cannabis abuse. Albania, Bulgaria, Estonia, Romania, the Russian Federation and Slovenia reported that heroin abuse had become a major concern, and Hungary saw increased intravenous use of the substance at an alarming rate. "Liquid heroin" or "kompot", which was produced from poppy straw, continued to be abused in Estonia, Latvia and Lithuania. The availability of methamphetamine showed a marked increase in Western Europe.

Cannabis continued to be the most widely trafficked drug in Europe, with Morocco the main source of cannabis resin and Albania a major source of cannabis herb. The Netherlands and Switzerland were becoming important sources of cannabis. Indoor cultivation remained a significant problem in Western Europe, where cannabis seeds and paraphernalia were sold via the Internet. Large areas under cultivation were eradicated in Lithuania and Ukraine.

An increase in the amount of heroin seized in Europe was attributed partly to higher interception rates in Central and Eastern European countries. Law enforcement agencies considered that the bulk of heroin seized in Europe had passed along the Balkan route. Most heroin came from South-West Asia, particularly Afghanistan, and some was from South-East Asia or Colombia.

The availability and demand for cocaine increased in Europe, and large amounts of the substance were smuggled from South America through Spain. Cocaine abuse increased in Belgium, France, Greece, Luxembourg, the Netherlands, Sweden, the United Kingdom and Eastern European countries.

Europe continued to be a major source of the illicitly manufactured amphetamines and amphetamine-type stimulants that appeared on illicit markets not only in the region but throughout the world. Amphetamine seizures in Europe increased only slightly, with the United Kingdom accounting for the bulk of those seizures. Significant seizures of Ecstasy were made in France, Germany, Spain and Switzerland.

The Board welcomed the adoption of new drug control legislation in Slovenia and legislation to prevent money-laundering in Albania, the Czech Republic, Estonia, Latvia and Liechtenstein. In September, Poland approved a bill that increased penalties for abusers and sellers of any type of drug. Switzerland initiated a national campaign to prevent drug abuse, Spain adopted a national drug strategy for 2000-2008, and Latvia, Lithuania and Ukraine launched national drug control strategies or programmes.

At the regional level, the EU Action Plan to Combat Drugs (2000-2004), which provided guidelines to implement the EU Drugs Strategy and addressed the improvement of drug coordination and the development of national drug coordination units in each EU member State, was endorsed by the European Council (Santa Maria da Feira, Portugal, June). The Board noted the efforts of the European Monitoring Centre for Drugs and Drug Addiction to collect and analyse drug-related data and to provide comparable data on the drug phenomenon; the Centre's work in assessing synthetic drugs that posed a serious threat to public health; and the large number of cooperative bilateral and regional agreements between European countries.

The Board sent missions to Albania, Bosnia and Herzegovina, Greece, Ireland, Portugal, the Russian Federation, Spain and Switzerland. It expressed concern about the weak institutional structures in Albania that made it attractive to drug traffickers; political developments in Bosnia and Herzegovina that had prevented unified and effective controls over narcotic drugs and psychotropic substances; and that the cultivation and sale of cannabis in Switzerland had developed into a significant grey area of business. The Board commended Greece for offering a wide range of treatment and rehabilitation programmes. It urged Ireland to update the national drug strategy to address the high level of abuse of cannabis and Ecstasy. In view of Spain's importance as a transit country for drugs smuggled into Europe, the Board encouraged the Government to strengthen its law enforcement activities and to dismantle drug-trafficking organizations.

Oceania

The availability of and demand for cocaine were, with the exception of Australia, low in Oceania. Seizure data indicated that the Pacific islands, such as Fiji and Tonga, were increasingly used as transit points for South American cocaine en route to Australia and New Zealand.

Trafficking in and abuse of methamphetamine in crystal form appeared to rise in some of the Pacific islands. In New Zealand, the demand for Ecstasy rose, and LSD continued to be a major problem, since it was illicitly imported mainly through the mail system from Western Europe and the west coast of North America. The sale and abuse of sodium oxybate, a psychoactive substance with hallucinogenic properties not under international control, increased significantly in New Zealand.

In Australia, illicit trafficking in and abuse of heroin continued to be serious problems. Seizure data indicated that the drug remained widely available, that its price had fallen and that its purity remained high. Most of the heroin seized by Australian customs authorities originated in East and South-East Asia. Sydney and Melbourne remained key entry points since they were primary international and domestic transportation hubs. Other countries in Oceania, such as New Zealand, did not appear to have a significant market for heroin. A seizure of 350 kilograms of heroin in Fiji indicated that the Pacific islands were vulnerable to trafficking.

A decrease in the illicit outdoor cultivation of cannabis in Australia was offset by an increase in the hydroponic cultivation of the substance. Illicit cultivation continued in New Caledonia, Papua New Guinea and to a limited degree in Fiji. In Papua New Guinea, cannabis was increasingly bartered for commercial goods and weapons.

In view of the focus on harm reduction in the drug abuse strategies of Australia and New Zealand, the Board stressed that harm reduction should not become a goal in itself and the strategy should not be adopted at the expense of a strong commitment to reduce the supply of and demand for illicit drugs. The Board noted that some Pacific island States, such as Samoa, had considered ways to strengthen their financial controls to ensure that their institutions were not used for money-laundering.

Regional organizations such as the Oceania Customs Organization and the South Pacific Forum played an important role in improving the coordination of action to implement the provisions of the international drug control treaties among the Pacific island States. Australia held consultations with New Zealand and Papua New Guinea, with a view to contributing to more harmonized approaches in Oceania.

Following a mission to Australia in April, the Board recommended that measures be taken to reduce the number of heroin abusers and encouraged the Government to further develop its treatment and rehabilitation programme, which thus far had focused on pharmaco-therapeutic assistance.

UN action to combat drug abuse

UN International Drug Control Programme

The United Nations International Drug Control Programme (UNDCP), established in 1991 [YUN 1991, p. 721] to promote the application of international drug control treaties and the development of drug control strategies, was a catalyst in stimulating action at the national, regional and international levels. The Executive Director described UNDCP's activities in a report to the Commission on Narcotic Drugs [E/CN.7/2001/7]. Through a portfolio of technical cooperation programmes supported by a network of field offices located in key regions and countries, it promoted subregional cooperation and furthered bilateral cooperation and direct consultations between Governments. In mounting a global response to the drug problem, UNDCP mobilized specialized agencies and other UN entities, international financial institutions, other intergovernmental organizations and civil society, particularly non-governmental organizations (NGOs). In addition, UNDCP assisted States in complying with the international drug control treaties; supported their efforts to implement initiatives to meet the objectives agreed upon at the twentieth special session of the General Assembly [YUN 1998, p. 1135]; assisted in improving judicial cooperation, particularly by providing training to law enforcement personnel, national administrations, judges, magistrates and prosecutors, as well as personnel working in demand reduction; and provided direct support in the prosecution of serious drug-trafficking offences, including money-laundering. In 2000, UNDCP launched a global illicit crops monitoring programme to assist countries in establishing monitoring systems that would produce internationally comparable data and benchmarks by which to measure progress towards the eradication goals set for 2008.

UNDCP served as the substantive secretariat of INCB. In cooperation with the Board and Governments, it monitored the international drug control system and the flow of precursors, and implemented programmes that contributed to the establishment of mechanisms and procedures for precursor control. UNDCP also served as the substantive secretariat of the Commission on Narcotic Drugs at its forty-third (2000) session (see p. 1197) and assisted it in initiating the process whereby States would report biennially on their efforts to meet the goals and targets for 2003 and 2008 set out in the Political Declaration, adopted by the General Assembly in resolution S-20/2 [YUN 1998, p. 1136].

Income to the UNDCP Fund for 2000-2001 was estimated at $131.2 million, which was 7.5 per cent less than in 1998-1999. UNDCP improved its efficiency in programme delivery, with 79 per cent going to programmes and 21 per cent to support activities.

In the area of research and laboratory activities, the UNDCP databases on estimates and long-term trend analysis, which provided comprehensive data on the worldwide drug problem and on trend analysis, became operational. UNDCP worked with Interpol and the World Customs Organization on the creation of a common and expanded database on individual seizure cases. It provided expertise and data to the Financial Action Task Force on Money Laundering to help estimate the magnitude of the problem; co-hosted a workshop on dynamic drug policy to understand and control drug epidemics; and, in cooperation with the European Centre for Social Welfare Policy and Research, undertook a project on demand reduction programmes and their impact on drug abuse. The project concluded with an expert group meeting and the establishment of a network of social science researchers who would evaluate the structures of drug control institutions. UNDCP developed international standards and guidelines to enhance Member States' capacity in drug testing and to promote collaboration between national laboratory services and law enforcement, judiciary and health authorities. In that regard, UNDCP provided technical support to drug-testing laboratories in Benin and Cape Verde, and to UNDCP training centres in China, Ghana and Trinidad and Tobago.

UNDCP continued to promote the mainstreaming of drug control issues into the work of other agencies. Activities included collaboration with the Food and Agriculture Organization of the United Nations (FAO) and the PanAmerican Health Organization/World Health Organization (WHO) in alternative development in Colombia; joint UN programming for the rural development of the Bekaa valley in Lebanon; and the integration of a demand reduction component in activities undertaken by the Economic and Social Commission for Asia and the Pacific against sexual abuse and exploitation of minors in the Greater Mekong subregion. It continued to take part in the country-based common country assessment (CCA)/United Nations Development Assistance Framework (UNDAF), which was leading to more systematic joint programming. The third interparliamentarian meeting on drug control (Washington, D.C., February) was organized in cooperation with the United States Congress. In cooperation with the Asian Development Bank, UNDCP introduced drug control activities into rural development activities in the Lao People's Democratic Republic.

UNDCP, through its Global Youth Network against Drug Abuse and the UNDCP and WHO Global Initiative on Primary Prevention of Substance Abuse, continued to support young people in finding solutions to drug abuse problems. It supported research activities on possible linkages between drug abuse and HIV/AIDS, and was active in the International Partnership against AIDS in Africa, where, in collaboration with other UN agencies, it implemented several global, regional and national programmes that addressed HIV/AIDS and drug abuse.

ECONOMIC AND SOCIAL COUNCIL ACTION

On 27 July [meeting 43], the Economic and Social Council, on the recommendation of the Commission on Narcotic Drugs [E/2000/28], adopted **resolution 2000/17** without vote [agenda item 14 (d)].

Promotion of the design of national and regional prevention programmes through an interdisciplinary approach

The Economic and Social Council,

Recalling the United Nations Convention against Illicit Traffic in Narcotic Drugs and Psychotropic Substances of 1988,

Bearing in mind the Declaration on the Guiding Principles of Drug Demand Reduction, and in particular the Action Plan for the Implementation of the Declaration on the Guiding Principles of Drug Demand Reduction,

Stressing the need for interdisciplinary teams to promote national and regional prevention programmes, taking into account the specificities and distinguishing features of each region and country, with the aim of promoting health and individual and social well-being and raising awareness, through positive messages, of the consequences of drug abuse with regard to the achievement of that aim,

Noting the need for exchange of information on efforts in this field to ensure the effectiveness of international cooperation and solidarity,

Having considered the *Report of the International Narcotics Control Board for 1999,* which points to the need to continue work on the design of policies to reduce the demand for narcotic drugs and psychotropic substances,

1. *Urges* the United Nations International Drug Control Programme, subject to the availability of voluntary contributions, to support States and regional bodies in the design, through an interdisciplinary approach, of national and regional prevention programmes, taking into account the specificities and distinguishing features of each region and country, with the aim of promoting health and individual and social well-being and raising awareness, through positive messages, of the consequences of drug abuse with regard to the achievement of that aim;

2. *Urges* Member States to promote the establishment of interdisciplinary approaches, as well as multidisciplinary teams, to pursue, in the context of demand reduction, the objectives set out in paragraph 1 above;

3. *Calls* for the promotion of information and education programmes that will raise awareness of the risks of drug abuse, taking into account differences in gender, culture and education among the target groups, with special attention being paid to children and young people, and will reflect sound, precise and balanced data;

4. *Requests* the Secretary-General to transmit the text of the present resolution to all Governments for consideration.

Sub-Saharan Africa

UNDCP expanded the programme portfolio for Southern and Eastern Africa with a comprehensive regional framework integrating demand reduction, control measures, judicial development and cooperation. It initiated an African umbrella programme for demand reduction to support the development of drug abuse and HIV prevention programmes in various subregions. Renewed efforts were taken to develop law enforcement expertise and capacity. The OAU database on African drug control experts, training centres and research institutes, developed with UNDCP support, was in its final phase. In cooperation with the Southern African Development Community, UNDCP initiated, in October, a regional legal assistance programme for the 19 States of Southern and Eastern Africa and, in cooperation with the EU, assisted in the formulation of national drug control strategies for Benin, the Central African Republic, Côte d'Ivoire, Guinea and Togo. Training was provided to national drug control coordinators from Central and Western Africa. National drug control plans were finalized in Kenya, Madagascar and the United Republic of Tanzania.

UNDCP supported the development of networks of local demand reduction experts in East-ern and Western Africa. In Southern Africa, the first of 10 community centres for counselling, treatment and rehabilitation of drug users in South Africa was inaugurated. UNDCP facilitated efforts to determine the extent of drug abuse by providing for rapid situation assessments in Angola, Côte d'Ivoire, Ghana, Malawi, Nigeria, Senegal and South Africa. In Burkina Faso, it provided training to community leaders and social workers in drug abuse prevention and, in East Africa, it assisted NGOs in improving their outreach programmes at the grass-roots level.

In an effort to suppress illicit drug trafficking, UNDCP, in cooperation with INCB and WHO, worked towards strengthening the capacity of national authorities in Ethiopia, Kenya, Uganda and the United Republic of Tanzania to better control the supply and distribution of licit narcotic drugs and psychotropic substances. In cooperation with the Universal Postal Union, UNDCP launched an initiative to counter the increasing use of the mail system for drug trafficking and other organized crime and, in cooperation with the Customs Cooperation Council (World Customs Organization), undertook a programme to enhance the interdiction capacity of law enforcement agencies at major ports in Eastern and Southern Africa. Technical and advisory support was provided to assess the extent of cannabis cultivation in the region.

North Africa and the Middle East

In the Middle East, UNDCP initiated a subregional drug control programme to support the efforts of States in the Eastern Mediterranean to counter the drug problem. It signed a memorandum of understanding (MOU) on cooperation with the secretariat of the Council of Arab Ministers of the Interior to support judicial and other cooperation at the regional level. In May, UNDCP and the Naif Arab Academy for Security Sciences agreed on a programme in the Middle East to promote the sharing of expertise through joint training seminars, the exchange of information, studies and publications. UNDCP also supported the initiative of the Palestinian Authority to harmonize drug control legislation on the basis of the UNDCP model laws, and provided legal training to prosecutors in Egypt and the Syrian Arab Republic. Assessment missions were made to Algeria, the Libyan Arab Jamahiriya and the Sudan to draw up national drug control master plans.

In the area of drug abuse prevention and reduction, UNDCP assisted Middle Eastern Governments in assessing their capacities and needs for treatment and rehabilitation of drug abusers. In cooperation with the World Food Programme and the United Nations Children's Fund, UNDCP worked on cross-cutting issues, such as drug abuse among street children and promoting the establishment of networks of NGOs to support prevention initiatives. Training workshops on treatment and rehabilitation were held in the Palestinian Autonomous Areas and a seminar was conducted to share the findings of a rapid drug abuse assessment.

In Lebanon, UNDCP provided support to sustain the successful eradication of illicit poppy cultivation in the Bekaa valley, in cooperation with interested donors, other agencies and the Government. A training course on advanced law enforcement techniques was held and equipment provided to the Lebanese police to strengthen their interdiction capacity. In support of an initiative of Egypt, UNDCP conducted a baseline assessment of socio-economic structures in the main areas of illicit cultivation. UNDCP worked with Jordan to strengthen its drug law enforcement capacities, and provided specialized training courses to the United Arab Emirates on the control of precursors.

Central and Eastern Europe

In the Russian Federation, UNDCP completed the implementation of the first phase of a comprehensive programme on drug abuse prevention and countering drug-related organized crime. In Bosnia and Herzegovina, it assisted the Government in preparing new drug control legislation.

Regarding drug abuse prevention and reduction in Central Europe, UNDCP assisted with the training of health-care professionals; building a network of researchers and establishing a database on patterns of and trends in drug abuse; and, in cooperation with the International Labour Organization (ILO), promoting drug abuse prevention in the workplace. Demand reduction programmes were drawn up for Albania, Bosnia and Herzegovina, Bulgaria, Croatia, Romania and the former Yugoslav Republic of Macedonia (FYROM). Some 25 drug abuse treatment providers and health professionals from Belarus, the Republic of Moldova and the Russian Federation, with NGO assistance, were trained in modern techniques to treat drug addictions. UNDCP also initiated a school-based prevention programme in three Baltic States.

In an effort to suppress illicit trafficking in Central Europe, UNDCP provided technical support to enhance capacities for drug law enforcement in five States and continued to strengthen judicial cooperation between authorities of the region. With the support of Interpol and in co-operation with the Poland-Hungary Aid for the Reconstruction of the Economy programme of the European Commission, UNDCP assisted Bulgaria, Romania and FYROM in establishing drug intelligence units. UNDCP drew up a plan to support a policing approach emphasizing intelligence in Bosnia and Herzegovina, Bulgaria, Croatia, Romania, Slovenia and FYROM.

South Asia

In India, UNDCP provided training for data collection, the finalization of a rapid situation assessment, and the launching of a drug abuse monitoring system to collect information and plot trends. It granted technical support for the national household survey of drug abuse. UNDCP assisted Nepal to amend drug control legislation for compliance with international drug control treaties.

Two community-wide programmes in India were implemented to reduce and prevent drug abuse among the general population, high-risk groups and drug abusers on a nationwide scale, while support was mobilized for a high-risk group in north-eastern provinces. A five-year plan for drug abuse control was initiated in Bangladesh and material for advocacy and drug education was distributed to the Ministry of Education. In Sri Lanka, in cooperation with WHO, UNDCP provided training and support in data collection, preventive services and treatment and rehabilitation activities, and established a drug abuse monitoring system to cover general hospitals, prisons and outreach and drop-in centres.

The results of a 2000 survey on illicit opium poppy cultivation in north-eastern India were presented to the international community in New Delhi. UNDCP supported initiatives to foster cross-border cooperation between drug law enforcement agencies in India and Myanmar, which would be extended to include Bangladesh. A video on the control of precursors was produced and distributed to law enforcement institutions in India. In Bangladesh, 188 officials from the judiciary and police service received training to enhance inter-agency cooperation.

East Asia and the Pacific

The subregional action plan covering Cambodia, China, the Lao People's Democratic Republic, Myanmar, Thailand and Viet Nam, the signatories with UNDCP to a 1993 MOU, provided the framework for cooperation in drug control matters. The programmes pursued under the plan related to capacity-building, data collection, the dissemination of information, amphetamine-type stimulants, drug abuse and HIV/AIDS, precursor control, law enforcement training and cross-border cooperation. UNDCP was engaged in assisting Governments in East and South-East Asia to meet the challenge of illicit manufacture, trafficking and abuse of amphetamine-type stimulants. The Conference on Amphetamine-type Stimulants in East and South-East Asia (Tokyo, January), which recommended action for Governments to counter their illicit manufacture, trafficking and abuse, contributed to a landmark commitment to tackle the problem by ASEAN members and China, at a meeting convened by Thailand, ASEAN and UNDCP (Bangkok, 11-13 October).

UNDCP supported initiatives to prevent and reduce drug abuse, including six workshops that were held in Cambodia, China, Myanmar and Thailand on the methodology for conducting national drug abuse assessments and for data collection, and on the use of related software systems for data analysis. School surveys were conducted in the Lao People's Democratic Republic and Viet Nam. Initiatives to reduce drug abuse among selected highland ethnic minority groups were instituted across 17 sites in five countries. Demand reduction activities in the Lao People's Democratic Republic took place in the context of community-based alternative development initiatives, targeting areas affected by illicit opium cultivation; workshops on drug prevention were held following a national survey in the country; and a community-based programme in Xieng Khouang province, which included training for health volunteers and the supply of materials to the district detoxification centre, enhanced social services in the participating 55 villages. In Myanmar, where UNDCP continued to support preventive education, over 300 persons participated in the activities organized in cooperation with the NGO World Concern International. Community-level activities involved 27 villages and over 1,000 village participants. In Viet Nam, an educational curriculum for drug abuse prevention and materials for training primary school teachers were finalized. Other initiatives included a national forum on drug treatment and rehabilitation in Hanoi, a training course for master trainers and courses for treatment professionals.

Law enforcement activities to suppress illicit trafficking continued to constitute a major part of UNDCP's subregional cooperation. In collaboration with the World Customs Organization, most modules of the computer-based, interactive training programme in drug law enforcement were completed, and the training, management and evaluation system was improved following field-testing in northern Thailand. In other law enforcement programmes, UNDCP prepared model guidelines for police and customs interventions in countering illicit drug trafficking, in cooperation with Interpol and the World Customs Organization; delivered communications and training equipment for the Public Security Bureau Training School in the Yunnan province of China; and completed a subregional precursor control programme for East Asia. In the Lao People's Democratic Republic, a programme to strengthen overall drug control capacity continued with the establishment of a comprehensive data collection system. In Viet Nam, interdiction capacities were enhanced through the procurement of telecommunications and drug-detection equipment. To strengthen the judicial and prosecutorial capacity in the region, five national workshops were conducted for judges, prosecutors and senior investigators in Cambodia, the Lao People's Democratic Republic, Myanmar, Thailand and Viet Nam. UNDCP provided legal advice to authorities in Cambodia, the Lao People's Republic and Viet Nam on updating or drafting new drug control legislation.

In its efforts to assist in eliminating illicit crop cultivation, UNDCP launched an in-depth study of alternative development in Thailand to review and document the experiences of a country with a long record of activity in the subregion. In Myanmar, an initiative was under way that included agricultural development, income-generating activities and a programme of immunization covering over 90 per cent of children in 236 villages. A community-based programme for drug demand reduction was completed and teachers were trained in school management and introduced to new teaching methods and education materials. Alternative development activities in the Lao People's Democratic Republic reduced dependence on opium production and consumption. The pilot phase of Viet Nam's four-year alternative development programme targeting the poppy-cultivating Ky Son district was completed.

West and Central Asia

UNDCP continued its work in Afghanistan, which in 2000 accounted for 79 per cent of global opium production. Working closely with the "six plus two" group (the six States bordering Afghanistan, plus the Russian Federation and the United States) and donor countries to address the illicit production of opium, UNDCP convened a technical meeting (Vienna, May), followed by a high-level meeting (New York, September), which endorsed a regional plan of action to increase cooperation between States bordering Afghanistan. Training on programme planning was offered to officials from drug control–related institutions in Iran (March and September). In Turkey, UNDCP supported the creation of the Turkish International Academy against Drugs and Organized Crime, established to address the needs of 22 countries in the region.

Demand reduction, with the focus on abuse of opiates, particularly heroin, was an integral part of UNDCP's pilot programme for Afghanistan. An assessment of the drug abuse problem in rural areas was undertaken; training courses in drug awareness and abuse prevention were organized; a day-care drop-in centre for heroin addicts in Peshawar was established; and a community-based treatment, rehabilitation and prevention programme in a refugee camp near Peshawar was launched. In Iran, UNDCP organized four workshops to address the role of NGOs in drug abuse prevention, harm reduction, the social impact of drug abuse, and devising a strategy to reduce drug demand. In Pakistan, it supported the implementation of the national drug control master plan and the launching of a rapid assessment of the drug abuse situation. A rapid situation assessment programme was initiated in Central Asia to address the drug problem from a regional perspective, and training was provided to enhance the mass media's capability to raise public awareness of the adverse effects of drug trafficking and abuse.

The UNDCP annual opium poppy survey of Afghanistan indicated a 10 per cent decrease in poppy cultivation over 1999. In Kandahar province and three UNDCP target districts where alternative development assistance was provided, there was a reduction of about 50 per cent. In July, the Taliban issued a total ban on opium poppy cultivation during the 2000/01 planting season. UNDCP would monitor the implementation of the ban through the annual poppy survey to assess the impact on cultivation and production. UNDCP cooperated with Pakistan in the formulation of a strategy for a programme for the Dir district, where opium poppy cultivation had been eliminated, in order to sustain the achievement and to continue development assistance. In Central Asia, following mapping of the extent of illicit cultivation in Kazakhstan, Kyrgyzstan and Tajikistan, results showed that cooperation between the three Governments and UNDCP had led to a reduction in illicit opium poppy cultivation.

UNDCP initiated the establishment of a so-called security belt around Afghanistan to contain and reduce the alarming flow of drugs trafficked from the country into neighbouring countries and to stop precursor chemicals used in heroin manufacture from reaching clandestine laboratories. In that regard, UNDCP established regional coordination mechanisms to increase the efficiency and effectiveness of regional law enforcement activities. National programmes included strengthening border controls and cross-border cooperation, improving the analysis of information and training customs and border personnel. An international conference on enhancing security and stability in Central Asia (Tashkent, Uzbekistan, October), sponsored by the Office for Drug Control and Crime Prevention (ODCCP) of the Secretariat and the Organization for Security and Cooperation in Europe (OSCE), endorsed a set of priorities for cooperation between Central Asian States in the areas of drug control, organized crime and terrorism. UNDCP organized the Central Asian Conference on Diversion of Chemicals into Illicit Drug Trafficking (Bishkek, Kyrgyzstan, November) to foster cooperation on the phenomenon. In Tajikistan, the provision of $2.6 million in UNDCP assistance for the establishment of a drug control agency led to a 70 per cent increase in drug seizures in 2000.

Latin America and the Caribbean

In 2000, UNDCP continued to support cooperation in the Caribbean in regional law enforcement programmes, including judicial cooperation and demand reduction programmes. UNDCP participated in the process instituted by the Permanent Central American Commission for the Eradication of the Illicit Production, Traffic, Consumption, and Use of Drugs and Psychotropic Substances to facilitate regional cooperation in drug control by focusing on legal and judicial assistance, drug abuse prevention and advocacy.

In Central America, UNDCP cooperated with national drug control bodies, NGOs, other UN agencies, the media and private enterprise to reduce drug demand. The UNDCP programme for Central America included projects in drug abuse prevention with both Governments and NGOs, the provision of legal advice and judicial training and assistance to forensic laboratories. In the Caribbean, a regional communication and advocacy programme on the theme "sports against drugs" was launched. Other initiatives included a public information programme undertaken with the Caribbean News Agency; community-level activities led by the Caribbean Council of Churches; support for the training of trainers in methods of improving coordination and delivery of health and family life education programmes; and the conduct of rapid assessment surveys in Barbados and Trinidad and Tobago. A survey of drug treatment and rehabilitation in prisons was completed in the Bahamas, and treatment services were provided, along with training and equipment, to Trinidad and Tobago. At the subregional level, UNDCP promoted common methods and standards for epidemiological surveillance under a project based on an MOU signed by Argentina, Bolivia, Chile, Peru, Uruguay and UNDCP. In Nicaragua, a baseline study towards establishing a prevention programme for children and adolescents at risk was drawn up. In Peru, UNDCP continued to assist the Government in school-based prevention. An ongoing initiative in Bolivia on prevention was carried out in 36 municipalities. Support was granted to create multisectoral committees for drug control and to implement regional abuse prevention plans in Colombia. Brazil continued to implement UNDCP-suggested drug abuse and HIV/AIDS prevention activities, mostly financed by the Government with World Bank support. In April, UNDCP initiated a multisectoral drug control programme in Cuba. A UN inter-agency demand reduction programme was initiated in Guyana, and the Dominican Republic was assisted in extending and decentralizing its drug abuse prevention activities to provinces throughout the country.

UNDCP supported Bolivia, Colombia and Peru in formulating three individual business plans that combined the elimination of illicit drug crops with alternative development measures. Collectively, the three plans consisted of 18 projects, 12 of which were being implemented. In total, UNDCP support for alternative development in the Andean region rose from $4.1 million in mid-1998 to $11.5 million in mid-2000.

In the area of illicit drug trafficking, UNDCP assisted the Caribbean Customs Law Enforcement Council (CCLEC) to establish a regional clearance system for the control of movement of vessels, with pilot workstations in Saint Lucia, Trinidad and Tobago, and Puerto Rico. Through CCLEC, it provided training in risk profiling and targeting techniques to customs and port authorities in Curaçao, the Dominican Republic, Guyana, Haiti, Jamaica, and Trinidad and Tobago. UNDCP facilitated the consultation process for the Caribbean Treaty to Suppress Illicit Maritime Trafficking, initiated by the Netherlands, by holding a preparatory conference (Curaçao, November), and assisted the Legal Affairs Committee of the Caribbean Community (CARICOM) to finalize the Caribbean Treaty on Mutual Legal Assistance in Criminal Matters. In El Salvador, Honduras, Mexico and Nicaragua, members of the judiciary received training in the judicial aspects of drug control and investigation. UNDCP assisted the Dominican Republic in the development of a national judicial database, and provided it with expert advice during key trials involving drug trafficking and money-laundering. Under the subregional forensic laboratory programmes for Mexico, the Caribbean and Central America, UNDCP provided equipment to analyse illicit drugs and their precursors, fellowships to train laboratory personnel and training courses to upgrade laboratory services. A drug control programme was initiated in Cuba to provide expert advice in the design of a drug control curriculum for the police academy. UNDCP supported national law enforcement programmes in Bolivia, Brazil, Colombia and Ecuador, through the provision of training programmes, telecommunication devices and computers.

Administrative and budgetary matters

The Commission on Narcotic Drugs, at its March session (see p. 1197), had before it a January note by the Secretariat [E/CN.7/2000/10] that drew the Commission's attention to the need to focus on programme support cost arrangements, the integrated financial information system and the 2002-2005 medium-term plan.

In its review of programme support cost arrangements, the note stated that, in view of the high level of earmarking and the decline in the general-purpose balance of the UNDCP Fund, it was necessary to reconsider the appropriate level of programme support charges applied to projects, and that the Commission should authorize charging up to 13 per cent in programme support charges on all UNDCP projects. Those charges should be authorized at the beginning of the 2000-2001 biennium. In March [E/2000/28], the Commission decided to reconsider the issue of programme support charges in 2001. The Secretariat reported that its costs of the development of an integrated financial information system would be presented in the context of a revised budget for 2000-2001, for submission to the Commission at its forty-fourth (2001) session, should a revised budget be required, or in the context of the final budget for 2000-2001, for submission to the reconvened forty-fourth (2001) session. The installation, adaptation and implementation of the system was scheduled to begin in February. The work plan envisaged an 11-month implementation period. As to the 2002-2005 medium-term plan, the report stated that the Secretary-General had proposed joining the programmes on international drug control and on crime prevention and criminal justice, forming one programme on international drug control and crime prevention. Thus, there would be one programme with four subprogrammes for drug control and one subprogramme for crime prevention and criminal justice, all under the heading of the Office for Drug Control and Crime Prevention of the Secretariat. The four subprogrammes on international drug control of the proposed 2002-2005 medium-term plan were the same as the 1998-2001 plan, which had been revised to incorporate new and expanded mandates for UNDCP flowing from the twentieth special session of the General Assembly in 1998.

In a November report on the proposed revised biennial support and programme budget for 2000-2001 for the UNDCP Fund [E/CN.7/2001/9], the UNDCP Executive Director stated that the revised total Fund budget proposal amounted to $187.6 million, compared to $200 million contained in the initial 2000-2001 Fund budget. The revised Fund budget comprised the programme budget ($148.3 million), the biennial support budget ($35.2 million) and agency support costs ($4.1 million). The revised programme budget amounted to $148.3 million, compared to the initial programme budget of $157 million, which represented a decrease of 5.5 per cent, reflecting resource allocation trends that affected major programmes, mainly in Afghanistan, Myanmar and Peru. The revised support budget amounted to $35.2 million, compared to the initial budget of $36.2 million, representing a decrease of 2.8 per cent attributable to a volume decrease of $0.8 million and a cost decrease of $0.2 million. Total resources budgeted at $187.6 million for 2000-2001 were covered by Fund balances and estimated income of $211.5 million, leaving a balance of $23.9 million over and above the planned budget for 2000-2001, to fund ongoing programmes into 2002-2003. Compared to the initial plan, the revised one was reduced by $12.4 million, or 6.2 per cent, with proportionate decreases in programme and support, so that the plan maintained the balance in the use of resources, with 79 per cent going to programmes and 21 per cent to support activities. Reviewing the funding situation, the report predicted that sufficient funds would be available, mainly as a result of increased income, to cover the proposed budgets. However, the bulk of the increase had been, and was expected to continue to be, special-purpose resources, despite efforts by UNDCP to obtain more general-purpose resources from traditional and non-traditional sources. Therefore, a better balance between general- and special-purpose income was needed to respond to new programme opportunities and to sustain a minimum level necessary for the biennial support budget. In addition, with the reduction in Fund balances, a timing gap arose between project implementation and funding.

A November report of the UNDCP Executive Director on the proposed outline for 2002-2003 for the UNDCP Fund [E/CN.7/2001/8] stated that the proposed outline amounted to $198,254,600, an increase of $10,663,900, or 5.6 per cent, compared with the revised budget for 2000-2001. The estimate of $206,071,900 in resources available in the outline for 2002-2003 reflected a decrease of $5,435,100, compared with the revised estimate for 2000-2001. That decrease was a combination of a reduction of $13,696,100 in the opening balance offset by a modest estimated increase in income of $8,261,000. Income was estimated at $152,496,000 for 2002-2003, compared with $144,235,000 for 2000-2001. The report stated that about 90 per cent of the resources was provided by the UNDCP Fund and 10 per cent was from the regular budget. There had been a marked turnaround from 1999 onwards, with the Fund budget increasing significantly because of higher programme delivery.

Commission on Narcotic Drugs

The Commission on Narcotic Drugs held its forty-third session in Vienna from 6 to 15 March, during which it adopted 11 resolutions and one decision and recommended to the Economic and Social Council for adoption three draft resolutions and two draft decisions.

The Commission agreed to convene a ministerial-level segment in 2003 and 2008 to coincide with the target dates to meet the objectives decided upon at the special session of the General Assembly in 1998 [YUN 1998, p. 1135].

By a 15 March resolution [res. 43/1], the Commission streamlined the annual reports questionnaire and requested the UNDCP Executive Director to revise it, taking into account the results of a technical expert meeting (Lisbon, Portugal, January). He was asked to test the resulting draft questionnaire in countries with various levels of development with regard to data-collection capacity and to submit a draft in 2001.

Further action taken by the Commission is described below.

By **decision 2000/240** of 27 July, the Economic and Social Council took note of the Commission's report on its forty-third session [E/2000/28] and approved the provisional agenda and documentation for the forty-fourth (2001) session, on the understanding that informal intersessional meetings would be held in Vienna, at no additional cost, to finalize the items to be included in the provisional agenda and the documentation requirements for the forty-fourth session.

Demand reduction

At its forty-third session, the Commission on Narcotic Drugs considered reduction of illicit demand for drugs. It had before it a report of the

UNDCP Executive Director [YUN 1999, p. 1165] on follow-up to the Action Plan for the Implementation of the Declaration on the Guiding Principles of Drug Demand Reduction and a note by the Secretariat on the world situation with regard to drug abuse [YUN 1999, p. 1188].

By a 15 March resolution [res. 43/2] on follow-up to the Action Plan [YUN 1999, p. 1157], the Commission requested UNDCP to provide guidance and assistance for the development of demand reduction strategies and programmes in line with the Declaration [YUN 1998, p. 1137], and to facilitate the sharing of information on best practices in several areas. It called upon UNDCP, when preparing the regular budget proposals for the 2002-2003 biennium, to allocate adequate resources to allow it to fulfil its role in the implementation of the Action Plan, and called upon Member States to implement the Action Plan.

Drug abuse

In a 15 March resolution on enhancing assistance to drug abusers [res. 43/3], the Commission urged Member States to develop services for early detection, counselling, treatment, relapse prevention, aftercare and social reintegration, and to find strategies and increase access to services designed to reach drug abusers. It invited Member States to exchange with other Member States and relevant national and international bodies information on their strategies, programmes and services, and called for the provision of voluntary contributions for the implementation of the Action Plan for the Implementation of the Declaration on the Guiding Principles of Drug Demand Reduction. The Commission asked the UNDCP Executive Director to take into account the efforts taken by Governments when preparing, for submission in 2001, the biennial report on follow-up to the twentieth special session of the General Assembly [YUN 1998, p. 1135].

A Commission resolution of the same date [res. 43/4] urged States to assign priority to activities aimed at preventing drug and inhalant abuse among children, and to implement prevention programmes, training plans, grass-roots activities and treatment and rehabilitation projects targeted at children and young people, and special prevention projects targeted at children in difficult circumstances, particularly street children and children affected by conflict situations. UNDCP was requested to report in 2001 on the situation with regard to drug abuse among children and on prevention and treatment programmes.

Illicit cultivation and trafficking

By a 15 March resolution [res. 43/6], the Commission urged UNDCP to continue to provide

assistance, subject to the availability of voluntary contributions, to countries that had eradicated and continued to eradicate illicit crops, and that were seeking to avoid their relocation, through the implementation of sustainable alternative development programmes.

A Commission resolution of the same date [res. 43/5] encouraged interested Governments to develop regional maritime agreements on cooperation to suppress illicit maritime trafficking in narcotic drugs and psychotropic substances, and requested UNDCP to provide technical support to the negotiation processes. It supported UNDCP efforts to facilitate coordination by States parties, under article 17 of the 1988 Convention against Illicit Traffic in Narcotic Drugs and Psychotropic Substances [YUN 1988, p. 690], of ways to ensure more effective suppression of maritime drug trafficking and encouraged States parties to consider establishing a mechanism to respond to requests subject to national procedures.

Another 15 March Commission resolution [res. 43/8] outlined a series of measures for States to prevent the diversion of controlled pharmaceuticals and illicitly obtained precursor chemicals involving technologies based on the Internet.

Secretariat report. A December report by the Secretariat [E/CN.7/2001/5] provided an overview of global trends and patterns in illicit drug production and trafficking and of action taken by the Commission's subsidiary bodies. The report, which was based on information received from Governments in the annual reports questionnaires submitted to UNDCP and reports on individual significant seizure cases, also drew on information received from the International Criminal Police Organization, the Customs Cooperation Council, INCB and the Inter-American Drug Abuse Control Commission. The report stated that the global supply of heroin declined in 2000, mainly because of a decline in opium production in Afghanistan from over 5,700 tons in 1999 to some 4,700 tons in 2000. Afghanistan was also responsible for the production peak in 1999, though the overproduction was not passed on to Western Europe, the main consumer region, where prices and seizures of heroin remained stable in many countries. Enormous seizure increases were, however, noted in countries surrounding Afghanistan. In East and South-East Asia, China emerged as an important conduit for opiate trafficking. It was estimated that cocaine production continued at stable levels, with Bolivia and Peru indicating decreases, while estimates for Colombia reflected further increases. In 1999, seizures of cocaine rose in both major consumer regions, the United States and Western Europe.

Production and trafficking of amphetamine-type stimulants, mainly methamphetamine, rose rapidly in East and South-East Asia. In North America, the trafficking of methamphetamine continued, but the main concern was related to Ecstasy-type substances, imported in large quantities from Western Europe. Trafficking in amphetamine-type stimulants within Western Europe stabilized. The report also provided an overview of action taken by the Commission's subsidiary bodies (see below).

Regional cooperation

By a 15 March resolution on enhancing regional cooperation through a regional database on drug-related crimes [res. 43/7], the Commission, taking note of the threat posed by the increasing illicit cultivation of, and trafficking in, narcotic drugs in South-West Asia and the proceedings of the first International Conference of Drug Liaison Officers (Tehran, Iran, 17-18 January), invited the States concerned to continue to hold meetings of drug liaison officers in South-West Asia. It called on States to establish a point of contact to ensure the timely sharing of operational intelligence, and requested the UNDCP Executive Director to ensure assistance to establish in Tehran a South-West Asian regional database on drug-related crimes.

During the year, three of the Commission's subsidiary bodies, following a review of drug-trafficking trends and regional and subregional cooperation, addressed drug law enforcement issues of priority concern. The thirty-fifth session of the Subcommission on Illicit Drug Traffic and Related Matters in the Near and Middle East (Antalya, Turkey, 26-30 June) [UNDCP/SUBCOM/2000/6] adopted recommendations on measures for law enforcement agencies to mobilize community support for anti-drug objectives; the elimination or reduction of corrupt practices by drug law enforcement personnel; and measures to prevent illicit traffic including smuggling through the mail and express services, and the diversion of precursors. The Subcommission reviewed progress made in implementing resolutions adopted by the twentieth special session of

the General Assembly, and recommended to the Commission the adoption of a draft resolution on enhancing regional cooperation on drug control through training, and the approval of a draft resolution on international cooperation for the control of narcotic drugs for adoption by the Economic and Social Council. It brought to the Commission's attention a resolution on the control of acetic anhydride, a precursor frequently used in the illicit manufacture of heroin.

The Tenth Meeting of Heads of National Drug Law Enforcement Agencies (HONLEA), Latin America and the Caribbean (Ottawa, Canada, 3-6 October) [UNDCP/HONLAC/2000/4] examined major regional drug-trafficking trends and countermeasures and adopted recommendations on demand reduction, psychotropic substances and precursors. The Twenty-fourth Meeting of HONLEA, Asia and the Pacific (Yangon, Myanmar, 14-17 November) [UNDCP/HONLAP/2000/5] analysed the drug situation with respect to regional and subregional cooperation and made recommendations on illicit traffic in, and consumption of, heroin; the impact of electronic crime on drug-trafficking strategy; the control of stimulants; and illicit traffic by sea.

UN inter-agency coordination

The Subcommittee on Drug Control of the Administrative Committee on Coordination (ACC), at its eighth session (Vienna, 28 and 29 September) [ACC/2000/17], considered a draft ACC guidance note for UN system activities to counter the drug problem. The Secretariat had suggested that the draft be finalized with the intention of providing authoritative guidance to UN country teams in their coordination of and support to various levels of intervention, from assessments and plans to technical cooperation programmes and projects in their country/countries of operation.

The Subcommittee endorsed a draft UN system position paper on preventing HIV transmission among drug abusers, which was annexed to the report.

Chapter XV

Statistics

In 2000, the United Nations continued its statistical work programme. The 24-member Statistical Commission, at its thirty-first session, adopted the methodological references to the tourism satellite account developed by the World Tourism Organization and noted the launching of PARIS 21—the Partnership in Statistics for Development in the Twenty-first Century—which aimed to build statistical capacity by helping to develop well-managed statistical systems. The Commission, having reviewed the work of a number of established bodies and international organizations, made specific recommendations regarding the implementation of the 1993 System of National Accounts and the production of statistical handbooks and manuals. It recognized the United Nations Statistics Division's ongoing efforts to make crucial information and materials available using the Internet, and welcomed the production of international trade statistics on CD-ROM.

The Commission stressed the need for continuous dialogue between producers of statistics and policy makers, effective partnerships at the national level and the accuracy of data.

The Subcommittee on Statistical Activities of the Administrative Committee on Coordination met in September.

Work of Statistical Commission

The Statistical Commission held its thirty-first session in New York from 29 February to 3 March 2000 [E/2000/24]. Action taken included the adoption of the draft methodological references to the tourism satellite account and, in follow-up to UN conferences and summits, reiteration of the need to lessen the reporting burden of countries by reducing the number of data requests sent by international organizations. The Commission stressed the importance of coordination among and within international organizations and of statistical capacity-building; took note of the launching of the PARIS 21 initiative—the Partnership in Statistics for Development in the Twenty-first Century [E/CN.3/2001/24]; and expressed support for the Economic Commission for Europe (ECE) ini-

tiative to strengthen capacity-building in social statistics in connection with the General Assembly's special session on the five-year review of the 1995 World Summit for Social Development to be held in June (see p. 1011).

Having reviewed work being undertaken by groups of countries and international organizations in economic, social and environment statistics, the Commission made recommendations for the contents of the compilers' manual for international merchandise trade statistics; gave directions concerning the milestone assessment of the implementation of the 1993 System of National Accounts (SNA); requested the Intersecretariat Working Group on National Accounts (ISWGNA) to consider a number of specific issues at its April meeting; gave specific directions regarding the content of the International Labour Organization (ILO) *Manual on Consumer Price Indices*, the process of revision of the System of Integrated Environmental and Economic Accounting, and the schedule for completing the *Handbook on Integrated Environmental and Economic Accounting*; and recommended that the next round of the global International Comparison Programme be postponed for at least one year so that a number of steps it had specified could be taken.

The Commission endorsed recommendations for future work on the International Standard Industrial Classification of All Economic Activities, made by the Expert Group on International Economic and Social Classifications, and provided specific directions for that work. With regard to the Special Data Dissemination Standard (SDDS) and the General Data Dissemination System of the International Monetary Fund (IMF), the Commission urged IMF to reinforce the effective partnerships between statistical agencies, central banks and ministries of finance formed as a result of the data standards initiative; expressed concern about the planned extension of SDDS, stating that there was an opportunity cost in terms of the further development of other data systems and stressing the need for priorities and flexibility when implementing the standards; and requested IMF to take the outcomes of the data quality debate into account when reviewing SDDS.

Having considered information regarding the United Nations Development Programme (UNDP) *Human Development Report* (see p. 805), the Commission requested its Chairman to set up a group of statistical experts to prepare, in conjunction with UNDP, a report on the accuracy of the statistical information in the *Report.*

In relation to the planned work of the Statistics Division, the Commission took note of the draft medium-term plan for 2002-2005, the work programme for the biennium 2000-2001, the proposed 2000-2001 schedule of expert groups and workshops, and the activities to be undertaken under the Development Account in 2000 and 2001.

The Commission brought to the attention of the Economic and Social Council actions taken or planned as a follow-up to requests made at the Council's high-level and coordination segments and its 1999 resolutions, in particular the development of a multi-year programme of work for the Commission for the period 2000-2003.

By **decision 2000/228** of 26 July, the Council took note of the Commission's 2000 report, decided that the Commission's thirty-second session should be held in New York from 6 to 9 March 2001 and approved the provisional agenda and documentation for that session.

Economic statistics

National accounts

The Statistical Commission had before it a report of the Secretary-General on the milestone assessment of the implementation of the 1993 SNA by Member States [E/CN.3/2000/3]. The report provided background information on the definition and measurement method of the milestones for implementation of the 1993 SNA; a summary table, by region, of the milestone assessment for member countries covering the period 1993-1998; a general analysis of the assessment results, as well as of the changes that occurred over the preceding three years; and a discussion of what the implementation of the 1993 SNA meant. Annexed to the report was a fact sheet on milestones.

The Commission, while recognizing that the milestone analysis based on the full implementation of the 1993 SNA provided useful information, emphasized the need for additional data, such as evaluation of timeliness, periodicity, direct measurement and conceptual adherence. It also noted that the current analysis showed a lack of progress in the implementation for a large number of countries that needed to be addressed.

The Commission also had before it the report of the 1999 meeting of the Task Force on National Accounts [E/CN.3/2000/2] [YUN 1999, p. 1194].

The Commission requested the high-level group of ISWGNA to reconsider if the current definition of implementation of the 1993 SNA was suitable for all countries and to determine whether a core set of accounts could be defined. It requested ISWGNA, at its April meeting, to consider the items discussed in the Commission with regard to future work on gross domestic product (GDP) volume measures and the link between national accounts data and employment, and to re-examine the mechanism for updating the 1993 SNA. The Commission further requested ISWGNA to continue to give special attention in its work programmes to the needs of the countries listed at milestone levels 0 and 1. The Statistics Netherlands initiative to host a workshop on GDP volume and price measurement, in cooperation with the Statistical Office of the European Communities (Eurostat), was welcomed.

At its April 2000 meeting [E/CN.3/2001/7], the Task Force on National Accounts addressed issues raised by the Commission with respect to the current milestone assessment of countries and made proposals for an alternative approach. Included in the proposals was the identification of three main dimensions that needed to be examined or re-examined in order to better assess to what extent countries had implemented the 1993 SNA: the scope of the accounts; compliance with 1993 SNA concepts; and quality issues. The report also provided information on the frequency of updates; treatment of mobile phone licences; and topics that were candidates for updates of the 1993 SNA: the accrual accounting of interest; treatment of interest under conditions of high inflation; and the cost of transferring ownership of assets.

The Commission took note of the standard integrated presentation of the work programmes of ISWGNA in support of SNA implementation; information provided on handbooks and manuals being developed by "city groups" (see p. 1203); and reports on areas where further and/or new conceptual and methodological work was being carried out.

International trade statistics

Having considered the report of the Task Force on International Trade Statistics [E/CN.3/2000/4], the Statistical Commission restated its request that the treatment of electronic commerce in international trade statistics be clarified, particularly in terms of its coverage and methods of data collection, and noted that the issue would be addressed at the next meeting of the Task Force and in the compilers' manual that was being prepared. It welcomed the data set of international trade statistics analysed according to the Central Product Classification (CPC) produced on a CD-ROM by the Statistics Division for test use by economists and statisticians and requested the

Division to provide user feedback as part of a review of the usefulness of CPC data for analytical purposes. The Commission expressed concern that the liberalization of trade and the consequent reduced incentive to secure accurate records of trade transactions could impact negatively on the quality of international trade statistics. It requested the Task Force to address the issue, to consider alternative sources of international trade statistics to supplement the customs-based data, and to reflect the outcomes in the compilers' manual.

Service statistics

The Commission had before it the report of the Task Force on Statistics of International Trade in Services [E/CN.3/2000/5], which stated that the UN Statistics Division and IMF had circulated the draft manual on statistics of international trade in services to the statistical organizations of all Member countries for a worldwide review.

The Commission welcomed the substantial progress made on the manual, noting that it provided a useful framework for guiding future work in a new area of statistics. It noted, however, that the information on extended balance-of-payments classification of services required more detail than most statistical offices could provide and also required careful consideration of the way in which resident and non-resident definitions were utilized in the description of services traded. The Commission suggested that, in practice, trade in services data might be collected by national offices at a more aggregated level.

Finance statistics

In its report on its 1999 meeting (Basel, Switzerland, 17-18 June) [E/CN.3/2000/6], the Task Force on Finance Statistics stated that it had drawn up an outline for revised and expanded guidelines on external debt statistics for compilers and users. The Statistical Commission supported the Task Force's work, in particular that on further developing creditor-side data. It noted that obtaining quality data from financial institutions was essential for that work and that implementing disclosure standards might be an important prerequisite.

International Comparison Programme

In response to a 1999 Statistical Commission request [YUN 1999, p. 1195], the World Bank submitted a report on measures to improve the effectiveness of the International Comparison Programme (ICP) [E/CN.3/2000/7], which was a follow-up to a 1999 consultant's evaluation [YUN 1999, p. 1195]. The report reviewed the objectives of the organizational structure and output of ICP, highlighted areas where significant progress had been made in addressing issues raised in the consultant's evaluation, flagged areas where further progress could be made and outlined practical steps towards addressing outstanding issues.

The Commission noted the support of many countries and international agencies for a viable ICP and the efforts made by the international and supranational agencies to address their reservations. It suggested steps to be taken regarding the reservations on quality, timeliness, credibility and transparency of ICP, as identified in reports of consultants, and recommended that the next round of the global ICP be postponed by at least one year so that the suggested steps could be implemented.

The Commission empowered the Chairman to constitute a group of friends to review the implementation plan and to report back to the Commission's 2001 session.

SDDS and GDDS

The Statistical Commission had before it an IMF report on the Special Data Dissemination Standard (SDDS) and the General Data Dissemination System (GDDS), and issues of data quality [E/CN.3/2000/8], which described the strengthening of SDDS in the wake of recent financial crises, the application of the data dissemination standards, data quality and the status of GDDS.

The Commission welcomed the response of the IMF Statistics Department to its 1999 request to enhance the consultation process [YUN 1999, p. 1192], and acknowledged the contribution made by SDDS to the improvement of data in the economic and financial area. It re-emphasized the importance of early involvement of national statistical agencies in the further development of SDDS and GDDS; stressed the need for effective partnerships at the national level between statistical agencies, central banks and ministries of finance for the successful implementation of the dissemination standards; expressed its concern about the planned extension of SDDS, noting that there was an opportunity cost in terms of the further development of other data systems; and stressed the need for priorities and a certain degree of flexibility when implementing the standards.

The Commission also welcomed the debate on data quality stimulated by IMF, invited IMF to build on existing experiences and expertise in countries and regions, and asked IMF to take the outcomes of the data quality debate into account when SDDS was being reviewed in the future. The

Commission also stressed the importance of continuous dialogue between producers of statistics and policy makers, agreed on the need for further capacity-building and resources for the implementation of the standards, and welcomed IMF's intention to integrate GDDS into its regular technical cooperation programme.

Other economic statistics

City groups

The Commission had before it a report of seven city groups in the area of economic statistics [E/CN.3/2000/9] and an addendum [E/CN.3/2000/9/Add.1] containing the report of the Expert Group on Intangibles.

The city group report described the meetings, activities and future work of the Canberra (Australia) Group on Household Income Statistics; the Delhi (India) Group on Informal Sector Statistics; the Expert Group on Capital Stock Statistics; the Ottawa (Canada) Group on Price Indexes; the Paris Group on Labour and Compensation; the Round Table on Business Survey Frames; and the Voorburg (Netherlands) Group on Service Statistics.

The Commission welcomed the progress made by the groups, reiterated the importance of making information about the groups widely available and encouraged them to publish their documents on the Internet. It suggested that the Ottawa Group consider the implications of the increase in e-commerce on price indicators and invited the Voorburg Group to address the difficulties that developing countries encountered when attempting to collect data on the services sector.

With regard to the report of the Expert Group on Intangibles, the Commission noted that the Organisation for Economic Cooperation and Development (OECD) would continue its work on intangible assets and the information economy but decided that such work should no longer be reported to the Commission under the city group agenda item.

IWGPS

The Intersecretariat Working Group on Price Statistics (IWGPS) met several times, formally and informally, during 2000 to review progress on the preparation of the manuals on consumer price indices (CPI) and on producer price indices (PPI) [E/CN.3/2001/12]. There was agreement on a common outline for the two manuals and free exchange of information and relevant texts between the two processes; draft chapters had been prepared and the editing process had been established. The technical expert group on PPI held its second meeting in Madrid, Spain, in September, when first drafts of seven chapters of the PPI manual were reviewed.

The Statistical Commission encouraged the inclusion in the manual on CPI of technical guidelines for implementation.

Tourism satellite account

The Statistical Commission had before it the report of the World Tourism Organization on the tourism satellite account (TSA) and related methodological outputs [E/CN.3/2000/11]; the draft TSA [PROV/ST/ESA/STAT/SER.F/80]; and the draft update of the UN/World Tourism Organization *Recommendations on Tourism Statistics*, including the provisional list of tourism-specific products [PROV/ST/ESA/STAT/SER.M/83/Rev.1].

The report presented the statistical design of a TSA and an update of *Recommendations on Tourism Statistics*, and described the process that had been followed in developing those products, including by the Enzo Paci World Conference on the Measurement of the Economic Impact of Tourism (Nice, France, 15-18 June 1999).

The Commission adopted the methodological references to the draft TSA, as amended, and requested the World Tourism Organization, OECD and Eurostat to make the approved changes and include in the draft TSA the list of tourism-specific products contained in the draft update of *Recommendations on Tourism Statistics*, and to publish the document as soon as possible in cooperation with the Statistics Division. Although the Commission welcomed the draft update of *Recommendations on Tourism Statistics*, reflecting the changes necessary for consistency with the TSA, the 1993 SNA and the fifth edition of the IMF *Balance of Payments*, including the list of tourism-specific products contained in the draft update, it deferred detailed consideration pending further consultations and review by the World Tourism Organization. It requested that organization, OECD and Eurostat to continue their cooperation in the field and to provide consistent technical advice and data requests to countries. It welcomed ILO's offer to present, at the Commission's 2001 session, a report on its work on developing a labour statistics supplement to the TSA.

Environment statistics

The Commission had before it the report of the London Group on Environmental Accounting [E/CN.3/2000/12], which summarized progress on the revision of the System of Integrated Environmental and Economic Accounting (SEEA) and presented the planned future work programme.

The Commission welcomed the proposed extensive consultation process with the international community during the revision of SEEA, and recommended that the handbook on integrated environmental and economic accounting be submitted to it for approval at its 2001 session, while noting that due to time constraints the document would be available in English only.

Social statistics

The Siena Group for Social Statistics (Maastricht, Netherlands, 22-24 May) [E/CN.3/2001/5] discussed the theme "Accounting in social statistics and indicators for social development".

Gender issues

The Commission had before it the report of the Secretary-General on the implementation plan of a project on gender issues in the measurement of paid and unpaid work [E/CN.3/2000/13], which described the rationale and objectives of the project and its major expected outputs. The project was developed with UNDP and the International Development Research Centre (Canada). The report was in follow-up to a recommendation contained in the 1995 Platform for Action adopted by the Fourth World Conference on Women [YUN 1995, p. 1169] regarding the need to improve data collection on the full contribution of women and men to the economy, including in the informal sector.

The Commission recognized the importance of the work on the measurement of paid and unpaid work by the Secretariat as set out in the report, and noted the additional related work being carried out by various countries and agencies, particularly on time-use surveys.

Development indicators

The Commission had before it a report of the Secretary-General on the harmonization and rationalization of development indicators in the UN system [E/CN.3/2000/15], which described the Statistics Division's activities in support of the two-day informal meeting of the Economic and Social Council in 1999 on basic indicators for the integrated and coordinated implementation of and follow-up to the major UN conferences and summits [YUN 1999, p. 1352].

Proposed activities to strengthen the efforts of the Division in statistical capacity and common indicators in line with Council resolution 1999/55 [YUN 1999, p. 1353] included: working with countries, international organizations and UN agencies in the harmonization of common indicators; working with OECD on developing indicators on means of implementation; identifying

countries' capacities to respond to the requests of international agencies in terms of the burden imposed on countries' reporting systems, quality of data produced and deviation from other national priorities; a comprehensive analysis of the statistical requirements originated by the monitoring needs of the recent international conferences and summits and comparison of those requirements with the statistical capacity of countries; support for statistical capacity-building in order to enable countries routinely to produce relevant data; and working with UN organizations in completing a development indicators web site.

The Commission expressed support for the Secretariat's efforts towards harmonization and rationalization of basic indicators, reiterated the need to lessen the reporting burden of countries by reducing the number of data requests sent by international organizations and stressed the importance of coordination among and within international organizations and ·of statistical capacity-building. The Commission noted the launch of the PARIS 21 initiative—the Partnership in Statistics for Development in the Twenty-first Century. PARIS 21 was a new global consortium of policy makers, statisticians and users of statistical information in support of development. It aimed to build statistical capacity as the foundation for effective development policies by helping to develop well-managed statistical systems that were appropriately resourced. The Commission noted that unless the necessary resources for capacity-building were made available, it would not be possible to meet the demands for data made by policy makers.

International economic and social classifications

The Commission had before it a report of the Secretary-General on international economic and social classifications [E/CN.3/2000/17], which provided an overview of how the Commission's 1999 recommendations concerning international statistical classifications [YUN 1999, p. 1197] had been addressed. Annexed to the report were the conclusions of a meeting of the Expert Group on International Economic and Social Classifications and the summary action plan of the newly formed Technical Subgroup for updating and future revision of the International Standard Industrial Classification of All Economic Activities (ISIC) and the Central Product Classification.

The Commission endorsed the recommendations for future work on ISIC, as outlined in the report of the Expert Group, and noted that the concerns raised regarding the appropriate level of detail of an international classification were determined by the need to allow for international comparison at aggregated levels, as well as the need for detailed development of national classifications. It also noted that a two-digit ISIC with regional adaptations could possibly serve those needs and referred the matter to the Expert Group for further consideration.

The Commission recommended that the definition and use of alternate aggregations in ISIC receive more attention as a way to satisfy analytical needs of users, emphasized the need for training materials and noted the already existing support of Member countries in that field. The Commission also noted that during the revision process of ISIC, more attention should be given to the definition and use of statistical units and the definition of core units as building blocks, and that, although currently focused on economic classifications, the Expert Group could also bring items relating to social classifications to the attention of the Commission. It further noted the Statistics Division's ongoing efforts to make crucial information and materials available on the Internet.

Other statistical activities

In reviewing other major developments in the work programme of the Statistics Division, the Commission took note of the draft medium-term plan for the period 2002-2005 [E/CN.3/2000/CRP.1], the proposed schedule of expert groups and workshops [E/CN.3/2000/L.4] and the activities to be undertaken under the Development Account [A/53/374/Add.1].

Coordination and integration of international statistical programmes

Having considered the report of the Administrative Committee on Coordination (ACC) Sub-committee on Statistical Activities on its 1999 session [YUN 1999, p. 1197] and the report of the Secretary-General on the global integrated presentation of the work of the international organizations in statistical methodology [E/CN.3/2000/20], the Commission took note of the latter report and welcomed the cooperative and supportive action that had been taken by ECE, OECD and Euro-stat in the context of the Conference of European Statisticians' integrated presentation of statistical work in that region.

Inter-agency cooperation

The ACC Subcommittee on Statistical Activities, at its thirty-fourth session (Washington, D.C., 20-22 September) [ACC/2000/16], noted, among other things, the outcome of the International Statistical Institute conference on measurement of electronic commerce (Singapore, 6-8 December 1999), agreeing that e-commerce provided challenges to statisticians in concepts, definitions and data collection. The Subcommittee also took note of the work being undertaken on the development indicators web page; recognized the importance of user/producer dialogues and requested the Statistics Division to explore the use of the existing General Assembly panel series in the promotion of dialogues; and expressed concern that OECD had issued the publication *Measuring the Role of Tourism in OECD Economies: The OECD Manual on Tourism Satellite Accounts and Employment* without sufficient references to the forthcoming joint UN/OECD/Eurostat/World Tourism Organization "TSA: Methodological References", which had been adopted with certain modifications by the Statistical Commission in March (see p. 1203).

PART FOUR

Legal questions

Chapter I

International Court of Justice

In 2000, the International Court of Justice (ICJ) delivered one Judgment, made 22 Orders and had 25 contentious cases pending before it.

The ICJ President, in a 26 October address to the General Assembly, explained that although the Court had adopted measures to respond to the increased caseload, those steps would not be sufficient to cope with the situation in coming years. He recalled that the proliferation of international tribunals and their overlapping jurisdictions gave rise to a serious risk to the cohesiveness of international law. The President observed that the international community was dependent on courts acting in the service of law.

Judicial work of the Court

During 2000, the Court delivered a Judgment on its jurisdiction in the case concerning the *Aerial Incident of 10 August 1999 (Pakistan v. India).*

The Court made Orders on requests for the indication of provisional measures made by the Democratic Republic of the Congo in the case concerning *Armed activities on the territory of the Congo (Democratic Republic of the Congo v. Uganda)* and the case concerning the *Arrest Warrant of 11 April 2000 (Democratic Republic of the Congo v. Belgium).*

The Court or its President made further Orders on the conduct of the proceedings in the cases concerning *Questions of Interpretation and Application of the 1971 Montreal Convention arising from the Aerial Incident at Lockerbie (Libyan Arab Jamahiriya v. United Kingdom)* and *(Libyan Arab Jamahiriya v. United States)*; *Oil Platforms (Iran v. United States)*; *Sovereignty over Pulau Litigan and Pulau Sipadan (Indonesia/Malaysia)*; *Ahmadou Sadio Diallo (Republic of Guinea v. Democratic Republic of the Congo)*; *Legality of Use of Force (Yugoslavia v. Belgium)*, *(Yugoslavia v. Canada)*, *(Yugoslavia v. France)*, *(Yugoslavia v. Germany)*, *(Yugoslavia v. Italy)*, *(Yugoslavia v. Netherlands)*, *(Yugoslavia v. Portugal)* and *(Yugoslavia v. United Kingdom)*; *Armed activities on the territory of the Congo (Democratic Republic of the Congo v. Burundi)*, *(Democratic Republic of the Congo v. Uganda)* and *(Democratic Republic of the Congo v. Rwanda)*; *Application of the Convention on the Prevention and Punishment of the Crime of Genocide (Croatia v. Yugoslavia)*; *Maritime Delimitation between Nicaragua and Honduras in the Caribbean Sea (Nicaragua*

v. Honduras); and *Arrest Warrant of 11 April 2000 (Democratic Republic of the Congo v. Belgium).*

ICJ activities in 2000 were covered in two reports to the General Assembly, for the periods 1 August 1999 to 31 July 2000 [A/55/4] and 1 August 2000 to 31 July 2001 [A/56/4]. On 26 October, the Assembly took note of the 1999/2000 report (**decision 55/407**).

Maritime delimitation and territorial questions (Qatar v. Bahrain)

Qatar instituted proceedings in 1991 [YUN 1991, p. 820] against Bahrain in respect of disputes relating to sovereignty over the Hawar Islands, sovereign rights over the shoals of Dibal and Qit'at Jaradah, and the delimitation of the maritime areas of the two States.

In 1992, a Memorial by Qatar and a Counter-Memorial by Bahrain were filed [YUN 1992, p. 982], as were their respective Reply and Rejoinder.

Following hearings, the Court delivered a Judgment on 1 July 1994 [YUN 1994, p. 1279].

The Court received a letter from Qatar on 30 November 1994 transmitting an "Act to comply with paragraphs (3) and (4) of the operative paragraph 41 of the Judgment of the Court dated 1 July 1994". On the same day, Bahrain transmitted a "Report of the State of Bahrain to the International Court of Justice on the Attempt by the Parties to Implement the Court's Judgment of 1 July 1994".

At a public sitting held on 15 February 1995, the Court delivered a Judgment on jurisdiction and admissibility [YUN 1995, p. 1305], by which it found that it had jurisdiction and that the Application of Qatar as formulated on 30 November 1994 was admissible.

In 1996, each Party filed a Memorial on the merits [YUN 1996, p. 1176]. Counter-Memorials of the Parties were filed on 23 December 1997 [YUN 1997, p. 1312].

On 17 March 1998, the President held a meeting to ascertain the views of the Parties on a procedure concerning the authenticity of documents produced by Qatar [YUN 1997, p. 1312]. By an Order of 30 March 1998 [YUN 1998, p. 1184], the Court fixed 30 September 1998 as the time limit for the filing of an interim report by Qatar on the authenticity of the documents and directed the filing of a Reply by each of the Parties within the time limit of 30 March 1999. In its interim report filed in September 1998, Qatar stated that it would not rely on the disputed documents for the purposes of the present case so as to enable the Court to address the merits of the case without further procedural complications. In December 1998, Qatar requested "a two-month extension of the time limit for the filing of a Reply by each of the Parties, to 30 May 1999" [ibid.].

In February 1999 [YUN 1999, p. 1202], the Court placed on record Qatar's decision to disregard the 82 documents annexed to its written pleadings, which had been challenged by Bahrain, and decided that the Replies yet to be filed by Qatar and by Bahrain would not rely on those documents. After filing their Replies within the extended time limit, Qatar and Bahrain submitted, with the approval of the Court, certain additional expert reports and historical documents.

At the conclusion of sittings held from 29 May to 29 June 2000 to hear oral arguments of the Parties, Qatar requested the Court to adjudge and declare that it had sovereignty over the Hawar Islands, and Dibal and Qit'at Jaradah shoals; and that Bahrain had no sovereignty over the island of Janan nor over Zubarah and that any claim by it concerning archipelago baselines and areas for fishing for pearls and swimming fish would be irrelevant for the purpose of maritime delimitation. Qatar also requested that the Court draw a single maritime boundary between the maritime areas of seabed, subsoil and superjacent waters appertaining to Qatar and Bahrain on the basis that Zubarah, the Hawar Islands and Janan appertained to it and not to Bahrain, that boundary being based on a delimitation agreement concluded between Bahrain and Iran in 1971, a decision of the United Kingdom of 23 December 1947 and a delimitation agreement concluded by Bahrain and Saudi Arabia in 1958. Bahrain's final submission asked the Court to adjudge and declare that it was sovereign over Zubarah and the Hawar Islands, including Janan and Hadd Janan, and that, in view of Bahrain's sovereignty over all the insular and other features, including Gasht and Dibal and Qit'at Jaradah, comprising the Bahraini archipelago, the maritime boundary between Bahrain and Qatar was as described in its Memorial.

The Court held deliberations on its Judgment.

Questions of interpretation and application of the 1971 Montreal Convention arising from the aerial incident at Lockerbie (Libyan Arab Jamahiriya v. United Kingdom) and (Libyan Arab Jamahiriya v. United States)

The Libyan Arab Jamahiriya instituted in 1992 [YUN 1992, p. 982] separate proceedings against the

United Kingdom and the United States in respect of a dispute over the interpretation and application of the 1971 Montreal Convention for the Suppression of Unlawful Acts against the Safety of Civil Aviation [YUN 1971, p. 739], which arose from its alleged involvement in the crash of Pan Am flight 103 over Lockerbie, Scotland, on 21 December 1988. In the Applications, Libya referred to the charging and indictment of two of its nationals by the Lord Advocate of Scotland and by a United States Grand Jury for having caused a bomb to be placed aboard Pan Am flight 103, which exploded, caused the aircraft to crash and killed all 270 persons aboard.

The United Kingdom and the United States, on 16 and on 20 June 1995, respectively [YUN 1995, p. 1306], filed preliminary objections to the jurisdiction of the Court to entertain Libya's Applications. Libya presented a written statement of its observations and submissions on the preliminary objections raised by the United Kingdom and the United States within the prescribed time limits set by the Court. Public sittings to hear the oral arguments of the Parties on the preliminary objections raised by the United Kingdom and the United States were held in October 1997 [YUN 1997, p. 1313].

At public sittings held on 27 February 1998 [YUN 1998, p. 1184], the Court delivered the two Judgments on the preliminary objections, by which it rejected the objection to jurisdiction raised by the United Kingdom and the United States on the basis of the alleged absence of a dispute between the Parties concerning the interpretation or application of the Montreal Convention; found that it had jurisdiction, on the basis of article 14, paragraph 1, of the Convention, to hear the disputes between Libya and the United Kingdom and Libya and the United States concerning the interpretation or application of the provisions of the Convention; rejected the objection to admissibility derived by the United Kingdom and the United States from Security Council resolutions 748(1992) [YUN 1992, p. 55] and 883(1993) [YUN 1993, p. 101]; found that the Applications filed by Libya on 3 March 1992 were admissible; and declared that the objection raised by both countries according to which the same Council resolutions had rendered the claims of Libya without object did not, in the circumstances of the case, have an excessively preliminary character.

The time limit of 30 December 1998 fixed by the Court [YUN 1998, p. 1185] for the filing of the Counter-Memorials of the United Kingdom and the United States was extended to 31 March 1999 following a proposal of the United Kingdom and the United States, which referred to diplomatic initiatives [ibid., p. 163], and after the views of Libya had been ascertained. The Counter-Memorials were filed within the time limit.

Taking account of the agreement of the Parties and the special circumstances of the case, the Court, by Orders of 29 June 1999 [YUN 1999, p. 1203], authorized the submission of a Reply by Libya and a Rejoinder by the United Kingdom and the United States, which fixed 29 June 2000 as the time limit for the filing of the Reply. The Court fixed no date for the filing of the Rejoinders; the representatives of the Respondent States had expressed the desire that no such date be fixed at that stage of the proceedings, "in view of the new circumstances consequent upon the transfer of the two accused to the Netherlands for trial by a Scottish court". Libya's Reply was filed within the prescribed time limit.

By Orders of 6 September 2000, the President of the Court, taking account of the Parties' views, fixed 3 August 2001 as the time limit for filing the Rejoinder of the United Kingdom and the United States. (See also p. 189.)

Oil platforms (Iran v. United States)

Iran instituted proceedings against the United States in 1992 [YUN 1992, p. 983] regarding a dispute in which Iran alleged that the destruction by United States warships, on 19 October 1987 and 18 April 1988, of three offshore oil production complexes owned and operated by the National Iranian Oil Company constituted a breach of international law and the 1955 Iran/United States Treaty of Amity, Economic Relations and Consular Rights. Iran requested the Court to rule on the matter.

Orders of the Court in 1992 [YUN 1992, p. 983] and 1993 [YUN 1993, p. 1183] fixed time limits for the filing of the Memorial by Iran and for a Counter-Memorial by the United States. Iran filed its Memorial, while the United States filed certain preliminary objections to the jurisdiction of the Court. In 1994 [YUN 1994, p. 1280], Iran presented a written statement of its observations and submissions on the United States objections, in accordance with an Order of the Court.

The Court delivered its Judgment in 1996 [YUN 1996, p. 1178], by which it rejected the preliminary objection of the United States and found that it had jurisdiction to entertain the claims made by Iran.

By an Order of 16 December 1996 [YUN 1996, p. 1178], the President of the Court fixed 23 June 1997 as the time limit for the filing of the Counter-Memorial of the United States. Within that time limit, the United States filed the Counter-Memorial and a counter-claim [YUN 1997, p. 1313].

In November and December 1997, Iran and the United States, respectively, submitted written observations on the question of the admissibility of the United States counter-claim.

In 1998 [YUN 1998, p. 1185], the Court found that the counter-claim presented by the United States in its Counter-Memorial was admissible. It further directed Iran to submit a Reply and the United States to submit a Rejoinder, fixing the time limits for those pleadings at 10 September 1998 and 23 November 1999, respectively.

In May 1998 [YUN 1998, p. 1185], the Vice-President of the Court, Acting President, extended, at the request of Iran and taking into account the views expressed by the United States, the time limits for Iran's Reply and the United States Rejoinder to 10 December 1998 and 23 May 2000, respectively. In December 1998, the Court further extended those time limits to 10 March 1999 for Iran's Reply and 23 November 2000 for the United States Rejoinder. Iran's Reply was filed within the time limit thus extended.

By an Order of 4 September 2000, the President of the Court extended, at the request of the United States and taking into account the agreement between the Parties, the time limit for filing the United States Rejoinder to 23 March 2001.

Application of the Convention on the Prevention and Punishment of the Crime of Genocide (Bosnia and Herzegovina v. Yugoslavia)

Bosnia and Herzegovina instituted proceedings in 1993 [YUN 1993, p. 1138] against the Federal Republic of Yugoslavia (Serbia and Montenegro) (FRY) for alleged violations of the 1948 Convention on the Prevention and Punishment of the Crime of Genocide, adopted by the General Assembly in resolution 260 A (III) [YUN 1948-49, p. 959]. The time limits were fixed for the filing of a Memorial by Bosnia and Herzegovina and a Counter-Memorial by FRY [YUN 1993, p. 1138]. The Memorial by Bosnia and Herzegovina was filed within the prescribed time limit [YUN 1994, p. 1281].

The time limit for the filing of the Counter-Memorial by FRY was extended in 1995 [YUN 1995, p. 1307]. Within the time limit, FRY filed certain preliminary objections. The objections related, first, to the admissibility of the Application and, second, to the jurisdiction of the Court to deal with the case. By virtue of the Rules of Court, proceedings on the merits were suspended. Pursuant to an Order of the Court [ibid.], Bosnia and Herzegovina presented a written statement of its observations and submissions on the preliminary objections raised by FRY, within the prescribed time limit.

The Court delivered its Judgment in 1996 on the preliminary objections [YUN 1996, p. 1179], by which it rejected the objections raised by FRY. In accordance with an Order of 23 July 1996 [ibid.], FRY filed a Counter-Memorial that included counter-claims against Bosnia and Herzegovina [YUN 1997, p. 1315].

Both Parties accepted in 1997 that their respective Governments would submit written observations on the question of the admissibility of the FRY counter-claims and did so. The Court found that the counter-claims submitted by FRY in its Counter-Memorial were admissible and directed Bosnia and Herzegovina to submit a Reply and FRY to submit a Rejoinder, fixing the time limits for those pleadings at 23 January and 23 July 1998, respectively. In January 1998 [YUN 1998, p. 1186], those time limits were extended to 23 April 1998 and 22 January 1999, respectively. The Reply of Bosnia and Herzegovina was filed within the prescribed time limit. The Court, in December 1998 [ibid.], extended the time limit for the filing of FRY's Rejoinder to 22 February 1999, which was filed within the time limit [YUN 1999, p. 1204].

Since then, several exchanges of letters took place concerning new procedural difficulties in the case.

Land and maritime boundary between Cameroon and Nigeria

Cameroon instituted proceedings against Nigeria in March 1994 [YUN 1994, p. 1281] in a dispute concerning the question of sovereignty over the peninsula of Bakassi and requested the Court to determine the course of the maritime frontier between the two States insofar as that frontier had not already been established in 1975. The Application was amended by an Additional Application in June 1994. Cameroon's Memorial was filed in 1995 [YUN 1995, p. 1308]. On 13 December 1995, within the time limit for the filing of its Counter-Memorial, Nigeria filed certain preliminary objections to the jurisdiction of the Court and to the admissibility of the claims of Cameroon.

In 1996 [YUN 1996, p. 1180], Cameroon presented a written statement of its observations and submissions on the preliminary objections raised by Nigeria. Following hearings in March 1996, the Court made an Order [ibid.] indicating that neither Party should take any action of any kind, and that both should lend every assistance to a fact-finding mission to be sent by the United Nations Secretary-General [YUN 1996, p. 146].

On 11 June 1998 [YUN 1998, p. 1187], the Court delivered its Judgment on the preliminary objections, by which it rejected seven of Nigeria's eight preliminary objections; declared that the eighth preliminary objection did not have, in the cir-

cumstances of the case, an exclusively preliminary character; and found that, on the basis of Article 36, paragraph 2, of the ICJ Statute, it had jurisdiction to adjudicate on the dispute and that the Application filed by Cameroon on 29 March 1994, as amended by the Additional Application of 6 June 1994, was admissible. The Court, having been informed of the views of the Parties, fixed 31 March 1999 as the time limit for the filing of the Counter-Memorial of Nigeria.

On 28 October 1998, Nigeria filed a request for an interpretation of the Court's Judgment on the preliminary objections [YUN 1998, p. 1187]. The request for interpretation formed a separate case, in which the Court delivered its Judgment on 25 March 1999 [YUN 1999, p. 1205].

On 23 February 1999 [YUN 1999, p. 1204], Nigeria requested an extension of the time limit for the deposit of its Counter-Memorial, as it did not know the scope of the case it had to answer on State responsibility until the outcome of its request for interpretation was known. By a letter of 27 February 1999, the Agent of Cameroon informed the Court that Cameroon was resolutely opposed to Nigeria's request, as its dispute with Nigeria called for a rapid decision.

In March 1999 [YUN 1999, p. 1204], the Court extended to 31 May 1999 the time limit for the filing of Nigeria's Counter-Memorial, which was filed within the time limit.

The Counter-Memorial included counter-claims. At the end of each section dealing with a particular sector of the frontier, Nigeria asked the Court to declare that the incidents referred to "engage the international responsibility of Cameroon, with compensation in the form of damages, if not agreed between the parties, then to be awarded by the Court in a subsequent phase of the case".

The seventh and final submission set out by Nigeria in its Counter-Memorial read as follows: "as to Nigeria's counter-claims as specified in . . . of this Counter-Memorial, [the Court is asked to] adjudge and declare that Cameroon bears responsibility to Nigeria in respect of those claims, the amount of reparation due therefor, if not agreed between the parties within six months of the date of judgment, to be determined by the Court in a further judgment". In June 1999 [YUN 1999, p. 1204], the Court found that Nigeria's counter-claims were admissible and formed part of the proceedings; decided that Cameroon should submit a Reply and Nigeria a Rejoinder, relating to the claims of both Parties; and fixed the time limits for those pleadings at 4 April 2000 and 4 January 2001, respectively.

On 30 June 1999, Equatorial Guinea filed an Application for permission to intervene in the case, stating that the purpose was to protect its legal rights in the Gulf of Guinea and to inform the Court of Equatorial Guinea's legal rights and interests so that they might remain unaffected as the Court proceeded to address the question of the maritime boundary between Cameroon and Nigeria. Equatorial Guinea clarified that it did not seek to intervene in those aspects of the proceedings that related to the land boundary between Cameroon and Nigeria, nor to become a Party to the case. It further stated that, although it would be open to a request to the Court from the three countries not only to determine the Cameroon-Nigeria maritime boundary but also to determine Equatorial Guinea's maritime boundary with those two States, Equatorial Guinea had made no such request and wished to continue to determine its maritime boundary with its neighbours by negotiation.

The Court fixed 16 August 1999 [YUN 1999, p. 1205] as the time limit for the filing of written observations on Equatorial Guinea's Application by Cameroon and Nigeria, which were filed within the prescribed time limits.

By an Order of 21 October 1999, the Court handed down its decision on Equatorial Guinea's Application for permission to intervene, by which it unanimously decided that Equatorial Guinea could intervene in the case, pursuant to Article 62 of the Statute, to the extent, in the manner and for the purposes set out in its Application for permission to intervene, and fixed the time limits for the filing of the written statement and the written observations at 4 April 2001 for the written statement of Equatorial Guinea and 4 July 2001 for the written observations of Cameroon and Nigeria.

Sovereignty over Pulau Ligitan and Pulau Sipadan (Indonesia/Malaysia)

On 2 November 1998 [YUN 1998, p. 1189], Indonesia and Malaysia jointly notified the Court of a Special Agreement between them, signed at Kuala Lumpur on 31 May 1997, which entered into force on 14 May 1998, in which they requested the Court "to determine on the basis of the treaties, agreements and any other evidence furnished by the Parties, whether sovereignty over Pulau Ligitan and Pulau Sipadan belongs to the Republic of Indonesia or to Malaysia". By an Order of 10 November 1998 [ibid.], the Court fixed 2 November 1999 and 2 March 2000, respectively, as the time limits for the filing by each of the Parties of a Memorial and a Counter-Memorial. The time limit for filing the Counter-Memorials was extended to 2 July 2000, by an Order of 14 September 1999 [YUN 1999, p. 1206].

The Memorials were filed within the time limit of 2 November 1999, as fixed by the Court's Order of 10 November 1998.

By an Order of 11 May 2000, the President of the Court, acting on a joint request of the Parties, extended the time limit for the filing of the Counter-Memorials to 2 August. The Counter-Memorials were filed within the extended time limit.

In October 2000, the President, having regard to the Special Agreement and taking account of the agreement between the Parties, fixed 2 March 2001 as the time limit for the filing of a Reply by each Party.

Ahmadou Sadio Diallo (Guinea v. Democratic Republic of the Congo)

On 28 December 1998 [YUN 1998, p. 1190], Guinea instituted proceedings against the Democratic Republic of the Congo (DRC) by an "Application with a view to diplomatic protection", in which it requested the Court to condemn the DRC for the grave breaches of international law perpetrated upon the person of a Guinean national, Ahmadou Sadio Diallo.

According to Guinea, Mr. Diallo, a businessman who had been a resident of the DRC for 32 years, was "unlawfully imprisoned by the authorities of that State" during two and a half months, "divested from his important investments, companies, bank accounts, movable and immovable properties, then expelled". The expulsion took place on 2 February 1996, as a result of his attempts to recover sums owed to him by the DRC (especially by Gécamines, a State enterprise and mining monopoly) and by oil companies operating in that country (Zaïre Shell, Zaïre Mobil and Zaïre Fina) by virtue of contracts concluded with businesses owned by him, namely Africom-Zaïre and Africontainers-Zaïre.

As a basis of the Court's jurisdiction, Guinea invoked its own declaration of acceptance of the compulsory jurisdiction of the Court of 11 November 1998 and the declaration of the DRC of 8 February 1989.

By an Order of 25 November 1999 [YUN 1999, p. 1206], the Court, taking into account the agreement of the Parties, fixed 11 September 2000 as the time limit for the filing of a Memorial by Guinea and 11 September 2001 for the filing of a Counter-Memorial by the DRC.

By an Order of 8 September 2000, the President of the Court, at Guinea's request and after the views of the other Party had been ascertained, extended to 23 March 2001 and 4 October 2002 the respective time limits for the Memorial and Counter-Memorial.

Vienna Convention on Consular Relations (Germany v. United States)

On 2 March 1999 [YUN 1999, p. 1206], Germany instituted proceedings against the United States in a dispute concerning alleged violations of the 1963 Vienna Convention on Consular Relations [YUN 1963, p. 510]. In its Application, Germany based the jurisdiction of the Court on Article 36, paragraph 1, of the Statute and on article I of the Optional Protocol concerning the Compulsory Settlement of Disputes, which accompanied the Vienna Convention and which provided that the "disputes arising out of the interpretation or application of the Convention shall be within the compulsory jurisdiction of the International Court of Justice".

In the Application, Germany stated that in 1982 the authorities of Arizona (United States) detained two German nationals, Karl and Walter LaGrand; that the individuals were tried and sentenced to death without having been informed, as was required under article 36, subparagraph 1 (b), of the Vienna Convention, of their rights under that provision (which required the competent authorities of a State party to advise, without delay, a national of another State party whom such authorities arrested or detained of the national's right to consular assistance guaranteed by article 36). Germany also alleged that the failure to provide the required notification precluded it from protecting its nationals' interests in the United States, as provided for by the 1963 Convention, at both the trial and the appeal level in the United States courts.

Germany stated that it had been, until very recently, the contention of the authorities of the State of Arizona that they had been unaware of the fact that Karl and Walter LaGrand were German nationals, and that it had accepted that contention as true. However, during the proceedings before the Arizona Mercy Committee on 23 February 1999, the State Attorney admitted that the authorities of the State of Arizona had indeed been aware since 1982 that the two detainees were German nationals. Germany further stated that Karl and Walter LaGrand, finally with the assistance of German consular officers, did claim violations of the Vienna Convention before the Federal District Court (the federal court of first instance). In addition, it claimed that the Court, applying the municipal law doctrine of "procedural default", decided that, because the individuals in question had not asserted their rights under the Vienna Convention in the previous legal proceedings at the state level, they could not assert them in the federal habeas corpus proceedings; and the intermediate federal appellate court, the last means of legal recourse in the United States available to them, had affirmed that decision.

Germany asked ICJ to adjudge and declare that: the United States, in arresting, detaining, trying, convicting and sentencing the LaGrands, had violated its international legal obligations to Germany, in its own right and in the exercise of its right of diplomatic protection of its nationals, as provided by articles 5 and 36 of the Vienna Convention; Germany was therefore entitled to reparation; the United States was under an international legal obligation not to apply the doctrine of "procedural default", or any other doctrine of its internal law, so as to preclude the exercise of the rights accorded under the Vienna Convention; and the United States was under an international obligation to carry out in conformity with the foregoing international legal obligations any future detention of or criminal proceedings against the LaGrands or any other German national in its territory, whether by a constituent, legislative, executive, judicial or other power, whether that power held a superior or subordinate position in the organization of the United States, and whether that power's functions were of an international or internal character. The foregoing international legal obligations held that: any criminal liability imposed on the LaGrands in violation of international legal obligations was void, and should be recognized as void by the United States legal authorities; the United States should provide reparation, in the form of compensation and satisfaction, for the execution of Karl LaGrand on 24 February 1999; the United States should restore the status quo ante in the case of Walter LaGrand, which meant re-establishing the situation that existed before the detention of, proceedings against and conviction and sentencing of Walter LaGrand, whose execution had been set for 3 March; and the United States should provide Germany a guarantee of the non-repetition of the illegal acts.

On 2 March [YUN 1999, p. 1207], Germany also submitted an urgent request for the indication of provisional measures, asking the Court to indicate that "the United States should take all measures at its disposal to ensure that Walter LaGrand is not executed pending the final decision in these proceedings, and should inform the Court of all the measures which it has taken in implementation of that Order"; it asked the Court moreover to consider its request as a matter of the greatest urgency "in view of the extreme gravity and immediacy of the threat of execution of a German citizen".

By a letter of the same date, the Vice-President of the Court addressed the United States Government in the following terms: "Exercising the functions of the presidency in terms of Articles 13 and 32 of the Rules of Court, and acting in conformity with Article 74, paragraph 4, of the said Rules, I hereby draw the attention of [the] Government [of the United States] to the need to act in such a way as to enable any Order the Court will make on the request for provisional measures to have its appropriate effects."

At a public sitting on 3 March, the Court rendered its Order on the request for the indication of provisional measures by which it indicated that: the United States should take all measures at its disposal to ensure that Walter LaGrand was not executed pending the final decision in the proceedings, and should inform the Court of all the measures which it had taken in implementation of the Order; and the United States should transmit the Order to the Governor of the State of Arizona. It decided that, until the Court had given its final decision, it would remain seized of the matters which formed the subject matter of the Order. Walter LaGrand was executed later that day.

Judge Oda appended a declaration to the Order and President Schwebel a separate opinion.

By an Order of 5 March 1999 [YUN 1999, p. 1207], the Court, taking into account the views of the Parties, fixed 16 September 1999 and 27 March 2000 as the time limits for the filing of the Memorial of Germany and the Counter-Memorial of the United States, respectively. The Memorial was filed within the prescribed time limit.

At the conclusion of oral proceedings held from 13 to 17 November 2000, Germany requested the Court to adjudge and declare that: the United States, by not informing the LaGrands, without delay and following their arrest, of their rights under the Vienna Convention, and by depriving Germany of the possibility of rendering consular assistance, violated its international legal obligations to Germany; the United States, by applying rules of its domestic law, which barred the LaGrands from raising their claims under the Vienna Convention, and by executing them, violated its international obligations to Germany; the United States, by failing to take all measures to ensure that Walter LaGrand was not executed pending the final decision of ICJ on the matter, violated its international legal obligations to comply with the Court's Order of 3 March; and the United States should assure Germany that it would not repeat the unlawful acts and that, in future cases of detention of or criminal proceedings against German nationals, the United States would ensure in law and in practice the effective exercise of the rights under the Convention, particularly in cases involving the death penalty. The United States asked the

Court to adjudge and declare that there was a breach of the United States obligation to Germany under the Vienna Convention, in that the United States authorities did not promptly notify the LaGrands as required, and that the United States had apologized to Germany for the breach and was taking substantial measures to prevent any recurrence; and all other claims and submissions of Germany were dismissed.

In 2000, the Court held deliberations on its Judgment.

Use of force (Yugoslavia v. Belgium), (Yugoslavia v. Canada), (Yugoslavia v. France), (Yugoslavia v. Germany), (Yugoslavia v. Italy), (Yugoslavia v. Netherlands), (Yugoslavia v. Portugal), (Yugoslavia v. Spain), (Yugoslavia v. United Kingdom) and (Yugoslavia v. United States)

FRY instituted proceedings on 29 April 1999 [YUN 1999, p. 1207] against Belgium, Canada, France, Germany, Italy, the Netherlands, Portugal, Spain, the United Kingdom and the United States for alleged violation of the obligation not to use force. In the cases against Belgium, Canada, the Netherlands, Portugal, Spain and the United Kingdom, FRY invoked the jurisdiction of the Court based on Article 36, paragraph 2, of the Statute and on article IX of the 1948 Convention on the Prevention and Punishment of the Crime of Genocide, adopted by the General Assembly in resolution 260 A (III) [YUN 1948-49, p. 959], and, in the cases against France, Germany, Italy and the United States, on article IX of the Convention and Article 38, paragraph 5, of the Rules of Court.

In its Applications, FRY stated that the disputes involved acts of the [Respondent State concerned] "by which it has violated the international obligation banning the use of force against another State, the obligation not to intervene in the internal affairs of another State, the obligation not to violate the sovereignty of another State, the obligation to protect the civilian population and civilian objects in wartime, the obligation to protect the environment, the obligation relating to free navigation on international rivers, the obligation regarding fundamental human rights and freedoms, the obligation not to use prohibited weapons, the obligation not to deliberately inflict conditions of life calculated to cause the physical destruction of a national group".

FRY requested the Court to adjudge and declare that [the Respondent State concerned] had acted against it by taking part in the bombing of the territory of FRY, breaching its obligation not to use force against another State; by taking part in the training, arming, financing, equipping and supplying of terrorist groups, i.e. the Kosovo Liberation Army, breaching its obligation not to intervene in the affairs of another State; by taking part in attacks on civilian targets, breaching its obligation to spare the civilian population and civilian objects; by taking part in destroying or damaging monasteries and cultural monuments, breaching its obligation not to commit any act of hostility directed against historical monuments, works of art or places of worship that constituted people's cultural or spiritual heritage; by taking part in the use of cluster bombs, breaching its obligation not to use prohibited weapons, i.e. weapons calculated to cause unnecessary suffering; by taking part in the bombing of oil refineries and chemical plants, breaching its obligation not to cause considerable environmental damage; by taking part in the use of weapons containing depleted uranium, breaching its obligation not to use prohibited weapons and not to cause far-reaching health and environmental damage; by taking part in killing civilians, destroying enterprises, communications, health and cultural institutions, breaching its obligation to respect the rights to life, to work, to information and to health care as well as other basic human rights; by taking part in destroying bridges on international rivers, breaching its obligation to respect freedom of navigation on international rivers; and by taking part in activities listed above, and in particular by causing enormous environmental damage and by using depleted uranium, breaching its obligation not to deliberately inflict on a national group conditions of life calculated to bring about its physical destruction, in whole or in part. In addition, the [Respondent State concerned] was responsible for the violation of the above international obligations; was obliged to stop immediately the violation of the above obligations vis-à-vis FRY; and was obliged to provide compensation for the damage to FRY and to its citizens and juridical persons.

Also on 29 April 1999 [YUN 1999, p. 1208], FRY submitted, in each of the cases, a request for the indication of provisional measures, asking the Court to indicate that "the [Respondent State concerned] shall cease immediately its acts of use of force and shall refrain from any act of threat or use of force" against FRY. Hearings on the requests for the indication of provisional measures were held between 10 and 12 May 1999.

At a public sitting on 2 June 1999, the Vice-President of the Court, Acting President, read the Orders, by which, in the cases *(Yugoslavia v. Belgium)*, *(Yugoslavia v. Canada)*, *(Yugoslavia v. France)*, *(Yugoslavia v. Germany)*, *(Yugoslavia v. Italy)*, *(Yugoslavia v. Netherlands)*, *(Yugoslavia v. Portugal)* and *(Yugoslavia v. United Kingdom)*, the Court rejected the requests for the indication of provisional measures and reserved the subsequent procedure for further decision. In the cases of *(Yugoslavia v. Spain)* and *(Yugoslavia v. United States of America)*, the Court—having found that it manifestly lacked jurisdiction to entertain FRY's Application; that it could not therefore indicate any provisional measure whatsoever in order to protect the rights invoked therein; and that, within a system of consensual jurisdiction, to maintain on the General List a case upon which it appeared certain that the Court would not be able to adjudicate on the merits would most assuredly not contribute to the sound administration of justice—rejected FRY's requests for the indication of provisional measures and ordered that those cases be removed from the List.

In each of the cases *(Yugoslavia v. Belgium)*, *(Yugoslavia v. Canada)*, *(Yugoslavia v. Netherlands)* and *(Yugoslavia v. Portugal)*, Judge Koroma appended a declaration to the Order of the Court; Judges Oda, Higgins, Parra-Aranguren and Kooijmans appended separate opinions; and Vice-President Weeramantry, Acting President, Judges Shi and Vereshchetin and Judge ad hoc Kreca appended dissenting opinions.

In each of the cases *(Yugoslavia v. France)*, *(Yugoslavia v. Germany)* and *(Yugoslavia v. Italy)*, Vice-President Weeramantry, Acting President, and Judges Shi, Koroma and Vereshchetin appended declarations to the Order of the Court; Judges Oda and Parra-Aranguren appended separate opinions; and Judge ad hoc Kreca appended a dissenting opinion.

In the case *(Yugoslavia v. Spain)*, Judges Shi, Koroma and Vereshchetin appended declarations to the Order of the Court; and Judges Oda, Higgins, Parra-Aranguren and Kooijmans and Judge ad hoc Kreca appended separate opinions.

In the case *(Yugoslavia v. United Kingdom)*, Vice-President Weeramantry, Acting President, and Judges Shi, Koroma and Vereshchetin appended declarations to the Order of the Court; Judges Oda, Higgins, Parra-Aranguren and Kooijmans appended separate opinions; and Judge ad hoc Kreca appended a dissenting opinion.

In the case *(Yugoslavia v. United States of America)*, Judges Shi, Koroma and Vereshchetin appended declarations to the Order of the Court; Judges Oda and Parra-Aranguren appended separate opinions; and Judge ad hoc Kreca appended a dissenting opinion.

By Orders of 30 June 1999 [YUN 1999, p. 1209], the Court, having ascertained the views of the Parties, fixed the time limits for the filing of the written pleadings in each of the eight cases maintained on the List as at 5 January 2000 for the Memorial of FRY and 5 July 2000 for the Counter-Memorial of the Respondent State concerned.

On 5 July 2000, within the time limit for filing its Counter-Memorial, each of the Respondent States in the eight cases maintained on the Court's List raised preliminary objections of lack of jurisdiction and admissibility. By virtue of Article 79, paragraph 3, of the Rules of Court, the proceedings on the merits were suspended when preliminary objections were filed; proceedings then had to be organized for the consideration of the preliminary objections in accordance with the Article's provisions.

By Orders of 8 September 2000, the Vice-President of the Court, Acting President, fixed 5 April 2001 as the time for filing, in each of the cases, of a written statement by FRY on the preliminary objections raised by the Respondent State concerned.

Armed activities on the territory of the Congo (Democratic Republic of the Congo v. Burundi), (Democratic Republic of the Congo v. Uganda) and (Democratic Republic of the Congo v. Rwanda)

The DRC instituted proceedings against Burundi, Uganda and Rwanda on 23 June 1999 [YUN 1999, p. 1209] for acts of armed aggression perpetrated in flagrant violation of the Charter of the United Nations and the Charter of the Organization of African Unity.

In its Applications, the DRC contended that "such armed aggression . . . involved inter alia violation of the sovereignty and territorial integrity of the [DRC], violations of international humanitarian law and massive human rights violations". The DRC sought the cessation of the aggression against it, which constituted a serious threat to peace and security in Central Africa in general and in the Great Lakes region in particular; reparation for acts of intentional destruction and looting; and restitution of national property and resources appropriated for the benefit of the respective Respondent States.

In the cases against Burundi and Rwanda, the DRC invoked as bases for the jurisdiction of the Court Article 36, paragraph 1, of the Statute, which provided that the jurisdiction of the Court comprised all cases which the parties referred to it and all matters specially provided for in the UN Charter or in treaties and conventions in force; the Convention against Torture and Other Cruel, Inhuman or Degrading Treatment or Punishment, adopted by the General Assembly by resolution 39/46 [YUN 1984, p. 813]; the Convention for the Suppression of Unlawful Acts against the Safety of Civil Aviation [YUN 1971, p. 739]; and Article 38, paragraph 5, of the Rules of Court, which contemplated the situation where a State filed an application against another State that had not accepted the jurisdiction of the Court. In the case against Uganda, the DRC based the jurisdiction on Article 36, paragraph 2, of the Statute.

The DRC requested the Court to adjudge and declare that: [the Respondent State concerned] was guilty of an act of aggression within the meaning of article 1 of Assembly resolution 3314(XXIX) [YUN 1974, p. 847] and of the jurisprudence of the Court, contrary to Article 2, paragraph 4, of the UN Charter; [the Respondent State concerned] committed repeated violations of the Geneva Conventions for the protection of war victims of 1949 and the two Additional Protocols of 1977 [YUN 1977, p. 706], in flagrant disregard of the elementary rules of international humanitarian law in conflict zones, and was also guilty of massive human rights violations in defiance of the most basic customary law; [the Respondent State concerned], by taking forcible possession of the Inga hydroelectric dam and deliberately and regularly causing massive electrical power cuts, in violation of the provisions of article 56 of the Additional Protocol of 1977, was responsible for very heavy loss of life in the city of Kinshasa (5 million inhabitants) and the surrounding area; and [the Respondent State concerned] had violated the Convention on International Civil Aviation signed in Chicago on 7 December 1944, the 1970 Convention for the Suppression of Unlawful Seizure of Aircraft and the 1971 Convention for the Suppression of Unlawful Acts against the Safety of Civil Aviation by shooting down, on 9 October 1998 at Kindu, a Boeing 727, the property of Congo Airlines, thereby killing 40 civilians.

The DRC requested the Court to adjudge and declare that: all armed forces of [the Respondent State concerned] participating in acts of aggression should forthwith vacate its territory; [the Respondent State concerned] should secure the immediate and unconditional withdrawal from Congolese territory of its nationals, both natural and legal persons; and the DRC was entitled to compensation from [the Respondent State concerned] in respect of all acts of looting, destruction, removal of property and persons and other unlawful acts attributable to [the Respondent State concerned], in respect of which the DRC reserved the right to determine at a later date the precise amount of the damage suffered, in addition to its claim for the restitution of all property removed.

In each of the cases against Burundi and Rwanda, the Court, by an Order of 21 October 1999 [YUN 1999, p. 1210], taking into account the agreement of the Parties, as expressed at a meeting between the President and the Agents of the Parties held on 19 October 1999, decided that the written proceedings should first address the questions of the jurisdiction of the Court to entertain the Application and of its admissibility and fixed 21 April 2000 as the time limit for the filing of a Memorial on those questions by Burundi and Rwanda, and 23 October 2000 for the filing of a Counter-Memorial by the DRC.

In the case against Uganda, the Court, taking into account the agreement of the Parties, as expressed at a meeting held with them by the President of the Court on 19 October 1999, fixed, by an Order of 21 October, 21 July 2000 as the time limit for the filing of a Memorial by the DRC and 21 April 2001 for the filing of a Counter-Memorial by Uganda.

On 19 June 2000, the DRC, in the case against Uganda, filed a request for the indication of provisional measures, stating that "since 5 June last, the resumption of fighting between the armed troops of . . . Uganda and another foreign army has caused considerable damage to the Congo and to its population" while "these tactics have been unanimously condemned, in particular by the United Nations Security Council". It also maintained that Uganda had pursued a policy of aggression, brutal armed attacks of oppression and looting. The DRC requested the Court to indicate the following provisional measures: Uganda must order its army to withdraw immediately and completely from Kisangani; Uganda must order its army to cease all fighting or military activity on DRC territory, withdraw immediately from the territory and desist from providing any support to any State, group, organization, movement or individual engaged or planning to engage in military activities on DRC territory; Uganda must take measures to ensure that any units, forces or agents under its authority or that enjoyed its support, together with organizations or persons which could be under its control, authority or influence, desist from committing or inciting the commission of war crimes or any other oppressive or unlawful act against all persons on DRC territory; Uganda must discontinue any act of disruption, interference or hampering actions intended to give the population of the occupied zones their fundamental human rights; Uganda must cease all illegal exploitation of the DRC's natural resources and any illegal transfer of assets, equipment or persons to its territory; and Uganda must respect the DRC's right to sovereignty, political independence and territorial integrity, and the fundamental rights and freedoms of persons on DRC territory.

Public sittings to hear the oral observations of the Parties on the request for the indication of provisional measures were held on 26 and 28 June 2000.

On 1 July 2000, the Court rendered its Order on the DRC's request for provisional measures, which stated that both Parties must, forthwith, prevent and refrain from any action, particularly armed action, which might prejudice the rights of the other Party in respect of whatever judgment the Court might render, or which might aggravate or extend the dispute before the Court or make it more difficult to resolve; both Parties must, forthwith, take measures to comply with all their obligations under international law; and both Parties must, forthwith, take measures to ensure full respect within the zone of conflict for fundamental human rights and for the applicable provisions of humanitarian law. Judges Oda and Koroma appended declarations to the Order.

Application of the genocide convention (Croatia v. Yugoslavia)

Croatia instituted proceedings against FRY on 2 July 1999 [YUN 1999, p. 1210] for alleged violations of the 1948 Convention on the Prevention and Punishment of the Crime of Genocide, adopted by the General Assembly in resolution 260 A (III) [YUN 1948-49, p. 959], said to have been committed between 1991 and 1995.

In its Application, Croatia contended that by "directly controlling the activity of its armed forces, intelligence agents, and various paramilitary detachments, on the territory of . . . Croatia, in the Knin region, eastern and western Slovenia, and Dalmatia, [Yugoslavia] is liable [for] the 'ethnic cleansing' of Croatian citizens from these areas . . . and is required to provide reparation for the resulting damage". It further alleged that, "by directing, encouraging, and urging Croatian citizens of Serb ethnicity in the Knin region to evacuate the area in 1995, as . . . Croatia reasserted its legitimate governmental authority . . . , [Yugoslavia] engaged in conduct amounting to a second round of 'ethnic cleansing'". Croatia invoked the jurisdiction of the Court based on Article 36, paragraph 1, of the Statute and on article IX of the Convention.

Croatia requested the Court to adjudge and declare that FRY breached its legal obligations towards Croatia under articles I, II (a, b, c, d), III (a, b, c, d, e), IV and V of the 1948 Convention; and that FRY had an obligation to pay to Croatia, in its own right and as *parens patriae* for its citizens, reparations for damages to persons and property, as well as to the Croatian economy and environment caused by the foregoing violations of international law, in a sum to be determined by the Court. Croatia reserved the right to introduce to the Court at a future date a precise evaluation of the damages.

By an Order of 14 September 1999, the Court took account of an agreement of the Parties expressed on 13 September and fixed 14 March 2000 as the time limit for the filing of the Memorial of Croatia and 14 September 2000 for the filing of the Counter-Memorial of FRY.

In 2000, at Croatia's request, the President of the Court extended the time limits twice: in March, to 14 September 2000 for the Memorial of Croatia and 14 September 2001 for the Counter-Memorial of FRY, and again in June, to 14 March 2001 for the Memorial and to 16 September 2002 for the Counter-Memorial.

Aerial incident (Pakistan v. India)

Pakistan instituted proceedings against India on 21 September 1999 [YUN 1999, p. 1210] regarding a dispute in which Pakistan alleged that on 10 August India destroyed a Pakistani aircraft. Pakistan founded the jurisdiction of the Court on Article 36, paragraphs 1 and 2, of the Statute and the declarations whereby the two Parties had recognized the Court's compulsory jurisdiction. In November, the Agent of India filed preliminary objections to the assumption of jurisdiction by the Court on the basis of Pakistan's Application. During a November meeting between the President of the Court and representatives of the Parties, held pursuant to Article 31 of the Rules of Court, the Parties provisionally agreed to request the Court to determine separately the question of its jurisdiction. The agreement was subsequently confirmed in writing by both Parties. By an Order of 19 November, the Court, taking into account the agreement, decided that the written pleadings should first be addressed to the question of the jurisdiction of the Court to entertain the Application. The Court fixed 10 January 2000 and 28 February 2000, respectively, as the time limits for the filing of a Memorial by Pakistan and a Counter-Memorial by India, which were filed accordingly.

Following public hearings of the arguments of the Parties between 3 and 6 April 2000, the Court delivered its Judgment on jurisdiction on 21 June. By a vote of 14 to 2, the Court found that it had no jurisdiction to entertain the Application filed by Pakistan. Judges Oda and Koroma and Judge ad hoc Reddy appended separate opinions to the Judgment. Judge Al-Khasawneh and Judge ad hoc Pirzada appended dissenting opinions.

Maritime delimitation (Nicaragua v. Honduras)

On 8 December 1999 [YUN 1999, p. 1210], Nicaragua instituted proceedings against Honduras in respect of a dispute concerning the delimitation of the maritime zones appertaining to each of those States in the Caribbean Sea. In its Applica-

tion, Nicaragua stated that it had maintained for decades the position that its maritime Caribbean border with Honduras had not been determined, while the position of Honduras allegedly was that a delimitation line was fixed by the King of Spain in an Arbitral Award of 23 December 1906, which was found valid and binding by ICJ on 18 November 1960 [YUN 1960, p. 536]. According to Nicaragua, the position adopted by Honduras had brought repeated confrontations and mutual capture of vessels of both nations in and around the general border area, and diplomatic negotiations had failed. Nicaragua founded jurisdiction of the Court on declarations under Article 36, paragraph 2, of the Court's Statute, by which both States accepted the compulsory jurisdiction of the Court, and also article XXXI of the American Treaty on Pacific Settlement (officially known as the "Pact of Bogotá"), signed on 30 April 1948, to which both Nicaragua and Honduras were parties.

Nicaragua requested the Court to determine the course of the single maritime boundary between areas of territorial sea, continental shelf and exclusive economic zone appertaining to Nicaragua and Honduras.

By an Order of 21 March 2000, the Court, taking into account the agreement of the Parties, fixed 21 March 2001 as the time limit for the filing of a Memorial by Nicaragua and 21 March 2002 for the filing of the Counter-Memorial by Honduras.

Arrest warrant of 11 April 2000 (Democratic Republic of the Congo v. Belgium)

On 17 October, the DRC filed an Application instituting proceedings against Belgium concerning an international arrest warrant issued on 11 April 2000 by a Belgian examining judge against the DRC's Acting Minister for Foreign Affairs, seeking his detention and subsequent extradition to Belgium for alleged crimes constituting grave violations of international humanitarian law. The warrant was transmitted to all States.

In its Application, the DRC noted that the warrant characterized the alleged facts as crimes of international law committed by action or omission against persons or property protected by the Geneva Conventions of 12 August 1949 and the Additional Protocols I and II to those Conventions [YUN 1977, p. 706], and as crimes against humanity, and cited the allegedly applicable Belgian Law of 16 June 1993 as amended by the Law of 10 February 1999 pertaining to the punishment of grave violations of international humanitarian law. The DRC stated that, according to the warrant's terms, the examining judge affirmed his competence to deal with facts allegedly committed on the territory of the DRC by a national of that State, without it having been alleged that the victims were of Belgian nationality, or that the facts constituted violations of the security or dignity of Belgium. It further observed that article 5 of the Belgian Law prescribed that "the immunity conferred by a person's official capacity does not prevent application of this Law" and that its article 7 established the universal applicability of the Law and the universal jurisdiction of Belgian courts in relation to "grave violations of international humanitarian law", which jurisdiction was not subject to the presence of the accused on Belgian territory.

The DRC maintained that article 7 of the Belgian Law and the warrant issued on the basis of that article constituted "a violation of the principle whereby a State may not exercise its authority on territory of another State and the principle of sovereign equality among all Members of the United Nations", as declared in Article 2, paragraph 1, of the UN Charter. It also maintained that article 5 and the arrest warrant contravened international law, insofar as they claimed to derogate from the diplomatic immunity of the Minister for Foreign Affairs of a sovereign State, "deriving from article 41, paragraph 2, of the Vienna Convention of 18 April 1961 on Diplomatic Relations" [YUN 1961, p. 512]. Accordingly, the DRC asked the Court to declare that Belgium should annul the warrant, and filed a request for the indication of a provisional measure seeking to have the warrant withdrawn forthwith.

Hearings on the request for an indication of provisional measures were held from 20 to 23 November. The DRC asked the Court to order Belgium to comply with international law; to cease and desist from any conduct that might exacerbate the dispute with the DRC; and to discharge the warrant issued against its Acting Foreign Minister. Belgium asked the Court to refuse the DRC's request for an indication of provisional measures and to remove the case from its List.

On 8 December, the Court rendered its Order on the request for an indication of provisional measures, by which the Court unanimously rejected Belgium's request to remove the case from the List and, by a vote of 15 to 2, found that the circumstances did not require it to exercise its power to indicate provisional measures. Judges Oda and Ranjeva appended declarations to the Order; Judges Koroma and Parra-Aranguren, separate opinions; Judge Rezek and Judge ad hoc Bula-Bula dissenting opinions; and Judge ad hoc Van den Wijngaert a declaration.

By an Order of 13 December, the President of the Court, taking account of the agreement of the Parties, fixed 15 March 2001 and 31 May 2001 as the time limits for the filing of the Memorial of the DRC and the Counter-Memorial of Belgium, respectively.

1999 advisory opinion

On 4 February, the Economic and Social Council took note of a letter from the Secretary-General to the Council President [YUN 1999, p. 1212] regarding implementation of an ICJ advisory opinion [ibid., p. 1211] on the difference relating to immunity from legal process of a Special Rapporteur of the Commission on Human Rights, and decided to remain seized of the matter (**decision 2000/208**).

Chapter II

International tribunals

In 2000, the International Tribunal for the Prosecution of Persons Responsible for Serious Violations of International Humanitarian Law Committed in the Territory of the Former Yugoslavia since 1991 (ICTY) instituted internal reforms and saw an increase in the number of so-called high-profile accused persons anticipated to stand trial.

The International Criminal Tribunal for the Prosecution of Persons Responsible for Genocide and Other Serious Violations of International Humanitarian Law Committed in the Territory of Rwanda and Rwandan Citizens Responsible for Genocide and Other Such Violations Committed in the Territory of Neighbouring States between 1 January and 31 December 1994 (ICTR) delivered two judgements involving convictions for genocide and crimes against humanity.

On 30 November, the Security Council, in an effort to expedite the Tribunals' cases, established a pool of ad litem judges in ICTY, who would serve with the permanent judges on a case-by-case basis, and enlarged the membership of the Appeals Chambers of both Tribunals. The Council amended the statutes of the Tribunals accordingly. ICTY and ICTR shared the same Chief Prosecutor and appellate chamber, but had separate Registrars and Deputy Prosecutors.

The Security Council, by **resolution 1315(2000)** (see p. 205), requested the Secretary-General to negotiate an agreement with Sierra Leone to create an independent special court to try crimes against humanity, war crimes and other serious violations of international humanitarian law.

International Tribunal for the Former Yugoslavia

In 2000, ICTY efforts to institute internal reforms included the creation of a Coordination Council and a Management Committee to enable the organs of the Tribunal—the Chambers, the Office of the Prosecutor and the Registry—to determine their longer-term judicial priorities together and to work more closely towards the accomplishment of the Tribunal's mission. The package of reforms was expected to allow ICTY to fulfil its mandate by 2008 instead of 2016.

In 2000, the activities of ICTY, established by Security Council resolution 827(1993) [YUN 1993, p. 440], were described in two reports to the Council and the General Assembly—one covering the period 1 August 1999 to 31 July 2000 [A/55/273-S/2000/777] and the other covering the period 1 August 2000 to 31 July 2001 [A/56/352-S/2001/865]. On 20 November, the Assembly took note of the 1999/2000 report (**decision 55/413**).

The Chambers

The judicial activity of the Chambers comprised trials, appellate proceedings, proceedings pertaining to the exercise of the primacy of the Tribunal and contempt proceedings. The Chambers also reviewed indictments submitted by the Prosecutor, issued arrest warrants, conducted hearings, and engaged in regulatory activities to improve trial procedures.

New trials and cases

Mitar Vasiljevic, detained by the multinational Stabilization Force (SFOR) on 25 January and charged with violations of the laws or customs of war and crimes against humanity, pleaded not guilty to all counts on 28 January. On 22 September, the accused entered a special defence of alibi. The prosecution filed its pre-trial brief on 11 December. The trial was scheduled for September 2001.

On 3 April, Momcilo Krajisnik was arrested by SFOR and charged with genocide, complicity in genocide, crimes against humanity, violations of the laws and customs of war and grave breaches of the Geneva Conventions for the protection of war victims of 12 August 1949 (Geneva Conventions). The accused, at his initial appearance on 7 April, pleaded not guilty to all charges. On 8 June, the defence filed two preliminary motions challenging the jurisdiction of the Tribunal and the form of indictment. The Appeals Chamber denied the accused's application for leave to appeal the decision concerning the form of the indictment, while the appeal against the decision on jurisdiction was pending.

Following his detention by SFOR on 21 April, Dragan Nikolic pleaded not guilty to 80 counts charged against him on 28 April relating to grave breaches of the Geneva Conventions, violations of the laws or customs of war and crimes against humanity for his alleged role in the mistreatment of detainees at the Susica camp (Bosnia and Herzegovina) where he was a commander in 1992.

Ongoing trials

Radoslav Brdanin and Momir Talic, both charged with genocide and crimes against humanity [YUN 1999, p. 1215], pleaded not guilty to all counts at a hearing on 11 January. On 28 April, Mr. Brdanin filed a motion for provisional release, which was denied by the Trial Chamber on 25 July, following a hearing, on the basis that it was not satisfied that, if released, he would appear for trial. Mr. Brdanin filed an application for leave to appeal the decision on 1 August, which the Appeals Chamber rejected on 7 September. On 8 December, Mr. Talic filed a motion for provisional release.

In the case of Kupreskic and Others [YUN 1998, p. 1194], the Trial Chamber rendered its judgement on 14 January. In January, notices of appeal were filed by Vladimir Santic, Drago Josipovic, Vlatko Kupreskic, Zoran Kupreskic and Mirjan Kupreskic. The prosecution also filed an appeal. Subsequently, the Appeals Chamber rendered a number of decisions on various procedural and evidentiary matters, primarily concerning the admission of additional evidence.

Following a plea of not guilty to an amended indictment in 1999 [YUN 1999, p. 1216], the defence in the case of General Radislav Krstic filed a new motion based on defects in the form of some paragraphs of the indictment and pointed out that it considered the acts specified in support of counts 7 and 8 (deportation, inhumane acts) as being identical to those used for count 6 (persecution). The Chamber rejected the motion on 28 January, and suggested that the parties present arguments on cumulative charging in their pre-trial briefs. The trial began on 13 March; the prosecution closed its case on 28 July and the defence on 13 December.

In the appeal of Zlatko Aleksovski against a 1999 judgement and sentence [YUN 1999, p. 1215], the Appeals Chamber, on 9 February, dismissed his appeal against conviction and allowed the prosecution's appeal against the sentence. Stating that a "revised sentence" would be considered, the Appeals Chamber ordered the accused's immediate return to custody and reserved its judgement on the prosecution's grounds of appeal against the judgement. It announced that a written reasoned judgement, including the revised sentence, would be issued. On 24 March, the Appeals Chamber rendered its written judgement and found the accused responsible for aiding and abetting the mistreatment of prisoners outside the prison compound at Kaonik, Bosnia and Herzegovina; however, the Appeals Chamber specified that it did not believe that the additional finding warranted any heavier sentence. As to the prosecution appeal against the initial sentence of two and a half years, the Appeals Chamber found that the Trial Chamber had erred when exercising its discretion by not having given sufficient weight to the gravity of the conduct of the appellant and by failing to treat his position as a commander as an aggravating feature. In imposing a revised sentence, the Appeals Chamber considered the element of double jeopardy, in that the appellant had had to appear for sentencing twice for the same conduct and also that he had been detained a second time after a period of release of nine months. The sentence was increased to seven years' imprisonment with deduction for the time already spent in custody. On 22 September, the accused was transferred to Finland to serve his sentence.

Regarding the three accused in the case of Kunarac and Others [YUN 1999, p. 1215], a redacted indictment against Zoran Vukovic was made public at the time of his arrest on 21 February. The other accused, Radomir Kovac and Dragoljub Kunarac, appeared with him. Their trial began on 20 March and concluded on 13 June. On 20 June, the accused filed a joint motion for judgement of acquittal on certain counts in the indictments against them. On 3 July, the Trial Chamber entered a judgement of acquittal in favour of Mr. Kunarac on count 13 of the third amended indictment, and held that Mr. Vukovic had no case to answer in relation to the allegations made by a witness. All remaining counts stood. On 3 April, the prosecution withdrew counts 14 to 17 against Mr. Kunarac. The defence case began on 4 July and concluded on 20 September. Rebuttal witnesses were heard on 23 October.

The trial of Kvocka and Others (Miroslav Kvocka, Mlado Radic, Zoran Zigic, Milojica Kos) [YUN 1998, p. 1192, & YUN 1999, p. 1216] began on 28 February. A fifth accused, Dragoljub Prcac, who was transferred to the Tribunal in March, pleaded not guilty to the charges against him. The cases against the five accused were joined on 14 April, with the agreement of the parties. The trial resumed on 2 May and, for the first time in the Tribunal's history, two of the accused, Messrs. Kvocka and Radic, chose to testify at the opening of the prosecution case, while Mr. Zigic made a declaration, not under oath, at the start of his defence case. The prosecution case concluded on 6 October, having called 46 witnesses. Four of the five defendants filed motions for acquittal. The Trial Chamber granted certain aspects of the motions, entering a judgement of acquittal in favour of Messrs. Kvocka, Kos, Radic and Prcac on parts of the indictment that concerned the Keraterm and Trnopolje camps, and in favour of all the defendants with respect to certain allegations in support of which no evidence had been presented by the prosecution.

Milorad Krnojelac, who pleaded not guilty to all charges against him in 1999 [YUN 1999, p. 1216], was charged in the second amended indictment of 2 March with 18 counts of crimes against humanity, violations of the laws and customs of war and grave breaches of the Geneva Conventions for his alleged role as warden of a camp in Foca municipality (Bosnia and Herzegovina) between April 1992 and August 1993. At the trial's start, the prosecution motion to withdraw all grave breach charges was granted by the Trial Chamber and the trial proceeded on the remaining 12 counts only. The prosecution filed its pre-trial brief on 16 October and the defence filed its brief on 25 October. The pre-trial conference was held on 26 October and the trial began on 30 October.

Following the 1998 sentencing and appeal of Anto Furundzija [YUN 1998, p. 1194], a hearing of the appeal took place on 2 March. In its judgement of 21 July, the Appeals Chamber unanimously rejected each ground of appeal, dismissed the appeal and affirmed the convictions and sentences. On 21 September, the accused was transferred to Finland to serve his sentence.

Following the trial of General Tihomir Blaskic [YUN 1999, p. 1216], the accused filed a notice of appeal on 17 March against the Trial Chamber's judgement of 2 March. Pursuant to requests by the parties, the Appeals Chamber ordered suspension of the briefing schedule pending the resolution of certain issues relating to the admission of additional evidence.

In the case of Dario Kordic and Mario Cerkez, charged in 1999 [ibid., p. 1215], the Prosecution's case-in-chief concluded on 10 March. On 30 March, the Trial Chamber heard defence motions for a judgement of acquittal, which were dismissed on 6 April. Mr. Kordic's defence began on 10 April. Mr. Cerkez's defence began on 24 July, with closing arguments heard on 14 and 15 December. The Trial Chamber dealt with a large number of applications from both parties relating to provisional release, the admission of affidavit evidence, the admission of transcripts from the other factually related cases and applications for judicial assistance relating to States and other entities. In an interlocutory appeal, the accused, on 17 March, sought to appeal an oral decision of 10 March by the Trial Chamber, which granted a prosecution motion that sought to admit into evidence certain affidavits and a formal statement. On 18 September, the Appeals Chamber directed the Trial Chamber to exclude the affidavits from evidence and to re-evaluate the admissibility of the formal statement.

In the case of Martinovic and Naletilic, Mladen Naletilic was transferred from Croatia to the custody of the Tribunal on 21 March and entered a plea of not guilty, as had the co-accused, Vinko Martinovic, in 1999 [YUN 1999, p. 1216]. A request by Mr. Naletilic to be interrogated under application of a polygraph was denied on 27 November. Also in November, the prosecution was granted leave to amend the indictment to better characterize the charges contained therein. The amendment gave rise to a new opportunity for the defence to file preliminary motions, and both accused challenged the new indictment by that mechanism. The trial was scheduled to begin in 2001.

Regarding the Celebici case [YUN 1996, p. 1186], the Appeals Chamber heard the oral arguments of the parties from 5 to 8 June on the appeal against the 1998 judgement [YUN 1998, p. 1193] of three of the convicted co-accused, Zdravko Mucic, Hazim Delic and Esad Landzo. The prosecution also had filed a notice of appeal against the judgement, challenging the acquittal of the fourth co-accused, Zejnil Delalic, in 1998 [ibid.].

The Appeals Chamber ordered the brief of Goran Jelisic, convicted and sentenced in 1999 [YUN 1999, p. 1216], to be filed by 7 August, the Response by 6 September and the Reply by 21 September. Both sides had appealed in 1999, the prosecution against acquittal on the genocide count and the accused against sentence on the counts to which he had pleaded guilty, together with a challenge to cumulative convictions.

On 15 September, the Trial Chamber decided that Dusko Sikirica, arrested by SFOR on 25 July, would be jointly tried with Dragan Kolundzija and Damir Dosen [YUN 1999, p. 1215]. On 13 October, the prosecution filed its second, revised pre-trial brief, taking into account the arrest of Mr. Sikirica. In November, the three accused filed their pre-trial briefs. At a status conference on 22 November, the prosecution clarified certain points in the amended indictment, and counsel for Messrs. Kolundzija and Sikirica confirmed their intention to offer, at trial, evidence on diminished mental responsibility and alibi, respectively.

The defence counsel initially assigned to General Stanislav Galic, who had pleaded not guilty to charges against him in 1999 [YUN 1999, p. 1215], was replaced in November. The new counsel, who was working towards an expeditious trial, requested five months to prepare.

Three of the five accused in the case of Simic and Others [YUN 1999, p. 1215] (Miroslav Tadic, Simo Zaric, Milan Simic) were granted provisional release in 2000. Stevan Todorovic, the fourth accused, remained in custody while pursuing various challenges to the legality of his arrest. On 29 November, the prosecution and the defence filed a confidential joint motion for consideration of a plea agreement between Mr. Todorovic and the Office of the Prosecutor, pursuant to which Mr. Todorovic would plead guilty to the charge of persecution and withdraw all pending motions, while the prosecution would withdraw the remaining charges under the indictment and request a sentence of 5 and 12 years' imprisonment. It was also a condition of the agreement that he would testify for the prosecution in other proceedings before the Tribunal. On 13 December, Mr. Todorovic entered a guilty plea to count 1 of the indictment. The matter was referred to the full Trial Chamber. The fifth accused, Blagoje Simic, remained at large.

In 2000, there was one request for review. On 18 June, Dusko Tadic filed a review of his case and proceedings [YUN 1999, p. 1216], pursuant to the Tribunal's Rules with reference to the finding by the Appeals Chamber on 31 January of contempt by his previous defence counsel. That decision was reached on the ground that the former counsel had put forward to the Appeals Chamber a case that was known to him to be false and had manipulated two witnesses. On 25 October, a bench of the Appeals Chamber granted the former counsel's application for leave to appeal.

In other action, Mr. Tadic was transferred to Germany on 31 October on the basis of an ad hoc agreement concluded on 17 October between ICTY and Germany. Germany, where Mr. Tadic was first arrested and detained before his transfer to ICTY custody, had not signed a formal agreement with the United Nations on the enforcement of ICTY sentences. The ad hoc agreement was signed following an exequatur decision by a Munich regional court of 6 September, which confirmed the 20-year prison sentence imposed by the Appeals Chamber on 26 January.

Communications. On 4 May [S/2000/381], Bosnia and Herzegovina expressed concern about a public visit with Slobodan Milosevic, the President of the Federal Republic of Yugoslavia (FRY) who was indicted by ICTY in 1999 [YUN 1999, p. 1214], by two representatives of the Security Council while on a mission to Kosovo. Bosnia and Herzegovina proposed a debate within the Council and the adoption of standards of appropriate protocol in dealing with individuals who denied the Tribunal's authority and, by extension, that of the Council and the United Nations.

On 28 November [A/55/657-S/2000/1136], the Russian Federation, referring to a 21 November statement by the Prosecutor to the effect that the Tribunal had no agreement with the North Atlantic Treaty Organization (NATO), cited the Tri-

bunal's third annual report [YUN 1996, p. 1185], which stated, "On 9 May 1996, a memorandum of understanding between the Tribunal and the Supreme Headquarters of Allied Powers of Europe (SHAPE) was signed by both parties. The memorandum spelled out the practical arrangements for support to the Tribunal and the detention and transfer of indictees to the Tribunal."

Composition of the Chambers

On 23 February [S/2000/188], the Secretary-General informed the Security Council President of the resignation for health reasons of Judge Wang Tieya (China), effective 31 March, and that China had presented the candidacy of Liu Daqun to replace him. Mr. Liu's curriculum vitae was annexed to the Secretary-General's letter. Following consultations with Council members, the President, on 3 March [S/2000/189], indicated his support of the Secretary-General's intention to appoint Mr. Liu. On 7 March [S/2000/195], the Secretary-General stated that he had received a corresponding letter from the General Assembly President and had appointed Mr. Liu, effective 1 April 2000, for the remainder of Judge Wang's term, due to expire on 16 November 2001.

On 23 December, the General Assembly decided that the item on the election of ICTY judges would remain for consideration during its resumed fifty-fifth (2001) session (**decision 55/458**).

Office of the Prosecutor

In 2000, the Office of the Prosecutor, in addition to its ongoing prosecution work, completed mass grave exhumations in Kosovo. During the year, one grave site was exhumed in Croatia and another six in Bosnia and Herzegovina.

The Prosecutor's investigative strategy continued to be to prosecute the leaders of the conflict, with lower-level perpetrators subject to local/domestic prosecutions. The Office called on States and relevant organizations to arrest fugitives in Republika Srpska (Bosnia and Herzegovina) and FRY.

Regarding cooperation, the change in Government in FRY, following elections in September (see p. 384), had a significant impact on the activities of the Office. The Belgrade field office was reopened and investigators were granted visas to enter FRY. In January, a headquarters agreement was concluded with Croatia for the establishment of an office in Zagreb. A request to exhume a mass grave in Gospic where Croats allegedly had killed Croatian Serbs in 1991 was complied with, and access was granted to various archives containing collections of documents critically important for ongoing trials and investigations. Cooperation with Republika Srpska remained unchanged, with no indication of any concrete move to apprehend fugitives known to be hiding there.

An advocacy training course was held in March for 24 prosecutors in the Office.

The Registry

The Registry of the Tribunal continued to exercise court management functions and provide administration and services to the Chambers and the Office of the Prosecutor. It also provided information to the media and the public, administered the legal aid system and supervised the Detention Unit. The Victims and Witnesses Section was part of the Registry, which was also responsible for budgetary matters.

France and Spain, on 25 February and 28 March, respectively, concluded the Agreement with the United Nations on the Enforcement of Sentences imposed by the Tribunal, allowing convicted persons to serve their sentences in those countries. The other nations that had signed agreements were Austria, Finland, Italy, Norway and Sweden.

In 2000, the ICTY Outreach Programme, with offices in The Hague and in Banja Luka and Sarajevo (Bosnia and Herzegovina) and Zagreb (Croatia), sought to ensure that the Tribunal's activities were transparent and accessible to the communities of the former Yugoslavia through conferences, seminars and workshops.

International Tribunal for Rwanda

The work of ICTR accelerated in 2000 and its output increased. In February, several of the Tribunal's Rules were amended with a view to expediting and shortening trials. Current investigations were concerned with central and local government figures, members of the armed forces, militias and civil defence, prominent businessmen, intellectuals, members of the clergy and media figures. ICTR played a significant role in developing international humanitarian and criminal law, as many of the substantive legal issues adjudicated by its Trial Chambers previously had not been decided; the emerging jurisprudence would serve as precedent and impetus for the International Criminal Court (see p. 1238) and the special court for Sierra Leone, envisioned in Security Council resolution 1315(2000) (see p. 205). In addition to its judicial work, the Tribunal remained seized of the process of na-

tional reconciliation in Rwanda, by carrying out various outreach programmes.

In 2000, the activities of ICTR, established by Security Council resolution 955(1994) [YUN 1994, p. 299], were covered in two reports to the Council and the General Assembly, for the periods 1 July 1999 to 30 June 2000 [A/55/435-S/2000/927] and 1 July 2000 to 30 June 2001 [A/56/351-S/2001/863 & Corr.1,2]. On 20 November, the Assembly took note of the 1999/2000 report (**decision 55/412**).

The Chambers

New trials and cases

On 29 January, Augustin Ndindiliyimana, former Chief of Staff of the Gendarmerie Nationale of Rwanda, was arrested in Belgium and subsequently transferred to the Tribunal's Detention Facility. At his initial appearance on 22 April, he pleaded not guilty to 10 counts charging him with genocide, crimes against humanity and violations of the Geneva Conventions.

Tharcisse Muvunyi, former Commander of the Ecole des sous-officiers, was arrested in the United Kingdom on 5 February and transferred to the Tribunal on 30 October. On 8 November, he pleaded guilty to the charges against him—five counts of genocide or, alternatively, complicity in genocide, direct and public incitement to commit genocide and crimes against humanity.

François Xavier Nzuwonemeye, former Commander of the Forty-second Battalion, was arrested on 15 February and transferred to the Tribunal from France on 23 May. He pleaded not guilty to charges of conspiracy to commit genocide, genocide, complicity in genocide, crimes against humanity and violations of the Geneva Conventions.

On 15 February, Innocent Sagahutu, former Second-in-Command of the Reconnaissance Battalion, was arrested in Denmark and subsequently transferred to ICTR on 24 November. At his initial appearance on 28 November, he pleaded not guilty to 12 counts charging him with complicity in genocide, crimes against humanity and violations of the Geneva Conventions.

Jean de Dieu Kamuhanda, former Minister for Culture and Education, was transferred from France on 7 March. On 23 March, at his initial appearance before the Tribunal, he pleaded not guilty to nine counts charging him with genocide and crimes against humanity.

Elizaphan Ntakirutimana [YUN 1998, p. 1202], a former clergyman accused in a case with Gerard Ntakirutimana, was transferred, following protracted legal proceedings in the United States, to the ICTR Detention Facility on 24 March. He made his initial appearance on 31 March and pleaded not guilty to two counts of genocide and crimes against humanity. At a status conference on 24 May, the trial of both accused was scheduled to begin in January 2001.

The trial of André Ntagerura, former Minister of Transport, Emmanuel Bagambiki, former Prefect of Cyangugu, and Samuel Imanishimwe, former Lieutenant in the Rwandan Armed Forces, jointly consolidated as the Cyangugu case in 1999 [YUN 1999, p. 1222], began on 18 September. They were charged with genocide and crimes against humanity.

The trial of Laurent Semanza [YUN 1999, p. 1223], former Bourgmestre of Bicumbi, charged with genocide and crimes against humanity, began on 16 October. On 3 November, the Trial Chamber issued its decision on the Prosecutor's motion to take judicial notice. By taking judicial notice of various factual matters of common knowledge and numerous documents, the Trial Chamber was able to expedite the trial.

Ongoing trials

On 27 January, Alfred Musema [YUN 1999, p. 1223] was convicted of genocide and of two counts of crimes against humanity (rape and extermination), and was sentenced to life imprisonment. He appealed against the judgement.

In a 6 April decision, the Appeals Chamber dismissed the appeal of Omar Serushago, confirming his 15-year imprisonment sentence [YUN 1999, p. 1221].

On 15 May, Georges Ruggiu, a former Belgian journalist who had pleaded not guilty in 1997 [YUN 1997, p. 1328], changed his plea to guilty. On 1 June, he was convicted of direct and public incitement to commit genocide and crimes against humanity (persecution). Neither he nor the Prosecutor appealed against the sentence of 12 years' imprisonment on each of the counts, to run concurrently.

Regarding the Kajelijeli case [YUN 1999, p. 1223], involving five senior officials of the 1994 interim Government of Rwanda, the Appeals Chamber rendered two decisions. On 10 August, an appeal was dismissed because the notice of appeal had been filed outside the prescribed time limits. In a second decision, on 12 December, the Appeals Chamber dismissed a motion to grant relief from dismissal of appeal (appeal against its 10 August decision) and confirmed its previous decision.

Following defence motions in 1999 for severance from consolidated cases, known as the government cases, involving eight accused, the Trial Chamber only granted the motion to sever filed by Juvénal Kajelijeli [YUN 1999, p. 1222]. In 2000,

the Trial Chamber, following a defence motion, ordered that Mr. Kajelijeli be tried separately.

The Trial Chamber heard closing submissions in September and October in the trial of Ignace Bagilishema [YUN 1999, p. 1223]. On 19 October, the trial was adjourned for the Trial Chamber's deliberations and preparation of its judgement.

On 19 October, the Appeals Chamber rendered its judgement in respect of the appeal filed by Jean Kambanda, former head of the interim Government, against his conviction and sentence of a single term of life imprisonment handed down in 1998 [YUN 1998, p. 1202]. It unanimously dismissed the eight grounds of appeal and affirmed the conviction and sentence.

In the case against Jean-Bosco Barayagwiza [YUN 1998, p. 1202], consolidated with that of Ferdinand Nahimana and Hassan Ngeze in 1999 [YUN 1999, p. 1222] as the media case, trial began on 26 October and continued to 9 November. The hearings would resume in 2001. On 31 March, the Appeals Chamber reviewed its decision ordering the release of Mr. Barayagwiza [ibid.] and ordered a continuation of the proceedings, while deciding that the accused would be entitled either to compensation if he was acquitted or to a reduction in the sentence if he was found guilty. Two appeals filed by Mr. Barayagwiza against two decisions rendered by the Trial Chamber on 11 April and 6 June, respectively, were dismissed by the Appeals Chamber on 12 September. The appeals raised objections in respect of matters pertaining to the temporal jurisdiction of the Tribunal and challenged the validity of the indictment. On 14 December, the Appeals Chamber dismissed a motion for review or reconsideration of its 31 March decision, on the basis that the motion lacked merit. On 13 December, the Appeals Chamber dismissed an appeal filed on 18 September because it did not satisfy the Tribunal's Rules.

From 30 October to 2 November, the Appeals Chamber heard oral arguments in the appeals by Clément Kayishema [YUN 1999, p. 1221], former Prefect of Kibuye, Obed Ruzindana [ibid.], former businessman in Kibuye Prefecture, and Jean-Paul Akayesu [YUN 1998, p. 1201], former Bourgmestre of Taba commune. It was planned that the three would be transferred to State prisons to serve their sentences as soon as a treaty between the United Nations and the State concerned was finalized and the detention facilities completed.

On 13 November, the Appeals Chamber dismissed an appeal filed by Gratien Kabiligi [YUN 1997, p. 1328] against the Trial Chamber's decision of 13 April, stating that the alleged irregularity pertaining to the pre-trial proceedings did not fall within the ambit of the Tribunal's Rules.

In 2000, the appeal in the case of Georges Anderson Rutaganda [YUN 1999, p. 1221], the Second Vice-President of the Interahamwe in Rwanda in 1994, was still pending.

Office of the Prosecutor

In 2000, the Office of the Prosecutor continued to implement and refine its strategy of investigating new cases, preparing existing cases for trial and conducting trials before the Trial Chambers. The period was also one of reorientation for the Office. New systems were introduced governing the formal opening of investigations, the assignment of senior trial attorneys to oversee and direct investigations and the allocation, to named individuals, of the responsibility for the preparation and conduct of investigations and prosecutions. The Appeals Section was reorganized, as was the Investigations Division. A special team within the Division tracked the whereabouts of accused persons still at large.

The Office increased the level of cooperation with authorities of countries other than Rwanda by seeking assistance in the investigation and prosecution of crimes committed in Rwanda. A greater level of understanding, coordination and cooperation with the authorities in Rwanda was also achieved.

On 10 May, the Investigations Unit organized a workshop on witness management issues within the Tribunal.

The Registry

The Registry continued to administer and service the Tribunal, emphasizing the provision of judicial and administrative support to the Chambers and the Office of the Prosecutor, as well as reforms in strategies and management systems.

On 31 August, the United Nations signed an agreement with Swaziland on the enforcement of ICTR sentences. Benin and Mali had also committed themselves to enforcing the sentences.

The Press and Public Affairs Unit continued to disseminate information about the Tribunal's mandate, organization and achievements. The Unit produced printed information materials for journalists in English, French, Kinyarwanda and Kiswahili.

The Tribunal's information centre *Umusanzu mu Bwiyunge* in Kigali, the focal point of its Outreach Programme, was inaugurated on 25 September. Also in September, 20 Rwandan judges attended a week-long seminar organized by the Tribunal in Arusha, United Republic of Tanzania.

Under the internship programme, 105 interns were placed in various sections and units of the Tribunal. To increase the participation of African students/lawyers in the programme, the University of Notre Dame (Illinois, United States) made a grant to cover their expenses.

The Witness and Victims Support Section—Defence completed an operational guidance manual to serve as a reference book for defence counsel and experts in witness protection, in the context of international criminal justice.

Functioning of the tribunals

Amendment of the statutes

In identical letters of 7 September [A/55/382-S/2000/865] to the General Assembly and the Security Council, the Secretary-General summarized three proposals of the ICTY President for reducing the time to complete the trials of those persons who were being, or would be in the future, prosecuted before it. The proposals had been endorsed by the Bureau of the Tribunals and unanimously adopted by the judges on 18 April.

The proposals involved conferring on senior legal officers at the Trial Chambers certain powers vested in judges to take decisions regarding the pre-trial process; creating a pool of ad litem judges, on which the Tribunals could draw, as needed, to put together new Trial Chambers to supplement the existing three Chambers; and enlarging the ICTY and ICTR Appeals Chambers by two additional judges drawn from the ICTR Trial Chambers. While the first proposal would not require Council action, the Assembly's approval would be required for the related increase in the Tribunals' budgets. Adoption of the second proposal would require the Council to amend the ICTY statute, while the adoption of the last would require the Council to amend the statutes of both Tribunals. Adoption of the latter two proposals would require the Assembly's approval of the related increase in the budgets of the Tribunals.

Annexed to the Secretary-General's letter were the ICTY President's complete plan of 12 May on ICTY operation, including his plan for reform, and a letter of 14 June from the ICTR President containing comments on the plan.

SECURITY COUNCIL ACTION

Following consultations among its members on 21 and 30 November [meetings 4229, 4240], the Security Council, on 30 November, unanimously adopted **resolution 1329(2000)**. The draft [S/2000/

1131| was prepared during consultations among Council members.

The Security Council,

Reaffirming its resolutions 827(1993) of 25 May 1993 and 995(1994) of 8 November 1994,

Remaining convinced that the prosecution of persons responsible for serious violations of international humanitarian law committed in the territory of the former Yugoslavia contributes to the restoration and maintenance of peace in the former Yugoslavia,

Remaining convinced also that in the particular circumstances of Rwanda the prosecution of persons responsible for genocide and other serious violations of international humanitarian law contributes to the process of national reconciliation and to the restoration and maintenance of peace in Rwanda and in the region,

Having considered the letter from the Secretary-General to the President of the Security Council dated 7 September 2000 and the letters annexed thereto dated 12 May 2000 from the President of the International Tribunal for the Prosecution of Persons Responsible for Serious Violations of International Humanitarian Law Committed in the Territory of the Former Yugoslavia since 1991, and 14 June 2000 from the President of the International Criminal Tribunal for the Prosecution of Persons Responsible for Genocide and Other Serious Violations of International Humanitarian Law Committed in the Territory of Rwanda and Rwandan Citizens Responsible for Genocide and Other Such Violations Committed in the Territory of Neighbouring States, between 1 January 1994 and 31 December 1994, addressed to the Secretary-General,

Convinced of the need to establish a pool of ad litem judges in the International Tribunal for the Former Yugoslavia and to increase the number of judges in the Appeals Chambers of the International Tribunals in order to enable the Tribunals to expedite the conclusion of their work at the earliest possible date,

Noting the significant progress being made in improving the procedures of the International Tribunals, and convinced of the need for their organs to continue their efforts to further such progress,

Taking note of the position expressed by the International Tribunals that civilian, military and paramilitary leaders should be tried before them in preference to minor actors,

Recalling that the International Tribunals and national courts have concurrent jurisdiction to prosecute persons for serious violations of international humanitarian law, and noting that the rules of procedure and evidence of the International Tribunal for the Former Yugoslavia provide that a Trial Chamber may decide to suspend an indictment to allow for a national court to deal with a particular case,

Taking note with appreciation of the efforts of the judges of the International Tribunal for the Former Yugoslavia, as reflected in annex I to the letter from the Secretary-General dated 7 September 2000, to allow competent organs of the United Nations to begin to form a relatively exact idea of the length of the mandate of the Tribunal,

Acting under Chapter VII of the Charter of the United Nations,

1. *Decides* to establish a pool of ad litem judges in the International Tribunal for the Prosecution of Persons Responsible for Serious Violations of International Humanitarian Law Committed in the Territory of the Former Yugoslavia since 1991 and to enlarge the membership of the Appeals Chambers of the International Tribunal for the Former Yugoslavia and the International Criminal Tribunal for the Prosecution of Persons Responsible for Genocide and Other Serious Violations of International Humanitarian Law Committed in the Territory of Rwanda and Rwandan Citizens Responsible for Genocide and Other Such Violations Committed in the Territory of Neighbouring States, between 1 January 1994 and 31 December 1994, and to this end decides to amend articles 12, 13 and 14 of the statute of the International Tribunal for the Former Yugoslavia and to replace those articles with the provisions set out in annex I to the present resolution, and decides also to amend articles 11, 12 and 13 of the statute of the International Tribunal for Rwanda and to replace those articles with the provisions set out in annex II to the present resolution;

2. *Decides also* that two additional judges shall be elected as soon as possible as judges of the International Tribunal for Rwanda, and decides, without prejudice to article 12, paragraph 4, of the statute of that Tribunal, that, once elected, they shall serve until the date of the expiry of the terms of office of the existing judges, and that for the purpose of that election the Security Council shall, notwithstanding article 12, paragraph 2 (c) of the statute, establish a list from the nominations received of not less than four and not more than six candidates;

3. *Decides further* that, once two judges have been elected in accordance with paragraph 2 above and have taken up office, the President of the International Tribunal for Rwanda shall, in accordance with article 13, paragraph 3, of the statute of the International Tribunal for Rwanda and article 14, paragraph 4, of the statute of the International Tribunal for the Former Yugoslavia, take the necessary steps as soon as practicable to assign two of the judges elected or appointed in accordance with article 12 of the statute of the International Tribunal for Rwanda to be members of the Appeals Chambers of the International Tribunals;

4. *Requests* the Secretary-General to make practical arrangements for the elections mentioned in paragraph 2 above, for the election as soon as possible of twenty-seven ad litem judges in accordance with article 13 ter of the statute of the International Tribunal for the Former Yugoslavia, and for the timely provision to the International Tribunal for the Former Yugoslavia and the International Tribunal for Rwanda of personnel and facilities, in particular, for the ad litem judges and the Appeals Chambers and related offices of the Prosecutor, and further requests him to keep the Council closely informed of progress in this regard;

5. *Urges* all States to cooperate fully with the International Tribunals and their organs in accordance with their obligations under resolutions 827(1993) and 955(1994) and the statutes of the International Tribunals, and welcomes the cooperation already extended to the Tribunals in the fulfilment of their mandates;

6. *Requests* the Secretary-General to submit to the Council, as soon as possible, a report containing an assessment and proposals regarding the date ending the

temporal jurisdiction of the International Tribunal for the Former Yugoslavia;

7. *Decides* to remain actively seized of the matter.

ANNEX I
Amendments to the statute of the International Tribunal for the Former Yugoslavia

Replace articles 12, 13 and 14 by the following:

Article 12
Composition of the Chambers

1. The Chambers shall be composed of sixteen permanent independent judges, no two of whom may be nationals of the same State, and a maximum at any one time of nine ad litem independent judges appointed in accordance with article 13 ter, paragraph 2, of the statute, no two of whom may be nationals of the same State.

2. Three permanent judges and a maximum at any one time of six ad litem judges shall be members of each Trial Chamber. Each Trial Chamber to which ad litem judges are assigned may be divided into sections of three judges each, composed of both permanent and ad litem judges. A section of a Trial Chamber shall have the same powers and responsibilities as a Trial Chamber under the statute and shall render judgement in accordance with the same rules.

3. Seven of the permanent judges shall be members of the Appeals Chamber. The Appeals Chamber shall, for each appeal, be composed of five of its members.

Article 13
Qualifications of judges

The permanent and ad litem judges shall be persons of high moral character, impartiality and integrity who possess the qualifications required in their respective countries for appointment to the highest judicial offices. In the overall composition of the Chambers and sections of the Trial Chambers, due account shall be taken of the experience of the judges in criminal law, international law, including international humanitarian law and human rights law.

Article 13 bis
Election of permanent judges

1. Fourteen of the permanent judges of the International Tribunal shall be elected by the General Assembly from a list submitted by the Security Council, in the following manner:

(a) The Secretary-General shall invite nominations for judges of the International Tribunal from States Members of the United Nations and non-member States maintaining permanent observer missions at United Nations Headquarters;

(b) Within sixty days of the date of the invitation of the Secretary-General, each State may nominate up to two candidates meeting the qualifications set out in article 13 of the statute, no two of whom shall be of the same nationality and neither of whom shall be of the same nationality as any judge who is a member of the Appeals Chamber and who was elected or appointed a judge of the International Criminal Tribunal for the Prosecution of Persons Responsible for Genocide and Other Serious Violations of International Humanitarian Law Committed in the Territory of Rwanda and Rwandan Citizens Responsible for Genocide and Other Such Violations Committed in the Territory of Neighbouring States, between 1 January 1994 and 31 December 1994 (hereinafter referred to as "The Inter-

national Tribunal for Rwanda") in accordance with article 12 of the statute of that Tribunal;

(c) The Secretary-General shall forward the nominations received to the Security Council. From the nominations received the Security Council shall establish a list of not less than twenty-eight and not more than forty-two candidates, taking due account of the adequate representation of the principal legal systems of the world;

(d) The President of the Security Council shall transmit the list of candidates to the President of the General Assembly. From that list the General Assembly shall elect fourteen permanent judges of the International Tribunal. The candidates who receive an absolute majority of the votes of the States Members of the United Nations and of the non-member States maintaining permanent observer missions at United Nations Headquarters, shall be declared elected. Should two candidates of the same nationality obtain the required majority vote, the one who received the higher number of votes shall be considered elected.

2. In the event of a vacancy in the Chambers amongst the permanent judges elected or appointed in accordance with this article, after consultation with the Presidents of the Security Council and of the General Assembly, the Secretary-General shall appoint a person meeting the qualifications of article 13 of the statute, for the remainder of the term of office concerned.

3. The permanent judges elected in accordance with this article shall be elected for a term of four years. The terms and conditions of service shall be those of the judges of the International Court of Justice. They shall be eligible for re-election.

Article 13 ter
Election and appointment of ad litem judges

1. The ad litem judges of the International Tribunal shall be elected by the General Assembly from a list submitted by the Security Council, in the following manner:

(a) The Secretary-General shall invite nominations for ad litem judges of the International Tribunal from States Members of the United Nations and non-member States maintaining permanent observer missions at United Nations Headquarters;

(b) Within sixty days of the date of the invitation of the Secretary-General, each State may nominate up to four candidates meeting the qualifications set out in article 13 of the statute, taking into account the importance of a fair representation of female and male candidates;

(c) The Secretary-General shall forward the nominations received to the Security Council. From the nominations received the Security Council shall establish a list of not less than fifty-four candidates, taking due account of the adequate representation of the principal legal systems of the world and bearing in mind the importance of equitable geographical distribution;

(d) The President of the Security Council shall transmit the list of candidates to the President of the General Assembly. From that list the General Assembly shall elect the twenty-seven ad litem judges of the International Tribunal. The candidates who receive an absolute majority of the votes of the States Members of the United Nations and of the non-member States maintaining permanent observer missions at United Nations Headquarters shall be declared elected;

(*e*) The ad litem judges shall be elected for a term of four years. They shall not be eligible for re-election.

2. During their term, ad litem judges will be appointed by the Secretary-General, upon request of the President of the International Tribunal, to serve in the Trial Chambers for one or more trials, for a cumulative period of up to, but not including, three years. When requesting the appointment of any particular ad litem judge, the President of the International Tribunal shall bear in mind the criteria set out in article 13 of the statute regarding the composition of the Chambers and sections of the Trial Chambers, the considerations set out in paragraphs 1 (*b*) and (*c*) above and the number of votes the ad litem judge received in the General Assembly.

Article 13 quater
Status of ad litem judges

1. During the period in which they are appointed to serve in the International Tribunal, ad litem judges shall:

(*a*) Benefit from the same terms and conditions of service mutatis mutandis as the permanent judges of the International Tribunal;

(*b*) Enjoy, subject to paragraph 2 below, the same powers as the permanent judges of the International Tribunal;

(*c*) Enjoy the privileges and immunities, exemptions and facilities of a judge of the International Tribunal.

2. During the period in which they are appointed to serve in the International Tribunal, ad litem judges shall not:

(*a*) Be eligible for election as, or to vote in the election of, the President of the Tribunal or the Presiding Judge of a Trial Chamber pursuant to article 14 of the statute;

(*b*) Have power:

(i) To adopt rules of procedure and evidence pursuant to article 15 of the statute. They shall, however, be consulted before the adoption of those rules;

(ii) To review an indictment pursuant to article 19 of the statute;

(iii) To consult with the President in relation to the assignment of judges pursuant to article 14 of the statute or in relation to a pardon or commutation of sentence pursuant to article 28 of the statute;

(iv) To adjudicate in pre-trial proceedings.

Article 14
Officers and members of the Chambers

1. The permanent judges of the International Tribunal shall elect a President from amongst their number.

2. The President of the International Tribunal shall be a member of the Appeals Chamber and shall preside over its proceedings.

3. After consultation with the permanent judges of the International Tribunal, the President shall assign four of the permanent judges elected or appointed in accordance with article 13 bis of the statute to the Appeals Chamber and nine to the Trial Chambers.

4. Two of the judges elected or appointed in accordance with article 12 of the statute of the International Tribunal for Rwanda shall be assigned by the President of that Tribunal, in consultation with the President of the International Tribunal, to be members of the Appeals Chamber and permanent judges of the International Tribunal.

5. After consultation with the permanent judges of the International Tribunal, the President shall assign such ad litem judges as may from time to time be appointed to serve in the International Tribunal to the Trial Chambers.

6. A judge shall serve only in the Chamber to which he or she was assigned.

7. The permanent judges of each Trial Chamber shall elect a Presiding Judge from amongst their number, who shall oversee the work of the Trial Chamber as a whole.

ANNEX II
Amendments to the statute of the
International Tribunal for Rwanda
Replace articles 11, 12 and 13 by the following:

Article 11
Composition of the Chambers

The Chambers shall be composed of sixteen independent judges, no two of whom may be nationals of the same State, who shall serve as follows:

(*a*) Three judges shall serve in each of the Trial Chambers;

(*b*) Seven judges shall be members of the Appeals Chamber. The Appeals Chamber shall, for each appeal, be composed of five of its members.

Article 12
Qualification and election of judges

1. The judges shall be persons of high moral character, impartiality and integrity who possess the qualifications required in their respective countries for appointment to the highest judicial offices. In the overall composition of the Chambers due account shall be taken of the experience of the judges in criminal law, international law, including international humanitarian law and human rights law.

2. Eleven of the judges of the International Tribunal for Rwanda shall be elected by the General Assembly from a list submitted by the Security Council, in the following manner:

(*a*) The Secretary-General shall invite nominations for judges from States Members of the United Nations and non-member States maintaining permanent observer missions at United Nations Headquarters;

(*b*) Within sixty days of the date of the invitation of the Secretary-General, each State may nominate up to two candidates meeting the qualifications set out in paragraph 1 above, no two of whom shall be of the same nationality and neither of whom shall be of the same nationality as any judge who is a member of the Appeals Chamber and who was elected or appointed a permanent judge of the International Tribunal for the Prosecution of Persons Responsible for Serious Violations of International Humanitarian Law Committed in the Territory of the former Yugoslavia since 1991 (hereinafter referred to as "the International Tribunal for the Former Yugoslavia") in accordance with article 13 bis of the statute of that Tribunal;

(*c*) The Secretary-General shall forward the nominations received to the Security Council. From the nominations received the Security Council shall establish a list of not less than twenty-two and not more than thirty-three candidates, taking due account of the adequate representation on the International Tribunal for Rwanda of the principal legal systems of the world;

(d) The President of the Security Council shall transmit the list of candidates to the President of the General Assembly. From that list the General Assembly shall elect eleven judges of the International Tribunal for Rwanda. The candidates who receive an absolute majority of the votes of the States Members of the United Nations and of the non-member States maintaining permanent observer missions at United Nations Headquarters, shall be declared elected. Should two candidates of the same nationality obtain the required majority vote, the one who received the higher number of votes shall be considered elected.

3. In the event of a vacancy in the Chambers amongst the judges elected or appointed in accordance with this article, after consultation with the Presidents of the Security Council and of the General Assembly, the Secretary-General shall appoint a person meeting the qualifications of paragraph 1 above, for the remainder of the term of office concerned.

4. The judges elected in accordance with this article shall be elected for a term of four years. The terms and conditions of service shall be those of the judges of the International Tribunal for the Former Yugoslavia. They shall be eligible for re-election.

Article 13
Officers and members of the Chambers
1. The judges of the International Tribunal for Rwanda shall elect a President.
2. The President of the International Tribunal for Rwanda shall be a member of one of its Trial Chambers.
3. After consultation with the judges of the International Tribunal for Rwanda, the President shall assign two of the judges elected or appointed in accordance with article 12 of the present statute to be members of the Appeals Chamber of the International Tribunal for the Former Yugoslavia and eight to the Trial Chambers of the International Tribunal for Rwanda. A judge shall serve only in the Chamber to which he or she was assigned.
4. The members of the Appeals Chamber of the International Tribunal for the Former Yugoslavia shall also serve as the members of the Appeals Chamber of the International Tribunal for Rwanda.
5. The judges of each Trial Chamber shall elect a Presiding Judge, who shall conduct all of the proceedings of that Trial Chamber as a whole.

Before adoption of the text, the Council President noted that four urgent issues remained, namely, the issues of geographical distribution, compensation of victims (see below), compensation of victims of miscarriage of justice and of persons unlawfully arrested or detained (see below), and gender balance.

Compensation

In September [S/2000/904] and October [S/2000/925], the Secretary-General transmitted to the Security Council reports of the ICTY and ICTR Presidents indicating that, according to their judges, the Tribunals should be able, in certain situations, to compensate persons wrongfully detained, prosecuted or convicted. Compensation would be awarded when a person had suffered punishment resulting from a final decision and the decision was reversed by the Tribunals or a pardon granted; when a detainee was subsequently acquitted by a final decision or released following a decision to terminate the proceedings against him/her in circumstances that revealed a miscarriage of justice; and when a person was arrested or detained in a manner that constituted a violation of the right to liberty and security of person and when the conduct that gave rise to the violation was legally imputed to the Tribunals and thus to the United Nations. The Presidents observed that the Council would be obliged to amend the Tribunals' statutes to empower them to deal with compensation issues.

However, in November [S/2000/1063], the ICTY President stated that the judges had concluded that conferring the power to order the payment of compensation to the victims of crimes that fell within ICTY's jurisdiction was not desirable, since it would significantly increase the workload of the Chambers and the length and complexity of trials, and raised questions about the funding of such awards. They suggested that the Council, or some other organ to which it might refer the matter, might consider mechanisms for the payment of compensation, such as the creation of an international compensation commission.

The ICTR President, in December [S/2000/1198], stated that the judges shared the same view concerning the implications of ICTR possessing such a power, but considered that the Tribunal, in tandem with other mechanisms, might be vested with a limited power to order the payment of compensation from a trust fund to victims who appeared as witnesses in trials. Adoption of that measure would require the Council to amend the Tribunal's statute.

Expert Group recommendations

In response to General Assembly resolutions 54/239 A [YUN 1999, p. 1220] and 54/240 A [ibid., p. 1225], the Secretary-General, in April [A/54/850], transmitted the comments of the Tribunals on the report of the Expert Group to Conduct a Review of the Effective Operation and Functioning of ICTY and ICTR [YUN 1999, p. 1219].

Of the 46 recommendations made by the Group, 16 had been implemented and 11 had been indicated as subject to further review. The Secretary-General said that two recommendations dealing with the possible realignment of the control of administrative functions were of particular importance in terms of his overall authority. The Group had expressed the view that, although dividing the Registry into two separate administrative structures with one integrated into the Office of the Prosecutor and the other servicing the Chambers might have budgetary implications, it should be seriously considered. The Secretary-General was of the view that the continuing delineation of his overall responsibility for the functioning of the respective Registries did not preclude further efforts being made to improve the quality of support given to the other two organs. To maintain a clear line of accountability, the Secretary-General had delegated authority under the UN Financial Regulations and Rules and Staff Regulations and Rules to the Registrars and other officers under their authority. Should the Security Council decide to revise the administrative elements in the respective statutes, the revision would need to be subject to a full understanding between the Assembly and the Council regarding their respective authorities before any changes could be effected with respect to delegation of authority.

The general observations of the Prosecutor and the ICTR Registry were annexed to the note.

In June [S/2000/597], the Secretary-General transmitted to the Council the report of the Expert Group [YUN 1999, p. 1219].

ACABQ action. Following consideration of the Secretary-General's note (see above), the Advisory Committee on Administrative and Budgetary Questions (ACABQ), in May [A/54/874], referring to the recommendations that affected the statutory roles of the Registries vis-à-vis the Chambers and the Prosecutor, recalled that, in recommending the establishment of the Expert Group, it had indicated that the review would be carried out in full respect of the Tribunals' statutes. Accordingly, unless the statutes were amended by the Security Council, ACABQ recommended that the current practice be followed and that the shortcomings that had led to the Expert Group's recommendations on the matter be resolved. It also recommended that the Secretary-General prepare the 2001 budget proposals for the Tribunals based on their existing structures.

The Committee proposed that the Secretary-General prepare a separate report in 2001, in the context of the budgets of the Tribunals, on the actions taken or to be taken in respect of the recommendations that remained under review. Furthermore, a comprehensive report should be submitted in 2001 on the results of the implementation of the Group's recommendations.

ACABQ observed that the Tribunals were independent entities, operating and functioning in different environments, and their practices might diverge. Thus, it cautioned against calling for complete harmonization in applying the Group's recommendations.

GENERAL ASSEMBLY ACTION

On 15 June [meeting 98], the General Assembly, on the recommendation of the Fifth (Administrative and Budgetary) Committee [A/54/678/Add.1], adopted **resolution 54/239 B** without vote [agenda item 142].

Financing of the International Tribunal for the Prosecution of Persons Responsible for Serious Violations of International Humanitarian Law Committed in the Territory of the Former Yugoslavia since 1991

The General Assembly,

Recalling its resolutions 53/212 and 53/213 of 18 December 1998, in which it requested the Secretary-General, with a view to evaluating the effective operation and functioning of the International Tribunal for the Prosecution of Persons Responsible for Serious Violations of International Humanitarian Law Committed in the Territory of the Former Yugoslavia since 1991 and the International Criminal Tribunal for the Prosecution of Persons Responsible for Genocide and Other Serious Violations of International Humanitarian Law Committed in the Territory of Rwanda and Rwandan Citizens Responsible for Genocide and Other Such Violations Committed in the Territory of Neighbouring States between 1 January and 31 December 1994, to conduct a review in full cooperation with the Presidents of the International Tribunals, without prejudice to the provisions of the statutes of the Tribunals and their independent character, and to report thereon to the relevant organs of the United Nations,

Recalling also its resolution 54/239 A of 23 December 1999, in which it requested the Secretary-General to obtain comments and observations from the International Tribunal for the Former Yugoslavia on the report of the Expert Group to conduct a review of the effective operation and functioning of the International Tribunals, and to submit them, through the Advisory Committee on Administrative and Budgetary Questions, to the General Assembly for consideration at its resumed fifty-fourth session,

1. *Takes note* of the report of the Expert Group to conduct a review of the effective operation and functioning of the International Tribunal for the Prosecution of Persons Responsible for Serious Violations of International Humanitarian Law Committed in the Territory of the Former Yugoslavia since 1991 and the International Criminal Tribunal for the Prosecution of Persons Responsible for Genocide and Other Serious Violations of International Humanitarian Law Committed in the Territory of Rwanda and Rwandan Citizens Responsible for Genocide and Other Such Violations Committed in the Territory of Neighbouring States between 1 January and 31 December 1994, established by the Secretary-General pursuant to General Assembly resolutions 53/212 and 53/213, and the note by the Secretary-General transmitting comments thereon;

2. *Endorses* the observations and recommendations contained in the report of the Advisory Committee on Administrative and Budgetary Questions;

3. *Requests* the Secretary-General to transmit to the Security Council for its consideration the report of the Expert Group, together with the note by the Secretary-General transmitting comments thereon;

4. *Welcomes* the recent improvements in the functioning of the International Tribunal for the Former Yugoslavia, and encourages continued efforts to that effect;

5. *Notes* that work is in hand to address areas where improvement is needed, including those noted by the Expert Group and the external and internal oversight bodies;

6. *Requests* the Secretary-General to report to the General Assembly at its fifty-fifth session, in the context of the budget of the International Tribunal for the Former Yugoslavia for 2001, reflecting the views of all organs of the Tribunal, on actions taken or to be taken to improve the functioning of the Tribunal, including in respect of the recommendations of the Expert Group that remain under review, to the extent that they can be implemented;

7. *Also requests* the Secretary-General to submit a comprehensive report on the results of the implementation of the recommendations of the Expert Group to the General Assembly at its fifty-sixth session;

8. *Notes* that the proposed budget for the International Tribunal for the Former Yugoslavia for 2000 did not include provision for all the forensic experts later determined to be needed, and emphasizes that the Secretary-General should ensure that the budget proposals for the Tribunal are adequate and conform with the applicable rules and regulations and the relevant General Assembly resolutions;

9. *Confirms* the appropriation that was approved on a provisional basis in its resolution 54/239 A.

Also on 15 June [meeting 98], the Assembly, on the recommendation of the Fifth Committee [A/54/679/Add.1], adopted **resolution 54/240 B** without vote [agenda item 143].

Financing of the International Criminal Tribunal for the Prosecution of Persons Responsible for Genocide and Other Serious Violations of International Humanitarian Law Committed in the Territory of Rwanda and Rwandan Citizens Responsible for Genocide and Other Such Violations Committed in the Territory of Neighbouring States between 1 January and 31 December 1994

The General Assembly,

Recalling its resolutions 53/212 and 53/213 of 18 December 1998, in which it requested the Secretary-General, with a view to evaluating the effective operation and functioning of the International Tribunal for the Prosecution of Persons Responsible for Serious Violations of International Humanitarian Law Committed in the Territory of the Former Yugoslavia since 1991 and the International Criminal Tribunal for the Prosecution of Persons Responsible for Genocide and Other Serious Violations of International Humanitarian Law Committed in the Territory of Rwanda and Rwandan Citizens Responsible for Genocide and Other Such Violations Committed in the Territory of Neighbouring States between 1 January and 31 December 1994, to conduct a review in full cooperation with the Presidents of the International Tribunals, without prejudice to the provisions of the statutes of the Tribunals and their independent character, and to report thereon to the relevant organs of the United Nations,

Recalling also its resolution 54/240 A of 23 December 1999, in which it requested the Secretary-General to obtain comments and observations from the International Tribunal for Rwanda on the report of the Expert Group to conduct a review of the effective operation and functioning of the International Tribunals, and to submit them, through the Advisory Committee on Administrative and Budgetary Questions, to the General Assembly for consideration at its resumed fifty-fourth session,

1. *Takes note* of the report of the Expert Group to conduct a review of the effective operation and functioning of the International Tribunal for the Prosecution of Persons Responsible for Serious Violations of International Humanitarian Law Committed in the Territory of the Former Yugoslavia since 1991 and the International Criminal Tribunal for the Prosecution of Persons Responsible for Genocide and Other Serious Violations of International Humanitarian Law Committed in the Territory of Rwanda and Rwandan Citizens Responsible for Genocide and Other Such Violations Committed in the Territory of Neighbouring States between 1 January and 31 December 1994, established by the Secretary-General pursuant to General Assembly resolutions 53/212 and 53/213, and the note by the Secretary-General transmitting comments thereon;

2. *Endorses* the observations and recommendations contained in the report of the Advisory Committee on Administrative and Budgetary Questions;

3. *Requests* the Secretary-General to transmit to the Security Council for its consideration the report of the Expert Group, together with the note by the Secretary-General transmitting comments thereon;

4. *Welcomes* the recent improvements in the functioning of the International Tribunal for Rwanda, and encourages continued efforts to that effect;

5. *Notes* that work is in hand to address areas where improvement is needed, including those noted by the Expert Group and the external and internal oversight bodies;

6. *Requests* the Secretary-General to report to the General Assembly at its fifty-fifth session, in the context of the budget of the International Tribunal for Rwanda for 2001, reflecting the views of all organs of the Tribunal, on actions taken or to be taken to improve the functioning of the Tribunal, including in respect of the recommendations of the Expert Group that remain under review, to the extent that they can be implemented;

7. *Also requests* the Secretary-General to submit a comprehensive report on the results of the implementation of the recommendations of the Expert Group to the General Assembly at its fifty-sixth session;

8. *Confirms* the appropriation that was approved on a provisional basis in its resolution 54/240 A.

OIOS review

In response to a request from the UN Controller, the Office of Internal Oversight Services (OIOS), in June [A/55/759], conducted an investigation into possible fee-splitting arrangements between defence counsel and indigent detainees at both Tribunals. The request to OIOS followed the 1999 report of the Expert Group to Conduct a Review of the Effective Operation and Functioning of ICTY and ICTR [YUN 1999, p. 1219].

OIOS investigators found evidence that several former defence counsels at both Tribunals either had been solicited and/or had accepted requests for fee-splitting arrangements. At ICTR, some defence teams had made gifts to their clients and their relatives; at both Tribunals, some teams had hired friends or relatives of their clients as defence investigators. Fee-splitting was linked with problems in verifying claims for indigence submitted by the suspect/accused; the process of selecting and changing assigned counsel; the fees paid to defence teams; and the use of frivolous motions and other delaying tactics before the Trial Chambers.

The information found by OIOS about possible ongoing fee-splitting arrangements needed to be further developed, refined and corroborated by specific investigative steps. Thus, OIOS would continue to pursue the issue in consultation with the Registries and would report as necessary.

OIOS made a series of recommendations, with which the Secretary-General concurred.

Financing

ICTY

Reports of Secretary-General. In response to General Assembly resolution 54/239 B (see p. 1232), the Secretary-General, in October [A/55/517 & Corr.1], submitted the proposed 2001 ICTY resource requirements, amounting to $112,464,300 gross ($100,180,800 net), reflecting an increase of $4,238,200 net and an additional 89 posts over the 2000 appropriation and authorized staffing level.

Pursuant to Assembly resolution 53/212 [YUN 1998, p. 1199], the Secretary-General, in November [A/55/623], presented the fifth annual budget performance report of ICTY for the year ended 31 December 1999, including actual performance indicators. Of the total net appropriation of $94,103,800, actual expenditures recorded for 1999 totalled $80,489,500, resulting in a reduction in requirements of $13,614,300. The 1999 budget was impacted by expanded investigations into the Kosovo conflict that were funded through the assessed budget and the ICTY trust fund; lower-than-anticipated usage of the Tribunal's three courtrooms; and absorption of half the expenditures of the Expert Group to Conduct a Review of the Effective Operation and Functioning of ICTY and ICTR [YUN 1999, p. 1219] within the ICTY 1999 budget.

In December [A/55/517/Add.1], the Secretary-General submitted supplementary resource requirements for 2001, arising from Security Council resolution 1329(2000) (see p. 1228), for the use of six ad litem judges in ICTY in 2001. The estimated additional requirements would amount to $5,280,900 gross ($4,899,400 net) with an additional 54 temporary posts, bringing the total resource requirements for 2001 to $117,745,200 gross ($105,080,200 net). Provisions related to the proposed two additional judges for the ICTY Appeals Chamber were included in the report on the financing of ICTR [A/55/512/Add.1] (see p. 1236).

ACABQ action. In November [A/55/642], ACABQ recommended that the General Assembly approve an appropriation of $108,487,700 gross ($96,443,900 net) for the operation of the Tribunal in 2001. The Committee summarized its recommendations regarding post reductions.

GENERAL ASSEMBLY ACTION

On 23 December [meeting 89], the General Assembly, on the recommendation of the Fifth Committee [A/55/691], adopted **resolution 55/225 A** without vote [agenda item 127].

Financing of the International Tribunal for the Prosecution of Persons Responsible for Serious Violations of International Humanitarian Law Committed in the Territory of the Former Yugoslavia since 1991

The General Assembly,

Taking note of the report of the Secretary-General on the financing of the International Tribunal for the Prosecution of Persons Responsible for Serious Violations of International Humanitarian Law Committed in the Territory of the Former Yugoslavia since 1991, the related report of the Advisory Committee on Administrative and Budgetary Questions and the oral statement made by the Chairman of the Advisory Committee to the Fifth Committee on 6 December 2000,

Recalling its resolution 47/235 of 14 September 1993 on the financing of the International Tribunal for the Former Yugoslavia and its subsequent resolutions thereon, the latest of which were resolutions 54/239 A of 23 December 1999 and 54/239 B of 15 June 2000,

Taking note of the report of the Secretary-General on the budget performance of the International Tribunal for the Former Yugoslavia for 1999 and the comments of the Advisory Committee thereon in its report,

Taking note also of Security Council resolution 1329(2000) of 30 November 2000 concerning the establishment of a pool of ad litem judges in the International Tribunal for the Former Yugoslavia,

1. *Endorses* the conclusions and recommendations contained in the report of the Advisory Committee on Administrative and Budgetary Questions, subject to the provisions of the present resolution;

2. *Decides* that the budget of the International Tribunal for the Prosecution of Persons Responsible for Serious Violations of International Humanitarian Law Committed in the Territory of the Former Yugoslavia since 1991 shall be biennialized, on an experimental basis, for the period 2002-2003, also decides to keep the matter of the biennialization under review, and requests

the Secretary-General to report to the General Assembly at its fifty-eighth session on the results of the experiment and the impact on the functioning of the Tribunal;

3. *Notes with satisfaction* that the benefits of this provisional reform could include the use of two-year employment contracts at the International Tribunal for the Former Yugoslavia;

4. *Welcomes* recent improvements in the functioning of the International Tribunal for the Former Yugoslavia, and encourages continued efforts to address areas where improvement is needed;

5. *Requests* the Secretary-General to provide in his proposed budget, with the involvement of all organs of the International Tribunal for the Former Yugoslavia, workload data for the budget period so as to give more justification for its resource requirements, and also requests the Secretary-General to include in his budget presentation information on budgetary requirements, including targets for recruitment, training, judicial scheduling and performance standards for support activities;

6. *Welcomes* the actions taken so far to address the issue of dilatory motions and pleadings, which have the effect of lengthening trial proceedings, and encourages the International Tribunal for the Former Yugoslavia to take further measures to improve the monitoring and oversight of defence counsel;

7. *Endorses* the recommendation of the Advisory Committee that judicial activities of the International Tribunal for the Former Yugoslavia should have priority over public relations activities and attendance at external meetings;

8. *Decides* to revert, at its resumed fifty-fifth session, to the consideration of resource requirements for the implementation of modifications to the statute of the International Tribunal for the Former Yugoslavia, without prejudice to the nomination and election of the ad litem judges;

9. *Decides also* to appropriate to the Special Account for the International Tribunal for the Prosecution of Persons Responsible for Serious Violations of International Humanitarian Law Committed in the Territory of the Former Yugoslavia since 1991 a total amount of 108,487,700 United States dollars gross (96,443,900 dollars net) for 2001;

10. *Decides further* that the financing of the appropriation for 2001 under the Special Account shall take into account the unused unencumbered balance of 5,873,600 dollars gross (5,414,300 dollars net) for 1999, interest and miscellaneous income of 3,412,000 dollars recorded for the biennium 1998-1999, the estimated unencumbered balance of 2.5 million dollars gross (2,227,000 dollars net) for 2000 and the estimated income of 77,200 dollars for 2001, which shall be set off against the aggregate amount of the appropriation, as detailed in the annex to the present resolution;

11. *Decides* to apportion the amount of 48,312,450 dollars gross (42,695,300 dollars net) among Member States in accordance with the scale of assessments applicable to the regular budget of the United Nations for 2001, as set out in its resolution 55/5 B of 23 December 2000;

12. *Decides also* to apportion the amount of 48,312,450 dollars gross (42,695,300 dollars net) among Member States in accordance with the scale of assessments applicable to peacekeeping operations for 2001;

13. *Decides further* that, in accordance with the provisions of its resolution 973(X) of 15 December 1955, there shall be set off against the apportionment among Member States, as provided for in paragraphs 11 and 12 above, their respective share in the Tax Equalization Fund of the estimated staff assessment income of 11,234,300 dollars approved for the International Tribunal for the Former Yugoslavia for 2001.

ANNEX
Financing of the International Tribunal for the Prosecution of Persons Responsible for Serious Violations of International Humanitarian Law Committed in the Territory of the Former Yugoslavia since 1991

	Gross	Net
	(United States dollars)	
Proposed budget for 2001 (A/55/517 and Corr.1)[a]	112,464,300	100,180,800
Less:		
Recommendations of the Advisory Committee on Administrative and Budgetary Questions (A/55/642)	(3,976,600)	(3,736,900)
Estimated appropriation	108,487,700	96,443,900
Add:		
Estimated unencumbered balance for 1999 that was taken into account and reduced from the assessment for 2000 (resolutions 54/239 A and B)	8,200,000	8,200,000
Less:		
Actual unencumbered balance for 1999	(14,073,600)	(13,614,300)
Interest and other miscellaneous income for the biennium 1998-1999 as at 31 December 1999	(3,412,000)	(3,412,000)
Estimated unencumbered balance for 2000	(2,500,000)	(2,227,000)
Estimated income for 2001	(77,200)	
Balance to be assessed for 2001	96,624,900	85,390,600
Including:		
Contributions assessed on Member States in accordance with the scale of assessments applicable to the regular budget of the United Nations for 2001	48,312,450	42,695,300
Contributions assessed on Member States in accordance with the scale of assessments applicable to peacekeeping operations for 2001	48,312,450	42,695,300

[a]The amount does not include provisions sought for ad litem judges (A/55/517/Add.1).

Also on 23 December, the Assembly decided that the item on ICTY financing would remain for consideration during its resumed fifty-fifth (2001) session (**decision 55/458**) and that the Fifth Committee should continue consideration of the item at that session (**decision 55/455**).

ICTR

Reports of Secretary-General. In October [A/55/512 & Corr.1], the Secretary-General submitted the proposed 2001 ICTR resource requirements, amounting to $95,056,600 gross ($86,616,600 net), reflecting an increase of $8,901,700 gross ($8,446,400 net) and 81 additional new posts.

In response to Assembly resolution 49/251 [YUN 1995, p. 1324], the Secretary-General, in November [A/55/622], submitted the fifth annual budget performance report of ICTR for the year ended 31 December 1999, including actual performance indicators. Expenditures for 1999 totalled $64,156,000 net, resulting in an unencumbered balance of $4,375,300 net, which consisted of reduced requirements of $3,525,600 net under the Registry and $918,400 net under the Office of the Prosecutor, offset by an overexpenditure of $68,700 under the Chambers.

In December [A/55/512/Add.1], the Secretary-General presented the supplementary resource requirements for 2001 arising from Security Council resolution 1329(2000) (see p. 1228), by which the Council approved the appointment of two additional judges to the Appeals Chambers of ICTR and ICTY. The estimated additional requirements amounted to $654,300 gross ($628,900 net), bringing the total resource requirements for 2001 to $95,710,900 gross ($87,245,500 net).

ACABQ action. In November [A/55/643], ACABQ reviewed ICTR financing and recommended that the General Assembly approve an appropriation of $93,520,500 gross ($85,178,700 net) for the operation of the Tribunal in 2001, representing a reduction of $1,536,100 gross ($1,437,900 net) from the estimate in the Secretary-General's proposal.

GENERAL ASSEMBLY ACTION

On 23 December [meeting 89], the General Assembly, on the recommendation of the Fifth Committee [A/55/692], adopted **resolution 55/226** without vote [agenda item 128].

Financing of the International Criminal Tribunal for the Prosecution of Persons Responsible for Genocide and Other Serious Violations of International Humanitarian Law Committed in the Territory of Rwanda and Rwandan Citizens Responsible for Genocide and Other Such Violations Committed in the Territory of Neighbouring States between 1 January and 31 December 1994

The General Assembly,

Taking note of the report of the Secretary-General on the financing of the International Criminal Tribunal for the Prosecution of Persons Responsible for Genocide and Other Serious Violations of International Humanitarian Law Committed in the Territory of Rwanda and Rwandan Citizens Responsible for Genocide and Other Such Violations Committed in the Territory of Neighbouring States between 1 January and 31 December 1994, the related report of the Advisory Committee on Administrative and Budgetary Questions and the oral statement made by the Chairman of the Advisory Committee to the Fifth Committee on 6 December 2000,

Recalling its resolution 49/251 of 20 July 1995 on the financing of the International Tribunal for Rwanda

and its subsequent resolutions thereon, the latest of which were resolutions 54/240 A of 23 December 1999 and 54/240 B of 15 June 2000,

Taking note of the report of the Secretary-General on the budget performance of the International Tribunal for Rwanda for 1999 and the comments of the Advisory Committee thereon in its report,

Taking note also of Security Council resolution 1329(2000) of 30 November 2000 concerning the election of two judges of the International Tribunal for Rwanda and the assignment of two of the judges elected or appointed in accordance with article 12 of the statute of the International Tribunal for Rwanda to be members of the Appeals Chamber of the International Tribunal for Rwanda and the International Tribunal for the Prosecution of Persons Responsible for Serious Violations of International Humanitarian Law Committed in the Territory of the Former Yugoslavia since 1991,

1. *Endorses* the conclusions and recommendations contained in the report of the Advisory Committee on Administrative and Budgetary Questions, subject to the provisions of the present resolution;

2. *Decides* that the budget of the International Criminal Tribunal for the Prosecution of Persons Responsible for Genocide and Other Serious Violations of International Humanitarian Law Committed in the Territory of Rwanda and Rwandan Citizens Responsible for Genocide and Other Such Violations Committed in the Territory of Neighbouring States between 1 January and 31 December 1994 shall be biennialized, on an experimental basis, for the period 2002-2003, also decides to keep the matter of the biennialization under review, and requests the Secretary-General to report to the General Assembly at its fifty-eighth session on the results of the experiment and the impact on the functioning of the Tribunal;

3. *Notes with satisfaction* that the benefits of this provisional reform could include the use of two-year employment contracts at the International Tribunal for Rwanda;

4. *Welcomes* recent improvements in the functioning of the International Tribunal for Rwanda, and encourages continued efforts to address areas where improvement is needed;

5. *Requests* the Secretary-General to provide in his proposed budget, with the involvement of all organs of the International Tribunal for Rwanda, workload data for the budget period so as to give more justification for its resource requirements, and also requests the Secretary-General to include in his budget presentation information on budgetary requirements, including targets for recruitment, training, judicial scheduling and performance standards for support activities;

6. *Welcomes* the actions taken so far to address the issue of dilatory motions and pleadings, which have the effect of lengthening trial proceedings, and encourages the International Tribunal for Rwanda to take further measures to improve the monitoring and oversight of defence counsel;

7. *Endorses* the recommendation of the Advisory Committee that the judicial activities of the International Tribunal for Rwanda should have priority over public relations activities and attendance at external meetings;

8. *Also endorses* the recommendation of the Advisory Committee in paragraph 23 of its report, and requests the Secretary-General to undertake a study, with the involvement of the International Tribunal for Rwanda, to indicate whether it is possible to state the likely date or dates for the completion of the mandate of the Tribunal, and to report thereon in the context of the next proposed budget;

9. *Requests* the Secretary-General to submit to the General Assembly at its fifty-sixth session a report on the likely long-term financial obligations of the United Nations with regard to the enforcement of sentences;

10. *Approves* the budgetary recommendations of the Advisory Committee as contained in paragraph 66 of its report and the additional budgetary recommendations of the Advisory Committee arising from Security Council resolution 1329(2000), as presented orally by the Chairman of the Advisory Committee to the Fifth Committee;

11. *Decides* to appropriate to the Special Account for the International Criminal Tribunal for the Prosecution of Persons Responsible for Genocide and Other Serious Violations of International Humanitarian Law Committed in the Territory of Rwanda and Rwandan Citizens Responsible for Genocide and Other Such Violations Committed in the Territory of Neighbouring States between 1 January and 31 December 1994 a total amount of 93,974,800 United States dollars gross (85,607,600 dollars net) for 2001;

12. *Decides also* that the financing of the appropriation for 2001 under the Special Account shall take into account the actual unencumbered balance of 2,937,000 dollars gross (1,988,700 dollars net) as at the end of 1999, and the estimated unencumbered balance of 2 million dollars gross (1,816,000 dollars net) which was taken into account in resolution 54/240 A, as well as the amount of 2,667,000 dollars gross (2,667,000 dollars net), being the interest and other miscellaneous income recorded for the biennium 1998-1999, which shall be set off against the aggregate amount of the appropriation, as detailed in the annex to the present resolution;

13. *Decides further* that the financing of the appropriation for 2001 under the Special Account shall also take into account an amount of 4,237,100 dollars gross (3,851,900 dollars net), being the estimated unencumbered balance as at the end of 2000, which shall also be set off against the aggregate amount of the appropriation, as detailed in the annex to the present resolution;

14. *Decides* to apportion the amount of 43,066,850 dollars gross (39,458,000 dollars net) among Member States in accordance with the scale of assessments applicable to the regular budget of the United Nations for 2001, as set out in its resolution 55/5 B of 23 December 2000;

15. *Decides also* to apportion the amount of 43,066,850 dollars gross (39,458,000 dollars net) among Member States in accordance with the scale of assessments applicable to peacekeeping operations for 2001;

16. *Decides further* that, in accordance with the provisions of its resolution 973(X) of 15 December 1955, there shall be set off against the apportionment among Member States, as provided for in paragraphs 14 and 15 above, their respective share in the Tax Equalization Fund of the estimated staff assessment income of 7,217,700 dollars approved for the International Tribunal for Rwanda for 2001.

ANNEX
Financing of the International Criminal Tribunal for the Prosecution of Persons Responsible for Genocide and Other Serious Violations of International Humanitarian Law Committed in the Territory of Rwanda and Rwandan Citizens Responsible for Genocide and Other Such Violations Committed in the Territory of Neighbouring States between 1 January and 31 December 1994

	Gross	Net
	(United States dollars)	
Proposed budget for 2001 (A/55/512 and Corr.1)	95,056,600	86,616,600
Add:		
Additional requirements arising from Security Council resolution 1329 (2000) (see A/55/512/Add.1)	654,300	628,900
Total proposed budget for 2001	95,710,900	87,245,500
Less:		
Recommendations of the Advisory Committee on Administrative and Budgetary Questions (A/55/643)	(1,536,100)	(1,437,900)
Additional Advisory Committee recommendations as presented orally by the Chairman of the Advisory Committee to the Fifth Committee at its 35th meeting on 6 December 2000	(200,000)	(200,000)
Estimated appropriation	93,974,800	85,607,600
Add:		
Estimated unencumbered balance for 1998-1999 that was taken into account and reduced from the assessment for 2000 (see resolution 54/240 A)	2,000,000	1,816,000
Less:		
Actual unencumbered balance for the biennium 1998-1999 as at 31 December 1999	(2,937,000)	(1,988,700)
Interest and other miscellaneous income for 1998-1999 as at 31 December 1999	(2,667,000)	(2,667,000)
Estimated unencumbered balance from the appropriation for 2000 as at the end of 2000	(4,237,100)	(3,851,900)
Balance to be assessed for 2001	86,133,700	78,916,000
Including:		
Contributions assessed on Member States in accordance with the scale of assessments applicable to the regular budget of the United Nations for 2001	43,066,850	39,458,000
Contributions assessed on Member States in accordance with the scale of assessments applicable to peacekeeping operations for 2001	43,066,850	39,458,000

Also on 23 December, the Assembly decided that the item on ICTR financing would remain for consideration during its resumed fifty-fifth (2001) session (**decision 55/458**).

Chapter III

Legal aspects of international political relations

Throughout 2000, the Preparatory Commission for the International Criminal Court, created by the 1998 United Nations Diplomatic Conference of Plenipotentiaries on the Establishment of an International Criminal Court to make arrangements for the coming into operation of the Court, finalized the draft texts of the first instruments necessary for the Court's functioning, namely, the rules of procedure and evidence, and the elements of crimes. The General Assembly welcomed that accomplishment, requested that the Commission be reconvened in 2001 to continue its mandate and called on all States to sign, ratify or accede to the 1998 Rome Statute of the International Criminal Court.

The International Law Commission kept under review topics suitable for the progressive development and codification of international law. The completed set of articles on nationality of natural persons in relation to the succession of States, which the Commission had presented in declaration form to the Assembly in 1999, could contribute to the future elaboration of a convention or other appropriate instrument, the Assembly acknowledged in 2000, and, in pursuit of that possibility, recommended its wide dissemination to Governments for their comments. The Assembly also established an ad hoc committee to further the Commission's work on jurisdictional immunities of States and their property.

In addition to existing anti-terrorist instruments, elaboration of the draft international convention for the suppression of acts of nuclear terrorism remained under consideration in the Ad Hoc Committee created by the Assembly for that purpose, and elaboration was begun in the Assembly's Sixth (Legal) Committee of a comprehensive convention on international terrorism. The Assembly condemned all terrorist acts as criminal and unjustifiable. The Security Council reiterated its own condemnation of such acts, irrespective of motive, as well as its readiness to take steps in accordance with the Charter of the United Nations to counter terrorist threats to international peace and security.

Following its consideration of information transmitted by several States through the Secretary-General on acts of violence against their diplomatic and consular missions and rep-

resentatives, the Assembly condemned such acts and urged their investigation and prevention, as well as enhancement of the protection and security of those missions.

Establishment of the International Criminal Court

Throughout 2000, the Rome Statute of the International Criminal Court, which in 1998 [YUN 1998, p. 1209] established the Court as a permanent institution with the power to exercise jurisdiction over persons for the most serious crimes of international concern—genocide, crimes against humanity, war crimes and the crime of aggression—remained open for signature at United Nations Headquarters, New York.

The Statute would enter into force after 60 States had become parties to it. As at 31 December, 139 States had signed it and 27 had become parties.

Preparatory Commission

In accordance with General Assembly resolution 54/105 [YUN 1999, p. 1227], the Preparatory Commission for the International Criminal Court, established by the 1998 United Nations Diplomatic Conference of Plenipotentiaries on the Establishment of an International Criminal Court [YUN 1998, p. 1209], held three sessions in New York in 2000: its fourth (13-31 March), fifth (12-30 June) and sixth (27 November–8 December), during which it continued drafting the instruments essential for the Court's functioning.

In March, the Preparatory Commission, in addition to holding consultations on the crime of aggression, devoted its efforts to completing the elaboration of the rules of procedure and evidence, and of the elements of crimes.

In June, the Commission adopted its report covering its work from the first to the fifth sessions [PCNICC/2000/1], with addenda containing the finalized draft texts of those two instruments [PCNICC/2000/1/Add.1,2]. To ensure linguistic consistency among the various language versions, the Commission agreed to allow delegations to submit only linguistic corrections to the Secretariat no later than 15 October 2000 for incorporation in the texts. In addition, the Commission took note of an oral report by the coordinator for the crime of aggression. It established a working group for each of the next three agenda items: the relationship agreement between the Court and the United Nations, the financial regulations of the Court, and the agreement on privileges and immunities of the Court. To facilitate its work, the Commission asked the Secretariat to prepare, for advanced distribution, purely technical drafts including only standard provisions for those instruments.

The Commission began its November/December session by appointing a coordinator for each of the three new items and ended it, on 8 December, by taking note of the coordinators' oral reports, including that by the coordinator for the item on the crime of aggression. The Commission also decided that the working group on the Court's financial regulations should consider issues relating to the composition, tasks and format of the committee on budget and finance of the Assembly of States Parties; rules dealing with drafting the Assembly's budget; establishment of trust funds and other funds; and elaboration of criteria for receiving and utilizing voluntary contributions. It designated contact points for the items on the rules of procedure for the Assembly of States Parties—for which it also appointed a working group and a coordinator—and a budget for the first financial year; and on the basic principles governing a relationship agreement to be negotiated between the Court and the United Nations.

GENERAL ASSEMBLY ACTION

On 12 December [meeting 84], the General Assembly, on the recommendation of the Sixth (Legal) Committee [A/55/612], adopted **resolution 55/155** without vote [agenda item 162].

Establishment of the International Criminal Court

The General Assembly,

Recalling its resolutions 47/33 of 25 November 1992, 48/31 of 9 December 1993, 49/53 of 9 December 1994, 50/46 of 11 December 1995, 51/207 of 17 December 1996, 52/160 of 15 December 1997, 53/105 of 8 December 1998 and 54/105 of 9 December 1999,

Noting that the Rome Statute of the International Criminal Court was adopted on 17 July 1998 and is open for signature in New York at United Nations Headquarters until 31 December 2000, and taking note of the Final Act of the United Nations Diplomatic Conference of Plenipotentiaries on the Establishment of an International Criminal Court done at Rome on 17 July 1998,

Recalling the United Nations Millennium Declaration adopted at the Millennium Assembly, in which

heads of State and Government stressed the importance of the International Criminal Court,

Noting in particular that the Conference decided to establish a Preparatory Commission for the Court, and that the Commission held three sessions in 1999, from 16 to 26 February, 26 July to 13 August and 29 November to 17 December, and three sessions in 2000, from 13 to 31 March, 12 to 30 June and 27 November to 8 December,

Bearing in mind the mandate of the Preparatory Commission, as set out in resolution F adopted by the Conference, with regard to the preparation of proposals for practical arrangements for the establishment and coming into operation of the Court,

Recalling, with regard to future work of the Preparatory Commission and related working groups, the decision agreed upon by the Commission, referred to in paragraph 14 of the summary of the proceedings of its fifth session, to establish three new working groups, in addition to the working group on the crime of aggression,

Recognizing the continuing need for making available adequate resources and secretariat services to the Preparatory Commission in order to enable it to discharge its functions efficiently and expeditiously,

Emphasizing the need to make the necessary arrangements for the commencement of the functions of the International Criminal Court in order to ensure its effective operation,

Noting that a growing number of States have deposited their instruments of ratification and that a significant number of States have signed the Statute,

1. *Reiterates* the historic significance of the adoption of the Rome Statute of the International Criminal Court;

2. *Calls upon* all States to consider signing, ratifying or acceding to the Rome Statute of the International Criminal Court, as appropriate, and encourages efforts aimed at promoting awareness of the results of the United Nations Diplomatic Conference of Plenipotentiaries on the Establishment of an International Criminal Court and of the provisions of the Statute;

3. *Welcomes* the important work accomplished by the Preparatory Commission in the completion of the part of the mandate relating to the draft texts of the rules of procedure and evidence and the elements of crimes, as required under resolution F, and notes in this respect the importance of the growing participation in the work of the working group on the crime of aggression;

4. *Requests* the Secretary-General to reconvene the Preparatory Commission, in accordance with resolution F, from 26 February to 9 March and from 24 September to 5 October 2001, to continue to carry out the mandate of that resolution and, in that connection, to discuss ways to enhance the effectiveness and acceptance of the Court;

5. *Also requests* the Secretary-General to make available to the Preparatory Commission secretariat services, including the preparation of working documents if so requested by the Commission, to enable it to perform its functions;

6. *Further requests* the Secretary-General to invite, as observers to the Preparatory Commission, representatives of organizations and other entities that have received a standing invitation from the General Assem-

bly, pursuant to its relevant resolutions, to participate in the capacity of observers in its sessions and work, and also to invite as observers to the Commission representatives of interested regional intergovernmental organizations and other interested international bodies, including the International Tribunal for the Former Yugoslavia and the International Tribunal for Rwanda;

7. *Notes* that non-governmental organizations may participate in the work of the Preparatory Commission by attending its plenary and its other open meetings, in accordance with the rules of procedure of the Commission, receiving copies of the official documents and making available their materials to delegates;

8. *Encourages* States to make voluntary contributions to the trust funds established pursuant to General Assembly resolutions 51/207 and 52/160, the mandates of which were expanded pursuant to Assembly resolution 53/105, towards meeting the costs of the participation in the work of the Preparatory Commission of the least developed countries and of those developing countries not covered by the trust fund established pursuant to resolution 51/207;

9. *Requests* the Secretary-General to report to the General Assembly at its fifty-sixth session on the implementation of the present resolution;

10. *Decides* to include in the provisional agenda of its fifty-sixth session the item entitled "Establishment of the International Criminal Court".

International Law Commission

The International Law Commission (ILC) held its fifty-second session in Geneva from 1 May to 9 June and from 10 July to 18 August. The thirty-sixth session of the International Law Seminar (10-28 July) was held during the session. It was attended by 24 participants, mostly from developing countries, who observed Commission meetings, attended specially arranged lectures and participated in working groups on specific topics.

At its session, ILC continued to consider the Special Rapporteurs' reports on proposals relating to draft articles or draft guidelines for the formulation of instruments on State responsibility, international liability for injurious consequences arising out of acts not prohibited by international law (prevention of transboundary damage from hazardous activities), unilateral acts of States, diplomatic protection and reservations to treaties (see below for details under those topics). It was assisted by working groups and a Drafting Committee. Draft articles proposed by the Special Rapporteurs assigned to report on those topics were reproduced in ILC's report on the work of its 2000 session [A/55/10].

In furtherance of cooperation with other bodies concerned with international law, ILC continued traditional information exchanges with the Inter-American Juridical Committee, the Asian-African Legal Consultative Committee, the European Committee on Legal Cooperation, the Committee of Legal Advisers on Public International Law of the Council of Europe, the International Court of Justice and the International Committee of the Red Cross (ICRC).

As called for by Assembly resolution 54/111 [YUN 1999, p. 1229], ILC took measures to enhance its efficiency and productivity. On the basis of agreed criteria for the selection of topics for inclusion in its long-term programme of work, it adopted the Planning Group's report listing the following items for inclusion, together with the corresponding syllabuses describing their possible contents: responsibility of international organizations, effects of armed conflict on treaties, shared natural resources of States, expulsion of aliens, and risk ensuing from fragmentation of international law. To facilitate membership attendance, it decided to split each session of its next five-year mandate (2002-2006) into two half sessions of equal duration. In principle, ILC would continue to meet in Geneva; to enhance its relationship with the Sixth Committee, however, one or two half sessions could be held in New York towards the middle of the mandate period. Unless significant reasons required otherwise, the length of sessions in the initial years of its mandate should be 10 weeks and 12 in the final years.

ILC decided that its next session, the last of the current mandate, would be a 12-week split session, at the United Nations Office at Geneva, from 23 April to 1 June and from 2 July to 10 August 2001.

GENERAL ASSEMBLY ACTION

On 12 December [meeting 84], the General Assembly, on the recommendation of the Sixth Committee [A/55/609], adopted **resolution 55/152** without vote [agenda item 159].

Report of the International Law Commission on the work of its fifty-second session

The General Assembly,

Having considered the report of the International Law Commission on the work of its fifty-second session,

Emphasizing the importance of furthering the codification and progressive development of international law as a means of implementing the purposes and principles set forth in the Charter of the United Nations and in the Declaration on Principles of International Law concerning Friendly Relations and Cooperation among States in accordance with the Charter of the United Nations,

Recognizing the desirability of referring legal and drafting questions to the Sixth Committee, including topics that might be submitted to the International Law Commission for closer examination, and of enabling the Sixth Committee and the Commission to further enhance their contribution to the progressive development of international law and its codification,

Recalling the need to keep under review those topics of international law which, given their new or renewed interest for the international community, may be suitable for the progressive development and codification of international law and therefore may be included in the future programme of work of the International Law Commission,

Welcoming the holding of the International Law Seminar, and noting with appreciation the voluntary contributions made to the United Nations Trust Fund for the International Law Seminar,

Stressing the usefulness of structuring the debate on the report of the International Law Commission in the Sixth Committee in such a manner that conditions are provided for concentrated attention to each of the main topics dealt with in the report,

Wishing to enhance further the interaction between the Sixth Committee as a body of governmental representatives and the International Law Commission as a body of independent legal experts, with a view to improving the dialogue between the two organs,

1. *Takes note* of the report of the International Law Commission on the work of its fifty-second session;

2. *Expresses its appreciation* to the International Law Commission for the work accomplished at its fifty-second session, in particular with respect to the topic "State responsibility", and encourages the Commission to complete its work on this topic during its fifty-third session, taking into account the views expressed by Governments during the debates in the Sixth Committee at the fifty-fifth session of the General Assembly, and any written comments that may be submitted by 31 January 2001;

3. *Draws the attention* of Governments to the importance for the International Law Commission of having their views on the various aspects involved in the topics on the agenda of the Commission, in particular on all the specific issues identified in chapter III of its report;

4. *Reiterates its invitation* to Governments, within the context of paragraph 3 above, to respond, to the extent possible, in writing by 28 February 2001 to the questionnaire and requests for materials on unilateral acts of States circulated by the Secretariat to all Governments on 30 September 1999 and 2 October 2000;

5. *Also reiterates its invitation* to Governments to submit the most relevant national legislation, decisions of domestic courts and State practice relevant to diplomatic protection in order to assist the International Law Commission in its work on the topic "Diplomatic protection";

6. *Recommends* that, taking into account the comments and observations of Governments, whether in writing or expressed orally in debates in the General Assembly, the International Law Commission continue its work on the topics in its current programme;

7. *Notes with appreciation* the work done by the International Law Commission at its fifty-second session on the topic "International liability for injurious consequences arising out of acts not prohibited by international law", and requests the Commission to resume consideration of the liability aspects of the topic as soon as the second reading of the draft articles on the prevention of transboundary damage from hazardous activities is completed, bearing in mind the interrelationship between the prevention and the liability aspects of the topic and taking into account developments in international law and comments by Governments;

8. *Takes note* of paragraphs 726 to 733 of the report of the International Law Commission with regard to its long-term programme of work, and the syllabuses on new topics annexed to the report;

9. *Invites* the International Law Commission to continue taking measures to enhance its efficiency and productivity;

10. *Takes note* of paragraphs 734 and 735 of the report with regard to the length, nature and place of future sessions of the International Law Commission, in which specific recommendations are made to continue to increase the efficiency and productivity of its work, to facilitate the attendance by its members and to enhance the relationship between the Commission and the Sixth Committee;

11. *Also takes note* of paragraph 736 of the report, and decides that the next session of the International Law Commission shall be held at the United Nations Office at Geneva from 23 April to 1 June and from 2 July to 10 August 2001;

12. *Stresses* the desirability of further enhancing the dialogue between the International Law Commission and the Sixth Committee, and in this context encourages, inter alia, the holding of informal discussions between the members of the Sixth Committee and those members of the Commission attending the fifty-sixth session of the General Assembly;

13. *Reiterates* its request in paragraph 11 of its resolution 54/111 of 9 December 1999, and emphasizes the need to implement cost-saving measures such as those described in paragraph 639 of the report of the International Law Commission on the work of its fifty-first session;

14. *Requests* the International Law Commission to continue to pay special attention to indicating in its annual report, for each topic, any specific issues on which expressions of views by Governments, either in the Sixth Committee or in written form, would be of particular interest in providing effective guidance for the Commission in its further work;

15. *Also requests* the International Law Commission to continue the implementation of article 16, paragraph *(e)*, and article 26, paragraphs 1 and 2, of its statute in order to further strengthen cooperation between the Commission and other bodies concerned with international law, having in mind the usefulness of such cooperation, and in that regard takes note with appreciation of comments made by the Commission in paragraphs 737 to 741 of its report;

16. *Notes* that consulting with national organizations and individual experts concerned with international law may assist Governments in considering whether to make comments and observations on drafts submitted by the International Law Commission and in formulating their comments and observations;

17. *Reaffirms* its previous decisions concerning the role of the Codification Division of the Office of Legal Affairs of the Secretariat and those concerning the summary records and other documentation of the International Law Commission;

18. *Notes with appreciation* the inclusion of information about the work of the International Law Commission on its web site;

19. *Expresses the hope* that the International Law Seminar will continue to be held in connection with the sessions of the International Law Commission and that an increasing number of participants, in particular from developing countries, will be given the opportunity to attend the Seminar, and appeals to States to continue to make urgently needed voluntary contributions to the United Nations Trust Fund for the International Law Seminar;

20. *Requests* the Secretary-General to provide the International Law Seminar with adequate services, including interpretation, as required, and encourages him to continue considering ways to improve the structure and content of the Seminar;

21. *Also requests* the Secretary-General to forward to the International Law Commission, for its attention, the records of the debate on the report of the Commission at the fifty-fifth session of the General Assembly, together with such written statements as delegations may circulate in conjunction with their oral statements, and to prepare and distribute a topical summary of the debate, following established practice;

22. *Requests* the Secretariat to circulate to States, as soon as possible after the conclusion of the session of the International Law Commission, chapter II of its report containing a summary of the work of that session and the draft articles adopted on either first or second reading by the Commission;

23. *Recommends* that the debate on the report of the International Law Commission at the fifty-sixth session of the General Assembly commence on 29 October 2001.

State succession

Pursuant to General Assembly resolution 54/112 [YUN 1999, p. 1230], the item "Nationality of natural persons in relation to the succession of States" was included in the agenda of the Assembly's fifty-fifth (2000) session to allow consideration of the final draft preamble and draft articles on that subject, which ILC had recommended for the Assembly's adoption in the form of a declaration in 1999 [ibid.].

GENERAL ASSEMBLY ACTION

On 12 December [meeting 84], the General Assembly, on the recommendation of the Sixth Committee [A/55/610], adopted **resolution 55/153** without vote [agenda item 160].

Nationality of natural persons in relation to the succession of States

The General Assembly,

Having considered chapter IV of the report of the International Law Commission on the work of its fifty-first session, which contains final draft articles on nationality of natural persons in relation to the succession of States,

Noting that the International Law Commission decided to recommend the draft articles to the General Assembly for their adoption in the form of a declaration,

Recalling its resolution 54/112 of 9 December 1999, in which it decided to consider at its fifty-fifth session the draft articles on nationality of natural persons in relation to the succession of States with a view to their adoption as a declaration,

Considering that the work of the International Law Commission on nationality of natural persons in relation to the succession of States would provide a useful guide for practice in dealing with this issue,

Acknowledging that the work of the International Law Commission on this topic could contribute to the elaboration of a convention or other appropriate instrument in the future, and reiterating its invitation, contained in its resolution 54/112, for Governments to submit comments and observations on the question of a convention on nationality of natural persons in relation to the succession of States,

1. *Expresses its appreciation* to the International Law Commission for its valuable work on nationality of natural persons in relation to the succession of States;

2. *Takes note* of the articles on nationality of natural persons in relation to the succession of States, presented by the International Law Commission in the form of a declaration, the text of which is annexed to the present resolution;

3. *Invites* Governments to take into account, as appropriate, the provisions contained in the articles in dealing with issues of nationality of natural persons in relation to the succession of States;

4. *Recommends* that all efforts be made for the wide dissemination of the text of the articles;

5. *Decides* to include in the provisional agenda of its fifty-ninth session an item entitled "Nationality of natural persons in relation to the succession of States".

ANNEX
Nationality of natural persons in relation to the succession of States

Preamble

Considering that problems of nationality arising from succession of States concern the international community,

Emphasizing that nationality is essentially governed by internal law within the limits set by international law,

Recognizing that in matters concerning nationality, due account should be taken both of the legitimate interests of States and those of individuals,

Recalling that the Universal Declaration of Human Rights of 1948 proclaimed the right of every person to a nationality,

Recalling also that the International Covenant on Civil and Political Rights of 1966 and the Convention on the Rights of the Child of 1989 recognize the right of every child to acquire a nationality,

Emphasizing that the human rights and fundamental freedoms of persons whose nationality may be affected by a succession of States must be fully respected,

Bearing in mind the provisions of the Convention on the Reduction of Statelessness of 1961, the Vienna Convention on Succession of States in Respect of Treaties of 1978 and the Vienna Convention on Succession of States in Respect of State Property, Archives and Debts of 1983,

Convinced of the need for the codification and progressive development of the rules of international law concerning nationality in relation to the succession of

States as a means for ensuring greater juridical security for States and for individuals,

Part I. General provisions

Article 1
Right to a nationality

Every individual who, on the date of the succession of States, had the nationality of the predecessor State, irrespective of the mode of acquisition of that nationality, has the right to the nationality of at least one of the States concerned, in accordance with the present articles.

Article 2
Use of terms

For the purposes of the present articles:

(a) "Succession of States" means the replacement of one State by another in the responsibility for the international relations of territory;

(b) "Predecessor State" means the State which has been replaced by another State on the occurrence of a succession of States;

(c) "Successor State" means the State which has replaced another State on the occurrence of a succession of States;

(d) "State concerned" means the predecessor State or the successor State, as the case may be;

(e) "Third State" means any State other than the predecessor State or the successor State;

(f) "Person concerned" means every individual who, on the date of the succession of States, had the nationality of the predecessor State and whose nationality may be affected by such succession;

(g) "Date of the succession of States" means the date upon which the successor State replaced the predecessor State in the responsibility for the international relations of the territory to which the succession of States relates.

Article 3
Cases of succession of States covered by the present articles

The present articles apply only to the effects of a succession of States occurring in conformity with international law and, in particular, with the principles of international law embodied in the Charter of the United Nations.

Article 4
Prevention of statelessness

States concerned shall take all appropriate measures to prevent persons who, on the date of the succession of States, had the nationality of the predecessor State from becoming stateless as a result of such succession.

Article 5
Presumption of nationality

Subject to the provisions of the present articles, persons concerned having their habitual residence in the territory affected by the succession of States are presumed to acquire the nationality of the successor State on the date of such succession.

Article 6
Legislation on nationality and other connected issues

Each State concerned should, without undue delay, enact legislation on nationality and other connected issues arising in relation to the succession of States consistent with the provisions of the present articles. It should take all appropriate measures to ensure that persons concerned will be apprised, within a reasonable time period, of the effect of its legislation on their nationality, of any choices they may have thereunder, as well as of the consequences that the exercise of such choices will have on their status.

Article 7
Effective date

The attribution of nationality in relation to the succession of States, as well as the acquisition of nationality following the exercise of an option, shall take effect on the date of such succession, if persons concerned would otherwise be stateless during the period between the date of the succession of States and such attribution or acquisition of nationality.

Article 8
Persons concerned having their habitual residence in another State

1. A successor State does not have the obligation to attribute its nationality to persons concerned who have their habitual residence in another State and also have the nationality of that or any other State.

2. A successor State shall not attribute its nationality to persons concerned who have their habitual residence in another State against the will of the persons concerned unless they would otherwise become stateless.

Article 9
Renunciation of the nationality of another State as a condition for attribution of nationality

When a person concerned who is qualified to acquire the nationality of a successor State has the nationality of another State concerned, the former State may make the attribution of its nationality dependent on the renunciation by such person of the nationality of the latter State. However, such requirement shall not be applied in a manner which would result in rendering the person concerned stateless, even if only temporarily.

Article 10
Loss of nationality upon the voluntary acquisition of the nationality of another State

1. A predecessor State may provide that persons concerned who, in relation to the succession of States, voluntarily acquire the nationality of a successor State shall lose its nationality.

2. A successor State may provide that persons concerned who, in relation to the succession of States, voluntarily acquire the nationality of another successor State or, as the case may be, retain the nationality of the predecessor State shall lose its nationality acquired in relation to such succession.

Article 11
Respect for the will of persons concerned

1. States concerned shall give consideration to the will of persons concerned whenever those persons are qualified to acquire the nationality of two or more States concerned.

2. Each State concerned shall grant a right to opt for its nationality to persons concerned who have appropriate connection with that State if those persons would otherwise become stateless as a result of the succession of States.

3. When persons entitled to the right of option have exercised such right, the State whose nationality they have opted for shall attribute its nationality to such persons.

4. When persons entitled to the right of option have exercised such right, the State whose nationality they have renounced shall withdraw its nationality from such persons, unless they would thereby become stateless.

5. States concerned should provide a reasonable time limit for the exercise of the right of option.

Article 12
Unity of a family

Where the acquisition or loss of nationality in relation to the succession of States would impair the unity of a family, States concerned shall take all appropriate measures to allow that family to remain together or to be reunited.

Article 13
Child born after the succession of States

A child of a person concerned, born after the date of the succession of States, who has not acquired any nationality, has the right to the nationality of the State concerned on whose territory that child was born.

Article 14
Status of habitual residents

1. The status of persons concerned as habitual residents shall not be affected by the succession of States.

2. A State concerned shall take all necessary measures to allow persons concerned who, because of events connected with the succession of States, were forced to leave their habitual residence on its territory to return thereto.

Article 15
Non-discrimination

States concerned shall not deny persons concerned the right to retain or acquire a nationality or the right of option upon the succession of States by discriminating on any ground.

Article 16
Prohibition of arbitrary decisions concerning nationality issues

Persons concerned shall not be arbitrarily deprived of the nationality of the predecessor State, or arbitrarily denied the right to acquire the nationality of the successor State or any right of option, to which they are entitled in relation to the succession of States.

Article 17
Procedures relating to nationality issues

Applications relating to the acquisition, retention or renunciation of nationality or to the exercise of the right of option, in relation to the succession of States, shall be processed without undue delay. Relevant decisions shall be issued in writing and shall be open to effective administrative or judicial review.

Article 18
Exchange of information, consultation and negotiation

1. States concerned shall exchange information and consult in order to identify any detrimental effects on persons concerned with respect to their nationality and other connected issues regarding their status as a result of the succession of States.

2. States concerned shall, when necessary, seek a solution to eliminate or mitigate such detrimental effects by negotiation and, as appropriate, through agreement.

Article 19
Other States

1. Nothing in the present articles requires States to treat persons concerned having no effective link with a State concerned as nationals of that State, unless this would result in treating those persons as if they were stateless.

2. Nothing in the present articles precludes States from treating persons concerned, who have become stateless as a result of the succession of States, as nationals of the State concerned whose nationality they would be entitled to acquire or retain, if such treatment is beneficial to those persons.

Part II. Provisions relating to specific categories of succession of States

Section 1. Transfer of part of the territory

Article 20
Attribution of the nationality of the successor State and withdrawal of the nationality of the predecessor State

When part of the territory of a State is transferred by that State to another State, the successor State shall attribute its nationality to the persons concerned who have their habitual residence in the transferred territory and the predecessor State shall withdraw its nationality from such persons, unless otherwise indicated by the exercise of the right of option which such persons shall be granted. The predecessor State shall not, however, withdraw its nationality before such persons acquire the nationality of the successor State.

Section 2. Unification of States

Article 21
Attribution of the nationality of the successor State

Subject to the provisions of article 8, when two or more States unite and so form one successor State, irrespective of whether the successor State is a new State or whether its personality is identical to that of one of the States which have united, the successor State shall attribute its nationality to all persons who, on the date of the succession of States, had the nationality of a predecessor State.

Section 3. Dissolution of a State

Article 22
Attribution of the nationality of the successor States

When a State dissolves and ceases to exist and the various parts of the territory of the predecessor State form two or more successor States, each successor State shall, unless otherwise indicated by the exercise of a right of option, attribute its nationality to:

(a) Persons concerned having their habitual residence in its territory; and

(b) Subject to the provisions of article 8:

(i) Persons concerned not covered by subparagraph (a) having an appropriate legal connection with a constituent unit of the predecessor State that has become part of that successor State;

(ii) Persons concerned not entitled to a nationality of any State concerned under subparagraphs *(a)* and *(b)* (i) having their habitual residence in a third State, who were born in or, before leaving the predecessor State, had their last habitual residence in what has become the territory of that successor State or having any other appropriate connection with that successor State.

Article 23
Granting of the right of option by the successor States

1. Successor States shall grant a right of option to persons concerned covered by the provisions of article 22 who are qualified to acquire the nationality of two or more successor States.

2. Each successor State shall grant a right to opt for its nationality to persons concerned who are not covered by the provisions of article 22.

Section 4. Separation of part or parts of the territory

Article 24
Attribution of the nationality of the successor State

When part or parts of the territory of a State separate from that State and form one or more successor States while the predecessor State continues to exist, a successor State shall, unless otherwise indicated by the exercise of a right of option, attribute its nationality to:

(a) Persons concerned having their habitual residence in its territory; and

(b) Subject to the provisions of article 8:

(i) Persons concerned not covered by subparagraph *(a)* having an appropriate legal connection with a constituent unit of the predecessor State that has become part of that successor State;

(ii) Persons concerned not entitled to a nationality of any State concerned under subparagraphs *(a)* and *(b)* (i) having their habitual residence in a third State, who were born in or, before leaving the predecessor State, had their last habitual residence in what has become the territory of that successor State or having any other appropriate connection with that successor State.

Article 25
Withdrawal of the nationality of the predecessor State

1. The predecessor State shall withdraw its nationality from persons concerned qualified to acquire the nationality of the successor State in accordance with article 24. It shall not, however, withdraw its nationality before such persons acquire the nationality of the successor State.

2. Unless otherwise indicated by the exercise of a right of option, the predecessor State shall not, however, withdraw its nationality from persons referred to in paragraph 1 who:

(a) Have their habitual residence in its territory;

(b) Are not covered by subparagraph *(a)* and have an appropriate legal connection with a constituent unit of the predecessor State that has remained part of the predecessor State;

(c) Have their habitual residence in a third State, and were born in or, before leaving the predecessor State, had their last habitual residence in what has remained part of the territory of the predecessor State or have any other appropriate connection with that State.

Article 26
Granting of the right of option by the predecessor and the successor States

Predecessor and successor States shall grant a right of option to all persons concerned covered by the provisions of article 24 and paragraph 2 of article 25 who are qualified to have the nationality of both the predecessor and successor States or of two or more successor States.

State responsibility

ILC, at its 2000 session [A/55/10], considered the comments and observations received from Governments on the draft articles on State responsibility provisionally adopted on first reading [YUN 1996, p. 1207] and the third report of the Special Rapporteur, James Crawford (Australia). That report continued the task, begun in 1998 [YUN 1998, p. 1213], of considering the draft articles in the light of comments by Governments and developments in State practice, judicial decisions and literature. It contained the Special Rapporteur's proposals for Part Two, Part Two bis and Part Four of the draft articles dealing, respectively, with the legal consequences of an internationally wrongful act of a State, the implementation of State responsibility and general provisions, with the recommendation that the Drafting Committee produce a complete text of the draft articles by the end of the session. He further recommended that Part Three, dealing with dispute settlement, be considered in general terms after adoption of the entire draft, since to include dispute settlement provisions would be pointless unless the draft was submitted to the General Assembly in the form of a convention.

ILC referred to the Drafting Committee the draft articles contained in: chapters I, II and III of Part Two, on general principles, forms of reparation and serious breaches of obligations to the international community as a whole, together with two footnote texts pertaining to chapter III; chapters I and II of Part Two bis, on invocation of the responsibility of a State and countermeasures; and Part Four. Having completed consideration of those chapters, the Drafting Committee provisionally adopted the entire set of draft articles. ILC took note of the Committee's report and requested transmittal of the provisionally adopted texts to Governments for their comments and observations, with a view to completing the second reading at its 2001 session.

International liability

In accordance with its 1999 decision to defer consideration of the question of international liability for injurious consequences arising out of acts not prohibited by international law [YUN 1999, p. 1231], ILC, at its 2000 session [A/55/10], proceeded to consider the sub-topic of the prevention of transboundary damage from hazardous activities. It heard the oral report of the working group assigned to examine the comments and observations received from five Governments on the set of 17 draft articles on the sub-topic, adopted on first reading in 1998 [YUN 1998, p. 1214]. On the basis of the working group's discussion, the Special Rapporteur, Pemmaraju Sreenivasa Rao (India), presented his third report containing a draft preamble and a revised set of draft articles on prevention, along with the recommendation that they be adopted as a framework convention. It addressed questions such as the scope of the topic, its relationship with liability, the relationship between an equitable balance of interests among States concerned and the duty of prevention, as well as the duality of the regimes of liability and State responsibility. ILC referred the draft preamble and articles to the Drafting Committee.

Unilateral acts of States

ILC, at its 2000 session [A/55/10], examined the third report on unilateral acts of States by Special Rapporteur Victor Rodríguez Cedeño (Venezuela), who, in preparing his report, took into account the comments made in the working group on the subject. He proposed new draft articles as follows: 1, on the definition of unilateral acts, to supersede the previous draft article 1 on the scope of draft articles; 2, on the capacity of States to formulate unilateral acts; 3, on persons authorized to formulate unilateral acts on behalf of the State; 4, on subsequent confirmation of an act formulated by a person not authorized for that purpose; and 5, on the invalidity of unilateral acts. He also proposed deletion of previous draft article 6, on expression of consent, and examined the question of silence and unilateral acts. ILC decided to refer new draft articles 1 to 4 to the Drafting Committee and new draft article 5 to the working group.

In addition, ILC had before it the Secretary-General's report containing the replies received from Governments to the questionnaire circulated by the Secretariat pursuant to General Assembly resolution 54/111 [YUN 1999, p. 1229] on their practice in respect of unilateral acts of States and their position on certain aspects of ILC's study of the topic. As only 12 States had replied, ILC agreed that the Secretariat should renew its appeal to Governments to respond to the questionnaire.

International State relations and international law

Jurisdictional immunities of States and their property

In accordance with General Assembly resolution 54/101 [YUN 1999, p. 1232], the open-ended working group of the Sixth Committee established under resolution 53/98 [YUN 1998, p. 1215] met in 2000 (New York, 6-10 November) to continue its work on the future form of the 1991 draft articles adopted by ILC on jurisdictional immunities of States and their property [YUN 1991, p. 829]. Among the documents before it were the 1991 draft articles, the related 1999 ILC report annexing its working group's report on the topic [YUN 1999, p. 1232], and comments submitted by Governments at the Assembly's invitation since 1992 [YUN 1992, p. 992], including those received from four Governments in 2000 [A/55/298].

The working group took up the outstanding substantive issues it had previously identified, namely: concept of a State for purposes of immunity; criteria for determining the commercial character of a contract or transaction; concept of a State enterprise or other entity in relation to commercial transactions; contracts of employment; and measures of constraint against State property. Discussions were based on an informal working paper containing a proposed text and alternative proposed texts for each of those issues. The working group Chairman issued his report on the group's deliberations in November [A/C.6/55/L.12], containing the revised draft article texts resulting from the exchange of views on the issues, suggestions for convening a more formal body to work towards a final document on the topic, as well as texts on the basic concepts and alternative articles that could serve as a basis for further discussions.

The Chairman also reported orally on the work accomplished by the group before the Sixth Committee during its consideration (15-16 November) of the Assembly's agenda item "Convention on jurisdictional immunities of States and their property".

GENERAL ASSEMBLY ACTION

On 12 December [meeting 84], the General Assembly, on the recommendation of the Sixth Committee [A/55/607], adopted **resolution 55/150** without vote [agenda item 157].

Convention on jurisdictional immunities of States and their property

The General Assembly,

Recalling its resolution 54/101 of 9 December 1999,

Having considered the report of the Working Group on Jurisdictional Immunities of States and Their Property of the International Law Commission, set forth in the annex to the report of the Commission on the work of its fifty-first session,

Having considered also the reports presented to the Sixth Committee by the Chairman of the open-ended working group of the Committee established under resolutions 53/98 of 8 December 1998 and 54/101,

Having considered further the report of the Secretary-General,

1. *Takes note with appreciation* of the report of the Working Group on Jurisdictional Immunities of States and Their Property of the International Law Commission, set forth in the annex to the report of the Commission on the work of its fifty-first session;

2. *Urges* States, if they have not yet done so, to submit their comments to the Secretary-General in accordance with General Assembly resolution 49/61 of 9 December 1994, and also invites States to submit in writing to the Secretary-General, by 1 August 2001, their comments on the reports of the open-ended working group of the Sixth Committee established under resolutions 53/98 and 54/101;

3. *Decides* to establish an Ad Hoc Committee on Jurisdictional Immunities of States and Their Property, open also to participation by States members of the specialized agencies, to further the work done, consolidate areas of agreement and resolve outstanding issues with a view to elaborating a generally acceptable instrument based on the draft articles on jurisdictional immunities of States and their property adopted by the International Law Commission at its forty-third session, and also on the discussions of the open-ended working group of the Sixth Committee and their results;

4. *Decides* that the Ad Hoc Committee shall meet for two weeks in March 2002;

5. *Also decides* to include in the provisional agenda of its fifty-sixth session the item entitled "Convention on jurisdictional immunities of States and their property".

International terrorism

Convention for suppression of nuclear terrorism

As decided by General Assembly resolution 54/110 [YUN 1999, p. 1238], the Ad Hoc Committee established by resolution 51/210 [YUN 1996, p. 1208] convened for its fourth session (New York, 14-18 February) [A/55/37] to continue to elaborate a draft international convention for the suppression of acts of nuclear terrorism and to address the question of convening a high-level conference under UN auspices to formulate a joint organized response of the international community to terrorism in all its forms and manifestations.

For the first item, the Committee had before it the 1998 revised draft text of the instrument [YUN 1998, p. 1216], as proposed by the Friends of the Chairman (composed of members of the Committee's Bureau). The coordinator of the consul-

tations on the draft, who had conducted intersessional bilateral consultations on the remaining issues relating to the scope of the convention, felt that, since the delegations' positions were not sufficiently close, it was not yet time to convene open-ended informal consultations to reach agreement on a text. Several delegations supported holding a high-level conference under UN auspices as described, which could focus on strengthening the existing framework of international cooperation and on preventive measures. Doubt was expressed, however, as to the practical benefits of such a conference. Alternate forums were suggested, such as a special Assembly session, or part of an Assembly session set aside for the purpose and attended at a high level, for which the Ad Hoc Committee could serve as the preparatory committee.

While the question of the elaboration of a comprehensive international convention on international terrorism was not before the Committee for consideration, it was pointed out that work on that instrument would be facilitated by the early completion of the Committee's current two agenda items. Meanwhile, a revised text of the proposed draft convention had been informally circulated by India for delegations' comments.

Measures to eliminate terrorism

Report of Secretary-General. In a July report with later addendum [A/55/179 & Add.1], prepared in response to General Assembly resolution 50/53 [YUN 1995, p. 1330], the Secretary-General described measures to eliminate international terrorism. The report contained information received on measures taken at the national and international levels by 24 States and eight international organizations and UN agencies and bodies in implementation of the 1994 Declaration on Measures to Eliminate International Terrorism, approved by resolution 49/60 [YUN 1994, p. 1294]. It listed 19 international instruments pertaining to terrorism, indicating the status of State participation in each. It provided information on workshops and training courses on combating crimes connected with international terrorism; texts of laws and regulations to prevent and suppress terrorism; and progress in the publication of a compendium of such texts.

Working group report. A working group of the Sixth Committee convened (New York, 25 September–6 October) to begin work on the elaboration of a comprehensive convention on international terrorism within a comprehensive legal framework of relevant conventions, in accordance with the Assembly's decision in resolution 54/110 [YUN 1999, p. 1238]. Documents before the group included the 1998 revised text of the draft convention on the suppression of acts of nuclear terrorism, together with the Ad Hoc Committee's report on its 2000 session [A/55/37]; and the revised version of the working document entitled "Draft comprehensive convention on international terrorism" [A/C.6/55/1] submitted by India.

The group conducted a first reading of the preamble and articles 1 to 22 of the draft convention. Discussions of those texts led to oral and written amendments and further revisions of some of the draft articles, subsequently annexed to the group's report to the Sixth Committee [A/C.6/55/L.2]. The group recommended continuation of its work on the draft comprehensive convention and of the coordinator's consultations on the draft international convention for the suppression of acts of nuclear terrorism.

Communications. Submitted to the Sixth Committee were a number of communications circulated to the General Assembly and the Security Council by individual or groups of Member States drawing attention to, among other matters: the conflict in Afghanistan that had turned that country into a training ground for various terrorist groups [A/55/86-S/2000/604]; the 5 July Dushanbe Declaration confirming the parties' resolve jointly to combat international terrorism and to conduct training in methods of combating terrorism [A/55/133-S/2000/682]; the renewed commitment of the G-8 group of countries to fight all forms of terrorism, including hostage-taking [A/55/162-S/2000/715]; the fact that terrorism and banditry in Central Asia and Chechnya (Russia), and the political and military confrontation in Afghanistan were links in the same chain [A/55/326-S/2000/834]; inclusion of the question of creating an international anti-terrorism centre in the joint programme of action of the group of States comprising Azerbaijan, Georgia, the Republic of Moldova, Ukraine and Uzbekistan [A/55/434-S/2000/926]; the 3 October Declaration on Strategic Partnership between India and the Russian Federation, whereby the parties agreed to cooperate in the fight against terrorism [A/55/473 & Corr.1]; the 11 October Bishkek Statement urging the expeditious settlement of the Afghan conflict, the main source of instability in the Central Asian region [A/55/533-S/2000/1054]; the 18 September communiqué of the Organization of the Islamic Conference circulated under various Assembly agenda items, among them measures to eliminate international terrorism [A/55/541-S/2000/1067]; and two separate terrorist attacks in Jerusalem and near Kfar Darom, south of Gaza [A/55/540-S/2000/1065, A/55/634-S/2000/1108].

GENERAL ASSEMBLY ACTION

On 12 December [meeting 84], the General Assembly, on the recommendation of the Sixth Committee [A/55/614], adopted **resolution 55/158** by recorded vote (151-0-2) [agenda item 164].

Measures to eliminate international terrorism

The General Assembly,

Guided by the purposes and principles of the Charter of the United Nations,

Recalling all General Assembly and Security Council resolutions on measures to eliminate international terrorism,

Convinced of the importance of the consideration of measures to eliminate international terrorism by the General Assembly as the universal organ having competence to do so,

Recalling the Declaration on the Occasion of the Fiftieth Anniversary of the United Nations,

Recalling also the United Nations Millennium Declaration,

Deeply disturbed by the persistence of terrorist acts, which have been carried out worldwide,

Stressing the need to strengthen further international cooperation between States and between international organizations and agencies, regional organizations and arrangements and the United Nations in order to prevent, combat and eliminate terrorism in all its forms and manifestations, wherever and by whomsoever committed, in accordance with the principles of the Charter, international law and relevant international conventions,

Mindful of the need to enhance the role of the United Nations and the relevant specialized agencies in combating international terrorism, and of the proposals of the Secretary-General to enhance the role of the Organization in this respect,

Recalling the Declaration on Measures to Eliminate International Terrorism, contained in the annex to resolution 49/60 of 9 December 1994, wherein the General Assembly encouraged States to review urgently the scope of the existing international legal provisions on the prevention, repression and elimination of terrorism in all its forms and manifestations, with the aim of ensuring that there was a comprehensive legal framework covering all aspects of the matter,

Taking note of the final document of the Thirteenth Ministerial Conference of the Movement of Non-Aligned Countries, held at Cartagena, Colombia, on 8 and 9 April 2000, which reiterated the collective position of the Movement of Non-Aligned Countries on terrorism and reaffirmed the previous initiative of the Twelfth Conference of Heads of State or Government of Non-Aligned Countries, held at Durban, South Africa, from 29 August to 3 September 1998, calling for an international summit conference under the auspices of the United Nations to formulate a joint organized response of the international community to terrorism in all its forms and manifestations, and other relevant initiatives,

Recalling its decision in resolution 54/110 of 9 December 1999 that the Ad Hoc Committee established by General Assembly resolution 51/210 of 17 December 1996 should address the question of convening a high-level conference under the auspices of the United Nations to formulate a joint organized response of the international community to terrorism in all its forms and manifestations,

Noting regional efforts to prevent, combat and eliminate terrorism in all its forms and manifestations, wherever and by whomsoever committed, including through the elaboration of and adherence to regional conventions,

Having examined the report of the Secretary-General, the report of the Ad Hoc Committee and the report of the Working Group of the Sixth Committee established pursuant to resolution 54/110,

1. *Strongly condemns* all acts, methods and practices of terrorism as criminal and unjustifiable, wherever and by whomsoever committed;

2. *Reiterates* that criminal acts intended or calculated to provoke a state of terror in the general public, a group of persons or particular persons for political purposes are in any circumstances unjustifiable, whatever the considerations of a political, philosophical, ideological, racial, ethnic, religious or other nature that may be invoked to justify them;

3. *Reiterates its call* upon all States to adopt further measures in accordance with the Charter of the United Nations and the relevant provisions of international law, including international standards of human rights, to prevent terrorism and to strengthen international cooperation in combating terrorism and, to that end, to consider in particular the implementation of the measures set out in paragraphs 3 *(a)* to *(f)* of resolution 51/210;

4. *Also reiterates its call* upon all States, with the aim of enhancing the efficient implementation of relevant legal instruments, to intensify, as and where appropriate, the exchange of information on facts related to terrorism and, in so doing, to avoid the dissemination of inaccurate or unverified information;

5. *Reiterates its call* upon States to refrain from financing, encouraging, providing training for or otherwise supporting terrorist activities;

6. *Reaffirms* that international cooperation as well as actions by States to combat terrorism should be conducted in conformity with the principles of the Charter, international law and relevant international conventions;

7. *Urges* all States that have not yet done so to consider, as a matter of priority, becoming parties to relevant conventions and protocols as referred to in paragraph 6 of resolution 51/210, as well as the International Convention for the Suppression of Terrorist Bombings, and the International Convention for the Suppression of the Financing of Terrorism, and calls upon all States to enact, as appropriate, domestic legislation necessary to implement the provisions of those conventions and protocols, to ensure that the jurisdiction of their courts enables them to bring to trial the perpetrators of terrorist acts, and to cooperate with and provide support and assistance to other States and relevant international and regional organizations to that end;

8. *Notes with appreciation and satisfaction* that, during the fifty-fourth session of the General Assembly and the Millennium Assembly, a number of States became parties to the relevant conventions and protocols referred to in paragraph 7 above, thereby realizing the objective of wider acceptance and implementation of those conventions;

9. *Reaffirms* the Declaration on Measures to Eliminate International Terrorism contained in the annex to

resolution 49/60 and the Declaration to Supplement the 1994 Declaration on Measures to Eliminate International Terrorism contained in the annex to resolution 51/210, and calls upon all States to implement them;

10. *Welcomes* the efforts of the Terrorism Prevention Branch of the Centre for International Crime Prevention in Vienna, after reviewing existing possibilities within the United Nations system, to enhance, through its mandate, the capabilities of the United Nations in the prevention of terrorism;

11. *Invites* States that have not yet done so to submit to the Secretary-General information on their national laws and regulations regarding the prevention and suppression of acts of international terrorism;

12. *Invites* regional intergovernmental organizations to submit to the Secretary-General information on the measures they have adopted at the regional level to eliminate international terrorism;

13. *Decides* that the Ad Hoc Committee established by General Assembly resolution 51/210 of 17 December 1996 shall continue to elaborate a comprehensive convention on international terrorism and shall continue its efforts to resolve the outstanding issues relating to the elaboration of a draft international convention for the suppression of acts of nuclear terrorism, as a means of further developing a comprehensive legal framework of conventions dealing with international terrorism, and that it shall keep on its agenda the question of convening a high-level conference under the auspices of the United Nations to formulate a joint organized response of the international community to terrorism in all its forms and manifestations;

14. *Also decides* that the Ad Hoc Committee shall meet from 12 to 23 February 2001 to continue the elaboration of a draft comprehensive convention on international terrorism, with appropriate time allocated to the continued consideration of outstanding issues relating to the elaboration of a draft international convention for the suppression of acts of nuclear terrorism, that it shall keep on its agenda the question of convening a high-level conference under the auspices of the United Nations to formulate a joint organized response of the international community to terrorism in all its forms and manifestations, and that the work shall continue during the fifty-sixth session of the General Assembly between 15 and 26 October 2001, within the framework of a working group of the Sixth Committee;

15. *Requests* the Secretary-General to continue to provide the Ad Hoc Committee with the necessary facilities for the performance of its work;

16. *Requests* the Ad Hoc Committee to report to the General Assembly at its fifty-fifth session in the event of the completion of the draft international convention for the suppression of acts of nuclear terrorism;

17. *Also requests* the Ad Hoc Committee to report to the General Assembly at its fifty-sixth session on progress made in the implementation of its mandate;

18. *Decides* to include in the provisional agenda of its fifty-sixth session the item entitled "Measures to eliminate international terrorism".

RECORDED VOTE ON RESOLUTION 55/158:

In favour: Algeria, Andorra, Angola, Antigua and Barbuda, Argentina, Armenia, Australia, Austria, Azerbaijan, Bahamas, Bahrain, Bangladesh, Barbados, Belarus, Belgium, Belize, Benin, Bolivia, Brazil, Brunei Darussalam, Bulgaria, Burkina Faso, Burundi, Cambodia, Cameroon, Canada, Chile, China, Colombia, Costa Rica, Côte d'Ivoire, Croatia, Cuba, Cyprus, Czech

Republic, Democratic People's Republic of Korea, Denmark, Djibouti, Dominican Republic, Ecuador, Egypt, El Salvador, Eritrea, Estonia, Ethiopia, Fiji, Finland, France, Gabon, Georgia, Germany, Ghana, Greece, Grenada, Guatemala, Guinea, Guyana, Haiti, Honduras, Hungary, Iceland, India, Indonesia, Iran, Ireland, Israel, Italy, Japan, Jordan, Kazakhstan, Kenya, Kuwait, Kyrgyzstan, Lao People's Democratic Republic, Latvia, Lesotho, Libyan Arab Jamahiriya, Liechtenstein, Lithuania, Luxembourg, Madagascar, Malaysia, Maldives, Mali, Malta, Marshall Islands, Mauritania, Mauritius, Mexico, Micronesia, Monaco, Mongolia, Morocco, Myanmar, Namibia, Nauru, Nepal, Netherlands, New Zealand, Nicaragua, Nigeria, Norway, Oman, Pakistan, Panama, Papua New Guinea, Paraguay, Peru, Philippines, Poland, Portugal, Qatar, Republic of Moldova, Romania, Russian Federation, Rwanda, Saint Lucia, San Marino, Saudi Arabia, Senegal, Sierra Leone, Singapore, Slovakia, Slovenia, South Africa, Spain, Sri Lanka, Sudan, Swaziland, Sweden, Thailand, The former Yugoslav Republic of Macedonia, Togo, Tonga, Trinidad and Tobago, Tunisia, Turkey, Uganda, Ukraine, United Arab Emirates, United Kingdom, United Republic of Tanzania, United States, Uruguay, Uzbekistan, Venezuela, Viet Nam, Yemen, Yugoslavia, Zambia, Zimbabwe.

Against: None.

Abstaining: Lebanon, Syrian Arab Republic.

On 23 December, the General Assembly, by **decision 55/458**, decided that the agenda item on measures to eliminate international terrorism remained for consideration during its resumed fifty-fifth (2001) session.

SECURITY COUNCIL ACTION

Prior to the foregoing General Assembly action, the Security Council, in the first of two meetings it held on 6 December [meeting 4242], heard an oral presentation by Hans Corell, Under-Secretary-General for Legal Affairs and the Legal Counsel, underscoring the highlights of a briefing note he had provided to the Council two days earlier on the role of the Council, the Assembly and the UN Secretariat in the progressive development of international law on terrorism in the 1990s.

The most prominent cases of international terrorism dealt with by the Council, he noted, had been those involving the Libyan Arab Jamahiriya, Afghanistan and the Sudan. He drew attention to the Council's unequivocal condemnation, embodied in its resolution 1269(1999) [YUN 1999, p. 1240], of all terrorist acts, methods and practices, regardless of their motivation. He cited the Assembly's efforts that led to its adoption of the 1994 Declaration on Measures to Eliminate International Terrorism [YUN 1994, p. 1294], the 1997 International Convention for the Suppression of Terrorist Bombings [YUN 1997, p. 1348] and the 1999 International Convention for the Suppression of the Financing of Terrorism [YUN 1999, p. 1233]. He said work was continuing on the drafting of additional anti-terrorism instruments, specifically, on nuclear terrorism, on the international community's organized response to all forms of terrorism and on a comprehensive convention.

Within the Secretariat, the Secretary-General reported annually on Member States' implementation of the 1994 Declaration, including the enactment of national laws and regulations to pre-

vent and suppress international terrorism, and was preparing a compendium of such laws. In addition, the Office of Legal Affairs would soon submit for publication a compilation of global and regional anti-terrorism conventions. That Office shared the work of preventing and combating terrorism with the Terrorism Prevention Branch of the Office for Drug Control and Crime Prevention in Vienna, the former focusing on legal and normative matters and the latter on research and technical cooperation.

Mr. Corell pointed out that standing in the way of enhanced international cooperation in the fight against terrorism were the problem of defining "terrorism", the political element, the links between terrorist and organized crime groups, and the perceived relationship between religion and terrorism in some parts of the world.

Following Mr. Corell's presentation, the Council President, at the second meeting on 6 December [meeting 4243], made statement **S/PRST/2000/38** on behalf of the Council:

> The Security Council takes note with appreciation of the briefing of Mr. Hans Corell, Under-Secretary-General for Legal Affairs, the Legal Counsel, regarding follow-up measures to resolution 1269(1999) of 19 October 1999.
> The Council is deeply concerned by the increase, in many regions of the world, of acts of terrorism in all its forms and manifestations. The Council reiterates its condemnation of all acts of terrorism, irrespective of motive, wherever and by whomever committed. It welcomes the efforts of the General Assembly and other organs of the United Nations in the field of combating international terrorism.
> The Council calls upon all States that have not done so to consider, as a matter of priority, becoming party to the existing anti-terrorism conventions.
> The Council reaffirms its resolution 1269(1999) and calls upon all States to implement its provisions fully and expeditiously.
> The Council reiterates its readiness, including on the basis of the relevant reports of the Secretary-General, as provided for in its resolution 1269(1999), to take necessary steps in accordance with its responsibilities under the Charter of the United Nations in order to counter terrorist threats to international peace and security.
> The Council will remain seized of this matter.

Additional Protocols I and II to the 1949 Geneva Conventions

In response to General Assembly resolution 53/96 [YUN 1998, p. 1220], the Secretary-General submitted a July report and later addendum [A/55/173 & Corr.1,2 & Add.1] on the status of the two 1977 Protocols Additional to the Geneva Conventions of 12 August 1949 and relating to the protection of victims of armed conflicts [YUN 1977, p. 706], as well as on measures taken to strengthen the existing body of international humanitarian law with respect to, among other things, its dissemination and full implementation at the national level, based on information received from a total of 17 States and ICRC. Annexed to the report was a list of 158 States parties to one or both of the Protocols as at 31 May 2000.

GENERAL ASSEMBLY ACTION

On 12 December [meeting 84], the General Assembly, on the recommendation of the Sixth Committee [A/55/605], adopted **resolution 55/148** without vote [agenda item 155].

Status of the Protocols Additional to the Geneva Conventions of 1949 and relating to the protection of victims of armed conflicts

The General Assembly,

Recalling its resolutions 32/44 of 8 December 1977, 34/51 of 23 November 1979, 37/116 of 16 December 1982, 39/77 of 13 December 1984, 41/72 of 3 December 1986, 43/161 of 9 December 1988, 45/38 of 28 November 1990, 47/30 of 25 November 1992, 49/48 of 9 December 1994, 51/155 of 16 December 1996 and 53/96 of 8 December 1998,

Having considered the report of the Secretary-General,

Thanking Member States and the International Committee of the Red Cross for their contribution to the report of the Secretary-General,

Convinced of the continuing value of established humanitarian rules relating to armed conflicts and the need to respect and ensure respect for these rules in all circumstances within the scope of the relevant international instruments, pending the earliest possible termination of such conflicts,

Stressing the possibility of making use of the International Fact-Finding Commission in relation to an armed conflict, pursuant to article 90 of Protocol I, and recalling that the International Fact-Finding Commission may, where necessary, facilitate, through its good offices, the restoration of an attitude of respect for the Geneva Conventions and the Protocol,

Stressing also the need for consolidating the existing body of international humanitarian law through its universal acceptance and the need for wide dissemination and full implementation of such law at the national level, and expressing concern about all violations of the Geneva Conventions and the two additional Protocols,

Noting with satisfaction the increasing number of national commissions and other bodies involved in advising authorities at the national level on the implementation, dissemination and development of international humanitarian law,

Mindful of the role of the International Committee of the Red Cross in offering protection to the victims of armed conflicts,

Noting with appreciation the continuing efforts of the International Committee of the Red Cross to promote and disseminate knowledge of international humanitarian law, in particular the Geneva Conventions and the two additional Protocols,

Recalling that the Twenty-sixth International Conference of the Red Cross and Red Crescent endorsed the recommendations of the Intergovernmental Group of Experts on the Protection of War Victims, including the recommendation that the depositary of the Geneva Conventions should organize periodic meetings of States parties to the Conventions to consider general problems regarding the application of international humanitarian law,

Welcoming the adoption, at The Hague on 26 March 1999, of a second Protocol to the 1954 Hague Convention for the Protection of Cultural Property in the Event of Armed Conflict,

Noting the celebration in 1999 at The Hague and at St. Petersburg of the centennial of the first International Peace Conference which highlighted the importance of the Geneva Conventions for the protection of victims of armed conflicts and the additional Protocols,

Acknowledging the fact that the Rome Statute of the International Criminal Court, adopted on 17 July 1998, includes the most serious crimes of international concern under international humanitarian law, and that the Statute, while recalling that it is the duty of every State to exercise its criminal jurisdiction over those responsible for such crimes, shows the determination of the international community to put an end to impunity for the perpetrators of such crimes and thus to contribute to their prevention,

Noting that international humanitarian law has been an important topic in the United Nations Decade for International Law, which came to an end in 1999, fifty years after the adoption of the Geneva Conventions, and acknowledging the usefulness of discussing in the General Assembly the status of international humanitarian law instruments relevant to the protection of victims of armed conflicts,

1. *Appreciates* the virtually universal acceptance of the Geneva Conventions of 1949, and notes the trend towards a similarly wide acceptance of the two additional Protocols of 1977;

2. *Appeals* to all States parties to the Geneva Conventions that have not yet done so to consider becoming parties to the additional Protocols at the earliest possible date;

3. *Calls upon* all States that are already parties to Protocol I, or those States not parties, on becoming parties to Protocol I, to make the declaration provided for under article 90 of that Protocol;

4. *Calls upon* all States that have not yet done so to consider becoming parties to the 1954 Convention for the Protection of Cultural Property in the Event of Armed Conflict and the two Protocols thereto, and to other relevant treaties on international humanitarian law relating to the protection of victims of armed conflict;

5. *Calls upon* all States parties to the Protocols Additional to the Geneva Conventions to ensure their wide dissemination and full implementation;

6. *Notes with appreciation* the Plan of Action adopted by the Twenty-seventh International Conference of the Red Cross and Red Crescent, in particular the reiteration of the importance of universal adherence to treaties on humanitarian law and their effective implementation at the national level;

7. *Affirms* the necessity of making the implementation of international humanitarian law more effective;

8. *Welcomes* the advisory service activities of the International Committee of the Red Cross in supporting efforts undertaken by Member States to take legislative and administrative action to implement international humanitarian law and in promoting the exchange of information on those efforts between Governments;

9. *Welcomes also* the increasing numbers of national commissions or committees for the implementation of international humanitarian law and for promoting the incorporation of treaties on international humanitarian law into national law and disseminating the rules of international humanitarian law;

10. *Welcomes further* the adoption of the Optional Protocol to the Convention on the Rights of the Child on the involvement of children in armed conflicts;

11. *Requests* the Secretary-General to submit to the General Assembly at its fifty-seventh session a report on the status of the additional Protocols relating to the protection of victims of armed conflicts, as well as on measures taken to strengthen the existing body of international humanitarian law, inter alia, with respect to its dissemination and full implementation at the national level, based on information received from Member States and the International Committee of the Red Cross;

12. *Decides* to include in the provisional agenda of its fifty-seventh session the item entitled "Status of the Protocols Additional to the Geneva Conventions of 1949 and relating to the protection of victims of armed conflicts".

Diplomatic relations

Protection of diplomatic and consular missions and representatives

As at 31 December 2000, the States parties to the following conventions relating to the protection of diplomats and diplomatic and consular relations were: 180 States parties to the 1961 Vienna Convention on Diplomatic Relations [YUN 1961, p. 512], 49 parties to the Optional Protocol concerning acquisition of nationality [ibid., p. 516] and 62 parties to the Optional Protocol concerning the compulsory settlement of disputes [ibid.].

The 1963 Vienna Convention on Consular Relations [YUN 1963, p. 510] had 165 parties, the Optional Protocol concerning acquisition of nationality [ibid., p. 512] had 38 and the Optional Protocol concerning the compulsory settlement of disputes [ibid.] had 45.

Parties to the 1973 Convention on the Prevention and Punishment of Crimes against Internationally Protected Persons, including Diplomatic Agents [YUN 1973, p. 775], numbered 106.

Report of Secretary-General. In a July report with later addenda [A/55/164 & Add.1-3], the Secretary-General transmitted information on serious violations of the protection, security and

safety of diplomatic and consular missions and representatives. Prepared pursuant to General Assembly resolution 53/97 [YUN 1998, p. 1222], the report contained summaries of such information received from a total of nine States (one of which reported twice), together with the texts of their reports; the comments received from States on measures needed to enhance protection, security and safety, in response to Assembly resolution 42/154 [YUN 1987, p. 1068]; and the status of State participation in the relevant conventions named above.

The Secretary-General also issued two addenda to his 1999 report on the subject [A/INF/54/5/Add.1,2].

ILC consideration. ILC at its fifty-second session [A/55/10] took up the first report on diplomatic protection by the Special Rapporteur for the topic, Christopher John R. Dugard (South Africa). The report consisted of three parts: an introduction to diplomatic protection, which examined the history and scope of the topic; draft articles 1 to 8, with commentaries; and an outline of further articles. Draft articles 1 to 8 addressed definition and scope of the topic and the nature and conditions under which diplomatic protection might be exercised, in particular the requirement of nationality and the modalities of diplomatic protection. Articles 2 and 4 raised a number of controversial issues, as did articles 5 to 8, on which the Special Rapporteur required ILC's views to guide him in his future work. To follow up on the discussions and suggestions made in plenary, ILC referred articles 1, 3 and 6 to open-ended informal consultations chaired by the Special Rapporteur. Following consideration of the resulting report, ILC referred draft articles 1, 3 and 5 to 8 to the Drafting Committee. It deferred to 2001 consideration of the addendum to the Special Rapporteur's report, which dealt with article 9 on continuous nationality and transferability of claims.

GENERAL ASSEMBLY ACTION

On 12 December [meeting 84], the General Assembly, on the recommendation of the Sixth Committee [A/55/606], adopted **resolution 55/149** without vote [agenda item 156].

Consideration of effective measures to enhance the protection, security and safety of diplomatic and consular missions and representatives

The General Assembly,

Having considered the reports of the Secretary-General,

Conscious of the need to develop and strengthen friendly relations and cooperation among States,

Convinced that respect for the principles and rules of international law governing diplomatic and consular relations is a basic prerequisite for the normal conduct of relations among States and for the fulfilment of the purposes and principles of the Charter of the United Nations,

Alarmed by the recent acts of violence against diplomatic and consular representatives, as well as against representatives of international intergovernmental organizations and officials of such organizations, which have endangered or taken innocent lives and seriously impeded the normal work of such representatives and officials,

Expressing sympathy for the victims of such illegal acts,

Recalling the Security Council resolutions and statements by the President of the Security Council in relation to flagrant violations of the protection, security and safety of diplomatic and consular missions and representatives, as well as missions and representatives of international intergovernmental organizations and officials of such organizations,

Concerned at the failure to respect the inviolability of diplomatic and consular missions and representatives,

Recalling that, without prejudice to their privileges and immunities, it is the duty of all persons enjoying such privileges and immunities to respect the laws and regulations of the receiving State,

Recalling also that diplomatic and consular premises must not be used in any manner incompatible with the diplomatic or consular functions,

Emphasizing the duty of States to take all appropriate measures as required by international law, including measures of a preventive nature, and to bring offenders to justice,

Welcoming measures already taken by States to this end in conformity with their international obligations,

Convinced that the role of the United Nations, which includes the reporting procedures established under General Assembly resolution 35/168 of 15 December 1980 and further elaborated in subsequent Assembly resolutions, is important in promoting efforts to enhance the protection, security and safety of diplomatic and consular missions and representatives,

1. *Takes note* of the reports of the Secretary-General;

2. *Strongly condemns* acts of violence against diplomatic and consular missions and representatives, as well as against missions and representatives of international intergovernmental organizations and officials of such organizations, and emphasizes that such acts can never be justified;

3. *Also strongly condemns* the recent acts of violence against such missions, representatives and officials, referred to in relevant reports under this item;

4. *Urges* States to strictly observe, implement and enforce the principles and rules of international law governing diplomatic and consular relations and, in particular, to ensure, in conformity with their international obligations, the protection, security and safety of the missions, representatives and officials mentioned in paragraph 2 above officially present in territories under their jurisdiction, including practical measures to prohibit in their territories illegal activities of persons, groups and organizations that encourage, instigate, organize or engage in the perpetration of acts against the security and safety of such missions, representatives and officials;

5. *Also urges* States to take all necessary measures at the national and international levels to prevent any acts

of violence against the missions, representatives and officials mentioned in paragraph 2 above and to ensure, with the participation of the United Nations where appropriate, that such acts are fully investigated with a view to bringing offenders to justice;

6. *Recommends* that States cooperate closely through, inter alia, contacts between the diplomatic and consular missions and the receiving State with regard to practical measures designed to enhance the protection, security and safety of diplomatic and consular missions and representatives and with regard to the exchange of information on the circumstances of all serious violations thereof;

7. *Urges* States to take all appropriate measures, in accordance with international law, at the national and international levels, to prevent any abuse of diplomatic or consular privileges and immunities, in particular serious abuses, including those involving acts of violence;

8. *Recommends* that States cooperate closely with the State in whose territory abuses of diplomatic and consular privileges and immunities may have occurred, including by exchanging information and providing assistance to its juridical authorities in order to bring offenders to justice;

9. *Calls upon* States that have not yet done so to consider becoming parties to the instruments relevant to the protection, security and safety of diplomatic and consular missions and representatives;

10. *Also calls upon* States, in cases where a dispute arises in connection with a violation of their international obligations concerning the protection of the missions or the security of the representatives and officials mentioned in paragraph 2 above, to make use of the means for peaceful settlement of disputes, including the good offices of the Secretary-General, and requests the Secretary-General, when he deems it appropriate, to offer his good offices to the States directly concerned;

11. *Requests* all States to report to the Secretary-General in accordance with paragraph 9 of resolution 42/154 of 7 December 1987;

12. *Requests* the Secretary-General to issue a report on the item, in accordance with paragraph 12 of resolution 42/154, containing also an analytical summary of the reports received under paragraph 11 above, on an annual basis, as well as to proceed with his other tasks pursuant to the same resolution;

13. *Decides* to include in the provisional agenda of its fifty-seventh session the item entitled "Consideration of effective measures to enhance the protection, security and safety of diplomatic and consular missions and representatives".

Treaties and agreements

Reservations to treaties

ILC, at its 2000 session [A/55/10], considered the fifth report of Special Rapporteur Alain Pellet (France) on the law and practice relating to reservations to treaties. The first part contained draft guidelines dealing with procedural matters regarding the alternatives to reservations and interpretative declarations and the second part with procedural matters regarding the formulation, modification and withdrawal of reservations and interpretative declarations. The texts in the first part were referred to the Drafting Committee, following which ILC adopted on first reading the five draft guidelines pertaining to reservations made under exclusionary clauses, unilateral statements made under an optional clause, unilateral statements providing for a choice between the provisions of a treaty and alternatives to reservations and to interpretative declarations.

ILC deferred consideration of the second part of the fifth report.

Treaties involving international organizations

The 1986 Vienna Convention on the Law of Treaties between States and International Organizations or between International Organizations [YUN 1986, p. 1006], which had not entered into force, had 32 parties as at 31 December 2000.

Registration and publication of treaties by the United Nations

During 2000, 1,047 international agreements and 1,215 subsequent actions were received by the Secretariat for registration or filing and recording. In addition, there were 709 registrations of formalities concerning agreements for which the Secretary-General performed depositary functions. Twelve issues of the *Monthly Statement of Treaties and International Agreements* were published.

Added to the *Treaty Series*, the UN publication of international agreements registered or filed and recorded in their original languages, with translations into English and French where necessary, were 112 volumes published during the year, covering such agreements through 1998. The Cumulative Index to the *Treaty Series* currently covered up to 1,600 volumes; volumes 26 to 28 were published in English and French in 2000.

Multilateral treaties

The UN *Treaty Series* (approximately 2,000 printed volumes) and the regularly updated status of multilateral treaties deposited with the Secretary-General were available on the Internet at the UN Treaty Collection web site (http://untreaty.un.org).

New multilateral treaties
concluded under UN auspices

The following treaties, concluded under UN auspices, were deposited with the Secretary-General during 2000:

Cartagena Protocol on Biosafety to the Convention on Biological Diversity, adopted in Montreal on 29 January 2000

European Agreement concerning the International Carriage of Dangerous Goods by Inland Waters (ADN), concluded at Geneva on 25 May 2000

Optional Protocol to the Convention on the Rights of the Child on the sale of children, child prostitution and child pornography, adopted by the UN General Assembly on 25 May 2000

Optional Protocol to the Convention on the Rights of the Child on the involvement of children in armed conflict, adopted by the General Assembly on 25 May 2000

United Nations Convention against Transnational Organized Crime, adopted by the General Assembly on 15 November 2000

Protocol to Prevent, Suppress and Punish Trafficking in Persons, Especially Women and Children, supplementing the United Nations Convention against Transnational Organized Crime, adopted by the General Assembly on 15 November 2000

Protocol against the Smuggling of Migrants by Land, Sea and Air, supplementing the United Nations Convention against Transnational Organized Crime, adopted by the General Assembly on 15 November 2000

International Coffee Agreement 2001, concluded at London on 28 September 2000

Regulation No. 110. Uniform provisions concerning the approval of: I. Specific components of motor vehicles using compressed natural gas (CNG) in their propulsion system; II. Vehicles with regard to the installation of specific components of an approved type for the use of compressed natural gas (CNG) in their propulsion system, adopted in Geneva on 28 December 2000

Regulation No. 111. Uniform provisions concerning the approval of tank vehicles of categories N and O with regard to rollover stability, adopted in Geneva on 28 December 2000

Multilateral treaties
deposited with the Secretary-General

The number of multilateral treaties for which the Secretary-General performed depositary functions was 530 at the end of 2000. During the year, 737 signatures were affixed to treaties for which he performed depositary functions and 1,073 instruments of ratification, accession, acceptance and approval were deposited. In addition, 1,100 communications containing observations or declarations and reservations were lodged upon signature, ratification or accession.

The following multilateral treaties in respect of which the Secretary-General acted as depositary came into force in 2000:

Optional Protocol to the Convention on the Elimination of All Forms of Discrimination against Women, adopted in New York on 6 October 1999

United Nations Convention on Independent Guarantees and Stand-by Letters of Credit, adopted in New York on 11 December 1995

Agreement concerning the Establishing of Global Technical Regulations for Wheeled Vehicles, Equipment and Parts which can be fitted and/or be used on Wheeled Vehicles, adopted in Geneva on 25 June 1998

Amendments to articles 3 (5) and 9 (8) of the Constitution of the Asia-Pacific Telecommunity, adopted in Colombo on 29 November 1991

Convention on the Transboundary Effects of Industrial Accidents, adopted in Helsinki on 17 March 1992

Information for 2000 regarding all multilateral treaties deposited with the Secretary-General was contained in *Multilateral Treaties Deposited with the Secretary-General: Status as at 31 December 2000,* Vols. I & II [ST/LEG/SER.E/19], Sales No. E.01.V.5.

(For the treaty-signing ceremony during the Millennium Summit, see p. 68.)

Chapter IV

Law of the sea

During 2000, the United Nations continued to promote the universal acceptance of the 1982 United Nations Convention on the Law of the Sea and the two related Agreements. The three institutions created by the Convention—the International Seabed Authority, the International Tribunal for the Law of the Sea and the Commission on the Limits of the Continental Shelf—held sessions during the year.

The United Nations Open-ended Informal Consultative Process on Oceans and the Law of the Sea, established in 1999 to facilitate the General Assembly's review of developments in ocean affairs, held its first session in May/June. The Assembly, in October, established four voluntary trust funds in an effort to assist States, especially developing States, in applying the Convention and Agreements.

UN Convention on the Law of the Sea

Signatures and ratifications

In 2000, Luxembourg, Maldives and Nicaragua ratified the United Nations Convention on the Law of the Sea (UNCLOS), bringing the number of parties to 135. The Convention, which was adopted by the Third United Nations Conference on the Law of the Sea in 1982 [YUN 1982, p. 178], closed for signature in 1984, having received 159 signatures, and entered into force on 16 November 1994 [YUN 1994, p. 1301].

Meeting of States Parties. The tenth Meeting of States Parties to the Convention (New York, 22-26 May) [SPLOS/60 & Corr.1] discussed the 1999 activities of the International Tribunal for the Law of the Sea [YUN 1999, p. 1246], proposals concerning the Tribunal's 2001 budget and other budgetary and financial questions and a proposal to establish a trust fund to help States in proceedings before the Tribunal. Also discussed were the activities of the International Seabed Authority; matters relating to the continental shelf; the role of the Meeting of States Parties regarding the implementation of UNCLOS; and the rules of procedure of Meetings of States Parties,

in particular rule 53, which dealt with decisions on questions of substance.

The States parties recommended that the General Assembly consider the establishment of a voluntary fund or funds to: assist States parties to meet their obligations under article 76 of the Convention; and provide training to developing countries for preparing their submissions to the Commission on the Limits of the Continental Shelf with respect to the limits of their continental shelf beyond 200 nautical miles [SPLOS/59]. The States parties further recommended the establishment of a voluntary fund to meet the costs of participation of Commission members from developing countries in Commission meetings [SPLOS/58].

With regard to the Tribunal, the States parties recommended that the Assembly consider establishing a voluntary trust fund to assist States with their proceedings in the Tribunal [SPLOS/57].

The Assembly took action on those recommendations in **resolution 55/7** of 30 October.

Agreement relating to the Implementation of Part XI of the Convention

During 2000, the number of States parties to the Agreement relating to the Implementation of Part XI of the Convention, which was adopted by the General Assembly in 1994 by resolution 48/263 [YUN 1994, p. 1301], reached 100. The Agreement, which entered into force on 28 July 1996 [YUN 1996, p. 1215], was to be interpreted and applied together with the Convention as a single instrument and, in the event of any inconsistency between the Agreement and Part XI of the Convention, the provisions of the Agreement would prevail. Any ratification or accession to the Convention after 28 July 1994 represented consent to be bound by the Agreement as well. States that were parties to the Convention prior to the Agreement's adoption had to deposit an instrument of ratification or accession to the Agreement separately.

Agreement on the conservation and management of straddling fish stocks and highly migratory fish stocks

As at 31 December 2000, the 1995 Agreement for the Implementation of the Provisions of the

Convention on the Law of the Sea of 10 December 1982 relating to the Conservation and Management of Straddling Fish Stocks and Highly Migratory Fish Stocks [YUN 1995, p. 1334] had been ratified or acceded to by 27 States. It would enter into force 30 days after the deposit of the thirtieth instrument of ratification or accession.

Institutions created by the Convention

International Seabed Authority

Through the International Seabed Authority, established by UNCLOS and the 1994 Implementing Agreement, States organized and conducted exploration and exploitation of the resources of the seabed and ocean floor and subsoil beyond the limits of national jurisdiction. As at 31 December 2000, the Authority had 135 members.

In 2000, the Authority held its sixth session in two parts (20-31 March and 3-14 July) in Kingston, Jamaica. The main achievement was the approval of the Regulations on Prospecting and Exploration for Polymetallic Nodules in the Area.

A preliminary round of discussions between the Authority and the Government of Jamaica, host country to the Authority, on the transfer of the title of the headquarters building from the Government to the Authority took place in May.

Also in May, the Authority signed a Memorandum of Understanding with the Intergovernmental Oceanographic Commission concerning cooperation in promoting the conduct of marine scientific research in the international seabed area.

As at 31 December, the Protocol on the Privileges and Immunities of the International Seabed Authority, adopted in 1998 [YUN 1998, p. 1226], had 28 signatories and four ratifications/accessions. The Protocol would enter into force 30 days after the date of deposit of the tenth instrument of ratification or accession.

International Tribunal for the Law of the Sea

The International Tribunal for the Law of the Sea held its ninth administrative session (6-17 March) and tenth session (18-29 September), both in Hamburg, Germany [SPLOS/63]. The Tribunal approved amendments to the Staff Rules, which were to enter into effect on 1 January 2001.

On 3 July, the official opening of the permanent premises of the Tribunal in Hamburg took place. The Tribunal started working from its permanent premises on 27 November.

In May, the tenth Meeting of States Parties to the Convention approved the Tribunal's budget for 2001, which totalled $8,090,900.

Regarding the Tribunal's judicial work, judgements were delivered in the *Camouco* case between Panama and France on 7 February and in the *Monte Confurco* case between Seychelles and France on 18 December. In the M/V *Saiga* (No. 2) case between Saint Vincent and the Grenadines and Guinea, the Tribunal received communications from Saint Vincent and the Grenadines on the issue of compliance with the judgement of the Tribunal of 1 July 1999 [YUN 1999, p. 1246]. In the southern bluefin tuna case involving Australia and New Zealand, New Zealand informed the Tribunal of its unintentional overcatch of southern bluefin tuna during the 1998/99 fishing year and of the steps it had taken to reduce its catch for the 1999/2000 season. Australia submitted comments on the issue.

On 23 August, Chile requested the appointment of an arbitrator to sit on an arbitral panel to consider the dispute between Chile and the European Community concerning swordfish stocks in the south-eastern Pacific Ocean. Subsequently, both parties agreed to submit the case to a special chamber of the Tribunal and no further action was taken on Chile's request.

Commission on the Limits of the Continental Shelf

In 2000, the Commission on the Limits of the Continental Shelf, established in 1997 [YUN 1997, p. 1362], held its seventh (1-5 May) and eighth (31 August–4 September) sessions in New York [A/56/58]. The 21-member Commission considered data and other material submitted by coastal States concerning the outer limits of the continental shelf in areas where those limits extended beyond 200 nautical miles; made recommendations to its member States; and provided scientific and technical advice on request.

The Commission, which usually met in private (closed) sessions, held an open meeting on the first day of its seventh session to flag the most important and challenging issues related to the establishment of the continental shelf beyond 200 miles. The meeting was also intended to give policy makers and legal advisers insight into the benefits that a coastal State might derive from the resources of the extended continental shelf and to explain to experts in marine sciences involved in the preparation of submissions to the Commission how the Scientific and Technical Guidelines should be applied.

In its closed session, the Commission discussed the issue of training and requested the United Nations Division of Ocean Affairs and the Law of the Sea to prepare a cost estimate for a five-day training course with a view to aiding States, especially developing States, to further develop the knowledge and skills for preparing submissions to the Commission. On 1 September, the Commission adopted an outline for a five-day training course and noted that interested Governments could adapt the course to suit particular needs. The Commission also considered the proposals of the Committee on Confidentiality on the Rules of Procedure and adopted them with amendments.

Other developments related to the Convention

Report of Secretary-General. In March, the Secretary-General submitted his annual report on oceans and the law of the sea covering developments relating to the implementation of the Convention and the related Agreements [A/55/61]. As requested in General Assembly resolution 54/33 [YUN 1999, p. 994], the Secretary-General also submitted the report to the newly established Open-ended Informal Consultative Process on Oceans and the Law of the Sea (see below) in order to assist in its deliberations.

The report discussed progress made in implementing the Convention and Agreements and described the work of the three institutions created by the Convention: the International Seabed Authority, the International Tribunal for the Law of the Sea and the Commission on the Limits of the Continental Shelf.

In addition to addressing questions of maritime space and States with special geographical characteristics, the Secretary-General dealt comprehensively with the shipping industry and navigation, an industry that had traditionally been self-regulating but had gained public attention due to projected increases in decommissioning, recycling and scrapping and their safety and environmental implications. In that connection, he gave an overview of the activities of the International Maritime Organization and the International Hydrographic Organization. With regard to crimes at sea, the Secretary-General stated that the maintenance of security against crimes at sea had placed a heightened demand on the enforcement capacity of States and posed a challenge that most States, especially developing and small island States, had not been able to meet. In that connection, he addressed piracy and armed robbery, drug trafficking, illegal traffic in hazardous wastes, smuggling of migrants and stowaways.

The Secretary-General went on to review the development and management of marine resources; the underwater cultural heritage; marine science and technology; the settlement of disputes; and capacity-building and information dissemination.

United Nations Open-ended Consultative Process

The United Nations Open-ended Informal Consultative Process on Oceans and the Law of the Sea, established by General Assembly resolution 54/33 [YUN 1999, p. 994], held its first meeting in New York from 30 May to 2 June 2000 [A/55/274]. The process was established to facilitate the Assembly's review of developments in ocean affairs by considering the foregoing report of the Secretary-General on oceans and the law of the sea and by suggesting particular issues for the Assembly's consideration, with an emphasis on identifying areas where coordination and cooperation at the intergovernmental and interagency levels should be enhanced.

The major areas of concern identified at the meeting were responsible fisheries management and the prevention of marine pollution and degradation. Those two elements were among a list of issues that the meeting agreed deserved the Assembly's attention.

GENERAL ASSEMBLY ACTION

On 30 October [meeting 44], the General Assembly adopted **resolution 55/7** [draft: A/55/L.10 & Corr.1 & Add.1] by recorded vote (143-2-4) [agenda item 34].

Oceans and the law of the sea

The General Assembly,

Recalling its resolutions 49/28 of 6 December 1994, 52/26 of 26 November 1997, 54/31 and 54/33 of 24 November 1999 and other relevant resolutions adopted subsequent to the entry into force of the United Nations Convention on the Law of the Sea ("the Convention") on 16 November 1994,

Recalling also its resolution 2749(XXV) of 17 December 1970, and considering that the Convention, together with the Agreement relating to the Implementation of Part XI of the United Nations Convention on the Law of the Sea of 10 December 1982 ("the Agreement"), provides the regime to be applied to the Area and its resources as defined in the Convention,

Emphasizing the universal and unified character of the Convention and its fundamental importance for the maintenance and strengthening of international peace and security, as well as for the sustainable use and development of the seas and oceans and their resources,

Reaffirming that the Convention sets out the legal framework within which all activities in the oceans and seas must be carried out and is of strategic importance as the basis for national, regional and global action in the marine sector, and that its integrity needs to be maintained, as recognized also by the United Nations Conference on Environment and Development in chapter 17 of Agenda 21,

Conscious of the importance of increasing the number of States parties to the Convention and the Agreement in order to achieve the goal of universal participation,

Conscious also that the problems of ocean space are closely interrelated and need to be considered as a whole,

Convinced of the need, building on arrangements established in accordance with the Convention, to improve coordination at the national level and cooperation and coordination at both intergovernmental and inter-agency levels, in order to address all aspects of oceans and seas in an integrated manner,

Recognizing the important role that the competent international organizations have in relation to ocean affairs, in implementing the Convention and in promoting sustainable development of the oceans and seas and their resources,

Taking note of the report of the Secretary-General, and reaffirming the importance of the annual consideration and review of developments relating to ocean affairs and the law of the sea by the General Assembly as the global institution having the competence to undertake such a review,

Taking note also of the outcome of the first meeting of the United Nations open-ended informal consultative process ("the Consultative Process"), established by the General Assembly in its resolution 54/33 in order to facilitate the annual review by the Assembly of developments in ocean affairs,

Mindful of the importance of the oceans and seas for the earth's ecosystem and for providing the vital resources for food security and for sustaining economic prosperity and the well-being of present and future generations,

Bearing in mind the contribution that major groups, as identified in Agenda 21, can make to raising awareness of the goal of the sustainable development of the oceans and seas and their resources,

Underlining the essential need for capacity-building to ensure that all States, especially developing countries, in particular least developed countries and small island developing States, are able both to implement the Convention and to benefit from the sustainable development of their marine resources, as well as to participate fully in global and regional forums and processes dealing with oceans and law of the sea issues,

Expressing serious concern at the increase in illegal, unreported and unregulated fishing, and recognizing the importance of strengthening cooperation to combat such activities, particularly through the relevant regional fisheries management organizations and arrangements,

Recalling that the role of international cooperation and coordination on a bilateral basis and, where applicable, within a subregional, interregional, regional or global framework is to support and supplement the national efforts of coastal States to promote the integrated management and sustainable development of coastal and marine areas,

Expressing its deep concern at the degradation of the marine environment, particularly from land-based activities, and emphasizing the need for international cooperation and for a coordinated approach at the national level to this problem, bringing together the many different economic sectors involved and protecting the ecosystems, and in this context reaffirming the importance of ensuring full implementation of the Global Programme of Action for the Protection of the Marine Environment from Land-based Activities,

Reiterating its concern at the degradation of the marine environment as a result of pollution from ships, in particular through the illegal release of oil and other harmful substances, and as a result of pollution by dumping of hazardous waste, including radioactive materials, nuclear waste and dangerous chemicals,

Recalling the importance of marine science in promoting the sustainable management of the oceans and seas, including in the assessment, conservation, management and sustainable use of fish stocks,

Emphasizing the need to ensure access of decision makers to advice and information on marine science and technology, as well as to the transfer of technology and support for the production and diffusion of factual information and knowledge for end-users, as appropriate,

Expressing concern once again at the continuing threat from piracy and armed robbery at sea, and in this context noting the letter from the Secretary-General of the International Maritime Organization to the Secretary-General of the United Nations drawing attention to the increasing number and seriousness of incidents of piracy and armed robbery at sea,

Reaffirming the importance of enhancing the safety of navigation, as well as the necessity for cooperation in this regard,

Emphasizing the importance of the protection of the underwater cultural heritage, and recalling in this context the provisions of article 303 of the Convention,

Noting the responsibilities of the Secretary-General under the Convention and related resolutions of the General Assembly, in particular resolutions 49/28 and 52/26, and in this context the expected increase in responsibilities of the Division for Ocean Affairs and the Law of the Sea of the Office of Legal Affairs of the Secretariat in view of the progress in the work of the Commission on the Limits of the Continental Shelf ("the Commission") and the anticipated receipt of submissions from States,

1. *Calls upon* all States that have not done so, in order to achieve the goal of universal participation, to become parties to the Convention and the Agreement;

2. *Reaffirms* the unified character of the Convention;

3. *Calls upon* States to harmonize, as a matter of priority, their national legislation with the provisions of the Convention, to ensure the consistent application of those provisions and to ensure also that any declarations or statements that they have made or make when signing, ratifying or acceding to the Convention are in conformity therewith and, otherwise, to withdraw any of their declarations or statements that are not in conformity;

4. *Encourages* States parties to the Convention to deposit with the Secretary-General charts and lists of geographical coordinates, as provided for in the Convention;

5. *Urges* the international community to assist, as appropriate, developing countries, in particular least developed countries and small island developing States, in the acquisition of data and the preparation of charts or lists of geographical coordinates for publication under articles 16, 22, 47, 75 and 84 of the Convention and in the preparation of information under article 76 and annex II to the Convention;

6. *Requests* the Secretary-General to convene the eleventh Meeting of States Parties to the Convention in

New York from 14 to 18 May 2001 and to provide the services required;

7. *Notes with satisfaction* the continued contribution of the International Tribunal for the Law of the Sea ("the Tribunal") to the peaceful settlement of disputes in accordance with Part XV of the Convention, underlines its important role and authority concerning the interpretation or application of the Convention and the Agreement, encourages States parties to the Convention to consider making a written declaration choosing from the means set out in article 287 for the settlement of disputes concerning the interpretation or application of the Convention and the Agreement, and invites States to note the provisions of annexes V, VI, VII and VIII to the Convention concerning, respectively, conciliation, the Tribunal, arbitration and special arbitration;

8. *Recalls* the obligations of parties to cases before a court or a tribunal referred to in article 287 of the Convention to ensure prompt compliance with the decisions rendered by such court or tribunal;

9. *Requests* the Secretary-General to establish a voluntary trust fund to assist States in the settlement of disputes through the Tribunal, and to report annually to the Meeting of States Parties to the Convention on the status of the fund;

10. *Invites* States, intergovernmental organizations, national institutions, non-governmental organizations, as well as natural and juridical persons, to make voluntary financial contributions to the fund;

11. *Encourages* States that have not yet done so to nominate conciliators and arbitrators in accordance with annexes V and VII to the Convention, and requests the Secretary-General to continue to update and circulate lists of these conciliators and arbitrators on a regular basis;

12. *Welcomes* the adoption of the Regulations on Prospecting and Exploration for Polymetallic Nodules in the Area by the Assembly of the International Seabed Authority ("the Authority") on 13 July 2000, and notes with satisfaction that the Authority is now in a position to proceed to issue contracts to the registered pioneer investors in accordance with the Convention, the Agreement and those Regulations;

13. *Appeals* to all States parties to the Convention to pay their assessed contributions to the Authority and the Tribunal in full and on time, and appeals also to all former provisional members of the Authority to pay any outstanding contributions;

14. *Calls upon* States that have not done so to consider ratifying or acceding to the Agreement on the Privileges and Immunities of the Tribunal and to the Protocol on the Privileges and Immunities of the Authority;

15. *Notes* the continuing progress in the work of the Commission, including the successful open meeting on 1 May 2000 aimed at assisting States in implementing the provisions of the Convention related to the establishment of the outer limits of the continental shelf beyond 200 nautical miles and facilitating the preparation of submissions to the Commission by coastal States regarding the outer limits of their continental shelf;

16. *Also notes* that the Commission has issued a basic flow chart on the preparation of submissions and has adopted an outline for a five-day training course on the delineation of the outer limits of the continental shelf beyond 200 nautical miles and for the preparation of submissions, and encourages concerned States and relevant international organizations and institutions to consider developing and making available such training courses;

17. *Recalls* that under article 4 of annex II to the Convention, a State intending to establish the outer limits of its continental shelf beyond 200 nautical miles is to submit particulars of such limits to the Commission within ten years of the entry into force of the Convention for that State;

18. *Requests* the Secretary-General to establish a voluntary trust fund to provide training for technical and administrative staff, and technical and scientific advice, as well as personnel, to assist developing States, in particular the least developed countries and small island developing States, for the purpose of desktop studies and project planning, and preparing and submitting information under article 76 and annex II to the Convention in accordance with the procedures of the Scientific and Technical Guidelines of the Commission on the Limits of the Continental Shelf, and to report annually to the General Assembly on the status of the fund;

19. *Invites* States, intergovernmental organizations and agencies, national institutions, non-governmental organizations and international financial institutions as well as natural and juridical persons to make voluntary financial or other contributions to the fund;

20. *Requests* the Secretary-General to establish a voluntary trust fund for the purpose of defraying the cost of participation of the members of the Commission from developing States in the meetings of the Commission, and invites States to contribute to the fund;

21. *Approves* the convening by the Secretary-General of the ninth session of the Commission in New York from 21 to 25 May 2001 and a tenth session, if necessary, starting on 27 August 2001 of a duration of three weeks in the event of a submission being filed, or of one week, depending on the workload of the Commission;

22. *Calls upon* bilateral and multilateral donor agencies to keep their programmes under review to ensure the availability in all States, particularly in developing States, of the economic, legal, navigational, scientific and technical capacities and skills necessary for the full implementation of the Convention and the sustainable development of the oceans and seas and their resources nationally, regionally and globally, and in so doing to bear in mind the rights of landlocked developing States;

23. *Requests* the Secretary-General, in cooperation with the competent international organizations and programmes, including the Food and Agriculture Organization of the United Nations, the International Labour Organization, the International Hydrographic Organization, the International Maritime Organization, the United Nations Development Programme, the United Nations Industrial Development Organization, the Intergovernmental Oceanographic Commission of the United Nations Educational, Scientific and Cultural Organization, the United Nations Environment Programme, the United Nations Conference on Trade and Development, the World Meteorological Organization and the World Bank, as well as representatives of regional development banks and the donor community, to review the efforts being made to build capacity as well as to identify the duplications that need to be avoided and the gaps that may need to be filled for ensuring consistent approaches, both nationally and

regionally, with a view to implementing the Convention, and to include a section on this subject in his annual report on oceans and the law of the sea;

24. *Urges* States to continue the development of an international plan of action on illegal, unregulated and unreported fishing for the Food and Agriculture Organization of the United Nations, as a matter of priority, and in this context recognizes the central role that regional and subregional fisheries organizations and arrangements will have in addressing this issue;

25. *Emphasizes* the importance of the implementation of Part XII of the Convention in order to protect and preserve the marine environment, including coastal areas, and its living marine resources against pollution and physical degradation;

26. *Acknowledges* the need to build national capacity for the integrated management of the coastal zone and for the protection of its ecosystem, and invites relevant parts of the United Nations system to promote these aims, including through the provision of the training and institutional support needed to achieve them;

27. *Calls upon* States to prioritize action on marine pollution from land-based sources as part of their national sustainable development strategies and local Agenda 21 programmes, in an integrated and inclusive manner, as a means of enhancing their support for the Global Programme of Action for the Protection of the Marine Environment from Land-based Activities, and calls for their active collaboration to ensure that the 2001 intergovernmental review will enhance the implementation of the Global Programme of Action;

28. *Calls upon* United Nations agencies and programmes identified in General Assembly resolution 51/189 of 16 December 1996 to fulfil their roles in support of the Global Programme of Action and to provide information to Governments for their consideration at the 2001 intergovernmental review of the Global Programme of Action and to the Secretary-General for his annual report on oceans and the law of the sea on their action in this regard and on other steps which could be taken to protect the marine environment;

29. *Invites* the United Nations Environment Programme and the World Bank, as part of the preparations for the 2001 review of the Global Programme of Action, to consult with Governments, representatives of the private sector, financial institutions and bilateral and multilateral donor agencies to review their involvement in the implementation of the Global Programme of Action and to consider, inter alia, what international support is needed to help overcome the obstacles to the preparation and implementation of national and local action programmes and how they can participate actively in partnership-building with developing countries for the transfer of the requisite technology in accordance with the Convention and taking into account the relevant parts of Agenda 21, capacity-building and funding for the implementation of the Global Programme of Action;

30. *Emphasizes* the importance of ensuring that adverse impacts on the marine environment are taken into account when assessing and evaluating development programmes and projects;

31. *Urges* States to take all practicable steps, in accordance with the International Convention for the Prevention of Pollution from Ships, 1973, as modified by the Protocol of 1978 relating thereto, to prevent pol-

lution of the marine environment from ships and, in accordance with the 1972 Convention on the Prevention of Marine Pollution by Dumping of Wastes and Other Matter, to prevent pollution of the marine environment by dumping, and further calls upon States to become parties to and to implement the 1996 Protocol to the 1972 Convention;

32. *Stresses* the need to consider as a matter of priority the issues of marine science and technology and to focus on how best to implement the many obligations of States and competent international organizations under Parts XIII and XIV of the Convention, and calls upon States to adopt, as appropriate and in accordance with international law, the necessary national laws, regulations, policies and procedures to promote and facilitate marine scientific research and cooperation;

33. *Urges* all States, in particular coastal States, in affected regions to take all necessary and appropriate measures to prevent and combat incidents of piracy and armed robbery at sea, including through regional cooperation, and to investigate or cooperate in the investigation of such incidents wherever they occur and bring the alleged perpetrators to justice, in accordance with international law;

34. *Calls upon* States, in this context, to cooperate fully with the International Maritime Organization, including by submitting reports on incidents to the organization and by implementing its guidelines on preventing attacks of piracy and armed robbery;

35. *Urges* States to become parties to the Convention for the Suppression of Unlawful Acts against the Safety of Maritime Navigation and its Protocol, and to ensure its effective implementation;

36. *Notes* the continued work of the United Nations Educational, Scientific and Cultural Organization towards a convention for the implementation of the provisions of the Convention, relating to the protection of the underwater cultural heritage, and re-emphasizes the importance of ensuring that the instrument to be elaborated is in full conformity with the relevant provisions of the Convention;

37. *Invites* Member States and others in a position to do so to contribute to the further development of the Hamilton Shirley Amerasinghe Memorial Fellowship Programme on the Law of the Sea established by the General Assembly in resolution 35/116 of 10 December 1980 and to support the training activities under the TRAIN-SEA-COAST Programme of the Division for Ocean Affairs and the Law of the Sea of the Office of Legal Affairs of the Secretariat;

38. *Expresses its appreciation* to the Secretary-General for the annual comprehensive report on oceans and the law of the sea, prepared by the Division for Ocean Affairs and the Law of the Sea, as well as for the other activities of the Division, in accordance with the provisions of the Convention and the mandate set forth in resolutions 49/28, 52/26 and 54/33;

39. *Requests* the Secretary-General to continue to carry out the responsibilities entrusted to him in the Convention and related resolutions of the General Assembly, including resolutions 49/28 and 52/26, and to ensure that appropriate resources are made available to the Division for Ocean Affairs and the Law of the Sea for the performance of such responsibilities under the approved budget for the Organization;

40. *Reaffirms* its decision to undertake an annual review and evaluation of the implementation of the Convention and other developments relating to ocean affairs and the law of the sea, taking into account resolution 54/33 establishing the consultative process to facilitate the review of developments in ocean affairs, and requests the Secretary-General to convene the second meeting of the Consultative Process in New York from 7 to 11 May 2001;

41. *Recommends* that, in its deliberations on the report of the Secretary-General on oceans and the law of the sea at its second meeting, the Consultative Process organize its discussions around the following areas:

(a) Marine science and the development and transfer of marine technology as mutually agreed, including capacity-building in this regard;

(b) Coordination and cooperation in combating piracy and armed robbery at sea;

42. *Requests* the Secretary-General to ensure more effective collaboration and coordination between the relevant parts of the Secretariat of the United Nations and the United Nations as a whole, in particular in ensuring the effectiveness, transparency and responsiveness of the Subcommittee on Oceans and Coastal Areas of the Administrative Committee on Coordination, and also requests the Secretary-General to include in his report suggestions on initiatives to improve coordination, in accordance with resolution 54/33, and encourages all United Nations bodies to help this process by drawing to the attention of the Secretariat and the Subcommittee those areas of their work which may, directly or indirectly, affect the work of other United Nations bodies;

43. *Also requests* the Secretary-General to bring the present resolution to the attention of heads of intergovernmental organizations, the specialized agencies and funds and programmes of the United Nations engaged in activities relating to ocean affairs and the law of the sea, and the Subcommittee on Oceans and Coastal Areas of the Administrative Committee on Coordination, drawing their attention to paragraphs of particular relevance to them, and underlines the importance of their input for the report of the Secretary-General on oceans and the law of the sea and of their participation in relevant meetings and processes;

44. *Invites* the competent international organizations, as well as funding institutions, to take specific account of the present resolution in their programmes and activities, and to contribute to the preparation of the comprehensive report of the Secretary-General on oceans and the law of the sea;

45. *Requests* the Secretary-General to establish a voluntary trust fund for the purpose of assisting developing countries, in particular least developed countries, small island developing States and landlocked developing States, in attending the meetings of the Consultative Process, and invites States to contribute to this fund;

46. *Also requests* the Secretary-General to report to the General Assembly at its fifty-sixth session on the implementation of the present resolution, including other developments and issues relating to ocean affairs and the law of the sea, in connection with his annual comprehensive report on oceans and the law of the sea, and to provide the report in accordance with the modalities set out in resolution 54/33;

47. *Decides* to include in the provisional agenda of its fifty-sixth session the item entitled "Oceans and the law of the sea".

ANNEX I
International Tribunal for the Law of the Sea Trust Fund

Terms of reference

Reasons for establishing the Trust Fund

1. Part XV of the United Nations Convention on the Law of the Sea ("the Convention") provides for the settlement of disputes. In particular, article 287 specifies that States are free to choose one or more of the following means:

(a) The International Tribunal for the Law of the Sea;

(b) The International Court of Justice;

(c) An arbitral tribunal;

(d) A special arbitral tribunal.

2. The Secretary-General already operates a Trust Fund for the International Court of Justice. The Permanent Court of Arbitration has established a Financial Assistance Fund. The burden of costs should not be a factor for States, in making the choices under article 287, in deciding whether a dispute should be submitted to the Tribunal or in deciding upon the response to an application made to the Tribunal by others. For these reasons, it was decided to create a Trust Fund for the International Tribunal for the Law of the Sea ("the Tribunal").

Object and purpose of the Trust Fund

3. This Trust Fund ("the Fund") is established by the Secretary-General in accordance with General Assembly resolution 55/7 and pursuant to the Agreement on Cooperation and Relationship between the United Nations and the Tribunal of 18 December 1997 (resolution 52/251, annex).

4. The purpose of the Fund is to provide financial assistance to States parties to the Convention for expenses incurred in connection with cases submitted, or to be submitted, to the Tribunal, including its Seabed Disputes Chamber and any other Chamber.

5. Assistance, which will be provided in accordance with the following terms and conditions, should only be provided in appropriate cases, principally those proceeding to the merits where jurisdiction is not an issue, but in exceptional circumstances may be provided for any phase of the proceedings.

Contributions to the Fund

6. The Secretary-General invites States, intergovernmental organizations, national institutions, nongovernmental organizations, as well as natural and juridical persons, to make voluntary financial contributions to the Fund.

Application for assistance

7. An application for assistance from the Fund may be submitted by any State party to the Convention. The application should describe the nature of the case which is to be, or has been, brought by or against the State concerned and should provide an estimate of the costs for which financial assistance is requested. The application should contain a commitment to supply a final statement of account of the expenditures made from approved amounts, to be certified by an auditor acceptable to the United Nations.

Panel of experts

8. The Secretary-General will establish a panel of experts, normally three persons of the highest professional standing, to make recommendations on each request. The task of each panel is to examine the application and to recommend to the Secretary-General the amount of the financial assistance to be given, the phase or phases of the proceedings in respect of which assistance is to be given and the types of expenses for which the assistance may be used.

Granting of assistance

9. The Secretary-General will provide financial assistance from the Fund on the basis of the recommendations of the panel of experts. Payments will be made against receipts showing expenditures made in respect of approved costs. The latter may include:

(a) Preparing the application and the written pleadings;

(b) Professional fees of counsel and advocates for written and oral pleadings;

(c) Travel and expenses of legal representation in Hamburg during the various phases of a case;

(d) Execution of an Order of Judgment of the Tribunal, such as marking a boundary in the territorial sea.

Application of the Financial Regulations and Rules of the United Nations

10. The Financial Regulations and Rules of the United Nations will apply to the administration of the Fund, including the procedures for audit.

Reporting

11. An annual report on the activities of the Fund, including details of the contributions to and disbursements from the Fund, will be made to the Meeting of States Parties to the Convention.

Implementing office

12. The Division for Ocean Affairs and the Law of the Sea of the Office of Legal Affairs is the implementing office for this Fund and provides the services for the operation of the Fund.

Offers of professional assistance

13. The implementing office also maintains a list of offers of professional assistance which may be made on a reduced fee basis by suitably qualified persons or bodies. If an applicant for assistance so requests, the implementing office will make the list of offers available to it for its consideration and decision; both financial and other assistance may be extended in respect of the same case or phase thereof.

Revision

14. The General Assembly may revise the above if circumstances so require.

ANNEX II
Trust fund for the purpose of facilitating the preparation of submissions to the Commission on the Limits of the Continental Shelf for developing States, in particular the least developed countries and small island developing States, and compliance with article 76 of the United Nations Convention on the Law of the Sea

Terms of reference, guidelines and rules

1. Reasons for establishing the Trust Fund

1. Promoting and developing the marine scientific and technological capacity of developing States, in particular the least developed countries and small island States, with a view to accelerating their social and economic development, is essential for the effective implementation of the United Nations Convention on the Law of the Sea of 10 December 1982 ("the Convention").

2. Coastal States intending to establish the outer limits of their continental shelf beyond 200 nautical miles from the baseline from which the breadth of their territorial sea is measured are required by article 76 of the Convention to submit the relevant data and information to the Commission on the Limits of the Continental Shelf ("the Commission"). In accordance with article 4 of annex II to the Convention, the particulars of such limits should be submitted to the Commission within ten years of the entry into force of the Convention for that State. For some States a submission should be made by 16 November 2004.

3. Developing States, in particular the least developed countries and small island developing States, may face difficulties in complying with the time limit for submissions to the Commission. The Trust Fund is intended to assist these States in complying with the requirements relating to a submission to the Commission.

4. Under article 3, paragraph 1 (b), of annex II to the Convention, the Commission may provide scientific and technical advice, if requested by the coastal States concerned, during the preparation of the data to be submitted in accordance with article 76.

5. The Commission has adopted an outline for a five-day training course in order to facilitate the preparation of submissions in accordance with its Scientific and Technical Guidelines. The course is to be developed and delivered by interested Governments, international organizations and institutions which possess the necessary expertise and facilities. The Commission has likewise prepared a basic flow chart illustrating the preparation of submissions by coastal States.

6. The delineation of the continental shelf of a coastal State in accordance with article 76 and annex II to the Convention and annex II to the Final Act of the Third United Nations Conference on the Law of the Sea ("the Final Act") requires a programme for hydrographic and geoscientific surveying and mapping of the continental margin. The complexity and scale, and hence the costs involved, of such a programme will vary greatly from State to State according to the different geographical and geophysical circumstances. A first approach will always involve an assessment of the particular case at hand, followed by planning of appropriate projects for further data acquisition. Such projects require the contracting of high-level scientific/technical expertise and modern technology. By nature, the costs involved in such data acquisition projects are substantial. In addition to contributing to the Voluntary Fund herein established, the international community should make every effort to facilitate the full implementation of article 76 both financially and in any other possible way or capacity.

7. The initial assessment and the project planning itself will require qualifications in hydrography and geosciences in addition to a full understanding of the relevant provisions of the Convention. The final preparation of a submission to the Commission also requires high-level expertise in geosciences and hydrography.

8. The United Nations has extensive experience in providing assistance to countries for their industrial and economic development. This experience could be extended and utilized to assist States in implementing their rights and obligations under article 76 of the Convention.

2. Objects and purpose of the Trust Fund

9. The Secretary-General, under the Financial Regulations and Rules of the United Nations, establishes the present Trust Fund ("the Fund"). The object of the Fund is to enable developing States, in particular the least developed coastal countries and small island developing States, to make an initial assessment of their particular case, make appropriate plans for further investigations and data acquisition, and to prepare the final submission documents when the necessary data have been acquired.

10. The data acquisition campaigns themselves are not the object of the Fund.

11. An initial assessment of the nature of the continental shelf of a coastal State is often made in the form of a desktop study, which is a review and compilation of all existing data and information. Decisions for further action and/or planning for further data acquisition and mapping projects will be based on such a study.

12. The purpose of the Fund is to provide, in accordance with the terms and conditions specified in the Financial Regulations and Rules of the United Nations:

(a) Training to the appropriate technical and administrative staff of the coastal State in question, in order to enable them to perform initial desktop studies and project planning, or at least to take full part in these activities;

(b) Funds for such studies and planning activities, including funds for advisory/consultancy assistance if needed.

13. The preparation of the final submission documents will have to meet the requirements of article 76 and annex II to the Convention (and for some States, annex II to the Final Act) and the Scientific and Technical Guidelines of the Commission. The training should take this into account and aim at enabling the State's personnel also to prepare most of these documents themselves. The preparation of the submission may induce costs that may be met by funds from the Fund (e.g. software and hardware equipment, technical assistance, etc.).

3. Contributions to the Fund

14. The Secretary-General invites States, intergovernmental organizations and agencies, national institutions, non-governmental organizations and international financial institutions as well as natural and juridical persons to make voluntary financial or other contributions to the Fund.

4. Application for financial assistance

15. An application for financial assistance from the Fund may be submitted by any developing State, in particular the least developed countries and small island developing States, who are Members of the United Nations and party to the Convention.

16. The purpose of the financial assistance applied for should be specified. Financial assistance may be sought for the following purposes:

(a) Training of technical and administrative staff;

(b) Desktop study or other means to make an initial assessment of the nature of the continental shelf and its limits;

(c) Working out of plans for the acquisition of necessary additional data and mapping projects;

(d) Preparation of final submission documents;

(e) Advisory/consultancy assistance related to the above points.

17. Detailed information under each of these purposes should be provided as follows:

(a) Training of technical and administrative staff:
The application shall be accompanied by:

(i) A specification of the goal of the training and which positions the trainees are intended to fill afterwards;

(ii) Information on the training institute(s) in question;

(iii) A copy of the training course(s);

(iv) The curriculum vitae of the trainees;

(v) An itemized statement of the estimated costs for which assistance is requested.

(b) Desktop study or other means to make an assessment of the nature of the continental shelf and its limits:
The application shall be accompanied by:

(i) A short description of the aim of the study;

(ii) An overview map of the area in question;

(iii) An overview, as complete as possible, of the database already available to the State;

(iv) An outline of how the work will be done and what tools are available (software and hardware);

(v) A specification of what will be done by the State's own staff, and what will be contracted for;

(vi) An itemized statement of the estimated costs for which assistance is requested.

(c) Working out of plans for the acquisition of necessary additional data and mapping projects:
The application shall be accompanied by:

(i) A summary of the status of knowledge of the continental margin, preferably based on a previous desktop study;

(ii) A preliminary assessment of the needs for specific additional data and/or information in accordance with the requirements of article 76 and annex II to the Convention, and annex II to the Final Act;

(iii) An itemized statement of the estimated costs for which assistance is requested.

(d) Preparation of final submission documents:
The application shall be accompanied by:

(i) A specification of what kind of assistance is needed;

(ii) An itemized statement of the estimated costs for which assistance is requested.

(e) Advisory/consultancy assistance related to the above points:
The application shall be accompanied by:

(i) A copy of the contract between the Government and the technical or scientific expert in question;

(ii) An itemized statement of the costs for which assistance is requested.

18. In all these cases the application shall be accompanied by an undertaking that the requesting State

shall supply a final statement of account providing details of the expenditures made from the approved amounts, to be certified by an auditor acceptable to the United Nations.

5. Consideration of applications

19. Each request for financial assistance shall be considered by the Division for Ocean Affairs and the Law of the Sea of the Office of Legal Affairs ("the Division"), which acts as the secretariat of the Commission.

20. The Division may engage an independent panel of experts of the highest moral standing to assist in the examination of applications on the basis of section 4 above and to recommend the amount of financial assistance to be given. However, no sitting Commission member should serve on this panel of experts. The Division shall prepare and circulate to Member States a list of prospective members of the panel of experts. Any member of the expert panel opposed by a Member State should not be included in the panel. The Division shall on an annual basis provide a list of the panel of experts as an annex to the annual report of the Secretary-General.

21. In considering the application, the Division shall be guided solely by the financial needs of the requesting developing State and availability of funds, with priority given to least developed countries and small island developing States, taking into account the imminence of pending deadlines.

22. Travel expenses and subsistence allowance are payable to independent experts engaged by the Division to consider applications.

6. Granting of assistance

23. The Secretary-General will provide financial assistance from the Fund on the basis of the evaluation and recommendations of the Division. Payments will be made against receipts evidencing actual expenditures for approved costs.

7. Application of article 5 of annex II to the Convention

24. Nationals of the coastal State making the submission who are members of the Commission and any Commission member who has assisted a coastal State by providing scientific and technical advice with respect to the delineation shall not be a member of the subcommission dealing with that submission but has the right to participate as a member in the proceedings of the Commission concerning the said submission. In an effort to promote transparency and to give full effect to article 5 of annex II to the Convention there should be full disclosure by Commission members, Trust Fund recipients and training sponsors to the Division of any pre-submission contacts.

8. Reporting requirements for full disclosure

25. Interested Governments, international organizations and institutions who provide any training for which any costs are reimbursed by this Fund are strongly encouraged to provide the complete list of participants to the Division.

26. Commission members who participate in any activities pursuant to this Fund shall disclose this information to the Division.

27. Upon submission to the Commission of its information on the limits of its continental shelf pursuant to article 76 of the Convention, a coastal State that has received assistance from this Fund shall disclose this information, including the involvement of any Commission members.

9. Application of the Financial Regulations and Rules of the United Nations

28. The Financial Regulations and Rules of the United Nations shall apply to the administration of the Fund. The Fund shall be subject to the auditing procedures provided therein.

10. Reporting to the General Assembly

29. An annual report on the activities of the Fund, including details of the contributions to and disbursements from the Fund, will be made to the General Assembly.

11. Implementing office

30. The Division for Ocean Affairs and the Law of the Sea of the Office of Legal Affairs is the implementing office for the Fund and will provide the services required for the operation of the Fund.

12. Revision

31. The General Assembly may revise the above if circumstances so require.

RECORDED VOTE ON RESOLUTION 55/7:

In favour: Algeria, Andorra, Angola, Antigua and Barbuda, Argentina, Armenia, Australia, Austria, Bahamas, Bahrain, Bangladesh, Barbados, Belarus, Belgium, Belize, Bolivia, Brazil, Brunei Darussalam, Bulgaria, Cambodia, Cameroon, Canada, Chile, China, Costa Rica, Côte d'Ivoire, Croatia, Cuba, Cyprus, Czech Republic, Denmark, Djibouti, Dominica, Dominican Republic, Egypt, Equatorial Guinea, Eritrea, Estonia, Ethiopia, Fiji, Finland, France, Gambia, Georgia, Germany, Ghana, Greece, Grenada, Guatemala, Guinea, Guyana, Haiti, Hungary, Iceland, India, Indonesia, Iran, Ireland, Israel, Jamaica, Japan, Jordan, Kazakhstan, Kenya, Kuwait, Lao People's Democratic Republic, Latvia, Lebanon, Lesotho, Libyan Arab Jamahiriya, Liechtenstein, Lithuania, Luxembourg, Malawi, Malaysia, Maldives, Mali, Malta, Marshall Islands, Mauritius, Mexico, Micronesia, Monaco, Mongolia, Morocco, Mozambique, Myanmar, Namibia, Nauru, Nepal, Netherlands, New Zealand, Nicaragua, Nigeria, Norway, Oman, Pakistan, Panama, Papua New Guinea, Paraguay, Philippines, Poland, Portugal, Qatar, Republic of Korea, Republic of Moldova, Romania, Russian Federation, Saint Lucia, Saint Vincent and the Grenadines, Samoa, San Marino, Saudi Arabia, Senegal, Sierra Leone, Singapore, Slovakia, Slovenia, Solomon Islands, South Africa, Spain, Sri Lanka, Sudan, Suriname, Sweden, Tajikistan, Thailand, The former Yugoslav Republic of Macedonia, Togo, Tonga, Trinidad and Tobago, Tunisia, Uganda, Ukraine, United Arab Emirates, United Kingdom, United Republic of Tanzania, United States, Uruguay, Viet Nam, Yemen, Zambia, Zimbabwe.

Against: Saint Kitts and Nevis, Turkey.

Abstaining: Colombia, Ecuador, Peru, Venezuela.

Division for Ocean Affairs and the Law of the Sea

During 2000, the Division for Ocean Affairs and the Law of the Sea of the Office of Legal Affairs continued to fulfil its role as the substantive unit of the Secretariat responsible for reviewing and monitoring all developments related to the law of the sea and ocean affairs, as well as for the implementation of the Convention and related General Assembly resolutions.

The Division undertook three major initiatives under its TRAIN-SEA-COAST (TSC) programme [YUN 1998, p. 1232], designed to build up in-country capacity to improve skills in integrated ocean and coastal management. It conducted the Fourth

Course Developers Workshop and Planning Meeting, at which participants learned how to apply the TSC pedagogic methodology in the course development process. As part of a second national-level initiative, the Rockefeller Brothers Fund provided support to the TSC programme in planning a course development unit in Indonesia and the training of one course developer. Also, in the South Pacific, the TSC programme began planning for the sixth TSC course development unit.

The fifteenth Hamilton Shirley Amerasinghe Memorial Fellowship, established in 1981 [YUN 1981, p. 139], was presented to Margaret N. Mwangi, Senior State Counsel in the Attorney-General's Office in Kenya, who intended to utilize the fellowship to pursue a programme of study in the control of marine pollution.

Chapter V

Other legal questions

In 2000, the Special Committee on the Charter of the United Nations and on the Strengthening of the Role of the Organization pursued its consideration of proposals relating to the maintenance of international peace and security, the peaceful settlement of disputes between States, the future of the Trusteeship Council and, as a priority, the implementation of the Charter provisions on assistance to third States affected by the application of sanctions under Chapter VII. The General Assembly requested the Committee to continue considering those proposals and ways to improve its working methods. It welcomed the Secretary-General's report on the findings of an ad hoc group on developing a methodology for assessing the consequences incurred by third States due to sanctions application.

The Committee on Relations with the Host Country, in a continuing effort to ensure harmonious relations between the UN diplomatic community and the host country (the United States), addressed complaints relating to the security of the permanent missions accredited to the United Nations and the safety of their personnel, the maintenance of conditions for the normal functioning of those missions, the movement, travel and visa applications of their personnel, and the implementation of the Agreement between the United Nations and the United States of America regarding the Headquarters of the United Nations. The Assembly hoped that the issues raised would continue to be resolved in a spirit of cooperation and in accordance with international law.

The United Nations Commission on International Trade Law (UNCITRAL), entrusted with furthering the progressive unification and harmonization of international trade law, made progress in preparing draft instruments or model or uniform laws and rules on several aspects of international commercial arbitration, notably on receivables financing. UNCITRAL's work on privately financed infrastructure projects, initiated in 1996, culminated in the adoption in 2000 of the UNCITRAL Legislative Guide on Privately Financed Infrastructure Projects, an accomplishment which the Assembly commended.

In other action, the Assembly noted the continuing efforts of the Asian-African Legal Consultative Committee towards strengthening the role of the United Nations and its various organs, including the International Court of Justice, through programmes and initiatives undertaken by that Committee.

International organizations and international law

Strengthening the role of the United Nations

Special Committee on UN Charter

Pursuant to General Assembly resolution 54/106 [YUN 1999, p. 1251], the Special Committee on the Charter of the United Nations and on the Strengthening of the Role of the Organization, during its meetings in New York from 10 to 20 April 2000 [A/55/33], continued to consider questions relating to the maintenance of international peace and security, the peaceful settlement of disputes between States, the future of the Trusteeship Council, the improvement of the Committee's working methods and the publications *Repertory of Practice of United Nations Organs* and *Repertoire of the Practice of the Security Council*. It gave priority consideration to the implementation of the Charter provisions on assistance to third States affected by the application of sanctions (see p. 1269).

Discussion of the first item was based on current or previously submitted working papers by the Russian Federation on: the revised (2000) basic conditions and standard criteria for the introduction of sanctions and other coercive measures and their implementation, section I of which was examined paragraph by paragraph; the urgent need for the elaboration of a draft declaration on the basic principles and criteria for the work of UN peacekeeping missions and mechanisms for the prevention and settlement of crises and conflicts (1997); and fundamentals of the legal basis for UN peacekeeping operations in the context of Chapter VI (pacific settlement of disputes) of the Charter (1998). The Russian Federation proposed that the Special Committees on the Charter and on Peacekeeping Operations hold a joint meeting, or set up a joint working group, to deliberate on the proposed key elements of the legal framework, thereby to arrive at a conclusion on the proposal.

Other working papers were submitted by Cuba (1998) on strengthening the role of the Organization and enhancing its effectiveness and by the Libyan Arab Jamahiriya (1998) on strengthening the role of the United Nations in the maintenance of international peace and security. A draft resolution by Belarus and the Russian Federation (1999) recommended that an advisory opinion be requested from the International Court of Justice on the legal consequences of the resort to force by States, either without prior Security Council authorization or outside the context of self-defence.

For its consideration of peaceful dispute settlement, the Special Committee had before it a revised (1998) proposal by Sierra Leone on the establishment of a dispute prevention and early settlement service, and an informal (1999) paper by the United Kingdom on elements for a resolution on dispute prevention and settlement. Both countries subsequently introduced a joint revised (2000) informal working paper containing a draft resolution recalling existing mechanisms (fact-finding and good-will missions, special envoys, observers, good offices, mediators and conciliators), including those created by major multilateral treaties, and taking note of a Secretariat paper [A/AC.182/2000/INF/2] on mechanisms established by the Assembly in the context of dispute prevention and settlement. Additional revisions were suggested during a paragraph-by-paragraph discussion of the draft.

The debate on proposals regarding the future of the Trusteeship Council brought three main views to the fore: that the Council be reconstituted as a trustee and guardian of the common heritage and common concerns of mankind, as proposed by Malta (1996) in the light of Assembly resolution 50/52 [YUN 1995, p. 1342] and of the Secretary-General's proposal for a new concept of trusteeship [YUN 1998, p. 582]; that the status quo be maintained, since the Council's historic mission had yet to be fulfilled; or that it be abolished, its mandate having indeed been fulfilled. Views were also expressed in favour of considering the item in the context of the Charter's reform and biennially rather than annually.

Regarding improving the Committee's work methods, Japan introduced a working paper proposing, among other measures, maximum use of conference services, procedures for submitting proposals, the preliminary evaluation of new proposals, setting priorities, medium- and long-

term work programmes, and holding periodic reviews of the Committee's work methods. Close contact was supported between the Special Committee and other bodies of the Organization dealing with various practical aspects of issues before the Committee, including holding joint meetings and information exchanges.

The Special Committee commended the Secretary-General's ongoing efforts to reduce or eliminate the backlog in the publication of the *Repertory of Practice of United Nations Organs* and *Repertoire of the Practice of the Security Council*, the main sources of information on the Charter's implementation and on the work of its organs.

Report of Secretary-General. As called for by Assembly resolution 54/106, the Secretary-General submitted an August report [A/55/340] describing the steps taken by the Secretariat to expedite the preparation of Supplements to the *Repertory* and the *Repertoire*, the up-to-date status of those publications, their placement on the Internet and action required to eliminate the current backlogs and prevent future ones. Also mentioned was the creation in May of a trust fund for updating the *Repertoire* with a generous contribution from the United Kingdom.

GENERAL ASSEMBLY ACTION

On 12 December [meeting 84], the General Assembly, on the recommendation of the Sixth (Legal) Committee [A/55/613 & Corr.1], adopted **resolution 55/156** without vote [agenda item 163].

Report of the Special Committee on the Charter of the United Nations and on the Strengthening of the Role of the Organization

The General Assembly,

Recalling its resolution 3499(XXX) of 15 December 1975, by which it established the Special Committee on the Charter of the United Nations and on the Strengthening of the Role of the Organization, and its relevant resolutions adopted at subsequent sessions,

Recalling also its resolution 47/233 of 17 August 1993 on the revitalization of the work of the General Assembly,

Recalling further its resolution 47/62 of 11 December 1992 on the question of equitable representation on and increase in the membership of the Security Council,

Taking note of the report of the Open-ended Working Group on the Question of Equitable Representation on and Increase in the Membership of the Security Council and Other Matters related to the Security Council,

Recalling the elements relevant to the work of the Special Committee contained in its resolution 47/120 B of 20 September 1993,

Recalling also its resolution 51/241 of 31 July 1997 on the strengthening of the United Nations system and its resolution 51/242 of 15 September 1997, entitled "Supplement to an Agenda for Peace", by which it adopted the texts on coordination and the question of sanctions imposed by the United Nations, which are annexed to that resolution,

Recalling further that the International Court of Justice is the principal judicial organ of the United Nations, and reaffirming its authority and independence,

Considering the desirability of finding practical ways and means to strengthen the Court, taking into consideration, in particular, the needs resulting from its increased workload,

Taking note of the report of the Secretary-General on the *Repertory of Practice of United Nations Organs* and *Repertoire of the Practice of the Security Council,*

Recalling its resolution 54/106 of 9 December 1999,

Having considered the report of the Special Committee on the work of its session held in 2000,

1. *Takes note* of the report of the Special Committee on the Charter of the United Nations and on the Strengthening of the Role of the Organization;

2. *Decides* that the Special Committee shall hold its next session from 2 to 12 April 2001;

3. *Requests* the Special Committee, at its session in 2001, in accordance with paragraph 5 of General Assembly resolution 50/52 of 11 December 1995:

(a) To continue its consideration of all proposals concerning the question of the maintenance of international peace and security in all its aspects in order to strengthen the role of the United Nations and, in this context, to consider other proposals relating to the maintenance of international peace and security already submitted or which may be submitted to the Special Committee at its session in 2001;

(b) To continue to consider on a priority basis the question of the implementation of the provisions of the Charter of the United Nations related to assistance to third States affected by the application of sanctions under Chapter VII of the Charter, taking into consideration the reports of the Secretary-General, the proposals submitted on this subject, the debate on the question which was held by the Sixth Committee at the fifty-fifth session of the General Assembly and the text on the question of sanctions imposed by the United Nations contained in annex II to Assembly resolution 51/242, and also the implementation of the provisions of Assembly resolutions 50/51 of 11 December 1995, 51/208 of 17 December 1996, 52/162 of 15 December 1997, 53/107 of 8 December 1998 and 54/107 of 9 December 1999;

(c) To continue its work on the question of the peaceful settlement of disputes between States and, in this context, to continue its consideration of proposals relating to the peaceful settlement of disputes between States, including the proposal on the establishment of a dispute settlement service offering or responding with its services early in disputes and those proposals relating to the enhancement of the role of the International Court of Justice;

(d) To continue to consider proposals concerning the Trusteeship Council in the light of the report of the Secretary-General submitted in accordance with General Assembly resolution 50/55 of 11 December 1995, the report of the Secretary-General entitled "Renewing the United Nations: a programme for reform" and the views expressed by States on this subject at the previous sessions of the General Assembly;

(e) To continue to consider, on a priority basis, ways and means of improving its working methods and enhancing its efficiency with a view to identifying widely acceptable measures for future implementation;

4. *Takes note* of subparagraphs *(a)* to *(h)* of paragraph 33 of the report of the Secretary-General, commends the Secretary-General for his continued efforts to reduce the backlog in the publication of the *Repertory of Practice of United Nations Organs,* and endorses the efforts of the Secretary-General to eliminate the backlog in the publication of the *Repertoire of the Practice of the Security Council;*

5. *Invites* the Special Committee at its session in 2001 to continue to identify new subjects for consideration in its future work with a view to contributing to the revitalization of the work of the United Nations, to discuss how to offer its assistance to the working groups of the General Assembly in this field and, in this regard, to consider ways and means of improving coordination between the Special Committee and other working groups dealing with the reform of the Organization, including the role of the Chairperson of the Special Committee for this purpose;

6. *Requests* the Special Committee to submit a report on its work to the General Assembly at the fifty-sixth session;

7. *Decides* to include in the provisional agenda of its fifty-sixth session the item entitled "Report of the Special Committee on the Charter of the United Nations and on the Strengthening of the Role of the Organization".

Assistance to third States affected by Chapter VII sanctions

Special Committee consideration. In the Special Committee debate on the implementation of the Charter provisions related to assistance to third States affected by sanctions [A/55/33], recognition was expressed for the Security Council's continuing efforts to enhance the vigilance of the application of sanctions, evaluate their humanitarian impact on vulnerable groups within the target States and on third States, streamline the working procedures of the sanctions committees and facilitate access to them by third States affected by the implementation of sanctions.

Attention was drawn to the 1998 ad hoc expert group proposals [YUN 1998, p. 1235] that obtained a large measure of support, namely: to draw up a list of potential effects of sanctions on third States; to prepare for the Council an assessment of the potential impact of sanctions on the targeted State and on third States; to entrust the Secretariat with monitoring the effects of sanctions and providing third States with technical assistance in preparing the explanatory materials to accompany their requests for consultations with the Council; and to appoint a special representative of the Secretary-General to undertake a full assessment of the consequences of sanctions incurred by the most severely affected third

States. It was suggested, however, that before embarking on a substantive discussion of the expert group's proposals, the Special Committee could benefit from the Secretary-General's forthcoming report to the General Assembly as to their political, financial and administrative feasibility.

Report of Secretary-General. The Secretary-General's August report with later addendum [A/55/295 & Add.1] noted that, in implementation of the proposals in the Council President's 1999 note [YUN 1999, p. 1252], sanctions committees concerned with arms and other sanctions regimes in Africa had taken steps to open communication channels with relevant bodies of the UN system and with regional and subregional organizations to improve monitoring of sanctions implementation. Other committees began to consider ways to enhance arrangements for exemptions to sanctions on religious grounds. While the committees sought to increase transparency of their work through detailed briefings by their chairpersons, the Secretariat took steps to ensure the timely availability of summary records of their formal meetings.

The report noted that the chairpersons of the sanctions committees concerned with the situations in Angola, Sierra Leone and the Kosovo province of the Federal Republic of Yugoslavia visited those countries to obtain first-hand accounts of the impact of sanctions regimes there; that, at the Council's request, the Secretary-General appointed expert bodies to collect information on the sources and methods of sanctions violations and to recommend measures to end them, such as the monitoring mechanism for the sanctions in Angola (see p. 158) and the panel of experts for Sierra Leone (see p. 204); and that the Sanctions Committee on Sierra Leone held public hearings to assess the role of diamonds in that country's conflict (see p. 203).

The Secretariat continued to provide support to ongoing efforts to facilitate the design of less blunt and more effective sanctions. Its capacity and modalities for implementing the intergovernmental mandates and recommendations of the 1998 ad hoc expert group were under review by several intergovernmental bodies concerned with assisting third States affected by the application of sanctions—a review on which the Secretary-General would base his views regarding the feasibility of implementing the expert group's recommendations. He concurred with the recommendation of the Office of Internal Oversight Services that, after intergovernmental agreement on a methodology for assessing the impact of sanctions on third States, the Department of Economic and Social Affairs and the Department of Political Affairs should review the required activities and capacity needed within the Secretariat. That review was to be the basis for proposed revisions to the medium-term plans of relevant intergovernmental bodies.

The report conveyed the views of the World Food Programme regarding the ad hoc expert group's report and related issues of international assistance; its addendum conveyed those of the United Nations Development Programme and the World Bank.

As to the continuing role of the Assembly, the Economic and Social Council and the Committee for Programme and Coordination (CPC) in assisting third States affected by the application of sanctions, the report cited Economic and Social Council action (see p. 879) and CPC's emphasis on the role of the Administrative Committee on Coordination in the implementation of the relevant intergovernmental mandates for mobilizing and monitoring economic assistance provided by the international community and the UN system to those States [A/55/16].

Security Council consideration. The Security Council President, by a January note [S/2000/27], announced the Council's agreement to elect chairpersons and vice-chairpersons of the following sanctions committees for a period running until 31 December 2000: Committee established by resolution 661(1990) concerning the situation between Iraq and Kuwait; Committee established pursuant to resolution 748(1992) concerning the Libyan Arab Jamahiriya; Committee established pursuant to resolution 751(1992) concerning Somalia; Committee established pursuant to resolution 864(1993) concerning the situation in Angola; Committee established pursuant to resolution 918(1994) concerning Rwanda; Committee established pursuant to resolution 985(1995) concerning Liberia; Committee established pursuant to resolution 1132(1997) concerning Sierra Leone; Committee established pursuant to resolution 1160(1998) concerning Kosovo; and Committee established pursuant to resolution 1267 (1999) concerning Afghanistan.

A further note of April by the President [S/2000/319] pointed to the Council's awareness of the existence of considerable recent scholarship on the subject of UN sanctions meriting its consideration, as well as of efforts by Canada, Germany, Switzerland and the United Kingdom, among others, in sponsoring reports and studies on specific aspects of UN sanctions. Taking account of the President's 1999 proposals for improving the work of the sanctions committees [YUN 1999, p. 1252], the Council decided to establish an informal working group to examine 11 issues from which to develop recommendations on how to improve the effectiveness of UN sanctions and to report by 30 November 2000.

GENERAL ASSEMBLY ACTION

On 12 December [meeting 84], the General Assembly, on the recommendation of the Sixth Committee [A/55/613 & Corr.1], adopted **resolution 55/157** without vote [agenda item 163].

Implementation of the provisions of the Charter of the United Nations related to assistance to third States affected by the application of sanctions

The General Assembly,

Concerned about the special economic problems confronting certain States arising from the carrying out of preventive or enforcement measures taken by the Security Council against other States, and taking into account the obligation of Members of the United Nations under Article 49 of the Charter of the United Nations to join in affording mutual assistance in carrying out the measures decided upon by the Security Council,

Recalling the right of third States confronted with special economic problems of that nature to consult the Security Council with regard to a solution of those problems, in accordance with Article 50 of the Charter,

Recognizing the desirability of the consideration of further appropriate procedures for consultations to deal in a more effective manner with the problems referred to in Article 50 of the Charter,

Recalling:

(*a*) The report of the Secretary-General entitled "An Agenda for Peace", in particular paragraph 41 thereof,

(*b*) Its resolution 47/120 A of 18 December 1992, entitled "An Agenda for Peace: preventive diplomacy and related matters", its resolution 47/120 B of 20 September 1993, entitled "An Agenda for Peace", in particular section IV thereof, entitled "Special economic problems arising from the implementation of preventive or enforcement measures", and its resolution 51/242 of 15 September 1997, entitled "Supplement to an Agenda for Peace", in particular annex II thereto, entitled "Question of sanctions imposed by the United Nations",

(*c*) The position paper of the Secretary-General entitled "Supplement to an Agenda for Peace",

(*d*) The statement by the President of the Security Council of 22 February 1995,

(*e*) The report of the Secretary-General prepared pursuant to the statement by the President of the Security Council regarding the question of special economic problems of States as a result of sanctions imposed under Chapter VII of the Charter,

(*f*) The annual overview reports of the Administrative Committee on Coordination for the period from 1992 to 2000, in particular the sections therein on assistance to countries invoking Article 50 of the Charter of the United Nations,

(*g*) The reports of the Secretary-General on economic assistance to States affected by the implementation of the Security Council resolutions imposing sanctions against the Federal Republic of Yugoslavia and General Assembly resolutions 48/210 of 21 December 1993, 49/21 A of 2 December 1994, 50/58 E of 12 December 1995, 51/30 A of 5 December 1996, 52/169 H of 16 December 1997 and 54/96 G of 15 December 1999,

(*h*) The reports of the Special Committee on the Charter of the United Nations and on the Strengthening of the Role of the Organization on the work of its sessions held in the years 1994 to 2000,

(*i*) The reports of the Secretary-General on the implementation of the provisions of the Charter related to assistance to third States affected by the application of sanctions under Chapter VII of the Charter,

(*j*) The report of the Secretary-General to the Millennium Assembly of the United Nations, in particular section IV.E thereof, entitled "Targeting sanctions",

(*k*) The United Nations Millennium Declaration, in particular paragraph 9 thereof,

Taking note of the most recent report of the Secretary-General, submitted in accordance with General Assembly resolution 54/107 of 9 December 1999,

Taking note also of the report of the Office of Internal Oversight Services on the in-depth evaluation of the United Nations programmes relating to global development trends, issues and policies, and global approaches to social and microeconomic issues and policies, and the corresponding subprogrammes in the regional commissions, in particular recommendation 3 contained therein, as approved by the Committee for Programme and Coordination, at its fortieth session,

Recalling that the question of assistance to third States affected by the application of sanctions has been addressed recently in several forums, including the General Assembly, the Security Council, the Economic and Social Council and their subsidiary organs,

Recalling also the measures taken by the Security Council, in accordance with the statement by the President of the Security Council of 16 December 1994, that, as part of the effort of the Council to improve the flow of information and the exchange of ideas between members of the Council and other States Members of the United Nations, there should be increased recourse to open meetings, in particular at an early stage in its consideration of a subject,

Recalling further the measures taken by the Security Council in accordance with the note by the President of the Security Council of 29 January 1999 aimed at improving the work of the sanctions committees, including increasing the effectiveness and transparency of those committees,

Stressing that, in the formulation of sanctions regimes, due account should be taken of the potential effects of sanctions on third States,

Stressing also, in this context, the powers of the Security Council under Chapter VII of the Charter and the primary responsibility of the Council under Article 24 of the Charter for the maintenance of international peace and security in order to ensure prompt and effective action by the United Nations,

Recalling that, under Article 31 of the Charter, any Member of the United Nations that is not a member of the Security Council may participate, without vote, in the discussion of any question brought before the Council whenever the latter considers that the interests of that Member are specially affected,

Recognizing that the imposition of sanctions under Chapter VII of the Charter has been causing special economic problems in third States and that it is necessary to intensify efforts to address those problems effectively,

Taking into consideration the views of third States which could be affected by the imposition of sanctions,

Recognizing that assistance to third States affected by the application of sanctions would further contribute to an effective and comprehensive approach by the international community to sanctions imposed by the Security Council,

Recognizing also that the international community at large and, in particular, international institutions involved in providing economic and financial assistance should continue to take into account and address in a more effective manner the special economic problems of affected third States arising from the carrying out of preventive or enforcement measures taken by the Security Council under Chapter VII of the Charter, in view of their magnitude and of the adverse impact on the economies of those States,

Recalling the provisions of its resolutions 50/51 of 11 December 1995, 51/208 of 17 December 1996, 52/162 of 15 December 1997, 53/107 of 8 December 1998 and 54/107 of 9 December 1999,

1. *Renews its invitation* to the Security Council to consider the establishment of further mechanisms or procedures, as appropriate, for consultations as early as possible under Article 50 of the Charter of the United Nations with third States which are or may be confronted with special economic problems arising from the carrying out of preventive or enforcement measures imposed by the Council under Chapter VII of the Charter, with regard to a solution of those problems, including appropriate ways and means for increasing the effectiveness of its methods and procedures applied in the consideration of requests by the affected States for assistance;

2. *Welcomes* the measures taken by the Security Council since the adoption of General Assembly resolution 50/51, most recently the note by the President of the Security Council of 17 April 2000, whereby the members of the Security Council decided to establish an informal working group of the Council to develop general recommendations on how to improve the effectiveness of United Nations sanctions, looks forward to the findings of the working group, in particular to those regarding the issues of unintended impacts of sanctions and assistance to States in implementing sanctions, and strongly recommends that the Council continue its efforts to further enhance the effectiveness and transparency of the sanctions committees, to streamline their working procedures and to facilitate access to them by representatives of States that find themselves confronted with special economic problems arising from the carrying out of sanctions;

3. *Requests* the Secretary-General to pursue the implementation of General Assembly resolutions 50/51, 51/208, 52/162, 53/107 and 54/107 and to ensure that the competent units within the Secretariat develop the adequate capacity and appropriate modalities, technical procedures and guidelines to continue, on a regular basis, to collate and coordinate information about international assistance available to third States affected by the implementation of sanctions, to continue developing a possible methodology for assessing the adverse consequences actually incurred by third States and to explore innovative and practical measures of assistance to the affected third States;

4. *Welcomes* the report of the Secretary-General containing a summary of the deliberations and main findings of the ad hoc expert group meeting on developing a methodology for assessing the consequences incurred by third States as a result of preventive or enforcement measures and on exploring innovative and practical measures of international assistance to the affected third States, and renews its invitation to States and relevant international organizations within and outside the United Nations system which have not yet done so to provide their views regarding the report of the ad hoc expert group meeting;

5. *Renews its request* to the Secretary-General to present to the General Assembly any further views that he may have, as appropriate, on the deliberations and main findings, including the recommendations, of the ad hoc expert group on the implementation of the provisions of the Charter related to assistance to third States affected by the application of sanctions, taking into account the views of States, the organizations of the United Nations system, international financial institutions and other international organizations, as well as the forthcoming report of the informal working group of the Security Council on general issues relating to sanctions;

6. *Reaffirms* the important role of the General Assembly, the Economic and Social Council and the Committee for Programme and Coordination in mobilizing and monitoring, as appropriate, the economic assistance efforts by the international community and the United Nations system on behalf of States confronted with special economic problems arising from the carrying out of preventive or enforcement measures imposed by the Security Council and, as appropriate, in identifying solutions to the special economic problems of those States;

7. *Takes note* of the decision of the Economic and Social Council, in its resolution 2000/32 of 28 July 2000, to continue consideration of the question of assistance to third States affected by the application of sanctions, invites the Council, at its organizational session for 2001, to make appropriate arrangements for this purpose within its programme of work for 2001, and decides to transmit the most recent report of the Secretary-General on the implementation of the provisions of the Charter related to assistance to third States affected by the application of sanctions, together with the relevant background materials, to the Council at its substantive session of 2001;

8. *Invites* the organizations of the United Nations system, international financial institutions, other international organizations, regional organizations and Member States to address more specifically and directly, where appropriate, special economic problems of third States affected by sanctions imposed under Chapter VII of the Charter and, for this purpose, to consider improving procedures for consultations to maintain a constructive dialogue with such States, including through regular and frequent meetings as well as, where appropriate, special meetings between the affected third States and the donor community, with the participation of United Nations agencies and other international organizations;

9. *Requests* the Special Committee on the Charter of the United Nations and on the Strengthening of the Role of the Organization, at its session in 2001, to continue to consider on a priority basis the question of the implementation of the provisions of the Charter related to assistance to third States affected by the application of sanctions under Chapter VII of the Charter, taking into consideration all of the related reports of the Secretary-General, in particular the 1998 report containing a summary of the deliberations and main findings of the ad hoc expert group meeting convened pursuant to paragraph 4 of General Assembly resolution 52/162, together with the most recent report of the Secretary-General on this question, the forthcoming report of the informal working group of the Security Council on general issues relating to sanctions, the proposals submitted on the question, the debate on the question in the Sixth Committee during the fifty-fifth session of the Assembly and the text on the question of sanctions imposed by the United Nations contained in annex II to Assembly resolution 51/242, as well as the implementation of the provisions of Assembly resolutions 50/51, 51/208, 52/162, 53/107 and 54/107 and the present resolution;

10. *Decides* to consider, within the Sixth Committee, or a working group of the Committee, at the fifty-sixth session of the General Assembly, further progress in the elaboration of effective measures aimed at the implementation of the provisions of the Charter related to assistance to third States affected by the application of sanctions under Chapter VII of the Charter;

11. *Requests* the Secretary-General to submit a report on the implementation of the present resolution to the General Assembly at its fifty-sixth session, under the agenda item entitled "Report of the Special Committee on the Charter of the United Nations and on the Strengthening of the Role of the Organization".

Cooperation with the Asian-African Legal Consultative Committee

As requested by General Assembly resolution 53/14 [YUN 1998, p. 1241], the Secretary-General submitted an August report on the status of cooperation between the United Nations and the Asian-African Legal Consultative Committee (AALCC) [A/55/221] since his 1998 report. In keeping with the cooperation framework agreed upon by the two organizations, both routinely held consultations and exchanged documentation and information on matters of common interest in the field of international law, including economic, environmental and humanitarian law.

The report provided details of AALCC representation at UN meetings and conferences, and UN representation at AALCC sessions; AALCC contributions towards strengthening the role of the United Nations and implementing the programme of the United Nations Decade of International Law (1990-1999), in furthering the work of the Assembly's Sixth Committee, notably on environmental law, dispute settlement and jurisdictional immunities of States and their proper-

ties, and in promoting the ratification and implementation of the United Nations Convention on the Law of the Sea; and AALCC activities in international economic cooperation for development, including monitoring the work of the World Trade Organization, and in the development of refugee law. Other issues before AALCC were environment and development, legal protection of migrant workers, extraterritorial application of national legislation in relation to sanctions imposed against third parties, and the deportation of Palestinians and other Israeli practices.

In his statement before the Assembly on 25 October [A/55/PV.39], the AALCC Secretary-General affirmed AALCC's commitment to share responsibility in promoting the effective implementation of various international legal instruments.

GENERAL ASSEMBLY ACTION

On 25 October [meeting 39], the General Assembly adopted **resolution 55/4** [draft: A/55/L.12 & Add.1] without vote [agenda item 22].

Cooperation between the United Nations and the Asian-African Legal Consultative Committee

The General Assembly,

Recalling its resolutions 36/38 of 18 November 1981, 37/8 of 29 October 1982, 38/37 of 5 December 1983, 39/47 of 10 December 1984, 40/60 of 9 December 1985, 41/5 of 17 October 1986, 43/1 of 17 October 1988, 45/4 of 16 October 1990, 47/6 of 21 October 1992, 49/8 of 25 October 1994, 51/11 of 4 November 1996 and 53/14 of 29 October 1998,

Having considered the report of the Secretary-General on cooperation between the United Nations and the Asian-African Legal Consultative Committee,

Having heard the statement made by the Secretary-General of the Asian-African Legal Consultative Committee on the steps taken by the Consultative Committee to ensure continuing, close and effective cooperation between the two organizations,

1. *Takes note with appreciation* of the report of the Secretary-General;

2. *Notes with satisfaction* the continuing efforts of the Asian-African Legal Consultative Committee towards strengthening the role of the United Nations and its various organs, including the International Court of Justice, through programmes and initiatives undertaken by the Consultative Committee;

3. *Also notes with satisfaction* the commendable progress achieved towards enhancing cooperation between the United Nations and the Consultative Committee in wider areas;

4. *Notes with appreciation* the decision of the Consultative Committee to participate actively in the programmes of the United Nations Decade of International Law and programmes on environment and sustainable development, as well as in the United Nations Diplomatic Conference of Plenipotentiaries on the Establishment of the International Criminal Court;

5. *Also notes with appreciation* the initiative and efforts the Consultative Committee will undertake to

promote the objectives and principles set out in the United Nations Millennium Declaration, including wider acceptance of multilateral treaties deposited with the Secretary-General;

6. *Requests* the Secretary-General to submit to the General Assembly at its fifty-seventh session a report on cooperation between the United Nations and the Consultative Committee;

7. *Decides* to include in the provisional agenda of its fifty-seventh session the item entitled "Cooperation between the United Nations and the Asian-African Legal Consultative Committee".

Host country relations

At five meetings held in New York between 9 March and 1 November 2000 [A/55/26], the Committee on Relations with the Host Country continued to consider the following aspects of relations between the UN diplomatic community and the United States, the host country: housing for diplomatic personnel; host country travel regulations; acceleration of immigration and customs procedures; and issues arising from the implementation of the Agreement between the United Nations and the United States of America regarding the Headquarters of the United Nations, contained in General Assembly resolution 169(II) [YUN 1947-48, p. 199]. Since there were no new developments regarding the use of diplomatic motor vehicles, parking and related matters, the working group established in 1997 to consider those issues [YUN 1997, p. 1376] did not meet in 2000, nor did the working group on indebtedness meet during the reporting period.

Housing for diplomatic personnel

On 9 March, the Committee Chairman indicated a likely problem with the landlord practice of requiring diplomats of permanent missions accredited to the United Nations to execute waivers of diplomatic immunity and, in the event of a systematic problem, suggested referring the matter to the working group on indebtedness. The Russian Federation asserted that such a demand was contrary to international law and tantamount to blackmail, adding that it would welcome state and federal assistance, particularly in respect of its difficulties in rebuilding its apartment complex in Riverdale (Bronx, New York). Expressing concern about reports that that practice was widespread, the United States urged Members to put allegations of discrimination in writing to enable investigation. Iraq confirmed that obtaining housing for its mission staff was problematic owing to the refusal of rental agencies to rent to them, even though Iraq had never had any problem with landlords. Malaysia echoed those difficulties.

Host country travel regulations

On 9 March, the Libyan Arab Jamahiriya called on the host country to facilitate travel within the United States, saying that the announced easing of travel restrictions had not occurred. It moreover referred to the restrictions on the movement of its mission personnel, who were currently confined to New York's five boroughs. Protesting also the host country's single-entry-visa policy, it urged the issuance of multiple-entry visas. Cuba stated that it was subject to similar restrictions and to delays in the granting of visas, and that the lack of multiple-entry visas had impeded the work of its representative on the Advisory Committee on Administrative and Budgetary Questions (ACABQ).

The host country pointed out that the restrictions on the Libyan Arab Jamahiriya were imposed in the proper exercise of national security, and that the visa application for Cuba's ACABQ representative had not been submitted to allow for the required 15-day processing period. Pursuant to the host Government's internal regulations, multiple-entry visas were available to citizens of some countries, not of all. The obligation of the host country was to issue visas to officials coming to the United Nations and the time or validity of their visas was for it to decide as it saw fit.

Cuba, referring to the written request required for the movement of its representatives 25 kilometres beyond the Headquarters district, said the host authorities' persistent invocation of national security did not reflect post-cold-war realities. The Russian Federation agreed that the outdated stereotypes used to justify claims of national security were unconvincing and placed too much weight on potential threats. The host country restated that it was not violating its obligations under the Headquarters Agreement or international law. Because the threat of international terrorism was real, concerns about national security should not be dismissed lightly. The United States maintained that it placed no impediments to the official business of missions or their staff; rejections were made only with respect to requests for personal travel.

The Committee urged the host country to remove the remaining travel restrictions in question as soon as possible.

Acceleration of immigration and customs procedures

In July, Iraq protested the late issuance of entry visas to its delegates, noting that such delay was particularly onerous with regard to special sessions and conferences. It referred to its 11 June complaint about the inhumane treatment of an Iraqi official applying for a visa, the United

States response to which provided no satisfactory explanation. The host country expressed surprise over the allegation, pointing out that the official in question had declined the government visa offered as she was not representing the Government and had therefore been granted a tourist visa, which required her to be photographed and fingerprinted. Neither those procedures nor the area in which they were conducted was inhumane or reserved for criminals. The host country confirmed its sovereign right to decide on the eligibility and procedures for entry into its territory and said it was very careful to ensure that visas were issued on time, especially when applications had been submitted on time.

The Committee anticipated that the host country would ensure timely issuance of entry visas to representatives of Member States, including to attend official UN meetings.

Implementation of Headquarters Agreement

On 26 July, Argentina, on behalf of the Latin American and Caribbean Group, expressed indignation over the lack of courtesy of the New York City police engaged in carrying out security arrangements for the upcoming Millennium Summit (see p. 47) and called on the local authorities to issue instructions to all appropriate levels to respect the members of the diplomatic community. Cuba's position was that security measures should not interfere with the ability of the permanent missions to do their work. The host country confirmed that it would make every effort to maintain open and free access to UN Headquarters, but that it was also necessary to accept the measures required to ensure the safety and security of the more than 150 heads of State expected at the Summit. The Committee appreciated the host country's efforts in that regard and anticipated that it would continue to take all steps necessary to prevent any interference with the missions' functioning.

On 28 August, Cuba, observing that the host country's denial of entry visas was a recurring problem for it, lamented that the President of Cuba's National Assembly had been denied a visa to attend the Conference of Presiding Officers of National Parliaments, to be convened at Headquarters (30 August–1 September) by the Inter-Parliamentary Union (IPU) in conjunction with the Millennium Assembly, because the Conference was not a UN meeting under the terms of the Headquarters Agreement. The Libyan Arab Jamahiriya regarded the denial as a violation of that Agreement, while Iraq urged a broader interpretation of it. China, Costa Rica, France, Honduras, Hungary, Mali, Mexico, the Russian Federation and Spain appealed to the host country to reconsider its position, given the close link between the Conference and the Millennium Assembly. The host country reaffirmed its position that the Agreement did not apply to the Conference and thus it had no obligation to issue the visas. However, it had decided, in response to the Secretary-General's appeal, to issue visas to two of the four parliamentarians of the Cuban National Assembly and would consider the appeals made, but reiterated that it had no obligation to issue the visas.

At the Committee Chairman's request, the Assistant Secretary-General in charge of the Office of Legal Affairs, on 1 September, orally delivered the Legal Counsel's opinion on the status of the Conference and the host country's obligations relative to the issuance of visas to the participants. The Legal Counsel concluded that, as the Conference was convened by IPU and not by the United Nations, it could not be considered a UN meeting and thus could not be deemed to constitute "official United Nations business" within the meaning of section 11 of the Headquarters Agreement. The denial of entry visas to the Conference invitees would not therefore constitute a violation of the host country's obligations under the Agreement. However, in view of General Assembly resolutions 53/13 [YUN 1998, p. 1341], 54/12 [YUN 1999, p. 1357] and 54/281 (see p. 1367) and of the fact that the Conference was being held in conjunction with the Millennium Summit, the Conference was clearly a UN-related meeting. Thus, while the host country could not be called upon to issue the visas as a matter of legal obligation, the nexus between the Conference and the United Nations was such that the host country could be expected to do so as a matter of courtesy. Since the Agreement did not specifically cover UN-related meetings and since such meetings might become increasingly common as relations between the United Nations and other international and non-governmental actors expanded, the Committee might wish to consider recommending to the General Assembly that it include an appropriate request to the host country in the context of its future resolutions welcoming meetings and conferences at Headquarters related to or held in conjunction with its sessions and work.

In noting the foregoing opinion, the Committee recommended that the host country take it into consideration in the future.

GENERAL ASSEMBLY ACTION

On 12 December [meeting 84], the General Assembly, on the recommendation of the Sixth Committee [A/55/611 & Corr.1], adopted **resolution 55/154** without vote [agenda item 161].

Report of the Committee on Relations with the Host Country

The General Assembly,

Having considered the report of the Committee on Relations with the Host Country,

Recalling Article 105 of the Charter of the United Nations, the Convention on the Privileges and Immunities of the United Nations, the Agreement between the United Nations and the United States regarding the Headquarters of the United Nations and the responsibilities of the host country,

Recalling also that, in accordance with paragraph 7 of General Assembly resolution 2819(XXVI) of 15 December 1971, the Committee should consider, and advise the host country on, issues arising in connection with the implementation of the Agreement between the United Nations and the United States regarding the Headquarters of the United Nations,

Recognizing that effective measures should continue to be taken by the competent authorities of the host country, in particular to prevent any acts violating the security of missions and the safety of their personnel,

1. *Endorses* the recommendations and conclusions of the Committee on Relations with the Host Country contained in paragraph 62 of its report;

2. *Notes* that the Committee has taken note of the opinion of the Legal Counsel of 1 September 2000 concerning the issuance of visas to participants in United Nations–related meetings and that, in this connection, the Committee has recommended that the host country take that opinion into consideration in the future;

3. *Considers* that the maintenance of appropriate conditions for the normal work of the delegations and the missions accredited to the United Nations is in the interest of the United Nations and all Member States, and requests the host country to continue to take all measures necessary to prevent any interference with the functioning of missions;

4. *Expresses its appreciation* for the efforts made by the host country, and hopes that the issues raised at the meetings of the Committee will continue to be resolved in a spirit of cooperation and in accordance with international law;

5. *Notes* that during the reporting period the travel controls previously imposed by the host country on staff of certain missions and staff members of the Secretariat of certain nationalities remained in effect, and requests the host country to consider removing such travel controls, and in this regard notes the positions of affected States, of the Secretary-General and of the host country;

6. *Also notes* that the Committee anticipates that the host country will continue to ensure the issuance, in a timely manner, of entry visas to representatives of Member States, pursuant to article IV, section 11, of the Agreement between the United Nations and the United States regarding the Headquarters of the United Nations, inter alia, for the purpose of their attending official United Nations meetings;

7. *Requests* the host country to continue to take steps to resolve the problem relating to the parking of diplomatic vehicles in a fair, balanced and non-discriminatory way, with a view to responding to the growing needs of the diplomatic community, and to continue to consult with the Committee on this important issue;

8. *Requests* the Secretary-General to remain actively engaged in all aspects of the relations of the United Nations with the host country;

9. *Requests* the Committee to continue its work in conformity with General Assembly resolution 2819(XXVI);

10. *Decides* to include in the provisional agenda of its fifty-sixth session the item entitled "Report of the Committee on Relations with the Host Country".

International economic law

Legal aspects of international economic law continued to be considered in 2000 by the United Nations Commission on International Trade Law (UNCITRAL) and by the Sixth Committee of the General Assembly.

International trade law

At its thirty-third session (New York, 12 June–7 July), UNCITRAL considered privately financed infrastructure projects, electronic commerce, assignment in receivables financing, insolvency, implementation of the 1958 Convention on the Recognition and Enforcement of Foreign Arbitral Awards (New York Convention) [YUN 1958, p. 390], transport law, endorsement of texts of other organizations, case law on UNCITRAL texts, training and technical assistance, status and promotion of UNCITRAL texts, and relevant General Assembly resolutions on the Commission's work. The report on the session [A/55/17] described action taken on those topics and annexed a list of related documents.

GENERAL ASSEMBLY ACTION

On 12 December [meeting 84], the General Assembly, on the recommendation of the Sixth Committee [A/55/608], adopted **resolution 55/151** without vote [agenda item 158].

Report of the United Nations Commission on International Trade Law on the work of its thirty-third session

The General Assembly,

Recalling its resolution 2205(XXI) of 17 December 1966, by which it created the United Nations Commission on International Trade Law with a mandate to further the progressive harmonization and unification of the law of international trade and in that respect to bear in mind the interests of all peoples, in particular those of developing countries, in the extensive development of international trade,

Reaffirming its conviction that the progressive harmonization and unification of international trade law, in reducing or removing legal obstacles to the flow of international trade, especially those affecting the developing countries, would contribute significantly to universal economic cooperation among all States on a basis of equality, equity and common interest and to the elimination of discrimination in international trade and, thereby, to the well-being of all peoples,

Emphasizing the need for higher priority to be given to the work of the Commission in view of the increasing value of the modernization of international trade law for global economic development and thus for the maintenance of friendly relations among States,

Stressing the value of participation by States at all levels of economic development and from different legal systems in the process of harmonizing and unifying international trade law,

Having considered the report of the Commission on the work of its thirty-third session,

Concerned that activities undertaken by other bodies of the United Nations system in the field of international trade law without coordination with the Commission might lead to undesirable duplication of efforts and would not be in keeping with the aim of promoting efficiency, consistency and coherence in the unification and harmonization of international trade law, as stated in its resolution 37/106 of 16 December 1982,

Stressing the importance of the further development of case law on United Nations Commission on International Trade Law texts in promoting the uniform application of the legal texts of the Commission and its value for government officials, practitioners and academics,

1. *Takes note with appreciation* of the report of the United Nations Commission on International Trade Law on the work of its thirty-third session;

2. *Commends* the Commission for the work on privately financed infrastructure projects, which culminated in the adoption of the UNCITRAL Legislative Guide on Privately Financed Infrastructure Projects, as well as the important progress made in its work on receivables financing;

3. *Appeals* to Governments that have not yet done so to reply to the questionnaire circulated by the Secretariat in relation to the legal regime governing the recognition and enforcement of foreign arbitral awards and, in particular, to the legislative implementation of the Convention on the Recognition and Enforcement of Foreign Arbitral Awards, done at New York on 10 June 1958;

4. *Invites* States to nominate persons to work with the private foundation established to encourage assistance to the Commission from the private sector;

5. *Reaffirms* the mandate of the Commission, as the core legal body within the United Nations system in the field of international trade law, to coordinate legal activities in this field and, in this connection:

(a) Calls upon all bodies of the United Nations system and invites other international organizations to bear in mind the mandate of the Commission and the need to avoid duplication of effort and to promote efficiency, consistency and coherence in the unification and harmonization of international trade law;

(b) Recommends that the Commission, through its secretariat, continue to maintain close cooperation with the other international organs and organizations, including regional organizations, active in the field of international trade law;

6. *Also reaffirms* the importance, in particular for developing countries, of the work of the Commission concerned with training and technical assistance in the field of international trade law, such as assistance in the preparation of national legislation based on legal texts of the Commission;

7. *Expresses the desirability* for increased efforts by the Commission, in sponsoring seminars and symposia, to provide such training and technical assistance, and, in this connection:

(a) Expresses its appreciation to the Commission for organizing seminars and briefing missions in Brazil, Cameroon, Côte d'Ivoire, Madagascar, Peru, the Russian Federation and South Africa;

(b) Expresses its appreciation to the Governments whose contributions enabled the seminars and briefing missions to take place, and appeals to Governments, the relevant bodies of the United Nations system, organizations, institutions and individuals to make voluntary contributions to the United Nations Commission on International Trade Law Trust Fund for Symposia and, where appropriate, to the financing of special projects, and otherwise to assist the secretariat of the Commission in financing and organizing seminars and symposia, in particular in developing countries, and in the award of fellowships to candidates from developing countries to enable them to participate in such seminars and symposia;

8. *Appeals* to the United Nations Development Programme and other bodies responsible for development assistance, such as the International Bank for Reconstruction and Development and the European Bank for Reconstruction and Development, as well as to Governments in their bilateral aid programmes, to support the training and technical assistance programme of the Commission and to cooperate and coordinate their activities with those of the Commission;

9. *Appeals* to Governments, the relevant bodies of the United Nations system, organizations, institutions and individuals, in order to ensure full participation by all Member States in the sessions of the Commission and its working groups, to make voluntary contributions to the trust fund for travel assistance to developing countries that are members of the Commission, at their request and in consultation with the Secretary-General;

10. *Decides*, in order to ensure full participation by all Member States in the sessions of the Commission and its working groups, to continue, in the competent Main Committee during the fifty-fifth session of the General Assembly, its consideration of granting travel assistance to the least developed countries that are members of the Commission, at their request and in consultation with the Secretary-General;

11. *Requests* the Secretary-General to strengthen the secretariat of the Commission within the bounds of the resources available so as to ensure and enhance the effective implementation of the programme of the Commission;

12. *Stresses* the importance of bringing into effect the conventions emanating from the work of the Commission for the global unification and harmonization of international trade law, and to this end urges States that have not yet done so to consider signing, ratifying or acceding to those conventions;

13. *Requests* the Secretary-General to submit to the General Assembly at its fifty-sixth session a report on the implications of increasing the membership of the

Commission, and invites Member States to submit their views on this issue;

14. *Expresses its appreciation* to Gerold Herrmann, Secretary of the United Nations Commission on International Trade Law since 1991, who will retire on 31 January 2001, for his outstanding and devoted contribution to the process of unification and harmonization of international trade law in general and to the Commission in particular.

Also on 12 December, the Assembly, by **decision 55/428**, decided to resume consideration of the legal aspects of international economic relations at its fifty-eighth (2003) session and to include in the provisional agenda of that session the item entitled "Progressive development of the principles and norms of international law relating to the new international economic order".

International commercial arbitration

Assignment in receivables financing

UNCITRAL began consideration of the draft articles of the 1999 draft convention on assignment in receivables financing [YUN 1999, p. 1264], postponing discussion of the title and preamble until it had considered the scope of the convention. The related documents before UNCITRAL included the report of the Working Group on International Contract Practices on its thirty-first session (Vienna, 11-22 October 1999), a compilation of comments by Governments and international organizations on the draft, and an article-by-article analytical commentary prepared by the Secretariat.

UNCITRAL requested a Secretariat drafting group to review draft articles 1 to 17 for consistency between the various language versions. Following its consideration of that group's report, UNCITRAL adopted articles 1 to 17 as revised, with the exception of the bracketed texts in those articles and of article 1, paragraph 5, and subject to consideration of certain issues in articles 7 and 17. It revised the title to read "Convention on Assignment of Receivables in International Trade", as well as the preamble. It was agreed that a commentary to the draft convention could explain that the term "international trade" was used in the widest possible sense and was intended to include trade, financial and consumer transactions.

In view of the changes made to articles 1 to 17, UNCITRAL referred the draft convention back to the Working Group with a request that it proceed expeditiously with considering all unsettled issues and effect purely drafting changes in those articles. The Working Group did so at its thirty-second session (Vienna, 11-22 December) and

adopted the draft convention as a whole, with the exception of the bracketed texts, and submitted it to UNCITRAL for final review in 2001. It was noted that the draft convention as adopted by the Working Group would be distributed to all States and interested international organizations for their comments, and that the Secretariat would prepare an analytical compilation of those comments for distribution in advance of UNCITRAL's 2001 session, as well as a revised version of the commentary to the draft convention.

Privately financed infrastructure projects

At its June/July session [A/55/17], UNCITRAL conducted a final examination of the latest revised draft of a legislative guide on privately financed infrastructure projects, as contained in a report by the Secretary-General. On 29 June, UNCITRAL adopted the draft guide in its entirety, subject to a number of amendments, together with the notes to the recommendations, which the Secretariat was authorized to finalize in the light of the current session's deliberations. As finalized, the Guide consisted of chapters I to VII, with a total of 71 recommendations, published under the title "UNCITRAL Legislative Guide on Privately Financed Infrastructure Projects". UNCITRAL asked the Secretariat to transmit the text to Governments and other interested bodies and to ensure its widest possible dissemination. It recommended that all States give it favourable consideration when revising or adopting legislation relevant to privately financed infrastructure projects.

The desirability or feasibility of preparing a model law or model legislative provisions on selected issues covered by the Legislative Guide was deferred to 2001. To assist UNCITRAL in making an informed decision on the matter, it was agreed that the Secretariat, in cooperation with other international organizations or financial institutions, should organize a colloquium to disseminate knowledge about the Legislative Guide or solicit the views of the widest possible spectrum of experts on the matter and report to UNCITRAL.

Electronic commerce

UNCITRAL considered the reports of the Working Group on Electronic Commerce on the work of its thirty-fifth (Vienna, 6-17 September 1999) and thirty-sixth (New York, 14-25 February 2000) sessions in preparation of draft uniform rules on electronic signatures. UNCITRAL noted that the Working Group had adopted the texts of articles 1 and 3 to 12, with some issues remaining to be clarified as a result of the Group's deletion of the notion of enhanced electronic signature from the rules. It expressed appreciation for the Group's efforts and the progress it had achieved. The Working Group was urged to complete work on the draft uniform rules at its thirty-seventh session and to review the draft guide to enactment to be prepared by the Secretariat.

In a preliminary exchange of views on future work in the field of electronic commerce, three possible topics were suggested: electronic contracting, considered from the perspective of the United Nations Sales Convention, which was generally felt to constitute a readily acceptable framework for online contracts dealing with the sale of goods; dispute settlement, to determine whether specific rules were needed to facilitate the increased use of online dispute settlement mechanisms; and dematerialization of documents of title, particularly in the transport industry. A study might be undertaken to assess the desirability and feasibility of establishing a uniform statutory framework to support the development of contractual schemes currently being set up to replace traditional paper-based bills of lading by electronic messages, which should not be restricted to maritime bills of lading but should also envisage other modes of transportation; outside the sphere of transport law, it might also deal with issues of dematerialized securities.

UNCITRAL agreed that the Working Group, upon completing its current task, would examine in 2001 some or all of the topics mentioned, as well as any additional topic, and make specific proposals for UNCITRAL's future work.

In view of the rapid development of electronic commerce, a considerable number of projects with a possible impact on that field were being planned or undertaken. The Secretariat was asked to carry out appropriate monitoring and to report to UNCITRAL as to how the function of coordination was being fulfilled to avoid duplication of work and to ensure harmony in the development of various projects. The area of electronic commerce was generally regarded as one in which UNCITRAL's coordination mandate could be exercised with particular benefit to the global community and deserved corresponding attention from the Working Group and the Secretariat.

Implementation of the 1958 New York Convention

UNCITRAL noted that, at the beginning of its June/July session, the Secretariat had received 59 replies to the questionnaire it had sent relating to the legal regime governing the recognition and enforcement of foreign awards in States parties to the 1958 Convention on the Recognition and Enforcement of Foreign Arbitral Awards (New York Convention) [YUN 1958, p. 390]. UNCITRAL called on the remaining States parties to submit their replies or to inform the Secretariat about any new developments since their previous replies to the questionnaire, and requested the Secretariat to present its findings based on an analysis of the information gathered.

UNCITRAL considered the report of the Working Group on Arbitration on its thirty-second session (Vienna, 20-31 March 2000), which began considering the priority items for future work in the area of international commercial arbitration entrusted to it in 1999 [YUN 1999, p. 1265] and exchanged preliminary views on other possible topics. UNCITRAL took note of the report and commended the work accomplished. It reaffirmed the Working Group's mandate to decide on the time and manner of dealing with those topics. It also called for coordination between the Working Group and the Advisory Group on the European Convention on International Commercial Arbitration of the Economic Commission for Europe and stated that the latter's work should not overlap UNCITRAL's work at the global level.

Case law on UNCITRAL texts

UNCITRAL noted the ongoing work under the system for the collection and dissemination of case law on UNCITRAL texts (CLOUT). It expressed appreciation to national correspondents for their valuable work in the collection of relevant decisions and arbitral awards and in the preparation of case abstracts, as well as to the Secretariat for compiling, editing, issuing and distributing case abstracts. It noted that, whereas 62 jurisdictions had appointed national correspondents, another 26 had not done so. Noting the importance of uniform reporting from all jurisdictions, UNCITRAL urged States that had not appointed a national correspondent to do so. Also noted was the significant increase in the number of States adhering to conventions or enacting legislation based on model laws drawn up by UNCITRAL. Concern was expressed that the resultant increase in the caseload would put the continuation of CLOUT at risk if the human and financial resources of the UNCITRAL secretariat were not correspondingly increased.

Transport law

UNCITRAL took note of a March report of the Secretary-General on possible future work in transport law, which described the progress of work carried out by the Comité maritime international (CMI) in cooperation with the Secretariat to solicit information, ideas and opinions as to problems in transport law arising in practice and possible solutions. It further took note of an oral report on behalf of CMI on the preliminary work accomplished and of a transport law colloquium being organized jointly by the Secretariat and CMI on 6 July in the context of the current UNCITRAL session. The colloquium's purpose was to gather ideas and expert opinions on problems arising in the international carriage of goods, in particular carriage by sea, for incorporation into a report to be presented in 2001, to allow UNCITRAL to take an informed decision on a course of action.

The Secretariat was requested to continue co-operating actively with CMI with a view to presenting at UNCITRAL's 2001 session a report identifying transport law issues for possible inclusion in UNCITRAL's work programme.

Endorsement of texts of other organizations

UNCITRAL had before it three reports by the Secretary-General requesting its endorsement for the worldwide use of the following: the new Rules on International Standby Practices (ISP98), sought by the Director of the Institute of International Banking Law and Practice, Inc., following endorsement of those rules by the Commission on Banking Technique and Practice of the International Chamber of Commerce (ICC); the ICC Uniform Rules for Contract Bonds (URCB); and Incoterms 2000, the official ICC rules for the interpretation of contractual trade terms. It was pointed out that in a number of countries not all of the ISP98 provisions would conform with existing legal rules. Nonetheless, it was agreed, in the context of legal instruments emanating from other international organizations, that "endorsement" should be interpreted as commendation of those instruments for use as a record of good international commercial practice; it should carry no implication, however, as to the instruments' conformity with existing law.

UNCITRAL adopted a decision endorsing the three instruments and commending their use in international trade and financing transactions.

Model law on corporate insolvency

UNCITRAL considered the report of the Working Group on Insolvency Law on the work of its twenty-second session (Vienna, 6-17 December 1999). As requested, the Group explored, in the light of current regulatory practices and laws, the feasibility of developing a universally acceptable model law or principles for insolvency regimes and sought to define the scope of issues to be included. To that end, the Group examined,

among other aspects, the key objectives of an insolvency regime and core features of a national regime, as well as various possible forms that a model instrument might take.

UNCITRAL agreed with the Group's conclusion that a single model insolvency law was neither feasible nor necessary and, as recommended by the Group, mandated it to prepare a comprehensive statement of key objectives and core features for a strong insolvency, debtor-creditor regime, including consideration of out-of-court restructuring, and a legislative guide containing flexible approaches to the implementation of such objectives and features, including a discussion of the possible alternative approaches and the perceived benefits and detriments of such approaches. A legislative guide similar to that adopted by UNCITRAL for privately financed infrastructure projects would be useful and could contain model legislative provisions where appropriate. The Group should be mindful of the work under way or already completed by other organizations, including the International Monetary Fund, the World Bank, the Asian Development Bank, the International Federation of Insolvency Professionals (INSOL International) and the International Bar Association (IBA). In order to obtain the views and benefit from the expertise of those organizations, a colloquium would be held before the Group's next session, which INSOL International and IBA offered to organize with the Secretariat.

Security interests

UNCITRAL considered work undertaken by other organizations in the field of security interests on the basis of an April report by the Secretary-General, which discussed developments in the area of security interests law in the last 25 years, identified trends and problems and suggested possible areas for future work. Among the suggestions made in the discussion was that, in view of the divergent policies of States, a flexible approach aimed at the preparation of a set of principles with a guide, rather than a model law, would be advisable. Furthermore, to ensure optimal benefits from law reform, any efforts on security interests would need to be coordinated with those on insolvency law.

UNCITRAL requested the Secretariat to prepare a study discussing in detail the problems in the field of secured credit law and possible solutions for consideration by the Commission in 2001. The study should draw and build on the work carried out by other organizations and take into account the need to avoid duplication of effort.

Training and technical assistance

UNCITRAL had before it a Secretariat note [A/CN.9/473] indicating training and technical assistance activities undertaken since its 1999 session and the direction of future activities. It reported that 12 seminars and briefing missions were held, financed from the UNCITRAL trust fund for symposiums, and that, for the remainder of 2000, only some requests from Africa, Asia, Latin America and Eastern Europe could be met due to insufficient resources.

UNCITRAL recommended that the General Assembly request the Secretary-General to increase substantially the human and financial resources of its secretariat to enable it fully to implement its training and technical assistance programme aimed at promoting understanding of international commercial law conventions, model laws and other legal texts and at helping Member States with commercial law reform and adoption of UNCITRAL texts. UNCITRAL reiterated its appeal to all States, international organizations and other interested entities for contributions to its trust fund for that purpose and suggested encouraging the private sector to do the same, since it benefited considerably from UNCITRAL's overall work in international trade law.

PART FIVE

Institutional, administrative and budgetary questions

Chapter I

Strengthening and restructuring of the United Nations system

In 2000, the United Nations introduced new measures to further the process of reform of the Organization, including the drafting of a human resources reform package, the elaboration of an information technology policy and the development of a capital master plan. In his report to the Millennium Summit of the General Assembly, the Secretary-General identified constraints preventing the Organization from being more modern and flexible. The Assembly, in the Summit Declaration, urged the Secretariat to make better use of its resources by adopting the best management practices and technology available.

The Secretary-General reported on the implementation of Assembly resolution 54/14 on measures adopted to improve procurement in the United Nations and in the field. He reviewed the work of the UN oversight bodies: the Office of Internal Oversight Services and the Joint Inspection Unit.

The Secretary-General reported some progress in the continuing discussions on increasing the membership of the Security Council within the Open-ended Working Group on the Question of Equitable Representation on and Increase in the Membership of the Security Council and Other Matters related to the Security Council. He made recommendations to further implement the resolutions of the Assembly and the Economic and Social Council on the restructuring and revitalization of the United Nations in the economic, social and related fields.

Programme of reform

General aspects

The Secretary-General continued to implement his programme for UN reform, first introduced in 1997 [YUN 1997, p. 1389]. In his annual report on the work of the Organization (see p. 3), he said that considerable progress had been made during 2000 towards achieving the goal of creating an organizational culture that was responsive and results-oriented. Important developments were the drafting of a human resources reform package, an information technology policy and a capital master plan.

The reform package in human resources proposed fundamental changes in accountability, mobility, recruitment, placement and promotion, and contractual mechanisms (see p. 1337). Other reforms called for improvements in human resource planning and performance management, the streamlining of rules and procedures, the enhancement of skills and competency development, better conditions of service and strengthening the administration of justice. The information technology policy addressed the introduction and management of new information technologies and their use as vehicles for the distribution and management of information. It would also allow for more effective dissemination of greater amounts of information within the United Nations. In that regard, the Department of Public Information implemented a range of innovations to increase the breadth and depth of communication about the United Nations and its work, especially the millennium promotional campaign under the theme "The United Nations Works", which explained how the Organization was addressing the main challenges of the twenty-first century (see p. 572). The long-term capital master plan advanced possible solutions and financing options for dealing with major repairs and refurbishment of the Headquarters complex (see p. 1405).

In other areas, efforts continued to improve the Organization's productivity in terms of the quality, impact and cost-effectiveness of UN programmes, central to which was efficient management. Efficiency and transparency in the procurement process increased. The process of simplifying and streamlining the rules and procedures of the Organization continued, as did preparations to shift to results-based budgeting (see p. 1295). However, the greatest challenge to improving management and productivity over the past three bienniums continued to be financial constraints.

In his March report to the Millennium Summit (see p. 55), entitled "We the peoples: the role of the United Nations in the twenty-first century" [A/54/2000], the Secretary-General said that, were the international community to create a new United Nations, its make-up would have to be different from the current one, whose structure reflected decades of mandates conferred by Member States and, in some cases, the legacy of political disagreements. While there was widespread consensus on the need to make the United Nations more modern and flexible, unless Member States were willing to contemplate real structural reform, severe limits to what the Organization could achieve would continue. UN resources were not commensurate with its global tasks, given the continuing stagnant budgets, nonpayment of dues and imposition of new mandates without additional resources for their execution. The United Nations could not do its job in many areas, because disagreements among Member States precluded the consensus needed for effective action. Moreover, the intrusive and detailed oversight that Member States exercised over programme activities made it difficult to maximize efficiency or effectiveness. To reduce the built-in bias towards institutional inertia afflicting the Organization's work and to facilitate the strategic redeployment of resources, the Secretary-General proposed time limits or "sunset provisions" for initiatives involving new organizational structures or major commitment of funds. A more people-oriented United Nations had to be more results-based, in both staffing and resource allocation.

The General Assembly, by **decision 54/489** of 5 September, included in the draft agenda of its fifty-fifth (2000) session the sub-item entitled "United Nations reform: measures and proposals".

The Assembly, in the Millennium Declaration adopted by **resolution 55/2** on 8 September (see p. 49), resolved to ensure that the Organization was provided on a timely and predictable basis with the resources needed to carry out its mandates. It urged the Secretariat to make the best use of those resources by adopting the best management practices and technologies available and by concentrating on those tasks reflecting the agreed priorities of Member States.

By **decision 55/458** of 23 December, the Assembly decided that the item on UN reform should remain for consideration during its resumed fifty-fifth (2001) session.

Managerial reform and oversight

Procurement

In response to General Assembly resolution 54/14 [YUN 1999, p. 1271], the Secretary-General in February reissued his 1999 report [ibid., p. 1273] to revise the definition of "exigency needs" as it pertained to procurement reform. As revised, the term meant "an exceptional compelling and emergent need, not resulting from poor planning or from concerns over the availability of funds, that will lead to serious damage, loss or injury to property or persons if not addressed immediately" [A/54/650].

By **decision 54/468** of 7 April, the Assembly endorsed the revised definition, with the insertion of the words "or management" between the words "poor planning" and "or from concerns".

Also in response to resolution 54/14, the Secretary-General submitted a May report on measures to improve procurement in the field (see p. 111), consideration of which the Assembly, by **decision 54/462 B** of 15 June, deferred to its fifty-fifth (2000) session. He further submitted a July report on procurement reform [A/55/127], detailing Secretariat initiatives in response to the concerns expressed in the same resolution. Most of those initiatives, which had been implemented and had produced the desired results, were aimed mainly at increasing transparency and evaluation objectivity in the bidding process, encouraging greater vendor participation from developing countries and countries with economies in transition, and increasing the cost-effectiveness of the Secretariat's procurement activities. The Secretary-General remained committed to ensuring that those positive developments were sustained and advanced.

The Advisory Committee on Administrative and Budgetary Questions, in an October report [A/55/458], encouraged the Secretary-General to include information on such initiatives in subsequent reports, as well as an indication of areas where further improvements could be achieved. The Procurement Division should ensure that its human and financial resources were adequate to allow full compliance with resolution 54/14.

Oversight

Internal oversight

The Secretary-General, in transmitting a report on the activities of the Office of Internal Oversight Services (OIOS) (see p. 1288), concurred that OIOS was recognized as an objective source of reliable information and as an agent of change in the Organization, in particular with regard to strengthening internal controls and management performance. He noted the continuing efforts of OIOS to improve relationships with management and Member States and to coordinate its programme with other oversight bodies, including the Board of External Auditors and the Joint Inspection Unit (JIU).

By **decision 54/320** of 2 March, the General Assembly, on the proposal of the Secretary-General [A/54/109], appointed Dileep Nair (Singapore) Under-Secretary-General for Internal

Oversight Services for one five-year fixed term, effective 24 April 2000.

In April, during its resumed fifty-fourth session, the Assembly considered OIOS reports on the following: the review of the programme and administrative practices of the secretariat of the International Trade Centre UNCTAD/WTO (United Nations Conference on Trade and Development/World Trade Organization) [YUN 1997, p. 1400] and related JIU comments [YUN 1998, p. 1259]; investigation into the alleged conflict of interest in the United Nations Centre for Human Settlements (Habitat) [YUN 1997, p. 1099] and JIU's comments thereon [YUN 1998, p. 1259]; the audits of the regional commissions [ibid., p. 918]; the review of programme management in the Crime Prevention and Criminal Justice Division [ibid., p. 1035]; audit of the second United Nations Conference on Human Settlements [ibid., p. 1022]; review of the procurement of Lysol by the Office of the United Nations High Commissioner for Refugees (UNHCR) [A/52/887]; inquiry into allegations of insufficient use of expertise in procurement planning of aviation services in peacekeeping missions [YUN 1998, p. 59]; audit of the commercial insurance programmes [ibid., p. 1363]; audit of the UN health insurance programme [ibid.]; investigation into allegations of theft of funds by an UNCTAD staff member (see p. 1318); review of common services in the United Nations [YUN 1999, p. 1376] and JIU's comments [ibid., p. 1377]; review of the Office for the Coordination of Humanitarian Affairs (OCHA) and JIU's comments [ibid., p. 828]; investigation into the field office in Lebanon of the United Nations Relief and Works Agency for Palestine Refugees in the Near East (see p. 450); management audit of the conference centres at the Economic Commission for Africa (ECA) and the Economic and Social Commission for Asia and the Pacific [ibid., p. 1380]; and investigation into allegations concerning an electronic commerce project at UNCTAD [ibid., p. 911].

GENERAL ASSEMBLY ACTION

On 7 April [meeting 95], the General Assembly, on the recommendation of the Fifth (Administrative and Budgetary) Committee [A/54/511/Add.2], adopted **resolution 54/257** without vote [agenda item 118].

Reports of the Office of Internal Oversight Services
The General Assembly,
Recalling its resolutions 48/218 B of 29 July 1994 and 54/244 of 23 December 1999,

1. *Takes note* of the following reports:
(*a*) Report of the Office of Internal Oversight Services on the audit of the commercial insurance programmes;
(*b*) Report of the Office of Internal Oversight Services on the audits of the regional commissions;

(*c*) Report of the Office of Internal Oversight Services on the audit of the second United Nations Conference on Human Settlements;
(*d*) Report of the Office of Internal Oversight Services on the audit of the United Nations health insurance programme;
(*e*) Report of the Office of Internal Oversight Services on the investigation into allegations of theft of funds by a staff member of the United Nations Conference on Trade and Development;
(*f*) Report of the Office of Internal Oversight Services on the review of common services in the United Nations and the comments of the Joint Inspection Unit thereon;
(*g*) Report of the Office of Internal Oversight Services on the investigation into the field office in Lebanon of the United Nations Relief and Works Agency for Palestine Refugees in the Near East;
(*h*) Report of the Office of Internal Oversight Services on the management audit of conference centres at the Economic Commission for Africa and the Economic and Social Commission for Asia and the Pacific;
(*i*) Report of the Office of Internal Oversight Services on the investigation into allegations concerning an electronic commerce project at the United Nations Conference on Trade and Development;
(*j*) Report of the Office of Internal Oversight Services on the review of the procurement of Lysol by the Office of the United Nations High Commissioner for Refugees;
(*k*) Report of the Office of Internal Oversight Services on the inquiry into allegations of insufficient use of expertise in procurement planning of aviation services in peacekeeping missions;

2. *Takes note also* of the report of the Office of Internal Oversight Services on the review of the Office for the Coordination of Humanitarian Affairs and the comments of the Joint Inspection Unit thereon;

3. *Requests* that, in future, the appropriate legislative mandates relating to the work of the Office for the Coordination of Humanitarian Affairs be included in the reports of the Office of Internal Oversight Services, and also requests that the appropriate legislative mandates be included as well in other future published reports of the Office of Internal Oversight Services;

4. *Takes note* of the report of the Office of Internal Oversight Services on the review of the programme and administrative practices of the secretariat of the International Trade Centre UNCTAD/WTO and the comments of the Unit thereon, reaffirming that the merging of the United Nations Conference on Trade and Development and the International Trade Centre has not been approved by the pertinent legislative bodies;

5. *Takes note also* of the report of the Office of Internal Oversight Services on the review of programme management in the Crime Prevention and Criminal Justice Division, reaffirming that the discontinuation of mandates on crime prevention and criminal justice is within the prerogative of the pertinent legislative bodies;

6. *Takes note further* of the report of the Office of Internal Oversight Services on the investigation into the alleged conflict of interest in the United Nations Centre for Human Settlements (Habitat) and the comments of the Unit thereon, reaffirming that the ap-

proval of amendments to the Staff Regulations of the United Nations and the ratification of amendments to the Staff Rules are the prerogative of Member States.

By **decision 54/478** of the same date, the Assembly deferred consideration of the item on the report of the Secretary-General on OIOS activities until its fifty-fifth (2000) session.

Report of Secretary-General. In October, the Secretary-General transmitted the sixth annual report of OIOS covering its activities from 1 July 1999 to 30 June 2000 [A/55/436].

OIOS issued 16 reports to the General Assembly during the reporting period. Those transmitted in 2000 were on: follow-up review of the programme and administrative practices of Habitat [A/54/764]; audit of contingent-owned equipment procedures and payments to troop-contributing countries [A/54/765 & Corr.1]; follow-up to the 1996 review of the programme and administrative practices of the United Nations Environment Programme (UNEP) [A/54/817]; audit of the Human Rights Field Operation in Rwanda [A/54/836]; strengthening the role of evaluation findings in programme design, delivery and policy directives [A/55/63]; programme performance of the United Nations for the 1998-1999 biennium [A/55/73]; and ways in which the full implementation and quality of mandated programmes and activities could be ensured and could be better assessed by and reported to Member States [A/55/85].

A continuing focus of OIOS was the full implementation of its recommendations. It thus maintained consultations with clients before finalizing its recommendations to ensure their usefulness and during implementation. During the reporting period, the Audit and Management Consulting Division issued 825 recommendations, of which 50 per cent were implemented; the Investigations Section had a 50 per cent implementation rate for its 106 recommendations; and, of the 37 recommendations of the Central Monitoring and Inspections Unit, 24 per cent were implemented. The Central Evaluation Unit issued 37 recommendations.

OIOS identified and recommended $17 million in cost savings and recoveries, and realized savings and recoveries amounting to $5.3 million, compared to $37.8 million and $23.5 million, respectively, in the previous reporting period. The decline was due to a heavier audit focus on policy and programmatic issues, compared to the previous reporting period, when a large portion of the savings and recoveries resulted from audits of the liquidation of large peacekeeping missions in Angola and the former Yugoslavia.

The report gave an overview of activities of the oversight priority areas for the reporting period: peacekeeping, humanitarian and related activities, human resources management and procurement. Besides expanding the audit coverage of the Department of Peacekeeping Operations, OIOS conducted audits at 11 field missions and of contingent-owned equipment procedures and payments to troop-contributing countries, of the global vehicle procurement project and of mission liquidations. The audit of the liquidation of peacekeeping operations revealed that the Department's field asset control system had not been fully implemented, leaving no common recording system for assets. It also needed to improve inventory controls, reassess policy for asset transfer to other missions or to the United Nations Logistics Base in Brindisi, Italy, and standardize procedures for the commercial disposal of assets.

The audits of UNHCR centred on programme management by UNHCR and its implementing partners, as well as its field office administration and finance. OIOS noted that the delayed closure of the previous year's projects remained an issue of concern. It found that, while some level of assurance could be obtained as to the completeness and accuracy of financial reports submitted to UNCHR by its implementing partners, that was not always the case. In many instances, the partners realized significant exchange-rate gains not properly reported in UNHCR project accounts or disclosed in financial reports. The lack of pertinent documentation in the field relating to the programme activities of international non-governmental organizations (NGOs) was a continuing problem for the auditors. The triennial review of OCHA showed that progress had been made in addressing gaps in the response to emergencies and in the advocacy of humanitarian concerns. However, rapid response to emergencies was still hindered by the absence of special UN administrative and financial rules and procedures suited to emergency situations. Audits of the Office of the Iraq Programme included those of the financial and administrative procedures and operational arrangements of the Office of the Humanitarian Coordinator in Iraq. Through a market survey of vendors in northern Iraq, OIOS found that the amounts paid by the Office were on average 61 per cent higher than the quotes obtained by OIOS. It further found only limited coordination of programme planning, and insufficient review and independent assessment of project implementation activities. As to its review of the Office of the United Nations High Commissioner for Human Rights, OIOS noted not only the need to improve administrative support services, but also the lack of criteria for determining the number of security staff, for hiring such staff or for monitoring their performance.

A follow-up audit of the recruitment process indicated that the Office of Human Resources Management had made progress towards reducing the recruitment timeline by one third, improving the management of the national competitive examination programme and updating the roster of candidates, introducing an electronic recruitment tracking system, and including core values and competencies in the vacancy announcement and interview process. Key recommendations for further improvement included establishing overall recruitment goals and strategies, provision of guidance to programme managers regarding gender balance and geographical distribution, and further refinement of benchmarks for monitoring recruitment activities.

Given the significance of procurement expenditures, a separate unit was established within the OIOS Audit and Management Consulting Division as the focal point for procurement audits. A second follow-up audit of procurement reform was carried out to verify that the recommendations of the group of high-level experts on procurement reform [YUN 1995, p. 1457] had been satisfactorily implemented.

As part of its oversight function, the Audit and Management Consulting Division started 148 audit assignments, issued 82 audit reports to senior management and provided five reports for the General Assembly. In addition, it issued 453 audit observations. Key audit recommendations related to programme/project management, cash management, personnel, payroll and travel, financial accounting/reporting, procurement, property management, information technology systems, and general administration and management.

The Investigations Section received 287 cases, compared to 247 in the previous reporting period, a 16 per cent increase. Thirty-eight cases were presented for administrative or disciplinary action, 22 of which were recommended for criminal prosecution by national law enforcement authorities. Of the 194 open cases as at 30 June, 25 per cent were located at UN Headquarters, 27 per cent in Africa, 28 per cent in Europe, 8 per cent in the Middle East and Asia and 4 per cent in the United States outside UN Headquarters. New inspections were carried out at OCHA, Habitat and UNEP, as well as an inspectoral visit to ECA.

In-depth evaluations were undertaken of global development trends, issues and policies, and global approaches to social and microeconomic issues and policies, and the corresponding subprogrammes in the regional commissions [E/AC.51/2000/2], and of the advancement of women programme [E/AC.51/2000/3]. Triennial reviews were conducted on the implementation of the recommendations of the Committee for Programme and Coordination at its thirty-seventh session [YUN 1997, p. 1487] on the evaluations of the Department of Humanitarian Affairs [E/AC.51/2000/5] and the statistics programme [E/AC.51/2000/4].

OIOS investigation rules and procedures

Responding to General Assembly resolution 54/244 [YUN 1999, p. 1274], the Secretary-General submitted an October report on rules and procedures to be applied for the investigation functions performed by OIOS [A/55/469]. The Secretary-General said that the OIOS Investigations Section operated in conformity with the United Nations Staff Rules and Regulations, as well as the provisions of Assembly resolutions 48/218 B [YUN 1994, p. 1362] and 54/244 and the provisions of the Secretary-General's bulletin of 7 September 1994 [ST/SGB/273] and the OIOS Manual, which together constituted the OIOS mandate. The Section adhered to that mandate with due regard for fairness and objectivity and commitment to the concept of accountability. If evidence showed that a staff member had violated laws or standards of ethical behaviour or was culpable of misconduct, waste, abuse or mismanagement, the Section would make recommendations to the concerned programme manager, which might include referral to a national jurisdiction for criminal prosecution and/or to the Office of Human Resources Management for disciplinary action. The Section would also work to exonerate staff wrongly or incorrectly accused. Investigative activities were conducted in such a way as to ensure the confidentiality of those making reports, the rights of staff members involved, protection from reprisals of those who contacted the Section and the interests of the Organization. Direction and supervision by the OIOS Under-Secretary-General also ensured the accountability of the Section's work.

On 23 December, the General Assembly decided that the item on the report of OIOS remained for consideration at its resumed fifty-fifth (2001) session (**decision 55/458**) and that the Fifth Committee should continue consideration of the item at that session (**decision 55/455**).

External oversight

Strengthening external oversight mechanisms

By **decision 54/469** of 7 April, the General Assembly took note of the Secretary-General's report on the views of the Board of Auditors on improvement of oversight functions of the United Nations [YUN 1994, p. 1365], and a JIU note containing its updated and additional views on the strengthening of external oversight mechanisms [YUN 1996, p. 1265].

Joint Inspection Unit

On 7 April, the General Assembly, in **resolution 54/255**, stressed the importance for the Joint Inspection Unit to use the most recent data available in its reports and called on the Secretary-General and the executive heads of UN system organizations to provide timely data to JIU. The Secretary-General should ensure the timely issuance of JIU reports and his related comments and those of the Administrative Committee on Coordination (ACC) to enable the Assembly and all the governing bodies to take prompt action thereon. The Assembly asked JIU to continue to improve its reports consistent with the requirements of its follow-up system.

In its thirty-second report to the General Assembly [A/56/34 & Corr.1], JIU gave an overview of its activities in 2000, during which it issued reports on: the administration of justice at the United Nations [A/55/57]; the use of consultants in the United Nations [A/55/59]; senior-level appointments in the United Nations, its programmes and funds [A/55/423]; review of management and administration in the United Nations Educational, Scientific and Cultural Organization [JIU/REP/2000/4]; UN system common services at Geneva, part II, case studies (International Criminal Court, Joint Medical Service, Training and Examination Section, Diplomatic Pouch Service, Joint Purchase Service) [A/55/856]; delegation of authority for management of human and financial resources in the UN Secretariat [A/55/857]; young Professionals in selected organizations of the UN system: recruitment, management and retention [A/55/798]; review of management and administration in the Registry of the International Court of Justice [A/55/834]; and strengthening the investigative function in the UN system organizations [JIU/REP/2000/9].

JIU continued to enhance further its functioning and impact. It established internal measures to expedite the preparation of its reports for issuance in advance of meetings of the legislative organs of participating bodies. That goal, however, was often hindered by, among other reasons, the tardiness of some of those bodies in providing JIU with requested information and/or comments. In its proposed 2002-2003 biennium programme budget, JIU introduced a new approach aimed at improving its research capacity by reallocating its professional post resources and by allowing more flexibility in the use of required expertise under short-term contracts.

The Secretary-General, in an August note [A/54/960], transmitted to the Assembly JIU's 2000 work programme and preliminary list of potential reports for 2001 and beyond.

GENERAL ASSEMBLY ACTION

On 23 December [meeting 89], the General Assembly, on the recommendation of the Fifth Committee [A/55/532], adopted **resolution 55/230** without vote [agenda item 116].

Reports of the Joint Inspection Unit

The General Assembly,

Recalling its resolution 54/16 of 29 October 1999,

1. *Takes note* of the annual report of the Joint Inspection Unit for 1999;

2. *Also takes note* of the programme of work of the Unit for 2000 and the preliminary list of potential reports for 2001 and beyond;

3. *Stresses* the importance of timely consideration of the reports of the Unit by all participating organizations;

4. *Looks forward* to the report requested in paragraph 6 of its resolution 54/16 concerning progress made in the implementation of the system of follow-up to the recommendations of the Unit;

5. *Recognizes* the critical role of legislative bodies, their secretariats and the Unit in the success of the implementation of the system;

6. *Takes note* of paragraphs 19 and 20 of the report of the Joint Inspection Unit for 1998 and reaffirms article 20 of the statute of the Unit and paragraph 182 of General Assembly resolution 54/249 of 23 December 1999, and in this regard requests the Secretary-General to submit the report of the Administrative Committee on Coordination on the budget proposals made by the Unit as required by the statute;

7. *Invites* the Unit to continue to develop interaction with other United Nations oversight bodies and to intensify relations with the oversight bodies of other participating organizations with a view to achieving better coordination and sharing best practices;

8. *Decides* to consider the annual reports of the Unit on an annual basis.

Intergovernmental machinery

Strengthening of the UN system

By **decision 54/490** of 5 September, the General Assembly included in the draft agenda of its fifty-fifth (2000) session the item entitled

"Strengthening of the United Nations system". By **decision 55/458** of 23 December, the Assembly decided that the item should remain for consideration during its resumed fifty-fifth (2001) session.

Revitalization of the work of the General Assembly

By **decision 54/491** of 5 September, the General Assembly included in the draft agenda of its fifty-fifth session the item entitled "Revitalization of the work of the General Assembly". By **decision 55/458** of 23 December, the Assembly decided that the item should remain for consideration during its resumed fifty-fifth (2001) session.

United Nations/private sector partnership

The Secretary-General, in a January note [A/54/700], transmitted to the General Assembly a JIU report analysing the lines along which a new partnership between the UN system and the private sector could be developed and how areas of mutual interest and benefit could translate into actions to improve understanding so as to better serve the goals of the Organization.

According to the report, the increasing interest by the two parties in each other was based on the recognition by the business community of the Organization's significant contribution to the creation of a favourable environment for private sector activities and UN acceptance of that sector's role as an essential partner in supporting economic growth and sustainable development. The private sector was already actively engaged in many UN activities. UN agencies, funds and programmes were trying to maximize the benefits from that engagement, while protecting themselves from its inherent risks. Those precautions, however, were not uniform throughout the system, and inconsistencies in their nature and application could undermine the image, credibility, integrity and legal immunity of the UN system. While the specificity of each agency, fund and programme might not allow for the establishment of system-wide guidelines, JIU believed that an increased information exchange and harmonization of procedures were required.

To that end, JIU recommended that participating organizations set realistic objectives and expectations for their partnership with the private sector, which their governing bodies should clearly enunciate, publicize and endorse. Their secretariats should carry out outreach programmes targeting the private sector, and designate a focal point or identify accessible units to serve the business community's information and assistance needs. Organizations should also ensure a UN presence at relevant business events, organize joint encounters and encourage wide private sector participation in their relevant activities, with special attention to enterprises in developing countries and/or those in transition.

The working group established by the Secretary-General's Senior Management Group to develop policy proposals should draft guidelines governing relations with the private sector, drawing on work already undertaken by some funds and programmes. UN agencies that had not done so should also adopt guidelines, taking account of the working group's activities; they should include a statement of principles and procedures for dealing with the private sector.

The United Nations should ensure the implementation of staff rule 101.6 relating to outside activities and interests of staff members, including the feasibility of extending rules for financial disclosures. Other participating organizations should examine whether their respective staff rules and regulations guaranteed that staff members did not hold a financial interest in commercial enterprises with which a partnership was envisaged. They should also ensure that bureaucratic procedures and lengthy response time did not discourage private sector initiatives. Mechanisms for sharing information and best practices with regard to relations with the private sector should be established to ensure consistency of policy and harmonization of relevant procedures throughout the UN system.

In June [A/54/700/Add.1], the Secretary-General transmitted to the Assembly ACC's comments on the JIU report.

The Assembly, in **resolution 55/215** of 21 December, invited the Secretary-General to seek the views of relevant partners, in particular the private sector, on how to enhance their cooperation with the United Nations.

Review of Security Council membership and related matters

The Open-ended Working Group on the Question of Equitable Representation on and Increase in the Membership of the Security Council and Other Matters related to the Security Council submitted a report on its work during five substantive sessions held between 6 March and 21 July [A/54/47]. At those sessions, discussion continued on the items under cluster I: decision-making, including the veto, the Council's expansion and periodic review of the enlarged Council; and those under cluster II: the Council's working methods and transparency of its work. Before the

Group were conference room papers on each cluster, prepared by its Bureau.

The Working Group adopted its work programme and completed a reading of the paper on cluster II at the first session (6-15 March). At the second (3-5 April), it continued consideration of that cluster on the basis of a revised consolidated paper incorporating paragraphs provisionally agreed and proposals made on the paper's 1999 version; it began reading the paper on cluster I, which, owing to that paper's inadequacies, was subsequently revised and considered at the third session (2-12 May). At the fourth session (12-14 June), the Group completed a reading of the revised cluster II paper; it was briefed by Secretariat officials regarding the time required for the preparation and processing of the Council's annual report to the General Assembly. At the fifth session (10-21 July), Italy submitted legal observations on the notion of permanent membership on the Council. The Group further revised the papers on clusters I and II. It also considered its report to the Assembly.

The Assembly, by **decision 54/488** of 5 September, took note of the Working Group's report. It welcomed progress so far achieved, as provisional agreement had been recorded on a large number of issues, and urged the Working Group to continue efforts during its fifty-fifth (2000) session to achieve progress on all aspects of equitable representation on and increase in the membership of the Security Council and other related matters.

The Assembly also decided to continue consideration of the subject during its fifty-fifth session and that the Working Group should continue its work, taking into account the progress achieved during the Assembly's forty-eighth (1993) to fifty-fourth (1999) sessions, as well as the views to be expressed at the fifty-fifth session, and report before the end of that session, including any agreed recommendations.

By **decision 55/458** of 23 December, the Assembly decided that the item should remain for consideration during its resumed fifty-fifth (2001) session.

Revitalization of the United Nations in the economic, social and related fields

The Secretary-General submitted a report, in June [A/55/180-E/2000/67 & Corr.1], on restructuring and revitalization of the United Nations in the economic, social and related fields and cooperation between the United Nations and the Bretton Woods institutions (the World Bank Group and the International Monetary Fund). It described progress in the implementation of

General Assembly resolutions 50/227 [YUN 1996, p. 1249] and 52/12 B [YUN 1997, p. 1392] and Economic and Social Council resolutions 1998/46 [YUN 1998, p. 1262] and 1999/51 [YUN 1999, p. 1281].

To promote further implementation of the Assembly resolutions, the Secretary-General recommended that the Assembly's Second (Economic and Financial) and Third (Social, Humanitarian and Cultural) Committees extend the practice of organizing a dialogue, when starting to consider an agenda item, with the heads of substantive departments, offices or agencies responsible for reporting requirements under that item; that ways of strengthening cooperation between those two Committees should continue to be explored, including the holding of joint panels on common issues and more frequent meetings of their two bureaux; that the Assembly discuss the Economic and Social Council report in plenary; and that the Second Committee's Bureau review the provisional agenda and further rationalize the methods of work of the Committee, including further clustering of agenda items, reducing the number of meetings, and adopting more omnibus or integrated resolutions.

The Secretary-General also recommended that the Council, in implementation of its resolutions, should further reflect on how it could better organize its debate on the functional commissions' reports and make its own report to the Assembly more amenable to review. It should request the commission bureaux to ensure the sharing of reports and documents among the commissions. The Council's Bureau might, when opportune, convene meetings of the functional commission chairpersons to exchange views on the direction of the commissions' work programmes and on issues of common interest. The Council might reiterate its request that the commissions ensure complementarity among their work programmes, which should take account of major UN events. To that end, the Secretary-General should submit to the commissions' next sessions background notes on those programmes, including proposals for possible linkages among them.

Other suggestions were for the Council to: hold informal dialogue on cross-cutting themes in order to benefit from the expertise of delegates attending a commission session and to broaden that commission's perspective on interrelated issues; examine ways to facilitate the participation of specialized NGOs not in consultative status with the Council in commission sessions of direct interest to their work; invite the functional commission bureaux to propose ways on how the commissions could contribute to efforts to assist

African countries and the least developed countries, particularly in the framework of the Third United Nations Conference on the Least Developed Countries in 2001 (see p. 808) and the review of the United Nations New Agenda for the Development of Africa in the 1990s in 2002; and reiterate its call to the functional commissions to report to it on the follow-up.

On cooperation between the United Nations and the Bretton Woods institutions, the Council should involve in its future joint meetings the chairpersons of the relevant functional commissions and of the Executive Boards of UN funds and programmes. It might extend similar partnership with the World Trade Organization and discuss the modalities for such cooperation and closely involve UNCTAD in that process.

By **decision 54/492** of 5 September, the Assembly decided to include in the draft agenda of its fifty-fifth (2000) session the item entitled "Restructuring and revitalization of the United Nations in the economic, social and related fields". By **decision 55/458** of 23 December, it decided that the item would remain for consideration at its resumed fifty-fifth (2001) session.

Chapter II

United Nations financing and programming

The improved United Nations financial situation of 1999 was not sustained in 2000, which saw a return to lower cash balances, higher unpaid assessments and increased debt owed to Member States contributing troops for peacekeeping operations. Unpaid assessments at the end of 2000 stood at $2.2 billion, compared to $1.8 billion at the end of 1999, despite the increase in the number of Member States paying their regular budget assessments in full and on time, which rose to 137 in 2000. The Secretary-General considered the situation worrisome, especially in the light of proposed new expenditures for peacekeeping, personnel safety and security and the capital master plan for refurbishing the United Nations Headquarters complex.

The General Assembly adopted revised budget appropriations totalling $2,533,125,400 for 2000-2001, compared to the approved initial appropriations of $2,535,689,200. It noted the Secretary-General's budget outline for 2002-2003 and invited him to prepare his proposed programme budget on the basis of a preliminary estimate of $2,515.3 million at revised 2000-2001 rates. The Assembly considered the experience of UN system organizations with results-based budgeting and decided that the measures proposed by the Secretary-General to enhance responsibility and accountability in implementing programme budgets should be put in place in a gradual and incremental fashion.

The Committee on Contributions continued to review the methodology for preparing the scale of assessments of Member States' contributions to the UN budget, as well as new proposals for arriving at the rates of assessments for non-member and new Member States. It also considered a number of measures to encourage the timely, full and unconditional payment of assessed contributions. On the Committee's recommendation, the Assembly granted a number of exemptions under Article 19 of the Charter of the United Nations.

The Assembly accepted the financial reports and audited financial statements of the Board of Auditors for the 1998-1999 biennium. It reviewed UN programme performance for 1998-1999 and endorsed the recommendations of the Committee for Programme and Coordination (CPC) for improving programme evaluation. It noted CPC's

and the Secretary-General's recommendations on ways in which the full implementation and the quality of mandated programmes and activities could be better ensured and assessed. It also adopted the proposed medium-term plan for 2002-2005.

Financial situation

By **decision 54/495** of 5 September, the General Assembly included in the draft agenda of its fifty-fifth (2000) session the item entitled "Improving the financial situation of the United Nations".

In October [A/55/504], the Secretary-General reported that the turnaround in the Organization's financial situation evidenced in 1999 did not continue in 2000. Despite the increased number of Member States paying their regular budget assessments in full, the year-end cash position remained dependent on one Member State. The budgets and unpaid assessments for the two international tribunals (for Rwanda and the former Yugoslavia) were increasing annually and the larger unpaid assessments for peacekeeping operations limited the availability of cash, while the debt owed to troop-contributing Member States for troops and contingent-owned equipment remained intractable. That was worrisome, in the light of the Secretary-General's proposed expansion of peacekeeping field operations, backstopping support for better security protection for UN staff and the approval of a capital master plan for the United Nations Headquarters complex.

As at 30 September, unpaid assessments for the regular budget, peacekeeping and the international tribunals totalled just over $3 billion, up 23 per cent from the previous year: $533 million for the regular budget, $2,500 million for peacekeeping ($676 million more than in 1999), and $54 million for the international tribunals ($19 million more than in 1999). The number of Member States paying their regular budget assessments in full continued to increase, rising, as at 20 October, to 137 Member States in respect of their 2000 assessments.

In an end-of-year review of the financial situation [A/55/504/Add.1], the Secretary-General confirmed that the Organization had failed to meet the forecasts based on the positive results of the previous year: cash was lower, unpaid assessments rose and debt owed to Member States increased. Aggregate cash amounted to $1 billion, almost $100 million lower than in 1999.

Unpaid assessments totalled $2.2 billion, reflecting an increase of about $500 million over the previous year's figure. Of that total, $222 million was for the regular budget (of which 89 per cent was owed by three Member States and the remaining 11 per cent by 43 others); $1,989 million for peacekeeping and $47 million for the tribunals. Debt to Member States for troops and contingent-owned equipment increased to $917 million, exceeding the levels of the preceding four years.

On 23 December, the General Assembly decided that the agenda items on improving the financial situation of the United Nations and on the review of the efficiency of its administrative and financial functioning would remain for consideration at its resumed fifty-fifth (2001) session (**decision 55/458**), and that the Fifth (Administrative and Budgetary) Committee should continue to consider those items at that session (**decision 55/455**).

UN budget

Results-based budgeting

In November [A/55/543], the Advisory Committee on Administrative and Budgetary Questions (ACABQ) examined the Secretary-General's 1999 reports and that of the Joint Inspection Unit (JIU) on results-based budgeting [YUN 1999, p. 1284]. ACABQ concluded that for many years it had found the budget presentation to be of uneven quality. While its financial aspects had been highly developed and refined, the same was not true on the programme side. The Secretary-General's proposals on results-based budgeting contained in his 1999 report attempted to build upon and strengthen the existing process of programme budgeting.

As to whether the Secretary-General's proposals were driven by financial constraints, ACABQ believed that the UN financial situation should not be the impetus to change budget methodology, practice and process. The introduction of new budget procedures should not be a means to reduce the budget or achieve savings, nor should it encourage the arbitrary setting of budgetary ceilings. Furthermore, the Secretary-General's proposals should not be so interpreted as to diminish his responsibility to justify fully the financial aspects of his budget proposals. Since those proposals incorporated much of current practice, ACABQ saw no immediate need to amend the financial regulations or the rules governing programme planning. Nor would its role or that of the Fifth Committee change in the consideration of the financial aspects of budget proposals. What was needed were improved planning, with the formulation of specific objectives and precise performance indicators; clear identification of external factors influencing UN operations; and giving priority to expanding and developing information technology and cost accounting systems to support new requirements adequately.

ACABQ observed that the Secretary-General's proposals could not be applied equally to all sections and activities of the programme budget. Modified techniques would have to be developed for performance analysis to remain valid and relevant. The basic terms employed in the proposals should be fully and precisely defined and consistently applied. Terminology should be harmonized with other UN entities, a comprehensive training programme in techniques to be developed should be organized, and staff should be given the opportunity to contribute to the budgeting system's further development. The process of budget innovation would be incremental, with refinement based on experience.

ACABQ recommended approval of the Secretary-General's proposal that the General Assembly request him to continue to develop performance indicators for use in all substantive and support programmes and to include them in all sections of the proposed programme budget for the 2002-2003 biennium. It also recommended approval of his amended proposal that the programme performance report for that biennium should contain, in addition to the current method of output measurement, an assessment of the Organization's performance in terms of expected accomplishments, using the achievement indicators to be included in the proposed 2002-2003 programme budget.

GENERAL ASSEMBLY ACTION

On 23 December [meeting 89], the General Assembly, on the recommendation of the Fifth Committee [A/55/532/Add.1 & Corr.1], adopted **resolution 55/231** without vote [agenda item 116].

Results-based budgeting

The General Assembly,

Recalling its resolutions 52/12 B of 19 December 1997 and 53/205 of 18 December 1998,

Recalling also the Regulations and Rules Governing Programme Planning, the Programme Aspects of the Budget, the Monitoring of Implementation and the Methods of Evaluation,

Having considered the report of the Secretary-General on results-based budgeting and the related addenda,

Having also considered the report of the Advisory Committee on Administrative and Budgetary Questions on the report of the Secretary-General

Having further considered the report of the Joint Inspection Unit on the experience of United Nations system organizations with results-based budgeting techniques, as well as the comments of the Secretary-General thereon,

Bearing in mind the intergovernmental, multilateral and international character of the United Nations,

1. *Reaffirms* its resolution 41/213 of 19 December 1986;

2. *Also reaffirms* the role of the General Assembly in carrying out a thorough analysis and approval of posts and financial resources, of resource allocation to all sections of the programme budget and of human resources policies, with a view to ensuring full and efficient implementation of all mandated programmes and activities and the implementation of policies in this regard;

3. *Further reaffirms* the respective mandates of the Advisory Committee on Administrative and Budgetary Questions and the Committee for Programme and Coordination in the consideration of the proposed programme budget;

4. *Endorses* the conclusions and recommendations contained in the report of the Advisory Committee, subject to the provisions of the present resolution;

5. *Notes* that the measures proposed by the Secretary-General and recommended by the Advisory Committee are intended to provide, in essence, a management tool that should enhance responsibility and accountability in the implementation of programmes and budgets;

6. *Decides* that these measures, as approved by the General Assembly in the present resolution, should be implemented in a gradual and incremental manner, in full compliance with the Regulations and Rules Governing Programme Planning, the Programme Aspects of the Budget, the Monitoring of Implementation and the Methods of Evaluation and the Financial Regulations and Rules of the United Nations;

7. *Requests* the Secretary-General to ensure that the expected accomplishments and indicators of achievement are directly and clearly linked to the objectives of the programmes and in accordance with the different nature of the activities of the programmes, taking into account rules 104.7 *(a)* and 105.4 *(a)* of the Regulations and Rules Governing Programme Planning;

8. *Also requests* the Secretary-General to ensure that expected accomplishments, indicators of achievement and objectives are defined, bearing in mind the direct link between inputs and outputs, and that inputs are commensurate with the needs of programmes, and taking into consideration the international character of the United Nations, the purposes of its Charter and its legislative mandates, as well as the fact that the objectives of the Organization may not be realized in one medium-term plan only;

9. *Further requests* the Secretary-General to ensure that, in presenting the programme budget, expected accomplishments and, where possible, indicators of achievement are included to measure achievements in the implementation of the programmes of the Organization and not those of individual Member States;

10. *Stresses* in this regard the need for continued improvement in the formulation of objectives, expected accomplishments and indicators of achievement with the full involvement of the relevant intergovernmental bodies;

11. *Decides* that the design of programme objectives in the context of the medium-term plan and in the programme budget should be enhanced as a key element of results-based budgeting, in order to reflect in a more accurate manner the mandates, policy objectives, orientation and priorities of the Organization, taking into account regulation 4.2 and rule 104.7 *(e)* of the Regulations and Rules Governing Programme Planning;

12. *Requests* the Secretary-General to keep the definition of terms and guidelines under review and to bring the question of definitions to the attention of the Consultative Committee on Administrative Questions of the Administrative Committee on Coordination, with a view to obtaining the views and comments of the appropriate bodies of the United Nations system of organizations in order to arrive at an agreed set of key terms and guidelines pertaining to the results-based format of the budget within the United Nations system;

13. *Stresses* that external factors specific to the objectives and expected accomplishments should be identified in the proposed programme budget and that assessment of performance should reflect, and not be distorted by, the impact of unforeseen external factors;

14. *Decides* that significant external factors should also be identified in the context of future medium-term plans in order to illustrate their impact on the achievements obtained by the different programmes;

15. *Also decides* that the proposed programme budget for the biennium 2002-2003 shall contain input data at the same level of detail as that provided in the programme budget for the biennium 2000-2001, in keeping with the responsibility of the Secretary-General to provide complete information in support of the financial aspects of his budget proposals;

16. *Notes* the observation of the Advisory Committee, in paragraph 16 of its report, that the Secretary-General already enjoys delegation of authority in programme delivery, in particular in the transfer of resources within sections of the budget;

17. *Decides* that any transfer of resources between post and non-post objects of expenditure would require the prior approval of the General Assembly;

18. *Stresses* that the use of indicators of achievement in the proposed programme budget and assessment of the performance of the Organization in terms of all the expected accomplishments should not constitute a method by which to adjust the level of approved resources, or of staff, and that requested resources should continue to be justified in terms of the requirements of output delivery;

19. *Emphasizes* that resources proposed by the Secretary-General should be commensurate with all mandated programmes and activities to ensure their full, effective and efficient implementation;

20. *Notes* that, in order to implement the present resolution, no revisions to the Financial Regulations and Rules of the United Nations or to the Regulations and Rules Governing Programme Planning, the Programme Aspects of the Budget, the Monitoring of Implementation and the Methods of Evaluation are currently required, and, in this regard, also notes that the application of rule 105.6 *(a)* of the Regulations and Rules Governing Programme Planning should continue to reflect the understanding that approval of the medium-term plan and the programme budget constitutes the reaffirmation of mandates reflected therein;

21. *Recognizes* the difficulty of achieving the results of complex and long-standing political activities within specific time frames;

22. *Reaffirms* that, in accordance with rule 104.7 *(b)* of the Regulations and Rules Governing Programme Planning, when an objective for Secretariat action cannot be achieved by the end of the plan period, both this longer-term objective and more specific objectives to be achieved within the plan period shall be set;

23. *Emphasizes* the need for the Secretariat to continue to improve its programme evaluation capacity, in order to implement fully the Regulations and Rules Governing Programme Planning by, inter alia, strengthening standard evaluation methodologies in accordance with article VII of the Regulations and Rules Governing Programme Planning;

24. *Stresses* that any proposals for additional flexibility in managing inputs during budget implementation, if approved by the General Assembly, should always be accompanied by increased accountability;

25. *Also stresses* that flexibility in terms of the use of resources should be exercised with strict respect for the norms and decisions established by the General Assembly and the Financial Regulations and Rules of the United Nations, in particular in regard to the limits imposed by the General Assembly in the allocation of resources for every section, the staffing table and the rules and procedures for personnel matters;

26. *Requests* the Secretary-General to undertake a detailed analysis of the information, management control and evaluation systems required to implement the proposals contained in his report, and of the capacity and limitations of existing systems, and to submit a report thereon to the General Assembly, through the Advisory Committee, at the time of submitting his proposed programme budget for the biennium 2002-2003;

27. *Stresses* that the intention of the Secretary-General to focus the evaluation of programme delivery on expected accomplishments should be implemented in a manner that is flexible and complementary to the existing evaluation system;

28. *Invites* the Secretary-General to take appropriate measures to develop on a continuous basis and to implement an adequate training programme to ensure that staff, as appropriate, are proficient in the concepts and techniques, including the formulation of expected accomplishments and indicators of achievement, as described in his report.

Budget for 1998-1999

By **decision 55/458** of 23 December, the General Assembly decided that the agenda item on the programme budget for the 1998-1999 biennium would remain for consideration during its resumed fifty-fifth (2001) session.

Budget for 2000-2001

Appropriations

By **decision 54/481** of 15 June, the General Assembly took note of the Secretary-General's 1997 report [YUN 1997, p. 1416] concerning additional expenditures referred to in paragraphs 10 and 11 of annex I to resolution 41/213 [YUN 1986, p. 1024] and the relevant ACABQ report [YUN 1997, p. 1416]. The Assembly requested the Secretary-General to keep it informed on issues pertaining to inflation and currency fluctuations in the context of the budget performance reports.

In the first performance report on the 2000-2001 programme budget [A/55/645 & Corr.1], submitted on 24 November, the Secretary-General identified adjustments to the budget owing to variations in inflation and exchange rates and in standards assumed in the calculation of the initial appropriations. Those adjustments yielded a reduction in expenditure of $40.5 million and an increase in income of $18.3 million. The revised estimates for the 2000-2001 biennium amounted to $2,115,575,400, compared to $2,174,390,300 approved in Assembly resolution 54/250 A [YUN 1999, p. 1303].

The performance report also took into account unforeseen and extraordinary expenses ($10,987,900) and decisions of policy-making organs ($3,633,700).

Those estimates were further revised in December [A/55/645/Add.1] to take into account notable changes in currency exchange rates. The revised estimates for the 2000-2001 biennium amounted to $2,120,651,100 (providing for a decrease in expenditure of $34,624,200 and an increase in income of $19,097,000).

ACABQ [A/55/7/Add.5 & Corr.1] recommended approval of the revised requirements of $2,501,047,000 under the expenditure sections and $380,395,900 under the income sections, resulting in net revised requirements of $2,120,651,100.

Also in December [A/C.5/55/35], the Secretary-General provided recosting of $90.7 million for outstanding items, and recommended that the related adjustments to the expenditure and income sections be reflected in the revised appropriations for the 2000-2001 biennium.

GENERAL ASSEMBLY ACTION

On 23 December [meeting 89], the General Assembly, on the recommendation of the Fifth Committee [A/55/713], adopted **resolutions 55/239 A-C** without vote [agenda item 117].

Programme budget for the biennium 2000-2001

A

Revised budget appropriations for the biennium 2000-2001

The General Assembly

Resolves that for the biennium 2000-2001 the amount of 2,535,689,200 United States dollars appropriated by it in its resolution 54/250 A of 23 December 1999 shall be adjusted by 2,563,800 dollars, as follows:

Section	Amount approved in resolution 54/250 A	Increase/ (decrease)	Revised appropriation
	(United States dollars)		
Part I. Overall policy-making, direction and coordination			
1. Overall policy-making, direction and coordination	47,675,100	338,000	48,013,100
2. General Assembly affairs and conference services	425,970,200	(16,946,100)	409,024,100
Total, part I	**473,645,300**	**(16,608,100)**	**457,037,200**
Part II. Political affairs			
3. Political affairs	137,756,000	30,088,700	167,844,700
4. Disarmament	14,067,900	(247,000)	13,820,900
5. Peacekeeping operations	76,094,700	(1,210,700)	74,884,000
6. Peaceful uses of outer space	3,667,700	(354,200)	3,313,500
Total, part II	**231,586,300**	**28,276,800**	**259,863,100**
Part III. International justice and law			
7. International Court of Justice	20,864,500	(257,800)	20,606,700
8. Legal affairs	34,522,300	(641,700)	33,880,600
Total, part III	**55,386,800**	**(899,500)**	**54,487,300**
Part IV. International cooperation for development			
9. Economic and social affairs	113,112,600	(680,800)	112,431,800
10. Africa: New Agenda for Development	5,883,400	(23,600)	5,859,800
11A. Trade and development	87,685,500	(6,311,900)	81,373,600
11B. International Trade Centre UNCTAD/WTO	19,248,700	(2,238,900)	17,009,800
12. Environment	8,743,400	(642,500)	8,100,900
13. Human settlements	13,757,400	(1,460,100)	12,297,300
14. Crime prevention and criminal justice	5,299,100	(477,800)	4,821,300
15. International drug control	15,037,800	(1,319,600)	13,718,200
Total, part IV	**268,767,900**	**(13,155,200)**	**255,612,700**

Section	Amount approved in resolution 54/250 A	Increase/ (decrease)	Revised appropriation
	(United States dollars)		
Part V. Regional cooperation for development			
16. Economic and social development in Africa	78,455,200	2,189,800	80,645,000
17. Economic and social development in Asia and the Pacific	57,031,600	(2,620,400)	54,411,200
18. Economic development in Europe	40,554,600	(3,140,000)	37,414,600
19. Economic and social development in Latin America and the Caribbean	78,857,500	(3,273,400)	75,584,100
20. Economic and social development in Western Asia	50,336,200	(1,754,800)	48,581,400
21. Regular programme of technical cooperation	41,995,300	(740,500)	41,254,800
Total, part V	**347,230,400**	**(9,339,300)**	**337,891,100**
Part VI. Human rights and humanitarian affairs			
22. Human rights	41,163,400	(2,095,700)	39,067,700
23. Protection of and assistance to refugees	41,940,000	(3,101,100)	38,838,900
24. Palestine refugees	21,667,900	1,507,500	23,175,400
25. Humanitarian assistance	18,841,800	(393,900)	18,447,900
Total, part VI	**123,613,100**	**(4,083,200)**	**119,529,900**
Part VII. Public information			
26. Public information	143,605,500	(1,071,000)	142,534,500
Total, part VII	**143,605,500**	**(1,071,000)**	**142,534,500**
Part VIII. Common support services			
27. Management and central support services	441,857,400	(8,288,300)	433,569,100
Total, part VIII	**441,857,400**	**(8,288,300)**	**433,569,100**
Part IX. Internal oversight			
28. Internal oversight	19,220,600	(469,900)	18,750,700
Total, part IX	**19,220,600**	**(469,900)**	**18,750,700**
Part X. Jointly financed administrative activities and special expenses			
29. Jointly financed administrative activities	7,844,300	176,200	8,020,500
30. Special expenses	53,001,200	1,510,500	54,511,700
Total, part X	**60,845,500**	**1,686,700**	**62,532,200**

Section	Amount approved in resolution 54/250 A	Increase/ (decrease)	Revised appropriation
	(United States dollars)		
Part XI. Capital expenditures			
31. Construction, alteration, improvement and major mainte- nance	42,617,400	7,149,900	49,767,300
Total, part XI	42,617,400	7,149,900	49,767,300
Part XII. Staff assessment			
32. Staff assessment	314,248,000	14,237,300	328,485,300
Total, part XII	314,248,000	14,237,300	328,485,300
Part XIII. Develop- ment Account			
33. Development Account	13,065,000	—	13,065,000
Total, part XIII	13,065,000	—	13,065,000
Grand total	2,535,689,200	(2,563,800)	2,533,125,400

B

Revised income estimates for the biennium 2000-2001

The General Assembly

Resolves that, for the biennium 2000-2001, the estimates of income of 361,298,900 United States dollars
approved by it in its resolution 54/250 B of 23 December 1999 shall be increased by 19,523,800 dollars, as follows:

Income section	Amount approved in resolution 54/250 B	Increase/ (decrease)	Revised appropriation
	(United States dollars)		
1. Income from staff as- sessment	318,911,500	14,213,700	333,125,200
Total, income section 1	318,911,500	14,213,700	333,125,200
2. General income	37,178,000	5,550,600	42,728,600
3. Services to the public	5,209,400	(240,500)	4,968,900
Total, income sections 2 and 3	42,387,400	5,310,100	47,697,500
Grand total	361,298,900	19,523,800	380,822,700

C

Financing of the appropriations for the year 2001

The General Assembly

Resolves that, for the year 2001:

1. Budget appropriations totalling 1,265,280,800
United States dollars and consisting of 1,267,844,600
dollars, being half of the appropriations initially approved for the biennium 2000-2001 in its resolution
54/250 C of 23 December 1999, less 2,563,800 dollars,
being the reduction approved by the General Assembly
in resolution A above, shall be financed in accordance
with regulations 5.1 and 5.2 of the Financial Regulations of the United Nations as follows:

(a) 51,899,313 dollars, consisting of:

(i) 21,193,700 dollars, being half of the estimated
income other than income from staff assessment
approved for the biennium 2000-2001 by the Assembly in its resolution 54/250 B of 23 December 1999;

(ii) Plus 5,310,100 dollars, being the increase approved by the Assembly in resolution B above;

(iii) 25,395,513 dollars, being the balance in the surplus account as at 31 December 1999;

(b) 1,213,381,487 dollars, being the assessment on
Member States in accordance with its resolution
55/5 B of 23 December 2000 on the scale of assessments for the year 2001;

2. There shall be set off against the assessment on
Member States, in accordance with the provisions of
General Assembly resolution 973(X) of 15 December
1955, their respective share in the Tax Equalization
Fund in the total amount of 179,097,566 dollars, con-
sisting of:

(a) 159,455,750 dollars, being half of the estimated
staff assessment income approved by the Assembly in
its resolution 54/250 B;

(b) Plus 14,213,700 dollars, being the estimated increase in income from staff assessment approved by the
Assembly in resolution B above;

(c) Plus 5,428,116 dollars, being the increase in income from staff assessment for the biennium
1998-1999 compared with the revised estimates approved by the Assembly in its resolution 54/247 B of 23
December 1999.

Other questions related to the 2000-2001 programme budget

In its deliberations on the agenda item on the
2000-2001 programme budget, the Fifth Committee considered a number of special subjects,
among them the revised estimates in respect of
Security Council matters and resulting from Economic and Social Council resolutions and decisions; the budget section of the International
Court of Justice (ICJ); the capital master plan; a
subvention to the United Nations Institute for
Disarmament Research (UNIDIR); the first performance report on the 2000-2001 budget; the
contingency fund; and the recosting of outstanding statements of programme budget implications and revised estimates (see sections below).

Other subjects concerned the report of the
Panel on United Nations Peace Operations (the
Brahimi report); UN personnel safety and secu-
rity; full-time officials, other than those of the
Secretariat, serving the General Assembly; the
Information Systems Coordination Committee;
and the International Research and Training In-
stitute for the Advancement of Women.

GENERAL ASSEMBLY ACTION

On 23 December [meeting 89], the General Assembly, on the recommendation of the Fifth Committee [A/55/713], adopted **resolution 55/238**
without vote [agenda item 117].

Questions relating to the programme budget for the biennium 2000–2001

The General Assembly,

I
Report of the Panel on United Nations Peace Operations

Having considered the report of the Secretary-General on resource requirements for implementation of the report of the Panel on United Nations Peace Operations and the related report of the Advisory Committee on Administrative and Budgetary Questions,

Taking full account of the report of the Special Committee on Peacekeeping Operations on the comprehensive review of the whole question of peacekeeping operations in all their aspects and General Assembly resolution 55/135 of 8 December 2000, endorsing the proposals, recommendation and conclusions of the Special Committee contained in its report,

Recalling its resolutions 45/258 of 3 May 1991, 47/218 A of 23 December 1992, 48/226 A of 23 December 1993, 48/226 B of 5 April 1994, 48/226 C of 29 July 1994, 49/250 of 20 July 1995, 50/11 of 2 November 1995, 50/221 A of 11 April 1996, 50/221 B of 7 June 1996, 51/226 of 3 April 1997, 51/239 A of 17 June 1997, 51/239 B and 51/243 of 15 September 1997, 52/220 of 22 December 1997, 52/234 and 52/248 of 26 June 1998, 53/12 A of 26 October 1998, 53/208 B of 18 December 1998, 53/12 B of 8 June 1999, 54/243 A of 23 December 1999 and 54/243 B of 15 June 2000 and its decisions 48/489 of 8 July 1994, 49/469 of 23 December 1994 and 50/473 of 23 December 1995,

Recalling also its resolutions 54/249 and 54/250 of 23 December 1999,

Recalling further its resolution 55/2 of 8 September 2000, by which it adopted the United Nations Millennium Declaration,

1. *Reaffirms* rule 153 of its rules of procedure;

2. *Agrees* with the views expressed by the Special Committee on Peacekeeping Operations in paragraphs 34 and 35 of its report on the comprehensive review of the whole question of peacekeeping operations in all their aspects;

3. *Endorses* the conclusions and recommendations contained in the report of the Advisory Committee on Administrative and Budgetary Questions, and requests the Secretary-General to ensure their full implementation;

4. *Decides* to appropriate an additional amount of 363,000 United States dollars under section 3, Political affairs, 37,200 dollars under section 27, Management and central support services, and 19,200 dollars under section 32, Staff assessment, to be offset by a corresponding amount (19,200 dollars) under income section 1, Income from staff assessment, of the programme budget for the biennium 2000-2001;

5. *Approves* the support account post and non-post requirements in the amount of 9,190,200 dollars gross (8,741,600 dollars net) for the period from 1 July 2000 to 30 June 2001;

6. *Agrees* with paragraph 36 of the report of the Special Committee relating to proper representation of troop-contributing countries in the Department of Peacekeeping Operations of the Secretariat;

7. *Underscores* the importance of consultation with troop-contributing countries from the early stages of mission planning;

8. *Expresses deep concern* over the delay in reimbursement of troop contributors, which can cause hardship to all troop- and equipment-contributing countries, and requests the Secretariat to expedite the processing of all claims and present a progress report in this regard during the first part of the resumed fifty-fifth session of the General Assembly;

9. *Notes* that the related resource requirements presented by the Secretary-General in his report on resource requirements for implementation of the report of the Panel on United Nations Peace Operations have been described by him as an emergency request, whereas, in terms of paragraph 11 of the report of the Advisory Committee, it was acknowledged that not all the proposals in the report of the Secretary-General on resource requirements for implementation of the report of the Panel could be classified as emergency requests;

10. *Regrets* that the report of the Secretary-General on resource requirements for implementation of the report of the Panel was not presented in accordance with rule 153 of its rules of procedures and with established practices, as pointed out in paragraph 3 of the report of the Advisory Committee, and requests the Secretary-General to comply strictly with those rules in the future;

11. *Notes* that the report of the Secretary-General on resource requirements for implementation of the report of the Panel has not been issued in compliance with the six-week rule;

12. *Takes note* of the intention of the Secretary-General to submit future reports to the General Assembly at its fifty-fifth and fifty-sixth sessions on the implementation of the recommendations in the report of the Panel, including the comprehensive review, requested by the Special Committee, of the management, structure, recruitment processes and interrelationships of all relevant elements within the Secretariat that play a role in peacekeeping operations;

II
Safety and security of United Nations personnel

Reaffirming its resolutions 54/249 and 54/250 of 23 December 1999 and its other relevant resolutions,

Having considered the report of the Secretary-General on safety and security of United Nations personnel, in particular its administrative and budgetary aspects, and the related report of the Advisory Committee on Administrative and Budgetary Questions,

1. *Endorses* the recommendations contained in the report of the Advisory Committee on Administrative and Budgetary Questions, subject to the provisions set forth in the present section;

2. *Decides* to consider the reclassification of the post of Deputy Security Coordinator from the D-1 level to the D-2 level in the context of its review of the proposed programme budget for the biennium 2002-2003;

3. *Also decides* to establish, effective 1 January 2001, eight additional Professional posts (two P-5 and six P-4) in the Office of the United Nations Security Coordinator at Headquarters;

4. *Further decides* to establish, effective 1 January 2001, eight additional security officer (Field Service)

posts (four P-4 and four P-3) and sixteen additional Local level posts;

5. *Decides* to appropriate the amount of 2,210,000 dollars under section 30, Special expenses, and the amount of 238,400 dollars under section 32, Staff assessment, to be offset by an equivalent amount under income section 1, Income from staff assessment, of the programme budget for the biennium 2000-2001, for the Secretary-General to undertake the immediate measures for the strengthening of the security management system of the United Nations;

6. *Requests* the Secretary-General, in his capacity as Chairman of the Administrative Committee on Coordination, to develop, in coordination with executive heads of the United Nations specialized agencies, funds and programmes, an effective mechanism for cost-sharing arrangements and, in this connection, to ensure that in future the costs of the security management system are included in the regular budget, to be managed by the United Nations, contingent upon a formal arrangement with the concerned agencies, funds and programmes for participation in the funding of security arrangements and reimbursement to the United Nations for services provided, under income section 2, General income, of the programme budget, and to submit proposals thereon to the General Assembly at its fifty-sixth session through the Advisory Committee, and decides that, in the meantime, the established cost-sharing arrangements between the United Nations and its specialized agencies, funds and programmes will remain in place until the Assembly decides otherwise;

7. *Also requests* the Secretary-General, when presenting future reports under these agenda items, to continue to ensure that separate reports are presented;

III
Revised estimates in respect of matters of which the Security Council is seized

Takes note of the report of the Secretary-General on the revised estimates in respect of matters of which the Security Council is seized, and concurs with the observations and recommendations of the Advisory Committee on Administrative and Budgetary Questions contained in paragraph 7 of its related report;

IV
Capital master plan

1. *Takes note* of the report of the Secretary-General on the capital master plan;

2. *Also takes note* of the related report of the Advisory Committee on Administrative and Budgetary Questions, and endorses the observations and recommendations contained therein;

3. *Authorizes* the Secretary-General, without prejudice to a final decision by the General Assembly on this issue, to proceed with the preparation of a comprehensive design plan and detailed cost analysis for the capital master plan, and decides to appropriate an amount of 8 million dollars under section 31, Construction, alteration, improvement and major maintenance, of the programme budget for the biennium 2000-2001 for this purpose;

4. *Requests* the Secretary-General to submit a report on the outcome of the comprehensive design plan and detailed cost analysis to the General Assembly as soon

as possible, including details of measures designed to protect the Organization from cost overruns;

5. *Calls upon* the Secretary-General to ensure that the preparation of a comprehensive design plan and detailed cost analysis for the capital master plan will identify all viable alternatives in the most cost-effective and efficient manner;

V
International Court of Justice

1. *Approves* an additional appropriation of 591,900 dollars under section 7, International Court of Justice, of the programme budget for the biennium 2000-2001 and an additional appropriation of 128,800 dollars under section 32, Staff assessment, offset by the same amount under income section 1, Income from staff assessment;

2. *Requests* the Joint Inspection Unit to expedite its report on the review of the management and administration of the International Court of Justice and to submit it, together with the comments of the Court thereon, for consideration by the General Assembly at its resumed fifty-fifth session;

VI
Request for a subvention to the United Nations Institute for Disarmament Research resulting from the recommendations of the Board of Trustees of the Institute on the programme of work of the Institute for 2001

Approves the recommendation for a subvention of 213,000 dollars for 2001 from the regular budget of the United Nations, on the understanding that no additional appropriation would be required under section 4, Disarmament, of the programme budget for the biennium 2000-2001;

VII
Conditions of service and compensation for officials, other than Secretariat officials, serving the General Assembly: full-time members of the International Civil Service Commission and the Chairman of the Advisory Committee on Administrative and Budgetary Questions

1. *Takes note* of the report of the Secretary-General entitled "Conditions of service and compensation for officials, other than Secretariat officials, serving the General Assembly: full-time members of the International Civil Service Commission and the Chairman of the Advisory Committee on Administrative and Budgetary Questions", and approves the suggestions outlined in paragraphs 8 to 10 and in paragraph 19 of the report;

2. *Decides* to undertake a detailed examination of the issue of compensation relativity in the context of the next five-year review of the conditions of service and compensation for the three officials;

3. *Reaffirms* the principle that the conditions of service of the three officials should be separate and distinct from those of the Secretariat;

VIII
Review of the Information Systems Coordination Committee

Takes note of the report of the Secretary-General on the review of the Information Systems Coordination Committee, and concurs with the observations and recommendations of the Advisory Committee on Administrative and Budgetary Questions in paragraph 9 of its related report;

IX
First performance report on the programme budget for the biennium 2000-2001

Having considered the first performance report of the Secretary-General on the programme budget for the biennium 2000-2001 and the related report of the Advisory Committee on Administrative and Budgetary Questions,

1. *Reaffirms* the budgetary process as approved in its resolution 41/213 of 19 December 1986 and as reaffirmed in its subsequent resolutions;

2. *Reaffirms also* its resolution 54/249 of 23 December 1999;

3. *Takes note* of the first performance report of the Secretary-General on the programme budget for the biennium 2000-2001 and the related report and recommendations of the Advisory Committee on Administrative and Budgetary Questions;

4. *Notes* the higher than budgeted vacancy rate relative to the rate approved by the General Assembly in its resolution 54/249, and requests the Secretary-General to take all appropriate measures to rectify this situation in an expeditious manner;

5. *Approves* a net decrease of 34,642,200 dollars in the appropriation approved for the biennium 2000-2001 and a net increase of 19,097,000 dollars in the estimates of income for the biennium, to be apportioned among expenditure and income sections, as indicated in the report of the Secretary-General;

X
Contingency fund

Notes that a balance of 224,300 dollars remains in the contingency fund;

XI
Recosting of outstanding statements of programme budget implications and revised estimates

Takes note of the report of the Secretary-General on recosting of outstanding statements of programme budget implications and revised estimates, and decides that the recosting and the related adjustments should be reflected in the revised appropriation for the biennium 2000-2001.

On 23 December, the Assembly decided that the item on the programme budget for 2000-2001 would remain for consideration at its resumed fifty-first (2001) session (**decision 55/458**) and that the Fifth Committee would continue consideration of the item at that session (**decision 55/455**).

Contingency fund

The contingency fund, established by General Assembly resolution 41/213 [YUN 1986, p. 1024], accommodated additional expenditures relating to each biennium that derived from legislative mandates not provided for in the proposed programme budget or from revised estimates. Guidelines for its use were annexed to Assembly resolution 42/211 [YUN 1987, p. 1098].

Reports of Secretary-General. In his reports of March [A/C.5/54/46] and December [A/C.5/55/34] to the Fifth Committee, the Secretary-General submitted consolidated statements of programme budget implications and revised estimates chargeable against the fund. The first statement, totalling $2,737,300, was superseded by the second, which totalled $16,138,400; the itemized amounts corresponded to those that the Committee had previously recommended. The Secretary-General indicated that the fund's balance for the biennium 2000-2001, as noted by Assembly resolution 54/251 [YUN 1999, p. 1305], was $16,362,700 as at 23 December 1999. Therefore, should the Committee recommend to the Assembly appropriation of the required amounts under the relevant sections of the programme budget, it should also request the Assembly to note that a balance of $224,300 would remain in the fund.

The Assembly, by **decision 54/480** of 15 June, deferred consideration of the relationship between the treatment of perennial activities in the programme budget and the use of the contingency fund until its resumed fifty-fifth (2001) session.

Revised estimates in respect of matters of which the Security Council was seized

In March [A/C.5/54/52], the Secretary-General submitted estimated resource requirements of $6,154,600 for two political missions to be charged against the $90,387,200 provided for special political missions, approved by General Assembly resolution 54/250 A [YUN 1999, p. 1303]. The ACABQ Chairman, in an oral report to the Committee [A/54/7/Add.1-14, annex], recommended approval of the proposed charge.

By **decision 54/477 A** of 7 April, the Assembly took note of the Secretary-General's report and the related ACABQ oral report, and approved the charge of $6,154,600 for the United Nations Peace-building Support Office in Guinea-Bissau and the United Nations Peace-building Support Office in the Central African Republic against the provision for special political missions under section 3, Political affairs, of the 2000-2001 programme budget. The Assembly noted that, consequently, the utilization of the provision for special political missions amounted to $61,517,700, leaving an uncommitted balance of $28,869,500.

The Secretary-General submitted further estimated resource requirements on 18 April [A/C.5/54/53] of $3,846,300 and on 3 May [A/C.5/54/57] of $710,600 relating to the mandate of the United Nations Office in Angola (UNOA), also chargeable against the provision for special political missions. ACABQ recommended that the Assembly approve those charges [A/54/7/Add.1-14].

By **decision 54/477 B** of 15 June, the Assembly noted the Secretary-General's reports, endorsed ACABQ's observations and recommendations and asked the Secretary-General to bring them to the attention of the Security Council President. It approved the charge of $4,556,900 for UNOA's extension against the provision for special political missions of the 2000-2001 programme budget, and noted that, consequently, the utilization of the provision amounted to $66,074,600, leaving an unallocated balance of $24,312,600.

In December [A/C.5/55/30], the Secretary-General sought an additional appropriation of $4,162,500 for five political missions relating to actions taken by the Council on the basis of requests from Governments and/or recommendations of the Secretary-General. ACABQ [A/55/7/Add.6] recommended an additional appropriation in that amount under section 3, Political affairs, of the 2000-2001 programme budget.

Revised estimates resulting from Economic and Social Council action

By a November report to the Fifth Committee [A/C.5/55/25 & Corr.1], the Secretary-General submitted revised cost estimates totalling $1,858,300 resulting from Economic and Social Council resolutions and decisions adopted in 2000 to be financed from existing provisions of the 2000-2001 programme budget. He drew attention to the additional requirement of $114,800 entailed by resolution 2000/22 for the annual meeting of a permanent forum on indigenous issues to be established in Geneva (see p. 731), for which no provision had been made in the 2000-2001 programme budget. Should the meeting take place in 2001 and in line with General Assembly resolution 40/243 [YUN 1985, p. 1256], which reaffirmed that UN bodies should meet at their respective headquarters, an appropriation in that amount, representing a charge against the contingency fund, should be made under section 22, Human rights, of the programme budget.

In a December addendum [A/C.5/55/25/Add.1], the Secretary-General requested further additional resource requirements totalling $770,400 under section 2, General Assembly affairs and conference services ($28,800), and section 22 ($741,600), arising from Council decision 2000/311, which established a human rights inquiry commission on violations of human rights in the occupied Palestinian territories (see p. 776).

ACABQ orally agreed before the Fifth Committee on 18 December [meeting 41] that $114,800 be authorized for the forum meeting and recommended acceptance of the amounts of $28,800

and $741,600 to be appropriated under sections 2 and 22, respectively, for the implementation of decision 2000/311 and to be charged against the contingency fund.

By **decision 55/456** of 23 December, the Assembly took note of the Secretary-General's reports on the revised estimates resulting from the Council's resolutions and decisions adopted at its 2000 substantive session and, with respect to the related ACABQ recommendations made orally, authorized the Secretary-General to enter into commitments not exceeding $856,400 for implementing the Council's resolutions and decisions. It requested him to report thereon to the fifty-sixth (2001) session of the Assembly in the context of its consideration of the second performance report on the 2000-2001 programme budget.

International Court of Justice

The Secretary-General submitted to the Fifth Committee in November [A/C.5/55/21] a proposal for an additional appropriation of $606,100 under section 7, International Court of Justice, of the 2000-2001 programme budget, owing to the dramatic and unexpected increase in the Court's caseload. Should the General Assembly approve the proposal, an additional appropriation of $131,200 would be required under section 32, Staff assessment, offset by the same amount under section 1, Income from staff assessment. ACABQ recommended Assembly approval of those proposals [A/55/7/Add.2].

Subvention to UNIDIR

In October [A/C.5/55/15], the Secretary-General transmitted for the General Assembly's approval a request for a subvention of $213,000 from the UN regular budget to UNIDIR, resulting from the recommendations of the Institute's Board of Trustees on the 2001 work programme.

Programme budget outline for 2002-2003

Report of Secretary-General. In July [A/55/186], the Secretary-General presented the proposed programme budget outline for 2002-2003, indicating a preliminary estimate of resources; sectoral priorities; real growth, positive or negative, compared with the previous budgets; and the size of the contingency fund expressed as a percentage of the overall level of resources. The preliminary estimate for the 2002-2003 biennium, expressed at 2000-2001 prices, amounted to $2,475.4 million.

The full biennial provision for posts partially funded in the current (2000-2001) biennium, namely, new posts at the Professional level and above and those approved for the Integrated Management Information System (IMIS) at offices away from Headquarters, would require an additional $13.2 million. One-time costs of $13.4 million in 2000-2001 relating to the secretariat of the Millennium Assembly, the special General Assembly sessions and related plenary meetings, a number of UN conferences, and the costs of the final development phase of IMIS would not be required. New resource requirements for 2002-2003 were projected at $30.1 million. In the light of the ongoing review of recommendations arising from the Brahimi report (see p. 83), no provision had yet been made for special political missions or for strengthening the security and safety of UN system personnel (see p. 1345). Those issues and their effects on the budget outline would be addressed at the Assembly's fifty-fifth (2000) session, when the relevant reports were available. To maximize output effectiveness of the resources committed, the Secretary-General intended to subject the proposed 2002-2003 programme budget to the most intensive review within the Secretariat, focusing on expected accomplishments with the resources committed.

The preliminary estimate before adjustment for the non-inclusion of special political missions represented an increase of $30.1 million, or 1.2 per cent compared with the initial appropriation for the 2000-2001 biennium. Once account was taken of that amount, the total preliminary estimate would represent a decrease of $60.3 million, or 2.4 per cent compared with the initial appropriation for 2000-2001.

Noting that the size of the contingency fund was set at 0.75 per cent of the overall resource level, the Secretary-General recommended that the fund level be set at $18.6 million for the 2002-2003 biennium.

CPC report. Having considered the proposed programme budget outline at the second part (21-29 August) of its fortieth session [A/55/16 & Corr.1,2], the Committee for Programme and Coordination (CPC) recommended that the Assembly further consider all aspects of the outline, taking into account: the preliminary estimate's adequacy for the full implementation of all mandated programmes and activities, including projects initiated in the 2000-2001 biennium; that full information on the preliminary estimate was not available in the outline; that Assembly resolution 53/206 [YUN 1998, p. 1284] requiring the inclusion of a provision in the budget outline for expenditures for special political missions related to

peace and security expected to be extended or approved in the course of the biennium; that the Secretary-General's review of possible obsolete activities should remain within the context of relevant Regulations and Rules Governing Programme Planning, the Programme Aspects of the Budget, the Monitoring of Implementation and the Methods of Evaluation; that Member States should demonstrate their commitment to the United Nations by meeting their financial obligations in full, on time and without conditions; CPC's recommended approval of the priorities in the 2002-2003 programme budget outline; and that the size of the contingency fund should be 0.75 per cent of the budget outline.

ACABQ report. ACABQ [A/55/685 & Corr.1], noting the omission of the requirements for special political missions in the proposed 2002-2003 programme budget outline, pointed out that, had the Secretary-General included a provision of $93.7 million at revised 2000-2001 rates, the preliminary estimates for the 2002-2003 biennium would have amounted to $2,515.3 million. ACABQ therefore recommended that, for the 2002-2003 biennium, the Assembly adopt a total preliminary estimate of $2,515,300 million at revised 2000-2001 rates.

GENERAL ASSEMBLY ACTION

On 23 December [meeting 89], the General Assembly, on the recommendation of the Fifth Committee [A/55/532/Add.1 & Corr.1], adopted **resolution 55/233** without vote [agenda item 116].

Proposed programme budget outline for the biennium 2002-2003

The General Assembly,

Reaffirming its resolution 41/213 of 19 December 1986 in which it, inter alia, requested the Secretary-General to submit in off-budget years an outline of the proposed programme budget for the following biennium,

Reaffirming also section VI of its resolution 45/248 B of 21 December 1990,

Recalling its resolution 53/214 of 18 December 1998,

Reaffirming rule 153 of its rules of procedure,

Having considered the report of the Secretary-General on the proposed programme budget outline for the biennium 2002-2003, the related recommendations of the Committee for Programme and Coordination and the recommendations contained in the report of the Advisory Committee on Administrative and Budgetary Questions,

1. *Takes note* of the report of the Committee for Programme and Coordination and the report and recommendations of the Advisory Committee on Administrative and Budgetary Questions;

2. *Reaffirms* that the proposed programme budget outline shall contain an indication of the following:

(a) Preliminary estimate of resources to accommodate the proposed programme of activities during the biennium;

(*b*) Priorities reflecting general trends of a broad sectoral nature;

(*c*) Real growth, positive or negative, compared with the previous budget;

(*d*) Size of the contingency fund expressed as a percentage of the overall level of resources;

3. *Also reaffirms* that the budget outline should provide a greater level of predictability of resources required for the following biennium, promote greater involvement of Member States in the budgetary process and thereby facilitate the broadest possible agreement on the programme budget;

4. *Notes* that the budget outline is a preliminary estimate of resources;

5. *Endorses* the recommendation of the Advisory Committee contained in paragraph 8 of its report, that provision should be made in the budget outline for expenditures for special political missions related to peace and security expected to be extended or approved in the course of the biennium;

6. *Decides* that the preliminary estimate of resources for the proposed programme budget for the biennium 2002-2003 should therefore include a provision for special political missions, in the amount of 93.7 million United States dollars at revised 2000-2001 rates, which should be reflected in the proposed programme budget for the biennium 2002-2003, and that additional requirements shall continue to be treated in accordance with the provisions of General Assembly resolution 41/213;

7. *Notes* that the preliminary estimates of the Secretary-General for the proposed programme budget did not include provision for the requirements for the biennium 2002-2003 for the implementation of the report of the Panel on United Nations Peace Operations, that those requirements remain under discussion by the General Assembly and that the requirements pertinent to the regular budget should be reflected in the programme budget for the biennium 2002-2003, subject to approval by the Assembly;

8. *Notes also* that the preliminary estimates of the Secretary-General for the proposed programme budget did not include provision for the requirements for the biennium 2002-2003 for safety and security of personnel, that those requirements remain under discussion by the General Assembly, and that the requirements pertinent to the regular budget should be reflected in the programme budget for the biennium 2002-2003, subject to approval by the Assembly;

9. *Invites* the Secretary-General to prepare his proposed programme budget for the biennium 2002-2003 on the basis of a total preliminary estimate of 2,515.3 million dollars at revised 2000-2001 rates;

10. *Decides* that the proposed programme budget for the biennium 2002-2003 shall contain provisions for recosting on the basis of the existing methodology;

11. *Decides also* that the priorities for the biennium 2002-2003 are the following:

(*a*) Maintenance of international peace and security;

(*b*) Promotion of sustained economic growth and sustainable development, in accordance with the relevant resolutions of the General Assembly and recent United Nations conferences;

(*c*) Development of Africa;

(*d*) Promotion of human rights;

(*e*) Effective coordination of humanitarian assistance efforts;

(*f*) Promotion of justice and international law;

(*g*) Disarmament;

(*h*) Drug control, crime prevention and combating international terrorism in all its forms and manifestations;

12. *Requests* the Secretary-General, having considered his preliminary indicative estimates contained in the proposed budget outline, when presenting the proposed programme budget for the biennium 2002-2003, to reflect the priorities as outlined in paragraph 11 above;

13. *Reiterates its request* to the Secretary-General to submit, in the proposed programme budget for the biennium 2002-2003, the total amount of resources that he should have at his disposal, from all sources of financing, in order to implement fully all mandated programmes and activities;

14. *Decides* that the contingency fund shall be set at the level of 0.75 per cent of the preliminary estimate, namely at 18.9 million dollars, and that this amount is in addition to the overall level of the preliminary estimate and is to be used in accordance with the procedures for the use and operation of the contingency fund.

Contributions

According to the Secretary-General's March report [A/55/504/Add.1], unpaid assessed contributions from Member States to the UN budget at the end of 2000 totalled $2.2 billion ($500 million more than the 1999 figure); unpaid regular budget assessments totalled $222 million ($22 million less than at the end of 1999); outstanding peacekeeping arrears totalled $2 billion (some $600 million more than in 1999); and unpaid assessments to the international tribunals were $166 million (compared with $32 million in 1999).

The number of Member States paying their regular budget assessment in full continued to grow, rising to 141 Members by the end of 2000, 15 more than the previous year.

Unforeseen and extraordinary expenses

Under specific circumstances, the Secretary-General was authorized by the General Assembly to enter into commitments for activities of an urgent nature, without reverting to it for approval.

In his first performance report on the 2000-2001 programme budget [A/55/645 & Corr.1], the Secretary-General informed the Assembly that, under the terms of resolution 54/252 [YUN 1999, p. 1309] on unforeseen and extraordinary expenses, he had entered into commitments totalling $10,987,900, of which $7,233,400 was for activities he had certified as relating to the maintenance of peace and security; $3,396,500 for commitments agreed to by ACABQ in respect of Security Council decisions; $345,000 for commitments certified by the ICJ President: and $13,000 for inter-organizational security measures.

Assessments

Assessment methodology

In March, the General Assembly, pursuant to decision 54/455 B [YUN 1999, p. 1313], resumed consideration of the agenda item on the scale of assessments and apportionment of expenses of the United Nations.

GENERAL ASSEMBLY ACTION

On 7 April [meeting 95], the General Assembly, on the recommendation of the Fifth Committee [A/54/685/Add.1], adopted **resolution 54/237 D** without vote [agenda item 125].

Scale of assessments for the apportionment of the expenses of the United Nations

The General Assembly,

I

Recalling its previous resolutions and decisions on the scale of assessments, in particular resolution 52/215 A of 22 December 1997,

Recalling also paragraph 1 of its resolution 48/223 C of 23 December 1993,

Having considered the report of the Committee on Contributions on the work of its fifty-ninth session,

Reaffirming Article 17 of the Charter of the United Nations and rule 160 of its rules of procedure,

1. *Reaffirms* the obligation of all Member States to bear the expenses of the United Nations, as apportioned by the General Assembly, in conformity with Article 17 of the Charter of the United Nations;

2. *Also reaffirms* the fundamental principle that the expenses of the Organization should be apportioned among Member States, broadly according to capacity to pay, as established in rule 160 of the rules of procedure of the General Assembly;

3. *Requests* the Secretary-General to ensure that Permanent Missions are furnished in good time with copies of the national accounts questionnaire to enable them to provide for the appropriate follow-up;

4. *Requests* the Committee on Contributions to submit to the General Assembly at its fifty-fifth session twelve proposals for a scale of assessments for the period 2001-2003 as follows:

(*a*) A proposal based on the methodology used in preparing the scale of assessments for 2000, including the phasing out of the scheme of limits in accordance with the provisions of General Assembly resolutions 48/223 B of 23 December 1993 and 52/215 A;

(*b*) A proposal to include the following elements and criteria:

(i) Data on gross national product;

(ii) A statistical base period of six years;

(iii) Conversion rates based on market exchange rates, except where that would cause excessive fluctuations and distortions in the income of some Member States, when price-adjusted rates of exchange or other appropriate conversion rates should be employed, taking due account of General Assembly resolution 46/221 B of 20 December 1991;

(iv) Debt burden adjustment based on the total debt stock;

(v) A low per capita income adjustment with a threshold per capita income limit of the average world per capita income for the statistical base period and a sliding gradient;

(vi) Redistribution of the adjustment to all Member States, consistent with the practice before 1979;

(vii) A minimum assessment rate of 0.001 per cent;

(viii) A maximum assessment rate of 25 per cent;

(ix) A maximum assessment rate for the least developed countries of 0.01 per cent;

(*c*) A proposal to include the following elements and criteria:

(i) Estimates of gross national product;

(ii) A statistical base period of six years;

(iii) Conversion rates as recommended by the Committee on Contributions, and as earlier spelled out in General Assembly resolution 46/221 B;

(iv) Debt burden adjustment based on the total debt stock;

(v) A low per capita income adjustment with a per capita income limit of the current threshold used by the World Bank for high-income countries (9,361 United States dollars), and a gradient of 80 per cent;

(vi) A minimum assessment rate of 0.001 per cent;

(vii) A ceiling rate of 25 per cent;

(viii) Individual rates of assessment for the least developed countries, not to exceed the current level of 0.01 per cent;

(*d*) A proposal to include the following elements and criteria:

(i) Gross national product as the base;

(ii) A statistical base period of three years, with automatic annual recalculation;

(iii) Debt burden adjustment based on actual principal repayments (debt flow);

(iv) Conversion rates based on market exchange rates, except where that would cause excessive fluctuations and distortions in the income of some Member States, when price-adjusted rates of exchange or other appropriate conversion rates should be employed, taking due account of General Assembly resolution 46/221 B;

(v) A two-tiered gradient for relief of Member States with a low per capita income; a gradient of 80 per cent for least developed countries and a gradient of 70 per cent for other Member States with a per capita income below the world average;

(vi) To address discontinuity, a phase-in mechanism, that is divided equally over the period 2001-2003, for the redistribution of points received from the low per capita income adjustment for Member States that cross the threshold from one scale period to the next (example: all other things being equal, if the assessment of a Member State was 1.000 per cent when it was below the threshold, in the next scale period it would increase to 1.067 per cent, 1.134 per cent and 1.200 per cent over three years instead of going directly to 1.200);

(vii) A minimum assessment rate of 0.001 per cent and a maximum rate for the least developed countries of 0.01 per cent;

(viii) A ceiling rate of 25 per cent;

(*e*) A proposal to include the following elements and criteria:

(i) Gross national product as the base;

(ii) A statistical base period of three years, with automatic annual recalculation;

(iii) Debt burden adjustment based on actual principal repayments (debt flow);

(iv) A two-tiered gradient for relief of Member States with a low per capita income; a gradient of 80 per cent for least developed countries and a gradient of 70 per cent for other Member States with a per capita income below the world average;

(v) Conversion rates based on market exchange rates, except where that would cause excessive fluctuations and distortions in the income of some Member States, when price-adjusted rates of exchange or other appropriate conversion rates should be employed, taking due account of General Assembly resolution 46/221 B;

(vi) To address discontinuity, a phase-in mechanism, that is divided equally over the 2001-2003 period, for the redistribution of points received from the low per capita income adjustment for Member States that cross the threshold from one scale period to the next (example: all other things being equal, if the assessment of a Member State was 1.000 per cent when it was below the threshold, in the next scale period it would increase to 1.067 per cent, 1.134 per cent and 1.200 per cent over three years instead of going directly to 1.200);

(vii) A minimum assessment rate of 0.001 per cent and a maximum rate for the least developed countries of 0.01 per cent;

(viii) A ceiling rate of 20 per cent;

(*f*) A proposal to include the following elements and criteria:

(i) Estimates of gross national product;

(ii) A statistical base period of six years;

(iii) Conversion rates as recommended by the Committee on Contributions, and as earlier spelled out in General Assembly resolution 46/221 B;

(iv) Debt burden adjustment based on the total debt stock;

(v) A low per capita income adjustment with a threshold per capita income limit of the average world per capita income for the statistical base period, and a gradient of 80 per cent without discrimination among Member States;

(vi) A minimum assessment rate of 0.001 per cent and no ceiling;

(vii) A maximum assessment rate for the least developed countries, not to exceed the current level of 0.01 per cent;

(viii) To limit to 25 per cent, for developing countries previously benefiting from its application, the effect of the end of the scheme of limits on an annual basis for the first four years of the post-transition period;

(*g*) A proposal to include the following elements and criteria:

(i) Use of gross national product data as a first approximation of capacity to pay;

(ii) A statistical base period of three years, with automatic annual recalculation;

(iii) Conversion rates based on market exchange rates, except where that would cause excessive fluctuations and distortions in the income of some Member States, when price-adjusted rates of exchange or other appropriate conversion rates should be employed, taking due account of General Assembly resolution 46/221 B;

(iv) No debt burden adjustments;

(v) A low per capita income adjustment with a threshold per capita income limit of the average world per capita income for the statistical base period, and a gradient of 75 per cent;

(vi) A minimum assessment rate of 0.001 per cent;

(vii) A maximum assessment rate of 25 per cent;

(viii) A maximum assessment rate for the least developed countries of 0.01 per cent;

(ix) No scheme of limits;

(*h*) A proposal to include the elements and criteria in subparagraphs (i) to (viii) and a response to subparagraph (ix) below:

(i) Estimates of gross national product;

(ii) A statistical base period of six years;

(iii) Conversion rates as recommended by the Committee on Contributions, and as earlier spelled out in General Assembly resolution 46/221 B;

(iv) Debt burden adjustment based on the total debt stock;

(v) A low per capita income adjustment with a threshold per capita income limit of the average world per capita income for the statistical base period, and a gradient of 80 per cent;

(vi) A minimum assessment rate of 0.001 per cent and a maximum assessment rate of 25 per cent;

(vii) A maximum assessment rate for the least developed countries not to exceed the current level of 0.01 per cent;

(viii) To limit to 25 per cent, for developing countries previously benefiting from its application, the effect of the end of the scheme of limits on an annual basis for the first four years of the post-transition period;

(ix) To examine the long-term implications of the present criteria for determining the threshold of the low per capita income adjustment, and to recommend possible alternatives with a view to maintaining in the long run the overall benefit for all developing countries and to avoiding the continuous exclusion of middle-income developing countries from the benefit of the adjustment;

(*i*) A proposal to include the following elements and criteria:

(i) Data on gross national product as a first approximation of capacity to pay;

(ii) A constant statistical base period of three years;

(iii) Conversion rates based on market exchange rates, except where that would cause excessive fluctuations and distortions in the income of some Member States, when price-adjusted rates of exchange or other appropriate conversion rates should be employed, taking due account of General Assembly resolution 46/221 B;

(iv) Debt burden adjustment based on actual principal payments;

(v) A low per capita income adjustment with a threshold per capita income limit of the average world per capita income for the statistical base period, and with gradients based on the gross national product share of each eligible country as follows:

   a. A gradient of 70 per cent for countries with a gross national product share of less than 1 per cent;

   b. A gradient of 40 per cent for countries with a gross national product share of 1 per cent or more but less than 3 per cent;

   c. A gradient of 10 per cent for countries with a gross national product share of 3 per cent or more;

(vi) Non-eligibility of the States permanent members of the Security Council for a low per capita income adjustment;

(vii) A minimum assessment rate of 0.001 per cent;

(viii) A maximum assessment rate of 25 per cent;

(ix) A maximum assessment rate for the least developed countries of 0.01 per cent;

(j) A proposal to include the following elements and criteria:

(i) The methodology used in preparing the scale of assessments for 2000, including the phasing out of the scheme of limits in accordance with the provisions of General Assembly resolutions 48/223 B and 52/215 A, except for the provisions in subparagraph (ii) below;

(ii) A maximum assessment rate of 22 per cent, with the points arising from the reduction of the maximum assessment rate from 25 per cent to be distributed only among Member States other than members of the Group of 77 and China;

(k) A proposal to include the following elements and criteria:

(i) Data on gross national product;

(ii) A statistical base period of three years;

(iii) Conversion rates based on market exchange rates, except where that would cause excessive fluctuations and distortions in the income of some Member States, when price-adjusted rates of exchange or other appropriate conversion rates should be employed, taking due account of General Assembly resolution 46/221 B;

(iv) Debt burden adjustment based on actual principal payments;

(v) A low per capita income adjustment with a threshold per capita income limit of the average world per capita income for the statistical base period, and with gradients based on the gross national product share of each eligible country as follows:

   a. A gradient of 80 per cent for countries with a gross national product share of less than 1 per cent;

   b. A gradient of 50 per cent for countries with a gross national product share of 1 per cent or more;

(vi) A minimum assessment rate of 0.001 per cent;

(vii) A maximum assessment rate of 22 per cent;

(viii) A maximum assessment rate for the least developed countries of 0.01 per cent;

(l) A proposal to include the following elements and criteria:

(i) Data on gross national product;

(ii) A statistical base period of three years;

(iii) Conversion rates based on market exchange rates, except where that would cause excessive fluctuations and distortions in the income of some Member States, when price-adjusted rates of exchange or other appropriate conversion rates should be employed, taking due account of General Assembly resolution 46/221 B;

(iv) A low per capita income adjustment with a threshold per capita income limit of the average world per capita income for the statistical base period and a gradient of 70 per cent;

(v) A minimum assessment rate of 2.5 per cent for the permanent members of the Security Council;

(vi) A minimum assessment rate of 0.001 per cent;

(vii) A maximum assessment rate of 22 per cent;

(viii) A maximum assessment rate for the least developed countries of 0.01 per cent;

II

5. *Requests* the Committee on Contributions, in the context of and with a view to improving the current methodology, to examine and report to the General Assembly the consequences of the sharply depressed levels of primary commodity prices in the international markets on commodity-dependent economies, and also the impact on those countries whose economies have the burden of hosting refugees;

6. *Also requests* the Committee on Contributions:

(a) To follow up on paragraph 30 of its report and to provide suggestions to the General Assembly at its fifty-fifth session on how to address the combined effects of the loss of the low per capita income adjustment and having to contribute to the adjustment for Member States still below the threshold;

(b) To provide suggestions to the General Assembly at its fifty-fifth session on how to deal with the effect of discontinuities experienced by Member States moving up through the low per capita income and the Member States just above the threshold;

(c) To examine the long-term implications of the present criteria for determining the threshold of the low per capita income adjustment, and to report on possible alternatives to the General Assembly at its fifty-fifth session;

7. *Welcomes* the agreement of the Committee on Contributions to consider more systematic criteria for and approaches to deciding when market exchange rates should be replaced for the purposes of preparing the scale of assessments, and looks forward to further reports.

Committee on Contributions. The Committee on Contributions, at its sixtieth session (New

York, 5-30 June) [A/55/11], considered measures to encourage the timely, full and unconditional payment of assessed contributions, the application of Article 19 of the Charter, whereby a Member would lose its vote in the Assembly if the amount of its arrears equalled or exceeded the amount of contributions due from it for the preceding two full years; the scale of assessments for 2001-2003; and the assessment of non-member and new Member States.

The Committee decided to review further in 2001 measures to encourage payment of assessed contributions, including the possible indexation of or interest on arrears, multi-year payment plans and the new assessed fund proposed at its 1999 session [YUN 1999, p. 1310]. It agreed that the multi-year payment plan could be a useful tool in reducing arrears for those Member States seeking a rescheduling of arrearage payments. Specific plans, which required Assembly approval, could be arranged between the Member States concerned and the Secretariat within guidelines established by the Assembly. The Committee asked the Secretary-General to submit a report on those questions, including additional measures to encourage the timely, full and unconditional payment of assessed contributions.

The Committee deferred further consideration of the tightening of the application of Article 19 pending policy guidance from the Assembly.

Following its examination of requests from seven Members for exemption under that Article, the Committee determined that the failure to pay arrears by Burundi, Georgia (whose intention to eliminate its arrears by 2007 was duly noted), Kyrgyzstan and the Republic of Moldova were due to conditions beyond their control and therefore recommended that they be permitted to vote in the Assembly until 30 June 2001.

Noting that it did not consider the failure of the Comoros, Sao Tome and Principe, and Tajikistan, which had benefited from exemption since 1996, to pay the required amount to avoid application of Article 19 as being beyond their control, the Committee stated that it was not in a position to recommend their further exemption.

Reservations expressed in the case of Sao Tome and Principe concerned its serious debt problem and the accumulation of arrears during the period of its over-assessment. Reservations were also expressed as to the overall consistency of the recommendations, since all seven Governments faced conditions over which they had limited control; a more relevant recommendation for them would have been for multi-year payment plans, subject to the Assembly's approval.

At the conclusion of the Committee's session, 35 Member States were in arrears in the payment of their assessed contributions under Article 19. Of that number, 30 had no vote in the Assembly: Burundi, Cape Verde, Central African Republic, Chad, Djibouti, Dominica, Ecuador, Gambia, Grenada, Guinea, Haiti, Iraq, Kyrgyzstan, Liberia, Madagascar, Mauritania, Niger, Republic of Moldova, Rwanda, Saint Lucia, Saint Vincent and the Grenadines, Sao Tome and Principe, Seychelles, Sierra Leone, Somalia, Togo, Turkmenistan, Vanuatu, Yemen and Yugoslavia. The other five Members—the Comoros and Tajikistan; the Congo and Guinea Bissau; and Georgia—had been permitted to vote until 30 June 2000, pursuant to, respectively, Assembly resolution 53/36 F [YUN 1999, p. 1312] and decisions 53/406 C [ibid., p. 1310] and 54/455 B [ibid., p. 1313].

The Committee noted that, in 1999, five Members had availed themselves of the opportunity afforded by Assembly resolution 52/215 A [YUN 1997, p. 1442] of paying the equivalent of $1.7 million in currencies other than United States dollars.

In reviewing the 12 proposals for a scale of assessments for the period 2001-2003, which the Assembly requested be presented at its fifty-fifth session, based on elements and criteria outlined in paragraphs 4 *(a)* to *(l)* of resolution 54/237 D (see p. 1306), the Committee observed a number of common elements among the proposals: they were based on gross national product (GNP), with a floor assessment rate of 0.001 per cent and a ceiling of 0.01 per cent for the least developed countries; and the provisions for conversion rates, although formulated differently, were consistent with the general approach it had recommended for the current (1998-2000) scale and used in the preparation of the machine scales. The Committee further observed that, of the 12 proposals, 10 included a debt-burden adjustment, using either the debt-stock or the debt-flow approach, 11 set the threshold for the low per capita income adjustment at the average level of total per capita GNP, while 10 provided explicitly or implicitly for the complete phase-out of the scheme of limits, and 11 had a ceiling: seven at 25 per cent, three at 22 per cent and one at 20 per cent. The results of the application of the proposals were set out in annexes to the Committee's report [A/55/11].

For those proposals and related provisions that the Committee had difficulty interpreting, it applied the relevant element from the current methodology in preparing the machine scales in annexes IV to XV to its report. It noted a representation from the Bahamas that clarified the nature of the sliding gradient referred to in paragraph 4 *(b)* of resolution 54/237 D. As to the phase-in mechanism contained in paragraphs 4 *(d)* and *(e)* for countries crossing the threshold between scale periods, the Committee assumed that points picked up by a Member State from the low per capita income adjustment as a result of being above the threshold should be divided into three equal parts. That Member's assessment would increase by one part each year. The Committee determined that the intention with regard to the phasing out of the scheme of limits was that the provisions of subparagraphs 4 *(f)* (viii) and 4 *(h)* (viii) would apply to the six developing countries that in 2000 had benefited from the provisions of paragraph 1 *(j)* of Assembly resolution 52/215 A [YUN 1997, p. 1442].

The Committee also considered elements of the methodology for preparing the scale of assessments, including the base period, low per capita income adjustment, the floor and ceilings, and the annual recalculation of the scale.

The Committee decided to examine further the question of the system of assessment of non-member States [YUN 1999, p. 1311] in 2001. It authorized its Chairman to bring to the Assembly's attention the assessment of Tuvalu in the event that the Assembly admitted that country into the United Nations before adopting the assessments scale for 2001-2003.

The Assembly President, on 17 July [A/C.5/55/2], transmitted to the Fifth Committee Chairman a 30 June letter from the Chairman of the Committee on Contributions submitting sections of its report on requests for exemption under Article 19 of the Charter and the corresponding recommendations.

Reports of Secretary-General. During the year, the Secretary-General reported to the Assembly President on payments made by certain Member States to reduce their level of arrears below that specified in Article 19, so that they could vote in the Assembly. As at 31 January [A/54/730], 52 Member States remained below the gross amount assessed for the preceding two full years (1998-1999). By 14 June [A/54/915], that number had been reduced to 35, and on 1 September [A/55/345], it stood at 26. As at 17 October [A/ES-10/38], only 16 Member States were in arrears under Article 19.

Communications. On 26 September [A/C.5/55/12], the Assembly President transmitted to the Fifth Committee Chairman a letter from Tajikistan requesting postponement of the implementation of Article 19 to the end of the Assembly's fifty-fifth session and enclosing a plan for a 10-year (2001-2010) phased reduction of its arrears, which, as at 1 August 2000, amounted to $1,356,443.

On 26 October [meeting 41], the General Assembly, on the recommendation of the Fifth Committee [A/55/521 & Add.1], adopted **resolution 55/5 A** and, on 23 December [meeting 89], **resolutions 55/5 B-F**, all without vote [agenda item 122].

Scale of assessments for apportionment of the expenses of the United Nations

A

The General Assembly,

Recalling its resolutions 52/215 B of 22 December 1997, 53/36 C of 18 December 1998 and 54/237 C of 23 December 1999,

Having considered the letter dated 17 July 2000 from the President of the General Assembly to the Chairman of the Fifth Committee transmitting a letter dated 30 June 2000 from the Chairman of the Committee on Contributions regarding the recommendations of the Committee on Contributions,

Having also considered the letter dated 26 September 2000 from the President of the General Assembly to the Chairman of the Fifth Committee transmitting a letter dated 25 September 2000 from the Permanent Representative of Tajikistan to the United Nations appending a letter from the Prime Minister of the Republic of Tajikistan,

Reaffirming the obligation of Member States under Article 17 of the Charter of the United Nations to bear the expenses of the Organization as apportioned by the General Assembly,

1. *Reaffirms* its role in accordance with the provisions of Article 19 of the Charter of the United Nations and the advisory role of the Committee on Contributions in accordance with rule 160 of the rules of procedure of the General Assembly;

2. *Urges* all Member States to pay their assessed contributions in full, on time and without imposing conditions, in order to avoid difficulties being experienced by the United Nations;

3. *Decides* that Burundi, the Comoros, Georgia, the Republic of Moldova, Sao Tome and Principe and Tajikistan should be permitted to vote in the General Assembly until 30 June 2001;

4. *Decides also* that Kyrgyzstan would be permitted to vote from 1 January until 30 June 2001 should it fall at that time in arrears under Article 19 of the Charter;

5. *Requests* the Secretary-General, in order to ensure the sound financing of the Organization, to review the implications of the calculation of assessed contributions in arrears for the purpose of the application of Article 19 of the Charter at the beginning of each calendar year and at the beginning of the financial peacekeeping period on 1 July of each year, and to report thereon to the General Assembly at the first part of its resumed fifty-fifth session;

6. *Decides*, subject to the outcome of negotiations in the General Assembly on the report of the Secretary-General and the recommendations of the Committee on Contributions thereon, as requested in paragraph 5 above, at the main part of its fifty-sixth session and subject to further decision on its implementation by the General Assembly, to compare arrears with the amount actually assessed and payable for the preceding two full

years for the purpose of the application of Article 19 of the Charter;

7. *Requests* the Committee on Contributions to consider further the indexation of arrears, interest on arrears, multi-year payment plans, early reimbursement to troop-contributing countries and further suggestions for measures to encourage the timely, full and unconditional payment of assessed contributions, taking into account the experience with incentives and sanctions for the payment of assessed contributions of other United Nations organizations and other multilateral and regional organizations, and to report thereon to the General Assembly at its fifty-sixth session;

8. *Calls upon* the Committee on Contributions to give more detailed information and adequate reasons and rationale when making its recommendations.

B

The General Assembly,

Recalling the United Nations Millennium Declaration, in which the Assembly resolved, inter alia, to ensure that the Organization is provided on a timely and predictable basis with the resources it needs to carry out its mandates,

Having considered the report of the Committee on Contributions,

1. *Decides* that the scale of assessments for the period 2001-2003 shall be based on the following elements and criteria:

(a) Estimates of the gross national product;

(b) Average statistical base periods of six and three years;

(c) Conversion rates based on market exchange rates, except where that would cause excessive fluctuations and distortions in the income of some Member States, when price-adjusted rates of exchange or other appropriate conversion rates should be employed, taking due account of General Assembly resolution 46/221 B of 21 December 1991;

(d) The debt-burden approach employed in the scale of assessments for the period 1995-1997;

(e) A low per capita income adjustment of 80 per cent, with the threshold per capita income limit of the average per capita gross national product of all Member States for the statistical base periods;

(f) A minimum assessment rate of 0.001 per cent;

(g) A maximum assessment rate for the least developed countries of 0.01 per cent;

(h) A maximum assessment rate of 22 per cent;

2. *Decides also* that the elements of the scale of assessments contained in paragraph 1 above will be fixed until 2006, subject to the provisions of resolution C below, in particular paragraph 2 of that resolution, and without prejudice to rule 160 of the rules of procedure of the General Assembly;

3. *Notes* that the application of the methodology outlined in paragraph 1 above will lead to a substantial increase in the rate of assessment of some Member States;

4. *Decides* to apply transitional measures to address those substantial increases;

5. *Notes* that the United States of America has decided to pay to the United Nations in 2001 an amount equal to 3 per cent of the amount assessed on Member States pursuant to General Assembly resolution 55/239 of 23 December 2000;

6. *Decides*, as an exceptional measure and notwithstanding the provisions of the Financial Regulations and Rules of the United Nations, that this amount should be credited against the assessed contributions of the other Member States for the programme budget for 2001, as reflected in annex I to the present resolution;

7. *Resolves* that the scale of assessments for the contribution of Member States to the regular budget of the United Nations for the years 2001, 2002 and 2003 shall be as contained in annex II to the present resolution;

8. *Resolves also* that:

(a) Notwithstanding the terms of financial regulation 5.5, the Secretary-General shall be empowered to accept, at his discretion and after consultation with the Chairman of the Committee on Contributions, a portion of the contributions of Member States for the calendar years 2001, 2002 and 2003 in currencies other than United States dollars;

(b) In accordance with financial regulation 5.9, States which are not Members of the United Nations but which participate in certain of its activities shall be called upon to contribute towards the 2001, 2002 and 2003 expenses of the Organization on the basis of the following rates:

Holy See	0.001
Switzerland	1.274

These rates represent the basis for the calculation of the flat annual fees to be charged to non-member States in accordance with General Assembly resolution 44/197 B of 21 December 1989.

ANNEX I

Member State	Final share of United States 3 per cent[a]
Afghanistan	0.0020
Albania	—
Algeria	0.0020
Andorra	—
Angola	—
Antigua and Barbuda	—
Argentina	0.0440
Armenia	—
Australia	0.0320
Austria	0.0326
Azerbaijan	—
Bahamas	—
Bahrain	—
Bangladesh	—
Barbados	—
Belarus	0.0010
Belgium	0.0378
Belize	—
Benin	—
Bhutan	—
Bolivia	—
Bosnia and Herzegovina	
Botswana	0.0010
Brazil	0.5290
Brunei Darussalam	0.0010

Member State	Final share of United States 3 per cent[a]	Member State	Final share of United States 3 per cent[a]
Bulgaria	—	Kiribati	—
Burkina Faso	—	Kuwait	0.0060
Burundi	—	Kyrgyzstan	—
Cambodia	—	Lao People's Democratic Republic	—
Cameroon	—	Latvia	—
Canada	—	Lebanon	—
Cape Verde	—	Lesotho	—
Central African Republic	—	Liberia	—
Chad	—	Libyan Arab Jamahiriya	0.0020
Chile	0.0470	Liechtenstein	0.0010
China	0.0590	Lithuania	0.0010
Colombia	0.0440	Luxembourg	0.0026
Comoros	—	Madagascar	0.0010
Congo	—	Malawi	0.0010
Costa Rica	—	Malaysia	0.0080
Côte d'Ivoire	—	Maldives	—
Croatia	0.0020	Mali	—
Cuba	0.0010	Malta	0.0010
Cyprus	0.0020	Marshall Islands	—
Czech Republic	0.0450	Mauritania	—
Democratic People's Republic of Korea	—	Mauritius	0.0010
Democratic Republic of the Congo	—	Mexico	0.0430
Denmark	0.0255	Micronesia (Federated States of)	—
Djibouti	—	Monaco	0.0010
Dominica	—	Mongolia	—
Dominican Republic	0.0010	Morocco	0.0020
Ecuador	0.0010	Mozambique	—
Egypt	0.0040	Myanmar	—
El Salvador	0.0010	Namibia	0.0010
Equatorial Guinea	—	Nauru	—
Eritrea	—	Nepal	—
Estonia	—	Netherlands	0.0598
Ethiopia	—	New Zealand	0.0040
Fiji	—	Nicaragua	—
Finland	0.0176	Niger	—
France	0.2199	Nigeria	0.0150
Gabon	—	Norway	—
Gambia	—	Oman	0.0030
Georgia	—	Pakistan	0.0020
Germany	0.3325	Palau	—
Ghana	—	Panama	0.0010
Greece	0.0185	Papua New Guinea	0.0010
Grenada	—	Paraguay	0.0010
Guatemala	0.0010	Peru	0.0050
Guinea	—	Philippines	0.0040
Guinea—Bissau	—	Poland	0.0840
Guyana	—	Portugal	0.0150
Haiti	—	Qatar	0.0020
Honduras	0.0010	Republic of Korea	0.4100
Hungary	0.0050	Republic of Moldova	—
Iceland	0.0020	Romania	0.0020
India	0.0130	Russian Federation	—
Indonesia	0.0070	Rwanda	—
Iran (Islamic Republic of)	0.0600	Saint Kitts and Nevis	—
Iraq	0.0300	Saint Lucia	—
Ireland	0.0097	Saint Vincent and the Grenadines	—
Israel	0.0160	Samoa	—
Italy	0.1716	San Marino	—
Jamaica	—	Sao Tome and Principe	—
Japan	—	Saudi Arabia	0.0220
Jordan	—	Senegal	0.0010
Kazakhstan	0.0010	Seychelles	—
Kenya	—	Sierra Leone	—

Member State	Final share of United States 3 per cent[a]
Singapore	0.0150
Slovakia	0.0020
Slovenia	0.0030
Solomon Islands	—
Somalia	—
South Africa	0.0170
Spain	0.0853
Sri Lanka	0.0010
Sudan	—
Suriname	—
Swaziland	—
Sweden	0.0343
Syrian Arab Republic	0.0020
Tajikistan	—
Thailand	0.0650
The former Yugoslav Republic of Macedonia	—
Togo	—
Tonga	—
Trinidad and Tobago	0.0010
Tunisia	0.0010
Turkey	0.0170
Turkmenistan	—
Tuvalu	—
Uganda	—
Ukraine	0.0020
United Arab Emirates	0.0080
United Kingdom of Great Britain and Northern Ireland	0.1883
United Republic of Tanzania	0.0010
United States of America	—
Uruguay	0.0180
Uzbekistan	0.0010
Vanuatu	—
Venezuela	0.0080
Viet Nam	0.0040
Yemen	—
Yugoslavia	0.0010
Zambia	—
Zimbabwe	0.0010
Total	**3.0000**

[a]3 per cent additional payment by the United States of America.

ANNEX II

Member State	Scale 2001	Scale 2002 (Percentage)	Scale 2003
Afghanistan	0.008	0.007	0.00900
Albania	0.003	0.003	0.00300
Algeria	0.070	0.071	0.07000
Andorra	0.004	0.004	0.00400
Angola	0.002	0.002	0.00200
Antigua and Barbuda	0.002	0.002	0.00200
Argentina	1.156	1.159	1.14900
Armenia	0.002	0.002	0.00200
Australia	1.636	1.640	1.62700
Austria	0.952	0.954	0.94700
Azerbaijan	0.004	0.004	0.00400
Bahamas	0.012	0.012	0.01200
Bahrain	0.018	0.018	0.01800
Bangladesh	0.010	0.010	0.01000
Barbados	0.009	0.009	0.00900
Belarus	0.019	0.019	0.01900
Belgium	1.136	1.138	1.12900

Member State	Scale 2001	Scale 2002 (Percentage)	Scale 2003
Belize	0.001	0.001	0.00100
Benin	0.002	0.002	0.00200
Bhutan	0.001	0.001	0.00100
Bolivia	0.008	0.008	0.00800
Bosnia and Herzegovina	0.004	0.004	0.00400
Botswana	0.010	0.010	0.01000
Brazil	2.231	2.093	2.39000
Brunei Darussalam	0.033	0.033	0.03300
Bulgaria	0.013	0.013	0.01300
Burkina Faso	0.002	0.002	0.00200
Burundi	0.001	0.001	0.00100
Cambodia	0.002	0.002	0.00200
Cameroon	0.009	0.009	0.00900
Canada	2.573	2.579	2.55800
Cape Verde	0.001	0.001	0.00100
Central African Republic	0.001	0.001	0.00100
Chad	0.001	0.001	0.00100
Chile	0.198	0.187	0.21200
China	1.541	1.545	1.53200
Colombia	0.186	0.171	0.20100
Comoros	0.001	0.001	0.00100
Congo	0.001	0.001	0.00100
Costa Rica	0.020	0.020	0.02000
Côte d'Ivoire	0.009	0.009	0.00900
Croatia	0.039	0.039	0.03900
Cuba	0.030	0.030	0.03000
Cyprus	0.038	0.038	0.03800
Czech Republic	0.189	0.172	0.20300
Democratic People's Republic of Korea	0.009	0.009	0.00900
Democratic Republic of the Congo	0.004	0.004	0.00400
Denmark	0.753	0.755	0.74900
Djibouti	0.001	0.001	0.00100
Dominica	0.001	0.001	0.00100
Dominican Republic	0.023	0.023	0.02300
Ecuador	0.025	0.025	0.02500
Egypt	0.081	0.081	0.08100
El Salvador	0.018	0.018	0.01800
Equatorial Guinea	0.001	0.001	0.00100
Eritrea	0.001	0.001	0.00100
Estonia	0.010	0.010	0.01000
Ethiopia	0.004	0.004	0.00400
Fiji	0.004	0.004	0.00400
Finland	0.525	0.526	0.52200
France	6.503	6.516	6.46600
Gabon	0.014	0.014	0.01400
Gambia	0.001	0.001	0.00100
Georgia	0.005	0.005	0.00500
Germany	9.825	9.845	9.76900
Ghana	0.005	0.005	0.00500
Greece	0.542	0.543	0.53900
Grenada	0.001	0.001	0.00100
Guatemala	0.027	0.027	0.02700
Guinea	0.003	0.003	0.00300
Guinea-Bissau	0.001	0.001	0.00100
Guyana	0.001	0.001	0.00100
Haiti	0.002	0.002	0.00200
Honduras	0.005	0.004	0.00500
Hungary	0.121	0.121	0.12000
Iceland	0.033	0.033	0.03300
India	0.343	0.344	0.34100
Indonesia	0.201	0.201	0.20000
Iran (Islamic Republic of)	0.253	0.236	0.27200

Member State	Scale 2001	Scale 2002 (Percentage)	Scale 2003
Iraq	0.127	0.102	0.13600
Ireland	0.296	0.297	0.29400
Israel	0.417	0.418	0.41500
Italy	5.094	5.104	5.06475
Jamaica	0.004	0.004	0.00400
Japan	19.629	19.669	19.51575
Jordan	0.008	0.008	0.00800
Kazakhstan	0.029	0.029	0.02800
Kenya	0.008	0.008	0.00800
Kiribati	0.001	0.001	0.00100
Kuwait	0.148	0.148	0.14700
Kyrgyzstan	0.001	0.001	0.00100
Lao People's Democratic Republic	0.001	0.001	0.00100
Latvia	0.010	0.010	0.01000
Lebanon	0.012	0.012	0.01200
Lesotho	0.001	0.001	0.00100
Liberia	0.001	0.001	0.00100
Libyan Arab Jamahiriya	0.067	0.067	0.06700
Liechtenstein	0.006	0.006	0.00600
Lithuania	0.017	0.017	0.01700
Luxembourg	0.080	0.080	0.08000
Madagascar	0.003	0.003	0.00300
Malawi	0.002	0.002	0.00200
Malaysia	0.237	0.237	0.23500
Maldives	0.001	0.001	0.00100
Mali	0.002	0.002	0.00200
Malta	0.015	0.015	0.01500
Marshall Islands	0.001	0.001	0.00100
Mauritania	0.001	0.001	0.00100
Mauritius	0.011	0.011	0.01100
Mexico	1.093	1.095	1.08600
Micronesia (Federated States of)	0.001	0.001	0.00100
Monaco	0.004	0.004	0.00400
Mongolia	0.001	0.001	0.00100
Morocco	0.045	0.045	0.04400
Mozambique	0.001	0.001	0.00100
Myanmar	0.010	0.010	0.01000
Namibia	0.007	0.007	0.00700
Nauru	0.001	0.001	0.00100
Nepal	0.004	0.004	0.00400
Netherlands	1.748	1.751	1.73800
New Zealand	0.242	0.243	0.24100
Nicaragua	0.001	0.001	0.00100
Nigeria	0.062	0.056	0.06800
Norway	0.650	0.652	0.64600
Oman	0.062	0.062	0.06100
Pakistan	0.061	0.061	0.06100
Palau	0.001	0.001	0.00100
Panama	0.018	0.018	0.01800
Papua New Guinea	0.006	0.006	0.00600
Paraguay	0.016	0.016	0.01600
Peru	0.119	0.119	0.11800
Philippines	0.101	0.101	0.10000
Poland	0.353	0.319	0.37800
Portugal	0.465	0.466	0.46200
Qatar	0.034	0.034	0.03400
Republic of Korea	1.728	1.866	1.85100
Republic of Moldova	0.002	0.002	0.00200
Romania	0.059	0.059	0.05800
Russian Federation	1.200	1.200	1.20000
Rwanda	0.001	0.001	0.00100
Saint Kitts and Nevis	0.001	0.001	0.00100

Member State	Scale 2001	Scale 2002 (Percentage)	Scale 2003
Saint Lucia	0.002	0.002	0.00200
Saint Vincent and the Grenadines	0.001	0.001	0.00100
Samoa	0.001	0.001	0.00100
San Marino	0.002	0.002	0.00200
Sao Tome and Principe	0.001	0.001	0.00100
Saudi Arabia	0.557	0.559	0.55400
Senegal	0.005	0.005	0.00500
Seychelles	0.002	0.002	0.00200
Sierra Leone	0.001	0.001	0.00100
Singapore	0.395	0.396	0.39300
Slovakia	0.043	0.043	0.04300
Slovenia	0.081	0.081	0.08100
Solomon Islands	0.001	0.001	0.00100
Somalia	0.001	0.001	0.00100
South Africa	0.410	0.411	0.40800
Spain	2.534	2.539	2.51875
Sri Lanka	0.016	0.016	0.01600
Sudan	0.006	0.006	0.00600
Suriname	0.002	0.002	0.00200
Swaziland	0.002	0.002	0.00200
Sweden	1.033	1.035	1.02675
Syrian Arab Republic	0.081	0.081	0.08000
Tajikistan	0.001	0.001	0.00100
Thailand	0.275	0.254	0.29400
The former Yugoslav Republic of Macedonia	0.006	0.006	0.00600
Togo	0.001	0.001	0.00100
Tonga	0.001	0.001	0.00100
Trinidad and Tobago	0.016	0.016	0.01600
Tunisia	0.031	0.031	0.03000
Turkey	0.443	0.444	0.44000
Turkmenistan	0.003	0.003	0.00300
Tuvalu	0.001	0.001	0.00100
Uganda	0.005	0.005	0.00500
Ukraine	0.053	0.053	0.05300
United Arab Emirates	0.204	0.204	0.20200
United Kingdom of Great Britain and Northern Ireland	5.568	5.579	5.53600
United Republic of Tanzania	0.004	0.004	0.00400
United States of America	22.000	22.000	22.00000
Uruguay	0.075	0.081	0.08000
Uzbekistan	0.011	0.011	0.01100
Vanuatu	0.001	0.001	0.00100
Venezuela	0.210	0.210	0.20800
Viet Nam	0.015	0.013	0.01600
Yemen	0.007	0.007	0.00600
Yugoslavia	0.020	0.020	0.02000
Zambia	0.002	0.002	0.00200
Zimbabwe	0.008	0.008	0.00800
Total	**100.000**	**100.000**	**100.00000**

C

The General Assembly,

Noting that the financial burdens resulting from the reformed scale of assessments for the regular budget for calendar year 2001 will be borne in part by a voluntary donation from the major contributor,

Urging and expecting all Member States currently in arrears to fulfil their duties under international law and to settle those arrears promptly and in full,

1. *Establishes*, as from 1 January 2001, a reduced ceiling of 22 per cent for the assessed contribution of any individual Member State;

2. *Decides* to review the position at the end of 2003 and, depending on the status of contributions and arrears, to determine all appropriate measures to remedy the situation, including adjustments of the ceiling in keeping with its resolution 52/215 A to D of 22 December 1997;

3. *Stresses* that the reduction of the maximum assessment rate referred to in paragraph 1 of resolution B above shall apply to the apportionment of the expenses of the United Nations and should have no automatic implication for the apportionment of the expenses of the specialized agencies or the International Atomic Energy Agency.

D

The General Assembly,

Recalling the recommendations of the Committee on Contributions contained in its reports on its fifty-ninth and sixtieth sessions,

1. *Takes note* of the decision of the Committee on Contributions to consider the system of assessment of non-member States further at its sixty-first session;

2. *Decides* that, from 2001, the flat annual fee percentage for the Holy See should be set at 25 per cent of the approved notional rate of assessment.

E

The General Assembly,

Recalling its resolutions 47/217 of 23 December 1992, 51/218 E of 17 June 1997, 55/1 of 5 September 2000 and 55/12 of 1 November 2000,

Recalling also the recommendations of the Committee on Contributions with respect to the assessment of Tuvalu as a non-member State,

1. *Decides* that the rate of assessment for Tuvalu, admitted to membership in the United Nations on 5 September 2000, should be 0.001 per cent for the year 2000;

2. *Decides also* that the rate of assessment for the Federal Republic of Yugoslavia, admitted to membership in the United Nations on 1 November 2000, should be 0.026 per cent for the year 2000;

3. *Decides further* that the contributions of Tuvalu and the Federal Republic of Yugoslavia for the regular budget and the International Tribunal for the Prosecution of Persons Responsible for Serious Violations of International Humanitarian Law Committed in the Territory of the Former Yugoslavia since 1991 and the International Criminal Tribunal for the Prosecution of Persons Responsible for Genocide and Other Serious Violations of International Humanitarian Law Committed in the Territory of Rwanda and Rwandan Citizens Responsible for Genocide and Other Such Violations Committed in the Territory of Neighbouring States between 1 January and 31 December 1994, for the year 2000 should be calculated on the basis of one twelfth of their relevant rates of assessment for the year 2000 per full calendar month of membership;

4. *Decides* that Tuvalu should be credited with a corresponding proportion of its non-member State assessment for the year 2000;

5. *Decides also* that the contributions of Tuvalu and the Federal Republic of Yugoslavia for the year 2000 should otherwise be applied to the same basis of assessment as for other Member States, except that, in the case of appropriations or apportionments approved by the General Assembly for the financing of peacekeeping operations, the contributions of Tuvalu and the Federal Republic of Yugoslavia, as determined by the group of Member States to which they may be assigned by the Assembly, should be calculated in proportion to the calendar year;

6. *Decides further* that the assessments of Tuvalu and the Federal Republic of Yugoslavia for the year 2000 should be taken into account as miscellaneous income in accordance with regulation 5.2 *(c)* of the Financial Regulations and Rules of the United Nations;

7. *Decides* that, in accordance with financial regulation 5.8, the advances of Tuvalu and the Federal Republic of Yugoslavia to the Working Capital Fund should be calculated by the application of their rates of assessment for the year 2000 to the authorized level of the Fund and should be added to the Fund, pending their incorporation in a 100 per cent scale for the Fund for 2002-2003;

8. *Notes* that the Federal Republic of Yugoslavia can be said to have a share in the Peacekeeping Reserve Fund, established pursuant to General Assembly resolution 47/217;

9. *Notes also* that, pursuant to General Assembly resolution 47/217, the assessment of Tuvalu for the Peacekeeping Reserve Fund should be calculated by the application of its first rate of assessment for peacekeeping operations to the authorized level of the Fund.

F

The General Assembly

1. *Decides* to continue the review of other matters to be considered at the sixty-first session of the Committee on Contributions during the resumed fifty-fifth session;

2. *Decides also* to continue consideration of the proposal for the re-establishment of the Ad Hoc Intergovernmental Working Group on the Implementation of the Principle of Capacity to Pay during its resumed fifty-fifth session.

On 23 December, the Assembly decided that the item on the scale of assessments for the apportionment of the expenses of the United Nations would remain for consideration at its resumed fifty-fifth (2001) session (**decision 55/458**) and that the Fifth Committee would continue consideration of the item at that session (**decision 55/455**).

Accounts and auditing

The General Assembly, at its resumed fifty-fourth (2000) session, considered the report of the Board of Auditors on UN peacekeeping operations from 1 July 1998 to 30 June 1999 [A/54/5, vol. II], the related ACABQ report [A/54/801] and the Secretary-General's report on the implementation of the Board's recommendations

[A/54/748]. On 15 June, the Assembly, by **resolution 54/13 C**, accepted the Board's report and approved all its recommendations and conclusions (see p. 106).

Board of Auditors report. The Chairman of the Board of Auditors transmitted to the General Assembly the financial reports and audited financial statements for the biennium ended 31 December 1999 on the United Nations [A/55/5, vol. I], and on the following UN entities: the International Trade Centre [A/55/5, vol. III], the United Nations University (UNU) [A/55/5, vol. IV], the United Nations Development Programme (UNDP) [A/55/5/Add.1], the United Nations Children's Fund (UNICEF) [A/55/5/Add.2], the United Nations Relief and Works Agency for Palestine Refugees in the Near East (UNRWA) [A/55/5/Add.3 & Corr.1], the United Nations Institute for Training and Research [A/55/5/Add.4], the voluntary funds administered by the Office of the United Nations High Commissioner for Refugees (UNHCR) [A/55/5/Add.5], the Fund of the United Nations Environment Programme [A/55/5/Add.6], the United Nations Population Fund (UNFPA) [A/55/5/Add.7], the United Nations Habitat and Human Settlements Foundation [A/55/5/Add.8], the United Nations International Drug Control Programme (UNDCP) [A/55/5/Add.9], the United Nations Office for Project Services (UNOPS) [A/55/5/Add.10], the International Criminal Tribunal for the Prosecution of Persons Responsible for Genocide and Other Serious Violations of International Humanitarian Law Committed in the Territory of Rwanda and Rwandan Citizens Responsible for Genocide and Other Such Violations Committed in the Territory of Neighbouring States between 1 January and 31 December 1994 [A/55/5/Add.11], and the International Tribunal for the Prosecution of Persons Responsible for Serious Violations of International Humanitarian Law Committed in the Territory of the Former Yugoslavia since 1991 [A/55/5/Add.12].

Introducing the reports in the Fifth Committee, the Chairman of the Board explained that the Board had had to qualify and restrict the scope of its audit opinion on the financial statements of UNDP, UNFPA, UNDCP and UNU: in the case of the first three because it had been unable to obtain sufficient evidence from Governments and non-governmental organizations that funds advanced for national execution projects had been expended for the purposes intended; in the case of UNDP, because of uncertainty over unidentified amounts of $11.1 million arising from bank reconciliations; and in UNU's case, because UNU had not made a provision against longstanding unpaid pledged contributions (some $10 million of which had been outstanding for

more than five years). The Board welcomed ACABQ's recommendation that the Assembly defer action on the financial statements of UNDP, UNDCP and UNFPA, pending certification by the Board that the issues noted had been resolved or that satisfactory progress was being made to resolve them.

Regarding the Board's previous recommendations, 69 per cent had been fully implemented by the organizations, 25 per cent were being implemented and only 6 per cent had yet to be implemented.

In the United Nations, IMIS Release 3 had not yet been fully developed to enable the consolidated financial statements to be prepared or to provide an adequate audit trail. Moreover, in four procurement-related arbitration cases, the United Nations had been judged liable to pay compensation totalling $12.2 million to contractors, mainly owing to deficiencies in the formulation, interpretation and implementation of contracts. In one contract for legal representation by an outside counsel, the level of the fee cap had been increased from $590,000 to $2,460,000 over approximately two years. On the other hand, the Board was pleased with the progress made by the secretariat of the International Civil Service Commission in implementing its previous recommendations.

In UNDP, the Board found that problems related to the implementation of IMIS had led to weaknesses in financial control, seriously delaying finalization of the Board's report. The same was true of UNFPA's financial reports. UNDP had also experienced liquidity problems, its total expenditure from regular resources having exceeded its total income by $188 million.

In UNRWA, the value of land and buildings had not been capitalized and had therefore not been included in the statement of assets and liabilities and fund balances as at 31 December 1999. The Board had decided, however, not to qualify its audit opinion pending the outcome of the revision of UNRWA's Financial Regulations.

In UNHCR, the decline in voluntary contributions from donor countries posed a liquidity risk, and in UNICEF, the financial regulations had been changed to reflect the new definition of programme expenditure approved by the Executive Board in September 1999.

In UNFPA, the Board of Auditors found that regular resource expenditure ($575.9 million) had exceeded income by some $51 million, causing the operational reserve to fall from $63 million to $24 million during the 1998-1999 biennium. In addition, the proportion of national execution expenditure covered by audit reports had decreased from 70 per cent in 1996-1997 to

50 per cent in 1998-1999. The Board was concerned about the deteriorating financial position of the Fund. It noted that ACABQ had strongly disagreed with UNFPA's intention to amend the rules governing the audit reports of executing agencies, agreeing with ACABQ that such a step would make the situation worse, as larger expenditures could be incurred without supporting audit reports.

The Board further found that UNDCP had neither received nor followed up audit reports covering the $17.9 million expenditure incurred on nationally executed activities during the 1996-1997 biennium; and, in respect of UNOPS, that the cost of relocating its headquarters was considerably higher than estimated ($16.8 million in June 2000 compared with the 1998 estimate of $7.3 million), in addition to finding weaknesses in internal control and delays in the preparation of its financial statements due to problems in the implementation of IMIS.

The Chairman said the Board wanted the foregoing findings highlighted because of their implications for the effective management of UN programmes in good economic conditions. He noted, however, that a number of the organizations cited had made progress in certain significant areas, proving that implementing the Board's recommendations could lead to substantial improvements in the organizations' financial situation.

In its report on the United Nations [A/55/5, vol. I], the Board noted that cases of fraud or presumptive fraud, involving a total sum of $568,752, had come to its notice during the 1998-1999 biennium. Three cases pertained to the United Nations Office at Nairobi and one to United Nations Headquarters. In two cases there was no loss to the Organization.

By a September note [A/55/364], the Secretary-General transmitted to the Assembly a summary of the Board's principal findings, conclusions and recommendations, classified by audit area. He also submitted the first report [A/55/380 & Add.1] on measures taken or to be taken to implement the Board's recommendations on the accounts for the biennium ended 31 December 1999, as well as for the biennium ended 31 December 1997 [A/55/80 & Add.1]. The Assembly also had before it ACABQ's comments on the Board's reports [A/55/487].

GENERAL ASSEMBLY ACTION

On 23 December [meeting 89], the General Assembly, on the recommendation of the Fifth Committee [A/55/689], adopted **resolution 55/220 A** without vote [agenda item 115].

Financial reports and audited financial statements, and reports of the Board of Auditors

The General Assembly,

Reaffirming its resolutions 50/222 of 11 April 1996, 51/218 E of 17 June 1997, 52/212 B of 31 March 1998, 53/204 of 18 December 1998, 53/221, section VIII, of 7 April 1999 and 54/13 B of 23 December 1999,

Having considered, for the period ended 31 December 1999, the financial reports and audited financial statements of the United Nations, the International Trade Centre UNCTAD/WTO, the United Nations University, the United Nations Development Programme, the United Nations Children's Fund, the United Nations Relief and Works Agency for Palestine Refugees in the Near East, the United Nations Institute for Training and Research, the voluntary funds administered by the United Nations High Commissioner for Refugees, the Fund of the United Nations Environment Programme, the United Nations Population Fund, the United Nations Habitat and Human Settlements Foundation, the Fund of the United Nations International Drug Control Programme, the United Nations Office for Project Services, the International Criminal Tribunal for the Prosecution of Persons Responsible for Genocide and Other Serious Violations of International Humanitarian Law Committed in the Territory of Rwanda and Rwandan Citizens Responsible for Genocide and Other Such Violations Committed in the Territory of Neighbouring States between 1 January and 31 December 1994, the International Tribunal for the Prosecution of Persons Responsible for Serious Violations of International Humanitarian Law Committed in the Territory of the Former Yugoslavia since 1991, the reports and audit opinions of the Board of Auditors, the concise summary of principal findings, conclusions and recommendations contained in the reports prepared by the Board of Auditors on the audit of the accounts, the reports of the Secretary-General on the measures taken to implement the recommendations of the Board of Auditors and the report of the Advisory Committee on Administrative and Budgetary Questions,

1. *Accepts* the financial reports and audited financial statements and the reports and audit opinions of the Board of Auditors regarding the above-mentioned organizations, subject to the provisions of the present resolution, with the exception of the financial statements of the United Nations Development Programme, the United Nations Population Fund and the Fund of the United Nations International Drug Control Programme;

2. *Approves* all the recommendations and conclusions contained in the reports of the Board of Auditors, and endorses the observations and recommendations contained in the report of the Advisory Committee on Administrative and Budgetary Questions;

3. *Decides* to defer action on the financial statements of the United Nations Development Programme, the United Nations Population Fund and the Fund of the United Nations International Drug Control Programme for the period ended 31 December 1999, pending certification by the Board of Auditors that satisfactory progress is being made towards removing the reasons for the qualified opinions or that the matter has been resolved, and decides to revert to this matter at its resumed fifty-fifth session;

4. *Commends* the Board of Auditors for the quality of its reports, in particular with respect to its comments on the management of resources;

5. *Requests* the Secretary-General and the executive heads of the funds and programmes of the United Nations to present their financial statements on time so that the Board of Auditors can audit them and submit its reports to the General Assembly in accordance with the six-week rule;

6. *Takes note* of the reports of the Secretary-General on the implementation of the recommendations of the Board of Auditors;

7. *Notes* that the first report of the Secretary-General on the implementation of the recommendations of the Board of Auditors on the accounts of the United Nations for the biennium ended 31 December 1999 did not comply with the provisions of General Assembly resolution 54/248 of 23 December 1999 regarding the inclusion of a footnote giving the reason for the late submission of a report;

8. *Requests* the Secretary-General to review the question of the term of office of the Board of Auditors and to report to the General Assembly at its resumed fifty-fifth session under the item entitled "Review of the efficiency of the administrative and financial functioning of the United Nations";

9. *Decides* to consider the reports of the Board of Auditors on the International Tribunal for the Prosecution of Persons Responsible for Serious Violations of International Humanitarian Law Committed in the Territory of the Former Yugoslavia since 1991 and the International Criminal Tribunal for the Prosecution of Persons Responsible for Genocide and Other Serious Violations of International Humanitarian Law Committed in the Territory of Rwanda and Rwandan Citizens Responsible for Genocide and Other Such Violations Committed in the Territory of Neighbouring States between 1 January and 31 December 1994 also under the agenda items relating to the financing of the Tribunals;

10. *Requests* the Secretary-General to prepare the financial reports and audited financial statements for the International Tribunal for the Former Yugoslavia and the International Criminal Tribunal for Rwanda in line with their budget cycles;

11. *Calls upon* the executive heads of the funds and programmes of the United Nations to improve their procurement practices, as appropriate, using the Procurement Division of the Office of Central Support Services of the Secretariat as a model in such areas as the posting of bids on the Internet and inviting all registered suppliers to bid;

12. *Requests* the Secretary-General and the executive heads of the funds and programmes of the United Nations, in conjunction with the Board of Auditors, to continue to evaluate what financial information should be presented in the financial statements and schedules and what should be presented in annexes to the statements in accordance with the United Nations accounting standards.

On 23 December, the Assembly decided that the item entitled "Financial reports and audited financial statements, and reports of the Board of Auditors" would remain for consideration during its resumed fifty-fifth (2001) session (**decision 55/458**) and that the Fifth Committee should continue consideration of the item at that session (**decision 55/455**).

Common accounting standards

The General Assembly, by **decision 54/479** of 15 June, took note of the Secretary-General's 1999 report on the Guidelines for Internal Control Standards [YUN 1999, p. 1314].

Internal control and accountability

Management irregularities causing financial losses

OIOS report. In June, the General Assembly had before it a note by the Secretary-General [A/53/811] transmitting the report of the Office of Internal Oversight Services (OIOS) on the investigation into allegations of theft of funds by a senior officer of the United Nations Conference on Trade and Development (UNCTAD). The investigation proved that the official had used his position to perpetrate at least 59 separate instances of theft between 1987 and 1996, without triggering any meaningful alarm. The illegal activities were discovered by accident when the officer was on sick leave in mid-1996. Of the nearly 730,000 Swiss francs (SwF) involved, SwF 495,000, or 68 per cent, was recovered. Since the officer's trial and conviction by the Swiss Court, efforts had been made to determine lapses within the United Nations Office at Geneva and UNCTAD that may have contributed to the longevity of the scheme, including deficiencies in management and operations, leading to the enactment of changes by both entities. OIOS also included in its report recommendations to enable them to recognize and identify fraud indicators so as to minimize the risk of repetition.

By **decision 54/462 B** of 15 June, the Assembly deferred consideration of the OIOS report.

Report of Secretary-General. In response to General Assembly resolution 53/225 [YUN 1999, p. 1315], the Secretary-General submitted a follow-up report on management irregularities causing financial losses to the Organization [A/54/793]. The report outlined procedures being developed by the Secretary-General for determining gross negligence and for the effective implementation of staff rule 112.3 for financial recovery. Those procedures called for the preliminary investigation of any alleged gross negligence by heads of departments/offices (or OIOS) and for proven gross negligence to be dealt with under revised Joint Disciplinary Committee procedures with an expanded Committee mandate and revised composition. The report also described recently introduced measures to make for a more effective accountability mechanism, including: a programme management plan to be submitted yearly by senior managers, identifying their goals, along with measurable performance indicators; an Accountability Panel to advise the Secretary-General on accountability matters; and a strengthened monitoring of delegated authority by the Department of Management. Measures to improve internal control had also been introduced. The Secretary-General believed that a comprehensive approach to accountability, backed up by those measures, would contribute significantly to detecting and preventing management irregularities.

Having considered the Secretary-General's report, ACABQ [A/55/499] pointed out that an efficiently functioning system for the administration of justice, as well as the successful implementation of a comprehensive system of accountability (see p. 1337) would be key to the eventual positive impact of the procedures.

By **decision 54/462 B** of 15 June, the Assembly deferred consideration of the Secretary-General's report on management irregularities causing financial losses to the Organization.

Administrative and budgetary coordination

ACC report. In October, the Administrative Committee on Coordination (ACC) submitted the sixth statistical report [A/55/525] on the budgetary and financial situation of the organizations in the UN system. The report compared data from the United Nations and 12 intergovernmental organizations, as well as six voluntarily funded bodies.

The tabulated data were grouped under: approved regular budget and assessed contributions for 1992-2001, including the percentage of assessments for 2000-2001; assessments voted and received for 1998-1999, and collection of assessed contributions for 1998-1999; working capital funds for 2000-2001; and expenditures from and receipts of voluntary contributions in 1998-1999.

ACABQ report. ACABQ, in its first report on its activities during the General Assembly's fifty-fourth session [A/55/7], stated that the reforms witnessed during its 1998 meetings with the specialized agencies and the International Atomic Energy Agency (IAEA) had intensified. There was greater emphasis on planning for results and personnel management reform, as well as focus on priority-setting, a better definition of objectives, performance monitoring and evaluation. Except for the World Intellectual Property Or-

ganization, the agencies had hardly had any real increase in their budgets. However, resources for development had decreased dramatically, including those managed by UNDP, while resources for emergency and humanitarian operations had increased. ACABQ noted that the planning and budgeting processes in some agencies were being reformed extensively, but cautioned that such reforms should not bring new rigidities or a lack of transparency or make those processes more costly. Regarding the reported difficulties of many agencies in establishing performance measurement standards, ACABQ said that, unless those standards were carefully identified and realistically set, reforms could lead to confusion, excessive reporting and high cost.

Noting that the effect of extensive budgetary constraints on a number of agencies had led to a search for efficiencies and reductions in support services, ACABQ warned that there was a limit to reducing those services without negatively impacting on programme implementation. Such reductions might lead to greater expenditure in the future, as in the case of the United Nations Educational, Scientific and Cultural Organization and UN Headquarters buildings, for which estimated rehabilitation costs had reached more than $400 million and $1 billion, respectively. It pointed out that emphasis on giving greater flexibility to programme managers should not compromise the need for accountability.

ACABQ also noted that less than full receipt of assessed and voluntary contributions rendered the implementation of plans and realization of objectives more difficult. It stressed the need for agencies to collaborate and learn from each other in the reform process, a first step being the harmonization of terminologies relating to planning, budgeting and human resources reform, especially in the area of results-based budgeting (see p. 1295). Agencies also needed to share lessons learned and experiences in the development of management information systems to implement, monitor, evaluate and report on programmes and other operations. Lack of coordination in that regard could lead to potentially costly duplicate systems. Evidence pointed to some systems that were developed and later abandoned or considerably modified, demonstrating inadequate identification of needs prior to system design and implementation, as well as underestimation of related costs and unrealistic investment in information technology, leading to more expenditure in attempts to correct those mistakes.

As to delegation of authority to the field, ACABQ said that to succeed, it had to be accompanied by central capacity to monitor field performance, using new technologies to avoid excessive paper reporting and attendant bureaucracy. Field offices should be provided with new equipment and technologies and qualified staff.

ACABQ also examined results-based budgeting, human resources reform and training, cooperation in the field for peacekeeping and humanitarian operations and UN offices and programmes.

By **decision 55/451** of 23 December, the Assembly took note of the ACABQ report and requested the Secretary-General to bring it to the attention of the executive heads of the specialized agencies and funds and programmes concerned.

On the same date, the Assembly decided that the item on the administrative and budgetary coordination of the United Nations with the specialized agencies and IAEA would remain for consideration during the resumed fifty-fifth (2001) session (**decision 55/458**) and that the Fifth Committee should continue consideration of the item at that session (**decision 55/455**).

Programme planning

Medium-term plan

Rules and regulations governing programme planning

By **decision 54/474** of 7 April, the General Assembly took note of the additional paragraph in rule 105.4 of the revised Regulations and Rules Governing Programme Planning, the Programme Aspects of the Budget, the Monitoring of Implementation and the Methods of Evaluation, contained in the Secretary-General's 1999 note [YUN 1999, p. 1316], and recommended that the Secretary-General, in promulgating the rule, add the following sentence at the end of the paragraph: "Expected accomplishments shall be objective, feasible and pertinent to the nature of, and work carried out by, each subprogramme.".

Medium-term plan 2002-2005

The Secretary-General's proposed medium-term plan for the period 2002-2005 [A/55/6/Rev.1], as a translation of legislative mandates into programmes and subprogrammes, provided the principal policy directives of the United Nations and served as a framework for the formulation of the biennial programme budgets within the plan period and for the evaluation of programmes. The plan comprised two parts: the first noted the challenges to be faced in the plan period, the

plan's policy orientation and strategy, its methodology and format, and its priorities; the second set out the 25 programmes under the responsibility of UN offices.

In his introduction to the plan, the Secretary-General said the broad range of challenges posed by globalization required an integrated, action-oriented response from the Organization, for which effective planning was essential. In his medium-term plan, the programmes and subprogrammes foreseen under peace and security were those aimed at the prevention, control and peaceful resolution of conflicts, in tandem with humanitarian and human rights programmes; disarmament; post-conflict peacekeeping operations through special political missions in support of peace-building activities, including electoral assistance where appropriate; and ensuring a smooth transition from humanitarian relief to reconstruction and development.

Economic and social programmes would continue to address development, environmental, financial, gender, human rights, poverty, population, technological and trade issues in the context of globalization. Follow-up action to the high-level international intergovernmental event on financing for development, envisaged for 2001, and action resulting from the General Assembly's consideration of "Globalization and interdependence", could provide impetus and guidance for a better handling of globalization and related development issues. Continuing work was foreseen for the regional commissions, UNCTAD and the Department of Economic and Social Affairs to assist in the integration of developing countries and countries with economies in transition into the world economy. Also reflected in the plan was an increased awareness of the need for gender-sensitive programmes, projects and activities; the interests, experiences, priorities and needs of both women and men had been taken into account in designing the subprogrammes, facilitating the eventual design of the activities to be implemented at the operational level of the programme budgets.

A theme common to most of the programmes was the intent to make maximum use of technological developments to enhance the effectiveness of UN activities. A number of programmes, among them the public information and humanitarian programmes, were already making extensive use of the Internet. The humanitarian programme had developed ReliefWeb as a major tool for coordinating humanitarian aid. To meet the growing incidence and devastating impact of natural disasters, the plan provided for programmes in the areas of disaster prevention and mitigation, humanitarian response and post-disaster recovery and rehabilitation.

The plan sought to improve the presentation of programmes by maintaining consistency in their structure and coherence in the formulation of their components so as to overcome the difficulties in assessing the degree of programme implementation and achievement stemming from the failure to distinguish true objectives from activities at the planning stage.

The priority areas identified by the Secretary-General for 2002-2005 were the same as those for 1998-2001: maintenance of international peace and security; promotion of sustained growth and sustainable development; development of Africa; promotion of human rights; effective coordination of humanitarian assistance efforts; promotion of justice and international law; disarmament; and drug control, crime prevention and combating international terrorism in all its forms and manifestations.

CPC consideration. At the first part of its fortieth session (New York, 5 June-1 July) [A/55/16], CPC, having examined the Secretary-General's proposed 2002-2005 medium-term plan, recommended that the Assembly adopt the introduction to the plan, subject to a number of observations. Among them were that the priorities for 2002-2005 should be as recommended by the Secretary-General; that the Assembly request the Secretary-General to report on the implications of the plan's new format on the cycle of planning, programming, budgeting, monitoring and evaluation in the context of the next biennial report on the review of the efficiency of the administrative and financial functioning of the United Nations; that indicators of achievement be included in the plan, where possible, and that a number of expected accomplishments and achievement indicators needed to be re-elaborated, explicitly to reflect their relation to the objectives and the distinctive nature of the programme activities; that the distinct responsibilities of the Secretariat and of Member States in relation to the expected accomplishments and achievement indicators be identified to illustrate the different natures of the programme objectives and to identify clearly some of the elements having a direct impact on the accomplishment of their objectives; that all mandates and activities pertinent to the programmes be included in the plan; and that the Assembly ensure the relevance of the legislative mandates with the respective programmes.

CPC presented conclusions and recommendations on 23 of the 25 proposed programmes.

Following completion of its consideration of paragraph 7.37 *(e)* of programme 7, Economic and social affairs, and of programme 19, Human rights, at the second part of its fortieth session (New York, 21-29 August), CPC recommended to the Assembly approval of programme 7, with certain modifications, and a careful review of programme 19.

Programme performance

In a May report on the programme performance of the United Nations for the 1998-1999 biennium [A/55/73], the Secretary-General analysed programme performance in terms of the implementation of outputs identified in the 1998-1999 budget narrative. He reflected modifications to the programme of work during implementation, including the introduction of new activities by legislative bodies and the Secretariat, provided explanations for the non-implementation of outputs and reviewed resources utilized broken down by sources of funding.

Under the 1998-1999 programme budget, a total of 27,098 outputs were committed for implementation, including 22,830 programmed quantifiable outputs, 457 carried over from the previous biennium, 2,079 added by legislative bodies and 1,732 initiated by the Secretariat. Of that total, 24,025 outputs were implemented, 1,148 outputs were postponed to the following biennium and 1,925 were terminated. Implementation utilized 34,589 work-months, comprising 70 per cent of all work-months available to the Secretariat, with the remaining 30 per cent devoted to international cooperation, inter-agency coordination and liaison and technical cooperation activities. The average implementation rate was 88 per cent, ranging from 68 per cent to 100 per cent among budget sections.

The Secretary-General said that the overall implementation rate of 88 per cent for all mandated outputs, the highest level in the past decade, was one of the tangible outcomes of the resolve to promote managerial efficiency and accountability in the ongoing implementation of his reform measures. OIOS believed that the strengthening of accountability through the performance planning and appraisal system, and the institutionalization of computerized programme performance monitoring and reporting systems at the departmental level, contributed to improved programme implementation.

The implementation rates also pointed to more flexibility and resourcefulness in programme management. While implementation of mandated outputs increased by 8 percentage points to 88 per cent compared to the previous biennium, the ratio of all implemented outputs to those initially programmed increased by 9 percentage points to 105 per cent. Three departments attained implementation rates as high as 144, 146 and 172 per cent, pointing to the strengthened managerial ability to respond to unforeseen programmatic demands and to mobilize resources efficiently to attain higher programme delivery.

Despite those positive results, performance management and monitoring could be improved, particularly by applying performance measurements in assessing the achievement of stated objectives, and providing sound information on resource utilization. A structured and more informative qualitative assessment of programme performance needed to be carried out. The timing, substance and impact of the performance report as a feedback mechanism for future programme planning and budgeting should be reviewed to enhance its value to overall programme performance. Best practices in performance monitoring would be strengthened as a managerial decision-making tool, supporting electronic-based monitoring systems would be further developed, and remaining redundancies and duplications would be identified and eliminated.

The Secretary-General noted that the acceptance of and expertise in reporting on programme performance varied considerably between departments and offices. OIOS would have to provide more guidance and training support to departments and offices, which could be translated into a detailed plan of action to assure that the programme performance report for the next biennium would be more informative, comprehensive and prepared more cost-effectively.

CPC consideration. CPC, in August [A/55/16], noted the high implementation rate achieved by the Secretariat and requested reporting entities that had not yet done so to establish viable and compatible monitoring systems. The Committee also noted that some of the qualitative assessments were too general and thus not very helpful in determining whether activities had resulted in expected outcomes. It looked forward to the further refinement of future programme performance reports, including ways in which full implementation and the quality of mandated programmes and activities could be ensured, and better assessed by and reported to Member States.

Evaluation and programme planning

OIOS reports. By an April note [A/55/63], the Secretary-General transmitted to the General Assembly an OIOS report that reviewed in-depth evaluations and self-evaluation activities during 1998-1999, highlighting several developments in UN evaluation practices. OIOS found that the situation had improved significantly compared

to that described two years earlier [YUN 1998, p. 1294]. It noted in particular the high-level ad hoc examinations of the fall of the safe area of Srebrenica in Bosnia and Herzegovina in 1995 [YUN 1999, p. 327], the operation and functioning of the International Criminal Tribunal for Rwanda and UN actions during the 1994 genocide in Rwanda [YUN 1994, p. 281]. Those reviews represented a deepening of the commitment at the highest levels of the Organization to learning lessons of experience through an objective and authoritative scrutiny of how the United Nations operated. The evaluation function was well established for large-scale field operations, such as those involving peacekeeping and refugees. In the political, economic and social and public information fields, solid evaluation work was being conducted on a wider scale than in previous bienniums. Conference and support services had also instituted more critical reviews and assessments.

CPC consideration. CPC, in June/July [A/55/16], recommended that future OIOS reports on evaluation should be more analytical, should assess whether the evaluation function was being effectively carried out, and should consider how it might be improved, in particular strengthening its role in programme design, delivery and policy directives. It stressed the need for the internal evaluation system to benefit from the work of existing external evaluation mechanisms so as to allow for more effective, independent and critical evaluations.

Other OIOS reports transmitted to CPC by the Secretary-General included: the in-depth evaluation of global development trends, issues and policies, and global approaches to social and microeconomic issues and policies, and the corresponding subprogrammes in the regional commissions [E/AC.51/2000/2]; the in-depth evaluation of the advancement of women programme [E/AC.51/2000/3]; and the triennial reviews of the implementation of CPC's recommendations made at its thirty-seventh (1997) session on the evaluations of the statistics programme [E/AC.51/2000/4] and of the Department of Humanitarian Affairs [E/AC.51/2000/5]. CPC's comments and recommendations on those reports were contained in the report of its fortieth session [A/55/16].

By **decision 54/475** of 7 April, the Assembly endorsed the conclusions and recommendations contained in CPC's report on the work of its thirty-ninth session [A/54/16] regarding evaluation, the reports of JIU and improving CPC's working methods and procedures. It decided to review further the electoral assistance programme in the context of its consideration of CPC's report on the work of its fortieth session on the relevant programme of the 1998-2001 medium-term plan.

United Nations financing and programming 1323

Reports of Secretary-General. Pursuant to Assembly resolution 53/207 [YUN 1998, p. 1294], the Secretary-General reported in June [A/55/85] on ways in which the full implementation and the quality of mandated programmes and activities could be ensured and better assessed by and reported to Member States. To ensure a more effective use of the programme performance report, a number of measures were proposed with respect to that report's format, content and timing. Additionally, programme managers were urged to use computerized monitoring systems for tracking the timely and effective implementation of their work and to establish assessment criteria for measuring expected accomplishments. The 2000-2001 performance report should provide systematic reporting on the qualitative aspects of programme performance, building on the experience reflected in the 1998-1999 report, including a presentation of achievement indicators of expected accomplishments set out in the 2000-2001 programme budget. Besides continuing to provide information on the delivery of programmed outputs, the programme performance report should focus mainly on the extent to which outputs implemented had led to the attainment of the expected accomplishments, thereby providing CPC with substantive information to assist it in its consideration of future programme budgets. It should also be presented using the measures proposed regarding format, content and timing; CPC would review that procedure with a view possibly to utilizing it over the period of the 2002-2005 medium-term plan (see p. 1320).

As requested by CPC (see p. 1321), the Secretary-General submitted to the Fifth Committee an October report [A/C.5/55/14] on the impact of the format of the medium-term plan on the programme planning, budgeting, monitoring and evaluation cycle. He indicated that, since the different phases of the programme planning, budgeting, monitoring and evaluation cycle were closely connected, the changed format of the proposed 2002-2005 medium-term plan would provide for effective implementation of the subsequent phases of the cycle.

GENERAL ASSEMBLY ACTION

On 23 December [meeting 89], the General Assembly, on the recommendation of the Fifth Committee [A/55/710], adopted **resolution 55/234** without vote [agenda item 118].

Programme planning
The General Assembly,

Recalling its resolutions 37/234 of 21 December 1982, 38/227 A of 20 December 1983, 41/213 of 19 December 1986 and 51/219 of 18 December 1996,

Having examined the proposed medium-term plan for the period 2002-2005,

Having considered the views expressed by Member States in the context of the review by the Main Committees of the General Assembly of the relevant programmes of the proposed medium-term plan for the period 2002-2005,

Having also considered the report of the Committee for Programme and Coordination on the work of its fortieth session,

Having further considered the report of the Secretary-General on the programme performance of the United Nations for the biennium 1998-1999, the note by the Secretary-General transmitting the report of the Office of Internal Oversight Services on strengthening the role of evaluation findings in programme design, delivery and policy directives, the report of the Secretary-General on ways in which the full implementation and the quality of mandated programmes and activities could be ensured and could be better assessed by and reported to Member States, as well as the report of the Secretary-General on the impact of the format of the medium-term plan on the programme planning, budgeting, monitoring and evaluation cycle,

I
Medium-term plan for the period 2002-2005

1. *Reaffirms* that the medium-term plan is the principal policy directive of the United Nations and shall serve as the framework for the next biennial programme budget;

2. *Also reaffirms* the importance of ensuring that the medium-term plan reflects all mandated programmes and activities;

3. *Stresses* the importance of ensuring that all legislative mandates are accurately translated into programmes;

4. *Also stresses* the need to continue considering the impact of the new format of the medium-term plan for 2002-2005 on the rest of the cycle;

5. *Notes* that some of the conclusions and recommendations of the Committee for Programme and Coordination at its thirty-ninth session, as adopted by the General Assembly in its resolution 54/236 of 23 December 1999, regarding revisions to the Regulations and Rules Governing Programme Planning, the Programme Aspects of the Budget, the Monitoring of Implementation and the Methods of Evaluation had not been fully reflected in the Secretary-General's bulletin containing the revised edition of the Regulations and Rules Governing Programme Planning;

6. *Requests* the Secretary-General to ensure that, in presenting the medium-term plan, expected accomplishments and, where possible, indicators of achievement are included to measure achievements in the implementation of the programmes of the Organization, not those of individual Member States;

7. *Stresses* that the Secretary-General, in formulating the strategy components of future medium-term plans, should clearly present the approach that will be taken, the type of activities to be carried out and the course of action proposed to achieve the objective desired and to ensure that in subsequent programme budgets planned activities are programmed and reflected in the outputs to be produced;

8. *Adopts* the proposed medium-term plan for the period 2002-2005, together with the relevant recommendations of the Committee and the additional conclusions and recommendations contained in the annex to the present resolution;

II
Programme performance report

1. *Takes note* of the report of the Secretary-General on the programme performance of the United Nations for the biennium 1998-1999;

2. *Endorses* the conclusions and recommendations of the Committee for Programme and Coordination regarding the report of the Secretary-General on the programme performance of the United Nations for the biennium 1998-1999;

3. *Takes note* of the recommendations of the Committee on the report of the Secretary-General on ways in which the full implementation and the quality of mandated programmes and activities could be ensured and could be better assessed by and reported to Member States;

4. *Recognizes* the need for clear statements of objectives, expected accomplishments and corresponding indicators of achievement in future medium-term plans and programme budgets in order to ensure better assessment of the implementation of programmes in the context of the biennial programme performance reports, in accordance with the Regulations and Rules Governing Programme Planning;

III
Other conclusions and recommendations of the Committee for Programme and Coordination

Endorses all other conclusions and recommendations of the Committee for Programme and Coordination on the work of its fortieth session.

ANNEX
Conclusions and recommendations on the proposed medium-term plan for the period 2002-2005
Programme 19 should read as follows:

Programme 19
Human rights

Overall orientation

19.1 The purpose of the United Nations human rights programme is to promote universal enjoyment of all human rights by giving practical effect to the will and resolve of the world community as expressed by the United Nations. Its mandate derives from Articles 1, 13 and 55 of the Charter of the United Nations, the Vienna Declaration and Programme of Action, adopted by the World Conference on Human Rights on 25 June 1993 and subsequently endorsed by the General Assembly in its resolution 48/121 of 20 December 1993, the mandate of the United Nations High Commissioner for Human Rights as defined in Assembly resolution 48/141 of the same date, international human rights instruments adopted by the United Nations and the resolutions and decisions of policy-making bodies. The programme is based on the principles and recommendations of the Vienna Declaration and Programme of Action.

19.2 The programme is under the responsibility of the United Nations High Commissioner for Human Rights, who performs her or his functions under the direction and authority of the Secretary-General in accordance with resolution 48/141. Its objectives are to provide the leading role on human rights issues and to emphasize the importance of human rights on the international and national agendas; to promote international cooperation for human rights; to stimulate and coordinate action across the whole United Nations system; to promote universal ratification and implementation of international standards and to assist in the development of new norms; to support human rights organs and treaty-monitoring bodies; to anticipate serious violations and react to violations; to emphasize preventive human rights action and to promote the establishment of national human rights infrastructures; to undertake human rights field activities and operations; and to provide education, information, advisory services and technical assistance in the field of human rights.

19.3 By the end of the period covered by the present medium-term plan, it is expected that the following will have been accomplished:

(*a*) A significant enhancement and strengthening of international cooperation in the field of human rights leading to increased effectiveness of international machinery, improved respect for human rights at the national level, through, inter alia, universal ratification of all international human rights treaties, the incorporation of those standards into the domestic legislation of States and the continuing adaptation of the United Nations human rights machinery to current and future needs in the promotion and protection of human rights, as reflected in the Vienna Declaration and Programme of Action;

(*b*) Major strengthening of coordination for human rights across the United Nations system, leading to a comprehensive and integrated approach to the promotion and protection of human rights based on the contribution of each of the United Nations organs, bodies and specialized agencies whose activities deal with human rights and on improved inter-agency cooperation and coordination;

(*c*) The adoption and implementation of an integrated and multidimensional strategy for the promotion and protection of the right to development, accompanied by a significant enhancement of support from relevant United Nations bodies for that purpose;

(*d*) Provision of the appropriate assistance by the Secretariat and the Office of the United Nations High Commissioner for Human Rights to ensure that the promotion and protection of all human rights are guided by the principles of impartiality, objectivity and non-selectivity, in the spirit of constructive international dialogue and cooperation;

(*e*) Compliance by the Office of the High Commissioner with the paramount consideration of securing the highest standards of efficiency, competence and integrity, and with due regard to the importance of recruiting the staff on as wide a geographical basis as possible, bearing in mind that the principle of equitable geographical distribution is compatible with the highest standards of efficiency, competence and integrity;

(*f*) A significant increase in the recognition of economic, social and cultural rights and in activities for their protection, including the integration of economic, social and cultural rights as human rights into the strategies and programmes of international organizations, agencies and financial and developmental institutions, the identification of measures of achievement showing success in respecting those rights and the adoption of a communication procedure relating to non-compliance with economic, social and cultural rights;

(g) The adoption and progressive implementation of an improved treaty-monitoring system dealing with multiple reporting obligations and based on a comprehensive national approach;

(h) The implementation of a strengthened system of special procedures based on harmonization and rationalization of work;

(i) The reinforcement of the United Nations as the unique worldwide forum for the discussion and resolution of human rights matters of international concern, with the participation of all relevant actors;

(j) The adoption of more efficient methods within the United Nations to promote and protect human rights, including by preventing human rights violations throughout the world and removing obstacles to the full realization of human rights;

(k) The implementation of a comprehensive United Nations programme to assist States, at their request, in developing and implementing national human rights plans of action strengthening, inter alia, national structures having an impact on democracy and the rule of law; to establish national institutions to give effect to the right to development and economic, social and cultural rights; and to assist States, at their request, within the respective mandates of the Secretariat and the Office of the High Commissioner, in the process of ratifying United Nations human rights instruments;

(l) Fulfilment of the mandates given to the Secretariat for giving appropriate assistance, according to the resolutions and decisions of the General Assembly, the Economic and Social Council and the Commission on Human Rights, to treaty bodies, intergovernmental and expert bodies, as well as the existing relevant voluntary trust funds;

(m) The full integration of the human rights of women and the girl child into the activities of the United Nations system as a whole and its human rights machinery in particular;

(n) The implementation of effective measures to promote equality, dignity and tolerance, to fight racism and xenophobia and to protect minorities, indigenous populations, migrant workers, the disabled and others, taking into account also the outcome of the World Conference against Racism, Racial Discrimination, Xenophobia and Related Intolerance, to be held in 2001;

(o) The establishment of effective programmes of education and public information and the strengthened contribution of non-governmental organizations, national institutions, grass-roots organizations and civil society in United Nations human rights activities at all levels, according to the legislative mandates in effect regarding these issues;

(p) The provision to States, United Nations bodies, experts and the academic community of high-quality research and analysis on human rights issues, including that dealing with emerging problems and the development of new standards and instruments.

Subprogramme 1
Right to development, research and analysis

Objectives and strategy

19.4 The primary objectives of this subprogramme will include the promotion and protection of the right to de-velopment. In this regard, the objectives will be to develop an integrated and multidimensional strategy for the implementation, coordination and promotion of the right to development in accordance with the Declaration on the Right to Development and subsequent mandates and the Vienna Declaration and Programme of Action, aimed at facilitating action to be taken by relevant bodies of the United Nations system, including treaty bodies, international development and financial institutions and non-governmental organizations, for the implementation of the right to development as an integral part of fundamental human rights, ensuring the realization of the right to development across the human rights programme and by specialized agencies and United Nations treaty bodies; to promote national implementation of the right to development through coordination with State-appointed officials; to identify obstacles at the national and international levels; and to promote awareness about the content and importance of the right to development, including through information and educational activities.

19.5 With regard to research and analysis, the objectives will be to strengthen respect for human rights by increasing knowledge, awareness and understanding of human rights issues through data collection, research and analysis. These objectives will be pursued within the framework of the indivisibility, interdependence and interrelatedness of all human rights and will be aimed at facilitating the implementation of standards, the work of treaty bodies, special rapporteurs and other bodies and the preparation of new standards; ensuring the recognition on the national and international levels of economic, social and cultural rights; promoting democracy and strengthening national human rights institutions and procedures for the rule of law; contributing to the elimination of racism, racial discrimination, xenophobia and new forms of discrimination; and strengthening the recognition of the human rights of women and children and the protection of vulnerable groups such as minorities, migrant workers and indigenous people.

Expected accomplishments

19.6 Expected accomplishments of the Secretariat would include:

(a) Wider integration and/or inclusion of the promotion and protection of the right to development, in particular across the human rights programme and the relevant programmes of work of the United Nations departments and/or offices and specialized agencies and of major international organizations and forums related to this issue;

(b) Major strengthening of coordination for human rights across the United Nations system, leading to a comprehensive and integrated approach to the promotion and protection of human rights based on the contribution of each of the United Nations organs, bodies and specialized agencies whose activities deal with human rights and also based on improved inter-agency cooperation and coordination;

(c) Strengthened efforts which will contribute to the elimination of racism, racial discrimination, xenophobia and related intolerance;

(d) Enhanced awareness, knowledge and understanding of all human rights, including the right to development;

(e) Wider recognition of the rights of women, children and persons belonging to minorities, migrant workers, indigenous people and persons with disabilities, and strengthening the protection of vulnerable groups.

Measurements of achievement

19.7 Measures of achievement are elements used as tools for determining, where possible, the extent to which the objectives and/or expected accomplishments have been achieved.

19.8 Measures of achievement of the Secretariat would include:

(a) The extent to which the right to development had been included in the work programmes of the departments and offices of the United Nations, the specialized agencies and other relevant intergovernmental organizations, providing compiled examples of concrete steps in that regard;

(b) The extent to which the mandates given to the Secretariat contained in resolutions and decisions adopted by the General Assembly, the Economic and Social Council and the Commission on Human Rights, had been fulfilled;

(c) The holding of seminars and workshops organized by the Office of the United Nations High Commissioner for Human Rights, in accordance with the relevant resolutions and decisions adopted by the General Assembly, the Economic and Social Council and the Commission on Human Rights, or in cooperation with the Office of the High Commissioner, and the extent to which they contributed to the fulfilment of the objectives of the subprogramme;

(d) The extent to which the activities of the Office of the High Commissioner contributed to increasing knowledge, awareness and understanding in order to advance the full realization of the right to development, in accordance with the Declaration on the Right to Development;

(e) Increased number of visitors to the web site of the Office of the High Commissioner;

(f) The number of new publications of the Office of the High Commissioner as well as their distribution, and the assessment by users of their quality and usefulness.

Subprogramme 2
Supporting human rights bodies and organs

Objectives and strategy

19.9 The objectives are to support the United Nations human rights bodies and organs and to facilitate their deliberations by ensuring and enhancing their effective functioning; to contribute to increasing the knowledge, expanding the awareness and promoting the importance of all international human rights treaties; to improve existing procedures through rationalization and streamlining, and the coordination of the participation of Governments, experts, specialized agencies, other international organizations, national institutions and non-governmental organizations in their work; and to ensure the analytical capacity of human rights treaty bodies for the review of State party reports under international treaties and for the processing of communications.

Expected accomplishments

19.10 Expected accomplishments of the Secretariat would include:

(a) The timely delivery of required and appropriate support to intergovernmental bodies, expert bodies and treaty bodies, inter alia, in order to contribute to reducing the backlog in the consideration by the reviewing mechanisms of the States parties' reports;

(b) The timely delivery of required and appropriate support to intergovernmental bodies, expert bodies and treaty bodies, inter alia, in order to contribute to reducing the backlog in the consideration by the reviewing mechanisms of complaints.

Measurements of achievement

19.11 Measures of achievement are elements used as tools for determining, where possible, the extent to which the objectives and/or expected accomplishments have been achieved.

19.12 Measures of achievement of the Secretariat would include:

(a) The quality and timeliness of services provided by the Office of the High Commissioner;

(b) A reduction in the time lag between the submission of a State party report and its examination by the relevant treaty body;

(c) A reduction in the time lag between the submission of a complaint and its review, as appropriate, by the relevant mechanisms;

(d) The number of reports prepared by the Secretariat in accordance with resolutions and decisions of the General Assembly, the Economic and Social Council and the Commission on Human Rights, and the extent to which they were presented in a timely manner, in compliance with the six-week rule for the issuance of documentation, for consideration by organs dealing with human rights.

Subprogramme 3
Advisory services, technical cooperation, support to human rights fact-finding procedures and field activities

Objectives and strategy

19.13 In the area of advisory services and technical cooperation, the objectives are to assist countries, at their request, in developing comprehensive national plans of action to promote and protect human rights and to provide advice and support to specific projects to promote respect for human rights; to develop a comprehensive and coordinated United Nations programme to help States in building and strengthening national structures for human rights promotion and protection; and to raise awareness and promote specialized knowledge about human rights through the organization of training courses, seminars and workshops, and the production of a wide range of educational, training and information material.

19.14 In the area of support to fact-finding bodies, the objectives are to ensure the effective functioning of human rights monitoring mechanisms by assisting special rapporteurs and representatives, experts and working groups mandated by policy-making bodies, including through the preparation of information regarding alleged violations and situations for review and the provision of support for missions and meetings; and to enhance the efficiency of action by policy-making bodies by providing analytical information on human rights situations.

19.15 With respect to field activities, the objective is to ensure the efficiency of field missions and presences through the maintenance of contacts with Governments, appropriate sectors of the United Nations system, international and regional organizations and others by supporting and developing such activities through the development of training programmes and materials for human rights field staff and training in human rights for the appropriate components of other United Nations field operations.

Expected accomplishments

19.16 Expected accomplishments of the Secretariat would include:

(*a*) Provision of advisory services and technical and financial assistance, at the request of the State concerned and, where appropriate, the regional human rights organizations, with a view to supporting actions and programmes in the field of human rights;

(*b*) Fulfilment of the mandates given to the Office of the High Commissioner in resolutions and decisions of the General Assembly, the Economic and Social Council and the Commission on Human Rights to support human rights monitoring mechanisms, such as special rapporteurs/representatives and expert and working groups mandated by policy-making bodies;

(*c*) Enhanced awareness, knowledge and understanding of all human rights, including the right to development.

Measurements of achievement

19.17 Measures of achievement are elements used as tools for determining, where possible, the extent to which the objectives and/or expected accomplishments have been achieved.

19.18 Measures of achievement of the Secretariat would include:

(*a*) The number of seminars, workshops and training courses held or supported by the Office of the High Commissioner; and the number of persons trained, participants in seminars and workshops and fellowships granted, as well as data on their geographical distribution, and the extent to which they contributed to the fulfilment of the objectives of the subprogramme;

(*b*) The number of requests from Member States and, where appropriate, from the regional human rights organizations, received and fulfilled by the Office of the High Commissioner for the provision of advisory services and technical and financial assistance, with a view to supporting actions and programmes in the field of human rights;

(*c*) The timeliness, significance and relevance of the advisory services and technical cooperation.

Legislative mandates

Programme 19
Human rights

General Assembly resolutions

48/121	World Conference on Human Rights
48/141	High Commissioner for the promotion and protection of all human rights
53/166	Comprehensive implementation of and follow-up to the Vienna Declaration and Programme of Action (Subprogrammes 1 and 2)
54/138	Violence against women migrant workers (Subprogrammes 1 and 2)
54/168	Respect for the principles of national sovereignty and non-interference in the internal affairs of States in their electoral processes (Subprogrammes 1 and 3)

54/169	Respect for the right to universal freedom of travel and the vital importance of family reunification (Subprogrammes 1 and 2)
54/173	Strengthening the role of the United Nations in enhancing the effectiveness of the principle of periodic and genuine elections and the promotion of democratization (Subprogrammes 1 and 3)
54/174	Strengthening United Nations action in the field of human rights through the promotion of international cooperation and the importance of non-selectivity, impartiality and objectivity
55/96	Promoting and consolidating democracy
55/101	Respect for the purposes and principles contained in the Charter of the United Nations to achieve international cooperation in promoting and encouraging respect for human rights and for fundamental freedoms and in solving international problems of humanitarian character
55/102	Globalization and its impact on the full enjoyment of all human rights
55/107	Promotion of a democratic and equitable international order

Economic and Social Council resolution

2000/22	Establishment of a Permanent Forum on Indigenous Issues

Economic and Social Council agreed conclusions

	Agreed conclusions 1998/2 on the coordinated follow-up to and implementation of the Vienna Declaration and Programme of Action

Commission on Human Rights resolutions

1994/95	World Conference on Human Rights (Subprogrammes 1 and 2)
2000/73	Composition of the staff of the Office of the United Nations High Commissioner for Human Rights

Subprogramme 1
Right to development, research and analysis

General Assembly resolutions

41/128	Declaration on the Right to Development
53/142	Strengthening of the rule of law
53/146	Human rights and extreme poverty
54/133	Traditional or customary practices affecting the health of women and girls
54/134	International Day for the Elimination of Violence against Women
54/135	Improvement of the situation of women in rural areas
54/137	Convention on the Elimination of All Forms of Discrimination against Women
54/141	Follow-up to the Fourth World Conference on Women and full implementation of the Beijing Declaration and the Platform for Action
54/148	The girl child
54/149	The rights of the child
54/150	International Decade of the World's Indigenous People
54/153	Measures to combat contemporary forms of racism, racial discrimination, xenophobia and related intolerance
54/154	Third Decade to Combat Racism and Racial Discrimination and the convening of the World Conference against Racism, Racial Discrimination, Xenophobia and Related Intolerance
54/155	Universal realization of the right of peoples to self-determination
54/159	Elimination of all forms of religious intolerance
54/160	Human rights and cultural diversity
54/162	Effective promotion of the Declaration on the Rights of Persons Belonging to National or Ethnic, Religious and Linguistic Minorities
54/163	Human rights in the administration of justice
54/164	Human rights and terrorism
54/167	Protection of and assistance to internally displaced persons
54/172	Human rights and unilateral coercive measures
54/175	The right to development

54/181	Enhancement of international cooperation in the field of human rights
55/66	Working towards the elimination of crimes against women committed in the name of honour
55/68	Elimination of all forms of violence against women, including crimes identified in the outcome document of the twenty-third special session of the General Assembly entitled "Women 2000: gender equality, development and peace for the twenty-first century"
55/86	Use of mercenaries as a means of violating human rights and impeding the exercise of the right of peoples to self-determination
55/89	Torture and other cruel, inhuman or degrading treatment or punishment
55/92	Protection of migrants
55/98	Declaration on the Right and Responsibility of Individuals, Groups and Organs of Society to Promote and Protect Universally Recognized Human Rights and Fundamental Freedoms
55/102	Globalization and its impact on the full enjoyment of all human rights
55/103	Question of enforced or involuntary disappearances
55/111	Extrajudicial, summary or arbitrary executions

Economic and Social Council resolution

1999/12	Racism, racial discrimination, xenophobia and related intolerance

Commission on Human Rights resolutions

1999/22	Effects on the full enjoyment of human rights of the economic adjustment policies arising from foreign debt and, in particular, on the implementation of the Declaration on the Right to Development
1999/25	Question of the realization in all countries of the economic, social and cultural rights contained in the Universal Declaration of Human Rights and in the International Covenant on Economic, Social and Cultural Rights, and study of special problems which the developing countries face in their efforts to achieve these human rights
1999/34	Impunity
1999/40	Traffic in women and girls
1999/46	Contemporary forms of slavery
1999/61	Question of the death penalty
1999/65	Fundamental standards of humanity
2000/10	The right to food
2000/36	Question of arbitrary detention
2000/38	The right to freedom of opinion and expression
2000/46	Integrating the human rights of women throughout the United Nations system
2000/61	Human rights defenders
2000/62	Promotion of the right to a democratic and equitable international order
2000/82	Effects of structural adjustment policies and foreign debt on the full enjoyment of all human rights, particularly economic, social and cultural rights

Subprogramme 2
Supporting human rights bodies and organs

General Assembly resolutions

2106 A (XX)	International Convention on the Elimination of All Forms of Racial Discrimination
2200(XXI)	International Covenant on Economic, Social and Cultural Rights, International Covenant on Civil and Political Rights and Optional Protocol to the International Covenant on Civil and Political Rights
39/46	Convention against Torture and Other Cruel, Inhuman or Degrading Treatment or Punishment
44/25	Convention on the Rights of the Child
53/138	Effective implementation of international instruments on human rights, including reporting obligations under international instruments on human rights

54/157	International Covenants on Human Rights
55/88	International Convention on the Protection of the Rights of All Migrant Workers and Members of Their Families

Economic and Social Council resolutions and decision

1503(XLVIII)	Procedure for dealing with communications relating to violations of human rights and fundamental freedoms
1979/36	Further promotion and encouragement of human rights and fundamental freedoms
1990/48	Enlargement of the Commission on Human Rights and the further promotion of human rights and fundamental freedoms
1999/256	Rationalization of the work of the Commission on Human Rights

Economic and Social Council agreed conclusions

	Agreed conclusions 1998/2 on the coordinated follow-up to and implementation of the Vienna Declaration and Programme of Action

Commission on Human Rights resolutions

2000/22	Cooperation with representatives of United Nations human rights bodies
2000/46	Integrating the human rights of women throughout the United Nations system

Subprogramme 3
Advisory services, technical cooperation, support to human rights fact-finding procedures and field activities

General Assembly resolutions

926(X)	Advisory services in the field of human rights
53/148	Regional arrangements for the promotion and protection of human rights
54/151	Use of mercenaries as a means of violating human rights and impeding the exercise of the right of peoples to self-determination
54/161	United Nations Decade for Human Rights Education, 1995-2004, and public information activities in the field of human rights
54/176	National institutions for the promotion and protection of human rights
54/180	Human rights and mass exoduses

Economic and Social Council resolution

1235(XLII)	Question of the violation of human rights and fundamental freedoms, including policies of racial discrimination and segregation and of apartheid in all countries, with particular reference to colonial and other dependent countries and territories

Commission on Human Rights resolutions

1995/53	Advisory services and the Voluntary Fund for Technical Cooperation in the Field of Human Rights
1998/74	Human rights and thematic procedures

By **decision 55/458**, also of 23 December, the Assembly decided that the item on programme planning would remain for consideration at its resumed fifty-fifth (2001) session.

UN International Partnership Fund

Pursuant to General Assembly decision 53/475 [YUN 1999, p. 1318], the Secretary-General reported on the status of the United Nations Fund for International Partnership (UNFIP) [A/55/763 & Corr.1], established in 1998 [YUN 1998, p. 1297] to manage the process of grant allocations through the United Nations Foundation (UNF), a public charity founded by Robert Edward Turner to channel a gift to the United Nations of 18 million shares of Time Warner stock valued at some $1 billion. The report provided data on the outcome of the three funding cycles for operations in 2000 and information on progress in each programmatic focus area.

The three UNF-approved funding rounds of grants were: the sixth round, approved on 23 March, totalling more than $17 million for 23 projects; the seventh round, approved on 24 July, totalling $42 million for 29 projects; and the eighth round, approved on 20 December, totalling $16 million for 13 projects, bringing the grants programmed for 2000 to some $75 million. By sector, grants were awarded for projects as follows: $43 million for population and women; $17 million for the environment; $9 million for peace, security, human rights and institu-

tional capacity-building; and $7 million for children's health. Total funding since inception of the UNFIP-UNF partnership to the end of 2000 amounted to $312 million for some 169 projects.

Responding to comments by the Board of Auditors, UNFIP took the following steps to reduce delays in the submission of project documents: it streamlined the project approval and signature process, replacing the current two-step process with a single project document; and introduced a sunset clause to enter into effect 60 days after project approval, with funding to be withdrawn for failure to submit a project document for UNFIP's signature within 120 days following Board approval.

The Secretary-General provided additional information on UNFIP activities in respect of the programme framework on children's health [A/54/664/Add.1], on population and women [A/54/664/Add.2] and on biodiversity [A/54/664/Add.3].

Chapter III

United Nations staff

In 2000, the General Assembly, through the International Civil Service Commission (ICSC), maintained continuous review of the conditions of service of the staff of the UN common system. It adopted a number of ICSC recommendations updating conditions of service, among them the base/floor salary scale, the common staff assessment scale, the post adjustment system, dependency allowances and the education grant. The Assembly took note of progress made in finalizing the draft standards of conduct for the international civil service and welcomed the adoption by ICSC of the integrated framework for human resources management.

The Secretary-General kept the Assembly abreast of the proposed review of ICSC as part of his ongoing programme for UN reform and reported on developments related to staff composition, the use of gratis personnel, consultants, individual contractors and retirees, the status of women in the Secretariat, regulations governing the status, rights and duties of the Secretary-General, non-Secretariat officials and experts on mission, and adherence to regulations governing standards of accommodation for air travel of UN officials.

The Office of Internal Oversight Services audited the Secretariat's recruitment process, while the Joint Inspection Unit (JIU) examined the process of senior-level appointments, assessed the implementation of delegation of authority to department and office heads and reviewed the machinery for the administration of justice in the United Nations, following which the Assembly amended the Statute of the United Nations Administrative Tribunal.

In the face of increasing threats and attacks against UN and associated personnel serving in the field, the Security Council and the Assembly stressed that the responsibility for the security and safety of such personnel lay primarily on the host Governments, which were strongly urged to take protective measures and to prosecute the perpetrators of such acts. In addition, the Secretary-General appointed a United Nations Security Coordinator to assist him in fulfilling his obligation to ensure the security of UN personnel.

The Assembly established the United Nations System Staff College, with effect from 1 January 2001, making it a system-wide knowledge management, training and learning establishment.

In other action, the Assembly approved changes to the pension adjustment system and amendments to the Regulations of the United Nations Joint Staff Pension Fund.

Conditions of service

International Civil Service Commission

The International Civil Service Commission (ICSC), a 15-member body established in 1974 by General Assembly resolution 3357(XXIX) [YUN 1974, p. 875], continued in 2000 to regulate and coordinate the conditions of service of the UN common system of salaries and allowances. The United Nations and 12 related organizations had accepted the ICSC statute: the International Labour Organization (ILO); the Food and Agriculture Organization of the United Nations (FAO); the United Nations Educational, Scientific and Cultural Organization; the World Health Organization; the International Civil Aviation Organization (ICAO); the Universal Postal Union; the International Telecommunication Union; the World Meteorological Organization; the International Maritime Organization; the World Intellectual Property Organization; the United Nations Industrial Development Organization; and the International Atomic Energy Agency (IAEA). One other organization, the International Fund for Agricultural Development, had not formally accepted the statute but participated fully in ICSC work.

ICSC held its fifty-first (Vienna, 3-20 April) and its fifty-second (New York, 17 July–4 August) sessions in 2000. At those sessions, it considered, in addition to organizational matters, the conditions of service applicable to both Professional and General Service categories of staff and those pertaining specifically either to the Professional and higher categories or to the General Service and other locally recruited categories.

The deliberations, recommendations and decisions of ICSC on those matters were detailed in its twenty-sixth annual report to the Assembly [A/55/30] (see sections below).

In a November statement on the administrative and financial implications of ICSC decisions and recommendations [A/55/629] for the 2000-2001 programme budget, the Secretary-General estimated the resultant increased requirements at $5,736,846, net of staff assessment.

GENERAL ASSEMBLY ACTION

On 23 December [meeting 89], the General Assembly, on the recommendation of the Fifth (Administrative and Budgetary) Committee [A/55/709], adopted **resolution 55/223** without vote [agenda item 124].

United Nations common system: report of the International Civil Service Commission

The General Assembly,

Having considered the report of the International Civil Service Commission for the year 2000 and the statement submitted by the Secretary-General on the administrative and financial implications of the decisions and recommendations contained in the report of the Commission,

Reaffirming its commitment to a single unified United Nations common system as the cornerstone for the regulation and coordination of the conditions of service of the United Nations common system,

Convinced that the common system constitutes the best instrument to secure staff of the highest standards of efficiency, competence and integrity for the international civil service, as stipulated under the Charter of the United Nations,

Reaffirming the central role of the Commission in the regulation and coordination of the conditions of service of the United Nations common system,

Reaffirming also the statute of the Commission,

I
Conditions of service applicable to both categories of staff

A. Framework for human resources management

Recalling its resolutions 51/216 of 18 December 1996, 52/216 of 22 December 1997, 53/209 of 18 December 1998 and 54/238 of 23 December 1999,

1. *Welcomes with appreciation* the work of the Commission with regard to the integrated framework for human resources management, which would assist organizations of the common system to carry forward human resources management reforms;

2. *Endorses* the conclusions of the Commission as contained in paragraph 19 of its report;

3. *Requests* the Commission to use the integrated framework as a guide to its future programme of work as contained in paragraph 18 of its report;

4. *Encourages* the organizations of the United Nations common system to use the integrated framework as a basis for their future work in human resources policies and procedures and to bring it to the attention of their governing bodies;

B. Standards of conduct for the international civil service

Recalling its resolutions 52/252 of 8 September 1998 and 54/238,

Takes note of the decisions of the Commission contained in paragraph 31 of its report, urges organizations to reach consensus on the draft standards of conduct for the international civil service in sufficient time so as to enable the Commission to finalize the text to be submitted to the General Assembly at its fifty-sixth session, and emphasizes that the proposed standards should ensure that the staff uphold the principles of integrity, impartiality and independence;

C. Review of pay and benefits system

Recalling its resolutions 51/216, 52/216 and 53/209,

1. *Takes note* of the work of the Commission in respect of the review of the pay and benefits system in the context of the integrated framework for human resources management;

2. *Takes note also* of the decision of the Commission to move forward with the review of the pay and benefits system in accordance with the modalities described in annex III to its report;

D. Recognition of language knowledge

Recalling section II.E of its resolution 48/224 of 23 December 1993 and section II.B of its resolution 53/209,

Takes note of the decision of the Commission to address the issue of recognition of language knowledge within the context of the comprehensive review of the pay and benefits system;

E. Education grant

Recalling section III.C of its resolution 54/238, by which it requested the Commission to complete the review of the methodology for the education grant and report the results to the General Assembly at its fifty-fifth session,

1. *Takes note* of the decisions and recommendations of the Commission in respect of the review of the methodology for the education grant as contained in paragraph 81 of its report;

2. *Urges* the organizations of the United Nations common system to harmonize their rules and regulations to ensure that the education grant is treated as a benefit payable to internationally recruited staff with expatriate status only;

3. *Approves* increases in the maximum reimbursement levels in five currency areas, as well as other adjustments to the management of expenses under the education grant, as contained in paragraph 93 of its report;

4. *Takes note* of the decisions of the Commission as contained in paragraphs 94 and 95 of its report;

F. Common scale of staff assessment

Recalling its resolutions 48/225 of 23 December 1993 and 51/216,

Takes note of the decisions of the Commission as contained in paragraph 102 of its report;

II
Conditions of service of staff in the Professional and higher categories

A. Noblemaire principle and its application

Recalling its resolution 44/198 of 21 December 1989 and other relevant resolutions,

1. *Reaffirms* the continued application of the Noblemaire principle;

2. *Also reaffirms* the need to continue to ensure the competitiveness of the conditions of service of the United Nations common system;

B. Grade equivalencies between the United States federal civil service and the United Nations common system

Recalling section I.A of its resolution 50/208 of 23 December 1995,

1. *Takes note* of the updated grade equivalency study undertaken in 2000 by the Commission with the United States federal civil service;

2. *Also takes note* of the decisions of the Commission in respect of the grade equivalency study undertaken in 2000 with the comparator civil service as contained in paragraph 149 of its report;

C. Evolution of the margin

Recalling section I.B of its resolution 52/216 and the standing mandate from the General Assembly, in which the Commission is requested to continue its review of the relationship between the net remuneration of the United Nations staff in the Professional and higher categories in New York and that of the comparator civil service (the United States federal civil service) employees in comparable positions in Washington, D.C. (referred to as "the margin"),

Recalling also section IX, paragraph 3, of its resolution 46/191 A of 20 December 1991, in which it requested the Commission to include in its work a review of the differences between the United Nations and the United States net remuneration at individual grade levels,

1. *Notes* that the margin between the net remuneration of United Nations staff in grades P-1 to D-2 in New York and that of officials in comparable positions in the United States federal civil service for 2000 is 113.3, based on the results of the grade equivalency study between the United Nations and the United States carried out in 2000;

2. *Also notes* from annex V to the report of the Commission that the United Nations/United States remuneration ratios range from 119.9 at the P-2 level to 105.5 at the D-2 level, and considers that this imbalance should be addressed in the context of the overall margin considerations established by the General Assembly;

D. Base/floor salary scale

Recalling section I.H of its resolution 44/198, by which it established a floor net salary level for staff in the Professional and higher categories by reference to the corresponding base net salary levels of officials in comparable positions serving at the base city of the comparator civil service (the United States federal civil service),

1. *Approves*, with effect from 1 March 2001, the revised base scale of gross and net salaries for staff in the Professional and higher categories, contained in the annex to the present resolution;

2. *Requests* the Commission, in the context of the review of the pay and benefits system, to review the firm linkage between the base/floor salary scale and the mobility and hardship allowance;

E. Dependency allowances

Recalling section II.F, paragraph 2, of its resolution 47/216 of 23 December 1992, in which it noted that the Commission would review the level of dependency allowances every two years,

Recalling also section I.F, paragraph 4, of its resolution 53/209, in which it requested the Commission to examine the methodology, rationale and scope of the allowances,

Noting that the review of dependency allowances carried out by the Commission reflected relevant changes in tax abatement and social legislation at the seven headquarters duty stations since 1998,

1. *Takes note* of the decision of the Commission with regard to the methodology, rationale and scope of the allowances;

2. *Approves*, with effect from 1 January 2001, an increase of 11.89 per cent in the children's allowance, including that for disabled children, and in the secondary dependant's allowance;

3. *Takes note* of the updated list of hard-currency duty stations for which the allowances are specified in local currency, as contained in annex VIII to the report of the Commission;

4. *Notes* that dependency allowances payable to eligible United Nations common system staff should be reduced by the amount of any direct payments received from a Government in respect of dependants;

F. Post adjustment matters

Recalling its request in section II.G of its resolution 48/224 regarding the conduct of place-to-place surveys at headquarters duty stations,

1. *Welcomes* the review of the operation of the post adjustment system carried out by the Commission;

2. *Takes note* of the decisions reached by the Commission as contained in paragraph 157 of its report;

III
Conditions of service of the General Service and other locally recruited categories

A. Survey of best prevailing conditions of employment in New York and Montreal

Recalling section II.A of its resolution 52/216, in which it reaffirmed that the Flemming principle should continue to serve as the basis for determining the conditions of service of the General Service and related categories and endorsed the revised methodology for surveys of best prevailing conditions of employment for these categories,

Takes note of the results of the salary surveys conducted in New York and Montreal, as reported in chapter V of the report of the Commission;

B. Review of the headquarters salary survey methodology: decisions of the International Labour Organization Administrative Tribunal regarding the phasing out of the language factor in Rome and Vienna

Recalling section III, paragraph 2, of its resolution 47/216 and section II.E of its resolution 48/224,

Takes note of the decision of the Commission with regard to the treatment of the language factor, as contained in paragraph 192 of its report;

IV
Strengthening the international civil service

Decides to defer consideration of the reports of the Secretary-General with a view to taking a decision on strengthening the international civil service at the first part of its resumed fifty-fifth session.

ANNEX

Salary scale for staff in the Professional and higher categories showing annual gross salaries and net equivalents after application of staff assessment[a]

(United States dollars)

(Effective 1 March 2001)

Level		I	II	III	IV	V	VI	VII	VIII	IX	X	XI	XII	XIII	XIV	XV
								Steps								
Under-Secretary-General																
USG	Gross	167,035														
	Net D	113,762														
	Net S	102,379														
Assistant Secretary-General																
ASG	Gross	151,840														
	Net D	104,341														
	Net S	94,484														
Director																
D-2	Gross	124,384	127,132	129,877	132,623	135,369	138,115									
	Net D	87,318	89,022	90,724	92,426	94,129	95,831									
	Net S	80,218	81,645	83,072	84,498	85,925	87,352									
Principal Officer																
D-1	Gross	109,894	112,245	114,598	116,944	119,297	121,648	124,002	126,352	128,702						
	Net D	78,334	79,792	81,251	82,705	84,164	85,622	87,081	88,538	89,995						
	Net S	72,407	73,687	74,967	76,245	77,525	78,796	80,018	81,240	82,460						
Senior Officer																
P-5	Gross	96,705	98,832	100,961	103,089	105,216	107,342	109,471	111,598	113,724	115,853	117,982	120,106	122,234		
	Net D	70,157	71,476	72,796	74,115	75,434	76,752	78,072	79,391	80,709	82,029	83,349	84,666	85,985		
	Net S	65,176	66,385	67,545	68,703	69,862	71,018	72,177	73,335	74,493	75,651	76,809	77,966	79,101		
First Officer																
P-4	Gross	79,780	81,733	83,680	85,627	87,579	89,527	91,571	93,645	95,723	97,795	99,869	101,947	104,019	106,095	108,171
	Net D	59,255	60,544	61,829	63,114	64,402	65,688	66,974	68,260	69,548	70,833	72,119	73,407	74,692	75,979	77,266
	Net S	55,180	56,364	57,543	58,722	59,902	61,080	62,259	63,439	64,617	65,796	66,949	68,082	69,210	70,340	71,470
Second Officer																
P-3	Gross	65,388	67,220	69,053	70,880	72,714	74,544	76,373	78,206	80,038	81,868	83,700	85,529	87,361	89,191	91,089
	Net D	49,756	50,965	52,175	53,381	54,591	55,799	57,006	58,216	59,425	60,633	61,842	63,049	64,258	65,466	66,675
	Net S	46,445	47,556	48,669	49,780	50,892	52,002	53,113	54,225	55,335	56,447	57,555	58,663	59,770	60,877	61,985
Associate Officer																
P-2	Gross	53,129	54,632	56,132	57,633	59,135	60,692	62,332	63,967	65,606	67,244	68,879	70,520			
	Net D	41,253	42,335	43,415	44,496	45,577	46,657	47,739	48,818	49,900	50,981	52,060	53,143			
	Net S	38,694	39,675	40,653	41,633	42,611	43,592	44,587	45,580	46,577	47,571	48,564	49,561			
Assistant Officer																
P-1	Gross	41,189	42,633	44,075	45,519	46,960	48,403	49,847	51,290	52,731	54,174					
	Net D	32,656	33,696	34,734	35,774	36,811	37,850	38,890	39,929	40,966	42,005					
	Net S	30,805	31,763	32,720	33,677	34,633	35,590	36,548	37,493	38,434	39,375					

D = Rate applicable to staff members with a dependent spouse or child.

S = Rate applicable to staff members with no dependent spouse or child.

[a]This scale will be implemented in conjunction with a consolidation of 5.1 per cent of post adjustment. There will be consequential adjustments in post adjustment indices and multipliers at all duty stations effective 1 March 2001. Thereafter, changes in post adjustment classifications will be implemented on the basis of the movements of the consolidated post adjustment indices.

Also on 23 December, the Assembly decided that the agenda item on the UN common system would remain for consideration during its resumed fifty-fifth (2001) session (**decision 55/458**) and that the Fifth Committee should continue to consider it at that session (**decision 55/455**).

Functioning of ICSC

Review of ICSC

In response to General Assembly resolution 54/238 [YUN 1999, p. 1321], the Secretary-General submitted, in October [A/55/526], a report identifying the specific reasons for the proposed review of ICSC [YUN 1998, p. 1300], its objectives and desired impact on the UN common system, the outcomes of previous reviews and the particular problems to be addressed.

The Secretary-General stated that the proposed review was an integral part of the current reform processes under way in all organizations of the common system to strengthen that system's capacity to meet effectively new and complex challenges facing it and the international civil service. Its goal was to reinforce and modernize the system and to determine how to maximize ICSC's contribution to those objectives. The review would examine specifically ICSC's mission, membership and functioning and reappraise the complex network of relationships built into its statute. Although the provisions of the ICSC statute had stood the test of time, it was important to keep them under review to ensure the continued fulfilment of their intent and their adaptability to changing needs and circumstances. The review should be an independent one. It should serve to enhance the Assembly's role as the legislative organ for the common system and ICSC's role in maintaining the strength of the system, as well as to ensure the capacity and technical expertise of ICSC to provide timely advice and guidance to its constituents on matters impacting on organizational change.

The Secretary-General invited the Assembly to proceed with the proposed review at its current session, in consultation with Member States, ICSC and its interlocutors.

Remuneration issues

Pursuant to the standing mandate in General Assembly resolution 52/216 [YUN 1992, p. 1055] and to resolution 54/238 [YUN 1999, p. 1321], ICSC continued to review the relationship between the net remuneration of UN staff in the Professional and higher categories (grades P-1 to D-2) in New York and that of the current comparator, the United States federal civil service employees in comparable positions in Washington, D.C. (referred to as the margin).

Whereas a remuneration margin of 113.8 was forecast for 2000, based on current grade equivalencies, the five-yearly grade equivalency study undertaken by ICSC during the year with the comparator civil service showed an agreement rate of 92 per cent and resulted in a revised margin of 113.3. As shown by annex V to the ICSC report, the net remuneration margin calculation, based on the incorporation of the study's results, yielded relatively high margin levels at lower common system grades and relatively low margin at higher grades. Following its consideration of the views of the common system's organizations and staff representatives and its review of specific issues related to the grade equivalencies and resultant remuneration comparisons, ICSC endorsed the results of the 2000 equivalency exercise for remuneration purposes and requested its secretariat to review the current methodology, with a view to streamlining the process so as to reduce administrative costs without jeopardizing the quality of future grade equivalency studies.

In view of the upward movement of the comparator civil service salaries as at 1 January 2000, ICSC recommended that, with effect from 1 March 2001, the current base/floor salary scale for the Professional and higher categories in the UN common system should be increased by 5.1 per cent through standard consolidation procedures, on a no-loss/no-gain basis. The proposed revised base/floor salary scale and associated staff assessment scale were set out in annexes VI and VII to the ICSC report [A/55/30].

On the basis of the 1997 revised methodology for surveys of best prevailing conditions of employment at Headquarters and non-Headquarters duty stations [YUN 1997, p. 1453], ICSC conducted a survey of best prevailing conditions of service for General Service and other locally recruited categories of staff at the ICAO duty station in Montreal, with a reference date of November 1999. The survey resulted in the recommendation of a new ICAO salary scale, as reproduced in annex IX to the ICSC report, and of revised rates for dependency allowances.

ICSC also conducted surveys of employment conditions for staff in the General Service, Language Teachers, Public Information Assistant, Trades and Crafts and Security Service categories in New York, with a reference date of 1 May 2000. The surveys resulted in increases of 2.92 per cent for the General Service and Public Information Assistant categories and of 7.66 per cent for the Security Service category. Accordingly, ICSC recommended revised salary scales for those categories, as reflected in annex X to its report. Since, based on available data, a valid salary comparison for the Trades and Crafts category was not possible, ICSC instructed its secretariat to continue data collection to permit meaningful analysis.

As a result of the application of the 1993 revised methodology for surveys of the best prevailing employment conditions at headquarters duty stations [YUN 1993, p. 1228] to the 1994 survey of General Service salaries at FAO and to the 1996 survey at IAEA, ICSC decided that the 4 per cent language factor previously applied to those duty stations should be phased out at an annual rate of 1 per cent. The FAO survey was challenged by some staff in the ILO Administrative Tribunal, as was the IAEA survey. The Tribunal had set aside FAO's implementation of the 1995 ICSC decision approving the FAO survey insofar as that decision reduced the language factor.

In its Judgement 1915 of 2 February 2000 pertaining to the IAEA complaint, the Tribunal, referring to the Flemming principle on which the survey methodologies were based, stated that what Flemming ordained was that General Service staff should have pay and other terms of employment that matched the best on offer at their duty station; and that it was right to adjust pay by a language factor when jobs that did not require proficiency in a second language were matched with jobs that did, but wrong when the matching was with outside posts requiring but not compensating proficiency in a second language. The Tribunal subsequently dismissed the two complaints.

In the light of the Tribunal Judgement, ICSC, on the proposal of its secretariat, decided that, at the next survey at duty stations where the local language was not a working language of the organization, employers should be carefully surveyed to find out what bonus or other payments, if any, were made to staff members required to work in a working language of the organization; and that the results of that determination should be appropriately reflected in the pay scales established by the survey.

Common staff assessment scale

In keeping with a 1997 recommendation of the United Nations Joint Staff Pension Board for a biennial update of the common staff assessment scale for all staff categories, for the determination of pensionable remuneration levels, ICSC, at its fifty-second session, conducted an examination of tax changes at the seven duty stations between 1997 and 1999. Finding only minimal tax increases or decreases at the relevant income levels, ICSC recommended the continued applica-

tion of the current scale and its review during the next comprehensive review of pensionable remuneration, which, for work programme reasons, was postponed from 2002 to 2004.

Post adjustment

ICSC continued at its fifty-first session to review the operation of the post adjustment system. It considered the report of its Advisory Committee on Post Adjustment Questions on the subject and approved its recommendations on the methodology to be applied in the 2000 round of cost-of-living (place-to-place) surveys at headquarters duty stations, Berne (Switzerland) and Washington, D.C. Those recommendations related to the simplification of the post adjustment index structure; updating the list of items and specifications for the basket of goods and services; the procedures for the establishment of expenditure weights; the treatment of United States dollar-driven expenditures and housing data collected from staff; the procedures for price collection at headquarters duty stations; the selection of outlets; and the timetable for the place-to-place surveys.

Other remuneration issues

Conditions of service and compensation for non-Secretariat officials serving the General Assembly

In accordance with the schedule established by General Assembly resolution 35/221 [YUN 1980, p. 1173], the Secretary-General submitted a December report [A/C.5/55/29] on the five-year review of the conditions of service of the Chairman of the Advisory Committee on Administrative and Budgetary Questions (ACABQ) and of the ICSC Chairman and Vice-Chairman. The report noted that, as at 1 January 2000, the annual net compensation of the ACABQ and ICSC Chairmen represented 90.4 per cent of the annual net salaries of the referenced senior Secretariat officials' level, as against 97 per cent obtaining at the last comprehensive review in 1996. To restore that compensation relativity, the Secretary-General recommended, in addition to the cost-of-living increase due on 1 January 2001, a 3.1 per cent increase in the current remuneration levels of the three officials, with a corresponding adjustment to their pensionable remuneration.

Therefore, based on the estimated 7 per cent movement in the consumer price index for New York and the recommended 3.1 per cent adjustment, the pensionable remunerations of the ACABQ and ICSC Chairmen should be revised from $176,400 to $194,599 and, of the ICSC Vice-

Chairman, from $166,950 to $184,174, as from 1 January 2001.

By **resolution 55/238, section VII** (see p. 1300), of 23 December, the General Assembly took note of the Secretary-General's report, approved his suggestions and decided to examine the issue of compensation relativity in the context of the next five-year review.

Dependency allowances

In the light of its biennial review of dependency allowances for the Professional and higher categories conducted in 2000, ICSC examined the methodology for those allowances and their basic rationale and scope [A/55/30]. It recommended to the General Assembly an increase in the children's allowance and in the secondary dependant's allowance to reflect the 11.89 per cent increase in the value of tax abatements and social legislation payments that occurred between January 1998 and January 2000. Thus, the revised annual amounts for duty stations in the United States and in countries where dependency allowances were fixed in United States dollars would be: $1,936 for the children's allowance and $3,872 for the disabled children's allowance; and $693 for the secondary dependant's allowance, all effective 1 January 2001. The current list of duty stations where those allowances were payable in local currencies was to be maintained. The financial implications of those recommendations were estimated at $2.8 million.

Education grant

ICSC action. As requested by the General Assembly in resolution 54/238 [YUN 1999, p. 1321], ICSC reviewed the methodology for determining the education grant levels and the issue of harmonizing other organizations' education grant practices with those of the United Nations.

ICSC recommended to the Assembly to continue the education grant as a benefit payable to internationally recruited staff with expatriate status; to ask the organizations to draw to the attention of their governing bodies the issue of harmonizing the staff rules and regulations governing education grant payments along the lines of those of the United Nations; and that further consideration of the grant's scope and purpose be conducted under the ongoing overall review of the pay and benefits system.

ICSC further recommended that, in areas where education-related expenses were incurred in Belgian francs, Irish pounds, Italian lire, Swiss francs and United States dollars in the United States, the levels of maximum admissible expenses and the maximum grant should be set as shown in table 1 of annex IV to the ICSC report [A/55/30]; the maximum amount of admissible expenses and the maximum grant should remain at the current levels for the following currencies: Austrian schilling, deutsche mark, Danish krone, Finnish markka, French franc, Japanese yen, Netherlands guilder, Norwegian krone, pound sterling, Spanish peseta, Swedish krona and United States dollar for expenses incurred in educational institutions outside the United States; the flat rates for boarding to be taken into account within the maximum admissible educational expenses and the additional amounts for reimbursement of boarding costs over and above the maximum grant payable to staff members at designated duty stations should be revised as shown in table 2 of annex IV; and the amount of the special education grant for each disabled child should be equal to 100 percent of the revised amounts of maximum allowable expenses for the regular grant. All of the foregoing measures were to be applicable as from the school year in progress on 1 January 2001.

ICSC maintained the two separate United States dollar areas and the special measures for China and Indonesia, which would allow organizations to reimburse 75 per cent of actual expenses up to and not exceeding the maximum expenditure level in force for the United States dollar/inside the United States. It would review the trigger point for adjusting the education grant during the review of the methodology for determining the grant level.

ICSC noted that the system-wide cost implications of the proposed increases were estimated at approximately $860,000 per year in respect of the increase in maximum admissible expenditure level and $186,000 per year in respect of the increase in boarding costs.

OIOS report. Pursuant to General Assembly resolutions 48/218 B [YUN 1994, p. 1362] and 54/244 [YUN 1999, p. 1274], the Secretary-General transmitted, in September [A/55/352 & Corr.1], a report of the Office of Internal Oversight Services (OIOS) on its proactive investigation of the education grant entitlement. The report noted that, of 16 cases of alleged fraudulent education grant claims brought to the attention of OIOS between 1995 and 1999, 10 were substantiated and resulted in the termination of five staff members, in the administrative or disciplinary action of three others and in the resignation of two. Two cases were unsubstantiated, with the staff involved fully cleared, and four were still under investigation. The cases of fraud involved the misappropriation of UN funds totalling $265,000, with the individual cases ranging from several thousand dollars to over $69,000 in one case.

The report also noted that, in 1998, some 1,300 United Nations Headquarters staff members submitted education grant claims for some 3,300 dependants. In that year, payments exceeded $25 million, or an average of some $19,000 per staff member.

The investigation indicated that the education grant entitlement was an area for potential fraud, and its administration prone to error and open to opportunistic behaviour.

OIOS therefore recommended that serious consideration be given to providing the entitlement on a lump-sum basis for each country in which a school was located, making for a streamlined processing of claims, reduced administrative costs and the risk of fraud, and more time for spot checks. Alternatively, claims processing could be centralized in one office at each of the duty stations. Other recommendations called for staff members to be required to produce proof of a private-tuition instructor's competence; and for an examination of the rule permitting staff to receive a special education grant for a disabled child attending a regular educational institution and not receiving specialized instruction for his or her disability.

Other staff matters

Personnel policies

Human resources management

ICSC action. At its fifty first session, ICSC reviewed the draft framework for human resources management, which was completed by the working group created in 1998 [YUN 1998, p. 1309] for that purpose. The framework identified the internal and external forces impacting on human resources strategies. It contained six major human resources areas: ethics and standards of conduct for the international civil service, compensation and benefits, employment, career management, good governance and human resources information management. It had been strengthened by the definitions developed for each area, the identification of core and non-core areas, the linkages to other components and the underlying guiding principles. Core areas were those that bound the UN family together in order to avoid competition in the employment of staff resulting from differences in the compensation package, promote common values of the international civil service and facilitate staff mobility across the system.

ICSC adopted the framework, set out in annex II to its report [A/55/30], as a guide for its future work programme. It recommended that the framework be drawn to the attention of the governing bodies of common system organizations and serve as the basis of their future work on human resources policies and procedures.

Reports of Secretary General. Responding to General Assembly resolutions 53/221 [YUN 1999, p. 1324] and 54/248 [ibid., p. 1368], the Secretary-General submitted a 1 August report [A/55/253 & Corr.1] setting out a comprehensive human resources management implementation programme, constituting the next step to his 1997 reform initiatives [YUN 1997, p. 1389] for strategic change to strengthen the Organization's management systems. The report described work in progress and actions taken or envisaged to realize the goal set for each of the following areas: human resources planning; streamlined rules and procedures; recruitment, placement and promotion; mobility; contractual arrangements; the administration of justice; competencies and continuous learning; performance management; career development; and conditions of service. Also described were measures to enhance accountability mechanisms, monitoring and control procedures integral to the proposed reforms.

The Secretary-General requested specific Assembly action in support of his proposed reform initiatives on recruitment, placement and promotion; mobility; and the amendment to the staff rule covering central review bodies, as set out, respectively, in annexes II, III and X of his report.

In a 3 August report [A/55/270], the Secretary-General delineated the continuum between responsibility, authority and accountability and presented the elements of an integrated accountability system. He outlined the measures taken to address the concerns regarding the overall system, as highlighted in his 1994 report [YUN 1994, p. 1358]. They included: improvements in planning and budgeting to clarify responsibility and performance expectations; revision and streamlining of regulations, rules and administrative issuances; improvements in the procurement process; issuance of new bulletins on organizational structure; implementation of updated regulations and rules governing the conduct of staff; the creation of the Senior Management Group and other coordination mechanisms, and of OIOS; development of information systems, such as the Integrated Management Information System (IMIS), and updating of programme monitoring tools; implementation of the Performance Appraisal System (PAS); improved management training; the introduction of a performance management plan for departmental heads focusing on planned programme and management objectives, expected performance standards and a review of achievements; strengthened monitoring by the Department of Management and by OIOS; and the creation of an accountability panel to advise the Secretary-General on accountability matters from a systemic perspective.

The Secretary-General said the Assembly might wish to take note of the mechanisms in place since 1994, including those discussed in the report, which together constituted the comprehensive accountability system for the Organization.

ACABQ report. Having reviewed the Secretary-General's reports (see above), ACABQ, in October [A/55/499], recommended: giving priority to the systematic rejuvenation of the Secretariat by retaining younger staff in the light of the Organization's age profile, and to the full development of the Human Resources Management Information System at Headquarters and in the field, since many of the proposed reforms depended on system-wide information dissemination; taking the importance of institutional memory and expertise into account when implementing staff mobility; giving staff requested to remain on mission assignment longer than two years the same guarantees concerning returning to posts as for absences of up to two years; discontinuing 11-month contracts to meet continuing needs and instituting strict controls to prevent the future misuse of general temporary assistance funds; and, when ICSC proposals were before the Assembly, taking account of the indispensability of a competitive package of conditions of service to the successful achievement of mobility and recruitment goals. ACABQ urged the Secretary-General to move expeditiously forward with his proposal to transfer operational and transactional processes from the Office of Human Resources Management (OHRM) to programme managers and to include in annex I to the Secretary-General's 3 August report dealing with measures to ensure accountability an additional element, namely, access to an impartial, fair system of international administration of justice.

The General Assembly, by **decision 54/460 B** of 7 April, deferred consideration of the agenda item entitled "Human resources management" until its fifty-fifth (2000) session. On 23 December, it decided that the item remained for consideration at its resumed fifty-fifth (2001) session (**decision 55/458**) and that the Fifth Committee should continue to consider it at that session (**decision 55/455**).

Draft standards of conduct for the international civil service

At its fifty-first session [A/55/30], ICSC reviewed the draft standards of conduct for the international civil service, as updated by a working group, with the full participation of the Coordinating Committee for International Staff Unions and Associations of the United Nations System (CCISUA) and the Federation of International Civil Servants' Associations (FICSA). Following further ICSC revisions to the draft and subject to final comments from the legal advisers of the common system's organizations, to ensure consistency of those revisions with their legal instruments and legislative frameworks, ICSC adopted the draft as revised and circulated it to the organizations and staff associations for their comments. However, in view of the request by the Consultative Committee on Administrative Questions for an opportunity to present the organizations' comments, ICSC postponed finalizing the draft to 2001.

Staff composition

In his September annual report on the Secretariat's staff composition [A/55/427 & Corr.1], the Secretary-General updated information on changes in the desirable range of posts for Member States and described measures taken to ensure equitable representation at the senior and policy-making levels. As at 30 June 2000, Secretariat staff numbered 13,164, fewer by 1,155 than at 30 June 1999, due to the reclassification of the United Nations Joint Staff Pension Fund as an inter-organizational body and thus to the separate listing of its staff and to the discontinuance of reporting on locally recruited General Service staff holding indefinite special mission appointments.

Of the 13,164 Secretariat staff, 4,390 were in the Professional and higher categories, 7,977 were in the General Service and related categories and 797 were project personnel; 7,470 were paid from the regular budget and 5,694 from extrabudgetary sources.

Staff in posts subject to geographical distribution numbered 2,389, of whom 936 were female (an increase of 1.1 per cent compared to 1999). Twenty-one Member States remained unrepresented in all staff categories and eight were underrepresented (compared to 24 and 13, respectively, in 1999). Appointments to posts subject to geographical distribution between 1 July 1999 and 30 June 2000 totalled 141. Of those, 9 (6.4 per cent) were nationals of unrepresented Member States, 32 (22.7 per cent) of underrepresented Member States, 97 (68.8 per cent) of within-range Member States and 3 (2.1 per cent) of overrepresented Member States. Changes in representation status were the result of appointments or separations from service, adjustments to desirable ranges due to an increase or decrease in the number of posts subject to geographical distribution and changes in the number of Member States, in the scale of assessments, in population and in the status of individual staff members.

The report also detailed information on the demographic profile, as well as on Secretariat staff movement from 1 July 1999 to 30 June 2000, racial discrimination and forecasts of anticipated retirements in 2000-2004.

Gratis personnel

Pursuant to General Assembly resolution 51/243 [YUN 1997, p. 1469], the Secretary-General submitted four quarterly reports on the status of types I and II gratis personnel accepted by the United Nations, indicating, inter alia, their nationality, functions and duration of service. The periods covered were 1 October–31 December 1999 [A/C.5/54/51], 1 January–31 March [A/C.5/54/54], 1 April–30 June [A/C.5/55/13] and 1 July–30 September 2000 [A/55/728], which included the annual report for the period from 1 October 1999 to 30 September 2000.

Type I gratis personnel, serving under an established regime, included interns, associate experts, technical cooperation experts obtained on non-reimbursable loans, and gratis personnel who served with the United Nations Special Commission (UNSCOM) and, as at 17 December 1999, with the United Nations Monitoring, Verification and Inspection Commission (UNMOVIC), which replaced UNSCOM. Among the type II gratis personnel were a commander, economists, forensic investigation and anthropology officers, inspectors and investigators, laboratory technicians, logistics and medical officers, a nurse and a technical adviser on water resources.

In the annual report, the Secretary-General indicated that between 30 September 1999 and 30 September 2000, the overall number of type I gratis personnel decreased from 629 to 412 (34.5 per cent). During that period, all type I gratis personnel serving with UNMOVIC (25 on 1 January) were phased out; secretariat-wide associate experts decreased from 290 to 250 (14 per cent); the number of interns fell from 296 to 151 (49 per cent); and the number of technical cooperation experts decreased from 18 to 11 (39 per cent). Information on associate and technical cooperation experts and interns, formerly reported separately, were currently consolidated under IMIS.

During the same period, the number of type II gratis personnel decreased from 101 to 43, a reduction of 57 per cent, and 68 per cent if compared with 1998 data. The bulk of type II gratis personnel engaged during September 1999 to September 2000 were with the International Tribunal for the Former Yugoslavia (ICTY). At the end of December 1999, the 92 forensic experts engaged by ICTY for deployment in the Kosovo province of the Federal Republic of Yugoslavia were phased out. However, in response to the Tribunal's request, the Secretary-General, in January [A/54/734], authorized ICTY to accept gratis personnel to complete all forensic investigations. As at September 2000, the number of such experts engaged numbered 41. All type II gratis personnel (20, including the 15 who had been extended and not reported) engaged by the Field Administration and Logistics Division of the Department of Peacekeeping Operations (DPKO) were separated by 1 June 2000. The United Nations Conference on Trade and Development engaged two gratis personnel from 1 October 1999 to 30 September 2000, both of whom were extended for another year. The Economic and Social Commission for Western Asia retained one type II gratis personnel.

Annexed to the report were tables providing information on the number of engagements and separations of type II gratis personnel, their distribution as at 30 September 2000, compared to the previous year, by number, nationality and duration of service, the nature of the functions performed by department or office and the ratio of gratis personnel to regular staff in departments or offices that engaged them. Information was also provided on the evolution of type I gratis personnel.

GENERAL ASSEMBLY ACTION

Following receipt of the Secretary-General's last 1999 quarterly report [A/C.5/54/51], the General Assembly, by **decision 54/471** of 7 April 2000, on the recommendation of the Fifth Committee [A/54/827], deferred consideration of the question of gratis personnel provided by Governments and other entities until the second part of its resumed fifty-fourth (2000) session.

On 15 June [meeting 98], the Assembly, on the recommendation of the Fifth Committee [A/54/827/Add.1], adopted **resolution 54/264** without vote [agenda items 118 & 164].

Gratis personnel provided by Governments

The General Assembly,

Reaffirming its resolutions 51/243 of 15 September 1997, 52/234 of 26 June 1998 and 53/218 of 7 April 1999,

Having considered the reports of the Secretary-General and the related reports of the Advisory Committee on Administrative and Budgetary Questions,

1. *Takes note* of the reports of the Secretary-General and the related reports of the Advisory Committee on Administrative and Budgetary Questions;

2. *Endorses* the observations of the Advisory Committee in its report, in particular paragraphs 2 and 4, and requests that all future proposals by the Secretary-General on gratis personnel and the subsequent implementation of legislative mandates be in full compliance with relevant General Assembly resolutions and fully respect the relevant policies, procedures and regulations of the United Nations;

3. *Stresses* the need for an effective monitoring system in the Office of Human Resources Management of the Secretariat with regard to delegation of authority for gratis personnel to offices away from Headquarters;

4. *Notes with concern* the inaccurate information provided in paragraph 8 of the report of the Secretary-General and clarified in paragraph 7 of his subsequent report with regard to the type II gratis personnel not reported previously by the United Nations Environment Programme;

5. *Recalls* the existing mandates under the relevant General Assembly resolutions on gratis personnel;

6. *Reaffirms* that the circumstances in which the Secretary-General can accept gratis personnel shall be in strict compliance with the provisions of its resolution 51/243, in particular paragraphs 4 and 9, and its resolution 52/234, in particular paragraph 10;

7. *Expresses its concern* that detailed and comprehensive information on the use of gratis personnel in the case of the International Tribunal for the Prosecution of Persons Responsible for Serious Violations of International Humanitarian Law Committed in the Territory of the Former Yugoslavia since 1991 was not provided, and in this regard requests the Secretary-General to submit all future reports on gratis personnel in strict compliance with the provisions of paragraph 15 of its resolution 52/234;

8. *Decides* to continue, at the main part of its fifty-fifth session, its consideration of the question of gratis personnel provided by Governments.

Consultants and individual contractors

Report of Secretary-General. Pursuant to section VIII of General Assembly resolution 53/221 [YUN 1999, p. 1328], the Secretary-General submitted his annual report, in August [A/55/321], on the hiring and use of consultants and individual contractors in 1999. The report expanded on the format of previous reports, in accordance with requests in resolution 51/226, section VI [YUN 1997, p. 1463].

The Secretary-General noted that, while data were available for Headquarters, it had not been possible to present information that was comparable on a worldwide basis regarding the type and nature of contracts of consultants and individual contractors because such data would not be available until the full deployment in 2001 of IMIS (Release III) at all duty stations. The nine statistical tables presented in the annex to the report provided an overview of the use of such persons

in terms of their status as retired or not retired, gender, educational levels, the numbers engaged, nationality, purpose of engagement, the number and duration of contracts, fees, the contracting department or office, occupational grouping, performance evaluations and aggregate data for each duty station on institutional or corporate contractors engaged under contracts or subcontracts entered into directly with the employer institution. In 1999, 2,382 consultants and 886 individual contractors were engaged, accounting for 3,220 and 1,643 separate contracts, respectively. Fees for both totalled $28.9 million, a decrease of $2.6 million from the total reported for 1998.

JIU report. The Secretary-General, by a March note [A/55/59], transmitted to the General Assembly the JIU report on the effective implementation of Assembly policy directives on the use of consultants in the United Nations. Among its conclusions, JIU stated that there was no mechanism to facilitate the implementation of at least two out of seven basic principles contained in the administrative instruction governing the use of consultants [ST/AI/1997/7]; that the programme budget was the proper vehicle through which to address Member States' concerns, as well as problems identified and solutions recommended by external and internal oversight bodies; and that ACABQ and the Committee for Programme and Coordination (CPC) could significantly contribute to the process if provided with comprehensive information on the planned and past use of consultancy.

Pending the suggested expedition of the consolidated database on the inventory of staff skills and development of an electronic information system covering all UN substantive programmes, JIU recommended that, in the interim, the Secretary-General should instruct OHRM and the Office of Programme Planning, Budget and Accounts (OPPBA) to review all consultancy requests, OHRM to ascertain if the required expertise was available in the Secretariat and advise department and office heads accordingly, and OPPBA to advise them of cases of duplication with Secretariat work already completed or in progress. He should include in his introduction to the proposed programme budget information on the level of resources requested under "consultants and experts" compared with previous bienniums and establish clear operational procedures for the treatment of consultants' travel expenses, whether as a sub-item of consultancy appropriations or as part of the travel budget of a given organizational unit, to prevent distorting geographical balance when awarding contracts. ACABQ and CPC should include in their reports on the programme budget a detailed assessment of the situation as to the level of regular budget and extrabudgetary resources for consultants.

Other recommendations called on the Secretary-General to study different methodologies to achieve geographical balance in the use of consultants and, pending its outcome, the Assembly should ask him to use the desirable ranges for Professional staff financed through the regular budget as a norm for the geographical distribution of consultancies. The Secretary-General should include in his annual report on consultants certain comparative data and data breakdown by developing countries and/or regional groups, as well as separate data sets for participants in advisory meetings. He should ensure the timely availability to the permanent missions to the United Nations of information on planned consultancy requirements. The Assembly was to review and evaluate all aspects of policy and practice based on either an expanded report of the Secretary-General to be presented to its fifty-seventh (2002) session or an in-depth review by the OIOS Central Evaluation Unit.

In his comments on the JIU recommendations [A/55/59/Add.1], the Secretary-General said OHRM was in the second phase of implementing the skills inventory project. A specific monitoring mechanism would be required for the recommended electronic information system, regarding which management would conduct a needs assessment study. Closer scrutiny of consultancy requests would require OPPBA to establish a new monitoring mechanism whose cost could outweigh its benefits. The programme budget presentation, which included separating resource requirements for consultants and experts, was under constant review by the Secretariat, ACABQ and the Assembly. It would have been helpful if JIU had further addressed the issue of assessing the situation as to the level of resources for consultants. The suggested mechanisms for handling consultants' travel expenses could only provide information on the basis of which geographical distribution could be monitored and would not constitute an operational procedure. The Secretariat would continue to make every effort to recruit consultants from as wide a geographical area as possible. Efforts would be made to disseminate information on consultancy needs directly to Member States. In addition to noting the recommendations on data presentation in his annual reports on consultants, the Secretary-General said it would have been helpful if JIU had given some specifics for the recommended omnibus reporting in 2002.

Status of women in the Secretariat

In his January report to the Commission on the Status of Women [E/CN.6/2000/4], the Secretary-General provided a statistical update as at 30 November 1999 of the gender distribution of staff at the Professional and higher levels in the UN Secretariat and in the organizations of the UN common system. He also outlined his strategy for achieving gender equality in the Secretariat, indicating that the 2000 work programme would assign priority to the elaboration and implementation of gender action plans in individual departments and offices.

Responding to General Assembly resolution 54/139 [YUN 1999, p. 1334], the Secretary-General submitted a September report [A/55/399 & Corr.1] reviewing the status of women in the Secretariat. According to the report, the number of women on appointments subject to geographical distribution increased significantly at the D-1 level, from 16 (6.8 per cent) in June 1990 to 73 (35.8 per cent) in June 2000; and at the P-5 level, from 73 (15.8 per cent) to 151 (33.1 per cent), a more-than-double increase. Nonetheless, women's overall representation in the Professional and higher categories had been modest: 936 women (39.2 per cent) out of 2,389 staff on appointments subject to geographical distribution as at 30 June 2000, compared to 919 (38.1 per cent) out of 2,410 as at 30 June 1999 [YUN 1999, p. 1333]. The increase was consistent with the average annual rate of 1 per cent at which women's representation had increased over the preceding 10 years.

The number of women on appointments of one year or more had increased from 1,542 (35.8 per cent) on 30 June 1999 to 1,601 (36.5 per cent) on 30 June 2000, only a 0.7 per cent increase. The largest increase had been at the P-5 level, rising from 212 (30 per cent) to 242 (32.6 per cent). The highest concentration of women remained at the P-3 level, followed by those at the P-4 level. Gender balance was finally realized at the P-2 level, where the percentage of women had risen from 48.2 per cent on 30 June 1999 to 50.1 per cent on 30 June 2000. While the percentage at the D-1 level neared a critical mass at 29.3 per cent, the overall increase at the senior and policy-making levels (D-1 and above) had been slight, from 24.4 per cent to only 24.7 per cent. The slowdown since the Secretary-General's 1999 report [YUN 1999, p. 1333] was cause for concern, particularly as the number of staff appointed and promoted to those levels had increased. Although the number of women at the P-4 and D-2 levels had increased slightly (from 454 to 458 and from 19 to 21, respectively), the overall percentage of women at those levels had declined since June 1999 (from 33.7 per cent to 33.5 per cent and from 21.6 per cent to 20.8 per cent, respectively) owing to the significantly greater increase in the number of men at those levels.

The Secretary-General asked for the cooperation of department and office heads in further elaborating the gender component of the 1999-2001 departmental action plans on human resources management. He emphasized that the managers' record in improving gender balance should be a critical factor in the appraisal of their performance. The Steering Committee for the Improvement of the Status of Women in the Secretariat also monitored the progress of departments and offices in meeting the goal of 50/50 gender distribution in the staffing of Professional and higher-level posts. OHRM had been working with a number of departments and offices to develop and implement programmes on various gender-related issues, including training on gender sensitivity and mainstreaming. Issues currently being addressed were the development of common policies on retaining women staff, especially through spousal employment assistance, the introduction of flexible working time and workplace arrangements, and the designation of focal points for women in UN peacekeeping missions.

Elements of the Secretary-General's strategy to be accorded priority in 2001 included the identification of sources of women candidates for vacancies in departmental action plans, the evaluation of progress made in improving women's representation based on the implementation of gender action plans, the refinement of strategies to increase the supply of suitably qualified women candidates and the examination of factors impeding Professional and General Service staff mobility. Increasing attention would be paid to implementing the work/family agenda and designing measures for enhancing the career development of General Service staff, the majority of whom were women. The Secretary-General warned, however, that progress in achieving gender equality would continue to be slow without the sustained support of Member States in proposing national recruitment sources for women candidates.

GENERAL ASSEMBLY ACTION

On 4 December [meeting 81], the General Assembly, on the recommendation of the Third (Social, Humanitarian and Cultural) Committee [A/55/595 & Corr.1,2], adopted **resolution 55/69** without vote [agenda item 107].

Improvement of the status of women in the United Nations system

The General Assembly,

Recalling Articles 1 and 101 of the Charter of the United Nations, as well as Article 8, which provides that the United Nations shall place no restrictions on the eligibility of men and women to participate in any capacity and under conditions of equality in its principal and subsidiary organs,

Recalling also the goal, contained in the Platform for Action adopted by the Fourth World Conference on Women, of the achievement of overall gender equality, particularly at the Professional level and above, by the year 2000,

Recalling further its resolution 54/139 of 17 December 1999 on the improvement of the status of women in the Secretariat,

Taking note of Commission on Human Rights resolution 2000/46 of 20 April 2000 on integrating the human rights of women throughout the United Nations system, in particular paragraph 11, in which the Commission recognizes that gender mainstreaming will strongly benefit from the enhanced and full participation of women, including at the higher levels of decision-making in the United Nations system,

Taking note also of the recommendations made by the women heads of State and Government and women heads of United Nations agencies at their meeting, held on 5 September 2000, just prior to the Millennium Summit of the United Nations, to improve female representation within the United Nations system, especially at senior levels,

Welcoming the decision of the Secretary-General to include, in the performance appraisal of managers, information on the opportunities presented for the selection of women candidates and on progress made in improving women's representation, including efforts made to identify women candidates,

Taking into account the continuing lack of representation or under-representation of women from certain countries, in particular from developing countries, including least developed countries and small island developing States, and from countries with economies in transition,

Taking note with appreciation of those departments and offices that have achieved the goal of gender balance, as well as of those departments that have met or exceeded the goal of 50 per cent in the selection of women candidates for vacant posts in the past year,

Welcoming progress made in improving the representation of women at some levels of the Secretariat, but expressing concern that progress in improving the representation of women at the senior and policy-making levels has slowed, that the percentage of women appointed and promoted to one particular level has declined, and also expressing concern at the slow incremental pace at which the overall representation of women in the Secretariat has increased,

Expressing concern that there are currently no women acting as special representatives or envoys,

Noting that the statistics on the representation of women in the organizations of the United Nations system are not fully up to date,

1. *Takes note with appreciation* of the report of the Secretary-General and the actions contained therein;

2. *Reaffirms* the urgent goal of achieving 50/50 gender distribution in all categories of posts within the United Nations system, especially at the senior and policy-making levels, with full respect for the principle of equitable geographical distribution, in conformity

with Article 101, paragraph 3, of the Charter of the United Nations, and also taking into account the continuing lack of representation or under-representation of women from certain countries, in particular developing countries and countries with economies in transition;

3. *Welcomes:*

(a) The ongoing personal commitment of the Secretary-General to meeting the goal of gender equality and his assurance that gender balance will be given the highest priority in his continuing efforts to bring about a new management culture in the Organization, including full implementation of the special measures for the achievement of gender equality;

(b) The pledge of the executive heads of the organizations of the United Nations system to intensify their efforts to meet the gender equality goals set out in the Beijing Declaration and Platform for Action;

(c) The actions agreed upon by the General Assembly at its twenty-third special session, entitled "Women 2000: gender equality, development and peace for the twenty-first century", to ensure the full and equal participation of women at all levels of decision-making in the United Nations system;

(d) The inclusion of the objective of improving gender balance in action plans on human resources management for individual departments and offices, and encourages further cooperation between heads of departments and offices, the Special Adviser on Gender Issues and Advancement of Women and the Office of Human Resources Management of the Secretariat in the implementation of these plans, which include specific targets and strategies for improving the representation of women in individual departments;

(e) The designation of focal points for women in United Nations peacekeeping operations, and requests the Secretary-General to ensure that the focal points are designated at a sufficiently high level and enjoy full access to senior management in the mission area;

(f) The continued provision of specific training programmes on gender mainstreaming and gender issues in the workplace, tailored to meet the special needs of individual departments, commends those heads of departments and offices who have launched gender training for their managers and staff, and strongly encourages those who have not yet organized such training to do so by the end of the biennium;

4. *Regrets* that the goal of 50/50 gender distribution will not be met by the end of the year 2000, and urges the Secretary-General to redouble his efforts to realize significant progress towards this goal in the near future;

5. *Expresses concern* that, in five departments and offices of the Secretariat, women still account for less than 30 per cent of staff, and encourages the Secretary-General to intensify his efforts to meet the goal of gender balance within all departments and offices of the Secretariat;

6. *Requests* the Secretary-General, in order, inter alia, to achieve the goal of 50/50 gender distribution with full respect for the principle of equitable geographical distribution, in conformity with Article 101, paragraph 3, of the Charter:

(a) To identify and attract suitably qualified women candidates, in particular in developing countries and countries with economies in transition, in other Member States that are unrepresented or under-represented in the Secretariat and in occupations in which women are under-represented;

(b) To continue to monitor closely the progress made by departments and offices in meeting the goal of gender balance and to ensure that the appointment and promotion of suitably qualified women will be no less than 50 per cent of all appointments and promotions until the goal of 50/50 gender distribution is met, inter alia, through full implementation of the special measures for women and the further development of monitoring and assessment mechanisms to meet targets for improving women's representation;

(c) To enable the Office of the Special Adviser on Gender Issues and Advancement of Women to monitor effectively and facilitate progress in the implementation of the departmental action plans for the achievement of gender balance and the special measures for women, inter alia, by ensuring access to the information required to carry out that work;

(d) To intensify his efforts to create, within existing resources, a gender-sensitive work environment supportive of the needs of his staff, both women and men, including the development of policies for flexible working time, flexible workplace arrangements and child-care and elder-care needs, as well as the provision of more comprehensive information to prospective candidates and new recruits on employment opportunities for spouses and the expansion of gender-sensitivity training in all departments, offices and duty stations;

(e) To strengthen further the policy against harassment, including sexual harassment, inter alia, by ensuring the full implementation of the guidelines for its application at Headquarters and in the field;

7. *Strongly encourages* the Secretary-General to appoint more women as special representatives and envoys to pursue good offices on his behalf, especially in matters related to peacekeeping, peace-building, preventive diplomacy and economic and social development, as well as in operational activities, including appointment as resident coordinators, and to appoint more women to other high-level positions;

8. *Encourages* the Secretary-General and the executive heads of the organizations of the United Nations system to continue to develop common approaches for retaining women, inter-agency mobility and the improvement of career development opportunities;

9. *Strongly encourages* Member States:

(a) To support the efforts of the United Nations and the specialized agencies to achieve the goal of 50/50 gender distribution, especially at senior and policy-making levels, by identifying and regularly submitting more women candidates for appointment to intergovernmental, judicial and expert bodies, by identifying and proposing national recruitment sources that will assist the organizations of the United Nations system in identifying suitable women candidates, in particular from developing countries and countries with economies in transition, and by encouraging more women to apply for positions within the Secretariat, the specialized agencies, funds and programmes and the regional commissions, including positions in areas in which women are under-represented, such as peacekeeping, peace-building and other non-traditional areas;

(b) To identify women candidates for assignment to peacekeeping missions and to improve the representation of women in military and civilian police contingents;

10. _Requests_ the Secretary-General to report on the implementation of the present resolution, inter alia, by providing up-to-date statistics on the number and percentage of women in all organizational units and at all levels throughout the United Nations system, and on the implementation of departmental action plans for the achievement of gender balance, to the Commission on the Status of Women at its forty-fifth session and to the General Assembly at its fifty-sixth session.

Regulations governing the status, basic rights and duties of the Secretary-General, non-Secretariat officials and experts on mission

In response to General Assembly resolution 52/252 [YUN 1998, p. 1318], the Secretary-General submitted for the Assembly's approval proposed draft regulations [A/54/695] governing the status, basic rights and duties of officials other than Secretariat officials performing services for the United Nations on a substantially full-time basis and experts on mission (annex I). The draft regulations were to form part of the terms of appointment of such officials, appointed through Assembly action or by other representative bodies. Also annexed were the draft regulation texts, together with a commentary to serve as an official guide on the scope and application of the individual regulations (annex II).

The report cited the relevant provisions of the 1946 Convention on the Privileges and Immunities of the United Nations, adopted by Assembly resolution 22 A (I) [YUN 1946-47, p. 100], as the basis for the special status of the above-described officials and revised article I of the Staff Regulations of the United Nations and chapter I of the 100 series of the Staff Rules, as revised with effect from 1 January 1999, as the bases for the proposed draft regulations.

Also in response to resolution 52/252, the Secretary-General submitted a February 2000 report [A/54/710] regarding the previously proposed development of a separate set of regulations and rules applicable to the Secretary-General of the United Nations. He stated that, in reviewing the Charter of the United Nations for that purpose, it had become apparent that, with the exception of the oath of office, the Charter provisions relating to the Secretary-General appropriately addressed his status, basic rights and duties. In view of those provisions and with the understanding that the Secretary-General would continue orally to make the declaration of office currently contained in staff regulation 1.1 (b) at

a public Assembly meeting, the Secretary-General believed that there was no need for additional regulations and rules as had been proposed.

Following receipt of the Secretary-General's report [A/54/695] during its resumed fifty-fourth (2000) session, the General Assembly, by **decision 54/472** of 7 April 2000, deferred consideration of the question of the proposed regulations governing the status, basic rights and duties of officials other than Secretariat officials and experts on mission until its fifty-fifth (2000) session.

On 23 December [meeting 89], the Assembly, on the recommendation of the Fifth Committee [A/55/690], adopted **resolution 55/221** without vote [agenda items 116 & 123].

> **Proposed regulations governing the status, basic rights and duties of officials other than Secretariat officials and experts on mission and regulations governing the status, basic rights and duties of the Secretary-General**
>
> _The General Assembly,_
>
> _Having considered_ the reports of the Secretary-General on the proposed regulations governing the status, basic rights and duties of officials other than Secretariat officials and experts on mission and on the regulations governing the status, basic rights and duties of the Secretary-General,
>
> 1. _Requests_ the Secretary-General to undertake consultations on the proposed regulations with the officials referred to in paragraph 1 (a) of his report on proposed regulations governing the status, basic rights and duties of officials other than Secretariat officials and experts on mission, in particular those who are elected by the General Assembly and its subsidiary organs, and to report thereon to the Assembly at its resumed fifty-fifth session, including on the following elements:
>
> (a) The compatibility of the proposed regulations with the statutes governing the officials referred to above;
>
> (b) The possible impact, if any, of the proposed regulations on the independence of those expert bodies;
>
> (c) The accountability mechanisms envisaged to enforce the proposed regulations;
>
> 2. _Also requests_ the Secretary-General, in the context of the report mentioned in paragraph 1 above, to submit additional information on whether the proposed regulations ensure the impartiality, neutrality, objectivity and accountability of the personnel referred to in paragraph 1 (b) of the report.

Staff rules and regulations

In accordance with staff regulation 12.3 providing that the full text of provisional staff rules and amendments should be reported annually to the General Assembly, the Secretary-General did so in his July report [A/55/168], which set out in an annex the amendments to the 100 and 200 series of the Staff Rules. The rationale for the amendments, which were of a technical nature, was also provided. The amendments to the 100 series related to the official travel of staff members on family visits, on separation from service, and authorized for medical, safety or security reasons or in other appropriate cases; official travel of a staff member's eligible family members; commutation of accrued annual leave; and last day for pay purposes. The amendments to the 200 series related to sick leave, official travel of project personnel, official travel of family members, family visit travel and appeals.

The Secretary-General recommended that the Assembly take note of the amendments, which he proposed to implement as from 1 January 2001.

Safety and security

SECURITY COUNCIL ACTION

On 9 February [meeting 4100], following consultations among Security Council members, the President made statement **S/PRST/2000/4** on behalf of the Council:

The Security Council is gravely concerned at continued attacks against United Nations and associated personnel, and humanitarian personnel, which are in violation of international law, including international humanitarian law.

The Council recalls its resolution 1265(1999) of 17 September 1999, and reaffirms the statements by its President of 31 March 1993, on the safety of United Nations forces and personnel deployed in conditions of strife, of 12 March 1997, on condemnation of attacks on United Nations personnel, of 19 June 1997, on the use of force against refugees and civilians in conflict situations, and of 29 September 1998, on protection for humanitarian assistance to refugees and others in conflict situations. The Council also recalls General Assembly resolution 54/192 of 17 December 1999, on the safety and security of humanitarian personnel and protection of United Nations personnel.

The Council further recalls the report of the Secretary-General on the strengthening of the coordination of emergency humanitarian assistance of the United Nations, and the addendum thereto, on the safety and security of humanitarian personnel and protection of United Nations personnel, and looks forward to the report of the Secretary-General pursuant to resolution 54/192 to be submitted to the General Assembly in May 2000, which should contain a detailed analysis and recommendations addressing the scope of legal protection under the Convention on the Safety of United Nations and Associated Personnel of 9 December 1994.

The Council notes with satisfaction the entry into force of the Convention on the Safety of United Nations and Associated Personnel, recognizes its importance for addressing the security of such personnel and recalls the relevant principles contained therein. The Council encourages all States to become party to and respect fully their obligations under the relevant instruments, including the abovementioned Convention.

The Council recalls that, on a number of occasions, it has condemned attacks and the use of force against United Nations and associated personnel, and humanitarian personnel. It strongly deplores the fact that incidents of violence have continued, leading to a rising toll of casualties among United Nations, associated and humanitarian personnel. The Council strongly condemns the acts of murder and various forms of physical and psychological violence, including abduction, hostage-taking, kidnapping, harassment and illegal arrest and detention to which such personnel have been subjected, as well as acts of destruction and looting of their property, all of which are unacceptable.

The Council also recalls that the primary responsibility for the security and protection of United Nations and associated personnel, and humanitarian personnel, lies with the host State. The Council urges States and non-State parties to respect fully the status of United Nations and associated personnel, and to take all appropriate steps, in accordance with the purposes and principles of the Charter of the United Nations and the rules of international law, to ensure the safety and security of United Nations and associated personnel, and humanitarian personnel, and underlines the importance of unhindered access to populations in need.

The Council urges States to fulfil their responsibility to act promptly and effectively in their domestic legal systems to bring to justice all those responsible for attacks and other acts of violence against such personnel, and to enact effective national legislation as required for that purpose.

The Council will continue to stress in its resolutions the imperative for humanitarian assistance missions and personnel to have safe and unimpeded access to civilian populations and, in this context, is prepared to consider taking all appropriate measures at its disposal to ensure the safety and security of such personnel.

The Council welcomes the inclusion as a war crime in the Rome Statute of the International Criminal Court of attacks intentionally directed against personnel involved in a humanitarian assistance or peacekeeping mission, as long as they are entitled to the protection given to civilians under the international law of armed conflict, and notes the role that the Court could play in bringing to justice those responsible for serious violations of international humanitarian law.

The Council expresses the view that improving the security of United Nations and associated personnel, and humanitarian personnel, may require, inter alia, the development and strengthening of all aspects of the current safety and security regime in place, as well as the adoption of effective action to address the impunity of those who commit crimes against such personnel.

The Council recognizes the importance of issuing clear, appropriate and feasible mandates for peacekeeping operations, to ensure that they are applied in a timely, efficient and objective manner, and of ensuring that all new and ongoing United Nations field operations, include appropriate modalities for the safety and security of United Nations and associated personnel, and humanitarian personnel. The Council underscores the fact that United Nations personnel have the right to act in self-defence.

The Council encourages the Secretary-General to complete the process of conducting a general and comprehensive review of security in peacekeeping operations, with a view to elaborating and undertaking further specific and practical measures to increase the safety and security of United Nations and associated personnel, and humanitarian personnel.

The Council considers it important that a comprehensive security plan be developed for every peacekeeping and humanitarian operation and that, during early elaboration and implementation of that plan, Member States and the Secretariat cooperate fully in order to ensure, inter alia, an open and immediate exchange of information on security issues.

The Council, bearing in mind the need to reinforce the responsibility of the host State for the physical security of United Nations and associated personnel, also underlines the importance of including in each status-of-forces agreement and status-of-missions agreement specific and practical measures based on the provisions of the Convention on the Safety of United Nations and Associated Personnel.

The Council recalls the obligations of all United Nations personnel and associated personnel, and humanitarian personnel, to observe and respect the national laws of the host State in accordance with international law and the Charter.

The Council believes it is essential to continue to strengthen security arrangements, to improve their management, and to allocate adequate resources to the safety and security of United Nations and associated personnel, and humanitarian personnel.

The Council President, by a November note [S/2000/1133], circulated a 24 October letter from the CCISUA and FICSA presidents, transmitting a petition signed by over 12,000 staff members asking for a special Council meeting to address safety and security problems faced by UN staff and associated personnel, especially on mission assignments.

Reports of Secretary-General (May and October). In response to General Assembly resolution 54/192 [YUN 1999, p. 1336], the Secretary-General issued a note in May [A/C.5/54/56], a report in October [A/55/494] and another in November (see p. 1347). In May, he proposed the establishment, under the regular budget, of a full-time post of United Nations Security Coordinator at the Assistant Secretary-General level, to respond to the most immediate needs for strengthening the security and safety of UN system personnel in the field. He would report on the associated cost requirements in the context of the budget perform-

ance report for the 2000-2001 biennium and submit to the Assembly a comprehensive plan for strengthening personnel security and safety in due course.

The Assembly, by **decision 54/462 B** of 15 June, deferred consideration of the Secretary-General's note on strengthening UN security coordination to its fifty-fifth session.

In October, the Secretary-General cited incidents of threats against UN and associated personnel that had occurred between 1 July 1999 and 30 June 2000, and gave a comprehensive account of the existing security management structure at Headquarters, at UN system organizations and in the field, as well as of recent initiatives for improvement.

The Secretary-General said the threats against UN personnel took the form of murder, physical assault and verbal abuse; abductions and hostage-taking; illegal arrests and detentions; storming and occupation of UN premises; and destruction and seizure or looting of UN vehicles and other property. Threats to life and of bodily injury were posed also by mines and unexploded ordnance. In addition, staff were subjected to routine denial of visas and the imposition of travel restrictions on certain of them based on nationality. To date, only three of the 177 cases of violent death of UN personnel had been brought to justice. The report's annex II listed 26 civilian personnel who had lost their lives since 1 July 1999, indicating their nationality, the employing UN agency, and the date, place and cause of death. Annex III chronologically listed 40 staff members who remained under arrest and detention or were missing as at 30 June 2000; the first on the list had been missing since 20 April 1980.

The responsibilities of the Coordinator's Office encompassed all security-related policy and procedural matters, including: ensuring a coherent UN response to any emergency in UN areas of operation; formulating recommendations for safeguarding UN staff and eligible dependants; coordinating, planning and implementing interagency security and safety programmes and training; acting as focal point for inter-agency cooperation on security matters; consulting organizations whose field operations would be affected by a security decision; assessing, on a continuing basis, the extent to which UN operations worldwide were vulnerable to security problems; and reviewing security plans for duty stations to ensure that each had an adequate state of preparedness.

The Coordinator's Office was also responsible for deciding on the relocation or evacuation of staff and their dependants from insecure areas; managing the malicious acts insurance policy, covering 30,000 staff in 78 duty stations; dealing with incidents of hostage-taking, arrest and detention of staff; developing and conducting security stress management training; investigating cases of staff deaths under suspicious circumstances; and coordinating security at 150 duty stations with 70,000 civilian staff and their dependants.

The operating budget of the Coordinator's Office was funded through cost-sharing arrangements among the organizations participating in the UN security management system, with the UN regular budget bearing approximately 18 per cent of the costs totalling $650,880 for 1999. A trust fund for voluntary contributions, set up in 1998, supplemented existing inter-agency funding mechanisms. As at 1 August 2000, the fund had received a total of only $1,210,500 and pledges from four countries.

The Secretary-General reported the appointment of the UN Security Coordinator, currently a senior official at the Under-Secretary-General level. Pending submission of proposals for the full requirements of the Office of the United Nations Security Coordinator for the 2002-2003 biennium, he proposed, as an interim measure, the strengthening of that Office at Headquarters and in the field, effective 1 January 2001, through specific resource requirements within the 2000-2001 programme budget amounting to $2,776,900, as detailed in annex I to the report.

Security arrangements of UN system organizations involved the appointment of a focal point responsible for security management within each organization, regular contact with its field offices and joint inter-agency security assessment missions, and liaising with the Coordinator's Office.

At field duty stations, the country-specific security plan was the primary tool for security preparedness. Each plan, updated annually, defined security responsibilities and actions to be taken in response to a security crisis, and provided for the internal relocation of locally recruited staff and their dependants to a safe area.

ACABQ report. Having examined the Secretary-General's October report [A/55/494], ACABQ, in December [A/55/658], pointed to the lack of information on lessons learned and measures taken to ensure accountability. It recommended against the proposed establishment of an Assistant Secretary-General post, as well as the support General Service post, and that consideration be given to relocating the Security Coordinator's Office within the Office of Central Support Services. In the context of the review of the proposed 2002-2003 programme budget, consideration might be given to upgrading the post of Deputy Security Coordinator from D-1 to D-2. ACABQ

supported the interim proposals for the establishment, effective 1 January 2001, of two P-5 and six P-4 level posts, with appropriate support staff at Headquarters; and six P-4, four P-3 and 20 local level posts for the field. It recommended that the request for 10 additional field security officers and 20 additional local level posts, which lacked supporting detail, be considered in the context of the proposed 2002-2003 programme budget. Consequently, the corresponding reduction in requirements would amount to $1,005,700.

In view of the foregoing, ACABQ recommended approval of an additional appropriation of $646,000 under section 30, Special expenses, of the 2000-2001 programme budget, and an additional appropriation of $95,600 under section 32, Staff assessment, to be offset by an equivalent amount under income section I, Income from staff assessment.

(For General Assembly action on the foregoing Secretary-General's report and related ACABQ comments, see **resolution 55/238, section II** (p. 1300).)

Report of Secretary-General (November). The Secretary-General, in November [A/55/637], analysed the scope of legal protection under the 1994 Convention on the Safety of United Nations and Associated Personnel, adopted by General Assembly resolution 49/59 [YUN 1994, p. 1289], which entered into force in 1999 [YUN 1999, p. 1336], as it applied in practice to UN operations, UN and associated personnel, and humanitarian and locally recruited personnel, and underscored the Convention's limitations. He recalled that, in his 1999 report to the Council [A/54/619-S/1999/957], he had pointed to the emerging consensus among Member States on the Convention's inadequacies and had recommended the development of a protocol extending the scope of its legal protection to all UN and associated personnel not currently covered.

Pending the conclusion of such a protocol, which might or might not be ratified by some or all of the States parties to the Convention, the Secretary-General suggested three measures for the Assembly's consideration, which, within the parameters of the Convention, would strengthen its protective regime and give it full effect. They included: a procedure to initiate a declaration by the Security Council or the Assembly of an exceptional risk to the safety of UN personnel, to bring within the ambit of the Convention's protective regime all UN operations conducted in risky, dangerous or volatile environments; designating the Secretary-General as the certifying authority for purposes of attesting to the fact of a "declaration" or an "agreement", and to the status of any of the UN and associated personnel; and incorporating the key provisions of the Convention in the status-of-forces or status-of-mission agreements concluded between the United Nations and States in whose territories peacekeeping operations were deployed.

GENERAL ASSEMBLY ACTION

On 19 December [meeting 86], the General Assembly adopted **resolution 55/175** [draft: A/55/L.64 & Add.1] without vote [agenda item 20].

Safety and security of humanitarian personnel and protection of United Nations personnel

The General Assembly,

Reaffirming its resolution 46/182 of 19 December 1991 on strengthening of the coordination of humanitarian emergency assistance of the United Nations,

Recalling its resolutions 53/87 of 7 December 1998 and 54/192 of 17 December 1999 on safety and security of humanitarian personnel and protection of United Nations personnel, as well as resolutions 52/167 of 16 December 1997 on safety and security of humanitarian personnel and 52/126 of 12 December 1997 on protection of United Nations personnel,

Taking note of the report of the Secretary-General on protection of civilians in armed conflicts, and of Security Council resolutions 1265(1999) of 17 September 1999 and 1296(2000) of 19 April 2000 and the recommendations made therein, as well as the statements by the President of the Security Council of 30 November 1999 on the role of the Security Council in the prevention of armed conflicts, of 13 January 2000 on humanitarian assistance to refugees in Africa, of 9 February 2000 on protection of United Nations personnel, associated personnel and humanitarian personnel in conflict zones, and of 9 March 2000 on humanitarian aspects of issues before the Security Council, and in this context also noting the range of views expressed during all open debates of the Security Council on these issues,

Taking note also of the report of the Special Committee on Peacekeeping Operations on the report of the Panel on United Nations Peace Operations and the report of the Secretary-General on the implementation of the report of the Panel,

Reaffirming the need to promote and ensure respect for the principles and rules of international humanitarian law,

Deeply concerned by the growing number of complex humanitarian emergencies in the past few years, in particular in armed conflicts and in post-conflict situations, which have dramatically increased the loss of human lives, in particular of civilians, the suffering of victims, flows of refugees and internally displaced persons, as well as material destruction, which disrupt the development efforts of the countries affected, in particular those of developing countries,

Concerned by the increasingly difficult context in which humanitarian assistance takes place in some areas, in particular the continuous erosion, in many cases, of respect for the principles and rules of international humanitarian law,

Deeply concerned by the dangers and security risks faced by humanitarian personnel and United Nations and its associated personnel at the field level, and mindful of the need to improve the current security management system in order to improve their safety and security,

Strongly deploring the rising toll of casualties among national and international humanitarian personnel and United Nations and its associated personnel in complex humanitarian emergencies, in particular in armed conflicts and in post-conflict situations,

Strongly condemning the acts of murder and other forms of violence, rape and sexual assault, intimidation, armed robbery, abduction, hostage-taking, kidnapping, harassment and illegal arrest and detention to which those participating in humanitarian operations are increasingly exposed, as well as attacks on humanitarian convoys and acts of destruction and looting of their property,

Strongly condemning also all recent incidents in many parts of the world in which humanitarian personnel have been deliberately targeted, and expressing profound regret at the deaths of all United Nations and other personnel involved in the provision of humanitarian assistance,

Recalling that primary responsibility under international law for the security and protection of humanitarian personnel and United Nations and its associated personnel lies with the Government hosting a United Nations operation conducted under the Charter of the United Nations or its agreements with relevant organizations,

Urging all other parties involved in armed conflicts, in compliance with their obligations under the 1949 Geneva Conventions and the Additional Protocols thereto, of 8 June 1977, to ensure the security and protection of all humanitarian and United Nations and its associated personnel,

Expressing concern that the occurrence of attacks and threats against humanitarian personnel and United Nations and its associated personnel is a factor that increasingly restricts the ability of the Organization to provide assistance and protection to civilians in fulfilment of its mandate and Charter,

Welcoming the inclusion of attacks intentionally directed against personnel involved in a humanitarian assistance or peacekeeping mission in accordance with the Charter as a war crime in the Rome Statute of the International Criminal Court, adopted on 17 July 1998, and noting the role that the Court could play in bringing to justice those responsible for serious violations of international humanitarian law,

Noting that the Convention on the Safety of United Nations and Associated Personnel, which entered into force on 15 January 1999, has been ratified by 46 Member States as at the present date,

Reaffirming the fundamental requirement that appropriate modalities for the safety and security of humanitarian and United Nations and its associated personnel be incorporated into all new and ongoing United Nations field operations,

Emphasizing the need to give further consideration to the safety and security of locally recruited humanitarian personnel, who account for the majority of casualties, and United Nations and its associated personnel,

Commending the courage and commitment of those who take part in humanitarian operations, often at great personal risk,

Guided by the relevant provisions on protection contained in the Convention on the Privileges and Immunities of the United Nations of 13 February 1946, the Convention on the Privileges and Immunities of the Specialized Agencies of 21 November 1947, the Convention on the Safety of United Nations and Associated Personnel, the Fourth Geneva Convention of 12 August 1949 and the Additional Protocols, and Amended Protocol II to the Convention on Prohibitions and Restrictions on the Use of Certain Conventional Weapons Which May Be Deemed to Be Excessively Injurious or to Have Indiscriminate Effects of 10 October 1980,

1. *Takes note* of the report of the Secretary General on safety and security of United Nations personnel;

2. *Urges* all States to take the necessary measures to ensure the full and effective implementation of the relevant principles and rules of international humanitarian law, as well as relevant provisions of human rights law related to the safety and security of humanitarian personnel and United Nations personnel;

3. *Also urges* all States to take the necessary measures to ensure the safety and security of humanitarian personnel and United Nations and its associated personnel and to respect and ensure respect for the inviolability of United Nations premises, which are essential to the continuation and successful implementation of United Nations operations;

4. *Calls upon* all Governments and parties in complex humanitarian emergencies, in particular in armed conflicts and in post-conflict situations, in countries in which humanitarian personnel are operating, in conformity with the relevant provisions of international law and national laws, to cooperate fully with the United Nations and other humanitarian agencies and organizations and to ensure the safe and unhindered access of humanitarian personnel in order to allow them to perform efficiently their task of assisting the affected civilian population, including refugees and internally displaced persons;

5. *Strongly condemns* any act or failure to act which obstructs or prevents humanitarian personnel and United Nations personnel from discharging their humanitarian functions, or which entails being subjected to threats, the use of force or physical attack frequently resulting in injury or death, and affirms the need to hold accountable those who commit such acts and, for that purpose, the need to enact national legislation, as appropriate;

6. *Urges* all States to ensure that any threat or act of violence committed against humanitarian personnel on their territory is fully investigated and to take all appropriate measures, in accordance with international law and national legislation, to ensure that the perpetrators of such acts are prosecuted;

7. *Requests* the Secretary-General to take the necessary measures to ensure full respect for the human rights, privileges and immunities of United Nations and other personnel carrying out activities in fulfilment of the mandate of a United Nations operation and to continue to consider ways and means in which to strengthen the protection of United Nations and other personnel carrying out activities in fulfilment of the mandate of a United Nations operation, notably by seeking the inclusion, in negotiations of headquarter and other mission agreements concerning United Na-

tions and its associated personnel, of the applicable conditions contained in the Convention on the Privileges and Immunities of the United Nations, the Convention on the Privileges and Immunities of the Specialized Agencies and the Convention on the Safety of United Nations and Associated Personnel;

8. *Calls upon* all States to provide adequate and prompt information in the event of arrest or detention of humanitarian personnel or United Nations personnel, to afford them the necessary medical assistance and to allow independent medical teams to visit and examine the health of those detained, and urges them to take the necessary measures to ensure the speedy release of United Nations and other personnel carrying out activities in fulfilment of the mandate of a United Nations operation who have been arrested or detained in violation of their immunity, in accordance with the relevant conventions referred to in the present resolution and applicable international humanitarian law;

9. *Calls upon* all other parties involved in armed conflicts, in compliance with their obligations under the 1949 Geneva Conventions and the Additional Protocols thereto, to ensure the safety and protection of humanitarian personnel and United Nations and its associated personnel, to refrain from abducting or detaining them in violation of their immunity under relevant conventions referred to in the present resolution and applicable international humanitarian law, and speedily to release, without harm, any abductee or detainee;

10. *Calls upon* all States to consider signing and ratifying the Rome Statute of the International Criminal Court;

11. *Reaffirms* the obligation of all humanitarian personnel and United Nations and its associated personnel to observe and respect the national laws of the country in which they are operating, in accordance with international law and the Charter of the United Nations;

12. *Calls upon* all States to promote a climate of respect for the security of United Nations and humanitarian personnel;

13. *Requests* the Secretary-General to take the necessary measures, falling within his responsibilities, to ensure that security matters are an integral part of the planning for existing and newly mandated United Nations operations and that such precautions extend to all United Nations and its associated personnel;

14. *Also requests* the Secretary-General to take the necessary measures to ensure that United Nations and other personnel carrying out activities in fulfilment of the mandate of a United Nations operation are properly informed about the conditions under which they are called to operate, including relevant customs and traditions in the host country, and the standards that they are required to meet, including those contained in relevant domestic and international law, and that adequate training in security, human rights and humanitarian law is provided so as to enhance their security and effectiveness in accomplishing their functions, and reaffirms the necessity for all other humanitarian organizations to provide their personnel with similar support;

15. *Stresses* the need to ensure that all United Nations staff members receive adequate security training prior to their deployment to the field, the need to attach a high priority to the improvement of stress coun-

selling services available to United Nations staff members, including through the implementation of a comprehensive security and stress management training programme for United Nations staff throughout the system, and the need to make available to the Secretary-General the means for this purpose;

16. *Encourages* all States to contribute to the Trust Fund for Security of Staff Members of the United Nations System;

17. *Reaffirms* the need to strengthen the Office of the United Nations Security Coordinator, and in this regard expresses its appreciation for the recommendation of the Secretary-General to appoint a full-time Security Coordinator so as to enable the Office to enhance its capacity in the discharge of its duties, in consultation with the Office for the Coordination of Humanitarian Affairs of the Secretariat and appropriate agencies within the Inter-Agency Standing Committee, and calls for expeditious consideration of the recommendation;

18. *Recognizes* the need for a strengthened and comprehensive security management system for the United Nations system, both at headquarter and field level, and requests the United Nations system, as well as Member States, to take all appropriate measures needed to that end;

19. *Encourages* all States to become parties to and respect fully their obligations under the relevant international instruments, including the Convention on the Safety of United Nations and Associated Personnel;

20. *Takes note* of the report of the Secretary-General on the scope of legal protection under the Convention on the Safety of United Nations and Associated Personnel, and decides that the Sixth Committee shall consider the report at the fifty-sixth session of the General Assembly, under an item entitled "Scope of legal protection under the Convention on the Safety of United Nations and Associated Personnel";

21. *Calls upon* all States to consider becoming parties to and to respect fully their obligations under the Convention on the Privileges and Immunities of the United Nations and the Convention on the Privileges and Immunities of the Specialized Agencies, which have been ratified so far by 140 States and 106 States, respectively;

22. *Recalls* the essential role of telecommunication resources in facilitating the safety of humanitarian personnel and United Nations and its associated personnel, calls upon States to consider signing and ratifying the 1998 Tampere Convention on the Provision of Telecommunication Resources for Disaster Mitigation and Relief Operations, and encourages them, pending the entry into force of the Convention, to facilitate, consistent with their national laws and regulations, the use of communications equipment in such operations;

23. *Requests* the Secretary-General to submit to it at its fifty-sixth session a comprehensive, updated report on the safety and security situation of humanitarian personnel and protection of United Nations personnel and on the implementation of the present resolution, including an account of the measures taken by Governments and the United Nations to prevent and respond to all individual security incidents that involve United Nations and its associated personnel.

ACC consideration. The Administrative Committee on Coordination (ACC), at its first regular session in 2000 (Rome, 6-7 April) [ACC/2000/4], reaffirmed that host Governments had the primary responsibility for UN personnel safety and security. It requested Governments that had not yet done so to ratify the 1994 Convention on the Safety of United Nations and Associated Personnel and the statute of the International Criminal Court [YUN 1998, p. 1209]. It endorsed the intention to achieve a more stable security funding system and called for the expeditious implementation of priority security measures, including those relating to field security officers, training and communications.

At its second regular session (New York, 27-28 October) [ACC/2000/20], ACC adopted a statement on staff security in which it expressed full support for the proposals and initiatives outlined in the Secretary-General's October report [A/55/494], particularly those designed to reinforce the Coordinator's Office. It also expressed concern at the brutal deaths of six UN staff over the previous six months. ACC acknowledged the need for stress counselling and agreed that no staff should be assigned to the field without security training.

Personnel practices and policies

Delegation of authority

JIU report. The Secretary-General, by a March note [A/55/857], transmitted a JIU report assessing progress in the delegation of authority for the management of human and financial resources in the United Nations Secretariat. JIU observed that, over the preceding few years, delegation of such authority appeared to be implemented on an ad hoc basis rather than according to a well thought-out strategy. Measures to decentralize administrative tasks had been presented as delegation, when, in many cases, managers had not been given additional decision-making powers and lacked effective guidance and support services.

JIU thus recommended that an overall action plan for delegation of authority be drawn up, based on a systematically developed concept that defined those areas of responsibility requiring retention of central authority and those where authority could be delegated. The action plan should contain the elements spelled out in the JIU recommendations calling for: clarity in the formulation of policies and procedures and instructions promulgated through the Secretary-General's bulletins and administrative instructions; the promulgation of an updated administrative instruction on delegation for the administration of the Staff Regulations and Rules to reflect the current situation, of revised Financial Regulations and Rules and of individual delegation orders; the establishment of a culture of clarity, transparency and communication; the empowerment of managers through specialized training and briefings, and adequate support services; access to information; monitoring capacity by which to gauge progress in the exercise of delegated authority; mechanisms for the performance evaluation of officials to whom authority was delegated and the establishment of an accountability system; and consultations with staff representatives.

Reports of Secretary-General. The Secretary-General, in his April comments on the report of JIU [A/55/857/Add.1], stated that events had overtaken many of its recommendations, and a number of reform initiatives affecting the delegation of financial management authority appeared to have been overlooked, among them the results-based budgeting process (see p. 1295) and the Secretariat's efforts to review and adjust administrative budgetary and programming procedures to reflect the new management culture resulting from the introduction of results-based budgeting.

While the Secretary-General generally agreed with the first recommendation, his 1 August report on human resources management reform (see p. 1337) contained elements of an overall plan that included the Performance Appraisal System (PAS) and the programme management plan, a new instrument requiring department heads to define clearly the goals and results to be achieved, together with measurable performance indicators. The measures described in his 1994 comprehensive system of accountability [YUN 1994, p. 1358] had been carried out and, where necessary, refined and improved. His 3 August report (see p. 1337) on accountability and responsibility underlined progress made since then, and highlighted recent changes supplementing existing accountability mechanisms to allow for the effective functioning of the currently established comprehensive system of accountability.

The Secretary-General concurred with the need to update his 1976 bulletin on the administration of the Staff Regulations and Rules [ST/SGB/151] and stated that a thorough review of the Financial Regulations and Rules was in progress. Steps towards establishing a Secretariat-wide culture of transparency and communication had been incorporated into the human resources management strategy. He shared the view that delegation of authority should be made generic through the issuance of bulletins or instructions. The provisions for delegating author-

ity to programme managers were contained in his 1997 bulletin [ST/SGB/1997/5]. It would merely require an amendment of the applicable rules to expand the existing structure. The Secretary-General endorsed the thrust of the recommended specialized training of managers, recognizing that they all needed constant and immediate access to relevant information. IMIS and the Integrated Monitoring and Documentation Information System, combined with the Internet, contributed towards meeting that need. To facilitate monitoring, a computerized tracking system was being developed for the departmental human resources action plan, as was an automated system of recruitment, placement and promotion. He concurred with the imperative for full and meaningful consultations with staff representatives, but stressed constructive and results-oriented dialogue.

Recruitment process

Pursuant to General Assembly resolutions 48/218 B [YUN 1994, p. 1362] and 54/244 [YUN 1999, p. 1274], the Secretary-General, in September [A/55/397], transmitted a report by OIOS assessing progress made towards reforming and refining specific elements of the UN recruitment process identified in its 1996 audit of the management of that process. While acknowledging the many OHRM reform initiatives, OIOS believed that those initiatives should be integrated into a strategic plan aimed at meeting evolving staffing needs and transforming the current cumbersome and time-consuming process into one more proactive and flexible. That need was urgent, given the increased number of retirements expected in the next few years.

Apart from pointing to the need for OHRM to address the policy issue of establishing overall recruitment goals and strategies, OIOS proposed specific actions to expedite and improve the management of the recruitment process. Key among them were to provide operational guidance to programme managers for implementing human resources targets in order to achieve geographic distribution and gender balance; to integrate individual recruitment approaches and monitor their achievement; to refine further the benchmarks for performance monitoring of recruitment; to conduct in-depth analyses of human resources statistics as a basis for strategic planning; to improve operational efficiency and effectiveness, particularly regarding roster management and circulation of vacancy announcements; and to evaluate the effectiveness of the current national competitive examination programme.

OIOS also made a preliminary assessment of OHRM's recent reform proposal on recruitment, promotion and placement, which addressed managerial accountability and empowerment and outlined a streamlined recruitment process, but many of whose operational details had not been developed at the time of audit. OIOS supported the approach and encouraged OHRM to pursue adoption of that proposal.

Senior-level appointments

By a September note [A/55/423], the Secretary-General transmitted a JIU report on senior-level appointments in the United Nations, its programmes and funds, proposing measures to improve the selection of candidates, recruitment transparency, the geographical distribution of senior-level posts and the streamlining of related policies and procedures. The report noted that senior echelon officials included the Deputy Secretary-General (DSG), equivalent in rank with the executive heads of the specialized agencies and major UN programmes and funds, department and office heads at the Under-Secretary-General (USG) and Assistant Secretary-General (ASG) levels, officials performing diplomatic or special-representative functions for the Secretary-General, Directors (D-2s) and Principal Officers (D-1s). Appointments to those positions fell under the Secretary-General's discretionary power and no standard recruitment or promotion procedures applied. Table 1 of the report showed that, between 30 June 1995 and 30 June 1998, the regional distribution of senior-level posts were: 82 (10 USGs and ASGs) for Western Europe, 64 (4 USGs and ASGs) for North America and the Caribbean, 58 (5 USGs and ASGs) for Africa, 50 (10 USGs and ASGs) for Asia and the Pacific, 27 (8 USGs and ASGs) for Latin America, 18 (1 USG) for the Middle East and 13 (1 USG) for Eastern Europe.

Distribution among countries in 1999 indicated that only 18 Member States (less than 10 per cent of the UN membership) encumbered 182 (57.6 per cent) of the total 316 senior-level posts; 70 others encumbered the remaining 134 (42.4 per cent). Ninety-seven Members (more than half of the UN membership, the majority of which were developing countries and those with economies in transition) held no senior-level post. In comparing the 1999 data with those of 1995, the report concluded that, in the previous five years, the geographical distribution of senior-level posts had been stable but could hardly be regarded as positive. Moreover, although the number of women at the D-1 level and above had increased by 61.4 per cent, from 57 to 92, between 1 July 1995 and 30 June 1999, the representation of women from developing countries and those

with economies in transition continued to be inadequate.

While none of the top echelon appointments had been officially acknowledged as a mistake or failure, authoritative UN analysts recognized that their performance over the years had been uneven. Table 2 on senior staff appraisal suggested that, since the implementation of the PAS, only one USG and one ASG had been appraised. A general conclusion that might be drawn was that the PAS was far from being universally applied.

In its examination of senior-level staff in major UN programmes and funds, the report observed an uneven geographical distribution, as well as diversity in appointment modalities, but saw no compelling reason to recommend uniformity in that regard.

The report's recommendations called on the Secretary-General to consult widely with Member States and to inform them of vacancies and required credentials before making appointments at the USG and ASG levels, and, in his report on the composition of the Secretariat, to provide information on D-2 appointments made, including nationality, gender and type of contract; to amend staff regulation 4.5 relating to the appointments of senior-level officials earlier described; to appoint candidates for D-2 posts according to four modalities outlined in the report; to ensure adequate representation of developing countries in senior-level posts; to heed the repeated General Assembly statements that no post should be considered the exclusive preserve of any Member State or group; to improve gender balance in USG and ASG appointments and to lay emphasis on better representation of women from developing countries and those with economies in transition; to exert efforts to select candidates for the positions of special representative, envoy and related positions based on geographical and gender balance; to report biannually to the Assembly on the application of the PAS to senior-level officials; and to call on the executive heads of UN programmes and funds to ensure senior-level recruitment on as wide a geographical basis as possible.

Employment of retirees

The Secretary-General, in October, submitted his 1998-1999 report [A/55/451] on the use of retired personnel. Prepared in response to General Assembly decision 51/408 [YUN 1996, p. 1329], the report described the guidelines and the 27 May 1999 administrative instruction [ST/AI/1999/5] governing retiree re-employment; general conditions and contractual arrangements; restrictions concerning former staff in receipt of a pension benefit, including remuneration limits; and monitoring by OHRM to ensure compliance by departments and offices.

The report provided statistical data on persons who had retired after the age of 60 and 62 years, excluding those engaged by the United Nations Joint Staff Pension Fund, which, since its reclassification as an inter-organizational body, was no longer included in reports on the Secretariat. The report indicated the number of retirees engaged, the type and category of engagement, the departments or offices involved, the retirees' nationality, gender, functions, age group, days worked and fees or salaries.

The report noted that retiree fees and salaries in 1998-1999 totalled $10.3 million, of which language services accounted for nearly $6.7 million. The average cost for each retiree increased from $17,620 in 1996-1997 to $18,642 in 1998-1999. As to the possible revision of the limits on the annual earnings of retirees (currently $22,000 and $40,000 for language-services staff), the Secretary-General would continue to monitor the impact of ceilings on the delivery of services, particularly in respect of language services, a field where retirees were the main source of expertise. He observed that any revision had to be weighed against the corresponding increase in the regular budget.

Compared to 1996-1997 figures, the number of separate engagements (contracts) in 1998-1999 rose to 551 (a 1.3 per cent increase); the number of retirees engaged rose to 342 (a 4.3 per cent increase). Over 47 per cent of those engaged were in the Professional and higher categories; 17 per cent were in the Field Service and General Service categories. Special service agreements for consultants and individual contractors made up over one third of the engagements.

The language services of the Secretariat's Department of General Assembly Affairs and Conference Services was the largest user of retired staff, accounting for 121 (or 31 per cent) of the total engagements for the biennium. Retirees engaged in language services worked 5,065 more days in 1998-1999 (a 33 per cent increase) than in 1996-1997; their fees and salaries rose to $4.4 million in 1998-1999 from $3.4 million during 1996-1997.

By nationality, the United States accounted for 58 engagements, followed by France (44), the United Kingdom (31), Egypt (27), Chile (23), Spain (21) and Argentina (10). By gender, 35 per cent of the retirees engaged were female. By function, 214 retirees were engaged in language-related services, 106 in administrative services and 64 in political, economic, social, environmental, humanitarian, advisory and technical assistance services. Forty-three per cent of the retirees engaged were in the 60-to-65 age group and some 35 per cent were in the 65-to-70 age group.

Staff College

In his October report on the United Nations Staff College project [A/55/369], the Secretary-General informed the General Assembly that, in accordance with resolution 54/228 [YUN 1999, p. 1340], he had established a three-member team that undertook an evaluation of the College project in Turin, Italy, and made recommendations for its future status, funding and operations upon concluding its pilot phase in December 2000.

The team's report, transmitted as an addendum to the Secretary-General's report [A/55/369/Add.1], provided previously reported background information on the College project [YUN 1999, p. 1339], the methodology used and the evaluation results. The team's assessment covered the relevance, quality and impact of the training and learning programmes and workshops conducted by the College; directions as to its future role; relationships with other training institutions; methodologies to create maximum impact in addressing new cross-sectoral challenges; future status and functioning; and governance and requirements. The assessment provided a positive basis for the continuation of the College, especially in the light of the growing demand for its services.

The team recommended that: the Staff College be accorded legal status, to be embodied in a statute approved by the Assembly, as a permanent system-wide institution, subject to review after three years, and be renamed the United Nations System Staff College; a system of governance to make the College accountable to a Governing Board be put in place and a three-year operational strategy be followed to phase out, reorient and realign progammes and activities; the College facilitate the creation of a cohesive management culture by positioning itself as a management and leadership development centre and a catalyst for change in the system through learning and knowledge management; and the College take a proactive leadership role in open and distance learning.

The Secretary-General endorsed the team's recommendations to institutionalize the College as a system-wide establishment, as did ACC. Subsequent inter-agency consultations, however, concluded that a sharper definition of the functions and programme of the College, as well as agreement on specific modalities of governance and funding, should be reached at the outset of its new proposed status. Accordingly, an inter-agency working group was being created to address the matter.

In the meantime, the Secretary-General recommended that the Assembly establish the United Nations System Staff College, with effect from 1 January 2002, as a system-wide knowledge management and learning institution for the UN system staff; and request submission of the final draft statute for the College for its review in 2001, to reflect the outcome of the further interagency consultations. Thereafter, a biennial report should be submitted to the Assembly on the work, activities and accomplishments of the College, including its collaboration with relevant UN institutions.

GENERAL ASSEMBLY ACTION

On 20 December [meeting 87], the General Assembly, on the recommendation of the Second (Economic and Financial) Committee [A/55/584], adopted **resolution 55/207** without vote [agenda item 97].

United Nations Staff College in Turin, Italy

The General Assembly,

Recalling the decision taken by the Secretary-General in January 1996 to establish in Turin, Italy, the United Nations Staff College project for an initial period of five years,

Recalling also its resolution 54/228 of 22 December 1999,

Reaffirming the importance of a coordinated United Nations system-wide approach to research and training based on an effective coherent strategy and an effective division of labour among the relevant institutions and bodies,

Welcoming the report of the Secretary-General and the report of the Independent Evaluation Team,

1. *Takes note with appreciation* of the work of the United Nations Staff College project, in particular with regard to strengthening the performance of the United Nations in the areas of economic and social development and international peace and security and in promoting a common United Nations management culture;

2. *Expresses its deep appreciation* to the International Labour Organization for the technical, logistical and administrative contributions provided by its International Training Centre in Turin;

3. *Decides* to establish the United Nations System Staff College, as at 1 January 2002 after the approval of its statute, as an institution for system-wide knowledge management, training and learning for the staff of the United Nations system, aimed, in particular, at the areas of economic and social development, peace and security and internal management of the system;

4. *Requests* the Secretary-General to continue consultations on an urgent basis with the Administrative Committee on Coordination and relevant United Nations organizations and to submit, as early as possible, a final draft of the statute for the College, reflecting, as appropriate, the outcome of those consultations on functions, governance and funding for review and approval by the General Assembly, preferably at its fifty-fifth session;

5. *Decides* that, after the establishment of the Staff College, a biennial report should be submitted to the General Assembly on the work, activities and accomplishments of the College, including its collaboration with other relevant United Nations institutions.

UN Joint Staff Pension Fund

In 2000, the number of participants in the United Nations Joint Staff Pension Fund (UNJSPF) increased from 68,935 to 74,432 (8 per cent); the number of periodic benefits in award increased from 46,200 to 48,069 (4 per cent). On 31 December, the breakdown of the periodic benefits in award was: 15,129 retirement benefits; 10,165 early retirement benefits; 6,498 deferred retirement benefits; 7,336 widows' and widowers' benefits; 8,069 children's benefits; 829 disability benefits; and 43 secondary dependants' benefits. In the course of the year, 4,150 lump-sum withdrawal and other settlements were paid.

The Fund was administered by the 33-member United Nations Joint Staff Pension Board, which held its fiftieth session (Geneva, 5-14 July) [A/55/9] to consider actuarial matters, including the twenty-fifth actuarial valuation of the Fund as at 31 December 1999; management of the Fund's investments and reports on the investment strategy and performance for the two-year period ending 31 March 2000; longer-term administrative arrangements of the Fund; entitlement to survivors' benefits for spouses and former spouses; reviews of several features of the pension adjustment system; and status of the proposed agreement between the Fund and the Government of the Russian Federation concerning the pension-related claims of former Fund participants from the former USSR. The Board also examined and approved the financial statements and schedules for the year ended 31 December 1999 and considered the report of the Board of Auditors on the accounts and operations of the Fund, a report on the internal audits of the Fund and, pursuant to the Board's observations, possible penalties in cases of fraud by participants and beneficiaries. In addition, the Board considered a proposed transfer agreement between the Fund and the World Trade Organization; an ICSC review of the common scale of staff assessment for pensionable remuneration purposes; the size and composition of the Pension Board and of its Standing Committee; and a change in the pension adjustment system consequent to a judgement of the United Nations Administrative Tribunal.

ACABQ, commenting on the Board's report in October [A/55/481], concurred with the Board that the current contribution rate of 23.7 per cent of pensionable remuneration be retained; and with its decision to confirm its two 1998 conditional decisions reported to the General Assembly: to change the interest rates applicable to lump-sum commutations of periodic benefits from 6.5 to 6 per cent with respect to contributory service performed as from 1 January 2001, and to reduce the threshold for effecting cost-of-living adjustments of pensions in award from 3 to 2 per cent, effective from the adjustment due on 1 April 2001. As to the Board's decision to establish a tripartite Working Group to review the Fund's benefit provisions, ACABQ hoped that the Group would focus on specific issues so as to be able to make precise recommendations.

ACABQ agreed with the Board's recommendations to add new subparagraphs (e) to article 35 bis and (h) to article 34 and revise article 45 of the Regulations of the Fund relating, respectively, to the divorced surviving spouse's benefit, continuation of surviving spouse's benefit after remarriage and establishment of a payment facility for meeting family maintenance obligations. It further agreed with the Board's decision relating to the Administrative Tribunal's judgement involving the application of the cost-of-living differential factor on an applicant's deferred retirement benefit, as well as with its consequent recommendation to amend paragraphs 4 and 5 of the UNJSPF pension adjustment system.

GENERAL ASSEMBLY ACTION

On 23 December [meeting 89], the General Assembly, on the recommendation of the Fifth Committee [A/55/703], adopted **resolution 55/224** without vote [agenda item 125].

United Nations pension system

The General Assembly,

Recalling its resolutions 51/217 of 18 December 1996 and 53/210 of 18 December 1998, and section V of its resolution 54/251 of 23 December 1999,

Having considered the report of the United Nations Joint Staff Pension Board for 2000 to the General Assembly and to the member organizations of the United Nations Joint Staff Pension Fund, the report of the Secretary-General on the investments of the Fund and the related report of the Advisory Committee on Administrative and Budgetary Questions,

I
Actuarial matters

Recalling section I of its resolution 53/210,

Having considered the results of the valuation of the United Nations Joint Staff Pension Fund as at 31 December 1999 and the observations thereon of the Consulting Actuary of the Fund, the Committee of Actuaries and the United Nations Joint Staff Pension Board,

1. *Takes note with satisfaction* of the improvement in the actuarial situation of the United Nations Joint Staff Pension Fund, from an actuarial surplus of 0.36 per cent of pensionable remuneration as at 31 December

1997 to an actuarial surplus of 4.25 per cent of pensionable remuneration as at 31 December 1999, and, in particular, of the opinions provided by the Consulting Actuary and the Committee of Actuaries, as reproduced in annexes IV and V, respectively, to the report of the United Nations Joint Staff Pension Board;

2. *Takes note* of the decision of the Board, in accordance with article 11 (a) of the Regulations of the Fund, to lower the interest rate used to determine lump-sum commutations, from the current 6.5 per cent to 6 per cent, with respect to contributory service performed as from 1 January 2001;

3. *Takes note also* that the Board has established a working group to undertake a fundamental review of the benefit provisions of the Fund, taking into account developments in staffing and remuneration policies in the member organizations and in pension arrangements at the national and international levels, and to make proposals to the Standing Committee of the Board in 2001 and subsequently to the Board in 2002, on the future long-term needs of the Fund and its constituent groups, for eventual submission by the Board to the General Assembly at its fifty-seventh session;

4. *Takes note further* of the observations of the Advisory Committee on Administrative and Budgetary Questions contained in paragraph 8 of its report;

5. *Concurs* with the Transfer Agreement with the World Trade Organization, approved by the Board under article 13 of the Regulations of the Fund, with a view to securing continuity of pension rights between the Fund and the World Trade Organization, as set out in annex VII to the report of the Board;

6. *Takes note* of the intention of the Board and the International Bank for Reconstruction and Development to pursue a new transfer agreement in the light of the changes made in the pension plan of the Bank and of the interim procedures that will be followed until a new agreement is concluded;

II
Pension adjustment system

Recalling section II of its resolution 53/210,

Having considered the reviews carried out by the United Nations Joint Staff Pension Board, as set out in paragraphs 186 to 200 of its report, of various aspects of the pension adjustment system,

1. *Takes note* of the results of the monitoring of the costs/savings of recent modifications of the two-track feature of the pension adjustment system and the intention of the United Nations Joint Staff Pension Board to continue to monitor those costs/savings every two years, on the occasion of the actuarial valuations of the Fund;

2. *Approves* changes in the pension adjustment system, as set out in annex I to the present resolution:

(a) To lower the threshold for implementing cost-of-living adjustments of pensions in award from 3 per cent to 2 per cent, with effect from the adjustment due on 1 April 2001;

(b) To modify, provisionally, paragraphs 4 and 5 of the provisions of the pension adjustment system, in order to implement Judgement No. 942 of the United Nations Administrative Tribunal, as described in section X, paragraphs 263 to 272, of the report of the Board, pending possible future proposals made by the Board to the General Assembly for changes in the pension adjustment system as regards adjustments of deferred retirement benefits;

III
Financial statements of the United Nations Joint Staff Pension Fund and report of the Board of Auditors

Having considered the financial statements of the United Nations Joint Staff Pension Fund for the biennium ended 31 December 1999, the audit opinion and report of the Board of Auditors thereon, the information provided on the internal audits of the Fund and the observations of the United Nations Joint Staff Pension Board,

1. *Notes with satisfaction* that the report of the Board of Auditors on the accounts of the United Nations Joint Staff Pension Fund for the biennium ended 31 December 1999 indicated that the financial statements presented fairly, in all respects, the financial position of the Fund and that the transactions tested as part of the audit were, in all significant respects, in accordance with the Financial Regulations of the United Nations and legislative authority;

2. *Takes note* of the observations of the Advisory Committee on Administrative and Budgetary Questions contained in paragraph 13 of its report;

IV
Longer-term administrative arrangements of the United Nations Joint Staff Pension Fund

Recalling section VII of its resolution 51/217, section V of its resolution 52/222, section V of its resolution 53/210 and section V of its resolution 54/251 concerning the administrative arrangements and expenses of the United Nations Joint Staff Pension Fund,

Having considered section VI of the report of the United Nations Joint Staff Pension Board, on the longer-term administrative arrangements of the Fund,

1. *Takes note* of the information, set out in paragraphs 117 to 154 of the report of the United Nations Joint Staff Pension Board, on the strategic plan for the operations of the United Nations Joint Staff Pension Fund, which addresses computer systems, process reengineering and technological improvements, the progress report on the enhancement of the role of the Geneva office of the Fund, the delegation of personnel and procurement decisions to the Fund and office space needs;

2. *Welcomes* the efforts under way to effect improvements in the administrative operations of the Fund through greater use of the latest developments in information technology, including electronic exchanges of information between the Fund and its member organizations, as well as with participants and beneficiaries of the Fund, using Internet/Intranet web sites;

3. *Requests* the Standing Committee of the Board, in submitting the budget proposals of the Fund for the biennium 2002-2003 and, if necessary, revised estimates for the current biennium, to provide detailed information on the costs and benefits related to phase I and phase II of the project, including timetables and the prioritizing of the various initiatives;

V
Entitlement to survivors' benefits for spouses and former spouses

Recalling paragraph 4 of section VIII of its resolution 51/217 and section VI of its resolution 53/210,

Having considered the further review undertaken by the United Nations Joint Staff Pension Board of issues related to the pension entitlements of spouses and former spouses, as set out in paragraphs 155 to 185 of its report,

1. *Approves* the amendment to article 35 bis of the Regulations of the United Nations Joint Staff Pension Fund, as set out in annex II to the present resolution, which would extend the provision for a divorced surviving spouse's benefit to divorced spouses of former participants who separated before 1 April 1999 and who meet all the other eligibility conditions in subparagraph *(b)* of article 35 bis;

2. *Also approves* the amendment to article 34 of the Regulations of the Fund, as set out in annex II to the present resolution, which would restore the surviving spouse's benefit that had been eliminated for those who had remarried prior to 1 April 1999, subject to recovery (with interest) of the lump-sum payment made at the time of remarriage;

3. *Further approves* an amendment to article 45 of the Regulations of the Fund, as set out in annex II to the present resolution, which would modify the payment facility approved in resolution 53/210 along the lines set out in paragraphs 172 to 177 of the report of the United Nations Joint Staff Pension Board;

4. *Approves*, with effect from 1 April 2001, the amendment to article 34 *(b)* of the Regulations of the Fund, as set out in annex II to the present resolution, which would eliminate the partial commutation option for participants electing to receive a deferred retirement benefit for the reasons set out in paragraphs 178 to 183 of the report of the Board;

5. *Takes note* of the responses to the arrangements approved in resolution 53/210 for the optional purchase of surviving spouses' benefits, on cost-neutral terms, in respect of marriage after separation from service;

6. *Requests* the Board to continue to monitor the experience with these issues and to report thereon to the General Assembly at its fifty-seventh session;

7. *Also requests* the Board to replace the study of benefits for domestic partnerships, as referred to in paragraphs 184 and 185 of its report, with a study on the existing rules and practices governing entitlements to survivors' pension benefits in international organizations, and to report thereon to the General Assembly at its fifty-seventh session;

VI
Status of the proposed agreement between the United Nations Joint Staff Pension Board and the Government of the Russian Federation

Recalling section IV of its resolution 51/217 and section III of its resolution 53/210,

Noting the information provided by the United Nations Joint Staff Pension Board in paragraphs 201 to 232 of its report and the additional information contained in official communications from the Government of the Russian Federation to the Chief Executive Officer of the Fund after the fiftieth session of the Board,

1. *Takes note* of the information provided by the Government of the Russian Federation on internal solutions being prepared with a view to addressing the concerns of Russian former participants in the United Nations Joint Staff Pension Fund;

2. *Appreciates* the efforts of the Board in addressing this issue;

VII
Other matters

1. *Takes note* of the observations of the United Nations Joint Staff Pension Board, as set out in paragraphs 233 to 240 of its report, on the review and conclusions reached by the International Civil Service Commission on the changes in average tax rates at the seven headquarters duty stations which formed the basis for the development of the current common scale of staff assessment for pensionable remuneration;

2. *Also takes note* of the review of the size and composition of the Board and the Standing Committee of the United Nations Joint Staff Pension Board and, in particular, the provisional allocation of the seat vacated by the former Interim Commission for the International Trade Organization effected upon the termination of its membership in the United Nations Joint Staff Pension Fund as at 31 December 1998, as described in paragraphs 241 to 252 of the report of the Board;

3. *Notes* that a further review of the size and composition of the Board and the Standing Committee will be undertaken in the first instance by the Standing Committee in 2001 and subsequently by the Board in 2002, addressing the issues set out in paragraph 252 of the report of the Board;

4. *Approves*, with effect from 1 January 2001, an amendment to article 6 of the Regulations of the Fund, as set out in annex II to the present resolution, which would set the terms of office for the elected members and alternate members of the United Nations Staff Pension Committee at four years, instead of the current three years;

5. *Also approves*, with effect from 1 January 2001, an amendment to article 14 of the Regulations of the Fund, as set out in annex II to the present resolution, which would set the frequency for audits of the operations of the Fund to be annual and for audit reports on the accounts of the Fund by the Board of Auditors to be submitted to the General Assembly every two years, instead of annually;

6. *Further approves*, with effect from 1 January 2001, an amendment to article 43 of the Regulations of the Fund, as set out in annex II to the present resolution, which would provide for the recovery of indebtedness to the Fund pursuant to observations made by the Board of Auditors and to the comments thereon by the Board, for the reasons given in paragraphs 257 to 262 of the report of the Board;

7. *Takes note* of the consequent amendment that would be made to administrative rule J.9 *(a)* of the Fund, as set out in paragraph 261 of the report of the Board;

VIII
Investments of the United Nations Joint Staff Pension Fund

1. *Takes note* of the report of the Secretary-General on the investments of the United Nations Joint Staff Pension Fund, as well as the observations of the United Nations Joint Staff Pension Board thereon in its report;

2. *Expresses its appreciation* to the Secretary-General and to the members of the Investments Committee for the investment performances of the Fund, which contributed significantly to the actuarial surplus of the Fund as at 31 December 1999;

3. *Requests* the Secretary-General to continue to explore investment possibilities by the Fund in the developing countries, taking into consideration General Assembly resolutions 36/119 A to C of 10 December 1981, and to report thereon to the Assembly at its fifty-seventh session;

4. *Takes note* of the observations of the Board of Auditors on the outstanding tax refunds due to the Fund from some Member States in respect of direct taxes imposed on the investment income of the Fund, as set out in paragraphs 20 to 24 of its report, which is reproduced in annex III to the report of the Board;

5. *Urges once again* those Member States which have outstanding balances on foreign tax accounts receivable to provide the reimbursement due to the Fund;

6. *Reiterates its request* to those Member States which do not grant tax exemptions to make all possible efforts to do so as soon as possible.

ANNEX I
Changes in the pension adjustment system of the United Nations Joint Staff Pension Fund

1. At the beginning of paragraph 4, after the words "Except as otherwise noted", add the following phrase within parentheses: "(e.g., in paragraphs 5 *(d)*, 10 and 27 below with regard to deferred retirement benefits)."

2. In paragraph 5, add the following new subparagraph *(d)*:

"*(d)* The cost-of-living differential factor in subparagraph 5 *(b)* (i) above shall not apply to deferred retirement benefits."

3. In paragraph 18, replace the words "3 per cent" with the words "2 per cent".

ANNEX II
Amendments to the Regulations of the United Nations Joint Staff Pension Fund

Article 6
Staff pension committees

In paragraph *(b)*, replace the words "three years" with the words "four years."

Article 14
Annual report and audit

Replace paragraph *(b)* with the following:

"*(b)* There shall be annual audits of the operations of the Fund, in a manner agreed between the United Nations Board of Auditors and the Board. An audit report on the accounts of the Fund shall be made every two years by the United Nations Board of Auditors; a copy of the audit report shall be included in the report under *(a)* above."

Article 3
Deferred retirement benefit

Replace paragraph *(c)* with the following:

"*(c)* The benefit may be commuted by the participant into a lump sum if the rate of the benefit at the normal retirement age is less than 300 dollars. Such commutation shall be equivalent to the full actuarial value of the benefit."

Article 34
Widow's benefit

1. In paragraph *(b)*, delete the following phrase at the end of the paragraph:

", or had commuted a deferred retirement benefit under article 30 *(c)*".

2. Add the following new paragraph *(h)*:

"*(h)* Notwithstanding the provisions of *(a)* and *(f)* above, with respect to a surviving spouse who had remarried prior to 1 April 1999 the benefit under *(a)* above shall be payable as from 1 January 2001, subject to recovery (with interest) of the lump sum payment that had been made to that surviving spouse upon remarriage, as provided for in the Regulations then in effect."

Article 35 bis
Divorced surviving spouse's benefit
Add the following new paragraph *(e)*:

"*(e)* The divorced spouse of a former participant who separated before 1 April 1999 and, in the opinion of the Chief Executive Officer of the Fund, met all the other eligibility conditions in *(a)* and *(b)* above shall be entitled as from 1 April 1999 to a benefit equal to twice the minimum surviving spouse's benefit under article 34 *(c)*, subject to the proviso that the amount of such benefit cannot exceed the amount payable to a surviving spouse of the former participant."

Article 43
Recovery of indebtedness to the Fund
Add the following text at the end of the article:

", including interest and costs, where appropriate."

Article 45
Non-assignability of rights
Replace the text of article 45 with the following:

"*(a)* A participant or beneficiary may not assign his or her rights under these Regulations. Notwithstanding the foregoing, the Fund may, to satisfy a legal obligation on the part of a participant or former participant arising from a marital or parental relationship and evidenced by an order of a court or by a settlement agreement incorporated into a divorce or other court order, remit a portion of a benefit payable by the Fund to such participant for life to one or more former spouses and/or a current spouse from whom the participant or former participant is living apart. Such payment shall not convey to any person a benefit entitlement from the Fund or (except as provided herein) provide any rights under the Regulations of the Fund to such person or increase the total benefits otherwise payable by the Fund.

"*(b)* To be acted upon, the requirement under the court order must be consistent with the Regulations of the Fund, as determined by the Chief Executive Officer of the Fund to be beyond any reasonable doubt, and on the basis of the available evidence. Once implemented, the assignment shall normally be irrevocable; however, a participant or former participant may request, upon satisfactory evidence based on a court order or a provision of a settlement agreement incorporated into a court decree, a new decision by the Chief Executive Officer that would alter or discontinue the payment or payments. Furthermore, such payment or payments shall cease following the death of the participant or former participant. If a designee predeceases the participant or former participant, the payments shall not com-

mence, or if they have commenced, shall cease upon the designee's death. In the event that the payment or payments have been diminished, discontinued, or have failed to commence or have ceased, the amount of the benefit payable to the participant or former participant shall be duly adjusted."

Also on 23 December, the Assembly, by **decision 55/458**, decided that the agenda item on the UN pension system would remain for consideration during its resumed fifty-fifth (2001) session.

Pension Fund investments

The market value of UNJSPF assets as at 31 December 2000 was $24.1 billion, a decrease of $1.8 billion from the previous year. For the year ending 31 December 2000, UNJSPF had a one-year annualized real rate of return of -6.2 per cent compared to -7.4 per cent for the benchmark. After adjustment for a 3.6 per cent rise in the consumer price index, the Fund's real rate of return was -9.6 per cent. Over periods of three and five years, it had a total return of 10.1 per cent and 10.5 per cent, while the benchmark had returns of 8.3 per cent and 8.9 per cent, respectively.

At the end of 2000, the Fund had 64.4 per cent of its assets in equities, 24.4 per cent in bonds, 4.5 per cent in real estate and 6.7 per cent in short-term assets and reserves. The book value of development-related investments was $1,101 million.

In September [A/C.5/55/3], the Secretary-General described the economic conditions prevailing in the reporting period ended 31 March 2000 and presented statistical information on the Fund's investment returns and diversification, including development-related investments. The figures were based on the audited financial statements for 1998 and 1999 and the unaudited appraisals up to 31 March 2000. Some of the data were updated to 30 June 2000 in order to provide the General Assembly with timely information.

Travel-related matters

In October, the Secretary-General submitted his annual report on standards of accommodation for air travel [A/55/488], which listed exceptions to those standards from 1 July 1999 to 30 June 2000.

During the period under review, the Secretary-General authorized 46 cases of first-class and 30 of business-class air travel as exceptions to the standards of accommodation. Included in the first group were the Deputy Secretary-General, the President of the General Assembly's fifty-fourth session and the Secretary-General's personal aide/security officer. The Secretary-General noted that, while continuous administrative oversight had kept exceptions at a minimum, they were unavoidable in certain cases.

Administration of justice

JIU report. By a June note [A/55/57], the Secretary-General transmitted to the General Assembly a JIU report on the administration of justice in the United Nations. It reviewed the UN machinery for the administration of justice, from its legal foundation to its functioning and impact, with a view to making recommendations to adjust it to the new management requirements.

Although its mandate exclusively concerned the United Nations, JIU considered that the issue demanded further consideration from a system-wide perspective. It found the UN justice system slow, costly and cumbersome, and, in several significant ways, far less effective than it could or should be. The system featured some informal procedures and two stages of formal recourse: the first stage involved the review of claims by internal joint bodies of staff members' peers whose role was advisory; the second was recourse to the United Nations Administrative Tribunal, whose decisions were binding. JIU noted that a high proportion of the internal bodies' advice was rejected by administrators so that deliberations served only to lengthen the procedure. Flaws in the system were compounded by the fact that the international civil service was not subject to any domestic legal system and thus might fail to benefit from dynamic labour legislation. Important international instruments were not incorporated into UN internal regulations and rules.

JIU recommended the creation of an office for the settlement of disputes and the administration of justice so as to increase the independence of the UN justice system. It should include an ombudsman function to replace the Panel on Discrimination and Other Grievances so as to strengthen the system's capacity for informal conciliation, mediation and negotiation. It further recommended amending article 9 of the Tribunal's Statute to eliminate restrictions on its authority, especially with regard to ordering the rescission of a contested decision and to deciding on the appropriate compensation amount; replacing the Joint Disciplinary Committee by a Committee for Professional Responsibility; and strengthening the Office of the Coordinator of the Panel of Counsel to enhance the availability of legal advice and staff representation. Recommended options for higher appeals included giving further consideration to reviving the advisory functions of the International Court of Justice (ICJ) in the internal recourse procedure and forging closer relationships between the Tribunal and other major tribunals in the UN system.

Report of Secretary-General. In his comments issued in August [A/55/57/Add.1] on the JIU report, the Secretary-General stated his belief that all relevant basic labour standards enshrined in the 1948 Universal Declaration of Human Rights, adopted by General Assembly resolution 217 A (III) [YUN 1948-49, p. 535], were fully reflected in the UN conditions of service; the standards set out in ILO instruments were generally not developed to address conditions of service of individuals working for Governments or international organizations. The Secretary-General stated that the recommendation on the creation of an office for the settlement of disputes and the administration of justice needed further clarification on how the specific change would improve the current system. He agreed that replacing the Panel on Discrimination with an ombudsman appeared to be an effective means of strengthening the informal mediation process. However, to accept the recommendation to allow the Tribunal to order specific performance and unlimited compensation would seriously restrict his authority as the Organization's chief administrative officer; in any case, the matter would require General Assembly consideration for subsequent amendment of the Tribunal's Statute. He said there was unanimous agreement that nominees for the Tribunal should possess high professional qualifications and relevant experience. The proposal to add a post of Deputy Secretary in the Tribunal secretariat due to the increasing workload needed supporting quantitative data and analysis to establish sufficient justification for such a recommendation to the Assembly.

The Secretary-General said it was not clear why JIU called for greater emphasis on the ethical aspects of cases by suggesting the replacement of the Joint Disciplinary Committee, since that Committee's mandate was to advise on disciplinary, not ethical, questions arising from staff misconduct. Nor did it identify the specific problems with the Committee that required remedy. As to the concern over the lack of some form of appellate mechanism which led to the suggestion to revive the advisory functions of ICJ, it was not clear why the Assembly's decision in resolution 50/54 [YUN 1995, p. 1422] to cease recourse to ICJ should be reversed.

On the need to strengthen the Office of the Coordinator of the Panel of Counsel, the Secretary-General acknowledged that providing legal backstopping to the Office seemed appropriate, adding that related proposals were being put forward as part of the ongoing human resources management reform. However, responsibility for determining resource requirements to improve the provision of legal advice and staff representation rested with the Secretary-General.

ACABQ report. Following its consideration of the JIU report and the Secretary-General's comments, ACABQ, in October [A/55/514], observed that the system for administering justice should be considered in the context of the Secretary-General's overall human resources management reform. While agreeing with the need for an independent Tribunal secretariat, ACABQ felt that that did not solve the problem and suggested that the Secretary-General revisit the issue. In the meantime, ACABQ requested the Tribunal's comments on the JIU report, on the Secretary-General's related comments and on the relevant section of his report on human resources reform [A/55/253] for transmittal to the Fifth Committee. ACABQ was of the opinion that the Tribunal's inability to order performance of an obligation seriously limited the staff's right to redress; the time had come to close that gap, existent since the Tribunal's inception. It expressed serious doubts as to the appropriateness of involving ICJ in staff disputes. On the suggested additional posts for the Tribunal and the Office of the Coordinator of the Panel of Counsel, ACABQ recommended that the Secretary-General make such staffing proposals in the context of his proposed programme budget for 2002-2003, based on updated supporting workload indicators.

Communication. The General Assembly President transmitted to the Fifth Committee a letter of 11 December [A/C.5/55/33] from Guinea-Bissau expressing deep concern over the treatment to which its only national on the Secretariat staff had been subjected by the Departments of Public Information and of Management. It requested that the Committee ask the Department of Management to review carefully the case of its national. Alternatively, it would urge that Department to meet with the staff member in question and his representatives to discuss the facts surrounding the decision being contested, in the presence of the Committee, ACABQ, JIU and Staff Committee representatives.

UN Administrative Tribunal

In its annual note to the General Assembly [A/INF/55/5], the United Nations Administrative Tribunal reported in December, through the Secretary-General, that it had delivered 46 judgements during 2000, relating to cases brought by staff against the Secretary-General or the executive heads of other UN bodies to resolve disputes involving terms of appointment and related issues and regulations. The Tribunal met in plenary in New York on 22 November and held two panel sessions (Geneva, 3 July–4 August; New York, 23 October–22 November).

GENERAL ASSEMBLY ACTION

On 12 December [meeting 84], the General Assembly, on the recommendation of the Sixth (Legal) Committee [A/55/615], adopted **resolution 55/159** without vote [agenda item 165].

Review of the Statute of the United Nations Administrative Tribunal

The General Assembly,

Acknowledging with gratitude the important contribution which the United Nations Administrative Tribunal ("the Tribunal") has made to the functioning of the United Nations system, and commending the members of the Tribunal on their valuable work,

Desiring to assist the Tribunal in carrying out its future work as effectively as possible,

Taking note of the report of the Joint Inspection Unit on the administration of justice at the United Nations,

Noting the need to consider the appropriateness of the establishment of an appeals mechanism in relation to the decisions of the Tribunal,

Recognizing that, in appointing members of the Tribunal, the General Assembly should take into account the need to ensure adequate representation on the Tribunal of the principal legal systems of the world and fair geographical representation, and bearing in mind the relevant provisions of the Charter of the United Nations,

1. *Decides* to amend the Statute of the United Nations Administrative Tribunal ("the Statute"), with effect from 1 January 2001, as follows:

(a) Article 3, paragraph 1, shall be amended to read as follows:

"The Tribunal shall be composed of seven members, no two of whom may be nationals of the same State. Members shall possess the requisite qualifications and experience, including, as appropriate, legal qualifications and experience. Only three members shall sit in any particular case";

(b) Article 3, paragraph 2, shall be amended to read as follows:

"The members shall be appointed by the General Assembly for four years and may be reappointed once. A member appointed to replace a member whose term of office has not expired shall hold office for the remainder of his or her predecessor's term, and may be reappointed once";

(c) A new article shall be inserted as article 8, to read as follows:

"Where the three members of the Tribunal sitting in any particular case consider that the case raises a significant question of law, they may, at any time before they render judgement, refer the case for consideration by the whole Tribunal. The quorum for a hearing by the whole Tribunal shall be five members";

(d) Former articles 8 to 13 of the Statute shall be renumbered 9 to 14, and references to those articles shall be amended accordingly;

(*e*) The pronouns "he" and "his", wherever they appear in the Statute, shall be amended to read "he or she" or "his or her", respectively;

(*f*) In article 7, paragraph 7, and in renumbered article 11, paragraph 4, references to "five official languages" shall be amended to read "six official languages";

2. *Also decides* that members serving on the Tribunal as at 1 January 2001 shall have their current term of office extended by one year, and that thereafter, provided that they have not served on the Tribunal for more than seven years, they may be reappointed once;

3. *Further decides* that the Statute, with effect from 1 January 2001, shall read as it appears in the annex to the present resolution.

ANNEX
Statute of the Administrative Tribunal of the United Nations

Article 1

A Tribunal is established by the present Statute to be known as the United Nations Administrative Tribunal.

Article 2

1. The Tribunal shall be competent to hear and pass judgement upon applications alleging non-observance of contracts of employment of staff members of the Secretariat of the United Nations or of the terms of appointment of such staff members. The words "contracts" and "terms of appointment" include all pertinent regulations and rules in force at the time of alleged non-observance, including the staff pension regulations.

2. The Tribunal shall be open:

(*a*) To any staff member of the Secretariat of the United Nations even after his or her employment has ceased, and to any person who has succeeded to the staff member's rights on his or her death;

(*b*) To any other person who can show that he or she is entitled to rights under any contract or terms of appointment, including the provisions of staff regulations and rules upon which the staff member could have relied.

3. In the event of a dispute as to whether the Tribunal has competence, the matter shall be settled by the decision of the Tribunal.

4. The Tribunal shall not be competent, however, to deal with any applications where the cause of complaint arose prior to 1 January 1950.

Article 3

1. The Tribunal shall be composed of seven members, no two of whom may be nationals of the same State. Members shall possess the requisite qualifications and experience, including, as appropriate, legal qualifications and experience. Only three members shall sit in any particular case.

2. The members shall be appointed by the General Assembly for four years and may be reappointed once. A member appointed to replace a member whose term of office has not expired shall hold office for the remainder of his or her predecessor's term, and may be reappointed once.

3. The Tribunal shall elect its President and its two Vice-Presidents from among its members.

4. The Secretary-General shall provide the Tribunal with an Executive Secretary and such other staff as may be considered necessary.

5. No member of the Tribunal can be dismissed by the General Assembly unless the other members are of the unanimous opinion that he or she is unsuited for further service.

6. In case of a resignation of a member of the Tribunal, the resignation shall be addressed to the President of the Tribunal for transmission to the Secretary-General. This last notification makes the place vacant.

Article 4

The Tribunal shall hold ordinary sessions at dates to be fixed by its rules, subject to there being cases on its list which, in the opinion of the President, justify holding the session. Extraordinary sessions may be convoked by the President when required by the cases on the list.

Article 5

1. The Secretary-General of the United Nations shall make the administrative arrangements necessary for the functioning of the Tribunal.

2. The expenses of the Tribunal shall be borne by the United Nations.

Article 6

1. Subject to the provisions of the present Statute, the Tribunal shall establish its rules.

2. The rules shall include provisions concerning:

(*a*) Election of the President and Vice-Presidents;

(*b*) Composition of the Tribunal for its sessions;

(*c*) Presentation of applications and the procedure to be followed in respect to them;

(*d*) Intervention by persons to whom the Tribunal is open under paragraph 2 of article 2, whose rights may be affected by the judgement;

(*e*) Hearing, for purposes of information, of persons to whom the Tribunal is open under paragraph 2 of article 2, even though they are not parties to the case; and generally,

(*f*) Other matters relating to the functioning of the Tribunal.

Article 7

1. An application shall not be receivable unless the person concerned has previously submitted the dispute to the joint appeals body provided for in the Staff Regulations and the latter has communicated its opinion to the Secretary-General, except where the Secretary-General and the applicant have agreed to submit the application directly to the Administrative Tribunal.

2. In the event of the joint body's recommendations being favourable to the application submitted to it, and insofar as this is the case, an application to the Tribunal shall be receivable if the Secretary-General has:

(*a*) Rejected the recommendations;

(*b*) Failed to take any action within thirty days following the communication of the opinion;

(*c*) Failed to carry out the recommendations within thirty days following the communication of the opinion.

3. In the event that the recommendations made by the joint body and accepted by the Secretary-General are unfavourable to the applicant, and insofar as this is the case, the application shall be receivable, unless the joint body unanimously considers that it is frivolous.

4. An application shall not be receivable unless it is filed within ninety days reckoned from the respective

dates and periods referred to in paragraph 2 above, or within ninety days reckoned from the date of the communication of the joint body's opinion containing recommendations unfavourable to the applicant. If the circumstance rendering the application receivable by the Tribunal, pursuant to paragraphs 2 and 3 above, is anterior to the date of announcement of the first session of the Tribunal, the time limit of ninety days shall begin to run from that date. Nevertheless, the said time limit on his or her behalf shall be extended to one year if the heirs of a deceased staff member or the trustee of a staff member who is not in a position to manage his or her own affairs files the application in the name of the said staff member.

5. In any particular case, the Tribunal may decide to suspend the provisions regarding time limits.

6. The filing of an application shall not have the effect of suspending the execution of the decision contested.

7. Applications may be filed in any of the six official languages of the United Nations.

Article 8

Where the three members of the Tribunal sitting in any particular case consider that the case raises a significant question of law, they may, at any time before they render judgement, refer the case for consideration by the whole Tribunal. The quorum for a hearing by the whole Tribunal shall be five members.

Article 9

The oral proceedings of the Tribunal shall be held in public unless the Tribunal decides that exceptional circumstances require that they be held in private.

Article 10

1. If the Tribunal finds that the application is well founded, it shall order the rescinding of the decision contested or the specific performance of the obligation invoked. At the same time, the Tribunal shall fix the amount of compensation to be paid to the applicant for the injury sustained should the Secretary-General, within thirty days of the notification of the judgement, decide, in the interest of the United Nations, that the applicant shall be compensated without further action being taken in his or her case, provided that such compensation shall not exceed the equivalent of two years' net base salary of the applicant. The Tribunal may, however, in exceptional cases, when it considers it justified, order the payment of a higher indemnity. A statement of the reasons for the Tribunal's decision shall accompany each such order.

2. Should the Tribunal find that the procedure prescribed in the Staff Regulations or Staff Rules has not been observed, it may, at the request of the Secretary-General and prior to the determination of the merits of the case, order the case remanded for institution or correction of the required procedure. Where a case is remanded, the Tribunal may order the payment of compensation, which is not to exceed the equivalent of three months' net base salary, to the applicant for such loss as may have been caused by the procedural delay.

3. In all applicable cases, compensation shall be fixed by the Tribunal and paid by the United Nations or, as appropriate, by the specialized agency participating under article 14.

Article 11

1. The Tribunal shall take all decisions by a majority vote.

2. Subject to the provisions of article 12, the judgements of the Tribunal shall be final and without appeal.

3. The judgements shall state the reasons on which they are based.

4. The judgements shall be drawn up, in any of the six official languages of the United Nations, in two originals, which shall be deposited in the archives of the Secretariat of the United Nations.

5. A copy of the judgement shall be communicated to each of the parties in the case. Copies shall also be made available on request to interested persons.

Article 12

The Secretary-General or the applicant may apply to the Tribunal for a revision of a judgement on the basis of the discovery of some fact of such a nature as to be a decisive factor, which fact was, when the judgement was given, unknown to the Tribunal and also to the party claiming revision, always provided that such ignorance was not due to negligence. The application must be made within thirty days of the discovery of the fact and within one year of the date of the judgement. Clerical or arithmetical mistakes in judgements, or errors arising therein from any accidental slip or omission, may at any time be corrected by the Tribunal either of its own motion or on the application of any of the parties.

Article 13

The present Statute may be amended by decision of the General Assembly.

Article 14

1. The competence of the Tribunal shall be extended to the staff of the Registry of the International Court of Justice upon the exchange of letters between the President of the Court and the Secretary-General of the United Nations establishing the relevant conditions.

2. The Tribunal shall be competent to hear and pass judgement upon applications alleging non-observance of the regulations of the United Nations Joint Staff Pension Fund arising out of the decision of the United Nations Joint Staff Pension Board submitted to the Tribunal by:

(*a*) Any staff member of a member organization of the Pension Fund which has accepted the jurisdiction of the Tribunal in Pension Fund cases who is eligible under article 21 of the regulations of the Fund as a participant in the Fund, even if his or her employment has ceased, and any person who has acceded to such staff member's rights upon his or her death;

(*b*) Any other person who can show that he or she is entitled to rights under the regulations of the Pension Fund by virtue of the participation in the Fund of a staff member of such member organization.

3. The competence of the Tribunal may be extended to any specialized agency brought into relationship with the United Nations in accordance with the provisions of Articles 57 and 63 of the Charter upon the terms established by a special agreement to be made with each such agency by the Secretary-General of the United Nations. Each such special agreement shall provide that the agency concerned shall be bound by

the judgements of the Tribunal and be responsible for the payment of any compensation awarded by the Tribunal in respect of a staff member of that agency and shall include, inter alia, provisions concerning the agency's participation in the administrative arrangements for the functioning of the Tribunal and concerning its sharing the expenses of the Tribunal.

4. The competence of the Tribunal may also be extended, with the approval of the General Assembly, to any other international organization or entity established by a treaty and participating in the common system of conditions of service, upon the terms set out in a special agreement between the organization or entity concerned and the Secretary-General of the United Nations. Each such special agreement shall provide that the organization or entity concerned shall be bound by the judgements of the Tribunal and be responsible for the payment of any compensation awarded by the Tribunal in respect of a staff member of that organization or entity and shall include, inter alia, provisions concerning its participation in the administrative arrangements for the functioning of the Tribunal and concerning its sharing the expenses of the Tribunal.

Chapter IV

Institutional and administrative matters

A number of institutional and administrative matters were reviewed by the United Nations in 2000. The General Assembly held its fifty-fifth session, designated the "Millennium Assembly of the United Nations", during which it held a Millennium Summit (6-8 September), attended by heads of State or Government. Earlier in the year, the Assembly resumed its fifty-fourth session, convened its twenty-third and twenty-fourth special sessions and resumed its tenth emergency special session. The Assembly granted observer status to the Economic Community of Central African States and the Inter-American Development Bank. Two States were admitted to United Nations membership, bringing the total number to 189.

During the year, the Security Council held 167 formal meetings to deal with regional conflicts, peacekeeping operations and a wide variety of other issues related to the maintenance of international peace and security.

The Economic and Social Council held its 2000 organizational session in New York in January and February and a resumed organizational session between 28 February and 16 June. It also held a special high-level meeting with the Bretton Woods institutions in April, its substantive session in New York in July and a resumed substantive session in October and November. The Council decided to establish as a subsidiary organ a permanent forum on indigenous issues, consisting of eight members to be nominated by Governments and elected by the Council, and eight members to be appointed by the Council President.

UN bodies concerned with administrative and coordination matters, including the Administrative Committee on Coordination, the Committee for Programme and Coordination and the Joint Inspection Unit, also continued their work during the year.

The Committee on Conferences examined requests for changes to the calendar of conferences and meetings for 2000, and again recommended measures to improve the use of conference-servicing resources. The Committee commended the efforts of the Department of Public Information in developing the UN web sites, noting also that it had become necessary for consideration to be given to Internet activity as an integral part of the Organization's work programme.

Progress was reported on the development of the Integrated Management Information System and the United Nations common system. Proposals were also made for improving facilities management of UN property worldwide and for a capital master plan for the renovation and refurbishing of the Headquarters facilities.

Institutional machinery

Admission to UN membership

During 2000, two States, Tuvalu and the Federal Republic of Yugoslavia, were admitted to the United Nations, bringing the total membership to 189.

Admission of Tuvalu

On 17 February [meeting 4103], the Security Council considered the application of Tuvalu for United Nations membership [A/54/699-S/2000/5]. China, speaking before the vote, stated that it attached great importance to Tuvalu's desire to join the United Nations, but in considering the application the most important thing was upholding the principles and purposes of the Charter and implementation of General Assembly resolution 2758(XXVI) [YUN 1971, p. 136]. On the basis of that principled position, although China could not support the Council's recommendation to the Assembly, it would not block it. It hoped that, after joining the United Nations, Tuvalu would strictly abide by the Charter and implement resolution 2758(XXVI).

The Council, acting on the recommendation of the Committee on the Admission of New Members [S/2000/70], adopted **resolution 1290(2000)** by vote (14-0-1).

The Security Council,
Having examined the application of Tuvalu for admission to the United Nations,
Recommends to the General Assembly that Tuvalu be admitted to membership in the United Nations.

VOTE ON RESOLUTION 1290(2000):

In favour: Argentina, Bangladesh, Canada, France, Jamaica, Malaysia, Mali, Namibia, Netherlands, Russian Federation, Tunisia, Ukraine, United Kingdom, United States.
Against: None.
Abstaining: China.

Following the adoption of the resolution, the Council President made statement **S/PRST/2000/6** congratulating Tuvalu on behalf of the Council members, who had taken note of Tuvalu's commitment to uphold the UN Charter and fulfil all of its obligations.

The Assembly, in **resolution 55/1** of 5 September, admitted Tuvalu to UN membership.

Admission of the Federal Republic of Yugoslavia

On 31 October [meeting 4215], the Security Council, acting on the application of the Federal Republic of Yugoslavia [A/55/528-S/2000/1043], adopted **resolution 1326(2000)** without vote. The draft [S/2000/1051] was prepared by the Committee on the Admission of New Members.

The Security Council,
Having examined the application of the Federal Republic of Yugoslavia for admission to the United Nations,
Recommends to the General Assembly that the Federal Republic of Yugoslavia be admitted to membership in the United Nations.

Following the adoption of the resolution, the Council President made statement **S/PRST/2000/30** congratulating the Federal Republic of Yugoslavia on behalf of the Council members, who had taken note of its commitment to uphold the UN Charter and fulfil all of its obligations.

The General Assembly, in **resolution 55/12** of 1 November, admitted the Federal Republic of Yugoslavia to membership in the United Nations.

On 23 December, the Assembly, by **decision 55/458**, decided that the item on the admission of new Members to the United Nations remained for consideration at its resumed fifty-fifth (2001) session.

General Assembly

The General Assembly met throughout 2000; it resumed and concluded its fifty-fourth session and held the major part of its fifty-fifth session, which was designated the "Millennium Assembly of the United Nations". The fifty-fourth session was resumed in plenary meetings on 1 February, 2, 10, 14 and 15 March, 3 and 7 April, 10 and 25 May, 15 June, 11 August and 5 September. The fifty-fifth session opened on 5 September and continued until its suspension on 23 December. As part of that session, a Millennium Summit was held from 6 to 8 September (see p. 47).

The Assembly also held its twenty-third special session on "Women 2000: gender equality, development and peace for the twenty-first century" from 5 to 10 June (see p. 1082), and the twenty-fourth special session on social development

from 26 June to 1 July (see p. 1011). It resumed the tenth emergency special session on 18 and 20 October to discuss "Illegal Israeli actions in Occupied East Jerusalem and the rest of the Occupied Palestinian Territory" (see p. 421).

Organization of Assembly sessions

2000 sessions

On 11 September, by **decision 55/401**, the General Assembly, on the recommendation of the General Committee [A/55/250 & Corr.1], adopted a number of provisions concerning the organization of its fifty-fifth session.

The General Committee's recommendations covered rationalization of the Assembly's work; closing date of the session; schedule of meetings; general debate; explanations of vote, right of reply, points of order and length of statements; records of meetings; concluding statements; resolutions; documentation; questions related to the programme budget; observances and commemorative meetings; special conferences; and meetings of subsidiary organs. The Committee made observations and proposals on the organization of future Assembly sessions and recommendations concerning the agenda.

The Assembly in resolution 53/239 [YUN 1999, p. 1270] had decided that its fifty-fourth session should close on 5 September, in the morning, and that the fifty-fifth session should open on the same date, in the afternoon. The Assembly also decided that the Millennium Summit should begin on 6 September.

The Assembly authorized the following bodies to meet during its fifty-fifth session: the Executive Board of the United Nations Development Programme (UNDP) and the United Nations Population Fund (UNFPA), and the Working Group on the Financing of the United Nations Relief and Works Agency for Palestine Refugees in the Near East (**decision 55/403 A** of 5 September); the Committee on Relations with the Host Country, the Committee on the Exercise of the Inalienable Rights of the Palestinian People, the Executive Board of the United Nations Children's Fund (UNICEF) and the Preparatory Committee for the High-level International Intergovernmental Event on Financing for Development (**decision 55/403 B** of 11 September); and the Special Committee on Peacekeeping Operations and its Working Group (**decision 55/403 C** of 25 October).

Millennium Summit

At its resumed fifty-fourth session, the General Assembly took a number of actions relating to the organization of the Millennium Summit (New York, 6-8 September).

On 15 March [meeting 93], the Assembly adopted **resolution 54/254** [draft: A/54/L.81/Rev.1] without vote [agenda item 49 (b)].

Millennium Summit of the United Nations

The General Assembly,

Recalling its resolution 53/202 of 17 December 1998, by which it decided, inter alia, to designate the fifty-fifth session of the General Assembly "The Millennium Assembly of the United Nations" and to convene, as an integral part of the Millennium Assembly, a Millennium Summit of the United Nations,

Recalling also its resolution 53/239 of 8 June 1999, by which it decided, inter alia, that the Millennium Summit should begin on 6 September 2000,

Reiterating that the year 2000 constitutes a unique and symbolically compelling moment to articulate and affirm an animating vision for the United Nations in the new era, and in this context endorsing the proposal of a co-chairmanship of the Millennium Summit,

Reiterating also that a Millennium Assembly would provide an opportunity to strengthen the role of the United Nations in meeting the challenges of the twenty-first century,

Having considered the report of the Secretary-General entitled "The Millennium Assembly of the United Nations: thematic framework for the Millennium Summit",

Mindful of the need for appropriate organizational preparations for the holding of the Millennium Summit,

1. *Decides* that the Millennium Summit shall be held from 6 to 8 September 2000 in New York under the overall theme "The role of the United Nations in the twenty-first century";

2. *Also decides* that the Millennium Summit will be composed of plenary meetings and of four interactive round-table sessions, with each interactive session to be held in concurrence with a plenary meeting;

3. *Further decides* that, owing to the unique symbolic moment of the Millennium Summit, the country of the President of the fifty-fourth session of the General Assembly and the country of the President of the fifty-fifth session of the Assembly will jointly preside over the Summit;

4. *Requests* the President of the General Assembly to hold consultations with all Member States in an open-ended process with a view to taking decisions on all outstanding issues relating to the Millennium Summit, including its outcome.

On 10 May [meeting 96], the Assembly adopted **resolution 54/261** [draft: A/54/L.83/Rev.1, as orally revised] without vote [agenda item 49 (b)].

Establishment of the list of speakers and organization of the round tables for the Millennium Summit of the United Nations

The General Assembly,

Recalling its resolution 53/202 of 17 December 1998, in which it decided, inter alia, to designate the fifty-fifth session of the General Assembly "The Millennium Assembly of the United Nations" and to convene, as an integral part of the Millennium Assembly, a Millennium Summit of the United Nations,

Recalling also its resolution 54/254 of 15 March 2000, in which it:

(a) Decided that the Millennium Summit should be held from 6 to 8 September 2000 in New York under the overall theme "The role of the United Nations in the twenty-first century",

(b) Decided that the Millennium Summit would be composed of plenary meetings and four interactive round-table sessions, with each interactive session to be held in concurrence with a plenary meeting,

(c) Decided that, owing to the unique symbolic moment of the Millennium Summit, the country of the President of the fifty-fourth session of the General Assembly and the country of the President of the fifty-fifth session of the Assembly would jointly preside over the Summit,

(d) Requested the President of the General Assembly to hold consultations with all Member States in an open-ended process with a view to taking decisions on all outstanding issues relating to the Millennium Summit, including its outcome,

Reiterating that a Millennium Summit would provide an opportunity to strengthen the role of the United Nations in meeting the challenges of the twenty-first century,

Having considered the report of the Secretary-General entitled "The Millennium Assembly of the United Nations: thematic framework for the Millennium Summit",

Bearing in mind the presentation by the Secretary-General of his report entitled "We the peoples: the role of the United Nations in the twenty-first century",

1. *Decides* that the Millennium Summit shall consist of a total of six meetings, on the basis of two meetings a day, as follows:

Wednesday, 6 September 2000, from 9 a.m. to 1 p.m. and from 3 p.m. to 6 p.m.;

Thursday, 7 September 2000, from 9 a.m. to 1 p.m. and from 3 p.m. to 6 p.m.;

Friday, 8 September 2000, from 9 a.m. to 1 p.m. and from 3 p.m. to 6 p.m.;

2. *Decides also* that the Millennium Summit shall hold four interactive round-table sessions, as follows:

Wednesday, 6 September 2000, from 3 p.m. to 6 p.m.;

Thursday, 7 September 2000, from 10 a.m. to 1 p.m. and from 3 p.m. to 6 p.m.;

Friday, 8 September 2000, from 10 a.m. to 1 p.m.;

3. *Decides further* that the list of speakers for the Millennium Summit and the modalities for the round tables shall be established in accordance with the procedure set forth in the annex to the present resolution.

ANNEX

Establishment of the list of speakers and organization of the round tables for the Millennium Summit of the United Nations

A

1. The list of speakers for the Millennium Summit will be established on the basis of six meetings. At the opening meeting, on Wednesday, 6 September 2000, the first speakers will be the two Co-Chairpersons of the Millennium Summit, the Secretary-General and the head of State or head of the delegation of the host country of the Organization. Therefore, the opening meeting will have 32 speaking slots. The morning meetings of Thursday, 7 September 2000, and Friday,

8 September 2000, will have 40 speaking slots. The Wednesday and Thursday afternoon meetings will have 30 speaking slots. The Friday afternoon meeting will have 20 speaking slots since the last hour will be devoted to the closing of the Millennium Summit.

2. The list of speakers for the Millennium Summit will be established initially as follows:

(a) The representative of the Secretary-General will draw one name from a box containing the names of all Member States, the Holy See and Switzerland, in their capacity as observer States, and Palestine, in its capacity as observer. This procedure will be repeated until all names have been drawn from the box, thus establishing the order in which participants will be invited to choose their meetings and select their speaking slots;

(b) Consultations will continue regarding the possible participation of one or more representatives of intergovernmental organizations, parliaments and civil society;

(c) Six boxes will be prepared, each one representing a meeting and each one containing numbers corresponding to speaking slots at that meeting;

(d) Once the name of a Member State, observer State, or Palestine, in its capacity as observer, has been drawn by the representative of the Secretary-General, that Member State, observer State, or Palestine, in its capacity as observer, will be invited first to choose a meeting and then to draw from the appropriate box the number indicating the speaking slot in the meeting.

3. The establishment of the initial list of speakers for the Millennium Summit as outlined in paragraph 2 above will take place at a meeting to be scheduled as soon as possible during the month of May 2000.

4. Subsequently, the list of speakers for each meeting will be rearranged in accordance with the established practice of the General Assembly when organizing each category of speakers, following the order resulting from the selection process outlined in paragraph 2 above:

(a) Heads of State will thus be accorded first priority, followed by heads of Government; vice-presidents, crown princes/princesses; the highest-ranking official of the Holy See and Switzerland, in their capacity as observer States, and Palestine, in its capacity as observer; ministers; and permanent representatives;

(b) In the event that the level at which a statement is to be made is subsequently changed, the speaker will be moved to the next available speaking slot in the appropriate category at the same meeting;

(c) Participants may arrange to exchange their speaking slots in accordance with the established practice of the General Assembly;

(d) Speakers who are not present when their speaking turn comes will be automatically moved to the next available speaking slot within their category.

5. In order to accommodate all speakers at the Millennium Summit, statements should be limited to five minutes, on the understanding that this will not preclude the distribution of more extensive texts.

B

6. The four round tables will have at least 40 seats each and will be chaired by a head of State or Government.

7. The chairpersons of three of the round tables will be from the three regions not represented by the two Co-Chairpersons of the Millennium Summit. Those three chairpersons will be selected by their respective regional groups in consultation with the President of the General Assembly. The choice of chairperson of the fourth round table will be subject to further consultations.

8. Following the selection of the chairpersons of the round tables, each regional group will determine which of its members will participate in each round table, ensuring that equitable geographical distribution will be maintained, allowing for some flexibility. The chairpersons of the regional groups will communicate to the President of the General Assembly the list of countries from their respective regions that will participate in each round table. Member States are encouraged to be represented at the round tables at the level of heads of State or Government.

9. All four round tables will cover the same overarching theme and sub-themes.

On 11 August [meeting 99], the Assembly adopted **resolution 54/281** [draft: A/54/L.87, as orally revised] without vote [agenda item 49 (b)].

Organization of the Millennium Summit of the United Nations

The General Assembly,

Recalling its resolution 53/202 of 17 December 1998, by which it decided, inter alia, to designate the fifty-fifth session of the General Assembly "The Millennium Assembly of the United Nations" and to convene, as an integral part of the Millennium Assembly, a Millennium Summit of the United Nations,

Recalling also its resolution 54/254 of 15 March 2000, in which it:

(a) Decided that the Millennium Summit should be held from 6 to 8 September 2000,

(b) Decided also that the Millennium Summit would be composed of plenary meetings and four interactive round-table sessions, with each interactive session to be held in concurrence with a plenary meeting,

(c) Decided further that, owing to the unique symbolic moment of the Millennium Summit, the country of the President of the fifty-fourth session of the General Assembly and the country of the President of the fifty-fifth session of the Assembly would jointly preside over the Summit,

(d) Requested the President of the General Assembly to hold consultations with all Member States in an open-ended process, with a view to taking decisions on all outstanding issues relating to the Millennium Summit, including its outcome,

Recalling further its resolution 54/261 of 10 May 2000, in which it:

(a) Decided that the Millennium Summit shall consist of a total of six meetings, on the basis of two meetings a day,

(b) Decided also that the Millennium Summit shall hold four interactive round-table sessions, the modalities for which shall be established in accordance with the following procedure:

(i) The four round tables will have at least forty seats each and will be chaired by a head of State or Government,

(ii) The chairpersons of three of the round tables will be from the three regions not represented by the two Co-Chairpersons of the Millennium Summit. Those three chairpersons will be selected by their respective regional groups in consultation with the President of the General Assembly. The choice of chairperson of the fourth round table will be subject to further consultations,

(iii) Following the selection of the chairpersons of the round tables, each regional group will determine which of its members will participate in each round table, ensuring that equitable geographical distribution will be maintained, allowing for some flexibility. The chairpersons of the regional groups will communicate to the President of the General Assembly the list of countries from their respective regions that will participate in each round table. Member States are encouraged to be represented at the round tables at the level of heads of State or Government,

(iv) All four round tables will cover the same overarching theme and sub-themes,

Bearing in mind that the list of speakers for the plenary meetings was established by the drawing of lots in accordance with the provisions contained in resolution 54/261,

Decides that the Millennium Summit shall be organized in accordance with the procedure set forth in the annex to the present resolution.

ANNEX
Organization of the Millennium Summit of the United Nations

1. Owing to the unique symbolic moment of the Millennium Summit, the two Co-Chairpersons, the head of State of the country of the President of the fifty-fourth session of the General Assembly (Namibia) and the head of State of the country of the President of the fifty-fifth session of the Assembly (Finland), will jointly preside over the Summit. The podium in the General Assembly Hall will have three seats to accommodate the two Co-Chairpersons and the Secretary-General. In the absence of one of the heads of State of these countries, the highest-ranking official in the delegation of these countries will sit instead.

2. The overarching theme of the Millennium Summit, "The role of the United Nations in the twenty-first century", will also be the agenda of the round tables. The heads of State and heads of Government would be free to discuss any sub-themes proposed in the report of the Secretary-General, those raised during the consultations, or any other matter they wish to address.

3. Pursuant to General Assembly resolution 54/261, it has been agreed that one of the four round tables will be chaired by the Group of African States. Thus, the four round tables will be chaired by the following four regional groups:

(a) African States;
(b) Asian States;
(c) Eastern European States;
(d) Latin American and Caribbean States.

4. Each head of State or head of Government or head of delegation attending the round tables may be accompanied by two advisers.

5. The composition of the four round tables will be subject to the principle of equitable geographical distribution. Thus, for each regional group, the distribution of its members for participation in each round table will be done in the following manner:

(a) For the round table to be held on Wednesday, 6 September, from 3 p.m. to 6 p.m.:
(i) African States: fifteen Member States;
(ii) Asian States: fifteen Member States;
(iii) Eastern European States: seven Member States;
(iv) Latin American and Caribbean States: ten Member States;
(v) Western European and other States: nine Member States;

(b) For the round table to be held on Thursday, 7 September, from 10 a.m. to 1 p.m.:
(i) African States: fifteen Member States;
(ii) Asian States: fifteen Member States;
(iii) Eastern European States: seven Member States;
(iv) Latin American and Caribbean States: ten Member States;
(v) Western European and other States: nine Member States;

(c) For the round table to be held on Thursday, 7 September, from 3 p.m. to 6 p.m.:
(i) African States: fifteen Member States;
(ii) Asian States: fifteen Member States;
(iii) Eastern European States: seven Member States;
(iv) Latin American and Caribbean States: ten Member States;
(v) Western European and other States: nine Member States;

(d) For the round table to be held on Friday, 8 September, from 10 a.m. to 1 p.m.:
(i) African States: fifteen Member States;
(ii) Asian States: fifteen Member States;
(iii) Eastern European States: seven Member States;
(iv) Latin American and Caribbean States: ten Member States;
(v) Western European and other States: nine Member States.

6. The round tables will be chaired in the following manner:

(a) The round table to be held on Wednesday, 6 September, from 3 p.m. to 6 p.m., will be chaired by His Excellency Mr. Goh Chok Tong, Prime Minister of the Republic of Singapore;

(b) The round table to be held on Thursday, 7 September, from 10 a.m. to 1 p.m., will be chaired by His Excellency Mr. Aleksander Kwasniewski, President of the Republic of Poland;

(c) The round table to be held on Thursday, 7 September, from 3 p.m. to 6 p.m., will be chaired by His Excellency Mr. Hugo Rafael Chávez Frías, President of the Bolivarian Republic of Venezuela;

(d) The round table to be held on Friday, 8 September, from 10 a.m. to 1 p.m., will be chaired by His Excellency Mr. Abdelaziz Bouteflika, President of the People's Democratic Republic of Algeria.

7. Member States that are not members of any of the regional groups may participate in different round tables to be determined in consultation with the President of the General Assembly. The Holy See and Switzerland, in their capacity as observer States, and Palestine, in its capacity as observer, as well as the intergovernmental organizations listed in paragraph 11 below, may also participate in different round tables to be determined also in consultation with the President of the General Assembly.

8. The list of participants in each round table will be made available as soon as possible.

9. The round tables would be closed to the media and the general public. Accredited delegates and observers will be able to follow the proceedings of the round tables via a closed-circuit television in the overflow room.

10. Summaries of the deliberations of the four round tables will be presented orally by the chairpersons of the round tables, individually or collectively, during the concluding plenary meeting of the Millennium Summit.

11. Pursuant to resolution 54/261, one or more representatives of intergovernmental organizations, parliaments and civil society may participate in the plenary meetings of the Millennium Summit, time permitting. In this connection, and without prejudice to other organizations which have observer status in the General Assembly, a representative of each of the following may be included in the list of speakers for the plenary meetings of the Summit:

League of Arab States
Organization of African Unity
European Commission
Organization of the Islamic Conference
Conference of Presiding Officers of National Parliaments
Millennium Forum.

12. In addition, a representative of the International Committee of the Red Cross and a representative of the Sovereign Military Order of Malta may also be included in the list of speakers for the plenary meetings of the Millennium Summit, time permitting.

13. Other than for Member States, the list of speakers for the plenary meetings of the Millennium Summit will be closed on Wednesday, 16 August 2000.

Credentials

The Credentials Committee, at its first meeting, on 1 November [A/55/537 & Corr.1], had before it a memorandum by the Secretary-General indicating that, as at 31 October, 134 Member States had submitted the formal credentials of their representatives. The Assistant Secretary-General for Legal Affairs said the Secretary-General would report later on the representatives of those Member States whose formal credentials had not yet been received.

The Committee also examined the credentials of Afghanistan, from which it had received two sets of credentials: a communication signed by Burhanuddin Rabbani, "President of the Islamic State of Afghanistan", presenting a delegation whose leader was described as "Permanent Representative to the United Nations"; and a communication signed by Mulla Mohammad Rabbani, "Chairman of the Ministers Council of the Islamic Emirate of Afghanistan", presenting a delegation led by a "Deputy Foreign Minister". The Committee deferred a decision on those credentials on the understanding that the current

representatives of the country accredited to the United Nations would continue to participate in the work of the Assembly.

The Committee adopted a resolution accepting the credentials received and recommended to the Assembly a draft resolution for adoption. On 6 November, the Assembly, by **resolution 55/16 A**, approved the first report of the Credentials Committee.

At its second meeting, on 4 December [A/55/537/Add.1], the Credentials Committee considered a 1 December memorandum by the Secretary-General indicating that formal credentials had been received from an additional 28 Member States. Information had also been communicated to the Secretary-General concerning representatives of 27 other Member States.

The Committee accepted the credentials received and recommended to the Assembly a draft resolution for adoption. On 6 December, the Assembly, by **resolution 55/16 B**, approved the second report of the Credentials Committee.

Agenda

During its resumed fifty-fourth session, the General Assembly took a number of actions relating to its agenda, which were listed in **decision 54/402 B**: it decided to consider, in plenary, a sub-item on the appointment of members of the Advisory Committee on Administrative and Budgetary Questions (ACABQ) in order to consider expeditiously the Secretary-General's note [A/54/101/Rev.1/Add.1]; to include an additional item on the financing of the United Nations Organization Mission in the Democratic Republic of the Congo; to consider an item on the implementation of the outcome of the Fourth World Conference on Women, in plenary, so as to consider two draft decisions [A/54/L.77, A/54/L.78]; to include an additional item on the review of the problem of HIV/AIDS in all its aspects in plenary; to reopen the item on cooperation between the United Nations and the Preparatory Commission for the Comprehensive Nuclear-Test-Ban Treaty Organization; to consider the items on social development, including questions relating to the world social situation and to youth, ageing, disabled persons and the family, in plenary, in order to consider a draft resolution [A/54/L.85], and on human rights questions, in plenary, so as to consider a draft resolution [A/54/L.84]; to examine the sub-item "High-level international intergovernmental consideration of financing for development" in plenary so as to act on a draft resolution [A/54/L.82]; and to reopen debate on the sub-item "Renewal of the dialogue on strengthening international economic cooperation for development through partnership" in plenary to enable it to consider a letter from the Chairman of the Second (Economic and Financial) Committee [A/54/952].

On 15 March, the Assembly, by **decision 54/467**, decided to reconsider the question of accreditation of non-governmental organizations (NGOs) to the twenty-third special session on women.

On 5 September, the Assembly decided to include the following in the draft agenda of its fifty-fifth session: a sub-item entitled "United Nations reform: measures and proposals" (**decision 54/489**); and items on strengthening of the UN system (**decision 54/490**), revitalization of the work of the General Assembly (**decision 54/491**), restructuring and revitalization of the United Nations in the economic, social and related fields (**decision 54/492**), the question of Cyprus (**decision 54/493**), improving the financial situation of the United Nations (**decision 54/495**), financing of the United Nations Operation in Somalia II (**decision 496**), financing of the United Nations Operation in Mozambique (**decision 54/497**), financing of the United Nations Mission in Haiti (**decision 54/498**), financing of the United Nations Observer Mission in Liberia (**decision 54/499**), financing of the United Nations Assistance Mission for Rwanda (**decision 54/500**), cooperation between the United Nations and the Preparatory Commission for the Comprehensive Nuclear-Test-Ban Treaty Organization (**decision 54/501**), and armed aggression against the Democratic Republic of the Congo (**decision 54/502**).

On 15 June, by **decision 54/462 B**, the Assembly, on the recommendation of the Fifth (Administrative and Budgetary) Committee, deferred until its fifty-fifth session consideration of: management irregularities causing financial losses to the Organization; improving the working methods of the Fifth Committee; UN security coordination; information technologies; reports of the Office of Internal Oversight Services (OIOS); and measures taken to improve procurement activities in the field.

On 7 April, the Assembly deferred consideration of the question of improving the Fifth Committee's working methods (**decision 54/470**), and gratis personnel provided by Governments and other entities (**decision 54/ 471**) until the second part of its resumed fifty-fourth session; and the proposed regulations governing the status, basic rights and duties of officials other than Secretariat officials and experts on mission until its fifty-fifth session (**decision 54/472**).

On 7 April (**decision 54/478**), the Assembly deferred consideration of the Secretary-General's report on the activities of OIOS, and, on 15 June, it deferred a decision on the question of the relocation of South Africa to the group of Member States set out in paragraph 3 *(c)* of Assembly resolution 43/232 [YUN 1989, p. 793] (**decision 54/486**).

On 11 September, by **decision 55/402 A**, the Assembly, on the recommendation of the General Committee [A/55/250 & Corr.1], adopted the agenda [A/55/251] and the allocation of agenda items [A/55/252] for the fifty-fifth session to the plenary or appropriate Main Committee. It deferred the questions of the Comorian island of Mayotte and of the Malagasy islands of Glorieuses, Juan de Nova, Europa and Bassas da India and included them in the provisional agenda of its fifty-sixth session.

On 28 September, by the same decision, the Assembly, on the recommendation of the General Committee [A/55/250/Add.1], included in the agenda of its fifty-fifth session the item entitled "Cooperation between the United Nations and the Economic Community of Central African States" and decided to consider it in plenary, as well as the item on crime prevention and criminal justice.

On 17 October, by the same decision, on the recommendation of the General Committee [A/55/250/Add.2], the Assembly decided to include the following additional items and to consider them in plenary: cooperation between the United Nations and the Organization for the Prohibition of Chemical Weapons; follow-up to the outcome of the Millennium Summit; and peace, security and reunification on the Korean peninsula. On 16 November, the Assembly, on the recommendation of the General Committee [A/55/250/Add.3], included an additional item on observer status for the Economic Community of Central African States in the Assembly and allocated it to the Sixth (Legal) Committee.

On 14 December, the Assembly deferred the item "Implementation of the resolutions of the United Nations" and included it in the provisional agenda of its fifty-sixth (2001) session (**decision 55/433**).

On 23 December, the Assembly decided to retain 80 items for consideration during the resumed fifty-fifth (2001) session (**decision 55/458**).

Second, Third and Fifth Committees

The General Assembly, by **decision 55/423** of 4 December, approved the organization of work of the Third (Social, Humanitarian and Cultural) Committee and its 2001-2002 biennial programme of work.

The Assembly, by **decision 55/449** of 20 December, approved the biennial programme of work of the Second Committee for 2001-2002 and, by **decision 55/454** of 23 December, approved the biennial programme of work of the Fifth Committee for 2001-2002.

Amendment to Assembly's rules of procedure

On 3 November [meeting 51], the General Assembly adopted **resolution 55/14** [draft: A/55/L.19] without vote [agenda item 61].

Amendment to rule 1 of the rules of procedure of the General Assembly

The General Assembly,

Recalling its resolution 51/241 of 31 July 1997, by which it adopted the recommendations of the Open-ended High-level Working Group on the Strengthening of the United Nations System as contained in the annex to the resolution,

Recalling in particular paragraph 17 of the annex to resolution 51/241, in which it decided, inter alia, that the plenary meetings of the General Assembly should be formally opened every year on the first Tuesday following 1 September,

Noting that the Monday immediately preceding the first Tuesday following 1 September falls on a United Nations holiday at Headquarters,

Mindful that, for practical reasons, the closing of the regular sessions of the General Assembly should be on a Monday, which should not be a holiday, and the opening of the regular sessions should be on the following day, that is to say, on a Tuesday,

Recalling its resolutions 52/232 of 4 June 1998, 53/224 of 7 April 1999 and 53/239 of 8 June 1999, by which it took ad hoc decisions concerning the opening and/or closing dates of the fifty-second, fifty-third, fifty-fourth and fifty-fifth sessions of the General Assembly,

Recalling also paragraph 2 of resolution 52/232, in which it decided that the International Day of Peace would continue to be observed on the opening day of the regular sessions,

1. *Decides* to amend rule 1 of the rules of procedure of the General Assembly to read: "The General Assembly shall meet every year in regular session commencing on the Tuesday following the second Monday in September";

2. *Also decides* that this amendment shall take effect as from 2001 and that, therefore, for that year, the fifty-fifth session of the General Assembly shall close on Monday, 10 September 2001, and the fifty-sixth session of the Assembly shall open on Tuesday, 11 September 2001.

Security Council

The Security Council held 167 formal meetings in 2000, adopted 50 resolutions and issued 41 presidential statements. It considered 49 agenda items (see APPENDIX IV). In September [A/55/366], the Secretary-General, in accordance with Article 12, paragraph 2, of the Charter of the United Nations and with the consent of the Council, notified the General Assembly of 36 matters relative to the maintenance of international peace and security that the Council had discussed since his previous annual notification [YUN 1999, p. 1346]. The Secretary-General also listed 65 matters that the Council had not discussed since then. On 16 October, the Assembly, by **decision 55/405**, took note of the Secretary-General's note.

By **decision 55/406** of 19 October, the Assembly took note of the Security Council's report for the period 16 June 1999 to 15 June 2000 [A/55/2].

By **decision 55/458** of 23 December, the Assembly decided that the item on the report of the Security Council remained for consideration during its resumed fifty-fifth (2001) session.

Documentation

Working methods and procedures

In February [S/2000/155], the Council President reported that new Council members would, at their request, be invited to observe the Council's informal consultations for one month immediately preceding their term of membership (i.e., with effect from 1 December) to acquaint themselves with the Council's activities. Each delegation should be represented at the level of permanent representative or deputy permanent representative.

In April [S/2000/319], the Council President reported the establishment, on a temporary basis, of an informal working group of the Council to develop general recommendations on how to improve the effectiveness of sanctions. The working group should report its findings to the Council by 30 November 2000.

Membership

The General Assembly continued to examine the question of expanding the Security Council's membership. It considered the report of the Open-ended Working Group on the Question of Equitable Representation on and Increase in the Membership of the Security Council and Other Matters related to the Security Council [A/54/47], established by Assembly resolution 48/26 [YUN 1993, p. 212].

On 5 September, the Assembly, by **decision 54/488**, took note of the Working Group's report and decided that it should continue its work and report before the end of the Assembly's fifty-fifth session.

In June [A/54/909], Belarus said that an increase in the Council's membership was a pivotal element of reform, and proposed measures and principles it said would facilitate the correction of the current imbalance in regional representation on the Council.

On 23 December, the Assembly, by **decision 55/458**, decided that the item on the question of equitable representation on and increase in the membership of the Council and related matters remained for consideration at its resumed fifty-fifth (2001) session.

Economic and Social Council

The Economic and Social Council held its organizational session for 2000 on 27 January and 1 and 4 February, a resumed organizational session on 28 February, 9 March, 3, 10 and 12 May and 16 June, and a special high-level meeting with the Bretton Woods institutions (the World Bank Group and the International Monetary Fund (IMF)) on 18 April, all in New York. The Council held its substantive session from 5 to 28 July and a resumed substantive session on 18 and 30 October and 22 November, also in New York.

On 27 January, the Council elected five members of its bureau for 2000—the President and four Vice-Presidents (see APPENDIX III). It also adopted the agenda of its organizational session [E/2000/2 & Add.1]. On 21 July (**decision 2000/225**), the Council suspended rule 22 of its rules of procedure and requested Felix Mbayu, Chargé d'affaires a.i. of the Permanent Mission of Cameroon, to preside over the general segment of the Council in lieu of Martin Belinga-Eboutou, Vice-President of the Council, who was unable to preside due to circumstances beyond his control.

On 4 February, the Council adopted the provisional agenda of its substantive session [E/2000/1] (**decision 2000/202**) and decided on the working arrangements for that session (**decision 2000/204**).

On 5 July, the Council adopted the agenda of its 2000 substantive session [E/2000/100] and approved the programme of work of the session [E/2000/L.6]; on 7 July, it approved requests by NGOs to be heard [E/2000/82] (**decision 2000/223**).

(For agenda lists, see APPENDIX IV.)

Sessions and segments

During 2000, the Economic and Social Council adopted 35 resolutions and 117 decisions. By **decision 2000/204** of 4 February, the Council decided that the high-level segment of its substantive session should be held from 5 to 7 July; the operational activities segment from 10 to 13 July; the coordination segment from 14 to 18 July;

the humanitarian affairs segment from 19 to 21 July; and the general segment from 21 to 28 July. It decided that 31 July should be devoted to the finalization of all outstanding matters and documents, while the session would conclude on 1 August with the adoption of proposals. By **decision 2000/205** of the same date, the Council decided that the high-level meeting with the Bretton Woods institutions should be held on 18 April.

By **decision 2000/217** of 3 May, the Council changed the schedule of the substantive session: the coordination segment would take place from 10 to 12 July and the operational activities segment from 13 to 18 July, with the high-level meeting on operational activities taking place on 17 July.

The work of the Council in 2000 was summarized in its report to the General Assembly [A/55/3/Rev.1]. On 4 (**decision 55/424**), 19 (**decision 55/436**) and 20 (**decisions 55/448** and **55/450**) December, the Assembly took note of various chapters of the report.

2000 and 2001 sessions

On 4 February, the Council decided that the theme of the humanitarian affairs segment of the 2000 substantive session should be "Strengthening the coordination of humanitarian response and the role of technology in mitigating the effects of natural disasters and other humanitarian emergencies, including conflicts, with particular reference to the displacement of persons arising therefrom" (**decision 2000/206**); for the item on regional cooperation, the theme would be "Follow-up to major United Nations conferences and summits: exchange of regional experiences" (**decision 2000/207**).

By **decision 2000/303** of 18 October, the Council agreed on the following themes for the 2001 substantive session: the high-level segment would be devoted to "The role of the United Nations system in supporting the efforts of African countries to achieve sustainable development", and the coordination segment would be devoted to "The role of the United Nations in promoting development, particularly with respect to access to and transfer of knowledge and technology, especially information and communication technologies, inter alia, through partnerships with relevant stakeholders, including the private sector".

Work programme

On 4 February, the Economic and Social Council considered its basic programme of work for 2000 and 2001 [E/2000/1]. By **decision 2000/203**, the Council took note of the list of questions for inclusion in the programme of work for the 2001 substantive session.

Restructuring issues

The Economic and Social Council continued consideration of the implementation of General Assembly resolutions 50/227 [YUN 1996, p. 1249] and 52/12 B [YUN 1997, p. 1392] on the restructuring and revitalization of the United Nations in the economic, social and related fields. It had before it the Secretary-General's reports on the restructuring and revitalization of the United Nations in the economic, social and related fields and co-operation with the Bretton Woods institutions [A/55/180-E/2000/67 & Corr.1]; an informal summary of the special high-level meeting with the Bretton Woods institutions [E/2000/79]; and the consolidated report on the work of the Council's functional commissions in 2000 [E/2000/85].

On 24 July, the Council deferred consideration of the matter to its resumed session of 2000.

Coordination, monitoring and cooperation

Institutional mechanisms

ACC activities

During 2000, the Administrative Committee on Coordination (ACC) considered ways to advance the goals and targets of the UN Millennium Declaration (see p. 49), adopted at the Millennium Summit of the General Assembly. In its annual overview report for 2000 [E/2001/55], ACC stated that the effective follow-up to the Declaration should be a key priority for the advocacy, policy development and operational activities of the system as a whole. The system-wide effort should encompass a strengthening and refinement of instruments for the sharing of information and for monitoring and measuring progress.

ACC continued consideration of the UN system response to the challenges of globalization. It recognized that all UN system organizations were actively engaged in addressing different dimensions of globalization and underscored the need to understand better interlinkages among those dimensions and to develop more integrated approaches among system organizations, as well as promote such approaches among Member States and in the international community. ACC also considered the health and social dimensions of globalization, including the role of civil society and bridging the digital divide. ACC agreed to

strengthen arrangements for a continuous exchange of information on experiences concerning interaction with civil society and to draw lessons from best practices. It agreed to pursue a wide range of ideas for bridging the digital divide and to update the ACC statement on universal access to basic communication and information services [YUN 1997, p. 566].

ACC also considered inter-agency follow-up to UN conferences and summits and UN response to long-term food security in the Horn of Africa. It endorsed the recommendations of a task force on the scope of the UN response to the challenge of eliminating food insecurity, including a strategy of broadening opportunities for sustainable livelihoods protecting the most needy and creating an enabling environment for reducing food insecurity and poverty.

Preparations for a number of major events of system-wide importance were also reviewed. The issue of staff security and safety remained high on the ACC agenda. It issued a statement [ACC/2000/20] supporting the Secretary-General's proposals for achieving more stable and secure funding of security expenditures and ensuring adequate levels of staff to manage security.

Also discussed were measures for the reform and renewal of ACC's own functioning. As part of those reforms, two new high-level committees (High-level Committee on Programmes and High-level Committee on Management) were established and mandated, in the first instance, to review ACC's subsidiary bodies. It also consolidated different secretariat capacities into a single secretariat, with co-locations in New York and Geneva. In October, the executive heads concluded that a new name for ACC would highlight both its function as a board concerned with fostering the unity of the entire UN system and its capacity of bringing together all its member organizations at the highest executive level. They therefore proposed, subject to the Economic and Social Council's concurrence, to modify its name to "United Nations System's Chief Executives Board (C.E.B.)".

ACC also considered assistance to countries invoking Article 55 of the Charter on assistance to third States affected by the application of sanctions.

ACC held two regular sessions during the year (Rome, Italy, 6-7 April; New York, 27-28 October). Its principal subsidiary bodies met as follows:

Organizational Committee (Rome, 8-10 March, 10 April; New York, 2-4 and 30 October); Consultative Committee on Administrative Questions (Personnel and General Administrative Questions), ninety-second (Vienna, 29-31 March) and ninety-third (Geneva, 22-23 June, and New York, 17 July) sessions;

High-level Committee on Management, first session (New York, 11-12 December); Consultative Committee on Administrative Questions (Financial and Budgetary Questions), ninety-first session (Montreal, Canada, 28 August-1 September); Consultative Committee on Programme and Operational Questions, sixteenth (Geneva, 29 February–2 March) and seventeenth (New York, 20-22 September) sessions.

Bodies on specific subjects met as follows:

Subcommittee on Oceans and Coastal Areas, eighth (The Hague, Netherlands, 19-21 January) and ninth (London, 26-28 July) sessions; Subcommittee on Nutrition, twenty-seventh session (Washington, D.C., 10-14 April); Inter-Agency Committee on Sustainable Development, fifteenth (New York, 24-25 January) and sixteenth (Geneva, 18-19 September) meetings; Inter-Agency Committee on Women and Gender Equality, fifth session (New York, 23-25 February); Ad Hoc Inter-Agency Meeting on Security (Bonn, Germany, 16-18 May); Subcommittee on Demographic Estimates and Projections, twenty-first session (Geneva, 27-29 June); Joint United Nations Information Committee, twenty-sixth session (Geneva, 11-13 July); Subcommittee on Statistical Activities, thirty-fourth session (Washington, D.C., 20-22 September); Subcommittee on Drug Control, eighth session (Vienna, 28-29 September); Subcommittee on Water Resources, twenty-first session (Bangkok, Thailand, 16-20 October); Information Systems Coordination Committee, eighth session (Geneva, 25-27 October).

Report for 1999

ACC's annual overview report for 1999 [E/2000/53] was considered on 22 June by the Committee for Programme and Coordination (CPC), which concurred with the approach pursued in its preparation. CPC recommended that ACC, while continuing to address the HIV/AIDS epidemic in Africa, should give attention to other geographical regions, particularly Asia, where it also took note of the Secretary-General's initiative. CPC noted the attention ACC continued to give to improving staff security. It emphasized the need for an intergovernmental process to study cooperation between the United Nations and the private sector. It stressed ACC's important role in mobilizing and monitoring economic assistance to States with special economic problems arising out of measures imposed by the Security Council and in supporting efforts of States affected by the developments in the Balkans for their economic recovery, structural adjustment and development.

The Committee recommended that ACC report on progress in the implementation of relevant intergovernmental mandates and that it review elements of its 2000 programme of work as they did not conform with legislative decisions.

The Economic and Social Council, by **decision 2000/291** of 28 July, took note of the ACC report.

Programme coordination

The Committee for Programme and Coordination held an organizational meeting on 2 May and its fortieth session from 5 June to 1 July and from 21 to 29 August, all in New York [A/55/16].

The Committee considered the programme performance of the United Nations for the 1998-1999 biennium and ways in which the full implementation and quality of mandated programmes and activities could be ensured and better assessed by and reported to Member States; the proposed medium-term plan for 2002-2005; an outline of the proposed programme budget for the biennium 2002-2003; evaluation; coordination questions, including ACC's annual report for 1999 (see above), the UN System-wide Special Initiative for the Implementation of the United Nations New Agenda for the Development of Africa in the 1990s (see p. 877), and the advancement of the women's programme (see p. 1123); a Joint Inspection Unit report entitled "Private sector involvement and cooperation with the United Nations system"; improving the working methods and procedures of the Committee; the provisional agenda for the forty-first session; and adoption of the report on its fortieth session.

By **decision 2000/292** of 28 July, the Economic and Social Council took note of CPC's report on the first part of its fortieth session.

Joint Inspection Unit

The Joint Inspection Unit (JIU) submitted its thirty-first report to the General Assembly covering 1 January to 31 December 1999 [A/55/34]. The report examined measures to further JIU's functioning and impact, relations and cooperation with participating organizations and other oversight bodies and follow-up on its reports and recommendations. Within the context of enhancing the functioning and impact of the Unit, the report noted that improvement in the handling of its reports by participating organizations was important. The Unit considered that serious consideration should be given in the future to providing it with adequate resources so as to allow it better to discharge its mandate. To remain relevant to its participating organizations, JIU recognized the need for keeping abreast of developments in their governing bodies, while gaining a better knowledge of the functioning of their secretariats. The Unit wanted to ensure that it was not perceived as a foreign mechanism. Its statutory role would therefore need to be stressed more forcefully. In that regard, it had embarked on a series of meetings with the secretariats of its participating organizations, which had proved useful in showing JIU's commitment to a mutually fruitful dialogue and to ensuring a better understanding and appreciation of its relevance.

The Unit intended to have in place as soon as possible a tracking system as part of the follow-up system approved by the General Assembly in resolution 54/16 [YUN 1999, p. 1277] and to include in its annual reports on a system-wide basis the status of approved recommendations that had not been implemented. Information compiled for reports produced during 1994-1999 showed that, although the majority of participating organizations submitted JIU reports regularly or fairly frequently to their legislative bodies, they were often taken up one to three years after their publication and there had not been many instances of those bodies making specific decisions on the recommendations contained in the reports. JIU stressed that it was vital for legislative organs of participating organizations to take specific action on each of the relevant recommendations.

GENERAL ASSEMBLY ACTION

On 7 April [meeting 95], the General Assembly, on the recommendation of the Fifth Committee [A/54/511/Add.2], adopted **resolution 54/255** without vote [agenda item 118].

Reports of the Joint Inspection Unit
The General Assembly,

Recalling Economic and Social Council resolution 1999/66 of 16 December 1999 on the report of the Joint Inspection Unit entitled "Review of the Administrative Committee on Coordination and its machinery",

Having considered the report of the Unit and the note by the Secretary-General transmitting his comments and those of the Administrative Committee on Coordination thereon,

Having considered also the report of the Unit entitled "The United Nations system common services at Geneva, part I, Overview of administrative cooperation and coordination" and the note by the Secretary-General transmitting his comments and those of the Administrative Committee on Coordination thereon, as well as the report of the Office of Internal Oversight Services on the review of common services in the United Nations,

1. *Takes note* of the report of the Joint Inspection Unit entitled "Review of the Administrative Committee on Coordination and its machinery" and the comments of the Secretary-General and the Administrative Committee on Coordination thereon contained in the note by the Secretary-General, with the exception of paragraph 42;

2. *Endorses* the recommendations of the Unit contained in its report entitled "The United Nations system common services at Geneva, part I, Overview of administrative cooperation and coordination" and the

comments of the Secretary-General and the Administrative Committee on Coordination thereon;

3. *Stresses* that pursuit of common services at Geneva should be one of many tools available to organizations and managers to obtain goods and services in the most efficient and effective manner;

4. *Invites* the Unit to continue to examine common services at other duty stations where the United Nations system offices and agencies are established, where feasible, and to report thereon to the General Assembly;

5. *Stresses* the importance for the Unit of using the most recent data available in its reports and, in this regard, calls upon the Secretary-General and the executive heads of the organizations of the United Nations system to provide timely data to the Unit;

6. *Calls upon* the Secretary-General, in coordination with the Unit, to ensure the timely issuance of the reports of the Unit and the related comments of the Secretary-General and the Administrative Committee on Coordination, in order to enable the General Assembly and all the governing bodies to take prompt action thereon;

7. *Encourages* the Secretary-General and the Administrative Committee on Coordination to take concrete steps to enhance common services, and invites legislative organs of other organizations to take similar action on the basis of the present resolution;

8. *Requests* the Unit to continue to improve its reports consistent with the requirements of its follow-up system approved by the General Assembly in resolution 54/16 of 29 October 1999, in particular the provisions of paragraph 4 of annex I to its annual report for the period from 1 July 1996 to 30 June 1997;

9. *Requests* the Secretary-General to report to the General Assembly at its fifty-sixth session on the measures taken in connection with paragraph 7 above.

Other coordination matters

Follow-up to international conferences

The Economic and Social Council, at its coordination segment in July, discussed the coordination of the policies and activities of the specialized agencies and other bodies of the UN system related to the assessment of the progress made within the UN system, through the conference reviews, in the promotion of an integrated and coordinated implementation of and follow-up to major UN conferences and summits in the economic, social and related fields.

The Council had before it a May report of the Secretary-General [E/2000/57], which assessed the progress made. It examined lessons learned from the five-year conference reviews and proposed ways to further improve those reviews in the light of the upcoming 10-year reviews. It also discussed progress in developing an integrated approach to conference implementation and ways to deepen UN system collaborative efforts in achieving common conference goals.

The report stated that the modalities and scope of the five-year reviews varied considerably. Their coverage was too wide-ranging, allowing insufficient time for functional commissions and preparatory committees to negotiate the draft outcomes. There was a temptation in some reviews to reopen agreed issues and, in a number of areas, the five-year span proved too short for adequate assessment. However, they did identify a number of issues to be addressed, such as the problem of resources and the HIV/AIDS epidemic, the need for collective action to offset globalization's negative social and economic consequences, the increasing inequality within and between countries, the importance of rehabilitating the public sector and the impact of conflicts and crises on social development.

The five-year reviews also addressed common themes and overarching conference goals, new challenges posed by globalization and HIV/AIDS, information technology and armed conflicts. According to the report, they did not build on each other, and their outcomes often repeated one another and were contradictory in approaches. In addition, guidance developed by the Council since 1995 on many cross-cutting themes had not always been fed into the reviews.

In terms of progress in developing an integrated approach to conference implementation, the five-year reviews showed that there continued to be strong political will towards that effort. However, much remained to be done to bring about real integration among policies and programmes, at the national level and in international development cooperation. Greater effort was needed to translate the integrated approach into effective action plans and strategies to implement conference outcomes. The reviews did not give very clear indications as to the extent to which Governments had developed "cross-sectoral" strategies. National strategies focused by and large on individual conferences and on such overarching goals as gender, poverty, the environment, health and education. Overall, the main challenges to integrated conference implementation continued to be the need to effectively incorporate economic, social and environmental concerns in the design of policies nationally and internationally, and to foster an enabling environment for development at national and international levels, particularly ensuring greater consistency among macroeconomic, trade, aid, financial, social and environmental policies, so that all supported agreed development goals.

On 27 July, the Council, in agreed conclusions 2000/2, noted that major UN conferences and summits of the 1990s had contributed towards the development of an integrated framework and a global partnership for development. It noted the progress made by the UN system to support an integrated and coordinated follow-up to major UN conferences and summits and encouraged the system to further strengthen its efforts in that regard. The Council was committed to ensuring that the upcoming reviews were effectively coordinated and would lead to substantial progress in the implementation of their goals, building on lessons learned and taking into account the outcome of earlier reviews.

The Council was of the view that a number of options, including those proposed by the Secretary-General, could be considered for ensuring an effective and comprehensive review and invited the relevant functional commissions to consider them and other possible options and to inform the Council in 2001 of the outcome of their discussion. It asked the Secretary-General to prepare a comprehensive report on the different options, including the views of the functional commissions, which, with other intergovernmental bodies, should identify the agenda and scope of the reviews for which they had primary responsibility. The reviews should ascertain lessons learned, constraints encountered and ways of overcoming them and the impact of new developments and challenges. The outcome document should be action-oriented and concise. The regional commissions should also be involved in the reviews. The Council reiterated the importance of relevant, accurate and timely statistics and indicators for evaluating the implementation of outcomes. UN system organizations should limit the information requested from Governments and prepare harmonized and simplified formats for use by Governments in preparing information on a single subject or cluster of subjects. The governing bodies of specialized agencies and organizations should be extensively involved in the review processes and ACC should bring to the attention of the Council coordination issues and common challenges to conference follow-up. ACC and its subsidiary bodies should also continue to broaden the task-manager approach in promoting integrated and coordinated follow-up to major UN conferences and summits, including reporting on cross-cutting themes. Ways should be examined for improving the participation of civil society in the review process. The Council encouraged further progress to integrate conference outcome implementation into country assistance programmes. National reports on conference follow-up should be used in determining programmes in countries. The Council encouraged the building of partnerships and networks in pursuit of conference goals, called on Governments to mobilize resources for implementing conference and summit goals and urged donor countries to strive to fulfil the agreed target of 0.7 per cent of their gross national product for overall official development assistance.

The Council, on 27 (**decision 2000/234**) and 28 (**decision 2000/290**) July, took note of the Secretary-General's report on the progress made in implementation of and follow-up to major UN conferences.

Conference indicators

In response to Economic and Social Council resolution 1999/55 [YUN 1999, p. 1353], the Secretary-General submitted a May report [E/2000/60] on progress made on basic indicators for the integrated and coordinated implementation of and follow-up to major UN conferences and summits at all levels. It provided details of progress achieved in networking and exchange of relevant information and metadata; further development of indicators as a means of implementation; harmonization and rationalization of conference indicators; identification of commonly used indicators and mobilization of resources to support national statistical capacity-building in developing countries; and coordination of statistical capacity-building programmes.

According to the report, the UN Statistics Division played an active role in promoting networking among relevant institutions with regard to statistics and basic indicators. At its thirty-first session (see p. 1200), the Statistical Commission agreed to the programme of activities for the newly created Statistical Development and Analysis Section of the Division to follow up on resolution 1999/55, work with other organizations in harmonizing common indicators and analyse the statistical requirements created by the monitoring needs of recent international conferences and summits. The ACC Subcommittee on Statistical Activities and the Division established an indicator web page, which would contain metadata on all conference indicators of international organizations and would constitute an analytical tool for identifying overlap, inconsistencies and gaps. Methodological work had been initiated in the development of standards for measuring such issues as poverty and the informal sector, highlighted by conferences and summits. Also, IMF, with the support of the Statistics Division, had initiated work on data quality. Regarding the identification of a limited number of commonly used indicators, work on the various existing indicator lists had progressed and there was a tendency towards convergence. The common country assessment (CCA) indicator framework, developed by the United Nations Development Group as the most recent and comprehensive in-

dicator framework following UN conferences and summits, was currently working in over 100 countries and would produce practical experience at the country level on the validity of the indicator list and help address some of the concerns voiced by countries. It was intended to feed back those country experiences into future review processes of the CCA indicator framework to design an indicator list that was useful and implementable.

Regarding statistical capacity-building, the report noted the creation of the PARIS21 initiative—the Partnership in Statistics for Development in the Twenty-first Century—which shared global knowledge and best practices and encouraged South-South cooperation in statistical capacity-building. The UN Secretariat, UN funding and specialized agencies and the Bretton Woods institutions had been active in a number of initiatives to support statistical capacity-building. However, the resources engaged for statistical capacity-building were still insufficient to face the problems of data gaps and data quality.

In conclusion, the Secretary-General stated that, although it would take some time for resolution 1999/55 to be fully implemented, some encouraging signs had emerged. There was widespread acceptance among international agencies of the need for better coordination, existing frameworks were being reviewed and there was a trend towards greater harmonization. The United Nations Development Assistance Framework–CCA indicator framework provided a unique basis for moving towards a core indicator set, as it was based on the outcome of all UN conferences and summits. However, it still had to be re-examined and validated in cooperation with national Governments and specialized agencies. Although international efforts to achieve better coordination would alleviate some of the problems related to basic indicators, the most pressing issue remained the lack of a sufficient development information infrastructure, and building national statistical capacity was the only way to address that problem in the long run.

By **decision 2000/290** of 28 July, the Council took note of the Secretary-General's report.

ECONOMIC AND SOCIAL COUNCIL ACTION

On 28 July [meeting 45], the Economic and Social Council adopted **resolution 2000/27** [draft: E/2000/L.30] without vote [agenda item 6].

Basic indicators for the integrated and coordinated implementation of and follow-up to major United Nations conferences and summits at all levels

The Economic and Social Council,

Recalling its decision 1998/290 of 31 July 1998 on basic indicators for the integrated and coordinated implementation of and follow-up to the major United Nations conferences and summits in the economic, social and related fields and section II of its resolution 1999/55 of 30 July 1999 on integrated and coordinated implementation of and follow-up to major United Nations conferences and summits,

1. *Takes note* of the report of the Secretary-General on progress on basic indicators for the integrated and coordinated implementation of and follow-up to major United Nations conferences and summits at all levels;

2. *Reaffirms* the important role that the functional commissions play in the integrated and coordinated follow-up to and evaluation of the implementation of the outcome of major United Nations conferences and summits;

3. *Also reaffirms* the recommendations contained in section II of its resolution 1999/55 and the importance of national efforts to build statistical capacity in all countries, including through statistical training, and of effective international support in this context for developing countries;

4. *Urges* countries, the United Nations funds and programmes, the Secretariat, bilateral funding agencies, the Bretton Woods institutions and regional funding agencies to work closely together to implement these recommendations and to mobilize the required resources and coordinate their efforts to support national statistical capacity-building in developing countries, in particular in least developed countries;

5. *Emphasizes* that the indicators used by the Secretariat in the context of the integrated and coordinated implementation of and follow-up to major United Nations conferences and summits should be developed with the full participation of all countries and approved by the relevant intergovernmental bodies;

6. *Calls upon* the United Nations funds and programmes, functional and regional commissions and specialized agencies to keep under review the full range of indicators used in their reports and information networks with full participation and ownership of Member States, with a view to avoiding duplication, as well as ensuring the transparency, consistency and reliability of these indicators;

7. *Requests* the executive boards of the United Nations funds and programmes, with the support of the Statistics Division of the Secretariat, to review as a matter of urgency the common country assessment indicator frameworks and report thereon to the Council at its substantive session of 2001;

8. *Invites* the Statistical Commission to serve as the intergovernmental focal point for the review of the indicators used by the United Nations system for the integrated and coordinated implementation of and follow-up to major United Nations conferences and summits at all levels, and the methodologies employed in formulating them, including in the context of the elaboration of the common country assessment, and to make recommendations with a view to facilitating future consideration by the Council;

9. *Reiterates its invitation* to the Statistical Commission, with the assistance of the Statistics Division of the Secretariat and in close cooperation with other relevant bodies of the United Nations system, including the Administrative Committee on Coordination, and, as appropriate, other relevant international organiza-

tions, to review, with a view to facilitating future consideration by the Council, the work undertaken in harmonizing and rationalizing basic indicators in the context of the follow-up to United Nations conferences and summits, taking fully into account the decisions taken in other functional and regional commissions and, in that process, to identify a limited number of common indicators from among those currently accepted and widely used by the States Members of the United Nations, in order to lessen the data provision burden on Member States, bearing in mind the work done so far in this area;

10. *Stresses* the need further to develop indicators on means of implementation to evaluate progress towards conference goals in creating an enabling environment for development;

11. *Urges* the Secretariat, in particular the Statistics Division, to accelerate, with the support of the Subcommittee on Statistical Activities of the Administrative Committee on Coordination, the promotion of networking among national and international institutions in the area of statistics and in the development and application of indicators agreed to in the relevant intergovernmental bodies relating to the follow-up to the United Nations conferences and summits, in the context of its role as the focal point in the United Nations system in this regard, as well as to facilitate the exchange of relevant information and metadata between the United Nations system and Member States;

12. *Requests* the Secretary-General to prepare a progress report on the implementation of section II of resolution 1999/55 and the present resolution, for consideration by the Council at its substantive session of 2002.

The UN and other organizations

Cooperation with organizations

Economic Cooperation Organization

In a July report [A/55/122], the Secretary-General described cooperation between the Economic Cooperation Organization and various UN bodies during 1999 and 2000. The Assembly took action on the report in **resolution 55/42** (see p. 941).

Council of Europe

In July [A/55/191], Italy requested the inclusion in the agenda of the General Assembly's fifty-fifth session of a supplementary item entitled "Cooperation between the United Nations and the Council of Europe". Annexed to the letter was an explanatory memorandum, describing the Council's mandate, structure and membership, as well as the background and legal basis for its cooperation with the United Nations and current cooperation arrangements. The memorandum said that the Council was in a position to make a substantial contribution to the United Nations in meeting an increasing number of challenges.

The Assembly took action on the question of cooperation with the Council of Europe in **resolution 55/3** (see p. 410).

Asian-African Legal Consultative Committee

An August report of the Secretary-General [A/55/221] outlined the various activities of the Asian-African Legal Consultative Committee in support of the work of the United Nations (see p. 1273).

The Assembly, in **resolution 55/4**, took action on that report.

Organization of the Islamic Conference

In response to General Assembly resolution 54/7 [YUN 1999, p. 1358], the Secretary-General submitted a September report on cooperation between the United Nations and the Organization of the Islamic Conference [A/55/368]. The two organizations continued consultations on political matters, especially ongoing peacemaking efforts, which had become an important dimension in their cooperation. A Vienna meeting of their secretariats from 11 to 13 July covered a number of topics, including the development of science and technology, trade and development, assistance to refugees, food security and agriculture, and investment mechanisms and joint ventures. They also considered proposals to enhance cooperation between them.

GENERAL ASSEMBLY ACTION

On 30 October [meeting 44], the General Assembly adopted **resolution 55/9** [draft: A/55/L.17] without vote [agenda item 24].

Cooperation between the United Nations and the Organization of the Islamic Conference

The General Assembly,

Recalling its resolutions 37/4 of 22 October 1982, 38/4 of 28 October 1983, 39/7 of 8 November 1984, 40/4 of 25 October 1985, 41/3 of 16 October 1986, 42/4 of 15 October 1987, 43/2 of 17 October 1988, 44/8 of 18 October 1989, 45/9 of 25 October 1990, 46/13 of 28 October 1991, 47/18 of 23 November 1992, 48/24 of 24 November 1993, 49/15 of 15 November 1994, 50/17 of 20 November 1995, 51/18 of 14 November 1996, 52/4 of 22 October 1997, 53/16 of 29 October 1998 and 54/7 of 25 October 1999,

Recalling also its resolution 3369(XXX) of 10 October 1975, by which it decided to invite the Organization of the Islamic Conference to participate in the sessions and the work of the General Assembly and of its subsidiary organs in the capacity of observer,

Having considered the report of the Secretary-General on cooperation between the United Nations and the Organization of the Islamic Conference,

Taking into account the desire of both organizations to continue to cooperate closely in the political, eco-nomic, social, humanitarian, cultural and technical fields and in their common search for solutions to global problems, such as questions relating to international peace and security, disarmament, self-determination, decolonization, fundamental human rights and economic and technical development,

Recalling the Articles of the Charter of the United Nations that encourage the activities through regional cooperation for the promotion of the purposes and principles of the United Nations,

Noting the strengthening of cooperation between the United Nations, its funds and programmes and specialized agencies and the Organization of the Islamic Conference, its subsidiary organs and its specialized and affiliated institutions,

Noting also the encouraging progress made in the ten priority areas of cooperation between the two organizations, as well as in the identification of other areas of cooperation between them,

Convinced that the strengthening of cooperation between the United Nations and other organizations of the United Nations system and the Organization of the Islamic Conference and its organs and institutions contributes to the promotion of the purposes and principles of the United Nations,

Welcoming the results of the general meeting of the organizations and agencies of the United Nations system and the Organization of the Islamic Conference and its subsidiary organs and specialized and affiliated institutions, held in Vienna from 11 to 13 July 2000,

Noting with appreciation the determination of both organizations to strengthen further the existing cooperation by developing specific proposals in the designated priority areas of cooperation, as well as in the political field,

1. *Takes note with satisfaction* of the report of the Secretary-General;

2. *Takes note* of the conclusions and recommendations adopted by the organizations and agencies of the United Nations system and the Organization of the Islamic Conference and its subsidiary organs and specialized and affiliated institutions;

3. *Notes with satisfaction* the active participation of the Organization of the Islamic Conference in the work of the United Nations towards the realization of the purposes and principles embodied in the Charter of the United Nations;

4. *Requests* the United Nations and the Organization of the Islamic Conference to continue to cooperate in their common search for solutions to global problems, such as questions relating to international peace and security, disarmament, self-determination, decolonization, fundamental human rights, social and economic development and technical cooperation;

5. *Welcomes* the efforts of the United Nations and the Organization of the Islamic Conference to continue to strengthen cooperation between the two organizations in areas of common concern and to review the ways and means for enhancing the actual mechanisms of such cooperation;

6. *Welcomes with appreciation* the continuing cooperation between the United Nations and the Organization of the Islamic Conference in the field of peacemaking and preventive diplomacy, and takes note of the close cooperation between the two organizations in

continuing the search for a peaceful and lasting solution to the conflict in Afghanistan;

7. *Welcomes* the efforts of the secretariats of the two organizations to strengthen information exchange, coordination and cooperation between them in areas of mutual interest in the political field and their ongoing consultations with a view to developing the modalities of such cooperation;

8. *Also welcomes* the periodic high-level meetings between the Secretary-General of the United Nations and the Secretary-General of the Organization of the Islamic Conference, as well as between senior secretariat officials of the two organizations, and encourages their participation in important meetings of the two organizations;

9. *Encourages* the specialized agencies and other organizations of the United Nations system to continue to expand their cooperation with the subsidiary organs and specialized and affiliated institutions of the Organization of the Islamic Conference, particularly by negotiating cooperation agreements, and invites them to multiply the contacts and meetings of the focal points for cooperation in priority areas of interest to the United Nations and the Organization of the Islamic Conference;

10. *Urges* the United Nations and other organizations of the United Nations system, especially the lead agencies, to provide increased technical and other forms of assistance to the Organization of the Islamic Conference and its subsidiary organs and specialized and affiliated institutions in order to enhance cooperation;

11. *Expresses its appreciation* to the Secretary-General for his continued efforts to strengthen cooperation and coordination between the United Nations and other organizations of the United Nations system and the Organization of the Islamic Conference and its subsidiary organs and specialized and affiliated institutions to serve the mutual interests of the two organizations in the political, economic, social and cultural fields;

12. *Requests* the Secretary-General to report to the General Assembly at its fifty-sixth session on the state of cooperation between the United Nations and the Organization of the Islamic Conference;

13. *Decides* to include in the provisional agenda of its fifty-sixth session the item entitled "Cooperation between the United Nations and the Organization of the Islamic Conference".

League of Arab States

In response to General Assembly resolution 54/9 [YUN 1999, p. 1355], the Secretary-General submitted a September report [A/55/401] on cooperation between the United Nations and the League of Arab States (LAS). The report summarized follow-up action on proposals agreed to at meetings between organizations of the UN system and LAS. A sectoral meeting on youth and employment between the United Nations and LAS was held in Beirut, Lebanon, from 23 to 25 May. A number of working papers were discussed and recommendations made for future action. Informal consultations were held on cooperation

between the political affairs departments of the two organizations.

On 30 October [meeting 44], the General Assembly adopted **resolution 55/10** [draft: A/55/L.18 & Add.1] without vote [agenda item 25].

Cooperation between the United Nations and the League of Arab States

The General Assembly,

Recalling its previous resolutions on cooperation between the United Nations and the League of Arab States,

Having considered the report of the Secretary-General on cooperation between the United Nations and the League of Arab States,

Recalling article 3 of the Pact of the League of Arab States, which entrusts the Council of the League with the function of determining the means whereby the League will collaborate with the international organizations which may be created in the future to guarantee peace and security and organize economic and social relations,

Noting the desire of both organizations to consolidate, develop and enhance further the ties existing between them in the political, economic, social, humanitarian, cultural, technical and administrative fields,

Taking into account the report of the Secretary-General entitled "An Agenda for Peace", in particular section VII, concerning cooperation with regional arrangements and organizations, and the "Supplement to an Agenda for Peace",

Convinced of the need for more efficient and coordinated utilization of available economic and financial resources in order to promote the common objectives of the two organizations,

Acknowledging the need for closer cooperation between the United Nations system and the League of Arab States and its specialized organizations in achieving the goals and objectives of the two organizations,

1. *Takes note with satisfaction* of the report of the Secretary-General;

2. *Commends* the continued efforts of the League of Arab States to promote multilateral cooperation among Arab States, and requests the United Nations system to continue to lend its support;

3. *Expresses its appreciation* to the Secretary-General for the follow-up action taken by him to implement the proposals adopted at the meetings between the representatives of the secretariats of the United Nations and other organizations of the United Nations system and the General Secretariat of the League of Arab States and its specialized organizations, including the sectoral meeting on youth and employment held in Beirut from 23 to 25 May 2000;

4. *Requests* the Secretariat of the United Nations and the General Secretariat of the League of Arab States, within their respective fields of competence, to intensify further their cooperation for the realization of the purposes and principles embodied in the Charter of the United Nations, the strengthening of international peace and security, economic and social development, disarmament, decolonization,

self-determination and the eradication of all forms of racism and racial discrimination;

5. *Requests* the Secretary-General to continue his efforts to strengthen cooperation and coordination between the United Nations and other organizations and agencies of the United Nations system and the League of Arab States and its specialized organizations in order to enhance their capacity to serve the mutual interests and objectives of the two organizations in the political, economic, social, humanitarian, cultural and administrative fields;

6. *Calls upon* the specialized agencies and other organizations and programmes of the United Nations system:

(a) To continue to cooperate with the Secretary-General and among themselves, as well as with the League of Arab States and its specialized organizations, in the follow-up of multilateral proposals aimed at strengthening and expanding cooperation in all fields between the United Nations system and the League of Arab States and its specialized organizations;

(b) To strengthen the capacity of the League of Arab States and of its institutions and specialized organizations to benefit from globalization and information technology and to meet the development challenges of the new millennium;

(c) To step up cooperation and coordination with the specialized organizations of the League of Arab States in the organization of seminars and training courses and in the preparation of studies;

(d) To maintain and increase contacts and improve the mechanism of consultation with the counterpart programmes, organizations and agencies concerned regarding projects and programmes in order to facilitate their implementation;

(e) To participate whenever possible with organizations and institutions of the League of Arab States in the execution and implementation of development projects in the Arab region;

(f) To inform the Secretary-General, not later than 30 June 2001, of the progress made in their cooperation with the League of Arab States and its specialized organizations and, in particular, of the follow-up action taken on the multilateral and bilateral proposals adopted at the previous meetings between the two organizations;

7. *Also calls upon* the specialized agencies and other organizations and programmes of the United Nations system to increase their cooperation with the League of Arab States and its specialized organizations in the priority sectors of energy, rural development, desertification and green belts, training and vocational education, technology, environment and information and documentation;

8. *Requests* the Secretary-General of the United Nations, in cooperation with the Secretary-General of the League of Arab States, to encourage periodic consultation between representatives of the Secretariat of the United Nations and of the General Secretariat of the League of Arab States in order to review and strengthen coordination mechanisms with a view to accelerating implementation of, and follow-up action on, the multilateral projects, proposals and recommendations adopted at the meetings between the two organizations;

9. *Recommends* that the United Nations and all organizations of the United Nations system make the greatest possible use of Arab institutions and technical expertise in projects undertaken in the Arab region;

10. *Reaffirms* that, in order to enhance cooperation and for the purpose of review and appraisal of progress, a general meeting between representatives of the United Nations system and the League of Arab States should be held once every two years and that joint inter-agency sectoral meetings should also be convened on a biennial basis to address priority areas of major importance to the development of the Arab States, on the basis of agreement between the United Nations system and the League of Arab States and its specialized organizations;

11. *Also reaffirms* the importance of holding the next general meeting on cooperation between the representatives of the secretariats of organizations of the United Nations system and of the General Secretariat of the League of Arab States and its specialized organizations during 2001;

12. *Requests* the Secretary-General to submit to the General Assembly at its fifty-sixth session a report on the implementation of the present resolution;

13. *Decides* to include in the provisional agenda of its fifty-sixth session the item entitled "Cooperation between the United Nations and the League of Arab States".

Organization of American States

In July [A/55/184], the Secretary-General reported on cooperation between the United Nations and the Organization of American States (see p. 258).

The General Assembly took action on that report in **resolution 55/15**.

Caribbean Community

The Secretary-General submitted an August report [A/55/215] on cooperation between the United Nations and the Caribbean Community (see p. 259).

The General Assembly took action on that report in **resolution 55/17**.

Inter-Parliamentary Union

In response to General Assembly resolution 54/12 [YUN 1999, p. 1357], the Secretary-General submitted an October report [A/55/409] describing the action taken by the United Nations and the Inter-Parliamentary Union (IPU) to secure parliamentary input to major UN events, as well as the parliamentary action, coordinated by IPU, to support or complement UN work in peace and security, economic and social development, international law and human rights, democracy, governance and gender issues. The report also highlighted the variety and scope of the cooperation between the two organizations, demonstrating the potential for a greater contribution by national parliaments, through IPU, to UN work and to disseminating an understanding of that work and ensuring the requisite follow-up. IPU held its first meeting of Presiding Officers of National Parliaments in New York from 30 August to 1 September as a prelude to the Millennium Summit. In its final declaration, which was submitted to the Summit, the Conference confirmed the need for increasing parliamentary contribution to the work of the UN system (see p. 65).

Working relations between the UN Secretariat and that of IPU had been strengthened, and several practical arrangements had been institutionalized in the course of the year to improve information sharing, logistical support and policy coordination. Reciprocal access to documentation and meeting information was facilitated. The UN Department of Public Information worked closely with the IPU secretariat to issue press releases and other products to promote joint initiatives between the two organizations. The Secretary-General expressed the hope that the increasingly close and productive relationship between them might soon be recognized through a new, strengthened and formalized relationship between IPU and the Assembly.

GENERAL ASSEMBLY ACTION

On 8 November [meeting 55], the General Assembly adopted **resolution 55/19** [draft: A/55/L.20 & Add.1, as orally revised] without vote [agenda item 26].

Cooperation between the United Nations and the Inter-Parliamentary Union

The General Assembly,

Recalling its resolution 54/12 of 27 October 1999, in which it expressed the wish that the cooperation between the United Nations and the Inter-Parliamentary Union be strengthened further,

Having considered the report of the Secretary-General, which takes stock of such cooperation over the last twelve months,

Noting with appreciation the resolutions adopted by the Inter-Parliamentary Union and its activities during the past year in support of the United Nations, as well as the recommendation contained in the aforementioned report that the increasingly close and productive relationship between the two organizations be recognized through a new and formalized relationship between the Inter-Parliamentary Union and the General Assembly,

Welcoming the Conference of Presiding Officers of National Parliaments which was held at United Nations Headquarters from 30 August to 1 September 2000 and which concluded with the unanimous adoption of the Declaration entitled "The Parliamentary vision for international cooperation at the dawn of the third millennium",

Recalling with satisfaction the United Nations Millennium Declaration in which Member States resolved to strengthen further cooperation between the United

Nations and national parliaments through their world organization, the Inter-Parliamentary Union, in various fields, including peace and security, economic and social development, international law and human rights and democracy and gender issues,

Recalling the unique inter-State character of the Inter-Parliamentary Union,

1. *Welcomes* the efforts made by the Inter-Parliamentary Union to provide for a greater parliamentary contribution and enhanced support to the United Nations, and calls for the cooperation between the two organizations to be consolidated further;

2. *Requests* the Secretary-General, in consultation with Member States and with the Inter-Parliamentary Union, to explore ways in which a new and strengthened relationship may be established between the Inter-Parliamentary Union, the General Assembly and its subsidiary organs, and to report thereon to the Assembly by May 2001;

3. *Also requests* the Secretary-General to submit a report to the General Assembly at its fifty-sixth session on the various aspects of cooperation between the United Nations and the Inter-Parliamentary Union;

4. *Decides* to include in the provisional agenda of its fifty-sixth session the item entitled "Cooperation between the United Nations and the Inter-Parliamentary Union".

On 23 December, the Assembly, by **decision 55/458**, decided that the item on cooperation between the United Nations and IPU would remain for consideration at its resumed fifty-fifth (2001) session.

Economic Community of Central African States

In September [A/55/233], Equatorial Guinea requested the inclusion of an additional item entitled "Cooperation between the United Nations and the Economic Community of Central African States" in the agenda of the fifty-fifth session of the General Assembly. An explanatory memorandum annexed to the letter detailed the activities of the organization (see p. 232). The Assembly, in **resolution 55/22**, requested the Secretary-General to establish cooperation between the two organizations.

Organization for Security and Cooperation in Europe

The Secretary-General submitted a report on cooperation between the United Nations and the Organization for Security and Cooperation in Europe [A/55/98] (see p. 407). The General Assembly, by **resolution 55/179**, took action on the report.

Organization of African Unity

The Secretary-General submitted a report [A/55/498] on activities undertaken in various areas to promote cooperation between the United Nations and the Organization of African Unity (see p. 230).

The General Assembly took action on the report in **resolution 55/218**.

Cooperation between the United Nations and the Black Sea Economic Cooperation Organization

On 20 December [meeting 87], the General Assembly, on the recommendation of the Second Committee [A/55/587], adopted **resolution 55/211** without vote [agenda item 100].

Cooperation between the United Nations and the Black Sea Economic Cooperation Organization

The General Assembly,

Recalling its resolution 54/5 of 8 October 1999, by which it granted observer status to the Black Sea Economic Cooperation Organization,

Recalling also that one of the purposes of the United Nations is to achieve international cooperation in solving international problems of an economic, social or humanitarian nature,

Recalling further the Articles of the Charter of the United Nations that encourage activities through regional cooperation for the promotion of the purposes and principles of the United Nations,

Bearing in mind that the Charter signed at the summit meeting at Yalta, Ukraine, on 5 June 1998, which transformed the Black Sea Economic Cooperation Organization into a regional economic organization with a legal identity on the international scene, and the Istanbul Summit Declaration, adopted on 17 November 1999 by the heads of State or Government of the States members of the Black Sea Economic Cooperation Organization, confirmed the commitment of the Organization to the promotion of effective economic, social and democratic reforms in the region by application of the pragmatic concept that economic cooperation is an effective confidence-building measure,

Convinced that the strengthening of cooperation between the United Nations and other organizations of the United Nations system and the Black Sea Economic Cooperation Organization contributes to the promotion of the purposes and principles of the United Nations,

1. *Takes note* of the Istanbul Summit Declaration adopted on 17 November 1999 by the heads of State or Government of the States members of the Black Sea Economic Cooperation Organization and of the desirability expressed therein of strengthening cooperation between the United Nations Secretariat and the Black Sea Economic Cooperation Organization;

2. *Invites* the Secretary-General of the United Nations to undertake consultations with the Secretary-General of the Black Sea Economic Cooperation Organization, with a view to promoting cooperation and coordination between the two Secretariats;

3. *Invites* the specialized agencies and other organizations and programmes of the United Nations system to cooperate with the Secretary-General of the United Nations and the Secretary-General of the Black Sea Economic Cooperation Organization in order to initiate consultations and programmes with that Organization and its associated institutions for the attainment of their objectives;

4. *Requests* the Secretary-General to submit to the General Assembly at its fifty-seventh session a report on the implementation of the present resolution;

5. *Decides* to include in the provisional agenda of its fifty-seventh session an item entitled "Cooperation between the United Nations and the Black Sea Economic Cooperation Organization".

Observer status

Inter-American Development Bank

On 12 December [meeting 84], the General Assembly, on the recommendation of the Sixth Committee [A/55/616], adopted **resolution 55/160** without vote [agenda item 171].

Observer status for the Inter-American Development Bank in the General Assembly

The General Assembly,

Wishing to promote cooperation between the United Nations and the Inter-American Development Bank,

1. *Decides* to invite the Inter-American Development Bank to participate in the sessions and the work of the General Assembly in the capacity of observer;

2. *Requests* the Secretary-General to take the necessary action to implement the present resolution.

Economic Community of Central African States

On 12 December [meeting 84], the General Assembly, on the recommendation of the Sixth Committee [A/55/648], adopted **resolution 55/161** without vote [agenda item 184].

Observer status for the Economic Community of Central African States in the General Assembly

The General Assembly,

Wishing to promote cooperation between the United Nations and the Economic Community of Central African States,

1. *Decides* to invite the Economic Community of Central African States to participate in the sessions and the work of the General Assembly in the capacity of observer;

2. *Requests* the Secretary-General to take the necessary action to implement the present resolution.

International Institute for Democracy and Electoral Assistance

On 14 August [A/55/226], Sweden requested the inclusion of an item entitled "Observer status for the International Institute for Democracy and Electoral Assistance in the General Assembly". In an explanatory memorandum, it stated that the objective of the Institute was to promote and advance sustainable democracy worldwide. An important feature of its democratization assistance was its partnership with other international organizations, including UNDP. It believed that increased cooperation with the United Nations in democracy and conflict management, the relationship between democratization, sustainable development and poverty eradication, democracy as a human right and capacity-building would be crucial. The Institute therefore considered it desirable to consolidate and strengthen links with the United Nations and that observer status in the General Assembly would be mutually beneficial.

By **decision 55/429** of 12 December, the Assembly deferred a decision on the request for observer status for the Institute until its fifty-sixth (2001) session.

Participation of organizations in UN work

Intergovernmental organizations

On 3 May, the Economic and Social Council, by **decision 2000/213**, having considered the applications of the Asian and Pacific Development Centre and the Inter-American Development Bank, decided that the organizations might participate on a continuing basis, without the right to vote, in the deliberations of the Council on questions within the scope of their activities.

Private sector cooperation with UN system

A January note by the Secretary-General transmitted a report of JIU on private sector involvement and cooperation with the UN system [A/54/700]. The report analysed the lines along which a new partnership between the UN system and the private sector could be developed and how areas of mutual interests and benefits could translate into actions to better serve the goals of the Organization as a whole. The report noted that the private sector was already actively engaged in many UN activities, based on the recognition by the business community of the UN's contribution to the establishment of a favourable environment for private sector activities and a thorough understanding and acceptance by all UN Member States of the private sector as a partner in supporting economic growth and sustainable development. However, the objectives and nature of the partnership needed to be further clarified. The report also described how UN agencies, funds and programmes were trying to maximize the benefits to be drawn from private sector engagement, while protecting themselves from the risks inherent in it. Those precautions were not uniform throughout the system and the inconsistencies in their nature and how they were applied could undermine the image, credibility, integrity and legal immunity of the UN system.

JIU recommended that UN system organizations should set realistic objectives and expectations for their private sector partnership; carry out programmes targeting the private sector; each designate a focal point or easily accessible units to serve and assist the business community; ensure a UN presence at relevant business events; and encourage private sector participation in their relevant activities. The working group established by the Secretary-General's Senior Management Group should draft guidelines on relations with the private sector. Taking into consideration the working group's deliberations, UN agencies that had not done so should adopt guidelines, which should include a statement of principles and procedures for dealing with the private sector. The United Nations should ensure the implementation of Staff Rule 101.6, including the feasibility of extending rules for financial disclosures. Other participating organizations should examine whether their respective staff rules and regulations were sufficient to guarantee that staff did not hold financial interest in commercial enterprises with which a partnership was envisaged. Participating organizations should ensure that bureaucratic procedures and lengthy response time did not discourage initiatives from the private sector, and mechanisms for sharing information and best practices should be established, using the ACC structure, to ensure consistency of policy and harmonization of procedures throughout the UN system.

In June [A/54/700/Add.1], ACC submitted its comments on the JIU report, endorsing the general thrust of JIU's recommendations.

Non-governmental organizations

Committee on NGOs

The Committee on Non-Governmental Organizations, at its resumed 1999 session (New York, 17-28 January 2000) [E/1999/109/Add.2 (Part I & Corr.1 & Part II)], considered new applications for consultative status with the Economic and Social Council, including applications deferred from its 1998 and 1999 regular sessions, as well as requests for reclassification. It recommended 62 organizations for consultative status, 11 for reclassification and one to maintain its current status. The Committee took note of 43 quadrennial reports covering the periods 1994-1997 and 1995-1998, with two reservations. It recommended three draft decisions for action by the Council.

The Committee also considered implementation of Council decision 1996/302 [YUN 1996, p. 1368] on NGOs on the Roster, reviewed its working methods as they related to implementation of Council resolution 1996/31 [ibid., p. 1360], including the process of accreditation of NGO representatives, and Council decision 1995/304 [YUN 1995, p. 1445] on arrangements for consultation with NGOs.

On 3 May (**decision 2000/216**), the Council noted the Committee's report on its resumed 1999 session and approved the provisional agenda and documentation for its 2000 session. On the same date (**decision 2000/214**), the Council granted general consultative status to two NGOs and special consultative status to 61 NGOs. It reclassified six organizations from special to general consultative status and five organizations from the Roster to special consultative status. The Council noted that the Committee did not recommend granting consultative status to three organizations and that it had closed its consideration of the application of the International Committee of Peace and Human Rights. Also on 3 May (**decision 2000/215**), the Council approved the request of 15 NGOs on the Roster for the purposes of the work of the Commission on Sustainable Development to expand their participation into other fields of the Council's work.

At its 2000 session (New York, 15-19 May and 12-23 June) [E/2000/88 (Part I & Part II & Corr.1)], the Committee recommended 37 organizations for consultative status, deferred consideration of 72 applications and recommended that one organization be reclassified from special to general consultative status. It adopted four draft decisions for action by the Council. The Committee also decided to suspend the consultative status of two organizations—the International Council of the Associations for Peace in the Continents (ASO-PAZCO) and the Transnational Radical Party—for three years each.

The Committee resumed consideration of the items it had discussed at its 1999 resumed session (see above). Concerning its working methods, the Committee noted that several of the mechanisms put in place did not function as smoothly as anticipated. In view of the various incidents reported involving abuses of the accreditation procedure, the Committee emphasized the importance of the Secretariat continuing to hold training sessions to better inform NGOs about accreditation procedures and the principles of consultative status set out in resolution 1996/31. The Secretariat should distribute guidelines and other informative materials related to the work of the Council and its subsidiary bodies, including rules for NGOs to follow, and organizations should limit the number of representatives they accredited to meetings. On the issue of national clearance, clarification was sought regarding cases of national NGOs registered in one country yet active in another, raising the question as to whether nationality would apply to the country

of registration or to the one in which it aimed its work. The Committee, noting that current procedure left the determination of its classification to the organization itself, agreed on the necessity of establishing an objective definition to distinguish between national and international organizations. It also decided that, since not all NGO representatives could afford the financial expenses of an extended stay in New York, it would consider hearing those representatives with the longest distance to travel at the beginning of each session.

The Committee approved the provisional agenda of its 2001 session.

On 20 (**decision 2000/224 A**) and 25 (**decision 2000/224 B**) July, the Council authorized the Committee to hold a resumed 2000 session for a half day on 21 and 27 July, respectively, to consider replies from those NGOs whose consultative status was recommended for suspension.

The Committee, at its resumed 2000 session (21 and 27 July) [E/2000/88 (Part I/Add.1 & Part II/Add.1)], considered a submission from ASOPAZCO but was unable to reach a consensus that the response provided enough grounds for the Committee to reconsider its earlier decision. By a roll-call vote of 9 against, 4 in favour and 2 abstentions, a motion to reconsider the Committee's proposal to the Council to suspend ASOPAZCO's consultative status was defeated. In the case of the Transnational Radical Party, the Committee invited it to submit a comprehensive response by 16 September and recommended that the Council authorize it to hold a 2000 resumed session during the week of 25 September to consider that response. The Committee recommended a draft decision to the Council for adoption.

On 28 July (**decision 2000/294**), the Council decided to take action on 18 October on the four draft decisions contained in the report of the Committee on the first and second parts of its 2000 session, on the understanding that no other meeting requiring the attendance of the experts dealing with NGOs, in particular those experts from the General Assembly's Third Committee, would be convened on the same date. It also decided, pending a decision to be taken at its resumed substantive session, that the privileges enjoyed by ASOPAZCO should be temporarily suspended.

On the same date (**decision 2000/295**), the Council approved the Committee's request to meet for one day during the week of 25 to 29 September to consider the Transnational Radical Party's response. At that meeting, held on 27 September [E/2000/88 (Part II/Add.2)], the Committee, having considered the comprehensive response provided by the Transnational Radical Party, rejected by a roll-call vote (12-5-2) the proposal to reconsider its earlier recommendation to the Council to suspend the organization's consultative status.

On 18 October (**decision 2000/307**), the Council suspended for three years the special consultative status of ASOPAZCO as of 28 July. On the same date (**decision 2000/306**), it granted special consultative status to 34 NGOs and Roster status to three NGOs. It reclassified one organization from special to general consultative status and decided not to grant consultative status to five organizations and to close consideration of the application of the Council for the Defence of Human Rights and Freedom. It requested the Hague Appeal for Peace and Dominicans for Justice and Peace to resubmit their applications when they would have fulfilled the mandatory qualifying period (two years), as well as Safari Club International, which should reapply under the name Safari Club International Foundation.

Also on the same date, the Council authorized the Committee to hold a resumed session from 15 to 26 January 2001 to complete the work of its 2000 session (**decision 2000/308**), and took note of the Committee's report on the first and second parts of its 2000 session and approved the provisional agenda for the 2001 session (**decision 2000/309**).

Requests for hearing

On 23 June, the Committee on NGOs heard requests from NGOs in consultative status to address the Economic and Social Council in connection with items on its agenda [E/2000/82]. The Committee recommended that certain specified NGOs should be heard, on behalf of other specified organizations, during the Council's high-level segment.

Participation of NGOs not in consultative status

By **decision 2000/310** of 18 October, the Economic and Social Council, as an interim measure, invited those NGOs accredited to the twenty-third and/or the twenty-fourth special sessions of the General Assembly to attend the forty-fifth (2001) session of the Commission on the Status of Women and the thirty-ninth (2001) session of the Commission for Social Development, provided they had started the process of applying for consultative status in accordance with Council resolution 1996/31 [YUN 1996, p. 1360].

Strengthening the Secretariat's NGO Section

In May [A/54/520/Add.1], the Secretary-General submitted a report outlining the human re-

sources requirements of the Secretariat's NGO Section, pursuant to General Assembly resolution 54/249 [YUN 1999, p. 1289]. The Secretary-General stated that those resources funded by the regular budget included five Professional and four General Service posts, and were supplemented by the service of volunteers equivalent to some 60 work-months annually (20 at the Professional and 40 at the General Service level). An annual increase of the current staff resources by 12 work-months at both the Professional and General Service levels would be required to enable the Section to carry out its work efficiently and optimize the NGO contribution and participation in UN work.

The Section had obtained some temporary relief through redeployment of staff from other areas in 2000 and efforts in that regard were continuing, but the assistance provided by volunteers and short-term staff had reached the point of having serious negative effects on the Section's work. The Secretary-General therefore proposed that the Section be strengthened by the establishment of one Professional (P-4) and one General Service post at an additional cost of $105,600 under section 9, Economic and social affairs, of the 2000-2001 programme budget.

Also in May [A/54/868], ACABQ recommended that the two new posts be established on a temporary basis in the 2000-2001 biennium and that the proposal be resubmitted in the context of the proposed programme budget for the 2002-2003 biennium. ACABQ reiterated its view that the Secretariat should submit a comprehensive report on the administrative and management implications of the large increase in NGOs involved in UN work, particularly on the impact of the growth on the UN programme budget, so as to allow ACABQ to ascertain the extent to which optimum use was made of current resources, as well as to evaluate such additional resources as might be proposed for the various units of the Secretariat working with NGOs.

GENERAL ASSEMBLY ACTION

On 15 June [meeting 98], the General Assembly, on the recommendation of the Fifth Committee [A/54/691/Add.2], adopted **resolution 54/265** without vote [agenda item 121].

Analysis of the organizational structure and the personnel and technical resources of the Non-Governmental Organizations Section of the Secretariat of the United Nations

The General Assembly,

Recalling its resolution 54/249 of 23 December 1999, in particular paragraph 93,

Having considered the report of the Secretary-General on an analysis of the organizational structure and the personnel and technical resources of the Non-

Governmental Organizations Section of the Secretariat of the United Nations, and the related report of the Advisory Committee on Administrative and Budgetary Questions,

Takes note of the report of the Secretary-General, and endorses the observations and recommendations contained in the report of the Advisory Committee on Administrative and Budgetary Questions.

Conferences and meetings

The Committee on Conferences held organizational meetings on 27 April and 25 July and its substantive session from 7 to 9 August [A/55/32]. The Committee examined requests for additions and changes to the approved calendar of conferences and meetings for 2000 [A/AC.172/2000/2] and the draft revised calendar for 2001. It considered the utilization of conference-servicing resources and facilities, requests for exceptions to General Assembly resolution 40/243 [YUN 1985, p. 1256], documentation- and publication-related matters, translation- and interpretation-related matters, information technology and its working methods. The Committee approved a request from the International Civil Service Commission to convene its fifty-first session from 3 to 20 April in Vienna rather than New York, and noted the decision of the Governing Council of the United Nations Environment Programme to convene its sixth special session from 29 to 31 May in Malmö, Sweden. It also approved requests of the Advisory Board on Disarmament Matters to convene its thirty-fifth session from 5 to 7 July in Geneva rather than New York, of the Commission on the Status of Women to hold a one-day resumed session and of the Preparatory Committee for the special session of the General Assembly on social development to convene a resumed session in June.

The Committee recommended that the Assembly adopt the draft revised calender of conferences and meetings for 2001 and authorize the Committee to make adjustments to the calender as a result of Assembly actions. The Committee noted that the Secretariat had taken into account the arrangements referred to in Assembly resolution 54/248 [YUN 1999, p. 1368] regarding the inclusion of Id al-Adha and Id al-Fitr in the list of official holidays and that no UN meetings should be held on those days, and concerning Orthodox Good Friday. It recommended that, when planning the calender of conferences and meetings, every effort should be made to avoid simultaneous peak periods at the various duty stations. It

requested the Secretariat to avoid scheduling meetings of intergovernmental bodies too closely to each other.

On 8 May [A/C.5/54/62], the Chairman of the Committee on Conferences proposed that the Committee's 2000 session be held in Nairobi as requested in Assembly resolution 54/248 [YUN 1999, p. 1368]. The Fifth Committee considered the request in May and June [A/54/690/Add.2], including a draft resolution [A/C.5/54/L.83], by which the Assembly would have authorized the holding of the session in Nairobi and the payment of travel expenses for one representative of each Member State of the Committee. The Fifth Committee postponed consideration of the draft resolution pending receipt of a statement on programme budget implications and a report from ACABQ.

The Assembly, by **decision 54/482** of 15 June, took note of the report of the Fifth Committee.

On 23 December [meeting 89], the General Assembly, on the recommendation of the Fifth Committee [A/55/702], adopted **resolution 55/222** without vote [agenda item 121].

Pattern of conferences

The General Assembly,

Recalling its relevant resolutions, including resolutions 40/243 of 18 December 1985, 43/222 A to E of 21 December 1988, 47/202 A to D of 22 December 1992, 48/222 A and B of 23 December 1993, 49/221 A to D of 23 December 1994, 50/11 of 2 November 1995, 50/206 A to F of 23 December 1995, 51/211 A to E of 18 December 1996, 52/214 of 22 December 1997, 53/208 A to E of 18 December 1998 and 54/248 of 23 December 1999 and its decisions 38/401 of 23 September 1983 and 52/468 of 31 March 1998,

Having considered the report of the Committee on Conferences, the reports of the Secretary-General and the note by the Secretariat on the distribution of documentation,

Having also considered the report of the Advisory Committee on Administrative and Budgetary Questions,

I
Calendar of conferences and meetings

1. *Notes with appreciation* the work of the Committee on Conferences, and takes note of its report, subject to the provisions of the present resolution;

2. *Approves* the draft revised calendar of conferences and meetings of the United Nations for 2001, as submitted by the Committee on Conferences, also subject to the provisions of the present resolution;

3. *Authorizes* the Committee on Conferences to make adjustments to the calendar of conferences and meetings for 2001 that may become necessary as a result of actions and decisions taken by the General Assembly at its fifty-fifth session;

4. *Reaffirms its decision* that the headquarters rule shall be adhered to by all bodies, and decides that waiv-

ers to the headquarters rule shall be granted solely on the basis of the calendar of conferences and meetings of the United Nations recommended by the Committee on Conferences for adoption by the General Assembly;

5. *Requests* the Committee on Conferences and the Secretary-General, when planning the calendar of conferences and meetings, to avoid simultaneous peak periods at the various duty stations and to avoid scheduling meetings of related intergovernmental bodies too close together;

6. *Notes with satisfaction* that the Secretariat took into account the arrangements referred to in General Assembly resolutions 53/208 A and 54/248 concerning Orthodox Good Friday and the official holidays of Id al-Fitr and Id al-Adha, and requests all intergovernmental bodies to observe those decisions when planning their meetings;

7. *Reaffirms* the provisions established by the General Assembly in its resolution 50/11 and reaffirmed in its resolution 54/64 of 6 December 1999 regarding multilingualism;

II
Utilization of conference-servicing resources and facilities

1. *Reiterates its request* to the Committee on Conferences to consult with those bodies that consistently utilized less than the applicable benchmark figure of their allocated resources for the past three sessions with a view to making appropriate recommendations in order to achieve the optimum utilization of conference-servicing resources;

2. *Requests* duty stations away from Headquarters to keep statistics of requests for servicing of meetings;

3. *Reiterates* that meetings of Charter and mandated bodies must be serviced as a priority;

4. *Decides* to include all necessary resources in the budget for the biennium 2002-2003 to provide interpretation services for meetings of regional and other major groupings of Member States upon request by those groups, on an ad hoc basis, in accordance with established practice, and requests the Secretary-General to submit to the General Assembly at its fifty-sixth session, through the Committee on Conferences, a report on the implementation of this decision;

5. *Notes* the importance of meetings of regional and other major groupings of Member States for the smooth functioning of the sessions of intergovernmental bodies, and requests the Secretary-General to ensure that, as far as possible, all requests for conference services for meetings of regional and other major groupings of Member States are met;

6. *Notes with appreciation,* in particular in view of the increased requests for meetings of regional and other major groupings of Member States, that services were provided for 84 per cent of the meetings requested by those groups, in spite of the difficulties experienced in the meetings programme in 2000, and that 100 per cent of the requests for facilities only were met;

7. *Notes with concern* the difficulties experienced by some Member States owing to the lack of conference services for some meetings of regional and other major groupings of Member States;

8. *Urges* intergovernmental bodies to spare no effort at the planning stage to take into account meetings of regional and other major groupings of Member

States, to make provision for such meetings in their programmes of work and to notify the conference services, well in advance, of any cancellations so that unutilized conference-servicing resources may, to the extent possible, be reassigned to meetings of regional and other major groupings of Member States;

9. *Requests* the Secretary-General to provide information on meetings of regional and other major groupings of Member States not serviced by conference services in the context of the proposed programme budget for the biennium 2002-2003;

10. *Also requests* the Secretary-General, when preparing budget proposals for conference services, to ensure that the level of resources proposed for temporary assistance is commensurate with the full demand for services, estimated on the basis of current experience;

11. *Notes* the initial steps taken by the Secretariat to establish a permanent interpretation service at the United Nations Office at Nairobi, and reaffirms that its decisions in section B, paragraph 24, of resolution 54/248 and in paragraph 180 of resolution 54/249 of 23 December 1999 should be fully implemented by January 2001;

12. *Notes with satisfaction* that the creation of a permanent interpretation service at Nairobi offers great potential for Nairobi as a venue for United Nations conferences and meetings, and takes note with appreciation of the efforts being made by the United Nations Office at Nairobi to attract more meetings to its facilities;

13. *Requests* the Secretary-General to continue to report on the utilization rates of interpretation services and conference facilities at all duty stations;

14. *Takes note* of the information in paragraphs 20 and 21 of the report of the Secretary-General concerning the improved utilization of conference facilities at the United Nations Office at Nairobi and the successful experience with respect to the events and meetings held there in April and May 2000;

15. *Requests* the Secretary-General to consider improving and modernizing the conference facilities at the United Nations Office at Nairobi in order to accommodate adequately major meetings and conferences, and to report thereon to the General Assembly at its fifty-sixth session, through the Committee on Conferences;

16. *Also requests* the Secretary-General to issue a revision of administrative instruction ST/AI/342 on the guidelines for the preparation of host government agreements falling under General Assembly resolution 40/243 prior to the substantive session of the Committee on Conferences in 2001, and to take into account administrative arrangements with respect to the United Nations Office at Nairobi;

17. *Welcomes* the fact that, despite various constraints, steps have been taken to increase the utilization of conference centres at the Economic and Social Commission for Asia and the Pacific and the Economic Commission for Africa, and notes the plans for the future in this regard;

18. *Notes with concern* the lack of sufficient operational guidance in the management of the conference centres at the Economic and Social Commission for Asia and the Pacific and the Economic Commission for Africa;

19. *Notes with deep concern* the inadequate staff structure and the insufficient financial resources allocated for the marketing of the conference centre of the Economic Commission for Africa;

20. *Requests* the Secretary-General to continue to explore all possible options to increase further the utilization of the conference centres at the Economic and Social Commission for Asia and the Pacific and the Economic Commission for Africa, and to report thereon to the General Assembly at its fifty-sixth session, through the Committee on Conferences;

III
Documentation- and publication-related matters

1. *Notes with deep concern* the low rate of compliance with the six-week rule for the issuance of documentation, and encourages the Secretary-General, in view of the impact of late submissions on the timely issuance of documents, to intensify recent efforts with respect to planning meetings and forecasting documentation;

2. *Reiterates its request* to the Secretary-General to ensure that documentation is available in accordance with the six-week rule for the distribution of documents simultaneously in the six official languages of the General Assembly;

3. *Requests* the Secretary-General to strengthen accountability and responsibility measures, where applicable, as requested in section C, paragraph 11, of its resolution 54/248, to correct the alarming situation concerning the submission of documentation consistent with the six-week rule, and requests him to submit a report thereon to the Assembly at its fifty-sixth session;

4. *Invites* intergovernmental bodies, during their organizational sessions or other appropriate periods before the commencement of their substantive work, to review with author departments the question of the availability of documentation for the proper functioning of those bodies, and to report thereon to the General Assembly at its fifty-sixth session through the Committee on Conferences;

5. *Decides* that there should not be any exemption to the rule that documents must be distributed in all official languages, and emphasizes the principle that all documents must be distributed simultaneously in all official languages before they are made available on United Nations web sites;

6. *Reiterates its request* that the Secretary-General direct all departments to include, where appropriate, the following elements in reports originating in the Secretariat:
   (a) A summary of the report;
   (b) Consolidated conclusions, recommendations and other proposed actions;
   (c) Relevant background information;

7. *Reiterates* that all documents submitted to legislative organs by the Secretariat and expert bodies for consideration and action should have conclusions and recommendations in bold print;

8. *Reiterates its request* to the Advisory Committee on Administrative and Budgetary Questions to submit its reports in accordance with paragraph 12 of General Assembly resolution 53/208 B;

9. *Reaffirms its decision* that, if a report is issued late, the reasons for the delay should be indicated when the report is introduced;

10. *Reiterates its decision* that, if a report is submitted late to conference services, the reasons therefor should be included in a footnote to the document;

11. *Encourages* chairpersons of intergovernmental bodies to institute time limits, when appropriate, for the introduction of standard documents by the Secretariat;

12. *Reiterates its request* to the Secretary-General to ensure that the texts of all new public documents, in all six official languages, and information materials of the United Nations are made available through the United Nations web site daily and are accessible to Member States without delay;

13. *Also reiterates its request* to the Secretary-General to publish, prior to the fifty-sixth session of the General Assembly, an updated version of the Financial Regulations and Rules of the United Nations in the six official languages of the Organization;

14. *Further reiterates its request* to the Secretary-General to publish, as a matter of priority, the Staff Regulations and Rules of the United Nations in the six official languages of the Organization, once their consolidation has been completed;

15. *Welcomes* the efforts of the Secretary-General to eliminate the backlog in the publication of the *Repertoire of the Practice of the Security Council*, and requests him to publish the current and future issues of the *Repertoire* in all six official languages;

16. *Notes* the recent progress in reducing delays in the issuance of summary records, and requests the Secretary-General to consider means, including increased cooperation within the Secretariat, to continue efforts to accelerate their issuance;

17. *Notes with concern* the comments of the Committee on Conferences contained in paragraph 112 of its report, and requests the Secretary-General to implement, as a matter of priority, the provision contained in paragraph 45 of annex II to its resolution 52/220 of 22 December 1997 and reiterated in paragraph 7 of its resolution 54/259 of 7 April 2000, and to report thereon to the General Assembly at its fifty-sixth session;

IV
Translation- and interpretation-related matters

1. *Reiterates its request* to the Secretary-General to continue the efforts to utilize new technologies, such as computer-assisted translation, remote translation, terminology databases and speech recognition, in the six official languages so as to enhance further the productivity of conference services, and to keep the General Assembly informed of the introduction and use of any other new technology;

2. *Also reiterates its request* to the Secretary-General to ensure that training opportunities in the six official languages are equally available to all language staff, including those at duty stations away from Headquarters;

3. *Requests* the Secretary-General, in exceptional cases where an interpreter is assigned to an interpretation booth for which he or she has not passed the requisite competitive examination of the Interpretation Service, to set up an internal examination with standards similar to those of the competitive examinations of the Interpretation Service, which the interpreter must pass before such assignment;

4. *Reiterates its understanding* that the introduction of remote interpretation is not intended to replace traditional interpretation systems without the explicit approval of the General Assembly;

5. *Reaffirms its decision* that, in the absence of a decision of the General Assembly to the contrary, the use of remote interpretation shall not constitute an alternative to the current institutionalized system of interpretation;

6. *Requests* the Secretary-General to ensure that trials of remote interpretation are not confined to specific duty stations and that each duty station is considered as both recipient and provider;

7. *Reaffirms its decision* that the use of remote interpretation should not affect the quality of interpretation or in itself lead to any further reduction in language posts, nor will it affect the equal treatment of the six official languages;

8. *Requests* the Secretary-General to ensure that future reports on the question of remote interpretation include an analysis of all costs of any proposed system, its impact on the working conditions of interpreters, the level of service provided to delegates, the satisfaction of delegations with the interpretation and the technical aspects of this method of interpretation;

9. *Also requests* the Secretary-General to ensure that efforts continue to be made to improve the quality control of language services at all duty stations;

10. *Takes note* of the technical difficulties and timing problems, referred to in paragraph 9 of the report of the Advisory Committee, regarding remote interpretation, and requests the Secretary-General to clarify further the technical issues involved;

11. *Requests* the Secretary-General to comply with paragraphs 33 to 36 of its resolution 53/208 A, and also requests the Secretary-General to submit to the Assembly at its fifty-sixth session, through the Committee on Conferences and the Advisory Committee, a report on possible measures to alleviate the excessive vacancy rates in language services at some duty stations and to ensure the required quality of conference services Secretariat-wide;

12. *Urges* the Secretary-General to continue his efforts to implement the system of incentives to attract language staff to duty stations with high vacancy rates, and requests him to submit a comprehensive report to the General Assembly at its fifty-sixth session analysing problems relating to recruitment in language services at all duty stations and proposing actions to address them;

13. *Reiterates its request* to the Secretary-General to ensure that translation, in principle, reflects the specificity of each language;

14. *Also reiterates its request* to the Secretary-General, in order to improve further the quality of translation of documents issued in the six official languages, to ensure continuous dialogue between translation staff and interpretation staff, among United Nations headquarters at New York, Geneva, Vienna and Nairobi, and between translation divisions and Member States with regard to the standardization of the terminology used;

15. *Further reiterates its request* to the Secretary-General to hold informational meetings in order to brief Member States periodically on the terminology used;

16. *Requests* the Secretary-General to conduct consultations, with Member States concerned, on the improvement of translation services;

V
Information technology

1. *Urges* the Secretary-General to fill expeditiously the three official posts in the Department of Public Information of the Secretariat relating to web sites in Arabic, Chinese and Russian, in accordance with paragraph 151 of General Assembly resolution 54/249;

2. *Requests* the Secretary-General to report to the General Assembly at its fifty-sixth session on policy issues regarding the translation of non-parliamentary and public information material into all official languages and the possibility of providing those materials on the United Nations web site in all official languages;

3. *Also requests* the Secretary-General to report to the General Assembly at its fifty-sixth session on the implementation of the new re-engineered optical disk system, referred to in paragraph 9 of his report;

VI

1. *Reaffirms* its decision 38/401 concerning the prohibition of smoking in small conference rooms and the discouragement of smoking in large conference rooms;

2. *Calls upon* representatives of Member States to abide strictly by its decision 38/401, and strongly encourages all users of United Nations conference facilities to refrain from smoking in order to avoid exposing non-smokers to involuntary passive smoking;

3. *Strongly discourages* smoking in the immediate vicinity of conference rooms.

By **decision 55/458** of 23 December, the Assembly decided that the item "Pattern of conferences" would remain for consideration at its resumed fifty-fifth (2001) session.

Intergovernmental meetings

At the request of host Governments, the main documents of intergovernmental conferences held in 2000 were transmitted to the Secretary-General for circulation to the General Assembly, the Security Council or both, as follows:

Thirteenth Ministerial Conference of the Movement of Non-Aligned Countries (Cartagena, Colombia, 8-9 April) [A/54/917-S/2000/580]; South Summit of the Group of 77 (Havana, Cuba, 10-14 April) [A/55/74]; Authority of Heads of State and Government of the Common Market for Eastern and Southern Africa (Mauritius, 17-19 May) [A/55/325]; Tenth Summit of the Heads of State and Government of the Group of Fifteen (Cairo, Egypt, 19-20 June) [A/55/139-S/2000/93]; seventy-second ordinary session of the Council of Ministers of the Organization of African Unity (OAU) (Lomé, Togo, 6-8 July) and thirty-sixth ordinary session of the Assembly of Heads of State and Government of OAU (Lomé, 10-12 July) [A/55/286]; meeting of Foreign Ministers of G-8 countries (Miyazaki, Japan, 13 July) [A/55/162-S/2000/715]; summit meeting of G-8 countries (Okinawa, Japan, 21-23 July) [A/55/257- S/2000/766]; Summit of Heads of State or Government of the

Southern African Development Community (Windhoek, Namibia, 6-7 August) [A/55/287]; meeting of heads of State of the Commonwealth of Independent States (Yalta, Ukraine, 18 August) [A/55/330]; twenty-fourth annual meeting of the Ministers for Foreign Affairs of the Group of 77 (New York, 15 September) [A/55/459]; annual coordination meeting of Ministers for Foreign Affairs of the States members of the Organization of the Islamic Conference (New York, 18 September) [A/55/541-S/2000/1067]; 103rd Inter-Parliamentary Conference of the Inter-Parliamentary Union (Amman, Jordan, 27 April–6 May) [A/54/968]; meeting of heads of State and Government and representatives of the 16 States members of the Pacific Island Forum (Tarawa, Kiribati, 27-30 October) [A/55/536]; ninth session of the Islamic Summit Conference (Doha, Qatar, 12-14 November) [A/55/716-S/2000/1236]; meeting of the heads of Government of the member States of the Central European Initiative (Budapest, Hungary, 25 November) [A/55/668].

Use of conference services

The Secretary-General submitted to the Committee on Conferences a July report on improved utilization of conference-servicing resources, including meeting statistics of UN organs for 1999 [A/AC.172/2000/3/Rev.1].

The Committee noted that the overall utilization factor for 1999 exceeded the benchmark of 80 per cent. For Vienna it remained at 88 per cent, in Geneva it decreased by three percentage points to 84 per cent, and in New York it increased by two percentage points to 79 per cent. The Committee noted, however, that only 59 per cent of the bodies sampled utilized 80 per cent or more of their available conference-servicing resources. It requested its Chairperson to continue to consult with the chairpersons of those bodies that had consistently utilized less than the applicable benchmark figure (80 per cent) of their allocated resources for the past three sessions and to make recommendations to achieve optimum utilization of conference-servicing resources. The Committee noted the new format for reporting on the utilization of conference services and that statistics for Nairobi were incorporated in the analytical tables.

Documents control

In response to General Assembly resolution 54/248 [YUN 1999, p. 1368], the Secretariat submitted a note [A/AC.172/2000/6] containing six proposals to improve the timely issuance of pre-session documentation. The first two proposals, which required action by the Secretariat, stipulated that three months prior to the opening of a session, the servicing secretariat, the substantive department and the Department of General Assembly Affairs and Conference Services should meet to review documentation forecasts, bearing in mind the 10-week rule and the requirement to report on the status of documentation; and substantive departments should prepare forecasts of the volume of documentation under preparation and be required to keep within those limits.

The other proposals, which required action by intergovernmental organizations, called for the rescheduling of the processing of documents by a particular intergovernmental organization in order to accommodate late submissions by that body; intergovernmental bodies should review their reporting cycles with a view to changing the periodicity to quarterly or biannual reports instead of annual reporting; they should authorize the submission of reports for processing in accordance with the 10-week rule even if all relevant information was not available, with subsequent addenda to the parent document; and in cases of recurrent late submissions, they should adjust the proposed programme of work, reorder agenda items and delay or postpone consideration of items or documents.

Those proposals were intended to serve as a basis for the formulation of more elaborate and refined recommendations to enable conference services to process documents and distribute them in a timely manner.

In August, the Committee on Conferences supported the implementation of the proposals requiring action by the Secretariat and recommended to the Assembly that the other recommendations be reformulated as recommendations to intergovernmental bodies. It asked the Secretariat to prepare guidelines on procedures for effective and efficient use of conference services and to continue to draft proposals for improving the timely issuance of pre-session documentation.

The Committee, having considered a conference room paper on compliance with the regulations regarding page limits, noted that, although the number and proportion of documents issued in accordance with those limits had increased, compliance continued to be only partial. It further noted that documents that were significantly in excess of the page limit, especially when submitted late, created an additional burden for the processing services and could jeopardize timely issuance and compromise quality. Efforts to further reduce the length of documents should therefore be concentrated on those cases in which page limits were applicable or desirable.

Optical disk system

In his May report on information technologies [A/54/849], the Secretary-General indicated that, since its establishment as the electronic repository of UN documents, the optical disk system (ODS) had ensured simultaneous retrieval in the six official languages. Disparities between languages, due partially to lags in the development of software for some languages by the computer industry, and affecting the Arabic and Russian versions, had been eliminated.

All language units of the Text-Processing Section were currently fully equipped to operate with MS Word. Updated macros had been developed and staff training was about to be completed. The frequency of use of MS Word was increasing daily and full production in it of all new documents in all languages would be achieved shortly.

In addition to facilitating retrieval, bringing all languages to the same level of technological advancement would allow for easier conversion of all language versions of documents to other formats. Moreover, ODS was being re-engineered to operate on more current technology based on magnetic disks, rather than optical platters, and Notes Domino. The implementation of that new system, to be completed by the end of 2000, would provide concurrent access to a much higher number of users than currently.

Cost-effectiveness of UN publications

The General Assembly, at its resumed fifty-fourth (2000) session, considered a JIU report entitled "United Nations publications: enhancing cost-effectiveness in implementing legislative mandates" [YUN 1997, p. 1504], a note by the Secretary-General containing his comments on the report [ibid.], the relevant chapter of the report of the Committee for Programme and Coordination on the work of its thirty-eighth session [YUN 1998, p. 1352] and a report of ACABQ on UN publications [ibid.].

GENERAL ASSEMBLY ACTION

On 7 April [meeting 95], the General Assembly, on the recommendation of the Fifth Committee [A/54/690/Add. 1], adopted **resolution 54/259** without vote [agenda item 124].

United Nations publications: enhancing cost-effectiveness in implementing legislative mandates

The General Assembly,

Having considered the report of the Joint Inspection Unit entitled "United Nations publications: enhancing cost-effectiveness in implementing legislative mandates", the note by the Secretary-General containing his comments thereon, the relevant chapter of the report of the Committee for Programme and Coordination on the work of its thirty-eighth session and the report of the Advisory Committee on Administrative and Budgetary Questions on United Nations publications,

Recalling paragraph 1 of section D of its resolution 52/214 of 22 December 1997, and taking into account the fact that the General Assembly has not taken any decision on the question of a cost-accounting system,

1. *Endorses* recommendations 2, 3, 10 and 16 to 18 contained in the report of the Joint Inspection Unit;

2. *Also endorses* recommendations 4 and 6 contained in the report of the Unit, subject to the conclusions and recommendations of the Committee for Programme and Coordination contained in paragraph 350 of its report;

3. *Further endorses* recommendations 13 and 15 contained in the report of the Unit, as modified by the Advisory Committee on Administrative and Budgetary Questions in paragraphs 19 and 21, respectively, of its report;

4. *Endorses* recommendation 14 contained in the report of the Unit, without prejudice to the traditional distribution of printed publications, taking into account paragraph 20 of the report of the Advisory Committee;

5. *Concurs* with paragraphs 22 and 23 of the report of the Advisory Committee;

6. *Looks forward* to the conclusions of the study mentioned in paragraph 43 of the note by the Secretary-General;

7. *Regrets* that the provision contained in paragraph 45 of annex II to its resolution 52/220 of 22 December 1997 has not been implemented, and requests the Secretary-General to implement this provision as a matter of priority and to report to it at its fifty-fifth session in the context of the item entitled "Pattern of conferences";

8. *Requests* that additional efforts be made to improve the linguistic quality and content of United Nations publications concomitantly in all six official languages;

9. *Requests* the Secretary-General to submit to the General Assembly, at its fifty-sixth session, a report on the implementation of the provisions of the present resolution.

Regional and other major groupings

Report of Secretary-General. In July [A/55/182], the Secretary-General, responding to General Assembly resolution 54/248 [YUN 1999, p. 1368], reported on the provision of interpretation services to meetings of regional and other major groupings of Member States. For the period 1 July 1999 to 30 June 2000, 100 per cent of requests for conference services to regional and other major groupings were met in Geneva and New York. Eighty-four per cent of requests for the provision of interpretation services were met.

Committee action. The Committee on Conferences took note of the Secretary-General's report. It urged intergovernmental bodies to spare no effort at the planning stage to take into account meetings of regional and other major groupings of Member States, to make provision for such meetings in their programmes of work and to notify conference services well in advance of any cancellations. It requested the Chairperson to write to the chairpersons of intergovernmental organizations, bringing to their attention the need to anticipate requests for meetings of regional and other major groupings during their sessions.

ACABQ report. In September [A/55/430], ACABQ, in its comments on the Secretary-General's report, noted that among the difficulties preventing the Secretariat from meeting all the requests for interpretation services was the reduction in the proposed 2000-2001 programme budget of temporary assistance funds. It was of the opinion that the issue of general temporary assistance should be addressed in the context of the preparation of the 2002-2003 programme budget and that the time had come to assess the implementation of General Assembly resolution 49/221 C [YUN 1994, p. 1404] endorsing the Secretary-General's report on the comprehensive study on conference services [ibid., p. 1403].

Improved coordination of conference services

The Committee on Conferences considered an oral report on improved coordination of conference services. The Committee was told that the high level of enthusiasm of the staff and close coordination between various departments at the UN Office at Nairobi contributed to its conference centre's success, and the proposal to separate conference services from administration at the Office would further enhance the profile of conference services. The workload trend of various meeting services in Vienna, including translation and interpretation services, was generally upward. However, the potential for further efficiency gains had been mostly exhausted and there were concerns about the need to find the right balance between budgetary resources and workload. Constraints identified included uneven workload distribution, late requests, an unfavourable post structure that did not offer attractive career prospects to staff and the imbalance between workload and personnel and budgetary resources.

Concerning the vacancy rates for UN language professionals, it was suggested that the problem should be viewed in terms of supply and demand. Interpreters, particularly those interpreting from Russian into English and French, were in very short supply and the Organization should urgently consider mounting its own training programmes to ensure a steady supply of suitable candidates.

The Committee noted the oral report on improved coordination of conference services and encouraged efforts to promote a more coordinated approach aimed at providing services from all duty stations more effectively and efficiently.

It requested the Secretary-General to submit a comprehensive report as soon as possible analysing such problems as recruitment in language services at all duty stations and proposals for addressing them. He should implement the system of incentives to attract language staff to duty stations with high vacancy rates and report on measures to develop further such a system. The Committee looked forward to the revision of administrative instruction ST/AI/324 on guidelines for the preparation of host government agreements falling under Assembly resolution 40/243 [YUN 1985, p. 1256] and, in that regard, asked the Secretary-General to take into account the administrative arrangements with respect to the UN Office at Nairobi.

Improved utilization of regional conference facilities

Bangkok and Addis Ababa

In August, pursuant to General Assembly resolution 54/248 [YUN 1999, p. 1368], the Committee on Conferences heard an oral report by the Secretariat on measures to increase utilization of regional conference centres, including the constraints that had affected the utilization of the centres in Bangkok, Thailand, and Addis Ababa, Ethiopia, and action taken to improve the situation.

The Committee, while noting the oral report, regretted that the written report requested was not yet available and agreed to keep the matter under review.

In September [A/55/410], the Secretary-General, in his written report, said that greater utilization of both centres beyond their current use to meet the conference requirements of the Economic and Social Commission for Asia and the Pacific (ESCAP) and the Economic Commission for Africa (ECA) had been constrained by several factors. Among them was uncertainty about the appropriate use of the facilities, particularly as venues for private sector and commercial events. Other related factors were the legal and administrative restrictions imposed on the use of UN premises vis-à-vis the invitation to the Secretary-General in section II of Assembly resolution 52/220 [YUN 1997, p. 1421] to develop new income-generating measures, and the request of the Committee on Conferences that the Secretariat prepare proposals for increased utilization of the conference facilities, including by non-UN entities. Other constraints included the very limited opportunities for re-routing meetings included in the UN calendar of conferences, inadequate staffing structures for the management of the centres, lack of funds for marketing and promotional activities and regional instability.

However, ESCAP and ECA had taken steps to staff and manage the centres more adequately and to provide resources for marketing operations. Promotional campaigns were being launched to attract more users, mainly among UN agencies, national institutions and intergovernmental and non-governmental organizations, but also private sector entities.

The Secretary-General concluded that the two facilities were relatively new and it would be reasonable to allow some five years for awareness of the centres to be built up and their reputation to be established. He noted that the utilization of both centres was increasing and estimated that, with support from the UN system and the provision of the necessary staff and financial resources, utilization should improve considerably in the foreseeable future.

Nairobi

In August [A/55/259], the Secretary-General submitted a report on improved utilization of conference facilities at the UN Office at Nairobi, Kenya, pursuant to General Assembly resolution 54/248 [YUN 1999, p. 1368]. The report contained the first results of the policy decisions set out in that resolution for Nairobi as a venue for UN conferences and meetings. It examined meeting activity, including statistical information, in Nairobi in 1999 and 2000 and projections for 2001 and projected the effect of the creation of a permanent interpretation service as a factor in attracting more meeting activity to the Office from 2001 onwards.

The number of meetings with interpretation held in Nairobi in 1999 was 254, compared to 140 in 1998 and 166 in 1997. Of that number, 32 were meetings of calender bodies, while the remaining 222 were meetings of intergovernmental and expert groups related both to the United Nations and other organizations. The number of events held without interpretation was much higher— 354. The number of UN meetings held in Nairobi from January to July 2000 was 52. If the trend of the year 2000 continued, the report said, the number of meetings with interpretation should not be less than 320—a utilization rate of 21 per cent. During the same period, 10 meetings were held at locations outside Nairobi, 8 of which were provided with interpretation.

The decision to create a permanent interpretation service in Nairobi would have a dramatic impact on meeting activities there. Information on the expected availability of interpretation as of 2001 had been circulated to all clients and there was strong indication that interest existed not only from Nairobi-based UN agencies, but also from non-UN entities. The creation of the service was well under way and the Secretary-General had approved the creation of a separate Division of Conference Services at Nairobi to manage the new interpretation service and the conference facilities and to be accountable for their efficient utilization.

In the first part of 2000, the UN Office at Nairobi hosted a series of major environmental events, which put to the test its ability to handle conferences not previously held there and to cope with unprecedented massive participation of NGOs, press and governmental delegations and observers. To make it possible to use the centre as a regular venue for major meetings, the project for modernizing the conference facilities should be reviewed in the light of that successful experience.

The Secretary-General concluded that the effect of the creation of an interpretation service at the UN Office at Nairobi from 1 January 2001 could be evaluated as the potential interpreter utilization rate against meetings held in Nairobi in 2000 with interpretation, meetings held outside Nairobi with interpretation, and Committee of Permanent Representatives meetings held in Nairobi over a 12-month period in English, which in future would be held with six-language interpretation. The figure was 300, the report said. It added that the creation of a permanent interpretation service offered great potential for Nairobi as a venue for UN conferences and meetings.

In August, the Committee on Conferences noted the potential for Nairobi as a venue for UN conferences and meetings and commended the close cooperation between the UN Office at Nairobi and the Department of General Assembly Affairs and Conference Services. It also took note of the efforts of the Office to attract more meetings to its facilities.

In September [A/55/430], ACABQ, in its comments on the Secretary-General's report, requested that the Fifth Committee be provided with a breakdown of the costs associated with the establishment of the team of interpreters for the creation of the permanent interpretation service in January 2001 as compared with interpretation costs in 1999.

UN web sites

The Committee on Conferences, having considered the Secretary-General's report on the multilingual development, maintenance and enrichment of UN web sites [A/AC.198/2000/7- A/AC.172/2000/4] (see p. 576), noted that it had become necessary to consider Internet activity as an integral part of the Organization's programme of work. Each content-providing office should make available web-specific content on the web sites as part of its regular programme of activity, as well as the necessary budgetary provisions. The Committee took note of the electronic display of the meetings programme at Geneva and encouraged the Secretariat to develop it at other duty stations.

In a May report on information technologies [A/54/849], the Secretary-General informed the General Assembly that, in accordance with resolution 54/249 [YUN 1999, p. 1289], steps were under way to fill the three Professional posts in the Department of Public Information relating to the web sites in Arabic, Chinese and Russian, which had been converted from general temporary assistance posts to regular budget posts. There would then be a Professional-level web site coordinator for the management and coordination of the web site in each of the official languages. Though that would not resolve the issue of parity treatment of languages, it was a first step in that direction. The fundamental issue of content creation on an equal basis in the six official languages would have to be revisited so as to decide on policy issues regarding the rendering of non-parliamentary and public information material into all official languages. Requiring parity in the official languages on the web site would also require that the concept of working languages in the Secretariat be reviewed.

Interpretation and translation matters

Remote interpretation

In July [A/55/134], the Secretary-General, responding to General Assembly resolution 54/248 [YUN 1999, p. 1368], reported on preparations for the second remote interpretation experiment, to be conducted between Geneva and Nairobi in 2000. The experiment, to be conducted during a full-scale intergovernmental meeting in all six official languages, was intended to build on the first one organized in 1999 between Geneva and Vienna [ibid., p. 1367] and to gather missing information on relevant technical, financial and human resources issues. It had been scheduled to take place from 8 to 12 May during the first substantive session of the Preparatory Committee for the Assembly's special session for the review and appraisal of the Habitat Agenda. However, because of technical, financial and logistic considerations, by 14 March it was concluded that making substantial financial commitments and further technical and staffing preparations were not prudent, since the

technical set-up risked not being in place in time. With no other planned meetings in Nairobi suitable for the experiment, preparations were suspended. Moreover, the establishment of a full-fledged interpretation service in Nairobi as of January 2001 (see p. 1394) had changed one of the basic considerations for the experiment—the relative availability of interpreters in different conference centres. Consideration would be given to setting up an experiment in Nairobi when a full team of interpreters was available there.

The Committee on Conferences took note of the Secretary-General's report and requested that it be kept informed of future activities in remote interpretation. The Committee reiterated its understanding that the introduction of remote interpretation was not intended to replace traditional systems without the explicit approval of the Assembly. It requested that future reports on the matter include an analysis of the cost of any proposed system and of its impact on the working conditions of interpreters. The Committee recommended that remote interpretation not be confined to specific duty stations, that each duty station be considered both as recipient and provider and that the Secretariat explore every opportunity for its introduction.

ACABQ, in a September report [A/55/430], expressed regrets that the experiment did not take place and urged the Secretariat to clarify the technical issues involved as quickly as possible.

New technologies

In August [A/AC.172/2000/5], the Secretary-General reported on the utilization of new technologies in translation and interpretation. He stated that the computer-assisted translation (CAT) project had entered its operational phase, which involved the selection of suitable documents to be processed simultaneously in all translation languages. Initial findings and potential benefits of CAT implementation indicated that the impact of its usage would become clear only after a longer period of operation, and the method of validation of translation memories consisting of material subject to revision after CAT processing might have cost implications. Its expansion would also require that all stages of document processing upstream of translation be performed electronically. However, whether or not CAT was expanded, the introduction of translation-memory technology would have had a positive impact in speeding up the transition from hard-copy-based referencing of translation jobs to electronic referencing, thus enhancing the efficiency of the process, allowing more thorough and comprehensive search and retrieval, eliminating the need to make thousands of photocopies for inclusion in reference folders and facilitating the provision of reference material to remote contractual translators.

Remote translation, initiated five years earlier, had become the norm at Headquarters, Geneva, Nairobi and Vienna. The technology used for remote translation had evolved and the transmission of files over the Internet was increasingly being replaced with transmission to and from a dedicated File Transfer Protocol (FTP) server, which offered greater speed and reliability. The possibility of transmitting files in Portable Document Format was currently being studied. Remote translation had resulted in considerable savings on travel and daily subsistence costs, allowed more flexibility and efficient use of staff resources and speedier delivery of translations if the time difference between the meeting and servicing locations was favourable. Drawbacks included delays in processing translations or the need to establish special shifts at the servicing location when the time difference was unfavourable and lack of direct contact with delegations and the substantive secretariat of the remotely serviced meeting. The Department of General Assembly Affairs and Conference Services was reviewing guidelines governing the allocation of responsibilities between major conference-servicing centres for the servicing of meetings away from such centres, with a view to replacing the current system, and consideration was being given to remotely translating material needed by an organ or body meeting in a major conference-servicing centre other than the location of its established headquarters.

Speech recognition technology, successfully tested in 1999 in Geneva, had been deployed at Headquarters in the Translation and Editorial Division and the Verbatim Reporting Service. Benefits of the introduction of the technology would accrue downstream of the translation process in text-processing units, where the transcription of translations, summary and verbatim records recorded on audio cassettes still constituted a significant portion of the total workload. Savings in overtime costs might be expected in the medium term.

Centrally maintained databases of terminology resources were held at all duty stations. The application of new technologies to the management of those terminology resources raised concerns about the need to convert selected databases to the format required for inclusion in CAT dictionaries and to ensure the widest possible access to all terminology resources at all duty stations. The digital recording of meeting proceedings had been implemented by the Verbatim Reporting Service to allow easy and speedy transmission of recordings of meetings proceedings, in the form of digital sound files playable on personal computers to remote freelance verbatim reporters, together with relevant reference material. The system, developed in-house at no significant cost, had significantly reduced the need to bring on board costly internationally recruited freelance verbatim reporters. A portable version of the system was recently developed and successfully tested. As an extension of the project, audio cassettes had been phased out as a means of distribution "takes" to in-house verbatim reporters. A similar approach was being contemplated for the distribution to précis-writers and translators of recorded proceedings of meetings of bodies entitled to summary records.

The Committee on Conferences encouraged the Secretary-General to continue efforts to introduce new technologies in conference services and welcomed the proposal to extend the service of dedicated FTP sites to other conference centres.

UN information systems

Review of Information Systems Coordination Committee

In November [A/55/619], the Secretary-General reported on the review of the ACC Information Systems Coordination Committee, as requested by the General Assembly in resolution 54/249 [YUN 1999, p. 1289]. The report summarized the state of the review of the Committee's role being carried out within the framework of the reform of the ACC machinery and presented the Secretary-General's views on the Committee's usefulness and future role. The Secretary-General considered that strengthened coordination of information and communications technology activities was essential for enabling the UN system to perform more efficiently and for ensuring that it was best equipped to mobilize that technology for development. The role envisaged, within the reform of ACC activities, for the new High-level Committee on Management and for the coordination mechanism, based on the work of the Information Systems Coordination Committee, confirmed the commitment of the executive heads of UN system organizations to take full advantage of those critical technologies. The limited resources of the United Nations made it essential that the coordination of information and communications technology activities be strengthened, and play a key role in the transformation of the organizations of the UN system into knowledge-based entities.

The Secretary-General fully endorsed the strengthening of UN system coordination activities being pursued within the ACC framework. The arrangements made would capitalize on the work done so far by the Committee and would be based on a prioritization of the existing work programmes of the Committee and new initiatives. Continuation of the Committee's activities was indispensable, the cost of which in the 2000-2001 programme budget amounted to $1,380,300. Taking into account the fact that each initiative would impact on the UN system at large, the Secretary-General considered that the level of expenditure and the related UN contribution were fully justified. He pointed out that the overall cost of coordinating information technology activities had remained stable over the past bienniums and the limited resources available for coordination were a major reason for the apparent limited progress. The Secretary-General recommended the continued funding of the UN contribution to the Committee for the 2000-2001 biennium and indicated his intention to reflect the appropriation adjustments in the first performance report for the biennium.

ACABQ, in a December report [A/55/7/Add.3], recommended the approval of the proposal to reinstate funding of the UN share of the Information Systems Coordination Committee in the budget for 2000-2001. It trusted, however, that the Secretary-General would set out clearly the Committee's programme of work, as well as its accomplishments, in the proposed programme budget for 2002-2003.

On 23 December, the General Assembly, by **resolution 55/238, section VIII**, took note of the Secretary-General's report and concurred with ACABQ's observations and recommendations.

International cooperation on informatics

In response to Economic and Social Council resolution 1999/58 [YUN 1999, p. 1372], the Secretary-General submitted a July report on international cooperation in the field of informatics [E/2000/94], summarizing activities carried out by the Ad Hoc Open-ended Working Group on Informatics. A major focus of discussion during the past year had been the use of information technology to provide services to the permanent missions to the United Nations without placing undue burden on the smaller missions. The Working Group alerted Member States to the year 2000 computer rollover problem and was kept informed regularly on the steps taken by the Secretariat and the UN system at large to achieve

compliance. The Working Group, in cooperation with the Information Technology Services Division, as well as with other agencies in the UN system, continued to improve and expand electronic information services to Member States and permanent missions and to assure that the technologies employed were abreast with technological development. The report also contained information on the various activities in the field of informatics carried out by Secretariat departments and UN funds and programmes.

ECONOMIC AND SOCIAL COUNCIL ACTION

On 28 July [meeting 45], the Economic and Social Council adopted **resolution 2000/28** [draft: E/2000/L.20] without vote [agenda item 7 (e)].

The need to harmonize and improve United Nations informatics systems for optimal utilization and accessibility by all States

The Economic and Social Council,

Aware of the interest of Member States in taking full advantage of information and communications technologies for the acceleration of economic and social development,

Recalling its previous resolutions on the need to harmonize and improve United Nations information systems for optimal utilization and access by all States, with due regard to all official languages,

Welcoming the report presented by the Chairman of the Ad Hoc Open-ended Working Group on Informatics on the progress achieved so far in fulfilling the mandate of the Working Group,

1. *Reiterates once again* the high priority that it attaches to easy, economical, uncomplicated and unhindered access for States Members of the United Nations, observers and non-governmental organizations accredited to the United Nations to the computerized databases and information systems and services of the United Nations, provided that the unhindered access of non-governmental organizations shall not prejudice the access of Member States and that it shall not impose an additional financial burden for the use of databases and other systems;

2. *Requests* the President of the Economic and Social Council to convene the Ad Hoc Open-ended Working Group on Informatics for one more year to enable it to carry out, from within existing resources, its work of facilitating the successful implementation of the initiatives being taken by the Secretary-General with regard to the use of information technology and of continuing the implementation of measures required to achieve its objectives; in this regard, the Working Group is requested to continue:

(a) To improve electronic connectivity via the Internet for all Member States in their capitals and at major United Nations locations, inter alia, through the enhanced connectivity of permanent missions to the Internet and United Nations databases;

(b) To improve the access of Member States to a wider range of United Nations information on economic and social, development and political issues and other substantive programming areas, and to have all official documents available via the Internet;

(c) To improve electronic links among Member States, the United Nations and the specialized agencies;

(d) To provide training for the staff of permanent missions to enable them to take advantage of the facilities being developed for Member States, in particular electronic mail and Internet web sites;

(e) To enhance the capacity of Member States to access United Nations data online, using low-cost telecommunications links or providing other modalities, for example, CD-ROM, whereby Member States can have access to specialized databases not available on the Internet;

(f) To make arrangements, as appropriate, to provide permanent missions of developing countries with the hardware platform to utilize Internet technology;

(g) To use videoconferencing to further communication and interaction between the United Nations, permanent missions and academic institutions;

(h) To intensify contacts with the private sector so as to bring its wealth of experience to bear on the work of the Working Group;

3. *Notes with appreciation* the fact that the efforts of the Working Group to draw the attention of Member States to the threat posed by the millennium bug were successful and that, as a result, international cooperation to address the problem of the millennium bug was also successful;

4. *Supports* the efforts of the Working Group to keep intact the network of national focal points that was established in connection with the millennium bug initiative, as a vehicle for the diffusion of best practices and lessons learned, in particular for the exchange of information on locally and regionally appropriate solutions, and in this regard appeals to countries and other sources to provide the extrabudgetary resources necessary to maintain the mailing list of the national focal points;

5. *Reiterates* the request made in paragraph 18 of the Ministerial Declaration entitled "Development and international cooperation in the twenty-first century: the role of information technology in the context of a knowledge-based global economy", adopted on 7 July 2000 at the high-level segment of its substantive session of 2000, that the Working Group make recommendations regarding the proposal contained in paragraph 11 of the report of the high-level panel of experts on information and communications technology, convened from 17 to 20 April 2000, that the United Nations create a task force on information and communications technologies;

6. *Requests* the Working Group to make recommendations to the Bureau of the Council on how the Council can carry out the tasks specified in paragraph 15 of the Ministerial Declaration for the enhancement of the United Nations role in promoting synergies and coherence of all efforts directed towards expanding the development impact of information and communications technologies;

7. *Requests* the Secretary-General to extend full cooperation to the Working Group and to give priority to implementing its recommendations;

8. *Calls upon* the Secretary-General to report to the Council at its substantive session of 2001 on the follow-up action taken on the present resolution, including the findings of the Working Group.

Year 2000 computer problem

In response to General Assembly resolution 54/114 [YUN 1999, p. 1373], the Secretary-General submitted a September report [A/55/387] that evaluated the outcome of the steps taken within the UN system and with Member States to resolve the year 2000 computer rollover problem. It also contained summaries of the submissions of the organizations within the UN system on their activities in that respect.

GENERAL ASSEMBLY ACTION

On 10 November [meeting 58], the General Assembly adopted **resolution 55/21** [draft: A/55/L.28 & Add.1] without vote [agenda item 44].

Global implications of the year 2000 date conversion problem of computers

The General Assembly,

Recalling its resolutions 52/233 of 26 June 1998, 53/86 of 7 December 1998 and 54/114 of 15 December 1999 on the global implications of the year 2000 date conversion problem of computers,

Welcoming the report of the Secretary-General on the evaluation of the outcome of the steps taken within the United Nations system and with Member States to resolve the year 2000 problem,

Recognizing that the effective operation of Governments, companies and other organizations was threatened by the year 2000 date conversion problem of computers, or "millennium bug",

Recognizing also the serious impact that the year 2000 problem could have had in all countries whose economies are increasingly interdependent,

Appreciating the establishment of a trust fund by the World Bank to assist in the efforts to resolve the year 2000 problem and the voluntary contributions made to it by the Member States,

Appreciating also the efforts of the Ad Hoc Open-ended Working Group on Informatics of the Economic and Social Council in raising the level of awareness of the year 2000 problem,

Noting that, as a result of the concerted international effort, the "millennium bug" caused no serious destruction of critical services on a national, regional or global level,

1. *Expresses its satisfaction* with the efforts of all Member States to solve the year 2000 problem before the rollover date of 31 December 1999, including by working to ensure that the private sector was fully engaged in addressing the problem and by tackling it in those systems under their own control;

2. *Commends* the unprecedented international cooperation which contributed to the successful outcome and the interest in providing mutual assistance so that all could succeed, created by the realization of the interdependence among nations;

3. *Also commends* the public-private partnerships that were forged and which showed that, faced with a threat that affected entire industries, private and public interest converged;

4. *Urges* the international community to draw lessons from the experience of the initiative to address the

year 2000 problem in dealing with complex global technical problems.

Integrated Management Information System

By **decision 54/473** of 7 April, the General Assembly took note of the Secretary-General's eleventh progress report on the Integrated Management Information System (IMIS) [YUN 1999, p. 1375], the project's revised completion date and the activities planned until then. It endorsed ACABQ's comments on the report [ibid., p. 1376] and asked the Secretary-General to submit a comprehensive final report on the project's implementation, including a full analysis of lessons learned and experience gained. It should also address a long-term strategy for further developing the system for consideration by the Assembly in 2001.

In his twelfth progress report on IMIS [A/55/632], the Secretary-General said that, with the successful implementation of payroll in September at Headquarters, and that of additional functions over the past 12 months, the development phase of IMIS—as per the initial plan—had been completed. Progress had been made on the implementation of the finance applications at offices away from Headquarters with the successful installation of that application at the UN offices in Geneva, Santiago and Nairobi. The usage of the system had increased at all duty stations, with more than 500 users a day on average. Improvements to the system to better meet the needs of offices away from Headquarters had been introduced, and major efforts had been made to strengthen the training facilities. Agreement had been reached in principle for the establishment of an IMIS common service for the long-term operation of the system, in cooperation with UNDP, UNFPA, UNICEF and the UN Office for Project Services. As recommended by ACABQ, IMIS was progressively being integrated into the Information and Technology Services Division. The system was exclusively maintained by the United Nations, as the main contractor had been completely phased out by the end of October. The overall expenditures remained within the approved budget of $77.6 million. The IMIS team was reviewing, in consultation with users, the areas in which to concentrate its efforts for further improvement of the system. Work had been initiated for upgrading of the technological platform to make the system more accessible through the World Wide Web. Other projects to be undertaken included research for a new tool for the reporting application, the consolidation of data, a review of requirements of peacekeeping missions for systematic application and archiving of the IMIS data.

Other matters

Common services

JIU and OIOS reports. At its resumed fifty-fourth session, the General Assembly considered the JIU report entitled "The United Nations system common services at Geneva, part I, Overview of administrative cooperation and coordination" [YUN 1999, p. 1376] and the Secretary-General's note transmitting his comments and those of ACC [A/54/635], as well as the OIOS report on the review of common services in the United Nations [YUN 1999, p. 1376] and JIU comments thereon [ibid., p. 1377].

On 7 April, the Assembly, in **resolution 54/255** (see p. 1375), endorsed the JIU recommendations and the comments of the Secretary-General and ACC thereon and invited JIU to continue to examine common services at other duty stations. By **decision 54/257** of the same date, it noted the OIOS report and the JIU comments thereon.

Report of Secretary-General. In response to Assembly resolution 54/249 [YUN 1999, p. 1289], the Secretary-General, in October [A/55/461], reported on a review of common services in the UN system carried out by the Task Force on Common Services, established in the context of reform [YUN 1997, p. 1389]. The Task Force, convened by the Assistant Secretary-General for Central Support Services, in his capacity as Executive Coordinator for Common Services, included representatives of Secretariat departments and UN funds and programmes. Eleven working groups were established in the areas of archives and records management, facilities management, financial services, IMIS, information technology and telecommunications, printing, personnel, procurement, security and safety, and travel and transportation services. The Task Force focused its attention on New York and worked closely with the United Nations Development Group (UNDG) on common services in country offices, the Inter-Agency Procurement Working Group and other inter-agency forums, as well as with JIU. Considerable progress had been made with major accomplishments evident in procurement, travel and transport services, human resources and IMIS.

According to the report, the most significant achievement of the Task Force was the creation of a culture of collaboration and an atmosphere conducive to common services. It had fostered a demand-driven approach that emphasized best practices, which, in turn, had led to concrete action and tangible results. The Task Force had also sought to build on common interests and concerns, and to harmonize policies and practices of the participating organizations.

A workshop on the common services evaluation framework was conducted in February to identify criteria for measuring performance in the implementation of common services. Work on developing performance measurements had begun and was focused on measuring performance with respect to the achievement of quality and standards specified, volume of services, the extent to which services were meeting expectations and cost-effectiveness. The travel and transport working group issued in July a draft set of generic performance indicators that were considered applicable to the participating organizations.

Future work would be aimed at the establishment of a joint UN archives and research centre and the harmonization of policies and procedures related to archives and record-keeping; new arrangements for shared accounting services, continuation of efforts to establish a common treasury support unit or an alternative mechanism, and improvements in the current inter-agency accounting mechanisms; the development and implementation of the remaining releases of IMIS, implementation of effective long-term joint governance mechanisms and field connectivity; simplification of financial rules and regulations on procurement, adoption of the value-for-money concept and codes of conduct for procurement, continued coordination with the Inter-Agency Procurement Working Group/the Inter-Agency Procurement Services Office in common procurement training and professional certification; harmonization of other staff entitlements, particularly with respect to hardship duty stations; and periodic service reviews of travel agency services, adoption of innovative best practices with respect to staff entitlements and harmonization of staff travel entitlements.

The practice of disseminating information updates to Vienna, Geneva, the regional commissions, the specialized agencies and UN offices away from New York, including the United Nations University, would be further broadened. Efforts would be made to establish concrete collaboration with UNDG in the development of common services at the country office level. Emphasis would be placed on ensuring policy and procedural coherence with actions taken at Headquarters and on supporting ongoing field-based common services efforts.

Participating organizations agreed to establish a two-year project, starting in September on a cost-shared basis, for a Common Services Support Unit in New York.

Notwithstanding that development, the Task Force on Common Services was at a crossroads. It would require a new mandate if tangible results beyond those identified for its future work were to be achieved, including the realization of the originally conceived common services facilities. Accordingly, the Task Force had introduced a two-year phase-out arrangement for the jointly funded Common Services Support Unit, without prejudice to its possible extension or expansion.

ACABQ recommended in November [A/55/7/ Add.1, para. 29] that the General Assembly take note of the Secretary-General's report and that it request him to report at its fifty-seventh session in 2002 on the progress made and decisions taken on the future of the Task Force.

UN insurance programmes

The General Assembly, by **resolution 54/257** of 7 April, took note of OIOS reports on the audits of the UN commercial insurance programmes and of UN health insurance programmes and JIU comments thereon [YUN 1998, p. 1363].

Outsourcing practices

The General Assembly considered an OIOS report on a review of outsourcing practices in the United Nations [YUN 1997, p. 1511] and a JIU report on the challenge of outsourcing for the UN system [ibid.], as well as ACC comments thereon [YUN 1998, p. 1364]. It also considered a report of the Secretary-General on outsourcing practices [YUN 1999, p. 1377] and the related report of ACABQ [ibid.].

GENERAL ASSEMBLY ACTION

On 7 April [meeting 95], the General Assembly, on the recommendation of the Fifth Committee [A/54/511/Add.2], adopted **resolution 54/256** without vote [agenda item 118].

Outsourcing practices in the United Nations

The General Assembly,

Having considered the report of the Office of Internal Oversight Services on the review of outsourcing practices at the United Nations, the report of the Joint Inspection Unit entitled "The challenge of outsourcing for the United Nations system" and the comments of the Administrative Committee on Coordination thereon, and the report of the Secretary-General on outsourcing practices in the United Nations and the related report of the Advisory Committee on Administrative and Budgetary Questions,

1. *Requests* the Secretary-General to ensure that programme managers are guided by the basic reasons for outsourcing, as indicated in paragraph 4 of his report,

and the goals, as indicated in paragraph 13 of the report;

2. *Endorses* the United Nations guidelines on outsourcing set out in the report of the Secretary-General, pending consideration of the report requested in paragraph 3 below;

3. *Requests* the Secretary-General to define, in a more detailed way and with justification, the criteria for decisions on which activities and services should or should not be outsourced, and to report thereon to the General Assembly at its fifty-fifth session.

In response to the above resolution, the Secretary-General submitted an August report [A/55/301] on outsourcing practices containing four specific criteria that might be considered when evaluation was made of whether or not an activity of the Organization was suitable for outsourcing. The criteria related to cost-effectiveness and efficiency, safety and security, maintaining the international character of the Organization, and maintaining the integrity of procurement procedures and process. The Secretary-General said that an activity might be outsourced only if it was demonstrated that all four criteria were met and the practice was in the overall interest of the Organization.

ACABQ, in its comments on the Secretary-General's report [A/55/479], said that it did not receive an adequate reply to a clarification it had sought on the scope of application covered by the report; that clarification should be provided to the Assembly's Fifth Committee.

GENERAL ASSEMBLY ACTION

On 23 December [meeting 89], the General Assembly, on the recommendation of the Fifth Committee [A/55/532/Add.1 & Corr.1], adopted **resolution 55/232** without vote [agenda item 116].

Outsourcing practices

The General Assembly,

Recalling its resolution 54/256 of 7 April 2000,

Having considered the report of the Secretary-General on outsourcing practices and the related report of the Advisory Committee on Administrative and Budgetary Questions,

1. *Requests* the Secretary-General to continue to ensure that programme managers are guided by the following four basic reasons for outsourcing:

(a) To acquire technical skills not readily available within the Organization, including accessing state-of-the-art technologies and expertise or acquiring needed flexibility to meet quickly changing circumstances;

(b) To achieve cost savings;

(c) To provide a source more effectively, efficiently or expeditiously;

(d) To provide an activity or service not needed on a long-term basis;

2. *Affirms* that at least the following three significant goals must be considered with regard to the use of outsourcing by the United Nations:

(a) To respect the international character of the Organization;

(b) To avoid a possible negative impact on staff;

(c) To ensure appropriate management and/or control over the activities or services that have been outsourced;

3. *Affirms also* the firm commitment of the United Nations to provide fair treatment on as wide a geographical basis as possible to all participants involved in United Nations procurement activities, including outsourcing;

4. *Requests* the Secretary-General to continue to consider outsourcing actively in accordance with the guidance and goals mentioned above and to ensure that programme managers satisfy all of the following criteria in their assessment of whether or not an activity of the Organization could be fully, or even partially, outsourced:

(a) Cost-effectiveness and efficiency: this is considered to be the most basic criterion; unless it can be adequately demonstrated that an activity can be done significantly more economically and, at the very least, equally efficiently, by an external party, outsourcing may not be considered;

(b) Safety and security: activities that could compromise the safety and security of delegations, staff and visitors may not be considered for outsourcing;

(c) Maintaining the international character of the Organization: outsourcing may be considered for activities where the international character of the Organization is not compromised;

(d) Maintaining the integrity of procedures and processes: outsourcing may not be considered if it will result in any breach of established procedures and processes;

5. *Also requests* the Secretary-General to report to the General Assembly at its fifty-seventh session on the following:

(a) Progress achieved with regard to the implementation of the provisions of the present resolution, including information on the location and type of outsourced activities and the reason therefor;

(b) The activities outsourced during the years 1999-2000, by providing similar detailed information as mentioned in paragraph 5 (a) of the present resolution;

6. *Requests* the Joint Inspection Unit to conduct a management audit review of outsourcing in the United Nations and the United Nations funds and programmes in accordance with existing practice and to report thereon to the General Assembly at its fifty-seventh session.

Use of private management consulting firms

The Secretary-General transmitted a JIU report entitled "Policies and practices in the use of the services of private management consulting firms in the organizations of the United Nations system" [A/54/702]. The report examined the policies and practices governing their use to determine what practical advantages and disadvantages had resulted and to draw conclusions regarding system-wide standards, guidelines and procedures, paying due regard to internal and external oversight services as a primary source of expertise in management, and to formulate recommendations for improving current policies and practices with a view to regulating the use of such firms.

The Inspectors concluded that it was a sound practice for the organizations to use outside expertise in support of their mandated programmes when such expertise was not available in-house. Management consulting firms, in particular, helped to gather experience, identified best practices and introduced new technologies. Organizations should first make every effort to ascertain that the expertise required was not available internally or that it was indeed more economical to have recourse to consulting firms, which were, as a rule, very costly. Noting that organizations in many cases appeared to choose firms from mostly Western countries, the report said firms from other countries and regions, including developing countries, should be given equal opportunity to bid for consulting contracts.

The report laid out elements that it said should be reflected in guidelines for subcontracting, feasibility studies, procedures and checklists for the call for bids and methods for evaluating potential consulting firms. The organizations should ensure adequate means to monitor as closely as possible the performance of management consulting firms, including their transfer of new management skills, and so as to ensure creation and preservation of institutional memory. They should conduct ex post facto evaluations of the performance and extent of implementation of the recommendations of those firms, especially cost-effective benefits and the impact of their work within the organization, and should share the results of such evaluations with other organizations. Organizations should also reinforce system-wide cooperation and coordination in using such firms by, among other things, sharing rosters of cost-effective firms with UN experience; guarding against possible conflicts of interest when awarding contracts or when hiring former agents or personnel of those firms; adopting a policy of rotating management consulting firms to ensure they derived the broadest possible benefits; and advertising for international biddings in as many official languages and in as many countries as possible.

Internal and external printing

In response to section X of General Assembly resolution 54/251 [YUN 1999, p. 1378], the Secretary-General submitted a comprehensive report on the Organization's internal and external printing practices [A/55/132]. The report pro-

vided quantitative information on the total cost of operating all printing facilities in New York and Geneva; the capacity of all the plants; the organizations' printing workload; the printing programme that was contracted out; and the comparative costs for in-house and external printing. It also contained information on measures taken to achieve economies of scale, including through the development of common services; those taken to ensure that outputs were measured in the same way throughout the system; and the potential for reducing the budget for printing as a result of reductions in hard-copy output. There were also data on printing activities at UN Headquarters in New York and in Geneva and information supplied by certain UN funds and programmes.

The report concluded that there had been a steady reduction in the Organization's internal and external printing programme at Headquarters and in Geneva over the last three bienniums. Internal printing had been reduced by 31 per cent in physical terms (page impressions) and by some 20 per cent in costs, while the external jobs were down by 35 per cent in dollar terms. The report said that reductions had resulted in better management of the Organization's publication activities and closer monitoring of requirements on the part of the users. Extensive introduction of modern technologies for the electronic storage of documentation and desktop publishing had also contributed to the reduction of paper output. The Secretariat would further streamline its printing practices to respond to the needs of the Organization and its Member States, as well as to General Assembly guidelines.

ACABQ urged the Secretary-General to continue to make the UN printing services an attractive option for the Organization's funds and programmes, which were also urged not to arbitrarily rule out recourse to them [A/55/7/Add.1]. ACABQ requested that it be kept informed about measures taken to improve the in-house publishing capacities of the UN Office at Geneva (UNOG) so that UN specialized agencies located in the city could increasingly use them. It suggested an independent technical evaluation of printing practices at UNOG, the costs of internal printing and outsourcing.

Measures to increase profitability of UN commercial activities

In response to General Assembly resolution 52/220 [YUN 1997, p. 1421], the Secretary-General submitted a November report [A/55/546], which identified a number of measures the Secretariat could take to boost sales and revenues, as well as attract more customers for UN commercial services. The report, largely based on an independent assessment conducted by a private consulting firm contracted by the Secretariat, covered the work of the UN Postal Administration, the guided tours, the UN Bookshop/publications, the Gift Centre, catering services and the newsstand. The report observed that the overall outlook and approach to the management of commercial activities at the United Nations needed to be changed if their profitability was to be increased. Those activities should be distinct from the Secretariat's core work and the Organization's overall non-commercial nature. It was also noted that the proposal for a new UN visitors' experience would lead to an increase in the number of visitors as well as the attendance registered by the various commercial activities. A strategic plan would be developed to communicate clearly the long-term vision in the planning of commercial activities and to coordinate efforts across those activities. New, adjusted management practices would be undertaken jointly by the Department of Public Information and the Office of Central Support Services, to which UN commercial entities currently reported, with a view to ensuring consistency and maximizing effectiveness and efficiency.

Marketing activities for each commercial area were extremely limited in financial as well as human resources, and there was a need for planned promotional coordination throughout the commercial operations. That process would include market research and development, product pricing and market placement, as well as order fulfilment and efficient product delivery mechanisms. The management of each commercial activity needed to carry out customer surveys, provide customer service training to staff and improve the services delivered. The Secretariat intended to look into the economic and substantive viability of outsourcing market research and client feedback from Member States, with a view to conducting those activities regularly. The mix of products available for sale, their presentation and the method of sales would all be redefined based on the information accessed through such surveys.

More systematic promotion of commercial activities by tour guides would be introduced, as would simple upgrading of the current signage to make it more user-friendly and easy to follow. During the next biennium, the Commercial Activities Service would look into developing web-based sales to boost sales and better promote the UN image. Management changes would be introduced to ensure that revenue and other financial information became available as required, thereby laying the foundation for better strategic management and planning. Those changes would be accompanied by a continued effort to address the issue of creating a service-oriented culture and raising the overall level of professionalism within those units directly involved in managing commercial services, while preserving the non-commercial nature of the United Nations.

The report also contained specific recommendations for the UN Postal Administration, the guided tours, the UN Bookshop/publications, the Gift Centre and the catering services.

ACABQ, in November [A/55/7/Add.1], said it intended to revert to the matter, since the Secretary-General suggested that the report should be reviewed in conjunction with his forthcoming report on the proposed new visitors' experience.

UN premises and property

Facilities management

ACABQ, in November [A/55/7/Add.1], considered the Secretary-General's report [YUN 1999, p. 1379] updating information on principal properties occupied by the United Nations worldwide. It welcomed the Secretary-General's efforts in exploring ways of coordinating a common approach to the management of UN buildings and land valued at some $5,186,900,000. ACABQ agreed with his approach towards the coordinating role of Headquarters in the overview of all UN facilities, and shared his view that the postponement, due to lack of resources, of preventive maintenance often increased the overall need for resources for emergency repairs at a later date. In that regard, it was of the view that the current level for major maintenance expenditures at UN-owned buildings was well below the minimum recommended industry standards. ACABQ indicated its intention to review the subprogramme, which would be fully detailed in the capital master plan (see p. 1405) and proposed programme budget for 2002-2003 and would make its recommendations accordingly.

Overseas Properties Management Information Exchange Network

The Secretary-General, in August [A/55/210], proposed the establishment of an Overseas Properties Management Information Exchange Network (OPMIEN) to facilitate the coordination of common concerns related to UN property and facilities worldwide, as recommended by the pilot seminar held in New York from 31 January to 8 February. It would be composed of an Organization-wide team of professionals from each duty station. The team would network and exchange information on best practices, common approaches and policy directives that would enhance the safety, reliability, efficiency and operations of the facilities, while integrating into the buildings infrastructure evolving technological innovations. The Office of Central Support Services, in collaboration with the team, would provide a coordinating role for monitoring information exchange and policy dissemination with respect to locations outside Headquarters. The report gave details of the functions of OPMIEN, its terms of reference, membership and budgetary, manpower and other resources.

The Secretary-General said that OPMIEN would develop and maintain a database of all land, buildings and property values, office and conference spaces and guidelines for consistent operations, environmental controls, facilities planning and budgeting. It would meet once a year at one of the duty stations. The funding and other resources required by it would be included in the regular budgets of the offices at each of the duty stations. Integrated alterations, improvements, major maintenance and construction programmes would be projected over a long-range planning period (10 to 15 years). Medium-term plans and biennial programme budget proposals would continue to be presented in the four- and two-year cycles, but with greater emphasis on the coordination and integration of programme elements and on budgetary consistency over longer periods. The Secretary-General would report to the General Assembly periodically on the specific activities and accomplishments of OPMIEN.

In November [A/55/7/Add.1], ACABQ stressed the importance of reliable and comprehensive databases in all major areas of facilities management. It stated that membership of the proposed OPMIEN should be organized in a way that would ensure efficiency.

Asbestos problem

In March [A/54/779], the Secretary-General submitted a report entitled "Review assessment and management of the asbestos problem at United Nations Headquarters", pursuant to General Assembly resolution 54/249 [YUN 1999, p. 1289]. According to the report, the UN Headquarters buildings were constructed when the use of asbestos-containing materials (ACMs) was common for thermal insulation of piping and ductwork, fireproofing/acoustic treatment of walls and ceilings, strengthening vinyl floor tiles and electrical insulation. The UNDC-I and UNDC-II buildings did not contain any ACMs since they were constructed when the use of such mate-

rials was already discouraged. All leased spaces in other Headquarters buildings were inspected for ACMs and proper abatement or containment procedures were followed prior to occupancy. All known ACMs in Headquarters buildings were currently maintained in a non-friable, or encapsulated, state by inspections, testing and engineering controls. Any ACMs that might become friable during maintenance, alteration or construction were removed or encapsulated, on an as-needed basis, in accordance with proper safety, monitoring and control measures.

There had been adequate funding in the 2000-2001 ($1 million) and previous bienniums to manage the required asbestos management and control programme. Industry standards and guidelines indicated that the practice of removing asbestos materials only when a planned or unplanned activity could disturb the material and leaving the rest of encapsulated ACMs alone was the recommended option for occupied buildings and had been found to pose minimum risk to the health and safety of occupants. Under the proposed extensive buildings renovation programme in the capital master plan (see p. 1405), when staff would be relocated from multiple floors, complete removal of all ACMs from occupied spaces would be undertaken.

ACABQ, in March [A/54/7/Add.12], recommended that information be provided on buildings in Geneva, Vienna, Nairobi and the locations of the regional commissions.

By **decision 54/476** of 7 April, the Assembly took note of the Secretary-General's report and endorsed ACABQ's recommendation.

In response to that recommendation, the Secretary-General submitted a July report [A/55/135], which provided an assessment of the existing conditions with regard to ACMs at UN buildings located in Addis Ababa, Bangkok, Beirut, Geneva, Nairobi, Santiago and Vienna. The assessment showed that the United Nations Office at Nairobi, and the Economic and Social Commission for Western Asia headquarters in Beirut, Lebanon, had no ACMs in their buildings, infrastructure elements and equipment, and hence no further action was required at those locations. Asbestos was used to different degrees in buildings at the United Nations Offices at Geneva and Vienna, and at the Economic Commission for Africa (ECA) headquarters in Addis Ababa, Ethiopia, the Economic Commission for Latin America and the Caribbean headquarters in Santiago, Chile, and the Economic and Social Commission for Asia and the Pacific headquarters in Bangkok, Thailand.

For all those facilities, applicable regulations of the host country were followed with regard to monitoring, engineering controls, removal and disposal of ACMs. The emphasis at all those facilities had been to conduct regular inspections, testing and indoor air quality monitoring to ensure that all ACMs remained encapsulated and did not become friable, and that the fibre count in the air remained well below industry-established safe threshold limits. Adequate engineering control measures were in place to make sure that the safety and health of the staff, delegates and visitors were not adversely affected by the presence of ACMs. In addition, any ACM that could become friable by maintenance, alterations, improvement or other activities was either removed or encapsulated by following established safety, monitoring and control measures.

There had been no known or documented cases of asbestos contamination or known adverse health effects from the release of asbestos fibres. All facilities had developed or were developing a programme of phased removal of ACMs over a multi-year period, consistent with safety, operations, space availability and budgetary considerations.

ACABQ, in November [A/55/7/Add.1], said it intended to review the asbestos problem at the UN Office at Vienna and to inform the Assembly accordingly. It expressed concern that no tests had been performed to determine the type of ACMs in Addis Ababa, but noted that a programme of bulk samples testing to determine the extent of the asbestos problem was being developed in co-ordination with Headquarters to commence in 2001.

Addis Ababa conference facilities

The Secretary-General submitted an October annual progress report [A/55/493] on the construction of conference facilities at ECA in Addis Ababa, which had begun on 29 April 1991. The project was closed and capitalized in the Organization's books on 30 June 2000, and no further reports on it would be submitted. The construction costs totalled $114,937,567. The uncommitted balance of $290,927 remained on the construction-in-progress account, which totalled $7,702,600 as of 30 June. The Secretary-General recommended retention of those funds, pending consideration of all related matters.

ACABQ recommended the acceptance by the General Assembly of the Secretary-General's requests [A/55/7/Add.7].

Capital master plan

A June report of the Secretary-General [A/55/117] reviewed the long-term capital master plan developed for the United Nations Head-

quarters complex in New York in accordance with the budget appropriation for the 1998-1999 biennium. The plan, which covered the buildings and land owned by the United Nations in New York, with the exception of the residence of the Secretary-General, reviewed the current condition of the facilities and assessed their requirements over a 25-year period. The master plan was based on several assumptions, including the fact that UN Headquarters would remain in its current New York location, and that the Headquarters complex should be energy efficient, free of hazardous materials and compliant with host city building, fire and safety codes and should provide full accessibility to all persons. Other assumptions were that Headquarters should meet all reasonable, modern-day security requirements and the most cost-effective and technologically viable method of implementation selected for all repair and refurbishment. The current condition of the Headquarters complex was unacceptable for continued use over the long term. The capital master plan outlined the work required to rectify the situation and provide a safe, secure, appropriate and energy-efficient facility for carrying out the vital business of the Organization.

The estimated cost for the capital master plan ranged from $875 million for a three-year option for the planned programme to $1,054 million for a 12-year option, exclusive of any financing or maintenance costs. Each option had advantages and disadvantages in terms of costs and the impact that the refurbishment programme would have on operations at Headquarters. The Secretary-General believed that the most practical and desirable approach was a six-year option, at an estimated cost of $964 million, under which 33 per cent of the Headquarters facility would be under construction at the same time and would require the availability of swing space at an estimated cost of between $62 million and $91 million. The Secretary-General also examined the option of complete demolition and reconstruction of the Headquarters buildings, which would cost an estimated $992 million. There would be additional costs for relocating the entire Secretariat staff for up to five years at an estimated $218 million, bringing the total cost to $1,210 million. In addition, there would be further costs for convening all meetings away from UN Headquarters, which would be substantial for the Organization. The report suggested three possible sources of funding for the capital master plan: special assessments; the programme budget; and voluntary contributions, in cash or in kind, from public and private sources.

The Secretary-General recommended that the General Assembly endorse in principle the proposed six-year plan; approve a special assessment of $8 million to cover the costs of the initial schematic design for the plan, including the swing space requirement to provide a detailed basis for its implementation; and request the Secretary-General to continue exploring all financing options for meeting the plan's costs, including its amortization over a 25-year period, and to submit no later than 2001 a comprehensive schedule and financing plan.

An ACABQ report [A/55/7/Add.4] welcomed the Secretary-General's report, stating that it expected that there would be close coordination with local authorities regarding health and safety requirements at all stages of the capital master plan. It recommended that the Secretary-General be authorized to proceed with the preparation of the comprehensive design plan and cost analysis and that an additional $8 million be appropriated under section 31, Construction, alteration, improvement and major maintenance, of the 2000-2001 programme budget. The General Assembly might wish to encourage the active participation of the host Government, as well as state and local authorities, in the project of comprehensive renovation of the UN Headquarters complex, including its funding. ACABQ required that the Secretariat provide information on the participation of host Governments and local authorities in maintaining UN assets in their respective countries. In response to that request, the Secretary-General submitted an addendum to his report [A/55/117/Add.1] containing the required information.

On 23 December, the Assembly, in **resolution 55/238, section IV** (see p. 1301), took note of the Secretary-General's report and approved the recommendations of ACABQ.

Security

The Ad Hoc Inter-Agency Meeting on Security (Bonn, Germany, 16-18 May) [ACC/2000/10] made a number of recommendations to ACC covering security training, communications, residential security measures, hostage incident management, security management in the field and the use of technology. It also discussed policy issues. The Meeting urged continuation of the "mobile training team" concept implemented by the Office of the UN Security Coordinator, and welcomed the proposal by the Office to establish four regional training centres. It requested UNICEF to establish a working group on communications and to review proposals made previously on minimum communications standards. It called for system-atic implementation of UN policy on hostage incident management by all UN agencies, and urged the Office of the UN Security Coordinator to take the lead role as the focal point for handling those questions. The Meeting also called on the Office to develop guidelines on the Organization's role as an intermediary. UN system agencies were advised to bring cases of domestic violence affecting staff to the attention of the Designated Official, the Field Security Officer or Agency Security Officer and, as appropriate, to the Office of the UN Security Coordinator.

Security arrangements in Geneva

In response to General Assembly resolution 54/249 [YUN 1999, p. 1289], the Secretary-General submitted an October report on security arrangements at the UN Office at Geneva [A/55/511]. The report stated that, in the light of the demonstrated vulnerability of the Palais des Nations, considerable efforts had been made to improve the efficiency of the security and to upgrade the level of protection in the most vulnerable areas. Some $767,800 in the 1998-1999 biennium and budgetary provision of $746,000 in the 2000-2001 biennium had been or were being utilized to improve overall security. Further security reinforcement work programmed for 2000 and 2001 included the installation of additional cameras for the video control system, additional remote-controlled metal shutters, the extension of the electronic access control system and reinforcement of further sections of the perimeter fencing and entrance gates.

However, the penetration of the compound by a well-organized group and its occupation of a conference room underscored the need to devise a joint security strategy with the Swiss authorities. Consequently, a task force comprising security specialists representing the Swiss Federal and Cantonal authorities and the UN Office at Geneva recommended close cooperation among the security services of both sides and the preparation of a jointly defined and coordinated response scenario for all types of incidents. It also proposed a security concept for the Office compound, which would include a reinforced perimeter, an intermediate buffer zone and providing the buildings proper with reinforced protection against forced entry. The estimated portion of funding the security concept, which was to borne by both sides, was some $2.7 million, which was $2 million higher than the amounts spent or allocated in the 1998-1999 and 2000-2001 bienniums. The Secretary-General intended to address the requirements for upgrading the security of the UN compound at Geneva in the context of the 2002-2003 programme budget.

PART SIX

Intergovernmental organizations related to the United Nations

Chapter I

International Atomic Energy Agency (IAEA)

In 2000, the International Atomic Energy Agency (IAEA) continued to act as a catalyst for the development and transfer of peaceful nuclear technologies; to build and maintain a worldwide nuclear safety regime; and to assist in efforts to prevent the proliferation of nuclear weapons.

The forty-fourth session of the IAEA General Conference (Vienna, 18-22 September) adopted resolutions on: strengthening international cooperation in nuclear, radiation and waste safety, and IAEA's technical activities; the safety of radioactive waste management and nuclear research reactors; strengthening the effectiveness of the safeguards system and application of the 1997 Model Protocol Additional to Safeguards Agreements [YUN 1997, p. 1519]; application of IAEA safeguards in the Middle East; safeguards inspections in the Democratic People's Republic of Korea and Iraq; the safety of transport of radioactive materials; measures against illicit trafficking in nuclear and other radioactive sources; and the production of potable water.

In 2000, IAEA membership remained at 130.

Activities

Nuclear safety

IAEA continued to provide nuclear safety services and assistance worldwide. In 2000, the Agency published safety requirements and safety guides for the design and operation of nuclear power plants and provided safety services regarding their siting, design and operation, the safety of research reactors and the regulatory aspects of nuclear safety. Safety missions were undertaken to the Czech Republic, France, Spain, Switzerland, Ukraine and the United States. Safety review missions to research reactors under project and supply agreements were carried out in Colombia, the Democratic Republic of the Congo, Indonesia, Malaysia, Morocco, the Philippines, Thailand and Viet Nam. Overall, IAEA reviews indicated a general improvement in the operational safety of nuclear power plants throughout the world, but the safety of research reactors continued to cause concern, prompting an expanded range of IAEA activities in that area.

IAEA launched the Review of Accident Management Programmes service and developed guidelines for the Peer Review of Operating Safety Performance Experience service. During the year, countries participating in the Incident Reporting System, operated jointly with the Nuclear Energy Agency of the Organisation for Economic Cooperation and Development (OECD/NEA), submitted 68 reports concerning unusual events at nuclear power plants, as well as actual and potential safety problems.

In 2000, the European Atomic Energy Community (EURATOM) acceded to the 1994 Convention on Nuclear Safety [YUN 1994, pp. 925 & 1417], bringing the total number of parties to 53.

Radiation safety

IAEA's radiation safety programme continued to focus on the development of a unified set of safety standards and their application; implementation of the Agency's radiation protection rules; and the provision of advice and services to member States. Peer reviews of national radiation safety infrastructure were conducted in 24 member States during 2000. Through the technical cooperation Model Project on strengthening radiation and waste-safety infrastructures, IAEA provided technical support and assistance to more than 50 States. Implementation of the action plan on the safety of radiation sources and the security of radioactive materials continued. A system for categorizing radiation sources was established and a new international Code of Conduct on the Safety and Security of Radioactive Sources was developed. An international conference of national regulatory bodies was organized by the Agency in Buenos Aires, Argentina, in December. IAEA, with other UN agencies, received requests for assessments of areas with possible residues of radioactive material in the Balkans and in the Middle East.

Nuclear power

In 2000, the nuclear power programme reflected the growing economic competitiveness arising from the liberalization of electricity markets around the world. A number of documents were published and databases further expanded, containing guidance on engineering and management practices for achieving improved safety, reliability and economic cost-effectiveness of nuclear power plants. IAEA launched the project on Innovative Nuclear Reactors and Fuel Cycles, which would build upon programme activities on new technologies and applications, including small and medium-sized reactors, high temperature modular gas-cooled reactors and desalination applications. IAEA provided technical support for preparations for nuclear plant projects in Africa, Asia, Europe and Latin America; life management of power plants in Europe and Latin America; personnel training and qualification in the Commonwealth of Independent States; and modernization of instrumentation and control in Europe and Latin America. During the year, two large regional projects were completed in Europe on improving operations management and inspection of WWER-440/100 nuclear reactors.

Nuclear fuel cycle

In 2000, IAEA and OECD/NEA published *Uranium 1999: Resources, Production and Demand*, considered to be the foremost world reference on uranium. It provided substantial new information from all major uranium-producing centres throughout the world, and analysed industry statistics and worldwide projections of nuclear energy growth and uranium requirements and supply. During the year, IAEA activities focused on uranium resources and production, including environmental issues, and on spent fuel technologies. In October, an international symposium in Vienna addressed the uranium production cycle and its impact on the environment.

Radioactive waste management

The radioactive waste management programme in 2000 emphasized waste minimization and facility decommissioning; the implementation of waste management initiatives, with a greater focus on disposal issues; technology transfer and information exchange; and international cooperation in the geological disposal of high-level and long-lived wastes. A scientific forum on waste management, organized during IAEA's General Conference in September, agreed that public acceptance of the technological solutions to the safe management of radioactive waste was critical. Other IAEA activities and documents focused on the application of waste management technologies and options for recycling waste.

Marine environment and water resources

Activities in the marine environment continued to focus on protection of the oceans and coastal seas through radioactivity monitoring and assessment, and the use of nuclear and isotopic techniques for understanding pollutant behaviour. The work programme emphasized capacity-building, quality assurance activities and education and training in marine environmental protection. The IAEA Marine Environment Laboratory in Monaco continued to serve as a focal point for training and research studies on the transfer of nuclear and non-nuclear contaminants in contrasting marine ecosystems. During the year, IAEA and the United Nations Educational, Scientific and Cultural Organization (UNESCO) launched the Joint International Isotopes in Hydrology Programme, designed to integrate isotope hydrology techniques into the water sector activities of member States.

Food and agriculture

Under its food and agriculture programme, IAEA transferred, through technical cooperation, techniques and strategies that resulted in a number of achievements in the area of food security. They included advances in controlling fruit flies through the use of the sterile insect technique (SIT); eradicating rinderpest with the help of immunoassay techniques; introducing better crop varieties developed through radiation and more efficient nitrogen-fixing tree species for improving soil fertility and crop production; and adopting food irradiation to improve food safety and securing plant health. Progress was also made in identifying new opportunities for harnessing nuclear techniques. A Food and Agriculture Organization of the United Nations (FAO)/ IAEA symposium (Vienna, October) addressed the use of nuclear techniques in integrated plant nutrient, water and soil management. IAEA also continued research and training activities related to improved plant breeding, animal production, pest control, and food and environmental protection.

Human health

In 2000, IAEA's human health programme focused on the prevention of malnutrition, detection of contaminant levels affecting humans, and diagnosis and management of cancer and nutritional, infectious and genetic disorders. In particular, it concentrated on the validation of new nuclear tools for diagnosing drug-resistant strains of malaria and tuberculosis and the use of nuclear techniques to screen newborns for thyroid deficiency. Radiotherapy techniques for the treatment of cancer were made more accessible, and the Agency assisted several member States in verifying the quality of radiation measurements.

Technical cooperation

In 2000, IAEA continued to implement its 1999-2000 technical cooperation programme and approved the programme for 2001-2002. Expenditure on technical cooperation totalled $11,435,725. Programme implementation in 2000 was higher than in 1999, with new obligations totalling $66 million.

IAEA's technical cooperation activities included helping Ethiopia to create a 12-year groundwater assessment programme, using isotope hydrology applications; similar work was ongoing in other countries. The Agency signed an agreement with the Organization of African Unity to combat jointly the tsetse fly using SIT, and supported the World Health Organization (WHO) in its initiatives against tuberculosis and malaria. In collaboration with WHO and national disease control programmes, IAEA embarked on a three-year project in 11 African countries to evaluate new diagnostic tools for drug-resistant strains of tuberculosis and malaria. The Agency also supported new applications for nuclear and isotope technologies, such as a project in Europe on humanitarian demining.

Safeguards responsibilities

All information available to IAEA in 2000 led to the conclusion that nuclear material and other items placed under safeguards remained in peaceful nuclear activities or were otherwise accounted for. Over 900 facilities and locations were under Agency safeguards or contained safeguarded material. As at 31 December, 224 safeguard agreements with 140 States (and with Taiwan Province of China) were in force. Safeguards agreements that satisfied the requirements of the 1968 Treaty on the Non-Proliferation of Nuclear Weapons, adopted by the General Assembly in resolution 2373(XXII) [YUN 1968, p. 17], were in force in 128 States. Protocols Additional to safeguards agreements [YUN 1997, p. 1519] for 57 States were approved by the Board of Governors. Eighteen such Protocols were in force.

During the year, 2,467 safeguard inspections were performed. However, IAEA was unable to fulfil its safeguards mandates in the Democratic People's Republic of Korea and Iraq (see PART ONE, Chapter IV).

Nuclear information

In January 2000, the Agency convened an industry forum in Vienna with the aim of broadening and enhancing its contacts with non-traditional partners. The forum allowed private sector representatives to exchange views with the IAEA secretariat on the future prospects for nuclear power and related applications. IAEA continued to increase user access to information in electronic formats and posted a series of information pages on its WorldAtom web site. IAEA published some 163 books, reports, journal issues and leaflets and distributed some 800 video products. Regional public information seminars were held in Brazil, Finland, Hungary, Romania and Thailand.

The International Nuclear Information System, with 122 participating members (103 countries and 19 international organizations), continued to collect and distribute bibliographic information on nuclear literature published in member States, as well as on texts not readily available through commercial channels.

Secretariat

At the end of 2000, IAEA secretariat staff totalled 2,173, including 912 in the Professional and higher categories and 1,261 in the General Service category.

Budget

The 2000 regular budget amounted to $199.3 million, of which $191 million was from assessed contributions by member States, $4 million from income from reimbursable work and $4.3 million from miscellaneous income. Actual budget expenditure amounted to $196.4 million. A total of $38.7 million in extrabudgetary funds was provided by member States, the United Nations, international organizations and other sources.

NOTE: For further information, see *Annual Report 2000*, published by IAEA.

HEADQUARTERS AND OTHER OFFICE

HEADQUARTERS

International Atomic Energy Agency
Wagramerstrasse 5
(P. O. Box 100, Vienna International Centre)
A-1400 Vienna, Austria
  Telephone: (43) (1) 26000
  Fax: (43) (1) 26007
  Internet: http://www.iaea.org/worldatom
  E-mail: Official.Mail@iaea.org

LIAISON OFFICE

International Atomic Energy Agency Liaison Office at the United Nations
1 United Nations Plaza, Room 1155
New York, NY 10017, United States
  Telephone: (1) (212) 963-6010, 6011, 6012
  Fax: (1) (212) 751-4117

Chapter II

International Labour Organization (ILO)

In 2000, the International Labour Organization (ILO) continued to promote social justice and economic stability and improve labour conditions. ILO's strategic objectives were to promote and realize fundamental principles and rights at work; create greater opportunities for women and men to secure decent employment and income; enhance the coverage and effectiveness of social protection; and strengthen tripartism and social dialogue.

In 2000, ILO membership increased to 175 with the admission of Kiribati.

Meetings

The eighty-eighth session of the International Labour Conference (ILC) (Geneva, 30 May–15 June) adopted a new international Maternity Protection Convention (No. 183), revising the Maternity Protection Convention (No. 103) and its accompanying Recommendation No. 95. The Conference took action to compel the Government of Myanmar to comply with the ILO Forced Labour Convention (No. 29).

Sectoral and other meetings convened in Geneva during 2000 included: Meeting of Experts on Safety in the Use of Insulation Wools (17-26 January); Symposium on Information Technologies in the Media and Entertainment Industries: Their Impact on Employment, Working Conditions and Labour-Management Relations (28 February–3 March); Joint Meeting on Lifelong Learning in the Twenty-first Century: The Changing Roles of Educational Personnel (10-14 April); Tripartite Meeting on the Social and Labour Impact of Globalization in the Manufacture of Transport Equipment (8-12 May); Tripartite Meeting on Moving to Sustainable Agricultural Development through the Modernization of Agriculture and Employment in a Globalized Economy (18-22 September); and Tripartite Meeting on Labour Practices in the Footwear, Leather, Textiles and Clothing Industries (16-20 October).

International standards

ILO activities with regard to Conventions and Recommendations during 2000 included standard-setting and the supervision and promotion of the application of standards. Supervisory

bodies reviewed existing procedures and standard-setting policy.

In June, ILC adopted a new international Maternity Protection Convention (No. 183) and Recommendation (No. 191).

ILO standards covered a broad spectrum of work-related issues, ranging from social security and occupational health and safety to basic workers' rights, such as the abolition of forced labour and child labour, and equality and freedom of association.

Employment and development

ILO continued in 2000 to help constituents combat unemployment and poverty through the creation of employment opportunities and improvement of existing jobs. ILO also provided advice and guidance to constituents on employment and labour market policies, as well as on their labour market information and statistical systems. Activities to promote employment included support to constituents to develop entrepreneurship through the creation of cooperatives and small and micro-enterprises, particularly by vulnerable groups.

Regarding human resources development, ILO emphasized the adaptation of training policy and delivery to the rapidly changing skill requirements and the special needs of vulnerable groups. It also responded to the needs of countries affected by conflict.

Field activities

In 2000, extrabudgetary expenditure on operational activities totalled $82.5 million compared to $78.2 million in 1999. The leading field of activity in terms of annual expenditure (representing 46 per cent of total expenditure) was the employment sector ($37.7 million), followed by the standards and fundamental principles and rights at work sector (28 per cent), and social protection– and social dialogue–related activities (9 and 13 per cent, respectively). Interregional and global activities accounted for some $19 million.

In terms of regional distribution, Africa accounted for 31 per cent of total expenditure ($25.5 million), Asia and the Pacific for 23 per cent ($19.3 million), and Latin America and the

Caribbean for 15 per cent ($12.6 million). Expenditure in Europe showed a decrease of 14 per cent, to $4.5 million, and the Arab States programme decreased 49 per cent, to $1.5 million in 2000.

Educational activities

The Turin Centre and the International Institute for Labour Studies, both autonomous institutions, reported to the ILO Governing Body. The Centre continued to carry out training and related activities in a wide range of technical areas as an integral part of ILO technical cooperation activities. The Institute continued to carry out research, encouraged networking related to emerging labour policy issues and acted as a catalyst for future ILO programme development. Institute activities on labour policy issues focused on an analysis of the relationships between social exclusion, labour institutions and poverty, and an exploration of the changing global organization of production and its social implications at the local level.

Secretariat

As at 31 December 2000, ILO employed a total of 2,259 full-time staff. Of those, 971 were in the Professional and higher categories and 1,288 were in the General Service category.

Budget

In June 1999, ILC adopted a budget of $467 million for the 2000-2001 biennium.

NOTE: For further information on ILO, see *Report of the Director-General, Activities of the ILO, 2000-2001.*

HEADQUARTERS, LIAISON AND OTHER OFFICES

HEADQUARTERS

International Labour Organization
4 Route des Morillons
CH-1211 Geneva 22, Switzerland
Telephone: (41) (22) 799-6111
Fax: (41) (22) 798-8685
Internet: http://www.ilo.org
E-mail: doscom@ilo.org

LIAISON OFFICE

International Labour Organization
Liaison Office with the United Nations
220 East 42nd Street, Suite 3101
New York, NY 10017, United States
Telephone: (1) (212) 697-0150
Fax: (1) (212) 697-5218
E-mail: newyork@ilo.org

ILO maintained regional offices in Abidjan, Côte d'Ivoire; Bangkok, Thailand; Geneva, Switzerland; and Lima, Peru.

Chapter III

Food and Agriculture Organization of the United Nations (FAO)

The Food and Agriculture Organization of the United Nations (FAO) continued to work towards the achievement of sustainable global food security by raising levels of nutrition and standards of living, improving agricultural productivity and advancing the condition of rural populations.

At its one hundred and nineteenth session (Rome, Italy, 20-25 November), the 49-member FAO Council decided to convene in November 2001 a world food summit to review progress towards the goal of the 1996 World Food Summit [YUN 1996, p. 1129] of reducing the number of hungry in the world from 800 million to 400 million by 2015. As lead agency in preparations for the International Year of Mountains in 2002, declared by the General Assembly in resolution 53/24 [YUN 1998, p. 994], FAO continued to work with other UN agencies, Governments and nongovernmental organizations to increase international awareness of the global importance of mountain peoples and ecosystems.

The FAO Director-General established the Panel of Eminent Experts on Ethics in Food and Agriculture to advise on issues related to accelerating technological development, changes in the resource base, and market and economic developments, in the context of their relevance to food security and sustainable rural development.

In 2000, FAO membership remained at 180 countries, plus the European Community.

World food situation

World cereal production in 2000 fell to 1,852 million tonnes, some 2 per cent below the previous year's level and below the average for the preceding five years. Factors contributing to the contraction in output ranged from natural disasters and low prices to government policies aimed at cutting excess supply. Global wheat production fell slightly to 586 million tonnes, mostly due to severe droughts in parts of Europe and North Africa and in several countries in Asia. Global output of coarse grains registered a 2 per cent drop to 869 million tonnes, mostly because of weather damage in parts of Asia and Europe. World rice output fell to 397 million tonnes, down by almost 3 per cent compared with 1999; however, it was still the second highest on record. The contraction was primarily due to diversification of crops in response to weak rice prices.

FAO's Global Information and Early Warning System, in cooperation with the World Food Programme (WFP), fielded an increasing number of crop and food supply assessment missions and issued 43 special alerts about impending food shortages. In response, some 29 emergency operations worth about $1.4 billion were jointly approved by FAO and WFP for food assistance to affected populations. The Inter-Agency Task Force on the Horn of Africa adopted a new strategy to break the cycle of chronic food insecurity in the region, which proposed ways to protect rural people from external shocks by broadening their livelihoods and enhancing their resilience.

Activities

Emergency assistance

FAO's Special Relief Operations Service (TCOR) continued to provide assistance to rehabilitate agriculture devastated by natural or human-induced calamities. In 2000, TCOR obtained $65 million to fund 114 projects in 42 countries, and $403 million for the execution of the agricultural component of the oil-for-food programme in Iraq (see p. 302).

Field programmes

Through its field programmes, FAO provided technical advice in food and agriculture, fisheries, forestry and rural development. Expenditures for the year totalled $353 million ($180 million for its emergency agricultural rehabilitation programme and $173 million for development and technical support). Thirty projects, prepared with assistance from the FAO Investment Centre, were approved for financing for total investments of $1.6 billion, including supporting loans of $1 billion from financing institutions.

The Special Programme for Food Security (SPFS) assisted developing countries, particularly low-income food-deficit countries, to improve national and household food security on an economically and environmentally sustainable basis. By October, SPFS was in operation in 61 countries in Africa, Asia, Europe, Latin America and Oceania.

Crops and livestock

FAO continued in 2000 to participate in activities related to plant biological diversity; crop management and diversification; seed production and improvement; crop protection; agricultural engineering; prevention of food losses; and food and agricultural industries. It also contributed to the development of animal production and health programmes through better resource utilization, improved processing and commercialization, and better control of animal diseases. Through the Global Rinderpest Eradication Programme, FAO tracked down the last pockets of the virus in Africa and Asia as part of its goal to eliminate the livestock disease by 2010.

Forestry

The FAO Forestry Department continued its work in forest resource management, forest policy and planning, and forest products. In 2000, the Global Forest Resources Assessment 2000, the most comprehensive collection of data on the state of the world's forest resources, was released. FAO also intensified support for national forest programmes and for international processes to promote sustainable forest management, including the United Nations Forum on Forests (see p. 979).

Fisheries

The FAO fisheries programme promoted sustainable development of responsible fisheries and contributed to food security through activities in fishery resources, policy, industries and information. Priorities included implementation of the FAO Code of Conduct for Responsible Fisheries.

Food standards and nutrition

In 2000, the Codex Alimentarius Commission, responsible for implementing the Joint FAO/World Health Organization Food Standards Programme, began developing standards for geneti-cally modified foods. The Commission also continued to develop standards, guidelines and other recommendations to protect consumer health and ensure fair practices in the food trade.

Environment and natural resources management

FAO continued activities aimed at achieving more productive and efficient use of the Earth's natural resources to meet current and future food and agricultural needs in a sustainable manner, concentrating on six main areas: natural resources assessment and planning; farming systems development; plant nutrition development and management; water development, management and conservation; soil management, conservation and reclamation; and sustaining the potential of natural resources.

Plant and animal genetic resources

FAO provided technical assistance in plant breeding, the safe movement of germ plasm and associated systems. It assisted its members to comply with the World Trade Organization Agreement on Trade-related Aspects of Intellectual Property Rights as it related to plant varieties, animal breeds, related technology and germ plasm.

Information

FAO continued to function as an information centre, collecting, analysing, interpreting and disseminating information through various media. The World Agricultural Information Centre provided immediate access to FAO's bibliographical information, documents and multimedia resources through the Internet and on CD-ROM.

Secretariat

As at 31 December 2000, FAO had a full-time staff of 3,442, of whom 1,350 were in the Professional or higher categories, and 2,092 were in the General Service category.

Budget

The regular programme budget for the 2000-2001 biennium was $650 million.

NOTE: For further information, see *The State of Food and Agriculture 2001.*

HEADQUARTERS AND OTHER OFFICES

Food and Agriculture Organization of the United Nations
Viale delle Terme di Caracalla
00100 Rome, Italy
 Telephone: (39) (06) 57051
 Fax: (39) (06) 5705 3152
 Internet: http://www.fao.org
 E-mail: FAO-HQ@fao.org

NEW YORK LIAISON OFFICE

Food and Agriculture Organization Liaison Office with the United Nations
1 United Nations Plaza, Room 1125
New York, NY 10017, United States
 Telephone: (1) (212) 963-6036
 Fax: (1) (212) 963-5425
 E-mail: FAO-LONY@field.fao.org

FAO also maintained liaison offices in Brussels, Geneva, Washington, D.C., and Yokohama, Japan; regional offices in Accra, Ghana; Bangkok, Thailand; Cairo, Egypt; and Santiago, Chile; and subregional offices in Apia, Samoa; Bridgetown, Barbados; Budapest, Hungary; Harare, Zimbabwe; and Tunis, Tunisia.

Chapter IV

United Nations Educational, Scientific and Cultural Organization (UNESCO)

The United Nations Educational, Scientific and Cultural Organization (UNESCO) continued in 2000 to promote cooperation in education, science, culture and communication among its member States.

The General Conference, which met biennially to decide on policy, programmes and budgetary matters, was scheduled to hold its thirty-first session in 2001. The 58-member Executive Board held its one hundred and fifty-ninth (9-26 May) and one hundred and sixtieth (9-25 October) sessions, both at UNESCO headquarters in Paris.

UNESCO membership remained at 188 in 2000.

Activities

Education

UNESCO, together with the United Nations Children's Fund, the United Nations Development Programme, the United Nations Population Fund and the World Bank, convened the World Education Forum (Dakar, Senegal, 26-28 April). The Forum adopted the Dakar Framework for Action, in which participants reaffirmed their commitment to achieving education for all by 2015, and entrusted UNESCO with the overall responsibility of coordinating international partners and sustaining their collaborative momentum. The Forum was the culmination of the Education for All 2000 Assessment, an in-depth evaluation of basic education. _The World Education Report 2000: The Right to Education: Towards Education for All throughout Life_ focused on education as a basic human right, the underlying principle of the Dakar Framework for Action.

An International Expert Meeting in Goa, India, led to the preparation of policy guidelines and an action plan for socio-culturally relevant science and technology education. The Joint International Labour Organization/UNESCO Committee of Experts on the Application of the Recommendations concerning Teaching Personnel (Geneva, 11-15 September) made several recommendations for improving the status of teachers worldwide. UNESCO contributed to the International Year for the Culture of Peace (2000) (see

p. 634) through its educational activities, and provided assistance for the elaboration of strategies to strengthen the teaching of human rights. UNESCO also addressed the development of technical and vocational education, the prevention of HIV/AIDS and drug abuse, and civics education.

In 2000, the Associated Schools Project network continued to expand, promoting activities such as experimentation in 130 countries. The programme involved 7,000 schools in 171 countries.

Sciences

Under its programme of sciences in the service of development, UNESCO continued to promote the advancement, sharing and transfer of knowledge. It emphasized the fostering of synergies between the exact and natural sciences and the social and human sciences.

Natural sciences

In 2000, UNESCO's activities continued to focus on the advancement, sharing and transfer of scientific and technological knowledge, the training of scientists and the provision of advisory services and training programmes on science and technology policy-making and planning. As the clearing house for follow-up activities to the 1999 World Conference on Science [YUN 1999, p. 1393], UNESCO worked towards the implementation of the Conference's recommendations.

Through the Abdus Salam International Centre for Theoretical Physics, operated jointly with the International Atomic Energy Agency, UNESCO provided research opportunities and advanced training in physics and applied mathematics to some 1,500 scientists from developing countries.

In the environmental sciences, UNESCO pursued activities related to natural disasters, terrestrial ecosystems, biological diversity, desertification, oceans, coastal areas and small islands, and marine, terrestrial and freshwater resources, as well as environmental education. The Man and Biosphere Programme, in partnership with the secretariat of the 1992 Convention on Biological Diversity [YUN 1992, p. 683], continued to promote the Ecosystem Approach. During 2000, the biosphere reserves network expanded, bringing the number of reserves to 391 in 94 countries; new reserves were nominated in India, Malawi and Pakistan. In 2000, UNESCO hosted the secretariat of the World Water Assessment Programme. Through its Intergovernmental Oceanographic Commission (IOC), UNESCO continued to play a key role in coordinating UN activities in ocean and coastal issues. The IOC Committee on International Oceanographic Data and Information Exchange, which included 57 national oceanographic data centres and designated national authorities, held its sixteenth session (Lisbon, Portugal, 30 October–9 November) to define new directions for the programme.

Social and human sciences

Activities in the social and human sciences included strengthening research and training capacities, mainly through the establishment of UNESCO chairs, networks and other mechanisms for inter-university cooperation, and building bridges between social scientists and decision makers under the programme called Management of Social Transformations. As part of its future-oriented studies, UNESCO established a Council on the Future, an advisory network for gathering views and recommendations from leading experts in the field. In addition, in a new report, *The World Ahead: Our Future in the Making*, UNESCO addressed issues such as population, water, desertification, poverty, development, women, cities, education, new technologies, the future of languages and Africa tomorrow. The organization also continued efforts to increase awareness about issues related to women and a culture of peace; tolerance and non-violence; human rights education; and the ethics of scientific knowledge and technology.

UNESCO promoted a culture of peace at the national, regional and international levels. As part of its observance of the International Year of Culture (see p. 634), it organized the Asian Women for a Culture of Peace Conference (Hanoi, Viet Nam, 6-9 December), in cooperation with Viet Nam and the Economic and Social Commission for Asia and the Pacific. The Conference was part of the preparations for the International Decade for a Culture of Peace and Non-Violence for the Children of the World (2001-2010), for which UNESCO had been designated as the lead agency by the General Assembly in resolution 55/47 (see p. 635).

Culture

In 2000, UNESCO's cultural development activities included a meeting of the Committee of Experts on the Strengthening of UNESCO's Role in Promoting Cultural Diversity in the Context of Globalization (Paris, 21-22 September); an international training workshop on the Living Human Treasures System (Seoul, South Korea, November); and several intercultural projects as part of preparations for the United Nations Year of Dialogue among Civilizations, 2001, declared by the General Assembly in resolution 53/22 [YUN 1998, p. 1031].

UNESCO continued to promote international and national standards for better protection of moveable and immovable cultural heritage. The Third Meeting of Governmental Experts on the Draft Convention on the Protection of Underwater Cultural Heritage was held at UNESCO headquarters in July. On 15 November, UNESCO marked the thirtieth anniversary of the 1970 Convention on the Means of Prohibiting and Preventing the Illicit Import, Export and Transfer of Ownership of Cultural Property. In addition, UNESCO published the International Code of Ethics for Dealers in Cultural Property and launched a fund for the return and restitution of cultural property.

A further 61 sites were inscribed on the World Heritage List, bringing the number of sites protected under the Convention for the Protection of the World Cultural and Natural Heritage to 690 in 122 States.

Communication

UNESCO promoted activities in favour of press freedom, notably through the worldwide celebration of World Press Freedom Day on 3 May. The UNESCO/Guillermo Cano World Press Freedom Prize was awarded in 2000 to Nizzar Nayyouf, a journalist from the Syrian Arab Republic recently released from prison. The organization supported independent media in areas of conflict, as well as in countries undergoing transition from an authoritarian to a democratic regime.

The need for greater affordable access to information, especially in developing countries, was highlighted during INFOethics 2000, UNESCO's third Congress on the challenges of cyberspace. UNESCO established a new Information Programme for All to bridge the gap between the information-rich and information-poor, and its communications advocacy, training and capacity-building activities in developing countries assisted a variety of media outlets and communications professionals.

The International Consultation Meeting of UNESCO Chairs in Communication (Mexico City, 10-11 July) agreed on a new medium-term plan of action, which called for research on the uses of new technologies in developing countries, information exchange over the Internet and public access to new communications technologies in Latin America and their impact on development.

Secretariat

As at 31 December 2000, UNESCO had a full-time staff of 2,348, of whom 1,090 were in the Professional or higher categories and 1,258 in the General Service category, drawn from 153 nationalities.

Budget

The UNESCO General Conference, at its 1999 session, approved a budget of $544,367,250 for the 2000-2001 biennium.

HEADQUARTERS AND OTHER OFFICES

HEADQUARTERS
UNESCO House
7, Place de Fontenoy
75352 Paris 07-SP, France
Telephone: (33) (1) 45-68-10-00
Fax: (33) (1) 45-67-16-90
Internet: http://www.unesco.org

NEW YORK LIAISON OFFICE
United Nations Educational, Scientific and Cultural Organization
2 United Nations Plaza, Room 900
New York, NY 10017, United States
Telephone: (1) (212) 963-5995
Fax: (1) (212) 963-8014
E-mail: newyork@unesco.org

UNESCO also maintained liaison offices in Geneva, Vienna and Washington, D.C.

Chapter V

World Health Organization (WHO)

In 2000, the World Health Organization (WHO) adopted a new corporate strategy that focused on reducing excess mortality and disability; reducing risk to human health; developing health systems that equitably improved health outcomes; and placing health at the centre of economic and development policy. The strategy also identified WHO's core functions: advocacy for health; information management; technical support; partnership-building; innovation; and the development and monitoring of norms and standards.

The World Health Assembly, WHO's governing body, at its fifty-third session (Geneva, 15-20 May), adopted resolutions on HIV/AIDS; the Global Alliance for Vaccines and Immunization; the draft framework convention on tobacco control (see p. 1170); the prevention and control of non-communicable diseases; the Stop Tuberculosis Initiative; and food safety. The issue of HIV/AIDS in Africa and its impact on peace and security was debated by the Security Council (see p. 81). WHO played a leading role in launching the global strategy to combat HIV/AIDS worldwide.

The one hundred and fifth session of the WHO Executive Board (Geneva, 24-29 January) endorsed the organization's new corporate strategy, recommended several resolutions for adoption by the World Health Assembly, and, among other things, took action regarding collaboration with non-governmental organizations and several other financial and management matters. At its one hundred and sixth session (Geneva, 22-23 May), the Board discussed smallpox eradication, the Roll Back Malaria Initiative, and the 2002-2003 programme budget as a key tool for implementation of the new corporate strategy, in addition to other management and financial matters.

The World Health Report 2000—Health Systems: Improving Performance offered new approaches to the analysis of health systems. The report focused on the essential functions and performance of health systems, including their responsiveness to people's needs and the equality of health financing.

In 2000, WHO membership remained at 191, with two associate members and four observers.

Health policy

During the year, WHO worked with national health authorities around the world to formulate better health-care policies, design more efficient health systems and deliver better health care, especially to those in greatest need. In March, the organization merged its programmes on non-communicable disease and social change and mental health into a single cluster covering chronic health conditions, accidents, disabilities, violence and mental health. WHO also launched a global strategy on mental health, as well as its global strategy on non-communicable diseases, and initiated its first world report on violence and health to raise awareness regarding the public health aspects of violence.

Health and development

In 2000, WHO established the Commission on Macroeconomics and Health, which brought together a group of the world's leading economists and economic policy makers to assess the linkages between health and development and between poverty and disease, with the aim of identifying the potential for better health as a contributor to human well-being and prosperity. The urgency of targeting the causes and consequences of health conditions that affected the poor and perpetuated poverty was also emphasized at the Third International Conference on Priorities in Health Care (Amsterdam, Netherlands, 22-24 November).

Disease trends and control efforts

New initiatives launched in 2000 by WHO to improve the health of poor people included: Roll Back Malaria; the Global Alliance for Vaccines and Immunization; Stop Tuberculosis; the International Partnership against AIDS in Africa (see p. 1166); Kick Polio Out of Africa; and Making Pregnancy Safer. Those new ventures brought in new WHO partners, broadening international efforts to improve global public health. As a result of those efforts, more than 190 countries and territories were expected to be polio-free by the end of 2000. WHO also succeeded in its global elimination target for leprosy by the end of 2000.

Secretariat

At the end of 2000, WHO employed a staff of 3,486, including 1,293 posts at the Professional and higher categories and 2,065 in the General Service category.

Budget

The World Health Assembly, in 1999, adopted a budget of $842,654,000 for the 2000-2001 biennium.

NOTE: For further details of WHO activities, see the *World Health Report 2000* and *2001*, published by the organization.

HEADQUARTERS AND OTHER OFFICES

HEADQUARTERS

World Health Organization
20, Avenue Appia
CH-1211 Geneva 27, Switzerland
Telephone: (41) (22) 791-21-11
Fax: (41) (22) 791-31-11
Internet: http://www.who.int/
E-mail: info@who.ch

WHO OFFICE AT THE UNITED NATIONS

2 United Nations Plaza
New York, NY 10017, United States
Telephone: (1) (212) 963-4388
Fax: (1) (212) 963-8565

WHO also maintained regional offices in Alexandria, Egypt; Copenhagen, Denmark; Harare, Zimbabwe; Manila, Philippines; New Delhi, India; and Washington, D.C.

Chapter VI

World Bank (IBRD and IDA)

The World Bank consisted of the International Bank for Reconstruction and Development (IBRD) and the International Development Association (IDA) (see below). Collectively, the following five institutions were known as the World Bank Group: IBRD, IDA, the International Finance Corporation, the Multilateral Investment Guarantee Agency (MIGA) and the International Centre for Settlement of Investment Disputes (ICSID).

In fiscal 2000 (1 July 1999–30 June 2000), the World Bank continued to promote sustainable economic development by providing loans, guarantees and related technical assistance for projects and programmes in developing nations. Within the context of the Bank's central objective of poverty reduction, key focal points of its assistance were economic management and private and financial sector development. Special attention was also given to human development, including the strengthening of health services, education and social protection, and environmental management.

IBRD began working with countries interested in piloting the Comprehensive Development Framework (CDF) [YUN 1999, p. 1398], which recognized the multidimensional nature of the challenges in poverty reduction and the need for extensive partnerships. The Bank's framework and strategies for poverty reduction were outlined in *The World Development Report 2000/2001*.

At the end of fiscal 2000, IBRD membership remained at 181.

Lending operations

Gross disbursement by IBRD totalled $13.3 billion, a decrease of nearly 25 per cent from fiscal 1999. The Bank's loan commitment also decreased to $10.9 billion for 97 new operations in 41 countries, a more than 50 per cent reduction from the previous fiscal year. Having reached peak levels in the wake of the 1997/98 financial crises, demand for IBRD funds subsided in 2000 as global financial markets recovered and emerging market economies regained access to private capital flows. Lending to IBRD "crisis borrowers"—Argentina, Brazil, Indonesia, the Republic of Korea, the Russian Federation and Thailand—which accounted for $13 billion in fiscal 1999, was down to $1.8 billion in fiscal 2000.

Compared to the preceding two fiscal years, the regional composition of commitments in fiscal 2000 shifted away from East Asia and slightly more towards Eastern Europe, Central Asia and Latin America. The five largest borrowers were Turkey ($1.8 billion), China ($1.7 billion), Brazil ($1.3 billion), Mexico ($1.2 billion) and Colombia ($941 million). Lending focused on strengthening the financial sector ($1.6 billion), improving public sector management ($1.5 billion) and meeting infrastructure needs ($1.8 billion).

International Development Association

Established in 1960 as the Bank's concessional lending arm, IDA provided interest-free loans and other services to low-income countries to reduce poverty and improve the quality of life. In 2000, 81 countries were eligible for IDA assistance. IDA credits to those countries totalled $4.4 billion.

At the end of 2000, IDA membership had increased to 161 countries.

Fiscal 2000 was the first of the three years of the twelfth replenishment of IDA (IDA-12), which provided resources for new financing commitments during fiscal 2000-2002. The IDA-12 replenishment of $20.5 billion included $11.6 billion of new donor funds, $8 billion of its own resources and IBRD's contribution of $0.9 billion. As at 30 June, available IDA-12 resources totalled 7.4 billion special drawing rights.

In fiscal 2000, total IDA lending commitments reached $4.4 billion for 126 operations in 52 countries, compared to $6.8 billion in the previous fiscal year. The size of new IDA operations averaged under $35 million in fiscal 2000, compared to $55 million for 1990-1999. The decline in IDA lending commitments in fiscal 2000 reflected the confluence of country-specific factors, especially policy and institutional performance and conflict situations in Africa and Asia, as well as an increasing focus on selectivity and aid effectiveness. The largest commitments were to India ($867 million), the United Republic of Tanzania ($330 million) and Viet Nam ($286 million). New IDA commitments to the Africa region stood at $2 billion, about the same as for fiscal 1999, but they constituted a higher share of total IDA lending and approached the 50 per cent target set by donors. Overall, sub-Saharan Africa accounted for almost half of IDA commitments.

The majority of IDA lending went to support for human development ($1.6 billion), followed by economic reform, recovery and private-sector development, largely in Africa ($0.7 billion), infrastructure needs ($0.6 billion) and assistance for agriculture and the environment ($0.5 billion).

Although IDA was legally and financially distinct from IBRD, it shared the same staff, and the projects it supported had to meet the same criteria as those supported by IBRD.

International Centre for Settlement of Investment Disputes

ICSID, established in 1966, continued to encourage foreign investment by providing international facilities for conciliation and arbitration of investment disputes. In 2000, 12 new cases were registered with the Centre. ICSID also undertook research and publishing activities in arbitration and foreign investment law.

In 2000, ICSID's membership totalled 131.

Multilateral Investment Guarantee Agency

MIGA, established in 1988, continued to encourage the flow of foreign direct investment to its developing member countries by providing investment guarantees against non-commercial risks. The Agency also provided technical assistance to help developing countries disseminate information on investment opportunities. MIGA had its own operating and legal staff, but drew on the Bank for administrative and other services. In 2000, MIGA had 152 members.

In fiscal 2000, MIGA issued $1.6 billion in guarantee coverage for a cumulative total of $7.1 billion.

World Bank Institute

In 2000, the World Bank Institute reached some 30,000 participants in nearly 150 countries through some 500 training activities. It scaled up its programmes through distance learning, global knowledge networks, extended partnerships, and by harnessing the newest learning technologies. A new initiative, the Global Development Learning Network (GDLN), provided clients with new learning opportunities through videoconferencing, the Internet and peer exchanges; 13 GDLN centres were operational and over 50 countries had expressed interest in the initiative. Demand for assistance in developing knowledge strategies was also expanding, as countries, such as China and Viet Nam, sought to use global and domestic knowledge more effec-

tively in support of economic and social development.

Co-financing

In fiscal 2000, co-financing amounted to $9.3 billion, a decrease of $2.1 billion compared to the previous year. Official bilateral and multilateral partners continued to be the largest source of co-financing, accounting for 59 per cent of the total share. Major co-financing partners included the Inter-American Development Bank ($2.6 billion); private sponsors ($2.2 billion); the Andean Development Corporation ($900 million); the Montreal Protocol Investment Fund ($230 million); the Global Environment Facility ($197 million); and European Union institutions ($165 million). By region, the majority of co-financing went to Africa (47 per cent), followed by Latin America and the Caribbean (41 per cent), East Asia and the Pacific (5 per cent), Europe and Central Asia (3 per cent), the Middle East and North Africa (2 per cent) and South Asia (2 per cent).

Financing activities

During fiscal 2000, IBRD raised $15.8 billion in medium- and long-term debt, compared to $22.4 billion the previous year. The majority of new funding continued to be initially swapped into floating rate United States dollars, with conversion to other currencies or fixed-rate funding being carried out subsequently in accordance with funding requirements.

As at 30 June 2000, outstanding borrowings totalled $114 billion, after swaps. The currency composition continued to be concentrated in United States dollars, with its share as at 30 June 2000 rising to 80 per cent of the borrowing portfolio, compared to 79 per cent as at 30 June 1999. Borrowing was carried out in 13 currencies, resulting in 148 transactions.

Capitalization

As at 30 June 2000, the total subscribed capital of IBRD was $188.6 billion, or 98 per cent of its authorized capital of $190.8 billion. Outstanding loans and callable guarantees totalled $120.1 billion, or 57 per cent of IBRD's statutory lending limit.

Income, expenditures and reserves

IBRD's gross revenues totalled $10 billion in fiscal 2000, compared with $9.8 billion in fiscal 1999. Net income amounted to $1.99 billion, up from $1.52 billion in fiscal 1999. Expenses decreased to $8.1 billion, compared to $8.2 billion a year earlier. Administrative costs fell to $935 million, from $965 million in 1999. At the end of fiscal 2000, the Bank's liquidity totalled $24.2 billion, a decrease of $5.8 billion compared to 1999. Its equity-to-loan ratio rose to 21.23 per cent as a result of higher net income and the increase in reserves.

Secretariat

As at 30 June 2000, IBRD's regular, fixed-term and long-term consultants, and long-term temporary staff in Washington, D.C., and local offices numbered approximately 8,000.

NOTE: For further details regarding the Bank's activities, see *The World Bank Annual Report 2000.*

HEADQUARTERS AND OTHER OFFICES

The World Bank
1818 H Street N.W.
Washington, D.C. 20433, United States
 Telephone: (1) (202) 473-1000
 Fax: (1) (202) 477-6391
 Internet: http://www.worldbank.org

Office of the Special Representative to the United Nations
809 UN Plaza, 9th floor
New York, NY 10017, United States
 Telephone: (1) (212) 963-6008
 Fax: (1) (212) 697-7020

The World Bank also maintained offices in Brussels, Frankfurt, Geneva, London, Paris, Sydney and Tokyo.

Chapter VII

International Finance Corporation (IFC)

The International Finance Corporation (IFC), part of the World Bank Group, continued in fiscal 2000 (1 July 1999–30 June 2000) to promote growth in developing countries by financing private sector investments, helping to mobilize capital in the international financial markets and providing technical assistance and advice to Governments and businesses. To address concerns about the environment and the social consequences of development, IFC made corporate responsibility a top priority in its investment and advisory activities.

In the aftermath of the global financial crises of the late 1990s, the Corporation helped companies to restructure and use capital more effectively. IFC increased its gross investment approvals by more than 10 per cent in fiscal 2000 and expanded investments in new sectors, such as information technology. Nearly 70 per cent of project approvals were for financial and infrastructure projects.

During fiscal 2000, IFC membership remained at 174.

Financial and advisory services

In fiscal 2000, IFC's Board of Directors approved a total of $5.8 billion in financing for 259 new projects in 81 countries, compared with 255 projects in 77 countries in fiscal 1999. Total project cost of the enterprises supported by IFC amounted to more than $21 billion, compared with $15.6 billion the previous year. In 2000, IFC approved investments in six countries for the first time: Armenia, Chad, Samoa, Saudi Arabia, the Syrian Arab Republic and Turkmenistan.

Organizational changes were undertaken during the fiscal year to ensure that IFC's investment, portfolio management and advisory operations were more closely aligned with strategic priorities. Several World Bank/IFC jointly managed departments, known as Global Product Groups, were created, with a focus on mining, oil, gas and chemicals, information and communication technologies, private sector advisory services, and small and medium-sized enterprises (SMEs).

Cumulative contributions to the IFC-managed technical assistance trust funds totalled $525 million in fiscal 2000, compared with a cumulative total of $451 million at the end of fiscal 1999. Projects supported by the funds during the year

included a study of industries and the convening of a private sector development conference in the West Bank and Gaza; an environment audit for a gold company in Tajikistan; the conversion of a not-for-profit organization to a microfinance bank in Cambodia; and a project aimed at turning small Moldovan banks into effective financing sources for SMEs.

Regional projects

IFC approved 259 projects in 81 countries and regions in fiscal 2000. It also reconfigured its regional structure.

In sub-Saharan Africa, IFC's priorities focused on support for private infrastructure development, expanding and strengthening financial institutions, and assisting indigenous entrepreneurs in building competitive businesses. It approved 80 projects in 25 countries in fiscal 2000, compared to 80 projects in 26 countries in fiscal 1999. As at 30 June 2000, IFC's committed portfolio, including loans and investments, totalled $1.48 billion, up from $1.33 billion in fiscal 1999.

In Asia and the Pacific, IFC continued to rehabilitate corporate and financial sectors in market economies and assisted the development of market institutions in transition economies. IFC initiated a programme to enhance the capital and technological base of existing clients and new ventures, and strengthened commercial banks and other financial intermediaries. In addition, it developed trade finance facilities to increase exports, and supported new venture funds. In fiscal 2000, IFC approved 54 projects in 12 countries of the region, compared to 33 projects in 8 countries in fiscal 1999. Its committed portfolio totalled $6.7 billion.

In the Middle East and North Africa, IFC focused on reducing constraints on private enterprise in order to foster economic development. It increased the capacity of its field offices in Cairo, Egypt, and the West Bank to undertake investment work. The Corporation approved 16 projects for 10 countries in fiscal 2000, compared to 22 projects in 8 countries in fiscal 1999. IFC's committed portfolio totalled $877 million.

In Europe and Central Asia, IFC was mainly active in Georgia, the Russian Federation and Ukraine where it built grass-roots programmes to help create and strengthen private enterprises through technical assistance in corporate governance, leasing and self-sustaining business centres. IFC activities aimed to attract further foreign investment throughout the region and build support for market reforms. Although the need for IFC as an investor was declining rapidly in Central Europe, it would continue to provide advice on the challenges facing private sector development and help countries prepare for integration into the European Union. Southern Europe presented a major development challenge, with only Croatia and Turkey reporting a per capita gross national product of more than $1,500. Significant progress was made on small-scale privatization in Central Asia, but results in the privatization of larger enterprises and in the financial sector were mixed. IFC approved 47 projects in 19 countries in fiscal 2000, compared with 61 projects in 19 countries the previous year. Its committed portfolio totalled $3.67 billion.

In Latin America and the Caribbean, lack of credit had created an unprecedented demand for multilateral development banks like IFC to provide investment financing to the private sector. IFC's regional strategy was aimed at helping private firms develop environmentally and socially responsible frontier sectors that previously had been in the hands of Governments, such as housing finance, transportation, water and sanitation, health and education. IFC also concentrated on building the domestic financial sector and directly supported middle-market firms in agribusiness, manufacturing and services. In fiscal 2000, IFC approved 58 projects in 15 countries, compared to the same number of projects in 16 countries in fiscal 1999. Its committed portfolio totalled $8.83 billion, compared to $8.23 billion in fiscal 1999.

Foreign Investment Advisory Service

The Foreign Investment Advisory Service (FIAS), jointly operated by IFC and the World Bank, continued to advise Governments on policies, law, regulations and procedures to increase inflows of productive foreign direct investment.

In fiscal 2000, FIAS completed 50 advisory projects, of which 16 were projects requiring a simple approval process and involving a small amount of resources. Twelve projects dealt with investment law reviews, four served groups of countries trying to coordinate investment policies and promotion activities, and eight dealt with the reduction of barriers to investment.

Financial performance

In fiscal 2000, IFC's net income increased to $380 million from $249 million in fiscal 1999. The loan portfolio generated net income of $67 million, while the net income from the equity and quasi-equity portfolios recovered to $188 million, after falling to $76 million in fiscal 1999, mainly because of lower loss provisioning in fiscal 2000. Net income from IFC's invested net worth and treasury activity totalled $153 million.

IFC's committed portfolio at the end of the fiscal year was $13.5 billion, up from $12.9 billion in fiscal 1999. The portfolio consisted of loans, equity investments, risk management products and guarantees in 1,333 companies in 113 countries.

Capital and retained earnings

As at 30 June 2000, IFC's net worth reached $5.8 billion, compared to $5.3 billion at the end of fiscal 1999.

Secretariat

As at 31 December 2000, IFC employed 1,875 staff, of whom 1,182 were in the Professional or higher categories and 693 were in the General Service category.

NOTE: For further details of IFC activities, see *International Finance Corporation 2000 Annual Report*, published by the Corporation.

HEADQUARTERS AND OTHER OFFICE

HEADQUARTERS

International Finance Corporation
2121 Pennsylvania Avenue, NW
Washington, DC 20433, United States
Telephone: (1) (202) 473-1000
Fax: (1) (202) 974-4384
Internet: http://www.ifc.org
E-mail: webmaster@ifc.org

NEW YORK OFFICE

International Finance Corporation
809 UN Plaza, 9th floor
New York, NY 10017, United States
Telephone: (1) (212) 963-6008
Fax: (1) (212) 697-7020

Chapter VIII

International Monetary Fund (IMF)

During 2000, the International Monetary Fund (IMF) promoted currency exchange stability; assisted in the establishment of a multilateral payments system; made its general resources temporarily available to members experiencing balance-of-payment difficulties; and helped to shorten the duration and lessen the degree of disequilibrium in members' international balances of payments. The IMF Executive Board acted during the year to transform its operation by increasing the transparency of members' policies and of IMF activities; developing and strengthening international standards of good practice; helping member countries strengthen their financial systems; involving the private sector in preventing and resolving financial crises; transforming the former enhanced structural adjustment facility into the poverty reduction and growth facility (PRGF), which made poverty reduction a key element of a growth-oriented strategy; and enhancing the Heavily Indebted Poor Countries (HIPC) Initiative to provide faster and broader debt relief.

During fiscal 2000 (1 May 1999–30 April 2000), IMF membership remained at 182.

IMF facilities and policies

IMF reassessed its lending policies and facilities in fiscal 2000 to ensure that they met member country needs, introduced new safeguards to protect its resources from potential misuse by member countries and to forestall instances of misreporting by its members, and discussed ways to help them adopt sound practices of external reserve management, as part of the broader effort to strengthen the global financial system.

The IMF Executive Board eliminated the buffer stock financing facility, the contingency element of the compensatory and contingency financing facility (CCFF), and supported currency stabilization funds and commercial bank debt and debt-service reduction operations. At the same time, the Board recommended modifications to other facilities, particularly the design of contingent credit lines and other precautionary facilities, to encourage greater efforts at crisis prevention.

The Fund provided concessional financial support to low-income countries under PRGF and through the HIPC Initiative.

Financial assistance

Demands for IMF financial support fell substantially during fiscal 2000, due to improved global economic and financial conditions and a return of investor confidence in many emerging market countries. Members' drawings of IMF general resources amounted to 6.3 billion special drawing rights (SDR) compared with SDR 21.4 billion in fiscal 1999.

Drawings consisted of SDR 5.7 billion under standby and extended arrangements; SDR 0.4 billion in emergency assistance for natural disasters and post-conflict countries; and SDR 0.2 billion under CCFF. Drawings under PRGF for poor countries fell to SDR 0.5 billion, compared with SDR 0.8 billion in fiscal 1999.

As at 30 April, 16 standby arrangements, 11 extended arrangements, and 31 PRGF arrangements were in effect with members, while outstanding IMF credit amounted to SDR 50.4 billion, compared with SDR 67.2 billion a year earlier.

Liquidity

The Fund's liquidity position improved substantially in 2000 as a result of increases in members' quotas under the Eleventh General Review [YUN 1999, p. 1404], and improved global economic and financial conditions.

As at 30 April, IMF's usable resources totalled SDR 108.2 billion, an increase of SDR 42.5 billion from fiscal 1999. Net uncommitted usable resources totalled SDR 74.8 billion at the end of fiscal 2000, compared with SDR 56.7 billion in fiscal 1999.

The Fund's liquid liabilities totalled SDR 48.8 billion, compared with SDR 63.6 billion a year earlier, while the ratio of the Fund's net uncommitted resources to its liabilities increased to 153 per cent at the end of April 2000 from 89.2 per cent a year earlier, reaching levels that prevailed before the onset of the 1997 Asian financial crisis.

SDR activity

In fiscal 2000, total transfers of SDRs declined to SDR 22.9 billion, from a peak of SDR 49.1 billion in fiscal 1999. That decline could be attributed largely to payments of Eleventh Review quota increases and delays in a number of large disbursements under arrangements with members during fiscal 2000.

Transfers of SDRs among participants and prescribed holders fell to SDR 7.8 billion in 2000, from SDR 19.4 billion a year earlier, mainly due to substantial decreases in transactions by agreement, and in the use of the same-day SDR borrowing facility by members paying the reserve asset portion of their Eleventh Review quota increases.

Transfers from participants to the general resources account (GRA) declined to SDR 7.1 billion from SDR 16.2 billion in fiscal 1999, reflecting a fall in quota payments, lower use of SDRs in repayments of IMF credit and a decline in charges. Drawings from IMF in SDRs amounted to SDR 3.6 billion during fiscal 2000, representing the largest category of transfers from the GRA, followed by remuneration payments of SDR 1.7 billion to members with creditor positions. Other transfers included the termination of the second special contingent account in December 1999, which led to the distribution of SDR 1 billion from the GRA to participants.

IMF's holdings of SDRs in the GRA declined to SDR 2.7 billion at the end of fiscal 2000, from SDR 3.6 billion a year earlier. Participants' holdings of SDRs increased correspondingly to SDR 18.1 billion as at 30 April, from SDR 17.4 billion a year earlier. The SDR holdings of industrial countries relative to their net cumulative allocations increased to 95 per cent at the end of fiscal 2000, from 94.6 per cent a year earlier; those of non-industrial countries increased to 62.5 per cent of their cumulative allocations, from 52.5 per cent a year earlier. The SDR holdings of prescribed holders also increased during fiscal 2000.

Policy on arrears

Total overdue financial obligations to IMF increased slightly during fiscal 2000 to SDR 2.32 billion, from SDR 2.3 billion a year earlier. No new cases of protracted arrears emerged in fiscal 2000, nor were any of the existing cases resolved, leaving seven member countries (Afghanistan, Democratic Republic of the Congo (DRC), Federal Republic of Yugoslavia, Iraq, Liberia, Somalia, Sudan) in protracted arrears.

As at 30 April, four countries (DRC, Liberia, Somalia, Sudan) were ineligible to use the Fund's general resources. Declarations of non-cooperation, a further step under the strengthened cooperative arrears strategy, were in effect with respect to the DRC and Liberia; a declaration of non-cooperation regarding the Sudan issued in September 1990 was lifted in August 1999.

Technical assistance and training

In fiscal 2000, technical assistance and training accounted for some 19 per cent of IMF's total administrative expenses. Demand for such assistance remained strong and continued to focus on the monetary, fiscal, statistical and legal aspects of macroeconomic management.

The IMF Institute continued to expand its training in different parts of the world. In 2000, it established the Joint China-IMF Training Programme and for the first time delivered a distance-learning course on financial programming and policies. The Institute also delivered several courses on financial sector issues.

Secretariat

As at 31 December 2000, IMF employed 2,455 staff members, of whom 1,727 were Professional staff and 728 assistant staff.

In March, the Executive Board named Horst Köhler (Germany) as Managing Director to succeed Michel Camdessus (France).

Budget

The Fund's administrative budget for fiscal 2000 was approved at $575.8 million and revised by a supplementary appropriation in January 2000 to $585.1 million. For the capital budget, $67.3 million was approved for projects beginning in fiscal 2000. Actual administrative expenses during the fiscal year totalled $583 million and capital project disbursements totalled $39.3 million, including $8.5 million for major building projects.

HEADQUARTERS AND OTHER OFFICES

HEADQUARTERS

International Monetary Fund
700 19th Street, NW
Washington, DC 20431, United States
 Telephone: (1) (202) 623-7000
 Fax: (1) (202) 623-4661
 Internet: http://www.imf.org
 E-mail: publicaffairs@imf.org

  IMF also maintained offices in Geneva, Paris and Tokyo.

IMF OFFICE, UNITED NATIONS, NEW YORK

International Monetary Fund
885 Second Avenue, 26th floor
New York, NY 10017, United States
 Telephone: (1) (212) 893-1700
 Fax: (1) (212) 893-1715

Chapter IX

International Civil Aviation Organization (ICAO)

The International Civil Aviation Organization (ICAO) continued in 2000 to promote the safety and efficiency of civil air transport by prescribing standards and recommending practices and procedures for facilitating civil aviation operations. Its objectives were set forth in annexes to the Convention on International Civil Aviation, adopted in Chicago, Illinois, United States, in 1944, known as the Chicago Convention.

In 2000, domestic and international scheduled traffic of the world's airlines increased to some 401 billion tonne-kilometres. The airlines carried about 1.65 billion passengers and some 30.2 million tonnes of freight. The passenger load factor on scheduled services in 2000 increased slightly to 71 per cent. Airfreight increased by 8.2 per cent to 117.6 billion tonne-kilometres, and airmail traffic increased by 5.4 per cent to 6 billion tonne-kilometres. Overall passenger/freight/mail tonne-kilometres increased by some 8 per cent and international tonne-kilometres by some 9 per cent.

The Council of ICAO held three regular sessions in 2000. In March, it appointed Renato Cláudio Costa Pereira (Brazil) as Secretary-General of ICAO for a second three-year term, effective 1 August 2000. The Council decided to convene, in 2001, a diplomatic conference to consider a draft Convention on International Interests in Mobile Equipment and an Aircraft Protocol thereto, which had been recommended by the ICAO Legal Committee. In June, the Council adopted revised text for ICAO's Strategic Action Plan. The Council in December adopted ICAO's Policies on Charges for Airports and Air Navigation Services.

Additionally, an ICAO task force began an implementation programme on an agreement reached in September by the Civil Aviation Administrations of China and Viet Nam. The agreement concerned the trial application of a revised route structure and airspace organization in the South China Sea area for a period of three years. Also in September, the Agreement of Cooperation between ICAO and the International Mobile Satellite Organization was signed in Montreal, Canada.

In 2000, ICAO membership remained at 185 countries.

Activities

Air navigation

ICAO continued to update and implement international specifications and regional plans, with particular emphasis on the introduction of communications, navigation and surveillance/air traffic management (CNS/ATM) systems. The specifications consisted of International Standards and Recommended Practices (SARPs) contained in 18 technical annexes to the 1944 Chicago Convention and Procedures for Air Navigation Services (PANS). Regional plans covered air navigation facilities and services required for implementation of CNS/ATM systems and other international air navigation elements in ICAO regions.

Five air navigation meetings, convened in Montreal, made recommendations to amend ICAO specifications. The Continuing Airworthiness Panel (10-21 January) developed provisions concerning the type certification process and restructured annex 8 to provide up-to-date broad aircraft design requirements upon which a detailed code of airworthiness could be based. The Aeronautical Telecommunication Network (ATN) Panel (7-18 February) developed amendments relating to ATN systems management, security and directory service. The Aeronautical Mobile Communications Panel (22-30 March) formulated provisions for aeronautical mobile satellite services, and proposals for the next-generation satellite communications systems. The Review of the General Concept of Separation Panel (8-19 May) proposed provisions relating to lateral and longitudinal separation of 55.5 kilometres and procedures for the use of automatic dependent surveillance for air traffic management. The Secondary Surveillance Radar Improvements and Collision Avoidance Systems Panel (11-22 September) recommended amendments concerning secondary surveillance radars with discrete addressing, associated data links and enhancements to the airborne collision avoidance system. The Council also adopted amendments to four technical annexes to the Chicago Convention and approved an amendment to one PANS document.

Other projects that were given special attention in 2000 included accident investigation; accident and incident data reporting; accident prevention; aerodromes; aerodrome rescue and fire fighting; aeronautical electromagnetic spectrum; aeronautical information services; assistance to civil aviation accident victims and their families; audio-visual aids; aviation environmental matters; aviation medicine; bird strikes to aircraft; CNS/ATM systems; controlled flight into terrain; flight safety and human factors; licensing/certification of aerodromes; aeronautical meteorology; personnel licensing and training; safety oversight; the TRAINAIR programme; and year 2000 planning.

Air transport

ICAO's air transport programmes were directed towards economic analysis, economic policy, forecasting and economic planning, collection and publication of air transport statistics, airport and route facility management, economic and organizational aspects of CNS/ATM systems, economic and coordination aspects of environmental protection and the promotion of greater facilitation in international air transport.

The Conference on the Economics of Airports and Air Navigation Services (Montreal, 19-28 June) adopted 30 recommendations, which revised guidance material on the management and operation of airports and air navigation services. The results of two studies, on cost recovery for search and rescue services and on the privatization of the provision of airport and air navigation services, were presented at the Conference.

The Technical Advisory Group on Machine Readable Travel Documents (Montreal, 6-8 September) adopted new specifications for machine readable passports. The Asia/Pacific (Bangkok, Thailand, 22-26 May) and the Caribbean/South American (Lima, Peru, 17-21 July) Traffic Forecasting Groups supported planning of air navigation services in their regions. Five workshops in the areas of air transport regulatory policy, forecasting and economic planning, economic aspects of planning and implementing CNS/ATM systems, and statistics, two seminars on air transport regulatory policy and a Facilitation Panel meeting were also held during the year.

ICAO participated in the review process launched by the World Trade Organization of the air transport services annex in the General Agreement on Trade in Services.

ICAO continued to provide secretariat services to three independent regional civil aviation bodies—the African Civil Aviation Commission, the European Civil Aviation Conference and the Latin American Civil Aviation Commission. It also maintained responsibilities for the administration of the Danish and Icelandic Joint Financ-

ing Agreements, to which 23 Governments were contracting parties in 2000. The two agreements were concerned with the provision in Greenland and Iceland of air traffic control, communications and meteorology facilities and services to North Atlantic flights.

The Aviation Security Panel (Montreal, 11-14 April) conducted a comprehensive review of annex 17 to adjust its structure and relevancy of SARPs and examined the problem of unruly passengers.

Legal matters

The ICAO Legal Committee's Subcommittee on International Interests in Mobile Equipment (aircraft equipment) held a third joint session (Rome, 20-31 March) with the Committee of Governmental Experts of the International Institute for the Unification of Private Law (UNIDROIT), which concluded examination of the texts of a draft Convention on International Interests in Mobile Equipment and a Protocol thereto. The texts were reviewed by the Legal Committee (Montreal, 28 August-8 September) and submitted to the ICAO Council with a recommendation to convene a diplomatic conference for their adoption. The Council decided to convene a diplomatic conference in 2001 under the joint auspices of ICAO and UNIDROIT.

At the third and fourth meetings of the Secretariat Study Group on Unruly Passengers (Montreal, 10-11 February, 26-27 October) a draft List of Offences and a draft Jurisdiction Clause were finalized and incorporated into a draft Model Legislation on Offences Committed on Board Civil Aircraft by Unruly or Disruptive Passengers.

Ratification of or adherence or succession to conventions and protocols on international air law concluded under ICAO auspices were registered in 2000.

Technical cooperation

In 2000, ICAO undertook 127 technical cooperation projects in 78 countries. The technical cooperation programmes, financed by the United Nations Development Programme (UNDP), trust funds, management service agreements and the Civil Aviation Purchasing Service, had total expenditures of $56.9 million. Some 36 per cent of that amount was provided by Governments to fund their own projects on the basis of cost sharing with UNDP.

ICAO had resident missions in 36 countries. A total of 565 fellowships were awarded in 2000, of which 526 were implemented. ICAO employed 364 experts from 43 countries, of whom 134 were on assignments under UNDP and 230 worked in trust fund projects. There were 87 Governments and organizations registered with ICAO in 2000 under its Civil Aviation Purchasing Services. Equipment purchases in 2000 totalled $20.5 million.

Secretariat

As at 31 December 2000, ICAO employed a total of 778 staff members, including 336 in the Professional and higher categories and 442 in the General Service and related categories.

Budget

Appropriations for the ICAO budget in 2000 were $53,765,000.

NOTE: For further details on the activities of ICAO in 2000, see *Annual Report of the Council, 2000.*

HEADQUARTERS AND REGIONAL OFFICES

International Civil Aviation Organization
999 University Street
Montreal, Quebec, Canada H3C 5H7
Telephone: (1) (514) 954-8219
Fax: (1) (514) 954-6077
Internet: http://www.icao.int
E-mail: icaohq@icao.int

ICAO maintained regional offices in Bangkok, Thailand; Cairo, Egypt; Dakar, Senegal; Lima, Peru; Mexico, D.F.; Nairobi, Kenya; and Paris, France.

Chapter X

Universal Postal Union (UPU)

In 2000, the Universal Postal Union (UPU) continued to promote a fast and reliable universal postal service at affordable prices through international collaboration among its member countries. UPU activities focused on postal reform and the future development of the Union, with special attention placed on the specific needs of developing countries.

UPU's 189 member countries remained the largest physical distribution network in the world, with some 6 million postal employees working in more than 700,000 post offices wordwide.

Activities of UPU organs

Universal Postal Congress

The Universal Postal Congress, UPU's supreme legislative authority, met every five years. It last convened in 1999 for the twenty-second Congress, held in Beijing, China [YUN 1999, p. 1408]. In 2000, the 25-member High-Level Group (HLG), established by the Congress to propose changes in UPU's structure, met four times; it was expected to make recommendations by the end of 2001. An Advisory Group, also established by the Congress and open to regional postal unions, non-governmental organizations and a number of postal administrations, met twice during the year, focusing on HLG's work.

Council of Administration

The Council of Administration, which ensured the continuity of the Union's work between Congresses and studied regulatory, administrative, legislative and legal issues of concern to the Union, held its annual session from 11 to 20 October at UPU Headquarters in Berne, Switzerland. It adopted several resolutions and recommendations, prepared a memorandum on principles and obligations for providing universal postal services, and signed a cooperation agreement with the World Savings Banks Institute.

Postal Operations Council

The Postal Operations Council (POC), which dealt with the operational, economic and commercial aspects of international postal services, assisted postal services to modernize and upgrade their products, including letter post, express mail service, parcels and postal financial services. At its annual session (Berne, 1-10 May), POC adopted decisions on the basic airmail conveyance rate, the supply of international reply coupons, the UPU initiative on e-business development, and the statutes and structural framework of the Quality of Service Fund, authorized by the 1999 Congress [YUN 1999, p. 1408] to help developing countries raise their quality of service pending the introduction of a new terminal dues system.

International Bureau

The International Bureau, under the supervision of the Council of Administration, was the area of the UPU secretariat that provided support, liaison, information and consultation to the postal administrations of member countries. It continued to act as a clearing house for the settlement of various inter-administration charges related to the exchange of postal items and international reply coupons. The Bureau undertook studies on developments in the postal environment, monitored the quality of postal service on a global scale and published information and statistics on international postal services.

A group of postal administration experts, after carrying out a six-month study, recommended that the Bureau be reorganized under seven centres of expertise. The proposed changes were accompanied by a number of proposals to reform management methods. The Council of Administration was informed of the Bureau's decisions and preparations were made to introduce the new structure early in 2001.

As at 31 December 2000, the permanent staff members of the Bureau numbered 151, of whom 60 were in the Professional and higher categories and 91 were in the General Service category.

Budget

Under the Union's self-financing system, contributions were payable in advance by member States based on the following year's budget. At its 2000 session, the Council of Administration approved a budget of 71.4 million Swiss francs for the 2001-2002 biennium.

NOTE: For further details of UPU activities, see *Universal Postal Union Annual Report 2000*, published by UPU.

HEADQUARTERS

Universal Postal Union
Weltpoststrasse 4
3015 Berne, Switzerland
Postal address: Union postale universelle
                  Case postale
                  3000 Berne 15, Switzerland
Telephone: (41) (31) 350-3111
Fax: (41) (31) 350-3110
Internet: http://www.upu.int
E-mail: ib.info@upu.int

Chapter XI

International Telecommunication Union (ITU)

The International Telecommunication Union (ITU) continued in 2000 to promote development and efficient operation of telecommunication systems and to provide technical assistance.

At its annual session, the ITU Council (Geneva, 19-28 July) discussed, among other things, international telecommunication regulations, and adopted several resolutions and decisions covering the Union's reform process and a variety of financial and institutional matters.

During the year, the Union staged ITU TELECOM AMERICAS 2000 (Rio de Janeiro, Brazil, 10-15 April), the fourth telecommunication exhibition and forum for the Americas. It also organized the ITU TELECOM ASIA 2000 (Hong Kong, China, 4-9 December), the fifth telecommunication exhibition and forum for Asia and the Pacific.

ITU membership remained at 189 in 2000.

Radiocommunication Sector

ITU's Radiocommunication Sector (ITU-R) developed operational procedures and technical characteristics for terrestrial and space-based wireless services and systems, established the global framework for managing the radio-frequency spectrum, and facilitated coordination of the frequencies and orbits used by communication, broadcasting and meteorological satellites.

In 2000, ITU-R organized two major radiocommunication meetings. The World Radiocommunication Conference (Istanbul, Turkey, 8 May-2 June), an international treaty-making forum, normally convened every two or three years, elicited widespread consensus on key issues. They included allocation of additional channels for broadcasting in Africa, Asia, Australasia and Europe; agreement on spectrum allocation for a new European satellite positioning service; finalization of spectrum-sharing arrangements between geostationary and non-geostationary satellite systems; and new allocations for emerging point-to-point and point-to-multipoint broadband wireless access technologies.

The Radiocommunication Assembly (Istanbul, 1-5 May) approved a number of recommendations on radio interface specifications and related spectrum requirements for International

Mobile Telecommunications 2000, which would provide a new global standard for harmonizing regional cellular systems as a basis for so-called "third generation" services, including fast data access, unified messaging and broadband multimedia in the form of new interactive services.

Telecommunication Standardization Sector

In 2000, the Telecommunication Standardization Sector (ITU-T) continued to foster seamless interconnection of the world's communication network and systems by developing internationally agreed technical and operating standards. ITU-T's work programme encompassed rapid developments in the global information infrastructure, including Internet Protocol networks and multimedia-based communications.

The four-yearly World Telecommunication Standardization Assembly (Montreal, Canada, 27 September–6 October) took a number of decisions designed to further streamline ITU's standards development process. New working methods were also adopted, as well as targets and deadlines for the transition to cost-oriented international settlement rates. In addition, the 14 ITU-T study groups, composed of experts from the public and private sectors, continued to develop technical specifications and operating parameters for equipment and systems covering every aspect of network operations.

Telecommunication Development Sector

The Telecommunication Development Sector (ITU-D) continued to promote investment and foster expansion of telecommunication infrastructure in developing countries. The Telecommunication Development Advisory Group, which advised ITU's Director in reviewing the priorities and strategies of ITU-D's activities, met twice in 2000, in March and October. At its first meeting, it discussed various issues, including the operational plan for 2000, study group matters and ITU-D reform. At its second meeting, it reviewed policy and strategic matters, such as Internet development. The Task Force on Gender Issues carried out its work on the main projects under implementation, including the development of a training curriculum on gender perspectives in telecommunication policy. The Telecommunication Development Bureau (BDT), the administrative arm of ITU-D, continued to provide assistance to countries in restructuring their telecommunication sectors by fostering institutional and organizational capacity through improved human resources development and management, using a range of cost-effective tools, such as tele-education and computer-based training. Major projects undertaken in 2000 included the Management Development for Telecommunications project, a public/private sector partnership programme comprising a series of workshops ranging from business planning to marketing, aimed at providing senior managers with the latest management techniques. In addition, BDT established five new Telecommunication Centres of Excellence to provide senior-level training in policy, management and technology in the developing world. During the year, ITU-D's workshops focused on the areas of fixed-mobile interconnection and Internet Protocol Telephony. The first development symposium for regulators was held to consider the emerging challenges prompted by the evolution of national, regional and global markets.

Secretariat

As at 31 December 2000, ITU had 769 staff members, comprising 5 elected officials, 301 in the Professional and higher categories and 463 in the General Service category.

Budget

The ITU budget for the 2000-2001 biennium amounted to 332,621,000 Swiss francs.

NOTE: For further details regarding ITU activities, see *ITU 2000 Annual Report,* published by the Union.

HEADQUARTERS

International Telecommunication Union
Place des Nations
CH-1211, Geneva 20, Switzerland
Telephone: (41) (22) 730-5111
Fax: (41) (22) 730-5939/733-7256
Internet: http://www.itu.int
E-mail: pressinfo@itu.int

Chapter XII

World Meteorological Organization (WMO)

The World Meteorological Organization (WMO), which celebrated its fiftieth anniversary in 2000, continued to facilitate cooperation in the generation and exchange of meteorological and hydrological information and the application of meteorology to aviation, shipping, water problems, agriculture and other activities. WMO also promoted operational hydrology and encouraged research and training in meteorology.

The WMO Executive Council, at its fifty-second session (Geneva, 16-26 May), reviewed WMO programmes and activities, including coordination in the UN system of geosciences and their applications for the benefit of humankind; free and unrestricted exchange of international meteorological and hydrological data and products; climate matters; hydrology and water resources; and the role and operation of national meteorological and hydrological services.

WMO membership remained at 179 States and six Territories in 2000.

World Weather Watch Programme

The World Weather Watch Programme (WWW), the backbone of WMO scientific and technical programmes, provided meteorological data and products needed by member States to run their meteorological services efficiently. WWW offered up-to-the-minute worldwide weather information through its Global Observing System, the Global Telecommunication System, the Global Data-processing System, and data management and system support activities, collectively known as the basic systems. WWW also included the Tropical Cyclone Programme, the Instruments and Methods of Observation Programme and WMO satellite and environmental emergency response activities.

World Weather Watch implementation

During the year, WWW's main activities focused on assessing the impact of the observing systems, particularly radiosondes, on numerical weather predictions; surveying the use of the Internet by national meteorological services; international exchange of meteorological data and products; and further implementation of advanced telecommunication technology for the collection and distribution of data. The twelfth

session of the WWW Commission for Basic Systems (Geneva, 29 November–8 December) reviewed the effectiveness of its new working structure.

Instruments and methods of observation

In 2000, activities were carried out to better meet users' needs regarding instrumentation and methods of observation. In August, the International Organizing Committee for the WMO Intercomparison of Global Positioning System Radiosondes met in Brasilia, Brazil, to prepare for a radiosonde test to be carried out in early 2001. The ninth International Pyrheliometer Comparison was held jointly with Regional Pyrheliometer Comparisons at the World Radiation Centre (Davos, Switzerland, 25 September–13 October). In all, 85 absolute pyrheliometers of various types were successfully calibrated. The WMO Technical Conference on Meteorological and Environmental Instruments and Methods of Observation (Beijing, China, 23-27 October) discussed a wide range of observing methodology issues.

Tropical Cyclone Programme

During the year, all the five regional tropical cyclone centres in Miami, Florida (United States), Nadi (Fiji), New Delhi (India), Réunion and Tokyo (Japan) accelerated the implementation of their respective regional cooperation programmes. Progress was made in implementing coordinated technical plans for tropical cyclone disaster mitigation, including training tropical cyclone forecasters. The booklet *Twenty years of progress and achievement of the WMO Tropical Cyclone Programme (1980-1999)* was published.

World Climate Programme

In 2000, as part of its responsibilities within the UN system, WMO contributed to a broad range of climate and environmental activities. As one of the UN agency task managers for the implementation of Agenda 21 [YUN 1992, p. 672], WMO, together with the United Nations Environment Programme, prepared a progress report on achievements of objectives regarding the protection of the atmosphere.

The Intergovernmental Panel on Climate Change, at its sixteenth session (Montreal, Canada, 1-8 May), completed three reports on land use change and forestry, emissions scenarios, and methodological and technological issues in technology transfer. It also completed a report on good practice guidance and uncertainty management for national greenhouse gas inventories.

During the year, the World Climate Applications and Services Programme focused on climate applications and services related to human health and energy. Support was provided for a World Health Organization seminar and workshop on climate change, variability and human health for small island States in Apia, Samoa. WMO co-sponsored the World Clean Energy Conference 2000 (Geneva, 24-28 January), and a number of regional climate outlook forums were held in many parts of the world.

World Climate Research Programme

The World Climate Research Programme, undertaken jointly by WMO, the International Council of Scientific Unions and the Intergovernmental Oceanographic Commission (IOC) of the United Nations Educational, Scientific and Cultural Organization (UNESCO), continued studies to provide the scientific basis for predictions of global and regional climate variations on all time-scales and made projections of the magnitude and rate of human-induced climate change. One of its principal projects was the climate variability and predictability study, which included a focused investigation of the variability of the American monsoon system. The Global Energy and Water Cycle Experiment continued the collection of global climatological datasets of key climate parameters.

Atmospheric Research and Environment Programme

The Atmospheric Research and Environment Programme continued to coordinate and encourage research in atmospheric and related sciences. The development of those activities was the responsibility of the Commission for Atmospheric Sciences (CAS). Programme activities in 2000 included an international workshop on long-range forecasting and its applications (Cairo, Egypt, 23-27 January); the fifth international cloud modelling workshop (Breckenridge, Colorado, United States, 7-11 August); the third session of the Science Steering Committee for the World Weather Research Programme (Vancouver, Canada, 7-12 September); and the twentieth session of the European Community Panel of Experts/ CAS Working Group on Physics and Chemistry of Clouds and Weather Modification Research (Geneva, 20-24 November).

The Global Atmosphere Watch continued to focus on improving data quality, availability and the overall performance of its global and regional measuring stations, which monitored atmospheric composition and the presence of greenhouse gases, ozone and harmful pollutants in support of international conventions on protecting the ozone layer and climate change. In 2000, a successful international Dobson spectrophotometer intercomparison was staged for the first time in Africa and a series of ozonesonde intercomparisons was conducted in Germany.

Applications of meteorology

Agricultural meteorology

In 2000, the Commission for Agricultural Meteorology held two meetings: on the impacts of agrometeorological applications for sustainable management of farming systems, forestry and livestock (Geneva, 11-14 September) and on communication of agrometeorological information (Geneva, 20-23 November). WMO co-sponsored international workshops on automated weather stations for applications in agriculture and water resources management: current use and future perspective (Lincoln, Nebraska, United States, 6-10 March) and on carbon sequestration, sustainable agriculture and poverty alleviation (Geneva, 30 August–1 September), as well as expert group meetings on early warning systems for drought preparedness and drought management (Lisbon, Portugal, 5-7 September) and on software for agroclimatic data management (Washington, D.C., 16-20 October). Roving seminars were held on geographical information systems and agro-ecological zoning (Kuala Lumpur, Malaysia, 8-19 May) and on agrometeorological data management and applications (Pretoria, South Africa, 19-30 June).

Aeronautical meteorology

In 2000, the Aeronautical Meteorology Programme held training events related to, among other things, the application of numerical weather prediction products to aviation and to the recovery of costs for aeronautical meteorological services. By year's end, more than 200 satellite broadcast terminals had been installed in nearly 150 countries.

Marine meteorology

In 2000, under the Marine Meteorology and Associated Oceanographic Activities Programme, it was agreed to establish a subset of the voluntary observing ships to provide the data and metadata necessary for climate observation, as a contribution to the Global Ocean Observing System/ Global Climate Observing System ocean climate module. In June, the second transition planning meeting for the joint WMO/IOC Technical Commission for Oceanography and Marine Meteorology, established to provide the institutional umbrella for all existing and future operational marine-related activities of WMO and IOC/ UNESCO, was held at UNESCO headquarters in Paris.

Public weather services

The Public Weather Services Programme continued to assist WMO members in the observation, monitoring and prediction of weather patterns. In 2000, a project was developed to make national meteorological services' warnings available to the media. Several training seminars and workshops were organized in different regions of the world with the objective of improving participants' national public weather services.

Hydrology and water resources

In 2000, the Hydrology and Water Resources Programme focused on promoting worldwide cooperation in the evaluation of water resources and the development of hydrological networks and services, including data collection and processing, hydrological forecasting and warnings, and the supply of meteorological and hydrological data for the design and management of water projects. A new associated programme of flood management was launched in collaboration with the Global Water Partnership. The WMO Commission for Hydrology held its eleventh session (Abuja, Nigeria, 6-16 November).

Technical cooperation

In 2000, WMO technical assistance, valued at $16.56 million, was financed by trust funds (32.6 per cent), the WMO Voluntary Cooperation Programme (47 per cent), the United Nations Development Programme (15.4 per cent) and the WMO regular budget (5.1 per cent).

Secretariat

As at 31 December 2000, the number of full-time staff employed by WMO totalled 264. Of those, 120 were in the Professional and higher categories and 144 were in the General Service category.

Budget

The WMO Executive Council, in 1999, approved a regular budget of 126,150,000 Swiss francs (SwF) for the 2000-2001 biennium. The Thirteenth World Meteorological Congress, also in 1999, approved a maximum expenditure of SwF 252,300,000 for the thirteenth financial period (2000-2003).

NOTE: For further details regarding WMO activities, see *World Meteorological Organization Annual Report 2000,* published by WMO.

HEADQUARTERS

World Meteorological Organization
7 bis, avenue de la Paix
(Case postale No. 2300)
CH-1211 Geneva 2, Switzerland
Telephone: (41) (22) 730-8111
Fax: (41) (22) 730-8181
Internet: http://www.wmo.ch
E-mail: ipa@gateway.wmo.ch

Chapter XIII

International Maritime Organization (IMO)

In 2000, the International Maritime Organization (IMO) continued to improve the safety of international shipping and to prevent marine pollution from ships. Its governing body, the IMO Assembly, held its most recent biennial session in 1999.

During the year, IMO membership increased to 158, with the admission of Tonga.

Activities in 2000

The IMO Council awarded the International Maritime Prize for 1999 to Ian Mills Williams, former manager for IMO relations at the Australian Maritime Safety Authority. The Prize was awarded annually to the person, organization or other entity judged to have done the most to advance IMO objectives.

Prevention of pollution

In March, IMO adopted a new Protocol on Preparedness, Response and Cooperation to Pollution Incidents by Hazardous and Noxious Substances, which aimed at providing a global framework for international cooperation in combating major incidents or threats of marine pollution from ships carrying hazardous and noxious substances, such as chemicals.

The Marine Environment Protection Committee, at its forty-fifth session in October, achieved the first, formal step towards a global timetable for accelerated phasing out of single-hull oil tankers. The Committee approved proposed amendments to the International Convention for the Prevention of Pollution from Ships, 1973, as modified by the Protocol of 1978 relating thereto (MARPOL 73/78), paving the way for the adoption of a revised regulation of MARPOL in April 2001.

IMO's Legal Committee, at its eighty-second session in October, adopted amendments to the 1992 Protocol to the International Convention on Civil Liability for Oil Pollution Damage and to the 1992 Protocol to the International Convention on the Establishment of an International Fund for Compensation for Oil Pollution Damage. The amendments raised the limits of compensation payable to victims of pollution by oil from oil tankers.

Ship security and safety at sea

On 1 January, a revised annex to the International Convention on Maritime Search and Rescue (SAR Convention), which was adopted in 1998, entered into force. It clarified the responsibilities of Governments, emphasizing a regional approach and coordination between maritime and aeronautical SAR operations.

A harmonized system of survey and certification covering international shipping regulations entered into force on 3 February. The system covered survey and certification requirements of the International Convention for the Safety of Life at Sea, 1974 (SOLAS), the International Convention on Load Lines, 1966, and MARPOL 73/78, as well as the International Code for the Construction and Equipment of Ships Carrying Dangerous Chemicals in Bulk, the Code for the Construction and Equipment of Ships Carrying Dangerous Chemicals in Bulk and the Code for the Construction and Equipment of Ships Carrying Liquefied Gases in Bulk.

At its seventy-third session in December, the Maritime Safety Committee adopted draft amendments to SOLAS. The amendments included a revised chapter on safety of navigation, which required passenger ships and ships other than passenger ships of 3,000 gross tonnage and upwards constructed on or after 1 July 2002 to carry voyage data recorders to assist in accident investigations; an updated High-Speed Craft Code 2000; a revised SOLAS chapter on fire protection, fire detection and fire extinction, and a new International Code for Fire Safety Systems; a new regulation that prohibited the new installation of materials which contained asbestos on all ships; and amendments to a 1988 SOLAS Protocol on the details of navigational systems and equipment referred to in the records of equipment.

The Committee approved the first list of countries deemed have given "full and complete effect" to the revised International Convention on Standards of Training, Certification and Watchkeeping for Seafarers, 1978. As at December, the list included 71 countries and one IMO associate member.

Secretariat

As at 31 December, IMO had 274 staff members; 113 were in the Professional and higher categories and 161 were in the General Service category.

Budget

The IMO Assembly, in 1999, approved budgetary appropriations of 36,612,200 pounds sterling for the 2000-2001 biennium, of which 18,155,000 pounds was for 2000 and 18,457,200 pounds was for 2001.

NOTE: For further information, see the organization's quarterly magazine, *IMO News*.

HEADQUARTERS

International Maritime Organization
4 Albert Embankment
London SE1 7SR, United Kingdom
Telephone: (44) (207) 735-7611
Fax: (44) (207) 587-3210
Internet: http://www.imo.org
E-mail: info@imo.org

Chapter XIV

World Intellectual Property Organization (WIPO)

The World Intellectual Property Organization (WIPO) continued development cooperation, norm-setting and registration activities to promote respect for the protection and use of intellectual properties. The organization's main areas of work continued to focus on strengthening the intellectual property systems of developing countries; promoting new or revised norms for the protection of intellectual property at the national, regional and multilateral levels; and facilitating the acquisition of intellectual property protection through international registration systems.

The governing bodies of WIPO and the Unions administered by the organization held their thirty-fifth series of meetings (Geneva, 25 September–3 October).

During 2000, WIPO membership increased to 175 States, with the accession of Belize and the Dominican Republic to the 1967 Convention establishing WIPO, amended in 1979. The number of States adhering to treaties administered by WIPO also increased: as at 31 December 2000, there were 160 States parties to the Paris Convention for the Protection of Industrial Property, 147 to the Berne Convention for the Protection of Literary and Artistic Works, and 109 to the Patent Cooperation Treaty (PCT).

Activities in 2000

Development cooperation

The primary focus of WIPO's work in 2000 was assisting developing countries in building infrastructures, developing human resources and implementing laws that enabled them to utilize effectively the intellectual property system for their economic, social and cultural development. To help bring developing countries into compliance with international standards, in particular the Agreement on Trade-related Aspects of Intellectual Property Rights (TRIPS Agreement) administered by the World Trade Organization, WIPO prepared 38 draft laws for 25 developing countries or regional organizations.

During the year, eight new nationally focused action plans (NFAPs) were launched. Established jointly between individual Governments and WIPO, NFAPs were aimed at helping developing

countries to reach a significantly higher level of efficient management and use of the national intellectual property system.

In 2000, WIPO created a new programme to focus specifically on the intellectual property needs of small and medium-sized enterprises, which produced four fifths of all goods and services worldwide. In addition, an ad hoc Advisory Panel on Privatization was established by WIPO to help ensure that intellectual property considerations were part of national privatization efforts in developing countries and countries in transition.

The WIPO Worldwide Academy, an Internet-based nine-module course established in 1998, continued to provide teaching, training and research services in intellectual property. In 2000, the Academy trained some 2,300 men and women and cooperated with the University of Turin, Italy, in launching the first postgraduate specialization course in intellectual property, and with the Raoul Wallenberg Institute and the University of Lund, Sweden, in a new joint master's degree programme in intellectual property and human rights.

Intellectual property law

In October 2000, the Advisory Committee on Enforcement of Industrial Property Rights met for the first time to consider the challenges faced by member States in enforcing those rights, and to develop recommendations for WIPO on how to promote more effective enforcement measures. The Committee agreed on several priorities for its future work, including the identification of difficulties, training needs and best practices in the enforcement of industrial property rights.

More than five years of negotiations in the Standing Committee on the Law of Patents culminated in the adoption of the Patent Law Treaty in June 2000, with the aim of reducing the cost of patent protection in multiple countries.

The Standing Committee on Copyright and Related Rights organized a Diplomatic Conference on the Protection of Audiovisual Performances (Geneva, 7-20 December). At the end of the Conference, the aim of which was to create a new international treaty safeguarding the rights of performers against unauthorized use of their performances in audiovisual media, negotiators from over 120 countries provisionally agreed on

19 of the 20 legal provisions of the treaty. Agreement could not be reached on the issue relating to the right of transfer, namely the question of how the performers' rights were acquired by the producers, whether by law or agreement.

The Standing Committee on the Law of Trademarks, Industrial Designs and Geographical Indications agreed on a set of measures to simplify and harmonize procedures relating to trademark licences. Discussions also continued on the protection of marks on the Internet.

Arbitration and Mediation Centre

The WIPO Arbitration and Mediation Centre continued to provide less expensive and speedier alternatives to costly court proceedings in commercial disputes involving intellectual property rights. In 2000, the Centre administered some 1,840 disputes, involving parties from 74 countries. In addition to its frequent workshops, the Centre also organized the International Conference on Dispute Resolution in Electronic Commerce (Geneva, 6-7 November). Some 300 participants discussed how electronic commerce was changing the ways in which business and the legal profession approached dispute resolution.

International registration activities

PCT. In 2000, just under 100,000 international applications were filed, representing an increase of 23 per cent over the total number for 1999 and the equivalent of some 8.5 million national patent applications.

Madrid Agreement. In the trademark system under the Madrid Agreement concerning the International Registration of Marks and its 1989 Protocol, the number of international registrations reached almost 23,000 in 2000, a 15 per cent increase compared with 1999.

Hague Agreement. Under the Hague Agreement concerning the International Deposit of Industrial Designs, the number of international deposits and renewals rose to 7,300 in 2000, an 8 per cent increase compared to 1999.

Secretariat

As at 31 December 2000, WIPO employed 783 staff members representing 84 countries; 264 were in the Professional or higher categories and 519 in the General Service category.

Budget

WIPO's principal sources of income in 2000 were fees paid by private sector users of the international protection services (85 per cent); sales of WIPO publications, fees for arbitration and mediation services and interest earnings (9 per cent); and contributions paid by member States (6 per cent). Budgeted income for the 2000-2001 biennium was 410 million Swiss francs (SwF). In 2000, the organization's budgeted income amounted to some SwF 260 million and budgeted expenditures totalled SwF 222 million.

NOTE: For further information on the organization, see *WIPO Annual Report 2000*, published by WIPO.

HEADQUARTERS AND OTHER OFFICE

HEADQUARTERS

World Intellectual Property Organization
34, chemin des Colombettes (P.O. Box 18)
CH-1211 Geneva 20, Switzerland
Telephone: (41) (22) 338-9111
Fax: (41) (22) 733-5428
Internet: http://www.wipo.int
E-mail: wipo.mail@wipo.int

WIPO OFFICE AT THE UNITED NATIONS

2 United Nations Plaza, Suite 2525
New York, NY 10017, United States
Telephone: (1) (212) 963-6813
Fax: (1) (212) 963-4801
E-mail: wipo@un.org

Chapter XV

International Fund for Agricultural Development (IFAD)

The International Fund for Agricultural Development (IFAD) continued in 2000 to promote the economic advancement of the rural poor, by improving the productivity of on- and off-farm activities and by designing and implementing innovative, cost-effective and replicable programmes.

The twenty-third session (Rome, 16-17 February) of the Governing Council approved the 2000 budget. The Executive Board held three regular sessions in 2000 (May, September, December); it approved loans for 27 projects and programmes, 22 grants and 11 contributions to debt reduction within the framework of the Heavily Indebted Poor Countries Initiative. The Board approved a programme of work for 2001 in the amount of $394 million for loans and grants under the Regular Programme. It also recommended that an administrative budget for 2001 totalling $53.3 million be transmitted to the twenty-fourth (2001) session of the Governing Council for approval.

As at 31 December 2000, IFAD membership remained at 161 countries, of which 22 were in List A (developed countries), 12 in List B (oil-exporting developing countries) and 127 in List C (other developing countries); 49 were in Sub-List C1 (Africa), 47 in Sub-List C2 (Europe, Asia and the Pacific) and 31 in Sub-List C3 (Latin America and the Caribbean).

Resources

The Consultation to Review the Adequacy of the Resources Available to IFAD recommended a fifth replenishment to support the Fund's operations in 2000-2002. As at December 2000, member States had pledged about $383 million. The fifth replenishment was to become effective during 2001 and could range from $460 million to $569 million.

Activities in 2000

Loans approved in 2000 and financed through IFAD totalled $409 million; another $32.8 million was in grants. The total cost of the 27 projects was estimated at $1,012.5 million, of which $276 million would be provided by other external financiers and $326.7 million by financiers in the recipient countries—primarily the Governments.

Regular Programme lending was distributed as follows: Asia and the Pacific, $127.5 million for six projects in 21 countries (31.2 per cent); Western and Central Africa, $83.2 million for seven projects in 24 countries (20.3 per cent); Eastern and Southern Africa, $73.3 million for five projects in 20 countries (17.9 per cent); Latin America and the Caribbean, $64 million for four projects in 28 countries (15.7 per cent); and the Near East and North Africa, $60.9 million for five projects in 22 countries (14.9 per cent).

During 2000, 36 projects were completed; thus the number of effective projects at the end of the year was 197.

Secretariat

As at 31 December 2000, the IFAD secretariat comprised 290 staff, including 132 staff in the Professional and higher categories and 158 in the General Service category.

Income and expenditure

The annual total of IFAD loans and grant operations at the end of 2000 was $52.7 million. IFAD's income on investments was minus $47 million and on loans it was $44.3 million, representing an annual income of minus $2.7 million. The total operating and administrative expenses for the year totalled $47.1 million.

NOTE: For further details on IFAD activities in 2000, see *Annual Report 2000*, published by the Fund.

HEADQUARTERS AND OTHER OFFICES

HEADQUARTERS

International Fund for Agricultural Development
Via del Serafico, 107
00142 Rome, Italy
  Telephone: (39) (06) 54591
  Fax: (39) (06) 5043463
  Internet: http://www.ifad.org
  E-mail: ifad@ifad.org

IFAD LIAISON OFFICES

1 United Nations Plaza, Room 1460
New York, NY 10017, United States
  Telephone: (1) (212) 963-0546
  Fax: (1) (212) 963-2787

1775 K Street, NW, Suite 410
Washington, DC 20006, United States
  Telephone: (1) (202) 331-9099
  Fax: (1) (202) 331-9366

Chapter XVI

United Nations Industrial Development Organization (UNIDO)

The United Nations Industrial Development Organization (UNIDO) continued to promote the sustainable industrial development of developing countries and countries with economies in transition. As a global forum on industrialization, UNIDO facilitated the spread of industrial information, knowledge, technology and investment.

The Industrial Development Board (IDB), at its twenty-second session (Vienna, 30-31 May), considered the financing, impact and status of implementation of UNIDO's integrated technical cooperation programmes in developing countries. At its twenty-third session (Vienna, 14-16 November), IDB discussed, among other things, UNIDO's integrated programmes, field representation, global forum activities, operational activities for development, the Global Environment Facility and other programme and budget matters. The ninth session of UNIDO's General Conference was scheduled for November 2001.

During the year, UNIDO membership increased to 169, with the admission of South Africa.

Global forum activities

In 2000, UNIDO, through its global forum activities, continued to offer industry policy advice; help build institutional capacity at the country and sectoral levels; provide industrial information through networking; act as a repository for industrial statistics; and provide advice and support in the areas of quality, standardization and metrology. Those activities included initiatives to understand the dynamics of the industrial development process and disseminate lessons learned through specialized meetings and publications covering a variety of industry-related issues. Special attention was placed on technology foresight, a policy-making tool aimed at harnessing technological innovation to support the strategic priorities of society. A UNIDO-organized meeting on the theme "Marginalization versus prosperity" was held in Venice, Italy, in September. Among other activities, a joint programme with the University of Oxford (United Kingdom) to fund research on African economic performance became operational in April 2000. Following the success of that programme, UNIDO drew up an

agreement with France's National Centre for Scientific Research to fund a number of industrial development activities in developing and transition economy countries. UNIDO also joined forces with the global telecommunications company Ericsson in an effort to introduce digital communications to small and rural industries in the world's poorest countries.

UNIDO co-sponsored the Asia-Pacific Forum on Industrial Development (Shanghai, China, 4-5 December), which reviewed the potential impact of China's entry into the World Trade Organization.

Integrated programmes

UNIDO provided technical cooperation through its integrated programmes, the major components of which were training, investment promotion, quality and standardization, and activities promoting cleaner industrial production and waste management. As at 31 December, 40 programmes and three country services were approved. Some 40 per cent of the programmes were for sub-Saharan Africa, 26 per cent for the Arab region and the remaining 34 per cent for programmes in Asia, Central and Eastern Europe and Latin America.

Investment promotion and institutional capacity-building

During the year, the Investment Promotion and Institutional Capacity-building Division focused on adding value to its services to developing countries and those with economies in transition through quality management, further integration of its branches' expertise and targeting of strategic alliances. Industrial policy formulation and implementation efforts focused on a mix of global forum and technical cooperation activities. To provide Internet-based access to information and knowledge on global trends and policy issues related to the dynamics of industrialization, UNIDO initiated construction of a knowledge base on industrial policies, strategies and best practices throughout the world. It also provided a wide range of industrial development policy advice to Ghana, Indonesia, Nigeria, Oman and Sri Lanka. UNIDO's International Technology Centres continued to act as outreach technology arms for services and international frameworks for cooperation in technology areas with cross-sectoral and wide economic impact. New programmes were launched with their assistance to support national efforts in technology upgrading of industrial sectors and capacity-building through North-South and South-South technology transfer and partnership. UNIDO also promoted the development of small and medium-sized enterprises with new programmes in Eritrea, Iran, Nepal and the United Republic of Tanzania, which focused specifically on women's entrepreneurship development strategies.

Environmental sustainability

In 2000, UNIDO's Sectoral Support and Environmental Sustainability Division established and reinforced partnership links with international conventions and funds, particularly in areas related to environment and energy.

As at 31 December, UNIDO was implementing 654 projects in 59 countries, valued at approximately $220 million, under the 1987 Montreal Protocol on Substances that Deplete the Ozone Layer [YUN 1987, p. 686]. Those activities corresponded to a phase-out of over 28,000 tons of ozone-depleting pollutants, of which 17,109 tons had already been eliminated. Three new National Cleaner Production Centres were established in Ethiopia, Kenya and Mozambique, bringing to 19 the total number of centres established since 1994.

Secretariat

As at 31 December 2000, UNIDO employed a total of 655 staff members: 260 were in the Professional or higher categories, 388 were in the General Service category and 7 were national officers.

Budget

The eighth (1999) session of the UNIDO General Conference approved the organization's 2000-2001 regular budget in the amount of $167.7 million. In 2000, new project approvals amounted to $76.9 million, compared with $81.6 million in 1999.

NOTE: For further information on UNIDO, see *Annual Report of UNIDO 2000*.

HEADQUARTERS AND OTHER OFFICES

HEADQUARTERS
United Nations Industrial Development Organization
Vienna International Centre
P.O. Box 300
A-1400 Vienna, Austria
  Telephone: (43) (1) 26026
  Fax: (43) (1) 269-26-69
  Internet: http://www.unido.org
  E-mail: unido@unido.org

LIAISON OFFICES

UNIDO Office at Geneva
Le Bocage
Pavillion 1/Palais des Nations
CH-1211 Geneva 10, Switzerland
  Telephone: (41) (22) 917-3367
  Fax: (41) (22) 917-0059

UNIDO Office in New York
1 United Nations Plaza, Room DC1-1110
New York, NY 10017, United States
  Telephone: (1) (212) 963-6890
  Fax: (1) (212) 964-4116

Chapter XVII

World Trade Organization (WTO)

In 2000, the World Trade Organization (WTO), the legal and institutional foundation of the multilateral trading system, continued to oversee the rules of international trade, settle trade disputes between Governments and organize trade negotiations.

During the year, WTO launched new negotiations on trade in agricultural products and services; adopted new measures to assist its least developed members; and made progress on issues arising from the Third (1999) WTO Ministerial Conference [YUN 1999, p. 1442], including renewed efforts to launch a comprehensive round of multilateral trade negotiations. The Fourth WTO Ministerial Conference, the organization's highest authority, was scheduled to take place in November 2001.

WTO's General Council, the body overseeing WTO's work between Conferences, continued to monitor the implementation and operation of the multilateral trading system embodied in the WTO Agreement [YUN 1995, p. 1515]. It examined, among other things, the internal transparency and effective participation of member States; and mandated negotiations on agriculture and services, accessions and electronic commerce.

During the year, WTO membership increased to 140 with the admission of Albania, Croatia, Georgia, Jordan and Oman.

General activities

The three working groups set up by the 1996 Ministerial Conference [YUN 1996, p. 1441] met during 2000. The Working Group on the Relationships between Trade and Investment, in June, October and November, examined the implications of the relationship between trade and investment for development and economic growth; and stocktaking and analysis of related international instruments and activities. The Working Group on Transparency in Government Procurement, in June and September, studied the definition and scope of government procurement; procurement methods; publication of information on national legislation and procedures; information on procurement opportunities; contract awards; bribery and corruption; dispute settlement procedures; technical cooperation; and special and differential treatment for developing countries. The Working Group on the Interac-

tion between Trade and Competition Policy, in June, October and November, discussed the relevance of WTO principles of national treatment, transparency and most-favoured-nation treatment to competition policy and vice versa; promoting technical cooperation; and the contribution of competition policy to achieving WTO objectives.

During the year, the Trade Policy Review Body carried out reviews of Bahrain, Bangladesh, Brazil, Canada, the European Union, Iceland, Japan, Kenya, Liechtenstein, Norway, Peru, Poland, the Republic of Korea, Singapore, Switzerland and the United Republic of Tanzania.

WTO continued to provide technical cooperation and training to developing countries and economies in transition to widen understanding of trade policy matters, the multilateral trading system, international law and other trade and development issues.

Trade in goods

The Council for Trade in Goods approved requests for and extensions of waivers from members in connection with the transposition of their schedules into the Harmonized Systems. It reviewed the operation of the Trade-related Investment Measures Agreement; adopted terms of reference under which 10 regional agreements were to be examined in the Committee on Regional Trade Agreements; and continued exploratory and analytical work on trade facilitation.

The Committee on Agriculture reviewed progress in the implementation of commitments under the Uruguay Round agriculture reform programme or resulting from WTO accession negotiations in market access, domestic support, export subsidies and export restrictions. Since 1995, the Committee had reviewed 1,033 notifications from member States. In 2000, the Committee commenced negotiations under article 20 of the Agreement on Agriculture on the continuation of the reform process.

The Committee on Sanitary and Phytosanitary Measures monitored implementation of the Agreement on the Application of Sanitary and Phytosanitary Measures, which set out the rights and obligations of members to ensure food safety, protect human health from plant- or animal-spread diseases, or protect plant and animal health from pests and diseases. In 2000, the Committee discussed trade concerns of members and considered the difficulties faced by developing countries, especially recognition of equivalence and the need for differential treatment. It developed guidelines on acceptable levels of health protection and monitored use of international standards.

Trade in services

In 2000, the Council for Trade in Services launched negotiations under article XIX of the General Agreement on Trade in Services, addressing, among other subjects, negotiating guidelines and procedures, assessment of trade in services, tourism services and modalities for the treatment of autonomous liberalization.

Intellectual property

The WTO Agreement on Trade-related Aspects of Intellectual Property Rights (TRIPS) provided for minimum international standards of protection in copyright, trademarks, geographic indications, industrial designs, patents, layout designs of integrated circuits and undisclosed information. During the year, the Council for TRIPS discussed the establishment of a multilateral system of notification and registration of geographical indications for wines and issues relevant to such a system for spirits; the extension of additional protection for geographical indications to products other than wines and spirits; exclusion from patentability of plants and animals other than micro-organisms; biological processes for the production of plants or animals other than non-biological and microbiological processes; and the scope and modalities for non-violation complaints and e-commerce.

Regional trade agreements

In 2000, the Committee on Regional Trade Agreements completed factual examination of 62 of the 86 regional trade agreements under its purview.

Trade and development

The Committee for Trade and Development, in 2000, examined special and differential treat-ment in favour of developing countries and their participation in world trade; implementation of WTO Agreements; technical cooperation and training; concerns and problems of small economies; the development dimension of electronic commerce; and market access for least developed countries.

Plurilateral agreements

The Committee on Government Procurement continued negotiations on the expansion of the coverage of the Agreement on Government Procurement, its simplification and improvement, especially adaptation related to advances in information technology, and elimination of discriminatory measures and practices that distorted open procurement.

The Agreement on Trade in Civil Aircraft eliminated all customs duties and other charges on imports of civil aircraft products and repairs, bound them at zero level, and required adaptation of end-use customs administration. Although part of the WTO Agreement, it remained outside the WTO framework. In 2000, signatories were unable to adopt a draft protocol rectifying the Agreement.

International Trade Centre

The International Trade Centre (ITC), operated jointly by WTO and the United Nations Conference on Trade and Development (see p. 900), continued to undertake technical cooperation activities as a follow-up to the Uruguay Round Agreements. ITC was also responsible for the management of the Integrated Technical Assistance Programme in Selected Least Developed Countries and Other African Countries.

Budget

The WTO budget for 2000 amounted to 125,386,460 Swiss francs.

Secretariat

At the end of 2000, WTO staff numbered 534.

NOTE: For further information on WTO activities, see the organization's *Annual Report 2000*.

HEADQUARTERS

World Trade Organization
Centre William Rappard
154, rue de Lausanne
CH-1211 Geneva 21, Switzerland
  Telephone: (41) (22) 739-5111
  Fax: (41) (22) 731-4206
  Internet: www.wto.org
  E-mail: enquiries@wto.org

Appendices

Appendix I

Roster of the United Nations

There were 189 Member States as at 31 December 2000.

MEMBER	DATE OF ADMISSION	MEMBER	DATE OF ADMISSION	MEMBER	DATE OF ADMISSION
Afghanistan	19 Nov. 1946	Egypt[2]	24 Oct. 1945	Malta	1 Dec. 1964
Albania	14 Dec. 1955	El Salvador	24 Oct. 1945	Marshall Islands	17 Sep. 1991
Algeria	8 Oct. 1962	Equatorial Guinea	12 Nov. 1968	Mauritania	27 Oct. 1961
Andorra	28 July 1993	Eritrea	28 May 1993	Mauritius	24 Apr. 1968
Angola	1 Dec. 1976	Estonia	17 Sep. 1991	Mexico	7 Nov. 1945
Antigua and Barbuda	11 Nov. 1981	Ethiopia	13 Nov. 1945	Micronesia (Federated	
Argentina	24 Oct. 1945	Fiji	13 Oct. 1970	States of)	17 Sep. 1991
Armenia	2 Mar. 1992	Finland	14 Dec. 1955	Monaco	28 May 1993
Australia	1 Nov. 1945	France	24 Oct. 1945	Mongolia	27 Oct. 1961
Austria	14 Dec. 1955	Gabon	20 Sep. 1960	Morocco	12 Nov. 1956
Azerbaijan	2 Mar. 1992	Gambia	21 Sep. 1965	Mozambique	16 Sep. 1975
Bahamas	18 Sep. 1973	Georgia	31 July 1992	Myanmar	19 Apr. 1948
Bahrain	21 Sep. 1971	Germany[3]	18 Sep. 1973	Namibia	23 Apr. 1990
Bangladesh	17 Sep. 1974	Ghana	8 Mar. 1957	Nauru	14 Sep. 1999
Barbados	9 Dec. 1966	Greece	25 Oct. 1945	Nepal	14 Dec. 1955
Belarus	24 Oct. 1945	Grenada	17 Sep. 1974	Netherlands	10 Dec. 1945
Belgium	27 Dec. 1945	Guatemala	21 Nov. 1945	New Zealand	24 Oct. 1945
Belize	25 Sep. 1981	Guinea	12 Dec. 1958	Nicaragua	24 Oct. 1945
Benin	20 Sep. 1960	Guinea-Bissau	17 Sep. 1974	Niger	20 Sep. 1960
Bhutan	21 Sep. 1971	Guyana	20 Sep. 1966	Nigeria	7 Oct. 1960
Bolivia	14 Nov. 1945	Haiti	24 Oct. 1945	Norway	27 Nov. 1945
Bosnia and Herzegovina	22 May 1992	Honduras	17 Dec. 1945	Oman	7 Oct. 1971
Botswana	17 Oct. 1966	Hungary	14 Dec. 1955	Pakistan	30 Sep. 1947
Brazil	24 Oct. 1945	Iceland	19 Nov. 1946	Palau	15 Dec. 1994
Brunei Darussalam	21 Sep. 1984	India	30 Oct. 1945	Panama	13 Nov. 1945
Bulgaria	14 Dec. 1955	Indonesia[4]	28 Sep. 1950	Papua New Guinea	10 Oct. 1975
Burkina Faso	20 Sep. 1960	Iran (Islamic Republic of)	24 Oct. 1945	Paraguay	24 Oct. 1945
Burundi	18 Sep. 1962	Iraq	21 Dec. 1945	Peru	31 Oct. 1945
Cambodia	14 Dec. 1955	Ireland	14 Dec. 1955	Philippines	24 Oct. 1945
Cameroon	20 Sep. 1960	Israel	11 May 1949	Poland	24 Oct. 1945
Canada	9 Nov. 1945	Italy	14 Dec. 1955	Portugal	14 Dec. 1955
Cape Verde	16 Sep. 1975	Jamaica	18 Sep. 1962	Qatar	21 Sep. 1971
Central African Republic	20 Sep. 1960	Japan	18 Dec. 1956	Republic of Korea	17 Sep. 1991
Chad	20 Sep. 1960	Jordan	14 Dec. 1955	Republic of Moldova	2 Mar. 1992
Chile	24 Oct. 1945	Kazakhstan	2 Mar. 1992	Romania	14 Dec. 1955
China	24 Oct. 1945	Kenya	16 Dec. 1963	Russian Federation[6]	24 Oct. 1945
Colombia	5 Nov. 1945	Kiribati	14 Sep. 1999	Rwanda	18 Sep. 1962
Comoros	12 Nov. 1975	Kuwait	14 May 1963	Saint Kitts and Nevis	23 Sep. 1983
Congo	20 Sep. 1960	Kyrgyzstan	2 Mar. 1992	Saint Lucia	18 Sep. 1979
Costa Rica	2 Nov. 1945	Lao People's Democratic		Saint Vincent and the	
Côte d'Ivoire	20 Sep. 1960	Republic	14 Dec. 1955	Grenadines	16 Sep. 1980
Croatia	22 May 1992	Latvia	17 Sep. 1991	Samoa	15 Dec. 1976
Cuba	24 Oct. 1945	Lebanon	24 Oct. 1945	San Marino	2 Mar. 1992
Cyprus	20 Sep. 1960	Lesotho	17 Oct. 1966	Sao Tome and Principe	16 Sep. 1975
Czech Republic[1]	19 Jan. 1993	Liberia	2 Nov. 1945	Saudi Arabia	24 Oct. 1945
Democratic People's		Libyan Arab Jamahiriya	14 Dec. 1955	Senegal	28 Sep. 1960
Republic of Korea	17 Sep. 1991	Liechtenstein	18 Sep. 1990	Seychelles	21 Sep. 1976
Democratic Republic of		Lithuania	17 Sep. 1991	Sierra Leone	27 Sep. 1961
the Congo	20 Sep. 1960	Luxembourg	24 Oct. 1945	Singapore[5]	21 Sep. 1965
Denmark	24 Oct. 1945	Madagascar	20 Sep. 1960	Slovakia[1]	19 Jan. 1993
Djibouti	20 Sep. 1977	Malawi	1 Dec. 1964	Slovenia	22 May 1992
Dominica	18 Dec. 1978	Malaysia[5]	17 Sep. 1957	Solomon Islands	19 Sep. 1978
Dominican Republic	24 Oct. 1945	Maldives	21 Sep. 1965	Somalia	20 Sep. 1960
Ecuador	21 Dec. 1945	Mali	28 Sep. 1960	South Africa	7 Nov. 1945

MEMBER	DATE OF ADMISSION	MEMBER	DATE OF ADMISSION	MEMBER	DATE OF ADMISSION
Spain	14 Dec. 1955	Trinidad and Tobago	18 Sep. 1962	United States of America	24 Oct. 1945
Sri Lanka	14 Dec. 1955	Tunisia	12 Nov. 1956	Uruguay	18 Dec. 1945
Sudan	12 Nov. 1956	Turkey	24 Oct. 1945	Uzbekistan	2 Mar. 1992
Suriname	4 Dec. 1975	Turkmenistan	2 Mar. 1992	Vanuatu	15 Sep. 1981
Swaziland	24 Sep. 1968	Tuvalu	5 Sep. 2000	Venezuela	15 Nov. 1945
Sweden	19 Nov. 1946	Uganda	25 Oct. 1962	Viet Nam	20 Sep. 1977
Syrian Arab Republic[2]	24 Oct. 1945	Ukraine	24 Oct. 1945	Yemen[8]	30 Sep. 1947
Tajikistan	2 Mar. 1992	United Arab Emirates	9 Dec. 1971	Yugoslavia (Federal Republic of)	1 Nov. 2000
Thailand	16 Dec. 1946	United Kingdom of Great Britain and Northern Ireland	24 Oct. 1945	Zambia	1 Dec. 1964
The former Yugoslav Republic of Macedonia	8 Apr. 1993			Zimbabwe	25 Aug. 1980
Togo	20 Sep. 1960	United Republic of Tanzania[7]	14 Dec. 1961		
Tonga	14 Sep. 1999				

[1]Czechoslovakia, which was an original Member of the United Nations from 24 October 1945, split up on 1 January 1993 and was succeeded by the Czech Republic and Slovakia.

[2]Egypt and Syria, both of which became Members of the United Nations on 24 October 1945, joined together—following a plebiscite held in those countries on 21 February 1958—to form the United Arab Republic. On 13 October 1961, Syria, having resumed its status as an independent State, also resumed its separate membership in the United Nations; it changed its name to the Syrian Arab Republic on 14 September 1971. The United Arab Republic continued as a Member of the United Nations and reverted to the name of Egypt on 2 September 1971.

[3]Through accession of the German Democratic Republic to the Federal Republic of Germany on 3 October 1990, the two German States (both of which became United Nations Members on 18 September 1973) united to form one sovereign State. As from that date, the Federal Republic of Germany has acted in the United Nations under the designation Germany.

[4]On 20 January 1965, Indonesia informed the Secretary-General that it had decided to withdraw from the United Nations. By a telegram of 19 September 1966, it notified the Secretary-General of its decision to resume participation in the activities of the United Nations. On 28 September 1966, the General Assembly took note of that decision and the President invited the representatives of Indonesia to take their seats in the Assembly.

[5]On 16 September 1963, Sabah (North Borneo), Sarawak and Singapore joined with the Federation of Malaya (which became a United Nations Member on 17 September 1957) to form Malaysia. On 9 August 1965, Singapore became an independent State and on 21 September 1965 it became a Member of the United Nations.

[6]The Union of Soviet Socialist Republics was an original Member of the United Nations from 24 October 1945. On 24 December 1991, the President of the Russian Federation informed the Secretary-General that the membership of the USSR in all United Nations organs was being continued by the Russian Federation.

[7]Tanganyika was admitted to the United Nations on 14 December 1961, and Zanzibar, on 16 December 1963. Following ratification, on 26 April 1964, of the Articles of Union between Tanganyika and Zanzibar, the two States became represented as a single Member: the United Republic of Tanganyika and Zanzibar; it changed its name to the United Republic of Tanzania on 1 November 1964.

[8]Yemen was admitted to the United Nations on 30 September 1947 and Democratic Yemen on 14 December 1967. On 22 May 1990, the two countries merged and have since been represented as one Member.

Appendix II

Charter of the United Nations and Statute of the International Court of Justice

Charter of the United Nations

NOTE: The Charter of the United Nations was signed on 26 June 1945, in San Francisco, at the conclusion of the United Nations Conference on International Organization, and came into force on 24 October 1945. The Statute of the International Court of Justice is an integral part of the Charter.

Amendments to Articles 23, 27 and 61 of the Charter were adopted by the General Assembly on 17 December 1963 and came into force on 31 August 1965. A further amendment to Article 61 was adopted by the General Assembly on 20 December 1971 and came into force on 24 September 1973. An amendment to Article 109, adopted by the General Assembly on 20 December 1965, came into force on 12 June 1968.

The amendment to Article 23 enlarges the membership of the Security Council from 11 to 15. The amended Article 27 provides that decisions of the Security Council on procedural matters shall be made by an affirmative vote of nine members (formerly seven) and on all other matters by an affirmative vote of nine members (formerly seven), including the concurring votes of the five permanent members of the Security Council.

The amendment to Article 61, which entered into force on 31 August 1965, enlarged the membership of the Economic and Social Council from 18 to 27. The subsequent amendment to that Article, which entered into force on 24 September 1973, further increased the membership of the Council from 27 to 54.

The amendment to Article 109, which relates to the first paragraph of that Article, provides that a General Conference of Member States for the purpose of reviewing the Charter may be held at a date and place to be fixed by a two-thirds vote of the members of the General Assembly and by a vote of any nine members (formerly seven) of the Security Council. Paragraph 3 of Article 109, which deals with the consideration of a possible review conference during the tenth regular session of the General Assembly, has been retained in its original form in its reference to a "vote of any seven members of the Security Council", the paragraph having been acted upon in 1955 by the General Assembly, at its tenth regular session, and by the Security Council.

WE THE PEOPLES
OF THE UNITED NATIONS
DETERMINED

to save succeeding generations from the scourge of war, which twice in our lifetime has brought untold sorrow to mankind, and

to reaffirm faith in fundamental human rights, in the dignity and worth of the human person, in the equal rights of men and women and of nations large and small, and

to establish conditions under which justice and respect for the obligations arising from treaties and other sources of international law can be maintained, and

to promote social progress and better standards of life in larger freedom,

AND FOR THESE ENDS

to practice tolerance and live together in peace with one another as good neighbours, and

to unite our strength to maintain international peace and security, and

to ensure, by the acceptance of principles and the institution of methods, that armed force shall not be used, save in the common interest, and

to employ international machinery for the promotion of the economic and social advancement of all peoples,

HAVE RESOLVED TO
COMBINE OUR EFFORTS TO
ACCOMPLISH THESE AIMS

Accordingly, our respective Governments, through representatives assembled in the city of San Francisco, who have exhibited their full powers found to be in good and due form, have agreed to the present Charter of the United Nations and do hereby establish an international organization to be known as the United Nations.

Chapter I
PURPOSES AND PRINCIPLES

Article 1

The Purposes of the United Nations are:

1. To maintain international peace and security, and to that end: to take effective collective measures for the prevention and removal of threats to the peace, and for the suppression of acts of aggression or other breaches of the peace, and to bring about by peaceful means, and in conformity with the principles of justice and international law, adjustment or settlement of international disputes or situations which might lead to a breach of the peace;

2. To develop friendly relations among nations based on respect for the principle of equal rights and self-determination of peoples, and to take other appropriate measures to strengthen universal peace;

3. To achieve international co-operation in solving international problems of an economic, social, cultural or humanitarian character, and in promoting and encouraging respect for human rights and for fundamental freedoms for all without distinction as to race, sex, language or religion; and

4. To be a centre for harmonizing the actions of nations in the attainment of these common ends.

Article 2

The Organization and its Members, in pursuit of the Purposes stated in Article 1, shall act in accordance with the following Principles:

1. The Organization is based on the principle of the sovereign equality of all its Members.

2. All Members, in order to ensure to all of them the rights and benefits resulting from membership, shall fulfil in good faith the obligations assumed by them in accordance with the present Charter.

3. All Members shall settle their international disputes by peaceful means in such a manner that international peace and security, and justice, are not endangered.

4. All Members shall refrain in their international relations from the threat or use of force against the territorial integrity or political independence of any state, or in any other manner inconsistent with the Purposes of the United Nations.

5. All Members shall give the United Nations every assistance in any action it takes in accordance with the present Charter, and shall refrain from giving assistance to any state against which the United Nations is taking preventive or enforcement action.

6. The Organization shall ensure that states which are not Members of the United Nations act in accordance with these Principles so far as may be necessary for the maintenance of international peace and security.

7. Nothing contained in the present Charter shall authorize the United Nations to intervene in matters which are essentially within the domestic jurisdiction of any state or shall require the Members to submit such matters to settlement under the present Charter; but this principle shall not prejudice the application of enforcement measures under Chapter VII.

Chapter II
MEMBERSHIP

Article 3

The original Members of the United Nations shall be the states which, having participated in the United Nations Conference on International Organization at San Francisco or having previously signed the Declaration by United Nations of 1 January 1942, sign the present Charter and ratify it in accordance with Article 110.

Article 4

1. Membership in the United Nations is open to all other peace-loving states which accept the obligations contained in the present Charter and, in the judgment of the Organization, are able and willing to carry out these obligations.

2. The admission of any such state to membership in the United Nations will be effected by a decision of the General Assembly upon the recommendation of the Security Council.

Article 5

A Member of the United Nations against which preventive or enforcement action has been taken by the Security Council may be suspended from the exercise of the rights and privileges of membership by the General Assembly upon the recommendation of the Security Council. The exercise of these rights and privileges may be restored by the Security Council.

Article 6

A Member of the United Nations which has persistently violated the Principles contained in the present Charter may be expelled from the Organization by the General Assembly upon the recommendation of the Security Council.

Chapter III
ORGANS

Article 7

1. There are established as the principal organs of the United Nations: a General Assembly, a Security Council, an Economic and Social Council, a Trusteeship Council, an International Court of Justice, and a Secretariat.

2. Such subsidiary organs as may be found necessary may be established in accordance with the present Charter.

Article 8

The United Nations shall place no restrictions on the eligibility of men and women to participate in any capacity and under conditions of equality in its principal and subsidiary organs.

Chapter IV
THE GENERAL ASSEMBLY

Composition

Article 9

1. The General Assembly shall consist of all the Members of the United Nations.

2. Each Member shall have not more than five representatives in the General Assembly.

Functions and Powers

Article 10

The General Assembly may discuss any questions or any matters within the scope of the present Charter or relating to the powers and functions of any organs provided for in the present Charter, and, except as provided in Article 12, may make recommendations to the Members of the United Nations or to the Security Council or both on any such questions or matters.

Article 11

1. The General Assembly may consider the general principles of co-operation in the maintenance of international peace and security, including the principles governing disarmament and the regulation of armaments, and may make recommendations with regard to such principles to the Members or to the Security Council or to both.

2. The General Assembly may discuss any questions relating to the maintenance of international peace and security brought before it by any Member of the United Nations, or by the Security Council, or by a state which is not a Member of the United Nations in accordance with Article 35, paragraph 2, and, except as provided in Article 12, may make recommendations with regard to any such questions to the state or states concerned or to the Security Council or to both. Any such question on which action is necessary shall be referred to the Security Council by the General Assembly either before or after discussion.

3. The General Assembly may call the attention of the Security Council to situations which are likely to endanger international peace and security.

4. The powers of the General Assembly set forth in this Article shall not limit the general scope of Article 10.

Article 12

1. While the Security Council is exercising in respect of any dispute or situation the functions assigned to it in the present Charter, the General Assembly shall not make any recommendation with regard to that dispute or situation unless the Security Council so requests.

2. The Secretary-General, with the consent of the Security Council, shall notify the General Assembly at each session of any matters relative to the maintenance of international peace and security which are being dealt with by the Security Council and shall similarly notify the General Assembly, or the Members of the United Nations if the General Assembly is not in session, immediately the Security Council ceases to deal with such matters.

Article 13

1. The General Assembly shall initiate studies and make recommendations for the purpose of:
   a. promoting international co-operation in the political field and encouraging the progressive development of international law and its codification;
   b. promoting international co-operation in the economic, social, cultural, educational and health fields, and assisting in the realization of human rights and fundamental freedoms for all without distinction as to race, sex, language or religion.

2. The further responsibilities, functions and powers of the General Assembly with respect to matters mentioned in paragraph 1 (b) above are set forth in Chapters IX and X.

Article 14

Subject to the provisions of Article 12, the General Assembly may recommend measures for the peaceful adjustment of any situation, regardless of origin, which it deems likely to impair the general welfare or friendly relations among nations, including situations resulting from a violation of the provisions of the present Charter setting forth the Purposes and Principles of the United Nations.

Article 15

1. The General Assembly shall receive and consider annual and special reports from the Security Council; these reports shall include an account of the measures that the Security Council has decided upon or taken to maintain international peace and security.

2. The General Assembly shall receive and consider reports from the other organs of the United Nations.

Article 16

The General Assembly shall perform such functions with respect to the international trusteeship system as are assigned to it under Chapters XII and XIII, including the approval of the trusteeship agreements for areas not designated as strategic.

Article 17

1. The General Assembly shall consider and approve the budget of the Organization.

2. The expenses of the Organization shall be borne by the Members as apportioned by the General Assembly.

3. The General Assembly shall consider and approve any financial and budgetary arrangements with specialized agencies referred to in Article 57 and shall examine the administrative budgets of such specialized agencies with a view to making recommendations to the agencies concerned.

Voting

Article 18

1. Each member of the General Assembly shall have one vote.

2. Decisions of the General Assembly on important questions shall be made by a two-thirds majority of the members present and voting. These questions shall include: recommendations with respect to the maintenance of international peace and security, the election of the non-permanent members of the Security Council, the election of the members of the Economic and Social Council, the election of members of the Trusteeship Council in accordance with paragraph 1 (c) of Article 86, the admission of new Members to the United Nations, the suspension of the rights and privileges of membership, the expulsion of Members, questions relating to the operation of the trusteeship system, and budgetary questions.

3. Decisions on other questions, including the determination of additional categories of questions to be decided by a two-thirds majority, shall be made by a majority of the members present and voting.

Article 19

A Member of the United Nations which is in arrears in the payment of its financial contributions to the Organization shall have no vote in the General Assembly if the amount of its arrears equals or exceeds the amount of the contributions due from it for the preceding two full years. The General Assembly may, nevertheless, permit such a Member to vote if it is satisfied that the failure to pay is due to conditions beyond the control of the Member.

Procedure

Article 20

The General Assembly shall meet in regular annual sessions and in such special sessions as occasion may require. Special sessions shall be convoked by the Secretary-General at the request of the Security Council or of a majority of the Members of the United Nations.

Article 21

The General Assembly shall adopt its own rules of procedure. It shall elect its President for each session.

Article 22

The General Assembly may establish such subsidiary organs as it deems necessary for the performance of its functions.

Chapter V

THE SECURITY COUNCIL

Composition

Article 23[1]

1. The Security Council shall consist of fifteen Members of the United Nations. The Republic of China, France, the Union of Soviet Socialist Republics, the United Kingdom of Great Britain and Northern Ireland and the United States of America shall be permanent members of the Security Council. The General Assembly shall elect ten other Members of the United Nations to be non-permanent members of the Security Council, due regard being specially paid, in the first instance to the contribution of Members of the United Nations to the maintenance of international peace and security and to the other purposes of the Organization, and also to equitable geographical distribution.

2. The non-permanent members of the Security Council shall be elected for a term of two years. In the first election of the non-permanent members after the increase of the membership of the Security Council from eleven to fifteen, two of the four additional members shall be chosen for a term of one year. A retiring member shall not be eligible for immediate re-election.

3. Each member of the Security Council shall have one representative.

Functions and Powers

Article 24

1. In order to ensure prompt and effective action by the United Nations, its Members confer on the Security Council primary responsibility for the maintenance of international peace and security, and agree that in carrying out its duties under this responsibility the Security Council acts on their behalf.

2. In discharging these duties the Security Council shall act in accordance with the Purposes and Principles of the United Nations. The specific powers granted to the Security Council for the discharge of these duties are laid down in Chapters VI, VII, VIII and XII.

3. The Security Council shall submit annual and, when necessary, special reports to the General Assembly for its consideration.

Article 25

The Members of the United Nations agree to accept and carry out the decisions of the Security Council in accordance with the present Charter.

Article 26

In order to promote the establishment and maintenance of international peace and security with the least diversion for armaments of the world's human and economic resources, the Security Council shall be responsible for formulating, with the assistance of the Military Staff Committee referred to in Article

47, plans to be submitted to the Members of the United Nations for the establishment of a system for the regulation of armaments.

Voting

Article 27[2]

1. Each member of the Security Council shall have one vote.

2. Decisions of the Security Council on procedural matters shall be made by an affirmative vote of nine members.

3. Decisions of the Security Council on all other matters shall be made by an affirmative vote of nine members including the concurring votes of the permanent members; provided that, in decisions under Chapter VI, and under paragraph 3 of Article 52, a party to a dispute shall abstain from voting.

Procedure

Article 28

1. The Security Council shall be so organized as to be able to function continuously. Each member of the Security Council shall for this purpose be represented at all times at the seat of the Organization.

2. The Security Council shall hold periodic meetings at which each of its members may, if it so desires, be represented by a member of the government or by some other specially designated representative.

3. The Security Council may hold meetings at such places other than the seat of the Organization as in its judgment will best facilitate its work.

Article 29

The Security Council may establish such subsidiary organs as it deems necessary for the performance of its functions.

Article 30

The Security Council shall adopt its own rules of procedure, including the method of selecting its President.

Article 31

Any Member of the United Nations which is not a member of the Security Council may participate, without vote, in the discussion of any question brought before the Security Council whenever the latter considers that the interests of that Member are specially affected.

Article 32

Any Member of the United Nations which is not a member of the Security Council or any state which is not a Member of the United Nations, if it is a party to a dispute under consideration by the Security Council, shall be invited to participate, without vote, in the discussion relating to the dispute. The Security Council shall lay down such conditions as it deems just for the participation of a state which is not a Member of the United Nations.

Chapter VI
PACIFIC SETTLEMENT OF DISPUTES

Article 33

1. The parties to any dispute, the continuance of which is likely to endanger the maintenance of international peace and security, shall, first of all, seek a solution by negotiation, enquiry, mediation, conciliation, arbitration, judicial settlement, resort to regional agencies or arrangements, or other peaceful means of their own choice.

2. The Security Council shall, when it deems necessary, call upon the parties to settle their dispute by such means.

Article 34

The Security Council may investigate any dispute, or any situation which might lead to international friction or give rise to a dispute, in order to determine whether the continuance of the dispute or situation is likely to endanger the maintenance of international peace and security.

Article 35

1. Any Member of the United Nations may bring any dispute, or any situation of the nature referred to in Article 34, to the attention of the Security Council or of the General Assembly.

2. A state which is not a Member of the United Nations may bring to the attention of the Security Council or of the General Assembly any dispute to which it is a party if it accepts in advance, for the purposes of the dispute, the obligations of pacific settlement provided in the present Charter.

3. The proceedings of the General Assembly in respect of matters brought to its attention under this Article will be subject to the provisions of Articles 11 and 12.

Article 36

1. The Security Council may, at any stage of a dispute of the nature referred to in Article 33 or of a situation of like nature, recommend appropriate procedures or methods of adjustment.

2. The Security Council should take into consideration any procedures for the settlement of the dispute which have already been adopted by the parties.

3. In making recommendations under this Article the Security Council should also take into consideration that legal disputes should as a general rule be referred by the parties to the International Court of Justice in accordance with the provisions of the Statute of the Court.

Article 37

1. Should the parties to a dispute of the nature referred to in Article 33 fail to settle it by the means indicated in that Article, they shall refer it to the Security Council.

2. If the Security Council deems that the continuance of the dispute is in fact likely to endanger the maintenance of international peace and security, it shall decide whether to take action under Article 36 or to recommend such terms of settlement as it may consider appropriate.

Article 38

Without prejudice to the provisions of Articles 33 to 37, the Security Council may, if all the parties to any dispute so request, make recommendations to the parties with a view to a pacific settlement of the dispute.

Chapter VII
ACTION WITH RESPECT TO THREATS TO THE PEACE,
BREACHES OF THE PEACE, AND ACTS OF AGGRESSION

Article 39

The Security Council shall determine the existence of any threat to the peace, breach of the peace, or act of aggression and shall make recommendations, or decide what measures shall be taken in accordance with Articles 41 and 42, to maintain or restore international peace and security.

Article 40

In order to prevent an aggravation of the situation, the Security Council may, before making the recommendations or deciding upon the measures provided for in Article 39, call upon the parties concerned to comply with such provisional measures as it deems necessary or desirable. Such provisional measures shall be without prejudice to the rights, claims or position of the parties concerned. The Security Council shall duly take account of failure to comply with such provisional measures.

Article 41

The Security Council may decide what measures not involving the use of armed force are to be employed to give effect to its decisions, and it may call upon the Members of the United Nations to apply such measures. These may include complete or partial interruption of economic relations and of rail, sea, air, postal, telegraphic, radio and other means of communication, and the severance of diplomatic relations.

Article 42

Should the Security Council consider that measures provided for in Article 41 would be inadequate or have proved to be inadequate, it may take such action by air, sea or land forces as may be necessary to maintain or restore international peace and security. Such action may include demonstrations, blockade, and other operations by air, sea, or land forces of Members of the United Nations.

Article 43

1.   All Members of the United Nations, in order to contribute to the maintenance of international peace and security, undertake to make available to the Security Council, on its call and in accordance with a special agreement or agreements, armed forces, assistance and facilities, including rights of passage, necessary for the purpose of maintaining international peace and security.

2.   Such agreement or agreements shall govern the numbers and types of forces, their degree of readiness and general location, and the nature of the facilities and assistance to be provided.

3.   The agreement or agreements shall be negotiated as soon as possible on the initiative of the Security Council. They shall be concluded between the Security Council and Members or between the Security Council and groups of Members and shall be subject to ratification by the signatory states in accordance with their respective constitutional processes.

Article 44

When the Security Council has decided to use force it shall, before calling upon a Member not represented on it to provide armed forces in fulfilment of the obligations assumed under Article 43, invite that Member, if the Member so desires, to participate in the decisions of the Security Council concerning the employment of contingents of that Member's armed forces.

Article 45

In order to enable the United Nations to take urgent military measures, Members shall hold immediately available national air-force contingents for combined international enforcement action. The strength and degree of readiness of these contingents and plans for their combined action shall be determined, within the limits laid down in the special agreement or agreements referred to in Article 43, by the Security Council with the assistance of the Military Staff Committee.

Article 46

Plans for the application of armed force shall be made by the Security Council with the assistance of the Military Staff Committee.

Article 47

1.   There shall be established a Military Staff Committee to advise and assist the Security Council on all questions relating to the Security Council's military requirements for the maintenance of international peace and security, the employment and command of forces placed at its disposal, the regulation of armaments, and possible disarmament.

2.   The Military Staff Committee shall consist of the Chiefs of Staff of the permanent members of the Security Council or their representatives. Any Member of the United Nations not permanently represented on the Committee shall be invited by the Committee to be associated with it when the efficient discharge of the Committee's responsibilities requires the participation of that Member in its work.

3.   The Military Staff Committee shall be responsible under the Security Council for the strategic direction of any armed forces placed at the disposal of the Security Council. Questions relating to the command of such forces shall be worked out subsequently.

4.   The Military Staff Committee, with the authorization of the Security Council and after consultation with appropriate regional agencies, may establish regional sub-committees.

Article 48

1.   The action required to carry out the decisions of the Security Council for the maintenance of international peace and security shall be taken by all the Members of the United Nations or by some of them, as the Security Council may determine.

2.   Such decisions shall be carried out by the Members of the United Nations directly and through their action in the appropriate international agencies of which they are members.

Article 49

The Members of the United Nations shall join in affording mutual assistance in carrying out the measures decided upon by the Security Council.

Article 50

If preventive or enforcement measures against any state are taken by the Security Council, any other state, whether a Member of the United Nations or not, which finds itself confronted with special economic problems arising from the carrying out of those measures shall have the right to consult the Security Council with regard to a solution of those problems.

Article 51

Nothing in the present Charter shall impair the inherent right of individual or collective self-defence if an armed attack occurs against a Member of the United Nations, until the Security Council has taken measures necessary to maintain international peace and security. Measures taken by Members in the exercise of this right of self-defence shall be immediately reported to the Security Council and shall not in any way affect the authority and responsibility of the Security Council under the present Charter to take at any time such action as it deems necessary in order to maintain or restore international peace and security.

Chapter VIII
REGIONAL ARRANGEMENTS

Article 52

1.   Nothing in the present Charter precludes the existence of regional arrangements or agencies for dealing with such matters relating to the maintenance of international peace and security as are appropriate for regional action, provided that such arrangements or agencies and their activities are consistent with the Purposes and Principles of the United Nations.

2.   The Members of the United Nations entering into such arrangements or constituting such agencies shall make every effort to achieve pacific settlement of local disputes through such regional arrangements or by such regional agencies before referring them to the Security Council.

3.   The Security Council shall encourage the development of pacific settlement of local disputes through such regional arrangements or by such regional agencies either on the initiative of the states concerned or by reference from the Security Council.

4.   This Article in no way impairs the application of Articles 34 and 35.

Article 53

1.   The Security Council shall, where appropriate, utilize such regional arrangements or agencies for enforcement action under its authority. But no enforcement action shall be taken under regional arrangements or by regional agencies

without the authorization of the Security Council, with the exception of measures against any enemy state, as defined in paragraph 2 of this Article, provided for pursuant to Article 107 or in regional arrangements directed against renewal of aggressive policy on the part of any such state, until such time as the Organization may, on request of the Governments concerned, be charged with the responsibility for preventing further aggression by such a state.

2.   The term enemy state as used in paragraph 1 of this Article applies to any state which during the Second World War has been an enemy of any signatory of the present Charter.

Article 54

The Security Council shall at all times be kept fully informed of activities undertaken or in contemplation under regional arrangements or by regional agencies for the maintenance of international peace and security.

Chapter IX
INTERNATIONAL ECONOMIC AND SOCIAL CO-OPERATION

Article 55

With a view to the creation of conditions of stability and well-being which are necessary for peaceful and friendly relations among nations based on respect for the principle of equal rights and self-determination of peoples, the United Nations shall promote:

   a.   higher standards of living, full employment, and conditions of economic and social progress and development;

   b.   solutions of international economic, social, health, and related problems; and international cultural and educational co-operation; and

   c.   universal respect for, and observance of, human rights and fundamental freedoms for all without distinction as to race, sex, language, or religion.

Article 56

All Members pledge themselves to take joint and separate action in co-operation with the Organization for the achievement of the purposes set forth in Article 55.

Article 57

1.   The various specialized agencies, established by intergovernmental agreement and having wide international responsibilities, as defined in their basic instruments, in economic, social, cultural, educational, health, and related fields, shall be brought into relationship with the United Nations in accordance with the provisions of Article 63.

2.   Such agencies thus brought into relationship with the United Nations are hereinafter referred to as specialized agencies.

Article 58

The Organization shall make recommendations for the co-ordination of the policies and activities of the specialized agencies.

Article 59

The Organization shall, where appropriate, initiate negotiations among the states concerned for the creation of any new specialized agencies required for the accomplishment of the purposes set forth in Article 55.

Article 60

Responsibility for the discharge of the functions of the Organization set forth in this Chapter shall be vested in the General Assembly and, under the authority of the General Assembly, in the Economic and Social Council, which shall have for this purpose the powers set forth in Chapter X.

Chapter X
THE ECONOMIC AND SOCIAL COUNCIL

Composition

Article 61[3]

1.   The Economic and Social Council shall consist of fifty-four Members of the United Nations elected by the General Assembly.

2.   Subject to the provisions of paragraph 3, eighteen members of the Economic and Social Council shall be elected each year for a term of three years. A retiring member shall be eligible for immediate re-election.

3.   At the first election after the increase in the membership of the Economic and Social Council from twenty-seven to fifty-four members, in addition to the members elected in place of the nine members whose term of office expires at the end of that year, twenty-seven additional members shall be elected. Of these twenty-seven additional members, the term of office of nine members so elected shall expire at the end of one year, and of nine other members at the end of two years, in accordance with arrangements made by the General Assembly.

4.   Each member of the Economic and Social Council shall have one representative.

Functions and Powers

Article 62

1.   The Economic and Social Council may make or initiate studies and reports with respect to international economic, social, cultural, educational, health, and related matters and may make recommendations with respect to any such matters to the General Assembly, to the Members of the United Nations, and to the specialized agencies concerned.

2.   It may make recommendations for the purpose of promoting respect for, and observance of, human rights and fundamental freedoms for all.

3.   It may prepare draft conventions for submission to the General Assembly, with respect to matters falling within its competence.

4.   It may call, in accordance with the rules prescribed by the United Nations, international conferences on matters falling within its competence.

Article 63

1.   The Economic and Social Council may enter into agreements with any of the agencies referred to in Article 57, defining the terms on which the agency concerned shall be brought into relationship with the United Nations. Such agreements shall be subject to approval by the General Assembly.

2.   It may co-ordinate the activities of the specialized agencies through consultation with and recommendations to such agencies and through recommendations to the General Assembly and to the Members of the United Nations.

Article 64

1.   The Economic and Social Council may take appropriate steps to obtain regular reports from the specialized agencies. It may make arrangements with the Members of the United Nations and with the specialized agencies to obtain reports on the steps taken to give effect to its own recommendations and to recommendations on matters falling within its competence made by the General Assembly.

2.   It may communicate its observations on these reports to the General Assembly.

Article 65

The Economic and Social Council may furnish information to the Security Council and shall assist the Security Council upon its request.

Article 66

1. The Economic and Social Council shall perform such functions as fall within its competence in connexion with the carrying out of the recommendations of the General Assembly.

2. It may, with the approval of the General Assembly, perform services at the request of Members of the United Nations and at the request of specialized agencies.

3. It shall perform such other functions as are specified elsewhere in the present Charter or as may be assigned to it by the General Assembly.

Voting

Article 67

1. Each member of the Economic and Social Council shall have one vote.

2. Decisions of the Economic and Social Council shall be made by a majority of the members present and voting.

Procedure

Article 68

The Economic and Social Council shall set up commissions in economic and social fields and for the promotion of human rights, and such other commissions as may be required for the performance of its functions.

Article 69

The Economic and Social Council shall invite any Member of the United Nations to participate, without vote, in its deliberations on any matter of particular concern to that Member.

Article 70

The Economic and Social Council may make arrangements for representatives of the specialized agencies to participate, without vote, in its deliberations and in those of the commissions established by it, and for its representatives to participate in the deliberations of the specialized agencies.

Article 71

The Economic and Social Council may make suitable arrangements for consultation with non-governmental organizations which are concerned with matters within its competence. Such arrangements may be made with international organizations and, where appropriate, with national organizations after consultation with the Member of the United Nations concerned.

Article 72

1. The Economic and Social Council shall adopt its own rules of procedure, including the method of selecting its President.

2. The Economic and Social Council shall meet as required in accordance with its rules, which shall include provision for the convening of meetings on the request of a majority of its members.

Chapter XI
DECLARATION REGARDING NON-SELF-GOVERNING TERRITORIES

Article 73

Members of the United Nations which have or assume responsibilities for the administration of territories whose peoples have not yet attained a full measure of self-government recognize the principle that the interests of the inhabitants of these territories are paramount, and accept as a sacred trust the obligation to promote to the utmost, within the system of international peace and security established by the present Charter, the well-being of the inhabitants of these territories and, to this end:

a. to ensure, with due respect for the culture of the peoples concerned, their political, economic, social, and educational advancement, their just treatment, and their protection against abuses;

b. to develop self-government, to take due account of the political aspirations of the peoples, and to assist them in the progressive development of their free political institutions, according to the particular circumstances of each territory and its peoples and their varying stages of advancement;

c. to further international peace and security;

d. to promote constructive measures of development, to encourage research, and to co-operate with one another and, when and where appropriate, with specialized international bodies with a view to the practical achievement of the social, economic, and scientific purposes set forth in this Article; and

e. to transmit regularly to the Secretary-General for information purposes, subject to such limitation as security and constitutional considerations may require, statistical and other information of a technical nature relating to economic, social, and educational conditions in the territories for which they are respectively responsible other than those territories to which Chapters XII and XIII apply.

Article 74

Members of the United Nations also agree that their policy in respect of the territories to which this Chapter applies, no less than in respect of their metropolitan areas, must be based on the general principle of good-neighbourliness, due account being taken of the interests and well-being of the rest of the world, in social, economic, and commercial matters.

Chapter XII
INTERNATIONAL TRUSTEESHIP SYSTEM

Article 75

The United Nations shall establish under its authority an international trusteeship system for the administration and supervision of such territories as may be placed thereunder by subsequent individual agreements. These territories are hereinafter referred to as trust territories.

Article 76

The basic objectives of the trusteeship system, in accordance with the Purposes of the United Nations laid down in Article 1 of the present Charter, shall be:

a. to further international peace and security;

b. to promote the political, economic, social, and educational advancement of the inhabitants of the trust territories, and their progressive development towards self-government or independence as may be appropriate to the particular circumstances of each territory and its peoples and the freely expressed wishes of the peoples concerned, and as may be provided by the terms of each trusteeship agreement;

c. to encourage respect for human rights and for fundamental freedoms for all without distinction as to race, sex, language, or religion, and to encourage recognition of the interdependence of the peoples of the world; and

d. to ensure equal treatment in social, economic, and commercial matters for all Members of the United Nations and their nationals, and also equal treatment for the latter in the administration of justice, without prejudice to the attainment of the foregoing objectives and subject to the provisions of Article 80.

Article 77

1. The trusteeship system shall apply to such territories in the following categories as may be placed thereunder by means of trusteeship agreements:

a. territories now held under mandate;
b. territories which may be detached from enemy states as a result of the Second World War; and
c. territories voluntarily placed under the system by states responsible for their administration.

2. It will be a matter for subsequent agreement as to which territories in the foregoing categories will be brought under the trusteeship system and upon what terms.

Article 78

The trusteeship system shall not apply to territories which have become Members of the United Nations, relationship among which shall be based on respect for the principle of sovereign equality.

Article 79

The terms of trusteeship for each territory to be placed under the trusteeship system, including any alteration or amendment, shall be agreed upon by the states directly concerned, including the mandatory power in the case of territories held under mandate by a Member of the United Nations, and shall be approved as provided for in Articles 83 and 85.

Article 80

1. Except as may be agreed upon in individual trusteeship agreements, made under Articles 77, 79 and 81, placing each territory under the trusteeship system, and until such agreements have been concluded, nothing in this Chapter shall be construed in or of itself to alter in any manner the rights whatsoever of any states or any peoples or the terms of existing international instruments to which Members of the United Nations may respectively be parties.

2. Paragraph 1 of this Article shall not be interpreted as giving grounds for delay or postponement of the negotiation and conclusion of agreements for placing mandated and other territories under the trusteeship system as provided for in Article 77.

Article 81

The trusteeship agreement shall in each case include the terms under which the trust territory will be administered and designate the authority which will exercise the administration of the trust territory. Such authority, hereinafter called the administering authority, may be one or more states or the Organization itself.

Article 82

There may be designated, in any trusteeship agreement, a strategic area or areas which may include part or all of the trust territory to which the agreement applies, without prejudice to any special agreement or agreements made under Article 43.

Article 83

1. All functions of the United Nations relating to strategic areas, including the approval of the terms of the trusteeship agreements and of their alteration or amendment, shall be exercised by the Security Council.

2. The basic objectives set forth in Article 76 shall be applicable to the people of each strategic area.

3. The Security Council shall, subject to the provisions of the trusteeship agreements and without prejudice to security considerations, avail itself of the assistance of the Trusteeship Council to perform those functions of the United Nations under the trusteeship system relating to political, economic, social, and educational matters in the strategic areas.

Article 84

It shall be the duty of the administering authority to ensure that the trust territory shall play its part in the maintenance of international peace and security. To this end the administering authority may make use of volunteer forces, facilities, and assistance from the trust territory in carrying out the obligations towards the Security Council undertaken in this regard by the administering authority, as well as for local defence and the maintenance of law and order within the trust territory.

Article 85

1. The functions of the United Nations with regard to trusteeship agreements for all areas not designated as strategic, including the approval of the terms of the trusteeship agreements and of their alteration or amendment, shall be exercised by the General Assembly.

2. The Trusteeship Council, operating under the authority of the General Assembly, shall assist the General Assembly in carrying out these functions.

Chapter XIII
THE TRUSTEESHIP COUNCIL

Composition

Article 86

1. The Trusteeship Council shall consist of the following Members of the United Nations:
   a. those Members administering trust territories;
   b. such of those Members mentioned by name in Article 23 as are not administering trust territories; and
   c. as many other Members elected for three-year terms by the General Assembly as may be necessary to ensure that the total number of members of the Trusteeship Council is equally divided between those Members of the United Nations which administer trust territories and those which do not.

2. Each member of the Trusteeship Council shall designate one specially qualified person to represent it therein.

Functions and Powers

Article 87

The General Assembly and, under its authority, the Trusteeship Council, in carrying out their functions, may:
   a. consider reports submitted by the administering authority;
   b. accept petitions and examine them in consultation with the administering authority;
   c. provide for periodic visits to the respective trust territories at times agreed upon with the administering authority; and
   d. take these and other actions in conformity with the terms of the trusteeship agreements.

Article 88

The Trusteeship Council shall formulate a questionnaire on the political, economic, social, and educational advancement of the inhabitants of each trust territory, and the administering authority for each trust territory within the competence of the General Assembly shall make an annual report to the General Assembly upon the basis of such questionnaire.

Voting

Article 89

1. Each member of the Trusteeship Council shall have one vote.

2. Decisions of the Trusteeship Council shall be made by a majority of the members present and voting.

Procedure

Article 90

1. The Trusteeship Council shall adopt its own rules of procedure, including the method of selecting its President.

2. The Trusteeship Council shall meet as required in accordance with its rules, which shall include provision for the convening of meetings on the request of a majority of its members.

Article 91

The Trusteeship Council shall, when appropriate, avail itself of the assistance of the Economic and Social Council and of the specialized agencies in regard to matters with which they are respectively concerned.

Chapter XIV
THE INTERNATIONAL COURT OF JUSTICE

Article 92

The International Court of Justice shall be the principal judicial organ of the United Nations. It shall function in accordance with the annexed Statute, which is based upon the Statute of the Permanent Court of International Justice and forms an integral part of the present Charter.

Article 93

1. All Members of the United Nations are *ipso facto* parties to the Statute of the International Court of Justice.

2. A state which is not a Member of the United Nations may become a party to the Statute of the International Court of Justice on conditions to be determined in each case by the General Assembly upon the recommendation of the Security Council.

Article 94

1. Each Member of the United Nations undertakes to comply with the decision of the International Court of Justice in any case to which it is a party.

2. If any party to a case fails to perform the obligations incumbent upon it under a judgment rendered by the Court, the other party may have recourse to the Security Council, which may, if it deems necessary, make recommendations or decide upon measures to be taken to give effect to the judgment.

Article 95

Nothing in the present Charter shall prevent Members of the United Nations from entrusting the solution of their differences to other tribunals by virtue of agreements already in existence or which may be concluded in the future.

Article 96

1. The General Assembly or the Security Council may request the International Court of Justice to give an advisory opinion on any legal question.

2. Other organs of the United Nations and specialized agencies, which may at any time be so authorized by the General Assembly, may also request advisory opinions of the Court on legal questions arising within the scope of their activities.

Chapter XV
THE SECRETARIAT

Article 97

The Secretariat shall comprise a Secretary-General and such staff as the Organization may require. The Secretary-General shall be appointed by the General Assembly upon the recommendation of the Security Council. He shall be the chief administrative officer of the Organization.

Article 98

The Secretary-General shall act in that capacity in all meetings of the General Assembly, of the Security Council, of the Economic and Social Council, and of the Trusteeship Council, and shall perform such other functions as are entrusted to him by these organs. The Secretary-General shall make an annual report to the General Assembly on the work of the Organization.

Article 99

The Secretary-General may bring to the attention of the Security Council any matter which in his opinion may threaten the maintenance of international peace and security.

Article 100

1. In the performance of their duties the Secretary-General and the staff shall not seek or receive instructions from any government or from any other authority external to the Organization. They shall refrain from any action which might reflect on their position as international officials responsible only to the Organization.

2. Each Member of the United Nations undertakes to respect the exclusively international character of the responsibilities of the Secretary-General and the staff and not to seek to influence them in the discharge of their responsibilities.

Article 101

1. The staff shall be appointed by the Secretary-General under regulations established by the General Assembly.

2. Appropriate staffs shall be permanently assigned to the Economic and Social Council, the Trusteeship Council, and, as required, to other organs of the United Nations. These staffs shall form a part of the Secretariat.

3. The paramount consideration in the employment of the staff and in the determination of the conditions of service shall be the necessity of securing the highest standards of efficiency, competence, and integrity. Due regard shall be paid to the importance of recruiting the staff on as wide a geographical basis as possible.

Chapter XVI
MISCELLANEOUS PROVISIONS

Article 102

1. Every treaty and every international agreement entered into by any Member of the United Nations after the present Charter comes into force shall as soon as possible be registered with the Secretariat and published by it.

2. No party to any such treaty or international agreement which has not been registered in accordance with the provisions of paragraph 1 of this Article may invoke that treaty or agreement before any organ of the United Nations.

Article 103

In the event of a conflict between the obligations of the Members of the United Nations under the present Charter and their obligations under any other international agreement, their obligations under the present Charter shall prevail.

Article 104

The Organization shall enjoy in the territory of each of its Members such legal capacity as may be necessary for the exercise of its functions and the fulfilment of its purposes.

Article 105

1. The Organization shall enjoy in the territory of each of its Members such privileges and immunities as are necessary for the fulfilment of its purposes.

2. Representatives of the Members of the United Nations and officials of the Organization shall similarly enjoy such privileges and immunities as are necessary for the independent exercise of their functions in connexion with the Organization.

3. The General Assembly may make recommendations with a view to determining the details of the application of paragraphs 1 and 2 of this Article or may propose conventions to the Members of the United Nations for this purpose.

Chapter XVII

TRANSITIONAL SECURITY ARRANGEMENTS

Article 106

Pending the coming into force of such special agreements referred to in Article 43 as in the opinion of the Security Council enable it to begin the exercise of its responsibilities under Article 42, the parties to the Four-Nation Declaration, signed at Moscow, 30 October 1943, and France, shall, in accordance with the provisions of paragraph 5 of that Declaration, consult with one another and as occasion requires with other Members of the United Nations with a view to such joint action on behalf of the Organization as may be necessary for the purpose of maintaining international peace and security.

Article 107

Nothing in the present Charter shall invalidate or preclude action, in relation to any state which during the Second World War has been an enemy of any signatory to the present Charter, taken or authorized as a result of that war by the Governments having responsibility for such action.

Chapter XVIII

AMENDMENTS

Article 108

Amendments to the present Charter shall come into force for all Members of the United Nations when they have been adopted by a vote of two thirds of the members of the General Assembly and ratified in accordance with their respective constitutional processes by two thirds of the Members of the United Nations, including all the permanent members of the Security Council.

Article 109[1]

1. A General Conference of the Members of the United Nations for the purpose of reviewing the present Charter may be held at a date and place to be fixed by a two-thirds vote of the members of the General Assembly and by a vote of any nine members of the Security Council. Each Member of the United Nations shall have one vote in the conference.

2. Any alteration of the present Charter recommended by a two-thirds vote of the conference shall take effect when ratified in accordance with their respective constitutional processes by two thirds of the Members of the United Na-

tions including all the permanent members of the Security Council.

3. If such a conference has not been held before the tenth annual session of the General Assembly following the coming into force of the present Charter, the proposal to call such a conference shall be placed on the agenda of that session of the General Assembly, and the conference shall be held if so decided by a majority vote of the members of the General Assembly and by a vote of any seven members of the Security Council.

Chapter XIX

RATIFICATION AND SIGNATURE

Article 110

1. The present Charter shall be ratified by the signatory states in accordance with their respective constitutional processes.

2. The ratifications shall be deposited with the Government of the United States of America, which shall notify all the signatory states of each deposit as well as the Secretary-General of the Organization when he has been appointed.

3. The present Charter shall come into force upon the deposit of ratifications by the Republic of China, France, the Union of Soviet Socialist Republics, the United Kingdom of Great Britain and Northern Ireland and the United States of America, and by a majority of the other signatory states. A protocol of the ratifications deposited shall thereupon be drawn up by the Government of the United States of America which shall communicate copies thereof to all the signatory states.

4. The states signatory to the present Charter which ratify it after it has come into force will become original Members of the United Nations on the date of the deposit of their respective ratifications.

Article 111

The present Charter, of which the Chinese, French, Russian, English, and Spanish texts are equally authentic, shall remain deposited in the archives of the Government of the United States of America. Duly certified copies thereof shall be transmitted by that Government to the Governments of the other signatory states.

IN FAITH WHEREOF the representatives of the Governments of the United Nations have signed the present Charter.

DONE at the city of San Francisco the twenty-sixth day of June, one thousand nine hundred and forty-five.

---

[1] Amended text of Article 23, which came into force on 31 August 1965.
(The text of Article 23 before it was amended read as follows:
1. The Security Council shall consist of eleven Members of the United Nations. The Republic of China, France, the Union of Soviet Socialist Republics, the United Kingdom of Great Britain and Northern Ireland and the United States of America shall be permanent members of the Security Council. The General Assembly shall elect six other Members of the United Nations to be non-permanent members of the Security Council, due regard being specially paid in the first instance to the contributions of Members of the United Nations to the maintenance of international peace and security and to the other purposes of the Organization, and also to equitable geographical distribution.
2. The non-permanent members of the Security Council shall be elected for a term of two years. In the first election of the non-permanent members, however, three shall be chosen for a term of one year. A retiring member shall not be eligible for immediate re-election.
3. Each member of the Security Council shall have one representative.)

[2] Amended text of Article 27, which came into force on 31 August 1965.
(The text of Article 27 before it was amended read as follows:
1. Each member of the Security Council shall have one vote.
2. Decisions of the Security Council on procedural matters shall be made by an affirmative vote of seven members.
3. Decisions of the Security Council on all other matters shall be made by an affirmative vote of seven members including the concurring votes of the permanent members; provided that, in decisions under Chapter VI, and under paragraph 3 of Article 52, a party to a dispute shall abstain from voting.)

[3] Amended text of Article 61, which came into force on 24 September 1973.
(The text of Article 61 as previously amended on 31 August 1965 read as follows:
1. The Economic and Social Council shall consist of twenty-seven Members of the United Nations elected by the General Assembly.
2. Subject to the provisions of paragraph 3, nine members of the Economic and Social Council shall be elected each year for a term of three years. A retiring member shall be eligible for immediate re-election.
3. At the first election after the increase in the membership of the Economic and Social Council from eighteen to twenty-seven members, in addition to the members elected in place of the six members whose term of office expires at the end of that year, nine

additional members shall be elected. Of these nine additional members, the term of office of three members so elected shall expire at the end of one year, and of three other members at the end of two years, in accordance with arrangements made by the General Assembly.

    4. Each member of the Economic and Social Council shall have one representative.)

[4] Amended text of Article 109, which came into force on 12 June 1968.
(The text of Article 109 before it was amended read as follows:
    1. A General Conference of the Members of the United Nations for the purpose of reviewing the present Charter may be held at a date and place to be fixed by a two-thirds vote of the members of the General Assembly and by a vote of any seven members of the Security Council. Each Member of the United Nations shall have one vote in the conference.
    2. Any alteration of the present Charter recommended by a two-thirds vote of the conference shall take effect when ratified in accordance with their respective constitutional processes by two thirds of the Members of the United Nations including all the permanent members of the Security Council.
    3. If such a conference has not been held before the tenth annual session of the General Assembly following the coming into force of the present Charter, the proposal to call such a conference shall be placed on the agenda of that session of the General Assembly, and the conference shall be held if so decided by a majority vote of the members of the General Assembly and by a vote of any seven members of the Security Council.)

Statute of the International Court of Justice

Article 1

The International Court of Justice established by the Charter of the United Nations as the principal judicial organ of the United Nations shall be constituted and shall function in accordance with the provisions of the present Statute.

Chapter I
ORGANIZATION OF THE COURT

Article 2

The Court shall be composed of a body of independent judges, elected regardless of their nationality from among persons of high moral character, who possess the qualifications required in their respective countries for appointment to the highest judicial offices, or are jurisconsults of recognized competence in international law.

Article 3

1. The Court shall consist of fifteen members, no two of whom may be nationals of the same state.

2. A person who for the purposes of membership in the Court could be regarded as a national of more than one state shall be deemed to be a national of the one in which he ordinarily exercises civil and political rights.

Article 4

1. The members of the Court shall be elected by the General Assembly and by the Security Council from a list of persons nominated by the national groups in the Permanent Court of Arbitration, in accordance with the following provisions.

2. In the case of Members of the United Nations not represented in the Permanent Court of Arbitration, candidates shall be nominated by national groups appointed for this purpose by their governments under the same conditions as those prescribed for members of the Permanent Court of Arbitration by Article 44 of the Convention of The Hague of 1907 for the pacific settlement of international disputes.

3. The conditions under which a state which is a party to the present Statute but is not a Member of the United Nations may participate in electing the members of the Court shall, in the absence of a special agreement, be laid down by the General Assembly upon recommendation of the Security Council.

Article 5

1. At least three months before the date of the election, the Secretary-General of the United Nations shall address a written request to the members of the Permanent Court of Arbitration belonging to the states which are parties to the present Statute, and to the members of the national groups appointed under Article 4, paragraph 2, inviting them to undertake, within a given time, by national groups, the nomination of persons in a position to accept the duties of a member of the Court.

2. No group may nominate more than four persons, not more than two of whom shall be of their own nationality. In no case may the number of candidates nominated by a group be more than double the number of seats to be filled.

Article 6

Before making these nominations, each national group is recommended to consult its highest court of justice, its legal faculties and schools of law, and its national academies and national sections of international academies devoted to the study of law.

Article 7

1. The Secretary-General shall prepare a list in alphabetical order of all the persons thus nominated. Save as provided in Article 12, paragraph 2, these shall be the only persons eligible.

2. The Secretary-General shall submit this list to the General Assembly and to the Security Council.

Article 8

The General Assembly and the Security Council shall proceed independently of one another to elect the members of the Court.

Article 9

At every election, the electors shall bear in mind not only that the persons to be elected should individually possess the qualifications required, but also that in the body as a whole the representation of the main forms of civilization and of the principal legal systems of the world should be assured.

Article 10

1. Those candidates who obtain an absolute majority of votes in the General Assembly and in the Security Council shall be considered as elected.

2. Any vote of the Security Council, whether for the election of judges or for the appointment of members of the conference envisaged in Article 12, shall be taken without any distinction between permanent and non-permanent members of the Security Council.

3. In the event of more than one national of the same state obtaining an absolute majority of the votes both of the General Assembly and of the Security Council, the eldest of these only shall be considered as elected.

Article 11

If, after the first meeting held for the purpose of the election, one or more seats remain to be filled, a second and, if necessary, a third meeting shall take place.

Article 12

1. If, after the third meeting, one or more seats still remain unfilled, a joint conference consisting of six members, three appointed by the General Assembly and three by the Security Council, may be formed at any time at the request of either the General Assembly or the Security Council, for the purpose of choosing by the vote of an absolute majority one name for each seat still vacant, to submit to the General Assembly and the Security Council for their respective acceptance.

2. If the joint conference is unanimously agreed upon any person who fulfils the required conditions, he may be included in its list, even though he was not included in the list of nominations referred to in Article 7.

3. If the joint conference is satisfied that it will not be successful in procuring an election, those members of the Court who have already been elected shall, within a period to be fixed by the Security Council, proceed to fill the vacant seats by selection from among those candidates who have obtained votes either in the General Assembly or in the Security Council.

4. In the event of an equality of votes among the judges, the eldest judge shall have a casting vote.

Article 13

1. The members of the Court shall be elected for nine years and may be re-elected; provided, however, that of the judges elected at the first election, the terms of five judges shall expire at the end of three years and the terms of five more judges shall expire at the end of six years.

2. The judges whose terms are to expire at the end of the above-mentioned initial periods of three and six years shall be chosen by lot to be drawn by the Secretary-General immediately after the first election has been completed.

3. The members of the Court shall continue to discharge their duties until their places have been filled. Though replaced, they shall finish any cases which they may have begun.

4. In the case of the resignation of a member of the Court, the resignation shall be addressed to the President of the Court for transmission to the Secretary-General. This last notification makes the place vacant.

Article 14

Vacancies shall be filled by the same method as that laid down for the first election, subject to the following provision: the Secretary-General shall, within one month of the occurrence of the vacancy, proceed to issue the invitations provided for in Article 5, and the date of the election shall be fixed by the Security Council.

Article 15

A member of the Court elected to replace a member whose term of office has not expired shall hold office for the remainder of his predecessor's term.

Article 16

1. No member of the Court may exercise any political or administrative function, or engage in any other occupation of a professional nature.

2. Any doubt on this point shall be settled by the decision of the Court.

Article 17

1. No member of the Court may act as agent, counsel, or advocate in any case.

2. No member may participate in the decision of any case in which he has previously taken part as agent, counsel, or advocate for one of the parties, or as a member of a national or international court, or of a commission of enquiry, or in any other capacity.

3. Any doubt on this point shall be settled by the decision of the Court.

Article 18

1. No member of the Court can be dismissed unless, in the unanimous opinion of the other members, he has ceased to fulfil the required conditions.

2. Formal notification thereof shall be made to the Secretary-General by the Registrar.

3. This notification makes the place vacant.

Article 19

The members of the Court, when engaged on the business of the Court, shall enjoy diplomatic privileges and immunities.

Article 20

Every member of the Court shall, before taking up his duties, make a solemn declaration in open court that he will exercise his powers impartially and conscientiously.

Article 21

1. The Court shall elect its President and Vice-President for three years; they may be re-elected.

2. The Court shall appoint its Registrar and may provide for the appointment of such other officers as may be necessary.

Article 22

1. The seat of the Court shall be established at The Hague. This, however, shall not prevent the Court from sitting and exercising its functions elsewhere whenever the Court considers it desirable.

2. The President and the Registrar shall reside at the seat of the Court.

Article 23

1. The Court shall remain permanently in session, except during the judicial vacations, the dates and duration of which shall be fixed by the Court.

2. Members of the Court are entitled to periodic leave, the dates and duration of which shall be fixed by the Court, having in mind the distance between The Hague and the home of each judge.

3. Members of the Court shall be bound, unless they are on leave or prevented from attending by illness or other serious reasons duly explained to the President, to hold themselves permanently at the disposal of the Court.

Article 24

1. If, for some special reason, a member of the Court considers that he should not take part in the decision of a particular case, he shall so inform the President.

2. If the President considers that for some special reason one of the members of the Court should not sit in a particular case, he shall give him notice accordingly.

3. If in any such case the member of the Court and the President disagree, the matter shall be settled by the decision of the Court.

Article 25

1. The full Court shall sit except when it is expressly provided otherwise in the present Statute.

2. Subject to the condition that the number of judges available to constitute the Court is not thereby reduced below eleven, the Rules of the Court may provide for allowing one or more judges, according to circumstances and in rotation, to be dispensed from sitting.

3. A quorum of nine judges shall suffice to constitute the Court.

Article 26

1. The Court may from time to time form one or more chambers, composed of three or more judges as the Court may determine, for dealing with particular categories of cases; for example, labour cases and cases relating to transit and communications.

2. The Court may at any time form a chamber for dealing with a particular case. The number of judges to constitute such a chamber shall be determined by the Court with the approval of the parties.

3. Cases shall be heard and determined by the chambers provided for in this Article if the parties so request.

Article 27

A judgment given by any of the chambers provided for in Articles 26 and 29 shall be considered as rendered by the Court.

Article 28

The chambers provided for in Articles 26 and 29 may, with the consent of the parties, sit and exercise their functions elsewhere than at The Hague.

Article 29

With a view to the speedy dispatch of business, the Court shall form annually a chamber composed of five judges which, at the request of the parties, may hear and determine cases by summary procedure. In addition, two judges shall be selected for the purpose of replacing judges who find it impossible to sit.

Article 30

1. The Court shall frame rules for carrying out its functions. In particular, it shall lay down rules of procedure.

2. The Rules of the Court may provide for assessors to sit with the Court or with any of its chambers, without the right to vote.

Article 31

1. Judges of the nationality of each of the parties shall retain their right to sit in the case before the Court.

2. If the Court includes upon the Bench a judge of the nationality of one of the parties, any other party may choose a person to sit as judge. Such person shall be chosen preferably from among those persons who have been nominated as candidates as provided in Articles 4 and 5.

3. If the Court includes upon the Bench no judge of the nationality of the parties, each of these parties may proceed to choose a judge as provided in paragraph 2 of this Article.

4. The provisions of this Article shall apply to the case of Articles 26 and 29. In such cases, the President shall request one or, if necessary, two of the members of the Court forming the chamber to give place to the members of the Court of the nationality of the parties concerned, and, failing such, or if they are unable to be present, to the judges specially chosen by the parties.

5. Should there be several parties in the same interest, they shall, for the purpose of the preceding provisions, be reckoned as one party only. Any doubt upon this point shall be settled by the decision of the Court.

6. Judges chosen as laid down in paragraphs 2, 3 and 4 of this Article shall fulfil the conditions required by Articles 2, 17 (paragraph 2), 20, and 24 of the present Statute. They shall take part in the decision on terms of complete equality with their colleagues.

Article 32

1. Each member of the Court shall receive an annual salary.

2. The President shall receive a special annual allowance.

3. The Vice-President shall receive a special allowance for every day on which he acts as President.

4. The judges chosen under Article 31, other than members of the Court, shall receive compensation for each day on which they exercise their functions.

5. These salaries, allowances, and compensation shall be fixed by the General Assembly. They may not be decreased during the term of office.

6. The salary of the Registrar shall be fixed by the General Assembly on the proposal of the Court.

7. Regulations made by the General Assembly shall fix the conditions under which retirement pensions may be given to members of the Court and to the Registrar, and the conditions under which members of the Court and the Registrar shall have their travelling expenses refunded.

8. The above salaries, allowances, and compensation shall be free of all taxation.

Article 33

The expenses of the Court shall be borne by the United Nations in such a manner as shall be decided by the General Assembly.

Chapter II

COMPETENCE OF THE COURT

Article 34

1. Only states may be parties in cases before the Court.

2. The Court, subject to and in conformity with its Rules, may request of public international organizations information relevant to cases before it, and shall receive such information presented by such organizations on their own initiative.

3. Whenever the construction of the constituent instrument of a public international organization or of an international convention adopted thereunder is in question in a case before the Court, the Registrar shall so notify the public international organization concerned and shall communicate to it copies of all the written proceedings.

Article 35

1. The Court shall be open to the states parties to the present Statute.

2. The conditions under which the Court shall be open to other states shall, subject to the special provisions contained in treaties in force, be laid down by the Security Council, but in no case shall such conditions place the parties in a position of inequality before the Court.

3. When a state which is not a Member of the United Nations is a party to a case, the Court shall fix the amount which that party is to contribute towards the expenses of the Court. This provision shall not apply if such state is bearing a share of the expenses of the Court.

Article 36

1. The jurisdiction of the Court comprises all cases which the parties refer to it and all matters specially provided for in the Charter of the United Nations or in treaties and conventions in force.

2. The states parties to the present Statute may at any time declare that they recognize as compulsory *ipso facto* and without special agreement, in relation to any other state accepting the same obligation, the jurisdiction of the Court in all legal disputes concerning:

a. the interpretation of a treaty;

b. any question of international law;

c. the existence of any fact which, if established, would constitute a breach of an international obligation;

d. the nature or extent of the reparation to be made for the breach of an international obligation.

3. The declarations referred to above may be made unconditionally or on condition of reciprocity on the part of several or certain states, or for a certain time.

4. Such declarations shall be deposited with the Secretary-General of the United Nations, who shall transmit copies thereof to the parties to the Statute and to the Registrar of the Court.

5. Declarations made under Article 36 of the Statute of the Permanent Court of International Justice and which are still in force shall be deemed, as between the parties to the present Statute, to be acceptances of the compulsory jurisdiction of the International Court of Justice for the period which they still have to run and in accordance with their terms.

6. In the event of a dispute as to whether the Court has jurisdiction, the matter shall be settled by the decision of the Court.

Article 37

Whenever a treaty or convention in force provides for reference of a matter to a tribunal to have been instituted by the League of Nations, or to the Permanent Court of International Justice, the matter shall, as between the parties to the present Statute, be referred to the International Court of Justice.

Article 38

1. The Court, whose function is to decide in accordance with international law such disputes as are submitted to it, shall apply:
   a. international conventions, whether general or particular, establishing rules expressly recognized by the contesting states;
   b. international custom, as evidence of a general practice accepted as law;
   c. the general principles of law recognized by civilized nations;
   d. subject to the provisions of Article 59, judicial decisions and the teachings of the most highly qualified publicists of the various nations, as subsidiary means for the determination of rules of law.
2. This provision shall not prejudice the power of the Court to decide a case *ex aequo et bono*, if the parties agree thereto.

Chapter III
PROCEDURE

Article 39

1. The official languages of the Court shall be French and English. If the parties agree that the case shall be conducted in French, the judgment shall be delivered in French. If the parties agree that the case shall be conducted in English, the judgment shall be delivered in English.
2. In the absence of an agreement as to which language shall be employed, each party may, in the pleadings, use the language which it prefers; the decision of the Court shall be given in French and English. In this case the Court shall at the same time determine which of the two texts shall be considered as authoritative.
3. The Court shall, at the request of any party, authorize a language other than French or English to be used by that party.

Article 40

1. Cases are brought before the Court, as the case may be, either by the notification of the special agreement or by a written application addressed to the Registrar. In either case the subject of the dispute and the parties shall be indicated.
2. The Registrar shall forthwith communicate the application to all concerned.
3. He shall also notify the Members of the United Nations through the Secretary-General, and also any other states entitled to appear before the Court.

Article 41

1. The Court shall have the power to indicate, if it considers that circumstances so require, any provisional measures which ought to be taken to preserve the respective rights of either party.
2. Pending the final decision, notice of the measures suggested shall forthwith be given to the parties and to the Security Council.

Article 42

1. The parties shall be represented by agents.
2. They may have the assistance of counsel or advocates before the Court.
3. The agents, counsel, and advocates of parties before the Court shall enjoy the privileges and immunities necessary to the independent exercise of their duties.

Article 43

1. The procedure shall consist of two parts: written and oral.

2. The written proceedings shall consist of the communication to the Court and to the parties of memorials, counter-memorials and, if necessary, replies; also all papers and documents in support.
3. These communications shall be made through the Registrar, in the order and within the time fixed by the Court.
4. A certified copy of every document produced by one party shall be communicated to the other party.
5. The oral proceedings shall consist of the hearing by the Court of witnesses, experts, agents, counsel, and advocates.

Article 44

1. For the service of all notices upon persons other than the agents, counsel, and advocates, the Court shall apply direct to the government of the state upon whose territory the notice has to be served.
2. The same provision shall apply whenever steps are to be taken to procure evidence on the spot.

Article 45

The hearing shall be under the control of the President or, if he is unable to preside, of the Vice-President; if neither is able to preside, the senior judge present shall preside.

Article 46

The hearing in Court shall be public, unless the Court shall decide otherwise, or unless the parties demand that the public be not admitted.

Article 47

1. Minutes shall be made at each hearing and signed by the Registrar and the President.
2. These minutes alone shall be authentic.

Article 48

The Court shall make orders for the conduct of the case, shall decide the form and time in which each party must conclude its arguments, and make all arrangements connected with the taking of evidence.

Article 49

The Court may, even before the hearing begins, call upon the agents to produce any document or to supply any explanations. Formal note shall be taken of any refusal.

Article 50

The Court may, at any time, entrust any individual, body, bureau, commission, or other organization that it may select, with the task of carrying out an enquiry or giving an expert opinion.

Article 51

During the hearing any relevant questions are to be put to the witnesses and experts under the conditions laid down by the Court in the rules of procedure referred to in Article 30.

Article 52

After the Court has received the proofs and evidence within the time specified for the purpose, it may refuse to accept any further oral or written evidence that one party may desire to present unless the other side consents.

Article 53

1. Whenever one of the parties does not appear before the Court, or fails to defend its case, the other party may call upon the Court to decide in favour of its claim.
2. The Court must, before doing so, satisfy itself, not only that it has jurisdiction in accordance with Articles 36 and 37, but also that the claim is well founded in fact and law.

Article 54

1. When, subject to the control of the Court, the agents, counsel, and advocates have completed their presentation of the case, the President shall declare the hearing closed.

2. The Court shall withdraw to consider the judgment.

3. The deliberations of the Court shall take place in private and remain secret.

Article 55

1. All questions shall be decided by a majority of the judges present.

2. In the event of an equality of votes, the President or the judge who acts in his place shall have a casting vote.

Article 56

1. The judgment shall state the reasons on which it is based.

2. It shall contain the names of the judges who have taken part in the decision.

Article 57

If the judgment does not represent in whole or in part the unanimous opinion of the judges, any judge shall be entitled to deliver a separate opinion.

Article 58

The judgment shall be signed by the President and by the Registrar. It shall be read in open court, due notice having been given to the agents.

Article 59

The decision of the Court has no binding force except between the parties and in respect of that particular case.

Article 60

The judgment is final and without appeal. In the event of dispute as to the meaning or scope of the judgment, the Court shall construe it upon the request of any party.

Article 61

1. An application for revision of a judgment may be made only when it is based upon the discovery of some fact of such a nature as to be a decisive factor, which fact was, when the judgment was given, unknown to the Court and also the party claiming revision, always provided that such ignorance was not due to negligence.

2. The proceedings for revision shall be opened by a judgment of the Court expressly recording the existence of the new fact, recognizing that it has such a character as to lay the case open to revision, and declaring the application admissible on this ground.

3. The Court may require previous compliance with the terms of the judgment before it admits proceedings in revision.

4. The application for revision must be made at latest within six months of the discovery of the new fact.

5. No application for revision may be made after the lapse of ten years from the date of the judgment.

Article 62

1. Should a state consider that it has an interest of a legal nature which may be affected by the decision in the case, it may submit a request to the Court to be permitted to intervene.

2. It shall be for the Court to decide upon this request.

Article 63

1. Whenever the construction of a convention to which states other than those concerned in the case are parties is in question, the Registrar shall notify all such states forthwith.

2. Every state so notified has the right to intervene in the proceedings; but if it uses this right, the construction given by the judgment will be equally binding upon it.

Article 64

Unless otherwise decided by the Court, each party shall bear its own costs.

Chapter IV
ADVISORY OPINIONS

Article 65

1. The Court may give an advisory opinion on any legal question at the request of whatever body may be authorized by or in accordance with the Charter of the United Nations to make such a request.

2. Questions upon which the advisory opinion of the Court is asked shall be laid before the Court by means of a written request containing an exact statement of the question upon which an opinion is required, and accompanied by all documents likely to throw light upon the question.

Article 66

1. The Registrar shall forthwith give notice of the request for an advisory opinion to all states entitled to appear before the Court.

2. The Registrar shall also, by means of a special and direct communication, notify any state entitled to appear before the Court or international organization considered by the Court, or, should it not be sitting, by the President, as likely to be able to furnish information on the question, that the Court will be prepared to receive, within a time limit to be fixed by the President, written statements, or to hear, at a public sitting to be held for the purpose, oral statements relating to the question.

3. Should any such state entitled to appear before the Court have failed to receive the special communication referred to in paragraph 2 of this Article, such state may express a desire to submit a written statement or to be heard; and the Court will decide.

4. States and organizations having presented written or oral statements or both shall be permitted to comment on the statements made by other states or organizations in the form, to the extent, and within the time limits which the Court, or, should it not be sitting, the President, shall decide in each particular case. Accordingly, the Registrar shall in due time communicate any such written statements to states and organizations having submitted similar statements.

Article 67

The Court shall deliver its advisory opinions in open court, notice having been given to the Secretary-General and to the representatives of Members of the United Nations, of other states and of international organizations immediately concerned.

Article 68

In the exercise of its advisory functions the Court shall further be guided by the provisions of the present Statute which apply in contentious cases to the extent to which it recognizes them to be applicable.

Chapter V
AMENDMENT

Article 69

Amendments to the present Statute shall be effected by the same procedure as is provided by the Charter of the United Nations for amendments to that Charter, subject however to any provisions which the General Assembly upon recommendation of the Security Council may adopt concerning the participation of states which are parties to the present Statute but are not Members of the United Nations.

Article 70

The Court shall have power to propose such amendments to the present Statute as it may deem necessary, through written communications to the Secretary-General, for consideration in conformity with the provisions of Article 69.

Appendix III

Structure of the United Nations

General Assembly

The General Assembly is composed of all the Members of the United Nations.

SESSIONS
Resumed fifty-fourth session: 1 February–5 September 2000.
Twenty-third special session: 5-10 June 2000.
Twenty-fourth special session: 26 June–1 July 2000.
Fifty-fifth session: 5 September–23 December 2000 (suspended).
Resumed tenth emergency special session: 18 and 20 October 2000 (suspended).

OFFICERS
Resumed fifty-fourth and twenty-third and twenty-fourth special sessions
President: Theo-Ben Gurirab (Namibia).[1]
Vice-Presidents:[2] Algeria, Bolivia, China, Congo, Côte d'Ivoire, Cuba, Democratic People's Republic of Korea, France, Grenada, Iceland, Iran, Iraq, Lithuania, Monaco, Nigeria, Russian Federation, Seychelles, Tajikistan, Thailand, United Kingdom, United States.

Fifty-fifth and resumed tenth emergency special sessions
President: Harri Holkeri (Finland).[3]
Vice-Presidents:[4] Belarus, Bhutan, Burkina Faso, China, Comoros, El Salvador, France, Gabon, Guinea, Haiti, Kuwait, Maldives, Mozambique, Russian Federation, Suriname, Tunisia, Turkey, United Kingdom, United States, Uzbekistan, Yemen.

The Assembly has four types of committees: (1) Main Committees; (2) procedural committees; (3) standing committees; (4) subsidiary and ad hoc bodies. In addition, it convenes conferences to deal with specific subjects.

Main Committees
Six Main Committees have been established as follows:

Disarmament and International Security Committee (First Committee)
Special Political and Decolonization Committee (Fourth Committee)
Economic and Financial Committee (Second Committee)
Social, Humanitarian and Cultural Committee (Third Committee)
Administrative and Budgetary Committee (Fifth Committee)
Legal Committee (Sixth Committee)

The General Assembly may constitute other committees, on which all Members of the United Nations have the right to be represented.

OFFICERS OF THE MAIN COMMITTEES

Resumed fifty-fourth session

Fourth Committee[5]
Chairperson: Sotirios Zackheos (Cyprus).
Vice-Chairpersons: Yuri Kazhura (Belarus), Matia Mulumba Semakula Kiwanuka (Uganda), Carlos Morales (Spain).
Rapporteur: Gualberto Rodríguez San Martín (Bolivia).

Fifth Committee[5]
Chairperson: Penny A. Wensley (Australia).
Vice-Chairpersons: Judith Maria Cardoze (Panama), Ahmed H. Darwish (Egypt), Amjad B. Sial (Pakistan).
Rapporteur: Jan Jaremczuk (Poland).

Twenty-third and twenty-fourth special sessions[6]

First Committee
Chairperson: Raimundo González (Chile).

Fourth Committee
Chairperson: Sotirios Zackheos (Cyprus).

Second Committee
Chairperson: Roble Olhaye (Djibouti) (twenty-fourth special session).
Acting Chairperson: Giovanni Brauzzi (Italy) (twenty-third special session).

Third Committee
Chairperson: Vladimir Galuška (Czech Republic) (twenty-third special session).
Acting Chairperson: Mónica Martínez (Ecuador) (twenty-fourth special session).

Fifth Committee
Chairperson: Penny A. Wensley (Australia).

Sixth Committee
Chairperson: Phakiso Mochochoko (Lesotho).

Ad Hoc Committee of the Whole of the Twenty-third Special Session[7]
Chairperson: Christine Kapalata (United Republic of Tanzania).
Vice-Chairpersons: Aicha Afifi (Morocco), Asith Bhattacharjee (India), Patricia Flor (Germany), Misako Kaji (Japan), Sonia R. Leonce-Carryl (Saint Lucia), Kirsten Mlacak (Canada), Rasa Ostrauskaite (Lithuania), Dubravka Šimonovic (Croatia).
Vice-Chairperson/Rapporteur: Mónica Martínez (Ecuador).

Ad Hoc Committee of the Whole of the Twenty-fourth Special Session[8]
Chairperson: Cristian Maquieira (Chile).
Vice-Chairpersons: Ion Gorita (Romania), Kheireddine Ramoul (Algeria), Koos Richelle (Netherlands).
Vice-Chairperson/Rapporteur: Bagher Asadi (Iran).
Ex-officio member: Zola Skweyiya (South Africa) (Chairperson of Commission for Social Development).

Fifty-fifth session[9]

First Committee
Chairperson: U Mya Than (Myanmar).
Vice-Chairpersons: Alberto Guani (Uruguay), Abdelkader Mesdoua (Algeria), Petra Schneebauer (Austria).
Rapporteur: Ratislav Gabriel (Slovakia).

Fourth Committee
Chairperson: Matia Mulumba Semakula Kiwanuka (Uganda).
Vice-Chairpersons: Patrick Albert Lewis (Antigua and Barbuda), Jelena Grcic Polic (Croatia), Julian Vassallo (Malta).
Rapporteur: Shingo Miyamoto (Japan).

Second Committee

Chairperson: Alexandru Niculescu (Romania).
Vice-Chairpersons: Anne Barrington (Ireland), Mauricio Escanero (Mexico), Navid Hanif (Pakistan).
Rapporteur: Ahmed Amaziane (Morocco).

Third Committee

Chairperson: Yvonne Gittens-Joseph (Trinidad and Tobago).
Vice-Chairpersons: Mostafa Alaei (Iran), Hazel de Wet (Namibia), Sarah Paterson (New Zealand).
Rapporteur: Anzhela Korneliouk (Belarus).

Fifth Committee

Chairperson: Gert Rosenthal (Guatemala).
Vice-Chairpersons: Jasminka Dinic (Croatia), Collen Vixen Kelapile (Botswana), Park Hae-yun (Republic of Korea).
Rapporteur: Eduardo Manuel da Fonseca Fernandes Ramos (Portugal).

Sixth Committee

Chairperson: Mauro Politi (Italy).
Vice-Chairpersons: Kenjika Linus Ekedede (Nigeria), Salah T. Suheimat (Jordan), Marcelo Vásquez (Ecuador).
Rapporteur: Drahoslav Štefánek (Slovakia).

Procedural committees

General Committee

The General Committee consists of the President of the General Assembly, as Chairperson, the 21 Vice-Presidents and the Chairpersons of the six Main Committees [at the twenty-third and twenty-fourth special sessions, the Chairperson of the Ad Hoc Committee of the Whole was also a member of the General Committee (dec. S-23/15 & S-24/15)].

Credentials Committee

The Credentials Committee consists of nine members appointed by the General Assembly on the proposal of the President.

Resumed fifty-fourth and twenty-third and twenty-fourth special sessions[10]
Austria, Bolivia, China, Philippines, Russian Federation, South Africa, Togo, Trinidad and Tobago, United States.

Fifty-fifth and resumed tenth emergency special sessions[11]
Bahamas, China, Ecuador, Gabon, Ireland, Mauritius, Russian Federation, Thailand, United States.

Standing committees

The two standing committees consist of experts appointed in their individual capacity for three-year terms.

Advisory Committee on Administrative and Budgetary Questions (ACABQ)

To serve until 31 December 2000: Ioan Barac (Romania); Hasan Jawarneh (Jordan); Mahamane Amadou Maiga (Mali); E. Besley Maycock, *Vice-Chairman* (Barbados); C. S. M. Mselle, *Chairman* (United Republic of Tanzania).
To serve until 31 December 2001: Nazareth A. Incera (Costa Rica); Ahmad Kamal (Pakistan); Rajat Saha (India); Juichi Takahara (Japan);[12] Nicholas A. Thorne (United Kingdom); Giovanni Luigi Valenza (Italy).
To serve until 31 December 2002: Gérard Biraud (France); Norma Goicochea Estenoz (Cuba); Vladimir V. Kuznetsov (Russian Federation); Susan M. McLurg (United States); Roger Tchoungui (Cameroon).

On 6 December 2000 (dec. 55/312), the General Assembly appointed the following for a three-year term beginning on 1 January 2001 to fill the vacancies occurring on 31 December

2000: Andrzej T. Abraszewski (Poland), Manlan Narcisse Ahounou (Côte d'Ivoire), Felipe Mabilangan (Philippines), E. Besley Maycock (Barbados), C. S. M. Mselle (United Republic of Tanzania).

Committee on Contributions

To serve until 31 December 2000: Sergio Chaparro Ruiz (Chile); Ihor V. Humenny (Ukraine); Nathan Irumba (Uganda);[13] David A. Leis (United States); Prakash Shah (India); Kazuo Watanabe (Japan).
To serve until 31 December 2001: Pieter Johannes Bierma (Netherlands); Uldis Blukis (Latvia); Paul Ekorong A Ndong (Cameroon); Neil Hewitt Francis (Australia); Bernardo Greiver (Uruguay); Henry Hanson-Hall, *Vice-Chairman* (Ghana).
To serve until 31 December 2002: Alvaro Gurgel de Alencar Netto (Brazil); Ju Kuilin (China);[14] Sergei I. Mareyev (Russian Federation); Angel Marrón (Spain); Park Hae-Yun (Republic of Korea); Ugo Sessi, *Chairman* (Italy).

On 6 December 2000 (dec. 55/309 B), the General Assembly appointed the following for a three-year term beginning on 1 January 2001 to fill the vacancies occurring on 31 December 2000: Petru Dumitriu (Romania), Chinmaya Gharekhan (India), Ihor V. Humenny (Ukraine), Gebhard Benjamin Kandanga (Namibia), David A. Leis (United States), Kazuo Watanabe (Japan). (Eduardo Iglesias (Argentina) was to serve from 1 January to 31 December 2001 [YUN 1998, p. 1437].)

Subsidiary and ad hoc bodies

The following is a list of subsidiary and ad hoc bodies functioning in 2000, including the number of members, dates of meetings/sessions in 2000, document numbers of 2000 reports (which generally provide specific information on membership), and relevant decision numbers pertaining to elections. (For other related bodies, see p. 1475.)

Ad Hoc Committee on the Elaboration of a Convention against Transnational Organized Crime

Sessions: Seventh, eighth, ninth, tenth and eleventh, Vienna, 17-28 January, 21 February–3 March, 5-16 June, 17-28 July, 2-28 October
Chairman: Luigi Lauriola (Italy) (acting in his personal capacity)
Membership: Open to all States
Reports: A/AC.254/25, A/AC.254/28, A/AC.254/31, A/AC.254/34, A/AC.254/38

Ad Hoc Committee established by General Assembly resolution 51/210 of 17 December 1996

Session: Fourth, New York, 14-18 February
Chairman: Rohan Perera (Sri Lanka)
Membership: Open to all States Members of the United Nations or members of the specialized agencies or of IAEA
Report: A/55/37

Ad Hoc Committee on the Indian Ocean

Meeting: Did not meet in 2000
Membership: 44

Advisory Committee on the United Nations Programme of Assistance in the Teaching, Study, Dissemination and Wider Appreciation of International Law

Session: Thirty-fifth, New York, 22 November
Chairman: Harold Adlai Agyeman (Ghana)
Membership: 25
Report: A/56/484

Board of Auditors

Sessions: Fifty-fourth, New York, 28-30 June; thirtieth special, Montreal, Canada, 31 October
Chairman: Sir John Bourn (United Kingdom)
Membership: 3
Decision: GA 55/313

Committee on Conferences

Sessions: New York, 27 April and 25 July (organizational), 7-9 August (substantive)
Chairman: Valeria María González Posse (Argentina)
Membership: 21
Report: A/55/32
Decision: GA 55/318

Committee on the Exercise of the Inalienable Rights of the Palestinian People

Meetings: Throughout the year
Chairman: Ibra Deguène Ka (Senegal)
Membership: 25
Report: A/55/35

Committee on Information

Session: Twenty-second, New York, 1-12 May
Chairman: Elhassane Zahid (Morocco)
Membership: 95 (97 from 8 December)
Report: A/55/21
Decision: GA 55/317

Committee on the Peaceful Uses of Outer Space

Session: Forty-third, Vienna, 7-16 June
Chairman: Raimundo González (Chile)
Membership: 61
Report: A/55/20

Committee on Relations with the Host Country

Meetings: New York, 9 March, 26 July, 28 August, 1 September, 1 November
Chairman: Sotirios Zackheos (Cyprus)
Membership: 19 (including the United States as host country)
Report: A/55/26

Committee for the United Nations Population Award

Meetings: New York, 22 February, 20 March
Chairman: José Luis Barbosa Leao Monteiro (Cape Verde)
Membership: 10 (plus 5 honorary members, the Secretary-General and the UNFPA Executive Director)
Report: A/55/419
Decision: ESC 2000/201 C

Disarmament Commission

Sessions: New York, 15 February and 26 June (organizational), 26 June–7 July (substantive), 1 December (organizational)
Chairman: Javad Zarif (Iran)
Membership: All UN Members
Reports: A/55/42, A/56/42

High-level Committee on the Review of Technical Cooperation among Developing Countries

Session: Did not meet in 2000
Membership: All States participating in UNDP

Intergovernmental Preparatory Committee for the Third United Nations Conference on the Least Developed Countries

Session: First, New York, 24-28 July
Chairman: Jacques Scavee (Belgium)
Membership: Open to all States members of UNCTAD
Report: A/CONF.191/2

International Civil Service Commission (ICSC)

Sessions: Fifty-first, Vienna, 3-20 April; fifty-second, New York, 17 July–4 August
Chairman: Mohsen Bel Hadj Amor (Tunisia)
Membership: 15
Report: A/55/30
Decision: GA 55/316

ADVISORY COMMITTEE ON POST ADJUSTMENT QUESTIONS
Session: Twenty-third, New York, 24-31 January
Chairman: Eugeniusz Wyzner (Poland)
Membership: 6

International Law Commission

Session: Fifty-second, Geneva, 1 May–9 June and 10 July–18 August
Chairman: Chusei Yamada (Japan)
Membership: 34
Report: A/55/10

Investments Committee

Meetings: Paris, 21-22 February; New York, 8-9 May; Geneva, 4-5 July; New York, 11-12 September, 20-21 November
Chairman: Emmanuel Noi Omaboe (Ghana)
Membership: 9
Decision: GA 55/314

Joint Advisory Group on the International Trade Centre UNCTAD/WTO

Session: Thirty-third, Geneva, 10-14 April
Chairman: Silvia Avila Seifert (Bolivia)
Membership: Open to all States members of UNCTAD and all members of WTO
Report: ITC/AG(XXXIII)/181

Joint Inspection Unit (JIU)

Chairman: Louis-Dominique Ouedraogo (Burkina Faso)
Membership: 11
Report: A/56/34 & Corr.1
Decision: GA 54/321

Office of the United Nations High Commissioner for Refugees (UNHCR)

EXECUTIVE COMMITTEE OF THE HIGH COMMISSIONER'S PROGRAMME
Session: Fifty-first, Geneva, 2-6 October
Chairman: Ali Khorram (Iran)
Membership: 57 (58 from 4 December)
Report: A/55/12/Add.1
Decisions: ESC 2000/201 B, 2000/302, GA 55/310

High Commissioner: Sadako Ogata

Panel of External Auditors

Membership: Members of the UN Board of Auditors and the appointed external auditors of the specialized agencies and IAEA

Preparatory Committee for the High-level International Intergovernmental Event on Financing for Development

Sessions: Organizational and resumed organizational, New York, 10 and 25 February, 27, 28 and 31 March and 30 May; first and resumed first, New York, 31 May and 2 June, 30 October and 16, 20 and 27 November
Co-Chairmen: Jørgen Bøjer (Denmark), Asda Jayanama (Thailand)
Membership: Open to all States
Report: A/55/28

Preparatory Committee for the Special Session of the General Assembly on Children

Sessions: Organizational, New York, 7-8 February; first, New York, 30 May–2 June
Chairperson: Patricia Durrant (Jamaica)
Membership: Open to all States Members of the United Nations and members of the specialized agencies
Report: A/55/43 (Parts I & II)

Preparatory Committee for the Special Session of the General Assembly entitled "World Summit for Social Development and beyond: achieving social development for all in a globalizing world"

Session: Second (final), New York, 3-14 April
Chairman: Cristian Maquieira (Chile)
Membership: Open to all States Members of the United Nations and members of the specialized agencies
Report: A/S-24/2

**Preparatory Committee for the World Conference against
Racism, Racial Discrimination,
Xenophobia and Related Intolerance**

Session: First, Geneva, 1-5 May
Chairperson: Absa Claude Diallo (Senegal)
Membership: Open to all States Members of the United Nations
and members of the specialized agencies
Report: A/CONF.189/PC.1/21 & Corr.1

**Special Committee on the Charter of the United Nations and on
the Strengthening of the Role of the Organization**

Meetings: New York, 10-20 April
Chairman: Saeid Mirzaee-Yengejeh (Iran)
Membership: Open to all States Members of the United Nations
Report: A/55/33

**Special Committee to Investigate Israeli Practices
Affecting the Human Rights of the Palestinian People
and Other Arabs of the Occupied Territories**

Meetings: Geneva, 16-17 March; Cairo, Egypt, 19-21 May; Am-
man, Jordan, 23-25 May; Damascus, Syrian Arab Republic,
26-30 May
Chairman: John de Saram (Sri Lanka)
Membership: 3
Reports: A/55/373, A/55/453

Special Committee on Peacekeeping Operations

Meetings: New York, 11-15 February (general debate), 16 Febru-
ary– 10 March (open-ended working group)
Chairman: Arthur C. I. Mbanefo (Nigeria)
Membership: 109
Report: A/54/839

**Special Committee to Select the Winners of
the United Nations Human Rights Prize**

Meeting: Did not meet in 2000
Membership: 5

**Special Committee on the Situation with regard to the
Implementation of the Declaration on the Granting of
Independence to Colonial Countries and Peoples**

Session: New York, 18 February, 24 and 28 March, 25 April (first
part); 5, 10-12, 17 and 20 July (second part)
Chairman: Peter D. Donigi (Papua New Guinea)
Membership: 24
Report: A/55/23

United Nations Administrative Tribunal

Sessions: Geneva, 3 July–4 August; New York, 23 October–
22 November
President: Hubert Thierry (France)
Membership: 7
Report: A/INF/55/5
Decision: GA 55/315

United Nations Capital Development Fund (UNCDF)

EXECUTIVE BOARD

The UNDP/UNFPA Executive Board acts as the Executive
Board of the Fund.

Managing Director: Mark Malloch Brown (UNDP Administrator)

**United Nations Commission on International
Trade Law (UNCITRAL)**

Session: Thirty-third, New York, 12 June–7 July
Chairman: Jeffrey Chan Wah Teck (Singapore)
Membership: 36
Report: A/55/17
Decision: GA 55/308

United Nations Conciliation Commission for Palestine

Membership: 3
Reports: A/55/329, A/56/290

United Nations Conference on Trade and Development (UNCTAD)

Session: Tenth, Bangkok, Thailand, 12-19 February
President: Supachai Panitchpakdi (Thailand)
Membership: Open to all States Members of the United Nations
or members of the specialized agencies or of IAEA
Report: TD/390

Secretary-General of UNCTAD: Rubens Ricupero

TRADE AND DEVELOPMENT BOARD

Sessions: Resumed twenty-third, twenty-fourth and twenty-
fifth executive, Geneva, 27 January, 24 March and 12 May,
22 September; forty-seventh, Geneva, 9-20 October
President: Philippe Petit (France) (executive sessions), Camilo
Reyes Rodriguez (Colombia) (forty-seventh session)
Membership: Open to all States members of UNCTAD
Reports: A/55/15, TD/B/47/11 (Vol. I) & Corr.1

*SUBSIDIARY ORGANS OF THE
TRADE AND DEVELOPMENT BOARD*

COMMISSION ON ENTERPRISE,
BUSINESS FACILITATION AND DEVELOPMENT

Session: Did not meet in 2000
Membership: Open to all States members of UNCTAD

COMMISSION ON INVESTMENT,
TECHNOLOGY AND RELATED FINANCIAL ISSUES

Session: Did not meet in 2000
Membership: Open to all States members of UNCTAD

*Intergovernmental Group of Experts
on Competition Law and Policy*
Session: Did not meet in 2000
Membership: Open to all States members of UNCTAD

*Intergovernmental Working Group of Experts on
International Standards of Accounting and Reporting*
Session: Seventeenth, Geneva, 3-5 July
Chairperson: Nelson Carvalho (Brazil)
Membership: 34
Report: TD/B/COM.2/25
Decisions: ESC 2000/201 C & F

COMMISSION ON TRADE IN
GOODS AND SERVICES, AND COMMODITIES

Session: Did not meet in 2000
Membership: Open to all States members of UNCTAD

WORKING PARTY ON THE
MEDIUM-TERM PLAN AND THE PROGRAMME BUDGET

Sessions: Thirty-fifth, Geneva, 13 and 20-21 March, 17-19
April; thirty-sixth, Geneva, 11-15 September
Chairperson: Y. Afanassiev (Russian Federation) (thirty-fifth ses-
sion), Federico Alberto Cuello (Dominican Republic) (thirty-
sixth session)
Membership: Open to all States members of UNCTAD
Reports: TD/B/47/3, TD/B/47/9

United Nations Development Fund for Women (UNIFEM)

CONSULTATIVE COMMITTEE
Session: Fortieth, New York, 13-14 January
Chairperson: Victoria Sandru (Romania)
Membership: 5
Decision: GA 55/311

Director of UNIFEM: Noeleen Heyzer
Deputy Director: Flavia Pansieri

United Nations Environment Programme (UNEP)

GOVERNING COUNCIL

Session: Sixth special (first Global Ministerial Environment Forum), Malmö, Sweden, 29-31 May
President: László Miklós (Slovakia)
Membership: 58
Report: A/55/25

Executive Director of UNEP: Klaus Töpfer

United Nations Institute for Disarmament Research (UNIDIR)

BOARD OF TRUSTEES

Session: Thirty-fourth, New York, 31 January–2 February; thirty-fifth, Geneva, 5-7 July
Chairman: Miguel Marín Bosch (Mexico)
Membership: 20, plus 1 ex-officio member (Director of UNIDIR)
Report: A/55/267

Director of UNIDIR: Patricia Lewis
Deputy Director: Christophe Carle

United Nations Institute for Training and Research (UNITAR)

BOARD OF TRUSTEES

Session: Thirty-eighth, Geneva, 26-28 April
Chairman: Arthur C. I. Mbanefo (Nigeria)
Membership: Not less than 11 and not more than 30, plus 4 ex-officio members
Reports: A/55/14, A/55/510

Executive Director of UNITAR: Marcel A. Boisard

United Nations Joint Staff Pension Board

Session: Fiftieth, Geneva, 5-14 July
Chairman: W. P. Scherzer (IAEA)
Membership: 33
Report: A/55/9

United Nations Relief and Works Agency for Palestine Refugees in the Near East (UNRWA)

ADVISORY COMMISSION OF UNRWA

Meeting: Amman, Jordan, 28 September
Chairman: Leo D'Aes (Belgium)
Membership: 10
Report: A/55/13

WORKING GROUP ON THE FINANCING OF UNRWA

Meetings: New York, 11 September, 6 October
Chairman: Mehmet U. Pamir (Turkey)
Membership: 9
Report: A/55/456

Commissioner-General of UNRWA: Peter Hansen
Deputy Commissioner-General: Dr. Mohamed Abdelmoumène (until 30 June), Karen Koning Abu Zayd (from 15 August)

United Nations Scientific Committee on the Effects of Atomic Radiation

Session: Forty-ninth, Vienna, 2-11 May
Chairman: L.-E. Holm (Sweden)
Membership: 21
Report: A/55/46

United Nations Staff Pension Committee

Meetings: New York, 9 February, 4 May, 1 December; Geneva, 4 July
Chairperson: Susan M. McLurg (United States) (February-July), Jean-Michel Jakobowicz (France) (December)
Membership: 12 members and 8 alternates
Decisions: GA 54/317 B, 55/319

United Nations University (UNU)

COUNCIL OF THE UNITED NATIONS UNIVERSITY

Session: Forty-seventh, Macao, China, 20-24 November
Chairperson: Jairam Reddy (South Africa)
Membership: 24 (plus 3 ex-officio members and the UNU Rector)

Rector of the University: Johannes A. van Ginkel

United Nations Voluntary Fund for Indigenous Populations

BOARD OF TRUSTEES

Session: Thirteenth, Geneva, 10-12 April
Chairperson: Victoria Tauli-Corpuz (Philippines)
Membership: 5
Reports: A/55/202, E/CN.4/Sub.2/AC.4/2000/4

United Nations Voluntary Fund for Victims of Torture

BOARD OF TRUSTEES

Session: Nineteenth, Geneva, 15-26 May
Chairman: Jaap Walkate (Netherlands)
Membership: 5
Report: A/55/178

United Nations Voluntary Trust Fund on Contemporary Forms of Slavery

BOARD OF TRUSTEES

Session: Fifth, Geneva, 7-10 February
Chairperson: Swami Agnivesh (India)
Membership: 5
Report: A/55/204

Security Council

The Security Council consists of 15 Member States of the United Nations, in accordance with the provisions of Article 23 of the United Nations Charter as amended in 1965.

MEMBERS
Permanent members: China, France, Russian Federation, United Kingdom, United States.
Non-permanent members: Argentina, Bangladesh, Canada, Jamaica, Malaysia, Mali, Namibia, Netherlands, Tunisia, Ukraine.

On 10 October 2000 (dec. 55/305), the General Assembly elected Colombia, Ireland, Mauritius, Norway and Singapore for a two-year term beginning on 1 January 2001, to replace Argentina, Canada, Malaysia, Namibia and the Netherlands whose terms of office were to expire on 31 December 2000.

PRESIDENT
The presidency of the Council rotates monthly, according to the English alphabetical listing of its member States. The following served as President during 2000:

Month	Member	Representative
January	United States	Richard C. Holbrooke
		Albert Gore
		Madeleine K. Albright
February	Argentina	Arnoldo M. Listre
		Rodríguez Giavarini
March	Bangladesh	Anwarul Karim Chowdhury
		Abdus Samad Azad

Month	Member	Representative
April	Canada	Robert R. Fowler
		Lloyd Axworthy
May	China	Wang Yingfan
June	France	Jean-David Levitte
July	Jamaica	Patricia Durrant
		Paul Robertson
August	Malaysia	Hasmy Agam
September	Mali	Moctar Ouane
		Alpha Oumar Konaré
October	Namibia	Martin Andjaba
		Theo-Ben Gurirab
November	Netherlands	A. Peter van Walsum
		Jozius van Aartsen
		Eveline Herfkens
December	Russian Federation	Sergey V. Lavrov

Military Staff Committee

The Military Staff Committee consists of the chiefs of staff of the permanent members of the Security Council or their representatives. It meets fortnightly.

Standing committees

Each of the three standing committees of the Security Council is composed of representatives of all Council members:

Committee of Experts (to examine the provisional rules of procedure of the Council and any other matters entrusted to it by the Council)
Committee on the Admission of New Members
Committee on Council Meetings Away from Headquarters

Subsidiary body

United Nations Monitoring, Verification and Inspection Commission (UNMOVIC)
Executive Chairman: Hans Blix.

Peacekeeping operations and special missions

United Nations Truce Supervision Organization (UNTSO)
Chief of Staff: Major-General Timothy Ford (until 31 March), Major-General Franco Ganguzza (from 1 April).

United Nations Military Observer Group in India and Pakistan (UNMOGIP)
Chief Military Observer: Major-General Jozsef Bali (until 3 March), Major-General Manuel Saavedra (from June).

United Nations Peacekeeping Force in Cyprus (UNFICYP)
Special Adviser to the Secretary-General on Cyprus: Alvaro de Soto.
Acting Special Representative of the Secretary-General and Chief of Mission: James Holger (until 31 May), Zbigniew Wlosowicz (from 1 June).
Force Commander: Major-General Victory Rana.

United Nations Disengagement Observer Force (UNDOF)
Force Commander: Major-General Cameron Ross (until 7 July), Major-General Bo Wranker (from 14 August).

United Nations Interim Force in Lebanon (UNIFIL)
Force Commander: Major-General Seth Kofi Obeng.

United Nations Iraq-Kuwait Observation Mission (UNIKOM)
Force Commander: Major-General John Augustine Vize.

United Nations Mission for the Referendum in Western Sahara (MINURSO)
Personal Envoy of the Secretary-General: James A. Baker III.
Special Representative of the Secretary-General: William Eagleton.
Force Commander: Brigadier-General Claude Buze.

United Nations Observer Mission in Georgia (UNOMIG)
Special Representative of the Secretary-General and Head of Mission: Dieter Boden.
Chief Military Observer: Major-General Anis Ahmed Bajwa.

United Nations Mission of Observers in Tajikistan (UNMOT) [15]
Special Representative of the Secretary-General and Head of Mission: Ivo Petrov.
Chief Military Observer: Brigadier-General John Hvidegaard.

United Nations Mission in Bosnia and Herzegovina (UNMIBH)
Special Representative of the Secretary-General and Coordinator of United Nations Operations in Bosnia and Herzegovina: Jacques Paul Klein.
Commissioner of the United Nations International Police Task Force: Detlef Buwitt (until 4 April), Vincent Coeurderoy (from 5 April).

United Nations Mission of Observers in Prevlaka (UNMOP)
Chief Military Observer: Lieutenant-Colonel Graeme Williams.

United Nations Civilian Police Mission in Haiti (MIPONUH) [16]
Special Representative of the Secretary-General and Head of Mission: Alfredo Lopes Cabral.

United Nations Mission in the Central African Republic (MINURCA) [17]
Force Commander and officer-in-charge of Mission: Major-General Barthélémy Ratanga.

United Nations Interim Administration Mission in Kosovo (UNMIK)
Special Representative of the Secretary-General: Bernard Kouchner.
Principal Deputy Special Representative: James Peter Covey.

United Nations Mission in Sierra Leone (UNAMSIL)
Special Representative of the Secretary-General and Head of Mission: Oluyemi Adeniji.
Force Commander: Major-General Vijay Kumar Jetley (until October), Lieutenant-General Daniel Ishmael Opande (from November).

United Nations Transitional Administration in East Timor (UNTAET)
Personal Representative of the Secretary-General for East Timor: Jamsheed K. A. Marker.
Special Representative of the Secretary-General and Transitional Administrator: Sergio Vieira de Mello.
Force Commander: Lieutenant-General Jaime de los Santos (until 21 July), Lieutenant-General Boonsrang Niumpradit (from 19 July).

United Nations Organization Mission in the Democratic Republic of the Congo (MONUC)
Special Representative of the Secretary-General and Head of Mission: Kamel Morjane.
Force Commander: Major-General Mountaga Diallo (from March).

United Nations Mission in Ethiopia and Eritrea (UNMEE) [18]
Special Representative of the Secretary-General: Legwaila Joseph Legwaila (from 29 September).
Force Commander: Major-General Patrick Cammaert (from 1 November).

Economic and Social Council

The Economic and Social Council consists of 54 Member States of the United Nations, elected by the General Assembly, each for a three-year term, in accordance with the provisions of Article 61 of the United Nations Charter as amended in 1965 and 1973.

MEMBERS

To serve until 31 December 2000: Algeria, Belarus, Belgium, Brazil, Colombia, Comoros, India, Italy, Lesotho, Mauritius, New Zealand, Oman, Pakistan, Poland, Saint Lucia, Sierra Leone, United States, Viet Nam.

To serve until 31 December 2001: Bolivia, Bulgaria, Canada, China, Czech Republic, Democratic Republic of the Congo, Denmark, Guinea-Bissau, Honduras, Indonesia, Morocco, Norway, Russian Federation, Rwanda, Saudi Arabia, Syrian Arab Republic, United Kingdom, Venezuela.

To serve until 31 December 2002: Angola, Austria, Bahrain, Benin, Burkina Faso, Cameroon, Costa Rica, Croatia, Cuba, Fiji, France, Germany, Greece, Japan, Mexico, Portugal, Sudan, Suriname.

On 12 October 2000 (dec. 55/306 A), the General Assembly elected the following for a three-year term beginning on 1 January 2001 to fill the vacancies occurring on 31 December 2000: Andorra, Argentina, Brazil, Egypt, Ethiopia, Georgia, Iran, Italy, Nepal, Netherlands, Nigeria, Pakistan, Peru, Republic of Korea, Romania, South Africa, Uganda, United States.

On 14 November (dec. 55/306 B), the Assembly elected Malta for the remaining term of office of Greece, beginning on 1 January 2001.

SESSIONS

Organizational session for 2000: New York, 27 January and 1 and 4 February.

Resumed organizational session for 2000: New York, 28 February, 9 March, 3, 10 and 12 May and 16 June.

Special high-level meeting with the Bretton Woods institutions: New York, 18 April.

Substantive session of 2000: New York, 5-28 July.

Resumed substantive session of 2000: New York, 18 and 30 October and 22 November.

OFFICERS

President: Makarim Wibisono (Indonesia).

Vice-Presidents: Martin Belinga-Eboutou (Cameroon), Bernd Niehous (Costa Rica), Gerhard Pfanzelter (Austria), Vladimir Sotirov (Bulgaria).

Subsidiary and other related organs

SUBSIDIARY ORGANS

The Economic and Social Council may, at each session, set up committees or working groups, of the whole or of limited membership, and refer to them any items on the agenda for study and report.

Other subsidiary organs reporting to the Council consist of functional commissions, regional commissions, standing committees, expert bodies and ad hoc bodies.

The inter-agency Administrative Committee on Coordination also reports to the Council.

Functional commissions

Commission on Crime Prevention and Criminal Justice
Session: Ninth, Vienna, 18-20 April
Chairman: Vladimiro Zagrebelsky (Italy)
Membership: 40
Report: E/2000/30
Decision: ESC 2000/201 C

Commission on Human Rights
Sessions: Fifty-sixth, Geneva, 20 March–28 April; fifth special, Geneva, 17-19 October
Chairperson: Shambhu Ram Simkhada (Nepal)
Membership: 53
Reports: E/2000/23 & Corr.1, E/2000/112
Decision: ESC 2000/201 C

SUBCOMMISSION ON THE PROMOTION AND PROTECTION OF HUMAN RIGHTS
Session: Fifty-second, Geneva, 31 July–18 August
Chairperson: Iulia Antoanella Motoc (Romania)
Membership: 26
Report: E/CN.4/2001/2

Commission on Narcotic Drugs
Session: Forty-third, Vienna, 6-15 March
Chairman: Mohammad S. Amirkhizi (Iran)
Membership: 53
Report: E/2000/28

Commission on Population and Development
Session: Thirty-third, New York, 27-30 March
Chairman: Simon B. Arap Bullut (Kenya)
Membership: 47
Report: E/2000/25
Decision: ESC 2000/201 C

Commission on Science and Technology for Development
Session: Did not meet in 2000
Membership: 33
Decisions: ESC 2000/201 C, E & F

Commission for Social Development
Session: Thirty-eighth, New York, 8-17 February and 14 and 17 March
Chairperson: Zola Skweyiya (South Africa)
Membership: 46
Report: E/2000/26 & Corr.1
Decision: ESC 2000/201 C

Commission on the Status of Women
Session: Forty-fourth, New York, 28 February–2 March
Chairperson: Dubravka Šimonovic (Croatia)
Membership: 45
Report: E/2000/27
Decision: ESC 2000/201 C

Commission on Sustainable Development
Sessions: Eighth (second part), New York, 24 April–5 May; ninth (first part), New York, 5 May
Chairman: Juan Mayr Maldonado (Colombia) (eighth session), Bedrich Moldan (Czech Republic) (ninth session)
Membership: 53
Reports: E/2000/29, E/2001/29
Decisions: ESC 2000/201 A, C & D

Statistical Commission
Session: Thirty-first, New York, 29 February–3 March
Chairman: Guest Charumbira (Botswana)
Membership: 24
Report: E/2000/24
Decision: ESC 2000/201 C

Regional commissions

Economic Commission for Africa (ECA)
Session: Did not meet in 2000
Membership: 53

Economic Commission for Europe (ECE)

Session: Fifty-fifth, Geneva, 3-5 May
Chairman: Harald Kreid (Austria)
Membership: 55
Report: E/2000/37

Economic Commission for Latin America and the Caribbean (ECLAC)

Session: Twenty-eighth, Mexico City, 3-7 April
Chairperson: Mexico
Membership: 41 members, 6 associate members
Report: E/2000/40

Economic and Social Commission for Asia and the Pacific (ESCAP)

Session: Fifty-sixth, Bangkok, Thailand, 1-7 June
Chairperson: Kamal Kharrazi (Iran)
Membership: 51 members (52 from 25 July), 9 associate members
Report: E/2000/39

Economic and Social Commission for Western Asia (ESCWA)

Session: Did not meet in 2000
Membership: 13

Standing committees

Commission on Human Settlements

Session: Did not meet in 2000
Membership: 58
Decision: ESC 2000/201 C

Committee on Non-Governmental Organizations

Session: New York, 15-19 May, 12-23 June, 21 and 27 July, 27 September
Chairman: Levent Bilman (Turkey)
Membership: 19
Reports: E/2000/88 (Part I) & (Part I)/Add.1 & (Part II) & (Part II)/ Corr.1 & (Part II)/Add.1,2
Decision: ESC 2000/201 C

Committee for Programme and Coordination (CPC)

Sessions: Fortieth, New York, 2 May (organizational), 5 June– 1 July (first part), 21-29 August (second part)
Chairman: Michel Tommo Monthe (Cameroon)
Membership: 34
Report: A/55/16
Decisions: ESC 2000/201 C, GA 55/307

Expert bodies

Ad Hoc Group of Experts on International Cooperation in Tax Matters

Meeting: Did not meet in 2000
Membership: 25

Committee for Development Policy

Session: Second, New York, 3-7 April
Chairman: Just Faaland (Norway)
Membership: 24
Report: E/2000/33

Committee on Economic, Social and Cultural Rights

Sessions: Twenty-second, twenty-third and twenty-fourth, Geneva, 25 April–12 May, 14 August–1 September, 13 November– 1 December
Chairman: Virginia Bonoan-Dandan (Philippines)
Membership: 18
Report: E/2001/22
Decision: ESC 2000/201 C

Committee on Energy and Natural Resources for Development

Session: Second, New York, 14-25 August
Chairman: Christian M. Katsande (Zimbabwe)
Membership: 24
Report: E/2000/32

Committee of Experts on the Transport of Dangerous Goods

Session: Twenty-first, Geneva, 4-13 December
Chairman: S. Benassai (Italy)
Membership: 23
Report: ST/SG/AC.10/27

United Nations Group of Experts on Geographical Names

Session: Twentieth, New York, 17-28 January
Membership: Representatives of the 22 geographical/linguistic divisions of the Group of Experts
Report: E/2000/49

Ad hoc bodies

Commission on Human Settlements acting as the preparatory committee for the special session of the General Assembly for an overall review and appraisal of the implementation of the Habitat Agenda

Session: First, Nairobi, Kenya, 8-12 May
Chairman: Germán García Durán (Colombia)
Membership: Open to all States
Report: A/55/121

Commission on the Status of Women acting as the preparatory committee for the special session of the General Assembly entitled "Women 2000: gender equality, development and peace for the twenty-first century"

Session: Third (final), New York, 3-17 March and 20 April (first part), 2 June (resumed)
Chairperson: Roselyn Ruth Asumwa Odera (Kenya) (March), Christine Kapalata (United Republic of Tanzania) (April and June)
Membership: Open to all States Members of the United Nations and members of the specialized agencies
Report: A/S-23/2 & Add.1

Administrative Committee on Coordination (ACC)

Sessions: Rome, Italy, 6-7 April; New York, 27-28 October
Chairman: The Secretary-General
Membership: Organizations of the UN system
Reports: ACC/2000/4, ACC/2000/20

Other related bodies

International Research and Training Institute for the Advancement of Women (INSTRAW)

BOARD OF TRUSTEES

Session: Twentieth, Santo Domingo, Dominican Republic, 4-6 April
President: Amaryllis Torres (Philippines)
Membership: 11
Report: E/2000/58
Decision: ESC 2000/201 C

Director of INSTRAW: Eleni Stamiris

Joint United Nations Programme on Human Immunodeficiency Virus/Acquired Immunodeficiency Syndrome (UNAIDS)

PROGRAMME COORDINATING BOARD

Meeting: Ninth, Geneva, 25-26 May
Chairperson: Osmo Soininvaara (Finland)
Membership: 22
Report: UNAIDS/PCB(9)/00.8
Decisions: ESC 2000/201 C & F

Executive Director of the Programme: Dr. Peter Piot

Permanent Forum on Indigenous Issues

Establishment: ESC resolution 2000/22 of 28 July
Membership: 16

United Nations Children's Fund (UNICEF)

EXECUTIVE BOARD

Sessions: First and second regular, New York, 31 January–
3 February, 18-22 September; annual, New York, 22-26 May
Chairman: Anwarul Karim Chowdhury (Bangladesh)
Membership: 36
Report: E/2000/34/Rev.1
Decision: ESC 2000/201 C

Executive Director of UNICEF: Carol Bellamy

United Nations Development Programme (UNDP)/
United Nations Population Fund (UNFPA)

EXECUTIVE BOARD

Sessions: First, second and third regular, New York, 24-28 and
31 January, 3-7 April, 25-29 September; annual, Geneva,
13-23 June
President: Vladimir Galuška (Czech Republic)
Membership: 36
Report: E/2000/35
Decision: ESC 2000/201 C

Administrator of UNDP: Mark Malloch Brown
Associate Administrator: Zéphirin Diabré
Executive Director of UNFPA: Dr. Nafis I. Sadik

United Nations Interregional Crime and Justice
Research Institute (UNICRI)

BOARD OF TRUSTEES

Session: Eleventh, Turin, Italy, 30 November–1 December
President: Adedokun A. Adeyemi (Nigeria)
Membership: 7 (plus 4 ex-officio members)

Director of UNICRI: Alberto Bradanini

United Nations Research Institute for Social Development (UNRISD)

BOARD OF DIRECTORS

Session: Thirty-eighth, Geneva, 3-4 July
Chairperson: Emma Rothschild (United Kingdom)
Membership: 11 (plus 7 ex-officio members)

Director of the Institute: Thandika Mkandawire

World Food Programme (WFP)

EXECUTIVE BOARD

Sessions: First, second and third regular, Rome, Italy, 8-10
February, 17-19 May, 23-26 October; annual, Rome, 22-25
May
President: Mohammad Saeed Nouri-Naeeni (Iran)
Membership: 36
Report: E/2001/36
Decision: ESC 2000/201 C

Executive Director of WFP: Catherine A. Bertini

Conference

Fifteenth United Nations Regional Cartographic Conference
for Asia and the Pacific

Session: Kuala Lumpur, Malaysia, 11-14 April
President: Dato' Abdul Majid Mohamed (Malaysia)
Attendance: 200 representatives and observers of 34 countries
and territories and 12 intergovernmental and international sci-
entific organizations
Report: E/CONF.92/1 (Sales No. E.01.I.2)

Trusteeship Council

Article 86 of the United Nations Charter lays down that the Trusteeship Council shall consist of the following:

Members of the United Nations administering Trust Territories;
Permanent members of the Security Council that do not adminis-
ter Trust Territories;
As many other members elected for a three-year term by the

General Assembly as will ensure that the membership of the
Council is equally divided between United Nations Members
that administer Trust Territories and those that do not.[19]

Members: China, France, Russian Federation, United Kingdom,
United States.

International Court of Justice

Judges of the Court

The International Court of Justice consists of 15 Judges
elected for nine-year terms by the General Assembly and the Security Council.

The following were the Judges of the Court serving in 2000,
listed in the order of precedence:

Judge	Country of nationality	End of term[20]
Gilbert Guillaume, *President*	France	2009
Shi Jiuyong, *Vice-President*	China	2003
Shigeru Oda	Japan	2003
Mohammed Bedjaoui	Algeria	2006
Raymond Ranjeva	Madagascar	2009
Géza Herczegh	Hungary	2003
Carl-August Fleischhauer	Germany	2003
Abdul G. Koroma	Sierra Leone	2003
Vladlen S. Vereshchetin	Russian Federation	2006
Rosalyn Higgins	United Kingdom	2009
Gonzalo Parra-Aranguren	Venezuela	2009
Pieter H. Kooijmans	Netherlands	2006
Francisco Rezek	Brazil	2006
Awn Shawkat Al-Khasawneh	Jordan	2009
Thomas Buergenthal [21]	United States	2006

Registrar: Eduardo Valencia-Ospina (until 5 February), Philippe
Couvreur (from 10 February).

Deputy Registrar: Jean-Jacques Arnaldez.

Chamber of Summary Procedure

Members: Gilbert Guillaume (ex officio), Shi Jiuyong (ex officio),
Géza Herczegh, Abdul G. Koroma, Gonzalo Parra-Aranguren.

Substitute members: Rosalyn Higgins, Awn Shawkat Al-
Khasawneh.

Chamber for Environmental Matters

Members: Gilbert Guillaume (ex officio), Shi Jiuyong (ex officio), Mohammed Bedjaoui, Raymond Ranjeva, Géza Herczegh, Francisco Rezek, Awn Shawkat Al-Khasawneh.

Parties to the Court's Statute

All Members of the United Nations are ipso facto parties to the Statute of the International Court of Justice. Also party to it is the following non-member: Switzerland.

States accepting the compulsory jurisdiction of the Court

Declarations made by the following States, a number with reservations, accepting the Court's compulsory jurisdiction (or made under the Statute of the Permanent Court of International Justice and deemed to be an acceptance of the jurisdiction of the International Court) were in force at the end of 2000:

Australia, Austria, Barbados, Belgium, Botswana, Bulgaria, Cambodia, Cameroon, Canada, Colombia, Costa Rica, Cyprus, Democratic Republic of the Congo, Denmark, Dominican Republic, Egypt, Estonia, Finland, Gambia, Georgia, Greece, Guinea, Guinea-Bissau, Haiti, Honduras, Hungary, India, Japan, Kenya, Lesotho,[22] Liberia, Liechtenstein, Luxembourg, Madagascar, Malawi, Malta, Mauritius, Mexico, Nauru, Netherlands, New Zealand, Nicaragua, Nigeria, Norway, Pakistan, Panama, Paraguay, Philippines, Poland, Portugal, Senegal, Somalia, Spain, Sudan, Suriname, Swaziland, Sweden, Switzerland, Togo, Uganda, United Kingdom, Uruguay, Yugoslavia.

United Nations organs and specialized and related agencies authorized to request advisory opinions from the Court

Authorized by the United Nations Charter to request opinions on any legal question: General Assembly, Security Council.
Authorized by the General Assembly in accordance with the Charter to request opinions on legal questions arising within the scope of their activities: Economic and Social Council, Trusteeship Council, Interim Committee of the General Assembly, ILO, FAO, UNESCO, ICAO, WHO, World Bank, IFC, IDA, IMF, ITU, WMO, IMO, WIPO, IFAD, UNIDO, IAEA.

Committees of the Court

BUDGETARY AND ADMINISTRATIVE COMMITTEE
Members: Gilbert Guillaume (ex officio) (Chair), Shi Jiuyong (ex officio), Mohammed Bedjaoui, Raymond Ranjeva, Carl-August Fleischhauer, Vladlen S. Vereshchetin, Pieter H. Kooijmans.

COMMITTEE ON THE COURT'S MUSEUM
Members: Pieter H. Kooijmans (Chair), Shigeru Oda, Raymond Ranjeva, Vladlen S. Vereshchetin.

COMMITTEE ON RELATIONS
Members: Gonzalo Parra-Aranguren (Chair), Géza Herczegh, Francisco Rezek, Awn Shawkat Al-Khasawneh.

COMPUTERIZATION COMMITTEE
Members: Rosalyn Higgins (Chair); open to all interested members of the Court.

LIBRARY COMMITTEE
Members: Abdul G. Koroma (Chair), Rosalyn Higgins, Pieter H. Kooijmans, Francisco Rezek.

RULES COMMITTEE
Members: Carl-August Fleischhauer (Chair), Shigeru Oda, Mohammed Bedjaoui, Géza Herczegh, Abdul G. Koroma, Rosalyn Higgins, Francisco Rezek, Thomas Buergenthal.

Other United Nations–related bodies

The following bodies are not subsidiary to any principal organ of the United Nations but were established by an international treaty instrument or arrangement sponsored by the United Nations and are thus related to the Organization and its work. These bodies, often referred to as "treaty organs", are serviced by the United Nations Secretariat and may be financed in part or wholly from the Organization's regular budget, as authorized by the General Assembly, to which most of them report annually.

Commission against Apartheid in Sports
Session: Has not met since 1992
Membership: 15

Committee on the Elimination of Discrimination against Women (CEDAW)
Sessions: Twenty-second, New York, 17 January–4 February; twenty-third, New York, 12-30 June
Chairperson: Aída González Martínez (Mexico)
Membership: 23
Report: A/55/38

Committee on the Elimination of Racial Discrimination (CERD)
Sessions: Fifty-sixth, Geneva, 6-24 March; fifty-seventh, Geneva, 31 July–25 August
Chairman: Michael E. Sherifis (Cyprus)
Membership: 18
Report: A/55/18

Committee on the Rights of the Child
Sessions: Twenty-third, twenty-fourth and twenty-fifth, Geneva, 10-28 January, 15 May–2 June, 18 September–6 October
Chairperson: Nafsiah Mboi (Indonesia)

Membership: 10
Reports: A/55/41, CRC/C/94, CRC/C/97, CRC/C/100

Committee against Torture
Sessions: Twenty-fourth, Geneva, 1-19 May; twenty-fifth, Geneva, 13-24 November
Chairman: Peter Burns (Canada)
Membership: 10
Reports: A/55/44, A/56/44

Conference on Disarmament
Meetings: Geneva, 17 January–24 March, 22 May–7 July, 7 August–22 September
President: Austria, Bangladesh, Belarus, Belgium, Brazil, Bulgaria (successively)
Membership: 61
Report: A/55/27

Human Rights Committee
Sessions: Sixty-eighth, New York, 13-31 March; sixty-ninth, Geneva, 10-28 July; seventieth, Geneva, 16 October–3 November
Chairperson: Cecilia Medina Quiroga (Chile)
Membership: 18
Reports: A/55/40, vol. I, A/56/40, vol. I

International Narcotics Control Board (INCB)
Sessions: Sixty-eighth and sixty-ninth, Vienna, 15-26 May and 30 October–16 November
President: Hamid Ghodse (Iran)
Membership: 13
Report: E/INCB/2000/1

Principal members of the United Nations Secretariat

(as at 31 December 2000)

Secretariat

The Secretary-General: Kofi A. Annan
Deputy Secretary-General: Louise Fréchette

Executive Office of the Secretary-General

Under-Secretary-General, Chef de Cabinet: S. Iqbal Riza
Under-Secretary-General, Special Adviser to the Secretary-General and Rector of the University for Peace: Maurice F. Strong
Assistant Secretary-General, Special Adviser: John Ruggie
Assistant Secretary-General for External Relations: Gillian M. Sorensen

Office of Internal Oversight Services

Under-Secretary-General: Dileep Nair

Office of Legal Affairs

Under-Secretary-General, Legal Counsel: Hans Corell
Assistant Secretary-General: Ralph Zacklin

Department of Political Affairs

Under-Secretary-General: Kieran Prendergast
Under-Secretary-General, Adviser for Special Assignments in Africa: Ibrahim A. Gambari
Assistant Secretaries-General: Ibrahima Fall, Danilo Türk

Department for Disarmament Affairs

Under-Secretary-General: Jayantha Dhanapala

Department of Peacekeeping Operations

Under-Secretary-General: Jean-Marie Guéhenno
Assistant Secretaries-General: Hédi Annabi, Michael Sheehan

Office for the Coordination of Humanitarian Affairs

Assistant Secretary-General, Emergency Relief Coordinator, a.i: Carolyn McAskie

Department of Economic and Social Affairs

Under-Secretary-General: Nitin Desai
Assistant Secretaries-General: Angela E. V. King, Patrizio M. Civili

Department of General Assembly Affairs and Conference Services

Under-Secretary-General: Yongjian Jin
Assistant Secretary-General: Federico Riesco-Quintana

Department of Public Information

Under-Secretary-General: Kensaku Hogen

Department of Management

Under-Secretary-General: Joseph E. Connor

OFFICE OF PROGRAMME PLANNING, BUDGET AND ACCOUNTS
Assistant Secretary-General, Controller: Jean-Pierre Halbwachs

OFFICE OF HUMAN RESOURCES MANAGEMENT
Assistant Secretary-General: Rafiah Salim

OFFICE OF CENTRAL SUPPORT SERVICES
Assistant Secretary-General: Toshiyuki Niwa

Office of the Iraq Programme

Under-Secretary-General, Executive Director: Benon V. Sevan
Assistant Secretary-General, Humanitarian Coordinator: Tun Myat

Economic Commission for Africa

Under-Secretary-General, Executive Secretary: K. Y. Amoako

Economic Commission for Europe

Under-Secretary-General, Executive Secretary: Danuta Hübner

Economic Commission for Latin America and the Caribbean

Under-Secretary-General, Executive Secretary: Jose Antonio Ocampo

Economic and Social Commission for Asia and the Pacific

Under-Secretary-General, Executive Secretary: Hak-Su Kim

Economic and Social Commission for Western Asia

Under-Secretary-General, Executive Secretary: Vacant

United Nations Centre for Human Settlements (Habitat)

Assistant Secretary-General, Executive Director: Anna Kajumulo Tibaijuka

United Nations Office at Geneva

Under-Secretary-General, Director-General of the United Nations Office at Geneva: Vladimir Petrovsky

Office of the High Commissioner for Human Rights

Under-Secretary-General, High Commissioner: Mary Robinson
Assistant Secretary-General, Deputy High Commissioner: Bertrand Gangapersaud Ramcharan

United Nations Office at Vienna

Under-Secretary-General, Director-General of the United Nations Office at Vienna and Executive Director of the United Nations Office for Drug Control and Crime Prevention: Giuseppe Arlacchi

International Court of Justice Registry

Assistant Secretary-General, Registrar: Philippe Couvreur

Secretariats of subsidiary organs, special representatives and other related bodies

International Trade Centre UNCTAD/WTO

Executive Director: J. Denis Bélisle

Office of the Secretary-General in Afghanistan and Pakistan

Under-Secretary-General, Special Envoy of the Secretary-General for Afghanistan: Lakhdar Brahimi
Assistant Secretary-General, Head of the Special Mission in Afghanistan: Francesc Vendrell

Office of the Special Adviser to the Secretary-General on International Assistance to Colombia

Under-Secretary-General, Special Adviser: Jan Egeland

Office of the Special Envoy of the Secretary-General for Myanmar

Under-Secretary-General, Special Envoy: Ismail Razali

Office of the Special Representative of the Secretary-General for Children and Armed Conflict

Under-Secretary-General, Special Representative: Olara A. Otunnu

Office of the Special Representative of the Secretary-General for the Great Lakes Region

Assistant Secretary-General, Special Representative: Berhanu Dinka

Office of the Special Representative of the Secretary-General for Tajikistan

Assistant Secretary-General, Special Representative: Ivo Petrov

Office of the United Nations High Commissioner for Refugees

Under-Secretary-General, High Commissioner: Sadako Ogata

Office of the United Nations Security Coordinator

Under-Secretary-General, United Nations Security Coordinator: Benon V. Sevan

Regional Coordinator for the Balkans

Under-Secretaries-General, Special Envoys of the Secretary-General: Carl Bildt, Eduard Kukan

Special Adviser to the Secretary-General on Africa

Under-Secretary-General, Special Adviser: Mohamed Sahnoun

Special Adviser to the Secretary-General on European Issues

Under-Secretary-General, Special Adviser: Jean-Bernard Merimée

Special Assignments in support of the Secretary-General's preventive and peacemaking efforts

Under-Secretary-General: Lakhdar Brahimi

Special Envoy of the Secretary-General

Under-Secretary-General, Special Envoy: Yuli Vorontsov

United Nations Children's Fund

Under-Secretary-General, Executive Director: Carol Bellamy
Assistant Secretaries-General, Deputy Executive Directors: Kul Gautam, André Roberfroid, Karin Sham Poo

United Nations Compensation Commission

Assistant Secretary-General, Executive Secretary: Rolf Goran Knutsson

United Nations Conference on Trade and Development

Under-Secretary-General, Secretary-General of the Conference: Rubens Ricupero
Assistant Secretary-General, Deputy Secretary-General of the Conference: Carlos Fortin Cabezas

United Nations Development Programme

Administrator: Mark Malloch Brown
Under-Secretary-General, Associate Administrator: Zéphirin Diabré
Assistant Secretary-General, Special Adviser to the Administrator: Richard Jolly
Assistant Administrator and Director, Bureau of Management: Jan Mattson
Assistant Administrator and Director, Bureau for Development Policy: Eimi Watanabe
Assistant Administrator and Regional Director, UNDP Africa: Abdoulie Janneh
Assistant Administrator and Regional Director, UNDP Arab States: Rima Khalaf Hunaidi
Assistant Administrator and Regional Director, UNDP Asia and the Pacific: Nay Htun
Assistant Administrator and Regional Director, UNDP Europe and the Commonwealth of Independent States: Anton Kruiderink
Assistant Administrator and Regional Director, UNDP Latin America and the Caribbean: Elena Martinez

United Nations Disengagement Observer Force

Assistant Secretary-General, Force Commander: Major-General Bo Wranker

United Nations Environment Programme

Under-Secretary-General, Executive Director: Klaus Töpfer
Assistant Secretary-General, Deputy Executive Director: Shafqat S. Kakakhel

United Nations Institute for Training and Research

Executive Director: Marcel A. Boisard

United Nations Interim Administration Mission in Kosovo

Under-Secretary-General, Special Representative of the Secretary-General: Bernard Kouchner
Assistant Secretary-General, Principal Deputy Special Representative of the Secretary-General: James Peter Covey
Assistant Secretaries-General, Deputy Special Representatives of the Secretary-General: Tom Koenigs, Dennis R. McNamara

United Nations Interim Force in Lebanon

Assistant Secretary-General, Force Commander: Major-General Seth Kofi Obeng

United Nations Iraq-Kuwait Observation Mission

Assistant Secretary-General, Force Commander: Major-General John Augustine Vize

United Nations Joint Staff Pension Fund

Assistant Secretary-General, Chief Executive Officer: Raymond Gieri

United Nations Military Observer Group in India and Pakistan

Chief Military Observer: Major-General Manuel Saavedra

United Nations Mission in Bosnia and Herzegovina

Under-Secretary-General, Special Representative of the Secretary-General and Coordinator of United Nations Operations in Bosnia and Herzegovina: Jacques Paul Klein
Commissioner of the United Nations International Police Task Force: Vincent Coeurderoy

United Nations Mission in Ethiopia and Eritrea

Under-Secretary-General, Special Representative of the Secretary-General: Legwaila Joseph Legwaila
Assistant Secretaries-General, Deputy Special Representatives of the Secretary-General: Cheikh Tidiane Gaye, Ian Martin
Force Commander: Major-General Patrick Cammaert

United Nations Mission of Observers in Prevlaka

Chief Military Observer: Lieutenant-Colonel Graeme Williams

United Nations Mission for the Referendum in Western Sahara

Under-Secretary-General, Personal Envoy of the Secretary-General: James A. Baker III
Under-Secretary-General, Special Representative of the Secretary-General: William Eagleton
Force Commander: Brigadier-General Claude Buze

United Nations Mission in Sierra Leone

Under-Secretary-General, Special Representative of the Secretary-General and Head of Mission: Oluyemi Adeniji
Assistant Secretary-General, Deputy Special Representative of the Secretary-General: Behrooz Sadry
Assistant Secretary-General, Force Commander: Lieutenant-General Daniel Ishmael Opande

United Nations Monitoring, Verification and Inspection Commission

Executive Chairman: Hans Blix

United Nations Observer Mission in Georgia

Assistant Secretary-General, Special Representative of the Secretary-General and Head of Mission: Dieter Boden
Chief Military Observer: Major-General Anis Ahmed Bajwa

United Nations Office for Project Services

Assistant Secretary-General, Executive Director: Reinhart Helmke

United Nations Organization Mission in the Democratic Republic of the Congo

Under-Secretary-General, Special Representative of the Secretary-General and Head of Mission: Kamel Morjane
Force Commander: Major-General Mountaga Diallo

United Nations Peacekeeping Force in Cyprus

Special Adviser to the Secretary-General on Cyprus: Alvaro de Soto
Force Commander: Major-General Victory Rana

United Nations Population Fund

Under-Secretary-General, Executive Director: Dr. Nafis I. Sadik
Deputy Executive Director, Policy and Administration: Kunio Waki
Deputy Executive Director, Programme: Kerstin Trone

United Nations Relief and Works Agency for Palestine Refugees in the Near East

Under-Secretary-General, Commissioner-General: Peter Hansen
Assistant Secretary-General, Deputy Commissioner-General: Dr. Mohamed Abdelmoumène

United Nations Special Coordinator for the Middle East Peace Process and Personal Representative of the Secretary-General to the Palestine Liberation Organization and the Palestine Authority

Under-Secretary-General, Special Coordinator and Personal Representative of the Secretary-General: Terje Roed-Larsen

United Nations Transitional Administration in East Timor

Under-Secretary-General, Special Representative of the Secretary-General for East Timor: Jamsheed K. A. Marker
Under-Secretary-General, Special Representative of the Secretary-General and Transitional Administrator: Sergio Vieira de Mello
Assistant Secretary-General, Deputy Special Representative of the Secretary-General for Governance and Public Administration: Jean-Christian Cady
Assistant Secretary-General, Deputy Special Representative of the Secretary-General for Humanitarian Assistance and Emergency Rehabilitation: Akira Takahashi
Assistant Secretary-General, Force Commander: Lieutenant-General Boonsrang Niumpradit
Assistant Secretary-General, Chief of Staff: Parameswaran Nagalingam

United Nations Truce Supervision Organization

Assistant Secretary-General, Chief of Staff: Major-General Franco Ganguzza

United Nations University

Under-Secretary-General, Rector: Johannes A. van Ginkel
Acting Director, World Institute for Development Economics Research: Matti Pohjola

---

On 31 December 2000, the total number of staff of the United Nations Secretariat with continuous service or expected service of a year or more was 14,312. Of these, 5,033 were in the Professional and higher categories, 820 were experts (200-series Project Personnel staff) and 8,459 were in the General Service and related categories.

---

[1]On 5 and 26 June 2000 (dec. S-23/12 and S-24/12), the Assembly decided that the President at its fifty-fourth session would serve in the same capacity at the twenty-third and twenty-fourth special sessions.

[2]On 5 and 26 June 2000 (dec. S-23/13 and S-24/13), the Assembly decided that the Vice-Presidents at its fifty-fourth session would serve in the same capacity at the twenty-third and twenty-fourth special sessions.

[3]Elected on 5 September 2000 (dec. 55/302).

[4]Elected on 5 September 2000 (dec. 55/304).

[5]The only Main Committees to meet at the resumed session.

[6]On 5 and 26 June 2000 (dec. S-23/14 and S-24/14), the Assembly decided that the Chairpersons of the Main Committees of the fifty-fourth session would serve in the same capacity at the twenty-third and twenty-fourth special sessions. In the absence of the Second Committee Chairperson at the twenty-third special session, a Vice-Chairperson served as Acting Chairperson; in the absence of the Third Committee Chairperson at the twenty-fourth special session, a Vice-Chairperson served as Acting Chairperson.

[7]Elected by the Assembly on 5 June 2000 (dec. S-23/15); other officers elected by the Ad Hoc Committee.

[8]Elected by the Assembly on 26 June 2000 (dec. S-24/15); other officers elected by the Ad Hoc Committee.

[9]Chairmen elected by the Committees; announced by the Assembly President on 5 September 2000 (dec. 55/303).

[10]On 5 and 26 June 2000 (dec. S-23/11 and S-24/11), the Assembly decided that the Credentials Committee for the twenty-third and twenty-fourth special sessions would have the same composition as that for the fifty-fourth session.

[11]Appointed on 5 September 2000 (dec. 55/301).

[12]Appointed on 1 February 2000 (dec. 54/312 B) to fill the vacancy created by the resignation of Fumiaki Toya (Japan).

[13]Appointed on 10 May 2000 (dec. 54/313 B) to fill the vacancy created by the resignation of David Etuket (Uganda).

[14]Resigned in August 2000; Wu Gang (China) was appointed on 16 October (dec. 55/309 A) to fill the resultant vacancy.

[15]Mandate expired on 15 May 2000.

[16]Mandate expired on 15 March 2000.

[17]Mandate expired on 15 February 2000.

[18]Established on 31 July 2000.

[19]During 2000, no Member of the United Nations was an administering member of the Trusteeship Council, while five permanent members of the Security Council continued as non-administering members.

[20]Term expires on 5 February of the year indicated.

[21]Elected by the General Assembly (dec. 54/310 B) and the Security Council on 2 March 2000 to fill the vacancy created by the resignation on 29 February of Stephen M. Schwebel (United States).

[22]Declaration deposited on 6 September 2000.

Appendix IV

Agendas of United Nations principal organs in 2000

This appendix lists the items on the agendas of the General Assembly, the Security Council and the Economic and Social Council during 2000. For the Assembly, the column headed "Allocation" indicates the assignment of each item to plenary meetings or committees.

Agenda item titles have been shortened by omitting mention of reports, if any, following the subject of the item. Where the subject matter of an item is not apparent from its title, the subject is identified in square brackets; this is not part of the title.

General Assembly

Agenda items considered at the resumed fifty-fourth session
(1 February–5 September 2000)

Item No.	*Title*	*Allocation*
2.	Minute of silent prayer or meditation.	Plenary
8.	Adoption of the agenda and organization of work.	Plenary
15.	Elections to fill vacancies in principal organs:	
	(c) Election of a member of the International Court of Justice.	Plenary
17.	Appointments to fill vacancies in subsidiary organs and other appointments:	
	(a) Appointment of members of the Advisory Committee on Administrative and Budgetary Questions;	[1]
	(b) Appointment of members of the Committee on Contributions;	5th
	(f) Appointment of a member of the United Nations Staff Pension Committee;	5th
	(h) Appointment of members of the Joint Inspection Unit;	Plenary
	(i) Appointment of the Under-Secretary-General for Internal Oversight Services.	Plenary
20.	Strengthening of the coordination of humanitarian and disaster relief assistance of the United Nations, including special economic assistance:	
	(b) Special economic assistance to individual countries or regions.	Plenary
22.	Building a peaceful and better world through sport and the Olympic ideal.	Plenary
38.	Question of equitable representation on and increase in the membership of the Security Council and related matters.	Plenary
49.	United Nations reform: measures and proposals:	
	(a) United Nations reform: measures and proposals;	Plenary
	(b) The Millennium Assembly of the United Nations.	Plenary
59.	Strengthening of the United Nations system.	Plenary
60.	Revitalization of the work of the General Assembly.	Plenary
61.	Restructuring and revitalization of the United Nations in the economic, social and related fields.	Plenary
63.	Question of Cyprus.	[2]
90.	Comprehensive review of the whole question of peacekeeping operations in all their aspects.	4th
97.	Macroeconomic policy questions:	
	(a) High-level international intergovernmental consideration of financing for development.	[3]
99.	Sustainable development and international economic cooperation:	
	(g) Renewal of the dialogue on strengthening international economic cooperation for development through partnership.	[3]
106.	Social development, including questions relating to the world social situation and to youth, ageing, disabled persons and the family.	Plenary[4]
110.	Implementation of the outcome of the Fourth World Conference on Women.	[5]
116.	Human rights questions:	
	(a) Implementation of human rights instruments.	[5]
117.	Financial reports and audited financial statements, and reports of the Board of Auditors.	5th
118.	Review of the efficiency of the administrative and financial functioning of the United Nations.	5th
119.	Programme budget for the biennium 1998-1999.	5th

Agenda of the twenty-third special session
(5-10 June 2000)

Item No.	Title	Allocation
1.	Opening of the session by the Chairman of the delegation of Namibia.	Plenary
2.	Minute of silent prayer or meditation.	Plenary
3.	Credentials of representatives to the twenty-third special session of the General Assembly:	
	(a) Appointment of the members of the Credentials Committee;	Plenary
	(b) Report of the Credentials Committee.	Plenary
4.	Election of the President.	Plenary
5.	Report of the Commission on the Status of Women acting as the preparatory committee for the twenty-third special session of the General Assembly entitled "Women 2000: gender equality, development and peace for the twenty-first century".	Plenary
6.	Organization of the session.	Plenary
7.	Adoption of the agenda.	Plenary
8.	Review and appraisal of progress made in the implementation of the twelve critical areas of concern in the Beijing Platform for Action.	Plenary[7]
9.	Further actions and initiatives for overcoming obstacles to the implementation of the Beijing Platform for Action.	Plenary[7]
10.	Adoption of the final documents.	Plenary

Agenda of the twenty-fourth special session
(26 June–1 July 2000)

Item No.	Title	Allocation
1.	Opening of the session by the Chairman of the delegation of Namibia.	Plenary
2.	Minute of silent prayer or meditation.	Plenary
3.	Credentials of representatives to the twenty-fourth special session of the General Assembly:	
	(a) Appointment of the members of the Credentials Committee;	Plenary
	(b) Report of the Credentials Committee.	Plenary
4.	Election of the President.	Plenary
5.	Report of the Preparatory Committee for the twenty-fourth special session of the General Assembly entitled "World Summit for Social Development and beyond: achieving social development for all in a globalizing world".	Plenary
6.	Organization of the session.	Plenary
7.	Adoption of the agenda.	Plenary
8.	Proposals for further initiatives for social development:	
	(a) Review and appraisal of progress since the World Summit for Social Development;	Plenary[8]
	(b) Proposals for further initiatives for the full implementation of the Copenhagen Declaration on Social Development and Programme of Action of the World Summit for Social Development.	Plenary[8]
9.	Adoption of the final document.	Plenary

Agenda of the fifty-fifth session
(first part, 5 September–23 December 2000)

Item No.	Title	Allocation
1.	Opening of the session by the Chairman of the delegation of Namibia.	Plenary
2.	Minute of silent prayer or meditation.	Plenary
3.	Credentials of representatives to the fifty-fifth session of the General Assembly:	
	(a) Appointment of the members of the Credentials Committee;	Plenary
	(b) Report of the Credentials Committee.	Plenary
4.	Election of the President of the General Assembly.	Plenary
5.	Election of the officers of the Main Committees.	Plenary
6.	Election of the Vice-Presidents of the General Assembly.	Plenary
7.	Notification by the Secretary-General under Article 12, paragraph 2, of the Charter of the United Nations.	Plenary
8.	Adoption of the agenda and organization of work.	Plenary

Item No.	Title	Allocation
9.	General debate.	Plenary
10.	Report of the Secretary-General on the work of the Organization.	Plenary
11.	Report of the Security Council.	Plenary
12.	Report of the Economic and Social Council.	Plenary, 4th, 2nd, 3rd, 5th
13.	Report of the International Court of Justice.	Plenary
14.	Report of the International Atomic Energy Agency.	Plenary
15.	Elections to fill vacancies in principal organs:	
	(a) Election of five non-permanent members of the Security Council;	Plenary
	(b) Election of eighteen members of the Economic and Social Council.	Plenary
16.	Elections to fill vacancies in subsidiary organs and other elections:	
	(a) Election of seven members of the Committee for Programme and Coordination;	Plenary
	(b) Election of seventeen members of the United Nations Commission on International Trade Law;	Plenary
	(c) Election of the United Nations High Commissioner for Refugees.	Plenary
17.	Appointments to fill vacancies in subsidiary organs and other appointments:	
	(a) Appointment of members of the Advisory Committee on Administrative and Budgetary Questions;	5th
	(b) Appointment of members of the Committee on Contributions;	5th
	(c) Appointment of a member of the Board of Auditors;	5th
	(d) Confirmation of the appointment of members of the Investments Committee;	5th
	(e) Appointment of members of the United Nations Administrative Tribunal;	5th
	(f) Appointment of members and alternate members of the United Nations Staff Pension Committee;	5th
	(g) Appointment of members of the International Civil Service Commission;	5th
	(h) Appointment of members of the Committee on Conferences;	Plenary
	(i) Appointment of the members of the Consultative Committee on the United Nations Development Fund for Women;	Plenary
	(j) Approval of the appointment of the United Nations High Commissioner for Human Rights.	Plenary
18.	Implementation of the Declaration on the Granting of Independence to Colonial Countries and Peoples.	Plenary, 4th
19.	Admission of new Members to the United Nations.	Plenary
20.	Strengthening of the coordination of humanitarian and disaster relief assistance of the United Nations, including special economic assistance:	
	(a) Strengthening of the coordination of emergency humanitarian assistance of the United Nations;	Plenary
	(b) Special economic assistance to individual countries or regions;	Plenary
	(c) Assistance to the Palestinian people;	Plenary
	(d) Emergency international assistance for peace, normalcy and reconstruction of war-stricken Afghanistan.	Plenary
21.	Cooperation between the United Nations and the Organization of American States.	Plenary
22.	Cooperation between the United Nations and the Asian-African Legal Consultative Committee.	Plenary
23.	Cooperation between the United Nations and the Caribbean Community.	Plenary
24.	Cooperation between the United Nations and the Organization of the Islamic Conference.	Plenary
25.	Cooperation between the United Nations and the League of Arab States.	Plenary
26.	Cooperation between the United Nations and the Inter-Parliamentary Union.	Plenary
27.	Cooperation between the United Nations and the Organization of African Unity.	Plenary
28.	Cooperation between the United Nations and the Economic Cooperation Organization.	Plenary
29.	Cooperation between the United Nations and the Organization for Security and Cooperation in Europe.	Plenary
30.	Implementation of the United Nations New Agenda for the Development of Africa in the 1990s, including measures and recommendations agreed upon at its mid-term review.	Plenary
31.	Elimination of coercive economic measures as a means of political and economic compulsion.	Plenary
32.	United Nations Year of Dialogue among Civilizations.	Plenary
33.	Culture of peace.	Plenary
34.	Oceans and the law of the sea:	
	(a) Consideration of elements relating to oceans and seas, including improvement of coordination and cooperation;	Plenary
	(b) Large-scale pelagic drift-net fishing, unauthorized fishing in zones of national jurisdiction and on the high seas, fisheries by-catch and discards, and other developments.	Plenary
35.	Necessity of ending the economic, commercial and financial embargo imposed by the United States of America against Cuba.	Plenary

Item No.	Title	Allocation
36.	Bethlehem 2000.	Plenary
37.	Implementation of the outcome of the World Summit for Social Development and of the special session of the General Assembly in this regard.	Plenary
38.	Zone of peace and cooperation of the South Atlantic.	Plenary
39.	Support by the United Nations system of the efforts of Governments to promote and consolidate new or restored democracies.	Plenary
40.	The situation in the Middle East.	
41.	Question of Palestine.	Plenary
42.	Special session of the General Assembly in 2001 for follow-up to the World Summit for Children.	Plenary
43.	The situation in Central America: procedures for the establishment of a firm and lasting peace and progress in fashioning a region of peace, freedom, democracy and development.	Plenary
44.	Global implications of the year 2000 date conversion problem of computers.	Plenary
45.	The situation in Bosnia and Herzegovina.	Plenary
46.	The situation in Afghanistan and its implications for international peace and security.	Plenary
47.	Assistance in mine action.	Plenary
48.	The situation of democracy and human rights in Haiti.	Plenary
49.	The situation in East Timor during its transition to independence.	Plenary
50.	Causes of conflict and the promotion of durable peace and sustainable development in Africa.	Plenary
51.	Question of the Falkland Islands (Malvinas).	Plenary, 4th
52.	Report of the International Tribunal for the Prosecution of Persons Responsible for Serious Violations of International Humanitarian Law Committed in the Territory of the Former Yugoslavia since 1991.	Plenary
53.	Report of the International Criminal Tribunal for the Prosecution of Persons Responsible for Genocide and Other Serious Violations of International Humanitarian Law Committed in the Territory of Rwanda and Rwandan Citizens Responsible for Genocide and Other Such Violations Committed in the Territory of Neighbouring States between 1 January and 31 December 1994.	Plenary
54.	Declaration of the Assembly of Heads of State and Government of the Organization of African Unity on the aerial and naval military attack against the Socialist People's Libyan Arab Jamahiriya by the present United States Administration in April 1986.	Plenary
55.	Armed Israeli aggression against the Iraqi nuclear installations and its grave consequences for the established international system concerning the peaceful uses of nuclear energy, the non-proliferation of nuclear weapons and international peace and security.	Plenary
56.	Consequences of the Iraqi occupation of and aggression against Kuwait.	Plenary
57.	Implementation of the resolutions of the United Nations.	Plenary
58.	Launching of global negotiations on international economic cooperation for development.	Plenary
59.	Question of equitable representation on and increase in the membership of the Security Council and related matters.	Plenary
60.	United Nations reform: measures and proposals:	
	(a) United Nations reform: measures and proposals;	Plenary
	(b) The Millennium Assembly of the United Nations.	Plenary
61.	Strengthening of the United Nations system.	Plenary
62.	Revitalization of the work of the General Assembly.	Plenary
63.	Restructuring and revitalization of the United Nations in the economic, social and related fields.	Plenary [9]
64.	Question of Cyprus.	
65.	Reduction of military budgets.	1st
66.	Development of good-neighbourly relations among Balkan States.	1st
67.	Maintenance of international security:	
	(a) Prevention of the violent disintegration of States;	1st
	(b) Stability and development of South-Eastern Europe.	1st
68.	Developments in the field of information and telecommunications in the context of international security.	1st
69.	Role of science and technology in the context of international security and disarmament.	1st
70.	Establishment of a nuclear-weapon-free zone in the region of the Middle East.	1st
71.	Conclusion of effective international arrangements to assure non-nuclear-weapon States against the use or threat of use of nuclear weapons.	1st
72.	Prevention of an arms race in outer space.	1st
73.	General and complete disarmament:	
	(a) Notification of nuclear tests;	1st

Item No.		Title	Allocation
	(b)	Establishment of a nuclear-weapon-free zone in Central Asia;	1st
	(c)	Mongolia's international security and nuclear-weapon-free status;	1st
	(d)	Measures to uphold the authority of the 1925 Geneva Protocol;	1st
	(e)	Preservation of and compliance with the Treaty on the Limitation of Anti-Ballistic Missile Systems;	1st
	(f)	Implementation of the Convention on the Prohibition of the Use, Stockpiling, Production and Transfer of Anti-personnel Mines and on Their Destruction;	1st
	(g)	Implementation of the Convention on the Prohibition of the Development, Production, Stockpiling and Use of Chemical Weapons and on Their Destruction;	1st
	(h)	Missiles;	1st
	(i)	Towards a nuclear-weapon-free world: the need for a new agenda;	1st
	(j)	Consolidation of peace through practical disarmament measures;	1st
	(k)	Transparency in armaments;	1st
	(l)	Assistance to States for curbing the illicit traffic in small arms and collecting them;	1st
	(m)	Reducing nuclear danger;	1st
	(n)	Nuclear-weapon-free southern hemisphere and adjacent areas;	1st
	(o)	Conventional arms control at the regional and subregional levels;	1st
	(p)	Regional disarmament;	1st
	(q)	Nuclear disarmament;	1st
	(r)	Follow-up to the advisory opinion of the International Court of Justice on the *Legality of the Threat or Use of Nuclear Weapons;*	1st
	(s)	Illicit traffic in small arms;	1st
	(t)	Observance of environmental norms in the drafting and implementation of agreements on disarmament and arms control;	1st
	(u)	Relationship between disarmament and development;	1st
	(v)	Convening of the fourth special session of the General Assembly devoted to disarmament;	1st
	(w)	Small arms.	1st
74.		Review and implementation of the Concluding Document of the Twelfth Special Session of the General Assembly:	
	(a)	Regional confidence-building measures: activities of the United Nations Standing Advisory Committee on Security Questions in Central Africa;	1st
	(b)	United Nations Regional Centre for Peace and Disarmament in Africa;	1st
	(c)	United Nations Regional Centre for Peace and Disarmament in Asia and the Pacific;	1st
	(d)	Convention on the Prohibition of the Use of Nuclear Weapons;	1st
	(e)	United Nations regional centres for peace and disarmament;	1st
	(f)	United Nations Regional Centre for Peace, Disarmament and Development in Latin America and the Caribbean;	1st
	(g)	United Nations Disarmament Information Programme;	1st
	(h)	United Nations disarmament fellowship, training and advisory services.	1st
75.		Review of the implementation of the recommendations and decisions adopted by the General Assembly at its tenth special session:	
	(a)	Report of the Disarmament Commission;	1st
	(b)	Report of the Conference on Disarmament;	1st
	(c)	Advisory Board on Disarmament Matters;	1st
	(d)	United Nations Institute for Disarmament Research;	1st
	(e)	Disarmament Week.	1st
76.		The risk of nuclear proliferation in the Middle East.	1st
77.		Convention on Prohibitions or Restrictions on the Use of Certain Conventional Weapons Which May Be Deemed to Be Excessively Injurious or to Have Indiscriminate Effects.	1st
78.		Strengthening of security and cooperation in the Mediterranean region.	1st
79.		Consolidation of the regime established by the Treaty for the Prohibition of Nuclear Weapons in Latin America and the Caribbean (Treaty of Tlatelolco).	1st
80.		Convention on the Prohibition of the Development, Production and Stockpiling of Bacteriological (Biological) and Toxin Weapons and on Their Destruction.	1st
81.		Comprehensive Nuclear-Test-Ban Treaty.	1st
82.		Effects of atomic radiation.	4th
83.		International cooperation in the peaceful uses of outer space.	4th

Item No.	Title	Allocation
84.	United Nations Relief and Works Agency for Palestine Refugees in the Near East.	4th
85.	Report of the Special Committee to Investigate Israeli Practices Affecting the Human Rights of the Palestinian People and Other Arabs of the Occupied Territories.	4th
86.	Comprehensive review of the whole question of peacekeeping operations in all their aspects.	4th
87.	Questions relating to information.	4th
88.	Information from Non-Self-Governing Territories transmitted under Article 73 *e* of the Charter of the United Nations.	4th
89.	Economic and other activities which affect the interests of the peoples of the Non-Self-Governing Territories.	4th
90.	Implementation of the Declaration on the Granting of Independence to Colonial Countries and Peoples by the specialized agencies and the international institutions associated with the United Nations.	4th
91.	Offers by Member States of study and training facilities for inhabitants of Non-Self-Governing Territories.	4th
92.	Macroeconomic policy questions:	
	(a) Trade and development;	2nd
	(b) Commodities;	2nd
	(c) External debt crisis and development;	2nd
	(d) Science and technology for development;	2nd
	(e) Financing of development, including net transfer of resources between developing and developed countries.	2nd
93.	Sectoral policy questions:	
	(a) Industrial development cooperation;	2nd
	(b) Business and development.	2nd
94.	Sustainable development and international economic cooperation:	
	(a) Implementation of the commitments and policies agreed upon in the Declaration on International Economic Cooperation, in particular the Revitalization of Economic Growth and Development of the Developing Countries, and implementation of the International Development Strategy for the Fourth United Nations Development Decade;	2nd
	(b) Integration of the economies in transition into the world economy;	2nd
	(c) Cultural development;	2nd
	(d) High-level dialogue on strengthening international economic cooperation for development through partnership;	2nd
	(e) Implementation of the outcome of the United Nations Conference on Human Settlements (Habitat II).	2nd
95.	Environment and sustainable development:	
	(a) Implementation of Agenda 21 and the Programme for the Further Implementation of Agenda 21;	2nd
	(b) Convention on Biological Diversity;	2nd
	(c) Water supply and sanitation;	2nd
	(d) Further implementation of the Programme of Action for the Sustainable Development of Small Island Developing States;	2nd
	(e) Implementation of the United Nations Convention to Combat Desertification in those Countries Experiencing Serious Drought and/or Desertification, particularly in Africa;	2nd
	(f) Promotion of new and renewable sources of energy, including the implementation of the World Solar Programme 1996-2005;	2nd
	(g) Protection of global climate for present and future generations of mankind.	2nd
96.	Operational activities for development.	2nd
97.	Training and research.	2nd
98.	Permanent sovereignty of the Palestinian people in the Occupied Palestinian Territory, including Jerusalem, and of the Arab population in the occupied Syrian Golan over their natural resources.	2nd
99.	Implementation of the first United Nations Decade for the Eradication of Poverty (1997-2006).	2nd
100.	Globalization and interdependence.	2nd
101.	High-level international intergovernmental consideration of financing for development.	2nd
102.	Third United Nations Conference on the Least Developed Countries.	2nd
103.	Social development, including questions relating to the world social situation and to youth, ageing, disabled persons and the family.	3rd
104.	Follow-up to the International Year of Older Persons.	3rd

Item No.	Title	Allocation
105.	Crime prevention and criminal justice.	Plenary, 3rd
106.	International drug control.	3rd
107.	Advancement of women.	3rd
108.	Implementation of the outcome of the Fourth World Conference on Women and of the special session of the General Assembly entitled "Women 2000: gender equality, development and peace for the twenty-first century".	3rd
109.	Report of the United Nations High Commissioner for Refugees, questions relating to refugees, returnees and displaced persons and humanitarian questions.	3rd
110.	Promotion and protection of the rights of children.	3rd
111.	Programme of activities of the International Decade of the World's Indigenous People.	3rd
112.	Elimination of racism and racial discrimination.	3rd
113.	Right of peoples to self-determination.	3rd
114.	Human rights questions:	
	(a) Implementation of human rights instruments;	3rd
	(b) Human rights questions, including alternative approaches for improving the effective enjoyment of human rights and fundamental freedoms;	3rd
	(c) Human rights situations and reports of special rapporteurs and representatives;	3rd
	(d) Comprehensive implementation of and follow-up to the Vienna Declaration and Programme of Action;	3rd
	(e) Report of the United Nations High Commissioner for Human Rights.	3rd
115.	Financial reports and audited financial statements, and reports of the Board of Auditors:	
	(a) United Nations;	5th
	(b) United Nations Development Programme;	5th
	(c) United Nations Children's Fund;	5th
	(d) United Nations Relief and Works Agency for Palestine Refugees in the Near East;	5th
	(e) United Nations Institute for Training and Research;	5th
	(f) Voluntary funds administered by the United Nations High Commissioner for Refugees;	5th
	(g) Fund of the United Nations Environment Programme;	5th
	(h) United Nations Population Fund;	5th
	(i) United Nations Habitat and Human Settlements Foundation;	5th
	(j) Fund of the United Nations International Drug Control Programme;	5th
	(k) United Nations Office for Project Services.	5th
116.	Review of the efficiency of the administrative and financial functioning of the United Nations.	5th
117.	Programme budget for the biennium 2000-2001.	5th
118.	Programme planning.	5th
119.	Improving the financial situation of the United Nations.	5th
120.	Administrative and budgetary coordination of the United Nations with the specialized agencies and the International Atomic Energy Agency.	5th
121.	Pattern of conferences.	5th
122.	Scale of assessments for the apportionment of the expenses of the United Nations.	5th
123.	Human resources management.	5th
124.	United Nations common system.	5th
125.	United Nations pension system.	5th
126.	Report of the Secretary-General on the activities of the Office of Internal Oversight Services.	5th
127.	Financing of the International Tribunal for the Prosecution of Persons Responsible for Serious Violations of International Humanitarian Law Committed in the Territory of the Former Yugoslavia since 1991.	5th
128.	Financing of the International Criminal Tribunal for the Prosecution of Persons Responsible for Genocide and Other Serious Violations of International Humanitarian Law Committed in the Territory of Rwanda and Rwandan Citizens Responsible for Genocide and Other Such Violations Committed in the Territory of Neighbouring States between 1 January and 31 December 1994.	5th
129.	Financing of the United Nations Angola Verification Mission and the United Nations Observer Mission in Angola.	5th
130.	Financing of the activities arising from Security Council resolution 687(1991):	
	(a) United Nations Iraq-Kuwait Observation Mission;	5th
	(b) Other activities.	5th
131.	Financing of the United Nations Mission in East Timor.	5th

Item No.	Title	Allocation
132.	Financing of the United Nations Mission in Sierra Leone.	5th
133.	Financing of the United Nations Interim Administration Mission in Kosovo.	5th
134.	Financing of the United Nations Transitional Administration in East Timor.	5th
135.	Financing of the United Nations Mission for the Referendum in Western Sahara.	5th
136.	Financing of the United Nations Mission of Observers in Tajikistan.	5th
137.	Financing of the United Nations Preventive Deployment Force.	5th
138.	Financing of the United Nations peacekeeping forces in the Middle East:	
	(a) United Nations Disengagement Observer Force;	5th
	(b) United Nations Interim Force in Lebanon.	5th
139.	Financing and liquidation of the United Nations Transitional Authority in Cambodia.	5th
140.	Financing of the United Nations Protection Force, the United Nations Confidence Restoration Operation in Croatia, the United Nations Preventive Deployment Force and the United Nations Peace Forces headquarters.	5th
141.	Financing of the United Nations Operation in Somalia II.	5th
142.	Financing of the United Nations Operation in Mozambique.	5th
143.	Financing of the United Nations Peacekeeping Force in Cyprus.	5th
144.	Financing of the United Nations Observer Mission in Georgia.	5th
145.	Financing of the United Nations Mission in Haiti.	5th
146.	Financing of the United Nations Observer Mission in Liberia.	5th
147.	Financing of the United Nations Assistance Mission for Rwanda.	5th
148.	Financing of the United Nations Mission in Bosnia and Herzegovina.	5th
149.	Financing of the United Nations Transitional Administration for Eastern Slavonia, Baranja and Western Sirmium and the Civilian Police Support Group.	5th
150.	Financing of the United Nations Support Mission in Haiti, the United Nations Transition Mission in Haiti and the United Nations Civilian Police Mission in Haiti.	5th
151.	Financing of the Military Observer Group of the United Nations Verification Mission in Guatemala.	5th
152.	Financing of the United Nations Mission in the Central African Republic.	5th
153.	Administrative and budgetary aspects of the financing of the United Nations peacekeeping operations:	
	(a) Financing of the United Nations peacekeeping operations;	5th
	(b) Relocation of South Africa to the group of Member States set out in paragraph 3 *(c)* of General Assembly resolution 43/232.	5th
154.	Progressive development of the principles and norms of international law relating to the new international economic order.	6th
155.	Status of the Protocols Additional to the Geneva Conventions of 1949 and relating to the protection of victims of armed conflicts.	6th
156.	Consideration of effective measures to enhance the protection, security and safety of diplomatic and consular missions and representatives.	6th
157.	Convention on jurisdictional immunities of States and their property.	6th
158.	Report of the United Nations Commission on International Trade Law on the work of its thirty-third session.	6th
159.	Report of the International Law Commission on the work of its fifty-second session.	6th
160.	Nationality of natural persons in relation to the succession of States.	6th
161.	Report of the Committee on Relations with the Host Country.	6th
162.	Establishment of the International Criminal Court.	6th
163.	Report of the Special Committee on the Charter of the United Nations and on the Strengthening of the Role of the Organization.	6th
164.	Measures to eliminate international terrorism.	6th
165.	Review of the Statute of the United Nations Administrative Tribunal.	6th
166.	Election of judges of the International Tribunal for the Prosecution of Persons Responsible for Serious Violations of International Humanitarian Law Committed in the Territory of the Former Yugoslavia since 1991.	Plenary
167.	Financing of the United Nations Organization Mission in the Democratic Republic of the Congo.	5th
168.	Programme budget for the biennium 1998-1999.	5th
169.	Scale of assessments for the apportionment of the expenses of United Nations peacekeeping operations.	5th
170.	Cooperation between the United Nations and the Council of Europe.	Plenary
171.	Observer status for the Inter-American Development Bank in the General Assembly.	6th

Item No.	Title	Allocation
172.	Observer status for the International Institute for Democracy and Electoral Assistance in the General Assembly.	6th
173.	Towards global partnerships.	Plenary
174.	The role of the United Nations in promoting a new global human order.	Plenary
175.	The role of diamonds in fuelling conflict.	Plenary
176.	Financing of the United Nations Mission in Ethiopia and Eritrea.	5th
177.	Cooperation between the United Nations and the Preparatory Commission for the Comprehensive Nuclear-Test-Ban Treaty Organization.	Plenary
178.	Armed aggression against the Democratic Republic of the Congo.	Plenary
179.	Review of the problem of human immunodeficiency virus/acquired immunodeficiency syndrome in all its aspects.	Plenary
180.	Cooperation between the United Nations and the Economic Community of Central African States.	Plenary
181.	Cooperation between the United Nations and the Organization for the Prohibition of Chemical Weapons.	Plenary
182.	Follow-up to the outcome of the Millennium Summit.	Plenary
183.	Peace, security and reunification on the Korean peninsula.	Plenary
184.	Observer status for the Economic Community of Central African States in the General Assembly.	6th

Agenda item considered at the resumed tenth emergency special session (18 and 20 October 2000)

Item No.	Title	Allocation
5.	Illegal Israeli actions in occupied East Jerusalem and the rest of the Occupied Palestinian Territory.	Plenary

Security Council

Agenda items considered during 2000

Item No. [10]	Title
1.	The situation in Africa: the impact of AIDS on peace and security in Africa.
2.	The situation in Croatia.
3.	Promoting peace and security: humanitarian assistance to refugees in Africa.
4.	The situation in Angola.
5.	The situation in Burundi.
6.	The situation concerning the Democratic Republic of the Congo.
7.	Admission of new Members.
8.	The situation in Georgia.
9.	The situation in the Middle East.
10.	The situation in Africa.
11.	The situation in East Timor.
12.	The situation in Sierra Leone.
13.	Protection of United Nations personnel, associated personnel and humanitarian personnel in conflict zones.
14.	The situation in the Central African Republic.
15.	Security Council resolutions 1160(1998), 1199(1998), 1203(1998), 1239(1999) and 1244(1999) [situation in Kosovo].
16.	Briefing by Mr. Carl Bildt, Special Envoy of the Secretary-General for the Balkans.
17.	The situation concerning Western Sahara.
18.	Election of a member of the International Court of Justice.
19.	Maintaining peace and security: humanitarian aspects of issues before the Security Council.
20.	The question concerning Haiti.
21.	The situation in Tajikistan and along the Tajik-Afghan border.
22.	The situation in Bosnia and Herzegovina.
23.	Maintenance of peace and security and post-conflict peace-building.
24.	The situation between Iraq and Kuwait.
25.	The situation in Guinea-Bissau.
26.	The situation in Afghanistan.
27.	The situation concerning Rwanda.

Item	
No.[10]	*Title*

28. General issues relating to sanctions.

29. Protection of civilians in armed conflict.

30. The situation between Eritrea and Ethiopia.

31. International Tribunal for the Prosecution of Persons Responsible for Serious Violations of International Humanitarian Law Committed in the Territory of the Former Yugoslavia since 1991; International Criminal Tribunal for the Prosecution of Persons Responsible for Genocide and Other Serious Violations of International Humanitarian Law Committed in the Territory of Rwanda and Rwandan Citizens Responsible for Genocide and Other Such Violations Committed in the Territory of Neighbouring States between 1 January and 31 December 1994.

32. The situation in Cyprus.

33. International Tribunal for the Prosecution of Persons Responsible for Serious Violations of International Humanitarian Law Committed in the Territory of the Former Yugoslavia since 1991.

34. The situation in Somalia.

35. The responsibility of the Security Council in the maintenance of international peace and security: HIV/AIDS and international peacekeeping operations.

36. The role of the Security Council in the prevention of armed conflicts.

37. Children and armed conflict.

38. Consideration of the draft report of the Security Council to the General Assembly.

39. Ensuring an effective role of the Security Council in the maintenance of international peace and security, particularly in Africa.

40. The situation in the Middle East, including the Palestinian question.

41. Women and peace and security.

42. Briefing by Judge Gilbert Guillaume, President of the International Court of Justice.

43. Briefing by Mrs. Sadako Ogata, United Nations High Commissioner for Refugees.

44. Ensuring an effective role of the Security Council in the maintenance of international peace and security.

45. No exit without strategy [closure or transition of peacekeeping operations].

46. Letter dated 10 November 2000 from the Chargé d'affaires a.i. of the Permanent Mission of Solomon Islands to the United Nations addressed to the President of the Security Council [situation in Solomon Islands].

47. Briefing by the Secretary-General.

48. The responsibility of the Security Council in the maintenance of international peace and security.

49. The situation in Guinea following recent attacks along its borders with Liberia and Sierra Leone.

Economic and Social Council

Agenda of the organizational and resumed organizational sessions for 2000
(27 January and 1 and 4 February; 28 February, 9 March, 3, 10 and 12 May and 16 June)

Item	
No.	*Title*

1. Election of the Bureau.

2. Adoption of the agenda and other organizational matters.

3. Basic programme of work of the Council.

4. Elections, nominations and confirmations.

Agenda of the substantive and resumed substantive sessions of 2000
(5-28 July; 18 and 30 October and 22 November)

Item	
No.	*Title*

1. Adoption of the agenda and other organizational matters.

High-level segment (5-7 July)

2. Development and international cooperation in the twenty-first century: the role of information technology in the context of a knowledge-based global economy.

Operational activities of the United Nations for international development cooperation segment

3. Operational activities of the United Nations for international development cooperation:

   (a) Follow-up to policy recommendations of the General Assembly and the Council:

(i) Resources and funding of the operational activities for development;

(ii) Simplification and harmonization of programming, operational and administrative procedures;

(iii) Progress report on the implementation of the triennial comprehensive policy review;

(b) Reports of the Executive Boards of the United Nations Development Programme/United Nations Population Fund, the United Nations Children's Fund and the World Food Programme.

Coordination segment

4. Coordination of the policies and activities of the specialized agencies and other bodies of the United Nations system related to the following themes:

    (a) Assessment of the progress made within the United Nations system, through the conference reviews, in the promotion of an integrated and coordinated implementation of and follow-up to major United Nations conferences and summits in the economic, social and related fields;

    (b) Coordinated implementation by the United Nations system of the Habitat Agenda.

Humanitarian affairs segment

5. Special economic, humanitarian and disaster relief assistance.

General segment

6. Integrated and coordinated implementation of and follow-up to major United Nations conferences and summits.

7. Coordination, programme and other questions:

    (a) Reports of coordination bodies;

    (b) Proposed medium-term plan for the period 2002-2005;

    (c) Long-term programme of support for Haiti;

    (d) Tobacco or health;

    (e) International cooperation in the field of informatics.

8. Implementation of General Assembly resolutions 50/227 and 52/12 B.

9. Implementation of the Declaration on the Granting of Independence to Colonial Countries and Peoples by the specialized agencies and the international institutions associated with the United Nations.

10. Regional cooperation.

11. Economic and social repercussions of the Israeli occupation on the living conditions of the Palestinian people in the occupied Palestinian territory, including Jerusalem, and the Arab population in the occupied Syrian Golan.

12. Non-governmental organizations.

13. Economic and environmental questions:

    (a) Sustainable development;

    (b) Public administration and finance;

    (c) Water supply and sanitation;

    (d) Cartography;

    (e) Population and development;

    (f) Statistics;

    (g) International cooperation in tax matters;

    (h) Functioning of the Commission on Science and Technology for Development, including its role in coordinating science and technology for development.

14. Social and human rights questions:

    (a) Advancement of women;

    (b) Social development;

    (c) Crime prevention and criminal justice;

    (d) Narcotic drugs;

    (e) United Nations High Commissioner for Refugees;

    (f) Implementation of the Programme of Action for the Third Decade to Combat Racism and Racial Discrimination;

    (g) Human rights.

[1] Allocated to the Fifth Committee at the first part of the session in 1999 but considered only in plenary meeting at the resumed session.

[2] Not allocated; consideration deferred to the fifty-fifth session.

[3] Allocated to the Second Committee at the first part of the session in 1999 but considered only in plenary meeting at the resumed session.

[4] Also allocated to the Third Committee at the first part of the session in 1999.

[5] Allocated to the Third Committee at the first part of the session in 1999 but considered only in plenary meeting at the resumed session.

[6] Item added at the resumed session.

[7] Also allocated to the Ad Hoc Committee of the Whole of the Twenty-third Special Session.

[8] Also allocated to the Ad Hoc Committee of the Whole of the Twenty-fourth Special Session.

[9] On 11 September 2000, the General Assembly adopted the General Committee's recommendation that the item be allocated at an appropriate time during the session.

[10] Numbers indicate the order in which items were taken up in 2000.

Appendix V

United Nations information centres and services

(as at 15 August 2002)

ACCRA. United Nations Information Centre
Gamel Abdul Nassar/Liberia Roads
(P.O. Box 2339)
Accra, Ghana
> *Serving:* Ghana, Sierra Leone

ADDIS ABABA. United Nations Information
Service, Economic Commission for Africa
P.O. Box 3001
Addis Ababa, Ethiopia
> *Serving:* Ethiopia, ECA

ALGIERS. United Nations Information Centre
9A Rue Emile Payen, Hudra
(Boîte Postale 823, Alger-Gare)
Algiers, Algeria
> *Serving:* Algeria

ANKARA. United Nations Information Centre
Birlik Mahallesi, 2 Cadde No. 11
(P.K. 407)
06610 Cankaya
Ankara, Turkey
> *Serving:* Turkey

ANTANANARIVO. United Nations Information Centre
22 Rue Rainitovo, Antasahavola
(Boîte Postale 1348)
Antananarivo, Madagascar
> *Serving:* Madagascar

ASUNCION. United Nations Information
Centre
Avda. Mariscal López esq. Saraví
Edificio Naciones Unidas
(Casilla de Correo 1107)
Asunción, Paraguay
> *Serving:* Paraguay

ATHENS. United Nations Information
Centre
36 Amalias Avenue
GR-10558 Athens, Greece
> *Serving:* Cyprus, Greece, Israel

BANGKOK. United Nations Information
Service, Economic and Social Commis-
sion for Asia and the Pacific
United Nations Building
Rajdamnern Avenue
Bangkok 10200, Thailand
> *Serving:* Cambodia, China, Lao Peo-
ple's Democratic Republic, Malaysia,
Singapore, Thailand, Viet Nam, ESCAP

BEIRUT. United Nations Information Cen-
tre/United Nations Information Service,
Economic and Social Commission for
Western Asia
UN House
Riad El-Solh Square
(P.O. Box 11-8575-4656)
Beirut, Lebanon
> *Serving:* Jordan, Kuwait, Lebanon,
Syrian Arab Republic, ESCWA

BOGOTA. United Nations Information Centre
Calle 100 No. 8A-55, Piso 10
Edificio World Trade Center - Torre "C"
(Apartado Aéreo 058964)
Bogotá 2, Colombia
> *Serving:* Colombia, Ecuador, Vene-
zuela

BONN. United Nations Information Centre
United Nations Premises in Bonn
Martin-Luther-King Strasse 8
D-53175 Bonn, Germany
> *Serving:* Germany

BRAZZAVILLE. United Nations Informa-
tion Centre
Avenue Foch, Case Ortf 15
(P.O. Box 13210 or 1018)
Brazzaville, Congo
> *Serving:* Congo

BRUSSELS. United Nations Information
Centre
UN House
14 Rue Montoyer
B-1000 Brussels, Belgium
> *Serving:* Belgium, Luxembourg, Neth-
erlands, European Union

BUCHAREST. United Nations Information
Centre
16 Aurel Vlaicu
(P.O. Box 1-701)
Bucharest 79362, Romania
> *Serving:* Romania

BUENOS AIRES. United Nations Information Centre
Junín 1940 (1er piso)
1113 Buenos Aires, Argentina
> *Serving:* Argentina, Uruguay

BUJUMBURA. United Nations Information Centre
117 Avenue de la Révolution
(Boîte Postale 2160)
Bujumbura, Burundi
> *Serving:* Burundi

CAIRO. United Nations Information
Centre
1 Osiris Street, Garden City
(Boîte Postale 262)
Cairo, Egypt
> *Serving:* Egypt, Saudi Arabia

COLOMBO. United Nations Information
Centre
202/204 Bauddhaloka Mawatha
(P.O. Box 1505, Colombo)
Colombo 7, Sri Lanka
> *Serving:* Sri Lanka

COPENHAGEN. United Nations Informa-
tion Centre
Midtermolen 3
DK-2100 Copenhagen East, Denmark
> *Serving:* Denmark, Finland, Iceland,
Norway, Sweden

DAKAR. United Nations Information
Centre
12 Avenue Léopold S. Senghor, Immeuble
UNESCO
(Boîte Postale 154)
Dakar, Senegal
> *Serving:* Cape Verde, Côte d'Ivoire,
Gambia, Guinea, Guinea-Bissau, Mauri-
tania, Senegal

DAR ES SALAAM. United Nations Infor-
mation Centre
Morogoro Road/Sokoine Drive
Old Boma Building (ground floor)
(P.O. Box 9224)
Dar es Salaam, United Republic of Tanzania
> *Serving:* United Republic of Tanzania

DHAKA. United Nations Information
Centre
IDB Bhaban (14th floor)
Begum Rokeya Sharani
Sher-e-Bangla Nagar
(G.P.O. Box 3658, Dhaka-1000)
Dhaka-1207, Bangladesh
> *Serving:* Bangladesh

GENEVA. United Nations Information Service, United Nations Office at Geneva
Palais des Nations
1211 Geneva 10, Switzerland

Serving: Bulgaria, Switzerland

HARARE. United Nations Information Centre
Sanders House (2nd floor)
First Street/Jason Moyo Avenue
(P.O. Box 4408)
Harare, Zimbabwe

Serving: Zimbabwe

ISLAMABAD. United Nations Information Centre
House No. 26, Street 88, G-6/3
(P.O. Box 1107)
Islamabad, Pakistan

Serving: Pakistan

JAKARTA. United Nations Information Centre
Gedung Surya (14th floor)
Jl. M. H. Thamrin Kavling 9
Jakarta 10350, Indonesia

Serving: Indonesia

KATHMANDU. United Nations Information Centre
Pulchowk, Patan
(P.O. Box 107, UN House)
Kathmandu, Nepal

Serving: Nepal

KHARTOUM. United Nations Information Centre
United Nations Compound
Gamma'a Avenue
(P.O. Box 1992)
Khartoum, Sudan

Serving: Somalia, Sudan

KINSHASA. United Nations Information Centre
Bâtiment Deuxième République
Boulevard du 30 Juin
B.P. 7248
Kinshasa 1, Democratic Republic of the Congo

Serving: Democratic Republic of the Congo

LAGOS. United Nations Information Centre
17 Kingsway Road, Ikoyi
(P.O. Box 1068)
Lagos, Nigeria

Serving: Nigeria

LA PAZ. United Nations Information Centre
Calle 14 esq. S. Bustamante
Edificio Metrobol II, Calacoto
(Apartado Postal 9072)
La Paz, Bolivia

Serving: Bolivia

LIMA. United Nations Information Centre
Lord Cochrane 130
San Isidro (L-27)
(P.O. Box 14-0199)
Lima, Peru

Serving: Peru

LISBON. United Nations Information Centre
Rua Latino Coelho 1
Edificio Aviz, Bloco A-1, 10°
1050-132 Lisbon, Portugal

Serving: Portugal

LOME. United Nations Information Centre
107 Boulevard du 13 Janvier
(Boîte Postale 911)
Lomé, Togo

Serving: Benin, Togo

LONDON. United Nations Information Centre
Millbank Tower (21st floor)
21-24 Millbank
London SW1P 4QH, England

Serving: Ireland, United Kingdom

LUSAKA. United Nations Information Centre
Revenue House (ground floor)
Cairo Road (Northend)
(P.O. Box 32905, Lusaka 10101)
Lusaka, Zambia

Serving: Botswana, Malawi, Swaziland, Zambia

MADRID. United Nations Information Centre
Avenida General Perón, 32-1
(P.O. Box 3400, 28080 Madrid)
28020 Madrid, Spain

Serving: Spain

MANAGUA. United Nations Information Centre
Palacio de la Cultura
(Apartado Postal 3260)
Managua, Nicaragua

Serving: Nicaragua

MANAMA. United Nations Information Centre
United Nations House
Building 69, Road 1901
(P.O. Box 26004, Manama)
Manama 319, Bahrain

Serving: Bahrain, Qatar, United Arab Emirates

MANILA. United Nations Information Centre
NEDA sa Makati Building
106 Amorsolo Street
Legaspi Village, Makati City, 1229
(P.O. Box 7285 ADC (DAPO), Pasay City)
Metro Manila, Philippines

Serving: Papua New Guinea, Philippines, Solomon Islands

MASERU. United Nations Information Centre
United Nations Road
UN House
(P.O. Box 301, Maseru 100)
Maseru, Lesotho

Serving: Lesotho

MEXICO CITY. United Nations Information Centre
Presidente Masaryk 29-6° piso
Col. Chapultepec Morales
11570 México, D.F., Mexico

Serving: Cuba, Dominican Republic, Mexico

MONROVIA. United Nations Information Centre
UNDP
Dubar Building
Monrovia, Liberia

Serving: Liberia

MOSCOW. United Nations Information Centre
4/16 Glazovsky pereulok
Moscow 121002, Russian Federation

Serving: Russian Federation

NAIROBI. United Nations Information Centre
United Nations Office
Gigiri
(P.O. Box 30552)
Nairobi, Kenya

Serving: Kenya, Seychelles, Uganda

NEW DELHI. United Nations Information Centre
55 Lodi Estate
New Delhi 110 003, India

Serving: Bhutan, India

OUAGADOUGOU. United Nations Information Centre
14 Avenue Georges Konseiga
Secteur No. 4
(Boîte Postale 135)
Ouagadougou 01, Burkina Faso

Serving: Burkina Faso, Chad, Mali, Niger

PANAMA CITY. United Nations Information Centre
Calle Gerardo Ortega y Ave. Samuel Lewis
Banco Central Hispano Building (1st floor)
(P.O. Box 6-9083 El Dorado)
Panama City, Panama

Serving: Panama

PARIS. United Nations Information Centre
1 Rue Miollis
75732, Paris Cedex 15, France

Serving: France

PORT OF SPAIN. United Nations Information Centre
2nd floor, Bretton Hall
16 Victoria Avenue
(P.O. Box 130)
Port of Spain, Trinidad, W.I.

Serving: Antigua and Barbuda, Bahamas, Barbados, Belize, Dominica, Grenada, Guyana, Jamaica, Netherlands Antilles, Saint Kitts and Nevis, Saint Lucia, Saint Vincent and the Grenadines, Suriname, Trinidad and Tobago

PRAGUE. United Nations Information Centre
nam. Kinskych 6
150 00 Prague 5, Czech Republic
Serving: Czech Republic

PRETORIA. United Nations Information Centre
Metro Park Building
351 Schoeman Street
(P.O. Box 12677)
Pretoria, South Africa
Serving: South Africa

RABAT. United Nations Information Centre
6 Angle Charii Ibnou Ziyad et Zankat Roudana
(Boîte Postale 601, Casier ONU, Rabat-Chellah)
Rabat, Morocco
Serving: Morocco

RIO DE JANEIRO. United Nations Information Centre
Palácio Itamaraty
Av. Marechal Floriano 196
20080-002 Rio de Janeiro, RJ Brazil
Serving: Brazil

ROME. United Nations Information Centre
Palazzetto Venezia
Piazza San Marco 50
00186 Rome, Italy
Serving: Holy See, Italy, Malta, San Marino

SANA'A. United Nations Information Centre
Street 5, off Al-Boniya Street
Handlal Zone, beside Handhal Mosque
(P.O. Box 237)
Sana'a, Yemen
Serving: Yemen

SANTIAGO. United Nations Information Service, Economic Commission for Latin America and the Caribbean
Edificio Naciones Unidas
Avenida Dag Hammarskjöld
Vitacura
(Avenida Dag Hammarskjöld s/n, Casilla 179-D)
Santiago, Chile
Serving: Chile, ECLAC

SYDNEY. United Nations Information Centre
46-48 York Street (5th floor)
(G.P.O. Box 4045, Sydney, N.S.W. 2001)
Sydney, N.S.W. 2000, Australia
Serving: Australia, Fiji, Kiribati, Nauru, New Zealand, Samoa, Tonga, Tuvalu, Vanuatu

TEHRAN. United Nations Information Centre
185 Gheammagham-Farahani St.
(P.O. Box 15875-4557, Tehran)
Tehran 15868, Iran
Serving: Iran

TOKYO. United Nations Information Centre
UNU Building (8th floor)
53-70 Jingumae 5-chome, Shibuya-ku
Tokyo 150-0001, Japan
Serving: Japan

TRIPOLI. United Nations Information Centre
Muzzafar Al-Aftas St.
Hay El-Andalous (2)
(P.O. Box 286)
Tripoli, Libyan Arab Jamahiriya
Serving: Libyan Arab Jamahiriya

TUNIS. United Nations Information Centre
61 Boulevard Bab-Benat
(Boîte Postale 863)
Tunis, Tunisia
Serving: Tunisia

VIENNA. United Nations Information Service, United Nations Office at Vienna
Vienna International Centre
Wagramer Strasse 5
(P.O. Box 500, A-1400 Vienna)
A-1220 Vienna, Austria
Serving: Austria, Hungary, Slovakia, Slovenia

WARSAW. United Nations Information Centre
A. Niepodleglosci 186
(P.O. Box 1, 02-514 Warsaw 12)
00-608 Warszawa, Poland
Serving: Poland

WASHINGTON, D.C. United Nations Information Centre
1775 K Street, N.W., Suite 400
Washington, D.C. 20006, United States
Serving: United States

WINDHOEK. United Nations Information Centre
372 Paratus Building
Independence Avenue
(Private Bag 13351)
Windhoek, Namibia
Serving: Namibia

YANGON. United Nations Information Centre
6 Natmauk Road
Yangon, Myanmar
Serving: Myanmar

YAOUNDE. United Nations Information Centre
Immeuble Tchinda, Rue 2044
Derrière camp SIC TSINGA
(Boîte Postale 836)
Yaoundé, Cameroon
Serving: Cameroon, Central African Republic, Gabon

For more information on UNICs, access the Internet: http://www.un.org/aroundworld/unics

Indexes

USING THE SUBJECT INDEX

To assist the researcher in reading and searching the *Yearbook* index, three typefaces have been employed.

ALL BOLD CAPITAL LETTERS are used for major subject entries, including chapter topics (e.g., **DEVELOPMENT, DISARMAMENT**), as well as country names (e.g., **TAJIKISTAN**), region names (e.g., **AFRICA**) and principal UN organs (e.g., **GENERAL ASSEMBLY**).

CAPITAL LETTERS are used to highlight major sub-topics (e.g., POVERTY), territories (e.g., MONTSERRAT), subregions (e.g., CENTRAL AMERICA) and official names of specialized agencies (e.g., UNIVERSAL POSTAL UNION) and regional commissions (e.g., ECONOMIC COMMISSION FOR EUROPE).

Regular body text is used for single entries and cross-reference entries, e.g., armed conflict, juvenile detention, social development.

1—An asterisk (*) next to a page number indicates the presence of a text (reproduced in full) of General Assembly, Security Council or Economic and Social Council resolutions and decisions, or Security Council presidential statements.

2—Entries, which are heavily cross-referenced, appear under key substantive words, as well as under the first word of official titles.

3—United Nations bodies are listed under major subject entries and alphabetically.

Subject Index

Index of resolutions and decisions

Resolution/decision numbers in italics indicate that the text is summarized rather than reprinted in full. (For dates of sessions, refer to Appendix III.)

General Assembly

Fifty-fourth session

GENERAL ASSEMBLY, 55th SESSION *(cont.)*

Index of 2000 Security Council presidential statements

Statement numbers in italics indicate that the text is summarized rather than reprinted in full.

How to obtain volumes of the *Yearbook*

Recent volumes of the *Yearbook* may be obtained in many bookstores throughout the world, as well as from United Nations Publications, Room DC2-853, United Nations, New York, N.Y. 10017, or from United Nations Publications, Palais des Nations, CH-1211 Geneva 10, Switzerland.

Older editions are available in microfiche.

Yearbook of the United Nations, 1999
Vol. 53. Sales No. E.01.I.4 $150.

Yearbook of the United Nations, 1998
Vol. 52. Sales No. E.01.I.1 $150.

Yearbook of the United Nations, 1997
Vol. 51. Sales No. E.00.I.1 $150.

Yearbook of the United Nations, 1996
Vol. 50. Sales No. E.97.I.1 $150.

Yearbook of the United Nations, 1995
Vol. 49. Sales No. E.96.I.1 $150.

Yearbook of the United Nations, 1994
Vol. 48. Sales No. E.95.I.1 $150.

Yearbook of the United Nations, 1993
Vol. 47. Sales No. E.94.I.1 $150.

Yearbook of the United Nations, 1992
Vol. 46. Sales No. E.93.I.1 $150.

Yearbook of the United Nations, 1991
Vol. 45. Sales No. E.92.I.1 $115.

Yearbook of the United Nations, 1990
Vol. 44. Sales No. E.98.I.16 $150.

Yearbook of the United Nations, 1989
Vol. 43. Sales No. E.97.I.11 $150.

Yearbook of the United Nations, 1988
Vol. 42. Sales No. E.93.I.100 $150.

Yearbook of the United Nations, 1987
Vol. 41. Sales No. E.91.I.1 $105.

Yearbook of the United Nations, 1986
Vol. 40. Sales No. E.90.I.1 $95.

Yearbook of the United Nations, 1985
Vol. 39. Sales No. E.88.I.1 $95.

Yearbook of the United Nations, 1984
Vol. 38. Sales No. E.87.I.1 $90.

Yearbook of the United Nations, 1983
Vol. 37. Sales No. E.86.I.1 $85.

Yearbook of the United Nations
Special Edition
UN Fiftieth Anniversary
1945-1995
Sales No. E.95.I.50 $95

The first 53 volumes of the *Yearbook of the United Nations* (1946-1999) are now available on CD-ROM in both single-user and network versions. Institutions can subscribe at $500 (single-user version) or $1,000 (network version). Special rates are available for individuals and least developed countries. For more information, contact United Nations Publications at the above address.

NOTES

NOTES

NOTES

NOTES

NOTES

NOTES

NOTES

NOTES

NOTES

NOTES

NOTES

NOTES

NOTES

NOTES